D0811078

WISDEN

CRICKETERS' ALMANACK

2005

EDITED BY MATTHEW ENGEL

WISDEN

CRICKETERS' ALMANACK

2005

142nd EDITION

Published by John Wisden & Co Ltd,
13 Old Aylesfield, Golden Pot,
Alton, Hampshire GU34 4BY

JOHN WISDEN & CO LTD
13 Old Aylesfield, Golden Pot, Alton, Hampshire GU34 4BY

Reader feedback: almanack@wisdengroup.com

Websites
www.cricinfo.com
www.wisden.com

WISDEN CRICKETERS' ALMANACK

Editor **Matthew Engel**
Deputy editors **Harriet Monkhouse** and **Hugh Chevallier**
Assistant editor **Paul Coupar**
Contributing editor **Lawrence Booth**
Chief statistician **Philip Bailey**
Design consultant **Peter Ward**
Production co-ordinator **Peter Bather**
Chief typesetter **Mike Smith**
Proofreaders **Gordon Burling, Simon Webber** and **Charles Barr**
Advertisement sales **Colin Ackehurst** and **James Milner** (020 7471 6960)
Publisher **Christopher Lane**

Typeset in Times New Roman and Univers by Lazertype (UK) Ltd, Colchester
Printed in Great Britain by William Clowes Ltd, Beccles, Suffolk

"Wisden" and its woodcut device are registered trademarks of John Wisden & Co Ltd

EDITIONS
Cased ISBN 0-947766-89-8 **£36**
Soft cover ISBN 0-947766-90-1 **£36**
Leatherbound ISBN 0-947766-91-X **£235**

Distributed by Macmillan Distribution Ltd
Distributed in Australia by Hardie Grant Books, Melbourne

A Taste of Wisden 2005

Cricket was the fortunate beneficiary of a brilliant flowering: the invincibles of Sobers, Lloyd and Richards were ruthless, athletic, haughty, joyful, violent and charismatic. It was a rare, perhaps unrepeatable, eruption of cricket energy.
Robert Winder on Cricket and Migration, page 29

* * *

He's Mr Spreadsheet. I've seen him sit on the bus in the middle of winter, turn to Duncan and say: "Edgbaston, June 14. When do you want to practise, morning or afternoon?" The reply came very slowly: "Phil... I... don't... care."
Malcolm Ashton on the England set-up, page 38

* * *

Harry Judd, who scored 252 runs last season, left Uppingham in 2003 to become full-time drummer in the pop group McFly. The summer ended well for the side, with four wins in the last five matches, but even better for Harry Judd: McFly topped the UK singles chart twice, with "Five Colours in Her Hair" and "Obviously".
Schools Cricket, page 992

* * *

Every so often an Australian summer comes along that stirs the senses. Days feel longer, traffic queues shorter, distractions like war and football slip away.
Christian Ryan on Cricket in Australia, page 1401

* * *

Regardless of how close it is, the reaction is always the same when an explosion reverberates during our regular Friday games at the newly constituted Baghdad Cricket Ground...
Cricket in Iraq, page 1526

* * *

"Malcolm Scott, the left-arm spinner, was bowling, and Bill was almost placing his field for him. He'd say 'No, you want that bloke at mid-wicket a bit squarer', and then he'd smash the ball over the chap's head anyway."
Obituaries, page 1632

LIST OF CONTRIBUTORS

Tanya Aldred
Andy Arlidge
Malcolm Ashton
Chris Aspin
Philip August
Charlie Austin
Sambit Bal
Steven Barnett
Richie Benaud
Benedict Bermange
Scyld Berry
Edward Bevan
Rahul Bhattacharya
Soumya Bhattacharya
Debashish Biswas
Paul Bolton
Mihir Bose
Liam Brickhill
Simon Briggs
Daniel Brigham
Colin Bryden
Don Cameron
Malcolm Conn
Mike Coward
Tony Cozier
Robert Craddock
John Curtis
Deb K. Das
Gareth A. Davies
Geoffrey Dean
Ralph Dellor
Norman de Mesquita
Mike Dickson
Philip Eden
Peter English

John Etheridge
Colin Evans
Stephen Fay
Paul Fearn
David Foot
Angus Fraser
David Frith
Ramachandra Guha
Julian Guyer
Gideon Haigh
Paul Haigh
David Hallett
David Hardy
Norman Harris
Jon Henderson
Paul Hiscock
Richard Hobson
Grenville Holland
Guy Jackson
Paul Jones
Abid Ali Kazi
Paul Kelso
Kate Laven
Alan Lee
Neil Leitch
David Llewellyn
Steven Lynch
Vic Marks
Christopher Martin-Jenkins
Mohandas Menon
Andrew Miller
Fazeer Mohammed
R. Mohan
Gerald Mortimer
Tony Munro

Brian Murgatroyd
Andrew Nickolds
Mark Pennell
Sarah Potter
Dileep Premachandran
Andrew Radd
S. Rajesh
David Rayvern Allen
Graham Russell
Christian Ryan
Carol Salmon
Andrew Samson
Derek Scott
Mike Selvey
Utpal Shuvro
Jasmer Singh
Rob Smyth
Rob Steen
John Stern
Pat Symes
Sa'adi Thawfeeq
Jenny Thompson
Gerry Vaidyasekera
Amit Varma
Anand Vasu
Michael Vockins
Mike Walters
John Ward
David Warner
Paul Weaver
Tim Wellock
Simon Wilde
Martin Williamson
Robert Winder
Graeme Wright

Photographers are credited next to the relevant picture. Special thanks to Patrick Eagar and Graham Morris.

Cartoons by Nick Newman, "Rip" and Punch.

Round the World Contributors to the Round the World section are listed after their articles.

The editor also acknowledges with gratitude assistance from the following: Andrew Barker, Marcus Berkmann, Keith Booth, Jeremy Brien, Robert Brooke, Gerry Byrne, Lynda Cole, Marion Collin, Andrew Collomosse, Bill Cook, cricketarchive.com, Brian Croudy, Prakash Dahatonde, Nigel Davies, Graham Dench, Christopher Douglas, Roderick Easdale, Robert Eastaway, John Ellison, Gulu Ezekiel, M. L. Fernando, Ric Finlay, Chris Florence, Bill Frindall, Stuart George, Keith Gerrish, Ghulam Mustafa Khan, Ray Goble, James Greenfield, Peter Griffiths, C. W. Haigh, Neil Harris, Col. Malcolm Havergal, Ed Hawkins, Keith Hayhurst, Brian Heald, Murray Hedgcock, Andrew Hignell, Brian Hunt, Vic Isaacs, Frank Keating, David Kendix, Rajesh Kumar, Rajneesh Gupta, Stephanie Lawrence, Robert Leach, Tony Lewis, Nirav Malavi, Mahendra Mapagunaratne, Ray Markham, Nick Mason, Colin Mills, Diana Morris, David Northwood, Steve Palmer, Francis Payne, William A. Powell, Peter Robinson, Shahid Hashmi, Alan Shiell, Mary Small, Graham Sprackling, Bruce Talbot, Gordon Vince, Charlie Wat, Marcus Williams, Robert Wood, Peter Wynne-Thomas, John Young and all our colleagues at *Cricinfo*, *The Wisden Cricketer* and *Wisden Cricket Asia*.

The production of *Wisden* would not be possible without the support and co-operation of many other cricket officials, county scorers, writers and lovers of the game. To them all, many thanks.

PREFACE

The *Daily Telegraph* review of the 2004 almanack concluded with the reassuring comment: "*Wisden* remains a reliably engrossing read." Then came the kicker: "Just don't expect it to look the same next year."

That was a reasonable response to two years of substantial changes to the corrections – and to meet the needs of our readers in the 21st century. ... not, however, an accurate prediction. In 2004 *Wisden* found a on the back of the title p.. and readers' changing requirements. To that ..d the book must continue to adapt – but, gradually,

I hope someone might write and comments, complaints, compliments, than ever: in its range of subject matter, the qua..;..tion is actually better looks, and the speed of its response. This year we have full coverage of ...ease write to us at the address ..., please write to us at the address wisdengroup.com.

..iting, its good England's tour of Southern Africa, which concluded in February only a week before the book went to the printers. I don't believe this compromises any of our traditional virtues.

Wisden always has to balance its twin roles: as a book published and primarily sold in the UK, and one with a global view of the game. So in part this volume celebrates the England team's remarkable achievements in 2004, and for the first time in 45 years names five Englishmen as Cricketers of the Year. It also has to retain a sense of perspective, and – after much debate – we concluded that our less venerable accolade (started in 2004, rather than 1889), the Leading Cricketer in the World, should go to Shane Warne.

Our new, rather hairy, publishing schedule is possible thanks to the calm, tolerance and hard work of two men at our typesetters, Lazertype: Peter Bather and Mike Smith, who have been associated with a combined total of 50 *Wisdens*. When they start to look worried about what we're attempting, I get worried.

Please forgive me if I end on a personal note: my son Laurie was born in 1992, just after I first became editor of *Wisden*. A year ago, he was diagnosed with a serious illness – on the day, as it happens, he intended to try out for the Under-12 team. The past year for us has been dominated by this crisis. More than ever I am grateful for, as well as to, all my family, Hilary, Laurie and Vika.

The core team behind the almanack – my deputies, Hugh Chevallier and Harriet Monkhouse, the assistant editor Paul Coupar and publisher Christopher Lane – have had to deal with the consequences too. Their magnificent professionalism has ensured that *Wisden* has come through. To me, their personal support and friendship have been every bit as important.

MATTHEW ENGEL
Newton St Margarets, Herefordshire, February 2005

CONTENTS

Part One
Comment

Part Two
World View

Part Three
The Players

Part Four
Records

Part Five
English Cricket

STATISTICS

INTERNATIONAL CRICKET IN ENGLAND

FRIZZELL COUNTY CHAMPIONSHIP

Review and Statistics 544

CHELTENHAM & GLOUCESTER TROPHY

TOTESPORT LEAGUE

TWENTY20 CUP

CAREER FIGURES

THE UNIVERSITIES

OTHER CRICKET IN THE BRITISH ISLES

Part Six
Overseas Cricket

Part Seven

History and Law

Part Eight

The Wisden Review

Part Nine

The Almanack

Opposite: Viewing figures. Cricket supporters in Kolkata squeeze in to catch sight of their heroes.
Picture by Jayanta Shaw, Reuters

PART ONE

Comment

NOTES BY THE EDITOR

Among the cricketers who visited Sri Lankan refugee camps in the aftermath of the Boxing Day tsunami that devastated the country's coastline was the fast bowler Chaminda Vaas. He listened to a man who told him how he had lost his seven-year-old daughter in the wave, even though he was cradling her in his arms. Then the man changed the subject: how *had* Sri Lanka managed to lose to New Zealand?

Vaas was taken aback and found it hard to understand how someone suffering such grief could care about a mere game. However, he concluded that it showed how much people "love their motherland, Sri Lanka, and its cricket". I think it tells us more than that about the human condition. And indeed the whole tsunami disaster may have taught everyone in cricket a great deal about the game's place in the scheme of things: its unimportance, and its importance.

Despite some early roughness at the edges, cricket responded wonderfully well to the tragedy that befell so much of Asia, including two of the game's most important countries, Sri Lanka and India (though the beach cricketers swept away on the Coromandel Coast of Tamil Nadu, remote from the journalistic hub of the crisis, received far less attention than the Sri Lankan victims). One can be somewhat sceptical about these great global outpourings of grief: the donors and the media move on to whatever comes next, and the sufferers are quickly forgotten. But people can only do their best, and cricket so far has done just that.

Our game is so time-consuming that those involved in it often forget there is a world outside, which may explain some of the wrong decisions administrators take. On this occasion, everyone remembered they were human beings. Let's hope we never forget that, or the tsunami victims.

On the field

When 2004 began, India were proving themselves a worthy match for mighty Australia in an away series, which is a remarkable turnaround. This even pleased many Australians, partly because they had reached the point where they wanted someone – *anyone* – to give them a decent contest, and partly because it offered some of them the chance to claim that the Border–Gavaskar Trophy was now the most important in world cricket and that the Ashes were irrelevant. Ah, these Aussies: they're obsessed with the Poms even as they deride us.

By the end of the year, that judgment looked a little shaky. In the return series, Australia regained their supremacy over India with far more ease than expected. And right through 2004, there was an insistent and extraordinary drumbeat that eventually could not be wholly ignored even in Sydney and Melbourne. England kept winning and winning and winning.

It is fair to claim that none of the 141 previous *Wisdens* has had a story of English success to report that can match this one. England played 13 Tests in 2004, won 11, including eight in a row, and lost none. Even the two draws (Antigua and Durban) were, in different ways, very special. If you look back in history to the greatest moments of English cricket, they were rarely sustained. The 1981 series against Australia was sandwiched between unsuccessful tours to the West Indies and India; even in the mid-1950s, when Australia were beaten three times running, England found it hard to subdue South Africa, and lost a home Test to the infant Pakistan.

Under the increasingly assured leadership of Michael Vaughan, England in 2004 rolled over West Indies, New Zealand, West Indies again and started a job on South Africa which they finished three weeks into 2005. (The only "but" came in one-day cricket.) This naturally led to talk about winning the Ashes, which may be as overexcited as the claims of England's irrelevance a year earlier.

At the end of 2003, Australia were starting to wobble. Their most reliable fast bowler, Glenn McGrath, was injured and, with Shane Warne banned, they lacked a spinner who could impose control as well as take wickets. The return of Warne in full cry is the biggest difference between Australia at the start of 2005 and a year earlier. That's why *Wisden* has chosen him as the Leading Cricketer in the World.

As things stand now, Australia seem to me still too close to the pinnacle of their game to lose to England this summer. But much can change. Battle is to be joined, and the anticipation of that kind of excitement keeps us all going: in England, Australia or a Sri Lankan refugee camp.

Sound the trumpets

Part of the English disease is that the nation takes too little pleasure from its successes. Win four series in a row, and bar-room moaners say: "Well, we haven't beaten the Aussies." Should Australia then fall, they will say: "Well, they're on the way down, aren't they?" As Margaret Thatcher once said, in another context: "Just rejoice."

England supporters need to enjoy what has been achieved so far and to congratulate those who have contributed to it, including a number of former players and officials who endured some very grim times themselves. Consistent, intelligent and sometimes even inspired selection policies (gosh, I never thought I'd write those words) have led to a settled team that has developed a spirit once associated with the best county sides.

A professional approach to coaching and motivation has brought the best out of the players once they are there: they have played with huge determination as well as skill. When the going got toughest, England got going. Then there is the overlay of luck that cannot be bought or manufactured: a handful of players with outstanding talent. Not everything is right. We will come to that. But it has been a fantastic year for England: their success has been significant and deserved.

The worst administrators in the world

The 2004 ICC Champions Trophy deserves to be ranked alongside the 1986 Commonwealth Games in Edinburgh and the 1996 Olympics in Atlanta in the list of Great Sporting Fiascos of our time. Edinburgh and Atlanta were flawed in execution; England's Champions Trophy was a terrible idea from the start – a turkey of a tournament. This was all said here a year ago. The International Cricket Council (ICC) and the England and Wales Cricket Board (ECB) must share the blame, and we will leave it at that.

But among the dozens of tricks they missed was the idea of lining up not merely all the players at an opening ceremony (which is fundamental) but the officials of all the competing countries as well. Had they done that, it would have made the point that the ICC and ECB, despite occasional appearances to the contrary, are not the worst administrations in cricket.

Let's consider the dozen countries who took part in the Champions Trophy. It would not be difficult to argue that a majority of their governing bodies could, in varying degrees, be categorised as either incompetent, corrupt, government-controlled or racist. The Kenya Cricket Association acquired a reputation so bad even by the standards of its own country – one of the most notoriously corrupt in Africa – that it was disbanded by the government. The USA Cricket Association has been appalling for years, and by the end of 2004 the ICC felt stung into sending it a letter of such vituperative splendour (quoted in our Cricket in the United States section on page 1521) that it should stand as a classic of its kind.

The Sri Lankan board's ex-president is still listed as a member of cricket's supreme body, the ICC executive board, and has continued to attend meetings, but only after receiving special bail arrangements from the courts (he faces charges relating to his alleged involvement with a gangster, who was shot dead in court). In January 2005, the AGM of the Indian board, the most powerful in the game, was closed in 30 seconds, having been preceded by elections that were at best suspect and at worst outrageous. And so on. In a way, this explains the ICC's complaisant attitude towards Zimbabwe, a full member with a seat at the table. Pick on them for maladministration, and where do you stop? But uniquely, there is evidence that Zimbabwean cricket is guilty on all four of the above counts.

Zimbabwe's rebel players may not be saintly victims, except in the sense that everyone suffering under Robert Mugabe's regime is a victim. And it may be that they will have been driven to submission by the time this is published, and that some kind of peace will have broken out. That might have solved the most visible of the country's cricketing problems – its inadequate team. It won't deal with what lies beneath.

The ICC managed to find a couple of judges who solemnly reported that Zimbabwean cricket is not racist, just as British governments always find some supine judge to blame someone else for a disaster. How can Zimbabwean cricket not be racist? The board's announced policy is racist. If it isn't racist, it would be the only institution in the whole damn country that isn't. That's not new: Rhodesia was a white racist country; Zimbabwe has turned that on its head. The racism might be a legitimate redress for past injustices (I think that's broadly true of UCB policies in South Africa), but non-merit selection is still racist. And in Zimbabwe, it has been executed with a peculiar mixture of malignancy and ham-fistedness. When the Mugabe regime falls, then – as with apartheid – something of the truth may come out. Those who collaborated with the regime's excesses, inside the country and out, might then feel some sense of shame. That includes cricket administrators.

Christmas Day at Headingley, anyone?

The most consistent fault of the game's rulers, however, is that they are rotten impresarios: they have lost any sense of when and how to present a cricket match. I have warmed to the Super Test and one-day Superseries between Australia and the Rest of the World scheduled for this October and (unlike some statisticians) think the world will still turn if the fixtures have official Test and one-day status. But why hold them in October, when Australia is not geared up for cricket watching? And why only one Test when this could have provided the best series of all time? There is too much dross on the fixture list, that's why.

In the meantime, we move on to the 2005 season in England, an absolutely lip smacking prospect, not least because it is an odd-numbered year when the midsummer months of June and July are (unlike any others in the two-year cycle) free of football, leaving a gap in the back pages and the public consciousness for cricket to burst through. And what better than a potentially close Ashes series?

But no. Locked into an inflexible TV schedule and an even more inflexible mindset, the ECB have come up with something else. They are filling the entire second half of June – traditional time for the Lord's Ashes Test – with a tournament dedicated to the thrilling proposition of discovering the two best one-day teams out of England, Australia and Bangladesh. The Ashes will not even start until July 21 (when football is limbering up, earlier than usual to make room for the 2006 World Cup) and will not finish until September 12, deep into the football season and, very likely, the weather that did for the Champions Trophy.

This year marks the sesquicentenary of *Wisden's* greatest editor, Sydney Pardon. And it seems right to quote somewhere in the Notes his most famous phrase "touched the confines of lunacy," which he used to describe the 1909 England selectors. The selectors have made themselves fireproof lately, but the rest of cricket is so target-rich that one holds that phrase like a card player with the ace of trumps, hardly knowing the right moment to deploy it. This would be it, except that someone has already played the joker. A leader in *The Times* described this scheduling as "total madness". And so it is.

The Gulf between us

It now seems almost certain (though it is as yet unconfirmed) that, after 96 years, the ICC will soon move from Lord's to pitch what will no doubt be a more palatial camp in Dubai. This is not an unreasonable decision, enabling it to maximise tax and cost advantages, and it will probably prove more symbolic than significant.

The main consequences will be for the ICC itself. Dubai is an excellent airline hub, a pleasant destination for a weekend break and a useful place for a single bloke to make some tax-free dosh before settling down back home. But not everyone would want to live there for ever, and it will be hard to retain top-line staff (and their spouses).

Dubai is also several hours from the nearest regular Test match venue, and an organisation which ordinary cricket followers already consider remote may become even more detached. The modern ICC is, in most respects, an improvement on its amateur predecessors. Since it is only a sum of its parts, it is no surprise that its political stances can be ugly. But it does have one overriding foible. No other governing body in sport is so determined to shove itself into the limelight. It must be a sign of deep insecurity.

The record for The Most Self-Referential Press Release in history seems to stand at 26 mentions of ICC in a 303-word document, dated July 15, 2004. This excludes all the guff at the top and bottom. I don't remotely blame the communications staff, who are apparently under orders from the executive board. I can understand why sporting organisations might wish to keep plugging their sponsors, but this relentless branding of everything with the ICC name is becoming absurd. It would be no surprise if one day it issued a release announcing that the game was henceforth to be known as criccet. Back off, guys: you'll feel better.

Part of the insecurity stems from the lack of cricketing clout at the top. Percy Sonn of South Africa, the next president, will be the fourth in a row to take the job without any significant background in the game except as a sporting politician. I have nothing against Sonn: he is apparently a very smart lawyer. But if the ICC were headed by someone who had a worldwide cricketing reputation, it might just feel less need to go round shouting "Look at us! We're important!"

Hiatus at the ECB

Compared to what goes on elsewhere, the follies of English cricket administration are comparatively mild. None the less, it was a grim year at the ECB. On the field, all was fresh and creamy. Inside the office, everything curdled. This was partly, but not entirely, due to the endless agonising about the visit to Zimbabwe – to go or not to go, that is the question – which cost the board an interesting and original marketing chairman in Des Wilson, who resigned on principle after his arguments for a moral stance were rejected. The chief executive, Tim Lamb, left wearily in September after eight years, and a whole cohort of junior officials went too, many for mundane reasons, but at a rate that suggested a deeply unhappy office. Very often, the lights were on and – as anyone who tried to phone them will confirm – almost nobody was home.

With the court in disarray, barons from the shires began throwing their weight around, as happened in the darker moments of English mediaeval history, with results we will discuss in a moment. The funding body Sport England began making threatening noises about English cricket's governance; and the ECB chairman, David Morgan, has been spending this spring-time trying to get the size of the management board down from 16 just to

12 or 14, the eight or ten more often construed as ideal for decisive action being unacceptable to the barons, and to prise away financial control from the counties. Last autumn, without an executive head, the board could not avoid a decision far more consequential than the fate of one piddling tour, and there was no dither: a firm, confident and very definite choice was made…

Reach for the Sky

English cricket followers will get substantial benefits from the deal whereby live cricket in England will cease to be shown on terrestrial television, starting from 2006, and instead move to the satellite network, Sky Sports. The insidious process by which Test match days have had to start earlier and earlier so that they finish in time for the evening schedules will cease. Coverage will no longer have to be interrupted to accommodate horse races or other irrelevances. Cricket will have the benefit of being covered by a network with a proven commitment to the game and a reasonably innovative approach to it (even if the commentary is often banal). The subsidiary deal with Channel Five, which is a terrestrial station, ensures that the highlights package will be shown in the early evening and not, as has increasingly happened on the present main Test match station Channel 4, after midnight and shortly before the mud wrestling.

Readers who are unfamiliar with British TV may not grasp the passion attached to this argument. While the BBC, which showed home Test matches until 1998, and Channel 4 are available to everyone on payment of an annual licence fee (and Five to most people), Sky Sports has to be purchased by subscription, costing about £400 a year. Only a minority of the population makes this payment, but, as defenders of the deal have pointed out, it is thought half the households with children do pay, and these are the people cricket is most anxious to get at.

And from what one can gather, the ECB ran short of options. The BBC did not bid at all; Channel 4 entered only half-heartedly; Sky made it clear that, while not demanding all or nothing, it wanted all or would pay a great deal less. ECB sources say the funding gap between the Sky deal and any alternative package would have been £20m per year, a quarter of the board's annual budget. What matters here is the politics, not the economics. Had the ECB management board accepted a lesser deal, the counties would almost certainly have rebelled. Those responsible would have been voted out at best, strung up from Father Time at worst. That's today's reality.

Let us now consider tomorrow's reality. The pattern of TV viewing is indeed changing, though not in the way the deal's instigators claim. Giles Clarke, the board's chief negotiator, described terrestrial television as "a dying form". But though all TV is indeed scheduled to be digital by 2012, there will still be mainstream channels, available to all viewers, and specialist ones for paying customers only. On Channel 4, Test matches have a peak audience of just over a million. No one knows what the figure might be on Sky: the company does not reveal such figures, partly, one suspects, because they are too small to be measurable by any available method; and partly because they would draw derisive laughter. All the anecdotal evidence and one's intuition suggest that Test matches only on Sky get noticed less than others.

Sky's business model does not depend on drawing large audiences. It makes money by accreting minorities who want different aspects of their service. Sky Sports will indeed give a good service to cricket lovers willing to pay the subscription. It will not, however, go beyond them. Cricket's post-war survival in Britain was driven by the BBC. Television and radio attracted not just the obvious audience, but drew in people who knew nothing about the game until they heard or glimpsed it by chance and were captivated. Sky will attract only the already committed.

Some argue that the prime-time highlights package will be a huge bonus, but these programmes really are a dying form, because viewers can now see so much live sport. Others claim football has not suffered from being on Sky, which spectacularly misses the point. A vast amount of football remains on mass audience TV, most especially the two biennial festivals of the game, the World Cup and the European Championship. The 2003 cricket World Cup was only on Sky, and there is little prospect of anything different in 2007.

We are talking about a situation where the overwhelming majority of the British population will never come across a game of cricket in their daily lives. Never, never, never, never. There will be short-term consequences as sponsors drift away; the longer-term effects will take a generation to unfold. Some believe these could be serious. I think we're looking at a potential catastrophe.

County cricket loses the plot

One of the arguments privately advanced for the Sky deal is that otherwise "several counties would have gone to the wall". This is something that has echoed down the ages: Derbyshire were supposedly going out of business in 1910; Northamptonshire almost crashed in 1929, shortly after Wall Street. Yet they have all proved remarkably resilient.

Let them go. This is not said the way the county game's enemies say it, but in the belief that if counties were pushed back on their own resources, they would emerge stronger, and with a clearer sense of purpose, than the subsidy junkies of today. Either the people of Derbyshire, Northamptonshire and Leicestershire (to choose only the most obvious examples) want county cricket or they don't. If the social security cheques from Test revenues dried up, the experience might prove not just salutary but liberating.

Four-day cricket played by moderate players on dead pitches is never likely to be a major 21st century public entertainment, but the county game is now in danger of sliding from its position at the margins of British life into total oblivion.

Some of this is old news. Some isn't. The very reforms credited with helping the England team have actually had a dire effect lower down: there are no local heroes any more because the best English players almost never play for their counties. And whereas England have learned the value of a settled side with its own *esprit de corps*, counties happily spend their subsidies flying in international allsorts who barely even know which side they are representing, never mind who their team-mates might be.

A few of the evils may be mitigated by the new system of using hand-outs to reward counties that develop their own players, and by a belated mini-tightening of the rules on overseas signings from 2006. And help may be at hand from a very unexpected source. The new draft European Constitution (Article III-182) recognises the "specific nature" of sport, implying that the Kolpak ruling, which has allowed counties to sign cricketers from anywhere that has a trade agreement with the EU, will be open to challenge.

But Brussels won't change the fact that the county game is increasingly unwatchable and pointless. Precisely as predicted here six years ago, the introduction of two divisions has forced counties into short-term signings instead of long-term development of players. And the fear of relegation made first-division cricket last summer absolutely wretched.

I did propose an idea to try to pep up county cricket by merging the Championship and the one-day league to create a real champion county, something the public would understand. It was endorsed by an ECB working party but rejected by the county chairmen, as a side-effect of their determination to stop the fixture list being slashed. "The Championship is a great competition," snorted their spokesman, Mike Soper, "and to muddle it up with one-day games seems completely stupid." Great competition? Are we on the same planet?

Anyway, on December 23 (a traditional date for burying bad news – there really was no one home at the ECB) Soper's own working party announced a new one-day cricketing set-up from 2006 rendering what was previously confused entirely incomprehensible. The one competition everyone could understand, the knockout cup, is to be abolished, which is a dreadful decision. Instead, there will be three competitions, indistinguishable to the naked eye except for their length: 20, 40 and 50 overs. If and when the sheen wears off Twenty20, as it probably will once international cricket muscles in, county cricket may then finally wither for good and all.

In the meantime club cricketers complain vociferously that the game is being run by the counties for their own benefit. "The ECB is not a national governing body," says Barrie Stuart-King of the Club Cricket Conference. "It's an 18-member private club." He sees no indications of improved grassroots funding as a result of the Sky deal, and claims that in 2005 counties are likely to spend an extra £4m flying in yet more overseas players.

However, at almost every level, clubs share this addiction to imports. The former England manager Micky Stewart did a survey for the ECB a decade ago and estimated there were 10,000 overseas players (i.e. who have come over specifically to play cricket) every summer in the English game. "To my knowledge there is very little difference now," he says. Both these figures – four million, 10,000 – may be on the high side, but the general points seem valid.

These players would range from fully fledged overseas professionals in the big leagues to Aussie and Kiwi lads who might play a bit, coach a bit, serve behind the club bar, and get a bit of cash in a brown envelope so they can backpack round Europe. It's all out of hand.

For keeps

Wisden 2004 contained an article, a slightly sentimental one I suppose, in which Pat Murphy lamented the decline of the wicket-keeper's craft. His point was vividly illustrated within 48 hours of publication: Chris Read was dropped from the England team in favour of Geraint Jones, regarded as an inferior wicket-keeper but a better batsman. This was done without the knowledge of the specialist selector, Rod Marsh, who was furious.

The 2000 version of the Laws contained a new provision restricting the use and nature of the webbing on keepers' gloves. This was included at the urging of Bob Taylor, who had noticed players deliberately catching the ball in the webbing rather than their palms, and sensed that the next step was going to be baseball mitts, enabling pretty much anyone with two hands to do the job.

This change barely slowed a global trend that threatens to become irreversible. In Australia, the arguments are even more bitter than in England: Darren Berry, the retired Victorian keeper rated by Shane Warne as the best he has ever seen, described the standard set by Adam Gilchrist and Parthiv Patel in the Chennai Test last year as "disgraceful".

And England's Jones may only be an interim choice: the future, one suspects, belongs to the batsman-keeper rather than the keeper-batsman. A young professional batsman with any kind of fielding aptitude would be well advised to see if he can keep wicket: it might make his career. The day may be approaching when wicket-keeper becomes no more than a quasi-specialist position, like a glorified first slip. The keeper's contribution is unquantifiable, so it doesn't get counted. Rather like the damage done by the Sky deal.

Let's get things straight

Unveiling the latest plans to regulate illegal bowling actions, Malcolm Speed, the ICC chief executive, said: "This issue has afflicted the game for over 60 years." History is not Speed's strong point. These Notes emerged out of the personal campaign to eradicate throwing conducted by Sydney Pardon more than a century ago. And since John Willes of Kent was no-balled for throwing (bowling round-arm rather than underarm) in 1822, the issue may truthfully be described as nearly 200 years old.

After much research involving biomechanics, hyperextension and other words not used much in Edwardian *Wisdens*, the ICC has announced a scheme that will allow all bowlers to straighten their arms by up to 15 degrees. This was attacked by some ex-players as giving licence to chuckers.

Any *Wisden* editor would hesitate to say anything that might be construed as a breach of the Pardon tradition, and I would hate to be seen as soft on throwing. But I invite opponents of the new scheme to conduct the following exercise. Listen carefully.

Sit in the bath and stretch your arm straight ahead of you. Then raise your forearm until the elbow is at right angles, as if flexing your biceps, Popeye-style. Then go back halfway between the two positions: that's 45 degrees. Then reduce that angle by a further two-thirds: that's 15 degrees. Can you tell if your arm's straight or not? Then imagine yourself wearing a long-sleeved shirt running in to bowl at full pace, and tell me if someone can judge a 15-degree arm movement from square leg. ICC has got this one right.

Matters spiritual

Both the ICC and MCC have acquired a taste lately for high-flown talk about "The Spirit of Cricket", and MCC now has an annual Cowdrey Lecture devoted to the subject. Last year it was given by Clive Lloyd, who used the occasion to call for much greater use of technology in all manner of umpiring decisions. "It is time to use technology to the fullest extent," he said. "There is a lot at stake in international cricket these days: what matters is that we get it right."

Well, up to a point. What matters is the spirit of cricket, which insists that – whether it is a playground or a Test ground – what's important is that the umpire's decision should be a fair one, and that the players should accept it. Personally, I would rather spend eight hours a day undergoing root-canal surgery than function as an international umpire, but it is gratifying that there are men willing to do the job and who are not rushing to have their lives made simpler the Lloyd way.

"I would like to have my skills tested. You know, the players' skills get tested in the match. Why not the officials?" said Simon Taufel, the ICC umpire of the year. "Players make mistakes, umpires make mistakes," said his colleague Billy Bowden. "Let's just get on and move on." Quite so. This does not preclude the sensible use of technology: there seems to be a case for further experiments with third umpires monitoring the front-foot law. But cricket is a game between humans, which should be controlled by humans.

It is possible that the argument may be ended for ever if the new trend towards self-regulation takes hold. The Australians have begun walking when they believe they are out. Maybe we soon won't need umpires at all. But I shall suspend judgment until we reach the final Test this summer with the Ashes series poised 2–2, the Test in the balance, when an out-of-form Aussie batsman, battling to maintain his place in the side, gets the thinnest of nicks while still in single figures. If he walks then, I will walk too: home from The Oval in my underpants.

Let the people go

There is no finer sight in cricket than a packed ground during an interval when the youngsters (of all ages) are allowed to spill over the boundary and play their own mini-Tests. In England, the Twenty20 has helped revive this lovely custom at many county grounds. In South Africa, it happily persists even at Test matches, and one local observer at the New Year Test thought the Newlands outfield had not been so full since Bill Lawry's tour of 1969-70.

It would be too much to expect this to happen at major English occasions. But this year we welcome a new ECB chief executive, David Collier, starting with a blank sheet of paper. So let me repeat the so far unavailing plea I made to his predecessor last year. If England win the Ashes at The Oval, or even if they don't, there is no reason on earth not to let the crowd share in the ceremonial. Don't block their view by erecting a stage facing the TV cameras, with snarling stewards standing on the boundary glowering at the paying spectators.

No one wants a return to the old mad free-for-all on to the field. But there are more than two options. Tell the crowd to wait ten minutes, then let them file on to the outfield to stand in front of the podium. The ECB has cut enough people out with its TV deal. In this small way, let's restore a grand tradition, and be inclusive.

Beware the sleeping dragon

Our article on betting in the Review section contains the staggering fact that the new internet betting exchanges now often take far more money on England Tests than they do on even the most important England football matches. This form of gambling is perfectly legal in Britain and pretty much unstoppable anywhere else the internet reaches. There is nothing intrinsically wrong with it either: betting adds spice to cricket, and exchange betting can be very spicy indeed. I am a participant, not a critic.

The figures can be extraordinary even for routine matches. The biggest exchange, Betfair, took more than £1m on the Essex–Glamorgan totesport League match last September. There was a reason for this: Glamorgan were already champions and fielding a weakened side; Essex were trying like mad to evade relegation. The shrewdies cleaned up over the internet, and in the betting shops of Cardiff. Nothing wrong with that, either.

But the line between that and the jiggery-pokery that came close to destroying international cricket a decade ago can be a thin one. And I suspect English cricket has not woken up to any of this. The ICC has an agreement with Betfair so that unusual betting patterns can be traced and potential match-fixing stamped on. The ECB has to be just as alert.

D'Oliveira for ever

A year ago I proposed in these Notes that Test matches between England and South Africa should have a permanent trophy to match the Ashes, the Wisden Trophy, the Border–Gavaskar and so on. I suggested naming it after Nelson Mandela. Instead, South Africa put up the Basil D'Oliveira Trophy, which was an infinitely more elegant and appropriate answer. Dolly is a son of the game, and of both nations.

The South African board said it was only for their home Tests, which would be meaningless. The series this winter showed yet again that when these two teams meet, they produce wonderful, well-fought contests (and also, let's say it again, that there is nothing in cricket, and few things in life, to beat a close five-Test series). The D'Oliveira Trophy should be at stake every time they meet.

Tempus fugit

In the Wanderers media centre, in the midst of the splendidly eventful January Test match between South Africa and England, I was passed one day by a familiar figure, bustling out of the TV commentary box, far too cross about something to say "Good morning". I did hear him say (to himself, I think) the words *"Extraordinary behaviour!"* in a voice reminiscent of Lady Bracknell or Bertie Wooster's Aunt Agatha.

Perhaps someone had put a mouse under his chair or uttered a profanity like "Darn!" or "Drat!" On November 24 this year, Ian Botham, the greatest tearaway ever to win the Ashes for England, will be 50. All England will be hoping the Ashes come back home before he gets there. In the meantime, go easy, Beefy. And welcome to middle age.

A Centennial Note

To return to Sydney Pardon – exactly a hundred years ago, he began his Editor's Notes for *Wisden 1905* as follows: "No serious matters of a controversial kind disturbed the cricket world during the past year." I thought about starting these Notes the same way. But then again, I thought not.

Cricket's Migrant Soul

ROBERT WINDER

The West Indies tour of England in the summer of 2004 was marked above all by an absence. There was a missing guest at the feast, and until the astonishing finale at The Oval, when the Champions Trophy ended in a raucous blare of trumpet and conch, it hovered over the summer like a rain cloud, or an elegy.

The sad fact, much remarked on by commentators, was that few of Britain's West Indians watched the games from the stands. At a time when Barbados and Antigua have become home matches for scarlet-faced Barmy foot-soldiers, the domestic venues were Caribbean-free. For atmosphere they relied on fancy dress: the grounds were alive with Elvis lookalikes, Heidi replicas, nuns and Vikings. The series felt like an extended rag week – there was none of the clamour that used to carry across the ocean the atmosphere of the tropics.

It could not be called a new phenomenon. After a noisy crescendo in the mid-1980s, the West Indian element in English stadiums has been dissolving for a generation. But now the silence was resounding: the exodus seemed complete. And it felt prompted by something more serious than a mere dip in the team's form. Form, as we are so often told, is temporary, and West Indies may rediscover it any day. But the evaporation of their English support felt deeper, like a permanent loss.

Some argued that the Caribbean game had been weakened by the Americanisation of the region, with its televised basketball, track-and-field scholarships and trim attention span. Perhaps the increasing disunity of the islands was generating a low-wattage team spirit, compared to the days when cricket was a rallying point for an archipelago of emerging nations. The poor form of the team certainly didn't help – who wanted to support such persistent losers? – but such fluctuations are hardly unusual. Just four years earlier, West Indies themselves had thrashed England in three days at Edgbaston to precipitate similar talk of England as a power in terminal decline.

So perhaps the answer lay not in the Caribbean but in England – in ticket prices that were too high for one of Britain's least affluent ethnic communities, or in the regulations mounted against the percussion for which West Indian fans were famous. Arguments such as these appealed to anyone who liked presuming that the establishment was barring the gate against colonial intruders. There was probably truth in all of these suggestions. And there were clues outside the game, too, in the social conditions that underpinned West Indian life in Britain.

The set text for such matters remains *Beyond a Boundary*, C. L. R. James's teasing assertion of cricket's importance in personal and national life. He

Setting the rhythm: West Indies supporters enjoy their team's first Test win in England, at Lord's in June 1950.

Picture by EMPICS

saw the game as an English pastime, designed to enact British virtues, but one that had been invaded and internalised by West Indians ("Eton or Harrow had nothing on us"). Excellence at cricket, he thought, could be an ennobling form of dissent, especially for liberated nations seeking fresh fields in which to excel. The thrill of outdoing the masters, on their own immaculate lawns, was extreme. When West Indies first won in England in 1950, Caribbean men danced in Piccadilly Circus. They didn't stop dancing for 40 years.

The Oval became a particular home-from-home. The pioneering migrants who crossed the Atlantic on the *Empire Windrush* in 1948 were sent to an underground shelter in Clapham, and directed to the Brixton Labour Exchange. So Lambeth, with The Oval at its heart, became a Caribbean locale. Would-be travellers could buy the *South London Press* on the harbour front in Kingston, Jamaica, just as they could buy *The Gleaner* on the Railton Road.

Cricket proved a vivid diversion for homesick migrants labouring in unfriendly factories and being cold-shouldered by colour-conscious landlords and employers. Those dreamy days at The Oval, with its exuberant orchestra of cans and bottles, the drumming and cheering, and the whiplash brilliance of the cricketers – if you closed your eyes you could almost have been back in Barbados. It was powerful medicine. In 1976, when Vivian Richards battered nearly three hundred runs across the parched brown outfield, the stands in front of the gasometers shook with West Indian glee.

THE CRICKET TEST...

The "cricket test", as applied to immigration, was invented (as little more than a throwaway line) in April 1990 by Norman Tebbit, the former Conservative minister and party chairman – improbably enough, in an interview with the *Los Angeles Times*. At the time Mr (now Lord) Tebbit was campaigning against unrestricted immigration from Hong Kong.

"A nation is a nation because of what it shares in common," he said, and complained that "a large proportion" of Britain's Asian population failed to pass his test. "Which side do they cheer for? It's an interesting test. Are you still harking back to where you came from, or where you are? And I think we've got real problems in that regard."

One of those who immediately rubbished the Tebbit argument was Tara Kumar Mukherjee, president of the Confederation of Indian Organizations (UK), who said: "Britain is our home and our first loyalty is to the UK. Politically, we are British, culturally we are Indian. Our job is to integrate into the British way of life without losing our Indian heritage. As to taking sides at cricket, Mr Tebbit should ask English settlers in Australia which side would they take when England is playing Test cricket."

...AND THE BOXING TEST

Despite its casual origins the Tebbit cricket test has an enduring power, especially to those offended by it. Baroness Amos, the Guyanese-born Leader of the House of Lords, attacked the idea when she gave a lecture in London on October 27, 2004, and came up with an alternative.

"I don't want to give Norman Tebbit's 'cricket test' any more credence by discussing it at length here," she said. "Suffice it to say that my two home teams ended up on the winning and the losing side in the recent one-day cricket final at The Oval.

"But let's face it, the 'cricket test' was never a question for Aussie cricket followers living in Britain… It was only for those of us supporting India, Pakistan, Sri Lanka, Bangladesh or the West Indies. It was about the loyalty of ethnic minorities to Britain. And it still depresses me that people give credit to it. Not least because it's such an incredibly 'un-British' test. Un-British because it just can't get past the colour of someone's skin.

"For me, 17-year-old Amir Khan [Britain's lightweight boxing silver medallist at the Athens 2004 Olympics] summed up the uniting of cultures on his return from Athens. He said: 'I'm Asian but I'm British – I was born here, I went to school here, all my mates are British and I'm proud to represent my country.' Call it the 'boxing test' if you like."

A generation later, there was hardly a Caribbean fan in sight to witness the capitulation of Brian Lara's 2004 team – just a few mournful elders staring into their drinks. Far from seeing cricket as a stage on which to swagger, today's black Britons saw cricket as a form of collusion or conformity. In media interviews, black spokesmen shrugged and said that cricket was simply not cool. And if you couldn't beat them, the saying seemed to go, then don't join them.

Added piquancy was given to the situation by the fact that, the following weekend, London's Afro-Caribbean population swayed through Notting Hill in a well-organised burst of migrant merry-making. The carnival was going strong, but cricket was neither invited nor included. The old idea that cricket was a West Indian game invented by the English had never seemed more like an anachronism.

The same can be said of some of the arguments surrounding the subject. In the many debates about Britain's West Indians, the fact that they are not "West Indian" is sometimes overlooked. They are British. They may be black, but they are no longer Caribbean. They sink or swim in the football-loving mainstream. There are many times more West Indian-descended sportsmen in football's Premiership than in county cricket. So it may not be a matter of them being too proud to endure the recent failures – on the contrary, they may not be West Indian enough.

> The disappearance of the West Indian fan is a commercial and cultural loss

History has installed them in a place where cricket has rarely gripped: in England's inner cities, where there are few pitches, fewer coaches, and enough racial animosity to lower anyone's spirits. That all is not well can be seen at a glance. In 2002, only 30% of Caribbean-descended children achieved five GCSE passes at school, against a national average of 51%, with 64% for the Indian community and 73% for the Chinese.

Television hates inert audiences: that is why it sponsors boundary placards and prizes for joke banners, and why its cameras seek out the wildest cheerleaders. So the disappearance of the West Indian fan is a commercial as well as a cultural loss. It is an especially keen setback for England fans. Not long ago, in the heyday of Clive Lloyd's fast-bowling quartets, they could look forward to a home-grown Holding or Marshall of their own. The size and fervour of the migrant population made it seem inevitable. More than a dozen players of Anglo-Caribbean descent have played Test cricket for England since Roland Butcher paved the way 24 years ago, but in the 1990s the flood slowed to a trickle, and now that appears to have dried up.

The English have a soft spot for narratives of decline, but it might be misleading to wonder, in the case of West Indian cricket, how far the mighty have fallen. The real surprise is that the team rose so high, that such a small and poor archipelago should have produced as many superlative sides as they did. In the years after liberation, cricket was the fortunate beneficiary of a brilliant flowering: the invincibles of Sobers, Lloyd and Richards were

And the beat goes on: in 1984 West Indian supporters are still celebrating. This time it's a 5–0 blitz.

Picture by Patrick Eagar

ruthless, athletic, haughty, joyful, violent and charismatic. It was a rare, perhaps unrepeatable, eruption of cricket energy.

In this light, it is no surprise that the spirit of cricket, its centre of gravity, should have moved on. Cricket has always had a migrant soul: the flame has been carried from country to country, from continent to continent, sometimes by rare individuals (Ranjitsinhji, D'Oliveira, Constantine) and sometimes by larger demographic commotions. No one should expect it to start standing still now.

Cricket – English cricket, at any rate – has often liked to portray itself as a reservoir of eternal verities, mostly of a rustic sort: the sound of willow on leather, the smell of mown grass, the splash of applause for an incoming batsman, the lethal rattle of bails, the aroma of cigars and the murmur of the crowd at Lord's. Modern cricket is changing rapidly, however, and supposedly stable qualities such as these – along with the imperial proposal that cricket is a byword for fair play and gentlemanly rectitude – are losing their hold. The game is shorter; crowds are noisier; run-rates are rising; fielding is more agile; and the umpire's decision is no longer final. These telling amendments may be symptoms of a deeper realignment. Beneath the local fluctuations and the press of modern marketing we can detect an insistent thrum.

This is only the latest in a sequence of such commotions. It is barely necessary to remind ourselves of cricket history in this of all publications, but to recap: the game matured in 18th-century Britain, and was escorted across the seas by imperial travellers and troops, who found it well-suited to hot climates and a stirring colonial pageant, fragrant with reminders of home. In Calcutta, Melbourne, Barbados and Cape Town, it became an emblem of British power: a calling, almost a vocation.

Wherever the game took root, it gained fresh accents or tendencies. Like a rare seedling transplanted into richer soils, it flowered in surprising ways, acquiring a subtle set of local characteristics which became, in the end, national clichés. West Indies brought free-flowing, beach-cricket euphoria and supernatural fast bowling. India contributed dextrous batsmen and guileful spinners. Pakistan gave us haughty and temperamental virtuosi, while Australia and South Africa continued to stand for a tough and busy approach – cricket as a white-knuckle virility test.

It wasn't always a question of sheer novelty: emerging nations often gave new life to old precepts. New Zealand aspired to an all-for-one team ethic that would have brought tears to the eyes of a Victorian Brigadier. The intimidating bowling of Clive Lloyd's West Indians was a new and improved version of Bodyline. And the shimmering strokeplay of the Sri Lankans who won the 1996 World Cup had distinct Caribbean echoes – Calypso cricket bathed in coconut milk. It has been a constant process of refreshment and renewal, and it is still going on today.

So what next? Unusually, it isn't hard to say. Cricket feels overwhelmingly an Indian sport – played by Indian players, cherished by Indian fans, spread by the Indian diaspora, administered by Indian magnates, and financed by Indian eyeballs, by the scale of the television audience in the subcontinent itself.

And the subcontinent is a historic engine of migration. The resulting diaspora is carrying the flame all over the world – even into cricket's proudest heartlands. There are now two dozen British Asian players in county cricket, compared to the remaining handful of Caribbean descent.

Quite why Britain's Indian and Pakistani children should have remained faithful to cricket, at a time when their West Indian compatriots have lapsed, is one of those questions to which there can be no simple answer. It could be to do with the fabled discipline of family life in these communities, or to the more energetic and alluring nationalisms at play in Delhi and Karachi. It may be simply that these are, to a greater extent than the West Indies, sporting monocultures where cricket has few rivals. (Unlike the other Test-playing nations, India, Pakistan and Sri Lanka make only a small dent in other sporting arenas.) Or it might be that the wider circumstances of life in Britain have proved helpful.

It is often said, by those unsympathetic to the idea of large-scale immigration, that immigrants should strive to "fit in" (when in Rome...). But the opposite may also be true – those who assimilate the least can end up fitting in as smoothly as anyone. Indian and Pakistani families in Britain have imported their own culture (religion, language, food and manners) with more enthusiasm and resolve than Caribbean peoples, whose heritage has in any case long since been fractured by slavery. The social and commercial trajectory of Indian and Pakistani life in Britain has also been more conducive to self-sufficiency: the corner shops and restaurants have grown into retail dynasties. All of which translates into an Indian, or subcontinental, ability to sustain themselves as independent enclaves, with their own priorities and tastes – including cricket.

Whatever the causes, the symptoms are inescapable. It only takes a brief look at *Wisden's* smallest print – at the entries for universities, schools and youth cricket – to see the vitality of Asian-inspired cricket. And a look at the Round the World section will reveal that this is a phenomenon extending to the furthest corners of the cricketing map. It even extends to the West Indies itself: more than half the Under-19 team that reached their World Cup final in 2004 were of Asian descent.

It goes without saying that the keepers of cricket's flame have the power to change it. Under English sovereignty the watchword was restraint. The West Indian influence rendered it a more vivacious and frightening affair: an ecstatic bullring. Under Indian guidance it may become more raucous still, and shorter. Whatever the consequences, cricket's torchbearers are now Asian. The game's migratory reflexes have carried us a long way.

Robert Winder is the author of Bloody Foreigners: The Story of Immigration to Britain (*Little, Brown*).

ENGLAND'S REVIVAL (1)

The Only Way Was Up

MIKE SELVEY

Spooky, isn't it, how, quite out of the blue, a tune can capture the moment? Just like that. So sitting there, as you do, pondering the vagaries of English cricket over the past couple of decades, suddenly, over the airwaves from a golden oldies radio station comes the sound of the Tremeloes from 1967 telling us that "Even The Bad Times Are Good". Then, blow me, if not ten minutes later, there are the Mamas and Papas making the pertinent observation that the darkest hour is in fact just before dawn.

Most English cricket followers have grown used to the notion that the darkest hour so far comes before an even darker one. They have become natural pessimists, with much to be pessimistic about. Clouds do not have silver linings: they build up into whopping great anvil-tops and it rains even harder. We glimpse the light down the tunnel and see only a freight train coming the other way. Glass half-full? Not on your life, someone has drunk the lot.

But it is not true. The bad times were good in their own way. Sometimes the failures actually dictated that events took a turn for the better. Serendipity: the discovery of new and pleasant things through chance.

Take, for instance, an incident at Lord's in early July 1981. The First Test against Australia has been lost, and the Second is sliding out of reach when England's champion is bowled, for his second nought in the game, and stomps off through the silent seething hostility of the Long Room, his captaincy in its death throes. That was indeed a dark hour, but it precipitated one of the most uplifting renaissances in cricket history. If Ian Botham's leadership was lying in the gutter at that stage, then as with Oscar Wilde, his career was looking at the stars.

And has English cricket, in all its years, sunk to the depths it managed in the latter 1980s, when in successive seasons England were trounced at home by West Indies and then gave up the Ashes with scarcely a whimper, to live only in hope of regaining them ever since?

Now, 1988 was a shocker. First came the infamous Rothley Romps, leading to tabloid revelations of high jinks, bare bums and barmaids at a Leicestershire hotel that resulted in the England captain Mike Gatting being sacked – although that was probably an expedient for Lord's officials who regretted not disciplining him for the previous winter's finger-wagging contest with Shakoor Rana at Faisalabad.

The trouble was, there was nowhere to go. The chairman of selectors Peter May dithered, appointing first of all John Emburey and then his own godson Chris Cowdrey. Finally though, from it all, emerged a man who was to lead

In a corner: David Gower faces the press at Old Trafford in 1989.

Picture by Patrick Eagar

by example and begin the process of instilling some backbone into the establishment. Graham Gooch, forgiven for his rebel forays to South Africa, led only briefly before David Gower got the job back, but the future was there.

First, though, came 1989, which was probably an even worse year without being lightened by barmaid stories. The nadir came at Old Trafford when David Boon swept the runs that regained the Ashes for Australia. Immediately prior to that came the news that a significant number of the England side had decided to abandon Test cricket and instead, under the leadership of the disgruntled Gatting, partake in another unofficial money-spinner to South Africa.

But the game has an immune system. Earlier that year, Angus Fraser, a future stalwart, had made his debut and became the first England bowler to dismiss Steve Waugh in a Test that summer, after he had scored a mere 393 runs in the series. After the defections, in came Mike Atherton. The end of the Ashes campaign brought with it the termination of Gower's captaincy and the appointment of Gooch once more, to take the side to the Caribbean, a cricketing war zone.

The response was a resounding win in the First Test at Jamaica, and the debuts of two more future captains in Nasser Hussain and Alec Stewart. Thus, from the carnage and probably even because of it, in the space of eight months, the careers had begun of four players who were to play 390 Tests, and captain England 114 times.

Gooch's period in charge lasted until a doleful resignation at Headingley in 1993 after the Ashes had once more been conceded to Australia. But if the cricket had brought only occasional shafts of sunlight, then he had brought some stability, and a boot-camp sense of discipline as a counterpoint to the laissez-faire that had preceded him. The ethos was changing.

Not that Atherton found it easy going. The next West Indies tour brought with it another failure, including the infamous 46 all out at Trinidad – although the consolation victory in Bridgetown, West Indies' first defeat there for 59 years, was an important milestone. Two winters later, South Africa ultimately proved too much on their home pitches, although Atherton's personal achievement in saving the game at the Wanderers was arguably Test cricket's greatest rearguard innings. The captain's relationship with Ray Illingworth, England's first supremo, was fractious, Illingworth being unable to translate his captaincy skills to management. England cricket at the highest level still lacked focus, and after a disastrous World Cup in 1996, Illingworth was replaced with the enthusiastic David Lloyd and, a year later, a more self-effacing chairman of selectors in David Graveney.

If another nadir was reached that winter in Zimbabwe (what has become known as the "we flippin' murdered 'em tour" after Lloyd's over-excited match report on a draw) then, in the background, the English game was about to undergo a fundamental overhaul that over the next eight years was to transform the way that the England team was regarded. The old TCCB, which once ran the game with a staff of a dozen, was replaced in 1997 by a far more elaborate operation, with

> England were still a metaphor for humiliating failure

a chief executive, Tim Lamb, and a high-profile chairman, Lord MacLaurin, the chairman of Tesco. MacLaurin viewed the England side as the shop window of the game, and its principal earner. Energies, he decided, should be diverted into maximising this to the benefit of everyone else.

England players were offered status not previously accorded them (beginning with the seemingly insignificant gesture of single rooms on tour). Lloyd and Atherton were given the forerunners of the backroom staff that surround the current national side. Counties were told that the England team – Team England as it came to be known – was to be prioritised.

But it was out of the depths of yet another crisis that the England team finally rose to the surface without sinking yet again. Stewart had been given the captaincy when Atherton resigned following another Caribbean failure, in 1997-98. But he never looked secure and, after England's miserable home World Cup in 1999, was replaced by the brooding, volcanic, Hussain. Immediately, a loss to New Zealand at home relegated England to the status of the world's worst team in the then unofficial Wisden World Championship. The boos that were directed at the new captain as he stood on the Oval balcony were merely a reflection of public derision: despite all the changes, the team was still a metaphor for humiliating failure.

Before Duncan Fletcher was appointed Lloyd's successor that summer, Hussain had never met him – which was lucky, because they might never have got on. But together, Hussain's volatility and drive and Fletcher's understated organisation and single-mindedness pulled England from the quagmire. Fletcher's ideas began to get credence and support. He wanted control over his players and it came in the form of central contracts, the argument in favour reinforced by previous failures. Today's England players regard themselves as just that, and it has transformed the way they play. Under the new captain Michael Vaughan, fitness has been taken to a new level.

Last summer's surprises were nearly all happy ones. Given a fair wind and fitness, the year might have finished successfully enough for England, with Hussain retiring at the end, and a hatful of runs for Mark Butcher and Graham Thorpe. Happenstance again interfered. A freak injury to Vaughan before the First Test brought a debut century for Andrew Strauss, and precipitated Hussain's departure in a blaze of glory.

A couple of bizarre injuries to Butcher let in Rob Key, who responded with a double-century. Finally, an injury to Thorpe gave Ian Bell his chance to make runs. Maybe in an ideal world, each would have been a triumph of selection rather than chance. But, with England, we take what we can get – and hope that all these signs of brightness really do constitute the dawn.

Mike Selvey has been cricket correspondent of The Guardian *since 1987, through thick and (more often) thin. He played three Tests for England, but they failed to win any of them.*

ENGLAND'S REVIVAL (2)

Goodbye Gin and Tonic: an Insider's View

Malcolm Ashton

Ten summers ago I was minding my own business, scoring for BBC TV alongside Ray Illingworth as summariser. Ray was then yanked out of the chair to become the England team "supremo". His power extended to picking his own backroom team for the 1995-96 tour to South Africa, and he asked me to join him as the official scorer.

He chose me simply because he knew me. The Illingworth reign was a brief one, but I managed to last for almost a decade, in which time my job was reinvented twice, and the entire management structure became wholly unrecognisable. The change behind the scenes has been vital in England's transformation into a competitive cricket team, and I was lucky enough to watch it happen, and play a bit-part role.

In hindsight, the Illingworth era marked the beginnings of the transformation, in that Ray had far more control over the playing side than previous managers. But in other respects, he ran things very much the old-fashioned way. Motivation? Three lions on the sweater should be motivation enough. Sports psychologist? They did without when he was playing. I was just an old-fashioned scorer, and the only pre-tour briefing I received was: "There may be some accounting work to do as well."

Illingworth and the captain, Mike Atherton, confined tactics and strategy to the evenings where, over a game of bridge, battle plans would be drawn up, accounts juggled, baggage sorted and disputes settled while Illingworth and Atherton took me and the team doctor to the cleaners. No fuss.

But very soon the notion of what a scorer did on tour began to change. I quickly took on the role of baggage-master, which is what the famous touring scorers of old, like Bill Ferguson and George Duckworth, also did. And with Bob Bennett in the West Indies in 1997-98, I devised a new system (which may be my most lasting legacy) of giving each player a baggage number – with the captain always No. 1 – so it was much easier to ensure the right bag went to the right room.

By my fourth tour, to Australia in 1998-99, Graham Gooch was the manager and David Lloyd the coach, and I found myself propelled into doing an entirely different job. Goochy didn't know me at the start and he was very circumspect. It was supposed to be a traditional tour, with Goochy in charge and Bumble underneath him. But the role of the coach was increasing all the time, and it was the playing side that interested Goochy, rather than the paperwork. So once he came to trust me, I ended up doing a lot of the routine

Tools of the trade: Malcolm Ashton analyses play at Lord's in 2002.

Picture by Patrick Eagar

administrative chores. Some players even started calling me "Manage". It wasn't acrimonious between manager and coach, though it was a bit confusing.

By the next winter, back in South Africa, this problem had been sorted out. The new team of Duncan Fletcher and Phil Neale had taken over and it soon became permanent. The coach was now in charge, not the administrator. So the overlap was between Phil's duties and mine. Phil won't delegate, and if I was getting up at 4.45 to supervise the bags for an early departure, he would insist on doing the same, which was stupid. But there's no job in the world he's more suited for, because he is an absolute master of detail, and I'm full of admiration for him. He's Mr Spreadsheet. I've seen him sit on the bus in the middle of winter, turn to Duncan and say: "Edgbaston, June 14. When do you want to practise, morning or afternoon?" The reply came, very slowly: "Phil... I... don't... care." Of course he would do eventually, but not in December.

So I was mainly back to just scoring again, because Phil was doing most of the baggage and all the accounts. My presence as scorer was still not universally popular back home. The county scorers, who had regarded an overseas tour as a perk just as a player might, had been upset by the appointment of an "outsider" right from the start, and even threatened to strike. I'm sure their grudge was against the board rather than me, though there was a very unpleasant incident at Hove where one scorer gave me a right bollocking in the umpires' room for taking the job, and I had to ask him if he wanted to continue the discussion outside. This was a stomach ache that never went away: every year there was a charade of the scorer's position being decided by interview, and every year I would get it.

But here we were in the new millennium, and county scoring had been computerised since 1993, and England were still using pen and paper, which felt a little strange. But at Chandigarh in 2001, Fletcher called me in and offered me a new job. He had watched what had happened in Australia, where John Buchanan had placed a lot of reliance on computer technology, and the scorer Mike Walsh had moved over to become the analyst. Now I was asked to do the same.

Actually, analyst is a misnomer. It should be called "logger". I sat down at the computer with special software that allowed me to get a picture from the TV output on to my laptop. I'd start it at the beginning of every run-up and stop it when the ball went dead. Before the next delivery I would then have to input the length of the ball (bouncer, short-pitched, back of a length, good length, full, yorker), the direction (leg side, on the stumps, in the channel or off side), the type of shot played, where the ball went and how many runs.

> **We'd never show them taking a wicket**

This would be used in two ways. I'd copy it on to a DVD so the players could pick out anything they wanted to see – all the bouncers from Bowler A, for instance. Then before a Test I would spend five or six hours putting together a Powerpoint presentation for Duncan to show the squad.

There was a formula for this. I'd collate all the fours and sixes we'd hit, and put music to it just to give the meeting an upbeat feel at the start. Then we'd show their batsmen and then their bowlers, in real time and slow motion. We'd always concentrate on the positive: we'd never show them taking a wicket.

This meant I wasn't doing any scoring at all: we began relying on local people, recommended by the home association. This worked very well, actually, especially in Asia where they are always very good. It's in places like New Zealand where they might make a pig's ear of things. But I did like to keep an eye on what was happening, and wherever we were, I would always take responsibility for Duckworth/Lewis calculations. Just in case.

Under Fletcher the whole of what came to be called "Team England" realised we had to be more professional, and up with the best. We couldn't just rely on good old skill and judgment. And he recognised what a tool computers could be. The analyst's job meant I was doing Tests at home as well as on tour, which worked out well for me, because the BBC had lost the ECB contract. But once again Australia were leading the way, and the next move wasn't such good news. Having appointed Mike Walsh at first, Australia decided that an assistant coach would be better employed hitting the keyboard as well as coaching. And the same happened to me. Duncan wanted an additional coach, and there was no money for an analyst as well. Fair dos: they gave me virtually 12 months' notice, but you'll forgive me being sceptical about whether a coach really wants to spend the match doing what I did.

All these regimes were very different: Raymond laid-back; Bumble always up and down; Duncan giving nothing away. He could be exasperating – you could work four hours on a presentation and he'd just say "We're not having a meeting" and that would be it, no apology or anything. But I've had some hilarious nights with him, and his was the most exhilarating era because you could sense everything coming right.

Managing a national cricket team is now a full-time occupation. Gone are the days when the tour manager was there as some kind of reward, appointed to play the ambassadorial role, dispense the gin and tonics, smooth the team's way through customs and sort out the occasional diplomatic shemozzle. Nowadays, the management team forms an integral part of the DNA of the side. For ten years I did my own small bit, formed one strand of that DNA if you like, and I loved almost all of it. I can't let go, and I've found myself texting Tim Boon on tour every day. This is my first winter home in ten years, and it's cold.

Malcolm Ashton was BBC TV scorer for home Tests from 1989 to 1999. He was England's winter tour scorer, and then analyst, between 1995 and 2004.

The Man Who Made Cricket Glow

RICHIE BENAUD

Keith Miller's statistics – a Test bowling average just under 23, a batting average just below 37 – are maybe those of a very good cricketer, but not a great one. Those who look at them, examine them closely and then give something of a wave of the hand, miss the point in the way some people now dismiss Victor Trumper. Trumper's batting average is ordinary compared to those who spent vastly more time at the crease, but much less time enthralling, entertaining, bemusing and imprinting themselves on the minds of cricket followers.

It was the same with Miller. In 1946 *Wisden* named him as the fastest bowler seen in England the previous summer. The war had just ended and the Victory Tests were played, and Miller was outstanding for the Australian Services' team with his prodigious hitting and innovative pace bowling. He became an overnight star in England, as he was to be in Australia after he returned and resumed playing Sheffield Shield. He became Australia's greatest all-round cricketer. To that you can add that he was also a much-loved character in both countries. His passing, on October 11, 2004, was an occasion for some sadness, but also for much raising of glasses to a man who captivated lovers of the game, not because of his statistics, but because he made cricket glow.

Miller was a one-off. I saw no one else in the time he played in Australian cricket who managed to be a great cricketer and a star at the same time. And that was without television, which began in Australia in 1956, the year he retired.

Everyone has heroes. Bradman was my first because, as a small boy, I listened on the giant-sized radio in Jugiong as he captained Australia and turned around a 0–2 deficit to a 3–2 victory in the 1936-37 Ashes series. Then Grimmett, because I saw him take six for 118 at the SCG in the first Sheffield Shield match I ever watched. After them it was Miller who, when playing for the Services against New South Wales, hit 105 off an attack which included Bill O'Reilly. Miller remained the hero even when I played in the same NSW and Australian side with him.

I was able to watch him at close quarters for the last six years of his career, and there were four things about him: skill, unpredictability, kindness and charisma. His skill, even when standing languidly at slip, was the reason young people do have heroes. As a batsman he made full use of his height and reach for the drive off both front and back foot. No one hit the ball harder. That didn't preclude him from the most delicate late cutting.

That mixture of grace and power was also the essence of his often devastating bowling. Miller's action was close to flawless, consisting of a wonderful delivery stride from a short run-up, his left arm high while looking

Majestic: Keith Miller in full flow for the Australians against the Duke of Norfolk's XI, at Arundel in April 1956.

Picture by Getty Images

over his left shoulder. He always had his bowling hand going in a full sweep past his front knee. He was genuinely fast, but also unorthodox in his thinking, always trying to stay two steps ahead of the batsmen. He had studied the art of swing by watching George Pope of Derbyshire and England, and there was no one who learned it better than Miller. With either bat or ball in hand, his thoughts were always attacking, a role model for any youngster watching either from the dressing-room or the Sydney Hill.

His approach to some matters, however, was less orthodox. In 1955-56, we twice played South Australia, the first time at the SCG and the second at the Adelaide Oval. In the Sydney match, Miller won the toss and then, bored with proceedings late in the day, closed our innings at 215 for eight. The South Australian openers successfully appealed against the light and "Nugget" was livid as he left the field. Also in our team was Peter Philpott. Like Miller, he lived in Manly, and Miller gave him a lift to the ground each morning. A few hours after that declaration, Miller's wife Peg gave birth to son Bob.

After a few celebratory drinks it was no wonder he was running late for the ground the next morning, and only remembered Philpott, standing on the Manly street corner, as he was speeding over the Harbour Bridge. Miller did a quick Jack Brabham U-turn, which was possible on the Bridge 50 years ago, and arrived at the SCG as I very slowly, and rather reluctantly, leading the team on to the field in his absence. Somehow, he and Philpott made it in time, whereupon Miller, from the Paddington End, proceeded to take seven for 12 to bowl out South Australia for 27.

Twenty-five days later, in Adelaide, South Australia won the toss and batted. It was an action-replay of Sydney with Miller bowling so superbly that they were five down for 31, with left-hander Tim Colley, making his debut, yet to face a ball. Three wickets and 30 times past the outside edge were enough for Keith, and he decided the crowd should have a bit more batting entertainment. He had a casual look around the field and waved to Norman O'Neill, who was also making his Sheffield Shield debut.

"Come and have a bowl, Normie, Colley hasn't faced a ball in Shield cricket."

"I've never bowled one, Nug."

"Should be a good contest!"

It was an interesting debut for both of them. Colley made 57 but only played three games in his career, O'Neill didn't take a wicket and made a duck, then became one of Australia's finest batsmen. Miller was an outstanding captain, the finest never to have captained Australia in an era where speech-making and public relations sometimes rated above all else with the aptly named Australian Board of Control.

But his kindness was overwhelming. It covered everyone from those in prominent places to the guy who worked at the fishmonger's stall down the road from where he lived in London. Others away from sport were recipients: people he knew in both England and Australia who might have been down on their luck, or simply having a bad trot. It extended as well to young cricketers trying to make a way in the sporting world, and it was my personal good fortune to have as mentors Miller and his two great friends, Arthur Morris and Ray Lindwall. For me, it was priceless luck that those three were there when I started in cricket.

He was sentimental too. Eight years ago I asked Nugget about the Victory Tests played when the war had just finished. The matches were fun, but sad as well because of those who weren't able to be there. He told me about one of the players, Graham Williams, the tall, broad-shouldered, bustling pace bowler, who was in the side having just been repatriated from a German prison camp after being shot down during the Libyan campaign. Williams had been four years in the camp and had spent most of that time teaching Braille to fellow prisoners, also to Germans blinded by the war.

Williams, as he walked slowly out to bat on the Lord's ground, looked around at the 30,000 spectators, most of whom had read his harrowing story in the newspapers and heard it on the wireless over the past few days. He was still tall but there was nothing broad-shouldered about Williams that day. He was gaunt. Miller said he would never forget that instant when Williams came out to bat. Thirty thousand rose to their feet and clapped softly from the moment he appeared until the moment he reached the centre of the ground. The only sound to be heard was that soft, unbroken applause.

Stepping out: a suave Miller arrives at a Chelsea function, 1956.

Picture by Getty Images

"It was the most touching thing I have ever seen or heard, almost orchestral in its sound and feeling. Whenever I think of it, tears still come to my eyes."

It was on that same ground, in 1956, that Keith had his greatest match during a series which eventually produced more joy for Jim Laker and England than Australia. With Ray Lindwall and Alan Davidson injured and Pat Crawford, Lindwall's replacement, breaking down in his fifth over, Miller and Ron Archer had to do the fast-bowling job with the assistance of medium-pacer Ken Mackay. Everyone played a part in the match but Miller, aged 36, was simply magnificent. He bowled 70 overs from the Pavilion End and took ten for 152, one of the finest fast-bowling performances I have ever seen. He loved Lord's and he did it proud that day.

But it didn't matter whether he was in the action or not. He made the game come alive simply by being on the field. It is a rare gift. That is charisma, and that was Keith Miller.

Richie Benaud played 63 Tests for Australia, 22 of them in the same team as Keith Miller. He has been present at more than 500 Tests, believed to be a world record, and remains chief commentator for both Channel 4 in the UK and Channel 9 in Australia.

THE TV EXECUTIVE'S DECISION IS FINAL (1)

The Power of Babel

MIHIR BOSE

A curious thing happened during the Champions Trophy final between England and West Indies at The Oval last summer. At various times during the match the scoreboard flashed messages in Sanskrit, an Indian language as dead as Latin. The Sanskrit words are part of the logo of Bharat Petroleum, an Indian oil company using the occasion to advertise to the audience back home, in the country that now provides 60% of world cricket's income.

Every second person watching cricket anywhere in the world is an Indian, and major cricket tournaments like the Champions Trophy or the World Cup could not exist without being sold to an Indian TV company. India is the classic case of the fat man inside a thin man trying to get out. Most of its population still lead lives only marginally changed by the passing centuries, but another 300 million of the 1.1 billion now count as middle-class. Most are not rich by western standards, but the sheer weight of numbers gives them phenomenal purchasing power. Cricket, particularly one-day cricket, is the great marketing tool for companies to reach them. Hence Sanskrit words flashed on the Oval scoreboard on a September afternoon.

The rise of the Indian television juggernaut is one of the great untold stories of cricket. In 1977, when the last major revolution in cricket took place, led by the Australian magnate Kerry Packer, India had barely entered the television age. There were fewer than 700,000 sets in a country whose population was already over 600 million: barely one per thousand. All that was  on offer was the state channel, Doordarshan, showing programmes about as professional and entertaining as those available in the Soviet bloc. Not a single ball of cricket had ever been televised in India.

Today there are still remote villages where people will gather to watch the one communal TV set: a flickering screen powered by an unreliable generator. But the *pan* shops, offering betel nuts and crackly radio commentary, now have competition from smart restaurants, often with large screens. And 80 million homes, containing maybe a third of the population, have their own sets. The 1977 schism came about because the Australian Cricket Board refused to consider Packer's offer of $US3.25m to show five years of cricket in Australia. In the autumn of 2004 Zee TV offered $308m for four years of cricket in India: a hundred times as much. Inflation cannot entirely explain this away.

Various factors came together to produce this explosion. By coincidence, they reached a critical mass together. The turning-point was 1991, when changes in cricket were matched by changes in society. That year, under pressure from the World Bank, India was forced to open up its economy and allow foreign investment into what had been one of the most protected markets on the planet. It was the year of the first Gulf War; suddenly Indians learned it was possible to follow world events on television rather than just through newspapers and cinema newsreels.

And that was also when cricket at last became one family: South Africa, having shed its apartheid past, was readmitted into the game and finally played a non-white country, launching its rebirth with a one-day series in India. That historic tour made the Indian board realise it had television rights, which it could sell. Before that, Doordarshan had televised big games within India but, far from paying anything, it had often demanded fees from the board to cover the cost of production.

Now two South African channels wanted to show the games. Amrit Mathur, an official who worked for then Indian board president Madhavrao Scindia, recalls: "We had to find out first who owned the rights and then how much

they were worth." Mathur discovered that they belonged to the Indian board, and that they were surprisingly valuable. So as South Africa realised what it is to play against someone outside the white commonwealth, the Indians realised that they were sitting on a goldmine.

They might never have dug for it but for the intervention of one man. Mark Mascarenhas, a Bangalore boy who went to live in Connecticut, was convinced cricket could make big money. He bought the rights for the 1996 World Cup held in the subcontinent, and guaranteed $10m to the host countries; he delivered $30m. At the time seasoned broadcasters thought Mascarenhas was mad. Hardly – he also became Sachin Tendulkar's agent and a big power in the game before his death in a car crash in 2002. And the Indian board's profits, as they ruthlessly commercialised the World Cup, enabled every major cricket ground in the country to be equipped with floodlights.

This was the turning-point for TV rights in general, and India in particular. By 1996 India had also gone from two channels to fifty, provided by more than 60,000 cable operators. Now there are 200 channels, and this Babel makes it easier to watch cricket, and even English football, than it is in England; I have watched Tottenham play Manchester City, a fixture not shown live at home, on a Saturday night in Darjeeling.

The government could not control this situation on the ground: there was no organised road digging, as in Britain or the USA – the companies just flung the wires over treetops and verandahs. They could not control the situation in the sky either, and two global media giants were now crucial players: Rupert Murdoch and the Disney Corporation. Murdoch owned Star, the Asian equivalent of Sky, and Disney had the sports channel ESPN. At first they competed furiously, then formed a curious and interesting alliance. They started a joint venture company called ESPN Star Sports and decided not to bid against each other, effectively carving up the cricket market. They

Street cricket: a pavement outside a New Delhi television showroom draws crowds for an India–Pakistan game.

Picture by Prakash Singh, AFP/Getty Images

continued to run their own separate sports channels, broadcast from Singapore, but divided up Indian cricket between them.

They have little else in common. ESPN remains a specialist sports channel, while Star is now the No. 1 TV company in India. Its programme *Who Wants to be a Crorepati?* (Who wants ten million rupees?), modelled on the UK's *Who Wants to be a Millionaire?* and hosted by the Bollywood star Amitabh Bachchan, is the country's most popular show. Doordarshan is still in the market and showed India's games from 1999 to 2003, paying $55m. To an extent this mirrored the triangular cricket television market in England in which the BBC, Channel 4 and Sky have all been regarded as potential bidders.

In Britain it makes a big difference to the audience who gets the rights, as each station has its own style, and Sky's coverage is still received by a minority. In India the audience is largely indifferent to which channel is showing the game. But the TV companies are not, and in 2000 the picture changed dramatically when another outfit, which had previously shown no interest, made the biggest bid cricket has ever seen.

The story of Zee TV is one of those extraordinary and very Indian tales. Its founder, Subhas Chandra, started making cooking oil when he was 19 and then earned money exporting grain to Russia. In 1992, a year after India opened up its markets, he set up Zee, funded by money from the Indian diaspora. For eight years Zee concentrated on films, sitcoms and the like. But in the summer of 2000, when the ICC met in Paris to allocate world rights for the 2003 and 2007

World Cups and other tournaments, Zee tabled the biggest bid in the history of the game: $660m, $110m more than the group backed by Rupert Murdoch.

Cricket decided to play safe. Murdoch seemed a more solid bet than Chandra, and the lower bid was accepted. Three years later, there was another surprising Indian intervention. This was from Sony, which for some years had been running a general entertainment channel with occasional forays into cricket, but now bid nearly $230m for the Indian rights for the 2003 and 2007 World Cups, an amazing amount given that the Murdoch company, the Global Communications Corporation, had struggled to sell coverage elsewhere. Outside India, the 2003 Cup was mainly on Murdoch-owned stations.

Sony showed the 2003 World Cup on its Max channel. With many of the top commentators contracted to ESPN Star, they had to bring in a relatively untried bunch of ex-cricketers, and the doyen, Sunil Gavaskar, had to spend

the World Cup broadcasting from a flat in Cape Town. Sony's chief executive, Kunal Dasgupta, was very clear about the logic of his bid: "Cricket is the only product in India which unites the whole country, north, south, east, west. It transcends class, religion, regional and language differences. You do not require words to explain Sachin Tendulkar or Rahul Dravid."

Sony Max

Just as Murdoch had used Premier League football in England to drive the sales of satellite dishes, and attract the free-spending young males who so delight advertisers, so Sony was using cricket. The same thought inspired Zee in the autumn of 2004, when the Indian Board began auctioning the rights for the next four years of international cricket. After a complex series of manoeuvres, Zee emerged on top with that bid of $308m, easily trumping ESPN Star, Doordarshan and Sony. But the tender document had said the rights would only go to a broadcaster that broadcasts cricket, which Zee so far has not. The case ended up in the Supreme Court, which in February 2005 ruled 3–2 against Zee, meaning the process had to start again. Sources inside the Indian board admit that it started the negotiations too late, and messed things up both strategically and legally. As a result, the Australian tour last autumn was almost blacked out.

Even more competitors could soon be on the scene: Ten, best-known as a company producing cricket broadcasts for other networks, has its own channel. In contrast to Britain, where TV rights may now remain with the same company for ever, all things are possible. Except, perhaps, order.

On the one hand, India's cricketers are the country's greatest stars. Individually and as a team, they are on TV adverts the whole time endorsing all the consumer products of the new India. Yet the game is still run in a chaotic and often inept manner. To that extent, India hasn't changed at all.

Mihir Bose is sports correspondent of the Daily Telegraph. *His 1986 book on Indian cricket,* A Maidan View, *is being revised and reissued this summer under the title* The Magic of Indian Cricket *(Taylor & Francis).*

THE TV EXECUTIVE'S DECISION IS FINAL (2)

Hello Sky, Goodbye World

STEVEN BARNETT

While cricket supporters reputedly jammed the England and Wales Cricket Board switchboard to vent their anger over the decision to move English Test cricket off Channel 4 and on to satellite television, the trade magazine *Broadcast* had a rather different angle. Its response to the news was headlined "C4's cricket loss frees 200 hours". For independent television producers and Channel 4's commissioning editors – not to mention its finance director – this was definitely not a bad-news story.

From the summer of 2006, not a single ball of live Test cricket will be available to viewers on free-to-air terrestrial television, for the first time in 60 years. This loss of mass exposure will without doubt have unfortunate consequences for promoting cricket amongst young and less devoted followers. The ECB decided to trade coverage for cash on the basis that this would not be for ever, and that when the next deal starts in 2010, cricket could again be widely available. This misunderstands the nature of the broadcasting world.

Dawn of the television age: wrapped up against the unseasonal August weather, cameramen record the 1946 England v India Test at The Oval.

Picture by Getty Images

When the ECB explained its reasoning – and in particular Channel 4's inability to match the four-year package of £220m primarily generated by BSkyB – a number of commentators condemned Channel 4 for its failure to commit itself to cricket. What they failed to appreciate was the unique difficulty of scheduling cricket in the heart of a mainstream TV channel that makes its living from selling commercials.

Cricket is a scheduler's nightmare. It takes up a huge amount of airtime, during most of which – to the uninitiated – not a great deal happens. It alienates large sections of the potential audience, especially women. Its finish time depends on the over-rate and is therefore unpredictable, which collides with the first rule of scheduling: always transmit your key early-evening shows at predictable times. In a competitive broadcasting environment, the early evening is critical to building audiences for the rest of the night. If two million switch on at 6 p.m. to watch *The Simpsons*, only to find an unknown Sri Lankan batsman playing for the close, they are unlikely to hang around. That is disastrous for the channel's revenue.

On top of that, there are the hours to fill when poor weather prevents play: the cricket lover isn't interested in time-fillers, and the non-believer thinks the cricket is on. So the channel loses twice over. Channel 4 can't even make do with old movies because it has a strict quota of original programming which would be severely compromised.

All these uncertainties have a cost, which in Channel 4's case is measurable. At its best, when England are doing well and a match is well poised, the channel can break even. At its worst, it loses money. Its original highlights package at 7.30 was drawing an average of 700,000 viewers instead of the usual 1.5 million. Sport is not part of its public service remit, which is defined by law and strictly monitored by the industry regulator Ofcom.

None of this diminished the enthusiasm with which Channel 4 embraced the game. To almost universal acclaim, it revolutionised coverage and demonstrated vividly how lazy and unimaginative the BBC's approach had become. From Hawkeye to regular and concise explanations of some of the more eccentric Laws, it made the game accessible and fun to watch.

It also demonstrated its commitment off the air. Part of the ECB's rationale in 1998, when it dumped the BBC, was that Channel 4 could exploit its trendy image to appeal to a new, younger and multicultural audience. And indeed the station has invested money in inner-city cricket programmes, teaching packs for schools, a community cricket ground in Lambeth, and themed cultural events encouraging ethnic Indian and West Indian communities to participate. It has kept its side of the bargain.

But over the next five years, the commercial environment will become much tougher. C4's new chief executive, Andy Duncan, has projected a funding gap of over £100m by 2012 and is already appealing to government for some kind of public subsidy for the first time in the channel's history. Against that kind of background, Channel 4 could hardly be blamed for not matching BSkyB's offer.

Unfortunately, the ECB doesn't seem to understand how difficult it will be to re-establish contact with terrestrial television. ITV's complete indifference to cricket – compared to rugby union, motor racing or European soccer – is one measure of the sport's lack of commercial viability. Channel Five may have committed itself to a highlights package at 7.15, but against *Coronation Street*, *EastEnders* and *Emmerdale* it will be lucky to attract an audience of half a million. Five certainly won't touch ball-by-ball coverage.

five

That leaves the non-commercial BBC, which for 60 years was televised cricket's natural home but this time did not even put in a bid. As it prepares for the decennial review of the BBC charter and makes its case for continued licence-fee funding, many cricket fans have been wondering why cricket should not be an integral part of the public service rationale. There are several reasons.

First, the new director-general, Mark Thompson, has made it clear he intends to move away from a populist approach. That means making more room for some of the core public service areas such as current affairs, documentaries, arts, music and children's programming. While cricket lovers may be keen to add their sport to the public service list, there are too many other programme areas being vacated by the commercial channels, and which the BBC is under growing pressure to prioritise.

Second, the BBC has existing obligations to sports which have stayed loyal or returned to it. Wimbledon tennis, rugby union, the FA Cup and football highlights all have a place in the BBC's sports pantheon. Once a sport takes itself off to a competitor, the BBC can't be expected to wait patiently in the wings for a change of mind; its sports resources and personnel will have been diverted elsewhere.

Third, schedules need to be filled. As *Test Match Special* producer Peter Baxter put it, "the problem with moving a sport off a mainstream channel is that the hole closes over". Commitments are made not just to other sports but to other programming areas, often with long lead times. Something in the current schedule – which will probably have built its own loyal audience – would have to make way, particularly for such a huge chunk of television time as Test cricket consumes.

B B C

Meanwhile, BSkyB has a very different agenda. With three dedicated sports channels, there is no shortage of airtime, and subscribers who are willing and able to pay upwards of £400 per year will see full coverage. More importantly, it is live and exclusive sport which drives the BSkyB business. After years of facing very little competition in the multichannel world, it is now finding life more difficult against Freeview, the BBC's digital offering which requires only a set-top box and no monthly subscription – but offers a much smaller range of channels. Sky's monthly rate of signing up new households has been declining and the number of Freeview homes accelerating. Exclusive Test cricket is a valuable carrot to persuade an additional tranche

In on the action: Ian Ward, then a Surrey player, wears a helmet complete with miniature camera in the 2003 Twenty20 Cup.

Picture by Patrick Eagar

of otherwise reluctant subscribers to join the BSkyB club and boost its subscription base.

This won't detract from the proven quality of Sky's coverage. But for Sky, as with all its exclusive sports, cricket is a commodity which it will want to buy as cheaply as possible next time around. And when the ECB starts looking in 2009 for competing bids from mainstream channels, it will be lucky to find any other potential takers for a sport which makes such enormous and unpredictable demands on airtime. Sky knows when it has a free run, and will be bidding accordingly – and the pot of gold which the ECB discovered this time round could prove to be a very short-lived cash bonanza.

There is one potential game-saving approach, which would depend on the government intervening to do what the ECB hasn't done and recognise the national significance of the game. Until 1998 home Test matches were among ten "listed events", the crown jewels of sport which were judged to be of such cultural value to the nation that live rights could not be sold exclusively to a non-terrestrial broadcaster. After intense lobbying from the ECB – and a much-touted "gentleman's agreement" between the board chairman Lord MacLaurin and the cabinet minister in charge of sport, culture secretary Chris Smith, that the game would not disappear from mainstream television – home Test matches were removed from the "A" list of protected events.

Unfortunately, the harsh reality of commercial life does not allow for agreements between gentlemen. So it is worth remembering the words of Chris Smith in June 1998 when he acceded to the request: "This is something for which the ECB and county cricket clubs have specifically asked. I expect to see their freedom used responsibly, with continued access for all viewers to a substantial proportion of live Test coverage. If those expectations are not fulfilled then I may, of course, need to review the listed criteria again."

Both Smith and MacLaurin have gone now, but it may be time for the government to act on Smith's threat. The English Rugby Football Union recognised its mistake in selling its Six Nations matches at Twickenham to BSkyB when live audiences allegedly plummeted to a tenth of their BBC1 size. The RFU understood the potential damage that was being done to maintaining a healthy grassroots interest in the sport, and reversed their decision. A rugby match is about one twenty-fifth the length of a Test match so the BBC could easily accommodate them. The same will not be true for cricket in 2009.

The current culture secretary, Tessa Jowell, is expected to move on after this year's general election. This may not be a great political issue, but cricket fans could certainly make their feelings known to the post-election guardian of the nation's cultural heritage. If cricket's governing body cannot be trusted to look after the best interests of our national game, some intense lobbying to have home Tests relisted might help the ECB recognise the dangers of its short-term thinking.

Steven Barnett is professor of communications at the University of Westminster. His books include Games and Sets, *an analysis of sport on television.*

Another Country:
Village Cricket Splits in Two

ALAN LEE

As a boy, my life revolved around the village cricket club. Indeed, the power of the attachment lasted well into adulthood and might never have slackened but for the intrusion of a job that diverted me to far pavilions. There was, about that club on the common in rural Hertfordshire, a spirit of community and camaraderie that I have never replicated in any subsequent environment.

It enveloped people's lives, dictated their diaries, and provided their social, as well as sporting, outlet. It fostered relationships, even marriages – fractured some, too. Matches were the focus, the headline items, but the idea that members did not meet from one weekend to the next was laughable. The club was the hub of life: our village, our soap opera.

It follows, nostalgia being the force it is, that when I set out last summer to discover the health of village cricket in the 21st century, I longed for every club to be as I remembered mine. And of course they weren't. How could they be? The beauty of the village game lies, as it has always done, in its infinite variety of settings and communities and characters.

There were trends apparent, though, some of them alarming to those of us with no desire to see everything quintessentially English expire. Despite its quaint image, village cricket reflects the world we live in. Sport in Britain is more competitive, more outwardly aggressive and less sociable than it was 30 years ago, and nowhere is immune. The incompetent overweight who once held his place because he was reliable, popular and happy to serve behind the bar every week is no longer necessarily tolerated. Characters are being lost, along with stalwart servants, putting the very future of many clubs in jeopardy.

Most villages now play in leagues, with the rigours of travel and player transience that this brings. The ambitious clubs continue to thrive, though with a sterner philosophy than was practised in my youth, but those that, by choice or circumstance, remain faithful to tradition are dropping in number and profile. Even more than before, their survival is dependent on the selfless work of one or two individuals.

My boyhood memories of early May are of Sundays that started clear blue – though seldom stayed that way – and of walking through the woods to be at the club by breakfast time. The pitch might need rolling, the pavilion sweeping, the scorebook brought up to date. The same few people were always there early. Although it scarcely occurred to me at the time, they did virtually all the work.

On a comparable May Sunday last year, I arrived at Godshill, a setting to match its name. This is a ground carved out of the New Forest. And shifting the ponies off the outfield, then sweeping up what ponies do, is

Wife of Deep-field, "NO, DARLING, DADDY CAN'T TALK TO YOU NOW;
WAIT UNTIL HE'S DROPPED THIS ONE!"

just one of the jobs that Alan Cousins does routinely and uncomplainingly before each game. Cousins is captain, groundsman, team and fixture secretary. He would doubtless run the bar if Godshill possessed such a luxury, but the rudimentary shack of a pavilion has no showers, electricity or phone line, and no evident hope of attaining them. Cricket survives because enough clubs still love visiting the place, and because Cousins works so hard to accommodate them. It is the more heroic for what is happening nearby: Fordingbridge, the nearest town, has seen its cricket club fold through lack of interest, and many Forest village teams have gone the same way.

Godshill is in Hampshire, but neighbouring Dorset is no better off. Of the 492 clubs who entered the 2004 National Village Cup (sponsored by npower and administered by *The Wisden Cricketer*), not one gave an address in Dorset. This does not mean that there is no village cricket played in the county, but it is indicative of the shrinkage. Perhaps, though, it also says something about apprehension, about a sense of reluctance to expose oneself to embarrassment? For the fact is that village cricket is no longer a comfortably uniform game. The span of standards, and of ambitions, is greater than at any time since the first shepherd boys whacked balls with their crooks.

The winners of the npower Cup in 2004 were Sully Centurions from Glamorgan, whose ground sits on the Barry peninsula, looking across the Bristol Channel. They were worthy winners. In all probability, this was the best team ever to play in the 33 years of the competition. But Sully, though physically and geographically a village, had outgrown the generally accepted criteria of village cricket. Having made swift and remarkable progress under the inspired leadership of a single, committed family – the Sylvesters – they not only played in the top league in Wales last year but won it, and the cup for good measure.

Several of the side had played for Wales. Four had played at Lord's before. Though they insist, heatedly, that none of their players is paid, some are certainly found accommodation and jobs. Sully are not alone in this – the best clubs around the country, towns and villages, now attract players this way – but, for them, the village cup was not so much a romantic adventure as a ruthless mission, duly accomplished. In the course of it, and in their eyes by doing nothing more heinous than playing competitively, Sully caused an uncomfortable stir, leaving a succession of opponents and some vocal observers disillusioned not only with the tournament but the direction in which village cricket was being taken.

There are those within English cricket's administration who may consider this to be an admirable sign of progress and wish for nothing more than the continued culling of the weakest clubs. Social cricket, in these eyes, is anathema, and it does not exist elsewhere in the world. The idea of village cricket in Australia would be derided. There, club players meet up to practise and to play, uncompromisingly hard in both cases. Lingering in a pavilion bar, chewing the fat with the opposition over a few pints, is simply not part of the psyche. Nor is the building of community spirit through a cricket club environment. The strong get on, the weak can go hang.

That, increasingly, is the norm here. Village cricket is splitting in two: the old and the new. But the old-style clubs cannot be allowed to vanish. Any further diminution of their numbers and influence will be detrimental to the game, for it will close another door of entry to the majority of teenagers, for whom schools cricket is already off the curriculum. One of the joys of my tour of Britain in search of the village game was seeing how many clubs now have highly developed colts sections, benefiting not only their own future but that of cricket in general. Shireshead & Forton from Lancashire (mainly famous for an M6 service station) was a shining example. There, a professor of environmental biology named Terry Mansfield was organising 70 boys at practice every weekend. Shireshead field three teams and it is their policy to have at least six Under-16s in the third XI. The future seems assured.

A grittier atmosphere awaited me at Hopkinstown in south Wales. This was a colliery village, devastated by the closure of the local pit in the late 1970s, and it is no exaggeration to say that village spirit was saved by the cricket club. Its pavilion, extended three times, is now a social centre, an arm around the shoulders of local youths who might otherwise run out of control. Here, they run teams from Under-11 upwards, all keenly subscribed. Hopkinstown is no rural idyll – indeed, it is as far away from the picture postcard stereotype of the village game as can be imagined. Yet it is the finest example I found of village cricket as community therapy.

If the village cup is a barometer of health for the game it represents, it is worrying that the entry has dropped from a peak of more than 800. The 2004 final, in which the more bucolic Exhall & Wixford (the dual names

The Young 'Un. "COME ON, IT'S AN EASY ONE! LUMMY, I COULD RUN TWO."
The Old 'Un. "COULD YER? THEN JUST RUN BACK AGAIN."

may themselves be signs of the times) from Warwickshire fought valiantly against Sully and the odds, was of startlingly high standard. This, the organisers acknowledge, was a mixed blessing. Measures have now been taken to redress the balance and any clubs playing in ECB Premier Leagues – including Sully – have been excluded from the 2005 competition.

The hope is that this will take the Cup back to the places where it truly belongs – places like Godshill, and the indefatigable Alan Cousins. He reminded me of similar men at my own club in Hertfordshire. The majority of village cricketers will always wish only to turn up with the pitch marked out, the sightscreens in place and the bar (where such a thing exists) fully stocked. Most clubs are still sustained by the efforts of a handful of people. Some things in village cricket are utterly unchanged. It's still the stage for local heroes.

Alan Lee spent the summer of 2004 visiting village cricket grounds for The Times, *as a break from his job as the paper's racing correspondent. He was its cricket correspondent from 1988 to 1999, and has written more than 30 books on the game.*

The cartoons, which appeared in Punch *in 1935 (Dropped Catch) and 1931, are reproduced by permission of punch.co.uk. Along with four other limited-edition village cricket cartoons, they can be obtained from the Lord's Taverners (0800 2793520).*

FIVE CRICKETERS OF THE YEAR

The Five Cricketers of the Year represent a tradition that dates back in Wisden *to 1889, making this the oldest individual award in cricket. The Five are picked by the editor, and the selection is based, primarily but not exclusively, on the players' influence on the previous English season. No one can be chosen more than once.*

The choice for 2005 comprises five English players for only the third time since the Second World War. The previous occasions were 1953 and 1960.

Ashley Giles

Vic Marks

The England selectors, once famous for trying players and hurriedly discarding them, no longer dispense with their cricketers lightly. The career of Ashley Giles is exemplification, and perhaps justification, of this policy.

At the start of the 2004 summer, Giles appeared to be on his last legs as an international cricketer. He had played 33 Tests, but was rarely dominant or, to many observers, convincing. After a barren tour of the Caribbean, he was treated with disdain by the New Zealand batsmen in the first innings at Lord's; at Headingley in the next Test he was wicketless, and "absolutely shattered".

"I hadn't contributed to the victory," he recalls. "I didn't feel part of the team. I was getting abuse from the crowd. I was reading in the press that Paul Collingwood's bowling would be of more use to England than mine. I was not happy." He told his wife: "I'm not sure how much longer I can take this."

At Trent Bridge before the Third Test he turned to the team's psychologist, Steve Bull, a familiar figure around the England camp, and a friend. Giles poured out his frustrations; Bull asked Giles to write down how he was feeling, how he was affected by the crowd's attitude and what his new goals were to be. It's a routine that he is unlikely to forsake for a while.

Whether the wonders of sports psychology did the trick, or his own inner steel, Giles's season was about to transform. Immediately, he was more relaxed: "Instead of fretting solely about where the next ball would land, I was thinking about field placements and different ways to disrupt batsmen." Giles took six wickets at Trent Bridge, and scored 81 unbeaten and vital runs.

That was just the start of a wondrous summer in which, contrary to all expectations, he became England's match-winner. In the following two Tests against West Indies he took 18 wickets. Suddenly he could arrive at a Test ground without eyeing the pitch apprehensively and wondering whether he would get a game. Giles took 31 Test wickets in the summer of 2004.

Three of them stick in his mind. There was the dismissal of Scott Styris when Giles was in the doldrums at Lord's. "Still bowling that negative stuff over the wicket?" goaded Styris upon his arrival at the crease. Giles stayed over the wicket, yielded nothing and soon had Styris snaffled at silly point in a spell that ensured his survival as a Test cricketer. At Trent Bridge he despatched Chris Cairns, a formidable slayer of spin bowling, with a delivery – from over the wicket, of course – which pitched leg and hit off stump. But the one to treasure was his 100th Test wicket, at Lord's.

Giles had never bowled to Brian Lara before, except in the nets at Warwickshire. In the second innings Lara shimmied down the pitch, misjudged the length, and the ball turned obligingly out of the rough and through the gate before hitting middle. Perfect. Giles was to torment all the West Indian left-handers throughout the series but to dismiss Lara in this manner highlighted his metamorphosis. Now the ball was dipping in the air and spinning upon arrival. For the first time in decades an English spinner dominated a home series.

Yet ASHLEY FRASER GILES, born on March 19, 1973, was never a spin bowler in his youth. In his teens he was a seamer, good enough to play for Guildford CC at 14 and arouse the interest of Surrey. A back problem compelled him to turn to spin, which was not in Surrey's plans. So after writing several letters to other counties, he arrived at Edgbaston as a 19-year-old untutored in his new role.

Soon, though, he became a reliable, engaging member of the Warwickshire side. He made fleeting appearances in the Championship-winning team of 1995 and was a regular thereafter. His Test debut was against the South Africans at Manchester in 1998, but it wasn't until the 2000-01 tour of Pakistan, where he took 17 wickets in three Tests, that he established himself in the England side. Since then no spinner has been preferred to him, though others have appeared whenever his troublesome Achilles tendon has flared up.

For much of the time his ability to muck in and to scramble a few runs down the order, coupled with a genial, open temperament, seemed the key reasons for his longevity (he became a close friend of Michael Vaughan before he was appointed England captain). Now Giles can be viewed as something of an innovator. He has become a leading proponent of the left-arm spinner bowling over the wicket to right-handers. In India in 2001-02 this produced cricket of almost unbearable tedium as he consistently pitched the ball 12 inches outside the leg stump of Sachin Tendulkar.

But after 2004, Giles can protest with some justification that this line of attack can be an aggressive option. He now bowls very close to the stumps and aims to pitch the ball on leg stump so that batsmen have to play. Left-arm spinners around the county circuit are increasingly copying the Giles way, but they may have to wait a while to replace him. Giles has come to view the 2004 season as a watershed: "the start of the rest of my career".

Steve Harmison

TANYA ALDRED

He is a shy home body with gangling limbs and a Newcastle United season ticket. But hand him a cricket ball and his limbs are awkward only to batsmen, bringing pace, bounce, height and menace. In 2004 Steve Harmison became England's keenest weapon in a generation. But what changed him from an unproven bowler of dubious backbone and fitness to Grievous Bodily Harmison (*The Sun*), not even he can pinpoint.

The second innings of the First Test at Sabina Park was his epiphany. On a March morning, with the disco booming and the home crowd waiting for some batting pyrotechnics, he was awesome. Six slips and a gully watched as his feet thudded into the Jamaican earth, and ball after ball spat off the spot – in less than two hours he had seven for 12, and West Indies had been humiliated. His confidence, a precarious thing, soared.

He finished the series with 23 wickets at 14.86, something of a hold over Brian Lara, and a spring in his step. It did not stop there. By August 2004 he was the No. 1 bowler in the world, the first Englishman to top the charts since their invention. He was at last hiding his disappointment that he was not Alan Shearer. England could hardly hide their glee.

STEPHEN JAMES HARMISON was born on October 23, 1978 in Ashington, an ex-mining town near Newcastle upon Tyne famous for producing the Charltons, Bobby and Jack. He was the second of five children, and something of a rum'un, hating school and being told what to do. He chalked up stumps in the yard and played a bit for his local club but – like most Ashington boys – young Harmison dreamed not of Lord's but St James' Park. For him too it was just a dream. But unlike the others, he had an alternative.

Geoff Cook, Durham's director of cricket, spotted him playing for Northumberland Under-16s and fast-tracked him into the Durham academy. At the very end of the 1996 season, aged 17, he made the first team. It was a chastening experience: Durham were walloped in two days by the champions Leicestershire, he took nought for 77 in nine overs, and *Wisden* grumbled about his selection. But England were hungry for young pace men, and called him up for an Under-19 tour of Pakistan. He came home early, profoundly homesick and with a bad back (later diagnosed as growing pains). It took him five years to recover from the experience.

He played for Durham without much enthusiasm, just the thought that it couldn't be any worse than the few turns he'd done as a labourer. He was plagued by injuries, but people began to see real potential hidden behind his chestnut curtains of hair. England first included him in a squad in 2000 but it was not until August 2002 that, nervous as you like and "a flimsy six foot five", he made his debut against India at Trent Bridge.

His England progress was on and off, much like his radar. On his bowling debut in Australia he served up seven wides in a row against the ACB

Chairman's team. Over the course of nine consecutive Tests he was nearly always fast, usually hostile and sometimes accurate – and by the end of the 2003 summer bowled with real fire against South Africa at The Oval.

Then England announced their central contracts: Harmison did not get one and was furious. Weeks later, he proved his stamina by bowling long and hard in the humidity of Dhaka to get England out of a spot of embarrassment. But he still came home early with an injury, and was welcomed by yet another chorus of whispers about both his physical and his mental strength. It was then that he joined forces with Paul Winsper, who used to coach at Durham but was now at Newcastle United. Harmison went to St James' Park four days a week and trained, not in free-kicks, but on strength, pounding his body mercilessly while mingling with his heroes.

When he arrived in West Indies early in 2004 he was strong as an ox. And from Sabina Park until the end of summer he has hardly put a foot wrong. He is as puzzled as anyone about why things suddenly clicked. "If I knew I'd have bottled it and be a rich man. I felt that it took me longer to adapt to international cricket than some people. Now I feel strong and as if I can handle a game of cricket, five-day Tests and long series. Before, I couldn't."

He certainly benefited from the tight-knit culture of the current England team – a set-up that gives people chances and the opportunity to grow into their role. The longer he was involved the more relaxed he felt, and the more relaxed he felt, the better he bowled. And he knows now he is lucky: "If I hadn't had cricket I wouldn't like to think what I'd have done."

It is not always easy. The South African tour of 2004-05 was very trying, and the confidence disappeared again. This time, there is a real belief that it will return. The homesickness is, if anything, getting worse, though. He misses his two young daughters. He does not like leaving the North-East. But he knows that he has to do it if he wants to be No. 1. And he does want that.

Robert Key

Hugh Chevallier

Ten tantalising runs from a first Test hundred, Rob Key headed for tea in the Lord's pavilion. Drained by the afternoon's humidity, he grabbed a few gulps of water before readying himself for the presentation of the England and West Indies teams to the Queen. He shook hands, then it was straight back out. He kept his concentration, but as he closed in on a century he felt the first stabs of a migraine – he knows dehydration can set one off – massing behind his left eye. Despite a slight blurring of vision, he whipped Fidel Edwards to mid-wicket and reached his hundred with a four, as he had his fifty and would his double. It was the happiest moment of Key's life.

He concedes he has played better – he was reprieved twice before making 60 – though 221 in a Lord's Test suggests something has gone right. In fact, most things went right in 2004. He unfurled a majestic hundred in Kent's opening game and in May transmuted his form from gold to platinum, stockpiling runs as though they were going out of circulation. In one sublime seven-innings sequence he passed 100 five times. So sure was his touch that he reached 1,000 first-class runs on June 2, the earliest for 16 years. He ended the season heading the averages with 1,896 at 79.

Against this backdrop, no one noticed his sketchy limited-overs form. Not even England, who oddly chose him for the NatWest Series. Key achieved little on the one-day stage but his dramatic county form had shot him to top of the list of Test understudies and, when Mark Butcher injured his neck, the call came. By his own admission, his timing, even at Lord's, was not as sweet as in May, and an indifferent performance at Edgbaston had critics carping about his technique a week after his double-hundred.

It brought out the fighter in Key – "he's got a bit of dog in him," said his former county captain Matthew Fleming – and in the Third Test at Old Trafford England had to scrap. Without a tenacious undefeated 93 from Key they might have lost. Fidel Edwards hurled it in short and eyeballed hard, but he rode it out. "In my mind, I'd come of age," Key recalls, the nearest this genuinely modest, affable man comes to a boast.

ROBERT WILLIAM TREVOR KEY was born in East Dulwich on May 12, 1979 into a family who lived sport. His father Trevor could turn his hand to any game, his mother Lyn played cricket for Kent Ladies, while his sister Elizabeth once took a hat-trick. The Keys live in Beckenham, where Kent meets London and even the primary schools still care about cricket. His own, Worsley Bridge, won both the Bromley and Kent Cups; he was chosen for the county Under-11s, and Alan Ealham, then in charge of youth teams at Kent, homed in and became his mentor. By 1998 Key was playing in the Under-19 World Cup, which England won. Later that summer, aged 19 years and ten days, he became Kent's fourth-youngest first-class centurion. A second hundred won him a place on the winter's A-tour to Zimbabwe and South Africa. Everything was falling into place.

Or was it? Without Ealham to push and inspire, the laid-back Key was happy to cruise – and good enough to get away with it. "I'd get a hundred and think: 'Now I've got three or four games to relax and enjoy it without any pressure.'"

Two events blasted away that attitude. The first was the 1999 PCA dinner when Alec Stewart approached the half-cut Key and told him to sort himself out. Few things had given Key as much pleasure as a drink or three with his friends. And it showed. For the first time in years, he had no overseas tour to focus on, and his plans amounted to a winter with his mates – "pretty much ruining myself, I suppose". He swapped the easy winter for a hard one with "Noddy" Holder, Justin Langer's batting coach in Perth, and for the first time became properly fit.

Then he met Rod Marsh in October 2001 as part of the first Academy intake. Initially, he queried the boot-camp regime; but he knuckled down. Having been pushed by Ealham, and then Stewart, Key was now driven by a craving for Marsh's praise, not common currency. His work-rate was as high as anyone's – and Marsh repaid him with the longed-for approbation. It proved a turning-point.

Injuries to others gave him his Test debut against India in 2002, and he did enough to squeeze on to the subsequent Ashes tour once Graham Thorpe pulled out. (After 15 Tests he is still to play as a first choice.) His hard-bitten Australian opponents discerned a new, steelier, slimmer Key, though the runs did not flow. They came in 2004.

Newspaper stories about his weight still rumble on like hunger pangs, though a glimpse at a photograph of him as a Kent teenager reveals how much he has shed. "I'm never going to look like an athlete," he acknowledges. But he is beginning to look like a hell of a cricketer. There are genuine signs that he can forge fitness, a phenomenal eye and a determination to eradicate technical faults with an Australian intensity. If so, England should benefit handsomely; if not, Kent may be the beneficiaries.

Andrew Strauss

JON HENDERSON

An England batsman who scores a hundred in his first Test is not necessarily signing on for a long and elevated career. Six men did so between the end of the Second World War and the start of 2004 – Billy Griffith, Peter May, Arthur Milton, John Hampshire, Frank Hayes and Graham Thorpe. But only the two Surrey men, May and Thorpe, went on to play more than ten Tests. All the more impressive, then, that Andrew Strauss, who made 112 in his maiden Test innings against New Zealand at Lord's last May, should advance from tyro to stalwart in the space of one English summer.

He had the cricketing advantage of a public-school education like May, and Ted Dexter, who preceded Strauss to Radley College. The England team of 2004 christened him Lord Brocket (a cocksure scapegrace of a celebrity aristocrat whose personality bears little resemblance to Strauss's). But his batting does not have the *hauteur* associated with May and Dexter. Without their tall, angular build, Strauss has developed a more utilitarian approach, which may be one reason why the selectors did not trust him with a Test cap until he was 27.

But left-handers often make effective batsmen without looking pretty, and Strauss soon made himself indispensable. Having helped to launch England's summer so successfully, he was at the wicket when they completed their seventh win out of seven, against West Indies at The Oval in August. In his first 14 Test innings, he made 590 runs – including another Lord's century, against West Indies – at an average of 45. He kept going in South Africa, where he often sustained an out-of-form England line-up almost single-handed.

That indispensability went beyond the Test team. His ability to accumulate quickly, through working rather than belting the ball, made him an ideal No. 4 in the one-day side. After watching that hundred against New Zealand, the former England captain Mike Brearley noted: "He is well organised, busy, plays very straight and scores runs in the right areas." Also on the credit side, Strauss, who shone as a fly-half at school and Durham University (fleetingly, he was tempted to pursue a career in rugby union) has good hands. As a schoolboy he kept wicket.

ANDREW JOHN STRAUSS was born on March 2, 1977 in Johannesburg, a son for sports-loving parents who already had three daughters. There is no known kinship with the composers (Johann the elder, Johann the younger, or Richard), but he accepts his surname will forever be accompanied in headlines by the word waltz. The family left South Africa when he was only six, in search of a less politically charged environment. Unlike other South African-born players who have come to England, no trace of accent or sentiment remains. The Stausses spent 18 months in Melbourne before settling in England in time for Strauss to be packed off to Caldicott, a preparatory school with a strong games-playing tradition.

As a schoolboy cricketer, he was constrained by remaining small for his age well into his teens, but established a pattern that defined his career until his call-up to the Test side: an instantly recognisable talent who always commanded attention, did not necessarily deliver spectacular results straight away, but came good eventually because of his diligence. "I suppose I was good but not out of the ordinary," he says. "I scored quickly without being stylish or flamboyant. My technique was what mattered."

Bert Robinson, Radley's veteran coach, taught both Dexter (although he admits that this was like trying to teach Einstein maths) and Strauss, who he describes as one of his most industrious pupils, always wanting just a little longer than anyone else against the bowling machine. At Durham University, another coach, the former England opener Graeme Fowler, is credited by Strauss with turning him into a player with an appreciation of what was required physically and technically to succeed in the first-class game, which he has done with gathering authority at Middlesex.

Strauss likes the Brearley assessment of him as a well-organised batsman. "For me, it's not about having big shots, it's about developing a game that works for me, knowing that, if a guy bowls in a certain area, I can hit it; otherwise I defend or leave it." He says he understands what Graham Gooch was getting at when he spoke about scoring 40,000 runs with three shots, twice as many as he would have made with six shots.

Test selection at the age of 27 was not, he reckons, yet another instance of England's selectors acting with exaggerated caution. "I wouldn't have been ready even two years ago. I've only been playing professional cricket since I was 21, whereas others started at 17." Nor does he underestimate the part luck played in his promotion to the Test side. An injury to Michael Vaughan offered the opening for the Lord's Test against New Zealand; then Nasser Hussain's impromptu retirement ended any doubt that he would be retained, although Hussain admits that Strauss's confident arrival led directly to his departure.

Luck is one thing, making the most of it is quite another. Over the past 12 months, Strauss wrung every last drop from his.

THANK YOU, THANK YOU, THANK YOU: The England players acknowledge the crowd as they emerge from the Centurion pavilion in January 2005 for the presentation after clinching their first Test series win in South Africa for 40 years.

Picture by Clive Mason, Getty Images

THE ECSTASY... Brian Lara claims back the world Test batting record by reaching 381 against England in Antigua in April 2004, just 185 days after he lost it to Matthew Hayden. He went on to score 400 not out.

Picture by Clive Rose, Getty Images

...AND THE OTHER THING: Lara is bowled for a duck by Andrew Flintoff during the Old Trafford Test in August 2004 as West Indies plunge to yet another defeat.
Picture by Hugh Routledge, The Times

FIVE CRICKETERS OF THE YEAR: Ashley Giles.

Picture by Patrick Eagar

FIVE CRICKETERS OF THE YEAR: Steve Harmison.

Picture by Patrick Eagar

FIVE CRICKETERS OF THE YEAR: Robert Key

Picture by Patrick Eagar

FIVE CRICKETERS OF THE YEAR: Andrew Strauss.

Picture by Patrick Eagar

FIVE CRICKETERS OF THE YEAR: Marcus Trescothick

Picture by Patrick Eagar

Marcus Trescothick

DAVID FOOT

There was a time, in the late 1990s, when Marcus Trescothick was unsure of his place in Somerset's Championship side. The runs had been coming more reluctantly, a new experience for someone whose still tender career had been aglow with often prodigious scoring. A natural, buoyant opener, he found himself descending in the order, and was starting to wonder if a change of county might help.

People were starting to murmur. Was he carrying too much weight? Did his approach and amiable features suggest he belonged, just a little too willingly, to the relaxed, less than competitive, Taunton ambience? Was his technique – which had served him so handsomely as he topped 1,000 runs for England Under-19 – robust enough? For all that left-handed brio and vigour, usually so exciting to the spectator, he could look vulnerable.

He knew what they were saying: that he needed to tighten his defence, to move his feet more and give the slips less hope as he pursued his boyish flirtations outside the off stump. And he admits now: "My diet was all wrong". He prefers to airbrush from the record his old nickname of "Banger", which referred to sausages, not his hitting. (His England team-mates call him, discreetly but boringly, "Tres".)

And it is true that a few of those reservations still persist. He will tell you that he hasn't changed his method that much. He reached a century in Johannesburg seemingly rooted to the spot. But he has built on his positive and instinctive assets. He is an undeniably powerful striker of the ball; he possesses an enviable shot-selection; he stands tall, physically and psychologically, these days for England. Duncan Fletcher, as has been well documented, detected some of those qualities in 1999 when he was looking after Glamorgan and they were playing Somerset. Trescothick cracked a hundred in his own, zestful way.

Still, his metamorphosis is remarkable. His Test and one-day record, since his senior international debut in 2000, reflects many signs of a changing persona – and reassuring confidence at the top of the order. He likes taking on fast bowlers. He bats without fear, occasionally too assured and impetuous when there is an innings to build. But fallibility is part of cricket's fascination. He has never been cowed by reputation; he demonstrated that when he carted Glenn McGrath for a quartet of fours in an over at Edgbaston during the Champions Trophy in September. In contrast, his (unavailing) 104 in the final was rigidly disciplined: "I really grafted it out," he says.

His ten Test centuries have been equally varied, and his 132 against New Zealand at Headingley in 2004 ranks with his best, beating the two he scored against West Indies at Edgbaston less than two months later. The one to cherish was surely the previous summer's 219 against South Africa at The Oval, made while he was still smarting from the criticism that he received at Headingley in the previous Test. That was when the umpires offered the batsmen the light with England flaying the bowling and, to general native dismay, Trescothick accepted it. England never regained the initiative.

Partly because of that, one imagines, he has a cool, though polite, relationship with the media. He has few extrovert traits, is inclined to be taciturn and is unceasingly serious and analytical about his game. He is better at dispensing boundaries than headlines. At dressing-room level, he is a strong team man. Colleagues like to have him at the other end, especially when it is the moment to start going for shots.

MARCUS EDWARD TRESCOTHICK was born on Christmas Day 1975, and was given his first bat when he was two. Cricket was an obsession in the family. Dad Martyn was opening bat (and regular century-maker), captain and chairman of Keynsham CC; mum Lin made the teas. Marcus, with puppy fat and slogger's muscles, hit his first hundred aged 11. Somerset coached and monitored him. When one of their junior sides didn't have a place for him, he played for the opposition and scored a century. His friends worked out that when he was 15, turning out for school, village and any other matches going, he actually scored 4,000 runs in a season.

Somerset's supporters quickly took to Marcus and liked to see him going out to bat with Mark Lathwell, a partnership sadly not to be sustained. Equally sad for them is the fact that Trescothick did not play a single Championship match for the county last summer. His affection for his native team remains strong. He was vice-captain under Jamie Cox and several times led the county. There are sentimental reasons why he hopes that one day, when his international career winds down, he can become Somerset's captain. That would offer the perfect sense of symmetry to his career.

Some pundits argue that he is better equipped technically to be a one-day player. "I enjoy both games equally," he says. "It's simply that you hit the ball in different areas for limited-overs cricket." Another "pundit", Shane Warne, implied that the Aussies would find him out in the Test matches, a psychological throwaway that Trescothick pondered in eloquent silence. He doesn't give much away, and remains happiest when parading his potent repertoire of shots, his occasional medium-paced seam, deputy wicket-keeping... and taking over from time to time as England's skipper. That leaves him fewer hours than he'd wish to spend with his wife Hayley and his close-knit family, or on the golf course.

Bent: A History of Chucking

DAVID FRITH

Across the ages, apart from match-fixing and political interference from outside its walls, cricket has wrestled with no more contentious issue than suspect bowling actions. The complaints against Arthur Mold which W. G. Grace piped through his whiskers in the 1890s were paraphrased and purpled up more than a century later by Nasser Hussain and directed at Muttiah Muralitharan. The 1998 edition of the *Wisden Book of Cricket Records* has a disconcerting *four page* list of bowlers who have been no-balled for throwing.

The pioneers of overarm bowling, before its legalisation in 1864, were dubbed "throwers" simply because they raised their arms above the permitted level. Earlier still, curious underhand deliveries, as purveyed by the Hambledon ace David Harris, involved kinky elbow movement, but nobody complained.

It was the turn of the century before cricket began to catch up with those who threw in the modern sense. Sydney Pardon, *Wisden* editor from 1891 to 1925, played a key role in eliminating the scourge of throwing when it first became rampant. He condemned the actions of Ernie Jones and Tom McKibbin after Australia's 1896 tour of England (adding a dollop of diplomacy by stating that it was all England's fault: the Australians were merely copying).

A big, fearless, itinerant Australian umpire, Jim Phillips, finished the job. Having called Jones once in a state match and once in a Melbourne Test during 1897-98, Phillips came over to England and dealt with somebody at the other end of the social scale, the eminent Mr C. B. Fry, whose action had been widely condemned. Encouraged, other umpires then called Fry. Editor Pardon was ecstatic. "A case of long-delayed justice," he called it. Fry thereafter concentrated on his batting.

But Phillips returned and dealt with a far more significant threat, the Lancashire and England fast bowler Arthur Mold, called by Phillips at Trent Bridge in 1900 and then again, 16 times in ten overs, at Old Trafford against Somerset the next year. Between the two seasons, the county captains had agreed not to use 14 bowlers regarded as suspect; Mold's captain, Archie MacLaren, was the one dissenter, so more direct action had become essential.

Film of Mold, recently discovered, reveals a bowling action seemingly without blemish. It was shot at Old Trafford in 1901, the day after Phillips had called him the last time. Mold was now conscious of being filmed, and was probably not only on his best behaviour but below his lethal top speed. Still, he vanished from first-class cricket, and thereafter reckoned that his career (1,673 low-cost wickets) amounted to nothing. The game was cleansed – for the time being.

Early offender: Arthur Mold in the flesh, and in the eye of "Rip", cartoonist of the *Evening News Cricket Annual* of 1901.

Picture (left) courtesy of David Frith

The outbreak of chucking more than half a century later was eventually put down just as dramatically and symbolically in 1963 by the no-balling of Ian Meckiff, the Australian left-armer, four times in an over by Col Egar in the Brisbane Test against South Africa. This was another intervention carried out by an umpire of strong character who knew he was backed by the administrators.

Forty years on, the issue has returned to the top of the agenda. And today, the International Cricket Council has devised a new system of dealing with the problem, the accent being on discreet behind-the-scenes action, thus commendably sparing erring bowlers any on-field humiliation. The complication is that the central figure in the latest "does he, doesn't he?" saga twirled his way to the top of the world's Test bowling table. At a time when international and racial tensions in cricket have been touchier than at any other point in history, the introduction of the name Muralitharan into a cricket discussion can be relied upon to divide any room outside Sri Lanka.

This scientific age has thrown up developments unimagined in Meckiff's day, let alone Mold's. While Eadweard Muybridge in the 1890s demonstrated, using 24 cameras, that horses do indeed have all four hooves off the ground during the gallop, so the modern 1,000-plus-frames-a-second television camera has allowed scientists to calibrate the movement in a bowler's elbow and shoulder joints. From this has sprung the ground-breaking finding that the arm of just about *every* bowler inadvertently flexes in the act of bowling.

A "levels of tolerance" scheme emerged whereby fast bowlers were permitted a maximum flex of ten degrees, medium-pacers 7.5 degrees, and

FIFTEEN ALL: WHY THE ICC FOUND A NEW ANGLE

ROB SMYTH

To some it represented the legalisation of chucking; to others, it was a sensible antidote to a noxious issue. Either way, the recommendation of the ICC Sub-Committee on Flawed Bowling Actions to bend the Law on throwing constituted the most radical action on the subject for decades.

The ICC's previous gloss on Law 24 (itself rewritten only five years ago) allowed bowlers to flex their arms during delivery: five degrees for spin bowlers, 7.5 for medium-pacers, and ten for fast bowlers. Now it is a standard-issue 15 degrees.

Conspiracy theorists noted that the new guidelines were uncomfortably close to the 14 degrees at which Muttiah Muralitharan's *doosra* – which was outlawed in 2004 – was measured. "I think it's been brought in through pressure from Sri Lanka and Murali's supporters," said Geoff Boycott. "It's a sad day for cricket that this pressure can allow Muralitharan to bowl whatever he wants."

But the reality is that nearly everyone's elbows turned out to be dirty. The panel found that almost all the great bowlers in history bent their arms. "While we watched the likes of McGrath, Pollock, Harmison and Donald, we quickly realised that the levels of tolerance were far too low," said panel member Angus Fraser. "All those bowlers possessed actions any youngster would be wise to copy, yet their bowling arms were nowhere near as straight as we anticipated."

Bruce Elliott, the biomechanics expert at the University of Western Australia who has been regularly consulted by the ICC, said the change is an inevitable response to technological advances: "People assumed everyone was zero degrees. If you had asked me two years ago I'd have guessed that five degrees was a reasonable number, but research has shown otherwise."

The consensus of expert advice suggested 15 degrees would accommodate any straightening which is purely a consequence of biomechanical forces – such as the hyperextension of an elbow joint – and is also the point at which the straightening becomes visible.

"Many will feel that, by allowing this, the ICC are legalising throwing," said Fraser. "They are not. All the information and opinion collected, along with the fact that is almost impossible to see the arm straighten with the naked eye until it reaches this angle, points to 15 degrees."

The recommendation was accepted by the ICC's committee of chief executives, meeting in Melbourne in February 2005. The review process is also to be overhauled and shortened. "This issue has afflicted the game for over 60 years. Try as it might, the sport has never properly come to terms with it," said the ICC's own chief executive Malcolm Speed. "Every time it comes up there are emotional reactions from people around the world based on fear and ignorance and I've no doubt we will see them all again this time. The reality is that this new process provides the game with a sensible way forward."

His figure of 60 years is a wild understatement, as David Frith's article shows. But his main point may be valid.

spinners five degrees. Biomechanical examination in Perth established that Muralitharan's bowling arm sometimes straightened 14 degrees. It was official. Under this ruling, he threw – sometimes, at least. Sri Lanka's cricket board immediately sought flexibility of another kind: Muralitharan's arm speed, it was claimed, was so swift that he should be given special dispensation to straighten the limb more than five degrees in delivering the ball. For the time being it was agreed that his *doosra* (off-spinner's googly) should be withheld from his repertoire. Batsmen find it hard enough to spot, so the umpires' job was complicated further with this added demand to detect any *doosra* slipped in.

Resentment boils over when bowlers are perceived not only to be transgressing but winning Test matches. England captain Peter May barred 1958-59 tour manager F. R. Brown from lodging an official complaint about Meckiff's action (which the bowler later amended, only to lose his effectiveness before reverting back).

May did not want England to be seen as squealing. But when Meckiff's six for 38 at Melbourne won an Ashes Test, a section of the English press gave vent to its indignation, which had been brewing at the sight of dubious bowling actions all across Australia. Predictably, the Poms were branded as whingers anyway.

This was a pointer to the seed of the problem, a seed which keeps regenerating. The longer a suspect bowler plays without remedial action, the greater the shock when the Laws finally catch up with him. "How could he be throwing?" they cry. "He's played all over the place for years and never been called!" Beside the point, M'Lud.

When Darrell Hair tried to emulate Phillips and Egar by calling Muralitharan for throwing at Melbourne in 1995, the response reached new heights of indignation. Media hysteria and threats to his person followed. The matter, Hair later wrote, had become "a political and religious hot potato". The claim that Muralitharan was incapable of straightening his arm (an echo of the bent-arm action of Australia's off-spinner Ian Johnson, whose name still brings a knowing smile from contemporaries) was brushed aside by Hair in his subsequent book.

Thereafter, the ICC kept umpire Hair well away from Sri Lanka's matches. But they couldn't stop him from revealing some embarrassing details in his book *Decision Maker*. A few days after he and his fellow umpire had filed reports to the ICC concerning the bowling actions of two other Sri Lankans, Kumar Dharmasena and Ruwan Kalpage, the ACB and the match referee instructed them not to call any Sri Lankan bowler. Hair indiscreetly wrote his book while still on the umpires panel, and his use of the word "diabolical" in respect of Muralitharan's action led to a warning from the ICC for "bringing cricket into disrepute".

However, feelings in Australia grew regardless. Another Australian umpire, Ross Emerson, called Muralitharan; even the prime minister, John Howard, eventually said that he was a chucker, and the man who was by then the leading Test wicket-taker of all time decided to give the 2004 tour of Australia a miss.

Unwelcome Test calls: Tony Lock (*left*) and Geoff Griffin both suffered humiliation on the international stage.

Pictures by Getty Images

New Zealander Ken Rutherford had written that the entire New Zealand team considered Muralitharan's action was not right from time to time, albeit unintentionally. "He just picked up an action when he was a little kid in backyard games... during the early days of his career when he could have corrected it, no one was around to coach him and correct him."

Therein lies the second alarming reality: bowlers' actions are innocently but eagerly copied by the juvenile masses. That was the greatest underlying danger of both Bodyline and the West Indies fast-bowling excesses of the 1980s (another period characterised by weak umpiring). Suddenly, every lad believed this was the way to play cricket. There is an enormous burden of responsibility on the shoulders of coaches, selectors and captains, as well as umpires.

Umpires have often looked in vain for the backing of the authorities who appointed them. The great Frank Chester was not alone in being convinced that South Africa's 1951 tourist Cuan McCarthy was a thrower, but the influential and incurable appeaser P. F. "Plum" Warner urged him to hold his fire, pleading: "These people are our guests." Chester thereafter gazed ostentatiously into the distance while standing at square leg whenever McCarthy bowled.

However, just a few years before Egar acted against Meckiff, another South African, Geoff Griffin, was central to one of the most grotesque chapters in Test history. He was a shaky selection for the England tour in 1960, having been called for throwing while playing for Natal. He was then no-balled by six different umpires in three of the lead-up matches in England, and in the Lord's Test's he was called 11 times by Frank Lee, and then

PROBABLES AND IMPROBABLES

The following are among the players no-balled for throwing

J. Willes   Kent v MCC at Lord's   1822
For bowling round-arm

E. Jones   on two occasions   1897-98
J. Phillips called Jones when bowling for Australia v England at Melbourne, the first instance in Tests

C. B. Fry   on four occasions   1898 and 1900

A. W. Mold   on two occasions   1900 and 1901
Phillips called Mold once in 1900 and then 16 times in ten overs a year later

G. H. T. Simpson-Hayward   Lord Brackley's XI v Barbados at Bridgetown   1904-05
For taking a shy at the wicket instead of bowling

D. J. Insole   Essex v Northamptonshire at Northampton   1952
"I was cross because Freddie Brown wouldn't declare, so I ran up and chucked one at him"

G. A. R. Lock   on five separate occasions   1952–1960

G. M. Griffin   on eight separate occasions   1958-59–1962-63
This includes one instance when he was no-balled 11 times for South Africa v England at Lord's, 1960

H. J. Rhodes   on four separate occasions   1960-65

I. Meckiff   on three separate occasions   1962-63–1963-64
He retired after being no-balled in his only over for Australia, v South Africa at Brisbane in 1963-64

S. M. Gavaskar   Rest of India v Karnataka at Ahmedabad   1974-75

G. A. Gooch   England XI v East Zone at Jamshedpur   1981-82
Impersonating J. E. Emburey

D. I. Gower   England v New Zealand at Nottingham   1986
Deliberate throw with the scores level

C. E. L. Ambrose   Leeward Islands v Trinidad at Pointe-à-Pierre   1987-88

M. Muralitharan   Sri Lanka v Australia at Melbourne   1995-96
Called seven times by D. B. Hair. He was also called by R. A. Emerson in two one-day internationals

R. W. T. Key   Kent v Somerset at Taunton   2001
Impersonating Shoaib Akhtar

Main source: Wisden Book of Cricket Records *(fourth edition)*

again by Syd Buller in the exhibition match that followed the early finish. This made the Australians fearful that their bowlers might be similarly humiliated, and for a time the 1961 Ashes tour was under threat. The two countries called a truce: the umpires were instructed to make private reports in the modern manner, and the Australian team were selected carefully.

Slower bowlers may profit from throwing just as effectively as the fast men. Much more than Johnson, the Australian off-spinner Jim Burke was a standing joke, although Peter May, for one, didn't think it funny when blatantly chucked out for 92 in a Sydney Test. Surrey and England left-arm match-winner Tony Lock became a thrower after protracted bowling at indoor nets, where the low roof caused him to abandon flight. When he knocked Doug Insole's stumps over in a county match, the bemused batsman enquired if he had been bowled or run out. In the West Indies in 1953-54, Lock became the first man to be called in a Test match since Ernie Jones. But it was not until 1959, after he saw film of himself bowling against New Zealand that Lock repented, remodelled his action, and extended his career.

So concerned were Sir Donald Bradman, Gubby Allen and other custodians of the game's welfare that bowlers were soon being spied upon – filmed from behind bushes as the campaign to clean up the game took priority. The small reels held at Lord's are not all labelled, but respectable bowlers such as Alec Bedser were among those filmed, presumably to establish what was legitimate, something to measure others by. Tom Graveney later wrote: "Throwers weren't new. They didn't suddenly appear in 1958, and they didn't all wear green caps. I had been thrown at for years by a few English county bowlers."

In the atmosphere of the time, almost everyone who did not have Alec Bedser's perfect action gave rise to suspicion, even Fred Trueman and Brian Statham. This was cricket's McCarthyite period. But realisation was now dawning that some bowlers were endowed with what was termed "hyper-extension" of the elbow – an ability to drop the extended forearm below the horizontal. The whippy Statham, who took 252 wickets for England, had this abnormality. Harold Rhodes had a similar arm formation, played in only two Tests, was called several times while playing for Derbyshire in the 1960s, and wrote an understandably bitter book.

Ernie Jones was no-balled only twice, which suggests he might have thrown only his extra-fast ball. These occasional throwers are hardest to sort out. England's Peter Loader was thought by many to throw his bouncer and his slower ball. Similarly with Charlie Griffith. He lumbered to the crease and bowled unexceptional medium-fast – until something almost invisible came down on the batsman. Brian Close later reflected that "you could almost put one hand in your pocket and play him... then one would come at you four yards quicker!"

In an age when freedom of speech was in much better health than subsequently, several major batsmen, Ken Barrington and Norm O'Neill among them, aired their anguish over Griffith's action, and Richie Benaud, recently retired as a player, was not exactly fêted in the Caribbean when he produced incriminating photographs. In the match in which a Griffith bouncer

And the debate rumbles on... The Australian fast bowler, Brett Lee (*left*), has suffered accusations of throwing, not as vociferous as those hurled at Muttiah Muralitharan.
Pictures by Hamish Blair, Getty Images and Patrick Eagar

almost killed the Indian captain Nari Contractor at Bridgetown, he was called for throwing, but not until an all-but-unnoticed one-off by Arthur Fagg in the West Indians' match against Lancashire in 1966 did it happen again.

Once more it was timid officialdom that had blocked potential action by conscientious umpires. Cec Pepper, a formidable Australian cricketer who settled in England and might have become the Jim Phillips of his day, was convinced that Griffith threw but, to his disgust, he was quietly asked by the rulers of the English game to do nothing.

Nowadays the threat of litigation is a concern to anyone discussing this issue. And the risk of losing sizeable professional earnings is a further consideration in persuading umpires that they have to be utterly certain that a bowler is transgressing. From Bobby Peel in the 1890s to a dozen or more whispered names today, the background hum seems always to have been there, often against bowlers who were never officially called at all. In the early 1900s, Australia's skipper Joe Darling dubbed Jack Saunders "the dirtiest chucker we ever had", but no umpire ever confirmed that.

Bowlers tend to protest their innocence to the grave. Aside from Lock, only one exception comes to mind. In 1999 the former West Indies spinner Sonny Ramadhin, in an interview with Peter Johnson in the *Daily Mail*, confessed that his faster ball was thrown: "Nowadays, the television cameras would have picked it up immediately... But I got away with it in every grade of cricket for 30 years." Ramadhin, who bowled with sleeves buttoned at the wrist, expressed doubts about Muralitharan's action, and marvelled that he had taken so many Test wickets.

After decades of muddled attempts to defenestrate erring bowlers, the ICC procedure has seemed to be close to perfection, apart from the clause permitting reported bowlers to continue playing while still undergoing remedial work. The ICC pursues a progressive scientific charter, though the precise effect remains unpredictable, especially with this increased licence for all to flex the bowling arm as much as 15 degrees. Over a century ago, Spofforth surprisingly suggested that bowlers should be allowed to throw, and the matter would soon sort itself out. Perhaps even the Demon himself did not quite know what he meant by that. Maybe we are about to see all manner of dart throwers and baseball pitchers entering the bowling ranks. It does feel as if something precious and fundamental is being torn from the heart of the game.

David Frith is a cricket journalist, author and historian. He was editor of The Cricketer *from 1972 to 1978 and of* Wisden Cricket Monthly *from its foundation in 1979 until 1996.*

SYDNEY PARDON 1855–1925

The Greatest Editor

MATTHEW ENGEL

One man is forever associated with this almanack, and the name Wisden is known wherever cricket is played. But in fact the history of the book is bound up with two completely different families – the Pardons and the Prestons – who between them provided the editor for more than half its 142 years.

Of these, one man stands out: Sydney Herbert Pardon, editor of *Wisden* for 35 years – from 1891 to his death – cricket correspondent of *The Times*, and senior partner of the Cricket Reporting Agency, known to everyone in sports journalism as Pardon's. It is fair to say that in the early years of the 20th century he was the embodiment of English cricket writing.

September 23, when the 2005 cricket season will still be dawdling to its close, will mark the 150th anniversary of Sydney Pardon's birth. Surrey will be playing Middlesex at The Oval. This was the ground where he grew up watching cricket and which he always seemed to love best. It may be a moment to reflect on what Pardon would have recognised (the essence of the game for sure, the gasometers and probably some of The Oval's remaining dark and unreconstructed corners), and what he would not (helmets, diving in the outfield, the absence of spinners, and Championship cricket as late as his birthday). One would like to believe that the sight somewhere in the press box of a *Wisden*, still going strong 80 years after his death, would please him. This almanack's continued existence owes more to Sydney Pardon than to anyone else.

It also owes much to another member of his family, and perhaps to a third. Sydney was the son of George Pardon, a well-known Victorian sportswriter whose splendid nom de plume was Captain Crawley. The captain functioned as John Wisden's ghost writer (Sydney would certainly recognise that sad trade today) and Wisden acknowledged his role in his book *Cricket, And How To Play It*. So it is possible that he had some unacknowledged role in the production of the early almanacks.

We do know that George's eldest son Charles helped rescue the book. By the mid-1880s it was barely spluttering into life, and the 1886 edition came out a year late. Charles Pardon grabbed the production end of the business by the scruff and brought out the almanack on time. It is hard to know what he might have achieved, because in 1890 he died, aged just 40, and the editorship passed to his younger brother.

"When he arrived, the almanack was a publication in disarray covering an area of parochial interest," Benny Green wrote of Sydney. "By the time he left, *Wisden* was one of the great almanacks of the world." Pardon's

SYDNEY PARDON IN WISDEN

1897   On a strike by professionals over pay...

The players were right in principle, but... their action was ill-judged and inopportune... Out of their revolt, however, I hope and believe that good will come. With England and Australia matches attracting such immense crowds of people, it is only right that the professionals should be liberally rewarded for their services.

1899   On C. B. Fry being called for throwing...

The no-balling of Mr Fry was only a case of long-delayed justice. As a matter of fact he ought never, after his caricature of bowling in the MCC and Oxford match at Lord's in 1892, to have been allowed to bowl at all.

1902   On throwing...

If the captains stick to their guns, we shall soon be entirely free from an evil of which not very long ago it seemed impossible to get rid.

1905   On a two-division County Championship...

The system which answers very well with football would not do at all for cricket. The idea of a county with the traditions of Surrey or Notts being relegated to the second-class as the result of one bad season could not be entertained for a moment.

1910   On England selectors...

Experts occasionally do strange things and this was one of the strangest. The idea of letting England go into the field in fine weather, on a typical Oval wicket, with no fast bowler except Sharp touched the confines of lunacy.

1911   On county finances...

There was a grave fear early in the autumn that Derbyshire as a first-class county club would cease to exist ... Cricket being one of the cheapest forms of amusement, it ought to be a simple matter for all who have the interest of their county club at heart to get new members.

1913   On tinkering...

Mr F. R. Spofforth made the astounding suggestion that the best way of improving cricket was to give two runs to the fielding side for every maiden over bowled. Never, I should think, has such an absurd proposition been put forward by a first-rate expert... Cricket does not stand in need of alterations. When played in the proper spirit – every match on its own merits – the game is as good as ever it was. It must not be tampered with to please people who vainly think that it can have the concentrated excitement of an hour-and-a-half's football.

1921   On the fixture list...

The whole cricket world would roar with laughter at the idea of a match between Northamptonshire and England, but where the Australians are concerned we take quite seriously fixtures just as absurd.

1922   On imports...

I object strongly to the importation of Australian players... Even at the risk of being described, as I have been before now, as a hide-bound Tory, I must affirm my belief that the two years' residential qualification is a great safeguard in preserving the true spirit of county cricket.

Research: Christopher Lane

special contribution – an act of genius, really – was to combine the virtues of an authoritative book of record, comparable to *Whitaker's* or *Who's Who*, with those of an elite journal of opinion. The Notes by the Editor grew out of his personal crusade against throwing. They turned into an institution he made powerful enough to endure to the present day.

Sydney Pardon

Pardon was a man of his time, of course. Much of his writing now seems a little quaint. But he was unflinching, and when he thought the Establishment was wrong he said so with a trenchancy by no means common among sportswriters of his day. But he was not just a sports writer: he wrote for *The Times* on music, the turf and the theatre, once contributing a seven-part series on Fifty Years of The Stage, in which he remembered Henry Irving and the old Lyceum. And he was sufficiently grand to have the title of cricket correspondent of *The Times*, but not have to sully himself with grubby match-reporting – and also to have his articles, in a paper that prided itself on its reporters' anonymity, published under the initials S. H. P., which everyone in cricket must have been able to identify.

Yet he was not an obviously grand man. He was small (a tradition among *Wisden* editors, that began with the "Little Wonder", John Wisden himself, and has somehow continued pretty much ever since) with – according to *The Times* obituary – "small feet, small hands and long tapering fingers which were never still and... small twinkling restless eyes".

Pardon was a bachelor, and the dynasty died with him. Pardon's agency, however, continued to dominate day-to-day cricket reporting until it was taken over by the Press Association in 1965, and even then his business heirs remained in charge of the almanack until Norman Preston died in 1980. The tradition, we hope, lives on now.

"He mourned over any England failure," wrote his immediate successor, Stewart Caine, in his tribute to Pardon in *Wisden 1926*, "yet, however keenly he might feel, nothing but sound and gracious criticism ever emanated from his pen. He treated his calling as a trust, and no power on earth could have made him write anything of which he was not absolutely convinced." No sportswriter could ask for a better epitaph.

Breaking the Silence

DAVID RAYVERN ALLEN

It was Grace who started it – just as he did so many things in cricket. Several years ago, while presenting a profile of W.G. for BBC Radio, I asked if anyone knew of the existence of a recording of the great man actually speaking. Nobody got in touch. There have been persistent reports that Grace's voice found its way on to those primitive wax cylinders first produced at the end of the 19th century, but so far nothing has turned up. All we have is C. B. Fry's insistence that from behind the mighty beard there came forth a "high-pitched squeaky voice". We cannot judge that for ourselves.

We can, however, ensure that future generations of cricketers can be heard as well as seen. The game is exhaustively recorded through art and artefacts, in recent years through video, and of course through written documentation. Oral history is a different question.

There are archives with audio holdings on the game, notably the Don Rowan Collection (put together by an enthusiastic amateur) at the British Library, and the BBC Sound Archive, which contains interviews with a number of famous figures from the past: Charles Kortright, Wilfred Rhodes and Sydney Barnes among them. But a broadcasting organisation cannot be custodian of cricket's heritage. The BBC's sheer volume of output in all fields means it has to take its own decisions about what or what not to keep. Inevitably, much valuable material has been irretrievably lost.

So it was put to MCC that there ought to be a national audio archive at the home of the game, Lord's. And they embraced the idea enthusiastically. A small team of professional interviewers have already started to tape conversations with cricketers and others connected with the game, asking them about their own time in cricket.

Modern stars are asked the same questions incessantly and get fed up. But many cricketers retire with their memories and thoughts on the game intact. They are never debriefed and can feel unrecognised. Consequently, some can feel disillusionment with and even bitterness towards the game they once loved. The aim is to redress such omissions by urging those who have helped make the game what it is create their own record for posterity.

Audio is an intimate and revelatory medium. The voice itself can tell so much more than the words. To hear Grace speak would be to gain matchless insight into the man. So begins a project which should be never-ending. And with luck, tomorrow's students of cricket will gain a deeper understanding of it.

David Rayvern Allen was a BBC radio producer from 1964 to 1993. His biography of E. W. Swanton, Jim, *was published in 2004. Please send suggestions for possible interviewees to him at 30 St Peter's Way, Chorleywood, Herts WD3 5QE (draproductions@hotmail.com).*

Hansie: The Making of a Martyr

ROB STEEN

Few things ring alarm bells more loudly than a newspaper story pinned on "a survey". But sometimes these can be very instructive. One such survey was conducted by the South African Broadcasting Corporation to discover the "100 Greatest South Africans". It was hardly a scientific study since the voting methods – phone, text and email – obviously favoured white South Africans rather than black.

Aware of the potential for embarrassment, the organisers decided in advance that Nelson Mandela would finish first. They did not plan the rest of the ballot well enough to reflect the new South Africa in quite the way they had hoped: Hendrik Verwoerd, the architect of apartheid, finished 14 places above Walter Sisulu, who helped demolish it. Most astonishing of all, to the casual observer, was the name in 11th place, only just behind President Thabo Mbeki and Bishop Desmond Tutu: Hansie Cronje, former captain of the South African cricket team and admitted match-fixer.

As beneficiaries of the estates of Elvis Presley, James Dean and Marilyn Monroe will attest, death can be less a full stop than a colon. And although Cronje was no global superstar, his story was a three-part drama that surpassed even Elvis or Marilyn: after the rise to fame came the disgrace, and only then the tragically early death – in a plane crash in June 2002, two years after he had been forced to admit taking bribes from bookmakers. This has given the Hansie story an extraordinary potency, especially among the Afrikaaner community from which he sprang, where he remains revered, not so much as a fallen hero but as a martyr.

His afterlife started with Leon Dorfling's Hawker Siddeley Project. Why not recover the wreckage of the 748 freighter on which Cronje hitched a last-minute ride, and exhibit it? Holidaymakers in Mossel Bay were soon paying canny Leon 20 rand (about £1.50) per gawk. Then came the opening ceremony for the 2003 World Cup at Newlands, where the caterers rebranded one of their most popular items. "The Gatsby", a huge and somewhat grotesque roll stuffed with ham, tomato and chips, metamorphosed into "The Hansie". Any symbolism seems to have been accidental, but the men do have something in common: Scott Fitzgerald invented a character who elevated money above honour.

But the process preceded the crash. The King commission of inquiry into match-fixing had barely completed its hearings when the rehabilitation programme kicked into gear. One TV channel aired a three-part homage/interview with an apologetic Cronje over successive evenings: his fee was reportedly in the region of one million rand. The *Hello*-style footage consisted largely of Cronje and his wife Bertha in their luxury home, or walking lovingly along a sun-kissed beach. In the final instalment Cronje and the interviewer,

Invisible presence: Hansie Cronje had died nearly a year earlier, but his name was hard to avoid at the 2003 World Cup in South Africa.

Picture by David Gray, Reuters

Michael Haysman, both in blue shirts and khaki trousers, stood either side of a roaring fireplace, glass of wine in hand and chatting amiably.

Barred from direct involvement in cricket, Cronje then undertook a series of speaking engagements around the country, set up by a marketing arm of Castle Lager, co-sponsors of the Test team then and now. The audiences were almost exclusively white, middle-class and male: the nucleus of the Rainbow Nation's audience for cricket and rugby. And the talks sold out.

Cronje was widely seen as a victim, who was punished cruelly for his misdemeanours while others involved, especially Australians, escaped. Many took at face value his assertion that he had never tried to lose a match for his country. Others are adamant he was picked on while black government officials get away with corruption. The foreign currency in Cronje's cupboard – for which he went unpunished – is seen as an irrelevance.

The victim thesis, strong enough while Cronje was alive, grew wings after he died. A year after the crash, there came an *Observer* article headlined "Was Hansie Cronje murdered?" "Many senior police officers believe he may have been – and they are working covertly to prove it," said the author, Daniel Murt. "A lot of people wanted Cronje dead," claimed one investigator. "It suits the police to have a closed case." This theory is pooh-poohed by most sources – after all, Cronje only took the plane at the last minute – and was ignored by the official inquiry. But it all helps the myth. "Pictures of Cronje remain on office desks," wrote Murt, "statues are erected in his honour, team-mates proclaim his virtues, his image is emblazoned across T-shirts, and the making of his martyrdom continues to grow."

But this has strange effects. The *Cape Times* recently ran an article headlined "Hansie killed my mother", in which a woman blamed her parent's death on

Cronje's misdemeanours and the way they had shattered her belief system. Yet the belief systems of white South Africans, and the Afrikaaner community in particular, have endured many shocks over the past decade or so. They have already been obliged to disavow their former political leaders. Who would ever have expected they would have to disavow a cricket captain too?

"Afrikaaners do feel embattled, especially on the sporting front, now that there are noises from parliamentary committees that their days are numbered in sport," explained Professor Bruce Murray, author of *Caught Behind*, a study of race and politics in South African cricket. "There is this sense that whites are being robbed of their cricket history. If you go to the corridor leading to the Long Room at the Wanderers, all the photographs of the old Springboks have been removed and replaced by bats from the World Cup. The grounds are being sanitised, and there's a denial of the white cricketing past."

Serving his memory – or serving Mammon? Leon Dorfling and the wreckage of Hansie Cronje's plane.

Picture by Jan Taljaard, Die Burger

Before the fall. A pensive Hansie Cronje in 1994.

Picture by Patrick Eagar

"There's a widespread feeling that Cronje owned up and came clean," Murray added, "and that it's always the South Africans who get the rough end of things." While that persists, the Cronje story will retain its power.

In November, it was reported that *The Fix*, a movie about match-rigging and Hansie's role in it, would be shot in India and South Africa in 2005. Cronje's elder brother, Frans, was dismissive. "I think they're running after the sensation," he charged, piqued that the family had not been consulted. "It's about how fragile mankind can be," explained the producer, Bonnie Rodini. Within days Frans himself would announce that the Cronjes had authorised a full-length biopic of Hansie, co-produced by Frans's own Cape Town-based company. Also in the pipeline was a biography by journalist Garth King, commissioned by the Cronjes.

Cue a plaintive family statement: "We still receive a great deal of communication... from people wanting to know more about Hansie's life and pledging their support. We hope that both the book and film will help those to attain some kind of closure regarding Hansie... the story is now ready to be told." The question is what you tell, and how you tell it.

Rob Steen is an author, freelance journalist and lecturer. His most recent book is 500-1: The Miracle of Headingley '81.

Additional reporting by Peter Robinson and John Young.

The Tragedy that Brought Us Together

CHARLIE AUSTIN

Boxing Day is traditionally a day of cricketing celebration, the biggest of the year. At 00.58 GMT on December 26, 2004, Sri Lanka's batsmen were already in difficulties against New Zealand in Auckland; Pakistan's batsmen were up against the Australian bowlers and a crowd of more than 61,000 at the MCG; England and South Africa were sleeping off Christmas and readying for battle when morning reached Durban; the teams were just waking in Dhaka, preparing for a game that produced a Bangladesh victory over India which would, on a normal day, have been a famous one.

This great global festival of the game went ahead as planned. It was only when the Sri Lankan players returned to their hotel rooms, and switched on their televisions, that the routine despondency of defeat was replaced by a genuine horror, something almost beyond human comprehension

For 00.58 was the moment when a violent underwater earthquake, the largest to hit the planet for 40 years, ruptured the fault line between the tectonic plates north and west of Indonesia. This jolted the seabed vertically and displaced hundreds of cubic miles of water, creating an underwater wave that was to carve a path of destruction across the vast expanse of the Indian Ocean.

The wave, travelling at up to 500 miles per hour, sped south-east towards the Indonesian province of Aceh, north towards Thailand's beach resorts, and west to Sri Lanka, south India, the Andamans and the Maldives. As it reached shallower waters it slowed and gathered strength, pulling back the normal shoreline by up to 50 yards in some places, leaving fish and lobsters flapping in the mud, before surging inland. At 03.36 GMT – 9.36 in the morning local time – the initial wave smashed into the east coast of Sri Lanka, reaching more than a mile inland in low-lying areas, then circling around the island to find new targets to destroy.

The First XI from Harrow School in England were warming up in readiness for a sweltering day's cricket at the Galle International Stadium – against a combined Richmond/Mahinda schools team – hoping to emulate some of the heroics of the England team which memorably saved a Test there just over a year earlier. "We were about half an hour from starting our game and were warming up," Stephen Jones, the Harrow coach, told the BBC. "Fortunately, we were doing fielding drills right in front of the pavilion – had we been doing them anywhere else on the field we would have been in trouble.

"I remember the level of noise going up and a colleague's wife and daughter screamed at us to watch out. It probably took only five minutes, maybe ten, for the water to get to about five metres deep."

Fortunately, the famous Dutch fort that overlooks the ground had achieved a defensive feat which cannot have been in the builders' minds. It sheltered

Comment

Muttiah Muralitharan helps with the distribution of food aid in the aftermath of the tsunami.

Picture by Giuseppe Cacace, Getty Images

the players from the full force of the wave. The frothing backwash surged around the fort and caught them in a pincer, but slowly enough for them to seek refuge. The water kept coming, and within minutes the boys were surrounded by swirling waters carrying fishing trawlers, upturned vehicles and piles of scrap metal and rubble. "We headed for the pavilion," said Jones, "but I actually went back to collect the kit bag. At that stage I did not see it as a life-threatening situation. When the water was around two metres deep, I realised it was serious. Then the team bus started floating towards the pavilion."

The two frightened teams sheltered in the solid two-storey pavilion for over two hours while the water destroyed the stadium, pulling down stands, gutting the indoor nets and covering the green outfield with salty sludge. Behind the pavilion, luckily out of the boys' view, the town's central bus station was ripped apart and hundreds were drowned. A few miles away a train carrying 1,200 people was plucked off its tracks and engulfed. Julian Ayer, whose stepson was in the Harrow team, was swept to his death as he was driven from his hotel to watch his son play. Another father was carried deep inland but amazingly survived and was found the next day.

In Auckland, the Sri Lankan players watched CNN red-eyed throughout the night, rightly scared for the safety of their families. Sanath Jayasuriya's 60-year-old mother Breeda was shopping for vegetables in the market at Matara, a fishing town on Sri Lanka's southern tip, when the waves poured over the beach. She was plucked from the water by a bystander, but badly injured. Upul Chandana's mother also had a lucky escape and then watched in horror as one of her rescuers was dragged to his death by the sea. Nuwan Zoysa's aunt and three relatives of Dilhara Fernando's wife also died. Local cricketers suffered too. In Hambantota, another fishing town on the south coast, the waves were so powerful that the whole seaside town centre was reduced to rubble. Seven players from the town's promotion-seeking Division Two club were washed away.

In India the wave hit hardest in Tamil Nadu, along the Coromandel Coast. At the town of Cuddalore, just south of Pondicherry, the children head for the Silver Beach every Sunday morning with rubber balls and coconut palm bats. Distraught parents looked on powerless as the waves dragged many to their deaths. "I saw my sons running but the next moment the waves hit them," said K. Manikandan, a local fisherman. "The beach was their playground. This was where they were born and brought up. How could this beach become their deathbed?" he asked. Manikandan had bought them a new bat from the market just two days before.

Ajit, a boy of nine, told *The Times*: "We saw the cricket people running forward, the waves were following them and attacked them. The waves went out 15 seconds later and we didn't see any of the cricketers in the water. They were all covered." On the small islands of the Coromandel Coast, the devastation was even worse. At the island village of MGR Thittu, 30 beach cricketers were reported to have been swept away; their families eventually left home and were taken into a refugee camp on the mainland.

Yet it took time for the world to wake up to the scale of this catastrophe. The estimated death toll rose steadily, but slowly, until the figure topped the 150,000 mark. Cricket was not alone in being slow to grasp what had happened. Sri Lanka Cricket, the game's governing body there, did not get a grip for a full three days, upsetting their players by refusing to abandon the New Zealand tour. The team's request to return home to their families was callously turned down on the grounds that the tour's cancellation would precipitate a fine from the International Cricket Council, of the sort with which England were threatened when they were trying to avoid going to Zimbabwe. Eventually, it emerged that the board, despite a media release to the contrary, had not even consulted the ICC, which was willing to support cancellation. At that point Sri Lanka Cricket had to acknowledge its misjudgment and call off the tour.

On the whole, the game reacted as swiftly as anyone. Galvanised by Tim May, head of FICA, the international cricketers' federation, the world's players gathered in Melbourne only 15 days after the tragedy to play the first World Cricket Tsunami Appeal match between an Asian XI and a World XI. More than 70,000 people turned up to see a game involving all the world's leading players, except from the England and South African Test teams who were in the midst of a hectic series. Even Muttiah Muralitharan forgot his reservations about bowling in Australia, and he was cheered when he came on to bowl. About £5.7m was raised in pledges, television rights and ticket sales for World Vision, a non-governmental organisation providing survival kits to tsunami-

Making do: boys in a refugee camp at Port Blair on the Andaman Islands, badly affected by the tsunami, use a makeshift bat.

Picture by Jayanta Shaw, Reuters

hit communities throughout the region. An online auction of the players' shirts also raised £216,000.

FICA followed up by organising a three-match limited-over series between a New Zealand team and a World XI captained by Shane Warne, as a replacement for the postponed Sri Lankan series. It failed to spark as a spectacle, partly because several of the World XI were so obviously rusty after a lack of practice, but raised another valuable £417,000. Other matches were pencilled in for later in the year, including a Twenty20 fixture between an Asian XI and a World XI on June 20 at The Oval.

There were a host of smaller efforts too. MCC donated £25,000 to the rebuilding of Galle's stadium. This was estimated to cost £2.25m and take at least a year, but later assessments were pessimistic that it would ever happen. Bollywood film stars and cricketers linked up for a game in Mumbai, and Thatcham Town Cricket Club from the Thames Valley League announced a 24-hour tour of all 18 first-class county headquarters to collect memorabilia for an auction.

In Sri Lanka, the players' arrival home after the disaster was marked by a flurry of fundraising led by Muralitharan, who had himself narrowly missed being caught up in the wave. Murali, who was in Sri Lanka recovering from shoulder surgery, was driving south from Colombo to attend a children's charity function. But midway through the two-hour journey, alerted by the agitated sea and fleeing cars, he turned around and sped back to the capital. However, a bus carrying 50 children to the function was swept into the sea without trace.

> **Murali was a big enough star to speak out**

The incident propelled Murali into action in partnership with the United Nation's World Food Programme, with whom he was already a goodwill ambassador. The WFP had large food stores in Colombo but no transport in the early stages for distribution. Personally organising the hire of private lorries, with assistance from team-mates Mahela Jayawardene and Kumar Sangakkara, Muralitharan led three separate relief convoys to different parts of the country.

The food was only part of the effort; the cricketers brightened the mood amongst the traumatised refugees. For children, the delight created by a surprise meeting with one of their heroes cut through some of the post-disaster depression. They crowded around excitedly, seizing any piece of scrap paper for an autograph and asking a stream of questions about their on-field exploits.

Muralitharan's crusade included a willingness to use his voice. Most cricketers are apolitical in Sri Lanka, worried about upsetting bigwigs, but Murali was a big enough star to speak out, warning about corruption and political discrimination in the aid distribution process. Sure enough, there was a backlash and wild allegations against him – in one publication he was accused of being a secret agent for the Tamil Tigers.

Sri Lanka Cricket launched their own emergency relief programme called Cricket Aid, a two-tiered campaign that was to set up four emergency camps for about 2,000 people and then permanent housing in themed "Cricket Villages" for 200 families who had lost their homes. Volunteers from cricket clubs helped staff the camps, the first of which was set up in Matara.

Predictably for an administration that is perennially politicised, Sri Lanka Cricket's scheme was not universally embraced. Thilanga Sumathipala, the former board president embroiled in an alleged immigration fraud involving a high-profile gangster, was appointed chairman. And Arjuna Ranatunga, Sri Lanka's former captain who is now a cabinet minister, lambasted the project for being nothing more than an opportunistic vehicle to rebuild Sumathipala's shattered reputation.

Ranatunga's view was shared by many but voiced by few. The Cricket Aid programme was worryingly over-obsessed with PR from the start. A pretentious (and expensive) launch was then followed by behind-the-scenes bullying of the players, some of whom were urged not to support Muralitharan's work, which was deflecting publicity from the board's own scheme, or raise funds for their own projects.

The Sri Lankan politicking, distasteful as it was, did not detract from the main facts. Against a tragedy of this scale, cricket becomes trivial. But for many of the people affected by the catastrophe, cricket is not just a triviality: it is part of their being. The game could help, and it did.

Charlie Austin is Sri Lankan correspondent of Cricinfo.

Opposite: Ours! In Mumbai, Adam Gilchrist grasps the Border–Gavaskar Trophy regained by Australia in November.
Picture by Hamish Blair, Getty Images

PART TWO

World View

WORLD CRICKET IN 2004

The Year of the Big Two

SIMON WILDE

Few, if any, have disputed Australia's right to be regarded as the world's best Test team since they toppled West Indies in 1995. But who exactly were their nearest rivals? This provided more debate. Was it South Africa, or Pakistan, or India? All had laid claim at various times. But the overriding feature of world cricket in 2004 was that there could be little argument as to who were the two best sides in the world. They were Australia and England.

In terms of figures, **England** were the Test team of the year. They won 11 of their 13 matches and remained unbeaten, a singular achievement in an age of so much international cricket, while Australia won ten, drew three and lost one – but only after failing by 14 runs to reach a target of 107 on a ropy pitch in Mumbai when they had already achieved a long-standing ambition of winning a series in India.

After nearly 20 years of variable performances, and more failures than successes, England, under an experienced coach in Duncan Fletcher and a newish captain in Michael Vaughan, finally gelled into a settled and efficient outfit. They emphatically won their first series in the Caribbean for 36 years – a process they began by routing West Indies in Jamaica for 47, their lowest-ever total – before winning all seven home Tests against New Zealand and West Indies, their first whitewashes in series of three or more games since 1978. They were probably thwarted only by Durban's fading light from taking the two wickets they needed to become the first side in history to win 12 Tests in a year (their 11 left them equal with the great West Indies side of 1984).

Australia's ten wins equalled their own best tally set in 2002, and by winning two series on the subcontinent they arguably won in more demanding conditions than England. They were into whitewashes too and, despite

TEST MATCHES IN 2004

	Tests	Won	Lost	Drawn	% won	% lost	% drawn
England	13	11	0	2	**84.62**	0.00	15.38
Australia	14	10	1	3	**71.43**	7.14	21.43
India	12	6	3	3	**50.00**	25.00	25.00
Sri Lanka	11	4	5	2	**36.36**	45.45	18.18
New Zealand	10	3	6	1	**30.00**	60.00	10.00
Pakistan	7	2	5	0	**28.57**	71.43	0.00
Zimbabwe	4	1	2	1	**25.00**	50.00	25.00
South Africa	11	2	4	5	**18.18**	36.36	45.45
West Indies	12	1	8	3	**8.33**	66.67	25.00
Bangladesh	8	0	6	2	**0.00**	75.00	25.00
Totals	51	40	40	11	78.43	78.43	21.57

conceding first-innings deficits in all three games, inflicted the first 3–0 whitewash Sri Lanka had ever suffered on their own soil. Australia continued to score faster than their rivals in Tests, but only just: their rate of 3.55 put them slightly ahead of West Indies on 3.51 and England on 3.49.

It was the first time England had gone unbeaten in Tests since 1970 (when they played only twice); the only side to have gone unbeaten in as many matches in a year were the 1987 Pakistanis, who won only three of the 13 games they played. England called on only 18 players, and their four leading bowlers – Steve Harmison, Matthew Hoggard, Andrew Flintoff and Ashley Giles – took 195 wickets between them, not far behind the 219 netted by Australia's front-line quartet of Glenn McGrath, Jason Gillespie, Michael Kasprowicz and Shane Warne. Finally, it seemed, England were living close to opponents they had so long aspired to match.

As it happened, in Tests, England faced neither Australia nor India (who after their performance in the 2003-04 series began the year looking like Australia's nearest challengers), but they beat both in the one-day arena, Australia resoundingly in the ICC Champions Trophy to end a run of 14 defeats at the hands of their oldest enemy, and India twice in the three-match NatWest Challenge. England's defeat by a young West Indies side in the Champions Trophy final, in which they were unexpectedly thwarted by a ninth-wicket stand of 71 between Courtney Browne and Ian Bradshaw, was one of their few setbacks.

India's form in fact was unexceptional, though their triumph in winning Test and one-day series in Pakistan made up for much. Largely for political reasons, they had not made a full tour of their neighbours for more than 14 years and were indebted to their batsmen for coming away with their first win in a major series abroad since 1993. However, hopes of a repeat performance at home in the return series with Australia evaporated as a spate of injuries affected both sides but took heavier toll of the hosts, who badly missed the talismanic Sachin Tendulkar and captain Sourav Ganguly in two matches apiece, their batsmen managing just one century between them in four games. India won nothing of note apart from the glorious mission to Pakistan. And the gloss was even taken off that by Pakistan subsequently beating them four times in one-dayers.

TEST MATCHES IN 2004

(excluding Zimbabwe and Bangladesh matches)

	Tests	Won	Lost	Drawn	% won	% lost	% drawn
England.	13	11	0	2	**84.62**	0.00	15.38
Australia	14	10	1	3	**71.43**	7.14	21.43
India.	10	4	3	3	**40.00**	30.00	30.00
Pakistan.	7	2	5	0	**28.57**	71.43	0.00
Sri Lanka	9	2	5	2	**22.22**	55.56	22.22
South Africa.	11	2	4	5	**18.18**	36.36	45.45
New Zealand	8	1	6	1	**12.50**	75.00	12.50
West Indies	10	0	8	2	**0.00**	80.00	20.00
Totals	41	32	32	9	78.05	78.05	21.95

National pride: at Rawalpindi in April, India beat Pakistan by an innings and 131 runs to secure the series. Danish Kaneria and Asim Kamal head for the pavilion; the Indians for cloud nine.

Picture by Arko Datta, Reuters

The dominance of England and Australia amounted to a return to cricket's pre-1960s order when both were rarely beaten by anyone except each other. The rest struggled to string together respectable results, at least in Tests. After losing so heavily to Australia, an event that triggered Hashan Tillekeratne's resignation as Test captain, **Sri Lanka** rallied to beat South Africa at home and draw in Pakistan. They also remained competitive in one-dayers in Asia, winning two triangular events and crushing South Africa 5–0, but their year ended in utter distress with the tsunami disaster that devastated their island and killed around 30,000. The stadium at Galle was wrecked. Within days, the team had abandoned a tour of New Zealand to return home.

In cricketing terms, it was an especially difficult year for **Pakistan**, **South Africa** and **West Indies**, all of whom changed coaches in efforts to spark revivals, West Indies turning to the Australian Bennett King as their first overseas coach. There was a sense that all of them possessed more talent than was reflected in results and that modernisation in administration, selection and preparation – of the kind that had taken place first in Australia and then England – was overdue.

Things were not helped in the Caribbean by the impact of another natural disaster, with hurricane Ivan creating havoc in Grenada, home to an impressive new ground at St George's earmarked to stage six second-phase matches at the 2007 World Cup. Brian Lara, the West Indies captain, said the disaster brought his team together and contributed to their shock victory in the ICC Champions Trophy. Earlier in the year, Lara himself gave his people a lift by taking advantage of a featherbed pitch in Antigua and a weary England attack to make a single-minded – and successful – mission to regain from Australia's Matthew Hayden possession of the Test record score. Equally importantly, Lara's 400 not out prevented West Indies suffering their first-ever whitewash at home and possibly saved Lara's captaincy.

New Zealand were another side to enjoy little success in the Test arena but they were usually a force to be reckoned with in limited-overs internationals. They won the one-day triangular in England, trounced Pakistan and South Africa, and held Australia 1–1 in Australia.

The biggest concern for the International Cricket Council was that its vision of spreading cricket's gospel suffered a series of heavy blows, with Zimbabwe and Bangladesh, the two newest Test recruits, and Kenya, the last side awarded one-day international status, all facing severe difficulties.

ONE-DAY INTERNATIONALS IN 2004

	ODIs	Won	Lost	NR	% won	% lost
New Zealand	25	19	4	2	**82.61**	17.39
Australia	26	19	5	2	**79.17**	20.83
Sri Lanka	28	20	8	0	**71.43**	28.57
England	21	12	8	1	**60.00**	40.00
West Indies	24	12	8	4	**60.00**	40.00
Pakistan	27	15	12	0	**55.56**	44.44
India	32	15	16	1	**48.39**	51.61
South Africa	18	5	12	1	**29.41**	70.59
Bangladesh	19	3	16	0	**15.79**	84.21
Zimbabwe	28	2	25	1	**7.41**	92.59
Kenya	2	0	2	0	**0.00**	100.00
Hong Kong	2	0	2	0	**0.00**	100.00
United Arab Emirates	2	0	2	0	**0.00**	100.00
USA	2	0	2	0	**0.00**	100.00
Totals	128	122	122	6		

For one-day internationals, the % won and lost excludes no results.

Zimbabwe cricket spent most of the year engulfed in an acrimonious dispute between the board and its experienced white players, including captain Heath Streak, which led to the rebel players, who had demanded changes in selection and administration, withdrawing from the team. They were not the first players to have fallen out with the board since 2000 but never had there been a protest involving such numbers. This left the board to pick a side to face Sri Lanka containing several novices under Tatenda Taibu (who become Test cricket's youngest-ever captain at 20), with predictable results. Sri Lanka won all five one-day matches easily, dismissing Zimbabwe for a record one-day low of 35 in the third match in Harare, and both Tests by an innings and plenty.

The prospect of even more lop-sided matches against Australia, who toured Zimbabwe a few weeks later, prompted the ICC to call an emergency meeting

of its executive board to consider whether the scheduled two Tests should
go ahead. Before it took place board officials from Australia and Zimbabwe
decided to cancel the Tests but proceed with the one-dayers, which Australia
duly won 3–0. Shortly afterwards, Zimbabwe were forced out of Test cricket
for the rest of the year, though they were allowed to continue playing one-
day internationals, to the irritation of England, who were obiliged – under
threat from the ICC – to undertake a one-day tour. They found this
unappealing in both moral and cricketing terms. But England won the series
4–0 and, like Australia, found trouble only in getting interested.

And little had changed by the end of the year. Attempts to resolve the
differences between the players and the board failed and several of the white
rebels left Zimbabwe to pursue careers elsewhere, although one former rebel,
Gavin Ewing, played for the new-look side.

TEST CENTURIES FOR EACH COUNTRY

		2004	2003
Australia		22	25
England		20	11
South Africa		16	16
Sri Lanka		15	5
West Indies		15	13
India		11	8
New Zealand		9	8
Pakistan		6	8
Bangladesh		4	2
Zimbabwe		1	3
Total		119	99

Reservations had been expressed for some time that neither Zimbabwe
nor Bangladesh provided worthwhile Test opposition. Support for them
among television and sponsorship companies in particular was on the wane.
The ICC's executive board meeting in October heard three proposals for
revising the future tours programme that all involved the two of them being
restricted to playing Tests at home on the basis that routine beatings abroad
were hindering, rather than helping, their development.

Bangladesh actually showed modest signs of progress on the field. They
deservedly drew with West Indies in St Lucia, where they achieved their
highest Test score of 416, and ended a five-year drought in one-dayers by
beating Zimbabwe, Hong Kong and India. The victory over India in Dhaka
was Bangladesh's first on home soil to set against 34 previous defeats, but
it was against a weakened Indian team.

Kenyan cricket was in no better shape than Zimbabwe's. Hopes that their
giant-killing run in the 2003 World Cup might be the start of a programme
of development that would culminate in an application for full Test status
proved ill-founded as Kenya, after a respectable debut in the Caribbean's

They just keep coming: Kumar Sangakkara passed 1,000 runs for the calendar year in both Tests and one-day internationals.

Picture by Hamish Blair, Getty Images

first-class competition, became engulfed in allegations of maladministration and corruption. Maurice Odumbe, a former Kenya captain, was found guilty of "inappropriate contact" with an Indian bookmaker and banned for five years; another 14 players were due to be summoned before the ICC's anti-corruption and security unit early in 2005. A group of leading players, including Steve Tikolo, the then captain, failed to attend training for the Intercontinental Cup, complaining that they were not getting their salaries.

Nor did the Champions Trophy do much to suggest cricket's church was broadening, with the four mice in the pews – Zimbabwe, Bangladesh, Kenya and the **United States** – losing every game and looking thoroughly out of place. Kenya lost nine wickets in the space of 63 balls to Pakistan.

Overall, bat continued ruthlessly to dominate ball. The year's tally of individual Test centuries was 119, yet another record, in 51 Tests, Michael Clarke bringing up the year's century with 141 in Brisbane on November 20. Damien Martyn, of Australia, scored six off his own bat. The figure for 2003, when there were fewer Tests because of the World Cup, was 99 in 44 (2.25 per match).

Nasser Hussain retired after scoring a match-winning century at Lord's and Stuart Carlisle also scored a hundred in what looked like being his final Test innings; as one of Zimbabwe's rebels, he dropped out of the team soon afterwards. Hussain's judgment was probably sound. He stepped down because Andrew Strauss had scored a century on debut as a stand-in and Hussain didn't want to get in his way: with Hussain gone, Strauss stayed in the team, made another three centuries before the year was out and on January 3, 2005, scored his 1,000th Test run, a record 228 days after his debut. Like Clarke, Strauss scored hundreds on his first Test appearances at home and abroad.

Even tail-enders enjoyed themselves. Eight hundreds were made from No. 7 (four for New Zealand) and two wicket-keepers, Mark Boucher of South Africa and Bangladesh's Khaled Mashud, scored them from No. 8. In the same game at St Lucia, Mashud's team-mate Mohammad Rafique, scored 111 at No. 9. Zaheer Khan of India set a new record for a No. 11 with 75, and Glenn McGrath recorded his maiden fifty in his 102nd Test.

Not everyone was content with a hundred. There were 14 double-centuries, and their mean figure was 258, boosted of course by Lara's exploits in Antigua. In Multan, Virender Sehwag pushed on to complete India's first-ever triple-century. Tendulkar and Kumar Sangakkara hit two double-hundreds each.

Eleven batsmen made 1,000 Test runs, the most in one year, beating the previous best of six recorded in each of the three previous years. Martyn, Justin Langer and Jacques Kallis all scored in excess of 1,200 runs and Hayden became the first to score 1,000 four years in a row. Sangakkara reached 1,000 runs in both Tests and one-dayers. Many were not just safe scorers but fast ones as well: Sehwag, for example, blazed his way to 309 off 375 balls against Pakistan and 164 off 228 against South Africa. His 1,141 runs came at the rate of 73.6 per 100 balls, the best of any specialist batsman.

The evidence of recent years was that batsmen had become increasingly hard to curb. In one-dayers this was plain from the frequency with which teams batting second met their targets. No wonder bowlers strove to find fresh ways to keep them in check, none more controversial than the spinner's "other one", or *doosra*. Some critics argued that this ball could not be purveyed legally, and super slo-mo television pictures only fuelled the debate.

The issue came to a head when Sri Lanka's Muttiah Muralitharan, whose methods had generated controversy for years, was reported by ICC match referee Chris Broad after the home series against Australia. For several weeks Murali's *doosra* became a *dontsra*, and the controversy took some of the shine from his feat of displacing Courtney Walsh as leading Test wicket-taker.

Murali, meanwhile, insisted there was nothing to change and went to great lengths to demonstrate that he did not unduly bend his arm delivering the *doosra,* bowling in the nets wearing a steel brace on his right arm. But when Australian prime minister John Howard labelled him a chucker, Murali withdrew from the reciprocal series in Australia on personal grounds, though he later said he would be happy to play there again. Murali missed two Tests there, and two more in Pakistan to undergo surgery on a cyst, all of which assisted Shane Warne – who enjoyed a productive year after playing no Tests in 2003 because of injury and a drugs ban – in relieving him of the world wicket-taking record in October.

LG ICC TEST CHAMPIONSHIP

(As at January 25, 2005)

		Matches/series	Points	Rating
1	Australia	45	5,933	132
2	England	49	5,396	110
3	India	39	4,209	108
4	Sri Lanka	35	3,613	103
5	Pakistan	31	3,145	101
6	South Africa . .	43	4,247	99
7	New Zealand . .	31	2,891	93
8	West Indies . . .	37	2,717	73
9	Zimbabwe	25	1,045	42
10	Bangladesh . . .	35	220	6

ICC ONE-DAY CHAMPIONSHIP

(As at December 31, 2004)

		Matches	Points	Rating
1	Australia	35	4,748	136
2	New Zealand . .	31	3,718	120
3	Sri Lanka	37	4,334	117
4	England	28	3,046	109
5	Pakistan	43	4,675	109
6	West Indies . . .	26	2,793	107
7	South Africa . .	29	2,929	101
8	India	37	3,639	98
9	Zimbabwe	32	1,860	58
10	Kenya.	8	204	26
11	Bangladesh . . .	28	83	3

Several other bowlers came under scrutiny, including Shoaib Malik, of Pakistan, who was reported more than once and barred from bowling until he completed remedial work, and Harbhajan Singh, whose *doosra* was reported during India's Test in Chittagong, a match which Broad also refereed.

With academic research throwing fresh light on the mechanics of bowling, the ICC ordered its cricket committee to re-examine the issue of what should and should not constitute a legal delivery. The committee effectively recommended handing power back to the on-field umpires by decreeing that all bowlers should be allowed to straighten their arms by up to 15 degrees above shoulder height during delivery, 15 degrees having been calculated as the smallest movement discernible to the naked eye.

Under tests conducted at the ICC Champions Trophy, 13 of the 23 slow bowlers monitored transgressed the previous permissible limit of five degrees for spinners (fast bowlers had been allowed ten degrees). The judgment cleared the way for Murali to resume bowling his *doosra*. The committee's recommendations, which also included switching supervision of a remedial action from the bowler's home board to the ICC, awaited the approval of the ICC's executive board in February 2005.

Amidst the welter of batting records, there were some notable bowling feats. Harmison's seven for 12 in Jamaica was the cheapest seven-wicket haul in Test history and Glenn McGrath's eight for 24 against Pakistan in Perth the cheapest eight-for since the 1890s. Michael Clarke, heralded for his batting, snapped up six for nine for Australia, the third-best six-for, in the absence of the injured Warne on Mumbai's dustbowl. Anil Kumble, Warne and Harmison all took more than 60 Test wickets in the year. Matthew Hoggard, Andrew Blignaut and James Franklin took Test hat-tricks (Blignaut's being the first for Zimbabwe at this level) while Harmison claimed one in one-day cricket.

ICC AWARDS

The International Cricket Council introduced its own awards in 2004, voted on by a panel of 50, including the ten Test captains, seven elite ICC referees and eight elite umpires. and presented at a ceremony in London in September. Indian batsman Rahul Dravid won the Sir Garfield Sobers Trophy as the ICC's Player of the Year, with 64 votes, while two all-rounders, England's Andrew Flintoff and South Africa's Jacques Kallis, won 44 each. Dravid was also named Test Player of the Year, with 82 votes to 53 for Australia's Matthew Hayden. Flintoff was One-Day International Player of the Year, with 58 votes, and Indian pace bowler Irfan Pathan was Emerging Player of the Year, with 100. Simon Taufel was Umpire of the Year, and New Zealand were named the team best exemplifying the Spirit of Cricket. A panel of five also selected two World XIs from the best players of the past 12 months. Their World Test XI was Matthew Hayden (Australia), Herschelle Gibbs (South Africa), Ricky Ponting (Australia), Rahul Dravid (India), Brian Lara (West Indies), Jacques Kallis (South Africa), Adam Gilchrist (Australia), Shane Warne (Australia), Jason Gillespie (Australia) and Steve Harmison (England); the World One-Day International XI was Adam Gilchrist (Australia), Sachin Tendulkar (India), Chris Gayle (West Indies), Ricky Ponting (Australia), Brian Lara (West Indies), Virender Sehwag (India), Jacques Kallis (South Africa), Andrew Flintoff (England), Shaun Pollock (South Africa), Chaminda Vaas (Sri Lanka) and Jason Gillespie (Australia). Ponting was named captain of both teams.

THE VIEW FROM THE TOP

A Golden Age, Yellowing at the Edges

GIDEON HAIGH

Late in 2004, Australia's national broadcaster screened a documentary series entitled *Rookies, Rebels and Renaissance*, reliving the tempestuous cricket summers of the 1980s, revelling in the body shirts, beards and boofy hair. For the uninitiated, though, one aspect of the narrative must have been especially arresting. Throughout the period, it was recalled, the Australian cricket team lost Test matches – by its standards, quite a lot.

Never mind the uninitiated: it was a surprise for the initiated to be so reminded. For as the tenth year of this baggy green and golden age unfolded, the chance of challenge seemed as remote as ever. South Africa and Pakistan, second and third on the ICC Test Championship in January, had stumbled. England, currently second and fantasising freely, have taken one "live" Test off their oldest rivals in 18 years. India, now third and briefly touted as a serious rival, had just been convincingly beaten on their home soil.

In 2004, in fact, Ricky Ponting sponsored a most unusual phenomenon: a revival following what was barely a decline. Steve Waugh's farewell series against India had been a two-cheer affair. Without the injured Glenn McGrath and the banned Shane Warne, Australia's attack had looked all thrust and no cut. Runs had come, as usual, in plenty – but, unusually for a home series, from both sides.

By the end of the year, Australia seemed to have acquired new life; it says much of Ponting's assurance that even Steve Waugh had virtually dropped from view. The country's first Tasmanian skipper placed his stamp on the team during its tour of Sri Lanka in February and March. Thrice Australia trailed on first innings to the home side, Murali, *doosra* and all. Thrice they surged back to win, the victory at Kandy being an escape as great in its way as the 1999 World Cup semi-final.

The stamp proved indelible. Comfortable victors in the rematch with Sri Lanka in the Australian north in July, the team then proceeded to win its first series in India since 1969, setting to rights its disappointments three years earlier. If Ponting himself did not enjoy a full share of these spoils because of a broken thumb, his fingerprints were all over the plans. His absence even had the serendipitous effect of expediting the rise of Michael Clarke – Australian cricket's latest and bonniest prospect.

When New Zealand and Pakistan took their licks in the home summer, there seemed alarmingly little of which to complain. Even Australia's on-field act had improved: only four of Ponting's men faced the ICC beak in 2004, two as a result of related fits of pique at Dambulla in February. Adam Gilchrist was ostentatiously walking, for heaven's sake, which in Australia hitherto has been as much of a solecism as admitting a partiality to Tony Greig's commentary.

Not everyone, however, was happy; as the poet Randall Jarrell once observed: "No matter how golden an age, there will always be someone complaining that everything looks too yellow." Success without a sense of struggle being a paltry thing, some critics, including an administrator as respected as Malcolm Gray and a past master as venerable as Greg Chappell, wondered aloud if Australian dominance risked alienating the public. A review of its strategic plan, completed in November by the smart management consultants McKinsey, then provided Cricket Australia with some evidence to support that theory: flat attendances, diminished ratings, only so-so growth in participation. "The game is not growing," conceded chief executive James Sutherland, "or certainly not at the rate we would like it to grow."

Most countries, of course, would kill to have the dilemmas posed by a surfeit of success, and some saw publicity for the report performing a subtler role, as a trial balloon ahead of the renegotiation of Cricket Australia's memorandum of understanding with the Australian Cricketers' Association; the current four-year deal between the board and the players' trade union is due to expire midway through 2005. For some time, administrators have been muttering *sotto voce* about the players' revenue rake-off. When *Business Review Weekly* magazine published its annual estimates of sporting incomes in December, half of the Australian team were said to be pulling down more than $A1m a year: Ponting ($A2.24m, around £910,000), Gilchrist ($A2m), Warne ($A1.45m), Brett Lee ($A1.3m), Matthew Hayden and McGrath ($A1.11m each). These numbers do not seem so extravagant given the public fame and recognition these players enjoy. The administrative argument runs, however, that without a healthy infrastructure, there is no fame to bestow.

There are strains in Australian cricket, too, that are deeper and longer-term. For much of the country's cricket history, for example, the first-grade or district club has been the game's principal organising unit, talent nursery and social institution – something implicitly recognised by the system under which board members of Cricket Australia are still chosen from club delegates elected to their associations. But the reality is that Test players now have precious little to do with their clubs; nor, increasingly, do promising juniors, given the sophistication of the programmes designed to identify and incubate talent. The implications of this steadily attenuating connection between cricket's higher and lower levels, with a concentration of riches and resources in the elite game, may not be appreciated for a generation.

Pressures have been discerned in the Australian set-up before, and prophecies issued that it would pull itself apart; the successes have always kept coming. One of the most provocative lessons of *Rookies, Rebels and Renaissance*, none the less, was how strategically motivating failure can be. Australian cricket's challenge will be recognising the need for change without the mandate that failure confers.

INTERNATIONAL WOMEN'S CRICKET IN 2004

Booming or Boring?

SARAH POTTER

In March 2004, at the National Stadium in Karachi, Pakistan opener Kiran Baluch bagged a coveted record. Her 242, compiled in 584 minutes, against West Indies became the highest individual score in women's Test cricket, eclipsing 214 by India's Mithali Raj at Taunton in 2002. In the same game, Pakistan captain Shaiza Khan collected 13 wickets, another Test record, including a hat-trick. And West Indies saved the match by scoring 440 after following on. Women's cricket across the globe must be in rude health.

Well, perhaps. The bald truth is that there are yawning gaps in standards. Pakistan had not even qualified for the World Cup in South Africa in March and April 2005. West Indies did but, like Sri Lanka and Ireland, were not expected to lift the trophy unless something jaw-droppingly improbable happened, such as the five major teams (Australia, New Zealand, England, India and South Africa) not turning up. Baluch, of course, could only play against what was before her. At least her innings had the chance to happen. Women's Test cricket is an endangered species.

Only three Test matches have been played worldwide since the end of the 2003 season. India met New Zealand in November 2003; Baluch's Test followed in March; and England played New Zealand in August. All three ended in stalemate. That New Zealand featured in two of them is odd, as they had avoided Test cricket since their tour of England in 1996.

Why so few? Partly cost, partly preference and partly, too, because it seems to be the modern perception that, if it isn't over in a day, nobody will be interested. I've heard that nasty little bouncer delivered from the lips of international coaches who ought to know better. Also, it has to be admitted, too many Tests end in draws. Boring, whisper the few who turn up to watch. The women have

Record-holder: Kiran Baluch hit 242 for Pakistan against West Indies, the highest score in women's Tests.

Picture by EMPICS

four, not five days, to nail a result, but lack of time is not the sole culprit. Simply put, not every team sets out to win.

So should women's Test cricket be killed off? Absolutely not. If international sides give up on 70 years of history, something more valuable than tradition will be lost. It's called credibility. Won't play it, or can't play it? The question may as well merge into one damning sneer.

The way forward, both for standards and acceptance, is to play more Tests. The International Women's Cricket Council is due to merge with the International Cricket Council in April 2005, during the women's World Cup, which the ICC has funded. It may seem like a small step for the men's governing body; it represents a thrilling shimmy for womankind.

If the similar marriage in 1998 between the old Women's Cricket Association and the England and Wales Cricket Board is anything to go by, the distaff side can tighten their thigh-pads for an exciting innings. Since then, the England team have been transformed beyond recognition (through their play, rather than the new sponsored trousers and wrap-around shades); grassroots women's cricket is healthier than at any time in its history (in 2003, the ECB announced that more than two million girls were playing cricket); a record number of clubs are affiliated (ECB figures showed a 33% increase in 2003) and – the key to it all – the growth is sustainable.

The necessary high-level merger throws up some tricky politics. Australia, New Zealand and Ireland are, like England, already fully affiliated to their men's governing bodies; South Africa and West Indies are in the throes of the process. India, Pakistan and Sri Lanka are not, but the ICC has stipulated that they must be. It is a particular problem for Pakistan. Two rival women's associations are in bitter dispute about who controls the game: how they can even open talks with the Pakistan Cricket Board is unclear.

The ICC has promised a period of transition in which these nations will, in theory, still be able to play Test cricket – if they want to. If they do not, another raft of countries will eventually emerge to take their places, courtesy of the ICC's power and money. In April and May 2004, for example, tournaments for emerging African nations were held in Uganda and Namibia, funded by the ICC. Such tournaments could never have happened on the IWCC's shoestring resources, and women stand to benefit from many more such development plans.

The broken records in Karachi may at first glance seem like the extra top-spin you put on the truth, but, all things considered, there is much to be cheerful about whenever the mind wanders during the tedious parts of the Test matches.

TEST AVERAGES, 2004

BATTING

(Qualification: 300 runs)

† *Left-handed batsman.*

	M	I	NO	R	HS	100s	Avge	SR	Ct/St
S. R. Tendulkar (I)	10	15	5	915	248*	3	91.50	56.10	5
J. H. Kallis (SA)	11	21	5	1,288	162	5	80.50	50.70	8
†G. P. Thorpe (E)	12	20	7	951	119*	4	73.15	48.94	12
V. Sehwag (I)	12	19	1	1,141	309	3	63.38	73.61	7
R. Dravid (I)	12	18	3	946	270	2	63.06	42.49	26
R. W. T. Key (E)	4	7	1	378	221	1	63.00	62.79	3
†A. J. Strauss (E)	9	18	2	971	137	4	60.68	50.89	14
†B. C. Lara (WI)	12	21	1	1,178	400*	3	58.90	61.38	13
H. H. Gibbs (SA)	7	14	1	751	192	2	57.76	53.33	5
†J. D. P. Oram (NZ)	10	16	4	690	126*	2	57.50	55.06	8
†S. T. Jayasuriya (SL)	11	20	0	1,130	253	4	56.50	70.01	6
D. R. Martyn (A)	14	26	2	1,353	161	6	56.37	51.97	6
†K. C. Sangakkara (SL)	11	20	0	1,114	270	3	55.70	63.62	20/4
†J. L. Langer (A)	14	27	0	1,481	215	5	54.85	54.91	9
†C. H. Gayle (WI)	12	22	1	1,135	141	4	54.04	71.24	10
A. Flintoff (E)	13	19	2	898	167	2	52.82	66.71	16
Younis Khan (P)	3	6	0	307	124	1	51.16	52.03	3
R. R. Sarwan (WI)	12	21	1	1,005	261*	3	50.25	53.11	14
M. J. Clarke (A)	8	13	1	596	151	2	49.66	57.08	11
†J. A. Rudolph (SA)	11	21	3	890	154*	3	49.44	42.38	4
M. S. Atapattu (SL)	11	20	0	966	249	4	48.30	54.14	8
N. Hussain (E)	5	9	2	334	103*	1	47.71	40.09	8
†S. Chanderpaul (WI)	10	18	3	715	128*	2	47.66	46.39	2
†S. P. Fleming (NZ)	10	17	1	737	202	2	46.06	51.18	12
†G. C. Smith (SA)	11	22	2	921	139	2	46.05	55.28	7
C. L. Cairns (NZ)	6	10	0	456	158	1	45.60	86.52	0
†S. C. Ganguly (I)	8	9	0	408	88	0	45.33	56.82	2
D. P. M. D. Jayawardene (SL)	11	20	1	861	237	2	45.31	48.20	23
†G. Gambhir (I)	5	7	0	307	139	1	43.85	61.89	4
†M. E. Trescothick (E)	13	26	3	1,004	132	4	43.65	54.09	18
†P. A. Patel (I)	7	9	1	349	69	0	43.62	51.55	19/3
†M. L. Hayden (A)	14	27	1	1,123	132	3	43.19	60.47	17
†S. M. Katich (A)	8	16	2	604	125	1	43.14	49.22	2
H. H. Dippenaar (SA)	5	10	2	343	110	1	42.87	38.40	5
S. B. Styris (NZ)	10	17	1	673	170	2	42.06	51.61	10
Yousuf Youhana (P)	7	13	0	539	112	2	41.46	60.49	2
R. T. Ponting (A)	10	19	2	697	98	0	41.00	56.99	12
†D. S. Lehmann (A)	12	20	0	803	153	2	40.15	61.86	3
Mohammad Ashraful (B)	8	15	2	520	158*	1	40.00	45.25	0
B. B. McCullum (NZ)	10	17	2	571	143	1	38.06	55.81	24/2
†A. C. Gilchrist (A)	14	25	3	837	144	3	38.04	75.06	58/8
Inzamam-ul-Haq (P)	6	10	0	372	118	2	37.20	48.06	5
M. P. Vaughan (E)	12	22	2	712	140	3	35.60	55.15	9
†M. A. Butcher (E)	9	17	3	498	79	0	35.57	40.19	6
G. O. Jones (E)	10	14	1	458	100	1	35.23	61.72	32/2
T. T. Samaraweera (SL)	10	18	3	516	100	1	34.40	36.21	11
†M. H. Richardson (NZ)	10	17	0	570	101	1	33.52	35.62	5
†D. S. Smith (WI)	6	11	1	322	108	1	32.20	50.31	6
V. V. S. Laxman (I)	12	16	0	513	178	1	32.06	55.70	12
†W. P. U. J. C. Vaas (SL)	11	18	6	369	69	0	30.75	46.88	3
†R. D. Jacobs (WI)	10	16	3	399	107*	1	30.69	52.56	30/3
Yasir Hameed (P)	6	12	1	313	91	0	28.45	53.87	6

	M	I	NO	R	HS	100s	Avge	SR	Ct/St
†Imran Farhat (P).	7	14	0	390	101	1	27.85	51.86	8
†Mohammad Rafique (B) . . .	8	15	1	377	111	1	26.92	67.68	3
Khaled Mashud (B)	8	15	2	349	103*	1	26.84	41.05	16/4
N. J. Astle (NZ).	7	12	0	314	64	0	26.16	48.53	7
T. M. Dilshan (SL).	9	15	2	333	104	1	25.61	49.85	8
A. F. Giles (E)	12	15	2	330	52	0	25.38	55.64	6
Rajin Saleh (B)	7	13	0	304	51	0	23.38	34.38	3
J. N. Gillespie (A)	14	23	7	314	54*	0	19.62	31.71	7

BOWLING

(Qualification: 10 wickets)

	Style	O	M	R	W	BB	5W/i	Avge	SR
G. D. McGrath (A).	RFM	363.3	119	868	47	8-24	2	18.46	46.40
M. Muralitharan (SL)	OB	359.3	71	1,035	47	6-45	5	22.02	45.89
M. S. Kasprowicz (A). . . .	RFM	406	93	1,116	47	7-39	2	23.74	51.82
S. J. Harmison (E)	RF	526.5	115	1,603	67	7-12	3	23.92	47.17
S. K. Warne (A)	LBG	578.4	123	1,685	70	6-125	5	24.07	49.60
I. K. Pathan (I)	LFM	324	89	919	38	6-51	3	24.18	51.15
A. Kumble (I)	LBG	613.2	127	1,838	74	8-141	6	24.83	49.72
P. T. Collins (WI).	LFM	259.3	46	871	35	6-53	1	24.88	44.48
J. N. Gillespie (A)	RF	514.3	129	1,369	55	5-56	1	24.89	56.12
S. T. Jayasuriya (SL).	SLA	164.4	40	383	15	5-34	1	25.53	65.86
Harbhajan Singh (I)	OB	338.4	64	976	38	7-87	4	25.68	53.47
A. Flintoff (E).	RFM	369.4	78	1,108	43	5-58	1	25.76	51.58
D. J. J. Bravo (WI).	RFM	128.4	25	419	16	6-55	1	26.18	48.25
J. E. C. Franklin (NZ). . . .	LFM	100.1	19	358	13	5-28	1	27.53	46.23
Shoaib Akhtar (P).	RF	192.5	26	737	26	5-60	3	28.34	44.50
D. N. T. Zoysa (SL)	LFM	180.2	45	570	20	5-20	1	28.50	54.10
W. P. U. J. C. Vaas (SL) . .	LFM	415.5	97	1,146	40	6-29	2	28.65	62.37
S. L. Malinga (SL).	RM	105.3	13	432	15	4-42	0	28.80	42.20
S. M. Pollock (SA).	RFM	470	129	1,274	43	4-32	0	29.62	65.58
R. R. Sarwan (WI).	LB	141	23	416	14	4-37	0	29.71	60.42
A. F. Giles (E).	SLA	392.5	75	1,140	38	5-57	2	30.00	62.02
M. J. Hoggard (E)	RFM	415.4	93	1,413	47	4-35	0	30.06	53.06
L. Balaji (I)	RFM	106	24	369	12	4-63	0	30.75	53.00
C. S. Martin (NZ)	RFM	246	50	895	29	6-76	4	30.86	50.89
H. M. R. K. B. Herath (SL)	SLA	187.5	38	560	18	4-64	0	31.11	62.61
C. L. Cairns (NZ)	RFM	191.5	31	675	21	5-79	1	32.14	54.80
D. L. Vettori (NZ)	SLA	450.2	104	1,224	38	6-28	4	32.21	71.10
Danish Kaneria (P).	LBG	318.3	48	964	29	7-118	2	33.24	65.89
M. Kartik (I).	SLA	174.3	34	511	15	4-44	0	34.06	69.80
A. Nel (SA)	RFM	161.5	43	513	15	5-87	1	34.20	64.73
S. P. Jones (E).	RF	226.1	39	814	23	5-57	1	35.39	59.00
M. Ntini (SA).	RF	437.4	73	1,394	39	5-49	1	35.74	67.33
C. H. Gayle (WI).	OB	164.2	35	439	12	5-34	1	36.58	82.16
T. L. Best (WI)	RF	183	25	601	16	3-37	0	37.56	68.62
Mohammad Rafique (B) . .	SLA	380.1	77	978	25	6-122	1	39.12	91.24
U. D. U. Chandana (SL) . .	LB	149.1	9	606	15	5-101	2	40.40	59.66
N. Boje (SA).	SLA	250.1	32	851	21	5-88	1	40.52	71.47
P. J. Wiseman (NZ).	OB	168.5	30	594	14	3-64	0	42.42	72.35
Zaheer Khan (I)	LFM	267.5	52	830	19	4-95	0	43.68	84.57
J. J. C. Lawson (WI).	RFM	100	12	446	10	4-94	0	44.60	60.00
J. H. Kallis (SA)	RFM	200	54	581	12	3-71	0	48.41	100.00
Mohammad Sami (P)	RF	224.3	34	837	16	4-71	0	52.31	84.18
F. H. Edwards (WI)	RF	295.4	33	1,231	22	4-70	0	55.95	80.63
J. D. P. Oram (NZ).	RM	292.5	78	751	13	3-36	0	57.76	135.15
Tapash Baisya (B)	RFM	195	28	761	13	3-133	0	58.53	90.00
C. D. Collymore (WI). . . .	RFM	243	62	662	10	2-24	0	66.20	145.80

MOST DISMISSALS BY A WICKET-KEEPER

66 (58ct, 8st)	A. C. Gilchrist (A)		20 (16ct, 4st)	Khaled Mashud (B)
34 (32ct, 2st)	G. O. Jones (E)		19 (17ct, 2st)	K. D. Karthik (I)
33 (30ct, 3st)	R. D. Jacobs (WI)		19 (15ct, 4st)	K. C. Sangakkara (SL)
26 (24ct, 2st)	B. B. McCullum (NZ)		18 (15ct, 3st)	Kamran Akmal (P)
23 (20ct, 3st)	M. V. Boucher (SA)		15 (11ct, 4st)	R. S. Kaluwitharana (SL)
22 (19ct, 3st)	P. A. Patel (I)		14 (12ct, 2st)	T. Taibu (Z)

Note: K. C. Sangakkara also held 5 ct in six Tests when not keeping wicket.

MOST CATCHES IN THE FIELD

26	R. Dravid (I)		12	S. P. Fleming (NZ)
23	D. P. M. D. Jayawardene (SL)		12	V. V. S. Laxman (I)
18	M. E. Trescothick (E)		12	R. T. Ponting (A)
17	M. L. Hayden (A)		12	G. P. Thorpe (E)
17	S. K. Warne (A)		11	M. J. Clarke (A)
16	A. Flintoff (E)		11	T. T. Samaraweera (SL)
14	R. R. Sarwan (WI)		10	C. H. Gayle (WI)
14	A. J. Strauss (E)		10	S. B. Styris (NZ)
13	B. C. Lara (WI)			

WOMEN'S TESTS IN 2003-04

At Vapi, November 27, 28, 29, 30, 2003. **Drawn.** Toss: India. **New Zealand 201-9 dec.** (H. M. Tiffen 66*) **and 102-4** (M. F. Fahey 60*); **India 277** (A. Jain 55, H. Kala 109; R. J. Steele 5-79).

This was the first Test New Zealand had played since they toured England in 1996. Test debuts: A. Sharma, N. Al Khader; N. J. Browne, M. F. Fahey, S. J. McGlashan, K. J. Martin, A. L. Mason, N. Scripps.

At Karachi, March 15, 16, 17, 18, 2004. **Drawn.** Toss: West Indies. **Pakistan 426-7 dec.** (Kiran Baluch 242, Sajjida Shah 98; F. Cummings 4-54) **and 58-2; West Indies 147** (Shaiza Khan 7-59) **and 440** (N. George 118, V. Felician 55, S. Power 57, J. Robinson 57; Shaiza Khan 6-167).

This was Pakistan's first Test since they toured England in 1979. Test debuts: Mariam Anwar, Urooj Mumtaz; West Indies (all). Kiran Baluch's 242 was the sixth and highest double-hundred in women's Tests; it lasted 584 minutes and 488 balls and included 38 fours, and she put on 241 for the first wicket with 16-year-old Sajjida Shah. Pakistan captain and leg-spinner Shaiza Khan took a first-innings hat-trick, only the second in women's Test cricket after Betty Wilson for Australia v England in 1957-58, to help enforce the follow-on. She finished with 13 wickets, beating the previous women's record of 11 in a Test. Nadine George scored West Indies' first Test century.

INDEX OF TEST MATCHES

Five earlier 2003-04 Test series – India v New Zealand, Australia v Zimbabwe, Pakistan v South Africa, Bangladesh v England, and Sri Lanka v England – all appeared in *Wisden 2004*.

ZIMBABWE v SRI LANKA, 2003-04

May 6	Harare	Sri Lanka won by an innings and 240 runs	1221
May 14	Bulawayo	Sri Lanka won by an innings and 254 runs	1224

ENGLAND v NEW ZEALAND, 2004

May 20	Lord's	England won by seven wickets	454
June 3	Leeds	England won by nine wickets	459
June 10	Nottingham	England won by four wickets	462

WEST INDIES v BANGLADESH, 2003-04

May 28	St Lucia	Drawn	1230
June 4	Kingston	West Indies won by an innings and 99 runs	1233

AUSTRALIA v SRI LANKA, 2004

July 1	Darwin	Australia won by 149 runs	1242
July 9	Cairns	Drawn	1244

ENGLAND v WEST INDIES, 2004

July 22	Lord's	England won by 210 runs	476
July 29	Birmingham	England won by 256 runs	480
August 12	Manchester	England won by seven wickets	485
August 19	The Oval	England won by ten wickets	488

SRI LANKA v SOUTH AFRICA, 2004

August 4	Galle	Drawn	1250
August 11	Colombo (SSC)	Sri Lanka won by 313 runs	1253

INDIA v AUSTRALIA, 2004-05

October 6	Bangalore	Australia won by 217 runs	1266
October 14	Chennai	Drawn	1268
October 26	Nagpur	Australia won by 342 runs	1271
November 3	Mumbai	India won by 13 runs	1274

BANGLADESH v NEW ZEALAND, 2004-05

October 19	Dhaka	New Zealand won by an innings and 99 runs	1279
October 26	Chittagong	New Zealand won by an innings and 101 runs	1281

PAKISTAN v SRI LANKA, 2004-05

October 20	Faisalabad	Sri Lanka won by 201 runs	1287
October 28	Karachi	Pakistan won by six wickets	1290

AUSTRALIA v NEW ZEALAND, 2004-05

November 18	Brisbane	Australia won by an innings and 156 runs	1302
November 26	Adelaide	Australia won by 213 runs	1304

INDIA v SOUTH AFRICA, 2004-05

November 20	Kanpur	Drawn	1293
November 28	Kolkata	India won by eight wickets	1296

BANGLADESH v INDIA, 2004-05

| December 10 | Dhaka | India won by an innings and 140 runs . . . . | 1323 |
| December 17 | Chittagong | India won by an innings and 83 runs . . . . | 1325 |

AUSTRALIA v PAKISTAN, 2004-05

December 16	Perth	Australia won by 491 runs	1313
December 26	Melbourne	Australia won by nine wickets	1316
January 2	Sydney	Australia won by nine wickets	1318

SOUTH AFRICA v ENGLAND, 2004-05

December 17	Port Elizabeth	England won by seven wickets	1059
December 26	Durban	Drawn	1062
January 2	Cape Town	South Africa won by 196 runs	1066
January 13	Johannesburg	England won by 77 runs	1069
January 21	Centurion	Drawn	1073

BANGLADESH v ZIMBABWE, 2004-05

| January 6 | Chittagong | Bangladesh won by 226 runs . . . . | 1154 |
| January 14 | Dhaka | Drawn . . . . | 1154 |

Opposite: Race you to 600! Shane Warne
and Muttiah Muralitharan kept swapping
the Test-wicket record throughout 2004.
Picture by Mark Dadswell, Getty Images

PART THREE

The Players

The Wisden Forty

The Wisden Forty, including the Leading Cricketer in the World, have been selected by Wisden *on the basis of their class and form shown in all cricket during the calendar year 2004. The selections were made in consultation with many of the world's most experienced cricket writers and commentators. In the end, though, they were* Wisden's *choices, guided by the statistics but not governed by them. The selection panel are no more infallible than any other selectors.*

THE LEADING CRICKETER IN THE WORLD, 2004

Shane Warne

GREG BAUM

In Shane Warne's prodigious career of spin, twist and revolution, no turn has been more startling than his comeback after a year's suspension to his former mastery at the venerable age of 34. In the soap opera of his life, the star was written out and wrote himself back in again, larger than before. But Warne's whole career has been about the inspiration he finds in the smell of the greasepaint and the roar of the crowd, and above all in the scale of the challenge.

He was thoughtless for a moment and idle for a year, and it was trying. The World Anti-Doping Authority, the Australian government and the cricket board were three of many forces who stayed on his back, and there were the several rods he made for himself, too, for he was never discreet. He remained in the limelight, but as a shadow. Some doubted that he could come back. Steve Waugh thought he would need time, but Terry Jenner, his mentor, felt he would return renewed.

His first step back was in a Victorian Second XI game at Melbourne's Junction Oval, a humble fixture suddenly made incongruously glamorous.

FIRST BOWLER TO EACH 50-WICKET MILESTONE IN TESTS

50	F. R. Spofforth	Australia v England at Sydney (Fourth Test)	1882-83
100	J. Briggs	England v Australia at Sydney (Fourth Test)	1894-95
150	S. F. Barnes	England v South Africa at Durban (First Test)	1913-14
200	C. V. Grimmett	Australia v South Africa at Johannesburg (Fourth Test) . . .	1935-36
250	F. S. Trueman	England v New Zealand at Christchurch (Third Test)	1962-63
300	F. S. Trueman	England v Australia at The Oval (Fifth Test)	1964
350	D. K. Lillee	Australia v Pakistan at Sydney (Fifth Test)	1983-84
400	R. J. Hadlee	New Zealand v India at Christchurch (First Test)	1989-90
450	C. A. Walsh	West Indies v England at Birmingham (First Test)	2000
500	C. A. Walsh	West Indies v South Africa at Port-of-Spain (Second Test) .	2000-01
550	**S. K. Warne**	**Australia v New Zealand at Adelaide (Second Test)** . . .	**2004-05**

Note: C. T. B. Turner (Australia) reached 100 wickets later in the same Test as Briggs.

The showman returns: Shane Warne at Galle, March 2004.
Photograph: Hamish Blair, Getty Images

He got hit for six an over in the second innings. But these were the wings, where he has never thrived; the selectors scarcely hesitated before putting him on the plane to Sri Lanka shortly afterwards.

Immediately, it was as if he had never been away, as he took ten wickets in each of his first two Tests. This was the big stage, and he was the big player. The Sri Lankans, who had played him deftly in the past, succumbed at home (26 wickets in three matches), and again in an off-season series in Australia (ten in two). India, previously fallow ground, also yielded wickets (14 in three) as Indian batsmen who had previously treated him with contempt now faltered.

More wickets ensued in home series against New Zealand (11 in two) and Pakistan (nine in two, plus five more in the first week of 2005), two countries who have never relished him. He ended with 70 wickets in 12 Tests in 2004, comparable to 1993 (72 in 16) and 1994 (70 in ten) when he was the new sensation. Warne missed matches against India in Sydney (still suspended) and Mumbai (injured) that on historical indications would have brought him many more wickets – without him, on a maverick pitch in Mumbai, Australia suffered their only defeat of the year.

He and Muttiah Muralitharan raced for the world record, and for a time shared it, until Muralitharan's personal boycott of Australia and another injury left Warne supremely alone. Meantime, he summered in England, leading Hampshire to their most successful season for more than a decade. Though he was on less money and attracted less fanfare than in a previous stint, his sheer zest for the game stood out amid the prevailing dullness. Warne was not a better bowler than before; that would have been impossible.

But he was at least as good, and that was itself a redoubtable achievement. Like Dennis Lillee before him, he reinvented the wheel. He bowled almost no flippers, nor many wrong 'uns, but depended on craft, wile and guile. He took wickets by skill, by force of personality, by subterfuge. Sometimes umpires were as transfixed as batsmen.

He was as indefatigable as ever, and as willing, maintaining his career average of around 46 overs a Test, and his economy rate of around 2.5 an over. Others – MacGill, Hogg, sometimes Katich – had served Australia well enough during Warne's absence, but Australia looked a complete side again with him back in it.

Everything was restored, even the melodrama that has characterised his career as surely as his wickets. He broke his thumb. He made tactless remarks about the advantages Muralitharan had enjoyed. After his successful return in Sri Lanka, he commented on how satisfying it was to play under a captain who had faith in spin in a crisis, an apparent jibe at the retired Waugh. He lived in the headlines, his old habitat.

After he appeared in the tsunami relief match at the MCG in January 2005, Australian captain Ricky Ponting hinted that Warne would come out of retirement in time for the 2007 World Cup if other spinners did not mature sufficiently. Warne, significantly, did not discount it. He has never tired of the thrill of the contest, nor the view from the top. He had missed a year and played a year, and there could be no doubt which year was preferable.

So the natural order of the last decade was restored, but at the end of 2004 all were reminded to presume nothing. Warne was assuredly back, but the ground at Galle on which he had made his return nine months earlier was in ruins.

THE FORTY

Of the 40 players chosen, 29 have retained their places from last year. The 11 dropped are Michael Bevan, Andy Bichel, Mark Boucher, Gary Kirsten, Brett Lee, Darren Lehmann, Stuart MacGill, Mushtaq Ahmed, Makhaya Ntini, Mark Richardson, and Steve Waugh. Kirsten, Richardson and Waugh all retired during 2004.

They have been replaced by Shivnarine Chanderpaul, Michael Clarke, Danish Kaneria, Harbhajan Singh, Steve Harmison, Sanath Jayasuriya, Mahela Jayawardene, Jacob Oram, Andrew Strauss, Graham Thorpe and Shane Warne.

The country-by-country breakdown is as follows:

Australia	10	(14)	South Africa	4	(7)
England	6	(3)	New Zealand	2	(2)
India	6	(5)	West Indies	2	(1)
Sri Lanka	5	(3)	Zimbabwe	1	(1)
Pakistan	4	(4)			

Wisden 2004 *numbers in brackets.*

SHIVNARINE CHANDERPAUL West Indies

No other player in world cricket was compared to an animal last year as often as Chanderpaul to a crab. Yet his game moved in two directions in 2004, and neither of them was sideways. First he regressed horribly during England's visit to the Caribbean, when his inelegance drew attention to his lack of runs, and cost him his place. Then he used the Bangladeshis as a route back into form for the return trip to England, where unbeaten innings of 128 and 97 at Lord's spared West Indies an even greater thrashing. Although he faded as the series wore on, his wicket became almost as vital to the England cause as that of Brian Lara. He also played a crucial role in West Indies' delightfully unexpected Champions Trophy triumph: a run-a-ball fifty to see off South Africa, followed by his side's top-score of 47 in the final – an innings that was forgotten amid the daring dusk raid by Courtney Browne and Ian Bradshaw.

2004: 10 Tests: 715 runs @ 47.66; no wicket for 0.
24 ODI: 668 runs @ 33.40; no wicket for 11.

MICHAEL CLARKE Australia

The blond streaks came from a bottle, but in everything else Clarke was an absolute natural. Having been made to wait what seemed like an eternity for his Test debut, he produced a performance for the annals with a wondrous 151 at Bangalore, imbuing it with an even greater lustre by pointedly and proudly swapping his helmet for the Baggy Green when in the nineties. His fresh face and fast feet breathed life into an ageing Australian team, and put a glint in the eye of world cricket: rarely had an Australian been taken so easily to hearts around the globe. If his youth damned him with inconsistency, it also blessed him with a striking fearlessness: through-out the year, Clarke thrived on the pressure points. He made two sparkling half-centuries at Nagpur, and a punishing 141 to wrench the  First Test at Brisbane away from New Zealand. Everything he touched turned to gold, including a remarkable and unlikely spell of six for nine at Mumbai. Twinkle-toed, deceptively powerful and so wonderfully talented, particularly against spin bowling, Clarke was the original smiling assassin. Batting's golden age seemed to have found its golden boy.

2004: 8 Tests: 596 runs @ 49.66; 6 wickets @ 6.16.
26 ODI: 615 runs @ 32.36; 9 wickets @ 34.55.

DANISH KANERIA   Pakistan

The torch of Pakistani leg-spin traditionally burns fiercely, and in 2004 it found a worthy carrier. Danish Kaneria may be as deadly a googly-merchant

as his predecessors Abdul Qadir and Mushtaq Ahmed, but he is largely cut from a different cloth: his action lacks their waspish grace, and instead he relies on height, control and mental strength. But at the end of the year he had the best average of the three. Kaneria's previous successes had been largely against Bangladesh, but now he went toe-to-toe with some of world cricket's finest players of spin. He chipped away at Sri Lanka to square the series in Karachi, and was one of the few Pakistan players to emerge with credit from the debacle in Australia. Afterwards, Shane Warne commented favourably.

2004:   6 Tests: 25 runs @ 8.33; 29 wickets @ 33.24.
              1 ODI: did not bat; 1 wicket @ 26.00.

RAHUL DRAVID   India

The Wall didn't quite come tumbling down, but Dravid regressed from the stratospheric standards of 2003. He was the ICC's inaugural Player of the Year – chiefly for his displays in Australia in 2003-04 – but struggled to influence the return series and made just one fifty in four Tests. Without the safety valve of Sachin Tendulkar below him for half the series, Dravid went into his shell: his strike-rate dropped from 51 in Australia to 27 at home. He still scored more one-day international runs than anyone else, and there were two trademark big Test hundreds. One – 160 against Bangladesh – was essentially meaningless; the other – a 12-hour 270 in a series decider in Pakistan when nobody else made a century – could barely have been of greater magnitude.

2004:   12 Tests: 946 runs @ 63.06.
              31 ODI (22 as wicket-keeper): 1,025 runs @ 39.42; 22 catches as keeper, 3 stumpings.

STEPHEN FLEMING   New Zealand

As a captain, Fleming had a mixed year. He very publicly outpsyched South Africa's Graeme Smith during a one-day international at Auckland, but for much of New Zealand's miserable series in England he cut a forlorn, helpless figure at slip, arms folded, lip bitten. A record of three wins out of ten, two of them against Bangladesh, damaged his carefully crafted reputation as world cricket's cleverest leader, and there were rumours of a power struggle with the new coach, John Bracewell. As a batsman, however, things could not have gone much better. For once, his Test conversion rate – past fifty four times, past a hundred twice – kept the critics off his back. And his form in black at the top of the one-day order was simply superlative, as was New Zealand's record of four defeats in 20 completed matches.

2004:   10 Tests: 737 runs @ 46.06.
         22 ODI: 921 runs @ 48.47.

ANDREW FLINTOFF   England

While he was busy lifting sixes and spirits, everything felt right in English cricket. Flintoff had first begun to apply his destructive talents on a regular basis in 2003, and in 2004 he kept going. A century in Antigua was followed by at least one score over 50 in the next seven Tests, including a monstrous

167 against West Indies at Edgbaston, when he hit seven of the 46 sixes he registered in both forms of the game in the calendar year. He was no less prolific in pyjamas: in six innings separated by the West Indies Tests, Flintoff made three centuries, and a 99 against India at The Oval, where he returned to the pavilion with the same broad grin he brought out in spectators. His bowling acquired new dimensions too, in spite of a bone spur on his

left ankle that prevented him from sending down a single over during the NatWest Series at home. He collected his first Test five-wicket haul in Barbados and, when he returned from injury, adopted a more probing, stump-threatening line. To top it all, his first child, Holly, arrived in September. By the end of the year, the talk was no longer of the new Botham. Thanks in no small part to Flintoff, the English game had finally moved on.

2004:   13 Tests: 898 runs @ 52.82; 43 wickets @ 25.76.
         14 ODI: 633 runs @ 57.54; 16 wickets @ 21.31.

HERSCHELLE GIBBS   South Africa

After turning 30 most people might embrace a quieter life but, even by Gibbs's helter-skelter standards, 2004 was a year full of incident. It began with two blockbusting hundreds against West Indies, took in injury, burn-out, an astonishingly poor run of form in Sri Lanka, and much soul-searching over whether he should tour India, for fear of reopening the Pandora's Box of match-fixing. Gibbs eventually pulled out and, when the new South African coach Ray Jennings called his performances "embarrassing", some felt his international career was done. But naked talent cannot be extinguished so easily, and Gibbs was fast-tracked into the side to face England after a finger injury; his (unavailing) 161 and 98 at Johannesburg in January 2005 put him right back among the best openers in world cricket. The fairground ride rumbled on.

2004:   7 Tests: 751 runs @ 57.76.
         18 ODI: 398 runs @ 23.41.

ADAM GILCHRIST   Australia

Gilchrist has always been the last player you should judge by statistics, and this year was no exception. In Test cricket in particular, he was an intoxicating mix of the binary and the breathtaking; as usual, his successes kept making

the difference. His gun-slinging 144 in Kandy, to end a horrendous trot of 14 runs in five innings, turned the Second Test against Sri Lanka, and he set the tone for triumphs over India and New Zealand with centuries in the first innings of the series. Gilchrist, the reluctant captain, covered capably for Ricky Ponting in Australia's series victory in India, and his gladiatorial exclamation upon victory at Nagpur was a defining image of the year. Gilchrist also made 66 Test dis-

missals – the next-best was 34 – and he remained the only man in world cricket who could score a 103-ball century, as he did in Bangalore, and prompt adjectives like "restrained". He was anything but when he blasted 172 against Zimbabwe, his highest one-day score, at Hobart, and nobody with 500 Test or one-day runs matched his strike-rate. Gilchrist may have been approaching his cricketing dotage, but he remained one of the true wonders of the cricket world.

2004:   14 Tests: 837 runs @ 38.04; 58 catches, 8 stumpings.
           21 ODI: 879 runs @ 43.95. 31 catches, 2 stumpings.

JASON GILLESPIE   Australia

Gillespie could no longer be labelled the world's most underrated bowler, mainly because it was now impossible not to give him the credit he deserved. He finally convinced everyone that he was more than Glenn McGrath's foil with a heroic performance in India, where his 20 wickets came at the far-from-subcontinental average of 16 and included a series-winning haul of nine for 80 at Nagpur. There, as everywhere else, a tight line combined with imaginative use of slower balls and leg-cutters proved enough. As Gillespie's mullet grew, so too did his prowess with the bat. An unbeaten half-century against New Zealand at Brisbane, his first in Tests, was followed by another against Pakistan at Melbourne. If Australia's work ethic was reflected in anything, it was in Gillespie's unlikely attempt to turn himself into an all-rounder.

2004:   14 Tests: 314 runs @ 19.62; 55 wickets @ 24.89.
           21 ODI: 56 runs @ 28.00; 33 wickets @ 21.84.

HARBHAJAN SINGH   India

Until his *doosra* was queried by the match referee Chris Broad, Harbhajan was well on the way to making up for the various disappointments of 2003. Not for the first time his opposition of choice were the Australians, who provided him with 11 wickets at Bangalore and a match-winning analysis of five for 29 on a Mumbai minefield. There was also seven for 87 against South Africa at Kolkata, just to prove that Harbhajan could beguile others too. His one-day success was limited to two meaner-than-mean performances against England. And he was left with a serious problem: the ICC had mooted a limit of 15 degrees of permissible straightening for bowlers of all types; his off-spinner's wrong 'un was believed to have been measured at 22.

2004:   7 Tests: 155 runs @ 17.22; 38 wickets @ 25.68.
        11 ODI: 62 runs @ 20.66; 13 wickets @ 32.00.

STEVE HARMISON   England

Few could have predicted that the man who pulled out of the Bangladesh tour in October 2003 amid snipes about a lack of fitness and commitment would rise to the top of the world rankings in 2004. Statistically speaking, it all began on a warm March morning at Sabina Park, when Harmison blew away West Indies for 47 with the astonishing figures of seven for 12. But the groundwork had been done over the previous six months in his training sessions at Newcastle United, which opened his eyes and the floodgates: he took 23 wickets at 14.86 in the Caribbean to provoke comparisons with Curtly Ambrose, 21 at 22.09 against New Zealand, and 17 at 29.52 in the return series with West Indies. His below-par performances in South Africa cost him his place at the top of the rankings, but England still hoped they had a tall, hostile, opening bowler capable of making the world's best batsmen duck and dive for a while to come. Harmison's 67 Test wickets beat Ian Botham's England calendar-year record of 66, set in 1978. And there was a one-day hat-trick, against India at Trent Bridge, to celebrate too. His star was so rapidly in the ascendant that he even felt able to withdraw from the one-day series in Zimbabwe on moral grounds. This time, no one questioned his commitment. *See also Five Cricketers of the Year, page 60.*

2004:   13 Tests: 116 runs @ 12.88; 67 wickets @ 23.92.
        17 ODI: 24 runs @ 12.00; 26 wickets @ 25.57.

MATTHEW HAYDEN   Australia

By most batsmen's standards, Hayden enjoyed a productive year. By his own, it was no more than adequate. Unusually for a player who prides himself on big hundreds, Hayden failed to make the most of his starts: on 12 occasions he reached double figures without going on to pass 50. The high point was a pair of hundreds against Sri Lanka at Cairns, but Hayden's only other three-figure score in Tests was an innings of 130 at Galle. His opening double act with Justin Langer dropped to the merely world-class from out-of-this-world. The two added 255 against Sri Lanka at Cairns and shared three other century stands, but an average partnership of 54 in 27 innings was less than they had come to expect. Even so, Hayden remained the opener bowlers feared most.

2004:   14 Tests: 1,123 runs @ 43.19.
        23 ODI: 946 runs @ 41.13.

INZAMAM-UL-HAQ   Pakistan

Like many Pakistan captains before him, Inzamam discovered that leadership is not all it is cracked up to be. He continued to rack up the hundreds – two in each form of the game – with ursine power but, by the time he was making one and nought at Perth in December, the knives were being sharpened. His partnership with the new coach, Bob Woolmer, looked convincing until Inzamam chose to bat first on a dank September morning in the semi-final of the Champions Trophy against West Indies, and the Australia tour was an unmitigated shambles – the "hardest" he had ever been on, admitted Inzamam. Bouncers and yorkers were one thing, and Inzamam dealt with those as well as ever. Calls for his resignation from former team-mates, a 3–0 whitewash, and claims that one of his players had raped a woman in Melbourne were quite another.

2004:   6 Tests: 372 runs @ 37.20.
           26 ODI: 911 runs @ 43.38.

SANATH JAYASURIYA   Sri Lanka

After years of relatively quiet performances, Jayasuriya returned to blow

bowlers off course. It was his most productive 12 months in Tests since the *annus mirabilis* of 1997, his runs came at a strike rate of over 70. There were the usual spurts of low scores that bedevil the touch player but, when his eye was in, he was seeing it like a football once again. Two innings stood out: a terrifying 131 that gave Australia quite a fright in Kandy, and a remarkable 253 against Pakistan at Faisalabad, when Jayasuriya added 101 for the ninth wicket with Dilhara Fernando – who contributed one. His gentle left-arm spin had a second wind, too: in the absence of Muralitharan, Jayasuriya shredded South Africa's top order in a series-winning burst at Colombo.

2004:   11 Tests: 1,130 runs @ 56.50; 15 wickets @ 25.53.
           25 ODI: 724 runs @ 31.47; 16 wickets @ 40.25.

MAHELA JAYAWARDENE   Sri Lanka

Few players have done so well for so long while attracting as little attention as Jayawardene, Sri Lanka's strokeplaying heir to Aravinda de Silva in the middle order. The *pièce de résistance* was a near-epic 237 out of a total of 486 in the draw against South Africa at Galle, but just as important was an innings of 82 to set up victory in that series in Colombo. But if Jayawardene enchanted with the ruthless wristiness of his strokeplay, he also infuriated:

in 20 Test innings, he was dismissed between 13 and 44 on 11 occasions. His one-day form was below par, although perhaps his most crucial contribution of the year came in the field. Jayawardene dropped Andrew Flintoff in the slips on one in the Champions Trophy: Flintoff went on to make a match-winning century.

2004:   11 Tests: 861 runs @ 45.31.
           28 ODI: 676 runs @ 32.19; no wicket for 16.

JACQUES KALLIS   South Africa

It was the year in which Kallis supplanted Rahul Dravid as world cricket's most immovable object. Throughout he was ensconced in a patch that was the deepest purple; it began with back-to-back 130 not outs against West

Indies, and ended with the innings of his life, a regal 162 against England at Durban. In between there was another big hundred in New Zealand, and a masterclass against India at Kolkata. So immaculate was his technique and so cold his blood that, once he got in, bowlers could usually forget it. The numbers were irresistible, but there remained something curiously loveless about Kallis's orgy of runs, and the

whispers that he batted for his average became increasingly voluble. His one-day form was no less impressive, but Kallis was swimming against the tide in a modest team: South Africa won just two of his 11 Tests and five of his 18 one-day internationals. Inevitably, something had to give. It wasn't his slip catching, which retained its bucket-handed brilliance, but his bowling: Kallis's strike-rate in Tests was exactly 100. A reluctant bowler at the best of times, he seemed now to be performing under duress. Opponents charged with the task of winkling him out knew how he felt.

2004:   11 Tests: 1,288 runs @ 80.50; 12 wickets @ 48.41.
           18 ODI: 770 runs @ 59.23; 11 wickets @ 39.63.

MICHAEL KASPROWICZ   Australia

There was a time when the Australian attack of Glenn McGrath, Jason Gillespie, Shane Warne and Brett Lee appeared to operate above a glass ceiling. But in 2004 Kasprowicz broke through in spectacular fashion, relegating Lee to the ranks of drinks bearer and stamping his own understated, roundish-arm style on the role of third seamer. At times, he could be truly destructive. At Darwin, he demolished Sri Lanka with seven for 39; at Perth, he cut through Pakistan with five for 30. And his one-day form was little short of astonishing. The days when Kasprowicz would be summoned to do the donkey-work on a gruelling tour of the subcontinent were gone. At 32, he was more like a seasoned thoroughbred.

2004:   13 Tests: 107 runs @ 6.29; 47 wickets @ 23.74.
           12 ODI: 11 runs @ 11.00; 26 wickets @ 14.46.

ANIL KUMBLE   India

If there were doubters before, there could be none now: this was the year Kumble cemented his place in the ranks of the all-time greats. No one claimed more than his 74 Test wickets, and no one could claim he had not earned them. His bunnies included the cream of Australia's batting: he dismissed both Simon Katich and Damien Martyn five times, Adam Gilchrist four, and Michael Clarke and Matthew Hayden three each. In all, Kumble's hurry-up assortment of top-spinners, googlies and the occasional leg-break accounted for 43 different Test batsmen. But three matches stood out: a 12-wicket haul in Steve Waugh's farewell game at Sydney, a further 13 in the truncated epic at Chennai, and the Dhaka Test against Bangladesh, when Kumble passed Kapil Dev's Indian record of 434 wickets. Tall, economical and ultra-competitive, he remained a captain's dream, even in his mid-30s.
2004:   12 Tests: 142 runs @ 12.90; 74 wickets @ 24.83.
      13 ODI: 26 runs @ 8.66; 8 wickets @ 68.87.

JUSTIN LANGER   Australia

It was the year in which the quiet achiever emerged from the hulking shadow of his opening partner Matthew Hayden – and everyone else, for that matter. Nobody scored more than Langer's 1,481 Test runs, and four of his five hundreds exceeded 160. There were fallow periods, most notably on the subcontinent, but at home he was irresistible, averaging 77 from seven Tests. That included the defining performance of his year, and probably his career: a fire-with-fire 191 in the First Test against Pakistan at Perth, when Australia were being charred like shrimps on the barby at 78 for five. The perception remained of Langer as the ugly sister of Australia's dazzling top seven, but his strike-rate of 54 for the year put him above some of cricket's great entertainers. More heads were being turned by the day.
2004:   14 Tests: 1,481 runs @ 54.85.

BRIAN LARA   West Indies

One moment made it all worthwhile. Six months after losing his Test record to Matthew Hayden, Lara wrenched it back with an extraordinary innings of 400 not out – against England, in Antigua, in a dead rubber, just like his first record. If it was a wonderful reaffirmation of a talent from a different plane, it also papered over the cracks of a difficult year. Lara had spent much of that England series in Steve Harmison's pocket; in six live Tests against England, Lara made one fifty, and looked as if he had an allergy to chin music. His one-day form, too, was inexplicably modest – his highest score was 59 – and there was much criticism of his captaincy as West Indies lurched from one knockout blow to the next. Rumours of his imminent sacking proved exaggerated, though: Lara passed 10,000 Test runs in the final Test in England, and then his troops grabbed a romantic victory in the Champions Trophy. A Caribbean cricket revival? At 35, Lara would not be around to see it through; but the events of Antigua and The Oval at last gave long-suffering West Indian supporters something to keep them going.
2004:   12 Tests: 1,178 runs @ 58.90.
      20 ODI: 484 runs @ 32.26.

V. V. S. LAXMAN   India

It was a year in which Laxman's pristine talent was soiled by the grubby limitations of mortality, and he had no answers. He began the year with an exquisite 178 at Sydney – an innings of such purity that, unthinkably, it outshone a Sachin Tendulkar double-century – but there was no mistaking the struggles that would follow. He continued his blistering Australian form with three hundreds in the VB Series, but then the house fell down around him. A match-winning century in the final one-day international in Pakistan was a reminder of Laxman's otherworldly ability, but there were just two fifties in his remaining 11 Tests, and he had a torrid time in the return series against Australia, against a vengeful Shane Warne. Anyone who had seen Laxman make batting look the easiest thing in the world had no idea what was going on. You suspected he felt the same way.

2004: 12 Tests: 513 runs @ 32.06.
       25 ODI: 837 runs @ 41.85.

GLENN McGRATH   Australia

Just when startled batsmen thought it was safe to enter the corridor once again, McGrath came back. The man who had spent his career cackling gleefully at the technical inadequacies of international batsmen spent 2004 having the last laugh on the critics who thought he was finished after his ankle injury. He blew away the cobwebs with a five-for on his return against Sri Lanka and then got down to the serious business of conquering India. A peach of an off-cutter to Rahul Dravid – perhaps the ball of the year – set the tone in the First Test in Bangalore, and throughout, McGrath produced his usual challenging mix of line, length and lip. He scaled two new peaks: a career-best eight for 24 against Pakistan at Perth and, most joyously and improbably of all, a carefree maiden Test fifty against New Zealand in Brisbane. Almost all his ambitions had been satisfied, but he showed no signs of letting up.

2004: 10 Tests: 97 runs @ 13.85; 47 wickets @ 18.46.
       9 ODI: no runs (not dismissed); 6 wickets @ 37.33.

DAMIEN MARTYN   Australia

It was hard to stand out in a team like Australia, but in 2004 Martyn managed it. Only Justin Langer scored more Test runs than Martyn's 1,353, a sequence that restored his career average to virtually 50, where it had not been since October 2002. Six Test hundreds – all six against subcontinental sides, five in winning causes and four on the subcontinent itself – told the tale of a man in the form of his life, and it would have been eight but for a pair of 97s. Martyn had never looked more at ease in the privileged but pressured No. 4 position. His one-day form was less glittering but, as he reached his 33rd birthday, he was cashing in just when the whispers might have started.

2004: 14 Tests: 1,353 runs @ 56.37; no wicket for 27.
       26 ODI: 611 runs @ 32.15.

MUTTIAH MURALITHARAN   Sri Lanka

He took 47 wickets in six Tests, and at various stages was the greatest wicket-taker in Test history. Yet 2004 was, in many ways, a year to forget for Muralitharan. As usual, there was one main reason. The chucking allegations that have followed every step of his career again threatened to overwhelm it when the ICC outlawed his *doosra*, only to change the rules and permit it later in the year. But there was more to it than that: a shoulder injury kept him out for five months; he was called cowardly for deciding not to tour Australia, where his long list of enemies extended to the prime minister; and, earlier in the year, he lost his long-awaited wrist-off with Shane Warne in March – despite taking 28 wickets in three Tests. Australia got after him, and Murali did not always know what to do. His economy rate – 2.87 – was his least stingy since 1992. That does not mean anyone wanted to face him. And his selfless, energetic response to the Sri Lankan tsunami enhanced his reputation as a human being.

2004: 6 Tests: 83 runs @ 11.85; 47 wickets @ 22.02.
13 ODI: 11 runs @ 5.50; 23 wickets @ 19.82.

JACOB ORAM   New Zealand

It was hard not to notice Oram in 2004, and not simply because of his 6ft

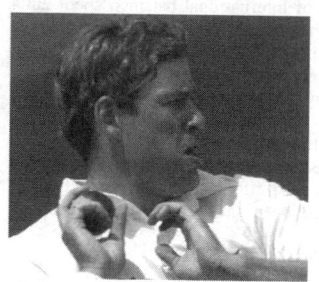

5in frame. In the space of a year, he had become a serious international all-rounder, despite a modest Test return with the ball. He began the year with scores of 119 not out and 90 against South Africa, faded slightly in England, then fought back with a vivacious unbeaten century against Australia in his first innings of the series at Brisbane. Oram's left-handed hitting – and he could hit the ball almost as powerfully as Andrew Flintoff – made him New Zealand's natural heir to Chris Cairns, while his rapid ascent provoked talk that he might one day succeed Stephen Fleming as captain. A consistent year with the white ball suggested good control; now he just needed to add penetration.

2004: 10 Tests: 690 runs @ 57.50; 13 wickets @ 57.76.
21 ODI: 221 runs @ 20.09; 32 wickets @ 24.09.

SHAUN POLLOCK   South Africa

Second only to Glenn McGrath, Pollock was turning, at 31, into the doyen of the seam-bowling fraternity, dispensing line, length and maidens – 129 out of 470 Test overs – with the affable certainty of an old don. If the wickets were a little more expensive in 2004, it was possibly because he did not make the batsmen play as much as usual, although six Test hauls of four in an innings suggested this was merely relative. His batting, though, fell away badly, with seven of his 16 Test innings in single figures – a significant factor in South Africa's decline. In the one-dayers he was steady rather than penetrative. But in both forms of the game he was still the South African bowler opposition batsmen looked to see off before tucking into the less parsimonious fare behind him.

2004: 11 Tests: 251 runs @ 17.92; 43 wickets @ 29.62.
18 ODI: 278 runs @ 39.71; 18 wickets @ 32.44.

RICKY PONTING   Australia

After the feast came the famine. Having scored 11 centuries for Australia in 2003, Ponting failed to reach three figures in 2004. He insisted it had nothing to do with him succeeding Steve Waugh as Test captain, but the statistics suggested otherwise: 11 of his 19 Test innings were between ten and 28, which hinted at a mind that was wandering to the bigger picture. That was hardly unreasonable: 2004 was the year in which Australia had the chance to exorcise not one but two subcontinental demons; though it seemed impossible, they reached another level under Ponting's captaincy. Whereas the Waugh vintage were happy to pummel the opposition into oblivion, leaving their jaw exposed in the process, Ponting's men chose to box clever. Subtlety was to be embraced, not pooh-poohed. It enabled them to win 3–0 in Sri Lanka, despite trailing on first innings every time, and to conquer the final frontier in India. Ponting missed the business end of that series with a fractured thumb, but in many ways the time off did him good. He returned for the Australian summer with his batteries recharged and, after a couple of near misses, began 2005 with that long-awaited first Test century as captain. When he turned it into a rampaging double-hundred, it was like 2003 all over again. Normal service had been resumed.

2004: 10 Tests: 697 runs @ 41.00.
24 ODI: 840 runs @ 38.18.

KUMAR SANGAKKARA   Sri Lanka

It was the year in which Sangakkara, the angry young man of Sri Lankan cricket, hinted tantalisingly at maturity. Where once a red mist undermined his talent, now he was a beacon of consistency in both forms of the game: only six of his 43 innings ended in single figures. But there were still vestiges of the past: Sangakkara was twice fined for breaching the ICC's code of conduct, and the penchant for losing his wicket to delusions of grandeur was still there. Few could argue with an average of over 50 in both forms of the game, however. Sangakkara mercilessly plucked 270 pieces of candy from the Zimbabwean babies at Bulawayo, and blasted 232 against South Africa in victory at Colombo. The only cloud was a series of unconverted starts against Australia; but even that was partially redeemed by a stunning 101 against them in a one-dayer in Colombo. Erudite, easy on the eye and increasingly engaging, Sangakkara was in serious danger of becoming likeable.

2004: 11 Tests (5 as wicket-keeper): 1,114 runs @ 55.70; no wicket for 4; 15 catches as keeper, 4 stumpings.
27 ODI (25 as wicket-keeper): 1,010 runs @ 53.15; 30 catches as keeper, 12 stumpings.

VIRENDER SEHWAG   India

When he was in full flow, there were few finer sights in world cricket in 2004 than Virender Sehwag at the crease, playing with a God-given instinct that left most mortals in his wake. Three innings stood out: 309 against

Pakistan at Multan – India's first Test triple-century – out of 509 while he was at the wicket; 155 out of 233 against Australia at Chennai; and 164 out of 294 against South Africa at Kanpur. Not even his glittering team-mates could hack the pace. There were times when Sehwag appeared to be playing in a bubble, apparently oblivious of the quality of the bowling or the context of the match. That made him

enchanting and exasperating in equal measure, although no captain in his right mind would have had it any other way. A moderate return in one-day cricket could not detract from Sehwag's standing as the most exciting opener in the world.

2004:   12 Tests: 1,141 runs @ 63.38; no wicket for 82.
27 ODI: 671 runs @ 25.80; 15 wickets @ 38.86.

SHOAIB AKHTAR   Pakistan

With Brett Lee's star falling, Shoaib established himself as the world's undisputed No. 1 fast bowler. Not that he ever doubted the fact himself. The scepticism came mostly from his countrymen: when Shoaib pulled up halfway through the pivotal Third Test against India with a wrist injury and back pain, some felt he was faking it – especially when he returned later to freewheel a 14-ball 28 – and an investigation was launched. A bone scan eventually cleared him, but some mud had stuck and the issue was raised again on the Australian tour. On the pitch, Pakistan lost five of Shoaib's six Tests. But with the suspicion remaining that his chief commitment was to his own cause, Shoaib would have been content with three first-innings five-fors and a strike-rate of 44. In his swaggering pomp – hair flapping, batsmen hopping, stumps flying – he remained the most visceral experience in world cricket. It was a shame his antics made it such a guilty pleasure.

2004:   6 Tests: 114 runs @ 10.36; 26 wickets @ 28.34.
23 ODI: 47 runs @ 6.71; 31 wickets @ 29.22.

GRAEME SMITH   South Africa

After the dream-sequence beginning to his captaincy career, Smith woke up to the harsh life of international cricket with a jolt in 2004. Reality bit fiercest on the subcontinent, where a declining South African side lost Test series to India and Sri Lanka. There was also a run of 11 defeats in 12 one-day internationals, the start of an ultimately fruitless struggle with England, and personal humiliation after some wily mind games from Stephen Fleming in Auckland. Yet for the most part, Smith continued to crunch runs aplenty. There was one minor epic: an unbeaten 125 to square the series in New Zealand that was made of granite. Smith yielded to no man physically, but he could be brought to his knees by more insidious means. By the end of the year, as Matthew Hoggard's in-swinger had him fumbling around his front pad time after time, even the runs had started to dry up. It was yet another cloud on an increasingly murky horizon.

2004:   11 Tests: 921 runs @ 46.05; 3 wickets @ 62.00.
            18 ODI: 652 runs @ 38.35; 3 wickets @ 47.33.

ANDREW STRAUSS   England

In January, Strauss was just another player England were keen to shoehorn into their one-day team; by December, he was one of the first names on every teamsheet. No Englishman had taken to international cricket so comfortably since Ian Botham. Not that the comparison went much further: Strauss's game was all about minimalism, based around three shots – cut, pull, drive – and an indecently even temperament. Fortune came his way with the freak injury to Michael Vaughan that gave him his debut, but from there he made his own luck: a nerveless debut century against New Zealand at Lord's was the prelude to a remarkable sequence of run-scoring. Records came and went: first man to score centuries in the first innings of his first three Test series; first man to score a century and a half-century in his first Tests at home and overseas. Only a low exposure to high-class spin bowling nagged against the sensation that Duncan Fletcher had unearthed a truly world-class talent from nowhere. Strauss's one-day form was barely less impressive. He became the heir to Graham Thorpe as England's finisher at No. 4, and his cameo in the Champions Trophy semi-final against Australia was nerveless. It was a microcosm of his year. *See also Five Cricketers of the Year, page 63.*

2004:   9 Tests: 971 runs @ 60.68.
            21 ODI: 655 runs @ 40.93; no wicket for 3.

HEATH STREAK   Zimbabwe

Streak's year was dominated by the murky politics of Zimbabwean cricket, and as such felt like an extended sabbatical. But the truth was that, with the possible exception of Australia, he would still have made every side in the world. Before he resigned the captaincy at the start of April, Streak showcased his world-class talents, first in the VB Series, then in the Harare Test against Bangladesh. He subsequently shone in his first match for Warwickshire with figures of 13 for 158 against Northamptonshire at Edgbaston – the best figures by a county debutant in the history of the Championship. But

injury intervened and, as his dispute with the Zimbabwe board rumbled on, the worry was that international cricket would lose one of its few high-class all-rounders.

2004: 2 Tests: 68 runs @ 68.00; 5 wickets @ 12.60.
      11 ODI: 317 runs @ 52.83; 22 wickets @ 19.04.

SACHIN TENDULKAR   India

Having spent his career delighting the purists, Tendulkar spent 2004 whipping the statisticians into a frenzy. In Tests, he played a remarkable three-card trick: 495 runs without being dismissed to start the year; then seven single-figure scores in eight innings either side of tennis elbow; finally normal service resumed with an average of 284 in the series in Bangladesh. Apart from a glorious, nothing-to-lose 55 against Australia on a Mumbai terror-track, watching Tendulkar became a colder experience: after his humbling 2003, he seemed to reject his bewitching fusion of majesty and human frailty in favour of a mechanical, robotic accumulation. The end – an average of 91 for the year – justified the means, but the game was the poorer for it.

2004: 10 Tests: 915 runs @ 91.50; 5 wickets @ 55.20.
      21 ODI: 812 runs @ 40.60; 19 wickets @ 24.26.

GRAHAM THORPE   England

England's Mr Fixit was at his DIY best in 2004. No longer the thrilling counter-attacker of old, Thorpe had become an utterly dependable, no-frills accumulator, especially when Tests were in the balance. Each of his four centuries almost doubled in value because of the context in which they were made: an unbeaten 119 in Barbados, where England's next-best score was 17; an undefeated 104 at Trent Bridge to make light of a target of 284; a brave 114 amid a lot of dross at Old Trafford; and a vital 118 not out at Durban that first insured against defeat, then so nearly set up one of the great comeback wins of all time. It was as though he only troubled to make runs when the situation was worthy of his attention. If Thorpe's fielding was beginning to fall prey to an ageing frame, his batting was the regular heartbeat of the middle order. Others took the breath away; Thorpe merely nudged and scampered at a steady pulse. And hardly anyone did it better.

2004: 12 Tests: 951 runs @ 73.15.

MARCUS TRESCOTHICK   England

Once again, Trescothick was England's leading run-scorer in Test cricket; once again, his achievement came with caveats. While his home form was still out of the top drawer – in seven Tests he hit 641 runs at 53.41 – he was less of a menace overseas, where he made 363 runs at 33.00. Had he not scorched a blistering 132 at Durban in his final innings of the year, the discrepancy would have been even more marked. Yet, overall, England would have been a much weaker side without him, and he struck up a harmonious partnership at the top of the order with his fellow left-hander Andrew Strauss, putting on over 150 on four occasions. He made twin centuries against West Indies at Edgbaston to atone for a miserable Test tour of the Caribbean, and continued to sparkle every now and then in the one-day game. A century in gloomy conditions in the final of the ICC Champions Trophy, when Ashley Giles's 31 was the next-highest score, should have been a match-winner. And his slip fielding, particularly off the fast bowlers, was world-class. Critics still noted a refusal to move his feet, but then they always have. Only against the fastest bowlers on the fastest pitches was this truly dangerous. *See also Five Cricketers of the Year, page 65.*

2004:   13 Tests: 1,004 runs @ 43.65; no wicket for 82.
             17 ODI: 670 runs @ 41.87; 2 wickets @ 36.00.

CHAMINDA VAAS   Sri Lanka

Vaas's reward for continuing to carry Sri Lanka's seam attack with his canny and reliable left-armers was a place in the ICC World Test and One-day XIs at their inaugural awards evening in September. If that raised a few eyebrows it was only because, in many people's eyes, Sri Lankan bowling remained synonymous with Muttiah Muralitharan – even when he was injured. But Vaas was as much the team man *par excellence* as he always has been, making regular incisions with the new ball and chipping in with useful runs down the order. His ability to swing it both ways meant that 45% of his Test victims were either caught behind or leg-before, while batsmen in the one-day game were rarely able to take liberties when faced with an economy rate of 3.83. It has been the story of Vaas's career.

2004:   11 Tests: 369 runs @ 30.75; 40 wickets @ 28.65.
             21 ODI: 105 runs @ 11.66; 37 wickets @ 18.72.

MICHAEL VAUGHAN   England

It was a year of confounded expectations. Just as few people thought Vaughan's captaincy could reach such ruthless heights, so nobody thought his batting could plumb such mundane depths. It will be remembered as the year in which he led England to a record eight consecutive wins, infusing the side with a strangely serene kind of steeliness, but also in which his batting lost its freedom, perhaps for ever. His three Test centuries, all against West Indies, and two in one Test at Lord's, were workmanlike affairs, and only two innings – 61 against New Zealand at Trent Bridge and 86 against Australia in the Champions Trophy semi-final – engaged the hairs on the back of the neck like the Vaughan of old. As his head fell over and he struggled desperately for form in South Africa, while also presiding over an outstanding victory, the comparisons with Mike Brearley gathered pace. It was a double-edged sword.

2004:   12 Tests: 712 runs @ 35.60; 1 wicket @ 116.00.
             21 ODI: 557 runs @ 30.94; 3 wickets @ 57.00.

SHANE WARNE   **Australia**

See the Leading Cricketer in the World, page 112.
2004:   12 Tests: 211 runs @ 11.72; 70 wickets @ 24.07.

YOUSUF YOUHANA   **Pakistan**

In a Pakistan batting line-up that blew hot and cold, Youhana was a warmingly
reassuring presence. It was typical of the team that his two Test centuries –
at Multan against India, and at Melbourne – were made in losing causes,
but his 72 at Lahore, also against India, helped set up a series-levelling win
and underlined his role, as he touched 30, as the team's elder statesman,
along with Inzamam-ul-Haq. But his value to the side was never more
apparent than during an innings of unobtrusive class to see off India in the
Champions Trophy at Edgbaston. And when Inzamam hurt his back in
Australia, Youhana took over as captain. Like many of his innings, that
generally went unnoticed.
2004:   7 Tests: 539 runs @ 41.46.
          27 ODI: 768 runs @ 36.57; no wicket for 1.

RETIREMENTS IN 2004

Twilight of the Revolutionaries

ANGUS FRASER

The crop of cricketers who retired in 2004 was a bumper one – at peak, this lot could have produced a very competitive XI to take on the Rest of the World, short only of a quality spinner. What's striking about these players is not just how good they were but how so many of them actually changed the game.

Steve Waugh's contribution to cricket was celebrated in an article in *Wisden 2004* (page 27). Now the author of that article has joined him as an ex-player. **Nasser Hussain** will not be remembered with that much affection by every cricketer. But he never gave a damn about that. He always intended to get where he was going by his own efforts, and he got there.

Nasser Hussain: "He always intended to get where he was going by his own efforts, and he got there."

Picture by Patrick Eagar

I never imagined he would make a captain. Before he got the England job, he always felt hard done by, always felt he was fighting, was never able to laugh at himself. But captaincy brought out the best in him. Suddenly he realised he was not the most important person in the field, and he was just what England wanted at the time. They needed discipline and direction, and in his dogmatic way he gave it to them. He was a very intelligent captain as well. His support for the players was total, and they in turn were won over.

As a batsman, he was limited because his technique was far from perfect. Anyone who opens the face as much as he did playing square on the off side is going to be vulnerable. But he built a pretty good Test career on the back of guts and determination. If he makes up his mind to do something, there is no way you will convince him otherwise, in cricket or anything else. That's why he had Ashley Giles bowling down the leg side to Tendulkar. Other captains would have wavered under the criticism, but he didn't give a monkey's. Then when he retired, he left on his own terms. And that was classic Nasser too.

Now that everyone talks casually about "reversing", it is easy to forget what a novelty it was when **Waqar Younis** and Wasim Akram perfected the art of reverse swing. I stood at square leg once and watched Waqar run in, and he was a magnificent sight. Facing him was a nightmare. I once had to have both my feet in boxes of ice because he'd whacked them so often. No one bowling reverse swing now can do it like him, because he did it at such pace that everything happened so late.

Michael Slater was a shocker to bowl at because he was one of the new breed of openers who thought nothing of hitting a bowler back over his head the very first ball of a Test match. He was one of the batsmen I least enjoyed bowling to because he could take the game away before you'd started. Remember Brisbane 1994-95? He hit Phil DeFreitas for two fours in the first over of the series, and that was the Ashes gone again. Once I called him a cane-cutter, West Indian slang for a slogger. The next ball he smashed me over extra-cover for four. Next thing I knew he was alongside me. "What are you doing?" I said grumpily. "Just cutting another piece of cane," he said, and strolled off.

Romesh Kaluwitharana was another opener of the same ilk. His opening partnerships with Sanath Jayasuriya at the 1996 World Cup completely changed the perception of how you batted in one-day cricket. **Mark Waugh** was one of the sweetest timers of a cricket ball you could ever see. He was wristy in the Asian way: all flicks and not a lot of foot movement. Nothing he did seemed hurried, even his slip-catching. It was as if he had all the time in the world to get into position. I don't know if it was his intention, but he was cool.

If Waugh was sublime, **Jack Russell** was ridiculous. The question that still puzzles me was whether everything he did (the teabags being used 20 times over; the Weetabix that had to be just so; the secret about where he lived; ordering chicken and celery every night, with the celery taken out) was genuine eccentricity or designed to cover his nerves. His corner of a

Jack Russell, amateur military historian, serial teabag reuser and wicket-keeper: on the 1995-96 tour of South Africa, he dressed as a British soldier on his visit to the site of the Battle of Isandhlwana.

Picture by Graham Morris

dressing-room looked a complete shambles, but actually everything was all meticulously placed.

And he was the best wicket-keeper I ever bowled to. He had these lovely soft hands which just enveloped the ball. It was like bowling into a big cushion, or a sponge that absorbed everything. He changed the game too, not with his teabags, but by standing up to the medium-pacers and controlling the game from there.

Adam Hollioake was another of the revolutionaries. He had an impact as an innovator in both one-day bowling and with his captaincy at Surrey. For years it was astonishing that they didn't win things. They needed a strong character to take charge and Adam was just that, physically and mentally, and he wouldn't take anything from anybody. He made the team the most important thing at The Oval. He was supremely confident, maybe over-confident, and at other counties he was seen as arrogant. This led people to believe he could be the future of the England team when he wasn't really good enough: his appointment as England one-day captain was a response to the force of his personality rather than his example. The death of his brother Ben led him to a different outlook on life. In the first season, this gave him and Surrey a motivation to do something special. Then he began to move on from cricket.

Gary Kirsten and **Mark Richardson** won't be missed by the crowds. But their team-mates will miss them. It must have been wonderful to be a bowler with them batting: you knew you could just put your feet up and wouldn't have to bowl for ages. Kirsten's century at Headingley in 2003 summed him up: he missed, got hit, missed it, nudged it, missed again... fantastic innings. Teams need players like that who score ugly runs but never give in. Richardson was much the same technically: he knew what he could do, and he didn't try to be flash. He was an innovator too in that he invented the snail-races against the slowcoach from the opposing side.

In an era without Russell and Alec Stewart, **Steve Rhodes** might have played a lot more games as England wicket-keeper. As it was, he got his England chances because he was one of Ray Illingworth's favourites. Illy was right to like him: he was a really dedicated and committed cricketer. **John Stephenson,** now head of cricket at MCC, was a one-Test wonder who reinvented himself from a batsman into an away-swinger, and turned that into a long and successful career. **Peter Martin** was an archetypal English seamer who technically had all the attributes of a very good bowler, but was too nice a man to upset people. **Peter Bowler** was a horrible pest to bowl at. Whatever shot he played it went to fine leg. Mind you, that got him 19,567 first-class runs.

These last four were all county cricketers, first and foremost, who built successful careers without playing much (or in Bowler's case, any) Test cricket. You have to wonder whether any of the people starting now will do the same. Twenty years ago, young cricketers still wanted to be cricketers, not to make a fortune. We'll miss players like them as much as we'll miss the superstars.

BIRTHS AND DEATHS

TEST CRICKETERS

Full list from 1876-77 to January 25, 2005

Abbreviations A: Australia. B: Bangladesh. E: England. I: India. NZ: New Zealand. P: Pakistan. SA: South Africa. SL: Sri Lanka. WI: West Indies. Z: Zimbabwe.

In the Test career column, dates in italics indicate seasons embracing two different years (i.e. non-English seasons). In these cases, only the first year is given, e.g. *1876* for 1876-77.

The totals of Tests played are complete up to January 25, 2005; the totals of one-day internationals are complete up to December 31, 2004.

The forename by which a player is known is underlined if it is not his first name.

Family relationships are indicated by superscript numbers; where the relationship is not immediately apparent from a shared name, see the notes at the end of this section.

	Country	Born	Died	Tests	Test Career	ODIs
Aamer Malik	P	3.1.1963		14	*1987–1994*	24
Aamir Nazir	P	2.1.1971		6	*1992–1995*	9
Aamir Sohail.	P	14.9.1966		47	*1992–1999*	156
Abdul Kadir.	P	10.5.1944	12.3.2002	4	*1964*	
Abdul Qadir	P	15.9.1955		67	*1977–1990*	104
Abdul Razzaq	P	2.12.1979		32	*1999 2004*	175
a'Beckett, Edward Lambert	A	11.8.1907	2.6.1989	4	*1928–1931*	
Abel, Robert	E	30.11.1857	10.12.1936	13	1888–1902	
Abid Ali, Syed................	I	9.9.1941		29	*1967–1974*	5
Absolom, Charles Alfred	E	7.6.1846	30.7.1889	1	*1878*	
Achong, Ellis Edgar	WI	16.2.1904	29.8.1986	6	*1929–1934*	
Ackerman, Hylton Deon	SA	14.2.1973		4	1997	
Adams, Andre Ryan	NZ	17.7.1975		1	*2001*	32
Adams, Christopher John	E	6.5.1970		5	1999	5
Adams, James Clive	WI	9.1.1968		54	*1991–2000*	127
Adams, Paul Regan.	SA	20.1.1977		45	*1995–2003*	24
Adcock, Neil Amwin Treharne	SA	8.3.1931		26	*1953–1961*	
Adhikari, Hemchandra Ramachandra ..	I	31.7.1919	25.10.2003	21	*1947–1958*	
Afaq Hussain	P	31.12.1939	25.2.2002	2	*1961–1964*	
Aftab Ahmed	B	10.11.1985		4	*2004*	8
Aftab Baloch.	P	1.4.1953		2	*1969–1974*	
Aftab Gul.	P	31.3.1946		6	*1968–1971*	
Afzaal, Usman	E	9.6.1977		3	2001	
Agarkar, Ajit Bhalchandra	I	4.12.1977		22	*1998–2004*	134
Agha Saadat Ali	P	21.6.1929	26.10.1995	1	*1955*	
Agha Zahid.	P	7.1.1953		1	*1974*	
Agnew, Jonathan Philip	E	4.4.1960		3	1984–1985	3
Ahangama, Franklyn Saliya	SL	14.9.1959		3	*1985*	1
Akram Khan	B	1.11.1968		8	*2000 2002*	44
Akram Raza.	P	22.11.1964		9	*1989–1994*	49
Alabaster, John Chaloner	NZ	11.7.1930		21	*1955–1971*	
Alamgir Kabir	B	10.1.1981		3	*2002–2003*	
Alderman, Terence Michael	A	12.6.1956		41	*1981–1990*	65
Alexander, Franz Copeland Murray ...	WI	2.11.1928		25	*1957–1960*	
Alexander, George	A	22.4.1851	6.11.1930	2	*1880–1884*	
Alexander, Harry Houston	A	9.6.1905	15.4.1993	1	*1932*	
Ali, Imtiaz	WI	28.7.1954		1	*1975*	
Ali, Inshan.	WI	25.9.1949	24.6.1995	12	*1970–1976*	
Ali, Kabir	E	24.11.1980		1	2003	1
Ali Hussain Rizvi	P	6.1.1974		1	*1997*	
Alim-ud-Din	P	15.12.1930		25	1954–1962	

[1] *Father and son(s).* [2] *Brothers.*

	Country	Born	Died	Tests	Test Career	ODIs
Ali Naqvi	P	19.3.1977		5	*1997*	
Allan, David Walter	WI	5.11.1937		5	*1961–1966*	
Allan, Francis Erskine	A	2.12.1849	9.2.1917	1	*1878*	
Allan, Peter John	A	31.12.1935		1	*1965*	
Allcott, Cyril Francis Walter	NZ	7.10.1896	19.11.1973	6	*1929–1931*	
Allen, David Arthur	E	29.10.1935		39	*1959–1966*	
Allen, *Sir* George Oswald Browning ("Gubby")	E	31.7.1902	29.11.1989	25	1930–*1947*	
Allen, Ian Basil Alston	WI	6.10.1965		2	*1991*	
Allen, Reginald Charles	A	2.7.1858	2.5.1952	1	*1886*	
Allom, Maurice James Carrick	E	23.3.1906	8.4.1995	5	*1929–1930*	
Allott, Geoffrey Ian	NZ	24.12.1971		10	*1995–1999*	31
Allott, Paul John Walter	E	14.9.1956		13	*1981–1985*	13
Alok Kapali	B	1.1.1984		16	*2002–2004*	43
Al Sahariar	B	23.4.1978		15	*2000–2003*	29
Amalean, Kaushik Naginda	SL	7.4.1965		2	*1985–1987*	8
[1, 2]Amarnath, Mohinder	I	24.9.1950		69	*1969–1987*	85
[1]Amarnath, Nanik ("Lala")	I	11.9.1911	5.8.2000	24	*1933–1952*	
[1, 2]Amarnath, Surinder	I	30.12.1948		10	*1975–1978*	3
[2]Amar Singh, Ladha	I	4.12.1910	20.5.1940	7	*1932–1936*	
Ambrose, Curtly Elconn Lynwall	WI	21.9.1963		98	*1987–2000*	176
Amerasinghe, Amerasinghe Mudalige Jayantha Gamini	SL	2.2.1954		2	*1983*	
Ames, Leslie Ethelbert George CBE	E	3.12.1905	26.2.1990	47	1929–*1938*	
Aminul Islam	B	2.2.1968		13	*2000–2002*	39
Amir Elahi	I, P	1.9.1908	28.12.1980	6	*1947–1952*	
Amiss, Dennis Leslie MBE	E	7.4.1943		50	*1966–1977*	18
Amla, Hashim Mahomed	SA	31.3.1983		3	*2004*	
Amre, Pravin Kalyan	I	14.8.1968		11	*1992–1993*	37
Anderson, James Henry	SA	26.4.1874	11.3.1926	1	*1902*	
Anderson, James Michael	E	30.7.1982		12	2003–*2004*	39
[1]Anderson, Robert Wickham	NZ	2.10.1948		9	*1976–1978*	2
[1]Anderson, William McDougall	NZ	8.10.1919	21.12.1979	1	*1945*	
Andrew, Keith Vincent	E	15.12.1929		2	*1954–1963*	
Andrews, Bryan	NZ	4.4.1945		2	*1973*	
Andrews, Thomas James Edwin	A	26.8.1890	28.1.1970	16	*1921–1926*	
Angel, Jo	A	22.4.1968		4	*1992–1994*	3
Anil Dalpat	P	20.9.1963		9	*1983–1984*	15
Ankola, Salil Ashok	I	1.3.1968		1	*1989*	20
Anurasiri, Sangarange Don	SL	25.2.1966		18	*1985–1997*	45
Anwar Hossain Monir	B	31.12.1981		1	*2003*	1
Anwar Hossain Piju	B	10.12.1983		1	*2002*	1
Anwar Hussain	P	16.7.1920	9.10.2002	4	*1952*	
Anwar Khan	P	24.12.1955		1	*1978*	
Appleyard, Robert	E	27.6.1924		9	*1954–1956*	
[2]Apte, Arvindrao Laxmanrao	I	24.10.1934		1	*1959*	
[2]Apte, Madhavrao Laxmanrao	I	5.10.1932		7	*1952*	
Aqib Javed	P	5.8.1972		22	*1988–1998*	163
Archer, Alfred German	E	6.12.1871	15.7.1935	1	*1898*	
[2]Archer, Kenneth Alan	A	17.1.1928		5	*1950–1951*	
[2]Archer, Ronald Graham	A	25.10.1933		19	*1952–1956*	
Arif Butt	P	17.5.1944		3	*1964*	
Armitage, Thomas	E	25.4.1848	21.9.1922	2	*1876*	
Armstrong, Warwick Windridge	A	22.5.1879	13.7.1947	50	*1901–1921*	
Arnold, Edward George	E	7.11.1876	25.10.1942	10	*1903–1907*	
Arnold, Geoffrey Graham	E	3.9.1944		34	1967–1975	14
Arnold, John	E	30.11.1907	4.4.1984	1	*1931*	
Arnold, Russel Premakumaran	SL	25.10.1973		44	*1996–2004*	128
Arnott, Kevin John	Z	8.3.1961		4	*1992*	13

[1] *Father and son(s).* [2] *Brothers.*

	Country	Born	Died	Tests	Test Career	ODIs
Arshad Ayub	I	2.8.1958		13	*1987–1989*	32
Arshad Khan	P	22.3.1971		8	*1997–2000*	48
Arthurton, Keith Lloyd Thomas	WI	21.2.1965		33	*1988–1995*	105
Arun, Bharathi	I	14.12.1962		2	*1986*	4
Arun Lal	I	1.8.1955		16	*1982–1988*	13
Asgarali, Nyron Sultan	WI	28.12.1920		2	*1957*	
Ashfaq Ahmed	P	6.6.1973		1	*1993*	3
Ashley, William Hare	SA	10.2.1862	14.7.1930	1	*1888*	
Ashraf Ali	P	22.4.1958		8	*1981–1987*	16
Asif Iqbal	P	6.6.1943		58	*1964–1979*	10
Asif Masood	P	23.1.1946		16	*1968–1976*	7
Asif Mujtaba	P	4.11.1967		25	*1986–1996*	66
Asim Kamal	P	31.5.1976		6	*2003–2004*	
Astill, William Ewart	E	1.3.1888	10.2.1948	9	*1927–1929*	
Astle, Nathan John	NZ	15.9.1971		66	*1995–2004*	188
Atapattu, Marvan Samson	SL	22.11.1970		79	*1990–2004*	225
Ata-ur-Rehman	P	28.3.1975		13	*1992–1996*	30
Atherton, Michael Andrew OBE	E	23.3.1968		115	*1989–2001*	54
Athey, Charles William Jeffrey	E	27.9.1957		23	*1980–1988*	31
Atif Rauf	P	3.3.1964		1	*1993*	
Atiq-uz-Zaman	P	20.7.1975		1	*1999*	3
[2]**Atkinson**, Denis St Eval	WI	9.8.1926	9.11.2001	22	*1948–1957*	
[2]**Atkinson**, Eric St Eval	WI	6.11.1927	29.5.1998	8	*1957–1958*	
Attewell, William	E	12.6.1861	11.6.1927	10	*1884–1891*	
Austin, Richard Arkwright	WI	5.9.1954		2	*1977*	
Azad, Kirtivardhan	I	2.1.1959		7	*1980–1983*	25
Azam Khan	P	1.3.1969		1	*1996*	6
Azeem Hafeez	P	29.7.1963		18	*1983–1984*	15
Azhar Khan	P	7.9.1955		1	*1979*	
Azhar Mahmood	P	28.2.1975		21	*1997–2001*	134
Azharuddin, Mohammad	I	8.2.1963		99	*1984–1999*	334
[2]**Azmat Rana**	P	3.11.1951		1	*1979*	2
Bacchus, Sheik Faoud Ahamul Fasiel . .	WI	31.1.1954		19	*1977–1981*	29
Bacher, Adam Marc	SA	29.10.1973		19	*1996–1999*	8
Bacher, Aron ("Ali")	SA	24.5.1942		12	*1965–1969*	
Badani, Hemang Kamal	I	14.11.1976		4	*2001*	40
Badcock, Clayvel Lindsay	A	10.4.1914	13.12.1982	7	*1936–1938*	
Badcock, Frederick Theodore	NZ	9.8.1897	19.9.1982	7	*1929–1932*	
Bahutule, Sairaj Vasant	I	6.1.1973		2	*2000–2001*	8
Baichan, Leonard	WI	12.5.1946		3	*1974–1975*	
Baig, Abbas Ali	I	19.3.1939		10	*1959–1966*	
Bailey, Robert John	E	28.10.1963		4	*1988–1989*	4
Bailey, Trevor Edward CBE	E	3.12.1923		61	*1949–1958*	
Bairstow, David Leslie	E	1.9.1951	5.1.1998	4	*1979–1980*	21
Bakewell, Alfred Harry	E	2.11.1908	23.1.1983	6	*1931–1935*	
Balaji, Lakshmipathy	I	27.9.1981		5	*2003*	24
Balaskas, Xenophon Constantine	SA	15.10.1910	12.5.1994	9	*1930–1938*	
Balderstone, John Christopher	E	16.11.1940	6.3.2000	2	*1976*	
Bandara, Charitha Malinga	SL	31.12.1979		1	*1997*	
Bandaratilleke, Mapa Rallage Chandima Niroshan	SL	16.5.1975		7	*1997–2001*	3
Banerjee, Sarobindu Nath	I	3.10.1911	14.10.1980	1	*1948*	
Banerjee, Subroto Tara ("Shute")	I	13.2.1969		1	*1991*	6
Banerjee, Sudangsu Abinash	I	1.11.1917	14.9.1992	1	*1948*	
Bangar, Sanjay Bapusaheb	I	11.10.1972		12	*2001–2002*	15
Banks, Omari Ahmed Clemente	WI	17.7.1982		8	*2002–2004*	3
[2]**Bannerman**, Alexander Chalmers	A	21.3.1854	19.9.1924	28	*1878–1893*	
[2]**Bannerman**, Charles	A	23.7.1851	20.8.1930	3	*1876–1878*	

[1] *Father and son(s).* [2] *Brothers.*

	Country	Born	Died	Tests	Test Career	ODIs
Baptiste, Eldine Ashworth Elderfield ..	WI	12.3.1960		10	*1983–1989*	43
Baqa Jilani, Mohammad	I	20.7.1911	2.7.1941	1	1936	
Barber, Richard Trevor	NZ	3.6.1925		1	*1955*	
Barber, Robert William	E	26.9.1935		28	1960–1968	
Barber, Wilfred	E	18.4.1901	10.9.1968	2	1935	
Bardsley, Warren	A	6.12.1882	20.1.1954	41	1909–1926	
Barlow, Edgar John............	SA	12.8.1940		30	*1961–1969*	
Barlow, Graham Derek	E	26.3.1950		3	*1976–1977*	6
Barlow, Richard Gorton	E	28.5.1851	31.7.1919	17	*1881–1886*	
Barnes, Sydney Francis	E	19.4.1873	26.12.1967	27	*1901–1913*	
Barnes, Sidney George	A	5.6.1916	16.12.1973	13	1938–1948	
Barnes, William	E	27.5.1852	24.3.1899	21	1880–1890	
Barnett, Benjamin Arthur........	A	23.3.1908	29.6.1979	4	1938	
Barnett, Charles John	E	3.7.1910	28.5.1993	20	1933–1948	
Barnett, Kim John	E	17.7.1960		4	1988–1989	1
Barratt, Fred................	E	12.4.1894	29.1.1947	5	*1929–1929*	
Barrett, Arthur George	WI	5.4.1942		6	*1970–1974*	
Barrett, John Edward	A	15.10.1866	6.2.1916	2	1890	
Barrington, Kenneth Frank......	E	24.11.1930	14.3.1981	82	1955–1968	
Barrow, Ivanhoe Mordred.......	WI	16.1.1911	2.4.1979	11	*1929–1939*	
Bartlett, Edward Lawson	WI	10.3.1906	21.12.1976	5	*1928–1930*	
Bartlett, Gary Alex............	NZ	3.2.1941		10	*1961–1967*	
Barton, Paul Thomas..........	NZ	9.10.1935		7	*1961–1962*	
Barton, Victor Alexander........	E	6.10.1867	23.3.1906	1	*1891*	
Basit Ali....................	P	13.12.1970		19	*1992–1995*	50
Bates, Willie	E	19.11.1855	8.1.1900	15	*1881–1886*	
Batty, Gareth Jon	E	13.10.1977		5	*2003*	6
Baugh, Carlton Seymour	WI	23.6.1982		5	*2002–2004*	6
Baumgartner, Harold Vane........	SA	17.11.1883	8.4.1938	1	*1913*	
Bean, George................	E	7.3.1864	16.3.1923	3	*1891*	
Beard, Donald Derek..........	NZ	14.11.1920	15.7.1982	4	*1951–1955*	
Beard, Graeme Robert..........	A	19.8.1950		3	*1979*	2
Beaumont, Rolland	SA	4.2.1884	25.5.1958	5	*1912–1913*	
Beck, John Edward Francis........	NZ	1.8.1934	23.4.2000	8	*1953–1955*	
Bedi, Bishan Singh	I	25.9.1946		67	*1966–1979*	10
Bedser, *Sir* Alec Victor	E	4.7.1918		51	1946–1955	
Begbie, Denis Warburton	SA	12.12.1914		5	*1948–1949*	
Bell, Alexander John	SA	15.4.1906	1.8.1985	16	1929–1935	
Bell, Ian Ronald	E	11.4.1982		1	2004	4
Bell, Matthew David	NZ	25.2.1977		13	*1998–2001*	7
Bell, William	NZ	5.9.1931	23.7.2002	2	*1953*	
[2]Benaud, John	A	11.5.1944		3	*1972*	
[2]Benaud, John OBE	A	6.10.1930		63	*1951–1963*	
Benjamin, Joseph Emmanuel	E	2.2.1961		1	1994	2
Benjamin, Kenneth Charlie Griffith ...	WI	8.4.1967		26	*1991–1997*	26
Benjamin, Winston Keithroy Matthew .	WI	31.12.1964		21	*1987–1994*	85
Bennett, Murray John	A	6.10.1956		3	*1984–1985*	8
Benson, Mark Richard..........	E	6.7.1958		1	1986	1
Bernard, David Eddison	WI	19.7.1981		1	*2002*	4
Berry, Robert................	E	29.1.1926		2	1950	
Best, Carlisle Alonza...........	WI	14.5.1959		8	*1985–1990*	24
Best, Tino la Bertram	WI	26.8.1981		8	*2002–2004*	6
Betancourt, Nelson............	WI	4.6.1887	12.10.1947	1	*1929*	
Bevan, Michael Gwyl	A	8.5.1970		18	*1994–1997*	232
Bhandari, Prakash	I	27.11.1935		3	*1954–1956*	
Bharadwaj, Raghvendrarao Vijay.....	I	15.8.1975		3	*1999*	10
Bhat, Adwai Ragharam	I	16.4.1958		2	*1983*	
Bichel, Andrew John...........	A	27.8.1970		19	*1996–2003*	67
Bicknell, Martin Paul	E	14.1.1969		4	1993–2003	7

[1] *Father and son(s).*   [2] *Brothers.*

	Country	Born	Died	Tests	Test Career	ODIs
Bikash Ranjan Das	B	14.7.1982		1	*2000*	
Bilby, Grahame Paul	NZ	7.5.1941		2	*1965*	
Binks, James Graham	E	5.10.1935		2	*1963*	
Binns, Alfred Phillip	WI	24.7.1929		5	*1952–1955*	
Binny, Roger Michael Humphrey	I	19.7.1955		27	*1979–1986*	72
Bird, Morice Carlos	E	25.3.1888	9.12.1933	10	*1909–1913*	
Birkenshaw, Jack	E	13.11.1940		5	*1972–1973*	
Birkett, Lionel Sydney	WI	14.4.1905	16.1.1998	4	*1930*	
Bishop, Ian Raphael	WI	24.10.1967		43	*1988–1997*	84
Bisset, *Sir* Murray.	SA	14.4.1876	24.10.1931	3	*1898–1909*	
Bissett, George Finlay	SA	5.11.1905	14.11.1965	4	*1927*	
Black, Marlon Ian.	WI	7.6.1975		6	*2000–2001*	5
Blackham, John McCarthy	A	11.5.1854	28.12.1932	35	*1876–1894*	
Blackie, Donald Dearness.	A	5.4.1882	18.4.1955	3	*1928*	
Blain, Tony Elston	NZ	17.2.1962		11	*1986–1993*	38
Blair, Robert William	NZ	23.6.1932		19	*1952–1963*	
Blakey, Richard John.	E	15.1.1967		2	*1992*	3
Blanckenberg, James Manuel	SA	31.12.1892	d unknown	18	*1913–1924*	
Bland, Kenneth Colin	SA	5.4.1938		21	*1961–1966*	
Blewett, Gregory Scott.	A	29.10.1971		46	*1994–1999*	32
Bligh *Hon.* Ivo Francis Walter [later 8th Earl of Darnley]	E	13.3.1859	10.4.1927	4	*1882*	
Blignaut, Arnoldus Mauritius	Z	1.8.1978		15	*2000–2003*	47
Blunt, Roger Charles.	NZ	3.11.1900	22.6.1966	9	*1929–1931*	
Blythe, Colin.	E	30.5.1879	8.11.1917	19	*1901–1909*	
Board, John Henry	E	23.2.1867	15.4.1924	6	*1898–1905*	
Bock, Ernest George	SA	17.9.1908	5.9.1961	1	*1935*	
Boje, Nico.	SA	20.3.1973		29	*1999–2004*	102
Bolton, Bruce Alfred	NZ	31.5.1935		2	*1958*	
Bolus, John Brian	E	31.1.1934		7	*1963–1963*	
Bond, Gerald Edward	SA	5.4.1909	27.8.1965	1	*1938*	
Bond, Shane Edward	NZ	7.6.1975		10	*2001–2002*	27
Bonnor, George John.	A	25.2.1855	27.6.1912	17	*1880–1888*	
Boock, Stephen Lewis	NZ	20.9.1951		30	*1977–1988*	14
Boon, David Clarence	A	29.12.1960		107	*1984–1995*	181
Booth, Brian Charles MBE.	A	19.10.1933		29	*1961–1965*	
Booth, Major William	E	10.12.1886	1.7.1916	2	*1913*	
Borde, Chandrakant Gulabrao	I	21.7.1933		55	*1958 1969*	
Border, Allan Robert.	A	27.7.1955		156	*1978–1993*	273
Bosanquet, Bernard James Tindal	E	13.10.1877	12.10.1936	7	*1903–1905*	
Bosch, Tertius	SA	14.3.1966	13.2.2000	1	*1991*	2
Botham, Ian Terence OBE	E	24.11.1955		102	*1977–1992*	116
Botten, James Thomas.	SA	21.6.1938		3	*1965*	
Boucher, Mark Verdon.	SA	3.12.1976		78	*1997–2004*	178
Bowden, Montague Parker	E	1.11.1865	19.2.1892	2	*1888*	
Bowes, William Eric	E	25.7.1908	5.9.1987	15	*1932–1946*	
Bowley, Edward Henry.	E	6.6.1890	9.7.1974	5	*1929–1929*	
Boyce, Keith David.	WI	11.10.1943	11.10.1996	21	*1970–1975*	8
Boycott, Geoffrey OBE	E	21.10.1940		108	*1964–1981*	36
Boyle, Henry Frederick	A	10.12.1847	21.11.1907	12	*1878–1884*	
[2]**Bracewell**, Brendon Paul.	NZ	14.9.1959		6	*1978–1984*	1
[2]**Bracewell**, John Garry.	NZ	15.4.1958		41	*1980–1990*	53
Bracken, Nathan Wade	A	12.9.1977		3	*2003*	17
[1]**Bradburn**, Grant Eric.	NZ	26.5.1966		7	*1990–2000*	11
[1]**Bradburn**, Wynne Pennell.	NZ	24.11.1938		2	*1963*	
Bradley, Walter Morris	E	2.1.1875	19.6.1944	2	*1899*	
Bradman, *Sir* Donald George, AC	A	27.8.1908	25.2.2001	52	*1928–1948*	
Brain, David Hayden.	Z	4.10.1964		9	*1992–1994*	23
Brandes, Eddo André	Z	5.3.1963		10	*1992–1999*	59

[1] *Father and son(s).*   [2] *Brothers.*

	Country	Born	Died	Tests	Test Career	ODIs
Brann, William Henry	SA	4.4.1899	22.9.1953	3	1922	
Braund, Leonard Charles	E	18.10.1875	23.12.1955	23	1901–1907	
Bravo, Dwayne James John	WI	7.10.1983		4	2004	19
Brearley, John Michael OBE	E	28.4.1942		39	1976–1981	25
Brearley, Walter	E	11.3.1876	30.1.1937	4	1905–1912	
Breese, Gareth Rohan	WI	9.1.1976		1	2002	
Brennan, Donald Vincent	E	10.2.1920	9.1.1985	2	1951	
Brent, Gary Bazil	Z	13.1.1976		4	1999–2001	48
Briant, Gavin Aubrey	Z	11.4.1969		1	1992	5
Briggs, John	E	3.10.1862	11.1.1902	33	1884–1899	
Bright, Raymond James	A	13.7.1954		25	1977–1986	11
Briscoe, Arthur Wellesley	SA	6.2.1911	22.4.1941	2	1935–1938	
Broad, Brian Christopher	E	29.9.1957		25	1984–1989	34
Brockwell, William	E	21.11.1865	30.6.1935	7	1893–1899	
Bromfield, Harry Dudley	SA	26.6.1932		9	1961–1965	
Bromley, Ernest Harvey	A	2.9.1912	1.2.1967	2	1932–1934	
Bromley-Davenport, Hugh Richard	E	18.8.1870	23.5.1954	4	1895–1898	
Brookes, Dennis	E	29.10.1915		1	1947	
Brown, Alan	E	17.10.1935		2	1961	
Brown, David John	E	30.1.1942		26	1965–1969	
Brown, Frederick Richard MBE	E	16.12.1910	24.7.1991	22	1931–1953	
Brown, George	E	6.10.1887	3.12.1964	7	1921–1922	
Brown, John Thomas	E	20.8.1869	4.11.1904	8	1894–1899	
Brown, Lennox Sidney	SA	24.11.1910	1.9.1983	2	1931	
Brown, Simon John Emmerson	E	29.6.1969		1	1996	
Brown, Vaughan Raymond	NZ	3.11.1959		2	1985	3
Brown, William Alfred	A	31.7.1912		22	1934–1948	
Browne, Courtney Oswald	WI	7.12.1970		14	1994–2001	32
Browne, Cyril Rutherford	WI	8.10.1890	12.1.1964	4	1928–1929	
Bruce, William	A	22.5.1864	3.8.1925	14	1884–1894	
Bruk-Jackson, Glen Keith	Z	25.4.1969		2	1993	1
Buckenham, Claude Percival	E	16.1.1876	23.2.1937	4	1909	
Burge, Peter John Parnell	A	17.5.1932	5.10.2001	42	1954–1965	
Burger, Christopher George de Villiers	SA	12.7.1935		2	1957	
Burgess, Mark Gordon	NZ	17.7.1944		50	1967–1980	26
Burke, Cecil	NZ	22.3.1914	4.8.1997	1	1945	
Burke, James Wallace	A	12.6.1930	2.2.1979	24	1950–1958	
Burke, Sydney Frank	SA	11.3.1934		2	1961–1964	
Burmester, Mark Greville	Z	24.1.1968		3	1992	8
Burn, Kenneth Edwin	A	17.9.1862	20.7.1956	2	1890	
Burton, Frederick John	A	2.11.1865	25.8.1929	2	1886–1887	
Burtt, Thomas Browning	NZ	22.1.1915	24.5.1988	10	1946–1952	
Butchart, Iain Peter	Z	9.5.1960		1	1994	20
[1]**Butcher,** Alan Raymond	E	7.1.1954		1	1979	1
Butcher, Basil Fitzherbert	WI	3.9.1933		44	1958–1969	
[1]**Butcher,** Mark Alan	E	23.8.1972		71	1997–2004	
Butcher, Roland Orlando	E	14.10.1953		3	1980	3
Butler, Harold James	E	12.3.1913	17.7.1991	2	1947–1947	
Butler, Ian Gareth	NZ	24.11.1981		8	2001–2004	15
Butler, Lennox Stephen	WI	9.2.1929		1	1954	
Butt, Henry Rigden	E	27.12.1865	21.12.1928	3	1895	
Butterfield, Leonard Arthur	NZ	29.8.1913	7.7.1999	1	1945	
Butts, Clyde Godfrey	WI	8.7.1957		7	1984–1987	
Buys, Isaac Daniel	SA	4.2.1895	d unknown	1	1922	
Bynoe, Michael Robin	WI	23.2.1941		4	1958–1966	
Caddick, Andrew Richard	E	21.11.1968		62	1993–2002	54
[1]**Cairns,** Bernard Lance	NZ	10.10.1949		43	1973–1985	78
[1]**Cairns,** Christopher Lance	NZ	13.6.1970		62	1989–2004	198

[1] Father and son(s). [2] Brothers.

	Country	Born	Died	Tests	Test Career	ODIs
Callaway, Sydney Thomas	A	6.2.1868	25.11.1923	3	*1891–1894*	
Callen, Ian Wayne	A	2.5.1955		1	*1977*	5
Calthorpe, *Hon.* Frederick Somerset Gough-	E	27.5.1892	19.11.1935	4	*1929*	
Camacho, George <u>Stephen</u>	WI	15.10.1945		11	*1967–1970*	
[2]**Cameron**, Francis James	WI	22.6.1923	10.6.1994	5	*1948*	
Cameron, Francis James MBE	NZ	1.6.1932		19	*1961–1965*	
Cameron, Horace Brakenridge	SA	5.7.1905	2.11.1935	26	*1927–1935*	
[2]**Cameron**, John Hemsley	WI	8.4.1914	13.2.2000	2	*1939*	
Campbell, Alistair Douglas Ross	Z	23.9.1972		60	*1992–2002*	188
Campbell, Gregory Dale	A	10.3.1964		4	1989–*1989*	12
Campbell, Sherwin Legay	WI	1.11.1970		52	*1994–2001*	90
Campbell, Thomas	SA	9.2.1882	5.10.1924	5	*1909–1912*	
Capel, David John	E	6.2.1963		15	1987–*1989*	23
Carew, George McDonald	WI	4.6.1910	9.12.1974	4	*1934–1948*	
Carew, Michael Conrad	WI	15.9.1937		19	1963–*1971*	
Carkeek, William	A	17.10.1878	20.2.1937	6	*1912*	
Carlisle, Stuart Vance	Z	10.5.1972		35	*1994–2003*	108
Carlson, Phillip Henry	A	8.8.1951		2	*1978*	4
Carlstein, Peter Rudolph	SA	28.10.1938		8	*1957–1963*	
Carr, Arthur William	E	21.5.1893	7.2.1963	11	*1922–1929*	
Carr, Donald Bryce OBE	E	28.12.1926		2	*1951*	
Carr, Douglas Ward	E	17.3.1872	23.3.1950	1	*1909*	
Carter, Claude Pagdett	SA	23.4.1881	8.11.1952	10	*1912–1924*	
Carter, Hanson	A	15.3.1878	8.6.1948	28	*1907–1921*	
Cartwright, Thomas William MBE	E	22.7.1935		5	*1964–1965*	
Catterall, Robert Hector	SA	10.7.1900	3.1.1961	24	*1922–1930*	
Cave, Henry Butler	NZ	10.10.1922	15.9.1989	19	*1949–1958*	
Challenor, George	WI	28.6.1888	30.7.1947	3	*1928*	
Chandana, Umagiliya Durage <u>Upul</u>	SL	7.5.1972		14	*1998–2004*	133
Chanderpaul, Shivnarine	WI	16.8.1974		80	*1993–2004*	161
Chandrasekhar, Bhagwat Subramanya	I	17.5.1945		58	*1963–1979*	1
Chang, Herbert Samuel	WI	22.7.1952		1	*1978*	
Chapman, Arthur <u>Percy</u> Frank	E	3.9.1900	16.9.1961	26	*1924–1930*	
Chapman, Horace William	SA	30.6.1890	1.12.1941	2	*1913–1921*	
[2,4]**Chappell**, Gregory Stephen MBE	A	7.8.1948		87	*1970–1983*	74
[2,4]**Chappell**, Ian Michael	A	26.9.1943		75	*1964–1979*	16
[2,4]**Chappell**, Trevor Martin	A	21.10.1952		3	*1981*	20
Chapple, Murray Ernest	NZ	25.7.1930	31.7.1985	14	*1952–1965*	
Charlton, Percie Chater	A	9.4.1867	30.9.1954	2	*1890*	
Charlwood, Henry Rupert James	E	19.12.1846	6.6.1888	2	*1876*	
Chatfield, Ewen John MBE	NZ	3.7.1950		43	*1974–1988*	114
Chatterton, William	E	27.12.1861	19.3.1913	1	*1891*	
Chauhan, Chetandra Pratap Singh	I	21.7.1947		40	*1969–1980*	7
Chauhan, Rajesh Kumar	I	19.12.1966		21	*1992–1997*	35
Cheetham, John Erskine	SA	26.5.1920	21.8.1980	24	*1948–1955*	
Chevalier, Grahame Anton	SA	9.3.1937		1	*1969*	
Chigumbura, Elton	Z	14.3.1986		4	*2003–2004*	15
Childs, John Henry	E	15.8.1951		2	*1988*	
Chipperfield, Arthur Gordon	A	17.11.1905	29.7.1987	14	*1934–1938*	
Chopra, Aakash	I	19.9.1977		10	*2003–2004*	
Chopra, Nikhil	I	26.12.1973		1	*1999*	39
Chowdhury, Nirode Ranjan	I	23.5.1923	14.12.1979	2	*1948–1951*	
[2]**Christiani**, Cyril Marcel	WI	28.10.1913	4.4.1938	4	*1934*	
[2]**Christiani**, Robert Julian	WI	19.7.1920	4.1.2005	22	*1947–1953*	
Christopherson, Stanley	E	11.11.1861	6.4.1949	1	*1884*	
Christy, James Alexander Joseph	SA	12.12.1904	1.2.1971	10	*1929–1931*	
Chubb, Geoffrey Walter Ashton	SA	12.4.1911	28.8.1982	5	*1951*	
Clark, Edward Winchester	E	9.8.1902	28.4.1982	8	*1929–1934*	

[1] *Father and son(s).* [2] *Brothers.*

	Country	Born	Died	Tests	Test Career	ODIs
Clark, Wayne Maxwell	A	19.9.1953		10	*1977–1978*	2
Clarke, Carlos Bertram OBE	WI	7.4.1918	14.10.1993	3	1939	
Clarke, Michael John	A	2.4.1981		9	*2004*	36
Clarke, Rikki	E	29.9.1981		2	*2003*	17
Clarke, Sylvester Theophilus	WI	11.12.1954	4.12.1999	11	*1977–1981*	10
Clay, John Charles	E	18.3.1898	12.8.1973	1	1935	
Cleverley, Donald Charles	NZ	23.12.1909	16.2.2004	2	*1931–1945*	
Close, Dennis Brian CBE	E	24.2.1931		22	*1949–1976*	3
Cochran, John Alexander Kennedy	SA	15.7.1909	15.6.1987	1	*1930*	
Coen, Stanley Keppel	SA	14.10.1902	28.1.1967	2	*1927*	
Colah, Sorabji Hormasji Munchersha	I	22.9.1902	11.9.1950	2	*1932–1933*	
Coldwell, Leonard John	E	10.1.1933	6.8.1996	7	*1962–1964*	
Colley, David John	A	15.3.1947		3	*1972*	1
Collinge, Richard Owen	NZ	2.4.1946		35	*1964–1978*	15
Collingwood, Paul David	E	26.5.1976		2	*2003*	63
Collins, Herbert Leslie	A	21.1.1888	28.5.1959	19	*1920–1926*	
[2]**Collins**, Pedro Tyrone	WI	12.8.1976		27	*1998–2004*	23
Collymore, Corey Dalanelo	WI	21.12.1977		14	*1998–2004*	56
Colquhoun, Ian Alexander	NZ	8.6.1924		2	*1954*	
Commaille, John McIllwaine Moore	SA	21.2.1883	28.7.1956	12	*1909–1927*	
Commins, John Brian	SA	19.2.1965		3	*1994*	
Compton, Denis Charles Scott CBE	E	23.5.1918	23.4.1997	78	*1937–1956*	
Coney, Jeremy Vernon MBE	NZ	21.6.1952		52	*1973–1986*	88
Congdon, Bevan Ernest OBE	NZ	11.2.1938		61	*1964–1978*	11
Coningham, Arthur	A	14.7.1863	13.6.1939	1	*1894*	
Connolly, Alan Norman	A	29.6.1939		29	*1963–1970*	1
Constantine, Learie Nicholas (later Baron Constantine of Maraval & Nelson)	WI	21.9.1901	1.7.1971	18	1928–1939	
Contractor, Nariman Jamshedji	I	7.3.1934		31	*1955–1961*	
Conyngham, Dalton Parry	SA	10.5.1897	7.7.1979	1	*1922*	
Cook, Cecil	E	23.8.1921	4.9.1996	1	*1947*	
Cook, Frederick James	SA	1870	30.11.1915	1	*1895*	
Cook, Geoffrey	E	9.10.1951		7	*1981–1982*	6
Cook, Nicholas Grant Billson	E	17.6.1956		15	*1983–1989*	3
Cook, Simon Hewitt	A	29.1.1972		2	*1997*	
Cook, Stephen James	SA	31.7.1953		3	*1992–1993*	4
Cooper, Alfred Henry Cecil	SA	2.9.1893	18.7.1963	1	*1913*	
Cooper, Bransby Beauchamp	A	15.3.1844	7.8.1914	1	*1876*	
[5]**Cooper**, William Henry	A	11.9.1849	5.4.1939	2	*1881–1884*	
Cope, Geoffrey Alan	E	23.2.1947		3	*1977*	2
Copson, William Henry	E	27.4.1908	14.9.1971	3	*1939–1947*	
Cork, Dominic Gerald	E	7.8.1971		37	*1995–2002*	32
Corling, Grahame Edward	A	13.7.1941		5	*1964*	
Cornford, Walter Latter	E	25.12.1900	6.2.1964	4	*1929*	
Cosier, Gary John	A	25.4.1953		18	*1975–1978*	9
Cottam, John Thomas	A	5.9.1867	30.1.1897	1	*1886*	
Cottam, Robert Michael Henry	E	16.10.1944		4	*1968–1972*	
Cotter, Albert	A	3.12.1884	31.10.1917	21	*1903–1911*	
Coulthard, George	A	1.8.1856	22.10.1883	1	*1881*	
Coventry, Hon. Charles John	E	26.2.1867	2.6.1929	2	*1888*	
Cowans, Norman George	E	17.4.1961		19	*1982–1985*	23
[1]**Cowdrey**, Christopher Stuart	E	20.10.1957		6	*1984–1988*	3
[1]**Cowdrey**, Michael Colin (later Baron Cowdrey of Tonbridge)	E	24.12.1932	4.12.2000	114	*1954–1974*	1
Cowie, John OBE	NZ	30.3.1912	3.6.1994	9	*1937–1949*	
Cowper, Robert Maskew	A	5.10.1940		27	*1964–1968*	
Cox, Joseph Lovell	SA	28.6.1886	4.7.1971	3	*1913*	
Coxon, Alexander	E	18.1.1916		1	*1948*	
Craig, Ian David	A	12.6.1935		11	*1952–1957*	

---

[1] *Father and son.* [2] *Brothers.* [5] *Great-grandfather and great-grandson.*

	Country	Born	Died	Tests	Test Career	ODIs
Cranston, James.	E	9.1.1859	10.12.1904	1	1890	
Cranston, Kenneth	E	20.10.1917		8	1947–1948	
Crapp, John Frederick	E	14.10.1912	15.2.1981	7	1948–*1948*	
Crawford, John Neville	E	1.12.1886	2.5.1963	12	1905–*1907*	
Crawford, William <u>Patrick</u> Anthony . . .	A	3.8.1933		4	1956–*1956*	
Crawley, John Paul	E	21.9.1971		37	1994–*2002*	13
Cremer, Alexander <u>Graeme</u>	Z	19.9.1986		2	2004	
Cresswell, George <u>Fenwick</u>.	NZ	22.3.1915	10.1.1966	3	1949–*1950*	
Cripps, Godfrey	SA	19.10.1865	27.7.1943	1	1891	
Crisp, Robert James	SA	28.5.1911	2.3.1994	9	1935–*1935*	
Crocker, Gary John.	Z	16.5.1962		3	1992	6
Croft, Colin Everton Hunte	WI	15.3.1953		27	1976–*1981*	19
Croft, Robert Damien Bale.	E	25.5.1970		21	1996–2001	50
Cromb, Ian Burns.	NZ	25.6.1905	6.3.1984	5	1931–*1931*	
Cronje, Wessel Johannes ("Hansie"). . .	SA	25.9.1969	1.6.2002	68	1991–*1999*	188
[2]**Crowe,** Jeffrey John	NZ	14.9.1958		39	1982–*1989*	75
[2]**Crowe,** Martin David MBE	NZ	22.9.1962		77	1981–*1995*	143
Cuffy, Cameron Eustace	WI	8.2.1970		15	1994–*2002*	41
Cullinan, Daryll John	SA	4.3.1967		70	1992–*2000*	138
Cummins, Anderson Cleophas	WI	7.5.1966		5	1992–*1994*	63
Cunis, Robert Smith	NZ	5.1.1941		20	1963–*1971*	
Curnow, Sydney Harry	SA	16.12.1907	28.7.1986	7	1930–*1931*	
Curtis, Timothy Stephen	E	15.1.1960		5	1988–1989	
Cuttell, Willis Robert	E	13.9.1864	9.12.1929	2	1898	
Da Costa, Oscar Constantine	WI	11.9.1907	1.10.1936	5	1929–*1934*	
Dahiya, Vijay.	I	10.5.1973		2	2000	19
Dale, Adam Craig.	A	30.12.1968		2	1997–*1998*	30
Dalton, Eric Londesbrough	SA	2.12.1906	3.6.1981	15	1929–*1938*	
Dani, Hemchandra Tukaram	I	24.5.1933	19.12.1999	1	1952	
Daniel, Wayne Wendell	WI	16.1.1956		10	1975–*1983*	18
Danish Kaneria	P	16.12.1980		23	2000–*2004*	10
D'Arcy, John William	NZ	23.4.1936		5	1958	
Darling, Joseph	A	21.11.1870	2.1.1946	34	1894–1905	
Darling, Leonard Stuart	A	14.8.1909	24.6.1992	12	1932–*1936*	
Darling, Warrick Maxwell	A	1.5.1957		14	1977–*1979*	18
Das, Shiv Sunder	I	5.11.1977		23	2000–*2001*	4
Dasgupta, Deep	I	7.6.1977		8	2001	5
Dassanayake, Pubudu Bathiya.	SL	11.7.1970		11	1993–*1994*	16
Davidson, Alan Keith	A	14.6.1929		44	1953–*1962*	
Davies, Eric Quail.	SA	26.8.1909	11.11.1976	5	1935–*1938*	
[2]**Davis,** Bryan Allan.	WI	2.5.1940		4	1964	
[2]**Davis,** Charles Allan.	WI	1.1.1944		15	1968–*1972*	
Davis, Heath-Ihi-O-Te-Rangi	NZ	30.11.1971		5	1994–*1997*	11
Davis, Ian Charles.	A	25.6.1953		15	1973–*1977*	3
Davis, Simon Peter	A	8.11.1959		1	1985	39
Davis, Winston Walter	WI	18.9.1958		15	1982–*1987*	35
Dawson, Alan Charles	SA	27.11.1969		2	2003	19
Dawson, Edward William	E	13.2.1904	4.6.1979	5	1927–*1929*	
Dawson, Oswald Charles	SA	1.9.1919		9	1947–*1948*	
Dawson, Richard Kevin James.	E	4.8.1980		7	2001–*2002*	
de Alwis, Ronald <u>Guy</u>	SL	15.2.1959		11	1982–*1987*	31
Dean, Harry.	E	13.8.1884	12.3.1957	3	1912	
Deane, Hubert Gouvaine	SA	21.7.1895	21.10.1939	17	1924–*1930*	
de Bruyn, Zander.	SA	5.7.1975		3	2004	
De Caires, Francis Ignatius.	WI	12.5.1909	2.2.1959	3	1929	
De Courcy, James Harry	A	18.4.1927	20.6.2000	3	1953	
DeFreitas, Phillip Anthony Jason.	E	18.2.1966		44	1986–1995	103
de Groen, Richard Paul	NZ	5.8.1962		5	1993–*1994*	12

[1] *Father and son(s).*   [2] *Brothers.*

	Country	Born	Died	Tests	Test Career	ODIs
Dekker, Mark Hamilton	Z	5.12.1969		14	*1993–1996*	23
Dell, Anthony Ross	A	6.8.1947		2	*1970–1973*	
de Mel, Ashantha Lakdasa Francis	SL	9.5.1959		17	*1981–1986*	57
Dempster, Charles Stewart	NZ	15.11.1903	14.2.1974	10	*1929–1932*	
Dempster, Eric William	NZ	25.1.1925		5	*1952–1953*	
Denness, Michael Henry	E	1.12.1940		28	*1969–1975*	12
Denton, David	E	4.7.1874	16.2.1950	11	*1905–1909*	
Depeiza, Cyril Clairmonte	WI	10.10.1927	10.11.1995	5	*1954–1955*	
Desai, Ramakant Bhikaji	I	20.6.1939	27.4.1998	28	*1958–1967*	
de Saram, Samantha Indika	SL	2.9.1973		4	*1999*	15
de Silva, Ashley Matthew	SL	3.12.1963		3	*1992–1993*	4
de Silva, Dandeniyage Somachandra	SL	11.6.1942		12	*1981–1984*	41
de Silva, Ellawalakankanamge Asoka Ranjit	SL	28.3.1956		10	*1985–1990*	28
de Silva, Ginigalgodage Ramba Ajit	SL	12.12.1952		4	*1981–1982*	6
de Silva, Karunakalage Sajeewa Chanaka	SL	11.1.1971		8	*1996–1998*	38
de Silva, Pinnaduwage Aravinda	SL	17.10.1965		93	*1984–2002*	308
de Silva, Sanjeewa Kumara Lanka	SL	29.7.1975		3	*1997*	11
de Silva, Weddikkara Ruwan Sujeewa	SL	7.10.1979		2	*2002*	
de Villiers, Abraham Benjamin	SA	17.2.1984		5	*2004*	
de Villiers, Petrus Stephanus ("Fanie")	SA	13.10.1964		18	*1993–1997*	83
Dewdney, David Thomas	WI	23.10.1933		9	*1954–1957*	
Dewes, John Gordon	E	11.10.1926		5	*1948–1950*	
Dexter, Edward Ralph	E	15.5.1935		62	*1958–1968*	
Dhanraj, Rajindra	WI	6.2.1969		4	*1994–1995*	6
Dharmasena, Handunnettige Deepthi Priyantha Kumar	SL	24.4.1971		31	*1993–2003*	141
Dias, Roy Luke	SL	18.10.1952		20	*1981–1986*	58
Dick, Arthur Edward	NZ	10.10.1936		17	*1961–1965*	
Dickinson, George Ritchie	NZ	11.3.1903	17.3.1978	3	*1929–1931*	
Dighe, Sameer Sudhakar	I	8.10.1968		6	*2000–2001*	23
Dilawar Hussain	I	19.3.1907	26.8.1967	3	*1933–1936*	
Dilley, Graham Roy	E	18.5.1959		41	*1979–1989*	36
Dillon, Mervyn	WI	5.6.1974		38	*1996–2003*	104
Dilshan, Tillekeratne Mudiyanselage	SL	14.10.1976		21	*1999–2004*	52
Dippenaar, Hendrik Human ("Boeta")	SA	14.6.1977		31	*1999–2004*	77
Dipper, Alfred Ernest	E	9.11.1885	7.11.1945	1	*1921*	
Divecha, Ramesh Vithaldas	I	18.10.1927	19.2.2003	5	*1951–1952*	
Dixon, Cecil Donovan	SA	12.2.1891	9.9.1969	1	*1913*	
Dodemaide, Anthony Ian Christopher	A	5.10.1963		10	*1987–1992*	24
Doggart, George Hubert Graham OBE	E	18.7.1925		2	*1950*	
D'Oliveira, Basil Lewis OBE	E	4.10.1931		44	*1966–1972*	4
Dollery, Horace Edgar	E	15.10.1914	20.1.1987	4	*1947–1950*	
Dolphin, Arthur	E	24.12.1885	23.10.1942	1	*1920*	
Donald, Allan Anthony	SA	20.10.1966		72	*1991–2001*	164
Donnan, Henry	A	12.11.1864	13.8.1956	5	*1891–1896*	
Donnelly, Martin Paterson	NZ	17.10.1917	22.10.1999	7	*1937–1949*	
Dooland, Bruce	A	1.11.1923	8.9.1980	3	*1946–1947*	
Doshi, Dilip Rasiklal	I	22.12.1947		33	*1979–1983*	15
Douglas, John William Henry Tyler	E	3.9.1882	19.12.1930	23	*1911–1924*	
Doull, Simon Blair	NZ	6.8.1969		32	*1992–1999*	42
Dowe, Uton George	WI	29.3.1949		4	*1970–1972*	
Dower, Robert Reid	SA	4.6.1876	15.9.1964	1	*1898*	
Dowling, Graham Thorne OBE	NZ	4.3.1937		39	*1961–1971*	
Downton, Paul Rupert	E	4.4.1957		30	*1980–1988*	28
Drakes, Vasbert Conniel	WI	5.8.1969		12	*2002–2003*	34
Draper, Ronald George	SA	24.12.1926		2	*1949*	
Dravid, Rahul	I	11.1.1973		86	*1996–2004*	245
Druce, Norman Frank	E	1.1.1875	27.10.1954	5	*1897*	

---

[1] *Father and son(s).* [2] *Brothers.*

	Country	Born	Died	Tests	Test Career	ODIs
Drum, Christopher James	NZ	10.7.1974		5	*2000–2001*	5
D'Souza, Antao	P	17.1.1939		6	*1958–1962*	
Ducat, Andrew	E	16.2.1886	23.7.1942	1	*1921*	
Duckworth, Christopher Anthony Russell	SA	22.3.1933		2	*1956*	
Duckworth, George	E	9.5.1901	5.1.1966	24	*1924–1936*	
Duff, Reginald Alexander	A	17.8.1878	13.12.1911	22	*1901–1905*	
Dujon, Peter Jeffrey Leroy	WI	28.5.1956		81	*1981–1991*	169
Duleepsinhji, Kumar Shri	E	13.6.1905	5.12.1959	12	*1929–1931*	
Dumbrill, Richard	SA	19.11.1938		5	*1965–1966*	
Duminy, Jacobus Petrus	SA	16.12.1897	31.1.1980	3	*1927–1929*	
Duncan, John Ross Frederick	A	25.3.1944		1	*1970*	
Dunell, Owen Robert	SA	15.7.1856	21.10.1929	2	*1888*	
Dunning, John Angus	NZ	6.2.1903	24.6.1971	4	*1932–1937*	
Dunusinghe, Chamara Iroshan	SL	19.10.1970		5	*1994–1995*	1
Du Preez, John Harcourt	SA	14.11.1942		2	*1966*	
Durani, Salim Aziz	I	11.12.1934		29	*1959–1972*	
Durston, Frederick John	E	11.7.1893	8.4.1965	1	*1921*	
Du Toit, Jacobus Francois	SA	2.4.1869	10.7.1909	1	*1891*	
Dyer, Dennis Victor	SA	2.5.1914	16.6.1990	3	*1947*	
Dyer, Gregory Charles	A	16.3.1959		6	*1986–1987*	23
Dymock, Geoffrey	A	21.7.1945		21	*1973–1979*	15
Dyson, John	A	11.6.1954		30	*1977–1984*	29
Eady, Charles John	A	29.10.1870	20.12.1945	2	*1896–1901*	
Ealham, Mark Alan	E	27.8.1969		8	*1996–1998*	64
Eastwood, Kenneth Humphrey	A	23.11.1935		1	*1970*	
Ebeling, Hans Irvine	A	1.1.1905	12.1.1980	1	*1934*	
Ebrahim, Dion Digby	Z	7.8.1980		23	*2000–2004*	78
Edgar, Bruce Adrian	NZ	23.11.1956		39	*1978–1986*	64
Edmonds, Philippe-Henri	E	8.3.1951		51	*1975–1987*	29
Edrich, John Hugh MBE	E	21.6.1937		77	*1963–1976*	7
Edrich, William John	E	26.3.1916	24.4.1986	39	*1938–1954*	
[2]**Edwards**, Fidel Henderson	WI	6.2.1982		15	*2003–2004*	4
Edwards, Graham Neil	NZ	27.5.1955		8	*1976–1980*	6
Edwards, John Dunlop	A	12.6.1860	31.7.1911	3	*1888*	
Edwards, Richard Martin	WI	3.6.1940		5	*1968*	
Edwards, Ross	A	1.12.1942		20	*1972–1975*	9
Edwards, Walter John	A	23.12.1949		3	*1974*	1
Ehsanul Haque	B	1.12.1979		1	*2002*	6
Ehtesham-ud-Din	P	4.9.1950		5	*1979–1982*	
Eksteen, Clive Edward	SA	2.12.1966		7	*1993–1999*	6
Elgie, Michael Kelsey	SA	6.3.1933		3	*1961*	
Elliott, Harry	E	2.11.1891	2.2.1976	4	*1927–1933*	
Elliott, Matthew Thomas Gray	A	28.9.1971		21	*1996–2004*	1
Ellison, Richard Mark	E	21.9.1959		11	*1984–1986*	14
Elworthy, Steven	SA	23.2.1965		4	*1998–2002*	39
Emburey, John Ernest	E	20.8.1952		64	*1978–1995*	61
Emery, Philip Allen	A	25.6.1964		1	*1994*	1
Emery, Raymond William George	NZ	28.3.1915	18.12.1982	2	*1951*	
Emery, Sidney Hand	A	16.10.1885	7.1.1967	4	*1912*	
Emmett, George Malcolm	E	2.12.1912	18.12.1976	1	*1948*	
Emmett, Thomas	E	3.9.1841	30.6.1904	7	*1876–1881*	
Enamul Haque, sen.	B	27.2.1966		10	*2000–2002*	29
Enamul Haque, jun.	B	5.12.1986		5	*2003–2004*	
Endean, William Russell	SA	31.5.1924	28.6.2003	28	*1951–1957*	
Engineer, Farokh Maneksha	I	25.2.1938		46	*1961–1974*	5
Ervine, Sean Michael	Z	6.12.1982		5	*2003–2003*	42
Evans, Alfred John	E	1.5.1889	18.9.1960	1	*1921*	

[1] *Father and son(s).*   [2] *Brothers.*

	Country	Born	Died	Tests	Test Career	ODIs
Evans, Craig Neil	Z	29.11.1969		3	1996–2003	53
Evans, Edwin	A	26.3.1849	2.7.1921	6	1881–1886	
Evans, Thomas Godfrey CBE	E	18.8.1920	3.5.1999	91	1946–1959	
Ewing, Gavin Mackie	Z	21.1.1981		2	2003	1
Fagg, Arthur Edward	E	18.6.1915	13.9.1977	5	1936–1939	
Fahim Muntasir	B	1.11.1980		3	2001–2002	3
Fairbrother, Neil Harvey	E	9.9.1963		10	1987–1992	75
Fairfax, Alan George	A	16.6.1906	17.5.1955	10	1928–1930	
Faisal Hossain	B	26.10.1978		1	2003	4
Faisal Iqbal	P	30.12.1981		10	2000–2002	17
Fane, Frederick Luther	E	27.4.1875	27.11.1960	14	1905–1909	
Farhan Adil	P	25.9.1977		1	2003	
Farnes, Kenneth	E	8.7.1911	20.10.1941	15	1934–1938	
Farooq Hamid	P	3.3.1945		1	1964	
Farrer, William Stephen	SA	8.12.1936		6	1961–1963	
Farrimond, William	E	23.5.1903	14.11.1979	4	1930–1935	
Farrukh Zaman	P	2.4.1956		1	1976	
Faulkner, George Aubrey	SA	17.12.1881	10.9.1930	25	1905–1924	
Favell, Leslie Ernest MBE	A	6.10.1929	14.6.1987	19	1954–1960	
Fazal Mahmood	P	18.2.1927		34	1952–1962	
Fazl-e-Akbar	P	20.10.1980		5	1997–2003	2
Fellows-Smith, Jonathan Payn	SA	3.2.1932		4	1960	
Fender, Percy George Herbert	E	22.8.1892	15.6.1985	13	1920–1929	
Ferguson, Wilfred	WI	14.12.1917	23.2.1961	8	1947–1953	
Fernandes, Maurius Pacheco	WI	12.8.1897	8.5.1981	2	1928–1929	
Fernando, Congenige Randhi Dilhara	SL	19.7.1979		16	2000–2004	62
Fernando, Ellekutige Rufus Nemesion Susil	SL	19.12.1955		5	1982–1983	7
Fernando, Kandana Arachchige Dinusha Manoj	SL	10.8.1979		2	2003	1
Fernando, Kandage Hasantha Ruwan Kumara	SL	14.10.1979		2	2002	5
Fernando, Thudellage Charitha Buddhika	SL	22.8.1980		9	2001–2002	17
Ferris, John James	A, E	21.5.1867	21.11.1900	9	1886–1891	
Fichardt, Charles Gustav	SA	20.3.1870	30.5.1923	2	1891–1895	
Fielder, Arthur	E	19.7.1877	30.8.1949	6	1903–1907	
Findlay, Thaddeus Michael MBE	WI	19.10.1943		10	1969–1972	
Fingleton, John Henry Webb OBE	A	28.4.1908	22.11.1981	18	1931–1938	
Finlason, Charles Edward	SA	19.2.1860	31.7.1917	1	1888	
Fisher, Frederick Eric	NZ	28.7.1924	19.6.1996	1	1952	
Fishlock, Laurence Barnard	E	2.1.1907	26.6.1986	4	1936–1946	
Flavell, John Alfred	E	15.5.1929	25.2.2004	4	1961–1964	
Fleetwood-Smith, Leslie O'Brien	A	30.3.1908	16.3.1971	10	1935–1938	
Fleming, Damien William	A	24.4.1970		20	1994–2000	88
Fleming, Stephen Paul	NZ	1.4.1973		89	1993–2004	229
Fletcher, Keith William Robert OBE	E	20.5.1944		59	1968–1981	24
Flintoff, Andrew	E	6.12.1977		45	1998–2004	80
Floquet, Claude Eugene	SA	3.11.1884	22.11.1963	1	1909	
[2]**Flower**, Andrew	Z	28.4.1968		63	1992–2002	213
[2]**Flower**, Grant William	Z	20.12.1970		67	1992–2003	219
Flowers, Wilfred	E	7.12.1856	1.11.1926	8	1884–1893	
Foley, Henry	NZ	28.1.1906	16.10.1948	1	1929	
Ford, Francis Gilbertson Justice	E	14.12.1866	7.2.1940	5	1894	
Foster, Frank Rowbotham	E	31.1.1889	3.5.1958	11	1911–1912	
Foster, James Savin	E	15.4.1980		7	2001–2002	11
Foster, Maurice Linton Churchill	WI	9.5.1943		14	1969–1977	2
Foster, Neil Alan	E	6.5.1962		29	1983–1993	48

[1] *Father and son(s).* [2] *Brothers.*

	Country	Born	Died	Tests	Test Career	ODIs
Foster, Reginald Erskine.	E	16.4.1878	13.5.1914	8	*1903–1907*	
Fothergill, Arnold James	E	26.8.1854	1.8.1932	2	*1888*	
Fowler, Graeme	E	20.4.1957		21	*1982–1984*	26
Francis, Bruce Colin.	A	18.2.1948		3	*1972*	
Francis, George Nathaniel	WI	11.12.1897	7.1.1942	10	*1928–1933*	
Francis, Howard Henry	SA	26.5.1868	7.1.1936	2	*1898*	
Francois, Cyril Matthew	SA	20.6.1897	26.5.1944	5	*1922*	
Frank, Charles Newton	SA	27.1.1891	25.12.1961	3	*1921*	
Frank, William Hughes Bowker	SA	23.11.1872	16.2.1945	1	*1895*	
Franklin, James Edward Charles	NZ	7.11.1980		6	*2000–2004*	30
Franklin, Trevor John	NZ	18.3.1962		21	*1983–1990*	3
Fraser, Angus Robert Charles	E	8.8.1965		46	*1989–1998*	42
Frederick, Michael Campbell	WI	6.5.1927		1	*1953*	
Fredericks, Roy Clifton	WI	11.11.1942	5.9.2000	59	*1968–1976*	12
Freeman, Alfred Percy.	E	17.5.1888	28.1.1965	12	*1924–1929*	
Freeman, Douglas Linford	NZ	8.9.1914	31.5.1994	2	*1932*	
Freeman, Eric Walter	A	13.7.1944		11	*1967–1969*	
Freer, Frederick Alfred William	A	4.12.1915	2.11.1998	1	*1946*	
French, Bruce Nicholas	E	13.8.1959		16	*1986–1987*	13
Friend, Travis John.	Z	7.1.1981		13	*2001–2003*	51
Fry, Charles Burgess	E	25.4.1872	7.9.1956	26	*1895–1912*	
Fuller, Edward Russell Henry	SA	2.8.1931		7	*1952–1957*	
Fuller, Richard Livingston	SA	30.1.1913	3.5.1987	1	*1934*	
Fullerton, George Murray	SA	8.12.1922	19.11.2002	7	*1947–1951*	
Funston, Kenneth James	SA	3.12.1925		18	*1952–1957*	
Furlonge, Hammond Allan	WI	19.6.1934		3	*1954–1955*	
Gadkari, Chandrasekhar Vaman.	I	3.2.1928	11.1.1998	6	*1952–1954*	
[1]**Gaekwad**, Anshuman Dattajirao	I	23.9.1952		40	*1974–1984*	15
[1]**Gaekwad**, Dattajirao Krishnarao	I	27.10.1928		11	*1952–1960*	
Gaekwad, Hiralal Ghasulal.	I	29.8.1923	2.1.2003	1	*1952*	
Gallage, Indika Sanjeewa	SL	22.11.1975		1	*1999*	3
Gallian, Jason Edward Riche	E	25.6.1971		3	*1995–1995*	
Gallichan, Norman	NZ	3.6.1906	25.3.1969	1	*1937*	
Gambhir, Gautam.	I	14.10.1981		5	*2004*	5
Gamsy, Dennis.	SA	17.2.1940		2	*1969*	
Gandhi, Devang Jayant	I	6.9.1971		4	*1999*	3
Gandotra, Ashok	I	24.11.1948		2	*1969*	
Ganesh, Doddanarasiah	I	30.6.1973		4	*1996*	1
Ganga, Daren	WI	14.1.1979		30	*1998–2003*	28
Ganguly, Sourav Chandidas	I	8.7.1972		79	*1996–2004*	266
Gannon, John Bryant	A	8.2.1947		3	*1977*	
Ganteaume, Andrew Gordon	WI	22.1.1921		1	*1947*	
Garner, Joel MBE	WI	16.12.1952		58	*1976–1986*	98
Garrett, Thomas William.	A	26.7.1858	6.8.1943	19	*1876–1887*	
Garrick, Leon Vivian	WI	11.11.1976		1	*2000*	3
Gaskin, Berkeley Bertram McGarrell . .	WI	21.3.1908	1.5.1979	2	*1947*	
Gatting, Michael William OBE.	E	6.6.1957		79	*1977–1994*	92
Gaunt, Ronald Arthur	A	26.2.1934		3	*1957–1963*	
Gavaskar, Sunil Manohar.	I	10.7.1949		125	*1970–1986*	108
Gay, Leslie Hewitt	E	24.3.1871	1.11.1949	1	*1894*	
Gayle, Christopher Henry.	WI	21.9.1979		47	*1999–2004*	106
Geary, George	E	9.7.1893	6.3.1981	14	*1924–1934*	
Gedye, Sidney Graham	NZ	2.5.1929		4	*1963–1964*	
Gehrs, Donald Raeburn Algernon	A	29.11.1880	25.6.1953	6	*1903–1910*	
Germon, Lee Kenneth.	NZ	4.11.1968		12	*1995–1996*	37
Ghavri, Karsan Devjibhai.	I	28.2.1951		39	*1974–1980*	19
Ghazali, Mohammad Ebrahim Zainuddin	P	15.6.1924	26.4.2003	2	*1954*	
Ghorpade, Jayasinghrao Mansinghrao. .	I	2.10.1930	29.3.1978	8	*1952–1959*	

[1] *Father and son(s).* [2] *Brothers.*

	Country	Born	Died	Tests	Test Career	ODIs
Ghulam Abbas	P	1.5.1947		1	1967	
Ghulam Ahmed	I	4.7.1922	28.10.1998	22	1948–1958	
Gibb, Paul Antony	E	11.7.1913	7.12.1977	8	1938–1946	
Gibbs, Glendon Lionel	WI	27.12.1925	21.2.1979	1	1954	
Gibbs, Herschelle Herman	SA	23.2.1974		64	1996–2004	156
Gibbs, Lancelot Richard	WI	29.9.1934		79	1957–1975	3
Gibson, Ottis Delroy	WI	16.3.1969		2	1995–1998	15
Giddins, Edward Simon Hunter	E	20.7.1971		4	1999–2000	
[2]Giffen, George	A	27.3.1859	29.11.1927	31	1881–1896	
[2]Giffen, Walter Frank	A	20.9.1861	28.6.1924	3	1886–1891	
Gifford, Norman MBE	E	30.3.1940		15	1964–1973	2
Gilbert, David Robert	A	29.12.1960		9	1985–1986	14
Gilchrist, Adam Craig	A	14.11.1971		65	1999–2004	198
Gilchrist, Roy	WI	28.6.1934	18.7.2001	13	1957–1958	
Giles, Ashley Fraser	E	19.3.1973		45	1998–2004	47
Gillespie, Jason Neil	A	19.4.1975		63	1996–2004	78
Gillespie, Stuart Ross	NZ	2.3.1957		1	1985	19
[2]Gilligan, Alfred Herbert Harold	E	29.6.1896	5.5.1978	4	1929	
[2]Gilligan, Arthur Edward Robert	E	23.12.1894	5.9.1976	11	1922–1924	
Gilmour, Gary John	A	26.6.1951		15	1973–1976	5
Gimblett, Harold	E	19.10.1914	30.3.1978	3	1936–1939	
Gladstone Morais, George	WI	14.1.1901	19.5.1978	1	1929	
Gladwin, Clifford	E	3.4.1916	10.4.1988	8	1947–1949	
Gleeson, John William	A	14.3.1938		29	1967–1972	
Gleeson, Robert Anthony	SA	6.12.1873	27.9.1919	1	1895	
Glover, George Keyworth	SA	13.5.1870	15.11.1938	1	1895	
Goddard, John Douglas Claude OBE	WI	21.4.1919	26.8.1987	27	1947–1957	
Goddard, Thomas William	E	1.10.1900	22.5.1966	8	1930–1939	
Goddard, Trevor Leslie	SA	1.8.1931		41	1955–1969	
Gomes, Hilary Angelo	WI	13.7.1953		60	1976–1986	83
Gomez, Gerald Ethridge	WI	10.10.1919	6.8.1996	29	1939–1953	
Gooch, Graham Alan OBE	E	23.7.1953		118	1975–1994	125
Goodwin, Murray William	Z	11.12.1972		19	1997–2000	71
Goonatillake, Hettiarachige Mahes	SL	16.8.1952		5	1981–1982	6
Gopalan, Morappakam Joysam	I	6.6.1909	21.12.2003	1	1933	
Gopinath, Coimbatarao Doraikannu	I	1.3.1930		8	1951–1959	
Gordon, Norman	SA	6.8.1911		5	1938	
Gough, Darren	E	18.9.1970		58	1994–2003	141
Gover, Alfred Richard MBE	E	29.2.1908	7.10.2001	4	1936–1946	
Gower, David Ivon OBE	E	1.4.1957		117	1978–1992	114
[2]Grace, Edward Mills	E	28.11.1841	20.5.1911	1	1880	
[2]Grace, George Frederick	E	13.12.1850	22.9.1880	1	1880	
[2]Grace, William Gilbert (W.G.)	E	18.7.1848	23.10.1915	22	1880–1899	
Graham, Henry	A	22.11.1870	7.2.1911	6	1893–1896	
Graham, Robert	SA	16.9.1877	21.4.1946	2	1898	
[2]Grant, George Copeland	WI	9.5.1907	26.10.1978	12	1930–1934	
[2]Grant, Rolph Stewart	WI	15.12.1909	18.10.1977	7	1934–1939	
Graveney, Thomas William OBE	E	16.6.1927		79	1951–1969	
Gray, Anthony Hollis	WI	23.5.1963		5	1986	25
Gray, Evan John	NZ	18.11.1954		10	1983–1988	10
Greatbatch, Mark John	NZ	11.12.1963		41	1987–1996	84
Greenough, Thomas	E	9.11.1931		4	1959–1960	
Greenidge, Alvin Ethelbert	WI	20.8.1956		6	1977–1978	1
Greenidge, Cuthbert Gordon MBE	WI	1.5.1951		108	1974–1990	128
Greenidge, Geoffrey Alan	WI	26.5.1948		5	1971–1972	
Greenwood, Andrew	E	20.8.1847	12.2.1889	2	1876	
[2]Gregory, David William	A	15.4.1845	4.8.1919	3	1876–1878	
[1, 2]Gregory, Edward James	A	29.5.1839	22.4.1899	1	1876	
Gregory, Jack Morrison	A	14.8.1895	7.8.1973	24	1920–1928	

[1] *Father and son(s).* [2] *Brothers.*

	Country	Born	Died	Tests	Test Career	ODIs
Gregory, Ross Gerald	A	28.2.1916	10.6.1942	2	*1936*	
[1]**Gregory,** Sydney Edward	A	14.4.1870	1.8.1929	58	*1890–1912*	
[2]**Greig,** Anthony William	E	6.10.1946		58	*1972–1977*	22
[2]**Greig,** Ian Alexander	E	8.12.1955		2	*1982*	
Grell, Mervyn George	WI	18.12.1899	11.1.1976	1	*1929*	
Grieve, Basil Arthur Firebrace	E	28.5.1864	19.11.1917	2	*1888*	
Grieveson, Ronald Eustace	SA	24.8.1909	24.7.1998	2	*1938*	
Griffin, Geoffrey Merton	SA	12.6.1939		2	*1960*	
Griffith, Adrian Frank Gordon	WI	19.11.1971		14	*1996–2000*	9
Griffith, Charles Christopher.	WI	14.12.1938		28	*1959–1968*	
Griffith, Herman Clarence	WI	1.12.1893	18.3.1980	13	*1928–1933*	
Griffith, Stewart Cathie CBE	E	16.6.1914	7.4.1993	3	*1947–1948*	
Grimmett, Clarence Victor	A	25.12.1891	2.5.1980	37	*1924–1935*	
Gripper, Trevor Raymond	Z	28.12.1975		20	*1999–2003*	8
Groube, Thomas Underwood	A	2.9.1857	5.8.1927	1	*1880*	
Grout, Arthur Theodore <u>Wallace</u> . . .	A	30.3.1927	9.11.1968	51	*1957–1965*	
Guard, Ghulam Mustafa	I	12.12.1925	13.3.1978	2	*1958–1959*	
Guest, Colin Ernest John	A	7.10.1937		1	*1962*	
Guha, Subrata	I	31.1.1946	5.11.2003	4	*1967–1969*	
Guillen, Simpson Clairmonte	WI, NZ	24.9.1924		8	*1951–1955*	
Gul Mahomed	I, P	15.10.1921	8.5.1992	9	*1946–1956*	
Gunasekera, Yohan	SL	8.11.1957		2	*1982*	3
Gunawardene, Dihan <u>Avishka</u>.	SL	26.5.1977		4	*1998–2003*	59
Guneratne, Ruslan Punyajith Wijesinghe	SL	26.1.1962		1	*1982*	
[2]**Gunn,** George.	E	13.6.1879	29.6.1958	15	*1907–1929*	
[2]**Gunn,** John Richmond	E	19.7.1876	21.8.1963	6	*1901–1905*	
Gunn, William	E	4.12.1858	29.1.1921	11	*1886–1899*	
[2]**Gupte,** Balkrishna Pandharinath	I	30.8.1934		3	*1960–1964*	
[2]**Gupte,** Subhashchandra Pandharinath. .	I	11.12.1929	31.5.2002	36	*1951–1961*	
Gursharan Singh	I	8.3.1963		1	*1989*	1
Gurusinha, Asanka Pradeep	SL	16.9.1966		41	*1985–1996*	147
Guy, John William	NZ	29.8.1934		12	*1955–1961*	
Habib, Aftab	E	7.2.1972		2	*1999*	
Habibul Bashar	B	17.8.1972		34	*2000–2004*	58
[1, 2]**Hadlee,** Dayle Robert	NZ	6.1.1948		26	*1969–1977*	11
[1, 2]**Hadlee,** *Sir* Richard John	NZ	3.7.1951		86	*1972–1990*	115
[1]**Hadlee,** Walter Arnold CBE	NZ	4.6.1915		11	*1937–1950*	
Hafeez, Abdul (see Kardar)						
Haig, Nigel Esmé.	E	12.12.1887	27.10.1966	5	*1921–1929*	
Haigh, Schofield.	E	19.3.1871	27.2.1921	11	*1898–1912*	
Hall, Alfred Ewart	SA	23.1.1896	1.1.1964	7	*1922–1930*	
Hall, Andrew James	SA	31.7.1975		14	*2001–2004*	43
Hall, Glen Gordon	SA	24.5.1938	26.6.1987	1	*1964*	
Hall, Wesley Winfield	WI	12.9.1937		48	*1958–1968*	
Halliwell, Ernest Austin	SA	7.9.1864	2.10.1919	8	*1891–1902*	
Hallows, Charles.	E	4.4.1895	10.11.1972	2	*1921–1928*	
Halse, Clive Gray	SA	28.2.1935	28.5.2002	3	*1963*	
Hamence, Ronald Arthur	A	25.11.1915		3	*1946–1947*	
Hamilton, Gavin Mark	E	16.9.1974		1	*1999*	5
Hammond, Jeffrey Roy	A	19.4.1950		5	*1972*	1
Hammond, Walter Reginald	E	19.6.1903	1.7.1965	85	*1927–1946*	
Hampshire, John Harry	E	10.2.1941		8	*1969–1975*	3
[2]**Hands,** Philip Albert Myburgh	SA	18.3.1890	27.4.1951	7	*1913–1924*	
[2]**Hands,** Reginald Harry Myburgh	SA	26.7.1888	20.4.1918	1	*1913*	
[1, 2]**Hanif Mohammad**	P	21.12.1934		55	*1952–1969*	
Hanley, Martin Andrew	SA	10.11.1918	2.6.2000	1	*1948*	
Hannan Sarkar	B	1.12.1982		17	*2002–2004*	20

---

[1] *Father and son(s).* [2] *Brothers.*

	Country	Born	Died	Tests	Test Career	ODIs
Hanumant Singh	I	29.3.1939		14	1963–1969	
Harbhajan Singh	I	3.7.1980		43	1997–2004	93
Hardikar, Manohar Shankar	I	8.2.1936	4.2.1995	2	1958	
Hardinge, Harold Thomas William	E	25.2.1886	8.5.1965	1	1921	
[1]Hardstaff, Joseph	E	9.11.1882	2.4.1947	5	1907	
[1]Hardstaff, Joseph, jun.	E	3.7.1911	1.1.1990	23	1935–1948	
Harford, Noel Sherwin	NZ	30.8.1930	30.3.1981	8	1955–1958	
Harford, Roy Ivan	NZ	30.5.1936		3	1967	
Harmison, Stephen James	E	23.10.1978		28	2002–2004	23
Haroon Rashid	P	25.3.1953		23	1976–1982	12
Harper, Roger Andrew	WI	17.3.1963		25	1983–1993	105
Harris, Chris Zinzan	NZ	20.11.1969		23	1992–2002	250
Harris, *Lord* [George Robert Canning]	E	3.2.1851	24.3.1932	4	1878–1884	
[1]Harris, Parke Gerald Zinzan	NZ	18.7.1927	1.12.1991	9	1955–1964	
Harris, Roger Meredith	NZ	27.7.1933		2	1958	
Harris, Terence Anthony	SA	27.8.1916	7.3.1993	3	1947–1948	
Harry, John	A	1.8.1857	27.10.1919	1	1894	
[2]Hart, Matthew Norman	NZ	16.5.1972		14	1993–1995	13
[2]Hart, Robert Garry	NZ	2.12.1974		11	2002–2003	2
Hartigan, Gerald Patrick Desmond	SA	30.12.1884	7.1.1955	5	1912–1913	
Hartigan, Roger Joseph	A	12.12.1879	7.6.1958	2	1907	
Hartkopf, Albert Ernst Victor	A	28.12.1889	20.5.1968	1	1924	
Hartland, Blair Robert	NZ	22.10.1966		9	1991–1994	16
Hartley, John Cabourn	E	15.11.1874	8.3.1963	2	1905	
[2]Harvey, Mervyn Roye	A	29.4.1918	18.3.1995	1	1946	
Harvey, Robert Lyon	SA	14.9.1911	20.7.2000	2	1935	
[2]Harvey, Robert Neil MBE	A	8.10.1928		79	1947–1962	
Harvinder Singh	I	23.12.1977		3	1997–2001	16
Hasan Raza	P	11.3.1982		5	1996–2002	16
Haseeb Ahsan	P	15.7.1939		12	1957–1961	
Hasibul Hussain	B	3.6.1977		5	2000–2001	32
Haslam, Mark James	NZ	26.9.1972		4	1992–1995	1
Hassett, Arthur Lindsay MBE	A	28.8.1913	16.6.1993	43	1938–1953	
Hastings, Brian Frederick	NZ	23.3.1940		31	1968–1975	11
Hathorn, Christopher Maitland Howard	SA	7.4.1878	17.5.1920	12	1902–1910	
Hathurusinghe, Upul Chandika	SL	13.9.1968		26	1990–1998	35
Hauritz, Nathan Michael	A	18.10.1981		1	2004	8
Hawke, *Lord* [Martin Bladen]	E	16.8.1860	10.10.1938	5	1895–1898	
Hawke, Neil James Napier	A	27.6.1939	25.12.2000	27	1962–1968	
Hayden, Matthew Lawrence	A	29.10.1971		64	1993–2004	103
Hayes, Ernest George	E	6.11.1876	2.12.1953	5	1905–1912	
Hayes, Frank Charles	E	6.12.1946		9	1973–1976	6
Hayes, John Arthur	NZ	11.1.1927		15	1950–1958	
Haynes, Desmond Leo	WI	15.2.1956		116	1977–1993	238
Hayward, Mornantau	SA	6.3.1977		16	1999–2004	21
Hayward, Thomas Walter	E	29.3.1871	19.7.1939	35	1895–1909	
Hazare, Vijay Samuel	I	11.3.1915	18.12.2004	30	1946–1952	
Hazlitt, Gervys Rignold	A	4.9.1888	30.10.1915	9	1907–1912	
[3]Headley, Dean Warren	E	27.1.1970		15	1997–1999	13
[3]Headley, George Alphonso MBE	WI	30.5.1909	30.11.1983	22	1929–1953	
[3]Headley, Ronald George Alphonso	WI	29.6.1939		2	1973	1
Healy, Ian Andrew	A	30.4.1964		119	1988–1999	168
[2]Hearne, Alec	E	22.7.1863	16.5.1952	1	1891	
[1, 2]Hearne, Frank	E, SA	23.11.1858	14.7.1949	6	1888–1895	
[1]Hearne, George Alfred Lawrence	SA	27.3.1888	13.11.1978	3	1922–1924	
[2]Hearne, George Gibbons	E	7.7.1856	13.2.1932	1	1891	
Hearne, John Thomas	E	3.5.1867	17.4.1944	12	1891–1899	
Hearne, John William	E	11.2.1891	14.9.1965	24	1911–1926	
Hegg, Warren Kevin	E	23.2.1968		2	1998	

[1] *Father and son.* [2] *Brothers.* [3] *Grandfather, father and son.*

	Country	Born	Died	Tests	Test Career	ODIs
Heine, Peter Samuel	SA	28.6.1928	4.2.2005	14	1955–1961	
Hemmings, Edward Ernest	E	20.2.1949		16	1982–1990	33
Henderson, Claude William	SA	14.6.1972		7	2001–2002	4
Henderson, Matthew	NZ	2.8.1895		1	1929	
Hendren, Elias Henry ("Patsy")	E	5.2.1889	4.10.1962	51	1920–1934	
Hendrick, Michael	E	22.10.1948		30	1974–1981	22
Hendriks, John Leslie	WI	21.12.1933		20	1961–1969	
Hendry, Hunter Scott Thomas Laurie . .	A	24.5.1895	16.12.1988	11	1921–1928	
Henry, Omar	SA	23.1.1952		3	1992	3
Herath, Herath Mudiyanselage Rangana Keerthi Bandara	SL	19.3.1978		7	1999–2004	6
Heseltine, Christopher	E	26.11.1869	13.6.1944	2	1895	
Hettiarachchi, Dinuka	SL	15.7.1976		1	2000	
Hibbert, Paul Anthony	A	23.7.1952		1	1977	
Hick, Graeme Ashley	E	23.5.1966		65	1991–2000	120
Higgs, James Donald	A	11.7.1950		22	1977–1980	
Higgs, Kenneth	E	14.1.1937		15	1965–1968	
Hilditch, Andrew Mark Jefferson	A	20.5.1956		18	1978–1985	8
Hill, Allen	E	14.11.1843	29.8.1910	2	1876	
Hill, Arthur James Ledger	E	26.7.1871	6.9.1950	3	1895	
Hill, Clement	A	18.3.1877	5.9.1945	49	1896–1911	
Hill, John Charles	A	25.6.1923	11.8.1974	3	1953–1954	
Hilton, Malcolm Jameson	E	2.8.1928	8.7.1990	4	1950–1951	
Ilime, Charles Frederick William	SA	24.10.1869	6.12.1940	1	1895	
Hindlekar, Dattaram Dharmaji	I	1.1.1909	30.3.1949	4	1936–1946	
Hinds, Ryan O'Neal	WI	17.2.1981		7	2001–2003	14
Hinds, Wavell Wayne	WI	7.9.1976		38	1999–2003	87
Hirst, George Herbert	E	7.9.1871	10.5.1954	24	1897–1909	
Hirwani, Narendra Deepchand	I	18.10.1968		17	1987–1996	18
Hitch, John William	E	7.5.1886	7.7.1965	7	1911–1921	
Hoad, Edward Lisle Goldsworthy	WI	29.1.1896	5.3.1986	4	1928–1933	
Hoare, Desmond Edward	A	19.10.1934		1	1960	
Hobbs, Sir John Berry	E	16.12.1882	21.12.1963	61	1907–1930	
Hobbs, Robin Nicholas Stuart	E	8.5.1942		7	1967–1971	
Hodges, John Robart	A	11.8.1855	d unknown	2	1876	
Hogan, Tom George	A	23.9.1956		7	1982–1983	16
Hogg, George Bradley	A	6.2.1971		4	1996–2003	52
Hogg, Rodney Malcolm	A	5.3.1951		38	1978–1984	71
Hoggard, Matthew James	E	31.12.1976		38	2000–2004	20
Hohns, Trevor Victor	A	23.1.1954		7	1988–1989	
Holder, Roland Irwin Christopher	WI	22.12.1967		11	1996–1998	37
Holder, Vanburn Alonza	WI	8.10.1945		40	1969–1978	12
Holding, Michael Anthony	WI	16.2.1954		60	1975–1986	102
Hole, Graeme Blake	A	6.1.1931	14.2.1990	18	1950–1954	
Holford, David Anthony Jerome	WI	16.4.1940		24	1966–1976	
Holland, Robert George	A	19.10.1946		11	1984–1985	2
Hollies, William Eric	E	5.6.1912	16.4.1981	13	1934–1950	
[2]**Hollioake**, Adam John	E	5.9.1971		4	1997–1997	35
[2]**Hollioake**, Benjamin Caine	E	11.11.1977	23.3.2002	2	1997–1998	20
Holmes, Errol Reginald Thorold	E	21.8.1905	16.8.1960	5	1934–1935	
Holmes, Percy	E	25.11.1886	3.9.1971	7	1921–1932	
Holt, John Kenneth Constantine	WI	12.8.1923		17	1953–1958	
Hondo, Douglas Tafadzwa	Z	7.7.1979		9	2001–2004	52
Hone, Leland	E	30.1.1853	31.12.1896	1	1878	
Hookes, David William	A	3.5.1955	19.1.2004	23	1976–1985	39
Hooper, Carl Llewellyn	WI	15.12.1966		102	1987–2002	227
Hopkins, Albert John Young	A	3.5.1874	25.4.1931	20	1901–1909	
Hopwood, John Leonard	E	30.10.1903	15.6.1985	2	1934	
Horan, Thomas Patrick	A	8.3.1854	16.4.1916	15	1876–1884	

[1] *Father and son(s).* [2] *Brothers.*

	Country	Born	Died	Tests	Test Career	ODIs
Hordern, Herbert Vivian	A	10.2.1883	17.6.1938	7	1910–1911	
Hornby, Albert Neilson	E	10.2.1847	17.12.1925	3	1878–1884	
²Horne, Matthew Jeffery	NZ	5.12.1970		35	1996–2002	50
²Horne, Philip Andrew	NZ	21.1.1960		4	1986–1990	4
Hornibrook, Percival Mitchell	A	27.7.1899	25.8.1976	6	1928–1930	
Horton, Martin John	E	21.4.1934		2	1959	
Hough, Kenneth William	NZ	24.10.1928		2	1958	
Houghton, David Laud	Z	23.6.1957		22	1992–1997	63
Howard, Anthony Bourne	WI	27.8.1946		1	1971	
Howard, Nigel David	E	18.5.1925	31.5.1979	4	1951	
²Howarth, Geoffrey Philip OBE	NZ	29.3.1951		47	1974–1984	70
²Howarth, Hedley John	NZ	25.12.1943		30	1969–1976	9
Howell, Henry	E	29.11.1890	9.7.1932	5	1920–1924	
Howell, William Peter	A	29.12.1869	14.7.1940	18	1897–1903	
Howorth, Richard	E	26.4.1909	2.4.1980	5	1947–1947	
Huckle, Adam George	Z	21.9.1971		8	1997–1998	19
Hudson, Andrew Charles	SA	17.3.1965		35	1991–1997	89
Hughes, Kimberley John	A	26.1.1954		70	1977–1984	97
Hughes, Mervyn Gregory	A	23.11.1961		53	1985–1993	33
²Humayun Farhat	P	24.1.1981		1	2000	5
Humphries, Joseph	E	19.5.1876	7.5.1946	3	1907	
Hunt, William Alfred	A	26.8.1908	30.12.1983	1	1931	
Hunte, *Sir* Conrad Cleophas	WI	9.5.1932	3.12.1999	44	1957–1966	
Hunte, Errol Ashton Clairmore	WI	3.10.1905	26.6.1967	3	1929	
Hunter, Joseph	E	3.8.1855	4.1.1891	5	1884	
Hurst, Alan George	A	15.7.1950		12	1973–1979	8
Hurwood, Alexander	A	17.6.1902	26.9.1982	2	1930	
Hussain, Nasser	E	28.3.1968		96	1989–2004	88
Hutchings, Kenneth Lotherington	E	7.12.1882	3.9.1916	7	1907–1909	
Hutchinson, Philip	SA	25.1.1862	30.9.1925	2	1888	
¹Hutton, *Sir* Leonard	E	23.6.1916	6.9.1990	79	1937–1954	
¹Hutton, Richard Anthony	E	6.9.1942		5	1971	
Hylton, Leslie George	WI	29.3.1905	17.5.1955	6	1934–1939	
Ibadulla, Khalid	P	20.12.1935		4	1964–1967	
Ibrahim, Khanmohammad Cassumbhoy	I	26.1.1919		4	1948	
Iddon, John	E	8.1.1902	17.4.1946	5	1934–1935	
Igglesden, Alan Paul	E	8.10.1964		3	1989–1993	4
Ijaz Ahmed, sen.	P	20.9.1968		60	1986–2000	250
Ijaz Ahmed, jun.	P	2.2.1969		2	1995	2
Ijaz Butt	P	10.3.1938		8	1958–1962	
Ijaz Faqih	P	24.3.1956		5	1980–1987	27
Ikin, John Thomas	E	7.3.1918	15.9.1984	18	1946–1955	
Illingworth, Raymond CBE	E	8.6.1932		61	1958–1973	3
Illingworth, Richard Keith	E	23.8.1963		9	1991–1995	25
Ilott, Mark Christopher	E	27.8.1970		5	1993–1995	
²Imran Farhat	P	20.5.1982		15	2000–2004	21
Imran Khan	P	25.11.1952		88	1971–1991	175
Imran Nazir	P	16.12.1981		8	1998–2002	61
Imtiaz Ahmed	P	5.1.1928		41	1952–1962	
Indrajitsinhji, Kumar Shri	I	15.6.1937		4	1964–1969	
Insole, Douglas John CBE	E	18.4.1926		9	1950–1957	
Intikhab Alam	P	28.12.1941		47	1959–1976	4
Inverarity, Robert <u>John</u>	A	31.1.1944		6	1968–1972	
Inzamam-ul-Haq	P	3.3.1970		97	1992–2004	328
Iqbal Qasim	P	6.8.1953		50	1976–1988	15
Irani, Jamshed Khudadad	I	18.8.1923	25.2.1982	2	1947	
Irani, Ronald Charles	E	26.10.1971		3	1996–1999	31
Iredale, Francis Adams	A	19.6.1867	15.4.1926	14	1894–1899	

¹ *Father and son(s).* ² *Brothers.*

	Country	Born	Died	Tests	Test Career	ODIs
Irfan Fazil	P	2.11.1981		1	*1999*	1
Ironmonger, Herbert	A	7.4.1882	1.6.1971	14	*1928–1932*	
Ironside, David Ernest James	SA	2.5.1925		3	*1953*	
Irvine, Brian Lee	SA	9.3.1944		4	*1969*	
Israr Ali	P	1.5.1927		4	*1952–1959*	
Iverson, John Brian	A	27.7.1915	24.10.1973	5	*1950*	
Jack, Steven Douglas	SA	4.8.1970		2	*1994*	2
Jackman, Robin David	E	13.8.1945		4	*1980–1982*	15
Jackson, Archibald Alexander	A	5.9.1909	16.2.1933	8	*1928–1930*	
Jackson, *Sir* Francis Stanley	E	21.11.1870	9.3.1947	20	*1893–1905*	
Jackson, Herbert Leslie	E	5.4.1921		2	*1949–1961*	
Jacobs, Ridley Detamore	WI	26.11.1967		65	*1998–2004*	147
Jadeja, Ajaysinhji	I	1.2.1971		15	*1992–1999*	196
¹Jahangir Khan, Mohammad	I	1.2.1910	23.7.1988	4	*1932–1936*	
Jai, Laxmidas Purshottamdas	I	1.4.1902	29.1.1968	1	*1933*	
Jaisimha, Motganhalli Laxmanarsu	I	3.3.1939	7.7.1999	39	*1959–1970*	
Jalal-ud-Dīn	P	12.6.1959		6	*1982–1985*	8
James, Kenneth Cecil	NZ	12.3.1904	21.8.1976	11	*1929–1932*	
James, Stephen Peter	E	7.9.1967		2	*1998*	
James, Wayne Robert	Z	27.8.1965		4	*1993–1994*	11
Jameson, John Alexander	E	30.6.1941		4	*1971–1973*	3
Jamshedji, Rustomji Jamshedji Dorabji.	I	18.11.1892	5.4.1976	1	*1933*	
Jardine, Douglas Robert	E	23.10.1900	18.6.1958	22	*1928–1933*	
Jarman, Barrington Noel	A	17.2.1936		19	*1959–1968*	
Jarvis, Arthur Harwood	A	19.10.1860	15.11.1933	11	*1884–1894*	
Jarvis, Malcolm Peter	Z	6.12.1955		5	*1992–1994*	12
Jarvis, Paul William	E	29.6.1965		9	*1987–1992*	16
Jarvis, Terrence Wayne	NZ	29.7.1944		13	*1964–1972*	
Javed Akhtar	P	21.11.1940		1	*1962*	
Javed Burki	P	8.5.1938		25	*1960–1969*	
Javed Miandad	P	12.6.1957		124	*1976–1993*	233
Javed Omar	B	25.11.1976		27	*2000–2004*	35
Jayantilal, Kenia	I	13.1.1948		1	*1970*	
Jayasekera, Rohan Stanley Amarasiriwardene	SL	7.12.1957		1	*1981*	2
Jayasuriya, Sanath Teran	SL	30.6.1969		94	*1990–2004*	333
Jayawardene, Denagamage Proboth Mahela de Silva	SL	27.5.1977		65	*1997–2004*	176
Jayawardene, Hewasandatchige Asiri Prasanna Wishvanath	SL	9.10.1979		5	*2000–2003*	3
Jeganathan, Sridharan	SL	11.7.1951	14.5.1996	2	*1982*	5
Jenkins, Roland Oliver	E	24.11.1918	21.7.1995	9	*1948–1952*	
Jenner, Terrence James	A	8.9.1944		9	*1970–1975*	1
Jennings, Claude Burrows	A	5.6.1884	20.6.1950	6	*1912*	
Jessop, Gilbert Laird	E	19.5.1874	11.5.1955	18	*1899–1912*	
John, Vinothen Bede	SL	27.5.1960		6	*1982–1984*	45
Johnson, Clement Lecky	SA	31.3.1871	31.5.1908	1	*1895*	
Johnson, David Jude	I	16.10.1971		2	*1996*	
Johnson, Hophnie Hobah Hines	WI	13.7.1910	24.6.1987	3	*1947–1950*	
Johnson, Ian William OBE	A	8.12.1917	9.10.1998	45	*1945–1956*	
Johnson, Leonard Joseph	A	18.3.1919	20.4.1977	1	*1947*	
Johnson, Neil Clarkson	Z	24.1.1970		13	*1998–2000*	48
Johnson, Richard Leonard	E	29.12.1974		3	*2003–2003*	10
Johnson, Tyrell Fabian	WI	10.1.1917	5.4.1985	1	*1939*	
Johnston, William Arras	A	26.2.1922		40	*1947–1954*	
Jones, Andrew Howard	NZ	9.5.1959		39	*1986–1994*	87
Jones, Arthur Owen	E	16.8.1872	21.12.1914	12	*1899–1909*	
Jones, Charles Ernest Llewellyn	WI	3.11.1902	10.12.1959	4	*1929–1934*	

---

¹ *Father and son(s).* ² *Brothers.*

	Country	Born	Died	Tests	Test Career	ODIs
Jones, Dean Mervyn	A	24.3.1961		52	*1983–1992*	164
Jones, Ernest	A	30.9.1869	23.11.1943	19	*1894–1902*	
Jones, Geraint Owen	E	14.7.1976		13	*2003–2004*	16
[1]Jones, Ivor Jeffrey	E	10.12.1941		15	*1963–1967*	
Jones, Prior Erskine Waverley	WI	6.6.1917	21.11.1991	9	*1947–1951*	
Jones, Richard Andrew	NZ	22.10.1973		1	*2003*	5
Jones, Samuel Percy	A	1.8.1861	14.7.1951	12	*1881–1887*	
[1]Jones, Simon Philip	E	25.12.1978		12	*2002–2004*	2
Joseph, David Rolston Emmanuel	WI	15.11.1969		4	*1998*	
Joseph, Sylvester Cleofoster	WI	5.9.1978		2	*2004*	9
Joshi, Padmanabh Govind	I	27.10.1926	8.1.1987	12	*1951–1960*	
Joshi, Sunil Bandacharya	I	6.6.1969		15	*1996–2000*	69
Joslin, Leslie Ronald	A	13.12.1947		1	*1967*	
Julian, Brendon Paul	A	10.8.1970		7	*1993–1995*	25
Julien, Bernard Denis	WI	13.3.1950		24	*1973–1976*	12
Jumadeen, Raphick Rasif	WI	12.4.1948		12	*1971–1978*	
Jupp, Henry	E	19.11.1841	8.4.1889	2	*1876*	
Jupp, Vallance William Crisp	E	27.3.1891	9.7.1960	8	*1921–1928*	
Jurangpathy, Baba Roshan	SL	25.6.1967		2	*1985–1986*	
Kabir Khan	P	12.4.1974		4	*1994*	10
Kaif, Mohammad	I	1.12.1980		7	*1999–2004*	81
Kallicharran, Alvin Isaac	WI	21.3.1949		66	*1971–1980*	31
Kallis, Jacques Henry	SA	16.10.1975		87	*1995–2004*	203
Kalpage, Ruwan Senani	SL	19.2.1970		11	*1993–1998*	86
[2]Kaluperuma, Lalith Wasantha Silva	SL	25.5.1949		2	*1981*	4
[2]Kaluperuma, Sanath Mohan Silva	SL	22.10.1961		4	*1983–1987*	2
Kaluwitharana, Romesh Shantha	SL	24.11.1969		49	*1992–2004*	189
Kambli, Vinod Ganpat	I	18.1.1972		17	*1992–1995*	104
Kamran Akmal	P	13.1.1982		10	*2002–2004*	13
Kanhai, Rohan Bholalall	WI	26.12.1935		79	*1957–1973*	7
[1]Kanitkar, Hrishikesh Hemant	I	14.11.1974		2	*1999*	34
[1]Kanitkar, Hemant Shamsunder	I	8.12.1942		2	*1974*	
Kapil Dev	I	6.1.1959		131	*1978–1993*	225
Kapoor, Aashish Rakesh	I	25.3.1971		4	*1994–1996*	17
Kardar, Abdul Hafeez	I, P	17.1.1925	21.4.1996	26	*1946–1957*	
Karim, Syed Saba	I	14.11.1967		1	*2000*	34
Karthik, Krishankumar Dinesh	I	1.6.1985		5	*2004*	2
Kartik, Murali	I	11.9.1976		8	*1999–2004*	17
Kasprowicz, Michael Scott	A	10.2.1972		30	*1996–2004*	30
Katich, Simon Mathew	A	21.8.1975		13	*2001–2004*	6
Keeton, William Walter	E	30.4.1905	10.10.1980	2	*1934–1939*	
Keith, Headley James	SA	25.10.1927	17.11.1997	8	*1952–1956*	
Kelleway, Charles	A	25.4.1886	16.11.1944	26	*1910–1928*	
Kelly, James Joseph	A	10.5.1867	14.8.1938	36	*1896–1905*	
Kelly, Thomas Joseph Dart	A	3.5.1844	20.7.1893	2	*1876–1878*	
Kemp, Justin Miles	SA	2.10.1977		3	*2000*	14
Kempis, Gustav Adolph	SA	4.8.1865	19.5.1890	1	*1888*	
Kendall, Thomas Kingston	A	24.8.1851	17.8.1924	2	*1876*	
Kennedy, Alexander Stuart	E	24.1.1891	15.11.1959	5	*1922*	
Kennedy, Robert John	NZ	3.6.1972		4	*1995*	7
Kenny, Ramnath Baburao	I	29.9.1930	21.11.1985	5	*1958–1959*	
Kent, Martin Francis	A	23.11.1953		3	*1981*	5
Kentish, Esmond Seymour Maurice	WI	21.11.1916		2	*1947–1953*	
Kenyon, Donald	E	15.5.1924	12.11.1996	8	*1951–1955*	
Kerr, John Lambert	NZ	28.12.1910		7	*1931–1937*	
Kerr, Robert Byers	A	16.6.1961		2	*1985*	4
Key, Robert William Trevor	E	12.5.1979		15	*2002–2004*	5
Khaled Mahmud	B	26.7.1971		12	*2001–2003*	68

[1] *Father and son(s).* [2] *Brothers.*

	Country	Born	Died	Tests	Test Career	ODIs
Khaled Mashud.	B	8.2.1976		33	*2000–2004*	88
Khalid Hassan.	P	14.7.1937		1	1954	
[1]**Khalid Wazir**	P	27.4.1936		2	1954	
Khan Mohammad	P	1.1.1928		13	*1952–1957*	
Killick, *Rev.* Edgar Thomas	E	9.5.1907	18.5.1953	2	1929	
Kilner, Roy	E	17.10.1890	5.4.1928	9	*1924–1926*	
King, Collis Llewellyn	WI	11.6.1951		9	1976–1980	18
King, Frank McDonald	WI	8.12.1926	23.12.1990	14	*1952–1955*	
King, John Herbert	E	16.4.1871	18.11.1946	1	1909	
King, Lester Anthony	WI	27.2.1939	9.7.1998	2	*1961–1967*	
King, Reon Dane	WI	6.10.1975		14	*1998–2001*	48
Kinneir, Septimus Paul	E	13.5.1871	16.10.1928	1	*1911*	
Kippax, Alan Falconer.	A	25.5.1897	4.9.1972	22	*1924–1934*	
Kirmani, Syed Mujtaba Hussein	I	29.12.1949		88	*1975–1985*	49
[2]**Kirsten,** Gary	SA	23.11.1967		101	*1993–2003*	185
[2]**Kirsten,** Peter Noel	SA	14.5.1955		12	*1991–1994*	40
Kirtley, Robert James	E	10.1.1975		4	*2003–2003*	11
Kishenchand, Gogumal	I	14.4.1925	16.4.1997	5	*1947–1952*	
Kline, Lindsay Francis	A	29.9.1934		13	*1957–1960*	
Klusener, Lance	SA	4.9.1971		49	*1996–2004*	171
Knight, Albert Ernest	E	8.10.1872	25.4.1946	3	*1903*	
Knight, Barry Rolfe	E	18.2.1938		29	*1961–1969*	
Knight, Donald John.	E	12.5.1894	5.1.1960	2	1921	
Knight, Nicholas Verity	E	28.11.1969		17	*1995–2001*	100
Knott, Alan Philip Eric	E	9.4.1946		95	*1967–1981*	20
Knox, Neville Alexander	E	10.10.1884	3.3.1935	2	1907	
Kotze, Johannes Jacobus	SA	7.8.1879	7.7.1931	3	*1902* 1907	
[2]**Kripal Singh,** Amritsar Govindsingh . .	I	6.8.1933	23.7.1987	14	*1955–1964*	
Krishnamurthy, Pochiah	I	12.7.1947	28.1.1999	5	*1970*	1
Kuggeleijn, Christopher Mary	NZ	10.5.1956		2	*1988*	16
Kuiper, Adrian Paul	SA	24.8.1959		1	*1991*	25
Kulkarni, Nilesh Moreshwar.	I	3.4.1973		3	*1997–2000*	10
Kulkarni, Rajiv Ramesh	I	25.9.1962		3	*1986*	10
Kulkarni, Umesh Narayan	I	7.3.1942		4	*1967*	
Kumar, Vaman Viswanath	I	22.6.1935		2	*1960–1961*	
Kumble, Anil.	I	17.10.1970		92	*1990–2004*	259
Kunderan, Budhisagar Krishnappa. . . .	I	2.10.1939		18	*1959–1967*	
Kuruppu, Don Sardha Brendon Priyantha	SL	5.1.1962		4	*1986–1991*	54
Kuruppuarachchi, Ajith Kosala	SL	1.11.1964		2	*1985–1986*	
Kuruvilla, Abey.	I	8.8.1968		10	*1996–1997*	25
Kuys, Frederick	SA	21.3.1870	12.9.1953	1	*1898*	
Labrooy, Graeme Fredrick	SL	7.6.1964		9	*1986–1990*	44
Laird, Bruce Malcolm.	A	21.11.1950		21	*1979–1982*	23
Laker, James Charles	E	9.2.1922	23.4.1986	46	*1947–1958*	
Lakshitha, Materba Kanatha Gamage Chamila Premanath	SL	4.1.1979		2	*2002–2002*	7
Lall Singh.	I	16.12.1909	19.11.1985	1	1932	
Lamb, Allan Joseph	E	20.6.1954		79	*1982–1992*	122
Lamba, Raman	I	2.1.1960	23.2.1998	4	*1986–1987*	32
Lambert, Clayton Benjamin	WI	10.2.1962		5	*1991–1998*	11
Lance, Herbert Roy.	SA	6.6.1940		13	*1961–1969*	
Langer, Justin Lee	A	21.11.1970		85	*1992–2004*	8
Langeveldt, Charl Kenneth.	SA	17.12.1974		1	*2004*	9
Langley, Gilbert Roche Andrews	A	14.9.1919	14.5.2001	26	*1951–1956*	
Langridge, James	E	10.7.1906	10.9.1966	8	*1933–1946*	
Langton, Arthur Chudleigh Beaumont .	SA	2.3.1912	27.11.1942	15	*1935–1938*	
Lara, Brian Charles	WI	2.5.1969		112	*1990–2004*	244

[1] *Father and son(s).*   [2] *Brothers.*

	Country	Born	Died	Tests	Test Career	ODIs
Larkins, Wayne	E	22.11.1953		13	*1979–1990*	25
Larsen, Gavin Rolf	NZ	27.9.1962		8	*1994–1995*	121
Larter, John David Frederick	E	24.4.1940		10	1962–1965	
Larwood, Harold MBE	E	14.11.1904	22.7.1995	21	*1926–1932*	
Lashley, Patrick Douglas	WI	11.2.1937		4	*1960–1966*	
Latham, Rodney Terry	NZ	12.6.1961		4	*1991–1992*	33
Lathwell, Mark Nicholas	E	26.12.1971		2	1993	
Laughlin, Trevor John	A	30.1.1951		3	*1977–1978*	6
Laver, Frank Jonas	A	7.12.1869	24.9.1919	15	1899–1909	
Law, Stuart Grant	A	18.10.1968		1	1995	54
Lawrence, David Valentine	E	28.1.1964		5	*1988–1991*	1
Lawrence, Godfrey Bernard	SA	31.3.1932		5	1961	
Lawry, William Morris	A	11.2.1937		67	1961–1970	1
Lawson, Geoffrey Francis	A	7.12.1957		46	*1980–1989*	79
Lawson, Jermaine Jay Charles	WI	13.1.1982		10	*2002–2004*	11
Laxman, Vangipurappu Venkata Sai . . .	I	1.11.1974		61	*1996–2004*	83
Leadbeater, Edric	E	15.8.1927		2	1951	
Lee, Brett	A	8.11.1976		37	*1999–2003*	91
Lee, Henry William	E	26.10.1890	21.4.1981	1	1930	
Lee, Philip Keith	A	15.9.1904	9.8.1980	2	*1931–1932*	
Lees, Warren Kenneth MBE	NZ	19.3.1952		21	1976–1983	31
Lees, Walter Scott	E	25.12.1875	10.9.1924	5	1905	
Legall, Ralph Archibald	WI	1.12.1925		4	1952	
Leggat, Ian Bruce	NZ	7.6.1930		1	1953	
Leggat, John Gordon	NZ	27.5.1926	9.3.1973	9	*1951–1955*	
Legge, Geoffrey Bevington	E	26.1.1903	21.11.1940	5	*1927–1929*	
Lehmann, Darren Scott	A	5.2.1970		27	*1997–2004*	110
le Roux, Frederick Louis	SA	5.2.1882	22.9.1963	1	1913	
Leslie, Charles Frederick Henry	E	8.12.1861	12.2.1921	4	1882	
Lever, John Kenneth MBE	E	24.2.1949		21	1976–1986	22
Lever, Peter	E	17.9.1940		17	1970–1975	10
Leveson Gower, *Sir* Henry Dudley Gresham	E	8.5.1873	1.2.1954	3	1909	
Levett, William Howard Vincent	E	25.1.1908	30.11.1995	1	1933	
Lewis, Anthony Robert CBE	E	6.7.1938		9	1972–1973	
Lewis, Clairmonte Christopher	E	14.2.1968		32	1990–1996	53
Lewis, Desmond Michael	WI	21.2.1946		3	1970	
Lewis, Percy Tyson	SA	2.10.1884	30.1.1976	1	1913	
Lewis, Rawl Nicholas	WI	5.9.1974		3	*1997–1998*	16
Leyland, Maurice	E	20.7.1900	1.1.1967	41	1928–1938	
Liaqat Ali Khan	P	21.5.1955		5	*1974–1978*	3
Liebenberg, Gerhardus Frederick Johannes	SA	7.4.1972		5	*1997–1998*	4
Lillee, Dennis Keith MBE	A	18.7.1949		70	*1970–1983*	63
Lilley, Arthur Augustus	E	28.11.1866	17.11.1929	35	1896–1909	
Lillywhite, James	E	23.2.1842	25.10.1929	2	1876	
[1]**Lindsay**, Denis Thomson	SA	4.9.1939		19	1963–1969	
[1]**Lindsay**, John Dixon	SA	8.9.1908	31.8.1990	3	1947	
Lindsay, Nevil Vernon	SA	30.7.1886	2.2.1976	1	1921	
Lindwall, Raymond Russell MBE	A	3.10.1921	22.6.1996	61	*1945–1959*	
Ling, William Victor Stone	SA	3.10.1891	26.9.1960	6	*1921–1922*	
Lissette, Allen Fisher	NZ	6.11.1919	24.1.1973	2	1955	
Liyanage, Dulip Kapila	SL	6.6.1972		9	*1992–2001*	16
Llewellyn, Charles Bennett	SA	26.9.1876	7.6.1964	15	*1895–1912*	
Lloyd, Clive Hubert OBE	WI	31.8.1944		110	*1966–1984*	87
Lloyd, David	E	18.3.1947		9	*1974–1974*	8
Lloyd, Timothy Andrew	E	5.11.1956		1	1984	3
Loader, Peter James	E	25.10.1929		13	*1954–1958*	
Lock, Alan Charles Ingram	Z	10.9.1962		1	1995	8

[1] *Father and son(s).* [2] *Brothers.*

	Country	Born	Died	Tests	Test Career	ODIs
Lock, Graham <u>Anthony</u> Richard	E	5.7.1929	29.3.1995	49	1952–1967	
Lockwood, William Henry	E	25.3.1868	26.4.1932	12	1893–1902	
Logie, Augustine Lawrence.	WI	28.9.1960		52	1982–1991	158
Lohmann, George Alfred.	E	2.6.1865	1.12.1901	18	1886–1896	
Lokuarachchi, Kaushal Samaraweera . .	SL	20.5.1982		4	2003–2003	12
Love, Hampden Stanley Bray	A	10.8.1895	22.7.1969	1	1932	
Love, Martin Lloyd	A	30.3.1974		5	2002–2003	
Loveridge, Greg Riaka.	NZ	15.1.1975		1	1995	
Lowry, Thomas Coleman	NZ	17.2.1898	20.7.1976	7	1929–1931	
Lowson, Frank Anderson	E	1.7.1925	8.9.1984	7	1951–1955	
Loxton, Samuel John Everett	A	29.3.1921		12	1947–1950	
Lucas, Alfred Perry.	E	20.2.1857	12.10.1923	5	1878–1884	
Luckhurst, Brian William	E	5.2.1939		21	1970–1974	3
Lundie, Eric Balfour.	SA	15.3.1888	12.9.1917	1	1913	
Lyons, John James	A	21.5.1863	21.7.1927	14	1886–1897	
Lyttelton, *Hon.* Alfred.	E	7.2.1857	5.7.1913	4	1880–1884	
McAlister, Peter Alexander	A	11.7.1869	10.5.1938	8	1903–1909	
Macartney, Charles George	A	27.6.1886	9.9.1958	35	1907–1926	
Macaulay, George Gibson	E	7.12.1897	13.12.1940	8	1922–1933	
Macaulay, Michael John	SA	19.4.1939		1	1964	
MacBryan, John Crawford William . . .	E	22.7.1892	14.7.1983	1	1924	
McCabe, Stanley Joseph	A	16.7.1910	25.8.1968	39	1930–1938	
McCague, Martin John	E	24.5.1969		3	1993–1994	
McCarthy, Cuan Neil	SA	24.3.1929	14.8.2000	15	1948–1951	
McConnon, James Edward.	E	21.6.1922	26.1.2003	2	1954	
McCool, Colin Leslie	A	9.12.1916	5.4.1986	14	1945–1949	
McCormick, Ernest Leslie	A	16.5.1906	28.6.1991	12	1935–1938	
McCosker, Richard Bede	A	11.12.1946		25	1974–1979	14
McCullum, Brendon Barrie	NZ	27.9.1981		10	2003–2004	57
McDermott, Craig John	A	14.4.1965		71	1984–1995	138
McDonald, Colin Campbell	A	17.11.1928		47	1951–1961	
McDonald, Edgar Arthur	A	6.1.1891	22.7.1937	11	1920–1921	
McDonnell, Percy Stanislaus.	A	13.11.1858	24.9.1896	19	1880–1888	
McEwan, Paul Ernest	NZ	19.12.1953		4	1979–1984	17
McGahey, Charles Percy	E	12.2.1871	10.1.1935	2	1901	
McGarrell, Neil Christopher.	WI	12.7.1972		4	2000–2001	17
MacGibbon, Anthony Roy	NZ	28.8.1924		26	1950–1958	
MacGill, Stuart Charles Glyndwr.	A	25.2.1971		33	1997–2004	3
McGirr, Herbert Mendelson	NZ	5.11.1891	14.4.1964	2	1929	
McGlew, Derrick <u>John</u>.	SA	11.3.1929	9.6.1998	34	1951–1961	
McGrath, Anthony	E	6.10.1975		4	2003	14
McGrath, Glenn Donald	A	9.2.1970		106	1993–2004	194
MacGregor, Gregor.	E	31.8.1869	20.8.1919	8	1890–1893	
McGregor, Spencer <u>Noel</u>	NZ	18.12.1931		25	1954–1964	
McIlwraith, John	A	7.9.1857	5.7.1938	1	1886	
McIntyre, Arthur John William.	E	14.5.1918		3	1950–1955	
McIntyre, Peter Edward.	A	27.4.1966		2	1994–1996	
Mackay, Kenneth Donald MBE.	A	24.10.1925	13.6.1982	37	1956–1962	
McKenzie, Graham Douglas	A	24.6.1941		60	1961–1970	1
McKenzie, Neil Douglas	SA	24.11.1975		41	2000–2003	59
McKibbin, Thomas Robert.	A	10.12.1870	15.12.1939	5	1894–1897	
McKinnon, Atholl Henry	SA	20.8.1932	2.12.1983	8	1960–1966	
MacKinnon, Francis Alexander	E	9.4.1848	27.2.1947	1	1878	
MacLaren, Archibald Campbell.	E	1.12.1871	17.11.1944	35	1894–1909	
McLaren, John William	A	22.12.1886	17.11.1921	1	1911	
Maclean, John Alexander.	A	27.4.1946		4	1978	2
McLean, Nixon Alexei McNamara. . . .	WI	20.7.1973		19	1997–2000	45
McLean, Roy Alastair	SA	9.7.1930		40	1951–1964	

---

[1] *Father and son(s).* [2] *Brothers.*

	Country	Born	Died	Tests	Test Career	ODIs
[2]McLeod, Charles Edward	A	24.10.1869	26.11.1918	17	*1894–1905*	
McLeod, Edwin George.	NZ	14.10.1900	14.9.1989	1	*1929*	
[2]McLeod, Robert William.	A	19.1.1868	14.6.1907	6	*1891–1893*	
McMahon, Trevor George	NZ	8.11.1929		5	*1955*	
McMaster, Joseph Emile Patrick	E	16.3.1861	7.6.1929	1	*1888*	
McMillan, Brian Mervin	SA	22.12.1963		38	*1992–1998*	78
McMillan, Craig Douglas.	NZ	13.9.1976		53	*1997–2004*	157
McMillan, Quintin	SA	23.6.1904	3.7.1948	13	*1929–1931*	
McMorris, Easton Dudley Ashton St John	WI	4.4.1935		13	*1957–1966*	
McRae, Donald Alexander Noel	NZ	25.12.1912	10.8.1986	1	*1945*	
McShane, Patrick George.	A	18.4.1858	11.12.1903	3	*1884–1887*	
McWatt, Clifford Aubrey.	WI	1.2.1922	20.7.1997	6	*1953–1954*	
Madan Lal	I	20.3.1951		39	1974–1986	67
Maddocks, Leonard Victor	A	24.5.1926		7	*1954–1956*	
Maddy, Darren Lee.	E	23.5.1974		3	*1999–1999*	8
Madondo, Trevor Nyasha.	Z	22.11.1976	11.6.2001	3	*1997–2000*	13
Madray, Ivan Samuel	WI	2.7.1934		2	*1957*	
Madugalle, Ranjan Senerath	SL	22.4.1959		21	*1981–1988*	63
Madurasinghe, Madurasinghe Arachchige Wijayasiri Ranjith	SL	30.1.1961		3	*1988–1992*	12
Maguire, John Norman	A	15.9.1956		3	*1983*	23
Mahanama, Roshan Siriwardene	SL	31.5.1966		52	*1985–1997*	213
Maharoof, Mohamed Farveez	SL	7.9.1984		4	*2003–2004*	17
Mahmood Hussain	P	2.4.1932	25.12.1991	27	*1952–1962*	
Mahwire, Ngonidzashe Blessing	Z	31.7.1982		6	*2002–2003*	3
Mailey, Arthur Alfred	A	3.1.1886	31.12.1967	21	*1920–1926*	
[1]Majid Khan	P	28.9.1946		63	*1964–1982*	23
Maka, Ebrahim Suleman	I	5.3.1922	d unknown	2	*1952*	
Makepeace, Joseph William Henry . . .	E	22.8.1881	19.12.1952	4	*1920*	
Malcolm, Devon Eugene	E	22.2.1963		40	*1989–1997*	10
Malhotra, Ashok Omprakash	I	26.1.1957		7	*1981–1984*	20
Malinga, Separamadu Lasith.	SL	4.9.1983		4	*2004–2004*	4
Mallender, Neil Alan.	E	13.8.1961		2	*1992*	
Mallett, Ashley Alexander	A	13.7.1945		38	*1968–1980*	9
Malone, Michael Francis	A	9.10.1950		1	*1977*	10
Maninder Singh	I	13.6.1965		35	*1982–1992*	59
[1]Manjrekar, Sanjay Vijay.	I	12.7.1965		37	*1987–1996*	74
[1]Manjrekar, Vijay Laxman.	I	26.9.1931	18.10.1983	55	*1951–1964*	
Manjural Islam	B	7.11.1979		17	*2000–2003*	34
Manjural Islam Rana.	B	4.5.1984		6	*2003–2004*	14
[1]Mankad, Ashok Vinoo	I	12.10.1946		22	*1969–1977*	1
[1]Mankad, Mulvantrai Himmatlal ("Vinoo").	I	12.4.1917	21.8.1978	44	*1946–1958*	
Mann, Anthony Longford.	A	8.11.1945		4	*1977*	
[1]Mann, Francis George CBE	E	6.9.1917	8.8.2001	7	*1948–1949*	
[1]Mann, Francis Thomas	E	3.3.1888	6.10.1964	5	*1922*	
Mann, Norman Bertram Fleetwood . . .	SA	28.12.1920	31.7.1952	19	*1947–1951*	
Mansell, Percy Neville Frank MBE	SA	16.3.1920	9.5.1995	13	*1951–1955*	
Mansoor Akhtar	P	25.12.1957		19	*1980–1989*	41
Mantri, Madhav Krishnaji	I	1.9.1921		4	*1951–1954*	
[2]Manzoor Elahi	P	15.4.1963		6	*1984–1994*	54
Maqsood Ahmed	P	26.3.1925	4.1.1999	16	*1952–1955*	
Maregwede, Alester	Z	5.8.1981		2	*2003*	9
Marillier, Douglas Anthony	Z	24.4.1978		5	*2000–2001*	48
Markham, Lawrence Anderson	SA	12.9.1924	5.8.2000	1	*1948*	
Marks, Victor James	E	25.6.1955		6	*1982–1983*	34
Marr, Alfred Percy	A	28.3.1862	15.3.1940	1	*1884*	
Marriott, Charles Stowell.	E	14.9.1895	13.10.1966	1	*1933*	

[1] *Father and son(s).* [2] *Brothers.*

	Country	Born	Died	Tests	Test Career	ODIs
Marsh, Geoffrey Robert.	A	31.12.1958		50	1985–1991	117
Marsh, Rodney William MBE	A	4.11.1947		96	1970–1983	92
Marshall, Hamish John Hamilton	NZ	15.2.1979		2	2000–2004	30
Marshall, Malcolm Denzil	WI	18.4.1958	4.11.1999	81	1978–1991	136
[2]**Marshall**, Norman Edgar	WI	27.2.1924		1	1954	
[2]**Marshall**, Roy Edwin.	WI	25.4.1930	27.10.1992	4	1951	
Martin, Christopher Stewart	NZ	10.12.1974		18	2000–2004	7
Martin, Frank Reginald	WI	12.10.1893	23.11.1967	9	1928–1930	
Martin, Frederick	E	12.10.1861	13.12.1921	2	1890–1891	
Martin, John Wesley	A	28.7.1931	16.7.1992	8	1960–1966	
Martin, John William	E	16.2.1917	4.1.1987	1	1947	
Martin, Peter James	E	15.11.1968		8	1995–1997	20
Martindale, Emmanuel Alfred	WI	25.11.1909	17.3.1972	10	1933–1939	
Martyn, Damien Richard	A	21.10.1971		53	1992–2004	159
Marx, Waldemar Frederick Eric.	SA	4.7.1895	2.6.1974	3	1921	
Masakadza, Hamilton	Z	9.8.1983		9	2001–2004	6
Mashrafe bin Mortaza	B	5.10.1983		16	2001–2004	14
Mason, John Richard.	E	26.3.1874	15.10.1958	5	1897	
Mason, Michael James.	NZ	27.8.1974		1	2003	5
Masood Anwar	P	12.12.1967		1	1990	
Massie, Hugh Hamon	A	11.4.1854	12.10.1938	9	1881–1884	
Massie, Robert Arnold Lockyer.	A	14.4.1947		6	1972–1972	3
Matambanadzo, Everton Zvikomborero	Z	13.4.1976		3	1996–1999	7
Matheson, Alexander Malcolm	NZ	27.2.1906	31.12.1985	2	1929 1931	
Mathias, Wallis	P	4.2.1935	1.9.1994	21	1955–1962	
Matsikenyeri, Stuart	Z	3.5.1983		6	2003–2004	37
Matthews, Austin David George	E	3.5.1904	29.7.1977	1	1937	
Matthews, Christopher Darrell	A	22.9.1962		3	1986–1988	
Matthews, Craig Russell	SA	15.2.1965		18	1992–1995	56
Matthews, Gregory Richard John.	A	15.12.1959		33	1983–1992	59
Matthews, Thomas James.	A	3.4.1884	14.10.1943	8	1911–1912	
Mattis, Everton Hugh	WI	11.4.1957		4	1980	2
May, Peter Barker Howard CBE	E	31.12.1929	27.12.1994	66	1951–1961	
May, Timothy Brian Alexander	A	26.1.1962		24	1987–1994	47
Maynard, Matthew Peter	E	21.3.1966		4	1988–1993	14
Mayne, Edgar Richard.	A	2.7.1882	26.10.1961	4	1912–1921	
Mayne, Lawrence Charles	A	23.1.1942		6	1964–1969	
Mbangwa, Mpumelelo.	Z	26.6.1976		15	1996–2000	29
Mead, Charles Philip.	E	9.3.1887	26.3.1958	17	1911–1928	
Mead, Walter.	E	1.4.1868	18.3.1954	1	1899	
Meale, Trevor	NZ	11.11.1928		2	1958	
Meckiff, Ian	A	6.1.1935		18	1957–1963	
Meherhomji, Khershedji Rustomji. . . .	I	9.8.1911	10.2.1982	1	1936	
Mehra, Vijay Laxman	I	12.3.1938		8	1955–1963	
Mehrab Hossain	B	22.9.1978		9	2000–2002	18
Meintjes, Douglas James	SA	9.6.1890	17.7.1979	2	1922	
Melle, Michael George.	SA	3.6.1930	28.12.2003	7	1949 1952	
Melville, Alan	SA	19.5.1910	18.4.1983	11	1938–1948	
Mendis, Louis Rohan Duleep	SL	25.8.1952		24	1981–1988	79
Mendonca, Ivor Leon	WI	13.7.1934		2	1961	
Merchant, Vijay Madhavji	I	12.10.1911	27.10.1987	10	1933–1951	
Merritt, William Edward	NZ	18.8.1908	9.6.1977	6	1929–1931	
Merry, Cyril Arthur	WI	20.1.1911	19.4.1964	2	1933	
Meuleman, Kenneth Douglas	A	5.9.1923	10.9.2004	1	1945	
Meuli, Edgar Milton	NZ	20.2.1926		1	1952	
Mhambrey, Paras Laxmikant	I	20.6.1972		2	1996	3
Middleton, James	SA	30.9.1865	23.12.1913	6	1895–1902	
Midwinter, William Evans	A, E	19.6.1851	3.12.1890	12	1876–1886	
Milburn, Barry Douglas.	NZ	24.11.1943		3	1968	

[1] *Father and son(s).* [2] *Brothers.*

	Country	Born	Died	Tests	Test Career	ODIs
Milburn, Colin.	E	23.10.1941	28.2.1990	9	1966–1968	
[2]Milkha Singh, Amritsar Govindsingh .	I	31.12.1941		4	1959–1961	
Miller, Audley Montague	E	19.10.1869	26.6.1959	1	1895	
Miller, Colin Reid.	A	6.2.1964		18	1998–2000	
Miller, Geoffrey	E	8.9.1952		34	1976–1984	25
Miller, Keith Ross MBE	A	28.11.1919	11.10.2004	55	1945–1956	
Miller, Lawrence Somerville Martin . . .	NZ	31.3.1923	17.12.1996	13	1952–1958	
Miller, Roy	WI	24.12.1924		1	1952	
Milligan, Frank William.	E	19.3.1870	31.3.1900	2	1898	
Millman, Geoffrey	E	2.10.1934		6	1961–1962	
Mills, Charles Henry	SA	26.11.1867	26.7.1948	1	1891	
Mills, John Ernest.	NZ	3.9.1905	11.12.1972	7	1929–1932	
Mills, Kyle David	NZ	15.3.1979		2	2004–2004	39
Milton, Clement Arthur	E	10.3.1928		6	1958–1959	
Milton, Sir William Henry	SA	3.12.1854	6.3.1930	3	1888–1891	
Minnett, Roy Baldwin	A	13.6.1888	21.10.1955	9	1911–1912	
Miran Bux	P	20.4.1907	8.2.1991	2	1954	
Mirando, Magina Thilan Thushara. . . .	SL	1.3.1981		1	2003	
Misbah-ul-Haq	P	28.5.1974		5	2000–2003	12
Misson, Francis Michael	A	19.11.1938		5	1960–1961	
Mitchell, Arthur.	E	13.9.1902	25.12.1976	6	1933–1936	
Mitchell, Bruce	SA	8.1.1909	2.7.1995	42	1929–1948	
Mitchell, Frank	E, SA	13.8.1872	11.10.1935	5	1898–1912	
Mitchell, Thomas Bignall.	E	4.9.1902	27.1.1996	5	1932–1935	
Mitchell-Innes, Norman Stewart	E	7.9.1914		1	1935	
Modi, Rustomji Sheryar.	I	11.11.1924	17.5.1996	10	1946–1952	
Mohammad Akram	P	10.9.1974		9	1995–2000	23
Mohammad Ashraful	B	9.9.1984		25	2001–2004	43
Mohammad Asif	P	20.12.1982		1	2004	
Mohammad Aslam.	P	5.1.1920		1	1954	
Mohammad Farooq	P	8.4.1938		7	1960–1964	
Mohammad Hafeez	P	17.10.1980		3	2003	22
Mohammad Hussain	P	8.10.1976		2	1996–1998	14
Mohammad Ilyas.	P	19.3.1946		10	1964–1968	
Mohammad Khalil.	P	11.11.1982		1	2004	
Mohammad Munaf	P	2.11.1935		4	1959–1961	
Mohammad Nazir	P	8.3.1946		14	1969–1983	4
Mohammad Rafique	B	5.9.1970		18	2000–2004	71
Mohammad Ramzan	P	25.12.1970		1	1997	
Mohammad Salim	B	15.10.1981		2	2003	1
Mohammad Sami	P	24.2.1981		18	2000–2004	66
Mohammad Sharif	B	12.12.1985		8	2000–2001	8
Mohammad Wasim	P	8.8.1977		18	1996–2000	25
Mohammad Zahid.	P	2.8.1976		5	1996–2002	11
Mohammed, Dave	WI	8.10.1979		2	2003–2004	
Mohanty, Debasis Sarbeswar.	I	20.7.1976		2	1997	45
Mohsin Kamal	P	16.6.1963		9	1983–1994	19
Mohsin Khan	P	15.3.1955		48	1977–1986	75
[2]Moin Khan	P	23.9.1971		69	1990–2004	219
Moir, Alexander McKenzie	NZ	17.7.1919	17.6.2000	17	1950–1958	
Mold, Arthur Webb.	E	27.5.1863	29.4.1921	3	1893	
Moloney, Denis Andrew Robert.	NZ	11.8.1910	15.7.1942	3	1937	
Mongia, Nayan Ramlal	I	19.12.1969		44	1993–2000	140
Moodie, George Horatio.	WI	26.11.1915	8.6.2002	1	1934	
Moody, Thomas Masson.	A	2.10.1965		8	1989–1992	76
Moon, Leonard James	E	9.2.1878	23.11.1916	4	1905	
Mooney, Francis Leonard Hugh	NZ	26.5.1921	8.3.2004	14	1949–1953	
More, Kiran Shankar.	I	4.9.1962		49	1986–1993	94
Morgan, Ross Winston	NZ	12.2.1941		20	1964–1971	

[1] *Father and son(s).* [2] *Brothers.*

	Country	Born	Died	Tests	Test Career	ODIs
Morkel, Denijs Paul Beck	SA	25.1.1906	6.10.1980	16	*1927–1931*	
Morley, Frederick	E	16.12.1850	28.9.1884	4	*1880–1882*	
Moroney, John	A	24.7.1917	1.7.1999	7	*1949–1951*	
Morris, Arthur Robert MBE.	A	19.1.1922		46	*1946–1954*	
Morris, Hugh	E	5.10.1963		3	1991	
Morris, John Edward.	E	1.4.1964		3	1990	8
Morris, Samuel	A	22.6.1855	20.9.1931	1	*1884*	
Morrison, Bruce Donald	NZ	17.12.1933		1	*1962*	
Morrison, Daniel Kyle.	NZ	3.2.1966		48	*1987–1996*	96
Morrison, John Francis MacLean	NZ	27.8.1947		17	*1973–1981*	18
Mortimore, John Brian	E	14.5.1933		9	*1958–1964*	
Moseley, Ezra Alphonsa	WI	5.1.1958		2	1989	9
Moses, Henry.	A	13.2.1858	7.12.1938	6	*1886–1894*	
Moss, Alan Edward.	E	14.11.1930		9	*1953–1960*	
Moss, Jeffrey Kenneth	A	29.6.1947		1	*1978*	1
Motz, Richard Charles	NZ	12.1.1940		32	*1961–1969*	
Moule, William Henry.	A	31.1.1858	24.8.1939	1	1880	
Moxon, Martyn Douglas	E	4.5.1960		10	*1986–1989*	8
Mpofu, Christopher Bobby	Z	27.11.1985		2	*2004*	3
Mubarak, Jehan.	SL	10.1.1981		4	*2002–2004*	7
[1]**Mudassar Nazar**	P	6.4.1956		76	*1976–1988*	122
Muddiah, Venatappa Musandra	I	8.6.1929		2	*1959–1960*	
Mufasir-ul-Haq	P	16.8.1944	27.7.1983	1	*1964*	
Mullally, Alan David. . . .	E	12.7.1969		19	*1996–2001*	50
Muller, Scott Andrew	A	11.7.1971		2	*1999*	
Munir Malik.	P	10.7.1934		3	*1959–1962*	
Munton, Timothy Alan	E	30.7.1965		2	1992	
Mupariwa, Tawanda	Z	16.4.1985		1	*2003*	5
Muralitharan, Muttiah	SL	17.4.1972		91	*1992–2004*	237
Murdoch, William Lloyd	A, E	18.10.1854	18.2.1911	19	*1876–1891*	
Murphy, Brian Andrew	Z	1.12.1976		11	*1999–2001*	31
Murray, Anton Ronald Andrew	SA	30.4.1922	17.4.1995	10	*1952–1953*	
Murray, Bruce Alexander Grenfell. . . .	NZ	18.9.1940		13	*1967–1970*	
Murray, David Anthony	WI	29.9.1950		19	*1977–1981*	10
Murray, Darrin James	NZ	4.9.1967		8	*1994*	1
Murray, Deryck Lance	WI	20.5.1943		62	*1963–1980*	26
Murray, Junior Randalph	WI	20.1.1968		33	*1992–2001*	55
Murray, John Thomas MBE.	E	1.4.1935		21	1961–1967	
Musgrove, Henry Alfred	A	27.11.1860	2.11.1931	1	*1884*	
Mushfiqur Rahman	B	1.1.1980		10	*2000–2004*	28
Mushtaq Ahmed	P	28.6.1970		52	*1989–2003*	144
Mushtaq Ali, Syed	I	17.12.1914		11	*1933–1951*	
[2]**Mushtaq Mohammad**	P	22.11.1943		57	*1958–1978*	10
Mutendera, David Travolta.	Z	25.1.1979		1	*2000*	9
Nadeem Abbasi	P	15.4.1964		3	1989	
Nadeem Ghauri	P	12.10.1962		1	1989	6
[2]**Nadeem Khan**	P	10.12.1969		2	*1992–1998*	2
Nadkarni, Rameshchandra Gangaram . .	I	4.4.1932		41	*1955–1967*	
Nafis Iqbal	B	31.1.1985		6	*2004*	9
Nagamootoo, Mahendra Veeren	WI	9.10.1975		5	*2000–2002*	24
Nagel, Lisle Ernest	A	6.3.1905	23.11.1971	1	*1932*	
Naik, Sudhir Sakharam	I	21.2.1945		3	*1974–1974*	2
Naimur Rahman	B	19.9.1974		8	*2000–2002*	29
Nanan, Rangy	WI	29.5.1953		1	*1980*	
Naoomal Jeoomal	I	17.4.1904	18.7.1980	3	*1932–1933*	
Narasimha Rao, Modireddy						
Venkateshwar	I	11.8.1954		4	*1978–1979*	
Nash, Dion Joseph	NZ	20.11.1971		32	*1992–2001*	81

[1] *Father and son(s).*   [2] *Brothers.*

	Country	Born	Died	Tests	Test Career	ODIs
Nash, Laurence John	A	2.5.1910	24.7.1986	2	*1931–1936*	
Nasim-ul-Ghani	P	14.5.1941		29	*1957–1972*	1
Naushad Ali	P	1.10.1943		6	*1964*	
Naved Anjum	P	27.7.1963		2	*1989–1990*	13
Naved Ashraf	P	4.9.1974		2	*1998–1999*	
Naved Latif	P	21.2.1976		1	*2001*	11
Naved-ul-Hasan	P	28.2.1978		2	*2004*	14
Navle, Janaradan Gyanoba	I	7.12.1902	7.9.1979	2	*1932–1933*	
Nawaz, Mohamed <u>Naveed</u>	SL	20.9.1973		1	*2002*	3
Nayak, Surendra Vithal	I	20.10.1954		2	*1982*	4
[2]**Nayudu,** Cottari Kanakaiya	I	31.10.1895	14.11.1967	7	*1932–1936*	
[2]**Nayudu,** Cottari Subbanna	I	18.4.1914	22.11.2002	11	*1933–1951*	
[1]**Nazar Mohammad**	P	5.3.1921	12.7.1996	5	*1952*	
[2]**Nazir Ali,** Syed	I	8.1.1906	18.2.1975	2	*1932–1933*	
Nazmul Hossain	B	5.10.1987		1	*2004*	6
Neblett, James Montague	WI	13.11.1901	28.3.1959	1	*1934*	
Nehra, Ashish	I	29.4.1979		17	*1998–2003*	55
Nel, Andre	SA	15.7.1977		11	*2001–2004*	22
Nel, John Desmond	SA	10.7.1928		6	*1949–1957*	
Newberry, Claude	SA	1889	1.8.1916	4	*1913*	
Newham, William	E	12.12.1860	26.6.1944	1	*1887*	
Newman, *Sir* Jack	NZ	3.7.1902	23.9.1996	3	*1931–1932*	
Newport, Philip John	E	11.10.1962		3	*1988–1990*	
Newson, Edward Serrurier OBE	SA	2.12.1910	24.4.1988	3	*1930–1938*	
Ngam, Mfuneko	SA	29.1.1979		3	*2000*	
Niaz Ahmed	P	11.11.1945	12.4.2000	2	*1967–1968*	
Nichols, Morris Stanley	E	6.10.1900	26.1.1961	14	*1929–1939*	
Nicholson, Frank	SA	17.9.1909	30.7.1982	4	*1935*	
Nicholson, Matthew James	A	2.10.1974		1	*1998*	
Nicolson, John Fairless William	SA	19.7.1899	13.12.1935	3	*1927*	
Nissanka, Ratnayake Arachchige <u>Prabath</u>	SL	25.10.1980		4	*2003*	23
Nissar, Mohammad	I	1.8.1910	11.3.1963	6	*1932–1936*	
Nitschke, Homesdale Carl	A	14.4.1905	29.9.1982	2	*1931*	
Nkala, Mluleki Luke	Z	1.4.1981		10	*2000–2004*	46
Noble, Montague Alfred	A	28.1.1873	22.6.1940	42	*1897–1909*	
Noblet, Geffery	A	14.9.1916		3	*1949–1952*	
Noreiga, Jack Mollinson	WI	15.4.1936	8.8.2003	4	*1970*	
Norton, Norman Ogilvie	SA	11.5.1881	27.6.1968	1	*1909*	
Nothling, Otto Ernest	A	1.8.1900	26.9.1965	1	*1928*	
[1]**Nourse,** Arthur <u>Dudley</u>	SA	12.11.1910	14.8.1981	34	*1935–1951*	
[1]**Nourse,** Arthur William ("Dave")	SA	26.1.1878	8.7.1948	45	*1902–1924*	
Ntini, Makhaya	SA	6.7.1977		54	*1997–2004*	103
Nunes, Robert <u>Karl</u>	WI	7.6.1894	22.7.1958	4	*1928–1929*	
Nupen, Eiulf Peter	SA	1.1.1902	29.1.1977	17	*1921–1935*	
Nurse, Seymour MacDonald	WI	10.11.1933		29	*1959–1968*	
Nyalchand, Shah	I	14.9.1919	3.1.1997	1	*1952*	
Oakman, Alan Stanley Myles	E	20.4.1930		2	*1956*	
O'Brien, Leo Patrick Joseph	A	2.7.1907	13.3.1997	5	*1932–1936*	
O'Brien, *Sir* Timothy Carew	E	5.11.1861	9.12.1948	5	*1884–1895*	
Ochse, Arthur Edward	SA	11.3.1870	11.4.1918	2	*1888*	
Ochse, Arthur Lennox	SA	11.10.1899	5.5.1949	3	*1927–1929*	
O'Connor, Jack	E	6.11.1897	22.2.1977	4	*1929–1929*	
O'Connor, John Denis Alphonsus	A	9.9.1875	23.8.1941	4	*1907–1909*	
O'Connor, Shayne Barry	NZ	15.11.1973		19	*1997–2001*	38
O'Donnell, Simon Patrick	A	26.1.1963		6	*1985–1985*	87
Ogilvie, Alan <u>David</u>	A	3.6.1951		5	*1977*	
O'Keeffe, Kerry James	A	25.11.1949		24	*1970–1977*	2
Old, Christopher Middleton	E	22.12.1948		46	*1972–1981*	32

[1] *Father and son(s).*   [2] *Brothers.*

	Country	Born	Died	Tests	Test Career	ODIs
Oldfield, Norman	E	5.5.1911	19.4.1996	1	1939	
Oldfield, William <u>Albert</u> Stanley MBE . .	A	9.9.1894	10.8.1976	54	*1920–1936*	
O'Linn, Sidney	SA	5.5.1927		7	*1960–1961*	
Olonga, Henry Khaaba	Z	3.7.1976		30	*1994–2002*	50
O'Neill, Norman Clifford	A	19.2.1937		42	*1958–1964*	
Ontong, Justin Lee	SA	4.1.1980		2	*2001–2004*	16
Oram, Jacob David Philip	NZ	28.7.1978		17	*2002–2004*	70
O'Reilly, William Joseph OBE	A	20.12.1905	6.10.1992	27	*1931–1945*	
Ormond, James	E	20.8.1977		2	*2001–2001*	
O'Sullivan, David Robert.	NZ	16.11.1944		11	*1972–1976*	3
Overton, Guy William Fitzroy.	NZ	8.6.1919	7.9.1993	3	*1953*	
Owens, Michael Barry.	NZ	11.11.1969		8	*1992–1994*	1
Owen-Smith, Harold Geoffrey.	SA	18.2.1909	28.2.1990	5	*1929*	
Oxenham, Ronald Keven	A	28.7.1891	16.8.1939	7	*1928–1931*	
Padgett, Douglas Ernest Vernon.	E	20.7.1934		2	*1960*	
Padmore, Albert Leroy	WI	17.12.1946		2	*1975–1976*	
Page, Milford Laurenson	NZ	8.5.1902	13.2.1987	14	*1929–1937*	
Pai, Ajit Manohar.	I	28.4.1945		1	*1969*	
Paine, George Alfred Edward	E	11.6.1908	30.3.1978	4	*1934*	
Pairaudeau, Bruce Hamilton.	WI	14.4.1931		13	*1952–1957*	
Palairet, Lionel Charles Hamilton	E	27.5.1870	27.3.1933	2	*1902*	
Palia, Phiroze Edulji	I	5.9.1910	9.9.1981	2	*1932–1936*	
Palm, Archibald William	SA	8.6.1901	17.8.1966	1	*1927*	
Palmer, Charles Henry CBE.	E	15.5.1919		1	*1953*	
Palmer, George Eugene	A	22.2.1859	22.8.1910	17	*1880–1886*	
Palmer, Kenneth Ernest MBE.	E	22.4.1937		1	*1964*	
Pandit, Chandrakant Sitaram.	I	30.9.1961		5	*1986–1991*	36
Panyangara, Tinashe.	Z	21.10.1985		3	*2003–2004*	16
Papps, Michael Hugh William.	NZ	2.7.1979		4	*2003–2004*	5
Parfitt, Peter Howard.	E	8.12.1936		37	*1961–1972*	
Park, Roy Lindsay	A	30.7.1892	23.1.1947	1	*1920*	
Parkar, Ghulam Ahmed.	I	25.10.1955		1	*1982*	10
Parkar, Ramnath Dhondu.	I	31.10.1946	11.8.1999	2	*1972*	
Parker, Charles Warrington Leonard. . .	E	14.10.1882	11.7.1959	1	*1921*	
Parker, George Macdonald	SA	27.5.1899	1.5.1969	2	*1924*	
[2]**Parker,** John Morton	NZ	21.2.1951		36	*1972–1980*	24
[2]**Parker,** Norman <u>Murray</u>	NZ	28.8.1948		3	*1976*	1
Parker, Paul William Giles	E	15.1.1956		1	*1981*	
Parkhouse, William <u>Gilbert</u> Anthony . .	E	12.10.1925	10.8.2000	7	*1950–1959*	
Parkin, Cecil Harry	E	18.2.1886	15.6.1943	10	*1920–1924*	
Parkin, Durant Clifford	SA	20.2.1873	20.3.1936	1	*1891*	
[1]**Parks,** James Horace	E	12.5.1903	21.11.1980	1	*1937*	
[1]**Parks,** James Michael.	E	21.10.1931		46	*1954–1967*	
Parore, Adam Craig	NZ	23.1.1971		78	*1990–2001*	179
Parry, Derick Recaldo	WI	22.12.1954		12	*1977–1979*	6
Parsana, Dhiraj Devshibhai	I	2.12.1947		2	*1978*	
Partridge, Joseph Titus	SA	9.12.1932	6.6.1988	11	*1963–1964*	
Pascoe, Leonard Stephen	A	13.2.1950		14	*1977–1981*	29
Passailaigue, Charles <u>Clarence</u>	WI	4.8.1902	7.1.1972	1	*1929*	
Patankar, Chandrakant Trimbak.	I	24.11.1930		1	*1955*	
[1]**Pataudi,** Iftikhar Ali Khan, Nawab of .	E, I	16.3.1910	5.1.1952	6	*1932–1946*	
[1]**Pataudi,** Mansur Ali Khan, Nawab of .	I	5.1.1941		46	*1961–1974*	
Patel, Brijesh Pursuram	I	24.11.1952		21	*1974–1977*	10
Patel, Dipak Narshibhai	NZ	25.10.1958		37	*1986–1996*	75
Patel, Jasubhai Motibhai	I	26.11.1924	12.12.1992	7	*1954–1959*	
Patel, Minal Mahesh	E	7.7.1970		2	*1996*	
Patel, Parthiv Ajay	I	9.3.1985		19	*2002–2004*	14
Patel, Rashid	I	1.6.1964		1	*1988*	1

[1] *Father and son(s).* [2] *Brothers.*

	Country	Born	Died	Tests	Test Career	ODIs
Pathan, Irfan Khan	I	27.10.1984		10	*2003–2004*	28
Patiala, Maharaja of (Yadavendra Singh)	I	17.1.1913	17.6.1974	1	*1933*	
Patil, Sadashiv Raoji	I	10.10.1933		1	*1955*	
Patil, Sandeep Madhusudan	I	18.8.1956		29	*1979–1984*	45
Patterson, Balfour <u>Patrick</u>	WI	15.9.1961		28	*1985–1992*	59
Payne, Thelston Rodney O'Neale.	WI	13.2.1957		1	*1985*	7
Paynter, Edward.	E	5.11.1901	5.2.1979	20	*1931–1939*	
Peall, Stephen Guy	Z	2.9.1969		4	*1993–1994*	21
Pearse, Charles <u>Ormerod</u> Cato	SA	10.10.1884	7.5.1953	3	*1910*	
Peate, Edmund	E	2.3.1855	11.3.1900	9	*1881–1886*	
Peebles, Ian Alexander Ross	E	20.1.1908	28.2.1980	13	*1927–1931*	
Peel, Robert.	E	12.2.1857	12.8.1941	20	*1884–1896*	
Pegler, Sidney James	SA	28.7.1888	10.9.1972	16	*1909–1924*	
Pellew, Clarence Everard	A	21.9.1893	9.5.1981	10	*1920–1921*	
Penn, Frank.	E	7.3.1851	26.12.1916	1	*1880*	
Perera, Anhettige <u>Suresh</u> Asanka	SL	16.2.1978		3	*1998–2001*	20
Perera, Panagodage Don <u>Ruchira</u> Laksiri	SL	6.4.1977		8	*1998–2002*	2
Perks, Reginald Thomas David	E	4.10.1911	22.11.1977	2	*1938–1939*	
Perry, Nehemiah Odolphus.	WI	16.6.1968		4	*1998–1999*	21
[2]**Pervez Sajjad**	P	30.8.1942		19	*1964–1972*	
Peterson, Robin John	SA	4.8.1979		5	*2003–2004*	21
Petherick, Peter James.	NZ	25.9.1942		6	*1976*	
Petrie, Eric Charlton	NZ	22.5.1927	14.8.2004	14	*1955–1965*	
Phadkar, Dattatraya Gajanan.	I	12.12.1925	17.3.1985	31	*1947–1958*	
Philipson, Hylton	E	8.6.1866	4.12.1935	5	*1891–1894*	
Phillip, Norbert	WI	12.6.1948		9	*1977–1978*	1
Phillips, Wayne Bentley	A	1.3.1958		27	*1983–1985*	48
Phillips, Wayne Norman.	A	7.11.1962		1	*1991*	
Philpott, Peter Ian.	A	21.11.1934		8	*1964–1965*	
Pierre, Lancelot Richard	WI	5.6.1921	14.4.1989	1	*1947*	
Pigott, Anthony Charles Shackleton . . .	E	4.6.1958		1	*1983*	
Pilling, Richard	E	5.7.1855	28.3.1891	8	*1881–1888*	
[2]**Pithey**, Anthony John	SA	17.7.1933		17	*1956–1964*	
[2]**Pithey**, David Bartlett	SA	4.10.1936		8	*1963–1966*	
Place, Winston	E	7.12.1914	25.1.2002	3	*1947*	
Playle, William Rodger	NZ	1.12.1938		8	*1958–1962*	
Plimsoll, Jack Bruce	SA	27.10.1917	11.11.1999	1	*1947*	
Pocock, Blair Andrew	NZ	18.6.1971		15	*1993–1997*	
Pocock, Patrick Ian	E	24.9.1946		25	*1967–1984*	1
Pollard, Richard	E	19.6.1912	16.12.1985	4	*1946–1948*	
Pollard, Victor	NZ	7.9.1945		32	*1964–1973*	3
[1, 2]**Pollock**, Peter Maclean	SA	30.6.1941		28	*1961–1969*	
[2]**Pollock**, Robert <u>Graeme</u>	SA	27.2.1944		23	*1963–1969*	
[1]**Pollock**, Shaun Maclean	SA	16.7.1973		92	*1995–2004*	221
Ponsford, William Harold MBE	A	19.10.1900	6.4.1991	29	*1924–1934*	
Ponting, Ricky Thomas	A	19.12.1974		85	*1995–2004*	209
Poole, Cyril John	E	13.3.1921	11.2.1996	3	*1951*	
Poore, Matt Beresford	NZ	1.6.1930		14	*1952–1955*	
Poore, Robert Montagu	SA	20.3.1866	14.7.1938	3	*1895*	
Pope, George Henry	E	27.1.1911	29.10.1993	1	*1947*	
Pope, Roland James	A	18.2.1864	27.7.1952	1	*1884*	
Pothecary, James Edward.	SA	6.12.1933		3	*1960*	
Pougher, Arthur <u>Dick</u>	E	19.4.1865	20.5.1926	1	*1891*	
Powell, Albert William.	SA	18.7.1873	11.9.1948	1	*1898*	
Powell, Daren Brentlyle	WI	15.4.1978		4	*2002–2002*	2
Powell, Ricardo Lloyd	WI	16.12.1978		2	*1999–2003*	102
Prabhakar, Manoj	I	15.4.1963		39	*1984–1995*	130
Prasad, Bapu Krishnarao <u>Venkatesh</u> . . .	I	5.8.1969		33	*1996–2001*	161
Prasad, Mannava Sri Kanth	I	24.4.1975		6	*1999*	17

[1] *Father and son(s).*   [2] *Brothers.*

	Country	Born	Died	Tests	Test Career	ODIs
Prasanna, Erapalli Anatharao Srinivas .	I	22.5.1940		49	*1961–1978*	
Pretorius, Dewald.	SA	6.12.1977		4	*2001–2003*	
Price, John Sidney Ernest.	E	22.7.1937		15	*1963–1972*	
Price, Raymond William	Z	12.6.1976		18	*1999–2003*	26
Price, Wilfred <u>Frederick</u> Frank	E	25.4.1902	13.1.1969	1	*1938*	
Prideaux, Roger Malcolm	E	31.7.1939		3	*1968–1968*	
Priest, Mark Wellings	NZ	12.8.1961		3	*1990–1997*	18
Prince, Ashwell Gavin.	SA	28.5.1977		7	*2001–2002*	3
Prince, Charles Frederick Henry	SA	11.9.1874	2.2.1949	1	*1898*	
Pringle, Christopher	NZ	26.1.1968		14	*1990–1994*	64
Pringle, Derek Raymond	E	18.9.1958		30	*1982–1992*	44
Pringle, Meyrick Wayne.	SA	22.6.1966		4	*1991–1995*	17
Procter, Michael John	SA	15.9.1946		7	*1966–1969*	
Promnitz, Henry Louis Ernest.	SA	23.2.1904	7.9.1983	2	*1927*	
Pullar, Geoffrey	E	1.8.1935		28	*1959–1962*	
Puna, Narotam.	NZ	28.10.1929	7.6.1996	3	*1965*	
Punjabi, Pananmal Hotchand	I	20.9.1921		5	*1954*	
Pushpakumara, Karuppiahyage						
Ravindra	SL	21.7.1975		23	*1994–2001*	31
Pycroft, Andrew John	Z	6.6.1956		3	*1992*	20
Qaiser Abbas.	P	7.5.1982		1	*2000*	
Qasim Omar.	P	9.2.1957		26	*1983–1986*	31
Quaife, William George	E	17.3.1872	13.10.1951	7	*1899–1901*	
Quinn, Neville Anthony.	SA	21.2.1908	5.8.1934	12	*1929–1931*	
Rabone, Geoffrey Osbourne	NZ	6.11.1921		12	*1949–1954*	
Rackemann, Carl Gray	A	3.6.1960		12	*1982–1990*	52
Radford, Neal Victor.	E	7.6.1957		3	*1986–1987*	6
Radley, Clive Thornton	E	13.5.1944		8	*1977–1978*	4
Rae, Allan Fitzroy.	WI	30.9.1922		15	*1948–1952*	
Rafiqul Islam	B	7.11.1977		1	*2002*	1
Ragoonath, Suruj	WI	22.3.1968		2	*1998*	
Rai Singh, Kanwar	I	24.2.1922		1	*1947*	
Rajindernath, Vijay	I	7.1.1928	22.11.1989	1	*1952*	
Rajinder Pal	I	18.11.1937		1	*1963*	
Rajin Saleh.	B	20.11.1983		14	*2003–2004*	27
Rajput, Lalchand Sitaram.	I	18.12.1961		2	*1985*	4
Raju, Sagi Lakshmi <u>Venkatapathy</u>	I	9.7.1969		28	*1989–2000*	53
Ramadhin, Sonny.	WI	1.5.1929		43	*1950–1960*	
Raman, Woorkeri Venkat	I	23.5.1965		11	*1987–1996*	27
Ramanayake, Champaka Priyadarshana						
Hewage.	SL	8.1.1965		18	*1987–1993*	62
Ramaswami, Cotar	I	16.6.1896	d unknown	2	*1936*	
Ramchand, Gulabrai Sipahimalani. . . .	I	26.7.1927	8.9.2003	33	*1952–1959*	
Ramesh, Sadagoppan.	I	16.10.1975		19	*1998–2001*	24
[2]**Ramiz Raja**	P	14.8.1962		57	*1983–1996*	198
[2]**Ramji,** Ladha	I	2.10.1902	20.12.1948	1	*1933*	
Ramnarine, Dinanath	WI	4.6.1975		12	*1997–2001*	4
Ramprakash, Mark Ravin	E	5.9.1969		52	*1991–2001*	18
Ranasinghe, Anura Nandana.	SL	13.10.1956	9.11.1998	2	*1981–1982*	9
[2]**Ranatunga,** Arjuna	SL	1.12.1963		93	*1981–2000*	269
[2]**Ranatunga,** Dammika.	SL	12.10.1962		2	*1989*	4
[2]**Ranatunga,** Sanjeeva	SL	25.4.1969		9	*1994–1996*	13
Ranchod, Ujesh	Z	17.5.1969		1	*1992*	3
Randall, Derek William	E	24.2.1951		47	*1976–1984*	49
Rangachari, Commandur						
Rajagopalachari.	I	14.4.1916	9.10.1993	4	*1947–1948*	
Rangnekar, Khanderao Moreshwar. . . .	I	27.6.1915	11.10.1984	3	*1947*	

[1] *Father and son.* [2] *Brothers.* [3] *Grandfather and grandson.*

	Country	Born	Died	Tests	Test Career	ODIs
Ranjane, Vasant Baburao	I	22.7.1937		7	*1958–1964*	
Ranjitsinhji, Kumar Shri	E	10.9.1872	2.4.1933	15	*1896–1902*	
Ransford, Vernon Seymour	A	20.3.1885	19.3.1958	20	*1907–1911*	
Rashid Khan	P	15.12.1959		4	*1981–1984*	29
Rashid Latif	P	14.10.1968		37	*1992–2003*	166
Rathore, Vikram	I	26.3.1969		6	*1996–1996*	7
Ratnayake, Rumesh Joseph	SL	2.1.1964		23	*1982–1991*	70
Ratnayeke, Joseph <u>Ravindran</u>	SL	2.5.1960		22	*1981–1989*	78
Ratra, Ajay	I	13.12.1981		6	*2001–2002*	12
Razdan, Vivek	I	25.8.1969		2	*1989*	3
Read, Christopher Mark Wells	E	10.8.1978		11	*1999–2003*	28
Read, Holcombe Douglas	E	28.11.1910	5.1.2000	1	*1935*	
Read, John <u>Maurice</u>	E	9.2.1859	17.2.1929	17	*1882–1893*	
Read, Walter William	E	23.11.1855	6.1.1907	18	*1882–1893*	
Reddy, Bharath	I	12.11.1954		4	*1979*	3
Redmond, Rodney Ernest	NZ	29.12.1944		1	*1972*	2
Redpath, Ian Ritchie MBE	A	11.5.1941		66	*1963–1975*	5
Reedman, John Cole	A	9.10.1865	25.3.1924	1	*1894*	
Reeve, Dermot Alexander OBE	E	2.4.1963		3	*1991*	29
Rege, Madhusudan Ramachandra	I	18.3.1924		1	*1948*	
Rehman, Sheikh <u>Fazalur</u>	P	11.6.1935		1	*1957*	
Reid, Bruce Anthony	A	14.3.1963		27	*1985–1992*	61
Reid, John Fulton	NZ	3.3.1956		19	*1978–1985*	25
Reid, John Richard OBE	NZ	3.6.1928		58	*1949–1965*	
Reid, Norman	SA	26.12.1890	6.6.1947	1	*1921*	
Reifer, Floyd Lamonte	WI	23.7.1972		4	*1996–1998*	2
Reiffel, Paul Ronald	A	19.4.1966		35	*1991–1997*	92
Relf, Albert Edward	E	26.6.1874	26.3.1937	13	*1903–1913*	
Renneberg, David Alexander	A	23.9.1942		8	*1966–1967*	
[2]**Rennie**, Gavin James	Z	12.1.1976		23	*1997–2001*	40
[2]**Rennie**, John Alexander	Z	29.7.1970		4	*1993–1997*	44
Rhodes, Harold James	E	22.7.1936		2	*1959*	
Rhodes, Jonathan Neil	SA	27.7.1969		52	*1992–2000*	245
Rhodes, Steven John	E	17.6.1964		11	*1994–1994*	9
Rhodes, Wilfred	E	29.10.1877	8.7.1973	58	*1899–1929*	
Riaz Afridi	P	21.1.1985		1	*2004*	
[2]**Richards**, Alfred Renfrew	SA	14.12.1867	9.1.1904	1	*1895*	
Richards, Barry Anderson	SA	21.7.1945		4	*1969*	
Richards, Clifton James ("Jack")	E	10.8.1958		8	*1986–1988*	22
Richards, *Sir* Isaac <u>Vivian</u> Alexander	WI	7.3.1952		121	*1974–1991*	187
[2]**Richards**, William Henry Matthews	SA	26.3.1862	4.1.1903	1	*1888*	
Richardson, Arthur John	A	24.7.1888	23.12.1973	9	*1924–1926*	
Richardson, David John	SA	16.9.1959		42	*1991–1997*	122
[2]**Richardson**, Derek Walter	E	3.11.1934		1	*1957*	
Richardson, Mark Hunter	NZ	11.6.1971		38	*2000–2004*	4
[2]**Richardson**, Peter Edward	E	4.7.1931		34	*1956–1963*	
Richardson, Richard Benjamin	WI	12.1.1962		86	*1983–1995*	224
Richardson, Thomas	E	11.8.1870	2.7.1912	14	*1893–1897*	
[4]**Richardson**, Victor York	A	7.9.1894	29.10.1969	19	*1924–1935*	
Richmond, Thomas Leonard	E	23.6.1890	29.12.1957	1	*1921*	
Rickards, Kenneth Roy	WI	22.8.1923	21.8.1995	2	*1947–1951*	
Ridgway, Frederick	E	10.8.1923		5	*1951*	
Rigg, Keith Edward	A	21.5.1906	28.2.1995	8	*1930–1936*	
Ring, Douglas Thomas	A	14.10.1918	23.6.2003	13	*1947–1953*	
Ritchie, Gregory Michael	A	23.1.1960		30	*1982–1986*	44
Rixon, Stephen John	A	25.2.1954		13	*1977–1984*	6
Rizwan-uz-Zaman	P	4.9.1961		11	*1981–1988*	3
Roach, Clifford Archibald	WI	13.3.1904	16.4.1988	16	*1928–1934*	
Roberts, Albert William	NZ	20.8.1909	13.5.1978	5	*1929–1937*	

[1] *Father and son(s).*   [2] *Brothers.*   [4] *Grandfather and grandsons.*

	Country	Born	Died	Tests	Test Career	ODIs
Roberts, Alphonso Theodore........	WI	18.9.1937	24.7.1996	1	*1955*	
Roberts, Anderson Montgomery Everton CBE	WI	29.1.1951		47	*1973–1983*	56
Roberts, Andrew Duncan Glenn	NZ	6.5.1947	26.10.1989	7	*1975–1976*	1
Roberts, Lincoln Abraham	WI	4.9.1974		1	*1998*	
Robertson, Gary Keith	NZ	15.7.1960		1	*1985*	10
Robertson, Gavin Ron...........	A	28.5.1966		4	*1997–1998*	13
Robertson, John Benjamin	SA	5.6.1906	5.7.1985	3	*1935*	
Robertson, John David Benbow	E	22.2.1917	12.10.1996	11	*1947–1951*	
Robertson, William Roderick	A	6.10.1861	24.6.1938	1	*1884*	
Robins, Robert *Walter* Vivian	E	3.6.1906	12.12.1968	19	*1929–1937*	
Robinson, Rayford Harold	A	26.3.1914	10.8.1965	1	*1936*	
Robinson, Richard Daryl	A	8.6.1946		3	*1977*	2
Robinson, Robert *Timothy*	E	21.11.1958		29	*1984–1989*	26
Rodriguez, William Vicente	WI	25.6.1934		5	*1961–1967*	
Rogers, Barney Guy	Z	20.8.1982		2	*2004*	7
Roope, Graham Richard James	E	12.7.1946		21	*1972–1978*	8
Root, Charles *Frederick*	E	16.4.1890	20.1.1954	3	*1926*	
Rorke, Gordon Frederick	A	27.6.1938		4	*1958–1959*	
Rose, Brian Charles.	E	4.6.1950		9	*1977–1980*	2
Rose, Franklyn Albert	WI	1.2.1972		19	*1996–2000*	27
Rose-Innes, Albert	SA	16.2.1868	22.11.1946	2	*1888*	
Routledge, Thomas William	SA	18.4.1867	9.5.1927	4	*1891–1895*	
[2]**Rowan**, Athol Matthew Burchell.....	SA	7.2.1921	22.2.1998	15	*1947 1951*	
[2]**Rowan**, Eric Alfred Burchell	SA	20.7.1909	30.4.1993	26	*1935–1951*	
Rowe, Charles *Gordon*............	NZ	30.6.1915	9.6.1995	1	*1945*	
Rowe, George Alexander	SA	15.6.1874	8.1.1950	5	*1895–1902*	
Rowe, Lawrence George.	WI	8.1.1949		30	*1971–1979*	11
Roy, Ambar	I	5.6.1945	19.9.1997	4	*1969*	
[1]**Roy**, Pankaj	I	31.5.1928	4.2.2001	43	*1951–1960*	
[1]**Roy**, Pranab	I	10.2.1957		2	*1981*	
Royle, Vernon Peter Fanshawe Archer..	E	29.1.1854	21.5.1929	1	*1878*	
Rudolph, Jacobus Andries	SA	4.5.1981		23	*2003–2004*	34
Rumsey, Frederick Edward	E	4.12.1935		5	*1964–1965*	
Rushmere, Mark Weir............	SA	7.1.1965		1	*1991*	4
Russell, Albert Charles	E	7.10.1887	23.3.1961	10	*1920–1922*	
Russell, Robert Charles ("Jack")	E	15.8.1963		54	*1988–1997*	40
Russell, William *Eric*...........	E	3.7.1936		10	*1961–1967*	
Rutherford, John Walter	A	25.9.1929		1	*1956*	
Rutherford, Kenneth Robert........	NZ	26.10.1965		56	*1984–1994*	121
Ryder, John.................	A	8.8.1889	3.4.1977	20	*1920–1928*	
[2]**Sadiq Mohammad**	P	3.5.1945		41	*1969–1980*	19
[2]**Saeed Ahmed**.................	P	1.10.1937		41	*1957–1972*	
Saeed Anwar.................	P	6.9.1968		55	*1990–2001*	247
Saggers, Martin John............	E	23.5.1972		3	*2003–2004*	
Saggers, Ronald Arthur	A	15.5.1917	17.3.1987	6	*1948–1949*	
[2]**St Hill**, Edwin Lloyd	WI	9.3.1904	21.5.1957	2	*1929*	
[2]**St Hill**, Wilton H.	WI	6.7.1893	d unknown	3	*1928–1929*	
Salah-ud-Din.................	P	14.2.1947		5	*1964–1969*	
Saleem Jaffer	P	19.11.1962		14	*1986–1991*	39
Salim Altaf	P	19.4.1944		21	*1967–1978*	6
[2]**Salim Elahi**	P	21.11.1976		13	*1995–2002*	48
Salim Malik	P	16.4.1963		103	*1981–1998*	283
Salim Yousuf.................	P	7.12.1959		32	*1981–1990*	86
Salisbury, Ian David Kenneth	E	21.1.1970		15	*1992–2000*	4
Salman Butt	P	7.10.1984		4	*2003–2004*	6
Samarasekera, Maitipage *Athula* Rohitha.	SL	5.8.1961		4	*1988–1991*	39

[1] *Father and son(s).*   [2] *Brothers.*

	Country	Born	Died	Tests	Test Career	ODIs
[2]**Samaraweera**, Dulip Prasanna	SL	12.2.1972		7	*1993–1994*	5
[2]**Samaraweera**, Thilan Thusara	SL	22.9.1976		24	*2001–2004*	14
Samuels, Marlon Nathaniel	WI	5.1.1981		19	*2000–2002*	53
Samuels, Robert George	WI	13.3.1971		6	*1995–1996*	8
Samuelson, Sivert Vause	SA	21.11.1883	18.11.1958	1	*1909*	
Sandham, Andrew	E	6.7.1890	20.4.1982	14	*1921–1929*	
Sandhu, Balwinder Singh	I	3.8.1956		8	*1982–1983*	22
Sanford, Adam	WI	12.7.1976		11	*2001–2003*	
Sangakkara, Kumar Chokshanada	SL	27.10.1977		44	*2000–2004*	123
Sanghvi, Rahul Laxman	I	3.9.1974		1	*2000*	10
Sanwar Hossain	B	5.8.1973		9	*2001–2003*	27
Saqlain Mushtaq	P	29.12.1976		49	*1995–2003*	169
Sarandeep Singh	I	21.10.1979		3	*2000–2001*	5
Sardesai, Dilip Narayan	I	8.8.1940		30	*1961–1972*	
Sarfraz Nawaz	P	1.12.1948		55	*1968–1983*	45
Sarwan, Ramnaresh Ronnie	WI	23.6.1980		50	*1999–2004*	73
Sarwate, Chandrasekhar Trimbak	I	22.6.1920	23.12.2003	9	*1946–1951*	
Saunders, John Victor	A	21.3.1876	21.12.1927	14	*1901–1907*	
Saxena, Ramesh Chandra	I	20.9.1944		1	*1967*	
Scarlett, Reginald Osmond	WI	15.8.1934		3	*1959*	
Schofield, Christopher Paul	E	6.10.1978		2	*2000*	
Schultz, Brett Nolan	SA	26.8.1970		9	*1992–1997*	1
Schultz, Sandford Spence	E	29.8.1857	18.12.1937	1	*1878*	
Schwarz, Reginald Oscar	SA	4.5.1875	18.11.1918	20	*1905–1912*	
[1]**Scott**, Alfred Homer Patrick	WI	29.7.1934		1	*1952*	
Scott, Henry James Herbert	A	26.12.1858	23.9.1910	8	*1884–1886*	
[1]**Scott**, Oscar Charles	WI	14.8.1892	15.6.1961	8	*1928–1930*	
Scott, Roy Hamilton	NZ	6.3.1917		1	*1946*	
Scott, Verdun John	NZ	31.7.1916	2.8.1980	10	*1945–1951*	
Scotton, William Henry	E	15.1.1856	9.7.1893	15	*1881–1886*	
Sealey, Benjamin James	WI	12.8.1899	12.9.1963	1	*1933*	
Sealy, James Edward Derrick	WI	11.9.1912	3.1.1982	11	*1929–1939*	
Seccull, Arthur William	SA	14.9.1868	20.7.1945	1	*1895*	
Sehwag, Virender	I	20.10.1978		31	*2001–2004*	106
Sekhar, Thirumalai Ananthanpillai	I	28.3.1955		2	*1982*	4
Selby, John	E	1.7.1849	11.3.1894	6	*1876–1881*	
Sellers, Reginald Hugh Durning	A	20.8.1940		1	*1964*	
Selvey, Michael Walter William	E	25.4.1948		3	*1976–1976*	
Sen, Probir Kumar	I	31.5.1926	27.1.1970	14	*1947–1952*	
Senanayake, Charith Panduka	SL	19.12.1962		3	*1990*	7
Sen Gupta, Apoorva Kumar	I	3.8.1939		1	*1958*	
Serjeant, Craig Stanton	A	1.11.1951		12	*1977–1977*	3
Sewell, David Graham	NZ	20.10.1977		1	*1997*	
Seymour, Michael Arthur	SA	5.6.1936		7	*1963–1969*	
Shabbir Ahmed	P	21.4.1976		7	*2003–2003*	29
Shackleton, Derek	E	12.8.1924		7	*1950–1963*	
Shadab Kabir	P	12.11.1977		5	*1996–2001*	3
Shafiq Ahmed	P	28.3.1949		6	*1974–1980*	3
[2]**Shafqat Rana**	P	10.8.1943		5	*1964–1969*	
Shah, Ali Hassimshah	Z	7.8.1959		3	*1992–1996*	28
Shahid Afridi	P	1.3.1980		15	*1998–2004*	191
Shahid Israr	P	1.3.1950		1	*1976*	
Shahid Mahboob	P	25.8.1962		1	*1989*	10
Shahid Mahmood	P	17.3.1939		1	*1962*	
Shahid Nazir	P	4.12.1977		8	*1996–1998*	17
Shahid Saeed	P	6.1.1966		1	*1989*	10
Shahriar Hossain	B	1.6.1976		3	*2000–2003*	20
Shakeel Ahmed, sen.	P	12.2.1966		1	*1998*	
Shakeel Ahmed, jun.	P	12.11.1971		3	*1992–1994*	2

[1] *Father and son.* [2] *Brothers.*

	Country	Born	Died	Tests	Test Career	ODIs
Shalders, William Alfred	SA	12.2.1880	18.3.1917	12	*1898–1907*	
Sharma, Ajay Kumar	I	3.4.1964		1	*1987*	31
Sharma, Chetan	I	3.1.1966		23	*1984–1988*	65
Sharma, Gopal.	I	3.8.1960		5	*1984–1990*	11
Sharma, Parthasarathy Harishchandra . .	I	5.1.1948		5	*1974–1976*	2
Sharma, Sanjeev Kumar	I	25.8.1965		2	*1988–1990*	23
Sharp, John.	E	15.2.1878	28.1.1938	3	*1909*	
Sharpe, Duncan Albert	P	3.8.1937		3	*1959*	
Sharpe, John William	E	9.12.1866	19.6.1936	3	*1890–1891*	
Sharpe, Philip John.	E	27.12.1936		12	*1963–1969*	
Shastri, Ravishankar Jayadritha	I	27.5.1962		80	*1980–1992*	150
Shaw, Alfred	E	29.8.1842	16.1.1907	7	*1876–1881*	
[5]**Sheahan,** Andrew <u>Paul</u>	A	30.9.1946		31	*1967–1973*	3
Shepherd, Barry Kenneth.	A	23.4.1937	17.9.2001	9	*1962–1964*	
Shepherd, John Neil	WI	9.11.1943		5	*1969–1970*	
Sheppard, *Rt. Rev. Lord* [David Stuart].	E	6.3.1929		22	*1950–1962*	
Shepstone, George Harold	SA	9.4.1876	3.7.1940	2	*1895–1898*	
Sherwell, Percy William.	SA	17.8.1880	17.4.1948	13	*1905–1910*	
Sherwin, Mordecai	E	26.2.1851	3.7.1910	3	*1886–1888*	
Shillingford, Grayson Cleophas	WI	25.9.1944		7	*1969–1971*	
Shillingford, Irvine Theodore	WI	18.4.1944		4	*1976–1977*	2
Shinde, Sadashiv Ganpatrao	I	18.8.1923	22.6.1955	7	*1946–1952*	
Shivnarine, Sewdatt	WI	13.5.1952		8	*1977–1978*	1
[1]**Shoaib Akhtar,**	P	13.8.1975		36	*1997–2004*	118
Shoaib Malik	P	1.2.1982		8	*2001–2004*	85
[1]**Shoaib Mohammad.**	P	8.1.1961		45	*1983–1995*	63
Shodhan, Roshan Harshadlal.	I	18.10.1928		3	*1952*	
Shrewsbury, Arthur.	E	11.4.1856	19.5.1903	23	*1881–1893*	
Shrimpton, Michael John Froud	NZ	23.6.1940		10	*1962–1973*	
Shuja-ud-Din Butt	P	10.4.1930		19	1954–*1961*	
Shukla, Rakesh Chandra	I	4.2.1948		1	*1982*	
Shuter, John	E	9.2.1855	5.7.1920	1	*1888*	
Shuttleworth, Kenneth.	E	13.11.1944		5	*1970–1971*	1
Sibanda, Vusimuzi	Z	10.10.1983		3	*2003–2004*	23
Siddiqui, Iqbal Rashid.	I	26.12.1974		1	*2001*	
[1]**Sidebottom,** Arnold	E	1.4.1954		1	*1985*	
[1]**Sidebottom,** Ryan Jay	E	15.1.1978		1	*2001*	2
Sidhu, Navjot Singh	I	20.10.1963		51	*1983–1998*	136
Siedle, Ivan Julian.	SA	11.1.1903	24.8.1982	18	*1927–1935*	
Sievers, Morris William	A	13.4.1912	10.5.1968	3	*1936*	
Sikander Bakht	P	25.8.1957		26	*1976–1982*	27
Silva, Kelaniyage <u>Jayantha</u>	SL	2.6.1973		7	*1995–1997*	1
Silva, Sampathawaduge <u>Amal</u> Rohitha. .	SL	12.12.1960		9	*1982–1988*	20
Silverwood, Christopher Eric Wilfred . .	E	5.3.1975		6	*1996–2002*	7
Simmons, Philip Verant	WI	18.4.1963		26	*1987–1997*	143
Simpson, Robert Baddeley	A	3.2.1936		62	*1957–1977*	2
Simpson, Reginald Thomas.	E	27.2.1920		27	*1948–1954*	
Simpson-Hayward, George Hayward . .	E	7.6.1875	2.10.1936	5	*1909*	
Sims, James Morton	E	13.5.1903	27.4.1973	4	*1935–1936*	
Sinclair, Barry Whitley	NZ	23.10.1936		21	*1962–1967*	
Sinclair, Ian McKay	NZ	1.6.1933		2	*1955*	
Sinclair, James Hugh.	SA	16.10.1876	23.2.1913	25	*1895–1910*	
Sinclair, Mathew Stuart	NZ	9.11.1975		25	*1999–2004*	43
Sincock, David John	A	1.2.1942		3	*1964–1965*	
Sinfield, Reginald Albert	E	24.12.1900	17.3.1988	1	*1938*	
Singh, Charran Kamkaran.	WI	27.11.1935		2	*1959*	
Singh, Rabindra Ramanarayan	I	14.9.1963		1	*1998*	136
Singh, Robin	I	1.1.1970		1	*1998*	
Sivaramakrishnan, Laxman	I	31.12.1965		9	*1982–1985*	16

[1] *Father and son(s).*   [2] *Brothers.*   [5] *Great-grandfather and great-grandson.*

	Country	Born	Died	Tests	Test Career	ODIs
Slack, Wilfred Norris.	E	12.12.1954	15.1.1989	3	*1985–1986*	2
Slater, Keith Nichol	A	12.3.1935		1	*1958*	
Slater, Michael Jonathon	A	21.2.1970		74	*1993–2001*	42
Sleep, Peter Raymond	A	4.5.1957		14	*1978–1989*	
Slight, James	A	20.10.1855	9.12.1930	1	*1880*	
Smailes, Thomas Francis	E	27.3.1910	1.12.1970	1	*1946*	
Small, Gladstone Cleophas	E	18.10.1961		17	*1986–1990*	53
Small, Joseph A.	WI	3.11.1892	26.4.1958	3	*1928–1929*	
Small, Milton Aster.	WI	12.2.1964		2	*1983–1984*	2
Smith, Alan Christopher CBE.	E	25.10.1936		6	*1962*	
Smith, Andrew Michael	E	1.10.1967		1	*1997*	
Smith, Cameron Wilberforce.	WI	29.7.1933		5	*1960–1961*	
Smith, Cedric Ivan James.	E	25.8.1906	9.2.1979	5	*1934–1937*	
Smith, Sir Charles Aubrey	E	21.7.1863	20.12.1948	1	*1888*	
Smith, Charles James Edward	SA	25.12.1872	27.3.1947	3	*1902*	
[2]**Smith**, Christopher Lyall	E	15.10.1958		8	*1983–1986*	4
Smith, David Bertram Miller	A	14.9.1884	29.7.1963	2	*1912*	
Smith, David Mark	E	9.1.1956		2	*1985*	2
Smith, David Robert	E	5.10.1934	17.12.2003	5	*1961*	
Smith, Denis	E	24.1.1907	12.9.1979	2	*1935*	
Smith, Devon Sheldon	WI	21.10.1981		10	*2002–2004*	7
Smith, Donald Victor.	E	14.6.1923		3	*1957*	
Smith, Dwayne Romel	WI	12.4.1983		6	*2003–2004*	20
Smith, Edward Thomas	E	19.7.1977		3	*2003*	
Smith, Ernest James	E	6.2.1886	31.8.1979	11	*1911–1913*	
Smith, Frank Brunton	NZ	13.3.1922	6.7.1997	4	*1946–1951*	
Smith, Frederick William	SA	31.3.1861	17.4.1914	3	*1888–1895*	
Smith, Graeme Craig.	SA	1.2.1981		33	*2001–2004*	56
Smith, Harry	E	21.5.1890	12.11.1937	1	*1928*	
Smith, Horace Dennis	NZ	8.1.1913	25.1.1986	1	*1932*	
Smith, Ian David Stockley	NZ	28.2.1957		63	*1980–1991*	98
Smith, Michael John Knight OBE	E	30.6.1933		50	*1958–1972*	
Smith, O'Neil Gordon ("Collie")	WI	5.5.1933	9.9.1959	26	*1954–1958*	
[2]**Smith**, Robin Arnold	E	13.9.1963		62	*1988–1995*	71
Smith, Steven Barry	A	18.10.1961		3	*1983*	28
Smith, Thomas Peter Bromley.	E	30.10.1908	4.8.1967	4	*1946–1946*	
Smith, Vivian Ian	SA	23.2.1925		9	*1947–1957*	
Smithson, Gerald Arthur	E	1.11.1926	6.9.1970	2	*1947*	
Snedden, Colin Alexander	NZ	7.1.1918		1	*1946*	
Snedden, Martin Colin	NZ	23.11.1958		25	*1980–1990*	93
Snell, Richard Peter.	SA	12.9.1968		5	*1991–1994*	42
[2]**Snooke**, Sibley John.	SA	1.2.1881	14.8.1966	26	*1905–1922*	
[2]**Snooke**, Stanley de la Courtte	SA	11.11.1878	6.4.1959	1	*1907*	
Snow, John Augustine	E	13.10.1941		49	*1965–1976*	9
Sobers, Sir Garfield St Aubrun	WI	28.7.1936		93	*1953–1973*	1
Sohoni, Sriranga Wasudev	I	5.3.1918	19.5.1993	4	*1946–1951*	
Solkar, Eknath Dhondu	I	18.3.1948		27	*1969–1976*	7
Solomon, Joseph Stanislaus	WI	26.8.1930		27	*1958–1964*	
Solomon, William Rodger Thomson	SA	23.4.1872	12.7.1964	1	*1898*	
Sood, Man Mohan	I	6.7.1939		1	*1959*	
Southerton, James	E	16.11.1827	16.6.1880	2	*1876*	
Sparling, John Trevor	NZ	24.7.1938		11	*1958–1963*	
Spearman, Craig Murray	NZ	4.7.1972		19	*1995–2000*	51
Spofforth, Frederick Robert	A	9.9.1853	4.6.1926	18	*1876–1886*	
Spooner, Reginald Herbert	E	21.10.1880	2.10.1961	10	*1905–1912*	
Spooner, Richard Thompson	E	30.12.1919	20.12.1997	7	*1951–1955*	
Srikkanth, Krishnamachari.	I	21.12.1959		43	*1981–1991*	146
Srinath, Javagal.	I	31.8.1969		67	*1991–2002*	229
Srinivasan, Thirumalai Echambadi.	I	26.10.1950		1	*1980*	2

[1] *Father and son(s).* [2] *Brothers.*

	Country	Born	Died	Tests	Test Career	ODIs
Stackpole, Keith Raymond MBE......	A	10.7.1940		43	*1965–1973*	6
Stanyforth, Ronald Thomas	E	30.5.1892	20.2.1964	4	*1927*	
Staples, Samuel James.............	E	18.9.1892	4.6.1950	3	*1927*	
Statham, John Brian CBE	E	17.6.1930	10.6.2000	70	*1950–1965*	
Stayers, Sven Conrad	WI	9.6.1937	6.1.2005	4	*1961*	
Stead, Gary Raymond	NZ	9.1.1972		5	*1998–1999*	
Steel, Allan Gibson..............	E	24.9.1858	15.6.1914	13	*1880–1888*	
Steele, David Stanley OBE.........	E	29.9.1941		8	*1975–1976*	1
Stephenson, John Patrick	E	14.3.1965		1	*1989*	
Stevens, Gavin Byron	A	29.2.1932		4	*1959*	
Stevens, Greville Thomas Scott	E	7.1.1901	19.9.1970	10	*1922–1929*	
Stevenson, Graham Barry...........	E	16.12.1955		2	*1979–1980*	4
[1]**Stewart**, Alec James OBE..........	E	8.4.1963		133	*1989–2003*	170
[1]**Stewart**, Michael James OBE	E	16.9.1932		8	*1962–1963*	
Stewart, Robert Burnard	SA	3.9.1856	12.9.1913	1	*1888*	
Steyn, Dale Willem	SA	27.6.1983		3	*2004*	
Steyn, Philippus Jeremia Rudolf	SA	30.6.1967		3	*1994*	1
Stirling, Derek Alexander..........	NZ	5.10.1961		6	*1984–1986*	6
Stoddart, Andrew Ernest	E	11.3.1863	3.4.1915	16	*1887–1897*	
[2]**Stollmeyer**, Jeffrey Baxter........	WI	11.4.1921	10.9.1989	32	*1939–1954*	
[2]**Stollmeyer**, Victor Humphrey.......	WI	24.1.1916	21.9.1999	1	*1939*	
Storer, William................	E	25.1.1867	28.2.1912	6	*1897–1899*	
[2]**Strang**, Bryan Colin.............	Z	9.6.1972		26	*1994–2001*	49
[2]**Strang**, Paul Andrew	Z	28.7.1970		24	*1994–2001*	95
Strauss, Andrew John	E	2.3.1977		12	*2004–2004*	22
Streak, Heath Hilton.............	Z	16.3.1974		59	*1993–2003*	183
Street, George Benjamin	E	6.12.1889	24.4.1924	1	*1922*	
Stricker, Louis Anthony...........	SA	26.5.1884	5.2.1960	13	*1909–1912*	
Strudwick, Herbert	E	28.1.1880	14.2.1970	28	*1909–1926*	
Strydom, Pieter Coenraad	SA	10.6.1969		2	*1999*	10
Stuart, Colin Ellsworth Laurie	WI	28.9.1973		6	*2000–2001*	5
[2]**Studd**, Charles Thomas...........	E	2.12.1860	16.7.1931	5	*1882–1882*	
[2]**Studd**, George Brown.............	E	20.10.1859	13.2.1945	4	*1882*	
Styris, Scott Bernard.............	NZ	10.7.1975		19	*2002–2004*	95
Su'a, Murphy Logo..............	NZ	7.11.1966		13	*1991–1994*	12
Subba Row, Raman CBE...........	E	29.1.1932		13	*1958–1961*	
Subramania, Venkataraman	I	16.7.1936		9	*1964–1967*	
Such, Peter Mark	E	12.6.1964		11	*1993–1999*	
Sugg, Frank Howe..............	E	11.1.1862	29.5.1933	2	*1888*	
Sunderam, Gundibali Rama	I	29.3.1930		2	*1955*	
Surendranath	I	4.1.1937		11	*1958–1960*	
Surti, Rusi Framroze............	I	25.5.1936		26	*1960–1969*	
Susskind, Manfred John...........	SA	8.6.1891	9.7.1957	5	*1924*	
Sutcliffe, Bert MBE	NZ	17.11.1923	20.4.2001	42	*1946–1965*	
Sutcliffe, Herbert	E	24.11.1894	22.1.1978	54	*1924–1935*	
Swamy, Venkataraman Narayan	I	23.5.1924	1.5.1983	1	*1955*	
Swetman, Roy	E	25.10.1933		11	*1958–1959*	
Symcox, Patrick Leonard	SA	14.4.1960		20	*1993–1998*	80
Symonds, Andrew...............	A	9.6.1975		2	*2003*	104
Taber, Hedley Brian	A	29.4.1940		16	*1966–1969*	
Taberer, Henry Melville...........	SA	7.10.1870	5.6.1932	1	*1902*	
Tahir Naqqash	P	6.7.1959		15	*1981–1984*	40
Taibu, Tatenda	Z	14.5.1983		18	*2001–2004*	71
Talat Ali Malik	P	29.5.1950		10	*1972–1978*	
Talha Jubair	B	10.12.1985		7	*2002–2004*	6
Tallon, Donald.................	A	17.2.1916	7.9.1984	21	*1945–1953*	
Tamhane, Narendra Shankar........	I	4.8.1931	19.3.2002	21	*1954–1960*	
[2]**Tancred**, Augustus Bernard	SA	20.8.1865	23.11.1911	2	*1888*	

[1] *Father and son(s).* [2] *Brothers.*

	Country	Born	Died	Tests	Test Career	ODIs
[2]Tancred, Louis Joseph	SA	7.10.1876	28.7.1934	14	*1902–1913*	
[2]Tancred, Vincent Maximillian	SA	7.7.1875	3.6.1904	1	*1898*	
Tapash Baisya	B	25.12.1982		20	*2002–2004*	43
[2]Tapscott, George Lancelot	SA	7.11.1889	13.12.1940	1	*1913*	
[2]Tapscott, Lionel Eric	SA	18.3.1894	7.7.1934	2	*1922*	
Tarapore, Keki Khurshedji	I	17.12.1910	15.6.1986	1	*1948*	
Tareq Aziz	B	4.9.1983		3	*2003–2004*	10
Taslim Arif	P	1.5.1954		6	*1979–1980*	2
[1]Tate, Frederick William	E	24.7.1867	24.2.1943	1	1902	
[1]Tate, Maurice William	E	30.5.1895	18.5.1956	39	*1924–1935*	
Tattersall, Roy	E	17.8.1922		16	*1950–1954*	
Taufeeq Umar	P	20.6.1981		22	*2001–2003*	18
Tauseef Ahmed	P	10.5.1958		34	*1979–1993*	70
Tavaré, Christopher James	E	27.10.1954		31	1980–1989	29
Tayfield, Hugh Joseph	SA	30.1.1929	24.2.1994	37	*1949–1960*	
Taylor, Alistair Innes	SA	25.7.1925		1	*1956*	
Taylor, Brendan Ross Murray	Z	6.2.1986		4	*2003–2004*	17
Taylor, Bruce Richard	NZ	12.7.1943		30	*1964–1973*	2
[2]Taylor, Daniel	SA	9.1.1887	24.1.1957	2	*1913*	
Taylor, Donald Dougald	NZ	2.3.1923	5.12.1980	3	*1946–1955*	
[2]Taylor, Herbert Wilfred	SA	5.5.1889	8.2.1973	42	*1912–1931*	
Taylor, Jaswick Ossie	WI	3.1.1932	13.11.1999	3	*1957–1958*	
Taylor, Jerome Everton	WI	22.6.1984		3	*2003–2003*	1
Taylor, John Morris	A	10.10.1895	12.5.1971	20	*1920–1926*	
Taylor, Jonathan Paul	E	8.8.1964		2	*1992–1994*	1
Taylor, Kenneth	E	21.8.1935		3	*1959–1964*	
Taylor, Leslie Brian	E	25.10.1953		2	1985	
Taylor, Mark Anthony	A	27.10.1964		104	*1988–1998*	113
Taylor, Peter Laurence	A	22.8.1956		13	*1986–1991*	83
Taylor, Robert William MBE	E	17.7.1941		57	*1970–1983*	27
Tendulkar, Sachin Ramesh	I	24.4.1973		120	*1989–2004*	342
Tennyson, *Lord* Lionel Hallam	E	7.11.1889	6.6.1951	9	*1913–1921*	
Terbrugge, David John	SA	31.1.1977		7	*1998–2003*	4
Terry, Vivian Paul	E	14.1.1959		2	1984	
Theunissen, Nicolaas Hendrik Christiaan de Jong	SA	4.5.1867	9.11.1929	1	*1888*	
Thomas, Grahame	A	21.3.1938		8	*1964–1965*	
Thomas, John Gregory	E	12.8.1960		5	*1985–1986*	3
Thompson, George Joseph	E	27.10.1877	3.3.1943	6	*1909–1909*	
Thompson, Patterson Ian Chesterfield	WI	26.9.1971		2	*1995–1996*	2
Thoms, George Ronald	A	22.3.1927	29.8.2003	1	*1951*	
Thomson, Alan Lloyd	A	2.12.1945		4	*1970*	1
Thomson, Jeffrey Robert	A	16.8.1950		51	*1972–1985*	50
Thomson, Keith	NZ	26.2.1941		2	*1967*	
Thomson, Nathaniel Frampton Davis	A	29.5.1839	2.9.1896	2	*1876*	
Thomson, Norman Ian	E	23.1.1929		5	*1964*	
Thomson, Shane Alexander	NZ	27.1.1969		19	*1989–1995*	56
Thornton, George	SA	24.12.1867	31.1.1939	1	*1902*	
Thorpe, Graham Paul	E	1.8.1969		98	*1993–2004*	82
Thurlow, Hugh Motley	A	10.1.1903	3.12.1975	1	*1931*	
Tillekeratne, Hashan Prasantha	SL	14.7.1967		83	*1989–2003*	200
Tindill, Eric William Thomas	NZ	18.12.1910		5	*1937–1946*	
Titmus, Frederick John MBE	E	24.11.1932		53	*1955–1974*	2
Tolchard, Roger William	E	15.6.1946		4	*1976*	1
Tomlinson, Denis Stanley	SA	4.9.1910	11.7.1993	1	*1935*	
Toohey, Peter Michael	A	20.4.1954		15	*1977–1979*	5
Toshack, Ernest Raymond Herbert	A	15.12.1914	11.5.2003	12	*1945–1948*	
[1]Townsend, Charles Lucas	E	7.11.1876	17.10.1958	2	*1899*	
[1]Townsend, David Charles Humphery	E	20.4.1912	27.1.1997	3	*1934*	

[1] *Father and son(s).* [2] *Brothers.*

	Country	Born	Died	Tests	Test Career	ODIs
Townsend, Leslie Fletcher	E	8.6.1903	17.2.1993	4	*1929–1933*	
Traicos, Athanasios John	SA, Z	17.5.1947		7	*1969–1992*	27
Travers, Joseph Patrick Francis	A	10.1.1871	15.9.1942	1	*1901*	
Tremlett, Maurice Fletcher	E	5.7.1923	30.7.1984	3	*1947*	
Trescothick, Marcus Edward	E	25.12.1975		59	2000–*2004*	92
Tribe, George Edward	A	4.10.1920		3	*1946*	
Trim, John	WI	25.1.1915	12.11.1960	4	*1947–1951*	
Trimborn, Patrick Henry Joseph	SA	18.5.1940		4	*1966–1969*	
[2]**Trott**, Albert Edwin	A, E	6.2.1873	30.7.1914	5	*1894–1898*	
[2]**Trott**, George Henry Stevens	A	5.8.1866	10.11.1917	24	*1888–1897*	
Troup, Gary Bertram	NZ	3.10.1952		15	*1976–1985*	22
Trueman, Frederick Sewards OBE	E	6.2.1931		67	1952–1965	
[2]**Trumble**, Hugh	A	12.5.1867	14.8.1938	32	1890–*1903*	
[2]**Trumble**, John William	A	16.9.1863	17.8.1944	7	*1884–1886*	
Trumper, Victor Thomas	A	2.11.1877	28.6.1915	48	*1899–1911*	
Truscott, Peter Bennetts	NZ	14.8.1941		1	*1964*	
Tsolekile, Thami Lungisa	SA	9.10.1980		3	*2004*	
[1]**Tuckett**, Lindsay	SA	6.2.1919		9	*1947–1948*	
[1]**Tuckett**, Lindsay Richard	SA	19.4.1885	8.4.1963	1	*1913*	
Tudor, Alex Jeremy	E	23.10.1977		10	*1998–2002*	3
Tuffey, Daryl Raymond	NZ	11.6.1978		22	*1999–2004*	73
Tufnell, Neville Charsley	E	13.6.1887	3.8.1951	1	*1909*	
Tufnell, Philip Clive Roderick	E	29.4.1966		42	*1990–2001*	20
Turnbull, Maurice Joseph Lawson	E	16.3.1906	5.8.1944	9	*1929–1936*	
Turner, Alan	A	23.7.1950		14	*1975–1976*	6
Turner, Charles Thomas Biass	A	16.11.1862	1.1.1944	17	*1886–1894*	
Turner, Glenn Maitland	NZ	26.5.1947		41	*1968–1982*	41
Tushar Imran	B	10.12.1983		3	*2002*	24
Twentyman-Jones, Percy Sydney	SA	13.9.1876	8.3.1954	1	*1902*	
Twose, Roger Graham	NZ	17.4.1968		16	*1995–1999*	87
[2]**Tyldesley**, Ernest	E	5.2.1889	5.5.1962	14	*1921–1928*	
[2]**Tyldesley**, John Thomas	E	22.11.1873	27.11.1930	31	*1898–1909*	
Tyldesley, Richard Knowles	E	11.3.1897	17.9.1943	7	*1924–1930*	
Tylecote, Edward Ferdinando Sutton . . .	E	23.6.1849	15.3.1938	6	*1882–1886*	
Tyler, Edwin James	E	13.10.1864	25.11.1917	1	*1895*	
Tyson, Frank Holmes	E	6.6.1930		17	1954–*1958*	
Ulyett, George	E	21.10.1851	18.6.1898	25	*1876–1890*	
Umar Gul	P	14.4.1984		5	*2003*	15
Umrigar, Pahlanji Ratanji	I	28.3.1926		59	*1948–1961*	
Underwood, Derek Leslie MBE	E	8.6.1945		86	*1966–1981*	26
Upashantha, Kalutarage Eric Amila . . .	SL	10.6.1972		2	*1998*–2002	12
Utseya, Prosper	Z	26.3.1985		1	*2003*	14
Vaas, Warnakulasuriya Patabendige Ushantha Joseph Chaminda	SL	27.1.1974		82	*1994–2004*	249
Valentine, Alfred Louis	WI	28.4.1930	11.5.2004	36	*1950–1961*	
Valentine, Bryan Herbert	E	17.1.1908	2.2.1983	7	*1933–1938*	
Valentine, Vincent Adolphus	WI	4.4.1908	6.7.1972	2	*1933*	
Vance, Robert Howard	NZ	31.3.1955		4	*1987–1989*	8
van der Bijl, Pieter Gerhard Vintcent . .	SA	21.10.1907	16.2.1973	5	*1938*	
van der Merwe, Edward Alexander . . .	SA	9.11.1903	26.2.1971	2	*1929–1935*	
van der Merwe, Peter Laurence	SA	14.3.1937		15	*1963–1966*	
Vandort, Michael Graydon	SL	19.1.1980		2	*2001–2002*	
van Jaarsveld, Martin	SA	18.6.1974		9	*2002–2004*	11
van Ryneveld, Clive Berrange	SA	19.3.1928		19	1951–*1957*	
Varnals, George Derek	SA	24.7.1935		3	*1964*	
Vaughan, Justin Thomas Caldwell	NZ	30.8.1967		6	*1992–1996*	18
Vaughan, Michael Paul	E	29.10.1974		55	*1999–2004*	60

[1] *Father and son(s).*   [2] *Brothers.*

	Country	Born	Died	Tests	Test Career	ODIs
Veivers, Thomas Robert	A	6.4.1937		21	*1963–1966*	
Veletta, Michael Robert John	A	30.10.1963		8	*1987–1989*	20
Vengsarkar, Dilip Balwant	I	6.4.1956		116	*1975–1991*	129
Venkataraghavan, Srinivasaraghavan	I	21.4.1946		57	*1964–1983*	15
Venkataramana, Margashayam	I	24.4.1966		1	*1988*	1
Verity, Hedley	E	18.5.1905	31.7.1943	40	*1931–1939*	
Vermeulen, Mark Andrew	Z	2.3.1979		8	*2002–2003*	32
Vernon, George Frederick	E	20.6.1856	10.8.1902	1	*1882*	
Vettori, Daniel Luca	NZ	27.1.1979		59	*1996–2004*	145
Viljoen, Dirk Peter	Z	11.3.1977		2	*1997–2000*	53
Viljoen, Kenneth George	SA	14.5.1910	21.1.1974	27	*1930–1948*	
Vincent, Cyril Leverton	SA	16.2.1902	24.8.1968	25	*1927–1935*	
Vincent, Lou	NZ	11.11.1978		15	*2001–2003*	62
Vine, Joseph	E	15.5.1875	25.4.1946	2	*1911*	
Vintcent, Charles Henry	SA	2.9.1866	28.9.1943	3	*1888–1891*	
Viswanath, Gundappa Rangnath	I	12.2.1949		91	*1969–1982*	25
Viswanath, Sadanand	I	29.11.1962		3	*1985*	22
[1]Vivian, Graham Ellery	NZ	28.2.1946		5	*1964–1971*	1
[1]Vivian, Henry Gifford	NZ	4.11.1912	12.8.1983	7	*1931–1937*	
Vizianagram, Maharaja Kumar of (Sir Vijaya Anand)	I	28.12.1905	2.12.1965	3	1936	
Voce, William	E	8.8.1909	6.6.1984	27	*1929–1946*	
Vogler, Albert Edward Ernest	SA	28.11.1876	9.8.1946	15	*1905–1910*	
Waddington, Abraham	E	4.2.1893	28.10.1959	2	*1920*	
[2]Wade, Herbert Frederick	SA	14.9.1905	23.11.1980	10	*1935–1935*	
[2]Wade, Walter Wareham	SA	18.6.1914	31.5.2003	11	*1938–1949*	
Wadekar, Ajit Laxman	I	1.4.1941		37	*1966–1974*	2
Wadsworth, Kenneth John	NZ	30.11.1946	19.8.1976	33	*1969–1975*	13
Wainwright, Edward	E	8.4.1865	28.10.1919	5	*1893–1897*	
Waite, John Henry Bickford	SA	19.1.1930		50	*1951–1964*	
Waite, Mervyn George	A	7.1.1911	16.12.1985	2	*1938*	
Wajahatullah Wasti	P	11.11.1974		6	*1998–1999*	15
Walcott, Sir Clyde Leopold	WI	17.1.1926		44	*1947–1959*	
Walcott, Leslie Arthur	WI	18.1.1894	27.2.1984	1	*1929*	
Walker, Brooke Graeme Keith	NZ	25.3.1977		5	*2000–2001*	11
Walker, Maxwell Henry Norman	A	12.9.1948		34	*1972–1977*	17
Walker, Peter Michael	E	17.2.1936		3	*1960*	
Wall, Thomas Welbourn	A	13.5.1904	26.3.1981	18	*1928–1934*	
Wallace, Philo Alphonso	WI	2.8.1970		7	*1997–1998*	33
Wallace, Walter Mervyn	NZ	19.12.1916		13	*1937–1952*	
Waller, Andrew Christopher	Z	25.9.1959		2	*1996*	39
Walmsley, Kerry Peter	NZ	23.8.1973		3	*1994–2000*	2
Walsh, Courtney Andrew	WI	30.10.1962		132	*1984–2000*	205
Walter, Kenneth Alexander	SA	5.11.1939		2	*1961*	
Walters, Cyril Frederick	E	28.8.1905	23.12.1992	11	*1933–1934*	
Walters, Francis Henry	A	9.2.1860	1.6.1922	1	*1884*	
Walters, Kevin Douglas MBE	A	21.12.1945		74	*1965–1980*	28
[2]Waqar Hassan	P	12.9.1932		21	*1952–1959*	
Waqar Younis	P	16.11.1971		87	*1989–2002*	262
Ward, Alan	E	10.8.1947		5	*1969–1976*	
Ward, Albert	E	21.11.1865	6.1.1939	7	*1893–1894*	
Ward, Francis Anthony	A	23.2.1906	25.3.1974	4	*1936–1938*	
Ward, Ian James	E	30.9.1972		5	*2001*	
Ward, John Thomas	NZ	11.3.1937		8	*1963–1967*	
Ward, Thomas Alfred	SA	2.8.1887	16.2.1936	23	*1912–1924*	
Wardle, John Henry	E	8.1.1923	23.7.1985	28	*1947–1957*	
Warnapura, Bandula	SL	1.3.1953		4	*1981–1982*	12

[1] *Father and son(s).* [2] *Brothers.*

	Country	Born	Died	Tests	Test Career	ODIs
Warnaweera, Kahakatchchi Patabandige Jayananda	SL	23.11.1960		10	*1985–1994*	6
Warne, Shane Keith	A	13.9.1969		120	*1991–2004*	193
Warner, *Sir* Pelham Francis	E	2.10.1873	30.1.1963	15	*1898–1912*	
Warr, John James	E	16.7.1927		2	*1950*	
Warren, Arnold	E	2.4.1875	3.9.1951	1	*1905*	
Washbrook, Cyril CBE	E	6.12.1914	27.4.1999	37	*1937–1956*	
Wasim Akram	P	3.6.1966		104	*1984–2001*	356
Wasim Bari	P	23.3.1948		81	*1967–1983*	51
Wasim Jaffer	I	16.2.1978		7	*1999–2002*	
[2]Wasim Raja	P	3.7.1952		57	*1972–1984*	54
Wassan, Atul Satish	I	23.3.1968		4	*1989–1990*	9
Watambwa, Brighton Tonderai	Z	9.6.1977		6	*2000–2001*	
Watkin, Steven Llewellyn	E	15.9.1964		3	*1991–1993*	4
Watkins, Albert John ("Allan")	E	21.4.1922		15	*1948–1952*	
Watkins, John Cecil	SA	10.4.1923		15	*1949–1956*	
Watkins, John Russell	A	16.4.1943		1	*1972*	
Watkinson, Michael	E	1.8.1961		4	*1995–1995*	1
Watson, Chester Donald	WI	1.7.1938		7	*1959–1961*	
Watson, Graeme Donald	A	8.3.1945		5	*1966–1972*	2
Watson, Shane Robert	A	17.6.1981		1	*2004*	27
Watson, William	NZ	31.8.1965		15	*1986–1993*	61
Watson, William James	A	31.1.1931		4	*1954*	
Watson, Willie	E	7.3.1920	23.4.2004	23	*1951–1958*	
Watt, Leslie	NZ	17.9.1924	15.11.1996	1	*1954*	
[2]Waugh, Mark Edward	A	2.6.1965		128	*1990–2002*	244
[2]Waugh, Stephen Rodger	A	2.6.1965		168	*1985–2003*	325
[1, 2]Wazir Ali, Syed	I	15.9.1903	17.6.1950	7	*1932–1936*	
[2]Wazir Mohammad	P	22.12.1929		20	*1952–1959*	
Webb, Murray George	NZ	22.6.1947		3	*1970–1973*	
Webb, Peter Neil	NZ	14.7.1957		2	*1979*	5
Webbe, Alexander Josiah	E	16.1.1855	19.2.1941	1	*1878*	
Weekes, *Sir* Everton de Courcy	WI	26.2.1925		48	*1947–1957*	
Weekes, Kenneth Hunnell	WI	24.1.1912	9.2.1998	2	*1939*	
Weerasinghe, Colombage Don Udesh Sanjeewa	SL	1.3.1968		1	*1985*	
Weir, Gordon Lindsay	NZ	2.6.1908	31.10.2003	11	*1929–1937*	
Wellard, Arthur William	E	8.4.1902	31.12.1980	2	*1937–1938*	
Wellham, Dirk Macdonald	A	13.3.1959		6	*1981–1986*	17
Wells, Alan Peter	E	2.10.1961		1	*1995*	1
Wesley, Colin	SA	5.9.1937		3	*1960*	
Wessels, Kepler Christoffel	A, SA	14.9.1957		40	*1982–1994*	109
Westcott, Richard John	SA	19.9.1927		5	*1953–1957*	
[2]Wettimuny, Mithra de Silva	SL	11.6.1951		2	*1982*	1
[2]Wettimuny, Sidath	SL	12.8.1956		23	*1981–1986*	35
Wharton, Alan	E	30.4.1923	26.8.1993	1	*1949*	
Whatmore, Davenell Frederick	A	16.3.1954		7	*1978–1979*	1
Whitaker, John James	E	5.5.1962		1	*1986*	2
White, Anthony Wilbur	WI	20.11.1938		2	*1964*	
White, Craig	E	16.12.1969		30	*1994–2002*	51
White, David John	NZ	26.6.1961		2	*1990*	3
White, David William	E	14.12.1935		2	*1961*	
White, Gordon Charles	SA	5.2.1882	17.10.1918	17	*1905–1912*	
White, John Cornish	E	19.2.1891	2.5.1961	15	*1921–1930*	
Whitelaw, Paul Erskine	NZ	10.2.1910	28.8.1988	2	*1932*	
Whitney, Michael Roy	A	24.2.1959		12	*1981–1992*	38
Whittall, Andrew Richard	Z	28.3.1973		10	*1996–1999*	63
Whittall, Guy James	Z	5.9.1973		46	*1993–2002*	147
Whitty, William James	A	15.8.1886	30.1.1974	14	1909–1912	

[1] *Father and son(s).*   [2] *Brothers.*

	Country	Born	Died	Tests	Test Career	ODIs
Whysall, William Wilfrid	E	31.10.1887	11.11.1930	4	*1924–1930*	
Wickremasinghe, Anguppulige Gamini Dayantha	SL	27.12.1965		3	*1989–1992*	4
Wickremasinghe, Gallage Pramodya	SL	14.8.1971		40	*1991–2000*	134
Wiener, Julien Mark	A	1.5.1955		6	*1979*	7
Wight, Claude Vibart	WI	28.7.1902	4.10.1969	2	*1928–1929*	
Wight, George Leslie	WI	28.5.1929	4.1.2004	1	*1952*	
Wijegunawardene, Kapila Indaka Weerakkody	SL	23.11.1964		2	*1991–1991*	26
Wijesuriya, Roger Gerard Christopher Ediriweera	SL	18.2.1960		4	*1981–1985*	8
Wijetunge, Piyal Kashyapa	SL	6.8.1971		1	*1993*	
Wiles, Charles Archibald	WI	11.8.1892	4.11.1957	1	*1933*	
Wilkinson, Leonard Litton	E	5.11.1916	3.9.2002	3	*1938*	
Willett, Elquemedo Tonito	WI	1.5.1953		5	*1972–1974*	
Willey, Peter	E	6.12.1949		26	*1976–1986*	26
Williams, Alvadon Basil	WI	21.11.1949		7	*1977–1978*	
Williams, Brad Andrew	A	20.11.1974		4	*2003*	25
Williams, David	WI	4.11.1963		11	*1991–1997*	36
Williams, Ernest Albert Vivian	WI	10.4.1914	13.4.1997	4	*1939–1947*	
Williams, Neil FitzGerald	E	2.7.1962		1	*1990*	
Williams, Stuart Clayton	WI	12.8.1969		31	*1993–2001*	57
Willis, Robert George Dylan MBE	E	30.5.1949		90	*1970–1984*	64
Willoughby, Charl Myles	SA	3.12.1974		2	*2003*	3
Willoughby, Joseph Thomas	SA	7.11.1874	11.3.1952	2	*1895*	
[2]**Wilson**, Clement Eustace Macro	E	15.5.1875	8.2.1944	2	*1898*	
Wilson, Donald	E	7.8.1937		6	*1963–1970*	
[2]**Wilson**, Evelyn Rockley	E	25.3.1879	21.7.1957	1	*1920*	
Wilson, John William	A	20.8.1921	13.10.1985	1	*1956*	
Wilson, Paul	A	12.1.1972		1	*1997*	11
Wimble, Clarence Skelton	SA	22.4.1861	28.1.1930	1	*1891*	
Winslow, Paul Lyndhurst	SA	21.5.1929		5	*1949–1955*	
Wiseman, Paul John	NZ	4.5.1970		22	*1997–2004*	15
Wishart, Craig Brian	Z	9.1.1974		25	*1995–2003*	89
Wishart, Kenneth Leslie	WI	28.11.1908	18.10.1972	1	*1934*	
Wood, Arthur	E	25.8.1898	1.4.1973	4	*1938–1939*	
Wood, Barry	E	26.12.1942		12	*1972–1978*	13
Wood, George Edward Charles	E	22.8.1893	18.3.1971	3	*1924*	
Wood, Graeme Malcolm	A	6.11.1956		59	*1977–1988*	83
Wood, Henry	E	14.12.1853	30.4.1919	4	*1888–1891*	
Wood, Reginald	E	7.3.1860	6.1.1915	1	*1886*	
Woodcock, Ashley James	A	27.2.1947		1	*1973*	1
Woodfull, William Maldon OBE	A	22.8.1897	11.8.1965	35	*1926–1934*	
Woods, Samuel Moses James	A, E	13.4.1867	30.4.1931	6	*1888–1895*	
Woolley, Frank Edward	E	27.5.1887	18.10.1978	64	*1909–1934*	
Woolley, Roger Douglas	A	16.9.1954		2	*1982–1983*	4
Woolmer, Robert Andrew	E	14.5.1948		19	*1975–1981*	6
Worrall, John	A	21.6.1860	17.11.1937	11	*1884–1899*	
Worrell, Sir Frank Mortimer Maglinne	WI	1.8.1924	13.3.1967	51	*1947–1963*	
Worthington, Thomas Stanley	E	21.8.1905	31.8.1973	9	*1929–1936*	
Wright, Charles William	E	27.5.1863	10.1.1936	3	*1895*	
Wright, Douglas Vivian Parson	E	21.8.1914	13.11.1998	34	*1938–1950*	
Wright, John Geoffrey MBE	NZ	5.7.1954		82	*1977–1992*	149
Wright, Kevin John	A	27.12.1953		10	*1978–1979*	5
Wyatt, Robert Elliott Storey	E	2.5.1901	20.4.1995	40	*1927–1936*	
Wynne, Owen Edgar	SA	1.6.1919	13.7.1975	6	*1948–1949*	
Wynyard, Edward George	E	1.4.1861	30.10.1936	3	*1896–1905*	
Yadav, Nandlal Shivlal	I	26.1.1957		35	*1979–1986*	7

[1] *Father and son(s).*   [2] *Brothers.*

	Country	Born	Died	Tests	Test Career	ODIs
Yadav, Vijay	I	14.3.1967		1	*1992*	19
Yajurvindra Singh	I	1.8.1952		4	*1976–1979*	
Yallop, Graham Neil	A	7.10.1952		39	*1975–1984*	30
Yardley, Bruce	A	5.9.1947		33	*1977–1982*	7
Yardley, Norman Walter Dransfield	E	19.3.1915	4.10.1989	20	*1938–1950*	
Yashpal Sharma	I	11.8.1954		37	*1979–1983*	42
Yasir Ali	P	15.10.1985		1	*2003*	
Yasir Hameed	P	28.2.1978		14	*2003–2004*	44
¹**Yograj** Singh	I	25.3.1958		1	*1980*	6
Yohannan, Tinu	I	18.2.1979		3	*2001–2002*	3
Young, Bryan Andrew	NZ	3.11.1964		35	*1993–1998*	74
Young, Harding Isaac	E	5.2.1876	12.12.1964	2	*1899*	
Young, John Albert	E	14.10.1912	5.2.1993	8	*1947–1949*	
Young, Richard Alfred	E	16.9.1885	1.7.1968	2	*1907*	
Young, Shaun	A	13.6.1970		1	*1997*	
²**Younis** Ahmed	P	20.10.1947		4	*1969–1986*	2
Younis Khan	P	29.11.1977		32	*1999–2004*	110
Yousuf Youhana	P	27.8.1974		56	*1997–2004*	181
Yuile, Bryan William	NZ	29.10.1941		17	*1962–1969*	
¹**Yuvraj** Singh	I	12.12.1981		6	*2003–2004*	111
Zaheer Abbas	P	24.7.1947		78	*1969–1985*	62
Zaheer Khan	I	7.10.1978		37	*2000–2004*	89
Zahid Fazal	P	10.11.1973		9	*1990–1995*	19
⁷**Zahoor** Elahi	P	1.3.1971		2	*1996*	14
Zakir Khan	P	3.4.1963		2	*1985–1989*	17
Zoehrer, Timothy Joseph	A	25.9.1961		10	*1985–1986*	22
Zondeki, Monde	SA	25.7.1982		1	*2003*	5
Zoysa, Demuni Nuwan Tharanga	SL	13.5.1978		30	*1996–2004*	88
Zulch, Johan Wilhelm	SA	2.1.1886	19.5.1924	16	*1909–1921*	
Zulfiqar Ahmed	P	22.11.1926		9	*1952–1956*	
Zulqarnain	P	25.5.1962		3	*1985*	16

See below for an explanation of family relationships not immediately apparent from a shared name.

Notes
In the same match, A. and G. G. Hearne played for England; their brother, F. Hearne, for South Africa.
The Waugh brothers are the only instance of Test-playing twins.
P. N. and G. Kirsten are half-brothers.
Amar Singh, L. is the brother of L. Ramji.
Azmat Rana is the brother of Shafqat Rana.
Chappell, G. S., Chappell I. M. and Chappell T. M. are the grandsons of V. Y. Richardson.
Collins, P. T. is the half-brother of F. H. Edwards.
Cooper, W. H. is the great-grandfather of A. P. Sheahan.
Edwards, F. H. is the half-brother of P. T. Collins.
Hanif Mohammad is the brother of Mushtaq Mohammad, Sadiq Mohammad and Wazir Mohammad, and the father of Shoaib Mohammad.
Jahangir Khan, M. is the father of Majid Khan.
Khalid Wazir is the son of S. Wazir Ali.
Majid Khan is the son of M. Jahangir Khan.
Manzoor Elahi is the brother of Salim Elahi and Zahoor Elahi.
Moin Khan is the brother of Nadeem Khan.
Mudassar Nazar is the son of Nazar Mohammad.
Mushtaq Mohammad is the brother of Hanif Mohammad, Sadiq Mohammad and Wazir Mohammad.
Nadeem Khan is the brother of Moin Khan.
Nazar Mohammad is the father of Mudassar Nazar.
Nazir Ali, S. is the brother of S. Wazir Ali.
Pervez Sajjad is the brother of Waqar Hassan.
Ramiz Raja is the brother of Wasim Raja.

---
¹ *Father and son(s).*   ² *Brothers.*

Ramji, L. is the brother of L. Amar Singh.
Richardson, V. Y. is the grandfather of G. S., I. M. and T. M. Chappell.
Sadiq Mohammad is the brother of Hanif Mohammad, Mushtaq Mohammad and Wazir Mohammad.
Saeed Ahmed is the half-brother of Younis Ahmed.
Salim Elahi is the brother of Manzoor Elahi and Zahoor Elahi.
Shafqat Rana is the brother of Azmat Rana.
Sheahan, A. P. is the great-grandson of W. H. Cooper.
Shoaib Mohammad is the son of Hanif Mohammad.
Waqar Hassan is the brother of Pervez Sajjad.
Wasim Raja is the brother of Ramiz Raja.
Wazir Ali, S. is the brother of S. Nazir Ali and the father of Khalid Wazir.
Wazir Mohammad is the brother of Hanif Mohammad, Mushtaq Mohammad and Sadiq Mohammad.
Yograj Singh is the father of Yuvraj Singh.
Younis Ahmed is the half-brother of Saeed Ahmed.
Yuvraj Singh is the son of Yograj Singh.
Zahoor Elahi is the brother of Manzoor Elahi and Salim Elahi.

ONE-DAY INTERNATIONAL CRICKETERS

The following players have appeared for Test-playing countries in one-day internationals by December 31, 2004, but had not represented their countries in Test matches by January 25, 2005:

England M. W. Alleyne (10), I. D. Austin (9), I. D. Blackwell (23), A. D. Brown (16), D. R. Brown (9), M. V. Fleming (11), P. J. Franks (1), I. J. Gould (18), A. P. Grayson (2), G. W. Humpage (3), T. E. Jesty (10), G. D. Lloyd (6), J. D. Love (3), M. A. Lynch (3), S. I. Mahmood (1), K. P. Pietersen (4), M. J. Prior (1), O. A. Shah (15), M. J. Smith (5), N. M. K. Smith (7), J. N. Snape (10), V. S. Solanki (31), G. P. Swann (1), J. O. Troughton (6), S. D. Udal (10), C. M. Wells (3), V. J. Wells (9), A. G. Wharf (11).

Australia G. A. Bishop (2), R. J. Campbell (2), M. J. Di Venuto (9), S. F. Graf (11), B. J. Haddin (7), I. J. Harvey (73), M. E. K. Hussey (1), S. Lee (45), R. J. McCurdy (11), K. H. MacLeay (16), J. P. Maher (26), G. D. Porter (2), J. D. Siddons (1), A. M. Stuart (3), G. S. Trimble (2), B. E. Young (6), A. K. Zesers (2).

South Africa S. Abrahams (1), D. M. Benkenstein (23), R. E. Bryson (7), D. J. Callaghan (29), D. N. Crookes (32), J-P. Duminy (5), J. C. Kent (2), L. J. Koen (5), J. A. Morkel (3), P. V. Mpitsang (2), S. J. Palframan (7), N. Pothas (3), C. E. B. Rice (3), M. J. R. Rindel (22), D. B. Rundle (7), T. G. Shaw (9), E. O. Simons (23), E. L. R. Stewart (6), R. Telemachus (33), M. N. van Wyk (1), C. J. P. G. van Zyl (2), H. S. Williams (7), M. Yachad (1).

West Indies H. A. G. Anthony (3), I. D. R. Bradshaw (16), D. Brown (3), B. St A. Browne (4), H. R. Bryan (15), R. S. Gabriel (11), R. C. Haynes (8), R. O. Hurley (9), K. C. B. Jeremy (6), R. S. Morton (2), M. R. Pydanna (3), R. Rampaul (17), D. J. G. Sammy (2), K. F. Semple (7), C. M. Tuckett (1), L. R. Williams (15).

New Zealand M. D. Bailey (1), B. R. Blair (14), C. E. Bulfin (4), T. K. Canning (3), P. G. Coman (3), C. D. Cumming (10), M. W. Douglas (6), P. G. Fulton (5), B. G. Hadlee (2), R. T. Hart (1), R. L. Hayes (1), P. A. Hitchcock (13), G. J. Hopkins (5), L. G. Howell (12), B. J. McKechnie (14), E. B. McSweeney (16), J. P. Millmow (5), C. J. Nevin (37), A. J. Penn (5), R. G. Petrie (12), R. B. Reid (9), S. J. Roberts (2), L. W. Stott (1), G. P. Sulzberger (3), A. R. Tait (5), M. D. J. Walker (3), R. J. Webb (3), J. W. Wilson (4), W. A. Wisneski (3).

India A. C. Bedade (13), A. Bhandari (2), Bhupinder Singh, sen. (2), G. Bose (1), V. B. Chandrasekhar (7), U. Chatterjee (3), N. A. David (4), P. Dharmani (1), M. S. Dhoni (3), R. S. Gavaskar (11), R. S. Ghai (6), Joginder Sharma (2), A. V. Kale (1), S. C. Khanna (10), G. K. Khoda (2), A. R. Khurasiya (12), T. Kumaran (8), J. J. Martin (10), A. Mishra (3), D. Mongia (49), S. P. Mukherjee (3), G. K. Pandey (2), J. V. Paranjpe (4), A. K. Patel (8), R. R. Powar (2), Randhir Singh (2), S. S. Raul (2), A. M. Salvi (4), L. R. Shukla (3), R. P. Singh (2), R. S. Sodhi (18), S. Somasunder (2), S. Sriram (8), Sudhakar Rao (1), P. S. Vaidya (4), J. P. Yadav (2).

Pakistan Aamer Hameed (2), Aamer Hanif (5), Akhtar Sarfraz (4), Arshad Pervez (2), Asif Mahmood (2), Bazid Khan (2), Faisal Athar (1), Ghulam Ali (3), Haafiz Shahid (3), Hasan Jamil (6), Iftikhar Anjum (2), Imran Abbas (2), Iqbal Sikandar (4), Irfan Bhatti (1), Javed Qadir (1), Junaid Zia (4), Kashif Raza (1), Mahmood Hamid (1), Mansoor Rana (2), Manzoor Akhtar (7), Maqsood Rana (1), Masood Iqbal (1), Moin-ul-Atiq (5), Mujahid Jamshed (4), Naeem Ahmed (1), Naeem Ashraf (2), Naseer Malik (3), Parvez Mir (3), Saadat Ali (8), Saeed Azad (4), Sajid Ali (13), Sajjad Akbar (2), Salim Pervez (1), Shahid Anwar (1), Shakil Khan (1), Sohail Fazal (2), Tanvir Mehdi (1), Wasim Haider (3), Yasir Arafat (2), Zafar Iqbal (8), Zahid Ahmed (2).

Sri Lanka J. W. H. D. Boteju (2), D. L. S. de Silva (2), G. N. de Silva (4), E. R. Fernando (3), T. L. Fernando (1), U. N. K. Fernando (2), J. C. Gamage (4), W. C. A. Ganegama (2), F. R. M. Goonatillake (1), P. W. Gunaratne (23), A. A. W. Gunawardene (1), P. D. Heyn (2), W. S. Jayantha (17), S. A. Jayasinghe (2), S. H. T. Kandamby (4), S. H. U. Karnain (19), K. M. D. N. Kulasekara (6), C. Mendis (1), A. M. N. Munasinghe (5), H. G. D. Nayanakantha (3), A. R. M. Opatha (5), S. P. Pasqual (2), K. G. Perera (1), H. S. M. Pieris (3), S. K. Ranasinghe (4), N. Ranatunga (2), N. L. K. Ratnayake (2), L. P. C. Silva (10), A. P. B. Tennekoon (4), M. H. Tissera (1), D. M. Vonhagt (1), A. P. Weerakkody (1), K. Weeraratne (11), S. R. de S. Wettimuny (3), R. P. A. H. Wickremaratne (3).

Zimbabwe R. D. Brown (7), C. K. Coventry (1), K. M. Curran (11), S. G. Davies (4), K. G. Duers (6), E. A. Essop-Adam (1), D. A. G. Fletcher (6), J. G. Heron (6), V. R. Hogg (2), A. J. Mackay (3), G. C. Martin (5), M. A. Meman (1), W. Mwayenga (3), G. A. Paterson (10), G. E. Peckover (3), E. C. Rainsford (5), P. W. E. Rawson (10), R. W. Sims (3).

Bangladesh Abdur Razzaq (5), Ahmed Kamal (1), Alam Talukdar (2), Aminul Islam, jun. (1), Anisur Rahman (2), Ather Ali Khan (19), Azhar Hussain (7), Faruq Ahmed (7), Faruq Chowdhury (2), Gazi Ashraf (7), Ghulam Faruq (3), Ghulam Nausher (9), Hafizur Rahman (2), Harunur Rashid (2), Jahangir Alam (3), Jahangir Badshah (5), Jamaluddin Ahmed (1), Mafizur Rahman (4), Mahbubur Rahman (1), Mazharul Haque (1), Minhazul Abedin (27), Moniruzzaman (2), Morshed Ali Khan (3), Nasir Ahmed (7), Neeyamur Rashid (2), Nurul Abedin (4), Rafiqul Alam (2), Raqibul Hassan (2), Saiful Islam (7), Sajjad Ahmed (2), Samiur Rahman (2), Shafiuddin Ahmed (11), Shahidur Rahman (1), Shariful Haq (1), Sheikh Salahuddin (6), Wahidul Gani (1), Zahid Razzak (3), Zakir Hassan (2).

A. Symonds appeared for Australia in 94 limited-overs internationals before making his Test debut.

BIRTHS AND DEATHS

OTHER CRICKETING NOTABLES

The following list shows the births and deaths of cricketers, and people associated with cricket, who have *not* played in Test matches.

Criteria for inclusion The following are included: all non-Test players who have either (1) been chosen as one of *Wisden's* Five Cricketers of the Year, or (2) scored 15,000 runs in first-class cricket, or (3) taken 1,000 first-class wickets, or (4) achieved 500 dismissals, or (5) reached *both* 10,000 runs *and* 500 wickets, or (6) achieved 10,000 runs or 500 wickets and have never played in the County Championship, or (7) taken 500 wickets if their career started in 1969 or later. It also includes (8) the leading players who flourished before the start of Test cricket and (9) all others deemed of sufficient merit or interest for inclusion, either because of their playing skill, their present position, their contribution to the game in whatever capacity or their fame in other walks of life.

Names Where players were normally known by a name other than their first, this is underlined.

Teams Where only one team is listed, this is normally the one for which the player made most first-class appearances. Additional teams are listed only if the player appeared for them in more than 20 first-class matches or if they are especially relevant to their career. School and university teams are not given unless especially relevant (e.g. for the schoolboys chosen as wartime Cricketers of the Year in the 1918 and 1919 *Wisdens*).

Abbreviations The following may not be obvious: ADBP – Agricultural Development Bank of Pakistan. HBFC – House Building Finance Corporation (Pakistan). KRL – Khan Research Laboratories (Pakistan). NBP – National Bank of Pakistan. OFS – Orange Free State (South Africa). PIA – Pakistan International Airlines. PNSC – Pakistan National Shipping Corporation.

	Teams	Born	Died
Abdur Raqib	Karachi, Habib Bank	18.11.1947	
Ackerman, Hylton Michael	Northants, W. Province	28.4.1947	
Adams, Percy Webster	Cheltenham, Sussex	5.9.1900	28.9.1962
Aird, Ronald MC	Hampshire	4.5.1902	16.8.1986
Secretary of MCC 1953–62; president of MCC 1968–69.			
Aislabie, Benjamin	Surrey	14.1.1774	2.6.1842
Secretary of MCC 1822–42; president of MCC 1823.			
Aitchison, *Rev.* James	Scotland	26.5.1920	13.2.1994
Alcock, Charles William	Secretary of Surrey 1872–1907	2.12.1842	26.2.1907
Editor, Cricket *magazine, 1882–1907. Captain of Wanderers and England football teams.*			
Aleem Dar	Lahore; ICC umpire	6.6.1968	
Alletson, Edwin Boaler	Nottinghamshire	6.3.1884	5.7.1963
Scored 189 in 90 minutes v Sussex at Hove in 1911.			
Alley, William Edward	NSW, Somerset; Test umpire	3.2.1919	26.11.2004
Alleyne, Mark Wayne MBE	Gloucestershire	23.5.1968	
Altham, Harry Surtees CBE	Surrey, Hampshire; historian	30.11.1888	11.3.1965
Coach at Winchester for 30 years; president of MCC 1959–60.			
Andrews, William Harry Russell	Somerset; coach	14.4.1908	9.1.1989
Arlott, Leslie Thomas <u>John</u> OBE	Broadcaster and writer	25.2.1914	14.12.1991
Armstrong, Norman Foster	Leicestershire	22.12.1892	19.1.1990
Arshad Pervez	Sargodha, Habib Bank	1.10.1953	
Ashdown, William Henry	Kent	27.12.1898	15.9.1979
The only cricketer to appear in English first-class cricket before and after the two wars.			
Ashley-Cooper, Frederick Samuel	Historian	22.3.1877	31.1.1932
Ashton, Sir Hubert	Camb. U., Essex; pres MCC 1960–61	13.2.1898	17.6.1979
Atkinson, Colin Ronald Michael CBE	Somerset	23.7.1931	25.6.1991
Atkinson, Graham	Somerset, Lancashire	29.3.1938	

	Teams	Born	Died
Austin, *Sir* Harold Bruce Gardiner	Barbados	15.7.1877	27.7.1943
Austin, Ian David	Lancashire	30.5.1966	
Aylward, James	Hampshire, All-England	1741	1827
Aymes, Adrian Nigel	Hampshire	4.6.1964	
Bailey, Jack Arthur	Essex; secretary of MCC 1974–87	22.6.1930	
Bainbridge, Philip	Gloucestershire, Durham	16.4.1958	
Baldwin, Herbert George	Surrey; Test umpire	16.3.1893	7.3.1969
Bannister, John David	Warwickshire; writer and broadcaster	23.8.1930	
Barclay, John Robert Troutbeck	Sussex	22.1.1954	
Barker, Gordon	Essex	6.7.1931	
Barling, Thomas Henry	Surrey	1.9.1906	2.1.1993
Barratt, Edward	Surrey	21.4.1844	27.2.1891
Bartlett, Hugh Tryon	Sussex	7.10.1914	26.6.1988
Bates, Leonard Ashton	Warwickshire	20.3.1895	11.3.1971
Bates, William <u>Ederick</u>	Yorkshire, Glamorgan	5.3.1884	17.1.1957
Beauclerk, *Rev. Lord* Frederick	Middlesex, Surrey, MCC	8.5.1773	22.4.1850
Bedser, Eric Arthur	Surrey	4.7.1918	
Beldam, George William	Middlesex; photographer	1.5.1868	23.11.1937
Beldam, William ("Silver Billy")	Hambledon, Surrey	5.2.1766	26.2.1862
Bellamy, Benjamin Walter	Northamptonshire	22.4.1891	22.12.1985
Bennett, Donald	Middlesex; coach	18.12.1933	
Bennett, George	Kent	12.2.1829	16.8.1886
Berry, Darren Shane	Victoria	10.12.1969	
Berry, Leslie George	Leicestershire	28.4.1906	5.2.1985
Berry, Scyld	Writer	28.4.1954	
Bestwick, William	Derbyshire; Test umpire	24.2.1875	2.5.1938
Bicknell, Darren John	Surrey, Nottinghamshire	24.6.1967	
Bird, Harold Dennis MBE	Yorkshire, Leicestershire; umpire	19.4.1933	
Blofeld, Henry Calthorpe OBE	Cambridge Univ; broadcaster	23.9.1939	
Bond, John David	Lancashire	6.5.1932	
Booth, Brian Joseph	Leicestershire	3.12.1935	
Booth, Roy	Yorkshire, Worcestershire	1.10.1926	
Boucher, James Chrysostom	Ireland	22.12.1910	25.12.1995
Bowden, Brent Fraser ("Billy")	ICC umpire	11.4.1963	
Bowell, Alexander	Hampshire	27.4.1880	28.8.1957
Bowler, Peter Duncan	Derbyshire, Somerset	30.7.1963	
Bowley, Frederick Lloyd	Worcestershire	9.11.1873	31.5.1943
Box, Thomas	Sussex	7.2.1808	12.7.1876
Boyes, George <u>Stuart</u>	Hampshire	31.3.1899	11.2.1973
Briers, Nigel Edwin	Leicestershire	15.1.1955	
Brittin, Janette Ann	England Women	4.7.1959	
Brooks, Edward William	Surrey	6.7.1898	10.2.1960
Brown, Anthony Stephen	Gloucestershire; administrator	24.6.1936	
Brown, Sydney Maurice	Middlesex	8.12.1917	28.12.1987
Bryan, Godfrey James CBE	Kent	29.12.1902	4.4.1991

The youngest player to hit a County Championship hundred, aged 17 years 247 days.

Bryan, John Lindsay	Kent, Cambridge Univ	26.5.1896	23.4.1985
Buchanan, John Marshall	Queensland; Australian coach 1999–	5.4.1953	
Bucknor, Stephen Anthony	ICC umpire	31.5.1946	

Umpire of 99 Tests up to January 2005, a record.

Bull, Frederick George	Essex	2.4.1875	16.9.1910
Buller, John <u>Sydney</u> MBE	Worcestershire; Test umpire	23.8.1909	7.8.1970
Burgess, Graham Iefvion	Somerset; umpire	5.5.1943	
Burns, Neil David	Somerset	19.9.1965	
Burnup, Cuthbert James	Kent	21.11.1875	5.4.1960
Buse, Herbert Francis Thomas	Somerset	5.8.1910	23.2.1992
Buss, Antony	Sussex	1.9.1939	
Buss, Michael Alan	Sussex	24.1.1944	
Byas, David	Yorkshire	26.8.1963	
Cadman, Samuel	Derbyshire	29.1.1877	6.5.1952

	Teams	Born	Died
Caesar, Julius	Surrey, All-England	25.3.1830	6.3.1878
Caffyn, William	Surrey	2.2.1828	28.8.1919
Calder, Harry Lawton	Cranleigh	24.1.1901	15.9.1995

The youngest-ever and longest-lived Wisden Cricketer of the Year.

	Teams	Born	Died
Cardus, *Sir* Neville	Writer	3.4.1888	27.2.1975
Carr, John Donald Middlesex; ECB director of cricket operations		15.6.1963	
Carrick, Phillip	Yorkshire	16.7.1952	11.1.2000
Chalk, Frederick *Gerald* Hudson	Kent	7.9.1910	17.2.1943
Chapple, Glen	Lancashire	23.1.1974	
Chester, Frank	Worcestershire; Test umpire	20.1.1895	8.4.1957

Stood in 48 Tests between 1924 and 1955, a record that lasted until 1992.

	Teams	Born	Died
Clark, Belinda Jane	Australia Women	10.9.1970	
Clark, David Graham	Kent; president of MCC 1977–78	27.1.1919	
Clarke, William	Nottinghamshire	24.12.1798	25.8.1856

Founded the All-England XI, Trent Bridge ground.

	Teams	Born	Died
Clarkson, Anthony	Somerset; umpire	5.9.1939	
Clayton, Geoffrey	Lancashire, Somerset	3.2.1938	
Clift, Patrick Bernard	Leicestershire	14.7.1953	3.9.1996
Cobbett, James	Surrey	12.1.1804	31.3.1842
Cobden, Frank Carroll	Cambridge Univ	14.10.1849	7.12.1932

Decided the 1870 University Match with a last-over hat-trick.

	Teams	Born	Died
Coe, Samuel	Leicestershire	3.6.1873	4.11.1955
Collier, David Gordon Chief Executive of ECB, 2005–		22.4.1955	
Collins, Arthur Edward Jeune	Clifton College	18.8.1885	11.11.1914

Made the highest score in any cricket, 628 in a house match in 1899.*

	Teams	Born	Died
Compton, Leslie Harry	Middlesex	12.9.1912	27.12.1984

England football international. Brother of Denis Compton.

	Teams	Born	Died
Conan Doyle, *Dr Sir* Arthur Ignatius	MCC	22.5.1859	7.7.1930

Creator of Sherlock Holmes; his only victim in first-class cricket was W. G. Grace.

	Teams	Born	Died
Connor, Cardigan Adolphus	Hampshire	24.3.1961	
Connor, Clare Joanne	England Women	1.9.1976	
Constable, Bernard	Surrey	19.2.1921	15.5.1997
Constant, David John	Kent, Leicestershire; Test umpire	9.11.1941	

36 seasons on first-class list 1969–2004, a record.

	Teams	Born	Died
Cook, Thomas Edwin Reed	Sussex	5.1.1901	15.1.1950
Cooper, Kevin Edwin	Nottinghamshire	27.12.1957	
Cornford, James Henry	Sussex	9.12.1911	17.6.1985
Corrall, Percy	Leicestershire	16.7.1906	23.2.1994
Cowley, Nigel Geoffrey	Hampshire; umpire	1.3.1953	
Cox, George, jun.	Sussex	23.8.1911	30.3.1985
Cox, George, sen.	Sussex	29.11.1873	24.3.1949
Cox, Jamie	Tasmania, Somerset	15.10.1969	
Cozier, Tony	Broadcaster and writer	10.7.1940	
Croom, Alfred John	Warwickshire	23.5.1896	16.8.1947
Curran, Kevin Malcolm	Zimbabwe, Glos, Northants	7.9.1959	
Cutmore, James Albert	Essex	28.12.1898	30.11.1985
Daft, Richard	Nottinghamshire, All-England	2.11.1835	18.7.1900
Dalmiya, Jagmohan	President of ICC 1997–2000	30.5.1940	
Daniell, John	Somerset	12.12.1878	24.1.1963
Davies, Dai	Glamorgan; Test umpire	26.8.1896	16.7.1976
Davies, Emrys	Glamorgan; Test umpire	27.6.1904	10.11.1975
Davies, Haydn George	Glamorgan	23.4.1912	4.9.1993
Davies, Jack Gale Wilmot *OBE* Kent; president of MCC 1985–86		10.9.1911	5.11.1992
Davis, Richard Peter Kent, Warwicks, Glos, Sussex, Leics		18.3.1966	29.12.2003
Davison, Brian Fettes Rhodesia, Leics, Tasmania, Gloucestershire		21.12.1946	
Dawkes, George Owen	Leicestershire, Derbyshire	19.7.1920	
Day, Arthur Percival	Kent	10.4.1885	22.1.1969
Dean, James, sen.	Sussex	4.1.1816	25.12.1881
Dennett, George	Gloucestershire	27.4.1880	14.9.1937
Deodhar, *Prof.* Dinakar Balwant	Maharashtra	14.1.1892	24.8.1993

	Teams	Born	Died
Dews, George	Worcestershire	5.6.1921	29.1.2003
Dodds, Thomas Carter ("Dickie")	Essex	29.5.1919	17.9.2001
Dorset, 3rd Duke of	Kent	24.3.1745	19.7.1799

Ambassador to France; organised tour of France 1789, abandoned due to revolution.

	Teams	Born	Died
Dudleston, Barry	Leicestershire; Test umpire	16.7.1945	
Dyson, Arnold Herbert	Glamorgan	10.7.1905	7.6.1978
Eagar, Edward <u>Desmond</u> Russell	Glos, Hants, administrator	8.12.1917	13.9.1977
Eagar, Edward <u>Patrick</u>	Photographer	9.3.1944	
East, David Edward	Essex; chief executive, 2000–	27.7.1959	
East, Raymond Eric	Essex	20.6.1947	
Eastman, Lawrence Charles	Essex	3.6.1897	17.4.1941
Edinburgh, *HRH Duke of*	President of MCC twice	10.6.1921	
Edrich, Geoffrey Arthur	Lancashire	13.7.1918	2.1.2004
Ehsan Mani	President, ICC 2003–	23.3.1945	
Ekanayake, Ajith Wijeratne	Kurunegala Youth	3.10.1965	
Elliott, Charles Standish MBE	Derbyshire; Test umpire	24.4.1912	1.1.2004
Evans, David Gwilym Lloyd	Glamorgan; Test umpire	27.7.1933	25.3.1990
Evans, Jeffrey Howard	Umpire	7.8.1954	
Fearnley, Charles <u>Duncan</u>	Worcestershire; bat-maker	12.4.1940	
"Felix" (Nicholas Wanostrocht)	Kent, Surrey, All-England	4.10.1804	3.9.1876

Batsman, artist, author (Felix on the Bat) and inventor of the Catapulta bowling machine.

	Teams	Born	Died
Ferguson, William Henry BEM	Scorer	6.6.1880	22.9.1957

Scorer and baggage-master for five Test teams on 43 tours over 52 years and "never lost a bag".

	Teams	Born	Died
Ferreira, Anthonie Michal	N. Transvaal, Warwickshire	13.4.1955	
Field, Frank Ernest	Warwickshire	23.9.1874	25.8.1934
Findlay, William	Lancashire	22.6.1880	19.6.1953

Secretary of Surrey 1907–19; secretary of MCC 1926–36.

	Teams	Born	Died
Firth, John D'Ewes Evelyn	Winchester, Oxford U, Nottinghamshire	21.1.1900	21.9.1957
Fitzpatrick, Cathryn Lorraine	Australia women	4.3.1968	
Fleming, Matthew Valentine	Kent	12.12.1964	
Fordham, Alan	Northants; ECB official	9.11.1964	
Foster, Henry Knollys	Oxford Univ, Worcestershire	30.10.1873	23.6.1950
Frindall, William Howard	Statistician	3.3.1939	
Frith, David Edward John	Writer	16.3.1937	
Gardner, Fred Charles	Warwickshire	4.6.1922	12.1.1979
Gibbons, Harold Harry Haywood	Worcestershire	8.10.1904	16.2.1973
Gibson, Clement Herbert	Sussex, Cambridge Univ, Argentina	23.8.1900	31.12.1976
Gillingham, *Canon* Frank Hay	Essex; broadcaster	6.9.1875	1.4.1953
Goel, Rajinder	Delhi, Haryana	20.9.1942	
Goonesena, Gamini	Ceylon, Nottinghamshire	16.2.1931	
Gore, Adrian Clements	Eton, Army	14.5.1900	7.6.1990
Gould, Ian James	Middlesex, Sussex; umpire	19.8.1957	
Grace, *Mrs* Martha	Mother and cricketing mentor of W.G.	18.7.1812	25.7.1884
Grace, William Gilbert	Gloucestershire; son of W.G.	6.7.1874	2.3.1905
Graveney, David Anthony	Gloucestershire, Somerset, Durham	2.1.1953	

Chairman of England selectors 1997–

	Teams	Born	Died
Gray, James Roy	Hampshire	19.5.1926	
Gray, Malcolm Alexander	President of ICC 2000–03	30.5.1940	
Green, David Michael	Lancashire, Gloucestershire	10.11.1939	
Green, *Major* Leonard	Lancashire	1.2.1890	2.3.1963
Gregory, Robert James	Surrey	26.8.1902	6.10.1973
Grieves, Kenneth James	New South Wales, Lancashire	27.8.1925	3.1.1992
Griffith, George	Surrey	20.12.1833	3.5.1879
Grundy, James	Nottinghamshire	5.3.1824	24.11.1873
Hair, Darrell Bruce	ICC umpire	30.9.1952	
Hall, Louis	Yorkshire	1.11.1852	19.11.1915
Hallam, Albert William	Lancashire, Nottinghamshire	12.11.1869	24.7.1940
Hallam, Maurice Raymond	Leicestershire	10.9.1931	1.1.2000
Hallows, James	Lancashire	14.11.1873	20.5.1910
Hamer, Arnold	Derbyshire	8.12.1916	3.11.1993

	Teams	Born	Died
Hardie, Brian Ross	Essex	14.1.1950	
Harper, Daryl John	ICC umpire	23.10.1951	
Harris, Charles Bowmar	Nottinghamshire	6.12.1907	8.8.1954
Harris, Michael John ("Pasty")	Middlesex, Notts; umpire	25.5.1944	
Harrison, Leo	Hampshire	8.6.1922	
Hartley, Alfred	Lancashire	11.4.1879	9.10.1918
Hartley, Peter John	Yorkshire, Hampshire; umpire	18.4.1960	
Harvey, Ian Joseph	Victoria, Gloucestershire, Yorkshire	10.4.1972	
Haygarth, Arthur	Sussex; historian	4.8.1825	1.5.1903
Hayward, Thomas	Cambridgeshire, All-England	21.3.1835	21.7.1876
Hearne, Thomas	Middlesex	4.9.1826	13.5.1900
Hedges, Bernard	Glamorgan	10.11.1927	
Hedges, Lionel Paget	Tonbridge, Kent, Oxford Univ, Glos	13.7.1900	12.1.1933
Henderson, Robert	Surrey	30.3.1865	29.1.1931
Herman, Oswald William	Hampshire; umpire	18.9.1907	24.6.1987
Hewett, Herbert Tremenheere	Somerset	25.5.1864	4.3.1921
Heyhoe-Flint, Rachael	England Women	11.6.1939	
Hide, Mary Edith ("Molly")	England Women	24.10.1913	10.9.1995
Hillyer, William Richard	Kent	5.3.1813	8.1.1861
First cricketer known to have performed the match double, 100 runs and ten wickets, in 1847.			
Hogg, Vincent Richard	Rhodesia/Zimbabwe; administrator	3.7.1952	
Holder, John Wakefield	Hampshire; Test umpire	19.3.1945	
Holmes, *Group Captain* Albert John	Sussex	30.6.1899	21.5.1950
Home of the Hirsel, Lord	Middx; President of MCC 1966–67	2.7.1903	9.10.1995
Prime Minister (as Sir Alec Douglas-Home) 1963–64.			
Horner, Norman Frederick	Warwickshire	10.5.1926	24.12.2003
Horton, Henry	Hampshire	18.4.1923	2.11.1998
Howard, Cecil Geoffrey	Middlesex; administrator	14.2.1909	8.11.2002
Hubble, John Charlton	Kent	10.2.1881	26.2.1965
Hughes, David Paul	Lancashire	13.5.1947	
Hughes, Simon Peter	Middx, Durham; broadcaster	20.12.1959	
Huish, Frederick Henry	Kent	15.11.1869	16.3.1957
Humpage, Geoffrey William	Warwickshire	24.4.1954	
Humphreys, Edward	Kent	24.8.1881	6.11.1949
Humphreys, Walter Alexander	Sussex, Hampshire	28.10.1849	23.3.1924
Hunt, Alma Victor OBE	Scotland, Bermuda	1.10.1910	3.3.1999
"The best cricketer ever to emerge from Bermuda" – Wisden.			
Hunter, David	Yorkshire	23.2.1860	11.1.1927
Hutchinson, James Metcalf	Derbyshire	29.11.1896	7.11.2000
Believed to be the longest-lived first-class cricketer at 103 years 344 days.			
Iddison, Roger	Yorkshire, Lancashire	15.9.1834	19.3.1890
Inchmore, John Darling	Worcestershire	22.2.1949	
Ingleby-Mackenzie, Alexander Colin David	Hampshire	15.9.1933	
President of MCC 1996–98.			
Inman, Clive Clay	Ceylon, Leicestershire	29.1.1936	
Hit 51 in eight minutes for Leicestershire v Nottinghamshire 1965.			
Iqbal Sikandar	Karachi, PIA	19.12.1958	
Iremonger, James	Nottinghamshire	5.3.1876	25.3.1956
Jackson, Guy Rolf	Derbyshire	23.6.1896	21.2.1966
Jackson, John	Nottinghamshire, All-England	21.5.1833	4.11.1901
Jackson, Percy Frederick	Worcestershire	11.5.1911	27.4.1999
Jackson, Victor Edward	NSW, Leicestershire	25.10.1916	30.1.1965
James, Cyril Lionel Robert	Writer	4.1.1901	31.5.1989
Jarvis, Kevin Bertram Sidney	Kent	23.4.1953	
Jayasinghe, Stanley	Ceylon, Leicestershire	19.1.1931	
Jeeves, Percy	Warwickshire	5.3.1888	22.7.1916
Jefferies, Stephen Thomas	Hants, Lancs, W. Province	8.12.1959	
Jennings, Raymond Vernon	Transvaal, N. Transvaal; South African coach 2004–	9.8.1954	
Jepson, Arthur	Nottinghamshire; Test umpire	12.7.1915	17.7.1997

	Teams	Born	Died
Jesty, Trevor Edward	Hampshire, Griqualand W, Surrey, Lancashire; umpire	2.6.1948	
Johnson, Graham William	Kent, Transvaal	8.11.1946	
Johnson, Paul	Nottinghamshire	24.4.1965	
Johnston, Brian Alexander CBE, MC	Broadcaster	24.6.1912	5.1.1994
Jones, Alan MBE	Glamorgan	4.11.1938	

Played once for England v Rest of the World, 1970, regarded at the time as a Test match.

	Teams	Born	Died
Jones, Allan Arthur	Sussex, Somerset, Middx, Glam; umpire	9.12.1947	
Jones, Eifion Wyn	Glamorgan	25.6.1942	
Julian, Raymond	Leicestershire; umpire	23.8.1936	
Key, *Sir* Kingsmill James	Surrey	11.10.1864	9.8.1932
Killick, Ernest Harry	Sussex	17.1.1875	29.9.1948
Kilner, Norman	Yorkshire, Warwickshire	21.7.1895	28.4.1979
King, John Barton	Philadelphia	19.10.1873	17.10.1965

"Beyond question the greatest all-round cricketer produced by America." – Wisden.

	Teams	Born	Died
Kitchen, Mervyn John	Somerset; Test umpire	1.8.1940	
Knight, Roger David Verdon	Surrey, Gloucestershire, Sussex	6.9.1946	
Secretary of MCC 1994–			
Knott, Charles James	Hampshire	26.11.1914	27.2.2003
Koertzen, Rudolf Eric	ICC umpire	26.3.1949	
Kortright, Charles Jesse	Essex	9.1.1871	12.12.1952
Krikken, Karl Matthew	Derbyshire	9.4.1969	
Kynaston, Roger	Middlesex; Secretary of MCC 1846–58	5.11.1805	21.6.1874
Lacey, *Sir* Francis Eden	Hants; Secretary of MCC 1898–1926	19.10.1859	26.5.1946
Lamb, Timothy Michael	Middlesex, Northants	24.3.1953	
Chief Executive of ECB, 1997–2004.			
Lambert, George Edward	Gloucestershire, Somerset	11.5.1918	31.10.1991
Lambert, Robert Hamilton	Ireland	18.7.1874	24.3.1956
Lambert, William	Surrey	1779	19.4.1851

The first batsman to score two hundreds in the same match.

	Teams	Born	Died
Lampitt, Stuart Richard	Worcestershire	29.7.1966	
Langford, Brian Anthony	Somerset	17.12.1935	
Langridge, John George MBE	Sussex; Test umpire	10.2.1910	27.6.1999
Lawrence, John	Somerset; coach	29.3.1914	10.12.1988
Leadbeater, Barrie	Yorkshire; umpire	14.8.1943	
Leary, Stuart Edward	Kent	30.4.1933	21.8.1988
Lee, Frank Stanley	Middlesex, Somerset; Test umpire	24.7.1905	30.3.1982
Lee, Garnet Morley	Nottinghamshire, Derbyshire	7.6.1887	29.2.1976
Lee, Peter Granville	Northamptonshire, Lancashire	27.8.1945	
Lefebvre, Roland Philippe	Somerset, Glamorgan, Holland	7.2.1963	
Lenham, Leslie John	Sussex; coach	24.5.1936	
Le Roux, Garth Stirling	Western Province, Sussex	4.9.1955	
Lester, Edward	Yorkshire; scorer	18.2.1923	
Lester, *Dr* John Ashby	Philadelphia	1.8.1871	3.9.1969
Lewis, Claude BEM	Kent; coach and scorer	27.7.1908	26.4.1993
Lilley, Ben	Nottinghamshire	11.2.1895	4.8.1950
Lillywhite, Fred	Sussex	23.7.1829	15.9.1866
Lillywhite, Frederick William	Sussex	13.6.1792	21.8.1854
Livingston, Leonard ("Jock")	NSW, Northamptonshire	3.5.1920	16.1.1998
Livsey, Walter Herbert	Hampshire	23.9.1893	12.9.1978
Llong, Nigel James	Kent; umpire	11.2.1969	
Lloyds, Jeremy William	Somerset, Gloucestershire; Test umpire	17.11.1954	
Lock, Herbert Christmas	Surrey; groundsman	8.5.1903	19.5.1978
Lockwood, Ephraim	Yorkshire	4.4.1845	19.12.1921
Long, Arnold	Surrey, Sussex	18.12.1940	
Longrigg, Edmund Fallowfield	Somerset	16.4.1906	23.7.1974
Lord, Thomas	Middlesex; founder of Lord's Cricket Ground	23.11.1755	13.1.1832
Love, James Derek	Yorkshire	22.4.1955	
Luckes, Walter Thomas	Somerset	1.1.1901	27.10.1982
Lynch, Monte Alan	Surrey, Gloucestershire	21.5.1958	

	Teams	Born	Died
Lyon, Beverley Hamilton	Gloucestershire	19.1.1902	22.6.1970
Lyon, Malcolm Douglas	Somerset	22.4.1898	17.2.1964
McCorkell, Neil Thomas	Hampshire	23.3.1912	
McCurdy, Rodney John	Victoria, E. Province	30.12.1959	
McEwan, Kenneth Scott	E. Province, Essex	16.7.1952	
McGilvray, Alan David	NSW; broadcaster	6.12.1909	17.7.1996
McIntyre, William	Lancashire	24.5.1844	13.9.1892
McKechnie, Brian John	Otago	6.11.1953	

Represented New Zealand at rugby and cricket (14 one-day internationals).

	Teams	Born	Died
MacLaurin of Knebworth, Lord	Chairman of ECB 1997–2002	30.3.1937	
MacLeay, Kenneth Hervey	W. Australia, Somerset	2.4.1959	
Majola, Khaya Eldridge	SA Council of Sport XI	17.5.1953	28.8.2000

Pioneer of non-racial cricket in South Africa.

	Teams	Born	Died
Majola, Mongezi Gerald	Chief executive, UCBSA	20.11.1959	
Manning, John Stephen	S. Australia, Northamptonshire	11.6.1923	5.5.1988
Mansoor Rana	Lahore, ADBP	27.12.1962	
Marchant, Francis	Kent	22.5.1864	13.4.1946
Marlar, Robin Geoffrey	Sussex; writer	2.1.1931	
Marner, Peter Thomas	Lancashire, Leicestershire	31.3.1936	
Marsh, Steven Andrew	Kent	27.1.1961	
Marshal, Alan	Queensland, Surrey	12.6.1883	23.7.1915
Martin, Sidney Hugh	Worcestershire, Natal	11.1.1909	17.2.1988
Martingell, William	Surrey	20.8.1818	29.9.1897
Martin-Jenkins, Christopher Dennis Alexander	Writer; broadcaster	20.1.1945	
Maru, Rajesh Jamandass	Hampshire	28.10.1962	
Mayer, Joseph Herbert	Warwickshire	2.3.1902	6.9.1981
Mendis, Gehan Dixon	Sussex, Lancashire	20.4.1955	
Mercer, John	Sussex, Glamorgan; coach and scorer	22.4.1893	31.8.1987
Merriman, Robert Frederick AO	Chmn, Cricket Australia 2001–	22.8.1935	
Metson, Colin Peter	Middlesex, Glamorgan	2.7.1963	
Meyer, Barrie John	Gloucestershire; Test umpire	21.8.1932	
Meyer, Rollo John Oliver OBE	Somerset	15.3.1905	9.3.1991
Millns, David James	Nottinghamshire, Leicestershire	27.2.1965	
Minshull, John	Kent, Surrey	c.1741	Oct 1793

Scorer of first recorded century: 107 for Duke of Dorset's XI v Wrotham, 1769.

	Teams	Born	Died
Mohammad Zahid	Bahawalpur, Allied Bank	12.8.1965	
Moles, Andrew James	Warwickshire	12.2.1961	
Moore, Denis Neville	Oxford Univ, Gloucestershire	26.9.1910	2.10.2003
Moore, Richard Henry	Hampshire	14.11.1913	1.3.2002
Moores, Peter	Sussex; coach	18.12.1962	
Morgan, Derek Clifton	Derbyshire	26.2.1929	
Morgan, Frederick David	Chairman of ECB 2003–	6.10.1937	
Mortensen, Ole Henrik	Denmark, Derbyshire	29.1.1958	
Morton, Arthur	Derbyshire	7.5.1883	19.12.1935
Moseley, Hallam Reynold	Somerset	28.5.1948	
Muncer, Bernard Leonard	Middlesex, Glamorgan; coach	23.10.1913	18.1.1982
Murrell, Harry Robert	Kent, Middlesex	19.11.1879	15.8.1952
Murtaza Hussain	Bahawalpur, KRL	20.12.1974	
Mycroft, William	Derbyshire	1.2.1841	19.6.1894
Mynn, Alfred	Kent, All-England	19.1.1807	1.11.1861
Nash, Malcolm Andrew	Glamorgan	9.5.1945	
Neale, Phillip Anthony	Worcestershire; England manager	5.6.1954	
Newman, John Alfred	Hampshire	12.11.1884	21.12.1973
Newstead, John Thomas	Yorkshire	8.9.1877	25.3.1952
Nicholas, Mark Charles Jefford	Hampshire; broadcaster	29.9.1957	
Nicholls, Ronald Bernard	Gloucestershire	4.12.1933	21.7.1994
Nixon, Paul Andrew	Leicestershire, Kent	21.10.1970	
Norman, Michael Eric John Charles	Northants, Leics	19.1.1933	
Nyren, John	Hampshire	15.12.1764	28.6.1837

Author of The Young Cricketer's Tutor, *1833.*

	Teams	Born	Died
Nyren, Richard	Hampshire	1734	25.4.1797
Proprietor Bat & Ball Inn, Broadhalfpenny Down.			
Oakes, Charles	Sussex	10.8.1912	
Oates, Thomas William	Nottinghamshire	9.6.1875	18.6.1949
Oldroyd, Edgar	Yorkshire	1.10.1888	27.12.1964
Ontong, Rodney Craig	Border, Glamorgan, N. Transvaal	9.9.1955	
Ormrod, Joseph *Alan*	Worcestershire, Lancashire	22.12.1942	
Outschoorn, Ladislaus	Worcestershire	26.9.1918	9.1.1994
Page, John *Colin* Theodore	Kent; coach	20.5.1930	14.12.1990
Palairet, Richard Cameron North	Somerset; administrator	25.6.1871	11.2.1955
Palmer, Roy	Somerset; Test umpire	12.7.1942	
Pardon, Sydney Herbert	Editor of *Wisden* 1891–1925	23.9.1855	20.11.1925
Parker, John Frederick	Surrey	23.4.1913	27.1.1983
Parks, Henry William	Sussex	18.7.1906	7.5.1984
Parks, Robert James	Hampshire	15.6.1959	
Parr, George	Nottinghamshire, All-England	22.5.1826	23.6.1891
Captain and manager of the All-England XI.			
Parsons, Gordon James	Leicestershire, OFS, Warwickshire	17.10.1959	
Parsons, *Canon* John Henry	Warwickshire	30.5.1890	2.2.1981
Partridge, Norman Ernest	Malvern, Cambridge U., Warwicks	10.8.1900	10.3.1982
Payton, Wilfred Richard Daniel	Nottinghamshire	13.2.1882	2.5.1943
Peach, Herbert *Alan*	Surrey; coach	6.10.1890	8.10.1961
Pearce, Thomas Neill	Essex; administrator	3.11.1905	10.4.1994
Pearson, Frederick	Worcestershire	23.9.1880	10.11.1963
Perkins, Henry	Cambridgeshire; secretary of MCC 1876–97	10.12.1832	6.5.1916
Perrin, Percival Albert	Essex	26.5.1876	20.11.1945
Phillips, Henry	Sussex	14.10.1844	3.7.1919
Pienaar, Roy Francois	Transvaal, N. Transvaal, W. Province, Natal	17.7.1961	
Pilch, Fuller	Norfolk, Kent	17.3.1804	1.5.1870
"The best batsman that has ever yet appeared" – Arthur Haygarth, 1862.			
Pilling, Harry	Lancashire	23.2.1943	
Piper, Keith John	Warwickshire	18.12.1969	
Pont, Keith Rupert	Essex; ECB director of development	16.1.1953	
Pooley, Edward	Surrey	13.2.1842	18.7.1907
Popplewell, *Hon. Sir* Oliver Bury	Camb U.; pres MCC 1994–96	15.8.1927	
Pressdee, James Stuart	Glamorgan, NE Transvaal	19.6.1933	
Preston, Kenneth Charles	Essex	22.8.1925	
Preston, Norman MBE	Editor of *Wisden* 1952–80	18.3.1903	6.3.1980
Prichard, Paul John	Essex	7.1.1965	
Pridgeon, Alan *Paul*	Worcestershire	22.2.1954	
Raees Mohammad	Karachi	24.12.1932	
His four brothers – Hanif, Mushtaq, Sadiq and Wazir – all played Test cricket.			
Rait-Kerr, *Colonel* Rowan Scrope	Europeans; sec. MCC 1936–52	13.4.1891	2.4.1961
Raja Afaq	Rawalpindi, ADBP	15.11.1956	
Rawson, Peter Walter Edward	Zimbabwe, Natal	25.5.1957	
Reeves, William	Essex; Test umpire	22.1.1875	22.3.1944
Relf, Robert Richard	Sussex	1.9.1883	28.4.1951
Revill, Alan Chambers	Derbyshire, Leicestershire	27.3.1923	6.7.1998
Reynolds, Brian Leonard	Northamptonshire	10.6.1932	
Rhodes, Albert Ennion Groucott	Derbyshire; Test umpire	10.10.1916	18.10.1983
Rice, Clive Edward Butler	Transvaal, Nottinghamshire	23.7.1949	
Riches, Norman Vaughan Hurry	Glamorgan	9.6.1883	6.11.1975
Ripley, David	Northamptonshire	13.9.1966	
Roberts, Frederick George	Gloucestershire; umpire	1.4.1862	7.4.1936
Roberts, William Braithwaite	Lancashire, Victory Tests	27.9.1914	24.8.1951
Robertson-Glasgow, Raymond Charles	Somerset; writer	15.7.1901	4.3.1965
Robins, Derrick Harold	Warwickshire; tour promoter	27.6.1914	3.5.2004
Robinson, Ellis Pembroke	Yorkshire, Somerset	10.8.1911	10.11.1998
Robinson, Emmott	Yorkshire; Test umpire	16.11.1883	17.11.1969
Robinson, Mark Andrew	Northamptonshire, Yorkshire, Sussex	23.11.1966	

	Teams	Born	Died
Robson, Ernest	Somerset	1.5.1870	23.5.1924
Roebuck, Peter Michael	Somerset; writer	6.3.1956	
Rogers, Neville Hamilton	Hampshire	9.3.1918	7.10.2003
Rose, Graham David	Somerset	12.4.1964	
Rotherham, Gerard Alexander	Rugby, Camb. U., Warwicks	28.5.1899	31.1.1985
Ryan, Francis	Hampshire, Glamorgan	14.11.1888	5.1.1954
Saadat Ali	HBFC, Pakistan Railways, United Bank	6.2.1955	
Sainsbury, Peter James	Hampshire	13.6.1934	
Sajid Ali	Karachi, National Bank	1.7.1963	
Sajjad Akbar	PNSC, Sargodha	1.3.1961	
Santall, Frederick Reginald	Warwickshire	12.7.1903	3.11.1950
Santall, Sydney	Warwickshire	10.6.1873	19.3.1957
Saville, Graham John	Essex; coach	5.2.1944	
Scott, Stanley Winckworth	Middlesex	24.3.1854	8.12.1933
Seccombe, Wade Anthony	Queensland	30.10.1971	
Sellers, Arthur Brian MBE	Yorkshire	5.3.1907	20.2.1981
Seymour, James	Kent	25.10.1879	30.9.1930
Shahid Anwar	Lahore, NBP	5.7.1968	
Sharp, George	Northamptonshire; Test umpire	12.3.1950	
Sharp, Harry Philip	Middlesex; scorer	6.10.1917	15.1.1995
Shaw, James Coupe	Nottinghamshire	11.4.1836	7.3.1888
Shepherd, David Robert MBE	Gloucestershire; ICC umpire	27.12.1940	
Shepherd, Donald John	Glamorgan	12.8.1927	
Shepherd, Thomas Frederick	Surrey	5.12.1889	13.2.1957
Shipman, Alan Wilfred	Leicestershire	7.3.1901	12.12.1979
Shipston, Frank William	Nottinghamshire	29.7.1906	
Believed to be the oldest living first-class cricketer at end of 2004.			
Shivalkar, Padmakar Kashinath	Bombay	14.4.1940	
Siddons, James Darren	Victoria, S. Australia	25.4.1964	
Sidwell, Thomas Edgar	Leicestershire	30.1.1888	8.12.1958
Silk, Dennis Raoul Whitehall CBE	Somerset	8.10.1931	
President of MCC 1992–94; chairman of TCCB 1994–96.			
Simmons, Jack MBE	Lancashire, Tasmania	28.3.1941	
Simons, Eric Owen	W. Province; S. African coach 2002–2004	9.3.1962	
Skelding, Alexander	Leicestershire; umpire	5.9.1886	17.4.1960
First-class umpire 1931–1958, when he was 72.			
Smales, Kenneth	Nottinghamshire	15.9.1927	
Small, John, sen.	Hampshire, All-England	19.4.1737	31.12.1826
Smedley, Michael John	Nottinghamshire	28.10.1941	
Smith, Edwin	Derbyshire	2.1.1934	
Smith, Haydon Arthur	Leicestershire	29.3.1901	7.8.1948
Smith, Michael John	Middlesex	4.1.1942	12.11.2004
Smith, Raymond	Essex	10.8.1914	21.2.1996
Smith, Sydney Gordon	Trinidad, Northamptonshire, Auckland	15.1.1881	25.10.1963
Smith, William Charles	Surrey	4.10.1877	15.7.1946
Speed, Malcolm Walter	Chief Executive of ICC 2001–	14.9.1948	
Spencer, Charles Terence	Leicestershire	18.8.1931	
Spencer, John	Sussex	6.10.1949	
Spencer, Thomas William OBE	Kent; Test umpire	22.3.1914	1.11.1995
Squires, Harry Stanley	Surrey	22.2.1909	24.1.1950
Staples, Arthur	Nottinghamshire	4.2.1899	9.9.1965
Steele, John Frederick	Leicestershire, Glamorgan; umpire	23.7.1946	
Stephenson, Franklyn Dacosta	Barbados, Notts, Sussex, OFS	8.4.1959	
Stephenson, George Robert	Hampshire	19.11.1942	
Stephenson, Harold William	Somerset	18.7.1920	
Stephenson, Heathfield Harman	Surrey, All-England	3.5.1832	17.12.1896
Captained first English team to Australia, 1861-62; umpired first Test in England, 1880.			
Stephenson, Lt-Col. John Robin CBE	Sec. MCC 1987–93	25.2.1931	2.6.2003
Stevens, Edward ("Lumpy")	Hampshire	c.1735	7.9.1819
Stewart, William James	Warwickshire	31.10.1934	

	Teams	Born	Died
Stone, James	Hampshire	29.11.1876	15.11.1942
Storey, Stewart James	Surrey; coach	6.1.1941	
Stovold, Andrew Willis	Gloucestershire	19.3.1953	
Street, James	Surrey	10.3.1839	17.9.1906
Studd, *Sir* John Edward Kynaston	Middlesex	26.7.1858	14.1.1944
Lord Mayor of London 1928–29; President of MCC 1930.			
Surridge, Walter Stuart	Surrey	3.9.1917	13.4.1992
Sutcliffe, William Herbert Hobbs	Yorkshire	10.10.1926	16.9.1998
Sutherland, James Alexander Vic.; CEO Cricket Australia 2001–	14.7.1965	
Suttle, Kenneth George	Sussex	25.8.1928	
Swanton, Ernest William CBE	Middlesex; writer	11.2.1907	22.1.2000
Tahir Rashid	Habib Bank, HBFC	21.11.1960	
Tarrant, Francis Alfred	Victoria, Middlesex	11.12.1880	29.1.1951
Taufel, Simon James Arthur	ICC umpire	21.1.1971	
Taylor, Brian	Essex	19.6.1932	
Taylor, Derek John Somerset	Somerset	12.11.1942	
Taylor, Derief David Samuel	Warwickshire; coach	10.9.1910	10.3.1987
Taylor, Neil Royston	Kent, Sussex	21.7.1959	
Taylor, Tom Launcelot	Cambridge Univ, Yorkshire	25.5.1878	16.3.1960
Tennekoon, Anura Punchi Banda	Sri Lanka	29.10.1946	
Thornton, Charles Inglis	Middlesex	20.3.1850	10.12.1929
Timms, Brian Stanley Valentine	Hampshire, Warwickshire	17.12.1940	
Timms, John Edward	Northamptonshire	3.11.1906	18.5.1980
Tissera, Michael Hugh	Sri Lanka	23.3.1939	
Todd, Leslie John	Kent	19.6.1907	20.8.1967
Tompkin, Maurice	Leicestershire	17.2.1919	27.9.1956
Trimble, Samuel Christy	Queensland	16.8.1934	
Tunnicliffe, John	Yorkshire	26.8.1866	11.7.1948
Turner, David Roy	Hampshire	5.2.1949	
Turner, Francis Michael MBE	Leicestershire; administrator	8.8.1934	
Turner, Robert Julian	Somerset	25.11.1967	
Turner, Stuart	Essex	18.7.1943	
Udal, Shaun David	Hampshire	18.3.1969	
Ufton, Derek Gilbert	Kent	31.5.1928	
van der Bijl, Vintcent Adriaan Pieter	Natal, Middx, Transvaal	19.3.1948	
van Geloven, Jack	Leicestershire; umpire	4.1.1934	21.8.2003
van Zyl, Cornelius Johannes Petrus Gerthardus	OFS, Glamorgan	1.10.1961	
Virgin, Roy Thomas	Somerset, Northamptonshire	26.8.1939	
Wade, Thomas Henry	Essex	24.11.1910	25.7.1987
Walden, Frederick Ingram ("Fanny")	Northants; Test umpire	1.3.1888	3.5.1949
Also played football for Tottenham Hotspur, Northampton Town and England; 5ft 2in tall.			
Walker, Isaac Donnithorne	Middlesex	8.1.1844	6.7.1898
Walker, Willis	Nottinghamshire	24.11.1892	3.12.1991
Walsh, John Edward	Leicestershire	4.12.1912	20.5.1980
Ward, William	Hampshire	24.7.1787	30.6.1849
Scorer of the first double-century: 278 for MCC v Norfolk, 1820.			
Wass, Thomas George	Nottinghamshire	26.12.1873	27.10.1953
Watson, Alexander	Lancashire	4.11.1844	26.10.1920
Watson, Frank	Lancashire	17.9.1898	1.2.1976
Watts, Patrick James	Northamptonshire	16.6.1940	
Webb, Rupert Thomas	Sussex	11.7.1922	
Webber, Roy	Statistician	23.7.1914	14.11.1962
Weigall, Gerald John Villiers	Kent; coach	19.10.1870	17.5.1944
Wells, Bryan Douglas ("Bomber")	Glos, Notts	27.7.1930	
Wells, Colin Mark	Sussex, Derbyshire	3.3.1960	
Wensley, Albert Frederick	Sussex	23.5.1898	17.6.1970
Wheatley, Oswald Stephen CBE	Warwickshire, Glamorgan	28.5.1935	
White, *Hon.* Luke Robert (Lord Annaly)	Middlesex, Victory Test	15.3.1927	30.9.1990
White, Robert Arthur	Middlesex, Nottinghamshire; umpire	6.10.1936	

	Teams	Born	Died
Whitehead, Alan Geoffrey Thomas	Somerset; Test umpire	28.10.1940	
Whitehead, Harry	Leicestershire	19.9.1874	14.9.1944
Whitington, Richard Smallpeice	S. Aust., Victory Tests; writer	30.6.1912	13.3.1984
Wight, Peter Bernard	Somerset; umpire	25.6.1930	
Wilkinson, Cyril Theodore Anstruther	Surrey	4.10.1884	16.12.1970
Hockey gold medallist at the 1920 Olympics.			
Willatt, Guy Longfield	Nottinghamshire, Derbyshire	7.5.1918	11.6.2003
Willsher, Edgar	Kent, All-England	22.11.1828	7.10.1885
Wilson, Arthur Edward ("Andy")	Gloucestershire	18.5.1910	29.7.2002
Wilson, Elizabeth Rebecca ("Betty")	Australia Women	21.11.1921	
Wilson, Jeffrey William	Otago	24.10.1973	
Represented New Zealand at rugby and cricket (four one-day internationals).			
Wilson, John Victor	Yorkshire	17.1.1921	
Wilson, Robert Colin	Kent	18.2.1928	
Wisden, John	Sussex	5.9.1826	5.4.1884
"The Little Wonder"; founder of Wisden Cricketers' Almanack, *1864.*			
Wood, Cecil John Burditt	Leicestershire	21.11.1875	5.6.1960
Woodcock, John Charles OBE	Writer; editor of *Wisden* 1981–86	7.8.1926	
Wooler, Wilfred	Glamorgan	20.11.1912	10.3.1997
Woolley, Claud Neville	Northamptonshire; Test umpire	5.5.1886	3.11.1962
Wootton, George	Nottinghamshire	16.10.1834	15.6.1924
Wright, Levi George	Derbyshire	15.6.1862	11.1.1953
Yachad, Mandy	Transvaal	17.11.1960	
Yarnold, Henry ("Hugo")	Worcestershire; Test umpire	6.7.1917	13.8.1974
Young, Douglas Martin	Worcestershire, Gloucestershire	15.4.1924	18.6.1993

HONOURS' LIST, 2004-05

In 2004-05, the following were decorated for their services to cricket:

Queen's Birthday Honours, 2004: C. J. Connor (England Women) MBE, W. H. Frindall (statistician; services to broadcasting and cricket) MBE.

Queen's Birthday Honours (Australia), 2004: J. A. Chapman (New South Wales Cricket Association) AM, P. D. Daffen (services to cricket administration) OAM, W. A. Deutrom (services to the Sri Lanka Cricket Foundation of Queensland) OAM, B. F. Freedman (services to cricket administration) OAM, D. A. Sloan (services to the Victorian Blind Cricket and Golf Association) OAM.

Queen's Birthday Honours (New Zealand), 2004: K. Ibadulla (Pakistan, Warwickshire, Otago and Tasmania) MNZM, C. Renwick (Auckland) MNZM, W. M. Wallace (Auckland and New Zealand) MNZM.

New Year's Honours, 2005: E. F. R. Pluck (Wanstead CC; services to cricket in Essex) MBE, G. R. Sandy (Hainault and Clayton CC; services to young people) MBE.

New Year's Honours (New Zealand), 2005: W. J. Henderson (services to cricket) MNZM.

Australia Day Honours, 2005: R. M. Artis (scorer; services to sport and the community) OAM, K. R. Miller (Victoria, New South Wales and Australia; services to sport as player, journalist and commentator, awarded posthumously, backdated to April 13, 2004) AM; M. E. Waugh (New South Wales and Australia) AM.

CRICKETERS OF THE YEAR, 1889–2005

1889   *Six Great Bowlers of the Year:* J. Briggs, J. J. Ferris, G. A. Lohmann, R. Peel, C. T. B. Turner, S. M. J. Woods.

1890   *Nine Great Batsmen of the Year:* R. Abel, W. Barnes, W. Gunn, L. Hall, R. Henderson, J. M. Read, A. Shrewsbury, F. H. Sugg, A. Ward.

1891   *Five Great Wicket-Keepers:* J. McC. Blackham, G. MacGregor, R. Pilling, M. Sherwin, H. Wood.

1892   *Five Great Bowlers:* W. Attewell, J. T. Hearne, F. Martin, A. W. Mold, J. W. Sharpe.

1893   *Five Batsmen of the Year:* H. T. Hewett, L. C. H. Palairet, W. W. Read, S. W. Scott, A. E. Stoddart.

1894   *Five All-Round Cricketers:* G. Giffen, A. Hearne, F. S. Jackson, G. H. S. Trott, E. Wainwright.

1895   *Five Young Batsmen of the Season:* W. Brockwell, J. T. Brown, C. B. Fry, T. W. Hayward, A. C. MacLaren.

1896   W. G. Grace.

1897   *Five Cricketers of the Season:* S. E. Gregory, A. A. Lilley, K. S. Ranjitsinhji, T. Richardson, H. Trumble.

1898   *Five Cricketers of the Year:* F. G. Bull, W. R. Cuttell, N. F. Druce, G. L. Jessop, J. R. Mason.

1899   *Five Great Players of the Season:* W. H. Lockwood, W. Rhodes, W. Storer, C. L. Townsend, A. E. Trott.

1900   *Five Cricketers of the Season:* J. Darling, C. Hill, A. O. Jones, M. A. Noble, Major R. M. Poore.

1901   *Mr R. E. Foster and Four Yorkshiremen:* R. E. Foster, S. Haigh, G. H. Hirst, T. L. Taylor, J. Tunnicliffe.

1902   L. C. Braund, C. P. McGahey, F. Mitchell, W. G. Quaife, J. T. Tyldesley.

1903   W. W. Armstrong, C. J. Burnup, J. Iremonger, J. J. Kelly, V. T. Trumper.

1904   C. Blythe, J. Gunn, A. E. Knight, W. Mead, P. F. Warner.

1905   B. J. T. Bosanquet, E. A. Halliwell, J. Hallows, P. A. Perrin, R. H. Spooner.

1906   D. Denton, W. S. Lees, G. J. Thompson, J. Vine, L. G. Wright.

1907   J. N. Crawford, A. Fielder, E. G. Hayes, K. L. Hutchings, N. A. Knox.

1908   A. W. Hallam, R. O. Schwarz, F. A. Tarrant, A. E. E. Vogler, T. G. Wass.

1909   *Lord Hawke and Four Cricketers of the Year:* W. Brearley, Lord Hawke, J. B. Hobbs, A. Marshal, J. T. Newstead.

1910   W. Bardsley, S. F. Barnes, D. W. Carr, A. P. Day, V. S. Ransford.

1911   H. K. Foster, A. Hartley, C. B. Llewellyn, W. C. Smith, F. E. Woolley.

1912   *Five Members of the MCC's Team in Australia:* F. R. Foster, J. W. Hearne, S. P. Kinneir, C. P. Mead, H. Strudwick.

1913   John Wisden: Personal Recollections.

1914   M. W. Booth, G. Gunn, J. W. Hitch, A. E. Relf, Hon. L. H. Tennyson.

1915   J. W. H. T. Douglas, P. G. H. Fender, H. T. W. Hardinge, D. J. Knight, S. G. Smith.

1916–17 No portraits appeared.

1918   *School Bowlers of the Year:* H. L. Calder, J. E. D'E. Firth, C. H. Gibson, G. A. Rotherham, G. T. S. Stevens.

1919   *Five Public School Cricketers of the Year:* P. W. Adams, A. P. F. Chapman, A. C. Gore, L. P. Hedges, N. E. Partridge.

1920   *Five Batsmen of the Year:* A. Ducat, E. H. Hendren, P. Holmes, H. Sutcliffe, E. Tyldesley.

1921   P. F. Warner.

1922   H. Ashton, J. L. Bryan, J. M. Gregory, C. G. Macartney, E. A. McDonald.

1923   A. W. Carr, A. P. Freeman, C. W. L. Parker, A. C. Russell, A. Sandham.

1924   *Five Bowlers of the Year:* A. E. R. Gilligan, R. Kilner, G. G. Macaulay, C. H. Parkin, M. W. Tate.

1925   R. H. Catterall, J. C. W. MacBryan, H. W. Taylor, R. K. Tyldesley, W. W. Whysall.

1926   J. B. Hobbs.

1927   G. Geary, H. Larwood, J. Mercer, W. A. Oldfield, W. M. Woodfull.

1928   R. C. Blunt, C. Hallows, W. R. Hammond, D. R. Jardine, V. W. C. Jupp.

1929   L. E. G. Ames, G. Duckworth, M. Leyland, S. J. Staples, J. C. White.

1930   E. H. Bowley, K. S. Duleepsinhji, H. G. Owen-Smith, R. W. V. Robins, R. E. S. Wyatt.

1931	D. G. Bradman, C. V. Grimmett, B. H. Lyon, I. A. R. Peebles, M. J. Turnbull.
1932	W. E. Bowes, C. S. Dempster, James Langridge, Nawab of Pataudi sen., H. Verity.
1933	W. E. Astill, F. R. Brown, A. S. Kennedy, C. K. Nayudu, W. Voce.
1934	A. H. Bakewell, G. A. Headley, M. S. Nichols, L. F. Townsend, C. F. Walters.
1935	S. J. McCabe, W. J. O'Reilly, G. A. E. Paine, W. H. Ponsford, C. I. J. Smith.
1936	H. B. Cameron, E. R. T. Holmes, B. Mitchell, D. Smith, A. W. Wellard.
1937	C. J. Barnett, W. H. Copson, A. R. Gover, V. M. Merchant, T. S. Worthington.
1938	T. W. J. Goddard, J. Hardstaff jun., L. Hutton, J. H. Parks, E. Paynter.
1939	H. T. Bartlett, W. A. Brown, D. C. S. Compton, K. Farnes, A. Wood.
1940	L. N. Constantine, W. J. Edrich, W. W. Keeton, A. B. Sellers, D. V. P. Wright.
1941–46	No portraits appeared.
1947	A. V. Bedser, L. B. Fishlock, V. (M. H.) Mankad, T. P. B. Smith, C. Washbrook.
1948	M. P. Donnelly, A. Melville, A. D. Nourse, J. D. Robertson, N. W. D. Yardley.
1949	A. L. Hassett, W. A. Johnston, R. R. Lindwall, A. R. Morris, D. Tallon.
1950	T. E. Bailey, R. O. Jenkins, John Langridge, R. T. Simpson, B. Sutcliffe.
1951	T. G. Evans, S. Ramadhin, J. A. Valentine, E. D. Weekes, F. M. M. Worrell.
1952	R. Appleyard, H. E. Dollery, J. C. Laker, P. B. H. May, E. A. B. Rowan.
1953	H. Gimblett, T. W. Graveney, D. S. Sheppard, W. S. Surridge, F. S. Trueman.
1954	R. N. Harvey, G. A. R. Lock, K. R. Miller, J. H. Wardle, W. Watson.
1955	B. Dooland, Fazal Mahmood, W. E. Hollies, J. B. Statham, G. E. Tribe.
1956	M. C. Cowdrey, D. J. Insole, D. J. McGlew, H. J. Tayfield, F. H. Tyson.
1957	D. Brookes, J. W. Burke, M. J. Hilton, G. R. A. Langley, P. E. Richardson.
1958	P. J. Loader, A. J. McIntyre, O. G. Smith, M. J. Stewart, C. L. Walcott.
1959	H. L. Jackson, R. E. Marshall, C. A. Milton, I. R. Reid, D. Shackleton.
1960	K. F. Barrington, D. B. Carr, R. Illingworth, G. Pullar, M. J. K. Smith.
1961	N. A. T. Adcock, E. R. Dexter, R. A. McLean, R. Subba Row, J. V. Wilson.
1962	W. E. Alley, R. Benaud, A. K. Davidson, W. M. Lawry, N. C. O'Neill.
1963	D. Kenyon, Mushtaq Mohammad, P. H. Parfitt, P. J. Sharpe, F. J. Titmus.
1964	D. B. Close, C. C. Griffith, C. C. Hunte, R. B. Kanhai, G. S. Sobers.
1965	G. Boycott, P. J. Burge, J. A. Flavell, G. D. McKenzie, R. B. Simpson.
1966	K. C. Bland, J. H. Edrich, R. C. Motz, P. M. Pollock, R. G. Pollock.
1967	R. W. Barber, B. L. D'Oliveira, C. Milburn, J. T. Murray, S. M. Nurse.
1968	Asif Iqbal, Hanif Mohammad, K. Higgs, J. M. Parks, Nawab of Pataudi jun.
1969	J. G. Binks, D. M. Green, B. A. Richards, D. L. Underwood, O. S. Wheatley.
1970	B. F. Butcher, A. P. E. Knott, Majid Khan, M. J. Procter, D. J. Shepherd.
1971	J. D. Bond, C. H. Lloyd, B. W. Luckhurst, G. M. Turner, R. T. Virgin.
1972	G. G. Arnold, B. S. Chandrasekhar, L. R. Gibbs, B. Taylor, Zaheer Abbas.
1973	G. S. Chappell, D. K. Lillee, R. A. L. Massie, J. A. Snow, K. R. Stackpole.
1974	K. D. Boyce, B. E. Congdon, K. W. R. Fletcher, R. C. Fredericks, P. J. Sainsbury.
1975	D. L. Amiss, M. H. Denness, N. Gifford, A. W. Greig, A. M. E. Roberts.
1976	I. M. Chappell, P. G. Lee, R. B. McCosker, D. S. Steele, A. A. Woolmer.
1977	J. M. Brearley, C. G. Greenidge, M. A. Holding, I. V. A. Richards, R. W. Taylor.
1978	I. T. Botham, M. Hendrick, A. Jones, K. S. McEwan, R. G. D. Willis.
1979	D. I. Gower, J. K. Lever, C. M. Old, C. T. Radley, J. N. Shepherd.
1980	J. Garner, S. M. Gavaskar, G. A. Gooch, D. W. Randall, B. C. Rose.
1981	K. J. Hughes, R. D. Jackman, A. J. Lamb, C. E. B. Rice, V. A. P. van der Bijl.
1982	T. M. Alderman, A. R. Border, R. J. Hadlee, Javed Miandad, R. W. Marsh.
1983	Imran Khan, T. E. Jesty, A. I. Kallicharran, Kapil Dev, M. D. Marshall.
1984	M. Amarnath, J. V. Coney, J. E. Emburey, M. W. Gatting, C. L. Smith.
1985	M. D. Crowe, H. A. Gomes, G. W. Humpage, J. Simmons, S. Wettimuny.
1986	P. Bainbridge, R. M. Ellison, C. J. McDermott, N. V. Radford, R. T. Robinson.
1987	J. H. Childs, G. A. Hick, D. B. Vengsarkar, C. A. Walsh, J. J. Whitaker.
1988	J. P. Agnew, N. A. Foster, D. P. Hughes, P. M. Roebuck, Salim Malik.
1989	K. J. Barnett, P. J. L. Dujon, P. A. Neale, F. D. Stephenson, S. R. Waugh.
1990	S. J. Cook, D. M. Jones, R. C. Russell, R. A. Smith, M. A. Taylor.
1991	M. A. Atherton, M. Azharuddin, A. R. Butcher, D. L. Haynes, M. E. Waugh.
1992	C. E. L. Ambrose, P. A. J. DeFreitas, A. A. Donald, R. B. Richardson, Waqar Younis.
1993	N. E. Briers, M. D. Moxon, I. D. K. Salisbury, A. J. Stewart, Wasim Akram.
1994	D. C. Boon, I. A. Healy, M. G. Hughes, S. K. Warne, S. L. Watkin.
1995	B. C. Lara, D. E. Malcolm, T. A. Munton, S. J. Rhodes, K. C. Wessels.
1996	D. G. Cork, P. A. de Silva, A. R. C. Fraser, A. Kumble, D. A. Reeve.

1997	S. T. Jayasuriya, Mushtaq Ahmed, Saeed Anwar, P. V. Simmons, S. R. Tendulkar.
1998	M. T. G. Elliott, S. G. Law, G. D. McGrath, M. P. Maynard, G. P. Thorpe.
1999	I. D. Austin, D. Gough, M. Muralitharan, A. Ranatunga, J. N. Rhodes.
2000	C. L. Cairns, R. Dravid, L. Klusener, T. M. Moody, Saqlain Mushtaq.

Cricketers of the Century D. G. Bradman, G. S. Sobers, J. B. Hobbs, S. K. Warne, I. V. A. Richards.

2001	M. W. Alleyne, M. P. Bicknell, A. R. Caddick, J. L. Langer, D. S. Lehmann.
2002	A. Flower, A. C. Gilchrist, J. N. Gillespie, V. V. S. Laxman, D. R. Martyn.
2003	M. L. Hayden, A. J. Hollioake, N. Hussain, S. M. Pollock, M. P. Vaughan.
2004	C. J. Adams, A. Flintoff, I. J. Harvey, G. Kirsten, G. C. Smith.
2005	A. F. Giles, S. J. Harmison, R. W. T. Key, A. J. Strauss, M. E. Trescothick.

Note: From 2000 to 2003 the award was made on the basis of all cricket round the world, not just the English season. This ended in 2004 with the start of *Wisden's* Leading Cricketer in the World award. Jayasuriya in 1997 was chosen for his "influence" on the English season, stemming from the 1996 World Cup.

CRICKETERS OF THE YEAR: AN ANALYSIS

The five players selected to be Cricketers of the Year for 2005 bring the number chosen since selection began in 1889 to 532. They have been chosen from 38 different teams as follows:

Derbyshire	13	Northants	13	Australians	68	Cranleigh School	1
Durham	1	Nottinghamshire	25	South Africans	24	Eton College	2
Essex	23	Somerset	18	West Indians	23	Malvern College	1
Glamorgan	10	Surrey	48	New Zealanders	8	Rugby School	1
Gloucestershire	17	Sussex	21	Indians	13	Tonbridge School	1
Hampshire	14	Warwickshire	20	Pakistanis	11	Univ. Coll. School	1
Kent	26	Worcestershire	15	Sri Lankans	4	Uppingham School	1
Lancashire	32	Yorkshire	41	Zimbabweans	1	Winchester College	1
Leicestershire	8	Oxford Univ.	6	Staffordshire	1		
Middlesex	27	Cambridge Univ.	10	Cheltenham College	1		

Notes: Schoolboys were chosen in 1918 and 1919 when first-class cricket was suspended due to war. The total of sides comes to 551 because 19 players played regularly for two teams (England excluded) in the year for which they were chosen. John Wisden, listed as a Sussex player, retired 50 years before his posthumous selection.

Types of Players

Of the 532 Cricketers of the Year, 269 are best classified as batsmen, 150 as bowlers, 79 as all-rounders and 34 as wicket-keepers or wicket-keeper/batsmen.

Nationalities

At the time they were chosen, 336 players (63.15%) were qualified to play for England, 79 for Australia, 36 West Indies, 34 South Africa, 14 Pakistan, 14 India, 12 New Zealand, 5 Sri Lanka and 2 Zimbabwe.

Note: Nationalities and teams are not necessarily identical.

Research: Robert Brooke

Opposite: The numbers man.
The Antigua scoreboard tells the story
as Brian Lara scales Test cricket's
batting summit all over again.
Picture by Clive Rose, Getty Images

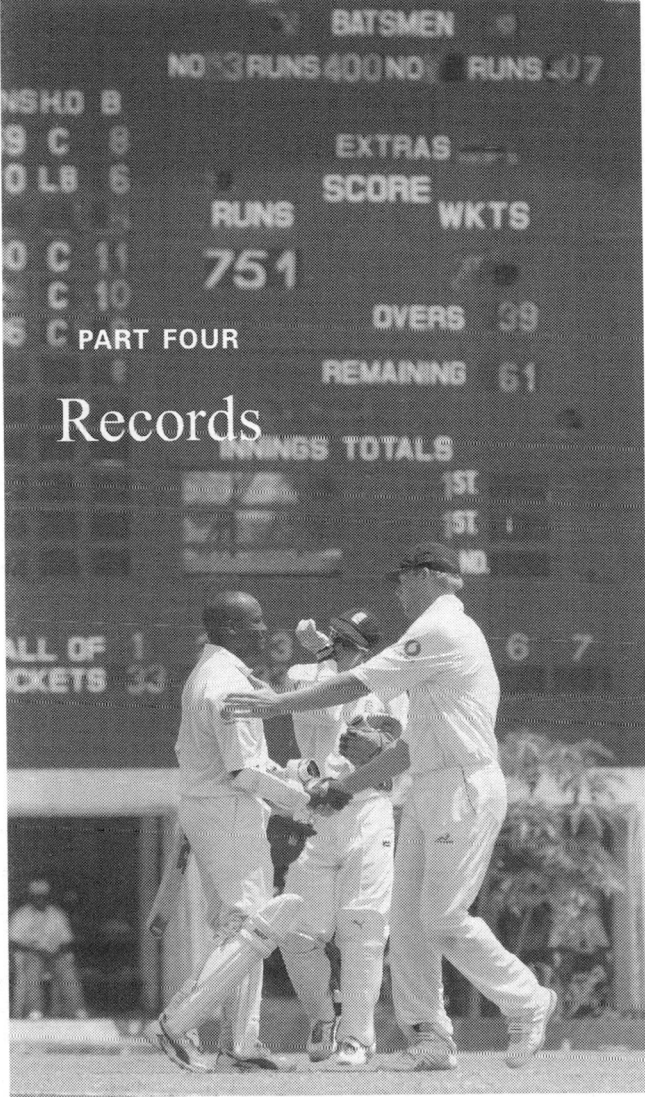

PART FOUR

Records

RECORDS

COMPILED BY PHILIP BAILEY

This section covers
- first-class records to December 30, 2004 (pages 202–240)
- Test records to January 25, 2005, the end of the South Africa v England series (pages 241–281)
- Test records series by series (pages 282–388)
- one-day international records to December 31, 2004 (pages 389–400)
- one-day records to September 25, 2004, the end of the season in England (pages 401–403)
- miscellaneous other records to September 25, 2004, the end of the season in England (pages 403–406)
- women's Test records to the end of the 2004 season in England (pages 407–408)

The sequence
- Test series records begin with those involving England, arranged in the order their opponents entered Test cricket (Australia, South Africa, West Indies, New Zealand, India, Pakistan, Sri Lanka, Zimbabwe, Bangladesh). Next come all remaining series involving Australia, then South Africa – and so on until Zimbabwe v Bangladesh records appear on pages 385–386

Notes
- Unless otherwise stated, all records apply only to first-class cricket. This is considered to have started in 1815, after the Napoleonic War
- mid-year seasons taking place outside England are given simply as 2002, 2003, etc.
- (E), (A), (SA), (WI), (NZ), (I), (P), (SL), (Z) or (B) indicates the nationality of a player or the country in which a record was made

See also
- up-to-date Test records on www.cricinfo.com
- Features of 2004 (pages 425–429)
- Overseas Features of 2003-04 and 2004 (pages 1004–1011)

CONTENTS

FIRST-CLASS RECORDS

BATTING RECORDS

BOWLING RECORDS

ALL-ROUND RECORDS

WICKET-KEEPING RECORDS

FIELDING RECORDS

TEAM RECORDS

TEST RECORDS

BATTING RECORDS

BOWLING RECORDS

ALL-ROUND RECORDS

WICKET-KEEPING RECORDS

FIELDING RECORDS

TEAM RECORDS

PLAYERS

UMPIRES

TEST SERIES

ONE-DAY INTERNATIONAL RECORDS

LIST A ONE-DAY RECORDS

MISCELLANEOUS RECORDS

WOMEN'S TEST RECORDS

FIRST-CLASS RECORDS

BATTING RECORDS

HIGHEST INDIVIDUAL INNINGS

In the history of first-class cricket, there have been **149** individual scores of 300 or more:

501*	B. C. Lara	Warwickshire v Durham at Birmingham.	1994
499	Hanif Mohammad	Karachi v Bahawalpur at Karachi	1958-59
452*	D. G. Bradman	NSW v Queensland at Sydney.	1929-30
443*	B. B. Nimbalkar	Maharashtra v Kathiawar at Poona	1948-49
437	W. H. Ponsford	Victoria v Queensland at Melbourne	1927-28
429	W. H. Ponsford	Victoria v Tasmania at Melbourne	1922-23
428	Aftab Baloch	Sind v Baluchistan at Karachi	1973-74
424	A. C. MacLaren	Lancashire v Somerset at Taunton.	1895
405*	G. A. Hick	Worcestershire v Somerset at Taunton	1988
400*	B. C. Lara	West Indies v England at St John's.	2003-04
394	Naved Latif	Sargodha v Gujranwala at Gujranwala	2000-01
385	B. Sutcliffe	Otago v Canterbury at Christchurch	1952-53
383	C. W. Gregory	NSW v Queensland at Brisbane	1906-07
380	M. L. Hayden	Australia v Zimbabwe at Perth.	2003-04
377	S. V. Manjrekar	Bombay v Hyderabad at Bombay	1990-91
375	B. C. Lara	West Indies v England at St John's.	1993-94
369	D. G. Bradman	South Australia v Tasmania at Adelaide	1935-36
366	N. H. Fairbrother	Lancashire v Surrey at The Oval	1990
366	M. V. Sridhar	Hyderabad v Andhra at Secunderabad	1993-94
365*	C. Hill	South Australia v NSW at Adelaide	1900-01
365*	G. S. Sobers	West Indies v Pakistan at Kingston	1957-58
364	L. Hutton	England v Australia at The Oval.	1938
359*	V. M. Merchant	Bombay v Maharashtra at Bombay	1943-44
359	R. B. Simpson	NSW v Queensland at Brisbane	1963-64
357*	R. Abel	Surrey v Somerset at The Oval	1899
357	D. G. Bradman	South Australia v Victoria at Melbourne	1935-36
356	B. A. Richards	South Australia v Western Australia at Perth.	1970-71
355*	G. R. Marsh	Western Australia v South Australia at Perth.	1989-90
355	B. Sutcliffe	Otago v Auckland at Dunedin	1949-50
353	V. V. S. Laxman	Hyderabad v Karnataka at Bangalore.	1999-2000
352	W. H. Ponsford	Victoria v NSW at Melbourne	1926-27
350	Rashid Israr	Habib Bank v National Bank at Lahore	1976-77
345	C. G. Macartney	Australians v Nottinghamshire at Nottingham	1921
344*	G. A. Headley	Jamaica v Lord Tennyson's XI at Kingston.	1931-32
344	W. G. Grace	MCC v Kent at Canterbury	1876
343*	P. A. Perrin	Essex v Derbyshire at Chesterfield	1904
341	G. H. Hirst	Yorkshire v Leicestershire at Leicester	1905
341	C. M. Spearman	Gloucestershire v Middlesex at Gloucester	2004
340*	D. G. Bradman	NSW v Victoria at Sydney	1928-29
340	S. M. Gavaskar	Bombay v Bengal at Bombay	1981-82
340	S. T. Jayasuriya	Sri Lanka v India at Colombo	1997-98
338*	R. C. Blunt	Otago v Canterbury at Christchurch	1931-32
338	W. W. Read	Surrey v Oxford University at The Oval	1888
337*	Pervez Akhtar	Railways v Dera Ismail Khan at Lahore.	1964-65
337*	D. J. Cullinan	Transvaal v Northern Transvaal at Johannesburg	1993-94
337	Hanif Mohammad	Pakistan v West Indies at Bridgetown	1957-58
336*	W. R. Hammond	England v New Zealand at Auckland	1932-33
336	W. H. Ponsford	Victoria v South Australia at Melbourne	1927-28
335*	M. W. Goodwin	Sussex v Leicestershire at Hove	2003
334*	M. A. Taylor	Australia v Pakistan at Peshawar	1998-99
334	D. G. Bradman	Australia v England at Leeds.	1930
333	K. S. Duleepsinhji	Sussex v Northamptonshire at Hove	1930

333	G. A. Gooch	England v India at Lord's	1990
332	W. H. Ashdown	Kent v Essex at Brentwood	1934
331*	J. D. Robertson	Middlesex v Worcestershire at Worcester	1949
331*	M. E. K. Hussey	Northamptonshire v Somerset at Taunton	2003
329*	M. E. K. Hussey	Northamptonshire v Essex at Northampton	2001
329	Inzamam-ul-Haq	Pakistan v New Zealand at Lahore	2002
325*	H. L. Hendry	Victoria v New Zealanders at Melbourne	1925-26
325	A. Sandham	England v West Indies at Kingston	1929-30
325	C. L. Badcock	South Australia v Victoria at Adelaide	1935-36
324*	D. M. Jones	Victoria v South Australia at Melbourne	1994-95
324	J. B. Stollmeyer	Trinidad v British Guiana at Port-of-Spain	1946-47
324	Waheed Mirza	Karachi Whites v Quetta at Karachi	1976-77
323	A. L. Wadekar	Bombay v Mysore at Bombay	1966-67
323	D. Gandhi	Bengal v Assam at Gauhati	1998-99
322*	M. B. Loye	Northamptonshire v Glamorgan at Northampton	1998
322	E. Paynter	Lancashire v Sussex at Hove	1937
322	I. V. A. Richards	Somerset v Warwickshire at Taunton	1985
321	W. L. Murdoch	NSW v Victoria at Sydney	1881-82
320	R. Lamba	North Zone v West Zone at Bhilai	1987-88
319	Gul Mahomed	Baroda v Holkar at Baroda	1946-47
318*	W. G. Grace	Gloucestershire v Yorkshire at Cheltenham	1876
317	W. R. Hammond	Gloucestershire v Nottinghamshire at Gloucester	1936
317	K. R. Rutherford	New Zealanders v D. B. Close's XI at Scarborough . .	1986
316*	J. B. Hobbs	Surrey v Middlesex at Lord's	1926
316*	V. S. Hazare	Maharashtra v Baroda at Poona	1939-40
316	R. H. Moore	Hampshire v Warwickshire at Bournemouth	1937
315*	T. W. Hayward	Surrey v Lancashire at The Oval	1898
315*	P. Holmes	Yorkshire v Middlesex at Lord's	1925
315*	A. F. Kippax	NSW v Queensland at Sydney	1927-28
315*	G. A. Hick	Worcestershire v Durham at Worcester	2002
315	M. A. Wagh	Warwickshire v Middlesex at Lord's	2001
314*	C. L. Walcott	Barbados v Trinidad at Port-of-Spain	1945-46
314*	Wasim Jaffer	Mumbai v Saurashtra at Rajkot	1996-97
313*	S. J. Cook	Somerset v Glamorgan at Cardiff	1990
313	H. Sutcliffe	Yorkshire v Essex at Leyton	1932
313	W. V. Raman‡	Tamil Nadu v Goa at Panjim	1988-89
312*	W. W. Keeton	Nottinghamshire v Middlesex at The Oval†	1939
312*	J. M. Brearley	MCC Under-25 v North Zone at Peshawar	1966-67
312	R. Lamba	Delhi v Himachal Pradesh at Delhi	1994-95
312	J. E. R. Gallian	Lancashire v Derbyshire at Manchester	1996
311*	G. M. Turner	Worcestershire v Warwickshire at Worcester	1982
311	J. T. Brown	Yorkshire v Sussex at Sheffield	1897
311	R. B. Simpson	Australia v England at Manchester	1964
311	Javed Miandad	Karachi Whites v National Bank at Karachi	1974-75
310*	J. H. Edrich	England v New Zealand at Leeds	1965
310*	M. E. K. Hussey	Northamptonshire v Gloucestershire at Bristol	2002
310	H. Gimblett	Somerset v Sussex at Eastbourne	1948
309*	S. P. James	Glamorgan v Sussex at Colwyn Bay	2000
309	V. S. Hazare	The Rest v Hindus at Bombay	1943-44
309	V. Sehwag	India v Pakistan at Multan	2003-04
308*	F. M. M. Worrell	Barbados v Trinidad at Bridgetown	1943-44
308*	D. Mongia	Punjab v Jammu and Kashmir at Jullundur	2000-01
307*	T. N. Lazard	Boland v W. Province at Worcester, Cape Province . .	1993-94
307	M. C. Cowdrey	MCC v South Australia at Adelaide	1962-63
307	R. M. Cowper	Australia v England at Melbourne	1965-66
306*	A. Ducat	Surrey v Oxford University at The Oval	1919
306*	E. A. B. Rowan	Transvaal v Natal at Johannesburg	1939-40
306*	D. W. Hookes	South Australia v Tasmania at Adelaide	1986-87
306	M. H. Richardson	New Zealanders v Zimbabwe A at Kwekwe	2000-01
305*	F. E. Woolley	MCC v Tasmania at Hobart	1911-12
305*	F. R. Foster	Warwickshire v Worcestershire at Dudley	1914

305*	W. H. Ashdown	Kent v Derbyshire at Dover.................	1935
305*	P. Dharmani	Punjab v Jammu and Kashmir at Ludhiana.........	1999-2000
304*	A. W. Nourse	Natal v Transvaal at Johannesburg	1919-20
304*	P. H. Tarilton	Barbados v Trinidad at Bridgetown............	1919-20
304*	E. D. Weekes	West Indians v Cambridge University at Cambridge..	1950
304	R. M. Poore	Hampshire v Somerset at Taunton...........	1899
304	D. G. Bradman	Australia v England at Leeds...............	1934
303*	W. W. Armstrong	Australians v Somerset at Bath	1905
303*	Mushtaq Mohammad	Karachi Blues v Karachi University at Karachi	1967-68
303*	Abdul Azeem	Hyderabad v Tamil Nadu at Hyderabad	1986-87
303*	S. Chanderpaul	Guyana v Jamaica at Kingston	1995-96
303*	G. A. Hick	Worcestershire v Hampshire at Southampton.......	1997
303*	D. J. Sales	Northamptonshire v Essex at Northampton........	1999
303*	N. V. Knight	Warwickshire v Middlesex at Lord's	2004
302*	P. Holmes	Yorkshire v Hampshire at Portsmouth	1920
302*	W. R. Hammond	Gloucestershire v Glamorgan at Bristol	1934
302*	Arjan Kripal Singh‡	Tamil Nadu v Goa at Panjim	1988-89
302*	B. J. Hodge	Leicestershire v Nottinghamshire at Nottingham	2003
302	W. R. Hammond	Gloucestershire v Glamorgan at Newport	1939
302	L. G. Rowe	West Indies v England at Bridgetown	1973-74
301*	E. H. Hendren	Middlesex v Worcestershire at Dudley	1933
301*	V. V. S. Laxman	Hyderabad v Bihar at Jamshedpur	1997-98
301*	P. G. Fulton	Canterbury v Auckland at Christchurch	2002-03
301*	J. P. Crawley	Hampshire v Nottinghamshire at Nottingham	2004
301	W. G. Grace	Gloucestershire v Sussex at Bristol	1896
300*	V. T. Trumper	Australians v Sussex at Hove..............	1899
300*	F. B. Watson	Lancashire v Surrey at Manchester	1928
300*	Imtiaz Ahmed	PM's XI v Commonwealth XI at Bombay	1950-51
300*	G. K. Khoda	Central Zone v South Zone at Panaji...........	2000-01
300*	M. L. Love	Queensland v Victoria at Melbourne (Junction Oval) .	2003-04
300*	Shoaib Khan	Peshawar v Quetta at Peshawar.............	2003-04
300*	Bazid Khan	Rawalpindi v Hyderabad at Hyderabad	2004-05
300	J. T. Brown	Yorkshire v Derbyshire at Chesterfield	1898
300	D. C. S. Compton	MCC v N. E. Transvaal at Benoni	1948-49
300	R. Subba Row	Northamptonshire v Surrey at The Oval..........	1958
300	Ramiz Raja	Allied Bank v Habib Bank at Lahore	1994-95

† *Played at The Oval because Lord's was required for Eton v Harrow.*

‡ *W. V. Raman and Arjan Kripal Singh scored triple-hundreds in the same innings, a unique occurrence.*

DOUBLE-HUNDRED ON DEBUT

227	T. Marsden	Sheffield & Leicester v Nottingham at Sheffield	1826
207	N. F. Callaway†	New South Wales v Queensland at Sydney	1914-15
240	W. F. E. Marx	Transvaal v Griqualand West at Johannesburg	1920-21
200*	A. Maynard	Trinidad v MCC at Port-of-Spain.............	1934-35
232*	S. J. E. Loxton	Victoria v Queensland at Melbourne...........	1946-47
215*	G. H. G. Doggart	Cambridge University v Lancashire at Cambridge	1948
202	J. Hallebone	Victoria v Tasmania at Melbourne	1951-52
230	G. R. Viswanath	Mysore v Andhra at Vijayawada.............	1967-68
260	A. A. Muzumdar	Bombay v Haryana at Faridabad	1993-94
209*	A. Pandey	Madhya Pradesh v Uttar Pradesh at Bhilai........	1995-96
210*	D. J. Sales	Northants v Worcestershire at Kidderminster	1996
200*	M. J. Powell	Glamorgan v Oxford University at Oxford.........	1997

† *In his only first-class innings. He was killed in action in France in 1917.*

TWO SEPARATE HUNDREDS ON DEBUT

148 and 111	A. R. Morris	New South Wales v Queensland at Sydney.....	1940-41
152 and 102*	N. J. Contractor	Gujarat v Baroda at Baroda	1952-53
132* and 110	Aamer Malik	Lahore A v Railways at Lahore	1979-80

TWO DOUBLE-HUNDREDS IN A MATCH

A. E. Fagg	244	202*	Kent v Essex at Colchester	1938

TRIPLE-HUNDRED AND HUNDRED IN A MATCH

G. A. Gooch	333	123	England v India at Lord's	1990

DOUBLE-HUNDRED AND HUNDRED IN A MATCH

C. B. Fry	125	229	Sussex v Surrey at Hove	1900
W. W. Armstrong	157*	245	Victoria v South Australia at Melbourne...	1920-21
H. T. W. Hardinge ...	207	102*	Kent v Surrey at Blackheath	1921
C. P. Mead	113	224	Hampshire v Sussex at Horsham........	1921
K. S. Duleepsinhji ...	115	246	Sussex v Kent at Hastings	1929
D. G. Bradman	124	225	Woodfull's XI v Ryder's XI at Sydney....	1929-30
B. Sutcliffe	243	100*	New Zealanders v Essex at Southend.....	1949
M. R. Hallam	210*	157	Leicestershire v Glamorgan at Leicester ...	1959
M. R. Hallam	203*	143*	Leicestershire v Sussex at Worthing	1961
Hanumant Singh	109	213*	Rajasthan v Bombay at Bombay	1966-67
Salah-ud-Din	256	102*	Karachi v East Pakistan at Karachi	1968-69
K. D. Walters	242	103	Australia v West Indies at Sydney	1968-69
S. M. Gavaskar	124	220	India v West Indies at Port-of-Spain.	1970-71
L. G. Rowe.........	214	100*	West Indies v New Zealand at Kingston ...	1971-72
G. S. Chappell......	247*	133	Australia v New Zealand at Wellington. . . .	1973-74
L. Baichan	216*	102	Berbice v Demerara at Georgetown	1973-74
Zaheer Abbas	216*	156*	Gloucestershire v Surrey at The Oval.....	1976
Zaheer Abbas	230*	104*	Gloucestershire v Kent at Canterbury.....	1976
Zaheer Abbas	205*	108*	Gloucestershire v Sussex at Cheltenham ...	1977
Saadat Ali.........	141	222	Income Tax v Multan at Multan	1977-78
Talat Ali	214*	104	PIA v Punjab at Lahore..............	1978-79
Shafiq Ahmad	129	217*	National Bank v MCB at Karachi	1978-79
D. W. Randall	209	146	Nottinghamshire v Middlesex at Nottingham	1979
Zaheer Abbas	215*	150*	Gloucestershire v Somerset at Bath	1981
Qasim Omar	210*	110	MCB v Lahore at Lahore	1982-83
A. I. Kallicharran...	200*	117*	Warwickshire v Northants at Birmingham..	1984
Rizwan-uz-Zaman ...	139	217*	PIA v PACO at Lahore	1989-90
G. A. Hick	252*	100*	Worcestershire v Glamorgan at Abergavenny	1990
N. R. Taylor	204	142	Kent v Surrey at Canterbury..........	1990
N. R. Taylor	111	203*	Kent v Sussex at Hove	1991
W. V. Raman	226	120	Tamil Nadu v Haryana at Faridabad	1991-92
A. J. Lamb	209	107	Northants v Warwicks at Northampton ...	1992
G. A. Gooch	101	205	Essex v Worcestershire at Worcester......	1994
P. A. de Silva	255	116	Kent v Derbyshire at Maidstone	1995
M. C. Mendis	111	200*	Colts CC v Singha SC at Colombo	1995-96
A. M. Bacher	210	112*	Transvaal v Griqualand West at Kimberley .	1996-97
H. H. Gibbs	200*	171	South Africans v India A at Nagpur.....	1996-97

M. L. Hayden	235*	119	Hampshire v Warwickshire at Southampton .	1997
G. S. Blewett.	169*	213*	Australian XI v England XI at Hobart	1998-99
A. Jadeja	136	202*	Haryana v Saurashtra at Rajkot.	1998-99
J. Cox	216	129*	Somerset v Hampshire at Southampton. . . .	1999
Mohammad Ramzan . .	205	102*	Faisalabad v Sargodha at Faisalabad.	2000-01
M. W. Goodwin	115	203*	Sussex v Nottinghamshire at Nottingham . .	2001
D. P. Fulton.	208*	104*	Kent v Somerset at Canterbury	2001
B. C. Lara.	221	130	West Indies v Sri Lanka at Colombo	2001-02
Minhazul Abedin	210	110	Chittagong v Dhaka at Mymensingh	2001-02
A. T. Rayudu.	210	159*	Hyderabad v Andhra at Secunderabad	2002-03
H. H. Kanitkar.	112	207*	Maharashtra v Services at Aurangabad	2003-04
M. J. Horne.	118	209*	Auckland v Northern Districts at Auckland .	2003-04

TWO SEPARATE HUNDREDS IN A MATCH

Eight times: Zaheer Abbas.

Seven times: W. R. Hammond.

Six times: J. B. Hobbs, G. M. Turner.

Five times: C. B. Fry, G. A. Gooch, M. L. Hayden, R. T. Ponting, M. R. Ramprakash.

Four times: D. G. Bradman, G. S. Chappell, J. Cox, J. H. Edrich, L. B. Fishlock, T. W. Graveney, C. G. Greenidge, H. T. W. Hardinge, E. H. Hendren, G. A. Hick, Javed Miandad, G. L. Jessop, S. G. Law, H. Morris, M. H. Parmar, P. A. Perrin, B. Sutcliffe, H. Sutcliffe.

Three times: C. J. Adams, Agha Zahid, L. E. G. Ames, Basit Ali, G. Boycott, I. M. Chappell, D. C. S. Compton, S. J. Cook, M. C. Cowdrey, D. Denton, P. A. de Silva, K. S. Duleepsinhji, M. T. G. Elliott, R. E. Foster, R. C. Fredericks, S. M. Gavaskar, W. G. Grace, G. Gunn, M. R. Hallam, Hanif Mohammad, M. J. Harris, T. W. Hayward, V. S. Hazare, D. W. Hookes, L. Hutton, A. Jones, D. M. Jones, P. N. Kirsten, R. B. McCosker, P. B. H. May, M. P. Maynard, C. P. Mead, T. M. Moody, Rizwan-uz-Zaman, R. T. Robinson, A. C. Russell, Sadiq Mohammad, J. T. Tyldesley, K. C. Wessels.

Notes: W. Lambert scored 107 and 157 for Sussex v Epsom at Lord's in 1817, and it was not until W. G. Grace made 130 and 102* for South of the Thames v North of the Thames at Canterbury in 1868 that the feat was repeated.

C. J. B. Wood, 107* and 117* for Leicestershire v Yorkshire at Bradford in 1911, and S. J. Cook, 120* and 131* for Somerset v Nottinghamshire at Nottingham in 1989, are alone in carrying their bats and scoring hundreds in each innings.

FOUR HUNDREDS OR MORE IN SUCCESSION

Six in succession: D. G. Bradman 1938-39; C. B. Fry 1901; M. J. Procter 1970-71.

Five in succession: B. C. Lara 1993-94/1994; E. D. Weekes 1955-56; M. E. K. Hussey 2003.

Four in succession: C. W. J. Athey 1987; M. Azharuddin 1984-85; M. G. Bevan 1990-91; G. S. Blewett 1998-99; A. R. Border 1985; D. G. Bradman 1931-32, 1948/1948-49; D. C. S. Compton 1946-47; N. J. Contractor 1957-58; S. J. Cook 1989; K. S. Duleepsinhji 1931; C. B. Fry 1911; C. G. Greenidge 1986; W. R. Hammond 1936-37, 1945/1946; H. T. W. Hardinge 1913; T. W. Hayward 1906; G. A. Hick 1998; J. B. Hobbs 1920, 1925; D. W. Hookes 1976-77; Ijaz Ahmed, jun. 1994-95; R. S. Kaluwitharana 1996-97; P. N. Kirsten 1976-77; J. G. Langridge 1949; C. G. Macartney 1921; K. S. McEwan 1977; P. B. H. May 1956-57; V. M. Merchant 1941-42; A. Mitchell 1933; Nawab of Pataudi sen. 1931; Rizwan-uz-Zaman 1989-90; L. G. Rowe 1971-72; Pankaj Roy 1962-63; Sadiq Mohammad 1976; Saeed Ahmed 1961-62; E. T. Smith 2003; M. V. Sridhar 1990-91/1991-92; H. Sutcliffe 1931, 1939; S. R. Tendulkar 1994-95; E. Tyldesley 1926; I. J. Ward 2002; W. W. Whysall 1930; F. E. Woolley 1929; Yasir Hameed 2002-03/2003; Younis Khan 1999-2000; Zaheer Abbas 1970-71, 1982-83.

Notes: T. W. Hayward (Surrey v Nottinghamshire and Leicestershire) and D. W. Hookes (South Australia v Queensland and New South Wales) are the only players listed above to score two hundreds in two successive matches. Hayward scored his in six days, June 4-9, 1906.

The most fifties in consecutive innings is ten – by E. Tyldesley in 1926, by D. G. Bradman in the 1947-48 and 1948 seasons and by R. S. Kaluwitharana in 1994-95.

MOST HUNDREDS IN A SEASON

Eighteen: D. C. S. Compton 1947.
Sixteen: J. B. Hobbs 1925.
Fifteen: W. R. Hammond 1938.
Fourteen: H. Sutcliffe 1932.
Thirteen: G. Boycott 1971; D. G. Bradman 1938; C. B. Fry 1901; W. R. Hammond 1933 and 1937; T. W. Hayward 1906; E. H. Hendren 1923, 1927 and 1928; C. P. Mead 1928; H. Sutcliffe 1928 and 1931.

Since 1969 (excluding G. Boycott – above)

Twelve: G. A. Gooch 1990.
Eleven: S. J. Cook 1991; Zaheer Abbas 1976.
Ten: G. A. Hick 1988; H. Morris 1990; M. R. Ramprakash 1995; G. M. Turner 1970; Zaheer Abbas 1981.

Note: The most achieved outside England is eight by D. G. Bradman in Australia (1947-48), D. C. S. Compton (1948-49), R. N. Harvey and A. R. Morris (both 1949-50) in South Africa, M. D. Crowe in New Zealand (1986-87), Asif Mujtaba in Pakistan (1995-96) and V. V. S. Laxman in India (1999-2000).

MOST DOUBLE-HUNDREDS IN A SEASON

Six: D. G. Bradman 1930.
Five: K. S. Ranjitsinhji 1900; E. D. Weekes 1950.
Four: Arun Lal 1986-87; C. B. Fry 1901; W. R. Hammond 1933, 1934; E. H. Hendren 1929-30; V. M. Merchant 1944-45; G. M. Turner 1971-72.
Three: L. E. G. Ames 1933; Arshad Pervez 1977-78; D. G. Bradman 1930-31, 1931-32, 1934, 1935-36, 1936-37, 1938, 1939-40; R. Dravid 2003-04; W. J. Edrich 1947; C. B. Fry 1903, 1904; M. W. Gatting 1994; G. A. Gooch 1994; W. R. Hammond 1928, 1928-29, 1932-33, 1938; J. Hardstaff jun. 1937, 1947; V. S. Hazare 1943-44; E. H. Hendren 1925; J. B. Hobbs 1914, 1926; B. J. Hodge 2004; M. E. K. Hussey 2001; L. Hutton 1949; D. S. Jadhav 2003-04; D. M. Jones 1991-92; A. I. Kallicharran 1982; V. G. Kambli 1992-93; P. N. Kirsten 1980; R. S. Modi 1944-45; D. Mongia 2000-01; Nawab of Pataudi sen. 1933; W. H. Ponsford 1927-28, 1934; W. V. Raman 1988-89; M. R. Ramprakash 1995; K. S. Ranjitsinhji 1901; I. V. A. Richards 1977; R. B. Simpson 1963-64; P. R. Umrigar 1952, 1959; F. B. Watson 1928.

Note: R. Dravid scored three double-hundreds in three different countries in 2003-04.

MOST DOUBLE-HUNDREDS IN A CAREER

D. G. Bradman	37	W. G. Grace	13	A. Sandham	11
W. R. Hammond	36	C. P. Mead	13	G. Boycott	10
E. H. Hendren	22	W. H. Ponsford	13	S. M. Gavaskar	10
H. Sutcliffe	17	J. T. Tyldesley	13	J. Hardstaff, jun.	10
C. B. Fry	16	P. Holmes	12	V. S. Hazare	10
G. A. Hick	**16**	Javed Miandad	12	I. V. A. Richards	10
J. B. Hobbs	16	R. B. Simpson	12	A. Shrewsbury	10
C. G. Greenidge	14	J. W. Hearne	11	R. T. Simpson	10
K. S. Ranjitsinhji	14	L. Hutton	11	G. M. Turner	10
G. A. Gooch	13	V. M. Merchant	11	Zaheer Abbas	10

Bold type denotes those who played in the calendar year 2004.

MOST HUNDREDS IN A CAREER

(50 or more)

		Total	Total 100th 100				
			Inns	Season	Inns	400+	300+	200+
1	J. B. Hobbs	197	1,315	1923	821	0	1	16
2	E. H. Hendren	170	1,300	1928-29	740	0	1	22
3	W. R. Hammond	167	1,005	1935	679	0	4	36
4	C. P. Mead	153	1,340	1927	892	0	0	13
5	G. Boycott	151	1,014	1977	645	0	0	10
6	H. Sutcliffe	149	1,088	1932	700	1	1	17
7	F. E. Woolley	145	1,532	1929	1,031	0	1	9
8	L. Hutton	129	814	1951	619	0	1	11
9	G. A. Gooch	128	990	1992-93	820	0	1	13
10 {	G. A. Hick	126	777	1998	574	1	3	16
{	W. G. Grace	126	1,493	1895	1,113	0	3	13
12	D. C. S. Compton	123	839	1952	552	0	1	9
13	T. W. Graveney	122	1,223	1964	940	0	0	7
14	D. G. Bradman	117	338	1947-48	295	1	6	37
15	I. V. A. Richards	114	796	1988-89	658	0	1	10
16	Zaheer Abbas	108	768	1982-83	658	0	0	10
17 {	A. Sandham	107	1,000	1935	871	0	1	11
{	M. C. Cowdrey	107	1,130	1973	1,035	0	1	3
19	T. W. Hayward	104	1,138	1913	1,076	0	1	8
20 {	G. M. Turner	103	792	1982	779	0	1	10
{	J. H. Edrich	103	979	1977	945	0	1	4
22 {	L. E. G. Ames	102	951	1950	915	0	0	9
{	E. Tyldesley	102	961	1934	919	0	0	7
{	D. L. Amiss	102	1,139	1986	1,081	0	0	3

Notes: In the above table, 200+, 300+ and 400+ include all scores above those figures. E. H. Hendren, D. G. Bradman and I. V. A. Richards scored their 100th hundreds in Australia; G. A. Gooch scored his in India. His record includes his century in South Africa in 1981-82, which is no longer accepted by the ICC. Zaheer Abbas scored his 100th in Pakistan. Zaheer Abbas and G. Boycott did so in Test matches.

J. W. Hearne	96	R. Abel	74	**J. L. Langer**	**67**
C. B. Fry	94	G. S. Chappell	74	J. D. Robertson	67
M. W. Gatting	94	D. Kenyon	74	P. A. Perrin	66
C. G. Greenidge	92	K. S. McEwan	74	K. C. Wessels	66
A. J. Lamb	89	Majid Khan	73	S. J. Cook	64
A. I. Kallicharran	87	**M. R. Ramprakash**	**73**	T. M. Moody	64
W. J. Edrich	86	Mushtaq Mohammad	72	R. G. Pollock	64
G. S. Sobers	86	J. O'Connor	72	R. T. Simpson	64
J. T. Tyldesley	86	W. G. Quaife	72	K. W. R. Fletcher	63
P. B. H. May	85	K. S. Ranjitsinhji	72	R. T. Robinson	63
R. E. S. Wyatt	85	D. Brookes	71	**M. G. Bevan**	**62**
J. Hardstaff, jun.	83	M. D. Crowe	71	G. Gunn	62
R. B. Kanhai	83	A. C. Russell	71	K. J. Barnett	61
S. M. Gavaskar	81	A. R. Border	70	D. L. Haynes	61
M. E. Waugh	**81**	D. Denton	69	R. A. Smith	61
Javed Miandad	80	**C. L. Hooper**	**69**	V. S. Hazare	60
M. Leyland	80	**D. S. Lehmann**	**69**	G. H. Hirst	60
B. A. Richards	80	M. J. K. Smith	69	R. B. Simpson	60
C. H. Lloyd	79	D. C. Boon	68	P. F. Warner	60
S. R. Waugh	**79**	**M. L. Hayden**	**68**	I. M. Chappell	59
K. F. Barrington	76	**S. G. Law**	**68**	A. L. Hassett	59
J. G. Langridge	76	R. E. Marshall	68	W. Larkins	59
C. Washbrook	76	R. N. Harvey	67	**M. P. Maynard**	**59**
H. T. W. Hardinge	75	P. Holmes	67	A. Shrewsbury	59

J. G. Wright 59	M. A. Atherton 54	J. E. Morris 52
A. E. Fagg 58	M. Azharuddin 54	**R. T. Ponting** **52**
P. H. Parfitt 58	D. J. Insole 54	D. W. Randall 52
W. Rhodes 58	W. W. Keeton 54	**J. Cox** **51**
S. R. Tendulkar **58**	W. Bardsley 53	E. R. Dexter 51
P. N. Kirsten 57	B. F. Davison 53	J. M. Parks 51
L. B. Fishlock 56	A. E. Dipper 53	W. W. Whysall 51
A. Jones 56	D. I. Gower 53	B. C. Broad 50
C. A. Milton 56	G. L. Jessop 53	G. Cox, jun. 50
C. W. J. Athey 55	H. Morris 53	H. E. Dollery 50
C. Hallows 55	James Seymour 53	K. S. Duleepsinhji 50
Hanif Mohammad 55	Shafiq Ahmad 53	H. Gimblett 50
D. M. Jones 55	E. H. Bowley 52	W. M. Lawry 50
B. C. Lara **55**	D. B. Close 52	Sadiq Mohammad 50
D. B. Vengsarkar 55	A. Ducat 52	F. B. Watson 50
W. Watson 55	**N. Hussain** **52**	

Bold type denotes those who played in the calendar year 2004.

Other Current Players

In addition to the above, the following who played in 2004 have scored 30 or more hundreds.

G. P. Thorpe 49	C. J. Adams 41	S. Chanderpaul 34
M. T. G. Elliott 48	D. R. Martyn 41	M. E. K. Hussey 34
Asif Mujtaba 46	Inzamam-ul-Haq 40	J. H. Kallis 34
G. Kirsten 46	Sajid Ali 38	N. V. Knight 34
M. S. Atapattu 45	M. P. Vaughan 37	A. Symonds 34
P. D. Bowler 45	A. D. Brown 36	B. J. Hodge 33
D. J. Bicknell 44	A. Flower 36	B. F. Smith 32
G. S. Blewett 43	V. V. S. Laxman 36	P. A. Cottey 31
J. P. Crawley 43	H. P. Tillekeratne 36	M. L. Love 31
R. Dravid 43	M. W. Goodwin 35	
D. J. Cullinan 42	V. G. Kambli 35	

MOST RUNS IN A SEASON

	Season	I	NO	R	HS	100s	Avge
D. C. S. Compton	1947	50	8	3,816	246	18	90.85
W. J. Edrich	1947	52	8	3,539	267*	12	80.43
T. W. Hayward	1906	61	8	3,518	219	13	66.37
L. Hutton	1949	56	6	3,429	269*	12	68.58
F. E. Woolley	1928	59	4	3,352	198	12	60.94
H. Sutcliffe	1932	52	7	3,336	313	14	74.13
W. R. Hammond	1933	54	5	3,323	264	13	67.81
E. H. Hendren	1928	54	7	3,311	209*	13	70.44
R. Abel	1901	68	8	3,309	247	7	55.15

Notes: 3,000 in a season has been surpassed on 19 other occasions (a full list can be found in *Wisden* 1999 and earlier editions). W. R. Hammond, E. H. Hendren and H. Sutcliffe are the only players to achieve the feat three times. K. S. Ranjitsinhji was the first batsman to reach 3,000 in a season, with 3,159 in 1899. M. J. K. Smith (3,245 in 1959) and W. E. Alley (3,019 in 1961) are the only players except those listed above to have reached 3,000 since World War II.

W. G. Grace scored 2,739 runs in 1871 – the first batsman to reach 2,000 runs in a season. He made ten hundreds including two double-hundreds, with an average of 78.25 in all first-class matches

The highest aggregate in a season since the reduction of County Championship matches in 1969 is 2,755 by S. J. Cook (42 innings) in 1991, and the last batsman to achieve 2,000 was M. R. Ramprakash (2,258 in 1995).

2,000 RUNS IN A SEASON MOST TIMES

17 times: J. B. Hobbs.
15 times: E. H. Hendren; H. Sutcliffe.
13 times: F. E. Woolley.

12 times: W. R. Hammond.
11 times: J. G. Langridge; C. P. Mead.
10 times: T. W. Hayward.

Note: Since the reduction of County Championship matches in 1969, G. A. Gooch is the only batsman to have reached 2,000 runs in a season five times.

1,000 RUNS IN A SEASON MOST TIMES

Includes overseas tours and seasons

28 times: W. G. Grace; F. E. Woolley.
27 times: M. C. Cowdrey; C. P. Mead.
26 times: G. Boycott; J. B. Hobbs.
25 times: E. H. Hendren.
24 times: D. L. Amiss; W. G. Quaife; H. Sutcliffe.
23 times: A. Jones.
22 times: T. W. Graveney; W. R. Hammond.
21 times: D. Denton; J. H. Edrich; G. A. Gooch; W. Rhodes .
20 times: D. B. Close; K. W. R. Fletcher; M. W. Gatting; G. Gunn; T. W. Hayward; James Langridge; J. M. Parks; A. Sandham; M. J. K. Smith; C. Washbrook.

Notes: F. E. Woolley reached 1,000 runs in 28 consecutive seasons (1907–1938), C. P. Mead in 27 (1906–1936).

Outside England, 1,000 runs in a season has been reached most times by D. G. Bradman (in 12 seasons in Australia).

Three batsmen have scored 1,000 runs in a season in each of four different countries: G. S. Sobers in West Indies, England, India and Australia; M. C. Cowdrey and G. Boycott in England, South Africa, West Indies and Australia.

HIGHEST AGGREGATES OUTSIDE ENGLAND

	Season	I	NO	R	HS	100s	Avge
In Australia D. G. Bradman	1928-29	24	6	1,690	340*	7	93.88
In South Africa J. R. Reid	1961-62	30	2	1,915	203	7	68.39
In West Indies E. H. Hendren	1929-30	18	5	1,765	254*	6	135.76
In New Zealand M. D. Crowe	1986-87	21	3	1,676	175*	8	93.11
In India C. G. Borde	1964-65	28	3	1,604	168	6	64.16
In Pakistan Saadat Ali	1983-84	27	1	1,649	208	4	63.42
In Sri Lanka R. P. Arnold	1995-96	24	3	1,475	217*	5	70.23
In Zimbabwe G. W. Flower	1994-95	20	3	983	201*	4	57.82
In Bangladesh Minhazul Abedin.	2001-02	15	1	1,012	210	3	72.28

Note: In more than one country, the following aggregates of over 2,000 runs have been recorded:

M. Amarnath (P/I/WI)	1982-83	34	6	2,234	207	9	79.78
J. R. Reid (SA/A/NZ)	1961-62	40	4	2,188	203	7	57.57
S. M. Gavaskar (I/P)	1978-79	30	6	2,121	205	10	88.37
R. B. Simpson (I/P/A/WI).	1964-65	34	4	2,063	201	8	68.76
M. H. Richardson (Z/SA/NZ) . .	2000-01	34	3	2,030	306	4	65.48

LEADING BATSMEN IN AN ENGLISH SEASON

(Qualification: 8 completed innings)

Season	Leading scorer	Runs	Avge	Top of averages	Runs	Avge
1946	D. C. S. Compton . . .	2,403	61.61	W. R. Hammond	1,783	84.90
1947	D. C. S. Compton . . .	3,816	90.85	D. C. S. Compton . . .	3,816	90.85
1948	L. Hutton	2,654	64.73	D. G. Bradman	2,428	89.92
1949	L. Hutton	3,429	68.58	J. Hardstaff	2,251	72.61
1950	R. T. Simpson	2,576	62.82	E. D. Weekes	2,310	79.65
1951	J. D. Robertson	2,917	56.09	P. B. H. May	2,339	68.79
1952	L. Hutton	2,567	61.11	D. S. Sheppard	2,262	64.62
1953	W. J. Edrich	2,557	47.35	R. N. Harvey	2,040	65.80
1954	D. Kenyon	2,636	51.68	D. C. S. Compton . . .	1,524	58.61
1955	D. J. Insole	2,427	42.57	D. J. McGlew	1,871	58.46
1956	T. W. Graveney	2,397	49.93	K. Mackay	1,103	52.52
1957	T. W. Graveney	2,361	49.18	P. B. H. May	2,347	61.76
1958	P. B. H. May	2,231	63.74	P. B. H. May	2,231	63.74
1959	M. J. K. Smith	3,245	57.94	V. L. Manjrekar	755	68.63
1960	M. J. K. Smith	2,551	45.55	R. Subba Row	1,503	55.66
1961	W. E. Alley	3,019	56.96	W. M. Lawry	2,019	61.18
1962	J. H. Edrich	2,482	51.70	R. T. Simpson	867	54.18
1963	J. B. Bolus	2,190	41.32	G. S. Sobers	1,333	47.60
1964	T. W. Graveney	2,385	54.20	K. F. Barrington	1,872	62.40
1965	J. H. Edrich	2,319	62.67	M. C. Cowdrey	2,093	63.42
1966	A. R. Lewis	2,198	41.47	G. S. Sobers	1,349	61.31
1967	C. A. Milton	2,089	46.42	K. F. Barrington	2,059	68.63
1968	B. A. Richards	2,395	47.90	G. Boycott	1,487	64.65
1969	J. H. Edrich	2,238	69.93	J. H. Edrich	2,238	69.93
1970	G. M. Turner	2,379	61.00	G. S. Sobers	1,742	75.73
1971	G. Boycott	2,503	100.12	G. Boycott	2,503	100.12
1972	Majid Khan	2,074	61.00	G. Boycott	1,230	72.35
1973	G. M. Turner	2,416	67.11	G. M. Turner	2,416	67.11
1974	R. T. Virgin	1,936	56.94	C. H. Lloyd	1,458	63.39
1975	G. Boycott	1,915	73.65	R. B. Kanhai	1,073	82.53
1976	Zaheer Abbas	2,554	75.11	Zaheer Abbas	2,554	75.11
1977	I. V. A. Richards	2,161	65.48	G. Boycott	1,701	68.04
1978	D. L. Amiss	2,030	53.42	C. E. B. Rice	1,871	66.82
1979	K. C. Wessels	1,800	52.94	G. Boycott	1,538	102.53
1980	P. N. Kirsten	1,895	63.16	A. J. Lamb	1,797	66.55
1981	Zaheer Abbas	2,306	88.69	Zaheer Abbas	2,306	88.69
1982	A. I. Kallicharran . . .	2,120	66.25	G. M. Turner	1,171	90.07
1983	K. S. McEwan	2,176	64.00	I. V. A. Richards	1,204	75.25
1984	G. A. Gooch	2,559	67.34	C. G. Greenidge	1,069	82.23
1985	G. A. Gooch	2,208	71.22	I. V. A. Richards	1,836	76.50
1986	C. G. Greenidge	2,035	67.83	C. G. Greenidge	2,035	67.83
1987	G. A. Hick	1,879	52.19	M. D. Crowe	1,627	67.79
1988	G. A. Hick	2,713	77.51	R. A. Harper	622	77.75
1989	S. J. Cook	2,241	60.56	D. M. Jones	1,510	88.82
1990	G. A. Gooch	2,746	101.70	G. A. Gooch	2,746	101.70
1991	S. J. Cook	2,755	81.02	C. L. Hooper	1,501	93.81
1992	{ P. D. Bowler	2,044	65.93	Salim Malik	1,184	78.93
	{ M. A. Roseberry	2,044	56.77			
1993	G. A. Gooch	2,023	63.21	D. C. Boon	1,437	75.63
1994	B. C. Lara	2,066	89.82	J. D. Carr	1,543	90.76
1995	M. R. Ramprakash . .	2,258	77.86	M. R. Ramprakash . . .	2,258	77.86
1996	G. A. Gooch	1,944	67.03	S. C. Ganguly	762	95.25
1997	S. P. James	1,775	68.26	G. A. Hick	1,524	69.27
1998	J. P. Crawley	1,851	74.04	J. P. Crawley	1,851	74.04
1999	S. G. Law	1,833	73.32	S. G. Law	1,833	73.32
2000	D. S. Lehmann	1,477	67.13	M. G. Bevan	1,124	74.93

Season	Leading scorer	Runs	Avge	Top of averages	Runs	Avge
2001	M. E. K. Hussey. . . .	2,055	79.03	D. R. Martyn	942	104.66
2002	I. J. Ward	1,759	62.82	R. Dravid	773	96.62
2003	S. G. Law	1,820	91.00	S. G. Law	1,820	91.00
2004	R. W. T. Key	1,896	79.00	R. W. T. Key	1,896	79.00

Notes: The highest average recorded in an English season was 115.66 (2,429 runs, 26 innings) by D. G. Bradman in 1938.

In 1953, W. A. Johnston averaged 102.00 from 17 innings, 16 not out.

25,000 RUNS

Dates in italics denote the first half of an overseas season; i.e. *1945* denotes the 1945-46 season.

		Career	R	I	NO	HS	100s	Avge
1	J. B. Hobbs	1905–34	61,237	1,315	106	316*	197	50.65
2	F. E. Woolley	1906–38	58,969	1,532	85	305*	145	40.75
3	E. H. Hendren	1907–38	57,611	1,300	166	301*	170	50.80
4	C. P. Mead	1905–36	55,061	1,340	185	280*	153	47.67
5	W. G. Grace	1865–1908	54,896	1,493	105	344	126	39.55
6	W. R. Hammond	1920–51	50,551	1,005	104	336*	167	56.10
7	H. Sutcliffe	1919–45	50,138	1,088	123	313	149	51.95
8	G. Boycott	1962–86	48,426	1,014	162	261*	151	56.83
9	T. W. Graveney	1948–*71*	47,793	1,223	159	258	122	44.91
10	G. A. Gooch	1973–2000	44,846	990	75	333	128	49.01
11	T. W. Hayward	1893–1914	43,551	1,138	96	315*	104	41.79
12	D. L. Amiss.	1960–87	43,423	1,139	126	262*	102	42.86
13	M. C. Cowdrey	1950–76	42,719	1,130	134	307	107	42.89
14	A. Sandham	1911–*37*	41,284	1,000	79	325	107	44.82
15	L. Hutton	1934–60	40,140	814	91	364	129	55.51
16	M. J. K. Smith.	1951–75	39,832	1,091	139	204	69	41.84
17	W. Rhodes.	1898–1930	39,802	1,528	237	267*	58	30.83
18	J. H. Edrich	1956–78	39,790	979	104	310*	103	45.47
19	R. E. S. Wyatt	1923–57	39,405	1,141	157	232	85	40.04
20	D. C. S. Compton . . .	1936–64	38,942	839	88	300	123	51.85
21	E. Tyldesley	1909–36	38,874	961	106	256*	102	45.46
22	J. T. Tyldesley	1895–1923	37,897	994	62	295*	86	40.66
23	K. W. R. Fletcher . . .	1962–88	37,665	1,167	170	228*	63	37.77
24	**G. A. Hick**	***1983–2004***	**37,505**	**777**	**76**	**405***	**126**	**53.50**
25	C. G. Greenidge	1970–92	37,354	889	75	273*	92	45.88
26	J. W. Hearne	1909–36	37,252	1,025	116	285*	96	40.98
27	L. E. G. Ames	1926–51	37,248	951	95	295	102	43.51
28	D. Kenyon	1946–67	37,002	1,159	59	259	74	33.63
29	W. J. Edrich	1934–58	36,965	964	92	267*	86	42.39
30	J. M. Parks	1949–76	36,673	1,227	172	205*	51	34.76
31	M. W. Gatting	1975–98	36,549	861	123	258	94	49.52
32	D. Denton	1894–1920	36,479	1,163	70	221	69	33.37
33	G. H. Hirst	1891–1929	36,323	1,215	151	341	60	34.13
34	I. V. A. Richards. . . .	*1971*–93	36,212	796	63	322	114	49.40
35	A. Jones	1957–83	36,049	1,168	72	204*	56	32.89
36	W. G. Quaife	1894–1928	36,012	1,203	185	255*	72	35.37
37	R. E. Marshall	*1945*–72	35,725	1,053	59	228*	68	35.94
38	G. Gunn	1902–32	35,208	1,061	82	220	62	35.96
39	D. B. Close	1949–86	34,994	1,225	173	198	52	33.26
40	Zaheer Abbas.	*1965–86*	34,843	768	92	274	108	51.54
41	J. G. Langridge	1928–55	34,380	984	66	250*	76	37.45
42	G. M. Turner	*1964–82*	34,346	792	101	311*	103	49.70
43	C. Washbrook	1933–64	34,101	906	107	251*	76	42.67

		Career	R	I	NO	HS	100s	Avge
44	M. Leyland	1920–48	33,660	932	101	263	80	40.50
45	H. T. W. Hardinge. . .	1902–33	33,519	1,021	103	263*	75	36.51
46	R. Abel.	1881–1904	33,124	1,007	73	357*	74	35.46
47	A. I. Kallicharran . .	1966–90	32,650	834	86	243*	87	43.64
48	A. J. Lamb	1972–95	32,502	772	108	294	89	48.94
49	C. A. Milton	1948–74	32,150	1,078	125	170	56	33.73
50	J. D. Robertson. . . .	1937–59	31,914	897	46	331*	67	37.50
51	J. Hardstaff, jun. . .	1930–55	31,847	812	94	266	83	44.35
52	James Langridge. . . .	1924–53	31,716	1,058	157	167	42	35.20
53	K. F. Barrington . . .	1953–68	31,714	831	136	256	76	45.63
54	C. H. Lloyd	1963–86	31,232	730	96	242*	79	49.26
55	Mushtaq Mohammad .	1956–85	31,091	843	104	303*	72	42.07
56	C. B. Fry	1892–1921	30,886	658	43	258*	94	50.22
57	D. Brookes	1934–59	30,874	925	70	257	71	36.10
58	P. Holmes	1913–35	30,573	810	84	315*	67	42.11
59	R. T. Simpson	1944–63	30,546	852	55	259	64	38.32
60	⎰ L. G. Berry	1924–51	30,225	1,056	57	232	45	30.25
	⎱ K. S. Suttle.	1949–71	30,225	1,064	92	204*	49	31.09
62	P. A. Perrin	1896–1928	29,709	918	91	343*	66	35.92
63	P. F. Warner	1894–1929	29,028	875	75	244	60	36.28
64	R. B. Kanhai	1954–81	28,774	669	82	256	83	49.01
65	J. O'Connor	1921–39	28,764	903	79	248	72	34.90
66	Javed Miandad	1973–93	28,647	631	95	311	80	53.44
67	T. E. Bailey.	1945–67	28,641	1,072	215	205	28	33.42
68	K. J. Barnett	1979–2002	28,593	784	76	239*	61	40.38
69	D. W. Randall	1972–93	28,456	827	81	237	52	38.14
70	E. H. Bowley	1912–34	28,378	859	47	283	52	34.94
71	B. A. Richards	1964–82	28,358	576	58	356	80	54.74
72	G. S. Sobers	1952–74	28,315	609	93	365*	86	54.87
73	A. E. Dipper	1908–32	28,075	865	69	252*	53	35.27
74	D. G. Bradman	1927–48	28,067	338	43	452*	117	95.14
75	J. H. Hampshire	1961–84	28,059	924	112	183*	43	34.55
76	P. B. H. May	1948–63	27,592	618	77	285*	85	51.00
77	R. T. Robinson	1978–99	27,571	739	85	220*	63	42.15
78	B. F. Davison	1967–87	27,453	766	79	189	53	39.96
79	Majid Khan	1961–84	27,444	700	62	241	73	43.01
80	A. C. Russell	1908–30	27,358	717	59	273	71	41.57
81	E. G. Hayes	1896–1926	27,318	896	48	276	48	32.21
82	A. E. Fagg	1932–57	27,291	803	46	269*	58	36.05
83	James Seymour	1900–26	27,237	911	62	218*	53	32.08
84	W. Larkins	1972–95	27,142	842	54	252	59	34.44
85	A. R. Border	1976–95	27,131	625	97	205	70	51.38
86	P. H. Parfitt	1956–73	26,924	845	104	200*	58	36.33
87	**M. E. Waugh. . . . . .**	***1985–2003***	**26,855**	**591**	**75**	**229***	**81**	**52.04**
88	G. L. Jessop	1894–1914	26,698	855	37	286	53	32.63
89	K. S. McEwan	1972–91	26,628	705	67	218	74	41.73
90	D. E. Davies	1924–54	26,564	1,032	80	287*	32	27.90
91	A. Shrewsbury	1875–1902	26,505	813	90	267	59	36.65
92	M. J. Stewart	1954–72	26,492	898	93	227*	49	32.90
93	C. T. Radley	1964–87	26,441	880	134	200	46	35.44
94	D. I. Gower	1975–93	26,339	727	70	228	53	40.08
95	C. E. B. Rice	1969–93	26,331	766	123	246	48	40.95
96	A. J. Stewart	1981–2003	26,165	734	81	271*	48	40.06
97	R. A. Smith.	1980–2003	26,155	717	87	209*	61	41.51
98	Younis Ahmed	1961–86	26,073	762	118	221*	46	40.48
99	P. E. Richardson	1949–65	26,055	794	41	185	44	34.60
100	D. L. Haynes	1976–96	26,030	639	72	255*	61	45.90
101	M. H. Denness	1959–80	25,886	838	65	195	33	33.48
102	S. M. Gavaskar	1966–87	25,834	563	61	340	81	51.46

		Career	R	I	NO	HS	100s	Avge
103	J. W. H. Makepeace. .	1906–30	25,799	778	66	203	43	36.23
104	W. Gunn	1880–1904	25,691	850	72	273	48	33.02
105	W. Watson	1939–64	25,670	753	109	257	55	39.86
106	G. Brown	1908–33	25,649	1,012	52	232*	37	26.71
107	G. M. Emmett	1936–59	25,602	865	50	188	37	31.41
108	J. B. Bolus	1956–75	25,598	833	81	202*	39	34.03
109	W. E. Russell	1956–72	25,525	796	64	193	41	34.87
110	C. W. J. Athey	1976–97	25,453	784	71	184	55	35.69
111	C. J. Barnett	1927–53	25,389	821	45	259	48	32.71
112	L. B. Fishlock	1931–52	25,376	699	54	253	56	39.34
113	D. J. Insole	1947–63	25,241	743	72	219*	54	37.61
114	J. M. Brearley	1961–83	25,185	768	102	312*	45	37.81
115	J. Vine	1896–1922	25,171	920	79	202	34	29.92
116	R. M. Prideaux	1958–74	25,136	808	75	202*	41	34.29
117	J. H. King	1895–1925	25,122	988	69	227*	34	27.33
118	J. G. Wright.	*1975–92*	25,073	636	44	192	59	42.35

Bold type denotes those who played in the calendar year 2004.

Note: Some works of reference provide career figures which differ from those in this list, owing to the exclusion or inclusion of matches recognised or not recognised as first-class by *Wisden*.

Other Current Players with 20,000 Runs

	Career	R	I	NO	HS	100s	Avge
M. R. Ramprakash	1987–2004	24,787	589	75	279*	73	48.22
M. P. Maynard	1985–2004	24,779	641	60	243	59	42.64
S. R. Waugh	*1984–2003*	24,052	551	88	216*	79	51.94
S. G. Law	1988–2004	23,099	507	56	263	68	51.21
C. L. Hooper	*1983–2004*	23,034	535	52	236*	69	47.68
D. S. Lehmann	1987–2004	21,822	416	28	255	69	56.24
G. P. Thorpe	1988–*2004*	21,350	547	77	223*	49	45.42
J. L. Langer.	*1991–2004*	21,251	461	43	274*	67	50.83
M. L. Hayden	*1991–2004*	20,701	424	42	380	68	54.19
N. Hussain	1987–2004	20,698	545	53	207	52	42.06

CAREER AVERAGE OVER 50

(Qualification: 10,000 runs)

Avge		Career	I	NO	R	HS	100s
95.14	D. G. Bradman	*1927–48*	338	43	28,067	452*	117
71.22	V. M. Merchant	*1929–51*	229	43	13,248	359*	44
67.46	Ajay Sharma	*1984–2000*	166	16	10,120	259*	38
65.18	W. H. Ponsford	*1920–34*	235	23	13,819	437	47
64.99	W. M. Woodfull	*1921–34*	245	39	13,388	284	49
61.33	**S. R. Tendulkar**	*1988–2004*	**334**	**36**	**18,278**	**248***	**58**
58.24	A. L. Hassett	*1932–53*	322	32	16,890	232	59
58.19	V. S. Hazare	*1934–66*	365	45	18,621	316*	60
57.66	**R. Dravid**	*1990–2004*	**320**	**46**	**15,801**	**270**	**43**
57.62	**R. T. Ponting**	*1992–2004*	**294**	**41**	**14,579**	**257**	**52**
57.22	A. F. Kippax	*1918–35*	256	33	12,762	315*	43
57.03	**M. G. Bevan**	*1989–2004*	**372**	**64**	**17,567**	**216**	**62**
56.83	G. Boycott	1962–86	1,014	162	48,426	261*	151
56.55	C. L. Walcott	*1941–63*	238	29	11,820	314*	40

Avge		Career	I	NO	R	HS	100s
56.37	K. S. Ranjitsinhji	1893–1920	500	62	24,692	285*	72
56.24	**D. S. Lehmann**	*1987–2004*	**416**	**28**	**21,822**	**255**	**69**
56.22	R. B. Simpson	1952–77	436	62	21,029	359	60
56.10	W. R. Hammond	1920–51	1,005	104	50,551	336*	167
56.02	M. D. Crowe	1979–95	412	62	19,608	299	71
55.51	L. Hutton	1934–60	814	91	40,140	364	129
55.34	E. D. Weekes	1944–64	241	24	12,010	304*	36
55.11	S. V. Manjrekar	1984–97	217	31	10,252	377	31
54.87	G. S. Sobers	1952–74	609	93	28,315	365*	86
54.74	B. A. Richards	1964–82	576	58	28,358	356	80
54.67	R. G. Pollock	1960–86	437	54	20,940	274	64
54.67	**V. V. S. Laxman**	*1992–2004*	**245**	**26**	**11,973**	**353**	**36**
54.24	F. M. M. Worrell	1941–64	326	49	15,025	308*	39
54.19	**M. L. Hayden**	*1991–2004*	**424**	**42**	**20,701**	**380**	**68**
53.78	R. M. Cowper	1959–69	228	31	10,595	307	26
53.67	A. R. Morris	1940–63	250	15	12,614	290	46
53.50	**G. A. Hick**	*1983–2004*	**777**	**76**	**37,505**	**405***	**126**
53.44	Javed Miandad	1973–93	631	95	28,647	311	80
52.86	D. B. Vengsarkar	1975–91	390	52	17,868	284	55
52.42	**J. H. Kallis**	*1993–2004*	**275**	**37**	**12,477**	**200**	**34**
52.32	Hanif Mohammad	1951–75	371	45	17,059	499	55
52.27	P. R. Umrigar	1944–67	350	41	16,154	252*	49
52.20	G. S. Chappell	1966–83	542	72	24,535	247*	74
52.04	**M. E. Waugh**	*1985–2003*	**591**	**75**	**26,855**	**229***	**81**
51.98	M. Azharuddin	1981–99	343	38	15,855	226	54
51.95	H. Sutcliffe	1919–45	1,088	123	50,138	313	149
51.94	**S. R. Waugh**	*1984–2003*	**551**	**88**	**24,052**	**216***	**79**
51.85	D. M. Jones	1981–97	415	45	19,188	324*	55
51.85	D. C. S. Compton	1936–64	839	88	38,942	300	123
51.54	Zaheer Abbas	1965–86	768	92	34,843	274	108
51.53	A. D. Nourse	1931–52	269	27	12,472	260*	41
51.51	**B. C. Lara**	*1987–2004*	**396**	**11**	**19,835**	**501***	**55**
51.46	S. M. Gavaskar	1966–87	563	61	25,834	340	81
51.44	W. A. Brown	1932–49	284	15	13,338	265*	39
51.43	**D. P. M. D. Jayawardene**	*1995–2004*	**212**	**17**	**10,029**	**274**	**29**
51.38	A. R. Border	1976–95	625	97	27,131	205	70
51.30	**A. Flower**	*1986 2004*	**320**	**57**	**13,494**	**232***	**36**
51.21	**S. G. Law**	*1988–2004*	**507**	**56**	**23,099**	**263**	**68**
51.16	**M. L. Love**	*1992–2004*	**283**	**29**	**12,997**	**300***	**31**
51.00	P. B. H. May	1948–63	618	77	27,592	285*	85
50.99	**M. E. K. Hussey**	*1994–2004*	**288**	**21**	**13,616**	**331***	**34**
50.95	N. C. O'Neill	1955–67	306	34	13,859	284	45
50.93	R. N. Harvey	1946–62	461	35	21,699	231*	67
50.90	W. M. Lawry	1955–71	417	49	18,734	266	50
50.90	A. V. Mankad	1963–82	326	71	12,980	265	31
50.83	**J. L. Langer**	*1991–2004*	**461**	**43**	**21,251**	**274***	**67**
50.80	E. H. Hendren	1907–38	1,300	166	57,611	301*	170
50.65	J. B. Hobbs	1905–34	1,315	106	61,237	316*	197
50.59	**D. R. Martyn**	*1990–2004*	**310**	**43**	**13,510**	**238**	**41**
50.58	K. C. Wessels	1973–99	539	50	24,738	254	66
50.58	S. J. Cook	1972–94	475	57	21,143	313*	64
50.53	**M. T. G. Elliott**	*1992–2004*	**326**	**26**	**15,160**	**203**	**48**
50.46	**Inzamam-ul-Haq**	*1985–2004*	**344**	**50**	**14,836**	**329**	**40**
50.37	**M. S. Atapattu**	*1989–2004*	**319**	**48**	**13,651**	**253***	**45**
50.36	**S. Chanderpaul**	*1991–2004*	**278**	**45**	**11,735**	**303***	**34**
50.22	C. B. Fry	1892–1921	658	43	30,886	258*	94

Note: G. A. Headley (*1927*–1954) scored 9,921 runs, average 69.86.

Bold type denotes those who played in the calendar year 2004.

FASTEST FIFTIES

Minutes

11	C. I. J. Smith (66)	Middlesex v Gloucestershire at Bristol	1938
13	Khalid Mahmood (56)	Gujranwala v Sargodha at Gujranwala	2000-01
14	S. J. Pegler (50)	South Africans v Tasmania at Launceston	1910-11
14	F. T. Mann (53)	Middlesex v Nottinghamshire at Lord's	1921
14	H. B. Cameron (56)	Transvaal v Orange Free State at Johannesburg . . .	1934-35
14	C. I. J. Smith (52)	Middlesex v Kent at Maidstone	1935

Note: The following fast fifties were scored in contrived circumstances when runs were given from full tosses and long hops to expedite a declaration: C. C. Inman (8 minutes), Leicestershire v Nottinghamshire at Nottingham, 1965; G. Chapple (10 minutes), Lancashire v Glamorgan at Manchester, 1993; T. M. Moody (11 minutes), Warwickshire v Glamorgan at Swansea, 1990; A. J. Stewart (14 minutes), Surrey v Kent at Dartford, 1986; M. P. Maynard (14 minutes), Glamorgan v Yorkshire at Cardiff, 1987.

FASTEST HUNDREDS

Minutes

35	P. G. H. Fender (113*)	Surrey v Northamptonshire at Northampton	1920
40	G. L. Jessop (101)	Gloucestershire v Yorkshire at Harrogate.	1897
40	Ahsan-ul-Haq (100*)	Muslims v Sikhs at Lahore	1923-24
42	G. L. Jessop (191)	Gentlemen of South v Players of South at Hastings	1907
43	A. H. Hornby (106)	Lancashire v Somerset at Manchester.	1905
43	D. W. Hookes (107)	South Australia v Victoria at Adelaide	1982-83
44	R. N. S. Hobbs (100)	Essex v Australians at Chelmsford.	1975

Notes: The fastest recorded authentic hundred in terms of balls received was scored off 34 balls by D. W. Hookes (above).

Research of the scorebook has shown that P. G. H. Fender scored his hundred from between 40 and 46 balls. He contributed 113 to an unfinished sixth-wicket partnership of 171 in 42 minutes with H. A. Peach.

E. B. Alletson (Nottinghamshire) scored 189 out of 227 runs in 90 minutes against Sussex at Hove in 1911. It has been estimated that his last 139 runs took 37 minutes.

The following fast hundreds were scored in contrived circumstances when full tosses, long hops etc were bowled deliberately to expedite a declaration: G. Chapple (21 minutes), Lancashire v Glamorgan at Manchester, 1993; T. M. Moody (26 minutes), Warwickshire v Glamorgan at Swansea, 1990; S. J. O'Shaughnessy (35 minutes), Lancashire v Leicestershire at Manchester, 1983; C. M. Old (37 minutes), Yorkshire v Warwickshire at Birmingham, 1977; N. F. M. Popplewell (41 minutes), Somerset v Gloucestershire at Bath, 1983.

FASTEST DOUBLE-HUNDREDS

Minutes

113	R. J. Shastri (200*)	Bombay v Baroda at Bombay	1984-85
120	G. L. Jessop (286)	Gloucestershire v Sussex at Hove	1903
120	C. H. Lloyd (201*)	West Indians v Glamorgan at Swansea	1976
130	G. L. Jessop (234)	Gloucestershire v Somerset at Bristol	1905
131	V. T. Trumper (293)	Australians v Canterbury at Christchurch	1913-14

FASTEST TRIPLE-HUNDREDS

Minutes

181	D. C. S. Compton (300)	MCC v N. E. Transvaal at Benoni	1948-49
205	F. E. Woolley (305*)	MCC v Tasmania at Hobart	1911-12
205	C. G. Macartney (345)	Australians v Nottinghamshire at Nottingham	1921
213	D. G. Bradman (369)	South Australia v Tasmania at Adelaide	1935-36

MOST RUNS IN A DAY BY ONE BATSMAN

390*	B. C. Lara	Warwickshire v Durham at Birmingham	1994
345	C. G. Macartney	Australians v Nottinghamshire at Nottingham	1921
334	W. H. Ponsford	Victoria v New South Wales at Melbourne	1926-27
333	K. S. Duleepsinhji	Sussex v Northamptonshire at Hove	1930
331*	J. D. Robertson	Middlesex v Worcestershire at Worcester	1949
325*	B. A. Richards	S. Australia v W. Australia at Perth	1970-71

Note: These scores do not necessarily represent the complete innings. See pages 160–162.
There have been another 13 instances of a batsman scoring 300 runs in a day (see *Wisden* 2003, pages 278–279, for full list).

LONGEST INNINGS

Mins

1,015	R. Nayyar (271)	Himachal Pradesh v Jammu and Kashmir at Chamba	1999-2000
970	Hanif Mohammad (337)	Pakistan v West Indies at Bridgetown	1957-58
	Hanif believes he batted 999 minutes.		
878	G. Kirsten (275)	South Africa v England at Durban	1999-2000
799	S. T. Jayasuriya (340)	Sri Lanka v India at Colombo	1997-98
797	L. Hutton (364)	England v Australia at The Oval	1938

1,000 RUNS IN MAY

	Runs	*Avge*
W. G. Grace, May 9 to May 30, 1895 (22 days)	1,016	112.88
Grace was 46 years old.		
W. R. Hammond, May 7 to May 31, 1927 (25 days)	1,042	74.42
Hammond scored his 1,000th run on May 28, thus equalling		
Grace's record of 22 days.		
C. Hallows, May 5 to May 31, 1928 (27 days)	1,000	125.00

1,000 RUNS IN APRIL AND MAY

	Runs	*Avge*
T. W. Hayward, April 16 to May 31, 1900	1,074	97.63
D. G. Bradman, April 30 to May 31, 1930	1,001	143.00
On April 30 Bradman was 75 not out.		
D. G. Bradman, April 30 to May 31, 1938	1,056	150.85
Bradman scored 258 on April 30, and his 1,000th run on May 27.		
W. J. Edrich, April 30 to May 31, 1938	1,010	84.16
Edrich was 21 not out on April 30. All his runs were scored at Lord's.		
G. M. Turner, April 24 to May 31, 1973	1,018	78.30
G. A. Hick, April 17 to May 29, 1988	1,019	101.90
Hick scored a record 410 runs in April, and his 1,000th run on May 28.		

MOST RUNS SCORED OFF AN OVER

(All instances refer to six-ball overs)

36	G. S. Sobers	off M. A. Nash, Nottinghamshire v Glamorgan at Swansea (six sixes)	1968
36	R. J. Shastri	off Tilak Raj, Bombay v Baroda at Bombay (six sixes)	1984-85
34	E. B. Alletson	off E. H. Killick, Nottinghamshire v Sussex at Hove (46604446; including two no-balls)	1911
34	F. C. Hayes	off M. A. Nash, Lancashire v Glamorgan at Swansea (646666)	1977
34†	A. Flintoff	off A. J. Tudor, Lancashire v Surrey at Manchester (64444660; including two no-balls)	1998
32	I. T. Botham	off I. R. Snook, England XI v Central Districts at Palmerston North (466466)	1983-84
32	P. W. G. Parker	off A. I. Kallicharran, Sussex v Warwickshire at Birmingham (466664)	1982
32	I. R. Redpath	off N. Rosendorff, Australians v Orange Free State at Bloemfontein (666644)	1969-70
32	C. C. Smart	off G. Hill, Glamorgan v Hampshire at Cardiff (664664)	1935
32	Khalid Mahmood	off Naved Latif, Gujranwala v Sargodha at Gujranwala (666662)	2000-01

† *Altogether 38 runs were scored off this over, the two no-balls counting for two extra runs each under ECB regulations.*

Notes: The following instances have been excluded from the above table because of the bowlers' compliance: 34 – M. P. Maynard off S. A. Marsh, Glamorgan v Kent at Swansea, 1992; 34 – G. Chapple off P. A. Cottey, Lancashire v Glamorgan at Manchester, 1993; 34 – F. B. Touzel off F. J. J. Viljoen, Western Province B v Griqualand West at Kimberley, 1993-94; 32 – C. C. Inman off N. W. Hill, Leicestershire v Nottinghamshire at Nottingham, 1965; 32 – T. E. Jesty off R. J. Boyd-Moss, Hampshire v Northamptonshire at Southampton, 1984; 32 – M. A. Ealham off G. D. Hodgson, Kent v Gloucestershire at Bristol, 1992; 32 – G. Chapple off P. A. Cottey, Lancashire v Glamorgan at Manchester, 1993. Chapple's 34 and 32 came off successive overs from Cottey.

There were 35 runs off an over received by A. T. Reinholds off H. T. Davis, Auckland v Wellington at Auckland 1995-96, but this included six no-balls (counting as two runs each), four byes and only 19 off the bat.

In a Shell Trophy match against Canterbury at Christchurch in 1989-90, R. H. Vance (Wellington), acting on the instructions of his captain, deliberately conceded 77 runs in an over of full tosses which contained 17 no-balls, and, owing to the umpire's understandable miscalculation, only five legitimate deliveries.

The greatest number of runs scored off an eight-ball over is 34 (40446664) by R. M. Edwards off M. C. Carew, Governor-General's XI v West Indians at Auckland, 1968-69.

MOST SIXES IN AN INNINGS

16	A. Symonds (254*)	Gloucestershire v Glamorgan at Abergavenny	1995
15	J. R. Reid (296)	Wellington v Northern Districts at Wellington	1962-63
14	Shakti Singh (128)	Himachal Pradesh v Haryana at Dharmsala	1990-91
13	Majid Khan (147*)	Pakistanis v Glamorgan at Swansea	1967
13	C. G. Greenidge (273*)	D. H. Robins' XI v Pakistanis at Eastbourne	1974
13	C. G. Greenidge (259)	Hampshire v Sussex at Southampton	1975
13	G. W. Humpage (254)	Warwickshire v Lancashire at Southport	1982
13	R. J. Shastri (200*)	Bombay v Baroda at Bombay	1984-85
12	Gulfraz Khan (207)	Railways v Universities at Lahore	1976-77
12	I. T. Botham (138*)	Somerset v Warwickshire at Birmingham	1985
12	R. A. Harper (234)	Northamptonshire v Gloucestershire at Northampton	1986
12	D. M. Jones (248)	Australians v Warwickshire at Birmingham	1989
12	U. N. K. Fernando (160)	Sinhalese SC v Sebastianites C and AC at Colombo	1990-91
12	D. N. Patel (204)	Auckland v Northern Districts at Auckland	1991-92
12	W. V. Raman (206)	Tamil Nadu v Kerala at Madras	1991-92
12	G. D. Lloyd (241)	Lancashire v Essex at Chelmsford	1996
12	Wasim Akram (257*)	Pakistan v Zimbabwe at Sheikhupura	1996-97

11	C. K. Nayudu (153)	Hindus v MCC at Bombay	1926-27
11	C. J. Barnett (194)	Gloucestershire v Somerset at Bath	1934
11	R. Benaud (135)	Australians v T. N. Pearce's XI at Scarborough	1953
11	R. Bora (126)	Assam v Tripura at Gauhati	1987-88
11	G. A. Hick (405*)	Worcestershire v Somerset at Taunton	1988
11	A. S. Jayasinghe (183)	Tamil Union v Burgher RC at Colombo	1996-97
11	N. J. Astle (222)	New Zealand v England at Christchurch	2001-02
11	C. L. Hooper (201)	Lancashire v Middlesex at Manchester	2003
11	I. D. Blackwell (247*)	Somerset v Derbyshire at Taunton	2003
11	M. L. Hayden (380)	Australia v Zimbabwe at Perth	2003-04
11	C. M. Spearman (133)	Central Districts v Auckland at Auckland	2003-04
11	D. J. Thornely (261*)	New South Wales v Western Australia at Sydney	2004-05

Note: F. B. Touzel (128*) hit 13 sixes for Western Province B v Griqualand West in contrived circumstances at Kimberley in 1993-94.

MOST SIXES IN A MATCH

20	A. Symonds (254*, 76)	Gloucestershire v Glamorgan at Abergavenny	1995
17	W. J. Stewart (155, 125)	Warwickshire v Lancashire at Blackpool	1959

MOST SIXES IN A SEASON

80	I. T. Botham	1985		49	I. V. A. Richards	1985
66	A. W. Wellard	1935		48	A. W. Carr	1925
57	A. W. Wellard	1936		48	J. H. Edrich	1965
57	A. W. Wellard	1938		48	A. Symonds	1995
51	A. W. Wellard	1933				

MOST BOUNDARIES IN AN INNINGS

	4s/6s			
72	62/10	B. C. Lara (501*)	Warwickshire v Durham at Birmingham	1994
68	68/–	P. A. Perrin (343*)	Essex v Derbyshire at Chesterfield	1904
65	64/1	A. C. MacLaren (424)	Lancashire v Somerset at Taunton	1895
64	64/–	Hanif Mohammad (499)	Karachi v Bahawalpur at Karachi	1958-59
57	52/5	J. H. Edrich (310*)	England v New Zealand at Leeds	1965
57	52/5	Naved Latif (394)	Sargodha v Gujranwala at Gujranwala	2000-01
55	55/–	C. W. Gregory (383)	NSW v Queensland at Brisbane	1906-07
55	53/2	G. R. Marsh (355*)	W. Australia v S. Australia at Perth	1989-90
55	51/3†	S. V. Manjrekar (377)	Bombay v Hyderabad at Bombay	1990-91
54	53/1	G. H. Hirst (341)	Yorkshire v Leicestershire at Leicester	1905
53	53/–	A. W. Nourse (304*)	Natal v Transvaal at Johannesburg	1919-20
53	45/8	K. R. Rutherford (317)	New Zealanders v D. B. Close's XI at Scarborough	1986
53	51/2	V. V. S. Laxman (353)	Hyderabad v Karnataka at Bangalore	1999-2000
53	52/1	M. W. Goodwin (335*)	Sussex v Leicestershire at Hove	2003
52	47/5	N. H. Fairbrother (366)	Lancashire v Surrey at The Oval	1990
51	51/–	W. G. Grace (344)	MCC v Kent at Canterbury	1876
51	47/4	C. G. Macartney (345)	Australians v Notts at Nottingham	1921
51	50/1	B. B. Nimbalkar (443*)	Maharashtra v Kathiawar at Poona	1948-49
51	49/2	G. A. Hick (315*)	Worcestershire v Durham at Worcester	2002
50	47/–‡	A. Ducat (306*)	Surrey v Oxford U. at The Oval	1919
50	46/4	D. G. Bradman (369)	S. Australia v Tasmania at Adelaide	1935-36
50	35/15	J. R. Reid (296)	Wellington v N. Districts at Wellington	1962-63
50	42/8	I. V. A. Richards (322)	Somerset v Warwickshire at Taunton	1985
50	50/	Shoaib Khan (300*)	Peshawar v Quetta at Peshawar	2003-04

† Plus one five.

‡ Plus three fives.

PARTNERSHIPS OVER 500

577 for 4th	V. S. Hazare (288) and Gul Mahomed (319), Baroda v Holkar at Baroda.	1946-47
576 for 2nd	S. T. Jayasuriya (340) and R. S. Mahanama (225), Sri Lanka v India at Colombo.	1997-98
574* for 4th	F. M. M. Worrell (255*) and C. L. Walcott (314*), Barbados v Trinidad at Port-of-Spain.	1945-46
561 for 1st	Waheed Mirza (324) and Mansoor Akhtar (224*), Karachi Whites v Quetta at Karachi.	1976-77
555 for 1st	P. Holmes (224*) and H. Sutcliffe (313), Yorkshire v Essex at Leyton.	1932
554 for 1st	J. T. Brown (300) and J. Tunnicliffe (243), Yorkshire v Derbyshire at Chesterfield	1898
502* for 4th	F. M. M. Worrell (308*) and J. D. C. Goddard (218*), Barbados v Trinidad at Bridgetown.	1943-44

HIGHEST PARTNERSHIPS FOR EACH WICKET

The following lists include all stands above 400; otherwise the top ten for each wicket.

First Wicket

561	Waheed Mirza and Mansoor Akhtar, Karachi Whites v Quetta at Karachi . . .	1976-77
555	P. Holmes and H. Sutcliffe, Yorkshire v Essex at Leyton	1932
554	J. T. Brown and J. Tunnicliffe, Yorkshire v Derbyshire at Chesterfield	1898
490	E. H. Bowley and J. G. Langridge, Sussex v Middlesex at Hove	1933
464	R. Sehgal and R. Lamba, Delhi v Himachal Pradesh at Delhi	1994-95
459	Wasim Jaffer and S. K. Kulkarni, Mumbai v Saurashtra at Rajkot	1996-97
456	E. R. Mayne and W. H. Ponsford, Victoria v Queensland at Melbourne	1923-24
451*	S. Desai and R. M. H. Binny, Karnataka v Kerala at Chikmagalur.	1977-78
431	M. R. J. Veletta and G. R. Marsh, Western Australia v South Australia at Perth	1989-90
428	J. B. Hobbs and A. Sandham, Surrey v Oxford University at The Oval. . . .	1926
425*	L. V. Garrick and C. H. Gayle, Jamaica v West Indies B at Montego Bay . .	2000-01
424	I. J. Siedle and J. F. W. Nicolson, Natal v Orange Free State at Bloemfontein	1926-27
421	S. M. Gavaskar and G. A. Parkar, Bombay v Bengal at Bombay	1981-82
418	Kamal Najamuddin and Khalid Alvi, Karachi v Railways at Karachi	1980-81
413	V. Mankad and Pankaj Roy, India v New Zealand at Madras	1955-56
406*	D. J. Bicknell and G. E. Welton, Notts v Warwickshire at Birmingham.	2000
405	C. P. S. Chauhan and M. S. Gupte, Maharashtra v Vidarbha at Poona	1972-73
403	Rizwan-uz-Zaman and Shoaib Mohammad, PIA v Hyderabad at Hyderabad .	1999-2000

Second Wicket

576	S. T. Jayasuriya and R. S. Mahanama, Sri Lanka v India at Colombo.	1997-98
475	Zahir Alam and L. S. Rajput, Assam v Tripura at Gauhati	1991-92
465*	J. A. Jameson and R. B. Kanhai, Warwicks v Gloucestershire at Birmingham	1974
455	K. V. Bhandarkar and B. B. Nimbalkar, Maharashtra v Kathiawar at Poona . .	1948-49
451	W. H. Ponsford and D. G. Bradman, Australia v England at The Oval	1934
446	C. C. Hunte and G. S. Sobers, West Indies v Pakistan at Kingston	1957-58
441	C. C. Bradfield and J. D. C. Bryant, Eastern Province v North West at Potchefstroom.	2002-03
438	M. S. Atapattu and K. C. Sangakkara, Sri Lanka v Zimbabwe at Bulawayo. .	2003-04
429*	J. G. Dewes and G. H. G. Doggart, Cambridge U. v Essex at Cambridge . . .	1949
426	Arshad Pervez and Mohsin Khan, Habib Bank v Income Tax at Lahore . . .	1977-78
417	K. J. Barnett and T. A. Tweats, Derbyshire v Yorkshire at Derby	1997
415	A. Jadeja and S. V. Manjrekar, Indians v Bowl XI at Springs	1992-93
403	G. A. Gooch and P. J. Prichard, Essex v Leicestershire at Chelmsford	1990

Third Wicket

467	A. H. Jones and M. D. Crowe, New Zealand v Sri Lanka at Wellington	1990-91
456	Khalid Irtiza and Aslam Ali, United Bank v Multan at Karachi	1975-76
451	Mudassar Nazar and Javed Miandad, Pakistan v India at Hyderabad	1982-83
445	P. E. Whitelaw and W. N. Carson, Auckland v Otago at Dunedin	1936-37
438*	G. A. Hick and T. M. Moody, Worcestershire v Hampshire at Southampton ..	1997
436*	D. L. Maddy and B. J. Hodge, Leicestershire v Loughborough UCCE at Leicester	2003
436	S. S. Das and S. S. Raul, Orissa v Bengal at Baripada	2001-02
434	J. B. Stollmeyer and G. E. Gomez, Trinidad v British Guiana at Port-of-Spain ..	1946-47
429*	J. A. Rudolph and H. H. Dippenaar, South Africa v Bangladesh at Chittagong	2003
424*	W. J. Edrich and D. C. S. Compton, Middlesex v Somerset at Lord's	1948
417	G. A. Hick and B. F. Smith, Worcestershire v Gloucestershire at Worcester ..	2004
413	D. J. Bicknell and D. M. Ward, Surrey v Kent at Canterbury............	1990
410*	R. S. Modi and L. Amarnath, India in England v The Rest at Calcutta	1946-47
409	V. V. S. Laxman and R. Dravid, South Zone v West Zone at Surat	2000-01
406*	R. S. Gavaskar and S. J. Kalyani, Bengal v Tripura at Agartala	1999-2000
405	A. Jadeja and A. S. Kaypee, Haryana v Services at Faridabad	1991-92

Fourth Wicket

577	V. S. Hazare and Gul Mahomed, Baroda v Holkar at Baroda............	1946-47
574*	C. L. Walcott and F. M. M. Worrell, Barbados v Trinidad at Port-of-Spain...	1945-46
502*	F. M. M. Worrell and J. D. C. Goddard, Barbados v Trinidad at Bridgetown..	1943-44
470	A. I. Kallicharran and G. W. Humpage, Warwicks v Lancs at Southport	1982
462*	D. W. Hookes and W. B. Phillips, South Australia v Tasmania at Adelaide ...	1986-87
448	R. Abel and T. W. Hayward, Surrey v Yorkshire at The Oval	1899
436	S. Abbas Ali and P. K. Dwevedi, Madhya Pradesh v Railways at Indore	1997-98
425*	A. Dale and I. V. A. Richards, Glamorgan v Middlesex at Cardiff	1993
424	I. S. Lee and S. O. Quin, Victoria v Tasmania at Melbourne	1933-34
411	P. B. H. May and M. C. Cowdrey, England v West Indies at Birmingham ...	1957
410	G. Abraham and P. Balan Pandit, Kerala v Andhra at Palghat	1959-60
402	W. Watson and T. W. Graveney, MCC v British Guiana at Georgetown	1953-54
402	R. B. Kanhai and K. Ibadulla, Warwicks v Notts at Nottingham..........	1968

Fifth Wicket

464*	M. E. Waugh and S. R. Waugh, New South Wales v Western Australia at Perth	1990-91
405	S. G. Barnes and D. G. Bradman, Australia v England at Sydney.........	1946-47
401	M. B. Loye and D. Ripley, Northamptonshire v Glamorgan at Northampton ..	1998
397	W. Bardsley and C. Kelleway, New South Wales v South Australia at Sydney.	1920-21
393	E. G. Arnold and W. B. Burns, Worcestershire v Warwickshire at Birmingham.	1909
391	A. Malhotra and S. Dogra, Delhi v Services at Delhi.	1995-96
385	S. R. Waugh and G. S. Blewett, Australia v South Africa at Johannesburg ...	1996-97
381	R. Nayyar and V. Sehwag, North Zone v South Zone at Agartala	1999-2000
377*	G. P. Thorpe and M. R. Ramprakash, England XI v South Australia at Adelaide	1998-99
376	V. V. S. Laxman and R. Dravid, India v Australia at Kolkata	2000-01

Sixth Wicket

487*	G. A. Headley and C. C. Passailaigue, Jamaica v Lord Tennyson's XI at Kingston	1931-32
428	W. W. Armstrong and M. A. Noble, Australians v Sussex at Hove	1902
411	R. M. Poore and E. G. Wynyard, Hampshire v Somerset at Taunton	1899
376	R. Subba Row and A. Lightfoot, Northamptonshire v Surrey at The Oval ...	1958
372*	K. P. Pietersen and J. E. Morris, Nottinghamshire v Derbyshire at Derby....	2001
371	V. M. Merchant and R. S. Modi, Bombay v Maharashtra at Bombay........	1943-44
365	B. C. Lara and R. D. Jacobs, West Indians v Australia A at Hobart	2000-01
356	W. V. Raman and A. Kripal Singh, Tamil Nadu v Goa at Panjim	1988-89
353	Salah-ud-Din and Zaheer Abbas, Karachi v East Pakistan at Karachi.......	1968-69
346	J. H. W. Fingleton and D. G. Bradman, Australia v England at Melbourne...	1936-37

Seventh Wicket

460	Bhupinder Singh, jun. and P. Dharmani, Punjab v Delhi at Delhi	1994-95
347	D. St E. Atkinson and C. C. Depeiza, West Indies v Australia at Bridgetown .	1954-55
344	K. S. Ranjitsinhji and W. Newham, Sussex v Essex at Leyton	1902
340	K. J. Key and H. Philipson, Oxford University v Middlesex at Chiswick Park	1887
336	F. C. W. Newman and C. R. N. Maxwell, Sir J. Cahn's XI v Leicestershire at Nottingham.	1935
335	C. W. Andrews and E. C. Bensted, Queensland v New South Wales at Sydney	1934-35
325	G. Brown and C. H. Abercrombie, Hampshire v Essex at Leyton	1913
323	E. H. Hendren and L. F. Townsend, MCC v Barbados at Bridgetown	1929-30
308	Waqar Hassan and Imtiaz Ahmed, Pakistan v New Zealand at Lahore	1955-56
301	C. C. Lewis and B. N. French, Nottinghamshire v Durham at Chester-le-Street	1993

Eighth Wicket

433	V. T. Trumper and A. Sims, A. Sims' Aust. XI v Canterbury at Christchurch	1913-14
313	Wasim Akram and Saqlain Mushtaq, Pakistan v Zimbabwe at Sheikhupura . .	1996-97
292	R. Peel and Lord Hawke, Yorkshire v Warwickshire at Birmingham	1896
291	R. S. C. Martin-Jenkins and M. J. G. Davis, Sussex v Somerset at Taunton . .	2002
270	V. T. Trumper and E. P. Barbour, New South Wales v Victoria at Sydney. . . .	1912-13
268	S. Sriram and M. R. Srinivas, Tamil Nadu v Punjab at Mohali	2002-03
263	D. R. Wilcox and R. M. Taylor, Essex v Warwickshire at Southend	1946
255	E. A. V. Williams and E. A. Martindale, Barbados v Trinidad at Bridgetown. .	1935-36
253	N. J. Astle and A. C. Parore, New Zealand v Australia at Perth	2001-02
249*	Shaukat Mirza and Akram Raza, Habib Bank v PNSC at Lahore	1993-94

Ninth Wicket

283	J. Chapman and A. Warren, Derbyshire v Warwickshire at Blackwell	1910
268	J. B. Commins and N. Boje, South Africa A v Mashonaland at Harare	1994-95
251	J. W. H. T. Douglas and S. N. Hare, Essex v Derbyshire at Leyton.	1921
249*†	A. S. Srivastava and K. Seth, Madhya Pradesh v Vidarbha at Indore.	2000-01
245	V. S. Hazare and N. D. Nagarwalla, Maharashtra v Baroda at Poona.	1939-40
244*	Arshad Ayub and M. V. Ramanamurthy, Hyderabad v Bihar at Hyderabad . .	1986-87
239	H. B. Cave and I. B. Leggat, Central Districts v Otago at Dunedin.	1952-53
232	C. Hill and E. Walkley, South Australia v New South Wales at Adelaide	1900-01
231	P. Sen and J. Mitter, Bengal v Bihar at Jamshedpur.	1950-51
230	D. A. Livingstone and A. T. Castell, Hampshire v Surrey at Southampton . . .	1962

† *276 unbeaten runs were scored for this wicket in two separate partnerships; after Srivastava retired hurt, Seth and N. D. Hirwani added 27.*

Tenth Wicket

307	A. F. Kippax and J. E. H. Hooker, New South Wales v Victoria at Melbourne	1928-29
249	C. T. Sarwate and S. N. Banerjee, Indians v Surrey at The Oval	1946
239	Aqeel Arshad and Ali Raza, Lahore Whites v Hyderabad at Lahore	2004-05
235	F. E. Woolley and A. Fielder, Kent v Worcestershire at Stourbridge.	1909
233	Ajay Sharma and Maninder Singh, Delhi v Bombay at Bombay.	1991-92
230	R. W. Nicholls and W. Roche, Middlesex v Kent at Lord's	1899
228	R. Illingworth and K. Higgs, Leicestershire v Northamptonshire at Leicester .	1977
219	D. J. Thornely and S. C. G. MacGill, New South Wales v Western Australia at Sydney.	2004-05
218	F. H. Vigar and T. P. B. Smith, Essex v Derbyshire at Chesterfield	1947
214	N. V. Knight and A. Richardson, Warwickshire v Hampshire at Birmingham .	2002

Note: There have been only 11 last-wicket stands of 200 or more, the 11th being 211 by M. Ellis and T. J. Hastings for Victoria v South Australia at Melbourne in 1902-03.

UNUSUAL DISMISSALS

Handled the Ball

There have been **50** instances in first-class cricket. The most recent are:

G. A. Gooch	England v Australia at Manchester	1993
A. C. Waller	Mashonaland CD v Mashonaland Under-24 at Harare	1994-95
K. M. Krikken	Derbyshire v Indians at Derby	1996
A. Badenhorst	Eastern Province B v North West at Fochville	1998-99
S. R. Waugh	Australia v India at Chennai	2000-01
M. P. Vaughan	England v India at Bangalore	2001-02
Tushar Imran	Bangladesh A v Jamaica at Spanish Town	2001-02
Al Sahariar	Dhaka v Chittagong at Dhaka	2003-04
Junaid Zia	Rawalpindi v Lahore at Lahore	2003-04

Obstructing the Field

There have been **19** instances in first-class cricket. T. Straw of Worcestershire was given out for obstruction v Warwickshire in both 1899 and 1901. The last occurrence in England involved K. Ibadulla of Warwickshire v Hampshire at Coventry in 1963. The most recent are:

Arshad Ali	Sukkur v Quetta at Quetta	1983-84
H. R. Wasu	Vidarbha v Rajasthan at Akola	1984-85
Khalid Javed	Railways v Lahore at Lahore	1985-86
C. Binduhewa	Singha SC v Sinhalese SC at Colombo	1990-91
S. J. Kalyani	Bengal v Orissa at Calcutta	1994-95
R. C. Rupasinghe	Rio v Kurunegala Youth at Colombo	2001-02

Hit the Ball Twice

There have been **20** instances in first-class cricket. The last occurrence in England involved J. H. King of Leicestershire v Surrey at The Oval in 1906. The most recent are:

Aziz Malik	Lahore Division v Faisalabad at Sialkot	1984-85
Javed Mohammad	Multan v Karachi Whites at Sahiwal	1986-87
Shahid Pervez	Jammu and Kashmir v Punjab at Srinagar	1986-87
Ali Naqvi	PNSC v National Bank at Faisalabad	1998-99
A. George	Tamil Nadu v Maharashtra at Pune	1998-99
Maqsood Raza	Lahore Division v PNSC at Sheikhupura	1999-2000

Timed Out

There have been **three** instances in first-class cricket:

H. Yadav	Tripura v Orissa at Cuttack	1997-98
V. C. Drakes	Border v Free State at East London	2002-03
A. J. Harris	Nottinghamshire v Durham UCCE at Nottingham	2003

BOWLING RECORDS

TEN WICKETS IN AN INNINGS

In the history of first-class cricket, there have been **77** instances of a bowler taking all ten wickets in an innings:

	O	M	R		
E. Hinkly (Kent)				v England at Lord's	1848
*J. Wisden (North)				v South at Lord's	1850
V. E. Walker (England)	43	17	74	v Surrey at The Oval	1859
V. E. Walker (Middlesex)	44.2	5	104	v Lancashire at Manchester	1865
G. Wootton (All England)	31.3	9	54	v Yorkshire at Sheffield	1865
W. Hickton (Lancashire)	36.2	19	46	v Hampshire at Manchester	1870
S. E. Butler (Oxford)	24.1	11	38	v Cambridge at Lord's	1871

Records

	O	M	R		
James Lillywhite (South)	60.2	22	129	v North at Canterbury	1872
A. Shaw (MCC)	36.2	8	73	v North at Lord's	1874
E. Barratt (Players)	29	11	43	v Australians at The Oval	1878
G. Giffen (Australian XI)	26	10	66	v The Rest at Sydney	1883-84
W. G. Grace (MCC)	36.2	17	49	v Oxford University at Oxford	1886
G. Burton (Middlesex)	52.3	25	59	v Surrey at The Oval	1888
†A. E. Moss (Canterbury)	21.3	10	28	v Wellington at Christchurch	1889-90
S. M. J. Woods (Cambridge U.)	31	6	69	v Thornton's XI at Cambridge	1890
T. Richardson (Surrey)	15.3	3	45	v Essex at The Oval	1894
H. Pickett (Essex)	27	11	32	v Leicestershire at Leyton	1895
E. J. Tyler (Somerset)	34.3	15	49	v Surrey at Taunton	1895
W. P. Howell (Australians)	23.2	14	28	v Surrey at The Oval	1899
C. H. G. Bland (Sussex)	25.2	10	48	v Kent at Tonbridge	1899
J. Briggs (Lancashire)	28.5	7	55	v Worcestershire at Manchester	1900
A. E. Trott (Middlesex)	14.2	5	42	v Somerset at Taunton	1900
A. Fielder (Players)	24.5	1	90	v Gentlemen at Lord's	1906
E. G. Dennett (Gloucestershire)	19.4	7	40	v Essex at Bristol	1906
A. E. E. Vogler (E. Province)	12	2	26	v Griqualand W. at Johannesburg	1906-07
C. Blythe (Kent)	16	7	30	v Northants at Northampton	1907
J. B. King (Philadelphia)	18.1	7	53	v Ireland at Haverford‡	1909
A. Drake (Yorkshire)	8.5	0	35	v Somerset at Weston-s-Mare	1914
W. Bestwick (Derbyshire)	19	2	40	v Glamorgan at Cardiff	1921
A. A. Mailey (Australians)	28.4	5	66	v Gloucestershire at Cheltenham	1921
C. W. L. Parker (Glos.)	40.3	13	79	v Somerset at Bristol	1921
T. Rushby (Surrey)	17.5	4	43	v Somerset at Taunton	1921
J. C. White (Somerset)	42.2	11	76	v Worcestershire at Worcester	1921
G. C. Collins (Kent)	19.3	4	65	v Nottinghamshire at Dover	1922
H. Howell (Warwickshire)	25.1	5	51	v Yorkshire at Birmingham	1923
A. S. Kennedy (Players)	22.4	10	37	v Gentlemen at The Oval	1927
G. O. B. Allen (Middlesex)	25.3	10	40	v Lancashire at Lord's	1929
A. P. Freeman (Kent)	42	9	131	v Lancashire at Maidstone	1929
G. Geary (Leicestershire)	16.2	8	18	v Glamorgan at Pontypridd	1929
C. V. Grimmett (Australians)	22.3	8	37	v Yorkshire at Sheffield	1930
A. P. Freeman (Kent)	30.4	8	53	v Essex at Southend	1930
H. Verity (Yorkshire)	18.4	6	36	v Warwickshire at Leeds	1931
A. P. Freeman (Kent)	36.1	9	79	v Lancashire at Manchester	1931
V. W. C. Jupp (Northants)	39	6	127	v Kent at Tunbridge Wells	1932
H. Verity (Yorkshire)	19.4	16	10	v Nottinghamshire at Leeds	1932
T. W. Wall (South Australia)	12.4	2	36	v New South Wales at Sydney	1932-33
T. B. Mitchell (Derbyshire)	19.1	4	64	v Leicestershire at Leicester	1935
J. Mercer (Glamorgan)	26	10	51	v Worcestershire at Worcester	1936
T. W. J. Goddard (Glos.)	28.4	4	113	v Worcestershire at Cheltenham	1937
T. F. Smailes (Yorkshire)	17.1	5	47	v Derbyshire at Sheffield	1939
E. A. Watts (Surrey)	24.1	8	67	v Warwickshire at Birmingham	1939
*W. E. Hollies (Warwickshire)	20.4	4	49	v Notts at Birmingham	1946
J. M. Sims (East)	18.4	2	90	v West at Kingston	1948
T. E. Bailey (Essex)	39.4	9	90	v Lancashire at Clacton	1949
J. K. Graveney (Glos.)	18.4	2	66	v Derbyshire at Chesterfield	1949
R. Berry (Lancashire)	36.2	13	102	v Worcestershire at Blackpool	1953
S. P. Gupte (President's XI)	24.2	7	78	v Combined XI at Bombay	1954-55
J. C. Laker (Surrey)	46	18	88	v Australians at The Oval	1956
J. C. Laker (England)	51.2	23	53	v Australia at Manchester	1956
G. A. R. Lock (Surrey)	29.1	18	54	v Kent at Blackheath	1956
K. Smales (Nottinghamshire)	41.3	20	66	v Gloucestershire at Stroud	1956
P. M. Chatterjee (Bengal)	19	11	20	v Assam at Jorhat	1956-57
J. D. Bannister (Warwickshire)	23.3	11	41	v Comb. Services at Birmingham§	1959
A. J. G. Pearson (Cambridge U.)	30.3	8	78	v Leics at Loughborough	1961
N. I. Thomson (Sussex)	34.2	19	49	v Warwickshire at Worthing	1964
P. J. Allan (Queensland)	15.6	3	61	v Victoria at Melbourne	1965-66
I. J. Brayshaw (W. Australia)	17.6	4	44	v Victoria at Perth	1967-68

	O	M	R			
Shahid Mahmood (Karachi Whites)	25	5	58	v Khairpur at Karachi	......	1969-70
E. E. Hemmings (International XI)	49.3	14	175	v West Indies XI at Kingston	..	1982-83
P. Sunderam (Rajasthan)	22	5	78	v Vidarbha at Jodhpur	....	1985-86
S. T. Jefferies (W. Province)	22.5	7	59	v Orange Free State at Cape Town		1987-88
Imran Adil (Bahawalpur)	22.5	3	92	v Faisalabad at Faisalabad	.....	1989-90
G. P. Wickremasinghe (Sinhalese)	19.2	5	41	v Kalutara at Colombo	....	1991-92
R. L. Johnson (Middlesex)	18.5	6	45	v Derbyshire at Derby	....	1994
Naeem Akhtar (Rawalpindi B)	21.3	10	28	v Peshawar at Peshawar	....	1995-96
A. Kumble (India)	26.3	9	74	v Pakistan at Delhi	....	1998-99
D. S. Mohanty (East Zone)	19	5	46	v South Zone at Agartala	.....	2000-01

Note: In addition, the following instances were achieved in 12-a-side matches:

	O	M	R			
E. M. Grace (MCC)	32.2	7	69	v Gents of Kent at Canterbury	..	1862
W. G. Grace (MCC)	46.1	15	92	v Kent at Canterbury	......	1873
†D. C. S. Hinds (A. B. St Hill's XII)	19.1	6	36	v Trinidad at Port-of-Spain	....	1900-01

* *J. Wisden and W. E. Hollies achieved the feat without the direct assistance of a fielder. Wisden's ten were all bowled; Hollies bowled seven and had three lbw.*
† *On debut in first-class cricket.*   ‡ *Pennsylvania.*   § *Mitchells & Butlers Ground.*

OUTSTANDING BOWLING ANALYSES

	O	M	R	W		
H. Verity (Yorkshire)	19.4	16	10	10	v Nottinghamshire at Leeds ..	1932
G. Elliott (Victoria)	19	17	2	9	v Tasmania at Launceston ...	1857-58
Ahad Khan (Railways)	6.3	4	7	9	v Dera Ismail Khan at Lahore	1964-65
J. C. Laker (England)	14	12	2	8	v The Rest at Bradford	1950
D. Shackleton (Hampshire)	11.1	7	4	8	v Somerset at Weston-s-Mare .	1955
E. Peate (Yorkshire)	16	11	5	8	v Surrey at Holbeck	1883
F. R. Spofforth (Australians)	8.3	6	3	7	v England XI at Birmingham .	1884
W. A. Henderson (North-Eastern Transvaal)	9.3	7	4	7	v Orange Free State at Bloemfontein .	1937-38
Rajinder Goel (Haryana)	7	4	4	7	v Jammu and Kashmir at Chandigarh	1977-78
N. W. Bracken (NSW)	7	5	4	7	v South Australia at Sydney ..	2004-05
V. I. Smith (South Africans)	4.5	3	1	6	v Derbyshire at Derby......	1947
S. Cosstick (Victoria)	21.1	20	1	6	v Tasmania at Melbourne....	1868-69
Israr Ali (Bahawalpur)	11	10	1	6	v Dacca U. at Bahawalpur ...	1957-58
A. D. Pougher (MCC)	3	3	0	5	v Australians at Lord's	1896
G. R. Cox (Sussex)	6	6	0	5	v Somerset at Weston-s-Mare .	1921
R. K. Tyldesley (Lancashire)	5	5	0	5	v Leicestershire at Manchester	1924
P. T. Mills (Gloucestershire)	6.4	6	0	5	v Somerset at Bristol	1928

MOST WICKETS IN A MATCH

19-90	J. C. Laker	England v Australia at Manchester	1956
17-48†	C. Blythe	Kent v Northamptonshire at Northampton.........	1907
17-50	C. T. B. Turner	Australians v England XI at Hastings	1888
17-54	W. P. Howell	Australians v Western Province at Cape Town	1902-03
17-56	C. W. L. Parker	Gloucestershire v Essex at Gloucester	1925
17-67	A. P. Freeman	Kent v Sussex at Hove	1922
17-89	W. G. Grace	Gloucestershire v Nottinghamshire at Cheltenham ...	1877
17-89	F. C. L. Matthews	Nottinghamshire v Northants at Nottingham	1923
17-91	H. Dean	Lancashire v Yorkshire at Liverpool	1913
17-91†	H. Verity	Yorkshire v Essex at Leyton	1933
17-92	A. P. Freeman	Kent v Warwickshire at Folkestone	1932
17-103	W. Mycroft	Derbyshire v Hampshire at Southampton	1876
17-106	G. R. Cox	Sussex v Warwickshire at Horsham	1926
17-106†	T. W. J. Goddard	Gloucestershire v Kent at Bristol	1939

17-119	W. Mead	Essex v Hampshire at Southampton.	1895
17-137	W. Brearley	Lancashire v Somerset at Manchester.	1905
17-137	J. M. Davison	Canada v USA at Fort Lauderdale.	2004
17-159	S. F. Barnes	England v South Africa at Johannesburg.	1913-14
17-201	G. Giffen	South Australia v Victoria at Adelaide	1885-86
17-212	J. C. Clay	Glamorgan v Worcestershire at Swansea	1937

† *Achieved in a single day.*

Note: H. Arkwright took 18-96 for MCC v Gentlemen of Kent in a 12-a-side match at Canterbury in 1861.

There have been 56 instances of a bowler taking 16 wickets in an 11-a-side match, the most recent being 16-119 by M. P. Bicknell for Surrey v Leicestershire at Guildford, 2000.

FOUR WICKETS WITH CONSECUTIVE BALLS

There have been **34** instances in first-class cricket. R. J. Crisp achieved the feat twice, for Western Province in 1931-32 and 1933-34. A. E. Trott took four in four balls and another hat-trick in the same innings of Middlesex v Somerset in 1907, his benefit match. Occurrences since the Second World War:

F. Ridgway	Kent v Derbyshire at Folkestone	1951
A. K. Walker‡	Nottinghamshire v Leicestershire at Leicester	1956
D. Robins†	South Australia v New South Wales at Adelaide	1965-66
S. N. Mohol	President's XI v Combined XI at Poona.	1965-66
P. I. Pocock	Surrey v Sussex at Eastbourne	1972
S. S. Saini†	Delhi v Himachal Pradesh at Delhi.	1988-89
D. Dias	W. Province (Suburbs) v Central Province at Colombo	1990-91
Ali Gauhar	Karachi Blues v United Bank at Peshawar	1994-95
K. D. James§	Hampshire v Indians at Southampton	1996
G. P. Butcher	Surrey v Derbyshire at The Oval	2000
Fazl-e-Akbar	PIA v Habib Bank at Lahore.	2001-02

† *Not all in the same innings.*

‡ *Having bowled Firth with the last ball of the first innings, Walker achieved a unique feat by dismissing Lester, Tompkin and Smithson with the first three balls of the second.*

§ *James also scored a century, a unique double.*

Notes: In their match with England at The Oval in 1863, Surrey lost four wickets in the course of a four-ball over from G. Bennett.

Sussex lost five wickets in the course of the final (six-ball) over of their match with Surrey at Eastbourne in 1972. P. I. Pocock, who had taken three wickets in his previous over, captured four more, taking in all seven wickets with 11 balls, a feat unique in first-class matches. (The eighth wicket fell to a run-out.)

HAT-TRICKS

Double Hat-Trick

Besides Trott's performance, which is mentioned in the preceding section, the following instances are recorded of players having performed the hat-trick twice in the same match, Rao doing so in the same innings.

A. Shaw	Nottinghamshire v Gloucestershire at Nottingham	1884
T. J. Matthews	Australia v South Africa at Manchester	1912
C. W. L. Parker	Gloucestershire v Middlesex at Bristol.	1924
R. O. Jenkins	Worcestershire v Surrey at Worcester.	1949
J. S. Rao	Services v Northern Punjab at Amritsar.	1963-64
Amin Lakhani	Combined XI v Indians at Multan	1978-79

Five Wickets in Six Balls

W. H. Copson	Derbyshire v Warwickshire at Derby	1937
W. A. Henderson	N.E. Transvaal v Orange Free State at Bloemfontein	1937-38
P. I. Pocock	Surrey v Sussex at Eastbourne	1972
Yasir Arafat	Rawalpindi v Faisalabad at Rawalpindi	2004-05

Yasir Arafat's five wickets were spread across two innings and interrupted only by a no-ball.

Most Hat-Tricks

Seven times: D. V. P. Wright.
Six times: T. W. J. Goddard, C. W. L. Parker.
Five times: S. Haigh, V. W. C. Jupp, A. E. G. Rhodes, F. A. Tarrant.
Four times: R. G. Barlow, A. P. Freeman, J. T. Hearne, J. C. Laker, G. A. R. Lock, G. G. Macaulay, T. J. Matthews, M. J. Procter, T. Richardson, F. R. Spofforth, F. S. Trueman.
Three times: W. M. Bradley, H. J. Butler, S. T. Clarke, W. H. Copson, R. J. Crisp, J. W. H. T. Douglas, J. A. Flavell, G. Giffen, D. W. Headley, K. Higgs, A. Hill, W. A. Humphreys, R. D. Jackman, R. O. Jenkins, A. S. Kennedy, W. H. Lockwood, E. A. McDonald, T. L. Pritchard, J. S. Rao, A. Shaw, J. B. Statham, M. W. Tate, H. Trumble, Wasim Akram, D. Wilson, G. A. Wilson.
Twice (current players only): D. G. Cork, K. J. Dean, Fazl-e-Akbar, D. Gough, A. Kumble, J. D. Lewry, A. Sheriyar, J. Srinath, Waqar Younis.

Hat-Trick on Debut

H. Hay	South Australia v Lord Hawke's XI at Unley, Adelaide.	1902-03
H. A. Sedgwick . . .	Yorkshire v Worcestershire at Hull	1906
R. Wooster.	Northamptonshire v Dublin University at Northampton.	1925
J. C. Treanor	New South Wales v Queensland at Brisbane.	1954-55
V. B. Ranjane	Maharashtra v Saurashtra at Poona	1956-57
Arshad Khan	Dacca University v East Pakistan B at Dacca	1957-58
N. Fredrick	Ceylon v Madras at Colombo	1963-64
J. S. Rao	Services v Jammu and Kashmir at Delhi	1963-64
Mehboodullah	Uttar Pradesh v Madhya Pradesh at Lucknow	1971-72
R. O. Estwick	Barbados v Guyana at Bridgetown	1982-83
S. A. Ankola	Maharashtra v Gujarat at Poona	1988-89
J. Srinath.	Karnataka v Hyderabad at Secunderabad	1989-90
S. P. Mukherjee . . .	Bengal v Hyderabad at Secunderabad	1989-90
S. M. Harwood. . . .	Victoria v Tasmania at Melbourne	2002-03

Notes: R. R. Phillips (Border) took a hat-trick in his first over in first-class cricket (v Eastern Province at Port Elizabeth, 1939-40) having previously played in four matches without bowling.

J. S. Rao took two more hat-tricks in his next match.

250 WICKETS IN A SEASON

	Season	O	M	R	W	Avge
A. P. Freeman	1928	1,976.1	423	5,489	304	18.05
A. P. Freeman	1933	2,039	651	4,549	298	15.26
T. Richardson	1895‡	1,690.1	463	4,170	290	14.37
C. T. B. Turner	1888†	2,427.2	1,127	3,307	283	11.68
A. P. Freeman	1931	1,618	360	4,307	276	15.60
A. P. Freeman	1930	1,914.3	472	4,632	275	16.84
T. Richardson	1897‡	1,603.4	495	3,945	273	14.45
A. P. Freeman	1929	1,670.5	381	4,879	267	18.27
W. Rhodes	1900	1,553	455	3,606	261	13.81
J. T. Hearne	1896‡	2,003.1	818	3,670	257	14.28
A. P. Freeman	1932	1,565.5	404	4,149	253	16.39
W. Rhodes	1901	1,565	505	3,797	251	15.12

† *Indicates 4-ball overs.* ‡ *5-ball overs.*

Notes: In four consecutive seasons (1928-31), A. P. Freeman took 1,122 wickets, and in eight consecutive seasons (1928-35), 2,090 wickets. In each of these eight seasons he took over 200 wickets.

T. Richardson took 1,005 wickets in four consecutive seasons (1894-97).

In 1896, J. T. Hearne took his 100th wicket as early as June 12. In 1931, C. W. L. Parker did the same and A. P. Freeman obtained his 100th wicket a day later.

200 WICKETS IN A SEASON MOST TIMES

Eight times: A. P. Freeman (in successive seasons – 1928 to 1935 – including 304 in 1928).
Five times: C. W. L. Parker.
Four times: T. W. J. Goddard.
Three times: J. T. Hearne, G. A. Lohmann, W. Rhodes, T. Richardson, M. W. Tate and H. Verity.

Note: The last bowler to reach 200 wickets in a season was G. A. R. Lock (212 in 1957).

100 WICKETS IN A SEASON MOST TIMES

(Includes overseas tours and seasons)

23 times: W. Rhodes.
20 times: D. Shackleton (in successive seasons – 1949 to 1968).
17 times: A. P. Freeman.
16 times: T. W. J. Goddard, C. W. L. Parker, R. T. D. Perks, F. J. Titmus.
15 times: J. T. Hearne, G. H. Hirst, A. S. Kennedy.

Note: Since the reduction of County Championship matches in 1969, D. L. Underwood (five times) and J. K. Lever (four times) are the only bowlers to have reached 100 wickets in a season more than twice. The highest aggregate in a season since 1969 is 134 by M. D. Marshall in 1982.

100 WICKETS IN A SEASON OUTSIDE ENGLAND

W		Season	Country	R	Avge
116	M. W. Tate	1926-27	India/Ceylon	1,599	13.78
113	Kabir Khan	1998-99	Pakistan	1,706	15.09
107	Ijaz Faqih	1985-86	Pakistan	1,719	16.06
106	C. T. B. Turner	1887-88	Australia	1,441	13.59
106	R. Benaud	1957-58	South Africa	2,056	19.39
105	Murtaza Hussain	1995-96	Pakistan	1,882	17.92
104	S. F. Barnes	1913-14	South Africa	1,117	10.74
104	Sajjad Akbar	1989-90	Pakistan	2,328	22.38
103	Abdul Qadir	1982-83	Pakistan	2,367	22.98

LEADING BOWLERS IN AN ENGLISH SEASON

(Qualification: 10 wickets in 10 innings)

Season	Leading wicket-taker	Wkts	Avge	Top of averages	Wkts	Avge
1946	W. E. Hollies	184	15.60	A. Booth	111	11.61
1947	T. W. J. Goddard	238	17.30	J. C. Clay	65	16.44
1948	J. E. Walsh	174	19.56	J. C. Clay	41	14.17
1949	R. O. Jenkins	183	21.19	T. W. J. Goddard	160	19.18
1950	R. Tattersall	193	13.59	R. Tattersall	193	13.59
1951	R. Appleyard	200	14.14	R. Appleyard	200	14.14
1952	J. H. Wardle	177	19.54	F. S. Trueman	61	13.78
1953	B. Dooland	172	16.58	C. J. Knott	38	13.71
1954	B. Dooland	196	15.48	J. B. Statham	92	14.13
1955	G. A. R. Lock	216	14.49	R. Appleyard	85	13.01
1956	D. J. Shepherd	177	15.36	G. A. R. Lock	155	12.46
1957	G. A. R. Lock	212	12.02	G. A. R. Lock	212	12.02
1958	G. A. R. Lock	170	12.08	H. L. Jackson	143	10.99
1959	D. Shackleton	148	21.55	J. B. Statham	139	15.01
1960	F. S. Trueman	175	13.98	J. B. Statham	135	12.31
1961	J. A. Flavell	171	17.79	J. A. Flavell	171	17.79

Season	Leading wicket-taker	Wkts	Avge	Top of averages	Wkts	Avge
1962	D. Shackleton	172	20.15	C. Cook	58	17.13
1963	D. Shackleton	146	16.75	C. C. Griffith	119	12.83
1964	D. Shackleton	142	20.40	J. A. Standen	64	13.00
1965	D. Shackleton	144	16.08	H. J. Rhodes	119	11.04
1966	D. L. Underwood	157	13.80	D. L. Underwood	157	13.80
1967	T. W. Cartwright	147	15.52	D. L. Underwood	136	12.39
1968	R. Illingworth	131	14.36	O. S. Wheatley	82	12.95
1969	R. M. H. Cottam	109	21.04	A. Ward	69	14.82
1970	D. J. Shepherd	106	19.16	Majid Khan	11	18.81
1971	L. R. Gibbs	131	18.89	G. G. Arnold	83	17.12
1972	{ T. W. Cartwright	98	18.64	I. M. Chappell	10	10.60
	{ B. Stead	98	20.38			
1973	B. S. Bedi	105	17.94	T. W. Cartwright	89	15.84
1974	A. M. E. Roberts	119	13.62	A. M. E. Roberts	119	13.62
1975	P. G. Lee	112	18.45	A. M. E. Roberts	57	15.80
1976	G. A. Cope	93	24.13	M. A. Holding	55	14.38
1977	M. J. Procter	109	18.04	R. A. Woolmer	19	15.21
1978	D. L. Underwood	110	14.49	D. L. Underwood	110	14.49
1979	{ D. L. Underwood	106	14.85	J. Garner	55	13.83
	{ J. K. Lever	106	17.30			
1980	R. D. Jackman	121	15.40	J. Garner	49	13.93
1981	R. J. Hadlee	105	14.89	R. J. Hadlee	105	14.89
1982	M. D. Marshall	134	15.73	R. J. Hadlee	61	14.57
1983	{ J. K. Lever	106	16.28	Imran Khan	12	7.16
	{ D. L. Underwood	106	19.28			
1984	R. J. Hadlee	117	14.05	R. J. Hadlee	117	14.05
1985	N. V. Radford	101	24.68	R. M. Ellison	65	17.20
1986	C. A. Walsh	118	18.17	M. D. Marshall	100	15.08
1987	N. V. Radford	109	20.81	R. J. Hadlee	97	12.64
1988	F. D. Stephenson	125	18.31	M. D. Marshall	42	13.16
1989	{ D. R. Pringle	94	18.64	T. M. Alderman	70	15.64
	{ S. L. Watkin	94	25.09			
1990	N. A. Foster	94	26.61	I. R. Bishop	59	19.05
1991	Waqar Younis	113	14.65	Waqar Younis	113	14.65
1992	C. A. Walsh	92	15.96	C. A. Walsh	92	15.96
1993	S. L. Watkin	92	22.80	Wasim Akram	59	19.27
1994	M. M. Patel	90	22.86	C. E. L. Ambrose	77	14.45
1995	A. Kumble	105	20.40	A. A. Donald	89	16.07
1996	C. A. Walsh	85	16.84	C. E. L. Ambrose	43	16.67
1997	A. M. Smith	83	17.63	A. A. Donald	60	15.63
1998	C. A. Walsh	106	17.31	V. J. Wells	36	14.27
1999	A. Sheriyar	92	24.70	Saqlain Mushtaq	58	11.37
2000	G. D. McGrath	80	13.21	C. A. Walsh	40	11.42
2001	R. J. Kirtley	75	23.32	G. D. McGrath	40	15.60
2002	{ M. J. Saggers	83	21.51	C. P. Schofield	18	18.38
	{ K. J. Dean	83	23.50			
2003	Mushtaq Ahmed	103	24.65	Shoaib Akhtar	34	17.05
2004	Mushtaq Ahmed	84	27.59	D. S. Lehmann	15	17.40

❝The sight of Warne equalling the record gave Cairns's unpretentious Bundaberg Rum Stadium a highlight worthy of Lord's on a balmy July evening or the MCG on Boxing Day."

The Sri Lankans in Australia, page 1240.

1,500 WICKETS

Dates in italics denote the first half of an overseas season; i.e. *1970* denotes the 1970-71 season.

		Career	*W*	*R*	*Avge*
1	W. Rhodes	1898–1930	4,187	69,993	16.71
2	A. P. Freeman	1914–36	3,776	69,577	18.42
3	C. W. L. Parker	1903–35	3,278	63,817	19.46
4	J. T. Hearne	1888–1923	3,061	54,352	17.75
5	T. W. J. Goddard	1922–52	2,979	59,116	19.84
6	W. G. Grace	1865–1908	2,876	51,545	17.92
7	A. S. Kennedy	1907–36	2,874	61,034	21.23
8	D. Shackleton	1948–69	2,857	53,303	18.65
9	G. A. R. Lock	1946–*70*	2,844	54,709	19.23
10	F. J. Titmus	1949–82	2,830	63,313	22.37
11	M. W. Tate	1912–37	2,784	50,571	18.16
12	G. H. Hirst	1891–1929	2,739	51,282	18.72
13	C. Blythe	1899–1914	2,506	42,136	16.81
14	D. L. Underwood	1963–87	2,465	49,993	20.28
15	W. E. Astill	1906–39	2,431	57,783	23.76
16	J. C. White	1909–37	2,356	43,759	18.57
17	W. E. Hollies	1932–57	2,323	48,656	20.94
18	F. S. Trueman	1949–69	2,304	42,154	18.29
19	J. B. Statham	1950–68	2,260	36,999	16.37
20	R. T. D. Perks	1930–55	2,233	53,770	24.07
21	J. Briggs	1879–1900	2,221	35,431	15.95
22	D. J. Shepherd	1950–72	2,218	47,302	21.32
23	E. G. Dennett	1903–26	2,147	42,571	19.82
24	T. Richardson	1892–1905	2,104	38,794	18.43
25	T. E. Bailey	1945–67	2,082	48,170	23.13
26	R. Illingworth	1951–83	2,072	42,023	20.28
27	{ N. Gifford	1960–88	2,068	48,731	23.56
	{ F. E. Woolley	1906–38	2,068	41,066	19.85
29	G. Geary	1912–38	2,063	41,339	20.03
30	D. V. P. Wright	1932–57	2,056	49,307	23.98
31	J. A. Newman	1906–30	2,032	51,111	25.15
32	†A. Shaw	1864–97	2,027	24,580	12.12
33	S. Haigh	1895–1913	2,012	32,091	15.94
34	H. Verity	1930–39	1,956	29,146	14.90
35	W. Attewell	1881–1900	1,951	29,896	15.32
36	J. C. Laker	1946–*64*	1,944	35,791	18.41
37	A. V. Bedser	1939–60	1,924	39,279	20.41
38	W. Mead	1892–1913	1,916	36,388	18.99
39	A. E. Relf	1900–21	1,897	39,724	20.94
40	P. G. H. Fender	1910–36	1,894	47,458	25.05
41	J. W. H. T. Douglas	1901–30	1,893	44,159	23.32
42	J. H. Wardle	1946–*67*	1,846	35,027	18.97
43	G. R. Cox	1895–1928	1,843	42,136	22.86
44	G. A. Lohmann	1884–*97*	1,841	25,295	13.73
45	J. W. Hearne	1909–36	1,839	44,926	24.42
46	G. G. Macaulay	1920–35	1,837	32,440	17.65
47	M. S. Nichols	1924–39	1,833	39,666	21.63
48	{ J. B. Mortimore	1950–75	1,807	41,904	23.18
	{ C. A. Walsh	*1981*–2000	1,807	39,233	21.71
50	C. Cook	1946–64	1,782	36,578	20.52
51	R. Peel	1882–99	1,752	28,442	16.23
52	H. L. Jackson	1947–63	1,733	30,101	17.36
53	J. K. Lever	1967–89	1,722	41,772	24.25
54	T. P. B. Smith	1929–52	1,697	45,059	26.55
55	J. Southerton	1854–79	1,681	24,290	14.44
56	A. E. Trott	*1892*–1911	1,674	35,317	21.09

		Career	W	R	Avge
57	A. W. Mold	1889–1901	1,673	26,010	15.54
58	T. G. Wass	1896–1920	1,666	34,092	20.46
59	V. W. C. Jupp	1909–38	1,658	38,166	23.01
60	C. Gladwin.	1939–58	1,653	30,265	18.30
61	M. D. Marshall	1977–95	1,651	31,548	19.10
62	W. E. Bowes.	1928–47	1,639	27,470	16.76
63	A. W. Wellard	1927–50	1,614	39,302	24.35
64	J. E. Emburey	1973–97	1,608	41,958	26.09
65	P. I. Pocock	1964–86	1,607	42,648	26.53
66	N. I. Thomson	1952–72	1,597	32,867	20.58
67	{ J. Mercer	1919–47	1,591	37,210	23.38
	{ G. J. Thompson	1897–1922	1,591	30,058	18.89
69	J. M. Sims	1929–53	1,581	39,401	24.92
70	{ T. Emmett	1866–88	1,571	21,314	13.56
	{ Intikhab Alam.	1957–82	1,571	43,474	27.67
72	B. S. Bedi	1961–81	1,560	33,843	21.69
73	W. Voce.	1927–52	1,558	35,961	23.08
74	A. R. Gover	1928–48	1,555	36,753	23.63
75	{ T. W. Cartwright	1952–77	1,536	29,357	19.11
	{ K. Higgs	1958–86	1,536	36,267	23.61
77	James Langridge	1924–53	1,530	34,524	22.56
78	J. A. Flavell	1949–67	1,529	32,847	21.48
79	E. E. Hemmings	1966–95	1,515	44,403	29.30
80	{ C. F. Root	1910–33	1,512	31,933	21.11
	{ F. A. Tarrant.	1898–1936	1,512	26,450	17.49
82	R. K. Tyldesley	1919–35	1,509	25,980	17.21

† *The figures for A. Shaw exclude one wicket for which no analysis is available.*

Note: Some works of reference provide career figures which differ from those in this list, owing to the exclusion or inclusion of matches recognised or not recognised as first-class by *Wisden*.

Current Players with 1,000 Wickets

	Career	W	R	Avge
P. A. J. DeFreitas.	1985–2004	1,236	34,403	27.83
A. A. Donald	1985–2003	1,216	27,680	22.76
Mushtaq Ahmed	1986–2004	1,080	28,205	26.11
M. P. Bicknell.	1986–2004	1,025	25,405	24.78
M. Muralitharan	1989–2004	1,015	19,388	19.10

ALL-ROUND RECORDS

HUNDRED AND TEN WICKETS IN AN INNINGS

V. E. Walker, England v Surrey at The Oval; 20*, 108; 10-74, 4-17	1859
W. G. Grace, MCC v Oxford University at Oxford; 104; 2-60, 10-49	1886

Note: E. M. Grace, for MCC v Gentlemen of Kent in a 12-a-side match at Canterbury in 1862, scored 192* and took 5-77 and 10-69.

DOUBLE-HUNDRED AND 16 WICKETS

G. Giffen, South Australia v Victoria at Adelaide; 271; 9-96, 7-70	1891-92

HUNDRED IN EACH INNINGS AND FIVE WICKETS TWICE

G. H. Hirst, Yorkshire v Somerset at Bath; 111, 117*; 6-70, 5-45	1906

HUNDRED IN EACH INNINGS AND TEN WICKETS

B. J. T. Bosanquet, Middlesex v Sussex at Lord's; 103, 100*; 3-75, 8-53 1905
F. D. Stephenson, Nottinghamshire v Yorkshire at Nottingham; 111, 117; 4-105, 7-117 1988

HUNDRED AND HAT-TRICK

K. D. James, Hampshire v Indians at Southampton. *Unique instance of 100 and four
  wickets in four balls* 1996
G. Giffen, Australians v Lancashire at Manchester 1884
W. E. Roller, Surrey v Sussex at The Oval. *Unique instance of 200 and hat-trick*. . . 1885
W. B. Burns, Worcestershire v Gloucestershire at Worcester. 1913
V. W. C. Jupp, Sussex v Essex at Colchester. 1921
R. E. S. Wyatt, MCC v Ceylon at Colombo 1926-27
L. N. Constantine, West Indians v Northamptonshire at Northampton 1928
D. E. Davies, Glamorgan v Leicestershire at Leicester. 1937
V. M. Merchant, Dr C. R. Pereira's XI v Sir Homi Mehta's XI at Bombay 1946-47
M. J. Procter, Gloucestershire v Essex at Westcliff-on-Sea. 1972
M. J. Procter, Gloucestershire v Leicestershire at Bristol. 1979

SEASON DOUBLES

2,000 Runs and 200 Wickets

| 1906 | G. H. Hirst | 2,385 runs and 208 wickets |

3,000 Runs and 100 Wickets

| 1937 | J. H. Parks | 3,003 runs and 101 wickets |

1,000 Runs and 100 Wickets

Sixteen times: W. Rhodes.
Fourteen times: G. H. Hirst.
Ten times: V. W. C. Jupp.
Nine times: W. E. Astill.
Eight times: T. E. Bailey, W. G. Grace, M. S. Nichols, A. E. Relf, F. A. Tarrant, M. W. Tate†,
F. J. Titmus, F. E. Woolley.
Seven times: G. E. Tribe.

† *M. W. Tate also scored 1,193 runs and took 116 wickets for MCC in first-class matches on the
1926-27 MCC tour of India and Ceylon.*

Note: R. J. Hadlee (1984) and F. D. Stephenson (1988) are the only players to perform the feat
since the reduction of County Championship matches. A complete list of those performing the
feat before then will be found on page 202 of the 1982 *Wisden.*
  T. E. Bailey (1959) was the last player to achieve 2,000 runs and 100 wickets in a season.
M. W. Tate (1925) was the last to reach 1,000 runs and 200 wickets. Full lists can be found in
Wisdens up to 2003.

Wicket-Keeper's Double

	Season	R	D		Season	R	D
L. E. G. Ames. . . .	1928	1,919	122	L. E. G. Ames . .	1932	2,482	104
L. E. G. Ames. . . .	1929	1,795	128	J. T. Murray	1957	1,025	104

20,000 RUNS AND 2,000 WICKETS

	Career	R	Avge	W	Avge	Doubles
W. E. Astill	1906–39	22,731	22.55	2,431	23.76	9
T. E. Bailey	1945–67	28,641	33.42	2,082	23.13	8
W. G. Grace	1865–1908	54,896	39.55	2,876	17.92	8
G. H. Hirst	1891–1929	36,323	34.13	2,739	18.72	14
R. Illingworth	1951–83	24,134	28.06	2,072	20.28	6
W. Rhodes	1898–1930	39,802	30.83	4,187	16.71	16
M. W. Tate	1912–37	21,717	25.01	2,784	18.16	8†
F. J. Titmus	1949–82	21,588	23.11	2,830	22.37	8
F. E. Woolley	1906–38	58,969	40.75	2,068	19.85	8

† *Plus one double overseas (see above).*

Current Player with 10,000 Runs and 1,000 Wickets

	Career	R	Avge	W	Avge	Doubles
P. A. J. DeFreitas	1985–2004	10,929	22.96	1,236	27.83	–

WICKET-KEEPING RECORDS

MOST DISMISSALS IN AN INNINGS

9 (8ct, 1st)	Tahir Rashid	Habib Bank v PACO at Gujranwala	1992-93
9 (7ct, 2st)	W. R. James*	Matabeleland v Mashonaland CD at Bulawayo	1995-96
8 (all ct)	A. T. W. Grout	Queensland v Western Australia at Brisbane	1959-60
8 (all ct)†	D. E. East	Essex v Somerset at Taunton	1985
8 (all ct)	S. A. Marsh‡	Kent v Middlesex at Lord's	1991
8 (6ct, 2st)	T. J. Zoehrer	Australians v Surrey at The Oval	1993
8 (7ct, 1st)	D. S. Berry	Victoria v South Australia at Melbourne	1996-97
8 (7ct, 1st)	Y. S. S. Mendis	Bloomfield v Kurunegala Youth at Colombo	2000-01
8 (7ct, 1st)	S. Nath§	Assam v Tripura at Guwahati	2001-02
8 (all ct)	J. N. Batty	Surrey v Kent at The Oval	2004

There have been **63** instances of seven dismissals in an innings. R. W. Taylor achieved the feat three times, and S. A. Marsh, K. J. Piper and Wasim Bari twice. One of Marsh's two instances was of eight dismssals – see above. A fuller list can be found in *Wisdens* before 2004. The most recent occurrences are:

7 (all ct)	R. D. Jacobs	West Indies v Australia at Melbourne	2000-01
7 (all ct)	N. D. Burns	Leicestershire v Somerset at Leicester	2001
7 (all ct)	R. J. Turner	Somerset v Northamptonshire at Taunton	2001
7 (all ct)	W. A. Seccombe	Queensland v New South Wales at Brisbane	2001-02
7 (all ct)	M. G. Croy	Otago v Auckland at Auckland	2001-02
7 (all ct)	Wasim Ahmed	Dadu v PWD at Karachi	2002-03
7 (all ct)	S. G. Clingeleffer	Tasmania v Western Australia at Perth	2003-04
7 (6ct, 1st)	C. O. Browne	Barbados v Jamaica at Kingston	2003-04
7 (all ct)	Adnan Akmal	Lahore Blues v Karachi Blues at Karachi	2004-05
7 (all ct)	G. J. Hopkins	New Zealand A v South Africa A at Centurion . . .	2004-05
7 (all ct)	Mohammad Kashif	Rawalpindi v Multan at Multan	2004-05
7 (all ct)	T. L. Tsolekile	Western Province Boland v Dolphins at Durban . . .	2004-05

* *W. R. James also scored 99 and 99 not out.* † *The first eight wickets to fall.*
‡ *S. A. Marsh also scored 108 not out.* § *On first-class debut.*

WICKET-KEEPERS' HAT-TRICKS

W. H. Brain, Gloucestershire v Somerset at Cheltenham, 1893 – three stumpings off successive balls from C. L. Townsend.

G. O. Dawkes, Derbyshire v Worcestershire at Kidderminster, 1958 – three catches off successive balls from H. L. Jackson.

R. C. Russell, Gloucestershire v Surrey at The Oval, 1986 – three catches off successive balls from C. A. Walsh and D. V. Lawrence (2).

MOST DISMISSALS IN A MATCH

13 (11ct, 2st)	W. R. James*	Matabeleland v Mashonaland CD at Bulawayo . .	1995-96
12 (8ct, 4st)	E. Pooley	Surrey v Sussex at The Oval	1868
12 (9ct, 3st)	D. Tallon	Queensland v New South Wales at Sydney	1938-39
12 (9ct, 3st)	H. B. Taber	New South Wales v South Australia at Adelaide .	1968-69
11 (all ct)	A. Long	Surrey v Sussex at Hove	1964
11 (all ct)	R. W. Marsh	Western Australia v Victoria at Perth	1975-76
11 (all ct)	D. L. Bairstow	Yorkshire v Derbyshire at Scarborough.	1982
11 (all ct)	W. K. Hegg	Lancashire v Derbyshire at Chesterfield	1989
11 (all ct)	A. J. Stewart	Surrey v Leicestershire at Leicester	1989
11 (all ct)	T. J. Nielsen	South Australia v Western Australia at Perth	1990-91
11 (10ct, 1st)	I. A. Healy	Australians v N. Transvaal at Verwoerdburg	1993-94
11 (10ct, 1st)	K. J. Piper	Warwickshire v Derbyshire at Chesterfield	1994
11 (all ct)	D. S. Berry	Victoria v Pakistanis at Melbourne	1995-96
11 (10ct, 1st)	W. A. Seccombe	Queensland v Western Australia at Brisbane	1995-96
11 (all ct)	R. C. Russell	England v South Africa (2nd Test) at Johannesburg	1995-96
11 (10ct, 1st)	D. S. Berry	Victoria v South Australia at Melbourne.	1996-97
11 (all ct)	Wasim Yousufi	Peshawar v Bahawalpur at Peshawar	1997-98
11 (all ct)	Aamer Iqbal	Pakistan Customs v Karachi Whites at Karachi . .	1999-2000
11 (10ct, 1st)	S. Nath†	Assam v Tripura at Guwahati.	2001-02
11 (all ct)	Wasim Ahmed	Dadu v PWD at Karachi.	2002-03
11 (7ct, 4st)	J. N. Batty	Surrey v Lancashire at Manchester	2004
11 (7ct, 4st)	M. S. Dhoni	India A v Zimbabwe Select XI at Harare	2004
11 (all ct)	Adnan Akmal	Lahore Blues v Karachi Blues at Karachi.	2004-05
11 (9ct, 2st)	M. S. Bisla	Himachal Pradesh v Saurashtra at Dharmasala. . .	2004-05

* W. R. James also scored 99 and 99 not out. † On first-class debut.

100 DISMISSALS IN A SEASON

128 (79ct, 49st)	L. E. G. Ames . . .	1929	104 (82ct, 22st)	J. T. Murray. . . .	1957
122 (70ct, 52st)	L. E. G. Ames . . .	1928	102 (69ct, 33st)	F. H. Huish	1913
110 (63ct, 47st)	H. Yarnold.	1949	102 (95ct, 7st)	J. T. Murray. . . .	1960
107 (77ct, 30st)	G. Duckworth . . .	1928	101 (62ct, 39st)	F. H. Huish	1911
107 (96ct, 11st)	J. G. Binks	1960	101 (85ct, 16st)	R. Booth.	1960
104 (40ct, 64st)	L. E. G. Ames . . .	1932	100 (91ct, 9st)	R. Booth.	1964

1,000 DISMISSALS

Dates in italics denote the first half of an overseas season; i.e. *1914* denotes the 1914-15 season.

			Career	*M*	*Ct*	*St*
1	1,649	R. W. Taylor	1960–88	639	1,473	176
2	1,527	J. T. Murray	1952–75	635	1,270	257
3	1,497	H. Strudwick.	1902–27	675	1,242	255
4	1,344	A. P. E. Knott	1964–85	511	1,211	133
5	**1,320**	**R. C. Russell**	**1981–2004**	**465**	**1,192**	**128**
6	1,310	F. H. Huish.	1895–1914	497	933	377
7	1,294	B. Taylor	1949–73	572	1,083	211
8	**1,263**	**S. J. Rhodes**.	**1981–2004**	**440**	**1,139**	**124**
9	1,253	D. Hunter.	1889–1909	548	906	347
10	1,228	H. R. Butt	1890–1912	550	953	275

			Career	M	Ct	St
11	1,207	J. H. Board	1891–*1914*	525	852	355
12	1,206	H. Elliott	1920–47	532	904	302
13	1,181	J. M. Parks	1949–76	739	1,088	93
14	1,126	R. Booth	1951–70	468	948	178
15	1,121	L. E. G. Ames	1926–51	593	703	418†
16	1,099	D. L. Bairstow	1970–90	459	961	138
17	1,096	G. Duckworth	1923–47	504	753	343
18	1,082	H. W. Stephenson	1948–64	462	748	334
19	1,071	J. G. Binks	1955–75	502	895	176
20	1,066	T. G. Evans	1939–69	465	816	250
21	1,046	A. Long	1960–80	452	922	124
22	1,043	G. O. Dawkes	1937–61	482	895	148
23	1,037	R. W. Tolchard	1965–83	483	912	125
24	1,017	W. L. Cornford	1921–47	496	675	342

Bold type denotes those who played in the calendar year 2004.

† *Record.*

Other Current Players with 500 Dismissals

		Career	M	Ct	St
905	W. K. Hegg	1986–2004	333	816	89
761	P. A. Nixon	1989–2004	265	703	58
730	R. J. Turner	1988–2004	241	681	49
661	A. C. Gilchrist	1992–2004	230	616	45
603	D. S. Berry	1989–2003	153	552	51
562	Tahir Rashid	1979–2003	181	501	61
530	Moin Khan	1986–2004	195	474	56
507	W. A. Seccombe	1992–2004	109	488	19

FIELDING RECORDS
excluding wicket-keepers

MOST CATCHES IN AN INNINGS

7	M. J. Stewart	Surrey v Northamptonshire at Northampton	1957
7	A. S. Brown	Gloucestershire v Nottinghamshire at Nottingham	1966

MOST CATCHES IN A MATCH

10	W. R. Hammond†	Gloucestershire v Surrey at Cheltenham	1928
8	W. B. Burns	Worcestershire v Yorkshire at Bradford	1907
8	F. G. Travers	Europeans v Parsees at Bombay	1923-24
8	A. H. Bakewell	Northamptonshire v Essex at Leyton	1928
8	W. R. Hammond	Gloucestershire v Worcestershire at Cheltenham	1932
8	K. J. Grieves	Lancashire v Sussex at Manchester	1951
8	C. A. Milton	Gloucestershire v Sussex at Hove	1952
8	G. A. R. Lock	Surrey v Warwickshire at The Oval	1957
8	J. M. Prodger	Kent v Gloucestershire at Cheltenham	1961
8	P. M. Walker	Glamorgan v Derbyshire at Swansea	1970
8	Masood Anwar	Rawalpindi v Lahore Division at Rawalpindi	1983-84
8	M. C. J. Ball	Gloucestershire v Yorkshire at Cheltenham	1994
8	J. D. Carr	Middlesex v Warwickshire at Birmingham	1995

† *Hammond also scored a hundred in each innings.*

MOST CATCHES IN A SEASON

78	W. R. Hammond	1928		69	P. M. Walker.	1960
77	M. J. Stewart.	1957		66	J. Tunnicliffe.	1895
73	P. M. Walker.	1961		65	W. R. Hammond	1925
71	P. J. Sharpe.	1962		65	P. M. Walker.	1959
70	J. Tunnicliffe	1901		65	D. W. Richardson.	1961
69	J. G. Langridge	1955				

Note: The most catches by a fielder since the reduction of County Championship matches in 1969 is 49 by C. J. Tavaré in 1978.

750 CATCHES

Dates in italics denote the first half of an overseas season; i.e. *1970* denotes the 1970-71 season.

			M					*M*
1,018	F. E. Woolley	1906–38	979		784	J. G. Langridge.	1928–55	574
887	W. G. Grace.	1865–1908	879		764	W. Rhodes.	1898–1930	1,107
830	G. A. R. Lock	1946–*70*	654		758	C. A. Milton	1948–74	620
819	W. R. Hammond.	1920–51	634		754	E. H. Hendren	1907–38	833
813	D. B. Close	1949–86	786					

Note: The most catches by a current player is 596 by G. A. Hick (*1983*–2004).

TEAM RECORDS

HIGHEST INNINGS TOTALS

1,107	Victoria v New South Wales at Melbourne	1926-27
1,059	Victoria v Tasmania at Melbourne	1922-23
952-6 dec.	Sri Lanka v India at Colombo.	1997-98
951-7 dec.	Sind v Baluchistan at Karachi.	1973-74
944-6 dec.	Hyderabad v Andhra at Secunderabad.	1993-94
918	New South Wales v South Australia at Sydney.	1900-01
912-8 dec.	Holkar v Mysore at Indore.	1945-46
912-6 dec.†	Tamil Nadu v Goa at Panjim	1988-89
910-6 dec.	Railways v Dera Ismail Khan at Lahore	1964-65
903-7 dec.	England v Australia at The Oval	1938
887	Yorkshire v Warwickshire at Birmingham	1896
868†	North Zone v West Zone at Bhilai.	1987-88
863	Lancashire v Surrey at The Oval	1990
855-6 dec.†	Bombay v Hyderabad at Bombay.	1990-91
849	England v West Indies at Kingston.	1929-30
843	Australians v Oxford & Cambridge U P & P at Portsmouth	1893
839	New South Wales v Tasmania at Sydney.	1898-99
826-4	Maharashtra v Kathiawar at Poona.	1948-49
824	Lahore Greens v Bahawalpur at Lahore.	1965-66
821-7 dec.	South Australia v Queensland at Adelaide	1939-40
815	New South Wales v Victoria at Sydney.	1908-09
811	Surrey v Somerset at The Oval	1899
810-4 dec.	Warwickshire v Durham at Birmingham	1994
807	New South Wales v South Australia at Adelaide.	1899-1900
805	New South Wales v Victoria at Melbourne	1905-06
803-4 dec.	Kent v Essex at Brentwood.	1934
803	Non-Smokers v Smokers at East Melbourne	1886-87
802-8 dec.	Karachi Blues v Lahore City at Peshawar	1994-95
802	New South Wales v South Australia at Sydney.	1920-21
801	Lancashire v Somerset at Taunton	1895

798	Maharashtra v Northern India at Poona..................	1940-41
793	Victoria v Queensland at Melbourne...................	1927-28
791-6 dec.	Karnataka v Bengal at Calcutta.....................	1990-91
790-3 dec.	West Indies v Pakistan at Kingston..................	1957-58
786	New South Wales v South Australia at Adelaide...........	1922-23
784	Baroda v Holkar at Baroda........................	1946-47
783-8 dec.	Hyderabad v Bihar at Secunderabad..................	1986-87
781-7 dec.	Northamptonshire v Nottinghamshire at Northampton........	1995
781	Lancashire v Warwickshire at Birmingham..............	2003
780-8	Punjab v Delhi at Delhi..........................	1994-95
777	Canterbury v Otago at Christchurch..................	1996-97
775	New South Wales v Victoria at Sydney.................	1881-82

† *Tamil Nadu's total of 912-6 dec. included 52 penalty runs from their opponents' failure to meet the required bowling rate. North Zone's total of 868 included 68, and Bombay's total of 855-6 dec. included 48.*

Note: The highest total in a team's second innings is 770 by New South Wales v South Australia at Adelaide in 1920-21.

HIGHEST FOURTH-INNINGS TOTALS

654-5	England v South Africa at Durban.....................	1938-39
	After being set 696 to win. The match was left drawn on the tenth day	
604	Maharashtra (*set 959 to win*) v Bombay at Poona..........	1948-49
576-8	Trinidad (*set 672 to win*) v Barbados at Port-of-Spain.......	1945-46
572	New South Wales (*set 593 to win*) v South Australia at Sydney....	1907-08
529-9	Combined XI (*set 579 to win*) v South Africans at Perth.......	1963-64
518	Victoria (*set 753 to win*) v Queensland at Brisbane.........	1926-27
513-9	Central Province (*won*) v Southern Province at Kandy........	2003-04
507-7	Cambridge University (*won*) v MCC and Ground at Lord's......	1896
506-6	South Australia (*won*) v Queensland at Adelaide...........	1991-92
503-4	South Zone (*won*) v England A at Gurgaon..............	2003-04
502-6	Middlesex (*won*) v Nottinghamshire at Nottingham.........	1925
502-8	Players (*won*) v Gentlemen at Lord's.................	1900
500-7	South African Universities (*won*) v Western Province at Stellenbosch......	1978-79

HIGHEST AGGREGATES IN A MATCH

Runs	Wkts		
2,376	37	Maharashtra v Bombay at Poona....................	1948-49
2,078	40	Bombay v Holkar at Bombay......................	1944-45
1,981	35	England v South Africa at Durban...................	1938-39
1,945	18	Canterbury v Wellington at Christchurch..............	1994-95
1,929	39	New South Wales v South Australia at Sydney...........	1925-26
1,911	34	New South Wales v Victoria at Sydney................	1908-09
1,905	40	Otago v Wellington at Dunedin....................	1923-24

In Britain

Runs	Wkts		
1,815	28	Surrey v Somerset at Taunton.....................	2002
1,808	20	Sussex v Essex at Hove.........................	1993
1,795	34	Somerset v Northamptonshire at Taunton..............	2001
1,723	31	England v Australia at Leeds.....................	1948
1,706	23	Hampshire v Warwickshire at Southampton.............	1997
1,665	33	Warwickshire v Yorkshire at Birmingham.............	2002
1,655	25	Derbyshire v Nottinghamshire at Derby...............	2001
1,650	19	Surrey v Lancashire at The Oval...................	1990
1,642	29	Nottinghamshire v Kent at Nottingham...............	1995

Runs	Wkts		
1,641	16	Glamorgan v Worcestershire at Abergavenny	1990
1,617	36	Essex v Glamorgan at Chelmsford	2004
1,614	30	England v India at Manchester	1990
1,614	26	Gloucestershire v Northamptonshire at Bristol	2002
1,606	34	Somerset v Derbyshire at Taunton	1996
1,603	28	England v India at Lord's	1990
1,601	29	England v Australia at Lord's	1930
1,601	35	Kent v Surrey at Canterbury	1995

LOWEST INNINGS TOTALS

12†	Oxford University v MCC and Ground at Oxford	1877
12	Northamptonshire v Gloucestershire at Gloucester	1907
13	Auckland v Canterbury at Auckland	1877-78
13	Nottinghamshire v Yorkshire at Nottingham	1901
14	Surrey v Essex at Chelmsford	1983
15	MCC v Surrey at Lord's	1839
15†	Victoria v MCC at Melbourne	1903-04
15†	Northamptonshire v Yorkshire at Northampton	1908
15	Hampshire v Warwickshire at Birmingham	1922
	Following on, Hampshire scored 521 and won by 155 runs.	
16	MCC and Ground v Surrey at Lord's	1872
16	Derbyshire v Nottinghamshire at Nottingham	1879
16	Surrey v Nottinghamshire at The Oval	1880
16	Warwickshire v Kent at Tonbridge	1913
16	Trinidad v Barbados at Bridgetown	1942-43
16	Border v Natal at East London (first innings)	1959-60
17	Gentlemen of Kent v Gentlemen of England at Lord's	1850
17	Gloucestershire v Australians at Cheltenham	1896
18	The Bs v England at Lord's	1831
18†	Kent v Sussex at Gravesend	1867
18	Tasmania v Victoria at Melbourne	1868-69
18†	Australians v MCC and Ground at Lord's	1896
18	Border v Natal at East London (second innings)	1959-60
19	Sussex v Surrey at Godalming	1830
19†	Sussex v Nottinghamshire at Hove	1873
19	MCC and Ground v Australians at Lord's	1878
19	Wellington v Nelson at Nelson	1885-86
19	Matabeleland v Mashonaland at Harare	2000-01

† *One man absent.*

Note: At Lord's in 1810, The Bs, with one man absent, were dismissed by England for 6.

LOWEST TOTALS IN A MATCH

34	(16 and 18) Border v Natal at East London	1959-60
42	(27 and 15) Northamptonshire v Yorkshire at Northampton	1908

Note: Northamptonshire batted one man short in each innings.

LOWEST AGGREGATE IN A COMPLETED MATCH

Runs	Wkts		
105	31	MCC v Australians at Lord's	1878

Note: The lowest aggregate since 1900 is 157 for 22 wickets, Surrey v Worcestershire at The Oval, 1954.

LARGEST VICTORIES

Largest Innings Victories

Inns and 851 runs:	Railways (910-6 dec.) v Dera Ismail Khan at Lahore	1964-65
Inns and 666 runs:	Victoria (1,059) v Tasmania at Melbourne	1922-23
Inns and 656 runs:	Victoria (1,107) v New South Wales at Melbourne	1926-27
Inns and 605 runs:	New South Wales (918) v South Australia at Sydney	1900-01
Inns and 579 runs:	England (903-7 dec.) v Australia at The Oval	1938
Inns and 575 runs:	Sind (951-7 dec.) v Baluchistan at Karachi	1973-74
Inns and 527 runs:	New South Wales (713) v South Australia at Adelaide	1908-09
Inns and 517 runs:	Australians (675) v Nottinghamshire at Nottingham	1921

Largest Victories by Runs Margin

685 runs:	New South Wales (235 and 761-8 dec.) v Queensland at Sydney	1929-30
675 runs:	England (521 and 342-8 dec.) v Australia at Brisbane	1928-29
638 runs:	New South Wales (304 and 770) v South Australia at Adelaide	1920-21
609 runs:	Muslim Commercial Bank (575 and 282-0 dec.) v WAPDA at Lahore . .	1977-78
585 runs:	Sargodha (336 and 416) v Lahore Municipal Corporation at Faisalabad . .	1978-79
573 runs:	Sinhalese SC (395-7 dec. and 350-2 dec.) v Sebastianites C and AC at Colombo	1990-91
571 runs:	Victoria (304 and 649) v South Australia at Adelaide	1926-27
562 runs:	Australia (701 and 327) v England at The Oval	1934
556 runs:	Nondescripts (397-8 dec. and 313-6 dec.) v Matara at Colombo	1998-99

Victory Without Losing a Wicket

Lancashire (166-0 dec. and 66-0) beat Leicestershire by ten wickets at Manchester . . 1956
Karachi A (277-0 dec.) beat Sind A by an innings and 77 runs at Karachi 1957-58
Railways (236-0 dec. and 16-0) beat Jammu and Kashmir by ten wickets at Srinagar . 1960-61
Karnataka (451-0 dec.) beat Kerala by an innings and 186 runs at Chikmagalur 1977-78

Notes: There have been 28 wins by an innings and 400 runs or more, the most recent being an innings and 425 runs by Allied Bank v Dadu at Karachi in 2002-03.

There have been 18 wins by 500 runs or more, the most recent being 533 runs by Chilaw Marians v Rio at Colombo in 2001-02.

There have been **29** wins by a team losing only one wicket, the most recent being by Windward Islands v Kenyans at St Vincent in 2003-04.

TIED MATCHES

Since 1948 a tie has been recognised only when the scores are level with all the wickets down in the fourth innings.

The following are the instances since then:

Hampshire v Kent at Southampton	1950
Sussex v Warwickshire at Hove	1952
Essex v Lancashire at Brentwood	1952
Northamptonshire v Middlesex at Peterborough	1953
Yorkshire v Leicestershire at Huddersfield	1954
Sussex v Hampshire at Eastbourne	1955
Victoria v New South Wales at Melbourne	1956-57
T. N. Pearce's XI v New Zealanders at Scarborough	1958
Essex v Gloucestershire at Leyton	1959
Australia v West Indies (First Test) at Brisbane	1960-61
Bahawalpur v Lahore B at Bahawalpur	1961-62
Hampshire v Middlesex at Portsmouth	1967
England XI v England Under-25 XI at Scarborough	1968
Yorkshire v Middlesex at Bradford	1973
Sussex v Essex at Hove	1974

South Australia v Queensland at Adelaide	1976-77
Central Districts v England XI at New Plymouth	1977-78
Victoria v New Zealanders at Melbourne	1982-83
Muslim Commercial Bank v Railways at Sialkot	1983-84
Sussex v Kent at Hastings	1984
Northamptonshire v Kent at Northampton	1984
Eastern Province B v Boland at Albany SC, Grahamstown	1985-86
Natal B v Eastern Province B at Pietermaritzburg	1985-86
India v Australia (First Test) at Madras	1986-87
Gloucestershire v Derbyshire at Bristol	1987
Bahawalpur v Peshawar at Bahawalpur	1988-89
Wellington v Canterbury at Wellington	1988-89
Sussex v Kent at Hove	1991
Nottinghamshire v Worcestershire at Nottingham	1993
Somerset v West Indies A at Taunton	†2002
Warwickshire v Essex at Birmingham	2003
Worcestershire v Zimbabweans at Worcester	2003

† *Somerset (453) made the highest total to tie a first-class match.*

MATCHES COMPLETED ON FIRST DAY

(Since 1946)

Derbyshire v Somerset at Chesterfield, June 11	1947
Lancashire v Sussex at Manchester, July 12	1950
Surrey v Warwickshire at The Oval, May 16	1953
Somerset v Lancashire at Bath, June 6 (H. F. T. Buse's benefit)	1953
Kent v Worcestershire at Tunbridge Wells, June 15	1960

SHORTEST COMPLETED MATCHES

Balls

350	Somerset (35 and 44) v Middlesex (86) at Lord's	1899
352	Victoria (82 and 57) v Tasmania (104 and 37-7) at Launceston	1850-51
372	Victoria (80 and 50) v Tasmania (97 and 35-2) at Launceston	1853-54
419*	England XI (82 and 26) v Australians (76 and 33-6) at Aston	1884
425	Derbyshire (180-0 dec. and forfeited second innings) v Northamptonshire (forfeited first innings and 181-2) at Northampton	1992
432	Victoria (78 and 67) v Tasmania (51 and 25) at Hobart	1857-58
435	Northamptonshire (4-0 dec. and 86) v Yorkshire (4-0 dec. and 88-5) at Bradford	1931
442*	Wellington (31 and 48) v Nelson (73 and 7-1) at Nelson	1887-88
445	Glamorgan (272-1 dec. and forfeited second innings) v Lancashire (forfeited first innings and 51) at Liverpool	1997
450	Bengal Governor's XI (33 and 59) v Maharaja of Cooch-Behar's XI (138) at Calcutta	1917-18

* *Match completed on first day.*

TEST RECORDS

Note: This section covers all Tests up to January 25, 2005.

BATTING RECORDS

HIGHEST INDIVIDUAL INNINGS

400*	B. C. Lara	West Indies v England at St John's	2003-04
380	M. L. Hayden	Australia v Zimbabwe at Perth	2003-04
375	B. C. Lara	West Indies v England at St John's	1993-94
365*	G. S. Sobers	West Indies v Pakistan at Kingston	1957-58
364	L. Hutton	England v Australia at The Oval	1938
340	S. T. Jayasuriya	Sri Lanka v India at Colombo (RPS)	1997-98
337	Hanif Mohammad	Pakistan v West Indies at Bridgetown	1957-58
336*	W. R. Hammond	England v New Zealand at Auckland	1932-33
334*	M. A. Taylor	Australia v Pakistan at Peshawar	1998-99
334	D. G. Bradman	Australia v England at Leeds	1930
333	G. A. Gooch	England v India at Lord's	1990
329	Inzamam-ul-Haq.	Pakistan v New Zealand at Lahore	2002
325	A. Sandham	England v West Indies at Kingston	1929-30
311	R. B. Simpson	Australia v England at Manchester	1964
310*	J. H. Edrich	England v New Zealand at Leeds	1965
309	V. Sehwag	India v Pakistan at Multan	2003-04
307	R. M. Cowper	Australia v England at Melbourne	1965-66
304	D. G. Bradman	Australia v England at Leeds	1934
302	L. G. Rowe	West Indies v England at Bridgetown	1973-74
299*	D. G. Bradman	Australia v South Africa at Adelaide	1931-32
299	M. D. Crowe	New Zealand v Sri Lanka at Wellington	1990-91
291	I. V. A. Richards	West Indies v England at The Oval	1976
287	R. E. Foster	England v Australia at Sydney	1903-04
285*	P. B. H. May	England v West Indies at Birmingham	1957
281	V. V. S. Laxman	India v Australia at Kolkata	2000-01
280*	Javed Miandad	Pakistan v India at Hyderabad	1982-83
278	D. C. S. Compton	England v Pakistan at Nottingham	1954
277	B. C. Lara	West Indies v Australia at Sydney	1992-93
277	G. C. Smith	South Africa v England at Birmingham	2003
275*	D. J. Cullinan	South Africa v New Zealand at Auckland	1998-99
275	G. Kirsten	South Africa v England at Durban	1999-2000
274*	S. P. Fleming	New Zealand v Sri Lanka at Colombo (PSS)	2003
274	R. G. Pollock	South Africa v Australia at Durban	1969-70
274	Zaheer Abbas	Pakistan v England at Birmingham	1971
271	Javed Miandad	Pakistan v New Zealand at Auckland	1988-89
270*	A. G. Headley	West Indies v England at Kingston	1934-35
270	D. G. Bradman	Australia v England at Melbourne	1936-37
270	R. Dravid	India v Pakistan at Rawalpindi	2003-04
270	K. C. Sangakkara	Sri Lanka v Zimbabwe at Bulawayo	2003-04
268	G. N. Yallop	Australia v Pakistan at Melbourne	1983-84
267*	B. A. Young	New Zealand v Sri Lanka at Dunedin	1996-97
267	P. A. de Silva	Sri Lanka v New Zealand at Wellington	1990-91
266	W. H. Ponsford	Australia v England at The Oval	1934
266	D. L. Houghton	Zimbabwe v Sri Lanka at Bulawayo	1994-95
262*	D. L. Amiss	England v West Indies at Kingston	1973-74
261*	R. R. Sarwan	West Indies v Bangladesh at Kingston	2003-04
261	F. M. M. Worrell	West Indies v England at Nottingham	1950
260	C. C. Hunte	West Indies v Pakistan at Kingston	1957-58
260	Javed Miandad	Pakistan v England at The Oval	1987
259	G. M. Turner	New Zealand v West Indies at Georgetown	1971-72
259	G. C. Smith	South Africa v England at Lord's	2003
258	T. W. Graveney	England v West Indies at Nottingham	1957

258	S. M. Nurse	West Indies v New Zealand at Christchurch . . .	1968-69
257*	Wasim Akram	Pakistan v Zimbabwe at Sheikhupura.	1996-97
257	R. T. Ponting.	Australia v India at Melbourne.	2003-04
256	R. B. Kanhai	West Indies v India at Calcutta.	1958-59
256	K. F. Barrington.	England v Australia at Manchester	1964
255*	D. J. McGlew	South Africa v New Zealand at Wellington	1952-53
254	D. G. Bradman	Australia v England at Lord's.	1930
253	S. T. Jayasuriya	Sri Lanka v Pakistan at Faisalabad	2004-05
251	W. R. Hammond	England v Australia at Sydney	1928-29
250	K. D. Walters	Australia v New Zealand at Christchurch	1976-77
250	S. F. A. F. Bacchus. . .	West Indies v India at Kanpur	1978-79
250	J. L. Langer	Australia v England at Melbourne.	2002-03

Note: The highest individual innings for Bangladesh is 158* by Mohammad Ashraful against India at Chittagong in 2004-05.

RECORD INDIVIDUAL INNINGS – THE ROAD TO 400

				Record held	
				Years	*Days*
165*	C. Bannerman	Australia v England at Melbourne	1876-77	7	150
211	W. L. Murdoch	Australia v England at The Oval	1884	19	124
287	R. E. Foster	England v Australia at Sydney	1903-04	26	111
325	A. Sandham	England v West Indies at Kingston . . .	1929-30	0	99
334	D. G. Bradman	Australia v England at Leeds	1930	2	263
336*	W. R. Hammond	England v New Zealand at Auckland . .	1932-33	5	144
364	L. Hutton	England v Australia at The Oval	1938	19	190
365*	G. S. Sobers	West Indies v Pakistan at Kingston . . .	1957-58	36	48
375	B. C. Lara	West Indies v England at St John's . . .	1993-94	9	175
380	M. L. Hayden	Australia v Zimbabwe at Perth	2003-04	0	185
400*	B. C. Lara	West Indies v England at St John's . . .	2003-04		

HUNDRED ON TEST DEBUT

C. Bannerman (165*)	Australia v England at Melbourne.	1876-77
W. G. Grace (152)	England v Australia at The Oval.	1880
H. Graham (107)	Australia v England at Lord's	1893
† K. S. Ranjitsinhji (154*) . . .	England v Australia at Manchester	1896
† P. F. Warner (132*)	England v South Africa at Johannesburg	1898-99
† R. A. Duff (104)	Australia v England at Melbourne.	1901-02
R. E. Foster (287)	England v Australia at Sydney	1903-04
G. Gunn (119).	England v Australia at Sydney	1907-08
† R. J. Hartigan (116)	Australia v England at Adelaide	1907-08
† H. L. Collins (104).	Australia v England at Sydney	1920-21
W. H. Ponsford (110)	Australia v England at Sydney	1924-25
A. A. Jackson (164)	Australia v England at Adelaide	1928-29
† G. A. Headley (176).	West Indies v England at Bridgetown	1929-30
J. E. Mills (117)	New Zealand v England at Wellington	1929-30
Nawab of Pataudi sen. (102) .	England v Australia at Sydney	1932-33
B. H. Valentine (136)	England v India at Bombay	1933-34
† L. Amarnath (118)	India v England at Bombay	1933-34
† P. A. Gibb (106)	England v South Africa at Johannesburg	1938-39
S. C. Griffith (140).	England v West Indies at Port-of-Spain	1947-48
A. G. Ganteaume (112). . . .	West Indies v England at Port-of-Spain	1947-48
† J. W. Burke (101*)	Australia v England at Adelaide	1950-51
P. B. H. May (138).	England v South Africa at Leeds	1951
R. H. Shodhan (110)	India v Pakistan at Calcutta	1952-53
B. H. Pairaudeau (115)	West Indies v India at Port-of-Spain	1952-53

†O. G. Smith (104)	West Indies v Australia at Kingston	1954-55
A. G. Kripal Singh (100*) . .	India v New Zealand at Hyderabad	1955-56
C. C. Hunte (142)	West Indies v Pakistan at Bridgetown	1957-58
C. A. Milton (104*)	England v New Zealand at Leeds	1958
†A. A. Baig (112)	India v England at Manchester	1959
Hanumant Singh (105)	India v England at Delhi	1963-64
Khalid Ibadulla (166)	Pakistan v Australia at Karachi	1964-65
B. R. Taylor (105)	New Zealand v India at Calcutta	1964-65
K. D. Walters (155)	Australia v England at Brisbane	1965-66
J. H. Hampshire (107)	England v West Indies at Lord's	1969
†G. R. Viswanath (137)	India v Australia at Kanpur	1969-70
G. S. Chappell (108)	Australia v England at Perth	1970-71
‡L. G. Rowe (214, 100*) . . .	West Indies v New Zealand at Kingston	1971-72
A. I. Kallicharran (100*) . . .	West Indies v New Zealand at Georgetown . . .	1971-72
R. E. Redmond (107)	New Zealand v Pakistan at Auckland	1972-73
†F. C. Hayes (106*)	England v West Indies at The Oval	1973
†C. G. Greenidge (107)	West Indies v India at Bangalore	1974-75
†L. Baichan (105*)	West Indies v Pakistan at Lahore	1974-75
G. J. Cosier (109)	Australia v West Indies at Melbourne	1975-76
S. Amarnath (124)	India v New Zealand at Auckland	1975-76
Javed Miandad (163)	Pakistan v New Zealand at Lahore	1976-77
†A. B. Williams (100)	West Indies v Australia at Georgetown	1977-78
†D. M. Wellham (103)	Australia v England at The Oval	1981
†Salim Malik (100*)	Pakistan v Sri Lanka at Karachi	1981-82
K. C. Wessels (162)	Australia v England at Brisbane	1982-83
W. B. Phillips (159)	Australia v Pakistan at Perth	1983-84
§M. Azharuddin (110)	India v England at Calcutta	1984-85
D. S. B. P. Kuruppu (201*) . .	Sri Lanka v New Zealand at Colombo (CCC) . .	1986-87
†M. J. Greatbatch (107*) . . .	New Zealand v England at Auckland	1987-88
M. E. Waugh (138)	Australia v England at Adelaide	1990-91
A. C. Hudson (163)	South Africa v West Indies at Bridgetown . . .	1991-92
R. S. Kaluwitharana (132*) .	Sri Lanka v Australia at Colombo (SSC)	1992-93
D. L. Houghton (121)	Zimbabwe v India at Harare	1992-93
P. K. Amre (103)	India v South Africa at Durban	1992-93
†G. P. Thorpe (114*)	England v Australia at Nottingham	1993
G. S. Blewett (102*)	Australia v England at Adelaide	1994-95
S. C. Ganguly (131)	India v England at Lord's	1996
†Mohammad Wasim (109*) . .	Pakistan v New Zealand at Lahore	1996-97
Ali Naqvi (115)	Pakistan v South Africa at Rawalpindi	1997-98
Azhar Mahmood (128*)	Pakistan v South Africa at Rawalpindi	1997-98
M. S. Sinclair (214)	New Zealand v West Indies at Wellington	1999-2000
†Younis Khan (107)	Pakistan v Sri Lanka at Rawalpindi	1999-2000
Aminul Islam (145)	Bangladesh v India at Dhaka	2000-01
†H. Masakadza (119)	Zimbabwe v West Indies at Harare	2001
T. T. Samaraweera (103*) . . .	Sri Lanka v India at Colombo (SSC)	2001
Taufeeq Umar (104)	Pakistan v Bangladesh at Multan	2001-02
†Mohammad Ashraful (114) . .	Bangladesh v Sri Lanka at Colombo (SSC) . .	2001-02
V. Sehwag (105)	India v South Africa at Bloemfontein	2001-02
L. Vincent (104)	New Zealand v Australia at Perth	2001-02
S. B. Styris (107)	New Zealand v West Indies at St George's . . .	2002
J. A. Rudolph (222*)	South Africa v Bangladesh at Chittagong	2003
‡Yasir Hameed (170, 105) . . .	Pakistan v Bangladesh at Karachi	2003
D. R. Smith (105*)	West Indies v South Africa at Cape Town	2003-04
A. J. Strauss (112)	England v New Zealand at Lord's	2004
M. J. Clarke (151)	Australia v India at Bangalore	2004-05

† *In his second innings of the match.*

‡ *L. G. Rowe and Yasir Hameed are the only batsmen to score a hundred in each innings on debut.*

§ *M. Azharuddin is the only batsman to score hundreds in each of his first three Tests.*

Notes: I.. Amarnath and S. Amarnath were father and son.

Ali Naqvi and Azhar Mahmood achieved the feat in the same innings.

Only Bannerman, Houghton and Aminul Islam scored hundreds in their country's first Test.

300 RUNS ON TEST DEBUT

314	L. G. Rowe (214, 100*)	West Indies v New Zealand at Kingston	1971-72
306	R. E. Foster (287, 19)	England v Australia at Sydney.	1903-04

DUCK ON TEST DEBUT

(Players with 2,500 Test runs who started with a duck in their first innings.)

†M. S. Atapattu	Sri Lanka v India at Chandigarh	1990-91
M. A. Atherton	England v Australia at Nottingham	1989
K. F. Barrington	England v South Africa at Nottingham	1955
K. W. R. Fletcher	England v Australia at Leeds	1968
H. A. Gomes	West Indies v England at Nottingham	1976
†G. A. Gooch	England v Australia at Birmingham	1975
L. Hutton	England v New Zealand at Lord's	1937
A. P. E. Knott	England v Pakistan at Nottingham	1967
M. Leyland	England v West Indies at The Oval	1928
Majid Khan	Pakistan v Australia at Karachi	1964-65
R. B. Richardson	West Indies v India at Bombay	1983-84
†Saeed Anwar	Pakistan v West Indies at Faisalabad.	1990-91
H. W. Taylor	South Africa v Australia at Manchester	1912
H. P. Tillekeratne	Sri Lanka v Australia at Hobart.	1989-90
V. T. Trumper	Australia v England at Nottingham.	1899
G. M. Turner	New Zealand v West Indies at Auckland	1968-69
G. R. Viswanath	India v Australia at Kanpur	1969-70
Wasim Akram	Pakistan v New Zealand at Auckland	1984-85

† *Made a pair.*

Notes: Atapattu made a duck and a single in his second Test, and another pair in his third.
  In his second innings, Viswanath made a hundred (see previous page).

TRIPLE-HUNDRED AND HUNDRED IN A TEST

G. A. Gooch (England)   333 and 123 v India at Lord's   1990

The only instance in first-class cricket. M. A. Taylor (Australia) scored 334 and 92 v Pakistan at Peshawar in 1998-99.*

DOUBLE-HUNDRED AND HUNDRED IN A TEST

K. D. Walters (Australia)	242 and 103 v West Indies at Sydney	1968-69
S. M. Gavaskar (India)	124 and 220 v West Indies at Port-of-Spain	1970-71
†L. G. Rowe (West Indies)	214 and 100* v New Zealand at Kingston	1971-72
G. S. Chappell (Australia)	247* and 133 v New Zealand at Wellington	1973-74
B. C. Lara (West Indies)	221 and 130 v Sri Lanka at Colombo (SSC).	2001-02

† *On Test debut.*

TWO SEPARATE HUNDREDS IN A TEST

Three times: S. M. Gavaskar.
Twice in one series: C. L. Walcott v Australia (1954-55).
Twice: †A. R. Border; G. S. Chappell; ‡P. A. de Silva; M. L. Hayden; G. A. Headley; H. Sutcliffe.

Once: W. Bardsley; D. G. Bradman; I. M. Chappell; D. C. S. Compton; R. Dravid; A. Flower; G. W. Flower; G. A. Gooch; C. G. Greenidge; A. P. Gurusinha; W. R. Hammond; Hanif Mohammad; V. S. Hazare; G. P. Howarth; Javed Miandad; A. H. Jones; D. M. Jones; R. B. Kanhai; G. Kirsten; B. C. Lara; A. Melville; L. R. D. Mendis; B. Mitchell; J. Moroney; A. R. Morris; E. Paynter; §L. G. Rowe; A. C. Russell; R. B. Simpson; G. S. Sobers; A. J. Stewart; M. E. Trescothick; G. M. Turner; M. P. Vaughan; Wajahatullah Wasti; K. D. Walters; S. R. Waugh; E. D. Weekes; §Yasir Hameed.

† *A. R. Border scored 150* and 153 against Pakistan in 1979-80 to become the first to score 150 in each innings of a Test match.*

‡ *P. A. de Silva scored 138* and 103* against Pakistan in 1996-97 to become the first to score two not out hundreds in a Test match.*

§ *L. G. Rowe's and Yasir Hameed's two hundreds were on Test debut.*

MOST DOUBLE-HUNDREDS

D. G. Bradman (A)	12	**R. Dravid (I)**	5	R. T. Ponting (A)	4
W. R. Hammond (E)	7	G. S. Chappell (A)	4	**S. R. Tendulkar (I)**	4
B. C. Lara (WI)	7	S. M. Gavaskar (I)	4	Zaheer Abbas (P)	4
M. S. Atapattu (SL)	6	C. G. Greenidge (WI)	4		
Javed Miandad (P)	6	L. Hutton (E)	4		

Bold type denotes those who have played Test cricket since January 1, 2004.

MOST HUNDREDS

S. M. Gavaskar (I)	34	**R. Dravid (I)**	18	P. B. H. May (E)	13
S. R. Tendulkar (I)	34	D. I. Gower (E)	18	**M. P. Vaughan (E).**	13
S. R. Waugh (A)	32	D. L. Haynes (WI)	18	J. H. Edrich (E)	12
D. G. Bradman (A)	29	D. C. S. Compton (E)	17	A. Flower (Z)	12
A. R. Border (A)	27	M. D. Crowe (NZ)	17	Hanif Mohammad (P)	12
B. C. Lara (WI)	26	D. B. Vengsarkar (I)	17	Ijaz Ahmed, sen. (P)	12
G. S. Sobers (WI)	26	M. A. Atherton (E)	16	**D. P. M. D. Jayawardene (SL)**	12
G. S. Chappell (A)	24	R. B. Richardson (WI)	16	A. I. Kallicharran (WI)	12
I. V. A. Richards (WI)	24	H. Sutcliffe (E)	16	A. R. Morris (A)	12
Javed Miandad (P)	23	**G. P. Thorpe (E)**	16	P. R. Umrigar (I)	12
M. Azharuddin (I)	22	**M. S. Atapattu (SL).**	15	J. G. Wright (NZ)	12
G. Boycott (E)	22	J. B. Hobbs (E)	15	**Yousuf Youhana (P).**	12
M. C. Cowdrey (E)	22	R. B. Kanhai (WI)	15	Zaheer Abbas (P)	12
W. R. Hammond (E)	22	Salim Malik (P)	15	M. Amarnath (I)	11
D. C. Boon (A)	21	A. J. Stewart (E)	15	D. L. Amiss (E)	11
R. N. Harvey (A)	21	C. L. Walcott (WI)	15	Asif Iqbal (P)	11
G. Kirsten (SA)	21	K. D. Walters (A)	15	**S. C. Ganguly (I)**	11
J. L. Langer (A)	21	E. D. Weekes (WI)	15	T. W. Graveney (E)	11
R. T. Ponting (A).	21	I. T. Botham (E)	14	D. M. Jones (A)	11
K. F. Barrington (E)	20	I. M. Chappell (A)	14	**D. R. Martyn (A)**	11
P. A. de Silva (SL)	20	D. J. Cullinan (SA)	14	Saeed Anwar (P)	11
G. A. Gooch (E)	20	**H. H. Gibbs (SA)**	14	R. J. Shastri (I)	11
M. L. Hayden (A)	20	**N. Hussain (E)**	14	**H. P. Tillekeratne (SL).**	11
Inzamam-ul-Haq (P)	20	**S. T. Jayasuriya (SL)**	14	M. W. Gatting (E)	10
J. H. Kallis (SA)	20	A. J. Lamb (E)	14	A. L. Hassett (A)	10
M. E. Waugh (A)	20	M. J. Slater (A)	14	G. A. Headley (WI)	10
C. G. Greenidge (WI)	19	G. R. Viswanath (I)	14	Mudassar Nazar (P)	10
L. Hutton (E)	19	**A. C. Gilchrist (A)**	13	Mushtaq Mohammad (P)	10
C. H. Lloyd (WI)	19	C. L. Hooper (WI)	13	R. B. Simpson (A)	10
M. A. Taylor (A)	19	W. M. Lawry (A)	13	**M. E. Trescothick (E)**	10

Note: The most hundreds for Bangladesh is 3 by **Habibul Bashar.**

Bold type denotes those who have played Test cricket since January 1, 2004.

MOST HUNDREDS AGAINST ONE TEAM

19	D. G. Bradman	Australia v England	
13	S. M. Gavaskar	India v West Indies	
12	J. B. Hobbs	England v Australia	

10	G. S. Sobers	West Indies v England	
10	S. R. Waugh	Australia v England	

MOST DUCKS

C. A. Walsh (West Indies) 43; **S. K. Warne (Australia) 30**; **G. D. McGrath (Australia) 29**; C. E. L. Ambrose (West Indies) and **M. Dillon (West Indies) 26**; **M. Muralitharan (Sri Lanka) 25**; D. K. Morrison (New Zealand) 24; B. S. Chandrasekhar (India) 23; **S. R. Waugh (Australia) 22**; **M. S. Atapattu (Sri Lanka)** and **Waqar Younis (Pakistan) 21**; M. A. Atherton (England) and B. S. Bedi (India) 20.

Bold type denotes those who have played Test cricket since January 1, 2004.

CARRYING BAT THROUGH TEST INNINGS

(Figures in brackets show team's total.)

A. B. Tancred	26* (47)	South Africa v England at Cape Town	1888-89
J. E. Barrett	67* (176)†	Australia v England at Lord's	1890
R. Abel	132* (307)	England v Australia at Sydney	1891-92
P. F. Warner	132* (237)†	England v South Africa at Johannesburg . . .	1898-99
W. W. Armstrong . .	159* (309)	Australia v South Africa at Johannesburg . . .	1902-03
J. W. Zulch	43* (103)	South Africa v England at Cape Town	1909-10
W. Bardsley	193* (383)	Australia v England at Lord's	1926
W. M. Woodfull . . .	30* (66)§	Australia v England at Brisbane	1928-29
W. M. Woodfull . . .	73* (193)‡	Australia v England at Adelaide	1932-33
W. A. Brown	206* (422)	Australia v England at Lord's	1938
L. Hutton	202* (344)	England v West Indies at The Oval	1950
L. Hutton	156* (272)	England v Australia at Adelaide	1950-51
Nazar Mohammad¶.	124* (331)	Pakistan v India at Lucknow	1952-53
F. M. M. Worrell . .	191* (372)	West Indies v England at Nottingham	1957
T. L. Goddard	56* (99)	South Africa v Australia at Cape Town	1957-58
D. J. McGlew	127* (292)	South Africa v New Zealand at Durban	1961-62
C. C. Hunte	60* (131)	West Indies v Australia at Port-of-Spain	1964-65
G. M. Turner	43* (131)	New Zealand v England at Lord's.	1969
W. M. Lawry	49* (107)	Australia v India at Delhi	1969-70
W. M. Lawry	60* (116)‡	Australia v England at Sydney	1970-71
G. M. Turner	223* (386)	New Zealand v West Indies at Kingston	1971-72
I. R. Redpath	159* (346)	Australia v New Zealand at Auckland	1973-74
G. Boycott	99* (215)	England v Australia at Perth	1979-80
S. M. Gavaskar . . .	127* (286)	India v Pakistan at Faisalabad	1982-83
Mudassar Nazar¶ . .	152* (323)	Pakistan v India at Lahore.	1982-83
S. Wettimuny	63* (144)	Sri Lanka v New Zealand at Christchurch .	1982-83
D. C. Boon	58* (103)	Australia v New Zealand at Auckland	1985-86
D. L. Haynes	88* (211)	West Indies v Pakistan at Karachi	1986-87
G. A. Gooch	154* (252)	England v West Indies at Leeds	1991
D. L. Haynes	75* (176)	West Indies v England at The Oval	1991
A. J. Stewart	69* (175)	England v Pakistan at Lord's	1992
D. L. Haynes	143* (382)	West Indies v Pakistan at Port-of-Spain	1992-93
M. H. Dekker	68* (187)	Zimbabwe v Pakistan at Rawalpindi	1993-94
M. A. Atherton . . .	94* (228)	England v New Zealand at Christchurch . . .	1996-97
G. Kirsten	100* (239)	South Africa v Pakistan at Faisalabad	1997-98
M. A. Taylor	169* (350)	Australia v South Africa at Adelaide	1997-98
G. W. Flower	156* (321)	Zimbabwe v Pakistan at Bulawayo	1997-98

Saeed Anwar	188* (316)	Pakistan v India at Calcutta	1998-99
M. S. Atapattu	216* (428)	Sri Lanka v Zimbabwe at Bulawayo	1999-2000
R. P. Arnold	104* (231)	Sri Lanka v Zimbabwe at Harare	1999-2000
Javed Omar	85* (168)†‡	Bangladesh v Zimbabwe at Bulawayo	2000-01

† *On debut.* ‡ *One man absent.* § *Two men absent.* ¶ *Father and son.*

Notes: G. M. Turner (223*) holds the record for the highest score by a player carrying his bat through a Test innings. He is also the youngest player to do so, being 22 years 63 days old when he first achieved the feat (1969).

D. L. Haynes, who is alone in achieving this feat on three occasions, also opened the batting and was last man out in each innings for West Indies v New Zealand at Dunedin, 1979-80.

750 RUNS IN A SERIES

	T	I	NO	R	HS	100s	Avge		
D. G. Bradman	5	7	0	974	334	4	139.14	A v E	1930
W. R. Hammond	5	9	1	905	251	4	113.12	E v A	1928-29
M. A. Taylor	6	11	1	839	219	2	83.90	A v E	1989
R. N. Harvey	5	9	0	834	205	4	92.66	A v SA	1952-53
I. V. A. Richards	4	7	0	829	291	3	118.42	WI v E	1976
C. L. Walcott	5	10	0	827	155	5	82.70	WI v A	1954-55
G. S. Sobers	5	8	2	824	365*	3	137.33	WI v P	1957-58
D. G. Bradman	5	9	0	810	270	3	90.00	A v E	1936-37
D. G. Bradman	5	5	1	806	299*	4	201.50	A v SA	1931-32
B. C. Lara	5	8	0	798	375	2	99.75	WI v E	1993-94
E. D. Weekes	5	7	0	779	194	4	111.28	WI v I	1948-49
†S. M. Gavaskar	4	8	3	774	220	4	154.80	I v WI	1970-71
B. C. Lara	6	10	1	765	179	3	85.00	WI v E	1995
Mudassar Nazar	6	8	2	761	231	4	126.83	P v I	1982-83
D. G. Bradman	5	8	0	758	304	2	94.75	A v E	1934
D. C. S. Compton	5	8	0	753	208	4	94.12	E v SA	1947
‡G. A. Gooch	3	6	0	752	333	3	125.33	E v I	1990

† *Gavaskar's aggregate was achieved in his first Test series.*
‡ *G. A. Gooch is alone in scoring 1,000 runs in Test cricket during an English season with 1,058 runs in 11 innings against New Zealand and India in 1990.*

MOST RUNS IN A CALENDAR YEAR

	T	I	NO	R	HS	100s	Avge	Year
I. V. A. Richards (WI)	11	19	0	1,710	291	7	90.00	1976
S. M. Gavaskar (I)	18	27	1	1,555	221	5	59.80	1979
R. T. Ponting (A)	11	18	3	1,503	257	6	100.20	2003
J. L. Langer (A)	14	27	0	1,481	215	5	54.85	2004
M. P. Vaughan (E)	14	26	2	1,481	197	6	61.70	2002
S. R. Tendulkar (I)	16	26	1	1,392	193	4	55.68	2002
M. L. Hayden (A)	14	25	3	1,391	203	5	63.22	2001
G. R. Viswanath (I)	17	26	3	1,388	179	5	60.34	1979
R. B. Simpson (A)	14	26	3	1,381	311	3	60.04	1964
D. L. Amiss (E)	13	22	2	1,379	262*	5	68.95	1974
R. Dravid (I)	16	26	3	1,357	217	5	59.00	2002
D. R. Martyn (A)	14	26	2	1,353	161	6	56.37	2004
B. C. Lara (WI)	10	19	1	1,344	209	5	74.66	2003
M. L. Hayden (A)	12	21	4	1,312	380	5	77.17	2003
S. M. Gavaskar (I)	18	32	4	1,310	236*	5	46.78	1983

Notes: M. Amarnath reached 1,000 runs in 1983 on May 3.

The only batsman to score 1,000 runs in a year before World War II was C. Hill of Australia: 1,061 in 1902.

MOST RUNS

		T	I	NO	R	HS	100s	Avge
1	A. R. Border (Australia).	156	265	44	11,174	205	27	50.56
2	**S. R. Waugh (Australia)**	**168**	**260**	**46**	**10,927**	**200**	**32**	**51.06**
3	S. M. Gavaskar (India).	125	214	16	10,122	236*	34	51.12
4	**B. C. Lara (West Indies)** . . .	**112**	**197**	**6**	**10,094**	**400***	**26**	**52.84**
5	**S. R. Tendulkar (India)**	**120**	**193**	**21**	**9,879**	**248***	**34**	**57.43**
6	G. A. Gooch (England)	118	215	6	8,900	333	20	42.58
7	Javed Miandad (Pakistan) . . .	124	189	21	8,832	280*	23	52.57
8	I. V. A. Richards (West Indies)	121	182	12	8,540	291	24	50.23
9	A. J. Stewart (England)	133	235	21	8,463	190	15	39.54
10	D. I. Gower (England)	117	204	18	8,231	215	18	44.25
11	G. Boycott (England).	108	193	23	8,114	246*	22	47.72
12	G. S. Sobers (West Indies) . . .	93	160	21	8,032	365*	26	57.78
13	M. E. Waugh (Australia)	128	209	17	8,029	153*	20	41.81
14	M. A. Atherton (England). . . .	115	212	7	7,728	185*	16	37.69
15	M. C. Cowdrey (England)	114	188	15	7,624	182	22	44.06
16	C. G. Greenidge (West Indies).	108	185	16	7,558	226	19	44.72
17	M. A. Taylor (Australia).	104	186	13	7,525	334*	19	43.49
18	C. H. Lloyd (West Indies) . . .	110	175	14	7,515	242*	19	46.67
19	D. L. Haynes (West Indies) . . .	116	202	25	7,487	184	18	42.29
20	D. C. Boon (Australia).	107	190	20	7,422	200	21	43.65
21	**R. Dravid (India). . . . .**	**86**	**146**	**18**	**7,363**	**270**	**18**	**57.52**
22	**G. Kirsten (South Africa)** . . .	**101**	**176**	**15**	**7,289**	**275**	**21**	**45.27**
23	W. R. Hammond (England). . .	85	140	16	7,249	336*	22	58.45
24	G. S. Chappell (Australia) . . .	87	151	19	7,110	247*	24	53.86
25	**Inzamam-ul-Haq (Pakistan)** .	**97**	**160**	**16**	**7,052**	**329**	**20**	**48.97**
26	D. G. Bradman (Australia) . . .	52	80	10	6,996	334	29	99.94
27	L. Hutton (England)	79	138	15	6,971	364	19	56.67
28	D. B. Vengsarkar (India).	116	185	22	6,868	166	17	42.13
29	**J. H. Kallis (South Africa)** . .	**87**	**147**	**24**	**6,833**	**189***	**20**	**55.55**
30	K. F. Barrington (England) . . .	82	131	15	6,806	256	20	58.67
31	**R. T. Ponting (Australia).** . . .	**85**	**138**	**18**	**6,657**	**257**	**21**	**55.47**
32	**G. P. Thorpe (England)**	**98**	**177**	**26**	**6,636**	**200***	**16**	**43.94**
33	**J. L. Langer (Australia)**	**85**	**145**	**6**	**6,401**	**250**	**21**	**46.05**
34	**S. T. Jayasuriya (Sri Lanka)** .	**94**	**160**	**13**	**6,388**	**340**	**14**	**43.45**
35	P. A. de Silva (Sri Lanka). . . .	93	159	11	6,361	267	20	42.97
36	R. B. Kanhai (West Indies). . .	79	137	6	6,227	256	15	47.53
37	M. Azharuddin (India)	99	147	9	6,215	199	22	45.03
38	R. N. Harvey (Australia)	79	137	10	6,149	205	21	48.41
39	G. R. Viswanath (India)	91	155	10	6,080	222	14	41.93
40	R. B. Richardson (West Indies)	86	146	12	5,949	194	16	44.39
41	D. C. S. Compton (England). .	78	131	15	5,807	278	17	50.06
42	Salim Malik (Pakistan).	103	154	22	5,768	237	15	43.69
43	**N. Hussain (England).**	**96**	**171**	**16**	**5,764**	**207**	**14**	**37.18**
44	C. L. Hooper (West Indies). . .	102	173	15	5,762	233	13	36.46
45	**S. P. Fleming (New Zealand).**	**89**	**154**	**10**	**5,663**	**274***	**8**	**39.32**
46	**M. L. Hayden (Australia)** . . .	**64**	**112**	**10**	**5,563**	**380**	**20**	**54.53**
47	M. D. Crowe (New Zealand). .	77	131	11	5,444	299	17	45.36
48	J. B. Hobbs (England)	61	102	7	5,410	211	15	56.94
49	K. D. Walters (Australia)	74	125	14	5,357	250	15	48.26
50	I. M. Chappell (Australia) . . .	75	136	10	5,345	196	14	42.42

Note: The leading aggregates for other countries are:

A. Flower (Zimbabwe)	63	112	19	4,794	232*	12	51.54
Habibul Bashar (Bangladesh) . . .	**34**	**67**	**1**	**2,299**	**113**	**3**	**34.83**

Bold type denotes those who have played Test cricket since January 1, 2004.

2,500 RUNS

ENGLAND

		T	I	NO	R	HS	100s	Avge
1	G. A. Gooch	118	215	6	8,900	333	20	42.58
2	A. J. Stewart	133	235	21	8,463	190	15	39.54
3	D. I. Gower	117	204	18	8,231	215	18	44.25
4	G. Boycott	108	193	23	8,114	246*	22	47.72
5	M. A. Atherton	115	212	7	7,728	185*	16	37.69
6	M. C. Cowdrey	114	188	15	7,624	182	22	44.06
7	W. R. Hammond	85	140	16	7,249	336*	22	58.45
8	L. Hutton	79	138	15	6,971	364	19	56.67
9	K. F. Barrington	82	131	15	6,806	256	20	58.67
10	**G. P. Thorpe**	**98**	**177**	**26**	**6,636**	**200***	**16**	**43.94**
11	D. C. S. Compton	78	131	15	5,807	278	17	50.06
12	**N. Hussain**	**96**	**171**	**16**	**5,764**	**207**	**14**	**37.18**
13	J. B. Hobbs	61	102	7	5,410	211	15	56.94
14	I. T. Botham	102	161	6	5,200	208	14	33.54
15	J. H. Edrich	77	127	9	5,138	310*	12	43.54
16	T. W. Graveney	79	123	13	4,882	258	11	44.38
17	A. J. Lamb	79	139	10	4,656	142	14	36.09
18	H. Sutcliffe	54	84	9	4,555	194	16	60.73
19	P. B. H. May	66	106	9	4,537	285*	13	46.77
20	E. R. Dexter	62	102	8	4,502	205	9	47.89
21	**M. E. Trescothick**	**59**	**113**	**10**	**4,430**	**219**	**10**	**43.00**
22	M. W. Gatting	79	138	14	4,409	207	10	35.55
23	A. P. E. Knott	95	149	15	4,389	135	5	32.75
24	**M. A. Butcher**	**71**	**131**	**7**	**4,288**	**173***	**8**	**34.58**
25	R. A. Smith	62	112	15	4,236	175	9	43.67
26	**M. P. Vaughan**	**55**	**99**	**8**	**4,023**	**197**	**13**	**44.20**
27	D. L. Amiss	50	88	10	3,612	262*	11	46.30
28	A. W. Greig	58	93	4	3,599	148	8	40.43
29	E. H. Hendren	51	83	9	3,525	205*	7	47.63
30	G. A. Hick	65	114	6	3,383	178	6	31.32
31	F. E. Woolley	64	98	7	3,283	154	5	36.07
32	K. W. R. Fletcher	59	96	14	3,272	216	7	39.90
33	M. Leyland	41	65	5	2,764	187	9	46.06
34	C. Washbrook	37	66	6	2,569	195	6	42.81

AUSTRALIA

		T	I	NO	R	HS	100s	Avge
1	A. R. Border	156	265	44	11,174	205	27	50.56
2	**S. R. Waugh**	**168**	**260**	**46**	**10,927**	**200**	**32**	**51.06**
3	M. E. Waugh	128	209	17	8,029	153*	20	41.81
4	M. A. Taylor	104	186	13	7,525	334*	19	43.49
5	D. C. Boon	107	190	20	7,422	200	21	43.65
6	G. S. Chappell	87	151	19	7,110	247*	24	53.86
7	D. G. Bradman	52	80	10	6,996	334	29	99.94
8	**R. T. Ponting**	**85**	**138**	**18**	**6,657**	**257**	**21**	**55.47**
9	**J. L. Langer**	**85**	**145**	**6**	**6,401**	**250**	**21**	**46.05**
10	R. N. Harvey	79	137	10	6,149	205	21	48.41
11	**M. L. Hayden**	**64**	**112**	**10**	**5,563**	**380**	**20**	**54.53**
12	K. D. Walters	74	125	14	5,357	250	15	48.26
13	I. M. Chappell	75	136	10	5,345	196	14	42.42
14	M. J. Slater	74	131	7	5,312	219	14	42.83
15	W. M. Lawry	67	123	12	5,234	210	13	47.15
16	R. B. Simpson	62	111	7	4,869	311	10	46.81

		T	I	NO	R	HS	100s	Avge
17	I. R. Redpath	66	120	11	4,737	171	8	43.45
18	K. J. Hughes	70	124	6	4,415	213	9	37.41
19	I. A. Healy	119	182	23	4,356	161*	4	27.39
20	**A. C. Gilchrist**	**65**	**94**	**16**	**4,109**	**204***	**13**	**52.67**
21	**D. R. Martyn**	**53**	**86**	**12**	**3,712**	**161**	**11**	**50.16**
22	R. W. Marsh	96	150	13	3,633	132	3	26.51
23	D. M. Jones	52	89	11	3,631	216	11	46.55
24	A. R. Morris	46	79	3	3,533	206	12	46.48
25	C. Hill	49	89	2	3,412	191	7	39.21
26	G. M. Wood	59	112	6	3,374	172	9	31.83
27	V. T. Trumper	48	89	8	3,163	214*	8	39.04
28	C. C. McDonald	47	83	4	3,107	170	5	39.32
29	A. L. Hassett	43	69	3	3,073	198*	10	46.56
30	K. R. Miller	55	87	7	2,958	147	7	36.97
31	W. W. Armstrong	50	84	10	2,863	159*	6	38.68
32	G. R. Marsh	50	93	7	2,854	138	4	33.18
33	K. R. Stackpole	43	80	5	2,807	207	7	37.42
34	N. C. O'Neill	42	69	8	2,779	181	6	45.55
35	G. N. Yallop	39	70	3	2,756	268	8	41.13
36	S. J. McCabe	39	62	5	2,748	232	6	48.21
37	G. S. Blewett	46	79	4	2,552	214	4	34.02

SOUTH AFRICA

		T	I	NO	R	HS	100s	Avge
1	**G. Kirsten**	**101**	**176**	**15**	**7,289**	**275**	**21**	**45.27**
2	**J. H. Kallis**	**87**	**147**	**24**	**6,833**	**189***	**20**	**55.55**
3	**H. H. Gibbs**	**64**	**110**	**5**	**5,053**	**228**	**14**	**48.12**
4	D. J. Cullinan	70	115	12	4,554	275*	14	44.21
5	W. J. Cronje	68	111	9	3,714	135	6	36.41
6	B. Mitchell	42	80	9	3,471	189*	8	48.88
7	**S. M. Pollock**	**92**	**131**	**31**	**3,120**	**111**	**2**	**31.20**
8	A. D. Nourse	34	62	7	2,960	231	9	53.81
9	H. W. Taylor	42	76	4	2,936	176	7	40.77
10	**M. V. Boucher**	**78**	**107**	**13**	**2,877**	**125**	**4**	**30.60**
11	**G. C. Smith**	**33**	**58**	**4**	**2,774**	**277**	**7**	**51.37**
12	J. N. Rhodes	52	80	9	2,532	117	3	35.66
13	E. J. Barlow	30	57	2	2,516	201	6	45.74
	T. L. Goddard	41	78	5	2,516	112	1	34.46

Note: K. C. Wessels scored 2,788 runs in 40 Tests: 1,761 (average 42.95) in 24 Tests for Australia, and 1,027 (average 38.03) in 16 Tests for South Africa.

WEST INDIES

		T	I	NO	R	HS	100s	Avge
1	**B. C. Lara**	**112**	**197**	**6**	**10,094**	**400***	**26**	**52.84**
2	I. V. A. Richards	121	182	12	8,540	291	24	50.23
3	G. S. Sobers	93	160	21	8,032	365*	26	57.78
4	C. G. Greenidge	108	185	16	7,558	226	19	44.72
5	C. H. Lloyd	110	175	14	7,515	242*	19	46.67
6	D. L. Haynes	116	202	25	7,487	184	18	42.29
7	R. B. Kanhai	79	137	6	6,227	256	15	47.53
8	R. B. Richardson	86	146	12	5,949	194	16	44.39
9	C. L. Hooper	102	173	15	5,762	233	13	36.46
10	**S. Chanderpaul**	**80**	**135**	**18**	**5,192**	**140**	**11**	**44.37**
11	E. D. Weekes	48	81	5	4,455	207	15	58.61

		T	I	NO	R	HS	100s	Avge
12	A. I. Kallicharran	66	109	10	4,399	187	12	44.43
13	R. C. Fredericks	59	109	7	4,334	169	8	42.49
14	F. M. M. Worrell	51	87	9	3,860	261	9	49.48
15	C. L. Walcott	44	74	7	3,798	220	15	56.68
16	**R. R. Sarwan**	**50**	**89**	**6**	**3,401**	**261***	**6**	**40.97**
17	P. J. L. Dujon	81	115	11	3,322	139	5	31.94
18	C. C. Hunte	44	78	6	3,245	260	8	45.06
19	H. A. Gomes	60	91	11	3,171	143	9	39.63
20	B. F. Butcher	44	78	6	3,104	209*	7	43.11
21	**C. H. Gayle**	**47**	**82**	**3**	**3,035**	**204**	**6**	**38.41**
22	J. C. Adams	54	90	17	3,012	208*	6	41.26
23	S. L. Campbell	52	93	4	2,882	208	4	32.38
24	**R. D. Jacobs**	**65**	**112**	**21**	**2,577**	**118**	**3**	**28.31**
25	S. M. Nurse	29	54	1	2,523	258	6	47.60

NEW ZEALAND

		T	I	NO	R	HS	100s	Avge
1	**S. P. Fleming**	**89**	**154**	**10**	**5,663**	**274***	**8**	**39.32**
2	M. D. Crowe	77	131	11	5,444	299	17	45.36
3	J. G. Wright	82	148	7	5,334	185	12	37.82
4	**N. J. Astle**	**66**	**113**	**9**	**3,906**	**222**	**9**	**37.55**
5	B. E. Congdon	61	114	7	3,448	176	7	32.22
6	J. R. Reid	58	108	5	3,428	142	6	33.28
7	**C. L. Cairns**	**62**	**104**	**5**	**3,320**	**158**	**5**	**33.53**
8	R. J. Hadlee	86	134	19	3,124	151*	2	27.16
9	**C. D. McMillan**	**53**	**88**	**10**	**3,078**	**142**	**6**	**39.46**
10	G. M. Turner	41	73	6	2,991	259	7	44.64
11	A. H. Jones	39	74	8	2,922	186	7	44.27
12	A. C. Parore	78	128	19	2,865	110	2	26.28
13	**M. H. Richardson**	**38**	**65**	**3**	**2,776**	**145**	**4**	**44.77**
14	B. Sutcliffe	42	76	8	2,727	230*	5	40.10
15	M. G. Burgess	50	92	6	2,684	119*	5	31.20
16	J. V. Coney	52	85	14	2,668	174*	3	37.57
17	G. P. Howarth	47	83	5	2,531	147	6	32.44

INDIA

		T	I	NO	R	HS	100s	Avge
1	S. M. Gavaskar	125	214	16	10,122	236*	34	51.12
2	**S. R. Tendulkar**	**120**	**193**	**21**	**9,879**	**248***	**34**	**57.43**
3	**R. Dravid**	**86**	**146**	**18**	**7,363**	**270**	**18**	**57.52**
4	D. B. Vengsarkar	116	185	22	6,868	166	17	42.13
5	M. Azharuddin	99	147	9	6,215	199	22	45.03
6	G. R. Viswanath	91	155	10	6,080	222	14	41.93
7	Kapil Dev	131	184	15	5,248	163	8	31.05
8	**S. C. Ganguly**	**79**	**128**	**12**	**4,901**	**173**	**11**	**42.25**
9	M. Amarnath	69	113	10	4,378	138	11	42.50
10	R. J. Shastri	80	121	14	3,830	206	11	35.79
11	**V. V. S. Laxman**	**61**	**98**	**10**	**3,795**	**281**	**7**	**43.12**
12	P. R. Umrigar	59	94	8	3,631	223	12	42.22
13	V. L. Manjrekar	55	92	10	3,208	189*	7	39.12
14	N. S. Sidhu	51	78	2	3,202	201	9	42.13
15	C. G. Borde	55	97	11	3,061	177*	5	35.59
16	Nawab of Pataudi jun.	46	83	3	2,793	203*	6	34.91
17	S. M. H. Kirmani	88	124	22	2,759	102	2	27.04
18	F. M. Engineer	46	87	3	2,611	121	2	31.08
19	**V. Sehwag**	**31**	**50**	**1**	**2,535**	**309**	**8**	**51.73**

PAKISTAN

		T	I	NO	R	HS	100s	Avge
1	Javed Miandad	124	189	21	8,832	280*	23	52.57
2	**Inzamam-ul-Haq**	**97**	**160**	**16**	**7,052**	**329**	**20**	**48.97**
3	Salim Malik.	103	154	22	5,768	237	15	43.69
4	Zaheer Abbas	78	124	11	5,062	274	12	44.79
5	Mudassar Nazar	76	116	8	4,114	231	10	38.09
6	Saeed Anwar	55	91	2	4,052	188*	11	45.52
7	**Yousuf Youhana**	**56**	**93**	**8**	**4,035**	**204***	**12**	**47.47**
8	Majid Khan	63	106	5	3,931	167	8	38.92
9	Hanif Mohammad	55	97	8	3,915	337	12	43.98
10	Imran Khan	88	126	25	3,807	136	6	37.69
11	Mushtaq Mohammad	57	100	7	3,643	201	10	39.17
12	Asif Iqbal	58	99	7	3,575	175	11	38.85
13	Ijaz Ahmed, sen.	60	92	4	3,315	211	12	37.67
14	Saeed Ahmed	41	78	4	2,991	172	5	40.41
15	Wasim Akram	104	147	19	2,898	257*	3	22.64
16	Ramiz Raja	57	94	5	2,833	122	2	31.83
17	Aamir Sohail	47	83	3	2,823	205	5	35.28
18	Wasim Raja	57	92	14	2,821	125	4	36.16
19	**Moin Khan**	**69**	**104**	**8**	**2,741**	**137**	**4**	**28.55**
20	Mohsin Khan	48	79	6	2,709	200	7	37.10
21	Shoaib Mohammad	45	68	7	2,705	203*	7	44.34
22	Sadiq Mohammad	41	74	2	2,579	166	5	35.81

SRI LANKA

		T	I	NO	R	HS	100s	Avge
1	**S. T. Jayasuriya**	**94**	**160**	**13**	**6,388**	**340**	**14**	**43.45**
2	P. A. de Silva	93	159	11	6,361	267	20	42.97
3	A. Ranatunga	93	155	12	5,105	135*	4	35.69
4	**M. S. Atapattu**	**79**	**137**	**14**	**4,873**	**249**	**15**	**39.61**
5	**D. P. M. D. Jayawardene** . . .	**65**	**106**	**8**	**4,738**	**242**	**12**	**48.34**
6	**H. P. Tillekeratne**	**83**	**131**	**25**	**4,545**	**204***	**11**	**42.87**
7	**K. C. Sangakkara**	**44**	**73**	**4**	**3,400**	**270**	**7**	**49.27**
8	R. S. Mahanama	52	89	1	2,576	225	4	29.27

ZIMBABWE

		T	I	NO	R	HS	100s	Avge
1	A. Flower	63	112	19	4,794	232*	12	51.54
2	**G. W. Flower**	**67**	**123**	**6**	**3,457**	**201***	**6**	**29.54**
3	A. D. R. Campbell	60	109	4	2,858	103	2	27.21

BANGLADESH: The highest aggregate is **2,299** (average 34.83) by **Habibul Bashar** in 34 Tests.

Bold type denotes those who have played Test cricket since January 1, 2004.

CAREER AVERAGE OVER 50

(Qualification: 20 innings)

Avge		T	I	NO	R	HS	100s
99.94	D. G. Bradman (A)	52	80	10	6,996	334	29
60.97	R. G. Pollock (SA)	23	41	4	2,256	274	7
60.83	G. A. Headley (WI)	22	40	4	2,190	270*	10
60.73	H. Sutcliffe (E)	54	84	9	4,555	194	16
59.23	E. Paynter (E)	20	31	5	1,540	243	4
58.67	K. F. Barrington (E)	82	131	15	6,806	256	20
58.61	E. D. Weekes (WI)	48	81	5	4,455	207	15
58.45	W. R. Hammond (E)	85	140	16	7,249	336*	22
57.78	G. S. Sobers (WI)	93	160	21	8,032	365*	26
57.52	**R. Dravid (I)**	**86**	**146**	**18**	**7,363**	**270**	**18**
57.43	**S. R. Tendulkar (I)**	**120**	**193**	**21**	**9,879**	**248***	**34**
56.94	J. B. Hobbs (E)	61	102	7	5,410	211	15
56.68	C. L. Walcott (WI)	44	74	7	3,798	220	15
56.67	L. Hutton (E)	79	138	15	6,971	364	19
56.63	**A. J. Strauss (E)**	**12**	**24**	**2**	**1,246**	**147**	**5**
55.55	**J. H. Kallis (SA)**	**87**	**147**	**24**	**6,833**	**189***	**20**
55.47	**R. T. Ponting (A)**	**85**	**138**	**18**	**6,657**	**257**	**21**
55.00	E. Tyldesley (E)	14	20	2	990	122	3
54.53	**M. L. Hayden (A)**	**64**	**112**	**10**	**5,563**	**380**	**20**
54.20	C. A. Davis (WI)	15	29	5	1,301	183	4
54.20	V. G. Kambli (I)	17	21	1	1,084	227	4
53.86	G. S. Chappell (A)	87	151	19	7,110	247*	24
53.81	A. D. Nourse (SA)	34	62	7	2,960	231	9
52.84	**B. C. Lara (WI)**	**112**	**197**	**6**	**10,094**	**400***	**26**
52.67	**A. C. Gilchrist (A)**	**65**	**94**	**16**	**4,109**	**204***	**13**
52.57	Javed Miandad (P)	124	189	21	8,832	280*	23
51.73	**V. Sehwag (I)**	**31**	**50**	**1**	**2,535**	**309**	**8**
51.62	J. Ryder (A)	20	32	5	1,394	201*	3
51.54	A. Flower (Z)	63	112	19	4,794	232*	12
51.37	**G. C. Smith (SA)**	**33**	**58**	**4**	**2,774**	**277**	**7**
51.12	S. M. Gavaskar (I)	125	214	16	10,122	236*	34
51.06	**S. R. Waugh (A)**	**168**	**260**	**46**	**10,927**	**200**	**32**
50.56	A. R. Border (A)	156	265	44	11,174	205	27
50.23	I. V. A. Richards (WI)	121	182	12	8,540	291	24
50.16	**D. R. Martyn (A)**	**53**	**86**	**12**	**3,712**	**161**	**11**
50.06	D. C. S. Compton (E)	78	131	15	5,807	278	17

Bold type denotes those who have played Test cricket since January 1, 2004.

FASTEST FIFTIES

Minutes			
28	J. T. Brown	England v Australia at Melbourne	1894-95
29	S. A. Durani	India v England at Kanpur	1963-64
30	E. A. V. Williams	West Indies v England at Bridgetown	1947-48
30	B. R. Taylor	New Zealand v West Indies at Auckland	1968-69
33	C. A. Roach	West Indies v England at The Oval	1933
34	C. R. Browne	West Indies v England at Georgetown	1929-30

The fastest fifties in terms of balls received (where recorded) are:

Balls			
26	I. T. Botham	England v India at Delhi	1981-82
27	Yousuf Youhana	Pakistan v South Africa at Cape Town	2002-03
30	Kapil Dev	India v Pakistan at Karachi (2nd Test)	1982-83
31	W. J. Cronje	South Africa v Sri Lanka at Centurion	1997-98
32	I. V. A. Richards	West Indies v India at Kingston	1982-83
32	I. T. Botham	England v New Zealand at The Oval	1986

Balls
33	R. C. Fredericks	West Indies v Australia at Perth	1975-76
33	Kapil Dev	India v Pakistan at Karachi	1978-79
33	Kapil Dev	India v England at Manchester	1982
33	A. J. Lamb	England v New Zealand at Auckland	1991-92
33	A. Flintoff	England v New Zealand at Wellington	2001-02

FASTEST HUNDREDS

Minutes
70	J. M. Gregory	Australia v South Africa at Johannesburg	1921-22
75	G. L. Jessop	England v Australia at The Oval	1902
78	R. Benaud	Australia v West Indies at Kingston	1954-55
80	J. H. Sinclair	South Africa v Australia at Cape Town	1902-03
81	I. V. A. Richards	West Indies v England at St John's	1985-86
86	B. R. Taylor	New Zealand v West Indies at Auckland	1968-69

The fastest hundreds in terms of balls received (where recorded) are:

Balls
56	I. V. A. Richards	West Indies v England at St John's	1985-86
67	J. M. Gregory	Australia v South Africa at Johannesburg	1921-22
69	S. Chanderpaul	West Indies v Australia at Georgetown	2002-03
71	R. C. Fredericks	West Indies v Australia at Perth	1975-76
74	Majid Khan	Pakistan v New Zealand at Karachi	1976-77
74	Kapil Dev	India v Sri Lanka at Kanpur	1986-87
74	M. Azharuddin	India v South Africa at Calcutta	1996-97
76	G. L. Jessop	England v Australia at The Oval	1902

FASTEST DOUBLE-HUNDREDS

Minutes
214	D. G. Bradman	Australia v England at Leeds	1930
217	N. J. Astle	New Zealand v England at Christchurch	2001-02
223	S. J. McCabe	Australia v England at Nottingham	1938
226	V. T. Trumper	Australia v South Africa at Adelaide	1910-11
234	D. G. Bradman	Australia v England at Lord's	1930
240	W. R. Hammond	England v New Zealand at Auckland	1932-33
241	S. E. Gregory	Australia v England at Sydney	1894-95
245	D. C. S. Compton . . .	England v Pakistan at Nottingham	1954

The fastest double-hundreds in terms of balls received (where recorded) are:

Balls
153	N. J. Astle	New Zealand v England at Christchurch	2001-02
211	H. H. Gibbs	South Africa v Australia at Cape Town	2002-03
212	A. C. Gilchrist	Australia v South Africa at Johannesburg	2001-02
220	I. T. Botham	England v India at The Oval	1982
222	V. Sehwag	India v Pakistan at Multan	2003-04
229	P. A. de Silva	Sri Lanka v Bangladesh at Colombo (PSS)	2002
231	G. P. Thorpe	England v New Zealand at Christchurch	2001-02
232	C. G. Greenidge	West Indies v England at Lord's	1984

FASTEST TRIPLE-HUNDREDS

Minutes
288	W. R. Hammond	England v New Zealand at Auckland	1932-33
336	D. G. Bradman	Australia v England at Leeds	1930

MOST RUNS SCORED OFF AN OVER

28	B. C. Lara (466444)	off R. J. Peterson	WI v SA at Johannesburg	2003-04
26	C. D. McMillan (444464)	off Younis Khan	NZ v P at Hamilton	2000-01

MOST RUNS IN A DAY

309	D. G. Bradman	Australia v England at Leeds	1930
295	W. R. Hammond	England v New Zealand at Auckland	1932-33
273	D. C. S. Compton	England v Pakistan at Nottingham	1954
271	D. G. Bradman	Australia v England at Leeds	1934

MOST SIXES IN A CAREER

C. L. Cairns (NZ)	87	M. L. Hayden (A)	68	
I. V. A. Richards (WI)	84	I. T. Botham (E)	67	
C. H. Lloyd (WI)	70	C. G. Greenidge (WI)	67	
B. C. Lara (WI)	69	C. L. Hooper (WI)	63	
A. C. Gilchrist (A)	68	Kapil Dev (I)	61	

Bold type denotes those who have played Test cricket since January 1, 2004.

SLOWEST INDIVIDUAL BATTING

0	in 101 minutes	G. I. Allott, New Zealand v South Africa at Auckland.... 1998-99
4*	in 110 minutes	Abdul Razzaq, Pakistan v Australia at Melbourne. 2004-05
7	in 123 minutes	G. Miller, England v Australia at Melbourne. 1978-79
9	in 132 minutes	R. K. Chauhan, India v Sri Lanka at Ahmedabad. 1993-94
10*	in 133 minutes	T. G. Evans, England v Australia at Adelaide. 1946-47
14*	in 165 minutes	D. K. Morrison, New Zealand v England at Auckland.... 1996-97
18	in 194 minutes	W. R. Playle, New Zealand v England at Leeds. 1958
19	in 217 minutes	M. D. Crowe, New Zealand v Sri Lanka at Colombo (SSC) 1983-84
25	in 242 minutes	D. K. Morrison, New Zealand v Pakistan at Faisalabad.. 1990-91
29*	in 277 minutes	R. C. Russell, England v South Africa at Johannesburg... 1995-96
35	in 332 minutes	C. J. Tavaré, England v India at Madras. 1981-82
60	in 390 minutes	D. N. Sardesai, India v West Indies at Bridgetown. 1961-62
62	in 408 minutes	Ramiz Raja, Pakistan v West Indies at Karachi. 1986-87
68	in 458 minutes	T. E. Bailey, England v Australia at Brisbane. 1958-59
99	in 505 minutes	M. L. Jaisimha, India v Pakistan at Kanpur. 1960-61
105	in 575 minutes	D. J. McGlew, South Africa v Australia at Durban. 1957-58
114	in 591 minutes	Mudassar Nazar, Pakistan v England at Lahore. 1977-78
146*	in 635 minutes	N. Hussain, England v South Africa at Durban. 1999-2000
163	in 720 minutes	Shoaib Mohammad, Pakistan v New Zealand at Wellington 1988-89
201*	in 777 minutes	D. S. B. P. Kuruppu, Sri Lanka v New Zealand at
		Colombo (CCC). 1986-87
275	in 878 minutes	G. Kirsten, South Africa v England at Durban. 1999-2000
337	in 970 minutes	Hanif Mohammad, Pakistan v West Indies at Bridgetown.. 1957-58

SLOWEST HUNDREDS

557 minutes	Mudassar Nazar, Pakistan v England at Lahore.	1977-78
545 minutes	D. J. McGlew, South Africa v Australia at Durban.	1957-58
535 minutes	A. P. Gurusinha, Sri Lanka v Zimbabwe at Harare	1994-95
516 minutes	J. J. Crowe, New Zealand v Sri Lanka at Colombo (CCC)	1986-87
500 minutes	S. V. Manjrekar, India v Zimbabwe at Harare	1992-93
488 minutes	P. E. Richardson, England v South Africa at Johannesburg	1956-57

Notes: The slowest hundred for any Test in England is 458 minutes (329 balls) by K. W. R. Fletcher, England v Pakistan, The Oval, 1974.

The slowest double-hundred in a Test was scored in 777 minutes (548 balls) by D. S. B. P. Kuruppu for Sri Lanka v New Zealand at Colombo (CCC), 1986-87, on his debut. It is also the slowest-ever first-class double-hundred.

PARTNERSHIPS OVER 400

576	for 2nd	S. T. Jayasuriya (340)/R. S. Mahanama (225) .	SL v I	Colombo (RPS)	1997-98
467	for 3rd	A. H. Jones (186)/M. D. Crowe (299)	NZ v SL	Wellington	1990-91
451	for 2nd	W. H. Ponsford (266)/D. G. Bradman (244) . .	A v E	The Oval	1934
451	for 3rd	Mudassar Nazar (231)/Javed Miandad (280*) .	P v I	Hyderabad	1982-83
446	for 2nd	C. C. Hunte (260)/G. S. Sobers (365*)	WI v P	Kingston	1957-58
438	for 2nd	M. S. Atapattu (249)/K. C. Sangakkara (270)	SL v Z	Bulawayo	2003-04
429*	for 3rd	J. A. Rudolph (222*)/H. H. Dippenaar (177*)	SA v B	Chittagong	2003
413	for 1st	V. Mankad (231)/Pankaj Roy (173)	I v NZ	Madras	1955-56
411	for 4th	P. B. H. May (285*)/M. C. Cowdrey (154) . .	E v WI	Birmingham	1957
405	for 5th	S. G. Barnes (234)/D. G. Bradman (234)	A v E	Sydney	1946-47

Note: 415 runs were added for the third wicket for India v England at Madras in 1981-82 by D. B. Vengsarkar (retired hurt), G. R. Viswanath and Yashpal Sharma.

HIGHEST PARTNERSHIPS FOR EACH WICKET

The following lists include all stands above 300; otherwise the top ten for each wicket.

First Wicket

413	V. Mankad (231)/Pankaj Roy (173)	I v NZ	Madras	1955-56
387	G. M. Turner (259)/T. W. Jarvis (182)	NZ v WI	Georgetown	1971-72
382	W. M. Lawry (210)/R. B. Simpson (201)	A v WI	Bridgetown	1964-65
368	G. C. Smith (151)/H. H. Gibbs (228).	SA v P	Cape Town	2002-03
359	L. Hutton (158)/C. Washbrook (195)	E v SA	Johannesburg	1948-49
338	G. C. Smith (277)/H. H. Gibbs (179).	SA v E	Birmingham	2003
335	M. S. Atapattu (207*)/S. T. Jayasuriya (188)	SL v P	Kandy	2000
329	G. R. Marsh (138)/M. A. Taylor (219)	A v E	Nottingham	1989
323	J. B. Hobbs (178)/W. Rhodes (179)	E v A	Melbourne	1911-12
301	G. C. Smith (139)/H. H. Gibbs (192).	SA v WI	Centurion	2003-04

Second Wicket

576	S. T. Jayasuriya (340)/R. S. Mahanama (225).	SL v I	Colombo (RPS)	1997-98
451	W. H. Ponsford (266)/D. G. Bradman (244).	A v E	The Oval	1934
446	C. C. Hunte (260)/G. S. Sobers (365*).	WI v P	Kingston	1957-58
438	M. S. Atapattu (249)/K. C. Sangakkara (270) . . .	SL v Z	Bulawayo	2003-04
382	L. Hutton (364)/M. Leyland (187).	E v A	The Oval	1938
369	J. H. Edrich (310*)/K. F. Barrington (163)	E v NZ	Leeds	1965
351	G. A. Gooch (196)/D. I. Gower (157).	E v A	The Oval	1985
344*	S. M. Gavaskar (182*)/D. B. Vengsarkar (157*) . . .	I v WI	Calcutta	1978-79
331	R. T. Robinson (148)/D. I. Gower (215)	E v A	Birmingham	1985
315*	H. H. Gibbs (211*)/J. H. Kallis (148*).	SA v NZ	Christchurch	1998-99
301	A. R. Morris (182)/D. G. Bradman (173*)	A v E	Leeds	1948

Third Wicket

467	A. H. Jones (186)/M. D. Crowe (299)	NZ v SL	Wellington	1990-91
451	Mudassar Nazar (231)/Javed Miandad (280*).	P v I	Hyderabad	1982-83
429*	J. A. Rudolph (222*)/H. H. Dippenaar (177*) . . .	SA v B	Chittagong	2003
397	Qasim Omar (206)/Javed Miandad (203*).	P v SL	Faisalabad	1985-86
370	W. J. Edrich (189)/D. C. S. Compton (208)	E v SA	Lord's	1947
352*‡	Ijaz Ahmed, sen. (211)/Inzamam-ul-Haq (200*) . . .	P v SL	Dhaka	1998-99
341	E. J. Barlow (201)/R. G. Pollock (175).	SA v A	Adelaide	1963-64
338	E. D. Weekes (206)/F. M. M. Worrell (167).	WI v E	Port-of-Spain	1953-54
336	V. Sehwag (309)/S. R. Tendulkar (194*)	I v P	Multan	2003-04
323	Aamir Sohail (160)/Inzamam-ul-Haq (177)	P v WI	Rawalpindi	1997-98
319	A. Melville (189)/A. D. Nourse (149).	SA v E	Nottingham	1947

316†	G. R. Viswanath (222)/Yashpal Sharma (140).....	I v E	Madras	1981-82
315	R. T. Ponting (206)/D. S. Lehmann (160)......	A v WI	Port-of-Spain	2002-03
308	R. B. Richardson (154)/I. V. A. Richards (178)....	WI v A	St John's	1983-84
308	G. A. Gooch (333)/A. J. Lamb (139)...........	E v I	Lord's	1990
303	I. V. A. Richards (232)/A. I. Kallicharran (97)....	WI v E	Nottingham	1976
303	M. A. Atherton (135)/R. A. Smith (175).......	E v WI	St John's	1993-94

† *415 runs were scored for this wicket in two separate partnerships; D. B. Vengsarkar retired hurt when he and Viswanath had added 99 runs.*

‡ *366 runs were scored for this wicket in two separate partnerships; Inzamam retired ill when he and Ijaz had added 352 runs.*

Fourth Wicket

411	P. B. H. May (285*)/M. C. Cowdrey (154)......	E v WI	Birmingham	1957
399	G. S. Sobers (226)/F. M. M. Worrell (197*).....	WI v E	Bridgetown	1959-60
388	W. H. Ponsford (181)/D. G. Bradman (304)......	A v E	Leeds	1934
353	S. R. Tendulkar (241*)/V. V. S. Laxman (178)...	I v A	Sydney	2003-04
350	Mushtaq Mohammad (201)/Asif Iqbal (175).....	P v NZ	Dunedin	1972-73
336	W. M. Lawry (151)/K. D. Walters (242)........	A v WI	Sydney	1968-69
322	Javed Miandad (153*)/Salim Malik (165).......	P v E	Birmingham	1992
288	N. Hussain (207)/G. P. Thorpe (138)...........	E v A	Birmingham	1997
287	Javed Miandad (126)/Zaheer Abbas (168).......	P v I	Faisalabad	1982-83
283	F. M. M. Worrell (261)/E. D. Weekes (129)......	WI v E	Nottingham	1950

288 runs were scored for this wicket in two separate partnerships for Pakistan v Bangladesh at Multan, 2001-02; Inzamam-ul-Haq retired hurt after adding 123 with Yousuf Youhana, who added a further 165 with Abdul Razzaq.*

Fifth Wicket

405	S. G. Barnes (234)/D. G. Bradman (234).......	A v E	Sydney	1946-47
385	S. R. Waugh (160)/G. S. Blewett (214).........	A v SA	Johannesburg	1996-97
376	V. V. S. Laxman (281)/R. Dravid (180).........	I v A	Kolkata	2000-01
332*	A. R. Border (200*)/S. R. Waugh (157*).......	A v E	Leeds	1993
327	J. L. Langer (144)/R. T. Ponting (197).........	A v P	Perth	1999-2000
322†	B. C. Lara (213)/J. C. Adams (94)............	WI v A	Kingston	1998-99
303	R. Dravid (233)/V. V. S. Laxman (148)........	I v A	Adelaide	2003-04
293	C. L. Hooper (233)/S. Chanderpaul (140)......	WI v I	Georgetown	2001-02
281	Javed Miandad (163)/Asif Iqbal (166).........	P v NZ	Lahore	1976-77
281	S. R. Waugh (199)/R. T. Ponting (104).........	A v WI	Bridgetown	1998-99

† *344 runs were scored for this wicket in two separate partnerships; P. T. Collins retired hurt when he and Lara had added 22 runs.*

Sixth Wicket

346	J. H. Fingleton (136)/D. G. Bradman (270)......	A v E	Melbourne	1936-37
317	D. R. Martyn (133)/A. C. Gilchrist (204*).....	A v SA	Johannesburg	2001-02
298*	D. B. Vengsarkar (164*)/R. J. Shastri (121*)....	I v A	Bombay	1986-87
282*	B. C. Lara (400*)/R. D. Jacobs (107*)........	WI v E	St John's	2003-04
281	G. P. Thorpe (200*)/A. Flintoff (137).........	E v NZ	Christchurch	2001-02
274*	G. S. Sobers (163*)/D. A. J. Holford (105*).....	WI v E	Lord's	1966
272	M. Azharuddin (199)/Kapil Dev (163).........	I v SL	Kanpur	1986-87
260*	D. M. Jones (118*)/S. R. Waugh (134*)........	A v SL	Hobart	1989-90
254	C. A. Davis (183)/G. S. Sobers (142)..........	WI v NZ	Bridgetown	1971-72
250	C. H. Lloyd (242*)/D. L. Murray (91).........	WI v I	Bombay	1974-75

Seventh Wicket

347	D. St E. Atkinson (219)/C. C. Depeiza (122)	WI v A	Bridgetown	1954-55
308	Waqar Hassan (189)/Imtiaz Ahmed (209)	P v NZ	Lahore	1955-56
248	Yousuf Youhana (203)/Saqlain Mushtaq (101*)	P v NZ	Christchurch	2000-01
246	D. J. McGlew (255*)/A. R. A. Murray (109)	SA v NZ	Wellington	1952-53
235	R. J. Shastri (142)/S. M. H. Kirmani (102)	I v E	Bombay	1984-85
225	C. L. Cairns (158)/J. D. P. Oram (90)	NZ v SA	Auckland	2003-04
221	D. T. Lindsay (182)/P. L. van der Merwe (76)	SA v A	Johannesburg	1966-67
217	K. D. Walters (250)/G. J. Gilmour (101)	A v NZ	Christchurch	1976-77
217	V. V. S. Laxman (130)/A. Ratra (115*)	I v WI	St John's	2001-02
197	M. J. K. Smith (96)/J. M. Parks (101*)	E v WI	Port-of-Spain	1959-60

Eighth Wicket

313	Wasim Akram (257*)/Saqlain Mushtaq (79)	P v Z	Sheikhupura	1996-97
253	N. J. Astle (156*)/A. C. Parore (110)	NZ v A	Perth	2001-02
246	L. E. G. Ames (137)/G. O. B. Allen (122)	E v NZ	Lord's	1931
243	R. J. Hartigan (116)/C. Hill (160)	A v E	Adelaide	1907-08
217	T. W. Graveney (165)/J. T. Murray (112)	E v WI	The Oval	1966
173	C. E. Pellew (116)/J. M. Gregory (100)	A v E	Melbourne	1920-21
170	D. P. M. D. Jayawardene (237)/W. P. U. J. C. Vaas (69)	SL v SA	Galle	2004
168	R. Illingworth (107)/P. Lever (88*)	E v I	Manchester	1971
168	H. H. Streak (127*)/A. M. Blignaut (91)	Z v WI	Harare	2003-04
161	M. Azharuddin (109)/A. Kumble (88)	I v SA	Calcutta	1996-97

Ninth Wicket

195	M. V. Boucher (78)/P. L. Symcox (108)	SA v P	Johannesburg	1997-98
190	Asif Iqbal (146)/Intikhab Alam (51)	P v E	The Oval	1967
163*	M. C. Cowdrey (128*)/A. C. Smith (69*)	E v NZ	Wellington	1962-63
161	C. H. Lloyd (161*)/A. M. E. Roberts (68)	WI v I	Calcutta	1983-84
161	Zaheer Abbas (82*)/Sarfraz Nawaz (90)	P v E	Lahore	1983-84
154	S. E. Gregory (201)/J. McC. Blackham (74)	A v E	Sydney	1894-95
151	W. H. Scotton (90)/W. W. Read (117)	E v A	The Oval	1884
150	E. A. E. Baptiste (87*)/M. A. Holding (69)	WI v E	Birmingham	1984
149	P. G. Joshi (52*)/R. B. Desai (85)	I v P	Bombay	1960-61
147	Mohammad Wasim (192)/Mushtaq Ahmed (57)	P v Z	Harare	1997-98

Tenth Wicket

151	B. F. Hastings (110)/R. O. Collinge (68*)	NZ v P	Auckland	1972-73
151	Azhar Mahmood (128*)/Mushtaq Ahmed (59)	P v SA	Rawalpindi	1997-98
133	Wasim Raja (71)/Wasim Bari (60*)	P v WI	Bridgetown	1976-77
133	S. R. Tendulkar (248*)/Zaheer Khan (75)	I v B	Dhaka	2004-05
130	R. E. Foster (287)/W. Rhodes (40*)	E v A	Sydney	1903-04
128	K. Higgs (63)/J. A. Snow (59*)	E v WI	The Oval	1966
127	J. M. Taylor (108)/A. A. Mailey (46*)	A v E	Sydney	1924-25
124	J. G. Bracewell (83*)/S. L. Boock (37)	NZ v A	Sydney	1985-86
120	R. A. Duff (104)/W. W. Armstrong (45*)	A v E	Melbourne	1901-02
118	N. J. Astle (222)/C. L. Cairns (23*)	NZ v E	Christchurch	2001-02

UNUSUAL DISMISSALS

Handled the Ball

W. R. Endean	South Africa v England at Cape Town.	1956-57
A. M. J. Hilditch	Australia v Pakistan at Perth	1978-79
Mohsin Khan	Pakistan v Australia at Karachi	1982-83
D. L. Haynes	West Indies v India at Bombay	1983-84
G. A. Gooch	England v Australia at Manchester	1993
S. R. Waugh	Australia v India at Chennai	2000-01
M. P. Vaughan	England v India at Bangalore	2001-02

Obstructing the Field

L. Hutton	England v South Africa at The Oval.	1951

Note: There have been no cases of Hit the Ball Twice or Timed Out in Test cricket.

BOWLING RECORDS

MOST WICKETS IN AN INNINGS

10-53	J. C. Laker	England v Australia at Manchester	1956
10-74	A. Kumble	India v Pakistan at Delhi	1998-99
9-28	G. A. Lohmann	England v South Africa at Johannesburg	1895-96
9-37	J. C. Laker	England v Australia at Manchester	1956
9-51	M. Muralitharan . . .	Sri Lanka v Zimbabwe at Kandy	2001-02
9-52	R. J. Hadlee	New Zealand v Australia at Brisbane	1985-86
9-56	Abdul Qadir	Pakistan v England at Lahore	1987-88
9-57	D. E. Malcolm	England v South Africa at The Oval	1994
9-65	M. Muralitharan . . .	Sri Lanka v England at The Oval.	1998
9-69	J. M. Patel	India v Australia at Kanpur	1959-60
9-83	Kapil Dev	India v West Indies at Ahmedabad	1983-84
9-86	Sarfraz Nawaz.	Pakistan v Australia at Melbourne	1978-79
9-95	J. M. Noreiga	West Indies v India at Port-of-Spain	1970-71
9-102	S. P. Gupte	India v West Indies at Kanpur	1958-59
9-103	S. F. Barnes	England v South Africa at Johannesburg	1913-14
9-113	H. J. Tayfield	South Africa v England at Johannesburg	1956-57
9-121	A. A. Mailey	Australia v England at Melbourne	1920-21
8-7	G. A. Lohmann. . . .	England v South Africa at Port Elizabeth	1895-96
8-11	J. Briggs	England v South Africa at Cape Town.	1888-89
8-24	G. D. McGrath	Australia v Pakistan at Perth	2004-05
8-29	S. F. Barnes	England v South Africa at The Oval	1912
8-29	C. E. H. Croft	West Indies v Pakistan at Port-of-Spain	1976-77
8-31	F. Laver.	Australia v England at Manchester	1909
8-31	F. S. Trueman	England v India at Manchester.	1952
8-34	I. T. Botham.	England v Pakistan at Lord's	1978
8-35	G. A. Lohmann	England v Australia at Sydney.	1886-87
8-38	L. R. Gibbs	West Indies v India at Bridgetown	1961-62
8-38	G. D. McGrath	Australia v England at Lord's	1997
8-43†	A. E. Trott	Australia v England at Adelaide.	1894-95
8-43	H. Verity	England v Australia at Lord's	1934
8-43	R. G. D. Willis	England v Australia at Leeds.	1981
8-45	C. E. L. Ambrose . . .	West Indies v England at Bridgetown	1989-90
8-51	D. L. Underwood. . .	England v Pakistan at Lord's	1974
8-52	V. Mankad	India v Pakistan at Delhi	1952-53
8-53	G. B. Lawrence	South Africa v New Zealand at Johannesburg	1961-62
8-53†	R. A. L. Massie	Australia v England at Lord's	1972
8-53	A. R. C. Fraser	England v West Indies at Port-of-Spain	1997-98
8-55	V. Mankad	India v England at Madras	1951-52
8-56	S. F. Barnes	England v South Africa at Johannesburg	1913-14

8-58	G. A. Lohmann. . . .	England v Australia at Sydney.	1891-92
8-58	Imran Khan	Pakistan v Sri Lanka at Lahore	1981-82
8-59	C. Blythe.	England v South Africa at Leeds	1907
8-59	A. A. Mallett	Australia v Pakistan at Adelaide.	1972-73
8-60	Imran Khan	Pakistan v India at Karachi.	1982-83
8-61†	N. D. Hirwani	India v West Indies at Madras	1987-88
8-64†	L. Klusener	South Africa v India at Calcutta	1996-97
8-65	H. Trumble.	Australia v England at The Oval	1902
8-68	W. Rhodes	England v Australia at Melbourne	1903-04
8-69	H. J. Tayfield	South Africa v England at Durban	1956-57
8-69	Sikander Bakht . . .	Pakistan v India at Delhi	1979-80
8-70	S. J. Snooke	South Africa v England at Johannesburg	1905-06
8-71	G. D. McKenzie . . .	Australia v West Indies at Melbourne	1968-69
8-71	S. K. Warne	Australia v England at Brisbane	1994-95
8-71	A. A. Donald	South Africa v Zimbabwe at Harare	1995-96
8-72	S. Venkataraghavan .	India v New Zealand at Delhi	1964-65
8-75†	N. D. Hirwani	India v West Indies at Madras	1987-88
8-75	A. R. C. Fraser . . .	England v West Indies at Bridgetown	1993-94
8-76	E. A. S. Prasanna . .	India v New Zealand at Auckland.	1975-76
8-79	B. S. Chandrasekhar.	India v England at Delhi	1972-73
8-81	L. C. Braund	England v Australia at Melbourne	1903-04
8-83	J. R. Ratnayeke	Sri Lanka v Pakistan at Sialkot	1985-86
8-84†	R. A. L. Massie . . .	Australia v England at Lord's	1972
8-84	Harbhajan Singh . . .	India v Australia at Chennai	2000-01
8-85	Kapil Dev	India v Pakistan at Lahore	1982-83
8-86	A. W. Greig	England v West Indies at Port-of-Spain	1973-74
8-86	J. Srinath	India v Pakistan at Calcutta.	1998-99
8-87	M. G. Hughes.	Australia v West Indies at Perth	1988-89
8-87	M. Muralitharan . . .	Sri Lanka v India at Colombo (SSC)	2001
8-92	M. A. Holding	West Indies v England at The Oval	1976
8-94	T. Richardson	England v Australia at Sydney.	1897-98
8-97	C. J. McDermott . . .	Australia v England at Perth	1990-91
8-103	I. T. Botham.	England v West Indies at Lord's.	1984
8-104†	A. L. Valentine	West Indies v England at Manchester	1950
8-106	Kapil Dev	India v Australia at Adelaide	1985-86
8-107	B. J. T. Bosanquet .	England v Australia at Nottingham	1905
8-107	N. A. Foster	England v Pakistan at Leeds	1987
8-109	P. A. Strang	Zimbabwe v New Zealand at Bulawayo	2000-01
8-112	G. F. Lawson	Australia v West Indies at Adelaide	1984-85
8-126	J. C. White.	England v Australia at Adelaide	1928-29
8-141	C. J. McDermott . . .	Australia v England at Melbourne	1985
8-141	A. Kumble.	India v Australia at Sydney.	2003-04
8-143	M. H. N. Walker . . .	Australia v England at Melbourne	1974-75
8-164	Saqlain Mushtaq . . .	Pakistan v England at Lahore	2000-01

† *On Test debut.*

Note: The best for Bangladesh is 7-95 by Enamul Haque, jun. against Zimbabwe at Dhaka in 2004-05.

OUTSTANDING BOWLING ANALYSES

	O	M	R	W		
J. C. Laker (E)	51.2	23	53	10	v Australia at Manchester.	1956
A. Kumble (I)	26.3	9	74	10	v Pakistan at Delhi	1998-99
G. A. Lohmann (E)	14.2	6	28	9	v South Africa at Johannesburg. . . .	1895-96
J. C. Laker (E)	16.4	4	37	9	v Australia at Manchester.	1956
G. A. Lohmann (E)	9.4	5	7	8	v South Africa at Port Elizabeth	1895-96
J. Briggs (E)	14.2	5	11	8	v South Africa at Cape Town	1888-89
S. J. Harmison (E)	12.3	8	12	7	v West Indies at Kingston	2003-04
J. Briggs (E)	19.1	11	17	7	v South Africa at Cape Town	1888-89
M. A. Noble (A)	7.4	2	17	7	v England at Melbourne	1901-02
W. Rhodes (E)	11	3	17	7	v Australia at Birmingham	1902
J. J. C. Lawson (WI)	6.5	4	3	6	v Bangladesh at Dhaka	2002-03

	O	M	R	W		
A. E. R. Gilligan (E)	6.3	4	7	6	v South Africa at Birmingham	1924
S. Haigh (E)	11.4	6	11	6	v South Africa at Cape Town	1898-99
Shoaib Akhtar (P)	8.2	4	11	6	v New Zealand at Lahore.	2002
D. L. Underwood (E)	11.6	7	12	6	v New Zealand at Christchurch. . . .	1970-71
S. L. V. Raju (I)	17.5	13	12	6	v Sri Lanka at Chandigarh	1990-91
H. J. Tayfield (SA)	14	7	13	6	v New Zealand at Johannesburg . . .	1953-54
C. T. B. Turner (A)	18	11	15	6	v England at Sydney.	1886-87
M. H. N. Walker (A)	16	8	15	6	v Pakistan at Sydney.	1972-73
E. R. H. Toshack (A)	2.3	1	2	5	v India at Brisbane	1947-48
H. Ironmonger (A)	7.2	5	6	5	v South Africa at Melbourne	1931-32
T. B. A. May (A)	6.5	3	9	5	v West Indies at Adelaide	1992-93
Pervez Sajjad (P)	12	8	5	4	v New Zealand at Rawalpindi	1964-65
K. Higgs (E)	9	7	5	4	v New Zealand at Christchurch	1965-66
P. H. Edmonds (E)	8	6	6	4	v Pakistan at Lord's	1978
J. C. White (E)	6.3	2	7	4	v Australia at Brisbane	1928-29
J. H. Wardle (E)	5	2	7	4	v Australia at Manchester	1953
R. Appleyard (E)	6	3	7	4	v New Zealand at Auckland	1954-55
R. Benaud (A)	3.4	3	0	3	v India at Delhi	1959-60

WICKET WITH FIRST BALL IN TEST CRICKET

	Batsman dismissed			
A. Coningham	A. C. MacLaren	A v E	Melbourne	1894-95
W. M. Bradley	F. Laver	E v A	Manchester.	1899
E. G. Arnold	V. T. Trumper	E v A	Sydney	1903-04
G. G. Macaulay	G. A. L. Hearne	E v SA	Cape Town	1922-23
M. W. Tate	M. J. Susskind	E v SA	Birmingham	1924
M. Henderson	E. W. Dawson	NZ v E	Christchurch	1929-30
H. D. Smith	E. Paynter	NZ v E	Christchurch	1932-33
T. F. Johnson	W. W. Keeton	WI v E	The Oval	1939
R. Howorth	D. V. Dyer	E v SA	The Oval	1947
Intikhab Alam	C. C. McDonald	P v A	Karachi	1959-60
R. K. Illingworth	P. V. Simmons	E v WI	Nottingham	1991
N. M. Kulkarni	M. S. Atapattu	I v SL	Colombo (RPS) . .	1997-98
M. K. G. C. P. Lakshitha	Mohammad Ashraful	SL v B	Colombo (SSC) . .	2002

HAT-TRICKS

F. R. Spofforth	Australia v England at Melbourne	1878-79
W. Bates.	England v Australia at Melbourne	1882-83
J. Briggs.	England v Australia at Sydney.	1891-92
G. A. Lohmann	England v South Africa at Port Elizabeth	1895-96
J. T. Hearne.	England v Australia at Leeds.	1899
H. Trumble	Australia v England at Melbourne	1901-02
H. Trumble	Australia v England at Melbourne	1903-04
T. J. Matthews† . . . . . }	Australia v South Africa at Manchester	1912
T. J. Matthews . . . . . . }		
M. J. C. Allom‡	England v New Zealand at Christchurch	1929-30
T. W. J. Goddard	England v South Africa at Johannesburg	1938-39
P. J. Loader.	England v West Indies at Leeds	1957
L. F. Kline	Australia v South Africa at Cape Town	1957-58
W. W. Hall	West Indies v Pakistan at Lahore	1958-59
G. M. Griffin	South Africa v England at Lord's	1960
L. R. Gibbs.	West Indies v Australia at Adelaide	1960-61
P. J. Petherick‡.	New Zealand v Pakistan at Lahore	1976-77
C. A. Walsh§.	West Indies v Australia at Brisbane	1988-89
M. G. Hughes§	Australia v West Indies at Perth	1988-89
D. W. Fleming‡	Australia v Pakistan at Rawalpindi	1994-95

S. K. Warne	Australia v England at Melbourne	1994-95
D. G. Cork	England v West Indies at Manchester	1995
D. Gough	England v Australia at Sydney	1998-99
Wasim Akram¶	Pakistan v Sri Lanka at Lahore	1998-99
Wasim Akram¶	Pakistan v Sri Lanka at Dhaka	1998-99
D. N. T. Zoysa	Sri Lanka v Zimbabwe at Harare	1999-2000
Abdul Razzaq	Pakistan v Sri Lanka at Galle	2000
G. D. McGrath	Australia v West Indies at Perth	2000-01
Harbhajan Singh	India v Australia at Kolkata	2000-01
Mohammad Sami	Pakistan v Sri Lanka at Lahore	2001-02
J. J. C. Lawson§	West Indies v Australia at Bridgetown	2002-03
Alok Kapali	Bangladesh v Pakistan at Peshawar	2003
A. M. Blignaut	Zimbabwe v Bangladesh at Harare	2003-04
M. J. Hoggard	England v West Indies at Bridgetown	2003-04
J. E. C. Franklin	New Zealand v Bangladesh at Dhaka	2004-05

† *T. J. Matthews did the hat-trick in each innings of the same match.*
‡ *On Test debut.*
§ *Not all in the same innings.*
¶ *Wasim Akram did the hat-trick in successive matches.*

FOUR WICKETS IN FIVE BALLS

M. J. C. Allom	England v New Zealand at Christchurch	1929-30
	On debut, in his eighth over: W-WWW	
C. M. Old	England v Pakistan at Birmingham	1978
	Sequence interrupted by a no-ball: WW-WW	
Wasim Akram	Pakistan v West Indies at Lahore (*WW-WW*)	1990-91

MOST WICKETS IN A TEST

19-90	J. C. Laker	England v Australia at Manchester	1956
17-159	S. F. Barnes	England v South Africa at Johannesburg	1913-14
16-136†	N. D. Hirwani	India v West Indies at Madras	1987-88
16-137†	R. A. L. Massie	Australia v England at Lord's	1972
16-220	M. Muralitharan	Sri Lanka v England at The Oval	1998
15-28	J. Briggs	England v South Africa at Cape Town	1888-89
15-45	G. A. Lohmann	England v South Africa at Port Elizabeth	1895-96
15-99	C. Blythe	England v South Africa at Leeds	1907
15-104	H. Verity	England v Australia at Lord's	1934
15-123	R. J. Hadlee	New Zealand v Australia at Brisbane	1985-86
15-124	W. Rhodes	England v Australia at Melbourne	1903-04
15-217	Harbhajan Singh	India v Australia at Chennai	2000-01
14-90	F. R. Spofforth	Australia v England at The Oval	1882
14-99	A. V. Bedser	England v Australia at Nottingham	1953
14-102	W. Bates	England v Australia at Melbourne	1882-83
14-116	Imran Khan	Pakistan v Sri Lanka at Lahore	1981-82
14-124	J. M. Patel	India v Australia at Kanpur	1959-60
14-144	S. F. Barnes	England v South Africa at Durban	1913-14
14-149	M. A. Holding	West Indies v England at The Oval	1976
14-149	A. Kumble	India v Pakistan at Delhi	1998-99
14-191	W. P. U. J. C. Vaas	Sri Lanka v West Indies at Colombo (SSC)	2001-02
14-199	C. V. Grimmett	Australia v South Africa at Adelaide	1931-32

† *On Test debut.*

Note: The best for South Africa is 13-165 by H. J. Tayfield against Australia at Melbourne, 1952-53, for Zimbabwe 11-255 by A. G. Huckle against New Zealand at Bulawayo, 1997-98, and for Bangladesh 12-200 by Enamul Haque, jun. against Zimbabwe at Dhaka, 2004-05.

MOST BALLS BOWLED IN A TEST

S. Ramadhin (West Indies) sent down 774 balls in 129 overs against England at Birmingham, 1957. It was the most delivered by any bowler in a Test, beating H. Verity's 766 for England against South Africa at Durban, 1938-39. In this match Ramadhin also bowled the most balls (588) in a Test or first-class innings, since equalled by Arshad Ayub, Hyderabad v Madhya Pradesh at Secunderabad, 1991-92.

MOST WICKETS IN A SERIES

	T	R	W	Avge		
S. F. Barnes	4	536	49	10.93	England v South Africa . . .	1913-14
J. C. Laker	5	442	46	9.60	England v Australia	1956
C. V. Grimmett	5	642	44	14.59	Australia v South Africa . .	1935-36
T. M. Alderman	6	893	42	21.26	Australia v England	1981
R. M. Hogg	6	527	41	12.85	Australia v England	1978-79
T. M. Alderman	6	712	41	17.36	Australia v England	1989
Imran Khan	6	558	40	13.95	Pakistan v India	1982-83
A. V. Bedser	5	682	39	17.48	England v Australia	1953
D. K. Lillee	6	870	39	22.30	Australia v England	1981
M. W. Tate	5	881	38	23.18	England v Australia	1924-25
W. J. Whitty	3	632	37	17.08	Australia v South Africa . .	1910-11
H. J. Tayfield	5	636	37	17.18	South Africa v England . . .	1956-57
A. E. E. Vogler	5	783	36	21.75	South Africa v England . . .	1909-10
A. A. Mailey	5	946	36	26.27	Australia v England	1920-21
G. D. McGrath	6	701	36	19.47	Australia v England	1997
G. A. Lohmann	3	203	35	5.80	England v South Africa . . .	1895-96
B. S. Chandrasekhar	5	662	35	18.91	India v England	1972-73
M. D. Marshall	5	443	35	12.65	West Indies v England . . .	1988

Notes: The most for New Zealand is 33 by R. J. Hadlee against Australia in 1985-86, for Sri Lanka 30 by M. Muralitharan against Zimbabwe in 2001-02, for Zimbabwe 22 by H. H. Streak against Pakistan in 1994-95, and for Bangladesh 17 by Mohammad Rafique against Pakistan in 2003 (all in three Tests).

75 WICKETS IN A CALENDAR YEAR

	T	R	W	Avge	5W/i	10W/m	Year
D. K. Lillee (A).	13	1,781	85	20.95	5	2	1981
A. A. Donald (SA)	14	1,571	80	19.63	7	–	1998
M. Muralitharan (SL) . . .	12	1,699	80	21.23	7	4	2001
J. Garner (WI)	15	1,604	77	20.83	4	–	1984
Kapil Dev (I)	18	1,739	75	23.18	5	1	1983
M. Muralitharan (SL) . . .	10	1,463	75	19.50	7	3	2000

MOST WICKETS

		T	Balls	R	W	Avge	5W/i	10W/m
1	S. K. Warne (Australia)	120	33,649	14,504	566	25.62	28	8
2	M. Muralitharan (Sri Lanka) . .	91	31,124	12,165	532	22.86	44	13
3	C. A. Walsh (West Indies)	132	30,019	12,688	519	24.44	22	3
4	G. D. McGrath (Australia)	106	24,751	10,309	481	21.43	25	3
5	A. Kumble (India)	92	29,015	12,371	444	27.86	28	6
6	Kapil Dev (India)	131	27,740	12,867	434	29.64	23	2
7	R. J. Hadlee (New Zealand) . . .	86	21,918	9,611	431	22.29	36	9
8	Wasim Akram (Pakistan)	104	22,627	9,779	414	23.62	25	5
9	C. E. L. Ambrose (West Indies) .	98	22,103	8,501	405	20.99	22	3

		T	Balls	R	W	Avge	5W/i	10W/m
10	I. T. Botham (England)	102	21,815	10,878	383	28.40	27	4
11	M. D. Marshall (West Indies) . .	81	17,584	7,876	376	20.94	22	4
12	**S. M. Pollock (South Africa) . .**	**92**	**21,032**	**8,195**	**374**	**21.91**	**16**	**1**
13	Waqar Younis (Pakistan)	87	16,224	8,788	373	23.56	22	5
14	Imran Khan (Pakistan)	88	19,458	8,258	362	22.81	23	6
15	D. K. Lillee (Australia).	70	18,467	8,493	355	23.92	23	7
16	A. A. Donald (South Africa) . .	72	15,519	7,344	330	22.25	20	3
17	R. G. D. Willis (England)	90	17,357	8,190	325	25.20	16	–
18	L. R. Gibbs (West Indies)	79	27,115	8,989	309	29.09	18	2
19	F. S. Trueman (England)	67	15,178	6,625	307	21.57	17	3
20	D. L. Underwood (England). . . .	86	21,862	7,674	297	25.83	17	6
21	C. J. McDermott (Australia). . . .	71	16,586	8,332	291	28.63	14	2
22	**W. P. U. J. C. Vaas (Sri Lanka)**	**82**	**18,132**	**8,045**	**269**	**29.90**	**9**	**2**
23	B. S. Bedi (India)	67	21,364	7,637	266	28.71	14	1
24	J. Garner (West Indies)	58	13,169	5,433	259	20.97	7	–
25	J. B. Statham (England)	70	16,056	6,261	252	24.84	9	1
26	M. A. Holding (West Indies) . . .	60	12,680	5,898	249	23.68	13	2
27	R. Benaud (Australia).	63	19,108	6,704	248	27.03	16	1
28	G. D. McKenzie (Australia). . . .	60	17,681	7,328	246	29.78	16	3
29	B. S. Chandrasekhar (India). . . .	58	15,963	7,199	242	29.74	16	2
30	**J. N. Gillespie (Australia)**	**63**	**12,932**	**6,060**	**241**	**25.14**	**8**	**–**
	⎧ A. V. Bedser (England)	51	15,918	5,876	236	24.89	15	5
31	⎨ J. Srinath (India)	67	15,104	7,196	236	30.49	10	1
	⎩ Abdul Qadir (Pakistan).	67	17,126	7,742	236	32.80	15	5
34	G. S. Sobers (West Indies)	93	21,599	7,999	235	34.03	6	–
35	A. R. Caddick (England).	62	13,558	6,999	234	29.91	13	1
36	D. Gough (England).	58	11,821	6,503	229	28.39	9	–
37	R. R. Lindwall (Australia).	61	13,650	5,251	228	23.03	12	–
38	**C. L. Cairns (New Zealand) . .**	**62**	**11,698**	**6,410**	**218**	**29.40**	**13**	**1**
39	C. V. Grimmett (Australia).	37	14,513	5,231	216	24.21	21	7
40	M. G. Hughes (Australia)	53	12,285	6,017	212	28.38	7	1
41	**Saqlain Mushtaq (Pakistan)** . .	**49**	**14,070**	**6,206**	**208**	**29.83**	**13**	**3**
	⎧ A. M. E. Roberts (West Indies) .	47	11,135	5,174	202	25.61	11	2
42	⎨ J. A. Snow (England)	49	12,021	5,387	202	26.66	8	1
	⎩ **H. H. Streak (Zimbabwe)**	**59**	**12,739**	**5,572**	**202**	**27.58**	**6**	**–**
45	J. R. Thomson (Australia)	51	10,535	5,601	200	28.00	8	–

Note: The most wickets for Bangladesh is:

Mohammad Rafique	**18**	**5,338**	**2,196**	**67**	**32.77**	**5**	**–**

Bold type denotes those who have played Test cricket since January 1, 2004.

100 WICKETS

ENGLAND

		T	Balls	R	W	Avge	5W/i	10W/m
1	I. T. Botham.	102	21,815	10,878	383	28.40	27	4
2	R. G. D. Willis	90	17,357	8,190	325	25.20	16	–
3	F. S. Trueman.	67	15,178	6,625	307	21.57	17	3
4	D. L. Underwood . . .	86	21,862	7,674	297	25.83	17	6
5	J. B. Statham	70	16,056	6,261	252	24.84	9	1
6	A. V. Bedser.	51	15,918	5,876	236	24.89	15	5
7	A. R. Caddick	62	13,558	6,999	234	29.91	13	1
8	D. Gough.	58	11,821	6,503	229	28.39	9	–
9	J. A. Snow.	49	12,021	5,387	202	26.66	8	1

		T	Balls	R	W	Avge	5W/i	10W/m
10	J. C. Laker	46	12,027	4,101	193	21.24	9	3
11	S. F. Barnes	27	7,873	3,106	189	16.43	24	7
12	A. R. C. Fraser	46	10,876	4,836	177	27.32	13	2
13	G. A. R. Lock	49	13,147	4,451	174	25.58	9	3
14	M. W. Tate	39	12,523	4,055	155	26.16	7	1
15	F. J. Titmus	53	15,118	4,931	153	32.22	7	–
16	J. E. Emburey.	64	15,391	5,646	147	38.40	6	–
17	H. Verity	40	11,173	3,510	144	24.37	5	2
18	C. M. Old	46	8,858	4,020	143	28.11	4	–
	M. J. Hoggard	**38**	**8,189**	**4,472**	**143**	**31.27**	**4**	**1**
20	A. W. Greig	58	9,802	4,541	141	32.20	6	2
21	P. A. J. DeFreitas. . . .	44	9,838	4,700	140	33.57	4	–
22	G. R. Dilley	41	8,192	4,107	138	29.76	6	–
23	T. E. Bailey	61	9,712	3,856	132	29.21	5	1
24	D. G. Cork	37	7,678	3,906	131	29.81	5	–
25	D. E. Malcolm	40	8,480	4,748	128	37.09	5	2
26	W. Rhodes	58	8,231	3,425	127	26.96	6	1
	A. F. Giles	**45**	**10,278**	**4,719**	**127**	**37.15**	**5**	**–**
28	P. H. Edmonds	51	12,028	4,273	125	34.18	2	–
29	D. A. Allen	39	11,297	3,779	122	30.97	4	–
	R. Illingworth.	61	11,934	3,807	122	31.20	3	–
31	P. C. R. Tufnell.	42	11,288	4,560	121	37.68	5	2
32	J. Briggs	33	5,332	2,095	118	17.75	9	4
33	G. G. Arnold	34	7,650	3,254	115	28.29	6	–
34	G. A. Lohmann	18	3,830	1,205	112	10.75	9	5
35	**S. J. Harmison**	**28**	**6,289**	**3,182**	**111**	**28.66**	**4**	**–**
36	**A. Flintoff**.	**45**	**7,907**	**3,828**	**110**	**34.80**	**1**	**–**
37	D. V. P. Wright	34	8,135	4,224	108	39.11	6	1
38	J. H. Wardle.	28	6,597	2,080	102	20.39	5	1
39	R. Peel	20	5,216	1,715	101	16.98	5	1
40	C. Blythe	19	4,546	1,863	100	18.63	9	4

AUSTRALIA

		T	Balls	R	W	Avge	5W/i	10W/m
1	**S. K. Warne**.	**120**	**33,649**	**14,504**	**566**	**25.62**	**28**	**8**
2	**G. D. McGrath**	**106**	**24,751**	**10,309**	**481**	**21.43**	**25**	**3**
3	D. K. Lillee	70	18,467	8,493	355	23.92	23	7
4	C. J. McDermott	71	16,586	8,332	291	28.63	14	2
5	R. Benaud	63	19,108	6,704	248	27.03	16	1
6	G. D. McKenzie	60	17,681	7,328	246	29.78	16	3
7	**J. N. Gillespie**	**63**	**12,932**	**6,060**	**241**	**25.14**	**8**	**–**
8	R. R. Lindwall	61	13,650	5,251	228	23.03	12	–
9	C. V. Grimmett	37	14,513	5,231	216	24.21	21	7
10	M. G. Hughes	53	12,285	6,017	212	28.38	7	1
11	J. R. Thomson	51	10,535	5,601	200	28.00	8	–
12	A. K. Davidson	44	11,587	3,819	186	20.53	14	2
13	G. F. Lawson	46	11,118	5,501	180	30.56	11	2
14	K. R. Miller	55	10,461	3,906	170	22.97	7	1
	T. M. Alderman	41	10,181	4,616	170	27.15	14	1
16	W. A. Johnston	40	11,048	3,826	160	23.91	7	–
	S. C. G. MacGill . . .	**33**	**8,729**	**4,611**	**160**	**28.81**	**10**	**2**
18	W. J. O'Reilly.	27	10,024	3,254	144	22.59	11	3
19	H. Trumble	32	8,099	3,072	141	21.78	9	3
20	**B. Lee**	**37**	**7,380**	**4,401**	**139**	**31.66**	**4**	**–**

		T	Balls	R	W	Avge	5W/i	10W/m
21	M. H. N. Walker....	34	10,094	3,792	138	27.47	6	–
22	A. A. Mallett......	38	9,990	3,940	132	29.84	6	1
23	B. Yardley........	33	8,909	3,986	126	31.63	6	1
24	R. M. Hogg.......	38	7,633	3,503	123	28.47	6	2
25	M. A. Noble......	42	7,159	3,025	121	25.00	9	2
26	B. A. Reid........	27	6,244	2,784	113	24.63	5	2
27	I. W. Johnson.....	45	8,780	3,182	109	29.19	3	–
28	P. R. Reiffel......	35	6,403	2,804	104	26.96	5	–
29	G. Giffen.........	31	6,457	2,791	103	27.09	7	1
30	A. N. Connolly.....	29	7,818	2,981	102	29.22	4	–
31	C. T. B. Turner.....	17	5,179	1,670	101	16.53	11	2

SOUTH AFRICA

		T	Balls	R	W	Avge	5W/i	10W/m
1	**S. M. Pollock......**	**92**	**21,032**	**8,195**	**374**	**21.91**	**16**	**1**
2	A. A. Donald......	72	15,519	7,344	330	22.25	20	3
3	**M. Ntini ....**	**54**	**11,402**	**5,929**	**199**	**29.79**	**7**	**1**
4	H. J. Tayfield......	37	13,568	4,405	170	25.91	14	2
	J. H. Kallis.......	**87**	**11,694**	**5,397**	**170**	**31.74**	**4**	**–**
6	**P. R. Adams .....**	**45**	**8,850**	**4,405**	**134**	**32.87**	**4**	**1**
7	T. L. Goddard.....	41	11,736	3,226	123	26.22	5	–
8	P. M. Pollock	28	6,522	2,806	116	24.18	9	1
9	N. A. T. Adcock	26	6,391	2,195	104	21.10	5	–

WEST INDIES

		T	Balls	R	W	Avge	5W/i	10W/m
1	C. A. Walsh	132	30,019	12,688	519	24.44	22	3
2	C. E. L. Ambrose ...	98	22,103	8,501	405	20.99	22	3
3	M. D. Marshall....	81	17,584	7,876	376	20.94	22	4
4	L. R. Gibbs.......	79	27,115	8,989	309	29.09	18	2
5	J. Garner.........	58	13,169	5,433	259	20.97	7	–
6	M. A. Holding.....	60	12,680	5,898	249	23.68	13	2
7	G. S. Sobers	93	21,599	7,999	235	34.03	6	–
8	A. M. E. Roberts ...	47	11,135	5,174	202	25.61	11	2
9	W. W. Hall	48	10,421	5,066	192	26.38	9	1
10	I. R. Bishop.......	43	8,407	3,909	161	24.27	6	–
11	S. Ramadhin......	43	13,939	4,579	158	28.98	10	1
12	A. L. Valentine.....	36	12,953	4,215	139	30.32	8	2
13	**M. Dillon ....**	**38**	**8,704**	**4,398**	**131**	**33.57**	**2**	**–**
14	C. E. H. Croft	27	6,165	2,913	125	23.30	3	–
15	C. L. Hooper......	102	13,794	5,635	114	49.42	4	–
16	V. A. Holder	40	9,095	3,627	109	33.27	3	–

NEW ZEALAND

		T	Balls	R	W	Avge	5W/i	10W/m
1	R. J. Hadlee.......	86	21,918	9,611	431	22.29	36	9
2	**C. L. Cairns ......**	**62**	**11,698**	**6,410**	**218**	**29.40**	**13**	**1**
3	**D. L. Vettori ......**	**59**	**14,900**	**6,592**	**188**	**35.06**	**11**	**2**
4	D. K. Morrison.....	48	10,064	5,549	160	34.68	10	–
5	B. L. Cairns.......	43	10,628	4,280	130	32.92	6	1
6	E. J. Chatfield	43	10,360	3,958	123	32.17	3	1
7	R. O. Collinge	35	7,689	3,393	116	29.25	3	–
8	B. R. Taylor.......	30	6,334	2,953	111	26.60	4	–
9	J. G. Bracewell.....	41	8,403	3,653	102	35.81	4	1
10	R. C. Motz	32	7,034	3,148	100	31.48	5	–

INDIA

		T	Balls	R	W	Avge	5W/i	10W/m
1	A. Kumble	92	29,015	12,371	444	27.86	28	6
2	Kapil Dev	131	27,740	12,867	434	29.64	23	2
3	B. S. Bedi	67	21,364	7,637	266	28.71	14	1
4	B. S. Chandrasekhar .	58	15,963	7,199	242	29.74	16	2
5	J. Srinath	67	15,104	7,196	236	30.49	10	1
6	Harbhajan Singh . . .	43	11,679	5,275	189	27.91	15	3
	E. A. S. Prasanna . . .	49	14,353	5,742	189	30.38	10	2
8	V. Mankad	44	14,686	5,236	162	32.32	8	2
9	S. Venkataraghavan . .	57	14,877	5,634	156	36.11	3	1
10	R. J. Shastri	80	15,751	6,185	151	40.96	2	–
11	S. P. Gupte.	36	11,284	4,403	149	29.55	12	1
12	D. R. Doshi	33	9,322	3,502	114	30.71	6	–
13	K. D. Ghavri	39	7,042	3,656	109	33.54	4	–
14	N. S. Yadav	35	8,349	3,580	102	35.09	3	–
15	Zaheer Khan.	37	6,823	3,677	101	36.40	3	–

PAKISTAN

		T	Balls	R	W	Avge	5W/i	10W/m
1	Wasim Akram	104	22,627	9,779	414	23.62	25	5
2	Waqar Younis	87	16,224	8,788	373	23.56	22	5
3	Imran Khan	88	19,458	8,258	362	22.81	23	6
4	Abdul Qadir.	67	17,126	7,742	236	32.80	15	5
5	Saqlain Mushtaq . . .	49	14,070	6,206	208	29.83	13	3
6	Mushtaq Ahmed	52	12,532	6,100	185	32.97	10	3
7	Sarfraz Nawaz	55	13,927	5,798	177	32.75	4	1
8	Iqbal Qasim	50	13,019	4,807	171	28.11	8	2
9	Shoaib Akhtar	36	6,386	3,569	144	24.78	11	2
10	Fazal Mahmood	34	9,834	3,434	139	24.70	13	4
11	Intikhab Alam	47	10,474	4,494	125	35.95	5	2
12	Danish Kaneria	23	6,191	3,006	102	29.47	8	2

SRI LANKA

		T	Balls	R	W	Avge	5W/i	10W/m
1	M. Muralitharan . . .	91	31,124	12,165	532	22.86	44	13
2	W. P. U. J. C. Vaas . .	82	18,132	8,045	269	29.90	9	2

ZIMBABWE

		T	Balls	R	W	Avge	5W/i	10W/m
1	H. H. Streak	59	12,739	5,572	202	27.58	6	–

BANGLADESH: The highest aggregate is **67** wickets, average 32.77, by **Mohammad Rafique** in 18 Tests.

Bold type denotes those who have played Test cricket since January 1, 2004.

BEST CAREER AVERAGES

(Qualification: 75 wickets)

Avge		T	W	Avge		T	W
10.75	G. A. Lohmann (E)	18	112	18.63	C. Blythe (E)	19	100
16.43	S. F. Barnes (E)	27	189	20.39	J. H. Wardle (E)	28	102
16.53	C. T. B. Turner (A)	17	101	20.53	A. K. Davidson (A)	44	186
16.98	R. Peel (E)	20	101	20.94	M. D. Marshall (WI)	81	376
17.75	J. Briggs (E)	33	118	20.97	J. Garner (WI)	58	259
18.41	F. R. Spofforth (A)	18	94	20.99	C. E. L. Ambrose (WI)	98	405
18.56	F. H. Tyson (E)	17	76				

BEST CAREER STRIKE-RATES

(Balls per wicket. Qualification: 75 wickets)

SR		T	W	SR		T	W
34.11	G. A. Lohmann (E)	18	112	45.42	F. H. Tyson (E)	17	76
41.65	S. F. Barnes (E)	27	189	45.46	C. Blythe (E)	19	100
43.49	Waqar Younis (P)	87	373	46.76	M. D. Marshall (WI)	81	376
44.34	**Shoaib Akhtar (P)**	**36**	**144**	47.02	A. A. Donald (SA)	72	330
44.52	F. R. Spofforth (A)	18	94	49.32	C. E. H. Croft (WI)	27	125
45.12	J. V. Saunders (A)	14	79	49.43	F. S. Trueman (E)	67	307
45.18	J. Briggs (E)	33	118				

Bold type denotes those who have played Test cricket since January 1, 2004.

BEST CAREER ECONOMY-RATES

(Runs per six balls. Qualification: 75 wickets)

ER		T	W	ER		T	W
1.64	T. L. Goddard (SA)	41	123	1.94	W. J. O'Reilly (A)	27	144
1.67	R. G. Nadkarni (I)	41	88	1.94	H. J. Tayfield (SA)	37	170
1.88	H. Verity (E)	40	144	1.95	A. L. Valentine (WI)	36	139
1.88	G. A. Lohmann (E)	18	112	1.95	F. J. Titmus (E)	53	153
1.89	J. H. Wardle (E)	28	102	1.97	S. Ramadhin (WI)	43	158
1.91	R. Illingworth (E)	61	122	1.97	R. Peel (E)	20	101
1.93	C. T. B. Turner (A)	17	101	1.97	A. K. Davidson (A)	44	186
1.94	M. W. Tate (E)	39	155	1.98	L. R. Gibbs (WI)	79	309

ALL-ROUND RECORDS

HUNDRED AND FIVE WICKETS IN AN INNINGS

England

A. W. Greig	148	6-164	v West Indies	Bridgetown	1973-74
I. T. Botham	103	5-73	v New Zealand	Christchurch	1977-78
I. T. Botham	108	8-34	v Pakistan	Lord's	1978
I. T. Botham	114	6-58 } 7-48 }	v India	Bombay	1979-80
I. T. Botham	149*	6-95	v Australia	Leeds	1981
I. T. Botham	138	5-59	v New Zealand	Wellington	1983-84

Australia

C. Kelleway	114	5-33	v South Africa .	Manchester . . .	1912
J. M. Gregory	100	7-69	v England	Melbourne. . . .	1920-21
K. R. Miller	109	6-107	v West Indies. .	Kingston	1954-55
R. Benaud	100	5-84	v South Africa .	Johannesburg . .	1957-58

South Africa

J. H. Sinclair	106	6-26	v England	Cape Town . . .	1898-99
G. A. Faulkner	123	5-120	v England	Johannesburg . .	1909-10
J. H. Kallis	110	5-90	v West Indies. .	Cape Town . . .	1998-99
J. H. Kallis	139*	5-21	v Bangladesh . .	Potchefstroom .	2002-03

West Indies

D. St E. Atkinson	219	5-56	v Australia. . . .	Bridgetown . . .	1954-55
O. G. Smith	100	5-90	v India	Delhi	1958-59
G. S. Sobers	104	5-63	v India	Kingston	1961-62
G. S. Sobers	174	5-41	v England	Leeds	1966

New Zealand

B. R. Taylor†	105	5-86	v India	Calcutta	1964-65

India

V. Mankad	184	5-196	v England	Lord's.	1952
P. R. Umrigar	172*	5-107	v West Indies. .	Port-of-Spain . .	1961-62

Pakistan

Mushtaq Mohammad	201	5-49	v New Zealand	Dunedin	1972-73
Mushtaq Mohammad	121	5-28	v West Indies. .	Port-of-Spain . .	1976-77
Imran Khan	117	6-98 } 5-82 }	v India	Faisalabad	1982-83
Wasim Akram	123	5-100	v Australia. . . .	Adelaide	1989-90

Zimbabwe

P. A. Strang	106*	5-212	v Pakistan	Sheikhupura. . .	1996-97

† *On debut.*

HUNDRED AND FIVE DISMISSALS IN AN INNINGS

D. T. Lindsay	182	6ct	SA v A.	Johannesburg	1966-67
I. D. S. Smith	113*	4ct, 1st	NZ v E.	Auckland	1983-84
S. A. R. Silva	111	5ct	SL v I	Colombo (PSS).	1985-86

100 RUNS AND TEN WICKETS IN A TEST

A. K. Davidson	44 80	5-135 } 6-87 }	A v WI.	Brisbane	1960-61
I. T. Botham	114	6-58 } 7-48 }	E v I	Bombay	1979-80
Imran Khan	117	6-98 } 5-82 }	P v I	Faisalabad	1982-83

1,000 RUNS AND 100 WICKETS

	Tests	Runs	Wkts	Tests for Double
England				
T. E. Bailey....................	61	2,290	132	47
†I. T. Botham..................	102	5,200	383	21
J. E. Emburey	64	1,713	147	46
A. Flintoff	**45**	**2,239**	**110**	**43**
A. F. Giles	**45**	**1,123**	**127**	**43**
A. W. Greig	58	3,599	141	37
R. Illingworth	61	1,836	122	47
W. Rhodes	58	2,325	127	44
M. W. Tate	39	1,198	155	33
F. J. Titmus	53	1,449	153	40
Australia				
R. Benaud....................	63	2,201	248	32
A. K. Davidson	44	1,328	186	34
G. Giffen	31	1,238	103	30
M. G. Hughes	53	1,032	212	52
I. W. Johnson.................	45	1,000	109	45
R. R. Lindwall................	61	1,502	228	38
K. R. Miller	55	2,958	170	33
M. A. Noble	42	1,997	121	27
S. K. Warne	**120**	**2,465**	**566**	**58**
South Africa				
T. L. Goddard	41	2,516	123	36
J. H. Kallis	**87**	**6,833**	**170**	**53**
S. M. Pollock	**92**	**3,120**	**374**	**26**
West Indies				
C. E. L. Ambrose..............	98	1,439	405	69
†C. L. Hooper.................	102	5,762	114	90
M. D. Marshall................	81	1,810	376	49
†G. S. Sobers.................	93	8,032	235	48
New Zealand				
J. G. Bracewell................	41	1,001	102	41
C. L. Cairns	**62**	**3,320**	**218**	**33**
R. J. Hadlee..................	86	3,124	431	28
D. L. Vettori	**59**	**1,482**	**188**	**47**
India				
Kapil Dev....................	131	5,248	434	25
A. Kumble	**92**	**1,550**	**444**	**56**
V. Mankad	44	2,109	162	23
R. J. Shastri	80	3,830	151	44
J. Srinath	67	1,009	236	67
Pakistan				
Abdul Qadir	67	1,029	236	62
Imran Khan...................	88	3,807	362	30
Intikhab Alam	47	1,493	125	41
Sarfraz Nawaz	55	1,045	177	55
Waqar Younis..................	87	1,010	373	86
Wasim Akram	104	2,898	414	45

	Tests	Runs	Wkts	Tests for Double
Sri Lanka				
W. P. U. J. C. Vaas.	**82**	**2,028**	**269**	**47**
Zimbabwe				
H. H. Streak.	**59**	**1,814**	**202**	**40**

Bold type denotes those who have played Test cricket since January 1, 2004.

† I. T. Botham (120 catches), C. L. Hooper (115) and G. S. Sobers (109) are the only players to have achieved the treble of 1,000 runs, 100 wickets and 100 catches.

WICKET-KEEPING RECORDS

MOST DISMISSALS IN AN INNINGS

7 (all ct)	Wasim Bari	Pakistan v New Zealand at Auckland	1978-79
7 (all ct)	R. W. Taylor	England v India at Bombay	1979-80
7 (all ct)	I. D. S. Smith	New Zealand v Sri Lanka at Hamilton . . .	1990-91
7 (all ct)	R. D. Jacobs	West Indies v Australia at Melbourne	2000-01
6 (all ct)	A. T. W. Grout	Australia v South Africa at Johannesburg .	1957-58
6 (all ct)	D. J. Lindsay	South Africa v Australia at Johannesburg .	1966-67
6 (all ct)	J. T. Murray	England v India at Lord's	1967
6 (5ct, 1st)	S. M. H. Kirmani . . .	India v New Zealand at Christchurch	1975-76
6 (all ct)	R. W. Marsh	Australia v England at Brisbane	1982-83
6 (all ct)	S. A. R. Silva	Sri Lanka v India at Colombo (SSC)	1985-86
6 (all ct)	R. C. Russell	England v Australia at Melbourne	1990-91
6 (all ct)	R. C. Russell	England v South Africa at Johannesburg . .	1995-96
6 (all ct)	I. A. Healy	Australia v England at Birmingham	1997
6 (all ct)	A. J. Stewart	England v Australia at Manchester	1997
6 (all ct)	M. V. Boucher	South Africa v Pakistan at Port Elizabeth .	1997-98
6 (all ct)	Rashid Latif	Pakistan v Zimbabwe at Bulawayo	1997-98
6 (all ct)	M. V. Boucher	South Africa v Sri Lanka at Cape Town . .	1997-98
6 (5ct, 1st)	†C. M. W. Read	England v New Zealand at Birmingham . .	1999

† *On debut.*

MOST STUMPINGS IN AN INNINGS

5	K. S. More	India v West Indies at Madras	1987-88

MOST DISMISSALS IN A TEST

11 (all ct)	R. C. Russell	England v South Africa at Johannesburg . .	1995-96
10 (all ct)	R. W. Taylor	England v India at Bombay	1979-80
10 (all ct)	A. C. Gilchrist	Australia v New Zealand at Hamilton	1999-2000
9 (8ct, 1st)	G. R. A. Langley . . .	Australia v England at Lord's	1956
9 (all ct)	D. A. Murray	West Indies v Australia at Melbourne	1981-82
9 (all ct)	R. W. Marsh	Australia v England at Brisbane	1982-83
9 (all ct)	S. A. R. Silva	Sri Lanka v India at Colombo (SSC)	1985-86
9 (8ct, 1st)	S. A. R. Silva	Sri Lanka v India at Colombo (PSS)	1985-86
9 (all ct)	D. J. Richardson	South Africa v India at Port Elizabeth . . .	1992-93
9 (all ct)	Rashid Latif	Pakistan v New Zealand at Auckland	1993-94
9 (all ct)	I. A. Healy	Australia v England at Brisbane	1994-95

9 (all ct)	C. O. Browne.	West Indies v England at Nottingham. . . .	1995
9 (7ct, 2st)	R. C. Russell	England v South Africa at Port Elizabeth .	1995-96
9 (8ct, 1st)	M. V. Boucher	South Africa v Pakistan at Port Elizabeth .	1997-98
9 (8ct, 1st)	R. D. Jacobs	West Indies v Australia at Melbourne. . . .	2000-01

Notes: S. A. R. Silva made 18 dismissals in two successive Tests.

The most stumpings in a match is 6 by K. S. More for India v West Indies at Madras in 1987-88.

J. J. Kelly (8ct) for Australia v England in 1901-02 and L. E. G. Ames (6ct, 2st) for England v West Indies in 1933 were the only wicket-keepers to make eight dismissals in a Test before World War II.

MOST DISMISSALS IN A SERIES

(Played in 5 Tests unless otherwise stated)

28 (all ct)	R. W. Marsh	Australia v England	1982-83
27 (25ct, 2st)	R. C. Russell	England v South Africa	1995-96
27 (25ct, 2st)	I. A. Healy	Australia v England (6 Tests)	1997
26 (23ct, 3st)	J. H. B. Waite	South Africa v New Zealand.	1961-62
26 (all ct)	R. W. Marsh	Australia v West Indies (6 Tests)	1975-76
26 (21ct, 5st)	I. A. Healy	Australia v England (6 Tests)	1993
26 (25ct, 1st)	M. V. Boucher	South Africa v England	1998
26 (24ct, 2st)	A. C. Gilchrist	Australia v England	2001
25 (23ct, 2st)	I. A. Healy	Australia v England	1994-95

Notes: S. A. R. Silva made 22 dismissals (21ct, 1st) in three Tests for Sri Lanka v India in 1985-86.

H. Strudwick, with 21 (15ct, 6st) for England v South Africa in 1913-14, was the only wicket-keeper to make as many as 20 dismissals in a series before World War II.

100 DISMISSALS

			T	*Ct*	*St*
1	395	I. A. Healy (Australia)	119	366	29
2	355	R. W. Marsh (Australia)	96	343	12
3	**298**	**M. V. Boucher (South Africa). . . . .**	**78**	**285**	**13**
4	**280**	**A. C. Gilchrist (Australia). . . . .**	**65**	**253**	**27**
5	270	P. J. L. Dujon (West Indies).	79	265	5
6	269	A. P. E. Knott (England).	95	250	19
7	241	A. J. Stewart (England).	82	227	14
8	228	Wasim Bari (Pakistan)	81	201	27
9 {	219	T. G. Evans (England)	91	173	46
	219	**R. D. Jacobs (West Indies).**	**65**	**207**	**12**
10	219	T. G. Evans (England)	91	173	46
11	201	A. C. Parore (New Zealand)	67	194	7
12	198	S. M. H. Kirmani (India)	88	160	38
13	189	D. L. Murray (West Indies)	62	181	8
14	187	A. T. W. Grout (Australia).	51	163	24
15	176	I. D. S. Smith (New Zealand)	63	168	8
16	174	R. W. Taylor (England).	57	167	7
17	165	R. C. Russell (England)	54	153	12
18	152	D. J. Richardson (South Africa)	42	150	2
19	151	A. Flower (Zimbabwe)	55	142	9
20	**147**	**Moin Khan (Pakistan)**	**66**	**127**	**20**
21	141	J. H. B. Waite (South Africa).	50	124	17
22 {	130	K. S. More (India).	49	110	20
	130	W. A. Oldfield (Australia)	54	78	52
	130	Rashid Latif (Pakistan)	37	119	11
25	**119**	**R. S. Kaluwitharana (Sri Lanka)**	**48**	**93**	**26**

26	112	J. M. Parks (England)	43	101	11
27	107	N. R. Mongia (India)	44	99	8
28	**106**	**K. C. Sangakkara (Sri Lanka)**	**31**	**92**	**14**
29	104	Salim Yousuf (Pakistan)	32	91	13
30	102	J. R. Murray (West Indies)	33	99	3

Notes: The records for P. J. L. Dujon and J. M. Parks each exclude two catches taken when not keeping wicket in two and three Tests respectively. A. J. Stewart's record excludes 36 catches taken in 51 Tests when not keeping wicket; A. C. Parore's excludes three in 11 Tests, A. Flower's nine in eight Tests and Moin Khan's one in three Tests when not keeping wicket; R. S. Kaluwitharana played one further Test when not keeping wicket without holding a catch; K. C. Sangakkara's record excludes 17 catches taken in 13 matches when not keeping wicket.

The most wicket-keeping dismissals for Bangladesh is **67 (Khaled Mashud** 59ct, 8 st in 33 Tests). H. P. Tillekeratne (Sri Lanka) has made 124 dismissals (122ct, 2st) in 83 Tests but only 35 (33ct, 2st) in 12 Tests as wicket-keeper (including one in which he took over during the match).

Bold type denotes those who have played Test cricket since January 1, 2004.

FIELDING RECORDS

(Excluding wicket-keepers)

MOST CATCHES IN AN INNINGS

5	V. Y. Richardson	Australia v South Africa at Durban	1935-36
5	Yajurvindra Singh	India v England at Bangalore	1976-77
5	M. Azharuddin	India v Pakistan at Karachi	1989-90
5	K. Srikkanth	India v Australia at Perth	1991-92
5	S. P. Fleming	New Zealand v Zimbabwe at Harare	1997-98

MOST CATCHES IN A TEST

7	G. S. Chappell	Australia v England at Perth	1974-75
7	Yajurvindra Singh	India v England at Bangalore	1976-77
7	H. P. Tillekeratne	Sri Lanka v New Zealand at Colombo (SSC)	1992-93
7	S. P. Fleming	New Zealand v Zimbabwe at Harare	1997-98
6	A. Shrewsbury	England v Australia at Sydney	1887-88
6	A. E. E. Vogler	South Africa v England at Durban	1909-10
6	F. E. Woolley	England v Australia at Sydney	1911-12
6	J. M. Gregory	Australia v England at Sydney	1920-21
6	B. Mitchell	South Africa v Australia at Melbourne	1931-32
6	V. Y. Richardson	Australia v South Africa at Durban	1935-36
6	R. N. Harvey	Australia v England at Sydney	1962-63
6	M. C. Cowdrey	England v West Indies at Lord's	1963
6	E. D. Solkar	India v West Indies at Port-of-Spain	1970-71
6	G. S. Sobers	West Indies v England at Lord's	1973
6	I. M. Chappell	Australia v New Zealand at Adelaide	1973-74
6	A. W. Greig	England v Pakistan at Leeds	1974
6	D. F. Whatmore	Australia v India at Kanpur	1979-80
6	A. J. Lamb	England v New Zealand at Lord's	1983
6	G. A. Hick	England v Pakistan at Leeds	1992
6	B. A. Young	New Zealand v Pakistan at Auckland	1993-94
6	J. C. Adams	West Indies v England at Kingston	1993-94
6	S. P. Fleming	New Zealand v Australia at Brisbane	1997-98
6	D. P. M. D. Jayawardene	Sri Lanka v Pakistan at Peshawar	1999-2000
6	M. E. Waugh	Australia v India at Chennai	2000-01
6	V. Sehwag	India v England at Leeds	2002
6	Taufeeq Umar	Pakistan v South Africa at Faisalabad	2003-04
6	D. P. M. D. Jayawardene	Sri Lanka v Zimbabwe at Harare	2003-04

MOST CATCHES IN A SERIES

15	J. M. Gregory	Australia v England	1920-21
14	G. S. Chappell	Australia v England (6 Tests)	1974-75
13	R. B. Simpson	Australia v South Africa	1957-58
13	R. B. Simpson	Australia v West Indies	1960-61
13	B. C. Lara	West Indies v England (6 Tests)	1997-98

100 CATCHES

Ct	T		Ct	T	
181	128	M. E. Waugh (Australia)	**112**	**168**	**S. R. Waugh (Australia)**
157	104	M. A. Taylor (Australia)	110	62	R. B. Simpson (Australia)
156	156	A. R. Border (Australia)	110	85	W. R. Hammond (England)
147	**112**	**B. C. Lara (WI)**	109	93	G. S. Sobers (West Indies)
129	**89**	**S. P. Fleming (NZ)**	108	125	S. M. Gavaskar (India)
122	87	G. S. Chappell (Australia)	**106**	**120**	**S. K. Warne (A)**
122	121	I. V. A. Richards (West Indies)	105	75	I. M. Chappell (Australia)
120	102	I. T. Botham (England)	105	99	M. Azharuddin (India)
120	114	M. C. Cowdrey (England)	103	118	G. A. Gooch (England)
119	**86**	**R. Dravid (I)**	**101**	**98**	**G. P. Thorpe (England)**
115	102	C. L. Hooper (West Indies)			

Note: The most catches in the field for other countries are South Africa **84** in 87 Tests (**J. H. Kallis**); Pakistan 93 in 124 Tests (Javed Miandad); Sri Lanka **89** in 72 Tests (**H. P. Tillekeratne**); Zimbabwe 60 in 60 Tests (A. D. R. Campbell); Bangladesh **19** in 34 Tests (**Habibul Bashar**). Tillekeratne's record excludes 35 dismissals in his Tests as wicket-keeper.

Bold type denotes those who have played Test cricket since January 1, 2004.

TEAM RECORDS

HIGHEST INNINGS TOTALS

952-6 dec.	Sri Lanka v India at Colombo (RPS)	1997-98
903-7 dec.	England v Australia at The Oval	1938
849	England v West Indies at Kingston	1929-30
790-3 dec.	West Indies v Pakistan at Kingston	1957-58
758-8 dec.	Australia v West Indies at Kingston	1954-55
751-5 dec.	West Indies v England at St John's	2003-04
735-6 dec.	Australia v Zimbabwe at Perth	2003-04
729-6 dec.	Australia v England at Lord's	1930
713-3 dec.	Sri Lanka v Zimbabwe at Bulawayo	2003-04
708	Pakistan v England at The Oval	1987
705-7 dec.	India v Australia at Sydney	2003-04
701	Australia v England at The Oval	1934
699-5	Pakistan v India at Lahore	1989-90
695	Australia v England at The Oval	1930
692-8 dec.	West Indies v England at The Oval	1995
687-8 dec.	West Indies v England at The Oval	1976
682-6 dec.	South Africa v England at Lord's	2003
681-8 dec.	West Indies v England at Port-of-Spain	1953-54
676-7	India v Sri Lanka at Kanpur	1986-87
675-5 dec.	India v Pakistan at Multan	2003-04
674-6	Pakistan v India at Faisalabad	1984-85
674	Australia v India at Adelaide	1947-48
671-4	New Zealand v Sri Lanka at Wellington	1990-91
668	Australia v West Indies at Bridgetown	1954-55
660-5 dec.	West Indies v New Zealand at Wellington	1994-95

The highest innings for the countries not mentioned above are:

563-9 dec.	Zimbabwe v West Indies at Harare	2001
488	Bangladesh v Zimbabwe at Chittagong	2004-05

HIGHEST FOURTH-INNINGS TOTALS

To win

418-7	West Indies (needing 418) v Australia at St John's	2002-03
406-4	India (needing 403) v West Indies at Port-of-Spain	1975-76
404-3	Australia (needing 404) v England at Leeds	1948
369-6	Australia (needing 369) v Pakistan at Hobart	1999-2000
362-7	Australia (needing 359) v West Indies at Georgetown	1977-78
348-5	West Indies (needing 345) v New Zealand at Auckland	1968-69
344-1	West Indies (needing 342) v England at Lord's	1984

To tie

347	India v Australia at Madras	1986-87

To draw

654-5	England (needing 696 to win) v South Africa at Durban	1938-39
429-8	India (needing 438 to win) v England at The Oval	1979
423-7	South Africa (needing 451 to win) v England at The Oval	1947
408-5	West Indies (needing 836 to win) v England at Kingston	1929-30

To lose

451	New Zealand (lost by 98 runs) v England at Christchurch	2001-02
445	India (lost by 47 runs) v Australia at Adelaide	1977-78
440	New Zealand (lost by 38 runs) v England at Nottingham	1973
417	England (lost by 45 runs) v Australia at Melbourne	1976-77
411	England (lost by 193 runs) v Australia at Sydney	1924-25
402	Australia (lost by 103 runs) v England at Manchester	1981

MOST RUNS IN A DAY (BOTH SIDES)

588	England (398-6), India (190-0) at Manchester (2nd day)	1936
522	England (503-2), South Africa (19-0) at Lord's (2nd day)	1924
509	Sri Lanka (509-9) v Bangladesh at Colombo (PSS) (2nd day)	2002
508	England (221-2), South Africa (287-6) at The Oval (3rd day)	1935

MOST RUNS IN A DAY (ONE SIDE)

509	Sri Lanka (509-9) v Bangladesh at Colombo (PSS) (2nd day)	2002
503	England (503-2) v South Africa at Lord's (2nd day)	1924
494	Australia (494-6) v South Africa at Sydney (1st day)	1910-11
475	Australia (475-2) v England at The Oval (1st day)	1934
471	England (471-8) v India at The Oval (1st day)	1936
458	Australia (458-3) v England at Leeds (1st day)	1930
455	Australia (455-1) v England at Leeds (2nd day)	1934
450	Australia (450) v South Africa at Johannesburg (1st day)	1921-22

MOST WICKETS IN A DAY

27	England (18-3 to 53 all out and 62) v Australia (60) at Lord's (2nd day)	1888
25	Australia (112 and 48-5) v England (61) at Melbourne (1st day)	1901-02

HIGHEST AGGREGATES IN A TEST

Runs	Wkts			Days played
1,981	35	South Africa v England at Durban	1938-39	10†
1,815	34	West Indies v England at Kingston	1929-30	9‡
1,764	39	Australia v West Indies at Adelaide	1968-69	5
1,753	40	Australia v England at Adelaide	1920-21	6
1,747	25	Australia v India at Sydney	2003-04	5
1,723	31	England v Australia at Leeds	1948	5

† *No play on one day.*   ‡ *No play on two days.*

LOWEST INNINGS TOTALS

26	New Zealand v England at Auckland	1954-55
30	South Africa v England at Port Elizabeth	1895-96
30	South Africa v England at Birmingham	1924
35	South Africa v England at Cape Town	1898-99
36	Australia v England at Birmingham	1902
36	South Africa v Australia at Melbourne	1931-32
42	Australia v England at Sydney	1887-88
42	New Zealand v Australia at Wellington	1945-46
42†	India v England at Lord's	1974
43	South Africa v England at Cape Town	1888-89
44	Australia v England at The Oval	1896
45	England v Australia at Sydney	1886-87
45	South Africa v Australia at Melbourne	1931-32
46	England v West Indies at Port-of-Spain	1993-94
47	South Africa v England at Cape Town	1888-89
47	New Zealand v England at Lord's	1958
47	West Indies v England at Kingston	2003-04

The lowest innings for the countries not mentioned above are:

53†	Pakistan v Australia at Sharjah	2002-03
63	Zimbabwe v West Indies at Port-of-Spain	1999-2000
71	Sri Lanka v Pakistan at Kandy	1994-95
87	Bangladesh v West Indies at Dhaka	2002-03

† *Batted one man short.*

FEWEST RUNS IN A FULL DAY'S PLAY

95	Australia (80), Pakistan (15-2) at Karachi (1st day, 5½ hours)	1956-57
104	Pakistan (0-0 to 104-5) v Australia at Karachi (4th day, 5½ hours)	1959-60
106	England (92-2 to 198) v Australia at Brisbane (4th day, 5 hours). *England were dismissed five minutes before the close of play, leaving no time for Australia to start their second innings.*	1958-59
111	South Africa (48-2 to 130-6 dec.), India (29-1) at Cape Town (5th day, 5½ hours)	1992-93
112	Australia (138-6 to 187), Pakistan (63-1) at Karachi (4th day, 5½ hours)	1956-57
115	Australia (116-7 to 165 and 66-5 after following on) v Pakistan at Karachi (4th day, 5½ hours)	1988-89
117	India (117-5) v Australia at Madras (1st day, 5½ hours)	1956-57
117	New Zealand (6-0 to 123-4) v Sri Lanka at Colombo (SSC) (5th day, 5¼ hours)	1983-84

In England

151	England (175-2 to 289), New Zealand (37-7) at Lord's (3rd day, 6 hours)	1978
158	England (211-2 to 369-9) v South Africa at Manchester (5th day, 6 hours)	1998
159	Pakistan (208-4 to 350), England (17-1) at Leeds (3rd day, 6 hours)	1971

LOWEST AGGREGATES IN A COMPLETED TEST

Runs	Wkts			Days played
234	29	Australia v South Africa at Melbourne............	1931-32	3†
291	40	England v Australia at Lord's...................	1888	2
295	28	New Zealand v Australia at Wellington	1945-46	2
309	29	West Indies v England at Bridgetown	1934-35	3
323	30	England v Australia at Manchester	1888	2

† *No play on one day.*

LARGEST VICTORIES

Largest Innings Victories

Inns & 579 runs	England (903-7 dec.) v Australia (201 & 123‡) at The Oval ..	1938
Inns & 360 runs	Australia (652-7 dec.) v South Africa (159 & 133) at Johannesburg.......................................	2001-02
Inns & 336 runs	West Indies (614-5 dec.) v India (124 & 154) at Calcutta	1958-59
Inns & 332 runs	Australia (645) v England (141 & 172) at Brisbane........	1946-47
Inns & 324 runs	Pakistan (643) v New Zealand (73 & 246) at Lahore.......	2002
Inns & 322 runs	West Indies (660-5 dec.) v New Zealand (216 & 122) at Wellington	1994-95
Inns & 310 runs	West Indies (536) v Bangladesh (139 & 87) at Dhaka	2002-03
Inns & 285 runs	England (629) v India (302 & 42†) at Lord's	1974
Inns & 264 runs	Pakistan (546-3 dec.) v Bangladesh (134 & 148) at Multan...	2001-02
Inns & 259 runs	Australia (549-7 dec.) v South Africa (158 & 132) at Port Elizabeth....................................	1949-50
Inns & 254 runs	Sri Lanka (713-3 dec.) v Zimbabwe (228 & 231) at Bulawayo.	2003-04

‡ *Two men absent in both Australian innings.* † *One man absent in India's second innings.*

Largest Victories by Runs Margin

675 runs	England (521 & 342-8 dec.) v Australia (122 & 66†) at Brisbane.....	1928-29
562 runs	Australia (701 & 327) v England (321 & 145‡) at The Oval........	1934
530 runs	Australia (328 & 578) v South Africa (205 & 171§) at Melbourne....	1910-11
491 runs	Australia (381 & 361-5 dec.) v Pakistan (179 & 72) at Perth........	2004-05
425 runs	West Indies (211 & 411-5 dec.) v England (71 & 126) at Manchester..	1976
409 runs	Australia (350 & 460-7 dec.) v England (215 & 186) at Lord's	1948
408 runs	West Indies (328 & 448) v Australia (203 & 165) at Adelaide........	1979-80
384 runs	Australia (492 & 296-5 dec.) v England (325 & 79) at Brisbane	2002-03
382 runs	Australia (238 & 411) v England (124 & 143) at Adelaide	1894-95
382 runs	Australia (619 & 394-8 dec.) v West Indies (279 & 352) at Sydney ...	1968-69
377 runs	Australia (267 & 581) v England (190 & 281) at Sydney	1920-21

† *One man absent in Australia's first innings; two men absent in their second.*
‡ *Two men absent in England's first innings; one man absent in their second.*
§ *One man absent in South Africa's second innings.*

TIED TESTS

West Indies (453 & 284) v Australia (505 & 232) at Brisbane.................	1960-61
Australia (574-7 dec. & 170-5 dec.) v India (397 & 347) at Madras	1986-87

MOST CONSECUTIVE TEST VICTORIES

16	Australia	1999-00–2000-01	7	England	1884-85–1887-88
11	West Indies	1983-84–1984-85	7	England	1928–1928-29
9	Sri Lanka	2001–2001-02	7	West Indies	1984-85–1985-86
9	South Africa	2001-02–2003	7	West Indies	1988–1988-89
8	Australia	1920-21–1921	7	Australia	2002-03
8	England	2004–2004-05			

MOST CONSECUTIVE TESTS WITHOUT VICTORY

44	New Zealand	1929-30–1955-56	23	New Zealand	1962-63–1967-68
34	Bangladesh	2000-01–2004-05	22	Pakistan	1958-59–1964-65
31	India	1981-82–1984-85	21	Sri Lanka	1985-86–1992-93
28	South Africa	1935–1949-50	20	West Indies	1968-69–1972-73
24	India	1932–1951-52			

WHITEWASHES

Teams winning every game in a series of four Tests or more:

Five-Test Series

Australia beat England	1920-21	West Indies beat England	1984
Australia beat South Africa	1931-32	West Indies beat England	1985-86
England beat India	1959	South Africa beat West Indies	1998-99
West Indies beat India	1961-62	Australia beat West Indies	2000-01

Four-Test Series

Australia beat India	1967-68	England beat West Indies	2004
South Africa beat Australia	1969-70		

Note: The winning team in each instance was at home, except for West Indies in England, 1984.

PLAYERS

YOUNGEST TEST PLAYERS

Years	Days			
14	227	Hasan Raza	Pakistan v Zimbabwe at Faisalabad	1996-97
15	124	Mushtaq Mohammad	Pakistan v West Indies at Lahore	1958-59
15	128	Mohammad Sharif	Bangladesh v Zimbabwe at Bulawayo	2000-01
16	189	Aqib Javed	Pakistan v New Zealand at Wellington	1988-89
16	205	S. R. Tendulkar	India v Pakistan at Karachi	1989-90

The previous table should be treated with extreme caution. All birthdates for Bangladesh and Pakistan (after Partition) must be regarded as questionable owing to deficiencies in record-keeping. Hasan Raza's age has been rejected by the Pakistan Cricket Board although no alternative has been offered. Suggestions that Enamul Haque jun. was 16 years 230 days old when he played against England in Dhaka in 2003-04 have been discounted by well-informed local observers, who believe he was 18.

The youngest Test players for countries not mentioned above are:

17	122	J. E. D. Sealy	West Indies v England at Bridgetown	1929-30
17	189	C. D. U. S. Weerasinghe	Sri Lanka v India at Colombo (PSS)	1985-86
17	239	I. D. Craig	Australia v South Africa at Melbourne	1952-53
17	352	H. Masakadza	Zimbabwe v West Indies at Harare	2001
18	10	D. L. Vettori	New Zealand v England at Wellington	1996-97
18	149	D. B. Close	England v New Zealand at Manchester	1949
18	340	P. R. Adams	South Africa v England at Port Elizabeth	1995-96

OLDEST PLAYERS ON TEST DEBUT

Years	Days			
49	119	J. Southerton	England v Australia at Melbourne	1876-77
47	284	Miran Bux	Pakistan v India at Lahore	1954-55
46	253	D. D. Blackie	Australia v England at Sydney	1928-29
46	237	H. Ironmonger	Australia v England at Brisbane	1928-29
42	242	N. Betancourt	West Indies v England at Port-of-Spain	1929-30
41	337	E. R. Wilson	England v Australia at Wellington	1920-21
41	27	R. J. D. Jamshedji	India v England at Bombay	1933-34
40	345	C. A. Wiles	West Indies v England at Manchester	1933
40	295	O. Henry	South Africa v India at Durban	1992-93
40	216	S. P. Kinneir	England v Australia at Sydney	1911-12
40	110	H. W. Lee	England v South Africa at Johannesburg	1930-31
40	56	G. W. A. Chubb	South Africa v England at Nottingham	1951
40	37	C. Ramaswami	India v England at Manchester	1936

Note: The oldest Test player on debut for New Zealand was H. M. McGirr, 38 years 101 days, v England at Auckland, 1929-30; for Sri Lanka, D. S. de Silva, 39 years 251 days, v England at Colombo (PSS), 1981-82; for Zimbabwe, A. C. Waller, 37 years 84 days, v England at Bulawayo, 1996-97; for Bangladesh, Enamul Haque, 35 years 58 days, v Zimbabwe at Harare, 2000-01. A. J. Traicos was 45 years 154 days old when he made his debut for Zimbabwe (v India at Harare, 1992-93) having played three Tests for South Africa in 1969-70.

OLDEST TEST PLAYERS

(Age on final day of their last Test match)

Years	Days			
52	165	W. Rhodes	England v West Indies at Kingston	1929-30
50	327	H. Ironmonger	Australia v England at Sydney	1932-33
50	320	W. G. Grace	England v Australia at Nottingham	1899
50	303	G. Gunn	England v West Indies at Kingston	1929-30
49	139	J. Southerton	England v Australia at Melbourne	1876-77
47	302	Miran Bux	Pakistan v India at Peshawar	1954-55
47	249	J. B. Hobbs	England v Australia at The Oval	1930
47	87	F. E. Woolley	England v Australia at The Oval	1934
46	309	D. D. Blackie	Australia v England at Adelaide	1928-29
46	206	A. W. Nourse	South Africa v England at The Oval	1924
46	202	H. Strudwick	England v Australia at The Oval	1926
46	41	E. H. Hendren	England v West Indies at Kingston	1934-35
45	304	A. J. Traicos	Zimbabwe v India at Delhi	1992-93
45	245	G. O. B. Allen	England v West Indies at Kingston	1947-48
45	215	P. Holmes	England v India at Lord's	1932
45	140	D. B. Close	England v West Indies at Manchester	1976

100 TEST APPEARANCES

168	**S. R. Waugh (Australia)**	116	D. B. Vengsarkar (India)
156	A. R. Border (Australia)	115	M. A. Atherton (England)
133	A. J. Stewart (England)	114	M. C. Cowdrey (England)
132	C. A. Walsh (West Indies)	**112**	**B. C. Lara (West Indies)**
131	Kapil Dev (India)	110	C. H. Lloyd (West Indies)
128	M. E. Waugh (Australia)	108	G. Boycott (England)
125	S. M. Gavaskar (India)	108	C. G. Greenidge (West Indies)
124	Javed Miandad (Pakistan)	107	D. C. Boon (Australia)
121	I. V. A. Richards (West Indies)	**106**	**G. D. McGrath (Australia)**
120	**S. R. Tendulkar (India)**	104	M. A. Taylor (Australia)
120	**S. K. Warne (Australia)**	104	Wasim Akram (Pakistan)
119	I. A. Healy (Australia)	103	Salim Malik (Pakistan)
118	G. A. Gooch (England)	102	I. T. Botham (England)
117	D. I. Gower (England)	102	C. L. Hooper (West Indies)
116	D. L. Haynes (West Indies)	**101**	**G. Kirsten (South Africa)**

Note: The most appearances for Sri Lanka is **94** by **S. T. Jayasuriya**, for New Zealand 86 by R. J. Hadlee, for Zimbabwe **67** by **G. W. Flower** and for Bangladesh **34** by **Habibul Bashar**.

Bold type denotes those who have played Test cricket since January 1, 2004.

MOST CONSECUTIVE TEST APPEARANCES

153	A. R. Border (Australia)	March 1979 to March 1994
107	M. E. Waugh (Australia)	June 1993 to October 2002
106	S. M. Gavaskar (India)	January 1975 to February 1987
87	G. R. Viswanath (India)	March 1971 to February 1983
86†	R. Dravid (India)	June 1996 to December 2004
85	G. S. Sobers (West Indies)	April 1955 to April 1972
84	S. R. Tendulkar (India)	November 1989 to June 2001
75	M. V. Boucher (South Africa)	February 1998 to August 2004
72	D. L. Haynes (West Indies)	December 1979 to June 1988
71	I. M. Chappell (Australia)	January 1966 to February 1976
69	M. Azharuddin (India)	April 1989 to February 1999
66	Kapil Dev (India)	October 1978 to December 1984
65	I. T. Botham (England)	February 1978 to March 1984
65†	A. C. Gilchrist (Australia)	November 1999 to January 2005
65	Kapil Dev (India)	January 1985 to March 1994
65	A. P. E. Knott (England)	March 1971 to August 1977

The most consecutive Test appearances for the countries not mentioned above are:

58†	J. R. Reid (New Zealand)	July 1949 to July 1965
56	A. D. R. Campbell (Zimbabwe)	October 1992 to September 2001
53	M. S. Atapattu (Sri Lanka)	June 1997 to July 2002
53	Javed Miandad (Pakistan)	December 1977 to January 1984

† *Complete Test career.*

> **"** When told, back in Colombo, that Warne had pulled level, Murali replied 'Oh, he's got it, has he? Well done. I've been out practising.' "
>
> The Sri Lankans in Australia, page 1244.

MOST TESTS AS CAPTAIN

	P	W	L	D		P	W	L	D
A. R. Border (A)	93	32	22	38*	**B. C. Lara (WI)**	40	10	23	7
C. H. Lloyd (WI)	74	36	12	26	Nawab of Pataudi jun. (I)	40	9	19	12
S. P. Fleming (NZ)	65	22	22	21	R. B. Simpson (A)	39	12	12	15
S. R. Waugh (A)	57	41	9	7	G. S. Sobers (WI)	39	9	10	20
A. Ranatunga (SL)	56	12	19	25	S. T. Jayasuriya (SL)	38	18	12	8
M. A. Atherton (E)	54	13	21	20	G. A. Gooch (E)	34	10	12	12
W. J. Cronje (SA)	53	27	11	15	Javed Miandad (P)	34	14	6	14
I. V. A. Richards (WI)	50	27	8	15	Kapil Dev (I)	34	4	7	22*
M. A. Taylor (A)	50	26	13	11	J. R. Reid (NZ)	34	3	18	13
G. S. Chappell (A)	48	21	13	14	D. I. Gower (E)	32	5	18	9
Imran Khan (P)	48	14	8	26	J. M. Brearley (E)	31	18	4	9
M. Azharuddin (I)	47	14	14	19	R. Illingworth (E)	31	12	5	14
S. M. Gavaskar (I)	47	9	8	30	I. M. Chappell (A)	30	15	5	10
N. Hussain (E)	45	17	15	13	E. R. Dexter (E)	30	9	7	14
S. C. Ganguly (I)	44	18	12	14	G. P. Howarth (NZ)	30	11	7	12
P. B. H. May (E)	41	20	10	11					

* One match tied.

Most Tests as captain of other countries:

	P	W	L	D
A. D. R. Campbell (Z)	21	?	12	7
Khaled Mashud (B)	12	0	12	0

Notes: A. R. Border captained Australia in 93 consecutive Tests.

W. W. Armstrong (Australia) captained his country in the most Tests without being defeated: ten matches with eight wins and two draws.

I. T. Botham (England) captained his country in the most Tests without ever winning: 12 matches with eight draws and four defeats.

Bold type denotes those who have been captains since January 1, 2004.

UMPIRES

MOST TESTS

		First Test	Last Test
99	**S. A. Bucknor (West Indies)**	**1988-89**	**2004-05**
86	**D. R. Shepherd (England)**	**1985**	**2004-05**
73	**S. Venkataraghavan (India)**	**1992-93**	**2003-04**
66	H. D. Bird (England)	1973	1996
59	**R. E. Koertzen (South Africa)**	**1992-93**	**2004-05**
58	**D. B. Hair (Australia)**	**1991-92**	**2004-05**
48	F. Chester (England)	1924	1955
48	**D. J. Harper (Australia)**	**1998-99**	**2004-05**
44	**D. L. Orchard (South Africa)**	**1995-96**	**2003-04**
42	C. S. Elliott (England)	1957	1974
39	R. S. Dunne (New Zealand)	1988-89	2001-02
38	**R. B. Tiffin (Zimbabwe)**	**1995-96**	**2003-04**
36	D. J. Constant (England)	1971	1988
36	S. G. Randell (Australia)	1984-85	1997-98
34	Khizar Hayat (Pakistan)	1979-80	1996-97
33	J. S. Buller (England)	1956	1969
33	A. R. Crafter (Australia)	1978-79	1991-92
32	R. W. Crockett (Australia)	1901-02	1924-25
31	D. Sang Hue (West Indies)	1961-62	1980-81
30	**E. A. R. de Silva (Sri Lanka)**	**2000**	**2003-04**

Bold type indicates umpires who have stood since January 1, 2004.

SUMMARY OF TESTS

To January 25, 2005

Opponents	Tests	Won by										Tied	Drawn
		E	A	SA	WI	NZ	I	P	SL	Z	B		
England Australia	306	95	125	–									86
South Africa	130	54	–	26									50
West Indies	134	38	–	–	52								44
New Zealand	88	41	–	–	–	7	–						40
India	91	33	–	–	–	–	16						42
Pakistan	60	16	–	–	–	–	–	10					34
Sri Lanka	15	7	–	–	–	–	–	–	4	–			4
Zimbabwe	6	3	–	–	–	–	–	–	–	–			3
Bangladesh	2	2	–	–	–	–	–	–	–	–	0	–	0
Australia South Africa	71	–	39	15									17
West Indies	99	–	45	–	32							1	21
New Zealand	43	–	20	–	–	7							16
India	68	–	32	–	–	–	15					1	20
Pakistan	52	–	24	–	–	–	–	11					17
Sri Lanka	18	–	11	–	–	–	–	–	1				6
Zimbabwe	3	–	3	–	–	–	–	–	–	0	–		0
Bangladesh	2	–	2	–	–	–	–	–	–	–	0	–	0
South Africa West Indies	15	–	–	10	2								3
New Zealand	30	–	–	16	–	4							10
India	16	–	–	7	–	–	3						6
Pakistan	11	–	–	5	–	–	–	2					4
Sri Lanka	15	–	–	8	–	–	–	–	2	–			5
Zimbabwe	5	–	–	4	–	–	–	–	–	0	–		1
Bangladesh	4	–	–	4	–	–	–	–	–	–	0	–	0
West Indies New Zealand	32	–	–	–	10	7							15
India	78	–	–	–	30	–	10						38
Pakistan	39	–	–	–	13	–	–	12					14
Sri Lanka	8	–	–	–	2	–	–	–	3	–			3
Zimbabwe	6	–	–	–	4	–	–	–	–	0	–		2
Bangladesh	4	–	–	–	3	–	–	–	–	–	0	–	1
New Zealand India	44	–	–	–	–	9	14						21
Pakistan	45	–	–	–	–	6	–	21					18
Sri Lanka	20	–	–	–	–	7	–	–	4	–			9
Zimbabwe	11	–	–	–	–	5	–	–	–	0	–		6
Bangladesh	4	–	–	–	–	4	–	–	–	–	0	–	0
India Pakistan	50	–	–	–	–	–	7	10					33
Sri Lanka	23	–	–	–	–	–	8	–	3	–			12
Zimbabwe	9	–	–	–	–	–	5	–	–	2	–		2
Bangladesh	3	–	–	–	–	–	3	–	–	–	0	–	0
Pakistan Sri Lanka	30	–	–	–	–	–	–	14	7	–			9
Zimbabwe	14	–	–	–	–	–	–	8	–	2	–		4
Bangladesh	6	–	–	–	–	–	–	6	–	–	0	–	0
Sri Lanka Zimbabwe	15	–	–	–	–	–	–	–	10	0	–		5
Bangladesh	3	–	–	–	–	–	–	–	3	–	0	–	0
Zimbabwe Bangladesh	8	–	–	–	–	–	–	–	–	4	1	–	3
	1,736	289	301	95	148	56	81	94	37	8	1	2	624

	Tests	Won	Lost	Drawn	Tied	% Won	Toss Won
England	832	289	240	303	–	34.73	398
Australia	662	301	176	183	2	45.46	335
South Africa	297	95	106	96	–	31.98	141
West Indies	415	148	125	141	1	35.66	219
New Zealand	317	56	126	135	–	17.66	162
India	382	81	126	174	1	21.20	194
Pakistan	307	94	80	133	–	30.61	144
Sri Lanka	147	37	57	53	–	25.17	80
Zimbabwe	77	8	43	26	–	10.38	45
Bangladesh	36	1	31	4	–	2.77	18

ENGLAND v AUSTRALIA

Series notes: England have won only one Test when the Ashes were still at stake (Birmingham 1997) in the last eight series between the sides... S. K. Warne needs 11 wickets in England to become the first man to take 100 Test wickets in an overseas country... Warne has 132 wickets against England, and needs 36 to break D. K. Lillee's record for Test wickets against one country... Since England last scored 500 in this fixture (Perth, 1986-87), Australia have exceeded 500 on 12 occasions – with five of those 12 in excess of 600... Australia have lost only one (1934) of their last 26 Tests at Lord's, and none of the last 17... In Ashes Tests since 1993, Australia have a conversion-rate of fifties to hundreds of 43% (50 × 100, 65 × 50); England's is 16% (16 × 100; 84 × 50)... In the last four series, Australia have won 15 out of 21 tosses... None of the last 14 Tests between the sides has been drawn... England have lost 14 and won only three of the 22 Tests in which they have put Australia in... Australia have won the last eight series between the sides – an Ashes record – and excluding one-off Tests there have been no drawn series since 1972.

		Captains					
Season	England	Australia	T	E	A	D	
1876-77	James Lillywhite	D. W. Gregory	2	1	1	0	
1878-79	Lord Harris	D. W. Gregory	1	0	1	0	
1880	Lord Harris	W. L. Murdoch	1	1	0	0	
1881-82	A. Shaw	W. L. Murdoch	4	0	2	2	
1882	A. N. Hornby	W. L. Murdoch	1	0	1	0	

THE ASHES

		Captains					
Season	England	Australia	T	E	A	D	Held by
1882-83	Hon. Ivo Bligh	W. L. Murdoch	4*	2	2	0	E
1884	Lord Harris[1]	W. L. Murdoch	3	1	0	2	E
1884-85	A. Shrewsbury	T. P. Horan[2]	5	3	2	0	E
1886	A. G. Steel	H. J. H. Scott	3	3	0	0	E
1886-87	A. Shrewsbury	P. S. McDonnell	2	2	0	0	E
1887-88	W. W. Read	P. S. McDonnell	1	1	0	0	E
1888	W. G. Grace[3]	P. S. McDonnell	3	2	1	0	E
1890†	W. G. Grace	W. L. Murdoch	2	2	0	0	E
1891-92	W. G. Grace	J. McC. Blackham	3	1	2	0	A
1893	W. G. Grace[4]	J. McC. Blackham	3	1	0	2	E
1894-95	A. E. Stoddart	G. Giffen[5]	5	3	2	0	E
1896	W. G. Grace	G. H. S. Trott	3	2	1	0	E
1897-98	A. E. Stoddart[6]	G. H. S. Trott	5	1	4	0	A
1899	A. C. MacLaren[7]	J. Darling	5	0	1	4	A
1901-02	A. C. MacLaren	J. Darling[8]	5	1	4	0	A
1902	A. C. MacLaren	J. Darling	5	1	2	2	A
1903-04	P. F. Warner	M. A. Noble	5	3	2	0	E
1905	Hon. F. S. Jackson	J. Darling	5	2	0	3	E
1907-08	A. O. Jones[9]	M. A. Noble	5	1	4	0	A
1909	A. C. MacLaren	M. A. Noble	5	1	2	2	A
1911-12	J. W. H. T. Douglas	C. Hill	5	4	1	0	E
1912	C. B. Fry	S. E. Gregory	3	1	0	2	E
1920-21	J. W. H. T. Douglas	W. W. Armstrong	5	0	5	0	A
1921	Hon. L. H. Tennyson[10]	W. W. Armstrong	5	0	3	2	A
1924-25	A. E. R. Gilligan	H. L. Collins	5	1	4	0	A
1926	A. W. Carr[11]	H. L. Collins[12]	5	1	0	4	E
1928-29	A. P. F. Chapman[13]	J. Ryder	5	4	1	0	E
1930	A. P. F. Chapman[14]	W. M. Woodfull	5	1	2	2	A
1932-33	D. R. Jardine	W. M. Woodfull	5	4	1	0	E
1934	R. E. S. Wyatt[15]	W. M. Woodfull	5	1	2	2	A
1936-37	G. O. B. Allen	D. G. Bradman	5	2	3	0	A
1938†	W. R. Hammond	D. G. Bradman	4	1	1	2	A

284   *Records*

Captains

Season	England	Australia	T	E	A	D	Held by
1946-47	W. R. Hammond[16]	D. G. Bradman	5	0	3	2	A
1948	N. W. D. Yardley	D. G. Bradman	5	0	4	1	A
1950-51	F. R. Brown	A. L. Hassett	5	1	4	0	A
1953	L. Hutton	A. L. Hassett	5	1	0	4	E
1954-55	L. Hutton	I. W. Johnson[17]	5	3	1	1	E
1956	P. B. H. May	I. W. Johnson	5	2	1	2	E
1958-59	P. B. H. May	R. Benaud	5	0	4	1	A
1961	P. B. H. May[18]	R. Benaud[19]	5	1	2	2	A
1962-63	E. R. Dexter	R. Benaud	5	1	1	3	A
1964	E. R. Dexter	R. B. Simpson	5	0	1	4	A
1965-66	M. J. K. Smith	R. B. Simpson[20]	5	1	1	3	A
1968	M. C. Cowdrey[21]	W. M. Lawry[22]	5	1	1	3	A
1970-71†	R. Illingworth	W. M. Lawry[23]	6	2	0	4	E
1972	R. Illingworth	I. M. Chappell	5	2	2	1	E
1974-75	M. H. Denness[24]	I. M. Chappell	6	1	4	1	A
1975	A. W. Greig[25]	I. M. Chappell	4	0	1	3	A
1976-77‡	A. W. Greig	G. S. Chappell	1	0	1	0	
1977	J. M. Brearley	G. S. Chappell	5	3	0	2	E
1978-79	J. M. Brearley	G. N. Yallop	6	5	1	0	E
1979-80‡	J. M. Brearley	G. S. Chappell	3	0	3	0	
1980‡	I. T. Botham	G. S. Chappell	1	0	0	1	—
1981	J. M. Brearley[26]	K. J. Hughes	6	3	1	2	E
1982-83	R. G. D. Willis	G. S. Chappell	5	1	2	2	A
1985	D. I. Gower	A. R. Border	6	3	1	2	E
1986-87	M. W. Gatting	A. R. Border	5	2	1	2	E
1987-88‡	M. W. Gatting	A. R. Border	1	0	0	1	
1989	D. I. Gower	A. R. Border	6	0	4	2	A
1990-91	G. A. Gooch[27]	A. R. Border	5	0	3	2	A
1993	G. A. Gooch[28]	A. R. Border	6	1	4	1	A
1994-95	M. A. Atherton	M. A. Taylor	5	1	3	1	A
1997	M. A. Atherton	M. A. Taylor	6	2	3	1	A
1998-99	A. J. Stewart	M. A. Taylor	5	1	3	1	A
2001	N. Hussain[29]	S. R. Waugh[30]	5	1	4	0	A
2002-03	N. Hussain	S. R. Waugh	5	1	4	0	A

In Australia			160	54	80	26	
In England			146	41	45	60	
Totals			306	95	125	86	

* *The Ashes were awarded in 1882-83 after a series of three matches which England won 2–1. A fourth match was played and this was won by Australia.*
† *The matches at Manchester in 1890 and 1938 and at Melbourne (Third Test) in 1970-71 were abandoned without a ball being bowled and are excluded.*
‡ *The Ashes were not at stake in these series.*

Notes: The following deputised for the official touring captain or were appointed by the home authority for only a minor proportion of the series:

[1]A. N. Hornby (First). [2]W. L. Murdoch (First), H. H. Massie (Third), J. McC. Blackham (Fourth). [3]A. G. Steel (First). [4]A. E. Stoddart (First). [5]J. McC. Blackham (First). [6]A. C. MacLaren (First, Second and Fifth). [7]W. G. Grace (First). [8]H. Trumble (Fourth and Fifth). [9]F. L. Fane (First, Second and Third). [10]J. W. H. T. Douglas (First and Second). [11]A. P. F. Chapman (Fifth). [12]W. Bardsley (Third and Fourth). [13]J. C. White (Fifth). [14]R. E. S. Wyatt (Fifth). [15]C. F. Walters (First). [16]N. W. D. Yardley (Fifth). [17]A. R. Morris (Second). [18]M. C. Cowdrey (First and Second). [19]R. N. Harvey (Second). [20]B. C. Booth (First and Third). [21]T. W. Graveney (Fourth). [22]B. N. Jarman (Fourth). [23]I. M. Chappell (Seventh). [24]J. H. Edrich (Fourth). [25]M. H. Denness (First). [26]I. T. Botham (First and Second). [27]A. J. Lamb (First). [28]M. A. Atherton (Fifth and Sixth). [29]M. A. Atherton (Second and Third). [30]A. C. Gilchrist (Fourth).

HIGHEST INNINGS TOTALS

For England in England: 903-7 dec. at The Oval 1938
              in Australia: 636 at Sydney 1928-29

For Australia in England: 729-6 dec. at Lord's 1930
              in Australia: 659-8 dec. at Sydney 1946-47

LOWEST INNINGS TOTALS

For England in England: 52 at The Oval 1948
              in Australia: 45 at Sydney 1886-87

For Australia in England: 36 at Birmingham 1902
              in Australia: 42 at Sydney 1887-88

DOUBLE-HUNDREDS

For England (10)

364	L. Hutton at The Oval	1938	231*	W. R. Hammond at Sydney	1936-37
287	R. E. Foster at Sydney	1903-04	216*	E. Paynter at Nottingham	1938
256	K. F. Barrington at Manchester	1964	215	D. I. Gower at Birmingham	1985
251	W. R. Hammond at Sydney	1928-29	207	N. Hussain at Birmingham	1997
240	W. R. Hammond at Lord's	1938	200	W. R. Hammond at Melbourne	1928-29

For Australia (23)

334	D. G. Bradman at Leeds	1930	232	S. J. McCabe at Nottingham	1938
311	R. B. Simpson at Manchester	1964	225	R. B. Simpson at Adelaide	1965-66
307	R. M. Cowper at Melbourne	1965-66	219	M. A. Taylor at Nottingham	1989
304	D. G. Bradman at Leeds	1934	212	D. G. Bradman at Adelaide	1936-37
270	D. G. Bradman at Melbourne	1936-37	211	W. L. Murdoch at The Oval	1884
266	W. H. Ponsford at The Oval	1934	207	K. R. Stackpole at Brisbane	1970-71
254	D. G. Bradman at Lord's	1930	206*	W. A. Brown at Lord's	1938
250	J. L. Langer at Melbourne	2002-03	206	A. R. Morris at Adelaide	1950-51
244	D. G. Bradman at The Oval	1934	201*	J. Ryder at Adelaide	1924-25
234	S. G. Barnes at Sydney	1946-47	201	S. E. Gregory at Sydney	1894-95
234	D. G. Bradman at Sydney	1946-47	200*	A. R. Border at Leeds	1993
232	D. G. Bradman at The Oval	1930			

INDIVIDUAL HUNDREDS

For England (212)

12: J. B. Hobbs.
9: D. I. Gower, W. R. Hammond.
8: H. Sutcliffe.
7: G. Boycott, J. H. Edrich, M. Leyland.
5: K. F. Barrington, D. C. S. Compton, M. C. Cowdrey, L. Hutton, F. S. Jackson, A. C. MacLaren.
4: I. T. Botham, B. C. Broad, M. W. Gatting, G. A. Gooch.

3: M. A. Butcher, E. H. Hendren, P. B. H. May, D. W. Randall, A. C. Russell, A. Shrewsbury, G. P. Thorpe, J. T. Tyldesley, M. P. Vaughan, R. A. Woolmer.

2: C. J. Barnett, L. C. Braund, E. R. Dexter, B. L. D'Oliveira, W. J. Edrich, W. G. Grace, G. Gunn, T. W. Hayward, N. Hussain, A. P. E. Knott, B. W. Luckhurst, K. S. Ranjitsinhji, R. T. Robinson, Rev. D. S. Sheppard, R. A. Smith, A. G. Steel, A. E. Stoddart, R. Subba Row, C. Washbrook, F. E. Woolley.

1: R. Abel, L. E. G. Ames, M. A. Atherton, R. W. Barber, W. Barnes, J. Briggs, J. T. Brown, A. P. F. Chapman, M. H. Denness, K. S. Duleepsinhji, K. W. R. Fletcher, R. E. Foster, C. B. Fry, T. W. Graveney, A. W. Greig, W. Gunn, J. Hardstaff, jun., J. W. Hearne, K. L. Hutchings, G. L. Jessop, A. J. Lamb, J. W. H. Makepeace, C. P. Mead, Nawab of Pataudi, sen., E. Paynter, M. R. Ramprakash, W. W. Read, W. Rhodes, C. J. Richards, P. E. Richardson, R. C. Russell, J. Sharp, R. T. Simpson, A. J. Stewart, G. Ulyett, A. Ward, W. Watson.

For Australia (264)

19: D. G. Bradman.

10: S. R. Waugh.

9: G. S. Chappell.

8: A. R. Border, A. R. Morris.

7: D. C. Boon, W. M. Lawry, M. J. Slater.

6: R. N. Harvey, M. A. Taylor, V. T. Trumper, M. E. Waugh, W. M. Woodfull.

5: C. G. Macartney, W. H. Ponsford.

4: W. W. Armstrong, P. J. Burge, I. M. Chappell, S. E. Gregory, A. L. Hassett, C. Hill, S. J. McCabe, R. T. Ponting, K. D. Walters.

3: W. Bardsley, G. S. Blewett, W. A. Brown, H. L. Collins, J. Darling, M. L. Hayden, K. J. Hughes, D. M. Jones, J. L. Langer, P. S. McDonnell, K. R. Miller, K. R. Stackpole, G. M. Wood, G. N. Yallop.

2: S. G. Barnes, B. C. Booth, R. A. Duff, R. Edwards, M. T. G. Elliott, J. H. Fingleton, A. C. Gilchrist, H. Graham, I. A. Healy, F. A. Iredale, R. B. McCosker, C. C. McDonald, G. R. Marsh, D. R. Martyn, W. L. Murdoch, N. C. O'Neill, C. E. Pellew, I. R. Redpath, J. Ryder, R. B. Simpson.

1: C. L. Badcock, C. Bannerman, G. J. Bonnor, J. W. Burke, R. M. Cowper, J. Dyson, G. Giffen, J. M. Gregory, R. J. Hartigan, H. L. Hendry, A. M. J. Hilditch, T. P. Horan, A. A. Jackson, C. Kelleway, A. F. Kippax, R. R. Lindwall, J. J. Lyons, C. L. McCool, C. E. McLeod, R. W. Marsh, G. R. J. Matthews, M. A. Noble, V. S. Ransford, A. J. Richardson, V. Y. Richardson, G. M. Ritchie, H. J. H. Scott, J. M. Taylor, G. H. S. Trott, D. M. Wellham, K. C. Wessels.

RECORD PARTNERSHIPS FOR EACH WICKET

For England

323 for 1st	J. B. Hobbs and W. Rhodes at Melbourne	....	1911-12
382 for 2nd†	L. Hutton and M. Leyland at The Oval	....	1938
262 for 3rd	W. R. Hammond and D. R. Jardine at Adelaide	....	1928-29
288 for 4th	N. Hussain and G. P. Thorpe at Birmingham	....	1997
206 for 5th	E. Paynter and D. C. S. Compton at Nottingham	....	1938
215 for 6th	{ L. Hutton and J. Hardstaff jun. at The Oval	....	1938
	{ G. Boycott and A. P. E. Knott at Nottingham	....	1977
143 for 7th	F. E. Woolley and J. Vine at Sydney	....	1911-12
124 for 8th	E. H. Hendren and H. Larwood at Brisbane	....	1928-29
151 for 9th	W. H. Scotton and W. W. Read at The Oval	....	1884
130 for 10th†	R. E. Foster and W. Rhodes at Sydney	....	1903-04

For Australia

329 for 1st	G. R. Marsh and M. A. Taylor at Nottingham.	1989
451 for 2nd†	W. H. Ponsford and D. G. Bradman at The Oval.	1934
276 for 3rd	D. G. Bradman and A. L. Hassett at Brisbane.	1946-47
388 for 4th†	W. H. Ponsford and D. G. Bradman at Leeds	1934
405 for 5th†	S. G. Barnes and D. G. Bradman at Sydney.	1946-47
346 for 6th†	J. H. Fingleton and D. G. Bradman at Melbourne	1936-37
165 for 7th	C. Hill and H. Trumble at Melbourne	1897-98
243 for 8th†	R. J. Hartigan and C. Hill at Adelaide	1907-08
154 for 9th†	S. E. Gregory and J. McC. Blackham at Sydney.	1894-95
127 for 10th†	J. M. Taylor and A. A. Mailey at Sydney.	1924-25

† *Record partnership against all countries.*

MOST RUNS IN A SERIES

England in England.	732 (average 81.33)	D. I. Gower	1985
England in Australia	905 (average 113.12)	W. R. Hammond	1928-29
Australia in England	974 (average 139.14)	D. G. Bradman	1930
Australia in Australia	810 (average 90.00)	D. G. Bradman	1936-37

TEN WICKETS OR MORE IN A MATCH

For England (38)

13-163 (6-42, 7-121)	S. F. Barnes, Melbourne.	1901-02
14-102 (7-28, 7-74)	W. Bates, Melbourne.	1882-83
10-105 (5-46, 5-59)	A. V. Bedser, Melbourne.	1950-51
14-99 (7-55, 7-44)	A. V. Bedser, Nottingham	1953
11-102 (6-44, 5-58)	C. Blythe, Birmingham	1909
11-176 (6-78, 5-98)	I. T. Botham, Perth	1979-80
10-253 (6-125, 4-128)	I. T. Botham, The Oval	1981
11-74 (5-29, 6-45)	J. Briggs, Lord's	1886
12-136 (6-49, 6-87)	J. Briggs, Adelaide	1891-92
10-148 (5-34, 5-114)	J. Briggs, The Oval	1893
10-215 (3-121, 7-94)	A. R. Caddick, Sydney	2002-03
10-104 (6-77, 4-27)†	R. M. Ellison, Birmingham	1985
10-179 (5-102, 5-77)†	K. Farnes, Nottingham	1934
10-60 (6-41, 4-19)	J. T. Hearne, The Oval	1896
11-113 (5-58, 6-55)	J. C. Laker, Leeds	1956
19-90 (9-37, 10-53)	J. C. Laker, Manchester	1956
10-124 (5-96, 5-28)	H. Larwood, Sydney	1932-33
11-76 (6-48, 5-28)	W. H. Lockwood, Manchester	1902
12-104 (7-36, 5-68)	G. A. Lohmann, The Oval	1886
10-87 (8-35, 2-52)	G. A. Lohmann, Sydney.	1886-87
10-142 (8-58, 2-84)	G. A. Lohmann, Sydney.	1891-92
12-102 (6-50, 6-52)†	F. Martin, The Oval.	1890
11-68 (7-31, 4-37)	R. Peel, Manchester	1888
15-124 (7-56, 8-68)	W. Rhodes, Melbourne	1903-04
10-156 (5-49, 5-107)†	T. Richardson, Manchester	1893
11-173 (6-39, 5-134)	T. Richardson, Lord's	1896
13-244 (7-168, 6-76)	T. Richardson, Manchester	1896
10-204 (8-94, 2-110)	T. Richardson, Sydney	1897-98

11-228 (6-130, 5-98)†	M. W. Tate, Sydney	1924-25
11-88 (5-58, 6-30)	F. S. Trueman, Leeds	1961
11-93 (7-66, 4-27)	P. C. R. Tufnell, The Oval	1997
10-130 (4-45, 6-85)	F. H. Tyson, Sydney	1954-55
10-82 (4-37, 6-45)	D. L. Underwood, Leeds	1972
11-215 (7-113, 4-102)	D. L. Underwood, Adelaide	1974-75
15-104 (7-61, 8-43)	H. Verity, Lord's	1934
10-57 (6-41, 4-16)	W. Voce, Brisbane	1936-37
13-256 (5-130, 8-126)	J. C. White, Adelaide	1928-29
10-49 (5-29, 5-20)	F. E. Woolley, The Oval	1912

For Australia (41)

10-151 (5-107, 5-44)	T. M. Alderman, Leeds	1989
10-239 (4-129, 6-110)	L. O'B. Fleetwood-Smith, Adelaide	1936-37
10-160 (4-88, 6-72)	G. Giffen, Sydney	1891-92
11-82 (5-45, 6-37)†	C. V. Grimmett, Sydney	1924-25
10-201 (5-107, 5-94)	C. V. Grimmett, Nottingham	1930
10-122 (5-65, 5-57)	R. M. Hogg, Perth	1978-79
10-66 (5-30, 5-36)	R. M. Hogg, Melbourne	1978-79
12-175 (5-85, 7-90)†	H. V. Hordern, Sydney	1911-12
10-161 (5-95, 5-66)	H. V. Hordern, Sydney	1911-12
10-164 (7-88, 3-76)	E. Jones, Lord's	1899
11-134 (6-47, 5-87)	G. F. Lawson, Brisbane	1982-83
10-181 (5-58, 5-123)	D. K. Lillee, The Oval	1972
11-165 (6-26, 5-139)	D. K. Lillee, Melbourne	1976-77
11-138 (6-60, 5-78)	D. K. Lillee, Melbourne	1979-80
11-159 (7-89, 4-70)	D. K. Lillee, The Oval	1981
11-85 (7-58, 4-27)	C. G. Macartney, Leeds	1909
11-157 (8-97, 3-60)	C. J. McDermott, Perth	1990-91
12-107 (5-57, 7-50)	S. C. G. MacGill, Sydney	1998-99
10-302 (5-160, 5-142)	A. A. Mailey, Adelaide	1920-21
13-236 (4-115, 9-121)	A. A. Mailey, Melbourne	1920-21
16-137 (8-84, 8-53)†	R. A. L. Massie, Lord's	1972
10-152 (5-72, 5-80)	K. R. Miller, Lord's	1956
13-77 (7-17, 6-60)	M. A. Noble, Melbourne	1901-02
11-103 (5-51, 6-52)	M. A. Noble, Sheffield	1902
10-129 (5-63, 5-66)	W. J. O'Reilly, Melbourne	1932-33
11-129 (4-75, 7-54)	W. J. O'Reilly, Nottingham	1934
10-122 (5-66, 5-56)	W. J. O'Reilly, Leeds	1938
11-165 (7-68, 4-97)	G. E. Palmer, Sydney	1881-82
10-126 (7-65, 3-61)	G. E. Palmer, Melbourne	1882-83
13-148 (6-97, 7-51)	B. A. Reid, Melbourne	1990-91
13-110 (6-48, 7-62)	F. R. Spofforth, Melbourne	1878-79
14-90 (7-46, 7-44)	F. R. Spofforth, The Oval	1882
11-117 (4-73, 7-44)	F. R. Spofforth, Sydney	1882-83
10-144 (4-54, 6-90)	F. R. Spofforth, Sydney	1884-85
12-89 (6-59, 6-30)	H. Trumble, The Oval	1896
10-128 (4-75, 6-53)	H. Trumble, Manchester	1902
12-173 (8-65, 4-108)	H. Trumble, The Oval	1902
12-87 (5-44, 7-43)	C. T. B. Turner, Sydney	1887-88
10-63 (5-27, 5-36)	C. T. B. Turner, Lord's	1888
11-110 (3-39, 8-71)	S. K. Warne, Brisbane	1994-95
11-229 (7-165, 4-64)	S. K. Warne, The Oval	2001

† *On first appearance in England–Australia Tests.*

Note: A. V. Bedser, J. Briggs, J. C. Laker, T. Richardson in 1896, R. M. Hogg, A. A. Mailey, H. Trumble and C. T. B. Turner took ten wickets or more in successive Tests. J. Briggs was omitted, however, from the England team for the first Test match in 1893.

SEVEN WICKETS OR MORE IN AN INNINGS

In addition to those listed above, the following have taken seven wickets or more in an innings:

For England

7-40	R. G. Barlow, Sydney	1882-83
7-44	R. G. Barlow, Manchester.	1886
7-60	S. F. Barnes, Sydney	1907-08
8-107	B. J. T. Bosanquet, Nottingham .	1905
8-81	L. C. Braund, Melbourne	1903-04
7-78	J. E. Emburey, Sydney	1986-87
7-68	T. Emmett, Melbourne	1878-79
7-71	W. H. Lockwood, The Oval. . . .	1899
7-17	W. Rhodes, Birmingham.	1902

7-40	J. A. Snow, Sydney	1970-71
7-57	J. B. Statham, Melbourne	1958-59
7-79	F. J. Titmus, Sydney.	1962-63
7-27	F. H. Tyson, Melbourne	1954-55
7-36	G. Ulyett, Lord's.	1884
7-50	D. L. Underwood, The Oval . . .	1968
7-78	R. G. D. Willis, Lord's.	1977
8-43	R. G. D. Willis, Leeds	1981
7-105	D. V. P. Wright, Sydney	1946-47

For Australia

7-148	A. Cotter, The Oval.	1905
7-117	G. Giffen, Sydney	1884-85
7-128	G. Giffen, The Oval.	1893
7-37	J. N. Gillespie, Leeds.	1997
7-69	J. M. Gregory, Melbourne	1920-21
7-105	N. J. N. Hawke, Sydney	1965-66
7-25	G. R. Hazlitt, The Oval . . . ,	1912
7-92	P. M. Hornibrook, The Oval . . .	1930
7-36	M. S. Kasprowicz, The Oval . . .	1997
7-55	T. K. Kendall, Melbourne	1876-77
7-64	F. J. Laver, Nottingham.	1905
8-31	F. J. Laver, Manchester.	1909
7-81	G. F. Lawson, Lord's	1981

7-63	R. R. Lindwall, Sydney	1946-47
8-141	C. J. McDermott, Manchester . .	1985
8-38	G. D. McGrath, Lord's.	1997
7-76	G. D. McGrath, The Oval	1997
7-76	G. D. McGrath, Leeds . , . . .	2001
7-153	G. D. McKenzie, Manchester. . .	1964
7-60	K. R. Miller, Brisbane	1946-47
7-100	M. A. Noble, Sydney	1903-04
7-189	W. J. O'Reilly, Manchester . . .	1934
8-43	A. E. Trott, Adelaide	1894-95
7-28	H. Trumble, Melbourne	1903-04
8-143	M. H. N. Walker, Melbourne. . .	1974-75

MOST WICKETS IN A SERIES

England in England	46 (average 9.60)	J. C. Laker	1956
England in Australia	38 (average 23.18)	M. W. Tate	1924-25
Australia in England	42 (average 21.26)	T. M. Alderman (6 Tests). .	1981
Australia in Australia	41 (average 12.85)	R. M. Hogg (6 Tests)	1978-79

WICKET-KEEPING – MOST DISMISSALS

	M	Ct	St	Total
†R. W. Marsh (Australia)	42	141	7	148
I. A. Healy (Australia)	33	123	12	135
A. P. E. Knott (England)	34	97	8	105
†W. A. Oldfield (Australia)	38	59	31	90
A. A. Lilley (England)	32	65	19	84
A. J. Stewart (England)	26	76	2	78
A. T. W. Grout (Australia).	22	69	7	76
T. G. Evans (England)	31	64	12	76

† *The number of catches by R. W. Marsh (141) and stumpings by W. A. Oldfield (31) are respective
records in England–Australia Tests.*

Note: Stewart held a further 6 catches in 7 matches when not keeping wicket.

SCORERS OF OVER 2,000 RUNS

	T	I	NO	R	HS	100s	Avge
D. G. Bradman	37	63	7	5,028	334	19	89.78
J. B. Hobbs.	41	71	4	3,636	187	12	54.26
A. R. Border.	47	82	19	3,548	200*	8	56.31
D. I. Gower	42	77	4	3,269	215	9	44.78
S. R. Waugh	46	73	18	3,200	177*	10	58.18
G. Boycott	38	71	9	2,945	191	7	47.50
W. R. Hammond	33	58	3	2,852	251	9	51.85
H. Sutcliffe.	27	46	5	2,741	194	8	66.85
C. Hill.	41	76	1	2,660	188	4	35.46
J. H. Edrich	32	57	3	2,644	175	7	48.96
G. A. Gooch	42	79	0	2,632	196	4	33.31
G. S. Chappell	35	65	8	2,619	144	9	45.94
M. A. Taylor	33	61	2	2,496	219	6	42.30
M. C. Cowdrey	43	75	4	2,433	113	5	34.26
L. Hutton	27	49	6	2,428	364	5	56.46
R. N. Harvey	37	68	5	2,416	167	6	38.34
V. T. Trumper	40	74	5	2,263	185*	6	32.79
D. C. Boon	31	57	8	2,237	184*	7	45.65
W. M. Lawry	29	51	5	2,233	166	7	48.54
M. E. Waugh	29	51	7	2,204	140	6	50.09
S. E. Gregory	52	92	7	2,193	201	4	25.80
W. W. Armstrong	42	71	9	2,172	158	4	35.03
I. M. Chappell	30	56	4	2,138	192	4	41.11
K. F. Barrington	23	39	6	2,111	256	5	63.96
A. R. Morris.	24	43	2	2,080	206	8	50.73

BOWLERS WITH 100 WICKETS

	T	Balls	R	W	5W/i	10W/i	Avge
D. K. Lillee	29	8,516	3,507	167	11	4	21.00
I. T. Botham	36	8,479	4,093	148	9	2	27.65
H. Trumble	31	7,895	2,945	141	9	3	20.88
S. K. Warne	26	7,792	3,040	132	7	2	23.03
R. G. D. Willis	35	7,294	3,346	128	7	0	26.14
G. D. McGrath	22	5,221	2,344	117	7	0	20.03
M. A. Noble	39	6,845	2,860	115	9	2	24.86
R. R. Lindwall	29	6,728	2,559	114	6	0	22.44
W. Rhodes	41	5,791	2,616	109	6	1	24.00
S. F. Barnes	20	5,749	2,288	106	12	1	21.58
C. V. Grimmett	22	9,224	3,439	106	11	2	32.44
D. L. Underwood	29	8,000	2,770	105	4	2	26.38
A. V. Bedser	21	7,065	2,859	104	7	2	27.49
G. Giffen	31	6,457	2,791	103	7	1	27.09
W. J. O'Reilly	19	7,864	2,587	102	8	3	25.36
C. T. B. Turner	17	5,195	1,670	101	11	2	16.53
R. Peel.	20	5,216	1,715	101	5	1	16.98
T. M. Alderman.	17	4,717	2,117	100	11	1	21.17
J. R. Thomson.	21	4,951	2,418	100	5	0	24.18

RESULTS ON EACH GROUND

In England

	Matches	England wins	Australia wins	Drawn
The Oval	33	15	6	12
Manchester	27	7	7	13†
Lord's	32	5‡	13	14
Nottingham	19	3	7	9
Leeds.	23	7	8	8
Birmingham	11	4	3	4
Sheffield.	1	0	1	0

† *Excludes two matches abandoned without a ball bowled.*
‡ *England have won only once (1934) since 1896.*

In Australia

	Matches	England wins	Australia wins	Drawn
Melbourne	52	19	26	7†
Sydney.	52	21	24	7
Adelaide.	28	8	15	5
Brisbane				
Exhibition Ground . .	1	1	0	0
Woolloongabba	17	4	9	4
Perth	10	1	6	3

† *Excludes one match abandoned without a ball bowled.*

ENGLAND v SOUTH AFRICA

Series notes: South Africa have failed to win any of their post-isolation series in England, despite leading each time... In their post-readmission Lord's Tests, South Africa have averaged 49.7 runs per wicket and England 21.0... South Africa have won only four of their last 20 Tests at home to England, and drawn 12... South Africa have failed to win in 12 attempts at The Oval and in five at Birmingham... S. M. Pollock needs nine wickets to become the first man to take 100 in this fixture... England lead 11–3 in the third Test of a series between the sides... There has been no play on seven days of the 15 scheduled between the sides at Centurion.

	Captains					
Season	England	South Africa	T	E	SA	D
1888-89	C. A. Smith[1]	O. R. Dunell[2]	2	2	0	0
1891-92	W. W. Read	W. H. Milton	1	1	0	0
1895-96	Lord Hawke[3]	E. A. Halliwell[4]	3	3	0	0
1898-99	Lord Hawke	M. Bisset	2	2	0	0
1905-06	P. F. Warner	P. W. Sherwell	5	1	4	0
1907	R. E. Foster	P. W. Sherwell	3	1	0	2
1909-10	H. D. G. Leveson Gower[5]	S. J. Snooke	5	2	3	0
1912	C. B. Fry	F. Mitchell[6]	3	3	0	0
1913-14	J. W. H. T. Douglas	H. W. Taylor	5	4	0	1
1922-23	F. T. Mann	H. W. Taylor	5	2	1	2
1924	A. E. R. Gilligan[7]	H. W. Taylor	5	3	0	2
1927-28	R. T. Stanyforth[8]	H. G. Deane	5	2	2	1
1929	J. C. White[9]	H. G. Deane	5	2	0	3
1930-31	A. P. F. Chapman	H. G. Deane[10]	5	0	1	4
1935	R. E. S. Wyatt	H. F. Wade	5	0	1	4
1938-39	W. R. Hammond	A. Melville	5	1	0	4
1947	N. W. D. Yardley	A. Melville	5	3	0	2
1948-49	F. G. Mann	A. D. Nourse	5	2	0	3

Captains

Season	England	South Africa	T	E	SA	D	Held by
1951	F. R. Brown	A. D. Nourse	5	3	1	1	
1955	P. B. H. May	J. E. Cheetham[11]	5	3	2	0	
1956-57	P. B. H. May	C. B. van Ryneveld[12]	5	2	2	1	
1960	M. C. Cowdrey	D. J. McGlew	5	3	0	2	
1964-65	M. J. K. Smith	T. L. Goddard	5	1	0	4	
1965	M. J. K. Smith	P. L. van der Merwe	3	0	1	2	
1994	M. A. Atherton	K. C. Wessels	3	1	1	1	
1995-96	M. A. Atherton	W. J. Cronje	5	0	1	4	
1998	A. J. Stewart	W. J. Cronje	5	2	1	2	
1999-2000	N. Hussain	W. J. Cronje	5	1	2	2	
2003	M. P. Vaughan[13]	G. C. Smith	5	2	2	1	

THE BASIL D'OLIVEIRA TROPHY

2004-05	M. P. Vaughan	G. C. Smith	5	2	1	2	E

	T	E	SA	D
In South Africa	73	28	17	28
In England	57	26	9	22
Totals	130	54	26	50

Notes: The following deputised for the official touring captain or were appointed by the home authority for only a minor proportion of the series:

[1]M. P. Bowden (Second). [2]W. H. Milton (Second). [3]Sir T. C. O'Brien (First). [4]A. R. Richards (Third). [5]F. L. Fane (Fourth and Fifth). [6]L. J. Tancred (Second and Third). [7]J. W. H. T. Douglas (Fourth). [8]G. T. S. Stevens (Fifth). [9]A. W. Carr (Fourth and Fifth). [10]E. P. Nupen (First), H. B. Cameron (Fourth and Fifth). [11]D. J. McGlew (Third and Fourth). [12]D. J. McGlew (Second). [13]N. Hussain (First).

HIGHEST INNINGS TOTALS

For England in England: 604-9 dec. at The Oval		2003
in South Africa: 654-5 at Durban		1938-39

For South Africa in England: 682-6 dec. at Lord's		2003
in South Africa: 572-7 at Durban		1999-2000

LOWEST INNINGS TOTALS

For England in England: 76 at Leeds		1907
in South Africa: 92 at Cape Town		1898-99

For South Africa in England: 30 at Birmingham		1924
in South Africa: 30 at Port Elizabeth		1895-96

DOUBLE-HUNDREDS

For England (5)

243	E. Paynter at Durban	1938-39	211	J. B. Hobbs at Lord's		1924
219	W. J. Edrich at Durban	1938-39	208	D. C. S. Compton at Lord's		1947
219	M. E. Trescothick at The Oval	2003				

For South Africa (6)

277	G. C. Smith at Birmingham	2003	236	E. A. B. Rowan at Leeds	1951
275	G. Kirsten at Durban	1999-2000	210	G. Kirsten at Manchester	1998
259	G. C. Smith at Lord's	2003	208	A. D. Nourse at Nottingham	1951

INDIVIDUAL HUNDREDS

For England (108)

7: D. C. S. Compton.
6: W. R. Hammond, H. Sutcliffe.
4: L. Hutton.
3: M. A. Atherton, M. C. Cowdrey, W. J. Edrich, N. Hussain, P. B. H. May, C. P. Mead, E. Paynter, A. J. Strauss, M. E. Trescothick, F. E. Woolley.
2: L. E. G. Ames, K. F. Barrington, M. A. Butcher, P. A. Gibb, E. H. Hendren, G. A. Hick, J. B. Hobbs, M. Leyland, A. C. Russell, G. P. Thorpe, E. Tyldesley, R. E. S. Wyatt.
1: R. Abel, G. Boycott, L. C. Braund, D. Denton, E. R. Dexter, J. W. H. T. Douglas, F. L. Fane, A. Flintoff, C. B. Fry, T. W. Hayward, A. J. L. Hill, D. J. Insole, F. G. Mann, P. H. Parfitt, J. M. Parks, G. Pullar, W. Rhodes, P. E. Richardson, R. W. V. Robins, R. T. Simpson, M. J. K. Smith, R. H. Spooner, A. J. Stewart, M. W. Tate, J. T. Tyldesley, B. H. Valentine, M. P. Vaughan, P. F. Warner, C. Washbrook, A. J. Watkins, H. Wood.

For South Africa (84)

7: B. Mitchell, A. D. Nourse, H. W. Taylor.
5: J. H. Kallis, G. Kirsten.
4: A. Melville.
3: R. H. Catterall, H. H. Gibbs, R. A. McLean.
2: K. C. Bland, D. J. Cullinan, E. L. Dalton, D. J. McGlew, R. G. Pollock, E. A. B. Rowan, G. C. Smith, G. C. White.
1: E. J. Barlow, M. V. Boucher, W. J. Cronje, A. B. de Villiers, H. H. Dippenaar, W. R. Endean, G. A. Faulkner, T. L. Goddard, C. M. H. Hathorn, P. N. Kirsten, L. Klusener, B. M. McMillan, H. G. Owen-Smith, A. J. Pithey, J. N. Rhodes, P. W. Sherwell, I. J. Siedle, J. H. Sinclair, P. G. van der Bijl, K. G. Viljoen, W. W. Wade, J. H. B. Waite, K. C. Wessels, P. L. Winslow.

RECORD PARTNERSHIPS FOR EACH WICKET

For England

359	for 1st	L. Hutton and C. Washbrook at Johannesburg	1948-49
280	for 2nd	P. A. Gibb and W. J. Edrich at Durban	1938-39
370	for 3rd†	W. J. Edrich and D. C. S. Compton at Lord's	1947
197	for 4th	W. R. Hammond and L. E. G. Ames at Cape Town	1938-39
237	for 5th	D. C. S. Compton and N. W. D. Yardley at Nottingham	1947
206*	for 6th	K. F. Barrington and J. M. Parks at Durban	1964-65
115	for 7th	J. W. H. T. Douglas and M. C. Bird at Durban	1913-14
154	for 8th	C. W. Wright and H. R. Bromley-Davenport at Johannesburg	1895-96
99	for 9th	A. Flintoff and S. J. Harmison at The Oval	2003
92	for 10th	A. C. Russell and A. E. R. Gilligan at Durban	1922-23

For South Africa

338	for 1st	G. C. Smith and H. H. Gibbs at Birmingham	2003
257	for 2nd	G. C. Smith and G. Kirsten at Lord's	2003
319	for 3rd	A. Melville and A. D. Nourse at Nottingham	1947
214	for 4th	H. W. Taylor and H. G. Deane at The Oval	1929
192	for 5th†	G. Kirsten and M. V. Boucher at Durban	1999-2000
171	for 6th	J. H. B. Waite and P. L. Winslow at Manchester	1955
123	for 7th	H. G. Deane and E. P. Nupen at Durban	1927-28
150	for 8th†	G. Kirsten and M. Zondeki at Leeds	2003
137	for 9th	E. L. Dalton and A. B. C. Langton at The Oval	1935
103	for 10th†	H. G. Owen-Smith and A. J. Bell at Leeds	1929

† *Record partnership against all countries.*

MOST RUNS IN A SERIES

England in England	753 (average 94.12)	D. C. S. Compton .	1947
England in South Africa.	656 (average 72.88)	A. J. Strauss	2004-05
South Africa in England.	714 (average 79.33)	G. C. Smith	2003
South Africa in South Africa. . . .	625 (average 69.44)	J. H. Kallis	2004-05

TEN WICKETS OR MORE IN A MATCH

For England (26)

11-110 (5-25, 6-85)†	S. F. Barnes, Lord's	1912
10-115 (6-52, 4-63)	S. F. Barnes, Leeds	1912
13-57 (5-28, 8-29)	S. F. Barnes, The Oval	1912
10-105 (5-57, 5-48)	S. F. Barnes, Durban	1913-14
17-159 (8-56, 9-103)	S. F. Barnes, Johannesburg	1913-14
14-144 (7-56, 7-88)	S. F. Barnes, Durban	1913-14
12-112 (7-58, 5-54)	A. V. Bedser, Manchester	1951
11-118 (6-68, 5-50)	C. Blythe, Cape Town	1905-06
15-99 (8-59, 7-40)	C. Blythe, Leeds	1907
10-104 (7-46, 3-58)	C. Blythe, Cape Town	1909-10
15-28 (7-17, 8-11)	J. Briggs, Cape Town	1888-89
13-91 (6-54, 7-37)†	J. J. Ferris, Cape Town	1891-92
10-122 (5-60, 5-62)	A. R. C. Fraser, Nottingham	1998
10-207 (7-115, 3-92)	A. P. Freeman, Leeds	1929
12-171 (7-71, 5-100)	A. P. Freeman, Manchester	1929
12-130 (7-70, 5-60)	G. Geary, Johannesburg	1927-28
11-90 (6-7, 5-83)	A. E. R. Gilligan, Birmingham.	1924
12-205 (5-144, 7-61)	M. J. Hoggard, Johannesburg	2004-05
10-119 (4-64, 6-55)	J. C. Laker, The Oval	1951
15-45 (7-38, 8-7)†	G. A. Lohmann, Port Elizabeth	1895-96
12-71 (9-28, 3-43)	G. A. Lohmann, Johannesburg	1895-96
10-138 (1-81, 9-57)	D. E. Malcolm, The Oval	1994
11-97 (6-63, 5-34)	J. B. Statham, Lord's	1960
12-101 (7-52, 5-49)	R. Tattersall, Lord's	1951
12-89 (5-53, 7-36)	J. H. Wardle, Cape Town.	1956-57
10-175 (5-95, 5-80)	D. V. P. Wright, Lord's	1947

For South Africa (8)

11-127 (6-53, 5-74)	A. A. Donald, Johannesburg	1999-2000
11-112 (4-49, 7-63)†	A. E. Hall, Cape Town	1922-23
10-220 (5-75, 5-145)	M. Ntini, Lord's	2003
11-150 (5-63, 6-87)	E. P. Nupen, Johannesburg	1930-31
10-87 (5-53, 5-34)	P. M. Pollock, Nottingham.	1965
12-127 (4-57, 8-70)	S. J. Snooke, Johannesburg	1905-06
13-192 (4-79, 9-113)	H. J. Tayfield, Johannesburg.	1956-57
12-181 (5-87, 7-94)	A. E. E. Vogler, Johannesburg	1909-10

† *On first appearance in England–South Africa Tests.*

Notes: S. F. Barnes took ten wickets or more in his first five Tests v South Africa and in six of his seven Tests v South Africa. A. P. Freeman and G. A. Lohmann took ten wickets or more in successive matches.

SEVEN WICKETS OR MORE IN AN INNINGS

In addition to those listed above, the following have taken seven wickets or more in an innings:

For England

7-46 A. R. Caddick, Durban 1999-2000	7-39 J. B. Statham, Lord's	1955
7-42 G. A. Lohmann, Cape Town. . 1895-96		

For South Africa

7-95 W. H. Ashley, Cape Town . . . 1888-89	7-65 S. J. Pegler, Lord's	1912
7-29 G. F. Bissett, Durban 1927-28	8-69 H. J. Tayfield, Durban	1956-57
7-84 G. A. Faulkner, The Oval . . . 1912	7-128 A. E. E. Vogler, Lord's	1907

MOST WICKETS IN A SERIES

England in England	34 (average 8.29)	S. F. Barnes	1912
England in South Africa	49 (average 10.93)	S. F. Barnes	1913-14
South Africa in England	33 (average 19.78)	A. A. Donald	1998
South Africa in South Africa . .	37 (average 17.18)	H. J. Tayfield	1956-57

ENGLAND v WEST INDIES

Series notes: England have won ten and lost none of the last 12 Tests between the sides… West Indies have never lost in eight Tests at Nottingham… In six Tests at St John's, West Indies have averaged 73.3 runs per wicket and England 32.4… Only one of West Indies' 52 Test wins over England has come in a lost series… West Indies' five wins at Manchester have all been emphatic: three by an innings, one by ten wickets, and the other by 425 runs… West Indies have won the toss in eight of the last 11 Tests – but have won none of them… In three Tests against England at St John's, B. C. Lara averages 432.

		Captains				
Season	*England*	*West Indies*	*T*	*E*	*WI*	*D*
1928	A. P. F. Chapman	R. K. Nunes	3	3	0	0
1929-30	Hon. F. S. G. Calthorpe	E. L. G. Hoad[1]	4	1	1	2
1933	D. R. Jardine[2]	G. C. Grant	3	2	0	1
1934-35	R. E. S. Wyatt	G. C. Grant	4	1	2	1
1939	W. R. Hammond	R. S. Grant	3	1	0	2
1947-48	G. O. B. Allen[3]	J. D. C. Goddard[4]	4	0	2	2
1950	N. W. D. Yardley[5]	J. D. C. Goddard	4	1	3	0
1953-54	L. Hutton	J. B. Stollmeyer	5	2	2	1
1957	P. B. H. May	J. D. C. Goddard	5	3	0	2
1959-60	P. B. H. May[6]	F. C. M. Alexander	5	1	0	4

THE WISDEN TROPHY

		Captains					
Season	*England*	*West Indies*	*T*	*E*	*WI*	*D*	*Held by*
1963	E. R. Dexter	F. M. M. Worrell	5	1	3	1	WI
1966	M. C. Cowdrey[7]	G. S. Sobers	5	1	3	1	WI
1967-68	M. C. Cowdrey	G. S. Sobers	5	1	0	4	E
1969	R. Illingworth	G. S. Sobers	3	2	0	1	E
1973	R. Illingworth	R. B. Kanhai	3	0	2	1	WI
1973-74	M. H. Denness	R. B. Kanhai	5	1	1	3	WI

Season	England	*Captains* West Indies	T	E	WI	D	Held by
1976	A. W. Greig	C. H. Lloyd	5	0	3	2	WI
1980	I. T. Botham	C. H. Lloyd[8]	5	0	1	4	WI
1980-81†	I. T. Botham	C. H. Lloyd	4	0	2	2	WI
1984	D. I. Gower	C. H. Lloyd	5	0	5	0	WI
1985-86	D. I. Gower	I. V. A. Richards	5	0	5	0	WI
1988	J. E. Emburey[9]	I. V. A. Richards	5	0	4	1	WI
1989-90‡	G. A. Gooch[10]	I. V. A. Richards[11]	4	1	2	1	WI
1991	G. A. Gooch	I. V. A. Richards	5	2	2	1	WI
1993-94	M. A. Atherton	R. B. Richardson[12]	5	1	3	1	WI
1995	M. A. Atherton	R. B. Richardson	6	2	2	2	WI
1997-98	M. A. Atherton	B. C. Lara	6	1	3	2	WI
2000	N. Hussain[13]	J. C. Adams	5	3	1	1	E
2003-04	M. P. Vaughan	B. C. Lara	4	3	0	1	E
2004	M. P. Vaughan	B. C. Lara	4	4	0	0	E

		T	E	WI	D
In England		74	25	29	20
In West Indies		60	13	23	24
Totals		134	38	52	44

† *The Second Test, at Georgetown, was cancelled owing to political pressure and is excluded.*
‡ *The Second Test, at Georgetown, was abandoned without a ball being bowled and is excluded.*

Notes: The following deputised for the official touring captain or were appointed by the home authority for only a minor proportion of the series:
[1]N. Betancourt (Second), M. P. Fernandes (Third), R. K. Nunes (Fourth). [2]R. E. S. Wyatt (Third). [3]K. Cranston (First). [4]G. A. Headley (First), G. E. Gomez (Second). •[5]F. R. Brown (Fourth). [6]M. C. Cowdrey (Fourth and Fifth). [7]M. J. K. Smith (First), D. B. Close (Fifth). [8]I. V. A. Richards (Fifth). [9]M. W. Gatting (First), C. S. Cowdrey (Fourth), G. A. Gooch (Fifth). [10]A. J. Lamb (Fourth and Fifth). [11]D. L. Haynes (Third). [12]C. A. Walsh (Fifth). [13]A. J. Stewart (Second).

HIGHEST INNINGS TOTALS

| For England in England: 619-6 dec. at Nottingham . . . . | 1957 |
| in West Indies: 849 at Kingston . . . . | 1929-30 |

| For West Indies in England: 692-8 dec. at The Oval. . . . . | 1995 |
| in West Indies: 751-5 dec. at St John's . . . . | 2003-04 |

LOWEST INNINGS TOTALS

| For England in England: 71 at Manchester. . . . . | 1976 |
| in West Indies: 46 at Port-of-Spain . . . . | 1993-94 |

| For West Indies in England: 54 at Lord's. . . . . | 2000 |
| in West Indies: 47 at Kingston . . . . | 2003-04 |

DOUBLE-HUNDREDS

For England (9)

325	A. Sandham at Kingston	1929-30	205*	E. H. Hendren at Port-of-Spain. .	1929-30
285*	P. B. H. May at Birmingham . . .	1957	205	L. Hutton at Kingston.	1953-54
262*	D. L. Amiss at Kingston	1973-74	203	D. L. Amiss at The Oval	1976
258	T. W. Graveney at Nottingham . .	1957	202*	L. Hutton at The Oval	1950
221	R. W. T. Key at Lord's	2004			

For West Indies (15)

400*	B. C. Lara at St John's	2003-04	223 C. G. Greenidge at Manchester. . 1984
375	B. C. Lara at St John's	1993-94	223 G. A. Headley at Kingston 1929-30
302	L. G. Rowe at Bridgetown.	1973-74	220 C. L. Walcott at Bridgetown . . 1953-54
291	I. V. A. Richards at The Oval. . .	1976	214* C. G. Greenidge at Lord's 1984
270*	G. A. Headley at Kingston	1934-35	209* B. F. Butcher at Nottingham . . . 1966
261	F. M. M. Worrell at Nottingham .	1950	209 C. A. Roach at Georgetown. . . . 1929-30
232	I. V. A. Richards at Nottingham .	1976	206 E. D. Weekes at Port-of-Spain . 1953-54
226	G. S. Sobers at Bridgetown	1959-60	

INDIVIDUAL HUNDREDS

For England (111)

6: M. C. Cowdrey, A. J. Lamb.

5: G. Boycott, G. A. Gooch, T. W. Graveney, L. Hutton.

4: D. L. Amiss, M. A. Atherton.

3: L. E. G. Ames, K. F. Barrington, A. W. Greig, P. B. H. May, R. A. Smith, A. J. Stewart, G. P. Thorpe, M. P. Vaughan.

2: D. C. S. Compton, E. R. Dexter, A. Flintoff, E. H. Hendren, P. E. Richardson, A. Sandham, M. E. Trescothick, C. Washbrook, P. Willey.

1: A. H. Bakewell, J. H. Edrich, T. G. Evans, K. W. R. Fletcher, G. Fowler, D. I. Gower, S. C. Griffith, W. R. Hammond, J. H. Hampshire, F. C. Hayes, G. A. Hick, J. B. Hobbs, N. Hussain, R. Illingworth, D. R. Jardine, R. W. T. Key, A. P. E. Knott, C. Milburn, J. T. Murray, J. M. Parks, W. Place, M. R. Ramprakash, J. D. Robertson, M. J. K. Smith, D. S. Steele, A. J. Strauss, R. Subba Row, E. Tyldesley, W. Watson.

For West Indies (117)

10: G. S. Sobers.

8: G. A. Headley, I. V. A. Richards.

7: C. G. Greenidge, B. C. Lara.

6: F. M. M. Worrell.

5: D. L. Haynes, R. B. Kanhai, C. H. Lloyd.

4: R. B. Richardson, C. L. Walcott.

3: R. C. Fredericks, C. L. Hooper, C. C. Hunte, L. G. Rowe, E. D. Weekes.

2: B. F. Butcher, S. Chanderpaul, H. A. Gomes, A. I. Kallicharran, S. M. Nurse, A. F. Rae, C. A. Roach, O. G. Smith.

1: J. C. Adams, K. L. T. Arthurton, I. Barrow, C. A. Best, G. M. Carew, C. A. Davis, P. J. L. Dujon, A. G. Ganteaume, C. H. Gayle, D. A. J. Holford, J. K. Holt, R. D. Jacobs, B. D. Julien, C. B. Lambert, R. R. Sarwan, D. S. Smith, K. H. Weekes.

RECORD PARTNERSHIPS FOR EACH WICKET

For England

212 for 1st	C. Washbrook and R. T. Simpson at Nottingham.	1950
291 for 2nd	A. J. Strauss and R. W. T. Key at Lord's	2004
303 for 3rd	M. A. Atherton and R. A. Smith at St John's	1993-94
411 for 4th†	P. B. H. May and M. C. Cowdrey at Birmingham	1957
150 for 5th	A. J. Stewart and G. P. Thorpe at Bridgetown.	1993-94
205 for 6th	M. R. Ramprakash and G. P. Thorpe at Bridgetown.	1997-98
197 for 7th†	M. J. K. Smith and J. M. Parks at Port-of-Spain	1959-60
217 for 8th	T. W. Graveney and J. T. Murray at The Oval.	1966
109 for 9th	G. A. R. Lock and P. I. Pocock at Georgetown	1967-68
128 for 10th	K. Higgs and J. A. Snow at The Oval	1966

For West Indies

298	for 1st†	C. G. Greenidge and D. L. Haynes at St John's	1989-90
287*	for 2nd	C. G. Greenidge and H. A. Gomes at Lord's	1984
338	for 3rd†	E. D. Weekes and F. M. M. Worrell at Port-of-Spain	1953-54
399	for 4th†	G. S. Sobers and F. M. M. Worrell at Bridgetown	1959-60
265	for 5th	S. M. Nurse and G. S. Sobers at Leeds....................	1966
282*	for 6th†	B. C. Lara and R. D. Jacobs at St John's..................	2003-04
155*	for 7th‡	G. S. Sobers and B. D. Julien at Lord's...................	1973
99	for 8th	C. A. McWatt and J. K. Holt at Georgetown	1953-54
150	for 9th	E. A. E. Baptiste and M. A. Holding at Birmingham	1984
70	for 10th	I. R. Bishop and D. Ramnarine at Georgetown	1997-98

† *Record partnership against all countries.*
‡ *231 runs were added for this wicket in two separate partnerships: G. S. Sobers retired ill and was replaced by K. D. Boyce when 155 had been added.*

TEN WICKETS OR MORE IN A MATCH

For England (12)

11-98 (7-44, 4-54)	T. E. Bailey, Lord's...........................	1957
11-110 (8-53, 3-57)	A. R. C. Fraser, Port-of-Spain.................	1997-98
10-93 (5-54, 5-39)	A. P. Freeman, Manchester....................	1928
13-156 (8-86, 5-70)	A. W. Greig, Port-of-Spain	1973-74
11-48 (5-28, 6-20)	G. A. R. Lock, The Oval	1957
10-137 (4-60, 6-77)	D. E. Malcolm, Port-of-Spain..................	1989-90
11-96 (5-37, 6-59)†	C. S. Marriott, The Oval	1933
10-142 (4-82, 6-60)	J. A. Snow, Georgetown	1967-68
10-195 (5-105, 5-90)†	G. T. S. Stevens, Bridgetown..................	1929-30
11-152 (6-100, 5-52)	F. S. Trueman, Lord's	1963
12-119 (5-75, 7-44)	F. S. Trueman, Birmingham	1963
11-149 (4-79, 7-70)	W. Voce, Port-of-Spain	1929-30

For West Indies (15)

10-127 (2-82, 8-45)	C. E. L. Ambrose, Bridgetown	1989-90
11-84 (5-60, 6-24)	C. E. L. Ambrose, Port-of-Spain...............	1993-94
10-174 (5-105, 5-69)	K. C. G. Benjamin, Nottingham	1995
11-147 (5-70, 6-77)†	K. D. Boyce, The Oval	1973
11-229 (5-137, 6-92)	W. Ferguson, Port-of-Spain	1947-48
11-157 (5-59, 6-98)†	L. R. Gibbs, Manchester	1963
10-106 (5-37, 5-69)	L. R. Gibbs, Manchester	1966
14-149 (8-92, 6-57)	M. A. Holding, The Oval	1976
10-96 (5-41, 5-55)†	H. H. H. Johnson, Kingston	1947-48
10-92 (6-32, 4-60)	M. D. Marshall, Lord's	1988
11-152 (5-66, 6-86)	S. Ramadhin, Lord's	1950
10-123 (5-60, 5-63)	A. M. E. Roberts, Lord's.....................	1976
11-204 (8-104, 3-100)†	A. L. Valentine, Manchester	1950
10-160 (4-121, 6-39)	A. L. Valentine, The Oval....................	1950
10-117 (4-43, 6-74)	C. A. Walsh, Lord's.........................	2000

† *On first appearance in England–West Indies Tests.*

Note: F. S. Trueman took ten wickets or more in successive matches.

SEVEN WICKETS OR MORE IN AN INNINGS

In addition to those listed above, the following have taken seven wickets or more in an innings:

For England

7-34 T. E. Bailey, Kingston 1953-54	7-50 W. E. Hollies, Georgetown 1934-35
8-103 I. T. Botham, Lord's 1984	7-103 J. C. Laker, Bridgetown 1947-48
7-43 D. G. Cork, Lord's 1995	7-56 James Langridge, Manchester . . 1933
8-75 A. R. C. Fraser, Bridgetown . . . 1993-94	7-49 J. A. Snow, Kingston 1967-68
7-12 S. J. Harmison, Kingston 2003-04	

For West Indies

7-69 W. W. Hall, Kingston 1959-60	7-49 S. Ramadhin, Birmingham 1957
7-53 M. D. Marshall, Leeds 1984	7-70 F. M. M. Worrell, Leeds 1957
7-22 M. D. Marshall, Manchester . . . 1988	

ENGLAND v NEW ZEALAND

Series notes: The teams' averages for runs per wicket in Tests between the sides are almost identical in England and New Zealand: in 47 Tests at home, England average 37.3 to New Zealand's 25.9: in 41 Tests away, England average 36.7 to New Zealand's 25.4… England have a 100% record from four Tests against New Zealand at Birmingham… England average 47.8 runs per wicket in Tests between the sides at Leeds, almost double New Zealand's 24.1… New Zealand's win at Lord's in 1999 was their only victory in 14 attempts… England have lost more Tests to New Zealand at home (four) than away (three)… In the 62 Tests where the team winning the toss have batted, England have won 32 and lost just three… None of the last 12 innings between the sides in New Zealand has spanned 100 overs – even though two of them exceeded 450… The home team have won only three of the last nine series.

Captains

Season	England	New Zealand	T	E	NZ	D
1929-30	A. H. H. Gilligan	T. C. Lowry	4	1	0	3
1931	D. R. Jardine	T. C. Lowry	3	1	0	2
1932-33	D. R. Jardine[1]	M. L. Page	2	0	0	2
1937	R. W. V. Robins	M. L. Page	3	1	0	2
1946-47	W. R. Hammond	W. A. Hadlee	1	0	0	1
1949	F. G. Mann[2]	W. A. Hadlee	4	0	0	4
1950-51	F. R. Brown	W. A. Hadlee	2	1	0	1
1954-55	L. Hutton	G. O. Rabone	2	2	0	0
1958	P. B. H. May	J. R. Reid	5	4	0	1
1958-59	P. B. H. May	J. R. Reid	2	1	0	1
1962-63	E. R. Dexter	J. R. Reid	3	3	0	0
1965	M. J. K. Smith	J. R. Reid	3	3	0	0
1965-66	M. J. K. Smith	B. W. Sinclair[3]	3	0	0	3
1969	R. Illingworth	G. T. Dowling	3	2	0	1
1970-71	R. Illingworth	G. T. Dowling	2	1	0	1
1973	R. Illingworth	B. E. Congdon	3	2	0	1
1974-75	M. H. Denness	B. E. Congdon	2	1	0	1
1977-78	G. Boycott	M. G. Burgess	3	1	1	1
1978	J. M. Brearley	M. G. Burgess	3	3	0	0
1983	R. G. D. Willis	G. P. Howarth	4	3	1	0
1983-84	R. G. D. Willis	G. P. Howarth	3	0	1	2
1986	M. W. Gatting	J. V. Coney	3	0	1	2
1987-88	M. W. Gatting	J. J. Crowe[4]	3	0	0	3
1990	G. A. Gooch	J. G. Wright	3	1	0	2
1991-92	G. A. Gooch	M. D. Crowe	3	2	0	1
1994	M. A. Atherton	K. R. Rutherford	3	1	0	2

Season	England	*Captains* New Zealand	T	E	NZ	D
1996-97	M. A. Atherton	L. K. Germon[5]	3	2	0	1
1999	N. Hussain[6]	S. P. Fleming	4	1	2	1
2001-02	N. Hussain	S. P. Fleming	3	1	1	1
2004	M. P. Vaughan[7]	S. P. Fleming	3	3	0	0
	In New Zealand		41	16	3	22
	In England		47	25	4	18
	Totals		88	41	7	40

Notes: The following deputised for the official touring captain or were appointed by the home authority for only a minor proportion of the series:

[1]R. E. S. Wyatt (Second). [2]F. R. Brown (Third and Fourth). [3]M. E. Chapple (First). [4]J. G. Wright (Third). [5]S. P. Fleming (Third). [6]M. A. Butcher (Third). [7]M. E. Trescothick (First).

HIGHEST INNINGS TOTALS

For England in England: 567-8 dec. at Nottingham	1994
in New Zealand: 593-6 dec. at Auckland	1974-75
For New Zealand in England: 551-9 dec. at Lord's	1973
in New Zealand: 537 at Wellington	1983-84

LOWEST INNINGS TOTALS

For England in England: 126 at Birmingham	1999
in New Zealand: 64 at Wellington	1977-78
For New Zealand in England: 47 at Lord's	1958
in New Zealand: 26 at Auckland	1954-55

DOUBLE-HUNDREDS

For England (7)

336* W. R. Hammond at Auckland	1932-33	210 G. A. Gooch at Nottingham	1994
310* J. H. Edrich at Leeds	1965	206 L. Hutton at The Oval	1949
227 W. R. Hammond at Christchurch	1932-33	200* G. P. Thorpe at Christchurch	2001-02
216 K. W. R. Fletcher at Auckland	1974-75		

For New Zealand (2)

222 N. J. Astle at Christchurch..... 2001-02 | 206 M. P. Donnelly at Lord's...... 1949

INDIVIDUAL HUNDREDS

For England (91)

4: M. A. Atherton, G. A. Gooch, D. I. Gower, W. R. Hammond, A. J. Stewart, G. P. Thorpe.

3: K. F. Barrington, I. T. Botham, J. H. Edrich, L. Hutton, A. J. Lamb, P. B. H. May.

2: L. E. G. Ames, D. L. Amiss, G. Boycott, D. C. S. Compton, M. C. Cowdrey, K. S. Duleepsinhji, K. W. R. Fletcher, J. Hardstaff, jun., N. Hussain, D. W. Randall, H. Sutcliffe.

1: G. O. B. Allen, T. E. Bailey, E. H. Bowley, B. C. Broad, M. H. Denness, E. R. Dexter, B. L. D'Oliveira, W. J. Edrich, A. Flintoff, G. Fowler, M. W. Gatting, A. W. Greig, G. O. Jones, B. R. Knight, A. P. E. Knott, G. B. Legge, C. A. Milton, P. H. Parfitt, C. T. Radley, P. E. Richardson, J. D. Robertson, P. J. Sharpe, R. T. Simpson, A. J. Strauss, C. J. Tavaré, M. E. Trescothick, C. Washbrook.

For New Zealand (47)

5: M. D. Crowe.
4: J. G. Wright.
3: N. J. Astle, B. E. Congdon, G. P. Howarth.
2: M. G. Burgess, C. S. Dempster, S. P. Fleming, V. Pollard, B. Sutcliffe.
1: J. G. Bracewell, J. V. Coney, J. J. Crowe, M. P. Donnelly, T. J. Franklin, M. J. Greatbatch, W. A. Hadlee, M. J. Horne, A. H. Jones, C. D. McMillan, J. E. Mills, M. L. Page, J. M. Parker, J. R. Reid, M. H. Richardson, K. R. Rutherford, B. W. Sinclair, I. D. S. Smith, S. B. Styris.

RECORD PARTNERSHIPS FOR EACH WICKET

For England

223	for 1st	G. Fowler and C. J. Tavaré at The Oval	1983
369	for 2nd	J. H. Edrich and K. F. Barrington at Leeds	1965
245	for 3rd	J. Hardstaff jun. and W. R. Hammond at Lord's	1937
266	for 4th	M. H. Denness and K. W. R. Fletcher at Auckland	1974-75
242	for 5th	W. R. Hammond and L. E. G. Ames at Christchurch	1932-33
281	for 6th†	G. P. Thorpe and A. Flintoff at Christchurch	2001-02
149	for 7th	A. P. E. Knott and P. Lever at Auckland	1970-71
246	for 8th†	L. E. G. Ames and G. O. B. Allen at Lord's	1931
163*	for 9th†	M. C. Cowdrey and A. C. Smith at Wellington	1962-63
59	for 10th	A. P. E. Knott and N. Gifford at Nottingham	1973

For New Zealand

276	for 1st	C. S. Dempster and J. E. Mills at Wellington	1929-30
241	for 2nd†	J. G. Wright and A. H. Jones at Wellington	1991-92
210	for 3rd	B. A. Edgar and M. D. Crowe at Lord's	1986
155	for 4th	M. D. Crowe and M. J. Greatbatch at Wellington	1987-88
180	for 5th	M. D. Crowe and S. A. Thomson at Lord's	1994
141	for 6th	M. D. Crowe and A. C. Parore at Manchester	1994
117	for 7th	D. N. Patel and C. L. Cairns at Christchurch	1991-92
104	for 8th	D. A. R. Moloney and A. W. Roberts at Lord's	1937
118	for 9th	J. V. Coney and B. L. Cairns at Wellington	1983-84
118	for 10th	N. J. Astle and C. L. Cairns at Christchurch	2001-02

† *Record partnership against all countries.*

TEN WICKETS OR MORE IN A MATCH

For England (8)

11-140 (6-101, 5-39)	I. T. Botham, Lord's	1978
10-149 (5-98, 5-51)	A. W. Greig, Auckland	1974-75
11-65 (4-14, 7-51)	G. A. R. Lock, Leeds	1958
11-84 (5-31, 6-53)	G. A. R. Lock, Christchurch	1958-59
11-147 (4-100, 7-47)†	P. C. R. Tufnell, Christchurch	1991-92
11-70 (4-38, 7-32)†	D. L. Underwood, Lord's	1969
12-101 (6-41, 6-60)	D. L. Underwood, The Oval	1969
12-97 (6-12, 6-85)	D. L. Underwood, Christchurch	1970-71

For New Zealand (5)

10-144 (7-74, 3-70)	B. L. Cairns, Leeds	1983
10-140 (4-73, 6-67)	J. Cowie, Manchester	1937
10-100 (4-74, 6-26)	R. J. Hadlee, Wellington	1977-78
10-140 (6-80, 4-60)	R. J. Hadlee, Nottingham	1986
11-169 (6-76, 5-93)	D. J. Nash, Lord's	1994

† *On first appearance in England–New Zealand Tests.*

Note: D. L. Underwood took 12 wickets in successive matches against New Zealand in 1969 and 1970-71.

SEVEN WICKETS OR MORE IN AN INNINGS

In addition to those listed above, the following have taken seven wickets or more in an innings:

For England

7-63	M. J. Hoggard, Christchurch . . . 2001-02	7-75 F. S. Trueman, Christchurch . . . 1962-63
7-35	G. A. R. Lock, Manchester 1958	7-76 F. E. Woolley, Wellington 1929-30

For New Zealand

7-143 B. L. Cairns, Wellington 1983-84

ENGLAND v INDIA

Series notes: The away side have won only one of the last 17 Tests between these teams... England have batted first in 40 of the 42 Tests against India in which they have won the toss... India have batted first in 43 out of 49... S. R. Tendulkar needs 317 runs to become the second Indian (after S. M. Gavaskar) to score 2,000 runs against one country... India have won their last two Tests at Leeds and have not lost there since 1967... England are unbeaten in seven Tests at Delhi and in six at Kanpur... India have failed to win in 16 Tests at Birmingham, Manchester and Nottingham... In Tests in India, A. Flintoff has been dismissed by three of the last four balls bowled to him by A. Kumble... England have won only five of the last 20 Tests at home to India, drawing 12.

		Captains				
Season	*England*	*India*	T	E	I	D
1932	D. R. Jardine	C. K. Nayudu	1	1	0	0
1933-34	D. R. Jardine	C. K. Nayudu	3	2	0	1
1936	G. O. B. Allen	Maharaj of Vizianagram	3	2	0	1
1946	W. R. Hammond	Nawab of Pataudi sen.	3	1	0	2
1951-52	N. D. Howard[1]	V. S. Hazare	5	1	1	3
1952	L. Hutton	V. S. Hazare	4	3	0	1
1959	P. B. H. May[2]	D. K. Gaekwad[3]	5	5	0	0
1961-62	E. R. Dexter	N. J. Contractor	5	0	2	3
1963-64	M. J. K. Smith	Nawab of Pataudi jun.	5	0	0	5
1967	D. B. Close	Nawab of Pataudi jun.	3	3	0	0
1971	R. Illingworth	A. L. Wadekar	3	0	1	2
1972-73	A. R. Lewis	A. L. Wadekar	5	1	2	2
1974	M. H. Denness	A. L. Wadekar	3	3	0	0
1976-77	A. W. Greig	B. S. Bedi	5	3	1	1
1979	J. M. Brearley	S. Venkataraghavan	4	1	0	3
1979-80	J. M. Brearley	G. R. Viswanath	1	1	0	0
1981-82	K. W. R. Fletcher	S. M. Gavaskar	6	0	1	5
1982	R. G. D. Willis	S. M. Gavaskar	3	1	0	2
1984-85	D. I. Gower	S. M. Gavaskar	5	2	1	2
1986	M. W. Gatting[4]	Kapil Dev	3	0	2	1
1990	G. A. Gooch	M. Azharuddin	3	1	0	2
1992-93	G. A. Gooch[5]	M. Azharuddin	3	0	3	0
1996	M. A. Atherton	M. Azharuddin	3	1	0	2
2001-02	N. Hussain	S. C. Ganguly	3	0	1	2
2002	N. Hussain	S. C. Ganguly	4	1	1	2
	In England		45	23	4	18
	In India		46	10	12	24
	Totals.		91	33	16	42

Notes: The 1932 Indian touring team was captained by the Maharaj of Porbandar but he did not play in the Test match.

The following deputised for the official touring captain or were appointed by the home authority for only a minor proportion of the series:

[1]D. B. Carr (Fifth). [2]M. C. Cowdrey (Fourth and Fifth). [3]Pankaj Roy (Second). [4]D. I. Gower (First). [5]A. J. Stewart (Second).

HIGHEST INNINGS TOTALS

For England in England: 653-4 dec. at Lord's 1990
          in India: 652-7 dec. at Madras 1984-85

For India in England: 628-8 dec. at Leeds 2002
         in India: 591 at Bombay 1992-93

LOWEST INNINGS TOTALS

For England in England: 101 at The Oval 1971
          in India: 102 at Bombay 1981-82

For India in England: 42 at Lord's 1974
         in India: 83 at Madras 1976-77

DOUBLE-HUNDREDS

For England (9)

333	G. A. Gooch at Lord's	1990	207 M. W. Gatting at Madras 1984-85
246*	G. Boycott at Leeds	1967	205* J. Hardstaff, jun. at Lord's 1946
217	W. R. Hammond at The Oval . . .	1936	201 G. Fowler at Madras 1984-85
214*	D. Lloyd at Birmingham	1974	200* D. I. Gower at Birmingham 1979
208	I. T. Botham at The Oval	1982	

For India (5)

224	V. G. Kambli at Bombay	1992-93	217 R. Dravid at The Oval 2002
222	G. R. Viswanath at Madras	1981-82	203* Nawab of Pataudi, jun. at Delhi . 1963-64
221	S. M. Gavaskar at The Oval	1979	

INDIVIDUAL HUNDREDS

For England (83)

5: I. T. Botham, G. A. Gooch.
4: G. Boycott, N. Hussain.
3: K. F. Barrington, M. C. Cowdrey, M. W. Gatting, A. W. Greig, A. J. Lamb, M. P. Vaughan.
2: D. L. Amiss, M. A. Atherton, M. H. Denness, K. W. R. Fletcher, D. I. Gower, T. W. Graveney, W. R. Hammond, L. Hutton, G. Pullar, R. A. Smith.
1: J. P. Crawley, E. R. Dexter, B. L. D'Oliveira, J. H. Edrich, T. G. Evans, G. Fowler, J. Hardstaff, jun., G. A. Hick, R. Illingworth, B. R. Knight, A. R. Lewis, C. C. Lewis, D. Lloyd, B. W. Luckhurst, P. B. H. May, P. H. Parfitt, D. W. Randall, R. T. Robinson, R. C. Russell, Rev. D. S. Sheppard, M. J. K. Smith, C. J. Tavaré, B. H. Valentine, C. F. Walters, A. J. Watkins, C. White, T. S. Worthington.

For India (73)

6: M. Azharuddin, S. R. Tendulkar.

5: D. B. Vengsarkar.

4: S. M. Gavaskar, R. J. Shastri, G. R. Viswanath.

3: R. Dravid, S. C. Ganguly, V. L. Manjrekar, V. M. Merchant, Nawab of Pataudi, jun., P. R. Umrigar.

2: V. S. Hazare, M. L. Jaisimha, Kapil Dev, B. K. Kunderan, Pankaj Roy.

1: A. B. Agarkar, L. Amarnath, A. A. Baig, D. Dasgupta, F. M. Engineer, Hanumant Singh, V. G. Kambli, S. M. H. Kirmani, V. Mankad, Mushtaq Ali, R. G. Nadkarni, S. M. Patil, D. G. Phadkar, V. Sehwag, N. S. Sidhu, Yashpal Sharma.

Notes: G. A. Gooch's match aggregate of 456 (333 and 123) for England at Lord's in 1990 is the record in Test matches and the only instance of a batsman scoring a triple-hundred and a hundred in the same first-class match. His 333 is the highest innings in any match at Lord's.

M. Azharuddin scored hundreds in each of his first three Tests.

RECORD PARTNERSHIPS FOR EACH WICKET

For England

225 for 1st	G. A. Gooch and M. A. Atherton at Manchester		1990
241 for 2nd	G. Fowler and M. W. Gatting at Madras		1984-85
308 for 3rd	G. A. Gooch and A. J. Lamb at Lord's		1990
266 for 4th	W. R. Hammond and T. S. Worthington at The Oval		1936
254 for 5th†	K. W. R. Fletcher and A. W. Greig at Bombay		1972-73
171 for 6th	I. T. Botham and R. W. Taylor at Bombay		1979-80
125 for 7th	D. W. Randall and P. H. Edmonds at Lord's		1982
168 for 8th	R. Illingworth and P. Lever at Manchester		1971
103 for 9th	C. White and M. J. Hoggard at Nottingham		2002
70 for 10th	P. J. W. Allott and R. G. D. Willis at Lord's		1982

For India

213 for 1st	S. M. Gavaskar and C. P. S. Chauhan at The Oval		1979
192 for 2nd	F. M. Engineer and A. L. Wadekar at Bombay		1972-73
316 for 3rd‡	G. R. Viswanath and Yashpal Sharma at Madras		1981-82
249 for 4th	S. R. Tendulkar and S. C. Ganguly at Leeds		2002
214 for 5th	M. Azharuddin and R. J. Shastri at Calcutta		1984-85
130 for 6th	S. M. H. Kirmani and Kapil Dev at The Oval		1982
235 for 7th†	R. J. Shastri and S. M. H. Kirmani at Bombay		1984-85
128 for 8th	R. J. Shastri and S. M. H. Kirmani at Delhi		1981-82
104 for 9th	R. J. Shastri and Madan Lal at Delhi		1981-82
63 for 10th	A. B. Agarkar and A. Nehra at Lord's		2002

† *Record partnership against all countries.*

‡ *415 runs were added between the fall of the 2nd and 3rd wickets: D. B. Vengsarkar retired hurt when he and Viswanath had added 99 runs.*

TEN WICKETS OR MORE IN A MATCH

For England (7)

10-78 (5-35, 5-43)†	G. O. B. Allen, Lord's	1936
11-145 (7-49, 4-96)†	A. V. Bedser, Lord's	1946
11-93 (4-41, 7-52)	A. V. Bedser, Manchester	1946
13-106 (6-58, 7-48)	I. T. Botham, Bombay	1979-80
11-163 (6-104, 5-59)†	N. A. Foster, Madras	1984-85
10-70 (7-46, 3-24)†	J. K. Lever, Delhi	1976-77
11-153 (7-49, 4-104)	H. Verity, Madras	1933-34

For India (5)

10-177 (6-105, 4-72)	S. A. Durani, Madras	1961-62
10-233 (7-115, 3-118)	A. Kumble, Ahmedabad	2001-02
12-108 (8-55, 4-53)	V. Mankad, Madras	1951-52
10-188 (4-130, 6-58)	Chetan Sharma, Birmingham	1986
12-181 (6-64, 6-117)†	L. Sivaramakrishnan, Bombay	1984-85

† *On first appearance in England–India Tests.*

Note: A. V. Bedser took 11 wickets in a match in each of the first two Tests of his career.

SEVEN WICKETS OR MORE IN AN INNINGS

In addition to those listed above, the following have taken seven wickets or more in an innings:

For England

7-80 G. O. B. Allen, The Oval	1936	8-31 F. S. Trueman, Manchester	1952

For India

7-86 L. Amar Singh, Madras	1933-34	8-79 B. S. Chandrasekhar, Delhi	1972-73

ENGLAND v PAKISTAN

Series notes: In 21 Tests between the sides in Pakistan, the team winning the toss – and the team batting first – have never won... The two are not unrelated: the team winning the toss have batted first in 20 out of 21 in Pakistan... Pakistan have won the last four tosses against England... Only one of the last nine series has been drawn (2001)... Over 80% of the matches in Pakistan have been drawn (17 out of 21), as against 44% in England (17 out of 39)... England lead Pakistan 10–4 when they have lost the toss – but are level at 6–6 when they have won it... Pakistan have not lost a series in England since 1982... England have never lost in five Tests where they have been put in – or in five more where they have put Pakistan in.

			Captains				
Season	*England*		*Pakistan*	*T*	*E*	*P*	*D*
1954	L. Hutton[1]		A. H. Kardar	4	1	1	2
1961-62	E. R. Dexter		Imtiaz Ahmed	3	1	0	2
1962	E. R. Dexter[2]		Javed Burki	5	4	0	1
1967	D. B. Close		Hanif Mohammad	3	2	0	1
1968-69	M. C. Cowdrey		Saeed Ahmed	3	0	0	3
1971	R. Illingworth		Intikhab Alam	3	1	0	2
1972-73	A. R. Lewis		Majid Khan	3	0	0	3
1974	M. H. Denness		Intikhab Alam	3	0	0	3
1977-78	J. M. Brearley[3]		Wasim Bari	3	0	0	3
1978	J. M. Brearley		Wasim Bari	3	2	0	1
1982	R. G. D. Willis[4]		Imran Khan	3	2	1	0
1983-84	R. G. D. Willis[5]		Zaheer Abbas	3	0	1	2
1987	M. W. Gatting		Imran Khan	5	0	1	4
1987-88	M. W. Gatting		Javed Miandad	3	0	1	2
1992	G. A. Gooch		Javed Miandad	5	1	2	2
1996	M. A. Atherton		Wasim Akram	3	0	2	1
2000-01	N. Hussain		Moin Khan	3	1	0	2
2001	N. Hussain[6]		Waqar Younis	2	1	1	0
	In England			39	14	8	17
	In Pakistan			21	2	2	17
	Totals.			60	16	10	34

Notes: The following deputised for the official touring captain or were appointed by the home authority for only a minor proportion of the series:
¹D. S. Sheppard (Second and Third). ²M. C. Cowdrey (Third). ³G. Boycott (Third). ⁴D. I. Gower (Second). ⁵D. I. Gower (Second and Third). ⁶A. J. Stewart (Second).

HIGHEST INNINGS TOTALS

For England in England: 558-6 dec. at Nottingham 1954
in Pakistan: 546-8 dec. at Faisalabad 1983-84

For Pakistan in England: 708 at The Oval 1987
in Pakistan: 569-9 dec. at Hyderabad. 1972-73

LOWEST INNINGS TOTALS

For England in England: 130 at The Oval 1954
in Pakistan: 130 at Lahore. 1987-88

For Pakistan in England: 87 at Lord's 1954
in Pakistan: 158 at Karachi 2000-01

DOUBLE-HUNDREDS

For England (2)

278	D. C. S. Compton at Nottingham	1954	205	E. R. Dexter at Karachi	1961-62

For Pakistan (5)

274	Zaheer Abbas at Birmingham. . .	1971	205	Aamir Sohail at Manchester. . . .	1992
260	Javed Miandad at The Oval	1987	200	Mohsin Khan at Lord's.	1982
240	Zaheer Abbas at The Oval	1974			

INDIVIDUAL HUNDREDS

For England (52)

4: K. F. Barrington, P. H. Parfitt.
3: D. L. Amiss, G. Boycott, M. C. Cowdrey, T. W. Graveney.
2: I. T. Botham, E. R. Dexter, M. W. Gatting, A. J. Stewart, G. P. Thorpe.
1: M. A. Atherton, C. W. J. Athey, B. C. Broad, D. C. S. Compton, J. P. Crawley, B. L. D'Oliveira, K. W. R. Fletcher, G. A. Gooch, N. V. Knight, A. P. E. Knott, B. W. Luckhurst, C. Milburn, G. Pullar, C. T. Radley, D. W. Randall, R. T. Robinson, R. T. Simpson, R. A. Smith, M. E. Trescothick, M. P. Vaughan.

For Pakistan (43)

4: Salim Malik.
3: Asif Iqbal, Hanif Mohammad, Inzamam-ul-Haq, Javed Burki, Mudassar Nazar, Mushtaq Mohammad.
2: Haroon Rashid, Javed Miandad, Mohsin Khan, Yousuf Youhana, Zaheer Abbas.
1: Aamir Sohail, Abdul Razzaq, Alim-ud-Din, Ijaz Ahmed, sen., Imran Khan, Intikhab Alam, Moin Khan, Nasim-ul-Ghani, Sadiq Mohammad, Saeed Anwar, Wasim Raja.

Note: Three batsmen – Majid Khan, Mushtaq Mohammad and D. L. Amiss – were dismissed for 99 at Karachi, 1972-73: the only instance in Test matches.

RECORD PARTNERSHIPS FOR EACH WICKET

For England

198 for 1st	G. Pullar and R. W. Barber at Dacca	1961-62
248 for 2nd	M. C. Cowdrey and E. R. Dexter at The Oval	1962
267 for 3rd	M. P. Vaughan and G. P. Thorpe at Manchester.	2001
188 for 4th	E. R. Dexter and P. H. Parfitt at Karachi.	1961-62
192 for 5th	D. C. S. Compton and T. E. Bailey at Nottingham.	1954
166 for 6th	G. P. Thorpe and C. White at Lahore	2000-01
167 for 7th	D. I. Gower and V. J. Marks at Faisalabad	1983-84
99 for 8th	P. H. Parfitt and D. A. Allen at Leeds	1962
76 for 9th	T. W. Graveney and F. S. Trueman at Lord's	1962
79 for 10th	R. W. Taylor and R. G. D. Willis at Birmingham.	1982

For Pakistan

173 for 1st	Mohsin Khan and Shoaib Mohammad at Lahore	1983-84
291 for 2nd†	Zaheer Abbas and Mushtaq Mohammad at Birmingham	1971
180 for 3rd	Mudassar Nazar and Haroon Rashid at Lahore	1977-78
322 for 4th	Javed Miandad and Salim Malik at Birmingham	1992
197 for 5th	Javed Burki and Nasim-ul-Ghani at Lord's.	1962
145 for 6th	Mushtaq Mohammad and Intikhab Alam at Hyderabad.	1972-73
112 for 7th	Asif Mujtaba and Moin Khan at Leeds	1996
130 for 8th	Hanif Mohammad and Asif Iqbal at Lord's	1967
190 for 9th†	Asif Iqbal and Intikhab Alam at The Oval	1967
62 for 10th	Sarfraz Nawaz and Asif Masood at Leeds	1974

† *Record partnership against all countries.*

TEN WICKETS OR MORE IN A MATCH

For England (2)

11-83 (6-65, 5-18)†	N. G. B. Cook, Karachi	1983-84
13-71 (5-20, 8-51)	D. L. Underwood, Lord's	1974

For Pakistan (6)

10-194 (5-84, 5-110)	Abdul Qadir, Lahore	1983-84
10-211 (7-96, 3-115)	Abdul Qadir, The Oval	1987
13-101 (9-56, 4-45)	Abdul Qadir, Lahore	1987-88
10-186 (5-88, 5-98)	Abdul Qadir, Karachi	1987-88
12-99 (6-53, 6-46)	Fazal Mahmood, The Oval	1954
10-77 (3-37, 7-40)	Imran Khan, Leeds	1987

† *On first appearance in England–Pakistan Tests.*

SEVEN WICKETS OR MORE IN AN INNINGS

In addition to those listed above, the following have taken seven wickets or more in an innings:

For England

8-34	I. T. Botham, Lord's	1978	7-50	C. M. Old, Birmingham	1978
7-66	P. H. Edmonds, Karachi	1977-78	7-56	J. H. Wardle, The Oval.	1954
8-107	N. A. Foster, Leeds	1987			

For Pakistan

7-52	Imran Khan, Birmingham	1982	8-164	Saqlain Mushtaq, Lahore	2000-01

ENGLAND v SRI LANKA

Series notes: M. Muralitharan has taken 69 wickets in this fixture, more than twice the next best on either side (W. P. U. J. C. Vaas, with 33)... D. P. M. D. Jayawardene is the leading scorer in this fixture with 877 runs... In Tests between the sides in Sri Lanka, the home side have won six out of eight tosses – but England have lost both matches when they won the toss... The team batting first have won just three and lost eight of the 15 matches... England scored in excess of 500 in their last three Tests at home to Sri Lanka – but have never managed it in 16 innings overseas... England average 44.8 runs per wicket at home, as opposed to 26.4 away... Sri Lanka, by contrast, average more in England (36.3) than at home (33.5).

Season	England	Captains	Sri Lanka	T	E	SL	D
1981-82	K. W. R. Fletcher		B. Warnapura	1	1	0	0
1984	D. I. Gower		L. R. D. Mendis	1	0	0	1
1988	G. A. Gooch		R. S. Madugalle	1	1	0	0
1991	G. A. Gooch		P. A. de Silva	1	1	0	0
1992-93	A. J. Stewart		A. Ranatunga	1	0	1	0
1998	A. J. Stewart		A. Ranatunga	1	0	1	0
2000-01	N. Hussain		S. T. Jayasuriya	3	2	1	0
2002	N. Hussain		S. T. Jayasuriya	3	2	0	1
2003-04	M. P. Vaughan		H. P. Tillekeratne	3	0	1	2
	In England			7	4	1	2
	In Sri Lanka			8	3	3	2
	Totals......................			15	7	4	4

HIGHEST INNINGS TOTALS

For England in England: 545 at Birmingham 2002
       in Sri Lanka: 387 at Kandy 2000-01

For Sri Lanka in England: 591 at The Oval 1998
       in Sri Lanka: 628-8 dec. at Colombo (SSC) 2003-04

LOWEST INNINGS TOTALS

For England in England: 181 at The Oval 1998
       in Sri Lanka: 148 at Colombo (SSC)..................... 2003-04

For Sri Lanka in England: 162 at Birmingham 2002
       in Sri Lanka: 81 at Colombo (SSC)..................... 2000-01

DOUBLE-HUNDREDS

For Sri Lanka (2)

213 S. T. Jayasuriya at The Oval ... 1998 | 201* M. S. Atapattu at Galle....... 2000-01

Highest score for England: 174 by G. A. Gooch at Lord's, 1991.

INDIVIDUAL HUNDREDS

For England (16)

2: M. A. Butcher, A. J. Stewart, G. P. Thorpe, M. E. Trescothick, M. P. Vaughan.
1: J. P. Crawley, G. A. Gooch, G. A. Hick, N. Hussain, A. J. Lamb, R. A. Smith.

For Sri Lanka (14)

3: D. P. M. D. Jayawardene.
2: M. S. Atapattu, P. A. de Silva.
1: R. P. Arnold, T. M. Dilshan, S. T. Jayasuriya, L. R. D. Mendis, T. T. Samaraweera, S. A. R. Silva, S. Wettimuny.

RECORD PARTNERSHIPS FOR EACH WICKET

For England

168 for 1st	M. E. Trescothick and M. P. Vaughan at Lord's	2002
202 for 2nd	M. E. Trescothick and M. A. Butcher at Birmingham.	2002
167 for 3rd	N. Hussain and G. P. Thorpe at Kandy	2000-01
128 for 4th	G. A. Hick and M. R. Ramprakash at The Oval	1998
92 for 5th	M. A. Butcher and A. J. Stewart at Manchester.	2002
87 for 6th	⎰ A. J. Lamb and R. M. Ellison at Lord's	1984
	⎱ A. J. Stewart and C. White at Kandy	2000-01
	⎰ A. Flintoff and G. J. Batty at Colombo (SSC)	2003-04
63 for 7th	A. J. Stewart and R. C. Russell at Lord's.	1991
102 for 8th	A. J. Stewart and A. F. Giles at Manchester	2002
53 for 9th	M. R. Ramprakash and D. Gough at The Oval	1998
91 for 10th	G. P. Thorpe and M. J. Hoggard at Birmingham	2002

For Sri Lanka

99 for 1st‡	R. S. Mahanama and U. C. Hathurusinghe at Colombo (SSC)	1992-93
92 for 2nd	M. S. Atapattu and K. C. Sangakkara at Galle	2000-01
262 for 3rd†	T. T. Samaraweera and D. P. M. D. Jayawardene at Colombo (SSC) .	2003-04
153 for 4th	D. P. M. D. Jayawardene and T. M. Dilshan at Kandy	2003-04
150 for 5th†	S. Wettimuny and L. R. D. Mendis at Lord's	1984
138 for 6th	S. A. R. Silva and L. R. D. Mendis at Lord's	1984
93 for 7th	K. C. Sangakkara and H. D. P. K. Dharmasena at Kandy	2000-01
53 for 8th	H. D. P. K. Dharmasena and W. P. U. J. C. Vaas at Kandy	2000-01
83 for 9th	H. P. Tillekeratne and M. Muralitharan at Colombo (SSC)	1992-93
64 for 10th	J. R. Ratnayeke and G. F. Labrooy at Lord's	1988

† *Record partnership against all countries.*
‡ *107 runs were scored for Sri Lanka's first wicket at Manchester in 2002, in two partnerships:*
M. S. Atapattu and R. P. Arnold put on 48 before Atapattu retired hurt, then Arnold and K. C. Sangakkara added a further 59.

TEN WICKETS OR MORE IN A MATCH

For Sri Lanka (2)

16-220 (7-155, 9-65)	M. Muralitharan, The Oval	1998
11-93 (7-46, 4-47)	M. Muralitharan, Galle.	2003-04

Note: The best match figures for England are 8-95 (5-28, 3-67) by D. L. Underwood at Colombo (PSS), 1981-82.

SEVEN WICKETS OR MORE IN AN INNINGS

In addition to those listed above, the following has taken seven wickets or more in an innings:

For England

7-70   P. A. J. DeFreitas, Lord's   1991

ENGLAND v ZIMBABWE

Series notes: All three of England's victories have been by an innings... Since scoring 376 in their first innings against England, Zimbabwe have failed to reach 300 in ten attempts... In the two Tests between the sides at Lord's, England average 44.3 runs per wicket and Zimbabwe 14.6... Spin bowlers have taken only 1.75 wickets per Test when the sides have met in England (seven in four matches) – and 12.5 per Test in Zimbabwe (25 in two).

Season	England	*Captains* Zimbabwe	T	E	Z	D
1996-97	M. A. Atherton	A. D. R. Campbell	2	0	0	2
2000	N. Hussain	A. Flower	2	1	0	1
2003	N. Hussain	H. H. Streak	2	2	0	0
	In England		4	3	0	1
	In Zimbabwe		2	0	0	2
	Totals		6	3	0	3

HIGHEST INNINGS TOTALS

For England in England: 472 at Lord's	2003
in Zimbabwe: 406 at Bulawayo.	1996-97
For Zimbabwe in England: 285-4 dec. at Nottingham	2000
in Zimbabwe: 376 at Bulawayo	1996-97

LOWEST INNINGS TOTALS

For England in England: 147 at Nottingham	2000
in Zimbabwe: 156 at Harare	1996-97
For Zimbabwe in England: 83 at Lord's	2000
in Zimbabwe: 215 at Harare	1996-97

HIGHEST INDIVIDUAL INNINGS

For England

137   M. A. Butcher at Lord's   2003

For Zimbabwe

148* M. W. Goodwin at Nottingham .   2000

INDIVIDUAL HUNDREDS

For England (7)

2: A. J. Stewart.
1: M. A. Atherton, M. A. Butcher, J. P. Crawley, G. A. Hick, N. Hussain.

For Zimbabwe (2)

1: A. Flower, M. W. Goodwin.

RECORD PARTNERSHIPS FOR EACH WICKET

For England

121 for 1st	M. A. Atherton and M. R. Ramprakash at Nottingham	2000
137 for 2nd	N. V. Knight and A. J. Stewart at Bulawayo.	1996-97
68 for 3rd	A. J. Stewart and N. Hussain at Bulawayo	1996-97
149 for 4th	G. A. Hick and A. J. Stewart at Lord's.	2000
148 for 5th	N. Hussain and J. P. Crawley at Bulawayo.	1996-97
149 for 6th	A. J. Stewart and A. McGrath at Chester-le-Street	2003
66 for 7th	A. McGrath and A. F. Giles at Lord's	2003
32 for 8th	⎰ C. P. Schofield and A. R. Caddick at Nottingham.	2000
	⎱ A. F. Giles and R. L. Johnson at Chester-le-Street	2003
57 for 9th	A. F. Giles and M. J. Hoggard at Lord's.	2003
28 for 10th	J. P. Crawley and P. C. R. Tufnell at Bulawayo.	1996-97

For Zimbabwe

20 for 1st	D. D. Ebrahim and M. A. Vermeulen at Lord's	2003
127 for 2nd	G. W. Flower and A. D. R. Campbell at Bulawayo	1996-97
129 for 3rd	M. W. Goodwin and N. C. Johnson at Nottingham	2000
122 for 4th	M. W. Goodwin and A. Flower at Nottingham	2000
29 for 5th	A. Flower and A. C. Waller at Bulawayo	1996-97
54 for 6th	S. M. Ervine and T. J. Friend at Chester-le-Street.	2003
79 for 7th	A. Flower and P. A. Strang at Bulawayo	1996-97
41 for 8th	A. Flower and H. H. Streak at Bulawayo	1996-97
51 for 9th	T. J. Friend and R. W. Price at Lord's	2003
31 for 10th	B. C. Strang and M. Mbangwa at Lord's	2000

BEST MATCH BOWLING ANALYSES

For England

7-42 (5-15, 2-27)†	E. S. H. Giddins, Lord's	2000

For Zimbabwe

7-186 (5-123, 2-63)†	P. A. Strang, Bulawayo	1996-97

† *On first appearance in England–Zimbabwe Tests.*

ENGLAND v BANGLADESH

Series notes: England's lowest innings total (295) is higher than Bangladesh's highest (255)... Bangladesh spinners have taken 50% of their side's wickets in this fixture (14 out of 28); England's spinners have managed only 8% (three of 39)... England's average opening partnership is 98.25; Bangladesh's is 8.75.

		Captains					
Season	*England*		*Bangladesh*	*T*	*E*	*B*	*D*
2003-04	M. P. Vaughan		Khaled Mahmud	2	2	0	0

HIGHEST INNINGS TOTALS

For England: 326 at Chittagong	2003-04
For Bangladesh: 255 at Dhaka	2003-04

LOWEST INNINGS TOTALS

For England: 295 at Dhaka 2003-04

For Bangladesh: 138 at Chittagong 2003-04

HIGHEST INDIVIDUAL INNINGS

For England

113   M. E. Trescothick at Dhaka 2003-04

For Bangladesh

58   Habibul Bashar at Dhaka 2003-04

INDIVIDUAL HUNDRED

For England (1)

1: M. E. Trescothick.

HUNDRED PARTNERSHIPS

For England

137 for 1st	M. E. Trescothick and M. P. Vaughan at Dhaka	2003-04
125 for 1st	M. E. Trescothick and M. P. Vaughan at Chittagong	2003-04
138 for 3rd	N. Hussain and G. P. Thorpe at Chittagong	2003-04
116 for 5th	N. Hussain and R. Clarke at Chittagong	2003-04

For Bangladesh

108 for 2nd	Hannan Sarkar and Habibul Bashar at Dhaka	2003-04

BEST MATCH BOWLING ANALYSES

For England

9-79 (5-35, 4-44)†   S. J. Harmison, Dhaka 2003-04

For Bangladesh

5-141 (3-84, 2-57)†   Mohammad Rafique, Dhaka 2003-04

† *On first appearance in England–Bangladesh Tests.*

> " Cricket Australia, having shortened its name from the Australian Cricket Board in June, appeared to have lopped several points off its IQ too."
> Cricket in Australia, page 1402.

AUSTRALIA v SOUTH AFRICA

Series notes: South Africa have not beaten Australia in six series since their return from isolation... Australia have won eight of the nine Tests between the teams at Cape Town... In 35 matches where they have won the toss, Australia have won 22 and lost just three... In 71 Tests between the sides, the team winning the toss have batted first 60 times... S. K. Warne is the only bowler in history to have taken 100 South African Test wickets – he has 101 from 18 Tests at 22.34.

		Captains				
Season	*Australia*	*South Africa*	*T*	*A*	*SA*	*D*
1902-03S	J. Darling	H. M. Taberer[1]	3	2	0	1
1910-11A	C. Hill	P. W. Sherwell	5	4	1	0
1912E	S. E. Gregory	F. Mitchell[2]	3	2	0	1
1921-22S	H. L. Collins	H. W. Taylor	3	1	0	2
1931-32A	W. M. Woodfull	H. B. Cameron	5	5	0	0
1935-36S	V. Y. Richardson	H. F. Wade	5	4	0	1
1949-50S	A. L. Hassett	A. D. Nourse	5	4	0	1
1952-53A	A. L. Hassett	J. E. Cheetham	5	2	2	1
1957-58S	I. D. Craig	C. B. van Ryneveld[3]	5	3	0	2
1963-64A	R. B. Simpson[4]	T. L. Goddard	5	1	1	3
1966-67S	R. B. Simpson	P. L. van der Merwe	5	1	3	1
1969-70S	W. M. Lawry	A. Bacher	4	0	4	0
1993-94A	A. R. Border	K. C. Wessels[5]	3	1	1	1
1993-94S	A. R. Border	K. C. Wessels	3	1	1	1
1996-97S	M. A. Taylor	W. J. Cronje	3	2	1	0
1997-98A	M. A. Taylor	W. J. Cronje	3	1	0	2
2001-02A	S. R. Waugh	S. M. Pollock	3	3	0	0
2001-02S	S. R. Waugh	M. V. Boucher	3	2	1	0
	In South Africa		39	20	10	9
	In Australia		29	17	5	7
	In England		3	2	0	1
	Totals		71	39	15	17

S Played in South Africa.   A Played in Australia.   E Played in England.

Notes: The following deputised for the official touring captain or were appointed by the home authority for only a minor proportion of the series:
[1]J. H. Anderson (Second), E. A. Halliwell (Third). [2]L. J. Tancred (Third). [3]D. J. McGlew (First). [4]R. Benaud (First). [5]W. J. Cronje (Third).

HIGHEST INNINGS TOTALS

For Australia in Australia: 578 at Melbourne.	1910-11
in South Africa: 652-7 dec. at Johannesburg	2001-02
For South Africa in Australia: 595 at Adelaide	1963-64
in South Africa: 622-9 dec. at Durban	1969-70

LOWEST INNINGS TOTALS

For Australia in Australia: 111 at Sydney.	1993-94
in South Africa: 75 at Durban	1949-50
For South Africa in Australia: 36† at Melbourne	1931-32
in South Africa: 85‡ at Johannesburg	1902-03
85‡ at Cape Town	1902-03

† *Scored 45 in the second innings, giving the smallest aggregate of 81 (12 extras) in Test cricket.*
‡ *In successive innings.*

DOUBLE-HUNDREDS

For Australia (7)

299* D. G. Bradman at Adelaide 1931-32
226 D. G. Bradman at Brisbane 1931-32
214* V. T. Trumper at Adelaide 1910-11
214 G. S. Blewett at Johannesburg .. 1996-97

205 R. N. Harvey at Melbourne 1952-53
204* A. C. Gilchrist at Johannesburg . 2001-02
203 H. L. Collins at Johannesburg .. 1921-22

For South Africa (5)

274 R. G. Pollock at Durban 1969-70
231 A. D. Nourse at Johannesburg .. 1935-36
209 R. G. Pollock at Cape Town ... 1966-67

204 G. A. Faulkner at Melbourne ... 1910-11
201 E. J. Barlow at Adelaide 1963-64

INDIVIDUAL HUNDREDS

For Australia (77)

8: R. N. Harvey.

4: D. G. Bradman, M. L. Hayden, M. E. Waugh.

3: W. Bardsley, J. H. Fingleton, A. L. Hassett, C. Hill, D. R. Martyn.

2: W. W. Armstrong, R. Benaud, B. C. Booth, A. C. Gilchrist, C. Kelleway, J. L. Langer, C. G. Macartney, S. J. McCabe, J. Moroney, A. R. Morris, R. T. Ponting, M. A. Taylor, V. T. Trumper, S. R. Waugh.

1: G. S. Blewett, W. A. Brown, J. W. Burke, A. G. Chipperfield, H. L. Collins, J. M. Gregory, W. M. Lawry, S. J. E. Loxton, C. C. McDonald, K. E. Rigg, J. Ryder, R. B. Simpson, K. R. Stackpole, W. M. Woodfull.

For South Africa (42)

5: E. J. Barlow, R. G. Pollock.

3: G. A. Faulkner, D. T. Lindsay.

2: G. Kirsten, D. J. McGlew, A. D. Nourse, B. A. Richards, J. H. Sinclair, J. H. B. Waite, J. W. Zulch.

1: K. C. Bland, W. J. Cronje, W. R. Endean, C. N. Frank, H. H. Gibbs, A. C. Hudson, B. L. Irvine, J. H. Kallis, A. W. Nourse, E. A. B. Rowan, S. J. Snooke, K. G. Viljoen.

RECORD PARTNERSHIPS FOR EACH WICKET

For Australia

233 for 1st	J. H. Fingleton and W. A. Brown at Cape Town	1935-36
275 for 2nd	C. C. McDonald and A. L. Hassett at Adelaide	1952-53
242 for 3rd	C. Kelleway and W. Bardsley at Lord's	1912
169 for 4th	M. A. Taylor and M. E. Waugh at Melbourne	1993-94
385 for 5th	S. R. Waugh and G. S. Blewett at Johannesburg	1996-97
317 for 6th	D. R. Martyn and A. C. Gilchrist at Johannesburg	2001-02
160 for 7th	R. Benaud and G. D. McKenzie at Sydney	1963-64
83 for 8th	A. G. Chipperfield and C. V. Grimmett at Durban	1935-36
78 for 9th	⎰ D. G. Bradman and W. J. O'Reilly at Adelaide	1931-32
	⎱ K. D. Mackay and I. Meckiff at Johannesburg	1957-58
82 for 10th	V. S. Ransford and W. J. Whitty at Melbourne	1910-11

For South Africa

176 for 1st	D. J. McGlew and T. L. Goddard at Johannesburg	....	1957-58
173 for 2nd	L. J. Tancred and C. B. Llewellyn at Johannesburg	....	1902-03
341 for 3rd	E. J. Barlow and R. G. Pollock at Adelaide	....	1963-64
206 for 4th	C. N. Frank and A. W. Nourse at Johannesburg	....	1921-22
129 for 5th	J. H. B. Waite and W. R. Endean at Johannesburg	....	1957-58
200 for 6th†	R. G. Pollock and H. R. Lance at Durban	....	1969-70
221 for 7th	D. T. Lindsay and P. L. van der Merwe at Johannesburg	....	1966-67
124 for 8th	A. W. Nourse and E. A. Halliwell at Johannesburg	....	1902-03
85 for 9th	R. G. Pollock and P. M. Pollock at Cape Town	....	1966-67
74 for 10th	B. M. McMillan and P. L. Symcox at Adelaide	....	1997-98

† *Record partnership against all countries.*

TEN WICKETS OR MORE IN A MATCH

For Australia (7)

14-199 (7-116, 7-83)	C. V. Grimmett, Adelaide.	....	1931-32
10-88 (5-32, 5-56)	C. V. Grimmett, Cape Town	....	1935-36
10-110 (3-70, 7-40)	C. V. Grimmett, Johannesburg	....	1935-36
13-173 (7-100, 6-73)	C. V. Grimmett, Durban	....	1935-36
11-24 (5-6, 6-18)	H. Ironmonger, Melbourne.	....	1931-32
12-128 (7-56, 5-72)	S. K. Warne, Sydney	....	1993-94
11-109 (5-75, 6-34)	S. K. Warne, Sydney		1997-98

For South Africa (3)

10-123 (4-80, 6-43)	P. S. de Villiers, Sydney	....	1993-94
10-116 (5-43, 5-73)	C. B. Llewellyn, Johannesburg	....	1902-03
13-165 (6-84, 7-81)	H. J. Tayfield, Melbourne	....	1952-53

Note: C. V. Grimmett took ten wickets or more in three consecutive matches in 1935-36.

SEVEN WICKETS OR MORE IN AN INNINGS

In addition to those listed above, the following have taken seven wickets or more in an innings:

For Australia

7-34 J. V. Saunders, Johannesburg . . . 1902-03

For South Africa

7-91 J. T. Partridge, Sydney 1963-64	7-23 H. J. Tayfield, Durban 1949-50
7-87 S. M. Pollock, Adelaide 1997-98	

AUSTRALIA v WEST INDIES

Series notes: There has not been a draw between the sides in the last 20 Tests... West Indies' last seven victories over Australia have come when they have fielded first... B. C. Lara is the only non-Englishman in the top ten Test run-scorers against Australia – he lies eighth with 2,470... West Indies have lost eight of the last ten matches in Australia; before that they lost only four in 21... G. D. McGrath needs three wickets to become the first bowler from any country to take 100 in Tests against West Indies... Of the top 18 bowling analyses in this fixture, 16 were recorded in Australia... Australia have won six of the last eight tosses in the West Indies.

		Captains						
Season	*Australia*		*West Indies*	*T*	*A*	*WI*	*T*	*D*
1930-31*A*	W. M. Woodfull		G. C. Grant	5	4	1	0	0
1951-52*A*	A. L. Hassett[1]		J. D. C. Goddard[2]	5	4	1	0	0
1954-55*W*	I. W. Johnson		D. St E. Atkinson[3]	5	3	0	0	2

THE FRANK WORRELL TROPHY

		Captains							
Season	*Australia*		*West Indies*	*T*	*A*	*WI*	*T*	*D*	*Held by*
1960-61*A*	R. Benaud		F. M. M. Worrell	5	2	1	1	1	A
1964-65*W*	R. B. Simpson		G. S. Sobers	5	1	2	0	2	WI
1968-69*A*	W. M. Lawry		G. S. Sobers	5	3	1	0	1	A
1972-73*W*	I. M. Chappell		R. B. Kanhai	5	2	0	0	3	A
1975-76*A*	G. S. Chappell		C. H. Lloyd	6	5	1	0	0	A
1977-78*W*	R. B. Simpson		A. I. Kallicharran[4]	5	1	3	0	1	WI
1979-80*A*	G. S. Chappell		C. H. Lloyd[5]	3	0	2	0	1	WI
1981-82*A*	G. S. Chappell		C. H. Lloyd	3	1	1	0	1	WI
1983-84*W*	K. J. Hughes		C. H. Lloyd[6]	5	0	3	0	2	WI
1984-85*A*	A. R. Border[7]		C. H. Lloyd	5	1	3	0	1	WI
1988-89*A*	A. R. Border		I. V. A. Richards	5	1	3	0	1	WI
1990-91*W*	A. R. Border		I. V. A. Richards	5	1	2	0	2	WI
1992-93*A*	A. R. Border		R. B. Richardson	5	1	2	0	2	WI
1994-95*W*	M. A. Taylor		R. B. Richardson	4	2	1	0	1	A
1996-97*A*	M. A. Taylor		C. A. Walsh	5	3	2	0	0	A
1998-99*W*	S. R. Waugh		B. C. Lara	4	2	2	0	0	A
2000-01*A*	S. R. Waugh[8]		J. C. Adams	5	5	0	0	0	A
2002-03*W*	S. R. Waugh		B. C. Lara	4	3	1	0	0	A
In Australia				57	30	18	1	8	
In West Indies				42	15	14	0	13	
Totals				99	45	32	1	21	

A Played in Australia.   W Played in West Indies.

Notes: The following deputised for the official touring captain or were appointed by the home authority for only a minor proportion of the series:
[1]A. R. Morris (Third). [2]J. B. Stollmeyer (Fifth). [3]J. B. Stollmeyer (Second and Third). [4]C. H. Lloyd (First and Second). [5]D. L. Murray (First). [6]I. V. A. Richards (Second). [7]K. J. Hughes (First and Second). [8]A. C. Gilchrist (Third).

HIGHEST INNINGS TOTALS

For Australia in Australia: 619 at Sydney	1968-69
in West Indies: 758-8 dec. at Kingston	1954-55
For West Indies in Australia: 616 at Adelaide	1968-69
in West Indies: 573 at Bridgetown	1964-65

LOWEST INNINGS TOTALS

For Australia in Australia: 76 at Perth	1984-85
in West Indies: 90 at Port-of-Spain	1977-78
For West Indies in Australia: 78 at Sydney	1951-52
in West Indies: 51 at Port-of-Spain	1998-99

DOUBLE-HUNDREDS

For Australia (9)

242	K. D. Walters at Sydney 1968-69	205	W. M. Lawry at Melbourne 1968-69
223	D. G. Bradman at Brisbane 1930-31	204	R. N. Harvey at Kingston 1954-55
216	D. M. Jones at Adelaide 1988-89	201	R. B. Simpson at Bridgetown . . . 1964-65
210	W. M. Lawry at Bridgetown. . . . 1964-65	200	S. R. Waugh at Kingston. 1994-95
206	R. T. Ponting at Port-of-Spain . . 2002-03		

For West Indies (6)

277	B. C. Lara at Sydney 1992-93	213	B. C. Lara at Kingston 1998-99
226	C. G. Greenidge at Bridgetown. . 1990-91	208	I. V. A. Richards at Melbourne . . 1984-85
219	D. St E. Atkinson at Bridgetown. 1954-55	201	S. M. Nurse at Bridgetown 1964-65

INDIVIDUAL HUNDREDS

For Australia (96)

7: S. R. Waugh.
6: K. D. Walters.
5: G. S. Chappell, I. M. Chappell.
4: W. M. Lawry, K. R. Miller, R. T. Ponting, I. R. Redpath, M. E. Waugh.
3: D. C. Boon, A. R. Border, R. N. Harvey, M. L. Hayden, J. L. Langer.
2: D. G. Bradman, R. M. Cowper, A. L. Hassett, K. J. Hughes, C. C. McDonald, W. H. Ponsford, G. M. Wood.
1: R. G. Archer, R. Benaud, B. C. Booth, G. J. Cosier, J. Dyson, A. C. Gilchrist, I. A. Healy, A. M. J. Hilditch, D. M. Jones, A. F. Kippax, D. S. Lehmann, R. R. Lindwall, R. B. McCosker, A. R. Morris, N. C. O'Neill, W. B. Phillips, C. S. Serjeant, R. B. Simpson, M. J. Slater, K. R. Stackpole, M. A. Taylor, P. M. Toohey, A. Turner, K. C. Wessels.

For West Indies (93)

9: R. B. Richardson.
8: B. C. Lara.
6: H. A. Gomes, C. H. Lloyd.
5: D. L. Haynes, R. B. Kanhai, I. V. A. Richards, C. L. Walcott.
4: C. G. Greenidge, A. I. Kallicharran, G. S. Sobers.
3: B. F. Butcher.
2: S. L. Campbell, S. Chanderpaul, P. J. L. Dujon, D. Ganga, G. A. Headley, S. M. Nurse.
1: F. C. M. Alexander, K. L. T. Arthurton, D. St E. Atkinson, C. C. Depeiza, M. L. C. Foster, R. C. Fredericks, C. L. Hooper, C. C. Hunte, F. R. Martin, L. G. Rowe, R. R. Sarwan, P. V. Simmons, O. G. Smith, J. B. Stollmeyer, E. D. Weekes, A. B. Williams, F. M. M. Worrell.

Note: F. C. M. Alexander and C. C. Depeiza scored the only hundreds of their first-class careers in a Test match.

RECORD PARTNERSHIPS FOR EACH WICKET

For Australia

382 for 1st†	W. M. Lawry and R. B. Simpson at Bridgetown	1964-65
298 for 2nd	W. M. Lawry and I. M. Chappell at Melbourne	1968-69
315 for 3rd†	R. T. Ponting and D. S. Lehmann at Port-of-Spain.	2002-03
336 for 4th	W. M. Lawry and K. D. Walters at Sydney	1968-69
281 for 5th	S. R. Waugh and R. T. Ponting at Bridgetown	1998-99
206 for 6th	K. R. Miller and R. G. Archer at Bridgetown	1954-55
134 for 7th	A. K. Davidson and R. Benaud at Brisbane	1960-61
137 for 8th	R. Benaud and I. W. Johnson at Kingston	1954-55
114 for 9th	D. M. Jones and M. G. Hughes at Adelaide	1988-89
97 for 10th	T. G. Hogan and R. M. Hogg at Georgetown	1983-84

For West Indies

250*	for 1st	C. G. Greenidge and D. L. Haynes at Georgetown	....	1983-84
297	for 2nd	D. L. Haynes and R. B. Richardson at Georgetown	....	1990-91
308	for 3rd	R. B. Richardson and I. V. A. Richards at St John's	....	1983-84
198	for 4th	L. G. Rowe and A. I. Kallicharran at Brisbane	....	1975-76
322	for 5th†‡	B. C. Lara and J. C. Adams at Kingston	....	1998-99
165	for 6th	R. B. Kanhai and D. L. Murray at Bridgetown	....	1972-73
347	for 7th†	D. St E. Atkinson and C. C. Depeiza at Bridgetown	....	1954-55
87	for 8th	P. J. L. Dujon and C. E. L. Ambrose at Port-of-Spain	....	1990-91
122	for 9th	D. A. J. Holford and J. L. Hendriks at Adelaide	....	1968-69
56	for 10th	J. Garner and C. E. H. Croft at Brisbane	....	1979-80

† *Record partnership against all countries.*

‡ *344 runs were added between the fall of the 4th and 5th wickets: P. T. Collins retired hurt when he and Lara had added 22 runs.*

TEN WICKETS OR MORE IN A MATCH

For Australia (15)

10-113 (4-31, 6-82)	M. G. Bevan, Adelaide	....	1996-97
11-96 (7-46, 4-50)	A. R. Border, Sydney	....	1988-89
11-222 (5-135, 6-87)†	A. K. Davidson, Brisbane	....	1960-61
11-183 (7-87, 4-96)†	C. V. Grimmett, Adelaide	....	1930-31
10-115 (6-72, 4-43)	N. J. N. Hawke, Georgetown	....	1964-65
10-144 (6-54, 4-90)	R. G. Holland, Sydney	....	1984-85
13-217 (5-130, 8-87)	M. G. Hughes, Perth	....	1988-89
11-79 (7-23, 4-56)	H. Ironmonger, Melbourne	....	1930-31
11-181 (8-112, 3-69)	G. F. Lawson, Adelaide	....	1984-85
10-127 (7-83, 3-44)	D. K. Lillee, Melbourne	....	1981-82
10-78 (5-50, 5-28)	G. D. McGrath, Port-of-Spain	....	1998-99
10-27 (6-17, 4-10)	G. D. McGrath, Brisbane	....	2000-01
10-159 (8-71, 2-88)	G. D. McKenzie, Melbourne	....	1968-69
10-113 (5-81, 5-32)	C. R. Miller, Adelaide	....	2000-01
10-185 (3-87, 7-98)	B. Yardley, Sydney	....	1981-82

For West Indies (4)

10-120 (6-74, 4-46)	C. E. L. Ambrose, Adelaide	....	1992-93
10-113 (7-55, 3-58)	G. E. Gomez, Sydney	....	1951-52
11-107 (5-45, 6-62)	M. A. Holding, Melbourne	....	1981-82
10-107 (5-69, 5-38)	M. D. Marshall, Adelaide	....	1984-85

† *On first appearance in Australia–West Indies Tests.*

SEVEN WICKETS OR MORE IN AN INNINGS

In addition to those listed above, the following have taken seven wickets or more in an innings:

For Australia

7-44	I. W. Johnson, Georgetown	1954-55	7-52	S. K. Warne, Melbourne	1992-93
7-104	S. C. G. MacGill, Sydney	2000-01	7-89	M. R. Whitney, Adelaide	1988-89

For West Indies

7-25	C. E. L. Ambrose, Perth	1992-93	7-54	A. M. E. Roberts, Perth	1975-76
7-78	J. J. C. Lawson, St John's	2002-03			

AUSTRALIA v NEW ZEALAND

Series notes: Pending the series in March 2005, New Zealand have never beaten Australia in 17 Tests when they have batted first... The team winning the toss have fielded in 60% of matches between the sides... They have never played more than a three-match series... Only one of the 27 victories has been in a losing series... In 24 Tests at home, Australia average 42.4 runs per wicket and New Zealand 27.9... In three Tests at Hobart, Australia average 63.0 and New Zealand 24.7 – but Australia have won only once... Eight of the last 17 innings in this fixture have been declared... In the last 12 Tests between the sides in Australia, only 19 of a possible 48 innings have been completed... In the last five series, Australia are unbeaten and have won nine out of 14 Tests... In the same period, New Zealand have won nine out of 14 tosses... New Zealand bowlers have taken eight of the top ten analyses in this fixture... S. K. Warne holds the record for Test wickets against New Zealand (86 at 24.84).

Season	Australia	*Captains* New Zealand	T	A	NZ	D
1945-46*N*	W. A. Brown	W. A. Hadlee	1	1	0	0
1973-74*A*	I. M. Chappell	B. E. Congdon	3	2	0	1
1973-74*N*	I. M. Chappell	B. E. Congdon	3	1	1	1
1976-77*N*	G. S. Chappell	G. M. Turner	2	1	0	1
1980-81*A*	G. S. Chappell	G. P. Howarth[1]	3	2	0	1
1981-82*N*	G. S. Chappell	G. P. Howarth	3	1	1	1

TRANS-TASMAN TROPHY

Season	Australia	*Captains* New Zealand	T	A	NZ	D	Held by
1985-86*A*	A. R. Border	J. V. Coney	3	1	2	0	NZ
1985-86*N*	A. R. Border	J. V. Coney	3	0	1	2	NZ
1987-88*A*	A. R. Border	J. J. Crowe	3	1	0	2	A
1989-90*A*	A. R. Border	J. G. Wright	1	0	0	1	A
1989-90*N*	A. R. Border	J. G. Wright	1	0	1	0	NZ
1992-93*N*	A. R. Border	M. D. Crowe	3	1	1	1	NZ
1993-94*A*	A. R. Border	M. D. Crowe[2]	3	2	0	1	A
1997-98*A*	M. A. Taylor	S. P. Fleming	3	2	0	1	A
1999-2000*N*	S. R. Waugh	S. P. Fleming	3	3	0	0	A
2001-02*A*	S. R. Waugh	S. P. Fleming	3	0	0	3	A
2004-05*A*	R. T. Ponting	S. P. Fleming	2	2	0	0	A
In Australia			24	12	2	10	
In New Zealand			19	8	5	6	
Totals			43	20	7	16	

A Played in Australia. N Played in New Zealand.

Notes: The following deputised for the official touring captain: [1]M. G. Burgess (Second). [2]K. R. Rutherford (Second and Third).

HIGHEST INNINGS TOTALS

For Australia in Australia: 607-6 dec. at Brisbane	1993-94
in New Zealand: 552 at Christchurch	1976-77
For New Zealand in Australia: 553-7 dec. at Brisbane	1985-86
in New Zealand: 484 at Wellington	1973-74

LOWEST INNINGS TOTALS

For Australia in Australia: 162 at Sydney.   1973-74
            in New Zealand: 103 at Auckland   1985-86

For New Zealand in Australia: 76 at Brisbane.   2004-05
            in New Zealand: 42 at Wellington   1945-46

DOUBLE-HUNDREDS

For Australia (5)

250	K. D. Walters at Christchurch. . . 1976-77	205	A. R. Border at Adelaide. 1987-88
247*	G. S. Chappell at Wellington . . . 1973-74	200	D. C. Boon at Perth 1989-90
215	J. L. Langer at Adelaide 2004-05		

Highest score for New Zealand: 188 by M. D. Crowe at Brisbane, 1985-86.

INDIVIDUAL HUNDREDS

For Australia (43)

5: A. R. Border.
4: J. L. Langer.
3: D. C. Boon, G. S. Chappell, K. D. Walters.
2: I. M. Chappell, A. C. Gilchrist, G. R. J. Matthews, M. J. Slater, M. A. Taylor, S. R. Waugh, G. M. Wood.
1: M. J. Clarke, M. T. G. Elliott, G. J. Gilmour, M. L. Hayden, I. A. Healy, G. R. Marsh, R. W. Marsh, R. T. Ponting, I. R. Redpath, K. R. Stackpole, M. E. Waugh.

For New Zealand (26)

3: M. D. Crowe.
2: B. E. Congdon, A. H. Jones, G. M. Turner, J. G. Wright.
1: N. J. Astle, C. L. Cairns, J. V. Coney, B. A. Edgar, S. P. Fleming, M. J. Greatbatch, B. F. Hastings, M. J. Horne, J. F. M. Morrison, J. D. P. Oram, J. M. Parker, A. C. Parore, J. F. Reid, K. R. Rutherford, L. Vincent.

Note: G. S. and I. M. Chappell each hit two hundreds at Wellington in 1973-74, the only instance of two batsmen on the same side scoring twin hundreds in the same Test.

RECORD PARTNERSHIPS FOR EACH WICKET

For Australia

224 for 1st	J. L. Langer and M. L. Hayden at Brisbane	2001-02
235 for 2nd	M. J. Slater and D. C. Boon at Hobart.	1993-94
264 for 3rd	I. M. Chappell and G. S. Chappell at Wellington	1973-74
184 for 4th	J. L. Langer and D. S. Lehmann at Adelaide.	2004-05
213 for 5th	G. M. Ritchie and G. R. J. Matthews at Wellington	1985-86
216 for 6th	M. J. Clarke and A. C. Gilchrist at Brisbane.	2004-05
217 for 7th†	K. D. Walters and G. J. Gilmour at Christchurch	1976-77
135 for 8th	A. C. Gilchrist and B. Lee at Brisbane	2001-02
69 for 9th	I. A. Healy and C. J. McDermott at Perth.	1993-94
114 for 10th	J. N. Gillespie and G. D. McGrath at Brisbane	2004-05

Win limited-edition Wisdens

Every year since 1995 *Wisden* has produced a de-luxe leatherbound version of the Almanack in a limited edition of 150 copies. Most owners of *Wisden* limited editions have enjoyed building a rare collection of these beautiful hand-bound books. The price of the 2005 limited edition is £235.

To have a chance of winning a run of three limited-edition Almanacks, fill in this form and post it before December 31, 2005 to the address shown. The answer to the competition question can easily be found in this year's *Wisden*. The first correct entry drawn will win the 2004, 2005 and 2006 limited editions of *Wisden*. The next ten correct entries will each win a year's subscription to *The Wisden Cricketer*.

Only one entry per person, please. The names of the winners will be announced in *Wisden* 2006.

Entry form
Q: Who are the current holders of the Wisden Trophy?

A: _____

Mr/Mrs/Ms/Title: _____

Name: _____

Address: _____

_____

Postcode: _____

Post this form before December 31, 2005, to:
Wisden Competition, SKS, P.O. Box 230, Plymouth PL1 2ZR.

☐ Please tick this box if you do not wish your name to be included on any mailing lists that may be passed to other companies.

the**wisden** cricketer

the complete cricket magazine

MARCH 2005
VOL. 2 NO. 6 £3.40

India v Pakistan
Rahul Dravid and Inzamam-ul-Haq
On rivalries and leadership

EXCLUSIVE INTERVIEW

MICHAEL VAUGHAN

"There's only one team under maximum pressure – and that's Australia"

+Nasser Hussain's verdict

under **21**

YOUTH SPECIAL
The world's top talents revealed

Sex, drugs, rock'n'roll
England's infamous NZ tour of '84

Women's Hour
Why England can lift the World Cup

the complete cricket magazine

For New Zealand

111	for 1st	M. J. Greatbatch and J. G. Wright at Wellington	1992-93
132	for 2nd	M. J. Horne and A. C. Parore at Hobart	1997-98
224	for 3rd	J. F. Reid and M. D. Crowe at Brisbane	1985-86
229	for 4th	B. E. Congdon and B. F. Hastings at Wellington	1973-74
97	for 5th	S. P. Fleming and C. D. McMillan at Hobart	2001-02
110	for 6th	S. P. Fleming and C. L. Cairns at Wellington	1999-2000
132*	for 7th	J. V. Coney and R. J. Hadlee at Wellington	1985-86
253	for 8th†	N. J. Astle and A. C. Parore at Perth	2001-02
73	for 9th	H. J. Howarth and D. R. Hadlee at Christchurch	1976-77
124	for 10th	J. G. Bracewell and S. L. Boock at Sydney	1985-86

† *Record partnership against all countries.*

TEN WICKETS OR MORE IN A MATCH

For Australia (2)

10-174 (6-106, 4-68)	R. G. Holland, Sydney	1985-86
11-123 (5-51, 6-72)	D. K. Lillee, Auckland	1976-77

For New Zealand (5)

10-106 (4-74, 6-32)	J. G. Bracewell, Auckland	1985-86
15-123 (9-52, 6-71)	R. J. Hadlee, Brisbane	1985-86
11-155 (5-65, 6-90)	R. J. Hadlee, Perth	1985-86
10-176 (5-109, 5-67)	R. J. Hadlee, Melbourne	1987-88
12-149 (5-62, 7-87)	D. L. Vettori, Auckland	1999-2000

SEVEN WICKETS OR MORE IN AN INNINGS

In addition to those listed above, the following have taken seven wickets or more in an innings:

For New Zealand

7-116 R. J. Hadlee, Christchurch . . . . . 1985-86 | 7-89 D. K. Morrison, Wellington 1992-93

AUSTRALIA v INDIA

Series notes: India have never won a series in Australia, and have won only one Test there since 1980-81... India have never won in ten Tests where they have put Australia in... R. T. Ponting averages 108.10 in seven Tests at home to India but only 12.28 in eight Tests away... S. R. Tendulkar is the top-scorer in this fixture with 1,859 runs, and needs 141 runs to become the second Indian (after S. M. Gavaskar) to score 2,000 runs against one country... None of the last 15 innings has reached 400... The six highest individual scores between the sides have all been scored since the turn of the century.

Captains

Season	Australia	India	T	A	I	T	D
1947-48*A*	D. G. Bradman	L. Amarnath	5	4	0	0	1
1956-57*I*	I. W. Johnson[1]	P. R. Umrigar	3	2	0	0	1
1959-60*I*	R. Benaud	G. S. Ramchand	5	2	1	0	2
1964-65*I*	R. B. Simpson	Nawab of Pataudi jun.	3	1	1	0	1
1967-68*A*	R. B. Simpson[2]	Nawab of Pataudi jun.[3]	4	4	0	0	0
1969-70*I*	W. M. Lawry	Nawab of Pataudi jun.	5	3	1	0	1
1977-78*A*	R. B. Simpson	B. S. Bedi	5	3	2	0	0
1979-80*I*	K. J. Hughes	S. M. Gavaskar	6	0	2	0	4
1980-81*A*	G. S. Chappell	S. M. Gavaskar	3	1	1	0	1
1985-86*A*	A. R. Border	Kapil Dev	3	0	0	0	3
1986-87*I*	A. R. Border	Kapil Dev	3	0	0	1	2
1991-92*A*	A. R. Border	M. Azharuddin	5	4	0	0	1

THE BORDER-GAVASKAR TROPHY

Season	Australia	Captains	India	T	A	I	T	D	Held by
1996-97*I*	M. A. Taylor		S. R. Tendulkar	1	0	1	0	0	I
1997-98*I*	M. A. Taylor		M. Azharuddin	3	1	2	0	0	I
1999-2000*A*	S. R. Waugh		S. R. Tendulkar	3	3	0	0	0	A
2000-01*I*	S. R. Waugh		S. C. Ganguly	3	1	2	0	0	I
2003-04*A*	S. R. Waugh		S. C. Ganguly	4	1	1	0	2	I
2004-05*I*	R. T. Ponting[4]		S. C. Ganguly[5]	4	2	1	0	1	A

	T	A	I	T	D
In Australia	32	20	4	0	8
In India	36	12	11	1	12
Totals	68	32	15	1	20

A Played in Australia. I Played in India.

Notes: The following deputised for the official touring captain or were appointed by the home authority for only a minor proportion of the series:
[1]R. R. Lindwall (Second). [2]W. M. Lawry (Third and Fourth). [3]C. G. Borde (First). [4]A. C. Gilchrist (First, Second and Third). [5]R. Dravid (Third and Fourth).

HIGHEST INNINGS TOTALS

For Australia in Australia: 674 at Adelaide	1947-48
in India: 574-7 dec. at Madras	1986-87
For India in Australia: 705-7 dec. at Sydney	2003-04
in India: 657-7 dec. at Kolkata	2000-01

LOWEST INNINGS TOTALS

For Australia in Australia: 83 at Melbourne	1980-81
in India: 93 at Mumbai	2004-05
For India in Australia: 58 at Brisbane	1947-48
in India: 104 in Mumbai	2004-05

DOUBLE-HUNDREDS

For Australia (8)

257	R. T. Ponting at Melbourne . .	2003-04	210	D. M. Jones at Madras	1986-87
242	R. T. Ponting at Adelaide . . .	2003-04	204	G. S. Chappell at Sydney	1980-81
223	J. L. Langer at Sydney	1999-2000	203	M. L. Hayden at Chennai	2000-01
213	K. J. Hughes at Adelaide . . .	1980-81	201	D. G. Bradman at Adelaide . .	1947-48

For India (4)

281	V. V. S. Laxman at Kolkata	2000-01	233	R. Dravid at Adelaide	2003-04
241*	S. R. Tendulkar at Sydney	2003-04	206	R. J. Shastri at Sydney	1991-92

INDIVIDUAL HUNDREDS

For Australia (71)

6: D. C. Boon.
4: A. R. Border, D. G. Bradman, R. N. Harvey, R. T. Ponting, R. B. Simpson.
3: M. L. Hayden, J. L. Langer.
2: I. M. Chappell, R. M. Cowper, A. C. Gilchrist, K. J. Hughes, D. M. Jones, D. R. Martyn, N. C. O'Neill, M. A. Taylor, S. R. Waugh, G. N. Yallop.

1: S. G. Barnes, J. W. Burke, G. S. Chappell, M. J. Clarke, L. E. Favell, A. L. Hassett, S. M. Katich, W. M. Lawry, A. L. Mann, G. R. Marsh, G. R. J. Matthews, T. M. Moody, A. R. Morris, G. M. Ritchie, A. P. Sheahan, K. R. Stackpole, K. D. Walters, M. E. Waugh, G. M. Wood.

For India (51)

8: S. M. Gavaskar.
7: S. R. Tendulkar.
4: V. V. S. Laxman, G. R. Viswanath.
2: M. Amarnath, M. Azharuddin, R. Dravid, V. S. Hazare, V. Mankad, V. Sehwag, R. J. Shastri, D. B. Vengsarkar.
1: N. J. Contractor, S. C. Ganguly, M. L. Jaisimha, Kapil Dev, S. M. H. Kirmani, N. R. Mongia, Nawab of Pataudi, jun., S. M. Patil, D. G. Phadkar, G. S. Ramchand, K. Srikkanth, Yashpal Sharma.

RECORD PARTNERSHIPS FOR EACH WICKET

For Australia

217	for 1st	D. C. Boon and G. R. Marsh at Sydney.	1985-86
236	for 2nd	S. G. Barnes and D. G. Bradman at Adelaide	1947-48
222	for 3rd	A. R. Border and K. J. Hughes at Madras	1979-80
178	for 4th	D. M. Jones and A. R. Border at Madras	1986-87
239	for 5th	S. R. Waugh and R. T. Ponting at Adelaide.	1999-2000
197	for 6th	M. L. Hayden and A. C. Gilchrist at Mumbai	2000-01
108	for 7th	S. R. Waugh and S. K. Warne at Adelaide	1999-2000
117	for 8th	S. M. Katich and J. N. Gillespie at Sydney.	2003-04
133	for 9th	S. R. Waugh and J. N. Gillespie at Kolkata.	2000-01
77	for 10th	A. R. Border and D. R. Gilbert at Melbourne	1985-86

For India

192	for 1st	S. M. Gavaskar and C. P. S. Chauhan at Bombay.	1979-80
224	for 2nd	S. M. Gavaskar and M. Amarnath at Sydney.	1985-86
159	for 3rd	S. M. Gavaskar and G. R. Viswanath at Delhi.	1979-80
353	for 4th†	S. R. Tendulkar and V. V. S. Laxman at Sydney.	2003-04
376	for 5th†	V. V. S. Laxman and R. Dravid at Kolkata	2000-01
298*	for 6th†	D. B. Vengsarkar and R. J. Shastri at Bombay.	1986-87
132	for 7th	V. S. Hazare and H. R. Adhikari at Adelaide.	1947-48
127	for 8th	S. M. H. Kirmani and K. D. Ghavri at Bombay.	1979-80
89	for 9th	I. K. Pathan and Harbhajan Singh at Bangalore.	2004-05
94	for 10th	S. M. Gavaskar and N. S. Yadav at Adelaide.	1985-86

† *Record partnership against all countries.*

TEN WICKETS OR MORE IN A MATCH

For Australia (12)

11-105 (6-52, 5-53)	R. Benaud, Calcutta	1956-57
12-124 (5-31, 7-93)	A. K. Davidson, Kanpur.	1959-60
12-166 (5-99, 7-67)	G. Dymock, Kanpur.	1979-80
10-168 (5-76, 5-92)	C. J. McDermott, Adelaide	1991-92
10-103 (5-48, 5-55)	G. D. McGrath, Sydney	1999-2000
10-91 (6-58, 4-33)†	G. D. McKenzie, Madras	1964-65
10-151 (7-66, 3-85)	G. D. McKenzie, Melbourne	1967-68
10-144 (5-91, 5-53)	A. A. Mallett, Madras	1969-70
10-249 (5-103, 5-146)	G. R. J. Matthews, Madras	1986-87
12-126 (6-66, 6-60)	B. A. Reid, Melbourne	1991 92
11-31 (5-2, 6-29)†	E. R. H. Toshack, Brisbane	1947-48
11-95 (4-68, 7-27)	M. R. Whitney, Perth.	1991-92

For India (11)

10-194 (5-89, 5-105)	B. S. Bedi, Perth	1977-78
12-104 (6-52, 6-52)	B. S. Chandrasekhar, Melbourne	1977-78
10-130 (7-49, 3-81)	Ghulam Ahmed, Calcutta	1956-57
13-196 (7-123, 6-73)	Harbhajan Singh, Kolkata	2000-01
15-217 (7-133, 8-84)	Harbhajan Singh, Chennai	2000-01
11-224 (5-146, 6-78)	Harbhajan Singh, Bangalore	2004-05
12-279 (8-141, 4-138)	A. Kumble, Sydney	2003-04
13-181 (7-48, 6-133)	A. Kumble, Chennai	2004-05
11-122 (5-31, 6-91)	R. G. Nadkarni, Madras	1964-65
14-124 (9-69, 5-55)	J. M. Patel, Kanpur	1959-60
10-174 (4-100, 6-74)	E. A. S. Prasanna, Madras	1969-70

† *On first appearance in Australia–India Tests.*

SEVEN WICKETS OR MORE IN AN INNINGS

In addition to those listed above, the following have taken seven wickets or more in an innings:

For Australia

7-72 R. Benaud, Madras	1956-57	7-38 R. R. Lindwall, Adelaide	1947-48
7-143 J. D. Higgs, Madras	1979-80	7-43 R. R. Lindwall, Madras	1956-57

For India

7-98 B. S. Bedi, Calcutta	1969-70	8-106 Kapil Dev, Adelaide	1985-86

AUSTRALIA v PAKISTAN

Series notes: Pakistan have lost their last nine Tests against Australia, three by an innings, two of those by an innings and 20 runs, and one by 491 runs... Australia have won 62% of Tests between the sides in Australia, but only 15% in Pakistan... Pakistan have won none of the 15 Tests played in Australia outside Sydney and Melbourne... Australia have won all five Tests between the teams at Perth... In four Tests at Brisbane, Australia average 59.3 runs per wicket and Pakistan 24.1... Pakistan have won five and lost none of the teams' eight Tests at Karachi... In the second Test of a series, Australia lead 9–1 from 16 Tests... S. K. Warne needs ten wickets, and G. D. McGrath 20, to become the first to take 100 in this fixture... Only two of the 35 victories in this fixture have been in a losing series – and both of those were in dead rubbers.

Season	Australia	Pakistan	T	A	P	D
		Captains				
1956-57P	I. W. Johnson	A. H. Kardar	1	0	1	0
1959-60P	R. Benaud	Fazal Mahmood¹	3	2	0	1
1964-65P	R. B. Simpson	Hanif Mohammad	1	0	0	1
1964-65A	R. B. Simpson	Hanif Mohammad	1	0	0	1
1972-73A	I. M. Chappell	Intikhab Alam	3	3	0	0
1976-77A	G. S. Chappell	Mushtaq Mohammad	3	1	1	1
1978-79A	G. N. Yallop²	Mushtaq Mohammad	2	1	1	0
1979-80P	G. S. Chappell	Javed Miandad	3	0	1	2
1981-82A	G. S. Chappell	Javed Miandad	3	2	1	0
1982-83P	K. J. Hughes	Imran Khan	3	0	3	0
1983-84A	K. J. Hughes	Imran Khan³	5	2	0	3
1988-89P	A. R. Border	Javed Miandad	3	0	1	2
1989-90A	A. R. Border	Imran Khan	3	1	0	2

	Captains					
Season	*Australia*	*Pakistan*	T	A	P	D
1994-95*P*	M. A. Taylor	Salim Malik	3	0	1	2
1995-96*A*	M. A. Taylor	Wasim Akram	3	2	1	0
1998-99*P*	M. A. Taylor	Aamir Sohail	3	1	0	2
1999-2000*A*	S. R. Waugh	Wasim Akram	3	3	0	0
2002-03*S/U*	S. R. Waugh	Waqar Younis	3	3	0	0
2004-05*A*	R. T. Ponting	Inzamam-ul-Haq[4]	3	3	0	0
	In Pakistan		20	3	7	10
	In Sri Lanka		1	1	0	0
	In United Arab Emirates		2	2	0	0
	In Australia		29	18	4	7
	Totals		52	24	11	17

A Played in Australia.   P Played in Pakistan.
S/U First Test played in Sri Lanka, Second and Third Tests in United Arab Emirates.

Notes: The following deputised for the official touring captain or were appointed by the home authority for only a minor proportion of the series:
[1]Imtiaz Ahmed (Second). [2]K. J. Hughes (Second). [3]Zaheer Abbas (First, Second and Third). [4]Yousuf Youhana (Second and Third).

HIGHEST INNINGS TOTALS

For Australia in Australia: 585 at Adelaide	1972-73
in Pakistan: 617 at Faisalabad	1979-80
in Sri Lanka: 467 at Colombo (PSS)	2002-03
in United Arab Emirates: 444 at Sharjah	2002-03

For Pakistan in Australia: 624 at Adelaide	1983-84
in Pakistan: 580-9 dec. at Peshawar	1998-99
in Sri Lanka: 279 at Colombo (PSS)	2002-03
in United Arab Emirates: 221 at Sharjah	2002-03

LOWEST INNINGS TOTALS

For Australia in Australia: 125 at Melbourne	1981-82
in Pakistan: 80 at Karachi	1956-57
in Sri Lanka: 127 at Colombo (PSS)	2002-03
in United Arab Emirates: 310 at Sharjah	2002-03

For Pakistan in Australia: 62 at Perth	1981-82
in Pakistan: 134 at Dacca	1959-60
in Sri Lanka: 274 at Colombo (PSS)	2002-03
in United Arab Emirates: 53 at Sharjah	2002-03

DOUBLE-HUNDREDS

For Australia (5)

334*	M. A. Taylor at Peshawar	1998-99	207	R. T. Ponting at Sydney	2004-05
268	G. N. Yallop at Melbourne	1983-84	201	G. S. Chappell at Brisbane	1981-82
235	G. S. Chappell at Faisalabad	1979-80			

For Pakistan (3)

237	Salim Malik at Rawalpindi	1994-95
211	Javed Miandad at Karachi	1988-89

210*	Taslim Arif at Faisalabad......	1979-80

INDIVIDUAL HUNDREDS

For Australia (62)

6: A. R. Border, G. S. Chappell.

4: J. L. Langer, R. T. Ponting, M. A. Taylor.

3: M. J. Slater, M. E. Waugh, S. R. Waugh, G. N. Yallop.

2: A. C. Gilchrist, K. J. Hughes, D. M. Jones, D. R. Martyn, R. B. Simpson.

1: J. Benaud, D. C. Boon, I. M. Chappell, G. J. Cosier, I. C. Davis, M. L. Hayden, R. B. McCosker, R. W. Marsh, N. C. O'Neill, W. B. Phillips, I. R. Redpath, G. M. Ritchie, A. P. Sheahan, K. D. Walters, K. C. Wessels, G. M. Wood.

For Pakistan (46)

6: Ijaz Ahmed, sen., Javed Miandad.

3: Asif Iqbal, Majid Khan, Mohsin Khan, Saeed Anwar.

2: Aamir Sohail, Hanif Mohammad, Sadiq Mohammad, Salim Malik, Zaheer Abbas.

1: Imran Khan, Inzamam-ul-Haq, Khalid Ibadulla, Mansoor Akhtar, Moin Khan, Mushtaq Mohammad, Qasim Omar, Saeed Ahmed, Salman Butt, Taslim Arif, Wasim Akram, Yousuf Youhana.

RECORD PARTNERSHIPS FOR EACH WICKET

For Australia

269 for 1st	M. J. Slater and G. S. Blewett at Brisbane	1999-2000
279 for 2nd	M. A. Taylor and J. L. Langer at Peshawar	1998-99
203 for 3rd	G. N. Yallop and K. J. Hughes at Melbourne.............	1983-84
217 for 4th	G. S. Chappell and G. N. Yallop at Faisalabad..........	1979-80
327 for 5th	J. L. Langer and R. T. Ponting at Perth	1999-2000
238 for 6th	J. L. Langer and A. C. Gilchrist at Hobart	1999-2000
185 for 7th	G. N. Yallop and G. R. J. Matthews at Melbourne	1983-84
117 for 8th	G. J. Cosier and K. J. O'Keeffe at Melbourne	1976-77
83 for 9th	J. R. Watkins and R. A. L. Massie at Sydney	1972-73
86 for 10th	S. K. Warne and S. A. Muller at Brisbane	1999-2000

For Pakistan

249 for 1st	Khalid Ibadulla and Abdul Kadir at Karachi	1964-65
233 for 2nd	Mohsin Khan and Qasim Omar at Adelaide	1983-84
223* for 3rd	Taslim Arif and Javed Miandad at Faisalabad	1979-80
192 for 4th	Younis Khan and Yousuf Youhana at Melbourne	2004-05
186 for 5th	Javed Miandad and Salim Malik at Adelaide	1983-84
196 for 6th	Salim Malik and Aamir Sohail at Lahore	1994-95
104 for 7th	Intikhab Alam and Wasim Bari at Adelaide.............	1972-73
111 for 8th	Majid Khan and Imran Khan at Lahore	1979-80
120 for 9th	Saeed Anwar and Mushtaq Ahmed at Rawalpindi..........	1998-99
87 for 10th	Asif Iqbal and Iqbal Qasim at Adelaide	1976-77

TEN WICKETS OR MORE IN A MATCH

For Australia (5)

10-111 (7-87, 3-24)†	R. J. Bright, Karachi	1979-80
10-135 (6-82, 4-53)	D. K. Lillee, Melbourne	1976-77
11-118 (5-32, 6-86)†	C. G. Rackemann, Perth	1983-84
11-77 (7-23, 4-54)	S. K. Warne, Brisbane	1995-96
11-188 (7-94, 4-94)	S. K. Warne, Colombo (PSS).................	2002-03

For Pakistan (6)

11-218 (4-76, 7-142)	Abdul Qadir, Faisalabad	1982-83
13-114 (6-34, 7-80)†	Fazal Mahmood, Karachi.	1956-57
12-165 (6-102, 6-63)	Imran Khan, Sydney	1976-77
11-118 (4-69, 7-49)	Iqbal Qasim, Karachi	1979-80
11-125 (2-39, 9-86)	Sarfraz Nawaz, Melbourne.	1978-79
11-160 (6-62, 5-98)†	Wasim Akram, Melbourne.	1989-90

† *On first appearance in Australia–Pakistan Tests.*

SEVEN WICKETS OR MORE IN AN INNINGS

In addition to those listed above, the following have taken seven wickets or more in an innings:

For Australia

7-75	L. F. Kline, Lahore 1959-60	8-59	A. A. Mallett, Adelaide 1972-73
8-24	G. D. McGrath, Perth 2004-05	7-187	B. Yardley, Melbourne 1981-82

For Pakistan

7-188 Danish Kaneria, Sydney 2004-05

AUSTRALIA v SRI LANKA

Series notes: Sri Lanka have never won in Australia... In eight Tests in Australia, Sri Lanka average 26.4 runs per wicket and Australia 47.4... Australia have batted first in 16 of the 18 matches between the sides... Sri Lanka have elected to field seven times out of nine, Australia have elected to bat first nine times out of nine – but their only defeat came when they did so, at Kandy... Australia have won both matches at Perth by an innings... Australia's last four victories in Sri Lanka have come after trailing on first innings.

		Captains				
Season	*Australia*	*Sri Lanka*	*T*	*A*	*SL*	*D*
1982-83*S*	G. S. Chappell	L. R. D. Mendis	1	1	0	0
1987-88*A*	A. R. Border	R. S. Madugalle	1	1	0	0
1989-90*A*	A. R. Border	A. Ranatunga	2	1	0	1
1992-93*S*	A. R. Border	A. Ranatunga	3	1	0	2
1995-96*A*	M. A. Taylor	A. Ranatunga[1]	3	3	0	0
1999-2000*S*	S. R. Waugh	S. T. Jayasuriya	3	0	1	2
2003-04*S*	R. T. Ponting	H. P. Tillekeratne	3	3	0	0
2004*A*	R. T. Ponting[2]	M. S. Atapattu	2	1	0	1
	In Australia		8	6	0	2
	In Sri Lanka		10	5	1	4
	Totals		18	11	1	6

A Played in Australia.   *S Played in Sri Lanka.*

Note: The following deputised for the official touring captain:
[1]P. A. de Silva (Third). [2]A. C. Gilchrist (First).

HIGHEST INNINGS TOTALS

For Australia in Australia: 617-5 dec. at Perth 1995-96
in Sri Lanka: 514-4 dec. at Kandy 1982-83

For Sri Lanka in Australia: 455 at Cairns 2004
in Sri Lanka: 547-8 dec. at Colombo (SSC). 1992-93

LOWEST INNINGS TOTALS

For Australia in Australia: 201 at Darwin 2004
in Sri Lanka: 120 at Kandy 2003-04

For Sri Lanka in Australia: 97 at Darwin 2004
in Sri Lanka: 154 at Galle 2003-04

DOUBLE-HUNDRED

For Australia (1)

219   M. J. Slater at Perth 1995-96

Highest score for Sri Lanka: 167 by P. A. de Silva at Brisbane, 1989-90.

INDIVIDUAL HUNDREDS

For Australia (26)

3: M. L. Hayden, D. M. Jones, S. R. Waugh.
2: J. L. Langer, D. S. Lehmann, D. R. Martyn, M. A. Taylor.
1: D. C. Boon, A. R. Border, A. C. Gilchrist, D. W. Hookes, T. M. Moody, R. T. Ponting, M. J. Slater, M. E. Waugh, K. C. Wessels.

For Sri Lanka (11)

2: M. S. Atapattu, A. P. Gurusinha, S. T. Jayasuriya.
1: P. A. de Silva, T. M. Dilshan, R. S. Kaluwitharana, A. Ranatunga, H. P. Tillekeratne.

RECORD PARTNERSHIPS FOR EACH WICKET

For Australia

255	for 1st	J. L. Langer and M. L. Hayden at Cairns	2004
170	for 2nd	K. C. Wessels and G. N. Yallop at Kandy	1982-83
200	for 3rd	A. C. Gilchrist and D. R. Martyn at Kandy	2003-04
206	for 4th	D. R. Martyn and D. S. Lehmann at Galle	2003-04
155*	for 5th	D. W. Hookes and A. R. Border at Kandy	1982-83
260*	for 6th	D. M. Jones and S. R. Waugh at Hobart.	1989-90
129	for 7th	G. R. J. Matthews and I. A. Healy at Moratuwa.	1992-93
107	for 8th	R. T. Ponting and J. N. Gillespie at Kandy	1999-2000
47	for 9th	A. C. Gilchrist and M. S. Kasprowicz at Darwin	2004
49	for 10th	I. A. Healy and M. R. Whitney at Colombo (SSC).	1992-93

For Sri Lanka

134 for 1st	M. S. Atapattu and S. T. Jayasuriya at Colombo (SSC)	2003-04
138 for 2nd	M. S. Atapattu and K. C. Sangakkara at Cairns	2004
125 for 3rd	S. T. Jayasuriya and S. Ranatunga at Adelaide	1995-96
230 for 4th	A. P. Gurusinha and A. Ranatunga at Colombo (SSC).	1992-93
116 for 5th	H. P. Tillekeratne and A. Ranatunga at Moratuwa.	1992-93
96 for 6th	A. P. Gurusinha and R. S. Kaluwitharana at Colombo (SSC)	1992-93
144 for 7th	P. A. de Silva and J. R. Ratnayeke at Brisbane	1989-90
47 for 8th	W. P. U. J. C. Vaas and K. S. Lokuarachchi at Kandy	2003-04
46 for 9th	H. D. P. K. Dharmasena and G. P. Wickremasinghe at Perth. . . .	1995-96
79 for 10th†	W. P. U. J. C. Vaas and M. Muralitharan at Kandy	2003-04

† *Record partnership against all countries.*

TEN WICKETS OR MORE IN A MATCH

For Australia (2)

10-159 (5-116, 5-43)	S. K. Warne, Galle	2003-04
10-155 (5-65, 5-90)	S. K. Warne, Kandy.	2003-04

For Sri Lanka (2)

11-212 (6-59, 5-153)	M. Muralitharan, Galle	2003-04
10-210 (5-109, 5-101)	U. D. U. Chandana, Cairns	2004

SEVEN WICKETS OR MORE IN AN INNINGS

For Australia

7-39   M. S. Kasprowicz, Darwin   2004

AUSTRALIA v ZIMBABWE

Series notes: Zimbabwe have won all three tosses – and lost all three matches… Australia average 64.3 runs per wicket and Zimbabwe 26.0… Australia's lowest innings score (403) exceeds Zimbabwe's highest (321)… Zimbabwe do lead 9–0 in one field, though. ducks.

Season	Australia	Captains Zimbabwe	T	A	Z	D
1999-2000Z	S. R. Waugh	A. D. R. Campbell	1	1	0	0
2003-04A	S. R. Waugh	H. H. Streak	2	2	0	0
	In Australia.		2	2	0	0
	In Zimbabwe.		1	1	0	0
	Totals		3	3	0	0

A Played in Australia.   Z Played in Zimbabwe.

HIGHEST INNINGS TOTALS

For Australia in Australia. 735-6 dec. at Perth	2003-04
in Zimbabwe: 422 at Harare.	1999-2000
For Zimbabwe in Australia: 321 at Perth.	2003-04
in Zimbabwe: 232 at Harare.	1999-2000

LOWEST INNINGS TOTALS

For Australia in Australia: 403 at Sydney 2003-04
          in Zimbabwe: 422 at Harare. 1999-2000

For Zimbabwe in Australia: 239 at Perth. 2003-04
          in Zimbabwe: 194 at Harare. 1999-2000

DOUBLE-HUNDRED

For Australia (1)

380   M. L. Hayden at Perth 2003-04

Highest score for Zimbabwe: 118 by S. V. Carlisle at Sydney, 2003-04.

INDIVIDUAL HUNDREDS

For Australia (5)

2: M. L. Hayden.
1: A. C. Gilchrist, R. T. Ponting, S. R. Waugh.

For Zimbabwe (1)

1: S. V. Carlisle.

HIGHEST PARTNERSHIPS

For Australia

233 for 6th	M. L. Hayden and A. C. Gilchrist at Perth	2003-04
207 for 4th	M. L. Hayden and S. R. Waugh at Perth	2003-04
151* for 2nd	M. L. Hayden and R. T. Ponting at Sydney.	2003-04
135 for 4th	R. T. Ponting and S. R. Waugh at Sydney.	2003-04
114 for 8th	S. R. Waugh and D. W. Fleming at Harare	1999-2000

For Zimbabwe

99 for 3rd   M. A. Vermeulen and S. V. Carlisle at Perth 2003-04

BEST MATCH BOWLING ANALYSES

For Australia

6-90 (0-25, 6-65)   S. M. Katich, Sydney 2003-04

For Zimbabwe

6-184 (6-121, 0-63)   R. W. Price, Sydney 2003-04

AUSTRALIA v BANGLADESH

Series notes: Australia average 87.5 runs per wicket and Bangladesh 18.3... Bangladesh have yet to dismiss Australia in a Test... In both the Tests between the sides, Australia have won the toss, fielded and won by an innings... Australia have taken a wicket every six overs in this fixture, Bangladesh every 24... S. C. G. MacGill has all three five-wicket hauls in this fixture... M. L. Hayden's average against Bangladesh (30.50) is the lowest of the nine nations he has played against.

Season	Australia	Captains	Bangladesh	T	A	B	D
2003*A*	S. R. Waugh		Khaled Mahmud	2	2	0	0

A Played in Australia.

HIGHEST INNINGS TOTALS

For Australia: 556-4 dec. at Cairns 2003

For Bangladesh: 295 at Cairns 2003

LOWEST INNINGS TOTALS

For Bangladesh: 97 at Darwin 2003

HIGHEST INDIVIDUAL INNINGS

For Australia

177   D. S. Lehmann at Cairns   2003

For Bangladesh

76   Hannan Sarkar at Cairns   2003

INDIVIDUAL HUNDREDS

For Australia (5)

2: D. S. Lehmann, S. R. Waugh.
1: M. L. Love.

HUNDRED PARTNERSHIPS

For Australia

141	for 3rd	J. L. Langer and D. S. Lehmann at Darwin	2003
250	for 4th	D. S. Lehmann and S. R. Waugh at Cairns	2003
174*	for 5th	S. R. Waugh and M. L. Love at Cairns	2003

For Bangladesh

108	for 2nd	Hannan Sarkar and Habibul Bashar at Cairns	2003

TEN WICKETS OR MORE IN A MATCH

For Australia (1)

10-133 (5-77, 5-56)   S. C. G. MacGill, Cairns   2003

Note: The best match figures for Bangladesh are 3-74 (3-74) by Mashrafe bin Mortaza at Darwin, 2003.

SOUTH AFRICA v WEST INDIES

Series notes: West Indies have never won a Test in South Africa, who lead 8–0 in home Tests, but are level at 2–2 away... Pending the series in 2004-05, West Indies trail 7–0 from nine Tests in which they have fielded first, but only 3–2 from six where they have batted first... South Africa have scored over 500 in the first innings of the last four Tests – before that neither side had done so in 11 Tests... South Africa have been bowled out in the second innings in only four of the 15 Tests between the sides; West Indies have been bowled out 12 times... The highest fourth-innings total to win a Test between the sides is 164 for six... J. H. Kallis is the leading run-scorer in this fixture, with 1,464... S. M. Pollock is the leading wicket-taker, with 65... B. C. Lara's 202 is the highest score between these sides – but the next 16 have all been made by South Africans... In two Tests at Centurion, South Africa have averaged 64.8 runs per wicket, more than double West Indies' 25.2.

Season	South Africa	Captains	West Indies	T	SA	WI	D
1991-92*W*	K. C. Wessels	R. B.	Richardson	1	0	1	0
1998-99*S*	W. J. Cronje		B. C. Lara	5	5	0	0

SIR VIVIAN RICHARDS TROPHY

Season	South Africa	Captains	West Indies	T	SA	WI	D	Held by
2000-01*W*	S. M. Pollock	C. L.	Hooper	5	2	1	2	SA
2003-04*S*	G. C. Smith		B. C. Lara	4	3	0	1	SA

	T	SA	WI	D
In South Africa	9	8	0	1
In West Indies	6	2	2	2
Totals	15	10	2	3

S Played in South Africa.   W Played in West Indies.

HIGHEST INNINGS TOTALS

For South Africa in South Africa: 658-9 dec. at Durban   2003-04
                            in West Indies: 454 at Bridgetown.   2000-01

For West Indies in South Africa: 427 at Cape Town.   2003-04
                            in West Indies: 387 at Bridgetown   2000-01

LOWEST INNINGS TOTALS

For South Africa in South Africa: 195 at Port Elizabeth   1998-99
                            in West Indies: 141 at Kingston   2000-01

For West Indies in South Africa: 121 at Port Elizabeth   1998-99
                            in West Indies: 140 at St John's.   2000-01

DOUBLE-HUNDREDS

For West Indies (1)

202   B. C. Lara at Johannesburg 2003-04

Highest score for South Africa: 192 by H. H. Gibbs at Centurion, 2003-04.

INDIVIDUAL HUNDREDS

For South Africa (22)

5: J. H. Kallis.
3: D. J. Cullinan, H. H. Gibbs, G. Kirsten.
2: M. V. Boucher, G. C. Smith.
1: A. C. Hudson, S. M. Pollock, J. N. Rhodes, J. A. Rudolph.

For West Indies (9)

2: C. H. Gayle, B. C. Lara, R. R. Sarwan.
1: S. Chanderpaul, R. D. Jacobs, D. R. Smith.

RECORD PARTNERSHIPS FOR EACH WICKET

For South Africa

301 for 1st	G. C. Smith and H. H. Gibbs at Centurion	....	2003-04
146 for 2nd	G. Kirsten and J. H. Kallis at Georgetown	....	2000-01
251 for 3rd	H. H. Gibbs and J. H. Kallis at Cape Town	....	2003-04
249 for 4th†	J. H. Kallis and G. Kirsten at Durban	....	2003-04
115 for 5th	G. Kirsten and J. N. Rhodes at Centurion	....	1998-99
92 for 6th	J. N. Rhodes and S. M. Pollock at Port Elizabeth	....	1998-99
92 for 7th	J. H. Kallis and M. V. Boucher at Centurion	....	1998-99
146 for 8th	M. V. Boucher and J. H. Kallis at Cape Town	....	2003-04
132 for 9th	S. M. Pollock and A. A. Donald at Bridgetown	....	2000-01
41 for 10th	R. J. Peterson and M. Ntini at Johannesburg	....	2003-04

For West Indies

126 for 1st	C. H. Gayle and D. Ganga at Cape Town	....	2003-04
88 for 2nd	C. H. Gayle and M. N. Samuels at Georgetown	....	2000-01
160 for 3rd	S. Chanderpaul and B. C. Lara at Durban	....	1998-99
174 for 4th	R. R. Sarwan and C. H. Gayle at Centurion	....	2003-04
116 for 5th	B. C. Lara and C. L. Hooper at Bridgetown	....	2000-01
113 for 6th	R. R. Sarwan and S. Chanderpaul at Durban	....	2003-04
81 for 7th	R. D. Jacobs and N. A. M. McLean at Centurion	....	1998-99
65 for 8th	R. D. Jacobs and N. A. M. McLean at Cape Town	....	1998-99
71 for 9th	R. D. Jacobs and M. Dillon at Port-of-Spain	....	2000-01
64 for 10th	R. D. Jacobs and M. Dillon at Cape Town	....	1998-99

† *Record partnership against all countries.*

BEST MATCH BOWLING ANALYSES

For South Africa

9-94 (5-28, 4-66)	S. M. Pollock, Kingston........................	2000-01

For West Indies

8-79 (2-28, 6-51)	C. E. L. Ambrose, Port Elizabeth.................	1998-99

SEVEN WICKETS OR MORE IN AN INNINGS

For West Indies

7-84 F. A. Rose, Durban 1998-99

SOUTH AFRICA v NEW ZEALAND

Series notes: New Zealand have never won a series against South Africa and have beaten them only once in 14 home Tests... South Africa average 46.1 runs per wicket away from home, well ahead of New Zealand's 27.6... All four of New Zealand's victories over South Africa have come when they have won the toss... South Africa have won all three matches between the sides at Durban... Six of the last eight victories in this fixture have been by the team fielding first.

Season	South Africa	*Captains* New Zealand	T	SA	NZ	D
1931-32*N*	H. B. Cameron	M. L. Page	2	2	0	0
1952-53*N*	J. E. Cheetham	W. M. Wallace	2	1	0	1
1953-54*S*	J. E. Cheetham	G. O. Rabone[1]	5	4	0	1
1961-62*S*	D. J. McGlew	J. R. Reid	5	2	2	1
1963-64*N*	T. L. Goddard	J. R. Reid	3	0	0	3
1994-95*S*	W. J. Cronje	K. R. Rutherford	3	2	1	0
1994-95*N*	W. J. Cronje	K. R. Rutherford	1	1	0	0
1998-99*N*	W. J. Cronje	D. J. Nash	3	1	0	2
2000-01*S*	S. M. Pollock	S. P. Fleming	3	2	0	1
2003-04*N*	G. C. Smith	S. P. Fleming	3	1	1	1
	In New Zealand		14	6	1	7
	In South Africa		16	10	3	3
	Totals.		30	16	4	10

N Played in New Zealand.   S Played in South Africa.

Note: The following deputised for the official touring captain:
  [1]B. Sutcliffe (Fourth and Fifth).

HIGHEST INNINGS TOTALS

For South Africa in South Africa: 471-9 dec. at Bloemfontein 2000-01
                 in New Zealand: 621-5 dec. at Auckland 1998-99

For New Zealand in South Africa: 505 at Cape Town. 1953-54
                 in New Zealand: 595 at Auckland. 2003-04

LOWEST INNINGS TOTALS

For South Africa in South Africa: 148 at Johannesburg 1953-54
                 in New Zealand: 223 at Dunedin. 1963-64

For New Zealand in South Africa: 79 at Johannesburg 1953-54
                 in New Zealand: 138 at Dunedin 1963-64

DOUBLE-HUNDREDS

For South Africa (3)

275* D. J. Cullinan at Auckland. . . . . 1998-99 | 211* H. H. Gibbs at Christchurch . . . 1998-99
255* D. J. McGlew at Wellington. . . . 1952-53 |

Highest score for New Zealand: 170 by S. B. Styris at Auckland, 2003-04.

INDIVIDUAL HUNDREDS

For South Africa (27)

3: J. H. Kallis, D. J. McGlew.
2: W. J. Cronje, D. J. Cullinan, H. H. Gibbs, G. Kirsten, R. A. McLean.
1: X. C. Balaskas, J. A. J. Christy, H. H. Dippenaar, W. R. Endean, N. D. McKenzie, B. Mitchell, A. R. A. Murray, D. J. Richardson, J. A. Rudolph, G. C. Smith, J. H. B. Waite.

For New Zealand (11)

2: J. R. Reid.
1: P. T. Barton, C. L. Cairns, P. G. Z. Harris, J. D. P. Oram, G. O. Rabone, B. W. Sinclair, M. S. Sinclair, S. B. Styris, H. G. Vivian.

RECORD PARTNERSHIPS FOR EACH WICKET

For South Africa

196	for 1st	J. A. J. Christy and B. Mitchell at Christchurch.	1931-32
315*	for 2nd†	H. H. Gibbs and J. H. Kallis at Christchurch	1998-99
183	for 3rd	G. Kirsten and D. J. Cullinan at Auckland	1998-99
171	for 4th	G. C. Smith and G. Kirsten at Wellington	2003-04
141	for 5th	D. J. Cullinan and J. N. Rhodes at Auckland	1998-99
126*	for 6th	D. J. Cullinan and S. M. Pollock at Auckland.	1998-99
246	for 7th†	D. J. McGlew and A. R. A. Murray at Wellington	1952-53
136	for 8th	N. D. McKenzie and N. Boje at Port Elizabeth	2000-01
60	for 9th	P. M. Pollock and N. A. T. Adcock at Port Elizabeth	1961-62
47	for 10th	D. J. McGlew and H. D. Bromfield at Port Elizabeth	1961-62

For New Zealand

126	for 1st	G. O. Rabone and M. E. Chapple at Cape Town.	1953-54
90	for 2nd	M. J. Horne and N. J. Astle at Auckland	1998-99
125	for 3rd	M. H. Richardson and S. B. Styris at Auckland	2003-04
171	for 4th	B. W. Sinclair and S. N. McGregor at Auckland	1963-64
176	for 5th	J. R. Reid and J. E. F. Beck at Cape Town.	1953-54
100	for 6th	H. G. Vivian and F. T. Badcock at Wellington.	1931-32
225	for 7th†	C. L. Cairns and J. D. P. Oram at Auckland	2003-04
113	for 8th	J. D. P. Oram and D. L. Vettori at Hamilton.	2003-04
87	for 9th	J. D. P. Oram and P. J. Wiseman at Hamilton	2003-04
57	for 10th	S. B. Doull and R. P. de Groen at Johannesburg	1994-95

† *Record partnership against all countries.*

TEN WICKETS OR MORE IN A MATCH

For South Africa (1)

11-196 (6-128, 5-68)†   S. F. Burke, Cape Town   1961-62

For New Zealand (1)

11-180 (6-76, 5-104)   C. S. Martin, Auckland.   2003-04

† *On first appearance in South Africa–New Zealand Tests.*

SEVEN WICKETS OR MORE IN AN INNINGS

For South Africa

8-53 G. B. Lawrence, Johannesburg . . 1961-62

SOUTH AFRICA v INDIA

Series notes: India have never won a Test in South Africa in nine attempts... The side batting first have won none and lost four of the last seven matches... Before that, the side batting first had won the previous five... Neither side has chased more than 163 in the final innings to win this fixture... The team winning the toss has won only one of the last seven Tests between the teams... South Africa average 42.6 runs per wicket when they win the toss, but only 27.2 when they lose it... S. R. Tendulkar is the only man to score 1,000 runs in this fixture, yet his average (37.14) is his lowest against any Test-playing nation.

			Captains				
Season	*South Africa*		*India*	*T*	*SA*	*I*	*D*
1992-93*S*	K. C. Wessels		M. Azharuddin	4	1	0	3
1996-97*I*	W. J. Cronje		S. R. Tendulkar	3	1	2	0
1996-97*S*	W. J. Cronje		S. R. Tendulkar	3	2	0	1
1999-2000*I*	W. J. Cronje		S. R. Tendulkar	2	2	0	0
2001-02*S*†	S. M. Pollock		S. C. Ganguly	2	1	0	1
2004-05*I*	G. C. Smith		S. C. Ganguly	2	0	1	1
	In South Africa			9	4	0	5
	In India			7	3	3	1
	Totals.			16	7	3	6

S Played in South Africa.   I Played in India.

† *The Third Test at Centurion was stripped of its official status by the ICC after a disciplinary dispute and is excluded.*

HIGHEST INNINGS TOTALS

For South Africa in South Africa: 563 at Bloemfontein   2001-02
               in India: 510-9 dec. at Kanpur   2004-05

For India in South Africa: 410 at Johannesburg   1996-97
              in India: 466 at Kanpur   2004-05

LOWEST INNINGS TOTALS

For South Africa in South Africa: 235 at Durban   1996-97
                  in India: 105 at Ahmedabad   1996-97

For India in South Africa: 66 at Durban   1996-97
              in India: 113 at Mumbai   1999-2000

HIGHEST INDIVIDUAL INNINGS

For South Africa

196   H. H. Gibbs at Port Elizabeth . . 2001-02

For India

169   S. R. Tendulkar at Cape Town . . 1996-97

INDIVIDUAL HUNDREDS

For South Africa (15)

3: G. Kirsten.
2: D. J. Cullinan, H. H. Gibbs, L. Klusener.
1: W. J. Cronje, A. J. Hall, A. C. Hudson, J. H. Kallis, B. M. McMillan, K. C. Wessels.

For India (12)

4: M. Azharuddin.
3: S. R. Tendulkar.
2: V. Sehwag.
1: P. K. Amre, R. Dravid, Kapil Dev.

RECORD PARTNERSHIPS FOR EACH WICKET

For South Africa

236	for 1st	A. C. Hudson and G. Kirsten at Calcutta	1996-97
212	for 2nd	G. Kirsten and D. J. Cullinan at Calcutta	1996-97
130	for 3rd	J. H. Kallis and N. D. McKenzie at Bloemfontein	2001-02
105	for 4th	H. H. Gibbs and H. H. Dippenaar at Port Elizabeth	2001-02
164	for 5th	J. H. Kallis and L. Klusener at Bangalore	1999-2000
144	for 6th	A. J. Hall and Z. de Bruyn at Kanpur	2004-05
121	for 7th	L. Klusener and M. V. Boucher at Bloemfontein	2001-02
147*	for 8th	B. M. McMillan and L. Klusener at Cape Town	1996-97
60	for 9th	P. S. de Villiers and A. A. Donald at Ahmedabad	1996-97
74	for 10th	B. M. McMillan and A. A. Donald at Durban	1996-97

For India

218	for 1st	V. Sehwag and G. Gambhir at Kanpur	2004-05
171	for 2nd	D. Dasgupta and R. Dravid at Port Elizabeth	2001-02
60*	for 3rd	R. Dravid and S. R. Tendulkar at Kolkata	2004-05
145	for 4th	R. Dravid and S. C. Ganguly at Johannesburg	1996-97
220	for 5th	S. R. Tendulkar and V. Sehwag at Bloemfontein	2001-02
222	for 6th	S. R. Tendulkar and M. Azharuddin at Cape Town	1996-97
76	for 7th	R. Dravid and J. Srinath at Johannesburg	1996-97
161	for 8th†	M. Azharuddin and A. Kumble at Calcutta	1996-97
80	for 9th	V. V. S. Laxman and A. Kumble at Port Elizabeth	2001-02
52	for 10th	A. B. Agarkar and M. Kartik at Mumbai	1999-2000

† *Record partnership against all countries.*

TEN WICKETS OR MORE IN A MATCH

For South Africa (2)

12-139 (5-55, 7-84)	A. A. Donald, Port Elizabeth	1992-93
10-147 (4-91, 6-56)	S. M. Pollock, Bloemfontein	2001-02

For India (1)

10-153 (5-60, 5-93)	B. K. V. Prasad, Durban	1996-97

SEVEN WICKETS OR MORE IN AN INNINGS

In addition to those listed above, the following have taken seven wickets or more in an innings:

For South Africa

8-64	L. Klusener, Calcutta	1996-97

For India

7-87	Harbhajan Singh, Kolkata	2004-05

SOUTH AFRICA v PAKISTAN

Series notes: S. M. Pollock is the top wicket-taker in this fixture, and needs 13 more to become the first man to 50... G. Kirsten is the top-scorer with 838 runs, comfortably ahead of the next-best (Taufeeq Umar: 593)... South Africa have batted first in nine of the 11 Tests between these sides... Both Pakistan's victories came when they lost the toss... Kirsten is the only man to have played in all 11 Tests between the sides... In home Tests, South Africa average 38.4 runs per wicket, almost double Pakistan's 21.2... In away Tests, however, South Africa average 32.0 and Pakistan 34.5... Azhar Mahmood averages 75.71 in six Tests against South Africa – and 16.08 in 15 Tests against everyone else.

Season	South Africa	Captains Pakistan	T	SA	P	D
1994-95S	W. J. Cronje	Salim Malik	1	1	0	0
1997-98P	W. J. Cronje	Saeed Anwar	3	1	0	2
1997-98S	W. J. Cronje[1]	Rashid Latif[2]	3	1	1	1
2002-03S	S. M. Pollock	Waqar Younis	2	2	0	0
2003-04P	G. C. Smith	Inzamam-ul-Haq[3]	2	0	1	1
	In South Africa		6	4	1	1
	In Pakistan		5	1	1	3
	Totals....................		11	5	2	4

S Played in South Africa. P Played in Pakistan.

Notes: The following deputised for the official touring captain or were appointed by the home authority for only a minor proportion of the series:
[1]G. Kirsten (First). [2]Aamir Sohail (First and Second). [3]Yousuf Youhana (First).

HIGHEST INNINGS TOTALS

For South Africa in South Africa: 620-7 dec. at Cape Town................. 2002-03
            in Pakistan: 403 at Rawalpindi...................... 1997-98

For Pakistan in South Africa: 329 at Johannesburg...................... 1996-97
            in Pakistan: 456 at Rawalpindi....................... 1997-98

LOWEST INNINGS TOTALS

For South Africa in South Africa: 225 at Durban.................... 1997-98
            in Pakistan: 214 at Faisalabad...................... 1997-98

For Pakistan in South Africa: 106 at Port Elizabeth 1997-98
            in Pakistan: 92 at Faisalabad 1997-98

DOUBLE-HUNDRED

For South Africa (1)

228   H. H. Gibbs at Cape Town 2002-03

Highest score for Pakistan: 136 by Azhar Mahmood at Johannesburg, 1997-98.

INDIVIDUAL HUNDREDS

For South Africa (7)

2: G. Kirsten.
1: H. H. Gibbs, J. H. Kallis, B. M. McMillan, G. C. Smith, P. L. Symcox.

For Pakistan (8)

3: Azhar Mahmood.
2: Taufeeq Umar.
1: Ali Naqvi, Imran Farhat, Saeed Anwar.

RECORD PARTNERSHIPS FOR EACH WICKET

For South Africa

368 for 1st†	G. C. Smith and H. H. Gibbs at Cape Town	2002-03
114 for 2nd	G. Kirsten and J. H. Kallis at Rawalpindi	1997-98
122 for 3rd	G. Kirsten and J. H. Kallis at Durban	2002-03
108 for 4th	H. H. Gibbs and G. Kirsten at Faisalabad	2003-04
90 for 5th	G. Kirsten and J. H. Kallis at Faisalabad	2003-04
157 for 6th	J. N. Rhodes and B. M. McMillan at Johannesburg	1994-95
106 for 7th	S. M. Pollock and D. J. Richardson at Rawalpindi	1997-98
174 for 8th	G. Kirsten and P. L. Symcox at Faisalabad	1997-98
195 for 9th†	M. V. Boucher and P. L. Symcox at Johannesburg	1997-98
71 for 10th	P. S. de Villiers and A. A. Donald at Johannesburg	1994-95

For Pakistan

137 for 1st	Taufeeq Umar and Imran Farhat at Faisalabad	2003-04
116 for 2nd	Taufeeq Umar and Younis Khan at Cape Town	2002-03
121 for 3rd	Taufeeq Umar and Inzamam-ul-Haq at Cape Town	2002-03
93 for 4th	Asif Mujtaba and Inzamam-ul-Haq at Johannesburg	1994-95
99 for 5th	Asim Kamal and Shoaib Malik at Lahore	2003-04
144 for 6th	Inzamam-ul-Haq and Moin Khan at Faisalabad	1997-98
35 for 7th	Salim Malik and Wasim Akram at Johannesburg	1994-95
40 for 8th	Inzamam-ul-Haq and Kabir Khan at Johannesburg	1994-95
80 for 9th	Azhar Mahmood and Shoaib Akhtar at Durban	1997-98
151 for 10th†	Azhar Mahmood and Mushtaq Ahmed at Rawalpindi	1997-98

† *Record partnership against all countries.*

TEN WICKETS OR MORE IN A MATCH

For South Africa (1)

10-108 (6-81, 4-27)†	P. S. de Villiers, Johannesburg	1994-95

For Pakistan (1)

10-133 (6-78, 4-55)	Waqar Younis, Port Elizabeth	1997-98

† *On first appearance in South Africa–Pakistan Tests.*

SEVEN WICKETS OR MORE IN AN INNINGS

For South Africa

7-128 P. R. Adams, Lahore 2003-04

SOUTH AFRICA v SRI LANKA

Series notes: M. Muralitharan has taken eight five-wicket hauls in an innings against South Africa – the rest of Sri Lanka have managed three between them... Sri Lanka have never won a Test in South Africa... Half of the ten victories in this fixture have been by an innings... Sri Lanka have won 11 out of 15 tosses... Six of South Africa's eight wins have come when they have lost the toss... Muralitharan has taken 82 wickets in 13 Tests between the sides; he needs 18 more to become the second bowler (after S. K. Warne) to take 100 South African wickets in Tests.

		Captains				
Season	*South Africa*	*Sri Lanka*	*T*	*SA*	*SL*	*D*
1993-94*SL*	K. C. Wessels	A. Ranatunga	3	1	0	2
1997-98*SA*	W. J. Cronje	A. Ranatunga	2	2	0	0
2000*SL*	S. M. Pollock	S. T. Jayasuriya	3	1	1	1
2000-01*SA*	S. M. Pollock	S. T. Jayasuriya	3	2	0	1
2002-03*SA*	S. M. Pollock	S. T. Jayasuriya[1]	2	2	0	0
2004*SL*	G. C. Smith	M. S. Atapattu	2	0	1	1
	In South Africa		7	6	0	1
	In Sri Lanka		8	2	2	4
	Totals....................		15	8	2	5

SA Played in South Africa. SL Played in Sri Lanka.

Note: The following deputised for the official captain:
[1]M. S. Atapattu (Second).

HIGHEST INNINGS TOTALS

For South Africa in South Africa: 504-7 dec. at Cape Town................. 2000-01
    in Sri Lanka: 495 at Colombo (SSC)..................... 1993-94

For Sri Lanka in South Africa: 323 at Centurion........................ 2002-03
    in Sri Lanka: 522 at Galle............................... 2000

LOWEST INNINGS TOTALS

For South Africa in South Africa: 200 at Centurion..................... 1997-98
    in Sri Lanka: 179 at Colombo (SSC)..................... 2004

For Sri Lanka in South Africa: 95 at Cape Town......................... 2000-01
    in Sri Lanka: 119 at Colombo (SSC)..................... 1993-94

DOUBLE-HUNDREDS

For Sri Lanka (2)

237 D. P. M. D. Jayawardene at Galle ... 2004 | 233 K. C. Sangakkara at Colombo (SSC) 2004

Highest score for South Africa: 180 by G. Kirsten at Durban, 2000-01.

INDIVIDUAL HUNDREDS

For South Africa (12)

5: D. J. Cullinan.
1: W. J. Cronje, G. Kirsten, L. Klusener, N. D. McKenzie, S. M. Pollock, J. N. Rhodes, J. A. Rudolph.

For Sri Lanka (8)

3: D. P. M. D. Jayawardene.
1: M. S. Atapattu, S. T. Jayasuriya, A. Ranatunga, K. C. Sangakkara, H. P. Tillekeratne.

RECORD PARTNERSHIPS FOR EACH WICKET

For South Africa

137 for 1st	K. C. Wessels and A. C. Hudson at Colombo (SSC)	1993-94
108 for 2nd	G. C. Smith and M. van Jaarsveld at Colombo (SSC)	2004
140 for 3rd	H. H. Gibbs and J. H. Kallis at Centurion	2002-03
116 for 4th	G. Kirsten and W. J. Cronje at Centurion	1997-98
86 for 5th	D. J. Cullinan and M. V. Boucher at Cape Town	2000-01
124 for 6th	L. Klusener and M. V. Boucher at Kandy	2000
132 for 7th	M. V. Boucher and S. M. Pollock at Centurion	2002-03
150 for 8th†	N. D. McKenzie and S. M. Pollock at Centurion	2000-01
45 for 9th	N. Boje and P. R. Adams at Kandy	2000
43 for 10th	L. Klusener and M. Hayward at Kandy	2000

For Sri Lanka

193 for 1st	M. S. Atapattu and S. T. Jayasuriya at Galle	2000
103 for 2nd	S. T. Jayasuriya and R. P. Arnold at Colombo (SSC)	2000
192 for 3rd	K. C. Sangakkara and D. P. M. D. Jayawardene at Colombo (SSC)	2004
118 for 4th	R. S. Mahanama and A. Ranatunga at Centurion	1997-98
121 for 5th	P. A. de Silva and A. Ranatunga at Moratuwa	1993-94
103 for 6th	A. Ranatunga and H. P. Tillekeratne at Moratuwa	1993-94
43 for 7th	P. A. de Silva and G. P. Wickremasinghe at Centurion	1997-98
170 for 8th†	D. P. M. D. Jayawardene and W. P. U. J. C. Vaas at Galle	2004
48 for 9th	G. P. Wickremasinghe and M. Muralitharan at Cape Town	1997-98
42 for 10th	H. P. Tillekeratne and M. Muralitharan at Centurion	2002-03

† *Record partnership against all countries.*

TEN WICKETS OR MORE IN A MATCH

For Sri Lanka (2)

13-171 (6-87, 7-84)	M. Muralitharan, Galle	2000
11-161 (5-122, 6-39)	M. Muralitharan, Durban	2000-01

Note: The best match figures for South Africa are 9-106 (5-48, 4-58) by B. N. Schultz at Colombo (SSC), 1993-94.

❝Few titles have been so overdue. None, surely, can have been so emotional."
Cricket in Australia, page 1402.

SOUTH AFRICA v ZIMBABWE

Series notes: South Africa have a 100% record in three Tests at Harare but drew their only Test at Bulawayo... Pending the series in March 2005, South Africa average 169.7 runs per wicket when they bat first, as against 46.3 when they field... In Tests between the sides in Zimbabwe, South Africa's average is 62.1 and Zimbabwe's 26.2... Zimbabwe have failed to bowl South Africa out in the last three Tests, and have managed it only twice in five Tests overall... In three Tests in Zimbabwe, J. H. Kallis averages 503.

		Captains				
Season	*South Africa*	*Zimbabwe*	*T*	*SA*	*Z*	*D*
1995-96Z	W. J. Cronje	A. Flower	1	1	0	0
1999-2000S	W. J. Cronje	A. D. R. Campbell	1	1	0	0
1999-2000Z	W. J. Cronje	A. Flower	1	1	0	0
2001-02Z	S. M. Pollock	H. H. Streak	2	1	0	1
	In Zimbabwe		4	3	0	1
	In South Africa		1	1	0	0
	Totals.....................		5	4	0	1

S Played in South Africa.   Z Played in Zimbabwe.

HIGHEST INNINGS TOTALS

For South Africa in South Africa: 417 at Bloemfontein 1999-2000
               in Zimbabwe: 600-3 dec. at Harare 2001-02

For Zimbabwe in South Africa: 212 at Bloemfontein. 1999-2000
             in Zimbabwe: 419-9 dec. at Bulawayo 2001-02

LOWEST INNINGS TOTALS

For South Africa in South Africa: 417 at Bloemfontein 1999-2000
               in Zimbabwe: 346 at Harare 1995-96

For Zimbabwe in South Africa: 192 at Bloemfontein. 1999-2000
             in Zimbabwe: 102 at Harare. 1999-2000

DOUBLE-HUNDRED

For South Africa (1)

220   G. Kirsten at Harare......... 2001-02

Highest score for Zimbabwe: 199* by A. Flower at Harare, 2001-02.

INDIVIDUAL HUNDREDS

For South Africa (7)

3: J. H. Kallis.
1: M. V. Boucher, H. H. Gibbs, A. C. Hudson, G. Kirsten.

For Zimbabwe (2)

2: A. Flower.

RECORD PARTNERSHIPS FOR EACH WICKET

For South Africa

256 for 1st	H. H. Gibbs and G. Kirsten at Harare	2001-02
199 for 2nd	G. Kirsten and J. H. Kallis at Harare	2001-02
181 for 3rd	J. H. Kallis and N. D. McKenzie at Bulawayo	2001-02
100 for 4th	J. H. Kallis and W. J. Cronje at Harare	1999-2000
60 for 5th	A. C. Hudson and J. N. Rhodes at Harare	1995-96
101 for 6th	A. C. Hudson and B. M. McMillan at Harare	1995-96
44 for 7th	M. V. Boucher and L. Klusener at Harare	1999-2000
148 for 8th	M. V. Boucher and S. M. Pollock at Harare	1999-2000
79 for 9th	B. M. McMillan and A. A. Donald at Harare	1995-96
54 for 10th	M. V. Boucher and P. R. Adams at Bloemfontein	1999-2000

For Zimbabwe

152 for 1st	A. D. R. Campbell and D. D. Ebrahim at Bulawayo	2001-02
51 for 2nd	M. H. Dekker and A. D. R. Campbell at Harare	1995-96
29 for 3rd	M. W. Goodwin and N. C. Johnson at Harare	1999-2000
186 for 4th	H. Masakadza and A. Flower at Harare	2001-02
97 for 5th	A. Flower and G. J. Whittall at Harare	1995-96
17 for 6th	A. Flower and G. J. Whittall at Harare	2001-02
47 for 7th	G. J. Whittall and H. H. Streak at Bulawayo	2001-02
43 for 8th	C. B. Wishart and H. H. Streak at Harare	1995-96
75 for 9th	A. Flower and T. J. Friend at Harare	2001-02
47 for 10th	A. Flower and D. T. Hondo at Harare	2001-02

TEN WICKETS OR MORE IN A MATCH

For South Africa (1)

11-113 (3-42, 8-71)†   A. A. Donald, Harare 1995-96

Note: The best match figures for Zimbabwe are 5-105 (3-68, 2-37) by A. C. I. Lock at Harare, 1995-96.

† *On first appearance in South Africa–Zimbabwe Tests.*

SOUTH AFRICA v BANGLADESH

Series notes: South Africa have won all four Tests by an innings... South Africa average 86.2 runs per wicket and Bangladesh 18.3... South Africa's lowest score (330) is higher than Bangladesh's highest (252)... Bangladesh have taken an average of only 5.25 wickets per Test... J. H. Kallis has scored 214 runs against Bangladesh without being dismissed... J. A. Rudolph averages 293 in this fixture.

		Captains					
Season	South Africa	Bangladesh	T	SA	B	D	
2002-03S	S. M. Pollock[1]	Khaled Mashud	2	2	0	0	
2003B	G. C. Smith	Khaled Mahmud	2	2	0	0	
	In South Africa		2	2	0	0	
	In Bangladesh		2	2	0	0	
	Totals		4	4	0	0	

S Played in South Africa. B Played in Bangladesh.

Note: The following deputised for the official captain:
[1]M. V. Boucher (First).

HIGHEST INNINGS TOTALS

For South Africa in South Africa: 529-4 dec. at East London 2002-03
in Bangladesh: 470-2 dec. at Chittagong 2003

For Bangladesh in South Africa: 252 at East London 2002-03
in Bangladesh: 237 at Chittagong 2003

LOWEST INNINGS TOTALS

For South Africa in Bangladesh: 330 at Dhaka 2003

For Bangladesh in South Africa: 107 at Potchefstroom 2002-03
in Bangladesh: 102 at Dhaka 2003

DOUBLE-HUNDREDS

For South Africa (2)

222* J. A. Rudolph at Chittagong. . . .   2003 | 200   G. C. Smith at East London. . . . 2002-03

Highest score for Bangladesh is 75 by Habibul Bashar at Chittagong, 2003.

INDIVIDUAL HUNDREDS

For South Africa (7)

2: G. Kirsten.
1: H. H. Dippenaar, H. H. Gibbs, J. H. Kallis, J. A. Rudolph, G. C. Smith.

HUNDRED PARTNERSHIPS

For South Africa

429*	for 3rd†	J. A. Rudolph and H. H. Dippenaar at Chittagong	2003
272	for 2nd	G. C. Smith and G. Kirsten at East London	2002-03
234	for 3rd	G. Kirsten and J. H. Kallis at Potchefstroom	2002-03
141	for 2nd	H. H. Gibbs and G. Kirsten at Potchefstroom	2002-03
107	for 5th	J. A. Rudolph and M. V. Boucher at Dhaka.	2003

For Bangladesh

131	for 2nd	Javed Omar and Habibul Bashar at Chittagong	2003

† *Record partnership against all countries.*

TEN WICKETS OR MORE IN A MATCH

For South Africa (1)

10-106 (5-37, 5-69)   P. R. Adams, Chittagong 2003

Note: The best match figures for Bangladesh are 6-77 by Mohammad Rafique at Dhaka, 2003.

WEST INDIES v NEW ZEALAND

Series notes: West Indies have won 12 of the last 15 tosses and 22 out of 32 overall... In seven home Tests outside Bridgetown and Kingston, West Indies have never won... In two Tests at Georgetown, New Zealand average 75.6 runs per wicket and West Indies 64.7.

		Captains				
Season	*West Indies*	*New Zealand*	*T*	*WI*	*NZ*	*D*
1951-52*N*	J. D. C. Goddard	B. Sutcliffe	2	1	0	1
1955-56*N*	D. St E. Atkinson	J. R. Reid[1]	4	3	1	0
1968-69*N*	G. S. Sobers	G. T. Dowling	3	1	1	1
1971-72*W*	G. S. Sobers	G. T. Dowling[2]	5	0	0	5
1979-80*N*	C. H. Lloyd	G. P. Howarth	3	0	1	2
1984-85*W*	I. V. A. Richards	G. P. Howarth	4	2	0	2
1986-87*N*	I. V. A. Richards	J. V. Coney	3	1	1	1
1994-95*N*	C. A. Walsh	K. R. Rutherford	2	1	0	1
1995-96*N*	C. A. Walsh	L. K. Germon	2	1	0	1
1999-2000*N*	B. C. Lara	S. P. Fleming	2	0	2	0
2002*W*	C. L. Hooper	S. P. Fleming	2	0	1	1
In New Zealand			19	7	6	6
In West Indies			13	3	1	9
Totals.			32	10	7	15

N Played in New Zealand   W Played in West Indies.

Notes: The following deputised for the official touring captain or were appointed by the home authority for only a minor proportion of the series:
[1] H. B. Cave (First). [2] B. E. Congdon (Third, Fourth and Fifth).

HIGHEST INNINGS TOTALS

For West Indies in West Indies: 564-8 at Bridgetown. 1971-72
     in New Zealand: 660-5 dec. at Wellington. 1994-95

For New Zealand in West Indies: 543-3 dec. at Georgetown. 1971-72
     in New Zealand: 518-9 dec. at Wellington. 1999-2000

LOWEST INNINGS TOTALS

For West Indies in West Indies: 107 at Bridgetown. 2002
     in New Zealand: 77 at Auckland. 1955-56

For New Zealand in West Indies: 94 at Bridgetown. 1984-85
     in New Zealand: 74 at Dunedin 1955-56

DOUBLE-HUNDREDS

For West Indies (6)

258	S. M. Nurse at Christchurch . . . 1968-69	208*	J. C. Adams at St John's 1995-96
214	L. G. Rowe at Kingston 1971-72	208	S. L. Campbell at Bridgetown . . 1995-96
213	C. G. Greenidge at Auckland . . . 1986-87	204	C. H. Gayle at St George's 2002

For New Zealand (3)

259	G. M. Turner at Georgetown. .	1971-72	214	M. S. Sinclair at Wellington . . 1999-2000
223*	G. M. Turner at Kingston. . . .	1971-72		

INDIVIDUAL HUNDREDS

For West Indies (34)

3: D. L. Haynes, L. G. Rowe, E. D. Weekes.

2: J. C. Adams, S. L. Campbell, C. G. Greenidge, A. I. Kallicharran, S. M. Nurse.

1: M. C. Carew, C. A. Davis, R. C. Fredericks, C. H. Gayle, A. F. G. Griffith, C. L. King, B. C. Lara, J. R. Murray, I. V. A. Richards, R. B. Richardson, R. G. Samuels, G. S. Sobers, J. B. Stollmeyer, C. L. Walcott, F. M. M. Worrell.

For New Zealand (23)

3: M. D. Crowe.

2: N. J. Astle, B. E. Congdon, B. F. Hastings, G. M. Turner.

1: M. G. Burgess, J. J. Crowe, B. A. Edgar, S. P. Fleming, R. J. Hadlee, G. P. Howarth, T. W. Jarvis, A. C. Parore, M. S. Sinclair, S. B. Styris, B. R. Taylor, J. G. Wright.

Notes: E. D. Weekes in 1955-56 made three hundreds in consecutive innings.

L. G. Rowe and A. I. Kallicharran each scored hundreds in their first two innings in Test cricket. Rowe and Yasir Hameed (for Pakistan v Bangladesh) are the only two batsmen to do so in their first match.

RECORD PARTNERSHIPS FOR EACH WICKET

For West Indies

276 for 1st	A. F. G. Griffith and S. L. Campbell at Hamilton		1999-2000
269 for 2nd	R. C. Fredericks and L. G. Rowe at Kingston		1971-72
221 for 3rd	B. C. Lara and J. C. Adams at Wellington		1994-95
162 for 4th	{ E. D. Weekes and O. G. Smith at Dunedin		1955-56
	{ C. G. Greenidge and A. I. Kallicharran at Christchurch		1979-80
189 for 5th	F. M. M. Worrell and C. L. Walcott at Auckland		1951-52
254 for 6th	C. A. Davis and G. S. Sobers at Bridgetown		1971-72
143 for 7th	D. St E. Atkinson and J. D. C. Goddard at Christchurch		1955-56
83 for 8th	I. V. A. Richards and M. D. Marshall at Bridgetown		1984-85
70 for 9th	M. D. Marshall and J. Garner at Bridgetown		1984-85
31 for 10th	T. M. Findlay and G. C. Shillingford at Bridgetown		1971-72

For New Zealand

387 for 1st†	G. M. Turner and T. W. Jarvis at Georgetown		1971-72
210 for 2nd	G. P. Howarth and J. J. Crowe at Kingston		1984-85
241 for 3rd	J. G. Wright and M. D. Crowe at Wellington		1986-87
189 for 4th	M. S. Sinclair and N. J. Astle at Wellington		1999-2000
144 for 5th	N. J. Astle and J. T. C. Vaughan at Bridgetown		1995-96
220 for 6th	G. M. Turner and K. J. Wadsworth at Kingston		1971-72
143 for 7th	M. D. Crowe and I. D. S. Smith at Georgetown		1984-85
136 for 8th	B. E. Congdon and R. S. Cunis at Port-of-Spain		1971-72
62* for 9th	V. Pollard and R. S. Cunis at Auckland		1968-69
45 for 10th	D. K. Morrison and R. J. Kennedy at Bridgetown		1995-96

† *Record partnership against all countries.*

TEN WICKETS OR MORE IN A MATCH

For West Indies (2)

11-120 (4-40, 7-80)	M. D. Marshall, Bridgetown		1984-85
13-55 (7-37, 6-18)	C. A. Walsh, Wellington		1994-95

For New Zealand (4)

10-100 (3-73, 7-27)†	C. L. Cairns, Hamilton	1999-2000
10-124 (4-51, 6-73)†	E. J. Chatfield, Port-of-Spain	1984-85
11-102 (5-34, 6-68)†	R. J. Hadlee, Dunedin	1979-80
10-166 (4-71, 6-95)	G. B. Troup, Auckland	1979-80

† *On first appearance in West Indies–New Zealand Tests.*

SEVEN WICKETS OR MORE IN AN INNINGS

In addition to those listed above, the following have taken seven wickets or more in an innings:

For West Indies

7-53   D. St E. Atkinson, Auckland . . . 1955-56

For New Zealand

7-74   B. R. Taylor, Bridgetown 1971-72

WEST INDIES v INDIA

Series notes: The away side have not won this series since 1983-84... The side winning the toss have won only two of the last 13 Tests between the sides... Of the 16 Tests in the last ten years, the team batting second have won only two... Nineteen centuries have been scored in the last eight West Indies–India Tests... These sides have drawn only two of their 17 Test series... All six Tests in Georgetown have been drawn... India have never won in 26 Tests in the Caribbean outside Port-of-Spain... West Indies have won seven out of eight Tests against India in Bridgetown... Eight of the top ten analyses in this fixture have been recorded by spinners.

	Captains					
Season	West Indies	India	T	WI	I	D
1948-49*I*	J. D. C. Goddard	L. Amarnath	5	1	0	4
1952-53*W*	J. B. Stollmeyer	V. S. Hazare	5	1	0	4
1958-59*I*	F. C. M. Alexander	Ghulam Ahmed[1]	5	3	0	2
1961-62*W*	F. M. M. Worrell	N. J. Contractor[2]	5	5	0	0
1966-67*I*	G. S. Sobers	Nawab of Pataudi jun.	3	2	0	1
1970-71*W*	G. S. Sobers	A. L. Wadekar	5	0	1	4
1974-75*I*	C. H. Lloyd	Nawab of Pataudi jun.[3]	5	3	2	0
1975-76*W*	C. H. Lloyd	B. S. Bedi	4	2	1	1
1978-79*I*	A. I. Kallicharran	S. M. Gavaskar	6	0	1	5
1982-83*W*	C. H. Lloyd	Kapil Dev	5	2	0	3
1983-84*I*	C. H. Lloyd	Kapil Dev	6	3	0	3
1987-88*I*	I. V. A. Richards	D. B. Vengsarkar[4]	4	1	1	2
1988-89*W*	I. V. A. Richards	D. B. Vengsarkar	4	3	0	1
1994-95*I*	C. A. Walsh	M. Azharuddin	3	1	1	1
1996-97*W*	C. A. Walsh[5]	S. R. Tendulkar	5	1	0	4
2001-02*W*	C. L. Hooper	S. C. Ganguly	5	2	1	2
2002-03*I*	C. L. Hooper	S. C. Ganguly	3	0	2	1
	In India		40	14	7	19
	In West Indies		38	16	3	19
	Totals.		78	30	10	38

I Played in India.   W Played in West Indies.

Notes: The following deputised for the official touring captain or were appointed by the home authority for only a minor proportion of the series:
[1]P. R. Umrigar (First), V. Mankad (Fourth), H. R. Adhikari (Fifth). [2]Nawab of Pataudi jun. (Third, Fourth and Fifth). [3]S. Venkataraghavan (Second). [4]R. J. Shastri (Fourth). [5]B. C. Lara (Third).

HIGHEST INNINGS TOTALS

For West Indies in West Indies: 631-8 dec. at Kingston 1961-62
in India: 644-8 dec. at Delhi 1958-59

For India in West Indies: 513-9 dec. at St John's. 2001-02
in India: 644-7 dec. at Kanpur 1978-79

LOWEST INNINGS TOTALS

For West Indies in West Indies: 140 at Bridgetown 1996-97
in India: 127 at Delhi. 1987-88

For India in West Indies: 81 at Bridgetown. 1996-97
in India: 75 at Delhi. 1987-88

DOUBLE-HUNDREDS

For West Indies (6)

256	R. B. Kanhai at Calcutta	1958-59	237	F. M. M. Worrell at Kingston	1952-53
250	S. F. A. F. Bacchus at Kanpur	1978-79	233	C. L. Hooper at Georgetown	2001-02
242*	C. H. Lloyd at Bombay	1974-75	207	E. D. Weekes at Port-of-Spain	1952-53

For India (5)

236*	S. M. Gavaskar at Madras	1983-84	205	S. M. Gavaskar at Bombay	1978-79
220	S. M. Gavaskar at Port-of-Spain	1970-71	201	N. S. Sidhu at Port-of-Spain	1996-97
212	D. N. Sardesai at Kingston	1970-71			

INDIVIDUAL HUNDREDS

For West Indies (93)

8: I. V. A. Richards, G. S. Sobers.

7: C. H. Lloyd, E. D. Weekes.

5: S. Chanderpaul, C. G. Greenidge, C. L. Hooper.

4: R. B. Kanhai, C. L. Walcott.

3: A. I. Kallicharran.

2: J. C. Adams, B. F. Butcher, C. A. Davis, R. C. Fredericks, D. L. Haynes, W. W. Hinds, A. L. Logie, A. F. Rae, R. B. Richardson, J. B. Stollmeyer.

1: S. F. A. F. Bacchus, R. J. Christiani, P. J. L. Dujon, H. A. Gomes, G. E. Gomez, J. K. Holt, C. C. Hunte, R. D. Jacobs, B. C. Lara, E. D. A. McMorris, B. H. Pairaudeau, M. N. Samuels, O. G. Smith, J. S. Solomon, A. B. Williams, S. C. Williams, F. M. M. Worrell.

For India (67)

13: S. M. Gavaskar.

6: D. B. Vengsarkar.

4: G. R. Viswanath.

3: M. Amarnath, C. G. Borde, Kapil Dev, D. N. Sardesai, N. S. Sidhu, S. R. Tendulkar, P. R. Umrigar.

2: R. Dravid, V. S. Hazare, V. V. S. Laxman, R. J. Shastri.

1: H. R. Adhikari, M. L. Apte, S. A. Durani, F. M. Engineer, A. D. Gaekwad, S. V. Manjrekar, V. L. Manjrekar, R. S. Modi, Mushtaq Ali, B. P. Patel, M. Prabhakar, A. Ratra, Pankaj Roy, V. Sehwag, E. D. Solkar.

RECORD PARTNERSHIPS FOR EACH WICKET

For West Indies

296	for 1st	C. G. Greenidge and D. L. Haynes at St John's	. . . .	1982-83
255	for 2nd	E. D. A. McMorris and R. B. Kanhai at Kingston	. . . .	1961-62
220	for 3rd	I. V. A. Richards and A. I. Kallicharran at Bridgetown	. . . .	1975-76
267	for 4th	C. L. Walcott and G. E. Gomez at Delhi	. . . .	1948-49
293	for 5th	C. L. Hooper and S. Chanderpaul at Georgetown	. . . .	2001-02
250	for 6th	C. H. Lloyd and D. L. Murray at Bombay	. . . .	1974-75
130	for 7th	C. G. Greenidge and M. D. Marshall at Kanpur	. . . .	1983-84
124	for 8th	I. V. A. Richards and K. D. Boyce at Delhi	. . . .	1974-75
161	for 9th†	C. H. Lloyd and A. M. E. Roberts at Calcutta	. . . .	1983-84
98*	for 10th	F. M. M. Worrell and W. W. Hall at Port-of-Spain	. . . .	1961-62

For India

201	for 1st	S. B. Bangar and V. Sehwag at Mumbai	. . . .	2002-03
344*	for 2nd†	S. M. Gavaskar and D. B. Vengsarkar at Calcutta	. . . .	1978-79
177	for 3rd	N. S. Sidhu and S. R. Tendulkar at Nagpur	. . . .	1994-95
172	for 4th	G. R. Viswanath and A. D. Gaekwad at Kanpur	. . . .	1978-79
214	for 5th	S. R. Tendulkar and V. V. S. Laxman at Kolkata	. . . .	2002-03
170	for 6th	S. M. Gavaskar and R. J. Shastri at Madras	. . . .	1983-84
217	for 7th	V. V. S. Laxman and A. Ratra at St John's	. . .	2001-02
120*	for 8th	R. Dravid and Sarandeep Singh at Georgetown	. . . .	2001-02
143*	for 9th	S. M. Gavaskar and S. M. H. Kirmani at Madras	. . . .	1983-84
64	for 10th	J. Srinath and S. L. V. Raju at Mohali	. . . .	1994-95

† *Record partnership against all countries.*

TEN WICKETS OR MORE IN A MATCH

For West Indies (4)

11-126 (6-50, 5-76)	W. W. Hall, Kanpur	. . . .	1958-59
11-89 (5-34, 6-55)	M. D. Marshall, Port-of-Spain	. . . .	1988-89
12-121 (7-64, 5-57)	A. M. E. Roberts, Madras	. . . .	1974-75
10-101 (6-62, 4-39)	C. A. Walsh, Kingston	. . . .	1988-89

For India (4)

11-235 (7-157, 4-78)†	B. S. Chandrasekhar, Bombay	. . . .	1966-67
10-223 (9-102, 1-121)	S. P. Gupte, Kanpur	. . . .	1958-59
16-136 (8-61, 8-75)†	N. D. Hirwani, Madras	. . . .	1987-88
10-135 (1-52, 9-83)	Kapil Dev, Ahmedabad	. . . .	1983-84

† *On first appearance in West Indies–India Tests.*

SEVEN WICKETS OR MORE IN AN INNINGS

In addition to those listed above, the following have taken seven wickets or more in an innings:

For West Indies

8-38	L. R. Gibbs, Bridgetown	. . . . . .	1961-62	9-95 J. M. Noreiga, Port-of-Spain . . .	1970-71
7-98	L. R. Gibbs, Bombay	. . . .	1974-75		

For India

7-162	S. P. Gupte, Port-of-Spain	. . . . .	1952-53	7-159 D. G. Phadkar, Madras	1948-49
7-48	Harbhajan Singh, Mumbai	. . . .	2002-03		

WEST INDIES v PAKISTAN

Series notes: The away side have not won this series since 1980-81... Pakistan have batted first in the last five Tests between the sides; before that West Indies batted first in the previous seven... In the last three series West Indies have failed to pass 400; Pakistan have managed it five times... West Indies have won none of their six Tests at Karachi, but are unbeaten in five at Lahore... Pakistan have won none of the nine Tests played in Bridgetown, Kingston and St John's... West Indies average 36.3 runs per wicket at home and 23.3 in Pakistan... Inzamam-ul-Haq has made 840 Test runs against West Indies, and needs 252 to overtake I. V. A. Richards as the top-scorer in this fixture... Pakistan lead 6–1 in the first Test of series between the sides, but West Indies lead 6–3 in the second Test and 4–1 in the third... The best figures in this fixture were returned by a West Indian (eight for 29 by C. E. H. Croft) but the 12 next-best analyses were all taken by Pakistanis.

Season	West Indies	*Captains* Pakistan	T	WI	P	D
1957-58*W*	F. C. M. Alexander	A. H. Kardar	5	3	1	1
1958-59*P*	F. C. M. Alexander	Fazal Mahmood	3	1	2	0
1974-75*P*	C. H. Lloyd	Intikhab Alam	2	0	0	2
1976-77*W*	C. H. Lloyd	Mushtaq Mohammad	5	2	1	2
1980-81*P*	C. H. Lloyd	Javed Miandad	4	1	0	3
1986-87*P*	I. V. A. Richards	Imran Khan	3	1	1	1
1987-88*W*	I. V. A. Richards[1]	Imran Khan	3	1	1	1
1990-91*P*	D. L. Haynes	Imran Khan	3	1	1	1
1992-93*W*	R. B. Richardson	Wasim Akram	3	2	0	1
1997-98*P*	C. A. Walsh	Wasim Akram	3	0	3	0
1999-2000*W*	J. C. Adams	Moin Khan	3	1	0	2
2001-02*U*	C. L. Hooper	Waqar Younis	2	0	2	0
In West Indies			19	9	3	7
In Pakistan			18	4	7	7
In United Arab Emirates			2	0	2	0
Totals			39	13	12	14

P Played in Pakistan.   W Played in West Indies.   U Played in United Arab Emirates.

Note: The following was appointed by the home authority for only a minor proportion of the series:

[1]C. G. Greenidge (First).

HIGHEST INNINGS TOTALS

For West Indies in West Indies: 790-3 dec. at Kingston	1957-58
in Pakistan: 493 at Karachi	1974-75
in United Arab Emirates: 366 at Sharjah	2001-02
For Pakistan in West Indies: 657-8 dec. at Bridgetown	1957-58
in Pakistan: 471 at Rawalpindi	1997-98
in United Arab Emirates: 493 at Sharjah	2001-02

LOWEST INNINGS TOTALS

For West Indies in West Indies: 127 at Port-of-Spain	1992-93
in Pakistan: 53 at Faisalabad	1986-87
in United Arab Emirates: 171 at Sharjah	2001-02
For Pakistan in West Indies: 106 at Bridgetown	1957-58
in Pakistan: 77 at Lahore	1986-87
in United Arab Emirates: 472 at Sharjah	2001-02

DOUBLE-HUNDREDS

For West Indies (3)

365*	G. S. Sobers at Kingston	1957-58	217	R. B. Kanhai at Lahore	1958-59
260	C. C. Hunte at Kingston	1957-58			

For Pakistan (1)

337　Hanif Mohammad at Bridgetown 1957-58

INDIVIDUAL HUNDREDS

For West Indies (26)

3: D. L. Haynes, C. L. Hooper, C. C. Hunte, G. S. Sobers.
2: I. V. A. Richards.
1: L. Baichan, P. J. L. Dujon, R. C. Fredericks, C. G. Greenidge, W. W. Hinds, B. D. Julien, A. I. Kallicharran, R. B. Kanhai, C. H. Lloyd, I. T. Shillingford, C. L. Walcott, E. D. Weekes.

For Pakistan (30)

3: Inzamam-ul-Haq, Yousuf Youhana.
2: Aamir Sohail, Hanif Mohammad, Javed Miandad, Majid Khan, Mushtaq Mohammad, Wasim Raja, Wazir Mohammad.
1: Asif Iqbal, Ijaz Ahmed, sen., Imran Khan, Imran Nazir, Imtiaz Ahmed, Rashid Latif, Saeed Ahmed, Salim Malik, Shahid Afridi, Younis Khan.

RECORD PARTNERSHIPS FOR EACH WICKET

For West Indies

182	for 1st	R. C. Fredericks and C. G. Greenidge at Kingston	1976-77
446	for 2nd†	C. C. Hunte and G. S. Sobers at Kingston	1957-58
169	for 3rd	D. L. Haynes and B. C. Lara at Port-of-Spain	1992-93
188*	for 4th	G. S. Sobers and C. L. Walcott at Kingston	1957-58
185	for 5th	E. D. Weekes and O. G. Smith at Bridgetown	1957-58
151	for 6th	C. H. Lloyd and D. L. Murray at Bridgetown	1976-77
74	for 7th	S. Chanderpaul and N. A. M. McLean at Georgetown	1999-2000
60	for 8th	C. L. Hooper and A. C. Cummins at St John's	1992-93
61*	for 9th	P. J. L. Dujon and W. K. M. Benjamin at Bridgetown	1987-88
106	for 10th†	C. L. Hooper and C. A. Walsh at St John's	1992-93

For Pakistan

298	for 1st†	Aamir Sohail and Ijaz Ahmed, sen. at Karachi	1997-98
190	for 2nd	Shahid Afridi and Younis Khan at Sharjah	2001-02
323	for 3rd	Aamir Sohail and Inzamam-ul-Haq at Rawalpindi	1997-98
174	for 4th	Shoaib Mohammad and Salim Malik at Karachi	1990-91
88	for 5th	Basit Ali and Inzamam-ul-Haq at St John's	1992-93
206	for 6th	Inzamam-ul-Haq and Abdul Razzaq at Georgetown	1999-2000
128	for 7th‡	Wasim Raja and Wasim Bari at Karachi	1974-75
94	for 8th	Salim Malik and Salim Yousuf at Port-of-Spain	1987-88
96	for 9th	Inzamam-ul-Haq and Nadeem Khan at St John's	1992-93
133	for 10th	Wasim Raja and Wasim Bari at Bridgetown	1976-77

† *Record partnership against all countries.*
‡ *Although Pakistan's seventh wicket added 168 runs against West Indies at Lahore in 1980-81, this comprised two partnerships. Imran Khan added 72* with Abdul Qadir (retired hurt) and a further 96 with Sarfraz Nawaz.*

TEN WICKETS OR MORE IN A MATCH

For Pakistan (4)

12-100 (6-34, 6-66)	Fazal Mahmood, Dacca	1958-59
11-121 (7-80, 4-41)	Imran Khan, Georgetown	1987-88
10-106 (5-35, 5-71)	Mushtaq Ahmed, Peshawar	1997-98
11-110 (6-61, 5-49)	Wasim Akram, St John's	1999-2000

Note: The best match figures for West Indies are 9-95 (8-29, 1-66) by C. E. H. Croft at Port-of-Spain, 1976-77.

WEST INDIES v SRI LANKA

Series notes: B. C. Lara has scored 1,125 runs in Tests between these teams, more than twice the next-best (S. T. Jayasuriya 506)... The team batting first have won only one of the eight Tests between the sides... Only seven of the 30 innings in this fixture have exceeded 300... There have been no away victories... West Indies have lost both matches where they won the toss and batted – and won both where they won the toss and fielded... H. P. Tillekeratne averages 206.00 at home to West Indies, and 11.33 away.

Season	West Indies	*Captains* Sri Lanka	T	WI	SL	D
1993-94*S*	R. B. Richardson	A. Ranatunga	1	0	0	1
1996-97*W*	C. A. Walsh	A. Ranatunga	2	1	0	1
2001-02*S*	C. L. Hooper	S. T. Jayasuriya	3	0	3	0
2003*W*	B. C. Lara	H. P. Tillekeratne	2	1	0	1
	In West Indies		4	2	0	2
	In Sri Lanka		4	0	3	1
	Totals		8	2	3	3

W Played in West Indies.   S Played in Sri Lanka.

HIGHEST INNINGS TOTALS

For West Indies in West Indies: 477-9 dec. at Gros Islet, St Lucia	2003
in Sri Lanka: 448 at Galle	2001-02
For Sri Lanka in West Indies: 354 at Gros Islet, St Lucia	2003
in Sri Lanka: 627-9 dec. at Colombo (SSC)	2001-02

LOWEST INNINGS TOTALS

For West Indies in West Indies: 147 at St Vincent	1996-97
in Sri Lanka: 144 at Galle	2001-02
For Sri Lanka in West Indies: 152 at St John's	1996-97
in Sri Lanka: 190 at Moratuwa	1993-94

> **❝** After bowling on four pancake-flat wickets against India, the home bowlers appreciated favourable conditions like desert explorers sighting a water fountain."
> The Sri Lankans in Australia, page 1242.

DOUBLE-HUNDREDS

For West Indies (2)

221 B. C. Lara at Colombo (SSC) .. 2001-02 | 209 B. C. Lara at Gros Islet, St Lucia 2003

For Sri Lanka (1)

204* H. P. Tillekeratne at Colombo
    (SSC) 2001-02

INDIVIDUAL HUNDREDS

For West Indies (6)

5: B. C. Lara.
1: W. W. Hinds.

For Sri Lanka (4)

2: H. P. Tillekeratne
1: M. S. Atapattu, K. C. Sangakkara.

RECORD PARTNERSHIPS FOR EACH WICKET

For West Indies

160	for 1st	S. L. Campbell and S. C. Williams at St John's	1996-97
80	for 2nd	D. Ganga and R. R. Sarwan at Galle	2001-02
194	for 3rd	R. R. Sarwan and B. C. Lara at Colombo (SSC).	2001-02
153	for 4th	B. C. Lara and C. L. Hooper at Galle.	2001-02
84	for 5th	R. B. Richardson and C. L. Hooper at Moratuwa	1993-94
41	for 6th	B. C. Lara and R. D. Jacobs at Kandy	2001-02
136	for 7th	B. C. Lara and O. A. C. Banks at Gros Islet, St Lucia.	2003
53	for 8th	R. I. C. Holder and C. E. L. Ambrose at St Vincent	1996-97
13	for 9th	W. K. M. Benjamin and C. E. L. Ambrose at Moratuwa.	1993-94
29*	for 10th	O. A. C. Banks and J. E. Taylor at Gros Islet, St Lucia	2003

For Sri Lanka

126*	for 1st	M. S. Atapattu and S. T. Jayasuriya at Gros Islet, St Lucia	2003
109	for 2nd	M. S. Atapattu and K. C. Sangakkara at Galle	2001-02
162	for 3rd	K. C. Sangakkara and D. P. M. D. Jayawardene at Galle.	2001-02
110	for 4th	S. T. Jayasuriya and A. Ranatunga at St John's.	1996-97
141	for 5th	R. P. Arnold and H. P. Tillekeratne at Colombo (SSC)	2001-02
165	for 6th	H. P. Tillekeratne and T. T. Samaraweera at Colombo (SSC)	2001-02
52	for 7th	K. C. Sangakkara and W. P. U. J. C. Vaas at Kingston	2003
19	for 8th	H. P. Tillekeratne and D. N. T. Zoysa at Colombo (SSC)	2001-02
42	for 9th	H. P. Tillekeratne and M. R. C. N. Bandaratilleke at Colombo (SSC)	2001-02
28	for 10th	W. P. U. J. C. Vaas and R. A. P. Nissanka at Gros Islet, St Lucia . . .	2003

TEN WICKETS OR MORE IN A MATCH

For Sri Lanka (3)

11-170 (6-126, 5-44)	M Muralitharan, Galle	2001-02
10-135 (4-54, 6-81)	M. Muralitharan, Kandy.	2001-02
14-191 (7-120, 7-71)	W. P. U. J. C. Vaas, Colombo (SSC).	2001-02

Note: The best match figures for West Indies are 9-85 (2-28, 7-57) by C. D. Collymore at Kingston, 2003.

WEST INDIES v ZIMBABWE

Series notes: West Indies have never lost a Test to Zimbabwe... The two matches between the sides at Harare are the only ones in which Zimbabwe have not been beaten... Zimbabwe do outscore West Indies in centuries – six to four – but the three highest scores are all by West Indians... C. B. Wishart and A. M. Blignaut have both been out twice in the 90s.

Season	West Indies	*Captains* Zimbabwe	T	WI	Z	D
1999-2000*W*	J. C. Adams	A. Flower	2	2	0	0
2001*Z*	C. L. Hooper	H. H. Streak	2	1	0	1
2003-04*Z*	B. C. Lara	H. H. Streak	2	1	0	1
	In West Indies..............		2	2	0	0
	In Zimbabwe...............		4	2	0	2
	Totals		6	4	0	2

W Played in West Indies.   Z Played in Zimbabwe.

HIGHEST INNINGS TOTALS

For West Indies in West Indies: 339 at Kingston 1999-2000
                          in Zimbabwe: 559-6 dec. at Bulawayo 2001

For Zimbabwe in West Indies: 308 at Kingston 1999-2000
                        in Zimbabwe: 563-9 dec. at Harare 2001

LOWEST INNINGS TOTALS

For West Indies in West Indies: 147 at Port-of-Spain..................... 1999-2000
                          in Zimbabwe: 128 at Bulawayo........................ 2003-04

For Zimbabwe in West Indies: 63 at Port-of-Spain 1999-2000
                        in Zimbabwe: 104 at Bulawayo........................ 2003-04

HIGHEST INDIVIDUAL SCORES

For West Indies

191   B. C. Lara at Bulawayo....... 2003-04

For Zimbabwe

127* H. H. Streak at Harare 2003-04

INDIVIDUAL HUNDREDS

For West Indies (4)

1: J. C. Adams, C. H. Gayle, C. L. Hooper, B. C. Lara.

For Zimbabwe (6)

1: A. D. R. Campbell, A. Flower, M. W. Goodwin, H. Masakadza, H. H. Streak, M. A. Vermeulen.

RECORD PARTNERSHIPS FOR EACH WICKET

For West Indies

214 for 1st	D. Ganga and C. H. Gayle at Bulawayo		2001
100 for 2nd	D. Ganga and S. Chanderpaul at Harare		2001
52 for 3rd	D. Ganga and B. C. Lara at Harare		2003-04
190 for 4th	B. C. Lara and R. R. Sarwan at Bulawayo		2003-04
100 for 5th	C. L. Hooper and M. N. Samuels at Bulawayo		2001
68 for 6th	S. Chanderpaul and R. D. Jacobs at Harare		2003-04
50 for 7th	{ R. R. Sarwan and N. C. McGarrell at Harare		2001
	{ S. Chanderpaul and V. C. Drakes at Harare		2003-04
148 for 8th	J. C. Adams and F. A. Rose at Kingston		1999-2000
26 for 9th	M. Dillon and C. D. Collymore at Bulawayo		2003-04
26 for 10th	{ W. W. Hinds and C. A. Walsh at Port-of-Spain		1999-2000
	{ C. D. Collymore and F. H. Edwards at Harare		2003-04

For Zimbabwe

164 for 1st†	D. D. Ebrahim and A. D. R. Campbell at Bulawayo		2001
91 for 2nd	A. D. R. Campbell and H. Masakadza at Harare		2001
169 for 3rd	H. Masakadza and C. B. Wishart at Harare		2001
176 for 4th	M. W. Goodwin and A. Flower at Kingston		1999-2000
42 for 5th	C. B. Wishart and S. Matsikenyeri at Harare		2003-04
79 for 6th	S. Matsikenyeri and T. Taibu at Harare		2003-04
154 for 7th†	H. H. Streak and A. M. Blignaut at Harare		2001
168 for 8th†	H. H. Streak and A. M. Blignaut at Harare		2003-04
34 for 9th	A. M. Blignaut and R. W. Price at Bulawayo		2003-04
54 for 10th	S. V. Carlisle and H. K. Olonga at Kingston		1999-2000

† *Record partnership against all countries.*

TEN WICKETS OR MORE IN A MATCH

For Zimbabwe

10-161 (6-73, 4-88)	R. W. Price, Harare		2003-04

Note: The best match figures for West Indies are 7-50 (4-42, 3-8) by C. E. L. Ambrose at Port-of-Spain, 1999-2000.

WEST INDIES v BANGLADESH

Series notes: Hannan Sarkar has been dismissed by the first ball of three of the four Tests between the sides, each time by P. T. Collins... Bangladesh have batted first in all four Tests between the sides... Bangladesh have recorded 17 ducks to West Indies' two.

		Captains					
Season	West Indies		Bangladesh	T	WI	B	D
2002-03*B*	R. D. Jacobs		Khaled Mashud	2	2	0	0
2003-04*W*	B. C. Lara		Habibul Bashar	2	1	0	1
	In West Indies			2	1	0	1
	In Bangladesh			2	2	0	0
	Totals			4	3	0	1

B Played in Bangladesh. W Played in West Indies.

HIGHEST INNINGS TOTALS

For West Indies in West Indies: 559-4 dec. at Kingston   2003-04
     in Bangladesh: 536 at Dhaka   2002-03

For Bangladesh in West Indies: 416 at Gros Islet, St Lucia   2003-04
     in Bangladesh: 212 at Chittagong   2002-03

LOWEST INNINGS TOTALS

For West Indies in West Indies: 352 at Gros Islet, St Lucia   2003-04
     in Bangladesh: 296 at Chittagong   2002-03

For Bangladesh in West Indies: 176 at Kingston.   2003-04
     in Bangladesh: 87 at Dhaka   2002-03

DOUBLE-HUNDRED

For West Indies (1)

261* R. R. Sarwan at Kingston 2003-04

Highest score for Bangladesh: 113 by Habibul Bashar at Gros Islet, St Lucia, 2003-04.

INDIVIDUAL HUNDREDS

For West Indies (5)

2: R. R. Sarwan.
1: S. Chanderpaul, C. H. Gayle, B. C. Lara.

For Bangladesh (3)

1: Habibul Bashar, Khaled Mashud, Mohammad Rafique.

RECORD PARTNERSHIPS FOR EACH WICKET

For West Indies

131	for 1st	C. H. Gayle and W. W. Hinds at Dhaka	2002-03
87	for 2nd	C. H. Gayle and R. R. Sarwan at Gros Islet, St Lucia.	2003-04
179	for 3rd	B. C. Lara and R. R. Sarwan at Kingston.	2003-04
176	for 4th	R. R. Sarwan and M. N. Samuels at Dhaka	2002-03
262*	for 5th	R. R. Sarwan and S. Chanderpaul at Kingston.	2003-04
99	for 6th	D. Ganga and R. D. Jacobs at Chittagong.	2002-03
38	for 7th	R. D. Jacobs and V. C. Drakes at Chittagong.	2002-03
40	for 8th	R. D. Jacobs and D. B. Powell at Dhaka.	2002-03
34	for 9th	R. D. Jacobs and P. T. Collins at Dhaka	2002-03
17	for 10th	P. T. Collins and J. J. C. Lawson at Chittagong	2002-03

For Bangladesh

44	for 1st	Hannan Sarkar and Al Sahariar at Chittagong.	2002-03
121	for 2nd	Javed Omar and Habibul Bashar at Gros Islet, St Lucia	2003-04
50	for 3rd	Habibul Bashar and Rajin Saleh at Gros Islet, St Lucia	2003-04
120	for 4th†	Habibul Bashar and Manjural Islam Rana at Kingston	2003-04
26	for 5th	Mohammad Ashraful and Alok Kapali at Chittagong	2002-03
73	for 6th	Alok Kapali and Khaled Mashud at Dhaka	2002-03

73 for 7th	Alok Kapali and Enamul Haque at Chittagong	2002-03
87 for 8th†	Mohammad Ashraful and Mohammad Rafique at Gros Islet, St Lucia	2003-04
74 for 9th†	Khaled Mashud and Tapash Baisya at Gros Islet, St Lucia	2003-04
46 for 10th†	Mohammad Rafique and Tareq Aziz at Gros Islet, St Lucia.	2003-04
46 for 10th†	Tapash Baisya and Tareq Aziz at Kingston.	2003-04

† *Record partnership against all countries.*

BEST BOWLING MATCH ANALYSES

For West Indies

9-117 (3-64, 6-53)   P. T. Collins, Kingston   2003-04

For Bangladesh

6-117 (4-72, 2-45)   Tapash Baisya, Chittagong.   2002-03

NEW ZEALAND v INDIA

Series notes: The away team have won none of the last 17 Tests between the sides... Five of New Zealand's nine wins over India have come in the second Test of the series... New Zealand have lost only one of the last 11 Tests between the sides... The team batting first have won none of the last 15... In the last series in India the teams averaged 53.4 runs per wicket – more than three times as many as in the last series in New Zealand (16.2)... India are unbeaten in four Tests at Auckland, but have never won in four Tests at Christchurch.

		Captains					
Season	New Zealand		India	T	NZ	I	D
1955-56*I*	H. B. Cave		P. R. Umrigar[1]	5	0	2	3
1964-65*I*	J. R. Reid		Nawab of Pataudi jun.	4	0	1	3
1967-68*N*	G. T. Dowling[2]		Nawab of Pataudi jun.	4	1	3	0
1969-70*I*	G. T. Dowling		Nawab of Pataudi jun.	3	1	1	1
1975-76*N*	G. M. Turner		B. S. Bedi[3]	3	1	1	1
1976-77*I*	G. M. Turner		B. S. Bedi	3	0	2	1
1980-81*N*	G. P. Howarth		S. M. Gavaskar	3	1	0	2
1988-89*I*	J. G. Wright		D. B. Vengsarkar	3	1	2	0
1989-90*N*	J. G. Wright		M. Azharuddin	3	1	0	2
1993-94*N*	K. R. Rutherford		M. Azharuddin	1	0	0	1
1995-96*I*	L. K. Germon		M. Azharuddin	3	0	1	2
1998-99*N*†	S. P. Fleming		M. Azharuddin	2	1	0	1
1999-2000*I*	S. P. Fleming		S. R. Tendulkar	3	0	1	2
2002-03*N*	S. P. Fleming		S. C. Ganguly	2	2	0	0
2003-04*I*	S. P. Fleming		S. C. Ganguly[4]	2	0	0	2
	In India			26	2	10	14
	In New Zealand			18	7	4	7
	Totals.			44	9	14	21

I Played in India.   N Played in New Zealand.

† *The First Test at Dunedin was abandoned without a ball being bowled and is excluded.*

Notes: The following deputised for the official touring captain or were appointed by the home authority for a minor proportion of the series:
[1]Ghulam Ahmed (First). [2]B. W. Sinclair (First). [3]S. M. Gavaskar (First). [4]R. Dravid (Second).

HIGHEST INNINGS TOTALS

For New Zealand in New Zealand: 502 at Christchurch................. 1967-68
             in India: 630-6 dec. at Mohali 2003-04

For India in New Zealand: 482 at Auckland 1989-90
          in India: 583-7 dec. at Ahmedabad......................... 1999-2000

LOWEST INNINGS TOTALS

For New Zealand in New Zealand: 94 at Hamilton.................... 2002-03
            in India: 124 at Hyderabad 1988-89

For India in New Zealand: 81 at Wellington 1975-76
         in India: 83 at Mohali 1999-2000

DOUBLE-HUNDREDS

For New Zealand (2)

239   G. T. Dowling at Christchurch.   1967-68 | 230*   B. Sutcliffe at Delhi   1955-56

For India (6)

231	V. Mankad at Madras	1955-56	222	R. Dravid at Ahmedabad	2003-04
223	V. Mankad at Bombay......	1955-56	217	S. R. Tendulkar at Ahmedabad	1999-2000
223	P. R. Umrigar at Hyderabad ..	1955-56	200*	D. N. Sardesai at Bombay ...	1964-65

INDIVIDUAL HUNDREDS

For New Zealand (27)

3: G. T. Dowling, B. Sutcliffe, J. G. Wright.
2: J. R. Reid, G. M. Turner.
1: N. J. Astle, C. L. Cairns, M. D. Crowe, J. W. Guy, G. P. Howarth, A. H. Jones, C. D. McMillan, J. M. Parker, J. F. Reid, M. H. Richardson, I. D. S. Smith, S. B. Styris, B. R. Taylor, L. Vincent.

For India (36)

4: R. Dravid.
3: S. C. Ganguly, V. L. Manjrekar, S. R. Tendulkar.
2: M. Azharuddin, S. M. Gavaskar, V. Mankad, Nawab of Pataudi, jun., Pankaj Roy, D. N. Sardesai.
1: S. Amarnath, C. G. Borde, A. G. Kripal Singh, V. V. S. Laxman, G. S. Ramchand, S. Ramesh, V. Sehwag, N. S. Sidhu, P. R. Umrigar, G. R. Viswanath, A. L. Wadekar.

RECORD PARTNERSHIPS FOR EACH WICKET

For New Zealand

231	for 1st	M. H. Richardson and L. Vincent at Mohali	2003-04
155	for 2nd	G. T. Dowling and B. E. Congdon at Dunedin.............	1967-68
222*	for 3rd	B. Sutcliffe and J. R. Reid at Delhi	1955-56
160	for 4th	R. G. Twose and C. D. McMillan at Hamilton.............	1998-99
140	for 5th	C. D. McMillan and A. C. Parore at Hamilton.............	1998-99
137	for 6th	C. D. McMillan and C. L. Cairns at Wellington	1998-99
163	for 7th	B. Sutcliffe and B. R. Taylor at Calcutta.................	1964-65
137	for 8th	D. J. Nash and D. L. Vettori at Wellington	1998-99
136	for 9th†	I. D. S. Smith and M. C. Snedden at Auckland	1989-90
61	for 10th	J. T. Ward and R. O. Collinge at Madras	1964-65

For India

413	for 1st†	V. Mankad and Pankaj Roy at Madras	1955-56
204	for 2nd	S. M. Gavaskar and S. Amarnath at Auckland	1975-76
238	for 3rd	P. R. Umrigar and V. L. Manjrekar at Hyderabad	1955-56
281	for 4th	S. R. Tendulkar and S. C. Ganguly at Ahmedabad	1999-2000
182	for 5th	R. Dravid and S. C. Ganguly at Ahmedabad	2003-04
193*	for 6th	D. N. Sardesai and Hanumant Singh at Bombay	1964-65
128	for 7th	S. R. Tendulkar and K. S. More at Napier	1989-90
144	for 8th	R. Dravid and J. Srinath at Hamilton	1998-99
105	for 9th	{ S. M. H. Kirmani and B. S. Bedi at Bombay	1976-77
		{ S. M. H. Kirmani and N. S. Yadav at Auckland............	1980-81
57	for 10th	R. B. Desai and B. S. Bedi at Dunedin	1967-68

† *Record partnership against all countries.*

TEN WICKETS OR MORE IN A MATCH

For New Zealand (2)

11-58 (4-35, 7-23)	R. J. Hadlee, Wellington	1975-76
10-88 (6-49, 4-39)	R. J. Hadlee, Bombay.......................	1988-89

For India (3)

10-134 (4-67, 6-67)	A. Kumble, Kanpur	1999-2000
11-140 (3-64, 8-76)	E. A. S. Prasanna, Auckland	1975-76
12-152 (8-72, 4-80)	S. Venkataraghavan, Delhi....................	1964-65

SEVEN WICKETS OR MORE IN AN INNINGS

In addition to those listed above, the following have taken seven wickets or more in an innings:

For New Zealand

7-65 S. B. Doull, Wellington 1998-99

For India

7-128 S. P. Gupte, Hyderabad........ 1955-56

NEW ZEALAND v PAKISTAN

Series notes: New Zealand have won only one, and lost 12, of 21 Tests against Pakistan when they have batted first... Seven of the last 12 wins in this fixture, and ten of the last 19, have been achieved by sides trailing on first innings... Eight of the nine double-centuries in this fixture have been made by Pakistanis... In two Tests against New Zealand, Shoaib Akhtar has taken 17 wickets at an average of 5.23, with a wicket every 16.52 balls... Seven of the 17 were out for ducks, and nine of the 17 bowled... D. L. Vettori has taken four wickets in three matches at an average of 100.25... New Zealand have failed to win in six Tests at Wellington and six at Karachi... Four of New Zealand's wins have come when they won the toss and fielded: in such games they trail 5–4; in others they trail 16–2.

Captains

Season	New Zealand	Pakistan	T	NZ	P	D
1955-56P	H. B. Cave	A. H. Kardar	3	0	2	1
1964-65N	J. R. Reid	Hanif Mohammad	3	0	0	3
1964-65P	J. R. Reid	Hanif Mohammad	3	0	2	1
1969-70P	G. T. Dowling	Intikhab Alam	3	1	0	2
1972-73N	B. E. Congdon	Intikhab Alam	3	0	1	2
1976-77P	G. M. Turner¹	Mushtaq Mohammad	3	0	2	1
1978-79N	M. G. Burgess	Mushtaq Mohammad	3	0	1	2
1984-85P	J. V. Coney	Zaheer Abbas	3	0	2	1
1984-85N	G. P. Howarth	Javed Miandad	3	2	0	1

Captains

Season	New Zealand	Pakistan	T	NZ	P	D
1988-89*N†*	J. G. Wright	Imran Khan	2	0	0	2
1990-91*P*	M. D. Crowe	Javed Miandad	3	0	3	0
1992-93*N*	K. R. Rutherford	Javed Miandad	1	0	1	0
1993-94*N*	K. R. Rutherford	Salim Malik	3	1	2	0
1995-96*N*	L. K. Germon	Wasim Akram	1	0	1	0
1996-97*P*	L. K. Germon	Saeed Anwar	2	1	1	0
2000-01*N*	S. P. Fleming	Moin Khan²	3	1	1	1
2002*P‡*	S. P. Fleming	Waqar Younis	1	0	1	0
2003-04*N*	S. P. Fleming	Inzamam-ul-Haq	2	0	1	1

		T	NZ	P	D
In Pakistan	....	21	2	13	6
In New Zealand	....	24	4	8	12
Totals	....	45	6	21	18

N Played in New Zealand.   P Played in Pakistan.

† *The First Test at Dunedin was abandoned without a ball being bowled and is excluded.*
‡ *The Second Test at Karachi was cancelled owing to civil disturbances.*

Note: The following deputised for the official touring captain:
¹J. M. Parker (Third). ²Inzamam-ul-Haq (Third).

HIGHEST INNINGS TOTALS

For New Zealand in New Zealand: 563 at Hamilton.....................	2003-04
in Pakistan: 482-6 dec. at Lahore	1964-65
For Pakistan in New Zealand: 616-5 dec. at Auckland....................	1988-89
in Pakistan: 643 at Lahore	2002

LOWEST INNINGS TOTALS

For New Zealand in New Zealand: 93 at Hamilton.....................	1992-93
in Pakistan: 70 at Dacca	1955-56
For Pakistan in New Zealand: 104 at Hamilton	2000-01
in Pakistan: 102 at Faisalabad	1990-91

DOUBLE-HUNDREDS

For New Zealand (1)

204* M. S. Sinclair at Christchurch . . 2000-01

For Pakistan (8)

329	Inzamam-ul-Haq at Lahore	2002	203*	Hanif Mohammad at Lahore ...	1964-65
271	Javed Miandad at Auckland....	1988-89	203*	Shoaib Mohammad at Karachi ..	1990-91
209	Imtiaz Ahmed at Lahore	1955-56	203	Yousuf Youhana at Christchurch	2000-01
206	Javed Miandad at Karachi	1976-77	201	Mushtaq Mohammad at Dunedin	1972-73

INDIVIDUAL HUNDREDS

For New Zealand (26)

3: J. F. Reid.
2: M. G. Burgess, M. D. Crowe.
1: M. D. Bell, J. V. Coney, B. A. Edgar, S. P. Fleming, M. J. Greatbatch, B. F. Hastings, G. P. Howarth, W. K. Lees, S. N. McGregor, R. E. Redmond, J. R. Reid, M. H. Richardson, B. W. Sinclair, M. S. Sinclair, S. A. Thomson, G. M. Turner, D. L. Vettori, J. G. Wright, B. A. Young.

For Pakistan (48)

7: Javed Miandad.

5: Shoaib Mohammad.

3: Asif Iqbal, Hanif Mohammad, Inzamam-ul-Haq, Majid Khan, Mushtaq Mohammad.

2: Ijaz Ahmed, sen., Sadiq Mohammad, Saeed Anwar, Salim Malik.

1: Basit Ali, Imran Nazir, Imtiaz Ahmed, Mohammad Ilyas, Mohammad Wasim, Moin Khan, Mudassar Nazar, Saeed Ahmed, Saqlain Mushtaq, Waqar Hassan, Younis Khan, Yousuf Youhana, Zaheer Abbas.

Note: Mushtaq and Sadiq Mohammad both hit hundreds at Hyderabad in 1976-77, the fourth time – after the Chappells (thrice) – that brothers had each scored hundreds in the same Test innings.

RECORD PARTNERSHIPS FOR EACH WICKET

For New Zealand

181 for 1st	M. H. Richardson and M. D. Bell at Hamilton	2000-01
195 for 2nd	J. G. Wright and G. P. Howarth at Napier	1978-79
178 for 3rd	B. W. Sinclair and J. R. Reid at Lahore	1964-65
147 for 4th	C. D. McMillan and S. P. Fleming at Hamilton.	2000-01
183 for 5th	M. G. Burgess and R. W. Anderson at Lahore	1976-77
145 for 6th	J. F. Reid and R. J. Hadlee at Wellington.	1984-85
186 for 7th	W. K. Lees and R. J. Hadlee at Karachi	1976-77
125 for 8th	S. P. Fleming and D. L. Vettori at Hamilton	2003-04
99 for 9th	D. L. Vettori and D. R. Tuffey at Hamilton	2003-04
151 for 10th†	B. F. Hastings and R. O. Collinge at Auckland	1972-73

For Pakistan

172 for 1st	Ramiz Raja and Shoaib Mohammad at Karachi	1990-91
262 for 2nd	Saeed Anwar and Ijaz Ahmed, sen. at Rawalpindi	1996-97
248 for 3rd	Shoaib Mohammad and Javed Miandad at Auckland	1988-89
350 for 4th†	Mushtaq Mohammad and Asif Iqbal at Dunedin	1972-73
281 for 5th†	Javed Miandad and Asif Iqbal at Lahore	1976-77
217 for 6th†	Hanif Mohammad and Majid Khan at Lahore.	1964-65
308 for 7th	Waqar Hassan and Imtiaz Ahmed at Lahore	1955-56
89 for 8th	Anil Dalpat and Iqbal Qasim at Karachi	1984-85
78 for 9th	Inzamam-ul-Haq and Shoaib Akhtar at Lahore	2002
65 for 10th	Salah-ud-Din and Mohammad Farooq at Rawalpindi	1964-65

† *Record partnership against all countries.*

TEN WICKETS OR MORE IN A MATCH

For New Zealand (1)

11-152 (7-52, 4-100)	C. Pringle, Faisalabad	1990-91

For Pakistan (11)

10-182 (5-91, 5-91)	Intikhab Alam, Dacca	1969-70
11-130 (7-52, 4-78)	Intikhab Alam, Dunedin	1972-73
11-130 (4-64, 7-66)†	Mohammad Zahid, Rawalpindi	1996-97
10-171 (3-115, 7-56)	Mushtaq Ahmed, Christchurch.	1995-96
10-143 (4-59, 6-84)	Mushtaq Ahmed, Lahore	1996-97
11-78 (5-48, 6-30)	Shoaib Akhtar, Christchurch	2003-04
10-106 (3-20, 7-86)	Waqar Younis, Karachi	1990-91
12-130 (7-76, 5-54)	Waqar Younis, Faisalabad	1990-91
10-128 (5-56, 5-72)	Wasim Akram, Dunedin	1984-85
11-179 (4-60, 7-119)	Wasim Akram, Wellington	1993-94
11-79 (5-37, 6-42)†	Zulfiqar Ahmed, Karachi	1955-56

† *On first appearance in New Zealand–Pakistan Tests.*

Note: Waqar Younis's performances were in successive matches.

SEVEN WICKETS OR MORE IN AN INNINGS

In addition to those listed above, the following have taken seven wickets or more in an innings:

For New Zealand

7-87   S. L. Boock, Hyderabad 1984-85

For Pakistan

7-99   Mohammad Nazir, Karachi . . . . 1969-70 | 7-74   Pervez Sajjad, Lahore. 1969-70

NEW ZEALAND v SRI LANKA

Series notes: Pending the 2004-05 series, the team batting first have won six and lost only one of the last 15 matches between these sides... New Zealand's three highest individual scores have come against Sri Lanka... S. P. Fleming needs 54 runs to become the first to score 1,000 in Tests between the teams... Sri Lanka's only victory in New Zealand came at Napier... New Zealand have won only three of the last 15 Tests between these sides, having won four of the first five... Sri Lanka have won none of the five Tests in which they have inserted New Zealand... New Zealand have won the toss in seven of the last nine Tests..

		Captains					
Season	*New Zealand*		*Sri Lanka*	*T*	*NZ*	*SL*	*D*
1982-83*N*	G. P. Howarth		D. S. de Silva	2	2	0	0
1983-84*S*	G. P. Howarth		L. R. D. Mendis	3	2	0	1
1986-87*S*†	J. J. Crowe		L. R. D. Mendis	1	0	0	1
1990-91*N*	M. D. Crowe[1]		A. Ranatunga	3	0	0	3
1992-93*S*	M. D. Crowe		A. Ranatunga	2	0	1	1
1994-95*N*	K. R. Rutherford		A. Ranatunga	2	0	1	1
1996-97*N*	S. P. Fleming		A. Ranatunga	2	2	0	0
1997-98*S*	S. P. Fleming		A. Ranatunga	3	1	2	0
2003*S*	S. P. Fleming		H. P. Tillekeratne	2	0	0	2
	In New Zealand			9	4	1	4
	In Sri Lanka			11	3	3	5
	Totals			20	7	4	9

N Played in New Zealand.   S Played in Sri Lanka.

† *The Second and Third Tests were cancelled owing to civil disturbances.*

Note: The following was appointed by the home authority for only a minor proportion of the series:

   [1]. D. S. Smith (Third).

HIGHEST INNINGS TOTALS

For New Zealand in New Zealand: 671-4 at Wellington   1990-91
      in Sri Lanka: 515-7 dec. at Colombo (PSS)   2003

For Sri Lanka in New Zealand: 497 at Wellington   1990-91
      in Sri Lanka: 483 at Colombo (PSS)   2003

LOWEST INNINGS TOTALS

For New Zealand in New Zealand: 109 at Napier	1994-95
in Sri Lanka: 102 at Colombo (SSC)	1992-93
For Sri Lanka in New Zealand: 93 at Wellington	1982-83
in Sri Lanka: 97 at Kandy.	1986-87

DOUBLE-HUNDREDS

For New Zealand (3)

299	M. D. Crowe at Wellington	1990-91
274*	S. P. Fleming at Colombo (PSS) .	2003

267*	B. A. Young at Dunedin	1996-97

For Sri Lanka (2)

267	P. A. de Silva at Wellington	1990-91

201*	D. S. B. P. Kuruppu at Colombo (CCC)	1986-87

INDIVIDUAL HUNDREDS

For New Zealand (14)

3: A. H. Jones.
2: M. D. Crowe, S. P. Fleming.
1: J. J. Crowe, R. J. Hadlee, C. D. McMillan, J. F. Reid, K. R. Rutherford, J. G. Wright, B. A. Young.

For Sri Lanka (13)

3: A. P. Gurusinha.
2: P. A. de Silva, R. S. Mahanama, H. P. Tillekeratne.
1: R. L. Dias, D. P. M. D. Jayawardene, R. S. Kaluwitharana, D. S. B. P. Kuruppu.

Note: A. H. Jones and A. P. Gurusinha, on opposing sides, each hit two hundreds at Hamilton in 1990-91, the second time this had happened in Tests, after D. C. S. Compton and A. R. Morris, for England and Australia at Adelaide in 1946-47.

RECORD PARTNERSHIPS FOR EACH WICKET

For New Zealand

161	for 1st	T. J. Franklin and J. G. Wright at Hamilton	1990-91
172	for 2nd	M. H. Richardson and S. P. Fleming at Colombo (PSS)	2003
467	for 3rd†‡	A. H. Jones and M. D. Crowe at Wellington.	1990-91
240	for 4th	S. P. Fleming and C. D. McMillan at Colombo (RPS)	1997-98
151	for 5th	K. R. Rutherford and C. Z. Harris at Moratuwa	1992-93
246*	for 6th†	J. J. Crowe and R. J. Hadlee at Colombo (CCC).	1986-87
47	for 7th	D. N. Patel and M. L. Su'a at Dunedin	1994-95
79	for 8th	J. V. Coney and W. K. Lees at Christchurch	1982-83
43	for 9th	A. C. Parore and P. J. Wiseman at Galle	1997-98
52	for 10th	W. K. Lees and E. J. Chatfield at Christchurch	1982-83

For Sri Lanka

102	for 1st	R. S. Mahanama and U. C. Hathurusinghe at Colombo (SSC)	. . . . .	1992-93
138	for 2nd	R. S. Mahanama and A. P. Gurusinha at Moratuwa	. . . .	1992-93
159*	for 3rd§	S. Wettimuny and R. L. Dias at Colombo (SSC)	. . . .	1983-84
192	for 4th	A. P. Gurusinha and H. P. Tillekeratne at Dunedin	. . . .	1994-95
133	for 5th	D. P. M. D. Jayawardene and H. P. Tillekeratne at Colombo (PSS)	. .	2003
109*	for 6th¶	R. S. Madugalle and A. Ranatunga at Colombo (CCC)	. . . .	1983-84
109	for 6th	D. S. B. P. Kuruppu and R. S. Madugalle at Colombo (PSS)	. . . . .	1986-87
137	for 7th	R. S. Kaluwitharana and W. P. U. J. C. Vaas at Dunedin	. . . . . .	1996-97
73	for 8th	H. P. Tillekeratne and G. P. Wickremasinghe at Dunedin	. . . . . .	1996-97
31	for 9th	{ G. F. Labrooy and R. J. Ratnayake at Auckland	. . . .	1990-91
		{ S. T. Jayasuriya and R. J. Ratnayake at Auckland	. . . .	1990-91
71	for 10th	R. S. Kaluwitharana and M. Muralitharan at Colombo (SSC)	. . . . .	1997-98

† *Record partnership against all countries.*
‡ *Record third-wicket partnership in first-class cricket.*
§ *163 runs were added for this wicket in two separate partnerships: S. Wettimuny retired hurt and was replaced by J. R. Ratnayeke when 159 had been added.*
¶ *119 runs were added for this wicket in two separate partnerships: R. S. Madugalle retired hurt and was replaced by D. S. de Silva when 109 had been added.*

TEN WICKETS OR MORE IN A MATCH

For New Zealand (1)

10-102 (5-73, 5-29)	R. J. Hadlee, Colombo (CCC)	1983-84

For Sri Lanka (1)

10-90 (5-47, 5-43)†	W. P. U. J. C. Vaas, Napier	1994-95

† *On first appearance in New Zealand–Sri Lanka Tests.*

NEW ZEALAND v ZIMBABWE

Series notes: New Zealand have won four of the last five Tests between the sides... The team winning the toss have batted first in the last six matches, and nine of 11 overall... The team batting first have won only two out of 11 Tests between these sides.

		Captains				
Season	New Zealand	Zimbabwe	T	NZ	Z	D
1992-93Z	M. D. Crowe	D. L. Houghton	2	1	0	1
1995-96N	L. K. Germon	A. Flower	2	0	0	2
1997-98Z	S. P. Fleming	A. D. R. Campbell	2	0	0	2
1997-98N	S. P. Fleming	A. D. R. Campbell	2	2	0	0
2000-01Z	S. P. Fleming	H. H. Streak	2	2	0	0
2000-01N	S. P. Fleming	H. H. Streak	1	0	0	1
	In New Zealand		5	2	0	3
	In Zimbabwe		6	3	0	3
	Totals		11	5	0	6

N Played in New Zealand. Z Played in Zimbabwe.

HIGHEST INNINGS TOTALS

For New Zealand in New Zealand: 487-7 dec. at Wellington	2000-01
in Zimbabwe: 465 at Harare	2000-01
For Zimbabwe in New Zealand: 340-6 dec. at Wellington	2000-01
in Zimbabwe: 461 at Bulawayo	1997-98

LOWEST INNINGS TOTALS

For New Zealand in New Zealand: 251 at Auckland 1995-96
in Zimbabwe: 207 at Harare 1997-98

For Zimbabwe in New Zealand: 170 at Auckland 1997-98
in Zimbabwe: 119 at Bulawayo 2000-01

DOUBLE-HUNDRED

For Zimbabwe (1)

203* G. J. Whittall at Bulawayo. 1997-98

Highest score for New Zealand: 157 by M. J. Horne at Auckland, 1997-98.

INDIVIDUAL HUNDREDS

For New Zealand (11)

2: N. J. Astle, C. L. Cairns, M. J. Horne, C. D. McMillan.
1: M. D. Crowe, R. T. Latham, C. M. Spearman.

For Zimbabwe (6)

2: G. W. Flower, G. J. Whittall.
1: K. J. Arnott, D. L. Houghton.

RECORD PARTNERSHIPS FOR EACH WICKET

For New Zealand

214	for 1st	C. M. Spearman and R. G. Twose at Auckland	1995-96
127	for 2nd	R. T. Latham and A. H. Jones at Bulawayo	1992-93
71	for 3rd	A. H. Jones and M. D. Crowe at Bulawayo	1992-93
243	for 4th†	M. J. Horne and N. J. Astle at Auckland	1997-98
222	for 5th†	N. J. Astle and C. D. McMillan at Wellington.	2000-01
82*	for 6th	A. C. Parore and L. K. Germon at Hamilton	1995-96
108	for 7th	C. D. McMillan and D. J. Nash at Wellington.	1997-98
144	for 8th	C. L. Cairns and D. J. Nash at Harare.	2000-01
78	for 9th	A. C. Parore and D. L. Vettori at Bulawayo	2000-01
27	for 10th	C. D. McMillan and S. B. Doull at Auckland.	1997-98

For Zimbabwe

156	for 1st	G. J. Rennie and G. W. Flower at Harare.	1997-98
107	for 2nd	K. J. Arnott and A. D. R. Campbell at Harare	1992-93
70	for 3rd	A. Flower and G. J. Whittall at Bulawayo	1997-98
130	for 4th	G. J. Rennie and A. Flower at Wellington	2000-01
131	for 5th	A. Flower and G. J. Whittall at Harare	2000-01
151	for 6th	G. J. Whittall and H. H. Streak at Harare	2000-01
91	for 7th	G. J. Whittall and P. A. Strang at Hamilton	1995-96
94	for 8th	A. D. R. Campbell and H. H. Streak at Wellington	1997-98
46	for 9th	G. J. Crocker and M. G. Burmester at Harare.	1992-93
40	for 10th	G. J. Whittall and E. Z. Matambanadzo at Bulawayo	1997-98

† *Record partnership against all countries.*

TEN WICKETS OR MORE IN A MATCH

For Zimbabwe (2)

11-255 (6-109, 5-146)	A. G. Huckle, Bulawayo	1997-98
10-158 (8-109, 2-49)	P. A. Strang, Bulawayo.	2000-01

Note: The best match figures for New Zealand are 8-85 (4-35, 4-50) by S. B. Doull at Auckland, 1997-98.

NEW ZEALAND v BANGLADESH

Series notes: New Zealand have won all four matches by an innings... New Zealand have been dismissed only once in the four matches... New Zealand have never failed to reach 300; Bangladesh have never reached it... No Bangladeshi innings has lasted for 100 overs... D. L. Vettori has taken 26 wickets in this fixture, double the next-best (C. L. Cairns with 13)... Left-arm spinners have taken over 60% of the wickets in Tests in Bangladesh (34 out of 56).

		Captains				
Season	*New Zealand*	*Bangladesh*	*T*	*NZ*	*B*	*D*
2001-02*N*	S. P. Fleming	Khaled Mashud	2	2	0	0
2004-05*B*	S. P. Fleming	Khaled Mashud	2	2	0	0
	In New Zealand		2	2	0	0
	In Bangladesh		2	2	0	0
	Totals.		4	4	0	0

B Played in Bangladesh.   N Played in New Zealand.

HIGHEST INNINGS TOTALS

For New Zealand in New Zealand: 365-9 dec. at Hamilton 2001-02
              in Bangladesh: 545-6 at Chittagong 2004-05

For Bangladesh in New Zealand: 205 at Hamilton 2001-02
              in Bangladesh: 262 at Chittagong 2004-05

LOWEST INNINGS TOTALS

For New Zealand in Bangladesh: 402 at Dhaka 2004-05

For Bangladesh in New Zealand: 108 at Hamilton 2001-02
              in Bangladesh: 126 at Dhaka 2004-05

DOUBLE-HUNDRED

For New Zealand (1)

202   S. P. Fleming at Chittagong 2004-05

Highest score for Bangladesh: 67 by Mohammad Ashraful at Dhaka, 2004-05.

INDIVIDUAL HUNDREDS

For New Zealand (4)

1: S. P. Fleming, B. B. McCullum, C. D. McMillan, M. H. Richardson.

RECORD PARTNERSHIP

For New Zealand

104 for 1st	M. H. Richardson and M. J. Horne at Wellington	2001-02
63 for 2nd	M. S. Sinclair and S. P. Fleming at Dhaka.	2004-05
204 for 3rd	S. P. Fleming and S. B. Styris at Chittagong	2004-05
130 for 4th	S. P. Fleming and C. D. McMillan at Wellington.	2001-02
190 for 5th	M. H. Richardson and C. D. McMillan at Hamilton.	2001-02
89 for 6th	M. H. Richardson and C. L. Cairns at Hamilton.	2001-02
71 for 7th	B. B. McCullum and D. L. Vettori at Dhaka.	2004-05
57 for 8th	B. B. McCullum and J. E. C. Franklin at Dhaka	2004-05
20 for 9th	B. B. McCullum and P. J. Wiseman at Dhaka	2004-05
31 for 10th	P. J. Wiseman and I. G. Butler at Dhaka	2004-05

For Bangladesh

39 for 1st	Javed Omar and Al Sahariar at Hamilton.	2001-02
32 for 2nd	Javed Omar and Aftab Ahmed at Chittagong	2004-05
60 for 3rd	Habibul Bashar and Aminul Islam at Hamilton	2001-02
115 for 4th	Rajin Saleh and Mohammad Ashraful at Dhaka	2004-05
26 for 5th	{ Habibul Bashar and Sanwar Hossain at Hamilton	2001-02
	{ Javed Omar and Alok Kapali at Chittagong , , , , , , , , , , , , , , ,	2004-05
49 for 6th	Rajin Saleh and Khaled Mashud at Chittagong	2004-05
38 for 7th	Khaled Mashud and Mushfiqur Rahman at Chittagong	2004-05
39 for 8th	Mushfiqur Rahman and Mohammad Rafique at Chittagong	2004-05
49 for 9th	Khaled Mashud and Mashrafe bin Mortaza at Wellington	2001-02
45 for 10th	Tapash Baisya and Enamul Haque, jun. at Chittagong	2004-05

TEN WICKETS OR MORE IN A MATCH

For New Zealand (1)

12-170 (6-70, 6-100)   D. L. Vettori, Chittagong 2004-05

Note: The best match figures for Bangladesh are 6-122 (6-122) by Mohammad Rafique at Dhaka, 2004-05.

INDIA v PAKISTAN

Series notes: India's two victories in 2003-04 were their first in Pakistan after 20 without success. Pending the scheduled 2004-05 series, two-thirds of Tests between these sides have been drawn (33 out of 50)... The last six Tests have all had positive results, with three won by each team; before that there were 15 draws out of 16... India's runs-per-wicket average is almost the same at home and away: 34.0 in India, 35.9 in Pakistan... Pakistan's, by contrast, is 44.9 at home and 29.6 in India.

		Captains				
Season	*India*	*Pakistan*	*T*	*I*	*P*	*D*
1952-53*I*	L. Amarnath	A. H. Kardar	5	2	1	2
1954-55*P*	V. Mankad	A. H. Kardar	5	0	0	5
1960-61*P*	N. J. Contractor	Fazal Mahmood	5	0	0	5
1978-79*P*	B. S. Bedi	Mushtaq Mohammad	3	0	2	1
1979-80*I*	S. M. Gavaskar[1]	Asif Iqbal	6	2	0	4
1982-83*P*	S. M. Gavaskar	Imran Khan	6	0	3	3
1983-84*I*	Kapil Dev	Zaheer Abbas	3	0	0	3
1984-85*P*	S. M. Gavaskar	Zaheer Abbas	2	0	0	2
1986-87*I*	Kapil Dev	Imran Khan	5	0	1	4
1989-90*P*	K. Srikkanth	Imran Khan	4	0	0	4

		Captains					
Season	*India*		*Pakistan*	*T*	*I*	*P*	*D*
1998-99*I*	M. Azharuddin		Wasim Akram	2	1	1	0
1998-99*I*†	M. Azharuddin		Wasim Akram	1	0	1	0
2003-04*P*	S. C. Ganguly[2]		Inzamam-ul-Haq	3	2	1	0
	In India	. . . .		27	5	4	18
	In Pakistan	. . . .		23	2	6	15
	Totals	. . . .		50	7	10	33

I Played in India. P Played in Pakistan.

† *This Test was part of the Asian Test Championship and was not counted as part of the preceding bilateral series.*

Note: The following was appointed by the home authority for only a minor proportion of the series: [1]G. R. Viswanath (Sixth). [2]R. Dravid (First and Second).

HIGHEST INNINGS TOTALS

For India in India: 539-9 dec. at Madras	1960-61
in Pakistan: 675-5 dec. at Multan	2003-04
For Pakistan in India: 487-9 dec. at Madras	1986-87
in Pakistan: 699-5 at Lahore	1989-90

LOWEST INNINGS TOTALS

For India in India: 106 at Lucknow.	1952-53
in Pakistan: 145 at Karachi	1954-55
For Pakistan in India: 116 at Bangalore	1986-87
in Pakistan: 158 at Dacca	1954-55

DOUBLE-HUNDREDS

For India (4)

309	V. Sehwag at Multan	2003-04	218	S. V. Manjrekar at Lahore	1989-90
270	R. Dravid at Rawalpindi	2003-04	201	A. D. Gaekwad at Jullundur	1983-84

For Pakistan (6)

280*	Javed Miandad at Hyderabad	1982-83	215	Zaheer Abbas at Lahore	1982-83
235*	Zaheer Abbas at Lahore	1978-79	210	Qasim Omar at Faisalabad	1984-85
231	Mudassar Nazar at Hyderabad	1982-83	203*	Shoaib Mohammad at Lahore	1989-90

INDIVIDUAL HUNDREDS

For India (36)

5: S. M. Gavaskar, P. R. Umrigar.
4: M. Amarnath.
3: M. Azharuddin, R. J. Shastri.
2: S. V. Manjrekar, S. R. Tendulkar, D. B. Vengsarkar.
1: C. G. Borde, R. Dravid, A. D. Gaekwad, V. S. Hazare, S. M. Patil, V. Sehwag, R. H. Shodhan, K. Srikkanth, G. R. Viswanath, Yuvraj Singh.

For Pakistan (46)

6: Mudassar Nazar, Zaheer Abbas.
5: Javed Miandad.
3: Imran Khan, Salim Malik.
2: Aamer Malik, Hanif Mohammad, Saeed Ahmed, Shoaib Mohammad.
1: Alim-ud-Din, Asif Iqbal, Ijaz Faqih, Imran Farhat, Imtiaz Ahmed, Inzamam-ul-Haq, Mohsin Khan, Mushtaq Mohammad, Nazar Mohammad, Qasim Omar, Ramiz Raja, Saeed Anwar, Shahid Afridi, Wasim Raja, Yousuf Youhana.

RECORD PARTNERSHIPS FOR EACH WICKET

For India

200 for 1st	S. M. Gavaskar and K. Srikkanth at Madras	1986-87
135 for 2nd	N. S. Sidhu and S. V. Manjrekar at Karachi	1989-90
336 for 3rd†	V. Sehwag and S. R. Tendulkar at Multan	2003-04
186 for 4th	S. V. Manjrekar and R. J. Shastri at Lahore	1989-90
200 for 5th	S. M. Patil and R. J. Shastri at Faisalabad	1984-85
143 for 6th	M. Azharuddin and Kapil Dev at Calcutta	1986-87
155 for 7th	R. M. H. Binny and Madan Lal at Bangalore	1983-84
122 for 8th	S. M. H. Kirmani and Madan Lal at Faisalabad	1982-83
149 for 9th†	P. G. Joshi and R. B. Desai at Bombay	1960-61
109 for 10th	H. R. Adhikari and Ghulam Ahmed at Delhi	1952-53

For Pakistan

162 for 1st	Hanif Mohammad and Imtiaz Ahmed at Madras	1960-61
250 for 2nd	Mudassar Nazar and Qasim Omar at Faisalabad	1984-85
451 for 3rd†	Mudassar Nazar and Javed Miandad at Hyderabad	1982-83
287 for 4th	Javed Miandad and Zaheer Abbas at Faisalabad	1982-83
213 for 5th	Zaheer Abbas and Mudassar Nazar at Karachi	1982-83
207 for 6th	Salim Malik and Imran Khan at Faisalabad	1982-83
154 for 7th	Imran Khan and Ijaz Faqih at Ahmedabad	1986-87
112 for 8th	Imran Khan and Wasim Akram at Madras	1986-87
70 for 9th	{ Yousuf Youhana and Shoaib Akhtar at Multan	2003-04
	{ Mohammad Sami and Fazl-e-Akbar at Rawalpindi	2003-04
104 for 10th	Zulfiqar Ahmed and Amir Elahi at Madras	1952-53

† *Record partnership against all countries.*

TEN WICKETS OR MORE IN A MATCH

For India (5)

11-146 (4-90, 7-56)	Kapil Dev, Madras	1979-80
14-149 (4-75, 10-74)	A. Kumble, Delhi	1998-99
10-126 (7-27, 3-99)	Maninder Singh, Bangalore	1986-87
13-131 (8-52, 5-79)†	V. Mankad, Delhi	1952-53
13-132 (5-46, 8-86)	J. Srinath, Calcutta	1998-99

For Pakistan (7)

12-94 (5-52, 7-42)	Fazal Mahmood, Lucknow	1952-53
11-79 (3-19, 8-60)	Imran Khan, Karachi	1982-83
11-180 (6-98, 5-82)	Imran Khan, Faisalabad	1982-83
10-175 (4-135, 6-40)	Iqbal Qasim, Bombay	1979-80
10-187 (5-94, 5-93)†	Saqlain Mushtaq, Chennai	1998-99
10-216 (5-94, 5-122)	Saqlain Mushtaq, Delhi	1998-99
11-190 (8-69, 3-121)	Sikander Bakht, Delhi	1979-80

† *On first appearance in India–Pakistan Tests.*

SEVEN WICKETS OR MORE IN AN INNINGS

In addition to those listed above, the following have taken seven wickets or more in an innings:

For India

7-220 Kapil Dev, Faisalabad. . . . . . . 1982-83 | 8-85 Kapil Dev, Lahore. 1982-83

INDIA v SRI LANKA

Series notes: Sri Lanka have never won a Test in India... The team batting first have won none of the last ten Tests between the teams... In 11 Tests between the sides in India, India average 51.0 runs per wicket and Sri Lanka 24.4... S. R. Tendulkar has scored 1,124 runs against Sri Lanka and needs 129 more to overtake P. A. de Silva as the top-scorer in this fixture... Seven of the 11 victories in this fixture have been by an innings... India have batted first in five of the last six – but only won when they fielded first.

		Captains				
Season	*India*	*Sri Lanka*	*T*	*I*	*SL*	*D*
1982-83*I*	S. M. Gavaskar	B. Warnapura	1	0	0	1
1985-86*S*	Kapil Dev	L. R. D. Mendis	3	0	1	2
1986-87*I*	Kapil Dev	L. R. D. Mendis	3	2	0	1
1990-91*I*	M. Azharuddin	A. Ranatunga	1	1	0	0
1993-94*S*	M. Azharuddin	A. Ranatunga	3	1	0	2
1993-94*I*	M. Azharuddin	A. Ranatunga	3	3	0	0
1997-98*S*	S. R. Tendulkar	A. Ranatunga	2	0	0	2
1997-98*I*	S. R. Tendulkar	A. Ranatunga	3	0	0	3
1998-99*S†*	M. Azharuddin	A. Ranatunga	1	0	0	1
2001*S*	S. C. Ganguly	S. T. Jayasuriya	3	1	2	0
	In India		11	6	0	5
	In Sri Lanka		12	2	3	7
	Totals.		23	8	3	12

I Played in India. S Played in Sri Lanka.

† *This Test was part of the Asian Test Championship.*

HIGHEST INNINGS TOTALS

For India in India: 676-7 at Kanpur	1986-87
in Sri Lanka: 537-8 dec. at Colombo (RPS)	1997-98
For Sri Lanka in India: 420 at Kanpur.	1986-87
in Sri Lanka: 952-6 dec. at Colombo (RPS)	1997-98

LOWEST INNINGS TOTALS

For India in India: 288 at Chandigarh	1990-91
in Sri Lanka: 180 at Galle.	2001
For Sri Lanka in India: 82 at Chandigarh.	1990-91
in Sri Lanka: 198 at Kandy	1985-86

DOUBLE-HUNDREDS

For Sri Lanka (3)

340	S. T. Jayasuriya at Colombo (RPS) 1997-98	225 R. S. Mahanama at Colombo (RPS) 1997-98
242	D. P. M. D. Jayawardene at Colombo (SSC) 1998-99	

Highest score for India: 199 by M. Azharuddin at Kanpur, 1986-87.

INDIVIDUAL HUNDREDS

For India (30)

6: S. R. Tendulkar.
5: M. Azharuddin.
4: N. S. Sidhu.
3: S. C. Ganguly.
2: M. Amarnath, S. M. Gavaskar, V. G. Kambli, D. B. Vengsarkar.
1: R. Dravid, Kapil Dev, S. M. Patil, S. Ramesh.

For Sri Lanka (25)

5: P. A. de Silva.
3: S. T. Jayasuriya, D. P. M. D. Jayawardene, I. R. D. Mendis.
2: M. S. Atapattu, R. S. Mahanama.
1: R. L. Dias, R. S. Madugalle, A. Ranatunga, T. T. Samaraweera, K. C. Sangakkara, S. A. R. Silva, H. P. Tillekeratne.

RECORD PARTNERSHIPS FOR EACH WICKET

For India

171	for 1st	M. Prabhakar and N. S. Sidhu at Colombo (SSC)	1993-94
232	for 2nd	S. Ramesh and R. Dravid at Colombo (SSC)	1998-99
173	for 3rd	M. Amarnath and D. B. Vengsarkar at Nagpur	1986-87
256	for 4th	S. C. Ganguly and S. R. Tendulkar at Mumbai	1997-98
150	for 5th	S. R. Tendulkar and S. C. Ganguly at Colombo (SSC)	1997-98
272	for 6th	M. Azharuddin and Kapil Dev at Kanpur.	1986-87
78*	for 7th	S. M. Patil and Madan Lal at Madras	1982-83
70	for 8th	Kapil Dev and L. Sivaramakrishnan at Colombo (PSS).	1985-86
89	for 9th	S. C. Ganguly and A. Kuruvilla at Mohali	1997-98
30	for 10th	Zaheer Khan and B. K. V. Prasad at Colombo (SSC)	2001

For Sri Lanka

159	for 1st	S. Wettimuny and J. R. Ratnayeke at Kanpur	1986-87
576	for 2nd†	S. T. Jayasuriya and R. S. Mahanama at Colombo (RPS)	1997-98
218	for 3rd	S. T. Jayasuriya and P. A. de Silva at Colombo (SSC)	1997-98
216	for 4th	R. L. Dias and L. R. D. Mendis at Kandy	1985-86
144	for 5th‡	R. S. Madugalle and A. Ranatunga at Colombo (SSC)	1985-86
103	for 6th	P. A. de Silva and H. D. P. K. Dharmasena at Mohali	1997-98
194*	for 7th†	H. P. Tillekeratne and T. T. Samaraweera at Colombo (SSC)	2001
48	for 8th	P. A. de Silva and M. Muralitharan at Colombo (SSC).	1997-98
60	for 9th	H. P. Tillekeratne and A. W. R. Madurasinghe at Chandigarh	1990-91
64	for 10th	M. Muralitharan and P. D. R. L. Perera at Kandy	2001

† *Record partnership against all countries.*
‡ *Although Sri Lanka's fifth wicket added 176 runs against India at Colombo (SSC) in 1998-99, this comprised two partnerships. D. P. M. D. Jayawardene added 115* with A. Ranatunga (retired hurt) and a further 61 with H. P. Tillekeratne.*

TEN WICKETS OR MORE IN A MATCH

For India (3)

11-128 (4-69, 7-59)	A. Kumble, Lucknow.	1993-94
10-107 (3-56, 7-51)	Maninder Singh, Nagpur	1986-87
11-125 (5-38, 6-87)	S. L. V. Raju, Ahmedabad	1993-94

For Sri Lanka (1)

11-196 (8-87, 3-109)	M. Muralitharan, Colombo (SSC)	2001

INDIA v ZIMBABWE

Series notes: The nine highest individual scores in this fixture were all made at Nagpur or Delhi... Both of Zimbabwe's victories over India have come at Harare... India have won all three matches at Delhi... In two matches at Nagpur, India average 90.6 runs per wicket and Zimbabwe 37.6... The team batting second have won each of the last four Tests between the sides, despite losing the toss on each occasion.

Season	India	Captains Zimbabwe	T	I	Z	D
1992-93*Z*	M. Azharuddin	D. L. Houghton	1	0	0	1
1992-93*I*	M. Azharuddin	D. L. Houghton	1	1	0	0
1998-99*Z*	M. Azharuddin	A. D. R. Campbell	1	0	1	0
2000-01*I*	S. C. Ganguly	H. H. Streak	2	1	0	1
2001*Z*	S. C. Ganguly	H. H. Streak	2	1	1	0
2001-02*I*	S. C. Ganguly	S. V. Carlisle	2	2	0	0
	In India		5	4	0	1
	In Zimbabwe		4	1	2	1
	Totals.		9	5	2	2

I Played in India.   Z Played in Zimbabwe.

HIGHEST INNINGS TOTALS

For India in India: 609-6 dec. at Nagpur 2000-01
            in Zimbabwe: 318 at Bulawayo 2001

For Zimbabwe in India: 503-6 at Nagpur 2000-01
              in Zimbabwe: 456 at Harare 1992-93

LOWEST INNINGS TOTALS

For India in India: 354 at Delhi 2001-02
            in Zimbabwe: 173 at Harare. 1998-99

For Zimbabwe in India: 146 at Delhi 2001-02
              in Zimbabwe: 173 at Bulawayo 2001

DOUBLE-HUNDREDS

For India (3)

227 V. G. Kambli at Delhi........ 1992-93 | 200* R. Dravid at Delhi.......... 2000-01
201* S. R. Tendulkar at Nagpur..... 2000-01 |

For Zimbabwe (1)

232* A. Flower at Nagpur......... 2000-01

INDIVIDUAL HUNDREDS

For India (12)

3: R. Dravid, S. R. Tendulkar.
2: S. S. Das.
1: S. B. Bangar, S. C. Ganguly, V. G. Kambli, S. V. Manjrekar.

For Zimbabwe (6)

3: A. Flower.
1: A. D. R. Campbell, G. W. Flower, D. L. Houghton.

RECORD PARTNERSHIPS FOR EACH WICKET

For India

79	for 1st	S. S. Das and D. Dasgupta at Nagpur	2001-02
155	for 2nd	S. S. Das and R. Dravid at Nagpur	2000-01
249	for 3rd	R. Dravid and S. R. Tendulkar at Nagpur	2000-01
110*	for 4th	R. Dravid and S. C. Ganguly at Delhi	2000-01
120	for 5th	S. C. Ganguly and V. Sehwag at Delhi	2001-02
171	for 6th	S. R. Tendulkar and S. B. Bangar at Nagpur	2001-02
44	for 7th	R. Dravid and R. R. Singh at Harare	1998-99
72	for 8th	S. S. Dighe and Harbhajan Singh at Bulawayo	2001
19	for 9th	H. K. Badani and J. Srinath at Harare	2001
40	for 10th	J. Srinath and Harbhajan Singh at Harare	1998-99

For Zimbabwe

138	for 1st	G. J. Rennie and C. B. Wishart at Harare	1998-99
106	for 2nd	S. V. Carlisle and A. D. R. Campbell at Nagpur	2001-02
119	for 3rd	S. V. Carlisle and A. D. R. Campbell at Delhi	2000-01
209	for 4th	A. D. R. Campbell and A. Flower at Nagpur	2000-01
96	for 5th	A. Flower and G. W. Flower at Nagpur	2000-01
165	for 6th†	D. L. Houghton and A. Flower at Harare	1992-93
98*	for 7th	A. Flower and H. H. Streak at Nagpur	2000-01
46	for 8th	A. Flower and B. A. Murphy at Delhi	2000-01
59	for 9th	T. J. Friend and R. W. Price at Nagpur	2001-02
97*	for 10th†	A. Flower and H. K. Olonga at Delhi	2000-01

† *Record partnership against all countries.*

BEST MATCH BOWLING ANALYSES

For India

9-141 (4-81, 5-60) J. Srinath, Delhi 2000-01

For Zimbabwe

7-115 (3-69, 4-46) H. H. Streak, Harare 2001

INDIA v BANGLADESH

Series notes: The sides have yet to meet in a Test in India... India average 50.2 runs per wicket against Bangladesh's 22.2... India's lowest completed total (429) is bigger than Bangladesh's highest (400).

		Captains					
Season	*India*		*Bangladesh*	*T*	*I*	*B*	*D*
2000-01*B*	S. C. Ganguly		Naimur Rahman	1	1	0	0
2004-05*B*	S. C. Ganguly		Habibul Bashar	2	2	0	0
	In Bangladesh			3	3	0	0

B Played in Bangladesh.

HIGHEST INNINGS TOTALS

For India: 540 at Chittagong 2004-05

For Bangladesh: 400 at Dhaka.. 2000-01

LOWEST INNINGS TOTALS

For India: 429 at Dhaka 2000-01

For Bangladesh: 91 at Dhaka... 2000-01

DOUBLE-HUNDRED

For India (1)

248* S. R. Tendulkar at Dhaka 2004-05

Highest score for Bangladesh: 158* by Mohammad Ashraful at Chittagong, 2004-05.

INDIVIDUAL HUNDREDS

For India (3)

1: R. Dravid, G. Gambhir, S. R. Tendulkar.

For Bangladesh (2)

1: Aminul Islam, Mohammad Ashraful.

RECORD PARTNERSHIPS FOR EACH WICKET

For India

66 for 1st	S. S. Das and S. Ramesh at Dhaka......................	2000-01
259 for 2nd	G. Gambhir and R. Dravid at Chittagong.................	2004-05
61 for 3rd	R. Dravid and S. R. Tendulkar at Dhaka	2004-05
164 for 4th	S. R. Tendulkar and S. C. Ganguly at Dhaka	2004-05
59 for 5th	S. R. Tendulkar and V. V. S. Laxman at Dhaka...........	2004-05
48 for 6th	S. R. Tendulkar and K. D. Karthik at Dhaka	2004-05
121 for 7th	S. C. Ganguly and S. B. Joshi at Dhaka	2000-01
56 for 8th	S. B. Joshi and A. B. Agarkar at Dhaka	2000-01
75 for 9th	S. C. Ganguly and Harbhajan Singh at Chittagong........	2004-05
133 for 10th†	S. R. Tendulkar and Zaheer Khan at Dhaka	2004-05

For Bangladesh

48 for 1st	Javed Omar and Nafis Iqbal at Chittagong	2004-05
34 for 2nd	Shahriar Hossain and Habibul Bashar at Dhaka	2000-01
66 for 3rd	Habibul Bashar and Aminul Islam at Dhaka.	2000-01
70 for 4th	Habibul Bashar and Mohammad Ashraful at Chittagong	2004-05
115 for 5th	Mohammad Ashraful and Aftab Ahmed at Chittagong	2004-05
64 for 6th	Nafis Iqbal and Manjural Islam Rana at Dhaka.	2004-05
93 for 7th†	Aminul Islam and Khaled Mashud at Dhaka	2000-01
65 for 8th	Mohammad Ashraful and Mohammad Rafique at Dhaka.	2004-05
69 for 9th	Manjural Islam Rana and Tapash Baisya at Dhaka.	2004-05
40 for 10th	Nazmul Hossain and Talha Jubair at Chittagong	2004-05

† *Record partnership against all countries.*

TEN WICKETS OR MORE IN A MATCH

For India (1)

11-96 (5-45, 6-51) I. K. Pathan, Dhaka. 2004-05

Note: The best match figures for Bangladesh are 6-154 (6-132, 0-22) by Naimur Rahman at Dhaka, 2000-01.

PAKISTAN v SRI LANKA

Series notes: Six of Sri Lanka's seven victories have come away... They trail 8–6 in Tests in Pakistan and 5–1 in Sri Lanka... Sri Lanka have won the toss in the six of the last seven – and 11 of the last 14 – Tests between these teams... Six of Pakistan's 14 wins over Sri Lanka have been by an innings, but Sri Lanka have never beaten Pakistan by an innings... Sri Lanka have won only 14% of the matches between the sides in which they have won the toss and batted (two in 14), as against 60% when they have won the toss and fielded (three in five).

		Captains				
Season	Pakistan	Sri Lanka	T	P	SL	D
1981-82P	Javed Miandad	B. Warnapura[1]	3	2	0	1
1985-86P	Javed Miandad	L. R. D. Mendis	3	2	0	1
1985-86S	Imran Khan	L. R. D. Mendis	3	1	1	1
1991-92P	Imran Khan	P. A. de Silva	3	1	0	2
1994-95S†	Salim Malik	A. Ranatunga	2	2	0	0
1995-96P	Ramiz Raja	A. Ranatunga	3	1	2	0
1996-97S	Ramiz Raja	A. Ranatunga	2	0	0	2
1998-99P‡	Wasim Akram	H. P. Tillekeratne	1	0	0	1
1998-99B‡	Wasim Akram	P. A. de Silva	1	1	0	0
1999-2000P	Saeed Anwar[2]	S. T. Jayasuriya	3	1	2	0
2000S	Moin Khan	S. T. Jayasuriya	3	2	0	1
2001-02P‡	Waqar Younis	S. T. Jayasuriya	1	0	1	0
2004-05P	Inzamam-ul-Haq	M. S. Atapattu	2	1	1	0
In Pakistan			19	8	6	5
In Sri Lanka			10	5	1	4
In Bangladesh			1	1	0	0
Totals.			30	14	7	9

P Played in Pakistan. S Played in Sri Lanka. B Played in Bangladesh.

† *One Test was cancelled owing to the threat of civil disturbances following a general election.*
‡ *These Tests were part of the Asian Test Championship.*

Note: The following deputised for the official touring captain or were appointed by the home authority for only a minor proportion of the series:
[1]L. R. D. Mendis (Second). [2]Moin Khan (Third).

HIGHEST INNINGS TOTALS

For Pakistan in Pakistan: 555-3 at Faisalabad. 1985-86
          in Sri Lanka: 600-8 dec. at Galle. 2000
          in Bangladesh: 594 at Dhaka 1998-99

For Sri Lanka in Pakistan: 528 at Lahore 2001-02
          in Sri Lanka: 467-5 at Kandy 2000

LOWEST INNINGS TOTALS

For Pakistan in Pakistan: 182 at Rawalpindi 1999-2000
          in Sri Lanka: 132 at Colombo (CCC). 1985-86

For Sri Lanka in Pakistan: 149 at Karachi. 1981-82
          in Sri Lanka: 71 at Kandy 1994-95

DOUBLE-HUNDREDS

For Pakistan (4)

211	Ijaz Ahmed, sen. at Dhaka.	1998-99	203*	Javed Miandad at Faisalabad . . .	1985-86
206	Qasim Omar at Faisalabad.	1985-86	200*	Inzamam-ul-Haq at Dhaka.	1998-99

For Sri Lanka (3)

253	S. T. Jayasuriya at Faisalabad . . .	2004-05	207*	M. S. Atapattu at Kandy	2000
230	K. C. Sangakkara at Lahore. . . .	2001-02			

INDIVIDUAL HUNDREDS

For Pakistan (25)

5: Inzamam-ul-Haq.
3: Salim Malik, Younis Khan.
2: Ijaz Ahmed, sen., Saeed Anwar, Wajahatullah Wasti.
1: Haroon Rashid, Javed Miandad, Mohsin Khan, Moin Khan, Qasim Omar, Ramiz Raja, Wasim Akram, Zaheer Abbas.

For Sri Lanka (24)

8: P. A. de Silva.
4: S. T. Jayasuriya.
2: K. C. Sangakkara, H. P. Tillekeratne.
1: R. P. Arnold, M. S. Atapattu, R. L. Dias, A. P. Gurusinha, R. S. Kaluwitharana, A. Ranatunga, T. T. Samaraweera, S. Wettimuny.

RECORD PARTNERSHIPS FOR EACH WICKET

For Pakistan

156 for 1st	Wajahatullah Wasti and Shahid Afridi at Lahore	1998-99
151 for 2nd	Mohsin Khan and Majid Khan at Lahore	1981-82
397 for 3rd	Qasim Omar and Javed Miandad at Faisalabad	1985-86
178 for 4th	Wajahatullah Wasti and Yousuf Youhana at Lahore.	1998-99
132 for 5th	Salim Malik and Imran Khan at Sialkot	1991-92
124 for 6th	Inzamam-ul-Haq and Younis Khan at Karachi	1999-2000
120 for 7th	Younis Khan and Wasim Akram at Galle	2000
88 for 8th	Moin Khan and Waqar Younis at Karachi	1999-2000
145 for 9th	Younis Khan and Wasim Akram at Rawalpindi	1999-2000
90 for 10th	Wasim Akram and Arshad Khan at Colombo (SSC)	2000

For Sri Lanka

335	for 1st†	M. S. Atapattu and S. T. Jayasuriya at Kandy	2000
217	for 2nd	S. Wettimuny and R. L. Dias at Faisalabad	1981-82
176	for 3rd	U. C. Hathurusinghe and P. A. de Silva at Faisalabad	1995-96
240*	for 4th†	A. P. Gurusinha and A. Ranatunga at Colombo (PSS)	1985-86
143	for 5th	R. P. Arnold and R. S. Kaluwitharana at Lahore	1998-99
121	for 6th	A. Ranatunga and P. A. de Silva at Faisalabad.	1985-86
131	for 7th	H. P. Tillekeratne and R. S. Kalpage at Kandy.	1994-95
76	for 8th	P. A. de Silva and W. P. U. J. C. Vaas at Colombo (SSC)	1996-97
101	for 9th†	S. T. Jayasuriya and C. R. D. Fernando at Faisalabad	2004-05
73	for 10th	H. P. Tillekeratne and K. S. C. de Silva at Dhaka	1998-99

† *Record partnership against all countries.*

TEN WICKETS OR MORE IN A MATCH

For Pakistan (3)

10-190 (3-72, 7-118)	Danish Kaneria, Karachi	2004-05
14-116 (8-58, 6-58)	Imran Khan, Lahore	1981-82
11-119 (6-34, 5-85)	Waqar Younis, Kandy	1994-95

For Sri Lanka (1)

10-148 (4-77, 6-71)	M. Muralitharan, Peshawar	1999-2000

SEVEN WICKETS OR MORE IN AN INNINGS

In addition to those listed above, the following has taken seven wickets or more in an innings:

For Sri Lanka

8-83   J. R. Ratnayeke, Sialkot 1985-86

PAKISTAN v ZIMBABWE

Series notes: Zimbabwe have won the toss in 11 of the 14 Tests between the sides... Pakistan have a worse record at home to Zimbabwe (three wins and one defeat from seven matches) than away (five wins and one defeat from seven)... Zimbabwe are the only team with an innings win... The team batting first have won only one of the last eight matches between the sides... Pakistan lead 3–1 in Tests at Harare, but Zimbabwe have a greater runs-per-wicket average there (31.3 to 28.0).

	Captains					
Season	Pakistan	Zimbabwe	T	P	Z	D
1993-94P	Wasim Akram[1]	A. Flower	3	2	0	1
1994-95Z	Salim Malik	A. Flower	3	2	1	0
1996-97P	Wasim Akram	A. D. R. Campbell	2	1	0	1
1997-98Z	Rashid Latif	A. D. R. Campbell	2	1	0	1
1998-99P†	Aamir Sohail[2]	A. D. R. Campbell	2	0	1	1
2002-03Z	Waqar Younis	A. D. R. Campbell	2	2	0	0
	In Pakistan		7	3	1	3
	In Zimbabwe		7	5	1	1
	Totals		14	8	2	4

P Played in Pakistan.   Z Played in Zimbabwe.

† *The Third Test at Faisalabad was abandoned without a ball being bowled and is excluded.*

Notes: The following were appointed by the home authority for only a minor proportion of the series:
[1]Waqar Younis (First).   [2]Moin Khan (Second).

HIGHEST INNINGS TOTALS

For Pakistan in Pakistan: 553 at Sheikhupura 1996-97
in Zimbabwe: 403 at Bulawayo. 2002-03

For Zimbabwe in Pakistan: 375 at Sheikhupura 1996-97
in Zimbabwe: 544-4 dec. at Harare. 1994-95

LOWEST INNINGS TOTALS

For Pakistan in Pakistan: 103 at Peshawar 1998-99
in Zimbabwe: 158 at Harare. 1994-95

For Zimbabwe in Pakistan: 133 at Faisalabad 1996-97
in Zimbabwe: 139 at Harare 1994-95

DOUBLE-HUNDREDS

For Pakistan (1)

257* Wasim Akram at Sheikhupura . . 1996-97

For Zimbabwe (1)

201* G. W. Flower at Harare. 1994-95

INDIVIDUAL HUNDREDS

For Pakistan (7)

2: Inzamam-ul-Haq, Yousuf Youhana.
1: Mohammad Wasim, Taufeeq Umar, Wasim Akram.

For Zimbabwe (9)

3: G. W. Flower.
2: A. Flower.
1: M. W. Goodwin, N. C. Johnson, P. A. Strang, G. J. Whittall.

RECORD PARTNERSHIPS FOR EACH WICKET

For Pakistan

95	for 1st	Aamir Sohail and Shoaib Mohammad at Karachi (DS).	1993-94
118*	for 2nd	Shoaib Mohammad and Asif Mujtaba at Lahore	1993-94
180	for 3rd	Taufeeq Umar and Inzamam-ul-Haq at Harare	2002-03
127	for 4th	Younis Khan and Yousuf Youhana at Bulawayo.	2002-03
110	for 5th	Yousuf Youhana and Moin Khan at Bulawayo	1997-98
121	for 6th	Yousuf Youhana and Kamran Akmal at Bulawayo	2002-03
120	for 7th	Ijaz Ahmed, sen. and Inzamam-ul-Haq at Harare.	1994-95
313	for 8th†	Wasim Akram and Saqlain Mushtaq at Sheikhupura	1996-97
147	for 9th	Mohammad Wasim and Mushtaq Ahmed at Harare	1997-98
50*	for 10th	Yousuf Youhana and Waqar Younis at Lahore.	1998-99

For Zimbabwe

48*	for 1st	G. J. Rennie and G. W. Flower at Lahore.	1998-99
135	for 2nd†	M. H. Dekker and A. D. R. Campbell at Rawalpindi	1993-94
111	for 3rd	D. D. Ebrahim and G. W. Flower at Harare	2002-03
269	for 4th†	G. W. Flower and A. Flower at Harare	1994-95
277*	for 5th†	M. W. Goodwin and A. Flower at Bulawayo.	1997-98
72	for 6th	M. H. Dekker and G. J. Whittall at Rawalpindi.	1993-94
131	for 7th	G. W. Flower and P. A. Strang at Sheikhupura	1996-97
110	for 8th	G. J. Whittall and B. C. Strang at Harare.	1997-98
87	for 9th†	P. A. Strang and B. C. Strang at Sheikhupura	1996-97
29	for 10th	E. A. Brandes and S. G. Peall at Rawalpindi	1993-94

† *Record partnership against all countries.*

TEN WICKETS OR MORE IN A MATCH

For Pakistan (3)

10-155 (7-66, 3-89)	Saqlain Mushtaq, Bulawayo.	2002-03
13-135 (7-91, 6-44)†	Waqar Younis, Karachi (DS)	1993-94
10-106 (6-48, 4-58)	Wasim Akram, Faisalabad	1996-97

Note: The best match figures for Zimbabwe are 9-105 (6-90, 3-15) by H. H. Streak at Harare, 1994-95.

† *On first appearance in Pakistan–Zimbabwe Tests.*

PAKISTAN v BANGLADESH

Series notes: Bangladesh have batted first in all six Tests between the sides... Inzamam-ul-Haq averages 253 against Bangladesh in two Tests on his home ground at Multan... Pakistan have only been bowled out three times in six Tests, but have dismissed Bangladesh twice in each game... Yousuf Youhana has scored more runs (503) than anyone else against Bangladesh... Danish Kaneria has taken 34 Bangladesh wickets.

		Captains					
Season	*Pakistan*	*Bangladesh*	*T*	*P*	*B*	*D*	
2001-02P†	Waqar Younis	Naimur Rahman	1	1	0	0	
2001-02B	Waqar Younis	Khaled Mashud	2	2	0	0	
2003P	Rashid Latif	Khaled Mahmud	3	3	0	0	
	In Pakistan		4	4	0	0	
	In Bangladesh		2	2	0	0	
	Totals.		6	6	0	0	

P Played in Pakistan. B Played in Bangladesh.

† *This Test was part of the Asian Test Championship.*

HIGHEST INNINGS TOTALS

For Pakistan in Pakistan:	546-3 dec. at Multan	2001-02
in Bangladesh:	490-9 dec. at Dhaka.	2001-02

For Bangladesh in Pakistan: 361 at Peshawar 2003
in Bangladesh: 160 at Dhaka 2001-02

LOWEST INNINGS TOTALS

For Pakistan in Pakistan: 175 at Multan............................... 2003

For Bangladesh in Pakistan: 96 at Peshawar 2003
in Bangladesh: 148 at Chittagong (in both innings) 2001-02

DOUBLE-HUNDRED

For Pakistan (1)

204* Yousuf Youhana at Chittagong . 2001-02

Highest individual score for Bangladesh: 119 by Javed Omar at Peshawar, 2003.

INDIVIDUAL HUNDREDS

For Pakistan (12)

2: Abdul Razzaq, Inzamam-ul-Haq, Yasir Hameed, Yousuf Youhana.
1: Mohammad Hafeez, Saeed Anwar, Taufeeq Umar, Younis Khan.

For Bangladesh (2)

1: Habibul Bashar, Javed Omar.

Note: Yasir Hameed and L. G. Rowe (for West Indies v New Zealand) are the only two batsmen to score two hundreds in their first Test.

RECORD PARTNERSHIPS FOR EACH WICKET

For Pakistan

168	for 1st	Saeed Anwar and Taufeeq Umar at Multan	2001-02
134	for 2nd	Mohammad Hafeez and Yasir Hameed at Karachi	2003
80	for 3rd	Taufeeq Umar and Inzamam-ul-Haq at Multan	2001-02
165*	for 4th‡	Yousuf Youhana and Abdul Razzaq at Multan	2001-02
64	for 5th	Yousuf Youhana and Rashid Latif at Peshawar	2003
175	for 6th	Abdul Razzaq and Rashid Latif at Dhaka	2001-02
67	for 7th	Abdul Razzaq and Inzamam-ul-Haq at Dhaka................	2001-02
99	for 8th	Yousuf Youhana and Saqlain Mushtaq at Chittagong	2001-02
52	for 9th	Inzamam-ul-Haq and Umar Gul at Multan	2003
18*	for 10th	Yousuf Youhana and Danish Kaneria at Chittagong	2001-02

‡ *A total of 288 runs was added between the fall of Pakistan's third wicket and the end of the innings: Inzamam-ul-Haq retired hurt when he and Yousuf Youhana had added 123 runs.*

For Bangladesh

38	for 1st	Mehrab Hossain and Mohammad Ashraful at Dhaka	2001-02
167	for 2nd†	Javed Omar and Habibul Bashar at Peshawar	2003
130	for 3rd†	Javed Omar and Mohammad Ashraful at Peshawar	2003
111	for 4th	Habibul Bashar and Rajin Saleh at Karachi	2003
69	for 5th	Habibul Bashar and Sanwar Hossain at Chittagong	2001-02
62	for 6th	Rajin Saleh and Khaled Mashud at Multan	2003
27	for 7th	Aminul Islam and Khaled Mashud at Chittagong.	2001-02
45	for 8th	Habibul Bashar and Hasibul Hossain at Multan	2001-02
27	for 9th	{ Hasibul Hossain and Mohammad Sharif at Multan	2001-02
		{ Fahim Muntasir and Mohammad Sharif at Dhaka	2001-02
21	for 10th	Khaled Mashud and Manjural Islam at Chittagong.	2001-02

† *Record partnership against all countries.*

TEN WICKETS OR MORE IN A MATCH

For Pakistan (2)

12-94 (6-42, 6-52)†	Danish Kaneria, Multan	2001-02
10-80 (6-50, 4-30)	Shoaib Akhtar, Peshawar	2003

Note: The best match figures for Bangladesh are 7-105 (4-37, 3-68) by Khaled Mahmud at Multan, 2003.

† *On first appearance in Pakistan–Bangladesh Tests.*

SEVEN WICKETS OR MORE IN AN INNINGS

For Pakistan

7-77   Danish Kaneria, Dhaka. 2001-02

SRI LANKA v ZIMBABWE

Series notes: Zimbabwe have never beaten Sri Lanka... Sri Lanka have won all seven Tests at home to Zimbabwe... Zimbabwe passed 300 in their first three innings against Sri Lanka; since then they have managed it only once in 24 innings... Sri Lanka have scored over 500 in the first innings of four of the last five Tests between the sides, having failed to do so in either innings of the first ten Tests... Sri Lanka have never been dismissed for under 200 in this fixture... M. Muralitharan has taken more wickets in Tests against Zimbabwe than anyone, and needs 13 more to reach 100.

		Captains					
Season	*Sri Lanka*		*Zimbabwe*	*T*	*SL*	*Z*	*D*
1994-95Z	A. Ranatunga		A. Flower	3	0	0	3
1996-97S	A. Ranatunga	A. D. R. Campbell		2	2	0	0
1997-98S	A. Ranatunga	A. D. R. Campbell		2	2	0	0
1999-2000Z	S. T. Jayasuriya		A. Flower	3	1	0	2
2001-02S	S. T. Jayasuriya	S. V. Carlisle		3	3	0	0
2003-04Z	M. S. Atapattu		T. Taibu	2	2	0	0
	In Sri Lanka			7	7	0	0
	In Zimbabwe			8	3	0	5
	Totals			15	10	0	5

S Played in Sri Lanka.   Z Played in Zimbabwe.

HIGHEST INNINGS TOTALS

For Sri Lanka in Sri Lanka: 586-6 dec. at Colombo (SSC)................ 2001-02
in Zimbabwe: 713-3 dec. at Bulawayo 2003-04

For Zimbabwe in Sri Lanka: 338 at Kandy 1997-98
in Zimbabwe: 462-9 dec. at Bulawayo 1994-95

LOWEST INNINGS TOTALS

For Sri Lanka in Sri Lanka: 225 at Colombo (SSC) 1997-98
in Zimbabwe: 218 at Bulawayo........................ 1994-95

For Zimbabwe in Sri Lanka: 79 at Galle.............................. 2001-02
in Zimbabwe: 102 at Harare............................ 2003-04

DOUBLE-HUNDREDS

For Sri Lanka (4)

270	K. C. Sangakkara at Bulawayo	2003-04		223	M. S. Atapattu at Kandy	1997-98
249	M. S. Atapattu at Bulawayo ..	2003-04		216*	M. S. Atapattu at Bulawayo ..	1999-2000

For Zimbabwe (1)

266 D. L. Houghton at Bulawayo ... 1994-95

INDIVIDUAL HUNDREDS

For Sri Lanka (19)

5: M. S. Atapattu.
2: S. T. Jayasuriya, S. Ranatunga, K. C. Sangakkara, H. P. Tillekeratne.
1: R. P. Arnold, P. A. de Silva, T. M. Dilshan, A. P. Gurusinha, D. P. M. D. Jayawardene, T. T. Samaraweera.

For Zimbabwe (4)

2: A. Flower, D. L. Houghton.

RECORD PARTNERSHIPS FOR EACH WICKET

For Sri Lanka

281	for 1st	M. S. Atapattu and S. T. Jayasuriya at Harare...............	2003-04
438	for 2nd	M. S. Atapattu and K. C. Sangakkara at Bulawayo	2003-04
140	for 3rd	M. S. Atapattu and P. A. de Silva at Kandy	1997-98
178	for 4th	D. P. M. D. Jayawardene and T. M. Dilshan at Harare	1999-2000
114	for 5th	A. P. Gurusinha and H. P. Tillekeratne at Colombo (SSC)	1996-97
189*	for 6th†	P. A. de Silva and A. Ranatunga at Colombo (SSC)............	1997-98
136*	for 7th	T. T. Samaraweera and W. P. U. J. C. Vaas at Colombo (SSC)	2001-02
146	for 8th	T. T. Samaraweera and U. D. U. Chandana at Galle	2001-02
39	for 9th	M. F. Maharoof and D. N. T. Zoysa at Harare	2003-04
45	for 10th	D. N. T. Zoysa and M. Muralitharan at Harare	2003-04

For Zimbabwe

153 for 1st	S. V. Carlisle and T. R. Gripper at Galle	2001-02
40 for 2nd	G. J. Rennie and M. W. Goodwin at Colombo (SSC).	1997-98
194 for 3rd†	A. D. R. Campbell and D. L. Houghton at Harare	1994-95
121 for 4th	D. L. Houghton and A. Flower at Bulawayo	1994-95
101 for 5th	M. W. Goodwin and A. Flower at Harare.	1999-2000
100 for 6th	D. L. Houghton and W. R. James at Bulawayo	1994-95
125 for 7th	A. Flower and G. J. Whittall at Harare	1999-2000
84 for 8th	D. L. Houghton and J. A. Rennie at Bulawayo	1994-95
43 for 9th	J. A. Rennie and S. G. Peall at Bulawayo	1994-95
50 for 10th	D. T. Hondo and T. Panyangara at Harare	2003-04

† *Record partnership against all countries.*

TEN WICKETS OR MORE IN A MATCH

For Sri Lanka (2)

12-117 (5-23, 7-94)	M. Muralitharan, Kandy.	1997-98
13-115 (9-51, 4-64)	M. Muralitharan, Kandy.	2001-02

Note: The best match figures for Zimbabwe are 6-112 (2-28, 4-84) by H. H. Streak at Colombo (SSC), 1997-98.

SEVEN WICKETS OR MORE IN AN INNINGS

In addition to those listed above, the following has taken seven wickets or more in an innings:

For Sri Lanka

7-116 K. R. Pushpakumara, Harare . . . 1994-95

SRI LANKA v BANGLADESH

Series notes: M. Muralitharan has taken all four five-fors in this fixture... Muralitharan has taken 20 wickets in matches between the sides, nearly three times the next best (T. T. Samaraweera and W. R. S. de Silva, with seven each)... In all three Tests, the team winning the toss have fielded... The teams have never met outside Colombo... D. P. M. D. Jayawardene has made 150 (retired out) and nought in his two innings against Bangladesh.

		Captains					
Season	Sri Lanka		Bangladesh	T	SL	B	D
2001-02S†	S. T. Jayasuriya		Naimur Rahman	1	1	0	0
2002S	S. T. Jayasuriya		Khaled Mashud	2	2	0	0
		Totals.		3	3	0	0

S Played in Sri Lanka.

† *This Test was part of the Asian Test Championship.*

HIGHEST INNINGS TOTALS

For Sri Lanka: 555-5 dec. at Colombo (SSC) 2001-02

For Bangladesh: 328 at Colombo (SSC). 2001-02

LOWEST INNINGS TOTALS

For Sri Lanka: 373 at Colombo (SSC)...................................... 2002

For Bangladesh: 90 at Colombo (SSC) 2001-02

DOUBLE-HUNDREDS

For Sri Lanka (2)

206   P. A. de Silva at Colombo (PSS).   2002 | 201   M. S. Atapattu at Colombo (SSC) 2001-02

Highest score for Bangladesh: 114 by Mohammad Ashraful at Colombo (SSC), 2001-02.

INDIVIDUAL HUNDREDS

For Sri Lanka (5)

1: M. S. Atapattu, P. A. de Silva, S. T. Jayasuriya, D. P. M. D. Jayawardene, M. G. Vandort.

For Bangladesh (1)

1: Mohammad Ashraful.

HUNDRED PARTNERSHIPS

For Sri Lanka

234 for 5th†	P. A. de Silva and S. T. Jayasuriya at Colombo (PSS)	2002
172 for 2nd	M. G. Vandort and M. N. Nawaz at Colombo (SSC)	2002
171 for 3rd	M. S. Atapattu and D. P. M. D. Jayawardene at Colombo (SSC). . . .	2001-02
150 for 4th	K. C. Sangakkara and P. A. de Silva at Colombo (PSS)	2002
144 for 1st	M. S. Atapattu and S. T. Jayasuriya at Colombo (SSC).	2001-02
127 for 5th	S. T. Jayasuriya and T. T. Samaraweera at Colombo (SSC)	2002
125 for 2nd	M. S. Atapattu and K. C. Sangakkara at Colombo (SSC)	2001-02

For Bangladesh

126 for 5th†	Aminul Islam and Mohammad Ashraful at Colombo (SSC).	2001-02

† *Record partnership against all countries.*

TEN WICKETS OR MORE IN A MATCH

For Sri Lanka (2)

10-111 (5-13, 5-98)	M. Muralitharan, Colombo (SSC)	2001-02
10-98 (5-39, 5-59)	M. Muralitharan, Colombo (PSS).	2002

Note: The best match figures for Bangladesh are 4-144 (4-144) by Enamul Haque at Colombo (PSS), 2002.

ZIMBABWE v BANGLADESH

Series notes: Zimbabwe are the only team to lose a Test or a series to Bangladesh... Bangladesh trail 3–0 in Tests in Zimbabwe but are level at 1–1 at home... Zimbabwe have won the toss in six out of eight matches between the sides... The team batting first lost the first two Tests between the sides, but are unbeaten in the last six... Habibul Bashar is the leading scorer in this fixture with 578; Zimbabwe's best is 447 by T. Taibu.

		Captains				
Season	*Zimbabwe*	*Bangladesh*	*T*	*Z*	*B*	*D*
2000-01*Z*	H. H. Streak	Naimur Rahman	2	2	0	0
2001-02*B*	B. A. Murphy[1]	Naimur Rahman	2	1	0	1
2003-04*Z*	H. H. Streak	Habibul Bashar	2	1	0	1
2004-05*B*	T. Taibu	Habibul Bashar	2	0	1	1
	In Zimbabwe		4	3	0	1
	In Bangladesh		4	1	1	2
	Totals.		8	4	1	3

Z Played in Zimbabwe   B Played in Bangladesh.

Note: The following deputised for the official touring captain:

[1]S. V. Carlisle (Second).

HIGHEST INNINGS TOTALS

For Zimbabwe in Zimbabwe: 457 at Bulawayo   2000-01
            in Bangladesh: 542-7 dec. at Chittagong   2001-02

For Bangladesh in Zimbabwe: 331 at Harare.   2003-04
            in Bangladesh: 488 at Chittagong   2004-05

LOWEST INNINGS TOTALS

For Zimbabwe in Zimbabwe: 441 at Harare   2003-04
            in Bangladesh: 154 at Chittagong.   2004-05

For Bangladesh in Zimbabwe: 168 at Bulawayo.   2000-01
              168 at Bulawayo.   2003-04
            in Bangladesh: 107 at Dhaka   2001-02

HIGHEST INDIVIDUAL INNINGS

For Zimbabwe

153   T. Taibu at Dhaka   2004-05

For Bangladesh

121   Nafis Iqbal at Dhaka   2004-05

INDIVIDUAL HUNDREDS

For Zimbabwe (6)

1: S. V. Carlisle, A. Flower, T. R. Gripper, T. Taibu, G. J. Whittall, C. B. Wishart.

For Bangladesh (2)

1: Habibul Bashar, Nafis Iqbal.

RECORD PARTNERSHIPS FOR EACH WICKET

For Zimbabwe

108	for 1st	D. D. Ebrahim and T. R. Gripper at Chittagong..............	2001-02
129	for 2nd	T. R. Gripper and S. V. Carlisle at Bulawayo	2003-04
76*	for 3rd	S. V. Carlisle and G. W. Flower at Bulawayo	2003-04
149	for 4th	G. J. Whittall and A. Flower at Bulawayo	2000-01
150	for 5th	B. R. M. Taylor and T. Taibu at Dhaka	2004-05
137	for 6th	C. B. Wishart and D. A. Marillier at Dhaka	2001-02
119	for 7th	T. Taibu and E. Chigumbura at Chittagong................	2004-05
108	for 8th	H. H. Streak and T. J. Friend at Dhaka	2001-02
67	for 9th	T. Taibu and D. T. Hondo at Dhaka	2004-05
14	for 10th	B. A. Murphy and H. K. Olonga at Dhaka.................	2001-02

For Bangladesh

133	for 1st†	Javed Omar and Nafis Iqbal at Dhaka.....................	2004-05
122	for 2nd	Javed Omar and Habibul Bashar at Chittagong..............	2001-02
84	for 3rd	Javed Omar and Aminul Islam at Bulawayo	2000-01
119	for 4th	Habibul Bashar and Rajin Saleh at Chittagong	2004-05
85	for 5th	Rajin Saleh and Mohammad Ashraful at Harare	2003-04
97	for 6th†	Mohammad Ashraful and Mushfiqur Rahman at Harare	2003-04
69	for 7th	Khaled Mashud and Mohammad Rafique at Chittagong	2004-05
62	for 8th	Mohammad Rafique and Mashrafe bin Mortaza at Chittagong	2004-05
35	for 9th	Mashrafe bin Mortaza and Tapash Baisya at Dhaka...........	2004-05
46	for 10th†	Khaled Mashud and Manjural Islam at Harare	2003-04

† *Record partnership against all countries.*

TEN WICKETS OR MORE IN A MATCH

For Bangladesh (1)

12-200 (7-95, 5-105)   Enamul Haque, jun., Dhaka 2004-05

Note: The best match figures for Zimbabwe are 8-104 (4-41, 4-63) by G. W. Flower at Chittagong, 2001-02.

TEST GROUNDS

in chronological order

City and Ground	First Test Match		Tests
1 Melbourne, Melbourne Cricket Ground	March 15, 1877	A v E	97
2 London, Kennington Oval	September 6, 1880	E v A	87
3 Sydney, Sydney Cricket Ground (No. 1)	February 17, 1882	A v E	92
4 Manchester, Old Trafford	July 11, 1884	E v A	69
5 London, Lord's	July 21, 1884	E v A	108
6 Adelaide, Adelaide Oval	December 12, 1884	A v E	63
7 Port Elizabeth, St George's Park	March 12, 1889	SA v E	21
8 Cape Town, Newlands	March 25, 1889	SA v E	37
9 Johannesburg, Old Wanderers	March 2, 1896	SA v E	22
Now the site of Johannesburg Railway Station.			
10 Nottingham, Trent Bridge	June 1, 1899	E v A	51
11 Leeds, Headingley	June 29, 1899	E v A	65
12 Birmingham, Edgbaston	May 29, 1902	E v A	40
13 Sheffield, Bramall Lane	July 3, 1902	E v A	1
Sheffield United Football Club have built a stand over the cricket pitch.			

	City and Ground	*First Test Match*		*Tests*
14	Durban, Lord's	January 21, 1910	SA v E	4
	Ground destroyed and built on.			
15	Durban, Kingsmead	January 18, 1923	SA v E	32
16	Brisbane, Exhibition Ground	November 30, 1928	A v E	2
	No longer used for cricket.			
17	Christchurch, Lancaster Park	January 10, 1930	NZ v E	38
	Ground also known under sponsors' names; currently Jade Stadium.			
18	Bridgetown, Kensington Oval	January 11, 1930	WI v E	41
19	Wellington, Basin Reserve	January 24, 1930	NZ v E	42
20	Port-of-Spain, Queen's Park Oval	February 1, 1930	WI v E	53
21	Auckland, Eden Park	February 17, 1930	NZ v E	45
22	Georgetown, Bourda	February 21, 1930	WI v E	29
23	Kingston, Sabina Park	April 3, 1930	WI v E	40
24	Brisbane, Woolloongabba	November 27, 1931	A v SA	47
25	Bombay, Gymkhana Ground	December 15, 1933	I v E	1
	No longer used for first-class cricket.			
26	Calcutta (*now Kolkata*), Eden Gardens	January 5, 1934	I v E	33
27	Madras (*now Chennai*),			
	Chepauk (Chidambaram Stadium)	February 10, 1934	I v E	27
28	Delhi, Feroz Shah Kotla	November 10, 1948	I v WI	27
29	Bombay, Brabourne Stadium	December 9, 1948	I v WI	17
	Rarely used for first-class cricket.			
30	Johannesburg, Ellis Park	December 27, 1948	SA v E	6
	Mainly a football and rugby stadium, no longer used for cricket.			
31	Kanpur, Green Park (Modi Stadium)	January 12, 1952	I v E	19
32	Lucknow, University Ground	October 25, 1952	I v P	1
	Ground destroyed, now partly under a river bed.			
33	Dacca (*now Dhaka*),			
	Dacca (now Bangabandhu) Stadium	January 1, 1955	P v I	17
	Originally in East Pakistan, now Bangladesh.			
34	Bahawalpur, Dring (now Bahawal) Stadium	January 15, 1955	P v I	1
	Still used for first-class cricket.			
35	Lahore, Lawrence Gardens (Bagh-i-Jinnah)	January 29, 1955	P v I	3
	Still used for club and occasional first-class matches.			
36	Peshawar, Services Ground	February 13, 1955	P v I	1
	Superseded by new stadium.			
37	Karachi, National Stadium	February 26, 1955	P v I	37
38	Dunedin, Carisbrook	March 11, 1955	NZ v E	10
39	Hyderabad, Fateh Maidan			
	(Lal Bahadur Stadium)	November 19, 1955	I v NZ	3
40	Madras, Corporation Stadium	January 6, 1956	I v NZ	9
	Superseded by rebuilt Chepauk Stadium.			
41	Johannesburg, Wanderers	December 24, 1956	SA v E	26
42	Lahore, Gaddafi Stadium	November 21, 1959	P v A	35
43	Rawalpindi, Pindi Club Ground	March 27, 1965	P v NZ	1
	Superseded by new stadium.			
44	Nagpur, Vidarbha C.A. Ground	October 3, 1969	I v NZ	8
45	Perth, Western Australian C.A. Ground	December 11, 1970	A v E	32
46	Hyderabad, Niaz Stadium	March 16, 1973	P v E	5
47	Bangalore, Karnataka State C.A. Ground			
	(Chinnaswamy Stadium)	November 22, 1974	I v WI	15
48	Bombay (*now Mumbai*), Wankhede Stadium	January 23, 1975	I v WI	20
49	Faisalabad, Iqbal Stadium	October 16, 1978	P v I	22
50	Napier, McLean Park	February 16, 1979	NZ v P	3
51	Multan, Ibn-e-Qasim Bagh Stadium	December 30, 1980	P v WI	1
52	St John's (Antigua), Recreation Ground	March 27, 1981	WI v E	19
53	Colombo, P. Saravanamuttu Stadium	February 17, 1982	SL v E	9
54	Kandy, Asgiriya Stadium	April 22, 1983	SL v A	17
55	Jullundur, Burlton Park	September 24, 1983	I v P	1
56	Ahmedabad, Gujarat Stadium	November 12, 1983	I v WI	7

	City and Ground	First Test Match		Tests
57	Colombo, Sinhalese Sports Club Ground	March 16, 1984	SL v NZ	25
58	Colombo, Colombo Cricket Club Ground	March 24, 1984	SL v NZ	3
59	Sialkot, Jinnah Stadium	October 27, 1985	P v SL	4
60	Cuttack, Barabati Stadium	January 4, 1987	I v SL	2
61	Jaipur, Sawai Mansingh Stadium	February 21, 1987	I v P	1
62	Hobart, Bellerive Oval	December 16, 1989	A v SL	6
63	Chandigarh, Sector 16 Stadium	November 23, 1990	I v SL	1
	Superseded by Mohali ground.			
64	Hamilton, Seddon Park	February 22, 1991	NZ v SL	13
	Ground also known under various sponsors' names, including Trust Bank Park; currently Westpac Park.			
65	Gujranwala, Municipal Stadium	December 20, 1991	P v SL	1
66	Colombo, R. Premadasa (Khettarama) Stadium	August 28, 1992	SL v A	5
67	Moratuwa, Tyronne Fernando Stadium	September 8, 1992	SL v A	4
68	Harare, Harare Sports Club	October 18, 1992	Z v I	24
69	Bulawayo, Bulawayo Athletic Club	November 1, 1992	Z v NZ	1
	Superseded by Queens Sports Club ground.			
70	Karachi, Defence Stadium	December 1, 1993	P v Z	1
71	Rawalpindi, Rawalpindi Cricket Stadium	December 9, 1993	P v Z	8
72	Lucknow, K. D. "Babu" Singh Stadium	January 18, 1994	I v SL	1
73	Bulawayo, Queens Sports Club	October 20, 1994	Z v SL	15
74	Mohali, Punjab Cricket Association Stadium	December 10, 1994	I v WI	5
75	Peshawar, Arbab Niaz Stadium	September 8, 1995	P v SL	6
76	Centurion (*formerly Verwoerdburg*), Centurion Park	November 16, 1995	SA v E	9
77	Sheikhupura, Municipal Stadium	October 17, 1996	P v Z	2
78	St Vincent, Arnos Vale	June 20, 1997	WI v SL	1
79	Galle, International Stadium	June 3, 1998	SL v NZ	11
80	Springbok Park, Bloemfontein	October 29, 1999	SA v Z	3
	Ground also known under sponsor's name; currently Goodyear Park.			
81	Multan, Multan Cricket Stadium	August 29, 2001	P v B	3
82	Chittagong, Chittagong Stadium	November 15, 2001	B v Z	8
83	Sharjah, Sharjah Cricket Association Stadium	January 31, 2002	P v WI	4
84	St George's, Queen's Park New Stadium	June 28, 2002	WI v NZ	1
85	East London, Buffalo Park	October 18, 2002	SA v B	1
86	Potchefstroom, North West Cricket Stadium	October 25, 2002	SA v B	1
87	Chester-le-Street, Riverside Ground	June 5, 2003	E v Z	1
88	Gros Islet, St Lucia, Beausejour Stadium	June 20, 2003	WI v SL	2
89	Darwin, Marrara Cricket Ground	July 18, 2003	A v B	2
90	Cairns, Bundaberg Rum Stadium	July 25, 2003	A v B	2

ONE-DAY INTERNATIONAL RECORDS

Matches in this section do not have first-class status.

SUMMARY OF ONE-DAY INTERNATIONALS

1970-71 to December 31, 2004

	Opponents	Matches	Won by											Tied	NR
			E	A	SA	WI	NZ	I	P	SL	Z	B	Ass		
England	Australia	78	32	44	–	–	–	–	–	–	–	–	–	1	1
	South Africa	27	10	–	17	–	–	–	–	–	–	–	–	–	–
	West Indies	70	29	–	–	37	–	–	–	–	–	–	–	–	4
	New Zealand	54	25	–	–	–	25	–	–	–	–	–	–	1	3
	India	51	25	–	–	–	–	24	–	–	–	–	–	–	2
	Pakistan	53	31	–	–	–	–	–	21	–	–	–	–	–	1
	Sri Lanka	32	19	–	–	–	–	–	–	13	–	–	–	–	–
	Zimbabwe	30	21	–	–	–	–	–	–	–	8	–	–	–	1
	Bangladesh	4	4	–	–	–	–	–	–	–	–	0	–	–	–
	Associates	7	7	–	–	–	–	–	–	–	–	–	0	–	–
Australia	South Africa	56	–	29	24	–	–	–	–	–	–	–	–	1	2
	West Indies	105	–	47	–	55	–	–	–	–	–	–	–	2	1
	New Zealand	92	–	63	–	–	26	–	–	–	–	–	–	–	3
	India	80	–	49	–	–	–	27	–	–	–	–	–	–	4
	Pakistan	69	–	39	–	–	–	–	26	–	–	–	–	1	3
	Sri Lanka	55	–	36	–	–	–	–	–	17	–	–	–	1	1
	Zimbabwe	27	–	25	–	–	–	–	–	–	1	–	–	–	1
	Bangladesh	6	–	6	–	–	–	–	–	–	–	0	–	–	–
	Associates	9	–	9	–	–	–	–	–	–	–	–	0	–	–
South Africa	West Indies	33	–	–	21	11	–	–	–	–	–	–	–	–	1
	New Zealand	40	–	–	23	–	14	–	–	–	–	–	–	1	2
	India	46	–	–	28	–	–	16	–	–	–	–	–	–	2
	Pakistan	41	–	–	28	–	–	–	13	–	–	–	–	–	–
	Sri Lanka	39	–	–	18	–	–	–	–	19	–	–	–	1	1
	Zimbabwe	18	–	–	15	–	–	–	–	–	2	–	–	–	1
	Bangladesh	7	–	–	7	–	–	–	–	–	–	0	–	–	–
	Associates	11	–	–	11	–	–	–	–	–	–	–	0	–	–
West Indies	New Zealand	40	–	–	–	22	13	–	–	–	–	–	–	–	5
	India	76	–	–	–	46	–	28	–	–	–	–	–	1	1
	Pakistan	99	–	–	–	61	–	–	36	–	–	–	–	–	2
	Sri Lanka	39	–	–	–	23	–	–	–	15	–	–	–	–	1
	Zimbabwe	24	–	–	–	17	–	–	–	–	7	–	–	–	–
	Bangladesh	11	–	–	–	9	–	–	–	–	–	0	–	–	2
	Associates	8	–	–	–	7	–	–	–	–	–	–	1	–	–
New Zealand	India	72	–	–	–	–	33	35	–	–	–	–	–	–	4
	Pakistan	77	–	–	–	–	28	–	47	–	–	–	–	1	1
	Sri Lanka	56	–	–	–	–	29	–	–	24	–	–	–	1	2
	Zimbabwe	26	–	–	–	–	17	–	–	–	7	–	–	1	1
	Bangladesh	7	–	–	–	–	7	–	–	–	–	0	–	–	–
	Associates	6	–	–	–	–	6	–	–	–	–	–	0	–	–
India	Pakistan	95	–	–	–	–	–	33	58	–	–	–	–	–	4
	Sri Lanka	79	–	–	–	–	–	41	–	31	–	–	–	–	7
	Zimbabwe	47	–	–	–	–	–	37	–	–	8	–	–	–	2
	Bangladesh	14	–	–	–	–	–	13	–	–	–	1	–	–	–
	Associates	18	–	–	–	–	–	16	–	–	–	–	2	–	–
Pakistan	Sri Lanka	103	–	–	–	–	–	–	62	38	–	–	–	1	2
	Zimbabwe	34	–	–	–	–	–	–	30	–	2	–	–	1	1
	Bangladesh	18	–	–	–	–	–	–	17	–	–	1	–	–	–
	Associates	14	–	–	–	–	–	–	14	–	–	–	0	–	–
Sri Lanka	Zimbabwe	36	–	–	–	–	–	–	–	29	6	–	–	–	1
	Bangladesh	11	–	–	–	–	–	–	–	11	–	0	–	–	–
	Associates	8	–	–	–	–	–	–	–	7	–	–	1	–	–
Zimbabwe	Bangladesh	13	–	–	–	–	–	–	–	–	12	1	–	–	–
	Associates	18	–	–	–	–	–	–	–	–	15	–	1	–	2
Bangladesh	Associates	10	–	–	–	–	–	–	–	–	–	3	7	–	–
Associates	Associates	3	–	–	–	–	–	–	–	–	–	–	3	–	–
		2,202	203	347	192	288	198	270	324	204	68	6	15	19	68

Note: Associate Members of ICC who have played one-day internationals are Canada, East Africa, Holland, Hong Kong, Kenya, Namibia, Scotland, United Arab Emirates and USA. Sri Lanka, Zimbabwe and Bangladesh also played one-day internationals before being given Test status; these are not included among the Associates' results.

RESULTS SUMMARY OF ONE-DAY INTERNATIONALS

1970-71 to December 31, 2004 (2,002 matches)

	Matches	Won	Lost	Tied	No Result	% Won (excl. NR)
South Africa	318	192	114	4	8	62.58
Australia	577	347	208	7	15	62.36
West Indies.	505	288	197	5	15	59.28
Pakistan	603	324	261	6	12	55.32
England	406	203	189	2	12	51.77
India	578	270	281	3	24	49.00
Sri Lanka	458	204	235	3	16	46.49
New Zealand.	470	198	246	4	22	44.64
Zimbabwe.	273	68	193	4	8	26.41
Kenya	66	12	52	—	2	18.75
Canada.	9	1	8	—	—	11.11
United Arab Emirates . .	9	1	8	—	—	11.11
Holland	13	1	12	—	—	7.69
Bangladesh	101	6	93	—	2	6.06
USA	2	—	2	—	—	—
Hong Kong.	2	—	2	—	—	—
East Africa	3	—	3	—	—	—
Scotland.	5	—	5	—	—	—
Namibia	6	—	6	—	—	—

Note: Matches abandoned without a ball bowled are not included, except (from 2004) where the toss took place, in accordance with an ICC ruling. Such matches, like those called off after play began, are now counted as official internationals in their own right, even when replayed on another day. In the percentages of matches won, ties are counted as half a win.

BATTING RECORDS

MOST RUNS

		M	I	NO	R	HS	100s	Avge
1	**S. R. Tendulkar (India)**	**342**	**333**	**32**	**13,497**	**186***	**37**	**44.84**
2	**Inzamam-ul-Haq (Pakistan)** . .	**328**	**304**	**43**	**10,267**	**137***	**10**	**39.33**
3	**S. C. Ganguly (India)**.	**266**	**257**	**20**	**9,914**	**183**	**22**	**41.83**
4	**S. T. Jayasuriya (Sri Lanka)** . .	**333**	**324**	**14**	**9,896**	**189**	**18**	**31.92**
5	M. Azharuddin (India).	334	308	54	9,378	153*	7	36.92
6	P. A. de Silva (Sri Lanka)	308	296	30	9,284	145	11	34.90
7	**B. C. Lara (West Indies)**	**244**	**237**	**26**	**8,921**	**169**	**18**	**42.27**
8	Saeed Anwar (Pakistan)	247	244	19	8,824	194	20	39.21
9	D. L. Haynes (West Indies). . . .	238	237	28	8,648	152*	17	41.37
10	M. E. Waugh (Australia)	244	236	20	8,500	173	18	39.35
11	**R. Dravid (India)**	**245**	**224**	**27**	**7,751**	**153**	**9**	**39.34**
12	S. R. Waugh (Australia).	325	288	58	7,569	120*	3	32.90
13	A. Ranatunga (Sri Lanka)	269	255	47	7,456	131*	4	35.84
14	**R. T. Ponting (Australia)**	**209**	**204**	**26**	**7,422**	**145**	**15**	**41.69**
15	Javed Miandad (Pakistan).	233	218	41	7,381	119*	8	41.70
16	**M. S. Atapattu (Sri Lanka)** . . .	**225**	**219**	**26**	**7,296**	**132***	**11**	**37.80**
17	**J. H. Kallis (South Africa)** . . .	**203**	**194**	**36**	**7,267**	**139**	**13**	**45.99**
18	Salim Malik (Pakistan)	283	256	38	7,170	102	5	32.88

Note: The leading aggregates for other countries are:

	M	I	NO	R	HS	100s	Avge
A. Flower (Zimbabwe)	213	208	16	6,786	145	4	35.34
S. P. Fleming (New Zealand)	**229**	**220**	**19**	**6,539**	**134***	**6**	**32.53**
A. J. Stewart (England)	170	162	14	4,677	116	4	31.60
S. O. Tikolo (Kenya)	65	63	2	1,710	106*	1	28.03
Khaled Mashud (Bangladesh)	**88**	**82**	**16**	**1,275**	**54***	**0**	**19.31**

Bold type denotes those who played one-day internationals in the calendar year 2004.

BEST CAREER STRIKE-RATES BY BATSMEN

(Runs per 100 balls. Qualification: 500 runs)

SR		Position	M	I	R	Avge
105.54	**A. M. Blignaut (Z)**	9	47	36	533	19.03
104.88	B. L. Cairns (NZ)	9/8	78	65	987	16.72
103.35	**Shahid Afridi (P)**	2	191	183	4,125	23.57
99.43	I. D. S. Smith (NZ)	8	98	77	1,055	17.29
98.20	**R. L. Powell (WI)**	6	102	93	2,024	26.28
95.07	Kapil Dev (I)	7/6	225	198	3,783	23.79
94.87	**V. Sehwag (I)**	2	106	103	3,131	32.27
94.57	**A. C. Gilchrist (A)**	2	198	192	6,661	36.00
92.95	**A. Flintoff (E)**	5/6	80	71	2,111	35.18
90.64	**A. Symonds (A)**	5	104	79	2,287	36.88
90.20	I. V. A. Richards (WI)	4	187	167	6,721	47.00

Note: Position means a batsman's most usual position in the batting order.

Bold type denotes those who played one-day internationals in the calendar year 2004.

HIGHEST INDIVIDUAL INNINGS

194	Saeed Anwar	Pakistan v India at Chennai	1996-97
189*	I. V. A. Richards	West Indies v England at Manchester	1984
189	S. T. Jayasuriya	Sri Lanka v India at Sharjah	2000-01
188*	G. Kirsten	South Africa v UAE at Rawalpindi.	1995-96
186*	S. R. Tendulkar	India v New Zealand at Hyderabad	1999-2000
183	S. C. Ganguly	India v Sri Lanka at Taunton	1999
181	I. V. A. Richards	West Indies v Sri Lanka at Karachi	1987-88
175*	Kapil Dev	India v Zimbabwe at Tunbridge Wells.	1983
173	M. E. Waugh	Australia v West Indies at Melbourne	2000-01
172*	C. B. Wishart	Zimbabwe v Namibia at Harare.	2002-03
172	A. C. Gilchrist	Australia v Zimbabwe at Hobart	2003-04
171*	G. M. Turner	New Zealand v East Africa at Birmingham	1975
169*	D. J. Callaghan	South Africa v New Zealand at Verwoerdburg	1994-95
169	B. C. Lara	West Indies v Sri Lanka at Sharjah	1995-96
167*	R. A. Smith	England v Australia at Birmingham	1993
161	A. C. Hudson	South Africa v Holland at Rawalpindi.	1995-96
159*	D. Mongia	India v Zimbabwe at Guwahati	2001-02
158	D. I. Gower	England v New Zealand at Brisbane.	1982-83
154	A. C. Gilchrist	Australia v Sri Lanka at Melbourne	1998-99
153*	I. V. A. Richards	West Indies v Australia at Melbourne	1979-80
153*	M. Azharuddin	India v Zimbabwe at Cuttack	1997-98
153*	S. C. Ganguly	India v New Zealand at Gwalior	1999-2000

153*	C. H. Gayle	West Indies v Zimbabwe at Bulawayo..........	2003-04
153	B. C. Lara	West Indies v Pakistan at Sharjah	1993-94
153	R. Dravid	India v New Zealand at Hyderabad	1999-2000
153	H. H. Gibbs	South Africa v Bangladesh at Potchefstroom	2002-03
152*	D. L. Haynes	West Indies v India at Georgetown............	1988-89
152*	C. H. Gayle	West Indies v South Africa at Johannesburg......	2003-04
152	C. H. Gayle	West Indies v Kenya at Nairobi...............	2001
152	S. R. Tendulkar	India v Namibia at Pietermaritzburg...........	2002-03
151*	S. T. Jayasuriya	Sri Lanka v India at Mumbai	1996-97
150	S. Chanderpaul	West Indies v South Africa at East London	1998-99

Note: The highest individual scores for other countries are:

| 144 | K. O. Otieno | Kenya v Bangladesh at Nairobi.............. | 1997-98 |
| 101 | Mehrab Hossain | Bangladesh v Zimbabwe at Dhaka .... | 1998-99 |

MOST HUNDREDS

S. R. Tendulkar (I). . . . 37
S. C. Ganguly (I) 22
Saeed Anwar (P). 20
S. T. Jayasuriya (SL). . . 18
B. C. Lara (WI). 18
M. E. Waugh (A) 18
D. L. Haynes (WI). 17
R. T. Ponting (A) 15
N. J. Astle (NZ) 14
H. H. Gibbs (SA) 13

J. H. Kallis (SA) 13
G. Kirsten (SA). 13
M. S. Atapattu (SL) . . . 11
P. A. de Silva (SL). 11
C. G. Greenidge (WI). . . 11
I. V. A. Richards (WI) . . . 11
A. C. Gilchrist (A) 10
Ijaz Ahmed, sen. (P) . . . 10
Inzamam-ul-Haq (P). . . 10
Yousuf Youhana (P) . . . 10

Most hundreds for other countries:

G. A. Gooch (E) 8
M. E. Trescothick (E) . . 8
A. D. R. Campbell (Z). . . 7
K. O. Otieno (K) 2
Mehrab Hossain (B). . . . 1

Bold type denotes those who played one-day internationals in the calendar year 2004.

MOST HUNDREDS AGAINST ONE TEAM

Saeed Anwar.	7	Pakistan v Sri Lanka
S. R. Tendulkar	7	India v Australia
S. R. Tendulkar	7	India v Sri Lanka
D. L. Haynes.	6	West Indies v Australia
S. T. Jayasuriya	5	Sri Lanka v India
S. R. Tendulkar	5	India v Zimbabwe

HIGHEST PARTNERSHIP FOR EACH WICKET

258	for 1st	S. C. Ganguly and S. R. Tendulkar	I v K	Paarl	2001-02
331	for 2nd	S. R. Tendulkar and R. Dravid	I v NZ	Hyderabad	1999-2000
237*	for 3rd	R. Dravid and S. R. Tendulkar	I v K	Bristol	1999
275*	for 4th	M. Azharuddin and A. Jadeja	I v Z	Cuttack	1997-98
223	for 5th	M. Azharuddin and A. Jadeja	I v SL	Colombo (RPS)	1997-98
161	for 6th	M. O. Odumbe and A. V. Vadher	K v SL	Southampton	1999
130	for 7th	A. Flower and H. H. Streak	Z v E	Harare	2001-02
119	for 8th	P. R. Reiffel and S. K. Warne	A v SA	Port Elizabeth	1993-94
126*	for 9th	Kapil Dev and S. M. H. Kirmani	I v Z	Tunbridge Wells	1983
106*	for 10th	I. V. A. Richards and M. A. Holding	WI v E	Manchester	1984

BOWLING RECORDS

MOST WICKETS

		M	Balls	R	W	BB	4W/i	Avge
1	Wasim Akram (Pakistan).	356	18,186	11,812	502	5-15	23	23.52
2	Waqar Younis (Pakistan)	262	12,698	9,919	416	7-36	27	23.84
3	**M. Muralitharan (Sri Lanka).**	**237**	**12,871**	**8,103**	**366**	**5-15**	**18**	**22.13**
4	**W. P. U. J. C. Vaas (Sri Lanka)**	**249**	**12,219**	**8,407**	**322**	**8-19**	**10**	**26.10**
5	**A. Kumble (India)**	**259**	**13,817**	**9,854**	**321**	**6-12**	**10**	**30.69**
6	J. Srinath (India)	229	11,935	8,847	315	5-23	10	28.08
7	S. M. Pollock (South Africa) .	221	11,572	7,229	305	6-35	15	23.70
8	S. K. Warne (Australia)	193	10,600	7,514	291	5-33	13	25.82
9	**G. D. McGrath (Australia). . .**	**194**	**10,170**	**6,580**	**290**	**7-15**	**14**	**22.68**
10	Saqlain Mushtaq (Pakistan) . . .	169	8,770	6,275	288	5-20	17	21.78
11	A. A. Donald (South Africa) . .	164	8,561	5,926	272	6-23	13	21.78
12	**S. T. Jayasuriya (Sri Lanka) .**	**333**	**12,196**	**9,692**	**267**	**6-29**	**10**	**36.29**
13	Kapil Dev (India)	225	11,202	6,945	253	5-43	4	27.45
14	**H. H. Streak (Zimbabwe)** . .	**183**	**9,192**	**6,893**	**234**	**5-32**	**8**	**29.45**
15	C. A. Walsh (West Indies). . . .	205	10,822	6,918	227	5-1	7	30.47
16	C. E. L. Ambrose (West Indies)	176	9,353	5,429	225	5-17	10	24.12
17	**D. Gough (England)**	**141**	**7,560**	**5,425**	**213**	**5-44**	**12**	**25.46**
18	J. McDermott (Australia). . .	138	7,461	5,018	203	5-44	5	24.71
	A. B. Agarkar (India)	**134**	**6,649**	**5,653**	**203**	**6-42**	**9**	**27.84**
	C. Z. Harris (New Zealand). .	250	10,667	7,613	203	5-42	3	37.50

Note: The most wickets for other countries are:

	M	Balls	R	W	BB	4W/i	Avge
Khaled Mahmud (Bangladesh) . . .	**68**	**3,041**	**2,552**	**60**	**4-19**	**1**	**42.53**
Mohammad Rafique (Bangladesh)	**71**	**3,512**	**2,713**	**60**	**4-63**	**1**	**45.21**
T. M. Odoyo (Kenya).	**63**	**2,738**	**2,226**	**59**	**4-28**	**1**	**37.72**

Bold type denotes those who played one-day internationals in the calendar year 2004.

BEST CAREER STRIKE-RATES BY BOWLERS

(Balls per wicket. Qualification: 1,500 balls)

SR		M	W
28.60	**B. Lee (A)**	**91**	**160**
29.38	G. I. Allott (NZ)	31	52
29.58	L. S. Pascoe (A).	29	53
29.80	**Shoaib Akhtar (P)**	**118**	**186**
30.45	Saqlain Mushtaq (P)	169	288
30.52	Waqar Younis (P)	262	416
30.78	**M. S. Kasprowicz (A)**.	**30**	**50**

Bold type denotes those who played one-day internationals in the calendar year 2004.

BEST CAREER ECONOMY-RATES

(Runs conceded per six balls. Qualification: 50 wickets)

ER		M	W
3.09	J. Garner (WI)	98	146
3.28	R. G. D. Willis (E)	64	80
3.30	R. J. Hadlee (NZ).	115	158
3.32	M. A. Holding (WI)	102	142
3.40	A. M. E. Roberts (WI)	56	87
3.48	C. E. L. Ambrose (WI)	176	225

BEST BOWLING ANALYSES

8-19	W. P. U. J. C. Vaas	Sri Lanka v Zimbabwe at Colombo (SSC)	2001-02
7-15	G. D. McGrath	Australia v Namibia at Potchefstroom	2002-03
7-20	A. J. Bichel	Australia v England at Port Elizabeth	2002-03
7-30	M. Muralitharan	Sri Lanka v India at Sharjah	2000-01
7-36	Waqar Younis	Pakistan v England at Leeds	2001
7-37	Aqib Javed	Pakistan v India at Sharjah	1991-92
7-51	W. W. Davis	West Indies v Australia at Leeds	1983
6-12	A. Kumble	India v West Indies at Calcutta	1993-94
6-14	G. J. Gilmour	Australia v England at Leeds.	1975
6-14	Imran Khan	Pakistan v India at Sharjah	1984-85
6-15	C. E. H. Croft	West Indies v England at St Vincent.	1980-81
6-16	Shoaib Akhtar	Pakistan v New Zealand at Karachi	2002
6-18	Azhar Mahmood	Pakistan v West Indies at Sharjah.	1999-2000
6-19	H. K. Olonga	Zimbabwe v England at Cape Town	1999-2000
6-20	B. C. Strang	Zimbabwe v Bangladesh at Nairobi (Aga Khan) . .	1997-98
6-22	F. H. Edwards*	West Indies v Zimbabwe at Harare	2003-04
6-23	A. A. Donald	South Africa v Kenya at Nairobi (Gymkhana). . . .	1996-97
6-23	A. Nehra	India v England at Durban	2002-03
6-23	S. E. Bond	New Zealand v Australia at Port Elizabeth	2002-03
6-25	S. B. Styris	New Zealand v West Indies at Port-of-Spain	2002
6-25	W. P. U. J. C. Vaas	Sri Lanka v Bangladesh at Pietermaritzburg	2002-03
6-26	Waqar Younis	Pakistan v Sri Lanka at Sharjah.	1989-90
6-29	B. P. Patterson	West Indies v India at Nagpur	1987-88
6-29	S. T. Jayasuriya	Sri Lanka v England at Moratuwa	1992-93
6-30	Waqar Younis	Pakistan v New Zealand at Auckland	1993-94
6-35	S. M. Pollock	South Africa v West Indies at East London	1998-99
6-35	Abdul Razzaq	Pakistan v Bangladesh at Dhaka	2001-02
6-39	K. H. MacLeay	Australia v India at Nottingham.	1983
6-41	I. V. A. Richards	West Indies v India at Delhi	1989-90
6-42	A. B. Agarkar	India v Australia at Melbourne	2003-04
6-44	Waqar Younis	Pakistan v New Zealand at Sharjah.	1996-97
6-49	L. Klusener	South Africa v Sri Lanka at Lahore	1997-98
6-50	A. H. Gray	West Indies v Australia at Port-of-Spain	1990-91
6-59	Waqar Younis	Pakistan v Australia at Nottingham.	2001

* *Edwards is the first bowler to take six wickets on debut.*

Note: The best analyses for other countries are:

5-15	M. A. Ealham	England v Zimbabwe at Kimberley.	1999-2000
5-24	C. O. Obuya	Kenya v Sri Lanka at Nairobi	2002-03
5-31	Aftab Ahmed	Bangladesh v New Zealand at Dhaka	2004-05

HAT-TRICKS

Jalal-ud-Din	Pakistan v Australia at Hyderabad	1982-83
B. A. Reid	Australia v New Zealand at Sydney.	1985-86
Chetan Sharma	India v New Zealand at Nagpur	1987-88
Wasim Akram	Pakistan v West Indies at Sharjah	1989-90
Wasim Akram	Pakistan v Australia at Sharjah	1989-90
Kapil Dev	India v Sri Lanka at Calcutta	1990-91
Aqib Javed	Pakistan v India at Sharjah.	1991-92
D. K. Morrison	New Zealand v India at Napier.	1993-94
Waqar Younis	Pakistan v New Zealand at East London.	1994-95
Saqlain Mushtaq†	Pakistan v Zimbabwe at Peshawar	1996-97
E. A. Brandes	Zimbabwe v England at Harare.	1996-97
A. M. Stuart	Australia v Pakistan at Melbourne	1996-97
Saqlain Mushtaq	Pakistan v Zimbabwe at The Oval	1999
W. P. U. J. C. Vaas	Sri Lanka v Zimbabwe at Colombo (SSC)	2001-02

Mohammad Sami	Pakistan v West Indies at Sharjah	2001-02
W. P. U. J. C. Vaas‡	Sri Lanka v Bangladesh at Pietermaritzburg	2002-03
B. Lee	Australia v Kenya at Durban	2002-03
J. M. Anderson	England v Pakistan at The Oval	2003
S. J. Harmison	England v India at Nottingham	2004

† *Four wickets in five balls.*   ‡ *The first three balls of the match.*

WICKET-KEEPING AND FIELDING RECORDS

MOST DISMISSALS IN AN INNINGS

6 (all ct)	A. C. Gilchrist	Australia v South Africa at Cape Town	1999-2000
6 (all ct)	A. J. Stewart	England v Zimbabwe at Manchester	2000
6 (5ct, 1st)	R. D. Jacobs	West Indies v Sri Lanka at Colombo (RPS) .	2001-02
6 (5ct, 1st)	A. C. Gilchrist	Australia v England at Sydney	2002-03
6 (all ct)	A. C. Gilchrist	Australia v Namibia at Potchefstroom	2002-03
6 (all ct)	A. C. Gilchrist	Australia v Sri Lanka at Colombo (RPS) . . .	2003-04

MOST DISMISSALS

			M	*Ct*	*St*
1	326	**A. C. Gilchrist (Australia)**	198	287	39
2	287	**Moin Khan (Pakistan)**	219	214	73
3	265	**M. V. Boucher (South Africa)**	178	253	12
4	234	I. A. Healy (Australia)	168	195	39
5	220	Rashid Latif (Pakistan)	166	182	38
6	206	**R. S. Kaluwitharana (Sri Lanka)**	186	131	75
7	204	P. J. L. Dujon (West Indies)	169	183	21
8	189	**R. D. Jacobs (West Indies)**	147	160	29
9	{165	D. J. Richardson (South Africa)	122	148	17
	{165	A. Flower (Zimbabwe)	186	133	32
11	163	A. J. Stewart (England)	138	148	15
12	154	N. R. Mongia (India)	140	110	44
13	136	A. C. Parore (New Zealand)	150	111	25
14	124	R. W. Marsh (Australia)	92	120	4
15	119	**K. C. Sangakkara (Sri Lanka)**	79	88	31
16	103	Salim Yousuf (Pakistan)	86	81	22

Notes: The most for Bangladesh is **83** (63 ct, 20 st) in 88 matches by **Khaled Mashud**. The most for Kenya is **40** (26 ct, 14 st) in 46 matches by **K. O. Otieno**, who took one other catch in 17 one-day internationals when not keeping wicket.

A. J. Stewart's record excludes 11 catches taken in 32 one-day internationals when not keeping wicket; A. C. Gilchrist's excludes 5 in 29; A. Flower's 8 in 27; R. S. Kaluwitharana's 1 in 3; and K. C. Sangakkara's 19 in 44. R. Dravid (India) has made 164 dismissals (150 ct, 14 st) in 245 one-day internationals, but only 86 (72 ct, 14 st) in 74 as wicket-keeper (including one where he took over during the match).

Bold type denotes those who played one-day internationals in the calendar year 2004.

MOST CATCHES IN AN INNINGS

(Excluding wicket-keepers)

5	J. N. Rhodes	South Africa v West Indies at Bombay	1993-94
4	Salim Malik	Pakistan v New Zealand at Sialkot	1984-85
4	S. M. Gavaskar	India v Pakistan at Sharjah	1984-85
4	R. B. Richardson	West Indies v England at Birmingham	1991
4	K. C. Wessels	South Africa v West Indies at Kingston	1991-92
4	M. A. Taylor	Australia v West Indies at Sydney	1992-93

4	C. L. Hooper.	West Indies v Pakistan at Durban	1992-93
4	K. R. Rutherford	New Zealand v India at Napier	1994-95
4	P. V. Simmons	West Indies v Sri Lanka at Sharjah	1995-96
4	M. Azharuddin.	India v Pakistan at Toronto.	1997-98
4	S. R. Tendulkar	India v Pakistan at Dhaka	1997-98
4	R. Dravid	India v West Indies at Toronto	1999-2000
4	G. J. Whittall.	Zimbabwe v England at The Oval	2000
4	C. Z. Harris.	New Zealand v India at Colombo (RPS).	2001
4	Younis Khan	Pakistan v Zimbabwe at Harare	2002-03
4	M. Kaif	India v Sri Lanka at Johannesburg	2002-03
4	M. J. Clarke	Australia v India at Melbourne	2003-04
4	V. V. S. Laxman	India v Zimbabwe at Perth.	2003-04

Note: While fielding as substitute, J. G. Bracewell held 4 catches for New Zealand v Australia at Adelaide, 1980-81.

MOST CATCHES

Ct	M	
156	334	M. Azharuddin (India)
127	273	A. R. Border (Australia)
120	227	C. L. Hooper (West Indies)
111	325	S. R. Waugh (Australia)
110	**229**	**S. P. Fleming (New Zealand)**
109	213	R. S. Mahanama (Sri Lanka)
108	244	M. E. Waugh (Australia)
105	**333**	**S. T. Jayasuriya (Sri Lanka)**
105	245	J. N. Rhodes (South Africa)
102	**244**	**B. C. Lara (West Indies)**
101	**342**	**S. R. Tendulkar (India)**
100	187	I. V. A. Richards (West Indies)

Most catches for other countries:

Ct	M	
97	328	**Inzamam-ul-Haq (Pakistan)**
86	219	**G. W. Flower (Zimbabwe)**
64	120	G. A. Hick (England)
21	65	S. O. Tikolo (Kenya)
17	43	**Alok Kapali (Bangladesh)**
17	71	**Mohammad Rafique (Bangladesh)**

Bold type denotes those who played one-day internationals in the calendar year 2004.

TEAM RECORDS

HIGHEST INNINGS TOTALS

398-5	(50 overs)	Sri Lanka v Kenya at Kandy.	1995-96
376-2	(50 overs)	India v New Zealand at Hyderabad.	1999-2000
373-6	(50 overs)	India v Sri Lanka at Taunton.	1999
371-9	(50 overs)	Pakistan v Sri Lanka at Nairobi (Gymkhana)	1996-97
363-3	(50 overs)	South Africa v Zimbabwe at Bulawayo	2001-02
363-7	(55 overs)	England v Pakistan at Nottingham	1992
360-4	(50 overs)	West Indies v Sri Lanka at Karachi	1987-88
359-2	(50 overs)	Australia v India at Johannesburg.	2002-03
359-5	(50 overs)	Australia v India at Sydney.	2003-04
354-3	(50 overs)	South Africa v Kenya at Cape Town	2001-02
353-5	(50 overs)	India v New Zealand at Hyderabad.	2003-04
351-3	(50 overs)	India v Kenya at Paarl	2001-02

Note: The highest totals by other countries are:

349-9	(50 overs)	New Zealand v India at Rajkot	1999-2000
347-3	(50 overs)	Kenya v Bangladesh at Nairobi	1997-98
340-2	(50 overs)	Zimbabwe v Namibia at Harare	2002-03
272-8	(50 overs)	Bangladesh v Zimbabwe at Bulawayo	2000-01

HIGHEST TOTALS BATTING SECOND

344-8	(50 overs)	Pakistan v India at Karachi....................	2003-04
		(*Lost by 5 runs*)	
330-7	(49.1 overs)	Australia v South Africa at Port Elizabeth	2001-02
		(*Won by 3 wickets*)	
329	(49.3 overs)	Sri Lanka v West Indies at Sharjah.............	1995-96
		(*Lost by 4 runs*)	
326-8	(49.3 overs)	India v England at Lord's.....................	2002
		(*Won by 2 wickets*)	
325-5	(47.4 overs)	India v West Indies at Ahmedabad	2002-03
		(*Won by 5 wickets*)	
317	(48.4 overs)	India v Pakistan at Rawalpindi...............	2003-04
		(*Lost by 12 runs*)	
316-7	(47.5 overs)	India v Pakistan at Dhaka..................	1997-98
		(*Won by 3 wickets*)	
316-4	(48.5 overs)	Australia v Pakistan at Lahore...............	1998-99
		(*Won by 6 wickets*)	
315	(49.4 overs)	Pakistan v Sri Lanka at Singapore	1995-96
		(*Lost by 34 runs*)	

HIGHEST MATCH AGGREGATES

693-15	(100 overs)	Pakistan v India at Karachi.................	2003-04
664-19	(99.4 overs)	Pakistan v Sri Lanka at Singapore	1995-96
662-17	(99.3 overs)	Sri Lanka v West Indies at Sharjah.............	1995-96
660-19	(99.5 overs)	Pakistan v Sri Lanka at Nairobi (Gymkhana)	1996-97
656-10	(99.1 overs)	South Africa v Australia at Port Elizabeth	2001-02
655-19	(97 overs)	India v New Zealand at Rajkot	1999-2000
652-12	(100 overs)	Sri Lanka v Kenya at Kandy	1995-96
651-13	(99.3 overs)	England v India at Lord's....................	2002
650-15	(100 overs)	New Zealand v Australia at Auckland	1999-2000

LOWEST INNINGS TOTALS

35	(18 overs)	Zimbabwe v Sri Lanka at Harare	2003-04
36	(18.4 overs)	Canada v Sri Lanka at Paarl	2002-03
38	(15.4 overs)	Zimbabwe v Sri Lanka at Colombo (SSC)	2001-02
43	(19.5 overs)	Pakistan v West Indies at Cape Town	1992-93
45	(40.3 overs)	Canada v England at Manchester	1979
45	(14 overs)	Namibia v Australia at Potchefstroom	2002-03
54	(26.3 overs)	India v Sri Lanka at Sharjah	2000-01
54	(23.2 overs)	West Indies v South Africa at Cape Town	2003-04
55	(28.3 overs)	Sri Lanka v West Indies at Sharjah.............	1986-87
63	(25.5 overs)	India v Australia at Sydney..................	1980-81
64	(35.5 overs)	New Zealand v Pakistan at Sharjah.............	1985-86
65	(24 overs)	USA v Australia at Southampton	2004
68	(31.3 overs)	Scotland v West Indies at Leicester	1999
69	(28 overs)	South Africa v Australia at Sydney	1993-94
70	(25.2 overs)	Australia v England at Birmingham	1977
70	(26.3 overs)	Australia v New Zealand at Adelaide	1985-86

The lowest totals by other Test-playing countries are:

76	(30.1 overs)	Bangladesh v Sri Lanka at Colombo (SSC)	2002
76	(27.3 overs)	Bangladesh v India at Dhaka.................	2003
86	(32.4 overs)	England v Australia at Manchester	2001

LARGEST VICTORIES

256 runs	Australia (301-6 in 50 overs) v Namibia (45 in 14 overs) at Potchefstroom	2002-03
245 runs	Sri Lanka (299-5 in 50 overs) v India (54 in 26.3 overs) at Sharjah . . .	2000-01
233 runs	Pakistan (320-3 in 50 overs) v Bangladesh (87 in 34.2 overs) at Dhaka .	1999-2000
232 runs	Australia (323-2 in 50 overs) v Sri Lanka (91 in 35.5 overs) at Adelaide	1984-85
224 runs	Australia (332-5 in 50 overs) v Pakistan (108 in 36 overs) at Nairobi .	2002
217 runs	Pakistan (295-6 in 50 overs) v Sri Lanka (78 in 16.5 overs) at Sharjah .	2001-02
210 runs	New Zealand (347-4 in 50 overs) v USA (137 in 42.4 overs) at The Oval.	2004
209 runs	South Africa (263-4 in 50 overs) v West Indies (54 in 23.2 overs) at Cape Town	2003-04
208 runs	South Africa (354-3 in 50 overs) v Kenya (146 in 45.3 overs) at Cape Town	2001-02
208 runs	Australia (359-5 in 50 overs) v India (151 in 33.2 overs) at Sydney . . .	2003-04
206 runs	New Zealand (276-7 in 50 overs) v Australia (70 in 26.3 overs) at Adelaide	1985-86
206 runs	Sri Lanka (292-5 in 50 overs) v Holland (86 in 29.3 overs) at Colombo (RPS).	2002
202 runs	England (334-4 in 60 overs) v India (132-3 in 60 overs) at Lord's . . .	1975
202 runs	South Africa (305-8 in 50 overs) v Kenya (103 in 25.1 overs) at Nairobi	1996-97
202 runs	Zimbabwe (325-6 in 50 overs) v Kenya (123 in 36.5 overs) at Dhaka . .	1998-99
200 runs	India (276 in 49.3 overs) v Bangladesh (76 in 27.3 overs) at Dhaka . . .	2003

By ten wickets: there have been **24** instances of victory by ten wickets.

TIED MATCHES

There have been **19** tied one-day internationals. Australia have tied seven matches; Bangladesh are the only Test-playing country never to have tied. The most recent ties are:

Australia (213 in 49.2 overs) v South Africa (213 in 49.4 overs) at Birmingham . .	1999
Pakistan (196 in 49.4 overs) v Sri Lanka (196 in 49.1 overs) at Sharjah.	1999-2000
South Africa (226-8 in 50 overs) v Australia (226-9 in 50 overs) at Melbourne (CS)	2000
South Africa (259-7 in 50 overs) v Australia (259-9 in 50 overs) at Potchefstroom .	2001-02
Sri Lanka (268-9 in 50 overs) v South Africa (229-6 in 45 overs) at Durban (D/L method).	2002-03

OTHER RECORDS

MOST APPEARANCES

356 Wasim Akram (P)	325 S. R. Waugh (A)	**266 S. C. Ganguly (I)**
342 S. R. Tendulkar (I)	308 P. A. de Silva (SL)	262 Waqar Younis (P)
334 M. Azharuddin (I)	283 Salim Malik (P)	**259 A. Kumble (I)**
333 S. T. Jayasuriya (SL)	273 A. R. Border (A)	**250 C. Z. Harris (NZ)**
328 Inzamam-ul-Haq (P)	269 A. Ranatunga (SL)	250 Ijaz Ahmed, sen. (P)

Note: The most appearances for other countries are 245 by J. N. Rhodes (SA), **244** by **B. C. Lara** (WI), **219** by **G. W. Flower** (Z), 170 by A. J. Stewart (E), **88** by **Khaled Mashud** (B) and **65** by **S. O. Tikolo** (K).

Bold type denotes those who played one-day internationals in the calendar year 2004.

MOST APPEARANCES AGAINST ONE TEAM

75 P. A. de Silva	Sri Lanka v Pakistan	64 Javed Miandad	Pakistan v West Indies
72 S. T. Jayasuriya	**Sri Lanka v Pakistan**	64 Wasim Akram	Pakistan v West Indies
67 A. Ranatunga	Sri Lanka v Pakistan	61 A. R. Border	Australia v West Indies
65 D. L. Haynes	West Indies v Pakistan	61 R. B. Richardson	West Indies v Pakistan
64 M. Azharuddin	India v Pakistan	**60 Inzamam-ul-Haq**	**Pakistan v Sri Lanka**
64 D. L. Haynes	West Indies v Australia	60 S. R. Waugh	Australia v New Zealand

Bold type denotes those who played one-day internationals in the calendar year 2004.

CAPTAINS

England (406 matches; 24 captains)

N. Hussain 56; G. A. Gooch 50; M. A. Atherton 43; A. J. Stewart 41; M. W. Gatting 37; **M. P. Vaughan 34;** R. G. D. Willis 29; J. M. Brearley 25; D. I. Gower 24; A. J. Hollioake 14; M. H. Denness 12; I. T. Botham 9; K. W. R. Fletcher 5; J. E. Emburey 4; A. J. Lamb 4; D. B. Close 3; R. Illingworth 3; G. P. Thorpe 3; G. Boycott 2; N. Gifford 2; A. W. Greig 2; M. E. Trescothick 2; J. H. Edrich 1; A. P. E. Knott 1.

Australia (577 matches; 16 captains)

A. R. Border 178; S. R. Waugh 106; **R. T. Ponting 78;** M. A. Taylor 67; G. S. Chappell 49; K. J. Hughes 49; I. M. Chappell 11; S. K. Warne 11; I. A. Healy 8; **A. C. Gilchrist 7;** G. R. Marsh 4; G. N. Yallop 4; R. B. Simpson 2; R. J. Bright 1; D. W. Hookes 1; W. M. Lawry 1.

South Africa (318 matches; 6 captains)

W. J. Cronje 138; S. M. Pollock 90; K. C. Wessels 52; **G. C. Smith 34;** C. E. B. Rice 3; M. V. Boucher 1.

West Indies (505 matches; 17 captains)

I. V. A. Richards 108; R. B. Richardson 87; C. H. Lloyd 81; **B. C. Lara 79;** C. L. Hooper 49; C. A. Walsh 43; J. C. Adams 26; C. G. Greenidge 8; D. L. Haynes 7; R. D. Jacobs 4; **R. R. Sarwan 4;** M. A. Holding 2; R. B. Kanhai 2; D. L. Murray 2; S. L. Campbell 1; P. J. L. Dujon 1; A. I. Kallicharran 1.

New Zealand (470 matches; 17 captains)

S. P. Fleming 169; G. P. Howarth 60; M. D. Crowe 44; K. R. Rutherford 37; L. K. Germon 36; J. G. Wright 31; J. V. Coney 25; J. J. Crowe 16; M. G. Burgess 8; C. D. McMillan 8; G. M. Turner 8; C. L. Cairns 7; D. J. Nash 7; B. E. Congdon 6; G. R. Larsen 3; **D. L. Vettori 3;** A. H. Jones 2.

India (578 matches; 18 captains)

M. Azharuddin 174; **S. C. Ganguly 137;** Kapil Dev 74; S. R. Tendulkar 73; S. M. Gavaskar 37; D. B. Vengsarkar 18; A. Jadeja 13; K. Srikkanth 13; R. J. Shastri 11; **R. Dravid 10;** S. Venkataraghavan 7; B. S. Bedi 4; A. L. Wadekar 2; M. Amarnath 1; S. M. H. Kirmani 1; A. Kumble 1; V. Sehwag 1; G. R. Viswanath 1.

Pakistan (603 matches; 20 captains)

Imran Khan 139; Wasim Akram 110; Javed Miandad 62; Waqar Younis 62; **Inzamam-ul-Haq 40;** Moin Khan 34; Salim Malik 34; Rashid Latif 25; Aamir Sohail 22; Ramiz Raja 22; Zaheer Abbas 13; Saeed Anwar 10; Asif Iqbal 6; Abdul Qadir 5; Wasim Bari 5; Mushtaq Mohammad 4; **Yousuf Youhana 4;** Intikhab Alam 3; Majid Khan 2; Sarfraz Nawaz 1.

Sri Lanka (458 matches; 12 captains)

A. Ranatunga 193; S. T. Jayasuriya 118; L. R. D. Mendis 61; **M. S. Atapattu 35;** P. A. de Silva 18; R. S. Madugalle 13; B. Warnapura 8; **D. P. M. D. Jayawardene 4;** A. P. B. Tennekoon 4; R. S. Mahanama 2; D. S. de Silva 1; J. R. Ratnayeke 1.

Zimbabwe (273 matches; 11 captains)

A. D. R. Campbell 86; **H. H. Streak 68;** A. Flower 52; D. L. Houghton 17; **T. Taibu 17;** S. V. Carlisle 12; D. A. G. Fletcher 6; A. J. Traicos 6; B. A. Murphy 4; G. J. Whittall 4; G. W. Flower 1.

Bangladesh (101 matches; 9 captains)

Khaled Mashud 24; Aminul Islam 16; **Habibul Bashar 16;** Akram Khan 15; Khaled Mahmud 15; Gazi Ashraf 7; Naimur Rahman 4; Minhazul Abedin 2; **Rajin Saleh 2.**

Kenya (66 matches; 4 captains)

S. O. Tikolo 24; A. Y. Karim 21; M. O. Odumbe 20; T. M. Odoyo 1.

Associate Members (49 matches; 12 captains)

R. P. Lefebvre (Holland) 8; Sultan M. Zarawani (UAE) 7; J. V. Harris (Canada) 6; D. B. Kotze (Namibia) 6; G. Salmond (Scotland) 5; S. W. Lubbers (Holland) 4; B. M. Mauricette (Canada) 3; Harilal R. Shah (East Africa) 3; **Khurram Khan (UAE) 2; R. Sharma (Hong Kong) 2; R. W. Staple (USA) 2;** L. P. van Troost (Holland) 1.

Bold type denotes those who captained in one-day internationals in the calendar year 2004.

WORLD CUP RECORDS

WORLD CUP FINALS

1975	WEST INDIES (291-8) beat Australia (274) by 17 runs	Lord's
1979	WEST INDIES (286-9) beat England (194) by 92 runs.	Lord's
1983	INDIA (183) beat West Indies (140) by 43 runs	Lord's
1987	AUSTRALIA (253-5) beat England (246-8) by seven runs.	Calcutta
1992	PAKISTAN (249-6) beat England (227-9) by 22 runs	Melbourne
1996	SRI LANKA (245-3) beat Australia (241-7) by seven wickets	Lahore
1999	AUSTRALIA (133-2) beat Pakistan (132) by eight wickets	Lord's
2003	AUSTRALIA (359-2) beat India (234) by 125 runs	Johannesburg

TEAM RESULTS

	Rounds reached			Matches				
	W	F	SF	P	W	L	T	NR
Australia (8)	3	5	5	58	40	17	1	0
West Indies (8).	2	3	4	48	31	16	0	1
England (8).	0	3	5	50	31	18	0	1
India (8).	1	2	4	55	31	23	0	1
Pakistan (8).	1	2	5	53	29	22	0	2
New Zealand (8)	0	0	4	52	28	23	0	1
South Africa (4)	0	0	2	30	19	9	2	0
Sri Lanka (8).	1	1	2	46	17	27	1	1
Zimbabwe (6)	0	0	0	42	8	31	0	3
Kenya (3)	0	0	0	20	5	14	0	1
Bangladesh (2)	0	0	0	11	2	8	0	1
United Arab Emirates (1) .	0	0	0	5	1	4	0	0
Canada (2)	0	0	0	9	1	8	0	0
Holland (2)	0	0	0	11	1	10	0	0
East Africa (1).	0	0	0	3	0	3	0	0
Scotland (1).	0	0	0	5	0	5	0	0
Namibia (1).	0	0	0	6	0	6	0	0

The number of tournaments each team has played in is shown in brackets.

Note: Full World Cup Records may be found in the 2004 *Wisden*, and will return in 2006.

LIST A ONE-DAY RECORDS

List A is a concept, introduced by the Association of Cricket Statisticians and Historians, intended to provide an approximate equivalent in one-day cricket of first-class status. List A games comprise:

(a) One-day internationals.
(b) Other international matches (e.g. A-team internationals).
(c) Premier domestic one-day tournaments in Test-playing countries.
(d) Official tourist matches against the main first-class teams (e.g. counties, states, provinces and national Board XIs).

The following matches are excluded:

(a) Matches originally scheduled as less than 40 overs per side (e.g. Twenty20 games).
(b) World Cup warm-up games.
(c) Tourist matches against teams outside the major domestic competitions (e.g. universities).
(d) Festival games and pre-season friendlies.

Note: This section covers one-day cricket to the end of the 2004 season in England.

BATTING RECORDS

HIGHEST INDIVIDUAL INNINGS

268	A. D. Brown	Surrey v Glamorgan at The Oval	2002
222*	R. G. Pollock	Eastern Province v Border at East London	1974-75
206	A. I. Kallicharran	Warwickshire v Oxfordshire at Birmingham	1984
203	A. D. Brown	Surrey v Hampshire at Guildford	1997
202*	A. Barrow	Natal v SA African XI at Durban	1975-76
201	V. J. Wells	Leicestershire v Berkshire at Leicester	1996

MOST RUNS

	Career	M	I	NO	R	HS	100s	Avge
G. A. Gooch	1973–1997	614	601	48	22,211	198*	44	40.16
G. A. Hick	*1983–2004*	**590**	**572**	**83**	**20,437**	**172***	**39**	**41.79**
I. V. A. Richards	1973–1993	500	466	61	16,995	189*	26	41.96
S. R. Tendulkar	*1989–2004*	**419**	**408**	**46**	**16,710**	**186***	**47**	**46.16**
C. G. Greenidge	1970–1992	440	436	33	16,349	186*	33	40.56
A. J. Lamb	1972–1995	484	463	63	15,658	132*	19	39.14
D. L. Haynes	1976–1996	419	416	44	15,651	152*	28	42.07
K. J. Barnett	*1979–2004*	**526**	**499**	**54**	**15,543**	**136**	**17**	**34.92**

Bold type denotes those who have played since the start of 2003-04.

HIGHEST PARTNERSHIP FOR EACH WICKET

326* for 1st	Ghulam Ali/Sohail Jaffer, PIA v ADBP at Sialkot	2000-01
331 for 2nd	S. R. Tendulkar/R. Dravid, India v New Zealand at Hyderabad	1999-2000
309* for 3rd	T. S. Curtis/T. M. Moody, Worcestershire v Surrey at The Oval	1994
275* for 4th	M. Azharuddin/A. Jadeja, India v Zimbabwe at Cuttack	1997-98
267* for 5th	Minhazul Abedin/Khaled Mahmud, Bangladeshis v Bahawalpur at Karachi	1997-98
226 for 6th	N. J. Llong/M. V. Fleming, Kent v Cheshire at Bowdon	1999
170 for 7th	D. R. Brown/A. F. Giles, Warwickshire v Essex at Birmingham	2003
203 for 8th	Shahid Iqbal/Haaris Ayaz, Karachi Whites v Hyderabad at Karachi . . .	1998-99
130 for 9th	C. P. Schofield/G. I. Maiden, Lancashire v India A at Blackpool	2003
106* for 10th	I. V. A. Richards/M. A. Holding, West Indies v England at Manchester	1984

BOWLING RECORDS

BEST BOWLING ANALYSES

8-15	R. L. Sanghvi	Delhi v Himachal Pradesh at Una................	1997-98
8-19	W. P. U. J. C. Vaas	Sri Lanka v Zimbabwe at Colombo.............	2001-02
8-21	M. A. Holding	Derbyshire v Sussex at Hove.................	1988
8-26	K. D. Boyce	Essex v Lancashire at Manchester.............	1971
8-31	D. L. Underwood	Kent v Scotland at Edinburgh...............	1987
8-43	S. W. Tait	South Australia v Tasmania at Adelaide...........	2003-04
8-66	S. R. G. Francis	Somerset v Derbyshire at Derby................	2004

MOST WICKETS

	Career	M	B	R	W	BB	4W/i	Avge
Wasim Akram	1984–2003	594	29,719	19,303	881	5-10	46	21.91
A. A. Donald......	**1985–2003**	**458**	**22,856**	**14,942**	**684**	**6-15**	**38**	**21.84**
Waqar Younis	**1988–2003**	**412**	**19,841**	**15,098**	**675**	**7-36**	**44**	**22.36**
J. K. Lever	1968–1990	481	23,208	13,278	674	5-8	34	19.70
J. E. Emburey	1975–2000	536	26,399	16,811	647	5-23	26	25.98
I. T. Botham	1973–1993	470	22,899	15,264	612	5-27	18	24.94

Bold type denotes those who have played since the start of 2003-04.

WICKET-KEEPING AND FIELDING RECORDS

MOST DISMISSALS IN AN INNINGS

8 (5ct, 3st)	S. J. Palframan	Boland v Easterns at Paarl	1997-98
8 (all ct)	D. J. Pipe	Worcestershire v Hertfordshire at Hertford	2001
8 (all ct)	D. J. S. Taylor	Somerset v Combined Universities at Taunton...	1982
7 (6ct, 1st)	M. K. P. B. Kularatne	Galle v Colts at Colombo................	2001-02
7 (all ct)	I. Mitchell	Border v Western Province at East London.....	1998-99
7 (4ct, 3st)	Rizwan Umar	Sargodha v Bahawalpur at Sargodha	1991-92
7 (all ct)	A. J. Stewart	Surrey v Glamorgan at Swansea............	1994
7 (6ct, 1st)	R. W. Taylor	Derbyshire v Lancashire at Manchester	1975

MOST CATCHES IN AN INNINGS IN THE FIELD

5	Hasnain Raza	Bahawalpur v Pakistan Customs at Karachi........	2002-03
5	K. C. Jackson	Boland v Natal at Durban.................	1995-96
5	A. J. Kourie	Transvaal v Western Province at Johannesburg......	1979-80
5	V. J. Marks	Combined Universities v Kent at Oxford	1976
5	Mohammad Ramzan	PNSC v PIA at Karachi................	1998-99
5	J. N. Rhodes	South Africa v West Indies at Bombay...........	1993-94
5	J. M. Rice	Hampshire v Warwickshire at Southampton........	1978
5	Amit Sharma	Punjab v Jammu and Kashmir at Ludhiana........	1999-2000
5	J. W. Wilson	Otago v Auckland at Dunedin	1993-94
5	B. E. Young	South Australia v Tasmania at Launceston	2001-02

TEAM RECORDS

HIGHEST INNINGS TOTALS

438-5	(50 overs)	Surrey v Glamorgan at The Oval.................	2002
429	(49.5 overs)	Glamorgan v Surrey at The Oval.................	2002
424-5	(50 overs)	Buckinghamshire v Suffolk at Dinton..............	2002
413-4	(60 overs)	Somerset v Devon at Torquay...................	1990
411-6	(50 overs)	Yorkshire v Devon at Exmouth..................	2004
409-6	(50 overs)	Trinidad & Tobago v North Windward Islands at Kingston.	2001-02
408-4	(50 overs)	KRL v Sialkot at Sialkot.....................	2002-03
406-5	(60 overs)	Leicestershire v Berkshire at Leicester............	1996
405-4	(50 overs)	Queensland v Western Australia at Brisbane	2003-04
404-3	(60 overs)	Worcestershire v Devon at Worcester	1987
401-7	(50 overs)	Gloucestershire v Buckinghamshire at Wing	2003

LOWEST INNINGS TOTALS

23	(19.4 overs)	Middlesex v Yorkshire at Leeds..................	1974
30	(20.4 overs)	Chittagong v Sylhet at Dhaka...............	2002-03
34	(21.1 overs)	Saurashtra v Mumbai at Mumbai.................	1999-2000
35	(18 overs)	Zimbabwe v Sri Lanka at Harare................	2003-04
36	(25.4 overs)	Leicestershire v Sussex at Leicester	1973
36	(18.4 overs)	Canada v Sri Lanka at Paarl..................	2002-03
38	(15.4 overs)	Zimbabwe v Sri Lanka at Colombo	2001-02
39	(26.4 overs)	Ireland v Sussex at Hove.....................	1985

MISCELLANEOUS RECORDS

LARGE ATTENDANCES

Test Series

943,000	Australia v England (5 Tests)	1936-37

In England

549,650	England v Australia (5 Tests)	1953

Test Matches

††‡465,000	India v Pakistan, Calcutta......................	1998-99
350,534	Australia v England, Melbourne (Third Test)	1936-37

Note: Attendance at India v England at Calcutta in 1981-82 may have exceeded 350,000.

In England

158,000+	England v Australia, Leeds......................	1948
137,915	England v Australia, Lord's	1953

Test Match Day

‡100,000	India v Pakistan, Calcutta (first four days)..............	1998-99
90,800	Australia v West Indies, Melbourne (Fifth Test, second day) . . .	1960-61

Other First-Class Matches in England

93,000	England v Australia, Lord's (Fourth Victory Match, 3 days) . . .	1945
80,000+	Surrey v Yorkshire, The Oval (3 days)	1906
78,792	Yorkshire v Lancashire, Leeds (3 days)................	1904
76,617	Lancashire v Yorkshire, Manchester (3 days)	1926

One-Day Internationals

‡100,000	India v South Africa, Calcutta	1993-94
‡100,000	India v West Indies, Calcutta	1993-94
‡100,000	India v West Indies, Calcutta	1994-95
‡100,000	India v Sri Lanka, Calcutta (World Cup semi-final)	1995-96
‡100,000	India v Australia, Kolkata	2003-04
‡90,000	India v Pakistan, Calcutta	1986-87
‡90,000	India v South Africa, Calcutta	1991-92
87,182	England v Pakistan, Melbourne (World Cup final)	1991-92
86,133	Australia v West Indies, Melbourne	1983-84

† *Estimated.*
‡ *No official attendance figures were issued for these games, but capacity at Calcutta (now Kolkata) is believed to have reached 100,000 following rebuilding in 1993.*

LORD'S CRICKET GROUND

Lord's and the Marylebone Cricket Club were founded in London in 1787. The Club has enjoyed an uninterrupted career since that date, but there have been three grounds known as Lord's. The first (1787–1810) was situated where Dorset Square now is; the second (1809–13), at North Bank, had to be abandoned owing to the cutting of the Regent's Canal; and the third, opened in 1814, is the present one at St John's Wood. It was not until 1866 that the freehold of Lord's was secured by MCC. The present pavilion was erected in 1890 at a cost of £21,000.

HIGHEST INDIVIDUAL SCORES MADE AT LORD'S

333	G. A. Gooch	England v India	1990
316*	J. B. Hobbs	Surrey v Middlesex	1926
315*	P. Holmes	Yorkshire v Middlesex	1925
315	M. A. Wagh	Warwickshire v Middlesex	2001
303*	N. V. Knight	Warwickshire v Middlesex	2004

Note: The longest innings in a first-class match at Lord's was N. V. Knight's, which lasted 644 minutes.

HIGHEST TOTALS AT LORD'S

First-Class Matches

729-6 dec.	Australia v England	1930
682-6 dec.	South Africa v England	2003
665	West Indians v Middlesex	1939
653-4 dec.	England v India	1990
652-8 dec.	West Indies v England	1973

Minor Match

| 735-9 dec. | MCC and Ground v Wiltshire | 1888 |

BIGGEST HIT AT LORD'S

The only known instance of a batsman hitting a ball over the present pavilion at Lord's occurred when A. E. Trott, appearing for MCC against Australians on July 31, August 1, 2, 1899, drove M. A. Noble so far and high that the ball struck a chimney pot and fell behind the building.

MINOR CRICKET

HIGHEST INDIVIDUAL SCORES

628* A. E. J. Collins, Clark's House v North Town at Clifton College.
  A junior house match. His innings of 6 hours 50 minutes was spread over
  four afternoons 1899
566   C. J. Eady, Break-o'-Day v Wellington at Hobart 1901-02
515   D. R. Havewalla, B. B. and C. I. Railways v St Xavier's at Bombay 1933-34
506* J. C. Sharp, Melbourne GS v Geelong College at Melbourne 1914-15
502* Chaman Lal, Mehandra Coll., Patiala v Government Coll., Rupar at Patiala . . . 1956-57
485   A. E. Stoddart, Hampstead v Stoics at Hampstead. 1886
475* Mohammad Iqbal, Muslim Model HS v Islamia HS, Sialkot at Lahore 1958-59
466* G. T. S. Stevens, Beta v Lambda (University College School house match) at
  Neasden. 1919
459   J. A. Prout, Wesley College v Geelong College at Geelong 1908-09

Note: The highest score in a Minor County match is 323* by F. E. Lacey for Hampshire v Norfolk at Southampton in 1887; the highest in the Minor Counties Championship is 282 by E. Garnett for Berkshire v Wiltshire at Reading in 1908.

HIGHEST PARTNERSHIP

664* for 3rd   V. G. Kambli and S. R. Tendulkar, Sharadashram Vidyamandir School
  v St Xavier's High School at Bombay 1987-88

Note: Kambli was 16 years old, Tendulkar 14. Tendulkar made his Test debut 21 months later

RECORD HIT

The Rev. W. Fellows, while at practice on the Christ Church ground at Oxford in 1856, drove a ball bowled by Charles Rogers 175 yards from hit to pitch.

THROWING THE CRICKET BALL

140 yards 2 feet, Robert Percival, on the Durham Sands racecourse, Co. Durham . . .   c1882
140 yards 9 inches, Ross Mackenzie, at Toronto 1872
140 yards, "King Billy" the Aborigine, at Clermont, Queensland 1872

Note: Extensive research by David Rayvern Allen has shown that these traditional records are probably authentic, if not necessarily wholly accurate. Modern competitions have failed to produce similar distances although Ian Pont, the Essex all-rounder who also played baseball, was reported to have thrown 138 yards in Cape Town in 1981. There have been speculative reports attributing throws of 150 yards or more to figures as diverse as the South African Test player Colin Bland, the Latvian javelin thrower Janis Lusis, who won a gold medal for the Soviet Union in the 1968 Olympics, and the British sprinter Charley Ransome. The definitive record is still awaited.

COUNTY CHAMPIONSHIP

MOST APPEARANCES

762   W. Rhodes. . . . . . .   Yorkshire   1898–1930
707   F. E. Woolley. . . . .   Kent   1906–1938
668   C. P. Mead . . . . . .   Hampshire   1906–1936
617   N. Gifford . . . .   Worcestershire (484), Warwickshire (133)   1960–1988
611   W. G. Quaife . . . . .   Warwickshire   1895–1928
601   G. H. Hirst . . . .   Yorkshire   1891–1921

MOST CONSECUTIVE APPEARANCES

423   K. G. Suttle . . . . Sussex 1954–1969
412   J. G. Binks . . . . Yorkshire 1955–1969

Notes: J. Vine made 417 consecutive appearances for Sussex in all first-class matches (399 of them in the Championship) between July 1900 and September 1914.

J. G. Binks did not miss a Championship match for Yorkshire between making his debut in June 1955 and retiring at the end of the 1969 season.

UMPIRES

MOST COUNTY CHAMPIONSHIP APPEARANCES

570	T. W. Spencer.	1950–1980		496	**D. J. Constant**.	**1969–2004**
531	F. Chester	1922–1955		483	P. B. Wight	1966–1995
516	H. G. Baldwin	1932–1962		461	J. Moss.	1899–1929
500	**A. G. T. Whitehead** . .	**1970–2004**		452	A. Skelding	1931–1958

MOST SEASONS ON FIRST-CLASS LIST

36	**D. J. Constant**.	**1969–2004**		27	J. Moss.	1899–1929
35	**A. G. T. Whitehead** . .	**1970–2004**		26	W. A. J. West	1896–1925
31	K. E. Palmer	1972–2002		25	H. G. Baldwin	1932–1962
31	T. W. Spencer.	1950–1980		25	A. Jepson	1960–1984
30	R. Julian	1972–2001		25	J. G. Langridge.	1956–1980
30	P. B. Wight	1966–1995		25	B. J. Meyer	1973–1997
29	H. D. Bird	1970–1998		**25**	**R. Palmer**.	**1980–2004**
28	F. Chester	1922–1955				

Bold type denotes umpires who stood in the 2004 season.

WOMEN'S TEST RECORDS

Amended by MARION COLLIN to the end of the 2004 season in England

BATTING RECORDS

HIGHEST INDIVIDUAL INNINGS

242	Kiran Baluch	Pakistan v West Indies at Karachi	2003-04
214	M. Raj	India v England at Taunton.	2002
209*	K. L. Rolton	Australia v England at Leeds	2001
204	K. E. Flavell	New Zealand v England at Scarborough	1996
204	M. A. J. Goszko . . .	Australia v England at Shenley Park.	2001
200	J. Broadbent.	Australia v England at Guildford	1998
193	D. A. Annetts	Australia v England at Collingham.	1987
190	S. Agarwal.	India v England at Worcester	1986
189	E. A. Snowball. . . .	England v New Zealand at Christchurch	1934-35
179	R. Heyhoe-Flint . . .	England v Australia at The Oval	1976
177	S. C. Taylor.	England v South Africa at Shenley Park	2003
176*	K. L. Rolton	Australia v England at Worcester	1998

1,000 RUNS IN A CAREER

R	T		R	T	
1,935	27	J. A. Brittin (England)	1,110	13	S. Agarwal (India)
1,594	22	R. Heyhoe-Flint (England)	1,078	12	E. Bakewell (England)
1,301	19	D. A. Hockley (New Zealand)	1,007	14	M. E. Maclagan (England)
1,164	18	C. A. Hodges (England)			

BOWLING RECORDS

BEST BOWLING ANALYSES

8-53	N. David	India v England at Jamshedpur.	1995-96
7-6	M. B. Duggan . . .	England v Australia at Melbourne.	1957-58
7-7	E. R. Wilson. . . .	Australia v England at Melbourne.	1957-58
7-10	M. E. Maclagan. .	England v Australia at Brisbane	1934-35
7-18	A. Palmer.	Australia v England at Brisbane	1934-35
7-24	L. Johnston.	Australia v New Zealand at Melbourne	1971-72
7-34	G. E. McConway .	England v India at Worcester	1986
7-41	J. A. Burley	New Zealand v England at The Oval.	1966
7-51	L. C. Pearson . . .	England v Australia at Sydney	2002-03
7-59	Shaiza Khan	Pakistan v West Indies at Karachi	2003-04
7-61	E. Bakewell	England v West Indies at Birmingham	1979

11 WICKETS IN A MATCH

13-226	Shaiza Khan	Pakistan v West Indies at Karachi	2003-04
11-16	E. R. Wilson. . . .	Australia v England at Melbourne.	1957-58
11-63	J. Greenwood . . .	England v West Indies at Canterbury.	1979
11-107	L. C. Pearson . . .	England v Australia at Sydney	2002-03

50 WICKETS IN A CAREER

W	T		W	T	
77	17	M. B. Duggan (England)	60	19	S. Kulkarni (India)
68	11	E. R. Wilson (Australia)	57	16	R. H. Thompson (Australia)
63	20	D. F. Edulji (India)	55	15	J. Lord (New Zealand)
60	14	M. E. Maclagan (England)	50	12	E. Bakewell (England)

WICKET-KEEPING RECORDS

SIX DISMISSALS IN AN INNINGS

8	(6ct, 2st)	L. Nye	England v New Zealand at New Plymouth	1991-92
6	(2ct, 4st)	B. A. Brentnall .	New Zealand v South Africa at Johannesburg . . .	1971-72

EIGHT DISMISSALS IN A MATCH

9	(8ct, 1st)	C. Matthews . .	Australia v India at Adelaide	1990-91
8	(6ct, 2st)	L. Nye	England v New Zealand at New Plymouth	1991-92

25 DISMISSALS IN A CAREER

		T	Ct	St
58	C. Matthews (Australia)	20	46	12
36	S. A. Hodges (England)	11	19	17
28	B. A. Brentnall (New Zealand)	10	16	12
26	J. Smit (England)	16	24	2

TEAM RECORDS

HIGHEST INNINGS TOTALS

569-6 dec.	Australia v England at Guildford	1998
525	Australia v India at Ahmedabad	1983-84
517-8	New Zealand v England at Scarborough	1996
503-5 dec.	England v New Zealand at Christchurch	1934-35

LOWEST INNINGS TOTALS

35	England v Australia at Melbourne	1957-58
38	Australia v England at Melbourne	1957-58
44	New Zealand v England at Christchurch	1934-35
47	Australia v England at Brisbane	1934-35

Opposite: By George! Steve Harmison,
Rob Key and Andrew Flintoff celebrate a
golden summer at The Oval.
Picture by Tom Shaw, Getty Images

PART FIVE

English
Cricket

THE ENGLAND TEAM IN 2004

The Blessed Michael Inherits the Earth

SCYLD BERRY

It was on a Sunday morning in Kingston – March 14, 2004 to be exact – that England were transformed from being a competent, mid-table team into one of serious potential. A team equipped with two world-class cricketers. A team that was to go through the year unbeaten, equal a world record for the most Tests in a calendar year without defeat, and finally look as fit as the Southern Hemisphere teams.

When Nasser Hussain was England's captain, he never had a world-class bowler: between them Darren Gough and Andy Caddick made an excellent, complementary pair. But for reasons of height on the one hand and temperament on the other, neither could be hailed as a world-class strike bowler in himself. On that Sunday morning Michael Vaughan could not have been more blessed if he had been at church rather than Sabina Park: he became the first England captain to possess a match-winning strike bowler since David Gower in 1985, when Ian Botham lengthened his run for one last time and blew away 31 Australian batsmen in the six-Test series.

There had been indications that Steve Harmison was highly promising, but his progress, not unnaturally, had been gradual. From his Test debut against India in 2002 no batsman got after him, not even Australians, because his bounce was so steep. But he did not take wickets in any quantity until the second innings against South Africa at The Oval in 2003, when he took four for 33, after being dropped for the previous Test at Headingley: "make-or-break time" as Harmison later called it. Even then, it was mainly left-handed batsmen he troubled, as he could not move the ball away from right-handers. Progress continued in the First Test at Dhaka, when he kept a very consistent line outside off stump to the Bangladesh batsmen, all but one right-handers. There even discovered a hint of out-swing, as he and Hoggard between them led and virtually constituted England's attack.

Two steps forward were followed by one step back when Harmison went home after the Dhaka Test for reasons which some team-mates thought were more psychological than physical. He missed the Test series in Sri Lanka, where England missed him even more because they had no penetrative pace. But Harmison was not idle: the missing link was put into place while he trained with his football heroes at Newcastle United and improved his "core stability" (rather than weight-training, which would have strengthened his upper body but reduced the elasticity of his shoulders). Now he ran in the same way every time, and kept his shape in his chest-on delivery so that everything went in a straight line.

In the first innings at Kingston he pitched a yard too short and West Indies made a presentable total which England barely exceeded. In the second

There in black and white: Steve Harmison shows off a shirt (signed by the squad of Newcastle United, where he trained the previous winter) giving his Sabina Park figures. *Back row:* Nasser Hussain, James Anderson, Rikki Clarke, Matthew Hoggard, Gareth Batty, Chris Read. *Middle row:* Simon Jones, Michael Vaughan, Andrew Flintoff, Geraint Jones. *Front row:* Paul Collingwood, Mark Butcher, Marcus Trescothick, Ashley Giles.

Picture by Tom Shaw, Getty Images

innings his figures of seven for 12 were the cheapest seven-for in Test history: eight of those runs came from two edged boundaries by Devon Smith, and he had two chances dropped. The line was as good as it had been in Bangladesh, the pace was around 90mph, the stamina was now that of a Premiership footballer, and the temperament just right: consistently aggressive without ever getting overexcited.

Thereafter, Test cricket was a different game for Vaughan and England. Instead of shouting and hectoring as Hussain had felt forced to do, and setting defensive fields to contain batsmen and keep totals down, Vaughan just coolly threw the ball to Harmison. In the Second Test West Indies were cruising at 100 for nought shortly before lunch: by the interval they were reeling again with three men blasted out, including Brian Lara to a throat-ball. So it continued through the year – not least in Antigua where Lara, en route to 400, could not get him away even on an all-time featherbed. By August, Harmison was ranked the world's No. 1. If there was one criticism to be made, it was only one: that he did not follow up his spells of driving the batsman on to the back foot with sufficient yorkers or slower balls.

Following Harmison's example, his close friend Andrew Flintoff joined him as world-class, in both Test and one-day cricket. Until the Third Test in Barbados Flintoff was a defensive bowler: England's brake, the man who bowled back-of-a-length and kept the runs down. After the new bowling coach Troy Cooley had encouraged him to be more than a container, Flintoff roughed up Lara in the Barbados Test and finally took his first five-for. Thereafter, Vaughan had Harmison or Flintoff to attack with serious pace and bounce at one end, while Matthew Hoggard or Ashley Giles kept it tight at the other.

The calendar year also saw Flintoff progress from hitter to batsman. In the last Test of 2003 in Colombo had come the first signs that he might be able to build an innings, and now fulfilment was at hand. Instead of trying too hard to hit the ball, Flintoff just batted in an orthodox fashion and the ball went quite far enough. In eight consecutive Tests, until Port Elizabeth in December, he reached 50. He developed a special affinity with Geraint Jones the moment the new wicket-keeper took over from Chris Read in Antigua. While Flintoff drove straight, Jones hit square to either side (at least until Jones's runs dried up during the home series against West Indies, although his wicket-keeping steadily improved). But every England player seemed to prosper in Flintoff's company: finally fulfilled, he brought to the team's on-field chemistry the vital ingredient of cheerful extroversion which had been missing since Gough's decline.

Thus equipped, England found there was no limit to what they could achieve against a New Zealand side that was well-organised but had no strike bowler, and against a West Indies side that had two young strike bowlers but no organisation. Never before had England won seven Tests in one summer (they only got the chance to do so from 2000), or even six. In South Africa they extended the sequence to their best ever run of eight Test victories in a row, before being held to a draw from Durban.

Vaughan was not alone in finding Test and one-day cricket a slightly easier game for the presence of two world-class players: so did Giles, who now came on with four wickets down or so instead of one or none. Having remodelled his run-up, though not his action, in Asia the previous autumn, he was still not comfortable with his game in the West Indies. But it clicked into place during the Third Test against New Zealand when, from over the wicket, he bowled a ball which pitched on leg stump and hit the top of Chris Cairns's off.

From then on he seemed happy with what he was, basically a left-arm over-the-wicket bowler, although some spectators, or rather television commentators, continued to disagree. When bowling over the wicket, Giles got in so close to the stumps that he forced the right-handers to play, rather than bowling outside leg as he sometimes had under Hussain's captaincy. The proof of the pudding was in his summer haul of 31 Test wickets at 26 each, to go with Harmison's 38 at 25; in Giles dismissing all rivals to his place in England's one-day side; and in the Ball of the Summer, when he lured Lara from his crease at Lord's with a delivery that dipped, beat his drive and turned inside his bat to hit the stumps. Since pitches have been

Not a bad year: Duncan Fletcher allows himself a rare smile. In 2004, he could afford a few more than usual.

Picture by Graham Morris

covered no England spinner has enjoyed a home season anywhere near so successful.

For England to win 11 Tests out of 13, their batsmen still had to make runs, and they did, with ever increasing speed. In the West Indies the three key batsmen were Mark Butcher, Hussain and Graham Thorpe, grinding out heavy-duty contributions at three, four and five. Marcus Trescothick was troubled once the bowling touched 90mph and got under his ribs, so that his relatively poor run overseas (average 32) continued. But he returned to his best back home and had his revenge against West Indies when he made two hundreds in the Edgbaston Test.

During the home summer the runs were shared by all concerned – openers, middle order and those who followed – so that in all eight England batsmen made Test centuries, the injury-plagued Butcher the exception. Hussain retired after reaching his hundred in the opening Test against New Zealand: a moment of tumultuous triumph as he drove successive balls through the covers to bring up his hundred and then complete England's run-chase. The timing was right: he had flogged himself enough in the cause. As captain, Hussain had stopped the losing, just as Allan Border had when Australia's captain. Then Mark Taylor, and now Vaughan, took their teams to the next stage of being winners. Under Vaughan's consensual, self-governing style, the players took turns to give a motivational speech in the on-field huddles.

In the same Test, Andrew Strauss made his debut after a freak accident to Vaughan, who hurt his right knee playing a sweep in the nets; by New Year's Eve, such was his composure, Strauss had scored four hundreds and two 90s in his first nine Tests and was fast becoming England's third world-class player. He was another success for the current selectors' ability to detect class among county players, not just weight of runs, after coming to the attention of coach Duncan Fletcher's all-seeing eye.

Trescothick and Vaughan had made impressive starts to their England careers, but Strauss was a cut above as he made a hundred and 83 run out (largely by Hussain) on his debut. Strauss was helped by starting out on his home ground, and soon after his successful introduction to England's limited-overs side. This fuelled the theory that the one-day side was being expediently used to prepare players for Test cricket, when that role should have been undertaken by an England A side playing A Tests: if only the counties had been prepared to release their players and vote the funding.

Thorpe's key innings were his hundreds in Barbados – probably his best Test innings, although he himself rated more highly his comeback century at The Oval against South Africa after the turmoil of his marital break-up – and his hundred in the run-chase against New Zealand at Trent Bridge. But whenever England needed him, Thorpe was at the height of his nuggety powers, except for his back – and his slip fielding. It was not as fallible as Butcher's, but another welcome contribution came from Strauss when he moved into third slip, beside Flintoff at second and Trescothick at first, who were both as outstandingly consistent as the pace bowling itself.

Just as Strauss took over from Hussain, with Vaughan dropping down from opener to No. 4, so Robert Key took over from Butcher when he underwent a series of minor injuries. Although he scored a brilliant double-century against West Indies at Lord's, Key was not so convincing as Strauss: his hard-handed defensive technique against balls on and outside off stump suggested his future would more probably lie at No. 5 than No. 3. Vaughan himself was more relaxed by the time he reached South Africa, but during the summer was too tense to reproduce his pre-captaincy form. The one-day NatWest Series complicated matters for him as much as the birth of his first child in the middle of the Headingley Test: the more he tried in his one-day batting, the harder he tried to hit the ball and the more he edged to slip. By the West Indies Lord's Test he was nearing crisis point in the media's eyes at least but, after the enormous stand between Strauss and Key, he was able to find his touch slowly. In the second innings Vaughan rattled up a second hundred before his declaration; but he still had only one big game per series, compared to the succession of high scores before he became captain.

The drawback to England's batting was that too few batsmen went on to big, Australian or Indian-sized hundreds: the number of centuries was commendable, the size of them insufficient. In a summer when the Dukes ball would not swing, when pitches started dry and were built to last five days, when the opposing bowlers were either too slow or too young to be truly formidable, the only two batsmen to pass 140 were the two who should have been least expected to do so: Key with his 221 and Flintoff with 167.

Another criticism was that England were too slow out of the blocks. The pattern of the summer's Tests – or at least the three against New Zealand and the Old Trafford Test against West Indies – was that the matches were well-balanced after three days; then Harmison and Giles blew the opposition's second innings away and England knocked off the runs with commendable sang-froid. But England shouldn't have become quite so expert at chasing large fourth-innings totals: New Zealand, and West Indies at Old Trafford, shouldn't have scored quite so many first time round.

So one area for concern was the new-ball attack when England bowled first. Matthew Hoggard did not take a wicket in his opening spells against New Zealand: he was steady but hardly penetrative in taking nought for 109. When the ball swung for him, as in Barbados where he took a hat-trick, or again on the coast in South Africa, Hoggard deserved to open the attack. When it did not, as in England, he did his best work as a container, taking over Flintoff's old role, although not by means of back-of-a-length bounce but by bowling outside off-stump – sometimes to 7–2 fields – and pressurising batsmen into mistakes.

In one-day internationals England's progress was not so pronounced, but the year still ended with the makings of a very good team after the qualification of Kevin Pietersen and his debut in the controversial one-day series in Zimbabwe. They came from behind to draw 2–2 in the West Indies, then failed to qualify for the final of the NatWest Series. A significant factor was losing the toss: on the one occasion they won it they bowled first, and knocked off the runs easily against West Indies at Headingley.

The selectors, however, took time to get the team right. Too much faith was placed in Ian Blackwell, Rikki Clarke and Anthony McGrath, none of whom justified a place with bat or ball, although Clarke might come again. The tour to Zimbabwe allowed England to experiment in the absence of Flintoff, Harmison and Trescothick, and Pietersen in particular impressed with his batting, fielding and competitive attitude. Other features of England's one-day year were Strauss's new role as a No. 4 "finisher" in place of Thorpe; Flintoff's maturity as a batsman which enabled him to make his first one-day international hundreds as a specialist batsman when injury stopped him bowling; Harmison's new role as a wicket-taking new-ball bowler in succession to Gough; and, in Zimbabwe, Geraint Jones's brilliant hitting at No. 7 (after a brief go at No. 3 at home).

The highlights of England's one-day year came in the 2–1 victory over India in the NatWest Challenge, and the victory over Australia in the semi-final of the Champions Trophy at Edgbaston. England had lost 14 consecutive one-dayers to Australia but the newer and younger team, with fewer skeletons in the cupboard, were inspired by Trescothick and Vaughan in their run-chase, which was finished off by Strauss. Victory was achieved with sufficient panache to be added to the grains of hope that England would at long last win back the Ashes.

ENGLAND TEST AVERAGES IN CALENDAR YEAR 2004

BATTING AND FIELDING

	M	I	NO	R	HS	100s	Avge	SR	Ct/St
†G. P. Thorpe	12	20	7	951	119*	4	73.15	48.94	12
I. R. Bell	1	1	0	70	70	0	70.00	53.84	2
R. W. T. Key	4	7	1	378	221	1	63.00	62.79	3
†A. J. Strauss	9	18	2	971	137	4	60.68	50.89	14
A. Flintoff	13	19	2	898	167	2	52.82	66.71	16
N. Hussain	5	9	2	334	103*	1	47.71	40.09	8
†M. E. Trescothick. . . .	13	26	3	1,004	132	4	43.65	54.09	18
M. P. Vaughan	12	22	2	712	140	3	35.60	55.15	9
†M. A. Butcher	9	17	3	498	79	0	35.57	40.19	6
G. O. Jones	10	14	1	458	100	1	35.23	61.72	32/2
A. F. Giles	12	15	2	330	52	0	25.38	55.64	6
M. J. Hoggard	13	14	5	123	38	0	13.66	23.74	5
S. J. Harmison	13	14	5	116	36*	0	12.88	89.23	2
C. M. W. Read	3	3	0	36	20	0	12.00	40.90	6/1
†J. M. Anderson	3	4	2	23	12	0	11.50	36.50	2
†S. P. Jones	8	8	0	76	24	0	9.50	37.62	3
G. J. Batty	1	1	0	8	8	0	8.00	24.24	2
M. J. Saggers	2	2	0	0	0	0	0.00	0.00	0

† *Left-handed batsman.*

BOWLING

	Style	O	M	R	W	BB	5W/i	Avge	SR
S. J. Harmison	RF	526.5	115	1,603	67	7-12	3	23.92	47.17
A. Flintoff	RFM	369.4	78	1,108	43	5-58	1	25.76	51.58
A. F. Giles	SLA	392.5	75	1,140	38	5-57	2	30.00	62.02
M. J. Hoggard	RFM	415.4	93	1,413	47	4-35	0	30.06	53.06
J. M. Anderson	RFM	55.1	8	219	7	4-52	0	31.28	47.28
S. P. Jones	RF	226.1	39	814	23	5-57	1	35.39	59.00
M. J. Saggers	RFM	63	16	185	4	2-80	0	46.25	94.50
G. J. Batty	OB	52	4	185	2	2-185	0	92.50	156.00
M. P. Vaughan	OB	32	3	116	1	1-29	0	116.00	192.00
M. E. Trescothick. . . .	RM	23	3	82	0	–	–	–	–

ENGLAND PLAYERS IN 2004

The following 29 players (compared to 35 in 2003) appeared for England in Tests and one-day internationals in the calendar year 2004, when England played 13 Tests and 21 one-day internationals. All statistics refer to the full year, not the 2004 season.

JAMES ANDERSON   Lancashire

After the rocket-boosted rise in 2003, the return to terra firma in 2004. Anderson's biggest problem was that he was unsure about his place in the hierarchy. In Tests he fell behind Simon Jones and, briefly, Martin Saggers, before returning to favour with four wickets at The Oval. In the one-day game, he lost his place to Alex Wharf, seven years his senior, at the end of the summer. He then returned for the Zimbabwe one-dayers, only to suffer from an attack of the wides. Part of the problem was that Anderson kept being picked for England squads, but not teams, so he played little cricket. The upshot was he never established a rhythm: he conceded four runs an over in Tests, five in one-day internationals, and was cruelly exposed in the New Year during another comeback, this time at Johannesburg. His head seemed all over the place, literally and otherwise. At 22, time was on his side. But work was needed if his rip-roaring start was not to be forgotten.

2004:   3 Tests: 23 runs @ 11.50; 7 wickets at 31.28.
          12 ODI: 13 runs @ 13.00; 13 wickets at 35.61.

GARETH BATTY   Worcestershire

Batty began the year on Ashley Giles's shoulder in the race to be England's No. 1 spinner; by the end he was in his slipstream. He made only four appearances, took just four wickets all year, and ended with his Test and one-day bowling averages in the 60s. His most notable contribution was to bowl the deliveries from which Brian Lara passed 380 and reached 400 at Antigua in April. Batty remained a chipper squad member, but his opportunities were becoming fewer and further between.

2004:   1 Test: 8 runs @ 8.00; 2 wickets at 92.50.
           3 ODI: 1 run @ 1.00; 2 wickets at 49.00.

IAN BELL   Warwickshire

A storming run of form with Warwickshire brought Bell an England cap that was certainly not premature, and he took to international cricket instantly. He made half-centuries on his Test and one-day debuts, and though the latter was a freebie against Zimbabwe, his 70 against West Indies at The Oval was a cool, collected affair. With no obvious technical or temperamental shortcomings, Bell rapidly became the people's favourite among England's young batting pretenders. He surprisingly lost out to Paul Collingwood for the drinks-carrying role in South Africa, but was called up as cover for the injured Mark Butcher. Few doubted that his time would come.

2004:   1 Test: 70 runs @ 70.00.

           4 ODI: 163 runs @ 40.75; 3 wickets @ 3.00.

IAN BLACKWELL   Somerset

One man's renaissance is another man's regression. Blackwell was in the end a casualty of the rebirth of Ashley Giles, and his already tenuous grip on a place in England's one-day future loosened further. He bowled in only one match out of five, and his batting, intermittently lethal at county level, continually self-destructed. The England management appeared to have decided anyway that Blackwell's come-day go-day personal style was out of tune with the times.

2004:   5 ODI: 36 runs @ 9.00; 1 wicket @ 47.00.

MARK BUTCHER   Surrey

The benevolent half-smile that usually crosses Butcher's face was often replaced with a wry, weary one in 2004. Providence tested his easy-going nature to the full: there were freak injuries, poor form, and increasingly harsh media scrutiny. As observers cooed over England's new ruthlessness, there was a whiff of intolerance towards Butcher's languid-looking approach. But actually the year was a grind for Butcher, who was nowhere near his luscious touch of 2003. In the Caribbean in the spring, however, he showed he was more than a flash Harry, battling furiously to make crucial half-centuries in the first two Tests. He never got going against New Zealand, and missed the West Indies return – first with whiplash, then with a muscle pulled lifting a box at home. He had enough credit in the bank to walk back into the team in South Africa. A splendid 79, his smoothest innings of the year, was followed by three low scores. As the year ended and a wrist injury ruled him out of the Cape Town Test – and the rest of the series – Butcher was looking over Robert Key's shoulder rather than his own.

2004:   9 Tests: 498 runs @ 35.57.

RIKKI CLARKE   Surrey

After threatening to break through in 2003, Clarke went backwards in 2004, reaching double-figures in only one of his five one-day innings and never taking more than a single wicket per game. Part of the problem was that no one seemed quite sure about his role. In St Lucia in May, he batted at No. 8 and did not bowl; four days later at Bridgetown, he batted at No. 4 and sent down nine expensive overs. There were also whispers about his attitude, and his last chance came during the triangular NatWest Series. He failed to take it, and returned to the ranks with Surrey.

2004:   6 ODI: 33 runs @ 6.60; 3 wickets @ 43.66.

PAUL COLLINGWOOD   **Durham**

In a year that promised great strides, Collingwood stood still. He played no
Tests and, though he appeared in all 21 of England's one-day internationals,
he made only two fifties. The finisher's position at No. 4 was taken by
Andrew Strauss, and Collingwood's place in the side was starting to come
under threat until he made a splendidly unobtrusive 79 not out against India
at The Oval. He remained an important element of Team England – flexible,
phlegmatic, selfless – and was surprisingly selected ahead of Ian Bell for
the Test tour to South Africa. But he ended the year as he started it: in the
shadows. The future for a specialist substitute fielder with his 29th birthday
approaching did not seem especially enticing.

2004:   21 ODI: 363 runs @ 27.92; 9 wickets at 34.66.

ANDREW FLINTOFF   **Lancashire**

See *The Wisden Forty* (page 117)

ASHLEY GILES   **Warwickshire**

No other England player in 2004 plumbed such depths before touching such
heights. In the early part of the summer, after a bit-part contribution in the
Caribbean, Giles admitted that the stream of criticism from both the media
and spectators had almost persuaded him to quit the game. But a superb
spell on the fourth morning at Trent Bridge against New Zealand, including
a dream delivery to bowl Chris Cairns, and an unbeaten 36 later that day
as England chased down 284, injected new confidence. By the time West
Indies arrived, Giles had become England's banker. He took 18 wickets in
the first two Tests, as he finally reaped the rewards of tinkering with his
run-up and action the previous October in Bangladesh, and three more to
help set up victory in the Third. The competition might not have been fierce,
but Giles finished the summer as arguably the best left-arm spinner in the
world, not to mention a genuine Test No. 8. In South Africa, his batting
reputation grew and – with the wickets unfriendly – his bowling reputation
remained undamaged. References to the King of Spain (the inscription on
his benefit mug at Warwickshire should have read the King of Spin) were
now made with respect rather than ridicule.

See also *Five Cricketers of the Year* (page 58)

2004:   12 Tests: 330 runs @ 25.38; 38 wickets @ 30.00.
            12 ODI: 96 runs @ 24.00; 14 wickets @ 21.92.

DARREN GOUGH   **Essex**

Some felt Gough blustered his way back into England's one-day squad,
having been originally omitted for the Caribbean tour, and that he now
intimidated selectors the way he used to intimidate batsmen. That he now
found much harder. His returns were acceptable, but strip away Zimbabwe
and his average was pushing 40. At times, Gough looked like he was as
well: the mind was as inventive as ever, but the body was less willing and
there was a suspicion that – for the first time – even Gough was losing faith

in his magic powers. There was one champagne moment, however: against India at Lord's, Gough became the first Englishman to take 200 one-day international wickets. It was a nice reward for all those days of brains, bravado and belligerence. But the memories were becoming more distant.

2004: 20 ODI: 45 runs @ 11.25; 25 wickets at 29.24.

STEVE HARMISON   Durham

See *The Wisden Forty* (page 119)
See also *Five Cricketers of the Year* (page 60)

MATTHEW HOGGARD   Yorkshire

The general perception was of a year spent in the shadows of Steve Harmison, but that would be to underestimate Hoggard's wholeheartedly consistent contributions. He failed to take five wickets in an innings in 2004, yet rarely

performed badly, and his pitch-it-up swingers were the ideal foil to Harmison's bang-it-in rib-ticklers. Until he swept all before him with 12 wickets at Johannesburg at the start of 2005, his personal highlight was the middle-order hat-trick at Bridgetown, although a fourth-evening spell against New Zealand at Headingley and intelligent use of the new ball in the first two Tests in South Africa were equally vital. The weary trudge back to his mark

continued to belie a sound work ethic, which was reflected in his improved batting. Having worked his way up to No. 9, he got stuck in against West Indies to score 23 at Old Trafford and 38 at The Oval. It was this ability to make the most of limited resources that made Hoggard the archetypal Duncan Fletcher cricketer.

2004:   13 Tests: 123 runs @ 13.66; 47 wickets @ 30.06.

NASSER HUSSAIN   Essex

Hussain's part in England's stunning summer was small but perfectly formed. Without his farewell century against New Zealand at Lord's back in May, their momentum might never have gathered. True to type, Hussain's final gesture was full of theatre: after running out Andrew Strauss, whose first-innings hundred had persuaded Hussain to retire at the end of the game, he dug deep to produce an innings of grit and class, bringing the house down by moving to three figures with a cover-drive for four, then sealing victory next ball. After 96 Tests, 45 as the captain who put the spunk back into the English game, he would play no more. He moved straight into the commentary box with Sky, where he proved a wholehearted and engaging commentator, then ruffled feathers with the release of his no-holds-barred autobiography, *Playing With Fire*. There were moments during England's tour of the Caribbean earlier in the year when Hussain appeared to be doing precisely that. Faced with the lightning pace of Fidel Edwards and Tino Best, he produced a pair of crucial 58s in the first two Tests, batting for a minute short of ten and a half hours. Another half-century in Lara's Test at Antigua helped shepherd England to safety after they had followed on. The quality was still there. But Hussain's exit, like so much else in his career, was brilliantly judged.

2004:   5 Tests: 334 runs @ 47.71.

GERAINT JONES   Kent

The presence of Jones behind the stumps for most of the year was a sign of the times. Few doubted that Chris Read, the man he replaced for the Antigua Test in April and later usurped in the one-day team as well, was the more dextrous keeper. But Jones was regarded as so much better a batsman that the byes and occasional fumble still left him in credit. His first act as England's wicket-keeper was to observe Brian Lara's unbeaten 400 from close quarters, but from then on he made headlines of his own. He struck an instant rapport in the lower middle order with Andrew Flintoff, and hammered a stirring century in only his third Test, against New Zealand at Headingley. A penchant  for cross-bat shots over the infield briefly persuaded the selectors to try him at No. 3 and as opener in 2005, but it was at No. 7 in both forms of the game that he was at his counter-attacking best. A sprightly 73 at Durban meant he ended the year on a high, but the glovework remained fallible.

2004:   10 Tests: 458 runs @ 35.23; 32 catches, 2 stumpings.
              16 ODI: 264 runs @ 33.00; 25 catches.

SIMON JONES   Glamorgan

Given a second life as an international cricketer following his horrific injury at Brisbane in November 2002, Jones endeavoured to seize every day as if it was his last. Having seen the role of spearhead taken by Steve Harmison, Jones reinvented himself. Where once his USP was raw pace, now it was a hustling, wicket-to-wicket style which, allied to his natural reverse swing with the old ball, made him a real threat even on bland pitches. He played a crucial role in England's victories in Trinidad and Port Elizabeth, and his spell to Brendon McCullum on the fourth morning at Lord's was very special. Injury, and a subsequent lack of rhythm, made for a bleak midsummer, when he lost his place to James Anderson, but he was back in the thick of things in South Africa. The nagging doubt remained, however, as to just how much faith Michael Vaughan had in him.

2004:   8 Tests: 76 runs @ 9.50; 23 wickets at 35.39.
             2 ODI: did not bat; 3 wickets at 25.33.

ROBERT KEY   Kent

The face of the bat angled dangerously, and the cheeks reddened far too easily in the field – but Key's failings could not overrule the impression that here was a cricketer made of the right stuff. He replaced the injured Mark Butcher against West Indies, and his two substantial innings exhibited the hallmarks of Michael Vaughan's reign: the last-chance-saloon 221 at Lord's – the highest Test score by an Englishman for 14 years – was cold-eyed and merciless, and his match-winning 93 not out at Old Trafford oozed sangfroid. Key's Bunterish appearance made him an easy target for ridicule, but his cheery nature made him popular in the dressing-room, and he was fleet of foot against spin and cool of mind against raw pace. Only a wandering mind and an allergy to medium-pace dobbers counted against him.

See also *Five Cricketers of the Year* (page 61)
2004:   4 Tests: 378 runs @ 63.00.
             3 ODI: 43 runs @ 14.33.

JAMES KIRTLEY   Sussex

Having jerked so promisingly into life the previous year, Kirtley's England career threatened to breathe its last in 2004, when the mutterings about his action never quite stopped. He made just one, wicketless one-day appearance, in Georgetown, and his subsequent omission from England's party for the NatWest Series barely registered because of the furore over Chris Read's exclusion. A modest county season completed a forgettable year.

2004:   1 ODI: did not bat; no wicket for 28.

ANTHONY McGRATH   Yorkshire

England's experiment with McGrath as a batting all-rounder appeared to reach its natural conclusion in 2004. He bowled ten economical overs in the NatWest Series game against West Indies at Headingley, but McGrath – like Blackwell, like Clarke, like pretty much anyone in the world – appeared a poor substitute for Andrew Flintoff.

2004:   4 ODI: 23 runs @ 7.66; 2 wickets @ 24.50.

SAJID MAHMOOD   Lancashire

After shining brightly on the England A tour of India in February, the outwardly confident Mahmood was given his one-day debut at the age of just 22 against New Zealand at Bristol. The confidence went, and seven nervous overs in a side that was struggling for form were not the best way to advertise his ability. But with his genuine fast-bowler's physique, his genuine pace and his raw competitiveness, more was expected.

2004:   1 ODI: 1 run @ 1.00; no wicket for 56.

KEVIN PIETERSEN — Nottinghamshire

Few England debuts have been trailed so far in advance since Graeme Hick shuffled uncertainly to the crease to face West Indies in 1991. Pietersen shared Hick's southern African heritage – he qualified because of his English mother and switched because he objected to racial quotas. But he seemed unlikely to suffer Hick's inferiority complex, or his fallibility against the short ball.

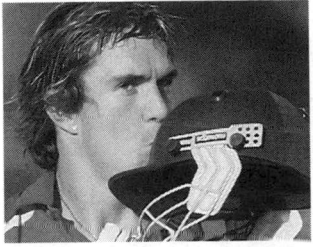

The confidence came through on the tour of Zimbabwe, where only a few hairy singles blighted an unbeaten 27 in his first game, at Harare. In his second, he added 120 for the sixth wicket with Geraint Jones, and he scored 104 in all before being dismissed – a first-ball flick to square leg at Bulawayo that brought a withering stare from his captain. But he hit the ball harder than any England batsman in 2004 bar Flintoff, whose injury worries in South Africa earned Pietersen a call for the one-day series with devastating effect. If he can shed his reputation as a troublemaker at his new county Hampshire, he could be denting boundary boards for years to come.

2004:   4 ODI: 104 runs @ 104.00; no wicket for 22.

MATTHEW PRIOR — Sussex

It was one of the most anonymous England debuts in living memory: the Johannesburg-born Prior, selected for the one-day tour to Zimbabwe when Marcus Trescothick was rested, took his international bow in the deadest of rubbers in Bulawayo. Yet his performance – a promising 35 – made him one of England's nerveless new boys. Having supped at the top table, Prior returned unnoticed to take his seat with the masses. He opened on his debut, and did not keep wicket. But he can, and he might, which may constitute worrying news for both Jones and Read.

2004:   1 ODI: 35 runs @ 35.00.

CHRIS READ — Nottinghamshire

The whispers at the end of 2003 that the England management were not happy with Read's lack of runs became a reality when he was replaced behind the stumps by Geraint Jones for the final Test in the West Indies. Read's glovework remained first-rate and he appeared to have safeguarded his one-day place with some typically feisty innings in the Caribbean, most notably a cathartic 27 in the opening game in Guyana, when he smacked Corey Collymore for three sixes in two overs to steer England to an unlikely win. At county level, he scored runs regularly, but the summer brought further disappointment when Read, to his evident disgust, was dumped from the one-day team too. A long winter as Jones's No. 2 followed.

2004:   3 Tests: 36 runs @ 12.00; 6 catches, 1 stumping.
       5 ODI: 85 runs @ 28.33; 4 catches.

MARTIN SAGGERS Kent

Saggers covered for Simon Jones in two Tests against New Zealand and his short England career ended with a whimper. At Headingley, he curved his first ball back in to bowl Mark Richardson, but his lack of pace made him increasingly easy meat for international-class batsmen.
2004: 2 Tests: 0 runs @ 0.00; 4 wickets at 46.25.

VIKRAM SOLANKI Worcestershire

Solanki's third coming as an England player was blighted by the same blemishes that ended the first two: poor concentration, fallibility outside off stump and a penchant for flattering to deceive. He was brought back after England's humbling midsummer in one-day cricket, as much for his elastic fielding as anything. But, after a promising start against India, he had a poor Champions Trophy. And though he made merry in Zimbabwe, crashing an 89-ball century at Bulawayo, the jury remained out.
2004: 10 ODI: 349 runs @ 34.90.

ANDREW STRAUSS Middlesex

See *The Wisden Forty* (page 127)
See also *Five Cricketers of the Year* (page 63)

GRAHAM THORPE Surrey

See *The Wisden Forty* (page 128)

MARCUS TRESCOTHICK Somerset

See *The Wisden Forty* (page 128)
See also *Five Cricketers of the Year* (page 65)

MICHAEL VAUGHAN Yorkshire

See *The Wisden Forty* (page 129)

ALEX WHARF Glamorgan

England's search for a bowling all-rounder took them to a 29-year-old

journeyman – crucial to Glamorgan's one-day team – who nobody had touted for selection until a few weeks earlier. But Wharf's startling impact – he scalped three of India's biggest guns in his first three overs on debut – suggested Duncan Fletcher had pulled another rabbit from the hat. A levelling-off was inevitable after that; Wharf went wicketless in the Champions Trophy and, despite a flurry of wickets in Zimbabwe, the suspicion that he was merely keeping the seat warm was hard to shake.
2004: 11 ODI: 16 runs @ 8.00; 13 wickets at 25.30.

FEATURES OF 2004

Double-Hundreds (19)

341††‡	C. M. Spearman	Gloucestershire v Middlesex at Gloucester.
303*	N. V. Knight	Warwickshire v Middlesex at Lord's.
301*	J. P. Crawley	Hampshire v Nottinghamshire at Nottingham.
262*	I. R. Bell	Warwickshire v Sussex at Horsham.
262‡	G. A. Hick	Worcestershire v Gloucestershire at Worcester.
262‡	B. J. Hodge	Leicestershire v Durham at Leicester.
250	J. Cox.	Somerset v Nottinghamshire at Nottingham.
244	J. W. M. Dalrymple.	Middlesex v Surrey at The Oval.
243	P. A. Jaques.	Yorkshire v Hampshire at Southampton.
240‡	B. J. Hodge	Leicestershire v Essex at Chelmsford.
237‡	C. M. Spearman	Gloucestershire v Warwickshire at Bristol.
222	W. I. Jefferson	Essex v Hampshire at Southampton.
221‡	B. J. Hodge	Leicestershire v Derbyshire at Oakham School.
221	R. W. T. Key	England v West Indies (First Test) at Lord's.
219	M. J. North	Durham v Glamorgan at Cardiff.
212	J. S. Foster	Essex v Leicestershire at Chelmsford.
204*‡	G. A. Hick	Worcestershire v New Zealanders at Worcester.
201*	M. J. Prior.	Sussex v Loughborough UCCE at Hove.
200	C. J. Adams.	Sussex v Northamptonshire at Hove.

† *County record.*
‡ *Hodge scored three double-hundreds, Hick and Spearman each scored two.*

Hundred on First-Class Debut

104	D. R. Fox	Oxford University v Cambridge University at Oxford.

Three Hundreds in Successive Innings

I. R. Bell (Warwickshire)	112 181 }	v Lancashire at Manchester;
	121	v Kent at Birmingham.
M. J. Clarke (Hampshire)	140 103 }	v Nottinghamshire at Nottingham;
	109	v Glamorgan at Cardiff.
D. J. Hussey (Nottinghamshire)	170	v Hampshire at Nottingham;
	116	v Essex at Southend;
	140	v Leicestershire at Nottingham.
M. R. Ramprakash (Surrey).	130 100* }	v Worcestershire at The Oval;
	134	v Lancashire at Whitgift School.

Hundred in Each Innings of a Match

I. R. Bell	112	181	Warwickshire v Lancashire at Manchester.
M. J. Clarke.	140	103	Hampshire v Nottinghamshire at Nottingham.
B. J. Hodge	105	158	Leicestershire v Glamorgan at Leicester.
B. L. Hutton	100	107	Middlesex v Kent at Southgate.
W. I. Jefferson	167	100*	Essex v Nottinghamshire at Nottingham.
R. W. T. Key	114	117*	Kent v New Zealanders at Canterbury.
M. L. Love	133*	161*	Northamptonshire v Worcestershire at Worcester.
S. D. Peters.	123	117	Worcestershire v Kent at Worcester.
M. R. Ramprakash . .	130	100*	Surrey v Worcestershire at The Oval.
M. E. Trescothick . . .	105	107	England v West Indies (Second Test) at Birmingham.
M. P. Vaughan	103	101*	England v West Indies (First Test) at Lord's.
M. J. Walker	157	100*	Kent v Sussex at Canterbury.

Carrying Bat through Completed Innings

M. T. G. Elliott	77*	Glamorgan (169) v Hampshire at Cardiff.
J. J. B. Lewis	35*	Durham (91) v Derbyshire at Chester-le-Street.
R. R. Montgomerie . .	60*	Sussex (195) v Lancashire at Hove.
M. J. Wood	66*	Yorkshire (160) v Somerset at Scarborough.

Hundred before Lunch

D. S. Lehmann .	15* to 120	Yorkshire v Durham at Chester-le-Street (3rd day).
M. A. Wagh . . .	105	Warwickshire v Cambridge UCCE at Cambridge (1st day).

Hundred with a Runner

S. R. Watson . . 112*   Hampshire v Somerset at Southampton.

Fastest Hundred

R. L. Johnson (101*) . . . 63 balls   Somerset v Durham at Chester-le-Street.

Four Sixes in Successive Balls

M. A. Ealham (139)   (off J. M. Dakin) Nottinghamshire v Leicestershire at Leicester.

First to 1,000 Runs

R. W. T. Key (Kent) on June 2.

Highest Partnerships

First Wicket
265   W. I. Jefferson/A. N. Cook, Essex v Leicestershire at Chelmsford.

Second Wicket
291   A. J. Strauss/R. W. T. Key, England v West Indies (First Test) at Lord's.
255   R. W. T. Key/E. T. Smith, Kent v Middlesex at Canterbury.
254   N. V. Knight/I. R. Bell, Warwickshire v Middlesex at Lord's.

Third Wicket
417   G. A. Hick/B. F. Smith, Worcestershire v Gloucestershire at Worcester.
299   D. J. Bicknell/K. P. Pietersen, Nottinghamshire v Derbyshire at Derby.
283   C. M. Spearman/C. G. Taylor, Gloucestershire v Middlesex at Gloucester.

260 runs were added by M. R. Ramprakash, J. G. E. Benning and A. D. Brown for Surrey's second wicket v Oxford UCCE at Oxford; Ramprakash retired hurt after 169 runs were added.

Fifth Wicket
298   E. C. Joyce/J. W. M. Dalrymple, Middlesex v Surrey at The Oval.
254   I. R. Bell/D. R. Brown, Warwickshire v Lancashire at Manchester.
243   J. N. Batty/A. D. Brown, Surrey v Gloucestershire at The Oval.
236   M. J. Walker/M. A. Carberry, Kent v Worcestershire at Canterbury.

Seventh Wicket
289*†   I. R. Bell/T. Frost, Warwickshire v Sussex at Horsham.
229   M. J. Prior/L. J. Wright, Sussex v Loughborough UCCE at Hove.

Eighth Wicket

198	J. D. Middlebrook/A. R. Adams,	Essex v Leicestershire at Leicester.
163	M. P. Maynard/R. D. B. Croft,	Glamorgan v Essex at Chelmsford.
158	S. R. Watson/S. D. Udal,	Hampshire v Somerset at Southampton.
154	M. A. Hardinges/R. J. Sillence,	Gloucestershire v Warwickshire at Bristol.

Ninth Wicket

157* A. W. Laraman/R. L. Johnson, Somerset v Durham at Chester-le-Street.

Tenth Wicket

120	D. J. Hussey/S. C. G. MacGill,	Nottinghamshire v Durham at Nottingham.
113	S. I. Mahmood/G. Keedy,	Lancashire v Sussex at Manchester.
106	T. J. Murtagh/J. Ormond,	Surrey v Middlesex at The Oval.
105	R. C. Irani/S. A. Brant,	Essex v Nottinghamshire at Southend.
104	M. R. Ramprakash/J. Ormond,	Surrey v Gloucestershire at Bristol.
103	M. A. Sheikh/N. G. E. Walker,	Derbyshire v Somerset at Derby.

† *County record.*

Eight Wickets in an Innings (1)

8-94 L. M. Daggett . . . . Durham UCCE v Durham at Chester-le-Street.

Twelve Wickets in a Match (4)

14-227	G. Keedy.	Lancashire v Gloucestershire at Manchester.
13-140	Mushtaq Ahmed	Sussex v Worcestershire at Hove.
13-158	H. H. Streak	Warwickshire v Northamptonshire at Birmingham.
13-186	Danish Kaneria.	Essex v Yorkshire at Chelmsford.

100 Wickets

No bowler took 100 wickets. The highest aggregate was 84 by Mushtaq Ahmed (Sussex).

Outstanding Innings Analysis

4–1–4–4 I. R. Bell. . . . . Warwickshire v Middlesex at Lord's.

Match Double (100 runs and 10 wickets)

G. R. Breese 35, 68; 5-41, 5-110 Durham v Yorkshire at Scarborough.

Wicket-Keeper's Match Double (100 runs and 10 dismissals)

J. N. Batty 129, 18*; 8 ct, 2 ct Surrey v Kent at The Oval.

Six Wicket-Keeping Dismissals in an Innings

8 ct†	J. N. Batty	Surrey v Kent at The Oval.
4 ct, 2 st . . .	J. N. Batty	Surrey v Lancashire at Manchester.
6 ct.	N. J. O'Brien	Kent v Middlesex at Canterbury.
5 ct, 1 st . . .	R. J. Turner	Somerset v Hampshire at Southampton.

† *County record.*

Nine Wicket-Keeping Dismissals in a Match

7 ct, 4 st . . .	J. N. Batty	Surrey v Lancashire at Manchester.
10 ct.	J. N. Batty	Surrey v Kent at The Oval.
7 ct, 2 st . . .	N. J. O'Brien	Kent v Middlesex at Canterbury.

Six Catches in a Match in the Field

6†   A. N. Cook....   Essex v Durham at Chester-le-Street.

† *Equalled county record.*

No Byes Conceded in Total of 500 or More

S. J. Adshead......   Gloucestershire v Worcestershire (619-6 dec.) at Worcester.
G. L. Brophy......   Northamptonshire v Lancashire (504-9 dec.) at Northampton.
R. D. Jacobs ......   West Indies v England (566-9 dec.) (Second Test) at Birmingham.
L. D. Sutton ......   Derbyshire v Leicestershire (534) at Oakham School.

Highest Innings Totals

708-9 dec.........   Essex v Leicestershire at Chelmsford.
695-9 dec.†......   Gloucestershire v Middlesex at Gloucester.
654-8 dec........   Somerset v Nottinghamshire at Nottingham.
642 ....   Essex v Glamorgan at Chelmsford.
641-4 dec........   Hampshire v Nottinghamshire at Nottingham.
634-9 dec........   Leicestershire v Durham at Leicester.
619-6 dec........   Worcestershire v Gloucestershire at Worcester.
618 ....   Sussex v Kent at Hove.
615 ....   Kent v Lancashire at Tunbridge Wells.
612 ....   Nottinghamshire v Hampshire at Nottingham.
608-7 dec........   Warwickshire v Middlesex at Lord's.
600-6 dec........   Warwickshire v Sussex at Horsham.

† *County record.*

Lowest Innings Totals

88 ....   Derbyshire v West Indians at Derby.
91 ....   Durham v Derbyshire at Chester-le-Street.
93 ....   Durham v Nottinghamshire at Chester-le-Street.
96 ....   Derbyshire v Nottinghamshire at Derby.

Highest Fourth-Innings Totals

453-9† ....   Durham v Somerset at Taunton (set 451).
429-5† ....   Kent v Worcestershire at Canterbury (set 429).
410 ....   Kent v Middlesex at Southgate (set 530).

† *County record.*

Match Aggregate of 1,500 Runs

1,617 for 36   Essex (642 and 165) v Glamorgan (587 and 223-6) at Chelmsford.
1,576 for 35   England (568 and 325-5 dec.) v West Indies (416 and 267) (First Test) at Lord's.
1,548 for 20   Hampshire (641-4 dec. and 295-6 dec.) v Nottinghamshire (612) at Nottingham.
1,532 for 39   Glamorgan (435 and 335) v Essex (437 and 325-9) at Cardiff.
1,522 for 35   Worcestershire (453 and 405-6 dec.) v Kent (420 and 244-9) at Worcester.

Large Margin of Victory

Glamorgan (333 and 468-9 dec.) v Leicestershire (255 and 137) at Cardiff by 409 runs (*County record*).

Most Extras in an Innings

b	l-b	w	n-b	
88	9	16	11	52	Sussex (618) v Kent at Hove.
70	0	11	15	44	Somerset (400-8 dec.) v Durham at Chester-le-Street.
63	5	13	5	40	Worcestershire (401) v Kent at Canterbury.
62	25	21	3	13	England (526) v New Zealand (Second Test) at Leeds.

Career Aggregate Milestones

15,000 runs	C. J. Adams
10,000 runs	D. P. Fulton, D. L. Hemp, B. J. Hodge, M. B. Loye, M. E. Trescothick, C. White.
1,000 wickets.	M. P. Bicknell, Mushtaq Ahmed.
500 wickets	A. J. Bichel, G. Chapple, R. J. Kirtley, M. M. Patel.

WALTER LAWRENCE TROPHY

The Walter Lawrence Trophy for the fastest first-class century in 2004 was won by Richard Johnson of Somerset, who reached 100 in 63 balls against Durham at Chester-le-Street on August 16. His nearest rival was Graham Napier of Essex, who reached his hundred in 78 balls against Nottinghamshire at Nottingham on September 18. Johnson received £5,000 from the trophy's sponsors, Aon, in a ceremony at Lord's celebrating the award's 70th anniversary. Silver medallions were also presented to six previous winners who were in attendance: Tom Graveney (1968), Robin Hobbs (1975), Mike Procter (1979), Roland Butcher (1987), Tom Moody (1990) and Paul Johnson (1993).

FIRST-CLASS AVERAGES, 2004

BATTING AND FIELDING

(Qualification: 8 completed innings)

† *Left-handed batsman.*

		M	I	NO	R	HS	100s	50s	Avge	Ct/St
1	R. W. T. Key (*MCC, Kent & England*)	16	27	3	1,896	221	9	3	79.00	8
2	G. B. Hogg (*Warwicks*)	12	13	3	706	158	1	7	70.60	6
3	D. J. Hussey (*Notts*)	17	23	4	1,315	170	7	2	69.21	24
4	I. R. Bell (*MCC, Warwicks & England*)	18	29	4	1,714	262*	6	7	68.56	12
5	M. R. Ramprakash (*Surrey*)	17	29	5	1,564	161	7	6	65.16	7
6	†S. Chanderpaul (*West Indians*)	6	12	3	583	128*	2	2	64.77	4
7	G. A. Hick (*Worcs*)	17	29	4	1,589	262	4	6	63.56	25
8	B. J. Hodge (*Leics*)	15	25	0	1,548	262	5	4	61.92	6
9	†I. D. Blackwell (*Somerset*)	11	16	2	864	131	2	6	61.71	5
10	D. J. Sales (*Northants*)	16	25	5	1,230	171	1	12	61.50	18
11	A. Flintoff (*England*)	7	11	1	603	167	1	6	60.30	7
12	†U. Afzaal (*Northants*)	16	28	5	1,365	167*	4	7	59.34	9
13	†D. S. Lehmann (*Yorks*)	7	11	1	592	120	1	5	59.20	2
14	†P. A. Jaques (*Yorks*)	11	19	0	1,118	243	3	5	58.84	11
15	†M. H. Richardson (*New Zealanders*)	6	11	1	583	101	1	3	58.30	4
16	R. C. Irani (*Essex*)	10	16	4	695	164	3	2	57.91	1
17	C. M. Spearman (*Glos*)	17	28	2	1,462	341	4	4	56.23	15
18	W. I. Jefferson (*Essex*)	17	29	1	1,555	222	6	5	55.53	15
19	†C. J. L. Rogers (*Derbys*)	6	11	2	498	156	1	3	55.33	6
20	†N. V. Knight (*Warwicks*)	16	30	6	1,324	303*	2	8	55.16	9
21	†M. J. Walker (*Kent*)	17	27	4	1,266	157	4	8	55.04	17
22	†G. P. Thorpe (*Surrey, MCC & England*)	10	17	3	770	114	2	4	55.00	7
23	†M. T. G. Elliott (*Glam*)	15	26	1	1,346	157	4	6	53.84	15
24	†S. P. Fleming (*New Zealanders*)	5	9	0	482	117	1	3	53.55	4
25	O. A. Shah (*Middx*)	17	30	5	1,336	140*	4	9	53.44	19
26	†M. E. Trescothick (*England*)	7	14	2	641	132	3	2	53.41	6
27	J. Cox (*Somerset*)	13	20	1	1,013	250	3	4	53.31	7
28	I. J. L. Trott (*Warwicks*)	17	28	6	1,170	115	1	10	53.18	12
29	A. D. Brown (*Surrey*)	15	24	2	1,155	170	4	6	52.50	15
30	K. P. Pietersen (*MCC & Notts*)	16	21	1	1,044	167	4	4	52.20	19
31	J. P. Crawley (*Hants*)	13	21	3	938	301*	1	5	52.11	4
32	J. S. Foster (*MCC & Essex*)	17	25	5	1,037	212	4	1	51.85	45
33	†C. H. Gayle (*West Indians*)	6	11	0	569	105	1	4	51.72	3
34	Hassan Adnan (*Derbys*)	18	31	4	1,380	140	3	8	51.11	11
35	S. G. Law (*Lancs*)	12	18	1	867	171*	3	1	51.00	17
36	C. M. W. Read (*Notts*)	13	18	2	807	130	2	6	50.43	35/3
37	D. R. Brown (*Warwicks*)	17	23	3	957	162	3	2	50.36	7
38	M. J. Wood (*Somerset*)	11	16	4	604	128*	2	3	50.33	5
39	†A. J. Strauss (*Middx & England*)	8	16	2	704	137	2	4	50.28	11
40	P. D. Bowler (*Somerset*)	16	27	6	1,034	187*	3	3	49.23	11
41	M. B. Loye (*Lancs*)	14	22	3	934	184	2	6	49.15	8
42	E. T. Smith (*Kent*)	18	30	4	1,277	189	4	5	49.11	6
43	J. E. R. Gallian (*Notts*)	17	25	2	1,121	190	3	8	48.73	16
44	M. A. Ealham (*Notts*)	16	20	2	871	139	4	4	48.38	13
45	C. J. Adams (*Sussex*)	16	25	4	1,003	200	4	2	47.76	14
46	B. F. Smith (*Worcs*)	16	25	3	1,036	187	2	7	47.09	17
47	†B. C. Lara (*West Indians*)	5	10	1	420	113*	1	2	46.66	10
48	M. J. Prior (*Sussex*)	18	26	1	1,158	201*	3	6	46.32	25/2
49	R. J. Warren (*Notts*)	13	19	2	784	134	2	6	46.11	4
50	M. P. Vaughan (*England*)	6	10	1	414	103	2	2	46.00	7

		M	I	NO	R	HS	100s	50s	Avge	Ct/St
51	S. C. Joseph (*West Indians*)	4	8	0	367	114	1	2	45.87	2
52	†E. C. Joyce (*Middx*)	14	25	2	1,055	134	2	7	45.86	12
53	A. McGrath (*Yorks*)	9	16	0	728	174	3	1	45.50	6
54	C. G. Taylor (*Glos*)	16	25	1	1,077	177	4	4	44.87	6
55	†D. L. Hemp (*Glam*)	17	29	4	1,120	102*	1	10	44.80	15
56	†S. A. Newman (*Surrey*)	17	30	1	1,277	131	3	9	44.03	11
57	M. J. Powell (*Warwicks & MCC*)	10	17	2	657	134	2	2	43.80	5
58	T. Frost (*Warwicks*)	17	19	6	568	135*	1	2	43.69	47/6
59	†P. N. Weekes (*Middx*)	16	26	3	1,001	118	2	9	43.52	14
60	†D. J. Bicknell (*Notts*)	17	26	1	1,080	175	5	1	43.20	4
61	M. P. Maynard (*Glam*)	15	24	3	906	163	3	4	43.14	14
62	†A. Flower (*MCC & Essex*)	17	29	3	1,121	172	2	6	43.11	18
63	†I. J. Ward (*Sussex*)	16	25	1	1,032	160	4	3	43.00	5
64	C. W. G. Bassano (*Derbys*)	14	22	3	814	123*	2	6	42.84	4
65	†M. A. Carberry (*Kent*)	12	19	4	639	112	2	4	42.60	5
66	J. C. Hildreth (*Somerset*)	13	20	2	760	108	2	5	42.22	12
67	A. J. Bichel (*Worcs*)	14	18	1	717	142	3	2	42.17	3
68	V. S. Solanki (*Worcs*)	13	18	0	757	107	1	6	42.05	10
69	†T. J. Murtagh (*Surrey*)	11	17	8	374	74*	0	4	41.55	8
70	D. P. Fulton (*Kent*)	16	28	1	1,106	122	5	3	40.96	21
71	D. C. Nash (*Middx*)	12	17	4	529	113	1	3	40.69	26/2
72	J. W. M. Dalrymple (*Middx*)	16	25	4	848	244	1	4	40.38	9
73	†B. L. Hutton (*Middx*)	16	29	1	1,129	126	5	3	40.32	23
74	T. H. C. Hancock (*Glos*)	9	13	1	481	77*	0	4	40.08	4
75	†J. J. Sayers (*Oxford UCCE & Yorks*)	8	13	0	518	147	1	4	39.84	1
76	N. Pothas (*Hants*)	16	24	3	834	131*	3	4	39.71	45/5
77	D. D. J. Robinson (*Leics*)	16	28	0	1,087	154	1	9	38.82	18
78	S. C. Moore (*Worcs*)	17	29	3	1,004	146	3	4	38.61	7
79	C. L. Hooper (*Lancs*)	13	21	3	693	115	2	4	38.50	19
80	M. J. Wood (*Yorks*)	16	27	2	955	123	1	7	38.20	24
81	N. J. Astle (*New Zealanders*)	6	10	1	343	93	0	3	38.11	1
82	S. J. Adshead (*Glos*)	15	23	7	609	61	0	4	38.06	39/2
83	†P. J. Franks (*Notts*)	17	22	5	634	57*	0	5	37.29	2
84	M. van Jaarsveld (*Northants*)	7	13	0	484	114	1	1	37.23	7
85	†J. D. Francis (*Somerset*)	10	16	1	554	110	2	3	36.93	6
86	M. A. Wagh (*Warwicks*)	17	30	2	1,033	167	2	5	36.89	16
87	†M. E. K. Hussey (*Glos*)	7	13	1	442	78	0	2	36.83	10
88	M. Burns (*Somerset*)	16	22	2	733	124*	1	4	36.65	17
89	A. P. Grayson (*Essex*)	6	10	0	365	119	1	2	36.50	0
90	†S. G. Koenig (*Middx & MCC*)	18	33	2	1,125	171	2	6	36.29	6
91	D. I. Stevens (*Leics*)	13	22	3	689	105	1	5	36.26	13
92	†A. F. Giles (*Warwicks & England*)	8	10	2	289	70	0	2	36.12	3
93	{ G. O. Jones (*Kent & England*)	11	13	1	433	101	2	1	36.08	34/3
	{ S. J. Rhodes (*Worcs*)	17	21	9	433	59*	0	2	36.08	44/4
95	R. R. Montgomerie (*Sussex*)	18	29	1	1,010	85	0	10	36.07	12
96	M. J. Powell (*Glam*)	16	27	2	900	124	1	7	36.00	14
97	†S. D. Thomas (*Glam*)	14	19	5	499	105*	1	3	35.64	8
98	†W. P. C. Weston (*Glos*)	17	28	1	961	135	2	4	35.59	18
99	M. J. Clarke (*Hants*)	12	20	0	709	140	3	2	35.45	20
100	A. Habib (*Essex*)	14	22	0	776	157	1	5	35.27	3
101	A. G. R. Loudon (*Kent*)	11	17	0	597	92	0	6	35.11	6
102	M. W. Goodwin (*Sussex*)	17	27	2	875	119	3	4	35.00	9
103	C. L. Cairns (*New Zealanders*)	6	10	0	349	82	0	4	34.90	0
104	S. D. Udal (*Hants*)	13	17	3	488	74	0	3	34.85	8
105	A. P. R. Gidman (*MCC & Glos*)	17	25	0	869	91	0	9	34.76	13
106	G. Chapple (*Lancs*)	14	22	1	726	112	2	4	34.57	3
107	J. N. Batty (*Surrey*)	17	29	2	933	145	3	3	34.55	50/6
108	†J. O. Troughton (*Warwicks*)	14	18	1	587	120	1	5	34.52	4
109	I. Dawood (*British Us & Yorks*)	9	14	5	310	75	0	1	34.44	13/2
110	†I. J. Sutcliffe (*Lancs*)	14	24	1	788	104	1	6	34.26	5

		M	I	NO	R	HS	100s	50s	Avge	Ct/St
111	B. B. McCullum (*New Zealanders*)	7	11	1	342	96	0	3	34.20	13/3
112	R. D. B. Croft (*Glam*)	17	25	4	712	138	2	1	33.90	2
113	J. Moss (*Derbys*)	12	20	2	608	147*	1	4	33.77	5
114	G. J. Muchall (*Durham*)	16	30	1	975	142*	1	5	33.62	14
115	G. R. Napier (*MCC & Essex*)	15	23	4	637	106*	1	5	33.52	7
116	J. D. Middlebrook (*Essex*)	16	24	2	723	115	2	3	32.86	4
117	A. J. Hall (*Worcs*)	12	19	2	558	81	0	5	32.82	16
118	†A. N. Cook (*MCC & Essex*)	14	24	2	718	126	1	5	32.63	21
119	M. J. Chilton (*Lancs*)	16	27	2	809	124*	2	2	32.36	9
120	G. L. Brophy (*Northants*)	16	25	2	744	181	1	4	32.34	27/2
121	†M. J. North (*Durham*)	17	31	1	969	219	2	4	32.30	8
122	M. J. Brown (*Hants*)	16	28	2	838	109*	2	6	32.23	12
123	D. L. Maddy (*Leics*)	17	30	2	900	145	1	7	32.14	24
124	G. J. Batty (*Worcs*)	12	18	3	470	133	1	2	31.33	7
125	S. D. Peters (*Worcs*)	17	29	0	907	123	3	3	31.27	13
126	†D. L. Vettori (*New Zealanders*)	6	8	0	250	77	0	2	31.25	1
127	R. Clarke (*Surrey*)	10	17	0	530	112	1	2	31.17	15
128	L. D. Sutton (*Derbys*)	16	27	3	747	131	1	2	31.12	34/3
129	†M. A. Butcher (*Surrey & England*)	7	14	1	403	184	1	1	31.00	3
130	C. D. McMillan (*New Zealanders*)	6	9	1	245	86	0	2	30.62	0
131	Azhar Mahmood (*Surrey*)	12	20	1	577	84	0	4	30.36	8
132	†J. H. K. Adams (*Loughborough UCCE & Hants*)	12	20	3	511	75	0	2	30.05	2
133 {	P. A. Cottey (*Sussex*)	11	17	0	510	185	1	0	30.00	7
	O. D. Gibson (*Leics*)	15	19	3	480	60*	0	4	30.00	5
135	T. B. Huggins (*Northants*)	9	14	2	355	82*	0	2	29.58	3
136	W. K. Hegg (*Lancs*)	12	17	3	412	54	0	1	29.42	23/5
137	†D. S. Smith (*West Indians*)	5	10	0	294	142	1	0	29.40	6
138	P. D. Collingwood (*Durham*)	6	11	0	322	68	0	3	29.27	5
139	†N. J. O'Brien (*Kent*)	14	19	4	439	69	0	3	29.26	33/5
140	G. Welch (*Derbys*)	16	25	4	609	115*	1	1	29.00	12
141	G. R. Breese (*Durham*)	14	25	1	685	165*	1	3	28.54	12
142	†N. J. Edwards (*Somerset*)	10	19	0	537	93	0	2	28.26	11
143	†A. Pratt (*Durham*)	14	25	3	618	68	0	4	28.09	33/2
144	O. A. C. Banks (*West Indians*)	5	10	2	224	47	0	0	28.00	1
145	M. P. Bicknell (*Surrey*)	13	19	3	447	47*	0	0	27.93	4
146	†M. A. Wallace (*Glam*)	17	28	0	776	105	1	3	27.71	41/3
147	T. W. Roberts (*Northants*)	17	29	2	748	89	0	6	27.70	12
148	†S. D. Stubbings (*Derbys*)	16	28	1	743	96	0	6	27.51	8
149	S. K. Warne (*Hants*)	12	16	2	381	57	0	1	27.21	9
150	M. H. W. Papps (*New Zealanders*)	5	9	0	241	126	1	1	26.77	4
151	R. R. Sarwan (*West Indians*)	6	12	0	319	139	1	1	26.58	7
152	J. G. E. Benning (*Surrey*)	6	11	1	265	123	1	0	26.50	1
153	B. J. M. Scott (*Middx*)	7	13	4	236	101*	1	0	26.22	8/3
154	L. R. Prittipaul (*Hants*)	5	9	0	231	49	0	0	25.66	3
155	D. J. J. Bravo (*West Indians*)	7	14	0	358	118	1	2	25.57	4
156	†A. G. Botha (*Derbys*)	11	18	2	405	103	1	1	25.31	5
157	J. J. B. Lewis (*Durham*)	17	31	1	757	127	1	4	25.23	7
158	L. E. Plunkett (*Durham*)	10	16	4	302	54	0	1	25.16	2
159	D. A. Kenway (*Hants*)	14	23	1	552	101	1	1	25.09	9
160	S. B. Styris (*New Zealanders*)	7	12	0	299	108	1	0	24.91	5
161 {	†M. J. Lumb (*Yorks*)	13	23	1	546	83	0	4	24.81	8
	I. J. Harvey (*Yorks*)	7	11	0	273	95	0	1	24.81	4
163	R. L. Johnson (*Somerset*)	15	14	2	297	101*	1	1	24.75	3
164	†J. W. Cook (*Northants*)	6	9	0	222	114	1	1	24.66	4
165	†J. L. Sadler (*Leics*)	14	25	2	566	95	0	3	24.60	7
166	R. K. J. Dawson (*Yorks*)	15	23	0	564	81	0	3	24.52	11
167	A. R. Adams (*Essex*)	7	8	0	196	124	1	0	24.50	4
168	D. G. Cork (*Lancs*)	14	20	2	437	109	1	2	24.27	17
169	A. Dale (*Glam*)	7	13	3	241	44	0	0	24.10	3

		M	I	NO	R	HS	100s	50s	Avge	Ct/St
170	†R. S. Clinton (*Loughborough UCCE & Surrey*)	7	12	1	265	73	0	2	24.09	10
	C. White (*Yorks*)	7	12	1	265	60	0	1	24.09	4
172	J. Hughes (*Glam*)	11	15	0	361	110	1	1	24.06	5
173	I. D. K. Salisbury (*Surrey*)	9	13	1	285	77	0	1	23.75	3
174	P. A. J. DeFreitas (*Leics*)	13	20	3	394	78	0	1	23.17	1
175	N. Peng (*Durham*)	10	18	0	417	88	0	3	23.16	6
176	R. J. Turner (*Somerset*)	16	18	3	346	46	0	0	23.06	61/4
177	A. J. Hollioake (*Surrey*)	11	19	1	412	106	1	2	22.88	6
178	†G. M. Hamilton (*Durham*)	8	15	1	320	58	0	2	22.85	3
179	M. G. N. Windows (*Glos*)	9	13	2	249	58	0	1	22.63	4
180	G. J. Smith (*Notts*)	13	12	3	201	35	0	0	22.33	2
181	Mushtaq Ahmed (*Sussex*)	17	24	5	424	62	0	2	22.31	6
182	†N. M. Carter (*Warwicks*)	14	15	4	245	95	0	1	22.27	3
183	G. P. Swann (*Northants*)	14	22	0	485	54	0	2	22.04	13
184	D. S. Harrison (*Glam*)	17	22	4	395	88	0	1	21.94	8
185	A. G. Wharf (*Glam*)	10	15	1	307	78	0	3	21.92	4
186	A. D. Mascarenhas (*Hants*)	16	24	2	477	104	1	0	21.68	8
187	Kadeer Ali (*Worcs*)	6	10	0	216	66	0	1	21.60	4
188	†M. A. Sheikh (*Derbys*)	13	18	6	259	42	0	0	21.58	1
189	G. D. Bridge (*Durham*)	11	18	3	321	52	0	1	21.40	1
190	A. I. Gait (*Derbys*)	14	25	1	509	81	0	2	21.20	12
191	K. J. Coetzer (*Durham*)	6	10	0	212	67	0	1	21.20	0
192	S. I. Mahmood (*Lancs*)	11	14	3	233	94	0	1	21.18	2
193	†J. K. Maunders (*Leics*)	11	22	0	461	116	1	2	20.95	6
194	A. W. Laraman (*Somerset*)	11	11	2	186	66*	0	1	20.66	5
195	A. R. Caddick (*Somerset*)	14	14	4	204	54	0	1	20.40	5
196	†P. A. Nixon (*Leics*)	12	21	3	361	63*	0	1	20.05	34/6
197	M. J. Powell (*Northants*)	7	12	0	239	49	0	0	19.91	2
198	Mohammad Akram (*Sussex*)	14	18	8	199	35*	0	0	19.90	2
199	C. T. Tremlett (*Hants*)	10	15	4	213	57	0	1	19.36	2
200	R. S. C. Martin-Jenkins (*Sussex*)	16	23	1	424	64*	0	2	19.27	6
201	†G. J. Pratt (*Durham*)	9	17	0	324	71	0	2	19.05	7
202	†I. D. Fisher (*Glos*)	11	17	0	320	45	0	0	18.82	4
203	C. E. W. Silverwood (*Yorks*)	7	10	2	150	37	0	0	18.75	3
204	M. J. Hoggard (*Yorks, MCC & England*)	13	18	5	239	89*	0	1	18.38	4
205	W. S. Kendall (*Hants*)	8	14	1	238	50	0	1	18.30	7
206	B. J. Phillips (*Northants*)	15	21	3	327	90	0	3	18.16	2
207	J. Louw (*Northants*)	16	22	3	342	63	0	1	18.00	8
208	†B. V. Taylor (*Hants*)	11	16	6	177	40	0	0	17.70	3
209	R. A. White (*Northants*)	5	9	0	158	52	0	1	17.55	3
210	J. Lewis (*Glos*)	16	15	4	193	34*	0	0	17.54	1
211	P. S. Jones (*Northants*)	8	9	1	139	37	0	0	17.37	1
212	J. Ormond (*Surrey*)	17	24	5	330	57	0	1	17.36	4
213	T. R. Ambrose (*Sussex*)	10	15	0	257	60	0	2	17.13	21/1
214	Shoaib Malik (*Glos*)	6	9	1	134	63	0	1	16.75	2
215	S. J. Cook (*Middx*)	12	15	0	251	40	0	0	16.73	6
216	C. W. Henderson (*Leics*)	16	21	3	295	63	0	2	16.38	6
217	R. J. Kirtley (*Sussex*)	13	18	5	212	53*	0	1	16.30	3
218	D. Gough (*Essex*)	7	10	1	144	50	0	1	16.00	0
219	†J. D. Lewry (*Sussex*)	11	14	4	159	72	0	1	15.90	2
220	N. Killeen (*Durham*)	13	22	5	269	35*	0	0	15.82	1
221	M. J. G. Davis (*Sussex*)	10	14	3	171	43	0	0	15.54	6
222	M. S. Mason (*Worcs*)	17	20	6	205	63	0	1	14.64	5
223	†C. T. Peploe (*Middx*)	8	12	2	140	28*	0	0	14.00	3
	M. S. Kasprowicz (*Glam*)	7	11	2	126	42	0	0	14.00	2
225	N. D. Doshi (*Surrey*)	9	13	3	134	29*	0	0	13.40	2
226	M. M. Patel (*Kent & MCC*)	13	19	1	238	44	0	0	13.22	1
227	S. C. G. MacGill (*Notts*)	15	12	2	126	28	0	0	12.60	3

		M	I	NO	R	HS	100s	50s	Avge	Ct/St
228	A. M. Davies (*Durham*)	10	17	8	110	29	0	0	12.22	2
229	T. T. Bresnan (*Yorks*)	10	15	3	143	35	0	0	11.91	3
230	Kabir Ali (*Worcs*)	8	9	1	93	31	0	0	11.62	2
231	J. D. C. Bryant (*Derbys*)........	9	16	1	169	30	0	0	11.26	3
232	S. M. Guy (*Yorks*)............	8	12	0	124	26	0	0	10.33	21/2
233	D. D. Masters (*Leics*)	6	9	1	74	31	0	0	9.25	3
234	J. F. Brown (*Northants*)	13	15	6	82	34	0	0	9.11	4
235	†S. A. Selwood (*Derbys*)	4	8	0	68	38	0	0	8.50	1
236	M. J. Saggers (*MCC, Kent & England*)	9	9	0	74	64	0	1	8.22	4
237	†N. A. M. McLean (*Somerset*)	10	11	3	61	22*	0	0	7.62	1
238 {	†G. Keedy (*Lancs*)	16	20	8	90	17	0	0	7.50	7
	C. E. Dagnall (*Leics*)	11	12	2	75	17	0	0	7.50	4
240	†R. J. Sidebottom (*Notts*)	10	10	2	49	15*	0	0	6.12	3
241	M. Hayward (*Middx*)	11	13	5	40	9	0	0	5.00	4
242	S. P. Kirby (*Yorks*)...........	13	16	5	39	14*	0	0	3.54	2

BOWLING

(Qualification: 10 wickets in 10 innings)

		Style	O	M	R	W	BB	5W/i	Avge
1	D. S. Lehmann (*Yorks*)	SLA	105.4	19	261	15	4-35	0	17.40
2	A. D. Mascarenhas (*Hants*).......	RM	404.2	132	1,046	56	6-25	4	18.67
3	A. M. Davies (*Durham*)	RFM	304.2	75	938	50	6-44	4	18.76
4	C. T. Tremlett (*Hants*)	RFM	268.2	56	867	39	4-29	0	22.23
5	S. D. Udal (*Hants*)	OB	247.4	40	869	39	6-79	1	22.28
6	D. Gough (*Essex*)	RFM	226.4	52	672	30	5-57	1	22.40
7	J. M. Anderson (*Lancs & England*) .	RFM	181.1	35	593	26	6-49	1	22.80
8	K. P. Dutch (*Somerset*).	OB	124	21	448	19	5-26	2	23.57
9	O. D. Gibson (*Leics*).	RFM	424.5	97	1,445	60	6-43	5	24.08
10	S. K. Warne (*Hants*)	LBG	411.5	88	1,231	51	6-65	3	24.13
11	A. R. Adams (*Essex*)...........	RFM	157.4	23	561	23	5-93	1	24.39
12	A. Flintoff (*England*)...........	RFM	193.2	41	588	24	3-25	0	24.50
13	J. Lewis (*Glos*).	RFM	472.4	121	1,440	57	7-72	4	25.26
14	S. J. Harmison (*England*)........	RF	301	64	966	38	6-46	1	25.42
15	Danish Kaneria (*Essex*)	LBG	563	123	1,609	63	7-65	4	25.53
16	C. White (*Yorks*).............	RFM	88.2	18	282	11	3-50	0	25.63
17	G. Keedy (*Lancs*)	SLA	645.3	122	1,849	72	7-95	6	25.68
18	C. E. W. Silverwood (*Yorks*)	RFM	174.3	33	570	22	3-18	0	25.90
19	N. A. M. McLean (*Somerset*)	RFM	322.1	62	1,127	43	6-79	3	26.20
20	N. D. Doshi (*Surrey*)	SLA	265.2	45	875	33	7-110	3	26.51
21	J. Louw (*Northants*)	RFM	463.3	89	1,591	60	5-44	3	26.51
22	C. E. Shreck (*Notts*)	RFM	235	51	823	31	6-46	2	26.54
23	J. A. R. Blain (*Yorks*).	RFM	188	26	804	30	4-38	0	26.80
24	A. F. Giles (*Warwicks & England*)..	SLA	362.1	79	939	35	5-57	2	26.82
25	I. R. Bell (*MCC, Warwicks & England*)	RM	149.4	34	438	16	4-4	0	27.37
26	Mushtaq Ahmed (*Sussex*)	LBG	791.2	164	2,318	84	7-73	6	27.59
27	D. S. Harrison (*Glam*)	RFM	480.3	123	1,584	57	5-48	3	27.78
28	N. Tahir (*Warwicks*)..........	RFM	207.4	33	791	28	4-43	0	28.25
29	R. J. Sidebottom (*Notts*)	LFM	258	59	859	30	5-86	1	28.63
30	M. M. Patel (*Kent & MCC*)	SLA	475	91	1,416	49	5-56	2	28.89
31	A. W. Laraman (*Somerset*)	RM	180.3	43	638	22	5-58	1	29.00
32	M. P. Bicknell (*Surrey*)	RFM	387	95	1,266	43	5-128	1	29.44
33	M. Hayward (*Middx*)	RF	289	54	918	31	4-41	0	29.44
34	G. J. Smith (*Notts*)	LFM	336.1	69	1,161	39	5-35	3	29.76
35	K. J. Dean (*Derbys*)	LFM	144	18	597	20	5-86	1	29.85
36	P. J. Franks (*Notts*)	RFM	352	68	1,287	43	7-72	2	29.93
37	Azhar Mahmood (*Surrey*)	RFM	336.3	77	1,138	38	5-54	1	29.94

		Style	O	M	R	W	BB	5W/i	Avge
38	D. G. Cork (*Lancs*)	RFM	332.5	59	1,144	38	7-120	3	30.10
39	D. A. Cosker (*Glam*)	SLA	174.1	42	513	17	3-40	0	30.17
40	M. S. Mason (*Worcs*)	RFM	597.1	181	1,582	52	5-62	1	30.42
41	S. J. Cook (*Middx*)	RFM	371	82	1,072	35	6-89	2	30.62
42	G. J. Batty (*Worcs*)	OB	492.1	129	1,381	45	7-52	2	30.68
43	A. G. R. Loudon (*Kent*)	OB	192.2	32	653	21	6-47	2	31.09
44	L. E. Plunkett (*Durham*)	RFM	247.5	37	964	31	6-74	1	31.09
45	M. J. Saggers (*MCC, Kent & England*)	RFM	259.5	72	717	23	4-43	0	31.17
46	J. D. Lewry (*Sussex*)	LFM	259.2	64	849	27	5-66	1	31.44
47	B. V. Taylor (*Hants*)	RFM	298.1	59	1,039	33	5-73	1	31.48
48	M. J. G. Davis (*Sussex*)	OB	235.3	40	662	21	4-57	0	31.52
49	C. E. Dagnall (*Leics*)	RFM	256.4	46	923	29	4-37	0	31.82
50	P. J. Martin (*Lancs*)	RFM	115.5	34	319	10	4-81	0	31.90
51	Kabir Ali (*Worcs*)	RFM	248	45	899	28	5-60	1	32.10
52	D. R. Brown (*Warwicks*)	RFM	425.4	97	1,293	40	5-53	2	32.32
53	M. J. Hoggard (*Yorks, MCC & England*)	RFM	385.5	80	1,360	42	4-32	0	32.38
54	M. N. Malik (*Worcs*)	RFM	204	35	781	24	5-88	1	32.54
55	T. T. Bresnan (*Yorks*)	RFM	160.3	39	557	17	3-32	0	32.76
56	Shabbir Ahmed (*Glos*)	RFM	169	38	605	18	4-96	0	33.61
57	G. Welch (*Derbys*)	RM	471.5	103	1,525	45	5-57	3	33.88
58	S. P. Jones (*Glam, MCC & England*)	RFM	310.1	53	1,155	34	5-77	2	33.97
59	R. H. Joseph (*Kent*)	RFM	165.2	31	648	19	3-47	0	34.10
60	P. A. J. DeFreitas (*Leics*)	RFM	343.4	81	1,064	31	4-49	0	34.32
61	R. L. Johnson (*Somerset*)	RFM	449.5	104	1,512	44	7-69	2	34.36
62	Mohammad Akram (*Sussex*)	RFM	432.1	76	1,581	46	4-85	0	34.36
63	R. K. J. Dawson (*Yorks*)	OB	379.4	71	1,255	36	5-40	1	34.86
64	M. F. Cleary (*Leics*)	RFM	230	27	946	27	7-80	2	35.03
65	R. D. B. Croft (*Glam*)	OB	674	146	2,006	57	4-52	0	35.19
66	S. C. G. MacGill (*Notts*)	LBG	410	80	1,408	40	7-109	2	35.20
67	C. W. Henderson (*Leics*)	SLA	469	132	1,373	39	7-74	2	35.20
68	G. D. Bridge (*Durham*)	SLA	235	60	680	19	4-64	0	35.78
69	I. D. Blackwell (*Somerset*)	SLA	345.1	85	972	27	7-90	2	36.00
70	A. G. Botha (*Derbys*)	SLA	291	62	938	26	5-55	1	36.07
71	A. R. Caddick (*Somerset*)	RFM	578.5	110	2,026	56	6-80	4	36.17
72	M. A. Sheikh (*Derbys*)	RM	298.3	69	945	26	4-9	0	36.34
73	S. R. G. Francis (*Somerset*)	RFM	295.5	51	1,201	33	5-42	2	36.39
74	B. J. Hodge (*Leics*)	OB	95.5	14	365	10	2-18	0	36.50
75	S. P. Kirby (*Yorks*)	RF	327.1	53	1,132	31	3-64	0	36.51
76	M. A. Ealham (*Notts*)	RM	317	90	952	26	4-43	0	36.61
77	J. Ormond (*Surrey*)	RFM	609.2	143	1,909	52	6-62	1	36.71
78	S. D. Thomas (*Glam*)	RFM	320.3	32	1,252	34	4-47	0	36.82
79	N. G. E. Walker (*Derbys*)	RFM	151.2	17	667	18	5-68	1	37.05
80	R. J. Kirtley (*Sussex*)	RFM	446.5	97	1,381	37	4-32	0	37.32
81	A. G. Wharf (*Glam*)	RFM	249.5	38	1,011	27	5-93	1	37.44
82	A. J. Hall (*Worcs*)	RFM	347	72	1,124	30	3-10	0	37.46
83	A. G. A. M. McCoubrey (*Essex*)	RFM	126.4	22	563	15	4-16	0	37.53
84	A. Khan (*Kent*)	RFM	170.3	24	756	20	4-47	0	37.80
85	B. J. Phillips (*Northants*)	RFM	408.3	107	1,175	31	5-106	1	37.90
86	P. D. Collingwood (*Durham*)	RM	137	37	455	12	3-49	0	37.91
87	G. R. Napier (*MCC & Essex*)	RM	403.3	65	1,595	42	5-56	1	37.97
88	J. W. M. Dalrymple (*Middx*)	OB	306.5	47	1,083	28	4-66	0	38.67
89	P. M. R. Havell (*Derbys*)	RFM	178.1	20	814	21	4-75	0	38.76
90	R. S. C. Martin-Jenkins (*Sussex*)	RFM	388.4	101	1,166	30	5-96	1	38.86
91	G. Chapple (*Lancs*)	RFM	374.4	80	1,128	29	5-136	1	38.89
92	G. P. Swann (*Northants*)	OD	403.2	71	1,168	30	4-94	0	38.93
93	D. Pretorius (*Warwicks*)	RFM	245	43	936	24	4-119	0	39.00
94	J. M. M. Averis (*Glos*)	RFM	285.2	51	1,099	28	6-32	2	39.25
95	A. D. Mullally (*Hants*)	LFM	245.4	69	711	18	6-68	1	39.50

	Style	O	M	R	W	BB	5Wi	Avge
96 C. L. Hooper (*Lancs*)	OB	234	51	595	15	4-56	0	39.66
97 G. R. Breese (*Durham*)	OB	307.4	44	1,163	28	5-41	2	41.53
98 P. C. Rofe (*Northants*)	RFM	167.5	42	505	12	4-109	0	42.08
99 J. F. Brown (*Northants*)	OB	584.3	133	1,523	36	5-113	1	42.30
100 M. S. Kasprowicz (*Glam*)	RFM	272.1	54	893	21	5-54	1	42.52
101 A. Sheriyar (*Kent*)	LFM	199.3	33	772	18	5-94	1	42.88
102 J. D. Middlebrook (*Essex*)	OB	394.3	57	1,459	34	5-26	1	42.91
103 F. H. Edwards (*West Indians*)	RF	139.2	14	610	14	5-22	2	43.57
104 T. J. Murtagh (*Surrey*)	RFM	243.3	50	873	20	5-74	1	43.65
105 C. T. Peploe (*Middx*)	SLA	242.2	59	745	17	4-65	0	43.82
106 S. I. Mahmood (*Lancs*)	RFM	230	26	1,010	23	4-59	0	43.91
107 M. M. Betts (*Middx*)	RFM	147.4	30	577	13	5-89	1	44.38
108 C. S. Martin (*New Zealanders*)	RFM	161.5	34	624	14	4-92	0	44.57
109 N. M. Carter (*Warwicks*)	LFM	367.4	79	1,209	27	4-50	0	44.77
110 P. N. Weekes (*Middx*)	OB	325.3	34	1,166	26	5-76	1	44.84
111 D. L. Maddy (*Leics*)	RM	169.2	24	686	15	2-41	0	45.73
112 J. Moss (*Derbys*)	RM	207.5	39	646	14	3-30	0	46.14
113 I. D. Fisher (*Glos*)	SLA	320.4	61	1,073	23	5-114	1	46.65
114 A. J. Bichel (*Worcs*)	RFM	398.5	75	1,549	33	5-87	2	46.93
115 I. D. K. Salisbury (*Surrey*)	LBG	222.1	39	660	13	3-30	0	50.76
116 M. A. Wagh (*Warwicks*)	OB	306.2	56	1,020	20	3-85	0	51.00
117 A. P. R. Gidman (*MCC & Glos*)	RM	210	39	827	16	2-12	0	51.68
118 G. B. Hogg (*Warwicks*)	SLC	297.2	54	956	18	4-90	0	53.11
119 M. C. J. Ball (*Glos*)	OB	183	25	609	11	3-96	0	55.36
120 S. A. Brant (*Essex*)	LFM	188.2	42	666	12	2-34	0	55.50
121 N. Killeen (*Durham*)	RFM	343.4	83	1,056	19	2-39	0	55.57
122 P. M. Hutchison (*Middx*)	LFM	182.4	28	645	11	3-50	0	58.63
123 P. S. Jones (*Northants*)	RFM	220	33	792	10	3-75	0	79.20

The following bowlers took ten wickets but bowled in fewer than ten innings:

	Style	O	M	R	W	BB	5Wi	Avge
C. H. Gayle (*West Indians*)	OB	66.1	13	189	10	5-34	1	18.90
L. M. Daggett (*Durham UCCE*)	RFM	66.1	5	236	12	8-94	1	19.66
M. W. Alleyne (*Glos*)	RM	66.3	19	227	11	5-71	1	20.63
S. R. Clark (*Middx*)	RFM	89	23	217	10	3-28	0	21.70
H. H. Streak (*Warwicks*)	RFM	159	29	522	24	7-80	2	21.75
J. E. C. Franklin (*New Zealanders & Glos*)	LFM	126.2	33	415	18	7-60	1	23.05
D. J. J. Bravo (*West Indians*)	RFM	146.4	29	486	20	6-55	1	24.30
D. B. Powell (*Derbys*)	RFM	70.3	14	253	10	6-49	1	25.30
Saqlain Mushtaq (*Surrey*)	OB	86.4	9	304	12	4-107	0	25.33
M. K. Munday (*Oxford UCCE*)	LB	60.3	13	257	10	4-36	0	25.70
C. B. Keegan (*Middx*)	RFM	161	29	550	20	5-36	2	27.50
C. L. Cairns (*New Zealanders*)	RFM	143.1	24	516	18	5-79	1	28.66
A. Symonds (*Kent*)	RM/OB	139.3	39	419	14	5-140	1	29.92
D. L. Vettori (*New Zealanders*)	SLA	173.1	22	612	20	5-92	1	30.60
S. M. J. Cusden (*Kent*)	RFM	100.3	17	404	13	4-68	0	31.07
A. B. Agarkar (*Middx*)	RFM	93.3	20	323	10	5-81	1	32.30
K. M. D. N. Kulasekara (*Sri Lanka A*)	RFM	102.1	15	407	12	6-109	1	33.91
C. G. Greenidge (*Northants*)	RFM	83.2	14	346	10	3-71	0	34.60
P. T. Collins (*West Indians*)	LFM	109	9	453	13	4-113	0	34.84
D. H. Wigley (*Loughborough UCCE*)	LFM	93	16	350	10	4-133	0	35.00
R. J. Logan (*Notts*)	RFM	75.1	9	353	10	4-34	0	35.30
A. P. Cowan (*Essex*)	RFM	148	39	463	13	3-44	0	35.61
J. J. C. Lawson (*West Indians*)	RF	105.3	13	471	13	4-94	0	36.23
A. J. Clarke (*Essex*)	RFM	131	25	444	12	3-53	0	37.00
Mohammad Sami (*Kent*)	RF	140	32	526	14	6-99	1	37.57
D. D. Masters (*Leics*)	RFM	149	29	533	14	4-74	0	38.07
I. G. Butler (*Kent*)	RF	101.3	11	446	11	4-114	0	40.54
R. W. Price (*Worcs*)	SLA	169.1	50	420	10	4-83	0	42.00
T. E. Savill (*Cambridge UCCE*)	RFM	96	10	435	10	3-93	0	43.50

	Style	O	M	R	W	BB	5W/i	Avge
M. M. M. Suraj (*Sri Lanka A*)	OB	134.4	21	498	11	5-40	1	45.27
P. J. McMahon (*Oxford UCCE, British Us* *& Notts*)	OB	172	36	551	12	4-68	0	45.91
O. A. C. Banks (*West Indians*)	OB	131	19	527	11	3-50	0	47.90
Mohammad Ali (*Derbys*)	LFM	116.4	18	486	10	4-75	0	48.60
L. Klusener (*Middx*)	RFM	170.3	18	673	13	4-89	0	51.76
Shoaib Malik (*Glos*)	OB	176	30	530	10	3-109	0	53.00
B. J. Trott (*Kent*)	RFM	153	23	538	10	4-109	0	53.80

BOWLING STYLES

LB	Leg-breaks (1)	**RFM**	Right-arm fast medium (82)
LBG	Leg-breaks and googlies (5)	**RM**	Right-arm medium (13)
LFM	Left-arm fast medium (13)	**SLA**	Slow left-arm (14)
OB	Off-breaks (24)	**SLC**	Slow left-arm chinamen (1)
RF	Right-arm fast (7)		

Note: The total comes to 160, because A. Symonds has two styles of bowling.

DATES OF WINNING COUNTY CHAMPIONSHIP

The dates on which the County Championship has been settled since 1979 are as follows:

			Final margin
1979	Essex	August 21	77 pts
1980	Middlesex	September 2	13 pts
1981	Nottinghamshire	September 14	2 pts
1982	Middlesex	September 11	39 pts
1983	Essex	September 13	16 pts
1984	Essex	September 11	14 pts
1985	Middlesex	September 17	18 pts
1986	Essex	September 10	28 pts
1987	Nottinghamshire	September 14	4 pts
1988	Worcestershire	September 16	1 pt
1989	Worcestershire	August 31	6 pts
1990	Middlesex	September 20	31 pts
1991	Essex	September 19	13 pts
1992	Essex	September 3	41 pts
1993	Middlesex	August 30	36 pts
1994	Warwickshire	September 2	42 pts
1995	Warwickshire	September 16	32 pts
1996	Leicestershire	September 21	27 pts
1997	Glamorgan	September 20	4 pts
1998	Leicestershire	September 19	15 pts
1999	Surrey	September 2	56 pts
2000	Surrey	September 13	20 pts
2001	Yorkshire	August 24	16 pts
2002	Surrey	September 7	44.75 pts
2003	Sussex	September 18	34 pts
2004	Warwickshire	September 6	16 pts

Note: The earliest date on which the Championship has been won since it was expanded in 1895 was August 12, 1910, by Kent.

INDIVIDUAL SCORES OF 100 AND OVER

There were **312** three-figure innings in 176 first-class matches in 2004, seven more than in 2003 when 178 first-class matches were played. Of these, 19 were double-hundreds, compared with 29 in 2003. The list includes 260 hundreds hit in the County Championship, compared with 238 in 2003.

R. W. T. Key (9)
118*	Kent v Glos, Bristol
114	
117*⎫	Kent v New Zealanders, Canterbury
173	Kent v Northants, Northampton
199	Kent v Surrey, The Oval
180	Kent v Lancs, Tunbridge Wells
221	England v West Indies, Lord's
131	Kent v Northants, Canterbury
131	Kent v Middx, Canterbury

D. J. Hussey (7)
107*	Notts v Oxford UCCE, Oxford
125	Notts v Yorks, Leeds
166*	Notts v Durham, Nottingham
170	Notts v Hants, Nottingham
116	Notts v Essex, Southend
140	Notts v Leics, Nottingham
124*	Notts v Essex, Nottingham

M. R. Ramprakash (7)
113*	Surrey v Oxford UCCE, Oxford
157	Surrey v Kent, The Oval
145*	Surrey v Warwicks, Guildford
161	Surrey v Northants, Northampton
130	
100*⎫	Surrey v Worcs, The Oval
134	Surrey v Lancs, Whitgift School

I. R. Bell (6)
262*	Warwicks v Sussex, Horsham
129	Warwicks v Middx, Lord's
155	Warwicks v Surrey, Guildford
112	
181 ⎬	Warwicks v Lancs, Manchester
121	Warwicks v Kent, Birmingham

W. I. Jefferson (6)
144	Essex v Cambridge UCCE, Cambridge
128	Essex v Leics, Chelmsford
222	Essex v Hants, Southampton
134	Essex v Durham, Colchester
167	
100*⎫	Essex v Notts, Nottingham

D. J. Bicknell (5)
150	Notts v Somerset, Bath
103	Notts v Hants, Nottingham
175	Notts v Derbys, Derby
142	Notts v Somerset, Nottingham
110	Notts v Essex, Nottingham

D. P. Fulton (5)
107	Kent v Worcs, Canterbury
109	Kent v Northants, Northampton
122	Kent v Sussex, Hove
121	Kent v Middx, Southgate
100	Kent v Warwicks, Birmingham

B. J. Hodge (5)
105	
158 ⎬	Leics v Glam, Leicester
240	Leics v Essex, Chelmsford
221	Leics v Derbys, Oakham School
262	Leics v Durham, Leicester

B. L. Hutton (5)
126	Middx v Warwicks, Lord's
108	Middx v Worcs, Worcester
100	
107 ⎬	Middx v Kent, Southgate
100	Middx v Northants, Northampton

C. J. Adams (4)
101	Sussex v Surrey, The Oval
144	Sussex v Warwicks, Horsham
200	Sussex v Northants, Hove
150*	Sussex v Lancs, Manchester

U. Afzaal (4)
167*	Northants v Sussex, Northampton
133*	Northants v Lancs, Liverpool
111	Northants v Middx, Northampton
100*	Northants v Glos, Northampton

A. D. Brown (4)
170	Surrey v Glos, The Oval
103	Surrey v Warwicks, Guildford
154	Surrey v Lancs, Manchester
123	Surrey v Sussex, Hove

M. T. G. Elliott (4)
114	Glam v Essex, Cardiff
157	Glam v Somerset, Swansea
103	Glam v Somerset, Taunton
125	Glam v Yorks, Leeds

J. S. Foster (4)
110*	MCC v Sussex, Lord's
212	Essex v Leics, Chelmsford
104*	Essex v Somerset, Taunton
188	Essex v Glam, Chelmsford

G. A. Hick (4)
204*   Worcs v New Zealanders, Worcester
262   Worcs v Glos, Worcester
158   Worcs v Warwicks, Birmingham
178   Worcs v Glos, Cheltenham

K. P. Pietersen (4)
167   Notts v Yorks, Leeds
107   Notts v Derbys, Nottingham
167   Notts v Essex, Southend
153   Notts v Derbys, Derby

O. A. Shah (4)
140*   Middx v Worcs, Worcester
103   Middx v Glos, Lord's
100   Middx v Northants, Northampton
108   Middx v Sussex, Hove

E. T. Smith (4)
116   Kent v Lancs, Tunbridge Wells
166   Kent v Sussex, Canterbury
156   Kent v Northants, Canterbury
189   Kent v Middx, Canterbury

C. M. Spearman (4)
139   Glos v Northants, Bristol
341   Glos v Middx, Gloucester
100   Glos v Middx, Lord's
237   Glos v Warwicks, Bristol

C. G. Taylor (4)
100   Glos v Middx, Gloucester
177   Glos v Surrey, The Oval
103   Glos v Worcs, Cheltenham
109   Glos v Lancs, Manchester

M. J. Walker (4)
151*   Kent v Worcs, Canterbury
157
100* }   Kent v Sussex, Canterbury
108   Kent v Middx, Canterbury

I. J. Ward (4)
115   Sussex v Northants, Northampton
160   Sussex v Warwicks, Horsham
107*   Sussex v Northants, Hove
148   Sussex v Middx, Lord's

J. N. Batty (3)
129   Surrey v Kent, The Oval
106   Surrey v Glos, The Oval
145   Surrey v Warwicks, Guildford

A. J. Bichel (3)
108   Worcs v Middx, Worcester
103*   Worcs v Glos, Cheltenham
142   Worcs v Northants, Worcester

P. D. Bowler (3)
127   Somerset v Derbys, Taunton
187*   Somerset v Essex, Chelmsford
138*   Somerset v Essex, Taunton

D. R. Brown (3)
106   Warwicks v Surrey, Guildford
162   Warwicks v Lancs, Manchester
108*   Warwicks v Northants, Northampton

M. J. Clarke (3)
140
103 }   Hants v Notts, Nottingham
109   Hants v Glam, Cardiff

J. Cox (3)
172   Somerset v Loughborough UCCE, Taunton
124   Somerset v Durham, Taunton
250   Somerset v Notts, Nottingham

M. A. Ealham (3)
139   Notts v Leics, Leicester
113*   Notts v Hants, Nottingham
104   Notts v Somerset, Nottingham

J. E. R. Gallian (3)
133   Notts v Yorks, Nottingham
190   Notts v Derbys, Nottingham
120*   Notts v Essex, Southend

M. W. Goodwin (3)
102   Sussex v MCC, Lord's
105   Sussex v Middx, Lord's
119   Sussex v Surrey, Hove

Hassan Adnan (3)
107*   Derbys v Somerset, Taunton
129*   Derbys v Notts, Nottingham
140   Derbys v Notts, Derby

R. C. Irani (3)
107   Essex v Yorks, Chelmsford
122*   Essex v Notts, Southend
164   Essex v Glam, Chelmsford

P. A. Jaques (3)
115   Yorks v Essex, Chelmsford
243   Yorks v Hants, Southampton
173   Yorks v Glam, Leeds

S. G. Law (3)
108   Lancs v Northants, Northampton
171*   Lancs v Sussex, Hove
159   Lancs v Worcs, Worcester

A. McGrath (3)
126   Yorks v Durham, Chester-le-Street
174   Yorks v Derbys, Derby
109   Yorks v Derbys, Leeds

M. P. Maynard (3)
163   Glam v Leics, Leicester
114   Glam v Leics, Cardiff
136   Glam v Essex, Chelmsford

S. C. Moore (3)
108* Worcs v Kent, Canterbury
111   Worcs v Middx, Lord's
146   Worcs v Surrey, Worcester

S. A. Newman (3)
100   Surrey v Oxford UCCE, Oxford
131   Surrey v Northants, The Oval
111   Surrey v Kent, Canterbury

S. D. Peters (3)
123
117 } Worcs v Kent, Worcester
108   Worcs v Surrey, Worcester

N. Pothas (3)
131* Hants v Derbys, Southampton
100   Hants v Yorks, Leeds
107   Hants v Leics, Leicester

M. J. Prior (3)
201* Sussex v Loughborough UCCE, Hove
123   Sussex v Kent, Hove
112   Sussex v Kent, Canterbury

A. Symonds (3)
107   Kent v Northants, Northampton
103   Kent v Worcs, Worcester
156* Kent v Warwicks, Beckenham

M. E. Trescothick (3)
132   England v New Zealand, Leeds
105
107 } England v West Indies, Birmingham

C. W. G. Bassano (2)
100   Derbys v Yorks, Derby
123* Derbys v Notts, Derby

I. D. Blackwell (2)
111   Somerset v Derbys, Derby
131   Somerset v Glam, Swansea

M. J. Brown (2)
102* Hants v Leics, Southampton
109* Hants v Glam, Southampton

M. A. Carberry (2)
104* Kent v Glos, Bristol
112   Kent v Worcs, Canterbury

S. Chanderpaul (2)
104* West Indians v Sri Lanka A, Shenley Park
128* West Indies v England, Lord's

G. Chapple (2)
102   Lancs v Kent, Tunbridge Wells
112   Lancs v Warwicks, Manchester

M. J. Chilton (2)
103   Lancs v Middx, Lord's
124* Lancs v Glos, Cheltenham

R. D. B. Croft (2)
138   Glam v Leics, Cardiff
125   Glam v Essex, Chelmsford

A. Flower (2)
172   Essex v Somerset, Taunton
119   Essex v Glam, Chelmsford

J. D. Francis (2)
109   Somerset v Yorks, Scarborough
110   Somerset v Hants, Taunton

J. C. Hildreth (2)
101   Somerset v Durham, Taunton
108   Somerset v Notts, Nottingham

C. L. Hooper (2)
115   Lancs v Northants, Northampton
100   Lancs v Worcs, Manchester

N. Hussain (2)
102   Essex v Glam, Cardiff
103* England v New Zealand, Lord's

G. O. Jones (2)
101   Kent v New Zealanders, Canterbury
100   England v New Zealand, Leeds

E. C. Joyce (2)
134   Middx v Cambridge UCCE, Cambridge
123   Middx v Surrey, The Oval

N. V. Knight (2)
303* Warwicks v Middx, Lord's
100   Warwicks v Northants, Birmingham

S. G. Koenig (2)
171   Middx v Lancs, Manchester
104* Middx v Worcs, Lord's

M. L. Love (2)
133*
161*} Northants v Worcs, Worcester

M. B. Loye (2)
101   Lancs v Middx, Lord's
184   Lancs v Warwicks, Stratford-on-Avon

J. D. Middlebrook (2)
101* Essex v Cambridge UCCE, Cambridge
115   Essex v Somerset, Taunton

D. Mongia (2)
111   Lancs v Glos, Cheltenham
108* Lancs v Warwicks, Manchester

M. J. North (2)
119   Durham v Derbys, Derby
219   Durham v Glam, Cardiff

R. T. Ponting (2)
112   Somerset v Yorks, Scarborough
117   Somerset v Glam, Taunton

M. J. Powell (2)
134   Warwicks v Kent, Beckenham
110   Warwicks v Surrey, Guildford

C. M. W. Read (2)
108*   Notts v Durham, Nottingham
130   Notts v Derbys, Nottingham

B. F. Smith (2)
187   Worcs v Glos, Worcester
127   Worcs v Kent, Worcester

A. J. Strauss (2)
112   England v New Zealand, Lord's
137   England v West Indies, Lord's

G. P. Thorpe (2)
104*   England v New Zealand, Nottingham
114   England v West Indies, Manchester

M. P. Vaughan (2)
103 }
101*}   England v West Indies, Lord's

M. A. Wagh (2)
105   Warwicks v Cambridge UCCE, Cambridge
167   Warwicks v Lancs, Stratford-on-Avon

R. J. Warren (2)
120   Notts v Durham, Chester-le-Street
134   Notts v Leics, Nottingham

P. N. Weekes (2)
118   Middx v Warwicks, Birmingham
102   Middx v Worcs, Lord's

W. P. C. Weston (2)
122   Glos v Warwicks, Birmingham
135   Glos v Surrey, Bristol

M. J. Wood (2)
128*   Somerset v Sri Lanka A, Taunton
113   Somerset v Notts, Nottingham

The following each played one three-figure innings:

A. R. Adams, 124, Essex v Leics, Leicester; Adnan Akram, 128, Cambridge UCCE v Middx, Cambridge.

G. J. Batty, 133, Worcs v Surrey, The Oval; C. S. Baugh, 150*, West Indians v Derbys, Derby; J. G. E. Benning, 128, Surrey v Oxford UCCE, Oxford; A. G. Botha, 103, Derbys v Durham UCCE, Derby; D. J. J. Bravo, 118, West Indians v Sri Lanka A, Shenley Park; G. R. Breese, 165*, Durham v Somerset, Taunton; G. L. Brophy, 181, Northants v Sussex, Hove; M. Burns, 124*, Somerset v Essex, Chelmsford; M. A. Butcher, 184, Surrey v Warwicks, Birmingham.

R. Clarke, 112, Surrey v Sussex, Hove; A. N. Cook, 126, Essex v Leics, Chelmsford; J. W. Cook, 114, Northants v Kent, Canterbury; D. G. Cork, 109, Lancs v Surrey, Whitgift School; P. A. Cottey, 115, Sussex v Kent, Hove; J. P. Crawley, 301*, Hants v Notts, Nottingham.

J. W. M. Dalrymple, 244, Middx v Surrey, The Oval.

S. P. Fleming, 117, New Zealand v England, Nottingham; A. Flintoff, 167, England v West Indies, Birmingham; D. R. Fox, 104, Oxford Univ v Cambridge Univ, Oxford; T. Frost, 135*, Warwicks v Sussex, Horsham.

C. H. Gayle, 105, West Indies v England, The Oval; A. P. Grayson, 119, Essex v Notts, Southend.

A. Habib, 157, Essex v Glam, Cardiff; D. L. Hemp, 102*, Glam v Derbys, Derby; G. B. Hogg, 158, Warwicks v Surrey, Birmingham; A. J. Hollioake, 106, Surrey v Middx, Lord's; J. Hughes, 110, Glam v Leics, Cardiff.

R. D. Jacobs, 117*, West Indians v Sri Lanka A, Shenley Park; R. L. Johnson, 101*, Somerset v Durham, Chester-le-Street; S. C. Joseph, 114, West Indians v Sri Lanka A, Shenley Park.

D. A. Kenway, 101, Hants v Derbys, Southampton.

B. C. Lara, 113*, West Indies v MCC, Arundel; D. S. Lehmann, 120, Yorks v Durham, Chester-le-Street; J. J. B. Lewis, 127, Durham v Essex, Colchester.

D. L. Maddy, 145, Leics v Glam, Cardiff; A. D. Mascarenhas, 104, Hants v Durham, Chester-le-Street; J. K. Maunders, 116, Leics v Durham, Chester-le-Street; J. Moss, 147*, Derbys v Durham, Chester-le-Street; G. J. Muchall, 142*, Durham v Yorks, Scarborough.

G. R. Napier, 106*, Essex v Notts, Nottingham; D. C. Nash, 113, Middx v Cambridge UCCE, Cambridge.

J. D. P. Oram, 103*, New Zealanders v Worcs, Worcester.

M. H. W. Papps, 126, New Zealanders v Kent, Canterbury; M. J. Powell, 124, Glam v Durham, Chester-le-Street.

M. H. Richardson, 101, New Zealand v England, Lord's; D. D. J. Robinson, 154, Leics v Yorks, Leicester; C. J. L. Rogers, 156, Derbys v Durham, Derby.

D. J. Sales, 171, Northants v Sussex, Hove; R. R. Sarwan, 139, West Indies v England, Birmingham; J. J. Sayers, 147, Oxford Univ v Cambridge Univ, Oxford; B. J. M. Scott, 101*, Middx v Northants, Lord's; A. Singh, 112*, Notts v Glam, Cardiff; D. S. Smith, 142, West Indians v MCC, Arundel; V. S. Solanki, 107, Worcs v Kent, Worcester; D. I. Stevens, 105, Leics v Hants, Leicester; S. B. Styris, 108, New Zealand v England, Nottingham; I. J. Sutcliffe, 104, Lancs v Northants, Northampton; L. D. Sutton, 131, Derbys v Essex, Derby.

S. D. Thomas, 105*, Glam v Hants, Southampton; I. J. L. Trott, 115, Warwicks v Kent, Beckenham; J. O. Troughton, 120, Warwicks v Glos, Bristol.

M. van Jaarsveld, 114, Northants v Kent, Northampton.

M. A. Wallace, 105, Glam v Derbys, Cardiff; S. R. Watson, 112*, Hants v Somerset, Southampton; D. F. Watts, 118*, Scotland v Ireland, Clontarf; G. Welch, 115*, Derbys v Leics, Oakham School; M. J. Wood, 123, Yorks v Derbys, Leeds; L. J. Wright, 100, Sussex v Loughborough UCCE, Hove.

M. H. Yardy, 115, Sussex v Surrey, Hove.

FASTEST HUNDREDS BY BALLS...

Balls	Mins		
63	69	R. L. Johnson	Somerset v Durham, Chester-le-Street
78	99	G. R. Napier	Essex v Notts, Nottingham
79	121	C. H. Gayle	West Indies v England, The Oval
80	109	A. R. Adams	Essex v Leics, Leicester
81	94	D. G. Cork	Lancs v Surrey, Whitgift School
81	112	D. J. Hussey	Notts v Oxford UCCE, Oxford
82	142	G. Chapple	Lancs v Warwicks, Manchester
82	120	M. A. Wagh	Warwicks v Cambridge UCCE, Cambridge
83	105	R. Clarke	Surrey v Sussex, Hove
89	114	B. C. Lara	West Indians v MCC, Arundel
90	116	M. J. Powell	Glam v Durham, Chester-le-Street
93	145	B. J. Hodge	Leics v Durham, Leicester
94	137	D. J. Hussey	Notts v Yorks, Leeds
94	128	M. J. North	Durham v Derbys, Derby
95	128	I. D. Blackwell	Somerset v Derbys, Derby
97	127	M. A. Carberry	Kent v Glos, Bristol
98	115	A. Symonds	Kent v Worcs, Worcester
100	181	G. O. Jones	Kent v New Zealanders, Canterbury

The fastest hundred in terms of minutes not in the above list was by C. G. Taylor (107 minutes, 124 balls) for Glos v Lancs at Manchester.

... AND THE SLOWEST

Balls	Mins		
363	470	J. Cox	Somerset v Notts, Nottingham
296	395	S. C. Moore	Worcs v Middx, Lord's
289	402	M. H. Richardson	New Zealand v England, Lord's
279	350	L. D. Sutton	Derbys v Essex, Derby
271	364	U. Afzaal	Northants v Middx, Northampton

TEN WICKETS IN A MATCH

There were **16** instances of bowlers taking ten or more wickets in first-class cricket in 2004, six fewer than in 2003. The list includes 15 in the County Championship.

N. D. Doshi (2)
11-182, Surrey v Lancs, Manchester; 10-183, Surrey v Sussex, Hove.

O. D. Gibson (2)
11-141, Leics v Notts, Leicester; 10-147, Leics v Essex, Leicester.

Mushtaq Ahmed (2)
10-149, Sussex v Middx, Lord's; 13-140, Sussex v Worcs, Hove.

The following each took ten wickets in a match on one occasion:

J. M. Anderson, 10-81, Lancs v Worcs, Manchester.
G. J. Batty, 10-113, Worcs v Northants, Northampton; G. R. Breese, 10-151, Durham v Yorks, Scarborough.
Danish Kaneria, 13-186, Essex v Yorks, Chelmsford
F. H. Edwards, 10-83, West Indians v Derbys, Derby.
G. Keedy, 14-227, Lancs v Glos, Manchester.
S. C. G. MacGill, 10-233, Notts v Essex, Southend; N. A. M. McLean, 11-124, Somerset v Yorks, Scarborough; Mohammad Sami, 10-138, Kent v Northants, Northampton.
H. H. Streak, 13-158, Warwicks v Northants, Birmingham.

PROFESSIONAL CRICKETERS' ASSOCIATION AWARDS

At the Professional Cricketers' Association annual dinner in September 2004, Andrew Flintoff was named NatWest Player of the Year and won the Reg Hayter Cup for his all-round role in England's magnificent summer. Ian Bell, whose form for Warwickshire led to his Test debut at The Oval, won the John Arlott Cup for the Costcutter PCA Young Player of the Year. Nasser Hussain, who had retired in May, received an ECB Special Merit Award. Paul Collingwood of Durham won the Slazenger Sheer Instinct Award and the Catch of the NatWest Series Award, both for a leaping one-handed catch at backward point to dismiss Ramnaresh Sarwan at Headingley. The PCA "In Safe Hands" Award, sponsored by Brit Insurance, was won by retiring wicket-keepers Jack Russell (Gloucestershire) and Steve Rhodes (Worcestershire). For the fourth year running, Neil Mallender received the Umpire of the Year award and Glamorgan won the MCC Spirit of Cricket Award. The totesport PCA in the Community Award went to former Sussex and Durham wicket-keeper Martin Speight. The PCA named two Dream Teams, sponsored by LBM: Four-day XI – Robert Key (Kent), Craig Spearman (Gloucestershire), Ian Bell (Warwickshire), Mark Ramprakash (Surrey) (*captain*), Usman Afzaal (Northamptonshire), Dougie Brown (Warwickshire), Chris Read (Nottinghamshire), Mushtaq Ahmed (Sussex), Johannes Louw (Northamptonshire), Mark Davies (Durham), Jon Lewis (Gloucestershire). One-day XI – Matthew Elliott (Glamorgan), Vikram Solanki (Worcestershire), Nick Knight (Warwickshire) (*captain*), Matthew Maynard (Glamorgan), Darren Maddy (Leicestershire), Andrew Flintoff (Lancashire), Paul Weekes (Middlesex), Matt Prior (Sussex), Alex Wharf (Glamorgan), Johannes Louw (Northamptonshire), Simon Cook (Middlesex).

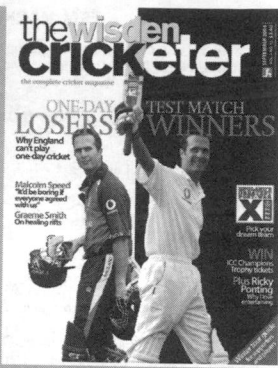

THE NEW ZEALANDERS IN ENGLAND, 2004

Review by Lawrence Booth

Few tours that finish with the captain holding aloft a trophy at Lord's are regarded as a let-down. This one was. New Zealand arrived in England with what looked suspiciously like a swagger after just two defeats in 13 Tests. Six weeks later, they were reeling from a 3–0 drubbing. Victory in the one-day triangular provided a glossy postscript, but it was like finding a penny after losing a fiver and New Zealand returned home feeling distinctly short-changed.

In advance, the Test series had the makings of a mini-classic. England were buzzing with expectation after their historic triumph in the Caribbean. But New Zealand had a point to prove, having long believed their 2–1 win in England in 1999 had never been given the credit it deserved. This time, the squad was older and wiser, Chris Cairns, playing his final Test series before concentrating exclusively on one-day internationals, reckoned it was the best ever to leave New Zealand. And at the helm stood a formidable pair: Stephen Fleming was widely hailed as Test cricket's canniest leader in the post-Steve Waugh era, while the coach, John Bracewell, had helped crown Gloucestershire one-day kings of the county circuit. A perceived wrong was set to be righted.

By the time England had chased down 284 at Trent Bridge to seal their first whitewash in a series of three or more Tests since 1978 – also against New Zealand – indignation had given way to frustration. An injury list of freakish proportions had reduced the bowling attack to a skeleton service, and awkward questions were being asked of the management. The decision to include six non-playing members in an initial party of 20 came under criticism, especially when Daniel Vettori tore a hamstring at Headingley to expose a complete lack of spin back-up. Meanwhile, rumours that Fleming and Bracewell were locked in a power struggle were strong enough to persuade Martin Snedden, the chief executive of New Zealand Cricket, to bring forward a trip to England to investigate for himself. Talk of infighting was played down, and Snedden emerged with a straightforward – but less comfortable – explanation for defeat. England, he ventured with refreshing candour, had simply been the better team. Bracewell's suggestion that the pitches had been prepared to suit the home side's taller, faster bowlers was exposed for what it was: a spurious piece of self-justification.

For Fleming, the result was the most bitter disappointment of his seven-year reign as captain. His only previous whitewash had occurred in 1999-2000 against Australia, who were in the middle of a world-record run of 16 Test wins at the time. This was far worse. For much of the series, he cut a forlorn figure, quietly seething at slip, arms folded, while his bowlers suffered stage fright or injuries or both. If looks could kill, Fleming would have been charged with mass murder.

The biggest blow was the realisation that Shane Bond, the only New Zealander capable of rattling the speedometer more ferociously than England's quicks, would not be fit for any of the Tests after a long lay-off because of a stress fracture of the back. But Bond's absence was merely the tip of an iceberg that would have sunk more buoyant sides than this. A combination of side strains, broken digits and pulled hamstrings meant that at various stages of the tour Jacob Oram, Craig McMillan, Michael Papps, Vettori, Chris Martin and Kyle Mills either were unable to perform to their full potential or missed Tests altogether. During the Second Test, New Zealand used five substitute fielders, but the nadir came in Nottingham, where Martin, who vied with Daryl Tuffey for the title of flop of the series, and the debutant Mills managed less than eight overs between them before breaking down. The situation recalled the Bangalore Test of 1988-89, when TV journalist Ken Nicholson and commentator Jeremy Coney had to be summoned to field after much of the squad was taken ill. "Everyone's a bit pissed off, really," was the succinct summation of opener Mark Richardson.

In the event, England's greater cohesion, firepower and self-belief meant they kept on winning the crucial sessions, and the three Tests followed an eerily similar pattern. Each time, New Zealand built up a position of strength, only to relinquish the advantage on the fourth day. A lack of penetration, stemming in part from an inability to find reverse swing, was one problem. But an inconsistent middle order was just as damaging: between them, New Zealand's third and fourth wickets totalled 117 runs in 12 attempts.

The top order, by contrast, was solidity itself. Richardson cemented his reputation as Test cricket's sticker nonpareil, batting and battling for a total of seven minutes short of 22 hours and scoring 369 runs, more than anyone else on either side. Fleming's productivity improved later in the series, and on average New Zealand lost their second wicket at an imposing 158.

Extended family: England's tight-knit unit of players and back-room staff celebrate a 3–0 clean sweep at a sunlit Trent Bridge.

Faced with potentially huge first-innings totals, England sides of the past might have wilted. But this one possessed Steve Harmison. After taking 23 wickets against West Indies, Harmison continued his rise up the world rankings by claiming a further 21 – nine more than the series' next-best, Cairns. Fleming likened his explosiveness to that of Brett Lee, but his consistency and miserliness – to say nothing of his gangling limbs and towering reach – confirmed what many observers had felt in the Caribbean: here was England's answer to Curtly Ambrose. He was tireless, too, and in three Tests sent down 169.2 overs, a country mile ahead of anyone else. "Harmison is outstanding," said Bracewell. "He has found international length... that middle length where as a batsman you don't know whether to go forward or back."

England's batting moved in one direction only, even if it took a bizarre injury to Michael Vaughan to harness its full potential. Three days before the start of the First Test at Lord's, Vaughan twisted his right knee in the nets. The captaincy passed – not without media misgivings – to Marcus Trescothick, and Vaughan's opening slot to Middlesex captain Andrew Strauss, who proceeded to hit 112 and 83 on a staggeringly assured debut. Nasser Hussain was so impressed that he made his mind up on the Sunday of that Test to retire, then bade farewell in style, with an emotional match-winning century. When he was gone, his old friend Graham Thorpe took over, easing England to victory at Trent Bridge with a masterful hundred, full of nurdles and wisdom. More than that, England discovered their best counter-attacking lower-middle-order partnership since Tony Greig and Alan Knott. At Lord's, Geraint Jones, more at home with the bat than with the gloves, helped Andrew Flintoff add 105 in 19 overs; at Headingley they put on 118 in 29. With Ashley Giles chipping in to make 81 unbeaten runs in the Third Test, England's batting order finally had some backbone.

Picture by Patrick Eagar

Leaving at the top: Nasser Hussain *(left)* ended his international career in glory at Lord's. At Trent Bridge, Chris Cairns bowed out of Test cricket with a lion-hearted nine for 187.

Pictures by Patrick Eagar

The new-found resilience meant that the memories of 1999 and 2001-02, when New Zealand twice fought back from 1–0 deficits, evaporated in the Nottingham sunshine. England had won six Tests out of seven and had been bowled out twice in only one of their last 13, at Colombo. Once he had recovered from injury, Vaughan's leadership – unruffled, sympathetic, authoritative – went from strength to strength.

While England celebrated their rebirth as a Test nation and excitedly, not to say inevitably, began the countdown to the 2005 Ashes, New Zealand embarked on the one-day leg of their tour. Things got worse before they got better. Defeat by lowly Derbyshire in a warm-up match provoked a heartfelt team meeting in which Gilbert Enoka, a sports psychologist who had worked extensively with the All Blacks, forced the players to undergo an uneasy bout of self-examination. That seemed to do the trick. They did not lose another game, a run which culminated in a crushing win over West Indies in what was, surprisingly, New Zealand's first one-day international at Lord's.

But behind the smiles lay a profound feeling of regret, and the words of Fleming after the chance of a Test series win had disappeared at Headingley best summed up the tour. "The penetration we had with the ball was pretty nil," he said through gritted teeth. Ultimately, it was a tour of missed opportunities.

NEW ZEALAND TOURING PARTY

S. P. Fleming (*captain*), N. J. Astle, S. E. Bond, C. L. Cairns, B. B. McCullum, C. D. McMillan, C. S. Martin, K. D. Mills, J. D. P. Oram, M. H. W. Papps, M. H. Richardson, S. B. Styris, D. R. Tuffey, D. L. Vettori.

M. S. Sinclair was called up as cover for McMillan before the Second Test. J. E. C. Franklin replaced the injured Bond before the Third Test. G. J. Hopkins also joined the first-class squad as cover for McCullum, who was due to leave during the following one-day series to be with his pregnant wife. I. G. Butler, C. Z. Harris and H. J. H. Marshall arrived for the one-day series, when Martin and Richardson went home. A. R. Adams joined the one-day party as cover.

Coach: J. G. Bracewell. *Manager:* L. M. Crocker. *Assistant coach:* V. F. Johnson. *Physiotherapist:* D. F. Shackel. *Medical co-ordinator:* W. Frost. *Video analyst:* Z. Hitchcock.

NEW ZEALAND TOUR RESULTS

Test matches – Played 3: Lost 3.
First-class matches – Played 7: Won 1, Lost 4, Drawn 2.
One-day internationals – Played 6: Won 4, No result 2. *Wins* – England (2), West Indies (2). *No result* – West Indies (2). *Abandoned* – England.
Other non-first-class matches – Played 3: Won 2, Lost 1.

TEST MATCH AVERAGES

ENGLAND – BATTING AND FIELDING

	T	I	NO	R	HS	100s	50s	Avge	Ct
†G. P. Thorpe	3	5	2	237	104*	1	1	79.00	3
†M. E. Trescothick	3	6	1	322	132	1	2	64.40	1
A. F. Giles	3	4	2	113	45*	0	0	56.50	0
A. Flintoff	3	4	0	216	94	0	3	54.00	2
G. O. Jones	3	4	0	195	100	1	0	48.75	14
†A. J. Strauss	3	6	0	273	112	1	2	45.50	4
M. P. Vaughan	2	3	0	84	61	0	1	28.00	4
†M. A. Butcher	3	6	1	105	59	0	1	21.00	2
M. J. Hoggard	3	3	0	24	15	0	0	8.00	1
S. J. Harmison	3	3	2	0	0*	0	0	0.00	2

Played in two Tests: M. J. Saggers 0, 0. Played in one Test: N. Hussain 34, 103* (3 ct); †S. P. Jones 4.

† *Left-handed batsman.*

BOWLING

	Style	O	M	R	W	BB	5W/i	Avge
S. J. Harmison	RF	169.2	44	464	21	4-74	0	22.09
A. Flintoff	RFM	104.5	24	291	10	3-60	0	29.10
A. F. Giles	SLA	114	21	302	9	4-46	0	33.55
S. P. Jones	RF	46	13	146	4	3-82	0	36.50
M. J. Hoggard	RFM	109	28	385	9	4-75	0	42.77
M. J. Saggers	RFM	63	16	185	4	2-80	0	46.25

Also bowled: M. E. Trescothick (RM) 2–0–3–0; M. P. Vaughan (OB) 3–0–8–0.

NEW ZEALAND – BATTING AND FIELDING

	T	I	NO	R	HS	100s	50s	Avge	Ct
†M. H. Richardson	3	6	0	369	101	1	2	61.50	2
†S. P. Fleming	3	6	0	308	117	1	1	51.33	4
B. B. McCullum	3	6	0	200	96	0	2	33.33	6
†J. D. P. Oram	3	6	1	160	67	0	1	32.00	3
S. B. Styris	3	6	0	191	108	1	0	31.83	3
C. L. Cairns	3	6	0	160	82	0	1	26.66	0
N. J. Astle.	3	6	0	138	64	0	1	23.00	1
†D. L. Vettori.	2	3	0	42	35	0	0	14.00	0
D. R. Tuffey.	2	4	1	29	14*	0	0	9.66	2
C. D. McMillan	2	4	0	36	30	0	0	9.00	0
C. S. Martin	3	6	3	10	7	0	0	3.33	1

Played in one Test: †J. E. C. Franklin 4*, 17 (1 ct); K. D. Mills 0, 8; M. H. W. Papps 86, 0.

† *Left-handed batsman.*

BOWLING

	Style	O	M	R	W	BB	5W/i	Avge
J. E. C. Franklin.	LFM	43.1	6	163	6	4-104	0	27.16
C. L. Cairns	RFM	97.3	15	379	12	5-79	1	31.58
S. B. Styris	RM	69.3	12	224	6	3-88	0	37.33
D. L. Vettori	SLA	69	8	205	4	2-69	0	51.25
C. S. Martin	RFM	80.5	18	314	6	3-94	0	52.33
D. R. Tuffey	RFM	66.1	14	246	3	1-28	0	82.00

Also bowled: C. D. McMillan (RM) 2–1–5–0; K. D. Mills (RM) 6–2–31–0; J. D. P. Oram (RM) 74.3–13–212–2; M. H. Richardson (SLA) 1–0–4–0.

NEW ZEALAND TOUR AVERAGES – FIRST-CLASS MATCHES

BATTING AND FIELDING

	M	I	NO	R	HS	100s	50s	Avge	Ct/St
†M. H. Richardson	6	11	1	583	101	1	3	58.30	4
†S. P. Fleming	5	9	0	482	117	1	3	53.55	6
†J. D. P. Oram	5	7	2	263	103*	1	1	52.60	3
N. J. Astle	6	10	1	343	93	0	3	38.11	1
C. L. Cairns	6	10	0	349	82	0	4	34.90	0
B. B. McCullum	7	11	0	342	96	0	3	34.20	13/3
†D. L. Vettori.	6	8	0	250	77	0	2	31.25	1
C. D. McMillan	6	9	1	245	86	0	2	30.62	0
K. D. Mills	2	4	2	57	42*	0	0	28.50	0
M. H. W. Papps	5	9	0	241	126	1	1	26.77	4
S. B. Styris	7	12	1	299	108	1	0	24.91	5
D. R. Tuffey	5	7	2	57	14*	0	0	11.40	5
C. S. Martin	6	9	5	13	7	0	0	3.25	2

Played in three matches: S. E. Bond 0, 7 (4 ct). Played in one match: †J. E. C. Franklin 4*, 17 (1 ct); G. J. Hopkins 71 (2 ct).

† *Left-handed batsman.*

BOWLING

	Style	O	M	R	W	BB	5W/i	Avge
J. E. C. Franklin.	LFM	43.1	6	163	6	4-104	0	27.16
C. L. Cairns	RFM	143.1	24	516	18	5-79	1	28.66
D. L. Vettori	SLA	173.1	22	612	20	5-92	1	30.60
C. S. Martin	RFM	161.5	34	624	14	4-92	0	44.57
S. B. Styris	RM	96.3	18	325	7	3-88	0	46.42
D. R. Tuffey	RFM	133.1	31	444	8	4-57	0	55.50

Also bowled: S. E. Bond (RF) 44–7–200–4; C. D. McMillan (RM) 9–3–30–0; K. D. Mills (RM) 31–6–117–3; J. D. P. Oram (RM) 95.4–19–319–3; M. H. Richardson (SLA) 6–0–28–1.

Note: Matches in this section which were not first-class are signified by a dagger.

†At Shenley Park, May 2. **New Zealanders won by 28 runs.** Toss: New Zealanders. **New Zealanders 275-5** (50 overs) (M. H. W. Papps 98, S. P. Fleming 75, N. J. Astle 47, S. B. Styris 34*; P. A. de Silva 3-35); **PCA Masters XI 247-6** (50 overs) (V. J. Wells 32, J. C. Adams 113*). *This match, against a Professional Cricketers' Association team mostly composed of retired players, was not part of the official tour programme.*

BRITISH UNIVERSITIES v NEW ZEALANDERS

At Cambridge, May 3, 4, 5. Drawn. Toss: British Universities. First-class debut: D. C. Shirazi.

Barely 35 overs' play was possible in the official opening match of the New Zealand tour. Rain wiped out the first two days entirely, but both teams forfeited an innings on the final morning to make a game of it. Wigley dismissed Papps first ball, and there was time for Astle, who had not played first-class cricket since October because of a knee injury, to unfurl 11 fours. Styris also struck out briefly, but he was caught behind off the first ball after lunch, and then the rain set in again.

Close of play: First day, No play; Second day, No play.

New Zealanders

New Zealanders forfeited their first innings.

M. H. Richardson lbw b Linley	. . . . . .	39
M. H. W. Papps lbw b Wigley	. . . .	0
N. J. Astle not out	. . . .	64
S. B. Styris c Dawood b Daggett	. . . . . .	22
L-b 2, w 1	. . . .	3

1/1 (2) 2/91 (1) 3/128 (4)   (3 wkts) 128

C. D. McMillan, *C. L. Cairns, †B. B. McCullum, J. D. P. Oram, D. L. Vettori, D. R. Tuffey and S. E. Bond did not bat.

Bowling: Wigley 12–2–40–1; Daggett 8.1–1–27–1; Linley 10–2–33–1; Marshall 3–1–20–0; McMahon 2–0–6–0.

British Universities

British Universities forfeited their first innings.

J. H. K. Adams (*Loughborough*), D. C. Shirazi (*Southampton Institute*), O. S. Anwar (*Oxford Brookes*), W. R. Smith (*Durham*), S J. Marshall (*Cambridge*), C. D. Nash (*Loughborough*), †I. Dawood (*Leeds Metropolitan*), P. J. McMahon (*Oxford*), *D. H. Wigley (*Loughborough*), L. M. Daggett (*Durham*) and T. E. Linley (*Oxford Brookes*).

Umpires: B. Dudleston and P. Willey.

WORCESTERSHIRE v NEW ZEALANDERS

At Worcester, May 7, 8, 9, 10. Drawn. Toss: Worcestershire.

Hick provided the highlight of a rain-hit match: on the final day, his 123rd first-class hundred moved him level with Denis Compton, and thus joint 11th in the list of century-makers. He finished with 204 – his 15th double, in 286 minutes – at a run a ball, his fifties taking 71, 54, 39 and 34 balls as he moved up through the gears, with 27 fours and eight sixes. Bond made a gentle return after his back injury, and Worcestershire captain Smith held the batting together on the opening day before the rain that had bedevilled the New Road spring (and had forced a switch to a used pitch for this game) returned at lunch on the second day. New Zealand finally got some batting practice on the third, when Oram rescued them from 168 for five and took them to a lead of 109. Hick overcame that in style, enabling Smith, who had spent two winters under Oram's captaincy at Central Districts, to declare again.

Close of play: First day, Worcestershire 163-3 (Smith 72, Kadeer Ali 26); Second day, Worcestershire 270-9 dec.; Third day, Worcestershire 0-1 (Moore 0, Hick 0).

Worcestershire

S. D. Peters c Richardson b Tuffey	9	– c McCullum b Bond	0
S. C. Moore c McCullum b Tuffey	18	– c McCullum b Styris	29
G. A. Hick c Bond b Vettori	36	– not out	204
*B. F. Smith c Fleming b Tuffey	92	– c Tuffey b Vettori	14
Kadeer Ali c Papps b Bond	27	– st McCullum b Vettori	8
A. J. Hall b Bond	7	– c Richardson b Oram	32
†D. J. Pipe c Bond b Tuffey	0	– c and b Vettori	8
S. J. Rhodes c Papps b Martin	14	– not out	7
M. S. Mason lbw b Vettori	12		
M. N. Malik not out	39		
M. A. Harrity not out	3		
B 4, l-b 1, w 6, n-b 2	13	B 5, l-b 3, n-b 8	16

1/28 (2) 2/29 (1) 3/98 (3)   (9 wkts dec.) 270   1/0 (1) 2/87 (2)   (6 wkts dec.) 318
4/176 (5) 5/188 (6) 6/192 (4)   3/132 (4) 4/197 (5)
7/193 (7) 8/224 (8) 9/226 (9)   5/261 (6) 6/277 (7)

Bowling: *First Innings*—Tuffey 21–8–57–4; Bond 15–4–46–2; Martin 14–3–41–1; Oram 11.1–3–56–0; Vettori 16–0–65–2. *Second Innings*—Bond 13–3–77–1; Martin 12–3–77–0; Tuffey 13–3–41–0; Oram 10–3–51–1; Styris 5–1–17–1; Vettori 14.4–3–47–3.

New Zealanders

M. H. Richardson lbw b Harrity	48	– not out	20
M. H. W. Papps c Hall b Mason	1	– lbw b Harrity	6
*S. P. Fleming c Rhodes b Harrity	23		
S. B. Styris c Rhodes b Moore	27		
C. D. McMillan c Mason b Hall	86		
†B. B. McCullum lbw b Harrity	4	– (3) not out	44
J. D. P. Oram not out	103		
D. L. Vettori c and b Malik	51		
D. R. Tuffey not out	14		
L-b 6, w 8, n-b 8	22	W 6, n-b 1	7

1/11 (2) 2/46 (3) 3/99 (4)   (7 wkts dec.) 379   1/12 (2)   (1 wkt) 77
4/156 (1) 5/168 (6)
6/251 (5) 7/350 (8)

S. E. Bond and C. S. Martin did not bat.

Bowling: *First Innings*—Mason 17–5–46–1; Harrity 22–3–111–3; Malik 19–3–57–1; Hall 12.3–2–52–1; Moore 4–0–28–1; Kadeer Ali 7–0–55–0; Hick 4–0–24–0. *Second Innings*—Mason 6–2–19–0; Harrity 7–1–31–1; Malik 6–1–10–0; Hall 4–0–17–0.

Umpires: R. J. Bailey and J. H. Hampshire.

KENT v NEW ZEALANDERS

At Canterbury, May 13, 14, 15, 16. Kent won by nine wickets. Toss: New Zealanders.

The New Zealanders had never beaten Kent in nine visits since 1927, but they had drawn the last six. The second sequence was emphatically halted 25 minutes after lunch on the final day, when Key became the third Kent batsman, after Colin Cowdrey and Peter Richardson, to score twin hundreds against a touring side. The upbeat ending rewarded spectators who had endured a dismal start of unashamed batting practice: Papps and Richardson, who batted for five mind-numbing hours, put on 244, a New Zealand first-wicket record against any county, before Stiff, a winter recruit from Yorkshire, removed both. Next day, in his first game since spinal surgery 14 months earlier, Patel claimed five wickets as the last eight fell for 79. Kent gained a narrow lead thanks to Key's enterprising strokeplay, which brought him 20 fours, while Jones warmed up for his home Test debut with five sixes and a run-a-ball century. New Zealand's top four then capitulated to Khan, and Kent had more than a day to score 189. Key and the patient Fulton almost got them unparted.

Close of play: First day, New Zealanders 297-2 (Astle 32, Styris 14); Second day, Kent 296-4 (Carberry 72, Jones 43); Third day, Kent 24-0 (Fulton 14, Key 10).

New Zealanders

M. H. Richardson b Stiff	92	– c Carberry b Khan	15
M. H. W. Papps lbw b Stiff	126	– lbw b Khan	2
N. J. Astle c Fulton b Patel	48	– b Khan	0
S. B. Styris c Walker b Khan	32	– lbw b Khan	12
C. D. McMillan c Jones b Khan	0	– lbw b Ferley	12
†B. B. McCullum lbw b Patel	4	– b Stiff	25
*C. L. Cairns c Smith b Patel	54	– st Jones b Ferley	73
D. L. Vettori c Jones b Patel	9	– b Patel	40
D. R. Tuffey b Patel	5	– c Jones b Sheryiar	9
S. E. Bond c Jones b Stiff	0	– c Carberry b Sheriyar	7
C. S. Martin not out	1	– not out	0
B 8, l-b 9, w 1, n-b 20	38	B 2, l-b 4, w 4, n-b 6	16
	409		**211**

1/244 (2) 2/253 (1) 3/330 (4) 4/334 (5)   409   1/8 (2) 2/8 (3) 3/24 (4) 4/41 (1)   211
5/339 (6) 6/342 (3) 7/386 (8)   5/41 (6) 6/81 (6) 7/130 (8)
8/405 (7) 9/405 (10) 10/409 (9)   8/158 (9) 9/178 (10) 10/211 (7)

Bowling: First Innings—Sheriyar 28–8–94–0; Khan 28–7–106–2; Stiff 20–2–88–3; Ferley 16–3–48–0; Patel 22.3–3–56–5. *Second Innings*—Sheriyar 15–2–45–2; Khan 11–2–50–4; Ferley 7.4–1–23–2; Stiff 6–1–32–1; Patel 13–1–55–1.

Kent

*D. P. Fulton c Tuffey b Martin	9	– st McCullum b Richardson	67
R. W. T. Key c McCullum b Vettori	114	– not out	117
E. T. Smith c Tuffey b Cairns	7	– not out	1
M. J. Walker c McCullum b Tuffey	32		
M. A. Carberry c McCullum b Martin	75		
†G. O. Jones c Bond b Martin	101		
M. M. Patel st McCullum b Vettori	44		
R. S. Ferley lbw b Bond	1		
A. Khan c Bond b Martin	16		
D. A. Stiff not out	3		
A. Sheryiar not out	4		
L-b 12, w 1, n-b 13	26	L-b 4	4

1/21 (1) 2/58 (3) 3/148 (4)   (9 wkts dec.) 432   1/174 (1)   (1 wkt) 189
4/185 (2) 5/307 (5) 6/365 (7)
7/387 (8) 8/412 (9) 9/427 (6)

Bowling: First Innings—Tuffey 23–2–76–1; Martin 21–3–92–4; Bond 16–0–77–1; Cairns 11–2–44–1; Vettori 15–1–100–2; Styris 4–0 26–0; McMillan 1–0–5–0. *Second Innings*—Tuffey 10–4–24–0; Martin 10–1–28–0; Cairns 5–1–11–0; Styris 7–0–35–0; Vettori 8–0–43 0; McMillan 6–2–20–0; Richardson 5–0–24–1.

Umpires: R. T. Robinson and G. Sharp.

ENGLAND v NEW ZEALAND

First npower Test

Mike Walters

At Lord's, May 20, 21, 22, 23, 24. England won by seven wickets. Toss: New Zealand.
Test debut: A. J. Strauss.

Rarely has Lord's witnessed a surge of affection for one of English cricket's grandees
to match the final flourish of Nasser Hussain's career, which concluded an extraordinary
sequence of events. The theory that a butterfly flapping its wings in Casablanca can
lead to a hurricane in Cuba found powerful supporting evidence in this compelling
match. It was a wonderful setting for anyone's farewell.

The first twist of a spellbinding plot came three days before a ball had been bowled
in anger. Vaughan, the England captain, attempted an innocuous sweep at a 19-year-
old net bowler, left-arm spinner Zac Taylor, collapsed in a heap and was carted from
the Nursery practice ground with a twisted right knee. The repercussions were
momentous: Trescothick stood in as captain for the first time in Tests and the Middlesex
captain Andrew Strauss, not named in the original 13-man squad, became only the
fourth player – after Australian Harry Graham (in 1893), England's John Hampshire
(1969) and India's Sourav Ganguly (1996) – to launch his Test career with a century
at Headquarters.

TOGETHER IN THE MIDDLE

England's most productive partnerships, opening pairs excluded

	T	I	Unbr.	Runs	Highest	100 stands	Avge
M. A. Butcher and N. Hussain	45	52	1	2,610	189	9	51.17
G. A. Gooch and D. I. Gower	39	45	0	2,271	351	8	50.46
K. F. Barrington and E. R. Dexter	29	36	2	2,265	246	6	66.61
N. Hussain and G. P. Thorpe	28	55	5	2,258	288	8	45.16
K. F. Barrington and M. C. Cowdrey . .	45	38	4	2,203	193	8	64.79
N. Hussain and A. J. Stewart	41	48	0	1,774	156	4	36.95
M. A. Atherton and A. J. Stewart	34	39	2	1,757	226	3	47.48
M. C. Cowdrey and P. B. H. May	26	32	1	1,687	411	6	54.41
D. C. S. Compton and L. Hutton	26	29	3	1,605	248	6	61.73
M. A. Butcher and M. E. Trescothick .	25	32	2	1,599	202	5	53.30

Updated to include England's series in South Africa, 2004-05.

But Strauss was not the only adhesive left-handed opener to make an impact. For
more than six hours on a stodgy first day, New Zealand's Richardson was a model of
obduracy. Prompted by fears of a terrorist attack, Lord's stewards had been ordered to
seal hampers and cool boxes left by spectators in the Coronation Garden for their
picnic lunches, but for 266 balls of torpor it was Richardson who might have been
removed from the premises as a suspect package. With delightful self-deprecation, he
described his 93 as "dour, pokey and proddy", but it was undeniably valuable. He was
robbed of a century by a poor lbw decision which disregarded an inside edge.

But that helped the innings perk up. There was Astle, with 11 fours in a 77-ball 64,
and Oram, with a similarly breezy 67 from 82 balls, and finally there was a performance
of awesome power and violence from Cairns. Four times in the space of ten deliveries,
Simon Jones, Harmison and Flintoff (twice) disappeared into the back of beyond. In

Running into trouble: Andrew Strauss (*far right*) heads for disaster after Nasser Hussain calls for a rash single to Chris Cairns at point.

Picture by Patrick Eagar

the process, Cairns surpassed Sir Vivian Richards's record of 84 sixes in Tests, and England's relief was palpable when he was last out, trying to hit Flintoff for a third straight six. He had ransacked 82 from 47 balls.

Without their fastest bowler, Bond, New Zealand's attack could hardly raise a gallop, and it was England's openers who made all the running with a fluent stand of 190 in 54 overs. Trescothick, punching 13 fours with the assurance of an immigration officer stamping passports, was finally beaten down the slope by Oram, 14 short of becoming only the third man to score a hundred in his first Test as England captain, after Archie MacLaren (1897-98) and Allan Lamb (1989-90). But Strauss, batting on his home ground and serenaded by the crowd warbling the "Blue Danube" in his honour, was not to be denied.

On 91, he enjoyed a miraculous slither of good fortune when his inside edge off Martin brushed off stump firmly enough to make the timber wobble but somehow failed to dislodge the bails. Another trail of scorched earth through the covers soon confirmed England's first centurion on debut since Graham Thorpe in 1993, and their superiority. But the applause was accompanied by a sense of wonder: Vaughan would have to come back, and Strauss could hardly be dropped. So who would make way? No one was considering the implications more clearly than a 36-year-old ex-captain already known to be close to retirement. Afterwards, the initiative slipped during a passage of hesitant batting and tighter bowling on the third morning, but Flintoff and Geraint Jones reclaimed it by hitting three sixes and 11 fours in a sparkling seventh-wicket stand of 105 in 19 overs, which led to a useful 55-run advantage.

With Richardson, a man whose batting fills the bars, in occupation again, the pendulum swung back towards New Zealand on the fourth morning. They clawed their way to a 125-run lead with nine wickets in hand. McCullum, promoted to No. 3 because Astle had flu, responded with 14 fours and was within a heartbeat of a maiden Test hundred when he was becalmed and then broken by Simon Jones's reverse swing. After his near miss in the first innings, Richardson was rewarded with a century second

NASSER HUSSAIN'S CAREER RECORD

Test career 1989-90–2004

	T	I	NO	R	HS	100s	Avge
(Won 35, Lost 33, Drew 28)	96	171	16	5,764	207	14	37.18
v Australia	23	45	4	1,581	207	2	38.56
v South Africa	14	26	3	1,010	146*	3	43.91
v West Indies	17	30	4	653	106	1	25.11
v New Zealand	10	17	2	698	106	2	46.53
v India	10	16	1	824	155	4	54.93
v Pakistan	6	10	2	267	64	0	33.37
v Sri Lanka	8	14	0	345	109	1	24.64
v Zimbabwe	6	9	0	198	113	1	22.00
v Bangladesh	2	4	0	188	95	0	47.00
As captain (W 17, L 15, D 13)	45	77	8	2,487	155	5	36.04
Not as captain (W 18, L 18, D 15)	51	94	8	3,277	207	9	38.10

Hussain bowled in one Test innings (5–0–15–0), at Durban in 1999-2000. He took 67 catches.

One-day internationals

	M	I	NO	R	HS	100s	Avge
1989-90–2002-03	88	87	10	2,332	115	1	30.28
(Won 37, Lost 49, Tied 1, NR 1)							
As captain (W 28, L 27, NR 1)	56	55	4	1,598	115	1	31.33
Not as captain (W 9, L 22, T 1)	32	32	6	734	93	0	28.23

Hussain never bowled in a one-day international. He took 40 catches.

First-class cricket 1987-2004

	M	I	NO	R	HS	100s	Avge
	334	545	53	20,698	207	52	42.06
Batting for Essex	189	298	26	11,982	206	31	44.05

	O	M	R	W	BB	Avge	Ct
First-class – bowling and fielding	52	3	323	2	1-38	161.50	350

One-day cricket 1987-2004

	M	I	NO	R	HS	100s	Avge
	364	339	47	10,732	161*	10	36.75

Hussain never bowled in one-day cricket. He took 161 catches.

---

time around; it occupied 309 balls and brought his time at the crease to more than 13 and a half hours.

Inexplicably, Trescothick ignored the second new ball and settled for the attrition of Giles, dutifully bowling over the wicket for 35 overs unchanged in a spell of three for 64, to suppress the scoring-rate. He could argue that negativity served its purpose, but it took three wickets in 19 balls from Harmison to end the charade. England eventually needed 282 from 95 overs to win – 64 more than they had ever managed in the fourth innings to win in 105 previous Lord's Tests.

At 35 for two, the chase began to look forlorn until Hussain – who had already decided, unknown to his team-mates, that this would be his final Test innings – marched out to join Strauss for his last hurrah. Strauss was the dominant partner in a 108-run stand and was on course for a century in each innings, a feat achieved on debut only by West Indian Lawrence Rowe and Pakistan's Yasir Hameed. Then he sacrificed himself in a Keystone Kops mix-up with Hussain. While the crestfallen Strauss would soon be mollified by the match award, Hussain was distraught after "doing a Boycott on the local lad" – a reference to Geoff Boycott running out Derek Randall against Australia at Trent Bridge 27 years earlier.

Only leading England to victory from the wreckage of Strauss's heartbreak would atone for Hussain's part in the catastrophe, and they were still 139 away. But few men are blessed with such willpower. Fortified by a succinct pep-talk from fellow warhorse

Thorpe – "Stop whinging and get on with it" – Hussain scrambled to his fifty in 158 deliveries before he was carried to glorious redemption, and the final curtain, on one last rush of adrenalin. His next fifty took only 45 balls; he reached his 14th Test hundred with a lofted on-drive and signature extra-cover drive off successive deliveries to level the scores, and the ovation had not subsided before he collared Martin through the covers again and swayed triumphantly into the sunset. Forgiveness rained down and, less than three days later, he confirmed what everybody had suspected from his nostalgic body language: after 96 Tests spanning 14 years, he was giving up the game in a blaze of glory.

Man of the Match: A. J. Strauss. *Attendance:* 125,890; *receipts* £2,086,368.

Close of play: First day, New Zealand 284-5 (Oram 64, Tuffey 2); Second day, England 246-2 (Butcher 22, Hoggard 0); Third day, New Zealand 134-1 (Richardson 46, McCullum 72); Fourth day, England 8-0 (Trescothick 1, Strauss 6).

New Zealand

M. H. Richardson lbw b Harmison	93	– c G. O. Jones b Harmison	101
*S. P. Fleming c Strauss b S. P. Jones	34	– c Hussain b Harmison	4
N. J. Astle c G. O. Jones b Flintoff	64	– (7) c G. O. Jones b Harmison	49
S. B. Styris c G. O. Jones b S. P. Jones	0	– c Hussain b Giles	4
C. D. McMillan lbw b Hoggard	6	– c Hussain b Giles	0
J. D. P. Oram c G. O. Jones b Harmison	67	– run out	4
D. R. Tuffey b Harmison	8	– (10) not out	14
C. L. Cairns c Harmison b Flintoff	82	– c Butcher b Giles	14
†B. B. McCullum b S. P. Jones	5	– (3) c G. O. Jones b S. P. Jones	96
D. L. Vettori b Harmison	2	– (9) c G. O. Jones b Harmison	5
C. S. Martin not out	1	– b Flintoff	7
B 9, l-b 6, w 2, n-b 7	24	B 14, l-b 16, n-b 8	38
	386		**336**

1/58 (2) 2/161 (3) 3/162 (4) 4/174 (5)   386
5/280 (1) 6/287 (6) 7/324 (7)
8/329 (9) 9/338 (10) 10/386 (8)

1/7 (2) 2/180 (3) 3/187 (4)   336
4/187 (5) 5/203 (6) 6/287 (1)
7/290 (7) 8/304 (9)
9/310 (8) 10/336 (11)

Bowling: *First Innings*—Hoggard 22–7–68–1; Harmison 31–7–126–4; Flintoff 21.4–7–63–2; S. P. Jones 23–8–82–3; Giles 5–0–32–0. *Second Innings*—Harmison 29–8–76–4; Flintoff 16.1–5–40–1; Hoggard 14–3–39–0; S. P. Jones 23–5–64–1; Giles 39–8–87–3.

England

*M. E. Trescothick c McCullum b Oram	86	– c and b Tuffey	2
A. J. Strauss c Richardson b Vettori	112	– run out	83
M. A. Butcher c McCullum b Vettori	26	– c Fleming b Martin	6
M. J. Hoggard c McCullum b Oram	15		
N. Hussain b Martin	34	– (4) not out	103
G. P. Thorpe b Cairns	3	– (5) not out	51
A. Flintoff c Richardson b Martin	63		
†G. O. Jones c Oram b Styris	46		
A. F. Giles c Oram b Styris	11		
S. P. Jones b Martin	4		
S. J. Harmison not out	0		
B 4, l-b 18, n-b 19	41	B 7, l-b 12, w 5, n-b 13	37
	441		**(3 wkts) 282**

1/190 (1) 2/239 (2) 3/254 (3) 4/288 (4)   441
5/297 (6) 6/311 (5) 7/416 (8)
8/428 (7) 9/441 (10) 10/441 (9)

1/18 (1) 2/35 (3)   (3 wkts) 282
3/143 (2)

Bowling: *First Innings*—Tuffey 26–4–98–0; Martin 27–6–94–3; Oram 30–8–76–2; Cairns 16–2–71–1; Vettori 21–1–69–2; Styris 4.3–0–11–2. *Second Innings*—Oram 15–4–39–0; Tuffey 10–3–32–1; Vettori 25–5–53–0; Martin 18–2–75–1; Styris 13–5–37–0; Cairns 6–0–27–0.

Umpires: D. B. Hair (Australia) and R. E. Koertzen (South Africa).
Third umpire: M. R. Benson. Referee: C. H. Lloyd (West Indies).

LEICESTERSHIRE v NEW ZEALANDERS

At Leicester, May 28, 29, 30, 31. New Zealanders won by 328 runs. Toss: New Zealanders. First-class debut: T. J. New.

The New Zealanders arrived still desperate for batting practice. They left with their first victory of the tour, but a batsman short; a blow to McMillan's hand, from Maddy, was to rule him out at Headingley. Leicestershire rested six regulars and gave a debut to England Under-19 wicket-keeper Tom New, while New Zealand also introduced a new keeper, Hopkins, who was to deputise for McCullum in the one-day series but batted with him here – both made fifties to follow up Astle's 93. For Leicestershire, only Maunders passed 23, but Fleming waived the follow-on. Batting again, he just missed a century, while Cairns hit five sixes, one of which struck a small boy on the ear, before Fleming declared 560 ahead on the third evening. Maunders made a second fifty, while Maddy, the acting-captain, resisted for more than four hours in a determined 87. But they could find little answer to Vettori's left-arm spin, which brought him his first five-wicket return in two and a half years.

Close of play: First day, New Zealanders 326-7 (Hopkins 40, Vettori 21); Second day, New Zealanders 13-0 (Papps 12, Fleming 1); Third day, Leicestershire 68-2 (Maunders 31, Maddy 14).

New Zealanders

M. H. W. Papps c Robinson b Dakin	0	– c Maddy b Dagnall 20
*S. P. Fleming c Robinson b Dagnall	56	– b Maddy 95
N. J. Astle lbw b Masters	93	
S. B. Styris c New b Brignull	2	– (3) lbw b Dagnall 13
C. D. McMillan c and b Masters	43	– (4) retired hurt 68
B. B. McCullum lbw b Dagnall	65	
C. L. Cairns c New b Masters	0	– (5) c Masters b Stevens 62
†G. J. Hopkins c Robinson b Brignull	71	
D. L. Vettori c New b Dagnall	31	– (6) c Maunders b Sadler 77
K. D. Mills not out	42	– (7) not out 7
C. S. Martin b Maddy	2	
B 1, l-b 5, w 2	8	B 6, l-b 4, w 3, n-b 2 15

1/0 (1) 2/95 (3) 3/104 (4) 4/198 (3)   413   1/38 (1) 2/64 (3)   (5 wkts dec.) 357
5/207 (5) 6/207 (7) 7/291 (6)   3/193 (2) 4/296 (5)
8/344 (9) 9/392 (8) 10/413 (11)   5/357 (6)

In the second innings McMillan retired hurt at 225.

Bowling: *First Innings*—Dakin 23–5–61–1; Masters 23–4–92–3; Dagnall 26–4–92–3; Brignull 19–0–78–2; Snape 6–1–23–0; Maddy 14–1–61–1. *Second Innings*—Dakin 12–1–57–0; Dagnall 21–0–90–2; Masters 12–2–43–0; Brignull 10–3–43–0; Maddy 6–1–36–1; Robinson 3–0–26–0; Stevens 4–0–30–1; Sadler 1.4–0–22–1.

Leicestershire

D. D. J. Robinson lbw b Martin	13	– c Hopkins b Martin 2
J. K. Maunders b Cairns	85	– c Hopkins b Mills 54
D. I. Stevens lbw b Cairns	14	– lbw b Mills 9
*D. L. Maddy lbw b Vettori	23	– c Fleming b Vettori 87
J. L. Sadler lbw b Vettori	15	– b Cairns 18
J. N. Snape lbw b Martin	0	– (7) c McCullum b Mills 5
†T. J. New b Vettori	18	– (6) c Papps b Vettori 2
J. M. Dakin b Cairns	10	– c Papps b Vettori 0
D. D. Masters c Styris b Cairns	3	– c Styris b Vettori 9
C. E. Dagnall c sub (D. R. Tuffey) b Vettori	2	– c Martin b Vettori 17
D. S. Brignull not out	0	– not out 0
L-b 10, n-b 11	21	B 12, l-b 5, w 2, n-b 10 . . 29

1/39 (1) 2/61 (3) 3/106 (4) 4/146 (5)   210   1/11 (1) 2/38 (3) 3/124 (2)   232
5/151 (6) 6/188 (2) 7/198 (7)   4/165 (5) 5/173 (6) 6/186 (7)
8/198 (8) 9/201 (10) 10/210 (9)   7/187 (8) 8/208 (9)
                                                            9/229 (4) 10/232 (10)

Bowling: *First Innings*—Martin 13–2–46–2; Mills 9–2–35–0; Styris 5–3–11–0; Cairns 13.4–4–48–4; Vettori 20–4–60–4. *Second Innings*—Martin 11–4–26–1; Mills 16–2–51–3; Cairns 16–2–34–1; Vettori 30.3–6–92–5; Styris 6–2–12–0.

Umpires: J. W. Holder and R. A. Kettleborough.

ENGLAND v NEW ZEALAND

Second npower Test

MIKE DICKSON

At Leeds, June 3, 4, 5, 6, 7. England won by nine wickets. Toss: England.

At a time when cricket's fight for wider public attention had rarely been more intense, there was no shortage of national debate surrounding this Test. It must be said, however, that the lines to radio phone-ins were not abuzz about an enthralling series, or the rise of Harmison to the world's elite, but more personal matters. Michael Vaughan's wife Nichola was due to give birth to their first child over the weekend of the match, and he announced that he would leave the field if necessary to be present.

And so was born a discussion that transcended mere sport: whether it was right for an England cricket captain to abandon his post to support his wife. It went on for two days until Vaughan ran off the field at 6.20 p.m. during Friday's elongated final session to drive to Sheffield, where Nichola had been admitted to hospital. A daughter, Tallulah Grace, arrived later in the evening, Vaughan was back on Saturday morning, and by Monday lunchtime he was also celebrating another series win to follow the Caribbean triumph.

> England's fast bowlers were, literally, dangerous

By then, the debate had switched from the baby's arrival to excited talk about England finally moulding a Test team ready to scale the peak of the world game. Progress, Vaughan acknowledged, was being made more swiftly than was thought possible the previous summer.

England made two changes. Vaughan himself returned from injury, a straight swap for the newly retired Hussain at No. 4, leaving Strauss in place as Trescothick's opening partner; and Kent's reliable swinger Martin Saggers replaced Simon Jones, who was ordered to rest his foot to prevent a stress fracture recurring (James Anderson, the next bowler in line, had a bruised heel). New Zealand brought in Papps for McMillan, who had a broken finger. Papps himself soon had a broken knuckle courtesy of Flintoff. On a wicket whose bounce was wholly unpredictable by the end, England's fast bowlers were, literally, dangerous.

Rain allowed only 19 overs' play on Thursday, when Vaughan, unsure how the pitch would turn out, put New Zealand in under overcast skies. Saggers dismissed Richardson, so immovable at Lord's, with his first delivery. Resuming on Friday, however, in more pleasant weather, Papps proved to be Richardson's successor in a line of obdurate New Zealand openers to frustrate England, broken knuckle or not. With Fleming, who reached his 41st Test fifty and for the 35th time failed to convert it to a hundred, he put together a hard-working 169-run partnership, helped by poor catching.

There was a generally lacklustre feel to England in the field. One theory was that they were distracted by the childbirth debate, another that they missed Hussain's abrasive presence. And it was a long day – too long, according to Butcher. To make up time,

The readiness is all: Marcus Trescothick gets into position to sweep Daniel Vettori during his first-innings hundred.

Picture by Patrick Eagar

15 overs were added to each day's allotment; on Friday and Sunday, this took seven and a half hours. Still, once Papps was removed England, especially Harmison and Flintoff, showed their pleasing new tendency to rein in opposition when they threatened to run away, and a priceless ability to extract maximum bounce from the conditions.

McCullum's rearguard fifty raised New Zealand to 409, but England trumped them. Trescothick, written off as just a one-day player by Shane Warne the previous week, responded with a magnificently aggressive 132 and shared another three-figure opening stand with Strauss, who again looked amazingly assured for a novice. On Sunday morning, when the ball was doing plenty, Thorpe and Flintoff built on this foundation in a partnership of understated importance. It was arguably Flintoff's most mature England innings to date, albeit against an underpowered attack who failed to exploit the conditions.

The most eye-catching contribution, however, came from Jones, who helped Flintoff add 118 for the sixth wicket. He had struggled with his glovework, but here he showed why he had been controversially promoted over Nottinghamshire's Chris Read, a superior wicket-keeper. Ruthlessly cutting and pulling for 15 fours and a six, he hit a maiden Test hundred in only his second full first-class season – and was out next over.

Meanwhile, New Zealand's injury list mounted. Papps could not field, Vettori went off after pulling a hamstring and Oram could not bowl because of a side strain. They were forced to call on Kyle Mills, Mathew Sinclair, unfit pace bowler Shane Bond, who was about to be sent home, the injured McMillan, and Rob Nicol, an Auckland batsman who happened to be in the crowd, as substitutes.

Having expected a first-innings lead, they conceded a deficit of 117 on a wicket getting steadily worse. Their morale was sinking while England's nose for a kill grew more refined. At the close of the fourth day, New Zealand were 15 behind with five

---

ENGLAND WICKET-KEEPERS WITH TEST HUNDREDS

L. E. G. Ames	8	R. C. Russell	2
A. J. Stewart	6	H. Wood	1
A. P. E. Knott	5	J. T. Murray	1
T. G. Evans	2	C. J. Richards	1
J. M. Parks	2	**G. O. Jones**	**1**

Stewart scored nine further Test hundreds when he was not keeping wicket.

---

wickets down, but Monday morning was still pregnant with possibilities. Hoggard, though, removed Styris with the 12th ball of the day and the batting quickly unravelled despite some brutal hitting from Oram. Papps appeared at No. 9 and lasted three balls; Vettori could not bat at all.

Hoggard, who had been under pressure after returning only three wickets in three innings, finished with four, but the contribution of Harmison, in his first Test at Headingley, could not be exaggerated: he created pressure for all the other bowlers as well as taking seven in the match. After England had knocked off the 45 needed before lunch, Fleming gave Harmison fulsome praise and described him as "more dynamic" than Glenn McGrath.

Man of the Match: G. O. Jones.   *Attendance:* 47,228; *receipts* £958,473.

Close of play: First day, New Zealand 41-1 (Papps 24, Fleming 3); Second day, New Zealand 351-6 (Cairns 41, McCullum 31); Third day, England 248-4 (Thorpe 7, Flintoff 4); Fourth day, New Zealand 102-5 (Styris 7, Oram 4).

New Zealand

M. H. Richardson b Saggers	13	– c Jones b Hoggard	40
M. H. W. Papps lbw b Flintoff	86	– (9) c Vaughan b Harmison	0
*S. P. Fleming c Vaughan b Harmison	97	– (2) c Strauss b Flintoff	11
N. J. Astle c Butcher b Saggers	2	– lbw b Hoggard	8
S. B. Styris c Jones b Harmison	21	– c Jones b Hoggard	19
J. D. P. Oram c Thorpe b Flintoff	39	– (7) not out	36
C. L. Cairns c Strauss b Harmison	41	– (8) lbw b Hoggard	10
†B. B. McCullum b Hoggard	54	– (3) c Trescothick b Harmison	20
D. L. Vettori b Harmison	35	– absent hurt	
D. R. Tuffey lbw b Hoggard	0	– (6) c Jones b Harmison	7
C. S. Martin not out	0	– (10) run out	0
B 5, l-b 14, w 2	21	B 4, l-b 4, n-b 2	10

1/33 (1) 2/202 (2) 3/215 (3) 4/215 (4)	409	1/39 (2) 2/75 (1) 3/77 (3)	161
5/263 (5) 6/293 (6) 7/355 (7)		4/84 (4) 5/91 (6) 6/118 (5)	
8/409 (8) 9/409 (10) 10/409 (9)		7/144 (8) 8/149 (9) 9/161 (10)	

Bowling: *First Innings*—Hoggard 27–6–93–2; Harmison 36.2–8–74–4; Flintoff 27–7–64–2; Saggers 30–6–86–2; Trescothick 2–0–3–0; Giles 19–1–67–0; Vaughan 2–0–3–0. *Second Innings* Hoggard 15–4–75–4; Harmison 16–5–57–3; Flintoff 6–0–16–1; Saggers 5–3–5–0.

England

M. E. Trescothick b Styris	132	– not out		30
A. J. Strauss c Tuffey b Vettori	62	– c Astle b Tuffey		10
M. A. Butcher lbw b Vettori	4	– not out		5
*M. P. Vaughan c Fleming b Styris	13			
G. P. Thorpe b Martin	34			
A. Flintoff c Martin b Styris	94			
†G. O. Jones c Fleming b Cairns	100			
A. F. Giles c Fleming b Martin	21			
M. J. Hoggard c McCullum b Tuffey	4			
M. J. Saggers c sub (S. E. Bond) b Cairns	0			
S. J. Harmison not out	0			
B 25, l-b 21, w 3, n-b 13	62			

1/153 (2) 2/174 (3) 3/229 (4) 4/240 (1)   526   1/18 (2)   (1 wkt) 45
5/339 (5) 6/457 (6) 7/491 (8)
8/526 (7) 9/526 (10) 10/526 (9)

Bowling: *First Innings*—Tuffey 26.1–7–88–1; Martin 30–9–127–2; Styris 27–5–88–3; Cairns 27–6–94–2; Vettori 23–2–83–2. *Second Innings*—Martin 4–1–17–0; Tuffey 4–0–28–1.

Umpires: S. A. Bucknor (West Indies) and S. J. A. Taufel (Australia).
Third umpire: N. J. Llong.   Referee: C. H. Lloyd (West Indies).

ENGLAND v NEW ZEALAND

Third npower Test

RICHARD HOBSON

At Nottingham, June 10, 11, 12, 13. England won by four wickets. Toss: New Zealand. Test debut: K. D. Mills.

For all the ups and downs along the way, a roller-coaster ride will always end in the same place. So too with this series. For the third time, New Zealand began strongly and held the advantage at various stages, only to dip for one last time in the final stretch. It took a nerveless hundred by Thorpe, his 14th in Test cricket, to complete what was described as a blackcapwash. And Fleming, New Zealand's highly regarded captain, could reflect on some unhelpful umpiring and injuries which restricted two of his front-line attack to 47 balls in the match.

In their stead, Cairns, who turned 34 on what proved to be the last day, coaxed his creaking body through a near-heroic effort to mark his Test farewell. He had brought this forward (though he continued in one-day cricket) because he wanted to bow out at Trent Bridge, his home from home as a Nottinghamshire overseas player. Despite the result and two failures with the bat – the crowd wanted to see a last swashbuckling innings – he could take pride from match figures of nine for 187, and seemed genuinely humbled when stewards lined up to form a guard of honour after the presentation ceremony.

Thorpe pipped him for the match award, but those who appreciate tales of the human spirit would have overlooked both. David Hopps's comparison of Ashley Giles to a wheelie bin, popularised via the radio by Henry Blofeld, had captured a general disregard for the slow left-armer, a decent sort who had considered giving up in the face of criticism. Now, the bin wheeled back, removing two of New Zealand's top three in the first innings, producing a peach of a ball to account for Cairns in the second, and then joining Thorpe for a match-winning partnership of 70 in 14 overs.

Singled out: Chris Cairns's last Test innings ends miserably, bowled by Ashley Giles for one.

Picture by Patrick Eagar

The folly of New Zealand's decision to include a single specialist slow bowler in their squad was exposed by the injury to Vettori. Their attack was unbalanced because they could not call up another spinner in time. James Franklin, left-arm seam, was drafted in from Rishton, of the Lancashire League, and Kyle Mills given a debut. England were unchanged, sticking with Saggers ahead of the centrally contracted Anderson, but, on a pitch which improved from the previous year against South Africa, they had to wait until the 52nd over for the first breakthrough, when Giles ended yet another obdurate effort by the limpet-like Richardson.

This time, Fleming completed his seventh Test hundred, whipping Saggers over mid-wicket for a second six, but a loose stroke brought his downfall after tea, and Harmison removed Astle and McMillan with successive deliveries as England made better use of the second new ball. Despite a hundred from Styris – like Fleming's, reached in 161 deliveries – New Zealand proved unable to construct a single substantial stand on Friday morning, when the ball swung and seamed more readily. Mills became Hoggard's 100th Test wicket and, four balls later, Martin his 101st.

However, Cairns and Franklin – introduced in the third over when Martin's hamstring went – made good use of the conditions as well. Effectively, the Vaughan–Trescothick opening partnership was restored, because they came together at 18 for two. Vaughan responded beautifully. Mills saw his first ball at this level race to the boundary and Vaughan reached his fifty in 49 deliveries with a six off Franklin, before becoming yet another victim of Cairns's slower ball. Soon after that, Mills joined Martin on the treatment table with a side strain.

Trescothick and Flintoff failed to build on half-centuries, and Thorpe was undone by one of three questionable decisions by Simon Taufel on the third day. A leg-side catch appeared to brush the thigh pad and, with Cairns and Franklin rising to their responsibilities, England needed some late clubbing by Giles to restrict the first-innings deficit to 65. Fleming and Richardson extended that until New Zealand were effectively 159 for nought. But once Giles's spin deceived Richardson – who had batted 21 hours 53 minutes in the series – the collapse was in motion. Fleming himself was given leg-before by Taufel offering no stroke to a ball going over the stumps, and Styris caught behind after swishing – and missing – against Harmison. The remaining five wickets realised 28 runs next morning. That still meant a target of 284: no side had ever won a Test at Trent Bridge chasing more than 247 in the fourth innings. Confidence grew when Cairns and Franklin claimed three wickets in the first 15 overs.

ENGLAND'S HIGHEST SUCCESSFUL TEST RUN-CHASES

332-7	(needing 332)	v Australia at Melbourne.	1928-29
315-4	(needing 315)	v Australia at Leeds.	2001
307-6	(needing 305)	v New Zealand at Christchurch	1996-97
298-4	(needing 297)	v Australia at Melbourne.	1894-95
284-6	**(needing 284)**	**v New Zealand at Nottingham**.	**2004**
282-9	(needing 282)	v Australia at Melbourne.	1907-08
282-3	**(needing 282)**	**v New Zealand at Lord's**.	**2004**
263-9	(needing 263)	v Australia at The Oval	1902
251-8	(needing 249)	v South Africa at Centurion.	1999-2000
247-2	(needing 247)	v South Africa at Nottingham.	1998
237-3	(needing 234)	v Australia at Melbourne.	1962-63
231-3	**(needing 231)**	**v West Indies at Manchester**	**2004**

But England were not about to go down with a prod and a poke. Butcher hit 12 fours, despite a broken finger, and Thorpe scored heavily between point and extra cover while presenting watertight defence in between. Jones helped him add 52 and Giles played even more forcefully in support. New Zealand's energy was spent by the time England claimed the extra half-hour on Sunday evening, with 25 needed. It took 21 balls. Thorpe completed a 163-ball hundred of concentrated study, and then England's first clean sweep in a three-match series for 26 years.

Man of the Match: G. P. Thorpe.　　　*Attendance:* 61,432; *receipts* £1,260,609.
Men of the Series: England – S. J. Harmison; New Zealand – M. H. Richardson.
Close of play: First day, New Zealand 295-4 (Styris 68, Oram 10); Second day, England 225-5 (Thorpe 30, Hoggard 0); Third day, New Zealand 190-5 (McMillan 28, Franklin 2).

New Zealand

M. H. Richardson c Vaughan b Giles	73	– lbw b Giles	49
*S. P. Fleming c Thorpe b Flintoff	117	– lbw b Flintoff	45
S. B. Styris c sub (B. M. Shafayat) b Giles	108	– (4) c Jones b Harmison	39
N. J. Astle b Harmison	15	– (5) lbw b Flintoff	0
C. D. McMillan lbw b Harmison	0	– (6) lbw b Harmison	30
J. D. P. Oram c Strauss b Saggers	14	– (8) c Flintoff b Harmison	0
C. L. Cairns c Thorpe b Saggers	12	– (9) b Giles	1
†B. B. McCullum c Hoggard b Harmison	21	– (3) c Flintoff b Giles	4
J. E. C. Franklin not out	4	– (7) c Jones b Flintoff	17
K. D. Mills c Jones b Hoggard	0	– c Harmison b Giles	8
C. S. Martin c Vaughan b Hoggard	2	– not out	0
B 2, l-b 14, n-b 2	18	B 1, l-b 21, n-b 3	25

1/163 (1) 2/225 (2) 3/272 (4) 4/272 (5)　384
5/308 (6) 6/331 (7) 7/366 (3)
8/377 (8) 9/382 (10) 10/384 (11)

1/94 (1) 2/106 (3) 3/126 (2)　218
4/134 (5) 5/185 (4) 6/198 (6)
7/198 (8) 8/208 (9)
9/210 (7) 10/218 (10)

Bowling: *First Innings*—Hoggard 25–6–85–2; Harmison 32–9–80–3; Flintoff 14–2–48–1; Saggers 22–5–80–2; Giles 27–6–70–2; Vaughan 1–0–5–0. *Second Innings*—Hoggard 6–2–25–0; Harmison 25–7–51–3; Saggers 6–2–14–0; Flintoff 20–3–60–3; Giles 24–6–46–4.

England

M. E. Trescothick c Styris b Franklin	63	– c and b Franklin	9
A. J. Strauss c McCullum b Cairns	0	– lbw b Cairns	6
M. A. Butcher c Styris b Franklin	5	– lbw b Cairns	59
*M. P. Vaughan lbw b Cairns	61	– lbw b Cairns	10
G. P. Thorpe c McCullum b Franklin	45	– not out	104
A. Flintoff lbw b Cairns	54	– c sub (H. J. H. Marshall) b Cairns	5
M. J. Hoggard c Styris b Franklin	5		
†G. O. Jones lbw b Styris	22	– (7) c Oram b Franklin	27
A. F. Giles not out	45	– (8) not out	36
M. J. Saggers b Cairns	0		
S. J. Harmison b Cairns	0		
B 2, l-b 5, n-b 12	19	B 4, l-b 16, n-b 8	28

1/1 (2) 2/18 (3) 3/128 (4) 4/140 (1) 319
5/221 (6) 6/244 (7) 7/255 (5)
8/295 (8) 9/301 (10) 10/319 (11)

1/12 (2) 2/16 (1) (6 wkts) 284
3/46 (4) 4/134 (3)
5/162 (6) 6/214 (7)

Bowling: *First Innings*—Martin 1.5–0–1–0; Cairns 23.3 5–79–5; Franklin 26.1–4–104–4; Mills 6–2 31–0; Oram 15–0–47–0; Styris 11–1–45–1; McMillan 2–1–5–0. *Second Innings*—Cairns 25–2–108–4; Franklin 17 2–59–2; Richardson 1–0–4–0; Oram 14.3–1–50–0; Styris 14–1–43–0.

Umpires: D. J. Harper (Australia) and S. J. A. Taufel (Australia).
Third umpire: M. R. Benson.   Referee: C. H. Lloyd (West Indies).

†At Derby, June 16. **Derbyshire won by four wickets.** Toss: Derbyshire. **New Zealanders** **258-7** (50 overs) (S. P. Fleming 102, S. B. Styris 56, C. D. McMillan 43); Derbyshire 259-6 (48.4 overs) (J. Moss 30, Hassan Adnan 113*, L. D. Sutton 41).
Fleming's 102 took 123 balls and included 13 fours; Hassan Adnan's 113 lasted 113 balls and included ten fours and a six.

†At Chelmsford, June 18 (day/night). **New Zealanders won by five wickets.** Toss: New Zealanders. Essex 243-3 (50 overs) (A. Habib 42, A. P. Grayson 57, R. C. Irani 72*, R. S. Bopara 40*); **New Zealanders 246-5** (38.3 overs) (N. J. Astle 41, H. J. H. Marshall 111, C. D. McMillan 52*).
Marshall's 111 took 97 balls and included 15 fours.

†At Northampton, June 20. **New Zealanders won by five runs (D/L method).** Toss: New Zealanders. **New Zealanders 253** (49.1 overs) (J. D. P. Oram 50, C. L. Cairns 46, B. B. McCullum 58, Extras 30; A. J. Shantry 5-37); **Northamptonshire 241-8** (48 overs) (M. van Jaarsveld 102, G. L. Brophy 57*).
First-team debut: C. J. R. Jennings (Northamptonshire). Northamptonshire's target was revised to 247 from 48 overs. Van Jaarsveld's 102 took 118 balls and included 12 fours.

New Zealand's matches against England and West Indies in the NatWest Series (June 24–July 10) appear on pages 492–503.

THE WEST INDIANS IN ENGLAND, 2004

REVIEW BY STEPHEN FAY

Two decades after the successive "blackwash" series that marked the high tide of Caribbean cricketing dominance, England completed a double rout of their own over West Indies so easily that English cricket lovers who had grown stoical in defeat started to take winning for granted. Having won a four-Test away series 3–0 earlier in the year, England swept the four at home, with Michael Vaughan's leadership of a relatively young team growing in skill and conviction all the time. Though he still lacked experience against hardened opposition from Australia and India, his team was beginning to expect to win even when the going was toughest.

THOSE LAZY, HAZY, CRAZY DAYS...

England's best Test summers

	Opponents	Tests	Won	Lost	Drawn
2004	**New Zealand/West Indies**	7	7	0	0
1959	India	5	5	0	0
1967	India/Pakistan	6	5	0	1
1978	Pakistan/New Zealand	6	5	0	1
1958	New Zealand	5	4	0	1
1962	Pakistan	5	4	0	1

The outlines of the two series were similar, England retaining the Wisden Trophy at the earliest opportunity. However, this time West Indian consolation was to come, not with one mega-innings from their captain Brian Lara, but in the one-day tournament that followed. West Indies' problem was that Lara had no confidence in this team, while his players, awed or fearful, were distanced from him and lacked confidence in themselves. There were talented young cricketers in the squad but, with one exception, they did not develop. It was emblematic of West Indies' predicament that, while the team and its managers criss-crossed England in a distinctively decorated bus, Lara usually travelled in a silver Mercedes lent him by an admirer.

They were destined not just to lose the series, but to be humiliated in a country where whole generations of cricket-lovers had grown up believing West Indies were invincible. Before the final Test, Lara came up with the notion that his side commonly restored their pride in the last match of a series they had already lost. In fact, they were blown away at The Oval. It was a whitewash.

The selectors relied on three inexperienced pace bowlers – Tino Best, Fidel Edwards and Jermaine Lawson – who, at 22, were still wet behind the ears. Corey Collymore, the only medium-fast bowler with experience of English wickets as a county overseas player, was originally left at home. They also gave a chance to even younger players, such as Dwayne Bravo and Dwayne Smith. It was a fragile-looking outfit that would need good leadership, great application and a lot of luck.

But the tour had a poor start, even before the team left home. Sir Vivian Richards, the chairman of selectors, had been accused of being an unsympathetic role model by some young players, and quit. Instead of spending the summer inside their tent and, in Lyndon Johnson's phrase, pissing out, he took a broadcast commentary job and regularly, but not unjustly, pissed in. Gus Logie's lack of authority as coach was clear from the start, and six weeks after the series he was gone. Tony Howard, the manager with the stern manner of a Barbadian preacher, promised he would make sure the young men behaved themselves. There were no scandals, though the players did spend much time at receptions ignoring their English hosts and chattering on mobile phones.

One early lesson for young West Indians with no experience of county cricket is that it can rain a lot in England in June. (Although the weather remained unusually wet, only one full day was lost during the Tests – in Manchester.) In the one-day tournament before the Tests, two of West Indies' games were washed away, but they reached the final against New Zealand by beating England at Lord's in the game that mattered most to them. It was a splendid affair, with brilliant centuries from Andrew Flintoff and Chris Gayle; to have

> **The first round went to England without a ball bowled**

won by seven wickets chasing 286 encouraged them to treat this one-day international as an augury for the Test series.

Before the First Test at Lord's, Lara tried to inflict a psychological wound on England. Vaughan, he said, turned to Steve Harmison whenever he needed a wicket, but he questioned whether Harmison could last the whole summer: "I don't know if they have a Plan B," he said. It did not take long to find out. Before the game began, Lara wounded himself.

The forecast was good but the morning was overcast and the ball might swing for an hour or two. He asked England to bat. The decision radiated unease. Did he fear for his top order against England's young pace bowlers in English conditions? If so, West Indies' best batsmen would interpret the decision as a vote of no confidence.

Whatever the reasoning, it was a serious error, and the first round went to England without a ball bowled. By the close of play, Best had taken one for 75 off 16 overs, Edwards none for 60 off 15. On the second day, Bravo and Pedro Collins picked up some wickets, but it had been a harrowing experience for them. Best bowled only three overs in the second innings and went home with a back injury after the Second Test at Edgbaston, where Edwards was omitted. West Indies' first-choice attack had disintegrated before England started their second innings at Lord's. Collymore was called up, but he could not be expected to put it together again.

Lara had begun the series with an average against England of 67.97. Now he owed his team one of his command performances: Daryl Harper, who mistakenly gave him caught behind when he was 11, prevented this in the

Punching above his weight: the unexpected star of the series, Ashley Giles, celebrates dismissing Chris Gayle at Lord's, with his friend and captain, Michael Vaughan.

Picture by Tom Shaw, Getty Images

first innings at Lord's, but a focused, highly concentrated performance on the final day might well have scrambled a draw. Instead, Lara went down the wicket to Ashley Giles and was beaten by a sharply turning ball that bowled him between bat and pad for 44, his second-best score at Lord's, where he had raised his average in three Tests to a mere 21.

It was scant consolation that Harmison's match figures were two for 150, because England's Plan B was the improbable figure of Giles, who took nine for 210 with his left-arm spin. Lara had lost something more than one Test. At Edgbaston, he was looking like his old self, and had reached 95 in a stand of 209 with Ramnaresh Sarwan. But Flintoff was bowling fast, and forcing Lara to make exaggerated foot movements across his stumps. He was finally drawn outside the off stump, where the bat flashed and edged a catch to second slip. Flintoff, who dismissed Lara for nought and seven in the Third Test at Old Trafford, had his measure. His only other innings of more than 50 was 79 in the final Test at The Oval. That was scored when all around him were losing their heads, and he managed to lose his last. In eight innings in four Tests, one of the world's greatest-ever batsmen scored 264 runs, averaging 33. He was a disappointment to the audience, his colleagues and, presumably, himself.

It was a shortfall that even Chanderpaul and Gayle, both of whom scored more heavily than any of the English batsmen, could not make up. Sarwan came and went, but Bravo at No. 6 performed manfully for a young lad. Even more impressive, he was the tourists' top wicket-taker with 16 at 26.18.

He was the one West Indian who was a better cricketer by the end of the summer. The performance of the bowlers was neatly encapsulated in the series averages, which were headed by Gayle, the opening bat, and Bravo. Of the pace attack, of whom so much had been hoped, only Collins managed ten wickets. But the poor bowlers had little help from Lara's field placing. When Flintoff entered, the fielders retreated: evidence of how much they feared him. When tailenders cut loose, Lara persisted with tired medium-pacers. Gayle's slow off-spin proved hard to score off, but Lara was perversely reluctant to bowl him.

The predicament of the team showed in the successive first-innings scores: 416, 336, 395 and 152. England, on the other hand, scored 568, 566, 330 and 470. Their only hiccough occurred at Old Trafford, where they were 65 behind on first innings. By the time they arrived at The Oval, West Indies were little more than a foil to set off compelling England performances. When Lara was caught at slip in the second innings, he received an ovation signifying regret that this would probably be his last Test in England, where his genius had been revealed so intermittently. It also looked like his last Test as captain.

England's batsmen scored eight hundreds, five more than in the West Indies. Vaughan, who had had a disappointing series with the bat against New Zealand, proved to himself that he could still score hundreds, with a brace at Lord's. He seemed to make runs when the team needed them most. Marcus Trescothick repeated the feat at Edgbaston, but his capricious approach to batting produced only 107 more runs in six innings. Andrew Strauss confirmed his place with his second Lord's Test hundred of the summer. Graham Thorpe buckled down at Old Trafford, when the team needed him to stay at the crease and score a hundred; it compensated for his increasingly unreliable and slow performances in the field.

> **Flintoff looked like the young Siegfried**

With a ginger beard, Andrew Flintoff looked like the young Siegfried, playing utterly without fear. His 167 at Edgbaston was the memorable performance of the series. The most decisive innings, however, was by Robert Key. Not his 221 at Lord's, but at Old Trafford, where he mocked West Indies' transitory hope of victory with a well-judged 93 out of 231 for three. When Thorpe was injured, Ian Bell made a purposeful debut at The Oval. Obviously, not all of them succeeded all the time, but two or three of the top order always did. These were heady days.

The only competition for places in a settled team was between James Anderson and Simon Jones for the last position in the attack. After the First Test, it went to Anderson. All the bowlers took wickets, and Giles surprised himself and his friends with 22. Flintoff moved on to play an offensive role, which was good timing, because he and Matthew Hoggard were indeed required as Plan B when Harmison's brilliant form briefly deserted him. Harmison took four for 337 in the first five innings of the series, and then bared his teeth again, taking 13 for 165 in the final three.

Leaps and bounds: Dwayne Bravo, whose improvement was West Indies' best news of the series, bowls at The Oval.

Picture by Patrick Eagar

There were no glaring weaknesses, and the only serious blemish was the fielding, and specifically the clumsiness of Geraint Jones behind the stumps. Although he had a quiet series at No. 7, he had earned his batting place; but there was no improvement in his principal role. The ground fielding was quick and neat, but chances were let slip by Thorpe, and Vaughan dropped a catch at Edgbaston so easy he quite forgot how to take it.

During this summer, Vaughan finally established a distinctive style of leadership: less driven than Nasser Hussain, and less judgmental. He was fortunate to inherit a side that had become more competitive, more reluctant to admit defeat, and with a developing self-belief. He nurtured these properties, and the team's confidence in him grew. They evidently liked playing for him. Vaughan's field placing showed a nice fusion of attack and defence, and his pace bowlers responded well to working in fairly short bursts. On the field, his body language was sympathetic. Off the field, he communicated freely with journalists without ever committing himself to strong opinions. He had established himself as England's leader; but his skill and resilience remained to be proved at the highest level of Test cricket.

WEST INDIAN TOURING PARTY

B. C. Lara (*captain*), R. R. Sarwan (*vice-captain*), O. A. C. Banks, C. S. Baugh, T. L. Best, D. J. J. Bravo, S. Chanderpaul, P. T. Collins, F. H. Edwards, C. H. Gayle, R. D. Jacobs, S. C. Joseph, J. J. C. Lawson, R. Rampaul, D. R. Smith, D. S. Smith.

Rampaul was replaced by C. D. Collymore and Best by D. Mohammed. I. D. R. Bradshaw, R. L. Powell and D. J. G. Sammy were selected only for the one-day series which preceded the Tests; Edwards, originally in the one-day party, was replaced by Lawson. Banks, Collins, Edwards and Joseph arrived for the first-class leg of the tour.

Coach: A. L. Logie. *Manager:* A. B. Howard. *Trainer:* R. Rogers. *Physiotherapist:* A. Simpson. *Analyst:* G. S. Smith. *Media liaison officer:* I. Khan.

WEST INDIAN TOUR RESULTS

Test matches – Played 4: Lost 4.
First-class matches – Played 7: Won 2, Lost 4, Drawn 1.
One-day internationals – Played 7: Won 2, Lost 3, No result 2. *Wins* – England (2). *Losses* – England, New Zealand (2). *No result* – New Zealand (2).
Other non-first-class matches – Played 4: Won 3, Lost 1. Abandoned 1.

TEST MATCH AVERAGES

ENGLAND – BATTING AND FIELDING

	T	I	NO	R	HS	100s	50s	Avge	Ct/St
A. Flintoff.	4	7	1	387	167	1	3	64.50	5
R. W. T. Key	4	7	1	378	221	1	1	63.00	3
†G. P. Thorpe.	3	5	0	286	114	1	2	57.20	3
M. P. Vaughan	4	7	1	330	103	2	1	55.00	3
†M. E. Trescothick	4	8	1	319	107	2	0	45.57	5
†A. J. Strauss.	4	8	1	317	137	1	1	45.28	7
M. J. Hoggard	4	5	2	83	38	0	0	27.66	1
S. J. Harmison	4	5	2	80	36*	0	0	26.66	0
G. O. Jones	4	5	0	116	74	0	1	23.20	13/2
A. F. Giles	4	5	0	106	52	0	1	21.20	3
†J. M. Anderson	3	4	2	23	12	0	0	11.50	2

Played in one Test: I. R. Bell 70 (2 ct); †S. P. Jones 4.

† *Left-handed batsman.*

BOWLING

	Style	O	M	R	W	BB	5W/i	Avge
A. Flintoff	RFM	88.3	17	297	14	3-25	0	21.21
A. F. Giles	SLA	186.1	41	509	22	5-57	2	23.13
S. J. Harmison . .	RF	131.4	20	502	17	6-46	1	29.52
M. J. Hoggard. . . .	RFM	126	24	492	16	4-83	0	30.75
J. M. Anderson . . .	RFM	55.1	8	219	7	4-52	0	31.28

Also bowled: S. P. Jones (RF) 25–6–99–1; M. E. Trescothick (RM) 2–0–7–0; M. P. Vaughan (OB) 4–0–17–0.

WEST INDIES – BATTING AND FIELDING

	T	I	NO	R	HS	100s	50s	Avge	Ct/St
†S. Chanderpaul	4	8	2	437	128*	1	2	72.83	2
†C. H. Gayle	4	8	0	400	105	1	3	50.00	3
R. R. Sarwan	4	8	0	267	139	1	1	33.37	6
†B. C. Lara	4	8	0	264	95	0	2	33.00	7
C. S. Baugh	2	4	0	111	68	0	1	27.75	2
D. J. J. Bravo	4	8	0	220	77	0	2	27.50	3
O. A. C. Banks	2	4	1	74	45	0	0	24.66	0
S. C. Joseph	2	4	0	85	45	0	0	21.25	1
†D. S. Smith	2	4	0	66	45	0	0	16.50	3
J. J. C. Lawson	2	4	3	9	4*	0	0	9.00	0
†R. D. Jacobs	2	4	0	33	32	0	0	8.25	8/1
P. T. Collins	3	6	1	35	19*	0	0	7.00	0
C. D. Collymore	3	6	1	33	10	0	0	6.60	0
F. H. Edwards	3	6	1	13	5	0	0	2.60	1

Played in one Test: T. L. Best 0, 3; D. Mohammed 23, 9; D. R. Smith 28.

† *Left-handed batsman.*

BOWLING

	Style	O	M	R	W	BB	5W/i	Avge
C. H. Gayle	OB	44.1	7	136	8	5-34	1	17.00
D. J. J. Bravo	RFM	128.4	25	419	16	6-55	1	26.18
P. T. Collins	LFM	84	8	347	10	4-113	0	34.70
J. J. C. Lawson	RF	68	10	320	8	4-94	0	40.00
C. D. Collymore	RFM	104	29	316	6	2-66	0	52.66

Also bowled: O. A. C. Banks (OB) 80–8–351–3; T. L. Best (RF) 24–2–118–1; F. H. Edwards (RF) 82.3–8–330–3; S. C. Joseph (OB) 2–0–8–0; D. Mohammed (SLC) 32–2–102–0; R. R. Sarwan (LB) 36–0–134–0; D. R. Smith (RM) 14–4–50–0.

WEST INDIAN TOUR AVERAGES – FIRST-CLASS MATCHES

BATTING AND FIELDING

	M	I	NO	R	HS	100s	50s	Avge	Ct/St
†S. Chanderpaul	6	12	3	583	128*	2	2	64.77	4
†C. H. Gayle	6	11	0	569	105	1	4	51.72	3
†R. D. Jacobs	4	7	2	242	117*	1	1	48.40	10/1
†B. C. Lara	5	10	1	420	113*	1	2	46.66	10
S. C. Joseph	4	8	0	367	114	1	2	45.87	2
C. S. Baugh	4	8	1	304	150*	1	1	43.42	10/2
†D. S. Smith	5	10	0	294	142	1	0	29.40	6
O. A. C. Banks	5	10	2	224	90	0	1	28.00	1
R. R. Sarwan	6	12	0	319	139	1	1	26.58	7
D. J. J. Bravo	7	14	0	358	118	1	2	25.57	4
D. R. Smith	4	7	0	130	55	0	1	18.57	1
C. D. Collymore	3	6	1	33	10	0	0	6.60	0
P. T. Collins	4	8	2	37	19*	0	0	6.16	2
J. J. C. Lawson	4	6	3	11	4*	0	0	3.66	2
F. H. Edwards	6	9	3	20	5*	0	0	3.33	2

Played in two matches: T. L. Best 0, 3 (1 ct); D. Mohammed 4, 23, 9 (1 ct).

† *Left-handed batsman.*

BOWLING

	Style	O	M	R	W	BB	5W/i	Avge
C. H. Gayle.	OB	66.1	13	189	10	5-34	1	18.90
D. J. J. Bravo.	RFM	146.4	29	486	20	6-55	1	24.30
D. R. Smith.	RM	54	12	163	5	3-4	0	32.60
T. L. Best.	RF	35	3	165	5	4-47	0	33.00
D. Mohammed.	SLC	60	10	171	5	3-47	0	34.20
P. T. Collins.	LFM	109	9	453	13	4-113	0	34.84
J. J. C. Lawson.	RF	105.3	13	471	13	4-94	0	36.23
F. H. Edwards	RF	139.2	14	610	14	5-22	2	43.57
O. A. C. Banks	OB	131	19	527	11	3-50	0	47.90
C. D. Collymore.	RFM	104	29	316	6	2-66	0	52.66

Also bowled: S. C. Joseph (OB) 7–1–23–0; R. R. Sarwan (LB) 39–1–145–0.

Note: Matches in this section which were not first-class are signified by a dagger.

†At Belfast, June 16. **West Indians won by 96 runs.** Toss: West Indians. **West Indians 242** (46.2 overs) (D. J. J. Bravo 45, B. C. Lara 106; A. C. Botha 3–42); **Ireland 146** (37.4 overs) (W. K. McCallan 32; R. Rampaul 3-25).
Lara scored his 106 in 99 balls, with 12 fours and four sixes.

†IRELAND v WEST INDIANS

At Belfast, June 17. Ireland won by six wickets. Toss: West Indians.
Ireland inflicted a humiliating defeat on the West Indians – just as they had 35 years earlier, when they skittled them for a meagre 25 on a trickier, emerald-green wicket. This time, they had to overhaul a demanding total. On a true pitch, West Indies lost Chanderpaul early on, regrouped, and then lurched from 118 for two to 133 for five. But Bravo seemed to dispel fears of embarrassment with an express unbeaten hundred from just 65 balls, and the West Indians ended on 292. John Mooney, a 22-year-old medium-pacer, claimed three for 67, and would have been cheaper but for ten wides. The Irish reply prospered from the start as Jason Molins and Jeremy Bray put on 111 for the first wicket. Molins gathered runs as briskly as Rampaul frittered them away, his seven overs costing 74. Ireland lost wickets, but stayed up with the rate as Niall O'Brien, the Kent reserve wicket-keeper, struck a run-a-ball fifty to ensure another famous victory. "Forget 1969; this is the game we will all be talking about now," said Peter Thompson, chief executive of the Irish Cricket Union. "It's a great day for Irish cricket."

West Indians

C. H. Gayle c O'Brien b Johnston.	31	*B. C. Lara c sub (G. Wilson) b Botha .	1
S. Chanderpaul c O'Brien b Johnston. . .	2	I. D. R. Bradshaw not out	7
D. S. Smith c McCallan b Mooney	42	B 6, l-b 2, w 21, n-b 4.	33
R. L. Powell c sub (G. Wilson) b Botha .	33		
D. J. G. Sammy c White b Mooney	3	1/5 (2) 2/46 (1) (7 wkts, 50 overs) 292
†R. D. Jacobs c Bray b Mooney	40	3/118 (4) 4/133 (3)
D. J. J. Bravo not out	100	5/133 (5) 6/264 (6) 7/268 (8)

R. Rampaul and J. J. C. Lawson did not bat.

Bowling: Johnston 7–1–29–2; Eagleson 7–2–40–0; Botha 10–0–67–2; Mooney 10–0–67–3; McCallan 10–1–33–0; White 6–0–48–0.

Ireland

*J. A. M. Molins b Rampaul	66	A. R. White not out	32
J. P. Bray st Jacobs b Gayle	71	B 3, l-b 8, w 9, n-b 8	28
A. C. Botha c Chanderpaul b Bradshaw	15		
†N. J. O'Brien not out	58	1/111 (1) 2/163 (3) (4 wkts, 46.5 overs) 295	
P. G. Gillespie run out	25	3/184 (2) 4/238 (5)	

W. K. McCallan, E. J. G. Morgan, D. T. Johnston, J. F. Mooney and R. L. Eagleson did not bat.

Bowling: Bradshaw 10–0–47–1; Rampaul 7–0–74–1; Powell 4–0–18–0; Lawson 10–0–53–0; Gayle 8.5–0–39–1; Sammy 2–0–19–0; Bravo 5–0–34–0.

Umpires: E. Cooke and P. White.

†At Hove, June 19 (day/night). **West Indians won by six wickets (D/L method).** Toss: Sussex. **Sussex 292-6** (50 overs) (M. J. Prior 37, M. W. Goodwin 90, T. R. Ambrose 79*); **West Indians 184-4** (21 overs) (C. H. Gayle 57, S. Chanderpaul 71*).
West Indies' target was revised first to 255 from 40 overs, and later to 181 from 23.

†At Beckenham, June 21. **West Indians won by 91 runs.** Toss: Kent. **West Indians 274-8** (48 overs) (S. Chanderpaul 60, R. R. Sarwan 79, B. C. Lara 68; M. J. Saggers 5-51); **Kent 183** (41.1 overs) (E. T. Smith 54, Extras 40; J. J. C. Lawson 4-59).
With a 7,000 capacity crowd waiting, the West Indians arrived at 11.06, 21 minutes after the scheduled start, due to traffic hold-ups. Lara made up for lost time by scoring his 68 off 53 balls.

†At Shenley Park, June 23. **Middlesex v West Indians. No result (abandoned).**

West Indies' matches against New Zealand and England in the NatWest Series (June 26–July 10) appear on pages 492–503.

MCC v WEST INDIANS

At Arundel, July 13, 14, 15. West Indians won by 29 runs. Toss: West Indians. First-class debut: M. H. Wessels.

Lara convalesced after a bout of flu by knocking off a dazzling 89-ball century, then retired saying he felt weak. He also complained of the weakness of the opposition, which included MCC's 39-year-old head of cricket, John Stephenson, and 18-year-old Riki Wessels, son of Kepler. But the "disappointing" side threatened to embarrass Lara when they almost chased down 278 in 78 overs. The 19-year-old Essex batsman Alastair Cook made a fine 89, and Stephenson himself passed 50 before coming to grief through a reverse sweep. On the opening day, Devon Smith had played a chanceless five-hour innings, adding 196 with Lara, as Hoggard and Jones sought to prove their fitness for the First Test. Hoggard collected eight wickets in the match and, with South African Charl Willoughby, reduced the tourists to 50 for five on the second day. MCC had conceded a lead of 120, after failing to build on a century stand between Cook and Koenig; Banks and Dwayne Smith snapped up the last five inside nine overs.

Close of play: First day, West Indians 373-6 (Banks 12, Collins 2); Second day, West Indians 115-5 (Gayle 60, Lara 34).

West Indians

C. H. Gayle c Cook b Jones	43	– c Powell b Jones	84
D. S. Smith c Cook b Stephenson	142	– c Koenig b Hoggard	3
D. J. J. Bravo st Wessels b Patel	4	– (6) lbw b Willoughby	1
*B. C. Lara retired ill	113	– (7) c Wessels b Hoggard	43
S. Chanderpaul lbw b Hoggard	0	– (4) c Wessels b Willoughby	10
D. R. Smith c Wessels b Hoggard	2	– (3) lbw b Hoggard	0
†C. S. Baugh b Patel	38	– (5) c Wessels b Hoggard	0
O. A. C. Banks c Thorpe b Hoggard	16	– b Willoughby	0
P. T. Collins lbw b Jones	2	– not out	1
F. H. Edwards not out	2	– c Stephenson b Willoughby	0
J. J. C. Lawson b Hoggard	0	– lbw b Willoughby	2
B 1, l-b 9, w 4, n-b 4	18	B 5, l-b 4, w 1, n-b 3	13

1/90 (1) 2/99 (3) 3/295 (5) 4/307 (6)   380   1/9 (1) 2/9 (3) 3/48 (4) 4/49 (5)   157
5/329 (5) 6/369 (7) 7/374 (9)   5/50 (6) 6/137 (7) 7/154 (8)
8/380 (8) 9/380 (11)   8/154 (1) 9/155 (10) 10/157 (11)

In the first innings Lara retired ill at 295-2.

Bowling: *First Innings*—Hoggard 18–6–32–4; Willoughby 24–7–66–0; Benkenstein 10–1–63–0; Jones 17–1–77–2; Patel 15–2–82–2; Cook 1–0–12–0; Stephenson 10–2–38–1. *Second Innings*—Hoggard 11–0–58–4; Willoughby 14.5–4–48–5; Jones 7–2–25–1; Patel 3–0–17–0.

MCC

S. G. Koenig c Lara b Lawson	79	– c Baugh b Collins	8
A. N. Cook lbw b Gayle	49	– c Baugh b Banks	89
M. J. Powell c Chanderpaul b Bravo	27	– lbw b Collins	0
G. P. Thorpe c Chanderpaul b Lawson	32	– c Lara b Collins	4
D. M. Benkenstein c Lawson b D. R. Smith	39	– c Collins b Lawson	9
*J. P. Stephenson lbw b Bravo	7	– c Lara b Banks	58
†M. H. Wessels lbw b Banks	1	– run out	34
M. M. Patel c Collins b Banks	4	– c Baugh b Lawson	4
S. P. Jones not out	2	– c D. S. Smith b Banks	2
M. J. Hoggard c sub b D. R. Smith	0	– b Lawson	25
C. M. Willoughby c Baugh b D. R. Smith	0	– not out	4
B 1, l-b 2, w 4, n-b 13	20	B 1, l-b 3, w 2, n-b 5	11

1/105 (2) 2/167 (3) 3/195 (1) 4/210 (4)   260   1/21 (1) 2/21 (3) 3/30 (4)   248
5/221 (6) 6/240 (7) 7/244 (9)   4/77 (5) 5/151 (2) 6/213 (6)
8/260 (5) 9/260 (10) 10/260 (11)   7/213 (7) 8/217 (8)
                                                    9/221 (9) 10/248 (10)

Bowling: *First Innings*—Collins 14–0–66–0; Edwards 8–0–49–0; Lawson 12–2–38–2; Gayle 6–1–19–1; Bravo 8–1–29–2; Banks 9–0–52–2; D. R. Smith 1–0–4–3. *Second Innings*—Collins 11–1–40–3; Edwards 14–2–66–0; D. R. Smith 9–0–33–0; Lawson 11.3–0–50–3; Banks 18–3–55–3.

Umpires: N. L. Bainton and J. H. Hampshire.

WEST INDIANS v SRI LANKA A

At Shenley Park, July 17, 18, 19. Drawn. Toss: West Indians. First-class debut: M. M. M. Suraj. The West Indians got plenty of batting practice ahead of the First Test. Three scored hundreds in their first innings, with one near-miss, and Chanderpaul added a fourth on the final day. Joseph was the first to complete three figures, with a six over mid-wicket; Bravo was the quickest, with 118 in 130 balls; and Jacobs got there during a 183-run stand with Banks, who smashed six sixes before falling for 90 in 85 balls. With three of the batsmen who had helped them win all their previous tour fixtures called up for the Asia Cup, Sri Lanka A could not quite respond in kind.

Daniel hit Edwards for three consecutive fours to get to his fifty, but Mubarak was the only other man to reach the mark. Best wrapped up the Sri Lankan innings on the final morning, when acting-captain Sarwan waived the follow-on. He failed to find form, but Chanderpaul made the most of the opportunity, accelerating as he progressed.

Close of play: First day, West Indians 351-6 (Jacobs 30, Banks 0); Second day, Sri Lanka A 271-6 (Jayawardene 16, Mirando 9).

West Indians

D. S. Smith c Gajanayake b Kulasekara	6	– c Kulasekara b Mirando 15
*R. R. Sarwan c Mubarak b Lokuarachchi	28	– b Mirando 3
S. C. Joseph b Lokuarachchi	114	– (5) lbw b Perera 68
S. Chanderpaul run out	32	– not out 104
D. J. J. Bravo c Mubarak b Prasad	118	– (6) c and b Perera 7
D. R. Smith run out	8	– (3) c Jayawardene b Mirando 37
†R. D. Jacobs not out	117	
O. A. C. Banks c Gajanayake b Mirando	90	– (7) not out 25
B 4, l-b 9, w 3, n-b 5	21	B 2, l-b 9, n-b 13 24

1/9 (1) 2/79 (2) 3/173 (4)   (7 wkts dec.) 534   1/12 (2) 2/45 (1)   (5 wkts dec.) 283
4/192 (3) 5/211 (6)   3/70 (3) 4/200 (5)
6/351 (5) 7/534 (8)   5/208 (6)

T. L. Best, F. H. Edwards and J. J. C. Lawson did not bat.

Bowling: *First Innings*—Mirando 24.1–2–96–1; Kulasekara 25–3–99–1; Prasad 19–5–94–1; Lokuarachchi 30–3–114–2; Suraj 22–3–118–0. *Second Innings*—Mirando 11.5–3–51–3; Kulasekara 7–1–35–0; Prasad 6–0–21–0; Suraj 17–2–74–0; Perera 16–0–67–2; Gajanayake 2–0–24–0.

Sri Lanka A

S. Kalawithigoda c Best b Bravo	27	K. M. D. N. Kulasekara c D. S. Smith
G. I. Daniel c Bravo b Edwards	72	b Best . 18
M. K. Gajanayake c D. S. Smith b Best .	29	M. M. M. Suraj b Best 0
*J. Mubarak c D. R. Smith b Banks	61	B 4, l-b 14, n-b 14 32
W. M. B. Perera c Jacobs b Banks	20	
†H. A. P. W. Jayawardene not out	48	1/92 (1) 2/114 (2) 3/192 (3) 346
K. S. Lokuarachchi c Edwards b Banks .	10	4/234 (4) 5/235 (5) 6/250 (7)
M. T. T. Mirando c Jacobs b Bravo	20	7/288 (8) 8/313 (9)
K. T. G. D. Prasad c Banks b Best	10	9/346 (10) 10/346 (11)

Bowling: Best 11–1–47–4; Edwards 10–1–82–1; Lawson 14–1–63–0; D. R. Smith 10–2–37–0; Bravo 10–3–38–2; Banks 12–2–50–3; Sarwan 3–1–11–0.

Umpires: R. K. Illingworth and J. W. Lloyds.

ENGLAND v WEST INDIES

First npower Test

STEVEN LYNCH

At Lord's, July 22, 23, 24, 25, 26. England won by 210 runs. Toss: West Indies. Test debut: D. J. J. Bravo.

England put aside their poor form of the one-day series to complete their fourth Test victory of the summer. The final margin was convincing, but the result was not sealed until the last morning, when Lara became a distinguished 100th Test victim for Giles. A sharply turning ball beat the advancing batsman and crashed into middle stump, bringing one of nine wickets in the match for a man who had admitted to thoughts of retirement earlier in the year, after injury problems and press criticism.

England's other hero was Key. He owed his place to an inattentive driver rear-ending Butcher's car in London traffic when he was on the way to his physio with a thigh injury. Whiplash forced Butcher to drop out, ending a run of 42 successive Tests, and Key grabbed the opportunity, driving and pulling powerfully. Meeting the Queen at tea on the first day, by which time he had 90, failed to put him off. He reached his maiden Test century and just kept going, passing Len Hutton's 196, the previous highest score for England against West Indies at Lord's, en route to 221. Dropped by Gayle off Edwards at 16 and reprieved on 58 when Smith, also at second slip, was unsure whether he had taken a catch off Best cleanly, Key faced 288 balls in 426 minutes, with 31 fours. The signature shots were chunky straight drives, one of which whistled back past Edwards before he could breathe, let alone stop it. But when Best tried to bowl short, Key pulled him effortlessly three times in an over.

He put on 291 in 60 overs with Strauss, surpassing England's previous second-wicket best against West Indies, 266 by Peter Richardson and Tom Graveney at Trent Bridge in 1957. Strauss departed after making his third century in as many internationals

TEST DOUBLE-HUNDREDS AT LORD'S

333	G. A. Gooch	England v India	1990
259	G. C. Smith	South Africa v England	2003
254	D. G. Bradman	Australia v England	1930
240	W. R. Hammond	England v Australia	1938
221	**R. W. T. Key**	**England v West Indies**	**2004**
214*	C. G. Greenidge	West Indies v England	1984
211	J. B. Hobbs	England v South Africa	1924
208	D. C. S. Compton	England v South Africa	1947
206*	W. A. Brown	Australia v England	1938
206	M. P. Donnelly	New Zealand v England	1949
205*	J. Hardstaff, jun.	England v India	1946
200	Mohsin Khan	Pakistan v England	1982

at Lord's, and then Key added a further 165 with Vaughan, who put some indifferent form behind him to record his 12th Test hundred, his second in successive innings against West Indies. By the end of the first day, when England had piled up 391 for two, Lara's decision to put them in already looked disastrous: the early clouds soon cleared and the pitch turned out to be blameless. Edwards and Best were fast but wayward. Although next day Collins belatedly found the right line for his in-swingers, as the last seven wickets tumbled for 41, it mattered little: England were 527 for three when the slide started.

With Harmison off-colour, West Indies made a bright start in reply, Gayle and Smith putting on 118 before both fell to Giles, who had rediscovered the teasing loop that had been missing since he remodelled his action during the winter. Then Lara was given out, caught behind off Giles, by umpire Harper when replays suggested the ball had only brushed his pad, and West Indies feared the worst. Lara was unimpressed by the decision, later issuing an oblique statement to explain why he tarried at the crease: "I still find it impossible not to walk when I know I'm out." But Chanderpaul, back to his crustacean best after an indifferent run, nudged and nurdled – and unfurled the occasional bent-kneed belt through the covers – to his 11th Test century. He shared a handy stand with the 20-year-old Dwayne Bravo, who flicked his first ball in Tests for four and made a polished 44, though he was becalmed in the forties for ten overs before swishing a lifter from one Jones through to the other. Chanderpaul then combined

Pivotal innings: Rob Key swivels, tonks Tino Best to leg and heads towards a Lord's double-hundred.

Picture by Patrick Eagar

with Jacobs and Banks to ensure that the follow-on was avoided. Flintoff, who had been given a cortisone injection in his injured heel and had not been expected to bowl, claimed three quick wickets at the end.

England built quickly on their lead of 152, Strauss and Trescothick adding 71 in 22 overs on the third evening. Next morning, Key was run out after a poor call from Vaughan, who made amends by gliding to his second century of the match, joining George Headley and Graham Gooch as the only batsmen to have achieved this in a Test at Lord's. Flintoff chimed in, blasting to fifty in 38 balls, with two huge sixes, and the declaration came when he was out, leaving West Indies an improbable target of 478 in around 130 overs. The early departures of Smith and Sarwan – jumping across his stumps and pinned leg-before cheaply by Hoggard for the second time in

HIGHEST TEST PARTNERSHIPS AT LORD'S

370 for 3rd	W. J. Edrich and D. C. S. Compton, England v South Africa	1947
308 for 3rd	G. A. Gooch and A. J. Lamb, England v India	1990
291 for 2nd	**A. J. Strauss and R. W. T. Key, England v West Indies**	**2004**
287* for 2nd	C. G. Greenidge and H. A. Gomes, West Indies v England	1984
274* for 6th	G. S. Sobers and D. A. J. Holford, West Indies v England.	1966
268 for 1st	J. B. Hobbs and H. Sutcliffe, England v South Africa.	1924
260 for 1st	M. A. Taylor and M. J. Slater, Australia v England	1993
257 for 2nd	G. C. Smith and G. Kirsten, South Africa v England	2003

the match – suggested one of the collapses in which they have specialised in recent years. But Gayle had other ideas, and took on Harmison in epic style. He lived dangerously: in one over, he edged Harmison between wicket-keeper and slip and then sliced a difficult chance to Thorpe in the gully. Gayle flashed 13 fours and a six in a thrilling display, but it seemed too good to last – and eventually, after hurtling to 81 out of 102, he inside-edged a yorker into his stumps and was gone.

England's main concerns on the fifth morning were drizzle, which delayed the start by ten minutes, and Lara, who had advanced confidently to 44 before Giles threaded that killer ball through the gate. Chanderpaul, reprieved first ball after gloving Giles to Key at short leg, was an immovable obstacle after that. He collected painful bruises to arm and knee, and ended just three short of emulating Vaughan's twin centuries, having stood unbeaten for ten hours 14 minutes in the match. But regular wickets at the other end ushered England to their seventh win in their last nine Tests against the once-mighty West Indies, and their third in a row against them at Lord's. The most memorable moment was the dismissal of Best, who had been greeted by Flintoff from slip with a cheery "Mind the windows, Tino!" as he prepared to face Giles. Best walked straight into the baited trap: the windows survived, but he did not – stumped for three after an inglorious swipe, which stood all summer as a symbol of West Indian naïveté and folly.

Man of the Match: A. F. Giles.   *Attendance:* 141,967; *receipts* £3,170,752.

Close of play: First day, England 391-2 (Key 167, Vaughan 36); Second day, West Indies 208-4 (Chanderpaul 41, Bravo 30); Third day, England 71-0 (Trescothick 34, Strauss 27); Fourth day, West Indies 114-3 (Lara 11, Chanderpaul 4).

England

M. E. Trescothick c Sarwan b Best	16	– b Collins.	45
A. J. Strauss c Jacobs b Banks	137	– c Sarwan b Collins	35
R. W. T. Key c Lara b Bravo	221	– run out	15
*M. P. Vaughan c Smith b Collins	103	– not out	101
G. P. Thorpe c Jacobs b Bravo	19	– c and b Gayle	38
A. Flintoff b Banks	6	– c Jacobs b Collins.	58
†G. O. Jones c Jacobs b Collins	4		
A. F. Giles c Smith b Collins	5		
M. J. Hoggard not out.	1		
S. P. Jones lbw b Collins.	4		
S. J. Harmison b Bravo.	4		
B 2, l-b 20, w 13, n-b 13	48	B 3, l-b 14, n-b 16	33
	568	(5 wkts dec.)	325

1/29 (1) 2/320 (2) 3/485 (3) 4/527 (5)   568
5/534 (6) 6/541 (7) 7/551 (8)
8/557 (4) 9/563 (10) 10/568 (11)

1/86 (1) 2/104 (2)   (5 wkts dec.) 325
3/117 (3) 4/233 (5)
5/325 (6)

Bowling: *First Innings*—Collins 24–2–113–4; Best 21–1–104–1; Edwards 21–2–96–0; Bravo 24.4–5–74–3; Banks 22–3–131–2; Sarwan 9–0–28–0. *Second Innings*—Best 3–1–14–0; Collins 14.4–1–62–3; Banks 26–1–92–0; Edwards 13–0–47–0; Bravo 7–0–28–0; Gayle 9–0–45–1; Sarwan 4–0–20–0.

West Indies

C. H. Gayle lbw b Giles	66	– b Harrison	81
D. S. Smith b Giles	45	– lbw b Giles	6
R. R. Sarwan lbw b Hoggard	1	– lbw b Hoggard	4
*B. C. Lara c G. O. Jones b Giles	11	– b Giles	44
S. Chanderpaul not out	128	– not out	97
D. J. J. Bravo c G. O. Jones b S. P. Jones	44	– c and b Giles	10
†R. D. Jacobs c G. O. Jones b Hoggard	32	– c Thorpe b Hoggard	1
O. A. C. Banks b Flintoff	45	– b Harrison	0
T. L. Best b Flintoff	0	– st G. O. Jones b Giles	3
P. T. Collins b Flintoff	0	– st G. O. Jones b Giles	2
F. H. Edwards b Giles	5	– c G. O. Jones b Flintoff	2
B 20, l-b 11, w 5, n-b 3	39	B 5, l-b 9, n-b 3	17

1/118 (2) 2/119 (1) 3/127 (3) 4/139 (4)　　416
5/264 (6) 6/327 (7) 7/399 (8)
8/399 (9) 9/401 (10) 10/416 (11)

1/24 (2) 2/35 (3) 3/102 (1)　　267
4/172 (4) 5/194 (6) 6/195 (7)
7/200 (8) 8/203 (9)
9/247 (10) 10/267 (11)

Bowling: *First Innings*—Hoggard 28–7–89–2; Harrison 21–6–72–0; S. P. Jones 17–3–70–1; Giles 40.4–5–129–4; Flintoff 10–4–25–3. *Second Innings*—Hoggard 14–2–65–2; Harrison 21–2–78–2; Giles 35–9–81–5; S. P. Jones 8–3–29–0; Flintoff 1.3–1–0–1.

Umpires: D. J. Harper (Australia) and R. E. Koertzen (South Africa).
Third umpire: N. J. Llong. Referee: R. S. Madugalle (Sri Lanka).

ENGLAND v WEST INDIES

Second npower Test

Hugh Chevallier

At Birmingham, July 29, 30, 31, August 1. England won by 256 runs. Toss: England.

Crushing defeat inside four days was further proof of West Indian cricket's descent into a vortex of despondency and failure. An abiding memory of this Test – a vignette that could stand for the series – was Lara, the captain, standing at mid-on and rolling his eyes in weary resignation as another wayward ball vanished to the rope. His face in his hands, mulling on the horror of it all, he steeled himself for the pain of it happening all over again. No consolation for the bowler, no word of advice; just lonely, anguished suffering.

In contrast, England went about their business with a *joie de vivre* that bubbled over into everything they did. Typifying this effervescence was Flintoff. Pounding in with the speedo in the high eighties, sweeping up sharp slip catches and swatting the ball to every corner, he did it all with a cheeky grin. And how Edgbaston loved it. In one act of glorious bravado, he lofted Lawson high into the top tier of the Ryder stand. A powerfully built middle-aged man stood up to take the catch. From a crowd of 20,000, Flintoff had somehow picked out his father, who muffed it: the only false move from a Flintoff in the entire Test. By the Sunday, only ten days after the series began, England had retained the Wisden Trophy.

With only two days' rest, West Indies had had little chance to regroup after Lord's, but they reshuffled their pace attack: Best had hurt his back and would fly home, while Edwards was thought too erratic. In came Lawson for his second Test since remodelling his action, and Collymore, talked up by Lara as providing the necessary discipline. England preferred Anderson's conventional swing to Simon Jones's reverse variety.

Only once, when Fred Trueman ran through Frank Worrell's 1963 tourists, had West Indies lost at Birmingham. Even in 2000, despite the rot seeping into Caribbean cricket, they flattened England by an innings. And Lara, part of that side, had made Edgbaston his home in 1994, his *annus mirabilis*, when he ransacked Durham for an unbeaten 501; Birmingham had happy memories.

He would have been unhappy to lose this toss, though. In the blink of an eye, the England openers had rocketed to 77 on a golden pitch shimmering with runs. Collymore failed to provide the promised control, although Lawson did rein in the scoring, whipping out Strauss in the process. Together with Bravo's ugly-but-effective line way outside off, they prevented England, 313 for five at the close, from disappearing out of sight. Even so, Trescothick had already made his way to an efficient century, the first against the West Indians in an Edgbaston Test since the famous Peter May–Colin Cowdrey stand in 1957.

Next morning, however, Flintoff and Jones broke gloriously, wantonly, loose. It was heady stuff, and it shattered the bowlers' spirits. Jones cut sharply and on-drove crisply, but Flintoff was on fire. It was payback time for all those occasions when Caribbean batsmen had toyed with the England attack as if they were small boys lobbing tennis balls. His innings reached its apogee shortly before its end. Now poor Banks was the

---

TWIN TEST HUNDREDS FOR ENGLAND

A. C. Russell	140 and 111 v South Africa at Durban	1922-23
H. Sutcliffe	176 and 127 v Australia at Melbourne	1924-25
W. R. Hammond	119* and 177 v Australia at Adelaide	1928-29
H. Sutcliffe	104 and 109* v South Africa at The Oval	1929
E. Paynter	117 and 100 v South Africa at Johannesburg	1938-39
D. C. S. Compton	147 and 103* v Australia at Adelaide	1946-47
G. A. Gooch	333 and 123 v India at Lord's	1990
A. J. Stewart	118 and 143 v West Indies at Bridgetown	1993-94
M. P. Vaughan	**103 and 101* v West Indies at Lord's**	**2004**
M. E. Trescothick	**105 and 107 v West Indies at Birmingham**	**2004**

---

one holding the tennis ball: the first delivery zoomed over long-on for six to bring up Flintoff's 150; the second whizzed over the rope at mid-wicket for six more; the third and fourth were dots; the fifth zipped to mid-wicket for another six that took him past his highest first-class score. And he nabbed a single off the last ball to retain the strike. Flintoff lost his wicket moments later but his 167 – an innings of pace, strength, variety and ebullience – was unforgettable: it came from 191 balls and included 17 fours and seven sixes. By then, Jones had long gone, but their 170-run stand for the sixth wicket had wrenched the game England's way. Before the declaration at 566 for nine, Harmison had time for a cameo unbeaten 31, including a deft reverse sweep off Banks and a Flintoffesque 4, 4, 6 off Lawson.

In a flash, Hoggard yanked out the West Indies openers, leaving Sarwan and Lara to pick up the pieces. Spontaneous applause erupted when Lara passed 15, followed by congratulation from Vaughan. The batsman looked perplexed. Word had leaked out he needed 15 to become the fourth player to 10,000 Test runs; as Lara well knew, it was 115. Minutes later, he did become the first to 1,000 Test runs in 2004 – it had taken him ten matches – but no one took it in. On the third morning he and Sarwan, batting resolutely and attractively, guided their stand to 209. England had bowled tidily, yet yearned for a wicket. Cue Flintoff. Lara, eager to stamp his authority, envisaged a rasping square drive. Instead, he slashed to second slip.

Chanderpaul had unbeaten scores of 101, 128 and 97 in his last three Test innings, so when Vaughan dropped a dolly from him, on 21, it might have been pricey.

There goes another... Brian Lara and Ridley Jacobs wince as Andrew Flintoff sends a ball from Omari Banks sailing into the Edgbaston crowd.

Picture by Patrick Eagar

It was not. Sarwan's wicket, the fourth to fall, at 297, hoisted the white flag. Giles, on his home ground and revelling in new-found self-belief, scooped up Chanderpaul and three others as seven wickets cascaded for 39 – six for just 13. The West Indies tailspin ended at 336.

England had found enough turn and indifferent bounce for them to forgo the follow-on. Their second innings, with one exception, was unconvincing, but to be fair, the convincing had come in their first. Trescothick was the bright spot; he reached his fifty before anyone else made double figures, and his thwacks to leg and occasional rocket through the covers maintained England's domination. He was eventually run out, having crafted his second canny hundred of the game. (Such feats seldom happened to England batsmen; now they happened twice in a week.) To be fair to West Indies, too, Lawson and Gayle bowled 27 sensible overs on the fourth morning.

Set 479 – a single more than at Lord's – with five sessions remaining, West Indies had nowhere to hide. Gayle briefly looked as if he would earn cricketing immortality by snatching five wickets, hitting a century and carrying his bat – not just in the same Test, but on the same day – before he was the fifth victim of the resurgent Giles, who took nine wickets for the second match running. Other than that, there was little fight left, and the vultures were already wheeling: Lara spent much of the post-match interviews fending off questions about resignation. Resigned? Yes. Resigning? Not yet.

Man of the Match: A. Flintoff.   *Attendance*: 66,875; *receipts* £1,622,398.
Close of play: First day, England 313-5 (Flintoff 42, Jones 27); Second day, West Indies 184-2 (Sarwan 87, Lara 74); Third day, England 148-3 (Trescothick 88, Thorpe 28).

England

M. E. Trescothick c Lara b Bravo	105	– run out	107
A. J. Strauss c Jacobs b Lawson	24	– c Jacobs b Lawson	5
R. W. T. Key c Lara b Collins	29	– c Gayle b Lawson	4
*M. P. Vaughan c and b Bravo	12	– c Gayle b Lawson	3
G. P. Thorpe c Jacobs b Collymore	61	– st Jacobs b Gayle	54
A. Flintoff lbw b Bravo	167	– c Bravo b Gayle	20
†G. O. Jones c Jacobs b Collymore	74	– b Lawson	4
A. F. Giles c Chanderpaul b Bravo	24	– b Gayle	15
M. J. Hoggard not out	15	– c Smith b Gayle	6
J. M. Anderson b Banks	2	– (11) not out	8
S. J. Harmison not out	31	– (10) lbw b Gayle	1
L-b 6, w 1, n-b 15	22	B 8, l-b 2, w 5, n-b 6	21

1/77 (2) 2/125 (3) 3/150 (4)   (9 wkts dec.) 566   1/24 (2) 2/37 (3) 3/52 (4)   248
4/210 (1) 5/262 (5) 6/432 (7)   4/184 (1) 5/195 (5) 6/214 (7)
7/478 (8) 8/522 (6) 9/525 (10)   7/226 (6) 8/234 (8)
9/239 (10) 10/248 (9)

Bowling: *First Innings*—Collins 18–1–90–1; Collymore 30–6–126–2; Lawson 23–4–111–1; Bravo 24–6–76–4; Banks 27–3–108–1; Sarwan 12–0–49–0. *Second Innings*—Collins 9–1–29–0; Collymore 9–2–33–0; Lawson 21–2–94–4; Bravo 6–1–28–0; Banks 5–1–20–0; Gayle 15 1–1–4–34–5.

West Indies

C. H. Gayle b Hoggard	7	– c Strauss b Giles	82
D. S. Smith c Giles b Hoggard	4	– c Trescothick b Hoggard	11
R. R. Sarwan b Flintoff	139	– c Strauss b Giles	14
*B. C. Lara c Thorpe b Flintoff	95	– c Flintoff b Giles	13
S. Chanderpaul c Key b Giles	45	– lbw b Giles	43
D. J. J. Bravo b Giles	13	– b Giles	0
†R. D. Jacobs c Trescothick b Hoggard	0	– c Anderson b Hoggard	0
O. A. C. Banks c Jones b Harmison	4	– not out	25
P. T. Collins c Flintoff b Giles	6	– lbw b Hoggard	0
C. D. Collymore lbw b Giles	2	– b Anderson	10
J. J. C. Lawson not out	0	– b Anderson	2
B 9, l-b 5, w 1, n-b 6	21	B 17, l-b 4, n-b 1	22

1/5 (2) 2/12 (1) 3/221 (4) 4/297 (3)   336   1/15 (2) 2/54 (3) 3/101 (4)   222
5/323 (6) 6/324 (7) 7/324 (5)   4/172 (5) 5/172 (6) 6/177 (1)
8/334 (9) 9/336 (8) 10/336 (10)   7/177 (7) 8/182 (9)
9/210 (10) 10/222 (11)

Bowling: *First Innings*—Hoggard 18–0–89–3; Harmison 14 1–64–1; Anderson 11–3–37–0; Giles 30.3–7–65–4; Flintoff 15–1–52–2; Vaughan 1–0–8–0; Trescothick 2–0–7–0. *Second Innings*—Hoggard 16–5–64–3; Harmison 5–1–29–0; Flintoff 5–1–19–0; Giles 21–9–57–5; Anderson 5.3–1–23–2; Vaughan 3–0–9–0.

Umpires: D. B. Hair (Australia) and S. J. A. Taufel (Australia).
Third umpire: J. W. Lloyds.   Referee: R. S. Madugalle (Sri Lanka).

DERBYSHIRE v WEST INDIANS

At Derby, August 5, 6, 7. West Indians won by 315 runs. Toss: West Indians. First-class debut: C. D. Paget.

The West Indians recovered from an alarmingly flippant start to inflict a heavy defeat. They batted with no sense of purpose on the first day: all out inside 41 overs, with 136 of their 223 scored in fours or sixes, and career-best figures for Dumelow. The umpires also had a word about frequent dissent, after which the bowling and fielding were equally aimless. The mood changed on the second day, as Edwards displayed genuine pace. Derbyshire's last six wickets fell for 29, after which Joseph and Baugh, who reached 150 before the declaration, made their cases for selection at Old Trafford. Joseph was bowled by Chris Paget, an off-spinner with two years remaining at Repton School. At 16 years and 277 days, he was the second-youngest player to appear for Derbyshire, after Fred Swarbrook (16 years 196 days) in 1967. Edwards took his match figures to ten for 83 when he dismissed Sutton, the only man to resist long in Derbyshire's feeble response.

Close of play: First day, Derbyshire 102-2 (Stubbings 37, Selwood 5); Second day, West Indians 293-6 (Baugh 110, Jacobs 25).

West Indians

C. H. Gayle b Havell	42	
S. C. Joseph c Sutton b Havell	23	– b Paget 77
D. S. Smith c Gunter b Dumelow	31	– (1) run out 31
D. J. J. Bravo c Sutton b Walker	3	– (3) b Paget 5
D. R. Smith c Gunter b Dumelow	55	– (4) c Walker b Paget 0
R. D. Jacobs c Gait b Dumelow	33	– (8) not out 59
*R. R. Sarwan lbw b Dumelow	6	– c Hassan Adnan b Dumelow 15
O. A. C. Banks c Sutton b Dumelow	6	– (6) c Hassan Adnan b Dumelow . . 12
†C. S. Baugh lbw b Gunter	5	– (5) not out 150
D. Mohammed c Sutton b Gunter	4	
F. H. Edwards not out	5	
L-b 7, w 1, n-b 2	10	B 5, l-b 6, w 2, n-b 6 19

1/52 (1) 2/85 (2) 3/103 (4) 4/109 (3)   **223**   1/41 (1) 2/80 (3)   (6 wkts dec.) **368**
5/159 (6) 6/182 (7) 7/209 (5)   3/82 (4) 4/178 (2)
8/210 (8) 9/214 (9) 10/223 (10)   5/199 (6) 6/217 (7)

Bowling: *First Innings*—Havell 10–1–47–2; Walker 6–0–44–1; Gunter 9.1–0–68–2; Dumelow 12–3–51–5; Paget 3–1–6–0. *Second Innings*—Havell 16–2–56–0; Walker 8–1–49–0; Gunter 12–1–58–0; Paget 17–1–63–3; Dumelow 28–5–131–2.

Derbyshire

A. I. Gait lbw b D. R. Smith	13	– lbw b Edwards 2
S. D. Stubbings c Sarwan b Edwards	56	– run out 5
Hassan Adnan c Baugh b Gayle	31	– lbw b Edwards 6
S. A. Selwood c Baugh b Edwards	5	– run out 0
J. D. C. Bryant b Edwards	10	– c Baugh b Edwards 2
*†L. D. Sutton c Baugh b Mohammed	36	– lbw b Edwards 27
N. R. C. Dumelow c Mohammed b Edwards	2	– lbw b D. R. Smith 12
N. E. L. Gunter b Edwards	2	– st Baugh b Mohammed 10
N. G. E. Walker st Baugh b Mohammed	7	– c Joseph b Mohammed 13
P. M. R. Havell b Mohammed	1	– b Edwards 1
C. D. Paget not out	0	– not out 0
B 4, l-b 5, w 7, n-b 9	25	B 4, l-b 4, n-b 2 10

1/26 (1) 2/80 (3) 3/104 (4) 4/131 (5)   **188**   1/7 (2) 2/8 (1) 3/13 (3)   **88**
5/159 (2) 6/172 (7) 7/178 (6)   4/15 (4) 5/16 (5) 6/42 (7)
8/186 (9) 9/188 (10) 10/188 (8)   7/69 (8) 8/85 (9)
    9/87 (10) 10/88 (6)

Bowling: *First Innings*—Edwards 16.2–1–61–5; D. R. Smith 11–2–23–1; Joseph 5–1–15–0; Gayle 9–4–14–1; Banks 12–6–19–0; Mohammed 17–6–47–3. *Second Innings*—Edwards 8.3–2–22–5; D. R. Smith 9–4–16–1; Gayle 7–1–20–0; Mohammed 11–2–22–2.

Umpires: R. A. Kettleborough and N. A. Mallender.

"This gave him a share of a strange world record..."
Bangladeshis in West Indies, page 1233.

ENGLAND v WEST INDIES

Third npower Test

PAUL COUPAR

At Manchester, August 12, 13, 14, 15, 16. England won by seven wickets. Toss: West Indies. Test debut: S. C. Joseph.

Beneath one of the few circles of blue in otherwise ugly skies, England won their sixth successive Test, the winning run coming with 27 overs to go, shortly before the long-forecast rain finally returned. They were piloted home by Key, continuing to enjoy his comeback as Butcher was kept out by a string of injuries. Key's success was the latest example of how things were falling right for England, where once they fell apart. Even the fickle and ill-tempered Manchester weather god smiled at the crucial moment.

Besides the weather, which washed away the second day, England had to overcome a stiffened West Indies. By the fourth evening, Lara's side had built a strong position – 153 ahead with nine wickets left – only for it to crumble beneath their feet. That left England chasing 231, tricky by historical standards, a breeze in their golden summer. Victory bolstered their new reputation for grit when things got tough: of the last eight Tests where they were either behind on first innings, or less than 30 ahead, they had won four and lost just one.

But the match provided a glimmer for West Indies – all the brighter because Lara, so often their crutch, made just seven runs. A battling performance confounded commentators predicting disaster. They arrived dispirited, 2–0 down, and their pre-match practice was condemned by Jonathan Agnew as the worst he had seen in 13 years as BBC cricket correspondent. They made four changes from Edgbaston: Antiguan opener Sylvester Joseph got his debut, replacing out-of-form Devon Smith; Baugh and Edwards came in for the injured Jacobs and Lawson; and Mohammed's wrist-spin was preferred to Banks's off-breaks. England were unchanged, and Flintoff beamed that he had not known a happier dressing-room.

> The batsman never arrived... Cynics suspected a ploy

But Lara was also able to smile a little when he won an important toss. In the previous Tests, England racked up 560-plus batting first: now West Indies, having handed over the opportunity at Lord's, had another chance to bat England out of the game on a dry pitch that was expected to deteriorate. In the end, they made it to lunch on the third day – helped by the rain – and totalled 395. Five batsmen got in but none played a telling innings, though Chanderpaul, with his open stance and off-side technique, and Bravo, classically correct, threatened to do it. They stood firm to add 157 on a surface where the occasional ball was already starting to leap or scuttle. But both edged behind in successive overs from Hoggard, leaving West Indies 275 for six when bad light stopped play. The wet second day was gloomy for a sell-out crowd and, despite the sunshine, much of the third was gloomy for England. They bowled too short, too often, and the ball flew off edge and middle as the tail added 120. Lunch was taken at the fall of the ninth wicket.

After the break, England's fielders emerged, ready to wrap up the innings. But the batsmen never arrived; Lara appeared at the pavilion door, waving to signify that he had declared. Word was that Collins – who had retired after being hit on the chin by a Flintoff bumper but indicated that he would resume – changed his mind at the last minute. Cynics suspected a ploy to stop the openers using the lunch break to psych up. Indeed, Trescothick fell second ball and, at 40 for three, England were in trouble.

That gave West Indies what Fletcher later called a "window of opportunity"; stronger opponents might have climbed through and stolen the game. As it was, England, and Thorpe in particular, banged it shut. He and Strauss, his equal in technique and temperament, calmly added 177, though Bravo removed Strauss and Flintoff before the close. Thorpe had already had a huge let-off: on 58, he lobbed a catch to Sarwan at point, who handled it like soap in a bath.

The match pivoted round that miss. Thorpe reached 114, despite a 93.7mph Edwards thunderbolt which broke his hand on 91. His innings was exactly what England needed. The pitch was grudging, the bowling straight – and in the case of the slingy Edwards terrifying. But somehow they weathered his brutal six-over morning spell, and Trescothick remained Edwards's only victim; some of his missing luck lighted on

---

ENGLAND'S TEST GROUNDS IN ORDER OF SOGGINESS

Most complete days of Test cricket lost at English grounds

	Complete days lost	Tests	= one day lost every x Tests
Manchester (1884–2004)	29	71	2.45
Nottingham (1899–2004)	10	51	5.10
Leeds (1899–2004)	12	65	5.42
Lord's (1884–2004)	19	108	5.68
The Oval (1880–2004)	14	87	6.21
Birmingham (1902–2004)	5	40	8.00

Note: Figures include two Manchester Ashes Tests (1890 and 1938) where not a ball was bowled. Neither Sheffield, Bramall Lane (one Test, 1902) nor Chester-le-Street (one Test, 2003) has lost a full day's play.

Research: Philip Bailey

Bravo, who took six for 55 with his medium-fast swingers. The night-watchman, Hoggard, supported Thorpe for 17 of the 22 overs bowled before lunch, a rate that later cost the West Indians 20% of their fee and Lara 40%. The innings included 18 wides, a Test record.

West Indies were still 65 ahead on first innings, and on the face of it were favourites. But no one really believed that, least of all the players. One false move triggered an avalanche of despairing batsmen, as the score plunged from 88 for one to 161 for nine. The collapse began with a suicidal drive from Gayle and a sprawling catch at long-on by Hoggard. Roared on by the capacity crowd, England's bowlers swarmed through the opening. Immediately, Vaughan brought back Flintoff. Lara hit the first ball of his spell for four, to become the fourth man to 10,000 Test runs, in his 111th Test and 195th innings, fewer than the other three: Sunil Gavaskar, Allan Border and Steve Waugh. But the third was a nasty lifter which he fended to slip: Flintoff had now dismissed him three times in 20 balls. After the colossus fell, the rest tumbled in a riot of poor shots. Harmison's four wickets made him the first Test bowler to take 50 in 2004.

England now had to score 231, a record to win in the fourth innings of an Old Trafford Test, while dodging the predicted showers. Their luck held. Key, all puffed-chest defiance in an unbeaten 93, led them home as the dark clouds loomed, bursting only during the lunch break. He was helped by curiously defensive fields, by Mohammed bowling just six overs of wrist-spin on a crumbling surface, and by his pal Flintoff, who was sensibly restrained in making a seventh fifty in successive Tests. Vaughan had already said Flintoff was currently the world's best player. It was a long time since England could have made such a claim, and the match ended with another unaccustomed statement. After their years battling with inadequate talent and despondency, coach Duncan Fletcher warned England they faced a new enemy – complacency.

Man of the Match: G. P. Thorpe.   *Attendance:* 62,624; *receipts* £1,189,124.

Close of play: First day, West Indies 275-6 (Baugh 9, Mohammed 0); Second day, No play; Third day, England 233-5 (Thorpe 89, Hoggard 3); Fourth day, West Indies 161-9 (Collymore 2, Edwards 0).

West Indies

C. H. Gayle c Strauss b Hoggard	5	– c Hoggard b Giles	42
S. C. Joseph c Thorpe b Harmison	45	– c Vaughan b Flintoff	15
R. R. Sarwan b Flintoff	40	– c Trescothick b Harmison	60
*B. C. Lara b Flintoff	0	– c Strauss b Flintoff	7
S. Chanderpaul c Jones b Hoggard	76	– c Vaughan b Flintoff	2
D. J. J. Bravo c Jones b Hoggard	77	– c Flintoff b Giles	6
†C. S. Baugh c Vaughan b Anderson	68	– c sub (A. N. Bressington) b Harmison	3
D. Mohammed c Strauss b Flintoff	23	– c Key b Giles	9
P. T. Collins not out	19	– b Harmison	8
C. D. Collymore b Hoggard	5	– not out	5
F. H. Edwards not out	4	– c Flintoff b Harmison	0
B 9, l-b 14, w 6, n-b 4	33	B 2, l-b 4, w 1, n-b 1	8

1/10 (1) 2/85 (3) 3/97 (4) (9 wkts dec.) 395	1/41 (2) 2/88 (1) 3/95 (4) 165
4/108 (2) 5/265 (6) 6/267 (5)	4/99 (5) 5/110 (6) 6/121 (7)
7/308 (8) 8/383 (10) 9/395 (7)	7/146 (8) 8/152 (3)
	9/161 (9) 10/165 (11)

In the first innings Collins retired hurt at 358.

Bowling. *First Innings*—Hoggard 22–3–83–4; Harmison 26–5–94–1; Flintoff 20–5–79–3; Anderson 11.3–1–49–1; Giles 15–0–67–0. *Second Innings*—Hoggard 7–0–21–0; Harmison 13.4–3–44–4; Flintoff 12–1–26–3; Giles 22–6–46–3; Anderson 5–1–22–0.

England

M. E. Trescothick c Sarwan b Edwards	0	– b Collymore	12
A. J. Strauss b Bravo	90	– c Chanderpaul b Collins	12
R. W. T. Key b Collymore	6	– not out	93
*M. P. Vaughan b Bravo	12	– c Lara b Gayle	33
G. P. Thorpe c Lara b Bravo	114		
A. Flintoff lbw b Bravo	7	– (5) not out	57
M. J. Hoggard c Sarwan b Collymore	23		
†G. O. Jones b Bravo	12		
A. F. Giles c and b Bravo	10		
S. J. Harmison lbw b Collins	8		
J. M. Anderson not out	1		
B 10, l-b 10, w 18, n-b 9	47	B 7, l-b 3, n-b 14	24

1/0 (1) 2/13 (3) 3/40 (4) 4/217 (2) 330	1/15 (1) 2/27 (2) (3 wkts) 231
5/227 (6) 6/283 (7) 7/310 (5)	3/111 (4)
8/321 (8) 9/322 (9) 10/330 (10)	

Bowling: *First Innings*—Edwards 18–2–68–1; Collymore 26–6–66–2; Bravo 26–6–55–6; Joseph 2–0–8–0; Gayle 4–1–7–0; Mohammed 26–2–77–0; Collins 10.2–1–29–1. *Second Innings*—Edwards 11–0–51–0; Collymore 16–7–33–1; Collins 8–2–24–1; Bravo 12–3–41–0; Mohammed 6–0–25–0; Gayle 8.4–0–32–1; Sarwan 4–0–15–0.

Umpires: Aleem Dar (Pakistan) and S. J. A. Taufel (Australia).
Third umpire: M. R. Benson.   Referee: R. S. Madugalle (Sri Lanka).

ENGLAND v WEST INDIES

Fourth npower Test

FAZEER MOHAMMED

At The Oval, August 19, 20, 21. England won by ten wickets. Toss: England. Test debut: I. R. Bell.

Four years after reclaiming the Wisden Trophy on the same ground, England administered a three-day whipping of West Indies that sealed a clean sweep of the series and emphasised the staggeringly swift decline of the Caribbean side from supremely professional invincibles to a temperamental, undisciplined rabble.

If the few hundred West Indian fans at The Oval took solace from avoiding defeat by an innings – just – they were clutching at straws, an act that had become Lara's preoccupation in his second term as captain. Yet there seemed little chance of any heroics saving West Indies. Vaughan's men were in no mood to let slip the opportunity to claim their own piece of history: a perfect record through the seven-Test summer. Seven consecutive wins equalled England's best-ever runs, from March 1885 to February 1888 and June 1928 to February 1929. It also extended their overall run to ten wins in 11 Tests, and consolidated a rise to second in the official rankings behind you-know-who.

A ragtag bunch masquerading as Test cricketers

Everything about this brief duel emphasised the gap in professional ethos between the teams. England's all-round strength, and strength in depth, allowed them to surge ahead on the few occasions when West Indies threatened parity; the tourists could offer only sparks of individual brilliance, which magnified the already glaring shortcomings in captaincy and team management.

Making the most of the first pitch of the series that offered reasonable bounce, Harmison took nine wickets. That included a devastating first-innings six for 46 which forced West Indies to follow on, 318 behind, late on the second day. Harmison had already played his part with the bat, helping England to reach 470 by smashing three sixes in a riotous career-best 36 not out.

Feeding off the confidence in the England camp, the 22-year-old Warwickshire batsman Ian Bell marked his Test debut (standing in for the injured Thorpe) with 70 runs, withstanding an early assault from Edwards. He added 146 with Vaughan, after England were listing at 64 for three early on the first afternoon. Lawson (who had replaced Collins), Edwards and the increasingly impressive Bravo had picked up one each. But with Collymore, whose ten overs in the morning cost just ten runs, not used in the second session, newcomer and captain were able to navigate to relatively calm waters before Lawson returned to end Bell's quest for a hundred, via a catch to the keeper.

Vaughan's confident 66 was terminated by a catch from Lara at first slip off Bravo, but Flintoff passed fifty for the eighth time in eight Tests and joined in another productive partnership with Jones. The ground was close to capacity before the start of the second day, with thousands looking forward to more spectacular strokeplay from the talismanic Flintoff. They were disappointed; in the first four overs, Jones edged to third slip to give Collymore a deserved wicket, and Flintoff's miscued pull off Edwards was caught by Lawson, tumbling as he ran back at mid-on.

With the danger man gone for 72 and England 321 for seven, West Indies proceeded to ignore the lessons of that early period of disciplined cricket. They put down three chances – all off Lawson – and reverted to the depressingly familiar role of a ragtag bunch masquerading as Test cricketers. Giles blazed his way to 52 while Hoggard produced another wholehearted effort to reach his best Test score, and Harmison rubbed

More than a handful: after a quiet series, Steve Harmison roared back to life at The Oval.

Picture by Patrick Eagar

salt in the wounds, adding 60 for the last wicket with Anderson. The innings finished as only the tenth in Test history in which all 11 batsmen got into double figures.

Teamwork like that could only be dreamed of by Lara. His cavalier 79, while all fell around him, betrayed his desperation more than it affirmed his faith. Crashing 14 fours in 93 balls, Lara gave glimpses of his masterful best, but such was his internal turmoil that he seemed unaware there was still one batsman to come when he was eighth out, to a top-edged hook off Harmison. His confusion probably owed something to the absence of Dwayne Smith, recalled to strengthen the batting but visiting a nearby hospital with a side injury. The capitulation Lara had witnessed at the other end was bewildering enough anyway. The entire innings lasted less than 37 overs.

All eight wickets that fell to bowlers went via catches behind square, the best being Key's to snare Chanderpaul's hook off Hoggard. A farcical run-out ended the innings, and Vaughan enforced the follow-on in the hope of completing the demolition quickly on the third day. Victory and the whitewash were indeed celebrated on a sunny Saturday, but not without some hard work. Having hammered all six deliveries of Hoggard's second over for fours – a unique occurrence in Tests – Gayle sped past fifty for the fourth time in the series before Joseph became Harmison's 100th Test victim and Sarwan the 101st, slashing to gully where Bell held a brilliant diving catch.

Any chance of West Indies at least gaining a measure of respect hinged on Gayle and Lara on the third morning. But Lara's demise for 15, caught by Trescothick at first slip off Anderson, signalled the beginning of the end. His prolonged acknowledgment of the crowd's ovation indicated that he believed this was his last Test in England,

---

DOUBLES ALL ROUND

Eleven batsmen reaching double figures in a Test innings

Lowest score

11	England (475) v Australia at Melbourne	1894-95
10	South Africa (385) v England at Johannesburg	1905-06
11	England (636) v Australia at Sydney	1928-29
10*	South Africa (358) v Australia at Melbourne	1931-32
11	Australia (575-8 dec.†) v India at Melbourne.................	1947-48
11	India (397) v Pakistan at Calcutta	1952-53
12	India (359) v New Zealand at Dunedin........................	1967-68
10*	India (524-9 dec.) v New Zealand at Kanpur..................	1976-77
10*	Australia (471) v Sri Lanka at Colombo (SSC)	1992-93
10	**England (470) v West Indies at The Oval**	**2004**

† *One man retired hurt.*

Research: M. L. Fernando

---

although his future as captain was also very much in doubt. This was his 23rd defeat in 40 Tests in charge, beating Allan Border's record of 22 losses; but Border led in 93 matches.

Gayle collected his sixth Test century, consecutive boundaries off Flintoff taking him to three figures from just 80 balls with 17 fours and a stunning six off Anderson over long-on. After one more four, however, the Lancashire pair had the last laugh: Anderson found the edge of Gayle's bat for Flintoff to take a sharp but nonchalant-looking catch at second slip. That meant West Indies were 155 for four, still 163 behind, and a swift end was expected. But Bravo survived a fearful blow on the helmet from Harmison to compile a half-century, while Chanderpaul was as resolute as ever.

Both were victims of dubious decisions that further dampened the mood of West Indian loyalists. They found their voices, briefly, when a four by Lawson meant England had to bat again. In the next over, Anderson yorked Edwards to finish with four wickets; Trescothick formalised another emphatic victory, only the fourth three-day finish at The Oval in 54 years since five-day cricket became the norm in 1950. The celebrations got going in earnest, while West Indies were left to pick up the pieces from another catastrophic campaign.

Man of the Match: S. J. Harmison.   *Attendance:* 62,468; *receipts* £1,922,124.

Men of the Series: England – A. Flintoff; West Indies – S. Chanderpaul.

Close of play: First day, England 313-5 (Flintoff 72, Jones 22); Second day, West Indies 84-2 (Gayle 59, Lara 1).

England

M. E. Trescothick c Sarwan b Edwards	30	– not out	4
A. J. Strauss c Edwards b Lawson	14	– not out	0
R. W. T. Key c Baugh b Bravo	10		
*M. P. Vaughan c Lara b Bravo	66		
I. R. Bell c Baugh b Lawson	70		
A. Flintoff c Lawson b Edwards	72		
†G. O. Jones c Sarwan b Collymore	22		
A. F. Giles c Lara b Bravo	52		
M. J. Hoggard c Joseph b Lawson	38		
S. J. Harmison not out	36		
J. M. Anderson b Gayle	12		
B 5, l-b 21, w 5, n-b 17	48		
	470	(no wkt)	**4**

1/51 (2) 2/64 (1) 3/64 (3) 4/210 (5)
5/236 (4) 6/313 (7) 7/321 (6)
8/408 (8) 9/410 (9) 10/470 (11)

Bowling: *First Innings*—Edwards 19–4–64–2; Collymore 23–8–58–1; Lawson 24–4–115–3; Bravo 29–4–117–3; Smith 14–3–50–0; Gayle 7.2–2–18–1; Sarwan 7–0–22–0. *Second Innings*—Edwards 0.3–0–4–0.

West Indies

C. H. Gayle c Jones b Harmison	12	– c Flintoff b Anderson	105
S. C. Joseph c Giles b Harmison	9	– c Jones b Harmison	16
R. R. Sarwan c Strauss b Flintoff	2	– c Bell b Harmison	7
*B. C. Lara c Bell b Harmison	79	– c Trescothick b Anderson	15
S. Chanderpaul c Key b Hoggard	14	– (6) c Jones b Giles	32
D. J. J. Bravo c Jones b Harmison	16	– (5) lbw b Hoggard	54
†C. S. Baugh c Strauss b Harmison	6	– (8) c Jones b Harmison	34
C. D. Collymore c Trescothick b Harmison	4	– (9) c Jones b Anderson	7
F. H. Edwards run out	0	– (10) b Anderson	2
J. J. C. Lawson not out	3	– (11) not out	4
D. R. Smith absent hurt		– (7) c Anderson b Flintoff	28
L-b 7	7	B 1, l-b 12, n-b 1	14
	152		**318**

1/19 (1) 2/22 (2) 3/26 (3)   1/73 (2) 2/81 (3) 3/126 (4)
4/54 (5) 5/101 (6) 6/118 (7)   4/155 (1) 5/237 (5) 6/265 (6)
7/136 (8) 8/149 (4) 9/152 (9)   7/285 (7) 8/312 (9)
                      9/314 (8) 10/318 (10)

Bowling: *First Innings*—Hoggard 9–2–31–1; Harmison 13–1–46–6; Flintoff 8–1–32–1; Anderson 6.5–0–36–0. *Second Innings*—Hoggard 12–5–50–1; Harmison 18–1–75–3; Giles 22–5–64–1; Flintoff 17–3–64–1; Anderson 15.2–2–52–4.

Umpires: D. B. Hair (Australia) and R. E. Koertzen (South Africa).
Third umpire: M. R. Benson.   Referee: R. S. Madugalle (Sri Lanka).

CEAT CRICKETER OF THE YEAR

Brian Lara was named CEAT International Cricketer of the Year for 2003-04 for his performances in Tests and limited-overs internationals in the 12 months to April 30, 2004. Lara was also CEAT's inaugural winner in 1995-96; since then, the award has gone to Venkatesh Prasad (India), Sanath Jayasuriya (Sri Lanka), Jacques Kallis (South Africa), Sourav Ganguly (India), Muttiah Muralitharan (Sri Lanka), who won two years running, and Ricky Ponting (Australia). Lara also won the awards for CEAT Batsman and Fielder of the Year; Muralitharan was named Bowler of the Year. Australia retained the team title for the third successive year.

THE NATWEST SERIES, 2004

Richard Hobson

Flawed selection and flawed batting meant that England failed to qualify for their own final for the second time since the NatWest Series began in 2000. It was a dismal effort by the hosts and, despite the clear supremacy of New Zealand, who completed only their third tournament win, a poor competition all round. Three of the nine group games were washed out and the remaining six were won by the side batting second. Only a wonderful match between England and West Indies at Lord's saved the event from being a total dud.

That contest was illuminated by a blistering hundred from Andrew Flintoff, which underlined how much England had come to rely on him. During his absence they lost horribly to both West Indies and New Zealand inside three days, when they were dismissed for a combined total of 248 runs. Initially ruled out of the series because of a bone spur on his left ankle, Flintoff was hastily recalled as a batsman only, with England denying that his early return would compromise a full recovery.

A world-class all-rounder balances a side, and the selectors were unable to conjure a plausible team even when they had half of him. Their attempts – a combination of Anthony McGrath, Ian Blackwell and Rikki Clarke – created more holes than they filled. The spare batsman, Robert Key, was a top-three rather than a middle-order player, so the experiment of using Geraint Jones at No. 3 was abandoned after two innings to accommodate him. This brought further criticism: if the wicket-keeper was to bat No. 7, then why ditch Chris Read after his success in the Caribbean two months earlier? The construction of the squad lacked foresight.

> The selectors
> were unable
> to conjure a
> plausible team

Problems also existed at the top of the order. A game did not pass without the captain, Michael Vaughan, being asked whether he intended to continue as an opener. He fell to a series of shots that were either ill-judged or badly executed, and his highest score in five innings was 14. Meanwhile, Marcus Trescothick, England's best one-day batsman, passed that only once. Flintoff notwithstanding, the biggest success was Steve Harmison, whose emergence in the shorter game astonished those who recalled his wayward bowling on the 2002-03 Ashes tour.

England coach Duncan Fletcher pointed once again, with some validity, to inexperience. It could not be coincidence that New Zealand included six players with 100 or more one-day appearances, and England only one: Darren Gough. During the tournament, Chris Gayle, the top run-scorer with 276, became the fourth member of the West Indies squad to reach that landmark. However, there were also good contributions from players such as Andrew

Strauss, Hamish Marshall and Dwayne Bravo (the leading wicket-taker with ten), who were in the early stages of their international careers.

New Zealand entered the tournament with heavy one-day series victories against Pakistan and South Africa to their credit. By the end, they had won 13 of their last 15 completed one-day matches. The top three of Stephen Fleming, Nathan Astle and Marshall scored 614 runs between them, and Jacob Oram, after a disappointing Test series, proved a consistent threat with the new ball. Their running between the wickets and fielding were rarely less than exemplary, not least in the final.

On that occasion, West Indies were made to look shoddy. Overall, though, Brian Lara could draw satisfaction at reaching a showpiece early in the tour, in what were alien conditions to a number of his squad. Like England, West Indies were forced to alter their batting order as Shivnarine Chanderpaul and Dwayne Smith struggled to counter early movement and bounce. But Ramnaresh Sarwan confirmed his reputation as one of the best middle-order batsmen of his type in the world, and a young bowling attack showed considerable promise in between occasional bouts of waywardness.

Note: Matches in this section were not first-class. Figures in brackets are balls received.

ENGLAND v NEW ZEALAND

At Manchester, June 24 (day/night). No result (abandoned). England 3 pts, New Zealand 3 pts.

The opening game of the series was due to clash with a much-hyped European Championship football quarter-final between England and Portugal. But as it happened, high winds and squally showers through the afternoon left little appetite for cricket, and the game was finally abandoned shortly after 6 p.m. – well before the kick-off.

NEW ZEALAND v WEST INDIES

At Birmingham, June 26. No result (D/L method). New Zealand 3 pts, West Indies 3 pts. Toss: New Zealand.

Rain proved a more potent opponent than the West Indian attack: New Zealand needed 43 runs from 7.2 overs, with eight wickets in hand, when a final downpour thwarted their push for victory. The game began as a 35-over contest at 2.25 p.m., but was interrupted after ten overs of West Indies' innings. Lara and Sarwan then added 56 in 29 balls, but New Zealand's adjusted target of 140 in 21 overs stood within reach against undisciplined bowling.

Attendance: 10,225; *receipts* £126,533.

West Indies

C. H. Gayle c McCullum b Oram	30	(49)
S. Chanderpaul lbw b Styris	14	(42)
D. R. Smith c McCullum b Styris	1	(3)
R. R. Sarwan not out	18	(9)
*B. C. Lara hit wkt b Cairns	36	(22)
R. L. Powell not out	1	(2)
L-b 10, w 11, n-b 1	22	

1/56 (2) (4 wkts, 21 overs) 122
2/59 (3)
3/59 (1) 4/115 (5) 10 overs: 39-0

D. J. J. Bravo, †R. D. Jacobs, I. D. R. Bradshaw, R. Rampaul and J. J. C. Lawson did not bat.

Bowling: Tuffey 5–1–10–0; Franklin 5–1–25–0; Cairns 4–0–18–1; Vettori 1–0–5–0; Oram 4–1–42–1; Styris 2–0–12–2.

New Zealand

*S. P. Fleming c Powell b Lawson	12	(10)	
N. J. Astle c Gayle b Lawson	13	(22)	
H. J. H. Marshall not out	24	(27)	
S. B. Styris not out	26	(26)	
L-b 5, w 14, n-b 3	22		

1/20 (1)   (2 wkts, 13.4 overs) 97
2/50 (2)   6 overs: 47-1

C. D. McMillan, J. D. P. Oram, C. L. Cairns, †B. B. McCullum, D. L. Vettori, D. R. Tuffey and J. E. C. Franklin did not bat.

Bowling: Rampaul 1.4–0–20–0; Bradshaw 4–0–19–0; Lawson 3–0–18–2; Bravo 2–0–13–0; Smith 2–0–15–0; Gayle 1–0–7–0.

Umpires: R. E. Koertzen (South Africa) and J. W. Lloyds.
Third umpire: N. J. Llong.   Referee: G. R. Viswanath (India).

ENGLAND v WEST INDIES

At Nottingham, June 27. West Indies won by seven wickets. West Indies 6 pts. Toss: West Indies. One-day international debut: G. O. Jones.

England collapsed to their lowest total in 15 one-day internationals at Trent Bridge, against an attack boasting just 52 appearances between them before this game. While conditions were hardly ideal for batting, they should not have been unfamiliar to a home side raised on spring-green seaming tracks. After both openers went inside the first three overs, the middle order failed to build on a stand of 82 in 15 overs between Jones and Strauss. Bravo and Rampaul jagged the ball around at medium-pace and profited from errors. A total of around 200 might have been enough on this pitch; instead, with most guns blazing, England were dismissed with nearly 12 overs left, their last eight falling for 63. Their early fielding matched their batting: Gayle and Chanderpaul were both reprieved in the slips against the new ball. Harmison bowled fiercly, but West Indies could afford to see him out of the attack and pick off runs against the others.

Man of the Match: D. J. J. Bravo.   *Attendance:* 15,358; *receipts* £454,357.

England

M. E. Trescothick c Lara b Bradshaw	0	(4)	
*M. P. Vaughan c Sarwan b Bradshaw	1	(6)	
†G. O. Jones b Rampaul	35	(45)	
A. J. Strauss c Jacobs b Bravo	43	(63)	
P. D. Collingwood c Jacobs b Rampaul	5	(13)	
A. McGrath c Gayle b Bravo	9	(16)	
I. D. Blackwell c Chanderpaul b Bravo	4	(7)	
R. Clarke lbw b Smith	11	(31)	
D. Gough b Lawson	13	(41)	
S. J. Harmison b Lawson	2	(4)	
J. M. Anderson not out	2	(5)	
B 4, l-b 5, w 8, n-b 5	22		

1/0 (1) 2/2 (2)   (38.2 overs) 147
3/84 (3) 4/102 (5)
5/104 (4) 6/115 (7)
7/118 (6) 8/139 (9)
9/145 (10) 10/147 (8)   15 overs: 78-2

Bowling: Bradshaw 10–3–32–2; Lawson 9–1–36–2; Bravo 10–2–26–3; Rampaul 6–0–34–2; Smith 3.2–1–10–1.

On the rampage: Ravi Rampaul removes Paul Collingwood for five, and England slide towards heavy defeat at Nottingham.

Picture by Graham Morris

West Indies

C. H. Gayle not out	60	(90)
S. Chanderpaul b McGrath	20	(54)
D. R. Smith c Trescothick b Anderson .	6	(9)
R. R. Sarwan c Trescothick b Anderson .	13	(12)
*B. C. Lara not out	32	(29)
L-b 4, w 13	17	

1/62 (2)   (3 wkts, 32.2 overs) 148
2/71 (3) 3/93 (4)   15 overs: 43-0

R. L. Powell, D. J. J. Bravo, †R. D. Jacobs, I. D. R. Bradshaw, R. Rampaul and J. J. C. Lawson did not bat.

Bowling: Gough 9–0–33–0; Harmison 10 2–29–0; Anderson 7.2–0–39–2; Clarke 4–0–30–0; McGrath 2–0–13–1.

Umpires: D. J. Harper (Australia) and M. R. Benson.
Third umpire: N. J. Llong.   Referee: G. R. Viswanath (India).

ENGLAND v NEW ZEALAND

At Chester-le-Street, June 29 (day/night). New Zealand won by seven wickets. New Zealand 6 pts. Toss: New Zealand. One-day international debut: G. J. Franklin.

As England practised under lights on the eve of the game, a thief entered the dressing-room to steal Gough's 17 credit cards and £1,200 from Vaughan's wallet. Things did not improve for England, who hopelessly misjudged their approach for the second time in three days. They batted like millionaires but were made to look like paupers by Franklin, himself having a more lucrative summer than he expected: his original plans were a stint in the leagues and a backpacking trip round Europe. He bowled his full quota of left-arm seam straight through to take a career-best five wickets. The last partnership survived the longest, but the crowd had already lost patience when Giles was seventh out, in only the 20th over. The booing was a little harsh on one of the few who was not culpable for his own demise. England's 101 was their second-lowest one-day total against New Zealand (after 89 at Wellington in 2001-02). They knocked off the runs with almost two-thirds of their overs unused, to leave a floodlit game completed before twilight.

Man of the Match: J. E. C. Franklin.   *Attendance:* 11,832; *receipts* £256,205.

England

M. E. Trescothick b Oram	14	(19)	S. J. Harmison not out	13	(30)	
*M. P. Vaughan b Franklin	12	(18)	J. M. Anderson b Vettori	11	(27)	
†G. O. Jones b Oram	5	(11)				
A. J. Strauss c Oram b Franklin	8	(29)	L-b 4, w 2, n-b 6	12		
P. D. Collingwood c Hopkins b Franklin	2	(7)	1/24 (1) 2/30 (2)	(32.5 overs) 101		
A. McGrath c Hopkins b Oram	12	(38)	3/37 (3) 4/44 (5)			
I. D. Blackwell lbw b Franklin	5	(11)	5/51 (4) 6/65 (7)			
A. F. Giles c Hopkins b Franklin	0	(1)	7/65 (8) 8/76 (9)			
D. Gough c Fleming b Cairns	7	(12)	9/78 (6) 10/101 (11)	15 overs: 51-4		

Bowling: Oram 10–0–23–3; Franklin 10–1–42–5; Cairns 10–2–27–1; Styris 2–1–4–0; Vettori 0.5–0–1–1.

New Zealand

*S. P. Fleming c Gough b Harmison	31	(34)	C. D. McMillan not out	15	(12)	
N. J. Astle lbw b Harmison	15	(27)				
H. J. H. Marshall c Giles b Harmison	5	(9)	L-b 7, w 2, n-b 5	14		
S. B. Styris not out	23	(27)	1/48 (1)	(3 wkts, 17.2 overs) 103		
			2/57 (2) 3/66 (3)	15 overs: 87-3		

J. D. P. Oram, C. L. Cairns, C. Z. Harris, D. L. Vettori, †G. J. Hopkins and J. E. C. Franklin did not bat.

Bowling: Gough 6–0–30–0; Harmison 7–0–38–3; Anderson 4.2–0–28–0.

Umpires: R. E. Koertzen (South Africa) and J. W. Lloyds.
Third umpire: M. R. Benson.   Referee: G. R. Viswanath (India).

ENGLAND v WEST INDIES

At Leeds, July 1 (day/night). England won by seven wickets. England 6 pts. Toss: England.

Nine days after declaring that Flintoff should rest his injured foot for a fortnight, England brought back their all-rounder as a specialist batsman, which spoke volumes for their desperation. A lop-sided team included only three front-line bowlers but, as Vaughan admitted, they got away with it. Harmison responded to the demands heaped upon his coat-hanger shoulders by recording what were then his best figures in a one-day international, and passed 96mph on the speed gun. Anderson, meanwhile, endorsed his own reputation as a bowler with a golden arm by making inroads with good and bad deliveries alike. The fielding, too, was much improved. Had Anderson held a sharp chance offered by Sarwan on nine, England's victory would have been more emphatic. Instead, Sarwan added 63 with Powell, until they went in successive overs. With Trescothick hinting at his powerful best and Strauss uninhibited in chasing a small target, England won in comfort. There was even a huge Flintoff six along the way.

Man of the Match: S. J. Harmison.   *Attendance:* 15,792; *receipts* £417,508.

West Indies

C. H. Gayle run out	23	(29)	I. D. R. Bradshaw c Jones			
S. Chanderpaul c Jones			b McGrath	12	(24)	
b Harmison	3	(4)	R. Rampaul c Anderson b Gough	10	(16)	
D. R. Smith c Jones b Harmison	2	(10)	J. J. C. Lawson not out	0	(1)	
R. R. Sarwan c Collingwood			L-b 4, w 9, n-b 1	14		
b Trescothick	46	(78)				
*B. C. Lara b Anderson	6	(22)	1/9 (1) 2/29 (3)	(40.1 overs) 159		
D. J. J. Bravo c Jones			3/29 (1) 4/40 (5)			
b Anderson	5	(14)	5/62 (6) 6/72 (7)			
†R. D. Jacobs b Anderson	2	(7)	7/135 (4) 8/137 (8)			
R. L. Powell b Harmison	36	(37)	9/159 (9) 10/159 (10)	15 overs: 40-4		

Bowling: Gough 8.1–2–23–1; Harmison 10–2–31–1; Anderson 8–1–37–3; McGrath 10–1–36–1; Trescothick 4–0–28–1.

England

M. E. Trescothick run out	55	(48)
*M. P. Vaughan c Gayle b Bravo	14	(25)
R. W. T. Key b Bravo	6	(12)
A. J. Strauss not out	44	(37)
A. Flintoff not out	21	(18)
L-b 8, w 4, n-b 8	20	

1/55 (2)   (3 wkts, 22 overs) 160
2/64 (3) 3/120 (1)   15 overs: 93-2

P. D. Collingwood, A. McGrath, †G. O. Jones, D. Gough, S. J. Harmison and J. M. Anderson did not bat.

Bowling: Bradshaw 6–0–29–0; Lawson 7–0–50–0; Bravo 4–0–29–2; Rampaul 3–0–28–0; Smith 2–0–16–0.

Umpires: D. J. Harper (Australia) and M. R. Benson.
Third umpire: J. W. Lloyds. Referee: G. R. Viswanath (India).

NEW ZEALAND v WEST INDIES

At Cardiff, July 3. New Zealand won by five wickets. New Zealand 5 pts, West Indies 1 pt. Toss: New Zealand.

New Zealand could not have imagined that victory would arrive so comfortably when West Indies reached 180 for three in the 37th over. At that stage, it seemed that the West Indians had shuffled their batting order to profitable effect, but the game turned against them once Bravo chipped Styris to mid-wicket. Panic set in against some canny bowling, and they lost their last seven wickets for just 36 to finish at least 30 short of expectations, with 22 balls remaining. Lara, promoting himself to open, gave the innings a cracking start, only to succumb to a slower ball from Cairns. A similar delivery accounted for Sarwan, the only other man to reach fifty. West Indies proceeded to give away 30 in wides and no-balls, and could not tighten the screw after Fleming and Styris went in quick succession. Marshall, a natural strokemaker, went against type, hitting only three fours in his unbeaten 75, but it was just what New Zealand required.

Man of the Match: H. J. H. Marshall.   *Attendance:* 8,025; *receipts* £120,867.

West Indies

C. H. Gayle c Hopkins b Cairns .	27	(58)
*B. C. Lara c Fleming b Cairns . .	58	(58)
R. R. Sarwan c Fleming b Cairns .	54	(67)
S. Chanderpaul c Hopkins		
b Butler .	21	(25)
D. J. J. Bravo c Astle b Styris . . .	15	(27)
R. L. Powell c and b Butler	7	(9)
D. R. Smith run out.	10	(23)
†C. S. Baugh c Hopkins		
b Franklin .	3	(11)
I. D. R. Bradshaw run out	0	(1)
T. L. Best not out	1	(3)
J. J. C. Lawson b Butler	4	(2)
L-b 5, w 5, n-b 6	16	

1/83 (2) 2/92 (1)   (46.2 overs) 216
3/132 (4) 4/180 (5)
5/190 (6) 6/199 (3)
7/207 (8) 8/208 (9)
9/212 (7) 10/216 (11)   15 overs: 66-0

Bowling: Oram 10–0–43–0; Franklin 6–0–37–1; Cairns 8–1–29–3; Vettori 8–0–36–0; Butler 8.2–2–0–41–3; Styris 6–0–25–1.

New Zealand

*S. P. Fleming c and b Bravo . . .	45	(62)
N. J. Astle c Chanderpaul		
b Lawson .	19	(34)
H. J. H. Marshall not out	75	(119)
S. B. Styris b Bravo.	3	(6)
C. D. McMillan c Lara b Bravo . .	22	(37)
J. D. P. Oram c Gayle b Lawson .	17	(21)
C. L. Cairns not out	4	(1)
L-b 5, w 26, n-b 4	35	

1/42 (2)   (5 wkts, 46 overs) 220
2/114 (1) 3/121 (4)
4/176 (5) 5/216 (6)   15 overs: 71-1

D. L. Vettori, †G. J. Hopkins, J. E. C. Franklin and I. G. Butler did not bat.

Bowling: Lawson 10–1–56–2; Bradshaw 10–1–34–0; Best 8–0–48–0; Bravo 8–0–36–3; Smith 7–0–30–0; Gayle 3–0–11–0.

Umpires: R. E. Koertzen (South Africa) and D. R. Shepherd.
Third umpire: N. J. Llong.   Referee: G. R. Viswanath (India).

ENGLAND v NEW ZEALAND

At Bristol, July 4. New Zealand won by six wickets. New Zealand 5 pts, England 1 pt. Toss: New Zealand. One-day international debut: S. I. Mahmood.

In contrast to their previous two heavy defeats, England could not be over-blamed for losing once Vaughan lost the toss on a bowler-friendly morning. That they got as many as 237 owed much to Flintoff, who recorded his first one-day international hundred in his 73rd appearance. His first fifty took 80 balls, his second 38, and he added 122 in 25 overs with Strauss. Both were reprieved early on by Marshall, and Flintoff's inauspicious beginning continued when he was struck on the helmet attempting evasive action against Butler. But he held on until the last over, hitting 11 fours and two sixes in all. Fleming and Astle, with exactly 400 one-day appearances between them after this game, opened New Zealand's reply with 122, and Marshall added 55 from 51 balls. The debutant Sajid Mahmood, from Lancashire, went for eight an over. It was not until Fleming reached 99 that New Zealand looked vulnerable. Then three wickets fell; he ran out Marshall before Styris and Fleming himself perished against Collingwood. But their side was already about to breast the tape.

Man of the Match: S. P. Fleming.   *Attendance:* 14,895; *receipts* £392,746.

England

M. E. Trescothick run out	1	(9)
*M. P. Vaughan c Harris b Oram	12	(31)
R. W. T. Key c Hopkins b Styris	18	(34)
A. J. Strauss c Astle b Butler	61	(86)
A. Flintoff b Butler	106	(121)
P. D. Collingwood c Hopkins b Oram	20	(20)
†G. O. Jones not out	1	(2)

S. I. Mahmood c Oram b Butler	1	(2)
B 1, l-b 2, w 9, n-b 5	17	

1/4 (1)   (7 wkts, 50 overs) 237
2/35 (2) 3/57 (3)
4/179 (4) 5/229 (6)
6/235 (5) 7/237 (8)   15 overs: 51-2

D. Gough, S. J. Harmison and J. M. Anderson did not bat.

Bowling: Oram 10–3–27–2; Franklin 8–0–53–0; Butler 10–0–57–3; Styris 9–0–34–1; Harris 8–0–37–0; Vettori 5–0–26–0.

New Zealand

*S. P. Fleming c Strauss b Collingwood	99	(126)
N. J. Astle b Harmison	53	(85)
H. J. H. Marshall run out	55	(51)
S. B. Styris c Trescothick b Collingwood	1	(4)
C. D. McMillan not out	3	(16)

J. D. P. Oram not out	10	(7)
B 1, l-b 4, w 8, n-b 7	20	

1/122 (2)   (4 wkts, 47.2 overs) 241
2/226 (3)
3/227 (4) 4/231 (1)   15 overs: 60-0

C. Z. Harris, D. L. Vettori, †G. J. Hopkins, J. E. C. Franklin and I. G. Butler did not bat.

Bowling: Gough 9–2–37–0; Harmison 9–2–38–1; Anderson 10–1–29–0; Mahmood 7–0–56–0; Collingwood 7.2–0–47–2; Vaughan 5–0–29–0.

Umpires: D. J. Harper (Australia) and M. R. Benson.
Third umpire: J. W. Lloyds.   Referee: G. R. Viswanath (India).

ENGLAND v WEST INDIES

At Lord's, July 6. West Indies won by seven wickets. West Indies 5 pts, England 1 pt. Toss: West Indies.

The close encounter that the competition desperately needed was graced by four wonderful innings, including a second hundred in three days by Flintoff and a match-winning 132 by Gayle. Despite the result, Flintoff's brutal display will be longer remembered. His 123 came from 104 balls with seven sixes, the most in a one-day innings by an England batsman, and eight fours. His 226-run partnership with Strauss, in 30 overs, was an all-wicket England record. Strauss

HIGHEST ONE-DAY PARTNERSHIPS FOR ENGLAND

226 for 4th	**A. J. Strauss and A. Flintoff v West Indies at Lord's**	**2004**
213 for 3rd	G. A. Hick and N. H. Fairbrother v West Indies at Lord's	1991
202 for 2nd	G. A. Gooch and D. I. Gower v Australia at Lord's	1985
200 for 1st	M. E. Trescothick and V. S. Solanki v South Africa at The Oval	2003

completed a maiden one-day international hundred in 115 balls, his second fifty spanning 31. The last ten overs brought 121 runs, 72 of them in four overs starting with the 45th; it was like listening to 20 minutes of crashing cymbals. But England's best batting of the tournament was not enough to keep them in it. They were jittery in the field and missed several possible chances as Gayle and the impish Sarwan put on 187, West Indies' all-wicket best against England. The loss of Lara in the 42nd over with 68 still required gave England hope. But Gayle accelerated after completing his ninth one-day international hundred from 141 balls, and when 16 came from the 47th over, bowled by Gough, West Indies were ahead of the game.

Man of the Match: C. H. Gayle.   *Attendance*: 27,829; *receipts* £825,719.

It seemed all right at the time: one Andrew, Strauss, congratulates another, Flintoff, on a brilliant century at Lord's. But it was not enough.

Picture by Patrick Eagar

England

M. E. Trescothick b Best	11	(11)		A. F. Giles not out	0	(0)
*M. P. Vaughan c Jacobs b Best	8	(21)				
R. W. T. Key b D. R. Smith	19	(51)		L-b 6, w 10, n-b 6	22	
A. J. Strauss c Bravo b Gayle	100	(116)				
A. Flintoff c Bradshaw b Gayle	123	(104)			(7 wkts, 50 overs)	285	

A. J. Strauss c Bravo b Gayle . . . 100 (116)
A. Flintoff c Bradshaw b Gayle . . 123 (104)
P. D. Collingwood c D. S. Smith
　　　　　　　b Gayle . 1 (2)
†G. O. Jones run out 1 (1)

A. F. Giles not out 0 (0)

L-b 6, w 10, n-b 6 22

1/14 (1)　　　(7 wkts, 50 overs) 285
2/27 (2) 3/54 (3)
4/280 (5) 5/284 (4)
6/284 (6) 7/285 (7)　　　15 overs: 38-2

D. Gough, S. J. Harmison and J. M. Anderson did not bat.

Bowling: Bradshaw 10–2–29–0; Best 10–1–42–2; Bravo 10–2–80–0; D. R. Smith 10–0–71–1; Gayle 10–0–57–3.

West Indies

C. H. Gayle not out. 132 (165)
D. S. Smith c Jones b Gough . . . 10 (18)
R. R. Sarwan c Jones b Anderson 89 (78)
*B. C. Lara c Jones b Anderson. . 10 (12)
R. L. Powell not out 33 (22)
　　　L-b 7, w 5 12

1/15 (2)　　(3 wkts, 49.1 overs) 286
2/202 (3) 3/218 (4)　　15 overs: 67-1

S. Chanderpaul, D. J. J. Bravo, D. R. Smith, †R. D. Jacobs, I. D. R. Bradshaw and T. L. Best did not bat.

Bowling: Gough 10–2–48–1; Harmison 10–0–51–0; Anderson 9.1–0–69–2; Giles 10–1–43–0; Vaughan 1–0–10–0; Collingwood 9–0–58–0.

Umpires: R. E. Koertzen (South Africa) and J. W. Lloyds.
Third umpire: N. J. Llong. Referee: G. R. Viswanath (India).

NEW ZEALAND v WEST INDIES

At Southampton, July 8. No result (abandoned). New Zealand 3 pts, West Indies 3 pts. Toss: West Indies. One-day international debut: D. J. G. Sammy.

With both sides assured of contesting the final, and heavy rain in the air, there was a subdued atmosphere around the Rose Bowl even when the umpires decreed a 4.30 p.m. start. At 4.29, rain broke through again, this time with terminal effect. A day later, the ICC confirmed their recent ruling that, because the captains had tossed, the game would count towards the records. Darren Sammy thus became the first player from St Lucia to represent West Indies – even though there was no play.

New Zealand

*S. P. Fleming, N. J. Astle, H. J. H. Marshall, S. B. Styris, C. D. McMillan, C. Z. Harris, D. L. Vettori, A. R. Adams, †G. J. Hopkins, D. R. Tuffey and I. G. Butler.

West Indies

C. H. Gayle, D. S. Smith, R. R. Sarwan, *B. C. Lara, D. J. J. Bravo, S. Chanderpaul, R. L. Powell, D. R. Smith, †R. D. Jacobs, D. J. G. Sammy and J. J. C. Lawson.

Umpires: D. J. Harper (Australia) and D. R. Shepherd.
Third umpire: M. R. Benson. Referee: G. R. Viswanath (India).

QUALIFYING TABLE

	Played	Won	Lost	No result	Bonus points	Points	Net run-rate
New Zealand	6	3	0	3	1	25	1.40
West Indies	6	2	2	2	2	18	−0.38
England	6	1	4	1	3	11	−0.59

Win = 5 pts; no result = 3 pts. One bonus point awarded either to the winning team for achieving victory with a run-rate 1.25 times that of the opposition or to the losing team for denying the winners a bonus point. Net run-rate is calculated by subtracting runs conceded per over from runs scored per over.

FINAL

NEW ZEALAND v WEST INDIES

At Lord's, July 10. New Zealand won by 107 runs. Toss: West Indies.

A one-sided final played out between showers made a fitting end to this unmemorable tournament. Lord's was roughly half-full when New Zealand completed their biggest one-day victory over West Indies at around 8 p.m. Many of the crowd had shuffled away after a particularly heavy shower some 90 minutes earlier, which threatened to take the match into a reserve day. At that point West Indies, who had selected nine batsmen, required 158 from 19 overs with five wickets left. But, on a slow pitch, New Zealand were in their element. Vettori completed his best one-day figures, five for 30, which were also the best in a one-day international at Lord's. He executed two run-outs as well in a brilliant team fielding performance. There was joy too for Harris, when he became the first New Zealander to take 200 wickets at this level – and the second all-rounder after Sanath Jayasuriya to combine this landmark with 4,000 runs. Fleming had been happy to buck the trend by batting first after losing the toss. Along with Astle and Marshall, he gave New Zealand another strong start, and McMillan manoeuvred the ball intelligently so that the loss of the last seven wickets for 49 runs in 58 balls was not decisive.

Man of the Match: D. L. Vettori. *Attendance:* 25,988; receipts £802,685.
Man of the Series: S. P. Fleming.

Down is up: Scott Styris clings on to a slip catch to remove Chris Gayle for four, to the delight of New Zealand captain Stephen Fleming.

Picture by Patrick Eagar

New Zealand

*S. P. Fleming c Gayle b Bravo	67	(66)	D. L. Vettori c D. R. Smith			
N. J. Astle c Gayle b Bravo	57	(81)	b Sarwan	6	(7)	
H. J. H. Marshall c Sarwan			†G. J. Hopkins run out	0	(0)	
b Gayle	44	(51)	I. G. Butler not out	0	(1)	
S. B. Styris c Powell			L-b 8, w 9, n-b 1	18		
b D. R. Smith	1	(4)				
C. D. McMillan c Chanderpaul			1/120 (1) 2/143 (2)	(49.2 overs) 266		
b Best	52	(53)	3/146 (4) 4/217 (3)			
C. L. Cairns st Jacobs b Sarwan	5	(10)	5/233 (6) 6/249 (5)			
J. D. P. Oram c Jacobs b Best	15	(22)	7/252 (8) 8/265 (9)			
C. Z. Harris c and b Sarwan	1	(2)	9/266 (7) 10/266 (10)	15 overs: 83-0		

Bowling: Best 7.2–0–57–2; Bradshaw 6–1–28–0; D. R. Smith 10–1–27–1; Bravo 10–0–67–2; Gayle 10–0–48–1; Sarwan 6–0–31–3.

West Indies

C. H. Gayle c Styris b Oram	4	(13)	I. D. R. Bradshaw run out	0	(1)	
D. S. Smith run out	44	(72)	T. L. Best not out	1	(1)	
R. R. Sarwan run out	19	(30)				
*B. C. Lara lbw b Vettori	30	(41)	L-b 2, n-b 3	5		
D. J. J. Bravo c Styris b Vettori	4	(14)				
S. Chanderpaul c McMillan			1/5 (1) 2/45 (3)	(41.2 overs) 159		
b Vettori	31	(44)	3/98 (2) 4/105 (4)			
R. L. Powell c Marshall b Vettori	18	(25)	5/106 (5) 6/144 (7)			
D. R. Smith lbw b Vettori	2	(7)	7/149 (8) 8/150 (9)			
†R. D. Jacobs c Cairns b Harris	1	(3)	9/150 (10) 10/159 (6)	15 overs: 54-2		

Bowling: Oram 8–2–26–1; Butler 6–0–25–0; Styris 5–0–22–0; Harris 10–0–45–1; Vettori 9.2–1–30–5; McMillan 3–0–9–0.

Umpires: R. E. Koertzen (South Africa) and D. R. Shepherd.
Third umpire: J. W. Lloyds. Referee: G. R. Viswanath (India).

NATWEST SERIES WINNERS

2000 England	2002 India	2004 New Zealand
2001 Australia	2003 England	

VODAFONE ENGLAND PLAYER OF THE YEAR AWARDS

Andrew Flintoff won the men's Vodafone England Cricketer of the Year Award in May 2004. The women's award went to opener Charlotte Edwards for her batting on the recent tour of South Africa. Steve Harmison won the men's Individual Performance of the Year for his match-winning seven for 12 to rout West Indies in the First Test at Kingston in March 2004, and Claire Taylor won the women's equivalent for her 177 in the First Test against South Africa at Shenley Park in August 2003.

VIDEOCON CUP, 2004

Australia took the Videocon Cup, staged in the Netherlands, by winning an exciting slow-burn final against Pakistan. But the tournament itself was a damp squib. Organised as a triangular quickie, with India the third team, as a warm-up for the Champions Trophy in England, it took place in Amsterdam's wettest August since 1912: all four games were affected, only two reached a result, and Sony Max, the Indian broadcasters, reportedly cut their payments from $2m to $1.5m for each of the competing teams' boards.

Australia refused to reschedule their two washed-out preliminary fixtures, and managed to qualify for the final without actually completing a game. The Royal Dutch Cricket Association were dependent on gate receipts for a share of the profits, but attendances dwindled after the opening game, between India and Pakistan, which drew the customary throng of expat Asians.

Note: Matches in this section were not first-class.

INDIA v PAKISTAN

At Amstelveen, August 21. Pakistan won by 66 runs (D/L method). Pakistan 6 pts. Toss: India.
In front of a sell-out crowd of 10,000, Pakistan jogged to victory on the back of a workmanlike display from Shoaib Malik. First, his restorative half-century gave the middle overs impetus; then, his efficient off-spin, in tandem with Shahid Afridi's leg-breaks, strangled India and removed their last seven wickets in 7.4 overs. Heavy morning rain had reduced the contest to 36 overs a side, and another shower made it 33. Before that, an economical first spell from Balaji harvested two wickets; afterwards, Abdul Razzaq led a charge that yielded 42 runs from the last three overs. Duckworth/Lewis revised India's target by a single run, and their reply started energetically. But the athletic run-out of Dravid, by Inzamam-ul-Haq of all people, brought a stutter, and there was no Tendulkar to marshal the middle order: he was out of the tournament with tennis elbow.
Man of the Match: Shoaib Malik.

Pakistan

Yasir Hameed c Dravid b Balaji	9	†Moin Khan not out	27
Shahid Afridi c Kaif b Agarkar	19		
Shoaib Malik c Kaif b Kumble	68	L-b 2, w 1, n-b 2	5
*Inzamam-ul-Haq c Dravid b Balaji	1		
Yousuf Youhana run out	28	1/22 (2) 2/52 (1) (6 wkts, 33 overs)	192
Abdul Razzaq not out	35	3/58 (4) 4/122 (5)	
Younis Khan c Dravid b Balaji	0	5/136 (3) 6/136 (7)	

Mohammad Sami, Shoaib Akhtar and Shabbir Ahmed did not bat.

Bowling: Pathan 7–0–57–0; Agarkar 7–0–40–1; Balaji 7–1–27–3; Ganguly 6–0–34–0; Kumble 6–0–32–1.

India

V. Sehwag c Shoaib Malik b Shabbir Ahmed	17	I. K. Pathan lbw b Shahid Afridi 1
*S. C. Ganguly c Yousuf Youhana b Abdul Razzaq	25	L. Balaji c Mohammad Sami b Shahid Afridi . 2
V. V. S. Laxman b Shoaib Malik	37	A. Kumble not out 1
†R. Dravid run out	0	L-b 1, w 3, n-b 1 5
Yuvraj Singh lbw b Shahid Afridi	13	
M. Kaif b Shahid Afridi	10	1/30 (1) 2/69 (2) (27 overs) 127
R. S. Gavaskar c Abdul Razzaq b Shoaib Malik	15	3/70 (4) 4/96 (3)
A. B. Agarkar c Yasir Hameed b Shoaib Malik	1	5/98 (5) 6/116 (6) 7/123 (8) 8/123 (7) 9/124 (9) 10/127 (10)

Bowling: Mohammad Sami 5–0–29–0; Shabbir Ahmed 5–0–22–1; Shoaib Akhtar 3–0–23–0; Abdul Razzaq 4–1–14–1; Shahid Afridi 6–0–20–4; Shoaib Malik 4–0–18–3.

Umpires: S. A. Bucknor (West Indies) and D. R. Shepherd (England).
Third umpire: J. W. Lloyds (England).   Referee: B. C. Broad (England).

AUSTRALIA v INDIA

At Amstelveen, August 23. No result. Australia 3 pts, India 3 pts. Toss: Australia.
Rain snuffed out the match two balls before the close of Australia's innings, already reduced to 32 overs by morning drizzle. In between, Clarke's assurance against the Indian bowlers eased Australia to a strong position, bringing 42 off 28 balls, including six fours, before Sehwag took off to hold him at deep mid-on. Balaji, from a shortened run, moved the ball both ways to snare three wickets.

Australia

M. L. Hayden c Ganguly b Balaji	29	G. B. Hogg not out 17
†B. J. Haddin c Balaji b Nehra	5	B. Lee not out 1
*R. T. Ponting lbw b Balaji	26	B 1, l-b 4, w 6, n b 1 12
D. R. Martyn b Sehwag	12	
A. Symonds c Dravid b Kumble	12	1/23 (2) 2/69 (1) (7 wkts, 31.4 overs) 175
D. S. Lehmann c Gavaskar b Kumble . . .	19	3/70 (3) 4/83 (5)
M. J. Clarke c Sehwag b Balaji	42	5/101 (4) 6/138 (6) 7/169 (7)

M. S. Kasprowicz and G. D. McGrath did not bat.

Bowling: Pathan 6.4–0–34–0; Nehra 6–0–44–1; Sehwag 6–0–35–1; Balaji 6–0–20–3; Kumble 7–0–37–2.

India

V. Sehwag, *S. C. Ganguly, V. V. S. Laxman, †R. Dravid, Yuvraj Singh, M. Kaif, R. S. Gavaskar, I. K. Pathan, L. Balaji, A. Kumble and A. Nehra.

Umpires: S. A. Bucknor (West Indies) and J. W. Lloyds (England).
Third umpire: D. R. Shepherd (England).   Referee: B. C. Broad (England).

AUSTRALIA v PAKISTAN

At Amstelveen, August 25. No result (abandoned). Australia 3 pts, Pakistan 3 pts.
With no toss made, this match did not count in the records. Heavy showers ensured India were eliminated and Australia won a place in the final without fielding once. The organisers suggested rescheduling the two washed-out games, and perhaps postponing the final for a day, but Australia said three matches in four days would be too taxing for their players.

QUALIFYING TABLE

	Played	Won	Lost	No result	Bonus points	Points	Net run-rate
Pakistan. . . .	2	1	0	1	1	9	2.00
Australia . . .	2	0	0	2	0	6	–
India.	2	0	1	1	0	3	–2.00

Win = 5 pts, no result = 3 pts. One bonus point awarded either to the winning team for achieving victory with a run-rate 1.25 times that of the opposition, or to the losing team for denying the winners a bonus point. Net run-rate is calculated by subtracting runs conceded per over from runs scored per over.

FINAL

AUSTRALIA v PAKISTAN

At Amstelveen, August 28. Australia won by 17 runs. Toss: Australia.

Delayed 90 minutes by drizzle, this game evolved into a low-scoring fizzer. On a slow pitch, Pakistan had their noses in front twice before the Australian machine won their fifth successive one-day tournament, a sequence including the World Cup. Disciplined early bowling, especially from Mohammad Sami, kept the usually browbeating Australian top order quiet. Consolidation came after Lehmann joined Hayden, who laboured for 105 balls to reach 50. Lehmann used his tactical nous to work the ball into gaps, before Symonds lashed it around to propel his side to 192. Pakistan began just as steadily, and at 93 for three were almost cruising. But the run-outs of Shoaib Malik and the dangerous Shahid Afridi off consecutive deliveries – with Yousuf Youhana the guilty partner both times – undermined hopes which finally crumbled when Youhana himself fell, with 32 needed off 45 and no one left to graft. Pakistanis were furious at the dismissals of Youhana and Inzamam-ul-Haq, both given out caught by umpire Shepherd. Chairman of selectors Wasim Bari said the decisions were like "target killings" and that it was "time for the inaccurate Shepherd to retire. His decisions were not only doubtful but disgraceful." This view was endorsed by Pakistan's most famous cricket columnist Omar Kureishi. "He [Shepherd] is an old man and his judgment in the final was very poor," he wrote. Shepherd was 63; Kureishi 77.

Man of the Match: A. Symonds.

Australia

M. L. Hayden c Yasir Hameed		M. J. Clarke c Inzamam-ul-Haq	
b Shoaib Akhtar .	59	b Shoaib Akhtar .	1
†B. J. Haddin b Mohammad Sami	10	G. B. Hogg run out	0
*R. T. Ponting c Imran Farhat			
b Abdul Razzaq .	25	B 1, l-b 5, w 5, n-b 4	15
D. S. Lehmann c Moin Khan			
b Shabbir Ahmed .	40	1/21 (2) 2/65 (3) (7 wkts, 50 overs) 192
A. Symonds b Shoaib Akhtar	36	3/126 (1) 4/183 (4)	
D. R. Martyn not out	6	5/189 (5) 6/192 (7) 7/192 (8)	

B. Lee, J. N. Gillespie and G. D. McGrath did not bat.

Bowling: Mohammad Sami 10–1–26–1; Shabbir Ahmed 8–1–25–1; Shoaib Akhtar 10–0–40–3; Abdul Razzaq 8–1–30–1; Shahid Afridi 6–0–20–0; Shoaib Malik 8–0–45–0.

Pakistan

Yasir Hameed b Lee	17	Shoaib Akhtar c Haddin b McGrath.... 2
Imran Farhat c Hayden b Symonds	17	Shabbir Ahmed not out 0
Shoaib Malik run out	36	
*Inzamam-ul-Haq c Haddin b Symonds .	7	B 6, 1-b 2, w 8 16
Yousuf Youhana c Haddin b Hogg.....	43	
Shahid Afridi run out	0	1/24 (1) 2/47 (2) 3/65 (4) (47.1 overs) 175
Abdul Razzaq c Clarke b Lehmann	26	4/93 (3) 5/93 (6) 6/154 (7)
†Moin Khan c Haddin b Gillespie.....	6	7/161 (5) 8/171 (9)
Mohammad Sami b Lehmann........	5	9/175 (8) 10/175 (10)

Bowling: McGrath 7.1–1–12–1; Gillespie 9–0–22–1; Lee 7–1–29–1; Hogg 7–0–43–1; Symonds 7–1–25–2; Lehmann 10–0–36–2.

Umpires: S. A. Bucknor (West Indies) and D. R. Shepherd (England).
Third umpire: M. R. Benson (England).   Referee: B. C. Broad (England).

FIFTY YEARS AGO

from WISDEN CRICKETERS' ALMANACK for 1955

ETON v HARROW, AT LORD'S, JULY 9, 10, 1954 – "Harrow won by nine wickets... Boisterous scenes, degenerating into rowdyism, followed, and water was poured from the Harrow dressing-room balcony on to Eton supporters trying to tear down the colours of the victors. A clergyman had his hat knocked off and kicked about."

NOTES BY THE EDITOR (Norman Preston) – "After waiting for twenty-two years, England have again won a rubber in Australia and retained the Ashes they retrieved at Kennington Oval in 1953. This is a great triumph for Len Hutton, the captain, and a great thing for English cricket. At last England are on top again and with so many excellent young players in the first-class counties, the team should be even stronger when Australia renew the challenge in England next year... This... struggle for the Ashes thrilled cricket lovers the world over. The issue was closer than the bare results indicate. As in England in 1953, one could rarely predict which way a match was likely to go. One day Australia looked to be on top; the next England would turn the tables. For the time being the ball has gained the mastery over the bat and generally youth, guided by the wise old head of Hutton, has taken command."

FIVE CRICKETERS OF THE YEAR, W. E. HOLLIES, – "When Donald Bradman walked to the wicket at Kennington Oval in August 1948, to play his last Test innings before retirement, he received one of the most tumultuous receptions known in cricket. A moment later the vast crowd sent up a united gasp of amazement as they saw Australia's champion bowled second ball without scoring. That triumphant moment for WILLIAM ERIC HOLLIES, the Warwickshire leg-break and googly bowler, marked but one spectacular incident in the career of a cricketer whose skill and unassuming cheerfulness could be taken as a model by all young players. Many other illustrious batsmen, and records by the score, have fallen to this fair-haired Peter Pan of Warwickshire cricket, but first, and always, he has remained a team-man to whom enjoyment brings its own reward."

SURREY IN 1954 – "When Surrey began their nineteenth Championship match at the end of July their prospects of becoming the first county for fifteen years to win the title three times in succession looked extremely slender. With ten matches to play they stood eighth in the table, 46 points behind Yorkshire the leaders... Then came a most remarkable transformation. By consistently dynamic cricket, Surrey swept aside all remaining opposition, taking 112 points from a possible 120 and finishing 22 points ahead of Yorkshire, the runners-up. In that period of thorough domination, Surrey raced to five victories in two days... The retention of the title came about through the supremacy of the attack, supported by fielding of uncommon excellence, together with the initiative and imagination of the captain, Surridge, who so accurately assessed the tactical risks and possibilities of each situation."

THE INDIANS IN ENGLAND, 2004

With preparation for the end-of-season Champions Trophy in mind, the ECB shifted the NatWest Challenge (the brief, bilateral complement to the triangular NatWest Series) from its midsummer home into early September. England's opponents were India, potentially one of the strongest limited-overs outfits in world cricket, providing both meaningful practice and additional revenue: these three games were sell-outs, as India's one-day internationals in England generally are.

Both teams had plenty at stake. England needed a fillip after failing to qualify for the final of the NatWest Series in early July, and their recent performances in the shorter game were at odds with their triumphant march through the Test summer. India too were keen to hit some sort of form

MOST WICKETS FOR ENGLAND IN ONE-DAY INTERNATIONALS

		Balls	Runs	BB	4W/i	Ave
224	**D. Gough**	**7,909**	**5,666**	**5-44**	10	25.29
145	I. T Botham.	6,271	4,139	4-31	3	28.54
115	P. A. J. DeFreitas	5,712	3,775	4-35	1	32.82
82	**A. Flintoff**	**2,807**	**1,966**	**4-14**	3	**23.97**
80	R. G. D. Willis.	3,595	1,968	4-11	4	24.60
76	J. E. Emburey	3,425	2,346	4-37	2	30.86
69	A. R. Caddick	2,937	1,965	4-19	3	28.47
67	M. A. Ealham	3,227	2,197	5-15	4	32.79
66	C. C. Lewis.	2,625	1,942	4-30	4	29.42
65	C. White.	2,364	1,726	5-21	1	26.55
63	A. D. Mullally	2,699	1,728	4-18	2	27.42
59	**J. M. Anderson**	**1,903**	**1,504**	**4-25**	**4**	**25.49**
59	N. A. Foster.	2,627	1,836	3-20	0	31.11

Figures correct at February 13, 2005. Gough also took 1-55 for an ICC World XI v ACC Asian XI at Melbourne in 2004-05.

before their Champions Trophy games, when they had a chance to gain revenge on Pakistan, who in recent weeks had got the better of them in both Colombo and Amstelveen. However, it emerged during this three-game challenge that throughout their short England tour the Indians would have to cope without Sachin Tendulkar, who was taking longer than expected to recover from tennis elbow.

The cricket was of a decent standard and, for England especially, there were several positives. Alex Wharf, plucked from the more obscure reaches of the county game, marked his international debut by removing three world-class batsmen, Steve Harmison grabbed a one-day best four for 22 and was player of the series, while Andrew Flintoff continued to strike terror into bowlers of all kinds. He was instrumental in England securing the series with a game to go and, when he was elsewhere for the third game, England promptly lost, despite Michael Vaughan ending a dire run with the bat that had brought him just 51 in seven one-day innings. And Darren Gough, believed by some to have passed his sell-by date, instead passed 200 one-day wickets for England.

Mohammad Kaif led the Indian batting and might perhaps have reached fifty in every game had his captain, Sourav Ganguly, not run him out in the third. Harbhajan Singh proved the value of quality spin, especially in the second game, at The Oval. But the Indians finished the short series with more questions asked than answered. Top of the list was the perennial "Who's going to be the wicket-keeper?" Rahul Dravid was in the games they lost, while the 19-year-old Dinesh Karthik made his debut in the successful third. But no one seemed sure this was the right answer.

INDIAN TOURING PARTY

S. C. Ganguly (*captain*), R. Dravid (*vice-captain*), A. B. Agarkar, L. Balaji, R. S. Gavaskar, Harbhajan Singh, M. Kaif, K. D. Karthik, A. Kumble, V. V. S. Laxman, A. Nehra, I. K Pathan, V. Sehwag, S. R. Tendulkar, Yuvraj Singh.

Coach: J. G. Wright. *Manager:* G. Dasgupta. *Bowling coach:* B. A. Reid. *Physiotherapist:* A. Leipus. *Trainer:* G. A. King. *Computer analyst:* B. Ramakrishnan.

INDIAN TOUR RESULTS

One-day internationals – Played 5: Won 2, Lost 3. *Wins* – England, Kenya. *Losses* – England (2), Pakistan.

Note: Matches in this section were not first-class.

Match reports by Julian Guyer

THE NATWEST CHALLENGE

ENGLAND v INDIA

First One-Day International

At Nottingham, September 1. England won by seven wickets. Toss: England. One-day international debut: A. G. Wharf.

Alex Wharf, a blunt-speaking Yorkshireman from Central Casting and the epitome of the journeyman pro, grabbed three wickets on debut to help set up an emphatic England win. Aged 29 and at his third county, Wharf was only in the squad because of injury to Kabir Ali, though he was the man in form, having taken six for five for Glamorgan v Kent three days earlier. He began unpromisingly with a no-ball, but with his fifth legitimate delivery persuaded Ganguly to miscue a pull to Jones. In Wharf's next over, Laxman edged behind, and in his third Dravid fell hooking: a respectable trio of victims with which to begin an international career. India, now 80 for four, never properly recovered. Kaif did produce a sensible fifty to see them to some sort of score, before Harmison wrapped up the innings in fine style. He became only the second England bowler to take a one-day international hat-trick, after James Anderson had removed the last three Pakistani batsmen at The Oval the previous summer. Harmison, though, was fortunate to gain his second wicket when umpire Shepherd ruled Balaji out after the ball came off his arm guard. Fresh from a hundred in the C&G Trophy final, Solanki made 52 on his first international outing for ten months, while Flintoff – the new Barnum – finished the match with a six off Kumble.

Man of the Match: A. G. Wharf. *Attendance:* 15,348; *receipts* £448,332.

India

V. Sehwag c Vaughan b Gough	4	L. Balaji c Flintoff b Harmison	0
*S. C. Ganguly c Jones b Wharf	24	A. Nehra c and b Harmison	0
V. V. S. Laxman c Jones b Wharf	29		
†R. Dravid c Gough b Wharf	13	L-b 6, w 5, n-b 3	14
Yuvraj Singh run out	4		
M. Kaif c Jones b Harmison	50	1/10 (1) 2/62 (2) 3/63 (3) (43.5 overs)	170
R. S. Gavaskar c Collingwood b Flintoff	20	4/80 (4) 5/89 (5) 6/129 (7)	
I. K. Pathan c and b Giles	3	7/143 (8) 8/170 (6)	
A. Kumble not out	9	9/170 (10) 10/170 (11) 15 overs: 76-3	

Bowling: Gough 7–2–29–1; Harmison 8.5–0–41–3; Flintoff 8–0–28–1; Wharf 8–0–30–3;
Giles 10–0–25–1; Collingwood 2–0–11–0.

England

M. E. Trescothick c Yuvraj Singh		A. Flintoff not out	34
b Balaji	33	L-b 1, w 7, n-b 3	11
V. S. Solanki lbw b Pathan	52		
*M. P. Vaughan b Balaji	0	1/63 (1) 2/65 (3) (3 wkts, 32.2 overs)	171
A. J. Strauss not out	41	3/128 (2) 15 overs: 65-2	

P. D. Collingwood, †G. O. Jones, A. F. Giles, A. G. Wharf, D. Gough and S. J. Harmison did not
bat.

Bowling: Pathan 10–0–53–1; Nehra 6–0–23–0; Balaji 10–1–37–2; Kumble 6.2–0–57–0.

Umpires: D. B. Hair (Australia) and D. R. Shepherd.
Third umpire: J. W. Lloyds.   Referee: M. J. Procter (South Africa).

ENGLAND v INDIA

Second One-Day International

At The Oval, September 3. England won by 70 runs. Toss: India.

For the first time since they beat Pakistan in the World Cup more than 18 months earlier, England
won a match batting first. Remarkably, it was the first time in their last 24 completed one-day
games that the team batting first had gone on to win. And, as had become commonplace, England
were heavily indebted to Flintoff. He came to the wicket with the score an uncertain 98 for three,
soon a precarious 105 for four. To begin with, Flintoff and Collingwood watchfully saw off the
bewitching Harbhajan Singh, whose exemplary spell of varied, suffocatingly accurate off-spin
threatened to stall England completely. But once he was bowled out, the shackles were broken and
the runs flowed. Towards the end they came in torrents: 100 gushed from the last ten overs, with
Flintoff giving a masterful display of clean hitting. As remarkable, though, was the joy radiating

HIGHEST PARTNERSHIPS FOR ENGLAND IN ONE-DAY INTERNATIONALS

226	for 4th	A. J. Strauss (100) and A. Flintoff (123) v WI at Lord's	2004
213	for 3rd	G. A. Hick (86*) and N. H. Fairbrother (113) v WI at Lord's	1991
202	for 2nd	G. A. Gooch (117*) and D. I. Gower (102) v A at Lord's	1985
200	for 1st	M. E. Trescothick (114*) and V. S. Solanki (106) v SA at The Oval	2003
193	for 1st	G. A. Gooch (91) and C. W. J. Athey (142*) v NZ at Manchester	1986
190*	for 3rd	C. J. Tavaré (83*) and A. J. Lamb (108*) v NZ at Sydney	1982-83
190	for 3rd	G. A. Hick (108) and N. Hussain (93) v A at Sydney	1998-99
185	for 1st	G. A. Gooch (56) and W. Larkins (124) v A at Hyderabad	1989-90
185	for 2nd	M. E. Trescothick (109) and N. Hussain (115) v I at Lord's	2002
176	for 2nd	D. L. Amiss (137) and K. W. R. Fletcher (68) v I at Lord's	1975
175	for 2nd	A. J. Stewart (87*) and N. Hussain (95) v B at Nairobi	2000-01
174	for 5th	A. Flintoff (99) and P. D. Collingwood (79*) v I at The Oval	2004

Pythonesque: Sourav Ganguly, without his bat, his wicket or much dignity after a mid-pitch muddle with V. V. S. Laxman at The Oval. Andrew Flintoff sees the funny side.

Picture by Paul Gilham, Getty Images

between batsman and crowd, who revelled in his success. But if the spectators were dismayed that, after slamming four sixes in his 93-ball innings, he fell aiming for a fifth that would have brought a century, Flintoff himself could hardly have seemed less concerned. Collingwood, initially outpacing his partner, contributed a healthy 79. In reply, India stuttered to ten for two when a run-out – so comic it might have been choreographed by Chaplin in harness with John Cleese – ended Ganguly's innings. He played Harmison into the off and called for a run. But he collided mid-pitch with Laxman and dropped his bat. On another day Flintoff's overarm throw from close range might have missed, but not in this golden season. An Indian-record last-wicket stand of 64 between Harbhajan and Balaji held things up before Flintoff, naturally, bowled Balaji. England had an unassailable 2–0 lead in the series.

Man of the Match: A. Flintoff.   *Attendance:* 14,806; *receipts* £526,167.

England

M. E. Trescothick c Balaji b Harbhajan Singh .	27
V. S. Solanki c Dravid b Sehwag.	48
*M. P. Vaughan c Dravid b Harbhajan Singh .	4
A. J. Strauss c Ganguly b Sehwag.	2
A. Flintoff c Dravid b Agarkar	99

P. D. Collingwood not out	79
†G. O. Jones not out.	12
B 1, l-b 5, w 28, n-b 2. . . .	36

1/71 (1) 2/93 (3)   (5 wkts, 50 overs) 307
3/98 (4) 4/105 (2)
5/279 (5)   15 overs: 93-1

A. F. Giles, A. G. Wharf, D. Gough and S. J. Harmison did not bat.

Bowling: Pathan 10–1–58–0; Balaji 8–0–77–0; Agarkar 6–0–60–1; Harbhajan Singh 10–2–14–2; Sehwag 10–0–51–2; Gavaskar 3–0–18–0; Yuvraj Singh 3–0–23–0.

India

*S. C. Ganguly run out	7	Harbhajan Singh not out	41
V. Sehwag lbw b Gough	0	L. Balaji b Flintoff	18
V. V. S. Laxman c Collingwood b Giles	33		
M. Kaif c Vaughan b Giles	51	L-b 11, w 11, n-b 5	27
†R. Dravid c Jones b Wharf	1		
Yuvraj Singh c Vaughan b Gough	24		
R. S. Gavaskar b Giles	13		
A. B. Agarkar c Trescothick b Gough	22		
I. K. Pathan c Vaughan b Gough	0		

1/2 (2) 2/10 (1) 3/99 (3) (46.3 overs) 237
4/102 (5) 5/113 (4) 6/143 (7)
7/169 (6) 8/169 (9)
9/173 (8) 10/237 (11) 15 overs: 82-2

Bowling: Gough 10–0–50–4; Harmison 8–0–51–0; Flintoff 7.3–1–31–1; Wharf 6–0–36–1; Giles 10–1–26–3; Vaughan 5–0–32–0.

Umpires: D. B. Hair (Australia) and M. R. Benson.
Third umpire: N. J. Llong. Referee: M. J. Procter (South Africa).

ENGLAND v INDIA

Third One-Day International

At Lord's, September 5. India won by 23 runs. Toss: India. One-day international debut: K. D. Karthik.

India ended a run of four defeats and a washout with an overdue, if not wholly convincing, victory. They limped past 200 thanks to a 93-run stand between Ganguly and the unflappable Dravid, who were alone in passing 14. Ganguly, occasionally at his lordly best, made 90, as he needed to after running out Kaif, the only Indian batsman in decent touch, for two. (If a call from Denis Compton was "the basis for negotiation", a shout from Ganguly is surely no more than talks about talks.) Harmison did most damage with a limited-overs career-best four for 22, while Gough became the first England bowler to 200 one-day international wickets when he removed Harbhajan Singh. Needing a fraction more than four an over, England, having won their last 13 games batting second, were clear favourites, but not at 62 for six. A partnership of 92 between Vaughan, putting a run of paltry one-day scores behind him, and Giles kept the game alive, though they were always behind the rate. Vaughan's innings was eventually ended by an acrobatic leg-side stumping by the 19-year-old debutant Dinesh Karthik and England – sorely missing Flintoff, who was with his girlfriend for the birth of their first child – were heading for defeat. Flintoff got a result, though: a daughter called Holly.

Man of the Match: S. C. Ganguly.   *Attendance:* 25,529; *receipts* £785,575.
Man of the Series: S. J. Harmison.

India

*S. C. Ganguly c Vaughan b Harmison	90	A. Kumble c Wharf b Gough	5
V. V. S. Laxman b Harmison	9	A. Nehra not out	2
M. Kaif run out	2		
V. Sehwag c and b Giles	1	L-b 5, w 10, n-b 4	19
R. Dravid c Collingwood b Harmison	52		
Yuvraj Singh c Giles b Wharf	9		
†K. D. Karthik c Jones b Harmison	1		
Harbhajan Singh c Vaughan b Gough	0		
I. K. Pathan b Wharf	14		

1/24 (2) 2/46 (3) 3/48 (4) (49.3 overs) 204
4/141 (1) 5/170 (6) 6/181 (7)
7/182 (8) 8/184 (5)
9/195 (10) 10/204 (9) 15 overs: 50-3

Bowling: Gough 10–0–41–2; Harmison 10–0–22–4; Wharf 9.3–0–41–2; Giles 10–0–43–1; Vaughan 5–0–23–0; Collingwood 5–0–29–0.

England

M. E. Trescothick c Laxman b Nehra	1	A. G. Wharf c Karthik b Yuvraj Singh	9
V. S. Solanki c Harbhajan Singh b Nehra	9	D. Gough b Nehra	10
*M. P. Vaughan st Karthik b Harbhajan Singh	74	S. J. Harmison not out	4
A. J. Strauss lbw b Pathan	2	L-b 11, w 4, n-b 1	16
A. McGrath lbw b Pathan	2		
P. D. Collingwood run out	4	1/5 (1) 2/22 (2) 3/27 (4) (48.2 overs) 181	
†G. O. Jones c Sehwag b Harbhajan Singh	11	4/29 (5) 5/48 (6) 6/62 (7) 7/154 (8) 8/155 (3)	
A. F. Giles c and b Harbhajan Singh	39	9/166 (9) 10/181 (10) 15 overs: 47-4	

Bowling: Pathan 9–0–32–2; Nehra 7.2–1–26–3; Kumble 10–1–36–0; Harbhajan Singh 10–1–28–3; Sehwag 6–0–24–0; Yuvraj Singh 6–0–24–1.

Umpires: D. B. Hair (Australia) and J. W. Lloyds.
Third umpire: M. R. Benson. Referee: M. J. Procter (South Africa).

India's matches against Kenya and Pakistan in the ICC Champions Trophy (September 11–19) appear on pages 515–538.

OVERSEAS PLAYERS IN 2004

In 2004, there was no limit on the number of overseas players each county could sign, subject to no more than two appearing in the same match. Durham used six overseas players during the season, Leicestershire, Nottinghamshire, Sussex and Worcestershire two each. The season also saw the arrival of the first Kolpak players, thanks to a European court judgment allowing citizens of countries which had trade agreements with the EU to play without being classed as foreigners.

Derbyshire J. Moss (A), D. B. Powell (WI), C. J. L. Rogers (A).
Durham A. M. Blignaut (Z), R. D. King (WI), M. J. North (A), Shoaib Akhtar (P), Tahir Mughal (P), S. W. Tait (A). *H. H. Gibbs (SA) withdrew unfit.*
Essex A. R. Adams (NZ), S. A. Brant (A), Danish Kaneria (P).
Glamorgan M. T. G. Elliott (A), M. S. Kasprowicz (A), M. L. Lewis (A).
Gloucestershire N. W. Bracken (A), J. E. C. Franklin (NZ), M. E. K. Hussey (A), Shabbir Ahmed (P), Shoaib Malik (P).
Hampshire M. J. Clarke (A), M. G. Dighton (A), S. M. Katich (A), S. K. Warne (A), S. R. Watson (A).
Kent M. G. Bevan (A), I. G. Butler (NZ), Mohammad Sami (P), Shahid Afridi (P), A. Symonds (A).
Lancashire C. L. Hooper (WI), S. G. Law (A), D. Mongia (I).
Leicestershire M. F. Cleary (A), B. J. Hodge (A). *G. J-P. Kruger (SA) withdrew unfit.* **Kolpak player** – C. W. Henderson (SA).
Middlesex A. B. Agarkar (I), S. R. Clark (A), M. Hayward (SA), L. Klusener (SA), G. D. McGrath (A).
Northamptonshire J. Louw (SA), M. L. Love (A), P. C. Rofe (A), M. van Jaarsveld (SA).
Nottinghamshire D. J. Hussey (A), S. C. G. MacGill (A). *D. R. Martyn (A) withdrew unfit.*
Somerset J. Cox (A), N. A. M. McLean (WI), R. T. Ponting (A).
Surrey Azhar Mahmood (P), G. S. Blewett (A), Saqlain Mushtaq (P), Zaheer Khan (I).
Sussex M. W. Goodwin (A), Mushtaq Ahmed (P).
Warwickshire G. B. Hogg (A), D. Pretorius (SA), H. H. Streak (Z).
Worcestershire A. J. Bichel (A), A. J. Hall (SA). **Kolpak player:** R. W. Price (Z).
Yorkshire I. J. Harvey (A), P. A. Jaques (A), D. S. Lehmann (A).

Scotland S. Sriram (I), Yasir Arafat (P).

THE NATWEST INTERNATIONAL

Note: This match was not first-class.

AUSTRALIA v PAKISTAN
One-Day International

At Lord's, September 4. Australia won by ten runs. Toss: Pakistan.

Under the same NatWest umbrella as the England–India series came a one-off 50-over game at Lord's between Australia and Pakistan arranged, according to one's outlook, with either practice or money in mind. For those with any kind of cricketing memory, this was a return to the scene of the dreadful 1999 World Cup final when Pakistan were crushed. Surprisingly, they fielded five survivors from that game, while supposedly stable Australia had just two: Ponting and Lehmann. The players were more concerned with recent history, though, and Pakistan ran Australia close for the second time in a week. Yet again Australia proved their expertise in getting out of a tight spot – in the previous match in the Netherlands the margin had been 17 runs – but there were signs that Australian success in the forthcoming Champions Trophy was not inevitable. With the white ball moving around early on, Australia were in trouble at 99 for three before Symonds, just as he had against Pakistan in the 2003 World Cup, retrieved the situation with a brawny hundred. Dropped on 24 and 82, Symonds helped himself to 17 off the last over, from Shoaib Akhtar, who struggled for control throughout. After the break, Kasprowicz, slower but far more accurate, gave a demonstration of intelligent fast-medium bowling as Pakistan collapsed to 66 for four. But a stand of 162 – a Pakistan fifth-wicket record – between Inzamam-ul-Haq and Yousuf Youhana sparked hopes of victory. Even when Symonds, bowling off-spin, had Inzamam caught at extra cover, leaving Pakistan to make 42 from 31 balls, the game seemed finely poised. However, some inspired fielding caused a collapse of five for 20, and Australia had beaten Pakistan for the fifth time out of six – the other game being a washout.

Man of the Match: A. Symonds.   *Attendance:* 20,285; *receipts* £447,432.

Australia

M. L. Hayden b Shahid Afridi	52	M. J. Clarke c Shoaib Malik		
†B. J. Haddin c Shoaib Malik		b Shoaib Akhtar	31	
b Mohammad Sami	13	S. R. Watson not out	7	
*R. T. Ponting lbw b Mohammad Sami	4	L-b 9, w 12, n-b 2	23	
D. R. Martyn c Imran Farhat				
b Shoaib Malik	26	1/19 (2) 2/30 (3)	(6 wkts, 50 overs)	269
A. Symonds not out	104	3/99 (1) 4/109 (4)		
D. S. Lehmann run out	9	5/148 (6) 6/236 (7)	15 overs: 72-2	

B. Lee, J. N. Gillespie and M. S. Kasprowicz did not bat.

Bowling: Mohammad Sami 10–1–56–2; Naved-ul-Hasan 9–0–46–0; Shoaib Akhtar 8–0–70–1; Abdul Razzaq 4–0–12–0; Shoaib Malik 10–0–36–1; Shahid Afridi 9–0–40–1.

Pakistan

Yasir Hameed c Hayden b Kasprowicz	47	Mohammad Sami b Kasprowicz	10	
Imran Farhat c Haddin b Lee	11	Shoaib Akhtar not out	2	
Shahid Afridi lbw b Gillespie	0			
Shoaib Malik c Lee b Kasprowicz	2	L-b 4, w 2, n-b 4	10	
*Inzamam-ul-Haq c Watson b Symonds	72			
Yousuf Youhana c Watson b Kasprowicz	88	(48.2 overs)	259	
Abdul Razzaq c and b Kasprowicz	15	1/30 (2) 2/45 (3) 3/50 (4)		
†Moin Khan c Martyn b Gillespie	0	4/66 (1) 5/228 (5)		
Naved-ul-Hasan run out	2	6/239 (6) 7/245 (7) 8/247 (9)		
		9/250 (8) 10/259 (10)	15 overs: 62-3	

Bowling: Gillespie 8–2–26–2; Lee 10–0–67–1; Kasprowicz 9.2–1–47–5; Lehmann 5–0–24–0; Symonds 5–0–31–1; Watson 9–0–47–0; Clarke 2–0–13–0.

Umpires: S. A. Bucknor (West Indies) and D. R. Shepherd.
Third umpire: J. W. Lloyds.   Referee: B. C. Broad.

ICC CHAMPIONS TROPHY, 2004

Review by Matthew Engel

As night fell, literally and figuratively, on The Oval and the longest English season in history, the West Indian No. 10 Ian Bradshaw smacked a ball from Alex Wharf to the boundary backward of point to secure victory in the fourth Champions Trophy, the tournament that veers between being the second most important in world cricket and a ludicrous waste of time.

It was a triumph that seemed improbable at the start of the competition – West Indies were the rank outsiders of the eight serious contenders – and almost impossible an hour earlier, when Bradshaw joined Courtney Browne with 71 still needed. England were traded at 100 to 1 *on* by punters on the internet betting exchange Betfair, i.e. a pound to a penny, and thus close to mathematical certainty. In cricket, that exists only after the game is over.

No one (except someone suckered into that kind of bet) can have begrudged West Indies their success. Their players raced on to the field with a mixture of delight and astonishment that might not have been seen on this ground since their cricketing ancestors won the Test series 54 years earlier which foreshadowed the rise of West Indies as a power in the game.

It was a personal triumph for their captain Brian Lara, the man who had suffered most abuse during their recent decline. Three days earlier, he had been struck on the neck by Shoaib Akhtar in the semi-final at Southampton and his participation in the final was by no means certain. But he produced an inspired performance in the field.

It was a strange, and rather inappropriate, climax to a summer and a year characterised by the relentless pummelling Lara's team had received from England. But there were wider issues here. The whole Caribbean was in the grip of a particularly dire hurricane season, in which a succession of storms had wrought death and destruction across several of the islands; now once again cricket could fulfil its historic destiny and bring the people of the region together in pride. The defeat maintained England's sorry record as the only member of the big eight (the Test-playing countries minus Zimbabwe and Bangladesh) never to win a global one-day tournament. West Indian cricket, however, was in greater need of this victory, at least as long as it did not kid their administrators into thinking the flabby complacency that has bedevilled the game there for a decade was now cured.

On the other hand, one couldn't help feeling that if West Indies were the answer, it must have been a damn silly question. The enthralling climax was entirely out of keeping with a terrible tournament that was ill-conceived and ill-executed in almost every particular. For sheer dreadfulness, the fourth Champions Trophy surpassed the third, which in Sri Lanka two years earlier had failed to produce a winner at all.

The International Cricket Council's hard-working publicity machine maintained a relentless flow of upbeat information, and at the closing

Who'd have thought it? Ian Bradshaw savours the moment that takes West Indies, outsiders at the start of the tournament, to the Champions Trophy. Courtney Browne comes over to congratulate.

Picture by Patrick Eagar

ceremony the president Ehsan Mani proudly announced that "over 100,000 spectators and tens of millions of television viewers around the world" had watched the 15 matches. Worldwide TV viewers are notoriously hard to assess, but that 100,000 figure is easy to break down.

Since the final was sold out, and India's two matches and Australia v New Zealand were crammed with expatriate supporters, it meant the attendance at the other 11 fixtures, including both semi-finals, ranged from the paltry to the pathetic. In keeping with the strained relations between the ICC and the hosts, the ECB, recriminations were muted but inevitable. It is not easy to apportion blame precisely for this fiasco, but between them the two governing bodies constituted a deadly combination.

The Champions Trophy began in 1998 as an altruistic endeavour, to raise funds for cricketing development. Thus sceptical countries (like England) were shamed into taking it seriously as a biennial mini-World Cup. In theory, the fourth renewal – its existence only confirmed when England agreed to knuckle down and tour Zimbabwe in November – fitted precisely into that category. All the world's leading players were present except Sachin Tendulkar and Muttiah Muralitharan (both injured) and Shane Warne and Graham Thorpe (retired from one-day internationals). Still, hardly anyone cared.

The event was slotted into the schedule as an afterthought. It has found a home in September, the only month when there is little international cricket. But there is a good reason for that: September is a lousy month for the game over most of the planet – it is the monsoon season in much of the subcontinent, including Mumbai and Kolkata; it is rainy in the Cape and hurricane time in the West Indies; it is too early in much of Australia, which is in any case distracted by its footy finals; and undoubtedly too late in England. (The weather in Zimbabwe might be just right, though.)

Clearly, a 16-day tournament involving all the major countries could have been a huge success in the English midsummer. The ICC said there was nothing to stop it being held then; but by the time England stupidly volunteered to host the tournament, too many commitments were in place. So the event began on September 10, when the children are back at school, and the season is usually winding down to its often sodden conclusion.

ECB officials insisted, sometimes tetchily, that September is statistically drier than both July and August. This is true, but meteorologically illiterate. Midsummer rain often comes from heat-induced storms and falls quickly and intensely. You don't have to be an expert to know the difference between that, and the endless drizzle of autumn. The probability of bad weather, combined with the near-certainty of morning dew and the absolute certainty of early dusk, meant the tournament was pedalling uphill from the start.

Unlucky? The organisers got the luck they deserved

The games had to start at 10.15, forcing spectators to buy premium rush-hour train tickets (on top of the £30–40 ticket prices) or get stuck in the morning traffic: before the ill-attended first semi-final – between England and Australia, no less – Edgbaston seemed the only unjammed area of Birmingham. The final finished in pitch dark at just 6.36 p.m.

As it happened, there was a heatwave that lasted until the eve of the opening match, and the weather perked up again the day after the final, which itself was played in ferocious wintry cold. Unlucky? You could say the organisers got the luck they deserved.

In such conditions, the toss became absurdly important. The West Indians probably won the final despite rather than because of winning the toss: they had to bat in the dark after fielding in the rain, with the ball like soap. But the conventional wisdom was overwhelming. All but two of the 15 toss-winners chose to field first, the Pakistanis proving a rare exception when they astoundingly chose to bat in their semi-final against West Indies. Bob Woolmer, the coach, said later the decision was prompted by advice from "high sources", which merely increased the speculation, and the Pakistan board chairman had to issue a clarification, insisting Woolmer had just meant people who knew the Rose Bowl well. Of the seven truly competitive matches, the team batting first won just one.

The poor timing was backed up by marketing that barely even approached the third-rate. The imaginative ideas employed to attract spectators to county Twenty20 matches were entirely forgotten. Nothing was spent on building

Line and length: the Rose Bowl struggled with numbers for the bigger games, and many queued for hours trying to leave after the Pakistan v West Indies semi-final.

the competition in the public consciousness. Astonishingly, for such a supposedly important competition, there was no attendant merchandising: not a T-shirt, not a key fob, not a souvenir mug. However, the shops round the grounds did have signs informing spectators they could not buy England shirts there – because the team sponsors, Vodafone, were competitors of one of the four event sponsors, Hutch.

This tied in with the one aspect of the Trophy that did get publicity. The ICC's obsession with the threat of "ambush marketing", a publicity stunt by a rival of one of the sponsors, led them to issue blood-curdling warnings to spectators not to carry in the wrong brand of cola or crisps. In vain did the ECB protest that no one really intended to bar spectators who happened to have a solitary bottle of Coke in their bag. But the ICC regulation was unequivocal; the damage was done, the public ridicule duly collected. Although no one was actually known to have been taken away and tortured by the stewards, a gateman at Southampton was spotted solemnly assisting a spectator pouring the wrong kind of drink into the right kind of bottle. Similar regulations were actually in force at the Ryder Cup in Detroit, which was being held simultaneously. But cricket, with its clod-hopping approach and snarling manner, reaped all the opprobrium.

Other parts of the organisation were equally dire: the Rose Bowl at Southampton, given the biggest test of its short life, proved sadly unready with desperate access problems, and some exasperated spectators claimed it took two miserable hours to get in and up to four hours to get away using the park-and-ride facility after the rained-off first day of the England–Sri Lanka match. Hampshire blamed a clash with the Southampton Boat Show, which caused mayhem on the M27. The Rose Bowl may be magnificent one day; but with hardly any cover and inadequate facilities and catering, it was an ill-judged selection for this event. For the convenience

Picture by Patrick Eagar

of the broadcasters, the event had to be confined to three grounds (and Lord's refused to get involved) so ticket sales were further hit because spectators in most places had famine, whereas those in Southampton and Birmingham had five games each, far more than they wanted or could afford.

A great deal might have been forgiven had the cricket been better. But the ICC's reach exceeded its grasp. By inviting 12 teams when only eight had any chance of being competitive, it created a tournament that had fewer matches than mismatches. The organisers chose to get the rubbish out of the way at the start. That meant the first eight games were all inevitably one-sided. The remnants of Zimbabwean cricket did provide a better account of themselves than expected, and gave Sri Lanka in particular some anxious moments. But they were still outclassed; Bangladesh and Kenya were both very poor, while the ageing Caribbean exiles billed as the United States, who only qualified in curious circumstances (see page 1380), would have been better employed in September playing the Cross Arrows on the Nursery Ground rather than being given a working over at the Rose Bowl by Australia in less than three hours. New Zealand's batsmen took 110 off the Americans in the last five overs.

Ricky Ponting, Australia's captain, made it clear he felt the USA should not have been there at all. "I'm not convinced the Champions Trophy or World Cup is the place for these sides to play," he said. Malcolm Speed, the ICC chief executive, insisted the Americans' inclusion would raise the profile of cricket in the US. A database trawl after the Australian match showed that, apart from some of the Florida papers which provide brief coverage of cricket for their Caribbean readers, only one major American newspaper gave the game a mention: the *Detroit Free Press* had one dismissive paragraph.

The real thing? Stewards at Edgbaston uncover a spectator trying to bring the wrong brand of cola into the ground. With Pepsi a main sponsor, others were banned.

Picture by Patrick Eagar

Despite the absence of crowds, behaviour did become an issue, when drunken Antipodeans decided to take on the stewards and charge the field after the Australia–New Zealand match. Six stewards were injured. There were also scuffles involving mischievous Indian interlopers at Pakistan v West Indies. These were at least displays of enthusiasm, which rarely recurred either at home or abroad, especially after India's exit. Some Indian TV advertising slots had to be slashed from up to 300,000 rupees (£3,600) for ten seconds to 50,000. The small Australian press corps complained their papers were uninterested, even before their team's defeat.

There were relatively few umpiring controversies. The innovation of wiring up umpires in some matches to the stump microphone made no obvious difference, and the decision to hand over calling of no-balls to the third umpire made no waves, though there were some signs of rebellion among the umpires themselves.

And of course, 15 cricket matches will produce happy memories that will linger: the joy of the West Indians at The Oval; Lara's effervescence in the field that day; the raw aggression of Shoaib Akhtar and Steve Harmison; the batting of Marcus Trescothick and Ramnaresh Sarwan; England's sudden realisation that they could and would beat Australia; the noise generated by the Indian and Pakistani spectators at Edgbaston; the enthusiasm of the young Zimbabweans and the all-round promise of young Elton Chigumbura, the one good thing yet to emerge from his country's trauma, cricketing and general.

But overall, the main memories will be of cold and wet, of organisational disasters and of the general sense of a doomed competition that did cricket far more harm than good, all of which was obvious and avoidable.

Leading run-scorers

M. E. Trescothick (E)	261	C. H. Gayle (WI)	139	M. P. Vaughan (E)	115
R. R. Sarwan (WI)	166	A. Flintoff (E)	129	B. C. Lara (WI)	114
N. J. Astle (NZ)	163	S. Chanderpaul (WI)	127		
P. D. Collingwood (E)	141	D. R. Martyn (A)	125		

Hundreds

145*	N. J. Astle	NZ v USA	at The Oval
104	A. Flintoff	E v SL	at Southampton
104	M. E. Trescothick	E v WI	at The Oval
101	H. H. Gibbs	SA v WI	at The Oval

Leading wicket-takers

A. Flintoff (E)	9	M. S. Kasprowicz (A)	7	J. D. P. Oram (NZ)	6
S. J. Harmison (E)	8	I. D. R. Bradshaw (WI)	6	Shoaib Akhtar (P)	6
C. H. Gayle (WI)	7	J. N. Gillespie (A)	6		

Leading wicket-keepers

G. O. Jones (E)	9 (all ct)	Moin Khan (P)	5 (all ct)
C. O. Browne (WI)	6 (4 ct, 2 st)	K. C. Sangakkara (SL)	4 (all ct)

Leading fielders

M. E. Trescothick (E)	5	D. Gough (E)	3	B. C. Lara (WI)	3
C. L. Cairns (NZ)	3	D. P. M. D. Jayawardene (SL)	3	D. J. G. Sammy (WI)	3

Note: Matches in this section were not first-class. Figures in brackets are balls received.

PRELIMINARY-ROUND MATCH REPORTS BY LIAM BRICKHILL, DANIEL BRIGHAM, HUGH CHEVALLIER, PAUL COUPAR, MATTHEW ENGEL, JENNY THOMPSON AND ANAND VASU. SEMI-FINAL REPORTS BY MATTHEW ENGEL AND HUGH CHEVALLIER. FINAL BY S. RAJESH.

POOL A

NEW ZEALAND v USA

At The Oval, September 10. New Zealand won by 210 runs. New Zealand 2 pts. Toss: USA. International debuts: all USA except C. B. Lambert (played for West Indies).

New Zealand's winning margin of 210 runs was their biggest in a one-day international and was based on a memorable hundred from Astle. The outfield was soggy and the conditions dank after heavy rain had delayed the start by over an hour. New Zealand struggled initially to adapt and failed to impress a three-figure crowd that had probably been expecting more records to be broken. The USA's new-ball pairing of Howard Johnson and Tony Reid, who both bowled batsman-friendly medium-pace, found enough swing to restrict New Zealand early on, and when Leon

Romero had Marshall caught at third man in the 13th over, the score was 43 for two. After a dawdling recovery, McMillan joined Astle at 211 for four in the 43rd, at which point both batsmen decided to avoid the slow outfield altogether and aim over the top. The plan worked spectacularly, with the pair lofting 13 sixes and hurrying the scorers with 136 runs in the final 7.4 overs of the innings. Astle recorded his 14th and highest one-day international hundred and pummelled 13 fours and six sixes, while McMillan launched seven of the 27 balls he faced over the ropes. The USA's reply was spirited but futile and, after reaching 52 without loss, they managed only 85 more.

Man of the Match: N. J. Astle.   *Attendance:* 4,500.

New Zealand

*S. P. Fleming c Romero b Reid .	15	(22)	C. D. McMillan not out 64 (27)
N. J. Astle not out.	145	(151)	
H. J. H. Marshall c Desai			L-b 10, w 21, n-b 3 . . . 34
b Romero .	11	(20)	
S. B. Styris c Aijaz Ali b Staple .	75	(78)	1/25 (1) (4 wkts, 50 overs) 347
C. L. Cairns c sub (D. L. Blake)			2/43 (3)
b Staple .	3	(5)	3/206 (4) 4/211 (5) 15 overs: 58-2

J. D. P. Oram, †B. B. McCullum, C. Z. Harris, D. L. Vettori and D. R. Tuffey did not bat.

Bowling: H. R. Johnson 7–1–43–0; Reid 10–0–37–1; Romero 4–0–52–1; Lambert 10–0–66–0; Rashid Zia 9–1–63–0; Staple 10–0–76–2.

USA

R. P. Alexander lbw b Oram	26	(47)	C. A. Reid b Vettori. 6 (12)
†M. R. Johnson c McCullum			H. R. Johnson not out 0 (5)
b Oram .	20	(18)	
L. C. Romero c Styris b Oram . .	0	(2)	L-b 3, w 15. 18
S. J. Massiah c McCullum b Oram	0	(2)	
*R. W. Staple lbw b Cairns.	0	(1)	1/52 (2) 2/52 (3) (42.4 overs) 137
C. B. Lambert c Cairns b Vettori .	39	(84)	3/52 (4) 4/55 (5)
J. H. Desai lbw b Vettori	16	(38)	5/63 (1) 6/99 (7)
Aijaz Ali c Styris b Harris	4	(5)	7/114 (8) 8/122 (6)
Rashid Zia c Cairns b Oram	8	(41)	9/132 (10) 10/137 (9) 15 overs: 64-5

Bowling: Tuffey 8–0–39–0; Oram 9.4–1–36–5; Cairns 5–0–16–1; Harris 10–2–29–1; Vettori 10–3–14–3.

Umpires: B. R. Doctrove (West Indies) and D. R. Shepherd (England).
Third umpire: D. B. Hair (Australia).   Referee: M. J. Procter (South Africa).

AUSTRALIA v USA

At Southampton, September 13. Australia won by nine wickets. Australia 2 pts. Toss: Australia. One-day international debuts: D. L. Blake, Nasir Javed.

In a tournament mired in mismatches, this was the biggest. To guard against a washout in Australia's decisive group game against New Zealand, Ponting formed a plan: insert the Americans and dash home quickly enough to boost Australia's run-rate above that of New Zealand. The scheme was executed in two hours 44 minutes, the only uncertainty being the toss. Ponting won that and, on a sluggish pitch and an outfield greased by overnight rain, the USA scraped 65 – the lowest total in the Champions Trophy's brief history. After Lee's second delivery yorked Mark Johnson, most Americans struggled to lay bat on ball. In total, four were lbw, two bowled, and they managed only 26 runs in front of square as Kasprowicz and Gillespie pinched four cheap wickets each. Even the suggestively named Massiah, with a relatively perky 23, could not redeem the innings, in which Extras came next with 14. It then took Australia 7.5 overs, full of premeditated charges, to win – the third-shortest one-day international run-chase. Afterwards, Ponting broke with the usual protocol and questioned whether "this is the place for sides like the USA to play".

Man of the Match: M. S. Kasprowicz.   *Attendance:* 500.

USA

R. P. Alexander c Gilchrist		
b Kasprowicz .	8	(28)
†M. R. Johnson b Lee	0	(1)
L. C. Romero run out	1	(5)
S. J. Massiah c Lehmann		
b Kasprowicz .	23	(42)
*R. W. Staple lbw b Kasprowicz .	4	(10)
C. A. Reid lbw b Kasprowicz	2	(5)
Rashid Zia lbw b Gillespie	1	(16)
Aijaz Ali c Gilchrist b Gillespie. .	1	(6)
Nasir Javed not out	2	(19)
D. L. Blake lbw b Gillespie	0	(2)
H. R. Johnson b Gillespie	9	(15)
L-b 2, w 7, n-b 5	14	

1/1 (2) 2/2 (3) 3/32 (1)   (24 overs) 65
4/38 (5) 5/46 (4) 6/46 (6)
7/49 (8) 8/53 (7) 9/53 (10) 10/65 (11)
15 overs: 47-6

Bowling: Lee 5–0–21–1; McGrath 6–1–13–0; Kasprowicz 7–1–14–4; Gillespie 6–1–15–4.

Australia

†A. C. Gilchrist not out	24	(25)
M. L. Hayden c M. R. Johnson		
b H. R. Johnson .	23	(17)
*R. T. Ponting not out	8	(8)
L-b 1, w 6, n-b 4	11	

1/41 (2)   (1 wkt, 7.5 overs) 66

D. S. Lehmann, A. Symonds, D. R. Martyn, M. J. Clarke, B. Lee, J. N. Gillespie, M. S. Kasprowicz and G. D. McGrath did not bat.

Bowling: H. R. Johnson 3–0–26–1; Reid 3 0–26–0; Blake 1–0–7–0; Rashid Zia 0.5–0–6–0.

Umpires: Aleem Dar (Pakistan) and B. F. Bowden (New Zealand).
Third umpire: S. A. Bucknor (West Indies). Referee: R. S. Madugalle (Sri Lanka).

AUSTRALIA v NEW ZEALAND

At The Oval, September 16. Australia won by seven wickets. Australia 2 pts. Toss: Australia.

A murderous innings from Symonds, who struck an unbeaten 71 from only 47 balls, with seven fours and four sixes, ultimately propelled Australia into the last four at the expense of their neighbours. But it was the bowling of McGrath that paved the way for a comprehensive victory. To mutterings about his declining powers, McGrath's first 23 deliveries had cost 24, but he responded just in time to trap Astle and then added Marshall and Styris in a wicket-to-wicket spell of three for three in 19 balls. With Kasprowicz claiming three scalps as well, New Zealand were reeling at 89 for seven, before McCullum marshalled some lower-order resistance, including a stand of 68 for the ninth wicket with Vettori – then a national record against any opposition. In the end, a total of 198 for nine on a sluggish pitch was a minor triumph. Gilchrist was out in the first over of Australia's reply, but Hayden eased his fears before Martyn and Symonds put together an increasingly violent century partnership. An otherwise jocular occasion, enlivened by some good-natured crowd interaction, was marred after the end of the match when drunken spectators staged a mini-pitch invasion and clashed with security guards, six of whom were injured.

Man of the Match: A. Symonds.   *Attendance:* 15,000.

New Zealand

*S. P. Fleming c Gillespie		
b Kasprowicz .	29	(51)
N. J. Astle lbw b McGrath	18	(19)
H. J. H. Marshall lbw b McGrath.	0	(2)
S. B. Styris c Clarke b McGrath .	0	(11)
C. D. McMillan run out	18	(27)
J. D. P. Oram		
c and b Kasprowicz .	15	(27)
C. L. Cairns lbw b Kasprowicz . .	0	(1)
C. Z. Harris c and b Lehmann. . .	26	(51)
†B. B. McCullum c Kasprowicz		
b Gillespie .	47	(68)
D. L. Vettori not out	29	(42)
K. D. Mills not out	3	(3)
L-b 4, w 7, n-b 2	13	

1/30 (2)   (9 wkts, 50 overs) 198
2/36 (3) 3/49 (4)
4/49 (1) 5/79 (6) 6/79 (7)
7/89 (8) 8/124 (8) 9/192 (9)   15 overs: 52-4

Bowling: McGrath 10–0–39–3; Gillespie 9–1–46–1; Kasprowicz 10–1–32–3; Watson 6–0–32–0; Symonds 10–2–29–0; Lehmann 5–0–16–1.

Australia

†A. C. Gilchrist b Oram	4	(5)
M. L. Hayden c Cairns b Harris	47	(73)
*R. T. Ponting b Styris	14	(29)
D. R. Martyn not out	60	(71)
A. Symonds not out	71	(47)
L-b 1, w 1, n-b 1	3	

1/4 (1)   (3 wkts, 37.2 overs) 199
2/49 (3) 3/99 (2)   15 overs: 65-2

D. S. Lehmann, M. J. Clarke, S. R. Watson, J. N. Gillespie, M. S. Kasprowicz and G. D. McGrath did not bat.

Bowling: Oram 9–2–34–1; Mills 5.2–0–34–0; Vettori 10–0–52–0; Styris 2–0–9–1; Cairns 3–0–17–0; Harris 7–1–36–1; McMillan 1–0–16–0.

Umpires: S. A. Bucknor (West Indies) and R. E. Koertzen (South Africa).
Third umpire: D. R. Shepherd (England).   Referee: R. S. Madugalle (Sri Lanka).

POOL B

BANGLADESH v SOUTH AFRICA

At Birmingham, September 12. South Africa won by nine wickets. South Africa 2 pts. Toss: Bangladesh. International debuts: Aftab Ahmed, Nazmul Hossain.

Rajin Saleh, aged 20 years 297 days, became the youngest captain in one-day international history because Habibul Bashar was injured, and took a decision that had older heads shaking. On a damp morning at Edgbaston he inexplicably decided to bat first. Rajin later argued that he thought the pitch would take spin as the day wore on, but South Africa's attack rendered such speculation irrelevant. In bowler-friendly conditions, Langeveldt and Ntini picked up three wickets apiece, and Bangladesh were blown away for only 93 – a total which would have been much lower but for the efforts of 19-year-old Nafis Iqbal, who hit a good-looking 40. Of the rest, only Khaled Mashud and Extras reached five. Despite the early loss of Gibbs, bowled for four during a bright opening spell from Tapash Baisya and the 16-year-old debutant Nazmul Hossain, South Africa then cantered home by nine wickets in a flurry of boundaries with more than 32 overs to spare.

Man of the Match: C. K. Langeveldt.   *Attendance:* 2,800.

Bangladesh

Javed Omar lbw b Langeveldt	4	(12)	Mohammad Rafique c Boje b Ntini	0	(2)
Mohammad Ashraful c Kallis b Langeveldt	4	(6)	Tapash Baisya c Boucher b Ntini	5	(6)
Nafis Iqbal c Gibbs b Boje	40	(59)	Nazmul Hossain not out	1	(13)
*Rajin Saleh c van Jaarsveld b Langeveldt	0	(2)	L-b 7, w 5, n-b 2	14	
Aftab Ahmed c Boucher b Pollock	0	(13)			
†Khaled Mashud c Smith b Boje	24	(65)	1/7 (2) 2/15 (1) (31.3 overs) 93		
Manjural Islam Rana b Boje	1	(11)	3/15 (4) 4/20 (5)		
Mushfiqur Rahman c Boje b Ntini	0	(2)	5/63 (3) 6/71 (7) 7/72 (8)		
			8/72 (9) 9/80 (10) 10/93 (6) 15 overs: 38-4		

Bowling: Pollock 6–1–15–1; Langeveldt 7–0–17–3; Ntini 9–2–19–3; Klusener 3–1–12–0; Boje 6.3–0–23–3.

South Africa

*G. C. Smith not out	42	(52)
H. H. Gibbs b Tapash Baisya	4	(11)
J. H. Kallis not out	40	(44)
B 5, w 2, n-b 1	8	

1/15 (2) (1 wkt, 17.5 overs) 94

15 overs: 70-1

J. A. Rudolph, M. van Jaarsveld, †M. V. Boucher, S. M. Pollock, L. Klusener, N. Boje, C. K. Langeveldt and M. Ntini did not bat.

Bowling: Tapash Baisya 6–0–39–1; Nazmul Hossain 6–1–17–0; Mohammad Rafique 3–0–9–0; Mushfiqur Rahman 2.5–0–24–0.

Umpires: J. W. Lloyds (England) and S. J. A. Taufel (Australia).
Third umpire: D. B. Hair (Australia). Referee: B. C. Broad (England).

BANGLADESH v WEST INDIES

At Southampton, September 15. West Indies won by 138 runs. West Indies 2 pts. Toss: Bangladesh.

Bangladesh were dumped out of the competition with an ease that disappointed their few hundred noisy fans, who entertained vague hopes of an upset. West Indies had just suffered humiliation in the Test series against England, but five new arrivals brought some vim: Hinds took part in an opening stand of 192; the tall Dillon took a career-best five for 29; and Darren Sammy began his international career (his "debut", also on this ground during the NatWest Series in July, had been a total washout) with two stunning catches, and three in total. However, Bangladesh had started the day tidily with the ball, even if they failed to break through: Gayle, who eventually feathered behind on 99, and Hinds were stubborn, lasting 40 overs thanks to three fumbled catches, but never commanding. By contrast, Lara was lordly. Only once had Bangladesh made as many as the 270 they needed now, and Dillon kept it that way, helping reduce a compliant top order to 26 for five.

Man of the Match: C. H. Gayle.   *Attendance:* 1,500.

West Indies

C. H. Gayle c Khaled Mashud b Tapash Baisya	99	(132)	S. Chanderpaul not out	18	(18)
W. W. Hinds c Nazmul Hossain b Tapash Baisya	82	(119)	L-b 6, w 12, n-b 2	20	
R. R. Sarwan not out	30	(26)	1/192 (2) (3 wkts, 50 overs) 269		
*B. C. Lara run out	20	(7)	2/201 (1) 3/232 (4) 15 overs: 62-0		

S. C. Joseph, D. J. J. Bravo, †C. O. Browne, M. Dillon, I. D. R. Bradshaw and D. J. G. Sammy did not bat.

Bowling: Tapash Baisya 10–0–58–2; Nazmul Hossain 10–1–44–0; Mushfiqur Rahman 10–0–40–0; Khaled Mahmud 10–1–57–0; Mohammad Rafique 10–0–64–0.

Bangladesh

Javed Omar c Sammy b Dillon	2	(7)	Khaled Mahmud not out	34	(51)
Mohammad Ashraful c Dillon b Bradshaw	10	(8)	Tapash Baisya c sub (R. O. Hinds) b Gayle	8	(16)
Nafis Iqbal b Dillon	2	(12)	Nazmul Hossain c Bravo b Gayle	4	(21)
*Rajin Saleh b Dillon	7	(9)	L-b 2, w 8	10	
Aftab Ahmed b Bravo	21	(44)			
†Khaled Mashud c Sammy b Dillon	0	(9)	1/13 (1) 2/15 (2) (39.3 overs) 131		
Mushfiqur Rahman c Joseph b Sammy	21	(41)	3/23 (3) 4/24 (4) 5/26 (6) 6/71 (5)		
Mohammad Rafique c Sammy b Dillon	12	(19)	7/71 (7) 8/94 (8) 9/105 (10) 10/131 (11) 15 overs: 39-5		

Bowling: Dillon 10–4–29–5; Bradshaw 10–2–25–1; Sammy 6–0–19–1; Bravo 9–0–44–1; Gayle 4.3–0–12–2.

Umpires: Aleem Dar (Pakistan) and J. W. Lloyds (England).
Third umpire: B. F. Bowden (New Zealand). Referee: B. C. Broad (England).

SOUTH AFRICA v WEST INDIES

At The Oval, September 18, 19. West Indies won by five wickets. West Indies 2 pts. Toss: West Indies.

West Indies edged into the semi-finals, courtesy of a rescue operation from their batsmen after rain had forced the match to spill over into the reserve day. Lara and Sarwan took charge once the openers had fallen early, before Chanderpaul, with a quickfire 51 off just 52 deliveries, majestically stroked his team home with seven balls to spare. It meant that South Africa's fine start went to waste. Smith and Gibbs had put on 102 for the first wicket after being asked to bat, with Gibbs going on to complete his 13th one-day international hundred – an innings he attributed to a good night's sleep following a pizza washed down by whisky. Rudolph's frisky 46 helped South Africa to a challenging 246 for six, before Pollock struck twice early on to maintain their advantage. West Indies consolidated with stands of 98 between Sarwan and Lara, and 83 between Sarwan and Chanderpaul. But with the asking-rate mounting, two successive towering leg-side sixes by Powell off Pollock in an over that cost 19 steadied their nerves.

Man of the Match: R. R. Sarwan. *Attendance:* 15,100.

Close of play: West Indies 20-0 (6 overs) (Gayle 12, W. W. Hinds 6).

South Africa

*G. C. Smith b Gayle	45	(64)	L. Klusener not out	12	(10)
H. H. Gibbs c Bravo b Gayle	101	(135)			
J. H. Kallis b Bravo	16	(33)			
J. A. Rudolph b Gayle	46	(39)	L-b 4, w 2	6	
M. van Jaarsveld c Powell b Bradshaw	0	(1)	1/102 (1) (6 wkts, 50 overs)	246	
S. M. Pollock not out	13	(11)	2/148 (3)		
†M. V. Boucher c Chanderpaul b Bradshaw	7	(7)	3/198 (2) 4/212 (5)		
			5/213 (4) 6/222 (7)	15 overs: 66-0	

N. Boje, C. K. Langeveldt and M. Ntini did not bat.

Bowling: Bradshaw 10–2–40–2; Collymore 9–0–53–0; Bravo 9–0–54–1; R. O. Hinds 10–0–35–0; Gayle 10–0–50–3; Powell 2–0–10–0.

West Indies

C. H. Gayle b Pollock	16	(19)	D. J. J. Bravo not out	4	(3)
W. W. Hinds lbw b Pollock	15	(30)	L-b 10, w 8, n-b 5	23	
R. R. Sarwan b Ntini	75	(99)			
*B. C. Lara b Boje	49	(85)	1/24 (1) (5 wkts, 48.5 overs)	249	
S. Chanderpaul not out	51	(52)	2/33 (2) 3/131 (4)		
R. L. Powell b Ntini	16	(10)	4/214 (3) 5/237 (6)	15 overs: 57-2	

†C. O. Browne, R. O. Hinds, I. D. R. Bradshaw and C. D. Collymore did not bat.

Bowling: Pollock 10–0–56–2; Langeveldt 7.5–2–41–0; Ntini 5–0–26–2; Klusener 10–1–32–0; Kallis 6–1–32–0; Boje 10–0–52–1.

Umpires: J. W. Lloyds (England) and D. R. Shepherd (England).
Third umpire: D. J. Harper (Australia). Referee: B. C. Broad (England).

POOL C

INDIA v KENYA

At Southampton, September 11. India won by 98 runs. India 2 pts. Toss: Kenya. One-day international debuts: R. G. Aga, M. A. Ouma.

The Rose Bowl metamorphosed into the subcontinent for this game. Klaxons and hooters blared incessantly and Asian voices roared amid a sky-blue sea of replica India one-day shirts, but for all the passion in the stands, the match flickered into life on the pitch. Tikolo won the toss and pleased the spectators by fielding, so virtually ensuring their idols would bat for 50 overs. Sehwag caused a few winces early on by scything across the line, but Ganguly and Laxman knuckled down on a curmudgeonly surface. The Kenyan bowlers put the ball in the right place, and just four boundaries came from the first 18 overs. But Ganguly upped the tempo before he was out aiming to run Martin Suji behind square, ten short of a fourth successive hundred against Kenya, and the Indian innings finished with a flourish the Kenyans had no hope of matching. Within nine overs, they had subsided to 21 for three. Maurice Ouma, a 21-year-old right-hander, batted intelligently on debut, though never threatened to do more than irritate. Rageb Aga, an all-rounder one year younger, endured a less happy baptism.

Man of the Match: S. C. Ganguly.   *Attendance:* 12,000.

India

*S. C. Ganguly b M. A. Suji....	90	(124)
V. Sehwag b Odoyo...........	17	(27)
V. V. S. Laxman st Otieno b Tikolo	79	(99)
Yuvraj Singh c Otieno b Odoyo..	9	(9)
M. Kaif not out	49	(29)
R. Dravid not out	30	(16)
B 4, l-b 5, w 3, n-b 4..	16	

1/30 (2)   (4 wkts, 50 overs) 290
2/191 (1)
3/204 (4) 4/213 (3)   15 overs: 55-1

†K. D. Karthik, A. B. Agarkar, Harbhajan Singh, I. K. Pathan and A. Nehra did not bat.

Bowling: M. A. Suji 10–2 42–1; Odoyo 10–1–43–2; Ongondo 5–0–27–0; Aga 9–0–70–0; Tikolo 10–0–53–1; Patel 3–0–21–0; T. O. Suji 3–0–25–0.

Kenya

†K. O. Otieno run out	0	(9)	M. A. Ouma c Karthik b Agarkar.	49	(93)
R. D. Shah c Karthik			B. J. Patel not out...........	40	(77)
b Harbhajan Singh .	33	(53)	M. A. Suji not out..........	6	(7)
*S. O. Tikolo lbw b Pathan.....	2	(10)			
H. S. Modi c Ganguly b Pathan..	5	(10)	B 10, l-b 9, w 19, n-b 4	42	
T. M. Odoyo c Karthik					
b Harbhajan Singh .	15	(42)	1/9 (1) 2/13 (3) (7 wkts, 50 overs) 192		
R. G. Aga c Ganguly			3/21 (4) 4/58 (2)		
b Harbhajan Singh .	0	(3)	5/62 (6) 6/74 (5) 7/166 (7) 15 overs: 46-3		

T. O. Suji and P. J. Ongondo did not bat.

Bowling: Pathan 6–1–11–2; Nehra 7–1–17–0; Agarkar 10–0–42–1; Harbhajan Singh 10–2–33–3; Ganguly 5–0–21–0; Yuvraj Singh 4–0–17–0; Sehwag 8–1–32–0.

Umpires: D. J. Harper (Australia) and R. E. Koertzen (South Africa).
Third umpire: Aleem Dar (Pakistan).   Referee: C. H. Lloyd (West Indies).

KENYA v PAKISTAN

At Birmingham, September 14, 15. Pakistan won by seven wickets. Pakistan 2 pts. Toss: Pakistan. One-day international debut: M. L. Patel.

An astonishing Kenyan collapse, in which they lost nine wickets for 27 in little more than ten overs, handed Pakistan victory after the weather had threatened to rob them of easy points. No play had been possible on the first day due to persistent rain, and the cloud cover on the reserve day hinted at further hold-ups. When one duly came after 20 overs, there was something close to relief among the predictably small crowd: Kenya had crawled to 64 for one against some listless bowling. But Pakistan re-emerged determined to demonstrate the difference in class, and Kenya tumbled to 94 all out. The unexpected destroyers were the spinners Shoaib Malik and Shahid Afridi, who ruined Kenya's hopes by taking advantage of a skiddy pitch, and batsmen who were leaving too many straight balls. Afridi finished with a career-best five for 11. Pakistan's reply was swift, as Yasir Hameed and Imran Farhat reached 70 in the 13th over.

Man of the Match: Shahid Afridi.   *Attendance:* 4,200.

Kenya

†K. O. Otieno lbw b Shoaib Malik	33	(73)
R. D. Shah c Shahid Afridi b Naved-ul-Hasan .	0	(2)
M. A. Ouma c Moin Khan b Shahid Afridi .	23	(63)
*S. O. Tikolo b Shoaib Malik . . .	0	(4)
H. S. Modi not out	18	(20)
T. M. Odoyo b Shahid Afridi . . .	0	(3)
B. J. Patel b Shahid Afridi	1	(14)
R. G. Aga b Shoaib Malik	1	(6)

M. L. Patel b Shahid Afridi.	0	(1)
M. A. Suji run out	0	(1)
P. J. Ongondo b Shahid Afridi . . .	2	(11)
L-b 5, w 5, n-b 6	16	

1/2 (2) 2/67 (3)   (32 overs) 94
3/67 (1) 4/70 (4) 5/71 (6)
6/78 (7) 7/85 (8) 8/90 (9)
9/90 (10) 10/94 (11)   15 overs: 43-1

Bowling: Mohammad Sami 5–2–14–0; Naved-ul-Hasan 6–0–19–1; Shoaib Akhtar 5–2–10–0; Abdul Razzaq 4–0–20–0; Shoaib Malik 6–1–15–3; Shahid Afridi 6–1–11–5.

Pakistan

Yasir Hameed c Otieno b Suji . . .	41	(48)
Imran Farhat not out	38	(45)
Shoaib Malik c Tikolo b Aga. . . .	0	(5)
Shahid Afridi b Aga.	3	(4)
Abdul Razzaq not out	7	(13)
L-b 1, w 2, n-b 3	6	

1/70 (1)   (3 wkts, 18.4 overs) 95
2/71 (3) 3/81 (4)   15 overs: 78-2

*Inzamam-ul-Haq, Yousuf Youhana, †Moin Khan, Naved-ul-Hasan, Mohammad Sami and Shoaib Akhtar did not bat.

Bowling: Suji 8–0–37–1; Odoyo 3–0–20–0; Ongondo 3.4–1–20–0; Aga 4–0–17–2.

Umpires: B. R. Doctrove (West Indies) and D. B. Hair (Australia).
Third umpire: R. E. Koertzen (South Africa).   Referee: C. H. Lloyd (West Indies).

INDIA v PAKISTAN

At Birmingham, September 19. Pakistan won by three wickets. Pakistan 2 pts. Toss: Pakistan.

At last the tournament came alive as the one match-up in world cricket that can draw a one-day crowd any time, anywhere, filled Edgbaston with noisy fans who paid up to £150 for £35 tickets. The game gave them fair value: it was fraught with the sort of tension and momentum-swings that low-scoring matches can sometimes inspire. After being put in, India's batsmen, so often the engine-room of their side, soon found themselves struggling at 28 for three, which became 106 for six in the 34th over. But an innings from Dravid which began in timid defiance

Thundering in: Shoaib Akhtar bowled at consistently terrifying pace throughout the tournament, blasting out four Indian batsmen at Edgbaston.

Picture by Patrick Eagar

and bloomed into belligerence – he held Shoaib Akhtar's fiery glares and occasionally told him where to get off – provided a gleam of hope, as did some joyous biffing by Agarkar. A total of 200 was defensible, and Pathan kept Indian hopes alive, swinging the ball with real control to reduce Pakistan to 27 for three. Inzamam-ul-Haq and Yousuf Youhana, captain and vice-captain, steadied the ship with a stand of 75, but India kept chipping away and at 152 for six Asian pride was up for grabs. Enter Shahid Afridi, held back until No. 8, to thrash two mighty sixes and provide impetus for the final push. Youhana, composed and canny, hardly put a foot wrong throughout his innings, and eased Pakistan to victory with four balls to spare. India, meanwhile, had to cope with the humiliation of being dumped out of the competition by their arch-rivals, who in the space of two months had beaten them in Sri Lanka, Holland and now England.

Man of the Match: Yousuf Youhana. *Attendance:* 19,800.

India

*S. C. Ganguly c Moin Khan b Mohammad Sami	0	(5)	
V. Sehwag c Shoaib Malik b Naved-ul-Hasan	10	(20)	
V. V. S. Laxman c Shoaib Malik b Naved-ul-Hasan	3	(9)	
M. Kaif c Moin Khan b Shoaib Akhtar	27	(59)	
†R. Dravid c and b Naved-ul-Hasan	67	(108)	
Yuvraj Singh c Moin Khan b Shoaib Akhtar	0	(3)	
R. S. Gavaskar c Moin Khan b Abdul Razzaq	13	(43)	
A. B. Agarkar c Yousuf Youhana b Naved-ul-Hasan	47	(50)	
I. K. Pathan c Yousuf Youhana b Shoaib Akhtar	6	(8)	
Harbhajan Singh not out	3	(3)	
A. Nehra c Shahid Afridi b Shoaib Akhtar	0	(2)	
L-b 10, w 3, n-b 11	24		

1/1 (1) 2/10 (3) (49.5 overs) 200
3/28 (2) 4/73 (4) 5/73 (6)
6/106 (7) 7/188 (5) 8/193 (8)
9/199 (9) 10/200 (11)   15 overs: 47-3

Bowling: Mohammad Sami 9–1–50–1; Naved-ul-Hasan 9–1–25–4; Abdul Razzaq 10–0–27–1; Shoaib Akhtar 9.5–1–36–4; Shahid Afridi 2–0–23–0; Shoaib Malik 10–0–29–0.

Pakistan

Yasir Hameed c Nehra b Pathan . .	15	(29)	
Imran Farhat c Dravid b Pathan . .	0	(4)	
Shoaib Malik c Dravid b Pathan .	5	(7)	
*Inzamam-ul-Haq c Dravid			
b Agarkar .	41	(79)	
Yousuf Youhana not out	81	(114)	
Abdul Razzaq b Sehwag	9	(21)	
†Moin Khan c Yuvraj Singh			
b Nehra .	10	(13)	

Shahid Afridi c Sehwag
           b Yuvraj Singh .   25 (12)
Naved-ul-Hasan not out 5 (17)
    B 2, l-b 5, w 3   10

1/1 (2)   (7 wkts, 49.2 overs) 201
2/10 (3) 3/27 (1)
4/102 (4) 5/127 (6)
6/152 (7) 7/187 (8)   15 overs: 39-3

Mohammad Sami and Shoaib Akhtar did not bat.

Bowling: Pathan 9–1–34–3; Nehra 10–0–45–1; Agarkar 10–2–33–1; Harbhajan Singh 10–1–37–0; Ganguly 4–0–17–0; Sehwag 4–0–22–1; Yuvraj Singh 2.2–0–6–1.

Umpires: R. E. Koertzen (South Africa) and S. J. A. Taufel (Australia).
Third umpire: S. A. Bucknor (West Indies).   Referee: C. H. Lloyd (West Indies).

POOL D

ENGLAND v ZIMBABWE

At Birmingham, September 10, 11. England won by 152 runs. England 2 pts. Toss: Zimbabwe.

England overcame a nervous beginning and eventually intimidated their young opponents before winning easily. This dull contest provided a dismal showcase for the start of the competition and was watched by barely 3,000 on the rain-hit opening day (and a few hundred when it resumed on the Saturday), almost certainly the lowest crowd ever to attend an England one-day international at home. Those who did turn up booed the opening ceremony, such as it was, with cries of "Get on with it!" as the ICC president, Ehsan Mani, shook hands with the teams before the delayed start. Things got rapidly worse from there. Tinashe Panyangara, Zimbabwe's 18-year-old opening bowler, bowled seven wides in his first over. None the less, the England batsmen, looking decidedly under-motivated, struggled to build a total against a side that showed considerable spirit and athleticism. They were saved, perhaps not coincidentally, by the two players least sure of their place: Solanki and Collingwood, whose canny second-day innings – his customary placements leavened by three sixes, two in successive balls off Hondo – took England to the brink of 300 and well out of Zimbabwe's reach. Harmison, bowling with and like the wind, and Flintoff were far too good for the Zimbabwean batsmen in these damp conditions. But a fighting innings from another of their 18-year-olds, Elton Chigumbura, impressed England, and delayed them. A handful of protesters opposed to the Zimbabwean regime sat quietly in the stands, but in the cold found it hard to maintain the formation they needed to show off their one-letter T-shirts reading MUGABE OUT. Eventually, this just became MUABO.

Man of the Match: P. D. Collingwood.   *Attendance:* 5,600.
Close of play: England 198-5 (38 overs) (Collingwood 35, Jones 23).

England

M. E. Trescothick c Taylor			
b Hondo .	10	(15)	
V. S. Solanki lbw b Sibanda	62	(81)	
*M. P. Vaughan c Vermeulen			
b Rainsford .	17	(13)	
A. J. Strauss c Taibu b Rainsford .	25	(30)	
A. Flintoff c Hondo b Panyangara	6	(8)	
P. D. Collingwood not out	80	(93)	
†G. O. Jones b Hondo	38	(43)	

A. F. Giles run out 23 (22)
A. G. Wharf not out 4 (2)

      L-b 5, w 22, n-b 7   34

1/21 (1)   (7 wkts, 50 overs) 299
2/54 (3) 3/114 (4)
4/123 (5) 5/159 (2)
6/220 (7) 7/295 (8)   15 overs: 94-2

D. Gough and S. J. Harmison did not bat.

Bowling: Panyangara 10–0–86–1; Hondo 9–0–66–2; Rainsford 10–0–43–2; Chigumbura 5–1–36–0; Utseya 10–0–35–0; Sibanda 3–0–12–1; Matsikenyeri 3–0–16–0.

Zimbabwe

S. Matsikenyeri c Collingwood			
b Gough .	4	(12)	
B. R. M. Taylor lbw b Gough . . .	6	(19)	
V. Sibanda b Flintoff	28	(56)	
D. D. Ebrahim c Jones b Harmison	3	(7)	
M. A. Vermeulen c Jones			
b Harmison .	0	(4)	
*†T. Taibu hit wkt b Giles	40	(61)	
E. Chigumbura not out.	42	(47)	
T. Panyangara b Harmison	1	(8)	
P. Utseya c Gough b Flintoff. . . .	5	(16)	

D. T. Hondo c Trescothick
b Flintoff . 0 (2)
E. C. Rainsford c Jones b Giles. . 4 (6)

L-b 3, w 7, n-b 4. 14

(39 overs) 147

1/14 (2) 2/23 (1) (39 overs) 147
3/26 (4) 4/26 (5)
5/64 (3) 6/106 (6)
7/120 (8) 8/142 (9)
9/142 (10) 10/147 (11)   15 overs: 42-4

Bowling: Gough 8–2–24–2; Harmison 10–3–29–3; Wharf 7–0–45–0; Flintoff 6–1–11–3; Giles 8–1–35–2.

Umpires: S. A. Bucknor (West Indies) and S. J. A. Taufel (Australia).
Third umpire: B. F. Bowden (New Zealand). Referee: R. S. Madugalle (Sri Lanka).

SRI LANKA v ZIMBABWE

At The Oval, September 14. Sri Lanka won by four wickets. Sri Lanka 2 pts. Toss: Sri Lanka,
On a chilly day, Sri Lanka made hard work of victory in what proved to be the closest thing to an upset in the competition. At 162 for six, they still needed 30 more to see off Zimbabwe's motley but spirited collection of youngsters, only for their extra experience and the depth of their batting to steer them to an unconvincing win. It was hard luck on Chigumbura, who had shone for Zimbabwe with a sparkling all-round performance, but his fine 57 and three-wicket haul were not quite enough to upset the form book. Early on, it had been business as usual as Zimbabwe slumped to 85 for six, before a strong rearguard action, led by the defiant Chigumbura, dragged them to 191 and into the realms of respectability. Sri Lanka's run-chase got off to a disastrous start, with both openers dismissed in single figures. But Atapattu anchored the innings with a steady 43, and although Zimbabwe continued to chip away at the middle order, the winning runs came with more than six overs remaining.

Man of the Match: E. Chigumbura.   *Attendance:* 2,500.

Zimbabwe

B. R. M. Taylor c Chandana			
b Maharoof .	13	(34)	
S. Matsikenyeri c Sangakkara			
b Zoysa .	16	(22)	
V. Sibanda c Jayawardene b Vaas .	9	(27)	
D. D. Ebrahim c Chandana			
b Zoysa .	3	(14)	
M. A. Vermeulen c Sangakkara			
b Maharoof .	17	(29)	
*†T. Taibu c Sangakkara			
b Maharoof .	16	(34)	
E. Chigumbura lbw b Chandana. .	57	(71)	

T. Panyangara c Atapattu b Zoysa. 8 (35)
P. Utseya c Jayawardene
b Chandana . 31 (28)
D. T. Hondo not out. 0 (0)
E. C. Rainsford b Jayasuriya 3 (4)
B 4, l-b 8, w 3, n-b 3 . . 18

1/23 (2) 2/43 (1) (49.1 overs) 191
3/47 (3) 4/61 (4)
5/76 (5) 6/85 (6)
7/120 (8) 8/184 (9)
9/188 (7) 10/191 (11)   15 overs: 48-3

Bowling: Vaas 10–0–42–1; Zoysa 10–2–19–3; Maharoof 9–1–38–3; Jayasuriya 9.1–1–28–1; Chandana 9–0–39–2; Dilshan 2–0–13–0.

> **❝** He hit four fours, a six and a seagull at short third man."
>
> Sussex in 2004, page 773.

Sri Lanka

D. A. Gunawardene c Vermeulen b Panyangara	4	(4)	D. P. M. D. Jayawardene lbw b Chigumbura	28	(43)	
S. T. Jayasuriya c Taibu b Hondo	2	(5)	T. M. Dilshan not out	25	(28)	
*M. S. Atapattu c Taibu b Chigumbura	43	(80)	U. D. U. Chandana not out	20	(24)	
W. S. Jayantha c Ebrahim b Chigumbura	36	(41)	W 7, n-b 2	9		
†K. C. Sangakkara c Chigumbura b Sibanda	28	(40)				

1/4 (1)   (6 wkts, 43.5 overs) 195
2/10 (2) 3/54 (4)
4/99 (5) 5/141 (3) 6/162 (6)   15 overs: 66-3

W. P. U. J. C. Vaas, M. F. Maharoof and D. N. T. Zoysa did not bat.

Bowling: Panyangara 6–0–39–1; Hondo 9–0–27–1; Rainsford 10–0–46–0; Chigumbura 8.5–1–37–3; Sibanda 6–0–24–1; Utseya 4–0–22–0.

Umpires: D. J. Harper (Australia) and D. R. Shepherd (England).
Third umpire: S. J. A. Taufel (Australia).   Referee: M. J. Procter (South Africa).

ENGLAND v SRI LANKA

At Southampton, September 17, 18. England won by 49 runs (D/L method). England 2 pts. Toss: Sri Lanka.

In a summer of jaw-dropping innings from Flintoff, this hundred against Sri Lanka left spectators open-mouthed with wonder. It had its faults – Jayawardene should have caught him at slip for a single, and Chandana will hold more difficult chances than the one he spilled at deep mid-wicket when Flintoff made 25 – but it was magnificent. Its glory lay in its tempo. Flintoff arrived at a thorny 70 for three, treading warily as the grudging Rose Bowl pitch hindered timing. He had a watchful 21 when rain ended the first day, and just 27 after facing his 50th delivery next morning. But soon the thud of ball on boundary board boomed round the ground – except when Flintoff went aerial. He reached 51 off 69 deliveries, then drew breath for three dot balls. The next 18 he plundered for 53 as all the earlier Sri Lankan containment – the inexperienced Maharoof had led the way – counted for nought. Flintoff's clean hitting, especially strong down the ground, helped England cash in 78 from the last six overs. The fourth and last hundred of Flintoff's phenomenal international season was the only one-day century made at the Rose Bowl in 2004. Lost in the excitement were important contributions from Trescothick and Collingwood. On this icing-sugar wicket, England's 251 was worth 300-plus elsewhere. The Sri Lankan reply was quickly derailed by Harmison and the ubiquitous Flintoff, who grabbed the key wicket of Jayasuriya before rain returned for the last time. Atapattu later claimed Sri Lanka's depth of batting could still have won it had the weather held. Few agreed.

Man of the Match: A. Flintoff.   *Attendance:* 15,000.

Close of play: England 118-3 (32 overs) (Trescothick 64, Flintoff 21).

England

M. E. Trescothick run out	66	(98)	†G. O. Jones not out	2	(2)	
V. S. Solanki c Sangakkara b Maharoof	18	(26)	A. G. Wharf run out	0	(1)	
*M. P. Vaughan b Zoysa	5	(11)	A. F. Giles not out	0	(0)	
A. J. Strauss run out	7	(22)	L-b 2, w 8	10		
A. Flintoff b Vaas	104	(91)				
P. D. Collingwood c Jayawardene b Vaas	39	(49)				

1/29 (2)   (7 wkts, 50 overs) 251
2/44 (3) 3/70 (4) 4/123 (1)
5/217 (6) 6/250 (5) 7/250 (8)   15 overs: 52-2

D. Gough and S. J. Harmison did not bat.

Bowling: Vaas 10–1–51–2; Zoysa 10–0–61–1; Maharoof 10–1–19–1; Jayawardene 3–0–16–0; Chandana 9–0–64–0; Jayasuriya 4–0–23–0; Dilshan 4–0–15–0.

Sri Lanka

D. A. Gunawardene c Jones b Harmison	5	(16)
S. T. Jayasuriya c Gough b Flintoff	27	(32)
*M. S. Atapattu c Jones b Harmison	1	(7)
W. S. Jayantha c Jones b Flintoff	23	(38)
†K. C. Sangakkara not out	17	(40)

D. P. M. D. Jayawardene c and b Giles	7	(15)
T. M. Dilshan not out	2	(2)
L-b 5, w 2, n-b 6	13	

1/11 (1)   (5 wkts, 24 overs) 95
2/15 (3) 3/49 (2)
4/74 (4) 5/88 (6)   15 overs: 65-3

U. D. U. Chandana, W. P. U. J. C. Vaas, M. F. Maharoof and D. N. T. Zoysa did not bat.

Bowling: Gough 6–1–19–0; Harmison 6–1–21–2; Flintoff 5–0–21–2; Wharf 5–1–20–0; Giles 1–0–2–1; Collingwood 1–0–7–0.

Umpires: B. F. Bowden (New Zealand) and D. B. Hair (Australia).
Third umpire: B. R. Doctrove (West Indies). Referee: M. J. Procter (South Africa).

FINAL POOL TABLES

Pool A

	Played	Won	Lost	Points	Net run-rate
AUSTRALIA	2	2	0	4	3.23
New Zealand	2	1	1	2	1.60
USA	2	0	2	0	–5.12

Pool B

	Played	Won	Lost	Points	Net run-rate
WEST INDIES	2	2	0	4	1.47
South Africa	2	1	1	2	1.55
Bangladesh	2	0	2	0	–3.11

Pool C

	Played	Won	Lost	Points	Net run-rate
PAKISTAN	2	2	0	4	1.41
India	2	1	1	2	0.94
Kenya	2	0	2	0	–2.74

Pool D

	Played	Won	Lost	Points	Net run-rate
ENGLAND	2	2	0	4	2.71
Sri Lanka	2	1	1	2	–0.25
Zimbabwe	2	0	2	0	–1.88

Win = 2 pts. Net run-rate is calculated by subtracting runs conceded per over from runs scored per over.

SEMI-FINALS

ENGLAND v AUSTRALIA

At Birmingham, September 21. England won by six wickets. Toss: England.

England ended a run of 14 consecutive one-day defeats against Australia, achieving victory for the first time since January 17, 1999, with style and growing confidence. The match was a personal triumph for their captain, Vaughan, who had not even made the team at the time of the last win and came into this game besieged by criticism for his defects as a one-day player. Having scored just 147 in his ten previous innings of the summer in this form of cricket, he flayed the Australian attack for 86, and added 140 with Trescothick to put England on the victory road. Strauss played the most handsome strokes of the day to provide the finishing touch. Earlier, Vaughan had bowled his very occasional off-spin to excellent effect for its full ration of ten overs, which was brave captaincy and shrewd too, since the faster bowlers were largely ineffective on this slow wicket

Settling scores: after a string of poor one-day innings, Michael Vaughan comes good in the semi-final against Australia.

Picture by Clive Mason, Getty Images

once the ball softened. None the less, Harmison gave the Australians early notice that rumours about his speed and quality were true, and none of their batsmen was able to settle and play a big innings. In contrast, McGrath – hit for four fours in an over by Trescothick – creaked badly, leading to presumptuous speculation that he might be gone before Australia's return for the 2005 Ashes. Afterwards, both teams were keen to play down the game's long-term significance – Australia wishing to avoid alarm, and England complacency. They could not prevent the excited buzz among the crowd, such as it was. Instead of the customary full house for this fixture, only 8,700 endured a dry but bitterly cold day. Officials blamed the fact that the pairing was known less than 72 hours before the start.

Man of the Match: M. P. Vaughan.   *Attendance:* 8,700.

Australia

†A. C. Gilchrist c Trescothick			
b Gough .	37	(50)	
M. L. Hayden c Trescothick			
b Harmison .	17	(21)	
*R. T. Ponting c Gough b Giles . .	29	(41)	
D. R. Martyn c Trescothick			
b Vaughan	65	(91)	
D. S. Lehmann b Vaughan	38	(42)	
A. Symonds run out	0	(2)	
M. J. Clarke b Flintoff	42	(34)	

B. Lee b Gough	15	(17)
J. N. Gillespie b Gough	0	(1)
M. S. Kasprowicz not out	0	(2)
G. D. McGrath not out	0	(1)
B 3, l-b 4, w 7, n-b 2 . .	16	

1/44 (2)   (9 wkts, 50 overs) 259
2/69 (1) 3/114 (3)
4/189 (5) 5/190 (6) 6/210 (4)
7/249 (8) 8/249 (9) 9/258 (7)   15 overs: 76-2

Bowling: Gough 7–1–48–3; Harmison 10–0–53–1; Flintoff 10–0–56–1; Giles 10–0–40–1; Wharf 3–0–13–0; Vaughan 10–0–42–2.

England

M. E. Trescothick b Symonds . . .	81	(88)
V. S. Solanki lbw b Gillespie. . . .	7	(18)
*M. P. Vaughan c Hayden b Lee .	86	(122)
A. J. Strauss not out	52	(42)
A. Flintoff c Hayden b Lee.	16	(9)
P. D. Collingwood not out.	6	(4)
L-b 5, w 5, n-b 4	14	

1/21 (2)   (4 wkts, 46.3 overs) 262
2/161 (1)
3/227 (3) 4/249 (5)   15 overs: 89-1

†G. O. Jones, A. F. Giles, A. G. Wharf, D. Gough and S. J. Harmison did not bat.

Bowling: McGrath 8–0–46–0; Gillespie 8–0–32–1; Kasprowicz 10–0–52–0; Lee 8.3–0–65–2; Lehmann 6–0–28–0; Symonds 6–1–34–1.

Umpires: B. F. Bowden (New Zealand) and R. E. Koertzen (South Africa).
Third umpire: Aleem Dar (Pakistan).   Referee: M. J. Procter (South Africa).

PAKISTAN v WEST INDIES

At Southampton, September 22. West Indies won by seven wickets. Toss: Pakistan. One-day international debut: Salman Butt.

No match could have typified better the reputation of Pakistan and their captain for unpredictability. In the tournament's 13 previous games, only once, when Bangladesh disintegrated against South Africa, had the captain winning the toss chosen to bat. In cloudy conditions utterly suited to bowling, Inzamam-ul-Haq defied both form and logic. Lara could hardly disguise his delight as the batsmen struggled to cope. Pakistan lost the 19-year-old debutant Salman Butt (blooding him was another odd decision) in the first over, but somehow picked their way to 64 for one after 18 overs. Yasir Hameed was even threatening a big score when he risked a second run to third man and was beaten by Bravo's pinpoint throw. Thereafter, the batsmen fell like mown grass. Yasir hit six boundaries, his colleagues three between them as they plummeted to 131 all out. In mitigation, they could cite the cold, the damp and the pitch, though movement was never extreme. Shoaib Akhtar tore in at speeds of up to 95mph from the start of the West Indian reply, and blew away both openers. But despite murky light, Sarwan and Lara looked unhurried – until Shoaib unleashed a snorter of a short delivery that Lara misjudged. As he turned away, the ball slammed into his neck just behind his jaw and he collapsed to the ground. Lara wanted to continue, but dizziness prevented him. It emerged later that as Lara had walked out to bat, Shoaib had greeted him with a cheery "I'm going to kill you." It was a day when everything Pakistan did was ill-judged, and Sarwan calmly took West Indies to victory.

Man of the Match: R. R. Sarwan.   *Attendance:* 8,000

Pakistan

Yasir Hameed run out	39	(56)	Mohammad Sami b Collymore. . .	0	(4)
Salman Butt c Sarwan b Bradshaw	0	(2)	Shoaib Akhtar not out	0	(2)
Shoaib Malik c Browne b Bravo .	17	(58)			
*Inzamam-ul-Haq c Browne			L-b 4, w 15.	19	
b W. W. Hinds .	21	(44)			
Yousuf Youhana c Browne b Bravo	12	(28)	1/1 (2) 2/65 (1) (38.2 overs) 131		
Abdul Razzaq run out	6	(17)	3/71 (3) 4/100 (5)		
†Moin Khan lbw b W. W. Hinds .	0	(2)	5/109 (6) 6/111 (4)		
Shahid Afridi st Browne b Gayle .	17	(13)	7/112 (7) 8/116 (9)		
Naved-ul-Hasan b Collymore. . . .	0	(4)	9/125 (10) 10/131 (8) 15 overs: 57-1		

Bowling: Bradshaw 8–0–23–1; Collymore 9–2–24–2; Bravo 9–0–41–2; W. W. Hinds 10–0–27–2; R. O. Hinds 1–0–1–0; Gayle 1.2–0–11–1.

In the neck: Brian Lara keels over after being struck by a short ball from Shoaib Akhtar.
Picture by Patrick Eagar

West Indies

C. H. Gayle lbw b Shoaib Akhtar .	1	(8)	R. L. Powell not out	6	(11)
W. W. Hinds c and b Shoaib Akhtar	5	(12)			
R. R. Sarwan not out	56	(85)	B 2, l-b 10, w 9, n-b 1 .	22	
*B. C. Lara retired hurt	31	(30)			
S. Chanderpaul c Salman Butt			1/8 (1) (3 wkts, 28.1 overs) 132		
b Shoaib Malik .	11	(24)	2/20 (2) 3/102 (5) 15 overs: 76-2		

D. J. J. Bravo, R. O. Hinds, †C. O. Browne, I. D. R. Bradshaw and C. D. Collymore did not bat.

Lara retired hurt at 76.

Bowling: Shoaib Akhtar 7–1–18–2; Mohammad Sami 3–0–23–0; Naved-ul-Hasan 7–2–24–0; Abdul Razzaq 6–0–39–0; Shoaib Malik 5–0–15–1; Yousuf Youhana 0.1–0–1–0.

Umpires: D. B. Hair (Australia) and S. J. A. Taufel (Australia).
Third umpire: D. R. Shepherd (England).   Referee: R. S. Madugalle (Sri Lanka).

FINAL

ENGLAND v WEST INDIES

At The Oval, September 25. West Indies won by two wickets. Toss: West Indies.

A tournament full of insipid, forgettable moments ended with one of the most memorable finals in recent years, as West Indies scripted a soul-stirring fightback to put paid to England's hopes of winning their first one-day tournament of any significance. For a region devastated by various opponents on the cricket field, and by Hurricanes Ivan and Jeanne off it, this was a victory to savour. The reactions of the players immediately after Bradshaw struck the winning boundary told the story – the entire West Indian party roared on to the field in semi-darkness, hugging, kissing, and screaming, ecstatic yet bewildered by their achievement.

None of those wild celebratory scenes looked even remotely possible when West Indies slumped to 147 for eight in their quest for 218. The top-order batsmen had all perished – Chanderpaul the last of them for a dogged 47 – and England moved in to finish off the formalities as Bradshaw joined Browne. About the only thing in the batsmen's favour was the asking-rate, which was less than four and a half an over. Browne and Bradshaw – both from Barbados, although Browne was born just round the corner in Lambeth – capitalised on that, initially looking for no more than nudges and pushes. But a stand which started off as nothing more than irritant value for Vaughan slowly assumed more ominous proportions.

Sensing a shift in momentum, Vaughan turned to Harmison, his chief weapon through much of the summer. It seemed an unequal battle: Harmison hurtling down his deliveries at 96mph in dubious light against batsmen of little repute. Not only did they see him off – Browne even cracked a magnificent square-drive in his penultimate over – they also quelled the venom of Flintoff, who had earlier ripped apart the heart of the West Indian middle order. The other bowler who might have been a force, Gough, had a strangely lacklustre day, and suddenly Vaughan had run out of attacking options. In cold and overcast conditions, he had preferred seam to spin throughout, and as crunch time approached, he stuck to his guns, opting for Wharf over Giles, who did not bowl at all. Wharf went for only two in the 47th over. But with 12 needed from the last two, West Indies clinched it in style – Browne thumped Wharf over gully for four, before Bradshaw found the third-man fence to seal an unbelievable win.

The statistically minded in the England camp should have had a whiff of defeat in the moment Trescothick struck his eighth one-day century – this was the fifth to end in a losing cause. Trescothick, though, was the only one among England's specialist batsmen who solved the mystery of getting runs on an unusually bowler-friendly Oval pitch. Solanki and Vaughan were consumed early in the piece by Bradshaw, before West Indies found an unexpected hero in the middle overs. Exploiting the conditions to the hilt, Hinds kept a tight leash on the runs, and picked up three crucial middle-order wickets as well. Lara's alacrity at short mid-wicket had a huge hand in two of those, though – a fierce pull by Flintoff was scooped up left-handed and inches from the ground to give Lara his 100th catch in one-day internationals, while Jones's heave was intercepted with a perfectly timed leap. Trescothick stuck to his task, however, and with Giles chipping in with a valuable 31, England had put together a competitive total of 217.

That seemed more than sufficient when Harmison and Flintoff got in on the act with the ball. Solanki kept up the high level of fielding with a one-handed, leaping effort which took care of Hinds. A sharp return catch by Harmison dismissed Gayle, while Sarwan and Lara both perished off the outside edge. Chanderpaul offered stout resistance, but when he left, so did many West Indian supporters, believing the game to be over. Little did they realise that they would be missing the best part.

Man of the Match: I. D. R. Bradshaw.   *Attendance:* 18,600.

Player of the Tournament: R. R. Sarwan.

England

M. E. Trescothick run out	104	(124)	
V. S. Solanki c Browne b Bradshaw	4	(13)	
*M. P. Vaughan b Bradshaw	7	(18)	
A. J. Strauss run out	18	(33)	
A. Flintoff c Lara b W. W. Hinds	3	(6)	
P. D. Collingwood c Chanderpaul b W. W. Hinds	16	(40)	
†G. O. Jones c Lara b W. W. Hinds	6	(18)	
A. F. Giles c Lara c Bravo	31	(37)	
A. G. Wharf not out	3	(6)	
D. Gough st Browne b Gayle	0	(1)	
S. J. Harmison run out	2	(2)	
B 1, l-b 7, w 15	23		

1/12 (2) 2/43 (3) (49.4 overs) 217
3/84 (4) 4/93 (5)
5/123 (6) 6/148 (7)
7/211 (1) 8/212 (8)
9/214 (10) 10/217 (11) 15 overs: 63-2

Bowling: Bradshaw 10–1–54–2; Collymore 10–1–38–0; Gayle 9.4–0–52–1; Bravo 10–0–41–1; W. W. Hinds 10–3–24–3.

West Indies

C. H. Gayle c and b Harmison	23	(33)	
W. W. Hinds c Solanki b Harmison	3	(16)	
R. R. Sarwan c Strauss b Flintoff	5	(7)	
*B. C. Lara c Jones b Flintoff	14	(28)	
S. Chanderpaul c Vaughan b Collingwood	47	(66)	
D. J. J. Bravo c Jones b Flintoff	0	(7)	
R. O. Hinds c Jones b Trescothick	8	(19)	
R. L. Powell c Trescothick b Collingwood	14	(16)	
†C. O. Browne not out	35	(55)	
I. D. R. Bradshaw not out	34	(51)	
L-b 11, w 19, n-b 5	35		

C. D. Collymore did not bat.

1/19 (2) (8 wkts, 48.5 overs) 218
2/35 (3) 3/49 (1)
4/72 (4) 5/80 (6) 6/114 (7)
7/135 (8) 8/147 (5) 15 overs: 67-3

Bowling: Gough 10–1–58–0; Harmison 10–1–34–2; Flintoff 10–0–38–3; Wharf 9.5–0–38–0; Trescothick 3–0–17–1; Collingwood 6–0–22–2.

Umpires: R. E. Koertzen (South Africa) and S. J. A. Taufel (Australia).
Third umpire: D. B. Hair (Australia).   Referee: R. S. Madugalle (Sri Lanka).

CHAMPIONS TROPHY WINNERS

1998-99	South Africa	2002-03	India and Sri Lanka
2000-01	New Zealand	2004	West Indies

SRI LANKA A IN ENGLAND, 2004

When Jehan Mubarak's Sri Lanka A side arrived at Taunton for the last game of their month-long trip, they must have believed they would return home undefeated. Of their nine previous games, they had won eight and drawn just one, against the touring West Indians. Somerset, not the strongest county in the land, had rested almost all their familiar names, including the most famous of the lot: Ricky Ponting was sightseeing in Paris with his wife. But Sri Lanka A came a cropper against a Somerset side mainly of a similar age to themselves, and left for home with their tails between their legs. Or possibly not: rumour had it that the Taunton umpires reported the Sri Lankans to Lord's for persistent dissent.

Despite the intensity the Sri Lankans showed during their cricket, this visit by an overseas A side seemed to sink lower on the radar screen than most. The problems were not new: weak county sides, almost always resting their biggest names, played tired cricket in echoing grounds. And it wasn't just the counties who were dissatisfied. Michael Tissera, who turned out for Sri Lanka in the 1975 World Cup and now managed their A side, bemoaned the preponderance of one-day games. Because the tour coincided with the Twenty20 Cup for its first fortnight or more, counties were not prepared to lurch back into four-day mode for the benefit of the visitors. The result was a rapid succession of seven limited-overs games which, to their credit, Sri Lanka A won with great efficiency.

> Have a ball...
> those days
> are gone

Tissera, by reputation something of a disciplinarian, had demanded full commitment from the touring side: "It doesn't mean that you go to England, see all your friends, have a ball, play the odd match and come back. Those days are gone." And Tissera seemed pleased with what he got. Speaking at the end of the tour, he singled out Stan Nell, the newly appointed Australian coach, for praise: "Stan did a superb job as coach. He was very professional, very aggressive and he had that real Australian approach."

Given that a major aim of the tour was for three batsmen to hit form before the Asia Cup, the Sri Lankan management had every right to be satisfied. The three – Avishka Gunawardene, Saman Jayantha and Thilina Kandamby – flew home after the Sussex game with a stack of runs to their names. Gunawardene started with three successive fifties, Jayantha peaked with a commanding unbeaten 147 against Worcestershire, while Kandamby seemed keen to teach his hosts a thing or two about the Twenty20. Against Glamorgan, his undefeated 40 came off 20 balls. The bowling was tight if not especially penetrative, though in the first-class victory at Swansea, the 19-year-old off-spinner Mohamed Suraj enjoyed first-innings figures of five for 40. The leg-spinners Bathiya Perera and Kaushal Lokuarachchi arguably had more success with the bat than the ball.

SRI LANKA A TOURING PARTY

J. Mubarak (*captain*), S. H. T. Kandamby (*vice-captain*), G. I. Daniel, W. J. M. R. Dias, C. S. Fernando, M. K. Gajanayake, D. A. Gunawardene, W. S. Jayantha, H. A. P. W. Jayawardene, K. M. D. N. Kulasekara, K. S. Lokuarachchi, M. T. T. Mirando, W. M. B. Perera, K. T. G. D. Prasad, W. M. G. Ramyakumara, M. M. M. Suraj.

S. Kalawithigoda and B. M. A. J. Mendis reinforced the party when Gunawardene, Jayantha and Kandamby flew home to join the senior side.

Coach: S. Nell.   *Manager:* M. H. Tissera.   *Physiotherapist:* L. Thamal.

SRI LANKA A TOUR RESULTS

First-class matches – Played 3: Won 1, Lost 1, Drawn 1.
Non-first-class matches – Played 7: Won 7.

Note: Matches in this section which were not first-class are signified by a dagger.

†At Leicester, June 30. **Sri Lanka A won by 138 runs.** Toss: Sri Lanka A. **Sri Lanka A 291-7** (50 overs) (W. S. Jayantha 36, D. A. Gunawardene 68, S. H. T. Kandamby 49, H. A. P. W. Jayawardene 63*, M. T. T. Mirando 37*; G. G. Read 3-75, M. S. Panesar 3-42); **British Universities 153** (40.2 overs) (W. M. G. Ramyakumara 3-17, G. I. Daniel 3-8).

†At Leeds, July 3. **Sri Lanka A won by seven wickets.** Toss: Sri Lanka A. **Yorkshire 179-7** (35 overs) (P. A. Jaques 79; K. T. G. D. Prasad 3-31); **Sri Lanka A 180-3** (31 overs) (W. S. Jayantha 31, D. A. Gunawardene 61, G. I. Daniel 30).
Reduced to 35 overs a side. Yorkshire recovered from 51 for five.

†At Chester-le-Street, July 5. **Sri Lanka A won by 37 runs** (D/L method). Toss: Durham. **Sri Lanka A 210-5** (32 overs) (D. A. Gunawardene 59, G. I. Daniel 42, S. H. T. Kandamby 40, Extras 32); **Durham 199** (28.3 overs) (P. Mustard 36, G. J. Pratt 89).
County debut: C. Rushworth (Durham). Durham's target revised to 237 from 32 overs.
Showers interrupted Sri Lanka A's innings five times, but Gunawardene, unperturbed, hit his third successive fifty, while Kandamby walloped three sixes in his 22-ball innings. Ian Pattison bowled six overs at a cost of 60, including nine wides.

†At Worcester, July 7. **Sri Lanka A won by six wickets.** Toss: Sri Lanka A. **Worcestershire 245-4** (50 overs) (S. C. Moore 91, Kadeer Ali 48, Extras 30); **Sri Lanka A 249-4** (42.4 overs) (W. S. Jayantha 147*, G. I. Daniel 37).
Jayantha faced 137 balls and hit 21 fours and two sixes. Jehan Mubarak was dismissed after surviving a direct hit on the stumps at the bowler's end; he then attempted a single on the ricochet, but another direct hit ran him out at the other end.

†At Cardiff, July 9. **Sri Lanka A won by 141 runs.** Toss: Sri Lanka A. **Sri Lanka A 309-3** (50 overs) (W. S. Jayantha 97, G. I. Daniel 57, J. Mubarak 88*, S. H. T. Kandamby 40*); **Glamorgan 168** (39 overs) (I. J. Thomas 36, A. G. Wharf 42).
England bowler Simon Jones – making his comeback after injuring his foot in May – had figures of 10–0–67–0. Kandamby crashed four sixes (but no fours) from 20 balls.

†At Hove, July 12. **Sri Lanka A won by 95 runs.** Toss: Sri Lanka A. **Sri Lanka A 251-7** (50 overs) (G. I. Daniel 68, J. Mubarak 71, Extras 31; J. D. Lewry 3-39); **Sussex 156** (40.5 overs) (R. R. Montgomerie 32, P. A. Cottey 53, M. J. G. Davis 36*; W. J. M. R. Dias 3-24, W. S. Jayantha 3-36).

†At Canterbury, July 14. **Sri Lanka A won by four wickets.** Toss: Kent. **Kent 188-8** (43 overs) (M. A. Carberry 48, E. T. Smith 70); **Sri Lanka A 190-6** (37.3 overs) (W. M. G. Ramyakumara 36, J. Mubarak 31, W. M. B. Perera 43*; A. Khan 3-39).
Reduced to 43 overs a side.

At Shenley Park, July 17, 18, 19. SRI LANKA A drew with WEST INDIANS (see West Indian tour section).

GLAMORGAN v SRI LANKA A

At Swansea, July 21, 22, 23, 24. Sri Lanka A won by four wickets. Toss: Glamorgan.

The Sri Lankans' second victory in Wales in just over a fortnight gave them eight wins from their first nine matches, although this time Glamorgan, who had not lost a four-day match in 2004, gave them a better run for their money. An improved second-innings batting performance set the tourists a target of 254, and when they lurched to 156 for six, the outcome was in the balance. A 100-run partnership between Perera and Ramyakumara then settled the issue. On the first day, Glamorgan failed to take advantage of winning the toss on a good pitch, and plummeted from 111 for three to 169 all out against the off-spin of Mohamed Suraj. Contributions down the order gave the Sri Lankans a lead of 198, before five Glamorgan batsmen made fifties in their second innings. There were two more for the game was out, taking the total to 11, though none was converted into a hundred.

Close of play: First day, Sri Lanka A 178-3 (Mubarak 60, Perera 43); Second day, Glamorgan 118-1 (I. J. Thomas 57, Cosker 4); Third day, Sri Lanka A 29-1 (Kalawithigoda 5, Gajanayake 22).

Glamorgan

M. T. G. Elliott b Suraj	48	– c Fernando b Kulasekara	53
†M. A. Wallace c Ramyakumara b Kulasekara	11	– (7) st Fernando b Suraj	91
D. L. Hemp c Perera b Kulasekara	10	– (4) b Kulasekara	73
M. J. Powell b Dias	3	– (5) b Kulasekara	2
J. Hughes c Kalawithigoda b Suraj	44	– (6) lbw b Mubarak	50
I. J. Thomas c Mendis b Suraj	9	– (2) c Dias b Suraj	68
*R. D. B. Croft c Daniel b Perera	4	– (8) lbw b Suraj	37
S. D. Thomas c Daniel b Suraj	16	– (9) c and b Kulasekara	13
D. S. Harrison b Perera	3	– (10) not out	22
A. P. Davies lbw b Suraj	1	– (11) c Perera b Kulasekara	3
D. A. Cosker not out	6	– (3) c Fernando b Kulasekara	8
B 5, l-b 3, n-b 6	14	B 12, l-b 9, w 4, n-b 6	31
	169		**451**

1/26 (2) 2/44 (3) 3/51 (4) 4/111 (1) 5/125 (6) 6/134 (5) 7/142 (7) 8/162 (9) 9/162 (8) 10/169 (10)

1/113 (1) 2/125 (3) 3/157 (2) 4/166 (5) 5/273 (6) 6/275 (4) 7/383 (8) 8/419 (9) 9/430 (7) 10/451 (11)

Bowling: *First Innings*—Kulasekara 10–2–24–2; Dias 11–3–52–1; Ramyakumara 6 0–21–0; Suraj 15.4–5–40–5; Perera 11–2–24–2. *Second Innings*—Kulasekara 36 9–109–6; Dias 11–3–41–0; Daniel 8–0–30–0; Ramyakumara 13–2–56–0; Suraj 33–4–110–3; Perera 17–2–64–0; Mubarak 5–1–20–1.

Sri Lanka A

S. Kalawithigoda c Hemp b Harrison	0	– (2) c Powell b Davies	39
G. I. Daniel c Harrison b Cosker	55	– (1) b Harrison	1
M. K. Gajanayake c Wallace b Harrison	19	– c Wallace b S. D. Thomas	22
*J. Mubarak c Hemp b Harrison	66	– c Hemp b S. D. Thomas	2
W. M. B. Perera c Croft b S. D. Thomas	65	– not out	86
B. M. A. J. Mendis run out	5	– lbw b Croft	20
†C. S. Fernando b Croft	44	– c I. J. Thomas b Croft	8
W. M. G. Ramyakumara not out	60	– not out	67
W. J. M. R. Dias lbw b Cosker	23		
K. M. D. N. Kulasekara lbw b S. D. Thomas	21		
M M. M. Suraj c Cosker b S. D. Thomas	4		
L-b 3, w 1, n-b 1	5	B 1, l-b 5, n-b 5	11
	367	(6 wkts)	**256**

1/0 (1) 2/52 (3) 3/109 (2) 4/184 (4) 5/195 (6) 6/216 (5) 7/272 (7) 8/307 (9) 9/363 (10) 10/367 (11)

1/4 (1) 2/29 (3) 3/45 (4) 4/82 (2) 5/125 (6) 6/156 (7)

Bowling: *First Innings*—Harrison 20–3–76–3; Davies 15–2–48–0; S. D. Thomas 18.3–0–80–3; Cosker 22–3–93–2; Croft 21–4–67–1. *Second Innings*—Harrison 12–2–43–1; S. D. Thomas 12–2–45–2; Cosker 14–2–48–0; Croft 24–2–73–2; Davies 9–1–25–1; I. J. Thomas 1–0–6–0; Elliott 0.3–0–10–0.

Umpires: S. A. Garratt and P. Willey.

SOMERSET v SRI LANKA A

At Taunton, July 27, 28, 29, 30. Somerset won by 289 runs. Toss: Somerset.

Any hopes the young Sri Lankans had of completing their tour unbeaten ended in a flurry of expansive shots and bowling that was consistently too short. Victory on the last day was a timely way for Peter Bowler, taking over as captain, to celebrate his 41st birthday. He had an inexperienced team around him, but he used them profitably. In the first innings, Wood, still only 23, reached his sixth first-class hundred to suggest he was back in form; in the second, Edwards, a 20-year-old left-hander, came close to a century, while in between Andrew, also 20, returned career-best figures of four for 63. The win confirmed that Somerset's season – they had just handsomely beaten Yorkshire at Scarborough – had turned the corner. As for Sri Lanka A, despite a mature fighting 83 from the captain, Mubarak, a target of 517 was far beyond them. In slight mitigation, they had bad luck with injuries: wicket-keeper Jayawardene hurt himself on the opening morning and Gajanayake deputised behind the stumps, while Kulasekara cut his finger while cleaning his bat and could hardly bowl in the Somerset second innings. Umpires Kitchen and Bailey were believed to have reported the Sri Lankans to Lord's for the way they contested decisions.

Close of play: First day, Sri Lanka A 37–0 (Gajanayake 12, Daniel 24); Second day, Somerset 159–4 (Edwards 67, Bowler 13); Third day, Sri Lanka A 87–3 (Mubarak 18, Perera 8).

Somerset

N. J. Edwards c Gajanayake b Mirando	24	– lbw b Lokuarachchi	93
J. D. Francis c Gajanayake b Ramyakumara	35	– run out	7
M. J. Wood not out	128	– c Mendis b Mubarak	17
*P. D. Bowler c Gajanayake b Kulasekara	22	– (6) c Gajanayake b Ramyakumara	48
A. V. Suppiah c Mubarak b Lokuarachchi	33	– (4) lbw b Lokuarachchi	11
I. D. Blackwell run out	38	– (7) st Gajanayake b Suraj	81
A. W. Laraman c Mendis b Suraj	28	– (8) b Perera	1
†C. M. Gazzard c Gajanayake b Suraj	35	– (9) not out	44
W. J. Durston run out	5	– (5) c Gajanayake b Mirando	34
G. M. Andrew c Mubarak b Kulasekara	0	– c Gajanayake b Mirando	44
R. L. Johnson lbw b Kulasekara	0	– not out	22
B 8, l-b 9, w 2, n-b 5	24	B 5, l-b 2, w 2, n-b 8, p 5	22

1/46 (1) 2/88 (2) 3/127 (4) 4/214 (5)	372
5/268 (6) 6/315 (7) 7/357 (8)	
8/366 (9) 9/372 (10) 10/372 (11)	

1/26 (2) 2/60 (3) (9 wkts dec.)	424
3/75 (4) 4/125 (5)	
5/197 (1) 6/291 (6)	
7/298 (8) 8/323 (7) 9/397 (10)	

Bowling: *First Innings*—Mirando 11–3–24–1; Kulasekara 18–0–98–3; Ramyakumara 11–2–44–1; Mubarak 3–0–15–0; Lokuarachchi 8–1–47–1; Suraj 17–2–83–2; Perera 10–0–44–0. *Second Innings*—Mirando 17.5–0–109–2; Kulasekara 6.1–0–42–0; Ramyakumara 11–0–51–1; Mubarak 9–2–30–1; Lokuarachchi 25–6–62–2; Suraj 30–5–73–1; Perera 15–1–45–1.

> "Touts at St John's Wood tube for a county match? It seemed impossible, but there they were."
>
> Twenty20 Cup, page 881.

Sri Lanka A

M. K. Gajanayake c Durston b Andrew	13	– c Gazzard b Johnson	22
G. I. Daniel c Durston b Laraman	48	– c Durston b Johnson	1
B. M. A. J. Mendis lbw b Andrew	5	– c Edwards b Laraman	34
*J. Mubarak lbw b Andrew	23	– b Laraman	83
W. M. B. Perera c Gazzard b Edwards	3	– c and b Laraman	36
†H. A. P. W. Jayawardene c Bowler b Johnson	28	– (7) c Andrew b Durston	0
W. M. G. Ramyakumara lbw b Laraman	8	– (6) c and b Suppiah	15
K. S. Lokuarachchi c Gazzard b Johnson	91	– c Blackwell b Durston	5
M. T. T. Mirando c Durston b Johnson	0	– c Laraman b Suppiah	5
K. M. D. N. Kulasekara c Blackwell b Andrew	38	– c Wood b Durston	0
M. M. M. Suraj not out	11	– not out	14
L-b 6, w 2, n-b 4	12	L-b 5, w 5, n-b 2	12

1/39 (1) 2/54 (3) 3/94 (4) 4/98 (2)   280   1/12 (2) 2/35 (1) 3/72 (3)   227
5/98 (5) 6/113 (7) 7/156 (6)   4/141 (5) 5/164 (6) 6/165 (7)
8/156 (9) 9/254 (10) 10/280 (8)   7/177 (8) 8/183 (9)
                                       9/186 (10) 10/227 (4)

Bowling: *First Innings*—Johnson 16–2–73–3; Andrew 15–2–63–4; Durston 2–0–19–0; Laraman 12–0–72–2; Edwards 7–0–31–1; Blackwell 3–0–16–0. *Second Innings*—Johnson 12–2–32–2; Andrew 9–0–53–0; Suppiah 18–1–69–2; Laraman 12.3–5–34–3; Edwards 3–0–11–0; Durston 9–0 23 3.

Umpires: R. J. Bailey and M. J. Kitchen.

I ZINGARI RESULTS, 2004

Matches 23: Won 10, Lost 9, Drawn 4. Abandoned 2.

April 22	Eton College	Won by seven runs
May 2	Hampshire Hogs	Lost by 18 runs
May 9	Stragglers of Asia	Abandoned
May 15	Eton Ramblers	Won by 34 runs
May 22	Royal Armoured Corps	Drawn
May 30	Earl of Carnarvon's XI	Won by 15 runs
June 6	Defence Academy CC	Lost by 99 runs
June 12	RMA Sandhurst	Won by 97 runs
June 19	Harrow School	Lost by 52 runs
June 20	Guards CC	Abandoned
June 27	Hagley CC	Drawn
June 29	Winchester College	Lost by three wickets
July 9	Free Foresters	Lost by 119 runs
July 10	Green Jackets CC	Lost by seven wickets
July 11	Old Wykehamists	Lost by one run
July 18	Sir John Starkey's XI	Won by four runs
July 24	Willow Warblers	Won by six wickets
July 25	Duke of Norfolk's XI	Won by five wickets
July 31	Hurlingham CC	Won by seven wickets
August 1	Band of Brothers	Lost by five wickets
August 8	Lord Vestey's XI	Won by 50 runs
August 15	Sir Paul Getty's XI	Drawn
August 22	Bradfield Waifs	Won by 35 runs
August 28	South Wales Hunts	Lost by seven wickets
August 29	J. H. Pawle's XI	Drawn

FRIZZELL COUNTY CHAMPIONSHIP, 2004

Warwickshire regained the County Championship in 2004 after a nine-year gap. Their style, however, was far removed from the two blitzes, inspired by Brian Lara and Allan Donald respectively, that made them champions in both 1994 and 1995. This time, Nick Knight led a quietly competent team

that made up for its weaknesses, especially in bowling, by using the points system to maximum effect. They executed their strategy to perfection, and from the end of May were never headed, and hardly threatened.

They did it without winning a single match after July 24, and only five in all. No team has won the title with a lower percentage of wins. But they were also the first team to go through a county season undefeated since Surrey in 1999, and they achieved a minimum nine points from every match except one early-season rain-hit game against Gloucestershire.

Many people found Warwickshire's strategy dreary, but it was based essentially on consistently heavy, and rapid, scoring. They passed 400 in 11 of their 16 first innings, including 500 six times out of eight between mid-May and late July. Five of their players, led by Ian Bell, averaged more than 50. Past Championships have usually been won by outstanding attacks, but Warwickshire's leading wicket-taker was Dougie Brown, who took less than

two and a half wickets per game. In one respect, they were wholly traditional: champions need a slice of luck, and they won 13 tosses.

What was decidedly un-traditional was that all the other first-division counties spent more time worrying about relegation than they did about catching the front-runners. With a maximum of 12 points available for a draw, only 22 for even the most comprehensive win, and a third of the division destined to go down, avoidance of defeat became the highest objective more often than not, which led to much turgid cricket. Even **Kent**, the eventual runners-up, were in danger

Nick Knight

of falling off the tightrope after two defeats in late July. Internal problems plagued their season, but their batsmen – with Robert Key to the fore early and late – carried them through.

COUNTY CHAMPIONSHIP TABLE

Division One	Matches	Won	Lost	Drawn	Bonus Points Batting	Bowling	Penalty	Points
1 – Warwickshire (**5**). . . .	16	5	0	11	65	43	0	222
2 – Kent (**4**)	16	7	3	6	43	41	0	206
3 – Surrey (**3**)	16	5	5	6	60	42	0.5	195.5
4 – Middlesex (**6**).	16	4	4	8	48	43	0	179
5 – Sussex (**1**)	16	4	5	7	46	42	0	172
6 – Gloucestershire (**3**) . .	16	3	3	10	49	41	0	172
7 – Worcestershire (*1*) . . .	16	3	6	7	51	40	0	161
8 – Lancashire (**2**)	16	2	4	10	44	44	2	154
9 – Northamptonshire (*2*) .	16	1	4	11	35	41	0	134

Division Two	Matches	Won	Lost	Drawn	Bonus Points Batting	Bowling	Penalty	Points
1 – Nottinghamshire (**8**). .	16	9	2	5	66	40	0	252
2 – Hampshire (*8*)	16	9	2	5	42	40	0	228
3 – Glamorgan (*5*)	16	5	2	9	48	44	1.5	196.5
4 – Somerset (*7*).	16	4	5	7	47	44	0	175
5 – Essex (*7*).	16	3	6	7	50	45	0	165
6 – Leicestershire (**9**). . . .	16	4	5	7	39	42	1.5	163.5
7 – Yorkshire (*4*)	16	3	4	9	44	40	0	162
8 – Derbyshire (*9*)	16	1	6	9	36	40	0	126
9 – Durham (*6*)	16	2	8	6	28	41	2.5	118.5

2003 positions are shown in brackets: Division One in bold, Division Two in italic.

Win = 14 pts; draw = 4 pts. Penalties were deducted for slow over-rates.

Surrey had a diabolical start to the season, in the Championship as in all the other competitions. But their strength in depth got them out of trouble, and four wins out of the last five saw them into a clear third place. Captaincy was the biggest bugbear for **Middlesex** once Andrew Strauss was elevated into the England team and his deputy Owais Shah proved an unsuitable replacement. But Shah and Ben Hutton (the man eventually named for 2005) found form together to give them two vital wins in late July, at Worcester and at Southgate against Kent, which helped them into fourth place, their best position in seven years.

The unexpected 2003 champions, **Sussex**, predictably fell away and found themselves bottom in early June. They won only one game before the last week in July. But the drier wickets of late summer enabled Mushtaq Ahmed, the hero of their Championship year, to settle into his best rhythm. They were the last team with even a theoretical chance of catching Warwickshire before the mathematics became impossible. **Gloucestershire** came through their first season in the top division, thanks to three midsummer wins and the prolific form of Craig Spearman. They started the Cheltenham Festival, where the county's dreams of a title are always most vivid, in second place. They never won again, ending the festival by losing to the other first-division debutants, **Worcestershire**, after Graeme Hick produced one of his epics.

But Gloucestershire lived to fight again while Worcestershire, whose overseas bowlers failed to find consistency, did not. The biggest shock of

LOWEST PERCENTAGE OF WINS BY COUNTY CHAMPIONS

% Won	Year	Champions	Matches	Won	Lost	Drawn	Abandoned
31.25	**2004**	**Warwickshire . . .**	**16**	**5**	**0**	**11**	–
31.25*	1927	Lancashire	32	10	1	20	1
33.33	1985	Middlesex	24	8	4	12	–
35.71	1930	Lancashire	28	10	0	18	–
37.50	1970	Kent	24	9	5	10	–
37.50*	1987	Nottinghamshire . .	24	9	1	13	1
38.46	1899	Surrey	26	10	2	14	–
39.28	1968	Yorkshire	28	11	4	13	–

* The percentage shown is that of wins to scheduled matches. Excluding matches abandoned without a ball bowled, Lancashire's percentage in 1927 was 32.25 and Nottinghamshire's in 1987 was 39.13.

all came from **Lancashire**, who started out hot favourites, despite the 70 seasons that have passed since their last outright title. That sequence will now become at least 72, as they will not even get the chance to try in 2005.

They began the season as the enthusiasts expected, and were top of the table after four of the 16 games. But thereafter, their formidable battery of batsmen fired blanks, and they never won another match. Under the old system, eighth place would have been a mildly disappointing season (it was Lancashire's worst since 1997); with relegation, it was a disaster. Their exit leaves Kent and Surrey as the only ever-presents in the first division as it enters its sixth year. Relegation for **Northamptonshire** was less of a shock: they hit rock-bottom in June and stayed there.

Replacing these three will be **Nottinghamshire**, **Hampshire** and **Glamorgan**. Nottinghamshire were the outstanding second-division team, winning nine matches – mostly by wide margins – including five in a row before the midsummer break. They had the advantage of the overseas find of the season, the Australian batsman David Hussey, brother of the peripatetic Michael. Hampshire were inspired by Shane Warne, whose adventurous

WARWICKSHIRE'S FIRST-INNINGS SCORES

317	v Middlesex at Birmingham	April 16
139-6	v Gloucestershire at Birmingham	April 28
546	v Surrey at Birmingham	May 12
600-6 dec.	v Sussex at Horsham	May 19
405	v Worcestershire at Birmingham	May 25
608-7 dec.	v Middlesex at Lord's	June 2
524	v Northamptonshire at Birmingham	June 9
499	v Lancashire at Stratford-on-Avon	June 18
502-6 dec.	v Kent at Beckenham	June 23
537	v Surrey at Guildford	July 21
410	v Lancashire at Manchester	July 28
457	v Kent at Birmingham	August 11
350	v Gloucestershire at Bristol	August 19
346	v Sussex at Birmingham	August 24
460	v Worcestershire at Worcester	August 31
295	v Northamptonshire at Northampton	September 16

UNBEATEN CHAMPIONSHIP SEASONS

		Matches	Won	Lost	Drawn	Abandoned	Position
1900	Yorkshire	28	16	0	12	0	1
1904	Lancashire	26	16	0	10	0	1
1907	Nottinghamshire . . .	20	15	0	4	1	1
1908	Yorkshire	28	16	0	12	0	1
1925	Yorkshire	32	21	0	11	0	1
1926	Yorkshire	32	14	0	17	1	2
1928	Lancashire	30	15	0	15	0	1
	Yorkshire	26	8	0	18	0	4
1930	Lancashire	28	10	0	18	0	1
1969	Glamorgan	24	11	0	13	0	1
1972	Warwickshire	20	9	0	11	0	1
1973	Hampshire	20	10	0	10	0	1
1974	Lancashire	20	5	0	15	0	8
1998	Leicestershire	17	11	0	6	0	1
1999	Surrey	17	12	0	5	0	1
2004	**Warwickshire . . . . .**	**16**	**5**	**0**	**11**	**0**	**1**

captaincy and *joie de vivre* were in contrast to the general po-faced mood of county cricket. His bowling helped a bit too. Glamorgan, with a well-balanced, settled, mostly Welsh, side won four successive games before midsummer, and only one after that. But their promotion still came easily: they were well ahead of **Somerset**, who were galvanised by a brief visit from Australian captain Ricky Ponting. Somerset won none of their first nine, but four of the last seven.

Essex were a disappointing fifth, managing to lose regularly even when their Pakistani leg-spinner Danish Kaneria was raking in wickets. **Leicestershire**, at sixth, endured what in effect was their worst Championship season since 1991, and **Yorkshire's** hopes of a quick return to their rightful place were wrecked by their worst since 1992. **Derbyshire** and **Durham**, who have swapped the wooden spoon between them for the past four seasons, were the bottom two, though this time it was Durham who came last. Neither side won a single home game.

Pre-season betting (best available prices): *Division One* – 9-4 Lancashire; 100-30 Surrey; 6-1 Sussex; 9-1 Kent; 10-1 WARWICKSHIRE; 16-1 Worcestershire; 25-1 Middlesex; 33-1 Gloucestershire; 40-1 Northamptonshire.

Division Two – 3-1 Yorkshire; 5-1 Essex and NOTTINGHAMSHIRE; 9-1 Hampshire; 10-1 Somerset; 12-1 Glamorgan; 14-1 Leicestershire; 20-1 Durham; 66-1 Derbyshire.

Prize money

Division One
£105,000 for winners: WARWICKSHIRE.
£50,000 for runners-up: KENT.

Division Two
£40,000 for winners: NOTTINGHAMSHIRE.
£25,000 for runners-up: HAMPSHIRE.

Winners of each match (both divisions): £2,000.

SUMMARY OF RESULTS, 2004

DIVISION ONE

	Gloucestershire	Kent	Lancashire	Middlesex	Northamptonshire	Surrey	Sussex	Warwickshire	Worcestershire
Gloucestershire	–	L	D	W	D	W	D	D	L
Kent	D	–	W	W	W	D	W	D	W
Lancashire	D	D	–	D	D	L	L	D	W
Middlesex	D	W	D	–	D	W	L	L	D
Northamptonshire	D	L	D	D	–	W	D	D	L
Surrey	D	W	W	D	D	–	D	L	W
Sussex	L	W	L	L	D	D	–	D	W
Warwickshire	D	D	D	D	W	W	D	–	W
Worcestershire	W	D	D	L	D	D	D	D	–

DIVISION TWO

	Derbyshire	Durham	Essex	Glamorgan	Hampshire	Leicestershire	Nottinghamshire	Somerset	Yorkshire
Derbyshire	–	D	D	L	L	D	L	D	D
Durham	L	–	D	L	D	L	L	D	L
Essex	W	D	–	L	L	D	L	D	L
Glamorgan	D	D	D	–	L	W	D	W	D
Hampshire	D	W	L	D	–	W	L	W	D
Leicestershire	W	W	L	D	L	–	W	L	D
Nottinghamshire	W	W	W	D	D	D	–	L	D
Somerset	D	L	D	W	L	D	L	–	D
Yorkshire	D	L	W	L	D	L	L	L	–

Home teams listed on left, away teams across top; results are for home teams.

W = Won, L = Lost, D = Drawn.

Leaders: *Division One* – from April 19 Kent; May 10 Middlesex; May 14 Lancashire; May 22 Kent; May 27 Warwickshire. Warwickshire became champions on September 6.
Division Two – from April 19 Hampshire; April 24 Yorkshire; May 1 Hampshire; May 21 Nottinghamshire. Nottinghamshire became champions on September 16.

Bottom place: *Division One* – from April 19 Worcestershire; April 24 Gloucestershire; May 1 Worcestershire; May 21 Gloucestershire; June 4 Sussex; June 11 Northamptonshire.
Division Two – from April 19 Essex, Leicestershire, Nottinghamshire, Somerset and Yorkshire; April 24 Essex; May 1 Leicestershire; June 5 Somerset; June 10 Durham.

Scoring of Points

(*a*) For a win, 14 points plus any points scored in the first innings.

(*b*) In a tie, each side scores seven points, plus any points scored in the first innings.

(*c*) In a drawn match, each side scores four points, plus any points scored in the first innings (see also paragraph (*f*)).

(*d*) If the scores are equal in a drawn match, the side batting in the fourth innings scores seven points, plus any points scored in the first innings, and the opposing side scores four points plus any points scored in the first innings.

(*e*) First-innings points (awarded only for performances in the first 130 overs of each first innings and retained whatever the result of the match).

(i) A maximum of five batting points to be available: 200 to 249 runs – 1 point; 250 to 299 runs – 2 points; 300 to 349 runs – 3 points; 350 to 399 runs – 4 points; 400 runs or over – 5 points. Penalty runs awarded within the first 130 overs of each first innings count towards the award of bonus points.

(ii) A maximum of three bowling points to be available: 3 to 5 wickets taken – 1 point; 6 to 8 wickets taken – 2 points; 9 to 10 wickets taken – 3 points.

(*f*) If play starts when less than eight hours' playing time remains and a one-innings match is played, no first-innings points shall be scored. The side winning on the one innings scores 14 points. In a tie, each side scores seven points. In a drawn match, each side scores four points. If the scores are equal in a drawn match, the side batting in the second innings scores seven points and the opposing side scores four points.

(*g*) If a match is abandoned without a ball being bowled, each side scores four points.

(*h*) The side which has the highest aggregate of points shall be the Champion County of their respective division. Should any sides in the Championship table be equal on points, the following tie-breakers will be applied in the order stated: most wins, fewest losses, team achieving most points in head-to-head contests between teams level on points, most wickets taken, most runs scored. At the end of the season, the top three teams from the second division will be promoted and the bottom three teams from the first division will be relegated.

(*i*) The minimum over-rate to be achieved by counties will be 16 overs per hour. Overs will be calculated at the end of the match and penalties applied on a match-by-match basis. For each over (ignoring fractions) that a side has bowled short of the target number, 0.5 points will be deducted from their Championship total.

(*j*) A county which is adjudged to have prepared a pitch unfit for four-day first-class cricket will have 22 points deducted. A county adjudged to have prepared a poor pitch will have eight points deducted. This penalty will rise to 12 points if the county has prepared a poor or unfit pitch within the previous 12 months.

Under ECB playing conditions, two extras were scored for every no-ball bowled whether scored off or not, and one for every wide. Any runs scored off the bat were credited to the batsman, while byes and leg-byes were counted as no-balls or wides, as appropriate, in accordance with Law 24.13, in addition to the initial penalty.

CONSTITUTION OF COUNTY CHAMPIONSHIP

At least four possible dates have been given for the start of county cricket in England. The first, patchy, references began in 1825. The earliest mention in any cricket publication is in 1864 and eight counties have come to be regarded as first-class from that date, including Cambridgeshire, who dropped out after 1871. For many years, the County Championship was considered to have started in 1873, when regulations governing qualification first applied; indeed, a special commemorative stamp was issued by the Post Office in 1973. However, the Championship was not formally organised until 1890 and before then champions were proclaimed by the press; sometimes publications differed in their views and no definitive list of champions can start before that date. Eight teams contested the 1890 competition – Gloucestershire, Kent, Lancashire, Middlesex, Nottinghamshire, Surrey, Sussex and Yorkshire. Somerset joined in the following year, and in 1895 the Championship began to acquire something of its modern shape when Derbyshire,

Essex, Hampshire, Leicestershire and Warwickshire were added. At that point MCC officially recognised the competition's existence. Worcestershire, Northamptonshire and Glamorgan were admitted to the Championship in 1899, 1905 and 1921 respectively and are regarded as first-class from these dates. An invitation in 1921 to Buckinghamshire to enter the Championship was declined, owing to the lack of necessary playing facilities, and an application by Devon in 1948 was unsuccessful. Durham were admitted to the Championship in 1992 and were granted first-class status prior to their pre-season tour of Zimbabwe.

In 2000, the Championship was split for the first time into two divisions, on the basis of counties' standings in the 1999 competition. From 2000 onwards, the bottom three teams in Division One were relegated at the end of the season, and the top three teams in Division Two promoted.

COUNTY CHAMPIONS

The title of champion county is unreliable before 1890. In 1963, *Wisden* formally accepted the list of champions "most generally selected" by contemporaries, as researched by the late Rowland Bowen (See *Wisden 1959*, pp 91–98). This appears to be the most accurate available list but has no official status. The county champions from 1864 to 1889 were, according to Bowen: 1864 Surrey; 1865 Nottinghamshire; 1866 Middlesex; 1867 Yorkshire; 1868 Yorkshire; 1869 Nottinghamshire and Yorkshire; 1870 Yorkshire; 1871 Nottinghamshire; 1872 Nottinghamshire; 1873 Gloucestershire and Nottinghamshire; 1874 Gloucestershire; 1875 Nottinghamshire; 1876 Gloucestershire; 1877 Gloucestershire; 1878 undecided; 1879 Lancashire and Nottinghamshire; 1880 Nottinghamshire; 1881 Lancashire; 1882 Lancashire and Nottinghamshire; 1883 Nottinghamshire; 1884 Nottinghamshire; 1885 Nottinghamshire; 1886 Nottinghamshire; 1887 Surrey; 1888 Surrey; 1889 Lancashire, Nottinghamshire and Surrey.

Official champions

1890	Surrey
1891	Surrey
1892	Surrey
1893	Yorkshire
1894	Surrey
1895	Surrey
1896	Yorkshire
1897	Lancashire
1898	Yorkshire
1899	Surrey
1900	Yorkshire
1901	Yorkshire
1902	Yorkshire
1903	Middlesex
1904	Lancashire
1905	Yorkshire
1906	Kent
1907	Nottinghamshire
1908	Yorkshire
1909	Kent
1910	Kent
1911	Warwickshire
1912	Yorkshire
1913	Kent
1914	Surrey
1919	Yorkshire
1920	Middlesex
1921	Middlesex
1922	Yorkshire
1923	Yorkshire
1924	Yorkshire
1925	Yorkshire
1926	Lancashire
1927	Lancashire
1928	Lancashire
1929	Nottinghamshire
1930	Lancashire
1931	Yorkshire
1932	Yorkshire
1933	Yorkshire
1934	Lancashire
1935	Yorkshire
1936	Derbyshire
1937	Yorkshire
1938	Yorkshire
1939	Yorkshire
1946	Yorkshire
1947	Middlesex
1948	Glamorgan
1949	Middlesex / Yorkshire
1950	Lancashire / Surrey
1951	Warwickshire
1952	Surrey
1953	Surrey
1954	Surrey
1955	Surrey
1956	Surrey
1957	Surrey
1958	Surrey
1959	Yorkshire
1960	Yorkshire
1961	Hampshire
1962	Yorkshire
1963	Yorkshire
1964	Worcestershire
1965	Worcestershire
1966	Yorkshire
1967	Yorkshire
1968	Yorkshire
1969	Glamorgan
1970	Kent
1971	Surrey
1972	Warwickshire
1973	Hampshire
1974	Worcestershire
1975	Leicestershire
1976	Middlesex
1977	Middlesex / Kent
1978	Kent
1979	Essex
1980	Middlesex
1981	Nottinghamshire
1982	Middlesex
1983	Essex
1984	Essex
1985	Middlesex
1986	Essex
1987	Nottinghamshire
1988	Worcestershire
1989	Worcestershire
1990	Middlesex
1991	Essex
1992	Essex
1993	Middlesex
1994	Warwickshire
1995	Warwickshire
1996	Leicestershire
1997	Glamorgan
1998	Leicestershire
1999	Surrey
2000	Surrey
2001	Yorkshire
2002	Surrey
2003	Sussex
2004	Warwickshire

Notes: Since the Championship was constituted in 1890 it has been won outright as follows: Yorkshire 30 times, Surrey 18, Middlesex 10, Lancashire 7, Essex, Kent and Warwickshire 6, Worcestershire 5, Nottinghamshire 4, Glamorgan and Leicestershire 3, Hampshire 2, Derbyshire and Sussex 1. Durham, Gloucestershire, Northamptonshire and Somerset have never won.

The title has been shared three times since 1890, involving Middlesex twice, Kent, Lancashire, Surrey and Yorkshire.

Wooden Spoons: since the major expansion of the Championship from nine teams to 14 in 1895, the counties have finished outright bottom as follows: Derbyshire 13; Northamptonshire and Somerset 11; Glamorgan 9; Nottinghamshire and Sussex 8; Gloucestershire and Leicestershire 7; Worcestershire 6; Durham and Hampshire 5; Warwickshire 3; Essex and Kent 2; Yorkshire 1. Lancashire, Middlesex and Surrey have never finished bottom. Leicestershire have also shared bottom place twice, once with Hampshire and once with Somerset.

From 1977 to 1983 the Championship was sponsored by Schweppes, from 1984 to 1998 by Britannic Assurance, from 1999 to 2000 by PPP healthcare, in 2001 by CricInfo, and from 2002 by Frizzell.

COUNTY CHAMPIONSHIP – FINAL POSITIONS, 1890–2004

	Derbyshire	Essex	Glamorgan	Gloucestershire	Hampshire	Kent	Lancashire	Leicestershire	Middlesex	Northamptonshire	Nottinghamshire	Somerset	Surrey	Sussex	Warwickshire	Worcestershire	Yorkshire
1890	–	–	–	6	–	3	2	–	7	–	5	–	1	8	–	–	3
1891	–	–	–	9	–	5	2	–	3	–	4	5	1	7	–	–	8
1892	–	–	–	7	–	7	4	–	5	–	2	3	1	9	–	–	6
1893	–	–	–	9	–	4	2	–	3	–	6	8	5	7	–	–	1
1894	–	–	–	9	–	4	4	–	3	–	7	6	1	8	–	–	2
1895	5	9	–	4	10	14	2	12	6	–	12	8	1	11	6	–	3
1896	7	5	–	10	8	9	2	13	3	–	6	11	4	14	12	–	1
1897	14	3	–	5	9	12	1	13	8	–	10	11	2	6	7	–	4
1898	9	5	–	3	12	7	6	13	2	–	8	13	4	9	9	–	1
1899	15	6	–	9	10	8	4	13	2	–	10	13	1	5	7	12	3
1900	13	10	–	7	15	3	2	14	7	–	5	11	7	3	6	12	1
1901	15	10	–	14	7	7	3	12	2	–	9	12	6	4	5	11	1
1902	10	13	–	14	15	7	5	11	12	–	3	7	4	2	6	9	1
1903	12	8	–	13	14	8	4	14	1	–	5	10	11	2	7	6	3
1904	10	14	–	9	15	3	1	7	4	–	5	12	11	6	7	13	2
1905	14	12	–	8	16	6	2	5	11	13	10	15	4	3	7	8	1
1906	16	7	–	9	8	1	4	15	11	11	5	11	3	10	6	14	2
1907	16	7	–	10	12	8	6	11	5	15	1	14	4	13	9	2	2
1908	14	11	–	10	9	2	7	13	4	15	8	16	3	5	12	6	1
1909	15	14	–	16	8	1	2	13	6	7	10	11	5	4	12	8	3
1910	15	11	–	12	6	1	4	10	3	9	5	16	2	7	14	13	8
1911	14	6	–	12	11	2	4	15	3	10	8	16	5	13	1	9	7
1912	12	15	–	11	6	3	4	13	5	2	8	14	7	10	9	16	1
1913	13	15	–	9	10	1	8	14	6	4	5	16	3	7	11	12	2
1914	12	8	–	16	5	3	11	13	2	9	10	15	1	6	7	14	4
1919	9	14	–	8	7	2	5	9	13	12	3	5	4	11	15	–	1
1920	16	9	–	8	11	5	2	13	1	14	7	10	3	6	12	15	4
1921	12	15	17	7	6	4	5	11	1	13	8	10	2	9	16	14	3
1922	11	8	16	13	6	4	5	14	7	15	2	9	4	6	12	17	1
1923	10	13	16	11	7	5	3	14	8	17	2	9	4	6	12	15	1
1924	17	15	13	6	12	5	4	11	2	16	6	8	3	10	9	14	1

	Derbyshire	Essex	Glamorgan	Gloucestershire	Hampshire	Kent	Lancashire	Leicestershire	Middlesex	Northamptonshire	Nottinghamshire	Somerset	Surrey	Sussex	Warwickshire	Worcestershire	Yorkshire
1925	14	7	17	10	9	5	3	12	6	11	4	15	2	13	8	16	1
1926	11	9	8	15	7	3	1	13	6	16	4	14	5	10	12	17	2
1927	5	8	15	12	13	4	1	7	9	16	2	14	6	10	11	17	3
1928	10	16	15	5	12	2	1	9	8	13	3	14	6	7	11	17	4
1929	7	12	17	4	11	8	2	9	6	13	1	15	10	4	14	16	2
1930	9	6	11	2	13	5	1	12	16	17	4	13	8	7	15	10	3
1931	7	10	15	2	12	3	6	16	11	17	5	13	8	4	9	14	1
1932	10	14	15	13	8	3	6	12	10	16	4	7	5	2	9	17	1
1933	6	4	16	10	14	3	5	17	12	13	8	11	9	2	7	15	1
1934	3	8	13	7	14	5	1	12	10	17	9	15	11	2	4	16	5
1935	2	9	13	15	16	10	4	6	3	17	5	14	11	7	8	12	1
1936	1	9	16	4	10	8	11	15	2	17	5	7	6	14	13	12	3
1937	3	6	7	4	14	12	9	16	2	17	10	13	8	5	11	15	1
1938	5	6	16	10	14	9	4	17	2	15	12	7	3	8	13	11	1
1939	9	4	13	3	15	5	6	17	2	16	12	14	8	10	11	7	1
1946	15	8	6	5	10	6	3	11	2	16	13	4	11	17	14	8	1
1947	5	11	9	2	16	4	3	14	1	17	11	11	6	9	5	7	7
1948	6	13	1	8	9	15	5	11	3	17	14	12	2	16	7	10	4
1949	15	9	8	7	16	13	11	17	1	6	11	9	5	13	4	3	1
1950	5	17	11	7	12	9	1	16	14	10	15	7	1	13	4	6	3
1951	11	8	5	12	9	16	3	15	7	13	17	14	6	10	1	4	2
1952	4	10	7	9	12	15	3	6	5	8	16	17	1	13	10	14	2
1953	6	12	10	6	14	16	3	3	5	11	8	17	1	2	9	15	12
1954	3	15	4	13	14	11	10	16	7	7	5	17	1	9	6	11	2
1955	8	14	16	12	3	13	9	6	5	7	11	17	1	4	9	15	2
1956	12	11	13	3	6	16	2	17	5	4	8	15	1	9	14	9	7
1957	4	5	9	12	13	14	6	17	7	2	15	8	1	9	11	16	3
1958	5	6	15	14	2	8	7	12	10	4	17	3	1	13	16	9	11
1959	7	9	6	2	8	13	5	16	10	11	17	12	3	15	4	14	1
1960	5	6	11	8	12	10	2	17	3	9	16	14	7	4	15	13	1
1961	7	6	14	5	1	11	13	9	3	16	17	10	15	8	12	4	2
1962	7	9	14	4	10	11	16	17	13	8	15	6	5	12	3	2	1
1963	17	12	2	8	10	13	15	16	6	7	9	3	11	4	4	14	1
1964	12	10	11	17	12	7	14	16	6	3	15	8	4	9	2	1	5
1965	9	15	14	10	12	5	13	14	6	2	17	7	8	16	11	1	4
1966	9	16	14	15	11	4	12	8	12	5	17	3	7	10	6	2	1
1967	6	15	14	17	12	2	11	2	7	9	15	8	4	13	10	5	1
1968	8	14	3	16	5	2	6	9	10	13	4	12	15	17	11	7	1
1969	16	6	1	2	5	10	15	14	11	9	8	17	3	7	4	12	13
1970	7	12	2	17	10	1	3	15	16	14	11	13	5	9	7	6	4
1971	17	10	16	8	9	4	3	5	6	14	12	7	1	11	2	15	13
1972	17	5	13	3	9	2	15	6	8	4	14	11	12	16	1	7	10
1973	16	8	11	5	1	4	12	9	13	3	17	10	2	15	7	6	14
1974	17	12	16	14	2	10	8	4	6	3	15	5	13	9	1	11	11
1975	15	7	9	16	3	5	4	1	11	8	13	12	6	17	14	10	2
1976	15	6	17	3	12	14	16	4	1	2	13	7	9	10	5	11	8
1977	7	6	14	3	11	1	16	5	1	9	17	4	14	8	10	13	12
1978	14	2	13	10	8	1	12	6	3	17	7	5	16	9	11	15	4
1979	16	1	17	10	12	5	13	6	14	11	9	8	3	4	15	2	7
1980	9	8	13	7	17	16	15	10	1	12	3	5	2	6	14	11	6
1981	12	5	14	13	7	9	16	8	4	15	1	3	6	2	17	11	10
1982	11	7	16	15	3	13	12	2	1	9	4	6	5	8	17	14	10
1983	9	1	15	12	3	7	12	4	2	6	14	10	8	11	5	16	17

	Derbyshire	Durham	Essex	Glamorgan	Gloucestershire	Hampshire	Kent	Lancashire	Leicestershire	Middlesex	Northamptonshire	Nottinghamshire	Somerset	Surrey	Sussex	Warwickshire	Worcestershire	Yorkshire
1984	12	–	1	13	17	15	5	16	4	3	11	2	7	8	6	9	10	14
1985	13	–	4	12	3	2	9	14	16	1	10	8	17	6	7	15	5	11
1986	11	–	1	17	2	6	8	15	7	12	9	4	16	3	14	12	5	10
1987	6	–	12	13	10	5	14	2	3	16	7	1	11	4	17	15	9	8
1988	14	–	3	17	10	15	2	9	8	7	12	5	11	4	16	6	1	13
1989	6	–	2	17	9	6	15	4	13	3	5	11	14	12	10	8	1	16
1990	12	–	2	8	13	3	16	6	7	1	11	13	15	9	17	5	4	10
1991	3	–	1	12	13	9	6	8	16	15	10	4	17	5	1	2	6	14
1992	5	18	1	14	10	15	2	12	8	11	3	4	9	13	7	6	17	16
1993	15	18	11	3	17	13	8	13	9	1	4	7	5	6	10	16	2	12
1994	17	16	6	18	12	13	9	10	2	4	5	3	11	7	8	1	15	13
1995	14	17	5	16	6	13	18	4	7	2	3	11	9	12	15	1	10	8
1996	2	18	5	10	13	14	4	15	1	9	16	17	11	3	12	8	7	6
1997	16	17	8	1	7	14	2	11	10	4	15	13	12	8	18	4	3	6
1998	10	14	18	12	4	6	11	2	1	17	15	16	9	5	7	8	13	3
1999	9	8	12	14	18	7	5	2	3	16	13	17	4	1	11	10	15	6
2000	**9**	**8**	*2*	*3*	*4*	**7**	**6**	**2**	**4**	*8*	*1*	*7*	**5**	**1**	*9*	*6*	*5*	**3**
2001	*9*	*8*	**9**	**8**	**4**	*2*	*3*	**6**	*5*	*5*	*7*	**7**	**2**	**4**	*1*	**3**	*6*	**1**
2002	*6*	*9*	**1**	*5*	*8*	**7**	**3**	**4**	**5**	*2*	*1*	*3*	**8**	**1**	**6**	**2**	*4*	*9*
2003	*9*	*6*	**7**	*5*	**3**	*8*	**4**	**2**	*9*	*6*	**2**	*8*	**7**	**3**	**1**	**5**	*1*	*4*
2004	*8*	*9*	*5*	*3*	*6*	**2**	**2**	*8*	*6*	**4**	*9*	**1**	**4**	**3**	**1**	**5**	*7*	**7**

Note: For the 2000–2004 Championships, Division One placings are shown in bold, Division Two in italic.

MATCH RESULTS, 1864–2004

County	Years of Play	Played	Won	Lost	Drawn	Tied	% Won
Derbyshire	1871–87; 1895–2004	2,355	582	872	900	1	24.71
Durham	1992–2004	220	36	120	64	0	16.36
Essex	1895–2004	2,317	669	679	963	6	28.87
Glamorgan	1921–2004	1,851	415	624	812	0	22.42
Gloucestershire . . .	1870–2004	2,591	766	953	870	2	29.56
Hampshire	1864–85; 1895–2004	2,426	634	831	957	4	26.13
Kent	1864–2004	2,715	981	812	917	5	36.13
Lancashire	1865–2004	2,790	1,034	583	1,170	3	37.06
Leicestershire	1895–2004	2,284	521	826	936	1	22.81
Middlesex	1864–2004	2,494	920	631	938	5	36.88
Northamptonshire .	1905–2004	2,052	509	710	830	3	24.80
Nottinghamshire . .	1864–2004	2,624	792	712	1,119	1	30.18
Somerset	1882–85; 1891–2004	2,325	551	925	846	3	23.69
Surrey	1864–2004	2,871	1,141	633	1,093	4	39.74
Sussex	1864–2004	2,764	776	954	1,028	6	28.07
Warwickshire	1895–2004	2,297	630	658	1,007	2	27.42
Worcestershire . . .	1899–2004	2,239	570	768	899	2	25.45
Yorkshire	1864–2004	2,892	1,274	510	1,106	2	44.05
Cambridgeshire . . .	1864–69; 1871	19	8	8	3	0	42.10
		21,063	12,809	12,809	8,229	25	

Notes: Matches abandoned without a ball bowled are wholly excluded.

Counties participated in the years shown, except that there were no matches in the years 1915–18 and 1940–45; Hampshire did not play inter-county matches in 1868–69, 1871–74 and 1879; Worcestershire did not take part in the Championship in 1919.

COUNTY CHAMPIONSHIP STATISTICS FOR 2004

County	Runs	For Wickets	Avge	Runs	Against Wickets	Avge	RPF
Derbyshire (8)	7,609	239	31.83	7,440	188	39.57	0.80
Durham (9)	7,220	276	26.15	7,617	203	37.52	0.69
Essex (5)	8,544	234	36.51	8,676	247	35.12	1.03
Glamorgan (3)	8,048	222	36.25	8,258	239	34.55	1.04
Gloucestershire (6) . .	8,092	211	38.35	7,423	201	36.93	1.03
Hampshire (2)	7,623	229	33.28	6,902	256	26.96	1.23
Kent (2)	8,676	227	38.22	8,513	217	39.23	0.97
Lancashire (8)	7,865	229	34.34	8,229	236	34.86	0.98
Leicestershire (6) . . .	7,705	237	32.51	7,918	233	33.98	0.95
Middlesex (4)	8,420	233	36.13	8,820	235	37.53	0.96
Northamptonshire (9)	7,859	232	33.87	8,064	211	38.21	0.88
Nottinghamshire (1) .	8,599	193	44.55	8,166	241	33.88	1.31
Somerset (4)	7,639	191	39.99	8,403	245	34.29	1.16
Surrey (3)	9,132	254	35.95	8,399	230	36.51	0.98
Sussex (5)	7,228	226	31.98	8,124	238	34.13	0.93
Warwickshire (1) . . .	9,310	195	47.74	8,445	208	40.60	1.17
Worcestershire (7) . . .	8,247	214	38.53	8,812	245	35.96	1.07
Yorkshire (7)	7,472	245	30.49	7,079	214	33.07	0.92
	145,288	4,087	35.54	145,288	4,087	35.54	

2004 Championship positions are shown in brackets; Division One in bold, Division Two in italic.
Relative performance factor (RPF) is determined by dividing the average runs scored per wicket by the average runs conceded per wicket.

RUNS SCORED PER 100 BALLS IN THE COUNTY CHAMPIONSHIP, 2004

County	Run-rate/ 100 balls	County	Run-rate/ 100 balls
Derbyshire (8)	52.95	Middlesex (4)	54.25
Durham (9)	56.85	Northamptonshire (9)	50.22
Essex (5)	62.73	Nottinghamshire (1)	64.47
Glamorgan (3)	61.85	Somerset (4)	61.39
Gloucestershire (6)	55.25	Surrey (3)	62.09
Hampshire (2)	60.25	Sussex (5)	56.07
Kent (2)	59.46	Warwickshire (1)	58.26
Lancashire (8)	58.50	Worcestershire (7)	60.51
Leicestershire (6)	58.76	Yorkshire (7)	59.19
		2004 average rate	58.36

2004 Championship positions are shown in brackets: Division One in bold, Division Two in italic.

ECB PITCHES TABLE OF MERIT

First-Class Matches, Under-19 & Women's Tests and UCCE Matches

		Points	Matches	Average in 2004	Average in 2003
1	Surrey (1)	96	9	5.33	5.68
2	Somerset (3)	116	11	5.27	5.23
3	Kent (4)	94	9	5.22	5.00
4	Nottinghamshire (14=)	92	9	5.11	4.00

		Points	Matches	Average in 2004	Average in 2003
5	Glamorgan (10)	119	12	4.96	4.50
6	Lancashire (6)	87	9	4.83	4.81
7	Middlesex (2).	105	11	4.77	5.42
8	Leicestershire (17).	84	9	4.67	3.89
9	Warwickshire (11).	83	9	4.61	4.45
	⎧ Essex (9).	72	8	4.50	4.61
10	⎨ Gloucestershire (5)	81	9	4.50	4.94
	⎩ Worcestershire (16)	90	10	4.50	3.90
13	Derbyshire (7)	89	10	4.45	4.70
14	⎰ Northamptonshire (18)	75	9	4.17	3.75
	⎱ Sussex (8)	75	9	4.17	4.68
16	Yorkshire (14=).	103	13	3.96	4.00
17	Durham (12)	70	9	3.89	4.40
18	Hampshire (13).	66	9	3.67	4.13
	Durham UCCE.	20	2	5.00	5.00
	Cambridge UCCE	48	5	4.80	4.71
	Oxford UCCE	56	6	4.67	4.10
	Bradford/Leeds UCCE	36	4	4.50	4.75
	Loughborough UCCE.	26	3	4.33	4.00

ECB PITCHES TABLE OF MERIT

One-Day Matches

		Points	Matches	Average in 2004	Average in 2003
1	Somerset (2)	132	12	5.50	5.42
2	Surrey (1)	120	11	5.45	5.54
3	Yorkshire (6)	136	13	5.23	4.91
4	Glamorgan (7)	142	14	5.07	4.89
5	Nottinghamshire (16)	152	15	5.07	4.37
6	Essex (4).	111	11	5.05	5.21
7	⎰ Derbyshire (14).	138	14	4.93	4.50
	⎱ Kent (10).	138	14	4.93	4.85
9	Middlesex (3).	176	18	4.89	5.38
10	Lancashire (8)	116	12	4.83	4.88
11	Scotland (15)	94	10	4.70	4.45
12	Gloucestershire (11).	129	14	4.61	4.82
13	Warwickshire (5).	147	16	4.59	4.92
14	Sussex (9)	125	14	4.46	4.87
15	Worcestershire (18)	122	14	4.36	4.23
16	Leicestershire (12).	112	13	4.31	4.80
17	Hampshire (19).	83	10	4.15	4.20
18	Durham (13)	102	13	3.92	4.55
19	Northamptonshire (17)	92	12	3.83	4.36

In both tables 2003 positions are shown in brackets. Each umpire in a game marks the pitch on the following scale of merit: 6 – very good; 5 – good; 4 – above average; 3 – below average; 2 – poor; 1 – unfit.

The tables, provided by the ECB, cover major matches, including Tests, Under-19 internationals, women's internationals and UCCE games, played on grounds under the county or UCCE's jurisdiction. Middlesex pitches at Lord's are the responsibility of MCC.

The ECB points out that the tables of merit are not a direct assessment of the groundsmen's ability. Marks may be affected by many factors including weather, soil conditions and the resources available.

DERBYSHIRE

A new beginning? Or the beginning of the end?

GERALD MORTIMER

The face of the County Ground changed in 2004, but the struggles on the field, and the administrative dislocation off it, remained the same. Regulars at Derby have now waited since June 2002 to see their side win a Championship match, with the only victory of 2004 coming in Durham. Amid that, the club's chief executive John Smedley ended a long absence with work-related stress by leaving, claiming a lack of committee support. So, in his first full season as director of cricket, David Houghton faced many difficulties, exacerbated by a freakish series of injuries to important players. With so many critics ready to abolish a county or three, there is an undercurrent of fear for the future.

The season began with the decaying Grandstand, having already lost its familiar copper dome, being replaced by a modern wood-clad design modishly called the Gateway Centre. The club hoped it would symbolise a change in direction. Funded through grants and sales of land surrounding the ground, the complex includes an excellent indoor school, housing a long-awaited academy under former wicket-keeper Karl Krikken. Facilities for sponsors are also impressive, but it is far less successful as a pavilion, with too many blank windowless walls and the one good viewing area for members usually masked by sightscreens. The permanent floodlights, first used in August, are a significant improvement.

But, under the terms of the club's long-term lease from the city council, profits from the land sales can only be used on the *ground*; and Derbyshire's main problem is rebuilding the team. Injuries nipped before the start, when both Michael Di Venuto, due to succeed Dominic Cork as captain, and his fellow Tasmanian Damien Wright were ruled out. Chris Rogers, from Western Australia, was an instant success in the top order, but he only managed six first-class matches before returning home for treatment on a damaged shoulder. The arrival of the Victorian Jon Moss was delayed by his wedding, and he was then hampered by his back. Only in the second half of the summer did he make a substantial contribution.

Kevin Dean, the best bowler of recent seasons, laboured through the early months before accepting in July that knee surgery was the only answer. And, having started to find his way as a spinning all-rounder, Ant Botha suffered a serious groin injury. Even Mike Hendrick, who returned as bowling coach, was seen on crutches.

With a weakened side Derbyshire could seldom score enough runs or find penetration with the ball. Luke Sutton, who took over as captain, had an inevitably hard task and he earned considerable respect through his determined leadership. Only in the last month did the strain of pushing constantly uphill tell on the team, notably in a dreadful final-day collapse against Nottinghamshire in August. Sutton impressed Houghton sufficiently to retain the captaincy for 2005, even with Di Venuto returning. But his summer ended in tragedy when his intended bride was killed in a car crash.

Sutton created a good atmosphere but he needed better cricketers to form a successful unit. The vibrancy and class of Cork, who had joined Lancashire, were missed, and Graeme Welch and Hassan Adnan shouldered too heavy a burden. Adnan is an ECB-qualified Pakistani who gets the scoreboard moving without playing

Hassan Adnan

big shots, and is dedicated to the game. In all matches, he scored 2,027 runs. Of the other batsmen, only Chris Bassano achieved par, shrugging aside a lean 2003 in the Championship. Meanwhile, Welch scored a maiden century and was, as ever, a model professional, both as a supportive vice-captain and an uncomplaining opening bowler, a role for which he is not suited. Not much keeps him out of action, but he suffered the season's oddest injury when his son, practising John Travolta-style disco dancing, jabbed him in the eye. Mohammad Sheikh, freed by Warwickshire, bowled almost as wholeheartedly as Welch and was an effective lower-order batsman, while Nick Walker, engaged from Hertfordshire, had his moments without suggesting consistency. In total, 13 players made a county debut but none of them yet appeared a match-winner.

Nor was there any cheer to be found in limited-overs games. Derbyshire took the first exit from the C&G Trophy and were next to bottom in the totesport League, as they were in the Championship. Unhappily for already ailing finances, two of their three home Twenty20 matches fell on rainy evenings. If anything could go wrong, it did, even in the most routine matters. When Derbyshire changed their nickname for the 2005 League from Scorpions (the name of a lager produced by a former sponsor) to Phantoms (a vague reference to local employers Rolls-Royce), the email announcement sent via the ECB went seriously haywire, and some bemused newspapers received it 7,000 times in a day. At least the county got noticed.

Tom Sears, formerly Worcestershire's commercial director, was due to start as the new chief executive early in 2005. Among the players, Mohammad Ali, Andrew Gait, Neil Gunter, Rawait Khan and Steve Selwood were released, and only pre-existing contracts saved others. Houghton did sign a fellow Zimbabwean, the all-rounder Travis Friend, as a Kolpak player to strengthen the team. It need hardly be said that improvements are urgently needed on all fronts, though the presence of Houghton, a competent individual, is something to cling to.

DERBYSHIRE RESULTS

All first-class matches – Played 18: Won 2, Lost 7, Drawn 9.
County Championship matches – Played 16: Won 1, Lost 6, Drawn 9.

Frizzell County Championship, 8th in Division 2; Cheltenham & Gloucester Trophy, 2nd round;
totesport League, 9th in Division 2; Twenty20 Cup, 3rd in North Group.

COUNTY CHAMPIONSHIP AVERAGES

BATTING AND FIELDING

Cap		M	I	NO	R	HS	100s	50s	Avge	Ct/St
	C. J. L. Rogers§	6	11	2	498	156	1	3	55.33	6
2004	Hassan Adnan	16	28	4	1,247	140	3	7	51.95	7
	N. G. E. Walker	7	7	3	201	80	0	2	50.25	2
2002	C. W. G. Bassano	14	22	3	814	123*	2	6	42.84	4
2004	J. Moss§	11	19	2	608	147*	1	4	35.76	2
2002	L. D. Sutton	15	25	3	684	131	1	2	31.09	30/3
2001	G. Welch	16	25	4	609	115*	1	1	29.00	12
2001	S. D. Stubbings	14	25	1	643	96	0	5	26.79	8
	Mohammad Ali	4	6	1	110	50	0	1	22.00	1
	M. A. Sheikh	13	18	6	259	42	0	0	21.58	1
	A. I. Gait	12	22	1	425	81	0	1	20.23	9
2004	A. G. Botha	10	17	2	302	52	0	1	20.13	5
1998	K. J. Dean	7	10	4	117	35	0	0	19.50	3
	B. J. France	4	7	0	126	56	0	1	18.00	2
	P. M. R. Havell	6	8	6	30	13*	0	0	15.00	2
	J. D. C. Bryant	7	13	1	149	30	0	0	12.41	3
	S. A. Selwood	3	6	0	63	38	0	0	10.50	1
	N. R. C. Dumelow	3	4	0	36	18	0	0	9.00	0

Also batted: L. J. Goddard (1 match) 8 (5 ct); D. R. Hewson (2 matches) 0, 9; I. D. Hunter (1 match) 0, 6; C. D. Paget (3 matches) 7, 0; D. B. Powell§ (1 match) 17, 13 (1 ct).

§ *Overseas player.*

BOWLING

	O	M	R	W	BB	5W/i	Avge
K. J. Dean	144	18	597	20	5-86	1	29.85
N. G. E. Walker	137.2	16	574	17	5-68	1	33.76
G. Welch	471.5	103	1,525	45	5-57	3	33.88
M. A. Sheikh	298.3	69	945	26	4-9	0	36.34
P. M. R. Havell	122.1	7	640	16	4-75	0	40.00
A. G. Botha	252	43	874	21	4-66	0	41.61
Mohammad Ali	116.4	18	486	10	4-75	0	48.60
J. Moss	266.5	39	643	13	3-30	0	49.46

Also bowled: N. R. C. Dumelow 86–12–306–2; B. J. France 4–0–20–0; Hassan Adnan 37.3–2–154–1; D. R. Hewson 46–18–112–4; I. D. Hunter 14.3–1–52–3; C. D. Paget 36–4–137–0; D. B. Powell 29.1–2–132–2.

COUNTY RECORDS

Highest score for:	274	G. Davidson v Lancashire at Manchester	1896
Highest score against:	343*	P. A. Perrin (Essex) at Chesterfield	1904
Best bowling for:	10-40	W. Bestwick v Glamorgan at Cardiff	1921
Best bowling against:	10-45	R. L. Johnson (Middlesex) at Derby	1994
Highest total for:	645	v Hampshire at Derby	1898
Highest total against:	662	by Yorkshire at Chesterfield	1898
Lowest total for:	16	v Nottinghamshire at Nottingham	1879
Lowest total against:	23	by Hampshire at Burton upon Trent	1958

DERBYSHIRE DIRECTORY

ADDRESS

County Ground, Nottingham Road, Derby DE21 6DA (01332 383211; fax 01332 290251; email post@dccc.org.uk). **Website** www.dccc.org.uk.

GROUND

Derby: 1 mile E of town centre, to the N of Pentagon Island roundabout where A61 and A52 cross. Nearest station: Derby (1¼ miles).

OFFICIALS

Captain L. D. Sutton
Director of cricket D. L. Houghton
Director of academy K. M. Krikken
President D. K. Arnott

Chairman G. T. Bowring
Chief executive T. Sears
Head groundsman N. Godrich
Scorer J. M. Brown

PLAYERS

Players expected to reappear in 2005

	Former counties	Country	Born	Birthplace
Bassano Christopher Warwick Godfrey .		A (EU)	11.9.1975	*East London, SA*
Botha Anthony Greyvensteyn		SA (EU)	17.11.1976	*Pretoria*
Bryant James Douglas Campbell	Somerset	SA (EU)	4.2.1976	*Durban*
Dean Kevin James.		E	16.10.1975	†*Derby*
Di Venuto Michael James	Sussex	A	12.12.1973	*Hobart*
France Benjamin John		E	14.5.1982	*Brunei*
Goddard Lee James		E	22.10.1982	*Dewsbury*
Hassan Adnan		P (EU)	15.5.1975	*Lahore*
Havell Paul Matthew Roger.	Sussex	A (EU)	4.7.1980	*Melbourne*
Hewson Dominic Robert	Glos	E	3.10.1974	*Cheltenham*
Hunter Ian David	Durham	E	11.9.1979	*Durham*
Lungley Tom		E	25.7.1979	†*Derby*
Moss Jonathon		A	4.5.1975	*Sydney*
Paget Christopher David		E	2.11.1987	*Stafford*
Sheikh Mohamed Avez.	Warwicks	E	2.7.1973	*Birmingham*
Spendlove Benjamin Lee		E	4.11.1978	†*Belper*
Stubbings Stephen David		E	31.3.1978	*Huddersfield*
Sutton Luke David	Somerset	E	4.10.1976	*Keynsham*
Walker Nicholas Guy Eades		E	7.8.1984	*Enfield*
Welch Graeme	Warwicks	E	21.3.1972	*Durham*

Player due to join in 2005

***Friend** Travis John		Z (K)	7.1.1981	*Kwekwe*

* *Test player.* † *Born in Derbyshire.*

At Cardiff, April 16, 17, 18, 19. DERBYSHIRE drew with GLAMORGAN.

At Taunton, April 21, 22, 23, 24. DERBYSHIRE drew with SOMERSET.

DERBYSHIRE v DURHAM

At Derby, April 28, 29, 30, May 1. Drawn. Derbyshire 12 pts, Durham 7 pts. Toss: Derbyshire. Championship debuts: G. R. Breese, G. Onions.

The loss of the first two days to rain turned this into a scramble for bonus points, with two Western Australia team-mates dominating what play was possible. Chris Rogers, replacing Derbyshire's injured captain Michael Di Venuto for the season, batted with a poise and authority that promised much, showing crisp strokes based on a sound technique. His stand of 152 with Hassan Adnan gave the innings its substance. North, the other Western Australian, responded with a matching century for Durham but failed to find a partner. Still, full bonus points did not mean full satisfaction for Derbyshire: Dean, who broke down with knee trouble, became the fifth seamer on their injury list. Even Mike Hendrick, back at his old county as bowling coach, was struggling with a calf strain.

Close of play: First day, No play; Second day, No play; Third day, Derbyshire 311-4 (Rogers 151, Sutton 8).

Derbyshire

A. I. Gait c Pattison b Onions	37	A. G. Botha c Lewis b Davies	2
S. D. Stubbings c North b Onions	9	K. J. Dean not out	17
C. J. L. Rogers c A. Pratt b Plunkett	156	B 5, l-b 7	12
Hassan Adnan b Breese	72		
C. W. G. Bassano c Davies b Plunkett	22	1/14 (2) 2/103 (1)	(8 wkts dec.) 400
*†L. D. Sutton c Peng b Pattison	27	3/255 (4) 4/294 (5)	
D. R. Hewson c A. Pratt b Davies	9	5/326 (3) 6/344 (6)	
G. Welch not out	37	7/350 (7) 8/360 (9)	

N. G. E. Walker did not bat.

Bonus points – Derbyshire 5, Durham 2.

Bowling: Plunkett 26.3–4–71–2; Onions 27–7–99–2; Pattison 13–2–42–1; Davies 23–3–67–2; Bridge 14–3–40–0; Breese 17–2–69–1.

Durham

*J. J. B. Lewis b Walker	2	A. M. Davies lbw b Botha	0
M. J. North c sub b Botha	119	G. Onions not out	0
G. R. Breese lbw b Dean	15		
G. J. Pratt c Sutton b Welch	7	L-b 9, n-b 6	15
N. Peng b Walker	0		
I. Pattison lbw b Welch	23	1/5 (1) 2/45 (3) 3/62 (4)	232
†A. Pratt c Rogers b Welch	44	4/85 (5) 5/172 (6) 6/176 (2)	
L. E. Plunkett b Botha	7	7/226 (8) 8/232 (9)	
G. D. Bridge c Welch b Botha	0	9/232 (7) 10/232 (10)	

Bonus points – Durham 1, Derbyshire 3.

Bowling: Welch 18–2–64–3; Walker 11.3–3–55–2; Dean 3.3–1–13–1; Hewson 7–2–25–0; Botha 17.5–6–66–4.

Umpires: B. Leadbeater and J. F. Steele.

At Southampton, May 7, 8, 9, 10. DERBYSHIRE drew with HAMPSHIRE.

DERBYSHIRE v SOMERSET

At Derby, May 19, 20, 21, 22. Drawn. Derbyshire 11 pts, Somerset 10 pts. Toss: Derbyshire.

Derbyshire's winless run in home Championship matches stretched to 15 after a frustrating last day. John Francis reached 68 despite a broken finger, the Derbyshire old boy Blackwell made an unbeaten 64, and Somerset batted out a draw. Worse, Rogers left on a stretcher with torn ankle ligaments. It was a disappointing end after Derbyshire took a 60-run first-innings lead. Caddick, still optimistic about an England recall, grabbed six for 92, his best since the 2002-03 Ashes, but could not budge Nick Walker, who hit him for three impertinent sixes in an over. Walker's 80 (the highest ever by a Derbyshire No. 11, passing Martin Jean-Jacques's 73 on debut in 1986) demonstrated strength and a good eye, and five wickets reaffirmed his promise. However, Blackwell, after an unbeaten 247 in 2003, again punished Derbyshire, hitting a typically beefy 111 to keep the deficit manageable. Significantly, Moss injured his neck in holding a fine boundary catch to end the innings: it reduced Sutton's bowling options and helped persuade him to wait until the final morning before a cautious declaration.

Close of play: First day, Derbyshire 315-9 (Sheikh 7, Walker 45); Second day, Somerset 299-8 (Johnson 5, S. R. G. Francis 2); Third day, Derbyshire 344-6 (Sutton 37, Welch 21).

Derbyshire

A. I. Gait c Turner b S. R. G. Francis	12	– b Johnson	81
S. D. Stubbings lbw b Caddick	37	– c Turner b Blackwell	17
C. J. L. Rogers c Turner b S. R. G. Francis	8	– c Turner b Caddick	91
Hassan Adnan lbw b Caddick	45	– c S. R. G. Francis b Caddick	60
J. Moss c Edwards b Caddick	0	– (6) b Blackwell	9
C. W. G. Bassano c S. R. G. Francis b Caddick	83	– (5) b Caddick	16
*†L. D. Sutton c Turner b McLean	17	– c Caddick b S. R. G. Francis	41
G. Welch b Caddick	28	– not out	45
A. G. Botha b Caddick	20	– not out	12
M. A. Sheikh not out	22		
N. G. E. Walker b McLean	80		
L-b 4, w 1, n-b 10	15	L-b 9, w 2, n-b 4	15
	367	(7 wkts dec.)	**387**

1/31 (1) 2/41 (3) 3/103 (2) 4/107 (5)
5/112 (4) 6/156 (7) 7/214 (8)
8/256 (6) 9/264 (9) 10/367 (11)

1/73 (2) 2/135 (1) (7 wkts dec.) 387
3/231 (3) 4/270 (5)
5/283 (4) 6/289 (6) 7/360 (7)

Bonus points – Derbyshire 4, Somerset 3.

Bowling: *First Innings*—Caddick 30–9–92–6; Johnson 17–2–60–0; S. R. G. Francis 18–3–66–2; McLean 24.2–5–80–2; Blackwell 21–8–58–0; Hildreth 3–0–7–0. *Second Innings*—Caddick 34–4–119–3; Johnson 13–2–45–1; McLean 10–2–30–0; S. R. G. Francis 6.5–0–53–1; Blackwell 30–4–105–2; Hildreth 3–0–26–0.

Somerset

N. J. Edwards c Sutton b Walker	30	– b Walker	13
J. D. Francis c Sutton b Walker	1	– st Sutton b Botha	68
J. Cox lbw b Welch	36	– b Welch	16
J. C. Hildreth c Botha b Sheikh	31	– lbw b Sheikh	31
*M. Burns lbw b Walker	4	– not out	33
I. D. Blackwell c and b Welch	111	– not out	64
†R. J. Turner c Rogers b Botha	45		
R. L. Johnson b Walker	9		
A. R. Caddick lbw b Welch	9		
S. R. G. Francis not out	2		
N. A. M. McLean c Moss b Walker	4		
B 9, l-b 3, w 3, n-b 10	25	B 5, l-b 5, w 1, n-b 16	27
	307	(4 wkts)	**252**

1/2 (2) 2/55 (3) 3/101 (4) 4/101 (1)
5/110 (5) 6/281 (7) 7/287 (6)
8/297 (9) 9/303 (8) 10/307 (11)

1/42 (1) 2/64 (3) (4 wkts) 252
3/114 (4) 4/156 (2)

Bonus points – Somerset 3, Derbyshire 3.

Bowling: *First Innings*—Welch 28–12–79–3; Walker 19.5–7–68–5; Sheikh 22–5–68–1; Botha 22–6–76–1; Hassan Adnan 2–0–4–0. *Second Innings*—Welch 23–4–70–1; Walker 11–0–45–1; Sheikh 15–4–43–1; Botha 25–6–58–1; Hassan Adnan 4–1–26–0.

Umpires: A. A. Jones and J. F. Steele.

DERBYSHIRE v GLAMORGAN

At Derby, May 25, 26, 27, 28. Glamorgan won by 128 runs. Glamorgan 22 pts, Derbyshire 7 pts. Toss: Glamorgan. County debut: D. B. Powell.

Increasingly short of players, Derbyshire borrowed Daren Powell, a 26-year-old Jamaican seamer with four Tests for West Indies, from the local Belper Meadows club – once home to "The Demon", F. R. Spofforth. Powell proved a little less fiendish, with two for 132. On a placid pitch, Glamorgan capitalised on winning their sixth successive Championship toss, batting soundly right down the order as the attack laboured. Maynard's ten was the lowest score, making this the first case in England since 1997 of a first-class innings in which all eleven reached doubled figures. The reply then fell 82 short, with Stubbings and Hassan Adnan narrowly missing centuries; Adnan's obvious disagreement with the lbw decision against him earned an ECB reprimand. Welch carried Derbyshire's second-innings bowling, and inspired fleeting hope of an attainable target with three dismissals in 21 balls. But Hemp's first Championship century since September 2002 allowed Glamorgan to dictate terms. They declared 341 ahead, and at 66 for five it became a matter of survival for Derbyshire. The spinners Croft and Cosker worked their way through the top order, and Glamorgan clinched victory with 12 minutes to spare.

Close of play: First day, Glamorgan 408-7 (Harrison 13, Wharf 10); Second day, Derbyshire 253-3 (Stubbings 93, Bassano 43); Third day, Glamorgan 188-6 (Hemp 69, Harrison 3).

Glamorgan

M. T. G. Elliott c Sutton b Sheikh	77	– (2) c and b Dean	15
†M. A. Wallace b Welch	87	– (1) c Welch b Botha	46
D. L. Hemp b Sheikh	26	– not out	102
M. J. Powell lbw b Dean	56	– b Welch	6
M. P. Maynard st Sutton b Botha	10	– c Dean b Welch	17
A. Dale c Gait b Walker	40	– c Sutton b Welch	0
*R. D. B. Croft b Powell	43	– c Welch b Sheikh	16
D. S. Harrison b Dean	22	– c Sutton b Welch	24
A. G. Wharf c Powell b Dean	29	– c Gait b Welch	10
S. D. Thomas c Hassan Adnan b Powell	16	– not out	4
D. A. Cosker not out	21		
B 7, l-b 9, w 7, n-b 24	47	L-b 8, w 1, n-b 10	19

1/168 (2) 2/184 (1) 3/240 (3) 4/273 (5)   474
5/297 (4) 6/372 (6) 7/398 (7)
8/436 (8) 9/443 (9) 10/474 (10)

1/36 (2) 2/100 (1)   (8 wkts dec.) 259
3/120 (4) 4/144 (5)
5/144 (6) 6/176 (7)
7/218 (8) 8/240 (9)

Bonus points – Glamorgan 5, Derbyshire 3.

Bowling: *First Innings*—Powell 20.1–2–85–2; Walker 17–0–83–1; Dean 19–2–77–3; Welch 26–5–96–1; Sheikh 19–6–53–2; Botha 20–5–64–1. *Second Innings*—Powell 9–0–47–0; Walker 3–0–14–0; Dean 5–0–21–1; Welch 23.4–3–100–5; Sheikh 9–3–21–1; Botha 18–4–48–1.

> **❝**Onions and Mustard were appearing for the first time in Championship cricket, if not culinary history."
>
> Durham in 2004, page 582.

Derbyshire

S. D. Stubbings c Wallace b Harrison	96	– c Maynard b Croft	9
A. I. Gait c Elliott b Harrison	2	– c Wallace b Harrison	13
A. G. Botha c Wallace b Harrison	0	– lbw b Cosker	7
Hassan Adnan lbw b Cosker	95	– c Elliott b Wharf	55
C. W. G. Bassano c Maynard b Wharf	64	– c Maynard b Cosker	6
*†L. D. Sutton c Cosker b Thomas	24	– c Maynard b Cosker	4
G. Welch c Maynard b Croft	22	– b Harrison	45
M. A. Sheikh st Wallace b Cosker	17	– not out	9
K. J. Dean not out	25	– c Powell b Croft	8
D. B. Powell b Cosker	17	– b Cosker	13
N. G. E. Walker c Thomas b Croft	1	– b Wharf	16
B 2, l-b 14, w 5, n-b 8	29	B 8, l-b 6, n-b 14	28

1/7 (2) 2/13 (3) 3/177 (4) 4/267 (1)   **392**   1/21 (2) 2/31 (3) 3/33 (1)   **213**
5/281 (5) 6/323 (6) 7/335 (7)   4/53 (5) 5/66 (6) 6/139 (4)
8/367 (8) 9/389 (10) 10/392 (11)   7/161 (7) 8/173 (9)
                                                 9/187 (10) 10/213 (11)

Bonus points – Derbyshire 4, Glamorgan 3.

Bowling: *First Innings*—Harrison 25–9–58–3; Wharf 14–2–57–1; Thomas 23–3–87–1; Croft 39.4–12–79–2; Cosker 27–3–93–3; Dale 1–0–2–0. *Second Innings*—Harrison 10–4–23–2; Wharf 15.5–3–68–2; Croft 23–10–35–3; Cosker 26–13–40–3; Thomas 9–1–33–0.

Umpires: M. J. Harris and N. A. Mallender.

At Oakham School, June 2, 3, 4, 5. DERBYSHIRE lost to LEICESTERSHIRE by six wickets.

DERBYSHIRE v DURHAM UCCE

At Derby, June 9, 10, 11. Derbyshire won by an innings and five runs. Toss: Durham UCCE. First-class debuts: J. R. Chapman; G. G. Read. County debut: L. J. Goddard.

Botha enjoyed a memorable match as the students were thoroughly outplayed. He scored his maiden century and took five wickets in the university's second innings, becoming the first Derbyshire player to achieve this double since George Pope, against Northamptonshire at Chesterfield in 1937. Powell, bowling fast and straight, was just too much for Durham in their first innings: his six for 49 was a career-best. In reply, Hassan Adnan made an untroubled 96, helped by blunt-edged bowling and variable fielding. He and Botha sped toward a declaration, adding 169 in 32 overs. Although Bishop and Brown ended Derbyshire's hopes of a two-day victory, Botha showed good control with his left-arm spin, and the last seven wickets went down before lunch on the final day.

Close of play: First day, Derbyshire 164-3 (Hassan Adnan 16, Bryant 5); Second day, Durham UCCE 164-3 (Brown 58, Longhurst 22).

❝It was the essence of what John Buchanan had recently called 'Baggy Green cricket': relentless, immune to pressure and ultimately match-winning."
Australians in Sri Lanka, page 1168.

Durham UCCE

A. J. Maiden c Goddard b Havell	20	– b Botha	13
J. E. Bishop c Hassan Adnan b Powell	3	– c Gait b Havell	51
*W. R. Smith c Goddard b Powell	4	– c Gait b Botha	5
D. O. Brown c Hassan Adnan b Gunter	18	– lbw b Botha	65
N. J. Longhurst lbw b Gunter	10	– b Moss	22
S. C. Hollingsworth c Moss b Gunter	5	– c Moss b Botha	1
M. A. P. Dale lbw b Powell	44	– c sub b Powell	30
†P. W. Howells c Moss b Powell	0	– b Havell	11
J. W. Somerville-Hendrie b Powell	23	– lbw b Botha	2
G. G. Read not out	1	– b Powell	9
E. J. Carpenter b Powell	0	– not out	0
B 4, l-b 10, w 2, n-b 4	20	B 5, l-b 7, w 5	17

1/9 (2) 2/13 (3) 3/35 (4) 4/50 (5)   148   1/43 (1) 2/61 (3) 3/93 (2)   226
5/74 (6) 6/76 (1) 7/86 (8)   4/167 (5) 5/169 (6) 6/172 (4)
8/133 (9) 9/148 (7) 10/148 (11)   7/201 (8) 8/204 (9)
                                                           9/222 (7) 10/226 (10)

Bowling: *First Innings*—Powell 19.5–7–49–6; Havell 12–5–24–1; Gunter 13–3–52–3; Botha 10–6–9–0. *Second Innings*—Havell 18–5–47–2; Powell 21.3–5–72–2; Gunter 11–1–37–0; Botha 29–13–55–5; Moss 1–0–3–1.

Derbyshire

S. D. Stubbings lbw b Somerville-Hendrie	39	D. B. Powell run out		3
A. I. Gait c Howells b Smith	69	N. E. L. Gunter not out		15
*J. Moss c Howells b Brown	0	B 1, l-b 8, w 2, n-b 28		39
Hassan Adnan c and b Smith	96			
J. D. C. Bryant run out	8	1/110 (1) 2/113 (3)	(8 wkts dec.)	379
J. R. Chapman c Howells b Read	7	3/151 (2) 4/168 (5)		
A. G. Botha c Smith b Carpenter	103	5/175 (6) 6/344 (4)		
		7/350 (8) 8/379 (7)		

†L. J. Goddard and P. M. R. Havell did not bat.

Bowling: Bishop 20–4–67–0; Read 14–5–45–1; Somerville-Hendrie 5–0–34–1; Brown 13–0–94–1; Smith 20–3–83–2; Carpenter 12.1–1–47–1.

Umpires: N. L. Bainton and A. Clarkson.

At Derby, June 16. DERBYSHIRE beat NEW ZEALANDERS by four wickets (see New Zealand tour section).

At Nottingham, June 18, 19, 20, 21. DERBYSHIRE lost to NOTTINGHAMSHIRE by ten wickets.

DERBYSHIRE v ESSEX

At Derby, June 23, 24, 25, 26. Drawn. Derbyshire 9 pts, Essex 8 pts. Toss: Derbyshire.
    The first and last days were washed out, leaving both sides winless in the Championship. After three heavy defeats, Derbyshire needed to retrench but were forced to do so without Rogers, who returned to Australia for a shoulder operation that would end his season. He left to ringing praise: "Rogers is a gem of a player," said his coach David Houghton. Fortunately for Derbyshire, Moss, previously restricted by a displaced disc in his neck, began to show the form that made him such a force for Victoria. And Sutton continued to display great determination in charge of a leaking team, reaching his first century of the season and sharing three-figure partnerships with Moss and Botha. In dismally cold conditions, three Essex fielders sought comfort in bobble-hats. Although Welch took two wickets in his first spell of the reply, Flower and Irani, in only his second Championship game of 2004, had taken control when rain washed out the last day.
    Close of play: First day, No play; Second day, Derbyshire 274-6 (Sutton 79, Botha 23); Third day, Essex 222-3 (Flower 88, Irani 51).

Derbyshire

S. D. Stubbings lbw b Clarke	12	K. J. Dean not out	8
A. I. Gait b Napier	33	Mohammad Ali c Napier	
J. Moss lbw b Napier	79	b Middlebrook	10
Hassan Adnan b Napier	1		
C. W. G. Bassano c Foster b Napier	0	B 6, l-b 11, n-b 10	27
*†L. D. Sutton c Napier b Danish Kaneria	131		
G. Welch b Napier	26		389
A. G. Botha run out	52	1/23 (1) 2/66 (2) 3/68 (4)	
M. A. Sheikh c Jefferson		4/68 (5) 5/171 (3) 6/231 (7)	
b Danish Kaneria	10	7/335 (8) 8/363 (9)	
		9/371 (6) 10/389 (11)	

Bonus points – Derbyshire 4, Essex 3.

Bowling: Brant 18–3–65–0; Clarke 27–2–105–1; Danish Kaneria 40–10–88–2; Napier 23–8–56–5; Middlebrook 20.1–4–58–1.

Essex

W. I. Jefferson lbw b Welch	39	*R. C. Irani not out	51
A. N. Cook c Stubbings b Welch	34	B 3, l-b 4	7
A. Flower not out	88		
A. Habib c Stubbings b Welch	3	1/67 (2) 2/90 (1) 3/98 (4) (3 wkts) 222	

†J. S. Foster, J. D. Middlebrook, G. R. Napier, A. J. Clarke, S. A. Brant and Danish Kaneria did not bat.

Bonus points – Essex 1, Derbyshire 1.

Bowling: Mohammad Ali 14–0–48–0; Moss 12–2–39–0; Dean 7–0–30–0; Welch 14–3–40–3; Botha 11–0–31–0; Sheikh 4–2–16–0; Hassan Adnan 3–1–11–0.

Umpires: G. I. Burgess and J. H. Hampshire.

At Chester-le-Street, July 21, 22, 23. DERBYSHIRE beat DURHAM by 165 runs.

DERBYSHIRE v YORKSHIRE

At Derby, July 28, 29, 30, 31. Drawn. Derbyshire 12 pts, Yorkshire 11 pts. Toss: Derbyshire.
In a fine match with an exciting ending, McGrath shone brightest, producing career-best bowling and batting performances. On the last day, Yorkshire were set 358 in 83 overs, a target they had never scaled to win a game, and while McGrath was there it looked possible. He batted with great composure until splendidly caught at short extra cover with ten overs left and 76 needed. Yorkshire continued to attack, reducing the target to 34 from five with four wickets in hand, but when two of them fell quickly they stopped gambling. Even so, 341 for eight was their highest Championship fourth-innings total, beating 331 for eight against Middlesex at Lord's in 1910, when George Hirst led them to victory. The match had begun with Bassano scoring his first Championship century for almost two years, while McGrath picked off four of his partners and, finally, Bassano himself. However, McGrath was underused next morning as Derbyshire stretched their last-wicket stand to 56. In reply, Wood passed 50 for the seventh time in eight Championship innings, and Craven banished the danger of Yorkshire following on. But Derbyshire's lower order (stiffened on the last day by Bassano, batting No. 10 after problems caused by his diabetes) again prospered to set up a last-morning declaration.
Close of play: First day, Derbyshire 351-9 (Sheikh 10, Havell 0); Second day, Yorkshire 276-6 (Craven 44, Dawson 17); Third day, Derbyshire 251-7 (Botha 42, Sheikh 18).

Derbyshire

S. D. Stubbings c Gray b Kirby	51	– c Craven b Kirby	1
A. I. Gait b Blain	1	– b Blain	12
J. Moss lbw b Kirby	10	– c Gray b Blain	56
Hassan Adnan lbw b McGrath	86	– c Dawood b Kirby	41
C. W. G. Bassano b McGrath	100	– (10) b Kirby	25
J. D. C. Bryant c Wood b McGrath	5	– (5) c Dawood b Craven	20
*†L. D. Sutton lbw b McGrath	25	– (6) lbw b Craven	6
G. Welch lbw b McGrath	6	– (7) c and b Dawson	24
A. G. Botha c and b Blain	19	– (8) c Wood b Dawson	49
M. A. Sheikh c Dawood b Gray	42	– (9) not out	36
P. M. R. Havell not out	13	– not out	4
B 22, l-b 8, w 10, n-b 8	48	B 5, l-b 10, w 8, n-b 8	31

1/14 (2) 2/35 (3) 3/163 (1) 4/195 (4)   406   1/4 (1) 2/66 (2)   (9 wkts dec.) 305
5/205 (6) 6/281 (7) 7/293 (8)   3/79 (3) 4/126 (5)
8/324 (9) 9/350 (5) 10/406 (10)   5/134 (6) 6/174 (7)
                                    7/176 (4) 8/266 (8) 9/300 (10)

Bonus points – Derbyshire 5, Yorkshire 3.

Bowling: *First Innings*—Kirby 21–1–76–2; Blain 19–5–58–2; Harvey 21–4–73–0; Craven 11–1–51–0; Dawson 5–1–23–0; McGrath 22–7–39–5; Gray 19–2–56–1. *Second Innings*—Kirby 21–3–75–3; Harvey 15–4–38–0; Blain 11–1–58–2; McGrath 16–4–41–0; Craven 7–2–18–2; Dawson 16–5–45–2; Gray 5–0–13–0; Lumb 1–0–2–0.

Yorkshire

*M. J. Wood c Welch b Sheikh	89	– lbw b Welch	25
A. W. Gale c Stubbings b Havell	10	– c Bryant b Havell	3
A. McGrath lbw b Moss	18	– c Welch b Sheikh	174
M. J. Lumb b Gait b Sheikh	27	– run out	18
I. J. Harvey c Stubbings b Sheikh	19	– st Sutton b Botha	12
V. J. Craven not out	81	– b Moss	19
†I. Dawood lbw b Hassan Adnan	36	– not out	46
R. K. J. Dawson c Sutton b Moss	25	– c Botha b Moss	26
A. K. D. Gray c Stubbings b Welch	27	– b Welch	0
J. A. R. Blain c Gait b Botha	0	– not out	1
S. P. Kirby lbw b Botha	0		
B 5, l-b 14, w 1, n-b 2	22	B 6, l-b 2, w 7, n-b 2	17

1/19 (2) 2/65 (3) 3/125 (4) 4/166 (5)   354   1/8 (2) 2/104 (1)   (8 wkts) 341
5/173 (1) 6/250 (7) 7/312 (8)   3/129 (4) 4/161 (5)
8/353 (9) 9/354 (10) 10/354 (11)   5/208 (6) 6/282 (3)
                                      7/329 (8) 8/331 (9)

Bonus points – Yorkshire 4, Derbyshire 3.

Bowling: *First Innings*—Havell 14–0–85–1; Welch 23–7–54–1; Sheikh 20–4–68–3; Moss 30–7–73–2; Botha 20–6–51–2; Hassan Adnan 2–0–4–1. *Second Innings*—Welch 22–2–101–2; Havell 7–0–33–1; Moss 18.5–2–66–2; Sheikh 9–1–33–1; Botha 24–2–88–1; Hassan Adnan 2–0–12–0.

Umpires: A. Clarkson and T. E. Jesty.

At Derby, August 5, 6, 7. DERBYSHIRE lost to WEST INDIANS by 315 runs (see West Indian tour section).

At Leeds, August 12, 13, 14, 15. DERBYSHIRE drew with YORKSHIRE.

DERBYSHIRE v NOTTINGHAMSHIRE

At Derby, August 19, 20, 21, 22. Nottinghamshire won by an innings and 56 runs. Nottinghamshire 21 pts, Derbyshire 8 pts. Toss: Derbyshire. First-class debut: B. J. France.

A first-day partnership of 240 between Hassan Adnan and Bassano was as good as anything Derbyshire produced all summer: both batsmen scored centuries, and Adnan completed 1,000 Championship runs in an impressive first full county season. But their hard work counted for nothing. Only 12.3 overs were possible on the second day, and on the third Nottinghamshire hit back with commanding innings from Bicknell and Pietersen; Pietersen's century was his fifth in nine Championship innings against Derbyshire, who again paid for failing to follow up a recommendation while he was playing in South Africa. Welch bowled with great heart, but instead of playing 60 overs for a comfortable draw, his team-mates collapsed pathetically in the second innings. On a pitch that had produced 952 untroubled runs, they were rattled out in less than 40 overs by the seamers Smith and Harris. Omitted from Nottinghamshire's four-day side previously this season, Harris took four for one in a five-over burst, and bowled as he had for Derbyshire in 1996 when he earned an England A place.

Close of play: First day, Derbyshire 346-5 (Bassano 92); Second day, Derbyshire 399-7 (Bassano 123, Sheikh 4); Third day, Nottinghamshire 390-4 (Bicknell 159, Read 9).

Derbyshire

S. D. Stubbings c Singh b Franks	31	– b Harris ... 23
B. J. France c Read b Harris	9	– b Smith ... 12
J. Moss c Bicknell b Franks	30	– c Read b Smith ... 1
Hassan Adnan b Smith	140	– lbw b Smith ... 28
C. W. G. Bassano not out	123	– lbw b Harris ... 7
J. D. C. Bryant b Harris	8	– c Singh b MacGill ... 2
*†L. D. Sutton b Harris	6	– b Harris ... 0
G. Welch c Gallian b Harris	12	– b Harris ... 0
M. A. Sheikh not out	5	– not out ... 17
C. D. Paget (did not bat)		– lbw b Smith ... 0
P. M. R. Havell (did not bat)		– b Smith ... 1
B 2, l-b 23, w 1, n b 10	36	B 4, l-b 1 ... 5

		(7 wkts dec.)	400

1/32 (2) 2/70 (1) 3/93 (3)
4/333 (4) 5/346 (6)
6/356 (7) 7/390 (8)

1/33 (2) 2/35 (3) 3/47 (1)   96
4/61 (5) 5/64 (6) 6/65 (7)
7/65 (8) 8/90 (4)
9/90 (10) 10/96 (11)

Bonus points – Derbyshire 5, Nottinghamshire 2.

Bowling: *First Innings*—Smith 20–2–95–1; Harris 24–4–61–4; Franks 16.5–3–67–2; Ealham 17–5–44–0; MacGill 26–4–82–0; Pietersen 1–0–5–0; Hussey 4–0–21–0. *Second Innings*—Smith 11.1–2–35–5; Harris 13–6–22–4; MacGill 11–1–26–1; Franks 4–1–8–0.

Nottinghamshire

D. J. Bicknell c and b Havell	175
*J. E. R. Gallian c Hassan Adnan b Welch	8
A. Singh b Welch	14
K. P. Pietersen c Hassan Adnan b Havell	153
D. J. Hussey b Sheikh	15
†C. M. W. Read not out	90
M. A. Ealham b Welch	1
P. J. Franks lbw b Welch	0
G. J. Smith run out	35
S. C. G. MacGill c France b Welch	9
A. J. Harris not out	1
B 15, l-b 9, w 1, n-b 26	51

	(9 wkts dec.)	552

1/21 (2) 2/42 (3)
3/341 (4) 4/371 (5)
5/419 (1) 6/420 (7)
7/420 (8) 8/524 (9) 9/539 (10)

Bonus points – Nottinghamshire 5, Derbyshire 3.

Bowling: Welch 29–7–101–5; Havell 24–1–137–2; Sheikh 31–7–99–1; Moss 13 0–65–0; Paget 17–1–68–0; Hassan Adnan 13–0–58–0.

Umpires: M. J. Harris and P. J. Hartley.

DERBYSHIRE v LEICESTERSHIRE

At Derby, August 24, 25, 26, 27. Drawn. Derbyshire 4 pts, Leicestershire 5 pts. Toss: Leicestershire. Championship debut: T. J. New.

Play was possible for only 43 overs on the third afternoon, and Leicestershire's faint hopes of a late promotion push disappeared. In all cricket, including a washed-out pre-season friendly, Leicestershire had eight days' play scheduled for Derby in 2004: the weather allowed just 80.1 overs. When action was possible, they lost Cleary with a recurrence of an ankle problem and DeFreitas with a foot injury. Ben France, a 22-year-old left-hander recommended to Derbyshire by his Suffolk team-mate Devon Malcolm, scored a maiden first-class fifty in his second game.

Close of play: First day, No play; Second day, No play; Third day, Derbyshire 138-3 (Hassan Adnan 30, Moss 13).

Derbyshire

S. D. Stubbings b Gibson	0	J. Moss not out		13
B. J. France c Maddy b Henderson	56	L-b 5, w 7, n-b 2		14
J. D. C. Bryant st New b Hodge	25			
Hassan Adnan not out	30	1/0 (1) 2/78 (3) 3/103 (2)	(3 wkts)	138

C. W. G. Bassano, *†L. D. Sutton, G. Welch, M. A. Sheikh, C. D. Paget and N. G. E. Walker did not bat.

Bonus point – Leicestershire 1.

Bowling: Gibson 6–3–10–1; Dagnall 7–2–19–0; Cleary 2–0–17–0; DeFreitas 7.4–2–19–0; Maddy 2–0–16–0; Hodge 5–2–13–1; Henderson 9–2–25–1; Snape 4.2–1–14–0.

Leicestershire

D. D. J. Robinson, D. L. Maddy, *B. J. Hodge, D. I. Stevens, J. N. Snape, †T. J. New, O. D. Gibson, P. A. J. DeFreitas, M. F. Cleary, C. W. Henderson and C. E. Dagnall.

Umpires: N. G. Cowley and N. J. Llong.

At Chelmsford, September 9, 10. DERBYSHIRE lost to ESSEX by eight wickets.

DERBYSHIRE v HAMPSHIRE

At Derby, September 16, 17, 18, 19. Hampshire won by 91 runs. Hampshire 18 pts, Derbyshire 3 pts. Toss: Hampshire. Championship debuts: L. J. Goddard; C. C. Benham, G. A. Lamb.

On an appropriately bleak and windswept last day, Derbyshire completed 21 home fixtures, over two and a half seasons, without a Championship win, threatening their record of 22 (including one total washout) set between 1970 and 1972. Hampshire were already guaranteed second place, and introduced Chris Benham, a 21-year-old right-handed batsman who had risen through their junior sides, and the former Zimbabwe Under-19 all-rounder Greg Lamb, now qualified by residency. Both made impressive Championship debuts, Lamb scoring 94 and Benham 74. Welch again justified Derbyshire's undue reliance on him as a bowler with five for 57, his best of the summer; Havell also showed some penetration, but at a price. The second day was Derbyshire's eighth in the 2004 Championship with no play but the captains contrived a conclusion. Despite a sound innings from Bassano, Derbyshire never threatened their target of 321, as Udal bowled his off-spin with fine control. Their captain Luke Sutton missed the match following the death in a road accident of his girlfriend, Nia Walters; he intended to propose to her at the end of the season, and had already bought the ring. The club considered asking for the game to be cancelled; in the end it started after a minute's silence. Lee Goddard, a recent Loughborough graduate, stood in tidily for Sutton as wicket-keeper.

Close of play: First day, Hampshire 287-5 (Benham 64, Lamb 44); Second day, No play; Third day, Derbyshire 95-2 (Stubbings 35, Hassan Adnan 41).

Hampshire

J. H. K. Adams c Goddard b Welch	27	– not out	10
M. J. Brown c Goddard b Sheikh	57		
J. P. Crawley c Stubbings b Havell	18		
S. M. Katich c Goddard b Welch	22		
C. C. Benham c Sheikh b Havell	74		
†N. Pothas c France b Havell	12		
G. A. Lamb c Goddard b Welch	94	– (2) not out	7
A. D. Mascarenhas c Goddard b Welch	22		
*S. D. Udal c Stubbings b Sheikh	1		
C. T. Tremlett b Welch	0		
J. A. Tomlinson not out	12		
B 8, l-b 8, w 9, n-b 32	57	N-b 2	2
	396	(no wkt dec.)	**19**

1/56 (1) 2/93 (3) 3/157 (4) 4/157 (2)
5/196 (6) 6/309 (5) 7/363 (8)
8/364 (9) 9/367 (10) 10/396 (7)

Bonus points – Hampshire 4, Derbyshire 3.

Bowling: *First Innings*—Havell 24–2–113–3; Sheikh 28–5–76–2; Welch 31.1–7–57–5; Moss 26–5–75–0; Dumelow 13–2–39–0; France 4–0–20–0. *Second Innings*—Sheikh 1–0–1–0; Dumelow 4–0–5–0; Hassan Adnan 3.3–0–13–0.

Derbyshire

S. D. Stubbings not out	35	– lbw b Udal	34
B. J. France c Pothas b Tomlinson	2	– c Tremlett b Udal	12
J. D. C. Bryant b Tremlett	1	– c sub b Tremlett	23
Hassan Adnan not out	41	– lbw b Tremlett	5
J. Moss (did not bat)		– c Tomlinson b Udal	20
C. W. G. Bassano (did not bat)		– not out	64
†L. J. Goddard (did not bat)		– lbw b Mascarenhas	8
*G. Welch (did not bat)		– b Mascarenhas	12
M. A. Sheikh (did not bat)		– c Katich b Udal	14
N. R. C. Dumelow (did not bat)		– lbw b Udal	12
P. M. R. Havell (did not bat)		– c Mascarenhas b Udal	3
B 3, l-b 2, w 1, n-b 10	16	B 8, l-b 12, n-b 2	22
	(2 wkts dec.) **95**		**229**

1/8 (2) 2/19 (3)

1/38 (2) 2/52 (1) 3/79 (4)
4/80 (3) 5/110 (5) 6/148 (7)
7/164 (8) 8/203 (9)
9/221 (10) 10/229 (11)

Bowling: *First Innings*—Tremlett 9–1–24–1; Tomlinson 8–4–9–1; Mascarenhas 6–1–18–0; Adams 2–0–14–0; Udal 7–2–24–0; Lamb 3–2–1–0. *Second Innings*—Tremlett 16–1–60–2; Tomlinson 12–3–34–0; Udal 26.5–8–79–6; Mascarenhas 9–2–22–2; Lamb 2–0–14–0.

Umpires: J. W. Holder and V. A. Holder.

DURHAM

The sad folks Harmy left at home

TIM WELLOCK

The failure to score enough runs was a familiar theme for Durham, but a tale of the unexpected unfolded in the tribulations of a succession of overseas bowlers. It was ironic that this saga should run at the same time as Ashington's Stephen Harmison was elevated to No. 1 in the world bowling rankings. His England commitments meant he only played two one-day games for Durham. How they missed him. After showing signs of promise in 2003, they slumped back to the bottom of the Championship.

Excitement surrounded the anticipated arrival in early April of Herschelle Gibbs and Shoaib Akhtar. But injury forced Gibbs out, to be replaced by the Australian Marcus North, who had married a local girl and was in Durham as a club professional. Then Shoaib was delayed, as accusations by the Pakistan board that he had feigned injury led to an investigation. Even when he arrived, Durham quickly wished he hadn't. It was soon clear that he really was unfit, and he was also ill twice, playing only two of the first nine Championship games. Soon after an expensive spell helped ensure defeat in an important totesport game at Hove, Shoaib was summoned for Asia Cup duty and the management waved him a less-than-tearful farewell.

After turning to three stop-gaps – the ineffective Reon King, the trundling Tahir Mughal and the expensive Andy Blignaut – Durham finally welcomed Shaun Tait, a 21-year-old Australian fast bowler. Just when it seemed things couldn't get any worse, they did. Tait, winner of the Bradman Young Cricketer of the Year award in Australia, showed signs of genuine pace, but lost his run-up and his confidence. In two games he took none for 176 in 18 overs, including 26 no-balls, and was dropped.

Between them the five overseas bowlers took just 19 Championship wickets. In the totesport League Shoaib took 13 at 16.53, but his poor bowling in the away defeats by Scotland and Sussex undermined Durham's promotion bid. They did well to sustain it to the final match, when defeat by Yorkshire saw them finish sixth, one place higher than the previous season.

Local conditions did not help. Two home games were rained off in the League, and the Championship summer was the wettest of Durham's 13 in first-class cricket. After a golden week of run-scoring away from home in May, they returned to the slow Riverside wicket, and the run spree ended in a heavy defeat by Glamorgan. It was the first sign Durham were beginning to dislike playing at home, where problems with the root system on the square were producing pitches without the firm base required by strokemakers such as North and Gareth Breese, the Jamaican captain, who qualified to play via a Welsh father.

But, when he found a surface more to his liking at Taunton, Breese provided the highlight of the season – indeed one of the highlights of any Durham season – as they successfully chased 451 to win. He led the ascent, coming in at 95 for five and ending 165 not out. Buoyed by that triumph, Durham made their record score in the one-day league, 319 for three, at Worcester the next day.

Both Paul Collingwood and North hit centuries in that Worcester game, and they were not the only batsmen who had a sharp contrast between home and away form. Eight visiting batsmen scored Championship centuries at Riverside; Durham didn't manage any. Pitch re-laying began as soon as the

Mark Davies

season ended, but it was too late for Nicky Peng and Gary Pratt, who had been dropped from the four-day team. Along with Gordon Muchall, they had been expected to form the middle order in the prolonged absence of Collingwood on England duty. But only Muchall progressed. He topped the averages with 970 at 35.92, and scored 142 not out in glorious September sunshine at Scarborough – Durham's only other Championship win.

No one else could be satisfied, except Mark Davies. While the big-name bowlers suffered, he became the team's unsung hero. After years of cruel trouble with collapsed lungs, his fitness improved greatly and his form was outstanding. Bowling just a touch above medium-pace, he made his mark from the start of the season, becoming the first in the country to 50 Championship wickets before a side-strain kept him out for the last two months. Liam Plunkett, an increasingly quick 19-year-old from Middlesbrough, recovered from early-season injury to finish strongly, as did Breese. Otherwise, success was all too fleeting.

Dropping back to the bottom made changes inevitable. But it was too soon for the new chairman Clive Leach, who took over in July, to tinker with the management, so a switch of captain was the obvious route. Jon Lewis showed himself to be a fighter right up to the final match, during which it was announced that the Australian Mike Hussey, for two seasons captain of Northamptonshire, would take over in 2005. Lewis was disappointed, but he could be justifiably proud that, after four difficult years, he had survived longer than any of his predecessors. Along with Hussey, Durham unveiled the seamer Ashley Noffke, another experienced Australian who had flirted with the Test squad but was unlikely to play in the 2005 Ashes. And Durham also planned to add the South Africa international Dale Benkenstein as a Kolpak player. They were lower-profile names than those announced the previous winter but, after the experiences of 2004, that was perhaps no bad thing.

DURHAM RESULTS

All first-class matches – Played 17: Won 2, Lost 8, Drawn 7.
County Championship matches – Played 16: Won 2, Lost 8, Drawn 6.

Frizzell County Championship, 9th in Division 2; Cheltenham & Gloucester Trophy, 2nd round;
totesport League, 6th in Division 2; Twenty20 Cup, 5th in North Group.

COUNTY CHAMPIONSHIP AVERAGES
BATTING AND FIELDING

Cap		M	I	NO	R	HS	100s	50s	Avge	Ct/St
	G. J. Muchall	15	28	1	970	142*	1	5	35.92	13
	M. J. North§.	16	29	1	879	219	2	3	31.39	8
	Shoaib Akhtar§	2	4	1	94	46	0	0	31.33	2
	P. Mustard	3	5	0	148	60	0	1	29.60	9
1998	P. D. Collingwood . .	6	11	0	322	68	0	3	29.27	5
	G. R. Breese.	14	25	1	685	165*	1	3	28.54	12
1998	J. J. B. Lewis	16	29	1	729	127	1	4	26.03	7
2001	N. Peng	9	16	0	387	88	0	3	24.18	6
2001	A. Pratt	13	23	3	483	59	0	2	24.15	30/2
	I. Pattison.	3	4	0	92	33	0	0	23.00	3
	J. A. Lowe	2	4	0	91	41	0	0	22.75	2
	G. M. Hamilton. . . .	7	13	1	270	58	0	2	22.50	2
	A. M. Blignaut§ . . .	2	4	0	90	56	0	1	22.50	0
	G. D. Bridge.	10	16	3	291	52	0	2	22.38	1
	L. E. Plunkett	9	14	3	242	54	0	1	22.00	2
	K. J. Coetzer.	6	10	0	212	67	0	1	21.20	2
	G. J. Pratt	8	15	0	273	71	0	2	18.20	7
1999	N. Killeen	12	20	4	218	35*	0	0	13.62	1
	A. M. Davies	10	17	8	110	29	0	0	12.22	5
	P. Kumar	2	4	1	36	21	0	0	12.00	0
	G. Onions	7	10	4	60	20*	0	0	10.00	2
	R. D. King§	2	4	0	4	3	0	0	1.00	1

Also batted: Tahir Mughal§ (1 match) 0, 17*; S. W. Tait§ (2 matches) 0, 4.

§ *Overseas player.*

BOWLING

	O	M	R	W	BB	5W/i	Avge
A. M. Davies	304.2	75	938	50	6-44	4	18.76
L. E. Plunkett	225.5	35	902	27	6-74	1	33.40
P. D. Collingwood	137	37	455	12	3-49	0	37.91
G. R. Breese.	307.4	44	1,163	28	5-41	2	41.53
G. D. Bridge.	204	43	648	15	4-64	0	43.20
N. Killeen	323.4	81	1,012	19	2-39	0	53.26

Also bowled: A. M. Blignaut 42–3–200–4; K. J. Coetzer 1–0–2–0; G. M. Hamilton 64–9–249–5;
R. D. King 38.5–5–206–5; P. Kumar 42–5–219–6; G. J. Muchall 34–5–136–5; M. J. North
22.1–2–93–3; G. Onions 128.4–25–560–8; I. Pattison 39–7–129–2; Shoaib Akhtar
57.2–12–218–8; S. W. Tait 18–0–176–0; Tahir Mughal 19–4–54–2.

COUNTY RECORDS

Highest score for:	273	M. L. Love v Hampshire at Chester-le-Street	2003
Highest score against:	501*	B. C. Lara (Warwickshire) at Birmingham	1994
Best bowling for:	9-64	M. M. Betts v Northamptonshire at Northampton .	1997
Best bowling against:	8-22	D. Follett (Middlesex) at Lord's	1996
Highest total for:	645-6 dec.	v Middlesex at Lord's	2002
Highest total against:	810-4 dec.	by Warwickshire at Birmingham	1994
Lowest total for:	67	v Middlesex at Lord's	1996
Lowest total against:	56	by Somerset at Chester-le-Street	2003

DURHAM DIRECTORY

ADDRESS

County Ground, Riverside, Chester-le-Street, County Durham DH3 3QR (0191 387 1717; fax 0191 387 1616; email reception.durham@ecb.co.uk). **Website** www.durhamccc.org.uk.

GROUND

Chester-le-Street (Riverside): ¼ mile W of town centre between A167 and A1(M). Entrance is from roundabout off A167. Nearest station: Chester-le-Street (1 mile).

OFFICIALS

Captain 2004 – J. J. B. Lewis; 2005 – M. E. K. Hussey
Head coach M. D. Moxon
President Sir J. Stevens
Chairman 2004 – R. Jackson; 2005 – C. W. Leach

Chief executive D. Harker
Director of cricket G. Cook
Head groundsman D. Measor
Scorer B. Hunt

PLAYERS

Players expected to reappear in 2005

	Former counties	Country	Born	Birthplace
*Breese Gareth Rohan		WI (EU)	9.1.1976	Montego Bay, Jamaica
Bridge Graeme David		E	4.9.1980	†Sunderland
Coetzer Kyle James		E/SCO	14.8.1984	Aberdeen
*Collingwood Paul David		E	26.5.1976	†Shotley Bridge
Davies Anthony Mark		E	4.10.1980	†Stockton-on-Tees
*Hamilton Gavin Mark	Yorks	E/SCO	16.9.1974	Broxburn
*Harmison Stephen James		‡E	23.10.1978	Ashington
Killeen Neil		E	17.10.1975	†Shotley Bridge
Lewis Jonathan James Benjamin	Essex	E	21.5.1970	Isleworth
Lowe James Adam		E	4.11.1982	Bury St Edmunds
Muchall Gordon James		E	2.11.1982	Newcastle upon Tyne
Mustard Philip		E	8.10.1982	†Sunderland
Onions Graham		E	9.9.1982	†Gateshead
Peng Nicky		E	18.9.1982	Newcastle upon Tyne
Plunkett Liam Edward		E	6.4.1985	Middlesbrough
Pratt Andrew		E	4.3.1975	†Helmington Row
Pratt Gary Joseph		E	22.12.1981	†Bishop Auckland

Players due to join in 2005

	Former counties	Country	Born	Birthplace
Benkenstein Dale Martin		SA (EU)	9.6.1974	Salisbury, Zim.
Hussey Michael Edward Killeen	Nor, Glos	A	27.5.1975	Morley
Noffke Ashley Allan	Middlesex	A	30.4.1977	Nambour
Thorp Callum David		A (EU)	11.2.1975	Perth

* Test player.   † Born in Durham.   ‡ 12-month ECB contract.

DURHAM v DURHAM UCCE

At Chester-le-Street, April 10, 11, 12. Drawn. Toss: Durham. First-class debuts: G. Onions; W. F. Burnell, E. J. Carpenter, S. C. Hollingsworth, P. W. Howells. County debuts: G. M. Hamilton, M. J. North.

Having attracted only passing interest from first-class counties, Lee Daggett, a right-arm seamer from Ramsbottom in Lancashire, returned the remarkable figures for a student of eight for 94 from 29 accurate and lively overs. "He put as much into his last ball as the first," said his coach, fellow-Lancastrian Graeme Fowler. "He has no idea how good that performance was." However, the UCCE surrendered naively in their first innings to the occasional off-spin of Western Australia's Marcus North who, on his county debut, then made a carefree 60 to help stretch Durham's lead to 469. But the students held out 65 overs for the draw. There were three wickets for a jubilant Gavin Hamilton, also making his county debut, following a two-year bowling nightmare with Yorkshire. Durham's wicket-keeper, Andrew Pratt, left out for much of 2003 under orders to make more runs, top-scored in both innings.

Close of play: First day, Durham UCCE 24-1 (Dale 16, Smith 0); Second day, Durham 194-7 (A. Pratt 48, Plunkett 4).

Durham

*J. J. B. Lewis c Howells b Daggett	9	– lbw b Bishop.................... 19
M. J. North c Howells b Daggett	30	– lbw b Somerville-Hendrie....... 60
G. J. Muchall lbw b Bishop..............	5	– c Hollingsworth b Daggett........ 0
G. J. Pratt c Brown b Daggett	45	– b Somerville-Hendrie............ 6
N. Peng b Daggett	30	– c Smith b Somerville-Hendrie 0
G. M. Hamilton lbw b Daggett............	8	– b Brown 42
†A. Pratt c Hollingsworth b Daggett.......	67	– b Bishop..................... 68
G. D. Bridge lbw b Dale	30	– c Smith b Brown 0
L. E. Plunkett not out.................	33	– c Carpenter b Bishop............ 27
N. Killeen lbw b Daggett...............	22	– not out 29
G. Onions c Howells b Daggett	1	– not out 15
B 1, l-b 5, w 2, n-b 23	31	B 1, l-b 7, w 1, n-b 16 25

1/40 (1) 2/43 (2) 3/47 (3) 4/115 (5)	**311**	1/74 (2) 2/77 (3) (9 wkts dec.) **291**
5/129 (6) 6/156 (4) 7/211 (8)		3/86 (1) 4/87 (5)
8/269 (10) 9/303 (10) 10/311 (11)		5/90 (4) 6/186 (6)
		7/186 (8) 8/238 (7) 9/241 (9)

Bowling: *First Innings*—Bishop 18–3–63–1; Daggett 29–1–94–8; Somerville-Hendrie 21–5–60–0; Carpenter 14–1–54–0; Dale 8–0–34–1. *Second Innings*—Bishop 26–4–81–3; Daggett 17–2–64–1; Somerville-Hendrie 16–2–51–3; Brown 12–2–60–2; Carpenter 10–3–22–0; Smith 1–0–5–0.

Durham UCCE

M. A. P. Dale b North	48	– b Hamilton 19
W. F. Burnell lbw b Onions.............	1	– lbw b Plunkett 0
*W. R. Smith c Muchall b Plunkett........	22	– c A. Pratt b Muchall 48
D. O. Brown lbw b Bridge..............	2	– lbw b Hamilton 0
S. C. Hollingsworth b North	6	– c A. Pratt b Plunkett 23
J. E. Bishop not out	21	– b Hamilton 7
†P. W. Howells c A. Pratt b North.......	2	– not out 20
J. W. Somerville-Hendrie b North	5	– (10) not out 0
L. M. Daggett c Hamilton b Plunkett.......	7	– (8) b Bridge 4
E. J. Carpenter lbw b Bridge	0	– (9) lbw b Bridge 0
A. J. Maiden absent hurt		
B 3, l-b 4, n-b 12	19	L-b 5, n-b 6 11

1/20 (2) 2/69 (3) 3/76 (4) 4/93 (5)	**133**	1/1 (2) 2/67 (1) 3/67 (4) (8 wkts) **132**
5/96 (1) 6/98 (7) 7/104 (8)		4/77 (3) 5/95 (6) 6/127 (5)
8/122 (9) 9/133 (10)		7/132 (8) 8/132 (9)

Bowling: *First Innings*—Plunkett 10–1–26–2; Onions 10–1–26–1; Killeen 9–0–21–0; Hamilton 3–0–9–0; Bridge 19–8–25–2; Muchall 1–0–3–0; North 12–4–16–4. *Second Innings*— Plunkett 12–1–36–2; Onions 8–6–7–0; Hamilton 12–2–30–3; Killeen 11–2–23–0; Muchall 8–2–22–1; Bridge 12–9–7–2; G. J. Pratt 2–0–2–0.

Umpires: R. A. Kettleborough and B. Leadbeater.

At Southampton, April 16, 17, 18, 19. DURHAM lost to HAMPSHIRE by three wickets.

DURHAM v NOTTINGHAMSHIRE

At Chester-le-Street, April 21, 22, 23, 24. Nottinghamshire won by an innings and 80 runs. Nottinghamshire 22 pts, Durham 6 pts. Toss: Nottinghamshire. Championship debut: D. J. Hussey.

On a lifeless pitch, the 6ft 7in Shreck relied more on away-swing than bounce to take his nine wickets, which included a career-best six for 46 in Durham's shambolic second innings. On the final morning they lost their seven remaining batsmen in just 90 minutes. Earlier, they might also have done better than 350 in the first innings, but five of the lower-middle order fell between 48 and 54, Plunkett top-scoring from No. 8 with his maiden fifty. In reply, Warren always seemed to have time to choose his shots in making 120 off 152 balls as Nottinghamshire took a lead of 173. Many of his 19 fours went through the covers off the back foot, including the first two of five successive boundaries from the disconsolate Hamilton. After two years without a Championship wicket, Hamilton finally broke his duck – an important psychological step – only to find that damage to tendons in his thumb would keep him out most of the season.

Close of play: First day, Durham 175-5 (Peng 48, A. Pratt 5); Second day, Nottinghamshire 159-2 (Warren 50, Alleyne 0); Third day, Durham 30-3 (Muchall 9, Peng 0).

Durham

*J. J. B. Lewis b Smith	15	– b Smith	0
M. J. North lbw b Shreck	27	– b Shreck	0
G. J. Muchall c Alleyne b Franks	14	– c Pietersen b Shreck	16
G. J. Pratt lbw b Shreck	50	– c Alleyne b Shreck	8
N. Peng c Pietersen b Smith	51	– c Gallian b Shreck	0
G. M. Hamilton b Shreck	4	lbw b Smith	7
†A. Pratt c Pietersen b MacGill	53	– c Alleyne b Smith	6
L. E. Plunkett c Pietersen b Ealham	54	– c Gallian b Shreck	12
G. D. Bridge c Gallian b Franks	48	– lbw b Shreck	17
A. M. Davies not out	0	– not out	9
R. D. King b Ealham	1	– c Alleyne b Ealham	3
B 4, l-b 23, w 2, n-b 4	33	B 4, l-b 7, w 2, n-b 2	15

1/40 (1) 2/44 (2) 3/71 (3) 4/158 (4)   350   1/0 (1) 2/4 (2) 3/27 (4)   93
5/166 (6) 6/190 (5) 7/241 (7)   4/33 (5) 5/44 (3) 6/44 (6)
8/347 (8) 9/349 (9) 10/350 (11)   7/55 (7) 8/81 (9) 9/84 (8) 10/93 (11)

Bonus points – Durham 4, Nottinghamshire 3.

Bowling: *First Innings*—Smith 29–6–80–2; Shreck 31–6–92–3; Ealham 19.4–7–51–2; Franks 15–4–37–2; MacGill 12–3–59–1; Hussey 1–0–4–0. *Second Innings*—Smith 11–4–28–3; Shreck 16–4–46–6; Franks 2–1–3–0; Ealham 3.4–2–5–1.

Nottinghamshire

D. J. Bicknell lbw b Davies	41	S. C. G. MacGill not out	5
*J. E. R. Gallian c A. Pratt b Plunkett	58	C. E. Shreck c A. Pratt b King	0
R. J. Warren c Plunkett b Bridge	120		
†D. Alleyne c A. Pratt b Davies	27	B 12, l-b 6, w 3, n-b 12	33
K. P. Pietersen lbw b King	52		
D. J. Hussey b Muchall	76	1/61 (1) 2/159 (2) 3/233 (4)	523
M. A. Ealham c A. Pratt b Hamilton	36	4/276 (3) 5/356 (5) 6/434 (6)	
P. J. Franks run out	41	7/465 (7) 8/497 (8)	
G. J. Smith c A. Pratt b King	34	9/521 (9) 10/523 (11)	

Bonus points – Nottinghamshire 5, Durham 2 (130 overs: 493-7).

Bowling: King 24.3–5–120–3; Plunkett 26–3–119–1; Davies 26–9–78–2; Bridge 35–14–73–1; Hamilton 22–5–99–1; North 1–0–2–0; Muchall 3–0–14–1.

Umpires: I. J. Gould and M. J. Kitchen.

At Derby, April 28, 29, 30, May 1. DURHAM drew with DERBYSHIRE.

DURHAM v ESSEX

At Chester-le-Street, May 7, 8, 9, 10. Drawn. Durham 10 pts, Essex 9 pts. Toss: Essex. County debut: Tahir Mughal.

Much of this contest between two depleted sides was as grim as the weather that ensured a draw. Durham drafted in Tahir Mughal, a Pakistani seamer, from league cricket in Staffordshire, while a threadbare Essex attack allowed Muchall to rediscover form. He started scratchily, but managed 18 high-class fours in reaching 94, his best Championship score for nearly two years. Only 27 balls were squeezed between the showers on the second day, and Essex faced a sweating pitch on the third. Other than twice hitting Breese's off-spin for three successive boundaries, Hussain was watchful as he made 70, from 173 balls, after asking to open. But his concentration was broken when he was rapped on the hand, and he lunged at the next ball from the highly impressive Davies to be caught behind. Davies finished with five for 30, and Durham took a lead of 74, but lost quick wickets on the shortened last day and concentrated on avoiding defeat rather than pushing for victory.

Close of play: First day, Durham 332-9 (Killeen 24, Davies 11); Second day, Essex 6-0 (Cook 4, Hussain 0); Third day, Essex 241-7 (Stephenson 26, ten Doeschate 1).

Durham

*J. J. B. Lewis b Napier	8	– b McCoubrey	9
M. J. North c Cook b ten Doeschate	15	– lbw b McCoubrey	0
G. J. Muchall lbw b Stephenson	94	– c Jefferson b Stephenson	40
G. J. Pratt b Napier	43	– c Danish Kaneria b McCoubrey	1
N. Peng c Cook b ten Doeschate	6	– c Cook b Stephenson	1
G. R. Breese c Cook b Stephenson	42	– c Cook b Stephenson	4
†A. Pratt st Foster b Danish Kaneria	20	– c Habib b Danish Kaneria	19
I. Pattison c and b Danish Kaneria	26	– c Cook b Napier	10
Tahir Mughal lbw b Danish Kaneria	0	– not out	17
N. Killeen lbw b McCoubrey	26	– not out	9
A. M. Davies not out	14		
L-b 8, w 1, n-b 36	45	B 2, l-b 2, w 1, n-b 6	11

1/12 (1) 2/32 (2) 3/111 (4) 4/124 (5)	339	1/4 (2) 2/21 (1) (8 wkts dec.) 121
5/224 (6) 6/244 (3) 7/285 (7)		3/23 (4) 4/41 (5)
8/285 (9) 9/300 (8) 10/339 (10)		5/62 (3) 6/63 (6) 7/88 (8) 8/95 (7)

Bonus points – Durham 3, Essex 3.

Bowling: *First Innings*—Napier 23–6–62–2; McCoubrey 18–2–87–1; ten Doeschate 15–2–52–2; Danish Kaneria 23–5–83–3; Stephenson 11–2–47–2. *Second Innings*—Napier 11–4–25–1; McCoubrey 11–2–40–3; ten Doeschate 3–0–16–0; Stephenson 9–2–28–3; Danish Kaneria 3–1–8–1.

Essex

A. N. Cook c Muchall b Davies	20	Danish Kaneria c Lewis b Killeen	3
N. Hussain c A. Pratt b Davies	70	A. G. A. M. McCoubrey not out	0
W. I. Jefferson lbw b Tahir Mughal	31		
*A. Flower c A. Pratt b Davies	15	B 12, l-b 7, w 4, n-b 8	31
A. Habib c North b Pattison	8		
†J. S. Foster c Pattison b Breese	15	1/39 (1) 2/94 (3) 3/149 (2)	265
G. R. Napier c A. Pratt b Tahir Mughal	25	4/164 (4) 5/166 (5) 6/205 (7)	
J. P. Stephenson c North b Davies	40	7/239 (6) 8/256 (9)	
R. N. ten Doeschate c Muchall b Davies	7	9/265 (8) 10/265 (10)	

Bonus points – Essex 2, Durham 3.

Bowling: Tahir Mughal 19–4–54–2; Killeen 21.4–7–68–1; Davies 20–11–30–5; Pattison 12–4–30–1; Breese 13–1–64–1.

Umpires: R. A. Kettleborough and J. W. Lloyds.

At Taunton, May 12, 13, 14, 15. DURHAM beat SOMERSET by one wicket.

DURHAM v GLAMORGAN

At Chester-le-Street, May 19, 20, 21. Glamorgan won by 201 runs. Glamorgan 21 pts, Durham 4 pts. Toss: Glamorgan. First-class debut: P. Kumar.

A dry, untrustworthy pitch encouraged batsmen to go for their shots before the fatal ball arrived, and the match rushed to a three-day finish. Their bowling still depleted, Durham summoned Pallav Kumar, a seamer from Sunderland University – Indian-born, Carlisle-bred. In a nervous start he was pulled for four sixes, and Powell hit 19 muscular fours as he sped to a 90-ball century. Although Kumar salvaged three wickets, Glamorgan reached 393. Durham were 110 for seven before eking out 220, thanks largely to Muchall; frustratingly for them, Collingwood, their England-contracted batsman, was released from the Lord's Test squad but delayed on the M1. When he finally replaced Pattison as a full substitute on the third morning it was too late. Glamorgan pulled 438 ahead, and though Durham had successfully chased 451 the week before, that had been on a placid wicket at Taunton. Wharf, at 6ft 5in, emulated Harrison in the first innings, with five wickets, helping Glamorgan end their run of four Championship draws. Of 29 wickets taken by seamers, 26 fell to those operating from the Lumley End, where the bounce was uneven.

Close of play: First day, Durham 4-2 (North 4); Second day, Glamorgan 77-2 (Wallace 36).

Glamorgan

M. T. G. Elliott lbw b Davies	37	– (2) c Peng b Davies	35
†M. A. Wallace c A. Pratt b Davies	26	– (1) run out	36
D. L. Hemp c A. Pratt b Kumar	45	– (4) c Peng b Collingwood	25
M. J. Powell c Lewis b Killeen	124	– (5) c Collingwood b Davies	38
M. P. Maynard st A. Pratt b Breese	10	– (6) not out	54
A. Dale c and b Breese	15	– (7) c Muchall b Collingwood	0
*R. D. B. Croft c G. J. Pratt b Davies	81	– (8) lbw b Collingwood	6
D. S. Harrison c G. J. Pratt b Kumar	2	– (9) st A. Pratt b Breese	32
A. G. Wharf lbw b Kumar	2	– (10) b Breese	20
S. D. Thomas not out	30	– (3) c Peng b Killeen	5
D. A. Cosker c Pattison b Killeen	1		
L-b 12, w 2, n-b 6	20	L-b 4, n-b 10	14

1/66 (1) 2/73 (2) 3/206 (3) 4/239 (5)	393	1/60 (2) 2/77 (3) (9 wkts dec.) 265
5/261 (4) 6/295 (6) 7/308 (8)		3/86 (1) 4/153 (5)
8/326 (9) 9/388 (7) 10/393 (11)		5/157 (4) 6/157 (7)
		7/165 (8) 8/211 (9) 9/265 (10)

Bonus points – Glamorgan 4, Durham 3.

Bowling: *First Innings*—Killeen 22–6–62–2; Kumar 15–1–78–3; Davies 21–4–95–3; Pattison 14–1–57–0; Breese 26–6–85–2; Muchall 1–0–4–0. *Second Innings*—Killeen 22–4–53–1; Davies 17–2–71–2; Kumar 9–1–60–0; Collingwood 11–1–49–3; Breese 8.3–1–28–2.

Durham

*J. J. B. Lewis c Maynard b Harrison	0	– lbw b Wharf	51
M. J. North lbw b Harrison	13	– lbw b Harrison	9
N. Killeen c Dale b Harrison	0	– (9) b Croft	14
G. J. Muchall c Elliott b Harrison	93	– (3) b Thomas	27
G. J. Pratt c Elliott b Wharf	12	– (6) lbw b Croft	15
N. Peng c Dale b Wharf	3	– (5) c Hemp b Wharf	7
G. R. Breese c Thomas b Croft	11	– c Elliott b Wharf	4
†A. Pratt c Elliott b Thomas	4	– c Thomas b Wharf	59
I. Pattison c Powell b Harrison	33		
A. M. Davies c Wallace b Cosker	29	– not out	21
P. Kumar not out	13	– c Dale b Croft	0
P. D. Collingwood		– (4) c Wallace b Wharf	14
B 4, l-b 4, w 1	9	B 1, l-b 2, w 1, n-b 12	16

1/0 (1) 2/4 (3) 3/23 (2) 4/74 (5)   220   1/15 (2) 2/58 (3) 3/81 (4)   237
5/78 (6) 6/105 (7) 7/110 (8)   4/108 (5) 5/115 (1) 6/123 (7)
8/169 (4) 9/176 (9) 10/220 (10)   7/157 (6) 8/191 (9)
                                          9/223 (8) 10/237 (11)

Bonus points – Durham 1, Glamorgan 3.

Bowling: *First Innings*—Harrison 16–2–75–5; Wharf 13–4–31–2; Thomas 8–0–42–1; Croft 15–3–61–1; Cosker 1.5–0–3–1. *Second Innings*—Harrison 10–0–51–1; Wharf 17–1–93–5; Thomas 9–0–41–1; Croft 13–2–48–3; Cosker 2–1–1–0.

Umpires: D. J. Constant and N. G. Cowley.

At Nottingham, May 25, 26, 27, 28. DURHAM lost to NOTTINGHAMSHIRE by three wickets.

DURHAM v YORKSHIRE

At Chester-le-Street, June 8, 9, 10. Yorkshire won by 320 runs. Yorkshire 20 pts, Durham 3 pts. Toss: Yorkshire.

For the second successive match at Riverside, the visitors did not enforce the follow-on but still won by the third evening. Halfway through the season, Durham were now bottom of the second division. Wood scored fifties for Yorkshire in two fluent opening stands, supplemented by a diligent 224-ball century from McGrath in the first innings and a much quicker hundred by Lehmann in the second – his 20th in 70 first-class games for the county. Those healthy Yorkshire innings sandwiched a scanty 150 from Durham. Left needing 535 to win, or a day and a half's resistance to draw, only Collingwood and North, with a third-wicket stand of 119, stood out in the midst of feeble Durham batting. On a light-coloured and close-shaven strip, Dawson had match figures of nine for 115, highlighting the home side's lack of a specialist spinner. He turned the ball enough to trouble all the batsmen and took his first five-wicket haul since August 2002.

Close of play: First day, Durham 14-2 (Lewis 5); Second day, Yorkshire 156-4 (Lehmann 15, Lumb 0).

Yorkshire

M. J. Wood c Muchall b Shoaib Akhtar	55	– lbw b Collingwood	71
P. A. Jaques c Shoaib Akhtar b Davies	36	– c Shoaib Akhtar b Muchall	53
A. McGrath b Shoaib Akhtar	126	– c A. Pratt b Davies	8
D. S. Lehmann c A. Pratt b Killeen	9	– c Peng b Davies	120
M. J. Lumb lbw b Collingwood	28	– (6) c and b Davies	0
*C. White c Muchall b Collingwood	27	– (7) c Breese b North	31
†S. M. Guy b Breese	0	– (8) b Shoaib Akhtar	21
R. K. J. Dawson b Shoaib Akhtar	23	– (9) b North	15
T. T. Bresnan b Shoaib Akhtar	2	– (10) not out	4
N. D. Thornicroft c sub b Killeen	6		
S. P. Kirby not out	1	– (5) lbw b Collingwood	0
B 5, l-b 5, w 6, n-b 2	18	B 9, l-b 14, w 1, n-b 6	30

1/79 (2) 2/93 (1) 3/118 (4) 4/171 (5) 331 1/118 (2) 2/136 (3) (9 wkts dec.) 353
5/250 (6) 6/251 (7) 7/297 (8) 3/156 (1) 4/156 (5)
8/299 (9) 9/314 (10) 10/331 (3) 5/165 (6) 6/306 (4)
  7/306 (7) 8/333 (9) 9/353 (8)

Bonus points – Yorkshire 3, Durham 3.

Bowling: *First Innings*—Shoaib Akhtar 16.2–3–64–4; Killeen 21–9–69–2; Davies 16–3–66–1; Collingwood 17–8–41–2; Breese 23–3–74–1; North 4–2–7–0. *Second Innings*—Shoaib Akhtar 14–3–46–1; Killeen 17–5–40–0; Davies 19–3–51–3; Breese 14–1–78–0; Collingwood 16–3–53–2; Muchall 5–0–17–1; North 8–0–45–2.

Durham

*J. J. B. Lewis b Thornicroft	6	– c Guy b Kirby	14
M. J. North c McGrath b Kirby	1	– b Kirby	59
N. Killeen c Wood b Dawson	2	– (10) b Dawson	3
G. J. Muchall b Jaques b Thornicroft	20	– (3) c Lehmann b Thornicroft	1
P. D. Collingwood c Bresnan b Dawson	26	– (4) c Kirby b Dawson	65
N. Peng c Jaques b Dawson	37	– (5) c Jaques b Lehmann	0
G. J. Pratt c Guy b White	17	– (6) lbw b Dawson	5
G. R. Breese b White	6	– (7) lbw b White	7
†A. Pratt b Dawson	7	– (8) b White	24
Shoaib Akhtar c and b Dawson	7	– (9) not out	16
A. M. Davies not out	2	– c McGrath b Dawson	4
B 4, l-b 6, w 1, n-b 8	19	B 7, l-b 3, n-b 6	16

1/5 (2) 2/14 (3) 3/27 (1) 4/38 (4) 150 1/14 (1) 2/23 (3) 3/142 (2) 214
5/101 (6) 6/110 (5) 7/116 (8) 4/143 (5) 5/158 (4) 6/158 (6)
8/141 (7) 9/141 (9) 10/150 (10) 7/180 (7) 8/197 (8)
  9/202 (10) 10/214 (11)

Bonus points – Yorkshire 3.

Bowling: *First Innings*—Kirby 10–2–25–1; Thornicroft 8–2–27–2; Dawson 16.5–2–40–5; Bresnan 5–2–11–0; White 13–4–36–2; Lehmann 1–0–1–0. *Second Innings*—Kirby 13–5–26–2; Thornicroft 9–3–24–1; Dawson 20.2–4–75–4; Bresnan 4–1–17–0; White 10–1–39–2; Lehmann 9–2–23–1.

Umpires: J. H. Evans and N. J. Llong.

❝ Even umpire Kitchen shared his pleasure. 'Get rid of the old man,' he said, 'he used to pick the bails up and put them back on the stumps.' ❞

Gloucestershire in 2004, page 621.

At Cardiff, June 23, 24, 25, 26. DURHAM drew with GLAMORGAN.

At Chester-le-Street, July 5. DURHAM lost to SRI LANKA A by 37 runs (D/L method) (see Sri Lanka A tour section).

DURHAM v DERBYSHIRE

At Chester-le-Street, July 21, 22, 23. Derbyshire won by 165 runs. Derbyshire 17 pts, Durham 3 pts. Toss: Derbyshire. Championship debut: A. M. Blignaut.

Derbyshire completed their first Championship win in 11 months with a day to spare. In a heavy atmosphere suiting swing, 17 wickets fell on the first day, when both keepers took five catches. Three bowlers emerged with career-bests: Davies, Sheikh and Havell. Conditions would have been ideal, too, for the omitted Killeen, but Zimbabwean rebel Andy Blignaut – joining Durham on a month's contract – looked rusty in his first first-class game since February. He bowled five of the six no-balls that provided Derbyshire's first 12 runs. Their first-innings resistance came only from an eighth-wicket stand worth 90 between Welch and Botha. But Durham's total, the lowest of the Championship season, barely exceeded that; Lewis carried his bat for 35. Although conditions eased on the second day, Davies became the first to 50 first-class wickets by removing both openers – before a side-strain ended his season. Moss survived some airy drives to plunder his first Championship century. The declaration set Durham 445; having won chasing 451 in May, they had hopes at 210 for five at tea, but they were extinguished once North chipped to mid-on.

Close of play: First day, Durham 64-7 (Lewis 19, Bridge 0); Second day, Derbyshire 297-5 (Moss 132, Sutton 45).

Derbyshire

A. I. Gait c Collingwood	30	– c Pratt b Davies	21
S. D. Stubbings c Pratt b Davies	8	– lbw b Davies	18
J. Moss c Pratt b Davies	0	– not out	147
Hassan Adnan c North b Collingwood	4	– c Collingwood b Blignaut	29
J. D. C. Bryant c Muchall b Davies	3	– run out	30
S. A. Selwood c Pratt b Davies	8	– lbw b Bridge	11
*†L. D. Sutton b Davies	2	– b Onions	45
G. Welch c Pratt b Davies	59	– not out	23
A. G. Botha c Pratt b Blignaut	42		
M. A. Sheikh lbw b Bridge	1		
P. M. R. Havell not out	1		
B 8, l-b 2, w 1, n-b 26	37	B 8, l-b 1, w 1, n-b 6	16
	195	(6 wkts dec.)	**340**

1/36 (2) 2/36 (3) 3/45 (4) 4/56 (5)   1/31 (1) 2/46 (2)   (6 wkts dec.) 340
5/79 (1) 6/83 (6) 7/88 (7)   3/100 (4) 4/164 (5)
8/178 (9) 9/181 (10) 10/195 (8)   5/204 (6) 6/301 (7)

Bonus points – Durham 3.

Bowling: *First Innings*—Onions 15–4–35–0; Blignaut 11–2–43–1; Davies 18.5–6–44–6; Collingwood 12–3–27–2; Bridge 14–4–32–1; Muchall 3–2–4–0. *Second Innings*—Onions 20.4–4–80–1; Blignaut 15–1–48–1; Davies 14.2–2–38–2; Collingwood 12–4–47–0; Bridge 22–1–73–1; Breese 14–2–40–0; Muchall 1–0–5–0.

Durham

*J. J. B. Lewis not out	35	– b Sheikh	25
G. R. Breese c Sutton b Havell	6	– b Havell	4
G. J. Muchall c Sutton b Havell	7	– c Bryant b Sheikh	49
P. D. Collingwood c Sutton b Moss	9	– c Sutton b Welch	22
M. J. North c Sutton b Sheikh	3	– c Selwood b Welch	68
K. J. Coetzer c Sutton b Sheikh	0	– b Welch	5
†A. Pratt c Botha b Moss	1	– b Botha	42
A. M. Blignaut c Botha b Moss	3	– c Botha b Havell	19
G. D. Bridge run out	8	– lbw b Havell	9
A. M. Davies c Moss b Sheikh	1	– (11) not out	2
G. Onions b Sheikh	0	– (10) c Welch b Havell	11
L-b 4, n-b 14	18	B 1, l-b 5, w 1, n-b 16	23
	91		**279**

1/15 (2) 2/23 (3) 3/45 (4) 4/48 (5)
5/48 (6) 6/49 (7) 7/53 (8)
8/77 (9) 9/83 (10) 10/91 (11)

1/19 (2) 2/44 (1) 3/96 (4)
4/128 (3) 5/133 (6) 6/215 (5)
7/243 (7) 8/255 (8)
9/272 (9) 10/279 (10)

Bonus points – Derbyshire 3.

Bowling; *First Innings*—Havell 6–0–36–2; Welch 12–6–12–0; Sheikh 11–7–9–4; Moss 17–7–30–3. *Second Innings*—Havell 16 1–3–75–4; Welch 21–4–56–3; Sheikh 18–2–68–2; Moss 9–1–27–0; Botha 12–2–47–1.

Umpires: M. J. Kitchen and G. Sharp.

At Leicester, July 27, 28, 29, 30. DURHAM lost to LEICESTERSHIRE by an innings and 26 runs.

DURHAM v SOMERSET

At Chester-le-Street, August 13, 14, 15, 16. Drawn. Durham 5.5 pts (after 1.5 pt penalty), Somerset 12 pts. Toss: Durham. County debut: S. W. Tait.

After a first-day washout, it was still too wet to start on the second, despite glorious weather. Even so, Somerset might have won had they not delayed their declaration to collect maximum batting points, allowing No. 10 Johnson to bludgeon the season's fastest century, off 63 balls. Trailing by 169, Durham slipped to 47 for five with 13.2 overs left, but lost only one more wicket. Simon Francis had wrecked their first innings, and their latest import, Shaun Tait, Australia's Bradman Young Player of the Year, endured a nightmare English debut. There were early glimpses of his undoubted pace from a slingy action, but his huge delivery stride made him over-step four times in his first over. Tait never recovered, finishing with none for 113 in 12 overs, including 21 no-balls. During the last of Tait's four spells, Johnson cut loose, before hitting Bridge for sixes over long-on and square leg. Four more driven sixes followed; he also hit nine fours.

Close of play: First day, No play; Second day, No play; Third day, Somerset 127-4 (Ponting 36, Laraman 0).

Durham

*J. B. Lewis b S. R. G. Francis	8	– lbw b Andrew	25
G. R. Breese c Ponting b Laraman	10	– lbw b Johnson	5
G. J. Muchall c Turner b S. R. G. Francis	40	– c Andrew b S. R. G. Francis	4
M. J. North c Turner b S. R. G. Francis	4	– lbw b Laraman	7
K. J. Coetzer c sub b S. R. G. Francis	16	– c Burns b Andrew	6
G. M. Hamilton c J. D. Francis			
b S. R. G. Francis	41	– c Ponting b J. D. Francis	12
†A. Pratt c J. D. Francis b Laraman	16	– not out	24
G. D. Bridge c Turner b Johnson	8	– not out	0
L. E. Plunkett c Turner b Andrew	38		
N. Killeen not out	35		
S. W. Tait c Turner b Johnson	0		
L-b 4, w 3, n-b 8	15	B 2	2

1/9 (1) 2/29 (2) 3/34 (4) 4/86 (3)	231	1/15 (2) 2/26 (3) 3/33 (4) (6 wkts) 85
5/87 (5) 6/129 (7) 7/142 (8)		4/46 (1) 5/47 (5) 6/83 (6)
8/164 (6) 9/225 (9) 10/231 (11)		

Bonus points – Durham 1, Somerset 3.

Bowling: *First Innings*—Johnson 20.5–2–71–2; S. R. G. Francis 23–6–75–5; Laraman 19–7–30–2; Andrew 10–1–39–1; J. D. Francis 3–0–12–0. *Second Innings*—Johnson 7–3–11–1; S. R. G. Francis 16–5–34–1; Laraman 4–2–8–1; Andrew 6–2–24–2; J. D. Francis 2.3–1–4–1; Bowler 2–1–2–0.

Somerset

P. D. Bowler b Hamilton	30	G. M. Andrew c Breese b Muchall	15
J. D. Francis lbw b Killeen	14	R. L. Johnson not out	101
R. T. Ponting c Breese b Plunkett	50	L-b 11, w 11, n-b 44	70
M. J. Wood lbw b Hamilton	0		
*M. Burns b Bridge	8	1/45 (2) 2/103 (1) (8 wkts dec.) 400	
A. W. Laraman not out	66	3/103 (4) 4/119 (5)	
I. D. Blackwell lbw b Plunkett	0	5/151 (3) 6/151 (7)	
†R. J. Turner c Pratt b Killeen	46	7/219 (8) 8/243 (9)	

S. R. G. Francis did not bat.

Bonus points – Somerset 5, Durham 2.

Bowling: Tait 12–0–113–0; Plunkett 16–0–100–2; Killeen 18–4–62–2; Hamilton 12–2–28–2; Bridge 4–0–26–1; Muchall 3–1–15–1; Breese 6–1–42–0; North 0.3–0–3–0.

Umpires: G. I. Burgess and M. J. Harris.

At Colchester, August 18, 19, 20, 21. DURHAM drew with ESSEX.

DURHAM v HAMPSHIRE

At Chester-le-Street, August 24, 25, 26, 27. Drawn. Durham 8 pts, Hampshire 9 pts. Toss: Durham.
Saturated conditions prevented play on the first two days, then 15 wickets fell on the third before a further 50 minutes were lost to bad light and drizzle. Durham left out Tait, their Australian newcomer, because of his run-up problems, as well as wicket-keeper Pratt. Their replacements, Onions and Mustard, were appearing together for the first time in Championship cricket, if not culinary history. Mustard began by hitting a Warne full toss for six, but scored only one more run. Plunkett bowled superbly for a career-best six for 74 and frequently troubled Mascarenhas, who remained unusually restrained, but still equalled his highest score with 104 in 178 balls. Durham batted out time.

Close of play: First day, No play; Second day, No play; Third day, Hampshire 50-5 (Pothas 5, Mascarenhas 1).

Durham

*J. J. B. Lewis b Adams	29	– lbw b Mascarenhas	37
G. R. Breese c Pothas b Mascarenhas	6	– lbw b Bruce	6
G. J. Muchall lbw b Warne	47	– c Pothas b Mascarenhas	4
M. J. North c and b Mascarenhas	0	– not out	23
K. J. Coetzer c Taylor b Adams	6	– c Pothas b Warne	12
G. M. Hamilton c Adams b Mascarenhas	25	– not out	9
†P. Mustard st Pothas b Warne	7		
G. D. Bridge not out	51		
L. E. Plunkett b Udal	14		
N. Killeen c Kenway b Warne	0		
G. Onions lbw b Udal	11		
B 7, l-b 5, w 1, n-b 8	21	L-b 2, n-b 16	18

1/26 (2) 2/56 (1) 3/57 (4) 4/68 (5)   217   1/42 (2) 2/64 (3)   (4 wkts) 109
5/107 (3) 6/119 (7) 7/147 (6)   3/75 (1) 4/94 (5)
8/193 (9) 9/196 (10) 10/217 (11)

Bonus points – Durham 1, Hampshire 3.

Bowling: *First Innings*—Taylor 12–5–28–0; Bruce 6–1–33–0; Mascarenhas 21–5–48–3; Adams 8–4–16–2; Udal 8.1–0–27–2; Warne 21–8–53–3. *Second Innings*—Taylor 6–1–26–0; Bruce 5–0–27–1; Mascarenhas 9–4–21–2; Adams 2–0–10–0; Warne 7–1–23–1.

Hampshire

J. H. K. Adams c Breese b Plunkett	16	B. V. Taylor not out	17
M. J. Brown lbw b Killeen	0	J. T. A. Bruce b Bridge	0
J. P. Crawley c Mustard b Plunkett	1		
S. M. Katich c Mustard b Plunkett	27	B 6, l-b 6, n-b 8	20
D. A. Kenway c Mustard b Plunkett	0		
†N. Pothas b Hamilton	54		280
A. D. Mascarenhas b Bridge	104		
*S. K. Warne c Breese b Plunkett	41		
S. D. Udal b Plunkett	0		

1/4 (2) 2/7 (3) 3/32 (1)
4/36 (5) 5/49 (4) 6/136 (6)
7/210 (8) 8/210 (9)
9/280 (7) 10/280 (11)

Bonus points – Hampshire 2, Durham 3.

Bowling: Plunkett 20 1–74–6; Killeen 14–3–64–1; Onions 5–0–46–0; Hamilton 7–0–26–1; Bridge 20–5–58–2.

Umpires: J. H. Hampshire and J. F. Steele.

At Scarborough, September 1, 2, 3. DURHAM beat YORKSHIRE by 210 runs.

DURHAM v LEICESTERSHIRE

At Chester-le-Street, September 9, 10, 11, 12. Leicestershire won by six wickets. Leicestershire 22 pts, Durham 5 pts. Toss: Durham.

Confirmation came on the first day that, after a four-year reign, Lewis would hand over Durham's captaincy to Australian Mike Hussey, formerly Northamptonshire's captain, in 2005. Lewis bowed out by winning his sixth successive first-class toss, but Leicestershire were happy enough as they exploited bad moisture, then prospered with the bat next day. Maunders, who entered the match averaging 10.50 in the 2004 Championship, survived an uncertain start to make a 138-ball century. But he was upstaged by some imperious strokes from Stevens in a fluent 92. There was a hint of Jack Russell about left-handed wicket-keeper Tom New as he completed his maiden fifty. With Breese scoring 65 – his last 12 innings on the slow Riverside pitches had yielded 74 – Durham looked capable of setting a reasonable target. Once Mustard was sixth out, however, at 246, the last four surrendered tamely to Henderson. Leicestershire needed only 71, though rain made them wait until the final morning. Defeat ensured Durham's fifth wooden spoon in their 13 first-class seasons.

Close of play: First day, Leicestershire 66-0 (Robinson 37, Maddy 28); Second day, Leicestershire 462-7 (New 22, Henderson 4); Third day, Leicestershire 0-0 (Robinson 0, Maddy 0).

Durham

*J. J. B. Lewis lbw b Maunders	27	– b Gibson		14
J. A. Lowe c Stevens b Dagnall	9	– b Gibson		10
G. J. Muchall c Gibson b Dagnall	35	– lbw b Masters		43
M. J. North c Maddy b Masters	8	– c New b Dagnall		11
G. R. Breese c Robinson b Masters	5	– c Stevens b Henderson		65
G. M. Hamilton c New b Gibson	29	– lbw b Gibson		53
†P. Mustard c Robinson b Gibson	60	– lbw b Dagnall		40
G. D. Bridge c Sadler b Hodge	52	– c Dagnall b Henderson		5
L. E. Plunkett b Maddy	7	– not out		17
N. Killeen b Gibson	30	– b Henderson		0
G. Onions not out	20	– lbw b Henderson		0
B 2, l-b 6, n-b 8	16	B 1, l-b 17, n-b 4		22

1/33 (2) 2/51 (1) 3/62 (4) 4/68 (5) 298 1/18 (1) 2/41 (2) 3/75 (4) 280
5/114 (6) 6/143 (3) 7/200 (7) 4/95 (3) 5/188 (6) 6/246 (7)
8/224 (9) 9/251 (8) 10/298 (10) 7/259 (8) 8/263 (5)
9/272 (10) 10/280 (11)

Bonus points – Durham 2, Leicestershire 3.

Bowling: *First Innings*—Gibson 14.2–1–69–3; Dagnall 14–5–42–2; Maunders 9–6–11–1; Masters 16–5–62–2; Maddy 7–0–26–1; Henderson 18–5–62–0; Hodge 2–0–18–1. *Second Innings*—Gibson 19–1–70–3; Dagnall 18–3–73–2; Masters 19–5–54–1; Henderson 13.4–2–44–4; Maunders 2–0–12–0; Maddy 2–0–9–0.

Leicestershire

D. D. J. Robinson run out	65	– lbw b Muchall		38
D. L. Maddy lbw b Breese	70	– c Muchall b Plunkett		10
J. K. Maunders b Plunkett	116	– c Muchall b Plunkett		0
D. I. Stevens c Hamilton b Bridge	92	– not out		19
*B. J. Hodge c Mustard b Plunkett	46			
J. L. Sadler lbw b Breese	28	– (5) b Plunkett		0
†T. J. New not out	51	– (6) not out		0
O. D. Gibson lbw b Breese	0			
C. W. Henderson c Mustard b Killeen	4			
D. D. Masters lbw b Plunkett	1			
C. E. Dagnall b Breese	16			
B 2, l-b 10, w 1, n-b 6	19	B 1, l-b 1, n-b 2		4

1/101 (1) 2/161 (2) 3/311 (4) 4/402 (5) 508 1/31 (2) 2/31 (3) (4 wkts) 71
5/405 (3) 6/454 (6) 7/454 (8) 3/65 (1) 4/70 (5)
8/468 (9) 9/469 (10) 10/508 (11)

Bonus points – Leicestershire 5, Durham 3 (130 overs: 479-9).

Bowling: *First Innings*—Plunkett 33–9–104–3; Killeen 35–9–93–1; Onions 20–3–93–0; Muchall 7–1–21–0; Bridge 20–3–92–1; Breese 24.2–6–93–4. *Second Innings*—Plunkett 6.5–1–27–3; Onions 5–1–41–0; Muchall 1–0–1–1.

Umpires: J. W. Holder and N. A. Mallender.

ESSEX

Gough is not enough

PAUL HISCOCK

A riddle lay at the heart of Essex's cricket in 2004. After Championship relegation in 2003, their batsmen answered the demands of head coach Graham Gooch for greater application and performance, amassing 20 Championship hundreds – 16 more than the previous season. Essex also recruited two new international bowlers in Danish Kaneria and Darren Gough, and the leg-spinner Kaneria ended with most wickets in the second division.

But it added up to very little team success. Essex made their worst start to a Championship season since 1953, drawing a blank until the tenth game, and winning just three times in total. They never threatened the promotion places. And, in the totesport League, they avoided relegation only by beating the champions Glamorgan in the last match. "We underachieved big-time," concluded the captain Ronnie Irani.

So what happened? Well, the poor results were not such a riddle to those who watched Essex regularly in the field: the seam attack was unbalanced and clearly in desperate need of an incisive strike bowler. Gough played only seven Championship games between international commitments and periods resting his dodgy knee, Ashley Cowan was recovering from a serious operation, also on a knee, and Scott Brant, the Queensland left-arm seamer, had a wretched second year. Injuries followed by poor form left him with nine Championship wickets, before a damaged heel ensured a flight home in August. In the second division, only Derbyshire and Durham conceded bigger average totals than Essex, and the attack often squandered big scores – never more obviously than in September against Glamorgan, when the county scored 642 and lost.

That was one of several giant totals: Essex reached 400 eight times, and 11 players scored Championship hundreds. But the batting was still too inconsistent. The great success was the 6ft 10in opener Will Jefferson, who hit six centuries and 1,555 runs; only four men, all with international caps, scored more. James Foster passed 1,000 first-class runs for the first time and, with his keeping consistently good, looked a genuine all-rounder. That was welcome because a knee injury forced Irani to quit bowling. The problem limited his Championship appearances to nine, but in those games he averaged more than 63, topping the county averages, and he easily held down a place purely as an attacking batsman and perky captain.

Meanwhile, Kaneria carried the attack. He bowled 179 more overs than anyone else in the side, took 63 wickets in 11 Championship games, and was an overwhelming success. Often his efforts deserved a better result: in two successive June defeats at Chelmsford he took 22 wickets. In support, Gough managed 30 cheap victims but was often absent, while the New

Zealand all-rounder Andre Adams made an impact late in the summer. He arrived in July, after playing in the Lancashire League for Colne, and made a sensational Championship debut, when his 80-ball century set up Essex's first win of the season. Fiercely competitive, he proved a capable medium-pacer taking 23 wickets in seven matches, though neither he, nor the rest of the attack, was much helped by the fielders. A lack of mobility was compounded by the absence of an expert slip catcher. Many chances went through a sieve of a cordon, a perennial problem since Stuart Law left in 2001.

Will Jefferson

Evening cricket remained very popular in Essex, with near-capacity crowds for the Twenty20 matches and the six other floodlit games. There was, however, some criticism from members about a lack of Sunday one-day cricket at home. And there was no success to celebrate in anything.

This summer, supporters will have a new ground to visit: the future of the Southend Festival has been safeguarded, but the venue will switch from Southchurch Park – where first-class cricket was introduced in 1906 – to Garons Park. Built in 1996, with modern facilities, it will be the first new Championship venue in Essex since Harlow was briefly introduced in 1970.

Two other old familiars will be missing in 2005. Nasser Hussain retired in a blaze of glory with a Test century at Lord's which meant with hindsight that he finished his Essex career with a hundred, scored at Cardiff barely a week earlier. Hussain made his debut for Essex in 1987, but had played only 12 Championship games in the last five seasons because of international duties. John Stephenson was appointed MCC head of cricket in June, and ended his second spell at the county where he started in 1985. Aftab Habib also departed, replaced by Zimbabwean Grant Flower, who signed under the Kolpak regulations and joins his brother Andy at Chelmsford. He should stabilise the batting and offer a spin option in one-dayers, while his fielding will be a much-needed asset.

Essex are convinced the batsmen can do the job in 2005. The Flowers and Jefferson offer experienced backbone while there is plenty of potential in the youngsters Alastair Cook, Ravinder Bopara and Mark Pettini. However, they need much-improved pace bowling to support them, and in February they signed Alex Tudor from Surrey.

Nigel Fuller, *Wisden's* longest-serving county correspondent, has retired after covering Essex for us for 29 years.

ESSEX RESULTS

All first-class matches – Played 17: Won 4, Lost 6, Drawn 7.
County Championship matches – Played 16: Won 3, Lost 6, Drawn 7.

Frizzell County Championship, 5th in Division 2; Cheltenham & Gloucester Trophy, q-f;
totesport League, 6th in Division 1; Twenty20 Cup, q-f.

COUNTY CHAMPIONSHIP AVERAGES

BATTING AND FIELDING

Cap		M	I	NO	R	HS	100s	50s	Avge	Ct/St
1994	R. C. Irani.	9	15	4	694	164	3	2	63.09	1
2002	W. I. Jefferson	16	28	1	1,411	222	5	5	52.25	13
2001	J. S. Foster	16	24	4	927	212	3	1	46.35	39/5
2002	A. Flower	16	28	3	1,045	172	2	5	41.80	18
1996	A. P. Grayson.	6	10	0	365	119	1	2	36.50	0
2003	G. R. Napier	14	22	4	633	106*	1	5	35.16	6
2002	A. Habib.	13	21	0	722	157	1	4	34.38	3
1989	J. P. Stephenson	3	4	1	90	40	0	0	30.00	0
	A. N. Cook	12	21	2	568	126	1	4	29.89	18
2003	J. D. Middlebrook	15	22	1	583	115	1	3	27.76	4
2004	A. R. Adams§	7	8	0	196	124	1	0	24.50	4
	R. S. Bopara	4	6	0	103	34	0	0	17.16	5
2004	D. Gough	7	10	1	144	50	0	1	16.00	0
1997	A. P. Cowan	5	7	2	63	25	0	0	12.60	3
	A. J. Clarke.	4	6	0	50	28	0	0	8.33	1
2004	Danish Kaneria§.	11	13	7	47	13*	0	0	7.83	7
2003	S. A. Brant§	6	8	1	39	19	0	0	5.57	0
	A. G. A. M. McCoubrey	5	7	4	4	2*	0	0	1.33	0

Also batted: N. Hussain (cap 1989) (2 matches) 70, 0, 102 (2 ct); A. P. Palladino (2 matches) 0, 41; M. L. Pettini (2 matches) 67, 0, 10 (1 ct); R. N. ten Doeschate (1 match) 7.

§ *Overseas player.*

BOWLING

	O	M	R	W	BB	5W/i	Avge
D. Gough.	226.4	52	672	30	5-57	1	22.40
A. R. Adams	157.4	23	561	23	5-93	1	24.39
Danish Kaneria	563	123	1,609	63	7-65	4	25.53
A. P. Cowan	148	39	463	13	3-44	0	35.61
G. R. Napier.	366.2	61	1,444	39	5-56	1	37.02
J. D. Middlebrook	383.3	56	1,423	32	5-26	1	44.46

Also bowled: R. S. Bopara 24–1–108–0; S. A. Brant 167.2–36–597–9; A. J. Clarke 113–24–357–9; A. P. Grayson 40.1–2–167–0; A. Habib 7–1–18–0; A. G. A. M. McCoubrey 103.4–17–491–8; A. P. Palladino 34–5–158–3; J. P. Stephenson 55–7–223–8; R. N. ten Doeschate 18–2–68–2.

COUNTY RECORDS

Highest score for:	343*	P. A. Perrin v Derbyshire at Chesterfield	1904
Highest score against:	332	W. H. Ashdown (Kent) at Brentwood	1934
Best bowling for:	10-32	H. Pickett v Leicestershire at Leyton	1895
Best bowling against:	10-40	E. G. Dennett (Gloucestershire) at Bristol	1906
Highest total for:	761-6 dec.	v Leicestershire at Chelmsford	1990
Highest total against:	803-4 dec.	by Kent at Brentwood	1934
Lowest total for:	30	v Yorkshire at Leyton	1901
Lowest total against:	14	by Surrey at Chelmsford	1983

ESSEX DIRECTORY

ADDRESS

County Ground, New Writtle Street, Chelmsford CM2 0PG (01245 252420; fax 01245 254030; email administration.essex@ecb.co.uk). **Website** www.essexcricket.org.uk.

GROUNDS

Chelmsford: ¼ mile S of town centre at junction of A138 Parkway and A12 New London Road. Entrance in New Writtle Street. Nearest station: Chelmsford (½ mile).

Southend-on-Sea (Garons Park): Travelling E along Eastern Avenue, turn L at McDonald's roundabout. Ground adjacent to leisure centre. Nearest station: Prittlewell (1¼ miles).

Colchester: ½ mile S of town centre in Lower Castle Park. From A133 Cowdray Avenue R into Catchpool Road and then straight on into Sportsway. Nearest stations: Colchester or Colchester Town (both ¾ mile).

OFFICIALS

Captain R. C. Irani
Head coach G. A. Gooch
President D. J. Insole
Chairman N. R. A. Hilliard

Chief executive D. E. East
Chairman, cricket committee G. J. Saville
Head groundsman S. Kerrison
Scorers A. E. Choat; D. J. Norris

PLAYERS

Players expected to reappear in 2005

	Former counties	Country	Born	Birthplace
*Adams Andre Ryan		NZ	17.7.1975	Auckland
Bishop Justin Edward		E	4.1.1982	Bury St Edmunds
Bopara Ravinder Singh		E	4.5.1985	Forest Gate
Clarke Andrew John		E	9.11.1975	†Brentwood
Cook Alastair Nathan		E	25.12.1984	Gloucester
Cowan Ashley Preston		E	7.5.1975	Hitchin
*Danish Kaneria		P	16.12.1980	Karachi
Denning Nicholas Alexander		E	3.10.1978	Ascot
*Flower Andrew		Z (EU)	28.4.1968	Cape Town, SA
*Foster James Savin		E	15.4.1980	Whipps Cross
*Gough Darren	Yorks	E	18.9.1970	Barnsley
Grayson Adrian Paul	Yorks	E	31.3.1971	Ripon
*Irani Ronald Charles	Lancs	E	26.10.1971	Leigh
Jefferson William Ingleby		E	25.10.1979	Derby
Middlebrook James Daniel	Yorks	E	13.5.1977	Leeds
Napier Graham Richard		E	6.1.1980	†Colchester
Palladino Antonio Paul		E	29.6.1983	London
Pettini Mark Lewis		E	7.8.1983	Brighton
ten Doeschate Ryan Neil		SA (EU/NL)	30.6.1980	Port Elizabeth

Players due to join in 2005

	Former counties	Country	Born	Birthplace
*Flower Grant William	Leics	Z (K)	20.12.1970	Salisbury, Rhodesia
*Tudor Alex Jeremy	Surrey	E	23.10.1977	Kensington

* *Test player.* † *Born in Essex.*

At Cambridge, April 10, 11, 12. ESSEX beat CAMBRIDGE UCCE by 153 runs.

At Leeds, April 21, 22, 23, 24. ESSEX lost to YORKSHIRE by seven wickets.

ESSEX v SOMERSET

At Chelmsford, April 28, 29, 30, May 1. Drawn. Essex 6 pts, Somerset 12 pts. Toss: Somerset. County debut: Danish Kaneria.

With rain allowing just 40 overs on the first two days, a draw was always the likeliest outcome, though Somerset retained flickering hopes of success on the final afternoon when they enforced the follow-on and removed Jefferson first ball. But time and more bad weather were against them, and stalemate resulted. Dutch had been the engineer of Essex's plight, taking three for ten in 24 balls after the ever-vigilant Bowler had batted for 467 minutes to hit an unbeaten 187 from 383 balls. He shared an unbroken fourth-wicket stand of 232 with Burns, and together they negated the threat of Danish Kaneria, the Pakistani leg-spinner. Stephenson had a quiet game on his 300th first-class appearance, while injuries forced Somerset to field both first-team coach Kevin Shine and fitness coach Andy Hurry as substitutes on the final afternoon.

Close of play: First day, Somerset 87-1 (Bowler 49, Wood 19); Second day, No play; Third day, Essex 28-0 (Jefferson 16, Cook 12).

Somerset

P. D. Bowler not out		187
J. D. Francis c Pettini b Stephenson		18
M. J. Wood b Danish Kaneria		34
J. Cox c Jefferson b Brant		22
*M. Burns not out		124
B 1, l-b 11, w 1, n-b 2		15

1/32 (2) 2/127 (3)   (3 wkts dec.) 400
3/168 (4)

A. W. Laraman, †R. J. Turner, K. P. Dutch, R. L. Johnson, A. R. Caddick and N. A. M. McLean did not bat.

Bonus points – Somerset 3, Essex 1.

Bowling: Brant 32–7–85–1; Napier 31–5–99–0; Stephenson 13–0–43–1; Danish Kaneria 34.3–8–92–1; Middlebrook 11–0–63–0; Habib 3–0–6–0.

Essex

W. I. Jefferson c Francis b Dutch	85	– c Turner b McLean	0
A. N. Cook c Turner b McLean	20	– not out	20
*A. Flower run out	1	– not out	13
A. Habib c Cox b Dutch	25		
M. L. Pettini c Burns b Dutch	10		
†J. S. Foster not out	75		
J. D. Middlebrook c Turner b Caddick	8		
G. R. Napier b Caddick	0		
J. P. Stephenson c Burns b Dutch	6		
Danish Kaneria st Turner b Dutch	0		
S. A. Brant run out	1		
		W 1, n-b 2	3

1/62 (2) 2/64 (3) 3/124 (4) 4/131 (1)   231   1/0 (1)   (1 wkt) 36
5/144 (5) 6/173 (7) 7/173 (8)
8/200 (9) 9/204 (10) 10/231 (11)

Bonus points – Essex 1, Somerset 3.

Bowling: *First Innings*—Caddick 28–1–114–2; Johnson 6–5–2–0; Dutch 22–3–65–5; McLean 11–3–31–1; Laraman 6–2–19–0. *Second Innings*—McLean 5–1–18–1; Laraman 2–0–14–0; Dutch 3–1–4–0; Caddick 0.1–0–0–0.

Umpires: N. G. Cowley and A. A. Jones.

At Chester-le-Street, May 7, 8, 9, 10. ESSEX drew with DURHAM.

At Cardiff, May 12, 13, 14, 15. ESSEX drew with GLAMORGAN.

ESSEX v LEICESTERSHIRE

At Chelmsford, May 19, 20, 21, 22. Drawn. Essex 12 pts, Leicestershire 10 pts. Toss: Leicestershire.
Essex awarded caps to their new international bowlers, Gough and Danish Kaneria, on the first day, but the Chelmsford wicket proved a batsmen's paradise. Hodge dominated the Leicestershire innings with a flawless unbeaten 240 from 337 balls and 431 minutes, containing one six and 32 fours. But their total of 510 proved insignificant as Essex racked up the second-highest score in

HIGHEST TOTALS BY ESSEX

761-6 dec.	v Leicestershire at Chelmsford............................	1990
708-9 dec.	**v Leicestershire at Chelmsford**.........................	**2004**
692	v Somerset at Taunton.................................	1895
673	v Leicestershire at Leicester............................	1899
662-7 dec.	v Hampshire at Colchester.............................	1995
642	**v Glamorgan at Chelmsford**...........................	**2004**
621	v Leicestershire at Leicester............................	1991
616-5 dec.	v Surrey at The Oval.................................	1904
616	v Kent at Chelmsford................................	1988
609-4 dec.	v Derbyshire at Leyton...............................	1912
604-7 dec.	v Northamptonshire at Northampton......................	1921

their history. On day two 19-year-old Alastair Cook hit his maiden first-class hundred as he and Jefferson built Essex's first Championship double-century opening partnership since 1996. Day three saw Foster – who had never before managed three figures for Essex – reach 179 by the close, a score he converted into a maiden double on the last morning. His authoritative 212 lasted 284 deliveries and 337 minutes and included 24 fours and three sixes. Grayson, in his first appearance of the season after knee surgery, declared with at least 87 overs' cricket remaining and may have sensed victory when Leicestershire went to tea at 152 for five, still 46 adrift. But they eased into credit for the loss of one more wicket before the game was called off early.

Close of play: First day, Leicestershire 390-6 (Hodge 184, DeFreitas 13); Second day, Essex 291-2 (Jefferson 124); Third day, Essex 665-7 (Foster 179, Brant 5).

Leicestershire

D. D. J. Robinson b Gough..............	56	– lbw b Danish Kaneria.........	53
J. K. Maunders lbw b McCoubrey..........	22	– c Foster b Gough............	7
B. J. Hodge c Flower b Middlebrook........	240	– b Brant.................	5
D. L. Maddy c Flower b Danish Kaneria.....	5	– st Foster b Danish Kaneria.....	23
J. L. Sadler c Foster b Gough............	46	– b Danish Kaneria............	43
J. N. Snape c Cook b Brant.............	15	– not out.................	39
†P. A. Nixon lbw b Danish Kaneria.........	41	– c Foster b Gough............	10
*P. A. J. DeFreitas c Jefferson b Middlebrook....	47	– not out.................	15
O. D. Gibson c Cook b Middlebrook........	13		
C. W. Henderson not out................	10		
M. F. Cleary b Danish Kaneria...........	2		
B 1, l-b 7, w 1, n-b 4	13	B 10, l-b 3, n-b 4.......	17

1/30 (2) 2/131 (1) 3/162 (4) 4/267 (5)   510   1/23 (2) 2/34 (3)   (6 wkts) 212
5/287 (6) 6/367 (7) 7/464 (8)   3/86 (4) 4/121 (1)
8/486 (9) 9/502 (3) 10/510 (11)   5/147 (5) 6/167 (7)

Bonus points – Leicestershire 5, Essex 3.

Bowling: *First Innings*—Gough 18–4–61–2; Brant 20–3–96–1; McCoubrey 14–1–89–1; Danish Kaneria 41.5–7–139–3; Middlebrook 35–3–117–3. *Second Innings*—Gough 17–3–38–2; Brant 11–3–49–1; Danish Kaneria 31–14–42–3; Middlebrook 12–4–38–0; McCoubrey 10–2–26–0; Grayson 1–0–6–0.

Essex

W. I. Jefferson lbw b DeFreitas	128	S. A. Brant b Cleary	5
A. N. Cook b Cleary	126	Danish Kaneria not out	5
*A. P. Grayson lbw b Gibson	7	B 6, l-b 17, w 6, n-b 24	53
A. Flower b Cleary	22		
A. Habib c Nixon b DeFreitas	97	1/265 (2) 2/291 (3) (9 wkts dec.) 708	
†J. S. Foster c Nixon b Cleary	212	3/295 (1) 4/326 (4)	
J. D. Middlebrook b DeFreitas	3	5/510 (5) 6/530 (7)	
D. Gough c Cleary b Snape	50	7/630 (8) 8/666 (9) 9/708 (6)	

A. G. A. M. McCoubrey did not bat.

Bonus points – Essex 5, Leicestershire 1 (130 overs: 480-4).

Bowling: Gibson 28–4–97–1; DeFreitas 45–11–145–3; Henderson 29–4–111–0; Cleary 27.4–2–130–4; Hodge 16–2–52–0; Snape 20–2–78–1; Maddy 12–1–67–0; Robinson 1–0–5–0.

Umpires: V. A. Holder and T. E. Jesty.

At Taunton, May 25, 26, 27, 28. ESSEX drew with SOMERSET.

ESSEX v YORKSHIRE

At Chelmsford, June 2, 3, 4, 5. Yorkshire won by 137 runs. Yorkshire 21 pts, Essex 7 pts. Toss: Essex.

Darren Gough grabbed a wicket with his third ball against his old county, but Essex capitulated tamely to the gentle left-arm spin of Lehmann, who followed an important second-innings 86 with a spell of four for 21 in 52 balls late on the third day. Yorkshire claimed the extra half-hour, though they still needed 13 balls on the last morning to wrap things up. On the opening day, after Gough's early breakthrough, Jaques hit Yorkshire's first Championship hundred of 2004, against an attack without the out-of-form Australian Scott Brant, who was seeking advice from Troy Cooley, the England bowling coach, after being dropped. By contrast, Danish Kaneria was in fine fettle, spinning the ball sharply and returning figures of 13 for 186, the best for Essex since Mark Ilott took 14 for 105 against Northamptonshire at Luton in 1995. Kaneria's efforts, though, were scuppered by Essex's feeble third-day batting, and defeat meant Yorkshire had beaten them twice in six weeks. Irani, however, marked his first appearance of the season in this competition with his first Championship century since July 2002.

Close of play: First day, Essex 41-1 (Jefferson 30, Flower 7); Second day, Yorkshire 40-1 (Wood 26, Kirby 1); Third day, Essex 108-8 (Napier 3, Gough 11).

> "Gough and Hussain were team-mates in a solitary Championship match, having shared a dressing-room in 41 Tests."
> Glamorgan in 2004, page 604.

Yorkshire

M. J. Wood c Foster b Gough	0	– c Foster b Clarke	81
P. A. Jaques c Napier b Middlebrook	115	– c Foster b Gough	13
A. McGrath c Foster b Danish Kaneria	93	– (4) c Danish Kaneria b Gough	5
D. S. Lehmann c Foster b Danish Kaneria	27	– (5) lbw b Danish Kaneria	86
M. J. Lumb c Napier b Middlebrook	45	– (6) c and b Danish Kaneria	36
*C. White lbw b Danish Kaneria	1	– (7) lbw b Danish Kaneria	4
†S. M. Guy b Danish Kaneria	3	– (8) c Flower b Danish Kaneria	6
R. K. J. Dawson lbw b Danish Kaneria	49	– (9) lbw b Danish Kaneria	5
T. T. Bresnan not out	10	– (10) lbw b Danish Kaneria	0
C. E. W. Silverwood b Gough	3	– (11) not out	4
S. P. Kirby lbw b Danish Kaneria	0	– (3) b Danish Kaneria	1
B 8, l-b 7, n-b 2	17	L-b 7, w 1	8
	363		**249**

1/0 (1) 2/207 (2) 3/241 (4) 4/254 (3)   363
5/260 (6) 6/268 (7) 7/310 (5)
8/351 (8) 9/362 (10) 10/363 (11)

1/35 (2) 2/46 (3) 3/53 (4)   249
4/188 (1) 5/210 (5) 6/226 (7)
7/235 (6) 8/244 (8)
9/244 (10) 10/249 (9)

Bonus points – Yorkshire 4, Essex 3.

Bowling: *First Innings*—Gough 11–1–27–2; Napier 7–0–36–0; Clarke 9–2–42–0; Danish Kaneria 33.5–5–121–6; Middlebrook 27–1–122–2. *Second Innings*—Gough 21–7–54–2; Napier 8–0–54–0; Danish Kaneria 23.1–5–65–7; Middlebrook 12–0–40–0; Clarke 11–4–29–1.

Essex

W. I. Jefferson st Guy b Dawson	45	– c Wood b Silverwood	8
A. N. Cook c White b Kirby	0	– lbw b Silverwood	2
A. Flower c Jaques b Dawson	43	– c Lumb b Lehmann	37
A. Habib c Guy b Silverwood	80	– c Jaques b Lehmann	17
*R. C. Irani c Guy b Kirby	107	– c Wood b Lehmann	8
†J. S. Foster c White b Kirby	20	– lbw b Dawson	5
J. D. Middlebrook c McGrath b Lehmann	2	– (8) c Lumb b Dawson	4
G. R. Napier run out	13	– (9) c Jaques b Kirby	5
D. Gough b Silverwood	13	– (10) c Wood b Silverwood	15
A. J. Clarke c Jaques b Silverwood	12	– (7) lbw b Lehmann	0
Danish Kaneria not out	7	– not out	0
B 5, l-b 4, w 4, n-b 4	17	B 8, l-b 3, n-b 4	15
	359		**116**

1/12 (2) 2/81 (1) 3/118 (3) 4/226 (4)   359
5/260 (6) 6/265 (7) 7/318 (8)
8/326 (5) 9/348 (9) 10/359 (10)

1/9 (2) 2/18 (1) 3/56 (4)   116
4/70 (5) 5/77 (6) 6/82 (7)
7/93 (3) 8/95 (8)
9/116 (10) 10/116 (9)

Bonus points – Essex 4, Yorkshire 3.

Bowling: *First Innings*—Silverwood 22.3–1–84–3; Kirby 21–2–86–3; Dawson 32–7–101–2; Lehmann 20–4–61–1; Bresnan 6–2–16–0; White 3–2–2–0. *Second Innings*—Silverwood 7–1–18–3; Kirby 6.1–0–20–1; Dawson 19–6–32–2; Lehmann 17–2–35–4.

Umpires: M. J. Harris and R. Palmer.

ESSEX v HAMPSHIRE

At Chelmsford, June 9, 10, 11. Hampshire won by 114 runs. Hampshire 21 pts, Essex 3 pts. Toss: Hampshire.

Hampshire maintained their promotion push as Billy Taylor bowled them to victory inside three days with a career-best five for 73; for Essex, it was a second humiliating home defeat in under a week. The game began with a diligent innings from Crawley, who needed 50 deliveries to reach double figures and in all batted almost four and a half hours. He was three short of a hundred when winkled out by Gough, who ended with five wickets in a Championship innings for the first time in four years. But Essex had no one with Crawley's mindset and they were all out 195 behind on first innings. As the pitch began to add increasing turn to its earlier uneven bounce, Hampshire's batsmen also had a hard time against Danish Kaneria, who took his total to 22 wickets in his last two matches. But Essex produced another abject display when set 350 to win. The first six wickets managed only 108 – ten fewer than first time round – and although Napier smashed a quick unbeaten fifty, he had the advantage of not facing Warne, who bowled only four overs after suffering a cracked bone in his hand, facing Gough.

Close of play: First day, Hampshire 306-7 (Pothas 54, Udal 1); Second day, Hampshire 81-5 (Pothas 9, Taylor 6).

Hampshire

D. A. Kenway c Flower b Danish Kaneria	25	– lbw b Danish Kaneria	27
M. J. Brown b Napier	0	– c Cook b Danish Kaneria	29
J. P. Crawley c Cook b Gough	97	– c Foster b Danish Kaneria	0
M. J. Clarke c and b Danish Kaneria	69	– c Foster b Clarke	8
W. S. Kendall c Foster b Gough	19	– b Clarke	2
†N. Pothas lbw b Gough	57	– b Gough	12
A. D. Mascarenhas c and b Danish Kaneria	32	– (8) c Jefferson b Danish Kaneria	0
*S. K. Warne b Danish Kaneria	0	– (10) c Napier b Danish Kaneria	34
S. D. Udal not out	43	– run out	8
C. T. Tremlett b Gough	0	– (11) not out	0
B. V. Taylor c Foster b Gough	2	– (7) c Foster b Gough	22
B 1, w 4, n-b 4	9	B 4, l-b 8	12
	353		**154**

1/0 (2) 2/38 (1) 3/175 (4) 4/207 (5)
5/224 (3) 6/286 (7) 7/286 (8)
8/325 (6) 9/331 (10) 10/353 (11)

1/55 (1) 2/55 (3) 3/64 (4)
4/64 (2) 5/72 (5) 6/105 (6)
7/108 (9) 8/108 (8)
9/147 (9) 10/154 (10)

Bonus points – Hampshire 4, Essex 3.

Bowling: First Innings—Gough 23.5–6–57–5; Napier 19–3–68–1; Clarke 15–3–58–0; Danish Kaneria 35–4–108–4; Middlebrook 15 1 58–0; Bopara 1–0–3–0. *Second Innings*—Gough 13–2–36–2; Napier 6–1–26–0; Danish Kaneria 19.2–4–68–5; Clarke 11–6 12–?

Essex

W. I. Jefferson c Pothas b Taylor	15	– lbw b Taylor	26
A. N. Cook c Pothas b Tremlett	25	– c Kenway b Taylor	22
*A. Flower c Warne b Udal	1	– c Brown b Udal	0
A. Habib lbw b Warne	42	– c Pothas b Taylor	13
R. S. Bopara c Brown b Warne	17	– lbw b Mascarenhas	19
†J. S. Foster lbw b Tremlett	6	– b Taylor	39
J. D. Middlebrook not out	30	– b Taylor	0
G. R. Napier c Kendall b Mascarenhas	7	– not out	51
D. Gough c Clarke b Mascarenhas	4	– c sub b Udal	20
A. J. Clarke c Clarke b Tremlett	0	– c and b Udal	8
Danish Kaneria c Brown b Tremlett	1	– c Crawley b Udal	13
B 5, l-b 1, n-b 4	10	L-b 16, n-b 8	24
	158		**235**

1/28 (1) 2/29 (3) 3/73 (2) 4/105 (4)
5/106 (5) 6/118 (6) 7/140 (8)
8/144 (9) 9/150 (10) 10/158 (11)

1/48 (1) 2/51 (3) 3/51 (2)
4/74 (5) 5/108 (4) 6/108 (7)
7/141 (6) 8/184 (9)
9/199 (10) 10/235 (11)

Bonus points – Hampshire 3.

Bowling: First Innings—Tremlett 16.5–6 29–4; Taylor 16–3–39–1; Mascarenhas 6–3–12–2; Udal 10–2–32–1; Warne 14–6–40–2. *Second Innings*—Tremlett 11–1–54–0, Taylor 19–4–73–5; Udal 13.4–1–55–4; Mascarenhas 8–3–17–1; Warne 4–0–20–0.

Umpires: D. J. Constant and N. A. Mallender.

At Chelmsford, June 18 (day/night). ESSEX lost to NEW ZEALANDERS by five wickets (see New Zealand tour section).

At Derby, June 23, 24, 25, 26. ESSEX drew with DERBYSHIRE.

At Leicester, July 21, 22, 23, 24. ESSEX beat LEICESTERSHIRE by 48 runs.

ESSEX v NOTTINGHAMSHIRE

At Southend, July 28, 29, 30, 31. Nottinghamshire won by eight wickets. Nottinghamshire 22 pts, Essex 8 pts. Toss: Essex.

Nottinghamshire led the second division by 39 points after victory in this high-scoring match. MacGill set up the win with seven for 109 before Gallian – the fifth batsman to reach three figures – saw them home. The game had begun with Essex's first six scoring strokes all making the boundary, and when Grayson reached his first Championship hundred for almost three years, he became their tenth centurion of the summer. He and Jefferson put on 188 for the first wicket, but the middle order wobbled, and it needed a last-wicket stand between Irani and Brant of 105 – the best in 98 years since first-class cricket came to Southchurch Park – to guide Essex to maximum batting points. Brant had been in poor form, but he and his captain frustrated the bowlers for almost 29 overs. The Nottinghamshire reply then centred on a 45-over partnership between Pietersen and Hussey worth 212. At 383 for three a massive total was in prospect, but uneven bounce on the third morning prompted seven wickets to fall for 52, Adams following his century in the previous game with five wickets. Nottinghamshire led by just four, before MacGill turned the game their way. At the end of Essex's first innings, Pietersen reported the loss of an ear-stud. The groundstaff searched, but the groundsman, Stuart Kerrison, said it had probably been "crunched up" by the mower. There would be no chance to hunt for it in 2005. In the autumn Essex announced they would move the Southend festival to the newer ground at Garons Park.

Close of play: First day, Essex 355-9 (Irani 59, Brant 12); Second day, Nottinghamshire 370-3 (Pietersen 152, Hussey 112); Third day, Nottinghamshire 54-1 (Gallian 28, Warren 12).

Essex

W. I. Jefferson run out	75	– c Smith b MacGill	12
A. P. Grayson c and b Pietersen	119	– lbw b MacGill	35
A. Flower c Gallian b Pietersen	18	– lbw b Shreck	1
A. Habib b Smith	7	– c Read b Smith	48
*R. C. Irani not out	122	– c Ealham b MacGill	60
†J. S. Foster c Ealham b Smith	2	– not out	44
J. D. Middlebrook lbw b Ealham	30	– c Ealham b MacGill	8
G. R. Napier lbw b MacGill	8	– c Hussey b MacGill	13
A. R. Adams c Ealham b MacGill	1	– c Ealham b MacGill	14
A. P. Cowan b MacGill	6	– c Read b MacGill	0
S. A. Brant b Ealham	19	– run out	0
B 3, l-b 8, w 1, n-b 12	24	B 2, l-b 3, n-b 8	13

1/188 (1) 2/219 (2) 3/228 (3) 4/230 (4)   **431**   1/55 (2) 2/56 (1) 3/59 (3)   **248**
5/234 (6) 6/291 (7) 7/310 (8)   4/158 (4) 5/166 (5) 6/196 (7)
8/312 (9) 9/326 (10) 10/431 (11)   7/212 (8) 8/246 (9)
                                    9/246 (10) 10/248 (11)

Bonus points – Essex 5, Nottinghamshire 3.

Bowling: *First Innings*—Smith 24–6–80–2; Shreck 16–1–84–0; Ealham 17.1–5–57–2; Franks 16–3–52–0; MacGill 35–9–124–3; Pietersen 11–1–23–2. *Second Innings*—Smith 9–2–24–1; Franks 7–1–26–0; Shreck 9–2–38–1; MacGill 28–5–109–7; Ealham 5–0–18–0; Pietersen 7.5–1–28–0.

Nottinghamshire

D. J. Bicknell c Foster b Cowan	0	– lbw b Adams	13
*J. E. R. Gallian run out	74	– not out	120
R. J. Warren lbw b Napier	14	– c Foster b Middlebrook	36
K. P. Pietersen lbw b Adams	167	– not out	69
D. J. Hussey c Foster b Cowan	116		
†C. M. W. Read lbw b Adams	0		
M. A. Ealham c Flower b Cowan	17		
P. J. Franks c Foster b Adams	0		
G. J. Smith b Adams	8		
S. C. G. MacGill c Middlebrook b Adams	18		
C. E. Shreck not out	1		
B 6, l-b 3, w 3, n-b 8	20	L-b 2, w 6	8
	435	(2 wkts)	246

1/0 (1) 2/43 (3) 3/171 (2) 4/383 (5)   1/31 (1) 2/128 (3)
5/384 (6) 6/397 (4) 7/408 (7)
8/408 (8) 9/432 (10) 10/435 (9)

Bonus points – Nottinghamshire 5, Essex 3.

Bowling: *First Innings*—Cowan 24–5–70–3; Brant 14–3–48–0; Napier 14–1–65–1; Middlebrook 18–1–102–0; Adams 22.4–1–93–5; Grayson 11–0–48–0. *Second Innings*—Cowan 8–0–39–0; Adams 13–1–42–1; Brant 7–2–27–0; Middlebrook 15–3–62–1; Napier 4–0–24–0; Grayson 8.1–0–50–0.

Umpires: N. J. Llong and A. G. T. Whitehead.

At Southampton, August 3, 4, 5. ESSEX beat HAMPSHIRE by 384 runs.

ESSEX v DURHAM

At Colchester, August 18, 19, 20, 21. Drawn. Essex 9 pts, Durham 7 pts. Toss: Durham.

Amid heavy showers, which washed out the second and fourth days, Essex's hopes of promotion faded and Durham's grim luck with overseas players continued. Play started on the first afternoon and Lewis batted more than six hours for 127 against his old county, without quite recovering his best form, or ensuring a commanding total. Danish Kaneria quickly hit his stride on his return from the Asia Cup; by contrast, when Durham fielded, their Australian quick bowler, Shaun Tait, continued the nervous no-balling which blighted his debut against Somerset. His four-over opening spell cost 37, including three no-balls, and seven fours for Jefferson, who passed 1,000 Championship runs en route to 134. By the end of the third day, Essex had rushed past Durham's 268 (in almost half the overs), but heavy overnight rain turned the outfield to a lake on the last day, and play was impossible despite warm sunshine and a gentle breeze.

Close of play: First day, Durham 170-6 (Lewis 74, Bridge 0); Second day, No play; Third day, Essex 274-4 (Irani 7, Foster 0).

Durham

*J. J. B. Lewis st Foster b Danish Kaneria	127	L. E. Plunkett lbw b Middlebrook	7
G. R. Breese c Adams b Cowan	34	N. Killeen not out	6
G. J. Muchall c Foster b Cowan	0	S. W. Tait c Adams b Middlebrook	4
M. J. North c Habib b Gough	7	B 3, l-b 4, n-b 2	9
K. J. Coetzer lbw b Danish Kaneria	29		
G. M. Hamilton c Middlebrook b Adams	9		268
†A. Pratt lbw b Danish Kaneria	10		
G. D. Bridge c Jefferson b Danish Kaneria	26		

1/60 (2) 2/64 (3) 3/77 (4)
4/135 (5) 5/156 (6) 6/169 (7)
7/237 (8) 8/258 (1)
9/258 (9) 10/268 (11)

Bonus points – Durham 2, Essex 3.

Bowling: Gough 13–3–34–1; Cowan 21–8–42–2; Adams 25–5–77–1; Danish Kaneria 33–11–70–4; Middlebrook 9.5–2–38–2.

Essex

W. I. Jefferson lbw b Breese	134	†J. S. Foster not out		0
A. P. Grayson c Breese b Bridge	26	L-b 8, n-b 10		18
A. Flower c Plunkett b Hamilton	72			
A. Habib b Bridge	17	1/104 (2) 2/247 (3)		(4 wkts) 274
*R. C. Irani not out	7	3/254 (1) 4/274 (4)		

J. D. Middlebrook, A. P. Cowan, A. R. Adams, D. Gough and Danish Kaneria did not bat.

Bonus points – Essex 2, Durham 1.

Bowling: Tait 6–0–63–0; Plunkett 11–1–49–0; Killeen 11–4–31–0; Hamilton 9–0–57–1; Bridge 9–2–49–2; Breese 6–2–17–1.

Umpires: J. W. Holder and T. E. Jesty.

ESSEX v GLAMORGAN

At Chelmsford, September 2, 3, 4, 5. Glamorgan won by four wickets. Glamorgan 21 pts, Essex 8 pts. Toss: Essex.

After scoring 642 in their first innings Essex had this game under armed guard, not just lock and key. No side had ever lost a first-class match from such a position, but Essex did, making an unwelcome kind of history and, as the game slipped away, losing any realistic chance of promotion. They started imperiously, with three first-innings hundreds: a canny one from Flower, chastened after giving two chances before reaching 30, and more carefree efforts by Irani (also dropped) and Foster, who made 188. Croft conceded 203 in the innings, the first bowling double-century for Glamorgan. Halfway through the second day, Essex were finally all out, on the truest of true pitches, and their expectation of success grew firmer when they had Glamorgan in a mess at 188

HIGHEST INNINGS TOTALS BY LOSING TEAMS

642	**Essex (642 & 165) v Glamorgan (587 & 223-6) at Chelmsford**	**2004**
632	Northants (632 & 155) v Essex (497-7 dec. & 291-6) at Northampton	2002
614	New South Wales (614 & 152) v Victoria (502 & 265-3) at Sydney	1924-25
608	Wellington (608-9 dec. & 35-1 dec.) v N. Dist. (323-5 dec. & 322-7) at Hamilton	1998-99
604†	Maharashtra (407 & 604) v Bombay (651 & 714-8 dec.) at Poona	1948-49
597	Essex (597 & 97) v Derbyshire (548 & 149-1) at Chesterfield	1904
591	Sussex (591 & 312-3 dec.) v Essex (493-4 dec. & 412-3) at Hove	1993

† *Losing team batted second.*

Research: Philip Bailey.

for five. But it proved a topsy-turvy innings. Crucially, the linchpin Maynard was missed twice on 46 by Grayson, the first drop so simple that Grayson's team-mates stared in disbelief. Maynard went on to 136, and the last three wickets added 301 as Croft belted 125 from No. 9 and Harrison made a career-best 88 from No. 10. The Essex bowling was wayward but the pace of Glamorgan's scoring (396 came in the first two sessions of day three) meant Essex were batting again, just 55 ahead, on the third evening. By the close they were floundering at 101 for four, after a hostile spell of three wickets in 11 balls from the Australian fast bowler Mick Lewis. Next morning, Croft's off-spin proved almost as deadly, removing four batsmen quickly and at small cost: the last six wickets fell before lunch, for the addition of only 64 runs. Essex's rock-solid position had melted away like a mirage, and Glamorgan were left a minimum of 69 overs to make 221. They completed their task comfortably, with 22 balls to spare.

Close of play: First day, Essex 445-4 (Irani 145, Foster 95); Second day, Glamorgan 188-5 (Maynard 6, Hughes 0); Third day, Essex 101-4 (Flower 34, Foster 43).

Essex

W. I. Jefferson b Harrison	0	– lbw b Lewis	8
A. P. Grayson c Hemp b Croft	57	– c Hemp b Jones	5
A. Flower c Lewis b Jones	119	– c Hughes b Croft	48
*R. C. Irani c Wallace b Croft	164	– b Lewis	3
R. S. Bopara c Hemp b Jones	4	– c Wallace b Lewis	0
†J. S. Foster c Wallace b Jones	188	– c Hughes b Croft	45
J. D. Middlebrook lbw b Harrison	3	– b Lewis	34
G. R. Napier b Croft	50	– c Wallace b Jones	2
A. R. Adams lbw b Lewis	3	– c Harrison b Croft	6
A. P. Cowan b Jones	25	– c Lewis	0
Danish Kaneria not out	2	– not out	2
B 8, l-b 7, n-b 12	27	L-b 1, w 1, n-b 10	12

1/0 (1) 2/122 (2) 3/268 (3) 4/278 (5)   **642**   1/17 (1) 2/17 (2) 3/22 (4)   **165**
5/488 (4) 6/495 (7) 7/566 (8)   4/22 (5) 5/106 (6) 6/119 (3)
8/583 (9) 9/625 (10) 10/642 (6)   7/124 (8) 8/135 (9)
                                       9/138 (10) 10/165 (7)

Bonus points – Essex 5, Glamorgan 2 (130 overs: 529-6).

Bowling: *First Innings*—Harrison 25–3–101–2; Jones 25.2–3–100–4; Lewis 24–3–126–1; Thomas 21–3–86–0; Croft 58–9–203–3; Maynard 1–0–11–0. *Second Innings*—Jones 16–2–50–2; Lewis 9.1–0–39–4; Croft 19–1–52–4; Harrison 2–0–7 0; Thomas 4–0–16–0.

Glamorgan

D. D. Cherry c Bopara b Danish Kaneria	22	– (2) lbw b Danish Kaneria	17
†M. A. Wallace c Foster b Danish Kaneria	42	– (1) c Flower b Middlebrook	19
D. L. Hemp c Flower b Middlebrook	67	– not out	83
M. J. Powell c Bopara b Middlebrook	31	– run out	10
M. P. Maynard c Bopara b Adams	136	– lbw b Napier	32
M. L. Lewis lbw b Danish Kaneria	0		
J. Hughes c Foster b Cowan	11	– (6) st Foster b Danish Kaneria	24
S. D. Thomas b Danish Kaneria	22	– (7) c Middlebrook b Danish Kaneria	0
*R. D. B. Croft b Napier	125	– (8) not out	28
D. S. Harrison c Flower b Danish Kaneria	88		
S. P. Jones not out	0		
B 6, l-b 16, w 2, n-b 14, p 5	43	B 4, l-b 6	10

1/73 (2) 2/74 (1) 3/182 (3) 4/187 (4)   **587**   1/36 (1) 2/40 (2)   (6 wkts) **223**
5/188 (6) 6/235 (7) 7/286 (8)   3/58 (4) 4/113 (5)
8/449 (5) 9/587 (9) 10/587 (10)   5/153 (6) 6/153 (7)

Bonus points – Glamorgan 5, Essex 3.

Bowling: *First Innings*—Cowan 21–5–79–1; Adams 22–1–107–1; Danish Kaneria 47.2–6–193–5; Napier 12–0–82–1; Middlebrook 18–5–81–2; Grayson 5–1–5–0; Bopara 2–0–13–0. *Second Innings*—Cowan 6–3–15–0; Danish Kaneria 26.2–5–80–3; Middlebrook 18–3–60–1; Napier 7–0–26–1; Adams 5–1–19–0; Grayson 3–0–13–0.

Umpires: I. J. Gould and M. J. Kitchen.

ESSEX v DERBYSHIRE

At Chelmsford, September 9, 10. Essex won by eight wickets. Essex 17 pts, Derbyshire 3 pts. Toss: Derbyshire. County debut: I. D. Hunter.

Despite lying only two strips away from the history-making pitch used in the last game, this one was a bowler's delight. Twenty batsmen fell on the first day and the match was over late on the second. However, the duty pitch inspector, Tony Brown, blamed poor shot selection rather than a wicket which was firm underneath with a little dust on top. It did give spinners early help, and in the first innings Middlebrook took a season's best five for 26 with his off-breaks. Essex's reply to 192 then fell 25 short, though both Flower and Foster completed 1,000 first-class runs, representing a bumper season for the wicket-keeper Foster (who made the landmark for the first time) and a lean one for the batsman Flower. Ian Hunter, Derbyshire's new seamer from Durham, took a wicket with his third ball and three for 32 in all. Spin wrecked Derbyshire's second innings, before Jefferson and Cook put any vagaries in the pitch into perspective by scoring 103 for the first wicket, as Essex rattled to their target of 192 at almost five an over.

Close of play: First day, Essex 167.

Derbyshire

S. D. Stubbings c Stubbins b Palladino	0	– lbw b Napier 7
B. J. France b Napier	2	– b Danish Kaneria 33
J. Moss lbw b Adams	28	– lbw b Adams 11
Hassan Adnan c Cook b Middlebrook	58	– c Flower b Adams 3
C. W. G. Bassano c Foster b Adams	0	– c Cook b Middlebrook 34
*†L. D. Sutton lbw b Middlebrook	48	– c Bopara b Danish Kaneria 44
G. Welch c Jefferson b Adams	5	– c Cook b Middlebrook 0
M. A. Sheikh c Foster b Middlebrook	23	– lbw b Danish Kaneria 8
N. R. C. Dumelow c Cook b Middlebrook	6	– lbw b Danish Kaneria 0
I. D. Hunter b Middlebrook	0	– c Jefferson b Middlebrook 6
P. M. R. Havell not out	5	– not out 2
B 6, l-b 2, w 1, n-b 8	17	B 4, l-b 9, w 1, n-b 4 18

1/0 (1) 2/11 (2) 3/58 (3) 4/58 (5)   192
5/136 (4) 6/141 (7) 7/153 (6)
8/163 (9) 9/163 (10) 10/192 (8)

1/11 (1) 2/26 (3) 3/42 (4)   166
4/91 (2) 5/95 (5) 6/99 (7)
7/120 (8) 8/120 (9)
9/129 (10) 10/166 (6)

Bonus points – Essex 3.

Bowling: *First Innings*—Palladino 7–1–28–1; Napier 5–0–46–1; Adams 14–5–44–3; Bopara 6–0–20–0; Danish Kaneria 12–4–20–0; Middlebrook 14.3–5–26–5. *Second Innings*—Palladino 3–0–17–0; Napier 5–1–14–1; Adams 11–1–39–2; Danish Kaneria 22.4–9–36–4; Middlebrook 14–3–47–3.

Essex

W. I. Jefferson c Sutton b Hunter	0	– c Sutton b Moss 60
A. N. Cook c Sutton b Dumelow	22	– not out 68
A. Flower c Sutton b Havell	5	– c Sutton b Moss 0
*R. C. Irani c Bassano b Havell	0	– not out 43
R. S. Bopara lbw b Sheikh	29	
†J. S. Foster b Welch	22	
J. D. Middlebrook c Sutton b Welch	7	
G. R. Napier b Hunter	52	
A. R. Adams run out	10	
A. P. Palladino b Hunter	0	
Danish Kaneria not out	1	
B 1, l-b 7, n-b 11	19	B 8, l-b 6, w 1, n-b 8 23

1/0 (1) 2/13 (3) 3/21 (4) 4/35 (2)   167
5/66 (6) 6/82 (7) 7/145 (5)
8/159 (9) 9/166 (8) 10/167 (10)

1/103 (1) 2/103 (3)   (2 wkts) 194

Bonus points – Derbyshire 3.

Bowling: *First Innings*—Hunter 8.3–1–32–3; Havell 8–1–23–2; Dumelow 12–2–52–1; Welch 8–2–28–2; Sheikh 4–1–24–1. *Second Innings*—Hunter 6–0–20–0; Havell 7–0–38–0; Welch 7–1–21–0; Dumelow 10–1–58–0; Sheikh 3.3–0–24–0; Moss 6–2–19–2.

Umpires: B. Dudleston and P. Willey.

At Nottingham, September 16, 17, 18, 19. ESSEX lost to NOTTINGHAMSHIRE by three wickets.

GLAMORGAN

White-ball wizards

Edward Bevan

Glamorgan ticked off their main pre-season objectives by returning to the first division of the Championship, after a three-year absence, and by blazing to the one-day League title with such ease that it was all over with three games left. They also reached the semi-finals of the Twenty20 Cup, where they lost out to Leicestershire – the eventual winners. For a side so good at one-day cricket, failing at the third round of the C&G Trophy was a disappointment. This is a tournament Glamorgan have never won in its 42 seasons, but news that it would be played in 2005 with the white ball the team use so well was greeted at Sophia Gardens with interested smiles.

Robert Croft had a memorable year as captain, and as an imaginative leader he made a significant and bold contribution. He was hard when necessary, too. Six weeks before the season, he turned down a request by Jimmy Maher, scheduled to return as an overseas batsman, to miss the two opening Championship games for a friend's wedding in Brisbane. Maher was discarded, which opened the way for the return of the Victorian opener Matthew Elliott, who played for the county in 2000. Over the winter Elliott had enjoyed the most prolific season in the history of the Australian domestic competition, and he came close to maintaining that form, scoring 2,270 runs in all cricket and making a huge impact.

The grey backdrop of the traditional Welsh weather did not help Glamorgan's cause. Rain ate into almost every Championship game at home, with only 125 overs possible in the last two fixtures. They won four games in succession in May and June, but only one match in the second half of the season, at Chelmsford. This, though, will be remembered the longest. Essex piled up 642 in the first innings – and created a world record by losing. Croft, who had become the first Glamorgan bowler to concede more than 200 in an innings, led a spirited effort by the tail: the last three wickets added 301, and Croft reached 125 from No. 9.

That golden match was won with a side including ten players nurtured by the club – an ever-rarer occurrence as more and more counties employed more and more foreigners. As often as not in the Championship, Glamorgan fielded just one player who learned his cricket outside the UK. But Elliott often did the job of two lesser men. He hit four Championship hundreds and was equally destructive in the one-days, especially early in the season.

Glamorgan's 48 batting points were the third-best in Division Two but, in contrast to 2003, they did not rely on the lower order to bale them out. Mark Wallace began with a century against Derbyshire and uncomplainingly combined opening with keeping wicket, though his Championship average of 25.92 signalled that he was being asked to do too much. David Hemp, who had opened his stance at the crease more, was the only batsman other than Elliott to score 1,000 first-class runs.

Both Matthew Maynard and Michael Powell came close, Maynard playing as well as ever and scoring consistently in one-day cricket. He hit three first-class centuries, to beat the previous Glamorgan career record of 52 shared by Hugh Morris and Alan Jones. Powell's early form led to an emergency call-up for England's one-day squad in June, after which he fell away: a winter spent with the ECB Academy should iron out minor deficiencies in technique.

David Harrison

The bowling was strong, as shown in July when Simon Jones was released from the England squad but could not break into the county team to face Hampshire, a decision that raised many eyebrows. However, the incident caused no animosity between him and the club: Jones played in all six remaining games and made up for the loss of Michael Kasprowicz, who managed only seven Championship matches between Test commitments for Australia.

By contrast, Croft and the 23-year-old seamer David Harrison played throughout. Each took 57 first-class wickets, with Harrison joining Powell at the Academy. Meanwhile, Alex Wharf was an important part of the one-day successes, taking a hat-trick to win the League match at Warwickshire, and ending with an astonishing six for five in a losing cause against Kent at Cardiff. He held his own when selected for the England one-day side, and retained a place for the winter. Wharf was joined in Africa by Maynard, whose fielding expertise and eye for reading a game, always valued by the England coach Duncan Fletcher when he was in charge of Glamorgan, earned him the job of assistant coach to the England limited-overs squad.

After 16 summers in the first team, Adrian Dale announced his retirement, and emigrated to New Zealand. As a model professional with an exemplary attitude, he made a telling contribution to a club that is prospering. The development at Cardiff continues: in January, work started on building permanent floodlights at Sophia Gardens and eight day/night games are scheduled for this summer, along with the ground's fifth one-day international, another step towards the goal of staging Wales's first-ever Test match.

GLAMORGAN RESULTS

All first-class matches – Played 17: Won 5, Lost 3, Drawn 9.
County Championship matches – Played 16: Won 5, Lost 2, Drawn 9.

Frizzell County Championship, 3rd in Division 2; Cheltenham & Gloucester Trophy, 3rd round;
totesport League, winners in Division 1; Twenty20 Cup, s-f.

COUNTY CHAMPIONSHIP AVERAGES

BATTING AND FIELDING

Cap		M	I	NO	R	HS	100s	50s	Avge	Ct/St
2000	M. T. G. Elliott§ . . .	14	24	1	1,245	157	4	5	54.13	15
1994	D. L. Hemp	16	27	4	1,037	102*	1	9	45.08	12
1987	M. P. Maynard	15	24	3	906	163	3	4	43.14	14
1997	S. D. Thomas	13	17	5	470	105*	1	3	39.16	8
2000	M. J. Powell	15	25	2	895	124	1	7	38.91	13
1992	R. D. B. Croft.	16	23	4	671	138	2	1	35.31	1
2000	D. A. Cosker.	6	7	5	54	21*	0	0	27.00	7
	D. D. Cherry.	3	5	1	107	29	0	0	26.75	0
2003	M. A. Wallace.	16	26	0	674	105	1	2	25.92	37/3
1992	A. Dale	7	13	3	241	44	0	0	24.10	3
2000	A. G. Wharf.	10	15	1	307	78	0	3	21.92	4
	D. S. Harrison.	16	20	3	370	88	0	1	21.76	7
	J. Hughes.	10	13	0	267	110	1	0	20.53	5
2002	M. S. Kasprowicz§ .	7	11	2	126	42	0	0	14.00	2
2002	S. P. Jones	8	7	4	33	20	0	0	11.00	2

Also batted: A. P. Davies (1 match) 6; M. L. Lewis§ (3 matches), 0 (1 ct); I. J. Thomas (1 match) 29 (1 ct).

§ *Overseas player.*

BOWLING

	O	M	R	W	BB	5W/i	Avge
D. A. Cosker	138.1	37	372	15	3-40	0	24.80
D. S. Harrison.	448.3	118	1,465	53	5-48	3	27.64
S. P. Jones	215.1	31	808	26	5-77	2	31.07
R. D. B. Croft.	629	140	1,866	54	4-52	0	34.55
A. G. Wharf.	249.5	38	1,011	27	5-93	1	37.44
S. D. Thomas	290	30	1,127	29	4-47	0	38.86
M. S. Kasprowicz	272.1	54	893	21	5-54	1	42.52

Also bowled: A. Dale 13–2–42–0; A. P. Davies 31.4–4–130–2; M. T. G. Elliott 1–0–16–0; M. L. Lewis 53.1–5–253–6; M. P. Maynard 7–0–27–0.

COUNTY RECORDS

Highest score for:	309*	S. P. James v Sussex at Colwyn Bay	2000
Highest score against:	322*	M. B. Loye (Northamptonshire) at Northampton. .	1998
Best bowling for:	10-51	J. Mercer v Worcestershire at Worcester	1936
Best bowling against:	10-18	G. Geary (Leicestershire) at Pontypridd	1929
Highest total for:	718-3 dec.	v Sussex at Colwyn Bay	2000
Highest total against:	712	by Northamptonshire at Northampton	1998
Lowest total for:	22	v Lancashire at Liverpool	1924
Lowest total against:	33	by Leicestershire at Ebbw Vale	1965

GLAMORGAN DIRECTORY

ADDRESS

Sophia Gardens, Cardiff CF11 9XR (029 2040 9380; fax 029 2040 9390; email info@glamorgancricket.co.uk). **Website** www.glamorgancricket.com.

GROUNDS

Cardiff (Sophia Gardens): 1 mile NW of city centre between A4119 and River Taff. From city centre take A4119 over the Taff Bridge and filter R into Cathedral Road, then R into Sophia Close. Nearest station: Cardiff Central (1 mile).

Colwyn Bay: Situated in Rhos-on-Sea. From A55 (signposted Rhos-on-Sea), take B5115 Brompton Avenue, continuing on Llandudno Road, then R into Church Road and R into Penrhyn Avenue for ground on R. Nearest station: Colwyn Bay (1½ miles).

Swansea (St Helen's): 1 mile W of city centre on A4067 Oystermouth Road, which becomes Mumbles Road. Then R into Gorse Lane for St Helen's Ground. Nearest station: Swansea (1½ miles).

Abergavenny: ¼ mile NW of town centre. Take A40 Brecon Road then R into Avenue Road. Nearest station: Abergavenny (2 miles).

OFFICIALS

Captain R. D. B. Croft
First-team coach J. Derrick
President C. M. Brain
Chairman R. P. Russell
Chief executive M. J. Fatkin

Chairman, cricket committee R. Needham
Cricket secretary Mrs C. L. Watkin
Head groundsman L. A. Smith
Scorer/Archivist Dr A. K. Hignell

PLAYERS

Players expected to reappear in 2005

	Former counties	Country	Born	Birthplace
Cherry Daniel David		E	7.2.1980	†*Newport*
Cosker Dean Andrew		E	7.1.1978	*Weymouth*
*****Croft** Robert Damien Bale		E	25.5.1970	†*Morriston*
Davies Andrew Philip		E	7.11.1976	†*Neath*
*****Elliott** Matthew Thomas Gray	Yorks	A	28.9.1971	*Chelsea, Aus.*
Harrison Adam James		E	30.10.1985	†*Newport*
Harrison David Stuart.		E	30.7.1981	†*Newport*
Hemp David Lloyd.	Warwicks	E	8.11.1970	*Hamilton, Bermuda*
Hughes Jonathan		E	30.6.1981	†*Pontypridd*
*****Jones** Simon Philip		‡E	25.12.1978	†*Morriston*
*****Kasprowicz** Michael Scott	Essex, Leics	A	10.2.1972	*Brisbane*
*****Maynard** Matthew Peter		E	21.3.1966	*Oldham*
Powell Michael John		E	3.2.1977	†*Abergavenny*
Shaw Adrian David.		E	17.2.1972	†*Neath*
Thomas Ian James		E	9.5.1979	†*Newport*
Thomas Stuart <u>Darren</u>.		E	25.1.1975	†*Morriston*
Wallace Mark Alexander		E	19.11.1981	†*Abergavenny*
Wharf Alexander George.	Yorks, Notts	E	4.6.1975	*Bradford*

* *Test player.*   † *Born in Wales.*   ‡ *12-month ECB contract.*

GLAMORGAN v DERBYSHIRE

At Cardiff, April 16, 17, 18, 19. Drawn. Glamorgan 7 pts, Derbyshire 7 pts. Toss: Glamorgan. County debuts: A. G. Botha, J. D. C. Bryant, C. J. L. Rogers, M. A. Sheikh.

Glamorgan included eight players raised in Wales whereas Derbyshire fielded just one county-born cricketer, Kevin Dean, and six not qualified for England; one paper called it Wales v the Rest of the World. Despite the international talent, neither team gained a batting point on a pitch with enough early-season moisture to encourage the seamers – all told, rain lopped 137 overs from the first and third days. Mohammad Ali, known as Ali Bukhari when Glamorgan gave him a trial in 2001, took two wickets in his second over, and but for an undefeated 37 from Harrison, the last man, Glamorgan might never have passed 150. Ali also batted competently at No. 11 after Derbyshire lost six wickets for 31, and helped restrict the deficit to 11. Wallace then struck an entertaining century, enabling Croft to declare. He set Derbyshire 335 from a minimum of 84 overs but, after losing their openers for seven, they showed no interest in the target. Music from the Chinese State Circus, camped nearby, was an incongruous background noise.

Close of play: First day, Glamorgan 68-3 (Powell 26, Maynard 16); Second day, Glamorgan 23-0 (Elliott 3, Wallace 19); Third day, Glamorgan 277-3 (Powell 79, Maynard 39).

Glamorgan

M. T. G. Elliott c Welch b Mohammad Ali	4	– c Bryant b Welch	3
†M. A. Wallace run out	20	– b Welch	105
D. L. Hemp lbw b Mohammad Ali	0	– lbw b Dean	20
M. J. Powell b Dean	29	– b Botha	94
M. P. Maynard lbw b Dean	26	– not out	59
A. Dale c Gait b Dean	41	– not out	5
*R. D. B. Croft lbw b Dean	0		
S. D. Thomas lbw b Welch	0		
A. G. Wharf b Mohammad Ali	17		
M. S. Kasprowicz b Mohammad Ali	0		
D. S. Harrison not out	37		
L-b 5, n-b 6	11	B 2, l-b 16, w 3, n-b 16	37

1/12 (1) 2/12 (3) 3/38 (2) 4/75 (4)   185   1/23 (1) 2/99 (3)   (4 wkts dec.) 323
5/90 (5) 6/90 (7) 7/93 (8)   3/162 (2) 4/306 (4)
8/128 (9) 9/128 (10) 10/185 (6)

Bonus points – Derbyshire 3.

Bowling: *First Innings*—Mohammad Ali 16–2–75–4; Sheikh 10–0–40–0; Welch 12–6–24–1; Dean 10.3–2–41–4. *Second Innings*—Mohammad Ali 20–2 84–0; Sheikh 3–0–12–0; Welch 21–4–64–2; Dean 14–1–46–1; Botha 16.3–0–95–1; Hassan Adnan 1–0–4–0.

Derbyshire

A. I. Gait lbw b Thomas	31	– lbw b Wharf	4
S. A. Selwood b Wharf	2	– c Maynard b Kasprowicz	1
C. J. L. Rogers c Wallace b Kasprowicz	47	– lbw b Harrison	43
Hassan Adnan c Wallace b Wharf	36	– c Thomas b Wharf	42
J. D. C. Bryant b Thomas	6	– retired hurt	15
*†L. D. Sutton b Harrison	0	– not out	61
G. Welch lbw b Kasprowicz	1	– st Wallace b Croft	48
A. G. Botha lbw b Harrison	0	– not out	12
M. A. Sheikh not out	15		
K. J. Dean run out	0		
Mohammad Ali c Wharf b Thomas	21		
B 1, l-b 3, w 1, n-b 10	15	B 1, l-b 1, n-b 10	12

1/12 (2) 2/75 (1) 3/95 (3) 4/108 (5)   174   1/7 (1) 2/7 (2) 3/69 (3)   (5 wkts) 238
5/126 (6) 6/127 (7) 7/128 (8)   4/114 (4) 5/209 (7)
8/139 (4) 9/139 (10) 10/174 (11)

Bonus points – Glamorgan 3.

In the second innings Bryant retired hurt at 104.

Bowling: *First Innings*—Kasprowicz 17–6–48–2; Wharf 14–2–43–2; Harrison 13–5–31–2; Thomas 11.4–1–48–3. *Second Innings*—Kasprowicz 19–6–62–1; Wharf 19–5–54–2; Harrison 13.4–5–27–1; Thomas 15–2–46–0; Croft 14–3–40–1; Dale 3–1–7–0.

Umpires: M. R. Benson and B. Dudleston.

At Leicester, April 21, 22, 23, 24. GLAMORGAN drew with LEICESTERSHIRE.

At Cardiff, April 28, 29, 30 (not first-class). **Drawn.** Toss: Glamorgan. **Glamorgan 586-9 dec.** (D. L. Hemp 138, M. J. Powell 201 retired out, M. P. Maynard 80, R. D. B. Croft 77; S. J. Collier 4-107, D. J. Nolan 4-234). **Cardiff UCCE 174-1** (R. M. Lewis 70, S. Pope 69*).
   Glamorgan hit their runs at 5.7 an over: the students 2.4. Rain disrupted the second and third days.

At Nottingham, May 7, 8, 9, 10. GLAMORGAN drew with NOTTINGHAMSHIRE.

GLAMORGAN v ESSEX

At Cardiff, May 12, 13, 14, 15. Drawn. Glamorgan 10.5 pts (after 1.5 pt penalty), Essex 12 pts. Toss: Glamorgan. County debut: D. Gough.
   As the final over of this enthralling contest began, Essex's last pair needed 12 for victory, but Napier preferred caution, and the draw. The sixth and seventh deliveries of the over were no-balls, prompting suspicions that they were a deliberate attempt to get Napier interested, but the bowler, Wharf, denied this. Wharf certainly had no role in the other bizarre distraction: in the midst of all this, a male streaker broke the tension by rushing on and stealing umpire Palmer's hat. That morning, Croft had wisely decided to prolong Glamorgan's second innings rather than declare – and the resulting target of 334 from 69 overs ensured the game remained perfectly poised till the end. It had not seemed so delicately balanced when Essex, in answer to Glamorgan's 435, were 115 for five, still 171 short of avoiding the follow-on. But Habib, who went to his fifty and his hundred with straight sixes off Croft, hit his highest score since leaving Leicestershire and, thanks to support from Middlebrook and Napier, steered Essex to a two-run advantage. After contributions down the order from Glamorgan, Hussain led Essex's run-chase with an attacking innings before surrendering with a rash stroke. By then, though, he had done enough to ensure that, in what turned out to be his final innings for Essex before retirement, he would sign off from county cricket as he would nine days later from Tests – with a hundred. Flower too was guilty of failing to capitalise on a productive innings, but Thomas and Jones intelligently bowled a full length to restrict progress. Gough made his Essex debut, though on a placid pitch took only a couple of wickets. He and Hussain were thus team-mates in a solitary Championship match, having shared a dressing-room in 41 Tests.
   Close of play: First day, Glamorgan 346-8 (Wharf 6, Thomas 6); Second day, Essex 301-6 (Habib 131, Napier 9); Third day, Glamorgan 247-7 (Wharf 4, Thomas 11).

Glamorgan

M. T. G. Elliott b Middlebrook	114	– c Flower b Napier	11
†M. A. Wallace c Foster b Napier	0	– b Danish Kaneria	14
D. L. Hemp b Danish Kaneria	55	– c Foster b Napier	21
M. J. Powell st Foster b Danish Kaneria	21	– b Danish Kaneria	61
M. P. Maynard lbw b Napier	64	– c Flower b Middlebrook	63
A. Dale c Foster b Napier	44	– (10) not out	28
*R. D. B. Croft lbw b Danish Kaneria	14	– (6) c Cook b Middlebrook	27
D. S. Harrison b Gough	0	– (7) run out	2
A. G. Wharf b Middlebrook	78	– (8) b Middlebrook	35
S. D. Thomas c Hussain b Napier	23	– (9) c Hussain b Gough	39
S. P. Jones not out	0	– b Middlebrook	0
B 6, l-b 10, n-b 6	22	B 10, l-b 23, w 1	34
	435		**335**

1/4 (2) 2/147 (3) 3/195 (4) 4/207 (1)
5/319 (5) 6/324 (6) 7/327 (8)
8/340 (7) 9/404 (10) 10/435 (9)

1/27 (1) 2/46 (2) 3/58 (3)
4/159 (4) 5/217 (5) 6/223 (7)
7/233 (6) 8/291 (9)
9/335 (8) 10/335 (11)

Bonus points – Glamorgan 5, Essex 3 (130 overs: 432-9).

Bowling: *First Innings*—Gough 23–6–77–1; Napier 26–5–91–4; McCoubrey 13–4–59–0; Middlebrook 24.2–4–70–2; Danish Kaneria 47–9–111–3; Habib 3–1–11–0. *Second Innings*—Gough 16–2–61–1; Danish Kaneria 45–13–91–2; Napier 7–1–31–2; McCoubrey 3–0–27–0; Middlebrook 27–5–92–4.

Essex

A. N. Cook c Croft b Harrison	10	– c Wallace b Thomas	51
N. Hussain lbw b Harrison	0	– c Maynard b Thomas	102
W. I. Jefferson c Wallace b Harrison	4	– c Wallace b Jones	5
*A. Flower lbw b Wharf	38	– c Jones b Thomas	66
A. Habib b Harrison	157	– lbw b Thomas	2
†J. S. Foster c Maynard b Croft	17	– c Thomas b Jones	26
J. D. Middlebrook c Maynard b Thomas	80	– b Jones	28
G. R. Napier c Powell b Thomas	82	– not out	13
D. Gough c sub b Harrison	16	– c sub b Wharf	3
Danish Kaneria not out	13	– lbw b Wharf	0
A. G. A. M. McCoubrey lbw b Thomas	0	– not out	0
L-b 6, w 2, n-b 12	20	B 5, l-b 17, w 1, n-b 6	29
	437	(9 wkts)	**325**

1/1 (2) 2/10 (1) 3/25 (3) 4/88 (4)
5/115 (6) 6/285 (7) 7/365 (5)
8/401 (9) 9/437 (8) 10/437 (11)

1/124 (1) 2/138 (3)
3/215 (2) 4/228 (5)
5/249 (4) 6/287 (6)
7/311 (7) 8/316 (9) 9/316 (10)

Bonus points – Essex 5, Glamorgan 3.

Bowling: *First Innings*—Harrison 28–11–99–5; Thomas 19.3–1–85–3; Croft 21–1–95–1; Jones 22–3–75–0; Wharf 14–0–77–1. *Second Innings*—Harrison 11–1–63–0; Wharf 15–0–71–2; Croft 20–2–78–0; Thomas 11–0–47–4; Jones 12–0–44–3.

Umpires: R. Palmer and P. Willey.

> " So who would make way? No one was considering the implications more clearly than a 36-year-old ex-captain already known to be close to retirement."
>
> The New Zealanders in England, page 455.

At Chester-le-Street, May 19, 20, 21. GLAMORGAN beat DURHAM by 201 runs.

At Derby, May 25, 26, 27, 28. GLAMORGAN beat DERBYSHIRE by 128 runs.

GLAMORGAN v SOMERSET

At Swansea, June 2, 3, 4, 5. Glamorgan won by seven wickets. Glamorgan 21 pts, Somerset 4 pts. Toss: Somerset.

For the fourth time in five years, Glamorgan's trip to St Helen's brought Championship success, this time with almost two sessions to spare. Somerset won the toss, but gained little advantage as Harrison claimed a career-best five for 48 and Croft his 800th first-class wicket. Thanks to a splendid, big-hitting hundred from Elliott, Glamorgan sailed past Somerset's 229 with one wicket down. At 312 for three, they were in total control, going to subside to 388. A belligerent century from Blackwell in Somerset's second innings gave his bowlers a slim chance before Elliott again treated them with disdain, adding 109 with Hemp for the second wicket. These two fell to successive balls, but Glamorgan still ended the game with a flurry of boundaries. Johnson bowled just one second-innings over before leaving the field with a recurrence of a knee injury, and all told Caddick sent down 38 innocuous and wicketless overs. Before the third day, Somerset coach Kevin Shine was summoned to Taunton by the chief executive, Peter Anderson, to discuss strategy for the rest of the summer. There were rumours about his future but Anderson insisted: "There was no question of him being sacked."

Close of play: First day, Glamorgan 180-1 (Elliott 129, Hemp 26); Second day, Somerset 84-3 (Cox 38, Burns 22); Third day, Glamorgan 46-0 (Wallace 5, Elliott 37).

Somerset

P. D. Bowler lbw b Kasprowicz	4	– lbw b Kasprowicz	2
N. J. Edwards c Powell b Harrison	4	– c Wallace b Wharf	15
J. Cox c Wallace b Harrison	2	– c Cosker b Wharf	50
J. C. Hildreth c Cosker b Harrison	61	– c Hughes b Wharf	0
*M. Burns c and b Harrison	11	– c Hughes b Cosker	54
I. D. Blackwell c Cosker b Croft	64	– c Hemp b Croft	131
†R. J. Turner c Cosker b Harrison	2	– lbw b Cosker	18
K. P. Dutch lbw b Croft	31	– c Wallace b Harrison	27
R. L. Johnson c Cosker b Croft	17	– c Maynard b Croft	27
A. R. Caddick not out	9	– not out	22
N. A. M. McLean c Powell b Kasprowicz		– lbw b Croft	7
B 1, l-b 8, n-b 14	23	B 3, l-b 11, w 1, n-b 2	17
	229		**370**

1/10 (2) 2/12 (1) 3/16 (3) 4/71 (5)
5/94 (4) 6/112 (7) 7/196 (6)
8/200 (8) 9/227 (9) 10/229 (11)

1/8 (1) 2/28 (2) 3/28 (4)
4/125 (3) 5/152 (5) 6/202 (7)
7/266 (8) 8/324 (6)
9/345 (9) 10/370 (11)

Bonus points – Somerset 1, Glamorgan 3.

Bowling: *First Innings*—Kasprowicz 16.5–1–87–2; Harrison 17–5–48–5; Wharf 10–2–41–0; Croft 11–3–44–3. *Second Innings*—Kasprowicz 30–7–101–1; Harrison 20–4–57–1; Croft 38.4–12–78–3; Cosker 33–13–62–2; Wharf 16–3–58–3.

Glamorgan

M. T. G. Elliott c Johnson b Blackwell	157	– (2) c Turner b Dutch	87
†M. A. Wallace c Turner b McLean	22	– (1) c Edwards b McLean	5
D. L. Hemp c Turner b Johnson	66	– c Burns b Blackwell	57
M. J. Powell b McLean	36	– not out	21
M. P. Maynard c Hildreth b Dutch	25	– not out	31
J. Hughes c Turner b Johnson	35		
*R. D. B. Croft c Burns b McLean	6		
A. G. Wharf c Cox b McLean	0		
D. S. Harrison c Turner b Johnson	22		
M. S. Kasprowicz b Johnson	0		
D. A. Cosker not out	4		
L-b 13, n-b 2	15	B 4, l-b 1, n-b 6	11

1/53 (2) 2/233 (3) 3/253 (1) 4/312 (5)   388   1/49 (1) 2/158 (3)   (3 wkts) 212
5/314 (4) 6/324 (7) 7/324 (8)   3/158 (2)
8/367 (9) 9/367 (10) 10/388 (6)

Bonus points – Glamorgan 4, Somerset 3.

Bowling: *First Innings*—Caddick 25–1–93–0; Johnson 26.1–8–83–4; McLean 19–5–91–4; Dutch 25–8–85–1; Blackwell 7–2–23–1. *Second Innings*—Caddick 13–4–49–0; Johnson 1 0–10–0; McLean 12–1–62–1; Blackwell 13.5–1–52–1; Dutch 9–1–34–1.

Umpires: I. J. Gould and J. W. Holder.

GLAMORGAN v LEICESTERSHIRE

At Cardiff, June 9, 10, 11, 12. Glamorgan won by 409 runs. Glamorgan 20 pts, Leicestershire 5 pts. Toss: Glamorgan.

Five minutes before lunch on the final day Glamorgan won their fourth successive Championship match, their largest-ever victory in terms of runs. Croft had delayed his declaration until after tea on the previous evening, but his bowlers needed less than 51 overs to dismiss Leicestershire. On the opening day, Maynard hit his 53rd hundred for Glamorgan, beating the record he had shared with Alan Jones and Hugh Morris since reaching his 52nd in April. He had scored a century on debut against Yorkshire in 1985, when Peter Hartley held the catch that ended his innings. Hartley

LARGEST CHAMPIONSHIP WINS BY RUNS

483	Surrey (494 and 492-9 dec.) beat Leicestershire (361 and 142) at The Oval	2002
470	Sussex (309 and 307-5 dec.) beat Gloucestershire (66 and 80) at Hove	1913
429	Kent (224 and 343-4 dec.) beat Northamptonshire (92 and 46) at Dover.	1933
423	Lancashire (277 and 405) beat Somerset (193 and 66) at Liverpool.	1911
419	Somerset (344 and 264-6 dec.) beat Kent (116 and 73) at Bath	1937
409	**Glamorgan (333 and 468-9 dec.) beat Leicestershire (255 and 137) at Cardiff** .	**2004**

was there to see him again – this time as umpire. In Leicestershire's reply, Maddy struck his first Championship century since 2002 to keep the deficit down to 78. And when they had Glamorgan 96 for five in their second innings, they were in contention. But a sixth-wicket stand of 218 between Hughes, who hit a maiden first-class hundred, and Croft enabled Glamorgan to set a target of 547. Hughes's father had chosen the perfect day to hire a hospitality box.

Close of play: First day, Leicestershire 46-3 (Maddy 25, Henderson 8); Second day, Glamorgan 157-5 (Hughes 29, Croft 29); Third day, Leicestershire 51-2 (Hodge 23).

Glamorgan

M. T. G. Elliott c and b DeFreitas	31	– (2) b Dagnall	42
†M. A. Wallace c Nixon b Gibson	5	– (1) lbw b DeFreitas	19
D. L. Hemp c Hodge b Gibson	26	– c Nixon b DeFreitas	10
M. J. Powell c Maddy b Gibson	9	– st Nixon b Henderson	5
M. P. Maynard c Maddy b DeFreitas	114	– c Nixon b Cleary	13
J. Hughes c Nixon b Maddy	21	– c Nixon b Henderson	110
*R. D. B. Croft c Maddy b Gibson	20	– c Robinson b Henderson	138
A. G. Wharf b Gibson	0	– b Hodge	51
D. S. Harrison c Henderson b Maddy	42	– c Sadler b Henderson	21
M. S. Kasprowicz c Gibson b DeFreitas	42	– not out	14
D. A. Cosker not out	1	– not out	11
B 5, l-b 7, w 2, n-b 8	22	B 15, l-b 9, w 6, n-b 4	34

1/14 (2) 2/56 (1) 3/83 (4) 4/90 (3)　　　　333
5/117 (6) 6/165 (7) 7/169 (8)
8/248 (9) 9/332 (5) 10/333 (10)

1/52 (2) 2/70 (1)　　(9 wkts dec.) 468
3/79 (4) 4/83 (3)
5/96 (5) 6/314 (6)
7/411 (7) 8/439 (8) 9/445 (9)

Bonus points – Glamorgan 3, Leicestershire 3.

Bowling: *First Innings*—Gibson 19–3–80–5; Dagnall 18–2–60–0; Cleary 19–1–74–0; DeFreitas 13–4–44–3; Maddy 9–1–41–2; Henderson 3–0–22–0. *Second Innings*—Gibson 14–1–66–0; Dagnall 15–0–64–1; DeFreitas 14.1–1–51–2; Hodge 14–2–46–1; Henderson 45–9–146–4; Cleary 11.5–0–53–1; Maddy 5–0–18–0.

Leicestershire

D. D. J. Robinson lbw b Harrison	5	– (2) lbw b Kasprowicz	18
J. K. Maunders c Elliott b Kasprowicz	3	– (1) c Powell b Croft	8
B. J. Hodge b Harrison	5	– b Kasprowicz	61
D. L. Maddy c Powell b Cosker	145	– lbw b Harrison	3
C. W. Henderson c Harrison b Cosker	15	– (9) c Hughes b Croft	1
J. L. Sadler c Hemp b Croft	33	– (5) c Wallace b Harrison	1
†P. A. Nixon c Wallace b Harrison	4	– c and b Wharf	14
*P. A. J. DeFreitas c Wallace b Cosker	6	– (6) b Harrison	0
O. D. Gibson b Croft	15	– (8) c Wallace b Wharf	0
C. E. Dagnall c Elliott b Croft	1	– lbw b Wharf	5
M. F. Cleary not out	17	– not out	8
B 5, l-b 1	6	L-b 2, n-b 16	18

1/7 (1) 2/13 (2) 3/13 (3) 4/77 (5)　　　　255
5/129 (6) 6/146 (7) 7/166 (8)
8/184 (9) 9/194 (10) 10/255 (4)

1/22 (2) 2/51 (1) 3/59 (4)　　　137
4/63 (5) 5/63 (6) 6/98 (7)
7/100 (8) 8/105 (9)
9/120 (10) 10/137 (3)

Bonus points – Leicestershire 2, Glamorgan 3.

Bowling: *First Innings*—Kasprowicz 22–5–60–1; Harrison 18–8–49–3; Cosker 12.1–3–40–3; Croft 20–4–70–3; Wharf 7–0–30–0. *Second Innings*—Kasprowicz 16.3–5–43–2; Harrison 11–6–17–3; Wharf 9–1–37–3; Croft 11–5–20–2; Cosker 3–0–18–0.

Umpires: P. J. Hartley and A. A. Jones.

GLAMORGAN v DURHAM

At Cardiff, June 23, 24, 25, 26. Drawn. Toss: Durham. Glamorgan 9 pts, Durham 11 pts. First-class debut: K. J. Coetzer.

With Kasprowicz (who had taken nine in an innings against Durham twice in 2003) and Elliott both in Australia, the entire Glamorgan side was England-qualified; in fact, with the exception of Wharf, all were coached as youngsters at the club. Durham included two non-England qualified players: North, from Western Australia, struck a career-best 219, lasting 353 minutes and 288 balls and featuring 29 fours and two sixes, while Gareth Breese, a Jamaican with a Welsh father and a British passport, scored 76 after being promoted to open. Durham had also hoped to field the Pakistan fast bowler, Shoaib Akhtar, for just his third first-class appearance of the summer, but he returned to the team hotel with a virus. Kyle Coetzer, a 20-year-old born and raised in Aberdeen (his father is South African), scored a half-century on his first-class debut as Durham secured maximum batting points for the first time in 2004. Glamorgan were in danger of following on at 150 for seven – and were still not out of the woods after Wharf and Thomas put on 108, which at least earned two batting points. Rain prevented play on the first and last days.

Close of play: First day, No play; Second day, Durham 407-4 (North 190, Coetzer 62); Third day, Glamorgan 258-7 (Wharf 53, S. D. Thomas 52).

Durham

*J. J. B. Lewis b Harrison	27	A. M. Davies c Hemp b Croft		2
G. R. Breese b Cosker	76	G. Onions not out		0
G. J. Muchall lbw b S. D. Thomas	23			
M. J. North c I. J. Thomas b Croft	219	L-b 7		7
N. Peng b S. D. Thomas	28			
K. J. Coetzer lbw b Harrison	67	1/65 (1) 2/103 (3) 3/143 (2)		466
†A. Pratt b Harrison	9	4/234 (5) 5/422 (6) 6/438 (7)		
G. D. Bridge lbw b Croft	4	7/460 (4) 8/460 (8)		
N. Killeen b Cosker	4	9/466 (10) 10/466 (9)		

Bonus points – Durham 5, Glamorgan 3.

Bowling: Harrison 27–5–116–3; Wharf 18–3–79–0; S. D. Thomas 19–4–62–2; Croft 42–8–128–3; Cosker 23.1–1–74–2.

Glamorgan

I. J. Thomas b Bridge	29	A. G. Wharf not out		53
D. D. Cherry lbw b Breese	29	S. D. Thomas not out		52
D. L. Hemp b Killeen	37	B 4, l-b 9, n-b 2		15
M. P. Maynard lbw b Davies	17			
J. Hughes c and b Onions	7	1/42 (1) 2/105 (2) 3/105 (3)	(7 wkts)	258
†M. A. Wallace b Onions	0	4/121 (5) 5/121 (6)		
*R. D. B. Croft c Peng b Davies	19	6/145 (7) 7/150 (4)		

D. S. Harrison and D. A. Cosker did not bat.

Bonus points – Glamorgan 2, Durham 2.

Bowling: Killeen 15–2–50–1; Onions 11–2–34–2; Davies 13–3–31–2; Bridge 23–2–88–1; Breese 18–6–42–1.

Umpires: T. E. Jesty and J. F. Steele.

At Cardiff, July 9. GLAMORGAN lost to SRI LANKA A by 141 runs (see Sri Lanka A tour section).

At Swansea, July 21, 22, 23, 24. GLAMORGAN lost to SRI LANKA A by four wickets (see Sri Lanka A tour section).

GLAMORGAN v HAMPSHIRE

At Cardiff, July 29, 30, 31. Hampshire won by nine wickets. Hampshire 19 pts, Glamorgan 6 pts. Toss: Glamorgan.

Glamorgan controversially left out their England fast bowler Simon Jones, who had been released from the Edgbaston Test squad in time to play in this fixture. Glamorgan did not want to change a balanced attack, and England, while keen for Jones to play, said they could not tell a county who to pick. After discussions with the management, Jones accepted the decision. As it turned out, Glamorgan could have done with him, especially in Hampshire's second innings when an attack missing Wharf (with a hip injury) and Cosker (broken finger) could not interrupt the batsmen's waltz to victory. A Hampshire win looked unlikely when they ended the first day 16 for three, still 285 behind. But Clarke led a recovery with his third successive Championship century – a feat last achieved for Hampshire by Gordon Greenidge in 1986 – and Warne kept up the momentum with the ball. His second-innings six for 65 were his best figures of the summer, and he made everyone struggle except Elliott, his Victorian team-mate, who carried his bat, the seventh time since the war this feat has been achieved for Glamorgan.

Close of play: First day, Hampshire 16-3 (Crawley 0); Second day, Glamorgan 44-2 (Elliott 19, Powell 3).

Glamorgan

M. T. G. Elliott c Warne b Mascarenhas	54	– (2) not out 77
†M. A. Wallace c Clarke b Mullally	23	– (1) b Bruce 2
D. L. Hemp c Pothas b Mascarenhas	77	– b Warne 7
M. J. Powell c Crawley b Udal	72	– c Clarke b Warne 10
M. P. Maynard c Clarke b Bruce	7	– st Pothas b Warne 9
J. Hughes c Pothas b Bruce	23	– b Warne 7
*R. D. B. Croft b Warne	16	– c Clarke b Mascarenhas 1
A. G. Wharf lbw b Warne	0	– lbw b Mascarenhas 0
D. S. Harrison lbw b Udal	7	– c and b Mascarenhas 15
M. S. Kasprowicz lbw b Warne	0	– c Clarke b Warne 8
D. A. Cosker not out	3	– c Pothas b Warne 13
B 1, l-b 1, w 1, n-b 16 19		B 2, l-b 1, w 5, n-b 7, p 5 . . 20

1/56 (2) 2/145 (1) 3/182 (3) 4/200 (5) 301 1/2 (1) 2/37 (3) 3/75 (4) 4/89 (5) 169
5/256 (6) 6/287 (7) 7/289 (8)   5/97 (6) 6/100 (7) 7/100 (8)
8/291 (4) 9/291 (10) 10/301 (9)   8/120 (9) 9/130 (10) 10/169 (11)

Bonus points – Glamorgan 3, Hampshire 3.

Bowling: *First Innings*—Bruce 15-2-62-2; Mullally 13-3-45-1; Mascarenhas 18-5-69-2; Udal 13.5-2-46-2; Warne 27-5-77-3; Clarke 2-2-0-0. *Second Innings*—Bruce 9-1-27-1; Mullally 6-2-9-0; Mascarenhas 25-8-53-3; Warne 27.5-6-65-6; Udal 2-0-7-0.

Hampshire

D. A. Kenway lbw b Wharf	5	
M. J. Brown lbw b Harrison	6	– c Elliott b Kasprowicz 57
S. D. Udal c Powell b Harrison	3	
J. P. Crawley lbw b Croft	18	– (3) not out 45
M. J. Clarke c Cosker b Croft	109	
†N. Pothas c Powell b Kasprowicz	18	
J. H. K. Adams c Hemp b Kasprowicz	75	– (1) not out 65
A. D. Mascarenhas c Powell b Croft	2	
*S. K. Warne b Cosker	29	
J. T. A. Bruce run out	9	
A. D. Mullally not out	0	
B 2, l-b 8, w 2, n-b 12 24		B 2, l-b 2, n-b 2 6

1/11 (2) 2/16 (3) 3/16 (1) 4/76 (4) 298 1/99 (2) (1 wkt) 173
5/147 (6) 6/193 (5) 7/195 (8)
8/251 (9) 9/296 (10) 10/298 (7)

Bonus points – Hampshire 2, Glamorgan 3.

Bowling: *First Innings*—Kasprowicz 24–5–71–2; Harrison 20–8–52–2; Wharf 13–1–56–1; Croft 28–5–68–3; Cosker 10–3–41–1. *Second Innings*—Kasprowicz 13–2–49–1; Harrison 10–3–37–0; Croft 18.1–5–59–0; Elliott 1–0–16–0; Maynard 3–0–8–0.

Umpires: B. Dudleston and G. Sharp.

At Taunton, August 3, 4, 5. GLAMORGAN lost to SOMERSET by eight wickets.

At Southampton, August 11, 12, 13, 14. GLAMORGAN drew with HAMPSHIRE.

GLAMORGAN v YORKSHIRE

At Colwyn Bay, August 24, 25, 26, 27. Drawn. Glamorgan 5 pts, Yorkshire 4 pts. Toss: Glamorgan. First-class debut: R. M. Pyrah. Championship debut: M. L. Lewis.

Only 51 overs were bowled, a frustration which Glamorgan blamed on two weeks of almost continuous rain in the build-up, and David Byas, Yorkshire's director of cricket, blamed on inadequate covers. Either way, one of the run-ups remained prohibitively sodden. Yorkshire were desperate for a win, which would have taken them neck-and-neck with Glamorgan for the third promotion spot; instead, Glamorgan pulled one point further ahead. In the brief snatch of play on the third afternoon, Mick Lewis, the Victorian pace bowler who had replaced Kasprowicz for Glamorgan, took a wicket with his tenth ball in Championship cricket; also on debut, Richard Pyrah, a 21-year-old batsman from Dewsbury, withstood a testing spell from Jones. But after further rain, the captains shook hands in glorious last-morning sunshine, half an hour before the scheduled start.

Close of play. First day, No play; Second day, No play; Third day, Yorkshire 158-5 (Pyrah 25, Dawood 11).

Yorkshire

*M. J. Wood c Wallace b Lewis	5	†I. Dawood not out	11
P. A. Jaques lbw b Thomas	21		
A. McGrath c Maynard b Jones	46	B 4, l-b 1, w 1, n-b 16	22
J. J. Sayers c Powell b Harrison	18		
R. M. Pyrah not out	25	1/9 (1) 2/61 (2) 3/96 (3) (5 wkts) 158	
V. J. Craven c Wallace b Harrison	10	4/131 (4) 5/145 (6)	

R. K. J. Dawson, J. A. R. Blain, T. T. Bresnan and S. P. Kirby did not bat.

Bonus point – Glamorgan 1.

Bowling: Harrison 12–5–36–2; Lewis 7–0–25–1; Thomas 10–2–24–1; Jones 9–1–49–1; Croft 10–5–11–0; Maynard 3–0–8–0.

Glamorgan

M. T. G. Elliott, †M. A. Wallace, D. L. Hemp, M. J. Powell, M. P. Maynard, J. Hughes, *R. D. B. Croft, S. D. Thomas, M. L. Lewis, D. S. Harrison and S. P. Jones.

Umpires: B. Leadbeater and A. G. T. Whitehead.

At Chelmsford, September 2, 3, 4, 5. GLAMORGAN beat ESSEX by four wickets.

GLAMORGAN v NOTTINGHAMSHIRE

At Cardiff, September 10, 11, 12, 13. Drawn. Glamorgan 6 pts, Nottinghamshire 6 pts. Toss: Nottinghamshire.

After three summers in Division Two, Glamorgan were promoted at 10 a.m. on the final morning, when news came through on the internet that Somerset's game against Yorkshire at Taunton had been abandoned as a rainy draw. The weather frowned on Cardiff too, and only 74 overs were bowled. Singh celebrated a first century for Nottinghamshire, in only his fourth first-class appearance of the season. But when the game was abandoned an hour after learning of their promotion, Nottinghamshire were still 27 runs short of the third bonus point that would have secured the Division Two title.

Close of play: First day, No play; Second day, Nottinghamshire 165-6 (Singh 62, Franks 0); Third day, Nottinghamshire 273-6 (Singh 112, Franks 52).

Nottinghamshire

D. J. Bicknell c Wallace b Jones	3	M. A. Ealham lbw b Harrison	30
*J. E. R. Gallian b Harrison	10	P. J. Franks not out	52
A. Singh not out	112	L-b 4, n-b 16	20
K. P. Pietersen b Croft	20		
D. J. Hussey b Croft	11	1/7 (1) 2/13 (2) 3/49 (4)	(6 wkts) 273
†C. M. W. Read run out	15	4/77 (5) 5/103 (6) 6/162 (7)	

G. J. Smith, R. J. Sidebottom and S. C. G. MacGill did not bat.

Bonus points – Nottinghamshire 2, Glamorgan 2.

Bowling: Harrison 14–7–23–2; Jones 19–3–83–1; Lewis 13–2–63–0; Croft 23–2–77–2; Thomas 5–0–23–0.

Glamorgan

M. T. G. Elliott, †M. A. Wallace, D. L. Hemp, M. J. Powell, M. P. Maynard, J. Hughes, S. D. Thomas, *R. D. B. Croft, D. S. Harrison, S. P. Jones and M. L. Lewis.

Umpires: N. G. Cowley and J. H. Hampshire.

At Leeds, September 16, 17, 18, 19. GLAMORGAN drew with YORKSHIRE.

CRICKET SOCIETY AWARDS, 2004

The Cricket Society made four Wetherell Awards to all-round cricketers, to Robert Croft of Glamorgan (leading all-rounder in the first-class game), Jamie Dalrymple of Middlesex (leading young first-class all-rounder), Jack O'Sullivan of Merchant Taylors' School, Northwood (leading all-rounder in schools cricket) and Luke Harvey (leading all-rounder at Repton School). James Hildreth of Somerset won the Cricket Society's Most Promising Young Cricketer Award; Kathryn Brunt of Yorkshire won the women's equivalent. The Sir John Hobbs Jubilee Memorial Prize for the outstanding Under-16 schoolboy went to Greg Wood, of Queen Elizabeth's Grammar School, and the A. A. Thomson Fielding Prize for the best schoolboy fielder to Stuart Meaker of Cranleigh. The Don Rowan Memorial Trophy, for primary schools promoting cricket, was given to St Aidan's RC Primary School, Coulsdon, and the Christopher Box-Grainger Memorial Trophy for schools promoting cricket to under-privileged children went to Horizon School in Hackney.

GLOUCESTERSHIRE

Grim start, glorious finish

GRAHAM RUSSELL

Gloomy head-shaking turned into smiles as, defying all predictions, Gloucestershire stayed up in the Championship's first division, retained the C&G Trophy, and saw Craig Spearman hit the county's highest score. On top of this, the club managed to report their first profit in five years and buy back their Bristol headquarters, which they had sold in a leaseback arrangement in 1976.

Foreboding was understandable after the loss of several significant figures from 2003. John Bracewell, who had seen Gloucestershire to six one-day titles, had left to coach his native New Zealand; of two key overseas players, South Africa's Jonty Rhodes had retired, while Australian Ian Harvey took his considerable one-day skills to Yorkshire. With money tight, the county promoted internally, making club captain Mark Alleyne head coach while Chris Taylor unexpectedly became captain of the first-class side; they also held on to ageing players whose fitness was in doubt. Jack Russell, that cult figure among wicket-keepers, played three games, agreed an extension of his contract, and was then forced to retire by a chronic back condition. Adding to the sombre mood, Gerry Collis, a popular president, died suddenly in May.

It was a daunting inheritance for Taylor, whose first match in charge was a seven-wicket defeat by Kent. By the end of May, Gloucestershire were in the relegation zones of both first divisions. Even when they turned things round, with three Championship wins out of four in June carrying them into second place, the critical view was that they were punching above their weight, and they did end up having to fend off relegation. They redeemed a disastrous start in the totesport League – five defeats out of six – by winning five in a row to finish fifth. And an eight-wicket thrashing of Worcestershire in the C&G Trophy final confirmed their status as knockout kings.

As coach, Alleyne was seeking to graft that reputation on to the four-day side. Fascinated by tactics, he gave his players the edge to handle the more attritional first-division game through planning and close analysis of the opposition. His experience was always there for Taylor, and he continued to lead the one-day team.

Gloucestershire's Championship turnaround was epitomised when Spearman batted himself into history with a county record 341 against Middlesex at Gloucester. He was only the club's third triple-centurion, after W. G. Grace and Wally Hammond. A couple of months later, Spearman took 237 off champions-elect Warwickshire. With Philip Weston, he forged one of the most successful opening partnerships in the country: Spearman the aggressive right-hander, thinking of every ball as a potential scoring chance, the left-handed Weston more orthodox and conservative. They put on 227 against Middlesex, but their sheer consistency was highlighted by the C&G

Trophy: three stands in the seventies plus one of 118, all topped in the final as they demolished Worcestershire by reaching 141 in 27 overs. Together, they gave the top order a stability unknown for years.

It had been expected that Spearman, Alleyne's deputy in 2003, would become captain, but the cricket committee under Tony Brown reasoned that he would be more valuable focusing on his batting. Their strategy was spectacularly justified. Taylor's appointment was a surprise: in the last two seasons, his batting average

Craig Spearman

had been in the low twenties, and in 2003 the presence of Rhodes had restricted him to four Championship appearances. But with the responsibility of captaincy, he unearthed his earlier form to lead from the crease, making 1,077 with a mix of graft and style, and matched Spearman's four centuries and four fifties.

Alex Gidman made eight fifties but was held back by injuries to hand and foot. Matt Windows was disappointing; Tim Hancock dropped out of the Championship team for three months but found form in September and was awarded a benefit. From July, the batting was boosted by the Australian Mike Hussey, ever reliable but never quite finding those explosive hot spots. Five overseas players represented a profligate policy not to be repeated; the costs and frustrations swung thoughts towards domestic talent. The Yorkshire fast bowler Steve Kirby was signed for 2005.

The success of Stephen Adshead, rescued from the fringes of Leicestershire and Worcestershire to be Russell's understudy, hastened the trend. He had hoped for a few games as a batsman but, catapulted into the side, quickly showed an aptitude to boss the field, and much of Russell's durability with the bat. Seven not-outs boosted his average to 38.06, allied to 41 dismissals: a very solid first year.

Above all, this was a happy summer for the dressing-room. The one serious complaint surfaced from Jon Lewis, who felt he was over-bowled and short of back-up. But 57 wickets carried him close to the England touring party, and he ended speculation of a move to Warwickshire by signing a fresh three-year deal. Gloucestershire had persuaded Mike Smith to stay for one last summer, but he was picked only twice in the Championship, though he plunged Sussex to defeat with three wickets in ten balls at Arundel. With no other front-line bowler, the county plugged the gap with overseas players. But left-arm spinner Ian Fisher finished with 23 first-class wickets, and James Averis with 28; Averis also had the distinction of collecting the first hat-trick in a Lord's final for 30 years.

GLOUCESTERSHIRE RESULTS

All first-class matches – Played 17: Won 3, Lost 3, Drawn 11.
County Championship matches – Played 16: Won 3, Lost 3, Drawn 10.

Frizzell County Championship, 6th in Division 1; Cheltenham & Gloucester Trophy, winners;
totesport League, 5th in Division 1; Twenty20 Cup, 5th in Midlands/Wales/West Group.

COUNTY CHAMPIONSHIP AVERAGES

BATTING AND FIELDING

Cap		M	I	NO	R	HS	100s	50s	Avge	Ct/St
2002	C. M. Spearman . . .	16	27	2	1,424	341	4	4	56.96	15
2001	C. G. Taylor	16	25	1	1,077	177	4	4	44.87	6
1998	T. H. C. Hancock . .	8	12	1	441	77*	0	4	40.09	4
	S. J. Adshead	15	23	7	609	61	0	4	38.06	39/2
1990	M. W. Alleyne. .	4	5	1	149	77*	0	2	37.25	5
	M. E. K. Hussey§ . .	7	13	1	442	78	0	2	36.83	10
	W. P. C. Weston. . .	16	27	1	922	135	2	4	35.46	18
	J. E. C. Franklin§ . .	3	6	2	134	44	0	0	33.50	1
	A. P. R. Gidman . . .	15	23	0	745	82	0	8	32.39	12
1996	M. C. J. Ball	7	10	4	155	38	0	0	25.83	4
	Shabbir Ahmed§ . . .	6	6	4	51	34*	0	0	25.50	1
1998	M. G. N. Windows. .	8	12	2	240	58	0	1	24.00	4
2001	J. M. M. Averis. . . .	12	11	4	150	48*	0	0	21.42	2
	I. D. Fisher.	11	17	0	320	45	0	0	18.82	4
1998	J. Lewis.	16	15	4	193	34*	0	0	17.54	1
	Shoaib Malik§.	6	9	1	134	63	0	1	16.75	2

Also batted: N. W. Bracken§ (2 matches) 8, 13*; A. N. Bressington (2 matches) 58*, 19*;
M. A. Hardinges (1 match) 68* (3 ct); R. C. Russell (cap 1985) (1 match) 2; R. J. Sillence
(2 matches) 92, 4; A. M. Smith (cap 1995) (2 matches) 3*, 9 (1 ct).

§ *Overseas player. Gloucestershire have abandoned the traditional system of caps.*

BOWLING

	O	M	R	W	BB	5W/i	Avge
J. E. C. Franklin	83.1	27	252	12	7-60	1	21.00
J. Lewis.	472.4	121	1,440	57	7-72	4	25.26
Shabbir Ahmed	169	38	605	18	4-96	0	33.61
J. M. M. Averis	271.2	47	1,075	26	6-32	2	41.34
I. D. Fisher.	320.4	61	1,073	23	5-114	1	46.65
Shoaib Malik	176	30	530	10	3-109	0	53.00
M. C. J. Ball	169	23	564	10	3-96	0	56.40
A. P. R. Gidman	173	32	695	12	2-12	0	57.91

Also bowled: M. W. Alleyne 56.3–16–206–9; N. W. Bracken 39–12–106–5; A. N. Bressington
12–0–93–1; T. H. C. Hancock 31–6–98–0; M. A. Hardinges 30–4–120–1; M. E. K. Hussey
8–2–22–0; R. J. Sillence 52–19–135–5; A. M. Smith 42.4–12–120–6; C. G. Taylor 1–0–2–0;
W. P. C. Weston 4–2–8–1.

COUNTY RECORDS

Highest score for:	341	C. M. Spearman v Middlesex at Gloucester.	2004
Highest score against:	310*	M. E. K. Hussey (Northamptonshire) at Bristol . .	2002
Best bowling for:	10-40	E. G. Dennett v Essex at Bristol	1906
Best bowling against:	{10-66	A. A. Mailey (Australians) at Cheltenham	1921
	{10-66	K. Smales (Nottinghamshire) at Stroud	1956
Highest total for:	695-9 dec.	v Middlesex at Gloucester	2004
Highest total against:	774-7 dec.	by Australians at Bristol	1948
Lowest total for:	17	v Australians at Cheltenham	1896
Lowest total against:	12	by Northamptonshire at Gloucester	1907

GLOUCESTERSHIRE DIRECTORY

ADDRESS

County Ground, Nevil Road, Bristol BS7 9EJ (0117 910 8000; fax 0117 924 1193; email info@glosccc.co.uk). **Website** www.gloscricket.co.uk.

GROUNDS

Bristol (Nevil Road) 2 miles NW of city centre between A38 and M32 junction 2 via B4469 on Muller Road, L into Ralph Road, L then immediate R into Kennington Avenue then L into Nevil Road. Nearest stations: Montpelier (¾ mile), Bristol Parkway (2½ miles) and Temple Meads (2 miles).

Cheltenham (College): 1 mile S of town centre off A46 Bath Road in Thirlestaine Road. Signposted Cricket Festival from both M5 junctions. Nearest station: Cheltenham Spa (1 mile).

Gloucester (Archdeacon Meadow): ½ mile NW of city centre on A417 in St Oswald's Road S of railway line. Nearest station: Gloucester (½ mile).

OFFICIALS

Club captain M. W. Alleyne
Four-day captain C. G. Taylor
Head coach M. W. Alleyne
Director of development A. W. Stovold
President 2004 – G. F. Collis; 2005 – J. Higson

Chairman A. H. Haines
Chief executive T. E. M. Richardson
Chairman, cricket committee A. S. Brown
Head groundsman S. Williams
Scorer K. T. Gerrish

PLAYERS

Players expected to reappear in 2005

	Former counties	Country	Born	Birthplace
Adshead Stephen John	Leics, Worcs	E	29.1.1980	Redditch
Alleyne Mark Wayne		E	23.5.1968	Tottenham
Averis James Maxwell Michael		E	28.5.1974	†Bristol
Ball Martyn Charles John		E	26.4.1970	†Bristol
Fisher Ian Douglas	Yorks	E	31.3.1976	Bradford
Gidman Alexander Peter Richard		E	22.6.1981	High Wycombe
Hancock Timothy Harold Coulter. . . .		E	20.4.1972	Reading
Hardinges Mark Andrew.		E	5.2.1978	†Gloucester
Lewis Jonathan		E	26.8.1975	Aylesbury
Sillence Roger John		E	29.6.1977	Salisbury
*****Spearman** Craig Murray.		E	4.7.1972	Auckland, NZ
Taylor Christopher Glyn		E	27.9.1976	†Bristol
Weston William <u>Philip</u> Christopher . . .	Worcs	E	16.6.1973	Durham
Windows Matthew Guy Newman		E	5.4.1973	†Bristol

Players due to join in 2005

Ali Kadeer	Worcs	E	7.3.1983	Moseley
*****Chandana** Umagiliya Durage <u>Upul</u>. . .		SL	7.5.1972	Galle
Greenidge Carl Gary	Surrey, Northants	E	20.4.1978	Basingstoke
Kirby Steven Paul	Yorkshire	E	4.10.1977	Ainsworth

* *Test player.*   † *Born in Gloucestershire.*

GLOUCESTERSHIRE v KENT

At Bristol, April 16, 17, 18, 19. Kent won by seven wickets. Kent 16 pts, Gloucestershire 3 pts. Toss: Kent. First-class debuts: N. J. O'Brien, D. A. Stiff.

Philip Weston will find it hard to forget Gloucestershire's first ball in Division One: it was dead straight and knocked back his off stump as he played outside the line to Saggers. Taylor's debut as captain was also memorable. He was caught at point on 96, and then, after bravely agreeing to a pair of forfeited innings, saw Kent romp home. Rain and an overwhelmed drainage system restricted the first three days to 55 overs. Apart from Saggers, the Kent bowling was as green as the wicket, and there were 56 extras in a Gloucestershire total of 301: no-balls accounted for 32. David Stiff, a tall ex-England Under-19 seamer just released by Yorkshire, bowled five in his first two overs. After the forfeited innings, Kent were set a target of 302 in 80 overs. They were slightly anxious at 119 for three before Key and Carberry settled into a match-winning partnership. Both made assured unbeaten hundreds. Unusually for any county match in 2004, neither team included an official overseas player.

Close of play: First day, Gloucestershire 140-5 (Taylor 35, Russell 2); Second day, Gloucestershire 202-6 (Taylor 58, Bressington 29); Third day, No play.

Gloucestershire

W. P. C. Weston b Saggers	0	A. N. Bressington not out	58
C. M. Spearman c Stiff b Khan	27	M. C. J. Ball not out	28
T. H. C. Hancock c Fulton b Saggers	13	B 10, l-b 10, w 4, n-b 32	56
M. G. N. Windows lbw b Khan	11		
*C. G. Taylor c Carberry b Walker	96	1/0 (1) 2/28 (3) 3/60 (4)	(7 wkts dec.) 301
A. P. R. Gidman c Fulton b Saggers	10	4/73 (2) 5/123 (6)	
†R. C. Russell b Saggers	2	6/141 (7) 7/245 (5)	

J. M. M. Averis and J. Lewis did not bat.

Bonus points – Gloucestershire 3, Kent 2.

Bowling: Saggers 17.5–7–43–4; Khan 12–0–63–2; Sheriyar 13–2–60–0; Stiff 8–1–24–0; Tredwell 10–1–34–0; Walker 5–0–36–1; Carberry 3–0–21–0.

Gloucestershire forfeited their second innings.

Kent

Kent forfeited their first innings.

*D. P. Fulton lbw b Lewis	10	M. A. Carberry not out	104
R. W. T. Key not out	118	B 4	4
E. T. Smith b Lewis	36		
M. J. Walker c Windows b Gidman	30	1/18 (1) 2/66 (3) 3/119 (4)	(3 wkts) 302

J. C. Tredwell, †N. J. O'Brien, A. Khan, M. J. Saggers, D. A. Stiff and A. Sheriyar did not bat.

Bowling: Lewis 16.4–4–62–2; Averis 19–2–97–0; Bressington 6–0–55–0; Gidman 16–1–62–1; Ball 3–0–22–0.

Umpires: V. A. Holder and J. W. Lloyds.

GLOUCESTERSHIRE v LOUGHBOROUGH UCCE

At Bristol, April 21, 22, 23. Drawn. Toss: Loughborough UCCE. First-class debut: R. M. Wilkinson.

The poignancy of this soggy, low-key draw became clear only in hindsight. Two months later 40-year-old Jack Russell – one of the most cherished cricketers of his generation – announced that a chronic back injury had forced him and his famous battered sunhat into retirement, making this – barring unscheduled comebacks – his 465th and last first-class match. Because of rain and a wet outfield only one over was possible before 4 p.m. on the second day, by which time Loughborough opener Adams had already become Russell's 1,320th and final victim. The left-arm Smith, like Russell a seasoned craftsman, proved he had overcome his own back problems and gave a classic display of controlled seam bowling. Ten of his 11 completed overs were maidens; his two wickets on the third morning cost four. The afternoon brought an extended net for Gloucestershire's batsmen: only a scattering of spectators remained as Russell walked off 28 not out.

Close of play: First day, Loughborough UCCE 1-1 (Wilkinson 1, Atri 0); Second day, Loughborough UCCE 107-2 (Wilkinson 49, Benham 30).

Loughborough UCCE

R. M. Wilkinson lbw b Hancock	49	M. S. Panesar c Ball b Gidman	0
J. H. K. Adams c Russell b Averis	0	J. E. Anyon not out	2
V. Atri c Gidman b Averis	21		
C. C. Benham lbw b Smith	30	B 6, l-b 19, w 1, n-b 4	30
C. D. Nash lbw b Hancock	0		
†P. W. Harrison c Bressington b Smith	23		202
M. C. Rosenberg c sub b Ball	3		
P. D. Lewis b Alleyne	43		
*D. H. Wigley b Alleyne	1		

1/1 (2) 2/33 (3) 3/111 (1)
4/112 (4) 5/112 (5) 6/124 (7)
7/178 (8) 8/190 (9)
9/191 (10) 10/202 (6)

Bowling: Averis 14–4–24–2; Bressington 9–2–45–0; Alleyne 10–3–21–2; Smith 11.5–10–7–2; Gidman 8–1–28–1; Ball 14–2–45–1; Hancock 6–2–7–2.

Gloucestershire

C. M. Spearman c Harrison b Lewis	38	†R. C. Russell not out	28
W. P. C. Weston c Harrison b Wigley	39	A. N. Bressington not out	6
T. H. C. Hancock b Anyon	40	B 3, l-b 7, w 3	13
M. G. N. Windows lbw b Wigley	9		
A. P. R. Gidman c Harrison b Anyon	33	1/46 (1) 2/113 (3) 3/131 (4)	(6 wkts) 228
*M. W. Alleyne c Wigley b Anyon	22	4/154 (2) 5/187 (5) 6/202 (6)	

M. C. J. Ball, J. M. M. Averis and A. M. Smith did not bat.

Bowling: Wigley 13–1–53–2; Lewis 13–2–53–1; Anyon 15–3–57–3; Panesar 11–3–26–0; Wilkinson 5–0–27–0; Nash 1–0–2–0.

Umpires: A. A. Jones and R. T. Robinson.

At Birmingham, April 28, 29, 30, May 1. GLOUCESTERSHIRE drew with WARWICKSHIRE.

At Canterbury, May 7, 8, 9, 10. GLOUCESTERSHIRE drew with KENT.

GLOUCESTERSHIRE v NORTHAMPTONSHIRE

At Bristol, May 12, 13, 14, 15. Drawn. Gloucestershire 12 pts, Northamptonshire 6 pts. Toss: Gloucestershire.

Unsettled by the wet run-ups and their effect on his rhythm, Gloucestershire's new Pakistan pace bowler Shabbir Ahmed first switched ends and then, with four balls of his fifth over left, refused to continue. Following discussions, the umpires decided he was "incapacitated" which, under Law 22.7, allows another bowler to finish the over. No one could recall a similar replacement for reasons other than injury. "I've never seen anything like it," said Gloucestershire coach Mark Alleyne, "but Shabbir was struggling and I think the umpires got it right." So Gidman replaced Shabbir – and, while attempting his second delivery, promptly fell over. Shabbir tried again later but tweaked a hamstring and finally gave up, having bowled 13 no-balls in 16.2 overs. Averis, though, returned a magnificent career-best six for 32 in 19 overs, a standard matched only on the third day when Phillips of Northamptonshire took three wickets in 11 balls to keep Gloucestershire's lead to 256. For that they could largely thank Spearman, who made 139, an innings of sweet timing. It looked a winning advantage. But Powell and Roberts built an opening stand of 111 and made a draw look likely. After 165 overs of defiance, it became fact.

Close of play: First day, Gloucestershire 93-0 (Spearman 53, Weston 33); Second day, Gloucestershire 432-5 (Gidman 66, Shoaib Malik 51); Third day, Northamptonshire 232-2 (van Jaarsveld 73, Afzaal 36).

Northamptonshire

M. J. Powell c Spearman b Averis	21	– c Weston b Shoaib Malik	33
T. W. Roberts c Taylor b Lewis	16	– b Shoaib Malik	68
M. van Jaarsveld lbw b Gidman	7	– c Weston b Lewis	84
U. Afzaal st Adshead b Shoaib Malik	63	– run out	64
*D. J. Sales c Spearman b Averis	1	– lbw b Gidman	43
G. P. Swann b Averis	14	– lbw b Shoaib Malik	8
†G. L. Brophy b Averis	0	– c Spearman b Weston	58
J. Louw not out	26	– not out	34
B. J. Phillips c Shoaib Malik b Averis	6	– not out	0
P. S. Jones c Windows b Shoaib Malik	11		
J. F. Brown b Averis	0		
B 4, l-b 8, w 1, n-b 30	43	B 5, l-b 13, w 1, n-b 16	35

1/36 (2) 2/52 (1) 3/56 (3) 4/67 (5)   218   1/111 (1) 2/148 (2)   (7 wkts dec.) 427
5/90 (6) 6/102 (7) 7/189 (4)   3/253 (3) 4/294 (4)
8/200 (9) 9/213 (10) 10/218 (11)   5/322 (5) 6/324 (6) 7/420 (7)

Bonus points – Northamptonshire 1, Gloucestershire 3.

Bowling: *First Innings*—Shabbir Ahmed 16.2–3–78–0; Lewis 17–7–31–1; Averis 19–7–32–6; Gidman 8.4–1–35–1; Shoaib Malik 11–3–30–2. *Second Innings*—Lewis 35–13–60–1; Shabbir Ahmed 5–1–27–0; Averis 28–3–86–0; Gidman 30–10–78–1; Shoaib Malik 45–14–109–3; Hancock 19–5–41–0; Weston 3–1–8–1.

Gloucestershire

C. M. Spearman b Brown	139	J. Lewis c Sales b Phillips	7
W. P. C. Weston c Roberts b Phillips	36	Shabbir Ahmed not out	2
T. H. C. Hancock c Brophy b Brown	65		
M. G. N. Windows b Swann	31	B 6, l-b 14, n-b 10	30
*C. G. Taylor c Brophy b Phillips	18		
A. P. R. Gidman lbw b Louw	68	1/102 (2) 2/245 (1) 3/260 (3)	474
Shoaib Malik b Louw	63	4/298 (5) 5/335 (4) 6/439 (6)	
†S. J. Adshead lbw b Phillips	14	7/456 (7) 8/462 (9)	
J. M. M. Averis lbw b Phillips	1	9/471 (8) 10/474 (10)	

Bonus points – Gloucestershire 5, Northamptonshire 1 (130 overs: 410-5).

Bowling: Louw 35–12–81–2; Jones 39–7–115 0; Phillips 34.1–4–106–5; Brown 30–4–83–2; Swann 16–1–69–1.

Umpires: J. H. Evans and I. J. Gould.

At Worcester, May 18, 19, 20, 21. GLOUCESTERSHIRE lost to WORCESTERSHIRE by an innings and 86 runs.

GLOUCESTERSHIRE v SURREY

At Bristol, June 2, 3, 4. Gloucestershire won by six wickets. Gloucestershire 22 pts, Surrey 5 pts. County debut: N. D. Doshi. Toss: Surrey.

A toe injury for Gidman meant Gloucestershire's coach Alleyne made an unscheduled first-class appearance. He responded with his usual ringcraft and perseverance, taking five for 71 in the first innings, his best for three years. When he knocked back Shahid's off stump it marked his 400th first-class wicket for Gloucestershire; later he scored his 14,000th first-class run for them. After choosing to bat, Surrey's top order faltered and they relied on the tail to reach 298.

Rather petulant in the field, they had to endure a determined century from Weston, whose 135 lasted six hours 41 minutes. They found some consolation in the promising debut of Nayan Doshi, 25-year-old son of the Indian Test bowler Dilip, who has taken up his father's trade of left-arm spin and reduced the run rate to a dribble on the second afternoon. With a lead of 108, Gloucestershire were well on top, and Lewis then destroyed Surrey's second innings, taking the first seven wickets, more through swing than speed. Though a last-wicket stand of 104 forced Gloucestershire to bat again, it was still over in three days.

Close of play: First day, Gloucestershire 113-2 (Weston 41, Windows 14); Second day, Surrey 21-1 (Batty 7, Doshi 0).

Surrey

S. A. Newman b Shabbir Ahmed	18	– c Weston b Lewis ... 10
*†J. N. Batty b Lewis	5	– c Alleyne b Lewis ... 11
M. R. Ramprakash c Adshead b Alleyne	6	– (4) not out ... 64
R. Clarke c Weston b Alleyne	62	– (5) lbw b Lewis ... 12
A. D. Brown c Weston b Averis	5	– (6) b Lewis ... 0
N. Shahid b Alleyne	5	– (7) c Adshead b Lewis ... 0
Azhar Mahmood lbw b Averis	14	– (8) c Alleyne b Lewis ... 11
M. P. Bicknell not out	47	– (9) c Hancock b Shoaib Malik ... 26
T. J. Murtagh b Alleyne	25	– (10) c Adshead b Averis ... 0
J. Ormond c Alleyne b Shabbir Ahmed	11	– (11) c Taylor b Shabbir Ahmed ... 57
N. D. Doshi c Windows b Alleyne	0	– (3) c Adshead b Lewis ... 11
B 7, l-b 11, w 4, n-b 30	52	B 4, l-b 5, n-b 2 ... 11
	298	**213**

1/23 (1) 2/31 (2) 3/37 (3) 4/66 (5)   298
5/155 (4) 6/188 (6) 7/203 (7)
8/264 (9) 9/293 (10) 10/298 (11)

1/16 (1) 2/36 (3) 3/41 (2)   213
4/53 (5) 5/55 (6) 6/59 (7)
7/75 (8) 8/108 (9)
9/109 (10) 10/213 (11)

Bonus points – Surrey 2, Gloucestershire 3.

Bowling: *First Innings*—Lewis 14–6–43–1; Shabbir Ahmed 18–2–91–2; Alleyne 17.3–4–71–5; Averis 12–2–41–2; Shoaib Malik 10–0–34–0. *Second Innings*—Lewis 21–3–72–7; Shabbir Ahmed 15.2–3–48–1; Alleyne 6–2–24–0; Averis 6–0–24–1; Shoaib Malik 10–0–36–1.

Gloucestershire

C. M. Spearman lbw b Bicknell	4	– (2) c sub b Bicknell ... 28
W. P. C. Weston b Murtagh	135	– (1) lbw b Bicknell ... 10
T. H. C. Hancock c Batty b Clarke	43	– b Doshi ... 21
M. G. N. Windows b Azhar Mahmood	58	– not out ... 23
*C. G. Taylor c Brown b Bicknell	24	– c Clarke b Doshi ... 0
Shoaib Malik c Newman b Bicknell	1	– not out ... 12
M. W. Alleyne c Newman b Azhar Mahmood	51	
†S. J. Adshead c Ormond b Bicknell	30	
J. M. M. Averis lbw b Murtagh	14	
J. Lewis c Ramprakash b Murtagh	8	
Shabbir Ahmed not out	0	
B 5, l-b 12, w 1, n-b 20	38	L-b 2, n-b 10 ... 12
	406	**(4 wkts) 106**

1/7 (1) 2/86 (3) 3/196 (4) 4/248 (5)   406
5/250 (6) 6/338 (2) 7/356 (7)
8/388 (9) 9/404 (10) 10/406 (8)

1/34 (1) 2/51 (2)   (4 wkts) 106
3/87 (3) 4/91 (5)

Bonus points – Gloucestershire 5, Surrey 3.

Bowling: *First Innings*—Bicknell 34.2–11–107–4; Ormond 26–5–75–0; Clarke 9–0–58–1; Murtagh 21–5–78–3; Doshi 19–7–26–0; Azhar Mahmood 16–4–45–2. *Second Innings*—Bicknell 10–2–46–2; Ormond 4–1–21–0; Azhar Mahmood 5–2–14–0; Murtagh 3.4–0–13–0; Doshi 3–1–10–2.

Umpires: A. Clarkson and A. A. Jones.

GLOUCESTERSHIRE v MIDDLESEX

At Gloucester, June 9, 10, 11, 12. Gloucestershire won by ten wickets. Gloucestershire 22 pts, Middlesex 5 pts. Toss: Middlesex.

At 2.36 p.m. on the sunny third afternoon, Craig Spearman pushed through mid-wicket to reach the highest score in Gloucestershire's 135-year first-class history. It was two and a half years after he was lured back to cricket from a planned career in the City and 498 minutes after his epic innings began. Along the way he eclipsed two towering giants: the previous record-holder was W. G. Grace (318 not out against Yorkshire at Cheltenham in 1876); four balls earlier Spearman had passed Hobbs's record for the biggest first-class innings against Middlesex (316 not out for Surrey at Lord's in 1926). "You are talking about the father of cricket as he is known the world over," said Spearman, who admitted targeting Grace's record, "so it is quite something." Even

GLORY AT GLOUCESTER

Highest first-class innings for Gloucestershire:

341	**C. M. Spearman**	**v Middlesex at Gloucester (Archdeacon Meadow)** ...	**2004**
318*	W. G. Grace	v Yorkshire at Cheltenham	1876
317	W. R. Hammond	v Nottinghamshire at Gloucester (Wagon Works)	1936
302*	W. R. Hammond	v Glamorgan at Bristol	1934
302	W. R. Hammond	v Glamorgan at Newport.	1939
301	W. G. Grace	v Sussex at Bristol.	1896
290	W. R. Hammond	v Kent at Tunbridge Wells	1934
288	W. G. Grace	v Somerset at Bristol	1895
286	G. L. Jessop	v Sussex at Hove	1903

Highest first-class totals for Gloucestershire:

695-9 dec.	**v Middlesex at Gloucester (Archdeacon Meadow)**	**2004**
653-6 dec.	v Glamorgan at Bristol (Greenbank)	1928
643-5 dec.	v Nottinghamshire at Bristol.	1946
636	v Nottinghamshire at Nottingham.	1904
634	v Nottinghamshire at Bristol.	1898
627-2 dec.	v Oxford University at Oxford	1930
625-6 dec.	v Worcestershire at Dudley	1934
611-9 dec.	v Somerset at Taunton	2003

umpire Kitchen shared his pleasure. "Get rid of the old man," he said. "He used to pick up the bails and put them back on the stumps." When he finally nibbled a catch behind on 341, he had batted nearly nine hours, faced 390 balls and hit six sixes and 40 fours. Helped when Middlesex lost the sharpness of Hayward, who suffered an early ankle injury, Spearman played an innings of complete control and no chances: he drove, swept and generally mastered a Middlesex attack reduced to going through the motions and waiting for a mistake. He owed much to his opening partner Weston – they put on 227 together – to Taylor who hit his first hundred in nearly two years, and to Gidman, whose aggression eased the burden on Spearman as he approached the record. The final total of 695 was Gloucestershire's highest, and a beaten-down Middlesex failed to bat out the last day to safety. The win lifted Gloucestershire to third place. Earlier, Klusener and Weekes had made fifties in Middlesex's first innings (repeated in the second), but no one managed a punishing score. A total of 383 would have seen off defeat in most matches, on most pitches. But when the weather is kind, as it was here, Archdeacon Meadow's dry pitch and close-cropped outfield are perfect for the confident batsman. Enter Spearman...

Close of play: First day, Middlesex 333-6 (Dalrymple 49, Klusener 62); Second day, Gloucestershire 353-2 (Spearman 208, Taylor 28); Third day, Middlesex 151-2 (Shah 58, Joyce 71).

Middlesex

B. L. Hutton c Adshead b Lewis	14	– c Adshead b Lewis	6
S. G. Koenig lbw b Smith	45	– b Shabbir Ahmed	3
*O. A. Shah c Spearman b Gidman	34	– c Shabbir Ahmed b Lewis	72
E. C. Joyce c Weston b Shoaib Malik	28	– c Adshead b Shoaib Malik	71
P. N. Weekes c Adshead b Shabbir Ahmed	50	– lbw b Fisher	53
J. W. M. Dalrymple b Lewis	49	– lbw b Lewis	0
†D. C. Nash run out	12	– c Weston b Fisher	16
L. Klusener b Shabbir Ahmed	63	– not out	68
C. T. Peploe not out	28	– c Shoaib Malik b Fisher	28
P. M. Hutchison b Shabbir Ahmed	8	– lbw b Fisher	0
M. Hayward b Shabbir Ahmed	7	– b Shabbir Ahmed	1
B 6, l-b 10, w 1, n-b 28	45	B 12, l-b 16, w 2, n-b 10	40

1/28 (1) 2/102 (3) 3/112 (2) 4/176 (4)   383   1/17 (2) 2/21 (1) 3/155 (4)   358
5/212 (5) 6/243 (7) 7/334 (8)   4/195 (3) 5/197 (6) 6/224 (7)
8/334 (6) 9/357 (10) 10/383 (11)   7/263 (5) 8/357 (9)
                                                        9/357 (10) 10/358 (11)

Bonus points – Middlesex 4, Gloucestershire 3.

Bowling: *First Innings*—Lewis 30–10–88–2; Shabbir Ahmed 26.1–7–96–4; Smith 16–3–55–1; Gidman 6–0–30–1; Shoaib Malik 20–2–49–1; Fisher 19–4–49–0. *Second Innings*—Lewis 12–3–36–3; Shabbir Ahmed 17.1–4–69–2; Smith 3–0–11–0; Fisher 32–7–110–4; Shoaib Malik 30–3–104–1.

Gloucestershire

W. P. C. Weston c Weekes b Peploe	85	– (2) not out	3
C. M. Spearman c Nash b Hutton	341	– (1) not out	29
M. G. N. Windows c Nash b Weekes	6		
*C. G. Taylor c Nash b Peploe	100		
A. P. R. Gidman c Klusener b Hutton	51		
Shoaib Malik c Dalrymple b Joyce	0		
†S. J. Adshead not out	35		
I. D. Fisher c Hutton b Peploe	6		
J. Lewis c and b Weekes	12		
Shabbir Ahmed st Nash b Peploe	5		
A. M. Smith not out	3		
B 14, l-b 12, w 5, n-b 20	51	B 4, w 1, n-b 10	15

1/227 (1) 2/254 (3) 3/537 (4)   (9 wkts dec.) 695   (no wkt) 47
4/610 (5) 5/616 (6) 6/646 (2)
7/659 (8) 8/681 (9) 9/690 (10)

Bonus points – Gloucestershire 5, Middlesex 1 (130 overs: 587-3).

Bowling: *First Innings*—Hayward 9–1–37–0; Hutchison 22–4–91–0; Peploe 43–3–199–4; Klusener 23–1–116–0; Dalrymple 11–2–38–0; Weekes 13–0–62–2; Joyce 14–0–62–1; Shah 1–1–0–0; Hutton 13–1–64–2. *Second Innings*—Hutton 4–1–16–0; Peploe 3–0–12–0; Weekes 2–0–10–0; Koenig 2–1–1–0; Shah 0–0–4–0.

Umpires: J. W. Holder and M. J. Kitchen.

At The Oval, June 18, 19, 20 21. GLOUCESTERSHIRE drew with SURREY.

At Arundel, June 23, 24, 25. GLOUCESTERSHIRE beat SUSSEX by nine wickets.

GLOUCESTERSHIRE v LANCASHIRE

At Cheltenham, July 21, 22, 23, 24. Drawn. Gloucestershire 8 pts, Lancashire 11 pts. Toss: Lancashire. Championship debut: J. E. C. Franklin.

Two overseas players called up from the leagues starred in an intriguing game. India's Dinesh Mongia batted with style, joy and verve for a sparkling maiden county hundred, followed by a 52-ball 76. New Zealand left-arm seamer James Franklin grabbed seven for 60, the best innings return on Gloucestershire debut since Archibald Fargus took seven for 55 at Lord's in 1900. Three of his wickets came at 333, as Lancashire's last six fell for 42. A rain-shortened but eventful second day featured five umpires after Roy Palmer suffered a stomach bug, and there was another changeover when Anderson, released from the Lord's Test, came on as a replacement for Martin. The last man pair saved the follow-on, and Lancashire plundered more than five an over on the third day, before Hooper declared with Chilton one short of his career-best. But Gloucestershire survived 144 overs, with Adshead batting through the last 68, to secure a draw.

Close of play: First day, Lancashire 362-8 (Mongia 111, Martin 8); Second day, Gloucestershire 186-6 (Adshead 35, Fisher 0); Third day, Gloucestershire 48-1 (Weston 20, Hussey 20).

Lancashire

M. J. Chilton c Adshead b Franklin	69	– not out	124
I. J. Sutcliffe run out	10	– c and b Ball	61
M. B. Loye c Weston b Ball	90	– c Hussey b Averis	69
D. Mongia c Adshead b Franklin	111	not out	76
*C. L. Hooper c Franklin b Fisher	19		
†J. J. Haynes c Hussey b Franklin	24		
G. Chapple b Franklin	0		
D. G. Cork b Franklin	0		
S. I. Mahmood b Franklin	0		
P. J. Martin c Weston b Franklin	20		
G. Keedy not out	1		
B 4, l-b 8, n-b 19	31	B 4, l-b 12, n-b 8	24

1/20 (?) 2/160 (1) 3/215 (3) 4/263 (5)   **375**   1/115 (2) 2/230 (3)   (2 wkts dec.) **354**
5/333 (6) 6/333 (7) 7/333 (8)
8/341 (9) 9/362 (4) 10/375 (10)

J. M. Anderson did not bat.

Bonus points – Lancashire 4, Gloucestershire 3.

Bowling: *First Innings*—Lewis 24–4–66–0; Franklin 22.1–7–60–7; Averis 14–1–62–0; Gidman 7–1–27–0; Ball 25–3–70–1; Fisher 19–1–78–1. *Second Innings*—Lewis 14–3–71–0; Franklin 10–4–39–0; Averis 9–3–51–1; Ball 18–1–109–1; Fisher 15–0–68–0.

Gloucestershire

C. M. Spearman c Haynes b Chapple	9	– (2) c Loye b Anderson	8
W. P. C. Weston c and b Anderson	44	– (1) lbw b Hooper	65
M. E. K. Hussey lbw b Martin	5	– c Chilton b Hooper	44
*C. G. Taylor lbw b Cork	33	– b Anderson	74
A. P. R. Gidman b Cork	1	– c Sutcliffe b Hooper	21
J. E. C. Franklin c Haynes b Keedy	34	– (7) lbw b Anderson	0
†S. J. Adshead c Haynes b Cork	40	– (6) not out	57
I. D. Fisher c Haynes b Cork	1	– c Hooper b Keedy	31
M. C. J. Ball c Loye b Cork	8	– not out	29
J. M. M. Averis not out	10		
J. Lewis b Chapple	14		
B 5, l-b 11, w 1, n-b 18	35	B 11, l-b 12, n-b 14	37

1/19 (1) 2/28 (3) 3/93 (4) 4/99 (5)   **234**   1/11 (2) 2/112 (3)   (7 wkts) **366**
5/99 (2) 6/181 (6) 7/188 (8)   3/160 (1) 4/225 (5)
8/199 (7) 9/216 (9) 10/234 (11)   5/233 (4) 6/233 (7) 7/291 (8)

Bonus points – Gloucestershire 1, Lancashire 3.

Bowling: *First Innings*—Martin 6–1–24–1; Chapple 11.1–2–23–2; Cork 16–4–54–5; Mahmood 7–0–46–0; Anderson 19–5–40–1; Keedy 12–3–31–1. *Second Innings*—Anderson 28–9–95–3; Chapple 11–3–15–0; Keedy 48.4–14–95–1; Cork 15–4–50–0; Hooper 29–9–55–3; Mahmood 8–4–24–0; Mongia 4–1–9–0.

Umpires: P. J. Hartley and R. Palmer.
(M. W. Alleyne, M. Johnson and D. J. Constant deputised for Palmer).

THE REVEREND ARCHIBALD FARGUS

Archibald Fargus made the newspapers in 2004 because Heath Streak of Warwickshire was erroneously believed to have beaten his record of 12 for 87 on his Championship debut, achieved for Gloucestershire against Middlesex at Lord's in 1900. (In fact, Streak had previously appeared for Hampshire). Fargus was also remarkable for living on for 48 years after *Wisden* erroneously published his obituary in 1915, believing he had gone down with the ship on which he was chaplain. He actually missed the boat, and died in 1963, but *Wisden* did not report this until the Supplementary Obituaries of 1994.

GLOUCESTERSHIRE v WORCESTERSHIRE

At Cheltenham, July 28, 29, 30, 31. Worcestershire won by five wickets. Worcestershire 19 pts, Gloucestershire 8 pts. Toss: Gloucestershire.

Worcestershire overturned a 171-run deficit to defeat their neighbours, who last beat them in the Championship in 1995: this was the 12th defeat in 14 subsequent games. Hick helped to demolish a target of 361 with his second hundred of the season against Gloucestershire and tenth against them in all. It was his 126th in first-class cricket, equalling W. G. Grace. But Grace played into his 60th year: Hick was still 38. In 343 minutes, he hit 24 fours and three sixes. He shared a destructive stand of 189 with Bichel, who completed his second hundred in a week. Earlier, Alleyne – deputising for Taylor, injured in the field after a first-day century – had waived the follow-on. Batty had wheeled through 30 consecutive overs for four wickets and Gloucestershire surmised a flat, dry pitch would help their spinners on the last day. It never did.

Close of play: First day, Gloucestershire 392-8 (Alleyne 61, Ball 3); Second day, Gloucestershire 0-0 (Weston 0, Spearman 0); Third day, Worcestershire 100-1 (Moore 46, Hick 46).

Gloucestershire

C. M. Spearman c Batty b Mason	8	– (2) lbw b Kabir Ali	5
W. P. C. Weston b Kabir Ali	14	– (1) c Rhodes b Hall	30
M. E. K. Hussey c Hall b Mason	0	– lbw b Kabir Ali	68
*C. G. Taylor c and b Hall	103	– c Hick b Hall	7
A. P. R. Gidman c Bichel b Kabir Ali	70	– c Hall b Batty	25
†S. J. Adshead lbw b Batty	48	– c Smith b Kabir Ali	11
J. E. C. Franklin lbw b Batty	9	– not out	8
M. W. Alleyne not out	77	– (10) run out	11
I. D. Fisher run out	45	– (8) c Hall b Kabir Ali	0
M. C. J. Ball c Hick b Batty	38	– (9) lbw b Batty	5
J. Lewis lbw b Batty	1	– c Rhodes b Bichel	0
B 8, l-b 13, w 1, n-b 10	32	B 6, l-b 7, n-b 6	19
	445		**189**

1/14 (1) 2/14 (3) 3/36 (2) 4/132 (5)
5/229 (6) 6/251 (7) 7/299 (4)
8/387 (9) 9/443 (10) 10/445 (11)

1/14 (2) 2/63 (1) 3/81 (4)
4/142 (5) 5/160 (3) 6/161 (6)
7/161 (8) 8/172 (9)
9/187 (10) 10/189 (11)

Bonus points – Gloucestershire 5, Worcestershire 3.

Bowling: *First Innings*—Mason 29–8–82–2; Kabir Ali 22–4–86–2; Bichel 19–2–73–0; Hall 22–0–101–1; Batty 30.2–8–82–4. *Second Innings*—Batty 34–10–68–2; Kabir Ali 13–5–33–4; Mason 11–3–18–0; Bichel 11.1–4–26–1; Hall 10–3–31–2.

Worcestershire

S. D. Peters lbw b Lewis	19	– c Ball b Franklin	5
S. C. Moore lbw b Franklin	35	– lbw b Ball	53
G. A. Hick c Fisher b Gidman	26	– c Spearman b Fisher	178
*B. F. Smith c Gidman b Ball	56	– c Taylor b Ball	4
V. S. Solanki c Spearman b Gidman	7	– st Adshead b Fisher	3
A. J. Bichel c Adshead b Lewis	36	– not out	103
G. J. Batty c Weston b Lewis	30	– not out	3
A. J. Hall lbw b Lewis	0		
Kabir Ali not out	11		
†S. J. Rhodes b Ball	16		
M. S. Mason c Spearman b Lewis	4		
B 6, l-b 5, w 1, n-b 22	34	L-b 5, w 1, n-b 8	14

1/59 (2) 2/63 (1) 3/118 (3) 4/126 (5)	274
5/179 (4) 6/223 (6) 7/229 (8)	
8/236 (7) 9/259 (10) 10/274 (11)	

1/9 (1) 2/128 (2)	(5 wkts) 363
3/138 (4) 4/153 (5)	
5/342 (3)	

Bonus points – Worcestershire 2, Gloucestershire 3.

Bowling: *First Innings*—Lewis 18.5–6–38–5; Franklin 17–5–58–1; Gidman 8–1–50–2; Ball 19–3–62–2; Alleyne 8–3–23–0; Fisher 9–0–32–0. *Second Innings*—Lewis 19–3–72–0; Franklin 16–4–53–1; Alleyne 4–0–26–0; Ball 32–2–93–2; Fisher 19.1–1–100–2; Gidman 2–0–14–0.

Umpires: J. W. Holder and J. F. Steele.

At Lord's, August 3, 4, 5, 6. GLOUCESTERSHIRE drew with MIDDLESEX.

GLOUCESTERSHIRE v WARWICKSHIRE

At Bristol, August 19, 20, 21, 22. Drawn. Gloucestershire 12 pts, Warwickshire 10 pts. Toss: Warwickshire.

Spearman, who had beaten Grace's county record score in June, became the first home batsman to reach a Championship double-hundred at Bristol since Hammond made two in 1946. Scoring fluently on the leg side, Spearman hit 25 fours and four sixes in 373 minutes and 279 balls, with just one fierce chance to gully. A six over mid-wicket brought him his fourth first-class hundred of the summer; another saw him to 150. His mammoth innings finally ended on the third morning, when he drove a return catch. Sillence and Hardinges, both in their first Championship game of the season, then added 154 for the eighth wicket. A thigh strain meant Streak bowled only eight overs. On the first day, leaders Warwickshire were 78 for four before Troughton, recalled to their Championship side after eight weeks' absence, combined with Brown in a stand of 182. But after conceding a 242-run deficit, Warwickshire were content to keep their unbeaten record.

Close of play: First day, Gloucestershire 20-0 (Spearman 11, Weston 7); Second day, Gloucestershire 352-3 (Spearman 232, Gidman 40); Third day, Warwickshire 111-1 (Wagh 54, Trott 50).

Warwickshire

*N. V. Knight c Hardinges b Lewis	7	– b Lewis	0
M. A. Wagh c Gidman b Averis	17	– c Adshead b Averis	73
M. J. Powell c Hussey b Lewis	10	– (5) c Weston b Sillence	9
I. J. L. Trott c Adshead b Hardinges	21	– (3) c Spearman b Fisher	79
J. O. Troughton c Spearman b Fisher	120	– (4) lbw b Fisher	21
D. R. Brown c Hussey b Sillence	91	– c Taylor b Gidman	49
†T. Frost c Taylor b Sillence	2	– b Lewis	28
H. H. Streak c Spearman b Fisher	29	– c Hardinges b Lewis	4
N. M. Carter c Hardinges b Fisher	0	– (10) not out	0
N. Tahir not out	18	– (9) not out	11
D. Pretorius c Weston b Lewis	9		
B 1, l-b 10, w 1, n-b 14	26	B 5, l-b 3, w 2, n-b 24	34
	350	**(8 wkts)**	**308**

1/10 (1) 2/38 (2) 3/38 (3) 4/78 (4) 5/260 (6) 6/266 (7) 7/300 (5) 8/300 (9) 9/313 (8) 10/350 (11)

1/0 (1) 2/163 (2) 3/164 (3) 4/202 (5) 5/202 (4) 6/263 (7) 7/281 (8) 8/306 (6)

Bonus points – Warwickshire 4, Gloucestershire 3.

Bowling: *First Innings*—Lewis 23–7–59–3; Averis 18–3–89–1; Hardinges 17–2–78–1; Gidman 5–1–21–0; Sillence 14–4–50–2; Fisher 20–5–42–3. *Second Innings*—Lewis 27–6–89–3; Averis 15–4–57–1; Hardinges 13–2–42–0; Sillence 17–8–33–1; Fisher 36–20–50–2; Hussey 1–0–1–0; Taylor 1–0–2–0; Gidman 12–4–26–1.

Gloucestershire

C. M. Spearman c and b Troughton	237	R. J. Sillence lbw b Trott	92
W. P. C. Weston c Trott b Tahir	30	J. M. M. Averis not out	0
M. E. K. Hussey lbw b Troughton	26	B 3, l-b 11, w 1, n-b 2	17
I. D. Fisher c Frost b Pretorius	13		
A. P. R. Gidman c Powell b Wagh	47	**(8 wkts dec.)**	**592**
*C. G. Taylor b Brown	30		
†S. J. Adshead b Brown	32		
M. A. Hardinges not out	68		

J. Lewis did not bat.

1/99 (2) 2/190 (3) 3/229 (4) 4/363 (5) 5/368 (1) 6/427 (6) 7/434 (7) 8/588 (9)

Bonus points – Gloucestershire 5, Warwickshire 2 (130 overs: 459-7).

Bowling: Pretorius 20–2–84–1; Carter 23–1–93–0; Brown 31–9–84–2; Tahir 5–0–43–1; Wagh 28–3–107–1; Troughton 37–9–106–2; Powell 7–0–36–0; Streak 8–1–24–0; Trott 2–1–1–1.

Umpires: A. Clarkson and N. J. Llong.

At Northampton, August 24, 25, 26, 27. GLOUCESTERSHIRE drew with NORTHAMPTONSHIRE.

GLOUCESTERSHIRE v SUSSEX

At Bristol, September 9, 10, 11, 12. Drawn. Gloucestershire 7 pts, Sussex 7 pts. Toss: Gloucestershire. Championship debut: N. W. Bracken.

Seventeen wickets fell on the first day, though pitch liaison officer Raman Subba Row gave an old strip qualified approval. Taylor decided to bat but was one of four early wickets, three lbw. Gloucestershire limped to their lowest Championship total of 2004 before Averis dismissed the Sussex top four. The ball still swung and seamed after a blank second day: last pair Kirtley and Lewry claimed a slender 21-run lead, with 50 in eight overs, and were denied a batting point only by a catch to tell your grandchildren about – Hussey diving full stretch in the deep after a long chase. Spearman showed the pitch could be mastered, with seven fours and a six in his eighth half-century of the campaign, while Gidman and Hancock settled into their best Championship innings of the season. Gloucestershire resisted setting a target; flirting with relegation, they wanted to be sure of a draw and also faced penalty points for a slow over-rate – a regulation applying only once they had bowled for four hours or more in the match. So they batted on until lashing rain ended play on the final afternoon.

Close of play: First day, Sussex 116-7 (Davis 5, Mushtaq Ahmed 5); Second day, No play; Third day, Gloucestershire 205-4 (Hancock 32, Gidman 33).

Gloucestershire

C. M. Spearman lbw b Martin-Jenkins	12	– (2) lbw b Mushtaq Ahmed	65
W. P. C. Weston lbw b Kirtley	1	– (1) lbw b Kirtley	13
M. E. K. Hussey b Lewry	1	– lbw b Davis	37
*C. G. Taylor lbw b Lewry	0	– run out	15
T. H. C. Hancock c Ward b Martin-Jenkins	44	– not out	77
A. P. R. Gidman c Goodwin b Lewry	22	– c Martin-Jenkins b Davis	82
†S. J. Adshead b Mushtaq Ahmed	19	– not out	0
I. D. Fisher lbw b Kirtley	17		
J. M. M. Averis b Mushtaq Ahmed	14		
J. Lewis not out	27		
N. W. Bracken b Kirtley	8		
B 6, l-b 3, n-b 4	13	B 2, l-b 7, w 1, p 5	15

1/7 (2) 2/12 (3) 3/12 (4) 4/31 (1)   178   1/22 (1) 2/109 (3)   (5 wkts) 304
5/69 (6) 6/110 (7) 7/110 (5)   3/129 (2) 4/142 (4)
8/135 (8) 9/159 (9) 10/178 (11)   5/304 (6)

Bonus points – Sussex 3.

Bowling: *First Innings*—Kirtley 18.3–4–52–3; Lewry 13–6–27–3; Mushtaq Ahmed 23–5–64–2; Martin-Jenkins 12–6–24–2; Davis 3–1–2–0. *Second Innings*—Kirtley 17–4–46–1; Lewry 10–2–35–0; Martin Jenkins 17–3–74–0; Mushtaq Ahmed 34–10–68–1; Davis 17.2–0–67–2.

Sussex

I. J. Ward b Averis	16	R. J. Kirtley not out	20
R. R. Montgomerie b Averis	7	J. D. Lewry c Hussey b Averis	32
P. A. Cottey lbw b Averis	21		
M. W. Goodwin c Hussey b Averis	5	B 2, l-b 1, w 1, n-b 28	32
*C. J. Adams b Gidman	9		
†M. J. Prior c Adshead b Gidman	27	1/30 (1) 2/37 (2) 3/57 (4)	199
R. S. C. Martin Jenkins b Bracken	6	4/62 (3) 5/78 (5) 6/105 (6)	
M. J. G. Davis c Adshead b Lewis	11	7/109 (7) 8/135 (9)	
Mushtaq Ahmed c Gidman b Bracken	13	9/149 (8) 10/199 (11)	

Bonus points – Gloucestershire 3.

Bowling: Lewis 18–4–81–1; Bracken 17–6–58–2; Averis 10.2–1–45–5; Gidman 7–2–12–2.

Umpires: M. J. Harris and M. J. Kitchen.

At Manchester, September 16, 17, 18, 19. GLOUCESTERSHIRE drew with LANCASHIRE.

HAMPSHIRE

The leggie lights up the Rose Bowl

PAT SYMES

In the spring of 2004, as jubilant players sang their newly created club victory song "Glory, glory, we are Hampshire" down a mobile phone to the chairman on his yacht in the Caribbean, it became clear the face of county cricket in Hampshire had changed. It was not a club Philip Mead or Lionel Tennyson would have recognised, though the hedonistic Tennyson might have enjoyed the yacht. However, they would surely have approved of both the Rose Bowl, the club's imposing headquarters, and the impressive tally of wins in 2004.

This was Hampshire's best year in terms of results since they left Mead and Tennyson's county ground in 2000. The song (lyrics: Kendall and Prittipaul) was part of the forging of a new Hampshire ethos, which helped induce a togetherness and spirit missing since the break-up of Mark Nicholas's team of the 1980s. Players travelled to away matches by coach, and "gaffe of the day", chosen by the team, earned the culprit a fetching pink T-shirt for the evening.

While one man does not make a team, Shane Warne came close. Yacht-owning Rod Bransgrove fought with determination to persuade Warne to return as captain, talisman and master tactician, and Warne lit up Hampshire cricket as no man since Malcolm Marshall in his prime. After his year's suspension, the great leg-spinner approached the task of raising the club's playing profile with a gusto and depth of involvement which inspired consistent underperformers by exuberant example. Warne's pre-match team talks were more like battle cries, and his reward came with much-improved results in all competitions. While his 51 wickets in 12 Championship matches may not have been exceptional, his fierce desire to win every game and his sharp tactical acumen were major factors in Hampshire's success. His mere presence was often enough.

The new victory song was rendered most often, and with greatest relish, during a Championship campaign which led to promotion as runners-up. The total of nine wins, up by seven from 2003, was a fair reflection of Warne's influence, and there might have been two more, with Derbyshire and Glamorgan both clinging on for draws. The highlight of an efficient campaign, in which coach Paul Terry was an astute and thoughtful foil for the captain, was a remarkable victory at Taunton where Somerset, chasing 351, were 300 for three before Warne got among them. The low point was a crushing home defeat by Essex, the 384-run margin Hampshire's biggest-ever in terms of runs.

In the C&G Trophy, Hampshire lost narrowly to the eventual winners Gloucestershire; and they reached the quarter-finals of the Twenty20, despite struggling in the group stage when Warne was on Test duty. Attendances at the Rose Bowl reflected the national enthusiasm for the competition. In the top division of the one-day League, they somehow flirted with relegation and second place at the same time, so close were the teams. In the end, they finished third.

The state of the Rose Bowl wicket was again a topic of concern, in the dressing-rooms and beyond. Nigel Gray, the groundsman, worked hard to eradicate the uneven bounce and there was evidence of a gradual improvement. It is to Gray's credit that, little more than five years after cattle had grazed the same spot, the

Shane Warne

ground now hosts internationals. But the criticism that the pitch is too bowler-friendly was borne out by the national first-class averages, where four Hampshire bowlers finished in the top ten and only three batsmen appeared in the top 100.

Cruelly, the suspicions about the surface worked against Dimitri Mascarenhas, who missed out on an England one-day place despite an outstanding season; the selectors seemed to think he could only take wickets on the green, green grass of home, yet 26 of his 56 cheap victims in the Championship came in away matches. Chris Tremlett, when fit, showed potential beyond county level, while the off-spinner Shaun Udal, though inevitably overshadowed by Warne, enjoyed one of his best seasons as both bowler and batsman, at the age of 35.

Hampshire used four other Australians: batsmen Michael Dighton, Shane Watson and Simon Katich appeared only briefly; Michael Clarke, burdened by being described as the next Ricky Ponting, played 12 Championship games but reserved his best performances for away matches on more reliable surfaces. He illuminated a moderate season with three successive centuries. Nic Pothas was as reliable behind the stumps as he was in front of them; John Crawley's prominence in the averages owed everything to a high-class 301 not out in a run feast at Trent Bridge. No Hampshire player reached 1,000 runs, but many contributed when it mattered – not least a new opener in Michael Brown, formerly of Middlesex and Durham UCCE.

In 2005, Hampshire will play in both first divisions for the first time. But it is also an Ashes summer and Warne, the man who did so much to get them where they wanted, is likely to be otherwise occupied at the business end of the season. It is a huge gap to fill, despite good-quality signings in the hard-hitting Kevin Pietersen, lured from Nottinghamshire amid hot competition, and Sean Ervine, an ex-Zimbabwe all-rounder with an EU passport. But with Warne intending to return in years to come, the chairman has reason to expect more interruptions to his cruises.

HAMPSHIRE RESULTS

All first-class matches – Played 16: Won 9, Lost 2, Drawn 5.
County Championship matches – Played 16: Won 9, Lost 2, Drawn 5.

Frizzell County Championship, 2nd in Division 2; Cheltenham & Gloucester Trophy, 3rd round;
totesport League, 3rd in Division 1; Twenty20 Cup, q-f.

COUNTY CHAMPIONSHIP AVERAGES

BATTING AND FIELDING

Cap		M	I	NO	R	HS	100s	50s	Avge	Ct/St
2002	J. P. Crawley	13	21	3	938	301*	1	5	52.11	4
2003	N. Pothas	16	24	3	834	131*	3	4	39.71	45/5
2003	S. M. Katich§	4	5	0	183	66	0	1	36.60	3
2004	M. J. Clarke§	12	20	0	709	140	3	2	35.45	20
	J. H. K. Adams	8	15	3	425	75	0	2	35.41	1
1992	S. D. Udal	13	17	3	488	74	0	3	34.85	8
	M. J. Brown	16	28	2	838	109*	2	6	32.23	12
2000	S. K. Warne§	12	16	2	381	57	0	1	27.21	9
	L. R. Prittipaul	5	9	0	231	49	0	0	25.66	3
2001	D. A. Kenway	14	23	1	552	101	1	1	25.09	9
1998	A. D. Mascarenhas . .	16	24	2	477	104	1	0	21.68	8
2004	C. T. Tremlett	10	15	4	213	57	0	1	19.36	2
1999	W. S. Kendall	8	14	1	238	50	0	1	18.30	7
	B. V. Taylor	11	16	6	177	40	0	0	17.70	3
2000	A. D. Mullally	10	10	5	67	22*	0	0	13.40	1
	J. T. A. Bruce	4	5	1	10	9	0	0	2.50	1

Also batted: C. C. Benham (1 match) 74; G. A. Lamb (1 match) 94, 7*; J. A. Tomlinson (1 match) 12* (1 ct); S. R. Watson§ (1 match) 24, 112*.

§ *Overseas player.*

BOWLING

	O	M	R	W	BB	5W/i	Avge
A. D. Mascarenhas	404.2	132	1,046	56	6-25	4	18.67
C. T. Tremlett	268.2	56	867	39	4-29	0	22.23
S. D. Udal	247.4	40	869	39	6-79	1	22.28
S. K. Warne	411.5	88	1,231	51	6-65	3	24.13
B. V. Taylor	298.1	59	1,039	33	5-73	1	31.48
A. D. Mullally	245.4	69	711	18	6-68	1	39.50

Also bowled: J. H. K. Adams 19-6-61-2; J. T. A. Bruce 88-11-375-9; M. J. Clarke 42.1-8-160-1; J. P. Crawley 4-1-24-0; S. M. Katich 18-1-61-0; W. S. Kendall 12-2-44-2; D. A. Kenway 2-2-0-0; G. A. Lamb 5-2-15-0; L. R. Prittipaul 21-4-71-1; J. A. Tomlinson 20-7-43-1; S. R. Watson 8.4-2-28-0.

COUNTY RECORDS

Highest score for:	316	R. H. Moore v Warwickshire at Bournemouth . . .	1937
Highest score against:	303*	G. A. Hick (Worcestershire) at Southampton	1997
Best bowling for:	9-25	R. M. H. Cottam v Lancashire at Manchester . . .	1965
Best bowling against:	10-46	W. Hickton (Lancashire) at Manchester	1870
Highest total for:	672-7 dec.	v Somerset at Taunton	1899
Highest total against:	742	by Surrey at The Oval	1909
Lowest total for:	15	v Warwickshire at Birmingham	1922
Lowest total against:	23	by Yorkshire at Middlesbrough	1965

HAMPSHIRE DIRECTORY

ADDRESS

The Rose Bowl, Botley Road, West End, Southampton SO30 3XH (023 8047 2002; fax 023 8047 2122; email enquiries@rosebowlplc.com). **Website** www.hampshirecricket.com.

GROUND

Southampton (The Rose Bowl): 2½ miles NE of city centre from M27 junction 7 then A334 Charles Watts Way. Turn L Tollbar Way B3342 and L Botley Road B3035 for entrance. Nearest stations: Hedge End (2 miles) and Southampton Airport/Parkway (2 miles).

OFFICIALS

Captain S. K. Warne
Director of cricket T. M. Tremlett
First-team manager V. P. Terry
President A. C. D. Ingleby-Mackenzie
Chairman R. G. Bransgrove

Managing director N. S. Pike
Chairman, members committee R. J. Treherne
Head groundsman N. Gray
Scorer V. H Isaacs

PLAYERS

Players expected to reappear in 2005

	Former counties	Country	Born	Birthplace
Adams James Henry Kenneth		E	23.9.1980	†*Winchester*
Benham Christopher Charles		E	24.3.1983	*Frimley*
Brown Michael James	Middx	E	9.2.1980	*Burnley*
Bruce James Thomas Anthony		E	17.12.1979	*Hammersmith*
Clapp Dominic Adrian	Sussex	E	25.5.1980	*Southport*
*****Crawley** John Paul	Lancs	E	21.9.1971	*Maldon*
*****Katich** Simon Mathew	Durham, Yorks	A	21.8.1975	*Middle Swan*
Kenway Derek Anthony		E	12.6.1978	*Fareham*
Lamb Gregory Arthur		Z (EU)	4.3.1980	*Harare*
Mascarenhas Adrian Dimitri		E	30.10.1977	*Chiswick*
*****Mullally** Alan David	Hants, Leics	E	12.7.1969	*Southend-on-Sea*
Pothas Nic		SA (EU)	18.11.1973	*Johannesburg*
Prittipaul Lawrence Roland		E	19.10.1979	†*Portsmouth*
Taylor Billy Victor	Sussex	E	11.1.1977	†*Southampton*
Tomlinson James Andrew		E	12.6.1982	†*Winchester*
Tremlett Christopher Timothy		E	2.9.1981	†*Southampton*
Udal Shaun David		E	18.3.1969	†*Farnborough*
*****Warne** Shane Keith		A	13.9.1969	*Ferntree Gully*

Players due to join in 2005

	Former counties	Country	Born	Birthplace
*****Ervine** Sean Michael		Z (K)	6.12.1982	*Harare*
Logan Richard James	Northants, Notts	E	28.1.1980	*Stone*
Pietersen Kevin Peter	Notts	E	27.6.1980	*Uitenhage, SA*

* *Test player.*   † *Born in Hampshire.*

HAMPSHIRE v DURHAM

At Southampton, April 16, 17, 18, 19. Hampshire won by three wickets. Hampshire 18 pts, Durham 2 pts (after 1 pt penalty). Toss: Durham. County debuts: M. J. Brown, M. J. Clarke, B. V. Taylor; R. D. King. Championship debut: M. J. North.

Shane Warne's first match as Hampshire captain ended in victory – as pre-season hype demanded – though not before a youthful and understrength Durham had competed to the last. Hampshire needed just 109, yet Warne had to pad up and watch anxiously when Davies and Plunkett, after a day and a half had been lost to rain, exploited the damp conditions and reduced them to 52 for seven. As the sun emerged, however, Kendall and Mascarenhas subdued a tiring attack, put together an unbeaten stand of 60 and ensured that Hampshire won their opening Championship fixture for the first time since 1992. Davies, brisk and accurate, deserved match figures of nine for 87 for a Durham side without Collingwood, Harmison and the intended overseas pairing of Herschelle Gibbs and Shoaib Akhtar, who was temporarily, and ineffectively, replaced by the former West Indies pace bowler Reon King. The pitch, while unpredictable, was not as difficult as 32 wickets on the first two days indicated. Warne's fellow-Australian Michael Clarke, on his Hampshire debut, made a sumptuous 75.

Close of play: First day, Hampshire 195-5 (Clarke 73, Mascarenhas 0); Second day, Hampshire 13-2 (Taylor 1, Tremlett 0); Third day, No play.

Durham

*J. J. B. Lewis c Pothas b Tremlett	3	– c Pothas b Tremlett	50
M. J. North c Taylor b Warne	29	– lbw b Tremlett	4
G. J. Muchall c Warne b Mullally	0	– lbw b Mullally	1
G. J. Pratt c Warne b Mascarenhas	13	– c Clarke b Mullally	4
N. Peng lbw b Taylor	49	– b Warne	66
G. M. Hamilton c Brown b Mascarenhas	6	– b Warne	15
†A. Pratt c and b Mascarenhas	0	– c Kendall b Mascarenhas	20
G. D. Bridge c Warne b Tremlett	3	– b Warne	6
L. E. Plunkett not out	15	– c Tremlett b Warne	21
A. M. Davies c Brown b Taylor	0	– not out	6
R. D. King lbw b Warne	0	– b Warne	0
B 3, l-b 5, n-b 2	10	B 7, w 1	8
	128		**201**

1/3 (1) 2/6 (3) 3/30 (4) 4/65 (2)
5/83 (6) 6/85 (7) 7/88 (8)
8/123 (5) 9/127 (10) 10/128 (11)

1/6 (2) 2/11 (3) 3/19 (4)
4/130 (5) 5/130 (1) 6/164 (6)
7/168 (7) 8/190 (8)
9/199 (9) 10/201 (11)

Bonus points – Hampshire 3.

Bowling: *First Innings*—Mullally 12-3-26-1; Tremlett 11-6-10-2; Taylor 10-5-23-2; Mascarenhas 12-5-28-3; Warne 8.3-1-27-2; Clarke 1-0-6-0. *Second Innings*—Mullally 10-4-33-2; Tremlett 16-3-42-2; Mascarenhas 17-10-13-1; Warne 29-8-68-5; Clarke 6-1-24-0; Taylor 7-2-14-0.

““Instead of spending the summer inside West Indies' tent and, in Lyndon Johnson's phrase, pissing out, Richards took a broadcast commentary job and regularly, but not unjustly, pissed in."

West Indians in England, page 467.

Hampshire

D. A. Kenway c North b Davies	35	– lbw b Davies	9
M. J. Brown c A. Pratt b Davies	28	– c Hamilton b Plunkett	0
J. P. Crawley c G. J. Pratt b King	35	– (5) lbw b Plunkett	0
M. J. Clarke c G. J. Pratt b Davies	75	– (6) b Plunkett	0
W. S. Kendall c Muchall b King	0	– (7) not out	31
†N. Pothas lbw b Davies	10	– (8) lbw b Davies	11
A. D. Mascarenhas c Muchall b Plunkett	3	– (9) not out	33
*S. K. Warne c King b Plunkett	3		
C. T. Tremlett not out	8	– (4) b Davies	10
B. V. Taylor c Lewis b Davies	5	– (3) c A. Pratt b Plunkett	9
A. D. Mullally c Lewis b Davies	5		
L-b 6, w 2, n-b 6	14	L-b 7, n-b 2	9

1/55 (1) 2/80 (2) 3/165 (3) 4/167 (5)   221   1/11 (2) 2/13 (1)   (7 wkts) 112
5/192 (6) 6/199 (4) 7/203 (7)   3/23 (4) 4/24 (5)
8/203 (8) 9/208 (10) 10/221 (11)   5/26 (6) 6/39 (3) 7/52 (8)

Bonus points – Hampshire 1, Durham 3.

Bowling: *First Innings*—King 11–1–65–2; Plunkett 17–4–66–2; Davies 17.2–7–53–6; Hamilton 6–1–19–0; Bridge 5–1–12–0. *Second Innings*—Plunkett 18–5–48–4; Davies 15–7–34–3; King 3.2–0–21–0; Hamilton 1 0–2–0

Umpires: A. Clarkson and P. Willey.

HAMPSHIRE v LEICESTERSHIRE

At Southampton, April 28, 29, 30, May 1. Hampshire won by an innings and 18 runs. Hampshire 19 pts, Leicestershire 2 pts. Toss: Leicestershire.

Even the loss of the middle two days to rain could not prevent Hampshire from sweeping to victory over a feeble Leicestershire with almost ten overs to spare. Hampshire were already dominant by the end of the first day after Leicestershire failed to cope with a sporting pitch. Even so, there seemed little prospect of a result when play resumed under a watery sun on the last day. Yet Warne sensed a chance and instructed his batsmen to hurry towards a declaration. The Durham graduate Michael Brown responded with a maiden century, taking advantage of two lapses in the deep. Warne's declaration, 129 ahead, left Leicestershire 53 overs to save themselves, but Mascarenhas wobbled through the top order for Warne and Udal to polish off what remained. Hampshire's win, their second in two Championship matches, equalled their total from 16 in 2003.

Close of play: First day, Hampshire 93-1 (Brown 30, Kendall 32); Second day, No play; Third day, No play.

Leicestershire

D. D. J. Robinson b Mascarenhas	11	– b Mascarenhas	8
J. K. Maunders b Warne	34	– c Kendall b Mascarenhas	23
B. J. Hodge c Clarke b Tremlett	1	– (5) c Clarke b Warne	29
D. L. Maddy lbw b Udal	7	– (3) lbw b Mascarenhas	0
D. I. Stevens c Pothas b Mascarenhas	11	– (4) b Mascarenhas	3
J. L. Sadler lbw b Warne	1	– c Clarke b Tremlett	7
†P. A. Nixon c Pothas b Mascarenhas	0	– c Brown b Mascarenhas	3
*P. A. J. DeFreitas b Tremlett	24	– (9) c Clarke b Warne	0
C. W. Henderson lbw b Mullally	31	– (8) not out	13
D. D. Masters b Mullally	5	– b Udal	9
M. F. Cleary not out	8	– lbw b Udal	4
B 1, l-b 5	6	B 4, l-b 2, n-b 6	12

1/22 (1) 2/29 (3) 3/56 (4) 4/69 (5)   139   1/24 (1) 2/26 (3) 3/30 (4)   111
5/69 (2) 6/70 (7) 7/70 (6)   4/37 (2) 5/66 (6) 6/73 (7)
8/104 (8) 9/126 (10) 10/139 (9)   7/80 (5) 8/80 (9)
                                9/103 (10) 10/111 (11)

Bonus points – Hampshire 3.

Bowling: *First Innings*—Mullally 11–4–22–2; Tremlett 14–5–33–2; Mascarenhas 15–9–22–3; Udal 12–3–39–1; Warne 12–6–17–2. *Second Innings*—Mullally 11–4–18–0; Tremlett 9–1–35–1; Mascarenhas 10–5–22–5; Warne 11–4–26–2; Udal 2.4–2–4–2.

Hampshire

D. A. Kenway c Nixon b DeFreitas	23	*S. K. Warne not out		29
M. J. Brown not out	102			
W. S. Kendall c Nixon b Cleary	38	B 13, l-b 5, n-b 4		22
M. J. Clarke b Cleary	0			
L. R. Prittipaul st Nixon b Henderson	31	1/48 (1) 2/105 (3)	(6 wkts dec.)	268
†N. Pothas c Hodge b Cleary	21	3/105 (4) 4/175 (5)		
A. D. Mascarenhas run out	2	5/214 (6) 6/222 (7)		

S. D. Udal, C. T. Tremlett and A. D. Mullally did not bat.

Bonus points – Hampshire 2, Leicestershire 2.

Bowling: Cleary 17–4–57–3; DeFreitas 22–2–62–1; Masters 11–3–24–0; Henderson 12–1–65–1; Maddy 5–1–23–0; Hodge 5–0–19–0.

Umpires: I. J. Gould and M. J. Harris.

HAMPSHIRE v DERBYSHIRE

At Southampton, May 7, 8, 9, 10. Drawn. Hampshire 12 pts, Derbyshire 10 pts. Toss: Hampshire. Championship debut: J. Moss.

Derbyshire's last pair, Mohammad Ali and Nick Walker, survived 14 balls to achieve a draw and deny Hampshire a third Championship win in three starts. Warne accused Derbyshire of "negative tactics" and admitted his irritation had led him to delay his declaration until they could not win. Set 274 in 53 overs, Derbyshire had no choice but try to avoid defeat. Mascarenhas then took a career-best six for 25 as the batsmen wavered on another Rose Bowl wicket of uncertain bounce. Kenway and Pothas were responsible for Hampshire's position of power with first-innings hundreds against an attack badly missing Kevin Dean. In their reply, Derbyshire depended on a cultured 87 from Rogers and, although they were eight down before they saved the follow-on, they kept Hampshire's lead down to 95. Warne, whose declaration calculations were not helped by losing all bar 17 overs of the second day to rain, set off after the match for Australia's fraught tour of Zimbabwe. He left Hampshire in a healthier state than for some years but, on this occasion, regretting his uncharacteristic risk-aversion.

Close of play: First day, Hampshire 333-6 (Pothas 86, Warne 4); Second day, Hampshire 399-8 (Pothas 112, Tremlett 11); Third day, Derbyshire 279-8 (Botha 23, Mohammad Ali 12).

Hampshire

D. A. Kenway lbw b Botha	101	– c and b Welch	33
M. J. Brown lbw b Mohammad Ali	1	– c Sutton b Walker	1
W. S. Kendall run out	25	– c sub b Welch	19
M. J. Clarke c Sutton b Mohammad Ali	21	– c Rogers b Moss	45
L. R. Prittipaul c Sutton b Walker	40	– c Sutton b Mohammad Ali	25
†N. Pothas not out	131	– not out	22
A. D. Mascarenhas lbw b Moss	46	– b Moss	15
*S. K. Warne lbw b Mohammad Ali	4	– not out	10
S. D. Udal c Stubbings b Welch	27		
C. T. Tremlett c Sutton b Mohammad Ali	12		
B 5, l-b 3, w 1, n-b 2	11	B 3, l-b 3, n-b 2	8

1/9 (2) 2/53 (3) 3/104 (4)   (9 wkts dec.) 419   1/12 (2) 2/49 (1)   (6 wkts dec.) 178
4/185 (1) 5/203 (5) 6/322 (7)   3/66 (3) 4/128 (5)
7/334 (8) 8/378 (9) 9/419 (10)   5/128 (4) 6/152 (7)

A. D. Mullally did not bat.

Bonus points – Hampshire 5, Derbyshire 3.

Bowling: *First Innings*—Mohammad Ali 32.2–8–121–4; Welch 33–8–100–1; Moss 26–5–91–1; Walker 10–1–40–1; Botha 23–2–59–1. *Second Innings*—Mohammad Ali 14–3–61–1; Walker 5–0–27–1; Welch 8–0–51–2; Moss 5–0–33–2.

Derbyshire

S. D. Stubbings c Brown b Warne	24	– lbw b Mascarenhas	20
A. I. Gait b Mascarenhas	9	– c Kenway b Warne	20
C. J. L. Rogers c and b Udal	87	– c Warne b Mascarenhas	0
Hassan Adnan lbw b Tremlett	0	– c Kenway b Mascarenhas	0
J. Moss c Kenway b Tremlett	9	– b Mascarenhas	12
C. W. G. Bassano c Pothas b Prittipaul	53	– lbw b Tremlett	21
*†L. D. Sutton c Warne b Udal	8	– c Prittipaul b Mascarenhas	5
G. Welch c Pothas b Mullally	40	– b Tremlett	12
A. G. Botha b Udal	31	– lbw b Mascarenhas	0
Mohammad Ali c Brown b Tremlett	12	– not out	3
N. G. E. Walker not out	31	– not out	0
B 4, l-b 10, n-b 6	20	L-b 5, n-b 4	9

324   (9 wkts) 102

1/19 (2) 2/73 (1) 3/90 (4) 4/104 (5)
5/153 (3) 6/183 (7) 7/221 (6)
8/260 (8) 9/279 (10) 10/324 (9)

1/38 (1) 2/38 (3) 3/40 (4)
4/54 (2) 5/56 (5) 6/80 (7)
7/94 (6) 8/99 (8) 9/101 (9)

Bonus points – Derbyshire 3, Hampshire 3.

Bowling: *First Innings*—Tremlett 16–4–49–3; Mullally 20–4–58–1; Mascarenhas 10–4–25–1; Warne 26–8–75–1; Udal 23–2–78 3; Clarke 7–2–11–0; Prittipaul 5–0–14–1. *Second Innings*—Tremlett 11–3–23–2; Mullally 6–2–14–0; Mascarenhas 17–9–25–6; Prittipaul 2–0–11–0; Warne 14–7–18–1; Udal 3–0–6–0.

Umpires: J. H. Evans and R. Palmer.

At Leeds, May 12, 13, 14. HAMPSHIRE beat YORKSHIRE by 119 runs.

At Southampton, May 19, 20, 21 (not first-class). **Drawn.** Toss: Hampshire. **Hampshire 287** (G. A. Lamb 66, M. S. T. Stokes 57*) **and 255-4 dec.** (G. A. Lamb 90, D. C. Shirazi 51*); **Cardiff UCCE 302** (J. Hibberd 5-72) **and 89-4.**
First-team debuts: T. G. Burrows, J. Hibberd, K. J. Latouf; M. S. T. Stokes (Hampshire). County debuts: A. P. Hollingsworth, G. A. Lamb, D. C. Shirazi.
Hampshire collapsed from 177 for four to 188 for eight. In reply, four Cardiff batsmen reached 44, but none passed 48. In all, the game included eight scores in the forties.

HAMPSHIRE v NOTTINGHAMSHIRE

At Southampton, June 2, 3. Nottinghamshire won by an innings and 44 runs. Nottinghamshire 21 pts, Hampshire 3 pts. Toss: Hampshire.
Fifteen wickets tumbled on the first day, triggering a visit by pitch liaison officer Tony Brown, who saw another 15 fall next day, when Nottinghamshire wrapped up victory 17 overs before the scheduled close. But Brown concluded Hampshire's batsmen were to blame rather than the pitch. They were bowled out twice in less than 90 overs, giving Warne his first Championship defeat as captain and Nottinghamshire a big win in the contest between the second division's early pace-setters. Logan led the seam attack on the opening day, when Hampshire endured the extra annoyance of missing a bonus point by one run. However, Ealham and Hussey put worries about the pitch in perspective with a stand of 143 for the sixth wicket. (Hussey, caught at the wicket off a sharply rising Tremlett delivery, was officially reprimanded for dissent.) Facing a deficit of 157, Hampshire collapsed to the seamers for just 113. Logan finished with match figures of eight for 90.
Close of play: First day, Nottinghamshire 185-5 (Hussey 27, Ealham 25).

Hampshire

D. A. Kenway c Read b Smith	21	– c Read b Franks	23
M. J. Brown lbw b Logan	20	– b Smith	10
W. S. Kendall lbw b Ealham	0	– b Logan	21
M. J. Clarke b Logan	28	– c Ealham b Franks	7
J. P. Crawley c Hussey b Franks	25	– c Ealham b Franks	7
†N. Pothas c Hussey b Franks	26	– lbw b Logan	3
A. D. Mascarenhas c Read b Smith	9	– c Read b Smith	18
*S. K. Warne c Hussey b Franks	14	– c Bicknell b Logan	8
S. D. Udal c Read b Logan	36	– not out	8
C. T. Tremlett c Warren b Logan	11	– c Hussey b Logan	3
A. D. Mullally not out	5	– c Ealham b Smith	0
L-b 2, w 2	4	B 1, l-b 4	5
	199		**113**

1/36 (1) 2/40 (3) 3/73 (4) 4/98 (5)
5/98 (2) 6/124 (7) 7/139 (8)
8/156 (6) 9/194 (9) 10/199 (10)

1/29 (1) 2/33 (2) 3/62 (4)
4/66 (3) 5/76 (6) 6/78 (5)
7/95 (8) 8/109 (7)
9/112 (10) 10/113 (11)

Bonus points – Nottinghamshire 3.

Bowling: *First Innings*—Smith 17–6–52–2; Franks 14–5–43–3; Ealham 13–5–46–1; Logan 10.1–2–56–4. *Second Innings*—Smith 10.4–0–34–3; Ealham 4–2–5–0; Franks 10–0–35–3; Logan 11–2–34–4.

Nottinghamshire

D. J. Bicknell lbw b Mascarenhas	54	R. J. Logan not out	9
*J. E. R. Gallian c Kendall b Tremlett	9	S. C. G. MacGill c sub b Tremlett	4
R. J. Warren lbw b Tremlett	0		
K. P. Pietersen lbw b Udal	49	B 4, l-b 6, n-b 19	29
D. J. Hussey c Pothas b Tremlett	48		
†C. M. W. Read b Udal	5		**356**
M. A. Ealham c Pothas b Kendall	96	1/19 (2) 2/25 (3) 3/124 (1)	
P. J. Franks c Clarke b Warne	32	4/130 (4) 5/136 (6) 6/279 (7)	
G. J. Smith c Mascarenhas b Warne	21	7/291 (5) 8/331 (8)	
		9/340 (9) 10/356 (11)	

Bonus points – Nottinghamshire 4, Hampshire 3.

Bowling: Tremlett 22.2–3–102–4; Mullally 15–7–29–0; Mascarenhas 20–8–55–1; Warne 21–3–85–2; Udal 14–3–57–2; Kendall 2–0–12–1; Clarke 1–0–6–0.

Umpires: M. R. Benson and G. Sharp.

At Chelmsford, June 9, 10, 11. HAMPSHIRE beat ESSEX by 114 runs.

HAMPSHIRE v SOMERSET

At Southampton, June 18, 19, 20. Hampshire won by 275 runs. Hampshire 18 pts, Somerset 4 pts. Toss: Hampshire. Championship debut: S. R. Watson.

Hampshire, encountering only the flimsiest of resistance, cruised to their fifth Championship win just one ball after Udal – captain while Warne recovered from a broken hand – had requested the extra half-hour at the end of the third day. There were, however, mitigating factors for Somerset's poor performance: Parsons and Johnson were injured early on and could take no further part in the game; Johnson damaged his ankle by treading on the ball. Two Hampshire bowlers also broke down mid-over, but unlike the Somerset wounded, Shane Watson, on his Championship debut, and Mascarenhas were able to bat with the aid of runners (together adding 32 for the ninth wicket). Indeed Watson, the Tasmanian all-rounder, showed little discomfort in an unbeaten, chanceless 112 as he and Udal, dropped on nought, put on 158 against a depleted attack containing just two front-line bowlers. Udal eventually declared, setting Somerset's nine batsmen a target of 422. They lasted 40 overs, with only Dutch showing much permanence. Hampshire gained 14 points for a win, but were deprived of a third bowling point by Somerset's absentees.

Close of play: First day, Somerset 21-1 (Edwards 5); Second day, Hampshire 119-5 (Crawley 34, Watson 9).

Hampshire

D. A. Kenway c Parsons b Caddick	7	– c Dutch b Burns	31
M. J. Brown lbw b Caddick	81	– c Hildreth b Burns	23
J. P. Crawley c Turner b Francis	3	– b Francis	40
W. S. Kendall c Edwards b Caddick	13	– c Turner b Burns	5
M. J. Clarke c Turner b Caddick	18	– c Turner b Caddick	1
S. R. Watson st Turner b Dutch	24	– (7) not out	112
†R. J. Pothas c Cox b Dutch	16	– (8) b Francis	6
A. D. Mascarenhas c Turner b Francis	6	– (10) lbw b Francis	9
*S. D. Udal c Turner b Francis	50	– b Francis	74
C. T. Tremlett c Turner b Francis	57	– (11) not out	0
B. V. Taylor not out	4	– (6) lbw b Caddick	0
L b 9, w 2	11	B 4, l-b 12, w 7, n-b 10	33
	290	(9 wkts dec.)	**334**

1/12 (1) 2/31 (3) 3/67 (4) 4/111 (5) 5/146 (2) 6/164 (6) 7/169 (7) 8/175 (8) 9/255 (9) 10/290 (10)

1/48 (2) 2/71 (1) 3/97 (4) 4/103 (5) 5/107 (6) 6/125 (3) 7/131 (8) 8/289 (9) 9/321 (10)

Bonus points – Hampshire 2, Somerset 3.

Bowling. *First Innings*—Caddick 29–9–75–4; Johnson 13–2–38–0; Francis 20.1–5–57–4; Parsons 9–3–36–0; Dutch 20–2–75–2. *Second Innings*—Caddick 30–8–119–2; Francis 24–2–113–4; Burns 16–4–46–3; Dutch 4–1–20–0; Edwards 3–0–20–0.

Somerset

P. D. Bowler c Kenway b Tremlett	15	– c Crawley b Taylor	6
N. J. Edwards b Taylor	13	– lbw b Tremlett	0
J. Cox c Pothas b Mascarenhas	24	– lbw b Taylor	23
J. C. Hildreth c and b Udal	61	– c Pothas b Tremlett	14
*M. Burns c Mascarenhas b Tremlett	36	– c Kendall b Udal	30
†R. J. Turner c Pothas b Mascarenhas	4	– b Kendall	0
K. P. Dutch lbw b Mascarenhas	2	– lbw b Tremlett	60
A. R. Caddick not out	28	– c Pothas b Taylor	5
S. R. G. Francis c Kendall b Udal	8	– not out	0
K. A. Parsons absent hurt		– absent hurt	
R. L. Johnson absent hurt		– absent hurt	
B 3, l-b 3, w 2, n-b 4	12	B 6, l-b 2	8
	203		**146**

1/21 (1) 2/39 (2) 3/72 (3) 4/153 (4) 5/163 (6) 6/165 (7) 7/169 (5) 8/203 (9)

1/1 (2) 2/21 (1) 3/40 (3) 4/49 (4) 5/60 (6) 6/121 (5) 7/130 (8) 8/146 (7)

Bonus points – Somerset 1, Hampshire 2.

Bowling: *First Innings*—Taylor 15.2–3–62–1; Tremlett 18–6–44–2; Watson 8–4–2–28–0; Mascarenhas 10.3–1–45–3; Udal 6.5–1–17–2; Clarke 1–0–1–0. *Second Innings*—Tremlett 11.1–1–43–3; Taylor 15–2–38–3; Kendall 8–2–20–1; Udal 6–0–37–1.

Umpires: A. Clarkson and R. Palmer.

HAMPSHIRE v YORKSHIRE

At Southampton, June 23, 24, 25, 26. Drawn. Hampshire 9 pts, Yorkshire 10 pts. Toss: Yorkshire.
Phil Jaques became the first player to score a double-hundred for and against Yorkshire. His career-best 243 – which came from 299 balls, lasted 411 minutes and contained six sixes and 33 fours – eclipsed the 222 he made a year earlier against Yorkshire for Northamptonshire. He made full use of a true Rose Bowl wicket to score just under two-thirds of Yorkshire's runs off the bat; Craven was the only other player to pass 22. Mullally, who had taken just seven Championship wickets in

PROS AND CONS

Batsmen who have hit double-hundreds for and against the same team.

Seven players have achieved this feat in England:

J. P. Crawley (Hampshire)
C. B. Fry (Hampshire)
C. L. Hooper (Lancashire)
P. A. Jaques (Yorkshire)

P. B. H. May (Cambridge University)
W. L. Murdoch (Sussex)
M. R. Ramprakash (Surrey)

Ten players have achieved this feat outside England:

S. Amarnath (Delhi)
D. G. Bradman (NSW and South Australia)
G. W. Flower (Mashonaland)
R. N. Harvey (New South Wales)
V. S. Hazare (Baroda)

M. J. Horne (Auckland)
K. R. Miller (New South Wales)
A. W. Nourse (Natal, Transvaal and W. Province)
J. R. Reid (Otago)
R. B. Simpson (NSW and Western Australia)

Nourse is alone in hitting double-hundreds for and against three teams. Bradman and Simpson did so for two.

Research: Philip Bailey

2004, grabbed six for 68, while Pothas held five catches as a weakened Yorkshire surrendered a powerful position, losing their last seven wickets for 50. The quality of Jaques's innings became even clearer as Hampshire laboured to 182 for six, still 64 short of saving the follow-on. But Pothas and Udal extinguished any Yorkshire hopes in a flurry of boundaries before rain, which knocked out 201 overs – almost half the match allocation – had the last, unwelcome word.
Close of play: First day, Yorkshire 34-1 (Jaques 22, Taylor 5); Second day, Yorkshire 268-3 (Jaques 193, Craven 15); Third day, Hampshire 202-6 (Pothas 18, Udal 14).

Yorkshire

*M. J. Wood c Pothas b Tremlett	1	M. J. Hoggard c Pothas b Udal	1	
P. A. Jaques b Mullally	243	S. P. Kirby lbw b Mullally	0	
C. R. Taylor c Clarke b Udal	22			
M. J. Lumb c Pothas b Taylor	18	L-b 10, n-b 18	28	
V. J. Craven c Pothas b Mullally	41			
A. K. D. Gray c Pothas b Mullally	10	1/10 (1) 2/125 (3) 3/211 (4)	395	
†S. M. Guy c Taylor b Mullally	13	4/345 (2) 5/354 (5) 6/365 (6)		
R. K. J. Dawson b Mullally	7	7/378 (7) 8/385 (8)		
C. E. W. Silverwood not out	11	9/394 (10) 10/395 (11)		

Bonus points – Yorkshire 4, Hampshire 3.

Bowling: Tremlett 23–5–93–1; Taylor 25–8–56–1; Udal 21–2–78–2; Clarke 2–0–7–0; Mullally 31.4–13–68–6; Mascarenhas 22–6–71–0; Kendall 2–0–12–0.

> **"**If looks could kill, Fleming would have been charged with mass murder."
> The New Zealanders in England, page **445**.

Hampshire

D. A. Kenway c Guy b Kirby	12	*S. D. Udal b Gray	41
M. J. Brown c Guy b Hoggard	1	C. T. Tremlett not out	0
J. P. Crawley lbw b Craven	53	B 6, l-b 22, w 3, n-b 12	43
W. S. Kendall c Taylor b Craven	15		
M. J. Clarke c Dawson b Kirby	27		(8 wkts) 259
†N. Pothas c Dawson b Hoggard	45		
A. D. Mascarenhas c Craven b Hoggard	22		

A. D. Mullally and B. V. Taylor did not bat.

1/5 (2) 2/22 (1) 3/55 (4) (8 wkts) 259
4/119 (5) 5/137 (3) 6/182 (7)
7/253 (8) 8/259 (6)

Bonus points – Hampshire 2, Yorkshire 2.

Bowling: Hoggard 20.4–6–50–3; Silverwood 13–4–37–0; Kirby 14–4–44–2; Craven 8–2–29–2; Dawson 15–2–51–0; Gray 7–1–20–1.

Umpires: N. G. Cowley and A. G. T. Whitehead.

At Nottingham, July 23, 24, 25, 26. HAMPSHIRE drew with NOTTINGHAMSHIRE.

At Cardiff, July 29, 30, 31. HAMPSHIRE beat GLAMORGAN by nine wickets.

HAMPSHIRE v ESSEX

At Southampton, August 3, 4, 5. Essex won by 384 runs. Essex 22 pts, Hampshire 3 pts. Toss: Hampshire.

This was Essex's biggest first-class win in terms of runs and Hampshire's heaviest defeat, eclipsing their previous worst of 380, against Surrey at Northlands Road in 1896. The thrashing was especially painful for their captain Warne, who chose to field first and watched Essex compile 416 on what turned out to be one of the Rose Bowl's more reliable pitches. The Essex innings was a one-man show from opener Jefferson, who drove and pulled commandingly, at one stage hitting Bruce for four successive fours. Jefferson was finally ninth out for 222; the next-best score was 40. He hit 31 fours, mainly through the off side, and stayed 410 minutes and 300 balls – only 63 deliveries fewer than Hampshire lasted in reply. Wary of batting on a fourth-innings pitch, Essex did not impose the follow-on, and the decision proved correct when Hampshire lost five wickets for four runs and were all out for 149. As Essex were extending their lead in the second innings, Warne exchanged unpleasantries with the batsman Irani and both were called to a meeting next morning, with their coaches, to be warned by the umpires. Irani issued a statement denying reports that Warne had called him the "son of a whore".

Close of play: First day, Essex 416; Second day, Essex 116-3 (Grayson 63, Irani 12).

Essex

W. I. Jefferson c Pothas b Taylor	222	– lbw b Mullally	4
A. P. Grayson lbw b Bruce	7	– c Clarke b Bruce	75
A. Flower c Warne b Mullally	32	– c Pothas b Warne	33
A. Habib c Kenway b Warne	19	– c Pothas b Mascarenhas	0
*R. C. Irani c Pothas b Taylor	17	– c Pothas b Taylor	41
†J. S. Foster c Brown b Warne	40	– c Brown b Bruce	7
J. D. Middlebrook c Pothas b Bruce	0	– c Mascarenhas b Clarke	93
G. R. Napier c sub b Bruce	8	– not out	31
A. R. Adams st Pothas b Warne	22		
A. P. Cowan not out	21		
D. Gough lbw b Warne	0		
B 3, l-b 9, w 2, n-b 14	28	B 1, l-b 1, w 2, n-b 6	10

1/32 (2) 2/154 (3) 3/189 (4) 4/222 (5) 416   1/6 (1) 2/83 (3) (7 wkts dec.) 294
5/321 (6) 6/322 (7) 7/340 (8)   3/88 (4) 4/144 (2)
8/385 (9) 9/415 (1) 10/416 (11)   5/152 (6) 6/212 (5) 7/294 (7)

Bonus points – Essex 5, Hampshire 3.

Bowling: *First Innings*—Mullally 20–6–72–1; Bruce 19–3–74–3; Mascarenhas 3–1–5–0; Taylor 23–3–111–2; Warne 32–1–118–4; Clarke 6–1–24–0. *Second Innings*—Mullally 14–4–36–1; Bruce 13–1–62–2; Taylor 12–0–56–1; Mascarenhas 17–5–33–1; Warne 17–2–53–1; Clarke 6.1–0–52–1.

Hampshire

J. H. K. Adams b Napier	21	– c Cowan b Adams 23
M. J. Brown c Adams b Gough	13	– lbw b Gough 0
J. P. Crawley c Flower b Cowan	55	– c Jefferson b Napier 24
M. J. Clarke c Foster b Adams	18	– b Adams 18
D. A. Kenway c Foster b Adams	21	– b Napier 5
†N. Pothas c Foster b Adams	0	– c Foster b Cowan 12
A. D. Mascarenhas b Adams	0	– c Flower b Cowan 0
*S. K. Warne c Irani b Napier	21	– c Foster b Adams 0
J. T. A. Bruce b Gough	1	– c Adams b Cowan 0
A. D. Mullally b Cowan	15	– not out 19
B. V. Taylor not out	4	– lbw b Gough 40
L-b 2, n-b 6	8	L-b 4, n-b 4 8

1/25 (2) 2/48 (1) 3/75 (4) 4/122 (5)   177
5/122 (6) 6/122 (7) 7/149 (8)
8/156 (9) 9/164 (3) 10/177 (10)

1/9 (2) 2/44 (1) 3/50 (3)   149
4/64 (5) 5/84 (6) 6/88 (4)
7/88 (7) 8/88 (8)
9/88 (9) 10/149 (11)

Bonus points – Essex 3.

Bowling: *First Innings*—Gough 15–3–44–2; Cowan 17–3–45–2; Napier 14–2–40–2; Adams 14–1–46–4. *Second Innings*—Gough 8–2–39–2; Cowan 8–2–44–3; Napier 5–1–26–2; Adams 9–2–23–3; Middlebrook 3–0–13–0.

Umpires: G. I. Burgess and M. J. Harris.

HAMPSHIRE v GLAMORGAN

At Southampton, August 11, 12, 13, 14. Drawn. Hampshire 11 pts, Glamorgan 10 pts. Toss: Hampshire.

Darren Thomas made perhaps the biggest-ever impact on a first-class game by a twelfth man. Thomas started the game for Glamorgan before Simon Jones was released from England's squad for the Old Trafford Test, and he proved a mighty effective stopgap – taking four Hampshire wickets and belting a century, which included six reverse sweeps for four off Warne. When Jones finally arrived for the last day, he proved much less effective, bowling ten wicketless overs for 51. Those figures were parsimonious compared to Croft, who went for ten an over during a declaration-hurrying barrage from Brown and Crawley. Together they put on 130 in 12 overs, Brown reaching his century with a fifth six. Left a minimum of 55 overs to get 269 on the Rose Bowl's best strip of the season, Glamorgan fell away to 130 for eight against the spinners Warne and Udal, only for their ninth-wicket pair to deny a ring of close fielders and survive ten overs at the end. After the match, Thomas was at the centre of a controversy over how his innings should correctly be recorded. He ended the second day 105 not out but was at his grandfather's funeral, and unable to resume, on the rain-shortened third. The scorers originally thought his innings should therefore be recorded as "Retired – not out", because the funeral, under Law 2.9(a), constituted "an unavoidable cause" for absence. But the ECB worried this was unfair on Hampshire, who were denied the wicket of Thomas, a penalty which might have cost them a bonus point. The board said Thomas was "Retired – out", but later accepted the original verdict.

Close of play: First day, Hampshire 317-7 (Warne 32, Udal 1); Second day, Glamorgan 257-4 (Powell 62, Thomas 105); Third day, Hampshire 28-0 (Adams 11, Brown 10).

Hampshire

J. H. K. Adams run out	6	– c Powell b Croft	42
M. J. Brown b Thomas	90	– not out	109
J. P. Crawley lbw b Croft	47	– not out	70
M. J. Clarke c sub b Croft	5		
D. A. Kenway c Wallace b Kasprowicz	64		
†N. Pothas b Croft	26		
A. D. Mascarenhas c Elliott b Harrison	34		
*S. K. Warne c Hemp b Thomas	42		
S. D. Udal b Thomas	40		
A. D. Mullally c Wallace b Thomas	0		
B. V. Taylor not out	2		
B 4, l-b 5, n-b 4	13	B 1, l-b 13, n-b 6	20

1/6 (1) 2/116 (3) 3/146 (4) 4/178 (2)　　　369　　1/111 (1)　　　　(1 wkt dec.) 241
5/235 (6) 6/261 (5) 7/302 (7)
8/348 (8) 9/348 (10) 10/369 (9)

Bonus points – Hampshire 4, Glamorgan 3.

Bowling: *First Innings*—Kasprowicz 31–5–100–1; Harrison 20–4–51–1; Thomas 26.3–1–103–4; Dale 9–1–33–0; Croft 25–3–73–3. *Second Innings*—Kasprowicz 14–2–37–0; Harrison 18–8–58–0; Jones 10–1–51–0; Croft 8–0–81–1.

Glamorgan

M. T. G. Elliott c Pothas b Taylor	8	– (2) st Pothas b Warne	34
†M. A. Wallace c Mullally b Mascarenhas	27	– (7) lbw b Udal	9
D. L. Hemp b Mascarenhas	17	– b Warne	32
M. J. Powell lbw b Mascarenhas	89	– c Brown b Udal	26
M. P. Maynard c Udal b Mascarenhas	5	– c Clarke b Warne	0
S. D. Thomas retired not out	105		
J. Hughes c Pothas b Mascarenhas	3	– (6) b Warne	0
A. Dale b Taylor	15	– not out	4
*R. D. B. Croft not out	14	– (1) b Mascarenhas	18
D. S. Harrison b Taylor	0	– (9) lbw b Udal	0
M. S. Kasprowicz b Udal	18	– (10) not out	20
B 8, l-b 7, n-b 26	41	L-b 1, n-b 6	7

1/13 (1) 2/55 (2) 3/62 (3) 4/72 (5)　　　342　　1/35 (1) 2/85 (2)　　　(8 wkts) 150
5/287 (7) 6/290 (4) 7/311 (8)　　　　　　　　　3/98 (3) 4/98 (5)
8/311 (10) 9/342 (11)　　　　　　　　　　　　5/108 (6) 6/119 (7)
　　　　　　　　　　　　　　　　　　　　　　7/130 (4) 8/130 (9)

S. P. Jones did not bat.

Bonus points – Glamorgan 3, Hampshire 3.

In the first innings Thomas retired not out at 257.

Bowling: *First Innings*—Mullally 16–3–64–0; Taylor 21–5–64–3; Mascarenhas 24–6–64–5; Udal 8.5–1–48–1; Warne 22–1–87–0. *Second Innings*—Taylor 7–0–24–0; Mullally 3–0–16–0; Mascarenhas 14–4–44–1; Udal 16–6–39–3; Warne 18.5–12–26–4.

Umpires: N. J. Llong and N. A. Mallender.

At Taunton, August 18, 19, 20, 21. HAMPSHIRE beat SOMERSET by ten runs.

At Chester-le-Street, August 24, 25, 26, 27. HAMPSHIRE drew with DURHAM.

At Leicester, September 1, 2, 3, 4. HAMPSHIRE beat LEICESTERSHIRE by 86 runs.

At Derby, September 16, 17, 18, 19. HAMPSHIRE beat DERBYSHIRE by 91 runs.

KENT

An unhappy ship sails strange waters

MARK PENNELL

This was an odd season for Kent, runners-up in the Championship but relegated for the first time in the one-day league. While an inexperienced side were proud of seven Championship wins (two more than the winners, Warwickshire), 2004 will be remembered more as a bleak summer of unrest.

By the last game, the club were consulting solicitors to quell a members' revolt. Persistent stories of dressing-room infighting through the season were followed by the news that the stylish and consistent Ed Smith was leaving for Middlesex and, much more surprisingly, that Alex Loudon, promising as an off-spinner, batsman and potential captain, was going to Warwickshire. Both cited a lack of faith in Kent's coaching and management structure, prompting members to demand action. It was a sad end to a season of great promise. And when the St Lawrence Ground lime tree was blown down in the New Year, some might have sensed a hint of symbolism.

Before his third year of captaincy, David Fulton had asked supporters to move on from an earlier controversial departure, that of Mark Ealham in October 2003. "We have players with huge potential, but their time is now," he said. "If the present crop get an opportunity they must take it." The exhortation struck a chord: for the first time since Colin Cowdrey's class of 1964, Kent won their opening two Championship games, and Robert Key embarked on an unforgettable season.

Key raced to 1,000 runs on June 2, quicker than anyone in 16 years, won back his England place, scored a double-century against West Indies at Lord's, and remained the country's leading run-scorer, heading the averages with 1,896 at 79. Key, Matthew Walker (voted player of the season by supporters), Fulton and Smith made Kent the only county for which four batsmen scored 1,000 Championship runs. Australian Andrew Symonds played only five matches for 506 at 72; Walker and Smith also averaged 50-plus. Yet Kent scored only 43 batting points, the second-worst in their division. Their first-innings failings ultimately cost them the title: Warwickshire took 22 more batting points and their overall advantage was 16.

But there were also problems that cannot be expressed mathematically. The crisis emerged in early June, when a resounding win over Lancashire lifted Kent to second, with four wins from six starts, and they should have been in good heart at Worcester four days later. A bruised hand forced Fulton to drop out, delegating the captaincy to Smith. But as Worcestershire piled up 453, it became obvious that Smith was getting no support from Symonds or, to a lesser extent, Key. By mid-afternoon, the atmosphere had degenerated so much that Fulton attempted to take charge as twelfth man. The umpires told him he was flouting Law 2.3 (a substitute shall not act as captain) and he went off again. Smith's authority had been fatally undermined.

It had been arranged before the season that Smith would be the four-day vice-captain and Key the one-day vice-captain. Symonds, however, was not party to that and baulked at accepting Smith's authority. The aloof and intellectual Smith and the abrasive Symonds were never natural soulmates, but their mutual distaste soon got out of hand. A fortnight later, Symonds raised the stakes. As acting-captain for the Twenty20 campaign (with Key now away), he dropped Smith, who had scored fifties in his last two one-day games. Symonds's explosive 34-ball century against

Matthew Walker

Middlesex was not matched by his man-management and leadership skills, and Kent failed to reach the quarter-finals.

By then, former England captain Mike Denness had resigned as chairman of cricket, though it was not announced immediately. When it became public, he said he hoped to "send a message to the lads that I thought their behaviour was despicable". Graham Johnson, another Kent stalwart of the 1970s, took over, and disciplined Key and Symonds. But with Key on Test duty and Symonds injured, he was merely closing the stable door. Kent lost seven successive games from mid-July to August 1, by which time Michael Bevan had become their fifth overseas player of 2004. To their credit, Fulton, Smith and a much-changed side rose above the squabbles to get through their last six Championship games unbeaten, regaining the runners-up spot and raising hopes for the future.

The late run saw the emergence of fast bowlers Rob Joseph, born in Antigua, Simon Cusden and Matthew Dennington. Meanwhile, Irish wicket-keeper Niall O'Brien, who took over from England's Geraint Jones for much of the summer, was improving steadily. The return of Min Patel after spinal surgery helped mask disappointing first-class campaigns for two younger spinners, Rob Ferley and James Tredwell. The pair were more successful during the faltering one-day campaign: bowling in tandem, they often provided Fulton's only element of control. Poor fielding, wayward seam bowling and inconsistent batting formed a recipe for relegation.

Johnson held a post-season members' forum and announced that the club would appoint a director of cricket to oversee the existing three-man coaching team of Simon Willis, Paul Farbrace and Chris Stone. The job went to the former South Africa coach, Graham Ford. On the playing front, South African all-rounder Andrew Hall was signed as an overseas player; Simon Cook and Darren Stevens were drafted in from Middlesex and Leicestershire respectively. Fulton was reappointed captain, with Walker his deputy. Kent want success, and harmony.

THE END OF THE LIME

In the early hours of January 8, 2005, there were widespread storms across Britain, and summer afternoons at Canterbury felt very distant. But at some time in the darkness, Kent's most regular and durable spectator suddenly gave way. The cause of death was technically the howling gale and *ganoderma*, a heartwood fungus. In truth, it was just old age.

No one was about on such a night, and it was dawn before the body was discovered. "To be honest I'd been out in the middle sweeping the square for about 20 minutes when I looked up and thought 'Something's missing,'" said the head groundsman, Mike Grantham.

It was the lime tree, which had stood guard on the Old Dover Road boundary – at wide mid-wicket or deep backward point – ever since Kent first used the St Lawrence ground in 1847. It was already semi-mature then. It grew in stature, girth and reputation to become the most famous tree in cricket, matched only by Parr's elm at Trent Bridge, which was blown down in 1976.

But Parr's Tree was behind the stands. The St Lawrence lime was inside the boundary, and the Laws of Cricket had to be adapted to allow for it. Sir Charles Igglesden on *66 Years' Memories of Kent Cricket* (1947) refers to an incident in which a Hampshire batsman was caught off the tree. "Was the batsman out? He was given out as the tree was not the boundary. You can imagine the annoyance of the visiting team and the heated annoyance around the ground."

This episode apparently led to the local rule that hitting the tree is neither six nor out, but four. David Robertson, the Kent archivist, assumes this must have been before 1910, when the vague law regarding boundaries began to be tidied up.

Robertson's records suggest only three men have ever cleared the tree in first-class cricket: Sir Learie Constantine, playing for the West Indians in 1928, Jim Smith of Middlesex in 1939 and Carl Hooper, on his Kent debut in 1992. But in his book *Hit for Six,* the historian Gerald Brodribb tells the story of the renowned big-hitter, Colonel A. C. "Jacko" Watson of Sussex, who in 1925 reportedly drove "Tich" Freeman over the lime tree. It then bounced off the inside of a catering van and into the bushes, where it was found next winter with bits of china embedded in it.

The fall of the lime was a shock but not a surprise. Kent were aware the tree was ailing; they were also aware of "public liability issues" – what if it fell on the crowd in the middle of a one-day international? – and in 1999 E. W. Swanton planted a sapling close by, ready for this moment. That is now 15ft tall, and Kent were planning to shift it on to the field before the season to replace the fallen sentinel. The old tree is being cut up to provide souvenirs.

Some believe it a mistake to replace the old tree. The new lime could be damaged by a full-blooded shot; and, whereas everyone knew the old tree was there, a young one might not be obvious to a fielder, who could end up damaged himself. Others think the legend should be left alone, and that it won't be the same with the new tree. It won't, not for many decades.

In its glory: the St Lawrence lime in full leaf.
Picture courtesy of Kent County Cricket Club

After the storm: the sight that greeted the Kent groundsman on the morning of January 8, 2005.
Picture by Jean Owens

KENT RESULTS

All first-class matches – Played 18: Won 8, Lost 3, Drawn 7.
County Championship matches – Played 16: Won 7, Lost 3, Drawn 6.

Frizzell County Championship, 2nd in Division 1; Cheltenham & Gloucester Trophy, 3rd round;
totesport League, 8th in Division 1; Twenty20 Cup, 4th in South Group.

COUNTY CHAMPIONSHIP AVERAGES, BATTING AND FIELDING

Cap		M	I	NO	R	HS	100s	50s	Avge	Ct/St
2001	R. W. T. Key	10	17	1	1,274	199	6	2	79.62	4
1999	A. Symonds§	5	8	1	506	156*	3	1	72.28	6
2000	M. J. Walker	16	26	4	1,234	157	4	8	56.09	16
2001	E. T. Smith	16	27	2	1,269	189	4	5	50.76	5
1998	D. P. Fulton	15	26	1	1,030	122	5	2	41.20	20
	M. A. Carberry	10	17	3	555	112	2	3	39.64	3
	A. G. R. Loudon	10	17	0	597	92	0	6	35.11	6
	J. C. Tredwell	6	7	1	197	51*	0	1	32.83	7
	I. G. Butler§	5	8	2	185	68	0	1	30.83	2
	N. J. O'Brien	14	19	4	439	69	0	3	29.26	33/5
	M. J. Dennington	6	9	2	108	50*	0	1	15.42	2
	A. Khan	7	8	2	91	29	0	0	15.16	0
	M. G. Bevan§	4	7	0	90	66	0	1	12.85	2
	R. H. Joseph	7	9	3	77	26	0	0	12.83	3
1994	M. M. Patel	11	16	1	186	28	0	0	12.40	1
	S. M. J. Cusden	4	6	4	22	12*	0	0	11.00	2
	A. Sheriyar	6	7	4	32	12	0	0	10.66	0
2001	M. J. Saggers	6	7	0	74	64	0	1	10.57	4
	Mohammad Sami§	5	6	0	52	29	0	0	8.66	1
	R. S. Ferley	2	4	0	33	29	0	0	8.25	1
	B. J. Trott	5	7	1	28	12	0	0	4.66	1

Also batted: G. O. Jones (cap 2003) (2 matches) 0, 20*, 1 (3 ct); D. A. Stiff (4 matches) 4, 18, 5 (1 ct). § *Overseas player.*

BOWLING

	O	M	R	W	BB	5W/i	Avge
M. J. Saggers	152.5	43	410	15	4-43	0	27.33
M. M. Patel	421.3	85	1,206	41	5-138	1	29.41
A. Symonds	139.3	39	419	14	5-140	1	29.92
S. M. J. Cusden	100.3	17	404	13	4-68	0	31.07
A. G. R. Loudon	192.2	32	653	21	6-47	2	31.09
R. H. Joseph	165.2	31	648	19	3-47	0	34.10
Mohammad Sami	140	32	526	14	6-99	1	37.57
A. Sheriyar	156.3	23	633	16	5-94	1	39.56
I. G. Butler	101.3	11	446	11	4-114	0	40.54
A. Khan	131.3	15	600	14	4-47	0	42.85
B. J. Trott	153	23	538	10	4-109	0	53.80

Also bowled: M. G. Bevan 6–0–25–0; M. A. Carberry 27–0–157–2; M. J. Dennington 93–13–368–9; R. S. Ferley 28–2–121–3; D. A. Stiff 62–10–299–3; J. C. Tredwell 124.1–16–495–3; M. J. Walker 66–10–228–6.

COUNTY RECORDS

Highest score for:	332	W. H. Ashdown v Essex at Brentwood	1934
Highest score against:	344	W. G. Grace (MCC) at Canterbury	1876
Best bowling for:	10-30	C. Blythe v Northamptonshire at Northampton	1907
Best bowling against:	10-48	C. H. G. Bland (Sussex) at Tonbridge	1899
Highest total for:	803-4 dec.	v Essex at Brentwood	1934
Highest total against:	676	by Australians at Canterbury	1921
Lowest total for:	18	v Sussex at Gravesend	1867
Lowest total against:	16	by Warwickshire at Tonbridge	1913

KENT DIRECTORY

ADDRESS

St Lawrence Ground, Old Dover Road, Canterbury CT1 3NZ (01227 456886; fax 01227 762168; email jon.fordham.kent@ecb.co.uk). **Website** www.kentccc.com.

GROUNDS

Canterbury (St Lawrence Ground): 1 mile SE of city centre in Old Dover Road. Well signposted from A2 junction at Bridge. Nearest stations: Canterbury East (1 mile) and Canterbury West (1½ miles).

Maidstone (The Mote): 1 mile SE of town centre in Willow Way. From Upper Stone Street, L into Waterloo Street, R into St Philips Avenue and then L into Lower Road for Willow Way. Nearest stations: Maidstone East (1 mile) and Maidstone West (1¼ miles).

Tunbridge Wells (Nevill Ground): ¼ mile E of town centre. From A21 junction with A26 Quarry Hill Road at Mount Ephraim take L on A267 then L into Warwick Gate for Nevill Gate. Nearest station: Tunbridge Wells (¾ mile).

Beckenham: ¼ mile off A21 towards Bromley, R into A2015 Beckenham Hill Road, R Stumps Hill and then R into Worsley Bridge Road. Nearest stations: Lower Sydenham and Beckenham Junction (both ½ mile).

OFFICIALS

Captain D. P. Fulton	**Chief executive** P. E. Millman
Director of Cricket G. X. Ford	**Chairman, cricket committee** G. W. Johnson
President 2004 – B. W. Luckhurst;	**Head groundsman** M. Grantham
2005 – R. E. Collins	**Scorer** J. C. Foley
Chairman C. F. Openshaw	

PLAYERS

Players expected to reappear in 2005

	Former counties	Country	Born	Birthplace
Carberry Michael Alexander	Surrey	E	29.9.1980	Croydon
Cusden Simon Mark James		E	21.2.1985	†Canterbury
Dennington Matthew John.		E	16.10.1982	Durban, SA
Ferley Robert Steven.		E	4.2.1982	Norwich
Fulton David Paul		E	15.11.1971	Lewisham
*****Jones** Geraint Owen		‡E	14.7.1976	Kundiawa, Papua NG
Joseph Robert Hartman		E	20.1.1982	Antigua
*****Key** Robert William Trevor		E	12.5.1979	East Dulwich
Khan Amjad.	DEN (EU)	14.10.1980	Copenhagen
O'Brien Niall John	IRE (EU)	8.11.1981	Dublin
*****Patel** Minal Mahesh		E	7.7.1970	Bombay, India
*****Saggers** Martin John.	Durham	E	23.5.1972	King's Lynn
Sheriyar Alamgir	Leics, Worcs	E	15.11.1973	Birmingham
Stiff David Alexander		E	20.10.1984	Dewsbury
Tredwell James Cullum.		E	27.2.1982	†Ashford
Walker Matthew Jonathan		E	2.1.1974	†Gravesend

Players due to join in 2005

Cook Simon James.	Middlesex	E	15.1.1977	Oxford
*****Hall** Andrew James	Worcs	SA	31.7.1975	Johannesburg
Stevens Darren Ian	Leics	E	30.4.1976	Leicester

* *Test player.*   † *Born in Kent.*   ‡ *12-month ECB contract.*

At Bristol, April 16, 17, 18, 19. KENT beat GLOUCESTERSHIRE by seven wickets.

KENT v WORCESTERSHIRE

At Canterbury, April 21, 22, 23, 24. Kent won by five wickets. Kent 19 pts, Worcestershire 8 pts. Toss: Worcestershire.

Outmanoeuvred and outclassed for three days, Kent hit their stride on the fourth to reach a target of 429 and win a match they seemed certain to lose when their chase faltered to 33 for two on the third evening. It was their highest fourth-innings total (beating the 416 for six they made against Surrey at Blackheath in 1934), and the seventh-best to win in the history of the Championship. (It became the eighth-best after Durham won at Taunton in May – see table on page 736.) This was also Kent's first victory over Worcestershire in 11 Championship fixtures at Canterbury stretching back to August 1914 (although their next meeting here was not until 1970). On the first two days, steady if unspectacular contributions, bolstered by 63 extras, saw Worcestershire's first innings past 400; Sheriyar, with five wickets against his former county, was the most penetrative of a wayward attack. In reply, Fulton scored a century – his first since a career-threatening eye injury 12 months earlier – but he gained insufficient support, and Kent trailed by 112. A measured hundred from Moore allowed a declaration late on day three. Kent recovered from their poor start thanks initially to the night-watchman, Saggers, who hit a career-best 64 and shared two half-century stands. Once he had gone, Walker, with his best score in eight years, and Carberry, hitting a second hundred in successive games, seized the initiative. Growing in confidence all the while, they added 236 and guided Kent within sight of victory, which came with 21 balls to spare.

Close of play: First day, Worcestershire 212-5 (Solanki 32, Bichel 1); Second day, Kent 191-2 (Fulton 103, Walker 57); Third day, Kent 35-2 (Key 11, Saggers 2).

Worcestershire

S. D. Peters b Sheriyar	76	– c Walker b Sheriyar 29
S. C. Moore lbw b Khan	5	– not out 108
G. A. Hick c Tredwell b Saggers	38	– c Tredwell b Carberry 89
*B. F. Smith c Carberry b Khan	8	– not out 78
V. S. Solanki lbw b Stiff	84	
D. J. Pipe c Tredwell b Saggers	12	
A. J. Bichel c Smith b Tredwell	50	
†S. J. Rhodes not out	42	
M. S. Mason c Jones b Sheriyar	16	
S. A. Khalid c Fulton b Sheriyar	0	
M. N. Malik c Jones b Sheriyar	7	
B 5, l-b 13, w 5, n-b 40	63	B 4, l-b 4, n-b 4 12

1/6 (2) 2/85 (3) 3/130 (4) 4/183 (1)   401 1/52 (1) 2/183 (3)   (2 wkts dec.) 316
5/195 (6) 6/317 (5) 7/331 (7)
8/357 (9) 9/357 (10) 10/401 (11)

Bonus points – Worcestershire 5, Kent 3.

Bowling: *First Innings*—Saggers 26–9–70–1; Khan 20–2–100–2; Sheriyar 22.3–1–94–5; Stiff 17–3–68–1; Tredwell 16–2–51–1. *Second Innings*—Saggers 10–3–32–0; Khan 8–1–42–0; Sheriyar 10–1–49–1; Stiff 9–2–46–0; Tredwell 15–1–83–0; Carberry 8–0–56–1.

> " Fielding on the second morning, Tredwell and O'Brien had to protect themselves from a swarm of bees. The real venom, though, was in the Kent dressing-room."
>
> Worcestershire in 2004, page 797.

Kent

*D. P. Fulton c Hick b Mason	107	– b Mason	16
R. W. T. Key c Smith b Malik	13	– lbw b Malik	46
E. T. Smith c Solanki b Malik	0	– lbw b Mason	6
M. J. Walker lbw b Malik	70	– (5) not out	151
M. A. Carberry c Peters b Mason	10	– (6) b Malik	112
†G. O. Jones c Rhodes b Mason	0	– (7) not out	20
J. C. Tredwell not out	51		
A. Khan lbw b Malik	1		
M. J. Saggers lbw b Malik	1	– (4) lbw b Mason	64
D. A. Stiff b Bichel	4		
A. Sheriyar c Khalid b Mason	5		
B 6, l-b 9, w 2, n-b 10	27	B 5, l-b 5, n-b 4	14

1/30 (2) 2/30 (3) 3/198 (1) 4/221 (5) 289   1/17 (1) 2/33 (3) (5 wkts) 429
5/225 (6) 6/227 (4) 7/239 (8) 3/105 (2) 4/170 (4)
8/249 (9) 9/254 (10) 10/289 (11) 5/406 (6)

Bonus points – Kent 2, Worcestershire 3.

Bowling: *First Innings*—Bichel 24–5–74–1; Mason 23.3–8–55–4; Malik 20–3–88–5; Khalid 14–4–42–0; Hick 3–0–15–0. *Second Innings*—Bichel 21–2–101–0; Mason 24–6–86–3; Malik 19–3–93–2; Khalid 29.3–7–88–0; Solanki 16–1–51–0.

Umpires: T. E. Jesty and J. F. Steele.

At Oxford, April 28, 29, 30. KENT drew with OXFORD UCCE.

KENT v GLOUCESTERSHIRE

At Canterbury, May 7, 8, 9, 10. Drawn. Kent 5 pts, Gloucestershire 7 pts. Toss: Kent. Championship debut: Shabbir Ahmed.

The English spring had the final say as rain and its after-effects wiped out the last three days of a match that started with a bang: in 59 overs, 15 wickets clattered for 206 runs. Cloud cover and a healthy layer of grass aided the excellent Lewis, who finished with five for 46, after Shabbir Ahmed marked his Championship debut by removing Kent's first three. Symonds was top scorer, hitting 33 from 36 balls against his former club, as Kent crashed to 129 all out five overs after lunch. Gloucestershire revelled in the conditions too and quickly grabbed three wickets. There were signs of a Gloucestershire recovery in the guise of an unbeaten fifty stand between Taylor and Adshead, but when play ended for the last time, they were still two behind.

Close of play: First day, Gloucestershire 127-5 (Taylor 32, Adshead 15); Second day, No play; Third day, No play.

Kent

*D. P. Fulton c Gidman b Shabbir Ahmed	18	M. J. Saggers c Adshead b Averis	3
R. W. T. Key c Hancock b Shabbir Ahmed	11	Mohammad Sami lbw b Lewis	0
E. T. Smith c Gidman b Shabbir Ahmed	9	A. Sheriyar not out	0
A. Symonds c Adshead b Lewis	33	L-b 1, n-b 14	15
M. J. Walker b Lewis	21		
M. A. Carberry b Averis	4	1/26 (1) 2/33 (2) 3/42 (3)	129
†G. O. Jones c Ball b Lewis	1	4/77 (4) 5/82 (6) 6/89 (7)	
J. C. Tredwell c Adshead b Lewis	14	7/124 (5) 8/129 (8)	
		9/129 (9) 10/129 (10)	

Bonus points – Gloucestershire 3.

Bowling: Shabbir Ahmed 11–2–34–3; Lewis 12.3–1–46–5; Averis 12–1–39–2; Shoaib Malik 1–0–9–0.

Gloucestershire

W. P. C. Weston c and b Saggers	6	†S. J. Adshead not out	15
C. M. Spearman c Symonds b Saggers	42		
T. H. C. Hancock lbw b Sheriyar	0	B 4, l-b 4, n-b 2	10
Shoaib Malik c Jones b Symonds	18		
*C. G. Taylor not out	32	1/32 (1) 2/39 (3) 3/73 (4) (5 wkts) 127	
A. P. R. Gidman c Walker b Saggers	4	4/73 (2) 5/77 (6)	

Shabbir Ahmed, M. C. J. Ball, J. Lewis and J. M. M. Averis did not bat.

Bonus point – Kent 1.

Bowling: Saggers 10.5–2–30–3; Mohammad Sami 9–1–22–0; Sheriyar 8–0–41–1; Symonds 6–1–24–1; Tredwell 1–0–2–0.

Umpires: D. J. Constant and B. Leadbeater.

At Canterbury, May 13, 14, 15, 16. KENT beat NEW ZEALANDERS by nine wickets (see New Zealand tour section).

At Northampton, May 19, 20, 21, 22. KENT beat NORTHAMPTONSHIRE by 145 runs.

At The Oval, May 25, 26, 27, 28. KENT lost to SURREY by seven wickets.

KENT v LANCASHIRE

At Tunbridge Wells, June 2, 3, 4, 5. Kent won by seven wickets. Kent 22 pts, Lancashire 4 pts. Toss: Kent.

Kent's fourth Championship win of the summer, their first with maximum points, lifted them three places to second, behind Warwickshire. In a compelling, high-scoring contest, both Kent's total (615) and the match aggregate (1,408) were ground records for The Nevill. On a featherbed such as this, runs flowed from the word go: Key and Smith each hit first-day hundreds and shared a second-wicket stand of 229. When Key passed 94 with a cut to the boundary, he became the

---

FIRST TO 1,000 RUNS

1994	B. C. Lara (Warwickshire)	June 6
1995	D. Byas (Yorkshire)	June 29
1996	M. G. Bevan (Yorkshire)	June 24
1997	S. P. James (Glamorgan)	July 18
1998	J. L. Langer (Middlesex)	June 27
1999	S. G. Law (Essex)	July 14
2000	M. G. Bevan (Sussex)	July 31
2001	D. P. Fulton (Kent)	July 4
2002	M. E. K. Hussey (Northamptonshire)	July 19
2003	E. T. Smith (Kent)	July 15
2004	**R. W. T. Key (Kent)**	**June 2**

The last player to score 1,000 runs before June 2 was G. A. Hick of Worcestershire, on May 28, 1988.

---

first to 1,000 first-class runs for the summer – the earliest anyone had reached the landmark in 16 seasons. It was the third time in four years that a Kent batsman had been first and, like Key, both Fulton in 2001 and Smith in 2003 had got there against Lancashire. Kent's weakened bowling resources – Saggers was on Test duty, Mohammad Sami was hampered by a knee injury, and a hamstring strain left Patel bowling stilted donkey drops – should have helped Lancashire's tilt toward 466 and saving the follow-on. But a stunning catch by Symonds – umpire Burgess thought it the finest he had seen – at square leg, racing back and taking it over his shoulder, ended Hegg's resistance, and the last four went for 51. With five sessions remaining, Lancashire were batting again 308 in arrears. Chapple, who had earlier taken his 500th first-class wicket, hit a battling hundred as Symonds, turning from medium-pace to off-spin, claimed five for 140 from more than 50 overs. Needing just 88, Kent raced home in 20 overs. Though the rhododendrons were past their best, a healthy attendance of 8,939 produced The Nevill's highest gate receipts.

Close of play: First day, Kent 416-4 (Walker 9, Carberry 9); Second day, Lancashire 246-6 (Crook 25, Hegg 24); Third day, Lancashire 316-6 (Chapple 77, Hegg 20).

Kent

*D. P. Fulton b Crook	42	– c Cork b Chapple	14
R. W. T. Key lbw b Chapple	180	– b Hogg	44
E. T. Smith c Keedy b Hogg	116	– not out	21
A. Symonds b Crook	33	– c Law b Hogg	4
M. J. Walker c Hegg b Swann	72	– not out	4
M. A. Carberry c Hegg b Chapple	85		
†N. J. O'Brien b Keedy	0		
M. M. Patel c Chilton b Chapple	25		
Mohammad Sami c Hegg b Chapple	0		
D. A. Stiff lbw b Chapple	18		
A. Sheriyar not out	5		
B 9, l-b 18, w 4, n-b 8	39	N-b 4	4

1/83 (1) 2/312 (3) 3/398 (4) 4/402 (2) **615**   1/24 (1) 2/79 (2)   (3 wkts) **91**
5/556 (5) 6/561 (7) 7/580 (6)   3/83 (4)
8/580 (9) 9/602 (10) 10/615 (8)

Bonus points – Kent 5, Lancashire 1 (130 overs: 517-4).

Bowling: *First Innings*—Chapple 36.1–7–136–5; Cork 28–3–116–0; Hogg 17–2–52–1; Crook 25–1–117–2; Keedy 28–2–114–1; Chilton 7–0–23–0; Law 5–1–16–0; Swann 4–2–14–1. *Second Innings*—Chapple 4–0–26–1; Cork 5–0–26–0; Keedy 7–2–23–0; Hogg 4–1–16–2.

Lancashire

M. J. Chilton run out	37	– c Fulton b Patel	25
I. J. Sutcliffe lbw b Symonds	50	– lbw b Sheriyar	10
M. B. Loye c O'Brien b Symonds	1	– lbw b Symonds	34
S. G. Law c Walker b Symonds	17	– c Fulton b Patel	48
A. J. Swann lbw b Sheriyar	19	– b Symonds	6
G. Chapple c Walker b Stiff	28	– b Sheriyar	102
S. P. Crook lbw b Sheriyar	37	– c and b Symonds	68
*†W. K. Hegg c Symonds b Mohammad Sami	24	– b Symonds	44
K. W. Hogg c Walker b Mohammad Sami	4	– (10) c sub b Symonds	20
D. G. Cork not out	35	– (9) c Key b Sheriyar	1
G. Keedy c Walker b Mohammad Sami	4	– not out	3
B 4, l-b 9, n-b 38	51	B 4, l-b 9, w 5, n-b 16	34

1/83 (1) 2/96 (3) 3/124 (4) 4/131 (2) **307**   1/30 (2) 2/53 (1) 3/129 (3) **395**
5/183 (6) 6/201 (5) 7/256 (8)   4/129 (4) 5/135 (6) 6/288 (7)
8/267 (9) 9/267 (7) 10/307 (11)   7/360 (6) 8/362 (9)
  9/372 (8) 10/395 (10)

Bonus points – Lancashire 3, Kent 3.

Bowling: *First Innings*—Mohammad Sami 18–3–117–2; Sheriyar 15–4–57–2; Symonds 23–8–51–3; Stiff 9–1–58–2; Walker 2–0–11–0. *Second Innings*—Mohammad Sami 8–2–39–0; Sheriyar 20–3–72–3; Symonds 52.4–13–140–5; Patel 32–8–77–2; Stiff 8–0–54–0.

Umpires: G. I. Burgess and M. J. Kitchen.

At Worcester, June 9, 10, 11, 12. KENT drew with WORCESTERSHIRE.

At Beckenham, June 21. KENT lost to WEST INDIANS by 91 runs (see West Indian tour section).

KENT v WARWICKSHIRE

At Beckenham, June 23, 24, 25, 26. Drawn. Kent 7 pts, Warwickshire 12 pts. Toss: Warwickshire.
   Second entertained first in this top-of-the-table game, and although almost two days were lost to rain, there was no doubt who had the better of the draw: Warwickshire, the unbeaten leaders, who played all the cricket between showers. The first day was washed out, and near gale-force winds limited attendances for Worsley Bridge Road's second Championship fixture, 50 years after its first. Warned for running on the pitch, Mohammad Sami turned in a petulant and wicketless display that included 14 no-balls. The Warwickshire batsmen were more composed: Wagh was the sole casualty of the second day, and both Jonathan Trott and Powell, in his second innings of the summer, hit hundreds. They barely missed the in-form but injured Nick Knight, as Warwickshire claimed maximum batting points for the seventh successive game, going on to their highest total in Kent. A magnificent unbeaten 156 from Symonds failed to save the follow-on as his team-mates struggled to read Hogg's wrist-spin. Heavy rain an hour into the second innings saved further embarrassment and forced dozens of supporters to take refuge in the press marquee. Kent's compensation was that the club shop did a brisk trade in fleeces.
   Close of play: First day, No play; Second day, Warwickshire 334-1 (Powell 112, Trott 97); Third day, Kent 249-8 (Symonds 124, Mohammad Sami 8).

Warwickshire

M. J. Powell c Patel b Trott	134	N. M. Carter not out 1
M. A. Wagh c Symonds b Trott	86	
I. J. L. Trott c O'Brien b Saggers	115	B 3, l-b 6, n-b 32 41
I. R. Bell c Fulton b Patel	49	
J. O. Troughton st O'Brien b Patel	21	1/171 (2) 2/354 (3) (6 wkts dec.) 502
G. B. Hogg c Symonds b Patel	28	3/396 (1) 4/436 (5)
*D. R. Brown not out	27	5/453 (4) 6/490 (6)

†T. Frost, N. Tahir and A. Richardson did not bat.

Bonus points – Warwickshire 5, Kent 1 (130 overs: 434-3).

Bowling: Mohammad Sami 25–3–111–0; Saggers 24–5–63–1; Trott 32–7–102–2; Symonds 8–3–26–0; Loudon 17–1–88–0; Patel 33–8–103–3.

Kent

*D. P. Fulton c Powell b Tahir	15	– not out 5
M. A. Carberry lbw b Carter	13	– not out 14
E. T. Smith b Tahir	2	
A. Symonds not out	156	
M. J. Walker b Hogg	21	
A. G. R. Loudon c Trott b Hogg	9	
†N. J. O'Brien lbw b Hogg	13	
M. M. Patel b Hogg	24	
M. J. Saggers b Carter	0	
Mohammad Sami c Frost b Tahir	18	
B. J. Trott run out	0	
B 5, l-b 3, w 6, n-b 12	26	N-b 4 4

1/17 (2) 2/22 (3) 3/50 (1) 4/86 (5)   297   (no wkt) 23
5/108 (6) 6/146 (7) 7/215 (8)
8/218 (9) 9/296 (10) 10/297 (11)

Bonus points – Kent 2, Warwickshire 3.

Bowling: *First Innings*—Carter 19–7–44–2; Brown 10–2–31–0; Tahir 9–2–50–3; Wagh 2–0–4–0; Richardson 11–3–55–0; Hogg 22.2–3–90–4; Bell 2–0–15–0. *Second Innings*—Tahir 3–0–7–0; Brown 5–3–6–0; Richardson 6–4–4–0; Trott 3–2–6–0.

Umpires: J. H. Evans and P. Willey.

At Canterbury, July 14. KENT lost to SRI LANKA A by four wickets (see Sri Lanka A tour section).

At Hove, July 23, 24, 25, 26. KENT lost to SUSSEX by an innings and 45 runs.

At Southgate, July 28, 29, 30, 31. KENT lost to MIDDLESEX by 119 runs.

KENT v SUSSEX

At Canterbury, August 3, 4, 5, 6. Kent won by 236 runs. Kent 22 pts, Sussex 5 pts. Toss: Kent.

Dressing-room unrest, which had led to the resignation of Kent cricket chairman Mike Denness, was a constant undertone during Canterbury Week. But Kent put that aside on the field, and ended a seven-match losing streak in all cricket. It was their first victory over Sussex at Canterbury since 1972. International calls and injuries meant they selected only four capped players, but of those, Walker scored a century in each innings and Smith – at the centre of the politics – was only seven short of doing the same. They led Kent to 527 on a benign pitch, before an attack including four seamers with an average age of 22 bowled out Sussex inside 70 overs – wicket-keeper O'Brien dismissing five. Kent led by 195, even though Prior scored his second century against them in a fortnight. Fulton elected to rest his fledgling bowlers and let his batsmen take the plaudits for a second time, declaring on the third evening when Walker reached 100 again. Facing a target of 515, Sussex succumbed to the spinners. Patel claimed four, despite a calf strain, and Loudon three in a ten-ball spell to ease Kent home just after tea on the final day.

Close of play: First day, Kent 405-7 (Walker 83, Khan 16); Second day, Sussex 332; Third day, Sussex 21-0 (Ward 13, Montgomerie 8).

Kent

*D. P. Fulton lbw b Kirtley	4	– c Goodwin b Kirtley	13
E. T. Smith c Goodwin b Mohammad Akram	166	– c Martin-Jenkins b Kirtley	93
A. G. R. Loudon c Montgomerie b Wright	55	– c and b Mushtaq Ahmed	50
M. G. Bevan lbw b Kirtley	0	– b Mohammad Akram	8
M. J. Walker c Mohammad Akram b Mushtaq Ahmed	157	– not out	100
M. J. Dennington lbw b Mohammad Akram	0	– lbw b Kirtley	0
†N. J. O'Brien run out	30	– c Wright b Mohammad Akram	20
M. M. Patel b Mushtaq Ahmed	26		
A. Khan lbw b Mushtaq Ahmed	29		
R. H. Joseph c Prior b Mushtaq Ahmed	7	– (8) b Mushtaq Ahmed	6
S. M. J. Cusden not out	12	– (9) not out	3
B 13, l-b 20, n-b 8	41	B 8, l-b 11, w 3, n-b 4	26
	527	(7 wkts dec.)	**319**

1/15 (1) 2/212 (3) 3/215 (4) 4/285 (2)   527   1/101 (3) 2/140 (4)   (7 wkts dec.) 319
5/285 (6) 6/329 (7) 7/362 (8)   3/195 (2) 4/229 (1)
8/458 (9) 9/506 (10) 10/527 (5)   5/229 (6) 6/277 (7) 7/296 (8)

Bonus points – Kent 5, Sussex 2 (130 overs: 471-8).

In the second innings Fulton, when 2, retired hurt at 2 and resumed at 195.

Bowling: *First Innings*—Mohammad Akram 28–5–100–2; Kirtley 30–6–99–2; Martin-Jenkins 17–0–95–0; Mushtaq Ahmed 41.5–6–126–4; Wright 20–1–74–1. *Second Innings*—Mohammad Akram 19–3–85–2; Kirtley 16–1–52–3; Mushtaq Ahmed 35–3–119–2; Wright 7.5–1–22–0; Martin-Jenkins 5–0–22–0.

Sussex

I. J. Ward b Khan	20	– lbw b Joseph	14
R. R. Montgomerie c O'Brien b Dennington	70	– c Walker b Cusden	80
P. A. Cottey c O'Brien b Joseph	0	– c O'Brien b Dennington	49
M. W. Goodwin c Bevan b Dennington	28	– lbw b Patel	12
*C. J. Adams c O'Brien b Dennington	5	– lbw b Joseph	2
†M. J. Prior st O'Brien b Patel	112	– c Loudon b Patel	53
R. S. C. Martin-Jenkins lbw b Loudon	22	– c Fulton b Patel	23
L. J. Wright c Walker b Patel	0	– b Loudon	18
Mushtaq Ahmed b Joseph	45	– not out	2
R. J. Kirtley c O'Brien b Joseph	3	– c Fulton b Loudon	0
Mohammad Akram not out	6	– b Loudon	4
B 2, l-b 4, w 1, n-b 14	21	B 10, l-b 9, n-b 2	21
	332		**278**

1/32 (1) 2/39 (3) 3/70 (4) 4/92 (5)   332
5/231 (2) 6/270 (6) 7/270 (8)
8/298 (7) 9/313 (10) 10/332 (9)

1/22 (1) 2/102 (3) 3/145 (4)   278
4/147 (5) 5/209 (2) 6/235 (6)
7/268 (7) 8/272 (8)
9/274 (10) 10/278 (11)

Bonus points – Sussex 3, Kent 3.

Bowling: *First Innings*—Khan 9–0–47–1; Joseph 13.2–1–70–3; Cusden 10–1–61–0; Dennington 14–3–48–3; Patel 11–1–44–2; Loudon 12–2–56–1. *Second Innings*—Joseph 13–6–38–1; Dennington 12–2–41–1; Patel 35–9–75–4; Loudon 20–5–60–3; Cusden 9–1–45–1.

Umpires: A. Clarkson and A. A. Jones.

At Birmingham, August 11, 12, 13, 14. KENT drew with WARWICKSHIRE.

KENT v SURREY

At Canterbury, August 18, 19, 20, 21. Drawn. Kent 7 pts, Surrey 12 pts. Toss: Kent.

Kent's resilient late-order batting prevented defeat in a game that lost a day and a half to rain. Surrey's decision to bat on into the final morning in search of maximum batting points ultimately allowed them to wriggle off the hook: Dennington scored a maiden fifty as he and Butler frustrated Surrey with an unbroken ninth-wicket stand of 92. Butler had also saved Kent first time round, hitting a career-best 68 after joining Ferley at 121 for eight. They batted throughout the second morning and finally added 103, the first ninth-wicket century stand in a fixture dating back to 1828. In between the showers, the fluent Newman and his latest opening partner, Clinton, put on 170 for Surrey, and a brash 85 from Brown left them two and a half sessions to dismiss Kent. Ormond took three wickets in his opening spell: Smith bagged a pair, and Bevan recorded his third duck in five innings. Another three-wicket burst, from Azhar Mahmood, saw Kent eight down and still 34 behind. But Dennington and Butler proved inseparable.

Close of play: First day, Kent 136-8 (Ferley 6, Butler 9); Second day, Surrey 263-5 (Batty 30, Brown 6); Third day, Surrey 337-6 (Brown 44, Azhar Mahmood 19).

> **"** Surrey were long on shots and short on gumption."
>
> Middlesex in 2004, page 691.

Kent

*D. P. Fulton c Clarke b Azhar Mahmood	57	– c Clarke b Murtagh	42
E. T. Smith c Brown b Bicknell	0	– c Batty b Ormond	0
A. G. R. Loudon c Azhar Mahmood b Bicknell	18	– lbw b Ormond	8
M. G. Bevan b Bicknell	7	– c Clarke b Ormond	0
M. J. Walker b Azhar Mahmood	2	– c sub b Azhar Mahmood	57
†N. J. O'Brien c Batty b Azhar Mahmood	20	– lbw b Bicknell	5
M. J. Dennington c Batty b Murtagh	3	– not out	50
R. S. Ferley c Brown b Ormond	29	– b Azhar Mahmood	0
M. M. Patel b Azhar Mahmood	10	– c sub b Azhar Mahmood	2
I. G. Butler c Batty b Azhar Mahmood	68	– not out	48
R. H. Joseph not out	2		
B 3, l-b 5, n-b 2	10	B 3, l-b 6, w 1, n-b 12	22

1/9 (2) 2/43 (3) 3/71 (4) 4/85 (1)   226   1/6 (2) 2/26 (3) 3/34 (4)   (8 wkts) 234
5/94 (5) 6/99 (7) 7/111 (6)   4/107 (1) 5/120 (6)
8/121 (9) 9/224 (8) 10/226 (10)   6/134 (5) 7/134 (8) 8/142 (9)

Bonus points – Kent 1, Surrey 3.

Bowling: *First Innings*—Bicknell 22–3–72–3; Ormond 20–6–57–1; Azhar Mahmood 20.1–7–54–5; Murtagh 12–4–35–1. *Second Innings*—Bicknell 18–2–67–1; Ormond 22–6–65–3; Azhar Mahmood 20–8–55–3; Murtagh 12–6–25–1; Doshi 4–1–13–0; Brown 2–2–0–0.

Surrey

S. A. Newman c Walker b Dennington	111	M. P. Bicknell not out	14
R. S. Clinton lbw b Dennington	58	T. J. Murtagh not out	1
*†J. N. Batty b Patel	46	B 2, l-b 8, w 1, n-b 2	13
R. Clarke c Loudon b Patel	33		
M. R. Ramprakash b Dennington	9	1/170 (2) 2/179 (1) (8 wkts dec.) 402
J. Ormond b Joseph	8	3/234 (4) 4/247 (5)
A. D. Brown c O'Brien b Butler	85	5/256 (6) 6/309 (3)
Azhar Mahmood c Butler b Patel	24	7/367 (8) 8/397 (7)

N. D. Doshi did not bat.

Bonus points – Surrey 5, Kent 2.

Bowling: Butler 14–2–71–1; Joseph 16–2–76–1; Patel 30–2–96–3; Dennington 18–2–88–3; Loudon 16–1–47–0; Ferley 4–0–14–0.

Umpires: N. G. Cowley and A. G. T. Whitehead.

At Manchester, August 24, 25, 26, 27. KENT drew with LANCASHIRE.

KENT v NORTHAMPTONSHIRE

At Canterbury, September 3, 4, 5, 6. Kent won by 194 runs. Kent 22 pts, Northamptonshire 2 pts. Toss: Kent.

Key showed he had not lost the brilliant county form that won him back his Test place, by sprinting to his eighth hundred of the season, and Kent built three century stands on the way to 393 for three. Then Louw's stint with the new ball caused havoc and a collapse to 414 all out, two of the batsmen going to hospital. First, he fractured the right hand of Dennington, who ran a single before retiring; four balls later, Louw broke O'Brien's nose and gashed his forehead, which required seven stitches. Richard Piesley, an 18-year-old from the Kent Academy, replaced O'Brien behind the stumps and claimed four catches in the match. Kent had ample revenge, though: Northamptonshire were shot out inside 45 overs. But Fulton declined the follow-on, and Smith scored a delightful 156, with 19 fours and three sixes, to build a lead of 581. Cook responded with his first century in four years, and at 223 for two there were wild thoughts of victory. But only Sales held firm on the final day, when Cusden revelled in misty conditions to claim a career-best four for 68, wrapping up a home win shortly after lunch.

Close of play: First day, Kent 409-7 (Joseph 0); Second day, Kent 200-3 (Smith 79, Walker 4); Third day, Northamptonshire 281-3 (Afzaal 41, Sales 43).

Kent

*D. P. Fulton c Sales b Rofe	57	– b Phillips	39
R. W. T. Key c Louw b Swann	131	– c Brophy b Louw	17
E. T. Smith c Roberts b Phillips	70	– lbw b Louw	156
A. G. R. Loudon c Swann b Louw	60	– b Cook	51
M. J. Walker c Swann b Louw	63	– b Rofe	34
†N. J. O'Brien retired hurt	10		
M. J. Dennington retired hurt	1		
M. M. Patel b Phillips	1	– (6) not out	9
A. Khan lbw b Louw	3		
R. H. Joseph c Cook b Louw	0		
S. M. J. Cusden not out	5		
L-b 9, n-b 4	13	B 5, l-b 5, n-b 2	12

1/118 (1) 2/260 (3) 3/262 (2) 4/393 (4)   414   1/29 (2) 2/95 (1)   (5 wkts dec.) 318
5/400 (5) 6/409 (8) 7/409 (9) 8/414 (10)   3/184 (4) 4/292 (5)
                                            5/318 (3)

Bonus points – Kent 5, Northamptonshire 2.

In the first innings Dennington and O'Brien retired hurt at 405.

Bowling: *First Innings*—Louw 22.5–4–92–4; Rofe 19–2–78–1; Jones 15–1–67–0; Phillips 21–9–58–2; Swann 21–2–65–1; Cook 7–0–45–0. *Second Innings*—Louw 9.4–0–66–2; Rofe 11–1–48–1; Phillips 9–1–21–1; Jones 14–0–66–0; Swann 14–3–41–0; Cook 18–1–66–1.

Northamptonshire

T. W. Roberts b Cusden	16	– b Khan	0
J. W. Cook b Khan	4	– (3) b Loudon	114
T. B. Huggins c sub b Joseph	1	– (2) c Cusden b Joseph	44
U. Afzaal b Khan	34	– lbw b Patel	41
*D. J. Sales lbw b Walker	3	– c Key b Cusden	92
†G. L. Brophy lbw b Khan	10	– lbw b Khan	20
G. P. Swann b Khan	16	– c sub b Joseph	9
J. Louw c Fulton b Joseph	1	– (9) c sub b Cusden	0
B. J. Phillips b Cusden	12	– (8) b Cusden	4
P. S. Jones c sub b Patel	37	– b Cusden	4
P. C. Rofe not out	0	– not out	15
L-b 3, w 2, n-b 12	17	B 10, l-b 12, w 12, n-b 10	44

1/6 (2) 2/25 (1) 3/27 (3) 4/45 (5)   151   1/1 (1) 2/162 (2) 3/223 (3)   387
5/58 (6) 6/92 (7) 7/99 (4)   4/284 (4) 5/315 (6) 6/330 (7)
8/106 (8) 9/151 (9) 10/151 (10)   7/334 (8) 8/334 (9)
                                            9/344 (10) 10/387 (5)

Bonus points – Kent 3.

Bowling: *First Innings*—Joseph 13–6–38–2; Khan 11–3–47–4; Cusden 8–3–18–2; Walker 7–2–24–1; Patel 5.1–1–21–1. *Second Innings*—Joseph 22–4–71–2; Khan 16–2–53–2; Patel 33–8–102–1; Cusden 15.3–3–68–4; Walker 7–0–24–0; Loudon 18–3–47–1.

Umpires: J. W. Holder and R. Palmer.

KENT v MIDDLESEX

At Canterbury, September 16, 17, 18. Kent won by an innings and 49 runs. Kent 22 pts, Middlesex 4 pts. Toss: Middlesex.

Both sides were still competing for second place in the Championship: Kent's biggest win of the summer secured it, forcing Middlesex to settle for fourth. The young home attack conceded 26 in no-balls on the first day, but still dismissed Middlesex in 72 overs. O'Brien, recovered from his broken nose, caught the first six batsmen to fall, three off Cusden, and Joseph exploited afternoon cloud cover to take three in nine balls. But the bedrock of Kent's success lay in a stand of 255 in 49 overs between Key and Smith, which the umpires described as the best batting they had seen all season. Key made his ninth century of 2004, and Smith his highest, in his last Kent innings; he joined Middlesex three weeks later. Walker added a third hundred to help his side to a 300-run lead. The off-breaks of Dalrymple and Weekes claimed six wickets between them, and the pitch offered equal assistance to the home spinners. In rapidly fading light, Loudon used his own brand of *doosra* to secure a career-best six for 47 and complete victory on the third evening. It was also goodnight from him: he followed Smith through the Kent door, and joined Warwickshire.

Close of play: First day, Kent 163-1 (Key 69, Smith 74); Second day, Kent 473-6 (Walker 86, Joseph 8).

Middlesex

S. G. Koenig c O'Brien b Cusden	39	– c O'Brien b Cusden	28
B. L. Hutton c O'Brien b Cusden	16	– c Fulton b Patel	32
O. A. Shah c O'Brien b Walker	25	– c Joseph b Patel	14
*E. C. Joyce c O'Brien b Trott	20	– c Trott b Loudon	74
P. N. Weekes c O'Brien b Walker	12	– c Fulton b Loudon	29
J. W. M. Dalrymple not out	52	– st O'Brien b Loudon	20
†B. J. M. Scott c O'Brien b Cusden	4	– lbw b Loudon	0
S. J. Cook b Joseph	30	– b Loudon	15
C. T. Peploe lbw b Joseph	0	– c Cusden b Loudon	6
M. M. Betts b Joseph	0	– st O'Brien b Patel	5
M. Hayward b Loudon	0	– not out	0
L-b 9, w 2, n b 26	37	B 14, l-b 5, w 1, n-b 8	28
	235		**251**

1/60 (1) 2/91 (2) 3/115 (3) 4/143 (5)
5/147 (4) 6/177 (7) 7/230 (8)
8/232 (9) 9/234 (10) 10/235 (11)

1/67 (1) 2/85 (2) 3/100 (3)
4/155 (5) 5/183 (6) 6/183 (7)
7/213 (8) 8/223 (9)
9/251 (10) 10/251 (4)

Bonus points – Middlesex 1, Kent 3.

Bowling: *First Innings*—Joseph 11–2–47–3; Trott 14–4–37–1; Stiff 9–2–31–0; Cusden 12–1–37–3; Loudon 7–1–31–1; Walker 10–2–21–2; Patel 9–3–22–0. *Second Innings*—Joseph 7–1–26–0; Trott 10–1–31–0; Patel 31–5–89–3; Cusden 5–1–21–1; Stiff 2–1–18–0; Loudon 14.5–1–47–6.

Kent

*D. P. Fulton c Weekes b Cook	17		D. A. Stiff c Hutton b Dalrymple	5
R. W. T. Key c Betts b Weekes	131		B. J. Trott not out	4
E. T. Smith lbw b Betts	189			
A. G. R. Loudon b Dalrymple	8		B 14, l-b 15, w 5, n-b 6	40
M. J. Walker st Scott b Dalrymple	108			
†N. J. O'Brien c Scott b Cook	2			**535**
M. M. Patel c Koenig b Cook	5		1/18 (1) 2/273 (2) 3/293 (4)	
R. H. Joseph c Hutton b Weekes	26		4/448 (3) 5/451 (6) 6/459 (7)	
S. M. J. Cusden c Hutton b Dalrymple	0		7/522 (8) 8/525 (9)	
			9/526 (5) 10/535 (10)	

Bonus points – Kent 5, Middlesex 3.

Bowling: Cook 28–3–107–3; Hayward 19–0–81–0; Betts 21–2–72–1; Hutton 2–0–9–0; Weekes 23–1–91–2; Peploe 13–0–73–0; Dalrymple 19.4–1–66–4; Shah 3–0–7–0.

Umpires: M. J. Harris and J. F. Steele.

LANCASHIRE

Who wants to be a millionaire?

COLIN EVANS

Rarely have a team fallen so far below expectations. Pre-season favourites for their first outright Championship since 1934, Lancashire were relegated on September 17. In a straight fight to avoid the drop, Gloucestershire claimed the fifth point they needed to stay up at 4.35 p.m. There was barely a whimper from the few hundred fans gathered at Old Trafford for the last rites. It was all over, but really Lancashire had been dead and buried long before.

Where did it all go wrong? During their first match, at Northampton, one of the home players remarked: "Millionaire club. Bought a team to win the Championship and if they don't, they will have to take a long, hard look at themselves." In late April, Lancashire crushed title-holders Sussex in three days at Hove, only to have two points deducted for a slow over-rate. Chairman Jack Simmons fumed: "I hope it doesn't cost us the title." First-division survival hardly seemed part of the equation: three weeks later, they hammered Worcestershire to go top. But the millionaires ended up paupers. They failed to win another Championship game.

Injuries were a factor. Almost every senior player was hurt, some seriously. Glen Chapple suffered a bruised brain, Stuart Law missed seven weeks with back trouble, Carl Hooper's thumb was broken, Peter Martin played only six Championship matches because of a knee injury, Mal Loye strained an Achilles tendon, Warren Hegg pulled a hamstring... Lancashire called up 22 players for Championship duty. Even if team spirit remained high, there was no continuity, and young players found themselves under pressure.

"We can talk about injuries and other things," said manager Mike Watkinson, "but first up we have to admit we underperformed." In 2003, four men passed 1,000 Championship runs, and Lancashire stacked up 28 centuries. This time, not one reached 1,000 – Loye was closest, with 934 – and there were just 15 hundreds. Hooper suffered most from the strange malaise. He managed only two first-innings fifties – one in the opening match, one in the last – and seriously thought of asking to be dropped.

The lack of runs increased the demands on the seam attack, which buckled. Martin was often missing; James Anderson, who claimed ten wickets in the victory over Worcestershire, played only three more matches, and in two of those he arrived in mid-game after being released by England. That left new signing Dominic Cork, Glen Chapple and Sajid Mahmood. Cork was most successful, with a modest 38 wickets, but was too hit-and-miss; Chapple took only 12 wickets in seven games after his head injury; and Mahmood's confidence slipped after a fruitless one-day debut for England.

More and more responsibility fell on slow left-armer Gary Keedy, who thrived on it, with a career-best 72 victims, including 14 against Gloucestershire. The last Lancashire bowler to take 14 had been Muttiah Muralitharan in 1999, and the club turned to him again, hoping his spin would help to bounce them straight back to the top flight; he agreed to play half the 2005 season, subject to the Sri Lankan board's approval. Meanwhile, Australian Brad Hodge was lured from Leicestershire to the other overseas slot; Stuart Law's application for UK citizenship came through and converted him into an England-qualified player.

Gary Keedy

Lancashire's Championship trauma coincided with a strong challenge for one-day honours. But a glittering century from Michael Vaughan wrecked them in the C&G quarter-final against Yorkshire, during a dreadful mid-season sequence: eight losses and two draws out of ten games in all cricket, after nine wins and three draws in their first 12. They rallied in time to finish second in the totesport League, but Surrey edged the Twenty20 semi-final by a single run. But Lancashire did win their one competition of the season that day: the County Mascots' race.

It was Lancashire's third knife-edge semi-final defeat in as many years under Hegg's captaincy. Inevitably, he gave way after the season, disappointed that the only trophy he had lifted was for the National League's second division in 2003, but knowing he had given his all. "If anyone had told me at the start of my career that one day I would captain Lancashire, I would not have believed it," he said. "It was a great honour." Mark Chilton was named to succeed him, with Law as vice-captain.

Finally giving in to his knee injury, Martin announced his retirement. In a career spanning 16 seasons, he had taken 606 first-class wickets and played eight Tests and 20 one-day internationals. Chris Schofield gave Lancashire a tough decision. In 2000, he had played two Tests against Zimbabwe, as a leg-spinner who could bat a bit; in retrospect, that call-up may have done more harm than good. As his bowling deteriorated, he was fighting for his county place as a middle-order batsman. In three Championship games in 2004, he took a single wicket, though he made 99 against Warwickshire and fifties in each of two defeats by Surrey. It was not enough to secure a new contract. John Wood and Alec Swann were also released, and Mark Currie had already gone.

Lancashire continued to investigate the possibility of leaving Old Trafford for the eastern side of Manchester. A feasibility study was taking longer than expected, and they had not reached any conclusion by the end of the season. The average member seemed more concerned about building a new team than a new stadium.

LANCASHIRE RESULTS

All first-class matches – Played 16; Won 2, Lost 4, Drawn 10.
County Championship matches – Played 16; Won 2, Lost 4, Drawn 10.

Frizzell County Championship, 8th in Division 1; Cheltenham & Gloucester Trophy, q-f;
totesport League, 2nd in Division 1; Twenty20 Cup, s-f.

COUNTY CHAMPIONSHIP AVERAGES

BATTING AND FIELDING

Cap		M	I	NO	R	HS	100s	50s	Avge	Ct/St
	D. Mongia§	6	9	2	470	111	2	2	67.14	2
2002	S. G. Law§.	12	18	1	867	171*	3	1	51.00	17
2003	M. B. Loye.	14	22	3	934	184	2	6	49.15	8
2002	C. P. Schofield	3	6	0	279	99	0	3	46.50	0
2003	C. L. Hooper§.	13	21	3	693	115	2	4	38.50	19
1994	G. Chapple.	14	22	1	726	112	2	4	34.57	3
2003	I. J. Sutcliffe.	14	24	1	788	104	1	6	34.26	5
2002	M. J. Chilton	16	27	2	809	124*	2	2	32.36	9
	S. P. Crook.	4	5	0	157	68	0	1	31.40	1
1989	W. K. Hegg	12	17	3	412	54	0	1	29.42	23/5
2004	D. G. Cork.	14	20	2	437	109	1	2	24.27	17
	S. I. Mahmood	11	14	3	233	94	0	1	21.18	2
	A. R. Crook	2	4	0	68	27	0	0	17.00	0
2002	A. J. Swann	5	7	0	112	34	0	0	16.00	2
1994	P. J. Martin.	6	7	2	59	33*	0	0	11.80	0
	K. W. Hogg	4	7	0	72	23	0	0	10.28	0
	J. J. Haynes	4	5	0	48	24	0	0	9.60	12/2
2000	G. Keedy	16	20	8	90	17	0	0	7.50	7
	J. M. Anderson	4	4	1	6	3	0	0	2.00	1

Also batted: P. J. Horton (1 match) 22; O. J. Newby (1 match) 0*; J. Wood (cap 2003) (2 matches) 13*, 35 (1 ct).

§ *Overseas player.*

BOWLING

	O	M	R	W	BB	5W/i	Avge
J. M. Anderson	126	27	374	19	6-49	1	19.68
G. Keedy	645.3	122	1,849	72	7-95	6	25.68
D. G. Cork	332.5	59	1,144	38	7-120	3	30.10
P. J. Martin	115.5	34	319	10	4-81	0	31.90
G. Chapple	374.4	80	1,128	29	5-136	1	38.89
C. L. Hooper	234	51	595	15	4-56	0	39.66
S. I. Mahmood	230	26	1,010	23	4-59	0	43.91

Also bowled: M. J. Chilton 24–3–84–1; A. R. Crook 50–6–212–2; S. P. Crook 68.1–5–309–6; K. W. Hogg 71–10–259–5; S. G. Law 5–1–16–0; M. B. Loye 1–0–1–0; D. Mongia 50.2–9–157–5; O. J. Newby 35–6–107–2; C. P. Schofield 26.3–3–85–1; A. J. Swann 6–2–18–1; J. Wood 51–5–243–4.

COUNTY RECORDS

Highest score for:	424	A. C. MacLaren v Somerset at Taunton	1895
Highest score against:	315*	T. W. Hayward (Surrey) at The Oval	1898
Best bowling for:	10-46	W. Hickton v Hampshire at Manchester	1870
Best bowling against:	10-40	G. O. B. Allen (Middlesex) at Lord's	1929
Highest total for:	863	v Surrey at The Oval	1990
Highest total against:	707-9 dec.	by Surrey at The Oval	1990
Lowest total for:	25	v Derbyshire at Manchester	1871
Lowest total against:	22	by Glamorgan at Liverpool	1924

LANCASHIRE DIRECTORY

ADDRESS

County Cricket Ground, Old Trafford, Manchester M16 0PX (0161 282 4000; fax 0161 282 4100; email enquiries@lccc.co.uk). **Website** www.lccc.co.uk.

GROUNDS

Manchester (Old Trafford): 2 miles SW of city centre on E side of A56 in Old Trafford close to Manchester United football ground, entrance in Talbot Road. Nearest stations: Old Trafford (MetroLink Tram) (adjacent) and Manchester Piccadilly (2½ miles).

Liverpool: 4 miles SE of city centre between A561 and River Mersey. From A562 Speke Road continue on A561 Speke Boulevard, R on Garston Way for Aigburth Road. Nearest station: Aigburth (½ mile).

Blackpool: 1 mile inland from seafront. From A583 North Shore (Preston New Road), R into Gorse Road, then L into West Park Drive for Stanley Park. Nearest stations: Blackpool North (1 mile) and Blackpool South (¾ mile).

OFFICIALS

Captain 2004 – W. K. Hegg; 2005 – M. J. Chilton
Cricket manager M. Watkinson
President Sir D. Landau
Chairman J. Simmons

Chief executive J. Cumbes
Chairman, cricket committee G. Ogden
Head groundsman P. Marron
Scorer A. West

PLAYERS

Players expected to reappear in 2005

	Former counties	*Country*	*Born*	*Birthplace*
*Anderson James Michael.....		‡E	30.7.1982	†*Burnley*
Chapple Glen		E	23.1.1974	*Skipton*
Chilton Mark James		E	2.10.1976	*Sheffield*
*Cork Dominic Gerald	Derbys	E	7.8.1971	*Newcastle-under-Lyme*
Crook Andrew Richard		A (EU)	14.10.1980	*Modbury*
Crook Steven Paul		A (EU)	28.5.1983	*Modbury*
Currie Mark Robert		E	22.9.1979	†*Manchester*
*Flintoff Andrew		‡E	6.12.1977	†*Preston*
*Hegg Warren Kevin........		E	23.2.1968	†*Whitefield*
Hogg Kyle William		E	2.7.1983	*Birmingham*
Horton Paul James		E	20.9.1982	*Sydney, Aus.*
Keedy Gary.............	Yorks	E	27.11.1974	*Wakefield*
*Law Stuart Grant	Essex	E	18.10.1968	*Herston, Aus.*
Loye Malachy Bernard......	Northants	E	27.9.1972	*Northampton*
Mahmood Sajid Iqbal		E	21.12.1981	†*Bolton*
Newby Oliver James		E	26.8.1984	†*Blackburn*
Rees Timothy Martyn		E	4.9.1984	*Loughborough*
Sutcliffe Iain John	Leics	E	20.12.1974	*Leeds*
Yates Gary		E	20.9.1967	†*Ashton-under-Lyne*

Players due to join in 2005

	Former counties	*Country*	*Born*	*Birthplace*
Croft Steven John		E	11.10.1984	†*Blackpool*
Cross Gareth David........		E	20.6.1984	†*Bury*
Hodge Bradley John	Durham, Leics	A	29.12.1974	*Sandringham*
Marshall Simon James		E	20.9.1982	*Birkenhead*
*Muralitharan Muttiah.......	Lancs, Kent	SL	17.4.1972	*Kandy*

* Test player.   *† Born in Lancashire.*   *‡ 12-month ECB contract.*

At Northampton, April 16, 17, 18, 19. LANCASHIRE drew with NORTHAMPTONSHIRE.

At Hove, April 21, 22, 23. LANCASHIRE beat SUSSEX by ten wickets.

At Lord's, May 7, 8, 9, 10. LANCASHIRE drew with MIDDLESEX.

LANCASHIRE v WORCESTERSHIRE

At Manchester, May 12, 13, 14. Lancashire won by 219 runs. Lancashire 17 pts, Worcestershire 3 pts. Toss: Lancashire.

A bystander in the Caribbean Tests, Anderson released the pent-up frustration in his first Championship game for 12 months and earned his first ten-wicket haul. He and Keedy had nine each before Anderson trapped last man Malik. "I've bowled better and not taken as many, but I had a long bowl and that's what I really needed," he said. England coach Duncan Fletcher had requested his inclusion, though it meant dropping Mahmood, who looked promising in an earlier three-day win at Hove. Hegg had to make another hard choice when he won the toss, but batting first in helpful conditions for swing ultimately paid off. In a low-scoring match, Lancashire owed their slender first-innings lead to Loye, who fought off back spasms to score 55 out of 70 when he resumed in obvious discomfort. The real difference came in the second innings thanks to a stand of 168 between Hooper, who scored his second century of the season, and Sutcliffe, who just missed his. Worcestershire had never successfully chased more than 203 to win a Championship game at Old Trafford; needing 347, they folded. Lancashire went top of the embryonic table, Worcestershire stayed bottom.

Close of play: First day, Worcestershire 77-4 (Malik 0, Kadeer Ali 0); Second day, Lancashire 200-3 (Sutcliffe 81, Keedy 0).

Lancashire

M. J. Chilton c Hick b Hall	28	– lbw b Batty	12
I. J. Sutcliffe c Moore b Bichel	9	– c Rhodes b Hall	95
M. B. Loye not out	59	– (7) c Smith b Batty	20
S. G. Law c Kadeer Ali b Mason	8	– (3) c Kadeer Ali b Mason	0
C. L. Hooper c Peters b Mason	1	– (4) c Rhodes b Bichel	100
G. Chapple c Hall b Bichel	21	– c Rhodes b Mason	38
D. G. Cork b Hall	15	– (8) b Bichel	1
*†W. K. Hegg c Hick b Malik	15	– (9) not out	21
P. J. Martin c Hick b Malik	0	– (10) lbw b Malik	2
G. Keedy c Smith b Batty	7	– (5) c Rhodes b Batty	1
J. M. Anderson c Smith b Batty	0	– c Hick b Bichel	3
B 4, l-b 8, n-b 12	24	B 2, l-b 10	12

1/15 (2) 2/44 (4) 3/46 (5) 4/63 (1)   187   1/31 (1) 2/32 (3) 3/200 (4)   305
5/87 (6) 6/117 (7) 7/119 (8)   4/209 (5) 5/225 (2) 6/264 (6)
8/119 (9) 9/179 (10) 10/187 (11)   7/265 (8) 8/288 (7)
                                                          9/295 (10) 10/305 (11)

Bonus points – Worcestershire 3.

In the first innings Loye, when 4, retired hurt at 19 and resumed at 117.

Bowling: *First Innings*—Bichel 20–3–51–2; Mason 20–7–52–2; Malik 14–5–26–2; Hall 8–0–37–2; Batty 7–4–9–2. *Second Innings*—Bichel 20.2–6–64–3; Mason 25–8–60–2; Batty 37–8–111–3; Hall 15–5–34–1; Malik 13–3–24–1.

Worcestershire

S. D. Peters c Hegg b Keedy	41	– c Chilton b Anderson	10
S. C. Moore b Anderson	8	– st Hegg b Keedy	45
G. A. Hick b Anderson	3	– c Hooper b Anderson	4
*B. F. Smith c Law b Keedy	23	– c Keedy b Anderson	10
M. N. Malik b Anderson	2	– (11) lbw b Anderson	0
Kadeer Ali c Hegg b Anderson	0	– (5) c Cork b Keedy	6
A. J. Hall c Law b Keedy	34	– (6) lbw b Chapple	7
G. J. Batty lbw b Anderson	0	– (7) not out	31
A. J. Bichel b Anderson	3	– (8) c Hegg b Keedy	4
†S. J. Rhodes not out	19	– (9) lbw b Keedy	6
M. S. Mason st Hegg b Keedy	10	– (10) c Law b Keedy	4
B 1, l-b 2	3		
	146		127

1/18 (2) 2/36 (3) 3/76 (4) 4/77 (1)   146
5/77 (6) 6/88 (5) 7/94 (8)
8/102 (9) 9/125 (7) 10/146 (11)

1/22 (1) 2/26 (3) 3/40 (4)   127
4/61 (5) 5/77 (6) 6/90 (2)
7/112 (8) 8/120 (9)
9/126 (10) 10/127 (11)

Bonus points – Lancashire 3.

Bowling: *First Innings*—Martin 16–4–36–0; Anderson 17–2–49–6; Chapple 14–4–32–0; Cork 4–1–6–0; Keedy 8.2–3–20–4. *Second Innings*—Martin 3–1–8–0; Anderson 10.3–1–32–4; Keedy 19–4–62–5; Chapple 8–2–18–1; Hooper 2–1–7–0.

Umpires: D. J. Constant and P. J. Hartley.

At Bradford, May 19, 20, 21. LANCASHIRE beat BRADFORD/LEEDS UCCE by 71 runs

LANCASHIRE v MIDDLESEX

At Manchester, May 25, 26, 27, 28. Drawn. Lancashire 10 pts, Middlesex 10 pts. Toss: Middlesex. With Strauss resting after his heroic Test debut, Koenig got another chance, despite only 101 from seven Championship innings, and dominated the opening day. He drove Keedy for six to reach his first Championship hundred since July 2002 and closed on a career-best 170, although Anderson ripped out his middle stump first thing next morning to start a slide of five for 53. Lancashire were able to edge ahead on first innings thanks to Loye and Chilton, who almost completed his fourth hundred in four matches against Middlesex. The visiting captain Shah was jeered by the crowd for the time he spent shining the ball during a long spell from slow left-armer Peploe, and he raised more eyebrows by not taking a new ball for 126 overs. Once he did, a hostile spell from Hayward saw four men fall in seven overs, including Loye for 98. Hutton and Shah regained the lead before rain restricted the final day to 32 balls. The 73-year-old former Northamptonshire and England fast bowler Frank Tyson, on a visit from his Australian home, watched Hutton bat, and recalled playing with his grandfather Len on the Ashes tour of 1954-55. Tyson walked through the pavilion of his native county barely recognised. "After National Service, I wrote to Lancashire, but they said there were no vacancies."

Close of play: First day, Middlesex 323-5 (Koenig 170, Nash 45); Second day, Lancashire 253-2 (Loye 47, Law 32); Third day, Middlesex 117-2 (Shah 66).

Middlesex

B. L. Hutton c Anderson b Keedy	27	– lbw b Anderson	41
S. G. Koenig b Anderson	171	– b Anderson	7
*O. A. Shah st Hegg b Hooper	35	– not out	67
E. C. Joyce b Mahmood	0	– not out	7
P. N. Weekes lbw b Anderson	8		
J. W. M. Dalrymple lbw b Keedy	17		
†D. C. Nash not out	81		
L. Klusener lbw b Anderson	2		
C. T. Peploe c Hegg b Chapple	3		
P. M. Hutchison lbw b Mahmood	4		
M. Hayward c Hooper b Keedy	1		
B 6, l-b 21, w 2, n-b 4	33	B 4, w 3	7

1/92 (1) 2/180 (3) 3/183 (4) 4/198 (5)   382   1/8 (2) 2/117 (1)   (2 wkts) 129
5/237 (6) 6/329 (2) 7/347 (8)
8/362 (9) 9/379 (10) 10/382 (11)

Bonus points – Middlesex 4, Lancashire 2 (130 overs: 379-8).

Bowling: *First Innings*—Anderson 33–7–95–3; Chapple 34–9–60–1; Mahmood 17–3–58–2; Keedy 34.2–6–99–3; Hooper 15–3–43–1. *Second Innings*—Anderson 12–2–45–2; Chapple 9–3–17–0; Keedy 10–1–23–0; Mahmood 3–1–8–0; Hooper 9–1–32–0.

Lancashire

M. J. Chilton b Peploe	93	G. Keedy not out	3
I. J. Sutcliffe st Nash b Peploe	59	J. M. Anderson b Peploe	1
M. B. Loye c Joyce b Hayward	98		
S. G. Law lbw b Dalrymple	49		
C. L. Hooper c Joyce b Dalrymple	4	B 10, l-b 13, w 4, n-b 14	41
A. J. Swann b Hayward	34		
G. Chapple c Nash b Klusener	1	1/126 (2) 2/189 (1) 3/288 (4)	417
*†W. K. Hegg c Weekes b Dalrymple	34	4/300 (5) 5/370 (6) 6/371 (7)	
S. I. Mahmood lbw b Hayward	0	7/373 (3) 8/373 (9)	
		9/416 (8) 10/417 (11)	

Bonus points – Lancashire 4, Middlesex 2 (130 overs: 371-6).

Bowling: Hayward 21–5–39–3; Klusener 25–3–99–1; Peploe 50.1–16–80–3; Hutchison 9–2–35–0; Weekes 4–0–22–0; Dalrymple 37–4–117–3; Hutton 1–0–2–0.

Umpires: A. Clarkson and A. G. T. Whitehead.

At Tunbridge Wells, June 2, 3, 4, 5. LANCASHIRE lost to KENT by seven wickets.

LANCASHIRE v SUSSEX

At Manchester, June 9, 10, 11. Sussex won by eight wickets. Sussex 22 pts, Lancashire 4 pts. Toss: Sussex.

Lancashire suddenly looked fragile, and were powerless as Sussex, the struggling champions, finally won at the seventh attempt. Lancashire began the game by thinking Adams was caught on ten, and dropped him on 19; he went on to 150, his ninth century of 2004, and Sussex to 470. Next, Mohammad Akram removed Lancashire's top three for 22, and Kirtley struck Chapple on the helmet. "He was talking but you could see there was no one at home," said his partner, Law. Chapple was out soon afterwards; a scan revealed a bruised brain, but he played it down as "a thick head". Lancashire were 101 for nine before No. 10 Mahmood, once a big hitter in the Bolton League, provided wonderful entertainment, 94 off 66 balls, with three sixes and 13 fours. After a rain-break he was caught trying to reach a maiden century in the grand manner. When Lancashire followed on for the second match running, Akram was taken off for bowling beamers but Mushtaq Ahmed wound things up. Anderson, a full substitute for Crook after his release from the Test squad, could do little more than concede the winning runs on the third afternoon.

Close of play: First day, Sussex 458-9 (Adams 145); Second day, Lancashire 148-4 (Hooper 23, Keedy 0).

Sussex

I. J. Ward c Hooper b Chapple	84	– c Cork b Mahmood	26
R. R. Montgomerie c Chilton b Cork	5	– c Loye b Cork	0
M. W. Goodwin c Hooper b Mahmood	83	– not out	11
*C. J. Adams not out	150	– not out	3
M. J. Prior c Crook b Hooper	61		
†T. R. Ambrose c Hegg b Mahmood	8		
R. S. C. Martin-Jenkins c Cork b Mahmood	9		
R. J. Kirtley c Cork b Chapple	14		
Mushtaq Ahmed c Law b Cork	6		
Mohammad Akram lbw b Keedy	11		
J. D. Lewry b Cork	7		
B 3, l-b 14, w 1, n-b 14	32	B 4	4
	470	**(2 wkts)**	**44**

1/16 (2) 2/164 (3) 3/190 (1) 4/306 (5)   1/2 (2) 2/33 (1)
5/317 (6) 6/329 (7) 7/387 (8)
8/430 (9) 9/458 (10) 10/470 (11)

Bonus points – Sussex 5, Lancashire 3.

Bowling: *First Innings*—Chapple 23–2–110–2; Cork 27.3–4–85–3; Mahmood 19–1–102–3; Crook 7–0–50–0; Keedy 19–2–67–1; Hooper 14–2–39–1. *Second Innings*—Anderson 6.3–1–18–0; Cork 4–2–11–1; Mahmood 2–0–11–1.

Lancashire

M. J. Chilton c Prior b Mohammad Akram	9	– lbw b Mohammad Akram	21
A. J. Swann c Ambrose b Mohammad Akram	6	– lbw b Mushtaq Ahmed	27
M. B. Loye lbw b Mohammad Akram	0	– c Ambrose b Lewry	24
S. G. Law c Montgomerie b Mushtaq Ahmed	25	– b Mushtaq Ahmed	42
C. L. Hooper lbw b Martin-Jenkins	9	– lbw b Mushtaq Ahmed	55
G. Chapple c and b Lewry	21	– (8) c Martin-Jenkins b Mushtaq Ahmed	27
S. P. Crook c Montgomerie b Mushtaq Ahmed	9		
*†W. K. Hegg c Ambrose b Lewry	3	– (7) b Lewry	11
D. G. Cork c Montgomerie b Lewry	7	– c Akram b Kirtley	31
S. I. Mahmood c Adams b Kirtley	94	– c Lewry b Mushtaq Ahmed	24
G. Keedy not out	14	– (6) c Ambrose b Mohammad Akram	5
J. M. Anderson		– (11) not out	2
B 12, l-b 4, w 1	17	B 6, l-b 14, n-b 8	28
	214		**297**

1/11 (2) 2/11 (3) 3/22 (1) 4/47 (5)   1/46 (1) 2/70 (2) 3/90 (3)
5/73 (6) 6/90 (7) 7/91 (4)   4/142 (4) 5/175 (6) 6/203 (5)
8/100 (9) 9/101 (8) 10/214 (10)   7/207 (7) 8/247 (8)
9/284 (9) 10/297 (10)

Bonus points – Lancashire 1, Sussex 3.

Bowling: *First Innings*—Mohammad Akram 10–1–49–3; Lewry 16–8–32–3; Martin-Jenkins 7–3–30–1; Kirtley 8–1–23–1; Mushtaq Ahmed 14–0–64–2. *Second Innings*—Mohammad Akram 15.3–2–60–2; Kirtley 16–5–53–1; Martin-Jenkins 4–1–14–0; Lewry 13.3–3–45–2; Mushtaq Ahmed 22.2–2–105–5.

Umpires: J. H. Hampshire and V. A. Holder.

At Stratford-upon-Avon, June 18, 19, 20, 21. LANCASHIRE drew with WARWICKSHIRE.

LANCASHIRE v NORTHAMPTONSHIRE

At Liverpool, June 26, 27, 28, 29. Drawn. Lancashire 9 pts, Northamptonshire 11 pts. Toss: Lancashire. Championship debut: O. J. Newby.

In six visits to Aigburth since 1911, Northamptonshire had always batted first, and never won; rain ensured it was not seventh time lucky. After a first-day washout, Lancashire put them in again on a green-tinged pitch. With Martin suffering a swollen knee, their pace attack was far from first-choice and included the 19-year-old Blackburn-born seamer Oliver Newby for the first time. And just when Keedy's third-morning spell of four for 18 promised to put his side on top, Hegg chose to take the new ball: Afzaal—who dug in for more than six hours—and Jones responded by adding 73, a county last-wicket record against Lancashire. In reply, Loye struck six off his first ball, then scored only four more runs in the next 40. Cork made a maiden first-class fifty for Lancashire, and held two sharp slip catches, injuring his hand as he helped the impressive Newby to a first Championship wicket. Earlier, Jones fractured his foot, which would keep him out until August.

Close of play: First day, No play; Second day, Northamptonshire 257-5 (Afzaal 83, Phillips 4); Third day, Lancashire 214-6 (Cork 46, Crook 20).

Northamptonshire

T. W. Roberts c Law b Wood	14	– c Cork b Keedy	20
G. L. Brophy c Hegg b Crook	36	– b Mongia	67
M. van Jaarsveld lbw b Wood	7	– c Cork b Newby	0
U. Afzaal not out	133	– c Wood b Newby	20
*D. J. Sales c Hegg b Keedy	59		
G. P. Swann c Hegg b Crook	47		
B. J. Phillips c Loye b Keedy	5	– (5) not out	26
J. Louw lbw b Keedy	2		
†T. M. B. Bailey lbw b Keedy	2	– (6) not out	11
A. J. Shantry c Mongia b Keedy	5		
P. S. Jones c Sutcliffe b Mongia	35		
B 5, l-b 7	12	L-b 2	2

1/21 (1) 2/35 (3) 3/74 (2) 4/158 (5)   357   1/47 (1) 2/50 (3)   (4 wkts) 146
5/250 (6) 6/258 (7) 7/260 (8)   3/96 (4) 4/108 (2)
8/264 (9) 9/284 (10) 10/357 (11)

Bonus points – Northamptonshire 4, Lancashire 3.

Bowling: *First Innings*—Cork 25–5–69–0; Wood 18–2–70–2; Crook 12–2–33–2; Newby 26–6–75–0; Keedy 25–3–73–5; Mongia 8.4–0–25–1. *Second Innings*—Cork 6–1–19–0; Wood 3–0–20–0; Keedy 23–7–58–1; Newby 9–0–32–2; Mongia 11–6–14–1; Loye 1–0–1–0.

Lancashire

M. J. Chilton b Phillips	35	G. Keedy lbw b Louw	5
I. J. Sutcliffe lbw b Swann	48	O. J. Newby not out	0
M. B. Loye run out	10		
S. G. Law c Bailey b Swann	3	L-b 3, w 3	6
D. Mongia c Shantry b Swann	18		
*†W. K. Hegg c Roberts b Louw	30	1/76 (2) 2/94 (1) 3/97 (4)	284
D. G. Cork c Louw b Shantry	74	4/107 (3) 5/122 (5) 6/169 (6)
S. P. Crook c van Jaarsveld b Shantry	20	7/215 (8) 8/278 (9)
J. Wood c Sales b Louw	35	9/284 (7) 10/284 (10)

Bonus points – Lancashire 2, Northamptonshire 3.

Bowling: Louw 19.1–6–57–3; Shantry 21–6–67–2; Jones 8–1–32–0; Phillips 13–0–52–1; Swann 32–9–69–3; Afzaal 4–1–4–0.

Umpires: M. J. Harris and J. W. Holder.

At Cheltenham, July 21, 22, 23, 24. LANCASHIRE drew with GLOUCESTERSHIRE.

LANCASHIRE v WARWICKSHIRE

At Manchester, July 28, 29, 30, 31. Drawn. Lancashire 12 pts, Warwickshire 11 pts. Toss: Warwickshire.

Ian Bell burnished his growing reputation by becoming the first Warwickshire batsman since Brian Lara in 1994 to score a century in each innings against an authentic attack (David Hemp achieved the feat against declaration bowling in 1997). This took Bell's record in four first-class innings to 155, 96 not out, 112 and 181. Keedy had reduced the visitors to 92 for four before the evergreen Brown joined Bell to add 254, a ground record for the fifth wicket. The 34-year-old Brown also made his second hundred in successive games, and underlined his fitness by batting more than six hours, then opening the bowling. It was the ninth successive match in which Warwickshire had amassed over 400 in the first innings. But Lancashire gained a two-run lead, despite losing Loye when he damaged his Achilles tendon trying to cut Wagh. They fought back gamely as Chapple reached three figures in 82 balls, while Schofield, in his first Championship match of 2004, was a whisker away from a maiden hundred. Bell was even more expansive second time around until Cork ran him out from mid-wicket. The evenness of the contest ruled out a result and Mongia scored the game's fifth hundred as Lancashire batted out time.

Close of play: First day, Warwickshire 308-4 (Bell 106, Brown 120); Second day, Lancashire 167-3 (Sutcliffe 67, Schofield 3); Third day, Warwickshire 191-4 (Bell 103, Tahir 0).

Warwickshire

*N. V. Knight c Haynes b Chilton	25	– c Keedy b Cork	3
M. A. Wagh c and b Keedy	41	– c Haynes b Keedy	24
I. R. Bell c Hooper b Cork	112	– run out	181
I. J. L. Trott c Hooper b Keedy	9	– c Cork b Keedy	41
M. J. Powell lbw b Keedy	0	– c Cork b Keedy	0
D. R. Brown c Chapple b Keedy	162	– (7) c Keedy b Chapple	0
G. B. Hogg lbw b Cork	0	– (8) not out	72
†T. Frost c Haynes b Keedy	6		
N. M. Carter c Haynes b Mahmood	7	– not out	3
N. Tahir not out	12	– (6) lbw b Keedy	7
A. Richardson c Hooper b Schofield	17		
B 1, l-b 7, w 1, n-b 10	19	B 12, l-b 2, n-b 8	22
	410	(7 wkts dec.)	**353**

1/72 (1) 2/78 (2) 3/92 (4) 4/92 (5) 5/346 (3) 6/346 (7) 7/361 (8) 8/368 (9) 9/380 (6) 10/410 (11)

1/3 (1) 2/66 (2) 3/184 (4) 4/190 (5) 5/214 (6) 6/215 (7) 7/332 (3)

Bonus points – Warwickshire 4, Lancashire 3 (130 overs: 380-9).

Bowling: *First Innings*—Chapple 26–5–73–0; Cork 27–6–53–2; Mahmood 25–4–100–1; Chilton 12–2–39–1; Keedy 40–7–109–5; Schofield 6.3–1–13–1; Hooper 7–1–15–0. *Second Innings*—Chapple 17–1–68–1; Cork 9–2–24–1; Keedy 38–7–109–4; Mahmood 12–0–76–0; Schofield 11–0–43–0; Mongia 8–1–19–0.

> ❝Ben Hutton and the debutant Nick Compton added 127, the first Hutton–Compton century stand in any first-class match since their grandfathers Len and Denis put on 150 in the riot-torn Georgetown Test of 1953-54. The Worcester crowd did not throw bottles."
>
> Worcestershire in 2004, page 799.

Lancashire

M. J. Chilton b Carter	19	– b Brown	20
I. J. Sutcliffe lbw b Hogg	72	– c Frost b Brown	5
M. B. Loye retired hurt	44		
D. Mongia c and b Hogg	15	– (3) not out	108
*C. L. Hooper c Brown b Hogg	16	– (4) c Trott b Carter	11
C. P. Schofield c Wagh b Carter	99	– (5) b Wagh	40
G. Chapple b Hogg	112	– (6) not out	5
D. G. Cork b Wagh	23		
†J. J. Haynes lbw b Wagh	0		
S. I. Mahmood not out	3		
G. Keedy lbw b Wagh	0		
B 1, l-b 7, w 1	9	B 4, l-b 1	5

1/32 (1) 2/130 (4) 3/148 (5)   412   1/21 (2) 2/34 (1)   (4 wkts) 194
4/190 (2) 5/358 (6) 6/409 (7)   3/61 (4) 4/178 (5)
7/409 (8) 8/412 (9) 9/412 (11)

Bonus points – Lancashire 5, Warwickshire 3.

In the first innings Loye retired hurt at 99.

Bowling: *First Innings*—Carter 20–2–71–2; Brown 18–3–81–0; Wagh 30–7–86–3; Tahir 8–1–29–0; Hogg 25–2–107–4; Richardson 7–0–18–0; Bell 2–0–12–0. *Second Innings*—Brown 7–2–26–2; Carter 16–4–40–1; Wagh 15–4–56–1; Hogg 11–2–53–0; Tahir 3–1–14–0.

Umpires: I. J. Gould and R. A. Kettleborough.

At Whitgift School, August 11, 12, 13. LANCASHIRE lost to SURREY by an innings and 55 runs.

LANCASHIRE v KENT

At Manchester, August 24, 25, 26, 27. Drawn. Lancashire 7 pts, Kent 9 pts. Toss: Lancashire.
The August monsoon wrecked this game, whose first two days saw only 39 balls bowled. By now, Lancashire were in real trouble, eighth in the first division, with Hegg and Law injured and Hooper a shadow of his true self. In 2003, he had scored five Championship centuries, helping to break records galore; a second-ball duck in this match meant he had passed 32 only twice since May. Lancashire's brightest moments came from Mongia, who took a breathtaking, diving catch, running from long-off, to dismiss Loudon, then showed his class with the bat after Patel took three wickets in 15 balls.
Close of play: First day, Kent 15-0 (Fulton 7, Key 8); Second day, No play; Third day, Lancashire 70-5 (Mongia 15, Chapple 13).

Kent

*D. P. Fulton c Sutcliffe b Chapple	18	– c Haynes b Chapple	0
R. W. T. Key lbw b Mahmood	52	– st Haynes b Keedy	18
E. T. Smith c Haynes b Chapple	0	– not out	35
A. G. R. Loudon c Mongia b Keedy	45	– lbw b Mongia	34
M. J. Walker c Haynes b Hooper	61		
†N. J. O'Brien lbw b Keedy	19		
M. J. Dennington c Haynes b Keedy	15		
A. Khan lbw b Keedy	0		
M. M. Patel c Hooper b Cork	17		
I. G. Butler b Cork	19		
R. H. Joseph not out	7		
B 2, l-b 6, w 1, n-b 4	13	L-b 3, n-b 2	5

1/34 (1) 2/34 (3) 3/92 (2) 4/162 (4)   266   1/0 (1) 2/32 (2) 3/92 (4)   (3 wkts) 92
5/195 (6) 6/213 (5) 7/218 (8)
8/229 (7) 9/237 (9) 10/266 (10)

Bonus points – Kent 2, Lancashire 3.

Bowling: *First Innings*—Martin 15–6–41–0; Chapple 16–3–79–2; Cork 11–3–18–2; Mahmood 8–0–45–1; Keedy 21–4–62–4; Hooper 4–1–13–1. *Second Innings*—Chapple 5–0–18–1; Mahmood 6–0–20–0; Keedy 11–1–30–1; Cork 2–0–4–0; Hooper 8–0–16–0; Mongia 1.1–0–1–1.

Lancashire

M. J. Chilton c Fulton b Patel	26	P. J. Martin not out	33
I. J. Sutcliffe b Butler	5	G. Keedy c Joseph b Butler	2
M. B. Loye b Patel	4		
D. Mongia c and b Dennington	41	B 5, l-b 6, n-b 6	17
*C. L. Hooper lbw b Patel	0		———
†J. J. Haynes c Dennington b Joseph	0		184
G. Chapple c Fulton b Joseph	18	1/23 (2) 2/38 (3) 3/47 (1)	
D. G. Cork b Joseph	28	4/47 (5) 5/50 (6) 6/84 (7)	
S. I. Mahmood c Loudon b Butler	10	7/130 (8) 8/134 (4)	
		9/174 (9) 10/184 (11)	

Bonus points – Kent 3.

Bowling: Butler 6.3–2–10–3; Joseph 15–1–70–3; Khan 6–1–32–0; Patel 20–4–51–3; Loudon 3–3–0–0; Dennington 2–0–10–1.

Umpires: I. J. Gould and V. A. Holder.

LANCASHIRE v SURREY

At Manchester, September 2, 3, 4. Surrey won by 147 runs. Surrey 21 pts, Lancashire 5 pts. Toss: Surrey.

Lancashire collapsed for a dismal 129, their lowest Championship total of the season, to suffer their second three-day defeat in a month at Surrey's hands. With relegation looming, disgruntled fans made their feelings plain; Hegg, the captain and not-out batsman, had a quiet word with one of the most vociferous critics. Two Surrey players shone. On the opening day, Brown completed his set of centuries against the other 17 counties (Ramprakash and Hooper, also appearing in this game, had taken hundreds off all 18). He arrived at 58 for four, after Sajid Mahmood had surprised Butcher and Ramprakash with superb deliveries, and over five and three quarter hours steered Surrey to four batting points. Then slow left-armer Doshi had Lancashire's top order in trouble in what was becoming a spinners' match. Early turn meant Keedy had wheeled away for 38 overs on the first day; on the third, he and Hooper bowled Surrey out to keep the target down to 277. But Doshi, sharing the new ball, finished with a career-best 11 for 182.

Close of play: First day, Surrey 346-7 (Brown 144, Murtagh 63); Second day, Surrey 8-0 (Newman 8, Clinton 0).

Surrey

S. A. Newman lbw b Keedy	17	– lbw b Hooper	8
R. S. Clinton b Chapple	2	– c Mahmood b Hooper	35
M. A. Butcher c Hegg b Mahmood	30	– lbw b Keedy	33
M. R. Ramprakash lbw b Mahmood	3	– c Hooper b Keedy	0
*†J. N. Batty c Chapple b Hooper	36	– c Sutcliffe b Keedy	3
A. D. Brown lbw b Mahmood	154	– b Hooper	14
Azhar Mahmood c Cork b Keedy	18	– not out	58
M. P. Bicknell b Mahmood	14	– lbw b Keedy	2
T. J. Murtagh c Hooper b Cork	65	– c Law b Hooper	17
J. Ormond not out	4	– c Cork b Keedy	1
N. D. Doshi c Loye b Keedy	6	– c Law b Keedy	2
B 7, l-b 13	20	B 6, l-b 6	12
	———		———
	369		185

1/11 (2) 2/50 (3) 3/58 (1) 4/58 (4)   1/12 (1) 2/69 (3) 3/69 (4)
5/177 (5) 6/206 (7) 7/225 (8)   4/91 (2) 5/105 (6) 6/111 (5)
8/349 (9) 9/362 (6) 10/369 (11)   7/115 (8) 8/162 (9)
   9/167 (10) 10/185 (11)

Bonus points – Surrey 4, Lancashire 3 (130 overs: 368-9).

Bowling: *First Innings*—Chapple 16–3–46–1; Cork 16–4–37–1; Mahmood 20–4–59–4; Keedy 44.4–7–112–3; Hooper 25–3–66–1; Schofield 9–2–29–0. *Second Innings*—Mahmood 5–0–22–0; Keedy 31.2–7–95–6; Hooper 27–8–56–4.

Lancashire

M. J. Chilton lbw b Bicknell	6	– c Murtagh b Doshi	21
I. J. Sutcliffe c Clinton b Doshi	6	– c Batty b Doshi	11
M. B. Loye b Ormond	54	– b Doshi	1
S. G. Law c Batty b Doshi	34	– lbw b Doshi	24
C. L. Hooper st Batty b Doshi	0	– c Azhar Mahmood b Doshi	10
C. P. Schofield st Batty b Doshi	65	– c Batty b Ormond	4
G. Chapple c Batty b Bicknell	67	– st Batty b Ormond	8
D. G. Cork b Bicknell	0	– c Clinton b Ormond	3
*†W. K. Hegg c Batty b Doshi	18	– not out	17
S. I. Mahmood not out	11	– st Batty b Doshi	4
G. Keedy c Batty b Azhar Mahmood	4	– c Batty b Ormond	17
B 2, l-b 9, n-b 2	13	B 5, l-b 4	9

1/8 (1) 2/28 (2) 3/100 (4) 4/100 (5)   **278**   1/22 (2) 2/24 (3) 3/45 (1)   **129**
5/112 (3) 6/226 (7) 7/226 (8)   4/66 (4) 5/75 (5) 6/81 (6)
8/258 (6) 9/261 (9) 10/278 (11)   7/90 (7) 8/99 (8)
                                    9/104 (10) 10/129 (11)

Bonus points – Lancashire 2, Surrey 3.

Bowling: *First Innings*—Bicknell 15–4–38–3; Ormond 15–4–47–1; Azhar Mahmood 18–4–56–1; Doshi 31–6–125–5; Ramprakash 2–1–1–0. *Second Innings*—Bicknell 7–1–19–0; Doshi 20–3–57–6; Azhar Mahmood 7–0–22–0; Ormond 6.5–1–22–4.

Umpires: N. A. Mallender and J. F. Steele.

At Worcester, September 9, 10, 11, 12. LANCASHIRE drew with WORCESTERSHIRE.

LANCASHIRE v GLOUCESTERSHIRE

At Manchester, September 16, 17, 18, 19. Drawn. Lancashire 9 pts, Gloucestershire 10 pts. Toss: Gloucestershire.

In the battle to decide the third relegation spot, Gloucestershire started with a 17-point advantage; six would make them safe, while Lancashire needed victory by at least 17 points. It was settled at 4.35 p.m. on the second day, when Crook was caught on the boundary hooking Lewis, and pre-season Championship favourites Lancashire were left contemplating life in the lower division. The ECB had asked pitch liaison officer Phil Sharpe to act as referee and monitor any "extraordinary declaration" intended to deprive the bowling side of bonus points without enhancing the batting side's chances of winning. In fact, Taylor declared at 311 for eight – restricting Lancashire to two bowling points, and ensuring Gloucestershire needed only two themselves – after Sharpe indicated it would be acceptable. Lancashire manager Mike Watkinson thought they would have done the same. The controversy overshadowed Keedy's career-best seven for 95 on the first day, and six sixes from Cork on the second. After a Saturday washout, the match meandered to a draw in front of a small crowd, with Taylor unwilling to set a target. At least Keedy finished on a high note. Another seven wickets gave him 14 for 227, the best match figures by an English spinner since Martyn Ball, one of his victims, took 14 for 169 at Taunton in 1993; Keedy's total of 72 first-class wickets in the season was second only to Mushtaq Ahmed.

Close of play: First day, Lancashire 0-0 (Chilton 0, Sutcliffe 0); Second day, Lancashire 311; Third day, No play.

Gloucestershire

C. M. Spearman st Hegg b Keedy	34	– (2) c Chilton b Mahmood	5
W. P. C. Weston b Keedy	19	– (1) c Hegg b Keedy	27
M. E. K. Hussey c Law b Keedy	46	– b Keedy	45
*C. G. Taylor st Hegg b Keedy	60	– c Hooper b Crook	109
T. H. C. Hancock c Law b Keedy	61	– c Cork b Keedy	1
A. P. R. Gidman lbw b Keedy	0	– c Mahmood b Keedy	28
†S. J. Adshead not out	52	– c and b Hooper	8
I. D. Fisher c Law b Keedy	5	– c Hegg b Keedy	34
M. C. J. Ball b Chapple	6	– lbw b Keedy	1
J. Lewis (did not bat)		– b Keedy	8
N. W. Bracken (did not bat)		– not out	13
B 7, l-b 4, w 1, n-b 16	28	B 3, l-b 3, n-b 4	10

1/55 (1) 2/60 (2) 3/171 (3)   (8 wkts dec.) 311
4/181 (4) 5/181 (6) 6/278 (5)
7/288 (8) 8/311 (9)

1/10 (2) 2/72 (1) 3/97 (3)   289
4/105 (5) 5/169 (6) 6/177 (7)
7/248 (4) 8/252 (9)
9/272 (10) 10/289 (8)

Bonus points – Gloucestershire 3, Lancashire 2.

Bowling: *First Innings*—Chapple 13.2–1–35–1; Cork 8–0–29–0; Mahmood 6–0–34–0; Keedy 42–9–95–7; Crook 14–1–67–0; Hooper 17–4–40–0. *Second Innings*—Cork 2–0–7–0; Mahmood 5–0–14–1; Keedy 35–2–132–7; Crook 21–3–92–1; Hooper 10–0–38–1.

Lancashire

M. J. Chilton c Weston b Fisher	47	– c Taylor b Bracken	3
I. J. Sutcliffe c and b Ball	28	– c Adshead b Gidman	0
M. B. Loye c Hancock b Ball	4	– not out	45
S. G. Law c Weston b Fisher	11		
C. L. Hooper c Hussey b Fisher	77	– not out	43
G. Chapple b Ball	10		
A. R. Crook c Fisher b Lewis	17	– (4) c Hancock b Bracken	0
*†W. K. Hegg c Adshead b Fisher	5		
D. G. Cork not out	77		
S. I. Mahmood c Spearman b Fisher	3		
G. Keedy c Adshead b Bracken	9		
B 10, l-b 7, n-b 6	23	B 4, l-b 4	8

1/87 (1) 2/87 (2) 3/102 (4) 4/110 (3)   311
5/154 (6) 6/209 (7) 7/217 (8)
8/218 (5) 9/231 (10) 10/311 (11)

1/2 (2) 2/12 (1) 3/12 (4)   (3 wkts) 99

Bonus points – Lancashire 3, Gloucestershire 3.

Bowling: *First Innings*—Lewis 11–1–38–1; Bracken 15–4–36–1; Gidman 3–2–10–0; Fisher 29–6–114–5; Ball 28–8–96–3. *Second Innings*—Bracken 7–2–12–2; Gidman 5–1–16–1; Fisher 5–0–20–0; Ball 5–0–14–0; Hussey 4–1–13–0; Hancock 2–0–16–0; Weston 1–1–0–0.

Umpires: J. H. Hampshire and P. Willey.

COUNTY BENEFITS AWARDED FOR 2005

Essex	A. P. Grayson.	Nottinghamshire	J. E. R. Gallian.
Glamorgan	M. P. Maynard (Testimonial).	Somerset	Club Benefit.
		Surrey	M. A. Butcher.
Gloucestershire	T. H. C. Hancock.	Sussex	M. A. Robinson (Testimonial).
Hampshire	A. D. Mullally.		
Lancashire	G. Yates.	Warwickshire	D. R. Brown.
Northamptonshire	Club Centenary Appeal.	Yorkshire	M. P. Vaughan.

No benefit was awarded by Derbyshire, Durham, Kent, Leicestershire, Middlesex or Worcestershire.

LEICESTERSHIRE

Twenty is plenty

PAUL JONES

Late on the hot evening of August 7, after a dramatic and draining day, Jeremy Snape hit a boundary through mid-wicket to win the hippest trophy in English cricket for Leicestershire, just 11 months after they had limped to the end of a miserable 2003 season. The Twenty20 Cup, the county's first one-day trophy for 19 years, was a deserved reward for a club that put its heart and soul into making the competition a success on and off the pitch.

Compared with the usual scattering at Grace Road, the support for Twenty20 was phenomenal. The ground was jam-packed with 5,806 spectators for the zonal match against Nottinghamshire, and the two other home games were also well attended. The crowds were rewarded with sound, disciplined cricket, and the odd dash of batting brilliance from Brad Hodge and Darren Maddy.

Still almost everyone expected the little club to come unstuck at Edgbaston on finals day. But Maddy, the competition's heaviest scorer in 2004 with 356 runs, played another masterful innings in the semi-final. Hodge then took centre-stage in the final against Surrey. Under intense pressure he hit a glorious unbeaten 77 from 53 deliveries and, to the delight of many neutrals, Leicestershire chased down a taxing target of 169. It ended Surrey's unbeaten record in the Twenty20 and sparked scenes of unbridled joy.

Many associated with the club would have settled for less than that at the start of the 2004 season, after a wretched double relegation in 2003. Yet when Leicestershire ended the summer floating in the middle of both second divisions, and unceremoniously bundled out of the C&G Trophy by Devon, there was a lingering feeling that the squad assembled by director of cricket James Whitaker was capable of more.

At the halfway stage Leicestershire had a chance of pushing for double promotion. DeFreitas, a reluctant captain, decided things were settled enough by early July for him to stand down and concentrate on his bowling. Hodge was the obvious successor. But in the second half of the season Leicestershire failed to put together the strong run needed to catch up in the Championship, and in the one-day league they stuttered badly.

An inability to chase runs proved their undoing in the closing limited-overs games, where Leicestershire won none of their last six. The hangover from the Twenty20 included three defeats in ten days, which effectively ended their hopes. And volume of runs, or lack of it, was also the major problem in four-day cricket, which was especially disappointing because batting had been seen as a strength at the start of the summer.

Hodge escaped any criticism. He continued where he left off in 2003, and plundered 1,548 Championship runs, including five centuries. Three were converted into doubles, a Leicestershire record for a single season.

Those efforts should have formed the backbone of a series of big totals, but only four others managed a Championship hundred, and then only one each. Darren Robinson, in his first season with the club, proved a sound acquisition, scoring more than 1,000 Championship runs. But the batting flourished only occasionally, and at the end of the season Darren Stevens, once one of the county's brightest prospects, was released, and signed for Kent.

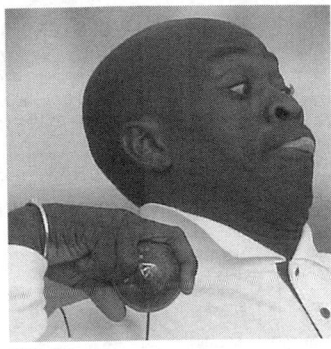

Ottis Gibson

Run-scoring was not the only problem. Promising positions too often eroded away, as Leicestershire left sides in deep trouble but failed to finish them. Essex, Yorkshire and Hampshire all squirmed off the hook at Grace Road. Still, 35-year-old Ottis Gibson, one of Whitaker's key signings, led the attack admirably, scored useful lower-order runs and surprised many who saw him as past his best. He bowled with accuracy and respectable pace to take five five-wicket hauls, and 60 Championship victims. Gibson, who had been signed as a player-coach, was so successful on the field that he had to catch up on some of his coaching work over the winter, when he formed part of a scheme to take cricket into local schools.

A second signing, the South African spinner Claude Henderson, was more controversial. In the spring of 2004, Leicestershire became the first county to dive through a new loophole which, in certain circumstances, allowed a county to field more than two overseas players. Although they were followed by other counties who took advantage of what became known as Kolpak signings, after the legal case which opened the loophole, Leicestershire bore the brunt of the anger of certain cricket followers. Whatever the rights and wrongs, Henderson certainly provided the wicket-taking spin option Leicestershire had lacked for a number of years; his 39 wickets helped repay the faith shown by Whitaker.

For 2005, Leicestershire suffered a setback when Hodge turned down a two-year contract and was lured away to Lancashire. Making the reverse journey was the Indian left-hander Dinesh Mongia, who had scored heavily in 2004 as a stopgap at Old Trafford. The new captain is to be H. D. Ackerman, the 32-year-old South African, given a three-year contract as another Kolpak player. And a replacement for Stevens was found in Aftab Habib, a member of the Championship-winning teams of the 1990s, who returned to Grace Road after three years at Essex. Leicestershire supporters hoped the return would prove auspicious.

LEICESTERSHIRE RESULTS

All first-class matches – Played 17: Won 4, Lost 6, Drawn 7.
County Championship matches – Played 16: Won 4, Lost 5, Drawn 7.

Frizzell County Championship, 6th in Division 2; Cheltenham & Gloucester Trophy, 2nd round; totesport League, 7th in Division 2; Twenty20 Cup, winners.

COUNTY CHAMPIONSHIP AVERAGES

BATTING AND FIELDING

Cap		M	I	NO	R	HS	100s	50s	Avge	Ct/St
2003	B. J. Hodge§	15	25	0	1,548	262	5	4	61.92	6
2000	J. M. Dakin	4	7	3	200	71*	0	1	50.00	1
	D. D. J. Robinson	15	26	0	1,072	154	1	9	41.23	15
2002	D. I. Stevens	12	20	3	666	105	1	5	39.17	13
	T. J. New	4	5	3	74	51*	0	1	37.00	8/1
1996	D. L. Maddy	16	28	2	790	145	1	6	30.38	23
	O. D. Gibson	15	19	3	480	60*	0	4	30.00	5
	M. F. Cleary§	11	14	8	179	38	0	0	29.83	3
2003	J. N. Snape	4	6	1	135	66	0	1	27.00	1
	J. L. Sadler	13	23	2	533	95	0	1	25.38	7
1986	P. A. J. DeFreitas	13	20	3	394	78	0	1	23.17	1
1994	P. A. Nixon	12	21	3	361	63*	0	1	20.05	34/6
	C. W. Henderson	16	21	3	295	63	0	2	16.38	6
	J. K. Maunders	10	20	0	322	116	1	0	16.10	5
	D. D. Masters	5	7	1	56	31	0	0	9.33	1
	C. E. Dagnall	10	10	2	56	16	0	0	7.00	4

Also batted: D. G. Brandy (1 match) 7, 4.

§ *Overseas player.*

BOWLING

	O	M	R	W	BB	5W/i	Avge
O. D. Gibson	424.5	97	1,445	60	6-43	5	24.08
C. E. Dagnall	209.4	42	741	24	4-37	0	30.87
P. A. J. DeFreitas	343.4	81	1,064	31	4-49	0	34.32
M. F. Cleary	230	27	946	27	7-80	2	35.03
C. W. Henderson	469	132	1,373	39	7-74	2	35.20
D. D. Masters	114	23	398	11	4-74	0	36.18
B. J. Hodge	95.5	14	365	10	2-18	0	36.50
D. L. Maddy	149.2	22	589	13	2-41	0	45.30

Also bowled: J. M. Dakin 102–22–372–7; J. K. Maunders 22–6–84–2; D. D. J. Robinson 4–0–38–0; J. L. Sadler 5–0–36–0; J. N. Snape 30.2–4–110–1; D. I. Stevens 13.2–1–50–2.

COUNTY RECORDS

Highest score for:	302*	B. J. Hodge v Nottinghamshire at Nottingham	2003
Highest score against:	341	G. H. Hirst (Yorkshire) at Leicester	1905
Best bowling for:	10-18	G. Geary v Glamorgan at Pontypridd	1929
Best bowling against:	10-32	H. Pickett (Essex) at Leyton	1895
Highest total for:	701-4 dec.	v Worcestershire at Worcester	1906
Highest total against:	761-6 dec.	by Essex at Chelmsford	1990
Lowest total for:	25	v Kent at Leicester	1912
Lowest total against: {	24	by Glamorgan at Leicester	1971
	24	by Oxford University at Oxford	1985

LEICESTERSHIRE DIRECTORY

ADDRESS

County Ground, Grace Road, Leicester LE2 8AD (0116 283 2128; fax 0116 244 0363; email enquiries@leicestershireccc.co.uk). **Website** www.leicestershireccc.co.uk.

GROUNDS

Leicester (Grace Road): 2 miles S of city centre close to A426. From Aylestone Road, turn L into Park Hill Drive or Duncan Road and then first L into Curzon Road. Nearest station: Leicester (2 miles).

Oakham: ¼ mile from town centre. From town, turn L into B668 Station Road then L into Kilburn Road for Oakham School entrance in Station Road. Nearest station: Oakham (¼ mile).

OFFICIALS

Captain 2004 – P. A. J. DeFreitas;
    2005 – H. D. Ackerman
Head coach P. Whitticase
Chairman R. C. N. Davidson

Director of Cricket J. J. Whitaker
Operations manager A. J. Mackay
Head groundsmen A. Ward and A. Whiteman
Scorer G. A. York

PLAYERS

Players expected to reappear in 2005

	Former counties	Country	Born	Birthplace
Brignull David Stephen		E	27.11.1981	*Forest Gate*
Cleary Mark Francis		A	19.7.1980	*Melbourne*
Dagnall Charles Edward	Warwicks	E	10.7.1976	*Bury*
*****DeFreitas** Phillip Anthony Jason	Leics, Lancs, Derbys	E	18.2.1966	*Scotts Head, Dominica*
*****Gibson** Ottis Delroy	Glamorgan	WI (EU)	16.3.1969	*Sion Hill, Barbados*
*****Henderson** Claude William		SA (K)	14.6.1972	*Worcester*
*****Maddy** Darren Lee		E	23.5.1974	†*Leicester*
Masters David Daniel	Kent	E	22.4.1978	*Chatham*
Maunders John Kenneth	Middx	E	4.4.1981	*Ashford, Middlesex*
New Thomas James		E	18.1.1985	*Sutton-in-Ashfield*
Nixon Paul Andrew	Leics, Kent	E	21.10.1970	*Carlisle*
Robinson Darren David John . .	Essex	E	2.3.1973	*Braintree*
Sadler John Leonard	Yorks	E	19.11.1981	*Dewsbury*
Snape Jeremy Nicholas	Northants, Glos	E	27.4.1973	*Stoke-on-Trent*

Players due to join in 2005

	Former counties	Country	Born	Birthplace
*****Ackerman** Hylton Deon		SA (K)	14.2.1973	*Cape Town*
*****Habib** Aftab	Middx, Essex	E	7.2.1972	*Reading*
Mongia Dinesh		I	17.4.1977	*Chandigarh*

* *Test player.*   † *Born in Leicestershire.*

LEICESTERSHIRE v GLAMORGAN

At Leicester, April 21, 22, 23, 24. Drawn. Leicestershire 8 pts, Glamorgan 12 pts. Toss: Glamorgan. County debuts: M. F. Cleary, O. D. Gibson, C. W. Henderson, D. D. J. Robinson.

The Australian Brad Hodge became the first batsman to record twin centuries for Leicestershire since 1965, though it was the left-arm spin of the South African, Claude Henderson, that almost turned the match their way on a dramatic final day. (Henderson was making his Leicestershire debut after being signed, controversially, under the Kolpak ruling, which allowed many non-EU passport holders to play county cricket as non-overseas players provided they had a work permit.)

TWO HUNDREDS IN A MATCH FOR LEICESTERSHIRE

C. J. B. Wood	107* and 117* v Yorkshire at Bradford...................	1911
J. H. King	111 and 100* v Northamptonshire at Leicester (Aylestone Road) ...	1913
C. S. Dempster	133 and 154* v Gloucestershire at Gloucester (Wagon Works)....	1937
L. G. Berry	165 and 111* v Essex at Clacton....................	1947
M. Tompkin	156 and 107* v Middlesex at Leicester.................	1952
M. R. Hallam	210* and 157 v Glamorgan at Leicester.................	1959
A. Wharton	129 and 108 v Middlesex at Leicester.................	1961
M. R. Hallam	203* and 143* v Sussex at Worthing..................	1961
M. R. Hallam	107* and 149* v Worcestershire at Leicester.............	1965
B. J. Booth	109 and 104 v Middlesex at Lord's..................	1965
B. J. Hodge	**105 and 158 v Glamorgan at Leicester**.................	**2004**

After rain allowed just 23 overs on the opening day, Maynard moved to a brisk and substantial hundred, allowing Glamorgan to declare on the second evening at 455 for seven. They strengthened their grip next day as Kasprowicz took five for 54 to help dismiss Leicestershire for 264, despite Hodge's defiance. Leicestershire fared better in the follow-on, as Hodge – continuing to bat fluently, except in the nineties when he was dropped by Wallace – found solid support from the night-watchman Henderson, and together they shared a stand of 130. Even so, a target of 163 should not have troubled Glamorgan, who set about their task confidently until coming up against Henderson. He found increasing turn and bounce to grab five wickets as Glamorgan plummeted from 73 for two to the brink of defeat at 121 for nine. The last pair batted out the final over.

Close of play: First day, Glamorgan 97-2 (Hemp 12, Powell 18); Second day, Leicestershire 50-2 (Hodge 18, Maddy 26); Third day, Leicestershire 124-5 (Hodge 42, Henderson 4).

Glamorgan

M. T. G. Elliott c Nixon b Gibson..........	37	– c Stevens b Henderson.........	33
†M. A. Wallace c Nixon b Gibson..........	20	– c Stevens b Henderson.........	15
D. L. Hemp lbw b Gibson.............	82	– (4) run out	9
M. J. Powell c Cleary b DeFreitas..........	55	– (5) c Robinson b Henderson.....	3
M. P. Maynard c Nixon b Dakin..........	163	– (6) b Dakin	11
A. Dale st Nixon b Hodge.............	41	– (7) c Stevens b Henderson......	6
*R. D. B. Croft not out..............	21	– (8) lbw b Gibson	6
S. D. Thomas c Stevens b Hodge	5	– (9) not out.	9
A. G. Wharf (did not bat).		– (3) c Maddy b Gibson.........	12
M. S. Kasprowicz (did not bat).		– c Maunders b Henderson.......	10
D. S. Harrison (did not bat).		– not out	0
B 1, l-b 3, w 5, n-b 22	31	B 3, l-b 5, w 1, n-b 2	11

1/50 (2) 2/77 (1) 3/145 (4)　　　(7 wkts dec.) 455
4/350 (3) 5/415 (5)
6/439 (6) 7/455 (8)

1/34 (2) 2/51 (3)　　　(9 wkts) 125
3/73 (1) 4/73 (4)
5/87 (6) 6/91 (5)
7/94 (7) 8/102 (8) 9/121 (10)

Bonus points – Glamorgan 5, Leicestershire 2.

Bowling: *First Innings*—DeFreitas 27–5–109–1; Dakin 21–3–79–1; Cleary 18–3–80–0; Gibson 23–4–97–3; Henderson 16–3–52–0; Maddy 2–0–7–0; Hodge 4.5–0–27–2. *Second Innings*—Gibson 11–2–38–2; Cleary 5–0–31–0; Henderson 15–9–28–5; Dakin 7–2–20–1.

Leicestershire

D. D. J. Robinson b Kasprowicz	0	– b Thomas	36
J. K. Maunders run out	0	– lbw b Wharf	5
B. J. Hodge c Harrison b Croft	105	– (4) run out	158
D. L. Maddy c Hemp b Kasprowicz	26	– (3) lbw b Wharf	28
D. I. Stevens lbw b Thomas	27	– c Wallace b Thomas	0
†P. A. Nixon c Powell b Croft	19	– c and b Kasprowicz	2
*P. A. J. DeFreitas c Elliott b Thomas	20	– (8) b Harrison	0
J. M. Dakin not out	23	– (9) b Kasprowicz	15
O. D. Gibson lbw b Kasprowicz	22	– (10) not out	20
C. W. Henderson b Kasprowicz	6	– (7) b Harrison	63
M. F. Cleary c Maynard b Kasprowicz	0	– c Thomas b Croft	3
L-b 8, n-b 8	16	B 13, l-b 2, n-b 8	23

1/0 (1) 2/0 (2) 3/53 (4) 4/102 (5)   264   1/12 (2) 2/45 (3) 3/100 (1)   353
5/136 (6) 6/199 (7) 7/221 (3)   4/106 (5) 5/114 (6) 6/244 (7)
8/258 (9) 9/264 (10) 10/264 (11)   7/244 (8) 8/322 (9)
                                                         9/343 (4) 10/353 (11)

Bonus points – Leicestershire 2, Glamorgan 3.

Bowling: *First Innings*—Kasprowicz 16.5–2–54–5; Wharf 10 0–63–0; Harrison 7–1–24–0; Thomas 15–1–73–2; Croft 16–4–42–2. *Second Innings*—Kasprowicz 27–5–88–2; Wharf 20–4–71–2; Harrison 23–6–61–2; Thomas 20–5–56–2; Croft 16.4–4–56–1.

Umpires: A. Clarkson and J. H. Evans.

At Southampton, April 28, 29, 30, May 1. LEICESTERSHIRE lost to HAMPSHIRE by an innings and 18 runs

At Bradford, May 7, 8, 9. LEICESTERSHIRE drew with BRADFORD/LEEDS UCCE.

LEICESTERSHIRE v NOTTINGHAMSHIRE

At Leicester, May 12, 13, 14, 15. Leicestershire won by 92 runs. Leicestershire 18 pts, Nottinghamshire 7 pts. Toss: Leicestershire.

Gibson finished with match figures of 11 for 141 to steer Leicestershire to their first Championship win of the season after another remarkable final day. A strongarm hundred from Ealham – his 139 included eight sixes, four in a row off Dakin – gave Nottinghamshire a first-innings advantage of 143, but solid batting down the order helped Leicestershire to 430 in their second innings. Robinson fell two short of a first century since leaving Essex, but was instrumental in setting Nottinghamshire 288, which always looked challenging. By the third-day close, they were two for two – and hopes of a recovery were wrecked next morning when they collapsed spectacularly to 22 for six against Leicestershire's experienced opening attack. The game seemed set for an early conclusion before Ealham and Franks dug in, inching Nottinghamshire back into contention at 180 for seven. But Gibson, who had come out of retirement to be Leicestershire's player/bowling coach, showed his charges how to operate by removing both batsmen, ending with six wickets and seeing Leicestershire over the line with something to spare.

Close of play: First day, Nottinghamshire 85-3 (Warren 34, Sidebottom 0); Second day, Leicestershire 94-2 (Robinson 36, Maddy 12); Third day, Nottinghamshire 2-2 (Gallian 1).

Leicestershire

D. D. J. Robinson lbw b Sidebottom	4	– c Hussey b MacGill	98
J. K. Maunders lbw b Shreck	0	– lbw b Sidebottom	0
B. J. Hodge b Ealham	30	– b Sidebottom	36
D. L. Maddy c Gallian b Shreck	3	– c Read b Ealham	53
J. L. Sadler b Shreck	62	– b Shreck	72
J. N. Snape lbw b Ealham	0	– c Read b Shreck	66
†P. A. Nixon c Hussey b Shreck	11	– c Read b Shreck	0
*P. A. J. DeFreitas c Hussey b Sidebottom	10	– c Read b Franks	10
O. D. Gibson not out	57	– st Read b Ealham	30
C. W. Henderson c Hussey b Shreck	4	– (11) not out	8
J. M. Dakin lbw b Sidebottom	32	– (10) c Pietersen b Sidebottom	34
L-b 8, w 2	10	B 14, l-b 8, w 1	23

1/3 (2) 2/9 (1) 3/18 (4) 4/61 (3)   223   1/3 (2) 2/55 (3) 3/175 (4)   430
5/63 (6) 6/102 (7) 7/124 (8)   4/221 (1) 5/310 (5) 6/318 (7)
8/128 (5) 9/136 (10) 10/223 (11)   7/337 (8) 8/373 (6)
                                   9/391 (9) 10/430 (10)

Bonus points – Leicestershire 1, Nottinghamshire 3.

Bowling: *First Innings*—Shreck 19–5–73–4; Sidebottom 19–7–52–4; Ealham 13–3–30–2; Franks 9–3–19–0; MacGill 10–1–41–0. *Second Innings*—Sidebottom 28.2–4–98–3; Shreck 31–7–87–3; Franks 22–5–92–1; Ealham 15–5–34–2; Pietersen 6–1–23–0; MacGill 23–3–74–1.

Nottinghamshire

D. J. Bicknell lbw b Gibson	17	– lbw b Gibson	0
*J. E. R. Gallian b Gibson	1	– b DeFreitas	24
R. J. Warren c Robinson b Gibson	72	– (4) b Gibson	7
K. P. Pietersen c Nixon b Dakin	32	– (5) lbw b DeFreitas	2
R. J. Sidebottom lbw b Gibson	0	– (3) lbw b Gibson	1
D. J. Hussey c Nixon b DeFreitas	5	– c Nixon b DeFreitas	0
†C. M. W. Read c Henderson b Maddy	31	– b Gibson	6
M. A. Ealham c Henderson b Maddy	139	– c Snape b Gibson	85
P. J. Franks c Maddy b DeFreitas	45	– c Sadler b Gibson	51
S. C. G. MacGill c Sadler b Gibson	1	– c Henderson b Maddy	10
C. E. Shreck not out	13	– not out	0
B 6, l-b 4	10	L-b 7, n-b 2	9

1/3 (2) 2/28 (1) 3/84 (4) 4/90 (5)   366   1/0 (1) 2/2 (3) 3/12 (4)   195
5/99 (6) 6/150 (3) 7/172 (7)   4/15 (5) 5/15 (6) 6/22 (7)
8/281 (9) 9/286 (10) 10/366 (8)   7/88 (2) 8/180 (9)
                                   9/191 (8) 10/195 (10)

Bonus points – Nottinghamshire 4, Leicestershire 3.

Bowling: *First Innings*—Gibson 24–8–98–5; Dakin 24–9–76–1; DeFreitas 26–8–81–2; Maddy 13.4–1–56–2; Henderson 17–6–33–0; Hodge 6–2–12–0. *Second Innings*—Gibson 17–7–43–6; DeFreitas 17–3–53–3; Henderson 16–7–31–0; Dakin 5–1–17–0; Maddy 11.2–2–35–1; Hodge 4–1–9–0.

Umpires: M. R. Benson and G. I. Burgess.

At Chelmsford, May 19, 20, 21, 22. LEICESTERSHIRE drew with ESSEX.

At Leicester, May 28, 29, 30, 31. LEICESTERSHIRE lost to NEW ZEALANDERS by 328 runs (see New Zealand tour section).

LEICESTERSHIRE v DERBYSHIRE

At Oakham School, June 2, 3, 4, 5. Leicestershire won by six wickets. Leicestershire 22 pts, Derbyshire 4 pts. Toss: Leicestershire.

First-class cricket returned to Rutland after four years, and Hodge gave another batting master-class. He took time to start, but went on first to a hundred – his 14th first-class century in 13 months – and then to a double, his second in a fortnight. Hodge faced 290 balls in 382 minutes, with 30 fours and four sixes, and was the cornerstone of Leicestershire's 534, their batsmen making the most of a good pitch and fast outfield. Derbyshire's did not, and were forced to follow on 243 behind. It could have been worse: their final three wickets added 156, their last producing 76 at breakneck speed thanks to a 32-ball 63 from Walker. Derbyshire's chances of saving the game were dented when a lifting delivery from Cleary struck Rogers above the eye, though Leicestershire's impetus was stalled by a maiden century from Welch, in his 11th season, and a stubborn fifty from Sutton. A burst from Cleary restored their belief, and he grabbed a career-best seven for 80. Leicestershire, who had 14 overs to chase 81, raced home with one to spare.

Close of play: First day, Leicestershire 383-4 (Hodge 189, Nixon 32); Second day, Derbyshire 72-4 (Bassano 1, Sutton 2); Third day, Derbyshire 123-4 (Sutton 18, Welch 0).

Leicestershire

D. D. J. Robinson c Welch b Botha	64	– c Hassan Adnan b Sheikh	29
J. K. Maunders c Sutton b Dean	28	– c sub b Sheikh	2
B. J. Hodge b Dean	221	– c Walker b Botha	29
D. L. Maddy run out	1	– (5) not out	12
J. L. Sadler c Walker b Botha	41	– (6) not out	0
†P. A. Nixon c Rogers b Sheikh	40	– (4) c sub b Botha	10
*P. A. J. DeFreitas b Welch	46		
O. D. Gibson b Dean	0		
C. W. Henderson c Bassano b Welch	35		
C. E. Dagnall c Bassano b Botha	15		
M. F. Cleary not out	11		
L-b 7, w 9, n-b 16	32	L-b 1	1

1/91 (2) 2/111 (1) 3/135 (4) 4/230 (5)   **534**   1/4 (2) 2/58 (1)   (4 wkts) **83**
5/422 (6) 6/428 (3) 7/436 (8)   3/61 (3) 4/75 (4)
8/503 (9) 9/508 (7) 10/534 (10)

Bonus points – Leicestershire 5, Derbyshire 2 (130 overs: 480-7).

Bowling: First Innings—Welch 35–8–141–2; Walker 18–2–82–0; Dean 29–3–111–3; Sheikh 35–11–97–1; Botha 24.4–3–92–3; Hassan Adnan 2–0–4–0. *Second Innings*—Dean 3–0–24–0; Sheikh 6–0–30–2; Botha 4–0–28–2.

Derbyshire

A. I. Gait c Maddy b Dagnall	6	– c Nixon b Cleary	24
S. D. Stubbings lbw b DeFreitas	50	– c Maddy b Henderson	66
C. J. L. Rogers lbw b Dagnall	0	– retired hurt	0
Hassan Adnan c Hodge b DeFreitas	5	– c Nixon b Cleary	0
C. W. G. Bassano c Robinson b Dagnall	62	– b Cleary	7
*†L. D. Sutton c Maddy b Dagnall	14	– lbw b Cleary	58
G. Welch c Maddy b DeFreitas	1	– not out	115
A. G. Botha lbw b Maddy	5	– c Nixon b Cleary	2
M. A. Sheikh run out	32	– c Robinson b DeFreitas	6
K. J. Dean st Nixon b Hodge	35	– c Nixon b Cleary	7
N. G. E. Walker not out	63	– b Cleary	10
L-b 4, w 2, n-b 12	18	B 1, l-b 13, n-b 14	28

1/46 (1) 2/46 (3) 3/68 (4) 4/69 (2)   **291**   1/57 (1) 2/57 (4) 3/73 (5)   **323**
5/101 (6) 6/112 (7) 7/135 (8)   4/119 (2) 5/249 (6) 6/261 (8)
8/172 (5) 9/215 (10) 10/291 (9)   7/275 (9) 8/297 (10) 9/323 (11)

Bonus points – Derbyshire 2, Leicestershire 3.

In the second innings Rogers retired hurt at 57-1.

Bowling: *First Innings*—Gibson 9.4–1–36–0; DeFreitas 17.2–7–37–3; Dagnall 14–5–37–4; Cleary 15–2–47–0; Maddy 11.4–1–59–1; Henderson 13–3–41–0; Hodge 6–1–30–1. *Second Innings*—DeFreitas 27–6–64–1; Dagnall 20–7–39–0; Henderson 36–16–71–1; Cleary 23.3–5–80–7; Hodge 6–0–29–0; Maddy 8–3–19–0; Maunders 1–0–7–0.

Umpires: D. J. Constant and P. Willey.

At Cardiff, June 9, 10, 11, 12. LEICESTERSHIRE lost to GLAMORGAN by 409 runs.

At Leeds, June 18, 19, 20, 21. LEICESTERSHIRE drew with YORKSHIRE.

At Taunton, June 23, 24, 25, 26. LEICESTERSHIRE drew with SOMERSET.

LEICESTERSHIRE v ESSEX

At Leicester, July 21, 22, 23, 24. Essex won by 48 runs. Essex 20 pts, Leicestershire 3 pts. Toss: Essex. Championship debut: A. R. Adams.

Essex's first Championship win of the season was set in motion by a blistering first-day century from New Zealand all-rounder Adams. They were struggling on 108 for seven until Adams joined Middlebrook to add 198 in 31 overs. He reached a stunning 80-ball century – then the fastest of the season – with his fourth six, and finally fell for 124 in 91 balls, with seven huge sixes, all but one off Henderson's left-arm spin, and 13 fours. Four wickets from Gough kept the initiative as Leicestershire conceded a lead of 125. Gibson claimed the first six wickets in Essex's second innings, which gave him ten in the match. But an eventual target of 398 looked well out of reach when Leicestershire closed the third day on 145 for five. Determined resistance from the lower order threatened one final twist. Gough took the new ball after lunch, however, to remove Sadler for 95, and finished the game shortly after tea with eight wickets, his best match return for Essex.

Close of play: First day, Leicestershire 64-3 (Robinson 27, Stevens 15); Second day, Essex 85-1 (Cook 55, Flower 11); Third day, Leicestershire 145-5 (Sadler 37, Nixon 3).

Essex

W. I. Jefferson c Maddy b Gibson	29	– b Gibson ... 11
A. N. Cook c Nixon b Cleary	0	– c Nixon b Gibson ... 55
A. Flower c Nixon b Dagnall	14	– b Gibson ... 12
A. Habib run out	13	– lbw b Dagnall ... 55
*R. C. Irani lbw b Gibson	6	– c Maddy b Gibson ... 49
†J. S. Foster b Dagnall	0	– lbw b Gibson ... 0
J. D. Middlebrook c Nixon b Dagnall	92	– b Gibson ... 0
G. R. Napier c Nixon b Dagnall	7	– c Robinson b Henderson ... 29
A. R. Adams b Gibson	124	– c Gibson b Dagnall ... 16
A. P. Cowan not out	5	– c Henderson b Maddy ... 6
D. Gough c Robinson b Gibson	11	– not out ... 12
L-b 5, w 1, n-b 15	21	B 6, l-b 14, w 3, n-b 4 ... 27

1/11 (2) 2/41 (1) 3/62 (3) 4/71 (4)   322   1/36 (1) 2/85 (2) 3/86 (3)   272
5/73 (6) 6/79 (5) 7/108 (8)   4/196 (5) 5/200 (6) 6/200 (7)
8/306 (7) 9/306 (9) 10/322 (11)   7/202 (4) 8/238 (9)
                           9/250 (10) 10/272 (8)

Bonus points – Essex 3, Leicestershire 3.

Bowling: *First Innings*—Cleary 14–0–76–1; Gibson 20.2–10–73–4; DeFreitas 4.2–1–11–0; Dagnall 19–1–71–4; Maddy 6.4–1–37–0; Henderson 7–2–49–0. *Second Innings*—Gibson 22–5–74–6; Cleary 5–0–20–0; Maddy 10–2–34–1; Dagnall 14–2–65–2; Hodge 1–0–5–0; DeFreitas 15–6–33–0; Henderson 7.1–3–21–1.

Leicestershire

D. D. J. Robinson lbw b Adams	33	– c Foster b Cowan	38
D. L. Maddy c Foster b Gough	1	– c Foster b Gough	25
*B. J. Hodge b Cowan	7	– c Cowan b Gough	4
J. L. Sadler b Gough	8	– lbw b Gough	95
D. I. Stevens c Flower b Napier	50	– run out	20
†P. A. Nixon lbw b Adams	11	– (7) lbw b Middlebrook	30
P. A. J. DeFreitas c Jefferson b Gough	38	– (8) lbw b Napier	39
O. D. Gibson c Cowan b Napier	14	– (9) run out	39
C. W. Henderson lbw b Gough	0	– (6) lbw b Adams	0
M. F. Cleary not out	14	– not out	27
C. E. Dagnall c Jefferson b Napier	0	– lbw b Gough	0
B 8, l-b 6, w 3, n-b 4	21	B 8, l-b 12, w 1, n-b 11	32
	197		**349**

1/15 (2) 2/22 (3) 3/39 (4) 4/99 (1)   1/54 (2) 2/60 (3) 3/107 (1)
5/115 (5) 6/153 (6) 7/165 (7)   4/136 (5) 5/140 (6) 6/218 (7)
8/165 (9) 9/197 (8) 10/197 (11)   7/256 (9) 8/305 (8)
      9/345 (9) 10/349 (11)

Bonus points – Essex 3.

Bowling: *First Innings*—Gough 22–7–55–4; Cowan 15–4–54–1; Napier 10–2–33–3, Adams 12–3–41–2. *Second Innings*—Gough 25.5–6–89–4; Cowan 28–9–75–1; Napier 26–6–85–1; Adams 10–2–30–1; Middlebrook 27–7–50–1.

Umpires: A. Clarkson and J. F. Steele.

LEICESTERSHIRE v DURHAM

At Leicester, July 27, 28, 29, 30. Leicestershire won by an innings and 26 runs. Leicestershire 22 pts, Durham 3 pts. Toss: Durham.

An imperious double-century was Hodge's third of the season, and fifth in all for Leicestershire – both county records. He now possessed three of their top five scores; this 262 was second only to his own 302 not out at Nottingham in 2003. Invited to bat, Hodge put his old side to the sword with his trademark strokeplay. He never took unnecessary risks, but Durham bowled short and wide to him with regularity and, whenever they did, he cut or pulled to the boundary. He added

MOST DOUBLE-HUNDREDS FOR LEICESTERSHIRE

5 B. J. Hodge
4 M. R. Hallam
3 V. J. Wells
2 L. G. Berry; J. H. King; A. E. Knight; J. J. Whitaker; C. J. B. Wood

N. E. Briers, S. Coe, W. J. Cronje, C. S. Dempster, B. Dudleston, D. I. Gower, A. Habib, D. L. Maddy, M. E. J. C. Norman, C. H. Palmer, A. T. Sharp, A. W. Shipman, P. V. Simmons, B. F. Smith, I. J. Sutcliffe and W. Watson have scored one double-hundred for Leicestershire.

223 with Stevens, and was already on 200 when bad light ended play in the 85th over. When he finally departed next day, he had batted 445 minutes and 299 balls: he hit 46 fours and two sixes, meaning almost three-quarters of his runs came in boundaries. Hodge eventually declared on 634 for nine, Leicestershire's fifth-highest total. Shortly before, Cleary was dismissed for the first time in all cricket since May 20, having scored 185 in 13 innings. Slow left-armer Henderson ran through Durham with seven wickets, and they followed on 415 behind. Muchall made a fight of it, falling in the nineties for the third time in 2004. But Leicestershire needed only 23 minutes of the final morning to complete victory and pull away from Durham at the bottom of the table.

Close of play: First day, Leicestershire 403-4 (Hodge 200, Nixon 0); Second day, Durham 194-7 (Coetzer 31, Plunkett 1); Third day, Durham 373-7 (Blignaut 52, Plunkett 24).

Leicestershire

D. D. J. Robinson c Muchall b Plunkett .	62	C. W. Henderson c and b Breese	9
D. L. Maddy c Pratt b Blignaut	11	C. E. Dagnall not out	4
*B. J. Hodge c Breese b Killeen	262		
J. L. Sadler lbw b Blignaut	21	B 1, l-b 11, w 1, n-b 16	29
D. I. Stevens lbw b Onions	84		
†P. A. Nixon c sub b Onions	22	1/32 (2) 2/120 (1) (9 wkts dec.) 634	
O. D. Gibson b Onions	21	3/179 (4) 4/402 (5)	
J. M. Dakin not out	71	5/478 (6) 6/510 (3)	
M. F. Cleary c North b Breese	38	7/510 (7) 8/603 (9) 9/615 (10)	

Bonus points – Leicestershire 5, Durham 2 (130 overs: 599-7).

Bowling: Plunkett 25.4–1–132–1; Blignaut 16–0–109–2; Killeen 24–4–81–1; Onions 23–4–110–3; Collingwood 14–4–52–0; Breese 27–4–114–2; Muchall 5–1–22–0; Coetzer 1–0–2–0.

Durham

*J. J. B. Lewis b Gibson	9	– b Dagnall	21
G. R. Breese lbw b Gibson	0	– c Nixon b Dagnall	43
G. J. Muchall c Stevens b Henderson	60	– c Maddy b Henderson	95
P. D. Collingwood c Maddy b Henderson	17	– c Robinson b Gibson	57
M. J. North lbw b Dagnall	48	– c Maddy b Gibson	5
K. J. Coetzer c Sadler b Henderson	33	– c and b Henderson	38
†A. Pratt st Nixon b Henderson	9	– c Nixon b Cleary	1
A. M. Blignaut st Nixon b Henderson	12	– b Gibson	56
L. E. Plunkett not out	19	– lbw b Cleary	26
N. Killeen c Sadler b Henderson	0	– run out	6
G. Onions c Nixon b Henderson	0	– not out	2
B 4, l-b 8	12	L-b 17, w 4, n-b 18	39

1/4 (2) 2/11 (1) 3/59 (4) 4/140 (5)	219	1/46 (1) 2/97 (2) 3/185 (4) 389
5/148 (3) 6/162 (7) 7/188 (8)		4/193 (5) 5/261 (6) 6/265 (7)
8/205 (6) 9/211 (10) 10/219 (11)		7/288 (3) 8/380 (8)
		9/386 (9) 10/389 (10)

Bonus points – Durham 1, Leicestershire 3.

Bowling: *First Innings*—Cleary 9–3–20–0; Gibson 19–4–62–2; Dakin 2–0–9–0; Henderson 25.4–7–74–7; Dagnall 8–1–42–1. *Second Innings*—Cleary 13–2–50–2; Gibson 16.3–2–67–3; Dakin 9–2–33–0; Dagnall 14–1–64–2; Henderson 36–11–104–2; Hodge 5–0–35–0; Maddy 3–0–16–0; Robinson 1–0–3–0.

Umpires: V. A. Holder and R. Palmer.

At Nottingham, August 11, 12, 13, 14. LEICESTERSHIRE drew with NOTTINGHAMSHIRE.

LEICESTERSHIRE v YORKSHIRE

At Leicester, August 19, 20, 21, 22. Drawn. Leicestershire 11 pts, Yorkshire 8 pts. Toss: Leicestershire. Championship debut: J. J. Sayers.

Badly needing a win to sustain their promotion hopes, Leicestershire were denied on the final day by some determined lower-order batting. Hodge had declared just before lunch, setting a target of 310 in 69 overs. Some felt he had delayed too long, but his side looked well on course when they reduced Yorkshire to 90 for six at tea, with a minimum of 36 overs remaining. Dawood, however, batted 156 minutes for an unbeaten 42, Dawson lasted 70 minutes for 19, and Blain faced 24 balls without scoring; they held out with two wickets in hand. Leicestershire had taken control on the first day, when Robinson made a maiden first-class century for the club, striking 23 fours in a five-hour 154. Only Gibson followed up properly, with a forceful 60, and most of the second day was lost to rain, but Yorkshire were in danger at six for seven, still 79 short of saving the follow-on. The first of two determined innings from Dawson ensured Leicestershire would bat again, setting up a tense last day.

Close of play: First day, Leicestershire 333-7 (DeFreitas 11, Gibson 24); Second day, Yorkshire 36-1 (Wood 20, McGrath 2); Third day, Leicestershire 61-4 (Hodge 27, Snape 5).

Leicestershire

D. D. J. Robinson lbw b McGrath	154	– c Wood b Bresnan 14
D. L. Maddy lbw b Craven	27	– b Bresnan 1
J. K. Maunders b Kirby	20	– lbw b Kirby................. 3
*B. J. Hodge b McGrath	24	– c Dawood b Blain........... 60
D. I. Stevens c Dawson b Kirby	48	– lbw b Kirby................. 2
J. N. Snape c Gale b Kirby	0	– c McGrath b Blain 15
†P. A. Nixon c and b McGrath	1	– not out 22
P. A. J. DeFreitas c Jaques b Bresnan	11	– not out 19
O. D. Gibson not out	60	
C. W. Henderson b Bresnan	1	
C. E. Dagnall lbw b Blain	6	
B 3, l-b 6, w 3, n-b 18	30	B 4, l-b 6, n-b 20..... 30

1/90 (2) 2/126 (3) 3/177 (4) 4/289 (5) 382	1/17 (2) 2/18 (1) (6 wkts dec.) 166
5/293 (6) 6/294 (7) 7/295 (1)	3/38 (3) 4/44 (5)
8/334 (8) 9/346 (10) 10/382 (11)	5/117 (4) 6/118 (6)

Bonus points – Leicestershire 4, Yorkshire 3.

Bowling: *First Innings*—Kirby 25–5–87–3; Blain 13–1–65–1; Bresnan 22–7–42–2; Craven 8–1–30–1; Dawson 23–3–84–0; McGrath 22–1–65–3. *Second Innings*—Bresnan 15–2–41–2; Kirby 16–5–60–2; Blain 6–0–19–2; McGrath 6–2–13–0; Dawson 5–1–18–0; Craven 0.4–0–5–0.

Yorkshire

*M. J. Wood c Maddy b Henderson	20	– (2) b Gibson 14
P. A. Jaques c Gibson b DeFreitas	11	– (1) c Robinson b Gibson 1
A. McGrath c Nixon b DeFreitas	2	– lbw b Dagnall 6
I. J. Sayers c Maddy b Henderson	35	– lbw b DeFreitas 18
A. W. Gale c Dagnall b Henderson	13	– c Robinson b Henderson 14
V. J. Craven lbw b Hodge	24	– lbw b Henderson 11
†I. Dawood c and b Hodge	2	– not out 42
R. K. J. Dawson c Nixon b DeFreitas	76	– c Maunders b Maddy 19
T. T. Bresnan c Maunders b Henderson	35	– b DeFreitas 4
J. A. R. Blain not out	3	– not out 0
S. P. Kirby c Stevens b DeFreitas	0	
B 5, l-b 11, n-b 2	18	L-b 14, n-b 4.......... 18

1/28 (2) 2/36 (1) 3/36 (3) 4/59 (5) 239	1/2 (1) 2/23 (3) 3/35 (2) (8 wkts) 147
5/98 (6) 6/102 (7) 7/154 (4)	4/63 (4) 5/73 (5) 6/90 (6)
8/232 (9) 9/237 (8) 10/239 (11)	7/125 (8) 8/145 (9)

Bonus points – Yorkshire 1, Leicestershire 3.

Bowling: *First Innings*—Gibson 20–5–55–0; DeFreitas 17.1–3–49–4; Henderson 32–16–41–4; Hodge 8–3–18–2; Dagnall 5–0–23–0; Maddy 6–3–19–0; Snape 6–1–18–0. *Second Innings*—Gibson 16–5–39–2; Henderson 23.5–10–26–2; Dagnall 7–3–11–1; DeFreitas 16–5–48–2; Hodge 3–0–7–0; Maddy 3–1–2–1.

Umpires: G. I. Burgess and J. H. Hampshire.

At Derby, August 24, 25, 26, 27. LEICESTERSHIRE drew with DERBYSHIRE.

LEICESTERSHIRE v HAMPSHIRE

At Leicester, September 1, 2, 3, 4. Hampshire won by 86 runs. Hampshire 20 pts, Leicestershire 5 pts. Toss: Hampshire.

Hampshire went into the game needing 16 points to secure promotion before Warne returned to Australia. That looked remote early on the first afternoon when they struggled to 78 for six. But Pothas led the recovery with a gutsy 107, sharing valuable stands with Warne and Tremlett as the last four wickets added 243. Leicestershire's reply also ran into early problems until Stevens fought back with a stylish century. Even so, Hampshire had a handy lead, and a better showing from the top order second time round enabled them to set a demanding target of 369 in 116 overs. Udal bowled Maddy with the first ball of the last morning, but Stevens and Hodge batted for the rest of the session, progressing to 201 for three shortly after lunch. Then Tremlett pinned Hodge lbw, and Stevens fell to Warne next ball. There was little to follow, and Hampshire were up.

Close of play: First day, Leicestershire 35-0 (Maunders 13, Maddy 19); Second day, Hampshire 56-1 (Brown 14, Crawley 18); Third day, Leicestershire 70-2 (Maddy 30, Stevens 27).

Hampshire

J. H. K. Adams c New b Maddy	16	– b Gibson	20
M. J. Brown c Stevens b Dakin	0	– b Masters	51
J. P. Crawley b Dakin	4	– b Masters	61
S. M. Katich c Dakin b Gibson	30	– c New b Gibson	66
L. R. Prittipaul c Masters b Henderson	9	– b Masters	4
†N. Pothas b Henderson	107	– lbw b Dakin	7
A. D. Mascarenhas c Maddy b Henderson	0	– c Maunders b Henderson	4
*S. K. Warne b Masters	57	– c Stevens b Henderson	42
S. D. Udal c New b Hodge	22	– c Stevens b Masters	39
C. T. Tremlett c Hodge b Henderson	48	– b Dakin	16
B. V. Taylor not out	8	– not out	4
L-b 9, w 3, n-b 8	20	B 3, l-b 6, n-b 6	15
	321		**329**

1/0 (2) 2/5 (3) 3/31 (1) 4/68 (4)   1/24 (1) 2/138 (3) 3/155 (2)
5/74 (5) 6/78 (7) 7/189 (8)   4/163 (5) 5/185 (6) 6/210 (7)
8/231 (9) 9/278 (6) 10/321 (10)   7/270 (8) 8/270 (4)
    9/317 (9) 10/329 (10)

Bonus points – Hampshire 3, Leicestershire 3.

Bowling: *First Innings*—Gibson 18–4–42–1; Dakin 17–2–66–2; Masters 16–2–59–1; Maddy 12–3–28–1; Henderson 25.4–4–103–4; Hodge 4–1–14–1. *Second Innings*—Gibson 20–8–38–2; Dakin 17–3–72–2; Maunders 2–0–9–0; Maddy 5–0–23–0; Henderson 37–9–88–2; Masters 20–3–74–4; Hodge 2–0–14–0; Sadler 1–0–2–0.

Leicestershire

J. K. Maunders lbw b Mascarenhas	13	– lbw b Mascarenhas	0
D. L. Maddy b Taylor	21	– b Udal	30
*B. J. Hodge lbw b Tremlett	26	– (5) lbw b Tremlett	74
D. I. Stevens c Mascarenhas b Tremlett	105	– c Pothas b Warne	70
J. L. Sadler c Udal b Mascarenhas	5	– (6) c Crawley b Warne	15
D. G. Brandy b Warne	7	– (3) c Katich b Tremlett	4
†T. J. New lbw b Udal	0	– (8) not out	22
O. D. Gibson c Pothas b Tremlett	50	– (7) b Warne	27
J. M. Dakin not out	21	– b Taylor	4
C. W. Henderson c Warne b Taylor	3	– lbw b Taylor	1
D. D. Masters st Pothas b Udal	1	– lbw b Taylor	0
B 8, l-b 9, w 1, n-b 12	30	B 7, l-b 12, w 4, n-b 12	35
	282		**282**

1/39 (2) 2/41 (1) 3/87 (3) 4/105 (5)   1/3 (1) 2/18 (3) 3/70 (2)
5/137 (6) 6/138 (7) 7/254 (4)   4/201 (5) 5/201 (4) 6/239 (7)
8/256 (8) 9/276 (10) 10/282 (11)   7/257 (6) 8/274 (9)
    9/282 (10) 10/282 (11)

Bonus points – Leicestershire 2, Hampshire 3.

Bowling: *First Innings*—Tremlett 14–3–49–3; Taylor 15–2–55–2; Warne 12–0–31–1; Mascarenhas 19–7–40–2; Udal 13.5–3–44–2; Prittipaul 6–1–17–0; Katich 9–1–29–0. *Second Innings*—Mascarenhas 14–5–38–1; Tremlett 14–1–44–2; Taylor 15.5–2–53–3; Udal 12–0–51–1; Warne 18–3–62–3; Adams 2–0–15–0.

Umpires: B. Dudleston and A. G. T. Whitehead.

At Chester-le-Street, September 9, 10, 11, 12. LEICESTERSHIRE beat DURHAM by six wickets.

LEICESTERSHIRE v SOMERSET

At Leicester, September 16, 17, 18, 19. Somerset won by 75 runs. Somerset 16 pts, Leicestershire 3 pts. Toss: Somerset.

There was little at stake for either side, with all three promotion places taken – and even less after rain had washed out the two middle days. The prolific Hodge had just turned down the offer of another two-year contract at Grace Road, and missed the game through injury. Little wonder the atmosphere was subdued at the start. Gibson did his best to lift spirits with five wickets, taking his total to 60, and Leicestershire would have been satisfied when they dismissed Somerset for 213 and reached 123 for three by the close. The rain made that irrelevant. Two declarations left Leicestershire to chase 275 in 65 overs: they failed to get close, despite Gibson hitting 11 fours and a six in a 49-ball 57. Caddick delivered the *coup de grâce*, which gave Somerset the consolation of fourth place.

Close of play: First day, Leicestershire 123-3 (Stevens 0, Sadler 1); Second day, No play; Third day, No play.

Somerset

M. J. Wood c Maddy b Gibson	35	– c New b Maunders	3
N. J. Edwards c Sadler b Masters	45	– c New b Stevens	33
*M. Burns c Maunders b DeFreitas	12	– b Stevens	26
J. C. Hildreth b DeFreitas	0	– not out	52
I. D. Blackwell c Maddy b Gibson	38	– not out	46
A. V. Suppiah c New b Masters	0		
A. W. Laraman c Dagnall b Gibson	12		
†R. J. Turner lbw b Gibson	1		
R. L. Johnson c Maddy b Henderson	11		
A. R. Caddick not out	19		
S. R. G. Francis lbw b Gibson	15		
L-b 6, w 1, n-b 18	25	B 4, l-b 2, n-b 18	24
	213	**(3 wkts dec.)**	**184**

1/52 (1) 2/77 (3) 3/78 (4) 4/125 (2)
5/125 (6) 6/164 (5) 7/166 (8)
8/177 (9) 9/183 (7) 10/213 (11)

1/25 (1) 2/59 (2) (3 wkts dec.) 184
3/72 (3)

Bonus points – Somerset 1, Leicestershire 3.

Bowling: *First Innings*—Gibson 18–4–44–5; Dagnall 6–1–36–0; DeFreitas 7–1–44–2; Masters 10–2–28–2; Henderson 15–2–55–1. *Second Innings*—DeFreitas 3–0–19–0; Maunders 8–0–45–1; Stevens 13.2–1–50–2; Robinson 2–0–30–0; Sadler 4–0–34–0.

Leicestershire

D. D. J. Robinson c Wood b Johnson	59	– lbw b Caddick	20
*D. L. Maddy b Johnson	52	– b Johnson	2
J. K. Maunders c Laraman b Johnson	9	– b Francis	29
D. I. Stevens not out	0	– st Turner b Johnson	1
J. L. Sadler not out	1	– st Turner b Suppiah	27
†T. J. New (did not bat)		– run out	1
O. D. Gibson (did not bat)		– st Turner b Suppiah	57
P. A. J. DeFreitas (did not bat)		– c Blackwell b Caddick	6
C. W. Henderson (did not bat)		– lbw b Caddick	1
D. D. Masters (did not bat)		– b Caddick	31
C. E. Dagnall (did not bat)		– not out	9
N-b 2	2	B 4, l-b 7, w 2, n-b 2	15

1/89 (2) 2/121 (3) 3/122 (1)   (3 wkts dec.) 123

1/3 (2) 2/41 (1) 3/46 (4)   199
4/73 (3) 5/77 (6) 6/138 (5)
7/158 (7) 8/159 (9)
9/162 (8) 10/199 (10)

Bonus point – Somerset 1.

Bowling: *First Innings*—Caddick 6–2–12–0; Johnson 14–4–33–3; Blackwell 10–2–28–0; Francis 5–1–24–0; Laraman 3–0–26–0. *Second Innings*—Johnson 10–4–31–2; Caddick 16.2–1–69–4; Blackwell 8–2–25–0; Francis 5–2–27–1; Suppiah 7–0–36–2.

Umpires: N. G. Cowley and G. Sharp.

DATES OF FORMATION OF FIRST-CLASS COUNTIES

County	First known organisation	Present Club Original date	Reorganisation, if substantial	First-class status from
Derbyshire	1870	1870	–	1871
Durham	1874	1882	1991	1992
Essex	By 1790	1876	–	1895
Glamorgan	1861	1888	–	1921
Gloucestershire	1863	1871	–	1870
Hampshire	1849	1863	1879	1864
Kent	1842	1859	1870	1864
Lancashire	1864	1864	–	1865
Leicestershire	By 1820	1879	–	1895
Middlesex	1863	1864	–	1864
Northamptonshire	1820†	1878	–	1905
Nottinghamshire	1841	1841	1866	1864
Somerset	1864	1875	–	1882
Surrey	1845	1845	–	1864
Sussex	1836	1839	1857	1864
Warwickshire	1826	1882	–	1895
Worcestershire	1844	1865	–	1899
Yorkshire	1861	1863	1891	1864

Note: Derbyshire lost first-class status from 1888 to 1894, Hampshire between 1886 and 1894 and Somerset between 1886 and 1890.

† Town club.

MIDDLESEX

Captains galore

NORMAN DE MESQUITA

Middlesex had a difficult year in 2004 thanks to the England selectors discovering what the county's supporters already knew: that Andrew Strauss is a very good player. His elevation to international status, and the astonishing rapidity with which he secured his place, meant he played only one Championship match, so Middlesex had to find another captain.

Strauss's deputy, Owais Shah, was the first choice, but by mid-June the team were in the first division's relegation zone, and he was relieved of the post. The club management went so far as to describe his captaincy as "tactically naïve"; Shah himself thought he had done a good job – perhaps that was the problem. Ed Joyce took over for a fortnight before he was injured, and Ben Hutton became the fourth captain of the year, until Joyce's return. During his month in charge, Hutton did well, and the players seemed to respond to him. He was rewarded by getting the position full-time for 2005, as Strauss was expected to be absent again on England duty.

Given these unsettling circumstances, finishing fourth in the Championship's first division and winning the second division of the totesport League was an excellent result. The one-day league has not always seen Middlesex at their best, but they clinched the title with 12 wins to Worcestershire's 11, and possessed the leading run-scorer, wicket-taker and wicket-keeper in the whole competition in Paul Weekes, Simon Cook, whose 39 victims equalled the League record, and Ben Scott.

Weekes had a wonderful spell in mid-season – a century and six fifties in nine totesport innings – and the speed at which he scored was an important factor in the team's success. He also reached 1,000 Championship runs for the second time in his career, and was voted the Middlesex Player of the Year. Shah seemed at last to have discovered how to build an innings; his late-season form was outstanding – he made four hundreds after losing the captaincy – and he signed a new four-year contract. He and Hutton, who made five centuries, also passed 1,000 Championship runs, with Joyce and Sven Koenig getting there in all first-class cricket; no other county produced five thousand-run aggregates.

The bowling was less satisfactory. Middlesex had lined up Australian seamer Ashley Noffke for a third season, along with India's leg-spinner, Anil Kumble, but in January both withdrew, Noffke to rest his back and Kumble on his board's instructions. Instead, the club turned to South Africa for pace bowler Nantie Hayward and all-rounder Lance Klusener. Hayward did take 31 Championship wickets (only Cook, with 34, had more), but one never knew if it was going to be one of his good or bad days, and he had too many bad ones. He was re-signed for 2005, to be joined by New Zealand all-rounder Scott Styris.

It was hoped Hayward and Styris would be available for the whole season; in 2004, Middlesex fielded five overseas players in all, with short stints from Indian Ajit Agarkar and Australians Glenn McGrath and Stuart Clark. The comings and goings did not help, and neither did the Australian board's decision to allow McGrath to play only two Championship matches, when he had been signed for four. He showed what might have been by taking nine wickets. But the biggest disappointment was Klusener. He did win one League match, at Trent Bridge, with a

Paul Weekes

spectacular 22 runs off the last five balls, but usually batted too low in the order, and his bowling was sadly ineffectual. His 13 Championship wickets cost more than 50 each.

Chad Keegan took 20 in five Championship games until his season was ended in July by a back injury, and the opening attack looked thin without him. Another fast bowler whose fitness often let him down was Paul Hutchison. When available, he offered variety with his left-arm delivery. But the great need, as at most counties, was for a class spinner. Slow left-armer Chris Peploe looked promising, but his 17 wickets cost nearly 40 apiece and he was not developing as quickly as hoped.

Scott seemed to establish himself as first-choice keeper. His form, standing up to the seamers, was an important ingredient in the one-day campaign; David Nash's batting originally gave him the edge in first-class cricket, but he damaged a finger in early June. That gave Scott his chance and, though Nash returned, Scott displaced him before the end of the season, when he scored a maiden century against Northamptonshire. Another youngster who advanced was Jamie Dalrymple, who made 244 against Surrey, and it was good to see Nick Compton fit once more. In 2005, Middlesex again seemed likely to rely on the batting to earn as many bonus points as possible and ensure first-division survival.

Cook, deciding he would prefer a more rural lifestyle, moved to Kent, and will be missed, particularly in the limited-overs game. But Ed Smith travelled in the other direction, leaving Canterbury for Lord's. He was expected to open with Hutton, as a ready-made replacement for Koenig, who turned his back on the game after three productive years with Middlesex, to follow a financial career in his native South Africa. Meanwhile, the seamer Alan Richardson was signed from Warwickshire.

In November, the death of Mike Smith ended many years of service to the club. He made nearly 19,000 runs for Middlesex from 1959 to 1980, and more recently chalked up 11 seasons as the county scorer.

MIDDLESEX RESULTS

All first-class matches – Played 17: Won 4, Lost 4, Drawn 9.
County Championship matches – Played 16: Won 4, Lost 4, Drawn 8.

Frizzell County Championship, 4th in Division 1; Cheltenham & Gloucester Trophy, q-f;
totesport League, winners in Division 2; Twenty20 Cup, 5th in South Group.

COUNTY CHAMPIONSHIP AVERAGES

BATTING AND FIELDING

Cap		M	I	NO	R	HS	100s	50s	Avge	Ct/St
2000	O. A. Shah	16	29	5	1,280	140*	4	8	53.33	18
1993	P. N. Weekes.	16	26	3	1,001	118	2	9	43.52	14
2002	E. C. Joyce.	13	23	2	906	123	1	7	43.14	12
2003	B. L. Hutton.	16	29	1	1,129	126	5	3	40.32	23
2004	J. W. M. Dalrymple .	15	24	4	767	244	1	3	38.35	9
2002	S. G. Koenig	16	29	2	971	171	2	4	35.96	4
2000	D. C. Nash.	11	16	4	416	81*	0	3	34.66	26/2
	L. Klusener§.	6	8	1	170	68*	0	2	24.28	2
	B. J. M. Scott	6	11	3	190	101*	1	0	23.75	6/3
2003	C. B. Keegan	5	4	0	75	44	0	0	18.75	2
2003	S. J. Cook	11	14	0	243	40	0	0	17.35	5
	N. R. D. Compton . .	3	5	0	80	40	0	0	16.00	3
	C. T. Peploe	7	11	2	135	28*	0	0	15.00	3
	M. M. Betts	6	7	2	75	31*	0	0	15.00	2
	A. B. Agarkar§	3	4	2	27	22	0	0	13.50	2
	M Hayward§	11	13	5	40	9	0	0	5.00	4
	P. M. Hutchison. . . .	7	9	2	25	8	0	0	3.57	3

Also batted: T. F. Bloomfield (cap 2001) (1 match) 8; S. R. Clark§ (3 matches) 34, 11, 24; G. D. McGrath§ (2 matches) 24, 4, 0; A. J. Strauss (cap 2001) (1 match) 95, 19*; C. J. C. Wright (1 match) 0.

§ *Overseas player.*

BOWLING

	O	M	R	W	BB	5W/i	Avge
S. R. Clark	89	23	217	10	3-28	0	21.70
C. B. Keegan.	161	29	550	20	5-36	2	27.50
M. Hayward	289	54	918	31	4-41	0	29.61
S. J. Cook.	346	77	1,008	34	6-89	2	29.64
A. B. Agarkar	93.3	20	323	10	5-81	1	32.30
J. W. M Dalrymple . .	277.5	37	1,001	26	4-66	0	38.50
M. M. Betts	135.4	27	507	13	5-89	1	39.00
C. T. Peploe	212.2	51	672	17	4-65	0	39.52
P. N. Weekes	325.3	34	1,166	26	5-76	1	44.84
L. Klusener.	170.3	18	673	13	4-89	0	51.76

Also bowled: T. F. Bloomfield 20-3-55-1; P. M. Hutchison 160-25-551-9; B. L. Hutton 113-23-353-8; E. C. Joyce 32-2-135-1; S. G. Koenig 3-1-7-0; G. D. McGrath 100.4-41-215-9; D. C. Nash 2-0-8-0; O. A. Shah 18-4-54-1; C. J. C. Wright 20-3-50-0.

COUNTY RECORDS

Highest score for:	331*	J. D. Robertson v Worcestershire at Worcester . . .	1949
Highest score against:	341	C. M. Spearman (Gloucestershire) at Gloucester. .	2004
Best bowling for:	10-40	G. O. B. Allen v Lancashire at Lord's	1929
Best bowling against:	9-38	R. C. Robertson-Glasgow (Somerset) at Lord's. .	1924
Highest total for:	642-3 dec.	v Hampshire at Southampton	1923
Highest total against:	734-5 dec.	by Lancashire at Manchester.	2003
Lowest total for:	20	v MCC at Lord's	1864
Lowest total against: {	31	by Gloucestershire at Bristol	1924
	31	by Glamorgan at Cardiff	1997

MIDDLESEX DIRECTORY

ADDRESS

Lord's Cricket Ground, London NW8 8QN (020 7289 1300; fax 020 7289 5831; email enquiries@middlesexccc.com). **Website** www.middlesexccc.com.

GROUNDS

Lord's: in St John's Wood, just W of Regent's Park, accessed from A41 or A5 via St John's Wood Road. Nearest station: St John's Wood (Jubilee Line Underground) (½ mile).

Southgate: ¼ mile SW of town centre. At Betstyle Circus continue on A1003 Waterfall Road for ground on L side opposite Christ Church. Nearest stations: Southgate (Piccadilly Line Underground) (¾ mile) and New Southgate (1 mile).

Richmond: ¾ mile NW of town centre in Old Deer Park in Kew Road A307, S of Kew Gardens. Nearest station: Richmond (District Line Underground) (¾ mile).

Uxbridge: ¼ mile NE of town centre. From M40/A40 Swakeleys Roundabout take B467 Park Road, then first L into Gatting Way. Nearest station: Uxbridge (Metropolitan/Piccadilly Lines Underground) (¾ mile).

OFFICIALS

Captain B. L. Hutton
Head coach J. E. Emburey
President A. E. Moss
Chairman P. H. Edmonds
Secretary/chief executive V. J. Codrington

Chairman, cricket committee D. Bennett
Head groundsmen M. Hunt (Lord's)
S. Martin (Southgate)
Scorer 2004 – M. J. Smith

PLAYERS

Players expected to reappear in 2005

		Former counties	Country	Born	Birthplace
Betts	Melvyn Morris	Durham, Warwicks	E	26.3.1975	Sacriston
Bloomfield	Timothy Francis		E	31.5.1973	†Ashford
Compton	Nicholas Richard Denis		E	26.6.1983	Durban, SA
Dalrymple	James William Murray		E	21.1.1981	Nairobi, Kenya
*****Hayward**	Mornantau	Worcestershire	SA	6.3.1977	Uitenhage
Hutchison	Paul Michael	Yorks, Sussex	E	9.6.1977	Leeds
Hutton	Benjamin Leonard		E	29.1.1977	Johannesburg, SA
Joyce	Edmund Christopher		IRE (EU)	22.9.1978	Dublin
Keegan	Chad Blake		E	30.7.1979	Sandton, SA
Nash	David Charles		E	19.1.1978	Chertsey
Peploe	Christopher Thomas		E	26.4.1981	Hammersmith
Scott	Ben James Matthew	Surrey	E	4.8.1981	†Isleworth
Shah	Owais Alam		E	22.10.1978	Karachi, Pak.
*****Strauss**	Andrew John		‡E	2.3.1977	Johannesburg, SA
Weekes	Paul Nicholas		E	8.7.1969	Hackney
Wright	Christopher Julian Clement		E	14.7.1985	Chipping Norton

Players due to join in 2005

Richardson	Alan	Derbys, Warwicks	E	6.5.1975	Newcastle-under-Lyme
*****Smith**	Edward Thomas	Kent	E	19.7.1977	Pembury
*****Styris**	Scott Bernard		NZ	10.7.1975	Brisbane, Aus.

* Test player. † Born in Middlesex. ‡ 12-month ECB contract.

At Birmingham, April 16, 17, 18, 19. MIDDLESEX drew with WARWICKSHIRE.

MIDDLESEX v SURREY

At Lord's, April 21, 22, 23, 24. Middlesex won by six wickets. Middlesex 20 pts, Surrey 8 pts.
Toss: Middlesex.

Needing 297 to win in just over a day, Middlesex batted with control and intelligence for their first Championship win against Surrey since 1995. Their openers stayed together until just before lunch on the last morning, when Koenig, out for 62, was so annoyed he hurled his helmet at a dressing-room chair, only for it to bounce and shatter a window. The seats below were showered with broken glass, but fortunately their occupants had decided to go for lunch early. Koenig's opening partner Hutton (replacing Andrew Strauss, who was on England duty in the West Indies) then guided the innings till just before tea when at 222 for two victory was in sight. After the first innings, Surrey had a lead of 93, thanks largely to a century by Hollioake (which was to prove his last before retirement) and Azhar Mahmood's swing bowling. But they frittered it away in a second innings long on shots and short on gumption. Although no mention was made in the umpires' report, Middlesex later accused Surrey of ball-tampering. Their coach John Emburey even recorded covert video footage, but the ECB later declared it inconclusive.

Close of play: First day, Surrey 164-2 (Ramprakash 12, Benning 20); Second day, Middlesex 176-2 (Shah 77, Hutchison 2); Third day, Middlesex 32-0 (Koenig 18, Hutton 6).

Surrey

S. A. Newman c Weekes b Hayward	86	– c Cook b Hayward	18
*†J. N. Batty c Cook b Keegan	35	– c Keegan b Hayward	0
M. R. Ramprakash c Nash b Hutchison	29	– c Nash b Keegan	68
J. G. E. Benning b Hutchison	20	– lbw b Keegan	12
A. D. Brown c Nash b Hutchison	18	– c Weekes b Hutchison	4
A. J. Hollioake c Hutton b Keegan	106	– run out	4
Azhar Mahmood c Hutton b Keegan	14	– c Hutchison b Weekes	70
I. D. K. Salisbury c Hayward b Keegan	77	– c Nash b Keegan	13
Saqlain Mushtaq c Hutton b Keegan	2	– c Shah b Hayward	1
J. Ormond c Nash b Hayward	1	– not out	1
T. J. Murtagh not out	8	– b Hayward	0
B 3, l-b 16, w 1, n-b 2	22	B 2, l-b 9, w 1	12

1/119 (1) 2/130 (2) 3/167 (4) 4/189 (5)   418   1/4 (2) 2/22 (1) 3/48 (4)   203
5/220 (3) 6/253 (7) 7/378 (6)   4/59 (5) 5/71 (6) 6/184 (7)
8/383 (9) 9/384 (10) 10/418 (8)   7/191 (3) 8/202 (8)
                                   9/202 (10) 10/203 (11)

Bonus points – Surrey 5, Middlesex 3.

Bowling: *First Innings*—Keegan 22–0–138–5; Hayward 21–2–100–2; Cook 20–5–57–0; Hutchison 21–4–72–3; Hutton 2–0–5–0; Weekes 5–0–27–0. *Second Innings*—Keegan 18–4–47–3; Hayward 11–1–41–4; Hutchison 6–1–11–1; Cook 9–2–44–0; Weekes 10–0–49–1.

> **"**While the team and its managers criss-crossed England in a distinctively decorated bus, Lara usually travelled in a silver Mercedes lent him by an admirer."
>
> West Indians in England, page 466.

Middlesex

S. G. Koenig lbw b Azhar Mahmood	1	– c Hol lioake b Saqlain Mushtaq	62
B. L. Hutton b Salisbury	78	– c Batty b Saqlain Mushtaq	88
*O. A. Shah c Batty b Azhar Mahmood	93	– c Brown b Saqlain Mushtaq	65
P. M. Hutchison b Azhar Mahmood	2		
E. C. Joyce b Salisbury	45	– (4) c and b Saqlain Mushtaq	47
P. N. Weekes lbw b Azhar Mahmood	7	– not out	9
J. W. M. Dalrymple lbw b Ormond	0		
†D. C. Nash c Newman b Saqlain Mushtaq	26	– (5) not out	3
S. J. Cook c Benning b Saqlain Mushtaq	21		
C. B. Keegan c Newman b Saqlain Mushtaq	5		
M. Hayward not out	8		
B 6, l-b 8, w 2, n-b 18, p 5	39	B 3, l-b 9, n-b 14	26
	325	(4 wkts)	**300**

1/1 (1) 2/172 (2) 3/176 (4) 4/209 (3)
5/225 (6) 6/226 (7) 7/273 (8)
8/297 (5) 9/310 (10) 10/325 (9)

1/114 (1) 2/222 (2) (4 wkts) 300
3/273 (3) 4/291 (4)

Bonus points – Middlesex 3, Surrey 3.

Bowling: *First Innings*—Ormond 18–5–52–1; Azhar Mahmood 19–4–96–4; Murtagh 10–0–55–0; Saqlain Mushtaq 18.4–2–71–3; Salisbury 17–6–32–2. *Second Innings*—Ormond 17–3–39–0; Azhar Mahmood 15–2–43–0; Murtagh 5–0–22–0; Saqlain Mushtaq 24–1–107–4; Salisbury 21.4–2–77–0.

Umpires: V. A. Holder and R. Palmer.

MIDDLESEX v LANCASHIRE

At Lord's, May 7, 8, 9, 10. Drawn. Middlesex 10 pts, Lancashire 8 pts. Toss: Lancashire.

Strauss arrived back at dawn from the West Indies and, having made an important 66 in a one-day international two days earlier, now proved the man for the smaller occasion too. In dank and generally un-Caribbean weather Lancashire struggled to 236 on the first day, Keegan bowling better than he did against Surrey for a second successive five-wicket haul. Loye hit a solid 101 but then became part of a remarkable collapse: five wickets for ten runs in 25 balls. Middlesex capitalised, building a lead of 102, Strauss quickly readjusting to the conditions with a high-quality 95. The former Derbyshire captain Cork continued to enjoy his change of county and took his first seven-for since 1995, when he was playing against Lancashire rather than for them. But with 68 overs lost during the first two days, Lancashire did not bat again until just before lunch on the third. Their second effort was much better than their first, Chilton reaching a Lord's century for the second year running, but Hegg was never in a position to make a challenging declaration.

Close of play: First day, Middlesex 78-2 (Shah 34, Joyce 32); Second day, Middlesex 257-5 (Strauss 92, Nash 5); Third day, Lancashire 128-1 (Chilton 47, Loye 31).

Lancashire

M. J. Chilton lbw b Keegan	2	– c Joyce b Weekes	103
I. J. Sutcliffe c Klusener b Hayward	21	– lbw b Hayward	38
M. B. Loye c Shah b Keegan	101	– lbw b Weekes	60
S. G. Law lbw b Hutchison	33	– c Nash b Klusener	91
C. L. Hooper lbw b Hutchison	0	– not out	33
G. Chapple b Keegan	32	– c Nash b Klusener	17
K. W. Hogg b Hayward	1	– b Klusener	12
D. G. Cork lbw b Keegan	0	– b Klusener	4
*†W. K. Hegg c Joyce b Klusener	36	– not out	12
S. I. Mahmood lbw b Keegan	5		
G. Keedy not out	1		
L-b 4	4	B 8, l-b 17, n-b 6	31
	236	(7 wkts dec.)	**401**

1/8 (1) 2/26 (2) 3/104 (4) 4/104 (5)
5/193 (6) 6/194 (3) 7/194 (8)
8/194 (7) 9/203 (10) 10/236 (9)

1/75 (2) 2/180 (3) (7 wkts dec.) 401
3/293 (1) 4/331 (4)
5/353 (6) 6/373 (7) 7/377 (8)

Bonus points – Lancashire 1, Middlesex 3.

Bowling: *First Innings*—Keegan 20–3–36–5; Hayward 17–1–75–2; Klusener 13.5–1–60–1; Hutchison 14–2–40–2; Weekes 4–1–21–0. *Second Innings*—Keegan 23–6–70–0; Hayward 18–5–36–1; Hutchison 15–2–52–0; Klusener 23.4–1–89–4; Hutton 9–0–26–0; Weekes 21–4–77–2; Joyce 9–2–26–0.

Middlesex

S. G. Koenig lbw b Cork	3	– (2) not out	14
B. L. Hutton lbw b Cork	4		
O. A. Shah b Chapple	34		
E. C. Joyce c Hegg b Chapple	44		
*A. J. Strauss c Hegg b Chapple	95	– (1) not out	19
P. N. Weekes c Hooper b Cork	50		
†D. C. Nash lbw b Cork	19		
L. Klusener c Chilton b Cork	19		
C. B. Keegan c and b Cork	26		
P. M. Hutchison not out	7		
M. Hayward lbw b Cork	7		
B 1, l-b 11, n-b 18	30	L-b 2, n-b 6	8
	338	(no wkt)	41

1/3 (1) 2/10 (2) 3/78 (3) 4/119 (4)
5/252 (6) 6/266 (5) 7/294 (7)
8/301 (8) 9/326 (9) 10/338 (11)

Bonus points – Middlesex 3, Lancashire 3.

Bowling: *First Innings*—Chapple 27–7–83–3; Cork 31.3–6–120–7; Mahmood 11–2–48–0; Hogg 7–2–25–0; Keedy 10–3–35–0; Hooper 9–2–15–0. *Second Innings*—Hogg 5–2–16–0; Mahmood 5–2–17–0; Hooper 2–0–4–0; Keedy 1–0–2–0.

Umpires: G. I. Burgess and B. Dudleston.

At Cambridge, May 12, 13, 14. MIDDLESEX drew with CAMBRIDGE UCCE.

At The Oval, May 19, 20, 21, 22. MIDDLESEX drew with SURREY.

At Manchester, May 25, 26, 27, 28. MIDDLESEX drew with LANCASHIRE.

MIDDLESEX v WARWICKSHIRE

At Lord's, June 2, 3, 4, 5. Warwickshire won by an innings and eight runs. Warwickshire 22 pts, Middlesex 1 pt. Toss: Warwickshire.

Nick Knight played what may be regarded as the innings of his life, though spectators who sat through it might not remember it so kindly. Knight scored 303 not out, the fifth first-class triple-century at Lord's (after Percy Holmes, Jack Hobbs, Graham Gooch and his own team-mate, Mark Wagh, in this fixture three years earlier). Apart from his first 50 (off 57 balls) and his last (off 58), Knight's innings was a workmanlike one. He set out to bat Middlesex out of the game, no matter how long it took or how ugly it looked, and he succeeded. Although Warwickshire piled up 608 for seven in the first innings, Knight said the bowlers made them fight for every run on the second day. "That just makes it more pleasing," he added. He batted 644 minutes and faced 488 balls on a slow pitch, carefully selecting a relatively modest 32 fours. Warwickshire were also helped by some strange captaincy by Shah. Peploe, the best of Middlesex's nine bowlers, with two catches dropped in his first four overs, bowled only ten in all, while Klusener, the least effective, bowled 28. When Middlesex finally batted on the second evening, they lost two wickets inside four overs and three more before the close. They never recovered, although the second innings, after they followed on 445 behind, was much better. Hutton led the way with 126 and, at 307 for three at lunch on the final day, Middlesex even had hopes of a draw. But nobody could stay there long enough: Warwickshire got home with 17 full overs to spare. Five people kept wicket in the match as both original keepers were hurt: Ben Scott deputised for Nash, and Trott replaced Frost until Ian Clifford could arrive.

Close of play: First day, Warwickshire 348-1 (Knight 179, Bell 119); Second day, Middlesex 76-5 (Weekes 32, Nash 0); Third day, Middlesex 216-2 (Hutton 116, Joyce 20).

Warwickshire

*N. V. Knight not out	303	N. M. Carter c Shah b Weekes	13
M. A. Wagh c Weekes b Dalrymple	43	†T. Frost not out	11
I. R. Bell b Hayward	129	B 2, l-b 11, w 5, n-b 4	22
I. J. L. Trott c sub b Hayward	3		
J. O. Troughton lbw b Hayward	0	1/118 (2) 2/372 (3)　　　(7 wkts dec.) 608	
D. R. Brown c Hayward b Klusener	13	3/382 (4) 4/382 (5)	
G. B. Hogg c Hutchison b Dalrymple	71	5/406 (6) 6/556 (7) 7/579 (8)	

D. Pretorius and N. Tahir did not bat.

Bonus points – Warwickshire 5, Middlesex 1 (130 overs: 428-5).

Bowling: Hayward 26–4–82–3; Klusener 28–3–104–1; Hutchison 32–5–92–0; Hutton 12–1–45–0; Dalrymple 21.4–2–99–2; Peploe 10–2–33–0; Weekes 28–1–120–1; Shah 1–0–3–0; Joyce 4–0–17–0.

Middlesex

B. L. Hutton c Bell b Pretorius	17	– (2) lbw b Wagh	126
S. G. Koenig c Frost b Carter	1	– (1) c Brown b Wagh	57
*O. A. Shah b Carter	0	– c Hogg b Wagh	3
E. C. Joyce b Carter	5	– c sub b Brown	66
P. N. Weekes c Trott b Carter	70	– c Knight b Brown	62
J. W. M. Dalrymple st Frost b Brown	19	– c Hogg b Tahir	17
†D. C. Nash c Brown b Bell	29	– c sub b Pretorius	32
L. Klusener lbw b Bell	0	– lbw b Bell	12
C. T. Peploe c Frost b Bell	3	– not out	19
P. M. Hutchison b Bell	0	– c sub b Pretorius	0
M. Hayward not out	0	– c Carter b Pretorius	7
B 9, l-b 9, w 1	19	B 14, l-b 21, w 1	36

1/12 (2) 2/12 (3) 3/22 (4) 4/28 (1)	163	1/167 (1) 2/173 (3) 3/243 (2)　437
5/72 (6) 6/155 (7) 7/155 (8)		4/339 (4) 5/340 (5) 6/362 (6)
8/163 (9) 9/163 (10) 10/163 (5)		7/393 (8) 8/411 (7)
		9/421 (10) 10/437 (11)

Bonus points – Warwickshire 3.

Bowling: *First Innings*—Pretorius 11–2–29–1; Carter 16.3–2–50–4; Brown 11–3–33–1; Tahir 9–1–29–0; Bell 4–1–4–4. *Second Innings*—Pretorius 27.3–6–86–3; Carter 29–9–64–0; Tahir 12–3–38–1; Brown 18–4–46–2; Wagh 30–2–85–3; Bell 8–3–14–1; Troughton 6–1–16–0; Hogg 23–8–53–0.

Umpires: B. Dudleston and T. E. Jesty.

At Gloucester, June 9, 10, 11, 12. MIDDLESEX lost to GLOUCESTERSHIRE by ten wickets.

MIDDLESEX v WORCESTERSHIRE

At Lord's, June 18, 19, 20, 21. Drawn. Middlesex 11 pts, Worcestershire 9 pts. Toss: Middlesex.
Before the match Middlesex sacked Owais Shah as acting-captain after failing to win in the Championship since April. Their chief executive, Vinny Codrington, described Shah's decisions as "tactically naïve" and announced Ed Joyce as the new stand-in. He won the toss, and his team, which had appeared rudderless, at least seemed to have a purpose, which was avoiding three successive defeat. And they succeeded. Batting first on an easy-paced pitch, Hutton and Koenig achieved their aim of crease occupation, staying together till midway through the afternoon. Koenig reached a determined century before retiring with a pulled thigh muscle. Poor Shah did not last long but Joyce's 82 gave an early hint that responsibility would not affect his form. Weekes did even better, his 102 continuing a rich run, and the innings lasted till tea on the second day. The only surprise of the heavily rain-affected Worcestershire reply was that Hick did not equal W. G. Grace with a 126th first-class hundred, to the chagrin of a camera crew poised to record the moment. Moore, however, did manage a slow century as the match dribbled to a draw.

Close of play: First day, Middlesex 299-2 (Joyce 59, Weekes 11); Second day, Worcestershire 46-1 (Moore 23, Hick 16); Third day, Worcestershire 170-1 (Moore 73, Hick 77).

Middlesex

B. L. Hutton c Rhodes b Batty	90	– not out		3
S. G. Koenig not out	104			
O. A. Shah lbw b Mason	12	– not out		5
*E. C. Joyce c Rhodes b Hall	82			
P. N. Weekes b Solanki	102			
J. W. M. Dalrymple c Peters b Solanki	41			
L. Klusener c Mason b Solanki	2			
†B. J. M. Scott lbw b Solanki	11	– (2) lbw b Bichel		0
S. J. Cook c Mason b Solanki	24			
C. B. Keegan c Batty b Kabir Ali	0			
T. F. Bloomfield b Kabir Ali	8			
B 4, l-b 14, n-b 14	32			

1/167 (1) 2/190 (3) 3/335 (4) 4/439 (6)   508   1/1 (2)   (1 wkt)   8
5/445 (7) 6/468 (5) 7/475 (8)
8/476 (10) 9/476 (11) 10/508 (9)

Bonus points – Middlesex 4, Worcestershire 1 (130 overs: 354-3).

In the first innings Koenig, when 104, retired hurt at 275 and resumed at 496.

Bowling: *First Innings*—Mason 35-8-87-1; Kabir Ali 32-9-84-2; Hall 32-7-92-1; Bichel 27-7-69-0; Batty 33-6-107-1; Moore 3-0-11-0; Solanki 13.4-3-40-5. *Second Innings*—Bichel 3-0-6-1; Kabir Ali 2-1-2-0.

Worcestershire

S. D. Peters c Cook b Keegan	6	†S. J. Rhodes st Scott b Dalrymple	12	
S. C. Moore c sub b Cook	111	M. S. Mason not out	0	
G. A. Hick b Klusener	86			
*B. F. Smith lbw b Klusener	12	B 9, l-b 14, n-b 4	27	
V. S. Solanki b Klusener	8			
A. J. Hall c sub b Cook	28		399	
G. J. Batty run out	52			
A. J. Bichel c sub b Bloomfield	53			
Kabir Ali c Dalrymple b Weekes	4			

1/6 (1) 2/186 (3) 3/200 (4)
4/218 (5) 5/268 (2) 6/271 (6)
7/378 (8) 8/378 (7)
9/399 (10) 10/399 (9)

Bonus points – Worcestershire 4, Middlesex 3.

Bowling: Keegan 24-7-78-1; Cook 25-6-69-2; Bloomfield 20-3-55-1; Klusener 26-5-60-3; Dalrymple 17-5-64-1; Weekes 14.2-3-47-1; Hutton 3-2-3-0.

Umpires: N. J. Llong and J. W. Lloyds.

At Shenley Park, June 23. MIDDLESEX v WEST INDIANS. No result (abandoned) (see West Indian tour section).

At Worcester, July 22, 23, 24, 25. MIDDLESEX beat WORCESTERSHIRE by six wickets.

MIDDLESEX v KENT

At Southgate, July 28, 29, 30, 31. Middlesex won by 119 runs. Middlesex 21 pts, Kent 3 pts. Toss: Middlesex. County debuts: M. G. Bevan, R. H. Joseph.

Although they fell some way short of a world-record fourth-innings winning total of 530, Kent battled into the final half-hour. For Middlesex, it was a hard day's work on a pitch that favoured batsmen to the end; they still needed five wickets at tea. Kent might even have prevailed had

Bevan, their latest import, who added 162 with Fulton, survived into the afternoon. Instead, Hutton completed his second win in two Championship games as captain, and his side supplanted Kent in third place. He handled the bowling well, the team responded with enthusiasm, and he proved his form was unaffected with twin centuries, the first instance of his career, which gave him three in four innings. Loudon's off-spin unexpectedly curtailed Middlesex on the opening day, but Kent's first innings was more predictably wrecked by McGrath, in the first of two Championship matches the ACB allowed him to play during his month's stay. It was partly to conserve his strength that Hutton waived the follow-on, setting up the huge target instead.

Close of play: First day, Kent 0-0 (Fulton 0, Carberry 0); Second day, Middlesex 162-0 (Hutton 72, Koenig 86); Third day, Kent 137-2 (Fulton 63, Bevan 52).

Middlesex

*B. L. Hutton c O'Brien b Patel	100	– c Carberry b Patel	107
S. G. Koenig b Joseph	31	– run out	86
N. R. D. Compton c O'Brien b Butler	2	– c O'Brien b Joseph	16
O. A. Shah b Trott	60	– c O'Brien b Joseph	3
P. N. Weekes c Walker b Patel	45	– lbw b Patel	54
J. W. M. Dalrymple c Bevan b Loudon	31	– c Fulton b Butler	27
†D. C. Nash not out	26	– c Loudon b Patel	23
S. J. Cook c Walker b Loudon	0	– b Patel	29
A. B. Agarkar b Loudon	0	– not out	1
M. M. Betts c and b Loudon	7		
G. D. McGrath c Fulton b Loudon	24		
B 3, l-b 5, w 1, n-b 16	25	B 12, l-b 8, n-b 4	24

1/68 (2) 2/109 (3) 3/186 (1) 4/228 (4)   351   1/163 (2) 2/207 (3)   (8 wkts dec.) 370
5/285 (5) 6/297 (6) 7/305 (7)   3/213 (4) 4/237 (1)
8/305 (9) 9/317 (10) 10/351 (11)   5/302 (6) 6/316 (5)
                                     7/353 (7) 8/370 (8)

Bonus points – Middlesex 4, Kent 3.

Bowling: *First Innings*—Butler 15–1–62–1; Trott 15–2–67–1; Joseph 20–3–55–1; Patel 32–8–106–2; Loudon 17.3–3–53–5. *Second Innings*—Butler 14–1–68–1; Trott 10–1–34–0; Patel 33.2–3–94–4; Joseph 11–1–50–2; Loudon 24–4–88–0; Bevan 3–0–16–0.

Kent

*D. P. Fulton c Nash b Cook	8	– c Hutton b McGrath	121
M. A. Carberry c Shah b Cook	0	– c Nash b Cook	1
E. T. Smith c Weekes b McGrath	63	– c Koenig b Cook	9
M. G. Bevan lbw b Dalrymple	9	– c Hutton b Weekes	66
M. J. Walker not out	50	– lbw b Weekes	28
A. G. R. Loudon b McGrath	4	– lbw b Shah	44
†N. J. O'Brien c Agarkar b Dalrymple	12	– not out	67
M. M. Patel c Agarkar b Cook	28	– b Dalrymple	14
I. G. Butler lbw b McGrath	1	– c sub b Dalrymple	14
R. H. Joseph b McGrath	0	– lbw b Dalrymple	10
B. J. Trott c Nash b Betts	8	– lbw b Weekes	0
L-b 1, n-b 8	9	B 13, l-b 8, n-b 15	36

1/4 (2) 2/17 (1) 3/67 (4) 4/96 (3)   192   1/2 (2) 2/20 (3) 3/182 (4)   410
5/106 (6) 6/121 (7) 7/167 (8)   4/236 (5) 5/268 (1) 6/340 (6)
8/168 (9) 9/168 (10) 10/192 (11)   7/366 (8) 8/386 (9)
                                    9/405 (10) 10/410 (11)

Bonus points – Middlesex 3.

Bowling: *First Innings*—McGrath 22–7–59–4; Dalrymple 15–2–52–2; Cook 14–3–33–3; Agarkar 4–0–27–0; Betts 4.3–0–14–1; Weekes 2–0–6–0. *Second Innings*—McGrath 30–10–71–1; Cook 11–3–46–2; Agarkar 17–6–53–0; Dalrymple 24–5–51–3; Weekes 44.3–7–128–3; Betts 8–1–31–0; Shah 3–0–9–1.

Umpires: J. H. Evans and N. A. Mallender.

MIDDLESEX v GLOUCESTERSHIRE

At Lord's, August 3, 4, 5, 6. Drawn. Middlesex 9 pts, Gloucestershire 9 pts. Toss: Middlesex.

Fear of relegation led to defensive cricket, even though the teams started third and second in the table. Once a violent storm had taken 59 overs out of the first day (a further 31 were lost on the third), both seemed to accept there was not enough time to force a result on a slow pitch. Middlesex missed Strauss and McGrath (ordered to rest by their respective boards), and the injured Keegan, but Agarkar claimed three wickets in 19 balls on the opening day. Gloucestershire batted with no sense of urgency – Weston hit six fours in six hours – but still had a chance of enforcing the follow-on when Middlesex were 98 for six. That was averted by Shah, who batted superbly for his second first-class century of the season, and Nash. Hutton declared on securing a second batting point, 94 behind, but there was no response from Taylor on the last day, when he and Spearman had a prolonged net. Frederik Klokker, an MCC Young Cricketer from Denmark, kept wicket in the final session after Nash had a back spasm.

Close of play: First day, Gloucestershire 133-4 (Weston 39, Adshead 9); Second day, Middlesex 66-3 (Shah 10, Hutchison 2); Third day, Gloucestershire 12-0 (Spearman 8, Weston 4).

Gloucestershire

W. P. C. Weston c Dalrymple b Agarkar	98	– (2) c Nash b Agarkar		7
C. M. Spearman c Nash b Cook	16	– (1) lbw b Weekes		100
M. E. K. Hussey c Koenig b Agarkar	43	– c Shah b Agarkar		0
*C. G. Taylor lbw b Franklin	8	– c Dalrymple b Weekes		91
A. P. R. Gidman b Agarkar	1	– b Dalrymple		56
†S. J. Adshead c Shah b Cook	19	– b Dalrymple		37
J. E. C. Franklin c Compton b Cook	44	– not out		39
I. D. Fisher c Nash b Dalrymple	28	– c Hutton b Dalrymple		28
M. C. J. Ball c Cook b Agarkar	7	– not out		2
J. M. M. Averis not out	28			
J. Lewis c Koenig b Weekes	21			
B 6, l-b 3, w 3, n-b 22	34	B 19, l-b 5, n-b 16		40

1/28 (2) 2/107 (3) 3/119 (4) 4/121 (5)   347   1/39 (2) 2/39 (3)   (7 wkts dec.) 400
5/157 (6) 6/250 (7) 7/256 (1)   3/209 (1) 4/224 (4)
8/268 (9) 9/314 (8) 10/347 (11)   5/326 (5) 6/333 (6) 7/393 (8)

Bonus points – Gloucestershire 3, Middlesex 3.

Bowling: *First Innings*—Cook 30–7–63–3; Agarkar 29–7–81–5; Betts 13–3–49–0; Hutchison 9 –0–39–0; Hutton 11–2–21–0; Weekes 18.2–1–50–1; Dalrymple 10–2–35–1. *Second Innings*—Agarkar 9–1–28–2; Cook 8–0–31–0; Betts 7–2–20–0; Hutchison 6–0–37–0; Dalrymple 25–0–141–3; Weekes 28–2–91–2; Hutton 6–2–8–0; Shah 3–0–20–0.

Middlesex

*B. L. Hutton c Hussey b Franklin	1	S. J. Cook c Gidman b Lewis		8
S. G. Koenig run out	36	A. B. Agarkar not out		4
N. R. D. Compton c Gidman b Lewis	2			
O. A. Shah lbw b Franklin	103	B 10, l-b 3, w 1, n-b 17		31
P. M. Hutchison c Adshead b Lewis	3			
P. N. Weekes lbw b Franklin	4	1/7 (1) 2/20 (3) 3/61 (2)	(8 wkts dec.)	253
J. W. M. Dalrymple b Averis	2	4/67 (5) 5/84 (6) 6/98 (7)		
†D. C. Nash not out	59	7/237 (4) 8/249 (9)		

M. M. Betts did not bat.

Bonus points – Middlesex 2, Gloucestershire 2.

Bowling: Lewis 21.5–9–48–3; Franklin 18–7–42–3; Averis 16–3–40–1; Gidman 7–1–33–0; Fisher 14–2–32–0; Ball 17–1–43–0; Hussey 1–0–2–0.

Umpires: J. H. Hampshire and A. G. T. Whitehead.

MIDDLESEX v SUSSEX

At Lord's, August 10, 11, 12, 13. Sussex won by 143 runs. Sussex 20 pts, Middlesex 4 pts. Toss: Sussex.

McGrath was allowed out for his second and last Championship game for Middlesex, but it was his opposite number, Mushtaq Ahmed, who took ten wickets and ensured victory for Sussex, still trapped in the relegation zone. McGrath did bowl six consecutive maidens on the opening afternoon, but Ward and Goodwin added 222 in just over two hours. Only two wickets had fallen in the two sessions possible on the first day, but there were 16 on the second: the visitors lost their last seven in 15 overs, and only Joyce passed 25 for Middlesex. Sussex led by 102 on first innings, but struggled against Cook when they resumed. On the second: the home batsmen to build a significant partnership as Mushtaq again proved too clever for the home batsmen.

Close of play: First day, Sussex 252-2 (Ward 120, Goodwin 99); Second day, Middlesex 195-8 (Scott 11, Betts 13); Third day, Middlesex 48-1 (Koenig 23, Shah 8).

Sussex

I. J. Ward lbw b Betts	148	– run out	28
R. R. Montgomerie lbw b Cook	4	– lbw b Cook	34
P. A. Cottey c Shah b Betts	25	– c Shah b Cook	42
M. W. Goodwin c and b Weekes	105	– c Joyce b Hutton	6
*C. J. Adams lbw b Cook	14	– c Hutton b Cook	54
†M. J. Prior c Dalrymple b Hutton	4	– lbw b Dalrymple	0
M. J. G. Davis c Scott b McGrath	5	– c Hutton b Cook	6
Mushtaq Ahmed b McGrath	1	– c Shah b Cook	0
R. J. Kirtley c Hutton b Betts	0	– c Hutton b McGrath	9
Mohammad Akram not out	2	– c Dalrymple b Betts	2
J. D. Lewry b McGrath	1	– not out	0
B 1, l-b 3, w 1	5	B 8, l-b 4, w 1, n-b 2	15
	314		**196**

1/4 (2) 2/48 (3) 3/270 (4) 4/293 (5)   314   1/51 (2) 2/66 (1) 3/83 (4)   196
5/300 (6) 6/306 (1) 7/310 (7)   4/167 (5) 5/167 (6) 6/179 (3)
8/311 (8) 9/313 (9) 10/314 (11)   7/179 (8) 8/183 (7)
                                 9/196 (10) 10/196 (9)

Bonus points – Sussex 3, Middlesex 3.

Bowling: *First Innings*—McGrath 28.2–15–44–3; Cook 19–5–69–2; Betts 19–6–39–3; Hutton 8–2–31–1; Weekes 16–2–58–1; Dalrymple 12–1–43–0; Joyce 4–0–26–0. *Second Innings*—McGrath 20.2–9–41–1; Cook 19–4–51–5; Betts 14.5–4–41–1; Hutton 10–2–24–1; Dalrymple 7–1–27–1.

Middlesex

B. L. Hutton c Prior b Mohammad Akram	14	– c Cottey b Mushtaq Ahmed	10
S. G. Koenig c Prior b Kirtley	9	– c Cottey b Mushtaq Ahmed	23
O. A. Shah lbw b Mushtaq Ahmed	25	– not out	60
*E. C. Joyce c Prior b Mushtaq Ahmed	69	– c Cottey b Mushtaq Ahmed	2
J. W. M. Dalrymple lbw b Mohammad Akram	8	– c Adams b Mohammad Akram	10
D. C. Nash lbw b Mushtaq Ahmed	11	– lbw b Mushtaq Ahmed	0
†B. J. M. Scott c Adams b Mushtaq Ahmed	13	– (8) b Kirtley	7
S. J. Cook c sub b Mushtaq Ahmed	17	– (9) b Mushtaq Ahmed	19
P. N. Weekes b Kirtley	11	– (7) b Mohammad Akram	1
M. M. Betts not out	22	– c Montgomerie b Kirtley	5
G. D. McGrath lbw b Mushtaq Ahmed	4	– c Adams b Kirtley	0
B 4, l-b 5	9	B 3, l-b 2, w 3, n-b 10	18
	212		**155**

1/24 (2) 2/24 (1) 3/96 (3) 4/114 (5)   212   1/28 (1) 2/53 (2) 3/57 (4)   155
5/137 (6) 6/137 (4) 7/163 (8)   4/79 (5) 5/80 (6) 6/81 (7)
8/178 (9) 9/206 (7) 10/212 (11)   7/111 (8) 8/138 (9)
                               9/151 (10) 10/155 (11)

Bonus points – Middlesex 1, Sussex 3.

Bowling: *First Innings*—Mohammad Akram 15–5–55–3; Kirtley 22–5–56–2; Lewry 4–0–26–0; Mushtaq Ahmed 24.5–3–66–5. *Second Innings*—Mohammad Akram 15–4–30–2; Kirtley 19.2–6–37–3; Mushtaq Ahmed 27–6–83–5.

Umpires: N. G. Cowley and J. W. Holder.

At Northampton, August 18, 19, 20, 21. MIDDLESEX drew with NORTHAMPTONSHIRE.

At Hove, September 4, 5, 6. MIDDLESEX beat SUSSEX by five wickets.

MIDDLESEX v NORTHAMPTONSHIRE

At Lord's, September 9, 10, 11, 12. Drawn. Middlesex 11 pts, Northamptonshire 8 pts. Toss: Middlesex. County debut: A. R. White.

This draw confirmed that Northamptonshire would be relegated while Middlesex remained in the first division. The opening day saw three home batsmen make half-centuries, but it was a maiden hundred from Scott on the second that lifted Middlesex to a formidable 425. Northamptonshire were soon 12 for three, and temporarily lost Sales when Clark struck him on the thumb two runs later. He returned and his team did enough to avert the follow-on by a whisker. Joyce's declaration set a target of 356 in 86 overs for an unlikely victory. Huggins overcame severe toothache to hit a career-best 82 and added 169 with Sales, despite some fiery pace from Hayward, who probably bowled as well as he had all season, for little reward. But the chase was called off with 132 required from 12. Koenig said farewell to Lord's with a fifty, and signed off by bowling the final over.

Close of play: First day, Middlesex 280-6 (Scott 31, Cook 15); Second day, Northamptonshire 139-4 (Sales 13, Brophy 42); Third day, Middlesex 167-3 (Joyce 37, Weekes 20).

Middlesex

B. L. Hutton c Brophy b Louw	7	– (2) st Brophy b Brown	31
S. G. Koenig c Brophy b Rofe	6	– (1) c Afzaal b Brown	51
O. A. Shah c Afzaal b Rofe	85	– c Cook b Brown	24
*E. C. Joyce c Roberts b Rofe	71	– c Sales b Rofe	59
P. N. Weekes c Rofe b Louw	54	– c Cook b Rofe	38
J. W. M. Dalrymple lbw b Louw	1	– c Brown b Rofe	2
†B. J. M. Scott not out	101	– not out	1
S. J. Cook lbw b Rofe	40		
C. T. Peploe c Brophy b Louw	21		
S. R. Clark b Brown	24		
M. Hayward c Louw b Brown	0		
L-b 10, w 5	15	B 1, l-b 3, w 2	6

1/12 (2) 2/14 (1) 3/170 (3) 4/177 (4)   425   1/82 (1) 2/87 (2)   (6 wkts dec.) 212
5/182 (6) 6/259 (5) 7/320 (8)   3/122 (3) 4/202 (5)
8/352 (9) 9/415 (10) 10/425 (11)   5/207 (6) 6/212 (4)

Bonus points – Middlesex 4, Northamptonshire 2 (130 overs: 387-8).

Bowling: *First Innings*—Louw 34–8–112–4; Rofe 35–7–109–4; Phillips 23–7–78–0; Cook 8–2–19–0; Brown 36.4–8–87–2; White 3–0–10–0. *Second Innings*—Louw 9–3–35–0; Rofe 7.5–2–23–3; Phillips 7–1–22–0; Brown 18–2–65–3; White 5–0–23–0; Cook 5–0–28–0; Afzaal 3–0–12–0.

Northamptonshire

T. B. Huggins c Joyce b Cook	4	– (2) not out	82
T. W. Roberts lbw b Clark	0	– (1) c Hayward b Cook	11
J. W. Cook c Scott b Clark	8	– lbw b Cook	0
U. Afzaal b Hayward	62	– c Joyce b Hayward	12
*D. J. Sales b Clark	22	– c Cook b Hutton	90
†G. L. Brophy c and b Hutton	81	– not out	5
A. R. White c Shah b Dalrymple	22		
B. J. Phillips c and b Hutton	30		
J. Louw c Scott b Hayward	32		
P. C. Rofe c Peploe b Hutton	1		
J. F. Brown not out	0		
B 6, l-b 7, w 1, n-b 6	20	B 8, l-b 12, n-b 4	24

1/4 (2) 2/8 (1) 3/12 (3) 4/117 (4)   282   1/14 (1) 2/18 (3)   (4 wkts) 224
5/161 (5) 6/210 (6) 7/210 (7)   3/43 (4) 4/212 (5)
8/272 (8) 9/282 (10) 10/282 (9)

Bonus points – Northamptonshire 2, Middlesex 3.

In the first innings Sales, when 1, retired hurt at 14 and resumed at 117.

Bowling: *First Innings*—Cook 20–4–68–1; Clark 22–6–51–3; Peploe 14–5–46–0; Hayward 21.3–5–54–2; Dalrymple 17–5–35–1; Hutton 9–6–14–3; Shah 2–1–1–0. *Second Innings*—Cook 12–8–11–2; Clark 10–5–24–0; Hayward 14–5–30–1; Hutton 13–3–47–1; Peploe 7–3–14–0; Dalrymple 10–0–45–0; Weekes 7–1–27–0; Koenig 1–0–6–0.

Umpires: M. R. Benson and A. A. Jones.

At Canterbury, September 16, 17, 18. MIDDLESEX lost to KENT by an innings and 49 runs.

WOMBWELL CRICKET LOVERS' SOCIETY AWARDS, 2004

Andrew Strauss, the Middlesex batsman who scored a century on Test debut, was voted George Spofforth Cricketer of the Year by members of the Wombwell Cricket Lovers' Society. England leader Michael Vaughan was named Brian Sellers Captain of the Year, and also won the Dr Taylor Award for the Best Performance in Yorkshire–Lancashire Matches. Andrew Flintoff received the Denis Compton Memorial Award for Flair. Other award-winners were: C. B. Fry Young Cricketer of the Year – Ian Bell of Warwickshire; Arthur Wood Wicket-Keeper of the Year – James Foster of Essex; Les Bailey Most Promising Young Yorkshire Player – Joe Sayers; Learie Constantine Award for Best Fielder in the C&G Final – Mike Hussey of Gloucestershire; Ted Umbers Services to Yorkshire Cricket – the late Jack Sokell. The J. M. Kilburn Cricket Writers of the Year were Stephen Chalke and Derek Hodgson, and Geoffrey Boycott was the Jack Fingleton Commentator of the Year.

NORTHAMPTONSHIRE

Gone south

ANDREW RADD

Optimists – not traditionally a majority at Wantage Road – might have been disappointed at Northamptonshire's showing in 2004; for realists, it was much in line with expectations. The loss of Mike Hussey, their talisman for three seasons, Phil Jaques and Andre Nel indicated the team would struggle to hold its own in first-division cricket. They went straight down again in the County Championship, where just one win was their worst showing since 1939, and only escaped relegation in the totesport League courtesy of a last-ball victory at Canterbury in their final fixture. Interest in the knockouts was short-lived.

When he was appointed first-team manager for the 2003 season, former South African captain Kepler Wessels swiftly made clear a desire to assemble his own side, rather than rely on players inherited from his predecessors, John Emburey and Bob Carter. No surprise, then, that the most successful batsman and bowler – Usman Afzaal and Johann Louw – were Wessels's own recruits, benefiting from his total support throughout the campaign. Others were not so fortunate. Graeme Swann, a free spirit not always on the same wavelength as Wessels, turned down a new contract and joined Nottinghamshire. The under-used Adam Shantry moved to Warwickshire and Carl Greenidge to Gloucestershire, while Toby Bailey and Mark Powell were released and Craig Jennings, a talented pace bowler from the Academy, was allowed to leave after initially agreeing terms.

Swann, the club's only senior England player in a decade (and that in a solitary one-day international), wrote in his last regular column for the Northampton *Chronicle & Echo* that Northamptonshire stood "in danger of losing its identity as the county's cricket club, unless there is a conscious effort to rebuild the sense of pride and kinship for the town and people". The fact that Bailey and Powell – like Swann, county-born – were also going, coupled with Wessels's criticisms of locally produced cricketers for not taking their opportunities, caused anger and consternation in some quarters.

The rebuilding process began before the season's end. Two Australians were named as overseas players for 2005: Martin Love, who scored 394 first-class runs in two games, including twin unbeaten centuries at Worcester, after replacing Martin van Jaarsveld, and Damien Wright, who made half a dozen appearances a year earlier. Left-arm seamer Charl Pietersen and wicket-keeper/batsman Riki Wessels, Kepler's son, joined Louw as South African-born Kolpak signings. Irish all-rounder Andrew White had come on board in September, and Bilal Shafayat subsequently followed Afzaal from Trent Bridge. It left Tim Roberts as the only county-born player in the likely first-team squad – a far cry from the final Championship fixture of 2000, when the side contained half a dozen.

Wessels could point to the results as his justification. Northamptonshire's single Championship win was over Surrey, on August 1, and failed to lift them off the bottom of the first division. Five successive League defeats transformed them from title contenders to relegation candidates. Of the regular batsmen, only Afzaal and new captain David Sales could be satisfied. Afzaal topped 1,800 runs in the Championship and League combined, hit four first-class centuries and displayed a fierce commitment. Sales averaged over 60 in the Championship and formed a close

Johann Louw

working relationship with Wessels; only once, when excessive caution on the final afternoon allowed Sussex to escape with a draw, could their tactics be seriously questioned. A lack of solidity at the top of the order, where Roberts failed to convert any of his promising starts into a Championship hundred, did not help, though Tom Huggins showed promise later on.

After a slow start, Louw's old-fashioned virtues – line and length, and a big heart – brought outstanding results. His 60 first-class wickets were the most by a Northamptonshire seamer for four years, and he dismissed 34 batsmen in the League, beating Alan Hodgson's county record of 30 in 1976. Ben Phillips remained fit and turned in some handy all-round displays.

But the two potential Championship match-winners, off-spinners Swann and Jason Brown, found fewer surfaces to suit them in a wet summer, especially away from home, and proved altogether less effective than the previous season. Between them, they managed 66 Championship wickets – Brown alone had 65 in 2003 – at more than 40 apiece. In support of a limited but hard-working attack, the catching could be sadly fallible. Wessels's preference for Gerard Brophy over Bailey behind the stumps apparently owed more to his run-scoring potential than his glovework.

The winds of change rattled the windows of the committee room, too. In August, John Scopes resigned as chairman of the cricket sub-committee, concerned that it was becoming irrelevant; a review of the management structure had proposed handing effective responsibility for all playing matters to Wessels, who signed a new three-year contract, and chief executive Mark Tagg, who had succeeded Steve Coverdale in April. Officials were also left to address serious issues – financial and managerial – arising from fraud by a former employee. Susan Woodward was jailed in November for stealing £82,000 by forging cheques, and the club were suing her for the loss of nearly a quarter of a million pounds. On and off the field, Northamptonshire's future felt more than ever like a journey into the unknown.

NORTHAMPTONSHIRE RESULTS

All first-class matches – Played 17: Won 1, Lost 4, Drawn 12.
County Championship matches – Played 16: Won 1, Lost 4, Drawn 11.

Frizzell County Championship, 9th in Division 1; Cheltenham & Gloucester Trophy, q-f;
totesport League, 4th in Division 1; Twenty20 Cup, 6th in Midlands/Wales/West Group.

COUNTY CHAMPIONSHIP AVERAGES

BATTING AND FIELDING

Cap		M	I	NO	R	HS	100s	50s	Avge	Ct/St
	M. L. Love§	2	4	3	394	161*	2	1	394.00	3
1999	D. J. Sales	16	25	5	1,230	171	1	12	61.50	18
	U. Afzaal	16	28	5	1,365	167*	4	7	59.34	9
	M. van Jaarsveld§ . .	7	13	0	484	114	1	1	37.23	7
	G. L. Brophy	15	24	2	744	181	1	4	33.81	27/2
	T. B. Huggins	8	13	2	342	82*	0	2	31.09	3
	T. W. Roberts	16	29	2	748	89	0	6	27.70	10
2003	J. W. Cook	5	8	0	204	114	1	1	25.50	4
1999	G. P. Swann	13	21	0	435	54	0	1	20.71	12
	B. J. Phillips	15	21	3	327	90	0	3	18.16	2
	J. Louw§	16	22	3	342	63	0	1	18.00	8
	R. A White	4	8	0	139	52	0	1	17.37	3
	P. S. Jones	8	9	1	139	37	0	0	17.37	1
	M. J. Powell	6	11	0	190	48	0	0	17.27	1
2003	T. M. B. Bailey . . .	2	4	1	37	20	0	0	12.33	1/4
	P. C. Rofe§	5	6	4	20	15*	0	0	10.00	1
2000	J. F. Brown	13	15	6	82	34	0	0	9.11	4
	C. G. Greenidge . . .	3	4	1	13	8*	0	0	4.33	0

Also batted: C. M. Goode (1 match) 0; C. J. R. Jennings (1 match) 6; A. J. Shantry (2 matches) 2*, 0*, 5 (1 ct); A. R. White (2 matches) 22, 0.

§ *Overseas player.*

BOWLING

	O	M	R	W	BB	5W/i	Avge
J. Louw	463.3	89	1,591	60	5-44	3	26.51
B. J. Phillips	408.3	107	1,175	31	5-106	1	37.90
G. P. Swann	403.2	71	1,168	30	4-94	0	38.93
P. C. Rofe	167.5	42	505	12	4-109	0	42.08
J. F. Brown	584.3	133	1,523	36	5-113	1	42.30
P. S. Jones	220	33	792	10	3-75	0	79.20

Also bowled: U. Afzaal 51.3–7–196–4; G. L. Brophy 1–0–1–0; J. W. Cook 84–14–285–5; C. M. Goode 16–3–70–1; C. G. Greenidge 56.2–6–277–9; C. J. R. Jennings 14–3–64–1; T. W. Roberts 1–1–0–0; D. J. Sales 2–1–2–0; A. J. Shantry 35–10–110–3; M. van Jaarsveld 4–2–8–0; A. R. White 26–3–62–2; R. A. White 12–1–52–1.

COUNTY RECORDS

Highest score for:	331*	M. E. K. Hussey v Somerset at Taunton	2003
Highest score against:	333	K. S. Duleepsinhji (Sussex) at Hove	1930
Best bowling for:	10-127	V. W. C. Jupp v Kent at Tunbridge Wells	1932
Best bowling against:	10-30	C. Blythe (Kent) at Northampton	1907
Highest total for:	781-7 dec.	v Nottinghamshire at Northampton	1995
Highest total against:	670-9 dec.	by Sussex at Hove	1921
Lowest total for:	12	v Gloucestershire at Gloucester	1907
Lowest total against:	33	by Lancashire at Northampton	1977

NORTHAMPTONSHIRE DIRECTORY

ADDRESS

County Ground, Wantage Road, Northampton NN1 4TJ (01604 514455; fax 01604 514488; email post@nccc.co.uk). Website www.nccc.co.uk.

GROUNDS

Northampton (County Ground): 2 miles NE of town centre between A45 and A43. Turn L off Wellingborough Road A4500 at Abington Avenue. Nearest station: Northampton (2¼ miles).

Milton Keynes (Campbell Park): Located E of the centre and 1 mile from junction 14 of M1. The ground is on E side of Campbell Park. Turns S off H6 (A509) near V10 (A4146). Nearest station: Milton Keynes Central (1 mile).

Stowe School: 1½ miles NW of Buckingham. Take A422 Brackley Road, then R into Stowe Avenue for main entrance to school. Nearest stations: Bicester North (11½ miles), Bicester Town (12¼ miles), Milton Keynes Central (14½ miles).

OFFICIALS

Captain D. J. Sales
First-team coach K. C. Wessels
Director of academy D. J. Capel
President L. A. Wilson

Chairman S. G. Schanschieff
Chief executive M. J. Tagg
Head groundsman P. Marshall
Scorer A. C. Kingston

PLAYERS

Players expected to reappear in 2005

	Former counties	Country	Born	Birthplace
*Afzaal Usman	Notts	E	9.6.1977	Rawalpindi, Pak.
Brophy Gerard Louis		SA (EU)	26.11.1975	Welkom
Brown Jason Fred		E	10.10.1974	Newcastle-under-Lyme
Cook Jeffrey William		E	2.2.1972	Sydney, Aus.
Goode Christopher Martin		E	12.10.1984	†Kettering
Huggins Thomas Benjamin		E	6.3.1983	Peterborough
Jones Philip Steffan	Somerset	E	9.2.1974	Llanelli
Louw Johann		SA (K)	12.4.1979	Cape Town
*Love Martin Lloyd	Durham	A	30.3.1974	Mundubbera
Panesar Mudhsuden Singh		E	25.4.1982	Luton
Phillips Ben James.	Kent	E	30.9.1974	Lewisham
Roberts Timothy William	Lancs	E	4.3.1978	†Kettering
Sales David John		E	3.12.1977	Carshalton
White Andrew Roland		IRE (EU)	3.7.1980	Newtownards
White Robert Allan		E	15.10.1979	Chelmsford

Players due to join in 2005

		Country	Born	Birthplace
Pietersen Charl		SA (EU)	6.1.1983	Kimberley
Shafayat Bilal Mustapha	Notts	E	10.7.1984	Nottingham
Wessels Matthew Hendrik		A (EU)	12.11.1985	Queensland
Wright Damien Geoffrey.		A	25.7.1975	Casino

* *Test player.* † *Born in Northamptonshire.*

NORTHAMPTONSHIRE v LANCASHIRE

At Northampton, April 16, 17, 18, 19. Drawn. Northamptonshire 8 pts, Lancashire 12 pts. Toss: Lancashire. County debuts: U. Afzaal, P. S. Jones, J. Louw; D. G. Cork. Championship debut: T. B. Huggins.

The loss of the third day's play to rain cost Lancashire, pre-season Championship favourites, a likely win. Their campaign began inauspiciously when Alec Swann was pinned lbw by the third ball, but Sutcliffe and Law added 169 in 46 overs; Law's power and timing were sumptuous. Hooper also hit the ball hard in becoming the third century-maker – so hard that when Brown dropped a stinging return chance with Hooper 93, he required treatment. Northamptonshire's reply was initially built round Roberts, who came close to a maiden first-class hundred, against the club that released him in 2002. He enjoyed a reprieve on 23, the umpires disallowing an appeal for caught and bowled by Martin because the ball rebounded off the short-leg fielder's helmeted head. Northamptonshire lost their last six wickets for 51 on the final day and were forced to follow on. But the pitch was too slow, and the remaining time too short, for Lancashire to finish the job.

Close of play: First day, Lancashire 306-4 (Hooper 23, Chapple 20); Second day, Northamptonshire 142-2 (Roberts 85, Afzaal 22); Third day, No play.

Lancashire

A. J. Swann lbw b Louw	0	*†W. K. Hegg b Louw	45
I. J. Sutcliffe c Louw b Swann	104	P. J. Martin not out	2
M. J. Chilton c Brophy b Louw	46	L-b 10	10
S. G. Law c Sales b Louw	108		
C. L. Hooper c Afzaal b Swann	115	1/0 (1) 2/92 (3)	(9 wkts dec.) 504
G. Chapple b Phillips	55	3/261 (2) 4/270 (4)	
K. W. Hogg c Sales b Jones	0	5/377 (6) 6/378 (7)	
D. G. Cork b Swann	19	7/412 (8) 8/502 (9) 9/504 (5)	

G. Keedy did not bat.

Bonus points – Lancashire 5, Northamptonshire 2 (130 overs: 406-6).

Bowling: Louw 28–7–71–4; Jones 25–2–94–1; Phillips 31–6–112–1; Brown 37–7–110–0; Swann 26.2–4–95–3; Afzaal 2–0–12–0.

Northamptonshire

M. J. Powell lbw b Martin	26	– lbw b Hogg	48
T. B. Huggins c Swann b Chapple	5	– not out	38
T. W. Roberts lbw b Martin	89	– not out	15
U. Afzaal c Hooper b Hogg	51		
*D. J. Sales run out	84		
†G. L. Brophy c Sutcliffe b Hooper	17		
G. P. Swann lbw b Keedy	1		
J. Louw c Martin b Keedy	5		
B. J. Phillips c Cork b Hooper	0		
P. S. Jones not out	15		
J. F. Brown c Law b Keedy	0		
L-b 5	5	B 5, l-b 5, n-b 2	12

1/6 (2) 2/59 (1) 3/146 (3) 4/200 (4)	298	1/78 (1) (1 wkt) 113
5/247 (6) 6/248 (7) 7/260 (8)		
8/277 (9) 9/291 (5) 10/298 (11)		

Bonus points – Northamptonshire 2, Lancashire 3.

Bowling: *First Innings*—Martin 19–10–25–2; Chapple 17–5–50–1; Cork 15–3–51–0; Keedy 26.1–7–55–3; Hooper 22–10–50–2. *Second Innings*—Martin 5–1–12–0; Chapple 7–2–13–0; Hooper 12–2–19–0; Cork 2–0–13–0, Keedy 15–6–29–0; Hogg 5–0–14–1; Swann 1–0–3–0.

Umpires: N. G. Cowley and A. A. Jones.

NORTHAMPTONSHIRE v DURHAM UCCE

At Northampton, April 21, 22, 23. Drawn. Toss: Durham UCCE. First-class debuts: A. P. A. Clarke, N. J. Longhurst.

Rain washed out the first day and ruined this excuse for a contest. Both sides settled for early-season batting practice – primarily, in the students' case, of the forward defensive. They made 229 for eight in 105 overs, with William Burnell, a Northamptonshire trialist in 2003, and the Essex all-rounder Justin Bishop defying a below-strength county attack, which featured the seldom-seen spin of Roberts and White. Powell, leading Northamptonshire for the first time, then reached 49 as partners came and went in lacklustre procession. Swann provided welcome enterprise.

Close of play: First day, No play; Second day, Durham UCCE 229-8 (Howells 25, Daggett 0).

Durham UCCE

M. A. P. Dale c and b Cawdron	16	– not out	9
W. F. Burnell c Swann b Greenidge	49	– lbw b Anderson	7
*W. R. Smith c Powell b Cook	7	– not out	5
D. O. Brown c Bailey b Cook	0		
S. C. Hollingsworth c Bailey b White	30		
J. E. Bishop c Roberts b Anderson	66		
N. J. Longhurst c and b Roberts	29		
A. P. A. Clarke lbw b White	0		
†P. W. Howells not out	25		
L. M. Daggett not out	0		
B 1, l-b 3, w 1, n-b 2	7	W 1	1

1/29 (1) 2/38 (3) 3/38 (4) (8 wkts dec.) 229   1/17 (2) (1 wkt) 22
4/98 (2) 5/111 (5) 6/166 (7)
7/177 (8) 8/221 (6)

E. J. Carpenter did not bat.

Bowling: *First Innings*—Greenidge 22–6–58–1; Cawdron 20–7–46–1; Anderson 16–3–43–1; Cook 15–5–22–2; White 20–5–46–2; Roberts 12–6–10–1. *Second Innings*—Greenidge 5–2–11–0; Anderson 5–0–11–1.

Northamptonshire

*M. J. Powell c Howells b Brown	49	R. S. G. Anderson not out	33
T. B. Huggins b Daggett	13		
J. W. Cook b Brown	18	L-b 3, w 1, n-b 6	10
R. A. White c and b Bishop	19		
G. L. Brophy c and b Bishop	0	1/24 (2) 2/69 (3) (6 wkts dec.) 244	
G. P. Swann c Carpenter b Daggett	50	3/104 (4) 4/104 (5)	
†T. M. B. Bailey not out	52	5/112 (1) 6/176 (6)	

T. W. Roberts, M. J. Cawdron and C. G. Greenidge did not bat.

Bowling: Bishop 17–5–52–2; Daggett 12–1–51–2; Brown 14–3–48–2; Carpenter 17–6–32–0; Smith 14–1–39–0; Clarke 5.4–1–19–0.

Umpires: M. R. Benson and D. J. Constant.

At The Oval, April 28, 29, 30, May 1. NORTHAMPTONSHIRE drew with SURREY.

NORTHAMPTONSHIRE v SUSSEX

At Northampton, May 7, 8, 9, 10. Drawn. Northamptonshire 12 pts, Sussex 9 pts. Toss: Northamptonshire. Championship debut: M. van Jaarsveld.

Northamptonshire's caution on the last afternoon, when captain and coach seemed unwilling to back their bowlers, allowed the champions Sussex to escape. Sales delayed his declaration until

20 minutes before tea, leaving Sussex to make 299 or, more realistically, survive a minimum of 39 overs. Sussex lost Ward first ball to a full toss, and Brown took three wickets in five overs as the collapse became embarrassing – to both sides, after Sussex's eighth-wicket pair clung on. In the first innings, Northamptonshire had rallied from 186 for seven in fine style: Afzaal spent eight hours 22 minutes building a career-best 167. Phillips provided not just support, but the lion's share of a 136-run eighth-wicket stand. Ward's first century for Sussex restricted the deficit to 106.

Close of play: First day, Northamptonshire 294-7 (Afzaal 102, Phillips 58); Second day, Northamptonshire 387-9 (Afzaal 157, Brown 0); Third day, Northamptonshire 6-0 (Powell 6, Roberts 0).

Northamptonshire

M. J. Powell c Ambrose b Lewry	4	– b Martin-Jenkins	15
T. W. Roberts c Ambrose b Lewry	1	– lbw b Mohammad Akram	10
M. van Jaarsveld lbw b Mushtaq Ahmed	37	– lbw b Mushtaq Ahmed	27
U. Afzaal not out	167	– c Adams b Davis	25
*D. J. Sales lbw b Mushtaq Ahmed	27	– not out	72
G. P. Swann c Ward b Davis	54	– c Adams b Mushtaq Ahmed	40
†G. L. Brophy c and b Davis	4	– not out	0
J. Louw b Davis	0		
B. J. Phillips b Lewry	73		
P. S. Jones b Mushtaq Ahmed	12		
J. F. Brown not out	1		
B 9, l-b 11	20	L-b 1, n-b 2	3

1/2 (2) 2/19 (1) 3/56 (3)   (9 wkts dec.) 400
4/90 (5) 5/178 (6) 6/186 (7)
7/186 (8) 8/322 (9) 9/382 (10)

1/27 (2) 2/27 (1)   (5 wkts dec.) 192
3/68 (4) 4/92 (3) 5/192 (6)

Bonus points – Northamptonshire 5, Sussex 3.

Bowling: *First Innings*—Mohammad Akram 33.5–4–105–0; Lewry 25–8–78–3; Mushtaq Ahmed 32–6–119–3; Martin-Jenkins 19–6–44–0; Davis 19–5–34–3. *Second Innings*—Mohammad Akram 9–3–32–1; Lewry 9–4–23–0; Martin Jenkins 12–6–22–1; Mushtaq Ahmed 17–4–49–2; Davis 12–0–55–1; Adams 1 0–10–0.

Sussex

I. J. Ward c Louw b Swann	115	– b Louw	0
R. R. Montgomerie c van Jaarsveld b Brown	9	– c van Jaarsveld b Phillips	13
M. W. Goodwin b Brown	3	– c van Jaarsveld b Jones	21
*C. J. Adams st Brophy b Swann	11	– c Powell b Brown	15
†T. R. Ambrose c Sales b Swann	12	– c van Jaarsveld b Phillips	1
R. S. C. Martin-Jenkins c Sales b Brown	51	– c van Jaarsveld b Brown	1
M. J. Prior c Brophy b Swann	32	– lbw b Brown	6
M. J. G. Davis lbw b Brown	6	– not out	11
Mushtaq Ahmed lbw b Jones	27	– not out	1
Mohammad Akram run out	19		
J. D. Lewry not out	1		
B 4, l-b 4	8		

1/47 (2) 2/57 (3) 3/74 (4) 4/96 (5)   294
5/183 (1) 6/231 (6) 7/247 (7)
8/251 (8) 9/290 (9) 10/294 (10)

1/0 (1) 2/29 (3) 3/43 (2)   (7 wkts) 69
4/47 (5) 5/50 (6)
6/55 (4) 7/62 (7)

Bonus points – Sussex 2, Northamptonshire 3.

Bowling: *First Innings*—Jones 13–1–51–1; Louw 5.2–1–24–0; Phillips 12–6–24–0; Brown 39–6–93–4; Swann 34–6–94–4. *Second Innings*—Louw 6–0–19–1; Jones 5–3–11–1; Brown 16.4–6–20–3; Phillips 7–1–9–2; Swann 9–5–10–0.

Umpires: T. E. Jesty and N. A. Mallender.

At Bristol, May 12, 13, 14, 15. NORTHAMPTONSHIRE drew with GLOUCESTERSHIRE.

NORTHAMPTONSHIRE v KENT

At Northampton, May 19, 20, 21, 22. Kent won by 145 runs. Kent 19 pts, Northamptonshire 5 pts. Toss: Kent.

The extra speed of Mohammad Sami, who took ten for 138 in the match, proved decisive: although Northamptonshire dug in on a tired last-day pitch, they fell 13 overs short of a draw. Sami's first wicket of the game – van Jaarsveld gloving a rapid lifter to slip – set the tone, and he took three more, all beaten for pace, inside six deliveries in the first innings. In the second, he removed both openers during an awkward session on the third evening, then picked off van Jaarsveld's three most obstinate partners on the last day; van Jaarsveld himself occupied the crease for 91 dogged overs before hitting his wicket trying to cut. On the first day, the fall of Symonds, who hit a brutal 107, began a landslide – six Kent wickets in 13 overs. But they still managed a slender lead, which Key and Fulton turned into a formidable one in the second innings. They shared an opening stand of 222, Key hitting 173 before being caught attempting his fifth six. Another Symonds flourish and a declaration left Northamptonshire staring at 410 to win. Kent's third win in four games put them top of the Championship.

Close of play: First day, Northamptonshire 115-1 (Roberts 64, van Jaarsveld 42); Second day, Kent 103-0 (Fulton 50, Key 45); Third day, Northamptonshire 39-2 (van Jaarsveld 18, Louw 0).

Kent

*D. P. Fulton c Brophy b Louw	6	– b Afzaal	109
R. W. T. Key b Louw	16	– c Louw b Greenidge	173
E. T. Smith run out	35	– c Roberts b Swann	1
A. Symonds b Swann	107	– c Roberts b Afzaal	61
M. J. Walker c Brophy b Swann	8	– b Greenidge	21
M. A. Carberry lbw b Louw	22	– (7) not out	8
M. M. Patel c Sales b Louw	10	– (6) c Brown b Afzaal	11
†N. J. O'Brien not out	32		
J. C. Tredwell lbw b Swann	11		
M. J. Saggers run out	5		
Mohammad Sami c Louw b Brown	0		
L-b 2	2	B 2, l-b 9, w 2, n-b 8	21

1/22 (1) 2/25 (2) 3/120 (3) 4/142 (5)   254   1/222 (1) 2/223 (3)   (6 wkts dec.) 405
5/191 (4) 6/197 (6) 7/206 (7)   3/334 (5) 4/381 (2)
8/239 (9) 9/246 (10) 10/254 (11)   5/393 (5) 6/405 (6)

Bonus points – Kent 2, Northamptonshire 3.

Bowling: *First Innings*—Louw 11–4–33–4; Greenidge 7–0–48–0; Phillips 6–2–15–0; Brown 24.3–4–75–1; Swann 24–4–81–3. *Second Innings*—Louw 20–3–82–0; Greenidge 12–0–79–2; Phillips 10–1–36–0; Brown 21–2–69–0; Swann 27–6–63–1; Afzaal 15.1–1–65–3.

> **❝**Umpire Mallender earned himself the nickname 'Muddy' (pronounced the Yorkshire way, to rhyme with 'woody'), a reference to his usual comment on the state of the outfield.**❞**
>
> Bangladeshis in Zimbabwe, page 1149.

Northamptonshire

	First innings		Second innings	
M. J. Powell c O'Brien b Saggers	5	– c O'Brien b Mohammad Sami.	13
T. W. Roberts b Mohammad Sami	69	– b Mohammad Sami.	0
M. van Jaarsveld c Fulton b Mohammad Sami	46	– hit wkt b Patel	114
U. Afzaal c Walker b Patel	7	– (5) c Walker b Patel	11
*D. J. Sales c Key b Patel	70	– (6) lbw b Patel	12
G. P. Swann b Mohammad Sami	5	– (7) lbw b Mohammad Sami	42
†G. L. Brophy b Mohammad Sami	4	– (8) c Smith b Mohammad Sami	6
J. Louw c Mohammad Sami b Patel	8	– (4) lbw b Mohammad Sami	19
B. J. Phillips c O'Brien b Symonds	4	– c O'Brien b Mohammad Sami.	2
C. G. Greenidge not out	8	– b Saggers	5
J. F. Brown c Saggers b Symonds	11	– not out	4
B 5, l-b 3, w 1, n-b 4	13	B 8, l-b 14, w 6, n-b 8	36
	250		**264**

1/7 (1) 2/123 (3) 3/132 (2) 4/136 (4)
5/143 (6) 6/147 (7) 7/181 (8)
8/219 (9) 9/231 (5) 10/250 (11)

1/1 (2) 2/30 (1) 3/117 (4)
4/134 (5) 5/167 (6) 6/243 (7)
7/250 (3) 8/253 (9)
9/260 (8) 10/264 (10)

Bonus points – Northamptonshire 2, Kent 3.

Bowling: *First Innings*—Mohammad Sami 22–6–39–4; Saggers 15–4–34–1; Symonds 13.5–3–44–2; Patel 28–6–81–3; Tredwell 14–1–44–0. *Second Innings*—Mohammad Sami 31–11–99–6; Saggers 14–6–18–1; Tredwell 20–6–55–0; Patel 26–8–50–3; Symonds 9–3–20–0.

Umpires: A. Clarkson and P. J. Hartley.

At Hove, May 25, 26, 27, 28. NORTHAMPTONSHIRE drew with SUSSEX.

NORTHAMPTONSHIRE v WORCESTERSHIRE

At Northampton, June 2, 3, 4, 5. Worcestershire won by nine wickets. Worcestershire 19 pts, Northamptonshire 3 pts. Toss: Northamptonshire.

An anxious feeling of déjà vu troubled Wantage Road as a spin-friendly wicket brought an ECB pitch inspection. In the same fixture the previous year, Northamptonshire were deducted eight points for a "poor" pitch; any repeat would have meant a 12-point penalty. But the guidelines on turning wickets had been liberalised and, late on the second day, inspector Phil Sharpe decided no action was necessary. By then Worcestershire had already taken a firm grip thanks to Batty who, despite a sore spinning finger, produced a career-best seven for 52, including a spell of four wickets in eight balls either side of lunch on the first day, which reduced Northamptonshire to 123 for six. A solid response, led by Peters, gave Worcestershire a lead of 115. Though Afzaal dug in for Northamptonshire, too many others were careless when application was needed. After three and three-quarter hours' resistance Afzaal fell to Solanki -- his first Championship wicket for nearly four years – and Worcestershire were left chasing 150. Moore and Hick blunted the spinners and carefully saw them home 50 minutes into the final morning.

Close of play: First day, Worcestershire 119-1 (Peters 63, Hick 30); Second day, Northamptonshire 63-1 (Roberts 18, van Jaarsveld 8); Third day, Worcestershire 97-1 (Moore 47, Hick 32).

Northamptonshire

T. B. Huggins st Rhodes b Batty	51	– (2) c Smith b Batty	17
T. W. Roberts b Batty	30	– (1) lbw b Mason	22
M. van Jaarsveld c Smith b Batty	13	– c Rhodes b Batty	28
U. Afzaal c Moore b Mason	32	– b Solanki	57
*D. J. Sales b Batty	0	– c Solanki b Kabir Ali	22
G. P. Swann c Solanki b Batty	2	– c Moore b Kabir Ali	6
†G. L. Brophy b Batty	0	– c Smith b Khalid	25
J. Louw c Kabir Ali b Khalid	11	– c Solanki b Bichel	28
B. J. Phillips c Hick b Khalid	1	– c Solanki b Bichel	4
A. J. Shantry not out	2	– not out	0
J. F. Brown c Hick b Batty	21	– c and b Batty	3
L-b 2, n-b 12	14	B 30, l-b 3, w 1, n-b 18	52

1/56 (2) 2/88 (3) 3/113 (1) 4/113 (5) 177
5/123 (6) 6/123 (7) 7/141 (4)
8/153 (9) 9/154 (8) 10/177 (11)

1/45 (2) 2/67 (1) 3/99 (3) 264
4/140 (5) 5/156 (6) 6/208 (7)
7/239 (4) 8/258 (9)
9/261 (8) 10/264 (11)

Bonus points – Worcestershire 3.

Bowling: *First Innings*—Bichel 13–4–54–0; Kabir Ali 4–0–21–0; Batty 27–10–52–7; Mason 14–5–28–1; Khalid 9–2–20–2. *Second Innings*—Bichel 16–4–42–2; Mason 16–4–34–1; Batty 34.4–11–61–3; Kabir Ali 6–0–26–2; Khalid 20–4–53–1; Solanki 6–0–15–1.

Worcestershire

S. D. Peters lbw b Swann	63	– c Brophy b Phillips	8
S. C. Moore c Huggins b Brown	18	– not out	66
G. A. Hick b Swann	34	– not out	63
*B. F. Smith c van Jaarsveld b Swann	46		
V. S. Solanki run out	32		
G. J. Batty b Brown	36		
A. J. Bichel c and b Swann	21		
Kabir Ali lbw b Louw	24		
†S. J. Rhodes b Phillips	7		
M. S. Mason c Brophy b Shantry	1		
S. A. Khalid not out	1		
B 5, w 2, n-b 2	9	B 4, l-b 5, w 2, n-b 4	15

1/50 (2) 2/123 (3) 3/124 (1) 4/180 (5) 292
5/229 (4) 6/243 (6) 7/267 (7)
8/283 (9) 9/284 (10) 10/292 (8)

1/20 (1) (1 wkt) 152

Bonus points – Worcestershire 2, Northamptonshire 3.

Bowling: *First Innings*—Shantry 12–4–34–1; Louw 8.3–2–18–1; Swann 41–9–111–4; Brown 22–4–83–2; Phillips 20–7–41–1. *Second Innings*—Shantry 2–0–9–0; Phillips 5–1–14–1; Swann 22–1–51–0; Brown 19–5–38–0; Afzaal 6.5–1–31–0.

Umpires: V. A. Holder and A. G. T. Whitehead.

At Birmingham, June 9, 10, 11, 12. NORTHAMPTONSHIRE lost to WARWICKSHIRE by eight wickets.

At Northampton, June 20. NORTHAMPTONSHIRE lost to NEW ZEALANDERS by five runs (D/L method) (see New Zealand tour section).

At Liverpool, June 26, 27, 28, 29. NORTHAMPTONSHIRE drew with LANCASHIRE.

NORTHAMPTONSHIRE v SURREY

At Northampton, July 29, 30, 31, August 1. Northamptonshire won by six wickets. Northamptonshire 20 pts, Surrey 8 pts. Toss: Surrey.

A tussle between the bottom two sides kept alive Northamptonshire's hopes of avoiding relegation, and left Surrey – champions three times in five seasons – in peril. On a turning pitch, spinners Brown and Swann were bowling in tandem on the first morning, and Surrey were indebted to Ramprakash, whose 70th first-class century was a gem. Decisive footwork and some bold hitting over the top yielded a six and 19 fours in 282 balls. Even though the last five wickets fell for 46, Northamptonshire were still 140 behind when Doshi claimed their ninth wicket – his fourth – on the second evening. Then Sales and Brown added 70 vital runs. Surrey's confidence evaporated, and irresolute batting produced their lowest total of the season. Greenidge removed the openers, Ramprakash fell second ball, and the spinners did the rest. Roberts and White took Northamptonshire halfway to a target of 218, and their first Championship victory of 2004 was completed with two sessions to spare. It was a sad exit for Hollioake; this turned out to be his last first-class match before retirement.

Close of play: First day, Surrey 382-6 (Azhar Mahmood 21, Salisbury 13); Second day, Northamptonshire 304-9 (Sales 50, Brown 17); Third day, Northamptonshire 137-2 (Love 8, Bailey 7).

Surrey

S. A. Newman st Bailey b Brown	28	– lbw b Greenidge	4
R. Clarke c Roberts b Greenidge	11	– c Love b Greenidge	5
M. R. Ramprakash b Greenidge	161	– b Louw	0
J. G. E. Benning b Brown	2	– c Love b Brown	33
*†J. N. Batty st Bailey b Brown	61	– b Brown	4
A. J. Hollioake lbw b Louw	76	– b Brown	1
Azhar Mahmood run out	21	– c White b Brown	21
I. D. K. Salisbury b Brown	17	– c White b Swann	24
J. Ormond c White b Louw	15	– st Bailey b Swann	19
N. D. Doshi lbw b Brown	0	– st Bailey b Swann	20
P. J. Sampson not out	0	– not out	11
L-b 8, n-b 2	10	B 1, l-b 4	5
	402		**147**

1/18 (2) 2/55 (1) 3/57 (4) 4/237 (5)   402   1/5 (1) 2/10 (3) 3/18 (2) 4/46 (5)   147
5/328 (3) 6/356 (6) 7/382 (7)   5/51 (4) 6/52 (6) 7/87 (7)
8/392 (8) 9/402 (10) 10/402 (9)   8/109 (8) 9/134 (9) 10/147 (10)

Bonus points – Surrey 5, Northamptonshire 3.

Bowling: First Innings—Louw 17.1–1–68–2; Greenidge 12–1–66–2; Brown 47–10–113–5; Phillips 20–6– 46–0; Swann 20–3–76–0; White 4–0–25–0. *Second Innings*—Louw 6–1–28–1; Greenidge 5–1–13–2; Brown 23–5–51–4; Swann 22.3–2–50–3.

Northamptonshire

T. W. Roberts b Doshi	57	– c and b Azhar Mahmood	64
R. A. White lbw b Ormond	9	– b Ramprakash	52
M. L. Love c Ormond b Doshi	51	– not out	49
U. Afzaal c Batty b Salisbury	29	– (6) not out	16
*D. J. Sales not out	61		
G. P. Swann c Batty b Ormond	37	– (5) c Benning b Doshi	1
J. Louw b Azhar Mahmood	11		
B. J. Phillips b Azhar Mahmood	1		
†T. M. B. Bailey lbw b Doshi	4	– (4) lbw b Ramprakash	20
C. G. Greenidge c Hollioake b Doshi	0		
J. F. Brown c Clarke b Azhar Mahmood	34		
B 25, l-b 7, n-b 6	38	B 11, l-b 1, n-b 6	18
	332		**(4 wkts) 220**

1/20 (2) 2/124 (3) 3/147 (1) 4/179 (4)   332   1/111 (1) 2/125 (2)   (4 wkts) 220
5/235 (6) 6/252 (7) 7/254 (8)   3/161 (4) 4/162 (5)
8/262 (9) 9/262 (10) 10/332 (11)

Bonus points – Northamptonshire 3, Surrey 3.

Bowling: *First Innings*—Azhar Mahmood 22.4–5–46–3; Ormond 28–8–90–2; Sampson 2–0–14–0; Clarke 1–0–5–0; Doshi 31–6–103–4; Salisbury 15–2–42–1. *Second Innings*—Ormond 13.5–3–56–0; Azhar Mahmood 8–2–27–1; Hollioake 3–0–11–0; Doshi 27–7–58–1; Salisbury 7–0–21–0; Ramprakash 16–3–35–2.

Umpires: J. H. Hampshire and P. J. Hartley.

At Worcester, August 11, 12, 13, 14. NORTHAMPTONSHIRE drew with WORCESTERSHIRE.

NORTHAMPTONSHIRE v MIDDLESEX

At Northampton, August 18, 19, 20, 21. Drawn. Northamptonshire 9 pts, Middlesex 10 pts. Toss: Middlesex. County debuts: P. C. Rofe; S. R. Clark.

The talking point of the match came on the second afternoon, when Cook could have been out in three different ways off the same delivery from Louw. It struck the pad and, evidently, something else, then flew to Swann in the slips. Umpire Constant initially turned down an enquiry for lbw, while Swann threw down the stumps, with Cook possibly out of his ground. Then the captain, Sales, appealed for a catch, which was upheld after the umpires conferred. Rain, which docked 59 overs during the first and third days, coupled with a slow, lifeless pitch frustrated both sides. Hutton's fifth hundred of the summer occupied six and a half hours and carried him past 1,000 runs in a season for the first time, but the solid Afzaal batted even longer, sharing century partnerships with Sales and Louw to avert the follow-on. Middlesex batted more positively second time round, thanks to a cultured hundred from Shah. Joyce was not about to gamble, though, and left Northamptonshire a target of 267 in 48 overs. With Afzaal forced down the order by a hand injury, it was beyond them.

Close of play: First day, Middlesex 182-2 (Hutton 88, Peploe 0); Second day, Northamptonshire 89-3 (Afzaal 39, Sales 35); Third day, Middlesex 41-1 (Koenig 20, Shah 19).

Middlesex

B. L. Hutton c Swann b Louw	100	– c Swann b Louw		1
S. G. Koenig lbw b Rofe	28	– c Brophy b Louw		22
O. A. Shah c Brophy b Swann	62	– c Phillips b Rofe		100
C. T. Peploe lbw b Swann	4			
*E. C. Joyce c Afzaal b Phillips	23	– (4) lbw b Louw		0
P. N. Weekes c Sales b Phillips	44	– (5) b Louw		51
J. W. M. Dalrymple lbw b Louw	2	– (6) b Louw		11
†B. J. M. Scott c Brophy b Brown	31	– (7) not out		22
S. J. Cook c Swann b Louw	13			
S. R. Clark c Afzaal b Louw	34			
M. Hayward not out	0			
L-b 4	4	B 2, l-b 5, n-b 2		9

1/45 (2) 2/182 (3) 3/198 (4) 4/198 (1)   345   1/3 (1) 2/56 (2)   (6 wkts dec.) 216
5/257 (6) 6/260 (7) 7/272 (5)   3/56 (4) 4/159 (3)
8/303 (9) 9/337 (8) 10/345 (10)   5/185 (6) 6/216 (5)

Bonus points – Middlesex 3, Northamptonshire 3.

Bowling: *First Innings*—Louw 31.3–7–110–4; Rofe 24–6–66–1; Phillips 23–7–38–2; Brown 24–5–76–1; Swann 20–5–49–2; White 2–1–2–0. *Second Innings*—Rofe 12–3–38–1; Louw 12.5–2–44–5; Brown 17–3–50–0; Swann 12–0–50–0; Phillips 9–2–27–0.

Northamptonshire

T. W. Roberts c Joyce b Hayward	1	– run out	46
R. A. White b Cook	0	– c Shah b Hayward	3
M. J. Powell c and b Peploe	14	– b Peploe	0
U. Afzaal lbw b Hayward	111	– (8) c Joyce b Peploe	6
*D. J. Sales c Shah b Peploe	57	– (4) not out	73
†G. L. Brophy b Dalrymple	1	– st Scott b Cook	11
G. P. Swann c Hutton b Clark	32	– c Hutton b Hayward	2
B. J. Phillips c Scott b Clark	10	– (9) not out	0
J. Louw b Hayward	63	– (5) b Dalrymple	8
P. C. Rofe not out	0		
J. F. Brown b Hayward	0		
L-b 6	6	B 4, n-b 2	6

1/1 (1) 2/1 (2) 3/24 (3) 4/131 (5)   295   1/20 (2) 2/31 (3) 3/80 (1)   (7 wkts) 155
5/132 (6) 6/173 (7) 7/185 (8)   4/112 (5) 5/133 (6)
8/286 (4) 9/295 (9) 10/295 (11)   6/138 (7) 7/153 (8)

Bonus points — Northamptonshire 2, Middlesex 3.

Bowling: *First Innings*—Cook 23–6–53–1; Hayward 19.3–4–62–4; Peploe 28–10–66–2; Clark 19–5–47–2; Dalrymple 18–6–48–1; Weekes 2–0–13–0. *Second Innings*—Cook 9–2–16–1; Hayward 13–5–36–2; Peploe 10.4–2–43–2; Clark 7–1–21–0; Dalrymple 8–0–35–1.

Umpires: D. J. Constant and P. Willey.

NORTHAMPTONSHIRE v GLOUCESTERSHIRE

At Northampton, August 24, 25, 26, 27. Drawn. Northamptonshire 8 pts, Gloucestershire 8 pts. Toss: Gloucestershire.

A dour contest fizzled out when a target of 290 in 68 overs failed to tempt Gloucestershire, due to contest the C&G Trophy final the following day. Some early moisture in the pitch had persuaded Taylor to bowl, which paid off as his seamers reduced Northamptonshire to 45 for four, but Afzaal and Brophy led the recovery either side of a lengthy rain break. Afzaal was ninth out after a hard-working stay of six hours 20 minutes, as the last five wickets fell for 32. Gloucestershire also struggled, despite a solid 78 from Hussey on his return to Northampton, his home ground over the previous three seasons and the scene of so many personal triumphs. He eventually became Cook's third victim in the space of 18 deliveries, though Ball and Lewis earned a slender lead with a last-wicket stand of 55. Northamptonshire then produced the most fluent batting of the match; Afzaal completed a 190-ball century after his first-innings near miss, and Sales was able to declare. But Gloucestershire soon lost interest.

Close of play: First day, Northamptonshire 164-5 (Afzaal 70, Swann 17); Second day, Gloucestershire 129-5 (Hussey 58, Averis 0); Third day, Northamptonshire 236-3 (Afzaal 76, Sales 39).

Northamptonshire

T. W. Roberts b Lewis	7	– c Adshead b Lewis	33
J. W. Cook c Hussey b Averis	2	– c Adshead b Sillence	23
T. B. Huggins b Averis	0	– c Spearman b Ball	45
U. Afzaal c Adshead b Lewis	96	– not out	100
*D. J. Sales c Fisher b Sillence	10	– not out	82
†G. L. Brophy c Lewis b Fisher	34		
G. P. Swann c Averis b Fisher	29		
J. Louw c Hussey b Fisher	13		
B. J. Phillips c Adshead b Averis	1		
P. C. Rofe not out	0		
J. F. Brown c Adshead b Lewis	0		
B 3, l-b 8, w 1, n-b 18	30	B 5, l-b 9, n-b 10	24

1/14 (2) 2/14 (1) 3/24 (3) 4/45 (5)   222   1/56 (1) 2/64 (2)   (3 wkts dec.) 307
5/133 (6) 6/190 (7) 7/216 (8)   3/166 (3)
8/222 (9) 9/222 (4) 10/222 (11)

Bonus points – Northamptonshire 1, Gloucestershire 3.

Bowling: *First Innings*—Lewis 23.2–6–64–3; Averis 13–7–25–3; Sillence 14–4–33–1; Gidman 2.2–1–5–0; Fisher 31–11–63–3; Hussey 2–1–6–0; Ball 10–3–15–0. *Second Innings*—Lewis 12–0–62–1; Averis 18–1–84–0; Sillence 7–3–19–1; Fisher 16–2–55–0; Gidman 11–3–33–0; Ball 12–2–40–1.

Gloucestershire

W. P. C. Weston lbw b Louw	2	– (2) c Sales b Louw	6
C. M. Spearman c Brophy b Louw	20	– (1) c Afzaal b Brown	69
M. E. K. Hussey c Sales b Cook	78	– not out	49
*C. G. Taylor c Huggins b Phillips	20	– c Brophy b Brown	2
†S. J. Adshead c Swann b Louw	6	– (6) not out	13
I. D. Fisher lbw b Brown	17		
J. M. M. Averis c and b Brown	23		
A. P. R. Gidman c Brophy b Cook	1	– (5) lbw b Swann	13
R. J. Sillence c Brophy b Cook	4		
M. C. J. Ball not out	31		
J. Lewis c Brophy b Phillips	29		
L-b 3, n-b 6	9	B 3, l-b 1, n-b 4	8

1/12 (1) 2/29 (2) 3/79 (4) 4/92 (5) 240   1/33 (2) 2/96 (1)   (4 wkts) 160
5/123 (6) 6/171 (7) 7/176 (8)   3/105 (4) 4/138 (5)
8/180 (9) 9/185 (3) 10/240 (11)

Bonus points – Gloucestershire 1, Northamptonshire 3.

Bowling: *First Innings*—Louw 27–4–90–3; Rofe 17–4–58–0; Phillips 21.2–11–32–2; Cook 12–4–42–3; Brown 14–8–14–2; Swann 1–0–1–0. *Second Innings*—Louw 11–1–35–1; Rofe 11–6–20–0; Phillips 7–1–37–0; Brown 23–4–50–2; Swann 9–2–14–1; Cook 1–1–0–0.

Umpires: B. Dudleston and J. H. Evans.

At Canterbury, September 3, 4, 5, 6. NORTHAMPTONSHIRE lost to KENT by 194 runs.

At Lord's, September 9, 10, 11, 12. NORTHAMPTONSHIRE drew with MIDDLESEX.

NORTHAMPTONSHIRE v WARWICKSHIRE

At Northampton, September 16, 17, 18, 19. Drawn. Northamptonshire 9 pts, Warwickshire 9 pts. Toss: Warwickshire. Championship debuts: N. A. Warren, I. J. Westwood.

Warwickshire had plenty to celebrate. The match itself lacked sparkle – one side already champions, the other already relegated, and a full day lost to rain didn't help – but they received their trophy on the first evening and completed the Championship programme unbeaten. They were, however, dismissed for less than 300 for the first time. Northamptonshire threatened to embarrass them at 69 for five, but Dougie Brown continued to show his fighting qualities in his third hundred of the summer, with 22 fours in 172 balls. He shared the honours with Louw, who finished with 33 wickets in his last six games. Northamptonshire were denied a first-innings lead when six wickets tumbled for 35 to Championship debutant Nick Warren and – inevitably – Brown, who completed only the fourth five-wicket haul by a Warwickshire bowler in 2004. He hoped to reach 1,000 runs, too, but a second-innings duck left him 43 short. By then, the game was effectively dead and buried. There was time for Irish off-spinner Andrew White to claim his first two Championship victims as the season ended in an 11th draw for both teams: top-of-the-class, and dunces.

Close of play: First day, Warwickshire 276-8 (Brown 95, Streak 8); Second day, No play; Third day, Northamptonshire 233-7 (Sales 48, Louw 1).

Warwickshire

M. A. Wagh c Brophy b Louw	7	– b Phillips	19
I. J. Westwood c Brophy b Louw	3	– c Louw b White	38
I. R. Bell c Cook b Rofe	24	– (4) lbw b Brown	1
I. J. L. Trott b Brown	15	– (5) not out	38
*N. V. Knight b Louw	20	– (6) b White	3
M. J. Powell lbw b Cook	49	– (7) not out	5
J. O. Troughton c Sales b Brown	27		
D. R. Brown not out	108	– (3) c Afzaal b Phillips	0
†T. Frost b Phillips	23		
H. H. Streak b Louw	14		
N. A. Warren b Louw	0		
B 3, n-b 2	5	L-b 3, n-b 2	5

1/5 (2) 2/18 (1) 3/43 (3) 4/69 (5)   295   1/36 (1) 2/36 (3)   (5 wkts) 109
5/69 (4) 6/115 (7) 7/197 (6)   3/37 (4) 4/87 (2) 5/96 (6)
8/246 (9) 9/295 (10) 10/295 (11)

Bonus points – Warwickshire 2, Northamptonshire 3.

Bowling: *First Innings*— Louw 20.4–2–93–5; Rofe 28–9–63–1; Phillips 19–11–36–1; Brown 35–11–67–2; Cook 7–1–23–1; White 3–0–10–0. *Second Innings*—Louw 7–2–18–0; Rofe 3–2–2–0; Brown 26–8–47–1; Phillips 8–3–10–2; White 15–3–19–2; Sales 2–1–2–0; Afzaal 2.3–1–7–0; Roberts 1–1–0–0; Brophy 1–0–1–0.

Northamptonshire

T. W. Roberts c Wagh b Brown	46	P. C. Rofe c Bell b Brown	4
T. B. Huggins b Brown	34	J. F. Brown lbw b Brown	0
J. W. Cook lbw b Trott	51		
U. Afzaal c Frost b Wagh	19		
*D. J. Sales not out	72	L-b 6, w 1, n-b 4	11
†G. L. Brophy b Warren	23		
A. R. White lbw b Warren	0	1/79 (1) 2/84 (2) 3/129 (4)	265
B. J. Phillips c Frost b Warren	0	4/189 (3) 5/230 (6) 6/230 (7)	
J. Louw c Frost b Brown	5	7/232 (8) 8/255 (9)	
		9/265 (10) 10/265 (11)	

Bonus points – Northamptonshire 2, Warwickshire 3.

Bowling: Streak 17–?–62–0; Brown 20.3–3–53–5; Warren 17–3–60–3; Bell 5–2–17–0; Wagh 10–2–37–1; Troughton 3–0–10–0; Trott 8–1–20–1.

Umpires: D. J. Constant and B. Leadbeater.

COUNTY CAPS AWARDED IN 2004

Derbyshire	A. G. Botha, Hassan Adnan, J. Moss.
Essex	A. R. Adams, Danish Kaneria, D. Gough.
Hampshire	M. J. Clarke, C. T. Tremlett.
Lancashire	D. G. Cork.
Middlesex	J. W. M. Dalrymple.
Nottinghamshire	M. A. Ealham, D. J. Hussey, R. J. Sidebottom, R. J. Warren.
Surrey	Azhar Mahmood.
Sussex	Mohammad Akram, I. J. Ward.
Worcestershire*	M. N. Malik, R. W. Price.
Yorkshire	R. K. J. Dawson.

Worcestershire have replaced caps with colours awarded to all Championship players.
   No caps were awarded by Durham, Glamorgan, Kent, Leicestershire, Northamptonshire or Warwickshire.
   Gloucestershire and Somerset have abandoned the traditional system of awarding caps.

NOTTINGHAMSHIRE

A great year for the Gallian battalion

Paul Fearn

At the AGM in February 2004, Nottinghamshire's director of cricket, Mick Newell, announced his target for the season: promotion in both league competitions. Not many believed it possible. The county's form of 2003 had been miserable, and plenty of supporters dismissed Newell's talk as morale-boosting bluster. But by September his predictions had proved astute rather than overambitious.

A key part of Newell's strategy was to bring in what he called "winning characters": the all-rounder Mark Ealham from Kent, the batsman Anurag Singh from Worcestershire and the left-arm seamer Ryan Sidebottom from Yorkshire. It worked: Nottinghamshire *did* win far more matches, and each newcomer contributed. But so did the existing staff, who had struggled through 2003.

The team gelled best in the Championship, where they dominated Division Two. The triumph was built on batting, which was some turnaround from 2003 when the county's slide to eight for seven against Essex summed up a lean year. By contrast, Nottinghamshire had a reasonable claim to be the strongest batting side of the 2004 Championship: they won 66 batting points from a possible 80, and scored 26 hundreds – totals unmatched even by county champions Warwickshire.

That run-power helped bowlers too. "If the batting struggles," explained Newell, "the bowlers are frightened to get hit for four, and tense up. When you're pretty sure you can outscore anyone, they perform with much more confidence." Confidence equalled wickets – and nine wins. And even their nearest rivals Hampshire were thrashed inside two days when they ran into Nottinghamshire at their irrepressible best in June.

The batting eliminated a previous tendency to self-destruct, with Chris Read, Ealham and Paul Franks in the middle order getting the side out of trouble when the opposition appeared to have grabbed the advantage. Eight batsmen averaged more than 40 but the find of the season for Nottinghamshire, perhaps even the best find in county cricket, was the inexperienced Australian David Hussey. Brother of Michael, another man who has scored a few county runs, David had completed only one full season for Victoria when he was recruited to cover for Damien Martyn's international absences. That turned into an entire summer when Martyn was injured.

Hussey took his chance, rattling up 1,208 Championship runs – including six centuries – and finishing third in the national first-class averages. He also caught almost everything as part of a fly-paper slip cordon, taking 24 catches in all. Alongside the reliable slips, Read was peerless as a wicket-keeper, and a revelation with the bat. After some brutal treatment over the winter of 2003-04 from the England selectors, who doubted his run-scoring powers, he reacted by hitting two hundreds and averaging 50.

The pace attack profited from three luxuries: big totals, attacking fields and fresh limbs, a product of Newell's rotation system. All took decent hauls of wickets, as did the Australian leg-spinner Stuart MacGill, though he was less penetrative than in the past. Still, injuries and losses of form were far less frequent than in 2003 and, outside the bowling rota, the team was settled. When Jason Gallian, Darren Bicknell and Russell Warren experienced barren spells, they responded with big scores before their inclusion was seriously questioned.

David Hussey

All this helped Nottinghamshire blaze to five consecutive Championship wins in five weeks in May and June. They went top of the table on May 21 and were never headed. Promotion was guaranteed with three games left; the second-division title was clinched in the last match of the season, when Ronnie Irani of Essex was pinned lbw and Nottinghamshire grabbed their first bonus point. In the one-day league, performances were far less consistent, at least until a closing sprint of six successive unbeaten games (four wins and two washouts), which was just enough to win promotion in a neck-and-neck finish. Still, Nottinghamshire lost fewer games than any team in either division. Ealham was upgraded to opening bowler and proved particularly miserly when swinging the new white ball; Gallian was equally effective when facing it. But there was less success in the other one-day competitions.

For 2005, Nottinghamshire faced a dilemma over the captaincy: Gallian, despite his successful summer in charge, was due to be nudged aside for the New Zealand Test captain, Stephen Fleming. Initially miffed, Gallian soon came round to the idea. MacGill was released, replaced as overseas player by Fleming, and as No. 1 spinner by Graeme Swann, signed from Northamptonshire. Swann should also add depth to an already impressive lower-middle order, while David Hussey is due to return in both 2005 and 2006, unless he overdoes it and wins promotion to the Australian team.

After a disappointing year, Bilal Shafayat moved to Northamptonshire in search of first-team cricket. Richard Logan was released and the long-running Kevin Pietersen saga ended with him moving to Hampshire. Pietersen had been in dispute with Nottinghamshire since 2003, a feud which erupted when Gallian threw his kit off the Trent Bridge balcony, and continued into 2004, with Pietersen at one point threatening legal action for unfair dismissal, despite never actually being sacked. By the start of the season the rift seemed to have been bridged, and Pietersen indicated he might stay. But in October he finally turned his back on Trent Bridge.

NOTTINGHAMSHIRE RESULTS

All first-class matches – Played 17: Won 9, Lost 2, Drawn 6.
County Championship matches – Played 16: Won 9, Lost 2, Drawn 5.

Frizzell County Championship, winners in Division 2; Cheltenham & Gloucester Trophy, 3rd round;
totesport League, 3rd in Division 2; Twenty20 Cup, 4th in North Group.

COUNTY CHAMPIONSHIP AVERAGES

BATTING AND FIELDING

Cap		M	I	NO	R	HS	100s	50s	Avge	Ct/St
2004	D. J. Hussey§	16	22	3	1,208	170	6	2	63.57	24
2002	K. P. Pietersen.	14	19	1	965	167	4	3	53.61	17
1999	C. M. W. Read	13	18	2	807	130	2	6	50.43	35/3
	A. Singh	5	8	1	332	112*	1	2	47.42	3
1998	J. E. R. Gallian	16	24	2	1,032	190	3	7	46.90	16
2000	D. J. Bicknell	16	24	1	1,066	175	5	1	46.34	4
2004	M. A. Ealham.	15	19	1	819	139	3	3	45.50	13
2004	R. J. Warren	12	17	1	697	134	2	3	43.56	4
1999	P. J. Franks.	16	21	5	610	57*	0	5	38.12	2
	R. J. Logan.	3	4	2	45	25*	0	0	22.50	3
2001	G. J. Smith.	12	12	3	201	35	0	0	22.33	1
2002	S. C. G. MacGill§ . .	14	12	2	126	28	0	0	12.60	2
	C. E. Shreck.	7	6	4	16	13*	0	0	8.00	1
2004	R. J. Sidebottom . . .	10	10	2	49	15*	0	0	6.12	3

Also batted: D. Alleyne (3 matches) 27, 14*, 28 (8 ct); A. J. Harris (cap 2000) (2 matches) 1*, 13, 10; P. J. McMahon (1 match) 0*, 0 (1 ct); B. M. Shafayat (1 match) 13, 3.

§ *Overseas player.*

BOWLING

	O	M	R	W	BB	5W/i	Avge
C. E. Shreck.	216	42	793	29	6-46	2	27.34
R. J. Sidebottom	258	59	859	30	5-86	1	28.63
P. J. Franks.	341.1	67	1,251	42	7-72	2	29.78
G. J. Smith.	315.1	63	1,109	34	5-35	2	32.61
M. A. Ealham.	304	85	910	26	4-43	0	35.00
R. J. Logan	75.1	9	353	10	4-34	0	35.30
S. C. G. MacGill	400	74	1,395	39	7-109	2	35.76

Also bowled: D. J. Bicknell 39.4–2–135–6; A. J. Harris 67–15–196–9; D. J. Hussey 64.2–5–284–1; P. J. McMahon 43–4–169–3; K. P. Pietersen 81.5–7–365–7; B. M. Shafayat 2–0–16–0.

COUNTY RECORDS

Highest score for:	312*	W. W. Keeton v Middlesex at The Oval	1939
Highest score against:	345	C. G. Macartney (Australians) at Nottingham . . .	1921
Best bowling for:	10-66	K. Smales v Gloucestershire at Stroud	1956
Best bowling against:	10-10	H. Verity (Yorkshire) at Leeds	1932
Highest total for:	739-7 dec.	v Leicestershire at Nottingham	1903
Highest total against:	781-7 dec.	by Northamptonshire at Northampton	1995
Lowest total for:	13	v Yorkshire at Nottingham	1901
Lowest total against: {	16	by Derbyshire at Nottingham	1879
	16	by Surrey at The Oval	1880

NOTTINGHAMSHIRE DIRECTORY

ADDRESS

County Cricket Ground, Trent Bridge, Nottingham NG2 6AG (0115 982 3000; fax 0115 945 5730; email marketing.notts@ecb.co.uk). **Website** www.nottsccc.co.uk.

GROUNDS

Nottingham (Trent Bridge): 1½ miles S of city centre in West Bridgford S of bridge over River Trent at junction of A52 Grantham Road and A6011 Radcliffe Road and Bridgford Road. Nearest station: Nottingham (1 mile).

OFFICIALS

Captain S. P. Fleming
Director of cricket M. Newell
Director of academy C. M. Tolley
President J. B. Bolus
Chairman P. B. Pailing

Chief executive 2004 – D. G. Collier
Chairman, cricket committee S. F. Foster
Head groundsman S. Birks
Scorer G. Stringfellow

PLAYERS

Players expected to reappear in 2005

	Former counties	Country	Born	Birthplace
Alleyne David	Middx	E	17.4.1976	York
Bicknell Darren John	Surrey	E	24.6.1967	Guildford
Clough Gareth David	Yorks	E	23.5.1978	Leeds
*****Ealham** Mark Alan	Kent	E	27.8.1969	Willesborough
Franks Paul John		E	3.2.1979	†Mansfield
*****Gallian** Jason Edward Riche	Lancs	E	25.6.1971	Sydney, Aus.
Harris Andrew James	Derbys	E	26.6.1973	Ashton-under-Lyne
Hussey David John		A	15.7.1977	Morley (WA)
McMahon Paul Joseph		E	12.3.1983	Wigan
Patel Samit Rohit		E	30.11.1984	Leicester
Randall Stephen John		E	9.6.1980	†Nottingham
*****Read** Christopher Mark Wells	Glos	E	10.8.1978	Paignton
Shreck Charles Edward		E	6.1.1978	Truro
*****Sidebottom** Ryan Jay	Yorks	E	15.1.1978	Huddersfield
Singh Anurag	Warwicks, Worcs	E	9.9.1975	Kanpur, India
Smith Gregory James		SA (EU)	30.10.1971	Pretoria
Warren Russell John	Northants	E	10.9.1971	Northampton

Players due to join in 2005

	Former counties	Country	Born	Birthplace
*****Fleming** Stephen Paul	Middx, Yorks	NZ	1.4.1973	Christchurch
Swann Graeme Peter	Northants	E	24.3.1979	Northampton

* *Test player.* † *Born in Nottinghamshire.*

At Oxford, April 16, 17, 18. NOTTINGHAMSHIRE drew with OXFORD UCCE.

At Chester-le-Street, April 21, 22, 23, 24. NOTTINGHAMSHIRE beat DURHAM by an innings and 80 runs.

NOTTINGHAMSHIRE v YORKSHIRE

At Nottingham, April 28, 29, 30, May 1. Drawn. Nottinghamshire 11 pts, Yorkshire 8 pts. Toss: Yorkshire. County debut: R. J. Sidebottom.

Any chance of a result drained away with the torrential rain that fell throughout the first two days and turned the outfield into a lake. The third day saw lighter skies, and hard work from the groundstaff allowed Yorkshire to begin their pursuit of batting points after lunch. Smith had other ideas, removing White and Taylor with consecutive deliveries. Lehmann, though, was a tougher obstacle and he biffed and bashed in typical fashion either side of the wicket, while Dawson hit a battling half-century in fading light. He was last out on the final morning, leaving Nottinghamshire most of the day to chase bonus points of their own. Gallian and Bicknell shared an opening stand of 110, Gallian going on to a hundred of the highest quality, despatching straight drives and trademark clips through mid-wicket with immaculate timing. The lower order had pushed past 350 when Sidebottom, a winter signing from Headingley, was eighth out; Gallian promptly declared, denying Yorkshire a chance of maximum bowling points.

Close of play: First day, No play; Second day, No play; Third day, Yorkshire 246-9 (Dawson 74, Blain 19).

Yorkshire

M. J. Wood c Hussey b Shreck	15
*C. White c Gallian b Smith	4
C. R. Taylor lbw b Smith	0
D. S. Lehmann c Sidebottom b Smith	62
M. J. Lumb c Hussey b Ealham	16
I. J. Harvey c Alleyne b Sidebottom	35
†S. M. Guy b Franks	0
R. K. J. Dawson c Gallian b Shreck	81
T. T. Bresnan c Hussey b Sidebottom	0
C. E. W. Silverwood c and b Pietersen	14
J. A. R. Blain not out	28
L-b 4, w 1, n-b 4	9
	264

1/5 (2) 2/5 (3) 3/57 (1)
4/88 (4) 5/113 (5) 6/122 (7)
7/151 (6) 8/151 (9)
9/193 (10) 10/264 (8)

Bonus points – Yorkshire 2, Nottinghamshire 3.

Bowling: Smith 16–2–75–3; Shreck 16–2–55–2; Sidebottom 17–2–48–2; Franks 7–0–38–1; Ealham 12–3–38–1; Pietersen 4–1–6–1.

Nottinghamshire

D. J. Bicknell c Guy b Silverwood	41
*J. E. R. Gallian lbw b Lehmann	133
R. J. Warren b Dawson	9
K. P. Pietersen lbw b Bresnan	21
D. J. Hussey run out	18
M. A. Ealham c Lumb b Dawson	54
P. J. Franks c Lehmann b Harvey	44
†D. Alleyne not out	14
R. J. Sidebottom b Dawson	3
B 2, l-b 4, n-b 10	16
(8 wkts dec.)	**353**

1/110 (1) 2/151 (3)
3/212 (4) 4/212 (2)
5/260 (5) 6/335 (6)
7/336 (7) 8/353 (9)

G. J. Smith and C. E. Shreck did not bat.

Bonus points – Nottinghamshire 4, Yorkshire 2.

Bowling: Silverwood 17–2–66–1; Blain 14–1–87–0; Bresnan 12–1–55–1; Dawson 30.4–7–102–3; Lehmann 8–2–21–0; White 5–0–12–0; Harvey 3–2–4–1.

Umpires: N. A. Mallender and R. Palmer.

NOTTINGHAMSHIRE v GLAMORGAN

At Nottingham, May 7, 8, 9, 10. Drawn. Nottinghamshire 11 pts, Glamorgan 9 pts. Toss: Glamorgan.

Once again, rain – which stole 185 overs – had the biggest influence on a game most notable for Simon Jones making his first Championship start since 2002. He had to wait, though, as Glamorgan chose to bat: Hemp battled to 82 in overcast conditions perfect for Sidebottom, who swung his way to five wickets. Jones finally had the ball in his hand for the 14th over of the third day and looked keen to make up for lost time, producing a vicious opening delivery that Bicknell fended to point. The Nottinghamshire middle order looked in good touch, however, though none made the three-figure score their form promised. The lower order then knuckled down, aiming for 400, but MacGill's ill-judged decision to go for glory off his first ball scuppered that. The match petered out with Glamorgan facing 20 overs of spin, an exercise solely designed to allow Nottinghamshire to improve a slack over-rate.

Close of play: First day, Glamorgan 196-5 (Hemp 62, Croft 2); Second day, Glamorgan 274; Third day, Nottinghamshire 287-6 (Franks 16, Alleyne 10).

Glamorgan

M. T. G. Elliott c Alleyne b Franks	41	– c Hussey b MacGill	12
†M. A. Wallace c Hussey b Sidebottom	13	– c Alleyne b MacGill	24
D. L. Hemp c Gallian b Smith	82	– not out	23
M. J. Powell b Sidebottom	53	– not out	2
M. P. Maynard c Gallian b Ealham	11		
A. Dale c Alleyne b Ealham	2		
*R. D. B. Croft c Pietersen b Ealham	2		
S. D. Thomas c Pietersen b Sidebottom	13		
A. G. Wharf b Sidebottom	0		
D. S. Harrison not out	32		
S. P. Jones c Bicknell b Sidebottom	11		
B 1, l-b 4, w 3, n-b 6	14	L-b 2, n-b 10	12

1/30 (2) 2/72 (1) 3/167 (4) 4/180 (5) 274 1/16 (1) 2/65 (2) (2 wkts) 73
5/194 (6) 6/196 (7) 7/221 (8)
8/229 (9) 9/231 (3) 10/274 (11)

Bonus points – Glamorgan 2, Nottinghamshire 3.

Bowling: *First Innings*—Smith 18–5–56–1; Sidebottom 25.1–6–86–5; Franks 13–0–45–1; Ealham 20–8–55–3; MacGill 8–3–27–0. *Second Innings*—MacGill 10–2–32–2; Pietersen 8–0–33–0; Hussey 2–0–6–0.

Nottinghamshire

D. J. Bicknell c Hemp b Jones	20	R. J. Sidebottom not out	15
*J. E. R. Gallian c Elliott b Wharf	0	S. C. G. MacGill c Harrison b Croft	0
R. J. Warren lbw b Harrison	97		
K. P. Pietersen c Wharf b Thomas	70	B 4, l-b 4, w 2, n-b 4	14
D. J. Hussey c Wallace b Jones	55		
M. A. Ealham c Wharf b Jones	10	1/1 (2) 2/40 (1) 3/176 (3) 384
P. J. Franks b Croft	45	4/212 (4) 5/257 (5) 6/260 (6)
†D. Alleyne c Wallace b Thomas	28	7/328 (8) 8/351 (7)
G. J. Smith c Harrison b Jones	30	9/382 (9) 10/384 (11)

Bonus points – Nottinghamshire 4, Glamorgan 3.

Bowling: Harrison 17–0–64–1; Wharf 25–7–76–1; Thomas 19–2–82–2; Jones 25–5–98–4; Croft 26.1–9–56–2.

Umpires: V. A. Holder and M. J. Kitchen.

At Leicester, May 12, 13, 14, 15. NOTTINGHAMSHIRE lost to LEICESTERSHIRE by 92 runs.

At Leeds, May 19, 20, 21. NOTTINGHAMSHIRE beat YORKSHIRE by 244 runs.

NOTTINGHAMSHIRE v DURHAM

At Nottingham, May 25, 26, 27, 28. Nottinghamshire won by three wickets. Nottinghamshire 20 pts, Durham 6 pts. Toss: Durham.

This exciting game remained neck-and-neck until deep into the final day when Nottinghamshire nosed ahead on the line. On the first day, Durham reached 157 for one before MacGill took six successive wickets. Davies removed Bicknell before the close and tore through Nottinghamshire next day until the scoreboard read 153 for eight. But Hussey was still there, and, with Sidebottom

---

HIGHEST LAST-WICKET STANDS FOR NOTTINGHAMSHIRE

152 }	E. B. Alletson and W. Riley v Sussex at Hove	1911
152 }	U. Afzaal and A. J. Harris v Worcestershire at Nottingham	2000
140	S. J. Staples and T. L. Richmond v Derbyshire at Worksop	1922
136	H. Larwood and W. Voce v Sussex at Nottingham	1931
135	C. M. W. Read and R. D. Stemp v Hampshire at Southampton	2001
123	B. Dooland and A. K. Walker v Somerset at Nottingham	1956
120	**D. J. Hussey and S. C. G. MacGill v Durham at Nottingham**	**2004**

---

and then MacGill as his assistants, he produced a memorable exhibition of clinical and sustained hitting. At one stage, Lewis placed all nine fielders on the boundary at Nottingham, yet Hussey continued to pierce the gaps or clear the ropes, in all swatting seven sixes. MacGill's over-eagerness eventually left Hussey high and dry, but the last two wickets had more than doubled the score, and the two Australians had added 120 from 16 mesmerising overs. Now Franks grabbed centre-stage, claiming five Championship wickets for the first time since July 2002, though Durham fought back through dogged contributions from Collingwood and Gary Pratt. With the Nottinghamshire top order again looking shaky, Durham were back as favourites – until Read, with a century of immense class and maturity, dashed their hopes.

Close of play: First day, Nottinghamshire 6-1 (Gallian 0, Warren 1); Second day, Durham 36-0 (Lewis 16, North 19); Third day, Nottinghamshire 86-2 (Gallian 46, Pietersen 14).

Durham

*J. J. B. Lewis b Franks	77	– c Logan b Franks	16
M. J. North c Bicknell b Sidebottom	17	– c Read b Franks	44
G. J. Muchall c Hussey b Franks	60	– c Logan b Franks	18
P. D. Collingwood c Pietersen b MacGill	31	– c Warren b MacGill	68
N. Peng c Pietersen b MacGill	32	– b Logan	19
G. J. Pratt lbw b MacGill	14	– lbw b MacGill	71
G. R. Breese lbw b MacGill	0	– c Read b Franks	27
†A. Pratt not out	39	– c Sidebottom b Franks	5
N. Killeen c Franks b MacGill	16	– not out	3
A. M. Davies b MacGill	0	– b Logan	6
P. Kumar run out	2	– lbw b MacGill	21
B 5, l-b 5, n-b 2	12	B 3, l-b 10, w 4	17

1/47 (2) 2/157 (3) 3/166 (1) 4/203 (4)   300   1/40 (1) 2/73 (2) 3/88 (3)   315
5/235 (6) 6/235 (7) 7/246 (5)   4/120 (5) 5/228 (4) 6/257 (6)
8/288 (9) 9/295 (10) 10/300 (11)   7/279 (8) 8/283 (7)
                                         9/293 (10) 10/315 (11)

Bonus points – Durham 3, Nottinghamshire 3.

Bowling: *First Innings*—Smith 19.1–4–44–0; Logan 18–3–72–0; Sidebottom 17–6–40–1; Franks 15–5–53–2; MacGill 24–4–81–6. *Second Innings*—Smith 15–2–64–0; Sidebottom 14–3–64–0; Franks 21–9–41–5; Logan 18–1–79–2; MacGill 17.2–3–54–3.

Nottinghamshire

D. J. Bicknell lbw b Davies	0	– lbw b Collingwood ... 23
*J. E. R. Gallian c Breese b Davies	36	– c G. J. Pratt b Killeen ... 50
R. J. Warren c G. J. Pratt b Kumar	31	– lbw b Kumar ... 0
K. P. Pietersen c Collingwood b Kumar	0	– c North b Davies ... 19
D. J. Hussey not out	166	– c Lewis b Davies ... 35
†C. M. W. Read lbw b Davies	10	– not out ... 108
P. J. Franks c A. Pratt b Davies	12	– c A. Pratt b Breese ... 14
R. J. Logan c A. Pratt b Killeen	7	– c A. Pratt b Breese ... 4
G. J. Smith b Davies	2	– not out ... 28
R. J. Sidebottom lbw b Collingwood	13	
S. C. G. MacGill c A. Pratt b Davies	24	
B 8, l-b 9, w 1, n-b 6	24	B 1, l-b 8, n-b 4 ... 13

325   (7 wkts) 294

1/5 (1) 2/71 (3) 3/71 (4) 4/85 (2)   1/64 (1) 2/65 (3)
5/103 (6) 6/135 (7) 7/150 (8)   3/90 (2) 4/112 (4)
8/153 (9) 9/205 (10) 10/325 (11)   5/152 (5) 6/191 (7) 7/221 (8)

Bonus points – Nottinghamshire 3, Durham 3.

Bowling: *First Innings*—Killeen 23–8–81–1; Davies 22.5–2–78–6; Collingwood 14–3–42–1; Kumar 11–1–56–2; Breese 7–0–51–0. *Second Innings*—Davies 19–4–78–2; Killeen 18–0–74–1; Collingwood 15–4–57–1; Kumar 7–2–25–1; Breese 16.2–1–51–2.

Umpires: T. E. Jesty and A. A. Jones.

At Southampton, June 2, 3. NOTTINGHAMSHIRE beat HAMPSHIRE by an innings and 44 runs.

At Bath, June 9, 10, 11, 12. NOTTINGHAMSHIRE beat SOMERSET by seven wickets.

NOTTINGHAMSHIRE v DERBYSHIRE

At Nottingham, June 18, 19, 20, 21. Nottinghamshire won by ten wickets. Nottinghamshire 22 pts, Derbyshire 3 pts. Toss: Derbyshire.

Nottinghamshire won five consecutive Championship matches in a season for the first time since 1925, when they ended the summer with six in a row. This victory came with a dismissive pounding of a feeble Derbyshire, who offered little resistance until the game was all but lost. Nottinghamshire were inserted under grey skies, survived a testing first hour and then battered a toothless attack, which too often pitched short. Gallian completed a marathon 190 (his highest since leaving Lancashire), Pietersen made a confident 107 (his fourth century in five Championship games against Derbyshire) and Read a rasping 130 – his second successive Championship century at Trent Bridge and the ideal riposte to England selectors who had dropped him for his inadequate batting. Derbyshire keeled over in their first innings and were 75 for five in the follow-on at the third-day close, still 256 adrift. At last, in the guise of Hassan Adnan, they showed some backbone. His unbeaten hundred, combined with showers, seemed set to force an unlikely and largely undeserved draw until Shreck's persistence left Adnan partnerless, Nottinghamshire raced home from just three of the 11 overs available.

Close of play: First day, Nottinghamshire 244-2 (Gallian 101, Pietersen 92); Second day, Derbyshire 106-3 (Moss 55, Dean 0); Third day, Derbyshire 75-5 (Hassan Adnan 27, Botha 0).

Nottinghamshire

D. J. Bicknell lbw b Mohammad Ali	24	– not out	25
*J. E. R. Gallian c Mohammad Ali b Botha	190	– not out	1
R. J. Warren lbw b Dean	13		
K. P. Pietersen c Sutton b Sheikh	107		
D. J. Hussey c Gait b Sheikh	0		
†C. M. W. Read c Sutton b Dean	130		
M. A. Ealham c Gait b Botha	14		
P. J. Franks not out	27		
R. J. Logan not out	25		
B 4, l-b 11, w 2, n-b 4	21	N-b 2	2

1/37 (1) 2/69 (3) 3/286 (4) (7 wkts dec.) 551
4/286 (5) 5/485 (6)
6/489 (2) 7/504 (7)

(no wkt) 28

C. E. Shreck and S. C. G. MacGill did not bat.

Bonus points – Nottinghamshire 5, Derbyshire 2 (130 overs: 511-7).

Bowling: *First Innings*—Welch 28–1–101–0; Mohammad Ali 19.2–3–83–1; Sheikh 27–8–78–2; Dean 21–1–138–2; Moss 24–4–65–0; Botha 14–1–71–2. *Second Innings*—Welch 2–0–14–0; Mohammad Ali 1–0–14–0.

Derbyshire

A. I. Gait lbw b Shreck	0	– c MacGill b Shreck	5
S. D. Stubbings c Warren b Ealham	0	– c Pietersen b Ealham	0
J. Moss c Warren b Shreck	69	– c Pietersen b Shreck	20
Hassan Adnan b Franks	43	– not out	129
K. J. Dean run out	1	– (10) b MacGill	8
C. W. G. Bassano c Read b Ealham	3	– (8) c and b Shreck	52
*†L. D. Sutton not out	36	– (5) lbw b Shreck	8
G. Welch c Read b Franks	29	– (6) b Pietersen	9
A. G. Botha c Gallian b MacGill	9	– (7) lbw b Shreck	40
M. A. Sheikh b Franks	1	– (9) b Shreck	1
Mohammad Ali c Gallian b MacGill	14	– c Logan b MacGill	50
B 4, l-b 6, w 1, n-b 4	15	B 7, l-b 13, w 7, n-b 6	33

1/0 (2) 2/4 (1) 3/93 (4) 4/107 (5) 220
5/122 (3) 6/130 (6) 7/177 (8)
8/198 (9) 9/205 (10) 10/220 (11)

1/5 (2) 2/25 (1) 3/26 (3) 355
4/44 (5) 5/64 (6) 6/158 (7)
7/253 (8) 8/274 (9)
9/291 (10) 10/355 (11)

Bonus points – Derbyshire 1, Nottinghamshire 3.

Bowling: *First Innings*—Shreck 14–4–47–2; Ealham 12–3–35–2; Logan 10–1–69–0; Franks 14–5–43–3; MacGill 8.1–2–16–2; Pietersen 1–1–0–0. *Second Innings*—Shreck 25–5–103–6; Ealham 11–1–46–1; Franks 7–0–28–0; MacGill 25.5–5–89–2; Pietersen 6–1–26–1; Logan 8–0–43–0.

Umpires: V. A. Holder and B. Leadbeater.

> **❝**At the end of Essex's first innings, Pietersen reported the loss of an ear-stud. The groundstaff searched, but the groundsman, Stuart Kerrison, said it had probably been 'crunched up' by the mower."
>
> Essex in 2004, page 594.

NOTTINGHAMSHIRE v HAMPSHIRE

At Nottingham, July 23, 24, 25, 26. Drawn. Nottinghamshire 10 pts, Hampshire 11 pts. Toss: Hampshire.

Reluctant to risk defeat against one of their main second-division rivals, Nottinghamshire prepared a featherbed – which won, producing 1,548 runs and a triple centurion, Trent Bridge's second in successive seasons. Arriving after Kenway's third-ball dismissal, Crawley had reason to be grateful: his last Championship hundred had been in April 2002, when he made 272 on debut for Hampshire. His only two centuries for Hampshire were now the county's third and fifth-highest scores. He shared several massive stands, including 238 with Clarke – whose career-best 140 was his maiden

---

MATCHES WHERE BOTH TEAMS REACHED 600 IN FIRST INNINGS

Leicestershire (609-8 dec.) v Sussex (686-8) at Leicester	1900
MCC (626) v New South Wales (619) at Sydney.	1924-25
Maharashtra (675) v Bombay (650) at Poona	1940-41
Bijapur Famine XI (703) v Bengal Cyclone XI (673) at Bombay	1942-43
Queensland (613) v New South Wales (661) at Brisbane.	1963-64
Australia (656-8 dec.) v England (611) at Manchester	1964
Maharashtra (624-5 dec.) v Rajasthan (604) at Pune.	1970-71
Delhi (705) v Karnataka (707-8) at Delhi.	1981-82
Surrey (707-9 dec.) v Lancashire (863) at The Oval.	1990
Karnataka (791-6 dec.) v Bengal (652-9) at Calcutta	1990-91
Hampshire (641-4 dec.) v Nottinghamshire (612) at Nottingham	**2004**

Research: Philip Bailey

---

county century – and showed immense concentration over 565 minutes and 442 balls. Crawley struck 35 fours and two sixes, and finally converted his seventh double into his first triple. Warne immediately declared, on an intimidating 641, leaving Crawley 15 short of R. H. Moore's 67-year-old county record. Then it was the Hampshire bowlers' turn to suffer. Left-hander Bicknell took giant strides down the pitch to negate the spin of Warne, whose fellow Victorian team-mate, Hussey, had time to play back to everything except half-volleys. Ealham also cashed in as this became the third Championship match in history to feature two first-innings totals over 600. There was still time for Clarke to race to a second hundred, the sixth of the match, but certainly not for a result.

Close of play: First day, Hampshire 375-2 (Crawley 154, Clarke 130); Second day, Nottinghamshire 129-3 (Bicknell 55, Hussey 19); Third day, Nottinghamshire 534-6 (Ealham 79, Franks 25).

Hampshire

D. A. Kenway c Read b Shreck	0	– c Pietersen b Sidebottom	28
M. J. Brown c Read b Sidebottom.	74	– c Read b MacGill.	30
J. P. Crawley not out.	301		
M. J. Clarke c Hussey b Shreck	140	– (3) c Hussey b Pietersen	103
J. H. K. Adams st Read b MacGill	36	– (4) b Bicknell	16
†N. Pothas not out	56		
A. D. Mascarenhas (did not bat)		– (5) not out.	41
B. V. Taylor (did not bat).		– (6) b Pietersen	27
A. D. Mullally (did not bat).		– (7) c Hussey b Pietersen	0
S. D. Udal (did not bat)		– (8) not out.	23
B 4, l-b 9, w 1, n-b 20	34	B 8, l-b 9, n-b 10.	27

1/0 (1) 2/153 (2)   (4 wkts dec.) 641   1/61 (2) 2/69 (1)   (6 wkts dec.) 295
3/391 (4) 4/489 (5)   3/184 (4) 4/200 (3)
                                                    5/234 (6) 6/236 (7)

*S. K. Warne did not bat.

Bonus points – Hampshire 5, Nottinghamshire 1 (130 overs: 499-4).

Bowling: *First Innings*—Shreck 30–6–106–2; Sidebottom 25–4–108–1; Franks 20–3–102–0; Ealham 24–8–68–0; MacGill 27–0–114–1; Pietersen 7–0–56–0; Hussey 19.2–2–74–0. *Second Innings*—Sidebottom 10–3–32–1; Shreck 5–0–53–0; MacGill 14–4–35–1; Franks 4–1–21–0; Hussey 5–0–33–0; Pietersen 13–1–72–3; Bicknell 13–2–32–1.

Nottinghamshire

D. J. Bicknell c Pothas b Mullally 103	S. C. G. MacGill b Mullally 28
*J. E. R. Gallian run out 26	C. E. Shreck lbw b Udal 1
R. J. Warren lbw b Warne 21	
K. P. Pietersen c Brown b Warne 0	B 10, l-b 5, w 6, n-b 16 37
D. J. Hussey b Taylor 170	
†C. M. W. Read c Pothas b Taylor 75	1/63 (2) 2/93 (3) 3/93 (4) 612
M. A. Ealham not out 113	4/230 (1) 5/408 (6) 6/459 (5)
P. J. Franks c Pothas b Taylor 30	7/542 (8) 8/573 (9)
R. J. Sidebottom c Udal b Mascarenhas . . 8	9/611 (10) 10/612 (11)

Bonus points – Nottinghamshire 5, Hampshire 2 (130 overs: 514-6).

Bowling: Mullally 24–3–83–2; Taylor 33–4–159–3; Warne 39–5–133–2; Mascarenhas 28–7–81–1; Udal 22.2–1–93–1; Clarke 9–2–24–0; Crawley 4–1–24–0.

Umpires: N. L. Bainton and A. A. Jones.

At Southend, July 28, 29, 30, 31. NOTTINGHAMSHIRE beat ESSEX by eight wickets.

NOTTINGHAMSHIRE v LEICESTERSHIRE

At Nottingham, August 11, 12, 13, 14. Drawn. Nottinghamshire 12 pts, Leicestershire 8 pts. Toss: Nottinghamshire.

Nottinghamshire missed out on victory after losing a day to rain, but took another step towards promotion. They claimed full batting points for the fifth game running, thanks to Warren's first century since the opening Championship match in April and Hussey's third in three innings – a feat last achieved for Nottinghamshire in 1971, by Pasty Harris. Then Ealham took four wickets for the first time since moving to Trent Bridge and, when Leicestershire ended the second day on 142 for seven (with Ealham 11–3–13–4), another win was in sight. After the third-day washout it took another 20 overs to enforce the follow-on, before Robinson and Hodge ensured the draw. The match cost Nottinghamshire dearly in terms of injuries. Warren's season ended after his calf took a blow at short leg, Sidebottom limped off with a pulled hamstring, and Smith dislocated a finger dropping a catch. Director of cricket Mick Newell won a dressing-room race with Second XI manager Wayne Noon to act as 14th man for the last hour.

Close of play: First day, Nottinghamshire 356-5 (Warren 120, Read 10); Second day, Leicestershire 142-7 (Gibson 13, Henderson 12); Third day, No play.

Nottinghamshire

D. J. Bicknell b Cleary 2	G. J. Smith b Gibson 1
*J. E. R. Gallian b Maddy 66	S. C. G. MacGill b Gibson 2
R. J. Warren b Gibson 134	
K. P. Pietersen lbw b Cleary 0	B 2, l-b 11, n-b 12 25
D. J. Hussey c Robinson b Masters 140	
R. J. Sidebottom c Stevens b Hodge . . . 0	1/2 (1) 2/110 (2) 3/111 (4) 490
†C. M. W. Read b Gibson 62	4/341 (5) 5/342 (6) 6/387 (3)
M. A. Ealham run out 1	7/396 (8) 8/462 (7)
P. J. Franks not out 57	9/464 (10) 10/490 (11)

Bonus points – Nottinghamshire 5, Leicestershire 3.

Bowling: Cleary 22–3–66–2; Gibson 30–5–106–4; DeFreitas 29–5–107–0; Masters 22–3–97–1; Henderson 12–1–54–0; Maddy 6–0–30–1; Hodge 4–0–17–1.

Leicestershire

D. D. J. Robinson c Read b Smith	4	– b Hussey	88
D. L. Maddy c Pietersen b Ealham	51	– b Franks	31
D. I. Stevens b Ealham	13	– (5) c sub b MacGill	5
J. L. Sadler lbw b Ealham	4	– b MacGill	7
*B. J. Hodge lbw b Ealham	9	– (3) c Gallian b Franks	76
†P. A. Nixon c Ealham b Franks	18	– not out	17
P. A. J. DeFreitas c Read b Franks	4	– not out	8
O. D. Gibson lbw b Sidebottom	26		
C. W. Henderson c Pietersen b Sidebottom	37		
M. F. Cleary c Read b Smith	14		
D. D. Masters not out	9		
B 4, l-b 9, w 2, n-b 8	23	B 5, l-b 5, n-b 21	31

1/6 (1) 2/28 (3) 3/38 (4) 4/54 (5)	212	1/58 (2) 2/203 (3) (5 wkts) 263
5/100 (6) 6/104 (7) 7/121 (2)		3/228 (4) 4/238 (1)
8/183 (8) 9/188 (9) 10/212 (10)		5/238 (5)

Bonus points – Leicestershire 1, Nottinghamshire 3.

Bowling: *First Innings*—Smith 12.1–3–27–2; Sidebottom 16.4–4–37–2; Ealham 17–3–43–4; Franks 9–1–40–2; MacGill 10.2–1–48–0; Pietersen 1–0–4–0. *Second Innings*—Smith 11–1–48–0; Ealham 14–5–40–0; MacGill 28–10–66–2; Franks 13–1–68–2; Pietersen 3–0–24–0; Hussey 5–1–7–1.

Umpires: J. W. Lloyds and J. F. Steele.

At Derby, August 19, 20, 21, 22. NOTTINGHAMSHIRE beat DERBYSHIRE by an innings and 56 runs.

NOTTINGHAMSHIRE v SOMERSET

At Nottingham, September 3, 4, 5, 6. Somerset won by ten wickets. Somerset 22 pts, Nottinghamshire 4 pts. Toss: Nottinghamshire.

With promotion in their pockets, Nottinghamshire returned home looking to wrap up the title. But Cox and Blackwell had other ideas, and lifted Somerset to fourth place to maintain their own faint hopes of going up. Despite Ealham's third hundred of the season, the home batting was below par. Cox responded with a career-best 250, a thoroughbred innings lasting seven minutes short of nine hours and including 35 fours and a six in 428 balls. He shared double-century stands with Wood and Hildreth on a pitch offering no help to bowlers; Somerset's 654 for eight declared was the highest total on this ground since 1947. Off-spinner McMahon, in his first county game of 2004, stuck to his task, claiming Blackwell first ball, and the eighth bowler, Bicknell, got two with his occasional left-arm spin. Reverting to his usual weapon, the bat, Bicknell stroked 142, but was helpless to stop Blackwell, using the seamers' rough, from equalling his career-best seven for 90 against Glamorgan the previous month. He finished off Nottinghamshire on the final evening, and Somerset needed only a single to win.

Close of play: First day, Nottinghamshire 306-7 (Ealham 95, Smith 0); Second day, Somerset 349-2 (Cox 130, Hildreth 73); Third day, Nottinghamshire 134-1 (Bicknell 68, Harris 5).

Nottinghamshire

D. J. Bicknell c Turner b Johnson	6	– c Burns b Blackwell	142
*J. E. R. Gallian c Turner b Blackwell	68	– c Durston b Blackwell	55
A. Singh c Burns b Johnson	7	– (4) lbw b Johnson	1
D. J. Hussey c Caddick b Blackwell	25	– (5) c Bowler b Blackwell	7
B. M. Shafayat c Turner b Johnson	13	– (6) c Durston b Blackwell	3
†C. M. W. Read c Hildreth b Francis	59	– (7) c Cox b Durston	24
M. A. Ealham c Durston b Johnson	104	– (8) c Durston b Blackwell	44
P. J. Franks c Hildreth b Johnson	11	– (9) b Blackwell	6
G. J. Smith c Bowler b Caddick	8	– (10) not out	13
A. J. Harris lbw b Caddick	13	– (3) c Turner b Johnson	10
P. J. McMahon not out	0	– c Turner b Blackwell	0
L-b 10, w 5, n-b 8	23	B 4, l-b 4, n-b 4	12

1/13 (1) 2/29 (3) 3/77 (4) 4/122 (5)	**337**	1/121 (2) 2/164 (3) 3/172 (4)	**317**
5/143 (2) 6/273 (6) 7/297 (8)		4/201 (5) 5/207 (6) 6/242 (7)
8/322 (9) 9/329 (7) 10/337 (10)		7/256 (1) 8/288 (9)
		9/317 (8) 10/317 (11)

Bonus points – Nottinghamshire 3, Somerset 3.

Bowling: *First Innings*—Caddick 25.4–8–97–2; Johnson 25–9–69–5; Francis 19–3–66–1; Burns 2–0–8–0; Blackwell 38–16–64–2; Durston 5–1–23–0. *Second Innings*—Caddick 8–1–55–0; Johnson 21–5–64–2; Blackwell 43.3–17–90–7; Francis 17–2–50–0; Durston 19–5–50–1.

Somerset

P. D. Bowler c Read b Smith	2	– not out	1
M. J. Wood lbw b McMahon	113	– not out	0
J. Cox c Gallian b McMahon	250		
J. C. Hildreth c Hussey b Harris	108		
*M. Burns run out	34		
I. D. Blackwell c and b McMahon	0		
†R. J. Turner not out	41		
W. J. Durston b Bicknell	47		
R. L. Johnson c Ealham b Bicknell	8		
B 5, l-b 13, w 9, n-b 24	51		

1/2 (1) 2/205 (2) 3/412 (4)	(8 wkts dec.) **654**	(no wkt) **1**
4/499 (5) 5/500 (6) 6/581 (3)		
7/646 (8) 8/654 (9)		

S. R. G. Francis and A. R. Caddick did not bat.

Bonus points – Somerset 5, Nottinghamshire 1 (130 overs: 510-5).

Bowling: *First Innings*—Smith 22–4–99–1; Harris 30–5–113–1; Franks 22–2–80–0; McMahon 43–4–169–3; Ealham 18–4–64–0; Shafayat 2–0–16–0; Hussey 14–1–63–0; Bicknell 11.1–0–32–2. *Second Innings*—Bicknell 0.4–0–1–0.

Umpires: D. J. Constant and J. H. Evans.

At Cardiff, September 10, 11, 12, 13. NOTTINGHAMSHIRE drew with GLAMORGAN.

NOTTINGHAMSHIRE v ESSEX

At Nottingham, September 16, 17, 18, 19. Nottinghamshire won by three wickets. Nottinghamshire 20 pts, Essex 7 pts. Toss: Essex.

Nottinghamshire needed one point to confirm the Division Two title. They got it when Irani was lbw to Franks, prompting a standing ovation and champagne on the field; and it was Franks, the only player born in the county, who hit the winning runs in a thrilling last-ball finish. With promotion in Championship and League already secured, Nottinghamshire's relaxed attitude helped Jefferson hit 167. He punished anything over-pitched, despite looking far from convincing against the short ball. Rain claimed the second day – when Adams twisted his ankle – but Napier reached a maiden Championship century in 78 balls – the second-fastest of the season – before the captains agreed to try to engineer a result. Hussey smashed his seventh hundred of the summer before Nottinghamshire declared 199 behind, and Jefferson despatched some friendly declaration bowling for his sixth. Set 379 in 71 overs, Bicknell built the foundations but, though the run-rate kept up, Essex kept chipping away. The No. 8, Franks, needed two from the final delivery: he and Smith scrambled them to complete Nottinghamshire's ninth win of the summer.

Close of play: First day, Essex 357-6 (Middlebrook 14, Napier 12); Second day, No play; Third day, Essex 48-1 (Jefferson 26, Flower 8).

Essex

W. I. Jefferson b Bicknell	167	– not out	100
A. N. Cook c Read b Sidebottom	7	– lbw b Sidebottom	11
A. Flower c Read b Smith	56	– not out	61
*R. C. Irani lbw b Franks	16		
R. S. Bopara lbw b Ealham	34		
†J. S. Foster lbw b Smith	23		
J. D. Middlebrook c Read b Franks	14		
G. R. Napier not out	106		
A. P. Palladino lbw b Bicknell	41		
Danish Kaneria b Bicknell	0		
A. R. Adams absent hurt			
B 6, l-b 12, n-b 18	36	L-b 3, w 2, n-b 2	7

1/20 (2) 2/152 (3) 3/180 (4)   500   1/31 (2)   (1 wkt dec.) 179
4/261 (5) 5/298 (6) 6/339 (1)
7/357 (7) 8/500 (9) 9/500 (10)

Bonus points – Essex 5, Nottinghamshire 3.

Bowling: *First Innings*—Smith 25–6–97–2; Sidebottom 21–3–103–1; Franks 19–4–77–2; Ealham 13–4–37–1; MacGill 20–3–72–0; Pietersen 11–0–58–0; Bicknell 6.5–0–33–3; Hussey 2–0–5–0. *Second Innings*—Sidebottom 6–0–22–1; Smith 3–0–17–0; Bicknell 8–0–37–0; Hussey 10–0–69–0; MacGill 5.2–0–24–0; Pietersen 2–0–7–0.

Nottinghamshire

D. J. Bicknell lbw b Palladino	24	– c Foster b Napier	110
*J. E. R. Gallian lbw b Danish Kaneria	13	– c and b Danish Kaneria	57
A. Singh lbw b Danish Kaneria	21	– lbw b Danish Kaneria	89
K. P. Pietersen b Middlebrook	37	– b Napier	0
D. J. Hussey not out	124	– b Napier	1
†C. M. W. Read c Flower b Danish Kaneria	7	– b Palladino	49
M. A. Ealham b Danish Kaneria	1	– lbw b Danish Kaneria	10
P. J. Franks not out	50	– not out	22
G. J. Smith (did not bat)		– not out	16
B 14, l-b 7, w 1, n-b 2	24	B 12, l-b 10, w 1, n-b 2	25

1/34 (1) 2/46 (2) 3/97 (3)   (6 wkts dec.) 301   1/121 (2) 2/206 (1)   (7 wkts) 379
4/107 (4) 5/164 (6) 6/172 (7)   3/206 (4) 4/216 (5)
                                        5/299 (6) 6/316 (7) 7/339 (3)

S. C. G. MacGill and R. J. Sidebottom did not bat.

Bonus points – Nottinghamshire 3, Essex 2.

Bowling: *First Innings*—Palladino 9–2–38–1; Napier 10–1–43–0; Danish Kaneria 26–2–102–4; Bopara 6–1–24–0; Middlebrook 12.4–1–73–1. *Second Innings*—Palladino 15–2–75–1; Napier 17–0–105–3; Danish Kaneria 24–1–92–3; Middlebrook 6–0–37–0; Bopara 9–0–48–0.

Umpires: A. Clarkson and T. E. Jesty.

SOMERSET

More head-shaking in the Quantocks

David Foot

A final, unlikely flourish, when four Championship wins out of seven ensured fourth place in the bottom division, meant too little, and was certainly too late, at the end of another disappointing summer for Somerset. The brief but successful visit of Ricky Ponting – with his near-instant hundreds, plus enthusiasm, encouragement and on-field counsel – only emphasised what could have been achieved with more imagination and competitive zeal. As it was, the exasperation and head-shaking continued at Taunton. How, for instance, did Somerset allow Durham to score 453 for victory in the fourth innings? It was, once again, a season of too many such perplexing questions.

Yet the irony was that the county had started with what, theoretically at least, was one of the best seam attacks in the country. Andrew Caddick, Richard Johnson and Nixon McLean appeared to make up a formidable new-ball trio, but then came the injuries and the compromises. In a brave comeback from back surgery, Caddick occasionally recaptured his former movement and bounce and took 54 Championship wickets, but something had been lost, and he hoped in vain for a Test recall. Johnson also had his good days, one of them with the bat at Chester-le-Street in mid-August, when he braced those sturdy shoulders to smite and smear the fastest first-class century of the season.

But there were not enough high points for a club who can usually dredge up at least a handful of thrilling cameos to offset the pathological pessimism of the cognoscenti from the Quantocks. True, in addition to Ponting's transitory brilliance, there was a memorably crisp career-best 250 from Jamie Cox at Trent Bridge. And Blackwell also managed a career-best – twice: seven for 90 against Glamorgan, and the same again at Nottingham, where Somerset upset the eventual winners of the division with a ten-wicket victory. Blackwell's two hundreds, and a healthy number of blows to distant parts of the outfield, continued to endear him to the crowd; now he demonstrated his value as an old-fashioned slow left-armer, getting some turn from the worn regions of the pitch and giving a lesson in accuracy. As a bowler, he proved himself a match-winner.

Still, even loyal hearts often sagged. Wins were elusive, as were positive play and adventure when needed. There was, however, evidence of more uplifting days to come. James Hildreth was perhaps the discovery of the county summer, though his progress had been quietly nurtured over recent years. Now he emerged as a mature and exciting batsman, and in his second first-class match he hit a Durham attack including Shoaib Akhtar for 101 in 113 balls. Hildreth went for his shots and showed the kind of temperament that was not cowed by reputations. England have been monitoring him, and rightly so, but it would be sad if he were lost to the appreciative Somerset members, as Marcus Trescothick has been.

They have waved goodbye to two others already. Cox returned to Tasmania after six summers; he was a quiet, popular, talented man who scored runs with handsome orthodoxy. Peter Bowler left too, to take up a legal career. His worth as a county cricketer over 19 years was reflected in an impressive batting average of 40.51, the result of his calm, correct demeanour at the top of the order. Bowler was the oldest professional on the circuit,

Ricky Ponting

generous with advice and dependable in a crisis. He held many slip catches and, towards the end, put a few down. There were three centuries in his valedictory season; mischievously he went out with a battery of aggressive shots against Yorkshire.

Matthew Wood seems to have the credentials to replace Bowler as opener. The selectors quibbled unnecessarily about bringing him into the Championship side in 2004, and when given his chance he paraded his natural skills and concentration. John Francis, joining his brother from Hampshire, looked a capable newcomer and should grow in assurance. However, many supporters argued the county were too reluctant to gamble on the best young players. The talent is there – Somerset came top of the Second Eleven Championship.

Aside from that glimpse of hope, the club ended the summer with little to celebrate. Dressing-room morale was not as buoyant as the county tried to portray, and there were protracted contractual wrangles, largely over whether some long-established players should be given full or part-time contracts. Before the end of the season, the usual ritualistic criticism began, centring on head coach Kevin Shine and captain Michael Burns, which was especially hard on Burns, who had inherited the captaincy virtually by default.

Conscious of the need for a lucid, rejuvenated approach, the club formed a cricket review group late in the season, comprising three former captains – Roy Kerslake, Vic Marks and Brian Rose. After their initial recommendations, in late 2004, Somerset signed South Africa's gifted and strong-minded young captain, Graeme Smith, to lead them from May 2005. Partly on Smith's recommendation, another South African, the all-rounder Albie Morkel, was also signed. Off the field, Shine was shifted to the county, not wholly with conviction, insisted it was not a demotion – to the academy, and the second-team coach Mark Garaway was promoted, a jump which caused some surprise. Among his priorities will be an infinitely better approach to one-day cricket; in 2004, Somerset's eighth place in the second division of the League told its own eloquently nondescript story.

SOMERSET RESULTS

All first-class matches – Played 18: Won 5, Lost 5, Drawn 8.
County Championship matches – Played 16: Won 4, Lost 5, Drawn 7.

Frizzell County Championship, 4th in Division 2; Cheltenham & Gloucester Trophy, 3rd round;
totesport League, 8th in Division 2; Twenty20 Cup, 4th in Midlands/Wales/West Group.

COUNTY CHAMPIONSHIP AVERAGES

BATTING AND FIELDING

Cap		M	I	NO	R	HS	100s	50s	Avge	Ct/St
	R. T. Ponting§	3	4	1	297	117	2	1	99.00	7
2001	I. D. Blackwell	10	14	2	745	131	2	5	62.08	3
1995	P. D. Bowler	14	24	6	957	187*	3	3	53.16	9
1999	J. Cox§	12	19	1	841	250	2	4	46.72	6
	J. C. Hildreth	13	20	2	760	108	2	5	42.22	12
	J. D. Francis	8	13	1	500	110	2	3	41.66	6
	M. J. Wood	9	13	3	402	113	1	2	40.20	4
1999	M. Burns	15	21	2	732	124*	1	4	38.52	17
1999	K. A. Parsons	3	4	1	114	55	0	1	38.00	2
2001	K. P. Dutch	6	8	1	248	72	0	2	35.42	2
2001	R. L. Johnson	13	11	1	246	101*	1	1	24.60	3
	A. W. Laraman	9	8	2	144	66*	0	1	24.00	3
	N. J. Edwards	8	16	0	380	87	0	1	23.75	8
1994	R. J. Turner	15	17	3	319	46	0	0	22.78	61/4
1992	A. R. Caddick	13	13	4	192	54	0	1	21.33	5
	S. R. G. Francis . . .	11	10	6	46	15	0	0	11.50	6
2003	N. A. M. McLean§ .	10	11	3	61	22*	0	0	7.62	1

Also batted: G. M. Andrew (1 match) 15 (1 ct); W. J. Durston (1 match) 47 (4 ct); C. M. Gazzard (1 match) 18; A. V. Suppiah (1 match) 0.

§ *Overseas player. Somerset have abandoned the traditional system of caps.*

BOWLING

	O	M	R	W	BB	5W/i	Avge
K. P. Dutch	124	21	448	19	5-26	2	23.57
N. A. M. McLean	322.1	62	1,127	43	6-79	3	26.20
A. W. Laraman	134	26	486	15	5-58	1	32.40
I. D. Blackwell	342.1	85	956	27	7-90	2	35.40
A. R. Caddick	534.3	98	1,922	54	6-80	4	35.59
S. R. G. Francis	295.5	51	1,201	33	5-42	2	36.39
R. L. Johnson	389.5	90	1,323	36	7-69	2	36.75

Also bowled: G. M. Andrew 16–3–63–3; P. D. Bowler 2–1–2–0; M. Burns 40.4–6–149–3; W. J. Durston 24–6–73–1; N. J. Edwards 15.1–1–68–1; J. D. Francis 15.3–3–55–1; J. C. Hildreth 17–1–76–2; K. A. Parsons 37–7–183–0; R. T. Ponting 5–2–6–0; A. V. Suppiah 7–0–36–2; M. J. Wood 2–0–6–0.

COUNTY RECORDS

Highest score for:	322	I. V. A. Richards v Warwickshire at Taunton	1985
Highest score against:	424	A. C. MacLaren (Lancashire) at Taunton	1895
Best bowling for:	10-49	E. J. Tyler v Surrey at Taunton	1895
Best bowling against:	10-35	A. Drake (Yorkshire) at Weston-super-Mare	1914
Highest total for:	705-9 dec.	v Hampshire at Taunton.	2003
Highest total against:	811	by Surrey at The Oval	1899
Lowest total for:	25	v Gloucestershire at Bristol	1947
Lowest total against:	22	by Gloucestershire at Bristol	1920

SOMERSET DIRECTORY

ADDRESS

County Ground, St James's Street, Taunton TA1 1JT (01823 272946; fax 01823 332395; email info@somersetcountycc.co.uk). **Website** www.somersetcountycc.co.uk.

GROUNDS

Taunton: ¼ mile N of town centre in St James's Street. From A358 or A38 follow signs for town centre and cricket ground. Nearest station: Taunton (½ mile).

Bath: ¼ mile from city centre in William Street adjoining Bath RFC. From Great Pulteney Street take L into William Street for main entrance, or access by foot via towpath from River Avon. Nearest station: Bath Spa (½ mile).

OFFICIALS

Captain 2004 – M. Burns; 2005 – G. C. Smith
Head coach M. Garaway
Academy director K. J. Shine
President R. Kerslake
Chairman C. G. Clarke

Chief executive P. W. Anderson
Chairman, cricket committee V. J. Marks
Head groundsman P. Frost
Scorer G. A. Stickley

PLAYERS

Players expected to reappear in 2005

	Former counties	Country	Born	Birthplace
Andrew Gareth Mark		E	27.12.1983	†Yeovil
Blackwell Ian David	Derbys	E	10.6.1978	Chesterfield
Burns Michael	Warwicks	E	6.2.1969	Barrow-in-Furness
*****Caddick** Andrew Richard		E	21.11.1968	Christchurch, NZ
Durston Wesley John		E	6.10.1980	†Taunton
Dutch Keith Philip	Middx	E	21.3.1973	Harrow
Edwards Neil James		E	14.10.1983	Treliske
Francis John Daniel	Hants	E	13.11.1980	Bromley
Francis Simon Richard George . .	Hants	E	15.8.1978	Bromley
Gazzard Carl Matthew		E	15.4.1982	Penzance
Hildreth James Charles		E	9.9.1984	Milton Keynes
*****Johnson** Richard Leonard	Middx	E	29.12.1974	Chertsey
Laraman Aaron William	Middx	E	10.1.1979	Enfield
Parsons Keith Alan		E	2.5.1973	†Taunton
Parsons Michael		E	26.11.1984	†Taunton
*****Ponting** Ricky Thomas		A	19.12.1974	Launceston
Suppiah Arul Vivasvan		E	30.8.1983	Kuala Lumpur, Malaysia
*****Trescothick** Marcus Edward		‡E	25.12.1975	†Keynsham
Turner Robert Julian		E	25.11.1967	Malvern
Wood Matthew James		E	30.9.1980	Exeter

Players due to join in 2005

		Country	Born	Birthplace
Morkel Johannes <u>Albertus</u>		SA	10.6.1981	Vereeniging
*****Smith** Graeme Craig		SA	1.2.1981	Johannesburg

* *Test player.* † *Born in Somerset.* ‡ *12-month ECB contract.*

SOMERSET v LOUGHBOROUGH UCCE

At Taunton, April 10, 11, 12. Drawn. Toss: Somerset. First-class debuts: C. C. Benham, P. W. Harrison, M. C. Rosenberg. County debuts: J. D. Francis, T. A. Hunt.

Caddick and Johnson, two England bowlers eager to fight their way back into national reckoning after injury, were given an extensive bowl, though on this benign Taunton surface the students coped pretty well. They batted throughout a shortened opening day, which saw a fifty from Nash, before declaring next morning. Cox then stole the show with a big hundred – containing 27 fours and three sixes – that spilled over on to the last day and helped give Somerset a useful lead. There was time enough for Nash to hit a second fifty, but not for the match to get anywhere near a result. It was not an especially happy county debut for Thos Hunt, newly arrived from Middlesex: his match figures of two for 124 included 20 no-balls and six wides.

Close of play: First day, Loughborough UCCE 260-7 (Nash 54); Second day, Somerset 296-6 (Cox 144, Turner 16).

Loughborough UCCE

R. S. Clinton lbw b Laraman	19	– (2) retired hurt	15
J. H. K. Adams b Caddick	47	– (1) b Johnson	21
V. Atri lbw b Hunt	15	– c Edwards b Laraman	0
C. C. Benham c Bowler b Johnson	37	– not out	38
C. D. Nash b Johnson	63	– not out	54
†P. W. Harrison lbw b Francis	27		
M. C. Rosenberg c Cox b Hunt	3		
P. D. Lewis c Edwards b Caddick	15		
*D. H. Wigley not out	23		
M. S. Panesar not out	12		
B 8, l-b 3, w 4, n-b 28	43	L-b 10, w 2, n-b 14	26

1/29 (1) 2/68 (3) 3/136 (2)   (8 wkts dec.) 304   1/24 (3) 2/48 (1)   (2 wkts) 154
4/152 (4) 5/202 (6) 6/218 (7)
7/260 (8) 8/278 (5)

J. E. Anyon did not bat.

In the second innings Clinton retired hurt at 22.

Bowling: *First Innings*—Caddick 29.2–7–80–2; Johnson 24–6–69–2; Laraman 13–4–42–1; Hunt 17–2–85–2; Burns 3–0–6–0; Francis 6–2–11–1. *Second Innings*—Caddick 15–5–24–0; Johnson 8–4–15–1; Laraman 9–8–4–1; Francis 15–4–54–0; Hunt 11–2–39–0; Cox 1–0–8–0; Burns 1–1–0–0.

Somerset

P. D. Bowler lbw b Wigley	7	A. R. Caddick c Wigley b Rosenberg	12
J. D. Francis lbw b Wigley	12	T. A. Hunt not out	1
N. J. Edwards b Panesar	40		
J. Cox c Adams b Lewis	172	L-b 8	8
*M. Burns b Wigley	1		
M. J. Wood c Harrison b Panesar	57	1/16 (1) 2/19 (2) 3/101 (3)	379
A. W. Laraman b Wigley	13	4/102 (5) 5/237 (6) 6/268 (7)	
†R. J. Turner c Nash b Lewis	27	7/329 (8) 8/336 (4)	
R. L. Johnson lbw b Anyon	29	9/375 (9) 10/379 (10)	

Bowling: Wigley 31–6–133–4; Lewis 23–9–68–2; Anyon 15–5–62–1; Panesar 33–6–81–2; Rosenberg 6.1–0–27–1.

Umpires: J. H. Evans and R. K. Illingworth.

❝Umpire Burgess thought it the finest catch he had seen.**❞**

Kent in 2004, pages 650–651.

SOMERSET v DERBYSHIRE

At Taunton, April 21, 22, 23, 24. Drawn. Somerset 10 pts, Derbyshire 9 pts. Toss: Derbyshire. First-class debut: N. G. E. Walker.

Somerset's last-afternoon declaration seemed to reflect excessive caution by the captain, Burns, though he argued that the pitch was too good for generosity. His opposite number, Sutton, had earlier declared with Derbyshire 113 behind, but in return was set an unrealistic target of 284 in 37 overs. Derbyshire, already bereft of seam bowlers through injury and illness, lost another when Welch broke down with back trouble. Into the breach stepped Nick Walker, a 19-year-old pace bowler from Hertfordshire spotted by the new coach Dave Houghton, and he earned six wickets. Despite a first-day washout and the tame end, there were still moments to savour. Forty-year-old Bowler, who had chosen to defer his legal career for another year and was now the oldest player in county cricket, again demonstrated his tidy, unhurried style with a century. Hassan Adnan responded with a defiant hundred of his own, while Laraman took a career-best five for 58.

Close of play: First day, No play; Second day, Somerset 364-5 (Wood 56, Laraman 20); Third day, Somerset 24-0 (Bowler 18, Francis 6).

Somerset

P. D. Bowler c Gait b Dean	127	– c Rogers b Walker	28
J. D. Francis lbw b Dean	17	– lbw b Walker	36
N. J. Edwards c Bassano b Hewson	14	– c Welch b Dumelow	13
J. Cox c Gait b Walker	35	– c Welch b Hewson	6
*M. Burns c Dean b Walker	68	– c Rogers b Hewson	5
M. J. Wood c Hassan Adnan b Walker	66	– lbw b Hewson	26
A. W. Laraman c Hassan Adnan b Walker	20	– not out	29
†R. J. Turner lbw b Dean	10	– not out	22
R. L. Johnson lbw b Dean	1		
A. R. Caddick c Sutton b Dean	1		
N. A. M. McLean not out	1		
B 1, l-b 6, w 1, n-b 20	28	L-b 5	5

1/52 (2) 2/87 (3) 3/182 (4) 4/246 (1)   **388**   1/37 (1) 2/59 (3)   **(6 wkts dec.) 170**
5/319 (5) 6/367 (7) 7/383 (6)   3/70 (4) 4/86 (5)
8/386 (9) 9/387 (8) 10/388 (10)   5/117 (2) 6/126 (6)

Bonus points – Somerset 4, Derbyshire 3.

Bowling: *First Innings*—Walker 23–0–111–4; Welch 16–5–33–0; Dean 26–6–86–5; Hewson 21–8–48–1; Dumelow 22–2–92–0; Hassan Adnan 2–0–11–0. *Second Innings*—Dean 6–2–10–0; Walker 19–3–49–2; Hewson 18–8–39–3; Dumelow 25–5–60–1; Hassan Adnan 3–0–7–0.

Derbyshire

A. I. Gait lbw b Laraman	43	– not out	36
S. A. Selwood c Edwards b McLean	38	– c Turner b Caddick	3
C. J. L. Rogers c Turner b Laraman	8	– not out	58
Hassan Adnan not out	107		
C. W. G. Bassano c Turner b Caddick	8		
*†L. D. Sutton lbw b Laraman	6		
D. R. Hewson c Turner b Laraman	0		
G. Welch lbw b Edwards	9		
N. R. C. Dumelow c Burns b Laraman	18		
K. J. Dean not out	8		
B 8, l-b 3, w 1, n-b 18	30	L-b 6, w 1, n-b 8	15

1/84 (1) 2/98 (3) 3/98 (2)   **(8 wkts dec.) 275**   1/3 (2)   **(1 wkt) 112**
4/118 (5) 5/141 (6)
6/141 (7) 7/170 (8) 8/237 (9)

N. G. E. Walker did not bat.

Bonus points – Derbyshire 2, Somerset 2.

Bowling: *First Innings*—Caddick 19–6–61–1; Johnson 20–7–58–0; McLean 21–5–62–1; Laraman 16–4–58–5; Burns 3–0–9–0; Edwards 3–0–16–1. *Second Innings*—Caddick 8–1–27–1; McLean 5–1–15–0; Johnson 4–1–16–0; Laraman 4–0–13–0; Edwards 6–1–24–0; Francis 4–0–11–0.

Umpires: J. W. Lloyds and N. A. Mallender.

At Chelmsford, April 28, 29, 30, May 1. SOMERSET drew with ESSEX.

SOMERSET v DURHAM

At Taunton, May 12, 13, 14, 15. Durham won by one wicket. Durham 18 pts, Somerset 7 pts. Toss: Somerset.

Durham, second-best for three days, snatched the game from Somerset on the last in spectacular fashion when they reached a resolute and unlikely 453 to win in the tautest of finishes. At 95 for five, a Durham victory looked impossible, but an unbeaten century from Breese, only his second in first-class cricket, guided them home by one wicket. Before hitting the winning boundary, Breese – a Jamaican employed primarily for his off-spin – survived some uncomfortable overs from the

---

YOUNGEST CENTURIONS FOR SOMERSET

Years	days		
18	104	A. T. M. Jones (106) v Leicestershire at Leicester.	1938
18	175	M. E. Trescothick (121) v Surrey at Bath	1994
19	193	R. J. Bartlett (117*) v Oxford University at Oxford.	1986
19	**246**	**J. C. Hildreth (101) v Durham at Taunton**	**2004**
19	281	W. T. Greswell (100) v Middlesex at Lord's.	1909
19	317 ⎫	R. J. Harden (107) v Cambridge University at Taunton	1985
19	317 ⎭	N. J. Edwards (160) v Hampshire at Taunton	2003
19	337	S. G. U. Considine (130*) v Worcestershire at Taunton	1921
19	357	G. S. Chappell (148) v Middlesex at Weston-super-Mare	1968

Note: H. Gimblett was 20 years 211 days when he scored his famous 63-minute century v Essex at Frome in 1935.

HIGHEST FOURTH-INNINGS TOTALS TO WIN IN COUNTY CHAMPIONSHIP

502-6	Middlesex v Nottinghamshire at Nottingham (set 502)	1925
461-3	Nottinghamshire v Worcestershire at Worcester (set 458)	2001
455-8	Sussex v Gloucestershire at Hove (set 452)	1999
453-9	**Durham v Somerset at Taunton (set 451)**	**2004**
449-9	Worcestershire v Somerset at Bath (set 446)	1996
446-8	Hampshire v Gloucestershire at Southampton (set 445)	1990
442-6	Essex v Derbyshire at Derby (set 440)	1992
429-5	**Kent v Worcestershire at Canterbury (set 429)**	**2004**

Somerset pace bowlers, and his last partner Davies was nearly run out. Captaining Somerset in Burns's absence, Cox compiled a good-looking century in the second innings; he also received some criticism from spectators for declaring too early. "I stand by what I did," he countered: "I wanted to give our bowlers as much time as possible, and they were really unlucky." Caddick did manage five wickets, but Johnson, after grabbing seven in the first innings, went wicketless. The most encouraging aspect for Somerset was the hundred from James Hildreth, a Millfield old boy playing only his second Championship match. He revealed a mature temperament and a generous repertoire of shots.

Close of play: First day, Durham 9-0 (Lewis 9, North 0); Second day, Somerset 68-2 (Wood 6, Cox 2); Third day, Durham 174-5 (Peng 70, Breese 25).

Somerset

P. D. Bowler lbw b Collingwood	12	– lbw b Davies	25
N. J. Edwards lbw b Davies	23	– c Lewis b Davies	30
M. J. Wood lbw b Muchall	5	– c Collingwood b Killeen	7
*J. Cox c G. J. Pratt b Shoaib Akhtar	66	– c Killeen b North	124
J. C. Hildreth c A. Pratt b Shoaib Akhtar	101	– c Collingwood b Breese	72
K. A. Parsons lbw b Davies	55	– not out	36
†R. J. Turner lbw b Shoaib Akhtar	0		
K. P. Dutch b Killeen	72		
R. L. Johnson lbw b Killeen	1		
A. R. Caddick c Breese b Davies	8		
N. A. M. McLean not out	14		
B 1, l-b 6, w 9, n-b 2	18	B 8, l-b 7, w 1	16

1/42 (2) 2/42 (1) 3/52 (3) 4/222 (5)	**375**	1/59 (1) 2/62 (2) (5 wkts dec.) 310
5/223 (6) 6/223 (7) 7/350 (8)		3/77 (3) 4/217 (5)
8/352 (9) 9/354 (6) 10/375 (10)		5/310 (4)

Bonus points – Somerset 4, Durham 3.

Bowling: *First Innings*—Shoaib Akhtar 14–3–63–3; Killeen 19–5–52–2; Collingwood 14–4–50–1; Davies 22–6–55–3; Muchall 5–0–33–1; Breese 18–3–85–0; North 7–0–30–0. *Second Innings*—Shoaib Akhtar 13–3–45–0; Killeen 20–3–59–1; Davies 20–3–69–2; Collingwood 12–3–37–0; Breese 21–1–79–1; North 14–0–6–1.

Durham

*J. J. B. Lewis b Johnson	65	– c Turner b Caddick	2
M. J. North lbw b Johnson	20	– c Turner b Caddick	33
G. J. Muchall c Turner b Johnson	0	– b McLean	19
P. D. Collingwood c Hildreth b Johnson	9	– lbw b Caddick	4
N. Peng lbw b Caddick	0	– lbw b Caddick	88
G. J. Pratt c Turner b McLean	1	– c Edwards b Caddick	12
G. R. Breese c Turner b Johnson	41	– not out	165
†A. Pratt not out	46	– c Edwards b Dutch	25
Shoaib Akhtar b McLean	25	– c Wood b Dutch	46
N. Killeen lbw b Johnson	3	– b McLean	35
A. M. Davies c Turner b Johnson	10	– not out	4
B 2, l-b 5, n-b 8	15	L-b 16, n-b 4	20

1/46 (1) 2/46 (3) 3/60 (4) 4/70 (5)	**235**	1/10 (1) 2/57 (2) (9 wkts) 453
5/71 (6) 6/136 (7) 7/145 (1)		3/57 (3) 4/75 (4) 5/95 (6)
8/199 (9) 9/209 (10) 10/235 (11)		6/226 (5) 7/269 (8)
		8/357 (9) 9/433 (10)

Bonus points – Durham 1, Somerset 3.

Bowling: *First Innings*—Caddick 22–5–59–1; Johnson 23–4–69–7; McLean 18–3–52–2; Parsons 9–2–48–0. *Second Innings*—Caddick 42–8–149–5; Johnson 31.5–4–141–0; McLean 31–4–93–2; Parsons 2–0–13–0; Hildreth 1–0–4–0; Dutch 6–0–37–2.

Umpires: J. H. Hampshire and N. A. Mallender.

At Derby, May 19, 20, 21, 22. SOMERSET drew with DERBYSHIRE.

SOMERSET v ESSEX

At Taunton, May 25, 26, 27, 28. Drawn. Somerset 10 pts, Essex 12 pts. Toss: Essex.

Yet again, the Taunton pitch remained full of runs, while offering little for the bowlers. Middlebrook made the point with a confident maiden Championship hundred in the first innings, after Jefferson, the tall, eager opener, hit a stirring 95. Napier, too, was in the runs to help carry Essex to maximum batting points. Somerset's reply was not without merit, at least not from the late order. Between them Johnson – offering some compensation for modest bowling returns – Caddick and McLean added 141 in 16 overs to avert the follow-on and squeeze Essex's lead to just 61. Mindful of Durham's achievement on this ground a fortnight earlier but not of a poor forecast, Essex, bolstered by centuries from Flower and Grayson, reached 400 a second time. Challenged to make 475, Somerset were in danger of losing, but another timely and painstaking hundred from Bowler, rain stoppages and an obdurate contribution from Turner all thwarted Essex.

Close of play: First day, Somerset 11-1 (Edwards 11, Cox 0); Second day, Essex 52-2 (Grayson 13, Flower 10); Third day, Somerset 23-0 (Bowler 19, Edwards 4).

Essex

W. I. Jefferson b McLean	95	– b McLean	14
A. N. Cook c Turner b Caddick	8	– lbw b McLean	10
*A. P. Grayson c Edwards b Caddick	4	– b Blackwell	30
A. Flower b Caddick	42	– c Turner b Caddick	172
A. Habib lbw b Caddick	0	– b Blackwell	28
†J. S. Foster run out	37	– not out	104
J. D. Middlebrook c Parsons b Caddick	115	– b Caddick	1
G. R. Napier c Burns b Caddick	79	– c Bowler b Blackwell	9
A. J. Clarke c Edwards b McLean	2	– b Blackwell	28
S. A. Brant not out	6	– b McLean	0
A. G. A. M. McCoubrey not out	1	– b McLean	0
L-b 7, n-b 4	11	B 1, l-b 8, w 6, n-b 2	17

1/17 (2) 2/33 (3) 3/140 (4)   (9 wkts dec.) 400   1/22 (2) 2/29 (1) 3/100 (3)   413
4/140 (5) 5/162 (1) 6/205 (6)   4/150 (5) 5/329 (4) 6/335 (7)
7/380 (8) 8/383 (9) 9/393 (7)   7/353 (8) 8/391 (9)
                                        9/405 (10) 10/413 (11)

Bonus points – Essex 5, Somerset 3.

Bowling: *First Innings*—Caddick 24–5–80–6; Johnson 21–2–90–0; McLean 20.3–3–75–2; Parsons 17–2–86–0; Blackwell 13–3–44–0; Burns 3–0–18–0. *Second Innings*—Caddick 29–5–84–2; Johnson 26–7–79–0; McLean 26.1–4–87–5; Blackwell 39–4–146–3; Edwards 3–0–8–0.

Somerset

P. D. Bowler c Flower b Napier	0	– not out	138
N. J. Edwards c Foster b Clarke	26	– c Foster b Brant	19
J. Cox c Cook b Brant	86	– run out	3
J. C. Hildreth c Flower b McCoubrey	9	– b Middlebrook	41
*M. Burns c Foster b Clarke	32	– b Napier	6
I. D. Blackwell c and b Napier	3	– b Clarke	30
K. A. Parsons c Cook b Clarke	12	– c Foster b Clarke	11
†R. J. Turner lbw b McCoubrey	25	– not out	20
R. L. Johnson c Cook b Middlebrook	58		
A. R. Caddick c Clarke b Brant	54		
N. A. M. McLean not out	22		
B 4, l-b 3, w 3, n-b 2	12	L-b 2, w 1	3

1/0 (1) 2/40 (2) 3/51 (4) 4/144 (5)   339   1/44 (2) 2/56 (3)   (6 wkts) 271
5/147 (6) 6/162 (7) 7/198 (8)   3/131 (4) 4/156 (5)
8/198 (3) 9/291 (9) 10/339 (10)   5/192 (6) 6/209 (7)

Bonus points – Somerset 3, Essex 3.

Bowling: *First Innings*—Napier 16–7–52–2; Brant 17.3–1–87–2; Clarke 21–2–61–3; McCoubrey 10–1–52–2; Middlebrook 10–1–59–1; Grayson 4–0–21–0. *Second Innings*—Napier 22–1–84–1; Clarke 19–5–50–2; Brant 11–4–24–1; Grayson 8–1–24–0; McCoubrey 6–2–35–0; Middlebrook 17–2–52–1.

Umpires: J. H. Evans and P. J. Hartley.

At Swansea, June 2, 3, 4, 5. SOMERSET lost to GLAMORGAN by seven wickets.

SOMERSET v NOTTINGHAMSHIRE

At Bath, June 9, 10, 11, 12. Nottinghamshire won by seven wickets. Nottinghamshire 22 pts, Somerset 7 pts. Toss: Nottinghamshire.

Nottinghamshire, with their fourth successive Championship win, comfortably confirmed their position at the top of Division Two in a match that disappointed a Festival crowd hoping for a marked improvement from Somerset. Edwards, with some good luck among his good shots, and the increasingly impressive Hildreth at least hinted at better times ahead. And until rain came in the early evening on the opening day, Blackwell seemed intent on the fastest century of the season, reaching his fifty off just 30 balls. But Franks worked his way through the innings, ending with seven for 72, his best for four years, and then the match's dominant innings came from Bicknell, who took advantage of a nondescript attack to give Nottinghamshire a lead of 61, which proved decisive when Smith led the demolition of Somerset's second innings. A broken finger meant Gazzard could not keep wicket for Somerset on the last day, and Burns took over.

Close of play: First day, Somerset 318-5 (Blackwell 55, Gazzard 7); Second day, Nottinghamshire 266-4 (Bicknell 145); Third day, Nottinghamshire 23-0 (Bicknell 15, Gallian 5).

Somerset

P. D. Bowler c Read b Franks	39	– lbw b Ealham	25
N. J. Edwards c Hussey b Franks	87	– c Ealham b Franks	15
J. Cox c Read b Franks	1	– b Smith	63
J. C. Hildreth c Read b Franks	60	– b Smith	29
*M. Burns c Hussey b Franks	35	– c Hussey b Smith	24
I. D. Blackwell b Sidebottom	78	– lbw b Smith	9
†C. M. Gazzard c Read b Sidebottom	18	– absent hurt	
K. P. Dutch c Ealham b Franks	5	– (7) c MacGill b Sidebottom	22
A. R. Caddick c Singh b Smith	27	– (8) c Ealham b Smith	3
S. R. G. Francis not out	7	– (9) not out	5
N. A. M. McLean c Sidebottom b Franks	1	– (10) c Hussey b Sidebottom	0
B 4, l-b 15, w 14, n-b 8	41	B 8, l-b 6, w 9, n-b 2	25
	399		**220**

1/100 (1) 2/107 (3) 3/211 (4) 4/245 (2) 5/276 (5) 6/352 (7) 7/353 (6) 8/378 (8) 9/396 (9) 10/399 (11)

1/33 (2) 2/88 (1) 3/145 (4) 4/175 (5) 5/184 (3) 6/189 (6) 7/199 (8) 8/220 (7) 9/220 (10)

Bonus points – Somerset 4, Nottinghamshire 3.

Bowling: *First Innings*— Smith 25–4–105–1; Sidebottom 21–6–60–2; Ealham 13–3–56–0; Franks 24.2–5–72–7; MacGill 22–4–85–0; Hussey 2–1–2–0. *Second Innings*—Smith 17–4–49–5; Sidebottom 7.5–1–38–2; Franks 8–1–45–1; Ealham 15–3–46–1; MacGill 7–0–28–0.

Nottinghamshire

D. J. Bicknell b McLean	150	– c Burns b McLean	26
*J. E. R. Gallian b McLean	10	– c Hildreth b Caddick	10
A. Singh c Burns b Francis	55	– c Burns b Caddick	33
R. J. Warren b Blackwell	32	– not out	48
R. J. Sidebottom c and b Caddick	5		
D. J. Hussey c Hildreth b Francis	21	– (5) not out	35
†C. M. W. Read c Hildreth b Caddick	66		
M. A. Ealham c Burns b McLean	24		
P. J. Franks b Francis	54		
G. J. Smith c Burns b Francis	5		
S. C. G. MacGill not out	4		
B 9, l-b 4, w 3, n-b 18	34	B 2, l-b 1, w 1, n-b 4	8

1/18 (2) 2/177 (3) 3/257 (4) 4/266 (5)   460   1/36 (2) 2/40 (1)   (3 wkts) 160
5/278 (1) 6/304 (6) 7/359 (8)   3/114 (3)
8/427 (7) 9/441 (10) 10/460 (9)

Bonus points – Nottinghamshire 5, Somerset 3.

Bowling: *First Innings*—Caddick 36–4–156–2; McLean 24–6–78–3; Francis 25.1–1–106–4; Burns 6–2–28–0; Blackwell 22–5–79–1. *Second Innings*—Caddick 19–3–64–2; McLean 8–3–26–1; Francis 8.3–0–41–0; Blackwell 4–1–11–0; Dutch 3–1–15–0.

Umpires: A. G. T. Whitehead and P. Willey.

At Southampton, June 18, 19, 20. SOMERSET lost to HAMPSHIRE by 275 runs.

SOMERSET v LEICESTERSHIRE

At Taunton, June 23, 24, 25, 26. Drawn. Somerset 8 pts, Leicestershire 10.5 pts (after 1.5 pt penalty). Toss: Leicestershire.

In a fixture ravaged by bad weather with no play on the first and last days, there was still little to suggest Somerset had found the formula for success. Leicestershire always had the better of things – including the toss – and they productively went after Somerset's wayward and inadequate bowling, passing 400 without much trouble. Maddy, especially strong, and Robinson put on 158 for the first wicket, and after them came useful contributions from the lower middle order. Somerset's opening stand made 99, but it was a struggle to save the follow-on against the Australian seamer Cleary. Maddy played another poised innings but rain meant it was a lost cause.

Close of play: First day, No play; Second day, Somerset 45-0 (Bowler 24, J. D. Francis 18); Third day, Leicestershire 95-2 (Maddy 59, Stevens 12).

Leicestershire

D. D. J. Robinson b McLean	72	– c Laraman b McLean	21
D. L. Maddy c Turner b McLean	84	– not out	59
B. J. Hodge c Turner b Caddick	2	– b Caddick	1
J. L. Sadler c Cox b S. R. G. Francis	10		
D. I. Stevens c Hildreth b S. R. G. Francis	37	– (4) not out	12
†P. A. Nixon not out	63		
*P. A. J. DeFreitas c Caddick b McLean	13		
O. D. Gibson c Turner b McLean	16		
C. W. Henderson c Turner b Laraman	52		
M. F. Cleary not out	31		
L-b 7, w 3, n-b 12	22	N-b 2	2

1/158 (2) 2/167 (1) 3/167 (3)   (8 wkts dec.) 402   1/27 (1) 2/32 (3)   (2 wkts) 95
4/211 (4) 5/224 (5) 6/255 (7)
7/277 (8) 8/358 (9)

C. E. Dagnall did not bat.

Bonus points – Leicestershire 5, Somerset 2.

Bowling: *First Innings*—Caddick 28.5–7–103–1; McLean 22–0–100–4; S. R. G. Francis 19–2–118–2; Laraman 18–2–74–1. *Second Innings*—Caddick 10–1–31–1; McLean 6–2–18–1; S. R. G. Francis 7–1–32–0; J. D. Francis 3–1–14–0.

Somerset

P. D. Bowler lbw b Cleary	46	S. R. G. Francis lbw b DeFreitas	6
J. D. Francis c Maddy b Gibson	52	N. A. M. McLean c Nixon b Cleary	11
J. Cox c and b Dagnall	2		
J. C. Hildreth c Stevens b Dagnall	4	B 10, l-b 9, n-b 14	33
*M. Burns b Cleary	27		
M. J. Wood not out	33		262
A. W. Laraman c Nixon b Cleary	4		
†R. J. Turner c Robinson b Cleary	37		
A. R. Caddick c Nixon b Maddy	7		

1/99 (1) 2/113 (3) 3/121 (2) 4/121 (4) 5/170 (5) 6/182 (7) 7/202 (9) 8/236 (10) 9/257 (11) 10/262 (8)

Bonus points – Somerset 2, Leicestershire 3.

Wood, when 29, retired hurt at 185 and resumed at 257.

Bowling: DeFreitas 23–8–46–1; Gibson 28–8–83–1; Henderson 2–0–13–0; Dagnall 18–5–49–2; Cleary 16–2–50–5; Maddy 3–2–2–1.

Umpires: I. J. Gould and B. Leadbeater.

At Scarborough, July 21, 22, 23. SOMERSET beat YORKSHIRE by ten wickets.

At Taunton, July 27, 28, 29, 30. SOMERSET beat SRI LANKA A by 289 runs (see Sri Lanka A tour section).

SOMERSET v GLAMORGAN

At Taunton, August 3, 4, 5. Somerset won by eight wickets. Somerset 21 pts, Glamorgan 5 pts. Toss: Somerset.

It was significant that the brightest chapter of Somerset's season coincided with the arrival of the Australian captain, Ricky Ponting. This was their second successive Championship victory, and in each match Ponting scored a hundred with a handsome, eager array of strokes; his influence in field placings and general encouragement was also clear. No one, however, did more to win this game than Blackwell. First, he scored 98 from No. 6, taking Somerset 132 runs beyond Glamorgan's first innings; Jones – perhaps piqued after being excluded when available for the previous Championship match – took five wickets. But Blackwell bettered that with a career-best seven for 90 on the third day, at times making cunning use of the rough in a long, accurate spell. Somerset were left a target of 163, which caused no alarms. Before taking spin, the pitch had helped the pace bowlers, and Somerset inserted Glamorgan, for whom the opener Elliott was last out for a composed hundred. Then Ponting and Blackwell took over. During the match, Bowler, the oldest player on the circuit at 41, announced his retirement.

Close of play: First day, Somerset 143-1 (Bowler 51, Ponting 71); Second day, Glamorgan 97-0 (Wallace 53, Elliott 43).

Glamorgan

M. T. G. Elliott b McLean	103	– (2) b Blackwell	85
†M. A. Wallace c Turner b Johnson	0	– (1) b Blackwell	70
D. L. Hemp c Turner b Johnson	5	– c J. D. Francis b Blackwell	3
M. J. Powell c Hildreth b S. R. G. Francis	39	– c Ponting b Blackwell	0
M. P. Maynard c Ponting b S. R. G. Francis	4	– lbw b Johnson	25
J. Hughes c Ponting b S. R. G. Francis	5	– c J. D. Francis b Blackwell	1
*R. D. B. Croft c Turner b S. R. G. Francis	23	– b S. R. G. Francis	16
D. S. Harrison c and b S. R. G. Francis	4	– c Turner b Johnson	5
S. D. Thomas c Turner b McLean	54	– b Blackwell	52
M. S. Kasprowicz lbw b Blackwell	0	– c Bowler b Blackwell	14
S. P. Jones not out	0	– not out	2
B 4, l-b 2, n-b 19	25	B 9, l-b 5, w 5, n-b 2	21

1/8 (2) 2/14 (3) 3/85 (4) 4/99 (5)   262   1/126 (1) 2/136 (3) 3/136 (4)   294
5/113 (6) 6/166 (7) 7/170 (8)   4/188 (2) 5/196 (6) 6/196 (5)
8/262 (9) 9/262 (10) 10/262 (1)   7/202 (8) 8/263 (7)
                                          9/277 (9) 10/294 (10)

Bonus points – Glamorgan 2, Somerset 3.

Bowling: *First Innings*—McLean 19.3–3–73–2; Johnson 16–4–82–2; Laraman 9–0–39–0; S. R. G. Francis 15–6–42–5; Blackwell 8–2–20–1. *Second Innings*—McLean 1.5–0–12–0; Johnson 23–2–102–2; S. R. G. Francis 14.1–1–67–1; Blackwell 35.5–12–90–7; Laraman 4–0–9–0.

Somerset

P. D. Bowler c Wallace b Jones	86	– c Wallace b Harrison	55
J. D. Francis c and b Kasprowicz	12	– lbw b Croft	54
R. T. Ponting c Jones b Thomas	117	– not out	18
J. C. Hildreth c Hemp b Jones	0	– not out	32
*M. Burns lbw b Harrison	10		
I. D. Blackwell c Elliott b Jones	98		
A. W. Laraman c Wallace b Harrison	1		
†R. J. Turner c Maynard b Croft	36		
R. L. Johnson b Jones	9		
S. R. G. Francis not out	1		
N. A. M. McLean lbw b Jones	0		
B 1, l-b 7, n-b 16	24	B 1, l-b 1, w 1, n-b 2	5

1/19 (2) 2/229 (3) 3/231 (4) 4/235 (1)   394   1/103 (2) 2/111 (1)   (2 wkts) 164
5/267 (5) 6/279 (7) 7/364 (8)
8/391 (9) 9/394 (6) 10/394 (11)

Bonus points – Somerset 4, Glamorgan 3.

Bowling: *First Innings*—Kasprowicz 21–3–81–1; Harrison 18–2–62–2; Jones 19.5–1–94–5; Croft 30–8–87–1; Thomas 16–1–62–1. *Second Innings*—Kasprowicz 4–0–12–0; Croft 17.4–3–71–1; Jones 7–2–27–0; Thomas 4–0–25–0; Harrison 5–1–27–1.

Umpires: V. A. Holder and T. E. Jesty.

At Chester-le-Street, August 13, 14, 15, 16. SOMERSET drew with DURHAM.

"Resigned? Yes. Resigning? Not yet."
West Indians in England, page 482.

SOMERSET v HAMPSHIRE

At Taunton, August 18, 19, 20, 21. Hampshire won by ten runs. Hampshire 17 pts, Somerset 3 pts. Toss: Hampshire.

In a game truncated by rain, the two captains managed, through predetermined declarations, to introduce purpose and competition to the final day. Somerset were set 351 in 85 overs and gave every indication of scoring the runs. They were strongly placed on 300 for three, only to crumble miserably against Warne. He took four wickets, which gave him six for the innings, and played a cool hand in two of Somerset's three panicky run-outs. In taking Somerset to the brink, John Francis had batted particularly well for a century against his former county, while Burns showed a captain's resolution before he was run out. Somerset had begun the match without a regular spinner, which appeared justified as Caddick took four wickets in five overs after almost two months out with a foot injury. But rain washed away more than half of the first three days' play, hence the collusion.

Close of play: First day, Hampshire 114-2 (Crawley 32, Katich 15); Second day, Somerset 20-1 (Bowler 7, Cox 3); Third day, Hampshire 66-1 (Adams 11, Prittipaul 49).

Hampshire

J. H. K. Adams c Hildreth b Johnson	31	– not out	21
M. J. Brown c Wood b Caddick	17	– c Bowler b Hildreth	5
J. P. Crawley c Burns b Johnson	34		
S. M. Katich c Johnson b Caddick	38		
D. A. Kenway c Turner b Caddick	37	– (4) not out	21
†N. Pothas c Bowler b Caddick	5		
L. R. Prittipaul b Bowler b Johnson	44	– (3) c Caddick b Hildreth	49
A. D. Mascarenhas c Turner b Caddick	1		
*S. K. Warne c J. D. Francis b Laraman	47		
B. V. Taylor c Turner b Laraman	14		
J. T. A. Bruce not out	0		
B 8, l-b 6, w 1, n-b 18	33	W 3	3
	301	**(2 wkts dec.)**	**99**

1/31 (2) 2/72 (1) 3/116 (3) 4/167 (4)   1/7 (2) 2/67 (3)   (2 wkts dec.) 99
5/177 (6) 6/190 (5) 7/196 (3)
8/271 (7) 9/293 (9) 10/301 (10)

Bonus points – Hampshire 3, Somerset 3.

Bowling: First Innings—Johnson 26–9–61–3; Caddick 29–4–97–5; Laraman 17–3–67–2; S. R. G. Francis 20–5–62–0. *Second Innings*—Burns 10.4–0–40–0; Hildreth 10–1–39–2; J. D. Francis 3–1–14–0; Wood 2–0–6–0.

Somerset

P. D. Bowler not out	22	– b Mascarenhas	25
J. D. Francis c Bruce b Taylor	4	– c Katich b Warne	110
J. Cox not out	12	– c Pothas b Warne	20
J. C. Hildreth (did not bat)		– c Prittipaul b Warne	40
*M. Burns (did not bat)		– run out	79
R. L. Johnson (did not bat)		– b Warne	4
M. J. Wood (did not bat)		– run out	18
A. W. Laraman (did not bat)		– c Pothas b Warne	3
†R. J. Turner (did not bat)		– lbw b Warne	11
A. R. Caddick (did not bat)		– run out	0
S. R. G. Francis (did not bat)		– not out	1
N-b 12	12	B 2, l-b 8, w 2, n-b 22	29
	(1 wkt dec.) 50		**340**

1/10 (2)   (1 wkt dec.) 50   1/48 (1) 2/93 (3) 3/155 (4)   340
4/300 (2) 5/306 (6) 6/313 (5)
7/324 (8) 8/336 (9)
9/336 (10) 10/340 (7)

Bowling: *First Innings*—Bruce 5–0–13–0; Taylor 4–2–7–1; Prittipaul 4–2–13–0; Katich 6–0–11–0; Adams 5–2–6–0; Kenway 2–2–0–0. *Second Innings*—Taylor 15–2–55–0; Bruce 16–3–77–0; Mascarenhas 17–4–46–1; Prittipaul 2–1–9–0; Warne 30.4–1–127–6; Katich 3–0–21–0.

Umpires: M. J. Kitchen and B. Leadbeater.

At Nottingham, September 3, 4, 5, 6. SOMERSET beat NOTTINGHAMSHIRE by ten wickets.

SOMERSET v YORKSHIRE

At Taunton, September 10, 11, 12, 13. Drawn. Somerset 7 pts, Yorkshire 7 pts. Toss: Somerset. First-class debut: D. J. Wainwright.

Any Somerset optimists still hoping for promotion were disappointed when the match disappeared in the rain. No play was possible on the final day, undoing earlier efforts by the captains to bring about a meaningful end. Only 74.5 overs were bowled on the first two days, during which Jaques scored 95; he began an opening stand of 162 with a string of fours off Caddick, though the bowler got belated revenge. When they finally had their chance, on the third day, Somerset's openers replied with a substantial partnership of their own. Bowler, in his farewell before retirement, was appropriately full of orthodox merit, as he and Wood, master and pupil, put on an elegant 141 for the first wicket. When Somerset declared, still 183 behind, their supporters applauded Bowler's valedictory flourish, after 19 summers of county cricket. With Yorkshire stretching their lead rapidly on the third evening, presumably aiming for a declaration of their own, the rain returned. The downpours restricted David Wainwright, a 19-year-old from Pontefract, to just three overs of left-arm spin on his first-class debut.

Close of play: First day, Yorkshire 60-0 (Jaques 48, Sayers 10); Second day, Yorkshire 276-5 (Dawood 18, Dawson 0); Third day, Yorkshire 125-4 (Wood 26, Dawood 6).

Yorkshire

P. A. Jaques c Bowler b Caddick	95	– c Johnson b Francis	27
J. J. Sayers c Wood b Caddick	62	– c Francis b Laraman	46
M. J. Lumb lbw b Blackwell	4	– c Blackwell b Francis	0
*M. J. Wood c Turner b Johnson	46	– not out	26
R. M. Pyrah lbw b Johnson	39	– run out	8
†I. Dawood c Francis b Blackwell	31	– not out	6
R. K. J. Dawson c Bowler b Laraman	0		
T. T. Bresnan c Hildreth b Caddick	13		
D. J. Wainwright c Burns b Laraman	5		
M. J. Hoggard c Cox b Caddick	7		
S. P. Kirby not out	0		
B 8, l-b 4, n-b 10	22	L-b 4, n-b 8	12

1/162 (2) 2/167 (1) 3/171 (3) 4/246 (5)	**324**	
5/273 (4) 6/277 (7) 7/299 (6)		
8/304 (9) 9/323 (8) 10/324 (10)		

1/69 (1) 2/69 (3)	**(4 wkts)**	**125**
3/93 (2) 4/103 (5)		

Bonus points – Yorkshire 3, Somerset 3.

Bowling: *First Innings*—Caddick 19.3–1–94–4; Johnson 22–4–78–2; Francis 8–1–22–0; Blackwell 31–4–75–2; Laraman 13–3–43–2. *Second Innings*—Caddick 3–0–23–0; Johnson 3–0–30–0; Laraman 5–0–33–1; Francis 5–0–35–2.

Somerset

P. D. Bowler not out 75
M. J. Wood not out 62
　　　　　N-b 4   4
　　　　　　　　　　　　　　　　　　　　　　　——
　　　　　　　　　　　　(no wkt dec.) 141

J. Cox, J. C. Hildreth, *M. Burns, I. D. Blackwell, A. W. Laraman, †R. J. Turner, R. L. Johnson,
A. R. Caddick and S. R. G. Francis did not bat.

　Bowling: Hoggard 8–1–44–0; Kirby 10–2–38–0; Bresnan 4–0–25–0; Dawson 8–1–29–0;
Wainwright 3–1–5–0.

　　　　　　　　　　　Umpires: V. A. Holder and J. F. Steele.

At Leicester, September 16, 17, 18, 19. SOMERSET beat LEICESTERSHIRE by 75 runs.

THE PETER SMITH MEMORIAL AWARD

David Foot, author of the appreciation of Marcus Trescothick (page 65),
received a rare honour himself in 2004 when he was given the Peter
Smith Memorial Award from the Cricket Writers' Club. He is only the
second journalist (after former *Wisden* editor John Woodcock) to be
chosen for the accolade since it was instituted in 1992.

　The award, in memory of the club's former chairman, is given "for
services to presentation of cricket to the public". Foot has written on
cricket for *The Guardian* for 35 years and has been both Gloucestershire
and now Somerset correspondent of *Wisden*.

　Pat Gibson, chairman of the awards' subcommittee said of him:
"Everybody loves Footy and he's welcome in every press box in the
country. He represents the best of English cricket writing. In this day
and age, he still treasures the old-fashioned values of the game and
writes about them beautifully."

David Foot

Previous winners
1992 David Gower; 1993 John Woodcock; 1994 Brian Lara; 1995 Mark Taylor; 1996 the Sri
Lankan World Cup squad; 1997 Dickie Bird; 1998 Angus Fraser; 1999 Steve Waugh; 2000 Courtney
Walsh; 2001 No award; 2002 Jack Russell; 2003 Andy Flower and Henry Olonga.

SURREY

The thoroughbreds go lame

David Llewellyn

The discontent of the previous winter, when Surrey's senior players had objected to departing coach Keith Medlycott appointing wicket-keeper/batsman Jon Batty as captain, turned into an inglorious early summer of ignominy and underachievement. Surrey won only one of their first 11 Championship matches, and crashed out of the C&G Trophy with a shock defeat by Ireland. Not until it was too late did they function as a competitive unit, reaching their second successive Twenty20 Cup final and making a fight of it for the Championship runners-up spot. Batty can take some credit for this belated revival. But the damage had been done much earlier, leaving the new coach, Steve Rixon, with a Herculean headache.

Batty's situation was unenviable: leading a side which doubted he was the man for the job and following in the footsteps of Adam Hollioake, one of the county's more brilliant captains. The old hands' worst fears were quickly realised – Batty's three-dimensional role as captain, opener and keeper did prove too much. He eventually dropped to No. 5, although that was often above Alistair Brown and Hollioake, whose career averages were about ten runs higher than his. Batty did manage three hundreds and three more half-centuries, but by August his runs were drying up.

Thankfully, a collective spirit was by then manifesting itself in what had been a disgruntled, underperforming group of talented individuals. They wound up with four wins in their last five Championship matches. It saved Surrey from Championship relegation – indeed, they soared up to third – but they did go down in the totesport League which they won in 2003. And it was not enough to save Batty.

It was mystifying that Rixon, the Australian who had coached New Zealand and New South Wales, had not insisted on picking his own man when he first arrived. Still, he got his chance after Batty was sacked, and Mark Butcher looked a sound choice. He had stood in for Hollioake in 15 Championship matches between 1998 and 2003, winning ten and losing one – easily outdoing Batty's five victories and five defeats from 16. True, Butcher's one-day record was woeful, but he had a good cricketing brain and his squad's respect. Mark Ramprakash was to step in when Butcher was required by England.

The bowling, or lack of it, was a key factor in Surrey's poor season. No one claimed 50 Championship wickets, for the second year running. Rikki Clarke hardly bowled, and Tim Murtagh caught the eye with his free-swinging bat rather than 20 expensive wickets. Martin Bicknell was sometimes injured, although his 41st haul of five, containing his 1,000th first-class wicket, helped Surrey beat Kent. Jimmy Ormond was the linchpin, with 48 Championship victims; four more at Oxford gave him 52. He also played some stubborn innings. But too often he was obliged to bowl within himself: carrying the attack pretty much alone meant many long spells. It was noticeable that when he bowled shorter bursts, in tandem with Bicknell, Ormond generated more pace, bounce, aggression and wickets.

Leg-spinner Ian Salisbury, whose arm seemed to get lower as the season progressed, had a lean time. Saqlain Mushtaq, his off-spin partner, injured his knee in May, and never reappeared. Zaheer Khan, India's left-arm seamer, stood in briefly: he was in England on

Scott Newman

holiday, so could not get a work permit, and played two eminently forgettable games as an amateur. It was left to an astute mid-summer signing – Nayan Doshi, a left-arm spinner like his father, Indian Test player Dilip – to provide the variety and wickets, 33 in nine first-class games, which earned him a two-year contract. The arrival of Mohammad Akram from Sussex should add depth and pace to the attack in 2005, while Harbhajan Singh, the Indian off-spinner, should compensate for the loss of Saqlain.

The batting centred around the relentless run machine that is Ramprakash. Surrey's first three Championship victories were all ensured by his bat, and he completed 1,000 runs for the 14th time in his career. Brown turned a thin summer around and reached four figures, as did Scott Newman, whose consistency was reassuring in his first full season. Though Batty missed the mark, his 899 Championship runs were a personal best in eight seasons at The Oval. Murtagh's buccaneering, left-handed style, which wowed crowds at Guildford and Croydon, revealed his potential as an all-rounder, a role that the excellent Azhar Mahmood, who signed up for another year, filled with credit. The August debut of opener Richard Clinton, son of former Surrey stalwart Grahame, was another minor coup for Rixon; Clinton's showing in the last five games secured a place on the staff.

There was a handful of departures in September, the saddest being that of Alex Tudor, who had struggled for a couple of years with injury, and managed only half a dozen appearances in 2004. Hollioake, who had led Surrey to seven titles as captain, had already announced that this would be his final season; Nadeem Shahid retired after ten years with the county, and Saqlain would not be returning.

Surrey did claim one title, thanks to Bill Gordon, the ECB's Groundsman of the Year. In his first season in charge, after many years assisting the Brinds, he ensured that The Oval won the four-day award for the third time running.

SURREY RESULTS

All first-class matches – Played 17: Won 5, Lost 5, Drawn 7.
County Championship matches – Played 16: Won 5, Lost 5, Drawn 6.

Frizzell County Championship, 3rd in Division 1; Cheltenham & Gloucester Trophy, 2nd round;
totesport League, 9th in Division 1; Twenty20 Cup, finalists.

COUNTY CHAMPIONSHIP AVERAGES

BATTING AND FIELDING

Cap		M	I	NO	R	HS	100s	50s	Avge	Ct/St
2002	M. R. Ramprakash..	16	28	4	1,451	161	6	6	60.45	5
1991	G. P. Thorpe......	3	5	1	211	89	0	1	52.75	0
1994	A. D. Brown......	14	23	1	1,094	170	4	5	49.72	15
	S. A. Newman	16	28	1	1,162	131	2	9	43.03	9
	T. J. Murtagh	11	17	8	374	74*	0	4	41.55	8
1996	M. A. Butcher.....	4	8	0	298	184	1	0	37.25	1
2001	J. N. Batty	16	27	2	899	145	3	3	35.96	47/5
	R. Clarke........	10	17	0	530	112	1	2	31.17	15
2004	Azhar Mahmood§ ..	12	20	1	577	84	0	4	30.36	8
1989	M. P. Bicknell.....	12	18	3	415	47*	0	0	27.66	3
	R. S. Clinton	5	8	0	205	73	0	1	25.62	8
1998	I. D. K. Salisbury .	8	13	1	285	77	0	1	23.75	1
1995	A. J. Hollioake	10	17	1	377	106	1	2	23.56	6
2003	J. Ormond	16	24	5	330	57	0	1	17.36	4
	J. G. E. Benning ...	5	9	1	137	35*	0	0	17.12	2
1998	N. Shahid........	2	4	0	54	53	0	1	13.50	1
	N. D. Doshi	9	13	3	134	29*	0	0	13.40	2
	P. J. Sampson	2	4	2	13	11*	0	0	6.50	0
1998	Saqlain Mushtaq§ ..	3	4	0	17	14	0	0	4.25	1

Also batted: A. J. Tudor (cap 1999) (1 match) 0 (3 ct); Zaheer Khan§ (1 match) 2*.

§ *Overseas player.*

BOWLING

	O	M	R	W	BB	5W/i	Avge
Saqlain Mushtaq	86.4	9	304	12	4-107	0	25.33
N. D. Doshi	265.2	45	875	33	7-110	3	26.51
Azhar Mahmood	336.3	77	1,138	38	5-54	1	29.94
M. P. Bicknell.........	363	88	1,198	40	5-128	1	29.95
J. Ormond	580.2	138	1,800	48	6-62	1	37.50
T. J. Murtagh	243.3	50	873	20	5-74	1	43.65

Also bowled: J. G. E. Benning 6.3–0–37–0; A. D. Brown 13.3–3–43–0; R. Clarke 109.3–16–518–9; B. S. Clinton 1–0–9–0; A. J. Hollioake 60.3–6–237–6; M. R. Ramprakash 22–4–52–2; I. D. K. Salisbury 182.1–26–587–7; P. J. Sampson 34.3–4–154–6; A. J. Tudor 22–4–118–4; Zaheer Khan 26.4–2–101–1.

COUNTY RECORDS

Highest score for:	357*	R. Abel v Somerset at The Oval	1899
Highest score against:	366	N. H. Fairbrother (Lancashire) at The Oval	1990
Best bowling for:	10-43	T. Rushby v Somerset at Taunton	1921
Best bowling against:	10-28	W. P. Howell (Australians) at The Oval........	1899
Highest total for:	811	v Somerset at The Oval.................	1899
Highest total against:	863	by Lancashire at The Oval	1990
Lowest total for:	14	v Essex at Chelmsford................	1983
Lowest total against:	16	by MCC at Lord's	1872

SURREY DIRECTORY

ADDRESS

The Oval, Kennington, London SE11 5SS (020 7582 6660; fax 020 7735 7769; email enquiries@surreyccc.co.uk). **Website** www.surreycricket.com.

GROUNDS

The Oval: In South London on A23 just N of A202 Camberwell New Road and ½ mile S of Vauxhall Bridge. Nearest stations: Oval (Northern Line Underground) (adjacent) and Vauxhall (Victoria Line Underground and mainline) (⅓ mile).

Guildford: ¼ mile N of town centre in Woodbridge Road at junction with Wharf Road. Nearest station: Guildford (¾ mile).

Whitgift School: 1 mile S of Croydon town centre at junction of A23 Brighton Road and Nottingham Road. Nearest station: South Croydon (½ mile).

OFFICIALS

Captain 2004 – J. N. Batty;
          2005 – M. A. Butcher
Cricket manager S. J. Rixon
President 2004 – D. H. Newton
Chairman D. P. Stewart

Chief executive P. C. J. Sheldon
Cricket administration manager S. B. Howes
Head groundsman W. Gordon
Scorer K. R. Booth

PLAYERS

Players expected to reappear in 2005

	Former counties	Country	Born	Birthplace
*Azhar Mahmood		P	28.2.1975	*Rawalpindi*
Batty Jonathan Neil		E	18.4.1974	*Chesterfield*
Benning James Graham Edward . .		E	4.5.1983	*Mill Hill*
*Bicknell Martin Paul		E	14.1.1969	†*Guildford*
Brown Alistair Duncan		E	11.2.1970	*Beckenham*
*Butcher Mark Alan		‡E	23.8.1972	†*Croydon*
*Clarke Rikki		E	29.9.1981	*Orsett*
Clinton Richard Selvey	Essex	E	1.9.1981	*Sidcup*
Dernbach Jade		E	3.3.1986	*Johannesburg, SA*
Doshi Nayan Dilip		E	6.10.1978	*Nottingham*
Hodd Andrew John	Sussex	E	12.1.1984	*Chichester*
Murtagh Timothy James		E	2.8.1981	*Lambeth*
Newman Scott Alexander		E	3.11.1979	†*Epsom*
*Ormond James	Leics	E	20.8.1977	*Walsgrave*
*Ramprakash Mark Ravin	Middx	E	5.9.1969	*Bushey*
*Salisbury Ian David Kenneth	Sussex	E	21.1.1970	*Northampton*
Sampson Philip James		E	6.9.1980	*Manchester*
Scott Ben James Matthew		E	4.8.1981	*Isleworth*
*Thorpe Graham Paul		‡E	1.8.1969	†*Farnham*

Players due to join in 2005

*Harbhajan Singh		I	3.7.1980	*Jullundur*
*Mohammad Akram	Nor, Essex, Sussex	P (EU)	10.9.1974	*Islamabad*

* *Test player.*   † *Born in Surrey.*   ‡ *12-month ECB contract.*

At Oxford, April 10, 11, 12. SURREY drew with OXFORD UCCE.

SURREY v SUSSEX

At The Oval, April 16, 17, 18, 19. Drawn. Surrey 10 pts, Sussex 12 pts. Toss: Surrey.

In an intriguing test of strength, the new champions Sussex bettered their predecessors Surrey but failed to beat them. Midway through the last afternoon Surrey were seven down and still 101 behind before Newman, forced to bat No. 7 after a hamstring strain cut short his fielding, scored a gritty unbeaten 86 to stave off defeat. Otherwise, flashes of lightning rather than inspiration had to help Surrey on that last afternoon. After a rumble of thunder, the umpires briefly stopped play although there was no rain: new safety rules demanded that groundstaff were given time to get the covers on before being endangered by lightning. It was a frustration to Sussex, likely winners but for a wet third day. Adams, nursing his left elbow after an operation, made one of the less aggressive of his 38 first-class hundreds; and Ward, who left Surrey in 2003, reminded them of what they let go. They put Surrey's first innings in perspective – and Sussex on top. When he bowled Bicknell, Mushtaq Ahmed became the third current player (after Phil DeFreitas and Allan Donald) to 1,000 first-class wickets.

Close of play: First day, Sussex 75-0 (Ward 44, Montgomerie 24); Second day, Sussex 445-9 (Lewry 44, Mohammad Akram 12); Third day, No play.

Surrey

S. A. Newman c Ambrose b Mohammad Akram	14	– (7)	not out	86
*†J. N. Batty lbw b Lewry	10	– (1)	lbw b Martin-Jenkins	22
M. R. Ramprakash c Ward b Martin-Jenkins	25	–	lbw b Mohammad Akram	21
J. G. E. Benning c Mushtaq Ahmed b Martin-Jenkins	24	–	c Ambrose b Lewry	1
A. D. Brown lbw b Lewry	27	–	c Ambrose b Martin-Jenkins	13
A. J. Hollioake c Ambrose b Martin-Jenkins	4	–	c Adams b Martin-Jenkins	4
Azhar Mahmood c Montgomerie b Lewry	84	– (8)	b Mohammad Akram	0
M. P. Bicknell c Ambrose b Innes	45	– (9)	b Mushtaq Ahmed	37
I. D. K. Salisbury b Mushtaq Ahmed	40	– (2)	b Mohammad Akram	18
J. Ormond c Ambrose b Martin-Jenkins	27	–	c Ambrose b Mohammad Akram	19
T. J. Murtagh not out	0	–	not out	9
L-b 4	4		B 4, l-b 6, n-b 14	24
	304		**(9 wkts)**	**254**

1/24 (2) 2/24 (1) 3/65 (4) 4/78 (3) 5/84 (6) 6/121 (5) 7/227 (8) 8/245 (7) 9/304 (9) 10/304 (10)

1/33 (2) 2/51 (1) 3/52 (4) 4/75 (5) 5/79 (3) 6/79 (6) 7/88 (8) 8/188 (9) 9/229 (10)

Bowling: First Innings—Mohammad Akram 19-6-74-1; Lewry 18-4-60-3; Martin-Jenkins 20.5-4-59-4; Innes 11-3-35-1; Mushtaq Ahmed 13-1-72-1. *Second Innings*—Mohammad Akram 19.3-6-85-4; Lewry 16-5-46-1; Martin-Jenkins 20-7-47-3; Mushtaq Ahmed 14-2-54-1; Innes 4-0-12-0.

Sussex

I. J. Ward lbw b Murtagh	82
R. R. Montgomerie c Salisbury b Bicknell	25
M. W. Goodwin c Brown b Azhar Mahmood	2
*C. J. Adams lbw b Ormond	101
†T. R. Ambrose c Brown b Murtagh	56
M. J. Prior c Brown b Murtagh	36
R. S. C. Martin-Jenkins c Ormond b Bicknell	31
K. J. Innes lbw b Hollioake	22
Mushtaq Ahmed run out	17
J. D. Lewry c Batty b Salisbury	72
Mohammad Akram not out	31
B 1, l-b 12, w 1, n-b 4	18
	493

1/85 (2) 2/110 (3) 3/128 (1) 4/232 (5) 5/311 (6) 6/315 (4) 7/364 (7) 8/370 (8) 9/406 (9) 10/493 (10)

Bonus points – Sussex 5, Surrey 3 (130 overs: 468-9).

Bowling: Bicknell 24–4–87–2; Ormond 28–6–85–1; Azhar Mahmood 23–2–83–1; Salisbury 23.4–2–86–1; Murtagh 23–8–65–3; Benning 2–0–15–0; Hollioake 6–0–35–1; Brown 6–0–24–0.

Umpires: D. J. Constant and J. F. Steele.

At Lord's, April 21, 22, 23, 24. SURREY lost to MIDDLESEX by six wickets.

SURREY v NORTHAMPTONSHIRE

At The Oval, April 28, 29, 30, May 1. Drawn. Surrey 9 pts, Northamptonshire 6 pts. Toss: Northamptonshire.

Newman had already nailed himself into the opening slot with his sweet early-season form, which continued during his second first-class hundred of the season. Showing steely resolve to curb his attacking instincts, he made 131 and took his first class tally for April to 409, one short of Graeme Hick's record. Northamptonshire's captain, Sales, was made to pay heavily for choosing to field – only the third time in four years a captain had done so at The Oval in the Championship. However, the loss of more than two and a half days to rain guaranteed a draw. Given their shaky start to 2004, Surrey were glad to pocket maximum batting points.

Close of play: First day, Surrey 163-2 (Newman 90); Second day, No play; Third day, No play.

Surrey

S. A. Newman c Swann b Jones	131	M. P. Bicknell not out	9
*†J. N. Batty c Sales b Louw	28	I. D. K. Salisbury not out	4
M. R. Ramprakash c Sales b Jones	34	B 4, l-b 6, w 6, n-b 2	18
G. P. Thorpe c Sales b Louw	13		
A. D. Brown b Swann	28	1/93 (2) 2/163 (3) (7 wkts dec.) 403	
A. J. Hollioake c Brophy b Louw	73	3/218 (4) 4/235 (1)	
Azhar Mahmood c Swann b Jones	65	5/262 (5) 6/383 (7) 7/399 (6)	

Saqlain Mushtaq and J. Ormond did not bat.

Bonus points – Surrey 5, Northamptonshire 2.

Bowling: Jones 28–5–114–3; Louw 26.3–3–87–3; Phillips 21–2–100–0; Brown 7–1–48–0; Swann 9–0–44–1.

Northamptonshire

M. J. Powell b Ormond	11
T. B. Huggins b Bicknell	14
T. W. Roberts not out	22
U. Afzaal not out	15
N-b 2	2

1/27 (1) 2/27 (2) (2 wkts dec.) 64

*D. J. Sales, G. P. Swann, †G. L. Brophy, J. Louw, B. J. Phillips, P. S. Jones and J. F. Brown did not bat.

Bowling: Bicknell 9.3–3–29–1; Ormond 6–2–28–1; Azhar Mahmood 3–1–7–0.

Umpires: G. I. Burgess and P. Willey.

At Birmingham, May 12, 13, 14, 15. SURREY lost to WARWICKSHIRE by seven wickets.

SURREY v MIDDLESEX

At The Oval, May 19, 20, 21, 22. Drawn. Surrey 11 pts, Middlesex 12 pts. Toss: Surrey.

This draw was scarred by vandalism and marred by confrontations. After the recent corresponding fixture at Lord's, Middlesex had made allegations of ball-tampering (later dismissed) against Surrey, and tempers flared again at The Oval. As Surrey recovered on the first day, Middlesex wicket-keeper Nash apparently ran out Ormond, who was arguing with the bowler mid-pitch: the appeal was rejected. A disputed boundary catch – finally given as six to Murtagh – compounded matters. He and Ormond added 106 for the last wicket, giving Surrey two extra batting points and

---

FEWEST INNINGS TO 1,000 CAREER RUNS FOR SURREY

18	M. R. Ramprakash	2002	23	R. Clarke	2003
20	J. H. Edrich	1958	24	P. B. H. May	1951
20	**S. A. Newman**	**2004**	25	A. D. Brown	1993
22	D. G. W. Fletcher	1947			

Research: Brian Cowley and M. L. Pearce

Middlesex's complaints a further twist. The next bout of trouble came from outside. Day three was delayed until 4.15 p.m. due to rain and the fact that a section of the outfield had been mysteriously dug up overnight. Fortunately, turf could be transplanted from outside the boundary; unfortunately, the culprits were not caught. When play began Dalrymple, included only because of Strauss's England call-up, completed an assured 244, lasting 388 minutes and 306 balls, and including 38 powerful fours. He added 298 with Joyce and beat Denis Compton's 235 in 1946 as Middlesex's highest innings against Surrey. When Surrey's second innings began, 128 behind, there was a nose-to-nose confrontation between Batty and Nash (who was later disciplined by the ECB); they had to be separated by umpire Evans, dashing from square leg. Surrey survived the last day for a draw, but their winless run in all cricket stretched to 13, going back to September 2003.

Close of play: First day, Middlesex 23-0 (Hutton 10, Koenig 9); Second day, Middlesex 363-5 (Dalrymple 182, Nash 1); Third day, Surrey 11-1 (Newman 4).

Surrey

S. A. Newman c Keegan b Klusener	56	– run out	87
*†J. N. Batty lbw b Hayward	0	– lbw b Keegan	3
M. R. Ramprakash c Dalrymple b Hayward	89	– c Hutton b Weekes	66
R. Clarke c Hutchison b Klusener	2	– c Dalrymple b Keegan	12
A. D. Brown lbw b Hutchison	0	– not out	64
A. J. Hollioake c Shah b Hutchison	8	– not out	41
J. G. E. Benning c Nash b Hutchison	4		
M. P. Bicknell c Nash b Keegan	19		
I. D. K. Salisbury c Weekes b Klusener	25		
T. J. Murtagh not out	74		
J. Ormond c Joyce b Dalrymple	40		
B 5, l-b 8, w 11, n-b 18	42	B 9, l-b 12, n-b 6	27
	359	**(4 wkts dec.)**	**300**

1/18 (2) 2/98 (1) 3/104 (4) 4/104 (5) 5/118 (6) 6/126 (7) 7/172 (8) 8/229 (9) 9/253 (3) 10/359 (11)

1/11 (2) 2/166 (1) 3/174 (3) 4/186 (4) (4 wkts dec.)

Bonus points – Surrey 4, Middlesex 3.

Bowling: *First Innings*—Keegan 20-2-72-1; Hayward 20-2-72-2; Klusener 17-2-86-3; Hutchison 16-3-50-3; Weekes 13-2-57-0; Dalrymple 0.5-0-9-1. *Second Innings*—Keegan 20-6-46-2; Hayward 16-3-53-0; Hutchison 10-2-32-0; Weekes 20-3-53-1; Klusener

Middlesex

B. L. Hutton c Hollioake b Ormond . . .	15
S. G. Koenig c Batty b Ormond	9
*O. A. Shah lbw b Bicknell	0
E. C. Joyce c Clarke b Bicknell	123
P. N. Weekes c Batty b Ormond	7
J. W. M. Dalrymple b Murtagh	244
†D. C. Nash c Batty b Bicknell	12
L. Klusener lbw b Murtagh	4
C. B. Keegan c Bicknell b Murtagh	44

P. M. Hutchison not out 1
M. Hayward not out 0

B 5, l-b 8, w 5, n-b 10 28

1/27 (2) 2/28 (3)   (9 wkts dec.) 487
3/28 (1) 4/62 (5) 5/360 (4)
6/396 (7) 7/409 (8)
8/480 (6) 9/487 (9)

Bonus points – Middlesex 5, Surrey 3.

Bowling: Ormond 34–9–117–3; Murtagh 23–5–84–3; Bicknell 35–8–109–3; Salisbury 20–0–76–0; Clarke 12–1–65–0; Benning 1.3–0–5–0; Hollioake 4.3–0–18–0.

Umpires: J. H. Evans and G. Sharp.

SURREY v KENT

At The Oval, May 25, 26, 27, 28. Surrey won by seven wickets. Surrey 22 pts, Kent 4 pts. Toss: Surrey. Championship debuts: Zaheer Khan; M. J. Dennington.

This entertaining victory was Surrey's first in ten Championship matches since their dramatic fall from grace began the previous August. Batty, whose attempt to combine captaincy, wicket-keeping and opening had been criticised, again dropped to No. 5 and again thrived, scoring a century, and holding eight catches in Kent's first innings. This all-round feat had previously been achieved only by Steve Marsh, for Kent against Middlesex in 1991. Ramprakash was more subdued in making his 20th 150. The Surrey total of 479 was too much for Kent, with Azhar Mahmood swinging the ball prodigiously. Only Key stood firm, and when Kent followed on, 240 behind, he reached 199 before nicking a Bicknell away-swinger. It was Key's fourth hundred in six first-class innings. Still, Surrey's eventual target of 174 in 47 overs looked too small, not least to Kent. They chose to boost a sluggish over-rate by using occasional bowlers, avoiding a possible 2.5-point penalty but handing Surrey easy victory. In his 273rd first-class game, Bicknell took his 1,000th wicket – Matthew Dennington – and was presented with the ball on a plinth.

Close of play: First day, Surrey 306-3 (Ramprakash 123, Batty 120); Second day, Kent 181-5 (Key 78); Third day, Kent 254-4 (Key 134, Dennington 2).

Surrey

S. A. Newman lbw b Saggers	0	– c Saggers b Carberry	31
N. Shahid c Smith b Mohammad Sami	1	– lbw b Saggers	0
M. R. Ramprakash b Mohammad Sami	157	– not out	91
R. Clarke c Walker b Saggers	44	– c Saggers b Walker	15
*†J. N. Batty c Ferley b Khan	129	– not out	18
A. D. Brown st O'Brien b Ferley	79		
A. J. Hollioake lbw b Khan	2		
Azhar Mahmood b Ferley	27		
M. P. Bicknell c Smith b Ferley	6		
J. Ormond c O'Brien b Saggers	6		
Zaheer Khan not out.	2		
B 10, l-b 3, w 1, n-b 12	26	B 6, l-b 3, n-b 10	19

1/1 (2) 2/1 (1) 3/92 (4) 4/323 (5)   479
5/379 (3) 6/386 (7) 7/440 (8)
8/464 (9) 9/477 (6) 10/479 (10)

1/14 (2) 2/81 (1)   (3 wkts) 174
3/116 (4)

Bonus points – Surrey 5, Kent 3.

Bowling: *First Innings*—Mohammad Sami 24–6–75–2; Saggers 31.1–6–111–3; Dennington 21–5–71–0; Khan 27–3–102–2; Ferley 24–2–107–3. *Second Innings*—Mohammad Sami 3–0–24–0; Saggers 4–1–9–1; Khan 2.3–0–20–0; Dennington 6–0–21–0; Carberry 12–0–67–1; Walker 7–0–24–1.

Kent

*D. P. Fulton c Batty b Azhar Mahmood	30	– c sub b Azhar Mahmood	13
R. W. T. Key c Batty b Bicknell	86	– c Brown b Bicknell	199
E. T. Smith c Batty b Azhar Mahmood	25	– b Ormond	23
M. J. Walker c Batty b Azhar Mahmood	20	– lbw b Bicknell	0
M. A. Carberry c Batty b Azhar Mahmood	17	– c Brown b Ormond	61
M. J. Saggers c Batty b Clarke	1	– (10) b Bicknell	0
M. J. Dennington b Clarke	11	– (6) c Batty b Bicknell	12
†N. J. O'Brien c Brown b Clarke	15	– (7) c Batty b Clarke	21
R. S. Ferley c Batty b Bicknell	0	– (8) lbw b Bicknell	4
A. Khan not out	9	– (9) not out	22
Mohammad Sami c Batty b Bicknell	5	– c Shahid b Zaheer Khan	29
B 1, l-b 6, w 1, n-b 12	20	B 1, l-b 14, n-b 14	29

1/52 (1) 2/82 (3) 3/142 (4) 4/180 (5)   239
5/181 (6) 6/199 (2) 7/203 (7)
8/204 (9) 9/220 (8) 10/239 (11)

1/26 (1) 2/109 (3) 3/114 (4)   413
4/240 (5) 5/272 (6) 6/313 (7)
7/361 (2) 8/364 (8)
9/364 (10) 10/413 (11)

Bonus points – Kent 1, Surrey 3.

Bowling: *First Innings*—Zaheer Khan 11–2–53–0; Bicknell 21.4–6–51–3; Ormond 15–5–25–0; Azhar Mahmood 15–5–56–4; Clarke 11–2–47–3. *Second Innings*—Bicknell 34–8–128–5; Zaheer Khan 15.4–0–48–1; Azhar Mahmood 22–5–63–1; Ormond 44–14–97–2; Clarke 14–2–49–1; Ramprakash 2–0–7–0; Brown 2–1–6–0.

Umpires: I. J. Gould and B. Leadbeater.

At Bristol, June 2, 3, 4. SURREY lost to GLOUCESTERSHIRE by six wickets.

SURREY v GLOUCESTERSHIRE

At The Oval, June 18, 19, 20, 21. Drawn. Surrey 12 pts, Gloucestershire 11 pts. Toss: Surrey.

A rash of dropped catches in both innings ultimately cost Surrey dear, as did the loss of Bicknell to a groin strain in the second innings and a knee injury that restricted Ormond in the first. Taylor, dropped on 31, went on to his seventh first-class hundred, sharing century stands with Gidman and Averis. But this was nowhere near enough to worry Surrey: Batty underlined the benefits of his move down the order with a hundred, and Brown ended one of the most depressing periods of his career with his first century since September 2002, as Surrey steamed into a 230-run lead. Unfortunately, Brown's three drops at slip in the Gloucestershire second innings helped undo his good work: two were regulation, the third, and most crucial, was diving to his right. That reprieved Lewis on 23, when Gloucestershire were just four in front and enough overs still remained for Surrey to polish it off. But Lewis and Shabbir Ahmed contrived to hang in, after sterling resistance earlier by Fisher.

Close of play: First day, Surrey 2-1 (Newman 0); Second day, Surrey 419-5 (Brown 131, Bicknell 21); Third day, Gloucestershire 4-0 (Spearman 4, Weston 0).

Gloucestershire

W. P. C. Weston c Ormond b Bicknell	19	– (2) c and b Clarke	31
C. M. Spearman lbw b Ormond	0	– (1) lbw b Bicknell	30
M. G. N. Windows lbw b Ormond	6	– c Hollioake b Clarke	20
*C. G. Taylor c Brown b Murtagh	177	– c Batty b Ormond	9
A. P. R. Gidman lbw b Bicknell	62	– b Murtagh	25
Shoaib Malik c Hollioake b Murtagh	4	– lbw b Ormond	0
†S. J. Adshead c Batty b Murtagh	13	– lbw b Hollioake	28
I. D. Fisher c Hollioake b Ormond	5	– c sub b Hollioake	38
J. M. M. Averis not out	48	– b Ormond	0
J. Lewis c and b Murtagh	0	– not out	34
Shabbir Ahmed lbw b Murtagh	0	– not out	10
B 6, l-b 10, w 2, n-b 16	34	B 9, l-b 16, w 1, n-b 4	30

1/0 (2) 2/6 (3) 3/55 (1) 4/186 (5)   368   1/49 (1) 2/93 (3)   (9 wkts) 255
5/191 (6) 6/215 (7) 7/247 (8)   3/102 (2) 4/110 (4)
8/368 (4) 9/368 (10) 10/368 (11)   5/110 (6) 6/154 (5)
                                                       7/171 (7) 8/191 (9) 9/233 (8)

Bonus points – Gloucestershire 4, Surrey 3.

Bowling: *First Innings*—Bicknell 31–10 84–2; Ormond 16.3–2–78–3; Murtagh 16.5–1–74–5; Clarke 7.3–0–47–0; Salisbury 9–0–23–0; Hollioake 6–2–12–0; Doshi 11–1–34–0. *Second Innings*—Bicknell 13–4–39–1; Ormond 25–11–53–3; Murtagh 15–3–49–1; Clarke 18–6–38–2; Hollioake 10–1–38–2; Salisbury 11–6–10–0; Doshi 2–0–3–0.

Surrey

S. A. Newman c Gidman b Fisher	73	J. Ormond c Adshead b Shabbir Ahmed	39
A. J. Hollioake run out	0	T. J. Murtagh not out	33
M. R. Ramprakash c Weston b Lewis	5	N. D. Doshi b Lewis	15
R. Clarke c Adshead b Shabbir Ahmed	43	B 4, l-b 12, w 3, n-b 36	55
*†J. N. Batty c Averis b Fisher	106		
A. D. Brown c Spearman b Gidman	170		598
M. P. Bicknell c Adshead b Shabbir Ahmed	36	1/2 (2) 2/64 (3) 3/124 (1)	
I. D. K. Salisbury b Averis	23	4/138 (4) 5/381 (5) 6/440 (7)	

1/2 (2) 2/64 (3) 3/124 (1)
4/138 (4) 5/381 (5) 6/440 (7)
7/493 (8) 8/525 (6)
9/575 (9) 10/598 (11)

Bonus points – Surrey 5, Gloucestershire 3 (130 overs: 582-9).

Bowling: Lewis 26.4–3–120–2; Shabbir Ahmed 30–9–90–3; Gidman 13–0–75–1; Averis 22–1–124–1; Fisher 31–2–132–2; Shoaib Malik 10–0–41–0.

Umpires: M. R. Benson and T. E. Jesty.

At Worcester, June 23, 24, 25, 26. SURREY drew with WORCESTERSHIRE.

SURREY v WARWICKSHIRE

At Guildford, July 21, 22, 23, 24. Warwickshire won by seven wickets. Warwickshire 22 pts, Surrey 6 pts. Toss: Surrey.

Championship leaders Warwickshire won their fifth – and final – victory of the season, the second over Surrey. On both occasions Surrey followed on, which they did against no other team in 2004, and lost by seven wickets. There was also an echo of Warwickshire's previous trip to Woodbridge Road, in 1994, the last time Surrey chose to field here and the last time they lost. In this match a ground record of 537 was founded on a 214-run stand between Bell and Powell, equalling the all-wicket best by a visiting side at Guildford (also by Warwickshire, in 1992). Against an injury-ravaged attack, Powell scored his second successive Championship century and, with a thoughtful innings, Bell reached his third of the season despite chances on 25 and 64; Dougie Brown also reached three figures. An unbeaten 145 from Ramprakash could not save Surrey from following on, and they were soon 182 behind with seven wickets left. But Alistair Brown and Batty added 200; six individual hundreds equalled the record for a Surrey game, set in a three-day charity match against Middlesex in 1919. Bell, who like Knight passed 1,000 first-class runs, could have made it seven as Warwickshire achieved their target, but shared the strike and finished four short.

Close of play: First day, Warwickshire 390-5 (Brown 39, Tahir 4); Second day, Surrey 307-9 (Ramprakash 138, Doshi 5); Third day, Surrey 363-7 (Murtagh 47).

Warwickshire

*N. V. Knight c Azhar Mahmood b Ormond	36	– c Clarke b Sampson	21
M. A. Wagh c Clarke b Sampson	0	– b Ormond	4
I. R. Bell c Murtagh b Doshi	155	– not out	96
I. J. L. Trott c Brown b Sampson	25	– c Batty b Clarke	61
M. J. Powell lbw b Sampson	110	– not out	12
D. R. Brown c Clarke b Sampson	106		
N. Tahir c Batty b Ormond	4		
G. B. Hogg c Newman b Doshi	67		
†T. Frost lbw b Sampson	0		
A. Richardson c Newman b Doshi	1		
D. Pretorius not out	4		
B 10, l-b 11, w 4, n-b 4	29	B 2, l-b 3, n-b 8	13
	537	(3 wkts)	**207**

1/6 (2) 2/48 (1) 3/112 (4) 4/326 (3) 5/376 (5) 6/398 (7) 7/505 (8) 8/506 (9) 9/529 (10) 10/537 (6)

1/15 (2) 2/37 (1) 3/175 (4)

Bonus points – Warwickshire 5, Surrey 3 (130 overs: 533-9).

Bowling: *First Innings*—Ormond 31–7–90–2; Sampson 24.3–1–121–5; Murtagh 26–4–105–0; Azhar Mahmood 20–3–78–0; Doshi 25–0–101–3; Hollioake 4–0–21–0. *Second Innings*—Ormond 13–4–37–1; Azhar Mahmood 11–1–40–0; Sampson 8–3–19–1; Murtagh 6–2–22–0; Doshi 10–1–37–0; Hollioake 2–0–12–0; Clarke 2–0–22–1; Brown 3.3–0–13–0.

Surrey

S. A. Newman c Frost b Pretorius	9	– c Trott b Pretorius	13
R. Clarke b Brown	21	– b Brown	6
M. R. Ramprakash not out	145	– lbw b Pretorius	1
A. D. Brown c Frost b Wagh	25	– c Frost b Tahir	103
*†J. N. Batty c Frost b Richardson	1	– lbw b Pretorius	145
A. J. Hollioake c Powell b Hogg	33	– (7) lbw b Brown	9
Azhar Mahmood b Richardson	25	– (6) c Frost b Tahir	14
T. J. Murtagh c Wagh b Tahir	0	– c and b Brown	57
J. Ormond c Trott b Brown	30	– not out	12
P. J. Sampson b Tahir	1	– (11) c Wagh b Tahir	1
N. D. Doshi c Bell b Tahir	22	– (10) st Frost b Hogg	18
L-b 10, w 1, n-b 8	19	B 4, l-b 15, w 4, n-b 10	33
	331		**412**

1/10 (1) 2/38 (2) 3/102 (4) 4/111 (5) 5/183 (6) 6/232 (7) 7/233 (8) 8/283 (9) 9/288 (10) 10/331 (11)

1/14 (2) 2/15 (3) 3/24 (1) 4/224 (4) 5/252 (6) 6/269 (7) 7/363 (5) 8/377 (8) 9/411 (10) 10/412 (11)

Bonus points – Surrey 3, Warwickshire 3.

Bowling: *First Innings*—Pretorius 19.2–7–73–1; Brown 16–4–57–2; Bell 2–0–11–0; Richardson 19–4–62–2; Tahir 11.1–2–63–4; Hogg 8–0–46–1; Wagh 3–0–9–0. *Second Innings*—Pretorius 18–4–71–3; Brown 25–3–80–3; Tahir 18.3–1–84–3; Richardson 12–3–39–0; Hogg 13–2–48–1; Wagh 15–1–41–0; Bell 5–0–22–0; Trott 1–0–8–0.

Umpires: M. J. Harris and V. A. Holder.

At Northampton, July 29, 30, 31, August 1. SURREY lost to NORTHAMPTONSHIRE by six wickets.

SURREY v WORCESTERSHIRE

At The Oval, August 3, 4, 5, 6. Surrey won by 68 runs. Surrey 21 pts, Worcestershire 5 pts. Toss: Surrey. County debut: R. S. Clinton.

Surrey's second Championship win rescued them from the relegation zone, and marked the turning of a page in their history. Hollioake, who was omitted, announced his retirement from first-class cricket; Tudor's comeback proved to be his last first-class appearance before leaving the county; and the Loughborough student Richard Clinton, whose father Grahame opened for Surrey from 1979 to 1990, made a fine debut. Clinton, who had spent two seasons with Essex, was Newman's sixth opening partner in the 2004 Championship; they put on 90 in each innings. Ramprakash followed up with his fifth pair of twin centuries, and first for Surrey. Worcestershire's first innings fell away after Moore was struck above the eye by Ormond, who claimed his best Championship figures for Surrey in the second – only their fourth five-wicket return in this year's competition. But there was a remarkable fightback from 44 for six on the final day. Solanki and Gareth Batty (both just named in England's one-day squad, with team-mate Kabir Ali) added 168, and a maiden hundred for Batty, against his old county, briefly made a target of 410 seem possible. Ormond and Azhar Mahmood finally cleaned up after tea.

Close of play: First day, Surrey 299-4 (Ramprakash 96, Brown 17); Second day, Worcestershire 281-8 (Rhodes 34, Mason 13); Third day, Worcestershire 27-4 (Smith 4, Solanki 5).

Surrey

S. A. Newman c Hall b Malik	46	– c Rhodes b Mason	59
R. S. Clinton run out	73	– lbw b Batty	27
M. R. Ramprakash lbw b Mason	130	– not out	100
R. Clarke c Batty b Hall	36	– c Batty b Malik	47
*†J. N. Batty c Hick b Kabir Ali	8		
A. D. Brown c Rhodes b Mason	22	– (5) b Malik	25
J. G. E. Benning c Smith b Malik	6	– not out	35
Azhar Mahmood b Mason	25	– (6) run out	22
A. J. Tudor lbw b Kabir Ali	0		
J. Ormond b Kabir Ali	0		
N. D. Doshi not out	0		
B 2, l-b 21, w 2, n-b 4	29	B 5, l-b 4, w 1, n-b 4	14

1/90 (1) 2/176 (2) 3/233 (4) 4/254 (5) **375**   1/90 (2) 2/106 (1)   (5 wkts dec.) **329**
5/309 (6) 6/332 (7) 7/374 (8)   3/197 (4) 4/233 (5)
8/375 (9) 9/375 (10) 10/375 (3)   5/271 (6)

Bonus points – Surrey 4, Worcestershire 3.

Bowling: *First Innings*—Mason 25.2–10–89–3; Kabir Ali 25–5–93–3; Hall 21–6–55–1; Malik 19–4–71–2; Batty 13–2–44–0. *Second Innings*—Mason 11–4–38–1; Kabir Ali 12–1–73–0; Hall 12–3–33–0; Malik 12–0–76–2; Batty 19–2–85–1; Solanki 1.5–0–15–0.

❝From about 10 a.m. on March 28, a regular thud, rather than the roars associated with cricket in the subcontinent, began to emerge from Multan Cricket Stadium."

Indians in Pakistan, page 1204.

Worcestershire

S. D. Peters c Batty b Azhar Mahmood	74	– b Ormond ... 4
S. C. Moore c Azhar Mahmood b Tudor	76	– lbw b Ormond ... 5
G. A. Hick c Clinton b Tudor	39	– b Ormond ... 5
*B. F. Smith b Ormond	4	– (5) b Ormond ... 8
V. S. Solanki b Tudor	0	– (6) lbw b Ormond ... 86
A. J. Hall c Brown b Tudor	5	– (7) c Clarke b Azhar Mahmood ... 1
G. J. Batty b Clarke	12	– (8) b Ormond ... 133
Kabir Ali c Tudor b Azhar Mahmood	11	– (4) c Clinton b Azhar Mahmood ... 0
†S. J. Rhodes not out	46	– not out ... 59
M. S. Mason c Tudor b Azhar Mahmood	13	– b Azhar Mahmood ... 13
M. N. Malik c Brown b Ormond	0	– c Tudor b Azhar Mahmood ... 0
L-b 2, w 2, n-b 11	15	L-b 22, w 1, n-b 4 ... 27
	295	**341**

1/116 (1) 2/159 (3) 3/161 (5) 4/167 (4)　　　295
5/167 (6) 6/189 (8) 7/203 (7)
8/253 (2) 9/282 (10) 10/295 (11)

1/4 (1) 2/13 (2) 3/18 (4)　　　341
4/18 (3) 5/39 (5) 6/44 (7)
7/212 (6) 8/318 (8)
9/341 (10) 10/341 (11)

Bonus points – Worcestershire 2, Surrey 3.

In the first innings Moore, when 32, retired hurt at 144 and resumed at 189.

Bowling: *First Innings*—Ormond 23.2–4–63–2; Azhar Mahmood 19–4–83–3; Tudor 13–2–61–4; Clarke 12–3–62–1; Doshi 9–2–15–0; Clinton 1–0–9–0. *Second Innings*—Ormond 25–7–62–6; Azhar Mahmood 22.2–6–69–4; Tudor 9–2–57–0; Clarke 10–2–45–0; Benning 3–0–17–0; Doshi 14–2–60–0; Ramprakash 2–0–9–0.

Umpires: M. J. Kitchen and P. Willey.

SURREY v LANCASHIRE

At Whitgift School, August 11, 12, 13. Surrey won by an innings and 55 runs. Surrey 22 pts, Lancashire 4 pts. Toss: Lancashire.

The Mayor of Croydon, Brenda Kirby, unwittingly delayed play by walking in front of the sightscreen as Bicknell prepared to bowl his first delivery for six weeks. Before long, however, Lancashire were 21 for four, and Surrey had complete control of this scrap for first-division survival. Bicknell, Ormond and Azhar Mahmood were masterly with the ball, but the game belonged to Ramprakash, who was batting before tea. He scored his 73rd first-class century and his fifth in seven innings, becoming only the fifth batsman (after Tom Hayward, Jack Hobbs, Andy Ducat and Ian Ward) to make four hundreds in successive matches for Surrey. Victory launched them from sixth to third, while Lancashire's fate looked ever gloomier. They were missing six leading players, but the remnants barely competed until Cork reached his first hundred for the county, in 81 balls, smiting seven sixes. By then it was meaningless. Murtagh had also hit out, with five sixes in a thrilling fifty – one landed in the headmaster's tent, threatening the tea table. Murtagh later stunned everyone with a throw from 75 yards deep in square-leg territory to run out Chapple, hastening the three-day win.

Close of play: First day, Surrey 148-2 (Ramprakash 55, Clarke 13); Second day, Lancashire 57-3 (Haynes 18, Hooper 20).

Lancashire

M. J. Chilton c Clarke b Bicknell	2	– c Clinton b Bicknell	0
I. J. Sutcliffe b Ormond	0	– c Murtagh b Ormond	17
†J. J. Haynes c Batty b Ormond	2	– lbw b Bicknell	22
D. Mongia c and b Bicknell	12	– c Clarke b Ormond	0
*C. L. Hooper b Azhar Mahmood	32	– c Batty b Azhar Mahmood	51
C. P. Schofield c Clarke b Azhar Mahmood	69	– b Ormond	2
G. Chapple c Azhar Mahmood b Bicknell	36	– run out	5
D. G. Cork c Newman b Murtagh	2	– c Murtagh b Doshi	109
K. W. Hogg c Bicknell b Azhar Mahmood	23	– c Newman b Azhar Mahmood	12
S. I. Mahmood c Clarke b Azhar Mahmood	15	– c and b Doshi	31
G. Keedy not out	0	– not out	4
L-b 15, n-b 2	17	L-b 3, n-b 4	7

1/6 (1) 2/6 (2) 3/17 (3) 4/21 (4)	210	1/0 (1) 2/24 (2) 3/28 (4) 260
5/71 (5) 6/142 (7) 7/164 (8)		4/68 (3) 5/73 (6) 6/104 (5)
8/172 (6) 9/209 (9) 10/210 (10)		7/113 (7) 8/156 (9)
		9/231 (10) 10/260 (8)

Bonus points – Lancashire 1, Surrey 3.

Bowling: *First Innings*—Bicknell 15–3–41–3; Ormond 15–2–72–2; Murtagh 14–5–42–1; Azhar Mahmood 13.2–3–40–4. *Second Innings*—Bicknell 14–3–61–2; Ormond 18–4–60–3; Azhar Mahmood 16–5–61–2; Murtagh 12–4–25–0; Doshi 6.4–0–50–2.

Surrey

S. A. Newman st Haynes b Keedy	61	J. Ormond c Chapple b Hooper	10
R. S. Clinton c Chilton b Cork	1	N. D. Doshi not out	29
M. R. Ramprakash c Hooper b Keedy	134		
R. Clarke lbw b Cork	64	B 1, l-b 7, n-b 26	34
*†J. N. Batty c Keedy b Mahmood	15		
A. D. Brown b Cork	50	1/20 (2) 2/122 (1) 3/246 (4)	525
Azhar Mahmood b Chapple	30	4/284 (5) 5/330 (3) 6/375 (6)	
M. P. Bicknell c Hooper b Mahmood	41	7/399 (7) 8/442 (8)	
T. J. Murtagh c Chilton b Mongia	56	9/464 (10) 10/525 (9)	

Bonus points – Surrey 5, Lancashire 3.

Bowling: Chapple 26–8–72–1; Cork 24–2–110–3; Mahmood 29–3–131–2; Hogg 20–2–74–0; Keedy 27–3–96–2; Hooper 3–0–27–1; Mongia 0.3–0–7–1.

Umpires: J. H. Evans and R. Palmer.

At Canterbury, August 18, 19, 20, 21. SURREY drew with KENT.

At Manchester, September 2, 3, 4. SURREY beat LANCASHIRE by 147 runs.

At Hove, September 16, 17, 18, 19. SURREY beat SUSSEX by 37 runs.

GROUNDSMEN OF THE YEAR

In his first year as Surrey's head groundsman, Bill Gordon retained the ECB's Groundsman of the Year award, for the best pitches in three and four-day cricket, won by his predecessor, Paul Brind, in the previous two seasons. Philip Frost of Taunton was runner-up in this category and also won the one-day award, ahead of Andy Fogarty of Yorkshire. Beckenham CC in Kent, managed by Andy Pierson, was named the best county outground, followed by Whitgift School in Croydon, prepared by Matt Pullen. The award for the best UCCE ground was won by John Moden for the Fenner's Ground in Cambridge, with Richard Sula of The Parks in Oxford coming second.

SUSSEX

A softish landing

Andy Arlidge

After the giddy heights of the previous year, when Sussex won their very first Championship title, the 2004 season never quite got going. With every other county out to claim the champions' scalp, they struggled for momentum in a poor first half. Things might have panned out differently had they beaten Surrey in a rain-shortened opening game. But halfway through the season, they had only one first-class victory and were second-bottom of both the Championship first division and the totesport League's second division, above only Scotland. They had also made early exits from the other two one-day tournaments.

But Sussex finally found form in late July, winning three of their next four Championship matches and five out of six League games. Though they missed League promotion, they still had a slender chance of retaining the Championship title in early September when they were the last team capable of catching Warwickshire. Defeat by Middlesex prevented that, and they could not guarantee safety from relegation until the penultimate game, but ultimately fifth place was a fair reflection. Not enough players had performed at their best at the same time, but the late consolidation was a sound achievement.

Captain Chris Adams was the only batsman with 1,000 Championship runs, though Matt Prior, Ian Ward and Richard Montgomerie got there in all first-class cricket. Prior improved his wicket-keeping and successfully opened the batting in limited-overs cricket, to earn a call-up for England's one-day squad in Zimbabwe. It was Murray Goodwin's leanest Sussex season to date, however – he failed to reach four figures for the first time in four years – and nothing went right for Tim Ambrose, who was dropped after June.

That brought Tony Cottey back into the side, and he immediately scored 185 to set up an innings victory over Kent. It was one of the season's highlights, and started the surge up the table, but this was very nearly the end of the road for Cottey. He was released, along with Kevin Innes, in September. His departure after six years at Hove should increase opportunities for the likes of Ambrose and Mike Yardy to secure their places. The left-handed Yardy recorded a maiden hundred against Surrey, in the season's final match; his improved form, particularly in one-day cricket, persuaded Sussex to give him a two-year deal, and he planned to develop his play against spin in the subcontinent during the winter.

Once again, the focal point of the season was Mushtaq Ahmed's effervescent leg-spin. The director of cricket, Peter Moores, observed that Mushtaq seemed to be getting younger, and was delighted when he committed himself to stay for another two years. Mushtaq finished strongly, after having 30 Championship wickets at the halfway point: he claimed 23 in consecutive victories over Middlesex and Worcestershire, to raise the county's title hopes, and a final first-class total of 84 made him the country's leading wicket-taker for the second year running – the first bowler to repeat the feat since Derek Underwood in 1979.

Mott Prior

James Kirtley's form and confidence appeared to suffer after he was largely overlooked by England on their Caribbean tour. He struggled on his return in May. But he claimed his 500th first-class wicket in August, and closed the season looking more like his old self. Jason Lewry was less successful than in 2003, and Robin Martin-Jenkins also found it arduous at times. All-rounder Luke Wright, in his first season after joining from Leicestershire, emerged as an exciting one-day talent and showed composure belying his 19 years. Former Pakistan pace bowler Mohammad Akram took 46 first-class wickets but decided to leave halfway through a two-year contract, and promptly sealed a move to Surrey.

Moores might also have departed: he unexpectedly emerged in October as a leading candidate to succeed Gus Logie as West Indies coach. But he was pipped by Australia's Bennett King. The partnership between Moores and Adams has been the bedrock of Sussex's success in recent years, and should now continue through its eighth season in 2005. Adams is due to equal Arthur Gilligan, who led Sussex from 1922 to 1929, as the county's longest-serving captain since the 19th century, as well as the only one to bring home the Championship. He is already the longest-serving captain on the current Championship circuit. Adams passed 15,000 first-class runs in May, when he also completed a full set of centuries against all 18 counties by hitting 200 against Northamptonshire; he ended the season with 41 hundreds, and has announced that he wants 50 before retiring.

Moores became as accomplished at juggling finances as coaching when he was forced to trim the playing budget by £100,000. There were fears of another big loss, following a £360,000 deficit for the year ended October 2003; Sussex were heavily in debt because of interest payments on a loan to finance the new indoor school and improvements to the pavilion. But there was light at the end of the tunnel. The money had been loaned against their legacy from former club president Spen Cama, who died in 2001. Sussex are guaranteed 34% of the £22.3m probate value of the estate, plus further funds from the sale of a property company; the first payment should clear their debts.

SUSSEX RESULTS

All first-class matches – Played 18: Won 4, Lost 5, Drawn 9.
County Championship matches – Played 16: Won 4, Lost 5, Drawn 7.

Frizzell County Championship, 5th in Division 1; Cheltenham & Gloucester Trophy, 3rd round;
totesport League, 5th in Division 2; Twenty20 Cup, 6th in South Group.

COUNTY CHAMPIONSHIP AVERAGES

BATTING AND FIELDING

Cap		M	I	NO	R	HS	100s	50s	Avge	Ct/St
1998	C. J. Adams	16	25	4	1,003	200	4	2	47.76	14
2004	I. J. Ward	15	23	1	985	160	4	3	44.77	5
	M. H. Yardy	2	4	0	154	115	1	0	38.50	0
2003	M. J. Prior	16	23	0	852	123	2	5	37.04	21/2
1999	P. A. Cottey	9	13	0	466	185	1	0	35.84	7
1999	R. R. Montgomerie . . .	16	25	1	809	82	0	7	33.70	11
2001	M. W. Goodwin§	16	25	2	756	119	2	4	32.86	9
2003	Mushtaq Ahmed§	16	22	4	416	62	0	2	23.11	6
2000	R. S. C. Martin-Jenkins	15	21	1	412	64*	0	2	20.60	5
2004	Mohammad Akram . . .	13	17	7	198	35*	0	0	19.80	2
1996	J. D. Lewry	10	13	4	150	72	0	1	16.66	2
1998	R. J. Kirtley	12	17	4	209	53*	0	1	16.07	3
2002	M. J. G. Davis	9	12	2	156	43	0	0	15.60	5
2003	T. R. Ambrose	8	11	0	148	56	0	1	13.45	20/1

Also batted: K. J. Innes (2 matches) 22, 5, 3; L. J. Wright (1 match) 0, 18 (1 ct).

§ *Overseas player.*

BOWLING

	O	M	R	W	BB	5W/i	Avge
Mushtaq Ahmed	751.2	153	2,226	82	7-73	6	27.14
J. D. Lewry	231.2	62	732	25	5-66	1	29.28
M. J. G. Davis	219.3	37	637	19	4-57	0	33.52
Mohammad Akram	401.1	69	1,451	43	4-85	0	33.74
R. S. C. Martin-Jenkins .	358.4	91	1,082	29	5-96	1	37.31
R. J. Kirtley	424.5	89	1,336	33	4-32	0	40.48

Also bowled: C. J. Adams 10–2–35–0; K. J. Innes 32–5–109–3; R. R. Montgomerie 4–0–9–0;
L. J. Wright 27.5–2–96–1; M. H. Yardy 13–2–46–0.

COUNTY RECORDS

Highest score for:	335*	M. W. Goodwin v Leicestershire at Hove	2003
Highest score against:	322	E. Paynter (Lancashire) at Hove	1937
Best bowling for:	10-48	C. H. G. Bland v Kent at Tonbridge	1899
Best bowling against:	9-11	A. P. Freeman (Kent) at Hove	1922
Highest total for:	705-8 dec.	v Surrey at Hastings	1902
Highest total against:	726	by Nottinghamshire at Nottingham	1895
Lowest total for: {	19	v Surrey at Godalming	1830
	19	v Nottinghamshire at Hove	1873
Lowest total against:	18	by Kent at Gravesend	1867

SUSSEX DIRECTORY

ADDRESS

County Ground, Eaton Road, Hove BN3 3AN (01273 827100; fax 01273 771549; email fran.watson@sussexcricket.co.uk). **Website** www.sussexcricket.co.uk.

GROUNDS

Hove: ½ mile from seafront and 1 mile W of Brighton town centre in Eaton Road, Hove. Nearest station: Hove (½ mile).

Horsham: 1 mile S of town centre. From A281 Worthing Road, turn L into Cricketfield Road. Nearest station: Horsham (1 mile).

Arundel: 1 mile N of town centre within grounds of Arundel Park N of Castle. From A284 London Road follow signs for castle and cricket ground. Nearest station: Arundel (1 mile).

OFFICIALS

Captain C. J. Adams
Director of cricket P. Moores
President J. M. Parks
Chairman D. E. Green

Chief executive H. H. Griffiths
Chairman, cricket committee J. R. T. Barclay
Head groundsman D. J. Traill
Scorers M. J. Charman; J. Hartridge

PLAYERS

Players expected to reappear in 2005

	Former counties	Country	Born	Birthplace
*Adams Christopher John	Derbys	E	6.5.1970	*Whitwell*
Ambrose Timothy Raymond		A (EU)	1.12.1982	*Newcastle*
Davis Mark Jeffrey Gronow		SA (EU)	10.10.1971	*Port Elizabeth*
*Goodwin Murray William		Z/A	11.12.1972	*Salisbury, Rhodesia*
Hopkinson Carl Daniel		E	14.9.1981	†*Brighton*
*Kirtley Robert James		E	10.1.1975	†*Eastbourne*
Lewry Jason David		E	2.4.1971	†*Worthing*
Martin-Jenkins Robin Simon Christopher		E	28.10.1975	*Guildford*
Montgomerie Richard Robert	Northants	E	3.7.1971	*Rugby*
*Mushtaq Ahmed	Somerset, Surrey	P	28.6.1970	*Sahiwal*
Prior Matthew James		E	26.2.1982	*Johannesburg, SA*
Voros Jason Alexander		A (EU)	31.12.1976	*Canberra*
*Ward Ian James	Surrey	E	30.9.1972	*Plymouth*
Wright Luke James	Leics	E	7.3.1985	*Grantham*
Yardy Michael Howard		E	27.11.1980	*Pembury*

* *Test player.*   † *Born in Sussex.*

At Lord's, April 9, 10, 11, 12. SUSSEX drew with MCC (see Other Matches section.)

At The Oval, April 16, 17, 18, 19. SUSSEX drew with SURREY.

SUSSEX v LANCASHIRE

At Hove, April 21, 22, 23. Lancashire won by ten wickets. Lancashire 18 pts (after 2 pt penalty), Sussex 3 pts. Toss: Sussex.

The champions' home season got off to a wretched start: they lost by ten wickets inside three days. For the first time since July 2002, they failed to get a single batting point when they were bowled out for 195. Montgomerie carried his bat for a patient 60 as his colleagues fell regularly to the Lancashire seamers and retreated to the warmth of the pavilion on a bitter spring day. The weather got better, but Sussex never did. Law, averaging 169 in this fixture, improved on that with an unbeaten 171, during which anything outside off stump was ruthlessly punished. Lancashire took a 140-run lead and complete control. Sussex's second innings was worse than their first, crumbling from 90 for one to 163 all out. Lancashire's new recruit Cork made his presence felt, hustling out five for 58. Their only blot was being docked two points for a slow over-rate; captain Warren Hegg said he would take that in exchange for the victory.

Close of play: First day, Lancashire 51-1 (Sutcliffe 18, Loye 15); Second day, Sussex 51-0 (Ward 30, Montgomerie 16).

Sussex

I. J. Ward c Cork b Martin	0	– c Hegg b Martin	37
R. R. Montgomerie not out	60	– b Mahmood	27
M. W. Goodwin lbw b Cork	33	– lbw b Cork	14
*C. J. Adams c Cork b Mahmood	3	– c Loye b Mahmood	0
†T. R. Ambrose b Cork	0	– lbw b Cork	28
R. S. C. Martin-Jenkins c Loye b Chapple	29	– lbw b Cork	0
M. J. Prior b Chapple	11	– c Hegg b Chapple	33
K. J. Innes c Cork b Martin	5	– c Chilton b Cork	3
Mushtaq Ahmed c Hegg b Cork	21	– run out	2
J. D. Lewry c Loye b Mahmood	11	– b Cork	0
Mohammad Akram b Mahmood	4	– not out	1
L-b 3, w 1, n-b 14	18	B 7, l-b 1, n-b 10	18

1/0 (1) 2/71 (3) 3/76 (4) 4/79 (5)   195
5/120 (6) 6/132 (7) 7/137 (8)
8/161 (9) 9/184 (10) 10/195 (11)

1/64 (1) 2/90 (2) 3/90 (4)   163
4/96 (3) 5/96 (6) 6/153 (5)
7/157 (7) 8/162 (9)
9/162 (10) 10/163 (8)

Bonus points – Lancashire 3.

Bowling: *First Innings*—Martin 14–4–37–2; Chapple 15–4–52–2; Mahmood 13–1–41–3; Cork 13–0–61–3; Keedy 1–0–1–0. *Second Innings*—Martin 13–4–25–1; Chapple 15–2–37–1; Cork 13.5–2–58–5; Mahmood 9–1–35–2; Keedy 2–2–0–0.

" The Sri Lankans erupted and embraced their hero. However, of the 200 spectators present to witness the record, few appreciated its true significance."
Sri Lankans in Zimbabwe, page 1223.

Lancashire

M. J. Chilton b Mohammad Akram	5	– not out	10
I. J. Sutcliffe b Innes	45	– not out	14
M. B. Loye b Martin-Jenkins	15		
S. G. Law not out	171		
C. L. Hooper c Prior b Mushtaq Ahmed	34		
G. Chapple lbw b Mushtaq Ahmed	10		
D. G. Cork lbw b Innes	0		
*†W. K. Hegg c Prior b Mushtaq Ahmed	0		
P. J. Martin lbw b Mushtaq Ahmed	0		
S. I. Mahmood lbw b Mohammad Akram	9		
G. Keedy lbw b Mohammad Akram	0		
B 5, l-b 16, w 1, n-b 24	46		

1/8 (1) 2/57 (3) 3/120 (2) 4/229 (5)   335   (no wkt) 24
5/286 (6) 6/287 (7) 7/290 (8)
8/292 (9) 9/331 (10) 10/335 (11)

Bonus points – Lancashire 3, Sussex 3.

Bowling: *First Innings*—Mohammad Akram 25–3–79–3; Lewry 19–5–60–0; Martin-Jenkins 13–2–37–1; Innes 13–2–50–2; Mushtaq Ahmed 28–3–88–4. *Second Innings*—Lewry 4.5–0–12–0; Innes 4–0–12–0.

Umpires: N. J. Llong and A. G. T. Whitehead.

At Worcester, April 28, 29, 30, May 1. SUSSEX drew with WORCESTERSHIRE.

At Northampton, May 7, 8, 9, 10. SUSSEX drew with NORTHAMPTONSHIRE.

SUSSEX v LOUGHBOROUGH UCCE

At Hove, May 12, 13, 14. Drawn. Toss: Sussex. First-class debut: J. A. Voros. County debut: L. J. Wright.

On the last day, the thickest sea fret at a Hove match in years rescued Loughborough from probable defeat. When mist rolled in 90 minutes after lunch Kirtley, back from England's one-day squad in the Caribbean, had figures of 7–6–1–3, and Loughborough were 51 for four, chasing an unlikely 363. Play stopped, never to resume. In the first innings, Luke Wright (formerly with Leicestershire) became only the second post-war player (after Neil Taylor in 1997) to score a century on his Sussex debut. Wright picked up the dashing tempo set by his partner Prior, whose 201 not out occupied just 257 balls and 306 minutes. Prior hit 30 fours and two sixes, adding 229 with Wright. Sussex also bowled the students out for 201, with the left-arm seamer Jason Voros taking four for 40. Voros, born in Canberra to a Hungarian father, had hoped to play as an EU-qualified player but instead was still counted as "overseas" because Budapest bureaucrats had not yet processed a passport application apparently made six months earlier.

Close of play: First day, Loughborough UCCE 29-1 (Clinton 11, Walker 0); Second day, Sussex 89-3 (Montgomerie 43, Hopkinson 0).

Sussex

M. H. Yardy c Clinton b Wigley	13	– lbw b Wilkinson	31
R. R. Montgomerie c Nash b Lewis	5	– lbw b Nash	85
P. A. Cottey lbw b Lewis	2	– lbw b Panesar	3
†M. J. Prior not out	201		
T. R. Ambrose c Clinton b Lewis	10	– (4) lbw b Panesar	4
K. J. Innes c Lewis b Wigley	38		
C. D. Hopkinson b Wigley	0	– (5) c sub b Lewis	13
L. J. Wright c Panesar b Nash	100		
M. J. G. Davis not out	0	– (6) b Panesar	15
*R. J. Kirtley (did not bat)		– (7) not out	3
J. A. Voros (did not bat)		– (8) not out	3
B 10, l-b 6, w 6	22	B 3, l-b 5, w 1, n-b 6	15

1/18 (2) 2/20 (3) 3/20 (1)   (7 wkts dec.) 391
4/44 (5) 5/144 (6)
6/144 (7) 7/373 (8)

1/62 (1) 2/73 (3)   (6 wkts dec.) 172
3/83 (4) 4/117 (5)
5/163 (6) 6/167 (2)

Bowling: *First Innings*—Wigley 20–3–79–3; Lewis 11–1–58–3; Wilkinson 15–3–70–0; Clinton 2–0–21–0; Panesar 22–7–62–0; Walker 7–0–29–0; Adams 4–0–16–0; Nash 10–0–40–1. *Second Innings*—Wigley 17–4–45–0; Lewis 17–4–50–1; Panesar 20–7–28–3; Wilkinson 17–3–36–1; Nash 2–1–5–1.

Loughborough UCCE

J. H. K. Adams b Voros	14	– b Voros	4
R. S. Clinton lbw b Kirtley	26	– c Davis b Kirtley	0
G. W. Walker c Prior b Voros	5		
V. Atri c Innes b Yardy	30	– (3) not out	18
C. C. Benham c Yardy b Davis	21	– (4) c Prior b Kirtley	2
C. D. Nash c Montgomerie b Davis	17	– (5) lbw b Kirtley	0
†P. W. Harrison c Prior b Hopkinson	6	– (6) not out	21
R. M. Wilkinson c Prior b Voros	20		
P. D. Lewis not out	43		
*D. H. Wigley c Prior b Voros	10		
M. S. Panesar run out	0		
B 2, l-b 7	9	B 4, n-b 2	6

1/29 (1) 2/37 (3) 3/76 (2) 4/90 (4)   201
5/107 (5) 6/120 (7) 7/136 (6)
8/173 (8) 9/201 (10) 10/201 (11)

1/1 (2) 2/11 (1)   (4 wkts) 51
3/14 (4) 4/14 (5)

Bowling: *First Innings*—Kirtley 15–2–44–1; Voros 14.5–5–40–4; Davis 16–3–25–2; Innes 11–1–37–0; Yardy 5–1–18–1; Wright 6–2–8–0; Hopkinson 7–2–20–1. *Second Innings*—Kirtley 7–6–1–3; Voros 6–1–22–1; Innes 3.3–1–10–0; Hopkinson 3–0–14–0.

Umpires: R. J. Bailey and J. F. Steele.

SUSSEX v WARWICKSHIRE

At Horsham, May 19, 20, 21, 22. Drawn. Sussex 11 pts, Warwickshire 11 pts. Toss: Warwickshire.
An emphatic win for batsmen over bowlers was the nearest a slow pitch came to producing a result. In fact, the whole second day (reduced to 83 overs by a late thunderstorm) passed without a wicket, part of a long drought for bowlers in which 432 runs were added. Of all batsmen, the hardest to budge was Bell, who lasted ten minutes short of ten hours before Warwickshire finally declared at 600 on the second afternoon. Bell reached an unbeaten 262, becoming the county's youngest double-centurion, 39 days past his 22nd birthday, 89 days younger than F. R. Foster in 1911. Displaying a remorseless approach to accumulation, he faced 481 balls, 27 hit for four and six for six, adding 289 for the seventh wicket with Frost. Bell was already Warwickshire's youngest centurion, giving him a rare county double, held elsewhere only by J. N. Crawford for Surrey and

Cyril Washbrook for Lancashire. Ward and Adams were just as ruthless when Sussex set out towards 451 to avoid the follow-on, and both made big hundreds themselves. Adams was the most aggressive of the three, but made no attempt to open the game up by declaring behind, and when Sussex were bowled out just before lunch on the last day a draw was inevitable – to the disappointment of a small crowd enjoying the sun, which for once smiled on the Horsham Festival. During Warwickshire's first innings the umpires swapped the ball, believing it had been scuffed and scratched deliberately; the Sussex opening bowler Mohammad Akram was reported to the ECB and given a three-point punishment under the disciplinary code while Warwickshire were awarded five penalty runs, the first instance of a county being penalised for ball-tampering in four seasons since the new Law 42.3 was implemented.

Close of play: First day, Warwickshire 357-6 (Bell 147, Frost 14); Second day, Sussex 84-0 (Ward 34, Montgomerie 47); Third day, Sussex 464-7 (Davis 23, Mushtaq Ahmed 27).

Warwickshire

*N. V. Knight b Mohammad Akram	26	– c Kirtley b Davis	59
M. A. Wagh c Ambrose b Mohammad Akram	20	– lbw b Kirtley	14
I. R. Bell not out	262	– not out	62
I. J. L. Trott lbw b Mushtaq Ahmed	26	– not out	40
J. O. Troughton b Mushtaq Ahmed	10		
D. R. Brown c Prior b Mushtaq Ahmed	21		
G. D. Hogg c Adams b Mushtaq Ahmed	68		
†T. Frost not out	135		
B 1, l-b 5, w 1, n-b 20, p 5	32	B 7, n-b 6	13

1/49 (2) 2/62 (1) 3/108 (4) (6 wkts dec.) 600   1/57 (2) 2/91 (1) (2 wkts dec.) 188
4/140 (5) 5/166 (6) 6/311 (7)

A. Richardson, N. M. Carter and D. Pretorius did not bat.

Bonus points – Warwickshire 5, Sussex 2 (130 overs: 447-6).

Bowling: *First Innings*—Mohammad Akram 29–2–94–2; Kirtley 28–3–130–0; Martin-Jenkins 23.4–6–62–0; Mushtaq Ahmed 50–6–194–4; Davis 31–3–96–0; Adams 4–1–13–0. *Second Innings*—Mohammad Akram 6–1–33–0; Kirtley 10–4–23 1; Martin-Jenkins 10–2–36–0; Davis 19–1–68–1; Adams 5–1–12–0; Montgomerie 4–0–9–0.

Sussex

I. J. Ward b Pretorius	160	Mushtaq Ahmed lbw b Richardson	62
R. R. Montgomerie c Richardson b Wagh	61	Mohammad Akram b Brown	34
M. W. Goodwin b Wagh	9	R. J. Kirtley not out	8
*C. J. Adams c Frost b Richardson	144	B 9, l-b 8, n-b 10	27
†T. R. Ambrose c Knight b Pretorius	1		562
R. S. C. Martin-Jenkins b Pretorius	0		
M. J. Prior lbw b Brown	17		
M. J. G. Davis c Frost b Pretorius	39		

1/143 (2) 2/155 (3) 3/349 (1)
4/383 (5) 5/383 (6) 6/402 (4)
7/418 (7) 8/498 (8)
9/523 (9) 10/562 (10)

Bonus points – Sussex 5, Warwickshire 2 (130 overs: 482-7).

Bowling: Pretorius 33–7–119–4; Carter 29–6–104–0; Hogg 17–4–68–0; Brown 29.3–5–74–2; Richardson 25–7–82–2; Wagh 18–4–81–2; Troughton 6–0–17–0.

Umpires: B. Leadbeater and P. Willey.

---

66 'This is as low as it can get,' Lara commented at the presentation ceremony."
West Indians in South Africa, page 1108.

SUSSEX v NORTHAMPTONSHIRE

At Hove, May 25, 26, 27, 28. Drawn. Sussex 10 pts, Northamptonshire 12 pts. Toss: Northamptonshire.

A hot sun and another easy pitch made bowlers sweat buckets for meagre reward, and provided a result that gave neither side satisfaction: both remained winless in the Championship. Northamptonshire dominated this fixture, as they had done at home earlier in the month, batting for most of the first two days and scoring 570, but they lacked the firepower to press home their advantage. Their total was built round 171 by their captain Sales – who hit powerfully and brought up his 150 with a cut for six – and 181 from Brophy, who relied more on placement. Sales's counterpart, Adams, then outdid him by scoring his fourth double-century: 200 of Sussex's reply of 406, thriving as his team-mates struggled. Dropped on 43, he went on to survive 374 minutes in total, facing 330 balls, with two sixes and 29 fours. In doing so he became only the third batsman, after Mark Ramprakash and Carl Hooper, to score a century against all 18 counties. But when he clipped Phillips to square leg, it began a collapse of six wickets for 24, and Sussex failed by 15 to avert the follow-on. But Ward scored a century for the third Championship match running to ensure Sussex's safety.

Close of play: First day, Northamptonshire 315-5 (Sales 153, Brophy 36); Second day, Sussex 95-2 (Montgomerie 28, Adams 25); Third day, Sussex 31-0 (Ward 18, Montgomerie 8).

Northamptonshire

T. W. Roberts c Ambrose b Kirtley	10	B. J. Phillips c Prior b Martin-Jenkins . . 58
T. B. Huggins lbw b Martin-Jenkins	7	P. S. Jones c Ambrose b Martin-Jenkins . 7
M. van Jaarsveld b Martin-Jenkins	27	J. F. Brown not out 1
U. Afzaal c Goodwin b Mushtaq Ahmed	69	
*D. J. Sales lbw b Mushtaq Ahmed	171	B 6, l-b 16, w 2, n-b 4 28
J. W. Cook lbw b Davis	2	
†G. L. Brophy c Ambrose		1/10 (1) 2/44 (2) 3/53 (3) 570
b Martin-Jenkins	181	4/234 (4) 5/250 (6) 6/345 (5)
J. Louw c Montgomerie		7/395 (8) 8/527 (9)
b Mushtaq Ahmed	9	9/555 (10) 10/570 (7)

Bonus points – Northamptonshire 5, Sussex 2 (130 overs: 411-7).

Bowling: Kirtley 32–4–106–1; Lewry 32–4–123–0; Mushtaq Ahmed 49–12–143–3; Martin-Jenkins 26.1–5–96–5; Davis 27–8–80–1.

Sussex

I. J. Ward c and b Jones	33	– not out 107
R. R. Montgomerie lbw b Jones	82	– lbw b Phillips 30
M. W. Goodwin c Brophy b Phillips	1	– c Brophy b Louw 11
*C. J. Adams c Roberts b Phillips	200	– (7) not out 26
†T. R. Ambrose c Phillips b Afzaal	28	– b Huggins b Brown 0
R. S. C. Martin-Jenkins b Phillips	25	– b Phillips 13
M. J. Prior lbw b Phillips	0	– (4) c Afzaal b Brown 70
M. J. G. Davis c Sales b Jones	0	
Mushtaq Ahmed not out	8	
R. J. Kirtley b Louw	1	
J. D. Lewry b Louw	13	
B 4, l-b 6, w 3, n-b 2	15	B 2, l-b 2, w 4, n-b 6 14

1/58 (1) 2/63 (3) 3/215 (2) 4/330 (5)	406	1/64 (1) 2/79 (3) (5 wkts) 271
5/382 (4) 6/382 (7) 7/383 (8)		3/192 (4) 4/194 (5)
8/383 (6) 9/390 (10) 10/406 (11)		5/223 (6)

Bonus points – Sussex 4, Northamptonshire 3 (130 overs: 390-9).

Bowling: *First Innings*—Jones 27–4–75–3; Louw 18.2–4–85–2; Phillips 29–8–103–4; Brown 35–12–71–0; Cook 16–3–33–0; Afzaal 8–0–29–1. *Second Innings*—Louw 16–0–70–1; Jones 11–4–20–0; Cook 10–2–29–0; Brown 27–9–70–2; Phillips 14–2–34–2; Afzaal 10–3–36–0; van Jaarsveld 4–2–8–0.

Umpires: M. J. Kitchen and N. J. Llong.

At Manchester, June 9, 10, 11. SUSSEX beat LANCASHIRE by eight wickets.

At Hove, June 19 (day/night). SUSSEX lost to WEST INDIANS by six wickets (D/L method) (see West Indian tour section).

SUSSEX v GLOUCESTERSHIRE

At Arundel, June 23, 24, 25. Gloucestershire won by nine wickets. Gloucestershire 20 pts, Sussex 3 pts. Toss: Gloucestershire.

On a gale-tossed first day – cross-Channel ferries had to be cancelled – Sussex were blown away by Lewis. They finished defeated on the third evening, after another shaky innings, this time under a dome of brilliant blue. Though the conditions at the start were fierce, the pitch was sound and Lewis's five for 33 came thanks to a little movement off the seam, which happened rarely, and rash shots, which happened often. An assured 81 by Weston then helped give Gloucestershire a lead of 194, even though Mushtaq Ahmed, for the second match running, was again bowling with the mastery of 2003: he took five for 58 in 30 overs. When Sussex batted again, Ward looked rock-solid in his 69, but a mid-order collapse put paid to their hopes. They crashed from 113 for two to 115 for seven. This was largely induced by 36-year-old Smith, who had a burst of three for nought in ten balls. Since he did not play again before leaving Gloucestershire at the end of the season, this looked like his last hurrah – and it was a classic Smith performance, mixing his trademark in-swing with balls that held their line and nicked the outside edge. Though a breezy eighth-wicket stand of 88 between Martin-Jenkins and Mushtaq prevented an innings defeat, Gloucestershire raced to their third win out of four, which took them second in the table for the first time since 1998.

Close of play: First day, Gloucestershire 63-0 (Weston 34, Spearman 24); Second day, Sussex 8-0 (Ward 5, Montgomerie 2).

Sussex

I. J. Ward c Alleyne b Lewis	0	– lbw b Shabbir Ahmed	69
R. R. Montgomerie c Gidman b Lewis	6	– b Alleyne	15
M. W. Goodwin c Gidman b Lewis	28	– c Adshead b Alleyne	5
*C. J. Adams b Smith	6	– c Gidman b Smith	12
M. J. Prior c Adshead b Shabbir Ahmed	5	– lbw b Smith	0
†T. R. Ambrose c Adshead b Lewis	14	– c Spearman b Shabbir Ahmed	0
R. S. C. Martin-Jenkins c Adshead b Alleyne	2	– c Smith b Lewis	43
R. J. Kirtley c Adshead b Lewis	17	– c Gidman b Smith	0
Mushtaq Ahmed c Fisher b Alleyne	1	– c Adshead b Lewis	54
Mohammad Akram not out	5	– c Weston b Lewis	0
J. D. Lewry b Smith	7	– not out	5
B 1, l-b 8, n-b 6	15	L-b 2, w 1, n-b 12	15

1/0 (1) 2/25 (2) 3/42 (4) 4/47 (5)	**106**	1/65 (2) 2/81 (3) 3/113 (4)	**218**
5/54 (3) 6/73 (6) 7/75 (7)		4/113 (1) 5/113 (6) 6/115 (5)
8/77 (9) 9/99 (8) 10/106 (11)		7/115 (8) 8/203 (7)
		9/203 (10) 10/218 (9)

Bonus points – Gloucestershire 3.

Bowling: *First Innings*—Lewis 13–4–33–5; Shabbir Ahmed 14–3–33–1; Smith 9.4–3–20–2; Alleyne 7–2–11–2. *Second Innings*—Lewis 18.5–3–67–3; Shabbir Ahmed 16–4–39–2; Smith 14–6–34–3; Alleyne 11–3–45–2; Gidman 1–0–8–0; Fisher 2–0–23–0.

Gloucestershire

W. P. C. Weston c Ambrose b Mohammad Akram	81	– (2) run out 0
C. M. Spearman lbw b Lewry	36	– (1) not out. 21
M. G. N. Windows lbw b Mushtaq Ahmed	33	– not out 3
*C. G. Taylor c Ambrose b Mushtaq Ahmed . . .	12	
A. P. R. Gidman b Mohammad Akram.	26	
M. W. Alleyne c Adams b Lewry	10	
†S. J. Adshead lbw b Mushtaq Ahmed.	5	
I. D. Fisher st Ambrose b Mushtaq Ahmed	21	
J. Lewis lbw b Mushtaq Ahmed	8	
Shabbir Ahmed not out	34	
A. M. Smith b Kirtley	9	
B 4, l-b 19, n-b 2	25	L-b 1 1

1/83 (2) 2/140 (1) 3/172 (4) 4/177 (3)   **300**   1/20 (2)   (1 wkt) **25**
5/208 (6) 6/219 (5) 7/221 (7)
8/235 (9) 9/270 (8) 10/300 (11)

Bonus points – Gloucestershire 3, Sussex 3.

Bowling: *First Innings*—Mohammad Akram 20–3–86–2; Kirtley 15–5–34–1; Martin-Jenkins 18–4–38–0; Lewry 11–0–61–2; Mushtaq Ahmed 30–10–58–5. *Second Innings*—Kirtley 2–0–20–0; Martin-Jenkins 1.3–1–4–0.

Umpires: R. Palmer and G. Sharp.

At Hove, July 12. SUSSEX lost to SRI LANKA A by 95 runs (see Sri Lanka A tour section).

SUSSEX v KENT

At Hove, July 23, 24, 25, 26. Sussex won by an innings and 45 runs. Sussex 22 pts, Kent 5 pts. Toss: Kent.

Sussex eased their relegation fears with their first home win since clinching the title the previous September. A convincing innings victory owed much to Cottey, who had not batted in the Championship since then, but made up for lost time with an eight-hour 185. That helped Sussex reach 600 for the 12th time in their history – the sixth in three seasons – and their eventual 618 was a record for this fixture, beating Kent's 580 for nine in 1939. Fulton had chosen to bat on a slow, flat pitch, and made a workmanlike hundred, but the last six fell for 40. Cottey then celebrated his recall, sharing three century partnerships, the last with Prior, who made a sparkling 123 in 133 balls as they put on 202. Kent dropped four chances and conceded 88 extras, mainly no-balls from the fast bowlers. Only Essex had conceded more in the Championship, donating 98 to Northamptonshire in 1999. Patel earned five wickets, but the home spinners, Mushtaq Ahmed and Davis, finished with seven each. Cottey held the winning catch an hour after lunch on the final day.

Close of play: First day, Kent 300-8 (O'Brien 2, Butler 2); Second day, Sussex 396-4 (Cottey 114, Prior 78); Third day, Kent 99-3 (Walker 32, Carberry 1).

Kent

*D. P. Fulton st Prior b Mushtaq Ahmed	122	– c and b Davis	47
J. C. Tredwell c Kirtley b Mohammad Akram	17	– lbw b Martin-Jenkins	12
E. T. Smith b Mohammad Akram	79	– b Mushtaq Ahmed	4
M. J. Walker c Prior b Davis	17	– c Montgomerie b Mushtaq Ahmed	62
M. A. Carberry c Cottey b Davis	29	– c Montgomerie b Mohammad Akram	3
A. G. R. Loudon c Prior b Davis	14	– b Davis	34
†N. J. O'Brien lbw b Kirtley	6	– st Prior b Davis	11
M. M. Patel b Mushtaq Ahmed	2	– lbw b Mushtaq Ahmed	2
A. Khan b Mushtaq Ahmed	0	– c Cottey b Davis	27
I. G. Butler not out	16	– c Kirtley b Mushtaq Ahmed	17
A. Sheriyar c Adams b Kirtley	12	– not out	5
B 8, l-b 6, n-b 2	16	B 1, l-b 4, n-b 14	19
	330		**243**

1/51 (2) 2/173 (3) 3/204 (4) 4/264 (5)
5/290 (6) 6/292 (1) 7/294 (8)
8/294 (9) 9/304 (7) 10/330 (11)

1/37 (2) 2/50 (3) 3/94 (1)
4/108 (5) 5/171 (6) 6/181 (4)
7/185 (8) 8/193 (7)
9/228 (10) 10/243 (9)

Bonus points – Kent 3, Sussex 3.

Bowling: *First Innings*—Mohammad Akram 19–0–98–2; Kirtley 18.3–4–64–2; Martin-Jenkins 12–4–41–0; Mushtaq Ahmed 39–13–59–3; Davis 27–10–54–3. *Second Innings*—Mohammad Akram 14–4–38–1; Kirtley 13–1–38–0; Mushtaq Ahmed 42–12–94–4; Davis 19.1–3–57–4; Martin-Jenkins 9–2–11–1.

Sussex

I. J. Ward c Fulton b Sheriyar	6	R. J. Kirtley b Loudon	19
R. R. Montgomerie c Tredwell b Khan	20	Mohammad Akram c O'Brien b Patel	1
P. A. Cottey b Patel	185		
M. W. Goodwin b Patel	55	B 9, l-b 16, w 11, n-b 52	88
*C. J. Adams b Butler	57		
†M. J. Prior c Walker b Patel	123		**618**
R. S. C. Martin-Jenkins run out	25	1/21 (1) 2/43 (2) 3/179 (4)	
M. J. G. Davis not out	17	4/283 (5) 5/485 (6) 6/550 (7)	
Mushtaq Ahmed c Butler b Patel	22	7/553 (3) 8/582 (9)	
		9/617 (10) 10/618 (11)	

Bonus points – Sussex 5, Kent 2 (130 overs: 553-6).

Bowling: Butler 24–2–100–1; Sheriyar 27 3 120 1; Khan 20 3 94 1; Patel 39.4–6–138–5; Tredwell 18–0–88–0; Walker 3–0–5–0; Loudon 17–4–48–1.

Umpires: J. H. Hampshire and A. G. T. Whitehead.

At Canterbury, August 3, 4, 5, 6. SUSSEX lost to KENT by 236 runs.

At Lord's, August 10, 11, 12, 13. SUSSEX beat MIDDLESEX by 143 runs.

SUSSEX v WORCESTERSHIRE

At Hove, August 19, 20, 21, 22. Sussex won by seven wickets. Sussex 22 pts, Worcestershire 4 pts. Toss: Sussex. Championship debut: R. W. Price.

Mushtaq Ahmed collected 13 for 140, his best match analysis in England, to set up a third victory in four games for Sussex, who climbed out of the relegation zone while their opponents dropped into it. On a slow pitch, Mushtaq took six to enforce the follow-on, then seven for 73, his best innings figures for any of his three counties. Worcestershire did well to extend the argument into the fourth day after slumping to 155 for six, still 75 behind. Solanki led a revival but Sussex still reached their target shortly after lunch. Their first innings had stretched into the second afternoon. Prior, dropped on 24, shared a stand of 144 with Goodwin, and looked set to complete his fourth century of the season until he cracked Hall to backward point. After a mini-collapse of four for 20, Davis took charge as Worcestershire, having lost Bichel to a hip injury, struggled.

Close of play: First day, Sussex 289-4 (Goodwin 72, Prior 73); Second day, Worcestershire 196-8 (Rhodes 2, Price 5); Third day, Worcestershire 305-8 (Rhodes 17, Price 18).

Sussex

I. J. Ward c Hick b Bichel	2	– b Hall	1
R. R. Montgomerie c Rhodes b Price	69	– c Solanki b Batty	37
P. A. Cottey c Hall b Mason	34	– c Peters b Batty	45
M. W. Goodwin c Hick b Hall	85	– not out	8
*C. J. Adams c Rhodes b Batty	34	– not out	18
†M. J. Prior c Solanki b Hall	93		
R. S. C. Martin-Jenkins c Peters b Hall	7		
M. J. G. Davis c Rhodes b Mason	43		
Mushtaq Ahmed c Hick b Mason	0		
R. J. Kirtley c Hick b Price	36		
Mohammad Akram not out	18		
B 1, l-b 8, w 2	11	B 2	2

1/7 (1) 2/105 (2) 3/109 (3) 4/170 (5)   **432**   1/2 (1) 2/82 (3) 3/86 (2)   (3 wkts) **111**
5/314 (6) 6/328 (7) 7/329 (4)
8/334 (9) 9/391 (10) 10/432 (8)

Bonus points – Sussex 5, Worcestershire 3 (130 overs: 400-9).

Bowling: *First Innings*—Bichel 6.3–1–29–1; Mason 32.3–8–57–3; Hall 32.3–7–105–3; Batty 32–6–126–1; Price 28–5–91–2; Solanki 5–0–15–0. *Second Innings*—Hall 6–1–18–1; Mason 4–0–18–0; Batty 13–2–55–2; Price 10.1–2–18–0.

Worcestershire

S. D. Peters c Davis b Martin-Jenkins	28	– c Prior b Mohammad Akram	14
S. C. Moore c Adams b Mohammad Akram	4	– lbw b Mushtaq Ahmed	32
G. A. Hick c and b Mushtaq Ahmed	47	– c Montgomerie b Martin-Jenkins	12
B. F. Smith lbw b Mushtaq Ahmed	1	– b Mushtaq Ahmed	40
V. S. Solanki lbw b Mushtaq Ahmed	26	– b Mushtaq Ahmed	84
G. J. Batty lbw b Mushtaq Ahmed	28	– (7) lbw b Mushtaq Ahmed	6
A. J. Bichel c Prior b Mohammad Akram	29	– (6) lbw b Mushtaq Ahmed	0
A. J. Hall b Mushtaq Ahmed	11	– c Prior b Mushtaq Ahmed	60
*†S. J. Rhodes c Adams b Mohammad Akram	7	– c Goodwin b Mohammad Akram	35
R. W. Price lbw b Mushtaq Ahmed	6	– not out	31
M. S. Mason not out	0	– c Davis b Mushtaq Ahmed	1
B 8, l-b 5, n-b 2	15	B 7, l-b 11, w 1, n-b 6	25

1/13 (2) 2/49 (1) 3/58 (4) 4/105 (3)   **202**   1/20 (1) 2/63 (3) 3/78 (2)   **340**
5/120 (5) 6/171 (7) 7/177 (6)   4/145 (4) 5/145 (6) 6/155 (7)
8/190 (8) 9/202 (10) 10/202 (9)   7/242 (5) 8/265 (8)
                                      9/339 (9) 10/340 (11)

Bonus points – Worcestershire 1, Sussex 3.

Bowling: *First Innings*—Mohammad Akram 14.2–2–52–3; Kirtley 10–3–29–0; Mushtaq Ahmed 23–8–67–6; Martin-Jenkins 12–4–41–1. *Second Innings*—Mohammad Akram 24–2–83–2; Kirtley 23–3–98–0; Mushtaq Ahmed 38.2–12–73–7; Martin-Jenkins 14–1–37–1; Davis 10–1–31–0.

Umpires: J. H. Evans and I. J. Gould.

At Birmingham, August 24, 25, 26, 27. SUSSEX drew with WARWICKSHIRE.

SUSSEX v MIDDLESEX

At Hove, September 4, 5, 6. Middlesex won by five wickets. Middlesex 17 pts, Sussex 5 pts. Toss: Sussex.

Middlesex crowned Warwickshire champions by ending Sussex's slim hopes of retaining their title. On the second day, the visitors averted the follow-on with their last pair at the crease; on the third, they made the match's highest score to win. The first two days had seen 31 wickets fall, culminating with that of Hutton, for his fourth consecutive duck in all cricket. But Shah turned the game with his fourth hundred in six matches. He played Mushtaq Ahmed particularly well, striking him for a straight six, to go with 11 fours in a five-hour vigil, before he was finally pinned in front; by then, Middlesex needed only 25. Mushtaq bowled 37 overs in the run-chase, despite a blow to his right thumb. This had caused him to retire briefly when he top-scored in the Sussex innings with an unbeaten 49, in which he hit four fours, a six, and a seagull at short third man. Mushtaq had also given Martin-Jenkins useful support in the first innings when Sussex led by 142, before he and Kirtley, who returned his best figures for more than a year, dismissed Middlesex cheaply.

Close of play. First day, Middlesex 31-4 (Koenig 5, Peploe 0); Second day, Middlesex 4-1 (Koenig 0, Peploe 4).

Sussex

I. J. Ward b Hayward	3	– lbw b Cook	0
R. R. Montgomerie c Shah b Hayward	40	– c Shah b Clark	12
P. A. Cottey lbw b Clark	23	– c Scott b Cook	0
M. W. Goodwin c Joyce b Weekes	5	– b Clark	16
*C. J. Adams b Clark	26	– b Clark	25
†M. J. Prior c Dalrymple b Peploe	11	– c Shah b Peploe	12
M. H. Yardy c Hutton b Peploe	11	– lbw b Weekes	3
R. S. C. Martin-Jenkins not out	64	– c Shah b Peploe	0
Mushtaq Ahmed c Peploe b Weekes	48	– not out	49
R. J. Kirtley c Joyce b Peploe	3	– b Hayward	15
Mohammad Akram c Hayward b Peploe	18	– lbw b Weekes	7
B 6, l-b 5, w 3, n-b 6, p 5	25	N-b 2	2

1/3 (1) 2/56 (3) 3/70 (2) 4/84 (4) 277
5/97 (6) 6/129 (7) 7/129 (5)
8/213 (9) 9/239 (10) 10/277 (11)

1/0 (1) 2/0 (3) 3/24 (2) 141
4/31 (4) 5/58 (6) 6/67 (7)
7/68 (8) 8/94 (5)
9/132 (10) 10/141 (11)

Bonus points – Sussex 2, Middlesex 3.

In the second innings Mushtaq Ahmed, when 46, retired hurt at 131 and resumed at 132.

Bowling: *First Innings*—Cook 16–4–46–0; Hayward 17–5–59–2; Clark 21–5–46–2; Hutton 4–0–16–0; Peploe 18.3–4–65–4; Weekes 10–3–29–2. *Second Innings*—Cook 14–3–38–2; Hayward 12–3–20–1; Clark 10–1–28–3; Peploe 15–6–41–2; Weekes 6.4–1–14–2.

> **"**Those twilight thrillers that had made the Gillette Cup and NatWest Trophy final famous seemed the stuff of nostalgic memory. Despite their local boys' success, the folk from Cheltenham & Gloucester, in their fourth final as sponsors, looked mildly miffed with their rotten luck."
>
> Cheltenham & Gloucester Trophy, page 839.

Middlesex

B. L. Hutton lbw b Mohammad Akram	0	lbw b Kirtley	0
S. G. Koenig lbw b Mushtaq Ahmed	26	c Cottey b Mushtaq Ahmed	49
O. A. Shah c Mushtaq Ahmed b Kirtley	4	(4) lbw b Mushtaq Ahmed	108
*E. C. Joyce lbw b Martin-Jenkins	3	(5) c Prior b Martin-Jenkins	18
P. N. Weekes b Kirtley	19	(6) not out	50
C. T. Peploe c and b Mushtaq Ahmed	16	(3) lbw b Mushtaq Ahmed	7
J. W. M. Dalrymple not out	39	not out	14
†B. J. M. Scott c Cottey b Mushtaq Ahmed	0		
S. J. Cook b Mushtaq Ahmed	5		
S. R. Clark c Mushtaq Ahmed b Kirtley	11		
M. Hayward b Kirtley	9		
B 1, l-b 2	3	B 12, l-b 17, w 8, n-b 2 ..	39

1/0 (1) 2/5 (3) 3/8 (4) 4/31 (5)   135   1/0 (1) 2/17 (3) 3/113 (2) (5 wkts) 285
5/64 (6) 6/75 (2) 7/75 (8)   4/176 (5) 5/259 (4)
8/87 (9) 9/114 (10) 10/135 (11)

Bonus points – Sussex 3.

Bowling: *First Innings*—Mohammad Akram 1–0–4–1; Kirtley 18.3–7–32–4; Martin-Jenkins 11–3–30–1; Mushtaq Ahmed 21–3–66–4. *Second Innings*—Kirtley 20–7–34–1; Martin-Jenkins 15.3–6–29–1; Mushtaq Ahmed 37–5–137–3; Mohammad Akram 9–1–33–0; Yardy 9–2–23–0.

Umpires: P. J. Hartley and T. E. Jesty.

At Bristol, September 9, 10, 11, 12. SUSSEX drew with GLOUCESTERSHIRE.

SUSSEX v SURREY

At Hove, September 16, 17, 18, 19. Surrey won by 37 runs. Surrey 19 pts, Sussex 5 pts. Toss: Surrey.

These teams were among four competing for the runners-up spot. Kent clinched it but, after a fluctuating contest with a centurion in every innings, Surrey finished third, putting aside their early-season traumas with four wins out of five. Their left-arm spinner, Doshi, claimed a career-best seven wickets; ten in all gave him 21 in two matches. Victory seemed unlikely when Surrey plunged to 60 for five after choosing to bat. But Clarke used two lives to reach his first century for 13 months in just 83 balls, and had cracked 18 fours and three sixes when he played on to Mushtaq Ahmed. In response, Sussex opener Yardy (deputising for Ward, who was ill) compiled a maiden hundred before they collapsed and conceded a 12-run deficit. Then Brown led the way for Surrey but, after Lewry claimed five in an innings for the first time in a year, Sussex were left to score 324 in 80 overs. Goodwin put Sussex firmly on course at 242 for four. But Ormond took two wickets in successive overs, and the rest caved in to Doshi.

Close of play: First day, Sussex 126-3 (Yardy 69); Second day, Surrey 72-2 (Butcher 18, Ramprakash 21); Third day, Surrey 260-6 (Brown 93, Bicknell 5).

Surrey

S. A. Newman b Kirtley	0	– b Lewry	25
R. S. Clinton lbw b Kirtley	4	– lbw b Lewry	5
M. A. Butcher c Prior b Lewry	6	– c Prior b Martin-Jenkins	24
M. R. Ramprakash c Montgomerie b Kirtley	3	– lbw b Mushtaq Ahmed	51
*†J. N. Batty c Prior b Lewry	8	– c Prior b Davis	42
A. D. Brown c Martin-Jenkins b Mushtaq Ahmed	54	– b Lewry	123
R. Clarke b Mushtaq Ahmed	112	– lbw b Martin-Jenkins	5
M. P. Bicknell c Goodwin b Davis	40	– lbw b Kirtley	9
T. J. Murtagh c Goodwin b Davis	13	– not out	14
J. Ormond c Adams b Davis	22	– b Lewry	0
N. D. Doshi not out	11	– b Lewry	0
B 1, l-b 2, w 1, n-b 6	10	B 2, l-b 6, w 1, n-b 4	13

1/0 (1) 2/5 (2) 3/13 (3) 4/14 (4)   283   1/31 (1) 2/32 (2) 3/82 (3)   311
5/60 (5) 6/142 (6) 7/228 (7)   4/128 (4) 5/223 (5) 6/230 (7)
8/239 (8) 9/256 (9) 10/283 (10)   7/268 (8) 8/311 (6)
                                   9/311 (10) 10/311 (11)

Bonus points – Surrey 2, Sussex 3.

Bowling: *First Innings*—Kirtley 15–2–80–3; Lewry 16–7–30–2; Martin-Jenkins 5–0–40–0; Mushtaq Ahmed 21–3–81–2; Yardy 4–0–23–0; Davis 9–2–26–3. *Second Innings*—Kirtley 20–2–87–1; Lewry 16–3–66–5; Martin-Jenkins 19–4–67–2; Mushtaq Ahmed 17–2–51–1; Davis 10–1–32–1.

Sussex

M. H. Yardy c Batty b Doshi	115	– c Clinton b Doshi	25
R. R. Montgomerie lbw b Bicknell	25	– c Batty b Murtagh	0
P. A. Cottey c Butcher b Murtagh	8	– c Murtagh b Doshi	4
M. W. Goodwin lbw b Doshi	16	– b Ormond	119
*C. J. Adams b Doshi	40	– c and b Doshi	41
†M. J. Prior run out	12	– c Brown b Ormond	39
R. S. C. Martin-Jenkins c Batty b Ormond	23	– c Clinton b Doshi	12
M. J. G. Davis c Ramprakash b Ormond	9	– lbw b Doshi	1
Mushtaq Ahmed c Murtagh b Ormond	0	– c Batty b Doshi	16
R. J. Kirtley not out	0	– c Murtagh b Doshi	11
J. D. Lewry c Clinton b Ormond	0	– not out	1
B 5, l-b 7, n-b 6, p 5	23	B 3, l-b 9, w 1, n-b 4	17

1/47 (2) 2/83 (3) 3/126 (4) 4/210 (5)   271   1/2 (2) 2/12 (3) 3/49 (1)   286
5/239 (6) 6/239 (1) 7/266 (8)   4/158 (5) 5/242 (6) 6/243 (4)
8/266 (9) 9/271 (7) 10/271 (11)   7/246 (8) 8/263 (7)
                                 9/281 (10) 10/286 (9)

Bonus points – Sussex 2, Surrey 3.

Bowling: *First Innings*—Bicknell 13–7–26–1; Ormond 23.5–6–69–4; Clarke 8–0–49–0; Murtagh 10–1–37–1; Doshi 25–5–73–3. *Second Innings*—Ormond 28–6–98–2; Murtagh 12–1–35–1; Doshi 27.4–3–110–7; Clarke 5–0–31–0.

Umpires: B. Dudleston and N. J. Llong.

WARWICKSHIRE

In the not-so-grand manner

Paul Bolton

The manner in which Warwickshire clinched their sixth County Championship summed up their summer. The title was secured not in the grand manner, with victory on the pitch, but on a day off. They monitored events at Hove, where Middlesex ended Sussex's mathematical hopes of overhauling the leaders, via television and computer scores. The players staged champagne celebrations at a deserted Edgbaston for the sponsors' benefit. And a day later, they were relegated in the totesport League.

Warwickshire spent most of the season talking down their Championship prospects, as if they never quite believed they were good enough, but their understated efficiency paid dividends. They may have completed only five wins, a record low for any Championship-winning side – but they could not be faulted for playing the system. New captain Nick Knight was quick to appreciate that the points were weighted so that not losing was almost as important as winning. He was justifiably proud that Warwickshire were the first county since Surrey in 1999 to survive a season unbeaten.

They insured themselves against defeat through big first-innings totals – a sequence of ten consecutive 400-plus scores was a Championship record – which put the opposition on the defensive. Winning 13 tosses provided an obvious advantage, but they won the three games in which Knight called incorrectly. A total of 65 batting points was the highest in the first division, and only Lancashire bettered their 43 bowling points. They scored their runs at an average of 47.74 per wicket, but took their wickets at 40.60 apiece: the highest and most expensive figures respectively by any champion county.

There were only four five-wicket hauls – two by Dougie Brown and two by Zimbabwean Heath Streak – another record low for the title-winners. But Warwickshire did not depend on outstanding individual contributions. Their success was based on a strong team ethic and hard work, which Knight instilled from the moment he invited the rower Sir Steve Redgrave to speak to the squad in March.

Knight's luck with the toss meant he was rarely tested as a tactician, but he prepared his players mentally and struck up an effective relationship with John Inverarity, the unobtrusive director of coaching. He combined captaincy and his benefit without any obvious deterioration in form, passing 1,000 runs, including a maiden triple-century, for the fifth time.

Ian Bell finally converted promise into consistency with six centuries and almost 1,500 Championship runs, which earned him a Test cap. Jonathan Trott also reached four figures in the Championship; he made only one century, but ten more fifties, scoring his runs quickly and attractively, often demoralising attacks already softened up by Knight or Bell. Mark Wagh reached 1,000 in all first-class cricket, but tailed off badly after a purple patch in June, when he scored 416 in six Championship innings; his last 14 innings brought only 284. Michael Powell regained confidence after relinquishing the captaincy; he was one of nine men who made centuries. So was Australian Brad Hogg, some consolation for a disappointing summer bowling his left-arm chinamen, but he was not offered new terms.

Ian Bell

Reserve wicket-keeper Tony Frost grasped his opportunity when Keith Piper broke a finger in a preseason friendly. Ever-present in the Championship, he kept consistently and contributed valuable lower-order runs, notably a match-saving innings in the key game against Sussex at Edgbaston. No one typified Warwickshire's fighting spirit and refusal to admit defeat more than Brown, who enjoyed another outstanding all-round season. He contributed 911 Championship runs, mostly scored according to his side's needs, and 38 wickets.

Streak dismissed 13 Northamptonshire batsmen on debut, but struggled with injuries thereafter. Dewald Pretorius made little impact as a locum overseas bowler, but both were expected to return for a further two years, Pretorius as a Kolpak player. The find of the season, however, was 20-year-old Naqqash Tahir, a shy swing bowler from Birmingham, who announced himself with eight Worcestershire wickets on Championship debut. He wobbled the ball both ways and proved an important partnership-breaker. His progress came at the expense of Alan Richardson, who moved to Middlesex in November. The close-season signings of Adam Shantry, a left-arm seamer from Northamptonshire, and Kent all-rounder Alex Loudon were acknowledgement that Warwickshire needed to strengthen their bowling.

Graham Wagg, an England A all-rounder the previous winter, was restricted to one-day cricket by a back injury; he was then suspended for 15 months by the ECB and sacked by the county after testing positive for cocaine at the final League match in Bristol.

Defeat in that match soon resulted in relegation. Warwickshire's limited-overs form was inconsistent throughout. They went out of both knockouts in the space of three days in July, beaten by Worcestershire in the C&G semis and Glamorgan in the Twenty20 quarter-finals. But they proved their resilience by defeating Surrey at Guildford five days later, in what proved their last Championship win of the season.

Knight believed there was more to come from his emerging side. "This success came two years early, to be honest," he said. "I said at the start of the season that we had the nucleus of a very good side for two years' time, and I still firmly believe that to be the case."

WARWICKSHIRE RESULTS

All first-class matches – Played 17: Won 6, Drawn 11.
County Championship matches – Played 16: Won 5, Drawn 11.

Frizzell County Championship, winners in Division 1; Cheltenham & Gloucester Trophy, s-f;
totesport League, 7th in Division 1; Twenty20 Cup, q-f.

COUNTY CHAMPIONSHIP AVERAGES

BATTING AND FIELDING

Cap		M	I	NO	R	HS	100s	50s	Avge	Ct/St
2001	I. R. Bell	15	25	4	1,498	262*	6	4	71.33	6
	G. B. Hogg§.	11	12	2	662	158	1	7	66.20	4
1995	N. V. Knight	15	28	6	1,256	303*	2	8	57.09	9
	I. J. L. Trott	16	27	6	1,126	115	1	10	53.61	11
1995	D. R. Brown	16	21	3	911	162	3	2	50.61	7
1999	M. J. Powell	9	15	2	630	134	2	2	48.46	4
1999	T. Frost	16	18	5	488	135*	1	1	37.53	44/4
2000	M. A. Wagh	16	29	2	928	167	1	5	34.37	14
2002	J. O. Troughton	13	16	0	528	120	1	4	33.00	2
	H. H. Streak§	6	9	2	180	61	0	1	25.71	0
	N. M. Carter.	13	15	4	245	95	0	1	22.27	3
	N. Tahir.	11	12	5	150	49	0	0	21.42	1
2002	A. Richardson.	7	4	2	26	17	0	0	13.00	2
	D. Pretorius§.	9	6	3	31	14	0	0	10.33	1

Also batted: A. F. Giles (cap 1996) (1 match) 70; N. A. Warren (1 match) 0; I. J. Westwood
(1 match) 3, 38.

§ *Overseas player.*

BOWLING

	O	M	R	W	BB	5W/i	Avge
H. H. Streak.	159	29	522	24	7-80	2	21.75
I. R. Bell.	137.4	32	400	14	4-4	0	28.57
N. Tahir.	194.4	26	766	26	4-43	0	29.46
D. R. Brown.	412.4	91	1,273	38	5-53	2	33.50
D. Pretorius	245	43	936	24	4-119	0	39.00
N. M. Carter.	349.4	71	1,189	27	4-50	0	44.03
M. A. Wagh	281.4	44	977	18	3-85	0	54.27
G. B. Hogg	256.2	39	881	14	4-90	0	62.92

Also bowled: A. F. Giles 62–17–128–4; M. J. Powell 8–0–51–0; A. Richardson 144–28–532–6;
I. J. L. Trott 23–5–86–3; J. O. Troughton 123–27–344–3; N. A. Warren 17–3–60–3.

COUNTY RECORDS

Highest score for:	501*	B. C. Lara v Durham at Birmingham	1994
Highest score against:	322	I. V. A. Richards (Somerset) at Taunton.	1985
Best bowling for:	10-41	J. D. Bannister v Combined Services at Birmingham .	1959
Best bowling against:	10-36	H. Verity (Yorkshire) at Leeds	1931
Highest total for:	810-4 dec.	v Durham at Birmingham	1994
Highest total against:	887	by Yorkshire at Birmingham.	1896
Lowest total for:	16	v Kent at Tonbridge	1913
Lowest total against:	15	by Hampshire at Birmingham	1922

WARWICKSHIRE DIRECTORY

ADDRESS

County Ground, Edgbaston, Birmingham B5 7QU (0121 446 4422; fax 0121 446 4544; email info@edgbaston.com). **Website** www.thebears.co.uk.

GROUNDS

Birmingham (Edgbaston): 1¼ miles S of city centre in B4217 Edgbaston Road at junction with A441 Pershore Road. Close to A38 Bristol Road. Nearest stations: Birmingham New Street (1¾ miles), Birmingham Moor Street (1¼ miles) and Birmingham Snow Hill (2¼ miles).

Stratford-on-Avon: ½ mile SE of town centre and bounded by River Avon to W. From A41 London Road L into Swan's Nest Lane before bridge over canal and river. Nearest station: Stratford-on-Avon (1½ miles).

OFFICIALS

Captain N. V. Knight
Director of coaching J. Inverarity
President The Rt Hon. Lord Guernsey
Chairman W. N. Houghton

Chief executive D. L. Amiss
Head groundsman S. J. Rouse
Scorer D. Wainwright

PLAYERS

Players expected to reappear in 2005

	Former counties	Country	Born	Birthplace
Bell Ian Ronald		E	11.4.1982	†*Walsgrave*
Brown Douglas Robert		E/SCO	29.10.1969	*Stirling*
Carter Neil Miller		SA (EU)	29.1.1975	*Cape Town*
Frost Tony		E	17.11.1975	*Stoke-on-Trent*
***Giles** Ashley Fraser		‡E	19.3.1973	*Chertsey*
***Knight** Nicholas Verity	Essex	E	28.11.1969	*Watford*
Penney Trevor Lionel		E	12.6.1968	*Salisbury, Rhodesia*
Piper Keith John		E	18.12.1969	*Leicester*
Powell Michael James		E	5.4.1975	*Bolton*
Pretorius Dewald	Durham	SA (K)	16.12.1977	*Pretoria*
Trott Ian Jonathan Leonard		SA (EU)	22.4.1981	*Cape Town*
***Streak** Heath Hilton	Hants	Z	16.4.1974	*Bulawayo, Rhodesia*
Tahir Naqaash		E	14.11.1983	†*Birmingham*
Troughton Jamie Oliver		E	2.3.1979	*Camden*
Wagh Mark Anant		E	20.10.1976	†*Birmingham*
Warren Nicholas Alexander		E	26.6.1982	†*Moseley*
Westwood Ian James		E	13.7.1982	†*Birmingham*

Players due to join in 2005

		Country	Born	Birthplace
Loudon Alexander Guy Rushworth	Kent	E	6.9.1980	*Westminster*
Shantry Adam John	Northants	E	13.11.1982	*Bristol*

* *Test player.*   † *Born in Warwickshire.*   ‡ *12-month ECB contract.*

WARWICKSHIRE v MIDDLESEX

At Birmingham, April 16, 17, 18, 19. Drawn. Warwickshire 9 pts, Middlesex 12 pts. Toss: Warwickshire. County debuts: G. B. Hogg, D. Pretorius; M. M. Betts, M. Hayward.

The weather made it a gloomy start to the season. Most of the first day was lost and though no rain fell during playing hours on the third day, water had run off the flat sheets and under the covers on the Pavilion End run-up. That ensured a draw. After Warwickshire's seamers failed to capitalise on helpful conditions Middlesex punished them on the second day, with a fifth-wicket partnership of 175 between Weekes, who scored a punchy century, and Dalrymple. The final-day battle for bonus points was enlivened by attractive Warwickshire strokeplay, by Weekes's first five-wicket Championship haul since June 2001 and by the best weather of the match.

Close of play: First day, Middlesex 115-3 (Joyce 36, Weekes 12); Second day, Warwickshire 16-1 (Wagh 5, Bell 7); Third day, No play.

Middlesex

S. G. Koenig c Wagh b Richardson	10	– c Frost b Carter	2
B. L. Hutton c Frost b Brown	30	– c Knight b Trott	20
*O. A. Shah c Wagh b Brown	17	– not out	20
E. C. Joyce c Frost b Carter	39	– not out	10
P. N. Weekes b Brown	118		
J. W. M. Dalrymple c Bell b Pretorius	77		
†D. C. Nash st Frost b Wagh	55		
S. J. Cook lbw b Hogg	22		
M. M. Betts not out	31		
B 3, l-b 10, w 2, n-b 18	33	N-b 2	2

1/17 (1) 2/52 (3) 3/69 (2)   (8 wkts dec.) 432   1/12 (1) 2/27 (2)   (2 wkts dec.) 54
4/119 (4) 5/294 (6) 6/337 (5)
7/373 (8) 8/432 (7)

C. B. Keegan and M. Hayward did not bat.

Bonus points – Middlesex 5, Warwickshire 2.

Bowling: *First Innings*—Pretorius 20–5–95–1; Carter 20–5–59–1; Brown 25–7–65–3; Richardson 24–4–92–1; Bell 2–0–10–0; Hogg 22–5–45–1; Trott 3–0–22–0; Wagh 8.2–0–31–1. *Second Innings*—Carter 8–3–21–1; Bell 5–2–8–0; Trott 3–1–6–1; Hogg 6–2–15–0; Wagh 1–0–4–0.

Warwickshire

*N. V. Knight lbw b Keegan	4	– not out	5
M. A. Wagh c Nash b Weekes	78	– not out	19
I. R. Bell c Joyce b Hayward	12		
I. J. L. Trott c Hutton b Weekes	67		
J. O. Troughton c Betts b Weekes	4		
D. R. Brown b Hayward	42		
G. B. Hogg lbw b Weekes	51		
†T. Frost c Nash b Keegan	4		
N. M. Carter c Weekes b Keegan	18		
A. Richardson not out	8		
D. Pretorius c and b Weekes	1		
B 2, l-b 5, w 3, n-b 18	28		

1/8 (1) 2/27 (3) 3/157 (4) 4/167 (5)   317   (no wkt) 24
5/204 (2) 6/272 (7) 7/283 (8)
8/303 (9) 9/312 (6) 10/317 (11)

Bonus points – Warwickshire 3, Middlesex 3.

Bowling: *First Innings*—Keegan 14–1–63–3; Hayward 14–3–41–2; Betts 8–0–74–0; Cook 14–2–56–0; Weekes 20.4–1–76–5. *Second Innings*—Nash 2–0–8–0; Joyce 1–0–4–0; Weekes 1–0–5–0; Shah 1–0–7–0.

Umpires: N. A. Mallender and G. Sharp.

At Cambridge, April 21, 22, 23. WARWICKSHIRE beat CAMBRIDGE UCCE by 247 runs.

WARWICKSHIRE v GLOUCESTERSHIRE

At Birmingham, April 28, 29, 30, May 1. Drawn. Warwickshire 6 pts, Gloucestershire 11 pts. Toss: Warwickshire. County debut: S. J. Adshead.

When play eventually began on the third morning, Spearman and Weston tried to make up for lost time with a rumbustious opening partnership of 120. Spearman dominated the stand, his half-century coming from his 39th ball, hit for the first of five successive fours off Bell. But it was Weston who pressed on to a patient century, surviving a testing spell of left-arm wrist-spin from Hogg, who tried to compensate for a wayward Warwickshire seam attack. The innings faltered when Brown bowled a spell of 6–5–4–3, but Steve Adshead, the former Leicestershire and Worcestershire reserve wicket-keeper, marked his debut as replacement for the injured Jack Russell with a confident half-century. With the exception of Trott, whose superb timing brought 15 fours, Warwickshire's batsmen struggled before the rain returned.

Close of play: First day, No play; Second day, No play; Third day, Gloucestershire 314-4 (Taylor 13, Gidman 1).

Gloucestershire

C. M. Spearman c Hogg b Brown	77		†S. J. Adshead not out	56
W. P. C. Weston c Richardson b Pretorius	122		A. N. Bressington not out	19
T. H. C. Hancock c Frost b Carter	44		L-b 2, w 1, n-b 8	11
M. G. N. Windows c Knight b Pretorius	48			
*C. G. Taylor c Frost b Brown	22		1/120 (1) 2/198 (3)	(7 wkts dec.) 400
A. P. R. Gidman c Frost b Brown	1		3/296 (4) 4/309 (2)	
M. W. Alleyne lbw b Brown	0		5/322 (6) 6/322 (7) 7/335 (5)	

J. M. M. Averis and J. Lewis did not bat.

Bonus points – Gloucestershire 5, Warwickshire 2.

Bowling: Pretorius 18–4–69–2; Carter 13–2–57–1; Brown 26–12–75–4; Bell 4–1–34–0; Richardson 14–1–62–0; Hogg 20–5–61–0; Wagh 8.2–0–35–0; Troughton 3–2–5–0.

Warwickshire

*N. V. Knight lbw b Lewis	34		G. B. Hogg not out	8
M. A. Wagh c Adshead b Averis	0		†T. Frost not out	0
I. R. Bell c Adshead b Averis	0		L-b 3, n-b 4	7
I. J. L. Trott b Bressington	76			
J. O. Troughton c Adshead b Lewis	14		1/4 (2) 2/4 (3) 3/116 (4)	(6 wkts) 139
D. R. Brown c Alleyne b Lewis	0		4/120 (1) 5/124 (6) 6/139 (5)	

N. M. Carter, A. Richardson and D. Pretorius did not bat.

Bonus points – Gloucestershire 2.

Bowling: Lewis 12–5–21–3; Averis 7–0–40–2; Gidman 5–0–31–0; Bressington 6–0–38–1; Alleyne 3–2–6–0.

Umpires: J. W. Holder and V. A. Holder.

WARWICKSHIRE v SURREY

At Birmingham, May 12, 13, 14, 15. Warwickshire won by seven wickets. Warwickshire 22 pts, Surrey 5 pts. Toss: Warwickshire.

An imposing Warwickshire total allowed their bowlers to put Surrey under pressure on a strip which, because of the need to conserve the square for Edgbaston's heavy international fixture list, had already been used for two one-day games. Troughton made 77 – his best in first-class games since his confidence-sapping spell in the England one-day side in June 2003. He and Trott provided the early initiative. However, Hogg's first century in eight years – only the third of his first-class career – was the centrepiece. Particularly strong off his legs, he reached 100 in 103 balls, against increasingly dispirited bowling, putting on 191 for the seventh wicket with Giles. In reply, only Batty, with 92 spanning 108 overs, offered prolonged resistance, and Surrey followed on. Butcher, with a century, and Thorpe gave hopes of a draw. But those were dashed when Knight finally took the new ball: Surrey lost their last eight wickets in 23.3 overs. Warwickshire needed 171 in 41 overs, and they won with eight to spare after Saqlain Mushtaq hobbled in to bowl with a knee injury that was to sideline him for the season.

Close of play: First day, Warwickshire 358-6 (Hogg 69, Giles 17); Second day, Surrey 190-7 (Batty 37, Salisbury 1); Third day, Surrey 243-2 (Butcher 114, Thorpe 32).

Warwickshire

*N. V. Knight c Batty b Saqlain Mushtaq	28	– (2) not out	62
M. A. Wagh c Azhar Mahmood b Ormond	0	– (3) lbw b Saqlain Mushtaq	12
I. R. Bell c Ramprakash b Saqlain Mushtaq	34	– (4) b Saqlain Mushtaq	31
I. J. L. Trott lbw b Saqlain Mushtaq	61	– (5) not out	35
J. O. Troughton st Batty b Salisbury	77		
D. R. Brown c Ramprakash b Bicknell	44		
G. B. Hogg c Batty b Bicknell	158		
A. F. Giles c Azhar Mahmood b Salisbury	70		
†T. Frost c Batty b Bicknell	10		
N. M. Carter c Ramprakash b Bicknell	29	– (1) run out	24
D. Pretorius not out	2		
B 11, l-b 13, n-b 9	33	B 2, l-b 3, n-b 2	7

1/14 (2) 2/64 (1) 3/71 (3) 4/190 (4)   546   1/47 (1) 2/64 (3)   (3 wkts) 171
5/242 (5) 6/306 (6) 7/497 (7)   3/114 (4)
8/505 (8) 9/544 (10) 10/546 (9)

Bonus points – Warwickshire 5, Surrey 2 (130 overs: 480-6).

Bowling: *First Innings*—Bicknell 27.3–5–130–4; Ormond 29–2–103–1; Saqlain Mushtaq 32–5–77–3; Azhar Mahmood 20–4–94–0; Salisbury 32–8–97–2; Holioake 4–0–21–0. *Second Innings*—Bicknell 8–0–37–0; Ormond 4–0–30–0; Saqlain Mushtaq 12–1–49–2; Azhar Mahmood 1–0–6–0; Salisbury 7.5–0–44–0.

Surrey

S. A. Newman c Frost b Pretorius	28	– c Knight b Wagh	55
M. A. Butcher c Bell b Carter	0	– b Pretorius	184
M. R. Ramprakash c Wagh b Carter	11	– c Pretorius b Giles	35
G. P. Thorpe c Frost b Wagh	42	– c Frost b Pretorius	89
*†J. N. Batty not out	92	– b Pretorius	8
A. J. Holioake c and b Wagh	0	– c Frost b Carter	0
Azhar Mahmood lbw b Hogg	27	– c Knight b Carter	7
M. P. Bicknell lbw b Giles	37	– b Brown	21
I. D. K. Salisbury lbw b Giles	34	– c Wagh b Carter	0
J. Ormond c Carter b Giles	0	– not out	3
Saqlain Mushtaq c Brown b Hogg	14	– lbw b Brown	0
L-b 8, w 5	13	B 5, l-b 7	12

1/2 (2) 2/32 (1) 3/50 (3) 4/98 (4)   302   1/124 (1) 2/186 (3) 3/364 (4)   414
5/98 (6) 6/133 (7) 7/183 (8)   4/382 (5) 5/383 (6) 6/387 (2)
8/267 (9) 9/275 (10) 10/302 (11)   7/395 (7) 8/395 (9)
                            9/414 (8) 10/414 (11)

Bonus points – Surrey 3, Warwickshire 3.

Bowling: *First Innings*—Pretorius 11–2–47–1; Carter 9–5–22–2; Giles 35–13–55–3; Brown 4–0–14–0; Wagh 26–9–60–2; Hogg 24–0–87–2; Troughton 13–5–9–0. *Second Innings*—Pretorius 18–2–88–3; Carter 14–2–39–3; Bell 3–1–10–0; Giles 27–4–73–1; Brown 15.3–3–40–2; Hogg 18–2–65–0; Wagh 18–2–69–1; Troughton 6–0–18–0.

Umpires: J. W. Holder and N. J. Llong.

At Horsham, May 19, 20, 21, 22. WARWICKSHIRE drew with SUSSEX.

WARWICKSHIRE v WORCESTERSHIRE

At Birmingham, May 25, 26, 27. Warwickshire won by nine wickets. Warwickshire 22 pts, Worcestershire 7 pts. Toss: Worcestershire. Championship debut: N. Tahir.

Warwickshire were indebted to the visitors for helping them avoid a possible points deduction. Tom Moody, Worcestershire's director of cricket, contended the pitch was "unsuitable for first-class cricket." But Hick scored a brilliant century and Worcestershire's bowlers were woeful; the teams shared 784 runs in the first innings, and the wicket was marked only "below average". One of the few remaining strips at Edgbaston laid in the days of uncovered pitches, the dry surface produced unpredictable bounce from the start. But while most batsmen struggled, Hick mixed watchful defence and judicious attack, proving he could bully on bumpy tracks too; it took a run-out to remove him. Perversely, the second day produced 481 runs, at the time the most in the 2004 Championship, including a violent 95 from No. 9 Carter. Worcestershire surrendered tentatively in the second innings and then bowled too short, allowing Knight and Wagh to make a mockery of what should have been a testing target. Naqqash Tahir, a 20-year-old Birmingham-born right-arm seamer, took eight wickets in his first Championship match, including the prized scalp of Hick with an in-swinger.

Close of play: First day, Worcestershire 373-8 (Mason 8); Second day, Worcestershire 70-2 (Moore 30, Smith 5).

Worcestershire

S. D. Peters c Frost b Tahir	31	– b Brown		2
S. C. Moore c Trott b Brown	5	– c Froot b Tahir		30
G. A. Hick run out	158	– lbw b Tahir		29
*B. F. Smith c Knight b Brown	67	– lbw b Carter		41
V. S. Solanki lbw b Richardson	12	– c Bell b Tahir		21
G. J. Batty c Frost b Bell	22	– lbw b Tahir		1
A. J. Bichel c Brown b Bell	35	– lbw b Bell		28
†S. J. Rhodes c Frost b Tahir	3	– c Knight b Carter		7
M. S. Mason not out	14	– b Bell		7
M. N. Malik lbw b Tahir	0	– not out		0
M. A. Harrity lbw b Tahir	0	– b Bell		0
B 8, l-b 6, w 10, n-b 8	32	B 9, l-b 6, n-b 4		19

1/6 (2) 2/82 (1) 3/223 (4) 4/248 (5)	379	1/2 (1) 2/61 (3) 3/70 (2)	185
5/291 (6) 6/357 (3) 7/359 (7)		4/98 (5) 5/111 (6) 6/156 (4)
8/373 (8) 9/373 (10) 10/379 (11)		7/178 (8) 8/182 (7)
		9/185 (9) 10/185 (11)

Bonus points – Worcestershire 4, Warwickshire 3.

Bowling: *First Innings*—Carter 18–2–70–0; Brown 24–6–83–2; Richardson 17–2–87–1; Bell 26–4–55–2; Tahir 17–1–47–4; Wagh 2–0–10–0; Trott 2–0–13–0. *Second Innings*—Brown 7–0–40–1; Carter 12–1–44–2; Tahir 10–0–43–4; Richardson 9–0–31–0; Bell 7–3–12–3.

> ❝The captain was suffering from 'intra-articular pathology of the right hip joint noted by increased synovial fluid accumulation'. It was difficult to imagine Steve Waugh, that great champion of the primacy of the Border–Gavaskar Trophy, being undone by a little synovial fluid."
>
> Australians in India, page 1264.

Warwickshire

*N. V. Knight b Bichel	16	– b Moore	83
M. A. Wagh c Rhodes b Mason	22	– not out	63
I. R. Bell c Hick b Bichel	8	– not out	5
I. J. L. Trott b Mason	3		
J. O. Troughton c Rhodes b Bichel	67		
M. J. Powell lbw b Mason	49		
D. R. Brown c Malik b Mason	82		
†T. Frost b Bichel	27		
N. M. Carter c Batty b Bichel	95		
N. Tahir c Batty b Malik	16		
A. Richardson not out	0		
B 9, l-b 11	20	L-b 2, n-b 8	10

1/38 (1) 2/46 (2) 3/46 (3) 4/50 (4)   **405**   1/152 (1)   (1 wkt) **161**
5/174 (5) 6/174 (6) 7/271 (8)
8/330 (7) 9/370 (10) 10/405 (9)

Bonus points – Warwickshire 5, Worcestershire 3.

Bowling: *First Innings*—Bichel 20.1–3–126–5; Mason 22–6–80–4; Harrity 8–2–48–0; Malik 11–0–83–1; Batty 13–3–48–0. *Second Innings*—Bichel 8–0–51–0; Mason 6–2–10–0; Malik 8–1–21–0; Harrity 5–0–26–0; Batty 7–0–21–0; Moore 6.3–1–30–1.

Umpires: J. H. Hampshire and R. Palmer.

At Lord's, June 2, 3, 4, 5. WARWICKSHIRE beat MIDDLESEX by an innings and eight runs.

WARWICKSHIRE v NORTHAMPTONSHIRE

At Birmingham, June 9, 10, 11, 12. Warwickshire won by eight wickets. Warwickshire 22 pts, Northamptonshire 5 pts. Toss: Northamptonshire. County debut: H. H. Streak.

Heath Streak, recently sacked as Zimbabwe captain in politically charged circumstances, took out his frustrations on the Northamptonshire batsmen, and achieved the best figures by a player making his debut for a county in the Championship since Cec Parkin took 14 for 99 for Lancashire in 1914. Streak's figures of 13 for 158 were also the best for Warwickshire since the West Indian Tony Merrick took 13 for 115 v Lancashire in 1987. (This was not Streak's Championship debut as he played for Hampshire in 1995.) On a pitch that looked green-tinged but generally proved flat, he initially looked rusty in his first competitive game for five weeks. But once settled, he was rewarded for bowling straight, exploiting a little uneven bounce, and later finding reverse swing. Northamptonshire assisted with some loose batting, although Phillips, who scored 80 of his 90 in boundaries, made aggression pay. In reply, Knight and Frost capitalised on a rash of dropped catches and missed stumpings to bat Warwickshire into an impregnable position. When Knight was out, shortly after reaching a 34th first-class century, he had been involved in 529 consecutive Championship overs, having spent every minute of the previous match on the field. Sales ensured Warwickshire had to bat again; Streak, with three wickets in 14 balls, ensured their target would be tiny.

Close of play: First day, Warwickshire 13-0 (Knight 10, Wagh 3); Second day, Warwickshire 334-5 (Brown 36, Hogg 2); Third day, Northamptonshire 178-4 (Sales 55, Swann 16).

Good impressions: Heath Streak took 13 for 158, the best by a player making his debut for a county in the Championship since Cec Parkin grabbed 14 for 99 in 1914.
Picture of Streak by Hamish Blair, Getty Images

Northamptonshire

T. W. Roberts c Frost b Streak	18	– lbw b Streak	0
R. A. White c Wagh b Brown	18	– c Brown b Carter	8
M. van Jaarsveld lbw b Streak	46	– c Frost b Streak	48
U. Afzaal c Frost b Streak	21	– b Brown	37
*D. J. Sales b Streak	8	– c Trott b Carter	76
G. P. Swann b Carter	35	– b Streak	29
†G. L. Brophy b Carter	25	– run out	41
J. Louw lbw b Streak	38	– c Frost b Streak	10
B. J. Phillips c Carter b Streak	90	– lbw b Streak	0
P. S. Jones b Streak	18	– lbw b Streak	0
J. F. Brown not out	0	– not out	7
B 2, l-b 6, n-b 4	12	B 2, l-b 11, n-b 11	24

1/24 (1) 2/64 (2) 3/105 (3) 4/110 (4)   329   1/0 (1) 2/16 (2) 3/83 (3)   280
5/127 (5) 6/170 (6) 7/185 (7)   4/126 (4) 5/201 (6) 6/234 (5)
8/307 (8) 9/312 (9) 10/329 (10)   7/257 (8) 8/259 (9)
                                     9/261 (10) 10/280 (7)

Bonus points – Northamptonshire 3, Warwickshire 3.

Bowling: *First Innings*—Streak 21.5–4–80–7; Carter 20–8–60–2; Brown 15–4–46–1; Tahir 16–4–39–0; Bell 7–2–24–0; Hogg 6–1–19–0; Wagh 9–2–49–0; Troughton 2–1–4–0. *Second Innings*—Streak 21.5–2–78–6; Carter 25.1–5–67–2; Tahir 4–0–17–0; Wagh 3–0–14–0; Bell 11–8–10–0; Brown 23.1–5–73–1; Troughton 2–0–8–0.

Warwickshire

*N. V. Knight c Brophy b Phillips	100	– not out		56
M. A. Wagh b Phillips	92	– c Swann b Louw		10
I. R. Bell b Phillips	2	– b Louw		0
I. J. L. Trott lbw b Swann	44	– not out		22
J. O. Troughton c Brown b Louw	54			
D. R. Brown c Brophy b Jones	45			
G. B. Hogg c Swann b Phillips	20			
H. H. Streak b Swann	61			
†T. Frost not out	85			
N. M. Carter lbw b White	9			
N. Tahir c and b Swann	1			
B 3, l-b 4, n-b 4	11			

1/189 (2) 2/194 (1) 3/197 (3) 4/249 (4)   524   1/29 (2) 2/35 (3)   (2 wkts) 88
5/331 (5) 6/358 (7) 7/368 (6)
8/508 (8) 9/517 (10) 10/524 (11)

Bonus points – Warwickshire 5, Northamptonshire 2 (130 overs: 401-7).

Bowling: *First Innings*—Jones 31–5–115–1; Louw 27–6–83–1; Phillips 34–7–110–4; Brown 41–9–128–0; Swann 26.3–5–69–3; White 3–0–12–1. *Second Innings*—Louw 7–0–27–2; Jones 4–0–32–0; Phillips 5–1–14–0; Brown 1.4–0–15–0.

Umpires: I. J. Gould and J. F. Steele.

WARWICKSHIRE v LANCASHIRE

At Stratford-upon-Avon, June 18, 19, 20, 21. Drawn. Warwickshire 11 pts, Lancashire 12 pts. Toss: Warwickshire. County debut: D. Mongia. Championship debut: P. J. Horton.

First-class cricket returned to Stratford after 53 years, but Warwickshire's first Championship game at the pleasant Swan's Nest Lane ground, just across the river from the Royal Shakespeare Theatre, was hit by unseasonably cold, wet weather, and even hail, which blanketed the outfield in white on the third day. The match, Warwickshire's first home fixture outside Edgbaston in 12 years, attracted good crowds who were richly entertained as the opening day produced 495 runs.

NEW TO THE CIRCUIT

The following grounds have staged their first Championship matches since 1993:

Gloucester (Archdeacon Meadow)	Gloucestershire v Worcestershire	1993
Chester-le-Street (Ropery Lane)	Durham v Nottinghamshire	1993
Chester-le-Street (Riverside)	Durham v Warwickshire	1995
Southgate	Middlesex v Essex	1998
Southampton (Rose Bowl)	Hampshire v Worcestershire	2001
Whitgift School	Surrey v Nottinghamshire	2003
Stratford-upon-Avon	**Warwickshire v Lancashire**	**2004**

The short boundaries, excellent pitch and depleted Lancashire attack made things comfortable for Wagh, who led the way in taking Warwickshire past 400 for the sixth successive game. Loye's 184 in reply was less flamboyant, but insured Lancashire against a third successive defeat and ended Warwickshire's hopes of a fourth successive victory. Dinesh Mongia, the Indian batsman recruited from league cricket in Staffordshire as a late replacement for the injured Carl Hooper, scored a languid 89.

Close of play: First day, Warwickshire 495-9 (Tahir 22, Pretorius 1); Second day, Lancashire 299-3 (Loye 125, Mongia 70); Third day, Lancashire 505-8 (Wood 12).

Warwickshire

*N. V. Knight lbw b Keedy	53	– not out	67
M. A. Wagh c Law b Crook	167	– c Law b Wood	18
I. R. Bell c Law b Crook	49	– c Hegg b Keedy	1
I. J. L. Trott b Martin	54	– not out	36
J. O. Troughton c Law b Keedy	8		
D. R. Brown lbw b Mongia	16		
G. B. Hogg b Martin	56		
†T. Frost lbw b Martin	0		
N. M. Carter c Swann b Wood	32		
N. Tahir b Martin	26		
D. Pretorius not out	1		
B 11, l-b 5, w 1, n-b 20	37	N-b 2	2

1/141 (1) 2/295 (3) 3/304 (2) 4/313 (5) 499 1/46 (2) 2/47 (3) (2 wkts) 124
5/356 (6) 6/419 (4) 7/419 (8)
8/446 (7) 9/478 (9) 10/499 (10)

Bonus points – Warwickshire 5, Lancashire 3.

Bowling: *First Innings*—Martin 18.5–2–81–4; Wood 20–2–122–1; Chilton 5–1–22–0; Crook 18–2–78–2; Mongia 17–1–82–1; Keedy 26–5–98–2. *Second Innings*—Martin 6–1–30–0; Wood 10–1–31 1; Keedy 12–1–31–1; Swann 1–0–1–0; Crook 6.1–0–31 0.

Lancashire

M. J. Chilton c Wagh b Carter	13	P. J. Martin b Pretorius	2
A. J. Swann lbw b Bell	20	G. Keedy c Frost b Pretorius	0
M. B. Loye b Wagh	184		
S. G. Law c Frost b Tahir	44	B 5, l-b 14, w 3, n-b 22	44
D. Mongia lbw b Bell	89		
P. J. Horton c Frost b Carter	22	1/19 (1) 2/93 (2) 3/162 (4)	508
S. P. Crook c Knight b Tahir	23	4/333 (5) 5/381 (6) 6/409 (7)	
*†W. K. Hegg b Hogg	54	7/459 (3) 8/505 (8)	
J. Wood not out	13	9/508 (10) 10/508 (11)	

Bonus points – Lancashire 5, Warwickshire 2 (130 overs: 500-7).

Bowling: Pretorius 27.3–6–76–2; Carter 16–1–93–2; Tahir 20–5–47–2; Bell 18–1 66–2; Brown 9–1–34–0; Wagh 19–1–77–1; Hogg 21–2 66–1; Troughton 4–0–30–0.

Umpires: N. G. Cowley and G. Sharp.

At Beckenham, June 23, 24, 25, 26. WARWICKSHIRE drew with KENT.

At Guildford, July 21, 22, 23, 24. WARWICKSHIRE beat SURREY by seven wickets.

At Manchester, July 28, 29, 30, 31. WARWICKSHIRE drew with LANCASHIRE.

WARWICKSHIRE v KENT

At Birmingham, August 11, 12, 13, 14. Drawn. Warwickshire 12 pts, Kent 12 pts. Toss: Warwickshire.

A superb century from Bell, his fourth in five innings, was the highlight of a match intriguingly poised before rain, and inadequate covering, drowned it. A few days later, he was in England's Test squad. Bell placed and timed the ball sublimely and put behind him an indifferent record on his home ground: this was only his third hundred in 30 first-class matches at Edgbaston. His eight previous Championship innings there in 2004 had yielded just 92 runs; yet he had passed 92 runs elsewhere. Good support, especially from Powell, enabled Warwickshire to pass 400 for a record tenth consecutive first innings – but their attack was also put under pressure. In an unfettered opening stand, Fulton and Smith clobbered 26 fours in 25 overs before they were halted by a thunderstorm at tea. As in the opening match of the season, rain seeped under the covers, restricting the third day to 40 overs, in which Fulton completed his 25th century before Kent stumbled, losing four for 26. But Championship-best scores from Loudon and O'Brien, who hit four sixes, averted any risk of following on.

Close of play: First day, Warwickshire 338-4 (Powell 77, Brown 49); Second day, Kent 135-0 (Fulton 59, Smith 72); Third day, Kent 255-5 (Loudon 27).

Warwickshire

*N. V. Knight b Butler	18	– not out	63
M. A. Wagh c O'Brien b Butler	5	– b Loudon	33
I. R. Bell b Butler	121		
I. J. L. Trott c O'Brien b Patel	50	– not out	1
M. J. Powell c Fulton b Butler	96		
D. R. Brown c Fulton b Butler	49		
G. B. Hogg c Smith b Patel	63		
H. H. Streak b Joseph	2	– (3) c O'Brien b Loudon	11
†T. Frost c Joseph b Trott	25		
N. M. Carter c Fulton b Dennington	0		
N. Tahir not out	3		
B 6, l-b 9, w 4, n-b 6	25	B 1, n-b 14	15

1/22 (1) 2/29 (2) 3/167 (4) 4/234 (3) 457
5/339 (6) 6/394 (5) 7/397 (8)
8/439 (9) 9/439 (10) 10/457 (7)

1/79 (2) 2/115 (3) (2 wkts dec.) 123

Bonus points – Warwickshire 5, Kent 3.

Bowling: *First Innings*—Butler 24–3–114–4; Joseph 18–4–83–1; Trott 13–0–67–1; Dennington 15–1–60–1; Patel 23.2–5–57–2; Loudon 9–2–31–1; Walker 7–0–21–0; Bevan 3–0–9–0. *Second Innings*—Butler 4–0–21–0; Joseph 6–0–24–0; Loudon 12–2–30–2; Dennington 5–0–29–0; Walker 3–1–5–0.

Kent

*D. P. Fulton st Frost b Wagh	100	R. H. Joseph not out	19
E. T. Smith c Wagh b Tahir	95	B. J. Trott c Frost b Bell	4
A. G. R. Loudon c Frost b Carter	92		
M. G. Bevan lbw b Carter	0	B 4, l-b 9, w 1, n-b 8	22
M. J. Walker c Trott b Wagh	1		
M. J. Dennington lbw b Streak	16		420
†N. J. O'Brien c Frost b Streak	69		
M. M. Patel c Wagh b Streak	0		
I. G. Butler c Frost b Streak	2		

1/184 (2) 2/229 (1) 3/230 (4) 420
4/231 (5) 5/255 (6) 6/382 (7)
7/382 (8) 8/390 (9)
9/406 (3) 10/420 (11)

Bonus points – Kent 5, Warwickshire 3.

Bowling: Streak 23–4–85–4; Carter 19–4–85–2; Brown 11–1–52–0; Tahir 15–1–71–1; Hogg 20–1–58–0; Wagh 18–4–55–2; Bell 0.4–0–1–1.

Umpires: B. Dudleston and M. J. Kitchen.

At Bristol, August 19, 20, 21, 22. WARWICKSHIRE drew with GLOUCESTERSHIRE.

WARWICKSHIRE v SUSSEX

At Birmingham, August 24, 25, 26, 27. Drawn. Warwickshire 10 pts, Sussex 12 pts. Toss: Warwickshire.

Warwickshire would not clinch the Championship for ten more days, but it was effectively settled here in a tense final session. Sussex, 49 points behind with a game in hand, had to win to have any real chance of retaining their title, and came close when Warwickshire were 132 for seven, four runs short of avoiding an innings defeat, just before tea. Then Frost and Streak batted for 28 overs on a turning but slow pitch to frustrate them. Though it was hardly the form of champions-in-waiting, this rearguard action typified Warwickshire's resilience and determination to preserve their unbeaten record; still, it might not have sufficed had not 44 overs not been lost to rain on the opening day. They had spluttered to 346, their lowest completed innings since April, before Prior fluently led Sussex towards the advantage. Later, Kirtley exploited a tired attack and ragged fielding to extend the lead to 136, adding 70 with last man Mohammad Akram, and was left six short of his career-best with an overnight declaration. He soon made up for it with his 500th first-class wicket, bowling Wagh with an in-swinger.

Close of play: First day, Warwickshire 177-2 (Bell 84, Trott 12); Second day, Sussex 125-1 (Montgomerie 73, Cottey 9); Third day, Sussex 482-9 (Kirtley 53, Mohammad Akram 35).

Warwickshire

*N. V. Knight c Ward b Mohammad Akram . . .	65	– b Mushtaq Ahmed	23
M. A. Wagh c Ward b Mohammad Akram	6	– b Kirtley.	0
I. R. Bell b Kirtley.	87	– b Mohammad Akram.	6
I. J. L. Trott b Martin-Jenkins.	90	– c Goodwin b Mohammad Akram . .	0
M. J. Powell c Prior b Mohammad Akram	5	– lbw b Mohammad Akram. . . . . ,	39
J. O. Troughton c Martin-Jenkins b Kirtley	2	– c Davis b Martin-Jenkins	33
D. R. Brown c Adams b Martin-Jenkins	12	– c Prior b Mushtaq Ahmed	14
†T. Frost lbw b Mushtaq Ahmed.	48	– not out	45
H. H. Streak c Goodwin b Martin-Jenkins	2	– not out	27
N. Tahir not out.	3		
D. Pretorius lbw b Martin-Jenkins	14		
B 2, l-b 6, n-b 4	12	B 4, l-b 9, p 5	18

1/11 (2) 2/141 (1) 3/184 (3) 4/195 (5)   **346**
5/198 (6) 6/226 (7) 7/325 (8)
8/327 (4) 9/330 (9) 10/346 (11)

1/6 (2) 2/15 (3) 3/15 (4)   (7 wkts) **205**
4/66 (1) 5/98 (5)
6/121 (6) 7/132 (7)

Bonus points – Warwickshire 3, Sussex 3.

Bowling: *First Innings*—Mohammad Akram 27–5–94–3; Kirtley 32–7–75–2; Mushtaq Ahmed 27–3–74–1; Martin-Jenkins 21–5–62–4; Davis 13–0–33–0. *Second Innings*—Mohammad Akram 20–6–45–3; Kirtley 21–5–68–1; Martin-Jenkins 14–6–20–1; Mushtaq Ahmed 31–13–52–2; Davis 3–2–2–0.

Sussex

I. J. Ward lbw b Tahir	34	R. J. Kirtley not out	53
R. R. Montgomerie lbw b Streak.	78	Mohammad Akram not out.	35
P. A. Cottey run out	30		
M. W. Goodwin lbw b Streak	75	B 6, l-b 14.	20
*C. J. Adams c Trott b Pretorius	7		
†M. J. Prior b Bell	95	1/106 (1) 2/135 (2) (9 wkts dec.) **482**
R. S. C. Martin-Jenkins c Frost b Tahir .	26	3/181 (3) 4/190 (5)
M. J. G. Davis c Frost b Tahir	8	5/293 (4) 6/343 (6)
Mushtaq Ahmed c Tahir b Pretorius	21	7/363 (7) 8/372 (8) 9/412 (9)

Bonus points – Sussex 5, Warwickshire 3 (130 overs: 434-9).

Bowling: Streak 31–8–92–2; Pretorius 22–1–99–2; Brown 26–8–71–0; Tahir 24–4–81–3; Bell 24–4–57–1; Troughton 10–3–24–0; Powell 1–0–15–0; Wagh 5–0–23–0.

Umpires: G. I. Burgess and D. J. Constant.

At Worcester, August 31, September 1, 2, 3. WARWICKSHIRE drew with WORCESTERSHIRE.

At Northampton, September 16, 17, 18, 19. WARWICKSHIRE drew with NORTHAMPTONSHIRE.

ONE HUNDRED YEARS AGO

FROM WISDEN CRICKETERS' ALMANACK FOR 1905

DEATHS IN 1904 – "MR. FREDERICK GALE, well known to thousands of cricketers under his nom de plume of "The Old Buffer" – died on April 24th in the Charterhouse… Mr. Gale did not win fame as a player, but no one loved cricket more than he did, or supported it more keenly. He kept up his enthusiasm to the end, and even so recently as the season of 1903 he was to be seen at the Oval – bent in figure, but still full of vivacity. As a writer on the game he was prolific, several books and numberless magazine and newspaper articles coming from his pen."

THE SECOND-CLASS COUNTIES – "Three new county elevens – Suffolk, Norfolk and Cornwall – took part in the competition in 1904, the total number of counties engaged being thus brought up to twenty. Never in previous years were so many included. With an excellent all-round team, Northamptonshire for the second season in succession came out on top. They won ten out of the twelve matches they played, and obtaining 30 points out of a possible 36, finished up with a percentage of over 80. During the summer they made application for promotion to the first division, and were subsequently admitted into the first-class county championship."

DERBYSHIRE v ESSEX, AT CHESTERFIELD, JULY 18, 19, 20, 1904 – "In defeating Essex, Derbyshire accomplished the most phenomenal performance ever recorded in first-class cricket. They went in against a first innings of 597, got within 49, and ultimately won by nine wickets. Such an achievement has no parallel in the history of the game. Two batsmen covered themselves with distinction in the match – P. Perrin whose 343 not out was not only the highest innings of the season, but the fifth best ever… and Ollivierre who scored 321 for once out. Perrin obtained his runs in five hours and three-quarters, and hit no fewer than sixty-eight 4's". *(Perrin's 68 fours remains the most ever hit in a first-class innings, and the second-most boundaries hit – surpassed only by Brian Lara's 62 fours and ten sixes during his record 501 not out 90 years later.)*

YORKSHIRE v NOTTS (TIME-LIMIT MATCH), AT LEEDS, MAY 2, 3, 4, 1904 – "This was a match arranged to try a time-limit scheme, the chief conditions of which were that each innings should be limited to four hours and a quarter with the qualification that time lost on innings one and two was to be equally deducted from innings three and four; time saved on the first two innings being added to the third and fourth innings. The result was to be determined by the runs scored irrespective of the number of wickets lost. Unfortunately, the course of the play prevented the special regulations being really tested, the match ending early on the third morning in a victory for Yorkshire by 71 runs. The game, the main object of which was, of course, to render play more attractive, quite failed from that point of view, the attendance proving meagre to a degree."

GENTLEMEN v PLAYERS, THE LORD'S MATCH, JULY 4, 5, 6, 1904 – "Gentlemen v. Players at Lord's proved emphatically the match of the season. Played through from the first ball to the last in the keenest and most sportsmanlike way, it ended amid intense excitement late on the third afternoon in a victory for the Gentlemen by two wickets. The Gentlemen had not won at Lord's since 1899, and inasmuch as they were 156 runs behind on the first innings, their performance could fairly be described as wonderful."

LANCASHIRE IN 1904 – "The season of 1904 may without exaggeration be described as the brightest in the history of Lancashire cricket. The county not only won the championship, but as in 1881, earned that distinction without suffering a single defeat in the competition… Their record came out at sixteen wins and ten drawn games… There can be no question that Lancashire last summer possessed a very brilliant team, capable of first-rate work under all conditions of weather and wickets. Up to the end of July their match-winning power was remarkable, fifteen of their victories being gained during the first three months of the season… All-round efficiency was the secret of their success. Well armed at every point, the team were never found at a disadvantage."

WORCESTERSHIRE

The captain goes down, then the ship

JOHN CURTIS

County captains come and go in all kinds of mysterious ways. But what happened at Worcester in mid-August was particularly baffling. Ben Smith gave up the job, without notice or logical explanation, in the middle of a match against Northamptonshire. His deputy, 40-year-old Steve Rhodes, had to take charge for the rest of the game and the season, before he retired after 20 years as Worcestershire's first-choice keeper.

It was a confusing episode in a confused season which ended with the county – tipped by some as outsiders for the title – relegated in the Championship but promoted in the totesport League, and searching for two overseas players as well as a new captain and vice-captain.

Australia's Andy Bichel was released after three seasons at New Road, with South African all-rounder Andrew Hall allowed to go to Kent. Promising batsman Kadeer Ali sought fresh pastures at Gloucestershire and, though chief executive Mark Newton squashed rumours that Smith, Gareth Batty and Stephen Peters were looking to move, it appeared the dressing room was not completely harmonious.

Director of cricket Tom Moody had certainly hoped for a top-three finish in Worcestershire's first season in the Championship's top division. They ended June in fourth place, which might have been higher: Kent held out with nine wickets down, and rain denied an almost certain victory against Surrey. But Worcestershire learned that it was more difficult to recover from a below-par session than in Division Two, and ultimately paid for a lack of consistency. They seldom performed to their best when the Championship resumed in July, and went straight down, with only three wins. Worcestershire were unlucky in losing 11 out of 16 Championship tosses, including the last seven, which reduced their chance to shape games. But too often, they did not bat well in the first innings – they reached 400 in only five of them. Back-to-the-wall heroics, such as they produced on the final day at The Oval, brought fewer tangible rewards.

In contrast, Worcestershire bounced right up again in the one-day league after a single season in Division Two (they have yet to play in both first divisions in the same year): they finished runners-up, level on points with Middlesex but with one fewer win. They also reached the C&G Trophy final for the second year running, only to be bridesmaids to Gloucestershire again.

By then, Smith had stood down as captain. His timing, on the third morning of a four-day match, was a shock ("We were as stunned as anyone else," said a senior player). Apart from anything else, Worcestershire were already in the C&G final, and Smith might have been looking forward to lifting the club's first trophy in ten years. But he had never looked at ease since replacing Graeme Hick in 2003, and cited concern over his own form. Yet he was averaging 55 in the Championship when he quit, though his limited-overs record was poor. Vikram Solanki was eventually chosen to succeed him, with Gareth Batty his deputy. But there was no word about what might happen if England should again choose both together. The Zimbabwean slow left-armer Ray Price, who joined as a Kolpak player, seemed the obvious No. 3. Rhodes will be harder to replace, and not just behind the stumps, where his 1,263 first-class dismissals left him eighth in the all-time list, and included a record 1,095 for Worcestershire. His

Stephen Moore

calming presence and defiance in the lower order will also be sorely missed: he guarded his wicket almost with his life to the end.

Given Worcestershire's generally successful record with foreign imports, Bichel and Hall both underachieved in 2004, managing just 62 Championship wickets between them. Bichel looked as if he had gone one season too far: the determination and drive were still there, though the bowling had lost its edge. He did compensate with the bat, but it was his bowling skills that were really needed. Hall had back problems, and only started to find form during the final weeks.

Hick weighed in with 1,589 first-class runs at 63.56. Even at the age of 38, he remained a force in the county game, although he had become more vulnerable early on: he was dismissed for ten or less nine times in 29 innings. The big plus was Solanki, who finally translated his potential into consistent run-making in all forms of the game, after a change of attitude and technique. Opener Stephen Moore showed promise, reaching 1,004 first-class runs in his first full season, which helped to keep Kadeer Ali out after he fractured his elbow. In June, Moore's opening partner, Peters, scored three hundreds in successive Championship innings at New Road, but he managed only one half-century after that and dropped out of the one-day side.

Matt Mason was the only bowler to claim 50 first-class wickets, though by the end of the campaign the strain of a heavy workload – nearly 600 overs – was showing. Kabir Ali was restricted to eight Championship appearances between injuries, which blunted the team's cutting edge. The other main wicket-taker, with 45, was off-spinner Batty. Price joined in August, and was due to return for the next two seasons. In November, Worcestershire announced a major signing in pace star Shoaib Akhtar, due to be available from July 1. But Shoaib's record at Durham was patchy, and the need is for consistent wicket-takers.

WORCESTERSHIRE RESULTS

All first-class matches – Played 17: Won 3, Lost 6, Drawn 8.
County Championship matches – Played 16: Won 3, Lost 6, Drawn 7.

Frizzell County Championship, 7th in Division 1; Cheltenham & Gloucester Trophy, finalists;
totesport League, 2nd in Division 2; Twenty20 Cup, q-f.

COUNTY CHAMPIONSHIP AVERAGES

BATTING AND FIELDING

Cap/Colours		M	I	NO	R	HS	100s	50s	Avge	Ct/St
1986	G. A. Hick	16	27	3	1,349	262	3	6	56.20	25
2004	R. W. Price	3	5	2	146	76*	0	1	48.66	1
2002	B. F. Smith	15	23	3	930	187	2	6	46.50	17
2001	A. J. Bichel§	14	18	1	717	142	3	2	42.17	3
1998	V. S. Solanki	13	18	0	757	107	1	6	42.05	10
2003	S. C. Moore	16	27	3	957	146	3	4	39.87	7
1986	S. J. Rhodes	16	19	8	412	59*	0	2	37.45	42/4
2003	A. J. Hall§	11	17	2	519	81	0	5	34.60	15
2002	S. D. Peters	16	27	0	898	123	3	3	33.25	13
2002	G. J. Batty	12	18	3	470	133	1	2	31.33	7
2002	Kadeer Ali	5	8	0	181	66	0	1	22.62	4
2002	M. S. Mason	16	19	6	193	63	0	1	14.84	4
2002	Kabir Ali	8	9	1	93	31	0	0	11.62	2
2004	M. N. Malik	7	8	1	9	7	0	0	1.28	1

Also batted: M. A. Harrity (colours 2003) (3 matches) 0, 0; S. A. Khalid (colours 2003) (3 matches) 0, 1*, 6* (1 ct); D. J. Pipe (colours 2002) (2 matches) 12.

§ *Overseas player.*

Since 2002, Worcestershire have awarded county colours to all players making their Championship debut.

BOWLING

	O	M	R	W	BB	5W/i	Avge
M. S. Mason	574.1	174	1,517	51	5-62	1	29.74
G. J. Batty	492.1	129	1,381	45	7-52	2	30.68
M. N. Malik	179	31	714	23	5-88	1	31.04
Kadeer Ali	248	45	899	28	5-60	1	32.10
A. J. Hall	330.3	70	1,055	29	3-10	0	36.37
R. W. Price	169.1	50	420	10	4-83	0	42.00
A. J. Bichel	398.5	75	1,549	33	5-87	2	46.93

Also bowled: Kadeer Ali 14–1–51–1; M. A. Harrity 65–15–240–4; G. A. Hick 5–1–16–1; S. A. Khalid 86.3–17–277–4; S. C. Moore 23–3–99–2; S. D. Peters 2–0–12–0; V. S. Solanki 74.3–7–240–6.

COUNTY RECORDS

Highest score for:	405*	G. A. Hick v Somerset at Taunton	1988
Highest score against:	331*	J. D. Robertson (Middlesex) at Worcester	1949
Best bowling for:	9-23	C. F. Root v Lancashire at Worcester	1931
Best bowling against:	10-51	J. Mercer (Glamorgan) at Worcester	1936
Highest total for:	670-7 dec.	v Somerset at Worcester	1995
Highest total against:	701-4 dec.	by Leicestershire at Worcester	1906
Lowest total for:	24	v Yorkshire at Huddersfield	1903
Lowest total against:	30	by Hampshire at Worcester	1903

WORCESTERSHIRE DIRECTORY

ADDRESS

County Ground, New Road, Worcester WR2 4QQ (01905 748474; fax 01905 748005; email info@wccc.co.uk). **Website** www.wccc.co.uk.

GROUNDS

Worcester (New Road): ¼ mile SW of city centre S of River Severn on L side of New Road one-way system. Nearest stations: Worcester Foregate Street (½ mile) and Worcester Shrub Hill (1 mile).

Kidderminster: ½ mile E of town centre, at junction of Birmingham Road (A456) and Chester Road North (A449), then R into Offmore Lane. Nearest station: Kidderminster (½ mile).

OFFICIALS

Captain 2005 – V. S. Solanki
Director of cricket T. M. Moody
Academy director D. B. D'Oliveira
President 2004 – N. H. Whiting

Chairman J. W. Elliott
Chief executive M. S. Newton
Head groundsman T. R. Packwood
Scorers W. Clarke; N. Smith

PLAYERS

Players expected to reappear in 2005

	Former counties	Country	Born	Birthplace
*Ali Kabir		E	24.11.1980	*Moseley*
*Batty Gareth Jon	Yorks, Surrey	E	13.10.1977	*Bradford*
Davies Steven Michael		E	17.6.1986	†*Bromsgrove*
*Hick Graeme Ashley		E	23.5.1966	*Salisbury, Rhodesia*
Khalid Shaftab Ahmed		E	6.10.1982	*Lahore, Pak.*
Leatherdale David Antony		E	26.11.1967	*Bradford*
Malik Muhammad <u>Nadeem</u>	Notts	E	6.10.1982	*Nottingham*
Mason Matthew Sean		A (EU)	20.3.1974	*Claremont, Aus.*
Moore Stephen Colin		E	4.11.1980	*Johannesburg*
Peters Stephen David	Essex	E	10.12.1978	*Harold Wood*
Pipe David <u>James</u>		E	16.12.1977	*Bradford*
*Price Raymond William		Z (K)	12.6.1976	*Salisbury*
Smith Benjamin Francis	Leics	E	3.4.1972	*Corby*
Solanki Vikram Singh.		E	1.4.1976	*Udaipur, India*

Players due to join in 2005

	Former counties	Country	Born	Birthplace
*de Bruyn Zander.		SA	5.7.1975	*Johannesburg*
*Shoaib Akhtar	Somerset, Durham	P	13.8.1975	*Rawalpindi*
*Vaas Warnakulasuriya Patabendige Ushantha Joseph <u>Chaminda</u>	Hampshire	SL	27.1.1974	*Mattumagala*

* *Test player.*   † *Born in Worcestershire.*

At Worcester, April 10, 11, 12 (not first-class). **Worcestershire won by an innings and 224 runs.** Toss: Worcestershire. **Cardiff UCCE 118** (M. N. Malik 6-41) **and 164** (M. S. Mason 4-25, S. A. Khalid 4-47); **Worcestershire 506-9 dec.** (S. D. Peters 89, V. S. Solanki 84, D. K. H. Mitchell 83, S. J. Rhodes 87 retired out).

Each side named 12 players, of whom 11 could bat and 11 field. First-team debuts: S. M. Davies, D. K. H. Mitchell. County debut: M. N. Malik.

At Canterbury, April 21, 22, 23, 24. WORCESTERSHIRE lost to KENT by five wickets.

WORCESTERSHIRE v SUSSEX

At Worcester, April 28, 29, 30, May 1. Drawn. Worcestershire 4 pts, Sussex 4 pts. Toss: Sussex.

Only 17 overs were possible, on the final day, after the opening three were washed out without a ball bowled. The match eventually got under way as a one-innings affair at 12.30, and it seemed bizarre that the players should leave the field after only half an hour of action. It hardly mattered: the rain returned 35 minutes into the afternoon session. There was time for both Worcestershire openers to fall after Adams, unsurprisingly, put them in.

Close of play: First day, No play; Second day, No play; Third day, No play.

Worcestershire

Worcestershire forfeited their first innings.

S. D. Peters c Ambrose b Mohammad Akram	16	*B. F. Smith not out	8	
S. C. Moore b Lewry	12	L-b 1, n-b 2	3	
G. A. Hick not out	7			
		1/28 (2) 2/30 (1)	(2 wkts) 46	

V. S. Solanki, D. J. Pipe, A. J. Bichel, †S. J. Rhodes, M. S. Mason, M. N. Malik and M. A. Harrity did not bat.

Bowling: Mohammad Akram 9–1–37–1; Lewry 8–3–8–1.

Sussex

Sussex forfeited their first innings.

I. J. Ward, R. R. Montgomerie, P. A. Cottey, M. W. Goodwin, *C. J. Adams, M. J. Prior, †T. R. Ambrose, R. S. C. Martin-Jenkins, Mushtaq Ahmed, J. D. Lewry and Mohammad Akram.

Umpires: M. R. Benson and A. G. T. Whitehead.

At Worcester, May 7, 8, 9, 10. WORCESTERSHIRE drew with NEW ZEALANDERS (see New Zealand tour section).

At Manchester, May 12, 13, 14. WORCESTERSHIRE lost to LANCASHIRE by 219 runs.

WORCESTERSHIRE v GLOUCESTERSHIRE

At Worcester, May 18, 19, 20, 21. Worcestershire won by an innings and 86 runs. Worcestershire 22 pts, Gloucestershire 2 pts. Toss: Worcestershire.

Record-breaking batting by Hick and Smith earned Worcestershire their maiden victory in the Championship's first division. It moved them off the bottom of the table, to be replaced by Gloucestershire, who had not won at New Road since 1986. Hick started with a streaky edge for four, but moved ahead of Denis Compton in sole 11th place in the century-makers' list with his 124th hundred, and ninth against Gloucestershire – more than against any other side. Next morning, he completed his second 200 in ten days and 16th in all, to go joint fifth in the even more exclusive list of double-centurions. In all, Hick faced 397 balls, harvesting 35 fours and three sixes in eight hours 11 minutes. Smith made a county-best 187 as they added 417, an all-wicket record at New Road, though 21 short of Worcestershire's biggest, also for the third wicket, 438 by Hick and Tom Moody at Southampton in 1997. It was the joint tenth-highest stand for any wicket in the Championship. Gloucestershire's openers reached 55 before six wickets fell on the second evening. The resolute Gidman occupied 52 overs, but the top order collapsed again in the follow-on. Gidman scored a second fifty before becoming one of five victims for Mason.

Close of play: First day, Worcestershire 396-2 (Hick 183, Smith 166); Second day, Gloucestershire 108-6 (Gidman 0, Shoaib Malik 0); Third day, Gloucestershire 166-5 (Gidman 54).

Worcestershire

S. D. Peters c Weston b Gidman	20	G. J. Batty not out		7
S. C. Moore c Weston b Lewis	10	L-b 14, w 2, n-b 8		24
G. A. Hick c Spearman b Lewis	262			
*B. F. Smith lbw b Shoaib Malik	187	1/15 (2) 2/37 (1)	(6 wkts dec.)	619
V. S. Solanki c Windows b Shoaib Malik	74	3/454 (4) 4/554 (3)		
Kadeer Ali b Fisher	35	5/600 (5) 6/619 (6)		

†S. J. Rhodes, M. S. Mason, M. N. Malik and M. A. Harrity did not bat.

Bonus points – Worcestershire 5, Gloucestershire 1 (130 overs: 507-3).

Bowling: Lewis 32–10–73–2; Averis 33–6–139–0; Gidman 24–3–129–1; Shoaib Malik 39–8–118–2; Fisher 23.3–0–105–1; Hancock 10–1–41–0.

Gloucestershire

C. M. Spearman c Smith b Batty	62	– (2) c Moore b Harrity	0
W. P. C. Weston lbw b Malik	26	– (1) c Hick b Mason	12
T. H. C. Hancock c Hick b Malik	4	– b Mason	68
M. G. N. Windows c Hick b Batty	1	– lbw b Mason	0
*C. G. Taylor c Rhodes b Batty	7	– c Rhodes b Malik	28
J. M. M. Averis c Rhodes b Mason	2	– (10) b Mason	10
A. P. R. Gidman c Rhodes b Mason	54	– (6) b Mason	77
Shoaib Malik c Moore b Harrity	33	– (7) c Rhodes b Harrity	3
†S. J. Adshead c Peters b Malik	10	– (8) c Hick b Batty	61
I. D. Fisher c Solanki b Harrity	20	– (9) st Rhodes b Batty	11
J. Lewis not out	0	– not out	24
B 1, l-b 4, n-b 8	13	B 2, l-b 1, n-b 4	7

1/55 (2) 2/69 (3) 3/70 (4) 4/105 (1)	232	1/4 (2) 2/12 (1) 3/12 (4)	301
5/106 (5) 6/108 (6) 7/149 (8)		4/55 (5) 5/166 (3) 6/181 (7)
8/182 (9) 9/232 (10) 10/232 (7)		7/201 (6) 8/236 (9)
		9/264 (10) 10/301 (8)

Bonus points – Gloucestershire 1, Worcestershire 3.

Bowling: *First Innings*—Mason 21.2–9–46–2; Harrity 24–6–60–2; Malik 19–4–58–3; Batty 29–10–63–3. *Second Innings*—Mason 24–9–62–5; Harrity 28–7–106–2; Malik 15–4–52–1; Batty 24.4–11–48–2; Moore 4–1–10–0; Solanki 5–1–20–0.

Umpires: G. I. Burgess and N. A. Mallender.

At Birmingham, May 25, 26, 27. WORCESTERSHIRE lost to WARWICKSHIRE by nine wickets.

At Northampton, June 2, 3, 4, 5. WORCESTERSHIRE beat NORTHAMPTONSHIRE by nine wickets.

WORCESTERSHIRE v KENT

At Worcester, June 9, 10, 11, 12. Drawn. Worcestershire 12 pts, Kent 12 pts. Toss: Worcestershire. First-class debut: S. M. J. Cusden.

Last man Sheriyar kept out Batty's final over to deny Worcestershire, his former county. He and O'Brien survived 31 deliveries after Kent lost six wickets for 66 in the final session. When the teams had met in April, Kent won chasing 429, and this time Ben Smith batted on for ten overs on the fourth morning, raising the target to 439; with hindsight, he may have regretted it. The first three innings, however, had all passed 400. Peters became the first player to score twin centuries for Worcestershire since Hick in 1999, and both times Smith and Solanki backed him up. In between, Symonds reached 100 in 98 balls, before O'Brien scored a maiden fifty. On the last day, although Carberry was hit on the helmet and Key batted at No. 7 because of a migraine, Kent looked to be comfortably seeing out time. But Batty struck twice before tea to trigger their collapse. Fielding on the second morning, Tredwell and O'Brien had to protect themselves from a swarm of bees. The real venom, though, was in the Kent dressing-room: the opening day saw the start of a row that continued all season. Ed Smith, acting-captain for the injured Fulton, received so little support from his senior team-mates (especially Symonds) that Fulton attempted to take charge as a substitute, until the umpires told him this was against the Laws. The internal argument ultimately led to the resignation of cricket committee chairman Mike Denness and Smith's departure to Middlesex.

Close of play: First day, Worcestershire 356-7 (Batty 17); Second day, Kent 347-6 (Tredwell 23, O'Brien 40); Third day, Worcestershire 340-3 (Smith 108, Solanki 64).

Worcestershire

S. D. Peters c O'Brien b Sheriyar	123	–	c O'Brien b Walker	117
S. C. Moore b Symonds	15	–	lbw b Trott	4
G. A. Hick c Tredwell b Symonds	2	–	c Loudon b Trott	27
*B. F. Smith c Tredwell b Sheriyar	65	–	c Key b Trott	127
V. S. Solanki c O'Brien b Trott	107	–	c Walker b Trott	86
A. J. Hall b Cusden	12	–	not out	9
G. J. Batty b Cusden	36	–	c Symonds b Tredwell	14
A. J. Bichel c Tredwell b Sheriyar	0			
Kabir Ali c O'Brien b Symonds	31			
†S. J. Rhodes c O'Brien b Tredwell	8			
M. S. Mason not out	35			
B 2, l-b 7, w 2, n-b 8	19		B 5, l-b 14, w 2	21

1/54 (2) 2/60 (3) 3/179 (4) 4/272 (1)   453   1/4 (2) 2/80 (3)   (6 wkts dec.) 405
5/295 (6) 6/355 (5) 7/356 (8)   3/224 (1) 4/370 (4)
8/405 (7) 9/414 (9) 10/453 (10)   5/384 (5) 6/405 (7)

Bonus points – Worcestershire 5, Kent 3.

Bowling: *First Innings*—Sheriyar 31–7–106–3; Cusden 26–5–91–2; Symonds 27–8–114–3; Trott 29–4–78–1; Tredwell 13.2–3–54–1; Loudon 1–0–1–0. *Second Innings*—Sheriyar 10–2–34–0; Trott 24–1–109–4; Walker 15–5–57–1; Cusden 15–2–63–0; Tredwell 16.5–2–84–1; Loudon 4–0–26–0; Carberry 4–0–13–0.

❝ Headingley's new scoreboard was under construction and inquisitive fans were surprised to see 'REMOVERS' underneath TOTAL, WICKETS, etc.**"**

Yorkshire in 2004, page 812.

Kent

M. A. Carberry c Rhodes b Bichel	8	– c Rhodes b Kabir Ali	64
R. W. T. Key c Rhodes b Hall	29	– (7) st Rhodes b Batty	10
*E. T. Smith lbw b Mason	1	– c Mason b Batty	35
A. Symonds c Smith b Batty	103	– c Hick b Batty	9
M. J. Walker c Peters b Hall	62	– c Peters b Kabir Ali	14
A. G. R. Loudon c Moore b Hall	59	– c Moore b Hall	12
J. C. Tredwell c Hall b Mason	47	– (2) b Mason	45
†N. J. O'Brien c and b Kabir Ali	67	– not out	20
B. J. Trott lbw b Kabir Ali	0	– (10) c Hick b Bichel	12
A. Sheriyar run out	5	– (11) not out	0
S. M. J. Cusden not out	2	– (9) lbw b Hall	0
L-b 8, w 3, n-b 26	37	B 6, l-b 2, w 1, n-b 14	23

1/10 (1) 2/31 (3) 3/116 (2) 4/189 (4)   420
5/250 (5) 6/281 (6) 7/391 (8)
8/395 (9) 9/403 (10) 10/420 (7)

1/71 (2) 2/107 (3)   (9 wkts) 244
3/167 (4) 4/169 (1)
5/194 (5) 6/206 (6)
7/216 (8) 8/221 (9) 9/235 (10)

Bonus points – Kent 5, Worcestershire 3.

In the second innings Carberry, when 4, retired hurt at 32 and resumed at 71.

Bowling: First Innings—Bichel 24–6–121–1; Mason 20.2–4–83–2; Kabir Ali 18–2–93–2; Hall 11–2–53–3; Batty 22–6–57–1; Solanki 5–1–5–0. Second Innings—Mason 14–8–19–1; Kabir Ali 12–1–39–2; Hall 15–5–63–2; Bichel 14–3–55–1; Batty 29–14–60–3.

Umpires: N. G. Cowley and G. Sharp.

At Lord's, June 18, 19, 20, 21. WORCESTERSHIRE drew with MIDDLESEX.

WORCESTERSHIRE v SURREY

At Worcester, June 23, 24, 25, 26. Drawn. Worcestershire 12 pts, Surrey 4.5 pts (after 0.5 pt penalty). Toss: Worcestershire.

Worcestershire were denied victory when rain prevented any cricket on the final day until 5 p.m. The weather had interfered throughout; only seven overs were bowled on the opening day, and on the second morning the sun's glare, reflected off white sheeting serving as a sightscreen, halted play for 19 minutes while a tractor brought a screen from the King's School ground next door. Worcestershire had outgunned a dispirited-looking Surrey from the start and, on a lively pitch, Hall's spell of three for ten then prompted another Surrey collapse. With four wickets to get, and mindful of the forecast, Worcestershire requested the extra half-hour on the third day, but the umpires refused, a decision which assumed greater significance next day. Thorpe, at No. 7 because of a bad back, ensured a fortuitous draw.

Close of play: First day, Surrey 16-2 (Newman 12, Thorpe 0); Second day, Worcestershire 170-0 (Peters 92, Moore 73); Third day, Surrey 167-6 (Thorpe 17, Bicknell 1).

Surrey

S. A. Newman c Hall b Kabir Ali	23	– b Hall	65
M. A. Butcher c Rhodes b Kabir Ali	4	– c Solanki b Bichel	17
M. R. Ramprakash run out	0	– c Rhodes b Hall	13
G. P. Thorpe lbw b Kabir Ali	41	– (7) not out	26
*†J. N. Batty c Bichel b Mason	53	– c Smith b Batty	10
A. D. Brown c Rhodes b Kabir Ali	0	– lbw b Mason	31
A. J. Hollioake b Mason	16	– (4) b Hall	0
M. P. Bicknell lbw b Kabir Ali	3	– c Rhodes b Mason	9
I. D. K. Salisbury c Rhodes b Mason	8	– b Kabir Ali	2
J. Ormond c Rhodes b Mason	0	– not out	1
T. J. Murtagh not out	2		
B 1, l-b 4	5	B 4, l-b 9	13

1/6 (2) 2/14 (3) 3/35 (1) 4/87 (4) 155 1/45 (2) 2/83 (3) 3/83 (4) (8 wkts) 187
5/87 (6) 6/114 (7) 7/123 (8)   4/106 (1) 5/127 (5)
8/142 (9) 9/150 (10) 10/155 (5)   6/164 (6) 7/178 (8) 8/181 (9)

Bonus points – Worcestershire 3.

Bowling: *First Innings*—Mason 17.1–5–46–4; Kabir Ali 19–6–60–5; Hall 7–2–16–0; Bichel 4–0–28–0. *Second Innings*—Kabir Ali 16–2–65–1; Mason 22–7–47–2; Hall 8–3–10–3; Bichel 10–3–46–1; Batty 4–3–6–1.

Worcestershire

S. D. Peters c Newman b Hollioake	108	A. J. Hall not out	53
S. C. Moore c Batty b Hollioake	146	L-b 9, w 2, n-b 2	13
G. A. Hick c Batty b Hollioake	0		
*B. F. Smith not out	80	1/240 (1) 2/245 (3) (4 wkts dec.) 400
V. S. Solanki c Batty b Salisbury	0	3/270 (4) 4/271 (5)

G. J. Batty, A. J. Bichel, Kabir Ali, †S. J. Rhodes and M. S. Mason did not bat.

Bonus points – Worcestershire 5, Surrey 1.

Bowling: Bicknell 11–4–27–0; Ormond 31–5–109–0; Murtagh 22–1–107–0; Hollioake 21–3–69–3; Salisbury 18–0–79–1.

Umpires: B. Dudleston and P. J. Hartley.

At Worcester, July 7. WORCESTERSHIRE lost to SRI LANKA A by six wickets (see Sri Lanka A tour section).

WORCESTERSHIRE v MIDDLESEX

At Worcester, July 22, 23, 24, 25. Middlesex won by six wickets. Middlesex 22 pts, Worcestershire 4 pts. Toss: Middlesex. Championship debuts: A. B. Agarkar, N. R. D. Compton, C. J. C. Wright.

Middlesex claimed their second win of the Championship season with 20 balls to spare. They had been held up by Hall and Bichel, who scored his third first-class hundred. But the game had moved decisively in Middlesex's favour on the third evening, when Cook bowled a full length to capitalise on unpredictable bounce; three batsmen were lbw to deliveries that kept low, leaving Worcestershire 173 behind with six second-innings wickets left. On the opening day, Betts had exploited bowler-friendly conditions too, but that time Solanki and Hall came to the rescue. When Middlesex replied, Ben Hutton and the debutant Nick Compton added 127, the first Hutton-Compton century stand in any first-class match since their grandfathers Len and Denis put on 150 in the riot-torn Georgetown Test of 1953-54. The Worcester crowd did not throw bottles. Shah later provided backbone with a mature hundred, while Dalrymple really sparkled with some dazzling strokes. On the final day, Hall scored his second fifty of the match but, when he was last out, Middlesex needed only 104 off 29 overs. Another half-century stand from Hutton and Compton helped them ease to victory in Hutton's first Championship match as captain.

Close of play: First day, Worcestershire 263-6 (Solanki 82, Hall 63); Second day, Middlesex 260-3 (Shah 22, Weekes 32); Third day, Worcestershire 136-4 (Kadeer Ali 32, Bichel 53).

Worcestershire

S. D. Peters c Hutton b Betts	24	– lbw b Betts	13
S. C. Moore b Betts	33	– b Cook	20
G. A. Hick c Betts b Cook	10	– lbw b Cook	2
V. S. Solanki c Compton b Betts	92	– lbw b Cook	9
Kadeer Ali c Nash b Betts	0	– c Shah b Cook	36
A. J. Bichel c Weekes b Agarkar	28	– c Weekes b Dalrymple	108
G. J. Batty lbw b Betts	8	– c Nash b Cook	0
A. J. Hall c Nash b Agarkar	71	– c Compton b Betts	81
Kabir Ali run out	3	– c Nash b Cook	7
*†S. J. Rhodes not out	5	– c Hutton b Dalrymple	20
M. S. Mason c Nash b Agarkar	6	– not out	5
L-b 2, w 3, n-b 20	25	B 5, l-b 2, w 1, n-b 14	22
	305		**323**

1/59 (2) 2/72 (3) 3/78 (1) 4/78 (5)   1/33 (2) 2/35 (3) 3/37 (1)
5/127 (6) 6/147 (7) 7/280 (4)   4/47 (4) 5/162 (5) 6/162 (7)
8/293 (8) 9/294 (9) 10/305 (11)   7/230 (6) 8/247 (9)
                                            9/307 (10) 10/323 (8)

Bonus points – Worcestershire 3, Middlesex 3.

Bowling: *First Innings*—Agarkar 20.3–4–72–3; Cook 23–4–61–1; Betts 18–3–89–5; Wright 7–0–31–0; Hutton 6–1–22–0; Dalrymple 2–0–20–0; Weekes 2–0–8–0. *Second Innings*—Cook 32–6–89–6; Agarkar 14–2–62–0; Betts 23.1–5–78–2; Weekes 10–1–25–0; Wright 13–3–19–0; Dalrymple 14–1–43–2.

Middlesex

*B. L. Hutton b Batty	108	– b Batty	43
S. G. Koenig c Rhodes b Mason	37	– run out	11
N. R. D. Compton lbw b Batty	40	– c Kadeer Ali b Batty	20
O. A. Shah not out	140	– b Kabir Ali	10
P. N. Weekes b Kabir Ali	42	– not out	11
J. W. M. Dalrymple run out	84	– not out	0
†D. C. Nash c Hall b Kadeer Ali	12		
S. J. Cook c Peters b Batty	0		
A. B. Agarkar c Rhodes b Batty	22		
M. M. Betts c Peters b Batty	5		
C. J. C. Wright lbw b Batty	0		
B 7, l-b 7, w 1, n-b 20	35	L-b 6, w 2, n-b 2	10
	525		**(4 wkts) 105**

1/72 (2) 2/199 (3) 3/202 (1) 4/278 (5)   1/15 (2) 2/73 (3)   (4 wkts) 105
5/432 (6) 6/458 (7) 7/459 (8)   3/90 (4) 4/94 (1)
8/519 (9) 9/525 (10) 10/525 (11)

Bonus points – Middlesex 5, Worcestershire 1 (130 overs: 440-5).

Bowling: *First Innings*—Bichel 21–5–76–0; Mason 30–10–77–1; Kabir Ali 24–1–95–1; Hall 20–3–71–0; Batty 41.5–5–141–6; Solanki 12–1–36–0; Kadeer Ali 5–1–15–1. *Second Innings*—Mason 6–1–21–0; Bichel 6–0–27–0; Kabir Ali 6–0–29–1; Hall 2–0–10–0; Batty 5.4–2–12–2.

Umpires: G. I. Burgess and B. Leadbeater.

At Cheltenham, July 28, 29, 30, 31. WORCESTERSHIRE beat GLOUCESTERSHIRE by five wickets.

At The Oval, August 3, 4, 5, 6. WORCESTERSHIRE lost to SURREY by 68 runs.

WORCESTERSHIRE v NORTHAMPTONSHIRE

At Worcester, August 11, 12, 13, 14. Drawn. Worcestershire 11 pts, Northamptonshire 10 pts. Toss: Northamptonshire. First-class debuts: C. M. Goode, C. J. R. Jennings.

Worcestershire captain Ben Smith caused consternation by announcing on the third morning that he was resigning with immediate effect, saying he wanted to concentrate on his batting. Since he was averaging 55 in the Championship (though his one-day form had indeed fallen away), and Smith's leadership had not been a matter of particular debate, coach Tom Moody had to deny that there was any kind of internal dispute. No one could recall any precedent for a county captain quitting in mid-match. Rhodes took over for the last two days, and was eventually given the job for the rest of the season. On the field, the match was mainly memorable for two unbeaten centuries by Love in his second Championship game for Northamptonshire. His first was undermined because eight wickets fell for 60 at the other end; his fellow-Australian Bichel, left out of Worcestershire's previous match, claimed his best Championship figures since April 2002. After rain cut the second day to 16 overs, Bichel returned to the middle at 81 for five. His third hundred in successive Championship games, a career-best 142, saved the follow-on and set up a lead of 50, against an attack including two 19-year-old debutants. Northamptonshire lost half their side for 130 by the final morning, and Swann slammed the pavilion gate with his bat in disgust at being given out. But Love, who was dropped twice, shepherded them to a draw in a 181-run stand with Brophy.

Close of play: First day, Worcestershire 14-2 (Peters 5, Hick 0); Second day, Worcestershire 75-4 (Hick 17, Solanki 21); Third day, Northamptonshire 69-2 (Love 32, Afzaal 12).

Northamptonshire

T. W. Roberts c Solanki b Bichel	53	– lbw b Kabir Ali	10
R. A. White c Moore b Kabir Ali	49	– c Hall b Kabir Ali	0
M. L. Love not out	133	– not out	161
U. Afzaal c Rhodes b Mason	45	– c Smith b Batty	22
*D. J. Sales b Bichel	0	– c Smith b Hall	13
G. P. Swann lbw b Hall	16	– c Peters b Hall	10
†G. L. Brophy c Hall b Bichel	1	– c Rhodes b Mason	94
J. Louw lbw b Bichel	1	– not out	18
C. M. Goode lbw b Bichel	0		
C. J. R. Jennings b Mason	6		
C. G. Greenidge b Mason	0		
L-b 7	7	B 14, l-b 5, w 6, n-b 6	31
	311	(6 wkts dec.)	359

1/87 (1) 2/119 (2) 3/251 (4) 4/252 (5)
5/283 (6) 6/286 (7) 7/290 (8)
8/290 (9) 9/311 (10) 10/311 (11)

1/11 (2) 2/20 (1) (6 wkts dec.)
3/95 (4) 4/116 (5)
5/130 (6) 6/311 (7)

Bonus points – Northamptonshire 3, Worcestershire 3.

Bowling: *First Innings*—Mason 20–9–37–3; Kabir Ali 15–3–52–1; Bichel 19–0–87–5; Hall 22–6–57–1; Batty 16–0–49–0; Solanki 6–0–22–0. *Second Innings*—Mason 23–4–55–1; Kabir Ali 22–5–48–2; Bichel 12–1–55–0; Hall 17–4–38–2; Batty 20–6–76–1; Solanki 4–0–21–0; Moore 8–1–35–0; Peters 2–0–12–0.

Worcestershire

S. D. Peters c Afzaal b Louw	9	†S. J. Rhodes not out	4
S. C. Moore c Sales b Greenidge	0	M. S. Mason b Greenidge	1
Kabir Ali b Louw	2		
G. A. Hick b Louw	66	B 1, l-b 13, w 1, n-b 20	35
*B. F. Smith c Roberts b Louw	13		361
V. S. Solanki lbw b Goode	26	1/4 (2) 2/7 (3) 3/22 (1)	
A. J. Bichel lbw b Louw	142	4/40 (5) 5/81 (6) 6/205 (4)	
G. J. Batty c Love b Jennings	51	7/328 (8) 8/347 (7)	
A. J. Hall c Roberts b Greenidge	12	9/349 (9) 10/361 (11)	

Bonus points – Worcestershire 4, Northamptonshire 3.

Bowling: Louu 27–6–63–5; Greenidge 20.2–4–71–3; Goode 16–3–70–1; Jennings 14–3–64–1; Swann 17–4–66–0; White 3–0–13–0.

Umpires: N. L. Bainton and G. Sharp.

At Hove, August 19, 20, 21, 22. WORCESTERSHIRE lost to SUSSEX by seven wickets.

WORCESTERSHIRE v WARWICKSHIRE

At Worcester, August 31, September 1, 2, 3. Drawn. Worcestershire 11 pts, Warwickshire 11 pts. Toss: Warwickshire.

Warwickshire could have clinched the title with a win; instead they got another of the high-scoring draws that typified their season, and so had to wait three days longer. They ground out their 11th total of 400-plus in 2004, without a single century. And Brown became only their second bowler (after Streak) to take five in an innings in 2004 – and the first to reach 30 wickets. On a difficult pitch where the ball kept low, Zimbabwean left-arm spinner Price bowled a marathon 56 overs for less than two an over; his final match figures were six for 178 from 91. In reply, Worcestershire lost three wickets in seven overs, but recovered: Hick led the way, and a career-best 56-ball 63 from Mason improbably earned them maximum points. Even more improbably, Warwickshire set them 299 in 38 overs; Moore and Hick batted belligerently before it was called off with nine overs to go.

Close of play: First day, Warwickshire 298-6 (Troughton 16, Tahir 15); Second day, Worcestershire 161-3 (Hick 78, Kadeer Ali 56); Third day, Warwickshire 94-3 (Bell 13, Trott 0).

Warwickshire

*N. V. Knight c Smith b Price	37	– c Hick b Price	39
M. A. Wagh c Peters b Bichel	15	– b Price	40
I. R. Bell c Hick b Price	54	– c Kadeer Ali b Price	17
I. J. L. Trott c Smith b Mason	63	– (5) c Rhodes b Hall	51
M. J. Powell c Price b Malik	69	– (6) b Malik	43
J. O. Troughton c Rhodes b Malik	64	– (7) c Rhodes b Price	6
D. R. Brown c Hall b Bichel	3	– (8) not out	27
N. Tahir c Rhodes b Bichel	49	– (4) b Hick	0
†T. Frost lbw b Bichel	19	– c Hall b Malik	20
H. H. Streak not out	30		
N. M. Carter b Hall	13	– (10) not out	1
B 10, l-b 19, w 9, n-b 6	44	B 4, l-b 5, w 1	10
	460	(8 wkts dec.)	**254**

1/26 (2) 2/108 (3) 3/117 (1) 4/248 (5)
5/271 (4) 6/274 (7) 7/388 (6)
8/409 (8) 9/426 (9) 10/460 (11)

1/66 (1) 2/93 (2) 3/94 (4) 4/108 (3)
5/180 (5) 6/193 (7) 7/213 (6) 8/243 (9)

Bonus points – Warwickshire 4, Worcestershire 2 (130 overs: 368-6).

Bowling: *First Innings*—Mason 33–10–84–1; Bichel 29–5–108–4; Hall 24–7–74–1; Malik 16–3–68–2; Price 56–24–95–2; Kadeer Ali 1–0–2–0. *Second Innings*—Mason 12–4–36–0; Bichel 11–1–47–0; Malik 13–1–54–2; Price 35–9–83–4; Hick 2–1–1–1; Hall 10–1–24–1.

Worcestershire

S. D. Peters lbw b Streak	19	– c Troughton b Streak	9
S. C. Moore lbw b Brown	0	– not out	83
G. A. Hick b Brown	93	– not out	56
B. F. Smith c Powell b Streak	2		
Kadeer Ali c Frost b Brown	66		
A. J. Bichel c Frost b Troughton	36		
A. J. Hall c Trott b Brown	26		
*†S. J. Rhodes not out	44		
R. W. Price b Brown	32		
M. S. Mason b Streak	63		
M. N. Malik b Streak	0		
B 8, l-b 14, n-b 13	35	L-b 1, w 1, n-b 6	8

1/12 (2) 2/30 (1) 3/38 (4) 4/195 (5)   416   1/14 (1)   (1 wkt) 156
5/202 (3) 6/254 (6) 7/286 (7)
8/322 (9) 9/410 (10) 10/416 (11)

Bonus points – Worcestershire 5, Warwickshire 3.

Dowling: *First Innings*—Streak 29.2 8 81 4; Brown 32 3 89 5; Tahir 8–0–48–0; Wagh 7–2–11–0; Carter 20–2–71–0; Troughton 25–6–76–1; Bell 2–0–18–0. *Second Innings*—Streak 7–0–20–1; Brown 4–0–20–0; Tahir 2–0–16–0; Carter 3–0–35–0; Troughton 6–0–21–0; Wagh 6–1–33–0; Trott 1–0–10–0.

Umpires: M. J. Harris and A. A. Jones.

WORCESTERSHIRE v LANCASHIRE

At Worcester, September 9, 10, 11, 12. Drawn. Worcestershire 11 pts, Lancashire 12 pts. Toss: Lancashire. County debut: A. R. Crook.

The Yorkshire exile Steve Rhodes ended his 24-season career in typically gritty fashion, denying Lancashire a win that would have reinforced their hopes of avoiding relegation. But he was unable to prevent Worcestershire from going down themselves, after a single year in the top flight. In his 440th first-class match, Rhodes walked out for the last time with 17.3 overs and four wickets left. Two more fell, but he remained unbeaten, and departed to a standing ovation, with 1,263 dismissals – eighth in the all-time list – and 14,839 runs to his name. Worcestershire had lost the toss for the seventh Championship game in a row, and an imperious five-hour 159 from Law, with 24 fours and a six on a tediously slow pitch, helped Lancashire secure maximum batting points. Though rain reduced the second day to 16 overs, Cork's opening spell put Worcestershire in danger of following on. But Rhodes batted defiantly for 44 overs before declaring 51 behind. Lancashire finally set an ungenerous target of 294 in 47 overs. "I hope they come down with us," said Worcestershire's chief executive, Mark Newton. Next week he got his wish.

Close of play: First day, Lancashire 350-8 (Hegg 22, Mahmood 2); Second day, Lancashire 403-9 (Mahmood 24, Keedy 10); Third day, Lancashire 58-0 (Chilton 25, Sutcliffe 21).

> **"**Maynard hit a record 53rd hundred for Glamorgan... He had hit a century on debut against Yorkshire in 1985, when Peter Hartley held the catch that ended his innings. Hartley was there to see him again – this time as umpire.**"**
>
> Glamorgan in 2004, page 607.

Lancashire

M. J. Chilton b Bichel	3	– c Hick b Hall	30
I. J. Sutcliffe st Rhodes b Price	51	– c Rhodes b Hall	29
M. B. Loye c Rhodes b Mason	17	– lbw b Bichel	0
S. G. Law lbw b Bichel	159	– lbw b Hall	0
C. L. Hooper lbw b Hall	8	– not out	75
A. R. Crook c Rhodes b Khalid	27	– c Hall b Mason	24
G. Chapple c Peters b Price	50	– c Smith b Moore	63
*†W. K. Hegg c Hick b Bichel	43		
D. G. Cork c and b Bichel	8		
S. I. Mahmood not out	24		
G. Keedy not out	10		
L-b 3	3	B 4, l-b 8, w 1, n-b 8	21

1/5 (1) 2/47 (3) 3/101 (2)   (9 wkts dec.) 403   1/68 (2) 2/71 (1)   (6 wkts dec.) 242
4/128 (5) 5/183 (6) 6/291 (7)   3/71 (4) 4/71 (3)
7/326 (4) 8/348 (9) 9/381 (8)   5/124 (6) 6/242 (7)

Bonus points – Lancashire 5, Worcestershire 3.

Bowling: *First Innings*—Mason 29–5–102–1; Bichel 26.4–8–91–4; Hall 23–1–92–1; Price 31–10–79–2; Khalid 6–0–28–1; Kadeer Ali 4–0–8–0. *Second Innings*—Bichel 13–2–42–1; Hall 13–4–41–3; Khalid 8–0–46–0; Kadeer Ali 4–0–26–0; Price 9–0–54–0; Mason 4–2–8–1; Moore 1.3–0–13–1.

Worcestershire

S. D. Peters c Hooper b Cork	27	– lbw b Cork	3
S. C. Moore c Hooper b Chapple	14	– b Chapple	19
G. A. Hick lbw b Cork	6	– lbw b Chapple	7
B. F. Smith c Law b Cork	0	– b Mahmood	50
Kadeer Ali b Cork	11	– b Mahmood	27
A. J. Bichel b Mahmood	31	– c and b Keedy	10
A. J. Hall lbw b Keedy	70	– c Hegg b Keedy	39
*†S. J. Rhodes c Hegg b Keedy	53	– not out	19
R. W. Price not out	76	– lbw b Crook	1
M. S. Mason c Hegg b Keedy	0	– not out	0
S. A. Khalid not out	6		
B 15, l-b 10, n-b 33	58	B 4, l-b 9, w 1, n-b 10	24

1/43 (2) 2/49 (1) 3/55 (4)   (9 wkts dec.) 352   1/9 (1) 2/24 (3) 3/41 (2)   (8 wkts) 199
4/70 (3) 5/77 (5) 6/149 (6)   4/103 (5) 5/120 (4)
7/212 (7) 8/327 (8) 9/327 (10)   6/134 (6) 7/188 (7) 8/191 (9)

Bonus points – Worcestershire 4, Lancashire 3.

Bowling: *First Innings*—Mahmood 12–0–78–1; Cork 17–5–61–4; Chapple 14–6–30–1; Keedy 17–1–74–3; Hooper 16–4–39–0; Crook 11–1–45–0. *Second Innings*—Chapple 10–1–35–2; Cork 11–2–62–1; Mahmood 8–0–41–2; Hooper 3–0–21–0; Keedy 11–3–19–2; Crook 4–1–8–1.

Umpires: T. E. Jesty and B. Leadbeater.

YORKSHIRE

The malady lingers on

DAVID WARNER

With David Byas back at Headingley as director of cricket and Craig White installed as captain, Yorkshire began 2004 confident they had the know-how and the playing staff to make a big impression. They were wrong, and the club endured their worst season in 12 years.

The goal of promotion in both Championship and one-day league was missed, and in the Championship it was not even close. As in 2003, Yorkshire got off to a magnificent start, beating Essex convincingly at Headingley, but doubts about their resolve and strength soon surfaced.

In June they enjoyed a misleading month of rude health, picking up five wins and two rain-hit draws in all competitions. But by July, permanent sickness had set in, and they failed to win any of their last ten Championship matches. Seventh place in Division Two was an embarrassment, the club's lowest position since they finished 16th in 1992 – the equivalent in the single-division competition.

An injection of new blood late in the season eased the malady slightly and gave hope for the future. But by then the weather was so poor that meaningful recovery was almost impossible. Wins in the last three totesport League games meant Yorkshire would have been promoted had Nottinghamshire failed to win their last match. But Nottinghamshire did win, and Byas had no excuses, saying his side should not have left their fate in the hands of others.

The reasons for the demise were not hard to find, the principal one being that the fast bowlers were simply not up to the task. Ryan Sidebottom, released from his contract after falling out with the club in 2003, was badly missed; Steve Kirby was well short of his best, although still the most successful of the pace men; Chris Silverwood drifted into another long spell of injury; and Ian Harvey, signed from Gloucestershire amid great hopes, was only spasmodically fit and available, and even then gave little evidence of being a top all-rounder. His seven Championship wickets cost him 61.42 apiece, and his 273 runs came at just 24.81.

Byas was acutely aware of the need to sign at least one fast bowler for 2005 – and that was before the end of the season, when Kirby left. He had simply become dispirited and wanted a new start, which he found with Gloucestershire. White himself was due to continue for 2005, after any doubts about him as a leader were quickly dispelled. He applied himself diligently and received the support and respect of his players. Having shown great discipline with the bat, he was just beginning to cause problems with the ball again when injury struck. His season stopped abruptly in June and never got properly going again; his absence as leader and proven all-rounder was a major blow.

On the plus side, Yorkshire were splendidly served by Phil Jaques, the left-hander from New South Wales. He substituted for both first-choice overseas players (Harvey and Darren Lehmann) over the season and, in just 19 innings as a fill-in, scored 1,118 first-class runs. His greatest achievement was an effortless 243 while everyone else struggled on an unhelpful pitch at the Rose Bowl. It was the highest score ever made on the ground and Jaques's success brought a full-time contract for 2005.

Phil Jaques

Lehmann, between flitting back home, was his usual consistent self with the bat and more than useful with his round-armed spin bowling. And Richard Dawson, a rather more classical spinner, regained form and confidence, earning his county cap nearly three years after his first for England. But for a rainy end to the season, he would almost certainly have taken more than 36 Championship wickets.

Otherwise it was a case of scrabbling for small compensations. Anthony McGrath made valuable contributions when not lolling around as England's twelfth man in one-day internationals. Matthew Wood, after a slow start, was consistent without being prolific; Michael Lumb looked in need of a rest; and Simon Guy's form behind the stumps and with the bat caused concern.

With Guy struggling, Yorkshire gave a trial to Ismail Dawood, a 27-year-old keeper who had done the rounds elsewhere but, at Scarborough on July 21, made history by becoming the first British-born (Dewsbury, indeed) Asian to play Championship cricket for Yorkshire. That built on an earlier breakthrough, when Ajmal Shahzad, a nippy 18-year-old seam bowler from Bradford, played in the totesport League game against Worcestershire. Shahzad would have been given further opportunities if he had not been laid low with a bad back.

It therefore came as a surprise when in October Terry Rooney, the Labour MP for Bradford North, accused Yorkshire of "deep-rooted, embedded racism" during a parliamentary debate on social cohesion. The comments caused outrage at the club: if Rooney's view had ever been accurate, it certainly looked out of date in 2004.

But it was a glum year for Yorkshire followers, who fell back on age-old consolations. One of their own was captaining England. Lancashire were beaten twice – once in the Twenty20 and once when Michael Vaughan replaced his England sweater for a Yorkshire one and thrashed an epic 116 in the C&G. And there was a measure of comfort in knowing that the summer's deep depression extended across the Pennines: following Lancashire's relegation, the two fading giants will resume Championship hostilities in 2005.

YORKSHIRE RESULTS

All first-class matches – Played 16: Won 3, Lost 4, Drawn 9.
County Championship matches – Played 16: Won 3, Lost 4, Drawn 9.

Frizzell County Championship, 7th in Division 2; Cheltenham & Gloucester Trophy, s-f;
totesport League, 4th in Division 2; Twenty20 Cup, 6th in North Group.

COUNTY CHAMPIONSHIP AVERAGES

BATTING AND FIELDING

Cap		M	I	NO	R	HS	100s	50s	Avge	Ct/St
1997	D. S. Lehmann§ . . .	7	11	1	592	120	1	5	59.20	2
	P. A. Jaques§	11	19	0	1,118	243	3	5	58.84	11
1999	A. McGrath	9	16	0	728	174	3	1	45.50	6
2001	M. J. Wood.	16	27	2	955	123	1	7	38.20	24
	J. J. Sayers	5	9	0	311	62	0	3	34.55	0
	I. Dawood	8	14	5	310	75	0	1	34.44	12/2
	V. J. Craven	6	8	1	202	81*	0	1	28.85	2
	R. M. Pyrah	4	7	1	158	39	0	0	26.33	0
	C. R. Taylor	4	5	1	105	43*	0	0	26.25	1
2003	M. J. Lumb	13	23	1	546	83	0	4	24.81	8
	I. J. Harvey§	7	11	0	273	95	0	1	24.81	4
2004	R. K. J. Dawson . . .	15	23	0	564	81	0	3	24.52	11
1993	C. White	7	12	1	265	60	0	1	24.09	4
2000	M. J. Hoggard.	5	8	3	107	89*	0	1	21.40	2
1996	C. E. W. Silverwood.	7	10	2	150	37	0	0	18.75	3
	J. A. R. Blain	9	13	6	94	28*	0	0	13.42	1
	T. T. Bresnan	10	13	3	143	33	0	0	11.91	3
	A. W. Gale	4	7	0	78	29	0	0	11.14	2
	S. M. Guy	8	12	0	124	26	0	0	10.33	21/2
	M. A. K. Lawson. . .	3	5	1	33	14	0	0	8.25	1
2003	S. P. Kirby	13	16	5	39	14*	0	0	3.54	2

Also batted: A. K. D. Gray (2 matches) 10, 27, 0 (2 ct); N. D. Thornicroft (2 matches) 30, 4, 6 (1 ct); D. J. Wainwright (1 match) 5.

§ *Overseas player.*

BOWLING

	O	M	R	W	BB	5W/i	Avge
D. S. Lehmann	105.4	19	261	15	4-35	0	17.40
C. White	88.2	18	282	11	3-50	0	25.63
C. E. W. Silverwood. . .	174.3	33	570	22	3-18	0	25.90
J. A. R. Blain	188	26	804	30	4-38	0	26.80
T. T. Bresnan	160.3	31	557	17	3-32	0	32.76
R. K. J. Dawson	379.4	71	1,255	36	5-40	1	34.86
S. P. Kirby	327.1	53	1,132	31	3-64	0	36.51

Also bowled: V. J. Craven 51.4–8–191–6; A. K. D. Gray 31–3–89–2; I. J. Harvey 154–41–430–7; M. J. Hoggard 121.5–22–393–9; P. A. Jaques 2–0–18–0; M. A. K. Lawson 75.3–6–308–9; M. J. Lumb 1–0–2–0; A. McGrath 102–21–280–8; R. M. Pyrah 6–4–2–0; N. D. Thornicroft 44.2–10–168–6; D. J. Wainwright 3–1–5–0; M. J. Wood 1–0–1–0.

COUNTY RECORDS

Highest score for:	341	G. H. Hirst v Leicestershire at Leicester	1905
Highest score against:	318*	W. G. Grace (Gloucestershire) at Cheltenham. . . .	1876
Best bowling for:	10-10	H. Verity v Nottinghamshire at Leeds	1932
Best bowling against:	10-37	C. V. Grimmett (Australians) at Sheffield	1930
Highest total for:	887	v Warwickshire at Birmingham	1896
Highest total against:	681-7 dec.	by Leicestershire at Bradford	1996
Lowest total for:	23	v Hampshire at Middlesbrough	1965
Lowest total against:	13	by Nottinghamshire at Nottingham	1901

YORKSHIRE DIRECTORY

ADDRESS

Headingley Cricket Ground, Leeds LS6 3BU (0113 278 7394; fax 0113 278 4099; email cricket@yorkshireccc.org.uk). **Website** www.yorkshireccc.org.uk.

GROUNDS

Leeds (Headingley): 2¼ miles NW of city centre and ¼ mile SW of Headingley centre. From city centre take A660 to Headingley High Street for Kirkstall Lane and St Michael's Lane. Nearest stations: Headingley (½ mile), Burley Park (¾ mile) or Leeds (2½ miles).

Scarborough: 1 mile N of town centre in North Marine Road, close to seafront. From A165 Coastal Road, L into Peasholm Road for North Marine Road and signs for cricket ground. Nearest station: Scarborough (¾ mile).

OFFICIALS

Captain C. White
Director of cricket D. Byas
Batting coach K. Sharp
Bowling coach S. Oldham
President D. Jones

Chief executive C. J. Graves
Operations director G. Cope
Head groundsman A. W. Fogarty
Scorer J. T. Potter

PLAYERS

Players expected to reappear in 2005

	Former counties	Country	Born	Birthplace
Blain John Angus Rae	Northants	SCO (EU)	4.1.1979	*Edinburgh*
*****Blakey** Richard John		E	15.1.1967	†*Huddersfield*
Bresnan Timothy Thomas		E	23.7.1976	†*Dewsbury*
Dawood Ismail	Northants, Worcs, Glam	E	28.2.1985	†*Pontefract*
*****Dawson** Richard Kevin James		E	4.8.1980	†*Doncaster*
Gale Andrew William		E	28.11.1983	†*Dewsbury*
Guy Simon Mark		E	17.11.1978	†*Rotherham*
Harvey Ian Joseph	Glos	A	10.4.1972	*Wonthaggi*
*****Hoggard** Matthew James		‡E	31.12.1976	†*Leeds*
Jaques Philip Anthony	Northants	A	3.5.1979	*Wollongong*
Lawson Mark Anthony Kenneth		E	24.10.1985	†*Leeds*
Lumb Michael John		E	12.2.1980	*Johannesburg, SA*
*****McGrath** Anthony		E	6.10.1975	†*Bradford*
Pyrah Richard Michael		E	1.11.1982	†*Dewsbury*
Sayers Joseph John		E	5.11.1983	†*Leeds*
*****Silverwood** Christopher Eric Wilfred		E	5.3.1975	†*Pontefract*
Taylor Christopher Robert		E	21.2.1981	†*Leeds*
Thornicroft Nicholas David		E	23.1.1985	†*York*
*****Vaughan** Michael Paul		‡E	29.10.1974	*Manchester*
Wainwright David John		E	21.3.1985	†*Pontefract*
*****White** Craig		E	16.12.1969	†*Morley*
Wood Matthew James		E	6.4.1977	†*Huddersfield*

Player due to join in 2005

Lucas David Scott	Notts	E	19.8.1978	*Nottingham*

* *Test player.*   † *Born in Yorkshire.*   ‡ *12-month ECB contract.*

At Leeds, April 10, 11, 12 (not first-class). **Yorkshire won by 481 runs.** Toss: Bradford/Leeds UCCE. **Yorkshire 401** (C. White 53, C. R. Taylor 150, S. M. Guy 90; D. I. Jones 4-58) **and 350-2 dec.** (M. J. Wood 213*, M. J. Lumb 80); **Bradford/Leeds UCCE 98** (J. A. R. Blain 4-36) **and 172** (J. O. Siddall 75*).

First-team debut: A. W. Gale (Yorkshire). County debut: J. A. R. Blain.

Yorkshire's second-innings 350 came in just 46 overs. Hard as Wood tried to surrender his wicket by deliberately hitting the ball in the air, he ended unbeaten, on 213 from 129 balls, with 31 fours and seven sixes.

YORKSHIRE v ESSEX

At Leeds, April 21, 22, 23, 24. Yorkshire won by seven wickets. Yorkshire 22 pts, Essex 5 pts. Toss: Yorkshire. County debut: I. J. Harvey.

Yorkshire's new regime, under captain Craig White and director of cricket David Byas, got off to an excellent start. But the victory had to be taken in context: Essex, already without six key players, were further handicapped when Stephenson was rapped on the thumb by Craven in the first innings (and struggled thereafter) and McCoubrey was hit on the head by a fierce return drive from Harvey, and could not continue bowling. On a pitch that started green, Jefferson and Pettini batted well but Essex's other batsmen laboured, and Yorkshire took a 146-run lead. The Australian all-rounder Harvey made 95 on county debut as he and Lumb batted entertainingly in warm third-day sunshine. On the last day, with Essex six down and still one run behind, an early finish seemed likely. But Habib, the tail and undemanding bowling all combined to ensure that it was mid-afternoon when Yorkshire took the last wicket, and almost into the last hour when they reached their target of 128.

Close of play: First day, Essex 128-3 (Jefferson 60, Pettini 11); Second day, Yorkshire 146-2 (Taylor 31, Lehmann 26); Third day, Essex 145-6 (Habib 21, Middlebrook 2).

Essex

W. I. Jefferson c Lumb b Kirby	74	– lbw b Blain		20
A. N. Cook c Guy b Silverwood	5	– c Guy b Blain		52
*A. Flower lbw b Blain	7	– c White b Lehmann		29
A. Habib c Wood b Harvey	29	– c Lumb b Kirby		62
M. L. Pettini lbw b Lehmann	67	– b Lehmann		0
†J. S. Foster c Wood b Kirby	0	– c Guy b Silverwood		0
J. D. Middlebrook c Guy b Lehmann	25	– (8) c Harvey b Kirby		6
G. R. Napier c Silverwood b Craven	13	– (9) c Wood b Harvey		30
J. P. Stephenson not out	10	– (10) c Wood b Blain		34
S. A. Brant b Silverwood	6	– (7) c Wood b Silverwood		2
A. G. A. M. McCoubrey c Guy b Blain	1	– not out		2
B 1, l-b 10, n-b 14	25	B 5, l-b 9, n-b 22		36
	262			**273**

1/17 (2) 2/38 (3) 3/87 (4) 4/159 (1) 5/159 (6) 6/207 (7) 7/236 (5) 8/244 (8) 9/252 (10) 10/262 (11)

1/49 (1) 2/92 (2) 3/135 (3) 4/135 (5) 5/138 (6) 6/142 (7) 7/153 (8) 8/206 (9) 9/267 (4) 10/273 (10)

Bonus points – Essex 2, Yorkshire 3.

In the first innings Stephenson, when 6, retired hurt at 244-8 and resumed at 252.

Bowling: *First Innings*—Silverwood 23–7–44–2; Kirby 23–5–72–2; Blain 15.2–1–63–2; Harvey 17–8–24–1; Craven 9–1–28–1; Lehmann 10–3–20–2. *Second Innings*—Silverwood 20–5–60–2; Kirby 16.3–5–50–2; Blain 16.3–3–52–3; Harvey 13–2–32–1; Lehmann 11–2–25–2; Craven 6–1–20–0; White 9–2–20–0.

Yorkshire

M. J. Wood b Brant	16	– lbw b Brant	9
*C. White lbw b McCoubrey	60	– b Napier	39
C. R. Taylor b Napier	32	– not out	43
D. S. Lehmann c Jefferson b Stephenson	53	– b Middlebrook	26
M. J. Lumb c and b Middlebrook	76	– not out	0
I. J. Harvey lbw b Napier	95		
V. J. Craven c Jefferson b Stephenson	5		
†S. M. Guy c Flower b Napier	7		
C. E. W. Silverwood c Habib b Brant	37		
J. A. R. Blain lbw b Napier	0		
S. P. Kirby not out	0		
B 2, l-b 1, n-b 24	27	N-b 12	12

1/38 (1) 2/108 (2) 3/149 (3) 4/183 (4)   408   1/18 (1) 2/66 (2)   (3 wkts) 129
5/331 (5) 6/338 (7) 7/355 (8)   3/125 (4)
8/396 (6) 9/404 (10) 10/408 (9)

Bonus points – Yorkshire 5, Essex 3.

Bowling: *First Innings*—Brant 25.2–6–86–2; McCoubrey 18.4–3–76–1; Napier 28.2–5–119–4; Middlebrook 14–1–47–1; Stephenson 15–1–76–2; Habib 1–0–1–0. *Second Innings*—Brant 11.3–4–30–1; Napier 10–1–52–1; Stephenson 7–2–29–0; Middlebrook 3–0–18–1.

Umpires: B. Leadbeater and G. Sharp.

At Nottingham, April 28, 29, 30, May 1. YORKSHIRE drew with NOTTINGHAMSHIRE.

YORKSHIRE v HAMPSHIRE

At Leeds, May 12, 13, 14. Hampshire won by 119 runs. Hampshire 20 pts, Yorkshire 6 pts. Toss: Yorkshire. County debut: P. A. Jaques.

This was a keenly contested match on a typical Headingley pitch that kept producing balls of variable bounce. For two days both sides maintained tight discipline, but on the third Yorkshire let go of Hampshire's coat-tails. From a shaky 114 for five overnight, Hampshire added 199, helped by a stubborn 77 from Pothas and some erratic bowling. Yorkshire's target of 320 never looked possible, although Phil Jaques, their stopgap overseas player, made an attractive but ultimately futile 78. Last out, he was the fifth victim of the innings and 25th of the season for Mascarenhas, who was briefly the leading first-class wicket-taker. But Hampshire owed most to Pothas, whose responsible century on the first day gave them 322, as Yorkshire dropped five chances.

Close of play: First day, Yorkshire 40-1 (Wood 16); Second day, Hampshire 114-5 (Pothas 25, Mascarenhas 5).

Hampshire

D. A. Kenway c Jaques b Hoggard	4	– lbw b Silverwood	20
M. J. Brown lbw b Blain	13	– lbw b Blain	20
*W. S. Kendall c Wood b Blain	50	– c Guy b Silverwood	0
M. J. Clarke b Blain	11	– c Jaques b Silverwood	6
L. R. Prittipaul c Guy b Harvey	12	– lbw b Blain	17
†N. Pothas c Hoggard b Silverwood	100	– c Guy b White	77
A. D. Mascarenhas c Guy b Dawson	49	– c Lumb b Blain	25
S. D. Udal c and b Silverwood	21	– c McGrath b White	52
C. T. Tremlett b White	13	– b Dawson	35
B. V. Taylor c Harvey b Silverwood	12	– run out	7
A. D. Mullally not out	1	– not out	22
B 4, l-b 17, w 1, n-b 14	36	B 12, l-b 8, n-b 12	32

1/4 (1) 2/54 (2) 3/80 (4) 4/97 (5)   **322**
5/115 (3) 6/195 (7) 7/250 (8)
8/279 (9) 9/317 (6) 10/322 (10)

1/29 (1) 2/29 (3) 3/35 (4)   **313**
4/64 (5) 5/73 (2) 6/147 (7)
7/219 (6) 8/284 (9)
9/284 (8) 10/313 (10)

Bonus points – Hampshire 3, Yorkshire 3.

Bowling: *First Innings*—Hoggard 22–5–64–1; Silverwood 17–6–61–3; Blain 19–5–63–3; Harvey 14–4–32–1; McGrath 8–2–30–0; Dawson 6–1–26–1; White 8–1–25–1. *Second Innings*—Hoggard 15–1–60–0; Silverwood 15–3–47–3; Blain 14–1–76–3; White 11–1–46–2; Harvey 11–3–37–0; Dawson 5.4–1–27–1; McGrath 1–1–0–0.

Yorkshire

M. J. Wood c Clarke b Mullally	16	– c Kenway b Mascarenhas	45
*C. White c Clarke b Tremlett	17	– c Pothas b Taylor	10
A. McGrath c Pothas b Mascarenhas	37	– lbw b Tremlett	18
P. A. Jaques b Taylor	31	– c Kenway b Mascarenhas	78
M. J. Lumb c and b Udal	83	– c Clarke b Mascarenhas	0
I. J. Harvey c Udal b Tremlett	22	– c Clarke b Mascarenhas	4
†S. M. Guy b Kendall b Taylor	7	– c Prittipaul b Taylor	8
R. K. J. Dawson c Pothas b Tremlett	35	– b Taylor	8
C. E. W. Silverwood lbw b Udal	30	– b Tremlett	10
J. A. R. Blain lbw b Udal	6	– b Mascarenhas	1
M. J. Hoggard not out	2	– not out	1
B 9, l-b 8, w 5, n-b 8	30	L-b 3, n-b 14	17

1/40 (2) 2/40 (1) 3/110 (4) 4/116 (3)   **316**
5/170 (6) 6/193 (7) 7/246 (8)
8/295 (9) 9/305 (10) 10/316 (5)

1/35 (2) 2/79 (3) 3/85 (1)   **200**
4/85 (5) 5/89 (6) 6/130 (7)
7/150 (8) 8/172 (9)
9/181 (10) 10/200 (4)

Bonus points – Yorkshire 3, Hampshire 3.

Bowling: *First Innings*—Mullally 19–4–71–1; Tremlett 21–3–77–3; Mascarenhas 19–3–85–1; Taylor 14–4–46–2; Clarke 1–0–5–0; Prittipaul 2–0–7–0; Udal 4.4–1–8–3. *Second Innings*—Tremlett 15–3–56–2; Mullally 14–3–47–0; Taylor 13–2–50–3; Mascarenhas 13.5–2–44–5.

Umpires: T. E. Jesty and J. W. Lloyds.

YORKSHIRE v NOTTINGHAMSHIRE

At Leeds, May 19, 20, 21. Nottinghamshire won by 244 runs. Nottinghamshire 21 pts, Yorkshire 3 pts. Toss: Nottinghamshire.

Yorkshire's pace attack was worryingly thin after Silverwood withdrew before the game with an ankle problem and Blain and Harvey picked up injuries during play. Nottinghamshire, and Pietersen in particular, soon took control. On a pitch of increasingly low bounce, Pietersen made 167 from 255 balls – studious by his normal, brutal standard. His three sixes were late ornamentation. In reply, Sidebottom's pace and MacGill's leg-spin were too much and Yorkshire fell 229 behind. Despite that, Nottinghamshire did not fancy batting last and spurned the follow-on. Instead, a powerful 125 by Hussey left Yorkshire chasing 499. Batting nearly two days for a draw never looked possible. During the game Headingley's new scoreboard was under construction and inquisitive fans were surprised to see "REMOVERS" underneath TOTAL, WICKETS, etc. Closer inspection revealed REM.OVERS, with a minute full stop after the M, a minor irritant put right in time for the New Zealand Test. In the event, Yorkshire could have done with a couple of removers themselves – one at each end of the pitch.

Close of play: First day, Yorkshire 10-1 (White 6, Blain 0); Second day, Nottinghamshire 194-4 (Hussey 99).

Nottinghamshire

D. J. Bicknell run out	48	– lbw b Dawson	19
*J. E. R. Gallian c Guy b Blain	0	– c Guy b Thornicroft	13
R. J. Warren c Jaques b Blain	8	– b White	55
K. P. Pietersen b Bresnan	167	– (5) c Dawson b White	0
D. J. Hussey b Thornicroft	15	– (4) c Dawson b Bresnan	125
†C. M. W. Read st Guy b Dawson	59	– lbw b White	11
M. A. Ealham b White	6	– (7) c Thornicroft b Bresnan	34
P. J. Franks c Wood b Dawson	17	– c Guy b Bresnan	0
R. J. Sidebottom c Jaques b Bresnan	4	– not out	0
S. C. G. MacGill b Thornicroft	21		
C. E. Shreck not out	1		
B 13, l-b 22, n-b 12	47	B 4, l-b 2, n-b 6	12

1/7 (2) 2/35 (3) 3/91 (1) 4/124 (5)   **393**   1/25 (2) 2/39 (1)   (8 wkts dec.) **269**
5/265 (6) 6/288 (7) 7/327 (8)   3/188 (3) 4/194 (5)
8/371 (4) 9/372 (9) 10/393 (10)   5/215 (6) 6/261 (4)
                                          7/269 (7) 8/269 (8)

Bonus points – Nottinghamshire 4, Yorkshire 3.

Bowling: *First Innings*—Blain 15–3–66–2; Bresnan 19–2–81–2; Harvey 15–6–34–0; Thornicroft 9.3–2–37–2; McGrath 7–1–26–0; Dawson 18–2–74–2; White 12–3–40–1. *Second Innings*—Blain 0.1–0–5–0; Thornicroft 17.5–3–80–1; Bresnan 14.3–3–57–3; Dawson 13–3–48–1; McGrath 6–1–23–0; White 13–2–50–3.

Yorkshire

M. J. Wood b Sidebottom	4	– c Read b Sidebottom	9
*C. White c Hussey b Sidebottom	28	– lbw b Franks	44
J. A. R. Blain lbw b MacGill	6	– (11) not out	7
A. McGrath b Franks	1	– (3) lbw b Sidebottom	25
P. A. Jaques c Read b Franks	20	– (4) b MacGill	43
M. J. Lumb c Gallian b Sidebottom	4	– (5) c Read b Franks	4
I. J. Harvey lbw b MacGill	28	– (6) c Read b Franks	18
†S. M. Guy c Pietersen b MacGill	9	– (7) lbw b MacGill	26
R. K. J. Dawson lbw b MacGill	0	– (8) c Gallian b Ealham	40
T. T. Bresnan not out	21	– (9) st Read b MacGill	21
N. D. Thornicroft c Franks b Ealham	30	– (10) c sub b Ealham	4
L-b 10, w 1, n-b 2	13	B 4, l-b 7, n-b 2	13

1/9 (1) 2/31 (3) 3/40 (4) 4/52 (2)   **164**   1/31 (1) 2/76 (3) 3/99 (2)   **254**
5/62 (6) 6/75 (5) 7/84 (8)   4/111 (5) 5/141 (6) 6/157 (4)
8/84 (9) 9/125 (7) 10/164 (11)   7/212 (7) 8/222 (8)
                                          9/226 (10) 10/254 (9)

Bonus points – Nottinghamshire 3.

Bowling: *First Innings*—Shreck 4–0–9–0; Sidebottom 14–7–19–3; Ealham 8.3–3–18–1; MacGill 14–6–54–4; Franks 16–1–54–2. *Second Innings*—Franks 13–3–62–3; Sidebottom 16–3–52–2; Ealham 19–3–74–2; MacGill 14–1–55–3.

Umpires: B. Dudleston and J. W. Holder.

At Chelmsford, June 2, 3, 4, 5. YORKSHIRE beat ESSEX by 137 runs.

At Chester-le-Street, June 8, 9, 10. YORKSHIRE beat DURHAM by 320 runs.

YORKSHIRE v LEICESTERSHIRE

At Leeds, June 18, 19, 20, 21. Drawn. Yorkshire 9 pts, Leicestershire 9 pts. Toss: Leicestershire.
    With no play possible on the first day and only 72 overs squeezed between rain and hail on the next two, the match dwindled into a battle for bonus points. It was already the final morning when the first innings was completed, DeFreitas belying his 38 years, and top-scoring for Leicestershire with 78. He followed that with a 13-over spell and three key wickets. Cleary, the young Australian seamer, soaked up severe punishment but eventually got rid of Lumb, Yorkshire's last real hope of sneaking 300 and a third batting point. The draw ended a run of six successive Yorkshire wins in all cricket, which had rejuvenated their season. Earlier, they suffered another blow when their captain White pulled up with a hamstring strain in his fifth over.
    Close of play: First day, No play; Second day, Leicestershire 76-2 (Hodge 30, Sadler 6); Third day, Leicestershire 237-6 (DeFreitas 52, Gibson 0).

Leicestershire

D. D. J. Robinson c Lumb b Silverwood	22	
D. L. Maddy c Wood b Bresnan	9	
B. J. Hodge lbw b Silverwood	37	
J. L. Sadler c White b Silverwood	6	
D. I. Stevens b Kirby	67	
†P. A. Nixon c Guy b Bresnan	23	
*P. A. J. DeFreitas c Silverwood b Dawson	78	
O. D. Gibson c Wood b Bresnan	13	

C. W. Henderson c Wood b Kirby	1
C. E. Dagnall b Dawson	0
M. F. Cleary not out	2
B 8, l-b 4, w 1, n-b 18	31
	289

1/36 (2) 2/58 (1) 3/76 (4)
4/91 (3) 5/152 (6) 6/234 (5)
7/276 (8) 8/287 (9)
9/287 (7) 10/289 (10)

Bonus points – Leicestershire 2, Yorkshire 3.

Bowling: Silverwood 23–3–78–3; Kirby 26–5–85–2; Bresnan 23–3–88–3; White 4.2–2–12–0; Dawson 5.1–1–12–2; Lehmann 3.4–2–2–0.

Yorkshire

M. J. Wood c Hodge b DeFreitas	63	
P. A. Jaques lbw b Gibson	30	
C. R. Taylor b DeFreitas	8	
D. S. Lehmann c Cleary b DeFreitas	17	
M. J. Lumb c Gibson b Cleary	77	
†S. M. Guy c Nixon b Dagnall	24	
R. K. J. Dawson c Nixon b Maddy	17	
T. T. Bresnan c Robinson b Dagnall	9	
C. E. W. Silverwood b Dagnall	12	

S. P. Kirby b Cleary	0
*C. White not out	0
L-b 6, n-b 20	26
	283

1/58 (2) 2/79 (3) 3/113 (4)
4/140 (1) 5/210 (6) 6/235 (7)
7/268 (8) 8/274 (5)
9/281 (10) 10/283 (9)

Bonus points – Yorkshire 2, Leicestershire 3.

Bowling: Cleary 12–0–95–2; Gibson 12–2–58–1; DeFreitas 13–3–42–3; Dagnall 12.4–4–46–3; Henderson 3–0–14–0; Maddy 6–0–22–1.

Umpires: G. I. Burgess and M. J. Kitchen.

At Southampton, June 23, 24, 25, 26. YORKSHIRE drew with HAMPSHIRE.

At Leeds, July 3. YORKSHIRE lost to SRI LANKA A by seven wickets (see Sri Lanka A tour section).

YORKSHIRE v SOMERSET

At Scarborough, July 21, 22, 23. Somerset won by ten wickets. Somerset 22 pts, Yorkshire 5 pts. Toss: Yorkshire. First-class debuts: A. W. Gale, M. A. K. Lawson. Championship debut: R. T. Ponting.

David Byas, Yorkshire's director of cricket, described his side's performance as "woeful" after they crumpled on the third morning to a side they confidently expected to beat. Byas wanted 600 when Yorkshire batted first on an excellent pitch; he got 296, with Lehmann stranded on 90. In reply, the Australian captain Ponting lived up to his billing, making a superb hundred on his Championship debut. He hit 50 of the first 55 runs off the bat on the second morning, brought up his century with a six and was a sniff away from adding 100 before lunch when he fell. John

HUNDRED ON FIRST-CLASS DEBUT FOR SOMERSET

116*	B. L. Bisgood	v Worcestershire at Worcester	1907
123	H. Gimblett	v Essex at Frome	1935
141*	M. M. Walford†	v Indians at Taunton	1946
109*	P. B. Wight†	v Australians at Taunton	1953
104*	D. B. Close†	v Leicestershire at Leicester	1971
117*	R. J. Bartlett	v Oxford University at Oxford	1986
110*	A. N. Hayhurst†	v Glamorgan at Cardiff	1990
139	J. Cox†	v Cambridge University at Cambridge	1999
109*	J. D. C. Bryant†	v Loughborough UCCE at Taunton	2003
112	**R. T. Ponting†**	**v Yorkshire at Scarborough**	**2004**

† *Played first-class cricket for other sides before Somerset.*

Francis made a less domineering century, and helped add 197 for the second wicket. Although Somerset reached 451, 18-year-old Mark Lawson was impressive as the first specialist leg-spinner to play for Yorkshire since Eddie Leadbeater in 1956, but had little luck until he grabbed the last two wickets in successive balls. When Yorkshire began their second innings, 155 behind, McLean's controlled hostility soon had them in trouble again; he and Dutch shared the wickets, McLean ending with match figures of 11 for 124. Only Wood resisted, becoming the first Yorkshire opener to carry his bat since Geoff Boycott in 1985. Lawson was allowed to open the bowling for Somerset's brief second innings, on the off-chance of a debut hat-trick. The wicket-keeper Ismail Dawood became the first Yorkshire-born Asian to play Championship cricket for the county; he had previously appeared for Northamptonshire, Worcestershire and Glamorgan.

Close of play: First day, Somerset 58-1 (J. D. Francis 26, Ponting 15); Second day, Yorkshire 63-3 (Wood 25, Harvey 5).

❝'After National Service I wrote to Lancashire,' recalled Frank Tyson, 'but they said there were no vacancies.'**❞**

Lancashire in 2004, page 663.

Yorkshire

*M. J. Wood c Turner b Dutch	59	– not out	66
A. W. Gale lbw b McLean	0	– c Dutch b McLean	9
A. McGrath c Ponting b Dutch	48	– (4) c Laraman b Dutch	12
M. J. Lumb c Turner b McLean	10	– (3) c Turner b McLean	11
I. J. Harvey lbw b McLean	14	– b McLean	10
D. S. Lehmann not out	90	– c S. R. G. Francis b Dutch	36
†I. Dawood c Ponting b Laraman	8	– b Dutch	1
R. K. J. Dawson c McLean b Dutch	23	– c Burns b Dutch	0
C. E. W. Silverwood c Blackwell b McLean	26	– c Turner b McLean	3
M. A. K. Lawson lbw b McLean	11	– c Turner b McLean	1
S. P. Kirby lbw b McLean	0	– lbw b Dutch	7
L-b 1, n-b 6	7	L-b 2, n-b 2	4

1/3 (2) 2/101 (1) 3/110 (3) 4/129 (5)   296   1/19 (2) 2/35 (3) 3/54 (4)   160
5/144 (4) 6/174 (7) 7/227 (8)   4/73 (5) 5/114 (6) 6/116 (7)
8/272 (9) 9/286 (10) 10/296 (11)   7/116 (8) 8/131 (9)
    9/135 (10) 10/160 (11)

Bonus points – Yorkshire 2, Somerset 3.

Bowling: *First Innings*—McLean 22.5–6–79–6; S. R. G. Francis 10–2–50–0; Laraman 13–3–43–1; Blackwell 13–2–30–0; Dutch 21–2–87–3; Ponting 5–2–6–0. *Second Innings*—McLean 15–5–45–5; S. R. G. Francis 10–3–61–0; Laraman 1–0–10–0; Dutch 11–2–26–5; Blackwell 5–0–16–0.

Somerset

P. D. Bowler c Dawson b Silverwood	6	not out	1
J. D. Francis c Dawood b Silverwood	109	– not out	5
R. T. Ponting c Gale b Dawson	112		
J. C. Hildreth c Wood b Kirby	14		
*M. Burns st Dawood b Dawson	74		
I. D. Blackwell c Dawson b Lehmann	73		
A. W. Laraman c Lumb b Lehmann	9		
K. P. Dutch not out	29		
†R. J. Turner c Harvey b Dawson	1		
S. R. G. Francis b Lawson	1		
N. A. M. McLean c Dawson b Lawson	0		
B 4, l-b 6, w 5, n-b 8	23		

1/31 (1) 2/228 (3) 3/251 (4) 4/292 (2)   451   (no wkt) 6
5/405 (6) 6/415 (7) 7/430 (5)
8/436 (9) 9/451 (10) 10/451 (11)

Bonus points – Somerset 5, Yorkshire 3.

Bowling: *First Innings*—Silverwood 17–1–75–2; Kirby 17–1–92–1; Harvey 17–3–90–0; Dawson 19–4–79–3; Lawson 16.3–1–69–2; Lehmann 10–0–36–2. *Second Innings*—Lawson 0.4–0–6–0.

Umpires: R. A. Kettleborough and B. Dudleston.

At Derby, July 28, 29, 30, 31. YORKSHIRE drew with DERBYSHIRE.

YORKSHIRE v DERBYSHIRE

At Leeds, August 12, 13, 14, 15. Drawn. Yorkshire 12 pts, Derbyshire 7 pts. Toss: Yorkshire. Championship debut: C. D. Paget.

With only 86.3 overs possible over the first two days, Yorkshire did well to leave themselves a full day to bowl Derbyshire out, after making their opponents follow on 202 behind. But on a sluggish pitch, they lacked the necessary firepower. Earlier, Wood, who had passed 50 in seven of his last nine Championship innings, finally reached 100, and McGrath made a splendid 109, his second century in a fortnight against this opposition. Yorkshire managed 442, their best of the season, but one of the highlights was an excellent first spell from Derbyshire off-spinner Chris Paget, who had just finished his GCSEs at Repton. At 16 years 284 days, he was his county's youngest Championship cricketer. Bowling with a high action, Paget found both loop and a good length, and his first 25 deliveries cost just two runs. In reply, Blain took four for 38 as Derbyshire were skittled for 240, with only Hassan Adnan offering much resistance. His team-mates showed much more resolve when they followed on, Stubbings and Moss ensuring the draw.

Close of play: First day, Yorkshire 225-1 (Wood 100, McGrath 89); Second day, Yorkshire 321-4 (Lehmann 25, Craven 0); Third day, Derbyshire 240.

Yorkshire

*M. J. Wood c Havell b Sheikh......	123	J. A. R. Blain not out............ 28
A. W. Gale lbw b Moss...........	29	M. A. K. Lawson not out......... 6
A. McGrath c Sutton b Welch.......	109	
D. S. Lehmann lbw b Havell........	66	B 3, l-b 7, w 1, n-b 16..... 27
I. J. Harvey run out	16	
V. J. Craven b Welch............	11	1/64 (2) 2/254 (1) (8 wkts dec.) 442
†I. Dawood c Sutton b Welch.......	5	3/289 (3) 4/318 (5)
R. K. J. Dawson c Hassan Adnan		5/347 (6) 6/361 (7)
b Sheikh .	22	7/393 (4) 8/409 (8)

S. P. Kirby did not bat.

Bonus points – Yorkshire 5, Derbyshire 2.

Bowling: Havell 16–0–100–1; Welch 31–6–118–3; Sheikh 23–3–85–2; Moss 20–4–60–1; Paget 19–3–69–0.

Derbyshire

S. D. Stubbings c Wood b Harvey.........	37	– b Lehmann	58
A. I. Gait lbw b Harvey	0	– lbw b Blain	5
J. Moss b Blain	7	– run out	87
Hassan Adnan c Harvey b Kirby........	86	– c Wood b Blain	6
C. W. G. Bassano c Wood b Blain	35	– not out	29
J. D. C. Bryant b Blain................	1	– lbw b Dawson	10
*†L. D. Sutton c Kirby b Lawson	35	– not out	33
G. Welch b Blain	1	
M. A. Sheikh lbw b Harvey.............	0	
C. D. Paget lbw b Lehmann............	7	
P. M. R. Havell not out................	1	
B 5, l-b 12, w 1, n-b 12..........	30	B 4, l-b 6, w 3, n-b 4	17

1/20 (3) 2/76 (1) 3/76 (2) 4/175 (5)	240	1/24 (2) 2/139 (1) (5 wkts dec.) 245
5/187 (6) 6/191 (4) 7/202 (8)		3/159 (4) 4/163 (3)
8/210 (9) 9/232 (10) 10/240 (7)		5/190 (6)

Bonus points – Derbyshire 1, Yorkshire 3.

In the first innings Gait, when 0, retired hurt at 6 and resumed at 76-2.

Bowling: *First Innings*—Kirby 17–3–41–1; Harvey 17–4–38–3; Dawson 9–0–30–0; Blain 12–3–38–4; Lawson 11.2–1–39–1; McGrath 7–0–22–0; Lehmann 6–0–15–1. *Second Innings*—Kirby 13–4–25–0; Blain 10–1–28–2; Harvey 11–1–28–0; McGrath 7–2–21–0; Dawson 26–7–53–1; Craven 2–0–10–0; Lawson 13–1–48–0; Lehmann 10–2–22–1.

Umpires: D. J. Constant and I. J. Gould.

At Leicester, August 19, 20, 21, 22. YORKSHIRE drew with LEICESTERSHIRE.

At Colwyn Bay, August 24, 25, 26, 27. YORKSHIRE drew with GLAMORGAN.

YORKSHIRE v DURHAM

At Scarborough, September 1, 2, 3. Durham won by 210 runs. Durham 20 pts, Yorkshire 4 pts. Toss: Durham.

On the first day, Lawson took five for 62 with his leg-breaks, the best Championship figures by an 18-year-old for Yorkshire since Jackie Birkenshaw took five for 39 against Lancashire in 1959. The sight of early turn meant the arrival of a pitch inspector, Mike Denness, but he decided the spin was not excessive. However, Lawson's mature bowling (he even took a wicket with the googly) was the only comfort for Yorkshire, who were easily beaten by their bottom-of-the-table opponents. A fluent 142 from 206 balls by Muchall held Durham's first innings together and, when Yorkshire replied, they collapsed against the off-spin of Breese. He grabbed the first of two five-wicket hauls, to go with healthy contributions with the bat. Durham took a lead of 125, which they stretched to 500 in the second innings, before declaring with more than five sessions left. By the third evening, it was all over. After 48 Championship games and seven Tests, Dawson was awarded his Yorkshire cap.

Close of play: First day, Yorkshire 89-1 (Jaques 50, Sayers 16); Second day, Durham 253-5 (Hamilton 28, Mustard 6).

Durham

*J. J. B. Lewis c and b Bresnan	12	– c Dawood b Kirby	15
J. A. Lowe c Wood b Hoggard	31	– lbw b Hoggard	41
G. J. Muchall not out	142	– lbw b Dawson	18
M. J. North c Dawood b Bresnan	24	– lbw b Kirby	62
G. R. Breese lbw b Bresnan	35	– c Dawood b Lawson	68
G. M. Hamilton lbw b Lawson	2	– b Dawson	58
†P. Mustard c Dawood b Lawson	15	– c Lawson b Kirby	26
G. D. Bridge lbw b Lawson	8	– not out	46
L. E. Plunkett b Lawson	5	– c Dawood b Dawson	0
N. Killeen c Wood b Lawson	6	– c Dawood b Hoggard	20
G. Onions st Dawood b Dawson	16		
L-b 6, w 1, n-b 22	29	B 5, l-b 7, w 5, n-b 4	21
	325	(9 wkts dec.)	**375**

1/47 (1) 2/81 (2) 3/119 (4) 4/203 (5) 5/208 (6) 6/236 (7) 7/264 (8) 8/270 (9) 9/278 (10) 10/325 (11)

1/23 (1) 2/50 (3) 3/109 (2) 4/203 (4) 5/228 (5) 6/303 (7) 7/306 (6) 8/306 (9) 9/375 (10)

Bonus points – Durham 3, Yorkshire 3.

Bowling: *First Innings*—Hoggard 13–1–53–1; Kirby 14–0–80–0; Bresnan 11–1–32–3; Dawson 25–3–92–1; Lawson 19–2–62–5. *Second Innings*—Hoggard 16.4–1–47–2; Kirby 20–1–64–3; Dawson 29–6–115–3; Bresnan 13–4–52–0; Lawson 15–1–84–1; Wood 1–0–1–0.

Yorkshire

*M. J. Wood b Killeen	22	– c Onions b Breese	42
P. A. Jaques b Plunkett	66	– c North b Breese	53
J. J. Sayers c Lowe b Breese	54	– c Mustard b Breese	17
R. M. Pyrah b Plunkett	4	– b Breese	34
M. J. Lumb lbw b Breese	17	– c Muchall b Bridge	4
†I. Dawood not out	21	– c Mustard b Plunkett	75
R. K. J. Dawson c Muchall b Breese	6	– c Mustard b Bridge	13
T. T. Bresnan b Killeen	0	– lbw b Bridge	6
M. J. Hoggard b Bridge	6	– c Mustard b Bridge	0
M. A. K. Lawson c Lowe b Breese	1	– c and b Breese	14
S. P. Kirby c Bridge b Breese	0	– not out	14
L-b 2, w 1	3	B 1, l-b 6, w 1, n-b 10	18

1/56 (1) 2/120 (2) 3/126 (4) 4/155 (5)	**200**	1/98 (2) 2/113 (1) 3/137 (3)
5/170 (3) 6/176 (7) 7/177 (8)		4/142 (5) 5/174 (4) 6/203 (7)
8/199 (9) 9/200 (10) 10/200 (11)		7/213 (8) 8/225 (9)
		9/250 (10) 10/290 (6)

Bonus points – Yorkshire 1, Durham 3.

Bowling: *First Innings*—Plunkett 15–3–55–2; Killeen 16–6–39–2; Onions 2–0–22–0; Breese 13.3–1–41–5; Bridge 17–1–41–1. *Second Innings*—Plunkett 10.5–3–57–1; Killeen 7–2–34–0; Breese 35–3–110–5; Hamilton 7–1–18–0; Bridge 21–7–64–4.

Umpires: G. Sharp and P. Willey.

At Taunton, September 10, 11, 12, 13. YORKSHIRE drew with SOMERSET.

YORKSHIRE v GLAMORGAN

At Leeds, September 16, 17, 18, 19. Drawn. Yorkshire 12 pts, Glamorgan 12 pts. Toss: Yorkshire.
   Yorkshire completed their worst season since 1992, when they also finished 16th of the 18 counties (but in a single-division Championship). A win would have taken them two places higher, but they were denied by bad light and rain, which cost around two sessions' play, and by unadventurous captaincy. On the last day, Wood could have declared at the fall of the ninth wicket to set Glamorgan 225, in a minimum of 40 overs. Instead, Yorkshire batted on and the game died. Both first innings were remarkably similar: each side just topped 400 thanks to a left-handed Australian opener. Jaques, who made 173 despite energetic fast bowling from Jones, became the only Yorkshire batsman to pass 1,000 first-class runs for the season; in reply, Elliott scored a powerful 125. By the last morning Yorkshire, with their lead just 105 and six men down, were in considerable danger before Hoggard put in a long shift as night-watchman, for 89 not out, his maiden fifty in all cricket. Still, by allowing Hoggard to bat on, Yorkshire ensured a draw, when victory would have boosted their league position, and defeat would have made no difference.
   Close of play: First day, Yorkshire 341-5 (Dawood 9, Dawson 5); Second day, Glamorgan 286-5 (Hughes 19, Thomas 8); Third day, Yorkshire 104-4 (Pyrah 32, Hoggard 2).

Yorkshire

P. A. Jaques b Jones	173	– c Thomas b Harrison	9
J. J. Sayers lbw b Croft	56	– lbw b Harrison	5
M. J. Lumb c Wallace b Jones	55	– c Harrison b Thomas	13
*M. J. Wood c Wallace b Jones	3	– b Croft	30
R. M. Pyrah c Elliott b Croft	12	– c Wallace b Croft	36
†I. Dawood c Wallace b Davies	24	– (7) st Wallace b Croft	2
R. K. J. Dawson c Thomas b Croft	16	– (8) c Wallace b Thomas	58
T. T. Bresnan lbw b Davies	17	– (9) c Wallace b Jones	1
J. A. R. Blain c Elliott b Jones	4	– (10) b Harrison	10
M. J. Hoggard c Wallace b Jones	1	– (6) not out	89
S. P. Kirby not out	9	– lbw b Harrison	7
B 7, l-b 12, w 2, n-b 10	31	B 4, l-b 9, w 1, n-b 12	26

1/171 (2) 2/287 (1) 3/294 (4) 4/323 (3)   401   1/13 (2) 2/20 (1) 3/34 (3)   286
5/325 (5) 6/363 (7) 7/367 (6)   4/101 (4) 5/112 (5) 6/114 (7)
8/383 (9) 9/385 (10) 10/401 (8)   7/199 (8) 8/203 (9)
                                   9/233 (10) 10/286 (11)

Bonus points – Yorkshire 5, Glamorgan 3.

Bowling: *First Innings*—Harrison 17–3–75–0; Jones 24–5–77–5; Davies 24–3–95–2; Croft 31–8–93–3; Thomas 10–0–42–0. *Second Innings*—Harrison 20.5–2–73–4; Jones 26–5–60–1; Davies 7.4–1–35–0; Thomas 14.2–3–44–2; Croft 34–9–61–3.

Glamorgan

M. T. G. Elliott c Hoggard b Dawson	125	– (2) c Wood b Dawson	23
D. D. Cherry b Hoggard	21	(1) not out	18
D. L. Hemp b Blain	60	– not out	0
M. J. Powell c Dawood b Blain	5		
J. Hughes b Bresnan	20		
†M. A. Wallace lbw b Dawson	25		
S. D. Thomas b Kirby	41		
*R. D. B. Croft not out	31		
D. S. Harrison b Blain	15		
A. P. Davies c Bresnan b Blain	6		
S. P. Jones c Dawson b Hoggard	20		
B 5, l-b 6, w 1, n-b 29	41	B 1, l-b 7, w 2, n-b 4	14

1/92 (2) 2/217 (3) 3/223 (4) 4/233 (1)   410   1/50 (2)   (1 wkt) 55
5/271 (6) 6/301 (5) 7/341 (7)
8/371 (9) 9/383 (10) 10/410 (11)

Bonus points – Glamorgan 5, Yorkshire 3.

Bowling: *First Innings*—Hoggard 23.3–6–67–2; Kirby 18–2–65–1; Blain 19–1–110–4; Bresnan 12–3–40–1; Dawson 31–4–97–2; Jaques 2–0–18–0; Pyrah 6–4–2–0. *Second Innings*—Kirby 6–0–21–0; Hoggard 3–1–8–0; Blain 4–0–16–0; Dawson 2–0–2–1.

Umpires: A. A. Jones and R. A. Kettleborough.

CHELTENHAM & GLOUCESTER TROPHY, 2004

REVIEW BY PAUL COUPAR

Nothing in the 2004 Cheltenham & Gloucester Trophy could quite match the second round, when the bankers, schoolteachers and bricklayers of Ireland and Devon beat the full-time cricketers of Surrey and Leicestershire – the first time in this tournament's 42 seasons that two minor teams had toppled first-class opposition.

The competition lost much of its fizz after that. The winners Gloucestershire might disagree, but the trouble was they were now so accomplished in one-day cricket that no one could get close enough to produce a really dramatic game. The genius of Shane Warne gave them a scare in the third round: after that they made winning a fourth Trophy in six years look easy. And, for the ninth year running, the final failed to produce the kind of close classic that used to be commonplace.

Only one other team had enjoyed such a golden run in the competition: the Clive Lloyd-inspired Lancashire side of the early 1970s. Gloucestershire, with fewer stars, pounds in the bank and pretensions, were far more unlikely champions. But, taking in two wins in the now-defunct Benson and Hedges Cup, they had written the most successful chapter in English knockout cricket.

Despite their record, few tipped Gloucestershire from the start. Since winning in 2003, they had lost batting brawn and bowling brain in Ian Harvey, fielding genius in Jonty Rhodes and, latterly, their wicket-keeping heartbeat in Jack Russell. However, their focus on one-day cricket, and their detailed preparation, still set them apart. In particular, opposing bowlers failed to contain their openers, who racked up 71, 76, 118, 73 and 141. Typically, they had been carefully chosen as a non-matching pair – Craig Spearman right-handed and favouring back foot, Philip Weston left and favouring front. Tight

Philip Weston

bowling and some luck in the draw also helped: all their fixtures against first-class opposition were on their idiosyncratic pitch at Bristol until they reached their home from home at Lord's.

There they faced Worcestershire for the second year running. By 11.13 a.m., Worcestershire were staggering at eight for three and from that mess there was no real coming back, despite a face-saving and elegant century by Solanki. The occasion suffered in comparison with the buzz of Twenty20 finals day at Edgbaston three weeks before, which was gifted sunshine and two classic games.

Twenty20 was not the only rival attraction. The 2004 C&G, having lost its place as the season's symbolic bookend in 1999, had to compete with an unprecedented number of glossy volumes, all trying to grab attention. In a season lasting 25 weekends, England played on 18, the Twenty20 finals swallowed one, other one-day internationals one more. The resultant swamping effect, plus the downbeat final, led to a spate of newspaper articles claiming the Trophy was dying in the popular imagination.

CUP KINGS

Most successful six-year period in English knockout cricket:

		Wins	
Gloucestershire	1999–2004	6	2 × NatWest Trophy, 2 × C&G Trophy, 2 × B&H Cup
Middlesex	1983–1988	4	2 × NatWest Trophy, 2 × B&H Cup
Somerset	1978–1983	4	1 × Gillette Cup, 1 × NatWest Trophy, 2 × B&H Cup
Kent	1973–1978	4	1 × Gillette Cup, 3 × B&H Cup
Lancashire	1970–1975	4	4 × Gillette Cup

The attendance figures were not so conclusive. The final was watched by 20,824, slightly up on 2003 and only a shade down on Leicestershire v Northamptonshire in 1992 – another match between counties with small memberships. The repeat match-up and engineering works on the Paddington–Worcester line were also inhibiting factors. At the semi-final stage, almost the same number watched the 2004 games at Birmingham and Bristol as saw equivalent matches in 1999 and 2000.

The competition got off to an attention-grabbing (if absurdly early) start with the shocks at Clontarf and Exmouth: Ireland's win over mighty Surrey was a candidate for the tournament's biggest-ever shock. With Surrey gone, Lancashire – whose early-season one-day form contained hints of the Lloyd era – were the team to dodge. But in perhaps the best tie of the year, and the only Roses fixture outside the Twenty20, they lost their quarter-final to Yorkshire, despite scoring 286. Yorkshire were resurrected by England captain Michael Vaughan, who lit up Old Trafford with one of the best hundreds of a packed summer. The innings also highlighted what the Trophy largely missed: Vaughan's was one of only 14 appearances by players with England contracts.

For 2005, the Trophy will be limited to 32 teams, with the 18 first-class counties and four nations (Ireland, Scotland, Denmark and Holland) remaining, but the Minor Counties cut back to just ten, which was a surprising response to the events of 2004.

Same time, same place, same result... Gloucestershire celebrate victory over
Worcestershire in the 2004 C&G final at Lord's, an identical story to the year before.
Picture by Patrick Eagar

Prize money

£53,000 for winners: GLOUCESTERSHIRE.
£27,000 for runners-up: WORCESTERSHIRE.
£16,500 for each losing semi-finalist: WARWICKSHIRE, YORKSHIRE.
£11,500 for each losing quarter-finalist: ESSEX, LANCASHIRE, MIDDLESEX,
  NORTHAMPTONSHIRE.

For the 2004 competition, man of the match award winners received £1,500 in the final, £550 in
the semi-finals, £500 in the quarter finals, £400 in the third round, £300 in the second round and
£200 in the first round (played in 2003).

FIRST ROUND

All first-round matches for the 2004 competition were played in 2003. Details of these games can
be found in *Wisden 2004*, pages 791–792.

SECOND ROUND

At Canterbury, May 5, 6. **Kent won by nine wickets.** Toss: Kent. **Berkshire 143** (44.4 overs) (J. R. Wood 49; M. J. Saggers 4-6, A. Symonds 3-24); **Kent 144-1** (16.3 overs) (M. A. Carberry 51, R. W. T. Key 61*).

Man of the Match: M. J. Saggers.

This home match for Berkshire was moved to Canterbury after rain washed out play at Reading on May 5. Saggers ended with 7.4–5–6–4.

At Northampton, May 5, 6. **Northamptonshire won by 163 runs.** Toss: Cambridgeshire. **Northamptonshire 273** (49.1 overs) (G. P. Swann 50, M. van Jaarsveld 85, D. J. Sales 67; P. J. Swanepoel 3-42, N. T. Gadsby 3-44); **Cambridgeshire 110** (40.1 overs) (I. N. Flanagan 38; J. F. Brown 5-19, U. Afzaal 3-4).

Man of the Match: J. F. Brown.

This was a Cambridgeshire home game, moved to Northampton after no play was possible at March on the first day. Brown demolished the Cambridgeshire top order with his off-spin, and 10–1–19–5 were his best one-day figures.

At Alderley Edge, May 5. **Hampshire won by 89 runs.** Toss: Cheshire. **Hampshire 273-8** (50 overs) (W. S. Kendall 53, A. D. Mascarenhas 53, C. T. Tremlett 38*, Extras 34; S. J. Renshaw 3-68, J. P. Whittaker 4-45); **Cheshire 184** (47.5 overs) (S. Ogilby 36; L. R. Prittipaul 3-11).

Man of the Match: J. P. Whittaker.

An upset threatened until Hampshire recovered from 65 for five through a late assault. The last over, bowled by Simon Renshaw, for five years a Hampshire player, cost 27; Tremlett's 38 not out came from ten balls. In reply, every Hampshire player except the wicket-keeper bowled; Jason Whittaker, a Bolton schoolteacher, added 27 runs to the four for 45 he took with his seamers.

DERBYSHIRE v SOMERSET

At Derby, May 5. Somerset won by 14 runs. Toss: Derbyshire.

The seamer Simon Francis became the first Somerset bowler to take eight wickets in a limited-overs match, but he went for nearly seven an over, and admitted he would bowl better for much less reward. Their previous best was seven for 15 by Roland Lefebvre against Devon in 1990. Francis benefited from an increasingly frantic chase by Derbyshire, after a fluent partnership of 93 between Rogers and Hassan Adnan had suggested victory. A century by Cox, his highest in one-day games, gave Somerset a strong position, bolstered by 106 from the last ten overs; Derbyshire's bowling, with the honourable exception of Welch, was totally inadequate, and so was much of their fielding. Still, Rogers was in command until he hooked Parsons straight to long leg with just under 100 still needed. Adnan was also caught on the boundary and then panic set in. The last seven fell for 60, including five in 25 balls, as Somerset held their catches and Francis profited from some poor shots.

Man of the Match: J. Cox.

Somerset

*M. Burns run out	59	†R. J. Turner not out		2
J. D. Francis c Sutton b Welch	3			
C. M. Gazzard c Moss b Welch	9	L-b 13, w 11		24
J. Cox run out	131			
K. A. Parsons run out	3	1/9 (2) 2/40 (3)	(6 wkts, 50 overs)	290
K. P. Dutch b Welch	9	3/123 (1) 4/129 (5)		
A. W. Laraman not out	50	5/163 (6) 6/286 (4)		

S. R. G. Francis, A. R. Caddick and N. A. M. McLean did not bat.

Bowling: Mohammad Ali 10–0–63–0; Welch 10–1–38–3; Moss 10–2–56–0; Dumelow 9–0–55–0; Botha 5–0–28–0; Hewson 6–0–37–0.

Derbyshire

C. J. L. Rogers c Laraman b Parsons . . .	93	
A. I. Gait c Turner b S. R. G. Francis . .	17	
C. W. G. Bassano lbw b S. R. G. Francis	18	
Hassan Adnan c Parsons		
b S. R. G. Francis .	78	
J. Moss c Turner b Caddick	6	
*†L. D. Sutton c Turner		
b S. R. G. Francis .	0	
D. R. Hewson c J. D. Francis		
b S. R. G. Francis .	7	
G. Welch c Gazzard b S. R. G. Francis .	22	

A. G. Botha c McLean
      b S. R. G. Francis .   4
N. R. C. Dumelow c Gazzard
      b S. R. G. Francis .   5
Mohammad Ali not out   17
    L-b 3, w 4, n-b 2   9

1/55 (2) 2/100 (3)   (48.5 overs) 276
3/193 (1) 4/216 (4) 5/218 (6)
6/224 (5) 7/228 (7) 8/237 (9)
9/250 (10) 10/276 (8)

Bowling: Caddick 10–0–58–1; McLean 9–0–38–0; S. R. G. Francis 9.5–0–66–8; Laraman 8–0–36–0; Dutch 6–0–42–0; Parsons 6–0–33–1.

Umpires: J. W. Holder and B. Leadbeater.

DEVON v LEICESTERSHIRE

At Exmouth, May 5, 6. Devon won by virtue of losing fewer wickets. Toss: Devon.

This victory ranked with Devon's four consecutive Minor Counties titles in the mid-1990s as the highest point in their long history. Their first win against a first-class county, it was the 13th upset in the competition by a minor side and of those 13 this was the closest of all. After Leicestershire scraped together 156, Devon had reached 152 as Dakin prepared to bowl the last over. Two runs came from as many balls, but from the third, the linchpin Dawson was held at mid-on, exposing the last man, Aqeel Ahmed. After profiting from a wide, Ahmed scrambled a single off the fifth ball to level the scores and ensure the final ball was irrelevant. (Even if Dakin had taken a wicket – to leave both sides 156 all out – Devon would have won on higher 15-over score.) Dawson placed the win above any of his first-class achievements with Gloucestershire. Earlier, after the scheduled day had been washed out, Leicestershire struggled to adapt to a slow, club pitch of low bounce, losing their first five wickets for 58. Nixon made late face-saving runs but the total was still small for the conditions.

Man of the Match: R. I. Dawson.

Leicestershire

D. D. J. Robinson b Hancock	0	
D. I. Stevens c Lye b Court	14	
B. J. Hodge b Philander	20	
D. L. Maddy c and b Hancock	3	
J. L. Sadler b Dawson	10	
J. N. Snape b Court	28	
†P. A. Nixon not out	33	
*P. A. J. DeFreitas b Procter	0	
J. M. Dakin lbw b Procter	7	

O. D. Gibson lbw b Procter   20
C. W. Henderson b Aqeel Ahmed   2
    B 3, l-b 8, w 6, n-b 2   19

1/5 (1) 2/28 (3) 3/31 (4) (47.2 overs) 156
4/47 (2) 5/58 (5) 6/103 (6)
7/105 (8) 8/115 (9)
9/153 (10) 10/156 (11)

Bowling: Hancock 10–2–29–2; Philander 10–1–25–1; Court 10–1–23–2; Dawson 5–1–15–1; Aqeel Ahmed 5.2–0–27–1; Procter 7–0–26–3.

Devon

M. P. Hunt c Dakin b Henderson	17	A. J. Procter not out	2
D. F. Lye c Hodge b Dakin	14	Aqeel Ahmed not out	1
A. V. Suppiah lbw b DeFreitas	18		
*R. I. Dawson c Gibson b Dakin	42	L-b 10, w 6	16
A. J. Pugh b Gibson	1		
†C. M. Mole c Nixon b Gibson	0	1/27 (2) 2/50 (3) (9 wkts, 50 overs) 156		
N. D. Hancock c Hodge b Henderson	1	3/54 (1) 4/68 (5)	
D. G. Court c Henderson b Dakin	36	5/72 (6) 6/75 (7)	
V. D. Philander run out	8	7/128 (8) 8/149 (9) 9/154 (4)	

Bowling: Gibson 8–3–17–2; DeFreitas 10–3–16–1; Dakin 8–0–40–3; Henderson 10–2–27–2; Hodge 5–0–22–0; Snape 8–1–18–0; Maddy 1–0–6–0.

Umpires: R. K. Illingworth and R. Palmer.

At Bournemouth (Dean Park), May 5, 6. **Yorkshire won by eight wickets.** Toss: Yorkshire. **Dorset 97** (38.2 overs) (C. E. W. Silverwood 4-18); **Yorkshire 101-2** (16.5 overs) (M. J. Wood 71*).

Man of the Match: C. E. W. Silverwood.

After the first day was washed out, Silverwood decided the match inside 15 overs by taking four wickets in a hostile first spell on a lively pitch. Wood exploited a small boundary, and his 71 not out came from 58 balls.

DURHAM v SUSSEX

At Chester-le-Street, May 5, 6. Sussex won by 22 runs. Toss: Durham.

Injuries forced Durham to draft in their 41-year-old second-team coach Alan Walker for his first senior game in six years, only for him to tear his calf in the sixth over when attempting a diving stop. Play had finally begun at 4.10 p.m. after rain, and was held over with Sussex 87 for one in 18 overs; Durham's lack of bowling strength was obvious as Ward twice pulled sixes off the medium-pacer Pattison. Next day, however, Pattison's figures were 7–1–19–3 as Sussex slid tamely from 206 for three with ten overs left, to 245 all out. Early in Durham's reply, North hit four successive fours off Mohammad Akram, but wickets fell regularly. The hobbling Walker thrashed 23 not out from No. 11, but only narrowed Sussex's winning margin. Given the turgid pitch, a robust 68 off 70 balls by the Sussex captain Adams was enough for the match award.

Man of the Match: C. J. Adams.

Close of play: Sussex 87-1 (18 overs) (Ward 47, Goodwin 13).

Sussex

I. J. Ward c North b Pattison	54	J. D. Lewry c sub b North	2
M. J. Prior c North b Killeen	20	Mohammad Akram run out	1
M. W. Goodwin b Breese	47		
*C. J. Adams c A. Pratt b Pattison	68	B 1, l-b 6, w 4, n-b 2	13
†T. R. Ambrose c A. Pratt b Davies	14		
R. S. C. Martin-Jenkins c A. Pratt b Pattison	4	1/36 (2) 2/97 (1) (49.4 overs) 245		
		3/176 (3) 4/206 (5)	
K. J. Innes not out	14	5/219 (4) 6/220 (6)	
M. J. G. Davis run out	1	7/222 (8) 8/237 (9)	
Mushtaq Ahmed st A. Pratt b North	7	9/239 (10) 10/245 (11)	

Bowling: Killeen 9.4–2–27–1; Davies 8–1–41–1; Pattison 10–1–45–3; Muchall 5–0–31–0; Breese 8–0–49–1; North 9–0–45–2.

Durham

N. Peng c Ward b Mohammad Akram	0	M. Davies c Lewry b Mohammad Akram	3
M. J. North c Prior b Martin-Jenkins	30	N. Killeen run out	29
*J. J. B. Lewis lbw b Lewry	10	A. Walker not out	23
G. J. Pratt c Ambrose b Mushtaq Ahmed	10		
G. R. Breese run out	25	B 4, l-b 8, w 5, n-b 2	19
G. J. Muchall c Ambrose b Mohammad Akram	22		
†A. Pratt c Goodwin b Innes	44	1/2 (1) 2/42 (3) 3/46 (2) (48.4 overs) 223
I. Pattison c Martin-Jenkins b Mohammad Akram	8	4/77 (4) 5/83 (5) 6/151 (6) 7/159 (7) 8/164 (8) 9/175 (9) 10/223 (10)

Bowling: Mohammad Akram 10–0–61–4; Lewry 8–2–24–1; Martin-Jenkins 7.4–0–21–1; Mushtaq Ahmed 10–0–33–1; Davis 7–0–29–0; Innes 6–0–43–1.

Umpires: S. A. Garratt and J. W. Lloyds.

At Worcester, May 5, 6. **Worcestershire won by 18 runs (D/L method).** Toss: Herefordshire. **Worcestershire 279-8** (47 overs) (A. J. Hall 34, G. A. Hick 41, B. F. Smith 91, S. C. Moore 47; S. A. Roberts 3-36); **Herefordshire 146-4** (29 overs) (R. J. Hall 54*, I. Dawood 30).
Man of the Match: B. F. Smith.
Another complete first-day washout meant a move from the Minor County venue, the Luctonians ground, to Worcester in hope of play. They got just enough: Smith scored 91 from 88 balls and Herefordshire were 19 runs behind their retrospective target of 165 in 29 overs when the rain returned.

At Amstelveen, May 5. **Gloucestershire won by 72 runs.** Toss: Gloucestershire. **Gloucestershire 264-6** (50 overs) (C. M. Spearman 39, W. P. C. Weston 106, M. G. N. Windows 62); **Holland 192** (47.2 overs) (M. P. Mott 41, E. Schiferli 37; M. W. Alleyne 4-33).
Man of the Match: W. P. C. Weston.
One anonymous Gloucestershire player admitted qualms about the trip to hedonistic Amsterdam: "If you lose here," he was quoted as saying, "you feel like people will be asking what you've been up to." Weston's 127-ball 106 settled any nerves.

IRELAND v SURREY

At Clontarf, May 5, 6. Ireland won by five wickets. Toss: Ireland.
Surrey, double one-day champions in 2003, fielded eight internationals but lost comprehensively against an Ireland team captained by a City of London banker. Although Surrey's early season had been poor, and Ireland had beaten the touring Zimbabweans in 2003, it was still a major shock. The match began on an overcast and chilly Wednesday, so the crowd was sparse when Jason Molins put Surrey in. The highlights of a rain-interrupted innings were Brown's 67 off 49 balls and the wonderful catch at long-off that ended it, held by 17-year-old Eoin Morgan. From 155 for three after 30 overs Surrey were restricted to 261; Ireland's fielders completed nine good catches and a brilliant stumping, and the off-spinners, Kyle McCallan and Andrew White, slowed the scoring and took five wickets. More rain before Ireland could bat forced a second day, but with the weather and crowd both improved, Ireland were inspired. Their openers hit 103 in 20 overs, before a muscular 45 from South African Gerald Dros kept up the momentum. When the fifth wicket fell, they needed 39 in 43 balls. White and McCallan used just 33. The bar, deserted during the climax, quickly filled again. Nobody went home for many hours.
Man of the Match: A. R. White.
Close of play: Surrey 261.

Surrey

*†J. N. Batty c Bushe b Johnston	8	Saqlain Mushtaq c and b Botha	1
A. D. Brown c Morgan b Dros	67	J. Ormond not out	1
M. R. Ramprakash c and b McCallan	34		
A. J. Hollioake st Bushe b McCallan	52	B 1, l-b 6, w 4	11
J. G. E. Benning c Johnston b White	27		
Azhar Mahmood c Bray b White	13	1/42 (1) 2/97 (2) 3/145 (3) (49.5 overs) 261	
N. Shahid c Johnston b Botha	27	4/194 (4) 5/194 (5)	
I. D. K. Salisbury c and b White	4	6/218 (6) 7/228 (8)	
M. P. Bicknell c Morgan b Botha	16	8/248 (7) 9/260 (10) 10/261 (9)	

Bowling: Johnston 8–2–35–1; Eagleson 8–0–50–0; Botha 9.5–0–48–3; Dros 4–0–27–1; McCallan 10–1–51–2; White 10–0–43–3.

Ireland

*J. A. M. Molins b Azhar Mahmood	58	W. K. McCallan not out	18
J. P. Bray b Saqlain Mushtaq	52	L-b 3, w 15, n-b 6	24
A. C. Botha lbw b Salisbury	47		
G. Dros c Brown b Bicknell	45	1/103 (1) 2/137 (3) (5 wkts, 48.2 overs) 262	
P. G. Gillespie lbw b Azhar Mahmood	28	3/154 (2) 4/221 (4)	
A. R. White not out	20	5/223 (5)	

E. J. G. Morgan, D. T. Johnston, R. L. Eagleson and †J. A. Bushe did not bat.

Bowling: Bicknell 10–0–55–1; Ormond 9–0–48–0; Azhar Mahmood 9.2–0–60–2; Saqlain Mushtaq 10–0–34–1; Salisbury 8–0–44–1; Hollioake 2–0–18–0.

Umpires: N. J. Llong and G. Sharp.

At Lincoln Lindum, May 5. **Glamorgan won by 110 runs.** Toss: Lincolnshire. **Glamorgan 340-4** (50 overs) (R. D. B. Croft 143, M. T. G. Elliott 87, M. P. Maynard 36, Extras 32); **Lincolnshire 230-6** (50 overs) (S. A. Deitz 56, G. E. Welton 60, O. E. Burford 34*).
Man of the Match: R. D. B. Croft.
Croft and Elliott raced to 194 in 29 overs for the first wicket; Elliott's 87 took his one-day average in 2004 to 359. For Lincolnshire, Elliot Wilson's medium-pace went for 10–0–85–1; for Glamorgan, Kasprowicz ended with 7–3–8–0.

At Edinburgh, May 5. **Essex won by 45 runs.** Toss: Scotland. **Essex 272-3** (50 overs) (N. Hussain 85, W. I. Jefferson 97, A. Habib 32*); **Scotland 227** (48 overs) (S. Sriram 56, R. R. Watson 76; A. P. Cowan 3-47, Danish Kaneria 3-30).
Man of the Match: W. I. Jefferson.
Jefferson and Hussain added 163 for Essex's second wicket, but Scotland were briefly in touch until Sridharan Sriram, their 28-year-old Indian international batsman, was bowled.

At Birmingham, May 5, 6. **Warwickshire won by eight wickets.** Toss: Warwickshire. **Shropshire 119** (42.5 overs) (J. T. Ralph 38; D. R. Brown 4-30); **Warwickshire 121-2** (21 overs) (I. R. Bell 58*).
Man of the Match: I. R. Bell.
No play was possible at Wellington on the first day and two other Shropshire grounds were inspected before the ECB ruled the match should be moved to Edgbaston, a decision initially resisted by Shropshire. Bell's 58 came from 37 balls.

At Stone, May 5. **Lancashire won by 20 runs.** Toss: Staffordshire. **Lancashire 232** (47 overs) (M. B. Loye 37, I. J. Sutcliffe 41, M. J. Chilton 42; Imran Tahir 3-31); **Staffordshire 212-8** (50 overs) (D. Mongia 31, G. F. Archer 31, P. S. J. Goodwin 31, Imran Tahir 41*).
Man of the Match: Imran Tahir.
For the second year running, Staffordshire almost sprang a surprise. On a slow, low pitch Lancashire reached 100 in 17 overs but were strangled by Staffordshire's three spinners. However, neither the Indian Dinesh Mongia (who would play for Lancashire later in 2004) nor Graeme Archer, formerly with Nottinghamshire, could turn their starts into a match-winning innings.

At Lamphey, May 5, 6. **Middlesex won by 174 runs.** Toss: Wales. **Middlesex 277-6** (50 overs) (P. N. Weekes 66, J. W. M. Dalrymple 104*); **Wales 103** (41.1 overs) (A. J. Jones 42; M. M. Betts 4-15).

Man of the Match: J. W. M. Dalrymple.

Dalrymple's 104 occupied only 74 balls. Wales, replying on the second day after rain ended the first between innings, collapsed from 62 for one; Betts took 7–2–15–4.

At Westbury, May 5, 6. **Wiltshire v Nottinghamshire. No result (abandoned).**

The outfield was deemed too wet for play on either scheduled day, though many locals believed play might have been possible on the second. Regulations stated the match should then have gone to a bowl-out. But the ECB, fearing several games could be totally washed out, had already sanctioned replays if the teams agreed. The Westbury ground could not be prepared in time for the agreed rematch on May 17, so it was held at Trent Bridge.

SECOND ROUND REPLAY

At Nottingham, May 17. **Nottinghamshire won by six wickets.** Toss: Nottinghamshire. **Wiltshire 186-7** (50 overs) (J. C. Adams 43, Baqar Rizvi 47; P. J. Franks 3-27); **Nottinghamshire 189-4** (38.2 overs) (R. J. Warren 45*, C. M. W. Read 77*).

County debut: A. Singh.

Man of the Match: C. M. W. Read.

Nottinghamshire were 69 for four before Read took control. The Wiltshire medium-pacer James Hibberd ended with figures of 7–3–9–1.

THIRD ROUND

DEVON v YORKSHIRE

At Exmouth, May 26. Yorkshire won by 132 runs. Toss: Devon.

A clubhouse window was broken and several car bonnets dented during a riotous display of big hitting by both sides, a performance which delighted the estimated 2,000 crowd – except those left facing garage bills. It was a match of 24 sixes on a decent-sized ground; most would have been sixes at Edgbaston as well as Exmouth. Wood led the assault, showing impressive straight hitting and a keen eye for the short ball in a blistering 160 from 124 balls, including 23 fours and three sixes. It was Yorkshire's second-biggest limited-overs innings, after 191 by Darren Lehmann against Nottinghamshire at Scarborough in 2001, and their highest in this competition, beating Geoffrey Boycott's famous 146 in the 1965 final. Yorkshire topped 400 for the first time in one-day cricket, managing 13 sixes. On a flawless batting pitch Devon replied with 11 of their own, including three from Bobby Dawson whose half-century came from only 25 balls. Although Yorkshire's total was out of sight, the match ended fittingly when the last ball was whacked into the crowd by Procter.

Man of the Match: M. J. Wood.

Yorkshire

M. J. Wood b Pugh	160	†R. J. Blakey not out	10
*C. White c and b Hancock	6		
M. J. Lumb st Mole b Suppiah	77	B 1, l-b 7, w 8	16
P. A. Jaques c Pugh b Philander	55		
A. McGrath not out	64	1/28 (2) 2/172 (3) (6 wkts, 50 overs) 411	
A. W. Gale c Philander b Bishop	16	3/296 (1) 4/307 (4)	
T. T. Bresnan b Bishop	7	5/346 (6) 6/376 (7)	

R. K. J. Dawson, A. K. D. Gray and M. J. Hoggard did not bat.

Bowling: Hancock 10–1–68–1; Philander 10–1–68–1; Bishop 10–0–90–2; Procter 10–0–78–0; Suppiah 4–0–42–1; Court 3–0–22–0; Pugh 2–0–29–1; Dawson 1–0–6–0.

Devon

M. P. Hunt c and b Gray	43	A. J. Procter not out	9
†C. M. Mole c Blakey b Dawson	40	I. E. Bishop not out	0
A. V. Suppiah b White	36	L-b 3, w 5	8
*R. I. Dawson c Lumb b McGrath	52		
A. J. Pugh c Blakey b McGrath	6	1/78 (2) 2/90 (1)	(8 wkts, 50 overs) 279
N. D. Hancock c Wood b McGrath	23	3/153 (4) 4/159 (5)	
D. G. Court b Bresnan	47	5/186 (3) 6/216 (6)	
V. D. Philander c and b McGrath	15	7/267 (7) 8/273 (8)	

D. F. Lye did not bat.

Bowling: Hoggard 8–2–20–0; Bresnan 9–1–44–1; White 6–1–42–1; McGrath 9–0–56–4; Gray 8–0–78–1; Dawson 10–2–36–1.

Umpires: D. J. Constant and N. G. Cowley.

GLOUCESTERSHIRE v HAMPSHIRE

At Bristol, May 29. Gloucestershire won by three wickets. Toss: Hampshire

A grey sky and a pitch that proved surprisingly responsive to all kinds of bowling left Warne regretting his decision to bat first and bowl himself late. Hampshire collapsed to 91 for eight against the swing of Lewis, and were finished off by the guile of Alleyne. In between, a defiant fifty from Mascarenhas at least gave Hampshire something to bowl at. In reply, the Gloucestershire opener Spearman hit a fifty in 36 balls. In one Hamblin over he took 22 off the first five deliveries, and the next ball was a wide that went to the boundary for five more. But when Warne did come on, in the 22nd over, he spread unease like a miasma in the Gloucestershire dressing-room, taking four wickets, three of them leg-before, and having Shoaib Malik dropped. Lewis then played out an important steadying over, including two wides as Warne tried his flipper, and Shoaib saw the holders through.

Man of the Match: J. Lewis.

Hampshire

J. R. C. Hamblin c Adshead b Shabbir Ahmed	3	S. D. Udal c Smith b Alleyne	13
D. A. Kenway c Gidman b Lewis	0	C. T. Tremlett b Alleyne	24
*S. K. Warne c Adshead b Lewis	0	A. D. Mullally not out	0
J. P. Crawley c Adshead b Lewis	15	L-b 3, w 8, n-b 6	17
M. G. Dighton c Gidman b Smith	12	1/4 (2) 2/4 (3) 3/4 (1)	(46.1 overs) 154
W. S. Kendall c Spearman b Lewis	2	4/33 (5) 5/39 (4) 6/49 (6)	
†N. Pothas c Adshead b Smith	16	7/63 (7) 8/91 (9)	
A. D. Mascarenhas b Alleyne	52	9/151 (10) 10/154 (8)	

Bowling: Lewis 10–1–39–4; Shabbir Ahmed 10–2–25–1; Smith 10–3–25–2; Gidman 2–0–15–0; Alleyne 9.1–0–25–3; Shoaib Malik 5–0–22–0.

Gloucestershire

W. P. C. Weston b Warne	29	†S. J. Adshead lbw b Warne	0
C. M. Spearman b Mullally	50	J. Lewis not out	2
A. P. R. Gidman lbw b Mullally	6	B 1, l-b 2, w 14, n-b 2	19
M. G. N. Windows lbw b Warne	6		
Shoaib Malik not out	32	1/76 (2) 2/84 (3)	(7 wkts, 37.5 overs) 157
C. G. Taylor lbw b Warne	9	3/105 (4) 4/116 (1)	
*M. W. Alleyne c Kenway b Mullally	4	5/127 (6) 6/132 (7) 7/137 (8)	

Shabbir Ahmed and A. M. Smith did not bat.

Bowling: Tremlett 10–3–30–0; Mascarenhas 5–0–24–0; Hamblin 2–0–31–0; Udal 3–0–17–0; Mullally 9–1–29–3; Warne 8.5–1–23–4.

Umpires: J. F. Steele and P. Willey.

MIDDLESEX v GLAMORGAN

At Lord's, May 29. Middlesex won by six wickets. Toss: Middlesex.

For the third year running, a strong Glamorgan team were knocked out early by a remarkable innings. Jamie Dalrymple could not quite match Chris Bassano of Derbyshire, who rose from his sick bed to score 121 in 2003, or Ally Brown, who walloped a world-record 268 for Surrey the year before. But he was the key to Middlesex's successful pursuit of 257, in swinging conditions where par was around 220. Joyce and Dalrymple managed that score on their own, in a stand lasting 37.2 overs. Earlier, Elliott, in fine touch in one-day matches, had rebuilt Glamorgan's score after watching Keegan remove three of his partners, before getting one that nipped back when he was 85. Dalrymple bowled a strangling spell of medium-pace, and then cleared up the mess Middlesex were in at 23 for three by counter-attacking with his usual brisk drives. When he fell to the otherwise disappointing Jones, his stand with Joyce was just 14 short of the fourth-wicket record in the tournament. But the contest was over.

Man of the Match: J. W. M. Dalrymple.

Glamorgan

*R. D. B. Croft lbw b Keegan	1	D. S. Harrison not out	10
M. T. G. Elliott b Hayward	85	A. P. Davies not out	7
A. G. Wharf b Keegan	13	B 2, l-b 13, w 11	26
M. J. Powell c Weekes b Keegan	2		
M. P. Maynard c Hayward b Hutton	25	1/2 (1) 2/34 (3) (8 wkts, 50 overs) 256	
D. L. Hemp st Scott b Klusener	36	3/38 (4) 4/116 (5)	
A. Dale b Hayward	30	5/168 (2) 6/196 (6)	
†M. A. Wallace b Dalrymple	21	7/229 (8) 8/236 (7)	

S. P. Jones did not bat.

Bowling: Keegan 10–0–47–3; Hayward 10–0–55–2; Klusener 8–0–40–1; Cook 6–0–30–0; Weekes 6–1–30–0; Hutton 3–0–16–1; Dalrymple 7–0–23–1.

Middlesex

P. N. Weekes c Wallace b Davies	1	B. L. Hutton not out	12
*A. J. Strauss b Harrison	19	L-b 7, w 14	21
O. A. Shah lbw b Harrison	0		
E. C. Joyce not out	100	1/1 (1) 2/11 (3) (4 wkts, 46.1 overs) 260	
J. W. M. Dalrymple c Wallace b Jones	107	3/23 (2) 4/243 (5)	

L. Klusener, S. J. Cook, †B. J. M. Scott, C. B. Keegan and M. Hayward did not bat.

Bowling: Harrison 8–1–45–2; Davies 10–2–38–1; Wharf 7–0–30–0; Jones 9.1–0–64–1; Croft 10–0–55–0; Dale 2–0–21–0.

Umpires: B. Dudleston and R. Palmer.

NOTTINGHAMSHIRE v ESSEX

At Nottingham, May 29. Essex won by 184 runs. Toss: Nottinghamshire.

The morning dawned depressingly dark, a description that also summed up Nottinghamshire's mood by the end. Rain delayed the start and they chose to bowl, hoping to exploit any movement offered by pitch or cloud. The decision backfired hopelessly. It took 42 overs for them to get the first wicket, gifted when Jefferson holed out to long-off. By then he had 126, scored at faster than a run a ball against bowling that built no real pressure, and the opening stand of 248 was the best by Essex in any one-day competition (beating 239 by Graham Gooch and Brian Hardie on this ground in 1985). Chasing 310, Nottinghamshire roared to 42 in four overs but Franks was run out by a deflection at the non-striker's end, and the rest rolled over. The exception was Read, who wrecked Brant's figures with three sixes into – and over – the Fox Road Stand.

Man of the Match: W. I. Jefferson.

Essex

W. I. Jefferson c Pietersen b Clough	126	†J. S. Foster not out	18
*A. Flower c Smith b Ealham	106	B 1, l-b 11, w 12	24
R. C. Irani b Franks	17		
M. L. Pettini not out	18	1/248 (1) 2/269 (2) (4 wkts, 50 overs)	309
G. R. Napier c Clough b Franks	0	3/273 (3) 4/273 (5)	

A. P. Grayson, J. D. Middlebrook, A. J. Clarke, D. Gough and S. A. Brant did not bat.

Bowling: Smith 8–1–38–0; Franks 9–0–59–2; Sidebottom 8–1–34–0; Ealham 10–0–54–1; Clough 9–0–59–1; MacGill 3–0–32–0; Hussey 3–0–21–0.

Nottinghamshire

P. J. Franks run out	27	G. J. Smith b Brant	0
*J. E. R. Gallian c Foster b Napier	18	R. J. Sidebottom c Irani b Brant	9
D. J. Hussey c Foster b Napier	0	S. C. G. MacGill not out	7
K. P. Pietersen lbw b Napier	0	L-b 6, w 2	8
R. J. Warren b Gough	2		
†C. M. W. Read c Jefferson		1/45 (1) 2/45 (3) 3/45 (4) (21.2 overs)	125
b Middlebrook	46	4/52 (5) 5/52 (7) 6/68 (7)	
M. A. Ealham c Foster b Brant	8	7/75 (8) 8/75 (9)	
G. D. Clough lbw b Brant	0	9/92 (10) 10/125 (6)	

Bowling: Gough 6–0–28–1; Brant 7–0–54–4; Napier 4–1–11–3; Clarke 3–0–20–0; Middlebrook 1.2–0–6–1.

Umpires: N. G. Cowley and M. J. Harris.

SUSSEX v LANCASHIRE

At Hove, May 29. Lancashire won by 12 runs. Toss: Sussex.

Run-scoring was not easy on a relaid pitch, with the odd ball jumping off a length at both ends, and Sussex never looked like reaching Lancashire's 242. Loye and Chilton laid the foundations for Lancashire; Flintoff was chief embellisher – a ball he hit through a windscreen ended up studded with glass and had to be changed. In reply, Sussex made an awful start when Anderson hit Ward on the hand second ball and forced him to retire. Anderson's hostility helped Chapple take three quick wickets at the other end and Sussex were in effect 20 for four. A battling 51 by Adams and an unbeaten 61 from Martin-Jenkins took Sussex close, but Lancashire's unbeaten run in the season's one-day cricket never really looked threatened.

Man of the Match: M. J. Chilton.

Lancashire

M. B. Loye lbw b Mushtaq Ahmed	54	*†W. K. Hegg c Prior	
I. J. Sutcliffe c Wright b Martin-Jenkins	16	b Mohammad Akram	2
S. G. Law c Prior b Kirtley	19	K. W. Hogg not out	1
M. J. Chilton c Prior		B 3, l-b 8, w 5	16
b Mohammad Akram	62		
A. Flintoff lbw b Mushtaq Ahmed	35	1/28 (2) 2/68 (3) (7 wkts, 50 overs)	242
C. L. Hooper not out	30	3/117 (4) 4/191 (5)	
G. Chapple run out	7	5/216 (4) 6/233 (7) 7/236 (8)	

J. M. Anderson and S. I. Mahmood did not bat.

Bowling: Mohammad Akram 10–2–47–2; Martin-Jenkins 10–0–53–1; Kirtley 10–1–29–1; Wright 8–0–43–0; Yardy 2–0–15–0; Mushtaq Ahmed 10–0–44–2.

Sussex

I. J. Ward run out	2	Mohammad Akram run out	1
†M. J. Prior c Law b Chapple	8	R. J. Kirtley not out	18
R. R. Montgomerie c Law b Chapple	0		
M. W. Goodwin c Chilton b Chapple	0	B 6, l-b 6, w 22, n-b 6	40
*C. J. Adams b Mahmood	51		
M. H. Yardy c Chilton b Flintoff	27	1/10 (3) 2/16 (4) (9 wkts, 50 overs) 230	
R. S. C. Martin-Jenkins not out	61	3/20 (2) 4/84 (6)	
L. J. Wright b Flintoff	21	5/147 (5) 6/189 (8)	
Mushtaq Ahmed b Mahmood	1	7/192 (9) 8/192 (1) 9/199 (10)	

Ward, when 2, retired hurt at 2 and resumed at 192-7.

Bowling: Anderson 10–0–39–0; Chapple 10–3–44–3; Flintoff 10–1–28–2; Mahmood 10–1–57–2; Hogg 10–1–50–0.

Umpires: V. A. Holder and G. Sharp.

WARWICKSHIRE v KENT

At Birmingham, May 29. Warwickshire won by nine wickets. Toss: Warwickshire.

Wagh's maiden one-day century, in his 53rd match, was the centrepiece of a bloodless Warwickshire victory against demoralised opposition. Wagh was in danger of being stranded on 96 when he lost the strike with three needed for victory but, with plenty of overs left, Knight could afford to block three deliveries, allowing his partner to pull Sheriyar for six. Their match-winning stand of 183 for the second wicket made a mockery of a pitch that offered encouragement to the seamers. After overnight rain delayed the start, Kent prospered initially against a wayward opening spell from Pretorius. But he proved more effective later as five men fell in 11 overs, including Key – who looked in no trouble until run out from square leg. That left Fulton to sustain the innings, with a poorly supported 78.

Man of the Match: M. A. Wagh.

Kent

M. A. Carberry c Ostler b Brown	9	M. J. Saggers c Bell b Giles	4
R. W. T. Key run out	45	A. Sheriyar not out	2
E. T. Smith c Ostler b Pretorius	15		
M. J. Walker c Frost b Pretorius	10	L-b 3, w 12, n-b 2	17
*D. P. Fulton c Pretorius b Brown	78		
†G. O. Jones b Bell	0	1/38 (1) 2/78 (3) 3/78 (2) (49.4 overs) 211	
J. C. Tredwell c Carter b Pretorius	13	4/93 (4) 5/94 (6) 6/122 (7)	
M. J. Dennington b Giles	13	7/174 (8) 8/179 (9)	
Mohammad Sami b Wagh	5	9/204 (10) 10/211 (5)	

Bowling: Pretorius 10–1–43–3; Carter 7–2–35–0; Brown 9.4–1–31–2; Bell 10–2–33–1; Trott 3–0–16–0; Giles 7–0–32–2; Wagh 3–0–18–1.

Warwickshire

N. M. Carter c Carberry		
	b Mohammad Sami	24
M. A. Wagh not out		102
*N. V. Knight not out		74
	L-b 3, w 10, n-b 2	15
1/32 (1)	(1 wkt, 42.1 overs)	215

I. R. Bell, I. J. L. Trott, D. P. Ostler, T. L. Penney, D. R. Brown, A. F. Giles, †T. Frost and D. Pretorius did not bat.

Bowling: Mohammad Sami 8–0–43–1; Sheriyar 7.1–0–51–0; Saggers 6–0–34–0; Dennington 10–0–47–0; Tredwell 10–0–31–0; Walker 1–0–6–0.

Umpires: A. Clarkson and D. J. Constant.

WORCESTERSHIRE v SOMERSET

At Worcester, May 29. Worcestershire won by eight wickets. Toss: Somerset.

Worcestershire wrapped up victory in 42 overs – barely three hours' playing time – as the muscular hostility of Bichel made Somerset's decision to bat in overcast conditions look flawed. In fairness to the Somerset captain Burns, there was little sign of the drama to follow when Kabir Ali, in his comeback from a double hernia operation, conceded 29 in two overs, and the Somerset openers reached 41. However Ali's failure allowed Bichel the still-hard ball and he was almost unplayable in a spell of 7–1–17–4. All ten wickets tumbled for 54, with Mason and Leatherdale giving excellent support. Only Blackwell, limited by a blow to the hand, and the openers reached double figures, an effort Bichel himself dwarfed by making 38 not out, the best of the day, from No. 3. He and Batty hurried Worcestershire home in 14.3 overs.

Man of the Match: A. J. Bichel.

Somerset

C. M. Gazzard c Hick b Mason	10		A. R. Caddick b Leatherdale	5
M. E. Trescothick c Smith b Bichel	24		N. A. M. McLean not out	0
*M. Burns c Hick b Bichel	0			
J. Cox c Rhodes b Mason	5		L-b 5, w 8	13
K. A. Parsons c Solanki b Bichel	2			
I. D. Blackwell c Batty b Leatherdale	27		1/41 (2) 2/41 (3) 3/41 (1)	(27.3 overs) 95
K. P. Dutch lbw b Bichel	1		4/45 (5) 5/53 (4) 6/56 (7)	
†R. J. Turner c Solanki b Leatherdale	5		7/64 (8) 8/79 (9)	
R. L. Johnson lbw b Kabir Ali	3		9/95 (6) 10/95 (10)	

Bowling: Mason 8–2–16–2; Kabir Ali 8–1–48–1; Bichel 7–1–17–4; Leatherdale 4.3–1–9–3.

Worcestershire

S. D. Peters c Trescothick b McLean	7
V. S. Solanki b Caddick	16
A. J. Bichel not out	38
G. J. Batty not out	32
B 2, l-b 3, n-b 2	7

1/15 (1) 2/29 (2)   (2 wkts, 14.3 overs) 100

G. A. Hick, *B. F. Smith, S. C. Moore, D. A. Leatherdale, Kabir Ali, †S. J. Rhodes and M. S. Mason did not bat.

Bowling: Caddick 5–0–42–1; McLean 5–1–23–1; Johnson 4.3–1–30–0.

Umpires: J. H. Evans and T. E. Jesty.

IRELAND v NORTHAMPTONSHIRE

At Clontarf, May 30. Northamptonshire won by six wickets. Toss: Northamptonshire.

On paper, Northamptonshire were not as strong as Ireland's last victims, Surrey. In practice, they were much better. As in the last round, the weather was bad and interruptions meant van Jaarsveld did not hit the winning runs till 8.50 p.m. Ireland batted very well to reach 263, overcoming a slump to 37 for three and three rain breaks. Jeremy Bray hit his fourth successive fifty for Ireland, equalling a national record, and added 115 with Peter Gillespie. Late hitting roused the crowd and hopes of another upset. Only the seamer Jones prevented an even more imposing total, with two wickets in his first two overs and four in his last four to finish with his best one-day figures. However, van Jaarsveld soon dampened local spirits. In soggy conditions he hit an unbeaten 93 in 87 balls, sharing three stands of fifty or more, to take Northamptonshire home with more than eight overs to spare. The match had been delayed a day at the county's request to allow them more travel time.

Man of the Match: M. van Jaarsveld.

Ireland

*J. A. M. Molins lbw b Jones	9	P. J. K. Mooney not out	8
J. P. Bray run out	76	E. J. G. Morgan not out	13
A. C. Botha c Louw b Jones	6	L-b 5, w 5	10
G. Dros c Brophy b Louw	7		
P. G. Gillespie b Jones	66	1/9 (1) 2/20 (3) (8 wkts, 50 overs)	263
A. R. White c Swann b Jones	44	3/37 (4) 4/152 (2)	
D. T. Johnston c Sales b Jones	2	5/178 (5) 6/180 (7)	
W. K. McCallan b Jones	22	7/240 (6) 8/240 (8)	

†J. A. Bushe did not bat.

Bowling: Louw 9–1–50–1; Jones 10–0–56–6; Brown 10–0–39–0; Phillips 9–0–53–0; Swann 10–1–38–0; Cook 2–0–22–0.

Northamptonshire

T. W. Roberts b Botha	39	G. P. Swann not out	18
J. W. Cook c Bushe b Botha	17	B 1, l-b 5, w 16, n-b 2	24
M. van Jaarsveld not out	93		
U. Afzaal run out	27	1/64 (1) 2/74 (2) (4 wkts, 41.5 overs)	267
*D. J. Sales lbw b Botha	49	3/124 (4) 4/215 (5)	

†G. L. Brophy, J. Louw, B. J. Phillips, P. S. Jones and J. F. Brown did not bat.

Bowling: Johnston 9–0–61–0; Mooney 6–0–43–0; Botha 10–1–51–3; Dros 2–0–12–0; White 7–0–42–0; McCallan 7.5–0–52–0.

Umpires: M. R. Benson and G. I. Burgess.

QUARTER-FINALS

WORCESTERSHIRE v ESSEX

At Worcester, June 15. Worcestershire won by 21 runs. Toss: Worcestershire.

Both teams lost their fifth wicket at 75, and both totals were underpinned by expertly accumulated half-centuries, from Smith for Worcestershire and Flower for Essex. But Worcestershire had a crucial edge in their seam attack: Bichel and Mason marginally outbowled their Essex counterparts on a slow, seaming pitch. The surface was not ideal for one-day cricket, and the best stand of the match was just 76 between Smith and Leatherdale, who together provided Worcestershire's only real substance. When Essex took their turn, Bichel struck an early psychological blow by bowling Jefferson, who had made 97 and 126 in previous rounds. The required rate was never a problem for Essex, but the regular fall of wickets certainly was. Mason curtailed the middle order's attempts to support Flower, helped by three costly run-outs, two down to dead-eyed fielding, Bopara's to poor running. Bichel returned to grab two more wickets and take Worcestershire to a third one-day semi-final in three years.

Man of the Match: B. F. Smith.

Worcestershire

S. D. Peters c Foster b Brant	4	†S. J. Rhodes c Irani b Brant	15
V. S. Solanki c Cook b Danish Kaneria	32	Kabir Ali b Brant	11
A. J. Bichel b Gough	0	M. S. Mason not out	1
G. A. Hick c Napier b Bopara	14	B 2, l-b 4, w 5	11
*B. F. Smith c Middlebrook b Bopara	54		
A. J. Hall c Foster b Middlebrook	6	1/13 (1) 2/14 (3) 3/52 (4) (50 overs)	204
D. A. Leatherdale c Bopara b Danish Kaneria	42	4/54 (2) 5/75 (6) 6/151 (5) 7/170 (7) 8/178 (8)	
G. J. Batty b Gough	14	9/203 (10) 10/204 (9)	

Bowling: Gough 10–0–49–2; Brant 10–3–19–3; Napier 6–0–45–0; Bopara 4–0–18–2; Danish Kaneria 10–1–32–2; Middlebrook 10–1–35–1.

Essex

W. I. Jefferson b Bichel	19	Danish Kaneria c Peters b Leatherdale	2
A. Flower run out	58	S. A. Brant not out	3
A. N. Cook lbw b Mason	0		
*R. C. Irani c Leatherdale b Kabir Ali	1	L-b 5, w 5	10
†J. S. Foster c and b Mason	8		
R. S. Bopara run out	11	1/30 (1) 2/31 (3) 3/36 (4) (48.1 overs) 183
J. D. Middlebrook run out	47	4/57 (5) 5/75 (6) 6/116 (2)
G. R. Napier b Bichel	13	7/144 (8) 8/176 (7)
D. Gough c and b Bichel	11	9/179 (10) 10/183 (9)

Bowling: Bichel 9.1–1–27–3; Mason 10–0–32–2; Kabir Ali 6–1–29–1; Batty 10–1–35–0; Hall 7–0–31–0; Leatherdale 6–0–24–1.

Umpires: P. J. Hartley and A. G. T. Whitehead.

GLOUCESTERSHIRE v MIDDLESEX

At Bristol, June 16. Gloucestershire won by 16 runs. Toss: Middlesex.

Alleyne drew on years of experience as one of England's canniest one-day bowlers to squeeze Middlesex as they threatened Gloucestershire's moderate total of 239. Middlesex's chase had been jolted early by fielding heroics from Spearman, who held two sizzling catches at first slip and one in the outfield, but at 140 for four, the asking-rate was less than a run a ball. Then Alleyne appeared for the 35th over. He soon duped three vital batsmen, including the well-set Joyce and the menacing big-hitter Klusener – and Middlesex fell too far behind the rate. On an easy wicket with some bounce, Gloucestershire's openers gave them a racing start which they failed to maintain; Spearman (fresh from 341 against these opponents in the Championship five days earlier) and Weston both reached fifties in 52 balls. But they fell in a tumble of six wickets for 51 in 13 overs, caused by tight spin bowling, good catching and two direct hits.

Man of the Match: C. M. Spearman.

Gloucestershire

C. M. Spearman run out	62	J. Lewis b Hayward	1
W. P. C. Weston c Hutton b Weekes	54	Shabbir Ahmed not out	10
A. P. R. Gidman c and b Dalrymple	11	L-b 4, w 2, n-b 2	8
C. G. Taylor run out	9		
Shoaib Malik c Klusener b Dalrymple	43	1/118 (2) 2/132 (1) (8 wkts, 50 overs) 239
*M. W. Alleyne c Dalrymple b Weekes	0	3/136 (3) 4/144 (4)
†S. J. Adshead b Hayward	8	5/145 (6) 6/169 (7)
M. C. J. Ball not out	33	7/212 (5) 8/225 (9)

A. M. Smith did not bat.

Bowling: Keegan 8–0–54–0; Hayward 10–1–43–2; Klusener 8–1–28–0; Cook 4–0–32–0; Weekes 10–0–36–2; Dalrymple 10–0–42–2.

Middlesex

P. N. Weekes c Spearman b Lewis	9	S. J. Cook not out	32
*A. J. Strauss c Spearman b Shabbir Ahmed	12	†B. J. M. Scott not out	8
C. B. Keegan c Spearman b Smith	26	B 1, l-b 11, w 7, n-b 2	21
O. A. Shah c Adshead b Ball	24		
E. C. Joyce c Taylor b Alleyne	53	1/27 (2) 2/28 (1) (8 wkts, 50 overs) 223
J. W. M. Dalrymple run out	20	3/84 (3) 4/87 (4)
B. L. Hutton c Gidman b Alleyne	15	5/144 (6) 6/173 (7)
L. Klusener lbw b Alleyne	3	7/178 (8) 8/185 (5)

M. Hayward did not bat.

Bowling: Shabbir Ahmed 7–2–23–1; Lewis 6–0–27–1; Smith 9–0–34–1; Shoaib Malik 10–0–47–0; Ball 10–1–49–1; Alleyne 8–0–31–3.

Umpires: T. E. Jesty and M. J. Kitchen.

LANCASHIRE v YORKSHIRE

At Manchester, June 16. Yorkshire won by three wickets. Toss: Lancashire.

With no first-class Roses match in 2004, even more significance was loaded on to this clash. But, by the end, even diehard Lancastrians were standing to applaud Yorkshire's Michael Vaughan, the England captain, who hit a thrilling hundred widely acclaimed as one of the best seen in a one-day game at Old Trafford. The innings combined match-winning substance with dreamy elegance. Vaughan, whose poor one-day form for England was about to become a national issue, first led Yorkshire from the precipice of 85 for four, in a stand of 149 with Lehmann. Then, when Lehmann fell with 53 still needed from 51 balls, he finished the job in style, including two late sixes, the second a trademark pirouetting pull. Yorkshire won with 14 balls left, against an attack led by Mahmood, who found reverse swing and took three wickets. On a good pitch, Lancashire had looked set for a flimsy total, before the last ten overs. A massive 105 were added as Cork flayed 54 off 20 balls, before strutting from the crease while his last-ball six was still airborne.

Man of the Match: M. P. Vaughan.

Lancashire

M. B. Loye c Blakey b Silverwood	50	*†W. K. Hegg not out	3
M. J. Chilton c Wood b Bresnan	3	B 6, l-b 5, w 7, n-b 6	24
S. G. Law c Dawson b Silverwood	48		
A. J. Swann run out	38	1/17 (2) 2/82 (1)　　(5 wkts, 50 overs) 286	
C. L. Hooper lbw b Hoggard	66	3/113 (3) 4/195 (4)	
D. G. Cork not out	54	5/261 (5)	

P. J. Horton, P. J. Martin, S. I. Mahmood and J. M. Anderson did not bat.

Bowling: Hoggard 10–0–54–1; Bresnan 10–1–45–1; Silverwood 8–0–50–2; White 8–0–45–0; Dawson 4–0–30–0; Lehmann 7–0–32–0; McGrath 3–0–19–0.

Yorkshire

M. J. Wood c Cork b Mahmood	15	R. K. J. Dawson b Anderson	4
*C. White c Hegg b Mahmood	43	T. T. Bresnan not out	3
M. P. Vaughan not out	116	L-b 20, w 11, n-b 4	35
P. A. Jaques b Martin	5		
A. McGrath run out	0	1/54 (1) 2/75 (2)　　(7 wkts, 47.4 overs) 287	
D. S. Lehmann c Hegg b Mahmood	62	3/84 (4) 4/85 (5)	
†R. J. Blakey c Chilton b Anderson	4	5/234 (6) 6/245 (7) 7/269 (8)	

C. E. W. Silverwood and M. J. Hoggard did not bat.

Bowling: Anderson 10–0–56–2; Cork 8.4–0–50–0; Martin 8–0–40–1; Mahmood 10–0–56–3; Hooper 9–0–51–0; Chilton 2–0–14–0.

Umpires: J. W. Holder and B. Leadbeater.

WARWICKSHIRE v NORTHAMPTONSHIRE

At Birmingham, June 16. Warwickshire won by 73 runs. Toss: Northamptonshire.

Sales gifted Warwickshire first use of a flat pitch and they gratefully scored 343, in another of the ruthless batting performances that characterised their season. The innings was topped and tailed by explosive hitting from Carter and Hogg. The pinch-hitter Carter clobbered 43 from just 18 balls, including 28 (four fours and two sixes) from one Jones over, the most expensive in the competition's history. Later, Hogg, the Australian signed as a left-arm wrist-spinner but making more impact with the bat, raced to 94 from 61 balls in a stand of 159 with Trott. Warwickshire's fielders then supported the batsmen with excellent catching, and Northamptonshire predictably failed to keep up with a rate of almost seven an over. Sales did his best to make amends for his decision at the toss with a 48-ball fifty.

Man of the Match: G. B. Hogg.

Warwickshire

N. M. Carter c Roberts b Louw	43	G. B. Hogg not out		94
M. A. Wagh c Bailey b Louw	23	L-b 1, w 2		3
*N. V. Knight c and b Brown	47			
I. R. Bell c Swann b Phillips	68	1/39 (2) 2/68 (1)	(4 wkts, 50 overs)	343
I. J. L. Trott not out	65	3/182 (4) 4/184 (3)		

J. O. Troughton, D. R. Brown, A. F. Giles, †T. Frost and A. Richardson did not bat.

Bowling: Jones 10–0–75–0; Louw 10–0–83–2; Phillips 10–0–60–1; Swann 7–0–49–0; Cook 3–0–20–0; Brown 10–0–55–1.

Northamptonshire

J. W. Cook c Frost b Richardson	33	P. S. Jones not out		2
T. W. Roberts c Richardson b Brown	8	J. F. Brown b Brown		0
M. van Jaarsveld c Giles b Brown	28	L-b 7, w 8, n-b 4		19
U. Afzaal b Hogg	18			
*D. J. Sales c Bell b Giles	52	1/16 (2) 2/72 (1)	(43.5 overs)	270
G. P. Swann c Brown b Wagh	38	3/76 (3) 4/116 (4)		
B. J. Phillips c Carter b Wagh	33	5/156 (5) 6/217 (6)		
†T. M. B. Bailey c Hogg b Brown	19	7/233 (7) 8/268 (9)		
J. Louw b Brown	20	9/269 (8) 10/270 (11)		

Bowling: Carter 8–0–48–0; Brown 7.5–0–43–5; Richardson 7–1–46–1; Bell 2–0–8–0; Hogg 8–0–49–1; Giles 7–0–38–1; Wagh 4–0–31–2.

Umpires: B. Dudleston and G. Sharp.

SEMI-FINALS

GLOUCESTERSHIRE v YORKSHIRE

At Bristol, July 17. Gloucestershire won by five wickets. Toss: Yorkshire.

Gloucestershire breezed into yet another final, with five wickets and 23 balls to spare. Almost the only thing to go against them was the toss; in the field, their containing game plan worked and then Spearman made chasing 244 look very easy indeed. He batted throughout for 143, destroying Yorkshire with a range of drives and flicks on the up, in an innings he called his best in one-day cricket. His fifty came in 30 balls and hundred in 84. From 200 for four in 37 overs, Gloucestershire could hardly fail. It was bravura cup batting at its most potent. But the win might not have been so straightforward. Lehmann, newly back from Australia, was the only Yorkshire batsman who really tried to disrupt the holders' strategies in the field, searching the outfield intelligently and sneaking impish singles. He ended 80 not out from 90 balls; his main partner was Vaughan, who was at the low ebb of his season, outscored almost three to one by his partners and dismissed playing badly across the line. Though Harvey crashed 20 off ten balls, it came too late to lift Yorkshire to the par total of around 270. He could not make it up with the ball either, because his old Gloucestershire team-mates could read his variations.

Man of the Match: C. M. Spearman.

> **"** The poignancy of this soggy, low-key draw became clear only in hindsight."
> Gloucestershire in 2004, page 617.

Yorkshire

*M. J. Wood c Ball b Lewis	32	†R. J. Blakey not out	7
M. J. Lumb c Adshead b Alleyne	34		
M. P. Vaughan b Lewis	30	B 3, l-b 4, w 10, n-b 6	23
D. S. Lehmann not out	80		
A. McGrath c Taylor b Ball	15	1/47 (1) 2/90 (2) (6 wkts, 50 overs) 243	
I. J. Harvey c Hussey b Franklin	20	3/153 (3) 4/184 (5)	
T. T. Bresnan st Adshead b Smith	2	5/213 (6) 6/218 (7)	

R. K. J. Dawson, C. E. W. Silverwood and M. J. Hoggard did not bat.

Bowling: Franklin 10–0–60–1; Lewis 10–2–49–2; Smith 10–3–29–1; Alleyne 10–0–67–1; Ball 10–0–31–1.

Gloucestershire

W. P. C. Weston c Lehmann b Hoggard	16	*M. W. Alleyne not out	4
C. M. Spearman not out	143	B 3, l-b 3, w 6	12
M. E. K. Hussey b McGrath	35		
M. G. N. Windows b Hoggard	19	1/73 (1) 2/142 (3) (5 wkts, 46.1 overs) 247	
C. G. Taylor run out	10	3/189 (4) 4/205 (5)	
J. E. C. Franklin lbw b Harvey	8	5/233 (6)	

†S. J. Adshead, M. C. J. Ball, J. Lewis and A. M. Smith did not bat.

Bowling: Hoggard 10–2–33–2; Bresnan 5–0–41–0; Harvey 9–0–46–1; Silverwood 4–0–31–0; Dawson 4–0–29–0; Lehmann 9–0–38–0; McGrath 5.1–1–23–1.

Umpires: I. J. Gould and A. A. Jones.

WARWICKSHIRE v WORCESTERSHIRE

At Birmingham, July 17. Worcestershire won by 41 runs. Toss: Warwickshire.

Solanki dominated, first with a century of elegance and mature restraint, then with three catches and the run-out of Trott. The aggressive fielding was almost as important as the runs, as he helped snuff out an embryonic Warwickshire revival. The leaden morning skies had looked ideal for swing when Worcestershire were sent in, but Solanki and Moore (recovering from a poor run in the Twenty20) made them wait 32 overs for a breakthrough. Solanki began fluently, hitting seven of his eight fours in his first fifty, then adapted as the ball became soft and the bowling tighter. He also hit three sixes before losing his middle stump at the death. It was an intelligent performance which would help him win back his England one-day place. Warwickshire ignored their opponents' strategy of steady accumulation, and soon ran into trouble trying to force the pace. As they fell apart Knight was actually run out twice: the first occasion left Warwickshire 93 for three, the second (when he returned as runner for Trott) came in a final whirl of five wickets for 17. In between, Brown and Penney had threatened a comeback with a belligerent sixth-wicket stand of 84. But Penney tore a hamstring and Worcestershire exploited his lack of mobility, guaranteeing their second successive trip to Lord's.

Man of the Match: V. S. Solanki.

Worcestershire

V. S. Solanki b Brown	127	A. J. Bichel not out	10
S. C. Moore c Brown b Hogg	56	L-b 4, w 5	9
G. A. Hick c Hogg b Brown	5		
*B. F. Smith c Knight b Carter	23	1/146 (2) 2/159 (3) (4 wkts, 50 overs) 257	
D. A. Leatherdale not out	27	3/211 (4) 4/237 (1)	

A. J. Hall, G. J. Batty, †S. J. Rhodes, Kabir Ali and M. S. Mason did not bat.

Bowling: Carter 10–0–47–1; Brown 10–1–50–2; Richardson 6–1–33–0; Bell 5–0–18–0; Giles 9–0–45–0; Hogg 8–0–48–1; Wagh 2–0–12–0.

Warwickshire

N. M. Carter c Rhodes b Bichel	16	†T. Frost lbw b Hall 4
M. A. Wagh c Solanki b Hall	36	A. Richardson not out 0
N. V. Knight run out	37	
*I. R. Bell c Rhodes b Hall	0	B 1, l-b 3, w 3 7
G. B. Hogg c Batty b Mason	18	
T. L. Penney c Solanki b Batty	41	1/20 (1) 2/85 (2) 3/93 (3) (47.4 overs) 216
D. R. Brown lbw b Batty	47	4/108 (4) 5/115 (5)
A. F. Giles c Solanki b Bichel	10	6/199 (7) 7/208 (6)
J. J. L. Trott run out	0	8/208 (9) 9/216 (8) 10/216 (10)

Bowling: Bichel 9–0–48–2; Mason 10–1–45–1; Kabir Ali 10–1–40–0; Hull 8.4–0–37 3; Batty 9–0–38–2; Leatherdale 1–0–4–0.

Umpires: J. H. Hampshire and N. J. Llong.

FINAL

GLOUCESTERSHIRE v WORCESTERSHIRE

Paul Weaver

At Lord's, August 28. Gloucestershire won by eight wickets. Toss: Gloucestershire.

This reprise of the previous year's final was less hopelessly one-sided, but Gloucestershire's victory margin was even wider, and the result not in serious doubt for most of the day. The fact that the teams were the same as in 2003 detracted from the sense of occasion, as did around 7,000 empty seats, and the game maintained the recent anticlimactic pattern of Lord's finals. Those twilight thrillers that made the Gillette Cup and NatWest Trophy finals famous seemed the stuff of nostalgic memory. Despite their local boys' success, the folk from Cheltenham & Gloucester, in their fourth final as sponsors, looked mildly miffed with their rotten luck.

THE HUNDRED CLUB

Centuries at Lord's in the main county cup final (Gillette Cup/NatWest Trophy/C&G Trophy).

146	G. Boycott	Yorkshire v Surrey	1965
128*	M. T. G. Elliott	Yorkshire v Somerset	2002
126	C. H. Lloyd	Lancashire v Warwickshire	1972
124	D. M. Smith	Sussex v Warwickshire	1993
117	I. V. A. Richards	Somerset v Northamptonshire	1979
115	**V. S. Solanki**	**Worcestershire v Gloucestershire**..........	**2004**
111	G. Cook	Northamptonshire v Derbyshire	1981
110*	**W. P. C. Weston**	**Gloucestershire v Worcestershire**..........	**2004**
110	B. R. Hardie	Essex v Nottinghamshire	1985
104	Asif Din	Warwickshire v Sussex	1993

Worcestershire's determined attempt to make up for the year before also began unluckily. Kabir Ali, the pace bowler recently recalled to England's one-day squad, suffered a side injury and, on his last big occasion before retirement, Rhodes promptly lost the toss, though that did not seem as costly as usual, given what looked like a good batting pitch. But Lewis, in the form of his life, made expert use of the passing dew and the more permanent slope to give Gloucestershire an advantage they never lost. Lewis, achieving late movement, mostly down the hill and away from the right-handers, had Moore, Hick and Smith caught in the cordon inside 11 deliveries to leave Worcestershire in ruins at eight for three. Hick failed to score, as he had in 2003.

Grace in defeat: Vikram Solanki glides towards an elegant hundred in the C&G final, but cannot prevent another Gloucestershire triumph.

Picture by Patrick Eagar

The restoration work was done by Solanki and Leatherdale, who put on 194 for the fourth wicket. These are contrasting cricketers: the elegant, wristy Solanki, whose recent consistency had earned him an England recall, and Leatherdale the canny old pro. Solanki required 83 deliveries for his fifty, just 45 more for his hundred and then unleashed a fusillade of strokes before he was stumped for 115, including 14 fours. Leatherdale made 66 from 118 balls. A late flurry would have given Worcestershire a competitive total, but instead they collapsed again, just as they had at the start. Six wickets fell for 32 runs, with Averis completing a hat-trick, only the second in a domestic cup final, after Ken Higgs for Leicestershire in the 1974 Benson and Hedges. This one was split across two overs, which muted its impact.

With the pitch fundamentally flat and true, a total of 236 was unlikely to be enough against these opponents, and Spearman and Weston put on 141 for the first wicket to settle the destiny of the Trophy. Spearman, who normally starts quickly before accelerating, was more restrained but still hit nine fours in his 70 while Weston, released by Worcestershire in 2002, took comprehensive revenge by making an unbeaten 110 from 129 deliveries. As spectators drifted away, Gloucestershire eased home with 37 balls to spare to collect a seventh one-day trophy in six seasons (six cups and a League). Still, the game lasted almost two hours longer than the 2003 final, which concluded at 4.10. Despite losing Jonty Rhodes, Ian Harvey and Jack Russell since 2003, Gloucestershire were still too good. One-day cricket is supposed to be more capricious than the longer game, but when Gloucestershire are involved, matches are often about as balanced as Laurel and Hardy on a see-saw.

Man of the Match: V. S. Solanki.   *Attendance:* 20,824; *receipts:* £587,828.

Worcestershire

V. S. Solanki st Adshead b Ball	......	115
S. C. Moore c Adshead b Lewis	......	0
G. A. Hick c Adshead b Lewis	......	0
B. F. Smith c Hussey b Lewis	....	1
D. A. Leatherdale c Hancock b Averis	..	66
A. J. Bichel st Adshead b Ball	....	19
A. J. Hall c Hussey b Averis	....	1
G. J. Batty c Weston b Averis	....	1
*†S. J. Rhodes not out	....	1
M. S. Mason b Averis	....	1
R. W. Price not out	....	2
B 2, l-b 4, w 17, n-b 6	......	29

1/4 (2) 2/4 (3)   (9 wkts, 50 overs) 236
3/8 (4) 4/202 (1)
5/218 (5) 6/231 (6) 7/232 (8)
8/232 (7) 9/234 (10)   15 overs: 34-3

Bowling: Lewis 10–2–32–3; Averis 10–3–23–4; Alleyne 8–0–32–0; Gidman 7–1–40–0, Ball 9–0–65–2; Hussey 6–0–38–0.

Gloucestershire

W. P. C. Weston not out	....	110
C. M. Spearman c Rhodes b Batty	....	70
M. E. K. Hussey b Price	....	20
C. G. Taylor not out	....	22
B 3, l-b 2, w 6, n-b 4	......	15

1/141 (2) 2/171 (3)   (2 wkts, 43.5 overs) 237
15 overs: 83-0

A. P. R. Gidman, *M. W. Alleyne, †S. J. Adshead, M. C. J. Ball, T. H. C. Hancock, J. Lewis and J. M. M. Averis did not bat.

Bowling: Mason 10–0–40–0; Bichel 7–0–46–0; Hall 5–0–28–0; Leatherdale 2.5–0–25–0; Price 9–0–51–1, Batty 10–0–42–1.

Umpires: N. A. Mallender and P. Willey.

CHELTENHAM & GLOUCESTER TROPHY RECORDS

(Including Gillette Cup, 1963–80, and NatWest Trophy, 1981–2000)

65-over games in 1963; 60-over games 1964–98; 50-over games 1999–2004.

The first two rounds of the 2002 competition, played in 2001, are designated as 2001-02; similarly 2002-03 and 2003-04.

Batting

Highest individual scores: 268, A. D. Brown, Surrey v Glamorgan, The Oval, 2002; 206, A. I. Kallicharran, Warwickshire v Oxfordshire, Birmingham, 1984; 201, V. J. Wells, Leicestershire v Berkshire, Leicester, 1996; 180*, T. M. Moody, Worcestershire v Surrey, The Oval, 1994; 179, J. M. Dakin, Leicestershire v Wales, Swansea, 2001; 177, C. G Greenidge, Hampshire v Glamorgan, Southampton, 1975; 177, A. J. Wright, Gloucestershire v Scotland, Bristol, 1997; 176*, D. R. Clarke, Bedfordshire v Derbyshire Board XI, Dunstable, 2001-02. *In the final:* 146, G. Boycott, Yorkshire v Surrey, Lord's, 1965. (424 hundreds have been scored in the competition. The most hundreds in one tournament was 29 in 2002.)

Most runs: G. A. Gooch 2,547; R. A. Smith 2,377; G. A. Hick 2,337; K. J. Barnett 2,226; M. W. Gatting 2,148; A. J. Lamb 1,998; W. Larkins 1,990; C. W. J. Athey 1,988; D. L. Amiss 1,950.

Fastest hundred: G. D. Rose off 36 balls, Somerset v Devon, Torquay, 1990.

Most hundreds: R. A. Smith 8; G. A. Hick and C. L. Smith 7; G. A. Gooch 6; D. I. Gower, I. V. A. Richards and G. M. Turner 5.

Highest totals: 438-5, Surrey v Glamorgan, The Oval, 2002; 429, Glamorgan v Surrey, The Oval, 2002; 424-5, Buckinghamshire v Suffolk, Dinton, 2002-03; 413-4, Somerset v Devon, Torquay, 1990; 411-6, Yorkshire v Devon, Exmouth, 2004; 406-5, Leicestershire v Berkshire, Leicester, 1996; 404-3, Worcestershire v Devon, Worcester, 1987; 401-7, Gloucestershire v Buckinghamshire, Wing, 2003. *In the final:* 322-5, Warwickshire v Sussex, Lord's, 1993.

Highest total by a side batting first and losing: 327-8 (60 overs), Derbyshire v Sussex, Derby, 1997. *In the final:* 321-6 (60 overs), Sussex v Warwickshire, Lord's, 1993.

Highest totals by a side batting second: 429 (49.5 overs), Glamorgan lost to Surrey, The Oval, 2002; 350 (59.5 overs), Surrey lost to Worcestershire, The Oval, 1994; 339-9 (60 overs), Somerset lost to Warwickshire, Birmingham, 1995; 339 (49.1 overs), Kent lost to Somerset, Taunton, 2002. *In the final:* 322-5 (60 overs), Warwickshire beat Sussex, Lord's, 1993.

†Lowest completed totals: 39 (26.4 overs), Ireland v Sussex, Hove, 1985; 41 (20 overs), Cambridgeshire v Buckinghamshire, Cambridge, 1972; 41 (19.4 overs), Middlesex v Essex, Westcliff, 1972; 41 (36.1 overs), Shropshire v Essex, Wellington, 1974. *In the final:* 57 (27.2 overs), Essex v Lancashire, Lord's, 1996.

†Lowest total by a side batting first and winning: 98 (56.2 overs), Worcestershire v Durham, Chester-le-Street, 1968.

†Shortest innings: 10.1 overs (60-1), Worcestershire v Lancashire, Worcester, 1963.

†Matches rearranged on a reduced number of overs are excluded from the above.

Record partnerships for each wicket

311	for 1st	A. J. Wright and N. J. Trainor, Gloucestershire v Scotland at Bristol . .	1997
286	for 2nd	I. S. Anderson and A. Hill, Derbyshire v Cornwall at Derby	1986
309*	for 3rd	T. S. Curtis and T. M. Moody, Worcestershire v Surrey at The Oval . . .	1994
234*	for 4th	D. Lloyd and C. H. Lloyd, Lancashire v Gloucestershire at Manchester . .	1978
166	for 5th	M. A. Lynch and G. R. J. Roope, Surrey v Durham at The Oval	1982
226	for 6th	N. J. Llong and M. V. Fleming, Kent v Cheshire at Bowdon	1999
170	for 7th	D. R. Brown and A. F. Giles, Warwickshire v Essex at Birmingham . . .	2003
112	for 8th	A. L. Penberthy and J. E. Emburey, Northamptonshire v Lancashire at Manchester	1996
87	for 9th	M. A. Nash and A. E. Cordle, Glamorgan v Lincolnshire at Swansea . .	1974
81	for 10th	S. Turner and R. E. East, Essex v Yorkshire at Leeds	1982

Bowling

Most wickets: A. A. Donald 88; G. G. Arnold 81; C. A. Connor 80; J. Simmons 79.

Best bowling: 10.1-2-21-8, M. A. Holding, Derbyshire v Sussex, Hove, 1988; 11.1-2-31-8, D. L. Underwood, Kent v Scotland, Edinburgh, 1987; 9.5-0-66-8, S. R. G. Francis, Somerset v Derbyshire, Derby, 2004; 12-7-15-7, A. L. Dixon, Kent v Surrey, The Oval, 1967; 9.3-6-15-7, R. P. Lefebvre, Somerset v Devon, Torquay, 1990; 12-4-19-7, N. V. Radford, Worcestershire v Bedfordshire, Bedford, 1991; 9.5-1-27-7, D. Gough, Yorkshire v Ireland, Leeds, 1997. *In the final:* 6.2-1-18-6, G. Chapple, Lancashire v Essex, Lord's, 1996.

Most economical analysis: 12-9-3-1, J. Simmons, Lancashire v Suffolk, Bury St Edmunds, 1985.

Most expensive analysis: 9-0-108-3, S. D. Thomas, Glamorgan v Surrey, The Oval, 2002.

Four wickets in five balls: D. A. D. Sydenham, Surrey v Cheshire, Hoylake, 1964 (including hat-trick). There have been 13 other hat-tricks in the competition, including one in the final, by J. M. M. Averis, Gloucestershire v Worcestershire, Lord's, 2004.

Wicket-keeping and Fielding

Most dismissals: R. C. Russell 104 (87 ct, 17 st); S. J. Rhodes 82 (72 ct, 10 st); W. K. Hegg 68 (61 ct, 7 st); R. W. Taylor 66 (58 ct, 8 st); A. P. E. Knott 65 (59 ct, 6 st).

Most dismissals in an innings: 8 (all ct), D. J. Pipe, Worcestershire v Hertfordshire, Hertford, 2001; 7 (all ct), A. J. Stewart, Surrey v Glamorgan, Swansea, 1994.

Most catches by a fielder: M. C. J. Ball 30; G. A. Hick, W. Larkins and J. Simmons 27; M. W. Gatting and G. A. Gooch 26; G. Cook 25; N. H. Fairbrother and P. J. Sharpe 24.

Most catches by a fielder in an innings: There have been 11 instances of four catches in an innings.

Results

Largest victories in runs: Somerset by 346 runs v Devon, Torquay, 1990; Gloucestershire by 324 runs v Buckinghamshire, Wing, 2003; Sussex by 304 runs v Ireland, Belfast, 1996; Worcestershire by 299 runs v Devon, Worcester, 1987.

Victories by ten wickets (25): By Bedfordshire, Essex, Glamorgan, Hampshire (twice), Holland, Lancashire (twice), Middlesex, Northamptonshire, Nottinghamshire, Scotland, Somerset (twice), Surrey (twice), Sussex (twice), Warwickshire (twice), Yorkshire (five times).

Earliest finishes: both at 2.20 p.m. Worcestershire beat Lancashire by nine wickets at Worcester, 1963; Essex beat Middlesex by eight wickets at Westcliff, 1972.

Closest result: Leicestershire (204-9) beat Hampshire (204-9) by virtue of their higher total after 30 overs at Leicester in 1995. *In the final·* Derbyshire (235-6) beat Northamptonshire (235-9) on fewer wickets lost, 1981.

There have been 12 other instances of the scores finishing level. Six have involved Essex, who have won one and lost five.

Under competition rules the side which lost fewer wickets won; at Leicester in 1995, Leicestershire won by virtue of their higher total after 30 overs.

Match Awards

Most awards: G. A. Gooch and R. A. Smith 9; C. H. Lloyd and C. L. Smith 8.

WINNERS 1963–2004

Gillette Cup

		Man of the Match
1963	SUSSEX* beat Worcestershire by 14 runs.	N. Gifford†
1964	SUSSEX* beat Warwickshire* by eight wickets.	N. I. Thomson
1965	YORKSHIRE beat Surrey* by 175 runs.	G. Boycott
1966	WARWICKSHIRE* beat Worcestershire by five wickets.	R. W. Barber
1967	KENT* beat Somerset by 32 runs.	M. H. Denness
1968	WARWICKSHIRE* beat Sussex* by four wickets.	A. C. Smith
1969	YORKSHIRE beat Derbyshire* by 69 runs.	B. Leadbeater
1970	LANCASHIRE* beat Sussex by six wickets	H. Pilling
1971	LANCASHIRE* beat Kent by 24 runs.	Asif Iqbal†
1972	LANCASHIRE* beat Warwickshire by four wickets.	C. H. Lloyd
1973	GLOUCESTERSHIRE* beat Sussex by 40 runs.	A. S. Brown
1974	KENT* beat Lancashire by four wickets.	A. P. E. Knott
1975	LANCASHIRE* beat Middlesex by seven wickets.	C. H. Lloyd
1976	NORTHAMPTONSHIRE* beat Lancashire by four wickets.	P. Willey
1977	MIDDLESEX* beat Glamorgan by five wickets.	C. T. Radley
1978	SUSSEX* beat Somerset by five wickets.	P. W. G. Parker
1979	SOMERSET beat Northamptonshire* by 45 runs.	I. V. A. Richards
1980	MIDDLESEX* beat Surrey by seven wickets.	J. M. Brearley

NatWest Trophy

		Man of the Match
1981	DERBYSHIRE* beat Northamptonshire by losing fewer wickets with the scores level.	G. Cook†
1982	SURREY* beat Warwickshire by nine wickets.	D. J. Thomas
1983	SOMERSET beat Kent* by 24 runs.	V. J. Marks
1984	MIDDLESEX beat Kent* by four wickets.	C. T. Radley
1985	ESSEX beat Nottinghamshire* by one run.	B. R. Hardie
1986	SUSSEX* beat Lancashire by seven wickets.	D. A. Reeve
1987	NOTTINGHAMSHIRE* beat Northamptonshire by three wickets.	R. J. Hadlee
1988	MIDDLESEX* beat Worcestershire by three wickets.	M. R. Ramprakash
1989	WARWICKSHIRE beat Middlesex* by four wickets.	D. A. Reeve
1990	LANCASHIRE* beat Northamptonshire by seven wickets.	P. A. J. DeFreitas
1991	HAMPSHIRE* beat Surrey by four wickets.	R. A. Smith
1992	NORTHAMPTONSHIRE* beat Leicestershire by eight wickets.	A. Fordham
1993	WARWICKSHIRE* beat Sussex by five wickets.	Asif Din
1994	WORCESTERSHIRE* beat Warwickshire by eight wickets.	T. M. Moody
1995	WARWICKSHIRE beat Northamptonshire* by four wickets.	D. A. Reeve
1996	LANCASHIRE beat Essex* by 129 runs.	G. Chapple
1997	ESSEX* beat Warwickshire by nine wickets.	S. G. Law
1998	LANCASHIRE* beat Derbyshire by nine wickets.	I. D. Austin
1999	GLOUCESTERSHIRE beat Somerset* by 50 runs.	R. C. Russell
2000	GLOUCESTERSHIRE* beat Warwickshire by 22 runs (D/L method).	A. A. Donald†

Cheltenham & Gloucester Trophy

2001	SOMERSET* beat Leicestershire by 41 runs.	K. A. Parsons
2002	YORKSHIRE beat Somerset* by six wickets.	M. T. G. Elliott
2003	GLOUCESTERSHIRE* beat Worcestershire by seven wickets.	I. J. Harvey
2004	GLOUCESTERSHIRE* beat Worcestershire by eight wickets.	V. S. Solanki†

* Won toss. † On losing side.

TEAM RECORDS 1963–2004

	Rounds reached				Matches		
	W	F	SF	QF	P	W	L
Derbyshire	1	3	5	14	86*	45	41
Durham	0	0	0	2	52	18	34
Essex	2	3	6	17	94	54	40
Glamorgan	0	1	4	16	90	48	42
Gloucestershire	5	5	9	19	100	62	38
Hampshire	1	1	10	22	104	63	41
Kent	2	5	8	17	98	58	40
Lancashire	7	10	18	25	123	88	35
Leicestershire	0	2	5	17	90	48	42
Middlesex	4	6	13	23	110	72	38
Northamptonshire	2	7	10	22	105	65	40
Nottinghamshire	1	2	3	13	87	46	41
Somerset	3	7	12	20	107	68	39
Surrey	1	4	12	25	108*	67	41
Sussex	4	8	13	20	106	68	38
Warwickshire	5	11	19	25	124	87	37
Worcestershire	1	6	12	18	101	60	41
Yorkshire	3	3	9	20	97	58	39

* Derbyshire and Surrey totals each include a bowling contest after their first-round matches were abandoned in 1991; Derbyshire lost to Hertfordshire and Surrey beat Oxfordshire.

MINOR TEAM RECORDS

From 1964 to 1979 the previous season's top five Minor Counties were invited to take part in the competition. The tournamenet gradually expanded to embrace 60 teams by 1999, including all 20 Minor Counties and the County Board XIs. In 2005, only ten Minor Counties will play, plus Ireland, Scotland, Denmark and Holland and the first-class counties.

Wins by a minor team over a first-class county (13): Durham v Yorkshire (by five wickets), Harrogate, 1973; Lincolnshire v Glamorgan (by six wickets), Swansea, 1974; Hertfordshire v Essex (by 33 runs), 2nd round, Hitchin, 1976; Shropshire v Yorkshire (by 37 runs), Telford, 1984; Durham v Derbyshire (by seven wickets), Derby, 1985; Buckinghamshire v Somerset (by seven runs), High Wycombe, 1987; Cheshire v Northamptonshire (by one wicket), Chester, 1988; Hertfordshire v Derbyshire (2–1 in a bowling contest after the match was abandoned), Bishop's Stortford, 1991; Scotland v Worcestershire (by four runs), Edinburgh, 1998; Holland v Durham (by five wickets), Amstelveen, 1999; Herefordshire v Middlesex (by three wickets), Kingsland, 2001; Devon v Leicestershire (by losing fewer wickets with the scores level), Exmouth, 2004; Ireland v Surrey (by five wickets), Clontarf, 2004.

THE BENSON AND HEDGES CUP

The Benson and Hedges Cup, founded nine years after the Gillette Cup, was the junior of county cricket's two limited-overs knockouts. Matches were 55 overs a side until 1996, when they were cut to 50. For 1999 only, the top eight sides from the previous year's County Championship competed for the B&H Super Cup. The tournament was replaced by the Twenty20 in 2003, leaving Lancashire, who won four times, as the outstanding county.

		Gold Award
1972	LEICESTERSHIRE* beat Yorkshire by five wickets.	J. C. Balderstone
1973	KENT* beat Worcestershire by 39 runs.	Asif Iqbal
1974	SURREY* beat Leicestershire by 27 runs.	J. H. Edrich
1975	LEICESTERSHIRE beat Middlesex* by five wickets.	N. M. McVicker
1976	KENT* beat Worcestershire by 43 runs.	G. W. Johnson
1977	GLOUCESTERSHIRE* beat Kent by 64 runs.	A. W. Stovold
1978	KENT beat Derbyshire* by six wickets.	R. A. Woolmer
1979	ESSEX beat Surrey* by 35 runs.	G. A. Gooch
1980	NORTHAMPTONSHIRE* beat Essex by six runs.	A. J. Lamb
1981	SOMERSET* beat Surrey by seven wickets.	I. V. A. Richards
1982	SOMERSET* beat Nottinghamshire by nine wickets.	V. J. Marks
1983	MIDDLESEX beat Essex* by four runs.	C. T. Radley
1984	LANCASHIRE* beat Warwickshire by six wickets.	J. Abrahams
1985	LEICESTERSHIRE* beat Essex by five wickets.	P. Willey
1986	MIDDLESEX beat Kent by two runs.	J. E. Emburey
1987	YORKSHIRE* beat Northamptonshire, having taken more wickets with the scores tied.	J. D. Love
1988	HAMPSHIRE* beat Derbyshire by seven wickets.	S. T. Jefferies
1989	NOTTINGHAMSHIRE beat Essex* by three wickets.	R. T. Robinson
1990	LANCASHIRE beat Worcestershire* by 69 runs.	M. Watkinson
1991	WORCESTERSHIRE beat Lancashire* by 65 runs.	G. A. Hick
1992	HAMPSHIRE beat Kent* by 41 runs.	R. A. Smith
1993	DERBYSHIRE beat Lancashire* by six runs.	D. G. Cork
1994	WARWICKSHIRE* beat Worcestershire by six runs.	P. A. Smith
1995	LANCASHIRE beat Kent* by 35 runs.	P. A. de Silva†
1996	LANCASHIRE* beat Northamptonshire by 31 runs.	I. D. Austin
1997	SURREY beat Kent* by eight wickets.	B. C. Hollioake
1998	ESSEX beat Leicestershire* by 192 runs.	P. J. Prichard
1999‡	GLOUCESTERSHIRE* beat Yorkshire by 124 runs.	M. W. Alleyne
2000	GLOUCESTERSHIRE beat Glamorgan* by seven wickets.	M. P. Maynard†
2001	SURREY* beat Gloucestershire by 47 runs.	B. C. Hollioake
2002	WARWICKSHIRE* beat Essex by five wickets.	I. R. Bell

* Won toss. † On losing side. ‡ Super Cup.

TOTESPORT LEAGUE, 2004

The old Sunday league appeared to limp through 2004, under its 13th different name, and its eighth in nine years. The Twenty20 stole most of its

thunder (though not all the rain); its compromise 45-over formula pleased almost no one; and the mix of Sunday, floodlit and weekday daytime matches confused more or less everyone.

However, it did have a sponsor once again: cricket's first nationalised industry – the once staid Horserace Totalisator Board, now given a fashionable lower-case makeover as totesport. The league also had a dominant team, who thought hard about the peculiar requirements of the cricket, and honed them something close to perfection.

This was Glamorgan, who regained the title they won two years earlier with the utmost ease. They won 11 of their first 13 matches and clinched the title on August 22, in the 13th at Colwyn Bay when their captain Robert Croft scored a century to floor their nearest rivals Lancashire.

With nothing at stake for them, Glamorgan lost their last three fixtures. In two of these, however, there was a considerable amount at stake for some of cricket's punting fraternity who are customers of one of totesport's rivals, the internet betting exchange Betfair. First, the champions lost an amazing match to Kent, whose last-wicket pair put on 28 to clinch a low-scoring match, with the New Zealander Ian Butler hitting the six he needed off the last ball. This cost one gambler £49,950, though his potential winnings were only £50.

Robert Croft

And more than £1m was staked on Betfair for the final match against Essex, who needed to win to avoid relegation and duly did so, against much-weakened opposition. Some punters cottoned on to Glamorgan's selection plans in advance.

Mostly, though, the Welsh conquered the English at will. Their strategy was built round two pinch-hitters, Croft and Alex Wharf. One or other of these came good in seven of Glamorgan's wins. Otherwise, they had the experience and quality of the two Matthews, Elliott and Maynard. And their attack, which had Croft and Dean Cosker as highly effective spin back-up to a penetrative front line, used the white ball far more skilfully than anyone else.

Lancashire, like Glamorgan, won their first four games, culminating in a five-wicket win when these two giants clashed at Old Trafford. But Lancashire fell to pieces in nearly all the competitions after May and, though they recovered in this one, they had too much ground to make up.

Below these two, confusion reigned, with several teams uncertain whether they were contesting the title or relegation. Shane Warne's Hampshire started and finished well to be third, ahead of Northamptonshire, who had fantasies of their first-ever League title in mid-July after downing Glamorgan, then lost five in a row to flirt with the drop.

The relegated three in the end were unusually distinguished: Warwickshire, the county champions, Kent, the only team never previously out of the top grade in either divisional competition, and Surrey, the 2003 League champions, who never overcame a dismal start. They are to be replaced for 2005 by Middlesex, Worcestershire and Nottinghamshire. Middlesex, inspired by the batting form of Paul Weekes, took a commanding lead for the second division title after winning nine games out of ten between the start of May and mid-July.

Scotland, in their second League season, took no inspiration from the Welsh and again came last, without the early excitements that enlivened 2003. They lost their first seven, and beat only Durham and (in the final match) Derbyshire, though they had very near misses at Taunton and Worcester.

Overall, crowds for League matches were believed to have fallen slightly compared to 2003. Pending a final audit from the ECB, the total attendance was thought to have dropped back below the 400,000 mark, due in part to the worse weather.

But the tournament is in any case heading for yet another revamp in 2006. It will revert to the 40-over format, which most counties believe is more crowd-friendly, and be staged only in the second half of the season, after the break for the Twenty20. Instead of three-up and three-down, two counties will be automatically promoted and relegated, and there will be a play-off between the team that finishes seventh in the first division and the one finishing third in the second.

TOTESPORT LEAGUE

Division One	M	W	L	T	NR	Pts	Net run-rate
1 – Glamorgan Dragons (*5*)	16	11	5	0	0	44	4.07
2 – Lancashire Lightning (*1*)	16	9	6	0	1	38	–3.39
3 – Hampshire Hawks (*3*)	16	7	6	0	3	34	0.80
4 – Northamptonshire Steelbacks (*2*)	16	8	8	0	0	32	1.85
5 – Gloucestershire Gladiators (*2*)	16	7	7	1	1	32	3.33
6 – Essex Eagles (*3*)	16	6	6	1	3	32	0.99
7 – Warwickshire Bears (*4*)	16	7	8	0	1	30	4.59
8 – Kent Spitfires (*6*)	16	5	9	0	2	24	–6.46
9 – Surrey Lions (*1*)	16	4	9	0	3	22	–7.26

Division Two

	M	W	L	T	NR	Pts	Net run-rate
1 – Middlesex Crusaders (4)......	18	12	6	0	0	48	−0.11
2 – Worcestershire Royals (9).....	18	11	5	0	2	48	14.16
3 – Nottinghamshire Outlaws (5)...	18	9	4	1	4	46	9.73
4 – Yorkshire Phoenix (8).......	18	10	6	0	2	44	2.76
5 – Sussex Sharks (8)..........	18	9	7	1	1	40	7.90
6 – Durham Dynamos (7)........	18	9	7	0	2	40	2.49
7 – Leicestershire Foxes (7)......	18	7	8	0	3	34	−0.10
8 – Somerset Sabres (9).........	18	6	11	0	1	26	−1.66
9 – Derbyshire Scorpions (6).....	18	5	12	0	1	22	−16.04
10 – Scottish Saltires (10)........	18	2	14	0	2	12	−17.56

2003 positions are shown in brackets: Division One in bold, Division Two in italic.

The bottom three teams in Division One are relegated for 2005, the top three teams in Division Two are promoted. The bottom four counties in Division Two (excluding Scotland) play each other in the second round of the 2005 Cheltenham and Gloucester Trophy.

When two or more teams finished with an equal number of points, the positions were decided by a) most wins, b) higher net run-rate (runs scored per 100 balls minus runs conceded per 100 balls).

Prize money

Division One
£54,000 for winners: GLAMORGAN.
£27,000 for runners-up: LANCASHIRE.

Division Two
£20,000 for winners: MIDDLESEX.
£11,000 for runners-up: WORCESTERSHIRE.

Winners of each match (both divisions): £600.

Leading run-scorers: *P. N. Weekes* 807, M. T. G. Elliott 686, *V. S. Solanki* 653, *M. J. Prior* 641, E. T. Smith 618, *M. P. Maynard* 612, *M. W. Goodwin* 600, *J. E. R. Gallian* 580, N. V. Knight 568, *O. A. Shah* 561, *C. J. Adams* 557.

Leading wicket-takers: *S. J. Cook* 39, J. Louw 34, *C. W. Henderson* and *R. S. C. Martin-Jenkins* 28, A. G. Wharf 26, *S. C. G. MacGill* and G. R. Napier 25, *N. Killeen*, J. Lewis and S. I. Mahmood 24, A. P. Davies and G. P. Swann 23.

Most economical bowlers (runs per over, minimum 50 overs): *M. A. Ealham* 3.35, *N. Killeen* 3.56, M. S. Kasprowicz 3.65, G. P. Swann 3.77, A. D. Mascarenhas 3.84, *C. E. Dagnall* 3.86, J. Louw 3.93, *G. Welch* 3.95, *G. J. Smith* 4.00.

Leading wicket-keepers: *B. J. M. Scott* 32 (24 ct, 8 st), *P. A. Nixon* 31 (24 ct, 7 st), S. J. Adshead 24 (18 ct, 6 st), J. S. Foster 22 (20 ct, 2 st), *A. Pratt* 20 (18 ct, 2 st), *S. J. Rhodes* 20 (16 ct, 4 st), *L. D. Sutton* 20 (19 st, 1 st).

Leading fielders: D. J. Sales and *P. N. Weekes* 12, G. Chapple, *J. E. R. Gallian*, K. A. Parsons and *D. I. Stevens* 11, *G. J. Pratt* 10.

Players who appeared in Division Two are shown in italics.

" On the other hand, one couldn't help feeling that if West Indies was the answer, it must have been a damn silly question."

ICC Champions Trophy, page 515.

SUMMARY OF RESULTS, 2004

DIVISION ONE

	Essex	Glamorgan	Gloucestershire	Hampshire	Kent	Lancashire	Northamptonshire	Surrey	Warwickshire
Essex	–	W	T	W	W	N	W	N	W
Glamorgan	W	–	W	W	L	W	W	W	L
Gloucestershire	L	L	–	L	W	W	L	W	W
Hampshire	W	L	W	–	N	W	L	N	W
Kent	N	L	W	L	–	W	L	L	W
Lancashire	W	W	L	W	W	–	L	W	W
Northamptonshire	W	W	L	L	W	L	–	W	L
Surrey	W	L	L	N	L	L	W	–	W
Warwickshire	W	L	N	L	W	W	W	W	–

DIVISION TWO

	Derbyshire	Durham	Leicestershire	Middlesex	Nottinghamshire	Scotland	Somerset	Sussex	Worcestershire	Yorkshire
Derbyshire	–	W	N	L	L	W	L	L	W	L
Durham	W	–	N	W	W	W	L	W	W	N
Leicestershire	W	W	–	L	L	W	N	W	L	L
Middlesex	W	W	W	–	L	W	W	L	L	W
Nottinghamshire	L	L	W	L	–	W	W	N	W	W
Scotland	W	W	L	W	N	–	L	L	L	L
Somerset	W	L	W	L	L	W	–	L	L	L
Sussex	W	W	L	W	T	N	W	–	W	L
Worcestershire	W	L	W	W	N	W	W	W	–	L
Yorkshire	L	W	L	L	N	W	W	W	L	–

Home teams listed on left, away teams across top; results are for home teams. W = Won, L = Lost, T = Tied, N = No result.

DIVISION ONE

ESSEX

At Chelmsford, May 3. **Essex won by six runs.** Toss: Warwickshire. **Essex 89-2** (10 overs) (A. Flower 40*, N. Hussain 40*); **Warwickshire 83-6** (10 overs). *Essex 4 pts.*

Reduced to ten overs a side.

Miserable bank-holiday weather eventually abated, allowing a ten-over match in bright afternoon sunshine. Hussain then sparkled in what turned out to be his last home appearance before retirement. Playing with great fluency, he scored off 19 of the 21 balls he faced. Warwickshire lost wickets steadily against a disciplined attack, and needed 20 from the last over, bowled by Danish Kaneria. Jonathan Trott hit the first ball for six, but could not keep up the momentum. Middlebrook was the only bowler in the match to bowl two successive overs.

At Chelmsford, June 8 (day/night). **Essex won by 35 runs.** Toss: Essex. **Essex 211-4** (45 overs) (W. I. Jefferson 32, A. Flower 41, R. C. Irani 31, J. S. Foster 46*, R. S. Bopara 40*); **Hampshire 176** (41 overs) (J. P. Crawley 70*, M. J. Clarke 42; D. Gough 3-19). *Essex 4 pts.*

Essex ended a run of three League defeats to beat in-form Hampshire. Five Essex batsmen reached 30, though none made 50. Irani, on 31, suffered a back spasm and called for a runner. Two balls later, he instinctively set off for a single, hesitated, and – though runner and non-striker made their ground – was run out. Warne's nine overs cost 62. Gough then removed both Hampshire openers for ducks (there were three more in the innings), before Crawley and Clarke added 65 in 14 overs. Crawley hung on, but ran out of partners.

At Chelmsford, June 28 (day/night). **Tied.** Toss: Gloucestershire. **Gloucestershire 234-7** (45 overs) (W. P. C. Weston 65, M. G. N. Windows 30, C. G. Taylor 56, A. P. R. Gidman 34*; A. J. Clarke 3-40); **Essex 234-8** (45 overs) (W. I. Jefferson 34, R. S. Bopara 55, R. C. Irani 30, A. P. Grayson 39, G. R. Napier 32; M. C. J. Ball 3-59). *Essex 2 pts, Gloucestershire 2 pts.*

Essex, with four wickets in hand, began the last over requiring five runs. But Ball maintained a superb length, conceded just three off the first four deliveries and then held a fine return catch to dismiss Middlebrook. It meant Cowan needed two from the last ball, but he picked out Taylor at long-on, and Grayson was run out going for the second that would have won the match. It was the 12th time Essex had tied a League game – more than any other county.

At Southend, July 25. **Essex won by 30 runs.** Toss: Essex. **Essex 168** (44.2 overs) (J. S. Foster 39; J. Louw 4-30, B. J. Phillips 3-21); **Northamptonshire 138** (42.3 overs) (T. W. Roberts 33; G. R. Napier 4-23). *Essex 4 pts.*

A two-paced wicket and heavy cloud cover gave bowlers assistance throughout. Essex lost their first three wickets on 35 and then stumbled to 73 for six before a stand of 48 between Foster and Grayson. The game was evenly poised when Northamptonshire stood at 96 for five, but Napier scuppered the lower order with three wickets in three overs.

At Chelmsford, August 9 (day/night). **No result** (D/L method). Toss: Lancashire. **Essex 107-0** (21 overs) (W. I. Jefferson 49*, R. C. Irani 49*) v **Lancashire.** *Essex 2 pts, Lancashire 2 pts.*

Lancashire's target was revised to 110 in 13 overs.

Gloom meant the floodlights were used from the start, before the rain arrived. One straight drive by Irani hit Chapple on the ankle and rebounded to fell umpire Llong with a blow to the leg. Both recovered quickly, but the weather did not. A few dogged spectators waited four hours before the game was finally called off.

At Colchester, August 22. **Essex won by 35 runs.** Toss: Essex. **Essex 267-6** (45 overs) (W. I. Jefferson 97, R. C. Irani 98; A. G. R. Loudon 4-48); **Kent 232-7** (45 overs) (E. T. Smith 61, D. P. Fulton 39, A. G. R. Loudon 52, M. G. Bevan 52; G. R. Napier 4-25). *Essex 4 pts.*

Jefferson and Irani put on a dazzling 196 for the first wicket as Essex amassed a challenging total. Irani hit six sixes to Jefferson's two, though Jefferson scored noticeably quicker. Loudon's four for 48 was a one-day best. With three fifties from the top four, Kent reached 217 for two, but they were always behind the asking-rate. Five wickets fell for 14 runs in the final desperate thrash. Kent slipped deeper into trouble in the relegation zone; Essex inched closer to safety.

At Chelmsford, August 25 (day/night). **No result.** Toss: Essex. **Essex 135-5** (25.1 overs) (W. I. Jefferson 61*; M. P. Bicknell 3-21) v **Surrey.** *Essex 2 pts, Surrey 2 pts.*

Reduced to 32 overs a side.

With both counties in danger of dropping into the second division, neither was happy with a no-result. Surrey captain Batty believed conditions could have allowed a shortened reply under the lights, but his counterpart Irani – and, after much deliberation, the umpires – thought the run-ups too wet. In the little play there was, Jefferson hit another fifty and Batty held three catches behind the stumps, all off Bicknell.

At Chelmsford, September 6 (day/night). **Essex won by 163 runs.** Toss: Essex. **Essex 316-4** (45 overs) (W. I. Jefferson 39, R. C. Irani 158*, A. Flower 54); **Glamorgan 153** (26.3 overs) (M. J. Powell 54). *Essex 4 pts.*

Glamorgan, already champions, had nothing to lose – and fielded a weakened team. Word got round and Betfair, the internet betting exchange, reported more than £1m profit on this game. Essex would have been relegated had they not won, but their fifth home victory, their biggest-ever in the League, kept them up. Essex's total of 316 was also their League-best, beating the 310 they took off Glamorgan in 1983. Irani faced 145 balls in his imperious unbeaten 158, his highest one-day score, which included 17 fours and three sixes. Essex hit 54 from the last three overs, while Glamorgan lost a wicket to the first ball of their reply.

GLAMORGAN

At Cardiff, May 3. **Glamorgan won by seven wickets.** Toss: Glamorgan. **Northamptonshire 233-7** (45 overs) (G. P. Swann 66, U. Afzaal 61, D. J. Sales 53); **Glamorgan 234-3** (39.5 overs) (M. T. G. Elliott 112*, M. J. Powell 31, M. P. Maynard 71*). *Glamorgan 4 pts.*

County debut: M. van Jaarsveld (Northamptonshire).

This comfortable victory was Glamorgan's third win in three starts. Elliott lifted his aggregate in those games to 272 runs without being dismissed, sharing an unbroken fourth-wicket stand of 169 with Maynard. Swann had dominated the start of Northamptonshire's innings and reached 50 from 40 balls, but on a decent pitch Glamorgan made light work of their target.

At Cardiff, May 16. **Glamorgan won by six wickets.** Toss: Essex. **Essex 162-9** (45 overs) (W. I. Jefferson 30, J. D. Middlebrook 40, A. P. Cowan 31; A. P. Davies 3-35, A. G. Wharf 3-24); **Glamorgan 163-4** (37.5 overs) (A. G. Wharf 41, M. P. Maynard 45*, D. L. Hemp 31*). *Glamorgan 4 pts.*

Maynard and Hemp, sharing an unbroken 70-run partnership, guided Glamorgan to a fourth successive League win. After his prolific start to the season, Elliott was dismissed first ball. Earlier, Essex had made scant use of a good pitch. A mid-innings wobble saw them veer from 79 for three to 85 for six and, although Middlebrook and Cowan added 71, Essex's total was well below par.

At Swansea, June 6. **Glamorgan won by 33 runs.** Toss: Gloucestershire. **Glamorgan 250** (45 overs) (R. D. B. Croft 68, M. T. G. Elliott 33, M. P. Maynard 67; J. Lewis 3-53, M. W. Alleyne 3-52); **Gloucestershire 217** (39.3 overs) (M. G. N. Windows 55, Shoaib Malik 52, C. G. Taylor 32, Shabbir Ahmed 42). *Glamorgan 4 pts.*

Croft struck 68 from 45 balls as Glamorgan raced to 95 for one in the 16th over. Then Maynard, with just one boundary in his first 50, turned the start into a solid total. Gloucestershire stumbled to 27 for three before Windows and Shoaib Malik gave them a glimmer with a 93-run partnership. But both fell to the left-arm spin of Cosker and, though a robust 42 from 20 balls by Shabbir Ahmed was briefly threatening, Gloucestershire were well short.

At Cardiff, June 27. **Glamorgan won by nine wickets** (D/L method). Toss: Surrey. **Surrey 197-8** (45 overs) (S. A. Newman 43, J. N. Batty 51; A. P. Davies 3-36, R. D. B. Croft 3-34); **Glamorgan 94-1** (8.2 overs) (R. D. B. Croft 46, I. J. Thomas 38*). *Glamorgan 4 pts.*

Glamorgan's target was revised to 94 in 15 overs.

Glamorgan blazed to their seventh win out of eight after Croft and Thomas launched a ferocious assault on the revised target. After a modest four from the first over, they looted 53 off the next three as Croft struck seven successive fours. Surrey had subsided to 51 for four before Batty and Hollioake dragged them past 100. Even so, a total of 197 never looked adequate.

At Cardiff, July 28 (day/night). **Glamorgan won by seven wickets.** Toss: Hampshire. **Hampshire 174-9** (45 overs) (N. Pothas 40; A. P. Davies 4-30, R. D. B. Croft 3-30); **Glamorgan 176-3** (34.4 overs) (M. T. G. Elliott 81*, M. J. Powell 36, M. P. Maynard 31*). *Glamorgan 4 pts.*

Hampshire began disastrously as Davies removed the top four for 41, itself a slight improvement on 11 for three. The middle and lower order managed to set some sort of target, but it was no problem to a team that had mastered this form of cricket. Glamorgan lost Croft in the first over, but Elliott guided them to an emphatic victory, assisted by Powell (who scooped a no-ball over his and the wicket-keeper's head for a one-bounce four) and Maynard.

GLAMORGAN v LANCASHIRE

At Colwyn Bay, August 22. Glamorgan won by five wickets. Toss: Glamorgan. Glamorgan 4 pts. County debut: M. L. Lewis.

In front of a capacity 4,294 crowd at their northern outpost, Glamorgan made sure of their third League title by beating their nearest rivals, Lancashire. (It was the first time they had clinched the crown on Welsh soil: in both 1993 and 2002 celebrations began after winning at Canterbury.) As he had all summer, Croft led by example, dismissing Lancashire's two highest scorers before striking the second League century of his career. On a fast-scoring ground, Mongia and Schofield had put on a 96-run stand to rescue Lancashire from 62 for four. Glamorgan then slipped to 79 for three before Croft and Maynard steered them to 200 – and close to victory. These two, as well as Dale, who hit the winning runs, had all played in that 1993 game against Kent. There was one other survivor: Carl Hooper was on the losing side then as now.

Lancashire

M. J. Chilton c Powell b Harrison	17	K. W. Hogg c Croft b Lewis	15
I. J. Sutcliffe c Hemp b Lewis	10	†J. J. Haynes not out	4
D. G. Cork c S. D. Thomas b Harrison	7	B 8, l-b 3, w 11	22
D. Mongia c Hemp b Croft	58		
*C. L. Hooper c Dale b S. D. Thomas	5	1/25 (2) 2/38 (3)　　(7 wkts, 45 overs)	218
C. P. Schofield c Lewis b Croft	48	3/38 (1) 4/62 (5)	
G. Chapple not out	32	5/158 (4) 6/173 (6) 7/193 (8)	

S. I. Mahmood and P. J. Martin did not bat.

Bowling: Lewis 9–2–38–2; Harrison 8–1–34–2; Wharf 9–2–42–0; S. D. Thomas 3–0–15–1; Croft 9–0–42–2; Dale 7–0–36–0.

Glamorgan

*R. D. B. Croft b Mahmood	106	A. Dale not out	4
I. J. Thomas c Haynes b Martin	0	L-b 8, w 4, n-b 2	14
A. G. Wharf c Chilton b Martin	26		
M. J. Powell b Cork	0	1/9 (2) 2/74 (3)　　(5 wkts, 40.2 overs)	219
M. P. Maynard c Chapple b Hogg	63	3/79 (4) 4/200 (5)	
D. L. Hemp not out	6	5/209 (1)	

†M. A. Wallace, S. D. Thomas, M. L. Lewis and D. S. Harrison did not bat.

Bowling: Martin 9–1–43–2; Chapple 5–0–33–0; Cork 7–0–42–1; Mahmood 8.2–1–42–1; Hooper 3–0–10–0; Schofield 2–0–18–0; Hogg 6–0–23–1.

Umpires: V. A. Holder and N. A. Mallender.

GLAMORGAN v KENT

At Cardiff, August 29. Kent won by one wicket (D/L method). Toss: Glamorgan. Kent 4 pts.

Kent won an amazing victory when Ian Butler hit the last ball for six, the only shot that would do. It left Glamorgan unperturbed – they were already champions. But it threw a lifeline to Kent in their effort to avoid relegation, and it was a disaster for one poor (or maybe greedy) punter. After they lost their ninth wicket, a Kent win was being traded at odds of 999-1 on the betting exchange Betfair. Several happy punters collected, but one customer is known to have been on the wrong end, and lost £49,950 trying to win £50. Kent were 35 short of their target with three overs to go, then lost their ninth wicket, needing 28 to win in the last two overs. Butler hit hard, but as he faced the final ball – bowled by Adrian Dale in his last game before retiring – they were still six short. Butler lofted the full toss on to the roof of the dressing-rooms. Yet his was not the performance of the match: Wharf, getting sharp movement and varying his pace cleverly, ended with the cheapest six-for in limited-overs cricket; his full figures were 5–3–5–6, and from his last 22 balls he took five for two. Rain interrupted the Glamorgan innings in the ninth over and restricted the game to 25 overs a side, but Duckworth/Lewis calculations did not alter Kent's target.

Glamorgan

*R. D. B. Croft c Jones b Joseph	8	A. Dale not out	3
M. T. G. Elliott c Dennington b Joseph		I. J. Thomas not out	0
A. G. Wharf b Butler	44	L-b 7, w 4	11
M. J. Powell c Walker b Butler	0		
M. P. Maynard c Loudon b Ferley	2	1/10 (1) 2/47 (3) (7 wkts, 25 overs) 142
D. L. Hemp c Ferley b Dennington	40	3/47 (4) 4/56 (5)
†M. A. Wallace run out	16	5/115 (2) 6/123 (6) 7/141 (7)

M. L. Lewis and D. S. Harrison did not bat.

Bowling: Butler 5–1–11–2; Joseph 5–0–34–2; Dennington 4 0 30–1; Walker 3–0–19–0; Ferley 5–0–22–1; Loudon 3–0–19–0.

Kent

E. T. Smith c Hemp b Wharf	36	I. G. Butler not out	18
*D. P. Fulton lbw b Wharf	18	R. H. Joseph not out	3
A. G. R. Loudon run out	2		
R. W. T. Key b Wharf	5	B 8, l-b 1, w 1, n-b 2	12
M. J. Walker b Lewis	29		
†G. O. Jones b Wharf	0	1/46 (1) 2/50 (3) (9 wkts, 25 overs) 143
M. A. Carberry c Wallace b Wharf	19	3/61 (2) 4/64 (4)
R. S. Ferley c Wallace b Wharf	0	5/64 (6) 6/104 (7)
M. J. Dennington b Dale	1	7/104 (8) 8/113 (9) 9/115 (5)

Bowling: Lewis 5–0–39–1; Harrison 3–0–19–0; Wharf 5–3–5–6; Dale 5–0–34–1; Croft 4–0–19–0; Thomas 3–0–18–0.

Umpires: G. I. Burgess and T. E. Jesty.

At Cardiff, August 30. **Warwickshire won by four wickets.** Toss: Glamorgan. **Glamorgan 211-7** (45 overs) (A. G. Wharf 44, M. P. Maynard 63, D. L. Hemp 38); **Warwickshire 213-6** (41 overs) (N. V. Knight 40, I. J. L. Trott 45, I. R. Bell 35, G. B. Hogg 44). *Warwickshire 4 pts.*

Glamorgan, with little to play for, fielded a weakened team and suffered a second home defeat in two days. Warwickshire, who had survival on their minds, obtained special dispensation from Cricket Australia to include Hogg, who was in their Champions Trophy squad. On a slow pitch, Glamorgan scored steadily, with Maynard moving past 8,000 League runs. But 211 was not enough for an attack without Kasprowicz, Wharf and Davies to defend, and victory came with four overs in hand. To be sure of staying up, Warwickshire had to beat Gloucestershire in their final match.

GLOUCESTERSHIRE

At Bristol, May 2. **Glamorgan won by eight wickets.** Toss: Glamorgan. **Gloucestershire 213-8** (45 overs) (C. M. Spearman 46, M. G. N. Windows 79); **Glamorgan 216-2** (37.2 overs) (R. D. B. Croft 56, M. T. G. Elliott 91*, M. J. Powell 41). *Glamorgan 4 pts.*

County debut: Shabbir Ahmed (Gloucestershire).

Elliott shared stands of 98 with Croft and 92 with Powell as Glamorgan coasted home. Elliott's unbeaten 91 contained a six and 11 fours and came from 116 balls. Windows and Taylor put on 66 for Gloucestershire's fifth wicket to ensure a reasonable score, but they defended uncharacteristically badly.

At Bristol, May 16. **Gloucestershire won by 42 runs.** Toss: Gloucestershire. **Gloucestershire 257-6** (45 overs) (W. P. C. Weston 53, A. P. R. Gidman 70, M. G. N. Windows 46); **Surrey 215-9** (45 overs) (M. R. Ramprakash 73, R. Clarke 41, A. J. Hollioake 33). *Gloucestershire 4 pts.*

An elegant 73 from 91 balls by Ramprakash failed to rouse Surrey, who were still without a win in all cricket in 2004. On a surface faster than most Bristol pitches, Gloucestershire scored consistently down the order to set a tricky target. Ramprakash kept Surrey in the frame, but when he was bowled behind his legs by Shoaib Malik, self-confidence seeped away, in part because of two accurate throws from Taylor that ran out Hollioake and Batty.

At Bristol, May 23. **Hampshire won by four wickets.** Toss: Gloucestershire. **Gloucestershire 240-5** (45 overs) (C. M. Spearman 57, W. P. C. Weston 75, Shoaib Malik 51; S. K. Warne 4-27); **Hampshire 244-6** (43.3 overs) (J. R. C. Hamblin 42, S. K. Warne 48, M. G. Dighton 74). *Hampshire 4 pts.*

County debut: M. G. Dighton (Hampshire).

Warne flew in from Zimbabwe after Australia's Tests were cancelled – and promptly starred with ball and bat. The Gloucestershire openers had put on 88 when he had Spearman stumped in his first over and – unlike the other Hampshire bowlers – continued to cause trouble. Warne grabbed four for 27 from his nine overs; the only other wicket to fall was a run-out. In the Hampshire reply, he smashed a run-a-ball 48 and shared a partnership of 68 with the Tasmanian Michael Dighton, who was standing in for Michael Clarke.

At Gloucester, June 13. **Northamptonshire won by 109 runs.** Toss: Northamptonshire. **Northamptonshire 266-6** (45 overs) (T. W. Roberts 88, U. Afzaal 69; Shoaib Malik 3-28); **Gloucestershire 157** (36.4 overs) (M. G. N. Windows 33, M. W. Alleyne 30; G. P. Swann 4-21, J. F. Brown 3-27). *Northamptonshire 4 pts.*

Gloucestershire, the one-day specialists, were left two points adrift at the bottom of the table after slumping to a fifth defeat in six games. On a dry surface, they failed to cope with Northamptonshire's three spinners, who between them had figures of eight for 66 from 19.4 overs. Earlier, Roberts provided the backbone of a healthy Northamptonshire innings from 94 balls. He and Afzaal added 106 for the third wicket.

At Cheltenham, July 25. **Gloucestershire won by 102 runs** (D/L method). Toss: Gloucestershire. **Gloucestershire 211-9** (36 overs) (C. M. Spearman 46, M. E. K. Hussey 60, M. G. N. Windows 31; J. M. Anderson 3-41); **Lancashire 114** (29.2 overs) (J. Lewis 5-23, I. D. Fisher 3-34). *Gloucestershire 4 pts.*

Lancashire's target was revised to 217 in 36 overs.

Rain interrupted Gloucestershire in full flow. In the seventh over, they were 54 without loss, though when the game resumed as a 36-over contest, they could not quite recapture their fluency. Duckworth/Lewis raised Lancashire's task slightly, but once Lewis delighted a 4,000 crowd by yanking out the first four Lancashire batsmen in six overs, that was irrelevant.

At Cheltenham, August 1. **Gloucestershire won by six wickets.** Toss: Kent. **Kent 226-8** (45 overs) (E. T. Smith 70, M. G. Bevan 41; J. M. M. Averis 3-56); **Gloucestershire 230-4** (37.4 overs) (M. E. K. Hussey 107*, C. G. Taylor 60). *Gloucestershire 4 pts.*

Smith made his sixth half-century in seven one-day matches to steer Kent to a respectable 226 on a slow pitch. The Gloucestershire reply faltered early on but, once Hussey and Taylor were compiling 139 from 22 overs for the fourth wicket, the outcome was hardly in doubt. Hussey faced 105 balls for his unbeaten 107 and hit 11 fours and a six, which took him to his hundred. After winning just one of their first six League games, Gloucestershire had now won four on the trot.

At Bristol, August 13 (day/night). **Essex won by six wickets** (D/L method). Toss: Gloucestershire. **Gloucestershire 150-6** (33 overs) (W. P. C. Weston 38, C. G. Taylor 41*); **Essex 164-4** (32 overs) (A. Flower 58, A. P. Grayson 58*; J. M. M. Averis 3-28). *Essex 4 pts.*

Essex's target was revised to 164 in 33 overs.

Gloucestershire's run of five successive wins came to an end on a damp night. The match, a 40-over affair when play started late, was interrupted during the Gloucestershire innings, reducing it again to 33 overs. At 29 for three, Essex made an uncertain start towards their increased target. Then Flower and Grayson shared a measured stand of 113 in 22 overs – Flower hit just four fours and Grayson one. Essex's first away win lifted them off the foot of the table.

At Bristol, September 4. **Gloucestershire won by three wickets.** Toss: Gloucestershire. **Warwickshire 248-7** (45 overs) (I. J. L. Trott 70, I. R. Bell 76); **Gloucestershire 250-7** (44.2 overs) (W. P. C. Weston 38, M. E. K. Hussey 82, C. G. Taylor 30; D. R. Brown 3-48). *Gloucestershire 4 pts.*

A last-over victory meant Gloucestershire clung on to their place in the first division, while Warwickshire's fate would hang on other teams' results. Trott and Bell led Warwickshire to 248. Gloucestershire's confidence when chasing a target then paid off again, despite losing the influential Spearman for two. Hussey, however, stood firm to make a vital 82. As Streak began bowling the final over, Gloucestershire needed eight. Averis crashed fours either side of the wicket to keep them in the top flight.

HAMPSHIRE

At Southampton, May 2. **Hampshire won by 31 runs.** Toss: Hampshire. **Hampshire 184-7** (45 overs) (N. Pothas 64, W. S. Kendall 55*); **Essex 153** (43.1 overs) (S. K. Warne 3-21). *Hampshire 4 pts.*

This was Hampshire's fourth win out of four in all competitions. On a bowler-friendly pitch, they managed to defend a modest total, given some substance by a stand of 69 for the fourth wicket between Pothas and Kendall. Six of the Essex top seven made double figures, but none could reach 25 as Warne wove a mesmerising spell. Mascarenhas, run out for three in the Hampshire innings, was later disciplined by the ECB for showing dissent to an umpire.

At Southampton, May 31. **No result.** Toss: Kent. **Kent 169-9** (45 overs) (D. P. Fulton 39*; S. K. Warne 3-31) v Hampshire. *Hampshire 2 pts, Kent 2 pts.*

First-team debut: S. M. J. Cusden (Kent).

On an awkward pitch, Kent never mastered either Warne's guile – he held himself back until the 23rd over – or the bounce and movement obtained by the Hampshire seamers. A painstaking 39 off 47 balls by Fulton did ensure a reasonable total, but rain prevented Hampshire replying.

At Southampton, June 6. **Hampshire won by 28 runs.** Toss: Hampshire. **Hampshire 241-7** (45 overs) (D. A. Kenway 41, J. P. Crawley 68, M. J. Clarke 54, A. D. Mascarenhas 55); **Warwickshire 213** (43.4 overs) (G. B. Hogg 39; C. T. Tremlett 4-37, S. D. Udal 3-43). *Hampshire 4 pts.*

Mascarenhas arrived at 148 for three, struck a whirlwind 55 off 31 balls and helped Hampshire amass 91 off their last eight overs. It was enough to give them a match-winning total on a typically sluggish Rose Bowl wicket. The Warwickshire reply was going nowhere at 117 for six, but while Dougie Brown and Hogg were adding 66 in eight overs, the visitors had an outside chance. Tremlett then removed Brown – one of six Warwickshire batsmen dismissed in the 20s – to put paid to the revival.

At Southampton, July 11. **Lancashire won by one run.** Toss: Hampshire. **Lancashire 182-8** (45 overs) (D. G. Cork 57, W. K. Hegg 37; B. V. Taylor 3-51); **Hampshire 181-7** (45 overs) (M. J. Brown 35, S. R. Watson 54*; J. M. Anderson 3-26). *Lancashire 4 pts.*

Hampshire needed seven from the final over, bowled by Hooper, and managed five, meaning Watson's unbeaten 54 from 60 balls was in vain. During the Lancashire innings, Law, on 16, deflected a ball off his thigh-pad to the keeper. Umpire Evans interpreted Law's pacing at the wicket as him walking, and only then raised his finger, prompting an outburst from the batsman, who was so furious he was more than halfway to the pavilion before he heard Pothas telling him he had been recalled. He added just four to his score. Mascarenhas bowled an exemplary line for figures of 9–2–12–1.

At Southampton, July 18. **Northamptonshire won by five wickets.** Toss: Hampshire. **Hampshire 153** (45 overs) (G. A. Lamb 32); **Northamptonshire 157-5** (43.1 overs) (D. J. Sales 63). *Northamptonshire 4 pts.*

County debut: M. L. Love (Northamptonshire).

Sales, the one batsman to master the conditions, hit the only half-century of a low-scoring match. His 63 included sixes off Warne and Udal, and was enough to give Northamptonshire a sixth win in seven League games. Warne, just back from equalling the record for Test wickets in Australia, could not break through, and his nine overs cost 41. By contrast, his team-mate Taylor bowled his nine for 11.

At Southampton, August 9 (day/night). **No result (abandoned). Hampshire v Surrey.** *Hampshire 2 pts, Surrey 2 pts.*

At Southampton, August 15. **Glamorgan won by three wickets.** Toss: Glamorgan. **Hampshire 208** (37 overs) (J. H. K. Adams 40, J. P. Crawley 56; D. L. Hemp 3-11); **Glamorgan 209-7** (36 overs) (R. D. B. Croft 52, M. T. G. Elliott 79*; A. D. Mascarenhas 3-54). *Glamorgan 4 pts.*

Reduced to 37 overs a side.

Victory for Glamorgan took them within touching distance of the title. Hampshire batted aggressively – especially against Croft, whose six overs cost 60 runs – as Crawley hit a 48-ball 56. The end of their innings, however, was a triumph for Hemp, pressed into a rare bowl by injuries. His first over of up-and-down medium-pace had gone for 11; the batsmen set out to slog *his second too, and he bowled a triple wicket maiden, giving him League wickets for the first time since 1998. In the Glamorgan reply, Elliott battered through the innings for the fifth time in 11 matches. Croft handed out the treatment he had been given with a savage 52 off 37 balls.*

At Southampton, August 30. **Hampshire won by five wickets.** Toss: Gloucestershire. **Gloucestershire 230-6** (45 overs) (C. M. Spearman 42, C. G. Taylor 34, T. H. C. Hancock 38, S. J. Adshead 32*, M. W. Alleyne 42); **Hampshire 234-5** (44.3 overs) (J. P. Crawley 62, N. Pothas 83*; N. W. Bracken 3-37). *Hampshire 4 pts.*

County debut: N. W. Bracken (Gloucestershire).

Just 48 hours after winning the C&G Trophy, Gloucestershire were squeezed out by Hampshire, and remained in danger of relegation. They seemed set for victory when they had their opponents 98 for four, but Crawley and then Pothas, with an unbeaten 83 off 79 balls, guided Hampshire home in the last over. The Australian Nathan Bracken, having just joined Gloucestershire, took wickets with his seventh and tenth deliveries.

KENT

At Canterbury, April 25. **Kent won by one run.** Toss: Gloucestershire. **Kent 175-9** (45 overs) (R. S. Ferley 31); **Gloucestershire 174** (44.3 overs) (C. M. Spearman 63; Mohammad Sami 6-20). *Kent 4 pts.*

Despite touching down from Pakistan around 7 a.m. that morning and grabbing just a couple of hours' sleep, Mohammad Sami claimed six for 20 – including two in the last over – to clinch a tense win for Kent. Earlier, his colleagues had struggled for runs on a two-paced pitch, and at 51 for nought in reply Gloucestershire seemed well set. When Sami began the last over, two runs were needed with two wickets in hand. He had Lewis caught behind with his first ball and removed Mike Smith's off stump with his third to earn his night's rest. Though no one knew at the time, this was 40-year-old Jack Russell's last match for Gloucestershire before injury forced him into retirement. He scored just six and took no catches – but conceded no byes.

At Tunbridge Wells, June 6. **Kent won by 56 runs.** Toss: Kent. **Kent 301** (44.5 overs) (A. Symonds 146, M. J. Walker 61, Extras 37; S. I. Mahmood 4-42); **Lancashire 245** (42.2 overs) (S. G. Law 51, M. J. Chilton 32, G. Chapple 35, I. J. Sutcliffe 35; M. J. Walker 3-28). *Kent 4 pts.*

Symonds walloped a magnificent 146 – the highest limited-overs innings for Kent – from 110 balls, 17 of which disappeared for four and four for six. It was Symonds's second one-day hundred after the unbeaten 143 he hit for Australia against Pakistan in the 2003 World Cup. Kent ended up on 301, the best limited-overs total at The Nevill since West Sussex hit 314 (from 65 overs) in the first round of the 1963 Gillette Cup. Symonds and Walker shared a fourth-wicket stand of 170. Simon Cusden bowled Loye with the first ball of the Lancashire reply, his first ball at senior level. Defeat ended Lancashire's 100% record in the League.

At Beckenham, June 27. **Kent won by ten runs** (D/L method). Toss: Warwickshire. **Warwickshire 233-9** (45 overs) (M. A. Wagh 83, I. J. L. Trott 49; J. C. Tredwell 3-35); **Kent 140-2** (30 overs) (M. A. Carberry 32, E. T. Smith 81). *Kent 4 pts.*

A tight game went Kent's way under Duckworth/Lewis when thunderstorms ended play early. Warwickshire were eight for two, but Wagh – whose 83 came at exactly a run a ball – and Trott put on 134. Then the innings fell apart against Kent's spinners, who had combined figures of seven for 93 from 23 overs. Smith faced 100 balls for his 81 before being run out after a mix-up with Symonds.

At Maidstone, July 4. **No result.** Toss: Essex. **Kent 168-2** (27 overs) (M. A. Carberry 76, E. T. Smith 58*) v Essex. *Kent 2 pts, Essex 2 pts.*

Kent's strong position counted for nothing once persistent drizzle set in at the Mote. Carberry played fluently for a 57-ball 76 as he and Smith shared an opening stand of 135.

At Canterbury, July 18. **Surrey won by four wickets.** Toss: Surrey. **Kent 192-8** (34 overs) (E. T. Smith 61, A. G. R. Loudon 35); **Surrey 193-6** (33.4 overs) (M. R. Ramprakash 66, A. J. Hollioake 41*). *Surrey 4 pts.*

Reduced to 34 overs a side.

Rain barged in on Kent's third successive home League match, reducing it to a 34-over contest. Even more consistent than the weather was Smith, who hit his fifth one-day fifty on the trot. Surrey lost Brown to the first ball of their reply, but the patience of Ramprakash and the effervescence of Hollioake guided them to just their second win in the competition all season.

At Canterbury, July 20 (day/night). **Hampshire won by 22 runs.** Toss: Hampshire. **Hampshire 146** (42.3 overs) (A. D. Mascarenhas 79; A. Symonds 3-28); **Kent 124** (35.4 overs) (A. G. R. Loudon 34; S. K. Warne 3-24). *Hampshire 4 pts.*

A dry, reused wicket assisted the spinners, especially Warne, who inspired Hampshire to their first League win at Canterbury since 1976. Hampshire also owed much to Mascarenhas, who came in at 47 for five. That soon became 54 for six, but Mascarenhas hit a swashbuckling 79 off 93 balls with ten fours and a six. Next highest score was 17 from Extras. Kent reached 75 for two in some comfort, but Warne's introduction sparked the loss of eight wickets for 49. Kent's 124 was their lowest in the League against Hampshire.

At Canterbury, August 9. **Glamorgan won by ten runs** (D/L method). Toss: Kent. **Glamorgan 250-6** (42 overs) (M. T. G. Elliott 112, M. P. Maynard 66; M. J. Dennington 3-53); **Kent 93-2** (20 overs) (J. C. Tredwell 30*, E. T. Smith 40). *Glamorgan 2 pts.*

Kent's target was revised to 252 in 42 overs.

An exquisitely timed century from Elliott and a belligerent 66 by Maynard – together they added 112 in 20 overs – helped Glamorgan control this top v bottom encounter. Drizzle eight overs into the Welsh innings forced a reduction to 42 overs a side and later slightly increased Kent's target. Smith played some sublime shots in his 40, but Kent were behind the rate when rain returned. This match was moved from the Sunday – when a hundred or so spectators, who had not heard the news, turned up anyway – to the Monday because Glamorgan had qualified for Saturday's Twenty20 finals. Kent were also reported to have lost £12,000 through corporate hospitality cancellations.

At Canterbury, September 7 (day/night). **Northamptonshire won by four runs.** Toss: Northamptonshire. **Northamptonshire 219-7** (45 overs) (U. Afzaal 47, G. L. Brophy 42, B. J. Phillips 44*); **Kent 215-7** (45 overs) (E. T. Smith 106, A. G. R. Loudon 31; J. Louw 3-37). *Northamptonshire 4 pts.*

Kent were already doomed to the second division, but Northamptonshire had everything to play for. Victory would ensure survival at Warwickshire's expense; defeat would see them relegated. Unable to forge a fifty partnership, Northamptonshire relied on Kent old-boy Phillips for late-innings impetus; he hit 44 from 26 balls, including three sixes in the last over. Kent's reply was held together by Smith, who stroked his way to 106 off 128 balls with 12 fours and a six, but crucially fell to a stunning catch by Phillips in the penultimate over. Seven were needed from the last, but Louw, the division's leading wicket-taker, bowled Ferley with the final ball.

LANCASHIRE

At Manchester, May 2. **Lancashire won by three wickets.** Toss: Kent. **Kent 203** (44 overs) (E. T. Smith 36, R. S. Ferley 42; S. I. Mahmood 3-39); **Lancashire 207-7** (44.2 overs) (M. B. Loye 48, I. J. Sutcliffe 44, K. W. Hogg 37*). *Lancashire 4 pts.*

Calm batting from Hogg guided Lancashire home after they seemed to have lost their way. He came in at 142 for six, after Lancashire, in the space of 14 overs, had plummeted from 93 for nought, and hit a career-best 37 not out from 35 balls. Earlier, Kent had recovered from 128 for seven thanks to a stand of 54 between Ferley and Saggers. During the Kent innings Hegg became the second wicket-keeper, after Worcestershire's Steve Rhodes, to make 300 League dismissals, while Symonds was back in the middle eight days after his wedding in Australia. "I've got to pay for the wedding dress somehow," he explained.

At Manchester, May 16. **Lancashire won by seven wickets.** Toss: Hampshire. **Hampshire 189-9** (45 overs) (N. Pothas 45, M. J. Clarke 54; S. I. Mahmood 3-40); **Lancashire 192-3** (31.5 overs) (S. G. Law 83, M. J. Chilton 58*). *Lancashire 4 pts.*

County debut: S. R. Watson (Hampshire).

Both sides were unbeaten in all cricket, though the expected close game never materialised. Hampshire, cruising at 150 for three, were reeling at 152 for seven 12 balls later as Mahmood yanked out three batsmen without conceding a run. Mascarenhas showed what might have been by crashing 17 off the last over. Law, after scores of five and nought in the League, made 83 from 74 balls: "I was just glad to get into double figures," he said. Law was especially harsh on Udal, whose four overs cost 35.

At Manchester, May 23. **Lancashire won by five wickets.** Toss: Lancashire. **Glamorgan 210** (42.1 overs) (M. T. G. Elliott 32, A. G. Wharf 72, M. P. Maynard 35; S. I. Mahmood 4-39); **Lancashire 211-5** (34.5 overs) (M. B. Loye 42, I. J. Sutcliffe 30, S. G. Law 35, C. L. Hooper 49*). *Lancashire 4 pts.*

In another clash of two unbeaten sides, Lancashire won handsomely to move top of the first division. A maiden limited-overs fifty from Wharf led Glamorgan to a strong position but Mahmood struck back. He devastated the visitors with some lively bowling, using his yorker to good effect and ending with a one-day best four for 39 to give him 12 wickets in four League games. Hooper and Loye, each scoring at better than a run a ball, helped Lancashire to speed home with ten overs to spare. Both Glamorgan and Lancashire had won all their 2004 League games batting second.

At Manchester, June 25 (day/night). **Northamptonshire won by seven wickets.** Toss: Lancashire. **Lancashire 176** (44.1 overs) (M. J. Chilton 51; J. F. Brown 4-33); **Northamptonshire 180-3** (27.1 overs) (G. P. Swann 78, M. van Jaarsveld 65*). *Northamptonshire 4 pts.*

Plagued by a spate of injuries and bereft of confidence, Lancashire, who had begun the season with four successive League wins, slumped to a third consecutive defeat. Chilton, the only home batsman to pass 24, faced 100 balls for his 51. In Northamptonshire's reply, Wood split Graeme Swann's helmet with a bouncer. Swann staggered to the ground and needed treatment, though suffered no lasting effects. He hit Wood for a six two balls later and in all made 78 from just 57 balls. He was eventually caught by his elder brother Alec to complete a pair of symmetrical dismissals: Alec had earlier been caught by Graeme. Mike Watkinson, the Lancashire manager, admitted his team's performance was "embarrassing".

At Manchester, July 4. **Gloucestershire won by 18 runs.** Toss: Gloucestershire. **Gloucestershire 237-9** (45 overs) (C. M. Spearman 89, M. G. N. Windows 30, T. H. C. Hancock 53*); **Lancashire 219** (43.1 overs) (M. B. Loye 65, D. Mongia 40, W. K. Hegg 36, D. G. Cork 37; J. Lewis 4-30). *Gloucestershire 4 pts.*

Spearman welcomed Oliver Newby, on his League debut, by hammering him for four successive fours en route to 89 off 66 balls. When Spearman was third out, at 129 in the 22nd over, he had had ten fours and four sixes. Keedy, in only his fifth game in the competition since the end of the 2000 season, bowled nine overs for 31 to put the brake on Gloucestershire, but they sped up through a rapid half-century from Hancock. Hegg and Cork dragged Lancashire to within 33 of victory with five overs left, but then Lewis grabbed three wickets in six balls.

At Manchester, July 18. **Lancashire won by seven wickets.** Toss: Essex. **Essex 185-7** (45 overs) (R. C. Irani 102*); **Lancashire 186-3** (38.4 overs) (M. J. Chilton 59*, C. L. Hooper 50*). *Lancashire 4 pts.*

County debut: A. R. Adams (Essex).

Lancashire went for spin in a big way, getting a full 27 overs from Keedy, Mongia and Hooper, the stand-in captain, at a cost of 100 runs. However, Schofield, a possible fourth, was not risked. The strategy worked well, despite Irani batting superbly for an unbeaten century to rescue his side from 13 for three. He hit eight fours and three sixes from 130 balls, though Essex's total was nowhere near good enough. Chilton and Hooper put on a sensible, unbroken stand of 114 as Lancashire cruised home.

At Manchester, July 27 (day/night). **Lancashire won by two wickets.** Toss: Lancashire. **Warwickshire 251-5** (45 overs) (N. M. Carter 40, N. V. Knight 122*, G. B. Hogg 34); **Lancashire 255-8** (44 overs) (I. J. Sutcliffe 68, D. Mongia 104*, Extras 33). *Lancashire 4 pts.*

The tension in this high-scoring match was punctured in the penultimate over when Warwickshire's dilatory over-rate meant Lancashire were awarded six penalty runs. Rather than needing eight from eight balls, Lancashire required just two, and Mongia hit the winning boundary with an over to spare. Defeat was hard on Knight, who had scored a wonderful unbeaten 122 from 116 balls with nine fours and two sixes – only to be let down by wayward fielding. Mongia was his equal though, calmly steering Lancashire through the crisis of losing five wickets in five overs.

At Manchester, August 31 (day/night). **Lancashire won by 48 runs.** Toss: Lancashire. **Lancashire 244-9** (45 overs) (M. J. Chilton 52, S. G. Law 73, C. P. Schofield 69*; P. J. Sampson 3-48); **Surrey 196** (40.2 overs) (S. A. Newman 33, A. D. Brown 41; G. Chapple 3-32). *Lancashire 4 pts.*

A straightforward win ensured Lancashire would pick up £27,000 for finishing runners-up in the League. An elegant run-a-ball half-century from Law, playing his first match since mid-July, and a similarly paced innings from Schofield saw Lancashire to a decent total. For Surrey, already condemned to the second division, there was little to savour. In his last match before retirement, Adam Hollioake ended his hugely successful Surrey career with a smile, but could not make it a swansong to remember. He conceded 27 from three overs and was then stumped after giving Keedy the charge.

NORTHAMPTONSHIRE

At Northampton, April 25. **Lancashire won by five wickets.** Toss: Lancashire. **Northamptonshire 161-9** (45 overs) (G. L. Brophy 50*; M. J. Chilton 3-27); **Lancashire 162-5** (41 overs) (M. B. Loye 70, I. J. Sutcliffe 38; G. P. Swann 3-16). *Lancashire 4 pts.*

Lancashire eased home thanks to Loye, a Northamptonshire player until 2002. He reached 70 from just 53 balls and had taken his opening stand with Sutcliffe to 93 when he was bowled by Louw. Sutcliffe was lucky not to have gone the same way when, on nought, he played the ball on to his off stump but did not dislodge a bail. Alec Swann, another former Northamptonshire batsman, was bowled by his brother, Graeme, for a duck. The home team's total was something of a recovery from 71 for six.

At Northampton, May 23. **Northamptonshire won by 65 runs.** Toss: Northamptonshire. **Northamptonshire 211-5** (45 overs) (M. van Jaarsveld 36, U. Afzaal 66, D. J. Sales 51*; M. J. Saggers 3-30); **Kent 146** (40.1 overs) (E. T. Smith 51, R. S. Ferley 37*). *Northamptonshire 4 pts.*

Northamptonshire struggled against Saggers until Sales joined Afzaal in a fifth-wicket stand worth 96 in 16 overs. Afzaal hit just two of his 89 balls for four, while Sales, slightly more aggressive, managed three fours and a six off 55 balls. Steffan Jones then removed both openers in his second over, and Kent soon careered to 33 for five, only achieving respectability thanks to Ferley and Patel down the order. The scorers had problems when Smith's score advanced by seven: he had completed three runs when Northamptonshire contributed four overthrows.

At Northampton, June 6. **Northamptonshire won by eight wickets.** Toss: Essex. **Essex 151** (41.4 overs) (J. D. Middlebrook 38; B. J. Phillips 3-28); **Northamptonshire 155-2** (32.2 overs) (T. W. Roberts 47, M. van Jaarsveld 96*). *Northamptonshire 4 pts.*

Van Jaarsveld piloted Northamptonshire to a commanding win with a confident unbeaten 96 from 114 balls. He and Roberts put on 124 for the second wicket after losing Huggins to the first ball of the second over. Essex offered a feeble display with the bat: only Middlebrook and Foster made much impression as they led a recovery from 74 for five.

At Northampton, July 11. **Northamptonshire won by 17 runs.** Toss: Northamptonshire. **Northamptonshire 267-8** (45 overs) (T. W. Roberts 68, R. A. White 101); **Glamorgan 250** (44.3 overs) (M. T. G. Elliott 32, M. P. Maynard 117; J. Louw 3-45, G. P. Swann 3-39). *Northamptonshire 4 pts.*

Despite a magnificent fighting hundred from Maynard, Glamorgan narrowly lost for the second time in their nine League games. They seemed totally out of it at 125 for seven, but Maynard, who crashed eight fours and four sixes, and Wharf added 113 in 17 overs. The equation was down to 30 off two overs when Brown bowled Maynard to drag the game back towards Northamptonshire. Earlier, White, on his first one-day appearance of 2004, and his fellow-opener Roberts put on 124 on a turning pitch.

At Northampton, August 4 (day/night). **Warwickshire won by one wicket.** Toss: Northamptonshire. **Northamptonshire 172** (44.5 overs) (G. P. Swann 50, G. L. Brophy 46); **Warwickshire 176-9** (44.5 overs) (N. V. Knight 32, I. R. Bell 58; J. Louw 5-27). *Warwickshire 4 pts.*

Northamptonshire's slight hopes of catching Glamorgan at the top of the table were all but ended by this narrow defeat. After Louw had bowled intelligently to grab five wickets, Frost saw Warwickshire home off the penultimate ball when he hit Greenidge for four. Bell, with a watchful half-century, proved the difference, but he should have been stumped on 11: wicket-keeper Brophy removed a bail with his right glove though the ball was in his left. Earlier, Brophy and Swann put on 69 in 12 overs to rescue Northamptonshire from 59 for five.

At Northampton, August 8. **Gloucestershire won by 91 runs.** Toss: Gloucestershire. **Gloucestershire 200** (45 overs) (C. M. Spearman 40, M. E. K. Hussey 44, C. G. Taylor 39; J. Louw 4-41); **Northamptonshire 109** (35 overs) (I. D. Fisher 3-18). *Gloucestershire 4 pts.*

On a worn pitch marked "poor" by the umpires, Gloucestershire's top order ensured a good total. Hussey, returning to Wantage Road for the first time since leaving Northamptonshire in 2003, top scored. Louw sent down seven wides in his first three overs but recovered well. Northamptonshire responded with a spineless batting display, the spin of Fisher – whose three victims were all stumped by Adshead – and Taylor proving decisive. Taylor, whose off-breaks had claimed just one limited-overs wicket till now, took two for five from four overs.

At Milton Keynes, August 22. **Hampshire won by 67 runs.** Toss: Northamptonshire. **Hampshire 238-9** (45 overs) (S. M. Katich 58, G. A. Lamb 54, N. Pothas 70*; P. C. Rofe 3-46); **Northamptonshire 171** (41.5 overs) (G. P. Swann 59, G. L. Brophy 47*; S. D. Udal 4-46). *Hampshire 4 pts.*

Northamptonshire's first League visit to Campbell Park since 1997 produced a healthy crowd estimated at 3,000 but a fifth successive defeat. Pothas boosted Hampshire with an unbeaten 70 from 56 balls and added 78 in 12 overs with Lamb. Northamptonshire never recovered from the depths of 17 for four despite a robust 59 off 46 deliveries from Swann.

At Northampton, August 29. **Northamptonshire won by five wickets** (D/L method). Toss: Surrey. **Surrey 179-7** (41 overs) (A. D. Brown 54, Azhar Mahmood 67; P. C. Rofe 3-53); **Northamptonshire 191-5** (39.5 overs) (J. W. Cook 38, U. Afzaal 86*). *Northamptonshire 4 pts.*

Northamptonshire's target was revised to 189 in 41 overs.

Defeat meant that Surrey, League champions a year earlier, were condemned to second-division cricket for 2005; Northamptonshire would stay up if they won at Canterbury in their last game. By dropping both Afzaal and Cook in the same over, Surrey made life difficult for themselves. The unlucky bowler was Azhar Mahmood, who had earlier hit 67 from 85 deliveries as Surrey regrouped after slumping to 50 for five.

SURREY

At The Oval, April 25. **Glamorgan won by seven wickets.** Toss: Surrey. **Surrey 146** (42.3 overs) (I. D. K. Salisbury 59*; M. S. Kasprowicz 3-27, A. P. Davies 4-29); **Glamorgan 147-3** (22.3 overs) (M. T. G. Elliott 69*, M. J. Powell 64). *Glamorgan 4 pts.*

Surrey's poor start to the season continued with a heavy defeat by Glamorgan, who at one stage reduced the League champions to 36 for seven. Salisbury, with his first one-day fifty in a career spanning 15 years and 233 games, then put on 64 with Saqlain Mushtaq for the eighth wicket and 43 with Tim Murtagh for the last. Glamorgan needed just half their overs to reach their target; Powell made 64 from 40 balls as he and Elliott rattled off 124 in 17 overs.

At The Oval, May 3. **No result (abandoned). Surrey v Hampshire.** *Surrey 2 pts, Hampshire 2 pts.*

At The Oval, May 23. **Surrey won by 31 runs.** Toss: Essex. **Surrey 268** (43.3 overs) (S. A. Newman 106, J. N. Batty 66, G. R. Napier 4-45); **Essex 237** (42.5 overs) (A. Flower 70, Extras 38; J. Ormond 3-49, A. J. Hollioake 3-13). *Surrey 4 pts.*

County debut: Zaheer Khan (Surrey).

A maiden one-day hundred from Newman, who faced 104 balls, and a combative innings from Batty helped Surrey to a sizeable total, boosted by 12 penalty runs because of Essex's slow over-rate. In the opening over of the Essex reply, the India pace bowler Zaheer Khan, playing as an amateur because of problems with his work permit, removed both openers for ducks. This, Surrey's 11th game in all competitions in 2004, was their first win.

At The Oval, June 13. **Kent won by five wickets.** Toss: Kent. **Surrey 230-8** (45 overs) (M. R. Ramprakash 32, N. Shahid 61*); **Kent 234-5** (43.5 overs) (M. A. Carberry 50, A. G. R. Loudon 51, M. J. Walker 51*, D. P. Fulton 48). *Kent 4 pts.*

Loudon reached his first League fifty in his fifth innings to propel Kent towards victory. He faced 41 balls and was especially severe on the England bowler Clarke, whose only over cost 24 (four fours, a no-ball and a six off the resulting free hit). Carberry, formerly a Surrey player, and Walker made more measured half-centuries. Surrey, struggling at 143 for seven, owed much to a brisk innings from Shahid.

At The Oval, July 11. **Gloucestershire won by four wickets.** Toss: Surrey. **Surrey 176** (43.5 overs) (G. S. Blewett 36, G. P. Thorpe 39, Extras 30; M. W. Alleyne 4-39); **Gloucestershire 180-6** (38.1 overs) (W. P. C. Weston 40, M. G. N. Windows 63; R. Clarke 4-50). *Gloucestershire 4 pts.*

Surrey were six points adrift at the foot of the division after another poor performance. They plummeted from 117 for two to 176 all out – fewer than in any of their three recent Twenty20 games – as Alleyne cut through the lower order. In Gloucestershire's reply, Clarke removed the top four to claim a one-day best four for 50, but Windows, with a run-a-ball 63, helped steer the visitors home with few alarms.

At Guildford, July 25. **Surrey won by 90 runs.** Toss: Surrey. **Surrey 315-8** (45 overs) (J. G. E. Benning 71, M. R. Ramprakash 40, R. Clarke 70, A. D. Brown 46, Azhar Mahmood 56*; N. M. Carter 3-53); **Warwickshire 225** (34.3 overs) (I. R. Bell 89, J. O. Troughton 36; R. Clarke 3-34, A. J. Tudor 3-31). *Surrey 4 pts.*

The second-highest limited-overs total at the small Woodbridge Road ground was more than enough to see off Warwickshire. Five Surrey batsmen reached 40, none more powerfully than Azhar Mahmood, whose unbeaten 56 included five sixes – three in one over from Dougie Brown – and came from just 27 balls. Benning, with a limited-overs best, and Ramprakash put on 105 for the second wicket, while Clarke compiled a carefree 70 before being brilliantly caught by Jonathan Trott at mid-wicket. Bell resisted gamely, but no one else threatened to make a match of it.

At The Oval, July 27. **Surrey won by 39 runs.** Toss: Surrey. **Surrey 265-6** (45 overs) (J. G. E. Benning 50, R. Clarke 45, J. N. Batty 66, A. J. Hollioake 80*); **Northamptonshire 226** (41.3 overs) (G. P. Swann 38, J. Louw 36, B. J. Phillips 42; J. Ormond 4-48). *Surrey 4 pts.*

A third consecutive victory lifted Surrey off the bottom of the table and raised hopes of avoiding relegation. Benning scored a second successive League fifty, Batty smacked 66 at better than a run a ball and Hollioake an unbeaten 80 off 66 deliveries. Ormond then sliced through the ineffectual Northamptonshire reply; Phillips, at No. 9, showed up his batting colleagues.

At Whitgift School, August 15. **Lancashire won by eight wickets.** Toss: Lancashire. **Surrey 235-8** (45 overs) (A. J. Hollioake 66, A. J. Tudor 56; D. G. Cork 3-35); **Lancashire 238-2** (38.1 overs) (M. J. Chilton 115, I. J. Sutcliffe 102*). *Lancashire 4 pts.*

Hollioake marked his final appearance in a home game with a fifty, but although he and Tudor rescued Surrey from 72 for six with a stand of 128 in 21 overs, they were well beaten. Needing 236, Lancashire did not lose a wicket until they were 13 from victory: Chilton and Sutcliffe put on 223, a county-record opening stand in the League, against a weakened attack. Earlier, the Surrey batsman Newman, who began 2004 in cracking form, ended a run of three successive League ducks, but hardly convincingly: he made three.

WARWICKSHIRE

At Birmingham, April 25. **Hampshire won by 26 runs.** Toss: Warwickshire. **Hampshire 215-6** (45 overs) (M. J. Clarke 68, W. S. Kendall 30, A. D. Mascarenhas 33*, S. D. Udal 30*); **Warwickshire 189** (42.4 overs) (G. B. Hogg 35, G. G. Wagg 35; C. T. Tremlett 3-30). *Hampshire 4 pts.*

Udal brought the Hampshire innings to a resounding end by crashing an unbeaten 30 from just nine balls, five of which he hammered for four and one for six; in all, 54 runs came from their last four overs. Carter (9–0–18–2) was easily the most economical Warwickshire bowler. On a green-tinged pitch none of their batsmen settled for long, and despite Wagg hitting three successive sixes off Warne – his 35 came from 17 balls – the result was never in question.

At Birmingham, May 9. **Warwickshire won by 45 runs.** Toss: Warwickshire. **Warwickshire 240** (45 overs) (N. M. Carter 30, I. R. Bell 32, I. J. L. Trott 49, T. L. Penney 44; Azhar Mahmood 5-24); **Surrey 195** (41 overs) (J. N. Batty 52, Extras 44; D. Pretorius 4-36, N. M. Carter 3-37). *Warwickshire 4 pts.*

Batting was tricky under grey skies and on a moist pitch, but it was never as difficult as Surrey suggested when they slipped to seven for four. Four of the top five, including three England players, made ducks; Pretorius, who found late swing, removed three in six deliveries. Only a gritty 73-ball half-century from Batty prevented a massive defeat; after seven games as captain he had yet to lead Surrey to victory. Earlier, Azhar Mahmood took three wickets with the score 210, but by then Trott and Penney had ensured a solid total.

At Birmingham, May 31. **Glamorgan won by 13 runs.** Toss: Glamorgan. **Glamorgan 243-9** (45 overs) (R. D. B. Croft 54, M. J. Powell 73; M. A. Wagh 4-35); **Warwickshire 230** (44 overs) (M. A. Wagh 31, N. V. Knight 111; A. G. Wharf 4-35). *Glamorgan 4 pts.*

A switchback contest was brought to a sudden end in the penultimate over by a hat-trick from Wharf. Warwickshire needed 16 from their last 12 balls, with Knight still there after a flawless 108-ball century. But from Wharf's last three deliveries, Wagg skied to mid-off, Knight was caught trying to sweep and Pretorius missed a slog. Earlier, Glamorgan failed to build after Croft and Powell hit a belligerent 87 between the fifth over and the 15th. They were pegged back by spin, Wagh earning his best one-day figures.

At Birmingham, June 13. **Warwickshire won by 112 runs.** Toss: Warwickshire. **Warwickshire 310-5** (45 overs) (M. A. Wagh 69, N. V. Knight 92, G. B. Hogg 41*); **Lancashire 198** (39.3 overs) (P. J. Horton 42). *Warwickshire 4 pts.*

For the second Sunday running Lancashire conceded their highest League score. On a flat wicket they bowled too short to the in-form Knight, who made a superb 92 at a run a ball; in all cricket he had now scored 766 runs in 18 days. Knight and Wagh put on 147 for the second wicket, before Hogg blasted Warwickshire to their best total in the League. In reply, Lancashire's highest partnership was 45. Despite the absence of five senior players it was a shoddy Lancashire performance as their season began to disintegrate. Two of the withdrawals came during the warm-up, which meant an emergency summons from Liverpool for Paul Horton, who had not played a competitive first-team match before. He arrived ten overs into the game but recovered to bat calmly for the team's top score.

At Birmingham, July 4. **Warwickshire won by four wickets.** Toss: Northamptonshire. **Northamptonshire 233** (44.5 overs) (T. W. Roberts 112, J. Louw 32; H. H. Streak 3-51); **Warwickshire 235-6** (43.4 overs) (M. A. Wagh 70, G. B. Hogg 74). *Warwickshire 4 pts.*

Northamptonshire's run of four wins ended as they failed to capitalise on a century by opener Roberts and lost at Edgbaston for the third time in 23 days. After a flying start against Streak, they were pegged back by accurate spells from Bell and Hogg. Wagh's third consecutive fifty in the competition, and Hogg's aggression, ensured a straightforward win.

At Birmingham, July 11. **Warwickshire won by 54 runs.** Toss: Warwickshire. **Warwickshire 223** (43.5 overs) (N. V. Knight 51, G. B. Hogg 33, D. R. Brown 41; S. A. Brant 4-49); **Essex 169** (36.4 overs) (A. Flower 32; G. B. Hogg 5-23). *Warwickshire 4 pts.*

At 99 for two in the 16th over Essex were strong favourites but, for the second match in succession, Hogg and Bell held back the tide of runs. In 14 mid-innings overs in tandem, they conceded just 38; Hogg's teasing wrist-spin and googlies brought five wickets as the last eight batsmen fell for 70. Earlier, in conditions demanding caution, Warwickshire reached a good total, Knight making a patient 51 on return from a broken hand, and Brown rescuing his side from 151 for seven.

At Birmingham, August 15. **Warwickshire won by six wickets.** Toss: Warwickshire. **Kent 135** (37.5 overs) (M. G. Bevan 35; H. H. Streak 3-7); **Warwickshire 139-4** (24.1 overs) (N. V. Knight 36, I. R. Bell 51). *Warwickshire 4 pts.*

In a congested league table, with only six points between third place and eighth, both sides began tied second from bottom. Warwickshire were worried about playing on a drying wicket but the concerns proved unfounded: Kent's collapse to 17 for three and then 90 for six was largely down to superb bowling by Streak (6–3–7–3) and limp batting. There was also turn for their three spinners, who returned combined figures of five for 36 in 15.5 overs. Bell played by far the most fluent innings – 51 in 61 balls – and was called into England's Test squad the next day.

At Birmingham, August 17 (day/night). **No result** (D/L method). Toss: Gloucestershire. **Gloucestershire 192-7** (42 overs) (W. P. C. Weston 46, C. M. Spearman 43); **Warwickshire 31-2** (7.2 overs). *Warwickshire 2 pts, Gloucestershire 2 pts.*

Warwickshire's target was revised to 205 in 42 overs.

Hogg took two for 19 in nine overs, slowing Gloucestershire after an aggressive opening stand of 78 between Weston and Spearman. Warwickshire's reply was washed away 16 balls short of the ten overs needed for a result.

DIVISION TWO

DERBYSHIRE

At Derby, May 2. **Derbyshire won by six wickets.** Toss: Derbyshire. **Durham 207** (44.5 overs) (G. R. Breese 49, A. Pratt 53; G. Welch 4-26); **Derbyshire 208-4** (42.3 overs) (A. I. Gait 49, C. W. G. Bassano 41, Hassan Adnan 50*). *Derbyshire 4 pts.*

Welch preyed on tentative Durham batsmen, maintaining an exemplary line to grab four wickets. Deep in trouble at 63 for five, Durham were hauled round by Breese and Andrew Pratt, who put on 94 for the sixth wicket. In the Derbyshire reply, patient batting on a slow pitch – typified by a fifty from Hassan Adnan which contained just one boundary – brought a straightforward victory.

At Derby, May 23. **Somerset won by 114 runs.** Toss: Somerset. **Somerset 316-5** (45 overs) (M. Burns 73, C. M. Gazzard 157); **Derbyshire 202** (35.5 overs) (C. W. G. Bassano 85; K. A. Parsons 5-39). *Somerset 4 pts.*

Burns and Gazzard stamped Somerset's authority with an opening partnership of 125 in 20 overs, and Gazzard, a 22-year-old Cornishman, went on to take the game well beyond Derbyshire. His first senior century was a dazzling display, with 157 hit from 136 balls, including 14 fours and two sixes. Only Bassano made more than 26 in reply.

At Derby, June 6. **Middlesex won by eight wickets.** Toss: Derbyshire. **Derbyshire 161** (40.1 overs) (G. Welch 33; M. Hayward 3-36, S. J. Cook 3-27); **Middlesex 162-2** (32.1 overs) (P. N. Weekes 60*, E. C. Joyce 74*). *Middlesex 4 pts.*

A teatime announcement that "the future for Derbyshire is looking bright" (a reference to the club's plans to install permanent floodlights) seemed misguided as a feeble batting collapse brought a sixth defeat in seven one-day games. From 24 for one in the second over, Derbyshire folded to 74 for six, and a partial recovery by the lower-middle order was not enough. Weekes and Joyce led Middlesex home in an unbroken stand of 138.

At Derby, June 8. **Derbyshire won by 28 runs.** Toss: Derbyshire. **Derbyshire 182** (44.5 overs) (N. G. E. Walker 43, M. A. Sheikh 50*; Yasir Arafat 3-52); **Scotland 154** (39.4 overs) (D. F. Watts 45; P. M. R. Havell 3-28, M. A. Sheikh 3-26, A. G. Botha 3-24). *Derbyshire 4 pts.*

Only Sheikh stood between Derbyshire and embarrassment. After a vigorous start, they were strangled by Craig Wright's medium-pace (his figures of 9–6–7–2 were Scotland's most economical in the competition), losing six wickets for 21 in 11.3 overs. But Sheikh hit a brisk fifty from No. 9, then removed three of Scotland's top four to help defend a vulnerable total.

At Derby, June 27. **Derbyshire won by 18 runs** (D/L method). Toss: Derbyshire. **Derbyshire 215-8** (45 overs) (J. Moss 104, L. D. Sutton 58*; A. J. Hall 3-42); **Worcestershire 159-9** (32 overs) (V. S. Solanki 32; Mohammad Ali 3-34, A. G. Botha 3-26). *Derbyshire 4 pts.*

County debut: D. K. Taylor (Derbyshire). Worcestershire's target was revised to 178 in 32 overs. A first one-day century by Moss, backed up by tight bowling and fielding, brought a second League win in a row for Derbyshire. Moss survived three near-misses, the narrowest when Kabir Ali fell over the boundary after a spectacular catch; he and Sutton provided Derbyshire's only substance, adding 100 together. Botha and Mohammad Ali bowled well in reply, helped by direct hits to remove Solanki and Hick, and by a downpour in the interval, which slowed the outfield.

At Derby, July 18. **Sussex won by ten runs** (D/L method). Toss: Sussex. **Sussex 185** (44.4 overs) (M. W. Goodwin 38; J. Moss 3-47); **Derbyshire 166** (40.1 overs) (Hassan Adnan 51, G. Welch 40; M. J. G. Davis 4-40). *Sussex 4 pts.*

Derbyshire's target was revised to 177 in 41 overs.

Much of Sussex's innings took place in drizzle, and acceleration was risky on a sticky pitch. However, the Derbyshire attack was too threadbare to take real advantage. Sussex were not so impotent: Wright bowled a lively first spell and, as Hassan Adnan and Welch took Derbyshire into a match-winning position, Sussex hit back with four wickets in three overs, two to the off-spin of Davis.

At Derby, August 3 (day/night). **No result.** Toss: Derbyshire. **Leicestershire 201-8** (37.1 overs) (D. L. Maddy 78) **v Derbyshire.** *Derbyshire 2 pts, Leicestershire 2 pts.*

Maddy rediscovered his sizzling form of the Twenty20, hitting 60 of his run-a-ball 78 in forceful boundaries. Before heavy rain ended things, Stevens was bowled by a double-bouncer from Dumelow, and Adnan, whose off-breaks showed promise, undid two batsmen trying to reverse sweep.

At Derby, August 18 (day/night). **Nottinghamshire won by 24 runs** (D/L method). Toss: Derbyshire. **Derbyshire 172-7** (39 overs) (Hassan Adnan 57, L. D. Sutton 43*); **Nottinghamshire 82-1** (17 overs) (A. Singh 47*, D. J. Hussey 30*). *Nottinghamshire 4 pts.*

Nottinghamshire's target was revised to 175 in 39 overs.

Derbyshire's new permanent lights were switched on and they cut through a rainy evening with great clarity. Nottinghamshire were 24 ahead of the par score when the rain returned for the last time. Earlier, Hassan Adnan hit just three fours as he pinned together Derbyshire's interrupted innings. He was later capped, in recognition of his strong first season, along with Botha and Moss.

At Derby, August 29. **Yorkshire won by five wickets** (D/L method). Toss: Derbyshire. **Derbyshire 168-6** (34 overs) (J. Moss 75*; R. K. J. Dawson 3-22); **Yorkshire 175-5** (32.4 overs) (M. P. Vaughan 57, P. A. Jaques 62; M. A. Sheikh 3-25). *Yorkshire 4 pts.*

Yorkshire's target was revised to 173 in 34 overs.

For the fifth League match in a row, it rained at Derby. Moss batted through three interruptions to give Derbyshire something to defend. Two early wickets then raised home hopes; but Vaughan, released by England to get his eye in for the forthcoming internationals against India, dashed them. He and Jaques added 105 in 13.4 overs, to take Yorkshire within sight and keep their hopes of promotion alive.

DURHAM

At Chester-le-Street, April 25. **Durham won by 26 runs.** Toss: Durham. **Durham 200-7** (45 overs) (M. J. North 53, G. J. Pratt 42); **Nottinghamshire 174** (42 overs) (A. M. Davies 3-16, G. R. Breese 3-37). *Durham 4 pts.*

County debut: G. R. Breese (Durham).

Durham cast aside the humiliation of the previous day, when Nottinghamshire had skittled them for 93 in the Championship. This time, North held the innings together with a patient fifty on a tricky, slow pitch, before his team-mate Davies turned the match decisively with the ball. His three-wicket burst reduced Nottinghamshire from 51 for one to 64 for four. On his Durham debut, the Jamaican Gareth Breese followed up a useful 25 with three wickets.

At Chester-le-Street, May 31. **Durham won by seven wickets.** Toss: Derbyshire. **Derbyshire 82** (44.3 overs) (L. D. Sutton 43; Shoaib Akhtar 4-15); **Durham 83-3** (26.3 overs). *Durham 4 pts.*

Derbyshire scraped 82 runs in 44.3 overs, beating their own 87 in 2000 as the lowest League total against Durham. The first four to fall all made ducks, three to Shoaib on his return from a rib injury; it took a last-wicket stand of 41 to put into perspective a pitch with tennis-ball bounce. Davies ended with 9–2–10–0, Durham's most economical complete spell in the League. His record looked like being short-lived but, by taking the last wicket, Killeen could not complete his spell, ending with 8.3–7–5–2.

At Chester-le-Street, June 6. **Durham won by 25 runs.** Toss: Durham. **Durham 203-9** (45 overs) (G. J. Pratt 54, J. J. B. Lewis 37); **Scotland 178** (43.4 overs) (C. V. English 45; N. Killeen 4-24). *Durham 4 pts.*

First-team debut: J. D. Nel (Scotland).

On a slow wicket, Durham struggled to 114 for four after 35 overs, before Lewis led a surge with 37 off 26 balls. Scotland were ahead at 35 overs – 115 for six – but Shoaib Akhtar and Killeen returned and the last four wickets fell for 23.

At Chester-le-Street, July 4. **Durham v Leicestershire. No result (abandoned).** *Durham 2 pts, Leicestershire 2 pts.*

At Chester-le-Street, July 11. **No result.** Toss: Yorkshire. **Yorkshire 40-0** (9 overs) **v Durham.** *Durham 2 pts, Yorkshire 2 pts.*

Durham fielded their only 11 who were fit and available. Play was washed out after nine overs.

At Chester-le-Street, July 18. **Durham won by one wicket.** Toss: Durham. **Middlesex 191-6** (45 overs) (E. C. Joyce 70*, J. W. M. Dalrymple 58); **Durham 193-9** (44.5 overs) (M. J. North 59, G. R. Breese 52*). *Durham 4 pts.*

County debut: A. M. Blignaut (Durham).

Durham, stiffened by Blignaut, Collingwood and Harmison, more than stood up to the runaway leaders. In a tense finish on another grudging pitch, the last man Harmison went in with eight needed off seven balls: he lapped the two deliveries he faced for singles, and Breese cracked the penultimate ball for the winning four through square leg. A Middlesex attack missing their overseas players could not match the squeeze applied by Durham's Killeen, who had bowled four maidens in his first seven overs, before finishing with 9–4–25–2.

At Chester-le-Street, August 8. **Durham won by five wickets.** Toss: Worcestershire. **Worcestershire 205-7** (45 overs) (V. S. Solanki 37, S. C. Moore 93*, D. A. Leatherdale 41); **Durham 209-5** (43 overs) (N. Peng 34, J. J. B. Lewis 40, P. D. Collingwood 63*, A. Pratt 35*; M. N. Malik 3-42). *Durham 4 pts.*

Worcestershire had surged to five successive league wins but were mired on yet another slow, slow pitch. They lost momentum after slipping from 66 for no wicket to 82 for three; Moore took 144 balls for 93 not out. In reply, Durham coasted to 139 for two, careered to 157 for five against Nadeem Malik, then cruised once more, with Collingwood making a steadying 63 at a run a ball.

At Chester-le-Street, August 11 (day/night). **Somerset won by six wickets** (D/L method). Toss: Durham. **Durham 162-9** (45 overs) (G. M. Hamilton 66*; R. L. Johnson 3-25); **Somerset 147-4** (31.2 overs) (R. T. Ponting 83*). *Somerset 4 pts.*

Somerset's target was revised to 146 in 37 overs.

Rain, fog, faltering floodlights and frugal bowling – nothing could trouble Ponting. Somerset were struggling at ten for one in the sixth over but Ponting was a class apart, surviving Killeen, who ended with 6–3–6–1, to reach 83 and ensure that Somerset won with ease. Earlier, Durham's fear of batting under lights prompted them to take on Johnson in sultry afternoon heat. They failed and Johnson helped reduce them to 52 for five.

At Chester-le-Street, August 29. **Durham won by two wickets** (D/L method). Toss: Sussex. **Sussex 214-7** (45 overs) (I. J. Ward 72, M. H. Yardy 46, M. W. Goodwin 35); **Durham 159-8** (27.4 overs) (J. J. B. Lewis 48; R. S. C. Martin-Jenkins 3-25). *Durham 4 pts.*

Durham's target was revised to 159 in 28 overs.

Both counties' chances of promotion hung on victory and twice it looked as though Sussex would be smiling. First, rain stopped play straight after Durham lost Gary Pratt, a wicket which put them behind on Duckworth/Lewis. The rain finally abated, leaving a relieved home side chasing 90 more from 13 overs. That came down to an unlikely 15 off the last, to be bowled by Martin-Jenkins, who had taken three frugal wickets. But the seam bowler Plunkett surprised perhaps even himself: after Killeen took a single, he drove the next three balls for four, six and four.

LEICESTERSHIRE

At Leicester, May 2. **Leicestershire won by nine wickets.** Toss: Leicestershire. **Scotland 86** (37.4 overs); **Leicestershire 87-1** (19.5 overs) (D. D. J. Robinson 43*). *Leicestershire 4 pts.*

Scotland debuts: S. Sriram, Yasir Arafat.

Scotland began their season with their lowest League score. The ball jagged around on a seamer's pitch, and none of the Leicestershire attack conceded more than three an over: Cleary ended with 7–1–9–1. Scotland's bowlers could not match that.

At Leicester, May 3. **Leicestershire won by 33 runs.** Toss: Leicestershire. **Leicestershire 131-8** (20 overs) (J. N. Snape 33*; Mohammad Ali 3-22, G. Welch 3-22); **Derbyshire 98** (19.1 overs) (J. M. Dakin 3-17, C. W. Henderson 4-9). *Leicestershire 4 pts.*

County debut: J. Moss (Derbyshire). Reduced to 20 overs a side.

Derbyshire squandered the game through a collapse horrible even by their own grim standards. At 44 without loss they were on course, but six wickets fell for 13 runs to the spinners Henderson (4–0–9–4) and Hodge (4–0–11–2). After heavy morning rain cut the game to 20 overs each, Leicestershire stuttered early and made only a modest 131, despite Nixon blasting 29 in 16 balls, including four sixes, one reverse sweep.

At Leicester, May 16. **Nottinghamshire won by 43 runs.** Toss: Nottinghamshire. **Nottinghamshire 252-5** (45 overs) (J. E. R. Gallian 68, K. P. Pietersen 43, D. J. Hussey 30, C. M. W. Read 32*, M. A. Ealham 40*); **Leicestershire 209** (44.2 overs) (J. L. Sadler 31, J. N. Snape 64, P. A. Nixon 37; G. J. Smith 3-17). *Nottinghamshire 4 pts.*

Ealham and Read smashed 54 from Nottinghamshire's final five overs, turning a competitive score into a commanding one. Ealham hit 40 from 20 balls, including four sixes, then whipped out both Leicestershire openers; Stevens was stumped off what appeared to be a deliberate wide. From 13 for three, Leicestershire lagged far behind the rate.

At Oakham School, June 6. **Worcestershire won by 124 runs.** Toss: Worcestershire. **Worcestershire 261-8** (45 overs) (V. S. Solanki 101); **Leicestershire 137** (36.4 overs) (A. J. Hall 4-26). *Worcestershire 4 pts.*

Solanki towered above every other batsman: he hit 101 at a shade under a run a ball, and the next-best score was 27. Crucially, Leicestershire dropped him on 54; as it was, they were left 262 to chase, and were crushed under the pressure. Hall took advantage with four wickets, helped by swinging conditions and some tight support bowling. Defeat cost Leicestershire first place in the table.

At Leicester, June 27. **Middlesex won by six wickets** (D/L method). Toss: Middlesex. **Leicestershire 205** (44.5 overs) (D. L. Maddy 41, B. J. Hodge 47; P. A. Nixon 31; S. J. Cook 6-37); **Middlesex 187-4** (40.3 overs) (P. N. Weekes 90). *Middlesex 4 pts.*

Middlesex's target was revised to 187 in 42 overs.

Leicestershire made one of their best starts of the season, Dakin and Maddy putting on 77, but dwindled to a less-than-imposing 205. On a dreadfully slow pitch, Cook bowled with unstinting accuracy, removing Maddy and Hodge when well set before adding the last three batsmen to fall. He ended with six for 37, the best figures in the second division in 2004. Weekes calmly organised the chase, passing 50 for the sixth successive League match, and Middlesex were always in control, despite a late change to their target after a rain break.

At Leicester, July 11. **Leicestershire won by 48 runs.** Toss: Leicestershire. **Leicestershire 234-6** (45 overs) (B. J. Hodge 37, D. I. Stevens 33, J. L. Sadler 49, Extras 36); **Sussex 186** (42.1 overs) (C. J. Adams 47; C. E. Dagnall 3-21, C. W. Henderson 3-42, J. N. Snape 3-42). *Leicestershire 4 pts.*

The white ball nipped about sharply on a green-tinged pitch, and Sussex's bowlers struggled for control, contributing 24 wides to a total of 234. That always looked too big, a fact confirmed by Dagnall, who bowled superbly and allowed only seven scoring shots in nine overs. A stunning catch by the wicket-keeper Nixon removed the dangerous Adams, and at 136 for six Sussex were finished. The win was Leicestershire's first since May.

At Leicester, July 25. **Leicestershire won by 15 runs.** Toss: Durham. **Leicestershire 176-7** (39 overs) (B. J. Hodge 46, D. I. Stevens 44, J. N. Snape 32*); **Durham 161-8** (39 overs) (G. J. Pratt 55*). *Leicestershire 4 pts.*

Reduced to 39 overs a side.

After a hot streak in the Twenty20, Leicestershire won their fifth one-day game in six. On a slow pitch and under grey clouds, Hodge and Stevens batted well to add 95 in 21 overs for Leicestershire's third wicket. In reply, Durham began with a rash of boundaries but Dagnall once again bowled with great control. He took one for 17 in eight overs, and forced Durham into the late risk-taking which brought three decisive run outs.

At Leicester, August 18 (day/night). **Yorkshire won by 34 runs** (D/L method). Toss: Yorkshire. **Yorkshire 177-8** (32 overs) (I. J. Harvey 37, D. S. Lehmann 56); **Leicestershire 145** (30.3 overs) (R. K. J. Dawson 3-20). *Yorkshire 4 pts.*

First-team debut: R. M. Pyrah (Yorkshire). Leicestershire's target was revised to 180 in 32 overs. Leicestershire's hangover from their Twenty20 triumph continued: a third League defeat in ten days halted their push for promotion and boosted Yorkshire's. Lehmann hit a restorative if unconvincing 56 to help Yorkshire recover from 75 for three on a slow, spinning wicket. Batting under lights, Leicestershire also struggled for fluency, scraping a highest partnership of just 30. Dawson bowled seven tidy overs of off-spin and took three for 20.

At Leicester, August 29. **No result.** Toss: Leicestershire. **Somerset 205-7** (45 overs) (M. E. Trescothick 36, J. D. Francis 36, J. C. Hildreth 42, A. V. Suppiah 30; C. W. Henderson 3-19) v **Leicestershire.** *Leicestershire 2 pts, Somerset 2 pts.*

An astonishing downpour during the tea interval ended a meaningless match. Rain fell for less than 15 minutes but it bucketed, and huge pools formed on the outfield and square.

MIDDLESEX

At Lord's, April 25. **Sussex won by eight wickets.** Toss: Middlesex. **Middlesex 140** (37.4 overs) (E. C. Joyce 48; J. D. Lewry 3-26); **Sussex 143-2** (30.1 overs) (I. J. Ward 56*, M. J. Prior 70). *Sussex 4 pts.*

County debut: B. J. M. Scott (Middlesex).

On a pitch encouraging seam movement, Middlesex collapsed from 47 for one to 98 for eight. Joyce and Weekes, who made 25, were alone in passing 18. At 126 for nought, Sussex looked set for their first ten-wicket win in the League, but then Prior fell for a 77-ball 70, soon followed by Goodwin.

At Lord's, May 3. **Middlesex won by seven wickets.** Toss: Middlesex. **Durham 120-7** (20 overs) (J. J. B. Lewis 31*); **Middlesex 121-3** (18.5 overs) (B. L. Hutton 70*). *Middlesex 4 pts.*

County debut: L. Klusener (Middlesex). Reduced to 20 overs a side.

The recently renovated Lord's drainage system made a 20-over game – and a Middlesex win – possible, after hours of heavy rain. Needing to score at just above six an over, Middlesex's openers, Weekes and Hutton, flew to 51 after six and Hutton's unbeaten 70 in 65 balls shepherded them home. The South African Test player Lance Klusener had a difficult debut: 4–0–36–1.

At Lord's, May 31. **Middlesex won by six wickets.** Toss: Somerset. **Somerset 249-6** (45 overs) (M. Burns 39, K. A. Parsons 62*, I. D. Blackwell 69); **Middlesex 250-4** (43.4 overs) (P. N. Weekes 119*, B. L. Hutton 40, O. A. Shah 54). *Middlesex 4 pts.*

Parsons made a brisk 62, but also ran out the menacing Blackwell, who faced just 74 balls and may well have taken Somerset out of sight. As it was, Middlesex won with eight balls to spare, thanks to Weekes, who was dropped on 40, and hit 13 fours and three sixes in matching his best League score. Middlesex's fourth successive win left them joint leaders.

At Lord's, June 13. **Nottinghamshire won by 94 runs.** Toss: Nottinghamshire. **Nottinghamshire 294-6** (45 overs) (J. E. R. Gallian 109, K. P. Pietersen 32, D. J. Hussey 75); **Middlesex 200** (36.4 overs) (P. N. Weekes 65, O. A. Shah 42; K. P. Pietersen 3-14). *Nottinghamshire 4 pts.*

On a good pitch close to the Grand Stand boundary, Nottinghamshire's opener Gallian made a hundred in 115 balls, his first in one-day cricket since 1999. That stability allowed Hussey to blaze a carefree 75 in just 44 deliveries from No. 5. Middlesex also came out hitting – Sidebottom's first two overs disappeared for 30 – but hit a wall at 164 for three, when they lost three wickets in as many balls.

At Richmond, July 5. **Middlesex won by 127 runs.** Toss: Middlesex. **Middlesex 216-4** (45 overs) (O. A. Shah 105*, N. R. D. Compton 33); **Scotland 89** (25.4 overs) (Extras 34; S. J. Cook 3-18). *Middlesex 4 pts.*

First-team debut: G. Goudie (Scotland).

Shah played a second impressive League innings in two days. He batted watchfully on a slow, inconsistent pitch before helping smash 82 in the last ten overs. Scotland's reply would have been even worse but for 26 wides, as Middlesex won for the eighth time in nine League matches.

At Southgate, July 11. **Middlesex won by nine wickets.** Toss: Middlesex. **Derbyshire 182-8** (45 overs) (Hassan Adnan 57; M. Hayward 4-21); **Middlesex 183-1** (38.5 overs) (P. N. Weekes 80*, B. L. Hutton 34, A. J. Strauss 59*). *Middlesex 4 pts.*

On another pudding of a pitch, Weekes's batting form remained golden, and Derbyshire's shaky. Despite Keegan breaking down with back spasms, Derbyshire managed just 182, a total Middlesex overhauled with more than six overs left. Weekes passed fifty for the seventh time in nine League innings.

At Southgate, August 1. **Middlesex won by 16 runs.** Toss: Yorkshire. **Middlesex 273-6** (45 overs) (B. L. Hutton 34, O. A. Shah 125*, D. C. Nash 35, Extras 30); **Yorkshire 257-9** (45 overs) (A. W. Gale 45, A. McGrath 96*). *Middlesex 4 pts.*

An excellent slow-burning century by Shah roused a crowd of 3,000 and gave Middlesex just enough runs. He faced 126 deliveries and hit the last three balls, bowled by Bresnan, high over long-on for six. That barrage proved crucial: McGrath batted almost as well for Yorkshire but their last six batsmen contributed only 22.

At Lord's, August 9. **Middlesex won by 17 runs** (D/L method). Toss: Leicestershire. **Middlesex 215-9** (41.5 overs) (P. N. Weekes 38, B. L. Hutton 30, E. C. Joyce 31, J. W. M. Dalrymple 40, Extras 40; C. W. Henderson 4-45); **Leicestershire 117** (18.4 overs) (A. B. Agarkar 3-22). *Middlesex 4 pts.*

Leicestershire's target was revised to 135 in 20 overs.

Leicestershire had won the Twenty20 Cup two days earlier, but failed when rain left them another 20-over challenge. At 63 for two after nine overs they were coasting but, in fading light and on a damp pitch, Agarkar took three important wickets in ten balls; Middlesex's six-run penalty for a slow over-rate proved irrelevant. Earlier, Henderson removed four of the middle order to slow a zippy Middlesex start, which was boosted by 31 wides.

At Lord's, August 15. **Worcestershire won by 83 runs.** Toss: Worcestershire. **Worcestershire 261-7** (45 overs) (G. A. Hick 120, D. A. Leatherdale 63; S. J. Cook 5-34); **Middlesex 178** (37 overs) (B. J. M. Scott 42, O. A. Shah 54; G. J. Batty 3-41). *Worcestershire 4 pts.*

County debut: R. W. Price (Worcestershire).

Hick maintained Worcestershire's strong hopes of promotion, and became the most prolific century-maker in League history, beating Wayne Larkins's record of 14. Facing 115 balls, he added a revitalising 160 for the fourth wicket with Leatherdale and fell to Cook, whose five wickets took him to 34 for the season, a Middlesex record. In reply, Middlesex's chances perished at 131, when Shah fell.

NOTTINGHAMSHIRE

At Nottingham, May 2. **Nottinghamshire won by 104 runs.** Toss: Nottinghamshire. **Nottinghamshire 291-6** (45 overs) (R. J. Warren 81, K. P. Pietersen 38, D. J. Hussey 87*, M. A. Ealham 31); **Yorkshire 187** (34.4 overs) (C. White 59, I. J. Harvey 49; M. A. Ealham 3-43, S. C. G. MacGill 3-24). *Nottinghamshire 4 pts.*

Yorkshire were outclassed by a Nottinghamshire side bristling with intent. Warren's stubborn anchoring innings of 81 allowed Hussey to free his arms and crash 87 in 75 balls. Ealham followed that lead with an 18-ball 31. Yorkshire began their reply promisingly, reaching 76 without loss in the 12th over, but wilted, failing to build a partnership against tidy bowling.

At Nottingham, May 23. **Middlesex won by three wickets.** Toss: Nottinghamshire. **Nottinghamshire 207-7** (45 overs) (A. Singh 31, R. J. Warren 31, D. J. Hussey 31, C. M. W. Read 45*; C. B. Keegan 3-28); **Middlesex 211-7** (45 overs) (P. N. Weekes 57, L. Klusener 56*; S. C. G. MacGill 4-55). *Middlesex 4 pts.*

Despite the slow pitch, Nottinghamshire's 207 looked about 20 short, with only Read imposing himself, in a quickfire 45. In reply, Weekes started the way Read had finished, but in his first six overs MacGill spun out three batsmen for 18. By the last over, Middlesex's task looked impossible – 19 needed and MacGill to bowl. But, in one of the most exciting finishes of the summer, Klusener smashed him for 22 belligerent runs: 046624.

At Nottingham, May 31. **Nottinghamshire won by seven wickets.** Toss: Sussex. **Sussex 176** (44.5 overs) (M. J. Prior 34, C. J. Adams 56; G. J. Smith 4-28); **Nottinghamshire 180-3** (37.4 overs) (R. J. Warren 45, K. P. Pietersen 80*). *Nottinghamshire 4 pts.*

A flawless exhibition of glovework from Read left Nottinghamshire with an easy target. He completed five dismissals, all standing up to the wicket; most memorable of all was the dazzling wicket of Hopkinson, stumped after the seamer Clough fired down a leg-side wide at yorker length. In reply, Nottinghamshire were 37 for two before Pietersen made a dominant and unbeaten 80.

At Nottingham, July 4. **Derbyshire won by nine wickets.** Toss: Nottinghamshire. **Nottinghamshire 211-8** (45 overs) (J. E. R. Gallian 56, R. J. Warren 39, D. J. Hussey 33, M. A. Ealham 37; J. Moss 4-45); **Derbyshire 212-1** (40.2 overs) (C. W. G. Bassano 100*, J. Moss 92). *Derbyshire 4 pts.*

Each time Nottinghamshire looked to accelerate they were blocked by Moss, who removed three dangerous hitters in the middle order. Moss then converted the advantage into a straightforward win. He and Bassano built an unfussy opening stand of 184 in 36.3 overs, the second-highest partnership for Derbyshire in the League. Bassano faced 115 balls, Moss 117; in their frustration, Nottinghamshire tried eight different bowlers.

At Nottingham, July 11. **Nottinghamshire won by three wickets.** Toss: Somerset. **Somerset 204-9** (45 overs) (J. C. Hildreth 85, M. J. Wood 39; M. A. Ealham 3-22, G. J. Smith 3-50); **Nottinghamshire 208-7** (43.5 overs) (K. P. Pietersen 82*; S. R. G. Francis 3-24). *Nottinghamshire 4 pts.*

For the third time in 2004, Nottinghamshire bounced straight back from a League defeat. The 19-year-old Hildreth proved their main obstacle; ignoring tumbling wickets at the other end – Ealham removed the top three in a flash and Somerset were 73 for five – he showed glimpses of real promise in a 90-ball 85. Nottinghamshire also stuttered, to 31 for two, but Pietersen guided their chase calmly, sharing 50 partnerships with Read and Ealham.

At Cleethorpes, August 1. **Durham won by six wickets.** Toss: Durham. **Nottinghamshire 229-7** (45 overs) (R. J. Warren 31, D. J. Hussey 37, K. P. Pietersen 30, M. A. Ealham 56, G. D. Clough 40*; G. D. Bridge 3-14); **Durham 233-4** (42.4 overs) (M. J. North 121*). *Durham 4 pts.*

North turned a hard-fought scrap between promotion rivals into something approaching a rout. In an unbeaten 121 from 114 balls he despatched MacGill into neighbouring gardens for two of his four sixes, leading Durham home with 14 balls to spare. Earlier, Nottinghamshire were set for a huge score at 113 for two after 19 overs; they got only a decent one, after the left-arm spinner Bridge applied a squeeze to end with 9-4-14-3.

At Nottingham, August 15. **Nottinghamshire won by 20 runs.** Toss: Nottinghamshire. **Nottinghamshire 249-6** (45 overs) (J. E. R. Gallian 73, A. Singh 45, K. P. Pietersen 51, C. M. W. Read 31); **Leicestershire 229** (44.5 overs) (D. L. Maddy 75, J. N. Snape 37, S. C. G. MacGill 3-50). *Nottinghamshire 4 pts.*

Nottinghamshire began their make-or-break run of five matches in 12 days with a win. It left them six points behind third-placed Durham, with three games in hand. Gallian dropped anchor for 73, giving his middle order licence to speed toward 249. In reply, Harris took two wickets in his first over and Leicestershire were in tatters at four for three; MacGill and Read then combined for three stumpings, including Maddy.

At Nottingham, August 25 (day/night). **No result (abandoned). Nottinghamshire v Worcestershire.** *Nottinghamshire 2 pts, Worcestershire 2 pts.*

Heavy rain soused the Midlands and ended any hopes of play. Two points confirmed Worcestershire's promotion, and left Nottinghamshire with a clear objective – winning both remaining matches to guarantee third place.

At Nottingham, August 26. **Nottinghamshire won by three wickets.** Toss: Scotland. **Scotland 143** (38.5 overs) (D. R. Lockhart 46; S. C. G. MacGill 4-18); **Nottinghamshire 144-7** (36 overs) (A. Singh 67). *Nottinghamshire 4 pts.*

The previous night's rain stayed away, and Nottinghamshire took a rather nervous step towards Division One. It looked simple enough when MacGill tied the Scottish batsmen in knots and grabbed four for 18 in nine overs. But cavalier shots in reply led to two wobbles – three wickets for 15 runs, followed by five for 24 as Nottinghamshire closed on the target; Yasir Arafat ended with 9-2-18-2. Victory with nine overs – but only three wickets – in hand left Nottinghamshire needing victory at Taunton for promotion.

SCOTLAND

At Edinburgh, May 7. **Somerset won by 55 runs.** Toss: Somerset. **Somerset 248-7** (45 overs) (C. M. Gazzard 43, J. Cox 51, K. A. Parsons 53, Extras 33; P. J. C. Hoffmann 3-27); **Scotland 193** (40.1 overs) (D. F. Watts 33, S. Sriram 35, R. R. Watson 45; N. A. M. McLean 3-31, K. A. Parsons 3-42). *Somerset 4 pts.*

Scotland failed to repeat the upset of the 2003 fixture. Watson, the hero of that game, this time turned the match the other way. Scotland's hopes waxed as he and Sriram took Scotland to 124 for four, but Sriram was needlessly run out. Despite Watson making 45 in 49 balls, momentum was lost and the last six wickets fell for 51.

At Edinburgh, May 16. **Middlesex won by nine wickets.** Toss: Scotland. **Scotland 218-5** (45 overs) (S. Sriram 88*); **Middlesex 221-1** (28 overs) (P. N. Weekes 83, A. J. Strauss 107*). *Middlesex 4 pts.*

In ideal batting conditions, Scotland started quietly before hustling 83 runs off their last ten overs. But that effort was quickly overshadowed as Strauss scored 107 in 80 balls, and Weekes 83 in 81. Their opening stand of 196 took Middlesex to the brink and they won with a derisive 17 overs spare.

At Edinburgh, May 31. **Yorkshire won by 59 runs.** Toss: Scotland. **Yorkshire 199-8** (45 overs) (M. J. Wood 33, M. P. Vaughan 32; Asim Butt 3-47); **Scotland 140** (39.4 overs) (R. K. J. Dawson 4-20). *Yorkshire 4 pts.*

Scotland gave an excellent performance in the field, encouraged by a seaming pitch and, perhaps, by the Sky TV cameras. Asim Butt – a 36-year-old opening bowler playing his first League game – swung the ball to trap three batsmen, Wright went for less than three an over, and Yorkshire lost regular wickets. England captain Vaughan, in one of his two 2004 League games for Yorkshire, batted steadily. In reply, Scotland reached 61 for two after 15 overs but faded.

At Edinburgh, June 20. **Scotland won by six wickets.** Toss: Scotland. **Durham 189-7** (41 overs) (J. J. B. Lewis 34, G. J. Pratt 48); **Scotland 190-4** (39.3 overs) (C. J. O. Smith 79*, C. V. English 53*). *Scotland 4 pts.*

Reduced to 41 overs a side.

Having begun their League season with seven defeats, Scotland beat Durham comprehensively. After a rain-delayed start, Asim Butt bowled an inspirational opening spell of 8–2–24–2 for Scotland; although the sun was now shining, the pitch was slightly uneven and the first ten overs brought two wickets and just 28 runs. However, Lewis and Gary Pratt dug in for 19 overs, to build a third-wicket stand of 83 and prevent collapse. They seemed to have done enough when Shoaib rattled Scotland's top order, helping reduce them to 44 for four. But the innings was rebuilt by Colin Smith, a 31-year-old Aberdonian wicket-keeper, and Cedric English, a South African with experience at several first-class provinces. Together they added 146 for the fifth wicket, Scotland's second-biggest League stand; by the time Shoaib was brought back they had already made 70 and were too well entrenched. The remaining runs were picked off at ease, and Scotland won with nine balls to spare.

At Edinburgh, June 27. **No result.** Toss: Nottinghamshire. **Nottinghamshire 205-8** (45 overs) (P. J. Franks 49, R. J. Warren 30, K. P. Pietersen 51; Yasir Arafat 3-36) **v Scotland.** *Scotland 2 pts, Nottinghamshire 2 pts.*

A finely poised game was ruined by rain during the interval. For the fifth match in a row Scotland contained their opponents to around 200; Yasir Arafat, once a medium-pacer in Pakistan's one-day side, helped ensure only 52 runs were added in Nottinghamshire's last ten overs.

At Edinburgh, June 30. **Worcestershire won by nine runs.** Toss: Worcestershire. **Worcestershire 128** (22 overs) (V. S. Solanki 36, K. Ali 33; S. Sriram 3-17); **Scotland 119-7** (22 overs) (D. A. Leatherdale 3-28). *Worcestershire 4 pts.*

First-team debut: S. Bruce (Scotland). Scotland debut: F. L. Reifer.

Reduced to 22 overs a side.

In a 22-over match, Scotland dismissed a county side for only the second time but their batsmen threw away a winning position and were left with wickets in hand, but no overs. Persistent bowling reduced Worcestershire from 40 for one to 69 for six, and the stand-in keeper Lockhart then finished off the innings with three stumpings off the economical Sriram. In reply Scotland reached 45 for one but then lost wickets regularly.

At Edinburgh, August 1. **Leicestershire won by six wickets.** Toss: Leicestershire. **Scotland 222-9** (45 overs) (D. R. Lockhart 63, D. F. Watts 34, Yasir Arafat 33, C. M. Wright 35; O. D. Gibson 3-36); **Leicestershire 223-4** (42 overs) (D. D. J. Robinson 109*, D. L. Maddy 35, J. N. Snape 39*). *Leicestershire 4 pts.*

First-team debut: S. C. Coetzer (Scotland).

Two openers formed the cornerstone of their team's innings. Lockhart made 63 in 105 balls, but was overshadowed by Robinson, who oversaw the entire Leicestershire innings to make the winning hit with three overs to spare. He survived a difficult patch in the 60s to end 109 not out, from 138 balls.

At Edinburgh, August 15. **Sussex won by 114 runs.** Toss: Scotland. **Sussex 263-6** (45 overs) (M. H. Yardy 83, M. J. Prior 44, Extras 36; Yasir Arafat 3-49); **Scotland 149** (34.5 overs) (G. I. Maiden 32; Mushtaq Ahmed 4-46). *Sussex 4 pts.*

The second over of the match – when Asim Butt conceded 14, including three wides – set the tone for Scotland's worst home display of the season. The bowling and fielding were poor, and Sussex opener Yardy was not shifted till the score was 229. The last two overs of the innings cost 32, taking Sussex to the summer's highest League score at the Grange. In reply, Scotland's best stand was just 30.

At Edinburgh, September 5. **Scotland won by eight wickets.** Toss: Scotland. **Derbyshire 179** (42.3 overs) (Hassan Adnan 50, Extras 40; P. J. C. Hoffmann 3-25); **Scotland 182-2** (36.1 overs) (D. R. Lockhart 58, G. I. Maiden 33, R. R. Watson 42*, D. F. Watts 32*). *Scotland 4 pts.*

Scotland, buoyed by a win against Bangladesh two days earlier, completed one of the better weeks in their history with their most crushing win against professional opposition. It began with luck at the toss – the pitch was difficult at the start – and three early wickets, both openers falling in single figures to Hoffman's medium pace. An understrength attack then kept a stranglehold on the batsmen – one stand-in, 17-year-old Goudie, conceded less than three an over – despite giving away 40 extras. After a slow start to the reply, Watson and Watts at Nos 3 and 4 dominated completely; victory came with nearly nine overs left, and the only two wickets were the result of overambitious hook shots.

SOMERSET

At Taunton, April 25. **Somerset won by 109 runs.** Toss: Derbyshire. **Somerset 278-7** (45 overs) (J. D. Francis 39, M. Burns 97, C. M. Gazzard 31, K. A. Parsons 51); **Derbyshire 169** (36.1 overs) (A. I. Gait 39, G. Welch 40; N. A. M. McLean 3-21). *Somerset 4 pts.*

Put in on a warm spring afternoon, Somerset were quickly in the runs. Burns put on 97 for the first wicket with Francis and another 69 with Gazzard for the second. Then Parsons, whose half-century came at a run a ball, and Rob Turner – 24 off 16 deliveries – made sure the momentum was not lost. Derbyshire, on the other hand, never got going, thanks especially to some hostile fast bowling from McLean.

At Taunton, May 9. **Yorkshire won by 145 runs.** Toss: Somerset. **Yorkshire 284-9** (45 overs) (M. J. Wood 51, C. White 41, M. J. Lumb 36, A. McGrath 58, T. T. Bresnan 49); **Somerset 139** (34.5 overs) (J. Cox 69; T. T. Bresnan 3-31). *Yorkshire 4 pts.*

Two explosive innings book-ended a commanding Yorkshire total. The opener White found the middle of the bat immediately on an honest pitch – hitting 41 in 27 balls – and at the death Bresnan scored an even quicker 49. Perhaps more impressively, given the conditions, he then prised out three middle-order wickets, to leave Somerset 40 for four. No one stayed with Cox, who was eighth with the score 136 and the match long-since lost.

At Bath, June 13. **Somerset won by three wickets.** Toss: Somerset. **Leicestershire 263-7** (45 overs) (D. I. Stevens 83, J. N. Snape 50); **Somerset 265-7** (44.1 overs) (M. Burns 45, J. C. Hildreth 43, K. A. Parsons 73). *Somerset 4 pts.*

Keith Parsons ended Somerset's run of five defeats in all cricket. Dropped for their two previous Championship matches, he answered with 73 at a run a ball, taking Somerset within ten of victory; on a fast pitch, he drove with poise. Earlier, a fifth-wicket stand of 118 by Stevens and Snape rescued Leicestershire from 99 for four; Hodge edged a short ball into his face and fell on to his stumps; he was not fit enough to field. The bowler responsible, Francis, was by far Somerset's most economical, ending with 9–1–22–2.

At Taunton, June 27. **Durham won by 16 runs** (D/L method). Toss: Durham. **Durham 278-4** (45 overs) (N. Peng 62, J. J. B. Lewis 41, G. J. Pratt 67*, Shoaib Akhtar 32); **Somerset 210-9** (33.2 overs) (J. C. Hildreth 47, J. D. Francis 75; N. Killeen 3-19). *Durham 4 pts.*

Somerset's target was revised to 236 in 35 overs.

Two sides tied in mid-table on 16 points produced an appropriately close game. Durham made 278 in a start-stop-start innings: 91 flowed from the first 14 overs, slowing to a trickle from the next eight, before 62 came from the last six. Somerset then whittled their rain-altered target down to 65 off seven overs. But John Francis was run out for a 78-ball 75, and rain returned soon afterwards, leaving Somerset stranded behind the Duckworth/Lewis par score.

At Taunton, July 26. **Worcestershire won by 34 runs.** Toss: Worcestershire. **Worcestershire 225** (44.2 overs) (V. S. Solanki 122, S. J. Rhodes 33; N. A. M. McLean 4-35); **Somerset 191** (41.4 overs) (R. T. Ponting 46, J. C. Hildreth 31, J. D. Francis 38; K. Ali 3-28, A. J. Hall 3-24). *Worcestershire 4 pts.*

A fine century by Solanki underpinned Worcestershire's fourth successive League win. He batted from first over – cover-driving two successive fours – to last, when he was ninth out for 122 in 114 balls. Rhodes – 33 in 36 deliveries – provided the only support, after McLean wrecked the middle order. Chasing 226 on an unusual seaming pitch, Somerset needed 37 from five overs, but fell well short as Hall struck three times in the 41st over.

At Taunton, August 1. **Sussex won by six runs.** Toss: Sussex. **Sussex** 274-9 (45 overs) (I. J. Ward 33, M. H. Yardy 37, M. W. Goodwin 50, P. A. Cottey 50); **Somerset** 268-9 (45 overs) (J. D. Francis 79, R. T. Ponting 56, K. A. Parsons 54, I. D. Blackwell 33; P. A. Cottey 5-49). *Sussex 4 pts.*

Somerset lost their sixth successive League match but it was a close thing. With five overs left, they needed 45 with seven wickets in hand, but one batsman after another fell to Cottey's usually unthreatening off-breaks. He emerged with five for 49, a career-best. Earlier, Cottey added 102 for the fifth wicket with Goodwin, helping Sussex to 274, before three contrasting innings took Somerset close. John Francis dropped anchor for 79 in 113 balls, while Ponting and Parsons both scored at quicker than a run a ball.

At Taunton, August 22. **Somerset won by seven runs.** Toss: Somerset. **Somerset** 253-8 (45 overs) (J. Cox 63, J. C. Hildreth 53, M. J. Wood 56; C. M. Wright 5-44); **Scotland** 246 (44.2 overs) (G. I. Maiden 44, C. V. English 55, Yasir Arafat 55*; G. M. Andrew 4-48). *Somerset 4 pts.*

Around 1,000 spectators, one of Taunton's smallest one-day crowds for many years, watched the inexperienced off-spinner Andrew save Somerset. With Scotland needing eight from the tense last over, Andrew took their two remaining wickets in the first two balls. Earlier, the Scottish captain Wright profited from late slogging to collect their first five-wicket League haul. In reply, Yasir Arafat buzzed to an unbeaten 55 from No. 7, facing just 40 balls.

At Taunton, August 24 (day/night). **Middlesex won by 57 runs** (D/L method). Toss: Somerset. **Somerset** 179 (39.3 overs) (J. Cox 42, M. J. Wood 44; M. M. Betts 3-23); **Middlesex** 153-2 (28 overs) (P. N. Weekes 76*, A. J. Strauss 68). *Middlesex 4 pts.*

Reduced to 43 overs a side.

Somerset never recovered from the depths of 94 for five. Wood was last to go, run out when a drive from Simon Francis was deflected on to the stumps by Clark, and the total of 179 never looked adequate. So it proved, as Weekes and Strauss drove the spinners crisply in adding 143 for the second wicket. When rain arrived at 9.15 p.m., Middlesex had used just 28 overs to get within 26 runs of victory.

At Taunton, September 8. **Nottinghamshire won by 34 runs.** Toss: Nottinghamshire. **Nottinghamshire** 259-7 (45 overs) (J. E. R. Gallian 68, D. J. Hussey 39, P. J. Franks 64); **Somerset** 225 (42.5 overs) (K. A. Parsons 115*; G. J. Smith 3-35). *Nottinghamshire 4 pts.*

A century by Keith Parsons dragged out the wait, but Nottinghamshire achieved the win they needed for promotion. A blistering 64 from 37 balls by Franks gave their innings a late boost; in reply, Parsons held out for 114 deliveries before running out of partners. Somerset's next-best score was 24. Some spectators claimed that the wave of Parsons's bat on reaching 100 was directed at his detractors in the committee room.

SUSSEX

SUSSEX v LEICESTERSHIRE

At Horsham, May 23. Leicestershire won by one run. Toss: Sussex. Leicestershire 4 pts.

A 3,000 crowd at Horsham was wonderfully entertained by a match that produced more runs than any in League history. And at the end of it all, including 17 sixes, the game came down to a hair's breadth. Sussex needed 15 from Cleary's last over, then ten from the final two balls, but for almost the first time things did not go as the batsman's way. Yardy leg-glanced the penultimate ball to the rope, and hit another four off the last, not the six he needed. Earlier, Leicestershire blazed to a huge total thanks to 154 from Hodge, the county's highest-ever League score. Hodge shared stands of 165 with Maddy and 74 with Nixon and, after reaching a run-a-ball century, he hit with unstoppable power to pass 150 in just 17 more deliveries. Leicestershire's total of 324 was the second-highest conceded by Sussex in the League. But they came back stronger than any side in the history of the competition, with a record second innings of 323. The opener Ward led boldly, overseeing the addition of 269 runs, and sharing stands of 143 with Goodwin and 91 with Adams. He had made 136 in 120 balls, Sussex's second-highest League score, when he missed a cut off Henderson. Soon afterwards Adams fell, also trying to cut the left-arm spinner, and Sussex hopes ebbed, before rising again briefly.

Leicestershire

D. I. Stevens c Adams b Martin-Jenkins	12	J. L. Sadler not out	0
D. L. Maddy run out	95		
B. J. Hodge not out	154	B 1, l-b 8, w 16	25
†P. A. Nixon b Kirtley	30		
*P. A. J. DeFreitas c Ward		1/42 (1) 2/207 (2) (4 wkts, 45 overs) 324	
b Mohammad Akram	8	3/281 (4) 4/322 (5)	

J. N. Snape, D. D. J. Robinson, C. W. Henderson, D. S. Brignull and M. F. Cleary did not bat.

Bowling: Martin-Jenkins 9–1–38–1; Mohammad Akram 9–0–63–1; Kirtley 8–0–75–1; Yardy 5–0–31–0; Mushtaq Ahmed 7–0–53–0; Davis 7–0–55–0.

Sussex

I. J. Ward b Henderson	136	M. H. Yardy not out	14
†M. J. Prior c and b Cleary	16		
M. W. Goodwin c and b Snape	66	B 1, l-b 5, w 11, n-b 2	19
*C. J. Adams c Brignull b Henderson	45		
R. S. C. Martin-Jenkins c Hodge		1/35 (2) 2/178 (3) (5 wkts, 45 overs) 323	
b Cleary	10	3/269 (1) 4/284 (4)	
R. R. Montgomerie not out	17	5/296 (5)	

M. J. G. Davis, Mushtaq Ahmed, Mohammad Akram and R. J. Kirtley did not bat.

Bowling: DeFreitas 9–0–66–0; Cleary 9–0–60–2; Brignull 4–0–32–0; Snape 9–0–46–1; Henderson 6–0–54–2; Maddy 2–0–16–0; Hodge 6–0–43–0.

Umpires: J. H. Evans and P. Willey.

At Hove, June 6. **Sussex won by six runs.** Toss: Sussex. **Sussex 230-7** (45 overs) (I. J. Ward 47, M. W. Goodwin 81, C. J. Adams 35; A. R. Caddick 3-32); **Somerset 224-7** (45 overs) (M. Burns 62, J. Cox 71; R. S. C. Martin-Jenkins 3-37). *Sussex 4 pts.*
At 168 for two, with more than 11 overs to score 63 runs, Somerset were cruising. But Martin-Jenkins took two wickets in two overs and Sussex scraped home, ending a run of four League defeats. On a slow pitch Sussex had been 164 for two – with Goodwin facing 101 balls for 81 – but they had no well-set batsman during the closing overs. In reply, Burns and Cox took Somerset within reach of victory, in a 26-over second-wicket stand of 140.

At Arundel, June 27. **Yorkshire won by eight wickets.** Toss: Sussex. **Sussex 118** (32.1 overs) (M. J. Hoggard 3-35, V. J. Craven 3-13); **Yorkshire 119-2** (26.5 overs) (A. W. Gale 46, M. J. Wood 41*). *Yorkshire 4 pts.*
Yorkshire won with dismissive ease, after superb accurate opening spells by Hoggard and Bresnan left Sussex 43 for five in the 11th over. In reply, Gale and Wood added 92 for the second wicket, and Yorkshire won with 18.1 overs spare. They did so in dark blue kit, after Wood went out to toss in their intended yellow away shirt and was attacked by a swarm of insects.

At Hove, June 30 (day/night). **Sussex won by 99 runs.** Toss: Sussex. **Sussex 261-4** (45 overs) (M. J. Prior 119, C. J. Adams 81); **Durham 162-8** (45 overs) (G. J. Pratt 58*, Extras 30; R. S. C. Martin-Jenkins 3-16). *Sussex 4 pts.*
Durham missed the chance of going joint-top of Division Two, falling woefully short of a challenging total. Prior powered his way to 119 from 135 balls and shared in a superb third-wicket stand of 135 in 20 overs. Adams, his partner, fired 81 from 69 balls. After slumping to 58 for four in reply, Durham simply batted out overs; Martin-Jenkins's full figures were 7–1–16–3.

At Hove, July 4. **No result.** Toss: Scotland. **Sussex 57-2** (10.2 overs) **v Scotland.** *Sussex 2 pts, Scotland 2 pts.*

First-team debut: S. J. S. Smith (Scotland).

Sussex, with only two wins in seven games, saw their chance of beating the whipping boys disappear in the rain.

SUSSEX v NOTTINGHAMSHIRE

At Hove, July 21 (day/night). Tied. Toss: Nottinghamshire. Sussex 2 pts, Nottinghamshire 2 pts.

Nottinghamshire pinched a tie from a losing situation as Sussex collapsed dramatically under lights. Adams seemed to have timed the charge perfectly: after smashing the 42nd over, bowled by Logan, for 21, Sussex needed just 14. But in the penultimate over Logan had his revenge: Adams failed to clear point, after scampering a 98-ball 93, Davis fell to the next ball and, from the last, Martin-Jenkins lost his off stump. With the pressure rising, four were needed from Sidebottom's last over, with two wickets in hand. Off the second ball, Wright was run out attempting to run two, a pair of singles brought the scores level and, from the last delivery, Sidebottom produced a beauty that trimmed Kirtley's off bail. It sparked celebrations from Nottinghamshire, who had feared the work of Gallian and Warren, who shared an opening stand of 147 in 29 overs, would be wasted.

Nottinghamshire

*J. E. R. Gallian b Martin-Jenkins	77	M. A. Ealham not out	7
R. J. Warren c Cottey b Mushtaq Ahmed	78	B 1, l-b 8, w 9, n-b 2	20
D. J. Hussey c Adams b Wright	24		
K. P. Pietersen c and b Kirtley	39	1/147 (1) 2/180 (2) (4 wkts, 45 overs) 260	
†C. M. W. Read not out	15	3/197 (3) 4/249 (4)	

P. J. Franks, G. D. Clough, S. C. G. MacGill, R. J. Logan and R. J. Sidebottom did not bat.

Bowling: Kirtley 9–0–48–1; Wright 6–0–52–1; Martin-Jenkins 9–0–44–1; Yardy 3–0–22–0; Davis 9–0–45–0; Mushtaq Ahmed 9–0–40–1.

Sussex

I. J. Ward lbw b Logan	28	Mushtaq Ahmed not out	1
†M. J. Prior c Warren b Ealham	25	R. J. Kirtley b Sidebottom	1
M. H. Yardy c Ealham b Franks	24	B 4, l-b 13, w 13, n-b 4	34
*C. J. Adams c Clough b Logan	93		
M. W. Goodwin c Clough b Franks	38	1/54 (2) 2/62 (1) (45 overs) 260	
P. A. Cottey c Read b Franks	2	3/133 (3) 4/205 (5)	
M. J. G. Davis c Read b Logan	12	5/214 (6) 6/255 (4)	
L. J. Wright run out	1	7/255 (7) 8/257 (9)	
R. S. C. Martin-Jenkins b Logan	1	9/258 (8) 10/260 (11)	

Bowling: Ealham 9–0–41–1; Sidebottom 8–1–48–1; Logan 9–0–50–4; Clough 4–0–29–0; MacGill 9–0–38–0; Franks 6–0–37–3.

Umpires: N. G. Cowley and T. E. Jesty.

At Hove, August 8. **Sussex won by 84 runs.** Toss: Sussex. **Sussex 271-7** (45 overs) (I. J. Ward 49, M. J. Prior 59, M. H. Yardy 88*); **Derbyshire 187** (39 overs) (J. D. C. Bryant 42, G. Welch 82; R. J. Kirtley 3-11, R. S. C. Martin-Jenkins 4-39). *Sussex 4 pts.*

Derbyshire were spared heavier defeat by Welch, who arrived with the innings in tatters at 65 for six. He walloped 82 in 47 balls, with eight fours and five sixes, but the game was lost long before. Kirtley took the first three wickets, finishing with 6–2–11–3. Earlier, Ward and Prior were both dropped during an opening stand of 102, and Yardy hit a fluent 88 in 74 balls, as Sussex set an imposing target on a slow wicket.

At Hove, August 17 (day/night). **Sussex won by eight wickets** (D/L method). Toss: Worcestershire. **Worcestershire 203-8** (45 overs) (S. C. Moore 76, A. J. Bichel 42); **Sussex 99-2** (15.1 overs) (M. J. Prior 56*). *Sussex 4 pts.*

Sussex's target was revised to 96 in 17 overs.

Sussex continued their late surge for promotion. A fifth win in six games took them joint third with Durham, with two matches left. Worcestershire opener Moore pulled round a nosedive to 69 for four, with a battling 111-ball innings. With Sussex chasing a revised 117 in 20 overs, Prior and Goodwin added 51 in just six, a match-winning second-wicket partnership briefly interrupted by more rain.

At Hove, September 2 (day/night). **Sussex won by 132 runs.** Toss: Sussex. **Sussex 217-8** (45 overs) (M. W. Goodwin 91, C. D. Hopkinson 41; S. J. Cook 4-37); **Middlesex 85** (27.5 overs) (L. J. Wright 4-12, R. S. C. Martin-Jenkins 3-11, C. D. Hopkinson 3-40). *Sussex 4 pts.*

First-team debut: C. D. Whelan (Middlesex).

Sussex thrashed the new second-division champions, but the preceding defeat at Chester-le-Street had already ended their own promotion hopes. On a lifeless pitch Goodwin rescued Sussex from 54 for five, with 91 in 93 balls. Cook took four wickets to equal Adam Hollioake's record of 39 in a season but the others dropped too short. Middlesex also slumped early, and for them there was no recovery: their best partnership was 20 for the last wicket, and the England Under-19 all-rounder Wright ended with 7–3–12–4.

WORCESTERSHIRE

At Worcester, May 2. **Worcestershire won by 21 runs.** Toss: Sussex. **Worcestershire 239-5** (45 overs) (G. A. Hick 63, B. F. Smith 77, S. C. Moore 46*); **Sussex 218** (44.2 overs) (I. J. Ward 50, M. W. Goodwin 30, C. J. Adams 44; A. J. Bichel 4-60, M. N. Malik 4-42). *Worcestershire 4 pts.*

Having ended 2003 with a run of eight consecutive one-day defeats, Worcestershire turned over a new leaf. Their middle order proved resilient after Sussex reduced them to 55 for three on a lively wicket, Smith hitting a run-a-ball 77. His 50th one-day fifty helped steer Worcestershire to 239. At 188 for four, Sussex seemed on course, but then Bichel and Malik, backed up by Shaftab Khalid's economical off-spin, broke through.

At Worcester, May 4. **No result (abandoned).** Worcestershire v Nottinghamshire. *Worcestershire 2 pts, Nottinghamshire 2 pts.*

At Worcester, May 16. **Durham won by 94 runs.** Toss: Durham. **Durham 319-3** (45 overs) (N. Peng 65, M. J. North 110, P. D. Collingwood 102*); **Worcestershire 225-8** (45 overs) (S. C. Moore 51, S. J. Rhodes 71*; A. M. Davies 3-43). *Durham 4 pts.*

Durham, elated by successfully chasing 451 in the Championship at Taunton the day before, continued their briefly imperious batting form. They made 319 – their highest one-day score against a first-class side. North lifted five leg-side sixes in reaching 110 from 112 balls, but no one could match Collingwood. He scurried to Durham's fastest-ever century in 72 deliveries, only 48 coming in boundaries. With North, he added 156 for the second wicket. They were helped by injuries to Bichel and Hall, sunny skies and a flat pitch, but in reply, Worcestershire failed to use the conditions. They lost three wickets on 34 and, at 90 for six, were flirting with the heaviest League defeat of all time. Moore and Rhodes avoided that.

At Worcester, June 13. **Yorkshire won by six wickets.** Toss: Worcestershire. **Worcestershire 189** (44.5 overs) (V. S. Solanki 52, G. A. Hick 42); **Yorkshire 190-4** (43 overs) (C. White 41, P. A. Jaques 62). *Yorkshire 4 pts.*

On a pitch with the bounce and pace of plasticine, Worcestershire reached 51 for no wicket but thereafter failed to build a partnership; the spinners Dawson and Lehmann bowled 18 tight overs for a joint return of four for 60. Even Hick, who overtook Graham Gooch's 8,573 League runs, and now trailed only Kim Barnett, could not score freely. In reply, White showed patience in the face of two early wickets and a 13-ball wait to score, giving Jaques licence to hit a brisker 62.

At Worcester, July 4. **Worcestershire won by 64 runs** (D/L method). Toss: Worcestershire. **Worcestershire 238-7** (39 overs) (V. S. Solanki 59, S. C. Moore 40, G. A. Hick 52; G. M. Andrew 3-50); **Somerset 179** (35.5 overs) (K. P. Dutch 79*; M. N. Malik 3-20). *Worcestershire 4 pts.*

Somerset's target was revised to 244 in 39 overs.

Worcestershire made an intimidating total in their rain-interrupted innings, led in turn by Solanki and Hick. Both scored at around a run a ball against an injury-hit attack, and both were well set when removed by the off-spinner Andrew. In reply, Dutch hit 56 of his 79 in crisp boundaries, but Mason and Malik removed his partners.

At Worcester, July 21 (day/night). **Worcestershire won by 70 runs.** Toss: Worcestershire. **Worcestershire 252-4** (45 overs) (V. S. Solanki 55, G. A. Hick 107*); **Middlesex 182** (42.3 overs) (O. A. Shah 36, E. C. Joyce 65, Extras 32; M. S. Mason 3-32). *Worcestershire 4 pts.*
 County debuts: A. B. Agarkar, G. D. McGrath (Middlesex).

Worcestershire continued their strong run, beating the leaders to go joint third in the table. Again, Hick and Solanki dominated. Hick reached a 109-ball hundred in the last over, during which the Australian Test star Glenn McGrath, once of Worcestershire, conceded 15. In reply, Joyce and Shah added 107 for the third wicket, but were never up with the rate, and Middlesex's last eight wickets fell for 50. Solanki added two run outs and a reflex catch to his earlier 55 runs.

At Worcester, August 1. **Worcestershire won by 111 runs.** Toss: Worcestershire. **Worcestershire 248-7** (45 overs) (V. S. Solanki 35, B. F. Smith 50, A. J. Hall 70*); **Derbyshire 137** (33.4 overs) (S. A. Selwood 35; G. J. Batty 3-22). *Worcestershire 4 pts.*

After a slow start, Worcestershire rocketed towards a fifth successive win: Hall made 70 in 55 balls, Kabir Ali 22 in nine and they belted 42 off the last two overs from the Diglis End. The resulting total of 248 was well beyond Derbyshire. Batty bowled a fine spell of off-spin (8.4–0–22–3) and removed Selwood, the only batsman to pass 20.

At Worcester, August 24. **Worcestershire won by one run.** Toss: Scotland. **Worcestershire 131** (40.4 overs) (V. S. Solanki 35, B. F. Smith 50*; Yasir Arafat 4-22); **Scotland 130** (39.3 overs) (R. R. Watson 44; A. J. Hall 3-26). *Worcestershire 4 pts.*
 First-team debut: C. A. R. Coles (Scotland). Reduced to 42 overs a side.

Even on this green pitch Scotland should have won: with more than 22 overs left, they needed 53 runs with eight wickets in hand. But soon afterwards Watson was out and inexperienced batsmen failed under pressure. Only Yasir Arafat held firm. He was 22 not out when, with the tension high and the total two short, the last man Hoffman clipped into square leg's hands. Worcestershire themselves had lasted only 40.4 overs; the seamer Arafat took four for 22 in helpful conditions and Smith was stranded on 50. A total of 131 looked inadequate as Watson hit an aggressive 44, helping add 70 for the third wicket. But he fell to Hall who, along with Malik, then worked through a jittery line-up.

At Worcester, September 5. **Worcestershire won by five wickets.** Toss: Leicestershire. **Leicestershire 107** (26.4 overs) (O. D. Gibson 32; D. H. Wigley 4-37); **Worcestershire 111-5** (18.4 overs) (B. F. Smith 33*). *Worcestershire 4 pts.*

Worcestershire were already promoted (barring a victory of freakish proportions in Durham's game at Scarborough) and victory made sure of the £11,000 cheque for second place. On a bowler's pitch, the match lasted just 45.2 overs: Wigley took four of the Leicestershire top six for his best figures in senior cricket; Rhodes, in his last one-day match before retirement, signed off with a neat leg-side stumping of Masters. Worcestershire hit out in reply, scoring 92 in boundaries.

YORKSHIRE

At Leeds, April 25. **Leicestershire won by 145 runs.** Toss: Yorkshire. **Leicestershire 257-7** (45 overs) (J. L. Sadler 88, J. N. Snape 69, Extras 32; I. J. Harvey 3-38); **Yorkshire 112** (28 overs) (M. F. Cleary 3-17, C. W. Henderson 5-24). *Leicestershire 4 pts.*

Leicestershire had slipped to 44 for four when Snape joined Sadler. Together they added 165 in 25 overs, a League record for Leicestershire against Yorkshire. Sadler, who began his career at Headingley, hit 88 from 81 balls, a one-day best. Yorkshire started their reply even more atrociously, lurching first to ten for four, then 22 for five. With the issue all but settled, Henderson mopped up the last five wickets: his five for 24 were another Leicestershire v Yorkshire record.

At Leeds, May 3. **Yorkshire won by 75 runs.** Toss: Scotland. **Yorkshire 240-5** (45 overs) (C. White 36, D. S. Lehmann 88*); **Scotland 165** (37.5 overs) (R. R. Watson 38; J. A. R. Blain 3-34, D. S. Lehmann 3-34). *Yorkshire 4 pts.*

On the wrong end of thrashings in their first two League games, Yorkshire inflicted one of their own. Though tied down for a long period by Scotland's nagging medium-pacers, Lehmann eventually broke free as Yorkshire hammered 94 from their final ten overs. That gave them 240, a total well beyond Scotland on a grudging Headingley wicket.

At Leeds, May 16. **Yorkshire won by five wickets.** Toss: Sussex. **Sussex 267-9** (45 overs) (M. J. Prior 72, M. W. Goodwin 64, C. J. Adams 56); **Yorkshire 271-5** (44.2 overs) (M. J. Lumb 43, P. A. Jaques 105, A. McGrath 42). *Yorkshire 4 pts.*

Jaques took command of his first one-day match for Yorkshire, hitting a chanceless 105 from 87 balls. It set exactly the right pace, and Yorkshire reached a stiff target with four balls remaining. On an excellent surface, Sussex's top order had batted with a confidence that made 300-plus seem likely, but progress was slowed by an unusual hat-trick: Martin-Jenkins was bowled by Harvey and two successive run-outs followed.

At Leeds, May 23. **Worcestershire won by 39 runs.** Toss: Worcestershire. **Worcestershire 238-6** (45 overs) (V. S. Solanki 68, G. A. Hick 54, K. Ali 51); **Yorkshire 199** (43.3 overs) (M. J. Wood 46, C. White 31; M. N. Malik 3-53). *Worcestershire 4 pts.*

First-team debut: A. Shahzad (Yorkshire).

This was a historic day for Yorkshire, with the 18-year-old Bradford schoolboy Ajmal Shahzad becoming the first Yorkshire-born Asian to play first-team cricket for the county. Brought in at the last minute because of an injury crisis, Shahzad withstood an early onslaught from Solanki and Peters to concede only 35 runs from six consecutive overs. In reply, Wood and White rattled up 65 in ten overs, before two crazy run-outs and some poor strokes pulled the game from Yorkshire's grasp.

At Leeds, July 4. **Middlesex won by 29 runs.** Toss: Yorkshire. **Middlesex 209-7** (24 overs) (B. L. Hutton 41, O. A. Shah 81; V. J. Craven 4-50); **Yorkshire 180** (23.5 overs) (A. W. Gale 33, P. A. Jaques 70, T. T. Bresnan 39). *Middlesex 4 pts.*

County debut: C. J. C. Wright (Middlesex). Reduced to 24 overs a side.

The two reduced sides had both won six of their last seven League games. After rain cut the match to 24 overs each, Middlesex reached a massive 209 thanks to ebullient innings by Shah – 81 in 56 balls – and Hutton – 41 in 35. Yorkshire matched that pace as Jaques hit 70 in 46 deliveries, but struggled thereafter.

At Scarborough, July 25. **Yorkshire won by six wickets** (D/L method). Toss: Yorkshire. **Somerset 252-6** (41 overs) (K. P. Dutch 34, R. T. Ponting 113, J. C. Hildreth 32); **Yorkshire 255-4** (38.4 overs) (M. J. Wood 56, M. J. Lumb 71, A. W. Gale 70*, A. McGrath 39). *Yorkshire 4 pts.*

Yorkshire's target was revised to 254 in 41 overs.

After the preceding rout in the Championship match Yorkshire's batsmen found some gumption. Facing a commanding target, Wood and Lumb hit powerful fifties at better than a run a ball and Gale, the 20-year-old left-hander, finished the job with 2.2 overs spare. For Somerset, Ponting scored a second hundred in four days, hitting crisply on an Australian-style pitch. He reached 113 in 107 balls, but the score might have been much bigger: Blackwell, batting at No. 7, was left stranded on 22 not out from just 12.

At Leeds, August 10 (day/night). **Derbyshire won by 29 runs.** Toss: Yorkshire. **Derbyshire 128-5** (17 overs) (J. Moss 54*, Hassan Adnan 33); **Yorkshire 99-7** (17 overs). *Derbyshire 4 pts.*

Reduced to 17 overs a side.

The groundstaff transformed a waterlogged ground and made a 17-over match possible. As the ball darted about under the lights, Moss batted through for 54, although Derbyshire were helped by loose bowling – Kirby conceded nine wides in his first two overs. The Derbyshire attack were much better – Sheikh ended with 4-0-10-2 – and Yorkshire's reply never got going.

At Leeds, August 16. **No result** (D/L method). Toss: Nottinghamshire. **Nottinghamshire 141-4** (25 overs) (J. E. R. Gallian 39, A. Singh 45); **Yorkshire 9-3** (4 overs). *Yorkshire 2 pts, Nottinghamshire 2 pts.*

Yorkshire's target was revised to 180 in 25 overs.

Yorkshire were sinking fast when the third and final shower ended the contest. Aided by Kirby's waywardness, Gallian and Singh gave Nottinghamshire a fine start with a stand of 85. Chasing a revised target of 180, Yorkshire were nine for three when the rain returned after four overs.

At Scarborough, September 5. **Yorkshire won by three wickets.** Toss: Durham. **Durham 178-9** (45 overs) (G. M. Hamilton 76; M. J. Hoggard 3-52); **Yorkshire 181-7** (41.4 overs) (M. J. Wood 46, R. M. Pyrah 42; L. E. Plunkett 3-35). *Yorkshire 4 pts.*

A crowd of 5,025 watched this promotion decider: both sides needed to win and then hope Somerset beat Nottinghamshire on September 8. Yorkshire struck early and stayed on top, with Hoggard taking three for ten in his first 13 balls, and Durham slumping to 16 for four and then 79 for five. Hamilton made 76, equalling his best one-day score, against his old county, to give Durham something to bowl at. Yorkshire also stumbled early – Plunkett taking three wickets – and at 61 for four the result was suddenly in doubt. But, with plenty of overs in hand, Wood and Pyrah could take time to add a steadying 63 for the sixth wicket. It counted for little: Somerset lost – and so Yorkshire stayed in the second division.

LEAGUE RECORDS

*40 overs available in all games up to 1998, except for 1993, when teams played 50 overs;
45 overs 1999–2004.*

Batting

Highest individual scores: 203, A. D. Brown, Surrey v Hampshire, Guildford, 1997; 191, D. S. Lehmann, Yorkshire v Nottinghamshire, Scarborough, 2001; 176, G. A. Gooch, Essex v Glamorgan, Southend, 1983; 175*, I. T. Botham, Somerset v Northamptonshire, Wellingborough School, 1986.

Most runs: K. J. Barnett 9,002; G. A. Hick 8,964; G. A. Gooch 8,573; M. P. Maynard 8,027; C. W. J. Athey 7,526; W. Larkins 7,499; P. Johnson 7,225; D. W. Randall 7,062; R. A. Smith 7,050; D. L. Amiss 7,048; R. J. Bailey 7,031. **In a season:** T. M. Moody 917 for Worcestershire, 1991.

Most hundreds: G. A. Hick 15; W. Larkins 14; A. D. Brown and G. A. Gooch 12; C. J. Adams and C. G. Greenidge 11; T. M. Moody and R. A. Smith 10. 782 hundreds have been scored in the League. The most in one season is 59 in 2003.

Most sixes in an innings: I. T. Botham, 13, Somerset v Northamptonshire, Wellingborough School, 1986. **By a team in an innings:** 18, Derbyshire v Worcestershire, Knypersley, 1985, and Surrey v Yorkshire, Scarborough, 1994. **In a season:** I. V. A. Richards, 26, Somerset, 1977.

Highest total: 377-9, Somerset v Sussex, Hove, 2003 (45-overs match). **By a side batting second:** 323-5, Sussex v Leicestershire, Horsham, 2004 (45-overs match).

Highest match aggregate: 647-9, Leicestershire (324-4) v Sussex (323-5), Horsham, 2004 (45-overs match).

Lowest total: 23 (19.4 overs), Middlesex v Yorkshire, Leeds, 1974.

Shortest completed innings: 16 overs (59), Northamptonshire v Middlesex, Tring, 1974.

Record partnerships for each wicket

239	for 1st	G. A. Gooch and B. R. Hardie, Essex v Nottinghamshire at Nottingham ..	1985
273	for 2nd	G. A. Gooch and K. S. McEwan, Essex v Nottinghamshire at Nottingham .	1983
228*	for 3rd	M. W. Goodwin and C. J. Adams, Sussex v Middlesex at Hove	2003
219	for 4th	C. G. Greenidge and C. L. Smith, Hampshire v Surrey at Southampton ..	1987
220*	for 5th	C. C. Lewis and P. A. Nixon, Leicestershire v Kent at Canterbury	1999
167*	for 6th	C. L. Cairns and C. M. W. Read, Notts v Sussex at Nottingham	2003
164	for 7th	J. N. Snape and M. A. Hardinges, Gloucestershire v Notts at Leicester .	2001
116*	for 8th	N. D. Burns and P. A. J. DeFreitas, Leicestershire v Northants at Leicester	2001
105	for 9th	D. G. Moir and R. W. Taylor, Derbyshire v Kent at Derby	1984
82	for 10th	G. Chapple and P. J. Martin, Lancashire v Worcestershire at Manchester ..	1996

Bowling

Most wickets: J. K. Lever 386; J. E. Emburey 368; D. L. Underwood 346; J. Simmons 307; S. Turner 303; N. Gifford 284; E. E. Hemmings 281; R. K. Illingworth 273; J. N. Shepherd 267; G. C. Small 261; A. C. S. Pigott 260; I. T. Botham 256; M. V. Fleming 250. **In a season:** A. J. Hollioake, 39 for Surrey, 1996; S. J. Cook, 39 for Middlesex, 2004.

Best bowling: 8-26, K. D. Boyce, Essex v Lancashire, Manchester, 1971; 7-15, R. A. Hutton, Yorkshire v Worcestershire, Leeds, 1969; 7-16, S. D. Thomas, Glamorgan v Surrey, Swansea, 1998; 7-30, M. P. Bicknell, Surrey v Glamorgan, The Oval, 1999; 7-39, A. Hodgson, Northamptonshire v Somerset, Northampton, 1976; 7-41, A. N. Jones, Sussex v Nottinghamshire, Nottingham, 1986.

Most economical analysis: 8-8-0-0, B. A. Langford, Somerset v Essex, Yeovil, 1969.

Most expensive analyses: 9-0-99-1, M. R. Strong, Northamptonshire v Gloucestershire, Cheltenham, 2001; 8-0-96-1, D. G. Cork, Derbyshire v Nottinghamshire, Nottingham, 1993; 8 0 94 2, P. N. Weekes, Middlesex v Leicestershire, Leicester, 1994; 9-0-91-1, M. J. Cawdron, Northamptonshire v Gloucestershire, Bristol, 2002.

Hat-tricks: There have been 33 hat-tricks, five of them for Glamorgan.

Four wickets in four balls: A. Ward, Derbyshire v Sussex, Derby, 1970; V. C. Drakes, Nottinghamshire v Derbyshire, Nottingham, 1999.

Wicket-keeping and Fielding

Most dismissals: S. J. Rhodes 414 (318 ct, 96 st); W. K. Hegg 308 (266 ct, 42 st); R. J. Blakey 292 (244 ct, 48 st); R. C. Russell 291 (232 ct, 59 st); P. A. Nixon 268 (216 ct, 52 st); D. L. Bairstow 257 (234 ct, 23 st). **In a season:** G. O. Jones 33 (27 ct, 6 st) for Kent, 2003.

Seven dismissals in an innings: (6 ct, 1 st), R. W. Taylor, Derbyshire v Lancashire, Manchester, 1975.

Six catches in an innings: K. Goodwin, Lancashire v Worcestershire, Worcester, 1969; R. W. Taylor, Derbyshire v Lancashire, Manchester, 1975; K. M. Krikken, Derbyshire v Hampshire, Southampton, 1994; P. A. Nixon, Leicestershire v Essex, Leicester, 1994; G. O. Jones, Kent v Leicestershire, Canterbury, 2003; K. J. Piper, Warwickshire v Leicestershire, Birmingham, 2003.

Four stumpings in an innings: S. J. Rhodes, Worcestershire v Warwickshire, Birmingham, 1986, N. D. Burns, Somerset v Kent, Taunton, 1991 and R. J. Turner, Somerset v Kent, Taunton, 2002.

Most catches by a fielder: C. J. Adams 112; M. P. Maynard 109†; K. J. Barnett 107; M. W. Alleyne 106†; V. P. Terry 103; J. F. Steele 101; G. A. Gooch and P. N. Weekes 100. **In a season:** J. M. Rice, 16 for Hampshire, 1978.

† *M. P. Maynard also made 11 catches and four stumpings as a wicket-keeper; M. W. Alleyne took four catches as a wicket-keeper.*

Five catches in an innings: J. M. Rice, Hampshire v Warwickshire, Southampton, 1978.

Results

Largest victory in runs: Somerset by 220 runs v Glamorgan, Neath, 1990.

Victories by ten wickets (36): By Derbyshire, Durham, Essex (four times), Glamorgan (three times), Hampshire (twice), Kent, Lancashire (twice), Leicestershire (twice), Middlesex (twice), Northamptonshire, Nottinghamshire, Somerset (twice), Surrey (three times), Warwickshire (twice), Worcestershire (six times) and Yorkshire (three times).

This does not include those matches in which the side batting second was set a reduced target but does include matches where both sides faced a reduced number of overs.

Ties: There have been 61 tied matches. Essex have tied 12 times.

Shortest match: 1 hr 53 min (26.3 overs), Surrey v Leicestershire, The Oval, 1996.

WINNERS 1969–2004

John Player's County League

1969   Lancashire

John Player League

1970   Lancashire
1971   Worcestershire
1972   Kent
1973   Kent
1974   Leicestershire
1975   Hampshire
1976   Kent
1977   Leicestershire
1978   Hampshire
1979   Somerset
1980   Warwickshire
1981   Essex
1982   Sussex
1983   Yorkshire

John Player Special League

1984   Essex
1985   Essex
1986   Hampshire

Refuge Assurance League

1987   Worcestershire
1988   Worcestershire
1989   Lancashire
1990   Derbyshire
1991   Nottinghamshire

Sunday League

1992   Middlesex

AXA Equity & Law League

1993   Glamorgan
1994   Warwickshire
1995   Kent
1996   Surrey

AXA Life League

1997   Warwickshire

AXA League

1998   Lancashire

CGU National League

1999   Lancashire

Norwich Union National League

2000   Gloucestershire

Norwich Union League

2001   Kent
2002   Glamorgan

National League

2003   Surrey

totesport League

2004   Glamorgan

MATCH RESULTS 1969–2004

	P	W	L	T	NR	1st	2nd	3rd
Derbyshire	587	235	289	5	58	1	0	1
Durham	219	71	122	3	23	0	0	0
Essex	583	291	232	12	48	3	5*	5
Glamorgan	583	230	289	8	56	3	0	0
Gloucestershire	583	219	292	5	67	1	2	1
Hampshire	585	274	256	7	48	3	1	4
Kent	583	309	211	9	54	5	4	5
Lancashire	585	303	207	10	65	5	3	3
Leicestershire	585	256	255	5	69	2	3*	2
Middlesex	587	259	258	10	60	1	1	3
Northamptonshire	585	238	284	6	57	0	0	2
Nottinghamshire	587	251	277	5	54	1	3	1
Somerset	587	271	258	4	54	1	6*	0
Surrey	583	263	254	5	61	2	0	1
Sussex	587	249	272	7	59	1	2*	1
Warwickshire	583	259	258	7	59	3	2	3
Worcestershire	585	288	231	11	55	3	5	2
Yorkshire	585	265	265	3	52	1	2	1
Scotland	36	6	27	0	3	0	0	0

Table header spanning columns: *Matches* (P, W, L, T, NR) and *League positions* (1st, 2nd, 3rd).

* Includes one shared 2nd place in 1976.

TWENTY20 CUP, 2004

REVIEW BY HUGH CHEVALLIER

If imitation is the sincerest form of flattery, the ECB had good reason to glow with smug self-satisfaction over its successful new invention. Within months of Surrey winning the first Twenty20 Cup on a balmy summer evening in 2003, similar tournaments sprang up with similar success in Sri Lanka and South Africa. And Australia, though holding back from a domestic 20-over competition, were in the thick of moves to bring the Twenty20 format to the international stage.

They agreed to take on New Zealand in February – and England at Southampton in June. But even on the international front, the ECB had got there first, holding a women's 20-over game between England and New Zealand in early August 2004. Whichever way you looked at it, the Twenty20 bandwagon was zinging along at an impressive lick.

This was all the more impressive because in its second year the competition faced more problems. Rain, a total absentee in 2003, barged in on the party, washing out three games and ensuring that Messrs Duckworth and Lewis were involved in several more. There was a danger too that the novelty factor might have worn off.

Not a bit of it: cricket followers lapped it up in even greater numbers. Although the use of larger grounds tended to mean fewer sell-outs – 11 of the 46 preliminary games had capacity crowds, down from 15 in 2003 – the average gate was about 1,000 up at 5,800. This was in part due to an astonishing turn-out at Lord's for the Middlesex–Surrey game, when the crowd reached over 27,500. Not since these same teams met here in the 1953 Championship had so many watched county cricket outside a cup final.

Touts at St John's Wood tube for a county match? It seemed impossible, but there they were. And the crowds turned up everywhere: Durham, Worcestershire, Glamorgan all hosted sell-outs; Leicestershire filled seats at Grace

Darren Maddy

Road that had hardly seen a backside in years. The one change from the original format was the introduction in 2004 of quarter-finals. It seemed wrong to tinker, yet there was a strong case for reducing the number of

Holding on: Graeme Hick, 38 years young, dives headlong to take a phenomenal boundary catch to remove Matthew Maynard, for Worcestershire v Glamorgan.
Picture by David Davies, PA Photos

dead matches towards the end of the group stage – and by adding a tier to the knockout stages the organisers did so. Only three counties began the last round of matches with no chance of progress.

However, in October 2004 further changes were announced. These were of an altogether different magnitude, and clearly smacked of greed. From 2005, although the make-up of the three groups remains unchanged, counties will each play eight rather than five preliminary matches. This means each county will play three opponents twice and two opponents once. At a stroke, the number of qualifying games swelled from 45 to 72, a 60% increase which the ECB disingenuously described as "modest". The aim, they said, was to ensure that each county would stage a revenue-generating local derby each year. But it introduced a new complexity to what had been a commendably simple system, and an element of unfairness too in that some teams will be disadvantaged by playing strong opponents twice.

Up till now, the guiding principle of this format had been that small is beautiful: a compact game of cricket neatly fitted between the office and supper, with the whole competition wrapped up in no time. Mission creep has set in. Call the Twenty20 a milch cow or the goose that lays the golden egg: either way, the whiff of cooking meat is in the air.

The winners of the comparatively slimline 2004 competition were Leicestershire, propelled to glory by the bats of Darren Maddy – easily the heaviest scorer in the tournament with 356 – and Brad Hodge, who came second, though over 100 behind. Mark Cleary, their unassuming young seam

THE TWENTY20 EVOLVES

For many, the resounding success of 20-over cricket came as a surprise. In its first year, a few seasoned county professionals saw an opportunity for a mid-summer battery-recharge, and sat it out. Come 2004, everyone wanted a piece of the high-speed, high-energy action. Those once content to sit back were now clamouring to get picked. After years of playing in echoing, nine-tenths empty grounds, here was a chance to swagger in front of thousands, possibly even tens of thousands. The overriding difference between the first two years of the Twenty20 was that, second time round, everyone took it seriously.

Even Surrey, the undisputed masters of that first tournament, had not given the Twenty20 much priority. "Like many, we took it as a bit of a joke to begin with," admits Adam Hollioake, who led his side to victory in the inaugural final. A year on, it was a different matter.

SIX APPEAL

How batsmen are tending to cut out the fielders:

	2003	2004	Difference
Sixes	280	**342**	+62 (+22%)
Fours	1,396	**1,216**	−180 (−13%)

At Cardiff, Glamorgan held nets where players were encouraged to improvise. If the shot worked, and if the batsman felt confident, he was given carte blanche to use it for real. Michael Powell developed an audacious paddle over the wicket-keeper's head which, when successful, brought an almost certain boundary. But despite predictions that the classical cover-drive would become as endangered as the corncrake, many runs came courtesy of the coaching manual. The rule seemed to be: do what you're comfortable with. So Ian Thomas, Powell's team-mate, included a couple of reverse sweeps in his record unbeaten 116 at Taunton, but otherwise batted in conventional manner. Similarly, Hollioake and Kent's Andrew Symonds, two of the most productive of Twenty20 run-scorers, avoided shots such as the ramp or the paddle. Robert Croft, the Glamorgan captain, put it pithily: "This year there was less slapping."

A batsman may have the option to limit his repertoire, but not a bowler. "Once you've come to terms with the embarrassment of being hit out of the ground," said Hollioake self-deprecatingly, "ordinary bowlers like me have to mix it up and be as unpredictable as possible." Variation of pace has become *de rigueur* for all, but some are now heading into unlikely territory. In 2004, Somerset's Keith Dutch, by trade an off-spinner, experimented with a deliberate low, slow full toss that was never going to spin in any direction. David Byas, Yorkshire's thoughtful coach, believed that bowlers had to be streetwise to survive. "The crux is the ability to adapt and to think on your feet. You need to play smart cricket. Jeremy Snape is a good example: there's someone who brings craft to the game."

In Byas's eyes, however, "craft" is best exemplified by fielding. Twice in 2004, Yorkshire passed 200 and lost. Rather than blame the bowlers, though, he pointed to fielding as where improvement was most needed: "We have to work on our craft. We can raise our fielding by 20%. That would make the difference for us." Yet there are signs that the fielder actually played a lesser role in Twenty20 in 2004. As Hollioake says, "A lot of sides think fielding is it, but a six is a massive thing and cuts out the fielders all together. We targeted them; it was a cavalier tactic, but it worked for us."

bowler from South Australia, led the attack with 15 victims, giving him a strike-rate of one wicket every ten balls. But this was nothing compared to Surrey's Adam Hollioake, the Twenty20's leading wicket-taker for the second year running: he snatched 20, prising someone out at an astonishing rate of once every eight balls. These two bowlers met in the final, where somehow Leicestershire deciphered the riddle of Hollioake's variations in pace, and Hodge steered them to a surprise win – Surrey's first-ever defeat in the competition.

THE SUFFERERS

Most expensive bowling analysis

4–0–63–1	R. J. Kirtley	Sussex v Surrey at Hove
4–0–60–0	S. P. Kirby	Yorkshire v Lancashire at Leeds
4–0–51–0	I. D. Blackwell	Somerset v Northamptonshire at Taunton
4–0–48–0	J. Louw	Northamptonshire v Somerset at Taunton

Most runs conceded in an over

26	J. Louw	Northamptonshire v Somerset at Taunton
25	C. G. Greenidge	Northamptonshire v Worcestershire at Luton
25	D. L. Maddy	Leicestershire v Yorkshire at Leeds
24	M. J. Clarke	Hampshire v Surrey at The Oval
24	R. J. Logan	Nottinghamshire v Yorkshire at Nottingham

Most runs conceded in boundaries in the competition

130	S. D. Thomas (Glamorgan)	110 M. F. Cleary (Leicestershire)
116	A. J. Hall (Worcestershire)	106 B. J. Trott (Kent)
112	A. J. Hollioake (Surrey)	106 P. J. Sampson (Surrey)
110	S. R. G. Francis (Somerset)	

Perhaps the best match of the whole Twenty20 summer had come earlier on finals day when Surrey edged out Lancashire by a single, but there was no shortage of tension, drama and downright entertainment throughout the tournament. With indifferent weather, it was no shock that the average total fell slightly, but intriguingly the number of centuries rose from one in the first year to five in the second, with the familiar Graeme Hick of Worcestershire and the unsung Ian Thomas of Glamorgan sharing the top score of 116 not out. The most memorable innings, however, came in Kent's opening fixture, against Middlesex. Andrew Symonds was on three figures in a flash: he needed just 34 balls, scoring off every delivery bar two, before eventually falling for a 43-ball 112. But lightning did not strike twice and, without his explosive runs, Kent could not make the next stage.

Unlike 2003, several ECB-contracted cricketers – available because England failed to reach the final of the NatWest Series – joined in the jamboree. In the Roses clash, Andrew Flintoff of Lancashire and England came up against Ian Harvey of Yorkshire and Australia, a mouth-watering foretaste of the 2005 Ashes encounter at the Rose Bowl. Flintoff sparkled, though not as brightly as his fellow all-rounder Harvey, who belted his second Twenty20 hundred.

Larking about: Andy Bichel and Adam Hollioake indulge in mid-pitch mock fisticuffs in the quarter-final between Surrey and Worcestershire.
Picture by Clive Rose, Getty Images

In the competition's second year, there was less emphasis on off-field innovations and sideshows, though the well-travelled spectator could indulge in speed-dating at Lancashire, Worcestershire and Glamorgan, a wild-hair competition at Nottinghamshire (inspired by Ryan Sidebottom's flowing locks), a Wild West rodeo at Leicestershire and, arguably least appealing of all, a mass aerobics workout at Somerset. All 5,902 spectators at the Hampshire game at The Oval won free tickets to the upcoming New Zealand–USA match in the Champions Trophy because a wicket fell in the fifth over. Children could swap theirs for a free ice-cream; some adults cast envious eyes on their offspring.

Sussex preferred a 50-piece samba band, while Kent chose to plonk nicknames on their shirts. Ah, so that meteoric hundred was not hit by Symonds, after all, but by "Roy", a name which at least had an air of mystery, unlike those of his team-mates Keysy (Rob Key), Kiwi (Ian Butler) and Noisy (Alex Loudon). Gloucestershire, who laid on reflexology, felt they did not need to try so hard. Tom Richardson, their chief executive, said: "We found that once the cricket starts people want to watch that."

The Edgbaston final followed the girl-band formula adopted at Trent Bridge the year before, though an addition was the "npower derby". Seventeen mascots charged around the outfield, and the provisional winner was Roary, the Surrey lion. However, replays showed he had swapped his oversize paws for trainers and he was subsequently disqualified. Lanky, the Lancashire giraffe, was then pronounced victor, prompting one disconsolate Lancashire member to say "at least we've won something in 2004".

Prize money

£42,000 for winners: LEICESTERSHIRE.
£21,000 for runners-up: SURREY.
£10,000 for losing semi-finalists: GLAMORGAN, LANCASHIRE.
£5,000 for losing quarter-finalists: ESSEX, HAMPSHIRE, WARWICKSHIRE, WORCESTER-
SHIRE.

The following awards were made at the end of the group stages. In each category, the leading
player received £1,500 (or shared it if there was a tie); when an award was made for the second-
placed player (indicated by a dagger), he received £1,000 (or shared it if there was a tie).

Most runs: G. A. Hick (Worcestershire) 195; †P. A. Jaques (Yorkshire) 180.
Most sixes: A. J. Bichel (Worcestershire), M. A. Ealham (Nottinghamshire), G. A. Hick
  (Worcestershire), R. W. T. Key (Kent), M. R. Ramprakash (Surrey) 9.
Best strike-rate (minimum 48 balls faced): A. Symonds (Kent) 217.14.
Best all-rounder: A. J. Hollioake (Surrey), †A. D. Mascarenhas (Hants).
Best wicket-keeper: C. M. W. Read (Nottinghamshire).
Most wickets: A. J. Hollioake (Surrey) 14; †G. B. Hogg (Warwickshire), †A. D. Mascarenhas
  (Hampshire) 12.
Best economy-rate (minimum 48 balls bowled): D. Mongia (Lancashire) 4.25; †D. R. Brown
  (Warwickshire) 5.06.

Note: Performances in the quarter-finals, semi-finals and finals had no bearing on these awards.

Match award winners received £1,000 in the final, £500 in the semi-finals, £250 in the quarter-
finals and £200 in the group games.

FINAL GROUP TABLES

Midlands/Wales/West Group

	Played	Won	Lost	No result	Points	Net run-rate
GLAMORGAN	5	4	1	0	8	0.43
WORCESTERSHIRE	5	3	2	0	6	−0.27
WARWICKSHIRE*	5	3	2	0	6	0.61
Somerset	5	2	2	1	5	−0.38
Gloucestershire	5	1	3	1	3	−0.37
Northamptonshire	5	1	4	0	2	−0.46

North Group

	Played	Won	Lost	No result	Points	Net run-rate
LEICESTERSHIRE	5	3	1	1	7	0.21
LANCASHIRE	5	3	2	0	6	0.27
Derbyshire	5	2	2	1	5	−0.03
Nottinghamshire	5	2	3	0	4	−0.55
Durham	5	2	3	0	4	0.26
Yorkshire	5	2	3	0	4	−0.10

South Group

	Played	Won	Lost	No result	Points	Net run-rate
SURREY	5	4	0	1	9	2.13
HAMPSHIRE	5	3	2	0	6	0.32
ESSEX*	5	2	2	1	5	0.52
Kent	5	2	3	0	4	−0.20
Middlesex	5	1	3	1	3	−1.23
Sussex	5	1	3	1	3	−1.71

* *Warwickshire and Essex qualified as the most successful third-placed teams.*

*Where two or more counties finished with an equal number of points, the positions were decided
by (a) most wins (b) most points in head-to-head matches (c) net run-rate (runs scored per over
minus runs conceded per over) (d) most wickets taken per balls bowled in matches achieving a
result.*

MIDLANDS/WALES/WEST GROUP

At Northampton, July 2. **Glamorgan won by five wickets.** Toss: Northamptonshire. **Northamptonshire 162-5** (20 overs) (M. van Jaarsveld 61*); **Glamorgan 166-5** (19.1 overs) (M. P. Maynard 34, S. D. Thomas 43*). *Glamorgan 2 pts.*
　　Man of the Match: S. D. Thomas.　　　　　*Attendance:* 4,127.
　　Van Jaarsveld faced 48 balls for his unbeaten 61; Northamptonshire's next-highest score was 21 from Extras. Glamorgan, 102 for five in the 14th over, were catapulted to victory by an unbroken stand of 64 by Robert Croft and Thomas, whose contribution was a whirlwind 19-ball 43 not out including six fours and two sixes.

At Birmingham, July 2. **Warwickshire won by seven wickets** (D/L method). Toss: Warwickshire. **Somerset 120** (19.5 overs) (K. A. Parsons 31; G. B. Hogg 4-9); **Warwickshire 101-3** (9.3 overs) (N. M. Carter 42). *Warwickshire 2 pts.*
　　Warwickshire's target was revised to 101 in 16 overs.
　　County debut: N. D. Hancock.
　　Man of the Match: N. M. Carter.　　　　　*Attendance:* 5,500.
　　At 97 for four, Somerset seemed set for a reasonable total, but in 30 balls they scored just 23 runs while losing six wickets. Hogg claimed four of them for nine, at the time the cheapest four-for in the competition's short history. Carter then made light of a rain-revised target by striking five sixes in his 23-ball innings. Warwickshire apologised to Somerset for an off-putting comment ("Wooooooooooohhhh") made by George Gavin, their match announcer, while Dutch was bracing himself to catch a skier off Carter. Dutch held on.

At Worcester, July 2. **Worcestershire won by one run.** Toss: Gloucestershire. **Worcestershire 184-9** (20 overs) (G. A. Hick 73, A. J. Bichel 58*); **Gloucestershire 183-5** (20 overs) (S. J. Adshead 81, C. G. Taylor 36). *Worcestershire 2 pts.*
　　Man of the Match: A. J. Bichel.　　　　　*Attendance:* 4,900.
　　Making his first Twenty20 appearance after missing the 2003 games with a broken hand, Hick faced 52 balls; Bichel scorched his unbeaten 58 from 30, including five sixes. Gloucestershire stayed in the hunt thanks to a 56-ball innings from Adshead, who had left New Road in the close season, but he fell in the penultimate over with 17 needed. Gloucestershire required six off the last two balls to win on fewer wickets lost: Martyn Ball struck a four, but could manage just a single off the last, and a capacity crowd went home happy, none more so than Andrew Knight, a Herefordshire doctor, who pocketed £1,000 for catching a ball struck for six into the crowd.

At Luton, July 5. **Worcestershire won by 21 runs** (D/L method). Toss: Worcestershire. **Worcestershire 173-5** (20 overs) (G. A. Hick 116*); **Northamptonshire 80-8** (11 overs). *Worcestershire 2 pts.*
　　Northamptonshire's target was revised to 102 in 11 overs.
　　Man of the Match: G. A. Hick.　　　　　*Attendance:* 3,500.
　　A sell-out crowd watched Hick destroy the Northamptonshire bowling and set a record Twenty20 score (matched by Glamorgan's Ian Thomas the same day). No one else managed more than 16, but their main task was to give the strike to Hick, whose 65-ball innings contained 11 fours and six sixes, three in a row off Graeme Swann. The last over of the Worcestershire innings, bowled by Carl Greenidge, cost 25. Rain during the interval shortened the Northamptonshire reply, but without a batsman of Hick's class, they never threatened their revised target.

At Taunton, July 5. **Glamorgan won by eight wickets.** Toss: Glamorgan. **Somerset 193-8** (20 overs) (M. Burns 36, J. C. Hildreth 66); **Glamorgan 194-2** (19.3 overs) (I. J. Thomas 116*, D. L. Hemp 31*). *Glamorgan 2 pts.*
　　Man of the Match: I. J. Thomas.　　　　　*Attendance:* 3,500.
　　Ian Thomas's 116 not out, from 57 balls and with 11 fours and seven sixes, was his first century for Glamorgan at senior level. His boisterous innings became the new high for the Twenty20, shared with Graeme Hick. Earlier, Hildreth had hammered 66 off 33 balls to ensure a demanding target.

At Cardiff, July 8. **Warwickshire won by 26 runs.** Toss: Warwickshire. **Warwickshire 152-9** (20 overs) (G. B. Hogg 34; A. P. Davies 3-23); **Glamorgan 126** (19 overs) (M. P. Maynard 53; G. B. Hogg 4-30). *Warwickshire 2 pts.*
　　Man of the Match: G. B. Hogg.　　　　　*Attendance:* 2,900.

Glamorgan looked to be heading for a third successive win until they were mesmerised by Hogg's left-arm wrist-spin. He claimed four wickets for the second game running as Glamorgan plummeted from 75 for one to 87 for six. In all, they lost nine for 51 in 11 overs, with Tony Frost, Warwickshire's wicket-keeper, making a record four stumpings.

At Northampton, July 8. **Gloucestershire won by eight wickets.** Toss: Gloucestershire. **Northamptonshire 42-5** (5 overs) (J. M. M. Averis 3-7); **Gloucestershire 44-2** (4.1 overs). *Gloucestershire 2 pts.*
  Reduced to 5 overs a side.
  Man of the Match: T. H. C. Hancock.   *Attendance:* 2,500.
  Even for short-form cricket, this was reductio ad absurdum. Rain meant each bowler was allowed a single over, though Jon Lewis, with two for two, and Averis, with three for seven, squeezed a lot into their six deliveries. For Northamptonshire, van Jaarsveld concocted 27 off 14 balls, though Gloucestershire's Tim Hancock trumped him with 28 from 13. The match, which did not start until 7.25, lasted 39 minutes. This was Northamptonshire's third consecutive defeat.

At Bristol, July 9. **No result.** Toss: Gloucestershire. **Somerset 151** (19.1 overs) (M. J. Wood 50; I. D. Fisher 4-22) v **Gloucestershire**. *Gloucestershire 1 pt, Somerset 1 pt.*
  Attendance: 8,000.
  A downpour prevented Gloucestershire from capitalising on a good performance from their spinners: Fisher and Martyn Ball shared six wickets. Somerset had begun well, with Wood striking 50 from 38 balls, before subsiding from 101 for two to 151 all out.

At Birmingham, July 9. **Worcestershire won by three wickets.** Toss: Worcestershire. **Warwickshire 146** (19.5 overs) (J. O. Troughton 32, D. R. Brown 37; A. J. Bichel 3-36); **Worcestershire 150-7** (19.3 overs) (V. S. Solanki 50, B. F. Smith 34, A. J. Bichel 45*). *Worcestershire 2 pts.*
  Man of the Match: A. J. Bichel.   *Attendance:* 9,000.
  In front of their biggest crowd of the season, Warwickshire recovered from 69 for seven on the strength of a brisk innings from Brown. Worcestershire were 13 for two in no time, but Solanki and Smith steadied the ship with 58. Even so, they needed Bichel to clobber three sixes to secure their third successive victory. Bichel, subtly varying his pace on a slow pitch, had also plucked out three Warwickshire batsmen.

At Birmingham, July 12. **Northamptonshire won by four wickets.** Toss: Northamptonshire. **Warwickshire 123-7** (20 overs) (I. J. L. Trott 39, T. L. Penney 32*); **Northamptonshire 125-6** (19 overs) (G. P. Swann 35*; G. B. Hogg 3-12). *Northamptonshire 2 pts.*
  Man of the Match: G. P. Swann.   *Attendance:* 5,000.
  Johann Louw conceded just six runs from his four overs – the most economical Twenty20 analysis so far – as Warwickshire nose-dived to 36 for five. Making the most of a green pitch, Louw even served up a double-wicket-maiden. Trott and Penney then shored up the innings with a sixth-wicket stand of 60. Three wickets in Northamptonshire's reply took Hogg's Twenty20 tally to 12 at under seven each, but Swann attacked judiciously to secure victory.

At Taunton, July 13. **Somerset won by 34 runs.** Toss: Somerset. **Somerset 178-6** (20 overs) (K. P. Dutch 47, J. C. Hildreth 51, J. D. Francis 31); **Worcestershire 144-4** (20 overs) (D. A. Leatherdale 52*, A. J. Bichel 37*; A. W. Laraman 4-15). *Somerset 2 pts.*
  Man of the Match: A. W. Laraman.   *Attendance:* 4,000.
  Worcestershire had already qualified for the quarter-finals, but losing to Somerset, victors in just one of their last 15 games in all competitions, was a surprise. A 32-ball 51 from Hildreth was the cornerstone of the Somerset innings, though they relied as much on the bowling of Laraman, who reduced Worcestershire to 43 for four by the eighth over. Leatherdale and Bichel added 101 – a competition record for the fifth wicket – but never threatened to overhaul Somerset.

At Cardiff, July 14. **Glamorgan won by 32 runs.** Toss: Gloucestershire. **Glamorgan 162-7** (20 overs) (D. L. Hemp 43; J. Lewis 3-21, J. M. M. Averis 3-25); **Gloucestershire 130** (19.1 overs) (T. H. C. Hancock 56; A. G. Wharf 3-23). *Glamorgan 2 pts.*
  County debuts: J. E. C. Franklin, M. E. K. Hussey (both Gloucestershire).
  Man of the Match: A. G. Wharf.   *Attendance:* 4,225.
  Hemp kept the Glamorgan innings on course with a cool-headed 43 from 35 balls. In reply, Gloucestershire, batting in light drizzle throughout, were never in contention; only Hancock, with his second one-day fifty of the season, passed 16.

At Bristol, July 15. **Warwickshire won by losing fewer wickets with the scores level.** Toss: Gloucestershire. **Gloucestershire 135-7** (20 overs) (M. E. K. Hussey 32, J. E. C. Franklin 36; A. Richardson 3-13); **Warwickshire 135-5** (20 overs) (N. V. Knight 63). *Warwickshire 2 pts.*

   Man of the Match: N. V. Knight.   *Attendance:* 5,500.

   By the narrowest of margins, Warwickshire squeezed past Gloucestershire, took third place in the table and reached the quarter-finals. As the last over began in murky light, Warwickshire needed 13. Jonathan Trott then eased the pressure by hitting Mark Hardinge's fourth delivery for six. As Hardinge ran in to bowl the final ball, the scores were already tied, so guaranteeing Warwickshire's progress on the fewer-wickets-lost rule. Despite a drizzly day and gloomy forecast, a healthy crowd had earlier watched Knight hit a rapid fifty, Warwickshire's first in the 2004 competition.

At Taunton, July 15. **Somerset won by four runs.** Toss: Somerset. **Somerset 211-5** (20 overs) (M. E. Trescothick 56, K. P. Dutch 47, K. A. Parsons 37*); **Northamptonshire 207-5** (20 overs) (T. W. Roberts 39, M. van Jaarsveld 61, D. J. Sales 60*). *Somerset 2 pts.*

   County debut: R. T. Ponting (Somerset).
   Man of the Match: D. J. Sales.   *Attendance:* 4,547.

   Trescothick, making a rare non England appearance, enjoyed his first foray into Twenty20 with a brutal 29-ball 56 containing ten fours and two sixes. He and Dutch put on 118 for the first wicket, helping Somerset pass 200 for the first time in this competition. Carl Greenidge's two overs yielded 36, including five wides. While van Jaarsveld and Sales were together, Northamptonshire retained a chance, but 22 off the last over proved just too much. Blackwell's four overs cost 51 runs. The day after arriving from Australia, Ponting made 20. Neither side progressed to the quarter-finals.

At Worcester, July 15. **Glamorgan won by 20 runs** (D/L method). Toss: Glamorgan. **Glamorgan 140-6** (16 overs) (M. P. Maynard 44, M. A. Wallace 32*); **Worcestershire 120** (14.1 overs) (Kabir Ali 49; A. P. Davies 3-17). *Glamorgan 2 pts.*

   Worcestershire's target was revised to 141 in 16 overs.
   Man of the Match: Kabir Ali.   *Attendance:* 4,900.
   Worcestershire were definitely in the quarter-finals, but Glamorgan had to avoid defeat to be sure of joining them. Another capacity New Road crowd saw Maynard crash 44 before rain ended the Glamorgan innings after 16 overs. Duckworth/Lewis calculations left Worcestershire's target unchanged, but at 46 for eight, that seemed an irrelevance. Kabir Ali's 49 off 28 balls ultimately ensured respectability, but for a fleeting moment hinted at a phenomenal Worcestershire win. Glamorgan won the group and a home tie in the next round.

NORTH GROUP

At Derby, July 2. **Yorkshire won by one wicket** (D/L method). Toss: Derbyshire. **Derbyshire 133-8** (20 overs) (Hassan Adnan 32; M. J. Hoggard 3-23); **Yorkshire 108-9** (15 overs) (P. A. Jaques 36*). *Yorkshire 2 pts.*

   Yorkshire's target was revised to 108 in 15 overs.
   County debut: I. Dawood (Yorkshire).
   Man of the Match: P. A. Jaques.   *Attendance:* 3,500.
   Derbyshire managed only 11 boundaries on a slow pitch. Rain briefly interrupted Yorkshire's reply at 39 for three in the sixth over and, with nine balls left, they needed 23. Silverwood hit three consecutive fours before Jaques, dropped on 18, lofted a six in the last over, which also included byes, an overthrow, two run-outs and a scrambled single off the final ball. Had Adnan, at mid-off, hit the stumps with his throw, Hoggard would have been Yorkshire's fifth run-out, and victory would have been Derbyshire's.

At Manchester, July 2. **Leicestershire won by eight runs.** Toss: Lancashire. **Leicestershire 139-9** (19 overs) (D. L. Maddy 51; D. Mongia 3-19); **Lancashire 131-6** (19 overs) (D. Mongia 47). *Leicestershire 2 pts.*

   Reduced to 19 overs a side.
   Man of the Match: D. L. Maddy.   *Attendance:* 5,868.
   Maddy hammered 51 off 27 balls, but later Leicestershire batsmen found it difficult to score off Lancashire's trio of spinners, who had combined figures of seven for 58 from 11 overs.

Lancashire began so briskly that with 15 overs and ten wickets in hand the required rate was barely above six. But they too struggled against the slower bowlers – Jeremy Snape claimed two for 13 from his four overs – and although Mongia hit 47 off 36 deliveries, no one else could middle anything: Chris Schofield was unbeaten on four from 17 balls.

At Nottingham, July 2. **Nottinghamshire won by three wickets.** Toss: Nottinghamshire. **Durham 120** (19.4 overs) (P. Mustard 64); **Nottinghamshire 122-7** (19.1 overs) (K. P. Pietersen 67). *Nottinghamshire 2 pts.*

Man of the Match: K. P. Pietersen. *Attendance:* 3,868.

A confident 67 from Pietersen, who faced 48 balls, guided Nottinghamshire, at one stage reeling at five for three, to what became a comfortable win. In a game where the bowlers held sway, Pietersen and Mustard (the only Durham batsman to hit a boundary) were alone in passing 15. Ealham and Clough (for Nottinghamshire) and Bridge (for Durham) all bowled four overs at a cost of less than 20.

At Leicester, July 7. **Durham won by 41 runs.** Toss: Durham. **Durham 138-4** (20 overs) (J. J. B. Lewis 49*, G. J. Muchall 45*); **Leicestershire 97-9** (20 overs) (N. Killeen 4-7, G. R. Breese 4-14). *Durham 2 pts.*

Man of the Match: N. Killeen. *Attendance:* 4,124.

Leicestershire lost for the first time in the group stages, beaten by a side that had not won a Twenty20 game since their first match, in 2003. An unbroken stand of 80 between Lewis and Muchall steered Durham to 138, a decent total on a stodgy pitch. Then Killeen, with what was at the time the cheapest four-over spell in the competition, grabbed four of Leicestershire's top five in 12 balls to leave them 11 for four. Breese yanked out four more in nine balls before Mark Cleary, at No. 11, top-scored with a consolation 24 not out.

At Nottingham, July 7. **Nottinghamshire won by three wickets.** Toss: Nottinghamshire. **Yorkshire 207-7** (20 overs) (M. J. Wood 96*, A. W. Gale 38, T. T. Bresnan 35); **Nottinghamshire 210-7** (19.5 overs) (M. A. Ealham 91). *Nottinghamshire 2 pts.*

Man of the Match: M. A. Ealham. *Attendance:* 6,221.

Despite leaden skies and a biting wind, this was Twenty20 cricket at its exhilarating best. Wood struck an attractive unbeaten 96 off 62 balls as every Nottinghamshire bowler bar Ealham (one for 19 off four) went for more than seven an over. However, Wood was eclipsed by a barnstorming display from Ealham, who came to the wicket at 56 for four, faced just 35 deliveries and cracked five fours and nine sixes. He struck three successive sixes off Anthony McGrath, whose 17 balls cost 46. Nottinghamshire's 210 was the highest successful run-chase in the tournament's history.

At Derby, July 8. **Lancashire won by five wickets.** Toss: Lancashire. **Derbyshire 142-4** (20 overs) (C. W. G. Bassano 30, J. Moss 39); **Lancashire 144-5** (17.1 overs) (M. B. Loye 32, S. G. Law 31, D. Mongia 50; Mohammad Ali 3-27). *Lancashire 2 pts.*

Man of the Match: D. Mongia. *Attendance:* 1,800.

Dominic Cork's first visit back to Derby, where he spent 14 often controversial seasons, was overshadowed as his team-mate Mongia ended his spell as stand-in for the injured Carl Hooper in style. First he pegged back Derbyshire's scoring-rate – Moss had lashed a 26-ball 39 – with two for 15 from four overs, before steering Lancashire to within touching distance of their first win in 11 matches in all competitions; his 50 came from 34 balls. After 15 hours of rain leading up to the game, the groundstaff did well to ensure a match.

At Leeds, July 8. **Leicestershire won by ten runs.** Toss: Leicestershire. **Leicestershire 221-3** (20 overs) (B. J. Hodge 78, D. L. Maddy 111); **Yorkshire 211-6** (20 overs) (P. A. Jaques 92, A. McGrath 37, T. T. Bresnan 42; M. F. Cleary 3-43). *Leicestershire 2 pts.*

Man of the Match: D. L. Maddy. *Attendance:* 2,438.

For the second day running, Yorkshire passed 200 and lost. Leicestershire openers Maddy – with the Twenty20's fifth hundred – and Hodge put on 167, comfortably the highest for any wicket in the tournament's history, in 16 overs. Maddy faced 60 balls and crashed eight fours and six sixes; Hodge faced 49. Leicestershire's total equalled the competition record. Yorkshire needed 79 from the last four overs, and Jaques, hitting nine fours and five sixes off 49 balls, smashed 62 from the first three before both fell to boundary catches. In all, there were 56 boundaries, and ten of the 13 bowlers gave away more than ten an over.

At Chester-le-Street, July 9. **Lancashire won by five wickets.** Toss: Lancashire. **Durham 111-8** (20 overs) (A. Pratt 35); **Lancashire 112-5** (18.2 overs) (C. L. Hooper 49*). *Lancashire 2 pts.*

Man of the Match: C. L. Hooper.   *Attendance:* 5,700.

Hooper, back in the side after injury, and his fellow spinners Keedy and Schofield had combined figures of five for 34 from ten overs as the Durham innings petered out after a reasonable start. The openers were the only Durham batsmen to strike boundaries. Hooper was batting at three for two, and his class, rather than his clout, saw Lancashire home with a run-a-ball innings. This was the first county match at the Riverside to sell out.

At Nottingham, July 9. **Derbyshire won by nine runs.** Toss: Nottinghamshire. **Derbyshire 163-7** (20 overs) (J. Moss 68); **Nottinghamshire 154-8** (20 overs) (K. P. Pietersen 32). *Derbyshire 2 pts.*

Man of the Match: J. Moss.   *Attendance:* 6,700.

A 43-ball innings from Moss helped Derbyshire to a respectable if gettable total. In previous matches, Nottinghamshire's middle order had covered for earlier failings, but not this time. Pietersen was one of two victims for Ant Botha, the Derbyshire left-arm spinner, whose first over was a double-wicket-maiden. Nottinghamshire's first defeat in three starts was Derbyshire's first win in three.

At Chester-le-Street, July 13. **Derbyshire won by four wickets.** Toss: Derbyshire. **Durham 117-9** (20 overs) (G. J. Pratt 36; Mohammad Ali 3-24); **Derbyshire 118-6** (18.3 overs) (J. Moss 33, J. D. C. Bryant 41). *Derbyshire 2 pts.*

Man of the Match: J. D. C. Bryant.   *Attendance:* 5,500.

Brothers Andrew and Gary Pratt came together at nine for two and added 60 for the third wicket; there was little other substance in a Durham innings containing just six fours and no sixes. Derbyshire were always ahead of the rate.

At Leicester, July 13. **Leicestershire won by 40 runs.** Toss: Leicestershire. **Leicestershire 150-7** (20 overs) (D. I. Stevens 31); **Nottinghamshire 110** (19.2 overs) (M. F. Cleary 3-11, C. E. Dagnall 4-22). *Leicestershire 2 pts.*

Man of the Match: C. E. Dagnall.   *Attendance:* 5,806.

Grace Road was almost bursting at the seams for this local derby. Leicestershire compiled an adequate total, though no batsman dominated. Then Dagnall, bowling a full length, undid Nottinghamshire with four top-order wickets and a running catch to remove Chris Read.

At Leeds, July 14. **Yorkshire won by eight wickets.** Toss: Yorkshire. **Lancashire 168** (19.1 overs) (A. Flintoff 85; A. K. D. Gray 3-18); **Yorkshire 170-2** (17.5 overs) (I. J. Harvey 108*, P. A. Jaques 39). *Yorkshire 2 pts.*

Man of the Match: I. J. Harvey.   *Attendance:* 11,610.

Both sides opened the batting with their big guns. Flintoff, making his Twenty20 debut, entertained a large crowd with powerful strokeplay that brought ten fours and three sixes from 48 balls, but nobody else passed 20. Harvey then outdid Flintoff with a magnificent century, his second in the competition, though Yorkshire's first. In all, he faced 59 balls, cracking 16 fours and two sixes. Earlier, Steve Kirby had bowled four wicketless overs for 60, the second most expensive analysis in the competition's history. While fielding, Yorkshire captain Craig White damaged his left knee, an injury that ended his season.

At Derby, July 15. **Derbyshire v Leicestershire. No result** (abandoned). *Derbyshire 1 pt, Leicestershire 1 pt.*

A no-result saw Leicestershire through to the quarter-finals, but not Derbyshire.

At Chester-le-Street, July 15. **Durham won by seven wickets.** Toss: Yorkshire. **Yorkshire 126-7** (20 overs) (V. J. Craven 44*); **Durham 129-3** (18.2 overs) (P. Mustard 42, G. J. Pratt 35*). *Durham 2 pts.*

Man of the Match: P. Mustard.   *Attendance:* 5,750.

Durham, unable to progress to the quarter-finals, easily beat Yorkshire to ensure they also missed out. Failing to realise that slow Riverside pitches had produced fewer runs than at Headingley, Yorkshire recklessly gave away wickets. On his Twenty20 debut, Harmison bowled the dangerous Harvey with a slow yorker, finishing with one for 19 off four overs. Mustard's 42 came from 34 balls.

At Manchester, July 15. **Lancashire won by seven wickets.** Toss: Lancashire. **Nottinghamshire 79-5** (8 overs) (D. J. Hussey 33, C. M. W. Read 34*; D. G. Cork 3-9); **Lancashire 82-3** (6.5 overs) (A. Flintoff 31). *Lancashire 2 pts.*

Reduced to eight overs a side.

Man of the Match: D. G. Cork.   *Attendance:* 4,682.

The winners of this rain-shortened match would qualify for the next round. After six and a half overs, Nottinghamshire were a prosperous 71 for one; three balls later, they were 71 for four, and Cork had taken the second hat-trick in the Twenty20 – on the ground where in 1995 he had taken a Test hat-trick against West Indies. Then Flintoff, dropped on four, smashed 31 from just 11 balls, with four fours and two sixes, as Lancashire eased into the quarter-finals.

SOUTH GROUP

At Chelmsford, July 2 (day/night). **Essex won by 40 runs.** Toss: Hampshire. **Essex 135-9** (18 overs) (R. C. Irani 36; A. D. Mascarenhas 3-22); **Hampshire 95** (15 overs) (G. R. Napier 3-13, R. S. Bopara 3-18). *Essex 2 pts.*

Reduced to 18 overs a side.

Man of the Match: R. C. Irani.   *Attendance:* 6,519.

Irani's rapid 36 from 23 balls delighted a big crowd. Napier then claimed a wicket in each of his three overs as the Hampshire reply plummeted to 40 for six before the halfway stage. The only Hampshire batsman to pass 15 was John Crawley, who made 21 before becoming the first of Bopara's three victims, all clean bowled.

At Maidstone, July 2. **Kent won by seven wickets** (D/L method). Toss: Kent. **Middlesex 155-7** (18 overs) (C. B. Keegan 42); **Kent 157-3** (13.1 overs) (A. Symonds 112). *Kent 2 pts.*

Kent's target was revised to 157 in 18 overs.

County debuts: Shahid Afridi (Kent); D. L. S. van Bunge (Middlesex).

Man of the Match: A. Symonds.   *Attendance:* 3,000.

Symonds, dropped on 11, massacred the Middlesex bowling in outrageous style, reaching his hundred off the 34th ball he faced. He slowed a little thereafter, eventually falling for 112, at the time a Twenty20 record, from 43 deliveries including 18 fours and three sixes. When he was third out, at 143, Symonds had hit more than 82% of Kent's runs off the bat, and a home victory was a formality. Earlier, Martin Saggers took two for 14 from four overs to stifle the Middlesex innings, which was briefly interrupted by rain. After the restart, Keegan, with three sixes and three fours off 16 balls, ensured a potentially defensible total – but for Symonds.

43 BALLS OF MAYHEM

Andrew Symonds's innings, ball by ball:

4 2 1 0 4 2 4 6 1 4 4 1 2 4 4 4 1 4 4 4 4 2 2 2 1 4 6 1 0 4 1 6 4 4 0 4 0 0 4 0 3 0 W

At Hove, July 2 (day/night). **Surrey won by 100 runs.** Toss: Sussex. **Surrey 221-8** (20 overs) (S. A. Newman 38, A. D. Brown 45, M. R. Ramprakash 46, M. A. Butcher 35, Extras 32); **Sussex 121** (17.2 overs) (M. J. Prior 35; A. J. Hollioake 4-14). *Surrey 2 pts.*

County debut: G. S. Blewett (Surrey).

Man of the Match: A. J. Hollioake.   *Attendance:* 4,900.

Surrey began the defence of their title in supreme fashion, equalling the Twenty20's highest total and winning by a record margin. With 45 from 25 balls, Brown was especially brutal, while Ramprakash hit all his five fours off one Mohammad Akram over before being caught off the last ball. Shabby bowling made things more difficult for Sussex: eight wides and four no-balls gifted Surrey another two overs. James Kirtley was most culpable, and his figures of one for 63 proved to be the most expensive in the competition's first two years. Sussex reached 76 for one, but Nayan Doshi (4–0–11–2) and Hollioake smothered the scoring.

At The Oval, July 3. **Surrey won by 31 runs.** Toss: Surrey. **Surrey 198-5** (20 overs) (M. A. Butcher 53, M. R. Ramprakash 76*, A. J. Hol-ioake 44*; J. T. A. Bruce 3-21); **Hampshire 167-9** (20 overs) (S. D. Udal 37, A. D. Mascarenhas 47; A. J. Holioake 5-34). *Surrey 2 pts.*
    Man of the Match: A. D. Mascarenhas.   *Attendance:* 5,902.
    Holioake grabbed five wickets in the Twenty20 for the second time; only four others had managed it once, though a fifth, Mascarenhas, would do so six days later. Ramprakash hit seven sixes in his 42-ball innings, Holioake four in 20. Hopes of a Hampshire victory, never bright, were snuffed out once Mascarenhas departed to the 36th ball he faced.

At Maidstone, July 5. **Essex won by eight wickets.** Toss: Kent. **Kent 125** (19.2 overs) (S. A. Brant 4-20); **Essex 128-2** (15.3 overs) (R. C. Irani 64*, G. R. Napier 38). *Essex 2 pts.*
    Man of the Match: R. C. Irani.   *Attendance:* 3,500.
    The Kent batsmen, too keen to bash the life out of the ball, failed against a no-nonsense line from the Essex seamers. Napier conceded 17 from his four overs, Andy Clarke a single more, while Brant collected the wickets. Irani then stroked a 52-ball unbeaten 64 containing nine fours.

At Chelmsford, July 7 (day/night). **Essex v Surrey. No result** (abandoned). *Essex 1 pt, Surrey 1 pt.*
    Rain prevented any play and meant Surrey dropped a point for the first time ever in the competition.

At Richmond, July 7. **Middlesex v Sussex. No result** (abandoned). *Middlesex 1 pt, Sussex 1 pt.*

At The Oval, July 9. **Surrey won by three runs.** Toss: Surrey. **Surrey 185-7** (20 overs) (G. S. Blewett 32, M. A. Butcher 60); **Kent 182-9** (20 overs) (M. J. Walker 32, R. W. T. Key 66*; A. J. Holioake 3-37). *Surrey 2 pts.*
    Man of the Match: R. W. T. Key.   *Attendance:* 5,674.
    Victory for Surrey guaranteed them, barring freak results, a place in the quarter-finals. Butcher's second fifty in a row – he hit 60 from 40 balls – steered Surrey towards 185, a fair total, though their lowest of the 2004 competition thus far. Kent needed 18 off the last over, but crucially Key, who ended unbeaten on 66 from 38 balls with four fours and five sixes, lost the strike. Holioake had now taken 12 wickets in three games.

At Hove, July 9 (day/night). **Hampshire won by three wickets.** Toss: Sussex. **Sussex 67** (14.5 overs) (C. J. Adams 37*; A. D. Mascarenhas 5-14); **Hampshire 69-7** (19 overs). *Hampshire 2 pts.*
    Man of the Match: A. D. Mascarenhas.   *Attendance:* 4,200.
    Hampshire ended a run of six Twenty20 losses when Chris Tremlett hoisted Mark Davis for six, though they made heavy weather of the most undemanding of targets: Sussex's 67 was comfortably the lowest total in the competition. On a fast, bouncy pitch Sussex were undone by Mascarenhas, whose record figures included the competition's first hat-trick. His victims were Davis, Mushtaq Ahmed and Jason Lewry. Adams scored over half Sussex's runs, Luke Wright contributed 18 – and no one else could reach five. Hampshire in turn lurched to 16 for four before John Crawley, top-scorer with 14, arrested the slide. Martin-Jenkins and James Kirtley conceded seven and eight respectively from their four-over spells.

At Southgate, July 12. **Middlesex won by nine wickets.** Toss: Middlesex. **Essex 120-8** (20 overs) (A. Flower 47); **Middlesex 121-1** (18.2 overs) (P. N. Weekes 55*, O. A. Shah 48*). *Middlesex 2 pts.*
    Man of the Match: P. N. Weekes.   *Attendance:* 3,000.
    For Essex, only Flower came to grips with a slow Southgate pitch, as they limped to 120. Middlesex fared better and although Weekes, like Flower, made his runs at fewer than a run a ball, Shah sped merrily along. Middlesex's first win was Essex's first defeat of the 2004 competition.

At Southampton, July 13. **Hampshire won by 30 runs.** Toss: Hampshire. **Hampshire 170-7** (20 overs) (M. J. Clarke 46, A. D. Mascarenhas 52; S. J. Cook 3-25); **Middlesex 140-8** (20 overs) (P. N. Weekes 34, J. W. M. Dalrymple 31, L. Klusener 35*; C. T. Tremlett 3-20). *Hampshire 2 pts.*
    Man of the Match: A. D. Mascarenhas.   *Attendance:* 8,000.
    This was Mascarenhas's match. Watched by his father, Malik, he spanked a lightning half-century – his 52 came from 22 balls and included four sixes, three in the last over, from Dalrymple – before clogging up the Middlesex reply with one for 13 off four. Weekes took 16 overs to compile 34. Hampshire maintained a chance of reaching the next round; Middlesex did not.

At Canterbury, July 13. **Kent won by 47 runs.** Toss: Sussex. **Kent 163-6** (20 overs) (M. J. Walker 48*, R. W. T. Key 35); **Sussex 116** (19.5 overs) (I. G. Butler 3-19). *Kent 2 pts.*
County debut: I. G. Butler.
Man of the Match: I. G. Butler.   *Attendance: 4,919.*
  Both sides reached the halfway mark of their innings at 57 for four, but while Kent built on their foundation through Walker and Key (who pummelled three fours and three sixes from 21 balls), Sussex subsided to heavy defeat. Butler marked his debut with three catches in the deep and three economical wickets.

At Chelmsford, July 15 (day/night). **Sussex won by nine wickets.** Toss: Essex. **Essex 134-8** (20 overs) (L. J. Wright 3-39); **Sussex 136-1** (17 overs) (M. J. Prior 68*, C. J. Adams 38*). *Sussex 2 pts.*
Man of the Match: M. J. Prior.   *Attendance: 7,000.*
  Victory would have guaranteed Essex a home draw in the quarter-finals, but in front of a capacity crowd, they never got going. Even so, they did scrape through despite finishing third, inching out Derbyshire on run-rate. Sussex bowled tidily, Jason Lewry picked up two for 16 from four overs, and Essex had little to defend. Exactly 50 of Prior's 49-ball innings came in boundaries – 11 fours and a six – as he and Adams added an unbroken 112, a Twenty20 second-wicket record. It was Sussex's only win of the tournament.

At Southampton, July 15. **Hampshire won by 64 runs.** Toss: Kent. **Hampshire 177-3** (20 overs) (S. R. Watson 97*, M. J. Clarke 38); **Kent 113-9** (20 overs) (M. J. Walker 38; A. D. Mascarenhas 3-20). *Hampshire 2 pts.*
Man of the Match: S. R. Watson.   *Attendance: 9,100.*
  This game was effectively a knockout: the winner would progress, the loser almost certainly would not. Watson, who had managed 25 runs in his past four Twenty20 innings, needed a four off the 68th ball he faced – the last of the Hampshire innings – to reach a quality century, but managed only a single. Bruce then held a spectacular, tumbling catch running back at long-on to dismiss the dangerous Symonds and, against the accuracy of Mascarenhas, Kent never recovered from 20 for four. The crowd was at the time a Rose Bowl record.

At Lord's, July 15. **Surrey won by 37 runs.** Toss: Middlesex. **Surrey 183-5** (20 overs) (J. G. E. Benning 30, M. R. Ramprakash 38, A. J. Hollioake 65*); **Middlesex 146-7** (20 overs) (P. N. Weekes 33, L. Klusener 53; N. D. Doshi 3-26). *Surrey 2 pts.*
Man of the Match: A. J. Hollioake.   *Attendance: 27,509.*
  Nothing hung on this game – Surrey were already guaranteed a home tie in the next round and Middlesex were out – yet the first Twenty20 game at Lord's produced the biggest crowd to watch a county match, cup finals excepted, since these two sides met here in 1953. Tickets had sold out several days earlier, and the crowd did not quite reach the Lord's capacity of 28,000 only because the pavilion was not full. Ramprakash, a former Middlesex stalwart, was booed occasionally during his measured innings. Hollioake then cut loose with 65 off 41 deliveries. Middlesex were never in the hunt, though the crowd enjoyed Klusener striking 22 from Hollioake's first over. He fell in his second. Westminster Council, which stopped Lord's staging a match in 2003, monitored noise levels to appease anxious residents.

QUARTER-FINALS

At Cardiff, July 19. **Glamorgan won by five wickets.** Toss: Warwickshire. **Warwickshire 158-7** (20 overs) (G. B. Hogg 54; S. D. Thomas 3-32); **Glamorgan 161-5** (19 overs) (M. T. G. Elliott 48, D. L. Hemp 74).
Man of the Match: D. L. Hemp.   *Attendance: 6,000*
  A third-wicket stand of 118 between Elliott and Hemp dragged the game from Warwickshire, who had lost a C&G semi-final just two days earlier. Hogg held the Warwickshire innings together with a steady fifty, and when both Glamorgan openers went without scoring, the capacity crowd feared a repetition of Glamorgan's defeat in the group game. But Elliott, in his first Twenty20 match, and Hemp, with six fours and three sixes, pulled them round.

At Southampton, July 19. **Lancashire won by nine wickets.** Toss: Lancashire. **Hampshire 120-9** (20 overs) (M. J. Clarke 36, A. D. Mascarenhas 33*); **Lancashire 121-1** (16.3 overs) (M. B. Loye 64*).

Man of the Match: M. B. Loye.   *Attendance:* 8,900.

Lancashire barely broke sweat in crushing Hampshire. Clarke and the dependable Mascarenhas helped Hampshire past 100, but not far enough to set a meaningful target. Glen Chapple claimed two for 14 from his four overs. Shane Warne, electing to pinch-hit at No. 3 on his competition debut, spent six balls over his nought. He bowled efficiently, but Loye, sharing fifty stands with Steven Crook and Mark Chilton, guided Lancashire home with 21 balls unused.

At Leicester, July 19. **Leicestershire won by 14 runs.** Toss: Essex. **Leicestershire 180-6** (20 overs) (D. L. Maddy 84, D. I. Stevens 39); **Essex 166-7** (20 overs) (A. Flower 58, A. P. Grayson 55; M. F. Cleary 3-36).

Man of the Match: D. L. Maddy.   *Attendance:* 5,065.

A dazzling 84 from Maddy, who hit 12 fours and three sixes from 48 balls, piloted Leicestershire to a daunting total in front of a boisterous crowd. Essex lost Ronnie Irani to the first ball of their reply and Graham Napier later the same over, bowled by Cleary, on his 24th birthday. A fourth-wicket stand of 95 between Flower and Grayson never threatened to deny Leicestershire.

At The Oval, July 19. **Surrey won by 14 runs.** Toss: Surrey. **Surrey 145-7** (20 overs) (A. J. Hollioake 45*; M. N. Malik 3-23); **Worcestershire 131-8** (20 overs) (V. S. Solanki 33; A. J. Hollioake 3-31).

Man of the Match: A. J. Hollioake.   *Attendance:* 6,380.

At 50 for five ten overs into their innings, Surrey seemed likely to surrender their unbeaten record in the Twenty20. But a 29-ball onslaught from Hollioake brought 45 vital runs, allowing Surrey to set a reasonable target. Even so, Worcestershire looked favourites as they reached the halfway mark at 73 for two. Then Hollioake derailed them with the ball, seizing another three wickets to take his tally in the competition to 17, more than anyone else. Surrey marched on to finals day at Birmingham.

Finals Day Reports by Paul Coupar

SEMI-FINALS

LANCASHIRE v SURREY

At Birmingham, August 7. Surrey won by one run. Toss: Surrey.

This thrilling game ended with Lancashire falling an agonising one short of Surrey's 133 – the smallest total successfully defended in Twenty20 cricket. The winner of this was expected to win the tournament and, as expected, by the end there was only a hair's breadth between them. Lancashire needed two from the last ball, bowled by Azhar Mahmood. He distilled his experience of 134 one-day internationals into a full straight delivery. Schofield hit straight to mid-on and scrambled one, but was hopelessly short of the second – and all the built-up tension was suddenly released into roaring Surrey celebrations. The match had begun in blazing sunshine as a salvo of 32 in 15 balls by Brown sent Surrey racing away at ten an over. Flintoff, introduced in the sixth over, got him with a low full toss to stem the torrent, which became a trickle as the slow men (who cost just 57 in 11 overs) wrecked the batsmen's timing. But with Lancashire's reply beginning unconvincingly, Surrey's unprecedented task began to look possible – and with 40 needed from five they were shading it. They looked safer still when the 16th over, from Doshi, brought two wickets and just two runs. But it also brought the ebullient Cork. His 13-ball 25 sent the game swooping back towards Lancashire. However it swooped away again when, with ten needed from 11 balls, Cork misguidedly attempted a third six and got a top edge. He had been carried away on the adrenalin rush, which was forgivable – by that stage everyone had.

Man of the Match: Azhar Mahmood.

Taking it seriously: Lanky the giraffe won the npower mascots race for Lancashire after Surrey's lion (Roary) was disqualified.

Picture by Roger Wootton

Surrey

A. D. Brown b Flintoff	32	P. J. Sampson run out	0
J. G. E. Benning b Anderson	16	N. D. Doshi b Anderson	1
S. A. Newman c Mongia b Flintoff	12		
M. R. Ramprakash b Keedy	24	L-b 5, w 3	8
R. Clarke lbw b Keedy	18		
A. J. Hollioake c Hegg b Mongia	1	1/24 (2) 2/61 (1) 3/66 (3) (20 overs) 133
Azhar Mahmood c Chilton b Keedy	13	4/109 (5) 5/111 (4) 6/111 (6)
*†J. N. Batty c Chapple b Mongia	3	7/121 (8) 8/127 (7)
J. Ormond not out	5	9/128 (10) 10/133 (11)

Bowling: Anderson 4–0–28–2; Chapple 2–0–28–0; Flintoff 3–0–15–2; Hooper 4–0–26–0; Keedy 4–0–25–3; Mongia 3–0–6–2.

Lancashire

A. Flintoff c Brown b Azhar Mahmood	15	*†W. K. Hegg not out	3
S. P. Crook c sub b Clarke	12		
M. J. Chilton c and b Azhar Mahmood	11	L-b 6	6
D. Mongia c Batty b Sampson	15		
C. L. Hooper b Doshi	26	1/22 (1) 2/37 (3) (8 wkts, 20 overs) 132
G. Chapple lbw b Doshi	11	3/47 (2) 4/63 (4)
C. P. Schofield run out	8	5/94 (5) 6/95 (6)
D. G. Cork c Clarke b Hollioake	25	7/124 (8) 8/132 (7)

G. Keedy and J. M. Anderson did not bat.

Bowling: Azhar Mahmood 4–0–22–2; Clarke 4–0–31–1; Ormond 3–0–12–0; Sampson 1–0–5–1; Doshi 4–0–27–2; Hollioake 4–0–29–1.

Umpires: I. J. Gould and J. H. Hampshire.
Third umpire: N. J. Llong.

GLAMORGAN v LEICESTERSHIRE

At Birmingham, August 7. Leicestershire won by 21 runs. Toss: Leicestershire.

The crowd were still buzzing from the first semi 45 minutes before, so it was quite something that for the first 11 overs Maddy kept them almost as well entertained. He was on course for the highest Twenty20 score yet, when he was caught at deep backward square for a scintillating 40-ball 72. But Glamorgan were an inch away from a very different game: Maddy, on 13, gave a hard chance to which Elliott, diving forward at mid-on, got a fingertip. As it was, the first 12 overs brought 107, and Leicestershire jogged on comfortably for the rest of the innings, ending with 165 after the slow bowlers calmed the scoring. Glamorgan's batsmen never kept up with the pace. Their two stars were extinguished inside five overs, Maynard by a stunning airborne catch at third man, Elliott by a sharp run-out. The rest fell trying to hustle nine an over on a slowish pitch against disciplined bowling, leaving their noisy supporters to choose between Surrey and Leicestershire in the final.

Man of the Match: D. L. Maddy.

Leicestershire

*B. J. Hodge c Hemp b Croft	22	J. L. Sadler not out	1
D. L. Maddy c Hemp b Dale	72	L-b 4, w 1, n-b 2	7
D. I. Stevens c Dale b Croft	27		
J. N. Snape b Wharf	5	1/82 (1) 2/106 (2) (5 wkts, 20 overs) 165
†P. A. Nixon not out	14	3/129 (4) 4/135 (3)
O. D. Gibson c Elliott b Kasprowicz	17	5/161 (6)

J. M. Dakin, C. W. Henderson, M. F. Cleary and C. E. Dagnall did not bat.

Bowling: Kasprowicz 3–0–16–1; S. D. Thomas 3–0–35–0; Wharf 4–0–29–1; Dale 3–0–30–1; Croft 4–0–27–2; I. J. Thomas 3–0–24–0.

Glamorgan

M. P. Maynard c Sadler b Cleary	9	A. G. Wharf c Hodge b Cleary	2
I. J. Thomas b Cleary	3	M. S. Kasprowicz b sub b Gibson	2
M. T. G. Elliott run out	15		
D. L. Hemp c Hodge b Henderson	44	L-b 9, w 3, n-b 2	14
†M. A. Wallace c Snape b Maddy	22		
*R. D. B. Croft b Henderson	6	1/13 (1) 2/18 (2) 3/30 (3) (18.5 overs) 144
M. J. Powell c Sadler b Henderson	5	4/79 (5) 5/108 (6) 6/111 (4)
S. D. Thomas not out	20	7/120 (7) 8/131 (9)
A. Dale run out	2	9/133 (10) 10/144 (11)

Bowling: Cleary 3–0–20–3; Gibson 2.5–0–14–1; Dagnall 4–0–27–0; Dakin 1–0–7–0; Snape 2–0–19–0; Maddy 3–0–22–1; Henderson 3–0–26–3.

Umpires: J. H. Hampshire and N. J. Llong.
Third umpire: I. J. Gould.

FINAL

LEICESTERSHIRE v SURREY

At Birmingham, August 7 (day/night). Leicestershire won by seven wickets. Toss: Surrey.

Leicestershire's outfoxing of Surrey provided a fitting end to a brilliant day's cricket. In subcontinental heat and noise, their batsmen Hodge and Snape delighted their own supporters and most neutrals by pulling off a wily heist on what looked a secure vault. With 30 balls left, Surrey, unbeaten in Twenty20 history and masters at defending low scores, were favourites. Leicestershire needed 47, the ball was seaming, and Holliaoke, whose slower delivery was frustrating the key batsman Hodge, still had two overs left. But the game pivoted when Snape arrived in the 16th over. Crucially, he and Hodge spotted the sign Hollioake gave to the keeper to indicate the slower ball. And if they missed that, they agreed the non-striker would shout a warning if the keeper inched forward. By breaking the Surrey code, they unravelled the enigma of Hollioake. His first two overs cost nine; after the code-breaking, his third was crisply hit for 11. As he started his fourth, the penultimate of an enthralling game and the last big over of Hollioake's career, Leicestershire needed 20 off 12. With the tension now feverish, it disappeared for 16 as Snape smashed the slower ball for six over long-on and Hodge walloped a straight four. With the whole Leicestershire squad watching nervously on the boundary, arms round each other's shoulders, Snape finally cleared the pressure by hitting the first ball of the 20th over to the mid-wicket boundary. The cacophony of crowd noise, Hollioake's head-in-hands despair and the Leicestershire jig of triumph dispelled any remaining notion that the Twenty20 was a frivolity that did not really matter. Earlier Brown biffed 64 from 41 balls to help Surrey to 168, the highest total of the three games. On a day for spinners, only Henderson's three overs of canny left-arm tweakers stood between them and a more intimidating total. Brought on in the 13th over, he conceded just 15 and took two wickets, including Brown with his first ball. Still, many thought Surrey had just enough. Hodge, bat brimming with orthodox strokes, scored 77 in 53 balls to prove them wrong.

Man of the Match: B. J. Hodge.

Attendance (for all three matches on finals day): 18,172; receipts £399,798.

Surrey

A. D. Brown c Sadler b Henderson	64	*†J. N. Batty not out	1
J. G. E. Benning c Henderson b Gibson	5		
S. A. Newman c Cleary b Dagnall	21	B 6, l-b 6, w 10, n-b 2	24
M. R. Ramprakash not out	23		
R. Clarke c Cleary b Henderson	13	1/11 (2) 2/91 (3) (6 wkts, 20 overs) 168	
A. J. Hollioake c Hodge b Cleary	4	3/109 (1) 4/135 (5)	
Azhar Mahmood b Cleary	13	5/141 (6) 6/160 (7)	

J. Ormond, P. J. Sampson and N. D. Doshi did not bat.

Bowling: Cleary 4–0–38–2; Gibson 3–0–21–1; Dagnall 4–0–36–1; Maddy 2–0–16–0; Snape 4–0–30–0; Henderson 3–0–15–2.

Leicestershire

*B. J. Hodge not out	77	J. N. Snape not out	34
D. L. Maddy b Sampson	22	L-b 3, w 7	10
D. I. Stevens c Azhar Mahmood b Hollioake	20		
J. L. Sadler c Clarke b Hollioake	6	1/62 (2) 2/114 (3) (3 wkts, 19.1 overs) 169	
		3/122 (4)	

†P. A. Nixon, O. D. Gibson, D. G. Brandy, C. W. Henderson, M. F. Cleary and C. E. Dagnall did not bat.

Bowling: Azhar Mahmood 3.1–0–33–0; Clarke 2–0–27–0; Sampson 2–0–14–1; Ormond 4–0–30–0; Doshi 4–0–26–0; Hollioake 4–0–36–2.

Umpires: I. J. Gould and N. J. Llong.
Third umpire: J. H. Hampshire.

CAREER FIGURES

Players not expected to appear in county cricket in 2005.

BATTING

	M	I	NO	R	HS	100s	Avge	1,000r/season
R. S. G. Anderson	40	52	6	683	67*	0	14.84	0
V. Atri	9	16	3	422	98	0	32.46	0
T. M. B. Bailey	52	71	12	1,324	101*	1	22.44	0
P. D. Bowler	318	542	59	19,567	241*	45	40.51	10
D. G. Brandy	9	14	2	187	52	0	15.58	0
A. N. Bressington	9	9	6	125	58*	0	41.66	0
M. J. Cawdron	25	32	4	396	42	0	14.14	0
P. A. Cottey	277	448	51	14,567	203	31	36.69	8
V. J. Craven	33	55	6	1,206	81*	0	24.61	0
J. M. Dakin	79	119	14	2,937	190	5	27.97	0
A. Dale	251	413	35	12,586	214*	23	33.29	4
N. R. C. Dumelow	25	41	4	781	75	0	21.10	0
A. I. Gait	63	118	2	3,093	175	4	26.66	0
A. K. D. Gray	18	26	3	649	104	1	28.21	0
N. E. L. Gunter	7	8	3	74	20*	0	14.80	0
J. R. C. Hamblin	11	18	2	440	96	0	27.50	0
J. J. Haynes	20	29	4	491	80	0	19.64	0
R. J. E. Hindley	1	2	1	76	68*	0	76.00	0
A. J. Hollioake	173	263	21	9,376	208	18	38.74	2
N. Hussain	334	545	53	20,698	207	52	42.06	5
K. J. Innes	45	70	17	1,256	103*	1	23.69	0
C. J. R. Jennings	1	1	0	6	6	0	6.00	0
W. S. Kendall	140	230	25	6,822	201	10	33.27	3
R. M. Khan	18	31	1	611	91	0	20.36	0
S. G. Koenig	135	234	13	8,820	171	16	39.90	3
P. Kumar	2	4	1	36	21	0	12.00	0
C. G. Liptrot	30	36	11	303	61	0	12.12	0
A. G. A. M. McCoubrey	10	12	6	6	2*	0	1.00	0
P. J. Martin	213	246	61	3,594	133	2	19.42	0
Mohammad Ali	84	112	26	1,247	92	0	14.50	0
W. M. Noon	92	145	23	2,527	83	0	20.71	0
D. P. Ostler	205	336	25	10,856	225	16	34.90	6
I. Pattison	7	11	0	215	62	0	19.54	0
M. J. Powell (Northants)	27	44	3	1,024	108*	2	24.97	0
S. J. Rhodes	440	618	166	14,839	124	12	32.82	2
R. C. Russell	465	690	145	16,861	129*	11	30.93	1
N. C. Saker	2	3	0	6	5	0	2.00	0
C. P. Schofield	68	95	14	2,423	99	0	29.91	0
S. A. Selwood	25	48	1	901	99	0	19.17	0
N. Shahid	148	235	27	6,453	150	9	31.02	1
Z. K. Sharif	7	10	1	258	67	0	28.66	0
A. M. Smith	157	206	62	1,756	61	0	12.19	0
W. R. Smith	8	13	2	216	48	0	19.63	0
J. P. Stephenson	302	510	56	14,772	202*	25	32.53	5
P. J. Swanepoel	2	3	0	20	17	0	6.66	0
A. J. Swann	77	123	4	3,305	154	8	27.77	1
A. C. Thomas	1	—	—	—	—	—	—	0
M. Thorburn	6	5	1	35	12	0	8.75	0
M. J. Todd	1	1	1	6	6*	0	—	0
B. J. Trott	34	37	11	150	26	0	5.76	0
G. W. Walker	4	5	2	74	37*	0	24.66	0
T. Webley	12	21	2	601	104	1	31.63	0
D. H. Wigley	7	9	2	91	23*	0	13.00	0
J. Wood	115	163	24	1,762	64	0	12.67	0

BOWLING AND FIELDING

	R	W	BB	Avge	5W/i	10W/m	Ct/St
R. S. G. Anderson	3,452	122	6-34	28.29	8	1	7
V. Atri	–	–	–	–	–	–	5
T. M. B. Bailey	3	0	–	–	–	–	97/18
P. D. Bowler	2,051	34	3-25	60.32	–	–	232/1
D. G. Brandy	172	4	2-11	43.00	–	–	3
A. N. Bressington	584	17	4-36	34.35	–	–	4
M. J. Cawdron	1,848	74	6-25	24.97	6	1	5
P. A. Cottey	954	16	4-49	59.62	–	–	182
V. J. Craven	584	15	2-18	38.93	–	–	18
J. M. Dakin	5,572	162	5-86	34.39	1	–	22
A. Dale	8,274	217	6-18	38.12	4	–	107
N. R. C. Dumelow	2,132	41	5-51	52.00	3	1	5
A. I. Gait	–	–	–	–	–	–	55
A. K. D. Gray	1,359	30	4-128	45.30	–	–	16
N. E. L. Gunter	602	17	4-14	35.41	–	–	5
J. R. C. Hamblin	723	14	6-93	51.64	1	–	5
J. J. Haynes	–	–	–	–	–	–	47/4
R. J. E. Hindley	46	0	–	–	–	–	0
A. J. Hollioake	4,927	120	5-62	41.05	1	–	157
N. Hussain	323	2	1-38	161.50	–	–	350
K. J. Innes	2,461	79	4-41	31.15	–	–	15
C. J. R. Jennings	64	1	1-64	64.00	–	–	0
W. S. Kendall	736	15	3-37	49.06	–	–	118
R. M. Khan	28	0	–	–	–	–	10
S. G. Koenig	102	2	1-0	51.00	–	–	63
P. Kumar	219	6	3-78	36.50	–	–	0
C. G. Liptrot	2,212	69	6-44	32.05	2	–	11
A. G. A. M. McCoubrey	842	23	4-16	36.60	–	–	3
P. J. Martin	16,677	606	8-32	27.51	17	1	56
Mohammad Ali	8,607	264	6-37	32.60	11	2	26
W. M. Noon	34	0	–	–	–	–	195/20
D. P. Ostler	295	1	1-46	295.00	–	–	259
I. Pattison	295	7	3-41	42.14	–	–	5
M. J. Powell (Northants)	12	0	–	–	–	–	40
S. J. Rhodes	30	0	–	–	–	–	1,139/124
R. C. Russell	68	1	1-4	68.00	–	–	1,192/128
N. C. Saker	179	1	1-71	179.00	–	–	0
C. P. Schofield	5,347	171	6-120	31.26	4	–	40
S. A. Selwood	95	2	1-8	47.50	–	–	6
N. Shahid	2,146	45	3-91	47.68	–	–	153
Z. K. Sharif	532	9	4-98	59.11	–	–	2
A. M. Smith	13,158	533	8-73	24.68	22	5	31
W. R. Smith	127	2	2-83	63.50	–	–	6
J. P. Stephenson	12,782	392	7-44	32.60	11	1	182
P. J. Swanepoel	129	3	2-40	43.00	–	–	1
A. J. Swann	326	6	2-30	54.33	–	–	56
A. C. Thomas	–	–	–	–	–	–	1
M. Thorburn	523	12	2-53	43.58	–	–	1
M. J. Todd	92	1	1-92	92.00	–	–	0
B. J. Trott	2,999	88	6-13	34.07	4	1	8
G. W. Walker	190	1	1-92	190.00	–	–	2
T. Webley	357	6	2-57	59.50	–	–	4
D. H. Wigley	746	15	4-133	49.73	–	–	2
J. Wood	10,787	318	7-58	33.92	11	–	28

THE UNIVERSITIES, 2004

Reports by Ralph Dellor, David Hallett,
Grenville Holland and Guy Jackson

University cricket went back to the future in 2004 when MCC – 36 years after ceding control of the game in England – once again took these traditional breeding grounds for players under its wing.

The ECB, current rulers of the English game, seemed happy to get rid of what it appeared to regard as an expensive distraction. MCC, with fewer responsibilities and financial problems, was anxious to spend its funds on encouraging young cricketers. Tony Lewis, the chairman of the cricket committee, was prime mover of the idea, and the club took charge of the six University Centres of Cricketing Excellence (UCCEs) in the autumn. Immediately, each centre had its annual grant increased from £50,000 to £65,000 a year, guaranteed until 2007. The club also added a new dose of enthusiasm.

John Stephenson, the former Essex, Hampshire and England player, is in charge of the scheme in his new role as MCC's head of cricket. "It fits in nicely for us," said Stephenson, himself a Durham graduate. "We are looking to become more involved in areas that will benefit the game. It's an excellent idea to combine a good education and a good cricketing programme."

The new arrangement is not without potential pitfalls. The ECB will remain in charge of those areas where university cricket rubs up against professional cricket, and this is where difficulties most often occur. Theoretically, the UCCEs have control of their players until the end of June. But universities can find it hard to refuse a county coach with a long injury list and an ingratiating manner; after all, the players are generally anxious for county first-team cricket.

However, counties have been known to go to great lengths to get players released from student fixtures, then made them twelfth man for four days, giving the youngster the worst of both worlds. Some university officials worry that MCC will not have enough authority to deal with cases like this. "You have to hope common sense will prevail," said Stephenson.

The MCC deal should ensure the medium-term future for the six UCCEs, including those based in South Wales and Yorkshire, which do not have first-class status and have been struggling. The other four are generally regarded as successes, though the balance of power in university cricket has clearly shifted away from Durham, who dominated the 1990s, to Loughborough, where the new National Academy facilities provide an extra draw to aspiring cricketers. Durham faces particular problems in maintaining its cricketing status. Whereas Oxford and Cambridge both have associated ex-polytechnics which can offer less bookish students the opportunities and facilities once restricted to a narrow elite, Durham has abandoned its sports degree at Stockton and tightened its academic focus.

However, it was **Durham** who enjoyed the most reflected glory in 2004, when the university's old boy Andrew Strauss spectacularly established himself in the England team. And though they failed to win any of the trophies on offer, they also produced the outstanding bowling performance – statistically the best of the entire first-class season – when their seamer Lee Daggett bowled out the Durham county team in their local derby on April 10, the second day of the season. Daggett took eight for 94; though more than five months of the season was left, no one else in the country took more than seven in an innings.

Oxford broke Loughborough's three-year stranglehold on the two-day Inter-UCCE competition, winning the play-off at Lord's with three balls to spare. They also dominated their time-honoured rivals Cambridge in both first-class and one-day fixtures. Oxford's Yorkshireman, Joe Sayers, scored 144 from 127 balls in the one-day match against Cambridge at Lord's, 98 in the Loughborough match there next day and followed up with a knock of 147 in the four-day Varsity Match in The Parks. However, of the 14 men who played for the UCCE against the counties, Sayers was one of only six from the traditional Oxford University colleges; the team now depends heavily on the neighbouring Oxford Brookes University. The 178-year-old Varsity Match itself is restricted to students from the ancient rivals, an anomaly causing continued murmurs about its first-class status.

But Oxford are enthusiastic about the UCCE set-up. Graham Charlesworth, the coach, said he believes the last three captains, Jamie Dalrymple, Sayers and Paul McMahon, have developed leadership qualities that will equip them to become county captains at the very least in future years. McMahon, an off-spinner attached to Nottinghamshire, displayed admirable invention by electing to take the new ball himself in the Varsity Match. Short of quality seam bowlers, he decided his best chance of taking 20 wickets in the match was to rely on his slow bowlers to do the job, which they did.

The two **Cambridge** teams had contrasting fortunes. The UCCE partnership, much slower to bloom than at Oxford, now became dependent on the resources of its junior partner, Anglia Polytechnic University. This team started the final day of their season with a chance of winning the UCCE championship: chasing Durham's 262, they were 112 for no wicket, only for the rain to prevent any further play. Their only championship defeat was by Oxford, and that only on first innings, although they were saved by rain against Loughborough. However, the traditional university side had a difficult time. The Light Blues suffered from availability problems: Simon Marshall, outstanding for the previous two years, was one of several leading players studying for their finals, but did play the only innings of substance for Cambridge in both Varsity Matches.

Chris Scott, as coach to both Cambridge sides, increased the competitive nature of their games leading up to the Varsity Matches, and the overall results suggested his side was in better shape than for several seasons.

At **Loughborough**, an already strong squad was bolstered by some promising first-year students, such as Richard Clinton, who top-scored in the British Universities and UCCE finals and later played a role in Surrey's end-of-season resurgence. Certainly, they had the most depth: their second team beat a strong Leicestershire Second Eleven while the university first team was playing Gloucestershire. Loughborough headed the inaugural British Universities National Premier League A, and the ensuing championship knockout, played between the top three sides in Premier League A and the winners of the League B play-off; they beat Durham in the final at Southgate by 86 runs. Loughborough also lifted the women's title.

OXFORD

President: A. C. Smith (Brasenose)
Chairman: Dr S. R. Porter (St Cross College)
Head Coach: G. M. Charlesworth

Captain: P. J. McMahon (Trinity RC Nottingham and Wadham)
Oxford UCCE Captain for 2005: L. C. Parker (Oxford Brookes)
Oxford University Captain for 2005: P. J. McMahon (Trinity RC Nottingham and Wadham)

OXFORD UCCE/UNIVERSITY RESULTS

First-class matches – Played 4: Won 1, Drawn 3.

OXFORD UCCE v SURREY

At Oxford, April 10, 11, 12. Drawn. Toss: Oxford UCCE. First-class debuts: O. R. Hutton, J. P. T. Knappett, L. C. Parker. UCCE debut: A. K. Suman.

Surrey's new captain, Batty, and his predecessor, Hollioake, were the only county batsmen who failed to indulge themselves when invited to bat. There were three centuries, including Benning in his third first-class match. In contrast to the students' enthusiastic but unpenetrative bowling, the county attack boasted five Test bowlers; it was not a happy start for Oliver Hutton (brother of Ben, son of Richard and grandson of Sir Len) when a 108-run stand between Anwar and Knappett helped Oxford to a respectable 267, and Batty was uninterested in enforcing the follow-on anyway. He finally set a nominal target of 350. Defeat looked certain when a collapse of six for 17 left Oxford on 115 for eight, but a determined stand of 39 between two Under-19 internationals – England's McMahon and India's Suman – denied Surrey.

Close of play: First day, Surrey 452-5 (Brown 61); Second day, Surrey 62-1 (Batty 22, Hollioake 22).

Surrey

S. A. Newman b Munday	100	– b Linley	15
*†J. N. Batty c Hutton b Suman	10	– c Hutton b Suman	24
M. R. Ramprakash retired hurt	113		
J. G. E. Benning lbw b Munday	128	– (5) c Knappett b Linley	0
A. D. Brown not out	61		
A. J. Hollioake c Parker b McMahon	12	– (3) c Knappett b Linley	23
N. Shahid c Airey b Munday	11	– (4) not out	44
M. P. Bicknell (did not bat)		– (6) c Hutton b Munday	32
A. J. Tudor (did not bat)		– (7) not out	18
B 3, l-b 2, n-b 12	17	B 1, l-b 1, n-b 6	8

1/15 (2) 2/156 (1) 3/416 (4)   (5 wkts dec.) 452
4/433 (6) 5/452 (7)

1/25 (1) 2/65 (2)   (5 wkts dec.) 164
3/71 (3) 4/73 (5)
5/142 (6)

I. D. K. Salisbury and J. Ormond did not bat.

In the first innings Ramprakash retired hurt at 325.

Bowling: *First Innings*—Suman 18–1–75–1; Linley 18–3–78–0; Airey 13–1–75–0; Hutton 6–1–36–0; Munday 13.5–1–87–3; McMahon 23–1–83–1; Parker 1–0–13–0. *Second Innings*—Suman 12–2–43–1; Linley 13–3–44–3; Airey 7–2–25–0; Munday 6–0–20–1; McMahon 9–2–30–0.

Oxford UCCE

S. J. Hawinkels b Tudor	19	– lbw b Bicknell	24
J. J. Sayers c Ramprakash b Bicknell	0	– c Batty b Ormond	56
O. R. Hutton c Ramprakash b Tudor	5	– st Batty b Salisbury	18
L. C. Parker c Batty b Hollioake	27	– b Salisbury	5
O. S. Anwar c Salisbury b Bicknell	82	– c and b Salisbury	7
†J. P. T. Knappett c Bicknell b Ormond	45	– c Benning b Ormond	0
S. J. Airey not out	24	– c Batty b Ormond	0
*P. J. McMahon c Newman b Salisbury	19	– not out	10
T. E. Linley b Salisbury	8	– c Shahid b Benning	0
A. K. Suman run out	15	– not out	24
M. K. Munday c Newman b Salisbury	14		
B 1, l-b 3, w 1, n-b 4	9	L-b 4, n-b 6	10

1/15 (2) 2/19 (1) 3/24 (3) 4/66 (4)   267   1/40 (1) 2/78 (3)   (8 wkts) 154
5/174 (6) 6/188 (5) 7/210 (8)   3/98 (4) 4/106 (2) 5/112 (6)
8/230 (9) 9/253 (10) 10/267 (11)   6/112 (7) 7/112 (5) 8/115 (9)

Bowling: *First Innings*—Bicknell 16–7–43–2; Tudor 11–3–39–2; Ormond 16–2–75–1; Hollioake 12–1–36–1; Salisbury 19–4–43–3; Benning 7–3–27–0. *Second Innings*—Bicknell 8–0–25–1; Ormond 13–3–34–3; Hollioake 6–0–17–0; Salisbury 21–9–30–3; Benning 11–2–28–1; Shahid 3–3–0–0; Ramprakash 2–0–16–0.

Umpires: N. L. Bainton and J. W. Holder.

OXFORD UCCE v NOTTINGHAMSHIRE

At Oxford, April 16, 17, 18. Drawn. Toss: Nottinghamshire. First-class debut: M. A. Richards. County debuts: D. Alleyne, M. A. Ealham, D. J. Hussey.

Another full-strength county side rattled up the runs on the opening day, with the most spectacular batting coming from Nottinghamshire's new overseas player, David Hussey from Victoria. He reached his hundred in 81 balls, with nine fours and six sixes – three of them in one over from McMahon – though oddly he faced 47 more balls and only advanced to 107. Smith and Shreck reduced Oxford to 39 for five on the second morning, culminating with the wicket of Mali Richards, son of Sir Viv, whose only significant contribution on first-class debut was a fine catch at deep cover to dismiss Pietersen. But Airey dug in for four and a half hours. Gallian waived the follow-on, and his team had extended their lead to 312 before the third day was washed out.

Close of play: First day, Oxford UCCE 15-1 (Sayers 4, Airey 1); Second day, Nottinghamshire 106-2 (Alleyne 43, Warren 20); Third day, No play.

Nottinghamshire

D. J. Bicknell lbw b Linley	1	– c Sayers b Linley	13
*J. E. R. Gallian c Howard b Linley	89		
R. J. Warren c McMahon b Linley	67	– (4) not out	20
K. P. Pietersen c Richards b McMahon	62		
D. J. Hussey not out	107		
M. A. Ealham not out	52		
P. J. Franks (did not bat)		– (2) c Anwar b Linley	24
†D. Alleyne (did not bat)		– (3) not out	43
L-b 6, n-b 12	18	L-b 2, n-b 4	6

1/5 (1) 2/165 (2)   (4 wkts dec.) 396   1/29 (1) 2/50 (2)   (2 wkts) 106
3/176 (3) 4/291 (4)

G. J. Smith, S. C. G. MacGill and C. E. Shreck did not bat.

Bowling: *First Innings*—Suman 14–3–44–0; Linley 21–1–101–3; Airey 15–4–51–0; McMahon 16–1–103–1; Richards 8–0–45–0; Munday 5–0–46–0. *Second Innings*—Suman 7–1–37–0; Linley 9–5–25–2; Richards 7–3–17–0; McMahon 7–2–20–0; Munday 2–0–5–0.

Oxford UCCE

S. J. Hawinkels b Smith	9		A. K. Suman not out		1
J. J. Sayers c Alleyne b Smith	4		M. K. Munday c MacGill b Franks		0
S. J. Airey c Alleyne b Smith	72				
L. C. Parker lbw b Smith	0		B 2, l-b 9, w 1, n-b 12		24
O. S. Anwar b Shreck	9				
M. A. Richards lbw b Shreck	5				190
†W. O. F. Howard c Alleyne b MacGill	33		1/13 (1) 2/20 (2) 3/20 (4)		
*P. J. McMahon c Shreck b Hussey	25		4/29 (5) 5/39 (6) 6/90 (7)		
T. E. Linley c and b Smith	8		7/155 (8) 8/176 (9)		
			9/187 (3) 10/190 (11)		

Bowling: Smith 21–6–52–5; Shreck 19–9–30–2; MacGill 10–6–13–1; Franks 10.5–1–36–1; Ealham 13–5–42–0; Hussey 8 5 6 1.

Umpires: R. J. Bailey and A. G. T. Whitehead.

OXFORD UCCE v KENT

At Oxford, April 28, 29, 30. Drawn. Toss: Oxford UCCE. First-class debuts: P. J. Selvey-Clinton; J. L. Denly, M. J. Dennington.

The weather allowed only two overs of play in three days. One of Kent's two first-class debutants, Matthew Dennington, never got on the field; the other, Joe Denly, fell lbw to his first ball, from Suman.

Close of play: First day, Kent 9-1 (Carberry 9, Smith 0); Second day, No play.

Kent

M. A. Carberry not out	9		
J. L. Denly lbw b Suman	0		
*E. T. Smith not out	0		
1/3 (2)		(1 wkt)	9

A. G. R. Loudon, †G. O. Jones, J. C. Tredwell, M. J. Dennington, R. S. Ferley, A. Khan, D. A. Stiff and A. Sheriyar did not bat.

Bowling: Suman 1–0–3–1; Linley 1–0–6–0.

Oxford UCCE

J. P. T. Knappett, P. J. Selvey-Clinton, S. J. Airey, L. C. Parker, O. S. Anwar, M. A. Richards, †W. O. F. Howard, *P. J. McMahon, T. E. Linley, A. K. Suman and M. K. Munday.

Umpires: B. Dudleston and R. A. Kettleborough.

At Lord's, June 24. OXFORD UNIVERSITY beat CAMBRIDGE UNIVERSITY by eight wickets (see The University Matches, 2004)

At Lord's, June 25. OXFORD UCCE beat LOUGHBOROUGH UCCE by two wickets (see The Inter-UCCE Championship, 2004).

At Oxford, June 28, 29, 30. OXFORD UNIVERSITY beat CAMBRIDGE UNIVERSITY by an innings and 77 runs (see The University Matches, 2004).

CAMBRIDGE

President: Professor A. D. Buckingham (Pembroke)
Head Coach: C. J. Scott

Cambridge UCCE Captain for 2004 and 2005: T. Webley (King's College Taunton
and Anglia Polytechnic University)
Cambridge University Captain: A. Shankar (Bedford and Queens')
Cambridge University Captain for 2005: R. J. Mann (Ipswich and St John's)

CAMBRIDGE UCCE/UNIVERSITY RESULTS

First-class matches – Played 4: Lost 3, Drawn 1.

CAMBRIDGE UCCE v ESSEX

At Cambridge, April 10, 11, 12. Essex won by 153 runs. Toss: Essex. First-class debuts: C. T. Buckham, P. D. Edwards, T. D. C. Hembry, C. J. C. Wright.

Jefferson and Habib put Essex on top from the outset, with a 144-run opening partnership, and though the batting stuttered a little, with three wickets falling for eight runs, Jefferson continued to maintain control for four hours before retiring. Marshall, the leg-spinner, was the pick of the student attack, claiming three of the four wickets to fall to bowlers. He also had the top score, even if it was only 22, in a disappointing Cambridge reply, which never recovered from McCoubrey taking four wickets in 40 minutes. Essex reshuffled their order and Middlebrook took the opportunity to score a maiden century as they stretched their lead from 176 to 398. Again, McCoubrey quickly removed the openers, but Cambridge showed greater resolve on the final day, when Wright scored a fifty on debut.

Close of play: First day, Cambridge UCCE 19-2 (Arfan Akram 11); Second day, Cambridge UCCE 57-2 (Hembry 25, Webley 23).

Essex

W. I. Jefferson retired out	144	
A. Habib c Savill b Marshall	54	
*R. C. Irani c Park b Wright	1	
†M. L. Pettini c Park b Marshall	0	– (2) c Park b Wright 27
R. S. Bopara not out	40	– (1) lbw b Edwards 13
J. D. Middlebrook c Hembry b Marshall	39	– (3) not out. 101
J. P. Stephenson (did not bat)		– (4) not out. 71
B 5, l-b 6, w 1, n-b 2	14	L-b 2, n-b 8 10

1/144 (2) 2/151 (3) 3/152 (4)   (5 wkts dec.) 292   1/37 (1) 2/43 (2)   (2 wkts dec.) 222
4/238 (1) 5/292 (6)

R. N. ten Doeschate, A. J. Clarke, S. A. Brant and A. G. A. M. McCoubrey did not bat.

Bowling: *First Innings*—Savill 15–2–82–0; Wright 21–5–85–1; Edwards 16–2–52–0; Buckham 4–0–19–0; Marshall 20.5–2–42–3; Adnan Akram 1–0–1–0. *Second Innings*—Savill 7–0–38–0; Wright 12–1–46–1; Edwards 11–3–31–1; Marshall 14.1–3–45–0; Buckham 11–1–60–0.

❝'Come and have a bowl, Normie, Colley hasn't faced a ball in Shield cricket.' 'I've never bowled one, Nug.' 'Should be a good contest!'"

Richie Benaud, *The Man Who Made Cricket Glow*, page 43.

Cambridge UCCE

A. Shankar c Jefferson b McCoubrey	1	– c and b McCoubrey	4
Arfan Akram c Jefferson b McCoubrey	21	– c ten Doeschate b McCoubrey	0
T. D. C. Hembry b McCoubrey	3	– c Clarke b Brant	25
*T. Webley lbw b McCoubrey	0	– lbw b McCoubrey	23
Adnan Akram lbw b Brant	8	– lbw b ten Doeschate	12
S. J. Marshall b ten Doeschate	22	– b Middlebrook	37
†G. T. Park lbw b Clarke	21	– lbw b Brant	36
C. J. C. Wright b Clarke	6	– c McCoubrey b ten Doeschate	57
T. E. Savill b ten Doeschate	0	– b Middlebrook	18
P. D. Edwards not out	12	– b ten Doeschate	10
C. T. Buckham c McCoubrey b Clarke	8	– not out	4
B 10, l-b 3, w 1	14	B 3, l-b 8, w 2, n-b 6	19
	116		245

1/3 (1) 2/19 (3) 3/23 (4) 4/30 (2)   116
5/41 (5) 6/84 (7) 7/88 (6)
8/90 (9) 9/98 (8) 10/116 (11)

1/0 (2) 2/11 (1) 3/57 (4)   245
4/57 (3) 5/87 (5) 6/128 (6)
7/158 (7) 8/206 (9)
9/238 (10) 10/245 (8)

Bowling: *First Innings*—Brant 8–1–35–1; McCoubrey 7–2–16–4; Clarke 8–0–32–3; ten Doeschate 7–2–20–2. *Second Innings*—Brant 13–5–34 2; McCoubrey 16–3–56–3; ten Doeschate 11.5–3–29–3; Clarke 10–1–55–0; Stephenson 9–2–24–0; Middlebrook 11–1–36–2.

Umpires: M. J. Harris and R. T. Robinson.

CAMBRIDGE UCCE v WARWICKSHIRE

At Cambridge, April 21, 22, 23. Warwickshire won by 247 runs. Toss: Cambridge UCCE. First-class debuts: G. D. James, N. T. Lee; N. Tahir.

The students' bowling continued to pour away runs: the principal beneficiary was Wagh, who had averaged 86 against Loughborough in his Oxford days, and now scored 105 before lunch on the opening day, in 89 balls, and swiped a huge six over the Fenner's pavilion. When the students replied, 20-year-old seamer Naqaash Tahir opened his first-class career with a spell of 8–5–6–1, and they conceded a 230-run deficit. With the weather threatening, Warwickshire raced through 28 overs second time around before setting a target of 392. Tahir could not bowl because of a leg strain, so Knight turned to his ninth bowler, Troughton, who took his first first-class wickets: three for one in 14 balls. Arfan Akram batted down the order because of a virus, but lasted only eight balls before he had to go off again.

Close of play: First day, Cambridge UCCE 8-0 (Singh 8, James 0); Second day, Cambridge UCCE 7-0 (Singh 5, James 1).

Warwickshire

*N. V. Knight lbw b Edwards	21	– c Park b Savill	47
M. A. Wagh c Park b Savill	105		
J. O. Troughton lbw b Savill	2	– not out	57
I. R. Bell c Park b Savill	54	– (2) b Wright	4
I. J. L. Trott c Park b Wright	44		
†T. Frost not out	80		
D. R. Brown c Wright b Arfan Akram	46		
G. D. Hogg (did not bat)		– (4) not out	44
L-b 1, n-b 8	9	B 4, l-b 5	9
	(6 wkts dec.) 361		(2 wkts dec.) 161

1/47 (1) 2/79 (3) 3/156 (2)   (6 wkts dec.) 361
4/210 (4) 5/243 (5) 6/361 (7)

1/9 (2) 2/77 (1)   (2 wkts dec.) 161

G. G. Wagg, N. M. Carter and N. Tahir did not bat.

Bowling: *First Innings*—Wright 19–4–80–1; Edwards 16–4–72–1; Marshall 20–4–85–0; Savill 16–0–93–3; Arfan Akram 5.1–1–30–1. *Second Innings*—Wright 7–2–22–1; Edwards 11–1–57–0; Savill 5–0–22–1; Marshall 5–0–51–0.

Cambridge UCCE

A. Singh c Frost b Wagg	17	– c Troughton b Brown	8
G. D. James b Brown	8	– lbw b Wagg	1
T. D. C. Hembry c Frost b Tahir	0	– b Hogg	28
*T. Webley lbw b Hogg	28	– c Hogg b Wagh	29
Arfan Akram c Troughton b Bell	3	– (9) retired ill	0
S. J. Marshall c Trott b Wagg	15	– c Wagh b Bell	33
N. T. Lee lbw b Wagg	0	– b Troughton	15
†G. T. Park c Wagh b Tahir	15	– c Frost b Troughton	11
C. J. C. Wright st Frost b Wagh	28	– (5) c and b Hogg	5
T. E. Savill c Bell b Hogg	3	– st Frost b Troughton	0
P. D. Edwards not out	0	– not out	0
B 3, l-b 5, w 1, p 5	14	B 4, l-b 9, w 1	14

1/22 (1) 2/24 (3) 3/28 (2) 4/41 (5)   131
5/65 (6) 6/65 (7) 7/84 (4)
8/102 (8) 9/107 (10) 10/131 (9)

1/8 (2) 2/27 (1) 3/55 (3)   144
4/69 (5) 5/85 (4) 6/120 (6)
7/143 (8) 8/144 (7) 9/144 (10)

In the second innings Arfan Akram retired ill at 144-8.

Bowling: *First Innings*—Wagg 12–4–21–3; Bell 5–1–15–1; Trott 1–0–4–0; Carter 10–5–13–0; Tahir 13–7–25–2; Brown 6–4–2–1; Hogg 20–7–37–2; Wagh 2.4–1–1–1. *Second Innings*—Carter 8–3–7–0; Wagg 6–3–12–1; Brown 7–2–18–1; Trott 7–5–6–0; Wagh 22–11–42–1; Hogg 21–8–38–2; Bell 4–1–7–1; Troughton 2.2–1–1–3.

Umpires: N. L. Bainton and J. H. Hampshire.

CAMBRIDGE UCCE v MIDDLESEX

At Cambridge, May 12, 13, 14. Drawn. Toss: Cambridge UCCE. First-class debuts: T. F. C. Harvey, M. A. Kay; N. R. D. Compton.

At last the Cambridge batsmen got their act together and, with Shah unwilling to set a challenge, earned themselves a comfortable draw. Adnan Akram scored a maiden hundred, striking 20 fours and a six as he reached 128 in 133 balls, and his captain, Webley, fell only seven short of his second. He promptly declared, only two runs behind Middlesex, whose first-innings 359 had depended largely on a century from Nash, promoted to open, and 81 from Dalrymple, who had tormented Cambridge with a double-hundred in the 2003 Varsity Match. But the county batted on and on in their second innings, allowing Joyce to reach a career-best 134, and leaving an impossible target of 266 in two hours. The openers batted out time until the game was called off.

Close of play: First day, Cambridge UCCE 58-2 (Adnan Akram 36, Edwards 0); Second day, Middlesex 50-0 (Joyce 26, Koenig 20).

Middlesex

S. G. Koenig c Park b Savill	3	– (2) b Savill	64
D. C. Nash c and b Wright	113		
*O. A. Shah c Savill b Wright	56		
E. C. Joyce c Park b Savill	15	– (1) lbw b Harvey	134
J. W. M. Dalrymple c Wright b Harvey	81		
†B. J. M. Scott not out	38	– (4) c Kay b Harvey	8
N. R. D. Compton not out	25	– (5) not out	6
S. J. Cook (did not bat)		– (3) lbw b Savill	8
M. M. Betts (did not bat)		– (6) c Webley b Edwards	12
C. T. Peploe (did not bat)		– (7) c Park b Harvey	5
P. M. Hutchison (did not bat)		– (8) not out	0
L-b 6, n-b 22	28	B 13, l-b 6, w 1, n-b 6	26

1/7 (1) 2/122 (3) 3/158 (4) (5 wkts dec.) 359
4/259 (2) 5/321 (5)

1/179 (2) 2/195 (3) (6 wkts dec.) 263
3/233 (1) 4/236 (4)
5/253 (6) 6/260 (7)

Bowling: *First Innings*—Palladino 15–1–63–0; Savill 15–1–85–2; Edwards 13–0–68–0; Wright 16–2–70–2; Harvey 18–3–67–1. *Second Innings*—Palladino 13–1–46–0; Savill 13–0–40–2; Harvey 19–4–43–3; Edwards 16–2–61–1; Wright 8–2–26–0; Webley 3–0–13–0; Kay 4–0–13–0; Adnan Akram 2–1–2–0.

Cambridge UCCE

A. Singh lbw b Hutchison		0 – not out	38
G. D. James c Scott b Cook	21	– not out	33
Adnan Akram b Dalrymple	128		
P. D. Edwards c Koenig b Dalrymple	43		
*T. Webley c Scott b Hutchison	93		
T. F. C. Harvey c Shah b Joyce	21		
M. A. Kay c Cook b Joyce	21		
†G. T. Park not out	4		
L-b 4, n-b 22	26	B 4, n-b 6	10

1/6 (1) 2/58 (2) 3/187 (3)   (7 wkts dec.) 357   (no wkt) 81
4/254 (4) 5/311 (6)
6/345 (7) 7/357 (5)

C. J. C. Wright, T. E. Savill and A. P. Palladino did not bat.

Bowling: *First Innings*—Hutchison 16.4–2–76–2; Cook 19–4–49–1; Peploe 28–8–62–0; Betts 8–3–53–0; Dalrymple 24–9–66–2; Shah 4–1–13–0; Joyce 9–1–34–2. *Second Innings*—Cook 6–1–15–0; Hutchison 6–1–18–0; Betts 4–0–17–0; Dalrymple 5–1–16–0; Peploe 2–0–11–0.

Umpires: R. K. Illingworth and B. Leadbeater.

At Lord's, June 24. CAMBRIDGE UNIVERSITY lost to OXFORD UNIVERSITY by eight wickets (see The University Matches, 2004).

At Oxford, June 28, 29, 30. CAMBRIDGE UNIVERSITY lost to OXFORD UNIVERSITY by an innings and 77 runs (see The University Matches, 2004).

DURHAM

President: Dr J. G. Holland (St Hild & St Bede)
Hon. Treasurer: B. R. Lander (Hatfield)
Head Coach: G. Fowler

Captain: W. R. Smith (Bedford and Collingwood)

DURHAM UCCE RESULTS

First-class matches – Played 3: Lost 1, Drawn 2.

At Chester-le-Street, April 10, 11, 12. DURHAM UCCE drew with DURHAM.

At Northampton, April 21, 22, 23. DURHAM UCCE drew with NORTHAMPTONSHIRE.

At Derby, June 9, 10, 11. DURHAM UCCE lost to DERBYSHIRE by an innings and five runs.

At Southgate, June 14. DURHAM UCCE lost to LOUGHBOROUGH UCCE by 86 runs (see The British Universities Championship, 2004).

LOUGHBOROUGH

Director of Cricket: Dr G. A. M. Jackson
Head Coach: G. R. Dilley

Loughborough UCCE Captain: D. H. Wigley (St Mary's RC Menstom)

LOUGHBOROUGH UCCE RESULTS

First-class matches – Played 3: Drawn 3.

At Taunton, April 10, 11, 12. LOUGHBOROUGH UCCE drew with SOMERSET.

At Bristol, April 21, 22, 23. LOUGHBOROUGH UCCE drew with GLOUCESTERSHIRE.

At Hove, May 12, 13, 14. LOUGHBOROUGH UCCE drew with SUSSEX.

At Southgate, June 14. LOUGHBOROUGH UCCE beat DURHAM UCCE by 86 runs (see The British Universities Championship, 2004).

At Lord's, June 25. LOUGHBOROUGH UCCE lost to OXFORD UCCE by two wickets (see The Inter-UCCE Championship, 2004).

THE UNIVERSITY MATCHES, 2004

At Lord's, June 24 (not first-class). **Oxford University won by eight wickets.** Toss: Cambridge University. **Cambridge University 228** (47.3 overs) (S. J. Marshall 94; D. C. Gerard 5-29); **Oxford University 229-2** (44.1 overs) (J. J. Sayers 144*).

Marshall scored 94 from 105 balls, with six fours and three sixes, but Sayers replied with 144 not out from 127 balls, including 14 fours and six sixes. Oxford's fourth successive win at Lord's gave them a 6–4 lead in the one-day Varsity series.

OXFORD UNIVERSITY v CAMBRIDGE UNIVERSITY

At Oxford, June 28, 29, 30. Oxford University won by an innings and 77 runs. Toss: Cambridge University. First-class debuts: G. P. Doran, D. R. Fox, A. M. Upadhyay; V. Banerjee, C. M. Hillyard, A. R. I. Newman.

For the second year running, Oxford completed an innings victory with a day in hand. Marshall and Sayers reprised their one-day performances at Lord's, but the key player was the home captain, off-spinner McMahon, who shared the new ball, claimed seven in 72 overs, and just missed a maiden hundred. After Suman trapped Shankar first ball, McMahon bowled unchanged throughout the first innings, judging that, without quality seamers, spin was his best bet; leg-spinner Munday followed his lead by taking four. Only Marshall held out, batting three hours until he top-edged a pull looking to repeat his century from 2003. By the close, Oxford were only 39 behind with eight wickets left, and Sayers was nearing his second Varsity hundred in six days. He hit 21 fours in a chanceless 147, and Dan Fox made a century on his first-class debut while adding 168 with McMahon. Marshall's leg-spin produced three successive wicket-maidens – but only kept the deficit to 293, with two days to go. On a turning pitch, another leg-spinner, Wyatt, shared the spoils with McMahon and Munday: Cambridge subsided long before making Oxford bat again.

Close of play: First day, Oxford University 135-2 (Sayers 76, Hawinkels 18); Second day, Oxford University 467-9 (Doran 9, Munday 1).

Cambridge University

*A. Shankar (Bedford and Queens') lbw b Suman	0	– b McMahon	40
R. J. Mann (Ipswich and St John's) b McMahon	2	– b Munday	24
A. Singh (King Edward's Birmingham and Gonville & Caius) c Wyatt b Suman	8	– lbw b Wyatt	5
S. J. Marshall (Birkenhead and Pembroke) c Doran b Suman	98	– run out	13
T. E. Savill (Fernwood and Homerton) st McMahon	4	– st Doran b McMahon	29
C. M. Hillyard (Edinburgh Academy and Jesus) c Dalrymple b Munday	20	– c and b McMahon	11
A. R. I. Newman (John Henry Newman and Jesus) b Munday	0	– (10) c Upadhyay b Suman	17
D. J. Noble (Rugby and Emmanuel) c Doran b McMahon	10	– c Doran b Munday	14
V. Banerjee (King Edward's Birmingham and Downing) c Suman b Munday	19	– lbw b McMahon	13
A. C. S. Clarke (Kimberly CS and Downing) not out	7	– (7) c Upadhyay b Wyatt	22
†J. J. N. Heywood (Worth and Homerton) lbw b Munday	0	– not out	0
B 4, w 2	6	B 12, l-b 7, w 9	28
	174		**216**

1/0 (1) 2/6 (2) 3/28 (3) 4/37 (5) 5/102 (6) 6/106 (7) 7/147 (4) 8/148 (8) 9/174 (9) 10/174 (11)

1/49 (2) 2/57 (3) 3/91 (4) 4/98 (1) 5/138 (5) 6/157 (6) 7/173 (7) 8/190 (8) 9/216 (9) 10/216 (10)

Bowling: *First Innings*—Suman 19–7–44–3; McMahon 34–12–72–3; Wyatt 6–1–18–0; Munday 9.4–2–36–4. *Second Innings*—Suman 19.3–10–32–1; McMahon 38–14–68–4; Munday 24–10–63–2; Hawinkels 3–0–12–0; Wyatt 14–8–22–2.

Oxford University

P. J. Selvey-Clinton (Eltham and Keble) c Heywood b Clarke	6
J. J. Sayers (St Mary's RC Menston and Worcester) lbw b Newman	147
A. M. Upadhyay (Gnana Bodhini, St Joseph's C and St Anthony's) c Mann b Newman	34
S. J. Hawinkels (St Stithians, Island School Hong Kong and University) c Savill b Clarke	27
D. R. Fox (King Edward VI and Greyfriars) b Savill	104
S. H. Dalrymple (Radley and Christchurch) c Mann b Savill	13
*P. J. McMahon (Trinity RC Nottingham and Wadham) c Mann b Marshall	99
A. K. Suman (Sadar Patel Vidyalaya, St Stephen's C Delhi and Pembroke) b Marshall	5
†G. P. Doran (Blue Coat CS Walsall and St Edmund Hall) not out	9
A. A. Wyatt (Melbourne GS, Melbourne U. and New) b Marshall	1
M. K. Munday (Truro and Corpus Christi) not out	1
B 1, l-b 7, w 3, n-b 10	21
	(9 wkts dec.) 467

1/19 (1) 2/105 (3) 3/168 (4) 4/260 (2) 5/277 (6) 6/445 (5) 7/455 (7) 8/456 (8) 9/462 (10)

Bowling: Savill 25–7–75–2; Clarke 24–8–56–2; Marshall 33–8–81–3; Newman 14–1–70–2; Banerjee 34–6–107–0; Noble 13–2–70–0.

Umpires: R. K. Illingworth and A. A. Jones.

> **"**But in other respects, Illingworth ran things very much the old-fashioned way. Motivation? Three lions on the sweater ought to be motivation enough. Sports psychologist? They did without when he was playing."
>
> Malcolm Ashton, Goodbye Gin and Tonic, page 37.

OXFORD v CAMBRIDGE, NOTES

The University Match dates back to 1827. Altogether there have been 159 official matches, Cambridge winning 56 and Oxford 51, with 52 drawn. Since the war Cambridge have won ten times (1949, 1953, 1957, 1958, 1972, 1979, 1982, 1986, 1992 and 1998) and Oxford 12 (1946, 1948, 1951, 1959, 1966, 1976, 1984, 1993, 1995, 2001, 2003 and 2004). All other matches have been drawn; the 1988 fixture was abandoned without a ball being bowled. The first-class fixture was moved from its traditional venue at Lord's in 2001, to be staged alternately at Cambridge and Oxford, and a one-day game was played at Lord's instead.

One hundred and sixteen three-figure innings have been played in the University matches, 56 for Oxford and 60 for Cambridge. For the fullest lists see the 1940 and 1993 *Wisdens*. There have been three double-centuries for Cambridge (211 by G. Goonesena in 1957, 201 by A. Ratcliffe in 1931 and 200 by Majid Khan in 1970) and three for Oxford (238* by Nawab of Pataudi, sen. in 1931, 236* by J. W. M. Dalrymple in 2003 and 201* by M. J. K. Smith in 1954). Ratcliffe's score was a record for the match for only one day, before being beaten by Pataudi's. M. J. K. Smith and R. J. Boyd-Moss (Cambridge) are the only players to score three hundreds.

The highest totals in the fixture are 604 in 2002 by Cambridge, and 522-7 in 2003, 513-6 in 1996, 503 in 1900, 467-9 in 2004, 457 in 1947, 453-8 in 1931 and 453-9 in 1994, all by Oxford. The lowest totals are 32 by Oxford in 1878 and 39 by Cambridge in 1858.

F. C. Cobden, in the Oxford v Cambridge match in 1870, performed the hat-trick by taking the last three wickets and won an extraordinary game for Cambridge by two runs. Other hat-tricks, all for Cambridge, have been achieved by A. G. Steel (1879), P. H. Morton (1880), J. F. Ireland (1911) and R. G. H. Lowe (1926). S. E. Butler, in the 1871 match, took all ten wickets in the Cambridge first innings.

D. W. Jarrett (Oxford 1975, Cambridge 1976), S. M. Wookey (Cambridge 1975-76, Oxford 1978) and G. Pathmanathan (Oxford 1975-78, Cambridge 1983) gained Blues for both Universities.

A full list of Blues from 1837 may be found in Wisdens *published between 1923 and 1939. The lists thereafter were curtailed, covering more recent years only, and dropped after 1992.*

Note: Matches in the remaining University sections were not first-class.

OTHER UCCEs, 2004

UCCE away games appear in the county sections.

At Worcester, April 10, 11, 12. CARDIFF UCCE lost to WORCESTERSHIRE by an innings and 224 runs.

At Leeds, April 10, 11, 12. BRADFORD/LEEDS UCCE lost to YORKSHIRE by 481 runs.

At Cardiff, April 28, 29, 30. CARDIFF UCCE drew with GLAMORGAN.

At Bradford, May 7, 8, 9. **Drawn.** Toss: Bradford/Leeds UCCE. **Leicestershire 293-5 dec.** (J. K. Maunders 106, D. L. Maddy retired out 66); **Bradford/Leeds UCCE 182-6** (I. Dawood 90). *First-team debut: C. Liddle.*

At Bradford, May 19, 20, 21. **Lancashire won by 71 runs.** Toss: Bradford/Leeds UCCE. **Lancashire 296** (A. J. Swann 62, M. R. Currie 125) **and 178** (M. R. Currie 56; K. Ahmed 4-40); **Bradford/Leeds UCCE 247** (I. Dawood 117; C. P. Schofield 4-37) **and 156**.

At Southampton, May 19, 20, 21. CARDIFF UCCE drew with HAMPSHIRE.

THE INTER-UCCE CHAMPIONSHIP, 2004

TWO-DAY CHAMPIONSHIP

	Played	Won	Lost	Drawn	1st-inns points	Bonus points	Points
OXFORD	5	0	0	5*	40	33	78
LOUGHBOROUGH . . .	5	1	0	4	23	38	78
Bradford/Leeds.	5	0	0	5	20	38	58
Cambridge.	5	0	0	5	26	32	57†
Durham.	5	0	0	5*	13	22	39†
Cardiff	5	0	1	4	0	29	28†

* Includes one abandoned match. † 1 pt deducted for slow over-rate.
Outright win (with 1st-innings lead) = 17 pts; 1st-innings win in a drawn match = 10 pts; draw
or no result on 1st innings = 3 pts; abandoned 5 pts.
Up to four bonus points for batting and bowling were available in each innings.

WINNERS

2001	Loughborough	2003	Loughborough
2002	Loughborough	2004	Oxford

ONE-DAY UCCE CHALLENGE

At Lord's, June 25. **Oxford won by two wickets.** Toss: Loughborough. **Loughborough 294-7** (50 overs) (R. S. Clinton 130, Extras 58); **Oxford 298-8** (49.3 overs) (J. J. Sayers 98, L. C. Parker 57).

THE BRITISH UNIVERSITIES CHAMPIONSHIP, 2004

PREMIER LEAGUE A

	Played	Won	Lost	Points
LOUGHBOROUGH UCCE.	5	5	0	15
EXETER	5	3	2	9
DURHAM UCCE	5	3	2	9
Cambridge UCCE	5	2	3	6
Oxford UCCE.	5	2	3	6
Cardiff UCCE.	5	0	5	0

The top three teams advanced to the semi-finals, where they were joined by Bradford/Leeds UCCE, who beat St Mary's in the Premier League B play-off. Bradford/Leeds were promoted to Premier League A (expanded to seven teams) for 2005, and Cardiff UCCE retained their status after a walkover against St Mary's.

SEMI-FINALS

At Exeter, June 7. **Durham UCCE won by 22 runs.** Toss: Durham UCCE. **Durham UCCE 141-9** (50 overs); **Exeter 119** (47.2 overs) (J. Rawson 58; G. G. Read 4-9).

At Loughborough, June 7. **Loughborough UCCE won by three wickets.** Toss: Bradford/Leeds UCCE. **Bradford/Leeds UCCE 145-9** (50 overs); **Loughborough UCCE 146-7** (32.1 overs).

FINAL

At Southgate, June 14. **Loughborough UCCE won by 86 runs.** Toss: Loughborough UCCE. **Loughborough UCCE 211-8** (50 overs) (R. S. Clinton 68*); **Durham UCCE 125** (35.4 overs).

WINNERS 1927–2004

The UAU Championship was replaced by the British Universities Championship from 1995.

1927	Manchester	1958	Null and void	1981	Durham
1928	Manchester	1959	Liverpool	1982	Exeter
1929	Nottingham	1960	Loughborough Colls.	1983	Exeter
1930	Sheffield	1961	Loughborough Colls.	1984	Bristol
1931	Liverpool	1962	Manchester	1985	Birmingham
1932	Manchester	1963	Loughborough Colls.	1986	Durham
1933	Manchester	1964	Loughborough Colls.	1987	Durham
1934	Leeds	1965	Hull	1988	Swansea
1935	Sheffield	1966	{Newcastle / Southampton}	1989	Loughborough
1936	Sheffield			1990	Durham
1937	Nottingham	1967	Manchester	1991	Durham
1938	Durham	1968	Southampton	1992	Durham
1939	Durham	1969	Southampton	1993	Durham
1946	Not completed	1970	Southampton	1994	Swansea
1947	Sheffield	1971	Loughborough Colls.	1995	Durham
1948	Leeds	1972	Durham	1996	Loughborough
1949	Leeds	1973	{Leicester / Loughborough Colls.}	1997	Durham
1950	Manchester			1998	{Durham / Loughborough}
1951	Manchester	1974	Durham		
1952	Loughborough Colls.	1975	Loughborough Colls.	1999	Durham
1953	Durham	1976	Loughborough	2000	Loughborough
1954	Manchester	1977	Durham	2001	Loughborough
1955	Birmingham	1978	Manchester	2002	Loughborough
1956	Null and void	1979	Manchester	2003	Durham
1957	Loughborough Colls.	1980	Exeter	2004	Loughborough

Durham have won the Championship outright 17 times, Loughborough 15, Manchester 11, Sheffield 4, Exeter, Leeds and Southampton 3, Birmingham, Liverpool, Nottingham and Swansea 2, Bristol and Hull 1. Loughborough have shared the title twice; Durham, Leicester, Newcastle and Southampton once each.

UMPIRES FOR 2005

FIRST-CLASS UMPIRES

M. R. Benson, G. I. Burgess, D. J. Constant, N. G. Cowley, B. Dudleston, J. H. Evans, I. J. Gould, J. H. Hampshire, M. J. Harris, P. J. Hartley, J. W. Holder, V. A. Holder, T. E. Jesty, A. A. Jones, M. J. Kitchen, B. Leadbeater, N. J. Llong, J. W. Lloyds, N. A. Mallender, R. Palmer, G. Sharp, D. R. Shepherd, J. F. Steele, A. G. T. Whitehead, P. Willey. *Reserves:* R. J. Bailey, N. L. Bainton, S. A. Garratt, D. B. Hair, R. K. Illingworth, R. A. Kettleborough, R. T. Robinson.

MINOR COUNTIES UMPIRES

N. L. Bainton, T. Beale, S. F. Bishopp, S. Boulton, P. Brown, A. Bullock, D. L. Burden, P. D. Clubb, K. Coburn, D. Davis, M. Dixon, R. Dowd, H. Evans, J. H. James, D. Johnson, J. S. Johnson, R. Johnson, P. W. Joy, P. W. Kingston-Davey, S. W. Kuhlmann, G. Maddison, S. Z. Marszal, C. Martin, C. Megennis, M. P. Moran, C. G. Pocock, C. T. Puckett, G. P. Randall-Johnson, P. L. Ratcliffe, J. G. Reed, W. E. Smith, R. M. Sutton, D. G. Tate, J. M. Tythcott, T. J. Urben, M. C. White, J. Wilkinson. *Reserves:* M. L. Brown, M. Eggleston, M. J. Miller.

THE MCC IN 2004

Graeme Wright

While batting helmets remained optional on the Nursery ground, hard hats of a different kind were *de rigueur* at the other end of Lord's come September. Work had begun on the £8.2m renovation of the pavilion. The accounts and membership offices moved out after the West Indies Test match in late July, and by mid-September other MCC staff were joining them in winter billets in the Mound Stand.

The basement-to-balcony project, ranging from improved facilities for the disabled to a roof terrace linking the Pavilion's twin turrets, was expected to be completed in time for the 2005 season. With oil prices rising, the reinstatement of the fireplaces in the Long Room and Writing Room suggested forward thinking as much as respecting the intention of the original architect, Thomas Verity, that the pavilion should be a centrepiece with special character. There was no substance in speculation that this much-needed makeover was associated with the first ever election of a woman to the MCC committee: the former England captain Rachael Heyhoe-Flint.

Another departure from MCC's reactionary image was the nomination – and heartfelt approval – of Tom Graveney as President for 2004-05. He became the first Player (from the pre-1963 distinction of Gentlemen and Players) to hold this office. Among the most elegant batsmen of his generation, Graveney played 79 Tests for England, and in first-class cricket scored 47,793 runs, average 44.91. Of his predecessors as MCC President, only Lord (Colin) Cowdrey comes close to those career figures.

In April, Tony Dodemaide, MCC's Head of Cricket since 1999, returned to Australia to become CEO of the Western Australia Cricket Association, and he was replaced at the end of June by the Essex all-rounder and former Hampshire captain, John Stephenson. One of his first duties was to captain MCC in their first-class match against the West Indians at Arundel, where his second-innings fifty helped get his side to within 30 runs of victory. Back at the office, his in-tray included the six university Centres of Excellence (UCCEs), whose funding – £390,000 each year for three years – MCC have taken over from the ECB.

Reviving the traditional Lord's curtain-raiser against the champion county, last played in 1991, doubled MCC's first-class fixtures in 2004. Otherwise, the club put out teams for 410 fixtures against countries, minor counties, clubs, universities and schools, winning 147, losing 84 and drawing 79, with 100 abandoned because of the weather. A further eight games were cancelled. There were also tours to the United Arab Emirates and Oman, Gambia and Ghana, the USA, and Italy, but the visit to Indonesia, planned for August, was called off on Foreign Office advice. MCC's women, meanwhile, won six of their scheduled 16 games, lost four and drew one; four were abandoned and one was cancelled.

OTHER MATCHES, 2004

Note: Matches in this section which were not first-class are signified by a dagger.

MCC v SUSSEX

At Lord's, April 9, 10, 11, 12. Drawn. Toss: Sussex. First-class debut: A. J. Harrison. County debuts: Mohammad Akram, I. J. Ward.

For the first time since 1991, the season opened with MCC playing the reigning county champions, who made a rocky start on the chilly opening day. Ward's first innings since leaving Surrey was ended by 18-year-old Adam Harrison, a late call-up because Sajid Mahmood had gone to Pakistan for his sister's wedding. Only Montgomerie passed 35, batting nearly four hours before he was one of three victims in 13 balls for Tredwell. Rain reduced the second day to 34 overs, but Bell and Flower put MCC in control with a century stand, and Gidman shared another with Foster, who went on to a five-hour hundred, his second in first-class cricket, and extended the lead to 339 with the tail's assistance. But Sussex were more resilient the second time round, with Goodwin – acting-captain while Adams nursed an elbow injury – reaching his own century, and Prior running up a lively 92 in 113 balls. They were out of danger when bad light stopped play.

Close of play: First day, MCC 166-3 (Bell 70, Flower 40); Second day, MCC 266-5 (Gidman 42, Foster 0); Third day, Sussex 124-1 (Montgomerie 49, Goodwin 43).

Sussex

I. J. Ward c Key b Harrison	19	– c Foster b Saggers	28
R. R. Montgomerie c Pietersen b Tredwell	61	– c Pietersen b Saggers	50
*M. W. Goodwin c Cook b Gidman	17	– c Bell b Harrison	102
P. A. Cottey c Foster b Napier	20	– c Foster b Harrison	19
†T. R. Ambrose lbw b Gidman	35	– b Gidman	60
R. S. C. Martin-Jenkins c Napier b Saggers	12	– c Foster b Tredwell	0
M. J. Prior c Bell b Tredwell	13	– c Foster b Saggers	92
M. H. Yardy c Foster b Napier	4	– not out	37
Mushtaq Ahmed st Foster b Tredwell	6	– not out	2
J. D. Lewry c Bell b Napier	9		
Mohammad Akram not out	1		
L-b 3	3	B 1, l-b 6, n-b 2	9
	200	(7 wkts)	**399**

1/23 (1) 2/60 (3) 3/87 (4) 4/139 (5)   1/56 (1) 2/135 (2)   (7 wkts)
5/154 (6) 6/177 (7) 7/180 (2)   3/185 (4) 4/232 (3)
8/184 (8) 9/190 (9) 10/200 (10)   5/235 (6) 6/319 (5) 7/378 (7)

Bowling: *First Innings*—Saggers 16–4–55–1; Harrison 11–3–43–1; Gidman 13–3–41–2; Napier 13.1–1–38–3; Tredwell 9–2–20–3. *Second Innings*—Saggers 28–9–67–3; Harrison 14.4–0–65–2; Napier 24–3–113–0; Gidman 16–3–63–1; Tredwell 19–3–68–1; Bell 3–0–16–0.

MCC

A. N. Cook lbw b Mohammad Akram	12	J. C. Tredwell c Martin-Jenkins	
R. W. T. Key lbw b Lewry	13	b Mohammad Akram	40
I. R. Bell c Yardy b Lewry	88	A. J. Harrison not out	34
K. P. Pietersen b Martin-Jenkins	17	B 14, l-b 14, w 6, n-b 20	54
*A. Flower c Ambrose			
b Mohammad Akram	76		(8 wkts dec.) **539**
A. P. R. Gidman lbw b Mushtaq Ahmed	91	1/27 (2) 2/31 (1)	
†J. S. Foster not out	110	3/71 (4) 4/195 (3)	
G. R. Napier lbw b Mushtaq Ahmed	4	5/254 (5) 6/376 (6)	
		7/382 (8) 8/459 (9)	

M. J. Saggers did not bat.

Bowling: Lewry 28–2–117–2; Mohammad Akram 31–7–130–3; Martin-Jenkins 30–10–84–1; Mushtaq Ahmed 40–11–92–2; Yardy 15–1–71–0; Montgomerie 4–0–17–0.

Umpires: N. G. Cowley and M. J. Kitchen.

†At Cardiff, June 19. **England XI won by six wickets.** Toss: Wales. **Wales 222-8** (50 overs) (D. L. Hemp 52); **England XI 225-4** (39.2 overs) (R. W. T. Key 83, A. J. Strauss 92*).
This was the third NatWest Challenge match, played as a warm-up for England's one-day squad. The Wales team was drawn from Glamorgan, supplemented by Welsh exiles Tony Cottey of Sussex and Steffan Jones of Northamptonshire. England, led by Marcus Trescothick, took a 2–1 lead in the series. Key won the match award for his 83, from 95 balls, with seven fours and a six; Strauss hit 92 in 86 balls with 11 fours and a six. Together, they added 138 for the third wicket.

CHAMPIONS TROPHY WARM-UPS

†At Belfast, August 29. **Bangladeshis won by two wickets (D/L method).** Toss: Bangladeshis. **Ireland 179-5** (32 overs) (J. A. M. Molins 64); **Bangladeshis 206-8** (32 overs) (Nafis Iqbal 100).
The Bangladeshis' target was revised to 206 in 32 overs.

†At Limavady, August 30. **Bangladeshis won by 54 runs.** Toss: Bangladeshis. **Bangladeshis 231** (49.4 overs) (Khaled Mashud 51*; G. Cooke 5-55); **Ireland 177** (46.3 overs) (Khaled Mahmud 4-34).

†At Edinburgh, September 1. **Bangladeshis won by five wickets.** Toss: Scotland. **Scotland 142** (48.1 overs), **Bangladeshis 144-5** (31.5 overs) (Mohammad Ashraful 61).

†At Taunton, September 2. **New Zealanders won by 105 runs.** Toss: New Zealanders. **New Zealanders 275** (50 overs) (H. J. H. Marshall 56, C. L. Cairns 108; M. Parsons 6-30); **Somerset 170** (39.4 overs) (K. A. Parsons 58).

†At Edinburgh, September 3. **Scotland won by four wickets.** Toss: Scotland. **Bangladeshis 259-6** (50 overs) (Aftab Ahmed 80, Faisal Hossain 54); **Scotland 263-6** (50 overs) (R. R. Watson 83, D. F. Watts 50).

†At Imber Court, September 6. **Bangladeshis won by 70 runs.** Toss: Bangladeshis. **Bangladeshis 285-5** (50 overs) (Javed Omar 73, Nafis Iqbal 57, Rajin Saleh 73*); **USA 215-8** (50 overs) (R. W. Staple 57).

†At Shenley Park, September 8. **Sri Lankans won by 14 runs.** Toss: Sri Lankans. **Sri Lankans 171-9** (50 overs); **New Zealanders 157** (38.5 overs).

†At Imber Court, September 8. **USA won by four wickets.** Toss: Zimbabweans. **Zimbabweans 272-5** (50 overs) (V. Sibanda 66, S. Matsikenyeri 69, D. D. Ebrahim 61*); **USA 273-6** (49.4 overs) (S. Massiah 142*).

†At Walmley, September 9. **Pakistanis won by 24 runs. Pakistanis 227-9** (50 overs) (Younis Khan 51, Shahid Afridi 59; C. K. Langeveldt 4-34); **South Africans 203** (48.2 overs) (G. C. Smith 59; Abdul Razzaq 4-48).

†At Bournemouth, September 12. **No result.** Toss: West Indians. **West Indians 202-5** (43.1 overs) (S. C. Joseph 56, S. Chanderpaul 54*) **v Hampshire.**
County debut: C. C. Benham.

†At Shenley Park, September 12. **Sri Lankans won by 170 runs.** Toss: Sri Lankans. **Sri Lankans 261-9** (45 overs) (M. F. Maharoof 54); **National Recreational Cricket Conference XI 91** (34.1 overs).

THE MINOR COUNTIES, 2004

PHILIP AUGUST

For the third time in four years, the Minor Counties Championship was shared after the final failed to produce a winner. Devon, champions four times in the 1990s, drew with Bedfordshire, who thus also took half a crown, 32 years after their last outright title. The game lost more than a third of its overs to rain, and a similar fate befell the last two rounds of Championship matches. In the Eastern Division, the weather prevented any chance of Bedfordshire being caught by their rivals. And Devon's win over Wiltshire in the West was one of only two definite results from the last weekend.

Bedfordshire

For 2004, the Minor Counties Cricket Association introduced a new rule, allowing each county to field only one player with more than 40 first-class appearances. The change was in part a reaction to the domination of the 2003 batting averages by former first-class players, and was not universally popular. However, the MCCA does see its role as being to some extent developmental.

With a reduction in available places for the Cheltenham & Gloucester Trophy for 2005, counties once again had to qualify for the competition. It was agreed that the two finalists in the MCCA Knockout Trophy, together with the eight teams with most Championship points over the season, would be the ten to enter the draw.

The knockout final at Lord's saw Berkshire beat Northumberland by seven wickets with a comfortable 38 balls to spare, but the three-day Championship final between Devon and Bedfordshire at Exmouth featured some rather less comfortable incidents.

Devon

With more than a third of the allocated 322 overs lost to rain, the match ended in a draw, though it will be remembered by those present mainly for Devon's tactic of hurling the ball back to the wicket-keeper in every situation. This resulted in three Bedfordshire batsmen being hit, but no genuine apology. The umpires failed to intervene until the last afternoon when Andy Trott, rapped on the helmet by a throw from mid-on despite not attempting a run, strode over to the fielder, Arul Suppiah, to make his feelings known. The incidents did little to enhance the reputation of the Minor County game: the following day's headlines preferred the fracas to the cricket.

MINOR COUNTIES CHAMPIONSHIP, 2004

Eastern Division	P	W	L	T	D	Bonus Points Batting	Bowling	Total Points
Bedfordshire	6	3	0	0	3	17	19	96
Staffordshire	6	2	1	1	2	17	20	85
Buckinghamshire	6	2	1	0	3	18	20	82
Suffolk	6	2	1	0	3	17	21	82
Northumberland	6	2	1	0	3	13	21	78
Hertfordshire	6	2	2	0	2	14	20	74
Cumberland.	6	2	2	0	2	9	24	73
Norfolk	6	0	1	1	4	19	17	60
Cambridgeshire	6	0	3	0	3	14	18	44
Lincolnshire	6	0	3	0	3	15	16	41*

Western Division	P	W	L	T	D	Bonus Points Batting	Bowling	Total Points
Devon	6	5	1	0	0	18	17	115
Shropshire.	6	3	1	0	2	15	19	90
Wales.	6	3	2	0	1	20	15	87
Berkshire	6	2	1	0	3	17	21	82
Wiltshire.	6	2	2	0	2	14	22	76
Cornwall.	6	2	3	0	1	16	17	69
Cheshire.	6	1	1	0	4	14	17	63
Oxfordshire	6	2	3	0	1	7	18	61
Dorset	6	1	3	0	2	11	22	57
Herefordshire.	6	0	4	0	2	15	18	41

Final: Bedfordshire drew with Devon.

Win = 16 points; tie = 8 points; draw = 4 points.

* Two points deducted for a slow over-rate.

Bedfordshire won the Eastern Division on the strength of their first four games – and were the only county in either division to remain unbeaten. They failed to score the six they required from the final delivery to win their opening fixture against Staffordshire, but then beat Lincolnshire, Northumberland and Hertfordshire. And they gained enough points from the weather-disrupted last two games to secure the divisional title. After an unsuccessful season with Sussex, Shaun Rashid returned to lead the attack, and his hostile spell of eight for 55 at Sleaford routed Lincolnshire. However, a foot injury later in the season severely reduced his – and the side's – effectiveness. Andy Roberts headed the batting averages, finished second in the bowling and again led the side with vision. Jon Walford, a product of MCC Young Cricketers, scored over 400 runs in his debut season and batted with the elegance often associated with tall left-handers. Steve Watts, a young off-spinner, took 22 wickets and often bowled long spells, fielded beautifully and made runs down the order when required.

The new regulation restricting counties to one player with 40 or more first-class appearances did not find favour with **Staffordshire**, who had to choose between Kim Barnett and Graeme Archer. Barnett, as player-coach, was preferred, and Archer left for Cheshire. Staffordshire needed to win their last match to have a chance of overtaking Bedfordshire, but after playing themselves into a position of strength on the first day – Lincolnshire were 35 for four in reply to 320 – saw the last two washed out. At Longton in June, Staffordshire were set 204 to beat Norfolk, but were in trouble at 173 for nine. However, their last pair added 30 before Gareth Morris was bowled, and the match tied. Morris had taken five for 59 with his left-arm spin earlier in the game, but a football injury ruled him out for the remainder of the season. Paul Goodwin was an able replacement behind the stumps for the retired Mark Humphries and he scored a maiden hundred against Norfolk, while Phil Cheadle and Barnett shared a record first-wicket partnership of 244 in a successful run-chase against Suffolk. David Follett and David Womble were again the leading wicket-takers, but the young spinners Morris, Peter Scott and Andrew Johnson all showed promise, while 16-year-old Peter Wilshaw established himself in the middle order.

Buckinghamshire were one of six sides behind Bedfordshire to record two wins, and would have had a realistic chance of taking the title if their game against the eventual champions at Luton had not been badly affected by rain. There was, however, time for Bobby Sher, returning to play against his former county, to score a maiden century and then take six for 83 with his off-spin. With a 60-run lead and on a dry pitch taking spin, Buckinghamshire would have been favourites. Sher won the MCCA Frank Edwards Trophy for the season's best bowling average (minimum 15 wickets) with 20 at 19.25. The former Surrey coach, Keith Medlycott, joined the county and played purely as a batsman, scoring consistently throughout the season.

Suffolk celebrated 100 years of Minor County cricket, but rain in the last two games prevented them from mounting a challenge to win the division. Phil Caley, captain for 11 seasons, hit a career-best 150 not out against Staffordshire, though Ben France, who made his first-class debut for Derbyshire in August, was the top scorer with 566 runs; Andrew Mawson scored three hundreds in his aggregate of 427. Former England fast bowler Devon Malcolm took 25 wickets, ten more than Trevor Smith.

By reaching Lord's for the knockout final, **Northumberland** came close to their first honour since their formation in 1895 but, with no major innings from any of their batsmen, they failed to set Berkshire a challenging target. Bradley Parker was again a heavy scorer in the Championship, as was Adam Heather. Alan Worthy and Daniel Shurben, two newcomers, provided valuable stability to the batting order, while the medium-pace of Marc Symington, formerly with Durham, claimed 20 wickets, the most for the county. Northumberland benefited greatly from the return of captain and wicket-keeper Philip Nicholson, who had missed the majority of the 2003 season because of injury. Nicholson was an astute leader and batted with good common sense in the lower middle order.

Hertfordshire continued with their youth policy, seven players under the age of 20 making their debuts during the season. David Ward was again captain and the leading scorer, his runs coming at almost a run a ball, with more than 70% in boundaries. Perhaps the highlight actually came in a losing cause against Staffordshire, when Hertfordshire, facing defeat by tea on the second day, rallied as the injured Simon White put on 112 for the ninth wicket with Tony Skeggs. White then added 70 for the last wicket with debutant Johan Thisanayagam and set Staffordshire a testing target, which they reached in the last session, just before a violent thunderstorm.

Marcus Sharp replaced Steve O'Shaughnessy as captain of **Cumberland,** another county to face a dilemma over their former first-class players. In the end, Graham Lloyd and Ashley Metcalfe each played three matches. With several players lost to first-class counties, Cumberland opted to give youth a chance, and 22-year-old Rhys Williams responded by taking five for 45 on his debut against Cambridgeshire at Barrow. Ben Harrison, a 24-year-old, took three for 30 against Staffordshire at Stone, also on debut. Local-born David Barnes, aged 21, scored a maiden century against a Suffolk attack led by Devon Malcolm, while 23-year-old Dean Williams topped the list of Minor County wicket-keepers with 23 victims.

For the first time since 1987 **Norfolk** failed to win a competitive match. They came close in the tie against Staffordshire when 24-year-old medium-pacer Michael Eccles took 11 for 145, including seven for 74 in the second innings; the last of those seven tied the game. Eccles took 21 Championship wickets, Chris Brown 26 and captain Paul Bradshaw 15. Between them, Norfolk's other bowlers managed just eight, which explains the county's lack of success. Openers Carl Rogers and Carl Amos each scored two hundreds and exceeded 450 runs, with Rogers passing 7,000 Championship runs during the season. New signing Tony Penberthy lasted just one game before he was injured, and his replacement, the experienced Trevor Ward, did not provide the expected quantity of runs.

Cambridgeshire just managed to avoid finishing bottom of the Eastern Division. Pieter Swanepoel took four for 66 and debutant Bevis Moynan three for 46 as they bowled out the divisional winners for 213. Captain Ajaz Akhtar was injured in the opening game against Northumberland at Jesmond, but continued to play until the last two matches with what was eventually diagnosed as a stress fracture of the leg. Twenty-year-old John Mann captained in the last two games. Simon Kellett, who had scored heavily in previous seasons, broke a finger prior to the first match, with the much-travelled Danny Law taking over. Joe Grant returned following two seasons with Essex only to sustain a serious knee injury early in the season.

Lincolnshire, unbeaten champions in 2003, failed to win a single game in any competition, despite an almost identical squad. They lost their first three Championship games before a tense draw ended with Norfolk 19 runs from victory and Lincolnshire one wicket short. The last two games were ruined by the weather. On the bright side, 20-year-old Lincoln-born Robert Cook established himself in the team and scored 455 runs at an average of 65; he hit two centuries, 102 not out against Norfolk and 148 in the next game against Cumberland. Off-spinner Martin Dobson was the pick of the bowlers in an attack that lacked penetration. Captain Mark Fell, suffering from the knee injury that forced him to miss part of the previous season, played twice.

Devon's big moment of the year came at Exmouth, when they dramatically defeated first-class opposition for the first time, edging Leicestershire out of the C&G Trophy, by losing fewer wickets with the scores tied. With five wins, they won the Western Division with something to spare, and Neil Hancock, a 28-year-old Australian now England-qualified, contributed significantly in his debut season. He scored 363 runs at over 50 and claimed 33 wickets at under 25. He also took 11 catches. Captain Bobby Dawson was again the leading run-scorer with 598. He hit three hundreds, two in the same game against Wales, the first time the feat had been achieved for the county. He and David Lye, who made his maiden Championship hundred in that match at Pontypridd, set a county-record sixth-wicket stand of 229.

Former England one-day international all-rounder Neil Smith had a good first season with **Shropshire**. He took 19 wickets in 230 overs and scored 302 runs at an average of 43. Batting proved to be the county's strength: Jamie Ralph, Duncan Catterall and Guy Home all averaged over 50, with Ralph scoring 440 in just six innings.

For **Wales**, 2004 was a season of records. They made their highest totals in both Championship and one-day cricket: 421 for five against Herefordshire and 335 for two in 50 overs against Oxfordshire. Against Berkshire, Daniel Cherry hit 170, Wales's highest individual innings, and shared a record fourth-wicket stand of 221 with Ryan Watkins. Richard Grant, aged 20, scored 126 not out against Wiltshire as he and Adam Harrison created a new best for the eighth wicket of 140. In the same match, Carl Roberts took a hat-trick as Wales won by one wicket. Cherry, aged 24, scored 564 runs during the season, while 21-year-old Watkins scored 364 runs and took 16 wickets. Eleven players aged between 16 and 24 made their debuts, and it was their most successful year since 1997.

Victory at Lord's was the high note of a **Berkshire** season in which winning two of their first three Championship matches proved something of a false dawn. Mike O'Sullivan's five for 59 helped secure victory against Cornwall after hundreds from Richard Howitt and Paul Prichard. And in the win against Dorset, Carl Crowe, with six for 77, and Nick Denning, five for 84, were the match-winners. Tom Fray, 24, scored a fine hundred against Shropshire and shared an opening partnership of 216 with debutant Chris Ellison.

Wiltshire were satisfied with their season, qualifying for the 2005 C&G Trophy and reaching the semi-final of the MCCA knockout competition: they were denied a first Lord's appearance when they were dismissed for just 91 by Northumberland and went down by eight wickets. Baqar Rizvi was the leading batsman with 459 runs, while wicket-keeper Steve Perrin made his 100th Championship appearance during the season.

The highlight of a modest year for **Cornwall** was their first victory in Devon since 1979. They won by ten wickets at Exmouth with three batsmen – Gary Thomas, Ryan Driver and Tim Sharp – scoring hundreds in the same innings for the first time in the club's history. Thomas equalled Malcolm Dunstan's record of 12 hundreds for Cornwall, and Gary Rollins had match figures of ten for 118 on his Championship debut. Their other victory was a 116-run win over Oxfordshire at Truro when Driver scored 183 and 80 not out, and enjoyed match figures of ten for 111. Driver won the MCCA Wilfred Rhodes Trophy for the leading batting average (minimum six completed innings) over the season, with 545 runs at 90.83. He also claimed 18 wickets.

Cheshire won their first match in remarkable style, lost their second and then endured four rain-affected draws. They defeated Berkshire by 55 runs after being bowled out for 132 and conceding a deficit of 162. Captain Andrew Hall (not the South African Test player) scored 160 in the second innings and Robin Fisher took four for 37 with his left-arm spin to complete a notable win. The county signed Graeme Archer from Staffordshire, and he played in the last four matches, scoring 434 from six innings with two unbeaten hundreds.

Keith Arnold, in his last season as **Oxfordshire** captain, took his 600th Minor County wicket in the last match against Wales. At the other end of the age scale, two 18-year-olds made an impression, opening bowler Ryan Newhook taking a hat-trick against Herefordshire and Chris Smith scoring his maiden century, at Abergavenny. Wicket-keeper Ian Hawtin also scored his first hundred, against Shropshire, and his keeping set a high standard in the field, where Charlie Knightley was outstanding.

Dorset recorded their first Championship win in the four seasons of three-day cricket when they beat Herefordshire by two wickets. Reg Keates and Neil Harrison-Smith hit maiden hundreds, and a result was made possible thanks to two imaginative declarations after much interruption from the weather. Dorset lost their captain before a ball was bowled after a detached retina forced Sean Walbridge to retire. Tim Lamb (not the former ECB Chief Executive) took over, and Peter Deakin became the county's third skipper in the final game against Cornwall.

Herefordshire experienced their worst season since joining the Minor Counties Championship in 1992 and finished bottom of the division, with two draws and four defeats. On a positive note, a number of local youngsters were given an opportunity and Simon Roberts, aged 21, took 29 wickets in five matches. Another 21-year-old, David Exall, averaged over 35 in the middle order and Ed Rollings, a left-arm spinner, took six for 67 in the last match against Berkshire. Toby Whitmarsh, aged 22, took over as wicket-keeper from Ismail Dawood, signed by Yorkshire in mid-season, and once again captain Chris Boroughs was leading run-scorer, hitting two centuries in an aggregate of 446.

LEADING AVERAGES, 2004

BATTING

(Qualification: 8 completed innings, average 35.00)

	M	I	NO	R	HS	100s	Avge
R. I. Dawson (*Devon*)	7	11	2	598	143*	3	66.44
A. R. Roberts (*Bedfordshire*)	7	11	2	519	123	1	57.66
D. D. Cherry (*Wales*)	6	10	0	565	170	3	56.50
K. T. Medlycott (*Buckinghamshire*) ..	6	10	1	508	111	1	56.44
C. Amos (*Norfolk*)	6	12	2	556	121	2	55.60
B. Parker (*Northumberland*)	6	9	0	476	183	2	52.88
C. R. Borrett (*Norfolk*)	6	11	2	462	111	1	51.33

	M	I	NO	R	HS	100s	Avge
D. M. Ward (*Hertfordshire*)	6	9	0	443	111	2	49.22
K. J. Barnett (*Staffordshire*)	6	11	2	438	150*	1	48.66
Baqar Rizvi (*Wiltshire*)	6	11	1	459	96	0	45.90
C. J. Rogers (*Norfolk*)	6	12	2	456	142*	0	45.60
A. V. Suppiah (*Devon*)	5	8	0	360	108	1	45.00
C. W. Boroughs (*Herefordshire*)	6	10	0	446	142	2	44.60
C. Jones (*Cambridgeshire*)	6	10	0	435	103	1	43.50
D. N. Leech (*Cheshire*)	6	10	0	430	118	1	43.00
A. Worthy (*Northumberland*)	5	9	1	342	85	0	42.75
D. E. Barnes (*Cumberland*)	6	11	2	373	135	1	41.44
R. P. Harvey (*Staffordshire*)	5	10	0	411	160	1	41.10
M. C. Dobson (*Lincolnshire*)	6	10	0	393	115	1	39.30
J. A. Knott (*Bedfordshire*)	7	12	0	468	107	2	39.00
S. A. Twigg (*Cheshire*)	6	10	0	379	86	0	37.90
G. R. Treagus (*Dorset*)	6	10	1	340	96	0	37.77
A. J. Hall (*Cheshire*)	5	8	0	300	160	1	37.50
M. S. Coles (*Wiltshire*)	6	11	0	412	111	1	37.45
S. A. Richardson (*Cumberland*)	6	11	1	365	95	0	36.50
J. E. P. Walford (*Bedfordshire*)	7	12	1	401	91	0	36.45
I. A. Hawtin (*Oxfordshire*)	6	10	2	289	117*	1	36.12
A. T. Heather (*Northumberland*)	6	10	0	357	120	1	35.70
G. D. Freear (*Cambridgeshire*)	5	8	0	285	73	0	35.62
T. G. Sharp (*Cornwall*)	6	10	0	354	113	2	35.40

BOWLING

(Qualification: 10 wickets, average 25.00)

	O	M	R	W	BB	5W/i	Avge
G. A. Rollins (*Cornwall*)	42.2	9	118	10	5-50	2	11.80
A. C. McGarry (*Suffolk*)	64.5	24	135	10	4-37	0	13.50
R. T. Foley (*Wiltshire*)	89.1	22	218	14	5-36	1	15.57
Z. A. Sher (*Buckinghamshire*)	120	25	385	20	6-83	2	19.25
C. M. Roberts (*Wales*)	82.1	19	258	13	6-60	1	19.84
J. B. Windows (*Northumberland*) . .	72.4	11	248	12	6-57	1	20.66
A. R. Roberts (*Bedfordshire*)	154.4	55	396	19	5-57	1	20.84
S. A. Roberts (*Herefordshire*).	187.3	37	609	29	6-90	3	21.00
R. E. Watkins (*Wales*)	91	20	357	17	4-42	0	21.00
M. A. Sharp (*Cumberland*)	142	46	401	19	5-45	2	21.10
N. A. Denning (*Berkshire*).	137.3	34	487	23	5-50	2	21.17
R. W. Fisher (*Cheshire*)	172.4	54	408	19	4-37	0	21.47
M. C. Dobson (*Lincolnshire*)	103	27	302	14	4-47	0	21.57
A. Jones (*Devon*).	179.4	51	466	21	4-41	0	22.19
A. W. Thomas (*Buckinghamshire*) . .	82	15	298	13	5-73	1	22.92
A. J. Procter (*Devon*)	241.4	74	640	27	4-44	0	23.70
S. Rashid (*Bedfordshire*)	174.5	39	571	24	8-55	1	23.79
I. N. Flanagan (*Cambridgeshire*). . .	81	9	291	12	4-54	0	24.25
N. D. Hancock (*Devon*)	223.4	40	801	33	7-80	2	24.27
R. C. Driver (*Cornwall*)	150.3	38	447	18	6-51	1	24.83

> **"** Lancashire won their one competition of the season on Twenty20 finals day: the county mascots' race."
>
> Lancashire in 2004, page 659.

CHAMPIONSHIP FINAL

BEDFORDSHIRE v DEVON

At Exmouth, September 12, 13, 14. Drawn. Toss: Devon.

Devon were in command of the match three times, but on each occasion Bedfordshire fought back to gain respectability, and ultimately a draw. Neil Hancock found movement off the pitch throughout a marathon spell, but a last-wicket stand of 64 between Mark Patterson and Will Sneath ensured a decent Bedfordshire total after the left-handed Jon Walford had earlier played well. Bedfordshire's captain and leg-spinner Andy Roberts broke his thumb whilst batting. In reply, openers Arul Suppiah and Matt Hunt put on 162 at a brisk rate, but off-spinner Steve Watts and second-choice leg-spinner Andy Trott stopped the flow and took wickets. The Devon innings closed early on the third day with a lead of 74. At lunch, Bedfordshire were 30 for four – effectively for five with Roberts unable to bat – making Devon clear favourites. But Walford, now with a runner, made a second elegant half-century and Trott his highest score for Bedfordshire. They shared an unbeaten partnership of 140 as the game petered out into a draw. The game was marred by Devon's repeated throwing of the ball back to the keeper, even when no run was contemplated. Three times Bedfordshire batsmen were hit, and after Trott was clonked on the helmet by a throw from Arul Suppiah, he marched over to remonstrate, prompting an intervention from the umpires.

Man of the Match: A. J. Trott.

Close of play: First day, Bedfordshire 131-7 (Watts 0, Patterson 3); Second day, Devon 222-6 (Pugh 14, Anning 1).

Bedfordshire

A. Shankar b Hancock	4	– b Bishop	0
†J. A. Knott b Hancock	17	– lbw b Bishop	0
D. J. M. Mercer c Mole b Hancock	10	– b Procter	16
J. E. P. Walford c Dawson b Procter	52	– (6) not out	55
M. H. Steed lbw b Hancock	6	– (4) c Anning b Hancock	0
*A. R. Roberts c Dawson b Hancock	27		
A. J. Trott lbw b Hancock	3	– (5) not out	83
S. J. Watts lbw b Hancock	0		
M. W. Patterson c Hancock b Procter	43		
S. Rashid c Dawson b Procter	6		
W. E. Sneath not out	31		
B 2, l-b 3, w 4, n-b 6	15	L-b 2, n-b 14	16
	214	**(4 wkts)**	**170**

1/13 (1) 2/24 (2) 3/49 (3) 4/60 (5)
5/116 (6) 6/128 (4) 7/128 (7)
8/133 (8) 9/150 (10) 10/214 (9)

1/0 (1) 2/3 (2)
3/12 (4) 4/30 (3)

Bonus points – Bedfordshire 1, Devon 3.

Bowling: *First Innings*—Bishop 14–4–47–0; Hancock 30–5–80–7; Anning 2–0–12–0; Procter 16.3–2–52–3; Jones 6–1–18–0. *Second Innings*—Bishop 15–4–50–2; Hancock 15–2–70–1; Procter 13–2–33–1; Jones 9–5–11–0; Anning 1–0–4–0.

Devon

M. P. Hunt run out	45	I. E. Bishop b Watts	1
A. V. Suppiah b Watts	97	A. Jones not out	0
*R. I. Dawson b Watts	22		
A. J. Pugh c Mercer b Watts	32	B 8, l-b 10, w 3, n-b 12	33
†C. M. Mole lbw b Trott	5		
N. D. Hancock lbw b Trott	0	**(9 wkts)**	**288**
D. F. Lye lbw b Trott	7		
T. S. Anning not out	27		
A. J. Procter c Watts b Trott	19		

1/162 (1) 2/187 (2)
3/196 (3) 4/209 (5)
5/209 (6) 6/221 (7)
7/249 (4) 8/274 (9) 9/277 (10)

Bowling: Rashid 11–2–44–0; Patterson 13–0–56–0; Sneath 6–2–15–0; Watts 24–3–104–4; Trott 16–2–51–4.

Umpires: K. Coburn and M. P. Moran.

THE MINOR COUNTIES CHAMPIONS

1895	Norfolk / Durham / Worcestershire	1931	Leicestershire II	1973	Shropshire
		1932	Buckinghamshire	1974	Oxfordshire
		1933	Undecided	1975	Hertfordshire
1896	Worcestershire	1934	Lancashire II	1976	Durham
1897	Worcestershire	1935	Middlesex II	1977	Suffolk
1898	Worcestershire	1936	Hertfordshire	1978	Devon
1899	Northamptonshire / Buckinghamshire	1937	Lancashire II	1979	Suffolk
		1938	Buckinghamshire	1980	Durham
		1939	Surrey II	1981	Durham
1900	Glamorgan / Durham / Northamptonshire	1946	Suffolk	1982	Oxfordshire
		1947	Yorkshire II	1983	Hertfordshire
		1948	Lancashire II	1984	Durham
1901	Durham	1949	Lancashire II	1985	Cheshire
1902	Wiltshire	1950	Surrey II	1986	Cumberland
1903	Northamptonshire	1951	Kent II	1987	Buckinghamshire
1904	Northamptonshire	1952	Buckinghamshire	1988	Cheshire
1905	Norfolk	1953	Berkshire	1989	Oxfordshire
1906	Staffordshire	1954	Surrey II	1990	Hertfordshire
1907	Lancashire II	1955	Surrey II	1991	Staffordshire
1908	Staffordshire	1956	Kent II	1992	Staffordshire
1909	Wiltshire	1957	Yorkshire II	1993	Staffordshire
1910	Norfolk	1958	Yorkshire II	1994	Devon
1911	Staffordshire	1959	Warwickshire II	1995	Devon
1912	In abeyance	1960	Lancashire II	1996	Devon
1913	Norfolk	1961	Somerset II	1997	Devon
1914	Staffordshire†	1962	Warwickshire II	1998	Staffordshire
1920	Staffordshire	1963	Cambridgeshire	1999	Cumberland
1921	Staffordshire	1964	Lancashire II	2000	Dorset
1922	Buckinghamshire	1965	Somerset II	2001	Cheshire / Lincolnshire
1923	Buckinghamshire	1966	Lincolnshire		
1924	Berkshire	1967	Cheshire	2002	Herefordshire / Norfolk
1925	Buckinghamshire	1968	Yorkshire II		
1926	Durham	1969	Buckinghamshire	2003	Lincolnshire
1927	Staffordshire	1970	Bedfordshire	2004	Bedfordshire / Devon
1928	Berkshire	1971	Yorkshire II		
1929	Oxfordshire	1972	Bedfordshire		
1930	Durham				

† *Disputed. Most sources claim the Championship was never decided.*

MCCA KNOCKOUT TROPHY FINAL

At Lord's, September 6. **Berkshire won by seven wickets**. Toss: Berkshire. **Northumberland 237** (49.3 overs) (S. P. Naylor 4-48); **Berkshire 240-3** (43.4 overs) (J. R. Perkins 73, B. H. D. Mordt 72*, J. R. Wood 51).

A disappointing display from the Northumberland batsmen, none of whom showed the application needed to bat through the innings, resulted in a simple target. In contrast, Berkshire batted with composure and a touch of panache from Julian Wood, and they coasted to an easy win.

WINNERS 1983–2004

1983	Cheshire	1991	Staffordshire	1999	Bedfordshire
1984	Hertfordshire	1992	Devon	2000	Herefordshire
1985	Durham	1993	Staffordshire	2001	Norfolk
1986	Norfolk	1994	Devon	2002	Warwickshire Board XI
1987	Cheshire	1995	Cambridgeshire	2003	Cambridgeshire
1988	Dorset	1996	Cheshire	2004	Berkshire
1989	Cumberland	1997	Norfolk		
1990	Buckinghamshire	1998	Devon		

Note: Staged as the ECB 38-County Competition from 1999 to 2002.

SECOND ELEVEN CHAMPIONSHIP, 2004

Michael Vockins

Somerset improved on a mid-table finish in 2003 to win their first Second Eleven Championship since 1994 and their second since the competition began in 1959. They shared with Yorkshire, the previous champions, the distinction of finishing the season undefeated, but while Somerset won three of their six matches, Yorkshire claimed just two victories in eight games and slid down to eighth.

This was a truncated competition, with qualification for the Championship reduced to a minimum of six games, to be played after July 1, compared with the old minimum of ten. Counties were free to play more games before or after the July 1 deadline but only matches played in the second half of the season qualified as Championship matches.

Somerset were among the counties who took advantage of this scaling-down and played as few games as possible, whereas Lancashire, with 13, were the most active of the group of Test-ground counties who opted for a much fuller programme.

The thinking behind the new regulations was to allow more university and schools players, some of whom were already part of county academies, to be considered for selection. However, there have always been plenty of good young league players available in the early part of the season and it

SECOND ELEVEN CHAMPIONSHIP, 2004

	P	W	L	D	Bonus points Batting	Bowling	Ded	Points	Avge
1 – Somerset (7).	6	3	0	3	23	16	0	93	15.50
2 – Sussex (14)	9	4	1	4	25	31	0	128	14.22
3 – Lancashire (8)	13	6	1	6	37	36	0	181	13.92
4 – Warwickshire (12). . .	12	4	2	6	37	38	−0.5	154.5	12.88
5 – Nottinghamshire (9). .	12	4	2	6	33	39	0	152	12.67
6 – Essex (13)	8	3	2	3	25	18	0	97	12.13
7 – Leicestershire (11). . .	10	3	1	6	22	35	−3.0	120	12.00
8 – Yorkshire (1)	8	2	0	6	16	27	−0.5	94.5	11.81
9 – Gloucestershire (10). .	9	2	3	4	25	25	0	97	10.78
10 – Hampshire (3)	9	2	3	4	29	23	0	96	10.67
11 – Derbyshire (18).	9	1	3	5	22	31	0	87	9.67
12 – Middlesex (15)	7	1	2	4	17	16	−0.5	62.5	8.93
13 – Kent (2)	6	1	3	2	12	21	0	53	8.83
14 – Northamptonshire (4).	11	1	3	7	27	27	0	96	8.73
15 – Surrey (6)	12	2	5	5	28	29	−0.5	104.5	8.71
16 – Glamorgan (16).	6	0	1	5	14	8	0	42	7.00
17 – Durham (5)	9	0	4	5	19	24	0	63	7.00
18 – Worcestershire (17) . .	6	0	3	3	15	14	−0.5	40.5	6.75

2003 positions are shown in brackets.

Win = 14 pts; draw = 4 pts.

was hard to escape the feeling that the new regulations made little difference to the calibre of players involved. Indeed, the impression persisted that financial considerations played a significant part in some counties' decision to play fewer Championship games.

The new format led to a reduction in the total number of games by almost a fifth and the programme was further cut by rain. Doubts were raised in retrospect about whether such a programme could really be regarded as a true Championship. Without detracting from Somerset's achievement in winning half their games, is it valid to describe as champions a county that has only been tested six times? No successful company, even in this cost-cutting age, reduces the importance attached to research and development; yet county cricket, almost solely for short-term financial gain, cut its Second Eleven programme to the point where the average number of fixtures played by each of the 18 counties was nine. Dividing the teams into three regional leagues would provide a truer Championship.

In 2005, the number of teams competing in the Championship and Second Eleven Trophy will be increased to 19 by the inclusion – for the first time in the Championship – of the MCC Young Cricketers. It is a move, says John Stephenson, MCC's Head of Cricket, that will provide the Lord's-based youngsters "with tough opposition and will enable them to monitor their progress against cricketers of a standard to which they aspire". He added: "It will also give them the chance to put into practice the coaching they receive at Lord's and to play in front of county coaches, ultimately helping them to gain a county contract."

On the plus side, the reduction in Championship fixtures allowed some counties to join forces with a neighbouring county to play against another combined team. Kent, for instance, linked up twice with Middlesex and twice with Essex. Many felt that these non-Championship matches produced a high standard of cricket, and were valuable testing grounds. "Combined matches were a big success in two and three-day format and most counties seem keen to arrange some for the start of the 2005 season," said John Childs, the Essex assistant coach. Yet while the standard in such games will, generally, be high, one senses that in the long term, it will not always be possible to strike the right balance in selection or to ensure that every young professional is involved on a regular basis.

Somerset used their Second Eleven programme to provide competitive cricket for their young professionals and for senior players seeking to regain first team places, while also offering development opportunities for academy players. Runs came from Keith Parsons and Wes Durston and, of their bowlers, Simon Francis took ten wickets in the victory over Worcestershire. Their academy wicket-keeper/batsman Sam Spurway and opening bat Richard Timms impressed, as did Michael Parsons and all-rounder Robert Woodman.

Sussex chased Somerset home, winning four of their nine games and securing the runners-up spot with a breathtaking finish to their final game against Essex at Hove. Needing 324 to win, they edged home by one wicket with three balls to spare. Sussex's captain, Michael Yardy, who had succeeded the veteran Tony Cottey in mid-summer and whose powers of motivation were an asset, led the way with 143.

Lancashire won six of their 13 games but, on average points, came third in the table. Oliver Newby, their leading wicket-taker with 36 victims, scored 133 and took six for 90 against Derbyshire in September, and his partnership of 166 with his captain, Gary Yates, set a last-wicket record for the Championship. Simon Marshall's second-innings return of nine for 47 against Nottinghamshire at Worksop was second only to Bob Ratcliffe's 1974 Red Rose record at this level of nine for 35.

Warwickshire and **Nottinghamshire** both won four of their 12 games, Warwickshire's higher tally of batting points edging them ahead in the table. Former county captain Michael Powell's early-season haul of 749 runs at an average of 93.63 earned a recall to the first team and was a splendid example to the aspiring young professionals. Ian Westwood continued to show all-round promise. Nottinghamshire's most prolific run-maker was their wicket-keeper David Alleyne, while Andy Harris and Paul McMahon led the attack.

Essex and **Leicestershire** won the same number of games as the champions but finished in mid-table. Essex improved on their 2003 placing, and a different result in their close encounter with Sussex would have taken them even higher. In that game Essex's Zoheb Sharif scored a century and took a hat-trick, and he finished the season with 815 runs and 21 wickets. For Leicestershire, the benefit of playing on good pitches was a bonus: between them, eight batsmen scored nine hundreds.

Yorkshire played some intriguing cricket, not least in their final two games. Against Derbyshire at Headingley, they needed 319 from a minimum of 66 overs, and started badly before a fourth-wicket partnership of 145 between Simon Guy and Philip Holdsworth helped them home by three wickets with two overs to spare. Against Surrey at Purley, the boot was on the other foot. Chasing 385, Surrey lost their ninth wicket at 214 but, despite 12 bowling changes, a last-wicket partnership of 106 between Simon Crampton and Jade Dernbach kept the Yorkshire attack at bay.

Gloucestershire set off well, winning two of four early games, but failed to maintain the momentum, while **Hampshire** found run-scoring easier than wicket-taking. Both had identical records of two wins and three defeats in nine games. **Derbyshire** and **Middlesex** improved on their positions of 2003 but, for both, it was a frustrating season. Derbyshire's progress was often curtailed by poor weather, but notable performances from Lee Goddard and Ben France earned them county contracts. Ben Scott, who had joined Middlesex from Surrey in the close season, was their leading run-maker and performed well behind the stumps.

Kent won few batting points, although all-rounder Alex Loudon, who joined Warwickshire in the autumn, and Jamie Tredwell each scored over 400 runs. Spinners Rob Ferley and Tredwell were the leading wicket-takers. **Northamptonshire** were another county to give experience to academy players, nine appearing in the Championship. Mark Powell led the side well and the free-flowing batting of Rob White was a joy.

Surprisingly, **Surrey** finished in the lower reaches of the table. A young side and major injury problems made for a modest summer in terms of results but a rich one in experience gained. Sixteen-year-old Rory Hamilton-Brown hit 84 from 89 balls on his debut against Sussex and Andrew Hodd scored good runs and kept wicket splendidly.

Durham and **Glamorgan** failed to win a game, although three of Durham's youngsters, Philip Mustard, Kyle Coetzer and James Lowe, earned promotion to the senior side during the summer through the weight of their run-scoring. Bowlers Danny Evans, Luke Evans and Luke Anderson also made favourable impressions. The weather affected all or part of 12 of Glamorgan's scheduled 18 days' play but Dan Cherry, Ian Thomas and Ryan Watkins took their chance to impress with the bat, and fast bowler Adam Harrison again showed immense potential.

At the foot of the table, **Worcestershire**, for a second season, did not register a single victory, despite Kadeer Ali scoring an excellent double-hundred in their game against the eventual champions. However, their emphatic victory over Essex in the Second Eleven Trophy final provided the county with their first piece of silverware at this level since 1982. To win a competition in which Worcestershire have seldom progressed beyond the zonal rounds, was a welcome reversal of fortunes.

In the final, at New Road, Essex made 241, with Ryan ten Doeschate scoring a rapid 47. But it never looked enough, and with Stephen Moore hitting an undefeated century, Kadeer Ali 58 and Stephen Davies 37 not out, Worcestershire cruised home by eight wickets with more than six overs in hand.

LEADING AVERAGES, 2004

BATTING

(Qualification: 300 runs, average 40.00)

	M	I	NO	R	HS	100s	50s	Avge	Ct/St
M. G. N. Windows (*Gloucs*) . . .	3	5	2	397	185	1	3	132.33	0
Z. K. Sharif (*Essex*).	7	12	4	815	162*	3	2	101.88	4
M. J. Powell (*Warwicks*)	6	9	1	749	158*	4	1	93.63	6
R. E. Watkins (*Glam*)	5	8	3	404	136	2	1	80.80	2
J. J. Sayers (*Yorks*).	4	6	2	322	151*	1	2	80.50	4
G. P. Rees (*Glam*).	3	6	2	306	134	2	0	76.50	1
P. Mustard (*Durham*)	7	12	2	746	193	3	2	74.60	15/1
W. S. Kendall (*Hants*)	4	7	1	447	138*	2	2	74.50	2
B. J. M. Scott (*Middx*)	4	7	2	318	78*	0	4	63.60	7
Kadeer Ali (*Worcs*)	4	8	2	380	221	1	1	63.33	2
K. A. Parsons (*Somerset*)	4	6	0	374	133	1	3	62.33	3
S. Seadon (*Derbys, Soms, Warks*)	6	11	4	436	108*	1	2	62.28	2
A. N. Bressington (*Gloucs*) . . .	9	14	7	419	127*	1	1	59.86	4
M. H. Yardy (*Sussex*)	7	11	3	471	143	1	3	58.88	5
R. M. Pyrah (*Yorks*).	5	8	1	401	107	1	2	57.28	2
M. J. Powell (*Northants*).	5	8	0	436	116	1	3	54.50	3
J. K. Maunders (*Leics*).	5	8	1	377	150	1	2	53.85	5
G. P. Hodnett (*Gloucs*)	6	11	3	430	75*	0	5	53.75	4
C. P. Schofield (*Lancs*).	6	6	0	320	168	1	1	53.33	5
D. Alleyne (*Notts*).	10	16	0	853	159	1	8	53.31	23/5

	M	I	NO	R	HS	100s	50s	Avge	Ct/St
B. M. Shafayat (*Notts*)	8	13	1	632	110	2	3	52.66	8
D. C. Shirazi (*Hants*)	8	12	3	460	128*	1	3	51.11	5
L. R. Prittipaul (*Hants*)	5	10	3	352	96	0	3	50.29	3
A. R. Crook (*Lancs, Leics*)	11	19	4	749	127*	3	3	49.93	2
D. I. Stevens (*Leics*)	4	7	0	347	93	0	4	49.57	4
S. A. Walker (*Durham*)	6	10	3	343	93*	0	3	49.00	5
G. D. Clough (*Notts*)	6	9	2	339	118	1	1	48.42	7
C. C. Benham (*Hants*)	5	9	1	384	114	2	1	48.00	3
T. B. Huggins (*Northants*)	6	10	1	431	121	1	2	47.89	1
R. A. White (*Northants*)	7	11	1	476	118	2	0	47.60	7
A. J. Tudor (*Surrey*)	6	12	2	475	144*	2	1	47.50	3
A. W. Gale (*Yorks*)	4	7	0	331	116	1	1	47.28	2
S. R. Patel (*Notts*)	6	8	1	330	130	1	1	47.14	4
M. A. Hardinges (*Gloucs*)	6	10	1	423	82	0	3	47.00	5
P. J. Horton (*Lancs*)	10	14	1	599	142	1	4	46.08	3
S. A. Heather (*Sussex*)	6	10	1	409	104	2	1	45.44	5
C. P. Murtagh (*Surrey*)	10	18	4	625	120	1	4	44.64	3
M. H. Wessels (*Northants*)	10	14	3	490	88	0	3	44.54	17/1
N. Shahid (*Surrey*)	7	12	0	519	131	1	4	43.25	8
S. D. Snell (*Gloucs*)	9	12	2	432	144	1	2	43.20	18/3
T. J. New (*Leics*)	7	12	1	474	136*	1	2	43.09	24/1
S. M. Guy (*Yorks*)	6	9	2	300	107	1	1	42.85	11/3
N. J. Ferraby (*Leics*)	7	12	1	463	110*	1	3	42.09	2
A. J. Hodd (*Surrey*)	10	20	3	693	85	0	5	40.76	20/2
I. J. Westwood (*Warwicks*)	11	19	0	762	102	1	7	40.11	9

BOWLING

(Qualification: 10 wickets, average 25.00)

	O	M	R	W	BB	5W/i	Avge
C. E. W. Silverwood (*Yorks*)	61	15	132	10	3-22	0	13.20
J. A. R. Blain (*Yorks*)	71	16	200	15	7-22	1	13.33
A. J. Shantry (*Northants*)	98.5	30	257	18	5-16	2	14.28
S. R. G. Francis (*Somerset*)	40	6	150	10	6-100	1	15.00
C. E. Shreck (*Notts*)	62.2	12	185	11	5-63	1	16.81
R. S. Ferley (*Kent*)	145.4	44	353	21	7-50	2	16.81
S. J. Marshall (*Lancs*)	190	60	433	25	9-47	1	17.32
N. A. Warren (*Warwicks*)	77	18	226	13	4-31	0	17.38
D. Pretorius (*Warwicks*)	82	16	278	16	5-57	1	17.38
J. Wood (*Lancs*)	84	28	174	10	4-26	0	17.40
P. J. McMahon (*Notts*)	194.4	51	505	29	7-56	3	17.41
C. D. Nash (*Sussex*)	70.1	12	205	11	4-10	0	18.64
R. J. Logan (*Notts*)	85.4	18	303	15	8-32	1	20.20
I. D. Fisher (*Gloucs*)	136	43	329	16	5-32	2	20.56
A. P. Palladino (*Essex*)	97	19	305	14	4-57	0	21.79
O. J. Newby (*Lancs*)	271.1	65	796	36	6-90	1	22.11
D. J. Wainwright (*Yorks*)	140	32	399	18	4-21	0	22.16
A. J. Harris (*Notts*)	204.3	40	643	29	5-44	1	22.17
M. J. Metcalfe (*Hants*)	82	22	266	12	4-76	0	22.17
C. P. Schofield (*Lancs*)	121.2	26	381	17	5-97	1	22.41
A. R. Crook (*Lancs, Leics*)	323.1	63	1,018	44	7-57	4	23.13
D. D. Masters (*Leics*)	108.4	31	279	12	3-24	0	23.25
I. J. Westwood (*Warwicks*)	190.4	42	606	26	6-50	2	23.31
A. Richardson (*Warwicks*)	126.5	35	350	15	3-18	0	23.33
J. C. Tredwell (*Kent*)	139.2	40	328	14	4-39	0	23.43
C. T. Peploe (*Middx*)	178.4	50	510	21	7-63	3	24.29
J. A. G. Green (*Sussex*)	85.1	13	324	13	5-34	1	24.92

SECOND ELEVEN CHAMPIONS 1959–2004

1959	Gloucestershire	1975	Surrey	1990	Sussex
1960	Northamptonshire	1976	Kent	1991	Yorkshire
1961	Kent	1977	Yorkshire	1992	Surrey
1962	Worcestershire	1978	Sussex	1993	Middlesex
1963	Worcestershire	1979	Warwickshire	1994	Somerset
1964	Lancashire	1980	Glamorgan	1995	Hampshire
1965	Glamorgan	1981	Hampshire	1996	Warwickshire
1966	Surrey	1982	Worcestershire	1997	Lancashire
1967	Hampshire	1983	Leicestershire	1998	Northamptonshire
1968	Surrey	1984	Yorkshire	1999	Middlesex
1969	Kent	1985	Nottinghamshire	2000	Middlesex
1970	Kent	1986	Lancashire	2001	Hampshire
1971	Hampshire	1987	{ Kent	2002	Kent
1972	Nottinghamshire		{ Yorkshire	2003	Yorkshire
1973	Essex	1988	Surrey	2004	Somerset
1974	Middlesex	1989	Middlesex		

SECOND ELEVEN TROPHY, 2004

A Zone	Played	Won	Lost	No result	Points	Net run-rate
DURHAM..............	8	7	1	0	14	4.97
Derbyshire.............	8	4	1	3	11	3.55
Lancashire.............	8	3	2	3	9	11.64
Nottinghamshire	8	2	5	1	5	−7.30
Yorkshire..............	8	0	7	1	1	−8.63

B Zone	Played	Won	Lost	No result	Points	Net run-rate
NORTHAMPTONSHIRE	8	7	0	1	15	9.38
Middlesex	8	6	1	1	13	12.46
Warwickshire	8	2	5	1	5	−6.01
Leicestershire	8	1	5	2	4	−6.41
Minor Counties.	8	1	6	1	3	−9.76

C Zone	Played	Won	Lost	No result	Points	Net run-rate
WORCESTERSHIRE........	8	4	2	2	10	−0.37
Somerset...............	8	2	2	4	8	1.00
Glamorgan.............	8	3	3	2	8	−7.59
Gloucestershire	8	2	3	3	7	3.73
Hampshire..............	8	3	4	1	7	3.67

D Zone	Played	Won	Lost	No result	Points	Net run-rate
ESSEX	8	6	1	1	13	18.15
Sussex	8	6	1	1	13	17.51
MCCYC	8	2	4	2	6	−3.87
Kent.................	8	1	5	2	4	−15.78
Surrey................	8	2	6	0	4	−15.79

Semi-finals

At Worcester, August 9, 10. **Worcestershire won by nine wickets**. Toss: Northamptonshire.
Northamptonshire 100 (42 overs) (P. D. Trego 4-23); **Worcestershire 101-1** (21.1 overs) (S. C. Moore 80*).

Rain allowed only 26 overs on the first day.

At Billericay, August 9, 10. **Essex won by four wickets.** Toss: Durham. **Durham 247-9 (50 overs)** (J. A. Lowe 48, G. M. Hamilton 57, I. D. K. Pattison 50; A. G. A. M. McCoubrey 4-37, A. P. Palladino 3-76); **Essex 249-6** (49.3 overs) (Z. K. Sharif 66, T. J. Phillips 91*; G. M. Hamilton 3-63).

The match went into a second day after rain allowed just 80.3 overs on the first.

Final

At Worcester, September 6. **Worcestershire won by eight wickets.** Toss: Worcestershire. **Essex 241** (49.1 overs) (A. N. Cook 37, Z. K. Sharif 35, T. J. Phillips 33, R. N. ten Doeschate 47; M. N. Malik 3-27); **Worcestershire 242-2** (43.4 overs) (S. C. Moore 117*, Kadeer Ali 58, S. M. Davies 37*).

Moore faced 138 balls and hit 14 fours and a six.

Statistics provided by Keith Gerrish.

LEAGUE CRICKET, 2004

GEOFFREY DEAN

After six years of premier leagues, one of the great successes is said to be that the average age of top club players has fallen, increasing the chances of an England player emerging through the amateur system. And in 2004 the most eye-catching performance of all indeed came from a player of Test match calibre. Unfortunately, the player concerned was Kim Barnett, then approaching his 44th birthday, 15 years after his England career finished.

It was a sensational feat of hitting nonetheless. Barnett, playing for Checkley against Leek in a North Staffs & South Cheshire League match, swung all six balls of an over from Minor Counties off-spinner, Dave Cartledge, over a short leg-side boundary. But he was not quite finished. When Cartledge was immediately replaced by Barnett's old Derbyshire teammate, Tim Tweats, Barnett crashed his first three balls for sixes and took 29 off that over. "I hit all my sixes with slog-sweeps or terrible cow shots," Barnett modestly confessed. The match was drawn.

That was in April and, in a wet summer, it was hard for any league cricketer to top that, though there was a stunning bowling performance in the South Yorkshire League where Northowram Fields were bowled out for ten in 69 balls by Carlton. Needing 147 to win, they began by taking eight runs off the first seven balls of their innings whereupon Mark Schofield, the Carlton captain, muttered to the bowler, Kevin Watson: "This match could be over in no time". He was right. Watson took four for five and Phil Mullins five for four, a run out completing the debacle.

Across the Pennines, Daisy Hill's Faizal Afridi became the 13th bowler in Bolton Association history to claim all ten wickets, his haul costing just 29 against Standish, who fell 16 short of a target of 106. Another unusual feat happened in the Liverpool Competition where Ian Lawless of St Helens scored eight off one ball against Formby. He ran three to the third man boundary, risked a fourth on a weak return to a relay fielder, who then conceded four overthrows. Bootle were champions and won three other trophies, including the Lancashire Cricket Board Trophy when they defeated Westhoughton of the Bolton League in the final at Old Trafford.

Bowdon completed a hat-trick of Cheshire League titles, overhauling Oulton Park, who led by 39 points at the end of July but faded when Bowdon dismissed them for just 23. A similarly decisive downturn in form ended Spencer's hopes of winning the Surrey Championship. Clear leaders at the halfway stage, with six wins out of nine, they managed only one victory in their last nine matches. Weybridge retained their title, as did Saffron Walden in the Essex League after they won nine of their last ten games.

In the Sussex League, Brighton & Hove's failure to observe the ECB's directives on protecting young fast bowlers cost them the title. They had 26 points deducted after being found guilty on 13 counts of exceeding the seven-over spell limit with their 19-year old seamer, Matthew Wood, and finished 11 points behind Horsham.

For the first time since the system was introduced in 1999, the number of premier leagues declined. From a peak of 25 the previous two years, the family was reduced to 23 in 2004 when both Leicestershire and South Wales were downgraded to ECB-approved leagues. Neither was prepared to meet the ECB's minimum requirement of 110 overs per day, opting instead for 100 and forfeiting their grant.

In October, the ECB gave way and finally agreed that 100 overs was acceptable; both leagues were expected to regain their status in 2005. Frank Kemp, the board's operations manager for recreational cricket, admitted this would be seen as a climbdown, but added: "We are still insisting that the games are not straight win–lose cricket and are played in the traditional form. And there will be a differentiation in terms of reward: 100-over leagues will not receive the full grant."

Instances of bad behaviour by players were again commonplace, and the Nottinghamshire player Anurag Singh followed Shaun Udal and Stuart MacGill in receiving a high-profile ban. Playing for Cannock in the Birmingham League, Singh received a six-match ban for violent conduct after a confrontation with Greg Smith (not the Nottinghamshire player), Coventry & North Warwick's South African pro. Smith's team-mate, Sarfraz Pathan, received a four-match suspension for abusing Singh, who was also disciplined by his county. Smith was not charged.

In a much more serious case, Mazhar Iqbal of Smethwick was banned for ten years from all ECB Premier Leagues after he was convicted in court of assaulting West Bromwich Dartmouth's Paul Swainson in the middle of a Second XI game. Bill Tansell, chairman of the Birmingham League's disciplinary committee, admitted: "While there has been no noticeable increase in the amount of cases we have to deal with, there has in the severity of the incidents." Nick Archer, the League's general manager, said he did not believe Birmingham had a particular problem. "There is a tendency for people to be more aggressive, both verbally and physically. And I think it's the same across all Leagues," he said. Some officials believe first-class cricketers get targeted when they come down to club level; others think the big names approach club matches with the wrong attitude.

The ECB are planning a new recording system for penalties to try to bring about some consistency and to ensure erring players are tracked if they switch Leagues.

Chris Aspin writes: After 102 years, Lowerhouse, the only Lancashire League club not to have won a major trophy, finally achieved their ambition. Success came on their own ground in failing light at the Worsley Cup final, when Chris Bleazard struck a boundary which completed his second century in the competition and a six-wicket win over Haslingden. The crowd paid a record £4,591 at the gate.

Bleazard was also man of the match in a record-breaking semi-final against Enfield, who seemed sure of victory when they reached 310 for eight, with

South African professional Alviro Petersen hitting 148 off 121 balls, including ten sixes. Spearheaded by Bleazard's 91-ball 107, Lowerhouse won by three wickets with a ball to spare.

On the final afternoon of the Lancashire League season, Haslingden achieved their 12th Championship, and first for seven years, by a five-point margin from Church. Haslingden's Australian pro, Andrew McDonald, was injured during the first match, leaving the club to find substitutes for the rest of the season. One, New Zealander Chris Harris, struck a record five consecutive sixes at Todmorden. In the same match, team-mate Steve Dearden became only the fifth amateur since the war to complete the double of 500 runs and 50 wickets – Qasim Ali of Colne did it later on – and Michael Ingham achieved his ambition of scoring 1,000 runs against each of the 13 other clubs.

Church, for whom the Sri Lankan Ruwin Peiris scored 1,295 runs at 61.66, enjoyed their best season since 1962, when the West Indian pro Chester Watson bowled them to the title. They made a club record 306 for six (with Peiris scoring 172 not out) against East Lancs, only to lose when the visitors' professional, the South African Quinton Friend, hit 150. Rawtenstall's 42-year-old left-arm spinner, Keith Roscoe, who began his career with Bacup in 1979, became the fifth amateur to take 1,000 wickets.

The Todmorden pro, Gyanendra Pandey, and Petersen also passed 1,000 runs. Sixteen-year-old Visal Tripathi of Lowerhouse led the amateurs with 749, and Jonathan Clare scored 746 for Burnley, including 113 not out against Haslingden, which made him, at 17, the youngest century-maker since the league began. John Simpson, another 16-year-old, scored a maiden fifty and claimed five victims for Haslingden in a match, against Rawtenstall. Murali Kartik, the Ramsbottom pro, took 80 wickets at 9.72; his nearest rival was the Bacup amateur David Ormerod with 73 at 18.24.

Norden won the Central Lancashire League for the second time since joining in 1981, and finished 18 points ahead of much-improved Unsworth. The Pakistani Test player Asif Mujtaba scored 1,532 runs as the Norden pro and headed the bowling averages with 99 wickets at 12.70. Oldham's South African pro Martin Smith just eclipsed Mujtaba and was the only player to top 100 wickets, while Clinton Perren of Littleborough scored his 1,282 runs at an average of 106.83. John Hean and Alan Badenhorst, both of Unsworth, were the leading amateurs, with 945 runs and 67 wickets respectively.

After 11 seasons in the league, wooden spoonists Stand resigned to join the Lancashire County League. Six clubs applied for the vacant place.

ECB PREMIER LEAGUE TABLES, 2004

Birmingham & District Premier Cricket League

	P	W	L	Pts
Wellington	22	11	5	325
Barnt Green	22	12	4	318
Knowle & Dorridge	22	7	4	307
Himley	22	11	7	301
Moseley	22	9	7	274
Old Hill	22	9	5	268
Coventry & N. Warwicks	22	8	8	243
Halesowen	22	8	5	240
West Bromwich Dartmouth	22	6	9	233
Walsall	22	6	10	213
Water Orton	22	3	14	150
Cannock	22	3	15	135

Cheshire County Cricket League

	P	W	L	Pts
Bowdon	22	14	3	373
Oulton Park	22	11	4	354
Hyde	22	10	4	322
Chester Boughton Hall	22	10	7	308
Oxton	22	7	6	283
Widnes	22	6	5	267
Poynton	22	5	9	243
Neston	22	4	9	237
Nantwich	22	5	6	236
Alderley Edge	22	3	10	222
Macclesfield	22	5	12	213
Didsbury	22	3	8	212

Cornwall Premier League

	P	W	L	Pts
St Just	24	13	3	367
Truro	24	13	4	351
Falmouth	24	13	5	334
Grampound Road	24	9	5	304
Newquay	24	9	7	289
Werrington	24	6	10	233
Menheniot	24	5	12	227
Callington	24	5	13	202
Troon	24	2	16	145

Derbyshire Premier League

	P	W	L	Pts
Sandiacre Town	22	17	0	445
Quarndon	22	10	4	381
Ockbrook & Borrowash	22	9	4	363
Clifton	22	10	5	328
Chesterfield	22	10	6	309
Ilkeston Rutland	22	6	9	284
Sawley & Long Eaton Park	22	7	9	272
Staveley Welfare	22	6	7	248
Alvaston & Boulton	22	6	9	244
Denby	22	3	6	224
Wirksworth	22	2	15	175
Shipley Hall	22	2	14	174

Devon Cricket League

	P	W	L	Pts
Sandford	18	11*	2	278
Barton	18	10*	4	258
Torquay	18	10	3	243
Exmouth	18	7	6	224
Exeter	18	5	7	199
Plympton	18	7	7	198
Paignton	18	6	8	195
Budleigh Salterton	18	6	9	186
North Devon	18	2	9	139
Sidmouth	18	3	12	130

* Plus one tie.

East Anglian Premier Cricket League

	P	W	L	Pts
Vauxhall Mallards	17	10	3	296
Cambridge Granta	17	10	4	267
Godmanchester	17	7	5	233
Fakenham	17	7	5	216
Norwich	17	5	3	209
Swardeston	17	6	4	207
Clacton-on-Sea	17	4	5	175
Bury St Edmunds	17	4	6	163
Maldon	17	2	9	125
Mildenhall	17	1	12	73

Essex Premier League

	P	W	L	Pts
Saffron Walden	18	11	2	285
Wanstead	18	9	3	245
Hainault & Clayhall	18	8	2	239
Loughton	18	5	4	184
South Woodford	18	5	6	183
Gidea Park & Romford	18	5	6	180
Ilford	18	4	4	179
Westcliff-on-Sea	18	4	10	157
Shenfield	18	4	11	149
Fives & Heronians	18	2	9	133

Home Counties Premier Cricket League

	P	W	L	Pts
Henley	18	10	2	308
Banbury	18	8	3	283
Slough	18	8	3	282
High Wycombe	18	6	4	253
Reading	18	6	3	245
Basingstoke & N. Hants.	18	4	3	228
Oxford	18	3	7	191
Finchampstead	18	2	6	181
Radlett	18	2	7	146
Potters Bar	18	0	11	140

Kent Cricket League

	P	W	L	Pts
Bromley	18	7	3	234
St Lawrence	18	8	0	219
Whitstable	18	8	3	215
Beckenham	18	8	4	208
Bexley	18	6	1	203
Gore Court	18	5	6	174
Folkestone	18	5	7	154
Sevenoaks Vine	18	2	9	141
Lordswood	18	2	9	117
Broadstairs	18	1	10	109

†Leicestershire County Cricket League

	P	W	L	Pts
Kibworth	22	14	2	412
Leicester Ivanhoe	22	10	4	361
Loughborough Town	22	11	2	354
Market Harborough	22	10	2	330
Illston Abey	22	9	5	330
Syston Town	22	7	6	294
Barrow Town	22	8	12	266
Lutterworth	22	6	9	248
Broomleys	22	5	11	239
Billesdon	22	4	12	231
Barwell	22	3	14	213
Hinckley Town	22	3	11	198

† *ECB-approved but not a Premier League.*

Lincolnshire Cricket Board Premier League

	P	W	L	Pts	Avge
Bracebridge Heath	16	12	0	288	18.00
Market Deeping	14	9	3	200	14.29
Sleaford	19	13	4	268	14.11
Bourne	17	8	4	225	13.24
Messingham	17	8	7	202	11.88
Grimsby Town	15	5	6	165	11.00
Lindum	19	7	9	194	10.21
Owmby	17	7	7	157	9.24
Long Sutton	16	5	9	136	8.50
Boston	16	3	10	102	6.38
Grantham	18	3	11	112	6.22
Market Rasen	16	2	13	92	5.75

Liverpool & District Cricket Competition

	P	W	L	Pts
Bootle	22	14	3	347
Lytham	22	12	6	294
Northern	22	9	6	231
Leigh	22	7	5	226
Ormskirk	22	8	6	212
Wallasey	22	7	9	207
Sefton Park	22	7	7	190
New Brighton	22	6	12	183
Huyton	22	5	11	182
Northop Hall	22	5	8	178
Southport & Birkdale	22	5	8	173
Maghull	22	5	9	172

Middlesex County Cricket League

	P	W	L	Pts
Richmond	18	10	4	109
Brondesbury	18	9	3	105
Ealing	18	7	4	91
Winchmore Hill	18	6	4	74
Finchley	18	6	3	68
Stanmore	18	5	4	68
Hampstead	18	4	5	61
Teddington	18	3	7	50
Southgate	18	3	7	47
Barnes	18	1	13	17

Northamptonshire Cricket League

	P	W	L	Pts
Northants Cricket Academy	22	15	2	471
Finedon Dolben	22	14	5	418
Bedford Town	22	13	5	393
Northampton Saints	22	12	4	385
Peterborough Town	22	9	4	312
Old Northamptonians	22	7	4	308
Rushden Town	22	5	9	259
Stony Stratford	22	4	11	201
Horton House	22	3	10	197
Brixworth	22	2	11	181
Desborough Town	22	2	11	161
Rothwell Town	22	3	13	151

North East Premier Cricket League

	P	W	L	Pts
South Northumberland	22	10	2	365
Sunderland	22	11	4	360
Blaydon	22	10	2	337
Chester-le-Street	22	10	5	328
Benwell Hill	22	8	5	279
Stockton	22	6	8	265
Durham Cricket Academy	22	7	6	260
Newcastle	22	4	7	230
Gateshead Fell	22	4	8	216
Tynemouth	22	2	10	191
Norton	22	3	8	183
Philadelphia	22	2	12	141

Northern Cricket League

	P	W	L	Pts
Fleetwood	24	15	4	250
Netherfield	24	12	2	243
Darwen	24	11	4	220
Morecambe	24	12	6	203
Chorley	24	9	8	188
Kendal	24	9	8	179
Blackpool	24	9	6	178
Preston	24	8	11	171
St Annes	24	6*	9	169
Leyland Motors	24	5	9	154
Barrow	24	5	11	149
Lancaster	24	3*	10	126
Leyland & Farington	24	0	18	63

* *Plus one tie.*

North Staffs & South Cheshire League

	P	W	L	Pts
Longton	22	13	3	337
Stone	22	9	4	287
Little Stoke	22	9	5	269
Checkley	22	6	2	244
Audley	22	5	4	227
Betley	22	7	6	226
Leek	22	5	4	212
Moddershall	22	5	3	205
Porthill Park	22	4	8	187
Knypersley	22	2	6	168
Meir Heath	22	2	9	150
Caverswall	22	1	14	136

North Wales Premier League

	P	W	L	Pts
Llandudno	22	13	4	357
Hawarden Park	22	11	5	353
Bangor	22	10	4	333
Mold	22	10	9	330
Brymbo	22	9	3	284
Northop	22	9	9	278
St Asaph	22	8	10	258
Pontblyddyn	22	6	6	251
Mochdre	22	6	11	249
Llanrwst	22	6	11	230
Marchwiel & Wrexham	22	5	12	218
Llay Welfare	22	4	13	169

Nottinghamshire Cricket Board Premier League

	P	W	L	Pts
West Indian Cavaliers	22	13	1	317
Welbeck Colliery	22	10	5	305
Kimberley Institute	22	9	6	272
Caythorpe	22	9	5	266
Clifton Village	22	8	8	251
Wollaton	22	10	9	250
Collingham & District	22	8	5	240
Papplewick & Linby	22	6	8	237
Retford Cricket & Sports	22	6	7	199
Notts Unity Casuals	22	2	10	150
Calverton	22	3	10	143
Southwell	22	2	12	123

Southern Premier Cricket League

	P	W	L	Pts	Avge
South Wiltshire	16	11	4	276	17.25
Havant	14	8	4	222	15.86
BAT Sports	15	10	5	231	15.40
Hampshire Academy	16	9	5	236	14.75
Bashley	15	7	5	206	13.73
Bournemouth	17	9	7	233	13.71
Portsmouth	16	7	8	180	11.25
Andover	15	4	11	145	9.67
Liphook & Ripsley	15	4	10	123	8.20
Old Tautonians & Romsey	15	2	12	96	6.40

†South Wales Cricket League

	P	W	L	Pts	Avge
Sully Centurions	18	15	3	326	18.11
St Fagans	15	12	3	253	16.87
Cardiff	18	12	6	277	15.39
Newport	17	11	6	255	15.00
Abergavenny	20	12	8	280	14.00
Sudbrook	18	9	9	243	13.50
Usk	17	9	8	216	12.71
Pentyrch	18	6	12	195	10.83
Pontypridd	17	5	12	165	9.71
Penarth	19	7	12	182	9.58
Panteg	16	4	12	150	9.38
Chepstow	17	3	14	149	8.76

† *ECB-approved but not a Premier League.*

Surrey Championship

	P	W	L	Pts
Weybridge	18	11	3	150
Wimbledon	18	9	4	131
Spencer	18	7	6	102
Reigate Priory	18	6	4	100
Normandy	18	7	7	98
Esher	18	6	7	86
Malden Wanderers	18	6	6	85
Banstead	18	5	9	78
Avorians	18	4	10	59
Guildford	18	3	9	50

Sussex Cricket League

	P	W	L	Pts
Horsham	19	11*	3	383
Brighton & Hove	19	11	5	372†
Eastbourne	19	9	4	347
Chichester Priory Park	19	7*	5	308
Sussex Development XI	10	3	5	287‡
Hastings & St Leonard's	19	5*	5	281
Three Bridges	19	7	6	268
East Grinstead	19	4	3	257
Steyning	19	4	8	247
St James's Montefiore	19	3	10	209
Lewes Priory	19	3*	13	199

* *Plus one tie.*
† *Brighton & Hove had 26 points deducted for over-bowling 19-year-old Matthew Wood.*
‡ *Sussex Development XI's actual points total, 151, was multiplied by 1.9.*

West of England Premier League

	P	W	L	Pts	Avge
Cheltenham	14	13	0	270	19.29
Bath	13	10	1	204	15.69
Frenchay	15	8	5	172	11.47
Keynsham	15	6	5	152	10.13
Taunton	14	5	6	116	8.29
Corsham	15	4	6	122	8.13
Taunton St Andrews	14	4	4	92	6.57
Optimists & Clifton	15	3	7	72	4.80
Downend	13	2	10	43	3.31
Thornbury	14	0	11	27	1.93

Yorkshire ECB County Premier League

	P	W	L	Pts
York	26	11*	4	136
Sheffield Collegiate	26	12	2	135
Harrogate	26	9	4	130
Doncaster Town	26	5	3	125
Cleethorpes	26	6	3	121
Driffield Town	26	4*	5	99
Scarborough.	26	6*	5	97
Castleford	26	9	6	96
Yorkshire Academy	26	9	9	90
Barnsley	26	5*	6	87
Sheffield United	26	7	5	78
Rotherham Town.	26	3	11	50
Hull	26	3	13	42
Appleby Frodingham . . .	26	3	16	34

* Plus one tie.

The following leagues do not have ECB Premier League status:

LANCASHIRE LEAGUES

Lancashire League

	P	W	L	Pts
Haslingden	26	16	6	207
Church.	26	16	7	202
Ramsbottom	26	15	9	198
Rawtenstall	26	14	9	192
Lowerhouse	26	14*	10	179
Bacup	26	13	10	179
Nelson.	26	14	8	171
Colne	26	11*	12	156
East Lancashire . . .	26	10	13	154
Todmorden	26	12	11	142
Accrington	26	9	12	123
Rishton	26	5*	16	101
Enfield.	26	6	18	99
Burnley	26	4*	18	82

* Plus one tie.

Central Lancashire League

	P	W	L	Pts
Norden	28	22	3	109
Unsworth	28	17	7	91
Littleborough	28	17	8	87
Heywood	28	16	9	78
Oldham	28	15	9	78
Walsden	28	15	9	76
Rochdale	28	13	11	75
Middleton.	28	12	14	67
Crompton	28	11	10	66
Milnrow.	28	11	13	62
Werneth	28	9	14	56
Radcliffe	28	7	14	52
Ashton.	28	7	17	48
Royton.	28	5	21	31
Stand.	28	3	21	26

OTHER LEAGUE WINNERS, 2004

Airedale & Wharfedale	Bilton
Bolton Association	Elton
Bolton League	Westhoughton
Bradford	Pudsey Congs
Cambridgeshire	Cambridge St Giles
Central Yorkshire	Methley
Durham County	Evenwood
Durham Senior	Burnmoor
Hertfordshire	Knebworth Park
Huddersfield	Elland
Lancashire County	Prestwich
Merseyside	Ainsdale
North Essex	Colchester & East Essex
North Lancs & Cumbria	Furness
Northumberland &	
Tyneside Senior	Tynedale
North Yorks &	
South Durham	Guisborough
Pembrokeshire	Haverfordwest
Ribblesdale	Read
Saddleworth	Saddleworth
South Wales Association	Briton Ferry Steel
Two Counties	Sudbury
West Wales Association	Llanybydder
West Wales Conference	Gowerton
York Senior	Easingwold

NATIONAL CLUB CHAMPIONSHIP, 2004

A pair of big fish from two of league cricket's smaller ponds met in the final of the 2004 club championship (played for the Cockspur Cup) when Kibworth, of the Leicestershire Premier League, cruised past Ockbrook & Borrowash, of the Derbyshire Premier. Kibworth, an agglomerate of the neighbouring A6 villages of Kibworth Beauchamp and Kibworth Harcourt, is the smallest place yet to have produced a winner, with a population of only 3,500.

They were also the first champions from Leicestershire, never regarded as a hotbed of league cricket. Paradoxically, the dearth of strong local clubs was one of Kibworth's advantages: there are few options for top players who move into the area. Since the club returned to the county's highest division, and signed their first overseas player, in the early 1990s, they have lured four cricketers with first-class experience. These include the former Hampshire seamer Simon Renshaw – now selling medical supplies in Leicestershire – who played an important role in their success.

Kibworth swatted away romantic suggestions that this was a village side. "We are a very good cricket club playing in a village," said their secretary Paul Abbott, and they proved as much in a thrilling quarter-final against two-time winners Teddington of Middlesex. Chasing 201, Teddington were rock-solid favourites at 170 for three, with plenty of overs to spare, but collapsed to 189, with Renshaw taking five for 25.

Kibworth had momentum – they won both the Leicestershire League and the County Cup – and luck on their side. All their crucial games in the latter stages were at home, in front of crowds that touched 1,000. Add in a batting line-up where even the No. 11 had made a league 150, and the juggernaut proved unstoppable. It was certainly too much for Ockbrook, in their first year in the competition. Inspired to enter by 2003 winners Sandiacre, just nine miles down the road, and stiffened by three former county players in captain Trevor Smith, spinner Lian Wharton and batsman Johnny Owen, they stumbled just twice on the journey to Lord's.

In the fifth round, it took three late Wharton wickets to snatch victory from Michael Vaughan's old club, Sheffield Collegiate. And in the sixth, they edged a last-over thriller against Bootle. It was not so close in the September final, despite a steadfast all-round display from 17-year-old Jake Needham of the Derbyshire academy.

However, for every club such as Ockbrook joining the competition, slightly more were leaving. The entry, which reached a high of 512 clubs in the 1980s, has dropped to a low of 332 for 2005. (Though the best estimates indicate there are simply fewer clubs than 20 years ago.) However, most of the strongest clubs are still there, and in 2004 the event had a sponsor again: it returned to the embrace of Cockspur Rum, supporters in the golden days of the late 1980s. Cockspur provided £23,000 in prize money, some much-needed love and marketing oomph, and also a trip to Barbados for the winners. For once a rum deal did not mean bad news.

FINAL

KIBWORTH v OCKBROOK & BORROWASH

At Lord's, September 7. Kibworth won by five wickets. Toss: Ockbrook & Borrowash.

Kibworth became the first Leicestershire winners of the national club competition, but not before two acts of spiky defiance from Ockbrook's 17-year-old all-rounder Jake Needham. First, he made a stay-at-your-post 51, ended only by a running mix-up, as his team-mates struggled to make up for a slow start. Against some spruce spin bowling, none of the last eight managed more than 19. Then, with Kibworth needing just under four and a half an over, Needham interrupted their cruise to victory: he took two wickets in successive balls with his off-spin but, with the score already 157, it was too late. Kibworth's win, set up by a brisk opening stand of 61 in 11 overs, was completed after the wobble, by Renshaw. He steadied nerves, then swatted a six over mid-on for victory.

Man of the Match: J. Needham.

Ockbrook & Borrowash

†C. Dunn c Hanger b Mason	44	C. Windmill b Spiers ... 4
J. E. H. Owen c Sutliff b Spiers	23	N. J. Smith not out ... 1
J. Needham run out	51	
D. Hallack b Mason	1	L-b 8, w 9, n-b 4 ... 21
D. Wood c Sutliff b Smith	11	
*T. M. Smith c Ferraby b Mason	1	1/53 (1) 2/102 (2) (9 wkts, 45 overs) 194
I. J. Darlington st Thompson b Smith	10	3/104 (4) 4/139 (5)
P. J. Darlington c and b Spiers	8	5/142 (6) 6/154 (7)
L. J. Wharton not out	19	7/168 (3) 8/169 (8) 9/186 (10)

Bowling: Mahmood 5–1–19–0; Renshaw 7–2–26–0; Parkin 7–1–30–0; Spiers 8–2–35–3; Smith 9–1–35–2; Mason 9–0–41–3.

Kibworth

*M. D. R. Sutliff c T. M. Smith b Needham	45	T. J. Mason c I. J. Darlington b Needham	0
J. D. Hanger c T. M. Smith b I. J. Darlington	29	S. J. Renshaw not out	31
A. P. Smith not out	47	L-b 3, w 6, n-b 6 ... 15
N. J. Ferraby st Dunn b Needham	5	1/61 (2) 2/85 (1) (5 wkts, 41.3 overs) 197
R. A. Cobb b Needham	25	3/91 (4) 4/157 (5)
		5/157 (6)

G. S. Parkin, Aamir Mahmood, R. A. Spiers and †S. G. Thompson did not bat.

Bowling: N. J. Smith 8–0–36–0; T. M. Smith 5–0–29–0; I. J. Darlington 5.3–0–30–1; Needham 9–0–27–4; Windmill 7–0–41–0; Wharton 7–0–31–0.

Umpires: M. J. Charman and R. Rigby.

WINNERS 1969–2004

1969	Hampstead	1981	Scarborough	1993	Old Hill
1970	Cheltenham	1982	Scarborough	1994	Chorley
1971	Blackheath	1983	Shrewsbury	1995	Chorley
1972	Scarborough	1984	Old Hill	1996	Walsall
1973	Wolverhampton	1985	Old Hill	1997	Eastbourne
1974	Sunbury	1986	Stourbridge	1998	Doncaster Town
1975	York	1987	Old Hill	1999	Wolverhampton
1976	Scarborough	1988	Enfield	2000	Sheffield Collegiate
1977	Southgate	1989	Teddington	2001	Bramhall
1978	Cheltenham	1990	Blackpool	2002	Saffron Walden
1979	Scarborough	1991	Teddington	2003	Sandiacre Town
1980	Moseley	1992	Optimists	2004	Kibworth

npower VILLAGE CUP, 2004

The gulf between the strongest villages, hardened in some of Britain's roughest and toughest leagues, and the rest was wider than ever in the 2004 village cup. A competition that began on bucolic grounds across the country ended with victory at Lord's for the league champions of South Wales. Sully Centurions – whose full-strength line-up boasts 375 Welsh caps – swatted aside all-comers. But Sully will not defend their title in 2005, after the organisers decided to fence off the competition, and its beer-and-biffing philosophy, from the strongest league sides.

Plainly Sully were far too good for anyone else, and many argued they were also too good for village cricket. As well as the league they also won the South Wales Cup. Transferring their sharp-edged approach to Sundays, they blazed through the 492 other entrants, winning by massive margins. A 21-run victory, over Somerset's Timsbury in the second national round, was the closest they came to a scrape.

The resounding wins bred resentment, and a whispering campaign. However, no evidence was produced to back up claims that their players were paid, something the rules forbid, or otherwise ineligible. Though there were complaints of sledging in their semi-final against Findon, their players' behaviour at Lord's – when every opposition batsman was clapped to and from the crease – was exemplary. Sully were worthy winners, but of a competition they had outgrown.

The organisers, the *Wisden Cricketer* magazine, recognised that in late 2004, when they banned clubs who play in certain high-standard leagues. The new ruling will eliminate Sully, and at least 14 other teams, for 2005. Clubs who field in any competition a player contracted to a first-class county will also be thrown out, along with those who, in the view of the umpires and committee, fail to comply with the spirit of the game. "There have been an increasing number of complaints about behaviour," says the organiser Tim Brocklehurst. "If we receive similar complaints in future we will disqualify teams."

In 2004, Sully, from the outskirts of Barry in Wales, simply buried their opponents under piles of runs. The two Sylvester brothers – Jamie, a managing director, and Ryan – each scored two hundreds in Sully's eight games; Lloyd Smith (nicknamed Thierry by his team-mates after the Arsenal striker Henry), made another in the final. Sixteen-year-old Michael O'Shea also starred at Lord's: a batsman for England Under-19 and the son of a local policeman, he helped complete a phenomenal success story, of an ambitious club with a council-owned ground that has gone a long way fast.

At Lord's, Sully's 243 in 40 overs was way beyond Exhall & Wixford, a club from two riverside villages near Stratford-upon-Avon. They were overwhelming underdogs, maintaining a different approach from their opponents: "We won't be drinking orange juice before the final, put it that way," said captain Simon Hollands, a banker. Exhall deserved a drink: they were drawn away in every round, won the toss just once, and were hanging on by their fingertips often. Poor fielding – "We had our summer ball the night before…" explained their chairman – left them to chase down 285 in the first national round. In the quarter-final they were just a foot away from going out, but an attempted six in the last over was caught on the rope. And in the semi, against Sherriff Hutton Bridge of North Yorkshire, they were 40 for four before a great escape.

By contrast, there were the usual one-sided contests in the early rounds. Mark Oldham of Plumtree CC in Nottinghamshire scored 161 not out, the highest of the year, against North Wheatley. And the outstanding bowling figures were seven for 19, by Andrew Palmer for Stone against Sheepscombe.

In 2004, 492 clubs entered the competition, more than 300 down on the peak number. Partly that is because villages have got bigger – busting the limit of 3,000 inhabitants (now increased to 4,000). But partly it was because some smaller clubs had become wary of embarrassing thrashings. In 2005, the organisers hope to start luring the small fry back.

FINAL

EXHALL & WIXFORD v SULLY CENTURIONS

At Lord's, August 22. Sully Centurions won by 79 runs. Toss: Sully Centurions.

To the surprise of nobody, Sully Centurions' captain Jamie Sylvester ended his seventh appearance at Lord's by lifting the npower Village Cup. Sylvester asked Exhall to bowl on a slow pitch, but nothing else was sluggish as Sully raced to 243 in 40 overs – the second-highest total in 33 Village finals. The meat of the innings came from Lloyd Smith, once of Glamorgan Second XI, and Michael O'Shea of England Under-19, who piled on 174 for the third wicket. After two early wickets, the Exhall drum, brought to celebrate breakthroughs, fell silent until the 37th over. Smith eventually reached 113, hitting five sixes in a well-paced innings. No Exhall batsman could match his class. John Simpson landed a few punches, reaching his fifty with 6, 4, 6, before falling to new-ball bowler Ryan Sylvester, the pick of Sully's attack and brother of Jamie. Well before the end, Sully could afford to toy with their victims, spreading the bowling around while they were serenaded from the stands with loud choruses of "Bread of Heaven".

Sully Centurions

*J. P. J. Sylvester c Gwynn b Keen	10	N. A. Gage not out		0
R. W. Sylvester c Hollands b Keen	19	B 2, l-b 3, w 4		9
M. P. O'Shea b Gates	79			
L. A. Smith c Gates b Hollands	113	1/33 (2) 2/34 (1)	(4 wkts, 40 overs)	243
D. Eskins not out	13	3/208 (3) 4/237 (4)		

H. Williams, M. C. Thomas, T. Williams, G. Sullivan and †O. Lovering did not bat.

Bowling: Gates 9–0–39–1; Keen 9–1–34–2; J. Park 9–0–42–0; S. Hollands 9–0–70–1; Grinsted 2–0–25–0; M. Park 2–0–28–0.

Exhall & Wixford

M. Gwynn b T. Williams	22	L. Gates c Sullivan b H. Williams		9
*S. Hollands c J. P. J. Sylvester b Eskins	0	S. Keen not out		2
†G. Wickes run out	4			
J. Simpson b R. W. Sylvester	58	B 1, l-b 10, w 4		15
S. Carmichael st Lovering				
b J. P. J. Sylvester	18	1/3 (2) 2/15 (3)	(7 wkts, 40 overs)	164
M. Park c Gage b J. P. J. Sylvester	9	3/65 (1) 4/108 (5)		
T. Heneghan not out	27	5/116 (4) 6/128 (6) 7/151 (8)		

M. Grinsted and J. Park did not bat.

Bowling: R. W. Sylvester 9–1–20–1; Eskins 7–0–19–1; T. Williams 9–0–48–1; Gage 6–1–23–0; J. P. J. Sylvester 5–1–16–2; Sullivan 2–0–16–0; H. Williams 1–0–8–1; Thomas 1–0–3–0.

Umpires: S. F. Bishopp and J. F. H. Salisbury.

WINNERS 1972–2004

1972	Troon (Cornwall)	1990	Goatacre (Wiltshire)
1973	Troon (Cornwall)	1991	St Fagans (Glamorgan)
1974	Bomarsund (Northumberland)	1992	Hursley Park (Hampshire)
1975	Gowerton (Glamorgan)	1993	Kington (Herefordshire)
1976	Troon (Cornwall)	1994	Elvaston (Derbyshire)
1977	Cookley (Worcestershire)	1995	Woodhouse Grange (Yorkshire)
1978	Linton Park (Kent)	1996	Caldy (Cheshire)
1979	East Bierley (Yorkshire)	1997	Caldy (Cheshire)
1980	Marchwiel (Clwyd)	1998	Methley (Yorkshire)
1981	St Fagans (Glamorgan)	1999	Linton Park (Kent)
1982	St Fagans (Glamorgan)	2000	Elvaston (Derbyshire)
1983	Quarndon (Derbyshire)	2001	Ynystawe (Glamorgan)
1984	Marchwiel (Clwyd)	2002	Shipton-under-Wychwood (Oxfordshire)
1985	Freuchie (Fife)		
1986	Forge Valley (Yorkshire)	2003	Shipton-under-Wychwood (Oxfordshire)
1987	Longparish (Hampshire)		
1988	Goatacre (Wiltshire)	2004	Sully Centurions (Glamorgan)
1989	Toft (Cheshire)		

ECB OSCAs

The ECB announced the winners of the 2004 Outstanding Service to Cricket Awards for volunteers from recreational cricket in October. Richard Fox of Olton and West Warwickshire CC won the "Get Involved" award for re-establishing the club's youth section, coaching four age-groups and building up a team of 14 coaches. Khalda Shafiq of Newcastle City CC won the "Volunteering" award for revolutionising her club's administration, setting up a junior section and bringing down ethnic barriers. Neil Moore and Karl Brown of Willington CC, Durham won the "Make a Difference" award, for fund-raising and winning numerous grants, which helped to build a £300,000 new pavilion, gain ClubMark accreditation and change the club's culture. Graham Clarke of Attenborough CC won the "All-Rounder" award for 47 years of service in which he developed the clubhouse facilities and worked on the maintenance of the ground and machinery. Derek Hopkins of Bournemouth & District Cricket Association won the "Leagues and Boards" award after forming youth leagues, an over-50s league, running representative sides, initiating a double-wicket competition and producing the BDCA handbook for 28 years. Mark Reynolds of Chipping Sodbury CC won the "Youth" award for setting up the website, managing three age-group teams, and organising training and development of seven new coaches. The committee of Chorley CC won the "Cricket Force" award for saving their club from financial collapse, improving the ground and increasing use of the function room by 500%. In addition to the above seven categories, David English was given a special award for his work within recreational cricket over the years.

IRISH CRICKET, 2004

DEREK SCOTT

For the Irish team, 2004 was a year of euphoria and disappointment. Wonderful wins against Surrey and the touring West Indians brought euphoria; but last-ball defeat by Bangladesh and the failure to win the two major tournaments they entered were a sobering let-down.

In the European Championships in Holland, Ireland narrowly lost their first fixture when it was eventually decided by a bowl-out: an ECB XI won 2–1. Wins over Holland, Scotland and Denmark left Ireland in second place. Things began well in the new first-class Intercontinental Cup as Holland were beaten by an innings, which guaranteed the Irish a place in the semi finals if they avoided defeat by Scotland. They did not.

Since winning two titles in 1996, Ireland have taken part in 11 tournaments involving ICC Associates and won none. The current Irish team is good, though has still to prove itself. They have an ideal opportunity in 2005 when Ireland stages the ICC Trophy. Cricket is scheduled for 25 different venues around the island, from Muckamore in the North to Malahide in the Republic. No fewer than five Associates will qualify from this for the 2007 World Cup in the Caribbean.

Crucial to Irish hopes will be the availability of the four experienced players who have county contracts: Ed Joyce and Eoin Morgan at Middlesex, Niall O'Brien at Kent and Andrew White at Northamptonshire. But while counties are obliged to release players to Test teams, Ireland, with a small pool of good players and a far greater need, are concerned that their request, which comes only once every four years, will be ignored. ICC pressure may be required.

That bowl-out apart, Ireland played 12 matches in 2004, winning six and losing six. The two big wins came chasing demanding targets. In May they overhauled Surrey in the C&G, their best result against county opposition, successfully chasing 262 against a team of renowned strength. Against the West Indians in June, the target was even steeper: 293. Both times Jason Molins and Jeremy Bray provided the ideal start with century stands.

In the Intercontinental Cup, Ireland crushed Holland by an innings in Deventer, where, on his first-class debut, White scored 152 not out from 182 balls, including 86 in boundaries. It is believed to be the first instance in Holland of a hundred on first-class debut. It was a good year for White, who in 2004 reached three notable landmarks: 50 caps, 1,000 runs and 50 wickets. Naseer Shaukat, a pace bowler with first-class experience in his native Pakistan, took five for 30 in Holland's second innings and followed it with five for 60 against Scotland, though he could not prevent Ireland from slipping to the defeat which cost them a winter trip to the Middle East. This, the bowl-out and defeat in a three-day friendly with MCC were the low points of 2004.

As usual, Ireland's youth teams did very well. At the Under-19 World Cup in Bangladesh back in February, Ireland convincingly beat Canada,

Papua New Guinea and Uganda. They also gave the losing finalists West Indies a jolt by coming within six runs of a shock win in a high-scoring match. The Under-13, Under-15 and Under-19 teams all won European tournaments.

Ireland called on 21 players for their 12 matches. Bray hit 489 runs at 34.92, White 440 at 48.88, backed up by 14 wickets with his off-spin – enough to get him his contract with Northamptonshire. The captain, Molins, scored 392 runs at 35.63, while Trent Johnston and Andre Botha both had splendid all-round seasons. Johnston totalled 360 runs at 45 and grabbed 14 wickets at 23.43; Botha managed 256 at 18.28 and 17 at 26.76.

These all-rounders – the Australian Johnston and South African Botha – are two of many foreign players drawn to Ireland by the success of the "Celtic Tiger" economy. Bray (another Australian) and Naseer bring to four the leading members of the national team qualified either by residence or citizenship. It remains to be seen whether the Irish Cricket Union feel the need to put a limit on such players if the next generation of home-grown cricketers is not to be discouraged.

North Leinster, who won all four of their matches, took the Interprovincial Tournament. The 23rd Royal Liver All Ireland Cup saw Limavady win for a third time (following victories in 1994 and 1997), thus emulating the achievements of Lurgan and North Down. In the regional leagues, Bangor won the Northern Union title for the first time in their 70-year history.

Winners of Irish Leagues and Cups
Interprovincial Tournament: North Leinster; **Royal Liver Senior Irish Cup:** Limavady; **Leinster/Dublin Senior League:** North County (also won Short League); **Leinster/Dublin Senior Cup:** Clontarf; **Munster League:** Limerick; **Munster Cup:** Cork County; **Northern Union:** Bangor; **Northern Union Cup:** North Down; **North-West League:** Brigade; **North-West Cup:** Donemana; **Ulster Cup:** Donemana.

SCOTTISH CRICKET, 2004

NEIL LEITCH

Scotland's season had a glorious finish in November, when they captured the inaugural ICC Intercontinental Cup, their first global trophy, with an emphatic innings victory over Canada. However, their success in the three-day format was in marked contrast to their disappointments in one-day competitions, which gave Scotland's playing record a less convincing look. From a schedule of 34 matches – their most hectic season yet – they won just nine, lost 21 and drew two, with two games abandoned.

Scotland qualified for the finals of the first-class Intercontinental Cup by heading the European group. In June, they had the better of a draw with Holland in Aberdeen, but travelled to Dublin two months later fearing the worst: Ireland were fresh from a rare victory against Scotland in the European Championships and needed only a draw to qualify for the finals in the United Arab Emirates. But an unbroken partnership of 178, their best of the season,

Back row (*left to right*) – Peter Drinnen (*Technical Director*), Paul Hoffmann, Andrew Raselli (*Physio*), Cedric English, Gavin Hamilton, Fraser Watts, Dewald Nel, Gregor Maiden, Kyle Coetzer. Front row (*left to right*) – Colin Smith, John Blain, Asim Butt, Craig Wright, Ryan Watson, Douglas Lockhart, Tony Judd (*Coach*).

by Dougie Lockhart and Fraser Watts saw Scotland home in an otherwise low-scoring game.

Success in the November finals came with unexpected ease. At Abu Dhabi, Scotland aggregated more than 700 runs in their semi against a weakened Kenya and, although they could not force a win, comfortably progressed to the final at Sharjah, where they blew Canada away by an innings inside two days. All told, the batsmen compiled nine century stands in their four Intercontinental games, while all the bowlers thrived. John Blain won the match award in the final for his overall figures of seven for 55.

The domestic season had also finished on a high, when a last-ball victory over Bangladesh, Scotland's first modern success against a Test-playing country, was followed two days later by an eight-wicket win against Derbyshire in the totesport League, their most emphatic against professional opposition.

But Scottish smiles were not so evident earlier in the season. They had travelled to Dubai and Sharjah at the end of February for the ICC Six Nations Challenge with a squad including Dougie Brown, Gavin Hamilton and John Blain, all county players. Defeats by Holland and USA dashed hopes of Scotland reaching the Champions Trophy, played later in the season, and which would have provided much-needed revenue. Even worse was to follow in July's European Championships, held in Holland: an all-amateur squad could win just one match from four.

The main plank of the international season was the Scottish Saltires' second year in what had become the totesport League. All feared 2004 would be more challenging than the previous summer – and so it proved. Just two wins was a poor record, though several more victories could and should have been achieved if they had been better at converting promising positions into results. For their last season in the League – the three-year trial ends in 2005 – the Scots must build on the progress they made late in 2004. The Scots will, however, continue to have regular involvement in county one-day cricket. For 2006, they will be the tenth team in the northern conference of the reorganised C&G Trophy.

Scotland looked to subcontinental all-rounders for their overseas players in 2004: both Sridharan Sriram, from India, and the Pakistani Yasir Arafat had one-day international experience. Although they could not match the runs of the previous year's pair, Rahul Dravid and Jon Kent, they did contribute well with the ball. Sriram's off-breaks applied a brake in the middle of the innings, and Arafat's in-swinging yorkers proved effective later in the season. Sriram was called up by India A for their tour of Zimbabwe in July, but financial constraints, a continuing problem in 2004, prevented his replacement.

The star performer, though, was Ryan Watson, Zimbabwe-born but Scotland-qualified. With 936 runs and 46 wickets, he came close to what would have been a unique double for Scotland, and was named all-rounder of the year. Fraser Watts, who hit 925 runs, and captain Craig Wright, with 40 wickets, won the batting and bowling awards. Watts probably advanced more than any other player, progressing from a regular twelfth man to a key batsman, and he made two of the team's four centuries.

Off the field, Cricket Scotland appointed Roddy Smith, a former Scotland batsman, as their new chief executive, while the Australian Tony Judd continued as part-time coach during 2004. Funding was eventually secured to make the post full-time for 2005 and, with Judd wishing to retain his commitments to Greenock, Andy Moles, who had spent an unhappy time as coach to the Kenya team, was appointed in early January.

The District Championship, abandoned for several seasons, was resurrected thanks to the arrival of a new sponsor. Now called the Citylets National Tri-Series, it pitted three sides – the East Coast Crusaders, Western Warriors and Scottish Colts (a development team) – and aimed to give the country's best players practice before the start of the main representative season. The East Coast Crusaders emerged as winners of the rain-affected 45-over tournament.

Winners of Scottish Leagues and Cups
Scottish National Cricket League: *Premier Division* – Clydesdale; *North Division* – Aberdeenshire; *South Division* – Poloc. **Scottish Cup:** Greenock. **CricketScotland Trophy:** Huntly. **Small Clubs Cup:** Rossie Priory. **Border League:** St Boswells. **East of Scotland League:** West Lothian. **Strathmore Union (amalgamated with Perthshire League):** Mannofield. **Western Union:** Renfrew. **North of Scotland League:** Northern Counties. **West League Cup:** Ferguslie. **Rowan Cup:** Poloc. **Masterton Trophy:** Grange.

BANGLADESH UNDER-19 IN ENGLAND, 2004

GARETH A. DAVIES

For talented Bangladeshi players, the journey from street cricket to Test arena can be a short one, making Under-19 tours such as this trip to England in July and August an important staging-post. By September, three of the touring squad – Nafis Iqbal, Aftab Ahmed and Nazmul Hossain – had been promoted to the senior team for their opening Champions Trophy match, against South Africa at Edgbaston.

Nafis scored 40 of a total of 93 in that game, and Nazmul, listed as a 16-year-old, bowled a controlled opening spell. But the evidence of the Under-19 tour suggested few of their younger players were actually ready for full international cricket. "It's a real challenge to get runs or take wickets at that level of the game when you are still learning your trade," said their coach Richard McInnes, formerly of the Australian national academy.

Bangladesh lost the Test series 2–0 and, although they finished on top at the drawn final Test in Cardiff, McInnes admitted his players made the same mistakes time after time. "They make improvements," he said, "and then go out and shoot themselves in the foot, particularly the batsmen, and that doesn't give the bowlers the chance they need."

Given the pressure on their attack, Nadif Chowdhury, an unflappable left-arm spinner, was one of the discoveries of the tour. Despite having never played in a national age-group team before, he took 13 cheap wickets in the Test series, and helped make up for the troubles of the senior slow left-armer, Enamul Haque junior. Enamul, who had shown turn and control on his full Test debut against England in 2003, did not bowl well, and England's youngsters appeared to target him. His tour was ended by injury before the last Test.

With a smooth run-up that does not place unnecessary pressure on his body, despite an open-chested action, Shahadat Hossain proved a tall, naturally aggressive seamer. Discovered at a talent-spotting camp in the port city of Narayanganj, he has the right ingredients to become his country's long-awaited strike bowler.

Among the batsmen, Nafis Iqbal – who hit the headlines in 2003 by calling the spinners on England's senior tour of Bangladesh "very much ordinary" – proved himself a gutsy, aggressive player, despite managing only one fifty in the Tests.

Although three of the squad already had experience in full internationals, six were still considered Under-17s, which bodes well for the next Under-19 World Cup. These six included Shamsur Rahman, who averaged 41.66 in the Tests, and the wicket-keeper/batsman Mushfiqur Rahim, who made 88 at Taunton. Mushfiqur is already rated one of the most professional and best-prepared cricketers in Bangladesh. Their highest run-scorer was Aftab

Ahmed, who appeared to have the talent, if not yet the application, to succeed at a higher level.

However, McInnes identified a deeper problem. "There is something of a culture of submissiveness in Bangladesh, a hierarchical set-up," he said. "The boys I come across have often never been taught to think for themselves. They just do as they are told. We've been trying to get them into the state of mind that they must not be fazed by anyone. We have made some improvements, but it needs a cultural change. That could take ten – even 20 – years." Bangladesh are striving to fast-forward the process: the Under-19 squad trained for eight weeks together prior to this tour, and there could be major financial support available from wealthy companies and individuals. But most want to see results first.

Bangladesh's weaknesses made England's true strength hard to judge. Neither of their Test wins was utterly overwhelming and, in the Third, England conceded a lead of 161, before rain rescued them. "The results have been satisfying," said their coach Andy Pick, "and we've just done enough when we've needed to. But our performances have been a bit disappointing." The only truly dominant individual display was a double-hundred – the first for England Under-19 since Bilal Shafayat in 2002 – on his home ground by Somerset's James Hildreth, a positive, attacking batsman. Ravinder Bopara, the Essex all-rounder, took ten wickets at 14.80 with his medium-pace. At the end of the summer, none of the Under-19s were judged polished enough to win a full-time contract at the ECB Academy. For some Bangladeshis, the wait for senior recognition was not so long.

BANGLADESH UNDER-19 TOURING PARTY

Enamul Haque, jun. (*captain*), Aftab Ahmed, Ashim Chowdhury, Dhiman Ghosh, Ishraq Sonet, Mushfiqur Rahim, Nadif Chowdhury, Nafis Iqbal, Nazimuddin, Nazmul Hossain, Rubaiyat Huq, Shahadat Hossain, Shamsur Rahman, Shahriar Nafees, Talha Jubair.

Coach: R. McInnes.

BANGLADESH UNDER-19 TOUR RESULTS

Played 10: Won 4, Lost 3, Drawn 2, No Result 1. Abandoned 2.

Note: Matches in this section were not first-class.

At Loughborough University, July 20. **No result.** Toss: ECB Schools. **Bangladesh Under-19 290-9** (50 overs) (Dhiman Ghosh 93, Shahriar Nafees 79); **ECB Schools 133-6** (27.2 overs) (N. Prowting 75; Nadif Chowdhury 3-23).

At Loughborough University, July 21. **Bangladesh Under-19 won by four wickets.** Toss: ECB Schools. **ECB Schools 173** (49.3 overs) (P. Cook 47; Enamul Haque, jun. 3-23); **Bangladesh Under-19 177-6** (37.5 overs) (Nafis Iqbal 66).

At Loughborough University, July 23, 24, 25. **Bangladesh Under-19 won by nine wickets.** Toss: Development of Excellence XI. **Development of Excellence XI 337** (M. O'Shea 73, B. W. Harmison 118; Nadif Chowdhury 5-81) **and 224-4 dec.** (M. Ali 63, M. Boyce 65*); **Bangladesh Under-19 338-8 dec.** (Shahriar Nafees 76, Nafis Iqbal 93; M. Ali 4-82) **and 224-1** (Shahriar Nafees 99, Shamsur Rahman 88*).

Ben Harmison is brother of England fast bowler Stephen.

ENGLAND v BANGLADESH

First Under-19 Test

At Leeds, July 28, 29, 30. England Under-19 won by five wickets. Toss: England Under-19.

Glamorgan's Adam Harrison and Luke Wright, of Sussex, tore the tourists apart on an opening day of sultry skies and blazing bats. A series of inappropriate shots – Bangladesh lost five wickets before lunch, four to mistimed cuts or top-edged pulls – left them with a below-par 230. Shamsur Rahman remained staunch as his team-mates tumbled, and a grinding partnership of 78 for the ninth wicket restored some respectability. England fared marginally better in reply, with Essex players to the fore: left-hander Alastair Cook hit 11 fours in his 45 and Ravinder Bopara scored 59 before becoming part of a burst of wickets. Five went down for ten runs, but Wright made a steadying 78 to help England to a small lead; the parsimony of Nadif Chowdhury was rewarded with five wickets. After a solid start, his team-mates looked comfortable at 115 for two, but then rapidly slid to 156 all out. Bangladesh lost their last six for 24 runs, and England reached their target easily enough, despite another mini-collapse.

Close of play: First day, England Under-19 95-2 (Bopara 31, Hildreth 9); Second day, Bangladesh Under-19 126-4 (Aftab Ahmed 45, Nadif Chowdhury 1).

Bangladesh Under-19

Shahriar Nafees c Stiff b Cusden	16	– (2) lbw b Cusden	3
Nafis Iqbal c Lawson b Cusden	0	– (1) c Patel b Stiff	44
Aftab Ahmed c New b Harrison	6	– c New b Harrison	54
Shamsur Rahman c Hildreth b Harrison	68	– c Denly b Bopara	23
†Dhiman Ghosh c Lawson b Wright	11	– (7) c New b Bopara	15
Nadif Chowdhury c Hildreth b Bopara	6	– lbw b Harrison	2
Mushfiqur Rahim c Cook b Cusden	1	– (5) lbw b Patel	1
Ishraq Sonet c New b Cusden	8	– lbw b Patel	1
Nazmul Hossain c Lawson b Wright	33	– lbw b Patel	1
*Enamul Haque jun. c New b Wright	36	– not out	1
Shahadat Hossain not out	4	– c Patel b Bopara	0
B 11, l-b 10, w 13, n-b 7	41	B 5, l-b 2, n-b 4	11

1/1 (2) 2/36 (1) 3/44 (3) 4/69 (5)	230	1/3 (2) 2/57 (1) 3/115 (4) 156
5/82 (6) 6/110 (7) 7/143 (8)		4/123 (5) 5/132 (6) 6/141 (3)
8/143 (4) 9/221 (10) 10/230 (9)		7/146 (8) 8/154 (7)
		9/155 (9) 10/156 (11)

Bowling: *First Innings*—Stiff 10–0–22–0; Cusden 18–4–64–4; Harrison 17–5–42–2; Wright 11.3–4–26–3; Bopara 12–5–31–1; Lawson 6–1–23–0; Patel 3–2–1–0. *Second Innings*—Cusden 5–2–29–1; Harrison 10–2–31–2; Stiff 8–2–24–1; Patel 17–3–31–3; Wright 4–0–15–0; Bopara 8–3–19–3.

England Under-19

*A. N. Cook c Dhiman Ghosh b Nadif Chowdhury	45	– c Aftab Ahmed b Enamul Haque	57
J. L. Denly c Dhiman Ghosh b Nazmul Hossain	1	– b Shahadat Hossain	0
R. S. Bopara c Dhiman Ghosh b Nadif Chowdhury	59	– b Nadif Chowdhury	22
J. C. Hildreth c Dhiman Ghosh b Nadif Chowdhury	27	– c Shahadat Hossain b Nadif Chowdhury	14
S. R. Patel c Aftab Ahmed b Nadif Chowdhury	0	– b Enamul Haque	4
L. J. Wright c Nadif Chowdhury b Enamul Haque	78	– not out	14
†T. J. New c Aftab Ahmed b Nadif Chowdhury	0	– not out	3
M. A. K. Lawson c and b Enamul Haque	3		
A. J. Harrison c Mushfiqur Rahim b Ishraq Sonet	33		
S. M. J. Cusden not out	0		
D. A. Stiff run out	0		
B 14, l-b 3, w 5, n-b 1	23	L-b 1, w 1, n-b 2	4
	269	**(5 wkts)**	**118**

1/17 (2) 2/86 (1) 3/145 (4) 4/147 (5) 5/148 (3) 6/148 (7) 7/155 (8) 8/269 (9) 9/269 (6) 10/269 (11)

1/2 (2) 2/66 (3) 3/94 (4) 4/99 (5) 5/100 (1)

Bowling: First Innings—Nazmul Hossain 18–5–66–1; Shahadat Hossain 12–3–35–0; Nadif Chowdhury 22–7–89–5; Ishraq Sonet 7–1–22–1; Enamul Haque 22.4–9–40–2. *Second Innings*—Nazmul Hossain 3–0–13–0; Shahadat Hossain 2–0–9–1; Nadif Chowdhury 14–3–54–2; Enamul Haque 13.3–4–41–2.

Umpires: D. J. Constant and M. J. Harris.

At Sleaford, August 2, 3, 4. **Drawn.** Toss: Bangladesh Under-19. **Bangladesh Under-19 466-9 dec.** (Dhiman Ghosh 67, Aftab Ahmed 111, Rubaiyat Huq 62*; B. Smith 3-61) **and 200-4 dec.** (Shahriar Nafees 116); **Development of Excellence XI 233** (W. Gifford 70) **and 91-4.**

At Oakham School, August 7, 8. **Bangladesh Under-19 won by 237 runs.** Toss: Bangladesh Under-19. **Bangladesh Under-19 535** (98.3 overs) (Nafis Iqbal 266, Dhiman Ghosh 84, Nadif Chowdhury 55; D. Evans 3-93, G. White 3-127, N. Woods 3-59); **Development of Excellence XI 298-8** (104 overs) (R. Timms 64, S. Davies 52; Enamul Haque jun. 3-71).

ENGLAND v BANGLADESH
Second Under-19 Test

At Taunton, August 10, 11, 12, 13. England Under-19 won by eight wickets. Toss: Bangladesh Under-19.

"Sensational," said Bangladesh coach Richard McInnes, "one of the best innings I have ever had the pleasure of seeing." Unfortunately for McInnes, he was referring to the commanding, match-turning double-hundred from Somerset's James Hildreth, rather than a performance by one of his own players. A near flawless innings with an explosive conclusion, it hauled England out of a deepening hole: after a poor start to the second day, they were five first-innings wickets down and still 131 behind. Against a swinging ball on the first day, a stubborn, hard-fought innings of 88 from Mushfiqur Rahim, listed as 15, took Bangladesh towards 273. It was a grind, with Mark Turner bowling well and grabbing five for 57, though Mushfiqur perked things up with three sixes. Four of his team-mates got started, including Nafis Iqbal who had just been named in the ICC Champions Trophy squad, but none put down roots. No Englishman managed that either, and at 142 for five the embarrassment was growing. However, Hildreth and Steven Davies, the wicket-keeper from Worcestershire, got together on the second afternoon and put on 177 for the sixth wicket. Hildreth composed an innings in harmony with his team's needs: he began cautiously, seldom hitting the ball in the air, before launching into his shots when Davies fell and the tail was exposed. He passed 200 in a Nazmul Hossain over that disappeared for 25, including three sixes. In all, he batted 302 minutes, faced 255 balls and hit 29 fours and six sixes; his second hundred took just 76 deliveries. When he was finally last out England had a first-innings lead of 123. And when Bangladesh briefly threatened to drag the game back during an aggressive 88-run partnership for the fifth wicket, between Aftab Ahmed and Nadif Chowdhury, Hildreth and Davies struck again, this time as medium-fast bowler and wicket-keeper. Chowdhury was caught behind and, from 155 for five, Bangladesh capitulated. On the final morning, England breezed to the 56 runs required and took an unassailable 2–0 lead in the series.

Close of play: First day, England Under-19 33-0 (Cook 15, Denly 16); Second day, Bangladesh Under-19 13-1 (Shahriar Nafees 7, Aftab Ahmed 0); Third day, Bangladesh Under-19 171-7 (Nazmul Hossain 0).

Bangladesh Under-19

Shahriar Nafees c Patel b Harrison	26	– c Davies b Turner	8
Nafis Iqbal c Denly b Harrison	27	– c Davies b Wright	6
Aftab Ahmed c Davies b Bopara	12	– c Davies b Wright	91
Dhiman Ghosh c Davies b Bopara	11	– b Wright	10
Nazimuddin lbw b Bopara	35	– c Cook b Cusden	4
Nadif Chowdhury c Patel b Turner	36	– c Davies b Hildreth	33
†Mushfiqur Rahim lbw b Turner	88	– lbw b Munday	1
Nazmul Hossain c Davies b Turner	0	– c Davies b Turner	0
*Enamul Haque jun. c Davies b Turner	3	– (11) not out	0
Ashim Chowdhury c Cook b Turner	12	– (9) b Turner	4
Shahadat Hossain not out	6	– (10) b Turner	0
L-b 2, w 8, n-b 7	17	B 3, l-b 13, w 4, n-b 1	21
	273		**178**

1/38 (2) 2/63 (3) 3/69 (1) 4/84 (4)
5/152 (5) 6/158 (6) 7/160 (8)
8/167 (9) 9/228 (10) 10/273 (7)

1/8 (2) 2/25 (1) 3/38 (4)
4/67 (5) 5/155 (6) 6/167 (7)
7/171 (3) 8/177 (8)
9/177 (10) 10/178 (9)

Bowling: First Innings—Turner 20.4–5–57–5; Cusden 7–1–31–0; Harrison 14–5–35–2; Bopara 21–6–41–3; Wright 18–4–42–0; Patel 8–0–39–0; Munday 3–0–21–0; Cook 1–0–5–0. *Second Innings*—Turner 14.1–5–47–4; Wright 13–5–29–3; Bopara 10–3–24–0; Cusden 8–2–36–1; Patel 7–2–21–0; Hildreth 3–2–3–1; Munday 3–2–2–1.

England Under-19

*A. N. Cook c Aftab Ahmed b Shahadat Hossain	23	– not out	16
J. L. Denly c Dhiman Ghosh b Shahadat Hossain	16	– lbw b Nazmul Hossain	12
R. S. Bopara b Nadif Chowdhury	28	– c Dhiman Ghosh b Nazmul Hossain	16
J. C. Hildreth b Shahadat Hossain	210	– not out	3
L. J. Wright b Nadif Chowdhury	13		
S. R. Patel c Shahriar Nafees b Nadif Chowdhury	1		
†S. M. Davies c Dhiman Ghosh b Nazmul Hossain	71		
A. J. Harrison b Nazmul Hossain	1		
M. L. Turner c Nazmul Hossain b Nadif Chowdhury	4		
S. M. J. Cusden c sub b Nazmul Hossain	1		
M. K. Munday not out	1		
B 4, l-b 2, w 11, n-b 10	27	B 8, w 1	9
	396	(2 wkts)	**56**

1/33 (2) 2/54 (1) 3/103 (3) 4/140 (5)
5/142 (6) 6/319 (7) 7/326 (8)
8/348 (9) 9/357 (10) 10/396 (4)

1/18 (2) 2/44 (3)

Bowling: *First Innings*—Nazmul Hossain 24–4–101–3; Shahadat Hossain 10.1–1–58–3; Nadif Chowdhury 36–7–109–4; Enamul Haque 19–2–74–0; Ashim Chowdhury 14–3–48–0. *Second Innings*—Nazmul Hossain 4–0–27–2; Nadif Chowdhury 3.4–0–21–0.

Umpires: B. Leadbeater and A. G. T. Whitehead.

ENGLAND v BANGLADESH

Third Under-19 Test

At Cardiff, August 17, 18, 19, 20. Drawn. Toss: England Under-19.

Too late to save the series, but not to save some self-respect, Bangladesh fought tigerishly and enjoyed the upper hand throughout. On a rain-affected first day, England elected to bat on a slow pitch offering turn, and slumped to 58 for six: only Samit Patel, who struck an aggressive 65 from 68 balls, and a last-wicket stand of 32 gave them something that passed for a total. However, the weather was not kind to Bangladesh. The whole second day and much of the third were washed out. With all of their lower-middle order contributing, and England forced to use eight bowlers, they built a first-innings lead of 161, but by then it was well into the last day, and the draw was inevitable. England's coach Andy Pick was left more relieved than pleased: "Our players are more experienced than Bangladesh's and it's disappointing that gap hasn't been more evident."

Close of play: First day, Bangladesh Under 19 58-2 (Nafis Iqbal 39, Shamsur Rahman 4); Second day, No play; Third day, Bangladesh Under 19 201-5 (Nazimuddin 23, Nadif Chowdhury 11).

England Under-19

*A. N. Cook lbw b Ashim Chowdhury	36		
J. L. Denly run out	0	– (1) lbw b Rubaiyat Huq	7
M. M. Ali c Mushfiqur Rahim b Rubaiyat Huq	8	– not out	6
R. S. Bopara c Mushfiqur Rahim b Rubaiyat Huq	0		
†S. M. Davies lbw b Nadif Chowdhury	6		
S. R. Patel c Rubaiyat Huq b Nadif Chowdhury	65		
T. C. Smith b Ashim Chowdhury	1		
M. L. Turner b Shahadat Hossain	13		
S. M. J. Cusden b Shahadat Hossain	5		
D. A. Griffiths c Aftab Ahmed b Ashim Chowdhury	21		
M. K. Munday not out	15	– (2) not out	13
B 1, l-b 4, w 4, n-b 6	15	B 4, l-b 2, w 2	8
	185	**(1 wkt)**	**34**

1/0 (2) 2/20 (3) 3/25 (4) 4/48 (5) 5/56 (1) 6/58 (7) 7/97 (8) 8/125 (9) 9/153 (6) 10/185 (10)

1/13 (1)

Bowling: *First Innings*—Shahadat Hossain 16–5–70–2; Rubaiyat Huq 8–1–29–2; Nadif Chowdhury 15–6–51–2; Ashim Chowdhury 10.1–3–30–3. *Second Innings*—Shahadat Hossain 6–2–16–0; Rubaiyat Huq 6–3–12–1.

❝This was no ordinary players' dispute; it was obvious to anyone spending time in the country that forces were at work with the aim of getting rid of white cricketers."

Australians in Zimbabwe, page 1235.

Bangladesh Under-19

Nafis Iqbal c Davies b Cusden	56	Ashim Chowdhury run out	8
*Shahriar Nafees c Cook b Cusden	8	Shahadat Hossain b Ali	10
Aftab Ahmed c Davies b Cusden	7		
Shamsur Rahman b Bopara	34	B 9, l-b 11, w 7, n-b 10	37
Dhiman Ghosh b Bopara	48		
Nazimuddin b Bopara	65		346
Nadif Chowdhury run out	37	1/22 (2) 2/52 (3) 3/85 (1)	
†Mushfiqur Rahim not out	36	4/152 (4) 5/170 (5) 6/275 (7)	
Rubaiyat Huq c Cook b Cusden	0	7/286 (6) 8/287 (9)	
		9/327 (10) 10/346 (11)	

Bowling: Turner 17–1–56–0; Cusden 28–6–81–4; Griffiths 14–1–57–0; Munday 15–1–52–0; Bopara 13–4–33–3; Patel 7–2–26–0; Smith 4–1–14–0; Ali 3.3–1–7–1.

Umpires: R. Palmer and J. F. Steele.

At The Rose Bowl (Nursery Ground), Southampton, August 22. **Bangladesh Under-19 won by one run**. Toss: Hampshire Academy XI. **Bangladesh Under-19 219** (44.3 overs) (Nafis Iqbal 92, Dhiman Ghosh 54; J. A. Tomlinson 3-35); **Hampshire Academy XI 218** (47.2 overs) (J. J. McLean 105, M. W. Barnes 51; Shahadat Hossain 4-31; Talha Jubair 5-36).

At Arundel, August 24. **First one-day international: England Under-19 v Bangladesh Under-19. No result (abandoned).**
Heavy overnight rain saturated the pitch.

At Hove, August 26. **Second one-day international: England Under-19 won by eight wickets.** Toss: Bangladesh Under-19. **Bangladesh Under-19 189** (49.5 overs) (Shamsur Rahman 75; T. C. Smith 3-27); **England Under-19 191-2** (39.4 overs) (J. L. Denly 62 not out, J. C. Hildreth 53*).

At Hove, August 27. **Third one-day international: England Under-19 v Bangladesh Under-19. No result (abandoned).**
England Under-19 won the three-match series 1–0.

ENGLAND YOUTH CRICKET, 2004

Paul Coupar

Stars rising in the West? James Hildreth (*left*), already a regular in the Somerset team, blasted a rare double-hundred for England Under-19; Steven Davies, on Worcestershire's books, later captained the national squad.

If reflected glory can be counted as success, the ECB National Academy – the pinnacle of the England youth system – had an astonishingly good 2004. The Academy and its staff played a vital role in England's Test success. During his stint there Andrew Flintoff lost weight, grooved his action and became a Test bowler; the convivial Rob Key found drive in desire for the praise of Rod Marsh; Simon Jones rebuilt a knee withered after horrific injury. And it was only after working with Troy Cooley, then the Academy fast bowling coach, that Steve Harmison finally began converting promise into wickets.

Without the recent streamlining and professionalisation in player development, England's golden year could easily have been another lament for young hopes lost to bad backs, knackered knees and county-circuit comforts. Since 2001, when Marsh took over youth cricket, the ECB had been speculating – to the tune of £4.5m for the world's best facilities in Loughborough. Now they started accumulating.

In 2004, the last blocks were slotted into a genuine pyramid under the full Academy, when the final three ECB-accredited county academies completed their first winter's coaching. For the first time ever, the development of English young cricketers, at both county and national level, was under the ultimate regulation of the England coaching staff.

That was a big change. Previously, different organisations ran different parts of the system, with some young players ending up with national caps from four different organisations: the TCCB, the English Schools Cricket Association, the Headmasters' Conference and the National Association of

Young Cricketers. The old system was less a pyramid than a maze, and relations between national organisations – and the counties – were often suspicious.

Now there are three teams – Under-15, 17 and 19 – and one controlling organisation – the ECB. Each side has a full-time coach, and trains, usually at Loughborough, with the same aids as the Test side: specialists such as Cooley, physiotherapists, sports psychologists and, at Loughborough, video cameras. "The amount of a player's game you can change gets less as they get older," says the England Under-19 coach Andy Pick, "so there's no point in having all the facilities for the full Academy only."

Some of the first youngsters to climb the pyramid reached the **Under-19** side in 2004. They comfortably beat Bangladesh 2–0 in a series lit up by Somerset's James Hildreth, a nimble, decisive 19 year-old from Millfield School. He hammered the Bangladeshis to all parts of Taunton and became the sixth Englishman to hit a double-hundred in a youth Test. Already he has ignited the same excitement in the West Country as Marcus Trescothick ten years before.

DOUBLE-HUNDREDS FOR ENGLAND IN UNDER-19 TESTS

267	M. P. Dowman	England v West Indies at Hove	1993
260*	K. Sharp	England v West Indies at Worcester	1978
254	G. J. Muchall	England v India at Cardiff	2002
210	**J. C. Hildreth**	**England v Bangladesh at Taunton**	**2004**
206	M. E. Trescothick	England v India at Birmingham	1994
201*	B. M. Shafayat	England v India at Northampton	2002

Later in 2004, Hildreth received a part-time Academy contract, along with seven other outstanding young players. The new part-time status was introduced to plug the gap left by a change in selection policy for the full Academy, when its focus shifted from precocious talents towards players considered ready for Test cricket at the pull of the next hamstring. Part-time contracts also went to Steven Davies, a Worcestershire wicket-keeper/batsman, and the Glamorgan swing bowler Adam Harrison. They were joined by Alastair Cook of Essex, Liam Plunkett of Durham, David Stiff of Kent and Luke Wright of Sussex.

The current Under-19 arrangements are not without pitfalls. During the summer the England side and the counties often want players at the same time, and the system brought in to soften the clash can produce perverse results. England have first call, but only until a player has clocked up six points – one is awarded for each home "Test" or one-day series he plays. As a result the most gifted 16 and 17-year-olds often miss out on England selection, because coaches don't want them to get too many points too early.

In fact the **Under-17s** played little cricket of any description in 2004. A wet August ensured three washouts, as well as two wins (one rain-affected) and a defeat in their one-day games against county academies and MCC

Young Cricketers. Karl Brown thundered to the only two fifties; his Lancashire team-mate, the seamer Steven Mullaney, took the best figures, five for 35 against Durham Academy. He, along with three others, was later considered ready for the Under-19 tour of India.

England **Under-15** went unbeaten against two older and physically stronger sides: Scotland Under-17 and Trinidad Under-16. The leading four from that side won *Daily Telegraph*/Bunbury scholarships and a stint with the full academy over the winter – Billy Godleman, a punishing batsman from Middlesex, Stuart Meaker, a fast-bowling all-rounder from Surrey, Alex Wakely, a spinner from Northamptonshire, and Greg Wood, a wicket-keeper from Yorkshire.

They will be the last scholars overseen by Marsh. In September, he steps down after four years as director, leaving his chrome-and-glass academy and the successful Test side he helped build, to return to his grandchildren in Australia.

PRESIDENTS OF MCC SINCE 1946

1946	General Sir Ronald Adam, Bt.	1973-74	Lord Caccia
1947	Captain Lord Cornwallis	1974-75	HRH The Duke of Edinburgh
1948	Brig.-Gen. The Earl of Gowrie	1975-76	C. G. A. Paris
1949	HRH The Duke of Edinburgh	1976-77	W. H. Webster
1950	Sir Pelham Warner	1977-78	D. G. Clark
1951-52	W. Findlay	1978-79	C. H. Palmer
1952-53	The Duke of Beaufort	1979-80	S. C. Griffith
1953-54	The Earl of Rosebery	1980-81	P. B. H. May
1954-55	Viscount Cobham	1981-82	G. H. G. Doggart
1955-56	Field Marshal Earl Alexander of Tunis	1982-83	Sir Anthony Tuke
		1983-84	A. H. A. Dibbs
1956-57	Vis. Monckton of Brenchley	1984-85	F. G. Mann
1957-58	The Duke of Norfolk	1985-86	J. G. W. Davies
1958-59	Marshal of the RAF Viscount Portal of Hungerford	1986-87	M. C. Cowdrey
		1987-88	J. J. Warr
1959-60	H. S. Altham	1988-89	Field Marshal The Lord Bramall
1960-61	Sir Hubert Ashton	1989-90	The Hon. Sir Denys Roberts
1961-62	Col. Sir William Worsley, Bt.	1990-91	The Rt Hon. The Lord Griffiths
1962-63	Lt-Col. Lord Nugent	1991-92	M. E. L. Melluish
1963-64	G. O. B. Allen	1992-94	D. R. W. Silk
1964-65	R. H. Twining	1994-96	The Hon. Sir Oliver Popplewell
1965-66	Lt-Gen. Sir Oliver Leese, Bt.	1996-98	A. C. D. Ingleby-Mackenzie
1966-67	Sir Alec Douglas-Home	1998-2000	A. R. Lewis
1967-68	A. E. R. Gilligan	2000-01	Lord Alexander of Weedon
1968-69	R. Aird	2001-02	E. R. Dexter
1969-70	M. J. C. Allom	2002-03	Sir Timothy Rice
1970-71	Sir Cyril Hawker	2003-04	C. A. Fry
1971-72	F. R. Brown	2004-05	T. W. Graveney
1972-73	A. M. Crawley		

Since 1951, Presidents of MCC have taken office on October 1. Previously they took office immediately after the annual general meeting at the start of the season. From 1992 to 2000, Presidents were eligible for two consecutive years of office; since then the period has reverted to one year.

SCHOOLS CRICKET, 2004

REVIEW BY PAUL COUPAR

The decline of competitive cricket in British state schools – where Geoff Boycott once grafted and ground for Hemsworth Grammar and Ian Botham belted sixes for Buckler's Mead Secondary – has been going on for at least 20 years. Fixtures were cut by an estimated 70% in the 1980s, when many teachers, underpaid and overworked, refused to supervise sport after the home-time bell rang. Most fixtures were never re-established. The decline came to be seen as a regrettable but pretty much inevitable part of British cricket – like April showers, and bad beefburgers at Test matches. However, 2004 saw two powerful challenges to the mood of resignation.

The first came from the very top. In December, in response to the ballooning waistlines of British schoolchildren, Tony Blair announced the biggest changes in secondary-school sport for a generation. Out would go non-competitive physical jerks, squeezed into the statutory minimum two hours' PE a week. In would come traditional competitive sport, including cricket, with at least four hours a week to be offered. A ring-fenced £519m a year, or an average of £150,000 for each secondary school, would pay for the extra PE teachers needed. "I want to see competition between schools," said Tessa Jowell, the Secretary for Culture, Media and Sport. "We have to get beyond the politically correct nonsense of the 1980s that competition damages children."

The second powerful challenge came from the Cricket Foundation, a charity which ploughs money from first-class cricket into development. In May 2005, its director Nick Gandon, a former coach at Haileybury, plans to announce a huge campaign, with the goal of restoring competitive cricket to the heart of life in state schools. The numbers are impressive. The foundation aims to put £50m into schools; riches indeed in cricket, where a year's TV revenue for the ECB is around £55m.

Pitfalls remain for both projects. The Labour government have to win a forthcoming general election. The Cricket Foundation estimates no more than 30% of state schools play even the odd competitive game – the decline has made deep cuts.

So, in 2004, most regular, competitive matches were played by the 7% of children who attend private schools. And the best team was a familiar name with a long-standing sporting reputation: Millfield. They won 20 of their 22 games, mainly limited-overs, and enjoyed reflected glory when James Hildreth, a former pupil, scored two enchanting hundreds for Somerset. Millfield also lifted the Lord's Taverners Under-15 Cup, their ninth outright victory in 16 years (they have also shared the Trophy once). "Millfield were simply better than us," admitted the opposing coach from RGS High Wycombe.

Many others could sympathise. The school's only defeats came against a powerful Exeter University side, and Tonbridge – another institution that

Making history: Ajmal Shahzad of Woodhouse Grove became the first-ever Yorkshire-born Asian to break into the county first team.

Picture by Simon Wilkinson

prides itself on placing equal value on sport and studies. Their attack only twice failed to cut through the opposition, leading the side to a record 15 wins, from 17 games. Sutton Valence, under the former England bowler Alan Igglesden, also blazed through the summer, winning 13 games. They were one agonising last-ball finish from a 100% season, which would have been the first recorded by *Wisden* since at least 1980. With slightly lower percentages of victories – 15 from 20 – came Oundle, whose cutting edge was Patrick Foster, with 54 wickets at 9.07, the school's best total by a pace bowler since 1895, and Brighton College, the top dogs in 2003.

With much of the season played under dark May clouds, no batsman showed the obvious class of Bedford School's Alastair Cook in 2003. However, James Cole of Merchant Taylors', Crosby quietly accumulated his way to 959 runs at 119.87, the best average in the country, played several games for Lancashire seconds, and still modestly admitted that "I'm more of a wicket-keeper than a batsman." Another all-rounder was the country's heaviest run-scorer: Martin Walters of Harrow with 1,204 at 109.45.

However, there was something rather unusual about Walters. For a start he was 19 years old. And he arrived four months after the traditional start of the academic year, having already completed his schooling at Selborne College in East London, South Africa. It certainly raised eyebrows, especially in the run-up to the Lord's match against Harrow's age-old rivals at Eton: "We wish him every success with his single AS-level module," said the *Eton College Chronicle* impishly, "and a very happy 20th birthday next March."

Walters and Harrow were far from alone. Gleaming sports records look good in glossy school prospectuses, and more schools are taking more sports scholars for shorter and shorter stints. Some weaker schools reported that games have become futile – for everyone involved. There were certainly some big mismatches: early in the summer Bharghav Modha, another sixth-form sports scholar and a leg-spinner working with Terry Jenner on the ECB's spin coaching scheme, took ten for 19 for Oakham against Worksop.

For an unprecedented third year running, Tom Woolsey, a left-arm spinner from St Peter's, York, topped the country's list of wicket-takers, with 55. To get there, he laboured through 307 overs, 40 more than anyone else, before taking up a place at Cambridge University. More incisive, taking one wicket fewer in two-thirds of the overs was Foster of Oundle. However, the sharpest of all, and the most discussed schoolboy cricketer of 2004, was another Yorkshireman.

On May 23, Ajmal Shahzad made cricket history when he bowled six tidy overs in the totesport League for the Yorkshire Phoenix, becoming the first Yorkshire-born Asian to play for the county's first team. It was a symbolic and overdue moment, coming more than 30 years after migrants from the subcontinent began arriving in Yorkshire in large numbers. The county's operations director, Geoff Cope, called it "A magic day... It is a clear message that if you have the talent and work hard, you can play for Yorkshire, whatever your skin colour." By contrast, taking 19 wickets for Woodhouse Grove, even at the country's best average of 4.63, must have seemed prosaic. Only a back injury stopped him grabbing many more.

In August, Chris Paget, an off-spinner from Repton, followed Shahzad into first-team cricket. He became Derbyshire's youngest-ever Championship player, at 16 years 284 days, won praise from a hard judge in the county coach David Houghton and then returned home to wait for GCSE results. "I think it's going to be difficult to concentrate on my school work," said Paget as he contemplated spending two A-level summers trying to help salvage Derbyshire's struggling first team.

However, unarguably the best player in schools cricket in 2004 starred for King's, Macclesfield. Having contacted the school's opponents, MCC, in search of match practice as he recovered from injury, the New Zealand left-arm spinner Daniel Vettori bowled ten cheap overs for King's, hit a quick fifty and still had the energy to push the sightscreens at both ends.

Vettori had a rival in the fame game. After the 2004 season, Uppingham reported that they had to cope without one of their leading batsmen of recent years, Harry Judd, who cut short his studies at the end of 2003 to become the drummer in a boy-band McFly. By the end of the next season, McFly had enjoyed two No. 1 singles, and the adoration of thousands of teenage girls, which some would call greater fame than any number of Test caps.

Most would be happy with even one cap, including a remarkable young man who made his debut for Harrow. Five years ago Mumtaz Habib fled the Taleban and arrived from Afghanistan in England, with no formal education, English or knowledge of cricket. He landed lucky, and was taken by his state school to a net in a local leisure centre, where he showed an outstanding instinctive talent. "I saw this boy who could do everything," enthused Harrow's master in charge, Simon Halliday, who spotted Habib and arranged a full bursary. Statistically, the move improved Habib's chances of playing professionally by a multiple of around four. In 2005, Tony Blair and the Cricket Foundation hope to do something about that.

ETON v HARROW

At Lord's, June 26. Eton won by 20 runs. Toss: Eton.

A storming captain's innings from Eddie Nissen led Eton to their third successive victory over Harrow. Rain washed out the morning, and Nissen arrived at 47 for three. He reached 50 in 45 balls, then lashed 74, including four sixes, off his next 37. Mumtaz Habib, a 17-year-old Afghan refugee given a sixth-form scholarship at Harrow, took two wickets, one caught and bowled, plus two boundary catches. Needing six an over, Harrow were on course at 145 for one in the 24th: Hamish Morrison struck two sixes into the Tavern Stand and 11 runs. But he fell for a 72-ball 79 as Gyles Scott-Hayward struck twice in two overs. The skies darkened, the asking-rate rose and the last wicket tumbled at 7.37 p.m.

Eton

O. G. Williams b Harper	2	W. T. Dobson c Habib b Walters	9
A. H. Ball c Habib b Spencer	27	D. G. Taylor not out	1
E. C. A. Bruce c Roditi b Spencer	13		
H. C. L. Rawlinson c and b Habib	21	L-b 4, w 8, n-b 1	13
*E. F. J. Nissen not out	124		
G. O. A. Scott-Hayward c Northeast b Habib	29	1/9 2/46 3/47 (6 wkts, 40 overs) 239 4/88 5/167 6/214	

†G. D. G. George, H. G. Franks and N. C. R. Westoll did not bat.

Bowling: Roditi 8–0–54–0; Harper 8–0–40–1; Walters 8–1–34–1; Spencer 5–0–32–2; Morrison 8–0–61–0; Habib 3–0–14–2.

Harrow

W. J. Spencer st George b Franks	14	G. M. Harper not out	5
H. M. Morrison c Bruce b Scott-Hayward	79	†R. T. de Oliveira b Bruce	0
M. D. Walters c Bruce b Scott-Hayward	36	J. B. K. Roditi run out	1
M. Habib run out	4	B 1, l-b 6, w 23, n-b 3	33
C. G. M. Travers run out	22		
*H. R. Howe b Dobson	9	1/46 2/145 3/150 (37.5 overs) 219	
S. A. Northeast st George b Franks	2	4/152 5/183 6/194	
E. J. Turner b Bruce	14	7/196 8/216 9/216	

Bowling: Bruce 7–0–20–2; Ball 3–0–23–0; Taylor 4–0–22–0; Franks 8–1–42–2; Westoll 4–0–26–0; Dobson 6.5–0–48–1; Scott-Hayward 5–0–31–2.

Umpires: J. A. Carter and C. J. Dalton.

Of the 166 matches played between the two schools since 1805, Eton have won 55, Harrow 45 and 66 have been drawn. Matches during the two world wars are excluded from the reckoning. The fixture was reduced from a two-day, two-innings-a-side match to one day in 1982, and became a limited-overs fixture from 1999. Fifty centuries have been scored, the highest being 183 by D. C. Boles of Eton in 1904; M. C. Bird of Harrow is the only batsman to have made two hundreds in a match, in 1907. The highest score since the First World War is 161 not out by M. K. Fosh of Harrow in 1975, Harrow's last victory before 2000.

Note: The following five tables cover only those schools listed in the Schools A–Z section.

BATTING

BEST AVERAGE IN SCHOOLS CRICKET

(Qualification: 150 runs, 3 completed innings, average 70.00)

	I	NO	Runs	HS	100s	Avge
J. Cole (*Merchant Taylors', Crosby*)	14	6	959	140	5	119.87
M. D. Walters (*Harrow School*)	19	8	1,204	135*	5	109.45
T. Cledwyn (*Canford School*)	10	4	605	144*	3	100.83
B. A. C. Howell (*The Oratory School*)	12	4	802	143	3	100.25
W. J. F. Stebbings (*Gresham's School*)	13	5	794	132*	4	99.25
F. Qureshi (*Radley College*)	9	3	547	111*	2	91.16
P. B. Muchall (*Durham School*)	12	4	712	127	2	89.00
C. Martin (*Canford School*)	12	2	881	172*	3	88.10
L. Lewis (*Blundell's School*)	12	4	687	127	3	85.87
R. Timms (*Millfield School*)	19	7	1,021	130*	3	85.08
M. A. Gouldstone (*Denstone College*)	14	4	776	106*	1	77.60
J. E. L. Buttleman (*Felsted School*)	12	6	459	69*	0	76.50
A. S. Jackson (*Sutton Valence School*)	14	3	841	147	3	76.45
M. P. Surry (*Felsted School*)	15	5	745	158*	4	74.50

MOST RUNS IN SCHOOLS CRICKET

(Qualification: 750 runs)

	I	NO	Runs	HS	100s	Avge
M. D. Walters (*Harrow School*)	19	8	1,204	135*	5	109.45
R. L. Young (*Brighton College*)	19	2	1,031	134	1	60.64
R Timms (*Millfield School*)	19	7	1,021	130*	3	85.08
J. Cole (*Merchant Taylors', Crosby*)	14	6	959	140	5	119.87
R. J. Hamilton-Brown (*Millfield School*)	20	3	955	101	1	56.17
C. Martin (*Canford School*)	12	2	881	172*	3	88.10
A. S. Jackson (*Sutton Valence School*)	14	3	841	147	3	76.45
C. J. Huntington (*Felsted School*)	17	4	833	151*	3	64.07
C. J. Cargo (*Bangor GS*)	19	2	805	152*	3	47.35
B. A. C. Howell (*The Oratory School*)	12	4	802	143	3	100.25
W. J. F. Stebbings (*Gresham's School*)	13	5	794	132*	4	99.25
R. M. Farenheim (*Oundle School*)	16	3	786	116	3	60.46
H. M. Morrison (*Harrow School*)	17	0	779	148	5	45.82
M. A. Gouldstone (*Denstone College*)	14	4	776	106*	1	77.60
T. S. Bartram (*St Peters, York*)	19	4	755	100	1	50.33
J. W. K. Beeny (*Tonbridge School*)	18	0	755	111	1	41.94

BOWLING

BEST AVERAGE IN SCHOOLS CRICKET

(Qualification: 10 wickets, average 9.00)

	O	M	R	W	BB	Avge
A. Shahzad (*Woodhouse Grove*)	51	15	88	19	7-18	4.63
S. O. Knott (*Sutton Valence School*)	67.2	15	149	27	4-6	5.51
S. G. Street (*Bryanston School*)	40.3	13	93	16	5-17	5.81
J. M. Leach (*Rydal Penrhos*)	30	8	65	10	3-9	6.50
W. J. Elphinstone (*Glenalmond College*)	84	21	193	29	5-4	6.65
J. W. K. Beeny (*Tonbridge School*)	33.2	4	102	15	5-28	6.80

	O	M	R	W	BB	Avge
D. Northover (*King Edward VI Coll, Stourbridge*).	17.3	0	68	10	4-42	6.80
S. W. Ireland (*The Harvey GS, Folkestone*)	64	21	150	22	5-14	6.81
T. Fleming (*The Glasgow Academy*).	38	6	127	18	6-26	7.05
D. Hastings (*Epsom College*)	100	21	245	33	6-10	7.42
R. M. T. Clegg (*Barnard Castle School*)	44.5	10	104	14	5-19	7.42
P. R. Mann (*Bromsgrove School*)	103.4	47	192	25	6-0	7.68
R. E. M. Williams (*Marlborough College*).	133	36	279	34	7-19	8.20
J. W. Neale (*King Edward's School, Birmingham*).	140	54	291	35	7-18	8.31
W. Sabey (*RGS Guildford*)	64	19	112	13	4-13	8.61
L. Butcher (*Sir Joseph Williamson's Math. S*) . . .	80	22	244	28	5-2	8.71

MOST WICKETS IN SCHOOLS CRICKET

(Qualification: 35 wickets)

	O	M	R	W	BB	Avge
T. J. Woolsey (*St Peter's, York*)	307.2	71	946	55	6-36	17.20
P. J. Foster (*Oundle School*)	208	62	490	54	6-19	9.07
C. R. Firth (*Merchant Taylors', Crosby*)	181.3	26	663	48	7-44	13.81
D. A. Woods (*Manchester GS*)	267.2	65	663	46	7-25	14.41
R. M. R. Brathwaite (*Dulwich College*)	201.4	47	474	45	6-42	10.53
J. C. Douglas-Hughes (*Felsted School*)	199	37	615	44	5-57	13.97
O. C. Griffiths (*Malvern College*)	237	68	623	41	6-12	15.19
O. Taylor (*Millfield School*)	190.2	24	782	41	5-26	19.07
J. D. Warr (*Elizabeth College, Guernsey*)	200.5	48	525	40	7-19	13.12
J. Chandrakumar (*Chigwell School*)	111.4	21	365	36	6-19	10.13
J. P. P. O'Sullivan (*Merchant Taylors', Northwood*)	187	60	384	35	6-33	10.97
G. G. White (*Stowe School*).	154.3	34	439	35	8-33	12.54
J. W. Neale (*King Edward's School, Birmingham*).	140	54	291	35	7-18	8.31
C. D. Whalley (*Newcastle-under-Lyme School*). . .	136	33	349	35	6-41	9.97
C. F. Young (*Tonbridge School*)	135.1	36	355	35	4-19	10.14
J. E. Mugnaioni (*Abingdon School*)	119.1	25	437	35	5-19	12.48

OUTSTANDING SEASONS, 2004

(Qualification: 8 matches)

	P	W	L	T	D	A	%W
Abingdon School.	17	13	3	0	1	3	76.47
Brighton College.	20	15	3	0	2	0	75.00
Bromsgrove School	13	10	3	0	0	6	76.92
Eastbourne College	14	12	0	0	2	2	85.71
King Edward's School, Birmingham . . .	14	11	2	0	1	6	78.57
Langley Park School	10	8	2	0	0	0	80.00
Millfield School	22	20	2	0	0	2	90.91
Monmouth School.	13	10	2	0	1	4	76.92
Oundle School	20	15	0	0	5	3	75.00
Queen Elizabeth's Hospital	8	6	0	1	1	3	75.00
Sutton Valence School	14	13	1	0	0	4	92.86
Taunton School	13	10	2	0	1	2	76.92
Tonbridge School	17	15	2	0	0	2	88.24
West Buckland School	12	9	3	0	0	0	75.00

Note: Besides those listed above, the following schools were unbeaten: Felsted, Leeds GS, Loughborough GS, Oakham, St Peter's, Wrekin College.

SCHOOLS A–Z

Qualification for averages: 150 runs or ten wickets.

In the results line, A = abandoned without a ball bowled. An asterisk next to a name indicates captain. Schools provide their own reports.

Abingdon School
P17 W13 L3 D1 A3
Master i/c S. P. G. Spratling
Coach G. V. Palmer

This was Abingdon's most successful season in many a year. They were captained superbly by Mugnaioni and led with the bat by Stern, who hit two splendid centuries. The brightest highlights came in the last week: three wins from three at a festival in Lytham, and playing at Edgbaston, where Abingdon lost to an excellent Felsted team in the final of the new "20s" tournament.

Batting P. T. R. Stern 711 at 59.25; J. E. Mugnaioni* 326 at 32.60; G. W. A. Stern 399 at 26.60; W. F. C. Poole 164 at 23.42.

Bowling J. E. Mugnaioni 35 at 12.48; A. M. McKenzie 31 at 15.93; G. W. A. Stern 25 at 18.76; A. U. Rehman 18 at 23.44.

Aldenham School
P12 W4 L2 D6 A4
Master i/c A. P. Stephenson
Coach D. W. Goodchild

Lots of good games disappeared into the rain: Aldenham could easily have won four of the drawn matches had the weather not butted in.

Batting C. E. Woolley 292 at 58.40; M. Karani 219 at 27.37; A. Sharma 151 at 21.57.

Bowling A. Sharma 15 at 13.26; J. Thakrar 15 at 16.60.

Alloyn's School
P12 W7 L3 D2 A2
Master i/c R. N. Ody
Coach P. H. Edwards

There were pleasing performances in 2004 but all the players who made the averages were in the upper sixth. Next season will be a challenge.

Batting A. L. Fuller* 395 at 49.37; C. Morris 373 at 46.62.

Bowling C. O. Greenwood 17 at 16.00; A. L. Fuller 19 at 16.94; C. J. McGill 16 at 22.50.

Ampleforth College
P7 W3 L2 D2 A4
Master i/c G. D. Thurman

Many matches and practices were lost in a season blighted by horrendous weather. When the rain held off, Ampleforth played exciting cricket under the adventurous captaincy of Nick Ainscough. James Pawle led a strong batting line-up, including Tom Bromet and Charlie O'Kelly, who both have several years left. The bowling, though not as strong, was spearheaded by Alex Faulkner.

Batting J. R. W. Pawle 292 at 36.50; T. H. J. Bromet 264 at 33.00; C. D. E. O'Kelly 190 at 23.75.

Bowling A. C. M. Faulkner 21 at 20.14; I. A. F. Wright 12 at 33.08; D. A. Tulloch 10 at 41.10; P. E. Waller 10 at 46.90.

Ardingly College
P12 W5 L6 D1 A1
Master i/c R. A. King
Coach C. Waller

The season picked up after starting with six defeats in a row. After the end of May the college won five games, including against MCC. Several good youngsters provided great optimism for the future.

Batting B. C. Brown 482 at 40.16; G. Martin 433 at 36.08; E. Long 232 at 23.20.

Bowling S. C. J. Lambert 10 at 11.60; E. Long 14 at 20.78; G. Martin 12 at 27.50.

Arnold School
P9 W2 L5 D2
Master i/c M. Evans
Coach A. McKeown

Batting T. Muir* 168 at 24.00; J. Cain 208 at 23.11.

Bowling M. Cowburn 25 at 17.16; P. Moss 10 at 22.50.

Ashville College
P12 W3 L6 D3 A5
Master i/c I. M. Walker

Batting N. R. Gupta* 251 at 25.10; C. E. Silverton 225 at 25.00; C. J. Gill 269 at 24.45; B. D. M. Portlock 260 at 21.66; P. D. Wickham 211 at 17.58.

Bowling N. R. Gupta 14 at 18.85; M. H. Wickham 12 at 20.16.

Bancroft's School
P18 W12 L4 D2 A1

Master i/c J. K. Lever

Bancroft's won 12 matches – their best in more than 30 years – and against other schools they lost only to Ilford County High. The batting was strong, particularly Simon Miller who broke the school record with 180 not out against Colfe's. His unbroken second-wicket stand of 249 with 15-year-old Robin Thompson, was also a record. Thompson impressed in a top four that did most of the side's batting.

Batting S. C. Miller 696 at 69.60; C. P. Smith 365 at 40.55; R. N. Thompson 442 at 40.18; A. Wilkinson 267 at 33.37; F. S. Khan 157 at 17.44.

Bowling J. K. Lever 21 at 17.66; F. S. Khan 26 at 19.65; T. J. Saull 15 at 25.06.

Bangor Grammar School
P21 W10 L6 D5

Master i/c D. J. Napier
Coach C. C. J. Harte

Chris Cargo's 152 not out put the final gloss on a very enjoyable and often sunny season. Cargo, also an Ireland Under-21 hockey player, Cooper and Watterson all represented Ulster and Irish Schools in their final year, but the lack of batting support prevented better team results.

Batting C. J. Cargo 805 at 47.35; S. Cooper 607 at 37.93; G. S. J. Watterson 195 at 13.00.

Bowling G. S. J. Watterson 34 at 12.17; T. B. G. Speers 29 at 14.20; A. W. Titmus 16 at 14.25; P. J. S. Speers 26 at 18.61; S. P. Connell 18 at 22.44.

Barnard Castle School
P9 W3 L4 D2 A3

Master i/c B. C. Usher
Coach M. P. Speight

The team put together a good run at the end of the season, with young players making a big contribution.

Batting R. M. Batty 427 at 47.44; A. M. Sammons 159 at 31.80; R. J. Hopwood 167 at 20.87.

Bowling R. M. T. Clegg 14 at 7.42; J. P. M. Stewart 11 at 18.09; R. M. Batty 20 at 19.75.

Bedford School
P16 W5 L6 D5 A3

Master i/c J. J. Farrell
Coach D. W. Randall

Bedford had an encouraging season. While the bowling was dominated by the experienced Binnington and the increasingly impressive Patel, the batting was centred round Alex Wakely, who represented England Under-15, and Andrew Bird. Impressive wins were recorded over Uppingham, Haileybury and Harrow.

Batting A. G. Wakely 728 at 52.00; A. S. Bird 483 at 30.18; D. J. Binnington 300 at 30.00; A. A. Burrows 427 at 28.46; R. V. Patel 193 at 24.12; J. A. D. Wilson 162 at 14.72.

Bowling R. V. Patel 25 at 21.60; A. A. Burrows 10 at 26.20; D. J. Binnington 25 at 27.04; T. M. R. Elliott 10 at 36.10; O. J. Yew* 15 at 38.60.

Bedford Modern School
P15 W1 L10 D4 A1

Master i/c N. J. Chinneck

A very young side struggled, but the performances improved considerably through the season.

Batting R. M. Godfrey 368 at 26.28; C. W. Comer 338 at 22.53; L. A. Presswell 164 at 20.50; N. J. A. Brooks 282 at 20.14; G. J. Hill 189 at 15.75

Bowling P. Katechia 11 at 25.45; A. Cook 12 at 29.75; S. Kanungo 11 at 34.09; R. Chandarana 10 at 40.50; R. M. Godfrey 10 at 53.00.

Berkhamsted Collegiate School
P11 W3 L7 T1 A3

Master i/c S. J. Dight
Coach S. Collins

This was a very tough season, though it did not look it during a 229-run stand for the third wicket against Kimbolton; Haddock, a 14-year-old, scored 120, Newman made 88 and, with Berkhamsted chasing 273, the match finished in a tie. Chesters captained with great determination and empathy; eight of his side should return next year.

Batting R. G. Newman 213 at 42.60; O. B. S. Haddock 280 at 23.33; J. P. Kilgannon 196 at 16.33.

Bowling F. T. S. Rodwell 19 at 17.94; I. J. E. Dent 17 at 23.47; T. D. Chesters* 13 at 30.61.

Bethany School
P8 W1 L3 D4 A5

Master i/c S. Brown

Individual performances were better than team results. The young players – there were no upper-sixth formers – surpassed expectations and the lower order showed real courage and grit batting out for draws against hostile and accurate bowling.

Batting C. J. Hall* 162 at 23.14; T. J. Danby 152 at 21.71; D. R. Booth 157 at 19.62.

Bowling F. Florry 13 at 16.53; J. R. Dobson 12 at 19.33; D. R. Booth 10 at 33.30.

The Bishop's Stortford High School
P10 W5 L3 D2 A3

Master i/c A. L. Leyshon

Greg Milward marshalled a strong bowling attack well but the batsmen were inconsistent. A draw against an excellent Felsted side was almost as pleasing as the five wins, including one against St Andrew's Cathedral College from Sydney. Luke Padgett's 100 not out against St Edmund's College was a great achievement.

Batting L. T. Padgett 295 at 36.87; P. S. Reed 227 at 22.70.

Bowling A. A. Lewin 12 at 11.16; P. S. Reed 14 at 14.28; R. F. Horne 11 at 19.18; A. Willcox 12 at 21.08.

Bloxham School
P12 L6 D6

Master i/c N. C. W. Furley   **Coach** R. Kaufman

Four of the six defeats were very close, which was frustrating. The batting relied too heavily on the excellent Baig, while Rahman, bowling chinamen, carried the attack. For 2005, Loxton and Smith look good prospects.

Batting A. D. Baig* 416 at 46.22; T. M. Whiteside 216 at 21.60; A. H. Rahman 192 at 21.33; T. M. Loxton 190 at 21.11.

Bowling A. H. Rahman 20 at 19.90; A. D. Baig 10 at 22.90; R. J. Tysoe 11 at 24.00; D. Smith 10 at 25.60.

Blundell's School
P11 W7 L3 T1 A4

Master i/c C. L. L. Gabbitass

The captain Liam Lewis, who returns next year, was the star, closely followed by Adam Gingell, whose fiery pace bowling tested the best. Otherwise, the side was light on bowling and this contributed to defeats. Against West Buckland, Lewis and Joe Smith put on a school-record opening stand of 236; at the time, Smith was only 14.

Batting L. Lewis* 687 at 85.87; W. J. Gingell 230 at 32.85; J. Smith 289 at 32.11; A. Gingell 201 at 28.71; J. Menheneott 216 at 27.00.

Bowling A. Gingell 19 at 11.68; L. Lewis 17 at 16.23; J. Menheneott 10 at 16.50; M. Lancelles 11 at 20.00.

Bradfield College
P14 W8 L5 D1 A2

Master i/c D. J. Clark

A young team had an excellent season: all of the wins – but only two of the defeats – were comprehensive. Richard Morris was outstanding with the ball and often held the batting together too; George Trewby's off-spin was once again controlled; 14-year-old Hamza Riazuddin played the whole season and his bowling was impressively mature at times. Nick Woodroffe captained with aplomb.

Batting R. K. Morris 374 at 34.00; W. H. Chaloner 390 at 32.50; H. Riazuddin 240 at 20.00; N. S. Woodroffe* 205 at 18.63; D. J. Plume 168 at 16.80; J. J. Smith 164 at 16.40.

Bowling R. K. Morris 19 at 13.15; G. W. Trewby 23 at 13.82; J. J. Smith 11 at 14.00; H. Riazuddin 18 at 16.33; M. L. Hutton 12 at 16.33; N. S. Woodroffe 13 at 19.84; D. J. Plume 18 at 25.53.

Bradford Grammar School
P15 W3 L9 D3 A4

Master i/c A. G. Smith

This was a difficult season. Run-scoring proved the main problem and six of the nine defeats could have been reversed with a little more application and composure. Despite losing the captain Fergus Parish to injury for half the season, the bowling was fairly consistent, with Oliver Collinge impressive in his debut year.

Batting R. Kroon 365 at 26.07; J. M. Shaw 255 at 19.61; L. Stockill 197 at 16.41; F. L. Parish* 168 at 15.27.

Bowling F. L. Parish 12 at 13.58; O. Collinge 18 at 18.00; L. Stockill 18 at 22.72; S. R. Lawrence 10 at 25.00; J. L. Dangerfield 14 at 30.35.

Brentwood School
P13 W2 L9 D2 A4

Master i/c B. R. Hardie

Batting C. R. Prowting 376 at 47.00; T. M. Gamby 247 at 27.44; B. Washington 190 at 27.14; R. I. Bull 190 at 19.00; T. Azim 190 at 17.27.

Bowling K. Sohal 16 at 27.93; D. Gulrajani 12 at 35.58; T. Azim 11 at 38.09.

Brighton College

P20 W15 L3 D2

Master i/c M. J. Edmunds   **Coaches** J. Spencer/R. G. Halsall

Exams caused more disruption than ever but once again the sun shone on Brighton when it mattered, and the batsmen had a few great days. They chased down 289 against MCC and 359 against the old boys, both in 50-over matches. The opening pair of Marc Gardner and Richard Young put on 214 against Ardingly and 166 against MCC; and four players scored a century. Young became the fifth in college history to score 1,000 runs in a summer.

Batting R. L. Young 1,031 at 60.64; M. A. Thornely 637 at 57.90; K. P. Stevenson 224 at 56.00; M. A. L. Gardner* 679 at 39.94; J. S. Gatting 290 at 32.22; R. Sekhri 218 at 31.14.

Bowling A. P. S. Sumner 24 at 14.33; R. Sekhri 27 at 15.03; A. P. Thornely 26 at 18.15; C. G. Saville 13 at 19.53; M. A. Thornely 11 at 24.00.

Bristol Grammar School

P10 W4 L5 D1 A2

Masters i/c K. R. Blackburn/R. S. Jones   **Coach** C. Baxter

The season started with four poor defeats but ended with four wins from five games. Tom Parnell, returning after illness, was often the catalyst, with his determined and skilful batting, and much-improved leg-spin. No others stood out consistently but the batting was deep and the attack varied and effective.

Batting T. M. Parnell 385 at 55.00.

Bowling T. M. Parnell 11 at 21.27.

Bromsgrove School

P13 W10 L3 A6

Master i/c P. Greetham   **Coach** J. E. Brinkley

Philip Mann produced the performance of the season, indeed one of the performances of any season, to take 10–10–0–6 against Worcestershire Gents. He was consistent with the bat and accurate with his flattish off-breaks. Matthew Mullan scored two brilliant centuries between England Under-18 rugby commitments; Luke Radford, son of former England bowler Neal, showed promise; and Ben Dudley excelled as wicket-keeper with 17 dismissals. Bromsgrove won their own festival, against opposition including two county junior sides.

Batting M. J. Mullan 334 at 47.71; P. R. Mann* 401 at 44.55; B. Dudley 199 at 28.42; S. P. Robinson 277 at 25.18; L. J. Radford 193 at 24.12.

Bowling P. R. Mann 25 at 7.68; R. P. Young 11 at 9.54; B. Bales 18 at 15.77; J. Jones 19 at 15.89; D. Mumford 15 at 16.26; L. J. Radford 14 at 17.28.

Bryanston School

P13 W7 L5 D1 A1

Master i/c T. J. Hill   **Coach** P. J. Norton

The revelation was Street, a left-armer from the Under-14s, who ended with a superb average. After three limp performances, the batsmen started taking responsibility in the absence of the injured Dorset Under-17 all-rounder Tom Turney. Seven consecutive victories was the best sequence for over 15 years.

Batting J. E. Marshall 338 at 37.55; J. R. H. Gibbs 318 at 35.33; J. G. Scott-Bolton 237 at 21.54; L. C. Bettesworth 221 at 20.09; G. H. E. Macpherson* 180 at 20.00.

Bowling S. G. Street 16 at 5.81; J. G. Scott-Bolton 17 at 20.05; J. R. H. Gibbs 11 at 26.45; C. Cosgrove 11 at 36.18.

Canford School

P14 W8 L5 D1

Master i/c R. Wallis   **Coach** A. A. Mallett

This was a season of four outstanding individuals. Chris Martin batted brilliantly, even against quality attacks; his fellow opener Tom Cledwyn also made a century, overcoming serious injury to show skill and determination; fast bowler Tom Myatt took a wicket every 22 balls, and wicket-keeper Ollie McLaren provided stability at No. 3. Still, the overall record was slightly disappointing.

Batting T. Cledwyn* 605 at 100.83; C. Martin 881 at 88.10; O. McLaren 321 at 32.10; P. Colvin 177 at 19.66.

Bowling T. Myatt 33 at 11.60; S. Ridley 11 at 16.45; N. A. W. Summerson 11 at 24.00; N. D. Van Der Meulen 14 at 26.92.

Charterhouse

P15 W6 L7 D2 A1

Master i/c P. J. Deakin   **Coach** R. V. Lewis

There were two eye-catching individual performances in an otherwise ordinary season: Toby Lumsden took the most wickets for five seasons and James Wood scored heavily, including a magnificent 123 not out to beat Dulwich. Other highlights included bowling out the Free Foresters for 52, and the selection of Harry Hooper and James Wood for ECB schools sides.

Batting J. R. Wood 538 at 53.80; N. R. Wood 279 at 27.90; M. St H. Stimpson 340 at 26.15; J. H. P. Hooper* 323 at 24.84; J. H.Walker 255 at 19.61; H. G. C. Schofield 169 at 16.90; T. N. H. Lumsden 151 at 13.72.
Bowling T. N. H. Lumsden 31 at 15.93; P. H. Summers 13 at 18.38; W. J. I. Tetley 20 at 22.50; J. B. Hunter 12 at 27.75.

Cheltenham College
P13 W5 L5 D3 A5
Master i/c M. W. Stovold
Coach M. P. Briers
Disappointingly, five games were abandoned because of inclement weather. However, Mace captained the side very positively and there were good wins against Malvern, Clifton, Sherborne and Hilton College, South Africa.
Batting D. C. Hall 569 at 63.22; C. J. L. Sandbach 348 at 34.80; S. C. Mason 167 at 27.83; A. J. Sherwood 242 at 26.88; J. P. Mills 239 at 26.55; A. J. Brooksbank 214 at 23.77.
Bowling R. Islam 17 at 19.64; A. J. Brooksbank 20 at 23.30; S. C. Mason 10 at 26.70.

Chigwell School
P14 W8 L3 D3 A1
Master i/c D. N. Morrison
Coach F. C. Griffith
A good all-round team had a very successful season. Conditions throughout favoured bowlers, helping Chigwell's varied attack force eight wins; all three losses could easily have gone the other way. The school went on a first-ever overseas tour, to the West Indies, and won nine out of ten matches. That made up for the longest examination study period anyone could remember.
Batting N. Amin 339 at 33.90; Rohan Bhome 227 at 28.37; Rahul Bhome 378 at 27.00; M. Ditta 203 at 22.55; W. M. Higgins 190 at 19.00.
Bowling J. Chandrakumar 36 at 10.13; Rahul Bhome 26 at 11.61; N. Amin 13 at 17.00; S. P. Martin 10 at 24.40; Rohan Bhome 11 at 24.45; V. Skandakumar 10 at 25.30.

Chislehurst and Sidcup Grammar School
P9 W2 L5 D2 A5
Master i/c R. A. Wallbridge
Rain and exams devastated the first half of the season, but thankfully more games were played in the second. The stop-start schedule made it difficult for the captain, James Gritt, to build team spirit. However, once he achieved this, the results improved, including a resounding win against a strong Old Sedcopians XI.
Batting J. Ahmed 151 at 30.20.
Bowling J. West 10 at 10.10; M. J. Willoughby 11 at 14.90.

Christ College, Brecon
P8 W2 L5 D1 A4
Masters i/c N. C. Blackburn/C. J. Webber
Wet weather at key stages of the term meant that the season never really got going, but a young side – all but two should return in 2005 – still made significant progress. The highlight was a two-wicket victory over MCC, having bowled them out for 146, the first school win in 38 years of the fixture.
Batting D. R. L. Jones 177 at 35.40.
Bowling B. N. J. Painter 13 at 21.30.

Christ's College, Finchley
P7 W4 L2 D1 A9
Master i/c S. S. Goldsmith
The early season was almost wiped out by rain, the late season by illness of the teacher in charge, so the college played an unusually low number of matches. Chetan Depala was the outstanding all-rounder and his nine for seven against Whitefield School, in a district cup match, was the equal third-best in college history.
Batting C. C. Depala 317 at 52.83.
Bowling C. C. Depala 15 at 11.20.

Christ's Hospital
P13 W8 L3 D2 A1
Master i/c H. P. Holdsworth
Coach L. J. Lenham
Only unbeaten Eastbourne College put Christ's Hospital to the sword, as accurate bowling and supportive fielding brought many fine victories. Only one century and nine fifties were scored, which suggested bowler-friendly wickets and a team not over-reliant on individuals. Still, the excellent form of James Maxwell in the second half of term certainly helped. Under-15 quick bowler Michael Quest is already very quick and should take many wickets.

Sebastian Street (*left*), a 14-year-old left-arm seamer, took 16 wickets at incredibly low cost for Bryanston; Martin Walters, a South African sports scholar at Harrow, was the country's leading run-scorer.

Batting J. G. Maxwell 356 at 39.55; S. C. Crocker 251 at 31.37; J. B. Mitra* 298 at 29.80; G. K. Chamberlin 230 at 25.55; M. P. Davey 241 at 20.08.
Bowling J. T. Maddren 18 at 10.83; M. J. Quest 20 at 13.05; S. A. D. Millicheap 11 at 13.90; S. C. Crocker 19 at 15.36; P. C. P. Boardman 19 at 17.84.

Clayesmore School
Master i/c D. Rimmer   **P14 W2 L11 D1 A2**
                                           Coach P. Warren
Batting E. J. B. Lack* 473 at 31.53; J. D. Morton 269 at 20.69; D. Briggs 209 at 17.41; D. P. Voisey 195 at 16.25.
Bowling J. W. Balmforth 16 at 15.93; G. J. H. Howard 13 at 16.61; A. G. Merson 25 at 18.32; S. J. Hughes 12 at 24.83.

Clifton College
Master i/c J. C. Bobby   **P11 W3 L6 D2 A4**
                                         Coach P. W. Romaines
This frustrating season promised much but delivered little. Early poor weather meant fixtures were lost and pressure of examinations left the team unsettled and lacking the confidence to score runs. The bowling showed the potential to dismiss sides, but all too often there were simply not enough runs to play with.
Batting T. Read 183 at 36.60.
Bowling W. Greig 21 at 12.52; C. Lincoln 15 at 20.93; J. Innes 16 at 21.25.

Colfe's School
Master i/c G. S. Clinton   **P13 W3 L7 D3 A4**
For the first time ever a girl played for the Colfe's first team: Susie Rowe plays for Kent Women's Under-17 and is a member of the England Academy. No Clinton appeared in the first team, for the first time in ten years.
Batting B. White 250 at 31.25; O. W. H. Taylor 161 at 20.12.
Bowling J. T. Taylor 21 at 11.00; Y. J. Khan 14 at 23.71.

Cranbrook School
Master i/c A. J. Presnell   **P15 W10 L3 D2**
Peter Towner made a record 62nd appearance in the first team, a career in which he took 117 wickets. The team beat MCC for the first time in five years.

Batting P. Towner 458 at 45.80; C. Marriott* 391 at 43.44; O. Reynolds 330 at 41.25.
Bowling T. Cullen 26 at 9.07; P. Towner 20 at 12.80; C. Marriott 16 at 15.56.

Cranleigh School

P13 W5 L6 D2 A6

Master i/c W. N. Bennett   Coach S. D. Welch

This was a mixed season. In a young side, Meaker continued to show promise opening the bowling and was well supported by Prince, Moore and by excellent, sure-handed fielding. Jones and Cope both scored centuries, and Crump hit an undefeated 92 in the victory over MCC. But in too many games the weather had the last say.

Batting M. J. Crump 201 at 40.20; R. H. Jones* 454 at 37.83; A. C. Cope 453 at 37.75; J. B. Haynes 360 at 32.72; S. Meaker 157 at 22.42.
Bowling E. C. P. Prince 14 at 15.42; S. Meaker 10 at 16.00; B. I. S. Gilchrist 14 at 19.35; A. E. Kendrick 13 at 26.46; J. Moore 10 at 31.50.

Culford School

P17 W10 L2 D5 A2

Master i/c N. A. Weedon   Coach L. Dearlove

An outstanding season: Mark Burchett scored a school-record 614 runs and helped the side break the record for wins in the season. Only two of the team return next year.

Batting M. R. Burchett* 614 at 40.93; W. O. Williamson 242 at 34.57; O. W. Wade 334 at 33.40; R. J. Hobley 473 at 29.56; A. E. Gibson 169 at 24.14; M. I. Fronicke 220 at 22.00, M. J. Feezko 180 at 20.00; T. A. Orton 272 at 17.00.
Bowling M. R. Burchett 23 at 14.39; R. E. H. Dennis 10 at 14.70; O. W. Wade 15 at 17.73; M. J. Feczko 18 at 19.55; M. T. Fronicke 16 at 21.87; T. W. French 10 at 38.00.

Dauntsey's School

P14 W1 L9 D4 A2

Master i/c A. J. Palmer   Coach G. Shome

A young and relatively weak team struggled in both league games and against several adult sides. The bowling lacked control early on but gradually improved, while the batting was inconsistent. However, some young players showed promise: three fifth-formers scored fifties and one third-former played regularly and successfully. Team spirit remained strong throughout.

Batting A. J. M. Penny 207 at 18.81.
Bowling C. T. Jones 18 at 18.44; W. P. J. Whyte 17 at 20.11; S. E. Blackford* 12 at 21.58; A. J. M. Penny 11 at 32.36; M. R. Lomas 10 at 39.50.

Dean Close School

P12 W1 L8 D3

Master i/c B. A. Barton   Coach D. Trist

For a developing side, the highlight was a record partnership of 240 undefeated by captain Carlisle and Gaylard against King's School, Gloucester.

Batting L. Gaylard 364 at 40.44; A. Carlisle* 265 at 33.12; J. Johnson 224 at 24.88.
Bowling A. Carlisle 12 at 25.00; L. Gaylard 10 at 29.60; T. Knights Johnson 12 at 30.91.

Denstone College

P14 W5 L5 D4 A1

Master i/c S. J. Dean

Matt Gouldstone had a season to remember, scoring an excellent hundred and nine consecutive fifties. Several others put in telling performances: James Parker richly deserved his century against Wickersley; Tom Morgan's batting won the match against Bishop Vesey's in the dying overs; and James Young bowled with some fire. The College acquitted themselves well in a new fixture against Repton, beat MCC, and only lost a cracking contest against Old Denstonians after a spectacular diving catch.

Batting M. A. Gouldstone* 776 at 77.60; J. O. S. Parker 322 at 24.76.
Bowling M. A. Gouldstone 30 at 17.16; J. M. Young 13 at 23.23; R. A. Rouse 15 at 25.26; J. W. D. Sharp 13 at 32.92.

Dollar Academy

P13 W4 L8 D1

Master i/c J. G. A. Frost

The bowling and fielding was generally good but the batting was very disappointing early in the season. Although Dollar lost to MCC in the last over, Wilson scoring 92, they beat Daniel Stewart's & Melville College and George Watson's College.

Batting G. K. Wilson 312 at 26.00; N. A. Alston 208 at 16.00.
Bowling G. K. Wilson 16 at 14.93; N. A. Alston 19 at 15.63; R. J. Baird 10 at 25.90.

Dover College
P8 L7 D1

Master i/c D. C. Butler/L. G. Moors

The best moment of the season was Daniel Adams's century against the Old Dovorians – the first by a 14-year-old for many years. A tree was planted on the ground in commemoration, as college custom dictates when a century is scored or eight wickets are taken.

Batting No batsman scored 150 runs. The leading batsman was D. R. Adams, who scored 140 at 28.00.
Bowling No bowler took ten wickets. The leading bowler was M. E. Walsh, who took eight at 30.50.

Downside School
P7 W4 L3 A1

Master i/c N. J. Bryars
Coach G. J. Kenness

This was very much a rebuilding year for Downside after the excellent 2003. The captain, Oliver Mellotte, led with a series of outstanding personal performances. The growth and development of all players over the season was exceptional.

Batting M. Marland 189 at 63.00; M. N. Warriner 199 at 39.80; O. J. K. R. Mellotte* 236 at 39.33.
Bowling M. N. Warriner 10 at 12.30; W. L. R. Harris 10 at 14.70; O. J. K. R. Mellotte 12 at 14.75.

Duke of York's Royal Military School
P11 W6 L5 A3

Master i/c S. Salisbury
Coach N. J. Llong

Several tight finishes and some exciting cricket lit up the season. The senior players failed to produce consistently but all played with real enthusiasm. Ben Inshaw applied himself with the bat and three Inshaws – Jamie, an Under-14, Ben and Sam – played together for the last three games. Exams make it increasingly difficult to field the strongest side for much of the season.

Batting B. M. W. Inshaw 361 at 45.12; M. Gilbert* 259 at 25.90; S. T. S. Inshaw 150 at 13.63.
Bowling R. H. Kaye 16 at 17.87; D. Malla 12 at 24.41; B. Kirby 11 at 27.27.

Dulwich College
P20 W9 L7 D4 A2

Master i/c D. J. Cooper
Coach C. W. J. Athey

All too often Dulwich underachieved with the bat, which turned what should have been a very good season into a mediocre one. Ruel Brathwaite again bowled with genuine pace, hit the ball cleanly and looked the best all-rounder on Dulwich's circuit. The new 20-over tournament, "20s", was an exciting challenge, though the College lost to the eventual winners, Felsted.

Batting T. D. Roy 663 at 36.83; M. Kafle 445 at 27.81; R. M. R. Brathwaite 453 at 26.64; V. L. Cella 265 at 22.08; C. J. Owen* 375 at 19.73; L. P. Furst 150 at 15.00.
Bowling R. M. R. Brathwaite 45 at 10.53; L. P. Furst 26 at 15.53; V. L. Cella 13 at 17.46; C. W. A. Southern 14 at 20.85; C. J. Owen 26 at 24.53.

Durham School
P11 W7 L2 D2 A4

Master i/c M. Hirsch

Durham had a very good season. The team was well led by Ben Embleton, who could call on three good all-rounders in Paul Muchall, Dias and Tiffin, who are all available in 2005. So is 13-year-old Michael Turns who has been outstanding in his age group and played in the first team in 2004. Because of pressure of exams the fixture list has been eroded.

Batting P. B. Muchall 712 at 89.00; B. H. Embleton* 347 at 38.55; S. F. Tiffin 175 at 29.16; L. S. J. Flunder 156 at 22.28.
Bowling S. F. Tiffin 14 at 11.64; P. B. Muchall 19 at 19.52; P. J. Dias 14 at 25.78; C. H. A. Stevenson 10 at 30.80.

Eastbourne College
P14 W12 D2 A2

Master i/c N. L. Wheeler
Coach A. J. Burger

Jan-Berrie Burger, the Namibian World Cup batsman, coached an experienced side to the college's best season since records began. The team went unbeaten, bowling the opposition out to win all their first ten matches. Accurate seam bowling was the main strength, and no opposing side reached 200. But the fielding was also excellent and runs were scored at a fast rate.

Batting J. A. M. Toy* 595 at 49.58; D. J. Loman 377 at 37.70; R. E. P. Chilcott 311 at 28.27; J. P. Reid 323 at 24.84; W. J. Ripley 228 at 20.72; C. B. Chisholm 165 at 20.62.
Bowling C. B. Chisholm 30 at 10.03; W. J. Ripley 22 at 11.18; L. M. Winter 22 at 11.22; J. L. Cherrill 10 at 14.60; J. C. Farley 14 at 16.14.

The Edinburgh Academy

P19 W6 L12 D1

Master i/c M. J. De-G. Allingham

Stuart Cosh was the top player, performing well with bat and ball and leading the team with a quiet authority. Reaching the Ryden Lothians Schools Cup final for the third time in a row was one of the highlights of a mixed season, although the Academy lost to Fettes in an exciting final.

Batting S. G. Cosh 436 at 27.25; P. D. M. Loudon 207 at 15.92; P. Steward 218 at 13.62; H. Paton 171 at 12.21; T. A. Clark 183 at 11.43.

Bowling S. G. Cosh 26 at 15.26; C. R. Loudon 14 at 18.35; H. Paton 24 at 19.87; P. D. M. Loudon 16 at 21.37; N. J. Lyell 16 at 31.43.

Elizabeth College, Guernsey

P18 W10 L4 D4

Master i/c M. E. Kinder   **Coach** A. Bannerjee

The captain James Warr hit a century against St Peter's, York and his best bowling was an impressive seven for 19. Home games were 40 overs a side and all six were won, making the college champions of Weekend League Division Two. The Old Elizabethans were defeated by five wickets as a young team made encouraging progress.

Batting J. D. Warr* 450 at 37.50; P. J. Le Hegarat 341 at 31.00; I. A. J. Nussbaumer 340 at 26.15; G. Bett 190 at 14.61; F. K. Calderwood 156 at 14.18.

Bowling J. D. Warr 40 at 13.12; L. D. Nussbaumer 10 at 16.70; G. Bett 32 at 19.09; S. E. De La Rue 16 at 26.12; P. J. Le Hegarat 13 at 26.46.

Ellesmere College

P11 W3 L2 D6 A3

Master i/c P. J. Hayes

Ellesmere enjoyed a good season but could not convert a number of winning opportunities into victories. The highlights were Richard Baxter's 129 against Rydal and Nick Watson Jones's six for 37 in the victory over Ormskirk School.

Batting R. A. M. Baxter* 447 at 49.66; N. D. Watson Jones 228 at 25.33; D. A. M. Baxter 153 at 13.90.

Bowling N. D. Watson Jones 26 at 17.30, R. A. M. Baxter 12 at 18.08; D. A. M. Baxter 17 at 18.11.

Eltham College

P11 W7 L4

Master i/c D. R. Grinstead   **Coach** R. R. Hills

Batting R. J. Malcolm* 361 at 51.57; T. J. F. Goodyear 195 at 32.50; J. G. Harris 188 at 17.09.

Bowling B. Patel 15 at 12.60; R. J. Malcolm 16 at 12.81; K. Desai 15 at 16.53; A. M. Higginson 14 at 19.00.

Enfield Grammar School

P9 W4 L4 D1 A6

Master i/c M. Alder

Enfield were runners-up in the Middlesex Under-19 Cup.

Batting S. Levy 238 at 34.00; J. Plumb 177 at 22.12; T. Ludlam* 152 at 16.88.

Bowling E. Ripsher 13 at 16.30; J. Schott 10 at 17.10; J. MacDonald 11 at 19.45.

Epsom College

P12 W7 L3 D2 A2

Master i/c D. Campbell

This was a great turnaround after a poor 2003. It was basically a two man show: Hastings was devastating with the ball, and Lammiman was an outstanding all-rounder.

Batting R. D. A. Lammiman* 413 at 45.88; C. G. T. Pountney 200 at 25.00.

Bowling D. Hastings 33 at 7.42; A. Richardson 20 at 12.65; K. McDuff 16 at 17.62.

Eton College

P15 W7 L7 D1 A1

Master i/c R. D. Oliphant-Callum

Batting A. H. Dall 504 at 38.76; E. C. A. Bruce 473 at 29.56; G. O. A. Scott-Hayward 344 at 28.66; E. F. J. Nissen* 270 at 27.00; H. C. L. Rawlinson 409 at 27.26; O. G. Williams 326 at 21.73; G. D. G. George 186 at 15.50; W. T. Dobson 170 at 14.16.

Bowling E. C. A. Bruce 29 at 17.58; H. G. Franks 21 at 18.52; W. T. Dobson 16 at 27.37.

Exeter School

P15 W8 L5 D2 A3

Master i/c W. A. Hughes   **Coach** N. Adams

This was a very encouraging season, but sadly rain-affected. A young side competed well and should be stronger next year. The three bowlers with 20 or more wickets were outstanding; more will be expected with the bat in 2005.

Batting G. R. Chappell 303 at 27.54; J. E. Cooke 299 at 23.00; O. P. V. Rimmer 217 at 21.70; S. J. Yeo 264 at 20.30; A. J. L. Smith 195 at 16.25; S. Barlow 189 at 13.50.
Bowling G. R. Chappell 20 at 11.35; S. J. Yeo 27 at 13.00; S. Barlow 29 at 13.13; O. J. Kernick 14 at 24.07; A. J. L. Smith 17 at 24.35; A. T. Phillips* 12 at 24.41.

Felsted School
P16 W11 D5 A1

Master i/c C. S. Knightley
Coach N. J. Lockhart

The 2004 season was an outstanding success, with a talented side progressing rapidly after their tour of Australia. Unbeaten in the regular season, Felsted also won the final of "20s", a national 20-over competition, at Edgbaston. The side was expertly led by Joseph Buttleman, who returns in 2005 with all but two of the current team: Charles Douglas-Hughes and Peter Ward will be missed. Two unbroken opening partnerships – 277 and 274 by Christopher Huntington and 15-year old Matthew Surry – were the highest on record.

Batting J. E. L. Buttleman* 459 at 76.50; M. P. Surry 745 at 74.50; C. J. Huntington 833 at 64.07; G. J. Phillips 229 at 45.80; J. C. Douglas-Hughes 265 at 44.16; F. F. Blackwell 157 at 22.42; P. M. Ward 194 at 21.55.
Bowling J. C. Douglas-Hughes 44 at 13.97; J. E. L. Buttleman 34 at 14.58; P. M. Ward 23 at 16.00; N. P. Harrison 10 at 22.70; M. J. Drain 10 at 25.80.

Fettes College
P11 W6 L4 T1 A3

Master i/c C. Thomson
Coach B. Russell

This was a very encouraging season for a squad featuring seven fifth-formers and one fourth-former. There were some fine victories – including a thriller against Edinburgh Academy in the final of the Ryden Lothian Schools Cup – and only two defeats against schools. The tied game against Strathallan was a cracker but rain, and the lack of a festival, were major frustrations.

Batting S. K. MacLennan 290 at 41.42; R. J. C. Forsyth 339 at 30.81; D. N. R. Philip 207 at 25.87; A. C. S. Fyffe 237 at 23.70; E. C. R. Philip 177 at 19.66.
Bowling D. N. R. Philip 16 at 15.93; S. K. MacLennan 12 at 18.75; H. J. L. Boisseau 11 at 28.18; O. G. C. Hunt 12 at 29.33.

Forest School
P18 W10 L4 D4 A4

Master i/c S. Turner

Swainland, the captain and wicket-keeper, and Whorlow are members of the Essex Academy; both played for the county seconds and for South of England Under-17. A six-match tour of Barbados brought four victories and good pre-season preparation.

Batting G. Whorlow 540 at 54.00; A. Palmer 453 at 34.84; C. Swainland* 384 at 29.53; D. Hawkes 159 at 26.50; E. Murphy 264 at 24.00; J. Yeo 186 at 23.25; J. Palmer 264 at 22.00; D. Bhachu 186 at 18.60.
Bowling D. Hawkes 26 at 11.65; G. Whorlow 26 at 14.96; E. Murphy 19 at 16.15; J. Palmer 13 at 16.23; A. Ryatt 16 at 17.87.

Framlingham College
P11 W6 L3 D2 A2

Master i/c M. J. Marvell
Coach M. D. Robinson

A successful season owed much to team spirit and willingness to approach matches without fear of losing. The batting relied heavily on wicket-keeper John Wybar and on Robert Newton. In his first season he scored a century and four fifties. The captain, Mark Stacpoole, was the most incisive and economical of the bowlers, though Richard Sprake took a hat-trick against St Joseph's College. Prospects look bright.

Batting R. I. Newton 451 at 50.11; A. J. Wybar 454 at 45.40; M. J. Stacpoole* 290 at 36.25; C. E. Hicks 155 at 25.83.
Bowling M. J. Stacpoole 19 at 14.00; H. M. Dunham 10 at 14.70; R. W. Sprake 14 at 17.85; B. J. A. Davies 14 at 25.07.

Giggleswick School
P15 W5 L8 D2 A1

Master i/c P. Humphreys
Coach D. Fallows

Batting A. Macdonald 304 at 20.26; N. Hird* 186 at 16.90; M. Harrison 184 at 16.72; M. Hughes 249 at 16.60; S. Illingworth 164 at 14.90; J. Illingworth 168 at 12.00; G. Crosby 164 at 10.93.
Bowling M. Harrison 14 at 15.50; G. Crosby 21 at 15.66; N. Hird 19 at 17.73; M. Hughes 10 at 28.10; S. Illingworth 13 at 29.38.

The Glasgow Academy
P7 W5 L1 D1 A1
Master i/c A. G. Lyall   **Coach** V. Hariharan

Winning our own Sixes Tournament was the high point of a season characterised by playing positive cricket. Michael Hopkins and Gautham Hariharan took wickets with their swing bowling, Thomas Fleming with spin. Hariharan earned a Scotland Under-19 cap. The team also became the first Scottish side to win the Henry Grierson award, presented by the XL Club to their best school opponents (measured by various yardsticks – from skill to turnout).

Batting R. Kelso 277 at 39.57.
Bowling T. Fleming 18 at 7.05; M. W. J. Hopkins 16 at 9.62; G. Hariharan* 14 at 12.71.

Glenalmond College
P8 W5 L2 D1
Master i/c A. Norton

The college's bowling was excellent, the batting occasionally fragile: the two defeats came when the batsmen failed to reach modest targets. The 2004 side were particularly happy and cohesive.

Batting M. R. Harvey 195 at 32.50.
Bowling W. J. Elphinstone 29 at 6.65; P. A. D. Stoll 14 at 13.64.

Gordonstoun School
P13 W3 L6 D4
Master i/c J. Rufey

A season of development for Gordonstoun was characterised by good performances from players in the lower-sixth and below. The highlight was a win against MCC, and the season ended with a tour of English schools.

Batting M. S. Gregory 607 at 50.58; C. S. Geddie 489 at 48.90; E. Martin 329 at 36.55.
Bowling C. S. Geddie 22 at 16.68; M. S. Gregory 19 at 23.89.

Gresham's School
P14 W9 L1 D4 A2
Master i/c A. M. Ponder

This was Gresham's best-ever season. Will Stebbings broke every school batting record: the highest-ever aggregate in a season (794), the highest-ever average (99.25), most hundreds in a season (four), and highest overall average in the first eleven. Sixteen-year-old Felix Flower also had an outstanding all-round season: he now has over 1,000 runs for the first eleven with two seasons still to go.

Batting W. J. F. Stebbings 794 at 99.25; F. J. Flower 574 at 57.40; R. M. K. Steward* 434 at 43.40; A. C. G. Broom 278 at 39.71; C. L. Ponder 239 at 26.55; J. O. Elliott 211 at 23.44.
Bowling S. Foster 10 at 13.90; J. O. Elliott 18 at 15.00; R. M. K. Steward 21 at 19.28; H. G. Flower 17 at 21.58; F. J. Flower 12 at 28.33.

Haberdashers' Aske's School
P18 W8 L5 T1 D4 A6
Master i/c S. D. Charlwood   **Coach** B. R. Mahoney

A young side played well in patches but were unable to sustain consistency. Notable victories included local rivals Merchant Taylors', Northwood and Bedford Modern; Gavin Baker's century against the XL Club and a fine win against Exmouth CC on the annual Devon tour also stood out. The side contained two sets of brothers – Anish and Sheilan Patel, and Edward and Robert Clements.

Batting J. S. T. Williams 361 at 30.08; G. C. Baker 424 at 28.26; E. G. Clements 190 at 27.14; A. M. Patel* 310 at 25.83; R. G. Clements 191 at 21.22; R. Panoya 277 at 18.46.
Bowling R. G. Clements 30 at 16.13; A. M. Patel 17 at 22.70; M. F. Gray 21 at 22.76; G. C. Baker 14 at 26.92; E. G. Clements 10 at 42.60.

Haileybury
P11 W4 L6 D1 A1
Master i/c C. Igolen-Robinson   **Coach** G. P. Howarth

Another exciting year, with young talent, individual achievements and excellent team spirit. There were memorable wins against Scotch College, Melbourne, Marlborough College and MCC. Ed Rayfield, an Under-16, impressed with the new ball, and Ross Noach, an Under-15, opened the batting with great poise for a young player.

Batting T. O. Stewart* 433 at 43.30; G. C. George 286 at 26.00; R. Noach 283 at 23.58.
Bowling G. C. George 14 at 21.50; E. J. R. Rayfield 20 at 22.75; R. M. Woodburn 13 at 25.53.

Hampton School
P14 W9 L1 D4 A2

Master i/c E. M. Wesson

Most of the wins were comprehensive – as was the single defeat, against Harrow. Hampton generally set good targets, then a strong bowling attack, spearheaded by Tim Ayers, strangled sides. The fielding was energetic, David Sellick's wicket-keeping full of élan, and many excellent catches were taken. Although the all-rounder Akbar Ansari dominated, it was a genuine team, ably led by Adam Samways, one of the few upper-sixth formers.

Batting A. S. Ansari 595 at 66.11; A. D. Samways* 340 at 37.77; T. S. Roland-Jones 396 at 30.46; A. J. Darby 164 at 23.42; M. J. Bendelow 200 at 20.00; J. A. C. Stevenson 153 at 13.90.

Bowling T. H. A. Ayers 22 at 9.81; A. S. Ansari 30 at 14.13; T. Handel 14 at 15.42; S. J. Jewell 21 at 16.95; R. S. Brown 12 at 24.91.

Harrow School
P20 W12 L6 D2 A1

Master i/c S. J. Halliday   Coaches R. K. Sethi/S. A. Jones

A successful season included 12 wins, including the Cowdrey Cup for the first time, and a narrow defeat by Eton in an exciting Lord's match. Success was built on excellent batting: Martin Walters broke the school record with 1,204 runs, including five centuries and seven fifties, and Morrison scored 779 off just 854 balls. The bowling relied on the leg-spin of Spencer and the medium-pace of Walters, who bowled 339 overs between them.

Batting M. D. Walters 1,204 at 109.45; H. M. Morrison 779 at 45.82; W. J. Spencer 506 at 31.62; S. A. Northeast 328 at 25.23; M. Habib 253 at 23.00; C. G. M. Travers 192 at 16.00; H. R. Howe 170 at 15.45.

Bowling W. J. Spencer 28 at 21.32; H. M. Morrison 19 at 22.26; J. B. K. Roditi 17 at 24.29; G. M. Harper 15 at 24.73; M. D. Walters 22 at 24.81; M. Habib 10 at 29.20.

The Harvey Grammar School
P15 W7 L5 D3 A4

Master i/c P. J. Harding

The highlight of the season was the 111 Charles Hemphrey made against MCC. Aged 14, he is the youngest player to score a century for the first team since Les Ames in 1920.

Batting S. W. Ireland 192 at 32.00; C. R. Hemphrey 302 at 27.45; T. J. L. Squire 190 at 23.75; B. M. Washer* 209 at 20.90; D. J. Boughtwood 154 at 17.11; T. B. Vincent 152 at 16.88; P. C. G. Owen 184 at 16.72.

Bowling S. W. Ireland 22 at 6.81; S. D. Green 10 at 10.80; P. C. G. Owen 10 at 17.70.

Hereford Cathedral School
P14 W3 L9 D2 A7

Master i/c A. H. Connop   Coach R. P. Skyrme

Batting A. J. Aston 382 at 63.66; G. J. B. Jacobs 208 at 34.66; B. R. Owens 337 at 28.08; T. C. Austwick 151 at 25.16; N. A. Townson* 261 at 21.75; T. G. D. Bates 204 at 17.00; H. J. S. Orgee 151 at 15.10.

Bowling D. C. Turner 10 at 23.70; G. J. B. Jacobs 11 at 24.09; R. M. Wilson 12 at 24.83.

Hurstpierpoint College
P16 W6 L4 D6 A2

Master i/c C. W. Gray   Coach M. Scott

Tom Edwards's eight for 46 against Bloxham was the highlight, but 2004 was a mediocre season for an inexperienced side.

Batting T. J. Jarvis 437 at 31.21; J. O. S. Richings 232 at 29.00; T. B. Poole 192 at 27.42; T. S. Voller 347 at 24.78; C. F. J. Viggor 343 at 21.43; S. Sabharwal 248 at 19.07.

Bowling T. I. Edwards 31 at 12.09; T. J. Jarvis 18 at 17.22; S. Sabharwal 26 at 22.50; J. O. S. Richings 13 at 26.61.

Ipswich School
P11 W3 L5 D3 A3

Master i/c A. K. Golding   Coach R. E. East

Ipswich had only three victories, but one was against a very strong Brighton College side during the end-of-term festival at Edinburgh Academy.

Batting M. J. Hilton* 158 at 31.60; A. J. Dunlavey 258 at 28.66; E. C. Driver 294 at 26.72; T. E. Davey 201 at 20.10; D. P. J. Crame 150 at 13.63.

Bowling I. Khalid 21 at 21.20; M. J. Hilton 15 at 23.13; F. L. Pope 15 at 23.13; M. K. Karia 10 at 24.60.

The John Lyon School
P13 W3 L4 T1 D5 A4

Master i/c I. R. Parker   Coach I. Blanchett

This was a disappointing season because expectations for a young side were high. But most of the team return for 2005.

Batting D. Hawes 316 at 52.66; N. Ruparelia 256 at 23.27; N. Rughani 195 at 21.66.
Bowling K. Desai 20 at 15.50; N. Ruparelia 15 at 18.80; K. Vasa 11 at 19.00; N. Rughani 12 at 21.83.

The Judd School, Tonbridge
P11 W5 L1 D5 A2

Master i/c D. W. Joseph

The 2004 season will be remembered for the successful Easter tour of Barbados, and some very encouraging performances. The core of the side return next season, and will look to build on the improvements made in 2004.

Batting F. Quirk 234 at 33.42; R. Joynes 158 at 17.55.
Bowling I. Smith 19 at 15.00; J. Southwart 16 at 15.56.

Kimbolton School
P16 W5 L9 D2 A5

Master i/c A. G. Tapp   **Coach** J. Bently

The summer was dominated by two players. The captain Mark Ralph beat the school record with 181 not out against Dean Close, and Oliver Huggins scored three hundreds. Huggins's brother Tom, a Kimbolton old boy, made his first-class debut for Northamptonshire in 2004.

Batting M. J. Ralph* 677 at 56.41; O. J. Huggins 559 at 39.92; D. W. Payne 315 at 22.50; M. D. Fitter 226 at 20.54; C. J. Vine 170 at 15.45.
Bowling M. J. Ralph 23 at 21.95; T. P. Sarkies 11 at 32.27; H. M. Gillam 11 at 50.18.

King Edward VI College, Stourbridge
P6 W4 L1 D1 A6

Masters i/c M. L. Ryan/R. A. Williams

The weather totally washed out half the scheduled matches. Two records were broken against Bishop Vesey's Grammar School: Northover (84) and Griffiths (140) put on 229 off 171 balls for the second wicket, and the college totalled 287 for seven, from 40 overs. Mitesh Patel scored heavily in the reduced season, making 111 not out of 175 against Old Edwardians and averaging 99.

Batting W. Griffiths 195 at 39.00.
Bowling D. Northover 10 at 6.80.

King Edward VI School, Southampton
P8 W3 L4 D1 A3

Master i/c C. Surry

The school played fewer games than anyone could remember. The weather led to abandoned and disrupted early-season matches, and the lack of cricket prevented bowlers hitting a rhythm. However, Steve Rhodes was a surprise with his unorthodox medium-pace, and he also scored quick runs with Anderson and Clarke. Rhodes won the Holden Trophy for best all-rounder. Richardson's 116 against Taunton College was the season's highlight.

Batting A. P. Richardson* 273 at 39.00; S. Rhodes 222 at 31.71; B. Anderson 185 at 30.83; T. Clarke 174 at 24.85.
Bowling S. Rhodes 10 at 17.00.

King Edward VII & Queen Mary School, Lytham
P23 W12 L9 D2 A1

Master i/c A. M. Weston   **Coach** W. McSkimming

After only one win in 2003, the school managed a record 12 in 2004 – a fitting tribute to their master in charge, who later left to coach in New Zealand. James Atherton scored 726 runs, a record for a 16-year-old. The school finished with a tour of Malta, where the match against Stockport Grammar, cancelled in the north-west in June, was played in somewhat warmer conditions.

Batting J. A. Atherton 726 at 30.25; N. G. Jones 525 at 27.63; R. G. Openshaw* 445 at 24.72; S. Ormsby 440 at 20.00; D. P. Tufft 317 at 19.81; T. J. Shillito 336 at 17.68; P. Jackson 201 at 11.82.
Bowling R. G. Openshaw 29 at 17.48; N. G. Jones 31 at 17.67; J. R. Whittam 19 at 22.78; P. Jackson 20 at 25.65; S. Ormsby 23 at 28.82; C. H. Tong 14 at 35.07.

King Edward's School, Birmingham
P14 W11 L2 D1 A6

Master i/c M. D. Stead   **Coach** D. Collins

This very successful season culminated in victories over MCC (with joint-captain Simon Chase scoring 111 not out) and, the next day, over St Peter's College, Adelaide. Three spinners, James Neale, Vikas Katyal and Nick Chase, were at the heart of most of the successes.

Batting S. P. G. Chase* 493 at 49.30; J. W. E. Metcalfe 247 at 30.80; J. W. Neale 372 at 28.60; A. P. S. Holmes* 251 at 20.90; V. Katyal 287 at 20.50; N. R. Chase 158 at 13.16.
Bowling J. W. Neale 35 at 8.31; V. Katyal 22 at 10.90; J. W. E. Metcalfe 14 at 15.78; N. R. Chase 12 at 25.91.

King Edward's School, Witley
Master i/c G. D. M. Lane

P14 W4 L6 D4 A2

A mixed season improved in the second half as some young players moved into the first team. Among them was an Under-14 leg-spinner, George Tarrant, who took 13 wickets in three games, including six for 62 against MCC. Alex Manley captained an injury-hit side superbly, and led the way with the bat. Although the team lost more often than they would have liked, they enjoyed some great close finishes.

Batting S. E. B. Shuker 222 at 37.00; A. M. W. Manley* 410 at 29.28; D. Bird 151 at 12.58.

Bowling G. Tarrant 13 at 11.23; S. E. B. Shuker 10 at 15.50; B. Copeman 14 at 18.35.

King's College, Taunton
Master i/c R. Codd

P11 W5 L6

Coach D. R. Breakwell

As losing semi-finalists in the 2001 Lord Taverner's Colts Cup, much was expected of the group in the upper-sixth. But only Will Bell with the bat, and James Yeabsley and James Excell with the ball, contributed enough. Charlie Lenygon, a 16-year-old all-rounder, was the best young player. With the departure of Harvey Trump as master in charge, this is a period of transition.

Batting C. Lenygon 333 at 33.30; W. Bell 315 at 28.63; G. Webber 164 at 14.90.

Bowling C. Lenygon 18 at 12.22; A. Trollope 12 at 15.91; T. Yeabsley 14 at 23.35; J. Excell* 12 at 23.66.

King's College School, Wimbledon
Master i/c T. Howland

P10 W3 L4 D3 A6

Coach S. Davies

Batting A. W. Blake 185 at 46.25; R. H. C. Slater 301 at 33.44; E. A. Clarke 224 at 24.88; A. J. R. Simmonds* 170 at 21.25; N. J. E. Burberry 170 at 18.88.

Bowling N. J. E. Burberry 16 at 22.00; R. N. Jones 15 at 25.40; M. P. A. Gregory 14 at 30.28.

The King's School, Canterbury
Master i/c R. White

P15 W7 L7 D1

Coach A. G. E. Ealham

Batting was the main strength of the team and for the first time since the early 1970s three different players scored centuries – all of them good to watch. Toby Humphrey produced some fine early-season bowling, including a hat-trick, and was effective even after returning from serious injury. His successor as captain, Will Bruce, can turn matches with both his batting and his leg-spinners.

Batting W. U. Bruce 514 at 39.53; G. E. Sweetman 208 at 34.66; P. G. Dixey 307 at 34.11; M. E. B. Humphrey 344 at 28.66; P. R. Archer 255 at 25.50.

Bowling T. J. L. Humphrey* 29 at 11.03; D. H. Johnston 16 at 24.37; H. L. S. Simmons 10 at 32.30; W. U. Bruce 16 at 33.62; T. C. V. Wilson 10 at 34.30.

The King's School, Chester
Master i/c S. Neal

P8 W3 L3 D2 A6

Coach A. L. Shillinglaw

Nearly half the fixtures were abandoned this year. Bad weather is not the school's only problem: it is becoming increasingly difficult to field a genuine first team, and just four cricketers played in every match.

Batting F. G. Owen* 288 at 41.14; A. C. J. Sissons 257 at 32.12; B. E. Turner 191 at 31.83.

Bowling No bowler took ten wickets. The leading bowler was R. D. Pawson, who took eight at 26.87.

The King's School, Ely
Masters i/c T. Arrand/W. J. Marshall

P12 W3 L7 D2 A6

Batting R. N. W. Ransom 199 at 66.33; B. H. N. Howgego 345 at 38.33; J. W. Payne 228 at 22.80; H. C. Sperling 161 at 17.88.

Bowling H. C. Sperling 12 at 21.41; B. H. N. Howgego 11 at 27.18; A. R. M. Cooper 10 at 28.40.

The King's School, Macclesfield
Master i/c S. Moores

P16 W7 L3 D6 A5

An excellent season was marred only by the bad weather, especially during cricket fortnight, and increasing pressure on players, due to exams. Spinners provided the highlights of the season: 16-year-old James Barratt bowls left-arm orthodox; his 14-year-old brother Jonathan bowls leg-spin; and against MCC, the New Zealand left-arm spinner Daniel Vettori played for the school while recovering from injury. The opening bowler Jonathan Lee took an excellent seven-for, including a hat-trick, against RGS, Newcastle and Perring captained with great authority.

Batting T. J. Parfett-Manning 560 at 46.66; J. S. J. Perring* 474 at 39.50; K. Sawas 500 at 38.46; T. R. McIlvenny 157 at 31.40; E. Purdom 181 at 30.16; B. J. Harding 191 at 17.36.

Bowling J. P. Barratt 29 at 13.96; J. F. Lee 21 at 17.66; O. J. W. Kenyon 11 at 18.27; J. D. Barratt 30 at 19.46; A. R. Jackson 16 at 21.50.

King's School, Rochester
P14 W6 L6 D2 A2

Master i/c G. R. Williams

Several leading players were unavailable for part of the season – through injury or school outings – and the strongest side seldom played together. Ben Phillips and Chris Maurice are outstanding batsmen, but felt the pressure on many occasions. Generally, the bowling was ill-directed and untidy.

Batting W. M. Ballard 155 at 51.37; C. A. Maurice 502 at 45.64; R. L. Smith 271 at 45.17; B. D. Phillips* 437 at 36.42.

Bowling C. A. Maurice 18 at 13.94; J. A. W. Warner 14 at 14.85; M. E. Gilbert 13 at 16.23; S. J. Edmed 13 at 22.61.

The King's School, Tynemouth
P12 W5 L5 D2 A2

Masters i/c P. J. Nicholson/W. Ryan

Bryan Telfer bowled well with the new ball, and Philip Morse and Jamie Coates, a pair of left-arm spinners, built great pressure. Coates, still an Under-15, took eight for 97 against Barnard Castle, the best figures for King's in living memory. However, the batting was more fragile. Tom Pollock, leading run-maker for the third year running, will be missed, as will wicket-keeper Michael Conn. The season ended with a two-week tour of Barbados.

Batting T. J. K. Pollock* 245 at 35.00; M. P. Conn 169 at 16.90.

Bowling J. P. Coates 21 at 16.57; C. J. Simpson 10 at 16.60; B. C. Telfer 12 at 17.08; P. A. Morse 12 at 17.91.

The King's School, Worcester
P23 W12 L7 D4

Master i/c D. P. Iddon Coach A. A. D. Gillgrass

A successful tour to Barbados, with six wins from seven, finished a satisfactory season. A surprising brittleness in the batting was never really overcome, and it was left to a pleasingly varied bowling attack to achieve many wins.

Batting S. Cullen 557 at 32.76; S. P. Bilboe* 580 at 32.22; T. H. Weston 425 at 22.36; O. Bendall 343 at 21.43; H. Dimond 324 at 19.05.

Bowling K. M. McNally 19 at 15.15; W. M. Smith 30 at 15.30; S. Cullen 28 at 15.89; B. J. Ford 17 at 16.11; J. A. Kelly 21 at 16.80; T. K. Gwynne 11 at 18.00; T. P. Cullen 18 at 19.33.

Kingston Grammar School
P11 W3 L6 D2

Master i/c D. E. C. Wethey Coach A. Smith

This was a more successful season than many recently – and it could have been better still. The loss of captain Ben Collier hit hard, but the opener Ben Jones emerged as a real force, Sam Houlston's seam bowling was exciting and Jamal Chohan, still an Under-15, scored a fine 91 against Westminster. The greatest excitement came in beating Trinity School by two runs – having been bowled out for 67.

Batting B. M. Jones 315 at 39.37; D. M. Sangaran 154 at 15.40.

Bowling S. J. Houlston 17 at 11.76; C. N. H. Bennett 12 at 15.58.

Kingswood School
P9 W4 L3 D2

Master i/c G. Opie

This was a very frustrating season due to poor weather.

Batting D. Brown 230 at 32.86; T. Seddon 212 at 26.50; A. Hola-Perier 152 at 19.00.

Bowling L. Baxter 19 at 10.31; J. Gerrish 15 at 12.47; N. Yuon 16 at 16.37.

Lancing College
P10 W3 L5 D2 A3

Master i/c P. Richardson Coach R. J. Davies

This was a transitional year. Runs were hard to come by, although the seamer Johnson bowled consistently and Cowell captained with intelligence and skill. There were good wins against Ardingly and the Lancing old boys. Things look more promising for 2005.

Batting T. E. J. Bennett 153 at 21.85; D. K. Sriharan 150 at 18.75.

Bowling M. D. E. Johnson 16 at 11.93; H. J. Gane 17 at 15.17; A. D. Williams 12 at 16.50.

Langley Park School for Boys
P10 W8 L2

Master i/c D. Crouch Coach C. H. Williams

The only two losses were in cup semi-finals, but much of the summer was disrupted by examinations and the weather.

Batting B. Couldrey* 177 at 29.50; J. Smedley 154 at 25.66.

Bowling H. Tidman 13 at 11.15; J. Couldrey 10 at 18.80.

Leeds Grammar School
P14 W6 D8 A6

Master i/c R. Hill

The season was ruined by rained-off games. The team's unbeaten record was only seriously threatened in a tight last match against Sedbergh, but their high expectations remain unfulfilled. So does Toby Jacklin's realistic ambition of taking 100 wickets in his school career. Both were thwarted by the Yorkshire weather.

Batting D. T. Syers 508 at 63.50; D. I. Sweeting 160 at 40.00; T. R. E. James 303 at 37.87; D. J. Stokoe 276 at 30.66; O. L. A. Finerty 185 at 26.42.

Bowling T. J. Jacklin* 34 at 10.29; J. F. McGowan 10 at 20.10; D. I. Sweeting 11 at 22.09; S. Siddiqui 12 at 27.41.

The Leys School, Cambridge
P11 W5 L3 D3

Master i/c A. Batterham
Coach J. Coleman

Batting M. J. Sanders* 597 at 66.33; C. W. Yeoman 300 at 37.50; T. E. Hoy 346 at 28.83; W. Heald 181 at 20.11.

Bowling D. J. McCallum 11 at 17.18; J. C. D. Brooklyn 14 at 24.50; M. J. Sanders 13 at 27.53; G. W. Musson 10 at 29.00.

Liverpool College
P14 W2 L6 D6 A1

Master i/c A. Fox
Coach A. Saricar

Despite the results, this was a promising season for a very young side.

Batting D. Jackson 536 at 53.60.

Bowling L. Lynch 22 at 17.54.

Llandovery College
P8 W2 L5 D1 A4

Master i/c T. D. Marks

Batting D. Thomas 160 at 32.00; D. E. Phillips 170 at 21.25.

Bowling D. E. Phillips 10 at 25.30.

Lord Wandsworth College
P8 W3 L3 D2 A6

Master i/c M. C. Russell
Coach W. Haupfleisch

With six abandoned games it was difficult to find any consistency or know quite how good the team were. Several of the defeats were close. For the first time in memory the college conceded 300 runs – against Hampton – and scored over 300 – 335 for three against St. Edmund's.

Batting P. K. Knight* 344 at 49.14; M. D. Feeney 252 at 31.50; B. N. P. Colvin 184 at 23.00.

Bowling B. D. Cloete 12 at 16.33; P. K. Knight 14 at 20.85; N. C. Priggen 10 at 34.70.

Loughborough Grammar School
P12 W8 D4 A6

Master i/c H. T. Tunnicliffe
Coach M. Gidley

Loughborough were unbeaten throughout an excellent season, with contributions from all. Craig Ashcroft stood out as an opening batsman and Worrall was consistently aggressive in the middle order. All the bowlers performed well, with Gurney accurate and aggressive with the new ball when fit.

Batting C. Ashcroft 571 at 51.90; S. Bird 294 at 49.00; F. Baker 432 at 48.00; R. Worrall* 402 at 44.66; R. Williams 228 at 28.50.

Bowling C. Krarup 14 at 14.28; S. Bird 14 at 18.42; M. Ashcroft 16 at 23.81; F. Baker 13 at 26.07.

Magdalen College School, Oxford
P8 W4 L4 A6

Master i/c S. J. Curwood

Batting J. Sutton 152 at 38.00; N. Murray 170 at 34.00.

Bowling No bowler took ten wickets. The leading bowler was R. West, who took nine at 24.44.

Malvern College
P18 W7 L6 D5 A1

Master i/c A. J. Murtagh
Coach R. W. Tolchard

Batting M. J. Wright 435 at 33.46; O. M. Griffiths 467 at 33.35; T. P. H. Chappell 500 at 33.33; O. C. Powell 405 at 27.00; B. C. Raymond 204 at 13.60.

Bowling R. D. K. Price 33 at 14.42; O. C. Griffiths 41 at 15.19; O. C. Powell 15 at 17.53; B. C. Raymond 23 at 20.39; C. T. Griffiths 14 at 26.71.

Chris Firth (*left*) took 48 wickets, the third-highest in the country, for Merchant Taylors', Crosby; his team-mate James Cole hit five hundreds and had the country's highest average.

Manchester Grammar School
P15 W6 L1 D8 A4

Master i/c D. Moss
Batting N. T. Reid 547 at 49.72; D. T. G. Leeming 595 at 45.76; I. S. Azam 320 at 35.55; R. W. Wingate-Saul 300 at 33.33.
Bowling D. A. Woods 46 at 14.41; E. R. Simpson 19 at 15.94; N. T. Reid 21 at 19.71; C. J. Hemmings 16 at 20.12.

Marlborough College
P11 W5 L3 D3 A4

Master i/c N. E. Briers
Coach R. Ratcliffe
Marlborough made all the running in the drawn two-day colours match at Rugby, and there were excellent wins against Radley, Cheltenham, Sherborne and St Edward's, as well as Wiltshire. Robbie Williams, a fast bowler of exceptional talent, had an outstanding season: in only 11 matches he took 34 wickets, including seven for 19 against Wiltshire.
Batting T. J. Forsythe 197 at 49.25; H. A. Adair* 275 at 30.55; E. R. Kilbee 313 at 28.45; A. W. Montagu-Pollock 295 at 24.58; R. E. M. Williams 177 at 17.70.
Bowling R. E. M. Williams 34 at 8.20; T. J. M. Graham 21 at 18.52; H. J. L. Simonds 10 at 22.60.

Merchant Taylors' School, Crosby
P14 W9 L3 D2 A4

Master i/c R. J. A. Smith
Coaches S. Sutcliffe/R. J. Pickup/J. Marshall
Batting J. Cole* 959 at 119.87; W. K. Miles 351 at 25.07; C. R. Firth 312 at 24.00.
Bowling C. R. Firth 48 at 13.81; J. Cole 10 at 18.70; N. S. Connor 15 at 22.40.

Merchant Taylors' School, Northwood
P13 W5 L3 T2 D3 A6

Master i/c C. R. Evans-Evans
Coach H. C. Latchman
Kavit Patel and Jack O'Sullivan formed a strong pace attack, and Ashish Mehta proved a genuine wicket-keeper/batsman: all three return in 2005.
Batting J. P. P. O'Sullivan 630 at 63.00; A. G. Mehta 423 at 28.20; R. Lipsitz 241 at 26.77; T. Gatzen 208 at 17.33; M. J. Patel 165 at 11.00.
Bowling J. P. P. O'Sullivan 35 at 10.97; R. Murthy 13 at 12.76; J. D. Hershman 27 at 16.07; K. H. Patel* 32 at 21.43; M. J. Patel 12 at 29.91.

Merchiston Castle School

Master i/c C. V. Swan

P16 W11 L1 D4 A1
Coach C. V. English

Merchiston won 11 of their 12 games against other schools – taking their tally over the past two seasons to 23 out of 24. Around half those games were time matches. William Quin proved an excellent captain and opening bat, hitting 158 against King's, Gloucester while on tour. James Brownlee was penetrative with the new ball, bowling his away-swingers at a brisk pace for a 15-year-old.

Batting W. G. H. Quin* 528 at 44.00; J. P. Brownlee 246 at 30.75; M. R. Welch 255 at 28.33; R. J. Holroyd 273 at 27.30; D. I. McKerchar 172 at 21.50; D. J. W. Smith 244 at 17.42.

Bowling J. P. Brownlee 26 at 9.03; D. J. W. Smith 10 at 11.70; C. W. S. Legget 12 at 14.41; C. J. Hedley 12 at 15.83; R. M. S. Legget 15 at 17.60.

Mill Hill School

Master i/c S. T. Plummer

P13 W2 L6 D5 A3
Coach I. J. F. Hutchinson

Batting N. Bawany* 236 at 33.71; G. Jacobs 152 at 13.81.

Bowling L. O. Johnson 17 at 14.88; M. Z. H. Burney 10 at 23.90; T. J. Audley 11 at 27.18.

Millfield School

Master i/c R. M. Ellison

P22 W20 L2 A2
Coach M. R. Davis

Defeats by Tonbridge and Exeter University did not mar one of the most successful seasons in the school's history. Much of the credit must go to the captain Richard Timms.

Batting R. T. Timms* 1,021 at 85.08; R. J. Hamilton-Brown 674 at 56.17; N. Page 252 at 42.00; T. Parker 183 at 36.60; S. J. P. Parry 360 at 36.00; R. J. Lett 607 at 33.72; O. Taylor 200 at 22.22.

Bowling D. Livingstone 19 at 9.78; D. Muralitharan 17 at 18.82; O. Taylor 41 at 19.07; T. Parker 21 at 22.04; R. J. Hamilton-Brown 24 at 26.33; N. A. Williams 18 at 27.22.

Monkton Combe

Master i/c P. R. Wickens

P15 W7 L5 D3 A1

Batting P. Auld 516 at 43.00; R. N. B. Baddeley* 315 at 28.63; J. A. Lowde 337 at 28.08; D. J. Kelly 239 at 15.93; R. J. Neil 173 at 15.72; G. E. J. Cook 164 at 12.61.

Bowling R. N. B. Baddeley 25 at 13.64; P. Auld 26 at 13.65; J. M. Nish 11 at 18.73; J. H. Geake 16 at 18.99.

Monmouth School

Master i/c A. J. Jones

P13 W10 L2 D1 A4
Coach G. I. Burgess

Despite being hit by bad weather, Monmouth had a successful and exciting season, with only two defeats, one against a very strong Glamorgan Under-17 team. Everyone contributed, with Douglas Spencer keeping wicket immaculately and completing over 20 dismissals.

Batting H. T. Waters 425 at 53.12; K. D. Tudge 359 at 35.90; J. H. Greaves 248 at 35.42; M. T. Knight 261 at 32.62; L. S. Cronk* 288 at 26.18; G. J. Fury 185 at 20.55.

Bowling K. D. Tudge 14 at 13.85; H. T. Waters 14 at 18.92; D. R. Wilson 11 at 21.09; L. S. Cronk 18 at 22.61; J. D. D. Osborne 14 at 24.71.

Newcastle-under-Lyme School

Master i/c P. S. J. Goodwin

P12 W5 L4 D3 A1

The season was more historic than overwhelmingly successful. In Whalley the school could boast a champion bowler; his average was the second-best in the school's history. And against Wolverhampton Grammar, Howland took seven for 39, the ninth-best figures on record. Unfortunately, the batting was less consistent, although Wright's average was the fifth-best on record for the school.

Batting J. D. Wright 376 at 47.00; S. J. P. Howland* 194 at 21.55.

Bowling C. D. Whalley 35 at 9.97; S. J. P. Howland 15 at 20.80.

Norwich School

Master i/c T. J. W. Day

P10 W2 L3 T1 D4 A3
Coaches R. A. Bunting/M. S. Sinclair

The school's batting was strong, but the attack failed to bowl sides out and turn draws into wins. Matt Kelly made up an excellent opening pair with Phil Wilkins, and the experienced Charlie Webster hit two centuries. There was much excitement when Mathew Sinclair, the school professional, was called into New Zealand's injury-hit squad for the Third Test; later in the summer one of his predecessors, Gareth Hopkins, kept wicket in New Zealand's one-day side.

Batting C. J. M. Webster 341 at 56.83; M. J. Kelly* 404 at 50.50; P. J. Wilkins 238 at 34.00; S. C. Crook 163 at 23.28.

Bowling A. M. Russell 10 at 26.90; G. W. Alston 10 at 27.10.

 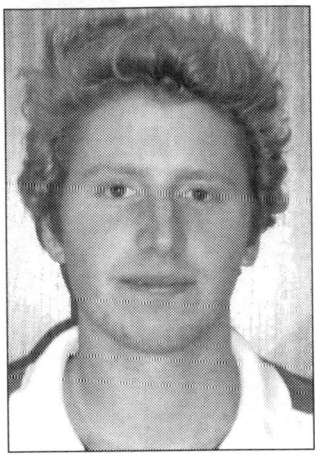

Jack O'Sullivan (*left*) of Merchant Taylors', Northwood averaged 63 with the bat and 10.97 with his fast-medium seamers; Calum Doutch of Queen's College, Taunton almost matched him, averaging 51.27 and 12.64.

Nottingham High School
P13 W4 L9 A6

Master i/c J. Lamb   **Coach** K. E. Cooper

Batting N. W. Nesbitt 183 at 45.75; N. D. Rose 507 at 39.00; S. C. Powell 221 at 31.57; J. M. Oldham 283 at 31.44; A. W. Mee 206 at 17.16; C. C. J. Nembhard 188 at 17.09; J. A. Coupland* 199 at 18.09.
Bowling N. D. Rose 13 at 23.23; F. A. Brown 11 at 36.63; S. Powell 10 at 39.40; M. W. Hallam 12 at 39.41.

Oakham School
P15 W9 T1 D5 A3

Master i/c F. C. Hayes   **Coach** D. S. Steele

The 2004 season continued the form of 2003: in 31 games, spread across two seasons, the school has not been beaten. Just as remarkably, Barghav Moda removed all ten batsmen for just 19 runs to beat Worksop College by eight wickets. Stuart Broad, son of ex-England batsman Chris, took three for 38 and made 67 not out in a nine-wicket win against Harrow.
Batting G. S. Sapal 595 at 59.50; S. C. J. Broad 591 at 59.10; M. W. Smith 154 at 51.33; P. G. Cook 325 at 36.11; S. P. Bevin 204 at 29.14.
Bowling P. G. Cook 10 at 13.20; B. Modha 25 at 15.80; M. C. Collier 14 at 19.50; S. C. J. Broad 16 at 23.75.

The Oratory School
P15 W10 L4 D1 A6

Master i/c P. L. Tomlinson   **Coach** J. B. K. Howell

A young side with just one player in the upper-sixth performed admirably and played positive cricket. Fifteen-year-old Benny Howell was the first boy in many years to average over 100, while England Under-16 batsman Dan Housego scored a wonderful century against MCC. Another 15 year-old, Michael Roberts, was top wicket-taker. It was the final year of Jonathan Howell's hugely successful spell as coach.
Batting B. A. C. Howell 802 at 100.25; D. M. Housego 618 at 51.50; P. L. Knox 205 at 29.28; M. D. T. Roberts 259 at 23.54; W. J. A. Macdonald 192 at 21.33.
Bowling M. D. T. Roberts 17 at 17.52; B. A. C. Howell 13 at 17.84; W. J. A. Macdonald 13 at 21.30; R. G. Ashton* 12 at 21.58.

Cameron Wake (*left*) hit 736 runs at 52.57 for Oundle, grabbed 30 wickets at 13.10, and played for ECB Schools; his team-mate Patrick Foster took 54 wickets – one behind the leading bowler.

Oundle School
P20 W15 D5 A3

Master i/c J. R. Wake
Coach V. d. M. Genis

Oundle won a record 15 games and their 75% success rate was the best for 126 years. Patrick Foster took more wickets than any seam bowler since 1895; the hard-hitting Robert Fahrenheim scored 2,536 runs in four years in the first team; Cameron Wake left with one of the best all-round records in school history and played for ECB Schools.

Batting R. M. Fahrenheim 786 at 60.46; C. J. Wake* 736 at 52.57; W. B. Wilson 401 at 33.41; J. W. R. Auld 363 at 30.25; M. K. Outar 415 at 29.64; G. P. Smith 275 at 27.50; J. E. Austen 165 at 20.62.

Bowling P. J. Foster 54 at 9.07; C. J. Wake 30 at 13.10; G. S. Krempels 30 at 16.73; J. E. Austen 16 at 29.56.

The Perse School, Cambridge
P17 W9 L3 D5 A1

Master i/c M. A. Judson
Coach D. C. Collard

Another highly successful season, with a record nine wins. Perse retained the County Under-19 Cup and Richard Hesketh broke the school record for runs by a fifth-former. The pace bowler Duncan Howells clean bowled 12 of his 27 victims.

Batting R. L. Hesketh 553 at 50.27; E. G. Pearson 255 at 31.87; A. P. Brookes 222 at 27.75; P. M. P. Frenay* 436 at 27.25; C. D. Rogers 228 at 20.72; O. J. Bassett 152 at 19.

Bowling D. E. Howells 27 at 18.03; R. L. Hesketh 24 at 22.25; A. S. Nathan 19 at 24.47; R. M. G. Bourne 21 at 25.85; A. R. L. Harris 16 at 28.37.

Plymouth College
P11 W5 L3 D3 A6

Master i/c G. C. Roderick

The highlight of 2004 was the four counties festival, held this year at Claysmore School, Dorset. The weather was good, much of the cricket excellent and Plymouth went unbeaten against Lord Wandsworth, Abbotsholme and the hosts. Philip Wass made 104 against Lord Wandsworth, and Charles Martin grabbed a hat-trick against Abbotsholme.

Batting P. Wass* 407 at 40.70; P. Garland 308 at 38.50; C. Martin 355 at 35.50.

Bowling B. Vince 15 at 20.13.

Pocklington School
P11 W2 L3 D6 A5

Master i/c D. Watton

Butcher's 12 wickets included a hat-trick.

Batting J. L. T. Bolam 495 at 55.00; C. L. Johnson 341 at 34.10; S. G. Butcher 254 at 28.22; A. V. Iyer 198 at 22.00; J. M. Hopwood 154 at 17.11.

Bowling A. V. Iyer 21 at 24.47; J. M. Butcher 12 at 28.50; D. A. Suddaby 10 at 31.40.

Portsmouth Grammar School
P12 W4 L7 D1

Master i/c D. Payne

Coach R. J. Maru

Batting E. J. Dickson-Lowe 273 at 27.30; D. M. Neville 216 at 24.00; M. A. Shaw* 226 at 22.60; S. A. Hodgson 183 at 18.30.

Bowling E. J. Dickson-Lowe 22 at 14.13; G. W. Morgan 10 at 18.00.

Prior Park College
P11 W6 L3 D2 A1

Master i/c T. J. J. Owens

Coach M. D. Browning

Good teamwork led to a very good season, with notable wins against MCC, Colston's and Dauntsey's and only one comprehensive defeat. Simon Williams was an outstanding leader and a constant threat to batsmen. But the undoubted star was 15-year-old James Campbell, who made four fifties and one score of 130, the highest in recent times for the college.

Batting J. R. A. Campbell 451 at 64.42; O. P. Lawson 158 at 31.60; A. R. Pynegar 188 at 23.50, M. J. Dann 161 at 20.12; K. J. Frere 163 at 18.11.

Bowling S. L. Williams* 20 at 10.65; K. P. Foley 13 at 14.07; M. J. Dann 13 at 21.53; K. J. Frere 10 at 22.30.

Queen Elizabeth's Hospital, Bristol
P8 W6 T1 D1 A3

Master i/c P. E. Joslin

Coach D. Forder

An experienced side, captained well by Ed Humphreys, went unbeaten. The bowling attack was led by Martin Jones and well supported by the younger Aaron Hemmings. The batting had good depth and there were fine contributions from Humphreys, Dan Chapman, Hassan Zaidi, John Sykes and John Colley. The most exciting game was a thrilling tie with Queen's, Taunton.

Batting E. J. Humphreys* 295 at 49.16; H. S. M. Zaidi 200 at 25.00; D. P. Chapman 158 at 22.57.

Bowling M. C. Jones 12 at 11.16; A. S. Hemmings 11 at 12.09.

Queen's College, Taunton
P13 W8 L2 T1 D2 A3

Master i/c A. S. Free

For the second season Calum Doutch led the side with great skill and by excellent example: he has been the college's most tactically astute leader of recent times. Doutch was supported by the all-round talents of Richard Catchpole, Oliver Stewart and Robert Dickins, though a young side bowled with greater confidence than they batted.

Batting C. H. Doutch* 564 at 51.27; O. J. Stewart 298 at 29.80; R. P. Dickins 201 at 25.12; R. S. E. Catchpole 226 at 20.54; F. I. Campbell-Wilson 199 at 15.30.

Bowling C. H. Doutch 17 at 12.64; R. S. E. Catchpole 10 at 14.20; O. J. Stewart 13 at 16.07; O. L. Scaife 10 at 16.10; A. R. Dodden 12 at 19.41; R. P. Dickins 13 at 20.23.

Radley College
P9 W5 L2 D2 A4

Master i/c A. J. T. Halliday

Coaches A. R. Wagner/A. G. Robinson

An enjoyable but short season, further truncated by four abandoned matches, was preceded by a tour to Malta.

Batting F. Qureshi 547 at 91.16; D. P. R. Clements 394 at 49.25; D. R. Dancy 153 at 38.25.

Bowling R. Haddon 14 at 16.57; O. J. W. Money 12 at 26.41.

Ratcliffe College
P11 L10 D1 A4

Master i/c R. M. Hughes

Coach M. J. Deane

Ratcliffe endured a very disappointing season, marred by bad weather, ever-increasing exam commitments and a lack of batting application. Those problems resulted in the only winless season in the 17 years Rik Hughes has been in charge of cricket. With all players bar one returning next year there is hope of improvement.

Batting J. A. Taylor* 277 at 25.18.

Bowling R. J. Cox 15 at 27.53.

Reading School
P10 W3 L2 D5 A4

Master i/c A. D. Walder

Coach M. Dawes

Batting let the side down, with potential not turned into runs, though the stop-start nature of the season – due to rain and examination breaks – did not help. The bowling strength of the team was clear but too many schools are reluctant to risk defeat in pursuit of victory and games can turn into non-events.

Batting G. J. Duncan* 289 at 32.11; A. P. Davidson 193 at 24.12.

Bowling A. P. Davidson 13 at 10.30; T. S. Vaal 27 at 14.40; M. D. Jubb 14 at 17.71; R. S. Mendhir 10 at 26.20.

Reed's School
P10 W4 L2 D4 A6

Master i/c M. R. Dunn

The best moments for a young side were beating MCC for the second time in three years and chasing down 285 against a powerful side from John Fisher School. Lucas Macdonald and Michael Wakefield set up the win with a school-record second-wicket partnership of 216; Macdonald finished 147 not out. Ben Bullock converted to bowling off-spinners and turned the ball prodigiously.

Batting M. P. Wakefield* 397 at 56.71; L. O. Macdonald 321 at 45.85; C. S. L. Mwanga-Magoye 178 at 44.50; S. Hussain 153 at 25.50.

Bowling M. P. Wakefield 18 at 18.22; S. Hussain 12 at 26.00; B. T. Bullock 19 at 26.47.

Repton School
P12 W7 L3 D2 A5

Master i/c F. P. Watson

Coach M. K. Kettle

Chris Paget, an off-spinner in the fifth-form, played four first-class matches for Derbyshire, becoming the county's youngest-ever Championship debutant and the 125th Reptonian to play first-class cricket. Luke Harvey's opening partnership with Ben Bridgen formed the heart of most big scores. The left-arm spinner Scott Chilman departed with 111 first-eleven wickets.

Batting B. D. Bridgen 546 at 60.66; A. J. Whiteley* 315 at 52.50; L. T. Harvey 460 at 46.00; A. W. Mace 254 at 36.28; C. D. Paget 172 at 28.66; J. E. Lamb 187 at 23.37.

Bowling L. T. Harvey 29 at 14.41; S. K. Chilman 11 at 23.45; A. W. Mace 12 at 27.25.

Rossall School
P16 W7 L8 D1

Master i/c A. Brunt

Rossall had a mixed year, with good victories against Stonyhurst and Arnold. The strengths were in the attack, with all bowlers contributing, and captaincy; in his third year as leader, Dingle was superb.

Batting R. V. Dingle* 408 at 29.14; P. F. Heald 389 at 27.78; F. Hameed 260 at 26.00; L. A. Dingle 305 at 23.46; J. B. Preston 268 at 22.33.

Bowling I. A. Swaine 27 at 13.18; L. A. Dingle 20 at 13.45; P. F. Heald 19 at 16.94; R. V. Dingle 32 at 17.40.

The Royal Grammar School, Colchester
P17 W3 L4 D10 A3

Master i/c R. L. Bayes

A poor record does not reflect the depth and resilience of the side. Due to an inability to take wickets quickly enough, there were too many draws when Colchester were well ahead. Omar Ahmed, still only 14, was the sole ever-present; Neil Davidson joined the school after playing for Zimbabwe Under-15 and hit the only hundred. James Warner's success with the ball and struggles with the bat were a surprise.

Batting N. Davidson 289 at 26.27; O. Ahmed 337 at 25.92; S. J. E. George 295 at 24.58; J. Warner* 325 at 21.66; G. L. Tuck 158 at 19.75; T. C. Overbury 208 at 17.33.

Bowling J. Warner 21 at 13.33; S. P. Rowe 14 at 16.85; J. J. Sandstra-Bennett 21 at 19.61; W. E. Stock 18 at 28.27; S. J. E. George 10 at 41.10.

The Royal Grammar School, Guildford
P14 W6 L4 D4

Master i/c S. B. R. Shore

Coach M. A. Lynch

Batting W. Sabey 419 at 41.90; C. Nelson 390 at 35.45; N. Symonds-Baig 178 at 22.25; P. Drake 199 at 22.11; A. Wilson* 181 at 20.11; C. Thomson 150 at 13.63.

Bowling W. Sabey 13 at 8.61; R. Colville 14 at 14.14; J. Thomas 13 at 17.23; S. Ackroyd 18 at 17.50; A. Wilson 13 at 26.61.

The Royal Grammar School, High Wycombe
P13 W5 L1 D7 A6

Master i/c S. J. Noyes

This was a stuttering, start-stop kind of season: eight matches out of 19 were rain-affected. A young side should come back stronger in 2005.

Batting L. Walker 437 at 39.72; J. Cousins 279 at 31.00; T. Collins 300 at 30.00; J. Cooper 234 at 29.25; J. Howlin* 218 at 19.81; J. Stevens 188 at 18.80.
Bowling T. Collins 18 at 13.00; L. Walker 15 at 22.73; J. Howlin 13 at 26.15.

The Royal Grammar School, Newcastle
P14 W5 L8 D1 A2

Master i/c O. L. Edwards
Batting M. C. Phillips* 530 at 48.18; I. A. Jones 290 at 36.25; G. R. Applegarth 397 at 28.35; R. G. Coughtrie 219 at 21.90.
Bowling C. R. Cleland 10 at 9.30; A. Sharma 18 at 18.11; R. A. Hopper 10 at 19.10; M. C. Phillips 15 at 20.40; I. A. Jones 10 at 21.20.

The Royal Grammar School, Worcester
P17 W8 L4 D5 A4

Master i/c M. D. Wilkinson
Liam O'Driscoll's fine batting was backed up by two centuries from fourth-former Nathan Newport (son of the coach and former England bowler, Phil) and excellent off-spin from Andrew Ford. It all culminated in a very good end to the season, including victory in the RGS Festival at High Wycombe.
Batting W. J. F. O'Driscoll 638 at 49.07; N. A. Newport 428 at 32.92; M. J. R. Illingworth 284 at 31.55; D. P. Harris* 345 at 26.53; S. C. Howell 265 at 17.66; G. W. R. Broadfield 217 at 14.46.
Bowling A. Ford 27 at 14.29; D. P. Harris 23 at 15.73; M. J. R. Illingworth 23 at 17.34; O. R. C. Butterworth 12 at 26.83; J. E. Dovey 13 at 27.07.

Rugby School
P14 W5 L3 D6 A1

Master i/c P. J. Rosser
Coach N. G. B. Cook
Despite no outstanding individual performances, 2004 was the most successful season for some years. The arrival of the former England slow left-armer Nick Cook as coach added dynamism and colour, and he brought out the best in each player. The school enjoyed a successful tour to Grenada in December.
Batting M. J. Wallis 205 at 25.62; G. W. Price 394 at 24.62; A. Davison 354 at 23.60; A. E. M. R. Jackson 305 at 19.06; T. B. M. Crawford* 235 at 16./8; R. C. R. Hardwick 184 at 15.33; F. D. H. MacLehose 199 at 15.30.
Bowling R. C. R. Hardwick 24 at 19.91; F. D. H. MacLehose 18 at 21.55; T. B. M. Crawford 13 at 22.84; J. O. Weaving 15 at 33.53; A. S. Cousens 11 at 43.36.

Rydal Penrhos, Colwyn Bay
P5 W4 L1

Master i/c M. T. Leach
A short season was further reduced by poor weather, and only a few players hit form. Joshua Leach, who has two years left at school, showed patience and maturity, while the captain, Andrew Fenby, always encouraged the younger players.
Batting J. M. Leach 186 at 46.50.
Bowling J. M. Leach 10 at 6.50.

St Albans School
P14 W8 L4 T2

Master i/c C. C. Hudson
The season was topped and tailed by pairs of defeats, but in between St Albans were unbeaten, including two ties, the first since 1976. Nick Lamb, in his third season as captain, played for Hertfordshire. His 28 wins as captain were a new school record. Gregory became only the second Under-16 to score 500 runs in a summer.
Batting N. J. Lamb* 401 at 66.83; S. G. Gregory 561 at 56.10; R. Vijh 179 at 25.57.
Bowling A. M. Addison 29 at 13.13; N. J. Lamb 23 at 13.60; R. W. Bateman 13 at 28.92; T. E. Cuppello 10 at 29.10.

St Benedict's School, Ealing
P12 W5 L4 D3 A1

Master i/c I. D. Stephen
All-rounder Huw Jones captained a successful side. The highlight was a six-wicket victory over MCC, the first in this long-running fixture. After three years in the team, opener Patrick Fallis finished 11th in the school's batting aggregates with 1,187 runs, while Jones totalled 76 wickets with his flighted leg-spin. Batting support came from Jeremy Kiernander and Ned Eckersley, a very promising Under-15 wicket-keeper/batsman. Ben Horan's medium-pace led the bowling, but the spinners, including Ravi Sidhu's off-breaks, took more wickets overall.
Batting P. A. Fallis 411 at 34.25; H. W. F. Jones* 358 at 32.54; J. E. Kiernander 253 at 25.30.
Bowling R. S. Sidhu 13 at 13.76; B. Horan 15 at 18.66; H. W. F. Jones 17 at 23.00; H. Orr-Ewing 11 at 24.45.

St Edmund's College, Ware
Master i/c T. W. Clark

P6 L4 D2 A2

A youthful, green side had a difficult time, though prospects look brighter for 2005, when Julian Jayawardena, the one outstanding performer of the summer, returns as captain. At times generating real pace, he grabbed 19 wickets in only six games. He also hit two fifties, though should perhaps have converted one into a century. A more substantial fixture list – and better weather – should give more scope for success. Jim Faithfull, who has now retired from running cricket here after 13 seasons, will be greatly missed.

Batting J. Jayawardena 164 at 27.33.
Bowling J. Jayawardena 19 at 9.84.

St Edmund's School, Canterbury
Master i/c M. C. Dobson

P11 W4 L7 A4

Coach H. L. Alleyne

St Edmund's finished the season with two outstanding run chases: against local rivals Kent College, they made 300 in 49.3 overs and, next day, a Danish Cricket Academy XI made 250 only for the belligerent St Edmund's batsmen to sail home in 27 overs. A talented group return in 2005, including the sons of two former Kent team-mates, Mark Benson and Chris Penn.

Batting J. S. Flood 153 at 38.25; M. T. Penn 181 at 30.16; J. J. Reed-Ashton 288 at 26.18; N. J. Copestake 252 at 25.20; O. J. Chalk 163 at 20.37; M. C. Craig 154 at 19.25; C. J. Plowman 151 at 16.77.
Bowling C. J. Plowman 16 at 18.50; C. E. Densham 10 at 23.20.

St Edward's School, Oxford
Master i/c J. Cope

P17 W7 L7 D3

Coach R. O. Butcher

After a poor start, St Edward's finished strongly. Freddie Hustler led the way with 31 wickets and formed a swift, hostile pairing with Murray Smith. John Barrett was the engine-room of the strong batting line-up with 513 runs.

Batting J. W. Barrett 513 at 39.46; N. D. Gleave 352 at 25.14; R. M. Smith* 300 at 23.07; H. J. Sutton 350 at 23.33; H. M. Redknap 224 at 20.36; D. R. Brewer 263 at 20.23; S. Farfan 152 at 16.88.
Bowling F. R. Hustler 31 at 13.38; R. M. Smith 26 at 14.76; R. T. A. Hazelton 15 at 21.00; M. E. Cunningham 17 at 21.64.

St George's College, Weybridge
Master i/c R. A. Ambrose

P17 W4 L6 D7 A4

Coach D. Ottley

A successful pre-season tour to Malta promised much, but the reality was rather more disappointing. However, the team has youth on its side, and there is real optimism for 2005.

Batting T. N. J. Doran 390 at 35.45; M. J. Ford 400 at 28.57; H. M. Grant 252 at 21.00; A. M. E. Willis 265 at 18.92; D. O. J. Holman 221 at 18.41; J. D. Hardman* 245 at 15.31.
Bowling H. M. Grant 26 at 16.38; D. W. McGahon 27 at 18.92; D. F. C. Pope 28 at 20.17; A. M. E. Willis 15 at 21.66.

St John's School, Leatherhead
Master i/c A. B. Gale

P13 W9 L4 A5

Coach I. Trott

Batting P. C. F. Scott 483 at 43.90; A. B. Lloyd 239 at 39.83; S. C. Barrett 277 at 34.62; P. D. Anderson* 285 at 25.90; K. D. S. Burge 262 at 23.81; P. M. Cohen 205 at 17.08.
Bowling P. M. Cohen 16 at 14.25; K. de Beer 13 at 15.30; S. W. Morton 11 at 16.18; P. N. Barrett 15 at 20.73; P. D. Anderson 18 at 22.50.

St Paul's School
Master i/c M. G. Howat

P13 W5 L1 D7

Coach A. G. J. Fraser

Strong batting was the secret of a decent summer, and only once was the side bowled out for less than 200. The bowling was tidy, but on good wickets sometimes lacked a cutting edge.

Batting A. Ashok 443 at 44.30; M. Maini 302 at 43.14; M. B. Kiernan* 352 at 39.11; M. E. Harries 250 at 35.71; J. J. Lofdahl 247 at 35.28; C. A. Elisha 372 at 33.81.
Bowling P. M. Newsome 15 at 30.80.

St Peter's School, York
Master i/c D. Kirby

P17 W10 D7 A2

This was an outstanding season for the school, who were unbeaten. The batting enjoyed real strength in depth with all-rounders Tom Bartram and James Wackett both averaging over 50. For the third year running, left-arm spinner Tom Woolsey took over 50 wickets, and he left with 183 first-team victims, way ahead of anyone else.

Off-spinner Chris Paget (*left*) made his Championship debut for Derbyshire shortly after finishing the fifth form at Repton; Sam Knott of Sutton Valence trailed only Ajmal Shahzad in the bowling averages, with 27 wickets at 5.51.

Batting J. M. Wackett 576 at 52.36; T. S. Bartram* 755 at 50.33; B. R. M. Hough 559 at 32.88; P. E. M. Puxon 256 at 28.44; T. J. Woolsey 328 at 27.33; I. D. Jarvis 197 at 21.88; J. Bairstow 256 at 21.33.
Bowling T. J. Woolsey 55 at 17.20; J. Bairstow 12 at 19.00; B. R. M. Hough 15 at 20.53; T. S. Bartram 20 at 25.20; H. J. Scott 11 at 39.45.

Sedbergh School
P15 W6 L4 D5 A2
Master i/c C. P. Mahon   **Coach** D. J. Fallows
Sedbergh tended either to win easily or lose narrowly. The outstanding individual was fifth former Michael Raikes, who passed 50 seven times and took 20 wickets, including a hat-trick against Kirkham School. The highlight was an end-of-season tour of Sri Lanka.
Batting M. K. Raikes 678 at 67.80; E. C. Parker* 321 at 32.10; O. J. Pimlott 256 at 21.33; D. G. Ford 242 at 20.16.
Bowling D. A. Clerey 16 at 10.00; W. P. Thornton 15 at 17.20; M. K. Raikes 20 at 21.35; A. J. Cowperthwaite 18 at 23.16; O. J. Pimlott 11 at 24.81.

Sevenoaks School
P15 W3 L10 D2 A2
Master i/c C. J. Tavaré
The batsmen did not make enough competitive scores, although the bowling ensured many matches were close-fought. The all-rounder Harry Florry enjoyed another good season; Simon Williams scored 230 runs in his last three innings; and Nick Tunnell was the most penetrative bowler. Four Under-14s represented the first team.
Batting S. J. Williams 397 at 49.62; H. S. R. Florry* 432 at 28.80; D. C. Franklin 156 at 15.60.
Bowling N. J. Tunnell 15 at 15.46; G. E. R. Alexander 16 at 19.75; H. S. R. Florry 13 at 28.61; C. J. Walker 10 at 28.80.

Shebbear College
P8 W1 L6 D1 A2
Master i/c A. Bryan
Batting C. A. Jenn 257 at 36.71.
Bowling C. A. Jenn 15 at 12.26; J. J. Corry* 10 at 19.90.

Sherborne School
P16 W9 L6 D1 A1

Master i/c G. D. Reynolds　　　　　　　　　　　　　Coach A. Willows

There is much enthusiasm for cricket at Sherborne and a young side achieved several good wins. Seamus Crawford led by example, including 164 not out against Sherborne Pilgrims, and was picked for England Under-17. Jack Jenkins, a young player, scored a match-winning 81 against Haileybury.

Batting S. A. Crawford* 493 at 41.08; J. H. C. Jenkins 255 at 28.33; A. A. Mackay-James 400 at 25.00; A. M. d'A. Willis 204 at 20.40; E. R. S. Kelly 219 at 19.90; M. H. Saunders 250 at 15.62.

Bowling S. A. Crawford 19 at 15.00; A. M. d'A. Willis 23 at 15.34; E. R. S. Kelly 10 at 17.00; C. H. O. Vollers 16 at 19.43; C. E. S. Clifton 16 at 20.25; P. B. Foster 17 at 20.41.

Shrewsbury School
P15 W8 L5 D2 A4

Master i/c A. Barnard

Shrewsbury were unbeaten until half-term, including wins over both Shropshire and Cheshire Under-17, but the season ebbed afterwards. James Gale bowled some excellent leg-spin and went on to play for Shropshire. James Taylor was selected for England Under-15 and promoted to the first team.

Batting T. Cox 315 at 31.50; I. Massey 297 at 27.00; J. S. Gale 253 at 25.30.

Bowling J. S. Gale 30 at 9.20; B. Marlow 16 at 17.75.

Simon Langton Grammar School
P8 W2 L4 D2 A2

Master i/c R. H. Green

A successful pre-season tour of Barbados should have been good preparation but a blunt-edged attack that leaked runs made victories scarce. In Barbados, the highlight was Freddie Phillips's 102 in a massive run-chase; at home, Jamie Morgan-Evans's 111 not out against the XL Club was scored in only 25 overs. Most players should return in 2005.

Batting J. Morgan-Evans 213 at 35.50.

Bowling No bowler took ten wickets. The leading bowler was P. Vinten*, who took seven at 22.00.

Sir Joseph Williamson's Mathematical School
P13 W9 L4

Master i/c D. J. Watson　　　　　　　　　　　　　Coach A. R. Hanman

This state-funded school played some excellent cricket in an enjoyable season. The first eleven were unlucky as they failed to retain two local trophies, losing in the semi-final of the Kent County Cup and the final of the League Cup. In total, the school's sides played 65 matches, and won 70% of them.

Batting D. R. Buckle 249 at 35.57; R. J. Sait 167 at 23.85; A. S. Ling* 186 at 23.25; C. J. Maguire 174 at 19.33.

Bowling L. Butcher 28 at 8.71; T. E. Hanman 23 at 9.82; L. Minshull 20 at 12.15.

Solihull School
P12 W4 L5 D3 A2

Master i/c S. A. Morgan　　　　　　　　　　　　　Coach C. Burrows

Batting J. Ord 537 at 44.75; S. Reddish 397 at 36.09; W. J. Mottram 238 at 26.44; B. J. Pugh* 209 at 22.41; J. Sammons 186 at 18.60.

Bowling W. J. Mottram 20 at 20.75; A. Madeley 18 at 22.94.

South Craven School
P8 W3 L2 D3 A3

Master i/c D. M. Birks　　　　　　　　　　　　　Coach D. A. Batty

Poor weather and cancellations marred a season which saw captain Matthew Walker make a school-record 39th first-team appearance, Michael Hebden score a maiden hundred, and several youngsters show talent, especially the captain's younger brother, Richard.

Batting M. J. Hebden 182 at 60.66.

Bowling M. Walker* 15 at 14.73.

Stockport Grammar School
P10 W3 L7 A5

Masters i/c R. Young/C. Wright　　　　　　　　　　　Coach D. J. Makinson

Bad weather could not diminish the positive attitude that ensured healthy competition for places. In the convincing win against Cheadle Hulme, Ben Garside claimed four for seven, while Scott Purdom hit 69 and grabbed three cheap wickets. During the very enjoyable tour to Malta, he went even better, stroking 71 and taking four for 13 against King Edward's, Lytham. Purdom aside, the key batsmen were Scott Trinder and Chris Jones, though the team must produce larger totals. The bowling fired only sporadically.

Batting C. Jones 169 at 28.16; S. Purdom 214 at 26.75.

Bowling S. Purdom 11 at 20.27.

Stowe School

Masters i/c J. A. Knott/C. Townsend

Eleven wins made for a fine season, if tempered by heavy losses to Radley and Oundle. Three players hit hundreds and two seized seven wickets or more in an innings. Stowe rounded things off nicely by hosting a highly successful four-team Twenty20 festival that used white balls, black stumps and coloured clothing. The players loved it, the cricket was exciting and it was a great way to finish the season – especially as Stowe won. Benefits included improved running and fielding skills.

Batting M. A. Nelson 529 at 52.90; A. G. F. Leon 421 at 42.10; H. D. L. Taylor 165 at 41.25; G. G. White* 391 at 27.92; A. D. Cossins 265 at 26.50.

Bowling G. G. White* 35 at 12.54; M. A. Nelson 23 at 14.39; C. J. W. Sheldon 13 at 18.46.

Strathallan School

Master i/c R. H. Fitzsimmons

Strathallan could make a case for having one of the stronger sides in Scotland. Led for a second year by the spinner Ross Anders, they lost only at the Dulwich festival, and to a powerful MCC side. Tom Hine scored two hundreds and Australian Sam Graves one, against Strathallans. Fifth former Jamie Cachia had a fine first season opening the batting, while Jono Becks often broke through the opposition's top order, three times taking five wickets in an innings. Charles Leadbetter's swing bowling was good support.

Batting S. Graves 375 at 41.66; T. W. F. Hine 392 at 39.20; J. D. Cachia 259 at 37.00.

Bowling J. F. Becks 28 at 13.35; R. Anders* 20 at 15.90; C. R. Leadbetter 16 at 16.81; S. Graves 10 at 29.50.

Sutton Valence School

Masters i/c W. D. Buck/A. P. Igglesden

Playing a mixture of declaration and limited-overs games, the team lost only once – and then off the last ball. The pace attack had a Caribbean flavour: Arl Richardson is the son of Richie, the former West Indies captain, while Orlando "Baby" Peters hails from Antigua. However, the leading bowlers were Sam Knott, whose left-arm swing accounted for 27 batsmen at under six, and Ben Spencer. Dominating the aggressive batting was wicket-keeper Ashley Jackson, who smashed three hundreds – and is now sixth in the list of school run-scorers.

Batting A. S. Jackson 841 at 76.45; E. P. Spencer 275 at 27.50; O. L. Peters 299 at 27.18; G. Palmer* 236 at 26.22.

Bowling S. O. Knott 27 at 5.51; B. T. Spencer 19 at 15.26; A. R. Richardson 17 at 15.47; A. R. Carr 11 at 15.72; O. L. Peters 13 at 22.38.

Taunton School

Master i/c S. T. Hogg

Taunton enjoyed an excellent season with many convincing victories under the astute leadership of James Hayward. James will captain the side again in 2005, with eight other regular players also returning. Eltham College, from Melbourne, Australia, were the only opponents to get on top of a strong bowling attack, chasing down 240 for victory in an end-of-season fixture.

Batting J. A. Hayward* 378 at 42.00; A. W. H. Carroll 353 at 39.22; J. W. Cooper 185 at 26.42; J. J. Bess 269 at 22.41.

Bowling A. D. C. Mason 21 at 10.71; H. C. P. Carpenter 21 at 11.76; A. W. H. Carroll 18 at 15.33; J. A. Hayward 16 at 16.81; E. G. Phelps 12 at 22.25.

Tiffin School

Master i/c M. J. Williams

Had they been able to polish off their opponents' last pairs, Tiffin might have won another four games. Despite other frustrations such as rain and exams, this was a good year. For Jonathan Mellett and Arun Harinath, it was outstanding: Mellett, in his first season in the team, claimed 32 wickets with his slow left-arm, while Harinath broke the school batting record for the second time in two years with a masterful 226 against Emanuel. He and Kapilan Balasubramaniam, who hit 136, added 318 for the second wicket, another school record. Harinath later played for ECB Schools South.

Batting A. Harinath* 642 at 64.20; K. Balasubramaniam 493 at 41.08; H. M. Vanderman 325 at 36.11; N. Desai 262 at 21.83; D. Patel 166 at 18.44.

Bowling J. S. Mellett 32 at 14.34; S. Selvarajan 12 at 15.58; H. E. Weale 11 at 24.63.

Tonbridge School

P17 W15 L2 A2

Master i/c J. Hodgson **Coach** N. Leamon

The first team set a new school record for wins in a season, thanks largely to an attack which bowled out the opposition in all but two of the matches. That was an outstanding achievement, given the excellent surfaces most games were played on.

Batting C. E. D. Makepeace 537 at 48.81; J. W. K. Beeny* 755 at 41.94; O. G. K. Howick 485 at 34.64; A. O. J. Shales 324 at 31.50; A. C. Howeson 227 at 22.70; E. J. Bonner 209 at 17.41; C. F. Young 172 at 15.63; C. M. M. Hill 151 at 15.10.

Bowling J. W. K. Beeny 15 at 6.80; C. F. Young 35 at 10.14; A. C. Howeson 10 at 12.50; O. G. K. Howick 32 at 14.09; C. M. M. Hill 25 at 15.24; H. S. C. Thomson 21 at 17.52; C. C. H. Hammond 13 at 26.30.

Trent College

P9 W5 L4 A4

Master i/c F. Seal **Coach** J. A. Afford

As well as nine 50-over games, the college played four 20-over matches, including a victory against England Women. A total of 300 for eight against Nottingham High School was the second-highest in college history. Spurr completed six catches and six stumpings.

Batting G. Johnston* 303 at 37.87; I. R. Smallwood 175 at 25.00; M. S. Spurr 154 at 19.25.

Bowling N. D. McKeown 14 at 17.14.

Trinity School, Croydon

P7 W1 L5 D1 A5

Master i/c M. D. Ferrao **Coach** R. H. Miller

Batting J. P. May 235 at 33.30; C. J. Turner 151 at 21.57.

Bowling D. Amin 10 at 15.40; J. P. May 10 at 16.60; T. E. Fox 10 at 18.30.

Truro School

P6 W3 L1 D2 A3

Master i/c A. Lawrence

Due to terrible weather only six games were finished, which was very disappointing.

Batting S. De Gruchy 251 at 50.20; R. J. Kendall 201 at 28.71; B. Pollard* 192 at 27.42.

Bowling No bowler took ten wickets. The leading bowler was R. J. Kendall, who took nine at 20.67.

University College School

P10 W3 L5 D2 A4

Master i/c S. M. Bloomfield **Coach** J. P. Cooke

UCS played much quality, competitive cricket but lacked support bowling to turn winning positions into victories.

Batting V. R. Nair 305 at 43.57; D. Patel 171 at 28.50; G. Gedroyc 235 at 26.11.

Bowling B. C. Bloom 25 at 12.04.

Uppingham School

P14 W5 L6 D3 A1

Master i/c C. C. Stevens **Coach** T. R. Ward

Most teams struggled to take wickets at Uppingham as the relaid square played beautifully. In the closing half of the season captain Jamie Sharrock returned from injury to boost a young side, who also missed another of 2003's better batsmen. Harry Judd, who scored 252 runs last season, left Uppingham in 2003 to become a full-time drummer in the pop group McFly. The summer ended well for the side, with four wins in the last five matches, but even better for Harry Judd: McFly topped the UK singles chart twice, with "Five Colours In Her Hair" and "Obviously".

Batting A. P. C. Collins 306 at 51.00; J. C. J. Sharrock* 209 at 29.85; S. W. Peters 330 at 27.50; H. A. Barton 313 at 24.07; M. T. Heslop 258 at 21.50.

Bowling T. G. C. Thornton 12 at 21.66; T. H. Higgs 14 at 27.21; B. R. Crowder 10 at 36.00.

Victoria College, Jersey

P14 W5 L5 D4 A2

Master i/c M. Smith **Coach** C. Minty

Captain Tom Minty took most wickets, scored most runs and captained the team fantastically well in a difficult season. Early in the summer, the side often failed to put good batting and good bowling together in the same match. But later on they clicked, beating Elizabeth College, Guernsey and playing superb cricket on tour to defeat Wellington School in a well-judged chase. After that, the weather wrecked things.

Batting T. E. Minty* 451 at 37.58; R. Mohanty 260 at 37.14; S. S. J. Dewhurst 336 at 25.84; O. Hughes 237 at 21.54; H. I. Maclachlan 154 at 19.25.

Bowling S. P. Warren 19 at 17.63; T. E. Minty 23 at 18.56; H. I. Maclachlan 15 at 20.20; T. G. Wherry 14 at 20.85.

Warwick School

P11 W4 L6 D1 A6

Master i/c G. A. Tedstone   **Coach** F. Klopper

Batting A. R. Wilkinson* 414 at 37.63; K. Chibber 249 at 24.90; R. L. Rigby 225 at 20.45; D. S. Dhillon 168 at 16.80.

Bowling D. S. Dhillon 10 at 9.50; A. D. R. Harris 13 at 15.61; A. R. Wilkinson 13 at 21.53; C. J. Carr 15 at 22.93; D. H. Wood 12 at 25.50.

Watford Grammar School

P8 W4 L1 D3 A3

Master i/c J. D. R. Williams   **Coach** P. C. Smith

Batting Z. A. Hussain 237 at 47.40; U. B. Nawaz 150 at 30.00.

Bowling C. M. Keppell 10 at 11.50; R. J. Willis 11 at 14.36; Z. A. Hussain 12 at 14.66.

Wellingborough School

P14 W7 L5 D2 A3

Master i/c L. M. Hilton   **Coach** N. Knight

A young team with a good work ethic won half their fixtures. Greg Evans scored heavily, and William Chudley was an invaluable all-rounder. Both players still have two more years in the first team.

Batting G. D. Evans 562 at 51.09; W. Chudley 332 at 25.53; S. Caunt 210 at 17.50; S. Singh 201 at 15.46.

Bowling G. Chudley 16 at 13.56; W. Chudley 27 at 15.81; N. Patel 14 at 17.21; S. Caunt 18 at 18.05.

Wellington College

P16 W5 L8 D3 A3

Masters i/c C. M. Oliphant-Callum/R. I. H. B. Dyer/T. J. Head

Coaches P. J. Lewington/N. A. Brett

Batting J. D. Atkinson 360 at 32.72; P. J. W. Young* 408 at 29.14; A. J. T. Briers 167 at 27.83; A. C. R. Digweed 193 at 27.57; J. A. Barker 161 at 26.83; B. J. E. Kingsnorth 285 at 25.90; R. M. D. Gotla 206 at 22.88; S. J. E. Stitcher 254 at 16.93; K. Singh 171 at 15.54; B. W. Marchant 167 at 13.91.

Bowling E. G. C. Young 21 at 28.80; P. J. W. Young 20 at 32.30; J. A. Barker 10 at 37.90.

Wellington School

P14 W2 L8 D4

Master i/c M. H. Richards

After an outstandingly successful 2003 this was a rebuilding year, with many young players contributing. Edward Young, who has three more years in the side, is a promising left-arm spinner.

Batting J. D. Crowther 239 at 39.83; S. C. Marsh 251 at 27.88; J. W. Clarkson 177 at 22.12.

Bowling S. C. Marsh 12 at 14.00; T. Collard 23 at 23.00; R. J. Collard 12 at 24.16.

Wells Cathedral School

P11 W2 L7 D2 A4

Master i/c M. C. H. Stringer   **Coach** R. J. Kitzinger

After 23 years as Master in Charge, Mike Stringer handed over to Richard Kitzinger.

Batting C. R. Dauncey 242 at 30.25; E. J. Chalmers 191 at 21.22; H. A. Lemanski 163 at 14.81.

Bowling B. A. Jones 14 at 16.35; M. P. Brandon* 14 at 20.28; C. R. Dauncey 11 at 22.27.

West Buckland School

P12 W9 L3

Master i/c L. Whittal-Williams   **Coach** M. T. Brimson

This was the best season for many years. Sixteen-year-old Daniel Bowser held together the batting and also bowled some useful left-arm spin. Jonathan Hickman recovered from missing last season with a shoulder injury and spearheaded the bowling. He had the best bowling figures in five of the 12 matches he played.

Batting D. J. Bowser 548 at 54.80; A. N. Loosemore 165 at 18.33; M. A. Stevens 160 at 17.77; S. F. Bowen 162 at 13.50.

Bowling J. C. Hickman* 26 at 11.34; D. J. Higgs 13 at 14.92; D. J. Bowser 14 at 16.71; C. M. Kingdom 13 at 20.15; T. I. Wallace 11 at 29.09.

Westminster School

P10 W5 L1 D4 A4

Master i/c J. D. Kershen

This was the first team's most successful season since 1987. They completed several demanding run-chases in a polished manner, and in the field fallible catching was compensated by the out-swing bowling of Low and the off-spin of Radhakrishnan.

Batting D. C. R. Bamford* 382 at 47.75; C. A. Cooke 309 at 51.5; D. H. S. Brodie 180 at 25.71.

Bowling R. H. C. Low 20 at 16.85; G. Radhakrishnan 19 at 22.94.

Whitgift School

P10 W2 L7 D1 A1

Master i/c D. M. Ward   Coach N. M. Kendrick

With an inexperienced side this season was always likely to be difficult. The best game by far was against a strong Tonbridge side; chasing just under 250, Whitgift finished 20 short, after an excellent 93 from Laurie Evans. In 2005, the school will be looking to turn tight finishes into victories.

Batting M. N. W. Spriegel* 346 at 49.42; L. Evans 346 at 38.44; S. Ratnayake 232 at 33.14.

Bowling M. N. W. Spriegel 17 at 17.23; M. I. McEwan 11 at 20.54; L. Evans 12 at 21.66.

Winchester College

P15 W6 L5 D4 A3

Master i/c C. J. Good   Coach B. L. Reed

A very good pre-season tour of the Caribbean, where the college won all seven of their games, was followed by a poor first half of term and a good second half.

Batting M. D. R. Skinner* 544 at 41.84; J. R. Irvine-Fortescue 450 at 32.14; J. M. Burridge 286 at 23.83; T. L. Hemmingway 247 at 22.45; H. Mohammed 267 at 20.53; S. R. A. Cheetham 195 at 19.5.

Bowling T. L. Hemmingway 25 at 18.96; J. A. Kenyon 17 at 20.35; R. N. Shipster 16 at 25.25; H. Mohammed 18 at 27.61.

Wolverhampton Grammar School

P10 W5 L2 D3 A6

Master i/c N. H. Crust   Coach T. King

In a season ruined by the weather, it was the bowling and fielding that will be remembered. Getting to the semi-final of the first-ever "20s" 20-over competition was an obvious highlight.

Batting C. J. Brook 184 at 36.80; J. R. Acaster 183 at 30.50; V. J. Wheeler 180 at 30.00; C. W. Lowe 160 at 16.00.

Bowling V. J. Wheeler 17 at 10.23; C. J. M. Mulvihill* 10 at 10.60; C. S. Adey 12 at 11.75; R. J. Browning 10 at 12.70; C. W. Lowe 11 at 13.27.

Woodbridge School

P10 L6 D4 A3

Master i/c R. J. H. Thorley

Batting J. J. C. Maclean 160 at 26.66; C. W. Tunstall 160 at 22.85; J. G. Bloomfield 174 at 21.75.

Bowling S. K. Lincoln 11 at 25.72.

Woodhouse Grove

P13 W7 L2 D4 A7

Master i/c R. I. Frost   Coach G. R. J. Roope

Quick bowler Ajmal Shahzad made history in May when he became the first Yorkshire-born Asian to play for the county first team. Ajmal also took 19 wickets in five games for Woodhouse Grove, before a back injury. Uzair Mahomed scored 131 not out on his debut and played for the Yorkshire Academy, while 14-year-old Tom Dalton followed up his 87 not out against QEGS Wakefield with a 35-ball 79 against Arnold, hitting 74 in boundaries. Woodhouse Grove lost only once to schoolboy opposition.

Batting U. Mahomed 428 at 47.55; A. Shahzad 456 at 45.60; T. K. Dalton 256 at 36.57; R. H. Haslam* 316 at 26.33; D. A. R. Blackburn 213 at 17.75.

Bowling A. Shahzad 19 at 4.63; T. I. Wellings 22 at 13.81; O. Wolfenden 18 at 17.16; U. Mahomed 13 at 19.53; J. J. Wheatley 13 at 22.46.

Worksop College

P16 W2 L8 D6 A3

Master i/c I. Parkin   Coach A. Kettleborough

A young but talented team had a poor season judged by results alone. There were encouraging performances against big schools but some naïve cricket was played at times. Caleb Mierkalns had a very good season for a 15-year-old.

Batting L. J. Carlisle 292 at 26.54; C. M. Mierkalns 401 at 25.06; S. Cowles 279 at 21.46; B. H. F. Stroud 298 at 21.28.

Bowling C. M. Mierkalns 17 at 17.05; D. D. Brown 18 at 18.11; I. H. Qadoos 24 at 19.95.

Wrekin College

P10 W5 D5 A4

Master i/c M. de Weymarn   Coach J. P. Dawson

The side developed beyond expectations and were particularly strong in batting: against Hereford Cathedral School the openers scored 100 in the first ten overs. Asif Sultan played for ECB Schools against Bangladesh; and is a member of the Derbyshire Academy. Jean-Paul Duminy, an exchange student at Wrekin in 2001, made his one-day international debut for South Africa against Sri Lanka.

Batting J. Hendricks 305 at 61.00; J. P. Andrews 365 at 52.14; A. Sultan 223 at 37.16.

Bowling N. Fern 11 at 12.81; A. Sultan 19 at 16.89; B. Summers* 16 at 17.68; J. Savage 10 at 22.30.

Wycliffe College
P8 W2 L5 D1 A1

Master i/c D. A. Pemberton
Coach M. J. Kimber

With only two departures, a young team have the potential to win many more matches in 2005. The outstanding performance was 92 not out by Harding against MCC.

Batting J. McGoldrick 158 at 31.60; R. Temple 158 at 26.33.
Bowling T. Williams 14 at 18.57; S. Russell 10 at 22.50.

YOUNG CRICKETER OF THE YEAR, 2004

Ian Bell was voted Young Cricketer of the Year by members of the Cricket Writers' Club. Surrey players have won the award eight times, Middlesex and Lancashire seven, and Yorkshire six. Worcestershire and Durham are the only first-class counties that have not had a winner.

1950 R. Tattersall (Lancs)	1978 D. I. Gower (Leics)
1951 P. B. H. May (Surrey)	1979 P. W. G. Parker (Sussex)
1952 F. S. Trueman (Yorks)	1980† G. R. Dilley (Kent)
1953 M. C. Cowdrey (OU & Kent)	1981 M. W. Gatting (Middx)
1954 P. J. Loader (Surrey)	1982 N. G. Cowans (Middx)
1955 K. F. Barrington (Surrey)	1983 N. A. Foster (Essex)
1956 B. Taylor (Essex)	1984 R. J. Bailey (Northants)
1957 M. J. Stewart (Surrey)	1985 D. V. Lawrence (Glos)
1958 A. C. D. Ingleby-Mackenzie (Hants)	1986 A. A. Metcalfe (Yorks)
1959 G. Pullar (Lancs)	J. J. Whitaker (Leics)
1960 D. A. Allen (Glos)	1987 R. J. Blakey (Yorks)
1961 P. H. Parfitt (Middx)	1988 M. P. Maynard (Glam)
1962 P. J. Sharpe (Yorks)	1989 N. Hussain (Essex)
1963 G. Boycott (Yorks)	1990 M. A. Atherton (Lancs)
1964 J. M. Brearley (CU & Middx)	1991 M. R. Ramprakash (Middx)
1965 A. P. E. Knott (Kent)	1992 I. D. K. Salisbury (Sussex)
1966 D. L. Underwood (Kent)	1993 M. N. Lathwell (Somerset)
1967 A. W. Greig (Sussex)	1994 J. P. Crawley (Lancs)
1968 R. M. H. Cottam (Kent)	1995 A. Symonds (Glos)
1969 A. Ward (Derbys)	1996 C. E. W. Silverwood (Yorks)
1970 C. M. Old (Yorks)	1997 B. C. Hollioake (Surrey)
1971 J. Whitehouse (Warwicks)	1998 A. Flintoff (Lancs)
1972 D. R. Owen-Thomas (CU & Surrey)	1999 A. J. Tudor (Surrey)
1973 M. Hendrick (Derbys)	2000 P. J. Franks (Notts)
1974 P. H. Edmonds (CU & Middx)	2001 O. A. Shah (Middx)
1975 A. Kennedy (Lancs)	2002 R. Clarke (Surrey)
1976 G. Miller (Derbys)	2003 J. M. Anderson (Lancs)
1977 I. T. Botham (Somerset)	2004 I. R. Bell (Warwicks)

Teams are those played for at the time.

† An extra award, in memory of Norman Preston, Editor of *Wisden* 1951–1980, was made to C. W. J. Athey (Yorks).

YOUTH CRICKET, 2004

UNDER-17

Under all too rare azure skies, the 2004 Under-17 County Championship was won by Warwickshire, in a style far more dramatic than their bloodless triumph in the senior version. After choosing to bat in the final at Bristol, on a good-looking Nevil Road pitch, Warwickshire were skittled by Surrey for 212, inside 82 of their allotted 100 overs. Only a century from Chris Cheslin prevented a rout. However, Surrey's failures kept the game alive: they lost key batsmen to poor shots and staggered to 45 for three. Laurie Evans made a revitalising 90 not out from No. 8 but, as the excitement rose, he ran out of partners with Surrey 12 short.

Warwickshire, like their seniors, fielded a formidable batting line-up. Omar Ali made 200 not out, the season's best, against Shropshire, and Nicholas James was the heaviest run-scorer overall. This suited the format of the competition. In the two-day group games, counties were awarded ten points for a first-innings lead and only five more for an outright win. The final was a straight limited-overs match.

This is now the highest-level county youth competition. The Under-19 Championship was disbanded at the end of 2002, followed by the ECB 38-County Cup at the end of 2003, after just one season as an Under-21 competition.

UNDER-15 CRICKET

The Under-15 Bunbury Festival was dominated by the West region, who beat Midlands in the final, and by the booming bat of the South's Billy Godleman. A powerful 15-year-old left-hander, Godleman hit 333 runs in four innings – 135 more than the previous year's top-scorer – and showed why he has already played eight games for Middlesex Second XI. David English, the competition organiser, rated Godleman's 143 against the West as the best innings at the festival in more than ten years.

It won Godleman a *Daily Telegraph*/Bunbury scholarship and a week at the full ECB Academy over the winter. Other scholarships went to Greg Wood, from Queen Elizabeth Grammar School, Wakefield, for spin bowling; Stuart Meaker, from Cranleigh School, for fast bowling; and Alex Wakely, from Bedford School, for wicket-keeping.

Torrential rain prevented Surrey defending their Lord's Taverners' Under-15 County Championship. Not a ball was bowled during the finals at Oundle School, where Yorkshire (northern champions) and Wales (western champions) joined Surrey. Given the round-robin format, a first-day washout scuppered the whole competition, and it was abandoned.

Big scorers with big futures? Omar Ali (*left*) piled up an unbeaten double-hundred for Under-17 champions Warwickshire; Billy Godleman, of Middlesex and the South, dominated the national Under-15 festival.

In the limited-overs Cup, Lancashire's strong attack bowled them to victory. In the final they restricted Middlesex to just 158 for nine in 50 overs, with Chris Tipper, an all-rounder from Hyde, ending with 5–1–8–2; later in 2004 he was called up by England Under-15. In reply, Christopher Clarke led Lancashire home with an unbeaten 79, the highest score at the finals, which also featured Warwickshire and Hampshire.

UNDER-14 CRICKET

Midlands ended the Under-14 Regional Festival, played for the first time at the Academy ground in Loughborough, with two wins from three games, though both were narrow scrapes. No single player grabbed hold of the week: there were no centuries and, despite often damp conditions, the leading wicket-taker was James Iles, with just eight from three games. A right-arm seamer from Maidstone Grammar, Iles was later selected as one of the youngest members of Kent's Academy.

UNDER-13 CRICKET

The Under-13 regional festival at King's College, Taunton produced far fewer runs than the sun-drenched 2003 competition. Aquib Zulfiqar, an opening batsman from Lancashire, bucked the trend, scoring 175 in three innings, comfortably the highest aggregate. He helped North win two of their three games: Midlands could produce nothing to match Zulfiqar's 120, and South were shot out short of a small target by Christopher France of Cheshire, who grabbed five for 40. But by far the outstanding bowler, with 12 wickets, was Jack Leach of West. He showed extraordinary control, having earlier in the summer bowled 52 dot balls in succession for Somerset Under-13 against Wales.

Warwickshire cruised the final of the Under-13 County Cup at Oundle School. They reached 175 for six in their 40 allotted overs; Yorkshire fired to 68 for one but then flopped to 115 all out against a strong attack. However, the performance of the tournament came in the third v fourth play-off, where Surrey's Daniel Newton batted all 40 overs for 137 not out, leading his side to a daunting 221 – and victory – against Devon. For the second year running, a declaration competition was also played, with eight regional groups but no national rounds, an attempt to encourage wicket-taking bowlers.

Millfield School, who had a successful summer even by their standards, won the David English/ESCA Under-13 Schools Cup. But for the second successive year a state school without a cricket field or nets reached the final. Under grey Headingley skies, Christchurch Middle School, from Stone in Staffordshire, were overawed, and skittled out for 49; Millfield won by ten wickets, and repeated their feat of 1997, lifting the schools cup at both Under-13 and Under-15 level.

After being left sponsorless and endangered in 2003, the cup was supported by David English of the Bunburys. In recognition of Christchurch's achievement, English arranged to buy them a net.

UNDER-11 CRICKET

Sion Mills Primary School, from County Tyrone in Northern Ireland, won the National Under-11 BBC Kwik Cricket final at Trent Bridge. Sion Mills, where cricket has flourished after being introduced in the 19th century by anglicised local mill owners, beat North Wooton Community School, from King's Lynn.

Eagle House from Berkshire failed by a whisker to defend their national hard-ball title, losing to Parkside Prep School from Surrey.

TEST MATCH SPECIAL UNDER-15 YOUNG CRICKETER OF THE YEAR

David Wheeldon, from Cheadle near Stoke-on-Trent, won the fifth BBC Test Match Special Under-15 Young Cricketer of the Year Award, decided by a panel of ECB national judges. A top-order batsman and effective off-spinner for England Under-15, he also played for Staffordshire County Board and attended the Worcestershire CCC County Academy. The previous winners were Samit Patel (Nottinghamshire), Adam Harrison (Glamorgan), Phillip Holdsworth (Yorkshire) and Ben Wright (Glamorgan).

WOMEN'S CRICKET, 2004

SARAH POTTER

NEW ZEALAND WOMEN IN ENGLAND, 2004

Hove, with its striped deckchairs and whirling seagulls, is an incongruous outpost for anything radical. That does not explain truthfully why only 500 spectators turned out to watch the world's first Twenty20 international, however: it was because it was played by women. England and New Zealand were rightly proud to have made history. Nail-biters did not have to chew their quicks as the tourists won by nine runs, but it was an innovative start to the tour.

It proved to be New Zealand's zenith, too, in a series encompassing five 50-over internationals and a single Test. The World Cup holders arrived in Hove with a fearsome reputation, and had just mauled Ireland in three one-day games. England, though, were the team who finally enhanced their stature. Led by Clare Connor, they beat New Zealand in a one-day series for the first time in 20 years, and more emphatically than the 3–2 margin suggests.

Despite victories at Northampton and a rain-affected Old Trafford, New Zealand were disappointing. They were less fit than England, tactically naïve and increasingly timid at the crease. The performances of Rebecca Steele, a 19-year-old left-arm spinner, and Louise Milliken, a 20-year-old seam bowler, were their only obvious consolations. Perhaps it would have been different had Emily Drumm – one of the world's great players – not been forced to stay at home because of work commitments.

None of that ought to lessen England's achievement. In their second season under coach Richard Bates, they developed the balance, power and confidence to challenge the best. No longer was the once brittle batting so perilously reliant on Charlotte Edwards and Claire Taylor. Several players made valuable contributions under pressure. Meanwhile, the bowling attack, led to good effect by left-arm seamer Lucy Pearson, gained added bite from 18-year-old Jenny Gunn.

Rosalie Birch influenced most games, either with the bat or her wily off-spin, but 19-year-old Isa Guha, a petite swing bowler, returned career-best figures of five for 22 at Derby and was chosen by Bates as England's Player of the Series. Steele, who claimed three wickets in each of the tourists' two wins, unsurprisingly took the New Zealand award.

Bad weather was the winner in the one-off Test at Scarborough, but England were again the classier, more thrusting unit. Laura Newton, who scored a maiden Test century, struck the only six in the seven matches. It swung thoughts full circle to things radical; why not bring in the boundaries for women's games? Sixes and fours, after all, are what the (missing) crowds want to see.

NEW ZEALAND TOURING PARTY

M. A. M. Lewis (*captain*), H. M. Tiffen (*vice-captain*), N. J. Browne, S. K. Burke, M. F. Fahey, P. B. Flannery, A. J. Green, A. M. Little, S. J. McGlashan, B. H. McNeill, A. L. Mason, L. E. Milliken, R. J. Rolls, R. J. Steele, H. M. Watson.
    Coach: M. J. F. Shrimpton.   *Manager:* C. A. Campbell.

NEW ZEALAND TOUR RESULTS

Matches – Played 14: Won 10, Lost 3, Drawn 1.

Note: Matches in this section were not first-class.

At Trinity CC, Dublin, July 22. **First one-day international: New Zealand won by 200 runs.**
Toss: New Zealand. **New Zealand 278-3** (50 overs) (R. J. Rolls 50, M. F. Fahey 66, M. A. M. Lewis 63); **Ireland 78** (36.1 overs).

At Merrion CC, Dublin, July 24. **Second one-day international: New Zealand won by 112 runs.**
Toss: Ireland. **New Zealand 272-5** (50 overs) (B. H. McNeill 88*); **Ireland 160** (44.3 overs) (I. M. Joyce 67*; A. J. Green 5-15).

At Merrion CC, Dublin, July 25. **Third one-day international: New Zealand won by 77 runs.**
Toss: New Zealand. **New Zealand 232-7** (50 overs) (H. M. Watson 115*); **Ireland 155** (45.1 overs) (Extras 51).
    New Zealand won the series with Ireland 3–0.

At Cambridge, July 29. **New Zealanders won by 47 runs.** Toss: Sussex. **New Zealanders 153-6** (20 overs); **Sussex 106-7** (20 overs).
    This was a Twenty20 match against newly-crowned county champions Sussex.

At Cambridge, July 30. **New Zealanders won by 128 runs.** Toss: MCC. **New Zealanders 279-7** (50 overs) (M. F. Fahey 87, H. M. Tiffen 74); **MCC 151-7** (50 overs).

At Horsham, August 2. **New Zealanders won by five wickets.** Toss: ECB Development XI. **ECB Development XI 222-4** (50 overs) (A. Brindle 123); **New Zealanders 223-5** (46 overs) (S. J. McGlashan 100*).

At Horsham, August 3. **New Zealanders won by 117 runs.** Toss: ECB Development XI. **New Zealanders 228-7** (50 overs) (M. A. M. Lewis 52); **ECB Development XI 111** (45.5 overs).

At Hove, August 5. **Twenty20 international: New Zealand won by nine runs.** Toss: New Zealand. **New Zealand 131-8** (20 overs) (R. A. Birch 4-27); **England 122-7**.

At Hove, August 6. **First one-day international: England won by 45 runs.** Toss: England. **England 221-9** (50 overs) (L. K. Newton 57); **New Zealand 176** (46.5 overs) (M. F. Fahey 64).

At Chelmsford, August 10 (day/night). **Second one-day international: England won by seven wickets.** Toss: New Zealand. **New Zealand 126** (46.2 overs) (J. L. Gunn 4-26, R. A. Birch 4-29); **England 127-3** (36 overs).

At Northampton, August 13. **Third one-day international: New Zealand won by five wickets.** Toss: England. **England 144-9** (50 overs), **New Zealand 147-5** (48.3 overs).

At Derby, August 15. **Fourth one-day international: England won by 38 runs.** Toss: New Zealand. **England 197-7** (50 overs) (C. M. Edwards 70, C. J. Connor 56*); **New Zealand 159-9** (50 overs) (I. T. Guha 5-22).

At Manchester, August 17. **Fifth one-day international: New Zealand won by 18 runs (D/L method).** Toss: England. **New Zealand 141-8** (46 overs); **England 129** (41 overs).
    Rain reduced the match to 46 overs a side, and further rain revised England's total to 148 in 46 overs. England won the one-day series 3–2.

ENGLAND v NEW ZEALAND

Test Match

At Scarborough, August 21, 22, 23, 24. Drawn. Toss: England. Test debuts: K. H. Brunt, J. L. Gunn; S. K. Burke, P. B. Flannery, R. J. Rolls.

The forked lightning that sizzled over the pavilion on the final afternoon provided more drama than the play. Downpours had already washed out the third day, and it was England who felt the more aggrieved. They had dismissed a tired and uncertain-looking New Zealand in 94 overs on the pedestrian opening day. Contrasting centuries by the openers, Charlotte Edwards and Laura Newton, underlined England's superiority. Newton, whose timing mocked the slow, low surface, reached her maiden Test hundred with her 14th four – she also had one six – when Edwards, usually the side's most free-flowing batsman, was still on 54. They put on 163 together and, although England then lost all ten wickets for 122 in the quest for quick runs, a lead of 70 ought to have been decisive. Then came the north-eastern monsoon. After some edgy defence on the closing morning, Maia Lewis ensured New Zealand's safety with a rearguard 60.

Player of the Match: L. K. Newton.

Close of play: First day, England 1-0 (Edwards 1, Newton 0); Second day, England 285; Third day, No play.

New Zealand

M. F. Fahey c Brindle b Guha	19	– b Brunt	39
P. B. Flannery lbw b Connor	46	– c Smit b Guha	18
*M. A. M. Lewis run out	17	– c Smit b Brunt	60
H. M. Tiffen lbw b Gunn	14	– not out	26
†R. J. Rolls lbw b Brunt	71	– not out	0
S. J. McGlashan b Birch	6		
A. L. Mason lbw b Guha	1		
N. J. Browne lbw b Pearson	23		
L. E. Milliken c Newton b Pearson	4		
S. K. Burke not out	1		
R. J. Steele c Newton b Gunn	0		
B 1, l-b 7, w 5	13	L-b 2, w 2, n-b 2	6

1/49 (1) 2/67 (2) 3/91 (4) 4/112 (3) 215   1/39 (2) 2/79 (1) (3 wkts) 149
5/125 (6) 6/126 (7) 7/199 (8)   3/148 (3)
8/205 (5) 9/211 (9) 10/215 (11)

Bowling: *First Innings*—Pearson 22–6–51–2; Gunn 9–3–18–2; Brunt 18–4–45–1; Guha 20–7–39–2; Birch 14–3–33–1; Connor 11–3–21–1. *Second Innings*—Pearson 17–6–31–0; Brunt 10–4–36–2; Gunn 10–2–23–0; Guha 8–2–33–1; Connor 8–3–15–0; Birch 4–0–8–0; Edwards 1.1–1–1–0.

England

C. M. Edwards lbw b Steele	117	I. T. Guha lbw b Steele	6
L. K. Newton c Rolls b Mason	103	K. H. Brunt not out	0
R. A. Birch c Steele b Burke	1		
*C. J. Connor c Browne b Mason	5	L-b 4, w 1, n-b 2	7
L. Greenway run out	12		
A. Brindle c Steele b Milliken	10	1/163 (2) 2/177 (3) 3/189 (4)	285
J. L. Gunn b Milliken	5	4/230 (5) 5/245 (6) 6/259 (7)	
†J. Smit run out	19	7/259 (1) 8/259 (9)	
L. C. Pearson lbw b Steele	0	9/277 (10) 10/285 (8)	

Bowling: Milliken 18–3–49–2; Steele 29–5–62–3; Browne 10–2–40–0; Burke 19–5–57–1; Mason 22–2–68–2; Flannery 1–0–5–0.

Umpires: S. A. Garratt and A. L. Roberts.

ENGLISH WOMEN'S CRICKET, 2004

The Super Fours, a tournament intended to prepare the nation's elite women players for international competition, kicked off its third season with a facelift, introducing coloured clothing, regional teams and a day of Twenty20 matches. The V Team, led by Laura Newton and made up of northern-based players, won both the Twenty20 competition, at the Rose Bowl in May, and the main trophy at Loughborough University in June.

Sussex, though, confirmed that the power base in the County Championship had shifted south, winning the tournament, held in Cambridge, for the second successive season. Clare Connor's side achieved the feat in emphatic style, winning five one-day matches in as many days. Surrey, who lost all their games, were relegated to Division Two, while Somerset pipped Berkshire by half a point to earn promotion. Durham, who finished bottom, dropped down to the Challenge Cup competition, which had replaced the third division, with Cheshire moving up. Sussex stayed on for an extra day, to play the New Zealanders at Fenner's in a Twenty20 match, to prepare the tourists for the inaugural Twenty20 international. New Zealand won by 47 runs.

Thrumpton, from Nottinghamshire, reached both the domestic club finals, and lost them both in one weekend. For the second year running, they lost the Premier League showdown, between the winners of the North and South divisions, to Brighton & Hove. Thrumpton's Jenny Gunn claimed four for ten, but Connor led Brighton to a convincing victory. The National Knockout Cup, against Kent Invicta, was a much closer contest, settled by just six runs. England opener Charlotte Edwards proved the decisive difference: she scored 38 out of Invicta's 108, and then broke Thrumpton hearts by taking four for 25 in ten overs of leg-spin.

The ECB Plate final, held on the same day, was a case of in with the old and out with the new. Shepperton, established in 1979, defeated Trafford, a mere four seasons old, by a whopping 217 runs, thanks to an unbeaten 109 from Jenny Tetley.

The age-group County Championship finals were both spoiled by August rains: Warwickshire and Sussex shared the Under-15 title, while Worcestershire and Kent were joint Under-17 champions.

In the same August week that the senior England side clinched their one-day series win over New Zealand, the Under-21 squad triumphed in the European Cup. Coached by Barbara Daniels, the former England player and administrator who oversaw the merger between the Women's Cricket Association and the ECB in 1998, the Under-21s defeated their counterparts from Scotland, Holland and Ireland, the host nation, to lift the trophy, before beating the senior Ireland team in two one-day matches.

Note: Matches in this section were not first-class.

SUPER FOURS, 2004

	Played	Won	Lost	Tied	Bonus Points	Points
V Team.	6	3	2	1	8	59
Super Strikers	6	3	3	0	8	53
Braves	6	3	3	0	2	47
Knight Riders	6	2	3	1	4	40

Win = 15 pts, tie = 6 pts.

FRIZZELL COUNTY CHAMPIONSHIP, 2004

Division One

	Played	Won	Lost	Bonus Points	Points
Sussex	5	5	0	46	106
Kent.	5	4	1	43.5	91.5
Yorkshire	5	3	2	36.5	72.5
Lancashire.	5	2	3	34	58
Nottinghamshire	5	1	4	34.5	46.5
Surrey	5	0	5	26	26

Division Two

	Played	Won	Lost	Bonus Points	Points
Somerset.	5	4	1	41	89
Berkshire	5	4	1	40.5	88.5
Staffordshire	5	3	2	36.5	72.5
Hampshire.	5	2	3	35	59
Middlesex	5	2	3	31.5	55.5
Durham	5	0	5	23	23

Win = 12 pts.

Surrey were relegated and Somerset promoted. Since 2003, Division Three had been replaced by a County Challenge Cup, featuring three groups; Group One winners Cheshire were promoted to Division Two, replacing Durham.

Group One: Cheshire 63.5 pts, Cumbria 31.5 pts, Derbyshire 26 pts, Leicestershire 6.5 pts.

Group Two: Northamptonshire 53 pts, Essex 27 pts, Norfolk 20 pts, Hertfordshire 19 pts.

Group Three: Warwickshire 62.5 pts, Worcestershire 49 pts, Wales 33 pts, Wiltshire 14 pts.

ECB NATIONAL LEAGUE FINAL, 2004

At Loughborough, September 4. **Brighton & Hove won by 77 runs.** Toss: Brighton & Hove. **Brighton & Hove 182-7** (50 overs) (J. L. Gunn 4-10); **Thrumpton 105** (49.1 overs).

ECB NATIONAL KNOCKOUT FINAL, 2004

At Loughborough, September 5. **Kent Invicta won by six runs.** Toss: Kent Invicta. **Kent Invicta 108** (35.5 overs); **Thrumpton 102-9** (40 overs) (C. M. Edwards 4-25).

ECB PLATE FINAL, 2004

At Loughborough, September 5. **Shepperton won by 217 runs.** Toss: Shepperton. **Shepperton 270-2** (40 overs) (M. Steele 55, J. Tetley 109*); **Trafford 53** (28.4 overs) (I. Cronje 5-12).

Opposite: Palmy days. Ed Smith of England A on the offensive against Karnataka at the Jain International Residential School Ground in Bangalore, February 2004. *Picture by Stu Forster, Getty Images*

PART SIX

Overseas Cricket

FEATURES OF 2003-04 AND 2004

Double-Hundreds (49)

400*†‡	B. C. Lara	West Indies v England (Fourth Test) at St John's.
380	M. L. Hayden	Australia v Zimbabwe (First Test) at Perth.
309	V. Sehwag	India v Pakistan (First Test) at Multan.
300*	M. L. Love	Queensland v Victoria at St Kilda.
300*	Shoaib Khan	Peshawar v Quetta at Peshawar.
270‡	R. Dravid	India v Pakistan (Third Test) at Rawalpindi.
270‡	K. C. Sangakkara	Sri Lanka v Zimbabwe (Second Test) at Bulawayo.
266*	Z. de Bruyn	Easterns v Griqualand West at Kimberley.
264	B. J. Hodge	Victoria v Indians at Melbourne.
261*	R. R. Sarwan	West Indies v Bangladesh (Second Test) at Kingston.
260*‡	D. S. Jadhav	India A v Kenyans at Nairobi.
257‡	R. T. Ponting	Australia v India (Third Test) at Melbourne.
251‡	D. S. Jadhav	Maharashtra v Madhya Pradesh at Pune.
250*	A. G. Puttick	Western Province v Griqualand West at Cape Town.
249	M. S. Atapattu	Sri Lanka v Zimbabwe (Second Test) at Bulawayo.
247	R. D. Shah	Kenyans v Pakistan A at Nairobi.
245	S. Chanderpaul	West Indians v Free State at Bloemfontein.
242‡	R. T. Ponting	Australia v India (Second Test) at Adelaide.
241*	S. R. Tendulkar	India v Australia (Fourth Test) at Sydney.
237	D. P. M. D. Jayawardene	Sri Lanka v South Africa (First Test) at Galle.
237	D. S. Lehmann	South Australia v New South Wales at Sydney.
234	T. R. Gripper	Manicaland v Mashonaland at Mutare.
233‡	R. Dravid	India v Australia (Second Test) at Adelaide.
232‡	K. C. Sangakkara	Sri Lanka v South Africa (Second Test) at Colombo.
228*‡	Y. Venugopal Rao	South Zone v England A at Gurgaon.
222‡	R. Dravid	India v New Zealand (First Test) at Ahmedabad.
219	C. H. Gayle	Jamaica v Leeward Islands at St Elizabeth.
218	Shahriar Hossain	Bangladesh A v DHA at Karachi.
216	M. G. Bevan	New South Wales v Tasmania at Sydney.
216	G. M. Strydom	Matabeleland v Manicaland at Bulawayo.
215*	K. D. Aphale	Maharashtra v Goa at Pune.
215*	A. S. Das	Bengal v Gujarat at Ahmedabad.
212*	D. J. Hussey	Victoria v New South Wales at Newcastle.
211*	S. L. Campbell	Barbados v Leeward Islands at St Thomas.
210	B. M. Rowland	Karnataka v Assam at Bangalore.
209*	M. J. Horne	Auckland v Northern Districts at Auckland.
207*	H. H. Kanitkar	Maharashtra v Services at Aurangabad.
207‡	D. S. Jadhav	Maharashtra v Himachal Pradesh at Ichalkaranji.
207	M. O. Odumbe	Kenyans v Leeward Islands at Anguilla.
206*	A. Jadeja	Delhi v Baroda at Vadodara.
205	Aamer Bashir	Multan v Hyderabad at Multan.
204	A. D. Soma	Manicaland v Matabeleland at Mutare.
203	S. G. Law	Queensland v Western Australia at Brisbane.
202*	D. A. Fitzgerald	South Australia v Tasmania at Hobart.
202‡	B. C. Lara	West Indies v South Africa (First Test) at Johannesburg.
201*	M. A. Aronstam	Northerns v Boland at Paarl.
201*	M. W. Goodwin	Western Australia v New South Wales at Sydney.
200*‡	D. S. Jadhav	Maharashtra v Orissa at Cuttack.
200*‡	Y. Venugopal Rao	India A v Kenyans at Nairobi.

† *National record.*

‡ *Jadhav scored four double-hundreds; Dravid three; Lara, Ponting, Sangakkara and Venugopal Rao all two.*

Hundred on First-Class Debut

143	Arshad Ali.	United Arab Emirates v Nepal at Sharjah.
151	F. Y. Fazal	Vidarbha v Jammu and Kashmir at Nagpur.
103	C. D. Hartley	Queensland v South Australia at Brisbane.
102	A. J. Nye	Queensland v New South Wales at Sydney.
106	H. P. Padmasanka	Nondescripts v Police at Colombo.
101*	C. A. Philipson.	Queensland v Tasmania at Hobart.
141	Usman Saeed	Rawalpindi v Multan at Rawalpindi.
120	Wajihuddin	Karachi Port Trust v National Bank at Rawalpindi.
152*	A. R. White.	Ireland v Holland at Deventer.

Three Hundreds in Successive Innings

M. T. G. Elliott (Victoria)	154*	v South Australia at Melbourne;
	166 102* }	v Tasmania at Melbourne.
S. Kalawithigoda (Colts)	110*	v Ragama at Colombo;
	114	v Kurunegala Youth at Kurunegala;
	110	v Sebastianites at Moratuwa.
H. H. Kanitkar (Maharashtra).	123*	v Goa at Pune;
	112 207* }	v Services at Aurangabad.
V. R. Mane (West Zone and Mumbai)	127*	v North Zone at Dharmasala;
	154	v Hyderabad at Mumbai;
	106	v Tamil Nadu at Chennai.
R. D. Shah (Kenyans).	135	v Uganda at Nairobi;
	124	v Pakistan A at Nairobi;
	247	v Pakistan A at Nairobi.
D. S. Smith (Windward Islands)	159	v Leeward Islands at St Maarten;
	180	v Kenyans at St Vincent;
	154	v West Indies B at St George's.

Hundred in Each Innings of a Match

Aamer Bashir	108	100*	Pakistan Customs v DHA at Karachi.
M. T. G. Elliott	166	102*	Victoria v Tasmania at Melbourne.
G. V. Grace	102	102*	North West v KwaZulu-Natal at Durban.
M. L. Hayden	117	132	Australia v Sri Lanka (Second Test) at Cairns.
M. J. Horne.	118	209*	Auckland v Northern Districts at Auckland.
H. H. Kanitkar	112	207*	Maharashtra v Services at Aurangabad.
G. J. Mail	128	152*	New South Wales v South Australia at Sydney.
K. P. Pietersen	104	115	England A v South Zone at Gurgaon.
P. S. A. N. Shiroman .	103	101	Sebastianites v Kurunegala Youth at Kurunegala.
G. M. Strydom.	128	104	Matabeleland v Manicaland at Mutare.
Yasir Hameed.	170	105	Pakistan v Bangladesh (First Test) at Karachi.
Yuvraj Singh	106	148	North Zone v East Zone at Mohali.

Carrying Bat through Completed Innings

S. A. Asnodkar.	126*	Goa (235) v Orissa at Cuttack.
S. L. Campbell.	211*	Barbados (432) v Leeward Islands at St Thomas.
A. S. Das	215*	Bengal (479) v Gujarat at Ahmedabad.
S. S. Das	124*	East Zone (283) v England A at Amritsar.
G. Gambhir	111*	North Zone (191) v West Zone at Dharmasala.
Imran Ahmed.	152*	Barisal (266) v Rajshahi at Barisal.
P. J. Ingram	105*	Central Districts (201) v Auckland at Auckland.
D. S. Jadhav	260*	India A (492) v Kenyans at Nairobi.
V. R. Mane	127*	West Zone (277) v North Zone at Dharmasala.
K. S. Rodrigo	83*	Ragama (190) v Bloomfield at Gampaha.
K. Waghela	95*	Saurashtra (228) v Orissa at Cuttack.

Most Sixes in an Innings

11   M. L. Hayden (380) . . . .   Australia v Zimbabwe (First Test) at Perth.
11   C. M. Spearman (133) . . . .   Central Districts v Auckland at Auckland.

Most Runs in Boundaries in an Innings

218 (38 × 4, 11 × 6)   M. L. Hayden (380) . . . . .   Australia v Zimbabwe (First Test) at Perth.
200 (50 × 4)   Shoaib Khan (300*) . . . . .   Peshawar v Quetta at Peshawar.

Long Innings

Mins
778   B. C. Lara (400*) . . . . . .   West Indies v England (Fourth Test) at St John's.
740   R. Dravid (270) . . . .   India v Pakistan (Third Test) at Rawalpindi.
731   D. S. Jadhav (251) . . . . . .   Maharashtra v Madhya Pradesh at Pune.
658   A. S. Das (215*) . . . .   Bengal v Gujarat at Ahmedabad.
635   D. S. Jadhav (200*) . . . . .   Maharashtra v Orissa at Cuttack.
635   S. C. Joseph (195) . . . . . .   Leeward Islands v Kenyans at Anguilla.
622   M. L. Hayden (380) . . . . .   Australia v Zimbabwe (First Test) at Perth.
613   S. R. Tendulkar (241*) . . .   India v Australia (Fourth Test) at Sydney.
610   M. L. Love (300*) . . . . . .   Queensland v Victoria at St Kilda.
607   D. A. Fitzgerald (202*) . . .   South Australia v Tasmania at Hobart.

Unusual Dismissals

Handled the Ball
Al Sahariar . . . .   Dhaka v Chittagong at Dhaka.
Junaid Zia . . . .   Rawalpindi v Lahore at Lahore.

First-Wicket Partnership of 100 in Each Innings

109   134   Taufeeq Umar/Imran Farhat, Pakistan v South Africa (First Test) at Lahore.
165   119   M. T. G. Elliott/J. L. Arnberger, Victoria v Queensland at Melbourne.
114   182   Salman Butt/Rizwan Aslam, Lahore v Hyderabad at Sheikhupura.

Highest Partnerships

First Wicket
309   D. S. Smith/R. K. Currency, Windward Islands v Kenyans at St Vincent.
301   G. C. Smith/H. H. Gibbs, South Africa v West Indies (Fourth Test) at Centurion.
281   M. S. Atapattu/S. T. Jayasuriya, Sri Lanka v Zimbabwe (First Test) at Harare.
255   J. L. Langer/M. L. Hayden, Australia v Sri Lanka (Second Test) at Cairns.

Second Wicket
438†   M. S. Atapattu/K. C. Sangakkara, Sri Lanka v Zimbabwe (Second Test) at Bulawayo.
369   C. T. Perren/S. G. Law, Queensland v Western Australia at Brisbane.
281   D. A. Fitzgerald/G. S. Blewett, South Australia v Tasmania at Hobart.
251   M. T. G. Elliott/B. J. Hodge, Victoria v Tasmania at Melbourne.
250   M. D. Bell/M. S. Sinclair, New Zealand A v Sri Lanka A at Queenstown.

Third Wicket
343   Jannisar Khan/Shoaib Khan, Peshawar v Quetta at Peshawar.
336   V. Sehwag/S. R. Tendulkar, India v Pakistan (First Test) at Multan.
288   R. N. Manyande/A. D. Soma, Manicaland v Matabeleland at Mutare.
286   T. J. Friend/C. B. Wishart, Midlands v Manicaland at Kwekwe.
284   R. S. Ricky/D. Mongia, Punjab v Uttar Pradesh at Meerut.
273*   K. D. Aphale/H. H. Kanitkar, Maharashtra v Goa at Pune.

270   S. M. Katich/S. R. Waugh, New South Wales v Tasmania at Hobart.
262   T. T. Samaraweera/D. P. M. D. Jayawardene, Sri Lanka v England (Third Test) at Colombo.
251   H. H. Gibbs/J. H. Kallis, South Africa v West Indies (Third Test) at Cape Town.

Fourth Wicket
353   S. R. Tendulkar/V. V. S. Laxman, India v Australia (Fourth Test) at Sydney.
313† R. P. Arnold/R. S. Kaluwitharana, Western Province v Uva Province at Colombo.
309* J. Moss/D. J. Hussey, Victoria v Western Australia at Perth.
276   G. M. Strydom/M. L. Nkala, Matabeleland v Manicaland at Bulawayo.

Fifth Wicket
359   S. Chanderpaul/R. D. Jacobs, West Indians v Free State at Bloemfontein.
347*† M. J. Horne/A. C. Barnes, Auckland v Northern Districts at Auckland.
303   R. Dravid/V. V. S. Laxman, India v Australia (Second Test) at Adelaide.
262* R. R. Sarwan/S. Chanderpaul, West Indies v Bangladesh (Second Test) at Kingston.
243   Y. Venugopal Rao/I. G. Srinivas, Andhra v Kerala at Visakhapatnam.
236   M. L. Love/J. R. Hopes, Queensland v Victoria at St Kilda.
229* Y. Venugopal Rao/A. T. Rayudu, India A v Kenyans at Nairobi.

Sixth Wicket
282* B. C. Lara/R. D. Jacobs, West Indies v England (Fourth Test) at St John's.
271   R. P. A. H. Wickremaratne/W. L. P. Fernando, Sinhalese v Ragama at Colombo.
246* Abdul Razzaq/Kamran Akmal, Lahore v Rawalpindi at Lahore.
233   M. L. Hayden/A. C. Gilchrist, Australia v Zimbabwe (First Test) at Perth.
229   Sharjeel Ashraf/Aamer Iqbal, DHA v Bangladesh A at Karachi.

Seventh Wicket
277   Shelzad Malik/Khalid Mahmood, Sialkot v Karachi at Sialkot.
250   C. J. Nevin/M. D. J. Walker, Wellington v Otago at Wellington.
225   C. L. Cairns/J. D. P. Oram, New Zealand v South Africa (Second Test) at Auckland.
218   C. D. Hartley/A. A. Noffke, Queensland v South Australia at Brisbane.
212   S. Sriram/K. D. Karthik, Tamil Nadu v Railways at Chennai.

Eighth Wicket
237† A. M. Blignaut/D. T. Hondo, Mashonaland v Manicaland at Mutare.
186   W. L. P. Fernando/F. H. S. M. Silva, Sinhalese v Panadura at Colombo.
170   D. P. M. D. Jayawardene/W. P. U. J. C. Vaas, Sri Lanka v South Africa (First Test) at Galle.
168   H. H. Streak/A. M. Blignaut, Zimbabwe v West Indies (First Test) at Harare.
163   A. Maregwede/R. W. Price, Midlands v Manicaland at Mutare.

Ninth Wicket
209   P. J. Wiseman/B. P. Martin, New Zealand A v Sri Lanka A at Christchurch.
182   Naved Ashraf/Iftikhar Anjum, ZTBL v Karachi Port Trust at Peshawar.
154   W. P. U. J. C. Vaas/M. R. C. N. Bandaratilleke, Uva Province v North Central Province at
      Dambulla.

Tenth Wicket
114   K. E. A. Upashantha/P. S. Liyanage, Colts v Burgher at Colombo.
103   J. A. Morkel/C. K. Langeveldt, South Africa A v Zimbabwe A at Bulawayo.

† *National record.*

Eight Wickets in an Innings (12)

9-74	Ali Asad	United Arab Emirates v Nepal at Sharjah *(on first-class debut).*
9-76	J. M. Davison.	Canada v USA at Fort Lauderdale *(second innings).*
8-28	F. Thomas	Windward Islands v Kenyans at St Vincent.
8-43	H. M. R. K. B. Herath. . .	Moors v Police at Colombo.
8-43	T. Taibu	Mashonaland v Midlands at Kwekwe.
8-54	U. Chatterjee	Bengal v Hyderabad at Kolkata.

8-59	C. P. Kulkarni	Maharashtra v Services at Aurangabad.
8-61	J. M. Davison	Canada v USA at Fort Lauderdale *(first innings)*.
8-67	Syed Russell	Khulna v Barisal at Barisal.
8-113	Azam Hussain	Karachi v Rawalpindi at Karachi.
8-129	V. A. Browne	Leeward Islands v Trinidad & Tobago at Pointe-à-Pierre *(on first-class debut)*.
8-141	A. Kumble	India v Australia (Fourth Test) at Sydney.

Twelve Wickets in a Match (12)

17-137	J. M. Davison	Canada v USA at Fort Lauderdale.
13-107	N. D. Hirwani	Madhya Pradesh v Haryana at Gwalior.
13-126	Ali Asad	United Arab Emirates v Nepal at Sharjah *(on first-class debut)*.
13-236	Azam Hussain	Karachi v Rawalpindi at Karachi.
12-47	P. Joubert	Northerns v Eastern Province at Port Elizabeth.
12-52	Saifullah Khan	Rajshahi v Dhaka at Rangpur.
12-102	S. S. Paul	India A v Zimbabwe A at Harare.
12-116	C. D. de Lange	Boland v Gauteng at Randjesfontein.
12-134	G. Vashisht	Haryana v Jammu and Kashmir at Rohtak.
12-160	L. Klusener	KwaZulu-Natal v Western Province at Cape Town.
12-192	Nasir Khan	DHA v Pakistan Customs at Karachi.
12-279	A. Kumble	India v Australia (Fourth Test) at Sydney.

Outstanding Innings Analyses

| 7.4–4–7–7 | Junaid Zia | Pakistan Customs v Bangladesh A at Karachi. |
| 4.4–3–3–5 | Vineet Sharma | Punjab v Andhra at Mohali. |

Hat-Tricks (6)

Alok Kapali	Bangladesh v Pakistan (Second Test) at Peshawar.
S. J. Benn	Barbados v Leeward Islands at St Thomas.
J. P. Bennett	West Indies B v Kenyans at Molyneux.
A. M. Blignaut	Zimbabwe v Bangladesh (First Test) at Harare.
M. J. Hoggard	England v West Indies (Third Test) at Bridgetown.
R. Ramkumar	Tamil Nadu v Karnataka at Bangalore.

Match Double (100 runs and 10 wickets)

| H. H. Streak | 107, 40; 4-49, 7-55 | Matabeleland v Mashonaland at Bulawayo. |

Six Wicket-Keeping Dismissals in an Innings

6 ct, 1 st	C. O. Browne	Barbados v Jamaica at Kingston.
7 ct	S. G. Clingeleffer	Tasmania v Western Australia at Perth.
6 ct	Aamer Iqbal	DHA v KRL at Karachi.
6 ct	M. S. Dhoni	Bihar v Vidarbha at Nagpur.
4 ct, 2 st	M. S. Dhoni	India A v Zimbabwe Select XI at Harare.
4 ct, 2 st	Hasibul Haque	Khulna v Sylhet at Sylhet.
4 ct, 2 st	R. S. Kaluwitharana	Western Province v Uva Province at Colombo.
6 ct	N. R. Mongia	Baroda v Punjab at Vadodara.
6 ct	K. O. Otieno	Kenyans v Pakistan A at Nairobi.
6 ct	T. L. Tsolekile	Western Province v Gauteng at Cape Town.

Nine Wicket-Keeping Dismissals in a Match

7 ct, 4 st	M. S. Dhoni	India A v Zimbabwe Select XI at Harare.
9 ct, 1 st	C. O. Browne	Barbados v Jamaica at Kingston.
9 ct, 1 st	K. H. Hibbert	Jamaica v Barbados at Kingston.
8 ct, 2 st	W. M. S. M. Perera	Sinhalese v Moors at Colombo.
10 ct	W. A. Seccombe	Queensland v Tasmania at Brisbane.
9 ct	M. S. Dhoni	Bihar v Vidarbha at Nagpur.
8 ct, 1 st	Hanif Malik	Pakistan Customs v WAPDA at Hyderabad.

There were ten wicket-keeping dismissals for Karachi against Peshawar at Karachi; Rashid Latif caught five in Peshawar's first innings, and Hasan Raza five more after taking over in their second.

Five Catches in an Innings in the Field

5	S. A. Khare	Vidarbha v Tripura at Agartala.
5	Wasim Jaffer	Mumbai v Tamil Nadu at Chennai.

Six Catches in a Match in the Field

7	M. L. Hayden	Australia v Sri Lanka (First Test) at Galle.
6	M. D. Bell	Wellington v Canterbury at Wellington.
6	D. P. M D. Jayawardene	Sri Lanka v Zimbabwe (First Test) at Harare.
6	Taufeeq Umar	Pakistan v South Africa (Second Test) at Faisalabad.
6	Wasim Jaffer	Mumbai v Kerala at Mumbai.
6	C. L. White	Victoria v Queensland at Brisbane.
6	C. L. White	Victoria v New South Wales at Melbourne.

No Byes Conceded in Total of 500 or More

W. Bossenger	Griqualand West v Easterns (528) at Kimberley.
M. V. Boucher	South Africa v New Zealand (595) (Second Test) at Auckland.
T. A. Bula	North West v Northerns (518-6 dec.) at Potchefstroom.
S. G. Clingeleffer	Tasmania v Western Australia (562-6 dec.) at Hobart.
H. A. P. W. Jayawardene . .	Sri Lanka v New Zealand A (570) at Lincoln.
R. S. Kaluwitharana	Western Province v North Central Province (547) at Colombo.
Kamran Akmal	Pakistan A v Kenyans (502) at Nairobi.
T. R. Peiris	Uva Province v Western Province (507-9 dec.) at Colombo.
M. S. K. Prasad	Andhra v Mumbai (504-6 dec.) at Vijayawada.
T. Taibu	Zimbabwe v Sri Lanka (713-3 dec.) (Second Test) at Bulawayo.

Highest Innings Totals

751-5 dec.	West Indies v England (Fourth Test) at St John's.
735-6 dec.	Australia v Zimbabwe (First Test) at Perth.
718-7.	Leeward Islands v Kenyans at Anguilla.
713-3 dec.	Sri Lanka v Zimbabwe (Second Test) at Bulawayo.
710	Victoria v Queensland at Melbourne.
705-7 dec.	India v Australia (Fourth Test) at Sydney.
683	Colts v Galle at Colombo.
675-5 dec.	India v Pakistan (First Test) at Multan.
658-9 dec.	South Africa v West Indies (Second Test) at Durban.
630-6 dec.	New Zealand v India (Second Test) at Mohali.
628-8 dec.	Sri Lanka v England (Third Test) at Colombo.
622	Moors v Air Force at Colombo.
618	West Indians v Free State at Bloemfontein.
613-3 dec.	Victoria v Western Australia at Perth.

613. . . . . . .   Mumbai v Tamil Nadu at Chennai.
610-7 dec. . . .   Multan v Hyderabad at Multan.
605-7 dec. . . .   Queensland v Victoria at St Kilda.
604-6 dec. . . .   South Africa v West Indies (Fourth Test) at Centurion.
600. . . . . . .   India v Pakistan (Third Test) at Rawalpindi.

Lowest Innings Totals

30 . . . .   Andhra v Punjab at Mohali.
30 . . . .   Bangladesh A v Pakistan Customs at Karachi.
47 . . . .   West Indies v England (First Test) at Kingston.
51 . . . .   Police v Galle at Colombo.
60 . . . .   Allied Bank v ZTBL at Rawalpindi.
63†. . . . . . .   DHA v KRL at Karachi.
63 . . . .   Central Districts v Wellington at Napier.
66 . . . .   Sylhet v Dhaka at Sylhet.
66†. . . . . . .   Singha v Air Force at Colombo.
67 . . . .   Moors v Air Force at Colombo.
67 . . . .   Khulna v Dhaka at Dhaka.
68 . . . .   Sui Gas v Karachi Port Trust at Peshawar.
70 . . . .   Eastern Province v Griqualand West at Kimberley.
70†. . . . . . .   University of West Indies Vice-Chancellor's XI v England XI at Kingston.
71 . . . .   Uttar Pradesh v Railways at Varanasi.
73†. . . . . . .   Nondescripts v Galle at Colombo.
73†. . . . . . .   Windward Islands v Trinidad & Tobago at Port-of-Spain.
73 . . . .   Moratuwa v Singha at Colombo.

† *One batsman absent or retired hurt.*

Highest Fourth-Innings Totals

513-9†. . . . .   Central Province v Southern Province at Kandy (set 512).
503-4 . . . . . .   South Zone v England A at Gurgaon (set 501).
495. . . . .   South Australia v New South Wales at Sydney (set 521).
471. . . . .   Southern Province v North Central Province at Galle (set 491).
455-7 . . . . . .   Victoria v New South Wales at Newcastle (set 455).

† *World record fourth-innings total to win a match.*

Match Aggregate of 1,500 Runs

1,747 for 25 . .   India (705-7 dec. and 211-2 dec.) v Australia (474 and 357-6) (Fourth Test) at Sydney.
1,648 for 28 . .   South Africa (532 and 335-3 dec.) v West Indies (427 and 354-5) (Third Test) at Cape Town.
1,617 for 31 . .   Queensland (362 and 445-8 dec.) v Western Australia (523 and 287-3) at Brisbane.
1,612 for 26 . .   Western Australia (562-6 dec. and 270-6 dec.) v Tasmania (384-5 dec. and 396-9) at Hobart.
1,532 for 32 . .   Western Australia (437 and 329-5 dec.) v Tasmania (380 and 386-7) at Perth.
1,508 for 36 . .   Australia (556 and 196) v India (523 and 233-6) (Second Test) at Adelaide.
1,507 for 35 . .   Rawalpindi (494 and 259) v Lahore (460 and 294-5) at Lahore.

Victory Losing One Wicket

Innings and 26 runs   Kenyans (152 and 179) v Windward Islands (357-1 dec.) at St Vincent.

Four Individual Hundreds in an Innings

New Zealand (630-6 dec.) v India (Second Test) at Mohali:
M. H. Richardson (145), L. Vincent (106), S. B. Styris (119), C. D. McMillan (100*).

Six or More Individual Fifties in an Innings

(Seven) Victoria (710) v Queensland at Melbourne:
  M. T. G. Elliott (155), J. L. Arnberger (90), B. J. Hodge (89), J. Moss (98), C. L. White (54), I. J. Harvey (62), D. S. Berry (61).

(Six) Colts (683) v Galle at Colombo:
  S. Kalawithigoda (126), S. I. Fernando (160), R. S. Kaluwitharana (53), H. G. J. M. Kulatunga (54), M. Pushpakumara (56), M. R. C. N. Bandaratilleke (68).

Zimbabwe (441) v Bangladesh (First Test) at Harare:
  D. D. Ebrahim (65), S. V. Carlisle (58), T. Taibu (59), S. M. Ervine (86), H. H. Streak (68), G. M. Ewing (71).

New Zealand A (570) v Sri Lanka A at Lincoln:
  M. D. Bell (92), J. M. How (92), M. S. Sinclair (50), L. Vincent (107), H. J. H. Marshall (60), J. E. C. Franklin (64*).

Easterns (563-9 dec.) v Boland at Benoni:
  S. G. Koenig (105), A. J. Seymore (51), Z. de Bruyn (64), P. de Bruyn (117), D. J. Cullinan (70), G. Toyana (73).

Most Extras in an Innings

b	l-b	w	n-b	pen	
78	13	18	6	41		Bangladesh A (452-9 dec.) v DHA at Karachi.
72	31	9	0	32		Lahore (427) v Sialkot at Sialkot.
68	23	13	7	25		North West (495-4) v Northerns at Potchefstroom.
61	21	15	7	13	5	Assam (306) v Rajasthan at Guwahati.
60	7	28	7	18		England (339) v West Indies (First Test) at Kingston.
60	18	11	12	19		Matabeleland (390) v Manicaland at Mutare.

Career Aggregate Milestones

20,000 runs	M. L. Hayden, N. Hussain, J. L. Langer, D. S. Lehmann, G. P. Thorpe.
15,000 runs	D. J. Cullinan, R. Dravid, S. C. Ganguly, H. H. Gibbs.
10,000 runs	C. L. Cairns, S. L. Campbell, S. Chanderpaul, M. W. Goodwin, U. C. Hathurusinghe, Mohammad Ramzan.
1,000 wickets	M. Muralitharan.
500 wickets	Arshad Khan, S. C. G. MacGill.
500 dismissals	Moin Khan.

ENGLAND IN THE WEST INDIES, 2003-04

Review by Christopher Martin-Jenkins

Having laboured hard for no reward in Sri Lanka before Christmas, Michael Vaughan's promising England team arrived in the Caribbean in February 2004 and performed even better than Australia had the previous year. They won the first three Tests, then held on for a draw in the final game on a supine pitch in Antigua, after Brian Lara had regained his Test batting record. In the course of an astonishing display of skill and willpower, he became the first batsman to reach 400 in a Test innings.

The feat gained precious time for Lara and his team of *ingénus* but he himself said that, in the context of the series, "it was nothing to rant and rave about". That is a matter of opinion. The fact remains that in all too short a span – Test schedules these days allow no time for the old slow-burning blue touchpaper that let a five-match series crackle into life – the dream that his side might bounce back from an embarrassing hammering

All eyes: Marcus Trescothick, the first of eight in the cordon, holds on to the catch, and West Indies hurtle towards catastrophe at Kingston. Adam Sanford is the batsman, Steve Harmison, inevitably, the bowler.

in South Africa was shattered by a united touring team playing harder, more disciplined and more thoughtful cricket.

The unexpectedly lively pitches produced for the first three Tests – a reaction to the bland surfaces on which Australia had built huge totals the previous year – played into the hands of the best group of England fast bowlers to have toured together for a long time. Impressively led by Steve Harmison, easily the most influential bowler on either side, they were arguably the best pack since the briefly invincible years of the 1950s, and certainly since John Snow, Jeff Jones and David Brown led the attack on England's last triumphant tour here in 1967-68.

West Indies' weakness against fierce fast bowling on helpful pitches, a bitter taste of the medicine doled out in giant spoonfuls by their own teams of the 1980s and 1990s, had been apparent when they relinquished the Wisden Trophy to England in 2000. If the events of this tour reflected the continuing struggle by West Indian cricket to catch up with developments in the rest of the world more than a sustained England revival, they nevertheless represented a further step in England's own desperate quest: to win back the Ashes.

The missing elements for England were obvious enough before a ball was bowled: no established spinner other than Ashley Giles, a reliable bowler

Picture by Patrick Eagar

but seemingly limited on pitches outside the subcontinent, and no young batsmen thrusting from below with unanswerable claims to oust the established top five. That said, the contemporary tour itinerary gives little chance to batting reserves unless someone gets injured. In past Caribbean series, England players expected to get hurt: this time, despite two very fast and promising 22-year-old bowlers from Barbados, Tino Best and Fidel Edwards, the senior batsmen emerged with no more than a few bruises. Paul Collingwood, seen as Nasser Hussain's most likely successor, played only three first-class innings.

The coach, Duncan Fletcher, had fought for Hussain's inclusion despite his vain struggle for form in Sri Lanka. In the event, the series would not have been won by England had it not been for the bravery and professional know-how of the three thirty-somethings in the middle order: Hussain himself, Mark Butcher and Graham Thorpe. The first two held the fort in the pivotal first innings of the first two Tests, and again when West Indies looked like gaining consolation on the final afternoon in St John's. Butcher played particularly fluently throughout the series, having almost missed the opening Test after twisting his ankle in the first warm-up match. But the best innings was played by Thorpe in the Third Test, at Bridgetown, where he repeated his hundred of 1997-98 in tougher circumstances. It was a canny, skilful, gritty performance that won the match award.

That could have been won by no one but Harmison in the first two Tests, a fact for which Durham's pale-faced assassin deserved most credit himself. His great natural talent, barely evident in so gangling a figure, might never have been developed, however, had it not been for the faith and patience shown by the most recent England selectors and the shrewd promptings of the back-up staff, led by Fletcher and valuably augmented by the fitness adviser Nigel Stockill and the bowling coach Troy Cooley. Between them, they drove home what was at stake, convinced Harmison of the need for greater stamina, and worked on keeping his naturally high action rhythmic and simple. Training sessions at Newcastle United FC paid handsome dividends.

He may never again produce an analysis quite like the seven for 12 that won the Sabina Park Test with startling suddenness on the fourth morning. But the performances that followed, notably a crucial spell before lunch on the opening day at Port-of-Spain after Chris Gayle had batted superbly for the first 25 overs, proved Harmison to be 14-carat rather than a mere flash of brass. Few cricketers have been so misunderstood, especially by the media. As a bowler, although everyone recognised his unusual pace from his teenage performances in north-eastern cricket, he was seen as hopelessly inconsistent. As a character, having married young, he appeared gauche, and unhappy to leave home and family. It was marvellous to behold the emergence not only of the most awkward English fast bowler since Bob Willis but also of a man whose quintessential English modesty was underpinned by a competitiveness that was never meretricious.

Matthew Hoggard had much the same qualities: a willingness to work hard and two large feet planted firmly on the ground – in wellington boots,

Taking a firm hold: England, spearheaded by Steve Harmison and Andrew Flintoff, keep their grip on the Wisden Trophy.

Picture by Graham Morris

to judge by his walk. His hat-trick on the Saturday of the Barbados Test, in humid conditions ideal for his out-swingers, was the second example of how one spell can decide a Test match.

In between, in Trinidad, came a first five-wicket Test haul for Simon Jones, a performance in which all cricketers could rejoice. The charismatic young Welshman's long and lonely fight for fitness, after suffering a serious and appallingly unlucky knee injury in the field at Brisbane in November 2002, was admirable. He was a marginal choice in the Test attack in front of Lancashire's James Anderson, who could, however, be all the better for a spell on the sidelines, after his swift rise from league to Test cricket the previous year and the inevitable fallow period that followed.

The fourth member of the fast-bowling quartet, Andrew Flintoff, had his most commanding all-round series yet. Using his great strength unstintingly, he was at once hostile and controlled. His catching at second slip was magnificent and by the end, although there were still technical faults to be worked on, he had justified his promotion to No. 6 in the batting order.

The series' most disappointing feature from an English viewpoint was the failure of the captain, Vaughan, and his opening partner, Marcus Trescothick, to give the team a stable start. They finally produced a partnership of substance in the second innings of the last match but, like Lara's record, saving the final game had to be seen in the context of a pitch that would have lasted for all of the 12 days that it had taken to decide the other three Tests.

At St John's, an all-Bajan West Indies attack bowled well together, especially the exuberant Best and the loose-armed Pedro Collins, to take advantage of opponents dazed and wearied by Lara's remorseless excellence. Flintoff's resolute if fortunate third Test century in the first innings and Vaughan's 140 in the second were the most important contributions in denying them.

Vaughan averaged 35 in the end but this was only his second hundred in 13 Tests since taking over the captaincy, both made in the cause of saving a game. Not surprisingly, it took him time to learn how to give as much thought to his own batting as he had to all aspects of leadership. Vaughan had averaged 31 in his first 16 Tests, 72 in the next 15, and 29 as captain before this innings. The hope was that this century might mark the start of the fourth phase of a career surprisingly mercurial for so classical a player and equable a character.

Trescothick finished the series in the paradoxical situation of needing runs in the one-day internationals to underpin his Test place, yet needing to bat less like a one-day cricketer in the five-day game in order to score more heavily and consistently. His sharp reactions at first slip and an innings of 88 at St John's – after being reprieved by an unsighted umpire before he had scored – only partially atoned for another disappointing tour.

Wanted: a foreign coach of stature, experience and clarity

Much the same could be said of Lara's extraordinary innings in relation to the earlier performances of his team. Playing on a neighbouring strip on the same square against the same opposition ten years to the month after the flawless 375 that first propelled him to stardom, he, too, might have been given out caught behind for nought (television replays were inconclusive about whether he had got a thin edge off Harmison). What followed, over the 13 hours in which he bent all bowlers to his will, was confirmation that, although he may seldom dominate like Viv Richards, Lara is the finest Caribbean strokemaker since Sobers. In this mood, too, his concentration and ability to eliminate risk bore comparison with Bradman, the only other batsman to have scored more than one Test triple-hundred.

Lara as leader was less of an open-and-shut case. He was polite and articulate with the media, supportive of his young team in selection meetings, and often very clever in his direction of them in the field – though after dislocating the little finger of his right hand in missing a slip catch in the First Test, he was unwilling to field close. Just occasionally, however, his tactics were unfathomable.

Still suffering pain from the finger, he dropped down the order in the second innings at Port-of-Spain. To some it looked like a retreat, which was nonsense, but it gave out negative pulses. More baffling was his reluctance to use Best and Edwards in tandem, particularly after lunch on the second day at Bridgetown when England, struggling at 73 for four, were allowed to settle down while Gayle bowled 11 overs in succession. Gayle is a steady enough off-spinner but Lara, not a Trinidadian for nothing, would

Bringing the bad news: the local press reports the West Indian rout in Bridgetown.

have been happier throughout the series had he been given a specialist spin bowler.

The lack of one good enough to demand inclusion was only one of a multitude of problems troubling the latest group of West Indian cricket administrators. During the series they replaced one manager, Ricky Skerritt, with another, Tony Howard, but frequent changes of captains, coaches and executives have done little to arrest the decline since the 1990s. This said, one sensible change for the near future would be a foreign coach of sufficient stature, experience and clarity to rise above regional differences, establish priorities and plot a sensible course.

Like their English counterparts (less so Australians), West Indian administrators seemed too much concerned about making money and too little about making cricketers. Talk of lavish new stadiums for the 2007

On top of the world, again: Brian Lara is cheered from the pitch at Antigua after hitting Test cricket's first quadruple-century.

Picture by Graham Morris

World Cup was heard almost everywhere. Generally, there would be more sense in updating and enlarging existing venues like Sabina Park, the Bourda and the Antigua Recreation Ground than in sinking millions of dollars into new ones where pitches might not bed down in time.

The levy of £160 on Test tickets for English visitors was another case in point. It did not prevent an invasion of some 10,000 England supporters, a good many of whom bypassed the surcharge by getting their tickets in the Caribbean from local buyers paying the proper price. There was a time when West Indian fans would not have been so happy to make a profit at the expense of missing the match.

In letters' columns and phone-in programmes, the home team was accused of lethargic practice routines, poor leadership, a lack of pride and passion, too much pay and too little hard work. There may be some truth in all of these, but they are familiar barbs against defeated cricket teams. The essential problems for Lara's side – as for many years they were for England – were brittle batting, fallible catching and a lack of penetrating bowlers of sufficient experience and fitness.

The 3–0 result in the Tests did not reflect any great difference in natural ability between the sides, a fact emphasised when, with several changes in both squads, the one-day games that survived poor weather produced two wins each.

For England, the distinctions between 50-over and five-day cricket were highlighted by the efforts of their two most influential players, Trescothick and Chris Read. For West Indies, Dwayne Smith demonstrated again, especially by his effortless six-hitting, an exciting talent that needs to be both tutored and encouraged by regular selection. Ramnaresh Sarwan, who had enjoyed that necessary faith from the selectors, batted with intelligence and authority, notably in St Lucia and in making a virtually faultless hundred at Bridgetown. Read, having lost his wicket-keeping place to Geraint Jones for the final Test despite immaculate work behind the stumps for eight Tests in succession, proved he could perform with the bat too. He won a game in Georgetown, reduced by rain to 30 overs, by means of three timely boundaries in succession when West Indies seemed to have capitalised on Shivnarine Chanderpaul's shrewd hitting.

Both matches in Port-of-Spain and one in Grenada were abandoned because of rain, the latter two without a ball bowled, but the sun shone on true pitches and a perfect outfield in St Lucia. The consequences were two successful run-chases by West Indies, ecstasy for capacity crowds on the most modern ground in the Caribbean, and the restoration of some lost pride. Appropriately, however, it was England who had the final word when Trescothick's barnstorming strokeplay on another good pitch in Barbados ensured that the side batting second won every completed game.

ENGLAND TOURING PARTY

M. P. Vaughan (Yorkshire) (*captain*), J. M. Anderson (Lancashire), G. J. Batty (Worcestershire), M. A. Butcher (Surrey), R. Clarke (Surrey), P. D. Collingwood (Durham), A. Flintoff (Lancashire), A. F. Giles (Warwickshire), S. J. Harmison (Durham), M. J. Hoggard (Yorkshire), N. Hussain (Essex), G. O. Jones (Kent), S. P. Jones (Glamorgan), C. M. W. Read (Nottinghamshire), G. P. Thorpe (Surrey), M. E. Trescothick (Somerset).

A. J. Strauss (Middlesex), originally picked for the one-day series only, was called up before the Tests as cover for Butcher and Thorpe. I. D. Blackwell (Somerset), D. Gough (Essex), R. J. Kirtley (Sussex) and A. McGrath (Yorkshire) replaced Butcher, Hoggard, Hussain, G. O. Jones, S. P. Jones and Thorpe for the one-day international series.

Coach: D. A. G. Fletcher. *Operations manager*: P. A. Neale. *Assistant coach (Test squad)*: T. J. Cooley. *Assistant coach (one-day squad)*: T. J. Boon. *Team analyst*: M. N. Ashton. *Physiotherapist (Test squad)*: K. A. Russell. *Physiotherapist (one-day squad)*: D. O. Conway. *Physiologist*: N. P. Stockill. *Media relations manager (Test squad)*: A. J. Walpole. *Media relations manager (one-day squad)*: M. C. K. Hodgson.

ENGLAND TOUR RESULTS

Test matches – Played 4: Won 3, Drawn 1.
First-class matches – Played 6: Won 5, Drawn 1.
One-day internationals – Played 5: Won 2, Lost 2, No result 1. Abandoned 2.
Other non-first-class matches – Played 1: Drawn 1. Abandoned 1.

TEST MATCH AVERAGES

WEST INDIES – BATTING AND FIELDING

	T	I	NO	R	HS	100s	50s	Avge	Ct
†B. C. Lara	4	7	1	500	400*	1	0	83.33	2
†R. D. Jacobs.	4	7	1	277	107*	1	1	46.16	10
†D. S. Smith	2	4	0	172	108	1	0	43.00	1
R. R. Sarwan	4	7	0	192	90	0	2	27.42	2
†C. H. Gayle	4	7	0	182	69	0	2	26.00	4
†R. O. Hinds	3	5	0	128	84	0	1	25.60	2
†S. Chanderpaul	3	6	0	101	50	0	1	16.83	0
T. L. Best	4	6	0	52	20	0	0	8.66	0
P. T. Collins	3	4	0	25	10	0	0	6.25	1
A. Sanford	2	4	0	4	1	0	0	1.00	3
F. H. Edwards	3	4	0	3	2	0	0	0.75	0
C. D. Collymore	4	6	6	15	6*	0	0	–	1

Played in two Tests: D. Ganga 11, 11, 10. Played in one Test: R. L. Powell 23; D. R. Smith 16, 14 (1 ct).

† *Left-handed batsman.*

BOWLING

	Style	O	M	R	W	BB	5W/i	Avge
T. L. Best	RF	96	14	301	12	3-37	0	25.08
P. T. Collins.	LFM	94	20	282	11	4-71	0	25.63
F. H. Edwards	RF	83.3	12	325	10	4-70	0	32.50

Also bowled: C. D. Collymore (RFM) 113–28–255–3; C. H. Gayle (OB) 48.5–15–98–2; R. O. Hinds (SLA) 72.2–18–148–4; R. L. Powell (OB) 8–0–36–0; A. Sanford (RFM) 52–8–182–3; R. R. Sarwan (LB) 24–3–53–3; D. R. Smith (RM) 9–0–30–1.

ENGLAND – BATTING AND FIELDING

	T	I	NO	R	HS	100s	50s	Avge	Ct
†G. P. Thorpe	4	6	3	274	119*	1	1	91.33	3
†M. A. Butcher	4	7	2	296	61	0	4	59.20	4
A. Flintoff	5	5	1	200	102*	1	0	50.00	7
M. P. Vaughan	4	8	1	245	140	1	0	35.00	2
N. Hussain	4	7	1	197	58	0	3	32.83	5
†M. E. Trescothick	4	8	1	166	88	0	1	23.71	7
†S. P. Jones	4	4	0	23	11	0	0	5.75	1
S. J. Harmison	4	4	0	21	13	0	0	5.25	0
M. J. Hoggard	4	4	2	10	9*	0	0	5.00	2

Played in three Tests: A. F. Giles 27, 37, 11 (2 ct); C. M. W. Read 20, 3, 13 (6 ct, 1 st). Played in one Test: G. J. Batty 8 (2 ct); G. O. Jones 38, 10*.

† *Left-handed batsman.*

BOWLING

	Style	O	M	R	W	BB	5W/i	Avge
S. J. Harmison	RF	139.5	41	342	23	7-12	2	14.86
M. J. Hoggard	RFM	106.4	24	326	13	4-35	0	25.07
A. Flintoff	RFM	102.2	21	297	11	5-58	1	27.00
S. P. Jones	RF	94	8	374	11	5-57	1	34.00

Also bowled: G. J. Batty (OB) 52–4–185–2; A. F. Giles (SLA) 31–2–137–2; M. E. Trescothick (RM) 19–3–72–0; M. P. Vaughan (OB) 14–0–62–0.

ENGLAND TOUR AVERAGES – FIRST-CLASS MATCHES

BATTING AND FIELDING

	M	I	NO	R	HS	100s	50s	Avge	Ct/St
†G. P. Thorpe	6	8	3	417	119*	1	3	83.40	3
†M. A. Butcher	5	8	2	313	61	0	4	52.16	6
A. Flintoff	5	6	1	204	102*	1	0	40.80	9
N. Hussain	5	8	1	283	86	0	4	40.42	6
M. P. Vaughan	5	9	1	311	140	1	1	38.87	2
†M. E. Trescothick	6	11	2	216	88	0	2	24.00	8
A. F. Giles	5	5	0	99	37	0	0	19.80	3
C. M. W. Read	5	5	0	45	20	0	0	9.00	8/1
M. J. Hoggard	6	6	3	25	10	0	0	8.33	3
†S. P. Jones	5	5	0	36	13	0	0	7.20	2
S. J. Harmison	5	5	0	21	13	0	0	4.20	0

Played in two matches: G. J. Batty 0, 5, 8 (5 ct); P. D. Collingwood 14, 20, 0 (2 ct); G. O. Jones 66, 38, 10* (5 ct). Played in one match: †J. M. Anderson 1*; R. Clarke 35, 8* (1 ct).

† *Left-handed batsman.*

BOWLING

	Style	O	M	R	W	BB	5W/i	Avge
S. J. Harmison	RF	155.5	45	371	27	7-12	2	13.74
J. M. Anderson	RFM	29.1	8	86	5	3-56	0	17.20
M. J. Hoggard	RFM	137	30	403	21	4-27	0	19.19
A. F. Giles	SLA	87	18	245	11	3-23	0	22.27
S. P. Jones	RF	106.2	10	417	17	5-57	1	24.52
A. Flintoff	RFM	112.2	25	320	11	5-58	1	29.09
G. J. Batty	OB	76	11	238	7	5-53	1	34.00

Also bowled: R. Clarke (RFM) 24-3-102-2; M. E. Trescothick (RM) 19-3-72-0; M. P. Vaughan (OB) 14-0-62-0.

Note: Matches in this section which were not first-class are signified by a dagger.

†At Kingston, March 1, 2, 3, 2004. **Drawn.** Toss: England XII. **England XII 320** (M. P. Vaughan 105, N. Hussain 65, C. M. W. Read 61) **and 259-6 dec.** (P. D. Collingwood 103, A. Flintoff 57); **Jamaica 281** (S. Findlay 51, M. D. Ventura 53) **and 106-6** (A. F. Giles 4-19).
This match did not have first-class status as each side named 12 players, of whom 11 could bat and 11 field. England later introduced a 13th player, Collingwood, as a full playing substitute for Mark Butcher, who sprained his ankle in the field. Vaughan scored his 105 in 89 balls, with 19 fours and a six.

UNIVERSITY OF WEST INDIES VICE-CHANCELLOR'S XI v ENGLAND XI

At Sir Frank Worrell Ground, Kingston, March 5, 6, 2004. England XI won by an innings and 85 runs. Toss: University of West Indies Vice-Chancellor's XI.

England wrapped up the inaugural first-class match at the Mona Bowl, on the University of West Indies campus, with a day to spare. Jason Haynes led the Vice-Chancellor's XI to 88 for two on the first afternoon; then Jones, making his England comeback 16 months after his knee injury at Brisbane, bowled him, sparking a collapse of seven wickets for 31 in 18 overs, three of them to Harmison. Though Trescothick was yorked first ball in England's reply, Vaughan and Hussain added 149, and Thorpe, who had left the field with back pains on the first morning, was able to bat for two and a half hours next day. The home side resumed 155 behind, and this time all nine wickets suddenly fell in 12 overs on a crumbling pitch – Tikolo, guesting alongside Kenyan team-mate Otieno, was absent ill. Butcher's sprained ankle had improved enough for him to join his colleagues in the nets on their day off.

Close of play: First day, England 152-2 (Hussain 76, Collingwood 1).

University of West Indies Vice-Chancellor's XI

*J. A. M. Haynes b Jones	45	– b Giles	11
†K. O. Otieno c Jones b Harmison	6	– c Collingwood b Hoggard	22
D. J. J. Bravo lbw b Hoggard	4	– lbw b Hoggard	0
S. O. Tikolo lbw b Harmison	23	– absent ill	
D. E. Bernard c Read b Giles	2	– (4) c Flintoff b Giles	14
T. A. Willett c Hussain b Giles	2	– (5) lbw b Giles	9
D. J. G. Sammy not out	17	– (6) c Read b Hoggard	0
R. P. O. Nurse b Harmison	1	– (7) b Jones	2
J. P. Bennett c Trescothick b Harmison	0	– (10) b Jones	0
R. O. Cunningham b Jones	5	– (8) not out	4
J. J. C. Lawson b Jones	0	– (9) c Flintoff b Jones	0
B 1, l-b 2, w 1, n-b 10	14	L-b 1, n-b 7	8

1/12 (2) 2/37 (3) 3/88 (1) 4/91 (4)   119
5/93 (5) 6/94 (6) 7/95 (8)
8/95 (9) 9/119 (10) 10/119 (11)

1/41 (2) 2/41 (1) 3/49 (3)   70
4/55 (4) 5/64 (6) 6/64 (5)
7/68 (7) 8/70 (9) 9/70 (10)

Bowling: *First Innings*—Hoggard 8–1–31–1; Harmison 11–3–17–4; Giles 17–6–26–2; Jones 10.2–2–40–3; Flintoff 5–4–2–0. *Second Innings*—Hoggard 7–2–10–3; Harmison 5–1–12–0; Flintoff 5–0–21–0; Giles 5–1–23–3; Jones 2–0–3–3.

England XI

M. E. Trescothick b Lawson	0	S. P. Jones b Cunningham	13
*M. P. Vaughan c Bravo b Cunningham	66	S. J. Harmison c Nurse b Cunningham	0
N. Hussain b Lawson	86		
P. D. Collingwood c Bravo b Bennett	14	B 13, l-b 2, w 1, n-b 13	29
G. P. Thorpe c Haynes b Willett	55		
A. Flintoff lbw b Bennett	4	1/0 (1) 2/149 (2) 3/166 (3)	274
†C. M. W. Read c Bernard b Bravo	0	4/190 (4) 5/198 (6) 6/200 (7)	
A. F. Giles lbw b Lawson	2	7/228 (8) 8/261 (5)	
M. J. Hoggard not out	5	9/274 (10) 10/274 (11)	

Bowling: Lawson 14–0–72–3; Bennett 11–2–32–2; Cunningham 11–5–37–3; Nurse 17–1–46–0; Tikolo 3–0–19–0; Bernard 5–0–14–0; Sammy 6–2–9–0; Bravo 7–3–15–1; Willett 5–0–15–1.

Umpires: C. Fletcher and N. A. Malcolm.

WEST INDIES v ENGLAND

First Test Match

ROB SMYTH

At Kingston, March 11, 12, 13, 14, 2004. England won by ten wickets. Toss: West Indies.

The denouement came like a bolt from the clear blue Kingston skies. For three days this was a gritty arm-wrestle of a match; then, on the fourth morning, West Indies collapsed for 47, their lowest total ever. Steve Harmison, bowling with cold-eyed purpose, finally came of age, taking the cheapest seven-wicket haul in Test history in a performance described by his captain Vaughan as "one of the greatest spells by an England bowler".

This was an exaggeration: only one batsman, Jacobs, got a real snorter. And Harmison himself felt he was to bowl better in Port-of-Spain five days later. No one played any truly appalling shots either, but the chips fell exactly where England wanted. The exception was the last-wicket partnership that inched West Indies past the symbolic mark of 46 – England's total when they were terrorised by Curtly Ambrose in Trinidad ten years earlier. Harmison's success, though spectacular, was a reward for getting the fundamentals right rather than sudden inspiration. After getting carried away and underpitching in the first innings, he simply increased his length, cut his pace a fraction, and concentrated on the basics. It worked, probably beyond his wildest dreams. Only two bowlers in Test history have taken more wickets in an innings more cheaply: George Lohmann and Johnny Briggs, with eight for seven and eight for 11, both for England in South Africa in the 19th century. The previous best seven-fors cost 17, a record shared by Briggs, Monty Noble and Wilfred Rhodes. The most recent of these feats came in 1902.

WEST INDIES' LOWEST TEST TOTALS

47	**v England at Kingston (lost by ten wickets)**	**2003-04**
51	v Australia at Port-of-Spain (lost by 312 runs)	1998-99
53	v Pakistan at Faisalabad (lost by 186 runs)	1986-87
54	v England at Lord's (lost by two wickets)	2000
61	v England at Leeds (lost by an innings and 39 runs)	2000
76	v Pakistan at Dacca (lost by 41 runs)	1958-59
77	v New Zealand at Auckland (lost by 190 runs)	1955-56
78	v Australia at Sydney (lost by 202 runs)	1951-52
82	v Australia at Brisbane (lost by an innings and 126 runs)	2000-01
86†	v England at The Oval (second innings) (lost by an innings and 237 runs) . .	1957
89†	v England at The Oval (first innings) (lost by an innings and 237 runs)	1957
90†	v Australia at Sydney (lost by an innings and 172 runs)	1930-31
91	v England at Birmingham (lost by 217 runs)	1963
94	**v England at Bridgetown (lost by eight wickets)**	**2003-04**
97	v England at Lord's (lost by an innings and 27 runs)	1933
97	v New Zealand at Hamilton (lost by nine wickets)	1999-2000
99	v Australia at Melbourne (lost by an innings and 122 runs)	1930-31

† *One man absent.*

England made three changes from the side pulverised in their last Test in Sri Lanka. Simon Jones, after 16 tortuous months, and Harmison returned from injury to play a Test together for the first time, while Hoggard's greater sobriety earned him the final place ahead of Anderson. With the possible qualification that Caddick was missing, this was the first time England had been able to select their best side since the successful tour of the subcontinent in 2000-01. West Indies' team selection centred around the Smiths: Devon returned in place of Ganga, while Dwayne dislocated a finger in the nets and was replaced by Ryan Hinds. Dillon and Drakes, their underachievement tolerated no longer, made way for another underachiever, Sanford, and the in-your-face Best.

The first day, as is customary for a series between these sides in the Caribbean, had a pack of virile young fast bowlers pummelling a bouncy castle of a pitch. But even this went against expectations: the bowlers were white and the pitch, by common consent, was the fastest and bounciest seen in the Caribbean for some time. When an emotional Jones snared Lara with his 13th ball back in Test cricket, England were on top. But Devon Smith and Hinds, a study in contrasts, took on the bullies in a fifth-wicket partnership of 122 in 25 overs. Smith, short and spiky, scythed at anything full and wide in the course of a mature maiden Test century; Hinds, tall, domineering and

In Harm's way: Shivnarine Chanderpaul falls to Steve Harmison as his amazing
spell takes shape.

Picture by Patrick Eagar

oozing machismo, simply planted his front foot and gave it some humpty. Giles eventually accounted for both – his only wickets of the series – and West Indies' final total of 311 felt like par.

Then England were introduced to the sheer, paint-stripping pace of Edwards: the openers were swept aside, and Butcher and Hussain could both have been out first ball. Butcher was then dropped on four by Sarwan at short leg, but slowly, surely, he and Hussain used their experience to weather a furious storm in a compelling passage of play. Life became easier after the Kookaburra ball lost its zing, and this odd couple became the most productive non-opening partnership in England's history, overtaking Graham Gooch and David Gower's 2,271 during a stand of 119. Butcher eventually fell in a manic mini-session after tea – three overs squeezed out between lengthy rain-breaks – but a more decisive blow came two balls earlier: he was dropped at first slip by Lara, who dislocated his finger in the process.

Lara was off the field on the third morning, when his deputy Sarwan allowed the game to drift. Despite that, run-scoring was never easy on another day severely interrupted by rain – except for Flintoff, who breezed emphatically to 46 off 50 balls until he was exasperatingly suckered by the leg-spin of Sarwan, inventively introduced by Lara on his return. With Edwards off the field nursing a side injury, Best bounded

HIGHEST FIRST-CLASS INNINGS IN WHICH EXTRAS WAS TOP-SCORER

374	Northamptonshire (Extras 73, L. Livingston 62) v Kent at Northampton .	1955
350-9 dec.	Western Australia (Extras 59, T. M. Moody 59) v Queensland at Brisbane	1989-90
342	Rawalpindi (Extras 66, Asif Mahmood 63) v Bahawalpur at Rawalpindi. .	1997-98
339	**England (Extras 66, M. A. Butcher 58, N. Hussain 58) v West Indies**	
	at Kingston	**2003-04**
324	Nottinghamshire (Extras 73, P. J. Franks 61) v Hampshire at Nottingham.	1999
319-8	Zimbabwe (Extras 65, D. L. Houghton 63) v Sri Lanka at Harare.	1994-95
315	England (Extras 59, D. I. Gower 47) v West Indies at Port of Spain	1985-86
309	National Bank (Extras 67, Akhtar Sarfraz 63) v Habib Bank at Karachi. .	1997-98
307	**Lancashire (Extras 51, I. J. Sutcliffe 50) v Kent at Tunbridge Wells . .**	**2004**

Penalty runs awarded for slow over-rates are ignored.

hyperactively into the role of attack leader, but useful contributions from the tail meant a lead of 28. Wayward bowling aided the cause: England's total was the highest in Test history in which Extras top-scored.

On the Sunday, that insignificant lead soon became mountainous. By the time West Indies restored parity, they had lost five wickets in seven overs and the game was up. Thorpe in the slips held a hot one from Gayle, a borderline lbw gave Sarwan a pair, Chanderpaul nutmegged himself, an uncomfortable Lara lasted only five balls and Hoggard clutched a scorching return catch from Smith that threatened to rearrange his face. By contrast, West Indies could not save their collective face: the second wave of five went down for six runs, and England danced giddily to victory inside three overs. Soon after the game had finished, though, some of the West Indies players were the ones dancing giddily in the stands, partying with their supporters as though ten-wicket defeats by England were all in a day's work.

Towards the end of the match, with eight in the cordon and Hussain at short leg, there was not one fielder in front of the bat. It felt quite absurd but, after totals of 54 and 61 in England in 2000 and now this, bowling out West Indies in double figures was in danger of becoming passé.

Man of the Match: S. J. Harmison.

Close of play: First day, West Indies 311-9 (Collymore 3, Edwards 1); Second day, England 154-3 (Hussain 41, Thorpe 1); Third day, West Indies 8-0 (Gayle 8, Smith 0).

West Indies

C. H. Gayle b Harmison	5	– c Thorpe b Harmison	9
D. S. Smith st Read b Giles	108	– c and b Hoggard	12
R. R. Sarwan lbw b Hoggard	0	– lbw b Harmison	0
*B. C. Lara c Flintoff b Jones	23	– (5) c Flintoff b Hoggard	0
S. Chanderpaul b Hoggard	7	– (4) b Harmison	0
R. O. Hinds c Butcher b Giles	84	– c Read b Jones	3
†R. D. Jacobs c Vaughan b Jones	38	– c Hussain b Harmison	15
T. L. Best lbw b Harmison	20	– c Read b Harmison	0
A. Sanford c Trescothick b Flintoff	1	– c Trescothick b Harmison	1
C. D. Collymore not out	3	– not out	2
F. H. Edwards c Flintoff b Hoggard	1	– c Trescothick b Harmison	0
L-b 6, w 1, n-b 14	21	L-b 4, n-b 1	5

1/17 (1) 2/22 (3) 3/73 (4) 4/101 (5)   **311**   1/13 (1) 2/13 (3) 3/15 (4)   **47**
5/223 (2) 6/281 (6) 7/289 (7)   4/16 (5) 5/21 (2) 6/41 (7)
8/300 (9) 9/307 (8) 10/311 (11)   7/41 (8) 8/43 (6) 9/43 (9) 10/47 (11)

Bowling: *First Innings*—Hoggard 18.4–3–68–3; Harmison 21–6–61–2; Flintoff 16–3–45–1; Jones 18–2–62–2; Giles 12–0–67–2; Vaughan 1–0–2–0. *Second Innings*—Hoggard 9–2–21–2; Harmison 12.3–8–12–7; Jones 4–1–10–1.

England

M. E. Trescothick b Edwards	7	– not out	6
*M. P. Vaughan c Lara b Edwards	15	– not out	11
M. A. Butcher c Jacobs b Edwards	58		
N. Hussain c sub (D. E. Bernard) b Best	58		
G. P. Thorpe c Sanford b Best	19		
A. Flintoff c Hinds b Sarwan	46		
†C. M. W. Read c Hinds b Best	20		
A. F. Giles b Sanford	27		
M. J. Hoggard not out	9		
S. P. Jones c Sanford b Hinds	7		
S. J. Harmison run out	13		
B 7, l-b 28, w 7, n-b 18	60	B 1, n-b 2	3

1/28 (1) 2/33 (2) 3/152 (3) 4/194 (5)   **339**   (no wkt) **20**
5/209 (4) 6/268 (6) 7/278 (7)
8/313 (8) 9/325 (10) 10/339 (11)

Bowling: *First Innings*—Collymore 26–7–55–0; Edwards 19.3–3–72–3; Best 19–1–57–3; Sanford 22–1–90–1; Hinds 11.5–2–18–1; Gayle 1–0–6–0; Sarwan 4–1–6–1. *Second Innings*—Best 1.3–0–8–0; Hinds 1–0–11–0.

Umpires: B. F. Bowden (New Zealand) and D. J. Harper (Australia).
Third umpire: E. A. Nicholls. Referee: M. J. Procter (South Africa).

WEST INDIES v ENGLAND

Second Test Match

JOHN STERN

At Port-of-Spain, March 19, 20, 21, 22, 23, 2004. England won by seven wickets. Toss: West Indies.

Less than a fortnight after the start of the series, England secured their main objective of the tour when they retained the Wisden Trophy, a prize they had barely sniffed for 27 years until 2000. The triumph could have come even quicker: they won after 23 minutes on the final morning of a match in which the equivalent of a whole day's play was lost to rain and bad light.

Brought low: Chris Gayle is the first of Simon Jones's five wickets in the second innings of the Port-of-Spain Test.

Picture by Graham Morris

Once again Harmison was the dominant figure in England's success, and was responsible for perhaps the crucial moment of the series. This came after West Indies had made an excellent start, with Gayle leading the charge in hot, sunny conditions on a pitch with far less pace than its Sabina Park predecessor. His century opening stand with Devon Smith, containing 82 in boundaries, came up in the 25th over. But at that point, clouds filled the blue sky and light rain started to fall. Harmison, whose first spell of six overs had gone for 27, had just changed ends and he got immediate results, dismissing Gayle, then Smith – and made it three in eight deliveries with the vital wicket of Lara. He hit him on the right hand with one that rose sharply from short of a length, then bounced him next ball: Lara could only fend towards gully as he took his eyes off it.

It was the first time in his career that Lara had made successive Test ducks. More significantly, it showed Harmison's earlier success was no fluke. Expectation might have lain heavily on his shoulders, but they were now broad enough for that; and he had a mental edge that enabled him to come back from a trying start to vanquish even his most formidable opponent. West Indies lunched uncomfortably on 110 for three and, after a couple of rain-breaks, Harmison completed his second five-wicket haul of the series; when he finished them off next morning, he had taken 13 in two innings. Arguably, this less bouncy, more uneven pitch was helpful to him since he had the ability to extract life from it in a way lesser bowlers could not.

England's reply followed the same pattern as the First Test. Both openers went cheaply, leaving Butcher and Hussain to repair the damage. West Indies were without Edwards, their most hostile bowler at Sabina; he was replaced by his half-brother, Collins, who took four wickets including Vaughan's second ball. But West Indies badly missed Edwards's skiddy relentlessness to back up Best's more intimidatory approach and Hussain, especially, revelled in conditions most players would have found difficult. Butcher was dropped on 20 by Chanderpaul at second slip off Collymore, as the two battled through the remaining 20 overs that survived the rain on the second day and kept on until the fourth over after lunch on the third, when Butcher was – wrongly, TV replays suggested – given out caught behind by umpire Bowden.

Out of the shadows, Jones produced a clenched fist

That brought in Thorpe, who emerged as the most fluent of England's three experienced middle-order batsmen, the "100 Club" as Hussain called them, a reference to their combined ages rather than their average. Having been seduced by a bouncer in Jamaica, Thorpe was peppered with short balls. But he pulled and hooked majestically, even with two men back on the leg-side boundary. One pull for four off Collins gave England first-innings lead shortly after tea. Thorpe's air of authority was punctured only when he was hit on the right hand by a beamer from Best. He was later struck on the head by a Sanford bouncer just after turning down an offer to go off for bad light. To Lara's annoyance, the light was offered again at the end of the over. His annoyance was obvious enough to cost him half his match fee. England had scored 103 in 36 overs in the last session to lead by 92 and, although they added only 19 more on the fourth morning, they were in complete control.

After a week in Harmison's shadow, Jones now took centre-stage, ripping out West Indies' top three in his first four overs. Coming on first change for Hoggard in the 13th over, he sent his first ball wide down the leg side, and it disappeared to the boundary. His second ball kept low and hit Gayle's off stump, and in his next over he had Devon Smith held at mid-off. When he trapped Sarwan leg-before playing back, Jones celebrated in confrontational clenched-fist style, which cost him, too, half his match fee.

Lara dropped himself down the order, promoting Jacobs to No. 4. While hardly sending out a message of confident defiance, the ploy worked to a degree, Jacobs and Chanderpaul adding 102 in 32 overs to put West Indies in front. Then Jones, in his second spell, removed Jacobs, and Lara emerged at No. 6, on a pair. He reached eight before Harmison was recalled and pinned Lara to his crease with his first ball, which swung back into the batsman. Umpire Harper took his time before giving a marginal – and momentous – lbw decision in England's favour. West Indies added only 38 more for the remaining five wickets; by dismissing Collins, Jones completed his first Test five-wicket haul.

England's target was 99, with 21 overs of the fourth evening to go. After losing Trescothick to the third ball of the innings, Vaughan and Butcher attempted to finish the job before the close, racing to 59 in the ninth over. But after Vaughan's dismissal, and much fractious discussion about the state of the light between batsmen, Lara and the umpires – this time, Lara seemed more enthusiastic about going off – England had to return on the last morning. Hussain was out to the second ball of the day and Thorpe dropped by Jacobs off the fifth, but victory was completed with ease as Butcher smashed three fours in five deliveries.

It was West Indies' sixth defeat out of seven on their captain's home ground. Immediately afterwards, Ricky Skerritt, the team manager for four years, announced his resignation, citing an inability "to instil in the entire team the fullest understanding of their obligations on and off the field to the people of the West Indies".

Man of the Match: S. J. Harmison.

Close of play: First day, West Indies 189-8 (Jacobs 29, Collins 6); Second day, England 54-2 (Butcher 25, Hussain 20); Third day, England 300-6 (Thorpe 81, Giles 28); Fourth day, England 71-2 (Butcher 32, Hussain 5).

West Indies

C. H. Gayle c Read b Harmison	62	– b Jones	16
D. S. Smith lbw b Harmison	35	– c Hoggard b Jones	17
R. R. Sarwan c Flintoff b Harmison	21	– lbw b Jones	13
*B. C. Lara c Giles b Harmison	0	– (6) lbw b Harmison	8
S. Chanderpaul c Read b Jones	2	– c Hussain b Flintoff	42
D. R. Smith c Hussain b Harmison	16	– (7) c sub (P. D. Collingwood) b Flintoff	14
†R. D. Jacobs run out	40	– (4) c Flintoff b Jones	70
T. L. Best c Read b Hoggard	1	– lbw b Hoggard	2
A. Sanford run out	1	– c Trescothick b Hoggard	1
P. T. Collins b Harmison	10	– b Jones	7
C. D. Collymore not out	3	– not out	0
L-b 7, w 6, n-b 4	17	B 1, l-b 3, w 5, n-b 10	19

1/100 (1) 2/110 (2) 3/110 (4) 4/113 (5)   **208**
5/142 (6) 6/143 (3) 7/148 (6)
8/165 (9) 9/202 (7) 10/208 (10)

1/34 (1) 2/45 (2) 3/56 (3)   **209**
4/158 (4) 5/171 (6) 6/194 (7)
7/195 (5) 8/200 (8)
9/205 (9) 10/209 (10)

Bowling: *First Innings*—Hoggard 15-3-38-1; Harmison 20.1-5-61-6; Flintoff 10-3-38-0; Giles 3-0-20-0; Jones 12-2-44-1. *Second Innings*—Hoggard 16-5-48-2; Harmison 16-5-40-1; Jones 15.2-5-57-5; Flintoff 12-1-27-2; Giles 7-1-29-0; Trescothick 1-0-4-0.

England

M. E. Trescothick c Sanford b Best	1	– b Best	4
*M. P. Vaughan lbw b Collins	0	– lbw b Sanford	23
M. A. Butcher c Jacobs b Best	61	– not out	46
N. Hussain b Best	58	– c Jacobs b Sanford	5
G. P. Thorpe c Gayle b Collins	90	– not out	13
A. Flintoff c and b D. R. Smith	23		
†C. M. W. Read lbw b Collins	3		
A. F. Giles c D. S. Smith b Collins	37		
M. J. Hoggard not out	0		
S. P. Jones b Gayle	1		
S. J. Harmison b Gayle	0		
B 5, l-b 20, w 3, n-b 17	45	B 4, l-b 3, n-b 1	8

1/2 (2) 2/8 (1) 3/128 (3) 4/186 (4)   **319**
5/218 (6) 6/230 (7) 7/315 (8)
8/318 (5) 9/319 (10) 10/319 (11)

1/8 (1) 2/59 (2) 3/71 (4)   (3 wkts) **99**

Bowling: *First Innings*—Collins 29–8–71–4; Best 28–5–71–3; Sanford 26–6–60–0; Collymore 24–7–39–0; D. R. Smith 9–0–30–1; Gayle 16.5–6–20–2; Sarwan 1–0–3–0. *Second Innings*—Best 4–0–27–1; Collins 4–0–25–0; Sanford 4–1–32–2; Collymore 3–1–8–0.

Umpires: B. F. Bowden (New Zealand) and D. J. Harper (Australia).
Third umpire: E. A. Nicholls. Referee: M. J. Procter (South Africa).

CARIB BEER XI v ENGLAND XI

At Three Ws Oval, Bridgetown, March 26, 27, 28, 2004. England XI won by eight wickets. Toss: Carib Beer XI.

England preserved their 100% first-class record on this tour at another university ground: the Three Ws Oval, close to Sir Frank Worrell's grave. The game provided Caribbean debuts for Batty, who claimed five wickets when he finally got a bowl, and Geraint Jones, who took the gloves while Read played as a batsman, then upstaged him with three sixes in a confident 66. Trescothick made a much-needed fifty and Thorpe maintained his form with 88. Anderson and Clarke also prospered in their first outing for three weeks, while Hoggard collected four in the first innings. On the last morning, Ganga, just recalled by West Indies, and Joseph advanced to 91 for one before the spinners took command. Lawson, the Test bowler recovering after injury, made England bat again, then dismissed his fifth victim of the match with the first delivery of the run-chase. Despite losing another wicket next over, England completed victory in 16 balls.

Close of play: First day, England 121-3 (Thorpe 25, Read 0); Second day, Carib Beer XI 51-1 (Ganga 17, Joseph 25).

Carib Beer XI

*D. Ganga c Jones b Anderson	25	– c and b Batty	39
X. M. Marshall c Batty b Hoggard	19	– c Jones b Anderson	4
S. C. Joseph c Butcher b Clarke	36	– c Hoggard b Giles	50
D. J. J. Bravo c Jones b Giles	2	– lbw b Batty	33
T. A. Willett lbw b Anderson	1	– c sub (S. J. Harmison) b Giles	21
†D. Ramdin c Jones b Clarke	7	– c Collingwood b Batty	4
O. A. C. Banks c Batty b Hoggard	17	– c Clarke b Batty	9
D. Mohammed c and b Giles	7	– c Jones b Batty	6
R. Rampaul b Hoggard	2	– c Butcher b Anderson	6
D. M. Washington not out	1	– (11) b Anderson	8
J. J. C. Lawson b Hoggard	0	– (10) not out	28
B 4, l-b 5, n-b 3	12	B 9, l-b 4, n-b 8	21

1/31 (2) 2/73 (1) 3/84 (4) 4/85 (5)   129   1/9 (2) 2/91 (3) 3/117 (1)   229
5/93 (6) 6/100 (3) 7/107 (8)   4/163 (5) 5/168 (4) 6/179 (6)
8/122 (9) 9/129 (7) 10/129 (11)   7/182 (7) 8/193 (8)
    9/195 (9) 10/229 (11)

Bowling: *First Innings*—Hoggard 11.2–3–27–4; Anderson 11–3–30–2; Clarke 11–2–38–2; Giles 15–5–25–2. *Second Innings*—Anderson 18.1–5–56–3; Clarke 13–1–64–0; Giles 19–4–34–2; Batty 24–7–53–5; Hoggard 4–0–9–0.

> **"**His face in his hands, mulling on the horror of it all, Lara steeled himself for the pain of it happening all over again."
>
> The West Indians in England, page 480.

England XI

*M. E. Trescothick b Banks	50	– (4) not out.	0
M. A. Butcher c Marshall b Washington	17		
P. D. Collingwood st Ramdin b Mohammed	20	– (1) c Ramdin b Lawson	0
G. P. Thorpe c sub (F. Thomas) b Willett	88		
C. M. W. Read c Ramdin b Mohammed	9		
†G. O. Jones c sub (R. D. Layne) b Lawson	66		
R. Clarke c Joseph b Lawson	35	– (2) not out.	8
A. F. Giles c Ramdin b Lawson	22		
G. J. Batty lbw b Lawson	0	– (3) b Rampaul	5
M. J. Hoggard b Mohammed	10		
J. M. Anderson not out	1		
B 8, n-b 21	29		
	347	**(2 wkts)**	**13**

1/30 (2) 2/72 (3) 3/120 (1) 4/142 (5)   347   1/0 (1) 2/7 (3)   (2 wkts) 13
5/259 (4) 6/285 (6) 7/325 (7)
8/325 (9) 9/336 (8) 10/347 (10)

Bowling: *First Innings*—Lawson 29–3–94–4; Washington 6–0–15–1; Rampaul 18–3–58–0; Mohammed 28–1–114–3; Banks 9–3–22–1; Bravo 5–1–22–0; Ganga 4–1–9–0; Willett 3–0–5–1. *Second Innings*—Lawson 1.4–0–13–1; Rampaul 1–1–0–1.

Umpires: T. Franklyn and M. Jones.

WEST INDIES v ENGLAND

Third Test Match

MATTHEW ENGEL

At Bridgetown, April 1, 2, 3, 2004. England won by eight wickets. Toss: England.

England stormed West Indies' once-impregnable fortress of Kensington Oval, just as they did almost precisely ten years earlier. On that occasion an overmatched team staged an improbable one-off smash-and-grab raid. But now the walls of the citadel have been demolished and pigeons haunt the empty halls. Against a well-marshalled invading force like Michael Vaughan's England there was no defence.

For much of this brief but compelling Test match, the two teams looked evenly matched. But England had the inner strength to come through their crises. Their bowling was effective, disciplined and – at moments – touched by magic. The West Indian batting, by contrast, was prone to regular outbreaks of wretchedness.

This was a total reversal of the old world order, and West Indies capitulated inside three days. England not merely clinched the series but made sure of their most successful Caribbean tour ever, with the whitewash still a possibility. As the moon rose over Kensington Oval on Saturday night, English supporters stood for hours yelling their support for each of the players in turn, even the reserves.

That was an outcrop of one of England's subsidiary advantages: it felt like a home Test. The West Indies board's differential pricing system failed to prevent the ground being entirely dominated by English holidaymakers. Most of them were too enervated by the heat and tension to do more than applaud politely at regular intervals. A minority maintained a cacophony of weird patriotic chants throughout.

Yet the game did not start well for England. Vaughan surprisingly opted to bowl first on a pitch with some bounce that most observers thought would play easily most of the game. They put down three slip catches on the opening day and, although Flintoff did get Lara (who this time accepted his responsibilities and came out at No. 3) caught in the gully for 36, Sarwan and Chanderpaul put together a fourth-wicket stand that took West Indies past tea in some comfort.

However, their batting line-up had become so fragile that it was now prone to crumple at the slightest touch. Once Harmison found his length in the evening session and had Sarwan caught at second slip, it was Flintoff's turn to collect the pickings – his first five in a Test innings, as the last seven wickets fell for 57.

If England fancied this set them up for a big lead, they were soon disillusioned. The return of Edwards to lead the West Indies attack gave their bowling an old-fashioned feel: a four-man pace attack, all Barbadian, with three of the four coming from the same small village, Boscobel, and two of them, Edwards and Collins, being half-brothers. And on a pitch that refused to calm down as expected, Edwards's skiddy 90mph pace took out the England top three with only 33 on the board. Steadily, the rest of their batting succumbed too. With one remarkable exception.

England's batting succumbed. With one remarkable exception

Thorpe, so often the linchpin of the England middle order, produced an innings of outstanding determination and quality. He held firm in defence and, when the bowlers dropped short, unleashed a series of high-class shots square of the wicket, receiving just enough help from the tail to reach his own century moments after the new ball was taken at 189 for nine. The last man Harmison stayed with him to add 39, which inched England into a psychologically vital two-run lead.

Thorpe also had help from a most unexpected quarter: the opposing captain. For 11 overs after lunch, Lara insisted on bowling Gayle's innocuous off-spin, even though he had four fast bowlers champing at the bit. It gave England important breathing space, though occasionally the batsmen must have been distracted by wondering what on earth Lara was playing at.

In theory, the game was now evenly poised. But the theory was quickly overwhelmed by the dynamic of the series. The third day was cloudy, with showers lurking. In English conditions, roared on by the English crowd, the most English bowler on display, Matthew Hoggard, emerged from his relative obscurity and sealed the game. Sarwan flicked wide outside off stump and handed a catch to gully. Next ball Hoggard produced a perfect in-swinger to trap Chanderpaul lbw on off stump, then moved one away to get Hinds caught at second slip. Hoggard became the tenth England bowler to take a Test hat-trick, the third to achieve the feat against West Indies after Peter Loader and Dominic Cork. It was not quite his first: he had taken one as a 14-year-old in the Dales Council third division.

Once the crowd had calmed down, which took a while, the rest was straightforward. West Indies were all out for 94, the fourth time in seven Tests England had bowled them out in two figures. The opening pair, Trescothick and Vaughan, put right one of England's few irritations of the series by finding a hint of form and scoring most of the runs between them. Vaughan paid tribute to West Indies' talent but summed up: "Every time they've got on top of us, we've dug ourselves out. But when the situation has been reversed, we have nailed the advantage down." This is the precise opposite of much of England's recent cricketing history.

Man of the Match: G. P. Thorpe.
Close of play: First day, England 20-1 (Vaughan 12, Butcher 3); Second day, West Indies 21-1 (Ganga 5, Lara 1).

West Indies

C. H. Gayle lbw b Hoggard	6	– b Harmison	15
D. Ganga lbw b Harmison	11	– c Thorpe b Hoggard	11
*B. C. Lara c Butcher b Flintoff	36	– c Vaughan b Harmison	33
R. R. Sarwan c Flintoff b Harmison	63	– c Giles b Hoggard	5
S. Chanderpaul c Thorpe b Flintoff	50	– lbw b Hoggard	0
R. O. Hinds c Jones b Harmison	5	– c Flintoff b Hoggard	0
†R. D. Jacobs c sub (P. D. Collingwood) b Flintoff	6	– c Butcher b Flintoff	1
T. L. Best c Butcher b Flintoff	17	– c Trescothick b Flintoff	12
P. T. Collins c Trescothick b Jones	7	– run out	1
C. D. Collymore not out	1	– not out	6
F. H. Edwards c Read b Flintoff	0	– c Hussain b Harmison	2
L-b 14, w 1, n-b 7	22	L-b 5, n-b 3	8

1/6 (1) 2/20 (2) 3/88 (3) 4/167 (4)   224
5/179 (6) 6/197 (7) 7/198 (5)
8/208 (9) 9/224 (8) 10/224 (11)

1/19 (1) 2/34 (2) 3/45 (4)   94
4/45 (5) 5/45 (6) 6/48 (7)
7/80 (8) 8/81 (9) 9/85 (3) 10/94 (11)

Bowling: *First Innings*—Hoggard 16–5–34–1; Harmison 18–6–42–3; Flintoff 16.2–2–58–5; Jones 16–1–55–1; Giles 9–1–21–0. *Second Innings*—Hoggard 14–4–35–4; Harmison 15.1–5–34–3; Flintoff 13–4–20–2.

England

M. E. Trescothick b Edwards	2	– c Jacobs b Collymore	42
*M. P. Vaughan c Jacobs b Edwards	17	– c Jacobs b Collymore	32
M. A. Butcher c Gayle b Edwards	5	– not out	13
N. Hussain c Collymore	17	– not out	0
G. P. Thorpe not out	119		
A. Flintoff c Collymore b Best	15		
†C. M. W. Read lbw b Edwards	13		
A. F. Giles c sub (A. N. Mayers) b Collins	11		
M. J. Hoggard lbw b Collins	0		
S. P. Jones c Sarwan b Best	4		
S. J. Harmison b Collins	3		
L-b 5, w 3, n-b 12	20	L-b 3, w 1, n-b 2	6

1/8 (1) 2/24 (3) 3/33 (2) 4/65 (4)   226
5/90 (6) 6/119 (7) 7/147 (8)
8/155 (9) 9/187 (10) 10/226 (11)

1/57 (2) 2/91 (1)   (2 wkts) 93

Bowling: *First Innings*—Edwards 20–4–70–4; Collins 23–6–60–3; Collymore 16–3–26–1; Hinds 4–1–7–0; Best 14–4–26–2; Gayle 13–3–32–0. *Second Innings*—Edwards 6–0–32–0; Best 3–0–18–0; Collymore 7–2–24–2; Collins 4–0–16–0.

Umpires: D. B. Hair (Australia) and R. E. Koertzen (South Africa).
Third umpire: B. R. Doctrove. Referee: M. J. Procter (South Africa).

> " As the Victorians sang their victory song they cleared a space for David Hookes and John Scholes, their much-loved coaches who had died in the previous 12 months."
> Cricket in Australia, page 1411.

WEST INDIES v ENGLAND

Fourth Test Match

TONY COZIER

At St John's, April 10, 11, 12, 13, 14, 2004. Drawn. Toss: West Indies. Test debut: G. O. Jones.

One hundred and eighty-five days after losing his position as scorer of Test cricket's highest innings, Brian Lara reclaimed the record from Matthew Hayden and became the first man to reach 400 in a Test. Nearly a year before Hayden accumulated 380 against Zimbabwe in October 2003, supplanting Lara's 375, Steve Waugh had predicted in print that Hayden would beat him one day. It required less genius to predict who was most likely to overtake Hayden, and it took Lara only 19 innings.

SAME MAN, SAME PLACE

Brian Lara's two world-record innings compared.

	Lara's 375 – April 16, 17, 18, 1994					Lara's 400* – April 10, 11, 12, 2004			
	Mins	*Balls*	*4s*	*6s*		*Mins*	*Balls*	*4s*	*6s*
50	154	121	7	–	50	115	61	7	–
100	232	180	16	–	100	192	131	13	–
150	327	240	22	–	150	281	199	18	–
200	440	311	27	–	200	391	260	22	1
250	515	377	32	–	250	479	323	27	2
300	610	432	38	–	300	576	404	34	2
350	721	511	42	–	350	678	494	39	3
					400	773	582	43	4
375	766	538	45	–	400*	778	582	43	4

Matthew Hayden scored his 380 against Zimbabwe in 622 minutes and 437 balls with 38 fours and 11 sixes. Lara's 501* for Warwickshire v Durham in 1994, still the world first-class record, lasted 474 minutes and 427 balls, with 62 fours and ten sixes.

Twenty-five minutes before lunch on the third day, he danced down the pitch to hoist Batty's invitingly flighted off-break into the stand for the six that lifted him past his own 375 and level with Hayden at 380. He then swept the next ball, flatter and ill-directed, to fine leg for four, to secure once more the record he had taken from another celebrated West Indian left-hander, Garry Sobers, on the same ground against the same opposition ten years earlier. It was the tenth time the record had changed hands; no one else had ever recovered it.

The reception this time was joyful enough, but less frenetic than first time round. There was no spectator invasion, as in 1994, except for an inappropriate appearance by a government entourage headed by the new prime minister of Antigua and Barbuda, Baldwin Spencer. As in Bridgetown, travelling England supporters formed the majority of the estimated 10,000 in the stands. They politely rejoiced that they were there to see history. Over in the popular, open section adjoining Independence Avenue, where hardly a pale face was to be seen, the celebrations were understandably more boisterous. The national flags of the independent Caribbean nations that somehow manage to find unity through their cricket team waved ecstatically. For the first time in the series, West Indian voices were no longer drowned out by the deafening, triumphant chants of the Barmy Army and their travelling accomplices.

In full cry: at Antigua, Brian Lara atoned for an otherwise meagre series with a bravura 400 not out.

Picture by Graham Morris

After handshakes from weary opponents, Lara again stooped to kiss the pitch – prepared under the supervision of Andy Roberts, the formidable fast bowler of an earlier era – that had once more favoured him.

Nor was he finished. He stated at the start of the third day that his aim was a total of 750, the highest ever conceded by England in their 820 Tests. Before that, he swept Batty to fine leg again for the single that raised Test cricket's first 400, and the tenth in all first-class cricket. Jacobs hit the next ball for four to take West Indies to 751, and Lara declared at the end of the over. He had batted two minutes short of 13 hours and faced 582 balls; there were four sixes – in 1994, he had none – and 43 fours.

WORDS (ALMOST) FAIL US

"All cricketdom arose yesterday to proclaim Brian Charles Lara as the all-conquering king of cricket."

Philip Spooner, *The Nation*, Barbados

"The equivalent of Neil Armstrong walking on the moon and going back into space ten years later to set foot on Mars."

Mike Walters, *Daily Mirror*

"IT'S A LARA LARA RUNS"

Headline, *The Sun*

"No amount of accolades can truly say how we feel about Lara."

Patrick Manning, prime minister of Trinidad & Tobago

"She cried and cried, she cried her eyes out – tears of joy, of course. We both cried."

Leasel Rovedas, mother of Lara's daughter Sydney

"Their whole first innings might have been geared around one individual performance, and they could have let a Test match slip because of it. They ran out of time in the game. That's not the way the Australian team plays."

Ricky Ponting, captain of Australia

"If I could chop my 400 four times, over the four Tests, in order to have won the series and celebrated with the Wisden Trophy, I would do so. I don't want to be remembered for records."

Lara, in an interview with the *Daily Telegraph*

He was so composed, so concentrated, so invincible that he surely could have carried on to 500, or 600 if he had been so minded. Geraint Jones, who had replaced Read as England wicket-keeper and thus had the closest vantage point, observed how fresh Lara looked throughout, hardly raising a sweat. Although he scored freely in all directions with his full range of strokes, he was, as in 1994, more calculating than extravagant.

Two other men were on the field during both record innings: England's Graham Thorpe, and Australian umpire Darrell Hair. Indeed, Hair had also officiated when Lara scored the first of his 25 Test hundreds – and the first of his seven doubles – 277 in Sydney in 1992-93. Yet, had Hair been persuaded by a convincing appeal for a catch at the wicket, Lara would not have scored a run. His fourth ball, from Harmison, his nemesis in earlier games, produced an indecisive drive. As Jones gathered, wicket-keeper, bowler and slips leapt in the certainty that there had been a thin edge. Hair shook his head, and television replays indicated he was correct.

There was nothing more that seriously tested the umpires' judgment. Lara offered one chance, a stinging, low straight drive off Batty that burst through the bowler's hands on its way to the boundary when he was 293. Only Harmison caused him the occasional bother – until his third warning for running on the pitch debarred him from bowling. By then, he had sent down 37 overs and Lara was 359.

As the series moved to Antigua, there were compelling circumstances to fire Lara's hunger and desire, conditions to accentuate his skill, and history to stir his imagination. For the second successive season, West Indies started the match considering the possible consequences of their first whitewash in a home series. A year earlier, they had impressively avoided it by amassing Test cricket's highest winning fourth-innings total to deny Australia; now, they were in danger of even greater humiliation by England, an old enemy for reasons not confined to cricket.

Lara's best score in the series to date was 36. He had been jumping around uncertainly at the crease in a vain effort to counter England's fast, bouncing bowling on fast, bouncing

HIGHEST TEST TOTALS AGAINST ENGLAND

751-5 dec.	**West Indies at St John's (drew)**	**2003-04**
729-6 dec.	Australia at Lord's (Australia won by seven wickets)	1930
708	Pakistan at The Oval (drew)	1987
701	Australia at The Oval (Australia won by 562 runs)	1934
695	Australia at The Oval (Australia won by an innings and 39 runs)	1930
692-8 dec.	West Indies at The Oval (drew).	1995
687-8 dec.	West Indies at The Oval (West Indies won by 231 runs)	1976
682-6 dec.	South Africa at Lord's (South Africa won by an innings and 92 runs) .	2003
681-8 dec.	West Indies at Port-of-Spain (drew)	1953-54
659-8 dec.	Australia at Sydney (Australia won by an innings and 33 runs)	1946-47
656-8 dec.	Australia at Manchester (drew)	1964
653-4 dec.	Australia at Leeds (Australia won by an innings and 148 runs)	1993
652-8 dec.	West Indies at Lord's (West Indies won by an innings and 226 runs) . .	1973

pitches. For the first time in his Test career, he had been dismissed without scoring in two successive innings; at his home ground, the Queen's Park Oval, he had slipped himself down to No. 6. As in his first term, which ended in resignation four years earlier, his captaincy was under critical scrutiny. "The next five days are very important in terms of my future as captain," he said beforehand. "No captain, no team, wants to go down for the first time in its history as losing all their Test matches at home."

He was clearly mentally ready for the challenge, even if he was still troubled by the finger he had dislocated in the First Test, which eliminated him from the first one-day international six days later. Lara was not the only one to appreciate a return to a benign pitch. Gayle and Sarwan also compensated for meagre series. Gayle thumped 12 fours in 69, Sarwan shared a third-wicket partnership of 232 with Lara, contributing a polished 90. After Powell, who had replaced the out-of-sorts Chanderpaul, and Hinds wasted opportunities to secure their tenuous places, the experienced Jacobs entered, with Lara 234, and followed in his slipstream for more than five hours to gather his third Test century. Their stand was worth 282, a sixth-wicket record for West Indies, at the declaration half an hour into the third afternoon.

There were some, notably Australia's captain Ricky Ponting, who criticised this delayed closure, claiming it disregarded the goal of winning the match. Lara's response was that his priority was to avoid the ignominy of an unprecedented whitewash. The Trinidad & Tobago government, which again lavished their most famous citizen with praise and gifts, was certain of the innings' significance. The prime minister, Patrick Manning, told Lara it was "symbolic of what we are capable of achieving when we harness our strengths and persevere with grit and determination in pursuit of excellence".

As it was, a minimum of 240 overs remained at the declaration. Had Lara not dropped a juggled catch at slip off Sarwan when Flintoff was 27 late on the third afternoon, West Indies would have been closer to a satisfying triumph to match that over Australia. Dropped again at 56 and 67, Flintoff spent nearly five and a half hours over an unbeaten century, skilfully ensuring that the last four wickets yielded 103. England did follow on but, without a genuine spinner, an omission later regretted by Lara, West Indies could make little impression in the second innings on a wearing pitch.

Vaughan and Trescothick put together an opening partnership of real substance for the first time in the series to steady England nerves. At 182, it was their highest to date. Vaughan compiled a fluent, composed century, his 11th in Tests, with 20 fours in nearly six hours; Trescothick, fortunate Hair did not detect his gloved deflection to Jacobs in Best's second over, played with increasing confidence for four hours.

Despite losing three wickets in the last session to the spin of Hinds and Sarwan, England were never in danger of the kind of collapse that led to their late defeat in the corresponding Test six years earlier. But they could not effect the series sweep to which they had been twice subjected by West Indies in the 1980s.

Man of the Match: B. C. Lara.　　　*Man of the Series:* S. J. Harmison.

Close of play: First day, West Indies 208-2 (Lara 86, Sarwan 41); Second day, West Indies 595-5 (Lara 313, Jacobs 47); Third day, England 171-5 (Flintoff 37, G. O. Jones 32); Fourth day, England 145-0 (Trescothick 74, Vaughan 61).

West Indies

C. H. Gayle c and b Batty	69	†R. D. Jacobs not out 107
D. Ganga lbw b Flintoff	10	B 4, l-b 5, w 2, n-b 5 16
*B. C. Lara not out	400	
R. R. Sarwan c Trescothick b Harmison	90	1/33 (2) 2/98 (1)　　　(5 wkts dec.) 751
R. L. Powell c Hussain b S. P. Jones	23	3/330 (4) 4/380 (5)
R. O. Hinds c and b Batty	36	5/469 (6)

T. L. Best, P. T. Collins, C. D. Collymore and F. H. Edwards did not bat.

Bowling: Hoggard 18–2–82–0; Harmison 37–6–92–1; Flintoff 35–8–109–1; S. P. Jones 29–0–146–1; Batty 52–4–185–2; Vaughan 13–0–60–0; Trescothick 18–3–68–0.

England

M. E. Trescothick c Jacobs b Best	16	– c Sarwan b Edwards	88
*M. P. Vaughan c Jacobs b Collins	7	– c Jacobs b Sarwan	140
M. A. Butcher b Collins	52	– c Gayle b Hinds	61
N. Hussain b Best	3	– b Hinds	56
G. P. Thorpe c Collins b Edwards	10	– not out	23
A. Flintoff not out	102	– c Lara b Sarwan	14
†G. O. Jones b Edwards	38	– not out	10
G. J. Batty c Gayle b Collins	8		
M. J. Hoggard c Jacobs b Collins	1		
S. P. Jones lbw b Hinds	11		
S. J. Harmison b Best	5		
B 1, l-b 5, w 4, n-b 22	32	B 4, l-b 7, w 3, n-b 16 ...	30

1/8 (2) 2/45 (1) 3/54 (4) 4/98 (3)	285	1/182 (1) 2/274 (2)　　　(5 wkts) 422
5/98 (5) 6/182 (7) 7/205 (8)		3/366 (3) 4/387 (4)
8/229 (9) 9/283 (11) 10/285 (10)		5/408 (6)

In the first innings S. P. Jones, when 11, retired hurt at 277 and resumed at 283.

Bowling: *First Innings*—Collins 26–4–76–4; Edwards 18–3–70–2; Collymore 19–5–45–0; Best 10.3–3–37–3; Hinds 17.3–7–29–1; Sarwan 7–0–18–0; Gayle 1–0–4–0. *Second Innings*—Best 16–1–57–0; Edwards 20–2–81–1; Collymore 18–3–58–0; Powell 8–0–36–0; Hinds 38–8–83–2; Gayle 17–6–36–0; Sarwan 12–2–26–2; Collins 8–2–34–0.

Umpires: Aleem Dar (Pakistan) and D. B. Hair (Australia).
Third umpire: B. R. Doctrove. Referee: M. J. Procter (South Africa).
J. J. Crowe (New Zealand) deputised for Procter on the 4th day.

†At Everest CC, Georgetown, April 16, 2004. **Guyana v England XI. No result (abandoned).**

THE CABLE & WIRELESS ONE-DAY SERIES

RICHARD HOBSON

†WEST INDIES v ENGLAND

First One-Day International

At Georgetown, April 18, 2004. England won by two wickets. Toss: England. One-day international debut: D. J. J. Bravo.

After England's only one-day warm-up match had been washed out two days previously, it was a near-miracle that play got under way here. Guyana retained its notoriety for wet weather, but helicopters assisted the drying process and a 30-over contest was possible. It had little to commend it until the penultimate over when Read – dropped from the Test team eight days earlier after a run of low scores – struck successive balls from Collymore for six, four and six. So, having needed 20 from the last ten balls, England entered the final over with just three required. Gough's eight-month absence from the international stage had not diminished his eye for a headline: he had claimed the game's first wicket and completed his recall by hitting the winning runs. With Lara resting his injured finger, West Indies owed their total to a curate's egg of an innings by Chanderpaul, 84 from 96 balls. He added 87 in 11 overs with Joseph. England's reply faltered after the drinks break against the variation of Gayle's spin, before Blackwell restored hope.

Man of the Match: C. M. W. Read.

West Indies

C. H. Gayle b Gough	2	(17)	†R. D. Jacobs not out	2	(4)
S. Chanderpaul c Clarke b Gough	84	(96)	B 1, l-b 7, w 10, n-b 1 .	19	
R. L. Powell c and b Flintoff	10	(12)			
*R. R. Sarwan lbw b Flintoff	0	(2)	1/7 (1) 2/25 (3) (5 wkts, 30 overs)	156	
D. R. Smith c Flintoff b Clarke	16	(18)	3/25 (4) 4/64 (5)		
S. C. Joseph not out	23	(32)	5/151 (2)	9 overs: 25-1	

D. J. J. Bravo, M. Dillon, R. Rampaul and C. D. Collymore did not bat.

Bowling: Gough 6–0–22–2; Harmison 6–0–34–0; Kirtley 6–0–28–0; Flintoff 6–2–22–2; Clarke 2–0–16–1; Trescothick 3–0–9–0; Collingwood 1–0–17–0.

England

M. E. Trescothick b Bravo	26	(53)	D. Gough not out	9	(10)
*M. P. Vaughan c Jacobs b Dillon	0	(3)	S. J. Harmison not out	0	(1)
A. J. Strauss b Bravo	29	(46)			
A. Flintoff c Jacobs b Gayle	8	(9)	L-b 4, w 14, n-b 2 .	20	
P. D. Collingwood c Smith b Gayle	10	(18)	1/1 (2) (8 wkts, 29.3 overs)	157	
I. D. Blackwell b Rampaul	27	(21)	2/60 (3) 3/75 (4)		
R. Clarke run out	1	(3)	4/75 (1) 5/108 (5) 6/119 (6)		
†C. M. W. Read b Gayle	27	(15)	7/120 (7) 8/154 (8)	9 overs: 36-1	

R. J. Kirtley did not bat.

Bowling: Dillon 6 0 35–1; Collymore 6–1–35–0; Bravo 6–0–31–2; Rampaul 6–0–32–1; Gayle 5.3–0–20–3.

Umpires: Aleem Dar (Pakistan) and E. A. Nicholls.
Third umpire: B. E. W. Morgan. Referee: J. J. Crowe (New Zealand).

"One six landed in the headmaster's tent, threatening the tea table."
Surrey in 2004, page 758.

†WEST INDIES v ENGLAND

Second One-Day International

At Port-of-Spain, April 24, 2004. No result. Toss: West Indies.

All eyes were on Lara's return for his first innings since the Test record in Antigua, but his home crowd were disappointed. Deafening cheers which greeted the emergence of West Indies' No. 4 subsided as soon as Sarwan became identifiable, and England could not claim another wicket before rain ended the already shortened game.

West Indies

C. H. Gayle c Collingwood			R. R. Sarwan not out	11	(13)
b Anderson .	20	(42)	L-b 6, w 9	15	
S. Chanderpaul c Read					
b Harmison .	3	(16)	1/28 (2)	(2 wkts, 16 overs) 57	
R. L. Powell not out	8	(25)	2/34 (1)	13 overs: 49-2	

*B. C. Lara, D. R. Smith, D. J. J. Bravo, †R. D. Jacobs, M. Dillon, R. Rampaul and C. D. Collymore did not bat.

Bowling: Gough 5–0–20–0; Harmison 7–1–16–1; Anderson 3–0–13–1; Flintoff 1–0–2–0.

England

M. E. Trescothick, *M. P. Vaughan, A. J. Strauss, A. Flintoff, P. D. Collingwood, I. D. Blackwell, R. Clarke, †C. M. W. Read, D. Gough, S. J. Harmison and J. M. Anderson.

Umpires: D. B. Hair (Australia) and B. R. Doctrove.
Third umpire: B. E. W. Morgan. Referee: J. J. Crowe (New Zealand).

†WEST INDIES v ENGLAND

Third One-Day International

At Port-of-Spain, April 25, 2004. No result (abandoned).

Vaughan wore only a slight smile as he reflected on a full programme of one-day cricket on a sunny Sunday back in England, but not a single ball bowled in Trinidad. The torrential rain was falling unseasonably early, but that was no consolation as England fell further behind in their plans to rebuild the one-day team.

†WEST INDIES v ENGLAND

Fourth One-Day International

At St George's, Grenada, April 28, 2004. No result (abandoned).

England did not even bother to leave their hotel for the ground, a 20-minute drive away, after overnight rain made abandonment a formality. The West Indies Cricket Board, meanwhile, were counting the cost of a third washout. Initial losses were estimated at around £400,000 and, though insured, the board faced an increase in premiums.

†WEST INDIES v ENGLAND

Fifth One-Day International

At Gros Islet, St Lucia, May 1, 2004. West Indies won by five wickets. Toss: West Indies. One-day international debut: I. D. R. Bradshaw.

For the first time since the Antigua Test 17 days earlier, cricket replaced the weather as the main concern, and West Indies achieved a convincing win. This came despite Trescothick's 130, his seventh one-day hundred and the highest limited-overs score against West Indies on their home turf. But his brilliant effort was quickly overshadowed by a shorter, sharper contribution – 44 in 28 balls from the precocious Dwayne Smith. The loss of Lara with West Indies 91 short of their target had left England in a strong position, and the home side began the last nine overs still 82 behind. But the next five went for 12, 10, 17, 14 and 17; during this sequence, Sarwan and Smith hit six sixes between them in 14 balls. Sarwan played the finisher's role to perfection, while a couple of Smith's whipped strokes over mid-wicket against Harmison recalled the young Viv Richards. On a good batting pitch with a sloping outfield, England's total of 281 was not quite as imposing as it looked. A direct hit by Chanderpaul finally accounted for Trescothick, while Dillon held Flintoff in comical fashion, at the third attempt, to end a useful supporting fifty.

Man of the Match: R. R. Sarwan.

England

M. E. Trescothick run out	130	(138)	R. Clarke b Gayle	6	(7)
*M. P. Vaughan c Jacobs			D. Gough not out	3	(4)
b Bradshaw	25	(29)	S. J. Harmison not out	3	(2)
A. J. Strauss b Dillon	10	(16)			
P. D. Collingwood c Jacobs			L-b 6, w 6, n-b 5	17	
b Rampaul	4	(14)			
A. Flintoff c Dillon b Bravo	59	(69)	1/43 (2) (8 wkts, 50 overs) 281		
I. D. Blackwell b Bravo	0	(1)	2/114 (3) 3/124 (4)		
†C. M. W. Read c Powell			4/234 (5) 5/235 (6) 6/249 (1)		
b Bradshaw	24	(25)	7/267 (8) 8/275 (7) 15 overs: 106-1		

J. M. Anderson did not bat.

Bowling: Bradshaw 10–0–58–2; Dillon 10–0–47–1; Bravo 8–0–57–2; Rampaul 9–0–48–1; Gayle 9–0–33–1; Powell 4–0–32–0.

West Indies

C. H. Gayle c Collingwood			D. R. Smith b Flintoff	44	(28)
b Anderson	36	(42)	D. J. J. Bravo not out	12	(6)
S. Chanderpaul c Read			L-b 2, w 10, n-b 1	13	
b Blackwell	40	(56)			
R. L. Powell b Anderson	29	(39)	1/62 (1) (5 wkts, 48 overs) 284		
R. R. Sarwan not out	73	(77)	2/102 (3) 3/115 (2)		
*B. C. Lara c Read b Harmison	37	(41)	4/191 (5) 5/271 (6) 15 overs: 74-1		

†R. D. Jacobs, I. D. R. Bradshaw, M. Dillon and R. Rampaul did not bat.

Bowling: Gough 9–1–45–0; Harmison 10–1–74–1; Flintoff 9–0–32–1; Anderson 10–0–66–2; Blackwell 7–0–47–1; Trescothick 3–0–18–0.

Umpires: Aleem Dar (Pakistan) and B. R. Doctrove.
Third umpire: E. A. Nicholls.   Referee: J. J. Crowe (New Zealand).

†WEST INDIES v ENGLAND

Sixth One-Day International

At Gros Islet, St Lucia, May 2, 2004. West Indies won by four wickets. Toss: West Indies.

For the second day running, and on the same pitch at the handsome Beausejour Stadium, West Indies sailed past a target of 280-plus with time to kill, giving them a 2–1 lead in the series with one to play. This time, their batting was most incendiary in the early stages: Chanderpaul and Powell blazed to 110 for one in the first 15 overs. Both fell soon afterwards, mistiming pulls against long-hops, to give England a sniff, but Sarwan and Lara stabilised the innings without fluster. Lara, on his 35th birthday, completed his fifty with successive fours driven against Gough, only to top-edge an attempted hook. With just 37 required from the last ten overs, however, Bravo and Jacobs could proceed without risk. Again, England had faltered in the last ten overs after laying a solid base. They took some comfort from an accomplished maiden international fifty by Strauss and a fluent one from Vaughan, narrowly run out by a direct hit by Powell from behind square.

Man of the Match: S. Chanderpaul.

England

M. E. Trescothick b Rampaul ...	29	(34)	
*M. P. Vaughan run out	67	(78)	
A. J. Strauss lbw b Gayle	67	(82)	
A. Flintoff c Chanderpaul			
b Bradshaw .	43	(47)	
P. D. Collingwood c Sarwan			
b Powell .	38	(34)	
†C. M. W. Read run out	11	(11)	
R. Clarke b Dillon	6	(9)	

G. J. Batty b Gayle 1 (3)
D. Gough not out 3 (2)
S. J. Harmison not out 0 (2)
L-b 3, w 10, n-b 2 15

J. M. Anderson did not bat.

1/57 (1)　　　(8 wkts, 50 overs) 280
2/141 (2) 3/199 (3)
4/251 (4) 5/258 (5) 6/273 (6)
7/276 (7) 8/276 (8)
15 overs: 73-1

Bowling: Rampaul 8–0–54–1; Dillon 10–0–59–1; Bradshaw 10–0–61–1; Bravo 5–0–25–0; Smith 5–0–30–0; Gayle 10–0–39–2; Powell 2–0–9–1.

West Indies

C. H. Gayle lbw b Gough	9	(10)	
S. Chanderpaul c Batty b Clarke .	63	(55)	
R. L. Powell c sub (A. McGrath)			
b Batty .	38	(32)	
R. R. Sarwan b Flintoff	28	(44)	
*B. C. Lara c Gough b Harmison .	57	(68)	
D. R. Smith c Strauss b Batty ...	18	(10)	

D. J. J. Bravo not out 33 (42)
†R. D. Jacobs not out 19 (22)
L-b 6, w 11 17

1/15 (1)　　(6 wkts, 47.1 overs) 282
2/112 (3) 3/113 (2) 4/185 (4)
5/206 (6) 6/244 (5)
15 overs: 110-1

I. D. R. Bradshaw, M. Dillon and R. Rampaul did not bat.

Bowling: Gough 8.1–0–67–1; Harmison 10–0–52–1; Anderson 4–0–27–0; Flintoff 9–0–55–1; Batty 9–0–40–2; Clarke 7–0–35–1.

Umpires: Aleem Dar (Pakistan) and E. A. Nicholls.
Third umpire: B. R. Doctrove. Referee: J. J. Crowe (New Zealand).

†WEST INDIES v ENGLAND

Seventh One-Day International

At Bridgetown, May 5, 2004. England won by five wickets. Toss: England.

In a direct reversal of St Lucia four days earlier, Trescothick eclipsed a century by Sarwan as England ended the tour by levelling the one-day series. Trescothick was at his most belligerent, standing tall to fire bullets through the off side. His 82 occupied a mere 57 balls, and he and Strauss hit six boundaries in succession during a thrilling stand of 87 in 11.2 overs. When Trescothick was stumped off a leg-side wide in the 18th over, England were already almost halfway to the target. Clarke's promotion to No. 4 proved unsuccessful, but so did Lara's attempt to stifle the innings by employing four slow bowlers. Strauss completed another composed half-century and Collingwood finished the job with one of his most productive innings of the winter. Read was there with him, having struck an earlier blow for the wicket-keeping union with a fine, left-handed catch to remove Lara. The England seamers bowled with discipline, especially early on, and it took a deceptively quick run-a-ball hundred from Sarwan to keep West Indies in contention.

Man of the Match: M. E. Trescothick. *Man of the Series:* M. E. Trescothick.

West Indies

C. H. Gayle b Anderson	41	(52)
S. Chanderpaul c Anderson b Harmison	3	(16)
R. L. Powell run out	9	(19)
R. R. Sarwan not out	104	(105)
*B. C. Lara c Read b Clarke	8	(28)
D. R. Smith lbw b Gough	39	(36)
D. J. J. Bravo b Flintoff	11	(19)
†R. D. Jacobs not out	32	(28)
L-b 6, w 5, n-b 3	14	

(6 wkts, 50 overs) 261

1/16 (2) 2/57 (3) 3/57 (1) 4/90 (5) 5/159 (6) 6/193 (7) 15 overs: 57-2

I. D. R. Bradshaw, M. Dillon and R. Rampaul did not bat.

Bowling: Gough 10–1–45–1; Harmison 10–0–51–1; Flintoff 10–1–45–1; Anderson 8–0–42–1; Clarke 9–0–50–1; Batty 3–0–22–0.

England

M. E. Trescothick st Jacobs b Gayle	82	(57)
*M. P Vaughan c Jacobs b Rampaul	14	(16)
A. J. Strauss b Bradshaw	66	(86)
R. Clarke c Smith b Bradshaw	9	(18)
A. Flintoff c and b Sarwan	11	(20)
P. D. Collingwood not out	46	(52)
†C. M. W. Read not out	23	(35)
L-b 5, w 6	11	

(5 wkts, 47.2 overs) 262

1/36 (2) 2/123 (1) 3/146 (4) 4/169 (5) 5/218 (3) 15 overs: 111-1

G. J. Batty, D. Gough, S. J. Harmison and J. M. Anderson did not bat.

Bowling: Dillon 9–0–67–0; Rampaul 4–0–32–1; Powell 6.2–0–35–0; Gayle 8–0–28–1; Bradshaw 10–0–46–2; Sarwan 9–0–38–1; Chanderpaul 1–0–11–0.

Umpires: Aleem Dar (Pakistan) and B. R. Doctrove.
Third umpire: E. A. Nicholls. Referee: J. J. Crowe (New Zealand).

Figures in brackets are balls received.

THE WISDEN TROPHY

The 100th edition of *Wisden Cricketers' Almanack* was published in 1963 and, to mark the occasion, John Wisden and Co presented the Wisden Trophy to the MCC. This was to be contested by England and West Indies, who were then emerging as a global power in the game. Like the Ashes urn, the Wisden Trophy has a permanent home in the Lord's museum, though, unlike the Ashes, it is taken out to be presented to victorious captains.

England and West Indies have played 30 Test series, the last 20 for the Wisden Trophy. Frank Worrell was the first captain to be presented with the trophy after West Indies won the 1963 series 3–1.

England won it in both 1967-68 and 1969, but the trophy was regained by West Indies in 1973, and they held it for the next 27 years. Including their two victories, away and home, in 2004, England have now won it three times in a row.

ENGLAND IN NAMIBIA, ZIMBABWE AND SOUTH AFRICA, 2004-05

REVIEW BY JOHN ETHERIDGE

England, under the calm yet increasingly bold captaincy of Michael Vaughan, won an often thrilling Test series 2–1 and secured their first victory in South Africa for 40 years. Admittedly, it was only their third Test tour to the country since M. J. K. Smith's team won in 1964-65, but that should not diminish their achievement. Only Australia, twice, had previously won a series in South Africa since their return from sporting isolation in 1991-92. It is a very tough country in which to win.

England failed to reach the standards they established in their demolitions of West Indies and New Zealand in 2004, yet this was a hugely determined performance in the face of a savage and unprecedented schedule – no touring team in history had previously been confronted by five Test matches in 40 days without a game of any description in between. Even David Morgan, the chairman of the ECB, said England must never again agree to such an itinerary, regardless of the financial benefits. Vaughan himself described the result as his best as captain, which is saying something because he had already presided over England's first win in the Caribbean for 36 years and an unprecedented seven victories out of seven during the English summer.

Vaughan's reasoning was that England won the Basil D'Oliveira Trophy without playing at their best, making it a triumph for mental resolve as much as for cricketing skill. Certainly, much of the excitement was generated because these were two flawed and often fatigued teams. England's weariness was obvious when they had to launch into a one-day series immediately afterwards without their star all-rounder, Andrew Flintoff, and lost it 4–1, though it was a series mainly notable for the stirring form of England's latest recruit from South Africa, Kevin Pietersen, who rode the boos from the fans he deserted to score three outstanding centuries.

By then, it was hard to remember this was a tour that started (after a couple of bunfights in Namibia) with England dragging themselves unwillingly on to a plane to Harare for a politically charged visit to Zimbabwe that was more or less unanimously unwanted. They nearly escaped when the Zimbabwean authorities banned an apparently arbitrary list of 13 cricket writers from entering the country, which appeared to give the ECB the excuse they needed to cancel the tour without reprisals from the ICC. The Zimbabweans backed down, to widespread regret, and, after the cancellation of the first one-day international, the visit passed off with less incident than feared. But it all added to the build-up of weariness for key members of the party.

Yet the players' spirit remained indomitable, at least until the final week of one-dayers. Andrew Strauss and Marcus Trescothick with the bat and Matthew Hoggard and Flintoff with the ball were their major players, but

Serial success: at Centurion, England celebrate winning the Basil D'Oliveira Trophy – and their fourth Test series in less than ten months. *Standing:* Gareth Batty, Chris Read, Steve Harmison, Geraint Jones, Ashley Giles, James Anderson, Matthew Hoggard, Jon Lewis, Ian Bell, Marcus Trescothick, Paul Collingwood, Rob Key. *Kneeling:* Andrew Strauss, Simon Jones, Michael Vaughan, Graham Thorpe, Andrew Flintoff.

Picture by Graham Morris

Vaughan's team usually found someone to produce something significant in times of need. Whether it was Simon Jones's stunning diving boundary catch and four-wicket burst in the First Test, or Graham Thorpe's vigil in the Fifth, there were telling contributions from all departments. The only one-sided Test was in Cape Town, the one England lost.

Followers of South African cricket regarded it as their most exciting home Test series since their comeback to the international arena. For England, it was their first five-Test overseas success since they retained the Ashes in 1986-87, and the victory instantly and inevitably cranked up by several notches the expectations for their forthcoming home series against Australia. Yet Vaughan and the coach, Duncan Fletcher, knew better than anybody that Australia would be unlikely to allow England to keep clambering off the canvas as happened on this tour – South Africa had a first-innings lead in each of the middle three Tests and still lost the series. The best teams nail down the coffin lid and dump half a ton of bricks on top for good measure.

The series was effectively decided on the final afternoon of the Fourth Test, when South Africa, thought to be safe from defeat at the start of the last day, were bowled out after lunch by Hoggard, who conducted a masterclass in the art of swing bowling. He found a tantalising length, and arced the ball away from the right-handed batsman to take seven for 61 and finish with match figures of 12 for 205, the best for England since Ian Botham in the Bombay Jubilee Test a quarter of a century earlier. Yet just as important was Vaughan's belief at the start of the day that England could win, rather than simply avoid defeat.

For South Africa, Jacques Kallis matched Strauss's three centuries, and his 162 in Durban was the innings of the series. With his patience, appetite for runs and textbook technique, Kallis was always the prized wicket: it was no coincidence that, when England bowled out South Africa in less than 60 overs in Johannesburg, Kallis was out first ball. South Africa used 18 players to England's 13, including three wicket-keepers and three opening partnerships. They chose a better-balanced side as the series progressed and one that did not unduly offend the proponents of their unofficial quota system, although in truth they could never quite decide on their best team, and there were tensions between the captain, Graeme Smith, and the selectors that became more overt during the one-day games.

FASTEST ENGLAND PLAYERS TO 1,000 TEST RUNS

	M	I	NO	HS	Avge	100s	50s	Seasons
H. Sutcliffe	9	12	2	176	100.00	5	4	1924 to 1924-25
L. Hutton	11	16	1	364	66.66	4	2	1937 to 1939
W. R. Hammond . . .	12	18	2	251	62.50	2	4	1927-28 to 1928-29
A. J. Strauss	**10**	**19**	**3**	**137**	**62.50**	**4**	**4**	**2004 to 2004-05**
D. I. Gower	13	20	2	142*	55.55	3	4	1978 to 1979
C. P. Mead.	15	21	3	182*	55.55	4	1	1911-12 to 1922-23
E. Paynter	14	21	5	216*	62.50	2	6	1931 to 1938-39

Research: Philip Bailey

Proven performers such as the mercurial Herschelle Gibbs and the wicket-keeper Mark Boucher came back into the side, and both Gibbs and the tyro A. B. de Villiers went close to registering a hundred in each innings of a Test. De Villiers, versatile and athletic, provided perhaps their best news of the series. But this was the least convincing South African team England have faced since the fixtures were resumed in 1994; when they did exert pressure, their self-belief appeared to desert them. Nor were they ever able to solve the problem of the soft underbelly of their middle-order batting, despite several changes of personnel. Smith even dropped himself to No. 5 in the final Test, as much to bolster the middle of the innings as to escape Hoggard, who had dismissed him lbw three times. Smith's series aggregate of 269 was fewer than the 277 he made in one innings at Edgbaston 18 months earlier. With the ball, Shaun Pollock was as immaculate as ever, and the tireless Makhaya Ntini was South Africa's leading bowler with 25 wickets; his aggression, wide angle of release and liberal use of the short ball infiltrated the techniques of a number of England batsmen, Vaughan and Andrew Flintoff among them. To hook or duck, that was the question.

IS THIS HARARE? NO, IT'S ANOTHER HOTEL

Paul Kelso

It was entirely in keeping with the ECB's unhappy handling of the Zimbabwe question over the years that the England team should have been stuck yet again in a luxury hotel hundreds of miles away when they should have been preparing to play international cricket.

Less than two years earlier, Nasser Hussain's squad had mooched in the Cullinan Hotel, Cape Town, while their employers searched in vain for a solution to the players' objections to visiting Harare for the World Cup. This time the gaudy Italianate Imperial Hotel in Johannesburg's northern suburbs was the venue for a stand-off prompted by the Zimbabwe government's refusal to accredit 13 British journalists, representing nine different media organisations – described as "political" rather than "*bona fide*" by one official. Those not meeting Zimbabwe's exacting standards included *The Times* and the *Daily Telegraph*.

The media ban, announced 24 hours before the squad were due to land in Harare, prompted an unlikely alliance between press and players. At a team meeting held in the first-class lounge at Jan Smuts airport just an hour before the scheduled departure, Michael Vaughan made it plain to ECB chairman David Morgan, already in Harare, that if the hacks weren't going, nor were the team.

As tour manager Phil Neale kindly collected boarding passes from the assembled media so our luggage could be rescued from the aircraft, you could not get a price on the tour going ahead – which only goes to confirm the players' more usual opinion of the press, i.e. we don't know what we're talking about. Next morning, as the players lounged round the Imperial's vast pool and their new allies discussed the merits of that evening's different flights to Heathrow, came news that Zimbabwe had climbed down. That night Morgan's emissary, John Carr, confirmed the tour was on.

David Morgan was delighted at having forced a change of heart in Harare, but in reality the *volte-face* had more to do with internecine feuding within the ruling party ZANU-PF than the ECB chairman's powers of diplomacy. Not that the players would have known it. Wearing the indifferent expressions that international cricketers adopt wherever they are, the squad spent the next ten days insulated from the country's politics and privations by the routine of playing and practising.

Transported from ground to hotel to golf course, they saw only sporadic graffiti and one pathetic early-morning protest to illustrate the deeper issues raised by this tour. The opening mismatch even took place in a festival atmosphere in front of several thousand Harareans who managed to find something to enjoy in it. The next three took place amid general indifference, even among the old Rhodesian diehards in the bars. Black and white alike knew that, whatever it was they were watching, it was not a genuine contest.

The players were not fooled either. The administrators present, including ICC president Ehsan Mani, may have believed this sad tour deserved to be called international cricket. Michael Vaughan certainly didn't.

Yet neither Pollock nor Ntini managed a five-wicket haul, and South Africa struggled to find reliable support bowling. Charl Langeveldt did take five for 46 at Newlands but could not play again because his hand was broken while batting. The pantomime villain Andre Nel, all staring and swearing, hissing and booing, could not appear until the Fifth Test because of injury and he promptly took six for 81 in England's first innings. Kallis could not bowl in the First Test because of an ankle injury and was reluctant thereafter, which also diminished South Africa's options. While his all-rounder rival, Flintoff, sent down more balls than any other England bowler, Kallis took just four wickets in the series in 96 overs. It was a crucial difference between the teams. South Africa's bowlers also struggled with England's left-handers. While Strauss, Trescothick and Thorpe averaged 72, 44 and 35 respectively, the right-handers Robert Key, Vaughan, Flintoff and Geraint Jones managed only 841 runs between them at 28 apiece.

The South African camp was not harmonious. The transformation issue remained divisive – should they pick their best team or offer as much encouragement as possible to the non-white communities? – and there were mutterings of discontent between some senior players and the eccentric coach, Ray Jennings. Jennings had already raised eyebrows when, as coach of South Africa A, he removed the fridge from the dressing-room and said his players could crawl on their hands and knees to drink warm water from a tap. In the event, he turned out to be not quite the madman he was portrayed as before the series began, yet some of his ideas were unusual to say the least. He recruited a couple of young tennis pros to serve balls at his batsmen in the nets, reaching speeds way in excess of anything real bowlers could manage. Bowlers who no-balled were punished by being forced to do laps of the ground, and Jennings frequently belted hand-stinging catches at his players from five yards away. It was on one such occasion, during the Wanderers Test, when Smith thought the catching practice had finished, that Jennings hit his captain on the side of his head. The England team, meanwhile, identified Smith as a hate figure, privately accusing him of hamming up the effects of that blow at the Wanderers, even though he had neurological advice warning him as to the possible consequences of another whack. Smith had plenty to say for himself on the field but perhaps England's rather illogical dislike of the opposition captain was their way of staying mean and moody.

At times, mainly because of the unrelenting itinerary, the series developed into a war of attrition. Bodies were tested by the heat and sheer volume of high-intensity cricket. Injuries had little time to heal. Strength of mind was as important as physical fitness. Steve Harmison was troubled by a calf strain in the final two Tests, and the toll on Flintoff's mighty body was enormous. Yet he still managed to withstand the soreness and crank up his pace to 90mph at times. Flintoff was always the bowler to whom Vaughan turned when he wanted control and to slow the scoring, so much so that he overbowled him at times.

The rescheduling which followed the cancellation of England's planned two-Test series in Zimbabwe left them with just one first-class warm-up

Silent protest: graffiti artists in Harare make their feelings known about England's tour of Zimbabwe.

Picture by Howard Burditt, Reuters

match before the First Test, a game they lost heavily to South Africa A. Chris Read, the reserve wicket-keeper, played just one day's cricket in two months; Gareth Batty, on tour a month longer, played four days. Coach Duncan Fletcher insisted claims that England were "undercooked" – the tour's buzzword – were not justified, because they won the opening Test in Port Elizabeth, but this had more to do with South Africa selecting an unbalanced team than any dynamic play on England's part. Indeed, the lack of coherent preparation affected some players throughout the series. Harmison, for example, was forced to try to discover his form in the Tests, instead of practice matches. He bowled far too short and seemed incapable of learning from the more probing length found by his new-ball partner, Hoggard. There was a technical flaw, too, with his left arm and shoulder pulling away too quickly in delivery, and Smith's pre-series claim that Harmison's confidence could be undermined proved startlingly accurate. Hyped as the world's No. 1 ranked bowler, who had taken 61 wickets in his previous 11 Tests in 2004, Harmison captured just nine wickets at 73.22 and finished it as No. 9. The old murmurings about his mental fragility and homesickness resurfaced, too. One factor could have been that his closest chum, Flintoff, had his fiancée and baby daughter with him for the entire tour and therefore had fewer chances to wrap a reassuring arm around Harmison's shoulder.

Apart from the usual Christmas and New Year family visits, the wives of Vaughan, Trescothick and Strauss also spent several weeks with their husbands. This was a new development. The tour of "no wives, no kids" to Zimbabwe and New Zealand in 1996-97 seemed a distant memory in these more liberated times. Mrs Strauss had plenty to applaud, too, because her husband was named man of the series and confirmed his emergence as a player with the technique and temperament to succeed at the highest level.

Strauss made three centuries and top-scored in six of England's first seven innings of the series, before the game had its revenge and he fell to earth with two ducks in the final three. During the Newlands Test, he reached 1,000 runs just 228 days after he became a Test cricketer, the quickest man to the landmark in history. Strauss has a method – compact, playing within his limitations and scoring heavily with the square cut, the pull and off his legs – which works, and he did not attempt to change at any time. Even South Africa's initial belief that Strauss was vulnerable from around the wicket was not proved; indeed, they eventually realised he was more susceptible to the ball angled across him from over the wicket, and he was caught behind or in the slips in each of his final four innings. Strauss scored 126 and 94 not out in the First Test victory and followed with further centuries in Durban and Johannesburg, where he played his most fluent innings, just a few miles from the suburb of Bedfordview, his home until the age of six. Strauss's aggregate of 656 was the highest aggregate for England in South Africa.

Trescothick also reached three figures in Durban and Johannesburg. His opening partnership of 273 with Strauss at Kingsmead – England's highest first-wicket stand since 1960 – transformed an astonishing match after they were bowled out for 139 in their first innings. The memory of the bad light there, which prevented England forcing home their recovery with a victory, was a strong motivation for Vaughan's attacking instincts two Tests later at the Wanderers. It was Trescothick's most productive overseas tour. His hand-eye co-ordination was such that South Africa's bowlers were unable to exploit foot movement which occasionally made it look as though he was standing in a tray of treacle.

Mark Butcher flew home because of a wrist injury after playing the first two Tests and was replaced in the team by Robert Key of Kent. Neither made an unanswerable case to retain the No. 3 position. Vaughan reached double figures in each of his first six innings in the series but never exceeded 20 until his brace of half-centuries in the Fourth Test at Johannesburg. Too often he prodded at the ball outside off stump or, unsettled by Ntini's short stuff, attempted his favoured pull-hook before he was set. Vaughan was fined his whole match fee – calculated at around £5,500 in these days of central contracts – for criticising the umpires for inconsistency over the interpretation of bad light at the Wanderers. Even then, his words were finely calculated and, overall, his leadership was superb. His understated style and desire for players to express themselves elicited blanket respect from his team. Vaughan has a streak of steel and is fiercely ambitious; the idea, mooted when he succeeded Nasser Hussain in 2003, that he might be too soft to captain England was made to seem ludicrous.

Thorpe made a century in Durban and 86 in Centurion but, at the age of 35, was generally less convincing than in the past. Flintoff, so immense with the ball, was less productive as a No. 6 batsman, frequently tossing away his wicket with a wishy-washy waft outside off stump, until his watchful 77 in the Fifth Test. Like Flintoff, Geraint Jones made a couple of half-centuries and always batted in a selfless way. He dropped at least three catches, usually because he did not seem to know where first slip was. Ashley Giles was steady enough with his left-arm spin, although rarely threatening. Indeed, he made at least as important a contribution with his batting, notably when he kick-started Trescothick into action on the final morning in Johannesburg.

Simon Jones took at least one wicket in every innings in which he bowled. He was fast at times and straighter than before – he is a cricketer with the knack of making things happen. James Anderson replaced him at the Wanderers in England's only unenforced change but, so badly did Anderson spray the ball and so bankrupt was his confidence, the decision was reversed for the Fifth Test. Because of the itinerary, the other back-up players – Batty, Read and Paul Collingwood – were little more than enthusiastic drinks waiters, nets performers and, at the Wanderers, emergency ball boys. When a team is successful and settled, the reserves lose out, especially on a tour with an itinerary like this. But that is one of the problems of success and, boy, are England grateful to have some of those.

ENGLAND TOURING PARTY

M. P. Vaughan (Yorkshire) (*captain*), M. E. Trescothick (Somerset) (*vice-captain*), J. M. Anderson (Lancashire), G. J. Batty (Worcestershire), M. A. Butcher (Surrey), P. D. Collingwood (Durham), A. Flintoff (Lancashire), A. F. Giles (Warwickshire), S. J. Harmison (Durham), M. J. Hoggard (Yorkshire), G. O. Jones (Kent), S. P. Jones (Glamorgan), R. W. T. Key (Kent), C. M. W. Read (Nottinghamshire), A. J. Strauss (Middlesex), G. P. Thorpe (Surrey).

I. R. Bell (Warwickshire) was added to the squad when Butcher, who injured his wrist, returned home during the Third Test. J. Lewis (Gloucestershire) was added as seam-bowling cover for the Fifth Test.

A party of 14 travelled to Zimbabwe for the one-day international series which preceded the South African tour. This consisted of Vaughan, Anderson, Batty, Bell, Collingwood, Giles, G. O. Jones, S. P. Jones and Strauss, plus D. Gough (Essex), K. P. Pietersen (Hampshire), M. J. Prior (Sussex), V. S. Solanki (Worcestershire) and A. G. Wharf (Glamorgan). Trescothick and Flintoff were rested and Harmison withdrew on conscientious grounds. For the one-day series in South Africa, Key, Read and Thorpe were replaced by Kabir Ali (Worcestershire), Gough, Solanki and Wharf. Pietersen was added to the squad as cover for Flintoff, who returned home after the Test series for an operation on a bone spur on his left ankle. Hoggard and S. P. Jones were also added, although Jones was sent home once it was established that Harmison would be fit later in the series.

Coach: D. A. G. Fletcher. *Operations manager:* P. A. Neale. *Assistant coach (Test squad):* M. Watkinson. *Assistant coach (one-day squad):* M. P. Maynard. *Bowling coach:* T. J. Cooley. *Team analyst:* T. J. Boon. *Physiotherapist (Test squad):* K. A. Russell. *Physiotherapist (one-day squad):* D. O. Conway. *Physiologist:* N. P. Stockill. *Team masseuse:* V. Byrne. *Media relations managers:* A. J. Walpole and D. A. Clarke.

ENGLAND TOUR RESULTS

Test matches – Played 5: Won 2, Lost 1, Drawn 2.
First-class matches – Played 6: Won 2, Lost 2, Drawn 2.
One-day internationals – Played 11: Won 5, Lost 4, Tied 1, No result 1. *Wins* – Zimbabwe (4), South Africa. *Losses* – South Africa (4). *Tie* – South Africa. *No result* – South Africa.
Other non-first-class matches – Played 4: Won 4.

TEST MATCH AVERAGES

SOUTH AFRICA – BATTING AND FIELDING

	T	I	NO	R	HS	100s	50s	Avge	Ct/St
J. H. Kallis	5	10	1	625	162	3	2	69.44	8
H. H. Gibbs	4	8	0	356	161	1	1	44.50	5
A. B. de Villiers	5	10	1	362	109	1	2	40.22	13/1
H. H. Dippenaar	3	6	0	207	110	1	0	34.50	3
†J. A. Rudolph	5	10	0	304	93	0	2	30.40	6
†G. C. Smith	5	10	1	269	74	0	3	29.88	9
†N. Boje	4	7	0	180	76	0	1	25.71	0
M. V. Boucher	2	4	0	95	64	0	1	23.75	8
S. M. Pollock	5	9	1	120	43	0	0	15.00	0
M. Ntini	5	9	3	89	26	0	0	14.83	2
D. W. Steyn	3	5	3	25	8	0	0	12.50	1
A. J. Hall	2	4	0	43	17	0	0	10.75	1
H. M. Amla	2	4	0	36	25	0	0	9.00	2

Played in one Test: Z. de Bruyn 6, 19; C. K. Langeveldt 5*; A. Nel 1*; T. L. Tsolekile 22, 0 (3 ct); M. van Jaarsveld 1, 49 (2 ct).

† *Left-handed batsman.*

BOWLING

	Style	O	M	R	W	BB	5W/i	Avge
A. Nel	RFM	41	12	105	6	6-81	1	17.50
C. K. Langeveldt	RFM	33	7	96	5	5-46	1	19.20
S. M. Pollock	RFM	222.1	83	503	21	4-32	0	23.95
M. Ntini	RF	221.3	49	627	25	4-50	0	25.08
D. W. Steyn	RF	100.2	16	416	8	2-26	0	52.00
N. Boje	SLA	137	31	430	6	4-71	0	71.66

Also bowled: Z. de Bruyn (RFM) 9–1–31–0; A. J. Hall (RFM) 52.2–7–176–3; J. H. Kallis (RFM) 96–20–303–4; G. C. Smith (OB) 36–7–121–2.

ENGLAND – BATTING AND FIELDING

	T	I	NO	R	HS	100s	50s	Avge	Ct
†A. J. Strauss	5	10	1	656	147	3	1	72.88	5
†M. E. Trescothick	5	10	0	448	180	2	0	44.80	11
†G. P. Thorpe	5	10	2	287	118*	1	1	35.87	4
M. P. Vaughan	5	10	2	246	82*	0	2	30.75	2
A. Flintoff	5	9	1	227	77	0	2	28.37	2
G. O. Jones	5	8	0	215	73	0	2	26.87	16
A. F. Giles	5	8	1	188	39	0	0	26.85	5
R. W. T. Key	3	6	0	153	83	0	1	25.50	2
†M. A. Butcher	2	4	0	97	79	0	1	24.25	0
S. J. Harmison	5	7	3	96	42	0	0	24.00	1
†S. P. Jones	4	5	1	64	24	0	0	16.00	2
M. J. Hoggard	5	7	2	20	7*	0	0	4.00	5

Played in one Test: †J. M. Anderson did not bat.

† *Left-handed batsman.*

BOWLING

	Style	O	M	R	W	BB	5W/i	Avge
A. Flintoff	RFM	201.2	42	574	23	4-44	0	24.95
M. J. Hoggard	RFM	200.3	37	663	26	7-61	2	25.50
S. P. Jones	RF	123.1	21	400	15	4-39	0	26.66
A. F. Giles	SLA	139.5	18	449	11	3-105	0	40.81
S. J. Harmison	RF	190.5	28	659	9	3-91	0	73.22

Also bowled: J. M. Anderson (RFM) 34–4–149–2; M. E. Trescothick (RM) 5–1–11–0; M. P. Vaughan (OB) 11–3–29–1.

ENGLAND TOUR AVERAGES – FIRST-CLASS MATCHES

BATTING AND FIELDING

	T	I	NO	R	HS	100s	50s	Avge	Ct
†A. J. Strauss.	6	12	1	706	147	3	2	64.18	7
†M. E. Trescothick	6	12	0	457	180	2	0	38.08	11
M. P. Vaughan	6	12	2	372	100	1	2	37.20	3
†G. P. Thorpe.	6	12	2	298	118*	1	1	29.80	5
G. O. Jones	6	10	0	282	73	0	2	28.20	18
R. W. T. Key	3	6	0	153	83	0	1	25.50	2
A. Flintoff.	6	11	1	252	77	0	2	25.20	3
A. F. Giles	6	10	1	212	39	0	0	23.55	6
S. J. Harmison	6	9	4	116	42	0	0	23.20	0
†S. P. Jones	5	7	2	100	31*	0	0	20.00	2
†M. A. Butcher	3	6	0	100	79	0	1	16.66	0
M. J. Hoggard	6	9	2	40	17	0	0	5.71	6

Played in one match: †J. M. Anderson did not bat.

† *Left-handed batsman.*

BOWLING

	Style	O	M	R	W	BB	5W/i	Avge
A. Flintoff	RFM	219.2	44	634	26	4-44	0	24.38
S. P. Jones	RF	146.1	22	485	19	4-39	0	25.52
M. J. Hoggard	RFM	223.3	42	750	28	7-61	2	26.78
A. F. Giles	SLA	149.5	20	494	13	3-105	0	38.00
S. J. Harmison	RF	219.5	32	779	11	3-91	0	70.81

Also bowled: J. M. Anderson (RFM) 34–4–149–2; M. E. Trescothick (RM) 5–1–11–0; M. P. Vaughan (OB) 11–3–29–1.

Note: Matches in this section which were not first-class are signified by a dagger.

†At Windhoek, November 21, 2004. **England XII won by 67 runs.** Toss: Namibia. **England XII 260-6** (42 overs) (M. P. Vaughan 89, A. J. Strauss 73); **Namibia 193-4** (42 overs) (D. Keulder 57, M. Karg 66).
   Each side named 12 players, of whom 11 could bat and 11 field.

†At Windhoek, November 23, 2004. **England XI won by seven wickets.** Toss: England XI. **Namibia 219-8** (50 overs) (G. Snyman 75); **England XI 220-3** (43.5 overs) (V. S. Solanki 82, I. R. Bell 51).

ONE-DAY INTERNATIONAL REPORTS BY PAUL KELSO

†ZIMBABWE v ENGLAND

First One-Day International

At Harare, November 28, 2004. England won by five wickets. Toss: England. One-day international debuts: C. B. Mpofu; I. R. Bell, K. P. Pietersen.

Shortly before 9.30 a.m., Michael Vaughan finally led an England team on to a Zimbabwean cricket field, three years after their last series in the country and just over 21 months since the acrimonious cancellation of their previous scheduled appearance, in the 2003 World Cup. He had strongly intimated that any attempt to politicise this series would have led to the team's withdrawal; fortunately neither Robert Mugabe nor any of his government officials showed up. Instead, around 3,000 spectators, black and white, piled in and by mid-afternoon were contributing to a festival atmosphere. Sadly, the mismatch failed to justify local interest. England made three changes to the side that lost the Champions Trophy final at The Oval in September: in came Pietersen and Bell for their one-day debuts, along with Anderson, in place of the resting Flintoff and Trescothick and the conscientious objector Harmison. Zimbabwe, with an average age below 21 and missing all the rebel white players sacked by the board earlier in the year, gave a debut to fast bowler Christopher Mpofu, a willowy 19-year-old discovered at a township class in 2003 by former West Indies pace man Ian Bishop. After Zimbabwe were inserted by Vaughan on a slow surface, the most notable contribution was Chigumbura's 47-ball 52, which turned a perilous 90 for five into a respectable 195. A clean striker of the ball armed with a thumping drive, Chigumbura was tipped by Phil Simmons, Zimbabwe's coach, as a future "world-beater" in the short game. England's run-chase was built round a half-century for Bell, who became the fifth Englishman – after Chris Broad, Martyn Moxon, Kim Barnett and Trescothick – to record debut fifties in both Tests and one-day internationals. His 75 off 115 balls anchored the innings, and a stand of 111 with Vaughan took England to the brink of victory before a late wobble saw four wickets fall for 43. Pietersen eventually hit the winning runs, but not before running out Collingwood and twice almost doing the same to Jones.

Man of the Match: I. R. Bell.

Zimbabwe

B. R. M. Taylor b Wharf	17	(31)	
S. Matsikenyeri c Pietersen			
b Gough	14	(26)	
V. Sibanda b Wharf	6	(17)	
D. D. Ebrahim b Giles	45	(90)	
M. A. Vermeulen run out	11	(34)	
*†T. Taibu b Gough	5	(14)	
E. Chigumbura c Collingwood			
b Anderson	52	(47)	
T. Panyangara lbw b Giles	1	(10)	

P. Utseya not out	11	(18)
D. T. Hondo run out	7	(10)
C. B. Mpofu b Gough	0	(1)
L-b 8, w 17, n-b 1	26	

1/36 (2) 2/45 (1)   (49.3 overs) 195
3/56 (3) 4/80 (5)
5/90 (6) 6/172 (4)
7/172 (7) 8/175 (8)
9/194 (10) 10/195 (11)   15 overs: 55-2

Bowling: Gough 9.3–0–34–3; Anderson 10–1–38–1; Wharf 10–2–38–2; Collingwood 10–0–41–0; Giles 10–0–36–2.

England

V. S. Solanki c Panyangara			
b Hondo	7	(19)	
I. R. Bell c Taibu b Taylor	75	(115)	
*M. P. Vaughan c Chigumbura			
b Matsikenyeri	56	(75)	
A. J. Strauss c and b Matsikenyeri	8	(14)	
K. P. Pietersen not out	27	(47)	

P. D. Collingwood run out	1	(2)
†G. O. Jones not out	7	(18)
L-b 3, w 9, n-b 4	16	

1/21 (1)   (5 wkts, 47.4 overs) 197
2/132 (3) 3/146 (4)
4/170 (2) 5/175 (6)   15 overs: 56-1

A. F. Giles, A. G. Wharf, D. Gough and J. M. Anderson did not bat.

Bowling: Panyangara 6–0–32–0; Mpofu 9.4–2–32–0; Hondo 6–0–26–1; Chigumbura 2–0–18–0; Utseya 10–0–39–0; Matsikenyeri 10–0–33–2; Taylor 4–0–14–1.

Umpires: B. G. Jerling (South Africa) and K. C. Barbour.
Third umpire: R. B. Tiffin. Referee: R. S. Mahanama (Sri Lanka).

†ZIMBABWE v ENGLAND

Second One-Day International

At Harare, December 1, 2004. England won by 161 runs. Toss: England. One-day international debut: G. M. Ewing.

An unchanged England shook off the torpor and nerves that tainted their opening display to hand out the second-heaviest defeat in Zimbabwe's one-day international history. On a livelier surface than that used for the opening game, Pietersen and Jones hit maiden one-day international half-centuries in a rollicking stand of 120 off 80 balls, which stood for four days as an England record for the sixth wicket against any opposition. Pietersen's innings had the air of an announcement. Arriving in the 26th over with England stuttering on 94 for three, he was initially studious, taking 40 balls over his first 16 runs, before opening up to finish with 77 from 76, including four fours and three sixes. In all, England thrashed 104 runs off the last ten overs, with Jones whacking 66 off only 46 deliveries, with six fours and two sixes. The hosts collapsed naively in pursuit of 264, losing all ten wickets for 62 after a promising opening stand of 40. Wharf, with four wickets, and Collingwood, with three, were the principal benefactors. Zimbabwe included Gavin Ewing, one of the less experienced of the group of rebel players, who had broken ranks in August and agreed to play for the country again.

Man of the Match: K. P. Pietersen.

England

V. S. Solanki st Taibu b Utseya	..	42	(71)	†G. O. Jones c Masakadza			
I. R. Bell c Ebrahim					b Panyangara	.	66	(46)
	b Panyangara	.	5	(16)	A. F. Giles not out	....	3	(5)
*M. P. Vaughan lbw b Panyangara		11	(21)		L-b 5, w 12, n-b 2	....	19	
A. J. Strauss b Ewing	....	33	(52)					
K. P. Pietersen not out	....	77	(76)	1/13 (2)	(6 wkts, 50 overs) 263		
P. D. Collingwood c Taibu				2/30 (3) 3/94 (1)			
	b Matsikenyeri	.	7	(15)	4/103 (4) 5/121 (6) 6/241 (7)	15 overs: 55-2		

A. G. Wharf, D. Gough and J. M. Anderson did not bat.

Bowling: Panyangara 10–1–61–3; Mpofu 10–0–51–0; Chigumbura 7–0–38–0; Utseya 10–0–35–1; Ewing 7–0–36–1; Matsikenyeri 4–0–18–1; Taylor 2–0–19–0.

Zimbabwe

S. Matsikenyeri c Vaughan				T. Panyangara c Solanki b Giles..		0	(5)
	b Anderson	.	17	(34)	P. Utseya not out	....	2	(24)
B. R. M. Taylor c Jones b Wharf	.	13	(26)	C. B. Mpofu c Collingwood			
D. D. Ebrahim c Vaughan					b Wharf	.	2	(28)
	b Collingwood	.	12	(24)				
M. A. Vermeulen c Pietersen					L-b 2, w 12, n-b 3	....	17	
	b Wharf	.	0	(2)				
H. Masakadza b Wharf	....	3	(9)	1/40 (1) 2/42 (2)	(36 overs) 102		
*†T. Taibu c and b Giles	......	32	(48)	3/42 (4) 4/53 (5)			
E. Chigumbura				5/78 (3) 6/89 (7)			
	c and b Collingwood	.	4	(9)	7/97 (6) 8/97 (9)			
G. M. Ewing c Anderson				9/97 (8) 10/102 (11)	15 overs: 63-4		
	b Collingwood	.	0	(10)				

Bowling: Gough 6–1–24–0; Anderson 7–1–24–1; Wharf 6–1–24–4; Collingwood 10–4–16–3; Giles 7–2–12–2.

Umpires: D. B. Hair (Australia) and R. B. Tiffin.
Third umpire: K. C. Barbour. Referee: R. S. Mahanama (Sri Lanka).

†ZIMBABWE v ENGLAND

Third One-Day International

At Bulawayo, December 4, 2004. England won by eight wickets. Toss: Zimbabwe. One-day international debut: S. P. Jones.

England moved into an unassailable 3–0 lead with their most emphatic performance of the trip on a near-perfect batting pitch. Solanki's second one-day century, an innings of elegance and power off front and back foot, dominated an opening stand of 138 with Bell, an England record against Zimbabwe, and rendered the result a formality. Zimbabwe might have put up more of a fight had they taken either of two chances offered by Solanki off successive balls when he had 37, or one by Bell on 16, but the rawness of the attack was plain as they wilted under the assault. Solanki went on to reach three figures from only 89 deliveries, with 14 fours and two sixes, while Bell and Vaughan both lodged fifties to ease England home with 41 balls to spare. Zimbabwe had been set on the path to a decent total by a maiden one-day half-century from Matsikenyeri, but two run-outs in two balls in the 40th over stalled progress. The fate of Chigumbura, run out without facing, summed up Zimbabwe's day: the last four balls of his only over were struck for four by Solanki.

Man of the Match: V. S. Solanki.

Zimbabwe

B. R. M. Taylor c G. O. Jones				
b S. P. Jones .	25	(54)		
S. Matsikenyeri c Anderson				
b Vaughan .	73	(97)		
D. D. Ebrahim c Collingwood				
b Wharf .	65	(94)		
M. A. Vermeulen run out	12	(13)		
E. Chigumbura run out.	0	(0)		
H. Masakadza b Giles	21	(24)		

*†T. Taibu c Anderson
b S. P. Jones . 24 (18)
P. Utseya not out. 4 (1)
T. Panyangara not out 0 (0)
B 1, l-b 3, w 9, n-b 1 . . 14

1/45 (1) (7 wkts, 50 overs) 238
2/143 (2) 3/164 (4) 4/165 (5)
5/203 (6) 6/227 (3) 7/234 (7) 15 overs: 45-0

D. T. Hondo and C. B. Mpofu did not bat.

Bowling: Wharf 8–1–30–1; Anderson 10–0–51–0; Collingwood 6–0–30–0; S. P. Jones 8–1–43–2; Giles 10–0–45–1; Vaughan 8–0–35–1.

England

V. S. Solanki c Hondo
b Matsikenyeri . 100 (91)
I. R. Bell c Taibu b Matsikenyeri . 53 (64)
*M. P. Vaughan not out 54 (75)
A. J. Strauss not out 22 (34)
W 5, n-b 5 10

1/138 (2) (2 wkts, 43.1 overs) 239
2/191 (1) 15 overs: 119-0

K. P. Pietersen, P. D. Collingwood, †G. O. Jones, A. F. Giles, A. G. Wharf, S. P. Jones and J. M. Anderson did not bat.

Bowling: Panyangara 5.1–0–37–0; Mpofu 6–0–46–0; Hondo 7–0–44–0; Chigumbura 1–0–16–0; Matsikenyeri 10–0–43–2; Utseya 10–0–35–0; Taylor 4–0–18–0.

Umpires: B. G. Jerling (South Africa) and K. C. Barbour.
Third umpire: R. B. Tiffin. Referee: R. S. Mahanama (Sri Lanka).

NO, HONEST, THE WEATHER'S LOVELY: Australia's Jason Gillespie looks on calmly as rain washes away the last day of their Test in Chennai, a game Australia looked destined to lose.

Picture by Hamish Blair, Getty Images

BEFORE THE WAVE... An aerial view of Galle International Stadium as it was in 2003.

Picture by Dominic Sansoni

...AND AFTER: The stadium as it was in the last week of December 2004, in the aftermath of the Indian Ocean tsunami.
Picture by Anuruddha Lokuhapuarachchi, Reuters

FACING A MOUNTAINOUS TOTAL: Cricket at 10,000ft on the way from Chitral to the Shandur Pass in Pakistan. The 21,000ft peak Buni Zum is in the background.
Picture by Basil Pao, from Himalaya by Michael Palin (Weidenfeld & Nicolson)

JAMMED SOLID... Lord's is full for its first Twenty20 fixture, Middlesex v Surrey on July 15. It was the biggest crowd for a county match there (cup finals excepted) in 51 years.

Picture by Philip Brown

...PLENTY OF ROOM: The United States team gets some support for their one-day international debut, against New Zealand in the Champions Trophy at The Oval. Not a lot, though.

Picture by Toby Melville, Reuters

PLAYING FOR BIG MONEY: Part of L. S. Lowry's two-part work, *The Cricket Match and a Cricket Sight Board*, which sold at Christie's in 2004 for £600,000.

By permission of the Lowry Estate; image supplied by Christie's Images Limited, 2004

†ZIMBABWE v ENGLAND

Fourth One-Day International

At Bulawayo, December 5, 2004. England won by 74 runs. Toss: England. One-day international debut: M. J. Prior.

A deeply unsatisfactory series concluded with yet another facile victory for England, watched from the stands by Heath Streak, the former Zimbabwe captain. England's inability to set totals as well as they chase them was evident as they stuttered to 104 for five in the 27th over. Better sides would have put them under pressure, but accomplished half-centuries from Vaughan, who hit his highest score in one-day internationals, and Geraint Jones ensured a total that was beyond the hosts. Vaughan's 90 not out came from 99 balls with only two fours and two sixes, while Jones's 80 took up just 75 deliveries. Their stand of 150 for the sixth wicket exceeded the record set four days earlier in Harare by Jones and Pietersen. England capped a fourth debutant, Matt Prior of Sussex, who was used as an opener but not in his other role of wicket-keeper. Batty was also given his first appearance of the series. England's contempt for the standard of opposition was evident as Vaughan used eight bowlers in Zimbabwe's innings, which featured a first one-day half-century for Masakadza. After the game, Vaughan said the retention of official status for Zimbabwe's under-strength side risked devaluing the currency of international cricket. Few who saw this series would have disagreed.

Man of the Match: G. O. Jones.   *Man of the Series:* M. P. Vaughan.

England

I. R. Bell c Matsikenyeri		P. D. Collingwood run out.	5 (15)
b Rainsford .	30 (15)	†G. O. Jones c Ebrahim	
M. J. Prior c Vermeulen		b Chigumbura .	80 (75)
b Rainsford .	35 (48)	G. J. Batty not out.	0 (0)
*M. P. Vaughan not out	90 (99)	W 3, n-b 1	4
A. J. Strauss c Chigumbura			
b Matsikenyeri .	17 (18)	1/55 (1) (6 wkts, 50 overs) 261	
K. P. Pietersen c Nkala		2/71 (2) 3/93 (4)	
b Matsikenyeri .	0 (1)	4/94 (5) 5/104 (6) 6/254 (7) 15 overs: 68-1	

A. G. Wharf, D. Gough and S. P. Jones did not bat.

Bowling: Panyangara 10–0–58–0; Rainsford 10–1–29–2; Nkala 3–0–35–0; Chigumbura 4–0–46–1; Utseya 10–0–33–0; Matsikenyeri 10–1–35–2; Taylor 3–0–25–0.

Zimbabwe

S. Matsikenyeri c G. O. Jones		T. Panyangara c Batty b Bell. . . .	13 (21)
b Gough .	10 (26)	P. Utseya not out.	12 (21)
B. R. M. Taylor c G. O. Jones		E. C. Rainsford b Bell	0 (2)
b Gough .	4 (13)		
D. D. Ebrahim lbw b Gough	0 (2)	L-b 2, w 13, n-b 3	18
M. A. Vermeulen c Collingwood			
b S. P. Jones .	5 (21)	1/8 (2) 2/8 (3) (48.4 overs) 187	
H. Masakadza b Collingwood . . .	66 (83)	3/22 (1) 4/43 (4)	
*†T. Taibu c Prior b Collingwood .	23 (57)	5/118 (6) 6/129 (5)	
E. Chigumbura b Bell	29 (35)	7/149 (8) 8/168 (7)	
M. L. Nkala c Pietersen b Gough .	7 (14)	9/187 (9) 10/187 (11) 15 overs: 49-4	

Bowling: Wharf 6–3–14–0; Gough 8–0–34–4; Collingwood 10–0–34–2; S. P. Jones 8–3–33–1; Batty 10–1–36–0; Pietersen 2–0–22–0; Bell 3.4–0–9–3; Strauss 1–0–3–0.

Umpires: D. B. Hair (Australia) and R. B. Tiffin.
Third umpire: K. C. Barbour.   Referee: R. S. Mahanama (Sri Lanka).

†At Randjesfontein, December 8, 2004. **England XI won by eight wickets (D/L method).** Toss: England XI. **N. F. Oppenheimer's XI 172-4** (39 overs) (N. C. Johnson 74); **England XI 190-2** (35.3 overs) (M. E. Trescothick 85*, R. W. T. Key 87).

Rain revised England's target to 185 off 39 overs. Johnson, the former Zimbabwe Test player, faced 58 balls, hitting seven fours and four sixes. Harmison's figures read 7–2–8–1. Trescothick, with eight fours and three sixes in 107 balls, and Key, with seven fours and five sixes off 85, put on 167 for the first wicket in 29 overs.

SOUTH AFRICA A v ENGLAND XI

At Potchefstroom, December 11, 12, 13, 2004. South Africa A won by seven wickets. Toss: South Africa A.

The rustiness of several of England's key players was badly exposed as they slumped to a crushing defeat in their only first-class match of the tour outside the Tests. Of the players who missed the Zimbabwe trip, Butcher, Thorpe and Flintoff contributed 39 runs, while Harmison could barely get going. England were sent on their way to defeat by a probing spell of swing bowling by Langeveldt, who took advantage of loose batting outside off stump to take five for 48; by the close of the first day, van Jaarsveld and Ontong had placed England's total in perspective with a stand of 106 in 21 overs. England fought back on day two, to keep their deficit to 56, only to lose their top three in five overs before tea and eventually collapse to 190, with only Vaughan's 149-ball century preventing a massacre. South Africa A's last-day victory march was interrupted first by thunder and lightning – the scoreboard indicated the players had left the field because of "dangerous weather" – then by rain. But they wrapped things up shortly after tea, with Vaughan left to reflect on what he described as "a kick up the arse".

Close of play: First day, South Africa A 133-2 (van Jaarsveld 58, Prince 7); Second day, England XI 154-7 (Vaughan 82, Hoggard 3).

England XI

M. E. Trescothick c Boucher b Mbhalati	7	–	lbw b Willoughby		2
A. J. Strauss c Ontong b Langeveldt	50	–	c Duminy b Mbhalati		0
M. A. Butcher c Boucher b Langeveldt	3	–	lbw b Willoughby		0
*M. P. Vaughan c Puttick b Morkel	26	–	c Boucher b Willoughby		100
G. P. Thorpe lbw b Langeveldt	0	–	b Willoughby		11
A. Flintoff c van Jaarsveld b Langeveldt	4	–	b Morkel		21
†G. O. Jones c Puttick b Morkel	41	–	c Boucher b Mbhalati		26
A. F. Giles c Boucher b Mbhalati	22	–	c van Jaarsveld b Thomas		2
M. J. Hoggard c Puttick b Langeveldt	17	–	c Prince b Langeveldt		3
S. P. Jones not out	31	–	c Prince b Langeveldt		5
S. J. Harmison b Willoughby	7	–	not out		13
B 5, l-b 4, w 3, n-b 5	17		L-b 2, w 1, n-b 4		7

1/44 (1) 2/47 (3) 3/79 (2) 4/79 (5) **225**
5/95 (6) 6/117 (4) 7/158 (8)
8/171 (7) 9/191 (9) 10/225 (11)

1/2 (1) 2/3 (2) 3/3 (3) **190**
4/29 (5) 5/64 (6) 6/109 (7)
7/125 (8) 8/164 (9)
9/176 (4) 10/190 (10)

Bowling: *First Innings*—Willoughby 10.1–3–40–1; Mbhalati 14–2–54–2; Langeveldt 15–3–48–5; Thomas 11–3–46–0; Morkel 8–3–28–2. *Second Innings*—Willoughby 14–2–63–4; Mbhalati 12–3–38–2; Langeveldt 12.1–5–25–2; Morkel 6–0–31–1; Thomas 6–1–15–1; Ontong 3–0–16–0.

South Africa A

A. G. Puttick b Harmison	4	– c G. O. Jones b S. P. Jones	45
M. van Jaarsveld c Thorpe b Flintoff	71	– c G. O. Jones b Hoggard	0
J. L. Ontong c Strauss b Giles	56	– c Giles b Harmison	23
*A. G. Prince c and b Flintoff	33	– not out	23
J-P. Duminy b Flintoff	7	– not out	25
†M. V. Boucher not out	26		
J. A. Morkel c Vaughan b Hoggard	47		
A. C. Thomas c Strauss b S. P. Jones	12		
C. K. Langeveldt lbw b Giles	4		
E. N. Mbhalati b S. P. Jones	1		
C. M. Willoughby c Hoggard b S. P. Jones	0		
L-b 7, w 1, n-b 12	20	L-b 12, w 3, n-b 4	19
	281	**(3 wkts)**	**135**

1/11 (1) 2/117 (3) 3/169 (4) 4/183 (2)   281   1/1 (2) 2/72 (1) 3/76 (3)   (3 wkts) 135
5/187 (5) 6/261 (7) 7/275 (8)
8/280 (9) 9/281 (10) 10/281 (11)

Bowling: First Innings—Hoggard 19–5–66–1; Harmison 17–3–69–1; S. P. Jones 15–1–49–3; Flintoff 13–1–50–3; Giles 9–2–40–2. *Second Innings*—Hoggard 4–0–21–1; Harmison 12–1–51–1; Flintoff 5–1–10–0; S. P. Jones 8–0–36–1; Giles 1–0–5–0.

Umpires: K. H. Hurter and L. H. Matroos.

SOUTH AFRICA v ENGLAND

First Test Match

Andrew Miller

At Port Elizabeth, December 17, 18, 19, 20, 21, 2004. England won by seven wickets. Toss: South Africa. Test debuts: A. B. de Villiers, D. W. Steyn.

Two made-to-measure innings from Strauss – the first painstaking, the second emphatic – carried England to an unprecedented eighth consecutive Test victory, as they eclipsed the seven in a row last achieved by Percy Chapman's team in 1928-29. Strauss's eight-Test career had now encompassed the entire record-breaking run and, by scoring 126 and an unbeaten 94 on his maiden appearance overseas, he became the first player to score centuries on debut against three consecutive opponents, after his performances against New Zealand and West Indies in the summer. Fittingly, he hit the winning runs as well, outscoring his partner Thorpe by 43 runs to eight as England surged to victory under rain-bearing skies on the final morning.

Though the margin of victory was convincing, the manner in which it was achieved was less so. England were never less than in control against a South African side in the throes of transition but, having entered the match on the back of a four-month break from Test cricket, they were not the same battle-hardened side that had played so gloriously in the summer. "Shoddy" was captain Michael Vaughan's word, particularly to describe their loss of the initiative on the third afternoon, when a collapse of four wickets in 16 balls allowed South Africa to claw themselves back into the game. It was a lapse that a stronger side might have seized upon.

With Kallis unable to bowl through injury, and Gibbs, Boje and Boucher all missing for a variety of personal and political reasons, South Africa's hopes rested on their captain, Smith. In England in 2003, Smith had set the agenda for the series with scores of 277, 85 and 259 in his first three innings. This time, however, Strauss caught him for a second-ball duck off Hoggard and, after losing the toss on a blustery day, England instantly had the wind in their sails. One moral victory quickly became two when Harmison, who lacked rhythm throughout the match, somehow bowled Kallis with a low full-toss. With their two best hopes out for nought, South Africa might have folded,

Careful driver: Andrew Strauss punches with characteristic neatness at Port Elizabeth, where he maintained his golden start in Test cricket.

Picture by Graham Morris

but Rudolph, with an eye-catching 93, and Dippenaar, who ground out a dour 110, added 112 for the fourth wicket. However, the decision to include Tsolekile ahead of Boucher meant South Africa's normally vestigial tail was significantly longer, and neither batsman ever quite dared dictate terms: South Africa's eventual total of 337 was a good 80 below par.

After their chastening defeat by South Africa A, England began cautiously too, as Strauss and Trescothick set about playing themselves in for the series with an opening stand of 152. The patient approach suited Strauss fine: he saw off a testing spell from Pollock before cashing in off the back foot as South Africa fed his favourite shots. Trescothick, however, was less settled and, after scratching around for over three hours for 47, he whipped across the line to give Steyn a memorable debut wicket. Raw, rapid and only 21, Steyn looked to have a big future. But he also bowled 16 no-balls in the innings, out of a team total of 35 – freebies South Africa could ill afford.

At 227 for one overnight, England were two good sessions from impregnability, but on the third day complacency quickly took hold. Strauss fell early to his only false stroke of the match and, after Thorpe was bowled round his legs by Smith's part-time off-spin, Ntini wrecked the middle order with three wickets in four balls. That included Butcher, playing his first Test since June, for 79 – an innings that began watchfully, ended with an impatient waft, and might have been a symbol for his team's general wastefulness. Had it not been for some lusty tail-end hitting, England would barely have secured a lead.

A total of 425 was a dominant position squandered, and by the close South Africa were right back in the game: they led by 11 with eight wickets standing, and Smith and Kallis – hungry for runs after their first-innings failures – at the crease. When Kallis was badly dropped next morning on 28 by Butcher at cover, South Africa's hopes soared, but the match soon lurched decisively back in England's favour, thanks to an inspirational sprawling catch at fine leg from Simon Jones. Diving full-stretch to remove Smith for 55, it was Jones's most committed moment in the field since his gruesome knee injury at Brisbane two years earlier, and the confidence instantly rubbed off on his bowling. After lunch he rediscovered his natural length – full, fast and reverse-swinging – and South Africa's last six wickets folded for 28. Jones's personal contribution was four for 14 in 40 balls, including Kallis for 61 and Pollock, given out caught behind off his pad, first ball.

England's target was 142 but, under heavy skies and with Pollock making the ball talk, they lost Trescothick, to the first ball of the innings, and Butcher, both for ducks, before Steyn detonated Vaughan's off stump with an unplayable leg-cutter to make it 50 for three. A feature of England's success in 2004, however, was their peerless batting in the fourth innings – this would be their ninth successful run-chase in 11 victories. And once the menace of the new ball had passed, South Africa's lack of a genuine spinner proved costly. Thorpe had his moments of unease against Smith, but Strauss was once again in utter command, as England rushed to within 49 runs of victory when bad light postponed their chase. After an anxious glance to the heavens, that requirement was ticked off in only 58 balls on the final morning.

Man of the Match: A. J. Strauss.

Close of play: First day, South Africa 273-7 (Dippenaar 79, Tsolekile 6); Second day, England 227-1 (Strauss 120, Butcher 24); Third day, South Africa 99-2 (Smith 33, Kallis 10); Fourth day, England 93-3 (Strauss 51, Thorpe 23).

South Africa

*G. C. Smith c Strauss b Hoggard	0	– (2) c S. P. Jones b Flintoff ... 55
A. B. de Villiers lbw b Flintoff	28	– (1) c and b Hoggard ... 14
J. A. Rudolph c G. O. Jones b Flintoff	93	– c Trescothick b Giles ... 28
J. H. Kallis b Harmison	0	– lbw b S. P. Jones ... 61
H. H. Dippenaar c Trescothick b S. P. Jones	110	– b Giles ... 10
Z. de Bruyn b Flintoff	6	– c Trescothick b Flintoff ... 19
S. M. Pollock c Trescothick b Hoggard	31	– c G. O. Jones b S. P. Jones ... 0
A. J. Hall b Hoggard	6	– run out ... 17
†T. L. Tsolekile c Flintoff b Giles	22	– b S. P. Jones ... 0
M. Ntini not out	2	– lbw b S. P. Jones ... 4
D. W. Steyn c Strauss b Giles	8	– not out ... 2
L-b 13, w 4, n-b 14	31	B 4, l-b 3, w 1, n-b 6, p 5 . 19

1/0 (1) 2/63 (2) 3/66 (4) 4/178 (3)   337   1/26 (1) 2/64 (3) 3/152 (2)   229
5/192 (6) 6/253 (7) 7/261 (8)   4/168 (5) 5/201 (4) 6/201 (7)
8/324 (5) 9/327 (9) 10/337 (11)   7/217 (6) 8/218 (9)
    9/224 (10) 10/229 (8)

Bowling: First Innings—Hoggard 20–4–56–3; Harmison 25–2–88–1; S. P. Jones 16–4–39–1; Flintoff 22–4–72–3; Giles 27.4–8–69–2. *Second Innings*—Hoggard 12–2–38–1; Harmison 14–1–54–0; Giles 15–2–39–2; Flintoff 15–2–47–2; S. P. Jones 13.1–3–39–4.

England

M. E. Trescothick b Steyn	47	– c Tsolekile b Pollock	0
A. J. Strauss c de Villiers b Pollock	126	– not out	94
M. A. Butcher c Tsolekile b Ntini	79	– c Smith b Ntini	0
*M. P. Vaughan c Smith b Hall	10	– b Steyn	15
G. P. Thorpe b Smith	4	– not out	31
A. Flintoff c Rudolph b Ntini	35		
†G. O. Jones c Dippenaar b Ntini	2		
A. F. Giles c Hall b Pollock	26		
M. J. Hoggard c Tsolekile b Hall	0		
S. P. Jones c and b Steyn	24		
S. J. Harmison not out	15		
L-b 21, w 1, n-b 35	57	L-b 3, n-b 2	5

1/152 (1) 2/238 (2) 3/249 (4) 4/267 (5)   425   1/0 (1) 2/11 (3) 3/50 (4)   (3 wkts) 145
5/346 (3) 6/353 (6) 7/353 (7)
8/358 (9) 9/394 (8) 10/425 (10)

Bowling: *First Innings*—Pollock 32–14–61–2; Ntini 28–6–75–3; Steyn 25.5–2–117–2; Hall 22–1–95–2; de Bruyn 9–1–31–0; Smith 10–3–25–1. *Second Innings*—Pollock 11–2–36–1; Ntini 6.4–1–24–1; Hall 9–1–14–0; Steyn 6–1–29–1; Smith 8–0–39–0.

Umpires: D. B. Hair (Australia) and S. J. A. Taufel (Australia).
Third umpire: I. L. Howell. Referee: C. H. Lloyd (West Indies).

SOUTH AFRICA v ENGLAND

Second Test Match

LAWRENCE BOOTH

At Durban, December 26, 27, 28, 29, 30, 2004. Drawn. Toss: South Africa.
The England players may not have been in the mood to agree as they waited in vain for the light to improve on the final evening, but this Test, as much as any in history, breathed fresh life into the cliché about cricket's glorious uncertainty. After two days, a South African victory seemed inevitable. Yet by tea on the fifth, England were favourites. For darkness to close in – with South Africa eight down and England itching to finish them off in the 15 overs that theoretically remained – was the final twist in a game grown dizzy with them.

The draw, confirmed at 4.45 p.m. beneath gloomy skies and the glare of the floodlights, ended England's run of eight wins, a national record that stretched back to May 2004 and victory over New Zealand at Lord's. It maintained their unbeaten record for 2004, and also local interest in a series which might have turned into a procession had England gone to Cape Town 2–0 up.

JUST FOR STARTERS

Highest opening partnerships in Tests for England

359	L. Hutton and C. Washbrook v South Africa at Johannesburg	1948-49
323	J. B. Hobbs and W. Rhodes v Australia at Melbourne	1911-12
290	G. Pullar and M. C. Cowdrey v South Africa at The Oval	1960
283	J. B. Hobbs and H. Sutcliffe v Australia at Melbourne	1924-25
273	**M. E. Trescothick and A. J. Strauss v South Africa at Durban**	**2004-05**
268	J. B. Hobbs and H. Sutcliffe v South Africa at Lord's	1924
234	G. Boycott and R. W. Barber v Australia at Sydney	1965-66

More in hope... England linger in the outfield on the last evening, waiting in vain for an improvement in the light, and a chance to polish off South Africa.
Picture by Graham Morris

When Hoggard bruised van Jaarsveld's outside edge nine overs before tea, South Africa were 183 for seven, and England were eyeing victory. But Pollock joined de Villiers in a fighting 27-over stand, adding 85 largely irrelevant runs and taking the match deep into the final session. Simon Jones gave England renewed hope with a direct hit from mid-on to prise out Pollock, but 11 balls later the umpires consulted – and that was that. Under the regulations agreed by the teams before the series, they were obliged to offer the batsmen the chance to come off once artificial light superseded natural, loosely defined as the moment the fielders began to cast four shadows instead of one. Since the lights had already been on for 20 minutes, England had to accept the decision; Vaughan's only grumble was that he had not been given the chance to use his slower bowlers.

Vaughan felt South Africa had "got out of jail", but admitted his side had only narrowly escaped from Alcatraz themselves. When England, invited to bat first, were bundled out for a feeble 139 in barely two sessions, they would have gladly accepted a draw. It was their lowest first-innings score since making 134 in the famous comeback win against West Indies at Lord's in 2000. But that was on a bouncy, seaming pitch: this one began with some life but soon flattened out.

Still, three South African wickets before the close gave England a glimmer, and next morning the fringe middle-order players caved in. Van Jaarsveld, in for the injured Dippenaar, was bowled by Flintoff; Amla (replacing de Bruyn) hung in grimly for 42 minutes before receiving a brute of a ball from Harmison; and de Villiers, given the wicket-keeping gloves to accommodate the return of Gibbs, spooned Jones tamely to mid-wicket.

At 118 for six, the game was loitering in no-man's land. But Kallis was still there on 42, and set about batting South Africa into the ascendancy. Always seen as more of a run-machine than a crowd-pleaser, he now played an innings worthy of Lara. Cautious at first, he scored 83 in the first two sessions of the second day, before plundering a masterful 66 runs in 20 overs after tea – a spectacle which might have been designed to silence critics who said he had no fourth gear. In all, Kallis batted four minutes over six hours, faced 264 balls and hit 21 fours and a hooked six off Flintoff. He supervised the addition of 214 runs for the last four wickets. Humid Durban was no place for fielding teams that start wilting, and England – missing Giles who was resting after his back went into spasm – just flopped.

South Africa led by 193, but England's openers batted out an 11-over session that evening, and on the third day set about one of Test cricket's most vivacious fightbacks. The tone was set in a five-over spell either side of the morning drinks: Trescothick, all drives and sweeps, and Strauss, preferring cuts and pulls, battered 50 runs off Boje and Steyn, to bring up their fourth century stand in nine Tests.

At lunch, the partnership was worth 137; at tea 223. By then, England led by 30 and both men had their centuries, reached in successive overs. For Strauss it was a fourth hundred in his ninth Test: among England batsmen, only Herbert Sutcliffe (four hundreds in his first seven Tests) and Peter Parfitt (four in eight) had started their Test career with as much aplomb. He and Trescothick were set to bat for the entire day, against an attack that was visibly losing faith in itself, but had to settle for a stand of 273 when Trescothick nibbled at the second new ball. It was England's highest opening partnership since 1960, when Colin Cowdrey and Geoff Pullar put on 290 against South Africa at The Oval, and their fifth-largest in all.

Yet still the game remained up for grabs. England began the fourth day with a lead of just 88, lost three wickets for 33, and could easily have folded. But this just set up the sort of mini-crisis that Thorpe relishes. With the help of a commendably restrained Flintoff and Geraint Jones, he chipped and chivvied South Africa out of the game. And this time there would be no coming back. When Flintoff fell for 60, snicking a long-hop from Smith, Jones took over, carving an impish 73. Thorpe's 16th Test hundred, after scraping just one run in the first innings, typified England's topsy-turvy batting: 570 for seven was their third-highest second-innings total.

AND NOW FOR SOMETHING COMPLETELY DIFFERENT

Biggest differences between a team's first and second innings in a Test match

551	Pakistan (106 & 657-8 dec.) drew with West Indies at Bridgetown	1957-58
497	New Zealand (174 & 671-4) drew with Sri Lanka at Wellington	1990-91
486	India (171 & 657-7 dec.) beat Australia at Kolkata.	2000-01
432	Zimbabwe (131 & 563-9 dec.) drew with West Indies at Harare	2001
431	West Indies (133 & 564-8) drew with New Zealand at Bridgetown	1971-72
431	**England (139 & 570-7 dec.) drew with South Africa at Durban**	**2004-05**
426	South Africa (506 & 80) lost to Australia at Melbourne.	1910-11
422	India (83 & 505-3 dec.) drew with New Zealand at Mohali	1999-2000
421	South Africa (199 & 620) beat Australia at Johannesburg	1966-67
420	Australia (586 & 166) lost to England at Sydney	1894-95
419	Australia (668 & 249) drew with West Indies at Bridgetown	1954-55
416	South Africa (156 & 572-7) drew with England at Durban	1999-2000
400	England (75 & 475) beat Australia at Melbourne	1894-95

Note: The above table includes only those matches where the lower total was a completed innings. The world record difference is 657 when Australia (729-6 dec. & 72-3) beat England at Lord's in 1930. The highest for England was 620 (636 & 16-2) in the win over Australia at Sydney in 1928-29.

Research: Philip Bailey

Set a notional 378, South Africa lost Smith that evening, and were four down by lunch the next day after loose off-side strokes from Gibbs and, more surprisingly, Kallis. Rudolph and van Jaarsveld steered them into calmer waters at 172 for four an hour after the break, before three wickets in five overs threatened to sink the ship. But de Villiers, who would complete a hard-earned maiden Test fifty, and Pollock held firm for nearly two hours, and the clouds came in. So England finished their golden year with 11 Test wins and two draws: only genius, in the form of Brian Lara's world-record 400 not out, and now the weather had denied them.

Man of the Match. J. H. Kallis.

Close of play: First day, South Africa 70-3 (Kallis 13); Second day, England 30-0 (Trescothick 7, Strauss 21); Third day, England 281-1 (Strauss 132, Butcher 1); Fourth day, South Africa 21-1 (Gibbs 11, Boje 4).

England

M. E. Trescothick c de Villiers b Ntini	18	– c de Villiers b Pollock	132
A. J. Strauss c Ntini b Boje	25	– c van Jaarsveld b Ntini	136
M. A. Butcher b Steyn	5	– c van Jaarsveld b Kallis	13
*M. P. Vaughan lbw b Ntini	18	– c de Villiers b Ntini	10
G. P. Thorpe lbw b Pollock	1	– not out	118
A. Flintoff c Amla b Pollock	0	– c de Villiers b Smith	60
†G. O. Jones c Rudolph b Ntini	24	– c Ntini b Boje	73
A. F. Giles c Rudolph b Steyn	10	– c de Villiers b Steyn	0
M. J. Hoggard not out	6		
S. P. Jones b Pollock	21		
S. J. Harmison b Pollock	0		
L-b 9, n-b 2	11	B 3, l-b 8, w 2, n-b 15	28

1/21 (1) 2/32 (3) 3/53 (2) 4/62 (5)   139   1/273 (1) 2/293 (2)   (7 wkts dec.) 570
5/64 (6) 6/80 (4) 7/93 (7)   3/306 (4) 4/314 (3)
8/113 (8) 9/139 (10) 10/139 (11)   5/428 (6) 6/560 (7) 7/570 (8)

Bowling: First Innings—Pollock 15.1–7–32–4; Ntini 13–2–41–3; Steyn 13–4–26–2; Kallis 7–4–10–0; Boje 9–2–21–1. *Second Innings*—Pollock 36–16–79–1; Ntini 37–4–111–2; Steyn 25.3–2–122–1; Boje 44–5–163–1; Kallis 25–4–57–1; Smith 5–1–27–1.

South Africa

*G. C. Smith c Flintoff b Harmison	9	– lbw b Hoggard	5
H. H. Gibbs b Hoggard	15	– c Giles b Harmison	36
J. A. Rudolph c Thorpe b Harmison	32	– (4) c Strauss b Giles	61
J. H. Kallis c sub (P. D. Collingwood) b Hoggard	162	– (5) c G. O. Jones b Harmison	10
M. van Jaarsveld b Flintoff	1	– (6) c Trescothick b Hoggard	49
H. M. Amla c G. O. Jones b Harmison	1	– (7) lbw b S. P. Jones	0
†A. B. de Villiers c Thorpe b S. P. Jones	14	– (8) not out	52
S. M. Pollock c G. O. Jones b Vaughan	43	– (9) run out	35
N. Boje c sub (P. D. Collingwood) b Hoggard	15	– (3) c Thorpe b Flintoff	10
M. Ntini c S. P. Jones b Flintoff	22	– not out	16
D. W. Steyn not out	7		
L-b 7, n-b 4	11	B 8, l-b 4, w 1, n-b 3	16

1/17 (1) 2/48 (2) 3/70 (3) 4/80 (5)   332   1/12 (1) 2/33 (3) 3/87 (2)   (8 wkts) 290
5/90 (6) 6/118 (7) 7/205 (8)   4/103 (5) 5/172 (4)
8/243 (10) 9/293 (10) 10/332 (4)   6/173 (7) 7/183 (6) 8/268 (9)

Bowling: First Innings—Hoggard 23–8–58–3; Harmison 28–3–91–3; Flintoff 23–5–66–2; S. P. Jones 18–1–81–1; Vaughan 10–2–29–1. *Second Innings*—Hoggard 19–3–58–2; Harmison 19–4–62–2; Flintoff 14–5–38–1; S. P. Jones 14–4–36–1; Giles 19–1–84–1; Vaughan 1–1–0–0.

Umpires: D. B. Hair (Australia) and S. J. A. Taufel (Australia).
Third umpire: K. H. Hurter. Referee: C. H. Lloyd (West Indies).

SOUTH AFRICA v ENGLAND

Third Test Match

ANDREW MILLER

At Cape Town, January 2, 3, 4, 5, 6, 2005. South Africa won by 196 runs. Toss: South Africa. Test debut: C. K. Langeveldt.

It was always going to be the big test of England's resolve – what would happen when the wheels stopped rolling? England's brakes had been applied with abrupt force in the closing moments at Durban. Sure enough, a week later at Newlands, the team hit the buffers with a resounding thud. One Test into 2005, and already they had suffered more defeats than in the whole of the previous year.

Those buffers mainly consisted of the immovable Kallis, who added another century of stultifying application to his masterful 162 at Durban. The absolute certainty of his shot-selection – or, more pertinently, non-selection – drew the sting from an England attack already weary after their exertions in the Second Test. And by batting purely for time (an alien concept to most modern Test cricketers) he ensured that, when England's turn to bat came on the second afternoon, they were already half-baked by five sessions in the January sun.

In the circumstances, there could have been few more opportune moments for Vaughan to end his extraordinary run of bad luck at the toss, and earn his bowlers an extra two days to recover. But, true to form, he called incorrectly for the 16th time in 22 Tests, and South Africa sensed a decisive shift in momentum. Three days earlier, they had been staring at a 2–0 deficit, the series almost certainly lost and the first whispers of the dreaded word "whitewash". But a new year really did bring resolution and Kallis merely resolved to be even more determined, so South Africa took tenacious advantage to inch along to 247 for four on an attritional first day.

That represented a promising start, but nothing more, and when Harmison launched the second morning with arguably the most venomous over of his career, it was clear that England had also taken heart from their effective, if not festive, opening day in the field. No one but Kallis could have survived the onslaught, which included a rap on the gloves and two near-decapitations, but survive he did, en route to a bloodlessly brilliant 149 – his eighth century in 14 Tests and his seventh in nine at home. In contrast to Durban, Kallis actually reined himself in for the closing stages of his innings, and hit only one boundary after reaching his hundred. It was left instead to Boje, who made 76 from 97 balls, to inject the required urgency, as the pair added 104 vital runs for the eighth wicket.

From an adequate 313 for seven, South Africa finished on an imposing 441, and by the close England, apparently incapable of tempering their attacking instincts to match

---

TAIL-END TERRORS

Test match No. 11s who have made the highest score of the innings

F. R. Spofforth	50	Australia (163) v England at Melbourne	1884-85
T. R. McKibbin	16	Australia (44) v England at The Oval	1896
A. E. E. Vogler	62*	South Africa (333) v England at Cape Town . .	1905-06
Asif Masood	30*	Pakistan (199) v West Indies at Lahore	1974-75
†A. M. J. G. Amerasinghe	34	Sri Lanka (215) v New Zealand at Kandy	1983-84
Talha Jubair	**31**	**Bangladesh (124) v India at Chittagong . . . .**	**2004-05**
S. J. Harmison	**42**	**England (304) v South Africa at Cape Town .**	**2004-05**

† *Amerasinghe performed the feat on debut.*

Like an eagle: Jacques Kallis swoops on an edge from Geraint Jones – and just holds on.

Picture by Clive Rose, Getty Images

the needs of the hour, were reeling from the loss of four key wickets. Once again their most successful performer was Strauss, who brought up his 1,000th Test run in just ten matches and 19 innings – a phenomenal rate that among Englishmen had been bettered only by Herbert Sutcliffe (12 innings), Len Hutton (16) and Wally Hammond (18). But in the day's penultimate over he dragged one on for 45, which – as a measure of England's inadequacies – was sufficient to make him their top-scorer for the fifth innings in succession.

The innings unravelled in dismal fashion on the third morning, as Langeveldt – pumped with adrenalin and anaesthetics – became the first South African since Lance Klusener in 1996-97 to take five wickets on debut. On the previous afternoon,

Langeveldt's left hand had been fractured by a Flintoff lifter, but it affected his performance not a jot. Relying on line, length and a modicum of movement, he scythed through England's batting, just as he had done for South Africa A earlier in the tour. The only resistance in a feeble total of 163 came from Giles, whose unbeaten 31 enabled him to become the ninth Englishman to achieve the Test double of 1,000 runs and 100 wickets, a feat that Flintoff would emulate later in the match.

With a lead of 278 and eight sessions to grind home the advantage, South Africa felt no obligation to enforce the follow-on, and instead condemned England to another frazzling in the outfield. In Kallis and Dippenaar, they had two batsmen tailor-made for such drip-drip tactics, and in a desperate third evening they added 75 dour runs in 32 overs. It was a soulless display that could have been counter-productive, but South Africa had gauged their opposition well: England are a team that like to get on with things, and their frustration was tangible. A comic collapse on the fourth morning proved the wisdom of this safety-first approach, as five wickets tumbled for the addition of 38 runs, but they were still able to declare with a lead of 500. The upshot was that England needed to survive for more than five sessions but, once Trescothick had fallen for a second-ball duck, another great escape was never remotely on the cards.

The dismissals of Key (who charged at Boje and was stumped) and Vaughan (who hooked Ntini to backward square leg) epitomised a team that simply no longer knew when the game was up, and it was left to Harmison to apply some gloss to another tatty performance. His hard-hitting, Test-best 42 brought the game back to life on the final afternoon, as he became only the seventh No. 11 to top-score in a Test innings. That meant, however, that for the first time in five years (since Lord's 2000, against West Indies), no England batsman had registered even a half-century in the match. After a run of unparalleled success, it was a dramatic reality check. About 5,000 English spectators in the ground, the most of the tour, had to endure what was perhaps England's most dismal overseas performance (outside Australia, anyway) since the last visit to Cape Town five years earlier. The Barmy Army were vocal to the end, especially when Harmison was in full cry too; the silent majority just suffered in the sun. And most were to go home before the good times rolled again.

Man of the Match: J. H. Kallis.

Close of play: First day, South Africa 247-4 (Kallis 81, Amla 21); Second day, England 95-4 (Thorpe 6, Hoggard 0); Third day, South Africa 184-3 (Kallis 60, Dippenaar 44); Fourth day, England 151-5 (Thorpe 22, G. O. Jones 2).

South Africa

*G. C. Smith c Trescothick b Giles	74	– lbw b Hoggard	2
H. H. Gibbs b Hoggard	4	– c G. O. Jones b Flintoff	24
J. A. Rudolph c G. O. Jones b S. P. Jones	26	– c Key b S. P. Jones	23
J. H. Kallis c G. O. Jones b Flintoff	149	– run out	66
H. H. Dippenaar b Giles	29	– c Vaughan b Flintoff	44
H. M. Amla lbw b Hoggard	25	– (7) c G. O. Jones b S. P. Jones	10
†A. B. de Villiers b Giles	21	– (8) c Giles b Harmison	10
S. M. Pollock c G. O. Jones b Flintoff	4	– (9) not out	3
N. Boje c G. O. Jones b Flintoff	76	– (6) run out	4
M. Ntini c Vaughan b Flintoff	0	– not out	0
C. K. Langeveldt not out	5		
B 4, l-b 15, w 3, n-b 6	28	B 7, l-b 12, w 10, n-b 7	36
	441	(8 wkts dec.)	222

1/9 (2) 2/70 (3) 3/145 (1) 4/213 (5) 5/261 (6) 6/308 (7) 7/313 (8) 8/417 (4) 9/417 (10) 10/441 (9)

1/2 (1) 2/62 (2) 3/101 (3) 4/184 (5) 5/190 (6) 6/203 (4) 7/215 (8) 8/219 (7)

Bowling: First Innings—Hoggard 32–7–87–2; Harmison 26–6–82–0; Flintoff 31.1–7–79–4; S. P. Jones 18–0–69–1; Giles 35–3–105–3. *Second Innings*—Hoggard 10–0–46–1; Harmison 19–3–55–1; Flintoff 18–1–46–2; Giles 13–2–41–0; S. P. Jones 9.3–4–15–2.

England

M. E. Trescothick c Gibbs b Ntini	28	– c Amla b Pollock	0
A. J. Strauss b Ntini	45	– lbw b Boje	39
R. W. T. Key c de Villiers b Pollock	0	– st de Villiers b Boje	41
*M. P. Vaughan c de Villiers b Langeveldt	11	– c Rudolph b Ntini	20
G. P. Thorpe c Rudolph b Langeveldt	12	– c de Villiers b Pollock	26
M. J. Hoggard c Smith b Ntini	1	– (9) not out	7
A. Flintoff c Gibbs b Ntini	12	– (6) c de Villiers b Pollock	20
†G. O. Jones c Smith b Langeveldt	13	– (7) c Kallis b Boje	38
A. F. Giles not out	31	– (8) c Kallis b Boje	25
S. P. Jones b Langeveldt	0	– c Kallis b Pollock	19
S. J. Harmison c Smith b Langeveldt	0	– c Dippenaar b Ntini	42
B 4, l-b 6	10	B 6, l-b 3, w 6, n-b 12	27

1/52 (1) 2/55 (3) 3/70 (4) 4/95 (2) 163 1/0 (1) 2/68 (2) 3/103 (3) 304
5/97 (6) 6/109 (7) 7/128 (8)   4/105 (4) 5/146 (6) 6/158 (5)
8/141 (5) 9/149 (10) 10/163 (11)   7/220 (8) 8/225 (7)
                    9/253 (10) 10/304 (11)

Bowling: *First Innings*—Pollock 17–5–36–1; Ntini 19–6–50–4; Langeveldt 16–4–46–5; Boje 4–1–15–0; Kallis 2–1–6–0. *Second Innings* Pollock 31–11–65–4; Ntini 24.4–6–49–2; Langeveldt 17–3–50–0; Boje 34–13–71–4; Kallis 15–4–49–0; Smith 2–0–11–0.

Umpires: S. A. Bucknor (West Indies) and D. J. Harper (Australia).
Third umpire: B. G. Jerling. Referee: C. H. Lloyd (West Indies).

SOUTH AFRICA v ENGLAND

Fourth Test Match

MATTHEW ENGEL

At Johannesburg, January 13, 14, 15, 16, 17, 2005. England won by 77 runs. Toss: England.

Most of the time, this Test resembled a well-run sightseeing tour (probably to a safari park, since this was definitely Big Game): it was always so varied and interesting no one objected that it seemed certain to lead them back exactly where they started. Then, just after lunch on the final day, the bus was hijacked by Hoggard, with a classical display of swing bowling. The draw all the shrewdies expected never happened, and England managed what eluded them in Durban. Once again, they found the onset of darkness harder to beat than South Africa, but this time they just managed it, and went 2–1 up.

It was their 12th Test win in ten months, and the most improbable of the lot. Vaughan's final-day declaration was a touch conservative, understandably so since his attack was in tatters: the spearhead Harmison had fallen so far that mid-match speculation suggested he might fly home; Flintoff seemed both wounded and distracted; Anderson had not played a first-class match since August, and it showed; even the spinner Giles was hurt. So Hoggard carried the team on his shoulders like Atlas. He bowled them to victory with seven for 61 and match figures of 12 for 205, England's best in 25 years.

It was an amazing and thrilling end to a match that often seemed four-sided. The two teams were contending against the ever-unpredictable Highveld summer weather, and the even more mysterious ICC regulations (copies almost unobtainable) and conditions of play. The pitch itself was a puzzle: Vaughan finally had some luck with the toss, but his response was not obvious. England expected the ball to swing, which explained the return of Anderson for Jones. (South Africa made another unforced wicket-keeping change, recalling Boucher and playing de Villiers as a specialist bat

On our way: Matthew Hoggard bowls Jacques Rudolph, on his way to a match-winning 12 for 205, England's best in 25 years.

Picture by Patrick Eagar

instead of Amla; Steyn replaced the injured Langeveldt.) Vaughan opted to bat, and was soon proved right: the bowlers quickly found themselves paying homage yet again to Strauss, who not merely scored his third century of the series but was England's top-scorer for the sixth time in seven innings – one extra boundary in Cape Town and it would have been seven out of seven.

Strauss's judgment and timing again looked flawless and, with hard-hitting support from Key, the ball kept racing along the fast outfield; England rocketed to 262 for two just after the new ball was taken. But during tea Ntini had been placed thigh-high in a barrel of ice by coach Ray Jennings to liven him up (it is thought he agreed to this) and it seemed to work. Strauss's departure, as the light declined, was not well timed; Thorpe quickly followed, and the middle order caved in when the next day dawned damp, Pollock and Ntini forming an alliance with the lowering clouds in two short early sessions to reduce England to 293 for seven. Vaughan was still there, grafting his way out of a mini-crisis for both himself and his team. In his first 129 minutes he only made 14, but his form and confidence gradually returned. After he had put on 82 in a rollicking ninth-wicket stand with Harmison, England were flying again.

The batsmen could see the ball all right but, with the floodlights on, the fielders were griping, apparently bothered by the light reflecting off it. The umpires gave in, and called the game off for the day just before a late burst of sunshine. Bob Willis, commentating on Sky TV, said umpire Bucknor, in his 98th Test, was "disgraceful" and should "sail off into the sunset". Vaughan said mildly: "All we ask for is consistency. We don't think it [the umpiring] has been consistent today." Referee Clive Lloyd couldn't fine Willis (though he later admonished South African commentators for not knowing the regulations). But he stamped on Vaughan by fining him his whole match fee, estimated at £5,500.

England declared overnight, expecting another damp day. In fact, the weather steadily improved, and large weekend crowds saw South Africa clamber back into the contest. Both Hoggard and Harmison were hopeless with the new ball: Harmison's figures were impressively economical, but that was mainly because the batsmen could leave almost everything alone. Then he damaged his calf and went off in mid-over. He came back on to the field later, but was evidently unfit to bowl even when it became legally possible, as Vaughan learned in an unusually public argument with the physio Kirk Russell (rough translation: "Can he bowl?" "No, he can't!" "Why the hell not?") with Harmison shrugging in the background.

Anderson *was* allowed to bowl, but had forgotten how. Luckily for England, Hoggard remembered, and began to work his way through the innings. At 184 for five, England were still in charge. But the South African batting order often seems bottomless, and Gibbs rediscovered his form, less traumatically than Vaughan, and eventually found an ally in the ever-perky Boucher, who was making it clear that, having regained his place, he intended to keep it. Anderson (in the course of a nine-ball over) somehow got rid of Boucher. Then came more drama: Jones, behind the stumps, damaged his left thumb and dropped both Gibbs and Boje in successive overs – the last on Saturday and the first on Sunday. Gibbs made another 25, Boje another 44, and a potentially useful England lead turned into a deficit of eight, with Gibbs making 161. By Sunday morning, England were so ragged that the occasional trundler Trescothick was used as first change with a still-newish ball. Yet the South African captain Smith's enjoyment of this was decidedly impaired: he had been concussed when hit during fielding practice.

Twice the sun went in… twice it came out again

England were still behind when Strauss finally failed, trying to drive Ntini's first ball. Trescothick, in his more accustomed role (all hands and eye, and no feet) and Vaughan saved them from meltdown. But on the final morning, they were only 189 on with half the side out; though the draw was hot favourite, a South African win seemed the most viable alternative. Trescothick put paid to that, charging on to 180, mainly supported by Giles, himself struggling with a right thumb dislocated when he had caught Rudolph two days earlier. Vaughan waited for Trescothick to get out before setting South Africa 325 in what seemed a notional 68 overs, because of the likelihood of bad light.

This was Hoggard's moment. He found the perfect length, swing in both directions and growing cracks in both the pitch and the batsmen's composure. Soon it was 18 for three, with Kallis nicking a slip catch first ball. Success re-energised England. Hoggard was dauntless; Flintoff gave staunch support; Harmison found enough inspiration at least to worry the batsmen, if not dismiss any. Gibbs, though, galloped to 98 in three hours through the gaps in the aggressive fields, and Smith shrugged off doctor's orders to march in at No. 8 and hold firm. England were anxiously scanning the clouds, and even sent out their spare players (most of whom had not set foot on a field in weeks) to act as ball boys in the absence of a last-day crowd. Twice the sun went in, and England groaned. Twice it came out again. At seven minutes to six, Hoggard induced a nick from last man Steyn. England had their first Test win at the Wanderers in 48 years, and one to rank among their most remarkable anywhere.

Man of the Match: M. J. Hoggard.

Close of play: First day, England 263-4 (Vaughan 9, Hoggard 0); Second day, England 411-8 (Vaughan 82, Harmison 30); Third day, South Africa 306-6 (Gibbs 136, Pollock 0); Fourth day, England 197-5 (Trescothick 101, Jones 1).

England

M. E. Trescothick c Boucher b Steyn	16	–	c Boucher b Ntini	180	
A. J. Strauss c Kallis b Pollock	147	–	c de Villiers b Ntini	0	
R. W. T. Key c Smith b Ntini	83	–	c Kallis b Ntini	19	
*M. P. Vaughan not out	82	–	c Boucher b Pollock	54	
G. P. Thorpe c Dippenaar b Ntini	0	–	c and b Kallis	1	
M. J. Hoggard c de Villiers b Ntini	5	–	(9) c Boucher b Kallis	0	
A. Flintoff c Smith b Ntini	2	–	(6) c Boucher b Pollock	7	
†G. O. Jones c Smith b Pollock	2	–	(7) c de Villiers b Pollock	13	
A. F. Giles c Gibbs b Steyn	26	–	(8) c Gibbs b Kallis	31	
S. J. Harmison not out	30	–	not out	3	
L-b 13, n-b 5	18		L-b 7, w 6, n-b 11	24	

1/45 (1) 2/227 (3) 3/262 (2)   (8 wkts dec.) 411
4/263 (5) 5/273 (6) 6/275 (7)
7/278 (8) 8/329 (9)

1/2 (2) 2/51 (3)   (9 wkts dec.) 332
3/175 (4) 4/176 (5)
5/186 (6) 6/222 (7)
7/272 (8) 8/274 (9) 9/332 (1)

J. M. Anderson did not bat.

Bowling: First Innings—Pollock 33–12–81–2; Ntini 34–8–111–4; Steyn 21–7–75–2; Kallis 22–2–79–0; Boje 14–2–52–0. *Second Innings*—Pollock 19–2–74–3; Ntini 20.1–2–62–3; Kallis 21–5–93–3; Steyn 9–0–47–0; Boje 12–0–49–0.

South Africa

*G. C. Smith lbw b Hoggard	29	–	(8) not out	67	
H. H. Gibbs c Hoggard b Anderson	161	–	lbw b Giles	98	
J. A. Rudolph c Giles b Hoggard	4	–	b Hoggard	2	
J. H. Kallis b Hoggard	33	–	c Trescothick b Hoggard	0	
H. H. Dippenaar c Trescothick b Flintoff	0	–	c Giles b Hoggard	14	
A. B. de Villiers c Giles b Hoggard	19	–	(1) lbw b Hoggard	3	
†M. V. Boucher c Strauss b Anderson	64	–	(6) c Jones b Hoggard	0	
S. M. Pollock lbw b Hoggard	0	–	(9) c Jones b Flintoff	4	
N. Boje run out	48	–	(7) c and b Hoggard	18	
M. Ntini b Giles	26	–	lbw b Flintoff	13	
D. W. Steyn not out	0	–	c Jones b Hoggard	8	
B 6, l-b 11, w 6, n-b 9	35		B 2, l-b 5, w 1, n-b 12	20	

1/64 (1) 2/75 (3) 3/138 (4) 4/149 (5)   419
5/184 (6) 6/304 (7) 7/306 (8)
8/358 (2) 9/399 (9) 10/419 (10)

1/10 (1) 2/18 (3) 3/18 (4)   247
4/80 (5) 5/86 (6) 6/118 (7)
7/163 (2) 8/172 (9)
9/216 (10) 10/247 (11)

Bowling: First Innings—Hoggard 34–2–144–5; Harmison 12.5–4–25–0; Anderson 28–3–117–2; Flintoff 30.1–8–77–1; Giles 8.1–0–25–1; Trescothick 5–1–11–0. *Second Innings*—Hoggard 18.3–5–61–7; Harmison 14–1–64–0; Flintoff 16–2–59–2; Anderson 6–1–32–0; Giles 5–0–24–1.

Umpires: Aleem Dar (Pakistan) and S. A. Bucknor (West Indies).
Third umpire: K. H. Hurter.   Referee: C. H. Lloyd (West Indies).

❝'He was talking,' said Law, 'but you could see there was no one at home.'❞

Lancashire in 2004, page 664.

SOUTH AFRICA v ENGLAND

Fifth Test Match

ANDREW MILLER

At Centurion, January 21, 22, 23, 24, 25, 2005. Drawn. Toss: England.

For the second time at Centurion, a rain-affected match involving England was given a fresh lease of life on the final afternoon by a tempting South African declaration. But whereas Hansie Cronje's gamble in 1999-2000 had been motivated by greed, Graeme Smith's was born purely of desperation. Trailing 2–1 in the series, South Africa's hopes of levelling the series by conventional means had not been helped by a first-day washout and, with England requiring only a draw for victory in the series, it was always going to take something remarkable to force a result.

To achieve that aim, Smith announced South Africa would "go for broke". In Nel, a combative, in-your-face fast bowler who took six wickets in his first appearance of the series following a back injury, and de Villiers, their fearless young strokemaker who hit 201 runs in the match, he had two men who responded magnificently. But for all their bold ambitions, South Africa ultimately fell short of the necessary resolve, and by dallying on the final morning when a declaration could have been a few lusty blows away, they allowed themselves just 44 overs in which to pull off a miracle. As if to highlight the extent of the missed opportunity, England then slumped to 20 for three. But Vaughan stood firm for over two hours for an unbeaten 26 to secure England's fourth series win in a row, and his fifth out of seven as captain. It had been his hardest-fought yet.

The blame for South Africa's reticence was pinned on their senior campaigner, Kallis – perhaps unfairly, given that he had carried their batting all series. His third century in four matches was another technically supreme performance that took his series tally to 625 runs – over 250 more than any of his team-mates – but he seemed not to share his captain's optimism on the final day that a result was still attainable. After reaching three figures, he added only 34 more in 16 overs by the declaration, as a succession of colleagues came and went in a frantic attempt to lift the run-rate. If Kallis was the scapegoat, then South Africa's other centurion, de Villiers, was their silver lining. Restored to the opening berth after his mid-series dalliance with the wicket-keeping gloves, he let a maiden Test century slip through his grasp in the first innings but, to the delight of his home crowd, made amends second time round, as he and Kallis cashed in on England's lack of urgency to add 227 for the third wicket. Aged 20 years and 11 months, he was South Africa's third-youngest centurion, behind Graeme Pollock and Tuppy Owen-Smith. Between them, de Villiers and Kallis helped turn a deficit of 112 into a target of 185, but there was too much at stake for England even to contemplate a shot at glory. Since readmission in 1992, only the Australians (twice) had managed to win a series on South African soil, while England had not been victorious there since M. J. K. Smith's team won 1–0 in 1964-65. Afterwards, Vaughan rightly hailed the achievement as the best moment he had known as captain.

Admittedly, England's task had been eased by the loss of the first day to the weather – their seventh blank day out of 11 in three Tests on the ground – although the Centurion groundstaff seemed to have done their bit for the cause. Presented with a vivid green wicket that had sweated for an extra 24 hours under the covers, England contemplated giving the Gloucestershire seamer Jon Lewis (flown out as emergency cover after the hard pounding at the Wanderers) a surprise debut, but in the end put their faith in the quartet that had carried them through the first three matches, recalling Simon Jones in place of Anderson. By the close of the first day, England had taken control of their destiny, although not in the expected fashion. The greenness of the wicket turned out to be the reddest of herrings; still, from 114 for one South Africa slumped to 247 for

Shattered: Jacques Kallis's stumps explode, as Andrew Flintoff yorks him for eight in the first innings.

Picture by Graham Morris

nine – which became 247 all out two balls into the next day – as Flintoff bent his back heroically on an unforgiving surface. He flew home immediately after the match for surgery on his troublesome left ankle but, in removing the cream of South Africa's line-up at a cost of 44 runs, he showed not a sign of his discomfort.

The weather remained in England's favour. Two spectacular thunderstorms limited the third day's play to just 46 overs, but England did their best to keep the contest alive. They donated three wickets for two runs to the new ball, and then lost Strauss shortly before the close with lightning striking all around. But by lunch the following morning the match seemed all but safe. Flintoff and Thorpe batted with supreme caution in a 141-run partnership, with Flintoff's half-century coming from 123 balls, the slowest of his international career. Nel, whose constant histrionics masked a skilful and controlled return to the side, finished with a career-best six for 81. By then, however, South Africa had conceded first-innings lead and, when Flintoff grabbed two quick wickets with the new ball, they looked in danger of losing the match as well. Kallis and de Villiers soon forced England to readjust their ambitions but, when it came to forging ambitions of their own, South Africa were unable to back up their words with deeds.

Man of the Match: A. B. de Villiers.   *Man of the Series:* A. J. Strauss.

Close of play: First day, No play; Second day, South Africa 247-9 (Hall 11, Nel 1); Third day, England 114-4 (Thorpe 32, Flintoff 0); Fourth day, South Africa 59-2 (de Villiers 20, Kallis 19).

South Africa

A. B. de Villiers lbw b Giles	92	– c Hoggard b S. P. Jones	109
H. H. Gibbs c G. O. Jones b Flintoff	14	– c G. O. Jones b Flintoff	4
J. A. Rudolph c Key b Hoggard	33	– (6) b Harmison	2
J. H. Kallis b Flintoff	8	– not out	136
*G. C. Smith c Trescothick b Flintoff	25	– c sub (P. D. Collingwood) b Harmison	3
†M. V. Boucher c Trescothick b S. P. Jones	25	– (7) c Trescothick b Hoggard	6
S. M. Pollock b Flintoff	0		
N. Boje c Thorpe b S. P. Jones	9		
A. J. Hall c Strauss b S. P. Jones	11	– (3) b Flintoff	9
M. Ntini c Hoggard b S. P. Jones	6		
A. Nel not out	1		
L-b 1, w 3, n-b 19	23	B 2, l-b 14, w 2, n-b 9	27

1/27 (2) 2/114 (3) 3/144 (4) 4/187 (1)   247   1/17 (2) 2/29 (3)   (6 wkts dec.) 296
5/200 (5) 6/200 (7) 7/222 (6)   3/256 (1) 4/267 (5)
8/237 (8) 9/245 (10) 10/247 (9)   5/277 (6) 6/296 (7)

Bowling: *First Innings*—Hoggard 18–4–64–1; Harmison 17–2–79–0; Flintoff 19–6–44–4; S. P. Jones 15.3–3–47–4; Giles 6–1–12–1. *Second Innings*—Hoggard 14–2–51–1; Flintoff 13–2–46–2; Giles 11–1–50–0; S. P. Jones 19–2–74–1; Harmison 16–2–59–2.

England

M. E. Trescothick run out	20	– b Ntini	7
A. J. Strauss c Boucher b Nel	44	– b Kallis b Ntini	0
R. W. T. Key c Boucher b Pollock	1	– lbw b Pollock	9
*M. P. Vaughan c Rudolph b Pollock	0	– not out	26
G. P. Thorpe b Nel	86	– c Gibbs b Ntini	8
A. Flintoff c Boucher b Hall	77	– not out	14
†G. O. Jones b Smith b Nel	50		
A. F. Giles b Nel	39		
M. J. Hoggard c Kallis b Nel	1		
S. P. Jones not out	0		
S. J. Harmison lbw b Nel	6		
B 1, l-b 22, w 8, n-b 4	35	L-b 7, n-b 2	9

1/27 (1) 2/29 (3) 3/29 (4) 4/114 (2)   359   1/0 (2) 2/16 (3)   (4 wkts) 73
5/255 (5) 6/257 (7) 7/335 (7)   3/20 (1) 4/45 (5)
8/351 (8) 9/352 (9) 10/359 (11)

Bowling: *First Innings*—Pollock 21–11–30–2; Ntini 28–8–92–0; Nel 29–7–81–6; Hall 16–3–58–1; Boje 19–7–59–0; Kallis 2–0–5–0; Smith 8–2–11–0. *Second Innings*—Nel 12–5–24–0; Ntini 11–6–12–3; Pollock 7–3–9–1; Smith 3–1–8–0; Hall 5.2–2–9–0; Boje 1–1–0–0; Kallis 2–0–4–0.

Umpires: Aleem Dar (Pakistan) and S. A. Bucknor (West Indies).
Third umpire: K. H. Hurter.   Referee: C. H. Lloyd (West Indies).

†At Kimberley, January 27, 2005. **England XI won by six wickets.** Toss: South Africa A. **South Africa A 251-8** (50 overs) (M. N. van Wyk 104, H. H. Dippenaar 66; Kabir Ali 4-40); **England XI 252-4** (42.2 overs) (I. R. Bell 87*, K. P. Pietersen 97).

Bell and Pietersen added 169 for England's fourth wicket in 27 overs; Pietersen hit nine fours and three sixes in 84 balls.

ONE-DAY INTERNATIONAL REPORTS BY RICHARD HOBSON

†SOUTH AFRICA v ENGLAND

First One-Day International

At Johannesburg, January 30, 2005. England won by 26 runs (D/L method). Toss: England.
  Despite losing three wickets inside the first 12 overs, England recovered sufficiently to stand well ahead of the Duckworth/Lewis mark when a thunderstorm broke over the Wanderers. Nobody seemed happier than Pietersen, who was there at the end after being loudly booed while walking out for his first innings against South Africa, the country he abandoned in frustration at a perceived lack of opportunities. His initial exchanges with the always theatrical Nel provided the most dramatic moments of the game, with Pietersen struggling nervously for 11 balls before getting off the mark. But otherwise the entertainment was a bit thin once Gough and Hoggard had exploited a dewy surface to reduce South Africa to 19 for three in the tenth over. The middle order fared a little better, and Boje upped the pace late on; but while a total of 175 for nine represented something of a recovery, it was still at least 30 short. Vaughan saw Pollock out of the attack and was in control by the time the rain set in for good.
  Man of the Match: M. P. Vaughan.

South Africa

*G. C. Smith c Strauss b Gough	1	(14)		M. Ntini not out	10	(11)
H. H. Gibbs c Pietersen b Hoggard	2	(4)		A. Nel not out	1	(1)
J. H. Kallis c Jones b Ali	5	(26)				
A. M. Bacher b Hoggard	4	(18)		B 3, l-b 11, w 4, n-b 1	19	
A. G. Prince lbw b Ali	22	(28)				
J. M. Kemp c Bell b Giles	24	(48)		1/3 (1) (9 wkts, 50 overs) 175		
†M. V. Boucher b Giles	17	(51)		2/5 (2) 3/19 (4)		
S. M. Pollock c Vaughan b Giles	37	(60)		4/41 (3) 5/49 (5) 6/83 (6)		
N. Boje b Gough	33	(40)		7/90 (7) 8/148 (9) 9/170 (8) 15 overs: 44-4		

  Bowling: Gough 10-2-27-2; Hoggard 10-2-35-2; Ali 8-1-29-2; Collingwood 7-0-21-0; Trescothick 8-0-31-0; Giles 7-0-18-3.

England

M. E. Trescothick c Kallis b Ntini	11	(11)
†G. O. Jones c Boucher b Pollock	8	(11)
*M. P. Vaughan not out	44	(70)
A. J. Strauss c Kemp b Nel	15	(26)
K. P. Pietersen not out	22	(33)
L-b 2, w 1	3	

1/19 (1)   (3 wkts, 25.1 overs) 103
2/21 (2) 3/44 (4)   15 overs: 46-3

I. R. Bell, P. D. Collingwood, A. F. Giles, Kabir Ali, D. Gough and M. J. Hoggard did not bat.

  Bowling: Pollock 8-3-19-1; Ntini 7-0-29-1; Nel 5-2-13-1; Kemp 3-0-25-0; Boje 1-0-8-0; Kallis 1.1-0-7-0.

  Umpires: S. A. Bucknor (West Indies) and I. L. Howell.
  Third umpire: K. H. Hurter. Referee: R. S. Madugalle (Sri Lanka).

†SOUTH AFRICA v ENGLAND

Second One-Day International

At Bloemfontein, February 2, 2005 (day/night). Tied. Toss: South Africa. One-day international debut: A. B. de Villiers.

Memories of great South African chokes from the past were rekindled as they failed to score three runs from the last six balls to win, producing the 20th tie in 2,219 one-day internationals, and South Africa's fifth in less than six years. The word "eventful" barely does justice to the last over. It began when Boucher swung a chest-high no-ball from the inexperienced Kabir Ali to the boundary, before pulling another full toss straight to Giles in the deep; continued with Prince

---

THE ONES THAT GOT AWAY

Tied one-day internationals involving South Africa

South Africa (213) tied with Australia (213)   Birmingham   1999
South Africa went out of the World Cup on net run-rate.

Australia (226-9) tied with South Africa (226-8) Melbourne (Colonial Stadium) . . .   2000
Australia scored 12 off the last over.

Australia (259-9) tied with South Africa (259-7) Potchefstroom   2001-02
Australia were 223-9 in the 46th over.

South Africa (229-6) tied with Sri Lanka (268-9) Durban   2002-03
South Africa went out of the World Cup after misunderstanding the Duckworth/Lewis calculations.

South Africa (270-8) tied with England (270-5) Bloemfontein   2004-05

Note: Chasing side listed first.

---

being run out by Bell; and ended with Hall stumped first ball on a dazed meander from the crease. England celebrated like winners, which they expected to be when Pietersen struck 108 not out from 96 balls, a maiden hundred for these three figures may have been the most passionate-looking ever witnessed on a cricket field. Pietersen's fifth-wicket stand of 92 from 79 balls with Collingwood appeared decisive, but Kallis and Gibbs manoeuvred the ball simply and effectively in mid-innings before Kemp upped the pace to produce the tense finale.

Man of the Match: K. P. Pietersen.

England

M. E. Trescothick b Pollock	37	(36)	I. R. Bell not out	11	(8)
†G. O. Jones c Ntini b Nel	20	(30)			
*M. P. Vaughan run out	42	(82)	L-b 3, w 5, n-b 2	10	
A. J. Strauss c Boucher b Hall	2	(9)			
K. P. Pietersen not out	108	(96)	1/52 (1) (5 wkts, 50 overs)	270	
P. D. Collingwood c de Villiers			2/60 (2) 3/67 (4)		
b Ntini	40	(41)	4/147 (3) 5/239 (6) 15 overs: 62-2		

A. F. Giles, Kabir Ali, D. Gough and M. J. Hoggard did not bat.

Bowling: Pollock 10–1–52–1; Ntini 10–0–51–1; Nel 10–0–54–1; Hall 10–0–50–1; Smith 2–0–10–0; Kallis 4–0–24–0; Kemp 4–0–26–0.

The passionate convert: at Bloemfontein, a delighted Kevin Pietersen reaches his maiden century for his adopted country, England.

Picture by Graham Morris

South Africa

*G. C. Smith c Jones b Hoggard .	25	(37)	A. G. Prince run out	0	(1)
A. B. de Villiers c sub			A. J. Hall st Jones b Ali	0	(1)
(V. S. Solanki) b Ali .	20	(38)	B 4, l-b 6, w 5, n-b 5 . .	20	
J. H. Kallis c Trescothick b Giles .	63	(78)			
H. H. Gibbs c Gough b Hoggard .	78	(101)	1/47 (1) (8 wkts, 50 overs) 270		
J. M. Kemp b Gough	32	(26)	2/51 (2) 3/185 (3)		
†M. V. Boucher c Giles b Ali . . .	15	(11)	4/237 (4) 5/239 (5) 6/268 (6)		
S. M. Pollock not out.	17	(12)	7/269 (8) 8/270 (9) 15 overs: 65-2		

M. Ntini and A. Nel did not bat.

Bowling: Gough 10–0–49–1; Hoggard 10–1–42–2; Ali 8–0–56–3; Collingwood 10–0–42–0; Giles 8–0–46–1; Trescothick 4–0–25–0.

Umpires: S. J. A. Taufel (Australia) and B. G. Jerling.
Third umpire: I. L. Howell. Referee: R. S. Madugalle (Sri Lanka).

†SOUTH AFRICA v ENGLAND

Third One-Day International

At Port Elizabeth, February 4, 2005 (day/night). South Africa won by three wickets. Toss: England.
Smith became the first South Africa captain to score a hundred in a one-day international. But his dismissal in the 43rd over, with his side still 54 short, raised thoughts of another stumble at the last fence. In Smith's own words there was "ecstasy and relief" when Boucher hit effectively, and Prince clipped the first ball of the final over from Gough for the winning boundary. It had been a challenging period for Smith, who awoke the day before to reports of disagreements among the selection panel on the back pages. Gibbs offered another solid innings in support and Smith played with character and power, though he was reprieved twice in the fifties when Trescothick dropped a simple catch and Jones missed a run-out after failing to collect a straightforward throw. All of England's top five had made a start without kicking on. Solanki top-scored on his recall in place of Vaughan, who had a virus, but the last ten overs produced only 58 runs.
Man of the Match: G. C. Smith.

England

*M. E. Trescothick c Smith b Nel	33	(43)	Kabir Ali not out	6	(6)
†G. O. Jones c and b Boje	39	(46)	D. Gough not out	3	(3)
V. S. Solanki c de Villiers b Nel .	66	(87)	B 2, l-b 8, w 1, n-b 4 . .	14	
A. J. Strauss c Prince b Pollock . .	35	(40)			
K. P. Pietersen c Gibbs b Nel . . .	33	(37)	1/49 (1) (8 wkts, 50 overs) 267		
P. D. Collingwood c Kallis b Ntini	22	(21)	2/99 (2) 3/156 (4)		
I. R. Bell c Smith b Ntini.	13	(16)	4/207 (3) 5/225 (5) 6/246 (6)		
A. F. Giles c Pollock b Ntini. . . .	3	(4)	7/253 (8) 8/257 (7) 15 overs: 74-1		

M. J. Hoggard did not bat.

Bowling: Pollock 10–0–44–1; Ntini 10–0–58–3; Nel 10–0–49–3; Boje 10–0–42–1; Kallis 7–0–45–0; Kemp 1–0–10–0; Smith 2–0–9–0.

South Africa

*G. C. Smith lbw b Giles.	105	(131)	†M. V. Boucher lbw b Gough . . .	33	(21)
A. B. de Villiers c Jones			S. M. Pollock not out.	4	(2)
b Hoggard .	16	(28)			
N. Boje c Giles b Ali.	20	(17)	B 3, l-b 5, w 3, n-b 2 . .	13	
J. H. Kallis c Pietersen					
b Collingwood .	3	(12)	1/45 (2) (7 wkts, 49.1 overs) 270		
H. H. Gibbs lbw b Gough	50	(60)	2/82 (3) 3/89 (4)		
J. M. Kemp b Collingwood	9	(8)	4/196 (5) 5/214 (6)		
A. G. Prince not out	17	(18)	6/214 (1) 7/257 (8) 15 overs: 80-1		

M. Ntini and A. Nel did not bat.

Bowling: Gough 9.1–1–46–2; Hoggard 9–1–66–1; Ali 10–1–39–1; Collingwood 10–0–54–2; Giles 9–0–40–1; Trescothick 2–0–17–0.

Umpires: S. A. Bucknor (West Indies) and B. G. Jerling.
Third umpire: K. H. Hurter.   Referee: R. S. Madugalle (Sri Lanka).

†SOUTH AFRICA v ENGLAND

Fourth One-Day International

At Cape Town, February 6, 2005. South Africa won by 108 runs. Toss: England.

As if tired of tight finishes, South Africa won convincingly after Kemp, with 57 from 36 balls, put the target beyond England's reach in a decisive climax to the first innings. Gibbs continued to relish his move down the order, completing his 14th one-day international hundred, from 114 balls, having added 143 for the third wicket with Kallis. For Ali, the hero four days earlier, this was a chastening experience, as his last two overs went for 36 runs, after he had conceded only 11 in his first six. But the performance of Harmison provided greater concern for England. The day before, he admitted he would rather have gone home after the Test series and now, recovered from a calf problem, he was not trusted for more than three overs in a spell. In contrast, Ntini, enjoying a good series, and Pollock made early inroads into the England innings, assisted by some loose driving. And when Pietersen succumbed attempting a third successive six against Boje the entertainment as well as the contest was over.

Man of the Match: H. H. Gibbs.

South Africa

*G. C. Smith lbw b Ali	16	(27)
A. B. de Villiers lbw b Gough	9	(14)
J. H. Kallis run out	71	(97)
H. H. Gibbs c Bell b Harmison	100	(115)
J. M. Kemp run out	57	(36)
A. G. Prince not out	14	(11)
L-b 6, w 18	24	

1/18 (2)   (5 wkts, 50 overs) 291
2/50 (1) 3/193 (3)
4/227 (4) 5/291 (5)   15 overs: 62-2

†M. V. Boucher, S. M. Pollock, N. Boje, M. Ntini and A. Nel did not bat.

Bowling: Gough 10–1–53–1; Harmison 10–0–65–1; Ali 10–1–58–1; Collingwood 5–0–24–0; Trescothick 1–0–12–0; Giles 10–0–52–0; Vaughan 4–0–21–0.

England

M. E. Trescothick b Ntini	13	(16)	D. Gough not out	9	(21)
†G. O. Jones c Boucher b Ntini	19	(20)	S. J. Harmison c Nel b Boje	4	(8)
*M. P. Vaughan c Kallis b Pollock	0	(6)			
A. J. Strauss c Prince b Nel	17	(25)	B 3, l-b 3, w 6	12	
K. P. Pietersen c de Villiers b Boje	75	(85)			
I. R. Bell c Boucher b Kallis	2	(8)	1/32 (2) 2/33 (3) (41.2 overs) 183		
P. D. Collingwood c Boucher			3/35 (1) 4/73 (4)		
b Pollock	11	(23)	5/92 (6) 6/127 (7)		
A. F. Giles c Pollock b Ntini	20	(31)	7/148 (5) 8/163 (9)		
Kabir Ali run out	1	(5)	9/175 (8) 10/183 (11) 15 overs: 67-3		

Bowling: Pollock 10–0–35–2; Ntini 9–1–29–3; Nel 6–0–27–1; Kallis 6–0–36–1; Kemp 2–0–9–0; Boje 8.2–0–41–2.

Umpires: S. J. A. Taufel (Australia) and I. L. Howell.
Third umpire: B. G. Jerling.   Referee: R. S. Madugalle (Sri Lanka).

†SOUTH AFRICA v ENGLAND

Fifth One-Day International

At East London, February 9, 2005 (day/night). South Africa won by seven runs. Toss: South Africa.

Comic-book baddie to a partisan crowd but an awesome presence to his team-mates, Pietersen completed the fastest hundred by an England player in a one-day international (69 deliveries) when he hit the last ball for his fourth six. Never before had England scored as many as 304 in a losing chase, and if Pietersen had engineered more of the strike late on he might have completed an extraordinary story. Giles and Ali also hit sixes and there was a moment when South Africa

---

GETTING THERE THE QUICK WAY

Fastest centuries (in terms of balls faced) in one-day internationals

Balls			
37	Shahid Afridi	Pakistan v Sri Lanka at Nairobi	1996-97
45	B. C. Lara	West Indies v Bangladesh at Dhaka	1999-2000
48	S. T. Jayasuriya	Sri Lanka v Pakistan at Singapore	1995-1996
62	M. Azharuddin	India v New Zealand at Baroda	1988-89
67	Basit Ali	Pakistan v West Indies at Sharjah	1993-94
67	J. M. Davison	Canada v West Indies at Centurion	2002-03
68	Ijaz Ahmed (sen.)	Pakistan v India at Lahore	1997-98
68	Yousuf Youhana	Pakistan v Zimbabwe at Harare	2002-03
69	V. Sehwag	India v New Zealand at Colombo	2001
69	**K. P. Pietersen**	**England v South Africa at East London**	**2004-05**

Pietersen's innings beat M. E. Trescothick (80 balls, v India, Kolkata, 2001-02) as the fastest century in a one-day international for England.

---

began to look alarmed. But Nel and Ntini exercised just enough control in the final overs to win the game, if not to stop Pietersen's personal triumph. Ultimately, poor bowling sent England to a defeat which meant South Africa could not lose the series. The England attack conceded 111 in the last ten overs, and Kemp, whose 80 came from 50 balls with seven sixes, was allowed to hit through his preferred leg side at will. Smith batted through the innings for 115 off 131 balls, moving from 50 to 100 without a boundary. Indeed, South Africa milked runs under little pressure in the middle stages after Kallis, with five fours from Ali's first over, contributed to a forceful start. The total was the highest in a one-day international at East London, and victory would have been more emphatic but for a missed stumping chance with Pietersen on 16.

Man of the Match: J. M. Kemp.

South Africa

*G. C. Smith not out	115	(131)	S. M. Pollock run out	2	(1)
A. B. de Villiers c Jones b Gough	2	(7)	N. Boje not out.	10	(4)
J. H. Kallis c sub (I. R. Bell)			L-b 3, w 4, n-b 4	11	
b Ali .	49	(53)			
H. H. Gibbs c Pietersen b Ali .	8	(12)	1/10 (2)	(7 wkts, 50 overs) 311	
A. G. Prince run out	34	(45)	2/100 (3) 3/119 (4)		
J. M. Kemp b Gough	80	(50)	4/181 (5) 5/298 (6)		
†M. V. Boucher b Gough	0	(1)	6/298 (7) 7/300 (8)	15 overs: 88-1	

M. Ntini and A. Nel did not bat.

Bowling: Gough 10–0–52–3; Hoggard 9–0–74–0; Ali 9–0–66–2; Collingwood 10–0–53–0; Trescothick 3–0–17–0; Giles 9–0–46–0.

England

M. E. Trescothick c Kemp b Pollock .	4	(20)	
†G. O. Jones c Gibbs b Nel	37	(47)	
*M. P. Vaughan c Prince b Boje. .	70	(94)	
A. J. Strauss run out	20	(29)	
K. P. Pietersen not out	100	(69)	
V. S. Solanki run out	19	(16)	
P. D. Collingwood lbw b Kallis . .	4	(4)	
A. F. Giles b Kallis	15	(7)	

M. J. Hoggard did not bat.

Kabir Ali run out 20 (15)
D. Gough not out 1 (1)

B 1, l-b 5, w 6, n-b 2 . . 14

1/22 (1)   (8 wkts, 50 overs) 304
2/61 (2) 3/117 (4)
4/179 (3) 5/224 (6) 6/236 (7)
7/254 (8) 8/290 (9)   15 overs: 59-1

Bowling: Pollock 10–1–35–1; Ntini 10–0–61–0; Kallis 10–0–62–2; Nel 10–0–69–1; Boje 8–0–54–1; Smith 2–0–17–0.

Umpires: S. A. Bucknor (West Indies) and I. L. Howell.
Third umpire: B. G. Jerling. Referee: R. S. Madugalle (Sri Lanka).

†SOUTH AFRICA v ENGLAND

Sixth One-Day International

At Durban, February 11, 2005 (day/night). No result (D/L method). Toss: South Africa.

South Africa were guaranteed victory in the series when heavy showers prevented England from chasing an adjusted target of 213 from 48 overs. But judging by the way Pollock and Ntini generated bounce and movement from a pitch freshened by drizzle they were facing a tall order in any case. Only Gibbs among the South Africans had appeared fully at ease – and there were four ducks in the innings. But Gibbs was able to share three successive half-century stands, and South Africa, having worked out that a score of around 225 would probably be enough, paced the innings accordingly. Thus, in one dull but tactically valid passage, the total moved from 78 to 127 entirely in singles. Gough caused problems with new ball and old, and Wharf marked his return with wickets from the first two balls of his second over. Again, though, South Africa found gaps a little too easily. Gibbs completed his second hundred in three innings just before the first break for rain.

South Africa

*G. C. Smith c Trescothick b Wharf .	1	(9)	
A. M. Bacher lbw b Ali	15	(35)	
J. H. Kallis c Strauss b Wharf . . .	0	(1)	
H. H. Gibbs c Collingwood b Ali .	118	(133)	
A. G. Prince c Collingwood b Giles .	27	(48)	
†M. V. Boucher c Ali b Wharf .	24	(32)	
J. M. Kemp c Strauss b Gough . .	0	(4)	
S. M. Pollock lbw b Collingwood .	0	(4)	

A. J. Hall b Ali. 10 (9)
M. Ntini c Strauss b Gough 0 (2)
A. Nel not out 2 (5)

B 4, l-b 4, w 3, n-b 3 . . 14

1/1 (1) 2/1 (3)   (46.3 overs) 211
3/53 (2) 4/114 (5)
5/169 (4) 6/171 (7)
7/180 (8) 8/208 (4)
9/208 (10) 10/211 (9)   15 overs: 53-3

Bowling: Gough 9–2–14–2; Wharf 9–1–48–3; Ali 8.3–0–44–3; Collingwood 5–0–35–1; Giles 10–0–38–1; Vaughan 5–0–24–0.

> ❝D'Oliveira scored 158 runs, 'against an attack comprising Prime Minister Johannes Vorster and South African apartheid at its most savage and corrupt, supported by the weight of the British establishment.'❞
>
> Ramachandra Guha, Cricket Books, page 1673.

England

M. E. Trescothick c Kallis b Pollock	1	(4)	
†G. O. Jones c Nel b Ntini	2	(12)	
*M. P. Vaughan not out	2	(6)	
A. J. Strauss not out	0	(0)	
L-b 1, w 1	2		

1/2 (1) 2/7 (2)   (2 wkts, 3.4 overs) 7

K. P. Pietersen, V. S. Solanki, P. D. Collingwood, A. F. Giles, Kabir Ali, A. G. Wharf and D. Gough did not bat.

Bowling: Pollock 2–1–2–1; Ntini 1.4–0–4–1.

Umpires: S. J. A. Taufel (Australia) and B. G. Jerling.
Third umpire: I. L. Howell.   Referee: R. S. Madugalle (Sri Lanka).

†SOUTH AFRICA v ENGLAND

Seventh One-Day International

At Centurion, February 13, 2005. South Africa won by three wickets. Toss: South Africa.

South Africa completed a 4–1 victory when Prince hit the winning runs from the last ball of the penultimate over. But the highlight came earlier when Pietersen rescued England from 68 for six with his third hundred of the series, during which he cleared the leg-side rope six times. His first fifty was a pedestrian affair, from 80 balls, but the second required only 24. Giles reached a one-day international best in support and the seventh-wicket stand of 104 ensured that another capacity crowd saw a contest not a capitulation. The result also meant that England went home from a tour – successful in its main purpose – with plenty of food for thought, both about their continuing problems in one-day cricket and Pietersen's potential challenge to the established Test players. South Africa were cruising in response to England's 240 until Smith and Gibbs fell in successive overs. Vaughan sought to attack, anticipating that a threatened storm would leave the result in the hands of Duckworth/Lewis. But the weather held out, and so did Prince, a whippet between the wickets. Having been booed from venue to venue, Pietersen received a more gracious ovation when he collected the man of the series award. In six innings he scored 454 runs from 430 balls at an average of 151.33; Flintoffesque and Bradmanesque all at once. He had also equalled Dennis Amiss's world record by reaching 500 runs in just nine innings.

Man of the Match: K. P. Pietersen.   *Man of the Series:* K. P. Pietersen.

England

M. E. Trescothick c Gibbs b Pollock	0	(2)	
†G. O. Jones c Kemp b Nel	14	(43)	
*M. P. Vaughan b Ntini	1	(5)	
A. J. Strauss c Boucher b Nel	15	(35)	
K. P. Pietersen b Hall	116	(110)	
V. S. Solanki c Smith b Boje	5	(13)	
P. D. Collingwood run out	10	(15)	
A. F. Giles b Ntini	41	(54)	
Kabir Ali b Hall	25	(19)	
A. G. Wharf not out	3	(4)	
S. J. Harmison b Hall	0	(2)	
W 7, n-b 3	10		

1/0 (1) 2/1 (3)   (49.5 overs) 240
3/32 (4) 4/36 (2)
5/54 (6) 6/68 (7)
7/172 (8) 8/225 (5)
9/240 (9) 10/240 (11)   15 overs: 36-3

Bowling: Pollock 10–1–36–1; Ntini 9–2–47–2; Nel 10–1–60–2; Hall 9.5–1–52–3; Boje 10–0–34–1; Kallis 1–0–11–0.

South Africa

*G. C. Smith c Solanki b Giles	47	(66)	N. Boje not out	1	(1)
A. J. Hall c Harmison b Wharf	23	(40)			
J. H. Kallis c Trescothick b Vaughan	36	(60)			
H. H. Gibbs lbw b Harmison	0	(2)	L-b 2, w 14, n-b 2	18	
A. G. Prince not out	62	(76)			
†M. V. Boucher run out	44	(40)	1/46 (2)	(7 wkts, 49 overs) 241	
J. M. Kemp c Giles b Ali	4	(7)	2/106 (1) 3/107 (4)		
S. M. Pollock c Collingwood			4/148 (3) 5/218 (6)		
b Wharf	6	(4)	6/228 (7) 7/236 (8)	15 overs: 60-1	

M. Ntini and A. Nel did not bat.

Bowling: Wharf 10–1–51–2; Harmison 10–0–55–1; Ali 9–0–48–1; Collingwood 5–0–25–0; Giles 10–0–38–1; Vaughan 5–0–22–1.

Umpires: S. A. Bucknor (West Indies) and B. G. Jerling.
Third umpire: I. L. Howell. Referee: R. S. Madugalle (Sri Lanka).

THE WEST INDIANS IN ZIMBABWE AND SOUTH AFRICA, 2003-04

Tony Cozier and John Ward

West Indies undertook their tour of southern Africa optimistic that they could finally end their abysmal overseas record. But their hopes, based on a stirring, if solitary, victory over Australia in the last of four home Tests six months earlier, their triumph over Sri Lanka in the brief series that followed, and the emergence of some young, obviously talented, players, came to nothing.

They were hard pressed to prevail even over Zimbabwe – along with Bangladesh the only team below them in the ICC ratings. West Indies scraped a draw in the First Test with their last pair together before winning the Second, and had to fight back from 2–1 down to take the one-day internationals 3–2.

Their inability to cope with the challenges of playing abroad was fully exposed in South Africa, where they were soundly beaten by opponents ruthlessly efficient in both forms of the game.

Three of their most promising young players – Omari Banks, Marlon Samuels and Jerome Taylor, for whom the tour would have provided invaluable experience – had to return home injured at the start of the South African leg. Of the others, only Ravi Rampaul, the 19-year-old fast bowler, made any advance, and he was not risked in any of the Tests.

> A crushing disappointment for Lara

When the team reported to a training camp in Antigua before the tour, coach Gus Logie publicly expressed his frustration at several players' lack of fitness. The consequence was a proliferation of disruptive injuries. Zimbabwe and South Africa were better physically prepared and had no such problems.

The outcome was a crushing disappointment for Brian Lara, especially as West Indies had endured defeat in all five Tests and six of the seven one-day internationals in South Africa during his first stint as captain five years earlier. A draw in one of the Tests and victory in one of the four completed internationals this time was only minimally better.

Lara himself maintained the form he had found after his reinstatement at the helm in March 2003, with 191 in the Test victory over Zimbabwe and two more hundreds in South Africa, where he averaged 66 in the Tests. In a high-scoring series on true pitches, Ramnaresh Sarwan and Chris Gayle had two hundreds each, Shivnarine Chanderpaul one, and 20-year-old Dwayne Smith, a surprise replacement for Samuels, an exhilarating, unbeaten 105 on debut that salvaged the only draw. Gayle could add two one-day hundreds in Zimbabwe and a third in South Africa.

Such scores were rendered irrelevant by ineffective and undisciplined bowling, along with catching and ground fielding that was an embarrassment set against the high standards of the Zimbabweans and South Africans. The

Constant presence: throughout the South African leg of the tour Jacques Kallis seemed immovable from the crease. He hit a hundred in all four Tests.

Picture by Getty Images

home batsmen took full advantage. In the six Tests, West Indies conceded two totals in excess of 600 and three more over 500. The pattern was set by Zimbabwe's 507 for nine declared at Harare, where their captain, Heath Streak, enhanced his considerable reputation as an all-rounder with a maiden Test hundred.

It was carried to exceptional heights in South Africa where Jacques Kallis, strong, sound and single-minded, accumulated hundreds in each of the four Tests, where he averaged 178, and two more plus an unbeaten 95 in the one-day internationals, where he averaged 180. There were also three Test hundreds for Herschelle Gibbs, two for Graeme Smith in his first home assignment as captain and one each for Gary Kirsten, Mark Boucher and Jacques Rudolph. South Africa's total of 12 hundreds in the series matched the Test record of Australia in the West Indies (1954-55) and Pakistan against India (1982-83) – but Australia played five matches to South Africa's four, and Pakistan had six. The 20 centuries scored by the two sides were one short of the record 21 of the West Indies–Australia 1954-55 series.

In spite of this glut of runs, South Africa's fast bowlers were seldom far away from a decisive wicket. The two fastest, Makhaya Ntini and Andre Nel, were the most penetrative: both had benefited from long hours in the nets refining their actions. Ntini's 29 wickets at 21 each helped make him Test cricket's leading wicket-taker for the calendar year 2003, with 59; Nel's 22 at 23 in his first full series included Lara's five times. As always, Shaun Pollock provided essential support by building pressure with his probing accuracy. In Zimbabwe, slow left-armer Ray Price had collected 19 wickets in two Tests – West Indies' leading wicket-taker, Fidel Edwards, managed 16 in six.

Sir Viv Richards, who had given his name to the trophy for the South African Test series, accompanied the team there as chief selector. He questioned the structure of the team management and criticised the attitude of certain players whom he accused of "playing games". These were among the factors that continued to keep West Indies in their undesirable position in the lower reaches of world cricket.

WEST INDIAN TOURING PARTY

B. C. Lara (*captain*), R. R. Sarwan (*vice-captain*), O. A. C. Banks, C. S. Baugh, S. Chanderpaul, C. D. Collymore, M. Dillon, V. C. Drakes, F. H. Edwards, D. Ganga, C. H. Gayle, W. W. Hinds, R. D. Jacobs, R. Rampaul, M. N. Samuels, J. E. Taylor.

At the start of the South African leg of the tour, because of injuries, Banks, Samuels and Taylor were replaced by A. Sanford, D. R. Smith and D. Mohammed. R. L. Powell was selected only for the one-day games in Zimbabwe and South Africa, replacing Ganga in Zimbabwe. I. D. R. Bradshaw, R. O. Hurley and K. J. Wilkinson replaced Baugh, Ganga and Hinds for the one-day internationals in South Africa.

Coach: A. L. Logie. *Manager:* R. O. Skerritt. *Assistant coach:* K. C. G. Benjamin. *Trainer:* R. Rogers. *Physiotherapist:* Mrs S. Liebenberg. *Analyst:* G. S. Smith.

WEST INDIAN TOUR RESULTS

Test matches – Played 6: Won 1, Lost 3, Drawn 2.
Win – Zimbabwe.
Losses – South Africa (3).
Draws – Zimbabwe, South Africa.
First-class matches – Played 10: Won 2, Lost 3, Drawn 5.
One-day internationals – Played 10: Won 4, Lost 5, No result 1. *Wins* – Zimbabwe (3), South Africa. *Losses* – Zimbabwe (2). South Africa (3). *No result* – South Africa.
Other non-first-class matches – Played 3: Won 3.

TEST MATCH AVERAGES – SOUTH AFRICA v WEST INDIES

SOUTH AFRICA – BATTING AND FIELDING

	T	I	NO	R	HS	100s	50s	Avge	Ct
J. H. Kallis	4	6	2	712	177	4	1	178.00	6
H. H. Gibbs	4	7	2	583	192	3	1	116.60	5
†G. C. Smith	4	7	1	418	139	2	0	69.66	1
†G. Kirsten	3	4	1	173	137	1	0	57.66	1
M. V. Boucher	4	5	1	192	122*	1	0	48.00	13
N. D. McKenzie	4	5	1	165	76	0	1	41.25	6
†J. A. Rudolph	4	6	0	220	101	1	0	36.66	1
S. M. Pollock	4	5	2	88	38*	0	0	29.33	4
M. Ntini	4	3	1	40	22*	0	0	20.00	1

Played in four Tests: A. Nel 0, 4 (1 ct). Played in two Tests: A. J. Hall 32 (2 ct). Played in one Test: P. R. Adams 0; †R. J. Peterson 25, 18* (2 ct); M. van Jaarsveld 73, 15 (1 ct).

† *Left-handed batsman.*

BOWLING

	Style	O	M	R	W	BB	5W/i	Avge
M. Ntini	RF	186.5	45	620	29	5-49	3	21.37
A. Nel	RFM	159.4	42	510	22	5-87	1	23.18
S. M. Pollock	RFM	181.2	50	464	16	4-31	0	29.00
J. H. Kallis	RFM	106	28	321	5	1-20	0	64.20

Also bowled: P. R. Adams (SLC) 41–4–173–0; A. J. Hall (RFM) 34.2–5–140–1; G. Kirsten (OB) 2–1–1–0; R. J. Peterson (SLA) 16–2–94–0; J. A. Rudolph (LBG) 34–4–141–1; G. C. Smith (OB) 15.4–2–48–0.

WEST INDIES – BATTING AND FIELDING

	T	I	NO	R	HS	100s	50s	Avge	Ct/St
†B. C. Lara	4	8	0	531	202	2	2	66.37	5
†C. H. Gayle	3	6	0	366	116	2	1	61.00	1
D. R. Smith	2	4	1	164	105*	1	0	54.66	0
R. R. Sarwan	4	8	0	392	119	2	1	49.00	4
†S. Chanderpaul	3	6	0	286	109	1	1	47.66	0
V. C. Drakes	4	7	0	157	67	0	1	22.42	0
†R. D. Jacobs	4	8	1	145	58	0	1	20.71	10/1
A. Sanford	2	3	1	33	18*	0	0	16.50	1
D. Ganga	4	8	0	122	60	0	1	15.25	3
M. Dillon	3	6	0	85	30	0	0	14.16	0
†W. W. Hinds	3	6	0	59	25	0	0	9.83	0
C. D. Collymore	2	4	2	18	13*	0	0	9.00	0
F. H. Edwards	4	7	4	16	10	0	0	5.33	1

Played in one Test: C. S. Baugh 21, 2; †D. Mohammed 36.

† *Left-handed batsman.*

BOWLING

	Style	O	M	R	W	BB	5W/i	Avge
W. W. Hinds	RM	48.4	7	215	5	3-79	0	43.00
R. R. Sarwan.	LB	73	3	266	6	2-55	0	44.33
A. Sanford	RFM	83.2	9	340	7	4-132	0	48.57
C. D. Collymore	RFM	61	10	228	4	2-118	0	57.00
F. H. Edwards	RF	134.4	9	648	8	3-132	0	81.00
M. Dillon	RFM	112	17	359	4	2-96	0	89.75
V. C. Drakes	RFM	148	22	459	5	2-113	0	91.80

Also bowled: D. Ganga (OB) 20–1–72–0; C. H. Gayle (OB) 26–3–112–0; D. Mohammed (SLC) 39–5–142–3; D. R. Smith (RM) 15–1–46–1.

Note: Matches in this section which were not first-class are signified by a dagger.

At Takashinga Sports Club, Harare, October 30, 31, November 1, 2003. **Drawn.** Toss: West Indians. **West Indians 404-5 dec.** (D. Ganga 110, S. Chanderpaul 102 retired out, M. N. Samuels 66*, R. D. Jacobs 55*) **and 343-6 dec.** (M. N. Samuels 147, D. Ganga 69*); **Zimbabwe A 242** (V. Sibanda 51, S. Matsikenyeri 84*; V. C. Drakes 5-66) **and 246-9** (C. N. Evans 59; J. E. Taylor 6-58).

Travis Friend was removed from the home attack during the first innings after bowling two accidental beamers.

ZIMBABWE v WEST INDIES

First Test Match

At Harare, November 4, 5, 6, 7, 8, 2003. Drawn. Toss: Zimbabwe. Test debuts: S. Matsikenyeri, V. Sibanda.

Against all expectations, Zimbabwe dominated an enthralling match to end a run of 11 consecutive Test defeats, and came heartbreakingly close to their first victory over a senior Test team since June 2001. It took a gallant last-wicket partnership between Jacobs and the inexperienced Edwards to save West Indies from humiliation: they safely played out the final 32 minutes and 71 deliveries.

Despite missing three senior players through injury – Grant Flower, Ervine and Hondo – Zimbabwe, who included two 20-year-old debutant batsmen, Vusimuzi Sibanda and Stuart Matsikenyeri, looked a far more organised side than the greenhorns who had performed so poorly in England. They were fortunate to win the toss, enabling them to take advantage of hot weather and an excellent batting pitch. But their top five fell for 154, mainly through lack of application against undisciplined bowling, before Taibu started a recovery with his former schoolmate, Matsikenyeri. Taibu was distraught to be dismissed for 83 but Streak carried on with a very correct and determined maiden Test century, in his 56th Test, a record. He added 168 with Blignaut, an eighth-wicket record for Zimbabwe, to ensure their ascendancy, even though West Indies were now bowling much better. Edwards, a "slinger" with deceptive pace and bounce, was the most impressive. Blignaut too just missed his century, brilliantly caught for 91, but Streak was able to declare at 507.

A freak incident delayed the start on the third day. As the pitch was being rolled, players were practising on the outfield; Gripper hit a ball right under the roller which left a deep indentation just short of a fast bowler's length to a left-hander. An auger was borrowed from the neighbouring golf club to replace the turf, play started one and a half hours late, and referee Gundappa Viswanath postponed lunch to allow a two-hour session. Lara earned widespread commendation for his positive approach and willingness to bat on the patched-up pitch. In the event, there were no problems and West Indies passed 200 with only three men out, but three quick wickets after tea swung the match further Zimbabwe's way. West Indies saved the follow-on with eight wickets down on the fourth morning before left-arm spinner Price completed figures of six for 73, the second-best recorded for his country.

BETTER LATE... MOST TESTS TO SCORE MAIDEN HUNDRED

56 (91 innings)   **H. H. Streak, 127*, Zimbabwe v West Indies at Harare** **2003-04**
51 (72 innings)   S. M. Pollock, 111, South Africa v Sri Lanka at Centurion   2000-01
49 (70 innings)   **D. L. Vettori, 137*, New Zealand v Pakistan at Hamilton** **2003-04**
48 (73 innings)   I. A. Healy, 102*, Australia v England at Manchester   1993
47 (84 innings)   A. D. R. Campbell, 102, Zimbabwe v India at Nagpur   2000-01

THWARTED! TESTS DRAWN WITH ONE WICKET TO FALL

England (294 and 153-5 dec.) v India (170 and 152-9) at Manchester   1946
West Indies (393 and 432-6 dec.) v Australia (366 and 273-9) at Adelaide   1960-61
West Indies (301 and 229) v England (297 and 228-9) at Lord's   1963
West Indies (414 and 264) v England (371 and 206-9) at Georgetown   1967-68
West Indies (276 and 616) v Australia (533 and 339-9) at Adelaide   1968-69
Pakistan (435 and 291) v West Indies (421 and 251-9) at Bridgetown   1976-77
Australia (343 and 305-3 dec.) v West Indies (280 and 258-9) at Kingston.   1977-78
India (300 and 361-1 dec.) v West Indies (327 and 197-9) at Calcutta   1978-79
New Zealand (317 and 286) v Australia (357 and 230-9) at Melbourne   1987-88
West Indies (174 and 391) v Pakistan (194 and 341-9) at Port-of-Spain   1987-88
Australia (400 and 138-2 dec.) v New Zealand (251-6 dec. and 223-9) at Hobart . . .   1997-98
Zimbabwe (507-9 dec. and 200-7 dec.) v West Indies (335 and 207-9) at Harare   **2003-04**
Sri Lanka (331 and 226) v England (235 and 210-9) at Galle   2003-04

Zimbabwe led by 172, but were unconvincing as they attempted to build towards a declaration. At the start of the final day, they were four down for 94, a lead of 266. When Wishart, who had looked in commanding form, fell early on, they might have promoted the hard-hitting Blignaut or Streak himself, but they decided to play safe, sending in Taibu as planned.

West Indies' eventual target was 373 in 83 overs, a difficult one made with the Lara factor in mind. He, however, had only a single to his credit when he was given lbw, not totally satisfactorily, to Streak, leaving his side reeling at 38 for three. After that, only one team could win.

The middle order, Jacobs included, played rather too freely for batsmen whose objective was saving the game. But only Streak and Price looked threatening with the ball, until Blignaut, who had been innocuous, suddenly produced an inspired spell, opening up the lower order and apparently propelling Zimbabwe towards victory. Price followed up with his tenth wicket of the match, but he was tiring and, when deteriorating light forced Streak to remove Blignaut, the last pair were able to play out the spin of Price and Gripper in the gloaming.

Man of the Match: H. H. Streak.

Close of play: First day, Zimbabwe 284-6 (Taibu 75, Streak 16); Second day, West Indies 11-0 (Gayle 6, Hinds 0); Third day, West Indies 241-6 (Chanderpaul 19, Drakes 0); Fourth day, Zimbabwe 94-4 (Wishart 25, Matsikenyeri 1).

Zimbabwe

	First Innings		Second Innings	
V. Sibanda c Jacobs b Edwards	18	– c Ganga b Collymore	16
T. R. Gripper c Lara b Taylor	41	– lbw b Drakes	26
M. A. Vermeulen c Hinds b Edwards	8	– c Chanderpaul b Edwards	2
S. V. Carlisle c Lara b Collymore	8	– lbw b Drakes	10
C. B. Wishart c Jacobs b Hinds	47	– b Drakes	34
S. Matsikenyeri c Jacobs b Edwards	57	– not out	46
†T. Taibu b Edwards	83	– b Drakes	21
*H. H. Streak not out	127	– (9) not out	7
A. M. Blignaut c Gayle b Drakes	91	– (8) c Jacobs b Collymore	13
R. W. Price lbw b Edwards	2		
N. B. Mahwire not out	1		
B 1, l-b 5, w 3, n-b 15	24	B 8, l-b 2, w 2, n-b 13	25
	(9 wkts dec.) 507		**(7 wkts dec.) 200**

1/26 (1) 2/35 (3) 3/58 (4)   1/21 (1) 2/27 (3)
4/112 (2) 5/154 (5) 6/233 (6)   3/60 (4) 4/90 (2)
7/314 (7) 8/482 (9) 9/495 (10)   5/107 (5) 6/152 (7) 7/175 (8)

Bowling: *First Innings*—Collymore 29–6–131–1; Edwards 34.3–3–133–5; Hinds 15–6–40–1; Drakes 34–4–85–1; Taylor 9.4–4–32–1; Gayle 19.2–6–38–0; Sarwan 9–0–35–0; Chanderpaul 1–0–7–0; Ganga 1–1–0–0. *Second Innings*—Collymore 15–2–59–2; Edwards 16–5–52–1; Drakes 20–2–67–4; Sarwan 1–0–12–0.

West Indies

	First Innings		Second Innings	
C. H. Gayle lbw b Streak	14	– c Taibu b Price	13
W. W. Hinds c Blignaut b Mahwire	79	– c Carlisle b Streak	24
D. Ganga b Mahwire	73	– b Price	16
*B. C. Lara c Mahwire b Price	29	– lbw b Streak	1
R. R. Sarwan lbw b Price	9	– st Taibu b Gripper	39
S. Chanderpaul lbw b Streak	36	– c Sibanda b Price	39
†R. D. Jacobs c Vermeulen b Price	5	– not out	60
V. C. Drakes c Streak b Price	31	– c Taibu b Blignaut	4
J. E. Taylor c Wishart b Price	9	– c Matsikenyeri b Blignaut	3
C. D. Collymore not out	11	– c Vermeulen b Price	1
F. H. Edwards c Matsikenyeri b Price	18	– not out	1
B 7, l-b 7, w 3, n-b 4	21	B 1, l-b 1, w 1, n-b 3	6
	335		**(9 wkts) 207**

1/50 (1) 2/127 (2) 3/179 (4) 4/211 (5)   1/37 (2) 2/37 (1)
5/215 (3) 6/240 (7) 7/290 (6)   3/38 (4) 4/73 (3)
8/294 (8) 9/309 (9) 10/335 (11)   5/103 (5) 6/171 (6)
7/184 (8) 8/194 (9) 9/204 (10)

Bowling: *First Innings*—Blignaut 14–3–68–0; Streak 28–9–74–2; Mahwire 25–7–75–2; Price 37.2–13–73–6; Matsikenyeri 2–0–10–0; Gripper 8–1–21–0. *Second Innings*—Streak 15–7–28–2; Blignaut 14–2–50–2; Price 38–11–88–4; Mahwire 2–0–10–0; Gripper 12–5–23–1; Matsikenyeri 2–0–6–0.

Umpires: B. F. Bowden (New Zealand) and S. J. A. Taufel (Australia).
Third umpire: K. C. Barbour. Referee: G. R. Viswanath (India).

ZIMBABWE v WEST INDIES

Second Test Match

At Bulawayo, November 12, 13, 14, 15, 16, 2003. West Indies won by 128 runs. Toss: West Indies.

This Test was memorable for one of Brian Lara's peerless innings, which proved the difference between the sides, and for abysmal batting on the fourth day, when 18 wickets fell for 205 runs.

Blown away at Bulawayo: Heath Streak conjures a wicked in-swinging yorker to despatch Brian Lara for a single in West Indies' second innings, but Zimbabwe still lost.

Picture by Howard Burditt, Reuters

Gayle had been West Indies' beacon: he seemed determined to shatter the bowlers' confidence from the start. West Indies rushed to 41 off the first seven overs, and Gayle made 47 in an opening stand of 73, his straight driving particularly fearsome. In the afternoon, Lara took over, racing to fifty in 53 balls and excelling in the cut, the sweep and the slash through the covers.

On the second day, Lara seemed deliberately to play the ball straighter, gaining many runs with drives between mid-on and mid-off. He and his partners targeted Price as the danger man, assaulting his left-arm spin for almost five an over. Price held up well and was again the backbone of the bowling; remarkably, his only maiden over was his last.

Lara's 22nd Test century arrived off 124 balls and, when he reached 107, he overtook Vivian Richards's aggregate of 8,540 to become West Indies' all-time highest scorer in Tests. He was eventually caught at second slip, trying to glide Blignaut to third man.

West Indies struck quickly when Zimbabwe batted, taking three wickets by the 14th over. But Vermeulen and Wishart fought back courageously. They added 154 before the more aggressive Wishart lost his nerve on the verge of a second Test century and was lbw, swinging across the line to Collymore. Vermeulen, handicapped by a thigh injury that restricted his trademark drives through the off side, was much more restrained but completed an admirable maiden Test hundred, batting over seven hours in all. Zimbabwe conceded a first-innings lead of 104, but dismissed Gayle with the first delivery of the second innings, when Streak moved a ball in off the seam to trap him just before the close of the third day.

A crumbling pitch could not account for the mayhem next day, when the West Indies batsmen displayed a serious lack of discipline and the Zimbabweans a similar lack of courage. The home side had begun with little hope of victory, but by mid-afternoon, to their own astonishment, they found themselves facing an attainable target. Streak and Blignaut cut through the West Indian top order like knives through butter: among the victims was Lara, bowled for a single by the ball of the series from Streak, a wicked in-swinging yorker that pierced his high backlift and knocked his middle stump out of the ground.

Zimbabwe seemed quite unprepared to chase 233, however. With Edwards unfit, Hinds showed how to succeed by bowling simple line and length, while the batsmen were all too ready to make mistakes. It was a major error for the experienced Streak to bat at No. 9, and he was stranded at the end. Nine wickets were down for 75 when, all too late, Streak and Mahwire dug in to suggest what could have been done, batting on 40 minutes into the final day before West Indies sealed their victory.

Man of the Match: B. C. Lara.

Close of play: First day, West Indies 282-3 (Lara 77, Sarwan 46); Second day, Zimbabwe 173-3 (Vermeulen 60, Wishart 86); Third day, West Indies 13-1 (Hinds 5, Ganga 8); Fourth day, Zimbabwe 90-9 (Streak 19, Mahwire 4).

West Indies

C. H. Gayle c Taibu b Blignaut	47	– lbw b Streak	0
W. W. Hinds st Taibu b Price	81	– c Carlisle b Price	28
D. Ganga c Matsikenyeri b Price	23	– c Carlisle b Blignaut	8
*B. C. Lara c Wishart b Blignaut	191	– b Streak	1
R. R. Sarwan c Vermeulen b Price	65	– c Wishart b Blignaut	9
S. Chanderpaul c Wishart b Price	15	– lbw b Streak	15
†R. D. Jacobs c Gripper b Streak	1	– c Blignaut b Price	10
O. A. C. Banks lbw b Blignaut	3	– c Vermeulen b Price	16
M. Dillon c Matsikenyeri b Price	19	– not out	27
C. D. Collymore not out	16	– b Price	0
F. H. Edwards c Taibu b Blignaut	0	– b Blignaut	0
B 1, l-b 12, w 2, n-b 5	20	B 5, l-b 3, w 4, n-b 2	14

1/73 (1) 2/146 (3) 3/161 (2) 4/351 (5)	481	1/0 (1) 2/17 (3) 3/21 (4) 4/51 (5)	128
5/389 (6) 6/394 (7) 7/422 (8)		5/51 (2) 6/82 (6) 7/82 (7)	
8/449 (4) 9/475 (9) 10/481 (11)		8/127 (8) 9/127 (10) 10/128 (11)	

Bowling: *First Innings*—Streak 24–4–87–1; Blignaut 20–4–86–4; Mahwire 15–3–79–0; Price 43–1–199–5; Gripper 5–1–17–0. *Second Innings*—Streak 15–2–39–3; Blignaut 14.4–6–29–3; Price 21–7–36–4; Mahwire 2–0–16–0.

Zimbabwe

V. Sibanda c and b Edwards	2	– c Lara b Dillon	0
T. R. Gripper b Dillon	1	– c Ganga b Banks	8
M. A. Vermeulen b Banks	118	– b Hinds	24
S. V. Carlisle b Edwards	11	– c Jacobs b Banks	9
C. B. Wishart lbw b Collymore	96	– c Jacobs b Hinds	13
S. Matsikenyeri b Collymore	8	(7) run out	5
†T. Taibu c Gayle b Collymore	27	– (8) lbw b Collymore	1
*H. H. Streak lbw b Dillon	3	– (9) not out	33
A. M. Blignaut lbw b Collymore	31	– (6) lbw b Banks	3
R. W. Price c Ganga b Banks	35	– b Collymore	4
N. B. Mahwire not out	8	– b Dillon	4
B 17, l-b 4, w 1, n-b 15	37		

1/5 (1) 2/10 (3) 3/31 (4) 4/185 (5)	377	1/0 (1) 2/32 (3) 3/33 (2) 4/54 (5)	104
5/201 (6) 6/279 (7) 7/289 (8)		5/56 (4) 6/62 (7) 7/63 (6)	
8/302 (3) 9/336 (9) 10/377 (10)		8/67 (8) 9/75 (10) 10/104 (11)	

Bowling: *First Innings*—Hinds 6–2–18–0; Edwards 15–3–48–2; Dillon 34–13–57–2; Collymore 24–5–70–4; Banks 41.1–13–106–2; Gayle 6–1–23–0; Sarwan 7–0–34–0. *Second Innings*—Dillon 8–2–17–2; Collymore 15–7–29–2; Hinds 9–2–20–2; Banks 15–2–35–3; Sarwan 2–1–3–0.

Umpires: R. E. Koertzen (South Africa) and S. J. A. Taufel (Australia).
Third umpire: I. D. Robinson. Referee: G. R. Viswanath (India).

†At Kwekwe, November 19, 2003. **West Indians won by seven wickets.** Toss: Zimbabwe A. **Zimbabwe A 239-8** (50 overs) (B. G. Rogers 54, A. Maregwede 69; W. W. Hinds 4-35); **West Indians 240-3** (39.1 overs) (W. W. Hinds 69 retired out, S. Chanderpaul 64 retired out, M. N. Samuels 51*).

†ZIMBABWE v WEST INDIES

First One-Day International

At Bulawayo, November 22, 2003. West Indies won by 51 runs (D/L method). Toss: West Indies. One-day international debuts: V. Sibanda; R. Rampaul.

"Bulawayo" means "place of slaughter", and Gayle and Lara made it live up to its name. The Zimbabwean bowling was not particularly poor, but no team in the world is a match for Lara in full flight. He hit 14 fours and three sixes in 82 balls, his second fifty taking just 23 balls. Gayle started more cautiously, but batted through the innings for a one-day best 153 not out in 160 balls, with 19 fours and two sixes. The best Zimbabwe could aim for was damage limitation. Sibanda hit a fifty on one-day debut, with some classy strokes, while Wishart showed the talent he had revealed all too rarely at international level. With rain approaching, West Indies turned to spin to ensure they completed the 25 overs required for a result.

Man of the Match: C. H. Gayle.

West Indies

W. W. Hinds c Taibu b Blignaut	28	†C. S. Baugh not out		3
C. H. Gayle not out	153			
*B. C. Lara run out	113	L-b 4, w 12, n-b 3		19
R. R. Sarwan run out	0			
S. Chanderpaul lbw b Ervine	8	1/77 (1) 2/253 (3)	(6 wkts, 50 overs)	347
M. N. Samuels st Taibu b Matsikenyeri	6	3/254 (4) 4/282 (5)		
R. L. Powell c Sibanda b Streak	17	5/289 (6) 6/328 (7)		

V. C. Drakes, M. Dillon and R. Rampaul did not bat.

Bowling: Streak 10–0–52–1; Blignaut 8–1–57–1; Brent 10–0–61–0; Ervine 7–0–75–1; Price 10–0–52–0; Gripper 2–0–15–0; Matsikenyeri 3–0–31–1.

Zimbabwe

V. Sibanda c Powell b Drakes	58
T. R. Gripper c Lara b Gayle	16
M. A. Vermeulen c Chanderpaul b Gayle	0
C. B. Wishart not out	72
A. M. Blignaut not out	10
L-b 2, w 4, n-b 11	17

1/40 (2) 2/40 (3)   (3 wkts, 34.5 overs)   173
3/150 (1)

S. Matsikenyeri, S. M. Ervine, †T. Taibu, *H. H. Streak, G. B. Brent and R. W. Price did not bat.

Bowling: Dillon 7.5–0–52–0; Drakes 4–0–15–1; Samuels 6–0–22–0; Gayle 10–1–21–2; Sarwan 3–0–23–0; Rampaul 4–0–38–0.

Umpires: R. E. Koertzen (South Africa) and K. C. Barbour.
Third umpire: I. D. Robinson. Referee: G. R. Viswanath (India).

†ZIMBABWE v WEST INDIES

Second One-Day International

At Bulawayo, November 23, 2003. Zimbabwe won by six wickets. Toss: West Indies.

The West Indian batsmen were transformed from Jekylls to Hydes overnight. The pitch was little different from the previous day's, perhaps yielding a little more turn and bounce. But they appeared complacent, and paid the penalty. Gayle and Lara, century-makers a day earlier, scored ten between them; only Samuels put up much of a fight against a well co-ordinated attack. As so often, though, Zimbabwe's top order wilted under the pressure of knowing victory was within their grasp. Four of the first five fell in single figures. Streak promoted himself to No. 6 to avoid a crisis, but the accolades went to Vermeulen, who played with languid calm for an unbeaten 66 in 79 balls to level the series.

Man of the Match: M. A. Vermeulen.

West Indies

W. W. Hinds c Taibu b Ervine	17	R. Rampaul c Wishart b Price		1
C. H. Gayle c Taibu b Blignaut	8	C. D. Collymore b Streak		2
*B. C. Lara lbw b Blignaut	2			
R. R. Sarwan run out	13	L-b 5, w 11		16
S. Chanderpaul c Streak b Brent	20			
M. N. Samuels not out	36	1/18 (2) 2/26 (3) 3/41 (1) (42.3 overs)		125
R. L. Powell c Taibu b Price	6	4/71 (5) 5/71 (4) 6/85 (7)		
†C. S. Baugh b Gripper	2	7/91 (8) 8/97 (9)		
V. C. Drakes c and b Gripper	2	9/110 (10) 10/125 (11)		

Bowling: Streak 6.3–1–18–1; Blignaut 7–0–27–2; Brent 8–1–18–1; Ervine 5–0–13–1; Price 10–2–16–2; Gripper 6–1–28–2.

Zimbabwe

V. Sibanda c Baugh b Drakes	0	*H. H. Streak not out		38
T. R. Gripper run out	6	L-b 1, w 2, n-b 4		7
M. A. Vermeulen not out	66			
C. B. Wishart c Sarwan b Collymore	8	1/8 (2) 2/8 (1) (4 wkts, 29.4 overs)		128
S. Matsikenyeri b Collymore	3	3/31 (4) 4/54 (5)		

S. M. Ervine, †T. Taibu, A. M. Blignaut, G. B. Brent and R. W. Price did not bat.

Bowling: Rampaul 10–2–47–0; Drakes 7–2–18–1; Collymore 7–1–27–2; Gayle 3–1–16–0; Samuels 2–0–10–0; Sarwan 0.4–0–9–0.

Umpires: R. E. Koertzen (South Africa) and I. D. Robinson.
Third umpire: K. C. Barbour. Referee: G. R. Viswanath (India).

†ZIMBABWE v WEST INDIES

Third One-Day International

At Harare, November 26, 2003. Zimbabwe won by 21 runs. Toss: West Indies.

Another mediocre performance by the disorganised West Indians helped Zimbabwe take a 2–1 lead, in a victory of discipline over flair. Zimbabwe should have exceeded 229 – they had five wickets in hand – but again started by playing safe. Vermeulen made the early running, with 66 in 70 balls, while Streak reached his tenth one-day fifty, surprisingly only his second in Zimbabwe. He and Taibu accelerated with 90 in 14 overs, but the target was well within West Indian capabilities. Gayle and Lara looked set to take them home, until Streak dismissed Lara with another superb yorker. They faltered, recovered, then faltered again as an ill-judged stroke by Samuels cost him his wicket; Powell fell next ball and after that Zimbabwe kept their grip.

Man of the Match: H. H. Streak.

Zimbabwe

V. Sibanda c Powell b Dillon	11	†T. Taibu not out	37
T. R. Gripper c and b Hinds	17	L-b 9, w 6, n-b 3	18
M. A. Vermeulen b Powell	66		
C. B. Wishart hit wkt b Drakes	7		
S. Matsikenyeri lbw b Hinds	8	1/22 (1) 2/53 (2) (5 wkts, 50 overs) 229	
*H. H. Streak not out	65	3/69 (4) 4/85 (5)	
		5/139 (3)	

S. M. Ervine, A. M. Blignaut, G. B. Brent and R. W. Price did not bat.

Bowling: Drakes 10–2–38–1; Dillon 10–2–32–1; Hinds 10–0–43–2; Collymore 10–0–39–0; Samuels 3–0–23–0; Powell 5–0–35–1; Gayle 2–0–10–0.

West Indies

W. W. Hinds c Taibu b Blignaut	13	M. Dillon b Streak	5
C. H. Gayle c Taibu b Blignaut	61	C. D. Collymore lbw b Ervine	2
R. R. Sarwan c Taibu b Streak	0		
*B. C. Lara b Streak	34	L-b 3, w 11, n-b 1	15
S. Chanderpaul c Sibanda b Price	19		
M. N. Samuels c Ervine b Blignaut	25	1/24 (1) 2/25 (3) 3/95 (4) (47.2 overs) 208	
R. L. Powell b Blignaut	0	4/120 (5) 5/164 (6)	
†R. D. Jacobs not out	25	6/164 (7) 7/170 (2)	
V. C. Drakes c Taibu b Ervine	9	8/184 (9) 9/205 (10) 10/208 (11)	

Bowling: Streak 9–0–45–3; Blignaut 10–0–43–4; Brent 7–1–37–0; Ervine 9.2–0–42–2; Price 10–2–27–1; Gripper 2–0–11–0.

Umpires: E. A. R. de Silva (Sri Lanka) and K. C. Barbour.
Third umpire: I. D. Robinson. Referee: G. R. Viswanath (India).

†ZIMBABWE v WEST INDIES

Fourth One-Day International

At Harare, November 29, 2003. West Indies won by 72 runs (D/L method). Toss: Zimbabwe. One-day international debut: F. H. Edwards.

The real West Indies stood up again, thanks to three magnificent performances. Gayle set the pace with a fifty of rare power and brilliance – three sixes and seven fours in 34 balls – while Hinds batted through the innings for his highest one-day score. Then Fidel Edwards unleashed a

FIVE WICKETS ON ONE-DAY INTERNATIONAL DEBUT

6-22	F. H. Edwards	West Indies v Zimbabwe at Harare	2003-04
5-21	A. I. C. Dodemaide	Australia v Sri Lanka at Perth	1987-88
5-26	S. H. U. Karnain	Sri Lanka v New Zealand at Moratuwa	1983-84
5-27	A. Codrington	Canada v Bangladesh at Durban	2002-03
5-29	A. A. Donald	South Africa v India at Calcutta	1991-92
5-67	T. C. B. Fernando	Sri Lanka v Zimbabwe at Sharjah	2001-02

deadly spell of swing, becoming the first bowler ever to take six wickets on his one-day international debut. The Zimbabwean bowlers should also have been able to use the humid conditions, which was why Streak bowled first, but the West Indian openers were the masters. There might have been a late onslaught too but rain curtailed the innings and amended Zimbabwe's target to 223 off 32 overs. Edwards's first ball was a superb yorker that uprooted Rogers's off stump, and he ripped through the top order, reducing Zimbabwe to 22 for five by the eighth over. Taibu and Ervine added 99 to regain some respectability.

Man of the Match: F. H. Edwards.

West Indies

W. W. Hinds not out 127
C. H. Gayle c Taibu b Ervine 51
*B. C. Lara c Taibu b Brent 14
R. R. Sarwan c Vermeulen b Streak 47
S. Chanderpaul not out 3
          W 13, n-b 1 14
                                          ———
1/96 (2) 2/124 (3)   (3 wkts, 45 overs) 256
3/231 (4)

R. L. Powell, †R. D. Jacobs, M. Dillon, C. D. Collymore, F. H. Edwards and R. Rampaul did not bat.

Bowling: Streak 8–0–46–1; Blignaut 8–0–47–0; Ervine 10–1–49–1; Brent 9–0–65–1; Price 10–0–49–0.

Zimbabwe

V. Sibanda c Jacobs b Edwards	7	S. M. Ervine not out	37
B. G. Rogers b Edwards	0	A. M. Blignaut not out	1
M. A. Vermeulen c Chanderpaul			
b Edwards .	6	B 4, l-b 5, w 8, n-b 1	18
C. B. Wishart lbw b Edwards	0		———
S. Matsikenyeri c Collymore b Edwards .	6	1/5 (2) 2/10 (1) (7 wkts, 32 overs) 150
*H. H. Streak c Powell b Gayle	9	3/10 (4) 4/15 (3)
†T. Taibu b Edwards	66	5/22 (5) 6/47 (6) 7/146 (7)

G. B. Brent and R. W. Price did not bat.

Bowling: Dillon 5–0–18–0; Edwards 7–1–22–6; Rampaul 6–0–35–0; Gayle 7–2–17–1; Powell 5–0–28–0; Hinds 2–0–21–0.

Umpires: E. A. R. de Silva (Sri Lanka) and I. D. Robinson.
Third umpire: K. C. Barbour.   Referee: G. R. Viswanath (India).

†ZIMBABWE v WEST INDIES

Fifth One-Day International

At Harare, November 30, 2003. West Indies won by eight wickets. Toss: Zimbabwe. One-day international debut: A. Maregwede.

With the series level, Zimbabwe succumbed to their traditional fault of capitulating under pressure and were overwhelmed. Again, the dominant figure was Gayle, who took four wickets and blasted another century off his favourite opponents. Zimbabwe were not doing too badly at 107 for two in the 23rd over, but Gayle sent them into terminal decline: they perished to one dismal stroke after another. West Indies' policy was domination rather than accumulation. Gayle and Hinds survived a couple of good overs from Streak and Blignaut before going into overdrive, not without luck. This time, Gayle needed only 75 balls to take himself to 112 not out and his team to a comprehensive win. Ervine did have the pleasure of extracting Lara's leg stump with a yorker.

Man of the Match: C. H. Gayle.   *Man of the Series*: C. H. Gayle.

Zimbabwe

V. Sibanda run out	8	G. B. Brent not out	10
B. G. Rogers c Jacobs b Dillon	34	R. W. Price lbw b Edwards	3
M. A. Vermeulen c Powell b Gayle	36		
C. B. Wishart c Jacobs b Gayle	16	B 1, l-b 5, w 19	25
A. Maregwede c Powell b Gayle	0		———
*H. H. Streak c Lara b Edwards	30	1/39 (1) 2/57 (2) 3/107 (4) (47.5 overs) 196
†T. Taibu c Sarwan b Powell	14	4/109 (5) 5/111 (3)
S. M. Ervine c Powell b Gayle	10	6/141 (7) 7/157 (8)
A. M. Blignaut st Jacobs b Powell	10	8/179 (6) 9/179 (9) 10/196 (11)

Bowling: Dillon 8–1–35–1; Edwards 8.5–0–60–2; Rampaul 6–2–17–0; Collymore 8–1–22–0; Gayle 10–1–24–4; Powell 7–0–32–2.

West Indies

W. W. Hinds c Price b Blignaut	......	13
C. H. Gayle not out	....	112
*B. C. Lara b Ervine	....	41
R. L. Powell not out	....	12
B 4, l-b 3, w 12	....	19

1/43 (1) 2/180 (3)   (2 wkts, 25.4 overs) 197

R. R. Sarwan, S. Chanderpaul, †R. D. Jacobs, M. Dillon, C. D. Collymore, F. H. Edwards and R. Rampaul did not bat.

Bowling: Streak 6–1–25–0; Blignaut 6–0–44–1; Ervine 4.4–0–35–1; Brent 3–0–25–0; Price 3–0–29–0; Rogers 3–0–32–0.

Umpires: E. A. R. de Silva (Sri Lanka) and K. C. Barbour.
Third umpire: I. D. Robinson.   Referee: G. R. Viswanath (India).

†At Randjesfontein, December 3, 2003. **West Indians won by 12 runs.** Toss: West Indians. **West Indians 241-4** (45 overs) (D. Ganga 70, S. Chanderpaul 53, B. C. Lara 53*); **N. F. Oppenheimer's XI 229-5** (45 overs).
Lara scored his 53 runs in 28 balls, with three fours and four sixes.

At Bloemfontein, December 5, 6, 7, 8, 2003. **Drawn.** Toss: West Indians. **West Indians 618** (R. R. Sarwan 51, B. C. Lara 72, S. Chanderpaul 245, R. D. Jacobs 149) **and 289-3 dec.** (D. Ganga 101*, C. S. Baugh 158*); **Free State 264** (J. F. Venter 79, D. du Preez 56; R. Rampaul 5-55) **and 97-2** (R. McLaren 53*).
Chanderpaul's 245 lasted 468 minutes and 369 balls and included 31 fours. He added 359 in 377 minutes with Jacobs for the West Indians' fifth wicket. Baugh scored 108 on the final morning, and in all 158 in 154 balls, including 18 fours and five sixes.

SOUTH AFRICA v WEST INDIES

First Test Match

At Johannesburg, December 12, 13, 14, 15, 16, 2003. South Africa won by 189 runs. Toss: South Africa.

South Africa capitalised on winning the toss on a hard, dry pitch that developed cracks which widened in the fierce, constant heat. They seized control on the first day when it was at its truest, and Smith's 132, in his first home Test as captain, followed by a commanding partnership between Kallis and van Jaarsveld, carried them to 368 for three. In spite of more controlled West Indian bowling and Lara's sixth Test double-century (the second in a losing cause), including a Test-record 28 in an over, they completed their victory 20 minutes before tea on the last day.

Smith and Gibbs set South Africa on the way with an opening stand of 149, and the removal of Gibbs – after an unusually restrained innings – and Rudolph in quick succession brought only temporary relief for West Indies. Kallis arrived, putting on 80

Going down fighting: Brian Lara pulls Makhaya Ntini for four on his way to a double-hundred, though it wasn't enough to prevent defeat.

Picture by Getty Images

with Smith, who finally edged the pacy but erratic Edwards low to first slip after hitting 22 fours off 184 balls. Kallis went on to add another 128 by the close with van Jaarsveld, who seized the chance offered by Gary Kirsten's decision to attend the birth of his son (delivered during the second day) to play with attractive ease.

West Indies were handicapped when Gayle, their only passable spinner, pulled up in the outfield with a torn right hamstring muscle; his further participation was restricted to hobbling through two innings down the order with a runner. But van Jaarsveld was lbw in the first over of the second day, from Dillon, who later produced one that kept low to bowl Kallis for a chanceless 158 featuring a six and 17 fours. West Indies eventually claimed the last seven wickets for 189, the final three through Hinds's medium-pace swing.

They made an encouraging start to their reply but, inevitably, it was left to Lara to eliminate the prospect of the follow-on. He started hesitantly, offering a low, but straightforward, chance to Pollock at first slip off Ntini when 15, but gradually found his customary timing and placement. There was little progress at the other end: Ganga needed over two hours to add 11 to his overnight 49 and Chanderpaul spent more than two and a half hours contributing 34 to a stand of 125. But Lara's momentum was building. His century was West Indies' first on South African soil, and his fusillade of two straight sixes and four fours in the third day's penultimate over, from Peterson, broke the New Zealander Craig McMillan's record for most runs in a Test match over. It also reduced the deficit to exactly 200. Next morning, he reached his double-hundred with his 32nd four – and drove the next ball, his 274th, to extra cover, to be ninth out. His latest masterpiece of an innings occupied seven hours 17 minutes.

MOST RUNS BY ONE BATSMAN IN A TEST OVER

28	B. C. Lara	off R. J. Peterson, WI v SA at Johannesburg (466444)....	**2003-04**
26	C. D. McMillan	off Younis Khan, NZ v P at Hamilton (444464).........	2000-01
24	J. F. M. Morrison	off Imran Khan, NZ v P at Karachi (2 x6 3 x4 – 8-ball over).	1976-77
24	A. M. E. Roberts	off I. T. Botham, WI v E at Port-of-Spain (462660*)......	1980-81
24	S. M. Patil	off R. G. D. Willis, I v E at Manchester (444*0444).......	1982
24	I. T. Botham	off D. A. Stirling, E v NZ at The Oval (464604).........	1986
24	I. D. S. Smith	off A. S. Wassan, NZ v I at Auckland (244266)..........	1989-90
24	Kapil Dev	off E. E. Hemmings, I v E at Lord's (006666)...........	1990
24	Yousuf Youhana	off N. Boje, P v SA at Cape Town (444426)............	2002-03
24	**C. H. Gayle**	off M. J. Hoggard, WE v E at The Oval (444444).......	**2004**

Note: Roberts ran a leg-bye off Botham's final ball. Patil's third four off Willis came from a no-ball.

South Africa's lead was 151 and, although Gibbs retired with a broken nose, when an edged hook off Drakes burst through his grille, they progressed to a second-innings declaration at more than three and a half runs an over. Smith challenged West Indies to score 378 off the remaining 100 overs.

If they found hope in their record 418 to beat Australia in Antigua seven months earlier, it was quickly quashed. Ntini despatched both openers and night-watchman Drakes before the close, and Pollock followed up next morning by removing Sarwan and Lara within the first seven overs.

Responding to the crisis of 43 for five, Chanderpaul abandoned his usual guise as steady accumulator and went into attack mode, stroking 13 fours in all directions to score 74 from 91 balls before he swung Pollock to long leg. Gayle thumped six fours in eight balls from Nel before the ninth had him taken at slip. Nel's version of the haka into the departing batsman's face cost him half his match fee, in a fine from referee Ranjan Madugalle. But South Africa's victory always looked assured.

Man of the Match: M. Ntini.   *Attendance:* 39,108.

Close of play: First day, South Africa 368-3 (Kallis 87, van Jaarsveld 69); Second day, West Indies 87-1 (Ganga 49, Sarwan 20); Third day, West Indies 363-6 (Lara 178, Dillon 6); Fourth day, West Indies 31-3 (Sarwan 6, Lara 0).

South Africa

*G. C. Smith c Lara b Edwards	132	– c sub (D. R. Smith) b Drakes	44
H. H. Gibbs b Collymore	60	– retired hurt	6
J. A. Rudolph c Lara b Drakes	2	– c Sarwan b Hinds	44
J. H. Kallis b Dillon	158	– lbw b Hinds	44
M. van Jaarsveld lbw b Dillon	73	– (6) run out	15
N. D. McKenzie c Jacobs b Edwards	8	– (8) not out	9
†M. V. Boucher c Ganga b Collymore	27	– (5) st Jacobs b Sarwan.........	18
S. M. Pollock c Jacobs b Hinds	30	– (7) b Collymore	10
R. J. Peterson c Jacobs b Hinds	25	– not out	18
A. Nel b Hinds	0		
M. Ntini not out	22		
B 4, l-b 7, w 4, n-b 9	24	B 2, l-b 3, w 6, n-b 7	18

1/149 (2) 2/160 (3) 3/240 (1) 4/372 (5)   561   1/72 (1) 2/145 (4)   (6 wkts dec.) 226
5/398 (6) 6/456 (7) 7/510 (4)   3/158 (3) 4/180 (5)
8/520 (8) 9/520 (10) 10/561 (9)   5/188 (6) 6/206 (7)

In the second innings Gibbs retired hurt at 42.

Bowling: *First Innings*—Edwards 27–3–102–2; Dillon 36–7–96–2; Collymore 26–2–118–2; Drakes 29–5–92–1; Ganga 4–0–26–0; Sarwan 9–0–37–0; Hinds 17.4–3–79–3. *Second Innings*—Edwards 13–0–60–0; Dillon 10–0–26–0; Drakes 10–2–21–1; Collymore 9–3–19–1; Sarwan 10–0–40–1; Hinds 11–0–55–2.

West Indies

W. W. Hinds c Peterson b Nel	10	– b Ntini	0
D. Ganga c Peterson b Nel	60	– lbw b Ntini	10
R. R. Sarwan c Boucher b Pollock	21	– (4) lbw b Pollock	8
*B. C. Lara c van Jaarsveld b Nel	202	– (5) b Pollock	5
S. Chanderpaul b Ntini	34	– (6) c Nel b Pollock	74
†R. D. Jacobs c Boucher b Ntini	4	– (7) b Nel	25
V. C. Drakes lbw b Kallis	21	– (3) b Ntini	6
M. Dillon b Ntini	13	– (9) b Ntini	7
C. H. Gayle c Kallis b Ntini	8	– (8) c Boucher b Nel	26
F. H. Edwards c McKenzie b Nel	0	– (11) not out	0
C. D. Collymore not out	1	– (10) lbw b Pollock	0
B 12, l-b 15, w 4, n-b 5	36	B 10, l-b 6, n-b 11	27
	410		**188**

1/43 (1) 2/94 (3) 3/141 (2) 4/266 (5)   410
5/278 (6) 6/314 (7) 7/380 (8)
8/405 (9) 9/409 (4) 10/410 (10)

1/5 (1) 2/18 (3) 3/25 (2)   188
4/41 (4) 5/43 (5) 6/141 (7)
7/168 (6) 8/176 (8)
9/188 (9) 10/188 (10)

Bowling: *First Innings*—Pollock 30–7–65–1; Ntini 32–9–94–5; Nel 32.5–11–78–3; Kallis 22–6–53–1; Peterson 13–2–76–0; Smith 4–0–17–0. *Second Innings*—Pollock 17–6–31–4; Ntini 14–4–53–4; Nel 13–3–49–2; Kallis 4–0–21–0; Peterson 3–0–18–0.

Umpires: D. B. Hair (Australia) and S. J. A. Taufel (Australia).
Third umpire: B. G. Jerling. Referee: R. S. Madugalle (Sri Lanka).

At East London, December 19, 20, 21, 22, 2003. **Drawn.** Toss: Border. **West Indians 278** (B. C. Lara 81, S. Chanderpaul 98; T. Henderson 5-57) **and 168-3** (R. R. Sarwan 71*); **Border 251** (P. C. Strydom 74; A. Sanford 5-53).

SOUTH AFRICA v WEST INDIES

Second Test Match

At Durban, December 26, 27, 28, 29, 2003. South Africa won by an innings and 65 runs. Toss: South Africa.

Lara's first disappointment in his 100th Test was losing the toss on a drizzly, overcast opening day which required floodlights throughout. The grassy pitch did not provide quite the movement expected when Smith sent West Indies in, but it did not take long for the psychological advantage to materialise: they lost five for 57 by lunch.

As the weather and the pitch improved, there was no way back. West Indies were further undermined by their atrocious fielding. As South Africa amassed their second-highest Test total, and highest on home soil, West Indies missed six chances, including two off Kirsten and one off Kallis, who both made centuries, as did Gibbs. Dashing, and defiant, second-innings hundreds by Sarwan and Chanderpaul saved some face for West Indies, but they lost by an innings with a day to spare. It was their seventh defeat in their seven Tests in South Africa.

While South Africa were back to full strength with the return of new father Kirsten, West Indies had to replace the injured Gayle and Collymore with reserve keeper Baugh, as a No. 6 batsman, and seam bowler Sanford, a recent addition to the squad.

Once more, Lara found himself mounting a rearguard action after South African pace swept aside the top half of the order, all to catches off the outside edge. He and Jacobs checked the collapse by adding 98. And after Lara fended from Ntini to first slip after nearly three hours' diligent application, the enterprising Drakes, with a maiden Test fifty, carried the innings into the second day, with help from his ninth-wicket partner Sanford.

It feels good. Makhaya Ntini is exultant after dismissing Shivnarine Chanderpaul on the first day of the Durban Test. He ended the game as 2003's leading wicket-taker in Tests.

Picture by Getty Images

Gibbs's 11th Test hundred meant South Africa were already 39 to the good with seven wickets standing by the close. Gibbs showed no ill effects from the broken nose sustained in the First Test as he and Kallis heaped misery on bowlers who found no consistency of line or length. He was livid with himself when he diverted a pull off Sanford into his stumps, having stroked 23 fours, mostly drives through the off side.

The match slipped away from West Indies early next morning. Kirsten was twice dropped off Dillon on his way to fifty, by Lara at first slip and Drakes at gully, while Kallis was badly missed by Drakes at long leg off Edwards, from a top-edged hook on 84. The two were ruthless as they overturned South Africa's 74-year-old fourth-wicket record, 214 between Herbie Taylor and "Nummy" Deane against England at The Oval, and had raised it to 249 when Kirsten top-edged a sweep off Sarwan to deep mid-wicket. He had just become the first South African to reach 7,000 Test runs, after completing his 20th hundred, another national record, in his 96th Test. Kirsten hit 20 fours, as did Kallis, who finally cut Dillon to point after eight hours.

By now, West Indies were simply waiting for the end of the innings, which they extended by dropping three more catches. Yet another humiliating defeat was in prospect at 130 for five on the fourth afternoon until Chanderpaul, who had been unable to field because of a strained leg muscle and was therefore prohibited from batting until No. 7, joined Sarwan, with Hinds as his runner. Sarwan had shaken off the effects of a stunning knock to the helmet from Ntini in the morning and, after Chanderpaul escaped a sharp, early chance to short leg off Rudolph's leg-break, the pair mounted an exciting, but ultimately irrelevant, counter-attack which added 113 in 35 overs.

HIGHEST TEST TOTALS BY SOUTH AFRICA

682-6 dec.	v England at Lord's (won by an innings and 92 runs)	2003
658-9 dec.	**v West Indies at Durban (won by an innings and 65 runs)**	**2003-04**
622-9 dec.	v Australia at Durban (won by an innings and 129 runs)	1969-70
621-5 dec.	v New Zealand at Auckland (drew)	1998-99
620	v Australia at Johannesburg (won by 233 runs)	1966-67
620-7 dec.	v Pakistan at Cape Town (won by an innings and 142 runs)	2002-03
604-6 dec.	**v West Indies at Centurion (won by ten wickets)**	**2003-04**
600-3 dec.	v Zimbabwe at Harare (won by nine wickets).	2001-02

Sarwan completed his third Test hundred and Chanderpaul his ninth, before both were dismissed by Ntini. Sarwan hit 18 fours in 225 balls, Chanderpaul a six and 20 fours in 173, but South Africa completed their mission with eight overs still available on the day.

Man of the Match: J. H. Kallis. *Attendance:* 27,763.

Close of play: First day, West Indies 232-8 (Drakes 40, Sanford 13); Second day, South Africa 303-3 (Kallis 74, Kirsten 16); Third day, West Indies 18-0 (Hinds 7, Ganga 4).

West Indies

W. W. Hinds c Boucher b Pollock	0	– b Nel	11
D. Ganga c Pollock b Ntini	6	– lbw b Pollock	12
R. R. Sarwan c Kallis b Pollock	4	– b Ntini	114
*B. C. Lara c Pollock b Ntini.	72	– c McKenzie b Hall	11
S. Chanderpaul c Hall b Ntini	0	– (7) c McKenzie b Ntini	109
C. S. Baugh c Kallis b Nel	21	– (5) c Ntini b Kallis	2
†R. D. Jacobs lbw b Nel	58	– (6) c Kirsten b Rudolph	15
V. C. Drakes c Boucher b Nel	67	– c Rudolph b Nel.	4
M. Dillon b Ntini.	6	– c Gibbs b Nel	0
A. Sanford c Hall b Ntini	15	– not out	18
F. H. Edwards not out	1	– c Boucher b Ntini.	5
L-b 6, n-b 8	14	L-b 16, w 1, n-b 11	28

1/0 (1) 2/4 (3) 3/15 (2) 4/17 (5)	**264**	1/31 (1) 2/32 (2) 3/78 (4) **329**
5/50 (6) 6/148 (7) 7/172 (4)		4/95 (5) 5/130 (6) 6/243 (3)
8/191 (9) 9/261 (8) 10/264 (10)		7/271 (8) 8/271 (9)
		9/317 (7) 10/329 (11)

Bowling: *First Innings*—Pollock 23–3–59–2; Ntini 25.5–8–66–5; Hall 10–2–51–0; Nel 13–4–43–3; Kallis 4–0–30–0; Rudolph 2–0–9–0. *Second Innings*—Pollock 22–9–42–1; Ntini 26–8–72–3; Nel 18–3–68–3; Hall 13–3–20–1; Kallis 11–3–20–1; Rudolph 23–3–91–1.

South Africa

*G. C. Smith c Sarwan b Edwards 14	A. J. Hall c sub (D. R. Smith) b Sarwan. 32	
H. H. Gibbs b Sanford 142	M. Ntini c Lara b Sanford 0	
J. A. Rudolph c Ganga b Sanford 36	B 1, l-b 8, w 6, n-b 23. 38	
J. H. Kallis c Sarwan b Dillon 177		
G. Kirsten c Drakes b Sarwan 137	1/38 (1) 2/99 (3) (9 wkts dec.) 658	
N. D. McKenzie c Jacobs b Drakes 32	3/267 (2) 4/516 (5)	
†M. V. Boucher lbw b Drakes. 12	5/562 (4) 6/572 (6)	
S. M. Pollock not out 38	7/599 (7) 8/649 (9) 9/658 (10)	

A. Nel did not bat.

Bowling: Dillon 33–5–111–1; Edwards 25–1–115–1; Sanford 38.2–4–170–3; Sarwan 21–2–65–2; Drakes 30–3–113–2; Hinds 13–2–50–0; Ganga 6–1–25–0.

Umpires: D. B. Hair (Australia) and S. J. A. Taufel (Australia).
Third umpire: I. L. Howell. Referee: R. S. Madugalle (Sri Lanka).

SOUTH AFRICA v WEST INDIES

Third Test Match

At Cape Town, January 2, 3, 4, 5, 6, 2004. Drawn. Toss: South Africa. Test debuts: D. Mohammed, D. R. Smith.

Both captains, being batsmen, described the pitch as "fabulous". It yielded 1,648 runs at 3.8 an over, for only 28 wickets, and there were seven individual hundreds, only the third time so many had been scored in one Test. Gayle powered to his from 79 balls – the ninth fastest recorded in Tests – and Kallis thumped five sixes in his third century in successive matches as South Africa sped towards a second-innings declaration. Yet none was more spectacular or significant than the last, Dwayne Smith's unbeaten run-a-ball 105 on debut. It not only ensured West Indies avoided their eighth successive Test defeat in South Africa but briefly raised the possibility of an incredible victory.

The 20-year-old Smith, a surprise choice as the injured Marlon Samuels's tour replacement, was playing only because Chanderpaul had a leg strain. When he entered 20 minutes after tea on the final day, another beating looked likely. Lara and Sarwan had been dismissed either side of the interval after a patient partnership of 156, more than 37 overs remained and, at 224 for four, the target of 441 was not an issue. Batting with what Lara called "the exuberance of youth", Smith launched an offensive that rapidly changed the balance of the contest. He was especially severe on Adams, but no bowler was spared as he rushed to 100 from 93 balls; his partners, Hinds and Jacobs, made 18 between them. Eventually, with only the bowlers to come, Lara decided victory was unrealistic. Once Smith passed his landmark, with 102 needed from 13 overs, he and Jacobs were instructed to play out time, the match ending in anticlimax with five overs remaining.

After South Africa won the toss for the third time, the left-handed Rudolph, who spent four and a half hours compiling his second Test hundred, and McKenzie laid the foundation for another large total with a stand of 142. They were both out to the left-handed wrist-spin of Dave Mohammed, another debutant, in the closing overs of the

Good impression: Dwayne Smith reaches a lightning hundred on debut.

Picture by Getty Images

day, and Pollock followed in the second over next morning. But West Indies lost their grip after Boucher, on 15, was bowled by an Edwards no-ball.

Boucher used the chance, and the conditions, to complete a century, stroking 21 fours and adding 146 with Kallis, who maintained his high-scoring form after resuming an innings interrupted on the first day by a blow to the forearm from Edwards. Boucher was unbeaten when South Africa were finally dismissed after passing 500 for the third match running.

The remaining 35 overs of the second day were utterly dominated by Gayle, returning after injury with a breathtaking display of clean hitting. A six and 19 fours (there were 20 in all) carried him to his hundred, which he reached out of 125 in the 23rd over, and Sarwan followed his lead with 39 from 43 balls as West Indies closed at 178 for one. Both were early victims next morning and it was once more left to Lara, with modest support down the order, to avoid the follow-on. On the way to his 24th Test hundred, Lara passed 9,000 runs in his 177th Test innings, two fewer than Tendulkar, who had got there in Sydney two days earlier. After striking 16 fours and a six, Lara was last out to his 238th ball, providing Nel with his first five-wicket return in Tests.

West Indies claimed two early wickets on the fourth day, then their cricket went to pieces as Gibbs and Kallis made merry under the floodlights. They added 251 in 59 overs, separated by weather interruptions. Between them, they belted seven sixes in the final session, when West Indies spilled four catches. Gayle was responsible for two but finally held one to account for Gibbs.

Graeme Smith's declaration gave his bowlers the entire last day to try to clinch a third win. They were stymied for over three hours by Lara and more than four by Sarwan, but the final, immovable obstacle was Dwayne Smith. It was the first time West Indies had escaped defeat in a Test in South Africa; the draw, however, was enough to give South Africa the series. Smith's hundred was the seventh of the match, a mark not reached in nearly half a century since the West Indies–Australia Test at Sabina Park in 1954-55. The only instance in a Test before that was the Trent Bridge Ashes match of 1938.

Man of the Match: J. H. Kallis.　　　　*Attendance:* 52,235.

Close of play: First day, South Africa 308-6 (Boucher 0, Pollock 2); Second day, West Indies 178-1 (Gayle 112, Sarwan 39); Third day, South Africa 38-0 (Smith 18, Gibbs 19); Fourth day, South Africa 335-3 (Kallis 130, Kirsten 10).

South Africa

*G. C. Smith c Lara b Sanford	42	– b Edwards	24
H. H. Gibbs c Jacobs b Sanford	33	– c Gayle b Sarwan	142
J. A. Rudolph lbw b Mohammed	101	– c Jacobs b Drakes	0
J. H. Kallis lbw b Sanford	73	– not out	130
G. Kirsten c Sanford b Edwards	16	– not out	10
N. D. McKenzie b Mohammed	76		
P. R. Adams b Edwards	0		
†M. V. Boucher not out	122		
S. M. Pollock c Jacobs b Edwards	9		
M. Ntini c Jacobs b Mohammed	18		
A. Nel c Jacobs b Sanford	4		
B 6, l-b 12, w 2, n-b 18	38	B 3, l-b 7, w 8, n-b 11	29

1/70 (2) 2/90 (1) 3/162 (5) 4/304 (3)	**532**	1/48 (1) 2/50 (3)　　(3 wkts dec.) **335**
5/305 (7) 6/305 (6) 7/315 (9)		3/301 (2)
8/461 (4) 9/513 (10) 10/532 (11)		

In the first innings Kallis, when 23, retired hurt at 120 and resumed at 315.

Bowling: *First Innings*—Drakes 26–7–64–0; Edwards 30–3–132–3; Sanford 37–4–132–4; Smith 2–0–4–0; Mohammed 33–5–112–3; Gayle 10–0–39–0; Hinds 7–2–31–0. *Second Innings*—Edwards 14–0–86–1; Sanford 8–1–38–0; Gayle 9–3–34–0; Drakes 20–0–68–1; Mohammed 6–0–30–0; Sarwan 19–1–69–1.

West Indies

C. H. Gayle lbw b Pollock	116	– c Gibbs b Ntini	32
D. Ganga b Nel	17	– c Boucher b Ntini	10
R. R. Sarwan c McKenzie b Nel	44	– c Gibbs b Ntini	69
*B. C. Lara b Nel	115	– c Boucher b Nel	86
W. W. Hinds c Boucher b Kallis	13	– b Pollock	25
D. R. Smith c Kallis b Nel	20	– not out	105
†R. D. Jacobs c Pollock b Ntini	23	– not out	9
V. C. Drakes c Boucher b Nel	20		
D. Mohammed c Kallis b Pollock	36		
A. Sanford run out	0		
F. H. Edwards not out	0		
B 6, l-b 7, n-b 10	23	B 2, l-b 7, w 2, n-b 7	18

1/126 (2) 2/183 (1) 3/187 (3) 4/224 (5) 427   1/28 (2) 2/47 (1) (5 wkts) 354
5/252 (6) 6/306 (7) 7/361 (8)   3/203 (4) 4/224 (3)
8/409 (9) 9/426 (10) 10/427 (4)   5/296 (5)

Bowling: *First Innings*—Pollock 24–6–88–2; Ntini 20–1–105–1; Nel 28.1–8–87–5; Kallis 21–8–64–1; Adams 19–1–70–0. *Second Innings*—Pollock 17–3–64–1; Ntini 21–4–82–3; Nel 21–5–57–1; Kallis 16–3–38–0; Adams 22–3–103–0; Rudolph 1–1–0–0; Kirsten 2–1–1–0.

Umpires: D. J. Harper (Australia) and S. Venkataraghavan (India).
Third umpire: I. L. Howell. Referee: R. S. Madugalle (Sri Lanka).

At Benoni, January 9, 10, 11, 12, 2004. **West Indians won by 33 runs**. Toss: West Indians. **West Indians 334** (C. H. Gayle 145) **and 263** (D. Ganga 51, R. R. Sarwan 72); **Easterns 313** (J. A. Morkel 132; R. Rampaul 4-63) **and 251** (A. J. Seymore 79).

Gayle scored 110 before lunch on the opening day, reaching his century in 74 balls with the 11th of his 17 fours; he also hit five sixes. Easterns were 169-8 in their first innings before No. 8 Albie Morkel and his younger brother Morne, who scored 44* at No. 10 on first-class debut, added 141 for the ninth wicket.

SOUTH AFRICA v WEST INDIES

Fourth Test Match

At Centurion, January 16, 17, 18, 19, 20, 2004. South Africa won by ten wickets. Toss: West Indies.

Lara won the toss for the first time and, encouraged by the grassiest pitch of the series and damp, overcast conditions that delayed the start by half an hour, chose to bowl. It made no difference. West Indies were overwhelmed by another huge South African total, almost half of it from openers Graeme Smith and Gibbs, who put on 301, a national record for any wicket against West Indies. They became the first pair to share three triple-hundred stands in Tests – all inside 13 months. Only their Indian contemporaries Dravid and Laxman, and Ponsford and Bradman 70 years earlier, have shared 300 stands even twice. Meanwhile, Kallis began to threaten further records by scoring his fourth hundred of the series.

South Africa gained a lead of 303 and had West Indies back in on the third evening. Hopes that they could salvage a draw, prompted by spirited hundreds from Sarwan and Gayle and the unsettled weather, swiftly disappeared as the last seven wickets tumbled for 75 on the last day. The 3.4 overs it took Smith and Gibbs to complete victory were a précis of the indiscipline that marked West Indies' cricket throughout the series. There were ten wides from Edwards – only two deliveries, but each went for four, the second sprayed in the general direction of fine leg to end the match – shoddy ground fielding and a remarkable catch by Dwayne Smith at long-on that was transformed into six when he stepped on to the rope.

West Indian confusion was evident from the start. Moments before the toss, Lara changed the chosen eleven, borrowing Graeme Smith's pen to insert Dillon on the team sheet instead of Sanford. This created the impression, never convincingly dispelled, that Lara was countermanding the instructions of Sir Viv Richards, the chief selector. With a little luck, the switch would have had quick returns: Gibbs was severely tested by Dillon's opening spell. As it was, Sarwan's off-target underarm throw from cover with Smith, on 23, well short of his ground was the only chance to separate the openers. Finally, Smith snicked Collymore to Jacobs two balls before the first day closed with nearly 23 overs remaining, in spite of the floodlights. During his five hours, Smith gathered 89 of his 139 runs on the leg side, where he hit both his sixes.

The floodlights were required again throughout the second day. Gibbs was just short of his third Test double-hundred when he cut Sarwan's leg-break to point. In nearly eight hours' occupation, he hit three sixes and 24 fours. Another Kallis hundred followed, chanceless, measured and seemingly inevitable. As always, his defence was tight and his judgment impeccable, yet he despatched loose deliveries with withering power: he took 31 runs from 17 balls just before the declaration.

Andre Nel must have been relieved when play – extended because of the shortened first day – was ended again by bad light. He just had time to be whisked off by helicopter to his wedding, arranged long before, at nearby Benoni. Nel was back next morning to join Ntini in harassing the West Indians with persistent pace. Only Gayle held them up, hitting a six and 14 typically powerful fours in three hours before he was one of Ntini's five victims.

Ntini struck Gayle painfully on the box when West Indies followed on, forcing him to retire for overnight recuperation. Ganga and Lara, lbw presenting no shot and out to Nel for the fourth successive innings, were permanent losses before the close of the third day.

South Africa's victory was delayed by a combination of rain and poor light, which restricted the fourth day to 64 overs, and determined batting by Sarwan and the returning Gayle, who closed with hundreds to their names and their partnership worth 164.

News of the death of David Hookes in Australia cast a pall of gloom over the final day. It was matched by the weather and the West Indian batting. After play was delayed for more than two hours by heavy and persistent rain, Gayle added just one run, Sarwan another 12. Only hearty hitting by Dillon and the tail ensured South Africa had to bat again. Given the nonsense that followed, it would have been better for West Indies if they hadn't.

Man of the Match: H. H. Gibbs.   *Attendance:* 44,220.

Man of the Series: M. Ntini.

Close of play: First day, South Africa 302-1 (Gibbs 139, Rudolph 1); Second day, West Indies 7-0 (Gayle 4, Ganga 2); Third day, West Indies 44-2 (Sarwan 7, Chanderpaul 12); Fourth day, West Indies 263-3 (Gayle 106, Sarwan 107).

South Africa

*G. C. Smith c Jacobs b Collymore	139	– not out	23
H. H. Gibbs c Ganga b Sarwan	192	– not out	8
J. A. Rudolph b Edwards	37		
J. H. Kallis not out	130		
G. Kirsten c and b Sarwan	10		
N. D. McKenzie c Lara b Dillon	40		
†M. V. Boucher c Edwards b Smith	13		
S. M. Pollock not out	1		
B 1, l-b 17, w 12, n-b 12	42	B 4, w 10, n-b 1	15

1/301 (1) 2/373 (3) 3/422 (2)   (6 wkts dec.) 604   (no wkt) 46
4/446 (5) 5/532 (6) 6/567 (7)

A. J. Hall, M. Ntini and A. Nel did not bat.

Bowling: *First Innings*—Dillon 31–5–109–1; Edwards 24–2–128–1; Drakes 33–5–101–0; Collymore 26–5–91–1; Gayle 7–0–39–0; Sarwan 14–0–55–2; Smith 13–1–42–1; Ganga 10–0–21–0. *Second Innings*—Dillon 2–0–17–0; Edwards 1.4–0–25–0.

West Indies

C. H. Gayle c McKenzie b Ntini	77	– c McKenzie b Ntini	107
D. Ganga c Kallis b Ntini	7	– b Ntini	0
R. R. Sarwan b Ntini	13	– lbw b Pollock	119
*B. C. Lara c Boucher b Nel	34	– lbw b Nel	6
S. Chanderpaul c Pollock b Nel	42	– c Gibbs b Kallis	27
D. R. Smith c Boucher b Kallis	39	– b Ntini	0
†R. D. Jacobs c Boucher b Nel	8	– lbw b Pollock	3
V. C. Drakes b Ntini	35	– c Gibbs b Pollock	4
M. Dillon b Ntini	30	– c Smith b Pollock	29
C. D. Collymore b Pollock	4	– not out	13
F. H. Edwards not out	0	– b Nel	10
L-b 7, n-b 5	12	B 4, l-b 11, w 7, n-b 8	30

1/22 (2) 2/37 (3) 3/139 (4) 4/142 (1)   301   1/18 (2) 2/32 (4) 3/99 (5)   348
5/195 (6) 6/224 (7) 7/241 (5)   4/273 (1) 5/277 (3) 6/278 (6)
8/280 (8) 9/301 (9) 10/301 (10)   7/284 (8) 8/309 (7)
                                9/322 (9) 10/348 (11)

In the second innings Gayle, when 14, retired hurt at 18-0 and resumed at 99.

Bowling: *First Innings*—Pollock 16.2–6–46–1; Ntini 20–7–49–5; Nel 18–6–64–3; Hall 11–0–65–0; Kallis 12–4–46–1; Smith 3–1–7–0; Rudolph 2–0–17–0. *Second Innings*—Pollock 32–10–69–4; Ntini 28–4–99–3; Nel 15.4–2–64–2; Kallis 16–4–49–1; Hall 0.2–0–4–0; Smith 8.4–1–24–0; Rudolph 6–0–24–0.

Umpires: D. R. Shepherd (England) and S. Venkataraghavan (India).
Third umpire: B. G. Jerling.   Referee: R. S. Madugalle (Sri Lanka).

---

†At Paarl, January 23, 2004 (day/night). **West Indians won by 65 runs.** Toss: West Indians. **West Indians 230-8** (50 overs) (C. H. Gayle 61); **South Africa A 165** (45.3 overs) (N. D. McKenzie 51).

†SOUTH AFRICA v WEST INDIES

First One-Day International

At Cape Town, January 25, 2004 (day/night). South Africa won by 209 runs. Toss: South Africa. One-day international debut: D. R. Smith.

"This is as low as it can get," Lara commented at the presentation ceremony. West Indies' 54 all out was indeed their worst total, and the margin of 209 runs their heaviest defeat, in their 482 one-day internationals, though Lara's team was to reach an even lower ebb in a Test against England less than two months later. Batting under lights at Newlands is usually a disadvantage, but it seemed as if the West Indian batsmen had never before seen a white ball swing and seam. As in the Test a week earlier, Lara was lbw padding up to Nel, and the last seven fell for 16 runs in 9.5 overs. An unbroken stand of 162 in 24 overs between Kallis – who hit his fifth hundred in successive international matches in 94 balls, including five sixes – and Rudolph was responsible for South Africa's healthy total. They could not have expected it would produce their biggest one-day win.

Man of the Match: J. H. Kallis.   *Attendance:* 18,218.

South Africa

*G. C. Smith b Hurley	53	J. A. Rudolph not out	61
H. H. Gibbs b Collymore	10	L-b 3, w 1, n-b 4	8
R. J. Peterson run out	21		
J. H. Kallis not out	109	1/32 (2) 2/64 (3) (4 wkts, 50 overs)	263
H. H. Dippenaar c Chanderpaul b Drakes	1	3/100 (1) 4/101 (5)	

†M. V. Boucher, S. M. Pollock, L. Klusener, A. Nel and M. Ntini did not bat.

Bowling: Dillon 8–2–40–0; Collymore 10–1–47–1; Gayle 9–0–46–0; Hurley 10–1–39–1; Drakes 10–1–64–1; Powell 3–0–24–0.

West Indies

C. H. Gayle c Smith b Pollock	4	M. Dillon c Boucher b Ntini		1
S. Chanderpaul c Rudolph b Nel	14	C. D. Collymore run out		0
*B. C. Lara lbw b Nel	2			
R. R. Sarwan lbw b Ntini	5	L-b 3, w 2, n-b 1		6
R. L. Powell c Boucher b Klusener	12			
D. R. Smith c Boucher b Klusener	1	1/10 (1) 2/16 (3) 3/21 (2)	(23.2 overs)	54
†R. D. Jacobs not out	6	4/38 (5) 5/40 (6) 6/40 (4)		
R O Hurley c Kallis b Klusener	2	7/43 (8) 8/49 (9)		
V. C. Drakes c Gibbs b Ntini	1	9/53 (10) 10/54 (11)		

Bowling: Pollock 6–2–9–1; Nel 6–1–18–2; Ntini 6–1–15–3; Klusener 5.2–2–9–3.

Umpires: D. B. Hair (Australia) and I. L. Howell.
Third umpire: B. G. Jerling. Referee: R. S. Madugalle (Sri Lanka).

†SOUTH AFRICA v WEST INDIES

Second One-Day International

At Port Elizabeth, January 28, 2004 (day/night). South Africa won by 16 runs. Toss: South Africa.
West Indies' most disciplined bowling and fielding performance of the tour restricted South Africa to 179 for seven before three suicidal run-outs denied them the chance of levelling the series. Dippenaar scored 83 to stabilise South Africa's innings but, even in conditions encouraging seam and swing, their total was modest. Then Lara, demoting himself to No. 5, was cut short by a direct underarm hit from Rudolph as he sought an improbable single to mid-off. The dawdling Sarwan was run out by Boucher's throw at the bowler's stumps, and Jacobs gambled with Gibbs's alacrity and lost. Only a last-wicket stand of 37 between Rampaul and Collymore, the highest of the innings, got West Indies anywhere near their target.
Man of the Match: H. H. Dippenaar. *Attendance:* 16,976.

South Africa

*G. C. Smith b Collymore	9	L. Klusener not out		7
H. H. Gibbs c Chanderpaul b Dillon	10	R. J. Peterson not out		0
J. H. Kallis c Collymore b Rampaul	16	L-b 2, w 2, n-b 5		9
H. H. Dippenaar c Sarwan b Collymore	83			
J. A. Rudolph c Rampaul b Gayle	14	1/15 (2) 2/20 (1)	(7 wkts, 50 overs)	179
†M. V. Boucher c and b Hurley	5	3/57 (3) 4/103 (5)		
S. M. Pollock b Collymore	26	5/110 (6) 6/164 (7) 7/177 (4)		

A. Nel and M. Ntini did not bat.

Bowling: Dillon 10–0–26–1; Collymore 10–2–25–3; Smith 6–0–27–0; Rampaul 9–0–33–1; Hurley 9–0–42–1; Gayle 6–1–24–1.

West Indies

C. H. Gayle c Dippenaar b Pollock	9	R. Rampaul c and b Klusener		24
S. Chanderpaul lbw b Pollock	2	C. D. Collymore not out		12
R. L. Powell lbw b Pollock	15			
R. R. Sarwan run out	12	L-b 13, w 9		22
*B. C. Lara run out	9			
D. R. Smith lbw b Kallis	24	1/4 (2) 2/24 (1) 3/29 (3)	(42.4 overs)	163
†R. D. Jacobs run out	15	4/58 (5) 5/74 (4) 6/96 (6)		
R. O. Hurley b Kallis	5	7/104 (7) 8/111 (8)		
M. Dillon lbw b Pollock	14	9/126 (9) 10/163 (10)		

Bowling: Pollock 10–2–26–4; Nel 7–0–36–0; Ntini 10–3–25–0; Klusener 7.4–0–35–1; Kallis 6–1–21–2; Peterson 2–0–7–0.

Umpires: Aleem Dar (Pakistan) and B. G. Jerling.
Third umpire: I. L. Howell. Referee: R. S. Madugalle (Sri Lanka).

†SOUTH AFRICA v WEST INDIES

Third One-Day International

At Durban, January 30, 2004 (day/night). No result (D/L method). Toss: West Indies.

Only Kingsmead's superior drainage and the industry of the groundstaff allowed play to start on time after two days of torrential rain, but the weather had the final say. Powell, with 50 in 71 balls, was the one West Indian batsman to come to terms with a damp pitch that, once more, assisted swing and seam. He was out before the first rain break, in the 28th over; a second break, in the 31st, trimmed ten overs from the innings. South Africa's target was set at 169 from 40 overs under the Duckworth/Lewis system but only five had been bowled when the rain set in for the last time.

Attendance: 20,286.

West Indies

C. H. Gayle c Gibbs b Nel	1	M. Dillon c Peterson b Kallis	0
S. Chanderpaul c Rudolph b Klusener	17	R. Rampaul not out	0
R. L. Powell c Dippenaar b Ntini	50	B 1, l-b 6, w 3	10
R. R. Sarwan c Dippenaar b Pollock	29		
*B. C. Lara c Boucher b Kallis	15	**1/3 (1) 2/52 (2) (8 wkts, 40 overs) 147**	
D. R. Smith c Pollock b Klusener	12	3/79 (3) 4/118 (4)	
†R. D. Jacobs not out	7	5/119 (5) 6/134 (6)	
R. O. Hurley b Kallis	6	7/146 (8) 8/146 (9)	

C. D. Collymore did not bat.

Bowling: Pollock 8–4–16–1; Nel 8–2–25–1; Ntini 6–0–23–1; Klusener 8–0–46–2; Peterson 7–0–22–0; Kallis 3–0–8–3.

South Africa

*G. C. Smith c Lara b Dillon	4
H. H. Gibbs c Lara b Dillon	7
J. H. Kallis not out	2
B 1, l-b 1	2

1/10 (1)   (1 wkt, 5 overs) 15

R. J. Peterson, H. H. Dippenaar, J. A. Rudolph, L. Klusener, †M. V. Boucher, S. M. Pollock, A. Nel and M. Ntini did not bat.

Bowling: Dillon 3–1–4–1; Collymore 2–0–9–0.

Umpires: D. B. Hair (Australia) and I. L. Howell.
Third umpire: B. G. Jerling.   Referee: R. S. Madugalle (Sri Lanka).

†SOUTH AFRICA v WEST INDIES

Fourth One-Day International

At Centurion, February 1, 2004. West Indies won by seven wickets. Toss: South Africa.

Challenged to score their highest one-day total against South Africa, West Indies did it with five overs to spare to complete their first international victory since leaving Zimbabwe two months earlier. Batsmen revelled in the first favourable conditions of the series, exploiting hot sunshine and a true pitch in the one daytime match of the five. Between them, the teams hit eight sixes and 53 fours, and amassed 597 runs from 95 overs. Kallis, with two sixes and seven fours, ended five short of yet another hundred. But Chanderpaul trumped him with 92 off 75 balls, and ran up 108 in 19 overs with Sarwan. They paved the way for Lara, who smashed 59 in 37 balls, a fitting finale to a welcome win.

Man of the Match: S. Chanderpaul.   *Attendance:* 16,759.

South Africa

*G. C. Smith b Gayle	46	L. Klusener not out 41
H. H. Gibbs c Smith b Dillon.	18	L-b 5, w 14, n-b 12. 31
R. J. Peterson c Gayle b Rampaul	36	
J. H. Kallis not out.	95	1/53 (2) 2/108 (1) (4 wkts, 50 overs) 297
H. H. Dippenaar b Sarwan	30	3/124 (3) 4/190 (5)

J. A. Rudolph, †M. V. Boucher, S. M. Pollock, M. Ntini and A. Nel did not bat.

Bowling: Dillon 9–0–58–1; Collymore 10–0–52–0; Hurley 10–0–65–0; Gayle 10–0–53–1; Rampaul 9–0–49–1; Sarwan 2–0–15–1.

West Indies

C. H. Gayle c Peterson b Pollock	26
S. Chanderpaul c Boucher b Pollock . . .	92
R. L. Powell b Kallis	34
R. R. Sarwan not out	77
*B. C. Lara not out	59
B 4, l-b 3, w 5	12

1/31 (1) 2/92 (3)   (3 wkts, 45 overs) 300
3/200 (2)

D. R. Smith, †R. D. Jacobs, R. O. Hurley, M. Dillon, R. Rampaul and C. D. Collymore did not bat.

Bowling: Pollock 10–0–40–2; Nel 6–0–63–0; Ntini 7–0–51–0; Kallis 7–0–37–1; Klusener 8–0–51–0; Peterson 6–0–45–0; Smith 1–0–6–0.

Umpires: Aleem Dar (Pakistan) and B. G. Jerling.
Third umpire: I. L. Howell.   Referee: R. S. Madugalle (Sri Lanka).

†SOUTH AFRICA v WEST INDIES

Fifth One-Day International

At Johannesburg, February 4, 2004 (day/night). South Africa won by four wickets. Toss: West Indies.
A capacity crowd was richly entertained by another batsmen's match which featured 614 runs and a last-over victory clinching the series 3–1 for South Africa. Both teams made their highest one-day scores against each other. Gayle and Chanderpaul laid the foundations with 193 in 39 overs, West Indies' second-biggest opening stand, and Powell's 24-ball 49 meant the last ten overs yielded 104. Gayle finished unbeaten on 152 off 153 balls, his eighth one-day international hundred, with three sixes and 12 fours. Once again, Kallis was at the heart of South Africa's pursuit. But he was out in the penultimate over from Rampaul, which yielded a solitary run, so eight were needed from the last, bowled by Gayle. Pollock benefited from misfields and, with the scores level, hoisted the fourth ball for six.
Man of the Match: J. H. Kallis.   *Attendance:* 28,091.   *Man of the Series:* J. H. Kallis.

West Indies

C. H. Gayle not out	152
S. Chanderpaul c Rudolph b Smith	85
*B. C. Lara c Ntini b Klusener.	11
R. L. Powell not out	49
L-b 1, w 4, n-b 2	7

1/193 (2) 2/212 (3)   (2 wkts, 50 overs) 304

R. R. Sarwan, D. R. Smith, †R. D. Jacobs, R. O. Hurley, M. Dillon, R. Rampaul and C. D. Collymore did not bat.

Bowling: Pollock 10–2–47–0; Ntini 7–1–41–0; Nel 10–0–60–0; Klusener 8–0–42–1; Peterson 3–0–22–0; Kallis 4–0–39–0; Smith 8–0–52–1.

South Africa

*G. C. Smith b Gayle	58	S. M. Pollock not out	12
H. H. Gibbs c Sarwan b Collymore	15		
J. H. Kallis c Chanderpaul b Rampaul	139	L-b 7, w 3, n-b 2	12
H. H. Dippenaar c Rampaul b Hurley	28		
J. A. Rudolph c Chanderpaul b Rampaul	35	1/31 (2) 2/133 (1) (6 wkts, 49.4 overs) 310	
L. Klusener c Lara b Collymore	4	3/187 (4) 4/277 (5)	
†M. V. Boucher not out	7	5/285 (6) 6/296 (3)	

R. J. Peterson, M. Ntini and A. Nel did not bat.

Bowling: Dillon 10–0–42–0; Hurley 9–0–56–1; Collymore 10–0–83–2; Rampaul 10–1–56–2; Gayle 9.4–0–61–1; Sarwan 1–0–5–0.

Umpires: D. B. Hair (Australia) and I. L. Howell.
Third umpire: B. G. Jerling. Referee: R. S. Madugalle (Sri Lanka).

LG ICC TEST RATINGS

Introduced in 1987, the Ratings have been sponsored successively by Deloitte, Coopers & Lybrand, and PricewaterhouseCoopers, and were taken over by the International Cricket Council, in association with LG, in January 2005. They rank Test cricketers on a scale up to 1,000 according to their performances in Test matches. The ratings take into account playing conditions, the quality of the opposition and the result of the matches. In August 1998, a similar set of ratings for one-day internationals was added (see page 1365).

The leading 15 batsmen and bowlers in the Test ratings after the 2004-05 Test series between South Africa and England which ended on January 25, 2005, were:

	Batsmen	Rating		Bowlers	Rating
1	J. H. Kallis (*South Africa*)	893	1	G. D. McGrath (*Australia*)	866
2	R. Dravid (*India*)	882	2	M. Muralitharan (*Sri Lanka*)	850
3	R. T. Ponting (*Australia*)	847	3	S. M. Pollock (*South Africa*)	840
4	B. C. Lara (*West Indies*)	845	4	Shoaib Akhtar (*Pakistan*)	811
5	D. R. Martyn (*Australia*)	830	5	A. Kumble (*India*)	780
6	V. Sehwag (*India*)	808	6	J. N. Gillespie (*Australia*)	774
7	S. R. Tendulkar (*India*)	778	7	M. Ntini (*South Africa*)	761
8	M. L. Hayden (*Australia*)	771	8	S. K. Warne (*Australia*)	732
9	K. C. Sangakkara (*Sri Lanka*)	752	9	S. J. Harmison (*England*)	703
10	A. J. Strauss (*England*)	751	10	M. J. Hoggard (*England*)	691
11	A. C. Gilchrist (*Australia*)	748	11	W. P. U. J. C. Vaas (*Sri Lanka*)	687
12	H. H. Gibbs (*South Africa*)	738	12	A. Flintoff (*England*)	686
13	Inzamam-ul-Haq (*Pakistan*)	730	13	Harbhajan Singh (*India*)	684
14	J. L. Langer (*Australia*)	728	14	Danish Kaneria (*Pakistan*)	668
15	S. T. Jayasuriya (*Sri Lanka*)	717	15	I. K. Pathan (*India*)	607

The following players have topped the ratings since they were launched on June 17, 1987. The date shown is that on which they first went top; those marked by an asterisk have done so more than once.

Batting: D. B. Vengsarkar, June 17, 1987; Javed Miandad*, February 28, 1989; R. B. Richardson*, November 20, 1989; M. A. Taylor, October 23, 1990; G. A. Gooch*, June 10, 1991; D. L. Haynes, May 6, 1993; B. C. Lara*, April 21, 1994; S. R. Tendulkar*, December 5, 1994; J. C. Adams, December 14, 1994; S. R. Waugh*, May 3, 1995; Inzamam-ul-Haq*, December 3, 1997; A. Flower, September 11, 2001; A. C. Gilchrist, May 5, 2002; M. L. Hayden*, October 12, 2002; M. P. Vaughan, April 13, 2003; R. T. Ponting, December 30, 2003; R. Dravid*, July 26, 2004; J. H. Kallis*, January 6, 2005.

Bowling: R. J. Hadlee*, June 17, 1987; M. D. Marshall*, June 21, 1988; Waqar Younis*, December 17, 1991; C. E. L. Ambrose*, July 26, 1992; S. K. Warne*, November 29, 1994; G. D. McGrath*, December 3, 1996; A. A. Donald*, March 30, 1998; S. M. Pollock*, November 1, 1999; M. Muralitharan*, January 7, 2002; S. J. Harmison, August 21, 2004.

THE INDIANS IN AUSTRALIA, 2003-04

REVIEW BY SAMBIT BAL

Every once in a while comes a special sporting contest that leaves behind a whiff of glory and magic. Australia and India played one such Test series in 2000-01; Kolkata was a match for the ages and Chennai not far behind. But ever so rarely comes a series that marks a turning point in history. It may be years or decades before the significance of India's tour of Australia in 2003-04 can be truly assessed, but in this series they announced themselves as a force in Test cricket, after years of living on promise and vain dazzle. They didn't quite end Australia's reign, but how close they came.

To expect anything to match Kolkata was a tough ask. Yet Adelaide, where India came back from the dead to win, was almost a replica. The quality of cricket was admittedly superior in 2000-01, because bowling was a factor then. This was a series decided by batsmen's rare mistakes; injury kept out leading bowlers from both sides, and the rest were blunted by the flatness of the pitches and a galaxy of batting talent. But throughout, the cricket was captivating, grand and redolent with meaning. It ended with a realignment of the world order: the Ashes and the Frank Worrell Trophy could keep their tradition, but the Border–Gavaskar Trophy had emerged as the worthiest in contemporary cricket. And yes, India kept it.

The 1–1 scoreline did not fully reveal India's gains. These have to be viewed through the prism of their wretched past. The last time they had won a Test series outside the subcontinent was in England in 1986, and not since 1980-81 had they won a Test in Australia (where they had lost seven of their last eight). Their previous tour had left deep scars, for they had come boasting a strong middle order and had sunk without a murmur. Meanwhile, under Steve Waugh, Australia had won 21 out of 25 Tests at home, losing a solitary dead-rubber Test against England the previous season. In a pre-series poll in *Wisden Asia Cricket*, optimists forecast that India would lose 1–3. Rain in the First Test at Brisbane was greeted with relief by many Indian fans, for it offered the hope of squeezing out a draw.

The Indian team was more sanguine. At the pre-series press conference, Sourav Ganguly, a stronger leader than either Mohammad Azharuddin or Sachin Tendulkar, his predecessors on Australian tours, put his and the team's reputations on the line, saying this was a test of their abilities: "After this tour, we will know how good we really are." It was a courageous statement for a man with a known susceptibility against quick bowling, but it was in keeping with the spirit of a team that had learned to shed its diffidence.

For Australia, the series meant a great deal more than the chance to keep their impressive home record intact. A legacy was at stake. Waugh, one of the most innovative of all Test captains, revealed beforehand that he would retire at the end of the series – an announcement whose timing would be questioned repeatedly. Waugh insisted that he had done it to end the

Arms and the man: Steve Waugh, on the shoulders of his team-mates, bids
farewell to the adoring Sydney crowd at the end of the Fourth Test. Waugh's
retirement from international cricket was a recurring theme of the series.

Picture by Adam Pretty, Getty Images

speculation; cynics saw a design to maximise the commercial potential of
a staged farewell. A spectacle it certainly was, with every city according
Waugh its own send-off complete with red rags (provided by the newspapers
to whom he was contracted), replicas of his good luck charm. It reached a
point where Waugh merely had to touch the ball for an eruption of mass
sentiment.

This was not unlike the reception reserved for Tendulkar at every ground
in India, and Waugh, a visionary and a doer, deserved every bit of it. Yet
when Damien Martyn ran himself out to save Waugh's wicket in the First
Test at Brisbane, commentators wondered whether his team-mates were
letting emotion affect their good sense. Waugh was uncharacteristically testy
at the post-match press conference, saying he had been hurt by the
"innuendos and conjecture", and remarking sarcastically that "even the red
rags are my fault".

But as the series wore on it became clear that what was affecting Australia
more was the absence of the injured Glenn McGrath, who had rarely allowed
the Indians a start in 1999-2000, claiming one of the openers in five innings
out of six. India's opening partnerships on that tour read 7 and 0, 11 and 5,
10 and 22. Also missing from action in the first two Tests was Brett Lee, who
on debut in 1999-2000 had harassed the Indians with pace and movement,
claiming 13 wickets in two matches. When he did return, for the Boxing Day
Test at the MCG, he cut a sorry figure, unable to land either the ball

consistently on a length or his foot behind the bowling crease. In the first innings of the two games he played, he bowled 28 no-balls, and at the SCG he was reduced to delivering from well behind the line. He did unleash a perfect in-swinging yorker that crashed into Ganguly's stumps on the second day, and he celebrated with gusto. But it was too late: India were 570 for five.

If there was less discussion about Australia missing Shane Warne, who was serving a 12-month drugs ban, it was because he had been collared by the Indians before. Warne remained a presence in the Channel Nine commentary box, occasionally straying into the press box to pick a bone with a journalist or two. Stuart MacGill, despite having taken wickets by the dozen against other opponents, turned out to be a poor replacement, and was a perennial source of boundary-balls.

So resplendent was India's top order through the series that it was difficult to guess what effect McGrath might have had. To start with, they had two openers with skill and steel. Virender Sehwag had been pushed up to open in 2002 because no place could be found for him in the middle order and he was too talented a player to sit on the bench. He had expressed reservations about his long-term future in the role, but returned from Australia with his reputation massively enhanced. Once asked, in Sunil Gavaskar's presence, to compare his own technique with the master's, Sehwag insouciantly replied that Gavaskar's technique belonged to that age while he played to the requirement of his. The same insouciance was evident in his batting as he carved the Australian bowlers around the vast MCG, scoring 195 breathless runs in a little over five hours before perishing as he tried to raise his double-hundred with a six. Aakash Chopra, Sehwag's resolute partner, averaged a meagre 23.25, but never failed in any of his first innings.

Chopra and Sehwag put on 61, 66, 141 and 123 in the four first innings. Before them, Waugh's team had conceded only one century opening partnership on home soil. By defying the new-ball bowlers, they eased the path for the middle order, India's best ever – in both substance and panache.

All the touring batsmen shone, none more dazzlingly than the contrasting pair of Rahul Dravid and V. V. S. Laxman. Yet India's first saviour was an unlikely one. Ganguly, the presumed weak link in the batting, arrived at the crease in Brisbane with the score reading 62 for three, and Dravid and Tendulkar gone in the space of four balls. He departed nearly five hours later, at 329 for six. His 144 was an emphatic assertion of authority, and Ganguly continued to lead by example through the series: he promoted himself during the dying overs of the third evening at Melbourne to protect Tendulkar's wicket at the risk of his own, whereas, in more favourable conditions at Sydney, he gave up his No. 5 spot to Laxman. The weather ensured a draw at the Gabba, but Ganguly's was a decisive innings nevertheless. Here was a team that looked adversity in the eye.

And so they did in the next Test, at Adelaide. They conceded 400 runs on the first day to Australia, and 556 in all in the first innings, and found themselves looking down the barrel at 85 for four on the second afternoon. Yet the matter was routine for Dravid and Laxman, who forged another 300-run partnership, just as at Kolkata, as if batting in a world of their own.

Star of Adelaide: Rahul Dravid powers on during the Second Test. He and V. V. S. Laxman shared a fifth-wicket stand of 303, the partnership that turned the match India's way. Adam Gilchrist watches Dravid's strokeplay, as he did for almost ten hours.

Picture by Hamish Blair, Getty Images

They so bedraggled their opponents that the Australian second innings was an exhibition of confusion. India, amazingly, were left with a target of 230 to win, which they achieved with another nerveless innings from Dravid. The defeat prompted John Buchanan to write a letter to his squad, questioning their commitment to the baggy green cap. And, not for the first time, a private missive from Buchanan found its way to the newspapers.

Like Adelaide, the Melbourne Test was decided by a couple of hours of bad batting. Ganguly bravely opted to bat on a pitch that Tony Ware, the curator, had described as the fastest in Australia. If anything, it was two-paced on the opening day, and Sehwag and Chopra were hit, ducking into bouncers that didn't climb enough. But an hour after tea, with Sehwag having scattered the Australian bowlers out of sight, India were in command and Waugh, in an eerie reprisal of his early dark years, was despairingly bowling bouncers. Even so, he produced the vital breakthrough. Dravid, until then serene and untroubled, fell for the leg trap, jabbing a flick to mid-wicket. From 278 for one, India collapsed to 366 all out.

If the collective splendour of the Indian batsmen captured the imagination, the individual exploits of Ricky Ponting, Australia's captain-in-waiting, invited awe. He had spoken about the sobering effects of marriage: at Adelaide and Melbourne, he demonstrated his maturity with back-to-back double-hundreds. The punch and crispness of his strokeplay remained, but the new Ponting was less impetuous, less prone to collaborate in his own dismissals, and keen to consolidate and work the angles when width was denied. At Melbourne, he hardly ever went down the wicket to Anil Kumble until he was in the 190s, ensuring that Australia didn't blow it.

The win at Melbourne set the series up for an extraordinary farewell to Waugh. But Sydney also provided the stage for the redemption of two other giants. From the moment Tendulkar was given out lbw to his third ball at Brisbane, he had had an awful series, with both his driving and self-belief gone astray. He rediscovered himself by limiting his scoring options by one-third: his 241 not out in the first innings featured not a single cover-drive, a stroke that had caused his dismissal a couple of times in the series. After an unbeaten half-century in the second innings, he raised his series average from 16.40 to 76.60. Kumble, a colossus most Indians fail to recognise, harvested 12 wickets, finishing with 24 overall, which made him the most successful bowler on either side. Overshadowing all else was Waugh's farewell.

But the Test, and the series, were drawn. It was ironic that Waugh, whose legacy to Test cricket was the virtual elimination of the draw, ended his career with one. But if India denied Waugh the captain a fitting end, they set the stage for one last scrap from Waugh the warrior batsman. A record fifth-day crowd watched as he made his way in for the final time, with Australia not yet out of danger at 170 for three. He began with a shovel-drive that could have got him out and minutes later the crowd gasped as a sweep flew off the edge to fall a few feet short of a fielder running in from deep square leg. But Waugh soon found his nerve, to hit a string of rasping boundaries, and a child held up a banner on Yabba's Hill: WAUGH RULES, OK.

He didn't rule his last series, but he played his part in saving it. The last hour of the match turned into a giant celebration. Willed on by the crowd and needled by young Parthiv Patel for one last blow ("Show some respect," Waugh countered, "you were in nappies when I made my debut."), he made a charge for the hundred and ended his career with a slog-sweep. It did make for a grand entry in the scorebooks: Waugh c Tendulkar b Kumble 80.

After an emotional parade around the ground on the shoulders of his team-mates, Waugh walked off, with two of his children in his arms, doting wife beside him, to applause heard around the cricket world. A glorious era had ended, and the promise of another was on the horizon. It was one hell of a series.

INDIAN TOURING PARTY

S. C. Ganguly (*captain*), R. Dravid (*vice-captain*), A. B. Agarkar, L. Balaji, A. Chopra, D. Dasgupta, Harbhajan Singh, A. Kumble, V. V. S. Laxman, A. Nehra, P. A. Patel, I. K. Pathan, S. Ramesh, V. Sehwag, S. R. Tendulkar, Zaheer Khan.

A. M. Salvi was originally selected but withdrew through injury before the tour and was replaced by Balaji. M. Kartik reinforced the party after the First Test. Harbhajan Singh had surgery on his finger after the Second Test and played no further part in the tour.

Coach: J. G. Wright. *Manager:* N. S. Yadav. *Bowling coach:* B. A. Reid. *Physiotherapist:* A. Leipus. *Trainer:* G. A. King.

INDIAN TOUR RESULTS

Test matches – Played 4: Won 1, Lost 1, Drawn 2.
First-class matches – Played 6: Won 1, Lost 1, Drawn 4.
One-day internationals – Played 10: Won 5, Lost 5. *Wins* – Zimbabwe (4), Australia.
  Losses – Australia (5).
Other non-first-class matches – Played 2: Won 1, Drawn 1.

TEST MATCH AVERAGES

AUSTRALIA – BATTING AND FIELDING

	T	I	NO	R	HS	100s	50s	Avge	Ct/St
R. T. Ponting	4	8	1	706	257	2	2	100.85	1
†S. M. Katich	4	6	1	353	125	1	2	70.60	3
†M. L. Hayden.	4	8	1	451	136	1	3	64.42	9
†J. L. Langer	4	8	0	369	121	2	1	46.12	3
S. R. Waugh	4	7	1	267	80	0	2	44.50	0
D. R. Martyn.	4	7	1	254	66*	0	1	42.33	3
J. N. Gillespie	3	5	2	110	48*	0	0	36.66	2
†A. C. Gilchrist	4	6	0	96	43	0	0	16.00	10/1
B. A. Williams	2	3	2	14	10*	0	0	14.00	1
A. J. Bichel	2	3	0	31	19	0	0	10.33	4
N. W. Bracken	3	3	1	9	6*	0	0	4.50	1
S. C. G. MacGill	4	5	1	2	1	0	0	0.50	2

Played in two Tests: B. Lee 8, 0.

† *Left-handed batsman.*

BOWLING

	Style	O	M	R	W	BB	5W/i	Avge
J. N. Gillespie	RF	139.1	41	377	10	4-65	0	37.70
S. M. Katich	SLC	51	5	215	5	2-22	0	43.00
B. A. Williams.	RF	79	24	225	5	4-53	0	45.00
A. J. Bichel.	RFM	70.4	10	295	6	4-118	0	49.16
S. C. G. MacGill	LBG	194.4	29	711	14	4-86	0	50.78
N. W. Bracken	LFM	128	38	351	6	2-12	0	58.50
B. Lee	RF	100.5	17	476	8	4-201	0	59.50

Also bowled: D. R. Martyn (RM) 9–1–27–0; R. T. Ponting (RM/OB) 1–0–4–0; S. R. Waugh
(RM) 31–5–82–1.

INDIA – BATTING AND FIELDING

	T	I	NO	R	HS	100s	50s	Avge	Ct/St
R. Dravid	4	8	3	619	233	1	3	123.80	4
V. V. S. Laxman	4	7	1	494	178	2	1	82.33	5
S. R. Tendulkar	4	7	2	383	241*	1	1	76.60	3
V. Sehwag.	4	8	0	464	195	1	1	58.00	8
†S. C. Ganguly	4	6	0	284	144	1	1	47.33	1
†P. A. Patel	4	6	1	160	62	0	1	32.00	8/3
A. Chopra	4	8	0	186	48	0	0	23.25	5

	T	I	NO	R	HS	100s	50s	Avge	Ct/St
Zaheer Khan	2	3	1	28	27	0	0	14.00	0
A. B. Agarkar	4	6	1	26	12	0	0	5.20	1
A. Kumble	3	3	0	15	12	0	0	5.00	1
A. Nehra	3	4	1	0	0*	0	0	0.00	2

Played in two Tests: †I. K. Pathan 1, 13* (1 ct). Played in one Test: Harbhajan Singh 19*; †M. Kartik did not bat.

† *Left-handed batsman.*

BOWLING

	Style	O	M	R	W	BB	5W/i	Avge
A. Kumble	LBG	206.1	28	710	24	8-141	3	29.58
A. B. Agarkar	RFM	154.5	23	596	16	6-41	1	37.25
Zaheer Khan	LFM	51	6	213	5	5-95	1	42.60
I. K. Pathan	LFM	68	7	266	4	2-80	0	66.50
A. Nehra	LFM	101	16	382	4	2-115	0	95.50

Also bowled: S. C. Ganguly (RM) 2–1–8–0; Harbhajan Singh (OB) 35–2–169–1; M. Kartik (SLA) 45–6–211–1; V. Sehwag (OB) 18–1–71–0; S. R. Tendulkar (RM/OB/LB) 28–0–141–3.

Note: Matches in this section which were not first-class are signified by a dagger.

At Melbourne, November 25, 26, 27, 2003. **Drawn.** Toss: Indians. **Indians 266-9 dec.** (S. Ramesh 87, S. R. Tendulkar 80, P. A. Patel 52*; M. W. H. Inness 4-64, C. L. White 4-59) and **116-2** (A. Chopra 55*); **Victoria 518-8 dec.** (B. J. Hodge 264, I. J. Harvey 71).
The Indians declared before the start of the second day's play, but a failure of communications meant both sides emerged to field. Hodge's 264 lasted 500 minutes and 380 balls and included 39 fours and a six; he shared three century partnerships.

†At Allan Border Field, Brisbane, November 29, 30, December 1, 2003. **Drawn.** Toss: Queensland Academy of Sport. **Queensland Academy of Sport 304-6 dec.** (L. A. Carseldine 112, C. A. Philipson 85; A. Kumble 4-74) and **208-6 dec.** (L. A. Carseldine 109*); **Indians 208-9 dec.** (V. V. S. Laxman 74) and **121-4.**
Each team named 12 players, of whom only 11 could bat and 11 bowl. Carseldine scored a hundred in each innings.

AUSTRALIA v INDIA

First Test Match

SAMBIT BAL

At Brisbane, December 4, 5, 6, 7, 8, 2003. Drawn. Toss: India. Test debut: N. W. Bracken.

The record books will show this Test as a rain-hit draw, but rarely do three days of play contain as much drama without a conclusion. Right from the toss the match twisted and turned, sprouted controversies, sprung surprises and, in hindsight, set the tone for the series. That India, notoriously slow starters, did not lose was a gain in itself.

Despite play being limited to 16 overs on the second day and just 38 balls on the third, the cricket was rarely uneventful. The unheralded Indian swing bowlers had rocked Australia on the fragmentary second day, triggering a sensational collapse – from 262 for two to 323 for nine – but an hour into the fourth, the match was winding down to a familiar script. After a resolute start, India had lost three wickets, including Dravid and Tendulkar in the space of four balls from Gillespie, and suddenly the follow-on mark, a mere 62 runs away, seemed miles distant. In walked Ganguly, carrying a history of grief against the quick stuff, to face the test of his life.

His first scoring shot was an edged three to third man, and he swished and missed once against Gillespie a couple of overs later. But for the next few hours he lorded it with a majesty that seemed to have deserted him in recent years. A few months before, he had sought advice from Greg Chappell; instead of talking technique, Chappell had talked mind. At Brisbane, Ganguly seemed powered as much by a renewal of self-belief as by his innate ability.

He added 65 with the steadfast Chopra, who was playing his first Test abroad, 146 at more than a run a minute with Laxman, who carried on from where he had left off against Australia in 2000-01, and a further 56 with Patel. There were fours hit all around the wicket, there were sizzling drives and cuts, neat deflections to the leg, and swivelled pulls to balls that were dug into his ribs. It was a gutsy, stirring, emotion-filled hundred, which took the Australians by surprise. Ganguly had been identified as a soft target but, when he was sixth out, India led by six runs and the entire stadium rose to salute him.

On the first morning, Ganguly had braved putting Australia in on a greenish pitch under overcast conditions, and his bowlers had made him look stupid. The atmosphere offered swing and the pitch afforded movement, yet Australia hit a string of boundaries

Waugh bore the brunt of criticism for a whole week

off loose balls and scored more than four an over on a rain-shortened day. While the strokemakers had fun, the hero was Langer, who ground out a hundred. Langer is underrated in Australia – some people are riled that he has more Test hundreds than Ian Chappell or Bill Lawry – but he is a gritty character who rarely fails to put away the bad ball. He was troubled by a few that cut back in to him, but never missed a chance to force the ball to the square boundaries when width was offered. Without him, Australia could have been in deep trouble.

Less than six overs were possible before lunch on the second day; sensationally, Australia lost three wickets in the last eight balls. These included Martyn, who punched Zaheer Khan to the covers and seemed happy with two until he saw Waugh charge down for the third, and sacrificed himself to save his captain – who trod on his own wicket two balls later. Martyn's gesture was an un-Australian thing to do, and Waugh bore the brunt of criticism for a whole week, during which reporters and commentators dug up statistics to show his sense of self-preservation in run-out situations. Waugh was vexed enough to hit back in the post-match press conference, but he did admit the fanfare over his farewell had been a distraction.

Play did not resume until late afternoon, but ten overs were enough for Zaheer and Agarkar to wangle four more wickets by bowling a fuller length, and Agarkar concluded the innings with one ball in the little play possible on the third day. But even 323 seemed a winning score until Ganguly and Laxman got together to make the match safe for India.

Australia trailed by 86, but Hayden fought back until he was caught on the boundary seeking what would have been a 98-ball hundred. He had already become the first man to score 1,000 Test runs in three consecutive calendar years. Waugh injected some excitement with a late declaration that left India a target of 199 in 23 overs. When both openers went cheaply to the debutant left-armer, Nathan Bracken, the move seemed to have paid off, at least as a psychological ploy. But Dravid turned it to his advantage, chalking up an unbeaten 43, his highest Test score to date in Australia. Though Ganguly would not claim a moral victory, India went to the next Test with a swagger and not a familiar limp.

Man of the Match: S. C. Ganguly.   *Attendance:* 52,905.

Close of play: First day, Australia 262-2 (Langer 115, Martyn 36); Second day, Australia 323-9 (Bracken 6, MacGill 1); Third day, India 11-0 (Chopra 5, Sehwag 5); Fourth day, India 362-6 (Patel 37, Agarkar 12).

Australia

J. L. Langer lbw b Agarkar	121	– (2) c Patel b Agarkar	0
M. L. Hayden c Laxman b Zaheer Khan	37	– (1) c Sehwag b Harbhajan Singh	99
R. T. Ponting c Patel b Zaheer Khan	54	– c Sehwag b Nehra	50
D. R. Martyn run out	42	– not out	66
*S. R. Waugh hit wkt b Zaheer Khan	0	– not out	56
S. M. Katich c Patel b Zaheer Khan	16		
†A. C. Gilchrist c Laxman b Zaheer Khan	0		
A. J. Bichel c Laxman b Agarkar	11		
J. N. Gillespie run out	8		
N. W. Bracken not out	6		
S. C. G. MacGill c Chopra b Agarkar	1		
B 4, l-b 7, w 2, n-b 14	27	B 4, n-b 9	13

1/73 (2) 2/162 (3) 3/268 (1) 4/275 (4)   323   1/6 (2) 2/146 (3)   (3 wkts dec.) 284
5/275 (5) 6/276 (7) 7/302 (8)   3/156 (1)
8/310 (6) 9/317 (9) 10/323 (11)

Bowling: *First Innings*—Zaheer Khan 23–2–95–5; Nehra 15–4–51–0; Agarkar 25.1–5–90–3; Harbhajan Singh 14–1–68–0; Ganguly 1–0–8–0. *Second Innings*—Zaheer Khan 3–0–15–0; Agarkar 12–3–45–1; Nehra 19–1–89–1; Harbhajan Singh 21–1–101–1; Tendulkar 2–0–9–0; Sehwag 5–1–21–0.

India

A. Chopra c Hayden b Gillespie	36	– c Langer b Bracken	4
V. Sehwag c Hayden b Bracken	45	– c Martyn b Bracken	0
R. Dravid c Hayden b Gillespie	1	– not out	43
S. R. Tendulkar lbw b Gillespie	0		
*S. C. Ganguly c Gillespie b MacGill	144		
V. V. S. Laxman c Katich b MacGill	75	– (4) not out	24
†P. A. Patel c Bichel b Gillespie	37		
A. B. Agarkar c Hayden b Bichel	12		
Harbhajan Singh not out	19		
Zaheer Khan b MacGill	27		
A. Nehra lbw b MacGill	0		
L-b 6, w 1, n-b 6	13	N-b 2	2

1/61 (2) 2/62 (3) 3/62 (4) 4/127 (1)   409   1/4 (2) 2/4 (1)   (2 wkts) 73
5/273 (6) 6/329 (5) 7/362 (8)
8/362 (7) 9/403 (10) 10/409 (11)

Bowling: *First Innings*—Gillespie 31–12–65–4; Bracken 26–5–90–1; Bichel 28–6–130–1; MacGill 26.1–4–86–4; Waugh 7–3–16–0; Katich 2–0–16–0. *Second Innings*—Gillespie 5–1–17–0; Bracken 4–1–12–2; MacGill 4–0–32–0; Bichel 3–0–12–0.

Umpires: S. A. Bucknor (West Indies) and R. E. Koertzen (South Africa).
Third umpire: P. D. Parker. Referee: M. J. Procter (South Africa).

AUSTRALIA v INDIA

Second Test Match

Sᴀᴍʙɪᴛ Bᴀʟ

At Adelaide, December 12, 13, 14, 15, 16, 2003. India won by four wickets. Toss: Australia. Test debut: I. K. Pathan.

After five breathless days it was difficult to decide what was more confounding. Just how had Australia managed to lose after scoring 556 by the second afternoon? Or how had India managed to win after being 85 for four in reply? Only once had a team scored more runs in the first innings of a Test and yet lost, and that 109-year-old record too belonged to Australia: they made 586 at Sydney in the Ashes opener of 1894-95, enforced the follow-on, and fell 11 short of the 177 needed to win.

So, did India win the match or did Australia lose it? The truth was somewhere in between. It was inevitable that a game yielding more than 1,500 runs would be decided by batting mistakes. Australia's inability to stick to their guns on the fourth day cost them the match. But it was as much a triumph of the Indian spirit, exemplified by none better than Dravid, who was on the field for most of the five days, batting 835 minutes and scoring 305 runs. He was last out in the first innings and there at the end to secure victory. It was a monumental effort, the finest performance by an Indian batsman in an overseas Test, because he made the difference.

TEST DOUBLE-HUNDRED FOR LOSING SIDE

242	**R. T. Ponting**	**Australia v India at Adelaide**	**2003-04**
222	N. J. Astle	New Zealand v England at Christchurch	2001-02
221	B. C. Lara†	West Indies v Sri Lanka at Colombo (SSC)	2001-02
214*	V. T. Trumper	Australia v South Africa at Adelaide	1910-11
209	R. G. Pollock	South Africa v Australia at Cape Town	1966-67
205	R. N. Harvey	Australia v South Africa at Melbourne	1952-53
204	G. A. Faulkner	South Africa v Australia at Melbourne	1910-11
203	D. L. Amiss	England v West Indies at The Oval	1976
203	M. L. Hayden	Australia v India at Chennai	2000-01
202*	L. Hutton	England v West Indies at The Oval	1950
202	**B. C. Lara**	**West Indies v South Africa at Johannesburg**	**2003-04**
201	S. E. Gregory	Australia v England at Sydney	1894-95

† *Lara also made 130 in the second innings.*

Research: Andrew Samson

The victory was all the more incredible because India had not won a Test in Australia in 23 years, and Australia had not lost a home Test of consequence in five – and because Australia had scored 400 runs on the first day, a record for any day on this ground. Ponting contributed 176 of those, and all the Australians exploited the short square boundaries on a flat pitch against an uninspired attack. It was a strange day, because wickets fell steadily, making the Indians believe they were in the match, but the runs came so fast that the wickets hardly mattered. Two before lunch on a batting pitch would have counted as a fair return if they had not cost 135 runs. Langer was a case in point. In one over from Kumble, he smashed two sixes and two fours, but he perished in the next trying another big one.

Ponting was an exception on a day of breezy cameos, though he was hardly sedate. For the most part, the Indians set a 7–2 or even 8–1 off-side field for him, yet he pierced it unfailingly: amazingly, his first 16 fours were all on the off. He reached 101 in just 117 balls, then scored his next 141 off 235, sluggish only by comparison with his team-mates. He hit 31 fours in all, and batted for eight hours 28 minutes, pausing to blow a kiss to his wife when he reached 200. No one had ever made as much as his 242 in a Test and gone on to lose.

Australia seemed set for at least 600 until Kumble finally had him caught at slip, and followed up with the last two wickets in the same over to restrict the innings to 556. Within a couple of hours it hardly seemed to matter.

Bichel, a controversial selection after a poor game in Brisbane, struck three vital blows. He bowled straight to a canny, defensive field set by Waugh (to Sehwag, there were no slips, only a gully) and India slumped from 66 without loss to 85 for four when Ganguly was run out. Laxman joined Dravid. It took Australia 94 overs to separate them. It was not quite Kolkata; there, they had added 376 for the fifth wicket, here it was a mere 303. That made them only the third pair to share two triple-century stands

Highs and lows: the Indian fielders congratulate Ajit Agarkar (*right*) after dismissing Ricky Ponting for a duck, his first for 50 innings. Agarkar ended with six for 41.

Picture by David Gray, Reuters

in Tests, after Bradman and Ponsford and, more recently, the South Africans Gibbs and Smith.

This time, it was Dravid's turn to score the double-hundred. He simply played everything on its merits, leaving every ball that carried the threat of an edge alone, while taking advantage of every scoring opportunity. After he played himself in, his cover-driving was sublime, and the only time he was in danger of getting out was when he top-edged a hook off Gillespie. But it sailed over backward square leg and brought up his hundred.

The law of a ball's merits does not apply to Laxman, who batted as he pleased, clipping balls square on the off side and sometimes fetching them from outside off to flick them past mid-wicket. The Australians had no idea where to bowl to him. He finally departed on the stroke of tea on the third day with India at 388, but Dravid was unshakeable and added 135 more with the tail before he was last out. He had batted all but six minutes of ten hours and hit 23 fours and a six in 446 balls; it was at the time his highest first-class score, and a Test record for India abroad. Australia's advantage had been whittled down to 33.

The Test took a decisive turn on the fourth day when a combination of weariness, tight bowling and a fatal urge to dominate the bowlers caused a dramatic Australian collapse. Agarkar bowled his best spell of the series, swinging the ball both ways, to account for Langer and Ponting, and thereafter every top-order batsman fell trying an aggressive stroke on a pitch that had slowed down. India were left to make 230 in 100 overs; Dravid redeemed a pledge to himself by being there to score the winning runs.

There was a minor scare when India lost their fourth wicket on 170, but Dravid sealed a historic victory by cutting MacGill to the cover boundary. Waugh chased the ball all the way, retrieved it from the gutter, handed it over to Dravid and said "Well played." Indeed.

Man of the Match: R. Dravid.   *Attendance:* 75,021.

Close of play: First day, Australia 400-5 (Ponting 176, Gilchrist 9); Second day, India 180-4 (Dravid 43, Laxman 55); Third day, India 477-7 (Dravid 199, Kumble 1); Fourth day, India 37-0 (Chopra 10, Sehwag 25).

Australia

J. L. Langer c Sehwag b Kumble	58	– lbw b Agarkar	10
M. L. Hayden c Patel b Pathan	12	– c Sehwag b Nehra	17
R. T. Ponting c Dravid b Kumble	242	– c Chopra b Agarkar	0
D. R. Martyn c Laxman b Nehra	30	– c Dravid b Tendulkar	38
*S. R. Waugh b Nehra	30	– c Dravid b Tendulkar	42
S. M. Katich c Sehwag b Agarkar	75	– c Nehra b Agarkar	31
†A. C. Gilchrist c Sehwag b Agarkar	29	– b Kumble	43
A. J. Bichel c Chopra b Kumble	19	– b Agarkar	1
J. N. Gillespie not out	48	– c Patel b Agarkar	3
B. A. Williams b Kumble	0	– not out	4
S. C. G. MacGill lbw b Kumble	0	– b Agarkar	1
B 1, l-b 7, w 1, n-b 4	13	B 2, l-b 2, w 1, n-b 1	6

1/22 (2) 2/135 (1) 3/200 (4) 4/252 (5)　　556
5/390 (6) 6/426 (7) 7/473 (8)
8/556 (3) 9/556 (10) 10/556 (11)

1/10 (1) 2/18 (3) 3/44 (2)　　196
4/109 (4) 5/112 (5) 6/183 (7)
7/184 (8) 8/188 (6)
9/192 (9) 10/196 (11)

Bowling: *First Innings*—Agarkar 26–1–119–2; Pathan 27–3–136–1; Nehra 25–3–115–2; Kumble 43–3–154–5; Sehwag 5–0–21–0; Tendulkar 1–0–3–0. *Second Innings*—Agarkar 16.2–2–41–6; Pathan 7–0–24–0; Nehra 7–2–21–1; Kumble 17–2–58–1; Tendulkar 6–0–36–2; Sehwag 3–0–12–0.

India

A. Chopra c and b Bichel	27	– lbw b Gillespie	20
V. Sehwag c Hayden b Bichel	47	– st Gilchrist b MacGill	47
R. Dravid c Bichel b Gillespie	233	– not out	72
S. R. Tendulkar c Gilchrist b Bichel	1	– lbw b MacGill	37
*S. C. Ganguly run out	2	– c Katich b Bichel	12
V. V. S. Laxman c Gilchrist b Bichel	148	– c Bichel b Katich	32
†P. A. Patel c Ponting b Katich	31	– b Katich	3
A. B. Agarkar c MacGill b Katich	11	– not out	0
A. Kumble lbw b MacGill	12		
I. K. Pathan c and b MacGill	1		
A. Nehra not out	0		
B 4, l-b 2, w 2, n-b 2	10	B 3, l-b 6, w 1	10

1/66 (1) 2/81 (2) 3/83 (4) 4/85 (5)　　523
5/388 (6) 6/447 (7) 7/469 (8)
8/510 (9) 9/518 (10) 10/523 (3)

1/48 (1) 2/79 (2)　　(6 wkts) 233
3/149 (4) 4/170 (5)
5/221 (6) 6/229 (7)

Bowling: *First Innings*—Gillespie 40.5–13–106–1; Williams 23–7–72–0; Bichel 28–3–118–4; MacGill 44–8–143–2; Katich 16–3–59–2; Waugh 9–2–15–0; Ponting 1–0–4–0. *Second Innings*—Gillespie 10.2–2–22–1; Williams 14–6–34–0; MacGill 24.4–3–101–2; Bichel 11.4–1–35–1; Katich 8–1–22–2; Waugh 4–0–10–0.

Umpires: R. E. Koertzen (South Africa) and D. R. Shepherd (England).
Third umpire: S. J. Davis.　Referee: M. J. Procter (South Africa).

At Hobart, December 19, 20, 21, 2003. **Drawn.** Toss: Australia A. **Australia A 311-5 dec.** (M. E. K. Hussey 67, C. J. L. Rogers 70, M. L. Love 94) **and 241-7 dec.** (M. J. Clarke 131*); **Indians 245** (M. J. Nicholson 4-25) **and 66-2.**

Clarke hit 12 fours and four sixes in 140 balls. In the Indians' second innings, opener Aakash Chopra took 64 minutes to get off the mark.

AUSTRALIA v INDIA

Third Test Match

MIKE COWARD

At Melbourne, December 26, 27, 28, 29, 30, 2003. Australia won by nine wickets. Toss: India.

Forfeiting a series lead from such an imposing first-day position will long haunt Ganguly and his minions. Opportunities to dictate to world cricket's superpower at the MCG come rarely. But at 329 for four after a rollicking Boxing Day, India were poised to press home the advantage so sensationally established at Adelaide ten days earlier. The abject submission of their batting on the second morning – the last six fell for 16 runs to a mostly unfamiliar attack – was an affront to Sehwag, who had given them a stunning start, and it cleared the way for a spectacular rally by the Australians.

Elite Indian batsmen have often been noted for their quiet demeanour and inscrutability, but Sehwag is representative of a new breed who boast a self-assuredness,

The form of his life: at Melbourne, Ricky Ponting blasts his second double-hundred in two Tests and, this time, ends on the winning side.

Picture by Hamish Blair, Getty Images

even cockiness. A daring opener, he has a simple philosophy and an uncomplicated style, playing by instinct and not by the book.

For five hours and 12 minutes he enthralled a first-day crowd of 62,613 – a record for India in Australia – his bold strokeplay bringing 25 fours and five sixes. He was as devastating on the drive and through the covers as he was through mid-wicket and the gully. Sehwag just missed a maiden Test double-hundred but his score of 195 was the highest by an Indian at the MCG, which was celebrating its 150th birthday with a spectacular $A430m makeover in advance of the Commonwealth Games in 2006.

While he could have been run out on five and should have been caught by Katich at 66, this was an innings of both brilliance and raw courage. Twice, Sehwag was hit on the helmet by Lee; each time, he barely flinched. In summers past, Indian openers would have wilted against such an attack on the body.

DOUBLE-HUNDREDS IN SUCCESSIVE TESTS

D. G. Bradman (Australia)	254 & 334 v England 1930
	304 & 244 v England 1934
	270 & 212 v England 1936-37
W. R. Hammond (England)	251 & 200 v Australia 1928-29
	227 & 336* v New Zealand 1932-33
V. G. Kambli (India)	224 v England 1992-93; 227 v Zimbabwe 1992-93
G. C. Smith (South Africa)	277 & 259 v England 2003
R. T. Ponting (Australia)	**242 & 257 v India 2003-04**

Such was Sehwag's authority he brought out the best in the emerging and capable Chopra. Their stand of 141 was India's first century opening partnership outside the subcontinent for nearly ten years. Chopra, playing just his fifth Test after being summoned against New Zealand in October, also showed he possessed courage to complement his poise. Following his departure, the redoubtable Dravid enabled Sehwag to advance the score to a startling 278 for one. India seemed destined for a score that would unsettle – even intimidate – the Australians, who had to cope with the combined pressures of a critical Test and the ongoing, exhausting Waugh valedictories.

India collapsed next morning, however, and Ponting, riding high after his glorious 242 in Adelaide, and Hayden moved swiftly to avert embarrassment. They pooled their formidable resources and added 234 for the second wicket before Hayden was lbw to the indefatigable Kumble for 136. Ponting completed his 20th Test century two overs later and, although he elicited only modest support from that point, he was in such sublime form that he reached 257, his third double. Before Adelaide, he had made 206 at Port-of-Spain in April; Don Bradman, in England in 1930, is the only other batsman to have scored three Test double-hundreds in a calendar year. With an unforgettable array of cuts, drives and thrilling trademark pulls and clips ahead of square, Ponting struck 25 fours (plus one all-run) in 458 balls, and batted for ten minutes shy of ten hours. He took the match away from India, much as Dravid and Laxman stole the Second Test from Australia.

Ponting rarely lapsed in concentration, even when the excitement surrounding Waugh's farewell reached fever pitch. On the third morning, the nation that halts for a horse race was stopped in its tracks when Waugh was struck above the left elbow by a short delivery from the enigmatic Agarkar. For one unsettling moment, as Waugh admitted later, he feared his distinguished career was to end in Melbourne and not his beloved Sydney the following week. He left the ground for treatment but, hard as nails, returned after lunch to assist Ponting in advancing the total beyond 500. Characteristically, he made light of the pain and received three standing ovations from a crowd of 33,256 – many there expressly to pay him tribute.

On the up: Brad Williams flies in at the MCG, where his pace brought five Indian wickets.

Picture by Mark Dadswell, Getty Images

Any lingering doubts as to the quality of India's cricket under duress were dispelled on the fourth day, although it must be said the batting after plucky Patel at No. 7 was lily-livered and inept. The tail's capitulation again undermined the splendid work of Dravid, who batted five and a half hours for 92, and Ganguly, who selflessly promoted himself ahead of Tendulkar in the closing overs of the third day, following the master's first-ball duck in the first innings. Demonstrably leading from the front, Ganguly showed his mettle by returning to the fray after receiving a nasty blow to the head from Williams, and compiling a neat 73. To the unrestrained delight of the entire Indian contingent, Tendulkar played with a quiet effectiveness for 44, suggesting better days might not be far away.

While the batsmen won the rave reviews, Kumble and MacGill, leg-spinners of vastly different styles, enjoyed a good deal of success. Though the Indians regretted risking their injured premier pace bowler Zaheer Khan, the Australians had reason to be pleased with the spirited showing of left-armer Bracken and the tearaway Williams.

But Ponting had the last word; when he swept the winning four to fine leg, he had 1,503 Test runs for the calendar year, a total exceeded only by Viv Richards and Sunil Gavaskar.

Man of the Match: R. T. Ponting. *Attendance:* 179,662.

Close of play: First day, India 329-4 (Ganguly 20, Laxman 6); Second day, Australia 317-3 (Ponting 120, Martyn 7); Third day, India 27-2 (Dravid 6, Ganguly 6); Fourth day, India 286.

India

A. Chopra c Katich b MacGill	48	– c Gilchrist b Bracken	4
V. Sehwag c Bracken b Katich	195	– c Williams b Lee	11
R. Dravid c Martyn b Waugh	49	– c Gilchrist b Lee	92
S. R. Tendulkar c Gilchrist b Lee	0	– (5) c Gilchrist b Williams	44
*S. C. Ganguly c Langer b Lee	37	– (4) b Bracken	73
V. V. S. Laxman c Hayden b MacGill	19	– c Hayden b MacGill	18
†P. A. Patel c Gilchrist b Bracken	0	– not out	27
A. B. Agarkar run out	0	– b Williams	1
A. Kumble c Langer b Williams	3	– lbw b Williams	0
Zaheer Khan not out	0	– c Hayden b Williams	1
A. Nehra c Gilchrist b MacGill	0	– c Hayden b MacGill	0
L-b 3, w 1, n-b 11	15	B 4, l-b 3, w 1, n-b 7	15
	366		**286**

1/141 (1) 2/278 (3) 3/286 (4) 4/311 (2)
5/350 (5) 6/353 (7) 7/353 (8)
8/366 (9) 9/366 (6) 10/366 (11)

1/5 (1) 2/19 (2) 3/126 (5)
4/160 (6) 5/253 (3) 6/258 (4)
7/271 (8) 8/271 (9)
9/277 (10) 10/286 (11)

In the second innings Ganguly, when 16, retired hurt at 39 and resumed at 160.

Bowling: *First Innings*—Lee 27–7–103–2; Bracken 28–6–71–1; Williams 20–6–66–1; MacGill 15–3–70–3; Katich 4–0–18–1; Waugh 9–0–35–1. *Second Innings*—Lee 22–3–97–2; Bracken 25–13–45–2; Williams 22–5–53–4; MacGill 26.5–5–68–2; Katich 4–0–16–0.

"It is roundly ignored, an anachronism, and a dusty one at that. But they were saying the same thing about five-day cricket not so long ago. And look what happened to that in 2003-04."
Cricket in Australia, page 1406.

Australia

J. L. Langer c Tendulkar b Agarkar	14	– lbw b Agarkar	2
M. L. Hayden lbw b Kumble	136	– not out	53
R. T. Ponting st Patel b Kumble	257	– not out	31
†A. C. Gilchrist c Nehra b Kumble	14		
D. R. Martyn c Patel b Agarkar	31		
*S. R. Waugh lbw b Kumble	19		
S. M. Katich c Chopra b Kumble	29		
B. Lee c Laxman b Kumble	8		
N. W. Bracken c and b Tendulkar	1		
B. A. Williams not out	10		
S. C. G. MacGill lbw b Agarkar	0		
B 4, l-b 8, w 5, n-b 17, p 5	39	B 4, l-b 2, w 1, n-b 4	11

1/30 (1) 2/264 (2) 3/295 (4) 4/373 (5)   558   1/9 (1)   (1 wkt) 97
5/437 (7) 6/502 (6) 7/535 (8)
8/542 (9) 9/555 (3) 10/558 (11)

In the first innings Waugh, when 0, retired hurt at 373-4 and resumed at 437.

Bowling: *First Innings*—Agarkar 33.2–5–115–3; Zaheer Khan 25–4–103–0; Nehra 29–3–90–0; Kumble 51–8–176–6; Tendulkar 13–0–57–1. *Second Innings*—Agarkar 7–2–25–1; Nehra 6–3–16–0; Kumble 6.2–0–43–0; Sehwag 3–0–7–0.

Umpires: B. F. Bowden (New Zealand) and D. R. Shepherd (England).
Third umpire: R. L. Parry.   Referee: M. J. Procter (South Africa).

AUSTRALIA v INDIA

Fourth Test Match

MATTHEW ENGEL

At Sydney, January 2, 3, 4, 5, 6, 2004. Drawn. Toss: India.

In strict cricketing terms, this should be remembered for the way India batted Australia out of the game, ensuring a drawn series, maintaining their hold on the Border–Gavaskar Trophy and consolidating their presumed new position as No. 1 contenders to Australia's crown. But cricket was a secondary feature of this extraordinary occasion, a mere backdrop. The contest was compelling enough, but it was taken over – hijacked almost – for a farewell the like of which cricket, normally a diffident kind of sport, had never seen.

Steve Waugh's 168th and positively last Test (no one would dare attempt a comeback after this) turned into one long wallow, starting with adulatory wrap-around newspaper souvenir supplements and culminating in Waugh being chaired round the SCG by his team-mates. John Williamson's nostalgic anthem "True Blue" competed with the roars of a record last-day crowd, many waving red rags, Waugh's customary comfort-object. No one had ever left the cricketing stage like this; no one had dared.

The show resulted from a benign (though presumably tacit) conspiracy between Cricket Australia, Waugh's personal management, the broadcasters Channel Nine, and the Murdoch press, to whom Waugh was contracted. Most cricketers, especially captains, go when the selectors choose: Waugh himself was forced out of the one-day captaincy in disagreeable circumstances two years earlier. By announcing his retirement date from Test cricket in advance, he controlled the timing. The other parties were able to leap aboard for the ride, and everyone cashed in. The total crowd of 181,063 had been surpassed at Sydney only by the 1946-47 Ashes Test, which lasted six days.

The Indians? They just dominated the Test match. The most important decision of the game was made by Ganguly, who called correctly and condemned Australia to the

Class will out: after a string of low scores, Sachin Tendulkar comes good – very good – at Sydney. His double-century was the fourth of the series.

Picture by Adam Pretty, Getty Images

field on a belting wicket, in extreme heat, with a weakened attack and less than 72 hours after the previous Test. The crowd had come to watch Waugh, and could indeed watch him throughout the first two days: standing at mid-off, issuing occasional instructions and – provided they didn't blink – bowling a couple of overs.

It was tough for Australia on the first day, which started with a blistering 72 from Sehwag and an outbreak of no-balls from Lee. But there were even more ominous features for Australia. They were set intently, behind the grille of his helmet, and they belonged to Tendulkar. Shrewd observers of the series sensed that he might impose himself in this Test, though no one would have guessed quite how. Tendulkar had thought through his problems to the point of cutting out one of his most distinguished strokes, abandoning the cover-drive and instead just waiting for the chance to hit to leg. He maintained this policy for ten hours 13 minutes and 436 deliveries, scoring an unbeaten 241, his highest first-class score and perhaps the highest ever made by a man still nowhere near his own top form. Twenty-eight of his 33 fours and 188 of his runs came on the leg side. His 32nd Test hundred matched Waugh; only Sunil Gavaskar, on 34, remained ahead. He was also the fourth man to reach 9,000 Test runs, two days ahead of Brian Lara in Cape Town.

Tendulkar put on 353, an Indian fourth-wicket record, with Laxman, whose 178 was of a different order: a lovely innings, full of perfectly timed caresses. The crowd never gave the partnership the credit it deserved, partly because they were obsessed with Waugh, partly because the over-elaborate Sydney scoreboard's failings meant only statisticians noted the 300 stand.

When Laxman was out, it was 547 for four, which in a normal series would be deemed unassailable. But Australia had scored 556 in Adelaide and lost, and Ganguly rightly decided to bat on and on, 39 minutes into the third day. This infuriated many

Australians, including the TV commentators, who had been anticipating the declaration minute by minute the previous evening.

It was yet another sign, however, that India were now playing cricket every bit as ruthlessly as Australia. When Ganguly finally gave over, at 705 for seven – India's highest Test total, and the second-highest conceded by Australia – the response was predictably savage. The Australian openers put on 147 and the once-introspective Langer played an innings so impertinently confident that he felt able to reach his hundred with a reverse sweep. At 214 for one, Australia might even have been sniffing first-innings lead.

However, the real difference between the teams lay not in the batting, nor in the fact that India had a spinner capable of maintaining control while Australia did not. MacGill had offered a four-ball almost every over; Kumble varied his pace while maintaining his line and was rewarded with eight for 141.

The third-day crowd were mostly interested in Waugh, who scored a cameo 40, after which they streamed out. Waugh himself was still intent on business and refused to doff his helmet, sensing this was not his real farewell innings. Less noticed, Katich became the fourth centurion of the game next day with an innings of lithe grace and huge promise, thus restricting India's lead to 231.

Again, Ganguly was criticised by pundits for not enforcing the follow-on, though again he was right: avoiding any risk of defeat before thinking of victory. Dravid and Tendulkar extended the lead to 442 before Kumble set to work again, sharing the new ball on the fourth evening. Realistically, Australia never had much chance of chasing that. But this match had long since left reality behind.

At 196 for four there was some danger of an Aussie defeat, but that presupposed a failure by Waugh. Not here, not today. He never quite got the century all Australia wanted – though his 15 fours were all cheered as if he had and certainly never glimpsed victory. But he batted with the ease and grace of a man at the peak of his career, flicking the ball to the off-side boundary whenever the spinners dropped short until he got to 80 and was caught, trying to hook Kumble for six, at deep square leg. "It shows that after 168 Tests you can still lose the plot under pressure," said Waugh.

Katich was staunch again; Kumble finished with 12 for 279. Their achievements were lost amid the hubbub. Then, cricket being cricket, Waugh finally slipped away, not quite to oblivion, merely to New South Wales v Victoria at Newcastle.

Man of the Match: S. R. Tendulkar.   *Attendance:* 181,063.

Man of the Series: R. Dravid.

Close of play: First day, India 284-3 (Tendulkar 73, Laxman 29); Second day, India 650-5 (Tendulkar 220, Patel 45); Third day, Australia 342-6 (Katich 51, Lee 0); Fourth day, Australia 10-0 (Langer 4, Hayden 1).

India

A. Chopra b Lee	45	– c Martyn b Gillespie	2
V. Sehwag c Gilchrist b Gillespie	72	– c Gillespie b MacGill	47
R. Dravid lbw b Gillespie	38	– not out	91
S. R. Tendulkar not out	241	– not out	60
V. V. S. Laxman b Gillespie	178		
*S. C. Ganguly b Lee	16		
†P. A. Patel c Gilchrist b Lee	62		
A. B. Agarkar b Lee	2		
I. K. Pathan not out	13		
B 4, l-b 5, w 4, n-b 25	38	L-b 3, w 1, n-b 7	11

1/123 (2) 2/128 (1) 3/194 (3)   (7 wkts dec.) 705   1/11 (1) 2/73 (2)   (2 wkts dec.) 211
4/547 (5) 5/570 (6)
6/671 (7) 7/678 (8)

A. Kumble and M. Kartik did not bat.

Bowling: *First Innings*—Lee 39.3–5–201–4; Gillespie 45–11–135–3; Bracken 37–13–97–0; MacGill 38–5–146–0; Waugh 2–0–6–0; Katich 17–1–84–0; Martyn 9–1–27–0. *Second Innings*—Lee 12.2–2–75–0; Gillespie 7–2–32–1; MacGill 16–1–65–1; Bracken 8–0–36–0.

Australia

J. L. Langer c Patel b Kumble	117	– c Sehwag b Kartik	47
M. L. Hayden c Ganguly b Kumble	67	– c Dravid b Kumble	30
R. T. Ponting lbw b Kumble	25	– c and b Pathan	47
D. R. Martyn c and b Kumble	7	– c sub (Yuvraj Singh) b Kumble	40
*S. R. Waugh c Patel b Pathan	40	– c Tendulkar b Kumble	80
S. M. Katich c Sehwag b Kumble	125	– not out	77
†A. C. Gilchrist b Pathan	6	– st Patel b Kumble	4
B. Lee c Chopra b Kumble	0		
J. N. Gillespie st Patel b Kumble	47	– (8) not out	4
N. W. Bracken c Agarkar b Kumble	2		
S. C. G. MacGill not out	0		
B 6, l-b 9, w 3, n-b 20	38	B 6, l-b 7, w 2, n-b 13	28

1/147 (2) 2/214 (1) 3/229 (3) 4/261 (4)   **474**   1/75 (2) 2/92 (1)   (6 wkts) **357**
5/311 (5) 6/341 (7) 7/350 (8)   3/170 (4) 4/196 (3)
8/467 (6) 9/473 (9) 10/474 (10)   5/338 (5) 6/342 (7)

Bowling: First Innings—Agarkar 25–3–116–0; Pathan 26–3–80–2; Kumble 46.5–7–141–8; Kartik 19–1–122–0; Ganguly 1–1–0–0. *Second Innings*—Agarkar 10–2–45–0; Kumble 42–8–138–4; Pathan 8–1–26–1; Kartik 26–5–89–1; Tendulkar 6–0–36–0; Sehwag 2–0–10–0.

Umpires: B. F. Bowden (New Zealand) and S. A. Bucknor (West Indies).
Third umpire: P. D. Parker. Referee: M. J. Procter (South Africa).

India's matches against Australia and Zimbabwe in the VB Series (January 9–February 8) appear on pages 1330–1342.

†At Canberra, January 28, 2004. **Indians won by one run.** Toss: Indians. **Indians 254-8** (50 overs) (H. K. Badani 100); **Prime Minister's XI 253-6** (50 overs) (M. J. North 74, C. Brown 80). *Steve Waugh led the Prime Minister's XI.*

ICC REFEREES' PANEL

In 1991, the International Cricket Council formed a panel of referees to enforce its Code of Conduct for Tests and one-day internationals, to impose penalties for slow over-rates, breaches of the Code and other ICC regulations, and to support the umpires in upholding the conduct of the game.

In March 2002, the ICC launched an elite panel of referees, on two-year full-time contracts, to act as its independent representatives in all international cricket. The panel was expanded from five to eight in April 2004, at which time a supplementary panel, created to provide cover during busy periods, was dropped. At the end of 2004, the chief referee was R. S. Madugalle (Sri Lanka), supported by B. C. Broad (England), J. J. Crowe (New Zealand), A. G. Hurst (Australia), C. H. Lloyd (West Indies), R. S. Mahanama (Sri Lanka), M. J. Procter (South Africa) and G. R. Viswanath (India). Broad, Crowe, Hurst and Mahanama joined the panel in April 2004, when Wasim Raja (Pakistan) left. The panel was sponsored by Emirates Airlines for three years from July 2002.

THE PAKISTANIS IN NEW ZEALAND, 2003-04

Don Cameron

Once again New Zealand cricket found itself embarrassed by the pitches produced for subcontinental touring teams. After the Indians glumly departed the previous year, having been reduced to rubble on one-sided green pitches, some officials and groundsmen were decent enough to offer a muted apology and set themselves the task of producing better, fairer pitches this time around. Mostly, they succeeded: the pitches were faster than 12 months before. But so were the opposition bowlers.

In both Tests New Zealand built strong positions only to see them dynamited late in the match by the rare skill of Pakistan's attack. In the First, at Hamilton, the New Zealanders ambled to 563 in their first innings but were torn apart in the second by the fast reverse swing of Mohammad Sami, and ended up grateful for a weather-assisted draw. But in the deciding Test there would be no escape. On a well-mannered pitch New Zealand again seemed safe, taking a first-innings lead of 170, but the fearsome Shoaib Akhtar then proved irresistible, bowling them out for 103. The 4–1 home win in the one-day series was small compensation. Some locals wondered what was so wrong with preparing greentops for their own medium-pacers.

The victorious Pakistanis brought a new attitude and appearance of togetherness. Their coach Javed Miandad worked them very hard in training and it showed in a notable improvement in the skill and confidence of their fielding. The squad quickly formed a united front on tour – despite having flown out in the wake of a row between Miandad and the chairman of selectors, Aamir Sohail – and those close to the party commented that some of the old, disruptive seniority problems had disappeared. Inzamam-ul-Haq led a team of equals. His own fitness and form steadily improved too.

> Off the field, Shoaib was their friendly, public face... On it, he was brutal

Off the field, Shoaib was their friendly public face – during the match against Auckland he joined the youngsters in their lunchtime outfield games. On it, he was brutal: he took 11 for 78 in his only Test, after six for 11 in his only previous Test innings against New Zealand, in 2002. "We don't get exposed to 150kph in-swingers that often," said Stephen Fleming later. "I don't think it was application or commitment that was missing – it came down to a skill issue." Fleming suggested hiring Wasim Akram to help his side decipher reverse swing.

Shoaib and Sami were not the only Pakistanis of disconcerting pace. In the shorter game, Abdul Razzaq scored runs at withering speed: in the third of the five one-day internationals, he blasted an unbeaten 50 from 26 balls; in the last, as Pakistan narrowly failed to chase 308, he crashed 89 from

40. This form of cricket has seen many daring and inventive big hitters, but perhaps Razzaq brought something new, adopting an open, baseball-hitter's stance, which allowed a scything rather than stroking bat, and splaying his front foot to the left to further open up his hitting range. Wherever New Zealand bowled, Razzaq smashed it. But his pyrotechnical art was not perfected until fifth game, by which time New Zealand's tight bowling had secured the series.

Still, the Pakistanis were content. Their fresh-faced side, in which Yasir Hameed and Shabbir Ahmed were also effective, looked like an emerging force in Test cricket – if it can be kept together. New Zealand sorely missed the injured fast bowler Shane Bond, but Ian Butler's six for 46 at Wellington offered hope that one day he and Bond might become a dominating fast-bowling pair. Fleming confirmed his new status as a confident strokemaker and his 192 in the first innings at Hamilton was perhaps the innings of the series. In terms of match sessions won, New Zealand probably finished ahead. They ended up disappointed, but not completely downcast.

PAKISTANI TOURING PARTY

Inzamam-ul-Haq (*captain*), Abdul Razzaq, Asim Kamal, Danish Kaneria, Imran Farhat, Mohammad Sami, Moin Khan, Salim Elahi, Shabbir Ahmed, Shoaib Akhtar, Shoaib Malik, Taufeeq Umar, Umar Gul, Yasir Hameed, Younis Khan, Yousuf Youhana.

Abdul Razzaq arrived late because of illness. Azhar Mahmood reinforced the party for the one-day internationals.

Coach: Javed Miandad.   *Manager:* Haroon Rashid.

PAKISTANI TOUR RESULTS

Test matches – Played 2: Won 1, Drawn 1.
First-class matches – Played 3: Won 1, Drawn 2.
One-day internationals – Played 5: Won 1, Lost 4.
Other non-first-class-match: Played 1: Won 1.

Note: Matches in this section which were not first-class are signified by a dagger.

At Eden Park Outer Oval, Auckland, December 14, 15, 16, 2003. **Drawn.** Toss: Pakistanis. **Pakistanis 318** (Imran Farhat 73, Yasir Hameed 96; B. G. K. Walker 5-55) **and 201-5** (Yousuf Youhana 67, Inzamam-ul-Haq 62); **Auckland 222** (R. J. Nicol 60; Danish Kaneria 5-70).

This match was moved from the main ground at Eden Park after rain interfered with the preparation of the wicket.

NEW ZEALAND v PAKISTAN

First Test Match

At Hamilton, December 19, 20, 21, 22, 23, 2003. Drawn. Toss: Pakistan.

When a team carefully stitches together a first innings of 563, victory or a dominating draw used to be considered the only possible outcomes. But cricket is changing: across the Tasman in Adelaide a week earlier, Australia had lost to India after scoring 556. And by the end of this Test, New Zealand were grateful for the bad light that confirmed the draw. If more than a day had not disappeared in drizzle and gloom they might well have lost.

Shortly before the start Shoaib Akhtar was forced to withdraw with a strained leg muscle, leaving Mohammad Sami as Pakistan's only sharp edge. Inzamam-ul-Haq still chose to bowl, perhaps thinking of the seaming Hamilton pitch of 2002-03 on which both India and New Zealand managed less than 100. But the watchful New Zealanders, having lost Vincent early, soon blunted what little menace bowling or pitch contained. It took a run-out, shortly after lunch, to remove Richardson and end his 101-run stand for the second wicket with Fleming.

A hundred for nine: New Zealand's No. 9, Daniel Vettori (*right*), is congratulated by Daryl Tuffey after making his maiden Test century.

Picture by Ross Setford, Fotopress

From then on only Danish Kaneria, the leg-spinner, showed any bite, and the score mounted steadily. But though Fleming reached his century, his sixth in Tests, after an industrious four hours, he lost four partners after tea. And when Hart fell to the new ball early next morning the New Zealanders were sizing up a mildly unsatisfactory total of perhaps 350. Then came Vettori – on his record something of a regular tailender but in ambition a Test all-rounder. Now even Fleming slipped into the shadows as Vettori unfurled a range of strokes of the purest quality. The partnership was worth 125 when Fleming played across a straight ball and was lbw on 192, after eight hours' defiance. Shortly afterwards Vettori reached his maiden hundred, from 131 balls with 20 fours, despatched to all points of the compass. The ninth wicket added another 99, and he was unbeaten on 137 when the frustrated attack finally ended the innings at 563.

TEST HUNDREDS BY BATSMEN AT NO. 9

173	I. D. S. Smith	New Zealand v India at Auckland	1989-90
160	C. Hill	Australia v England at Adelaide	1907-08
146	Asif Iqbal	Pakistan v England at The Oval	1967
137*	**D. L. Vettori**	**New Zealand v Pakistan at Hamilton**	**2003-04**
122	G. O. B. Allen	England v New Zealand at Lord's	1931
112	J. T. Murray	England v West Indies at The Oval	1966
111	S. M. Pollock	South Africa v Sri Lanka at Centurion	2000-01
111	**Mohammad Rafique**	**Bangladesh v West Indies at St Lucia**	**2003-04**
110	A. C. Parore	New Zealand v Australia at Perth	2001-02
106*	S. M. Pollock	South Africa v West Indies at Bridgetown	2000-01
102*	L. Klusener	South Africa v India at Cape Town	1996-97
100	J. M. Gregory	Australia v England at Melbourne	1920-21
100	R. R. Lindwall	Australia v England at Melbourne	1946-47

Pakistan worked solidly through the remaining session of the second day and on a gloomy, rain-shortened third, on which only 38.2 overs were possible. A delayed start on the fourth day left only 82 overs then too, but Tuffey's unflagging off-stump line gave New Zealand the edge and, at 285 for six, the follow-on still looked a possibility. Then a hero arrived in the shape of Moin Khan, a feisty wicket-keeper and a hardened battler, who savaged the bowling with a dazzling and sometimes impish range of strokes. Moin raced to a century in two hours, reaching the landmark with 4, 6, 4 off consecutive balls from Vettori, and also ended with 137. He found an unlikely lieutenant in Sami, who defended stolidly – scoring 25 in a seventh-wicket stand of 152.

New Zealand began the last day 104 ahead and with a feeling that another delayed start – there was no play before lunch – was the last blow to their chances. They ended it shaken by a nerve-racking collapse. Sami, who was clocked at nearly 96mph, showed the benefits of pace on a true pitch. After five overs' warm-up, he had Vincent and Fleming caught in the same over with away-swingers. Styris fended to slip, Umar Gul took two in two balls and suddenly New Zealand were 42 for five and sliding. There were further signs of panic when McMillan ran himself out. However, rain had pinched too much time for a result. Sami took two more wickets but could not break Oram's gritty defence. He and Tuffey survived until accepting the light, leaving New Zealand 96 for eight – and a touch relieved.

Man of the Match: S. P. Fleming.

Close of play: First day, New Zealand 295-6 (Fleming 125, Hart 7); Second day, Pakistan 118-2 (Yasir Hameed 36, Yousuf Youhana 24); Third day, Pakistan 227-4 (Inzamam-ul-Haq 38, Abdul Razzaq 12); Fourth day, New Zealand 4-0 (Richardson 4, Vincent 0).

New Zealand

M. H. Richardson run out	44	– c Moin Khan b Umar Gul	15
L. Vincent c Inzamam-ul-Haq b Shabbir Ahmed	8	– c Imran Farhat b Mohammad Sami	4
*S. P. Fleming lbw b Umar Gul	192	– c Moin Khan b Mohammad Sami	0
S. B. Styris c Taufeeq Umar b Danish Kaneria	33	– c Taufeeq Umar b Mohammad Sami	20
C. D. McMillan c Taufeeq Umar b Danish Kaneria	22	– run out	2
C. L. Cairns c Moin Khan b Shabbir Ahmed	11	– b Umar Gul	0
J. D. P. Oram b Shabbir Ahmed	6	– not out	23
†R. G. Hart c Yousuf Youhana b Shabbir Ahmed	10	– b Mohammad Sami	0
D. L. Vettori not out	137	– c Taufeeq Umar b Mohammad Sami	20
D. R. Tuffey b Umar Gul	35	– not out	1
I. G. Butler c Imran Farhat b Shabbir Ahmed	7		
B 4, l-b 12, w 9, n-b 33	58	L-b 4, w 1, n-b 6	11

1/16 (2) 2/117 (1) 3/217 (4) 4/249 (5)   563   1/13 (2) 2/13 (3) 3/42 (4)   (8 wkts) 96
5/266 (6) 6/274 (7) 7/314 (8)   4/42 (1) 5/42 (6) 6/47 (5)
8/439 (3) 9/538 (10) 10/563 (11)   7/52 (8) 8/95 (9)

Bowling: *First Innings*—Mohammad Sami 27–2–126–0; Shabbir Ahmed 43.2–9–117–5; Umar Gul 31–5–118–2; Abdul Razzaq 18–2–74–0; Danish Kaneria 32–6–112–2. *Second Innings*—Mohammad Sami 16–4–44–5; Shabbir Ahmed 10–7–10–0; Umar Gul 8.1–2–25–2; Danish Kaneria 4–2–6–0; Abdul Razzaq 3–1–7–0.

Pakistan

Imran Farhat c Hart b Oram	20	Shabbir Ahmed c Hart b Butler	8
Taufeeq Umar c Butler b Tuffey	27	Umar Gul c Vettori b Butler	3
Yasir Hameed lbw b Tuffey	80	Danish Kaneria not out	0
Yousuf Youhana c Vincent b Tuffey	28	L-b 4, w 11, n-b 21	36
*Inzamam-ul-Haq lbw b Tuffey	51		
Abdul Razzaq c Hart b Tuffey	48	1/47 (1) 2/55 (2) 3/134 (4) 4/209 (3)	463
†Moin Khan lbw b Oram	137	5/256 (5) 6/285 (6) 7/437 (8)	
Mohammad Sami c Hart b Vettori	25	8/453 (7) 9/462 (9) 10/463 (10)	

Bowling: Tuffey 33–8–87–5; Butler 23.4–6–113–2; Oram 23–7–55–2; Cairns 17–0–60–0; Vettori 36–3–117–1; Styris 12–4–27–0.

Umpires: S. J. Davis (Australia) and D. L. Orchard (South Africa).
Third umpire: A. L. Hill.   Referee: B. C. Broad (England).

NEW ZEALAND v PAKISTAN

Second Test Match

At Basin Reserve, Wellington, December 26, 27, 28, 29, 30, 2003. Pakistan won by seven wickets. Toss: New Zealand. Test debut: R. A. Jones.

The Second Test, like the First, produced a huge and improbable comeback – and this time there was no escape for New Zealand. Pakistan overturned a first-innings deficit of 170 to win comfortably. The fightback was sparked by a devastating spell of fast bowling by Shoaib Akhtar on the fourth morning: New Zealand lost seven wickets for eight runs, and with them the series.

Shot out: Shoaib Akhtar bowls Ian Butler for a duck to complete New Zealand's second-innings collapse at Wellington.

Picture by Ross Setford, Fotopress

Shoaib's success was tribute to the lonely hours of training he put in while recovering from a thigh problem at Hamilton. For New Zealand, Cairns was forced out through a late injury and Richard Jones, a 30-year-old from Wellington, was slotted into a recast batting order. Fleming was happy to bat first on a Basin Reserve pitch that, if not especially fast or bouncy, rewarded both batsmen and bowlers for hard work. But in murky conditions Shoaib made an immediate impact – bowling Vincent with his eighth ball and, after a long break for bad light, getting Fleming lbw with his 12th. Richardson again held firm, but no one at the other end matched his resolution. Early on the second day, New Zealand were 171 for six – with the second new ball already in the umpire's pocket.

But that only brought out New Zealand's dogged streak. Oram at last showed some batting form and Richardson was at his adhesive best until his considerable patience ran out just before lunch: his 82 lasted more than seven hours. But after the break Oram continued to use his reach well, before a lazy shot on 97, and Vettori chipped in with 44. He was helped by Inzamam-ul-Haq's odd decision to bowl the less threatening Danish Kaneria and Shabbir Ahmed for almost a whole session. New Zealand reached 366, and on the third day bolstered their position from useful to seemingly impregnable. Yousuf Youhana made a circumspect 60 before edging to slip and Pakistan's resilience went with him. With the second new ball in his hand, and a stiff Wellington northerly behind, Butler mixed full-length swing with well-directed throat balls to remove five batsmen in five overs. His final figures of six for 46 were a Test-match best. From 168 for four, Pakistan were 196 all out.

But that collapse would soon pale into insignificance. As midday approached on the fourth morning, New Zealand had a lead of 265, three wickets down and plenty of time to organise victory. Before 12.30 they were all out, having added just eight more. Richardson edged Shoaib behind, Styris was bowled by the next ball, and Tuffey was run out in the following over. Shabbir then joined in the carnage, pinning Oram and Vettori lbw, shortly before Shoaib finished the rout by bowling Hart and Butler. New Zealand had gone to pieces on a pitch without notable bounce or pace. Seldom had they encountered the incandescent fury of a bowler like Shoaib – swift run, long hair streaming, flying leap at the crease and true pace with a hint of in-swing. He took six for 30 in total and four for 16 on the day.

The New Zealanders were still dazed as Pakistan set out to score 274 for victory. Youhana and Inzamam were in control as the bowlers found none of the movement that gave Shoaib such a lethal advantage. Pakistan needed only 28 more runs at the scheduled close, but they left the field in fine weather without claiming the extra half-hour available. With an iffy forecast for the last day, Inzamam was so mortified by his mistake that he could not face breakfast the next morning.

Bad weather delayed the start, and when the players emerged they were forced off again by rain. Play restarted shortly before midday and this time Pakistan took no chances. They surged home in less than four overs, prompting a relieved Inzamam to look to the skies in thanks.

Man of the Match: Shoaib Akhtar.

Close of play: First day, New Zealand 151-5 (Richardson 53, Hart 3); Second day, Pakistan 52-2 (Taufeeq Umar 13, Yousuf Youhana 11); Third day, New Zealand 75-3 (Richardson 35, Tuffey 0); Fourth day, Pakistan 246-3 (Yousuf Youhana 73, Inzamam-ul-Haq 57).

"But the honour belonged to Bangladesh. Asked about his strategy for the next Test, the delighted Habibul replied: "Jamaica is far away, man. I'm not thinking about Jamaica tonight."

Bangladeshis in West Indies, page 1231.

New Zealand

M. H. Richardson c Yousuf Youhana b Shabbir Ahmed .	82	– c Moin Khan b Shoaib Akhtar . . .	41
L. Vincent b Shoaib Akhtar	0	– lbw b Shoaib Akhtar	4
*S. P. Fleming lbw b Shoaib Akhtar	0	– lbw b Danish Kaneria	24
R. A. Jones b Abdul Razzaq	16	– c Moin Khan b Shoaib Akhtar . . .	7
S. B. Styris c Moin Khan b Shoaib Akhtar	36	– (6) b Shoaib Akhtar	0
C. D. McMillan lbw b Shabbir Ahmed.	26	– (7) not out.	3
†R. G. Hart c Imran Farhat b Shoaib Akhtar . . .	19	– (10) b Shoaib Akhtar.	0
J. D. P. Oram c Moin Khan b Shabbir Ahmed . .	97	– lbw b Shabbir Ahmed	3
D. L. Vettori c Yasir Hameed b Mohammad Sami	44	– lbw b Shabbir Ahmed	0
D. R. Tuffey not out	9	– (5) run out	13
I. G. Butler c Moin Khan b Shoaib Akhtar	4	– b Shoaib Akhtar	0
B 5, l-b 14, w 3, n-b 11	33	L-b 4, w 1, n-b 3	8

1/1 (2) 2/1 (3) 3/41 (4) 4/94 (5)   366   1/8 (2) 2/43 (3) 3/73 (4) 4/95 (1)   103
5/145 (6) 6/171 (7) 7/247 (1)   5/95 (6) 6/96 (5) 7/101 (8)
8/327 (8) 9/361 (9) 10/366 (11)   8/102 (9) 9/103 (10) 10/103 (11)

Bowling: *First Innings*—Shoaib Akhtar 20.3–5–48–5; Mohammad Sami 30–12–64–1; Shabbir Ahmed 37–8–87–3; Danish Kaneria 32–5–86–0; Abdul Razzaq 23–6–62–1. *Second Innings*—Shoaib Akhtar 18–3–30–6; Shabbir Ahmed 17–5–20–2; Mohammad Sami 4–1–12–0; Danish Kaneria 9–2–18–1; Abdul Razzaq 5–1–19–0.

Pakistan

Imran Farhat c Hart b Oram	20	– c Hart b Oram	14
Taufeeq Umar c Oram b Tuffey	16	– lbw b Vettori	34
Yasir Hameed c Butler	3	– c Hart b Butler.	59
Yousuf Youhana c Fleming b Vettori	60	– not out	88
*Inzamam-ul-Haq lbw b Oram	34	– not out	72
Abdul Razzaq b Butler	26	
†Moin Khan c Vettori b Butler	19	
Mohammad Sami c Hart b Butler	4	
Shoaib Akhtar b Butler	0	
Shabbir Ahmed not out	0	
Danish Kaneria lbw b Butler	0	
B 4, l-b 3, w 1, n-b 6	14	B 4, l-b 2, n-b 4	10

1/27 (1) 2/30 (3) 3/60 (2) 4/112 (5)   196   1/37 (1) 2/75 (2)   (3 wkts) 277
5/168 (4) 6/171 (6) 7/194 (8)   3/156 (3)
8/195 (9) 9/196 (7) 10/196 (11)

Bowling: *First Innings*—Tuffey 24–9–46–1; Butler 20–6–46–6; Oram 22–5–49–2; Vettori 22–6–47–1; Styris 2–1–1–0. *Second Innings*—Tuffey 14–5–41–0; Butler 18.5–1–100–1; Oram 9–1–34–1; Styris 6–1–26–0; Vettori 23–5–59–1; McMillan 4–0–11–0.

Umpires: E. A. R. de Silva (Sri Lanka) and D. L. Orchard (South Africa).
Third umpire: D. B. Cowie. Referee: B. C. Broad (England).

†At Basin Reserve, Wellington, January 1, 2004. **Pakistanis won by 34 runs.** Toss: Pakistanis. **Pakistanis 258-9** (50 overs) (Younis Khan 63; L. J. Woodcock 4-38); **Wellington 224** (44.1 overs) (C. J. Nevin 80; Azhar Mahmood 4-41, Abdul Razzaq 4-33).

> **"**I don't know whether it's arrogance or what, but it's pretty dumb."
> England A in India, page 1374.

†NEW ZEALAND v PAKISTAN

First One-Day International

At Auckland, January 3, 2004. New Zealand won by four wickets. Toss: New Zealand.

On a tricky seaming pitch, New Zealand were relieved not to see Shoaib Akhtar – hit in the groin while practising without a box – and to win the toss. They put Pakistan in, and tight bowling left them 127 for six at 40 overs. But Moin Khan led a brilliant assault on some suspect death bowling, hitting 72 at a run a ball, and Pakistan salvaged a competitive 229. After losing Cumming in the second over, New Zealand were steadied by Fleming, and Styris played the backbone innings. As the required rate rose above seven, he answered with lofted drives and charged to his second one-day international century. Victory came with five balls left. Styris's hundred was reached almost in secret: the new scoreboard failed to track his progress.

Man of the Match: S. B. Styris.

Pakistan

Yasir Hameed b Oram	19	Abdul Razzaq run out	22
Imran Farhat b Cairns	24	Azhar Mahmood not out	26
Salim Elahi lbw b Styris	20	L-b 8, w 10	18
Yousuf Youhana c Styris b Oram	5		
Shoaib Malik c McCullum b Styris	4	1/47 (1) 2/55 (2) (7 wkts, 50 overs) 229		
*Inzamam-ul-Haq b Styris	19	3/60 (4) 4/79 (5)	
†Moin Khan not out	72	5/84 (3) 6/120 (6) 7/183 (8)	

Mohammad Sami and Shabbir Ahmed did not bat.

Bowling: Tuffey 10–1–49–0; Oram 10–3–28–2; Cairns 9–1–37–1; Adams 9–0–63–0; Styris 10–3–34–3; Vettori 2–0–10–0.

New Zealand

C. D. Cumming run out	1	J. D. P. Oram c Moin Khan	
*S. P. Fleming c Mohammad Sami		b Abdul Razzaq	3
b Azhar Mahmood	45	†B. B. McCullum not out	13
H. J. H. Marshall c Yasir Hameed			
b Shabbir Ahmed	14	L-b 16, w 20, n-b 2	38
S. B. Styris not out	101		
C. D. McMillan c Abdul Razzaq		1/8 (1) 2/35 (3) (6 wkts, 49.1 overs) 230		
b Shoaib Malik	12	3/102 (2) 4/141 (5)	
C. L. Cairns lbw b Shoaib Malik	3	5/151 (6) 6/156 (7)	

A. R. Adams, D. L. Vettori and D. R. Tuffey did not bat.

Bowling: Mohammad Sami 9.1–1–37–0; Shabbir Ahmed 10–1–53–1; Azhar Mahmood 10–0–35–1; Abdul Razzaq 10–0–61–1; Shoaib Malik 10–1–28–2.

Umpires: E. A. R. de Silva (Sri Lanka) and D. B. Cowie.
Third umpire: A. L. Hill. Referee: B. C. Broad (England).

†NEW ZEALAND v PAKISTAN

Second One-Day International

At Queenstown, January 7, 2004. Pakistan won by six wickets. Toss: Pakistan.

New Zealand's performance failed to match the ground's stunning setting. Once again they lost Cumming early, and spent the first half of the innings stumbling along. After 30 overs they were 104 for five, and only a dogged 91-run stand between Oram and McCullum allowed a respectable total of 235. Pakistan also lost an early wicket, but Imran Farhat began flowing into his strokes, even though the pitch still helped the seamers. The best of the Pakistan batting came when Yousuf Youhana joined him in a classical exhibition of nifty scoring through clever running and deft placements: had they cared to hurry, Pakistan would have won long before the 47th over.

Man of the Match: Yousuf Youhana.

New Zealand

C. D. Cumming lbw b Mohammad Sami	0	J. D. P. Oram b Mohammad Sami	54
*S. P. Fleming c Mohammad Sami		†B. B. McCullum not out	56
b Shoaib Malik	43	D. L. Vettori b Mohammad Sami	9
H. J. H. Marshall c Yousuf Youhana		D. R. Tuffey not out	3
b Shabbir Ahmed	10	L-b 2, w 13, n-b 1	16
S. B. Styris c Yousuf Youhana			
b Azhar Mahmood	10	1/1 (1) 2/25 (3) (8 wkts, 50 overs) 235	
C. D. McMillan c Moin Khan		3/53 (4) 4/79 (2)	
b Shoaib Malik	25	5/104 (6) 6/112 (5)	
C. L. Cairns b Abdul Razzaq	9	7/203 (7) 8/218 (9)	
I. G. Butler did not bat.			

Bowling: Mohammad Sami 10–0–52–3; Shabbir Ahmed 10–1–43–1; Azhar Mahmood 10–0–69–1; Abdul Razzaq 10–1–24–1; Shoaib Malik 10–0–45–2.

Pakistan

Yasir Hameed c Oram b Butler	2	Shoaib Malik not out	9
Imran Farhat c McMillan b Vettori	87	L-b 8, w 13, n-b 1	22
Salim Elahi c McCullum b Oram	14		
Yousuf Youhana not out	88	1/13 (1) 2/52 (3) (4 wkts, 47 overs) 236	
*Inzamam-ul-Haq c McCullum b Tuffey	14	3/195 (2) 4/224 (5)	

†Moin Khan, Abdul Razzaq, Azhar Mahmood, Mohammad Sami and Shabbir Ahmed did not bat.

Bowling: Tuffey 10–3–28–1; Butler 10–0–49–1; Oram 9–0–37–1; Cairns 4–0–28–0; Vettori 10–0–58–1; Styris 3–0–16–0; McMillan 1–0–12–0.

Umpires: E. A. R. de Silva (Sri Lanka) and A. L. Hill.
Third umpire: G. A. Baxter. Referee: B. C. Broad (England).

†NEW ZEALAND v PAKISTAN

Third One-Day International

At Christchurch, January 10, 2004. New Zealand won by seven wickets. Toss: New Zealand.

New Zealand chased this target as industriously as Pakistan had in Queenstown. In the case of Fleming, who hit a sublime match-winning century, there was a spot of panache too. On a much better batting pitch, Pakistan's top order hit flowing form, helped by grassed catches, before a collapse left them 190 for seven in the 43rd over. That only awoke Abdul Razzaq, lurking at No. 8. He opened his stance to swing like a baseball hitter, and used just 26 balls to hit a blistering 50 not out. Suddenly Pakistan had an imposing 255. But it was not half as imposing as Fleming's unbeaten 115, a majestic 135-ball innings. The middle order jogged comfortably in his shadow and New Zealand eased home with 22 balls to spare. It was Fleming's fifth one-day international hundred: all had underpinned successful run-chases. His sixth was to come the same way on the same ground the following month.

Man of the Match: S. P. Fleming.

Pakistan

Yasir Hameed c Styris b Oram	44	Shoaib Akhtar run out	2
Imran Farhat c McCullum b Mills	17	Mohammad Sami not out	0
Salim Elahi c Fleming b Styris	80		
Yousuf Youhana run out	36	L-b 2, w 2, n-b 1	5
*Inzamam-ul-Haq c McCullum b Tuffey	0		
Shoaib Malik c Fleming b Tuffey	0	1/50 (2) 2/72 (1) (9 wkts, 50 overs) 255	
†Moin Khan c Mills b Styris	10	3/144 (4) 4/144 (5)	
Abdul Razzaq not out	50	5/152 (6) 6/186 (7)	
Azhar Mahmood run out	11	7/190 (3) 8/234 (9) 9/247 (10)	

Bowling: Tuffey 10–2–45–2; Mills 10–0–58–1; Oram 10–0–48–1; Cairns 9–0–54–0; Vettori 8–0–34–0; Styris 3–0–14–2.

New Zealand

C. D. Cumming c Yasir Hameed		C. D. McMillan not out	36
b Mohammad Sami	3		
*S. P. Fleming not out	115	L-b 13, w 5, n-b 3	21
H. J. H. Marshall c Mohammad Sami			
b Shoaib Akhtar	64	1/10 (1) 2/158 (3) (3 wkts, 46.2 overs)	259
S. B. Styris b Shoaib Akhtar	20	3/188 (4)	

C. L. Cairns, J. D. P. Oram, †B. B. McCullum, D. L. Vettori, K. D. Mills and D. R. Tuffey did not bat.

Bowling: Shoaib Akhtar 10–0–43–1; Mohammad Sami 10–0–68–1; Azhar Mahmood 10–0–43–0; Abdul Razzaq 8–0–47–0; Shoaib Malik 8–0–40–1; Imran Farhat 0.2–0–5–0.

Umpires: D. B. Hair (Australia) and B. F. Bowden.
Third umpire: G. A. Baxter. Referee: B. C. Broad (England).

†NEW ZEALAND v PAKISTAN

Fourth One-Day International

At Napier, January 14, 2004. New Zealand won by eight wickets. Toss: New Zealand.

After the excellent pitch at Christchurch, the teams found a Napier wicket that started off ridiculously loaded towards bowlers. Fleming won the toss, forced Pakistan to bat and watched the ball seam and swing prodigiously. The seamers only had to bowl straight and wait, and not for long: Pakistan were out for 126, in 36.3 overs. But a last-wicket stand of 39 proved an omen: the pitch lost its sting and even Shoaib Akhtar could not bowl Pakistan back into the match, so New Zealand clinched the series. Cumming – so fallible in the three previous games – led the victory parade with an unbeaten 45. Oram was named New Zealand's man of the match for his bowling, the groundsman being ineligible.

Man of the Match: J. D. P. Oram.

Pakistan

Yasir Hameed c Styris b Mills	9	Shoaib Akhtar not out	27
Imran Farhat c McCullum b Oram	16	Mohammad Sami c Marshall b Vettori	6
Salim Elahi c McCullum b Mills	11		
Yousuf Youhana b Oram	4	B 1, l-b 8, w 9, n-b 2	20
*Inzamam-ul-Haq lbw b Cairns	0		
†Moin Khan c Cairns b Tuffey	15	1/20 (1) 2/49 (2) 3/49 (3) (36.3 overs)	126
Shoaib Malik c Tuffey b Cairns	0	4/53 (4) 5/53 (5) 6/57 (7)	
Abdul Razzaq c Styris b Tuffey	9	7/75 (6) 8/84 (9)	
Azhar Mahmood lbw b Tuffey	9	9/87 (8) 10/126 (11)	

Bowling: Tuffey 10–3–35–3; Mills 8–1–17–2; Oram 10–2–24–2; Cairns 7–1–38–2; Vettori 1.3–0–3–1.

New Zealand

C. D. Cumming not out	45	C. L. Cairns not out	25
*S. P. Fleming c Shoaib Malik			
b Azhar Mahmood	29	L-b 14, w 8, n-b 4	26
H. J. H. Marshall st Moin Khan			
b Shoaib Malik	2	1/84 (2) 2/87 (3) (2 wkts, 22.5 overs)	127

S. B. Styris, C. D. McMillan, J. D. P. Oram, †B. B. McCullum, D. L. Vettori, K. D. Mills and D. R. Tuffey did not bat.

Bowling: Shoaib Akhtar 7–1–27–0; Mohammad Sami 6–0–35–0; Shoaib Malik 4.5–2–19–1; Azhar Mahmood 5–0–32–1.

Umpires: D. B. Hair (Australia) and B. F. Bowden.
Third umpire: D. B. Cowie. Referee: B. C. Broad (England).

†NEW ZEALAND v PAKISTAN

Fifth One-Day International

At Westpac Stadium, Wellington, January 17, 2004 (day/night). New Zealand won by four runs.
Toss: New Zealand.

Though they lost the game, and the series 4–1, Pakistan were magnificent in a match that Abdul Razzaq turned into a spectacular. In just 40 balls of wonderful hitting he changed the near-impossible – 137 in 13 overs – into the very manageable – 14 from 11 balls. But after he holed out to a relieved long-off, the tail fell five short. The pitch, by reputation slow and bowler-friendly, was in fact splendid for strokeplay: Marshall and McMillan sent New Zealand racing past 200, before a fiery 20-ball 36 by Cairns – plus some poor fielding – helped them to 307. At 73 for four in reply, Pakistan looked lost. However, Inzamam-ul-Haq and Moin Khan carefully picked up the pace, before Razzaq exploded. He hit five thunderous sixes and nine fours. After the match, the umpires reported Shabbir Ahmed for a suspect bowling action.

Man of the Match: Abdul Razzaq.

New Zealand

C. D. Cumming b Mohammad Sami	31	A. R. Adams b Shoaib Akhtar	5
*S. P. Fleming c Shoaib Malik		J. D. P. Oram not out	18
b Mohammad Sami	16	D. L. Vettori not out	0
H. J. H. Marshall run out	84		
S. B. Styris c Moin Khan		L-b 3, w 1, n-b 13	17
b Azhar Mahmood	10		
C. D. McMillan c Shabbir Ahmed		1/47 (2) 2/57 (1) (8 wkts, 50 overs) 307	
b Azhar Mahmood	81	3/73 (4) 4/230 (5)	
C. L. Cairns run out	36	5/244 (3) 6/284 (6)	
†B. B. McCullum b Shoaib Akhtar	9	7/288 (7) 8/291 (8)	

K. D. Mills did not bat.

Bowling: Shoaib Akhtar 10–1–46–2; Shabbir Ahmed 10–0–63–0; Mohammad Sami 10–0–73–2; Azhar Mahmood 6–0–38–2; Shoaib Malik 10–0–55–0; Abdul Razzaq 4–0–29–0.

Pakistan

Yasir Hameed c McCullum b Oram	48	Mohammad Sami not out	3
Imran Farhat c Mills b Oram	8	Shabbir Ahmed run out	2
Azhar Mahmood b Mills	2		
Yousuf Youhana c McCullum b Mills	0	B 4, l-b 6, w 11, n-b 2	23
*Inzamam-ul-Haq run out	67		
†Moin Khan b Styris	52	1/34 (2) 2/53 (3) 3/57 (4) (49.3 overs) 303	
Abdul Razzaq c Marshall b Adams	89	4/73 (1) 5/171 (6)	
Shoaib Malik st McCullum b Vettori	0	6/265 (5) 7/266 (8)	
Shoaib Akhtar run out	9	8/294 (9) 9/294 (7) 10/303 (11)	

Bowling: Mills 9.3–1–65–2; Oram 10–2–28–2; Adams 9–0–69–1; Cairns 3–0–16–0; Vettori 10–0–62–1; Styris 8–0–53–1.

Umpires: D. B. Hair (Australia) and B. F. Bowden.
Third umpire: D. B. Cowie. Referee: B. C. Broad (England).

THE ZIMBABWEANS IN AUSTRALIA, 2003-04

The Zimbabweans, who had played two Tests in Australia in October chiefly notable for Matthew Hayden's Test-record 380 against them, returned in January to join Australia and India in the one-day triangular VB Series. Their only victory came in their opening warm-up game against Australia A, thanks to an unbeaten hundred from Stuart Carlisle.

ZIMBABWEAN TOURING PARTY

H. H. Streak (*captain*), T. Taibu (*vice-captain*), A. M. Blignaut, S. V. Carlisle, S. M. Ervine, G. W. Flower, I. J. Friend, D. T. Hondo, N. D. Mahwire, S. Matsikenyeri, R. W. Price, V. Sibanda, M. A. Vermeulen, C. B. Wishart.

D. D. Ebrahim replaced the injured Wishart, and Vermeulen was later forced to drop out of the squad with a fractured skull.

Coach: G. R. Marsh. *Manager:* M. A. Meman.
Bowling coach: B. A. Reid. *Physiotherapist:* B. I. Robinson.

ZIMBABWEAN TOUR RESULTS

One-day internationals – Played 8: Lost 7, No result 1. *Losses* – Australia (3), India (4). *No result* – Australia.
Other non-first-class matches – Played 3: Won 1, Lost 2.

Note: Matches in this section were not first-class.

At Perth, January 1, 2004 (day/night). **Zimbabweans won by eight runs.** Toss: Zimbabweans. **Zimbabweans 240** (49.5 overs) (S. V. Carlisle 100*); **Australia A 232** (49 overs) (S. E. Marsh 57; S. M. Ervine 4-44).

Carlisle carried his bat for 100* in 128 balls, with nine fours and a six. Australia A fought back from 66-6, thanks to a fifty from Shaun Marsh, son of Zimbabwe's coach, Geoff.

At Perth, January 4, 2004 (day/night). **Western Australia won by 70 runs.** Toss: Western Australia. **Western Australia 286-9** (50 overs) (S. W. Meuleman 67, M. W. Goodwin 77; S. M. Ervine 5-56); **Zimbabweans 216** (44.1 overs) (M. A. Vermeulen 55).

Vermeulen scored 55 in 35 balls, with 12 fours. Craig Wishart retired hurt with a knee injury that forced him out of the VB Series.

At Adelaide Oval, January 7, 2004 (day/night). **Australia A won by 119 runs.** Toss: Australia A. **Australia A 327-6** (50 overs) (M. J. North 115, M. J. Clarke 93); **Zimbabweans 208** (44 overs) (G. W. Flower 67, S. M. Ervine 51).

North scored 115 in 109 balls, with 14 fours and two sixes; Clarke scored 93 in 71 balls, with 11 fours and one six.

Zimbabwe's matches against Australia and India in the VB Series (January 11–February 3) appear on pages 1330–1342.

THE BANGLADESHIS IN ZIMBABWE, 2003-04

John Ward

This tour of Zimbabwe provided a possible turning point for Bangladeshi cricket. Under the guidance of Dav Whatmore, their new coach, they had taken obvious strides forward since a dismal 2003 World Cup and came close to embarrassing Pakistan in Multan five months earlier. But they were still looking for a first international victory since 1999. In Zimbabwe they found it, and the win clearly boosted their strength and determination.

The series was a basement battle: Zimbabwe, second-bottom in the ICC Test Championship, were probably weaker than at any point in the country's 11-year Test history, after the premature departure of many leading players, and their worries about bottom-placed Bangladesh became clear in their tense, laboured cricket for most of the First Test. But they ultimately won that match by a wide margin, and were far the superior team in the rain-ruined Second.

Perhaps Zimbabwe then went into the one-day series expecting an easy ride. This provided the opening Bangladesh needed, and they swept to a fine victory in the third one-dayer, the first game to escape the rain. It ended a drought lasting 47 one-day internationals and 28 Tests, since the dubious win over Pakistan at Northampton on May 31, 1999.

Shocked out of complacency, Zimbabwe lost confidence too, while the Bangladeshis were inspired. Visiting journalists said they had never seen their team play so well, and the two remaining games were close-fought and exciting. Bangladesh would have won both, but for the skill and cool temperament of Zimbabwe's captain, Heath Streak. He played decisive roles with both bat and ball, and Zimbabwe pinched the series 2–1. Despite that, Bangladesh left in high spirits.

The tour was scheduled for Zimbabwe's wettest season, and even Bulawayo, in comparatively dry Matabeleland, was drenched. The Test there was ruined, and two one-day internationals abandoned because of a water-logged ground. The weather often threatened in Harare too, but it stayed dry at the vital times. Otherwise the entire tour could have been a soggy disaster.

Bangladesh suffered from fragile batting, but their bowling was consistent, and the quality of fielding at times a revelation. The attack relied mainly on the seamer Mushfiqur Rahman and the left-arm spinner Mohammad Rafique, although Rafique was sent home before the final one-day match. During a practice session the new captain, Habibul Bashar, took the squad's junior left-arm spinner, Manjural Islam Rana, to his Zimbabwean counterpart Ray Price for some tips. Evidently feeling threatened, Rafique exploded. Habibul himself had a dismal time with the bat, apart from one fine innings of 61, which was vital to the precious win. But Bangladesh did not rely on outstanding individuals: they played well as a team.

BANGLADESHI TOURING PARTY

Habibul Bashar (*captain*), Rajin Saleh (*vice-captain*), Alamgir Kabir, Alok Kapali, Al Sahariar, Anwar Hossain Monir, Hannan Sarkar, Khaled Mashud, Manjural Islam, Manjural Islam Rana, Mohammad Ashraful, Mohammad Rafique, Mushfiqur Rahman, Shahriar Hossain, Tapash Baisya, Tareq Aziz.

Khaled Mahmud reinforced the party for the one-day internationals, during which Mohammad Rafique was sent home.

Coach: D. F. Whatmore. *Manager:* Latif Khan. *Physiotherapist:* J. Gloster. *Fitness trainer:* D. Woodford. *Computer analyst:* Nasir Ahmed.

BANGLADESHI TOUR RESULTS

Test matches – Played 2: Lost 1, Drawn 1.
First-class matches – Played 3: Won 1, Lost 1, Drawn 1.
One-day internationals – Played 3: Won 1, Lost 2. Abandoned 2.
Other non-first-class match – Played 1: No result 1.

Note: Matches in this section which were not first-class are signified by a dagger.

At Harare Country Club, Harare, February 14, 15, 16, 2004. **Bangladeshis won by 29 runs.** Toss: Bangladeshis. **Bangladeshis 199** (Shahriar Hossain 75) **and 174** (Mohammad Ashraful 59; D. T. Hondo 4-29); **Zimbabwe A 183** (G. M. Ewing 71; Alamgir Kabir 5-47) **and 161** (Tareq Aziz 6-46).

ZIMBABWE v BANGLADESH

First Test Match

At Harare, February 19, 20, 21, 22, 23, 2004. Zimbabwe won by 183 runs. Toss: Zimbabwe. Test debut: Manjural Islam Rana.

For most of the match there was little between the sides. The exception was Zimbabwe's glorious fourth evening, when their batsmen tore into the bowling, and their attack shattered the Bangladeshi batting, as Andy Blignaut veered the ball at pace to take his country's first Test hat-trick.

Zimbabwe had to overcome a nervous beginning, evidently induced by fear of losing to a team with such a bad record. After a delayed start, Gripper fell early, caught at slip off his first ball as he unwisely attempted a cut and was beaten by extra bounce. This persuaded Ebrahim and Carlisle to spurn risk as they ground out a century partnership. The rest largely followed their cautious example and the innings occupied most of the first two days. Mohammad Rafique bottled up an end for long periods, the outfield was heavy after considerable rain and – except for Ewing in his maiden Test fifty – the batting was often turgid. However, there were still unnecessary dismissals and, of the top four, only Carlisle was blameless. Six batsmen reached fifty but none went on to three figures.

In reply to Zimbabwe's 441, Shahriar Hossain and the middle order showed a determined response to three quick wickets. Mohammad Ashraful played beautifully for 98 and looked confident until he lashed at a wide ball from Streak and dragged it on. It was Streak's 200th Test wicket, almost three times as many as any other Zimbabwean.

Zimbabwe's second innings, building on a lead of 110, was another slow affair and Bangladesh began to harbour hopes of a draw. But finally, on the fourth evening, Taibu and Ervine decided it was safe to attack, both reaching their second fifty of the game. Ervine impressed observers, as he had in Australia, with upright confident strokeplay and powerful off-side driving. With Blignaut adding some meaty strokes, Zimbabwe were able to declare, leaving Bangladesh to make 353 – or bat out a day and 14 overs. In the brief session on the fourth evening, Streak could not bowl due to back spasms. But he did take the field, marshalling his troops and watching his fellow seamers rip through the Bangladesh top order, reducing them to 14 for five before the close.

The athletic Blignaut did most damage. In three balls, he trapped Hannan Sarkar lbw with an in-swinger, had Ashraful caught in the gully and then ripped one back off the pitch to Mushfiqur Rahman for a catch behind and the hat-trick. Television replays later appeared to show the ball hit pad only on its way to the keeper, but it was an extremely difficult decision for umpire Mallender. Blignaut managed just one more over before withdrawing with a thigh injury, which would keep him out of the next Test.

After the drama, the match again deteriorated into mediocrity as it took Zimbabwe until midway through the last day to winkle out the final five wickets, with Khaled Mashud playing a fine defiant innings. Taking the game as a whole, Zimbabwe's 183-run victory probably flattered them. But their golden afternoon showed what they could achieve when the force was with them.

Man of the Match: S. M. Ervine.

Close of play: First day, Zimbabwe 175-4 (Taibu 18, Ervine 25); Second day, Bangladesh 14-1 (Shahriar Hossain 8, Tapash Baisya 0); Third day, Bangladesh 313-9 (Manjural Islam Rana 30, Manjural Islam 3); Fourth day, Bangladesh 25-5 (Rajin Saleh 6, Manjural Islam Rana 4).

Zimbabwe

D. D. Ebrahim st Khaled Mashud b Mohammad Rafique .	65	– c Hannan Sarkar b Tapash Baisya .	31
T. R. Gripper c Habibul Bashar b Tapash Baisya	0	– c Khaled Mashud b Manjural Islam	5
S. V. Carlisle c and b Tapash Baisya	58	– run out	33
G. W. Flower c Hannan Sarkar b Mohammad Rafique .	5	– c Khaled Mashud b Tapash Baisya .	3
†T. Taibu lbw b Mohammad Rafique	59	– c Habibul Bashar b Mohammad Rafique .	58
S. M. Ervine c Hannan Sarkar b Tapash Baisya .	86	– c Tapash Baisya b Manjural Islam Rana .	74
*H. H. Streak c Khaled Mashud b Mushfiqur Rahman .	68		
A. M. Blignaut st Khaled Mashud b Mohammad Rafique .	7	– (7) b Manjural Islam Rana	32
G. M. Ewing c Khaled Mashud b Mushfiqur Rahman .		– (8) c Khaled Mashud b Mohammad Rafique .	1
R. W. Price c Rajin Saleh b Mushfiqur Rahman.	71	– (9) not out	1
D. T. Hondo not out	9		
B 1, l-b 7, w 3, n-b 2	0	L-b 2, w 2	4
	13		

1/0 (2) 2/107 (3) 3/130 (1) 4/133 (4)   441
5/258 (5) 6/299 (7) 7/306 (8)
8/412 (7) 9/433 (10) 10/441 (9)

1/12 (2) 2/50 (1)   (8 wkts dec.) 242
3/54 (4) 4/90 (3)
5/180 (5) 6/232 (6)
7/234 (8) 8/242 (7)

Bowling: *First Innings*—Manjural Islam 28–8–69–0; Tapash Baisya 36–6–133–3; Mushfiqur Rahman 24.2–8–75–3; Mohammad Rafique 57–11–121–4; Manjural Islam Rana 13–4–26–0; Mohammad Ashraful 2–1–9–0. *Second Innings*—Tapash Baisya 16–1–65–2; Manjural Islam 12–4–24–1; Mushfiqur Rahman 9–0–49–0; Mohammad Rafique 20–3–62–2; Manjural Islam Rana 7.2–0–40–2.

Bangladesh

Batsman	1st innings		2nd innings	
Hannan Sarkar lbw b Streak	4	– lbw b Blignaut	10
Shahriar Hossain lbw b Hondo	48	– lbw b Hondo	1
Tapash Baisya c Taibu b Streak	4	– (9) lbw b Price	2
*Habibul Bashar c Taibu b Blignaut	0	– (3) lbw b Hondo	0
Rajin Saleh b Price	49	– (4) st Taibu b Price	47
Mohammad Ashraful b Streak	98	– (5) c sub (T. J. Friend) b Blignaut	0
Mushfiqur Rahman b Streak	44	– (6) c Taibu b Blignaut	0
Manjural Islam Rana not out	35	– (7) c Gripper b Price	31
†Khaled Mashud c Taibu b Hondo	6	– (8) st Taibu b Price	61
Mohammad Rafique c Ervine b Hondo	3	– c and b Ewing	5
Manjural Islam c Taibu b Blignaut	5	– not out	1
B 1, l-b 11, w 8, n-b 15	35	B 5, l-b 1, n-b 5	11
	331		**169**

1/13 (1) 2/34 (3) 3/55 (4) 4/77 (2)
5/162 (5) 6/259 (6) 7/265 (7)
8/278 (9) 9/288 (10) 10/331 (11)

1/12 (2) 2/14 (3) 3/14 (1)
4/14 (5) 5/14 (6) 6/81 (4)
7/110 (7) 8/112 (9)
9/123 (10) 10/169 (8)

Bowling: *First Innings*—Streak 26.2–11–44–4; Blignaut 22.4–6–73–2; Ervine 12–2–52–0; Hondo 19.4–5–49–3; Price 25–4–79–1; Ewing 7–2–19–0; Gripper 3–2–3–0. *Second Innings*—Blignaut 4.1–1–22–2; Hondo 12–3–24–2; Ervine 12–3–34–0; Price 20.5–3–61–4; Ewing 8–3–27–1; Gripper 1–0–5–0.

Umpires: N. A. Mallender (England) and D. L. Orchard (South Africa).
Third umpire: I. D. Robinson.   Referee: Wasim Raja (Pakistan).

ZIMBABWE v BANGLADESH

Second Test Match

At Bulawayo, February 26, 27, 28, 29, March 1, 2004. Drawn. Toss: Zimbabwe.

Bangladesh avoided defeat for the second time in their 28-Test history, when persistent rain handed them a draw. Their only previous escape, against Zimbabwe at Dhaka in 2001-02, had also been rain-assisted. In the three weeks prior to this match, nearly a year's worth of rain soaked Bulawayo, and much of the south-eastern corner of the ground was waterlogged. Areas next to the square, where water ran off the covers, were also a major concern.

After tireless work by the curator Noel Peck and his staff, play was scheduled for the first afternoon, but another storm put paid to that and to the second day. The game finally began an hour before lunch on the third, after umpteen inspections; umpire Mallender earned himself the nickname "Muddy" (pronounced the Yorkshire way, to rhyme with "woody"), a reference to his usual comment on the state of the outfield.

When the teams were eventually named, Andy Blignaut, still feeling the thigh strain suffered in the previous Test, and Ewing were replaced by Friend and Blessing Mahwire, while Bangladesh also swapped seamers, the gentle-paced Alamgir Kabir replacing Manjural Islam.

Streak put Bangladesh in, hoping a crash of wickets might make a result possible. But the opening batsmen began with great determination. It took 37 minutes for the first runs off the bat. During the afternoon they opened up and were looking good until Shahriar Hossain slashed at Ervine and was caught behind.

That was virtually the end of Bangladesh's resistance. Wickets tumbled against a backdrop of approaching rain, which finally relieved them at 88 for five. The downpour was heavy, and more followed overnight, washing out day four. More hard work by the groundstaff meant the last day started on time, but a result was virtually out of the question.

Bangladesh subsided to 168: had Zimbabwe held their chances they could have been batting before lunch, and might still have had the glimmer of a chance. As it was, only batting practice remained. Carlisle hit his second Test hundred, nine years after his debut, and four months after making 118 against Australia at Sydney. There was little doubt which innings he will treasure more dearly. Zimbabwe had completely dominated the day and a half possible, which perhaps bred the overconfidence that cost them in the one-day series.

Close of play: First day, No play; Second day, No play; Third day, Bangladesh 88-5 (Manjural Islam Rana 5, Mushfiqur Rahman 0); Fourth day, No play.

Bangladesh

Hannan Sarkar b Ervine	25	
Shahriar Hossain c Taibu b Ervine	31	
*Habibul Bashar c Friend b Streak	4	
Rajin Saleh c Ervine b Hondo	6	
Mohammad Ashraful c Carlisle b Friend	1	
Manjural Islam Rana c Taibu b Price	39	
Mushfiqur Rahman lbw b Hondo	0	
†Khaled Mashud lbw b Ervine	9	

Tapash Baisya c Flower b Price	2
Mohammad Rafique not out	26
Alamgir Kabir c Ebrahim b Price	3
L-b 4, w 6, n-b 12	22

1/64 (2) 2/73 (3) 3/73 (1) 4/81 (5)   168
5/87 (4) 6/89 (7) 7/126 (8)
8/137 (9) 9/144 (6) 10/168 (11)

Bowling: Streak 15–9–19–1; Hondo 18–5–25–2; Ervine 15–4–44–3; Mahwire 10–2–36–0; Friend 9–2–20–1; Price 8.5–2–20–3.

Zimbabwe

D. D. Ebrahim c Hannan Sarkar b Tapash Baisya	2
T. R. Gripper c Khaled Mashud b Tapash Baisya	65
S. V. Carlisle not out	103

G. W. Flower not out	37
N-b 3	3

1/5 (1) 2/134 (2)   (2 wkts) 210

†T. Taibu, S. M. Ervine, *H. H. Streak, T. J. Friend, R. W. Price, N. B. Mahwire and D. T. Hondo did not bat.

Bowling: Tapash Baisya 15–3–43–2; Alamgir Kabir 8–1–39–0; Mushfiqur Rahman 10–1–36–0; Mohammad Rafique 20–7–53–0; Manjural Islam Rana 6–0–33–0; Mohammad Ashraful 1.2–0–6–0.

Umpires: N. A. Mallender (England) and D. L. Orchard (South Africa).
Third umpire: I. D. Robinson. Referee: Wasim Raja (Pakistan).

---

†At Kwekwe Sports Club, Kwekwe, March 3, 2004. **No result.** Toss: Bangladeshis. **Bangladeshis 96-5** (28.3 overs) **v Zimbabwe A.**
Heavy rain halted the match and a waterlogged outfield prevented any resumption.

†ZIMBABWE v BANGLADESH

First One-Day International

At Bulawayo, March 6, 2004. No result (abandoned).
The outfield was in such poor condition after yet more rain that the umpires abandoned the match as soon as they arrived at the ground early in the morning.

†ZIMBABWE v BANGLADESH

Second One-Day International

At Bulawayo, March 7, 2004. No result (abandoned).
The outfield remained soft and slippery, blighting faint hopes of a shortened game starting in the afternoon.

†ZIMBABWE v BANGLADESH

Third One-Day International

At Harare, March 10, 2004. Bangladesh won by eight runs. Toss: Zimbabwe.

Bangladesh ended almost five years of desperate longing by finally winning an international match. Zimbabwe seemed to be resting on their laurels after dominating the Tests, while their opponents were revived and played with growing self-belief. It was their first international win since the now-tainted World Cup match against Pakistan in 1999, which helped earn them the promotion to Test status they have done so little to justify. Zimbabwe were at least pleased that play was possible: to the relief of those who feared a series washout, Harare, usually wetter than Bulawayo, produced better weather and a surprisingly dry pitch. When Bangladesh were put in, Habibul Bashar played his one significant innings of the tour, digging in with his 20-year-old vice-captain, Rajin Saleh, for a century partnership after the openers fell cheaply. But for Zimbabwe really lost their grip when Mohammad Ashraful, with 51 in 32 balls, and the all-rounders were allowed to hammer 89 in the last ten overs. Rogers and Carlisle began a brisk reply with a partnership of 109 – but the stroll soon became a scramble. The middle order threw away wickets and, when Streak was taken by surprise and sent a hip-high full toss skywards, Zimbabwe were doomed. The steady bowling of Mushfiqur Rahman and Mohammad Rafique was crucial.

Man of the Match: Mohammad Ashraful.

Bangladesh

Alok Kapali c Taibu b Hondo	9	Khaled Mahmud run out	22
Shahriar Hossain c Rogers b Streak	2	†Khaled Mashud not out	11
*Habibul Bashar c Ebrahim b Flower	61	L-b 6, w 11, n-b 2	19
Rajin Saleh c Hondo b Ervine	57		
Mohammad Rafique run out	6	(7 wkts, 50 overs)	238
Mohammad Ashraful not out	51	1/14 (1) 2/20 (2)	
Mushfiqur Rahman run out	0	3/134 (3) 4/148 (5)	
		5/153 (4) 6/160 (7) 7/211 (8)	

Tapash Baisya and Tareq Aziz did not bat.

Bowling: Streak 10–2–34–1; Hondo 8.2–0–48–1; Ervine 10–1–54–1; Mahwire 4.4–2–30–0; Price 10–0–42–0; Flower 7–0–24–1.

Zimbabwe

G. W. Flower lbw b Tareq Aziz	2	D. D. Ebrahim b Mohammad Rafique	13
B. G. Rogers c Alok Kapali		S. Matsikenyeri b Tareq Aziz	20
b Mushfiqur Rahman	51	R. W. Price not out	20
S. V. Carlisle c Alok Kapali		D. T. Hondo b Tareq Aziz	0
b Mohammad Rafique	71	N. B. Mahwire not out	3
†T. Taibu c Khaled Mahmud		L-b 3, w 7, n-b 4	14
b Mushfiqur Rahman	2		
S. M. Ervine c sub (Hannan Sarkar)		1/12 (1) 2/121 (2) (9 wkts, 50 overs)	230
b Khaled Mahmud	4	3/129 (4) 4/139 (5)	
*H. H. Streak c Khaled Mashud		5/140 (3) 6/169 (7)	
b Tapash Baisya	30	7/199 (6) 8/226 (8) 9/226 (10)	

Bowling: Tapash Baisya 10–0–51–1; Tareq Aziz 6–0–38–3; Mushfiqur Rahman 10–0–30–2; Khaled Mahmud 10–0–57–1; Mohammad Rafique 10–1–33–2; Alok Kapali 4–0–18–0.

Umpires: B. G. Jerling (South Africa) and I. D. Robinson.
Third umpire: K. C. Barbour.   Referee: Wasim Raja (Pakistan).

" But now the walls of the citadel have been demolished and pigeons haunt the empty halls."
England in West Indies, page 1030.

Long time coming: Bangladesh are jubilant at their eight-run defeat of Zimbabwe, their first win in international cricket since the 1999 World Cup.

Picture by Howard Burditt, Reuters

†ZIMBABWE v BANGLADESH

Fourth One-Day International

At Harare, March 12, 2004. Zimbabwe won by 14 runs. Toss: Zimbabwe.

After their shock defeat, Zimbabwe's confidence had evaporated like morning dew, and their top order collapsed to 79 for five. Streak and Ervine began the recovery towards a competitive total, which might have been higher had not the powerful Blignaut been wasted at No. 9. When Bangladesh batted, Streak bowled his usual incisive opening spell, but faced problems when his new-ball partner Blignaut was first erratic, and then limped off. But Streak and Price were frugal enough and Bangladesh fell steadily behind the required rate. Their hopes expired in the 46th over, when Streak brilliantly ran out Mohammad Rafique. He finished with 45 runs, four wickets and two catches.

Man of the Match: H. H. Streak.

Zimbabwe

M. A. Vermeulen c Hannan Sarkar b Tareq Aziz	4	*H. H. Streak b Tapash Baisya	45
B. G. Rogers st Khaled Mashud b Mohammad Rafique	26	D. D. Ebrahim c Khaled Mashud b Tareq Aziz	33
S. V. Carlisle c Khaled Mashud b Tapash Baisya	10	A. M. Blignaut not out	28
G. W. Flower c Habibul Bashar b Mushfiqur Rahman	3	G. B. Brent not out	4
†T. Taibu c Tareq Aziz b Tapash Baisya	10	B 2, l-b 8, w 17, n-b 2	29
S. M. Ervine c Alok Kapali b Rajin Saleh	50	(8 wkts, 50 overs)	242

R. W. Price did not bat.

1/7 (1) 2/31 (3) 3/34 (4) 4/46 (5) 5/79 (2) 6/155 (6) 7/202 (7) 8/212 (8)

Bowling: Tareq Aziz 10–0–63–2; Tapash Baisya 10–0–45–3; Mushfiqur Rahman 10–0–37–1; Mohammad Rafique 10–0–34–1; Khaled Mahmud 5–0–30–0; Rajin Saleh 5–0–23–1.

Bangladesh

Hannan Sarkar c Brent b Streak	14	Tapash Baisya b Streak	0
Alok Kapali lbw b Streak	18	Tareq Aziz not out	11
*Habibul Bashar lbw b Streak	0		
Rajin Saleh c Streak b Brent	12	B 1, l-b 3, w 22	26
Mohammad Ashraful c Rogers b Price	31		
Mushfiqur Rahman c Ebrahim b Ervine	49	1/27 (1) 2/30 (3) 3/40 (2)	(49.2 overs) 228
†Khaled Mashud c Streak b Ervine	41	4/70 (4) 5/113 (5) 6/167 (6)	
Khaled Mahmud c Ebrahim b Brent	0	7/168 (8) 8/207 (9)	
Mohammad Rafique run out	26	9/211 (10) 10/228 (7)	

Bowling: Streak 10–1–30–4; Blignaut 3.5–0–19–0; Brent 9.1–1–32–2; Ervine 7.2–0–50–2; Flower 9–0–51–0; Price 10–0–42–1.

Umpires: B. G. Jerling (South Africa) and K. C. Barbour.
Third umpire: I. D. Robinson. Referee: Wasim Raja (Pakistan).

†ZIMBABWE v BANGLADESH

Fifth One-Day International

At Harare, March 14, 2004. Zimbabwe won by three wickets. Toss: Bangladesh.

Both sides began with century opening partnerships and both then suffered dramatic collapses. But Zimbabwe managed to pull out of their nosedive just in time, with the burly figure of Streak again proving the difference between the sides. Zimbabwe looked in trouble as Hannan Sarkar and the stand-in opener Manjural Islam Rana put on 105, helped by several missed chances. But then Bangladesh imploded, scuppered by loose shots under pressure and a couple of dubious umpiring decisions. Streak, testing but luckless in his opening spell, finished off the innings. In reply, Zimbabwe looked on course with an opening stand of 112, but their own fall was even more spectacular, six wickets tumbling for 12 runs. Khaled Mahmud took four, reflecting accuracy and enthusiasm rather than hostility. But, with 60 still needed, Streak stood firm, guiding his team to a series victory that would have been unlikely without him.

Man of the Match: Khaled Mahmud.   *Man of the Series:* H. H. Streak.

Bangladesh

Hannan Sarkar c Rogers b Price	59	Tapash Baisya c Carlisle b Streak	4
Manjural Islam Rana c Matsikenyeri b Flower	63	Tareq Aziz not out	2
Mohammad Ashraful c Taibu b Price	0	B 2, l-b 2, w 12	16
Rajin Saleh run out	21		
Alok Kapali c Taibu b Flower	8	1/105 (1) 2/105 (3)	(48.5 overs) 183
Mushfiqur Rahman c Taibu b Flower	3	3/153 (2) 4/155 (4)	
*Habibul Bashar c Carlisle b Brent	2	5/164 (5) 6/167 (7)	
†Khaled Mashud c Hondo b Streak	2	7/168 (6) 8/177 (9)	
Khaled Mahmud c Carlisle b Ervine	3	9/177 (8) 10/183 (10)	

Bowling: Streak 8.5–1–17–2; Hondo 3–0–22–0; Brent 9–1–42–1; Ervine 8–1–24–1; Price 10–0–38–2; Flower 10–0–36–3.

Zimbabwe

G. W. Flower c sub (Al Sahariar)		*H. H. Streak not out	31
b Khaled Mahmud .	59	D. D. Ebrahim run out	11
B. G. Rogers c Alok Kapali b Tareq Aziz	54	G. B. Brent not out	14
S. V. Carlisle c Khaled Mashud			
b Khaled Mahmud .	0	L-b 2, w 10, n-b 3.	15
S. Matsikenyeri lbw b Khaled Mahmud .	0		
†T. Taibu c Khaled Mashud		1/112 (1) 2/112 (3) (7 wkts, 42.3 overs)	185
b Khaled Mahmud .	0	3/119 (4) 4/119 (5)	
S. M. Ervine b Tareq Aziz .	1	5/120 (6) 6/124 (2) 7/157 (8)	

R. W. Price and D. T. Hondo did not bat.

Bowling: Tapash Baisya 10–0–58–0; Mushfiqur Rahman 6–0–32–0; Tareq Aziz 8–1–35–2; Khaled Mahmud 10–1–19–4; Manjural Islam Rana 8–1–35–0; Mohammad Ashraful 0.3–0–4–0.

Umpires: B. G. Jerling (South Africa) and I. D. Robinson.
Third umpire: K. C. Barbour. Referee: Wasim Raja (Pakistan).

BANGLADESH v ZIMBABWE, 2004-05

Full details of this Test series, and others too late for inclusion, will appear in *Wisden 2006.*

At Chittagong, January 6, 7, 8, 9, 10, 2005. **Bangladesh won by 226 runs.** Toss: Bangladesh. **Bangladesh 488** (Javed Omar 33, Nafis Iqbal 56, Habibul Bashar 94, Rajin Saleh 89, Khaled Mashud 49, Mohammad Rafique 69, Mashrafe bin Mortaza 48; C. B. Mpofu 4-109) **and 204-9 dec.** (Habibul Bashar 55; D. T. Hondo 3-61, E. Chigumbura 5-54); **Zimbabwe 312** (B. R. M. Taylor 39, T. Taibu 92, E. Chigumbura 71; Mashrafe bin Mortaza 3-59, Mohammad Rafique 5-65) **and 154** (H. Masakadza 56, B. R. M. Taylor 44; Enamul Haque, jun. 6-45).

Against a weakened Zimbabwe, Bangladesh won their first Test victory at the 35th attempt, after 31 defeats and three draws. Their total of 488 was their highest yet, despite containing no hundreds; 18-year-old slow left-armer Enamul Haque's 6-45 was their best innings return, until he beat it the following week.

At Dhaka, January 14, 15, 16, 17, 18, 2005. **Drawn.** Toss: Zimbabwe. **Zimbabwe 298** (S. Matsikenyeri 51, H. Masakadza 43, T. Taibu 85*, E. Chigumbura 34; Enamul Haque, jun. 7-95) **and 286** (B. R. M. Taylor 78, T. Taibu 153; Mashrafe bin Mortaza 3-51, Enamul Haque, jun. 5-105); **Bangladesh 211** (Javed Omar 34, Mohammad Rafique 56; D. T. Hondo 6-59) **and 285-5** (Javed Omar 43, Nafis Iqbal 121, Rajin Saleh 56*; T. Panyangara 3-28).

Enamul Haque became the first Bangladesh bowler to take seven wickets in a Test innings, or ten or more in a match; his 12-200 gave him 18 in the series, another Bangladesh record. Taibu's maiden Test hundred could not prevent Bangladesh from winning their first series victory.

THE AUSTRALIANS IN SRI LANKA, 2003-04

PAUL COUPAR

Just six weeks after being shaken at home by India, Australia arrived in Sri Lanka for their first Tests of the post-Waugh era amid whispers about the possible end of their long supremacy.

In fact, the outcome suggested this was not even the beginning of the beginning of the end. Under Ricky Ponting, Steve Waugh's successor as Test captain, Australia inflicted Sri Lanka's first-ever home whitewash in a three-Test series, and won the one-dayers 3–2. Four years earlier, Waugh had come here to suffer defeat and a broken nose, smashed in a fielding accident. This time it was Sri Lanka who lurched into crisis. Their Test captain, Hashan Tillekeratne, resigned. Their governing board, which had undergone five upheavals in as many years, was flirting with financial ruin, while its president, Thilanga Sumathipala, was on remand, mostly under guard in hospital, charged with passport fraud. Worst of all, their match-winner, Muttiah Muralitharan, was reported for chucking.

Still, it was not quite as balmy for Australia, or as bleak for Sri Lanka, as results hinted. None of the one-day games was a thrashing and, in the First Test at Galle, Sri Lanka's plan to parch the pitch and spin out the opposition was one Hayden epic away from success. They were 161 ahead on first innings before a dramatic turnaround. That Test set the pattern. In the Second, at Kandy, Australia scraped only 120 in their first innings, their worst total in six and a half years, but sneaked a win. In the Third, they were on course to leave Sri Lanka a derisory target before Langer and Katich set themselves in concrete at the crease.

The wins were triumphs of self-belief over probability, which dictated that Sri Lanka should have won at least once. On the first two days of the Tests Australia averaged 30 per wicket, and the Sri Lankans nearly 45. But on days three, four and five the Australians averaged more than 42 per wicket, the Sri Lankans less than 22. When the going got tough, Australia got going and Sri Lanka got nervy. "We were just so soft," said Tillekeratne.

He was right. The Sri Lankans lacked self-belief, not least Tillekeratne himself. His captaincy was often reactive and defensive, and lacked Ponting's firmness of purpose. Australian skill was equally decisive, however, in particular their batsmen's blunting of Muralitharan, who had terrorised England into crease-bound pad-play on their recent tour. The Australians used their feet. It took fighter-pilot courage, but it helped neuter the *doosra*, the ball which spat the wrong way, and it opened up scoring opportunities. They hit Muralitharan for 3.10 an over, and fielders stopping runs meant fewer huddling the bat. Murali still took 28 wickets at 23.17 – a record on the losing side in a three-match series – but he was contained. By the Second Test, he was bowling round the wicket to defensive, leg-side fields.

Things soon got far worse for him. As the Australian backpackers, who generated almost all the atmosphere at the Tests, noisily celebrated the clean sweep, referee Chris Broad announced his suspicion that the *doosra* was delivered with an illegal action. Some Sri Lankans alleged an Anglo-Saxon plot to trip Muralitharan, who finished the series on 513 Test wickets, four behind Shane Warne as they raced each other towards Courtney Walsh's world-record 519. The knockers gleefully said it invalidated Murali's whole career. A later biomechanical investigation by the University of Western Australia vindicated neither party, agreeing the *doosra* was illegal, but wondering why he should be singled out. "There are many finger spinners straightening more than the five degrees allowed," said Bruce Elliott, the biomechanics expert who led the investigation, "not just Murali." But the ICC confirmed that he could be no-balled for throwing if he continued to bowl it.

The series itself, unlike previous meetings, had been played in a refreshing "it's-only-a-game" spirit, epitomised by one-day captain Marvan Atapattu's remarkable sportsmanship in recalling Andrew Symonds to the wicket after he was given out lbw. But later it got ugly, especially in high places. Sri Lanka's board claimed (wrongly) that Broad and the Australians had been out "boozing" together. In May, the Sri Lankan prime minister, Mahinda Rajapakse, threatened to sue the ICC; Australia's, John Howard, publicly called Muralitharan a chucker. Embattled and tired, Murali refused to go on the reciprocal tour to Australia four months later.

It was a sad end to what should have been a celebration of two bowlers who had revived the art of spin. Both Murali and Warne began the series approaching 500 Test wickets, and the Great Race became an extraordinary sideshow, heavily pushed by the cash-strapped home board who hoped, mistakenly, it might boost abysmal Test attendances. The race was won by Warne. After his year-long ban for taking a prohibited drug, he returned better than before, ripping his leg-break a touch harder. Helped by receptive pitches, tight support bowling and a lean physique, he took 26 wickets at 20.03, and his control proved crucial on last-day pitches. Without him, Galle and Colombo might have been draws.

Australia's first-innings batting was often awful

But as well as regaining old strengths, Australia showed a few unfamiliar weaknesses. Their team selection seemed wacky. On a green pitch at Kandy they chose a second leggie, only to replace him with a third seamer on a desiccated wicket at Colombo. And Symonds's few overs of off-spin did not justify his selection over Simon Katich, dropped after a century in his last Test at Sydney. Meanwhile, the first-innings batting, which averaged 463 under Waugh, was often awful, scraping just 247 on average. Partly that was down to the pitches: sappy at Kandy, parched to suit Sri Lanka's spinners at Galle and Colombo. Mainly it was down to impatience.

Those failures seemed even odder when set against three glorious second-innings triumphs. Six of Australia's seven centuries came in the second innings, under extreme pressure and in draining heat. Darren Lehmann,

He's behind you! Shane Warne held off Muttiah Muralitharan and became the second player in history to reach 500 Test wickets.

Picture by Hamish Blair, Getty Images

previously a fringe player, was the pick. He scored 375 runs at 62.50 by using his feet and placing neatly or biffing over the in-field. Lehmann said the recent death of his friend David Hookes had changed his view on the importance of cricket and made him unafraid of failure. But all the batsmen except Symonds played match-changing innings.

For Sri Lanka, Chaminda Vaas bowled with subtle variation, especially at Kandy, and deserved more than 11 wickets. And Sanath Jayasuriya scored 294 largely counter-attacking runs at 49.00 and hit the bowling out of its groove. But they relied too heavily on these ageing players, and on Murali. With the uncertainty at board level, development of young players seemed to have been neglected.

It was a tricky series to judge. Should Sri Lanka be praised for getting on top or criticised for not staying there? And just how strong were the Australians? Ponting rightly said they played some of their best cricket for a long time. But they also played some of their flakiest.

AUSTRALIAN TOURING PARTY

R. T. Ponting (*captain*), A. C. Gilchrist (*vice-captain*), J. N. Gillespie, M. L. Hayden, M. S. Kasprowicz, S. M. Katich, J. L. Langer, B. Lee, D. S. Lehmann, S. C. G. MacGill, D. R. Martyn, W. A. Seccombe, A. Symonds, S. K. Warne, B. A. Williams.

Lee left the party during the First Test due to an ankle injury and was replaced by S. W. Tait. M. G. Bevan, M. J. Clarke, B. J. Haddin, I. J. Harvey and G. B. Hogg were part of the one-day squad and were replaced by Langer, Lehmann, MacGill, Seccombe and Warne for the Tests.

Coach: J. M. Buchanan. *Manager:* S. R. Bernard. *Assistant coach/performance analyst:* T. J. Nielsen. *Physiotherapist:* E. L. Alcott. *Physical performance manager:* J. A. Campbell.

AUSTRALIAN TOUR RESULTS

Test matches – Played 3: Won 3.
First-class matches – Played 4: Won 4.
One-day internationals – Played 5: Won 3, Lost 2.
Other non-first-class-match: Played 1: Won 1.

TEST MATCH AVERAGES

SRI LANKA – BATTING AND FIELDING

	T	I	NO	R	HS	100s	50s	Avge	Ct/St
†S. T. Jayasuriya.	3	6	0	294	131	1	2	49.00	2
T. T. Samaraweera.	2	4	1	145	53	0	1	48.33	2
†W. P. U. J. C. Vaas	3	6	2	156	68*	0	1	39.00	1
M. S. Atapattu	3	6	0	212	118	1	0	35.33	1
†H. P. Tillekeratne.	3	6	1	172	74*	0	1	34.40	2
D. P. M. D. Jayawardene . .	3	6	0	185	68	0	1	30.83	6
T. M. Dilshan	3	6	0	184	104	1	0	30.66	1
†K. C. Sangakkara	3	6	0	112	29	0	0	18.66	7/4
M. Muralitharan	3	6	2	55	43	0	0	13.75	4
†D. N. T. Zoysa	2	4	0	8	4	0	0	2.00	1

Played in one Test: U. D. U. Chandana 27, 43 (1 ct); H. D. P. K. Dharmasena 6, 0 (1 ct); †D. A. Gunawardene 13, 9; †H. M. R. K. B. Herath 3, 0 (1 ct); K. S. Lokuarachchi 15, 16.

† *Left-handed batsman.*

BOWLING

	Style	O	M	R	W	BB	5W/i	Avge
M. Muralitharan	OB	209.1	37	649	28	6-59	4	23.17
W. P. U. J. C. Vaas. . . .	LFM	130.2	22	377	11	3-93	0	34.27
D. N. T. Zoysa	LFM	64.3	15	233	6	4-54	0	38.83
H. M. R. K. B. Herath .	SLA	47.2	6	167	4	4-92	0	41.75

Also bowled: U. D. U. Chandana (LBG) 38.3–3–161–2; H. D. P. K. Dharmasena (OB) 44–5–152–2; T. M. Dilshan (OB) 8–4–15–0; S. T. Jayasuriya (SLA) 35.3–3–96–2; K. S. Lokuarachchi (LB) 12–2–33–0; T. T. Samaraweera (OB) 29.3–5–78–1.

AUSTRALIA – BATTING AND FIELDING

	T	I	NO	R	HS	100s	50s	Avge	Ct/St
†D. S. Lehmann	3	6	0	375	153	2	1	62.50	0
D. R. Martyn	3	6	0	333	161	2	0	55.50	2
†M. L. Hayden.	3	6	0	283	130	1	1	47.16	7
†A. C. Gilchrist	3	6	1	201	144	1	0	40.20	11/3
†J. L. Langer	3	6	0	241	166	1	0	40.16	3
R. T. Ponting	3	6	0	198	92	0	1	33.00	1
S. C. G. MacGill	2	3	2	25	17*	0	0	25.00	0
A. Symonds.	2	4	0	53	24	0	0	13.25	4
S. K. Warne.	3	6	0	79	32	0	0	13.16	3
J. N. Gillespie	3	6	2	35	11*	0	0	8.75	1
M. S. Kasprowicz	3	6	1	19	8	0	0	3.80	2

Played in one Test: †S. M. Katich 14, 86 (1 ct); B. A. Williams 0*, 2.

† *Left-handed batsman.*

BOWLING

	Style	O	M	R	W	BB	5W/i	Avge
D. S. Lehmann	SLA	38	4	101	6	3-42	0	16.83
S. K. Warne	LBG	168	37	521	26	5-43	4	20.03
M. S. Kasprowicz	RFM	107.5	20	302	12	4-83	0	25.16
J. N. Gillespie.	RF	110	25	316	10	4-76	0	31.60
S. C. G. MacGill.	LBG	55.2	7	232	5	4-74	0	46.40

Also bowled: S. M. Katich (SLC) 12–1–44–0; A. Symonds (OB) 24–4–85–1; B. A. Williams (RF) 24–5–67–0.

Note: Matches in this section which were not first-class are signified by a dagger.

†At Moratuwa, February 17, 2004. **Australians won by five wickets.** Toss: Sri Lanka Cricket President's XIII. **Sri Lanka Cricket President's XIII 283-8** (50 overs) (W. S. Jayantha 50, J. Mubarak 56); **Australians 284-5** (44.1 overs) (R. T. Ponting 57 retired out).

Each team named 13 players, of whom 11 could bat and 11 field. Three Australians retired out, including Ponting and Andrew Symonds, who launched a massive six through the press-box window en route to 47 in 34 balls.

†SRI LANKA v AUSTRALIA

First One-Day International

At Dambulla, February 20, 2004 (day/night). Australia won by 84 runs. Toss: Australia.

Sri Lanka matched Australia for much of the game but lost badly in the end: the recurring motif of the tour. After 30 overs they were 133 for three, where Australia had been 145 for two. But neither Sangakkara, who tickled behind, nor Jayawardene, beaten in the flight, could turn a fifty into a match-winning innings. Wickets clattered as the tail struggled with an asking-rate rising past ten an over on a slow, grudging pitch. Hogg took five wickets for just three runs in 14 balls. "Sri Lanka have to improve a lot," said Ponting afterwards. Earlier, his side made 262, smashing the ground record, against a team that had played a solitary one-day international in eight months. With the spinners on after six overs in shirt-drenching heat, Australia's openers rotated the strike and scored 104. Solid middle-order contributions were then eclipsed by a spectacular one from Symonds: 37 in 20 balls, including 19 off the last over.

Man of the Match: G. B. Hogg.

Australia

†A. C. Gilchrist c Atapattu b Chandana .	66	M. J. Clarke lbw b Muralitharan	. . . . . .	0
M. L. Hayden run out	40	G. B. Hogg not out		2
*R. T. Ponting c Dilshan b Jayasuriya . .	58	L-b 5, w 5, n-b 1		11
D. R. Martyn c and b Chandana	27			
M. G. Bevan st Kaluwitharana		1/104 (1) 2/114 (2)	(6 wkts, 50 overs) 262	
b Muralitharan .	21	3/189 (4) 4/207 (3)		
A. Symonds not out	37	5/239 (5) 6/239 (7)		

B. Lee, J. N. Gillespie and B. A. Williams did not bat.

Bowling: Vaas 3–0–19–0; Kulasekara 3–0–18–0; Dharmasena 10–0–49–0; Dilshan 5–0–28–0; Muralitharan 10–2–30–2; Chandana 10–0–47–2; Jayasuriya 9–0–66–1.

Sri Lanka

S. T. Jayasuriya run out	8	K. M. D. N. Kulasekara b Hogg		1
†R. S. Kaluwitharana run out	2	M. Muralitharan c Lee b Hogg		0
*M. S. Atapattu b Gillespie	1			
K. C. Sangakkara c Gilchrist b Lee	58	B 1, l-b 2, w 13, n-b 4		20
D. P. M. D. Jayawardene b Symonds . . .	61			
T. M. Dilshan not out	18	1/12 (1) 2/13 (2)	(43.3 overs) 178	
U. D. U. Chandana lbw b Hogg	9	3/24 (3) 4/145 (4)		
W. P. U. J. C. Vaas c Hayden b Hogg. . .	0	5/147 (5) 6/166 (7)		
H. D. P. K. Dharmasena st Gilchrist		7/170 (8) 8/170 (9)		
b Hogg .	0	9/178 (10) 10/178 (11)		

Bowling: Gillespie 6–2–14–1; Lee 8–1–31–1; Williams 5–0–28–0; Hogg 9.3–1–41–5; Clarke 5–0–21–0; Symonds 10–0–40–1.

Umpires: B. F. Bowden (New Zealand) and E. A. R. de Silva.
Third umpire: P. T. Manuel.   Referee: M. J. Procter (South Africa).

†SRI LANKA v AUSTRALIA

Second One-Day International

At Dambulla, February 22, 2004. Sri Lanka won by one run. Toss: Sri Lanka.

Vaas called this thrilling, uplifting one-day international the best of the 230 he had played. With just under ten overs left, it was on a knife-edge. On a tricky re-used pitch, Australia needed 56; the fourth wicket had just gone, but Symonds, capable of settling things in a few blows, looked ominous on ten. The pressure made what happened next the more remarkable. Symonds bottom-edged Dharmasena into his pad and umpire Manuel gave him lbw, but was quickly gripped by doubt. Tentatively, he suggested a recall, a decision he insisted was unconnected with non-striker Gilchrist's glove-hurling dissent. Despite a capacity crowd demanding a series-levelling win, the Sri Lankan captain, Atapattu, called Symonds back. His sportsmanship looked costly: Symonds edged Australia towards victory and they needed eight from the last over. But Vaas confounded Bevan's nous and Symonds's brawn with six pinpoint yorkers, and they finished two short. Sri Lanka should have been out of sight. From 121 without loss after 21 overs, they barely doubled their score, as overambitious batting handed five cheap wickets to Clarke and his occasional left-armers. In reply, Hayden and Ponting added 148 against Sri Lanka's six spinners.

Man of the Match: W. P. U. J. C. Vaas.

Sri Lanka

*M. S. Atapattu run out	47	H. D. P. K. Dharmasena run out	2
S. T. Jayasuriya lbw b Symonds	55	M. Muralitharan not out	2
K. C. Sangakkara c Bevan b Harvey	39		
D. P. M. D. Jayawardene c Ponting b Clarke	38	B 1, l-b 16, w 8, n-b 7	32
T. M. Dilshan b Clarke	11	1/121 (1) 2/122 (2) (49.5 overs) 245	
†R. S. Kaluwitharana run out	0	3/192 (4) 4/216 (3)	
U. D. U. Chandana c Gilchrist b Clarke	4	5/220 (6) 6/225 (7)	
R. P. Arnold lbw b Clarke	10	7/226 (5) 8/236 (9)	
W. P. U. J. C. Vaas c Lee b Clarke	5	9/242 (10) 10/245 (8)	

Bowling: Gillespie 7–0–36–0; Lee 6–0–39–0; Harvey 9–0–38–1; Symonds 10–0–45–1; Hogg 10–1–35–0; Clarke 7.5–0–35–5.

Australia

M. J. Clarke c Chandana b Vaas	0	M. G. Bevan not out	24
M. L. Hayden c Jayawardene b Dharmasena	93	B 1, l-b 7, w 9	17
*R. T. Ponting c Vaas b Chandana	69		
D. R. Martyn c Atapattu b Vaas	5	1/0 (1) 2/148 (3) (5 wkts, 50 overs) 244	
A. Symonds not out	36	3/170 (4) 4/190 (2)	
†A. C. Gilchrist c and b Vaas	0	5/192 (6)	

I. J. Harvey, G. B. Hogg, B. Lee and J. N. Gillespie did not bat.

Bowling: Vaas 10–0–48–3; Dilshan 6–0–32–0; Dharmasena 10–0–40–1; Muralitharan 10–0–49–0; Chandana 9–0–40–1; Arnold 2–0–9–0; Jayasuriya 3–0–18–0.

Umpires: B. F. Bowden (New Zealand) and P. T. Manuel.
Third umpire: M. G. Silva. Referee: M. J. Procter (South Africa).

†SRI LANKA v AUSTRALIA

Third One-Day International

At R. Premadasa Stadium, Colombo, February 25, 2004 (day/night). Australia won by five wickets.
Toss: Sri Lanka.

When Bevan fell in the 38th over, the capacity crowd erupted, expecting drama and hoping for a home win. But Symonds and Clarke made sure they got neither, with a cool-headed match-winning stand of 68. Earlier, Gillespie forced Sri Lanka's top three batsmen to fend fatally, and the score crawled to 54 for four in the 21st over. Only a diligent 80 from Jayawardene and dashing innings from the lower order changed the total from desperate to defensible. Australia's start was almost as bad, with Vaas striking twice in the third over. Martyn and Ponting, in vigorous form en route to his third successive fifty, put on 129, before three quick wickets meant the crowd got going. But so did Symonds and Clarke. For the second match running, Muralitharan went wicketless, supporting Ponting's claim that several Australians could spot his *doosra*.

Man of the Match: J. N. Gillespie.

Sri Lanka

*M. S. Atapattu b Gillespie	3	H. D. P. K. Dharmasena not out	24
S. T. Jayasuriya c Clarke b Gillespie	0	D. N. T. Zoysa not out	0
†K. C. Sangakkara c Hayden b Gillespie	15	B 1, l-b 8, w 3	12
D. P. M. D. Jayawardene run out	80		
R. P. Arnold c Clarke b Hogg	4	1/1 (2) 2/10 (1) (8 wkts, 50 overs) 226	
T. M. Dilshan c Gilchrist b Symonds	30	3/34 (3) 4/54 (5)	
U. D. U. Chandana run out	34	5/112 (6) 6/170 (4)	
W. P. U. J. C. Vaas c Hogg b Kasprowicz	24	7/182 (7) 8/218 (8)	

M. Muralitharan did not bat.

Bowling: Gillespie 10–1–36–3; Kasprowicz 10–2–37–1; Harvey 6–0–29–0; Hogg 10–0–41–1; Clarke 5–0–26–0; Symonds 9–0–48–1.

Australia

†A. C. Gilchrist c Jayawardene b Vaas	0	M. J. Clarke not out	31
M. L. Hayden c Muralitharan b Vaas	3	L-b 4, w 8, n-b 1	13
*R. T. Ponting b Vaas	63		
D. R. Martyn run out	62	1/3 (2) 2/4 (1) (5 wkts, 48.3 overs) 227	
A. Symonds not out	45	3/133 (3) 4/136 (4)	
M. G. Bevan run out	10	5/159 (6)	

I. J. Harvey, G. B. Hogg, M. S. Kasprowicz and J. N. Gillespie did not bat.

Bowling: Vaas 9–2–34–3; Zoysa 7.1–0–37–0; Dharmasena 6.5–0–31–0; Muralitharan 10–0–43–0; Chandana 7–0–36–0; Jayasuriya 8–0–40–0; Dilshan 0.3–0–2–0.

Umpires: B. F. Bowden (New Zealand) and E. A. R. de Silva.
Third umpire: M. G. Silva.   Referee: M. J. Procter (South Africa).

†SRI LANKA v AUSTRALIA

Fourth One-Day International

At R. Premadasa Stadium, Colombo, February 27, 2004 (day/night). Australia won by 40 runs. Toss: Australia. One-day international debut: W. S. Jayantha.

Another capacity crowd trudged into the sticky Colombo night disappointed, debating whether Kasprowicz had won the match, which clinched the series, or Sri Lanka's middle order had thrown it away. Once again the game was in the balance with 20 overs to go. That was almost exclusively thanks to Sangakkara, who peppered the off side, hit six fours in two hectic overs and rushed to his hundred in 106 balls. Local observers considered it his finest one-day innings. But he chased a wide one and no other Sri Lankan matched his fluency. Needing about five an over, they lost seven for 45, thanks to Kasprowicz finding seam movement, flashes outside off (which gave Gilchrist a record-equalling six catches for the fourth time) and a run-out. Australia had also collapsed. Two exquisite swivel-pulls off Vaas highlighted Ponting's form, so good that his final score of 67 – a fourth successive fifty – was a disappointment.

Man of the Match: M. S. Kasprowicz.

Australia

†A. C. Gilchrist c Sangakkara b Zoysa	14	M. S. Kasprowicz c Sangakkara	
M. L. Hayden c Zoysa b Vaas	15	b Chandana	0
*R. T. Ponting lbw b Muralitharan	67	J. N. Gillespie not out	8
D. R. Martyn c Zoysa b Lokuarachchi	1	L-b 3, w 12, n-b 6	21
A. Symonds c Jayantha b Muralitharan	53		
M. G. Bevan c and b Muralitharan	14	1/28 (1) 2/42 (2) 3/62 (4) (47.4 overs) 233	
M. J. Clarke c Dilshan b Chandana	36	4/136 (3) 5/177 (5)	
I. J. Harvey run out	4	6/201 (6) 7/205 (8)	
G. B. Hogg lbw b Chandana	0	8/205 (9) 9/206 (10) 10/233 (7)	

Bowling: Vaas 10–0–45–1; Zoysa 8–0–40–1; Lokuarachchi 8–0–40–1; Muralitharan 10–0–44–3; Jayasuriya 4–0–24–0; Chandana 7.4–0–37–3.

Sri Lanka

*M. S. Atapattu c Bevan b Hogg	19	W. P. U. J. C. Vaas c Gilchrist		
S. T. Jayasuriya c Gilchrist b Kasprowicz	0	b Kasprowicz	0	
†K. C. Sangakkara c Gilchrist		D. N. T. Zoysa lbw b Hogg	1	
b Kasprowicz	101	M. Muralitharan not out	2	
D. P. M. D. Jayawardene c Gilchrist				
b Gillespie	25	L-b 2, w 2	4	
W. S. Jayantha c Gilchrist b Harvey	1			
I. M. Dilshan run out	9	1/0 (2) 2/78 (1) 3/143 (4) (43.4 overs) 193		
U. D. U. Chandana c Gilchrist		4/148 (3) 5/150 (5)		
b Kasprowicz	13	6/158 (6) 7/189 (7)		
K. S. Lokuarachchi lbw b Kasprowicz	18	8/189 (9) 9/190 (8) 10/193 (10)		

Bowling: Gillespie 8–2–20–1; Kasprowicz 9–1–45–5; Harvey 7–0–34–1; Symonds 10–1–47–0; Hogg 6.4–0–32–2; Clarke 3–0–13–0.

Umpires: B. F. Bowden (New Zealand) and T. H. Wijewardene.
Third umpire: P. T. Manuel. Referee: M. J. Procter (South Africa).

†SRI LANKA v AUSTRALIA

Fifth One-Day International

At Sinhalese Sports Club, Colombo, February 29, 2004. Sri Lanka won by three wickets. Toss: Australia.

Too late to save the series, and against too depleted a side to have much psychological impact, Sri Lanka won another fluctuating match. Australia spent much of their innings rebuilding after Zoysa's miserly opening spell of two for 20 from eight overs. His accuracy and zip made scoring difficult, and frustration brought wickets: Haddin smashed him to mid-off, Gilchrist missed a drive, Katich tried for a non-existent second and Clarke top-edged Muralitharan's third delivery. It was soon 120 for six, and Symonds and Hogg could afford few risks, despite a good pitch, as they added a face-saving 76. In reply, Sangakkara's aggressive 37 raised noisy expectation in another capacity crowd. That became anxious quiet as Sri Lanka collapsed to 136 for seven, with 63 still wanted. But while Arnold froze in the spotlight, scratching 23 in 64 balls, Zoysa thrived. He played proper shots from No. 9 to take his side home after being neglected for 19 months before this series.

Man of the Match: D. N. T. Zoysa.   *Man of the Series: A. Symonds.*

Australia

*†A. C. Gilchrist lbw b Zoysa	18	G. B. Hogg not out	35	
B. J. Haddin c Jayasuriya b Zoysa	9	B. Lee not out	1	
M. J. Clarke c Dilshan b Muralitharan	16			
S. M. Katich run out	13	L-b 6, w 7, n-b 1	14	
D. R. Martyn b Chandana	38			
M. G. Bevan c Jayawardene		1/23 (2) 2/34 (1) (7 wkts, 50 overs) 198		
b Muralitharan	14	3/55 (4) 4/86 (3)		
A. Symonds c Arnold b Zoysa	40	5/117 (6) 6/120 (5) 7/196 (7)		

M. S. Kasprowicz and B. A. Williams did not bat.

Bowling: Zoysa 10–3–34–3; Kulasekara 10–0–50–0; Chandana 8–0–38–1; Dilshan 3–0–11–0; Jayasuriya 10–1–24–0; Muralitharan 9–0–35–2.

Sri Lanka

*M. S. Atapattu b Kasprowicz	0	U. D. U. Chandana c Katich b Symonds	4
S. T. Jayasuriya c Williams b Lee	13	D. N. T. Zoysa not out	47
†K. C. Sangakkara b Hogg	37		
D. P. M. D. Jayawardene c Clarke		L-b 6, w 11, n-b 2	19
b Williams	21		—
W. S. Jayantha b Kasprowicz	23	1/2 (1) 2/25 (2) (7 wkts, 47.5 overs) 202
T. M. Dilshan b Symonds	15	3/85 (4) 4/91 (3)
R. P. Arnold not out	23	5/117 (5) 6/126 (6) 7/136 (8)

K. M. D. N. Kulasekara and M. Muralitharan did not bat.

Bowling: Lee 9–1–52–1; Kasprowicz 9–2–20–2; Williams 9–1–29–1; Hogg 7–0–44–1; Clarke 4–0–17–0; Symonds 9.5–2–34–2.

Umpires: B. F. Bowden (New Zealand) and E. A. R. de Silva.
Third umpire: T. H. Wijewardene. Referee: M. J. Procter (South Africa).

At Colombo Cricket Club, Colombo, March 2, 3, 4, 2004. **Australians won by 245 runs.** Toss: Sri Lanka Cricket President's XI. **Australians 484-6 dec.** (R. T. Ponting 116, S. M. Katich 116, D. S. Lehmann 134) **and 250-4 dec.** (J. L. Langer 63, A. Symonds 119*); **Sri Lanka Cricket President's XI 166** (D. A. Gunawardene 70; B. Lee 4-29) **and 323** (T. T. Samaraweera 50, S. K. L. de Silva 92, W. M. G. Ramyakumara 67).

The President of Sri Lanka Cricket, Thilanga Sumathipala, was on remand for alleged passport fraud while the team representing him played here. All the Australians' centuries came at close to a run a ball. Lee's tour ended when he injured his left ankle in the second innings; Warne took 1–21 and 2–79 in his first match for Australia after a year-long drugs ban.

SRI LANKA v AUSTRALIA

First Test Match

At Galle, March 8, 9, 10, 11, 12, 2004. Australia won by 197 runs. Toss: Australia. Test debut: A. Symonds.

After the first innings of this fabulous Test, Sri Lanka's position looked as impregnable as the stone fort that dwarfs the Galle stadium. They had a lead of 161, the world's most complete spinner ready to bowl on an arid pitch, and history overwhelmingly in their favour – only nine Test sides since 1900 had overcome such a deficit and won. Ponting's honeymoon as Test captain looked likely to last around four days.

But Australia turned it round. The last Tests to see such a swing pivoted round a freakishly brilliant spell by Shoaib Akhtar for Pakistan against New Zealand at Wellington ten weeks earlier and a miraculous innings by V. V. S. Laxman for India against Australia at Kolkata in 2000-01. This time it was just hard cricket and self-belief that won it. In horrible heat, Hayden hit a century of little style but match-changing substance, and the middle order ground Sri Lanka into the dust. Warne and MacGill then bowled them out on the last afternoon. But it was Australia's batsmen who manufactured the win.

Australia made four changes to the side that had struggled against India's batsmen at Sydney two months before. Warne, available after a 12-month drugs ban, was predictably, and gladly, welcomed straight back. Kasprowicz was recalled in place of the injured Lee, and Lehmann stepped into Steve Waugh's huge shoes. English-born Andrew Symonds played as an off-spinning all-rounder; had he chosen England, his Test debut would probably have come much earlier. As it was, he had played a record 94 one-day internationals before he displaced poor Simon Katich who was dropped the Test after scoring a century.

THE COMEBACK KINGS

Teams winning a Test after conceding a first-innings lead of 150 or more:

Deficit

291	Australia (256) beat Sri Lanka (547-8 dec.) by 16 runs at Colombo (SSC) . . .	1992-93
274	India (171) beat Australia (445) by 171 runs at Kolkata	2000-01
261	England (325) beat Australia (586) by ten runs at Sydney	1894-95
236	Australia (75) beat South Africa (311) by five wickets at Durban	1949-50
227	England (174) beat Australia (401-9 dec.) by 18 runs at Leeds.	1981
182	India (237) beat Australia (419) by 59 runs at Melbourne	1980-81
177	Australia (190) beat England (367) by 54 runs at Manchester.	1961
171	England (133) beat South Africa (304) by 71 runs at Lord's	1955
170	**Pakistan (196) beat New Zealand (366) by seven wickets at Wellington** . . .	**2003-04**
163	Australia (144) beat England (307) by 72 runs at Sydney	1891-92
161	West Indies (329) beat Australia (490) by one wicket at Bridgetown	1998-99
161	**Australia (220) beat Sri Lanka (381) by 197 runs at Galle**.	**2003-04**
160	Australia (198) beat South Africa (358) by 169 runs at Melbourne	1931-32
158	Australia (348) beat South Africa (506) by 89 runs at Melbourne	1910-11

Note: In 1999-2000, England beat South Africa by two wickets at Centurion after declaring their first innings at 0–0, South Africa's first innings having totalled 248.

Research: Philip Bailey

Sri Lanka began with a clear plan: prepare a bone-dry pitch and pack the side with spinners, five in total. One visiting journalist, looking at the wicket set in a lush outfield, said it was the first time he'd seen a drought 22 yards long and three yards wide. It is not the normal response to a visit from Shane Warne, so it was risky but, for the first two days, it worked. The pitch did turn but only slowly, and too many Australian batsmen were over-keen to make an attacking statement. Lehmann reached the top score of 63 before being flummoxed by Muralitharan's *doosra*, one of his six victims for 59. Australia's 220 looked paltry.

In reply, Sri Lanka showed the patience Australia lacked. After a hot, tough second day they were 132 ahead, with four wickets standing and the match under control. Dilshan, who used his feet and a straight bat to make 104, continued his golden form from the England series. But in fading light he top-edged a pull against the second new ball. It was reward for the persevering attack and it kept the door an inch open for Australia.

On day three, the most gripping of a gripping series, they somehow prised it open. Sri Lanka's last wickets fell quickly, as Samaraweera, the final recognised batsman, made a poor 36 not out, neither shepherding the tail nor playing shots. Then, in blazing afternoon heat, and on a wearing pitch, Australia began the long trek towards safety. Hayden led the way. He put on 91 with Langer and 84 with Ponting, before running him out. It was as compelling as cricket gets: some of the world's best batsmen against Murali. Despite several scrapes, Hayden attacked sensibly and refused to let the bowler settle. By the close, he had 106 of Australia's 193 for two.

Hayden was finally caught at slip on the fourth morning. He had battled more than five hours for 130, using little more than the sweep shot, iron willpower and a multi-

Clean sweep: Matthew Hayden rarely tired of turning the ball behind square on the leg side.

Picture by Hamish Blair, Getty Images

coloured umbrella, brought on to provide welcome shade during breaks in play. Martyn then stockpiled runs unobtrusively, making his first Test hundred in two years. And Lehmann, less studious, followed three balls later. They were so successful that, despite five expensive wickets for Murali (giving him match figures of 11 for 212), Australia could even declare, 351 ahead.

Sri Lanka's spirits had wilted, and they managed just 154. Their demoralised batsmen fell to a masterly display of controlled leg-spin from Warne, in his first post-ban Test. As he approached 500 wickets, the "Warnie Wicket Count", painted on a bedsheet by the travelling Australian fans, ticked on, while the huge sign counting Murali's wickets was stuck on 496. They started the last day level. Atapattu fended a quicker ball – 497. Dilshan played inside the straight one – 498. Jayawardene edged to slip – 499. And finally, at 1.38 p.m., with the Dutch fort and most of Australia behind him, Warne found Tillekeratne's top edge and became only the second man in history, after Courtney Walsh, to 500. The last three wickets were a formality, though Dharmasena provided not only Warne's tenth victim of the match – one behind Murali – but Hayden's seventh catch, equalling the Test record. Australia won by 197 runs: comebacks don't come much more comprehensive.

Man of the Match: M. L. Hayden.

Close of play: First day, Sri Lanka 81-1 (Atapattu 29, Sangakkara 16); Second day, Sri Lanka 352-6 (Samaraweera 21, Chandana 20); Third day, Australia 193-2 (Hayden 106, Martyn 10); Fourth day, Sri Lanka 3-0 (Atapattu 0, Sangakkara 3).

Australia

J. L. Langer c Sangakkara b Dharmasena	12	– lbw b Jayasuriya	32
M. L. Hayden c Chandana b Muralitharan	41	– c Jayawardene b Muralitharan	130
*R. T. Ponting st Sangakkara b Chandana	21	– run out	28
D. R. Martyn c Jayawardene b Dharmasena	42	– c sub (K. S. Lokuarachchi) b Muralitharan	110
D. S. Lehmann b Muralitharan	63	– c and b Muralitharan	129
A. Symonds c Jayawardene b Muralitharan	0	– st Sangakkara b Muralitharan	24
†A. C. Gilchrist c Dharmasena b Muralitharan	4	– lbw b Chandana	0
S. K. Warne c Sangakkara b Vaas	23	– st Sangakkara b Muralitharan	0
J. N. Gillespie not out	4	– not out	11
M. S. Kasprowicz b Muralitharan	1	– not out	3
S. C. G. MacGill lbw b Muralitharan	0		
B 3, l-b 6	9	B 15, l-b 28, n-b 2	45

1/31 (1) 2/62 (2) 3/76 (3) 4/148 (4)   **220**   1/91 (1) 2/175 (3)   (8 wkts dec.) **512**
5/153 (6) 6/163 (7) 7/215 (5)   3/245 (2) 4/451 (4)
8/219 (8) 9/220 (10) 10/220 (11)   5/480 (5) 6/498 (6)
   7/498 (7) 8/498 (8)

Bowling: *First Innings*—Vaas 12–2–39–1; Dharmasena 20–4–52–2, Muralitharan 21.3–5–59–6; Chandana 14–1–59–1; Jayasuriya 1–0–2–0. *Second Innings*—Vaas 27–3–67–0; Dharmasena 24–1–100–0; Muralitharan 56–9–153–5; Dilshan 6–3–9–0; Jayasuriya 14.3–2–38–1; Chandana 24.3–2–102–1.

Sri Lanka

M. S. Atapattu b Gillespie	47	– c Hayden b Warne	16
S. T. Jayasuriya lbw b Warne	35	– (5) c Hayden b MacGill	5
†K. C. Sangakkara c and b Kasprowicz	22	– (2) lbw b Kasprowicz	7
D. P. M. D. Jayawardene c Hayden b Symonds	68	– (3) c Hayden b Warne	21
T. M. Dilshan c Langer b Kasprowicz	104	– (4) lbw b Warne	6
*H. P. Tillekeratne lbw b Warne	33	– c Symonds b Warne	25
T. T. Samaraweera not out	36	– b MacGill	15
U. D. U. Chandana c Gilchrist b Warne	27	– c Langer b MacGill	43
W. P. U. J. C. Vaas c Hayden b MacGill	0	– not out	10
H. D. P. K. Dharmasena c Hayden b Warne	6	– c Hayden b Warne	0
M. Muralitharan c and b Warne	0	– st Gilchrist b MacGill	0
B 2, n-b 1	3	B 4, w 1, n-b 1	6

1/53 (2) 2/92 (3) 3/123 (1) 4/198 (4)   **381**   1/14 (2) 2/41 (1) 3/49 (4)   **154**
5/298 (6) 6/323 (5) 7/369 (8)   4/56 (3) 5/56 (5) 6/89 (7)
8/372 (9) 9/381 (10) 10/381 (11)   7/119 (6) 8/153 (8)
   9/153 (10) 10/154 (11)

Bowling: *First Innings*—Gillespie 28–9–61–1; Kasprowicz 23–3–56–2; Warne 42.4–9–116–5; Symonds 19–3–68–1; MacGill 22–4–69–1; Lehmann 2–0–9–0. *Second Innings*—Warne 15–5–43–5; Gillespie 9–2–20–0; Kasprowicz 5–1–13–1; MacGill 16.2–2–74–4.

Umpires: R. E. Koertzen (South Africa) and D. R. Shepherd (England).
Third umpire: M. G. Silva. Referee: B. C. Broad (England).

---

66 Steve Waugh had predicted in print that Hayden would beat Lara one day. It needed less genius to predict who was most likely to overtake Hayden, and it took Lara only 19 innings."
England in West Indies, page 1033.

SRI LANKA v AUSTRALIA

Second Test Match

At Kandy, March 16, 17, 18, 19, 20, 2004. Australia won by 27 runs. Toss: Australia.

Australia won a thriller, taking the series 2–0. But it could easily have been 1–1: for the second tour in a row, Kandy was not quite dandy for Australia. In 1999-2000, they lost badly after Steve Waugh and Gillespie collided and were helicoptered to hospital. This time they scraped the win – but only after trying to throw it away.

By lunch on day two, both first innings were over. The pitch was not perfect, offering some seam movement, but the batting was horrid. Australia might have bowled first but were deterred by an ill-suited line-up, including two leg-spinners and no third seamer. Instead they batted, but not for long. Only Hayden managed more than 18. Two of the top seven padded up disastrously, two swished and edged, and Lehmann was bowled trying to leg-glance. Their 120 all out was Australia's lowest total yet against Sri Lanka, and their worst overall since they made 104 against Phil Tufnell on a crumbling Oval pitch in 1997.

THE 500 MEN

The three bowlers' records at the moment they took their 500th Test wicket

	Tests	Balls	Runs	Avge	S/R	Personal % of team's wickets
C. A. Walsh	129	28,833	12,336	24.67	57.66	24
S. K. Warne	108	30,201	12,771	25.54	60.40	26
M. Muralitharan . .	87	29,511	11,382	22.76	59.02	38

Sri Lankan smiles were doubly broad because, when Kasprowicz was bowled, local hero Muralitharan had his 500th wicket. Congratulatory banners unfurled in the ground, and firecrackers echoed off the green hillsides as news spread. But it proved a bittersweet game for Murali, partly because Warne had beaten him to 500 in the previous Test and claimed another ten here, and partly because fleet-footed Australian batting in the second innings forced him to retreat into a containing round-the-wicket line. The key battle of the series had been won.

That came later. Australia's feckless first innings had given Sri Lanka what Tillekeratne later called a "chance on a platter". But his batsmen turned up their noses. On a disastrous first afternoon, they plummeted to 92 for seven. The odd jagging ball demanded a straight bat: instead, three of the top four fell playing across the line, and the middle order were undone by Warne's subtleties.

However, on the madcap second morning Australia again offered free gifts. Kasprowicz was given an unusually long spell in search of a trophy fifth wicket, while Warne tossed the ball up and hoped for an outfield catch. Murali finally gave him one, but only after his slogging – which brought him three sixes – and Vaas's strokeplay had eked out 79, a record for Sri Lanka's last wicket. It meant a lead of 91.

That brought out Australia's fighting spirit. Gilchrist, in terrible form, volunteered to replace Ponting (who had ricked his back) at No. 3 and hit ruthlessly straight. He and Martyn put on exactly 200 and Martyn went on, and on... and on. He made a career-best 161, accumulating as assiduously as a squirrel in autumn, though lucky to survive three slip chances, and oversaw the addition of 416. It was the essence of what John Buchanan, Australia's coach, had recently called "Baggy Green cricket": relentless, immune to pressure and ultimately match-winning. When Martyn was last out, after nearly nine hours, shortly before lunch on day four, Sri Lanka faced a target of 352 – identical to Galle, but with two more sessions in hand.

What goes up... While Sanath Jayasuriya was batting, Sri Lanka had every chance of levelling the series at Kandy. Once he was gone, Australia were favourites.
Picture by Hamish Blair, Getty Images

Only two months before, and on a similar improving Kandy pitch, Central Province had scored a world-record 513 to win in the last innings. A reprise looked possible when Sri Lanka were 174 for three during the fourth afternoon and Jayasuriya was bullying MacGill in a shot-a-ball hundred. But, crucially, Jayasuriya cut to the keeper on 131, and late in the evening Warne bowled Dilshan, the last recognised batsman. Both teams faced a nervous night: Sri Lanka needed 51; Australia three wickets.

The Sri Lankan tail spent the evening practising on the outfield, and a bigger-than-normal crowd filed in next morning to cheer them on. Neither made much difference. Ponting set run-saving fields and gambled that Sri Lanka would crack under pressure. They did. The real tension lasted just three overs, when their final hope, Vaas, tried to hit Warne into the jungle past mid-wicket. With four men on the boundary it was a daft end to a superb innings. The last two wickets fell quickly. Warne ended with a fourth successive five-for; Sri Lanka ended distraught at another near-miss; and Ponting ended with a big grin, all the wider for being tinged with relief.

Man of the Match: S. K. Warne.

Close of play: First day, Sri Lanka 92-7 (Vaas 16, Zoysa 0); Second day, Australia 221-2 (Gilchrist 140, Martyn 64); Third day, Australia 320-5 (Martyn 104, Symonds 6); Fourth day, Sri Lanka 301-7 (Vaas 30, Lokuarachchi 13).

Australia

J. L. Langer lbw b Zoysa	3	– c Sangakkara b Zoysa	9
M. L. Hayden lbw b Muralitharan	54	– c and b Vaas	5
*R. T. Ponting lbw b Vaas	10	– (6) c Sangakkara b Vaas	27
D. R. Martyn lbw b Muralitharan	1	– st Sangakkara b Muralitharan	161
D. S. Lehmann b Zoysa	8	– lbw b Vaas	21
A. Symonds c Tillekeratne b Zoysa	6	– (7) lbw b Muralitharan	23
†A. C. Gilchrist c Sangakkara b Zoysa	0	– (3) lbw b Muralitharan	144
S. K. Warne c Muralitharan b Vaas	18	– c Zoysa b Muralitharan	6
J. N. Gillespie c Jayawardene b Muralitharan	8	– c Atapattu b Muralitharan	11
M. S. Kasprowicz b Muralitharan	0	– c Jayawardene b Zoysa	8
S. C. G. MacGill not out	8	– not out	17
B 1, l-b 3	4	B 2, l-b 7, n-b 1	10

1/25 (1) 2/47 (3) 3/50 (4) 4/60 (5)　　　　　120　　1/11 (2) 2/26 (1) 3/226 (3)　　　　　442
5/84 (6) 6/84 (7) 7/86 (2)　　　　　　　　　　　　　4/255 (5) 5/304 (6) 6/360 (7)
8/100 (9) 9/106 (10) 10/120 (8)　　　　　　　　　　7/376 (8) 8/393 (9)
　　　　　　　　　　　　　　　　　　　　　　　　9/408 (10) 10/442 (4)

Bowling: First Innings—Vaas 11.2–5–14–2; Zoysa 16–3–54–4; Muralitharan 15–4–48–4. *Second Innings*—Vaas 33–6–103–3; Muralitharan 50.3–8–173–5; Zoysa 33–11–102–2; Lokuarachchi 12–2–33–0; Jayasuriya 5–0–16–0; Dilshan 1–0–6–0.

Sri Lanka

M. S. Atapattu c Gilchrist b Kasprowicz	9	– lbw b Gillespie	8
S. T. Jayasuriya lbw b Kasprowicz	1	– c Gilchrist b Gillespie	131
D. A. Gunawardene lbw b Kasprowicz	13	– lbw b Kasprowicz	9
†K. C. Sangakkara c Symonds b Gillespie	5	– c and b Warne	29
D. P. M. D. Jayawardene c Symonds b Warne	17	– c Gilchrist b Gillespie	13
*H. P. Tillekeratne c Gilchrist b Warne	16	– (7) c Ponting b Warne	7
T. M. Dilshan lbw b Warne	0	– (6) b Warne	43
W. P. U. J. C. Vaas not out	68	– c Langer b Warne	45
D. N. T. Zoysa c Gilchrist b Kasprowicz	4	– (10) c Gilchrist b Gillespie	0
K. S. Lokuarachchi c Kasprowicz b Warne	15	– (9) lbw b Warne	16
M. Muralitharan c Symonds b Warne	43	– not out	4
B 8, l-b 9, n-b 3	20	B 4, l-b 14, n-b 1	19

1/6 (2) 2/34 (3) 3/39 (1) 4/49 (4)　　　　　211　　1/17 (1) 2/36 (3) 3/98 (4)　　　　　324
5/67 (5) 6/67 (7) 7/88 (6)　　　　　　　　　　　　　4/174 (5) 5/218 (2) 6/239 (7)
8/111 (9) 9/132 (10) 10/211 (11)　　　　　　　　　　7/274 (6) 8/319 (8)
　　　　　　　　　　　　　　　　　　　　　　　　9/320 (10) 10/324 (9)

Bowling: First Innings—Gillespie 12–4–25–1; Kasprowicz 24–5–83–4; Warne 20.1–3–65–5; Symonds 2–1–1–0; MacGill 5–1–20–0. *Second Innings*—Kasprowicz 17–1–55–1; Gillespie 20–1–76–4; Warne 21.1–2–90–5; Symonds 3–0–16–0; MacGill 12–0–69–0.

Umpires: S. A. Bucknor (West Indies) and D. L. Orchard (South Africa).
Third umpire: T. H. Wijewardene. Referee: B. C. Broad (England).

SRI LANKA v AUSTRALIA

Third Test Match

At Sinhalese Sports Club, Colombo, March 24, 25, 26, 27, 28, 2004. Australia won by 121 runs. Toss: Australia.

Within two hours of Australia completing the clean sweep, referee Chris Broad stated his suspicion that Muralitharan's wrong'un was a throw, and the game itself was almost forgotten in the roar of the reignited chucking debate. Broad, the former England Test batsman, claimed to have seen one particularly suspicious delivery during this match;

many suspected he had made up his mind previously and delayed the announcement to minimise disruption to the series.

It was not a bad game, but it suffered for being the last of an already-settled rubber. Australia were again in deep trouble, in effect 92 for five in the second innings, but by now they had amply proved their mental superiority under pressure. So it proved again. Langer and Katich built a do-or-die double-century stand, and the bowlers cut down the last Sri Lankan wicket in the penultimate over. Followers of the series were starting to feel like children jaded by *Boys' Own* comics: no matter how close the scrape, there was an inevitability about the outcome. "We need to show a bit of character when the going gets tough," said Tillekeratne as he pre-empted the selectors by resigning.

The opening three days were played in an eerie near-silence in front of a tiny crowd scarcely more animated than the travelling fans' inflatable wallabies. On the first, a nonchalant century by Lehmann gave Australia control. He was helped by a willingness to use his feet, by Ponting's punchy 92 and by Tillekeratne's cautious captaincy. By the afternoon, the spinners, including Muralitharan, had retreated to defensive 7–2 legside fields, on a pitch offering slow but significant turn. Murali took five wickets, but, in essence, was contained. The humidity was appalling, and Lehmann used his bat as a walking stick as well as a weapon. Even he admitted he was sometimes bored.

Sri Lanka then cancelled out Australia's 401 and took a lead of six. They came out hitting on the second afternoon and reached 50 by the eighth over. Early on, the seamers dropped too short, and later they could not get the ball dry enough to reverse-swing it. But in the first over of the third morning, Gillespie took two in two balls with brutes that slanted in and seamed away, and Kasprowicz snaked an inswinger through Atapattu's drive, ending an elegant century. An imposing 240 for two became 256 for five. But Tillekeratne dug in. There was a bizarre attempt to remove him, when Ponting appealed for hit wicket: replays showed the bail knocked off by Langer, who had crossed the wicket to change fielding position as the batsmen ran a single. He claimed obliviousness and was cleared of bringing the game into disrepute, fuelling the Sri Lankans' sense of injustice when Broad later reported Murali.

> Australian resilience was now almost superhuman

On the fourth morning, Australia's second innings was on the verge of collapse at 98 for five. But the resilience of their batting was now assuming almost superhuman status: they did not collapse. Langer, lucky to escape when caught at short leg on seven, and Katich, in his first Test of the series, were immovable and added 218 in 65 overs. Langer struggled badly, with the humidity, with his own poor form and with crippling cramp. He began, as so often, by scratching like a chicken in a farmyard but eked out 166 in six and three-quarter hours. He had spurred himself on, he later said, by repeating to himself Allan Border's famous goad to Dean Jones in Madras in 1986-87 – "Go off if you like… we'll get a real Australian out here." Katich's five-hour 86 was more assured. Australia set a target of 370 just before the end of the fourth day.

Victory for Sri Lanka was unlikely, a draw was not. But, despite stout resistance, they fell agonisingly short. With 40 overs left, Samaraweera and Jayawardene had defied the dusting pitch and reached 156 for two. But fortune smiled on Australia: as if Warne wasn't enough to cope with, Jayawardene, like Jayasuriya before him, got a bad decision. And after tea Warne finally broke through with four wickets. It had been grim work because of the heat, because Ponting was reluctant to crowd the bat and because there was no second main spinner. But Kasprowicz, persevering and perspiring, finally took the last wicket with eight balls left. It was a suitably close end to the least one-sided of whitewashes.

Man of the Match: D. S. Lehmann.   *Man of the Series:* S. K. Warne.

Close of play: First day, Australia 314-6 (Lehmann 104, Warne 7); Second day, Sri Lanka 239-2 (Atapattu 109, Jayawardene 29); Third day, Australia 80-3 (Langer 29); Fourth day, Sri Lanka 18-0 (Atapattu 5, Jayasuriya 13).

Australia

	First Innings		Second Innings	
J. L. Langer c Dilshan b Vaas	19	– b Vaas	166
M. L. Hayden c sub (U. D. U. Chandana) b Samaraweera	25	– lbw b Vaas	28
*R. T. Ponting c Muralitharan b Vaas	92	– c Samaraweera b Herath	20
D. R. Martyn c Sangakkara b Vaas	14	– (5) lbw b Vaas	5
D. S. Lehmann c Jayasuriya b Muralitharan	153	– (6) c Sangakkara b Muralitharan	1
S. M. Katich c and b Muralitharan	14	– (7) lbw b Muralitharan	86
†A. C. Gilchrist c Jayasuriya b Muralitharan	22	– (8) not out	31
S. K. Warne lbw b Muralitharan	32	– (9) c Samaraweera b Herath	0
J. N. Gillespie c Tillekeratne b Muralitharan	0	– (4) c Jayawardene b Muralitharan	1
M. S. Kasprowicz b Jayasuriya	4	– run out	3
B. A. Williams not out	0	– c and b Herath	2
B 13, l-b 9, n-b 4	26	B 11, l-b 11, w 4, n-b 6	32
	401		**375**

1/43 (1) 2/60 (2) 3/96 (4) 4/217 (3)   401
5/244 (6) 6/299 (7) 7/376 (8)
8/380 (9) 9/387 (10) 10/401 (5)

1/40 (2) 2/79 (3) 3/80 (4)   375
4/89 (5) 5/98 (6) 6/316 (1)
7/341 (7) 8/346 (9)
9/368 (10) 10/375 (11)

Bowling: *First Innings*—Vaas 26–3–93–3; Zoysa 3.3–1–23–0; Samaraweera 14.3–1–38–1; Muralitharan 37.1–6–123–5; Herath 23–5–75–0; Jayasuriya 11–1–27–1. *Second Innings*—Vaas 21–3–61–2; Zoysa 12–0–54–0; Muralitharan 29–5–93–3; Herath 24.2–1–92–4; Samaraweera 15–4–40–0; Jayasuriya 4–0–13–0; Dilshan 1–1–0–0.

Sri Lanka

	First Innings		Second Innings	
M. S. Atapattu b Kasprowicz	118	– b Kasprowicz	14
S. T. Jayasuriya c Gillespie b Lehmann	71	– c Katich b Lehmann	51
†K. C. Sangakkara c Gilchrist b Lehmann	22	– (5) b Warne	27
D. P. M. D. Jayawardene c Gilchrist b Gillespie	29	– c Gilchrist b Warne	37
T. M. Dilshan b Gillespie	0	– (6) c Martyn b Warne	31
*H. P. Tillekeratne not out	74	– (7) lbw b Gillespie	17
T. T. Samaraweera c Gilchrist b Gillespie	41	– (3) st Gilchrist b Lehmann	53
W. P. U. J. C. Vaas b Warne	24	– lbw b Warne	9
D. N. T. Zoysa st Gilchrist b Warne	3	– b Warne	1
H. M. R. K. B. Herath c Martyn b Warne	3	– lbw b Kasprowicz	0
M. Muralitharan c Warne b Kasprowicz	8	– not out	0
B 4, l-b 7, w 1, n-b 2	14	B 4, l-b 1, w 1, n-b 2	8
	407		**248**

1/134 (2) 2/175 (3) 3/240 (4) 4/240 (5)   407
5/256 (5) 6/327 (7) 7/378 (8)
8/381 (9) 9/390 (10) 10/407 (11)

1/45 (1) 2/92 (2) 3/156 (3)   248
4/181 (4) 5/191 (5) 6/232 (6)
7/245 (7) 8/247 (9)
9/248 (8) 10/248 (10)

Bowling: *First Innings*—Gillespie 23–3–96–3; Kasprowicz 22.1–5–58–2; Williams 19–5–48–0; Warne 36–7–115–2; Lehmann 19–2–50–3; Katich 8–0–29–0. *Second Innings*—Gillespie 18–6–38–1; Kasprowicz 16.4–5–37–2; Warne 33–11–92–4; Williams 5–0–19–0; Lehmann 17–2–42–3; Katich 4–1–15–0.

Umpires: S. A. Bucknor (West Indies) and D. L. Orchard (South Africa).
Third umpire: P. T. Manuel.   Referee: B. C. Broad (England).

THE SOUTH AFRICANS IN NEW ZEALAND, 2003-04

COLIN BRYDEN

South Africa's tour of New Zealand started and ended with victories. But in between it was tough going for a team who seldom lived up to their ranking as the second-best in Test and one-day cricket. New Zealand, on the other hand, proved themselves a competent, well-organised side able to shrug off the absence through injury of two leading players: the fast bowler, Shane Bond, and the experienced batsman, Nathan Astle.

The South Africans left for New Zealand just three days after completing Test and one-day series victories over West Indies at home. Coming at the end of a period of almost uninterrupted international cricket stretching back to August 2002, it was perhaps one tour too many. South Africa took the opening one-dayer, but New Zealand won the remaining five – the first time they had taken a series off the South Africans in either form of cricket.

The First Test, played on a poor pitch at Hamilton, was drawn, but a New Zealand series double was distinctly possible after their convincing win at Auckland. This was another first for New Zealand, who had never before defeated South Africa in a home Test. And there were more firsts, too: Stephen Fleming's side totalled 595, Scott Styris hit 170 and Chris Martin grabbed 11 for 180 – all uncharted waters for New Zealand against South Africa.

But at Wellington, where the South African bowlers found conditions more to their liking than the slow surfaces of Hamilton and Auckland, they squared the series. Graeme Smith, the South African captain, made a match-winning unbeaten century in the fourth innings after they had been set 234.

Coming of age: Jacob Oram (*left*) and Jacques Rudolph, two stars of the series.
Pictures by Clive Rose and Touchline, Getty Images

It was a particularly satisfying finish to the tour for Smith. In the early matches, his inexperience was exploited by Fleming, who launched a sledging campaign against him, and later said it had been a deliberate tactic to disconcert his opponent. Experience apart, Fleming held at least two more aces: his all-rounders performed much better than their counterparts, while Martin was the only bowler on either side able to deliver sustained bursts of wicket-taking deliveries.

During the Test series, six South African batsmen averaged over 50 but their last five, so long a guaranteed source of runs, suffered a rare collective failure. By contrast, Chris Cairns and Jacob Oram, who finished the series batting at Nos 7 and 8, were two of New Zealand's stars. The tall, phlegmatic Oram, who bats left-handed and bowls right, gave notice that he could become one of the finest all-rounders in the game.

Martin, recalled to the Test side at the age of 29 after an absence of almost two years, was a revelation. A record of 34 wickets at around 35 from 11 Tests did not suggest anything special, but he had prospered in domestic cricket and John Bracewell, the New Zealand coach, believed his ability to swing the ball away from left-handers would be valuable against a side with three in the top five. In any case, the Martin who lined up at Eden Park was a different proposition from the string-bean who made his debut against South Africa on New Zealand's 2000-01 tour, having added 9kg in weight and an extra yard or so of pace.

The drop-in surfaces were a mystery

South Africa made plenty of runs but not always when they needed them most: Smith and Herschelle Gibbs twice shared century opening partnerships, only to see the advantage dissipated. Jacques Rudolph did come of age with two excellent unbeaten innings: 154 in the second innings at Auckland and 93 in the first at Wellington, batting at No. 3. And Jacques Kallis maintained the form that had brought him four hundreds against West Indies, cracking his fifth in successive Tests at Hamilton, while Gary Kirsten made his last series a memorable one. Having revealed before the Tests began that he would retire at the end of the tour, he made a century at Hamilton, failed twice at Auckland (where he became the first South African to play in 100 Tests), but shared a match-clinching stand with Smith in his final innings.

New Zealand's batting strength came from No. 4 down, with Styris outstanding. He adapted his style to the demands of each game, in the First Test playing a long, patient innings, and in the Second setting up New Zealand's big total with sparkling strokeplay.

South Africa's attack lacked penetration: Makhaya Ntini and Shaun Pollock both looked stale, and the back-up bowling was largely unimpressive. The exception was Nicky Boje, who bowled his left-arm spin effectively in the victory at Wellington. However, New Zealand's slow left-armer, Daniel Vettori, could manage only four expensive victims in the first innings of the series – and then nothing more.

Throughout the series, pitches were a talking point. The drop-in surfaces used at rugby-cum-cricket grounds such as Auckland's Eden Park proved as much of a mystery to the home team as the tourists, while the condition of the pitch in Hamilton was plain unsatisfactory – so bad the umpires considered calling the game off prematurely.

SOUTH AFRICAN TOURING PARTY

G. C. Smith (*captain*), M. V. Boucher (*vice-captain*), P. R. Adams, N. Boje, H. H. Dippenaar, H. H. Gibbs, J. H. Kallis, G. Kirsten, L. Klusener, N. D. McKenzie, J. A. Morkel, A. Nel, M. Ntini, R. J. Peterson, S. M. Pollock, A. G. Prince, J. A. Rudolph, D. J. Terbrugge, M. van Jaarsveld.

M. Ngam was originally selected but withdrew because of injury and was replaced, for the Test series only, by Terbrugge. At the end of the one-day series, Adams, Kirsten, McKenzie and van Jaarsveld replaced Dippenaar, Klusener, Peterson and Prince.

Coach: E. O. Simons. *Manager:* T. J. Southey. *Assistant coach:* V. A. Barnes. *Physiotherapist:* S. Jabaar.

SOUTH AFRICAN TOUR RESULTS

Test matches – Played 3: Won 1, Lost 1, Drawn 1.
First-class matches – Played 4: Won 1, Lost 1, Drawn 2.
One-day internationals – Played 6: Won 1, Lost 5.
Other non first-class match – Played 1: Won 1.

TEST MATCH AVERAGES

NEW ZEALAND – BATTING AND FIELDING

	T	I	NO	R	HS	100s	50s	Avge	Ct
†J. D. P. Oram	3	4	1	283	119*	1	1	94.33	3
S. B. Styris	3	5	1	321	170	1	2	80.25	1
C. L. Cairns	3	4	0	296	158	1	1	74.00	0
B. B. McCullum	3	5	1	147	57	0	2	36.75	9
†S. P. Fleming	3	5	1	101	31*	0	0	25.25	4
†M. H. Richardson	3	5	0	110	45	0	0	22.00	1
†D. L. Vettori	3	4	1	66	53	0	1	22.00	0
M. H. W. Papps	3	6	1	86	59	0	1	17.20	5
C. S. Martin	2	3	2	2	1*	0	0	2.00	0

Played in two Tests: C. D. McMillan 19, 82 (2 ct); D. R. Tuffey 0, 13 (1 ct). Played in one Test: M. J. Mason 3, 0; M. S. Sinclair 74, 21; P. J. Wiseman 36.

† *Left-handed batsman.*

BOWLING

	Style	O	M	R	W	BB	5W/i	Avge
C. S. Martin	RFM	92.2	20	300	18	6-76	3	16.66
C. L. Cairns	RFM	94.2	16	296	9	4-60	0	32.88
J. D. P. Oram	RFM	119.3	36	256	7	2-60	0	36.57
S. B. Styris	RM	75	23	221	3	2-46	0	73.66
D. L. Vettori	SLA	146.2	26	454	4	4-158	0	113.50

Also bowled: C. D. McMillan (RM) 10.1–1–23–1; M. J. Mason (RFM) 22–5–105–0; D. R. Tuffey (RFM) 69–22–144–2; P. J. Wiseman (OB) 31–5–122–2.

SOUTH AFRICA – BATTING AND FIELDING

	T	I	NO	R	HS	100s	50s	Avge	Ct/St
†J. A. Rudolph	3	6	2	336	154*	1	2	84.00	0
J. H. Kallis	3	6	1	354	150*	1	2	70.80	2
†G. C. Smith	3	6	1	290	125*	1	1	58.00	1
H. H. Gibbs.	3	6	0	321	80	0	3	53.50	1
†G. Kirsten	3	6	1	250	137	1	1	50.00	0
†N. Boje	2	3	1	61	25	0	0	30.50	2
N. D. McKenzie	2	4	0	89	52	0	1	22.25	0
M. V. Boucher	3	4	0	36	22	0	0	9.00	7/1
S. M. Pollock.	3	4	0	35	10	0	0	8.75	2
M. Ntini	3	4	0	31	21	0	0	7.75	0

Played in two Tests: A. Nel 4*, 0 (1 ct). Played in one Test: P. R. Adams 7; D. J. Terbrugge 0, 2; M. van Jaarsveld 59, 13* (3 ct).

† *Left-handed batsman.*

BOWLING

	Style	O	M	R	W	BB	5W/i	Avge
N. Boje	SLA	75.4	11	248	9	4-65	0	27.55
S. M. Pollock	RFM	123.3	25	382	13	4-98	0	29.38
J. H. Kallis	RFM	56	13	183	5	3-71	0	36.60
M. Ntini.	RF	115	28	343	7	3-110	0	49.00
A. Nel	RFM	79	22	241	4	2-58	0	60.25

Also bowled: P. R. Adams (SLC) 48–12–120–2; N. D. McKenzie (RM) 3–0–9–0; J. A. Rudolph (LBG) 11–0–46–0; G. C. Smith (OB) 7–0–33–1; D. J. Terbrugge (RFM) 22–4–93–0.

Note: Matches in this section which were not first-class are signified by a dagger.

†At Hamilton, February 11, 2004 (day/night). **South Africans won by six wickets.** Toss: Northern Districts. **Northern Districts 114** (42.3 overs); **South Africans 115-4** (17.2 overs).

†NEW ZEALAND v SOUTH AFRICA

First One-Day International

At Auckland, February 13, 2004 (day/night). South Africa won by five wickets. Toss: South Africa. One-day international debut: M. H. W. Papps.

New Zealand, sent in on a slow, drop-in pitch, never really got going. Fleming did hit Nel for a four and six in the tenth over, but by the end of the next he had been run out by a direct hit from Ntini, fielding at short fine leg. Styris and Cairns added 91 for the fifth wicket, though both departed as they looked to lift the tempo. In reply, the South African openers laid an ideal foundation, allowing Dippenaar to play a solid anchor innings. Even so, the finish was tense: two wickets fell late on and Pollock struggled to make contact in the last over before South Africa slithered home with two balls to spare.

Man of the Match: G. C. Smith.

New Zealand

M. H. W. Papps c Boucher b Ntini	14	D. L. Vettori run out		6
*S. P. Fleming run out	30	K. D. Mills not out		1
H. J. H. Marshall c Boucher b Ntini	7	B 1, l-b 3, w 4, n-b 1		9
S. B. Styris c Ntini b Nel	60			—
C. D. McMillan c Boucher b Klusener	9	1/45 (2) 2/52 (1)	(8 wkts, 50 overs)	225
C. L. Cairns b Nel	58	3/55 (3) 4/79 (5)		
J. D. P. Oram c Nel b Klusener	15	5/170 (4) 6/191 (6)		
†B. B. McCullum not out	16	7/202 (7) 8/222 (9)		

D. R. Tuffey did not bat.

Bowling: Pollock 10–0–33–0; Ntini 10–1–41–2; Nel 10–1–42–2; Klusener 9–0–39–2; Peterson 8–0–42–0; Kallis 3–0–24–0.

South Africa

*G. C. Smith b Cairns	72	S. M. Pollock not out		5
H. H. Gibbs c McCullum b Vettori	43	B 2, l-b 4, w 6		12
J. H. Kallis lbw b Vettori	26			—
H. H. Dippenaar not out	44	1/86 (2) 2/149 (1)	(5 wkts, 49.4 overs)	226
J. A. Rudolph c and b Styris	24	3/149 (3) 4/209 (5)		
†M. V. Boucher b Tuffey	0	5/215 (6)		

L. Klusener, R. J. Peterson, M. Ntini and A. Nel did not bat.

Bowling: Tuffey 8.4–0–34–1; Mills 7–0–42–0; Oram 10–1–44–0; Vettori 10–1–37–2; Styris 10–1–35–1; Cairns 4–0–28–1.

Umpires: S. J. Davis (Australia) and D. B. Cowie.
Third umpire: A. L. Hill. Referee: G. R. Viswanath (India).

†NEW ZEALAND v SOUTH AFRICA

Second One-Day International

At Christchurch, February 17, 2004 (day/night). New Zealand won by five wickets. Toss: South Africa.

Rain meant the covers stayed on for most of the morning and delayed the start by 30 minutes. There was extravagant early movement off another drop-in pitch in a rugby stadium – and Smith's decision to bat seemed unwise. But he played a fighting innings, was well supported by the South African middle order, and 132 runs came from the last 20 overs. Ntini then struck twice in his first three overs before Fleming took over. He played superbly to make his sixth one-day international century, all of which had anchored successful run-chases. In the process, he became the first New Zealander to 6,000 one-day international runs. McMillan struck the ball firmly, and his century partnership with Fleming ensured New Zealand were always in touch with the required rate.

Man of the Match: S. P. Fleming.

South Africa

*G. C. Smith c Tuffey b Cairns	80	N. Boje lbw b Mills		2
H. H. Gibbs lbw b Mills	0	M. Ntini not out		9
J. H. Kallis b Tuffey	6	B 1, l-b 3, w 2, n-b 4		10
H. H. Dippenaar lbw b Vettori	36			—
J. A. Rudolph c Tuffey b Styris	42	1/1 (2) 2/28 (3)	(8 wkts, 50 overs)	253
†M. V. Boucher c and b Cairns	40	3/107 (4) 4/161 (5)		
L. Klusener c Cairns b Tuffey	8	5/204 (1) 6/218 (6)		
S. M. Pollock not out	20	7/223 (7) 8/231 (9)		

A. Nel did not bat.

Bowling: Tuffey 10–1–47–2; Mills 8–1–36–2; Oram 10–1–44–0; Cairns 8–0–35–2; Vettori 8–0–42–1; Styris 6–0–45–1.

New Zealand

M. H. W. Papps c Pollock b Ntini	2	C. L. Cairns not out	10
*S. P. Fleming c Nel b Ntini	108	B 1, l-b 6, w 9, n-b 5	21
†B. B. McCullum c Boucher b Ntini	2		
H. J. H. Marshall c Rudolph b Klusener	18	1/8 (1) 2/19 (3) (5 wkts, 45.1 overs)	255
S. B. Styris c Gibbs b Kallis	24	3/66 (4) 4/124 (5)	
C. D. McMillan not out	70	5/226 (2)	

J. D. P. Oram, D. L. Vettori, K. D. Mills and D. R. Tuffey did not bat.

Bowling: Pollock 8–0–42–0; Ntini 10–1–45–3; Klusener 8–0–55–1; Nel 7.1–1–45–0; Boje 7–0–41–0; Kallis 5–0–20–1.

Umpires: S. J. Davis (Australia) and A. L. Hill.
Third umpire: G. A. Baxter. Referee: G. R. Viswanath (India).

†NEW ZEALAND v SOUTH AFRICA

Third One-Day International

At Westpac Stadium, Wellington, February 20, 2004 (day/night). New Zealand won by five runs. Toss: South Africa. One-day international debut: J. A. Morkel.

This match had a soggy beginning but a fiery end. Floods were affecting the Wellington area, and heavy rain was falling the day before the game. The groundsman's task was made more difficult by the need to replace 740 square metres of turf damaged during a David Bowie concert less than a week before. Even though a helicopter aided the drying process, the match, reduced to a 38-over affair, began two and a half hours late. Papps, who made his first international half-century, and Fleming gave New Zealand a good start before South Africa fought back strongly, despite losing Pollock with a groin strain. Smith completed Pollock's over and bowled his off-spin steadily, though he kept himself on one over too long: the 35th cost 23. McCullum and Styris hit another 46 off the remaining three overs and shared an unbeaten stand of 84 from just 44 balls. Smith and Gibbs gave South Africa a chance, but New Zealand took control as five wickets fell between the 21st and 26th overs. When Mills began the last over, the South Africans needed a seemingly impossible 27. That became 18 off three balls, then six off one as Pollock slammed sixes over extra cover and mid-wicket. One more would do it. But Mills got his length right for the final ball, and Pollock could not score off a yorker.

Man of the Match: S. B. Styris.

New Zealand

M. H. W. Papps c Boucher b Kallis	67	†B. B. McCullum not out	41
*S. P. Fleming c Prince b Boje	43	L-b 9, w 6, n-b 2	17
C. L. Cairns run out	20		
J. D. P. Oram c Kallis b Smith	20	1/100 (2) 2/137 (3) (5 wkts, 38 overs)	254
S. B. Styris not out	45	3/163 (4) 4/165 (1)	
C. D. McMillan run out	1	5/170 (6)	

H. J. H. Marshall, D. L. Vettori, K. D. Mills and D. R. Tuffey did not bat.

Bowling: Pollock 5.5–1–8–0; Nel 5–0–38–0; Kallis 5–0–45–1; Ntini 6–0–48–0; Morkel 5–0–21–0; Boje 7–0–49–1; Smith 4.1–0–36–1.

South Africa

*G. C. Smith c Fleming b Styris	43	N. Boje run out	24
H. H. Gibbs c Cairns b Styris	69	S. M. Pollock not out	29
J. H. Kallis c McCullum b Vettori	16	L-b 5, w 2, n-b 2	9
J. A. Morkel run out	6		
H. H. Dippenaar c Fleming b Cairns	8	1/95 (1) 2/134 (3) (7 wkts, 38 overs)	249
†M. V. Boucher c and b Vettori	0	3/140 (2) 4/142 (4)	
A. G. Prince not out	45	5/142 (6) 6/153 (5) 7/203 (8)	

M. Ntini and A. Nel did not bat.

Bowling: Tuffey 5–1–38–0; Mills 7–0–56–0; Oram 6–0–41–0; Styris 8–0–44–2; Vettori 8–1–41–2; Cairns 4–0–24–1.

Umpires: S. J. Davis (Australia) and A. L. Hill.
Third umpire: G. A. Baxter.   Referee: G. R. Viswanath (India).

†NEW ZEALAND v SOUTH AFRICA

Fourth One-Day International

At Dunedin, February 25, 2004. New Zealand won by six wickets. Toss: New Zealand.

This game was planned for the day before, when Smith won the toss and decided to field, but rain and ferocious wind prevented any play on a bitterly cold day. It was not much better 22 hours later when Fleming won the toss and also chose to field. After a slow start by South Africa, Boje and Rudolph shared a fifth-wicket stand of 84 off 75 balls, but a total of 259 was not enough on a good pitch. Marshall, who put on 126 for the third wicket with Styris, anchored the innings before Cairns made sure with a flurry of big hitting, including three sixes, towards the end. Victory meant New Zealand, 3–1 up, were guaranteed a share of the series. However, the game was perhaps of as much consequence to administrators as players. Debate over whether the first day's toss constituted the start of the match caused the ICC to declare in July that in future it should do so, and all one-day internationals abandoned after the toss should count in the records. This game did not. Under NZC regulations, if the match had started on the first day, it would have continued on the second, rather than being superseded by a new match and new toss. The fresh start enabled Pollock, unfit at the first toss, to play.

Man of the Match: H. J. H. Marshall.

South Africa

*G. C. Smith c McCullum b Oram	37	
H. H. Gibbs lbw b Mason	16	
J. H. Kallis c Cairns b Oram	13	
H. H. Dippenaar b Cairns	18	
N. Boje b Styris	50	
J. A. Rudolph not out	70	
†M. V. Boucher c McMillan b Oram . . .	35	

S. M. Pollock c Vettori b Mills	5
L. Klusener not out	3
L-b 6, w 3, n-b 3	12

M. Ntini and A. Nel did not bat.

1/29 (2) 2/53 (3)   (7 wkts, 50 overs) 259
3/78 (1) 4/100 (4)
5/184 (5) 6/248 (7) 7/255 (8)

Bowling: Mason 10–1–46–1; Mills 10–1–53–1; Oram 10–1–51–3; Cairns 10–1–42–1; Vettori 5–0–28–0; Styris 5–0–33–1.

New Zealand

M. H. W. Papps c Boje b Ntini	29	
*S. P. Fleming c Pollock b Boje	51	
H. J. H. Marshall c Kallis b Ntini	74	
S. B. Styris c Klusener b Nel	69	
C. D. McMillan not out	6	

C. L. Cairns not out	29
L-b 2, w 2, n-b 2	6

1/71 (1) 2/102 (2)   (4 wkts, 49 overs) 264
3/228 (4) 4/230 (3)

J. D. P. Oram, †B. B. McCullum, D. L. Vettori, K. D. Mills and M. J. Mason did not bat.

Bowling: Pollock 10–2–33–0; Nel 10–0–60–1; Ntini 10–1–63–2; Klusener 8–0–39–0; Kallis 5–0–32–0; Boje 6–0–35–1.

Umpires: R. B. Tiffin (Zimbabwe) and A. L. Hill.
Third umpire: G. A. Baxter.   Referee: G. R. Viswanath (India).

†NEW ZEALAND v SOUTH AFRICA

Fifth One-Day International

At Auckland, February 29, 2004. New Zealand won by two runs (D/L method). Toss: South Africa.
Rain reduced this game to a 33-over contest played on the reserve day. Fleming unluckily fell to the only delivery he faced – the ball deflected off his thigh pad – and New Zealand were in trouble when Harris walked out at 73 for five. Recalled mainly for his bowling on slow pitches, he made an invaluable contribution with the bat before becoming Pollock's first victim of the series in the last over of the innings. Gibbs attacked from the word go, but fell to a diving catch by Harris at backward point. Klusener was aggressive, too, and South Africa had reached 40 for one in the sixth over, well ahead of the rate, when he was caught at deep mid-wicket. However, just 13 runs came in the next seven overs, and the ploy of using Morkel as a second pinch-hitter did not come off. More rain then cut a further four overs from the innings, leaving South Africa to get another 107 from 13.2 overs. As in Wellington, Mills bowled the last over, and, as in Wellington, caused New Zealand some anxiety. This time, South Africa needed 28, and looked out of it after managing just one from two balls. Then Boucher hit two sixes – one off a no-ball – to make victory possible. But the next delivery yielded only a single, and although Kallis hit the last two for six and four, New Zealand narrowly secured the series.

Man of the Match: C. Z. Harris.

New Zealand

H. J. H. Marshall b Ntini	18	D. L. Vettori not out	19
*S. P. Fleming c Kallis b Ntini	0	K. D. Mills not out	5
C. L. Cairns c Smith b Morkel	28	B 1, l-b 5, w 2, n-b 4	12
S. B. Styris c Smith b Klusener	16		
C. D. McMillan b Klusener	7	1/3 (2) 2/34 (1) (8 wkts, 33 overs) 193	
J. D. P. Oram run out	22	3/61 (4) 4/73 (5)	
C. Z. Harris c and b Pollock	55	5/73 (3) 6/127 (6)	
†B. B. McCullum b Ntini	11	7/154 (8) 8/182 (7)	

D. R. Tuffey did not bat.

Bowling: Pollock 7–0–36–1; Ntini 7–1–47–3; Klusener 6–0–30–2; Morkel 7–0–41–1; Boje 5–0–25–0; Kallis 1–0–8–0.

South Africa

*G. C. Smith b Oram	15	†M. V. Boucher not out	48
H. H. Gibbs c Harris b Tuffey	13	L-b 2, w 5, n-b 1	8
L. Klusener c Smith b Oram	14		
J. A. Morkel b Cairns	11	1/17 (2) 2/40 (3) (5 wkts, 29 overs) 175	
J. H. Kallis not out	58	3/48 (1) 4/64 (4)	
H. H. Dippenaar b Cairns	8	5/86 (6)	

J. A. Rudolph, S. M. Pollock, N. Boje and M. Ntini did not bat.

Bowling: Tuffey 6–0–37–1; Mills 6–1–63–0; Oram 6–2–20–2; Cairns 6–0–22–2; Harris 4–0–20–0; Styris 1–0–11–0.

Umpires: R. B. Tiffin (Zimbabwe) and D. B. Cowie.
Third umpire: G. A. Baxter.   Referee: G. R. Viswanath (India).

> **"**An injury list of freakish proportions had reduced the bowling attack to a skeleton service."
>
> The New Zealanders in England, page 445.

†NEW ZEALAND v SOUTH AFRICA

Sixth One-Day International

At Napier, March 2, 2004. New Zealand won by five wickets. Toss: South Africa.

Smith won the toss for the fifth time in six matches, and again made the wrong decision. (In fact he called right at Dunedin, too, but the game was washed out and Fleming won the toss on the reserve day.) This time he took first use of a pitch that looked good for batting but actually gave the New Zealand seamers assistance. An early finish seemed likely while South Africa were floundering to 29 for five, then 40 for six. Prince and Klusener repaired some damage, though the highest stand – a South African tenth-wicket record of 67 – came from Morkel and the hard-hitting Ntini. In reply, Papps, who had heard the previous day that he would be in New Zealand's Test squad for the first time, played a sound, technically correct innings and ensured a comfortable win.

Man of the Match: M. H. W. Papps.

South Africa

*G. C. Smith c McCullum b Tuffey	9	J. A. Morkel not out		23
H. H. Gibbs c McCullum b Mason	3	M. Ntini not out		42
J. H. Kallis c McCullum b Mason	0			
J. A. Rudolph c Marshall b Tuffey	3	B 1, l-b 3, w 7, n-b 1		12
A. G. Prince c and b Oram	47			
†M. V. Boucher c Fleming b Tuffey	0	1/8 (2) 2/11 (3)	(9 wkts, 50 overs)	186
S. M. Pollock c McCullum b Oram	7	3/15 (1) 4/20 (4)		
L. Klusener run out	35	5/29 (6) 6/40 (7)		
R. J. Peterson c McCullum b Oram	5	7/103 (8) 8/114 (5) 9/119 (9)		

Bowling: Tuffey 10–1–35–3; Mason 10–1–35–2; Oram 10–2–24–3; Cairns 7–0–33–0; Vettori 10–0–25–0; Harris 1–0–14–0; Styris 2–0–16–0.

New Zealand

M. H. W. Papps not out	92	C. Z. Harris not out		22
*S. P. Fleming run out	32	B 1, l-b 5, w 4, n-b 5		15
H. J. H. Marshall b Morkel	3			
S. B. Styris c Boucher b Pollock	10	1/58 (2) 2/63 (3)	(5 wkts, 46 overs)	190
C. L. Cairns b Peterson	10	3/85 (4) 4/115 (5)		
J. D. P. Oram c Klusener b Ntini	6	5/155 (6)		

†B. B. McCullum, D. L. Vettori, M. J. Mason and D. R. Tuffey did not bat.

Bowling: Pollock 7–0–37–1; Ntini 10–0–44–1; Klusener 7–2–27–0; Morkel 9–0–33–1; Kallis 4–0–15–0; Peterson 9–0–28–1.

Umpires: R. B. Tiffin (Zimbabwe) and A. L. Hill.
Third umpire: D. B. Cowie. Referee: G. R. Viswanath (India).

At Napier, March 5, 6, 7, 2004. **Drawn.** Toss: Central Districts. **South Africans 286-5 dec.** (N. D. McKenzie 100*, M. V. Boucher 58) **and 224-7 dec.** (L. J Hamilton 4-67); **Central Districts 239-6 dec.** (M. S. Sinclair 99, J. I. Englefield 77) **and 195-8** (J. I. Englefield 53*).

NEW ZEALAND v SOUTH AFRICA

First Test Match

At Hamilton, March 10, 11, 12, 13, 14, 2004. Drawn. Toss: South Africa. Test debuts: B. B. McCullum, M. H. W. Papps.

Speculation about the state of the pitch dominated the build-up to the match. The ground had been waterlogged during floods that hit North Island in February, and algae developed on the square, destroying most of the grass. The only serviceable pitch was

Undoing the damage: Mike George, fourth umpire for the Hamilton Test, watches groundsman Karl Johnson reverse illegal pitch repairs.

Picture by Getty Images

a new one, made of Kakanui soil imported from South Island. Officials from New Zealand Cricket considered a change of venue before giving Hamilton the go-ahead a week before the match.

The new surface proved slow, with low bounce, and both the South African openers were out before lunch, trying to force the pace. Rudolph and Kallis then played positively, taking the total past 200. The turning-point, though, came with the second new ball. Tuffey and Oram bowled superbly, becalming Kallis on 90 – ten short of a fifth century in successive Tests – for 20 balls. Kallis eventually managed a two off Oram but mistimed a hook to fine leg two deliveries later.

Kirsten played a typically composed innings without much support and was on 98 when Nel, the last man, joined him. Nel saw him to his 21st Test century, whereupon Kirsten went on the attack, smashing another 37 from 21 balls before he was last out, with the total a healthy 459.

Michael Papps, New Zealand's new opener, made an uncertain start before settling down to make a half-century on debut. But before he resumed his innings on the third morning a row broke out over the pitch. The South Africans told the referee, Clive

Lloyd, of repairs made to the surface, reinforcing their case by showing him photographs they had taken after play ended the previous evening. (They had been alerted to the patching of the wicket after overhearing a conversation.) Lloyd ordered that the repair work be undone, blaming the incident on "misunderstanding and miscommunication". The South Africans were also disconcerted to learn that a sightscreen had been improved after a complaint from the home team, though Lloyd had apparently given this his blessing.

The South Africans seemed in control when Cairns was sixth out at 225, but the tall, left-handed Oram showed excellent composure to make his first Test century, aided by some fine play from the lower order. New Zealand's other debutant, the Canterbury wicket-keeper, Brendon McCullum (Papps occasionally deputises for him in provincial cricket), played brightly for his fifty, Vettori hit one too, and Wiseman weighed in with 36. Oram was the common factor in all three stands, which either equalled – in the case of the seventh wicket – or beat existing records for New Zealand against South Africa. The total also surpassed the 505 they made in Cape Town in 1953-54, giving them a lead of 50, with more than a day and a half to go. One more record was teetering: Pollock had now equalled Allan Donald's record of 330 Test wickets for South Africa.

Although most of the pitch held together well, a crater (apparently unrelated to the controversial repair work) roughly 12 inches across appeared a couple of feet outside the left-handers' off stump. Vettori exploited it bowling to right-handers as well, but Kallis proved masterly at getting his body between the damaged area and his stumps. Even so, South Africa were still in some trouble at the end of the fourth day: 84 ahead with three wickets down. In truth, the pitch continued to play easily for right-handers, and Kallis moved smoothly to the century he had missed in the first innings, thus giving him a hundred in five successive Tests, one behind Don Bradman's record.

Things were trickier for left-handers. After lunch on the last day, Fleming took the second new ball against the left-handed Kirsten, and the umpires, concerned that conditions could become dangerous, asked Lloyd to join them in the middle. They toyed with abandoning the game before ruling it was safe to play on. There were, in fact, no major alarms, and the match petered out to a draw.

Man of the Match: J. H. Kallis.

Close of play: First day, South Africa 279-4 (Kirsten 31, Adams 7); Second day, New Zealand 102-2 (Papps 50, Styris 16); Third day, New Zealand 361-7 (Oram 49, Vettori 21); Fourth day, South Africa 134-3 (Kallis 56, McKenzie 11).

South Africa

*G. C. Smith c Oram b Vettori	25	– c McCullum b Tuffey	5
H. H. Gibbs c Styris b Vettori	40	– c McCullum b Wiseman	47
J. A. Rudolph c McCullum b Styris	72	– b Cairns	0
J. H. Kallis c Tuffey b Oram	92	– not out	150
G. Kirsten c Papps b Vettori	137	– (6) not out	34
P. R. Adams b Oram	7		
N. D. McKenzie lbw b Vettori	10	– (5) c Richardson b Wiseman	52
†M. V. Boucher lbw b Styris	22		
S. M. Pollock run out	10		
M. Ntini run out	21		
A. Nel not out	4		
B 1, l-b 5, w 1, n-b 12	19	B 12, l-b 5, n-b 8	25

1/51 (1) 2/79 (2) 3/211 (3) 4/271 (4)	459	1/15 (1) 2/16 (3) (4 wkts dec.) 313
5/281 (6) 6/305 (7) 7/364 (8)		3/108 (2) 4/215 (5)
8/379 (9) 9/415 (10) 10/459 (5)		

Bowling: *First Innings*—Tuffey 26–11–62–0; Oram 27–7–76–2; Cairns 18–2–52–0; Vettori 39.2–2–158–4; Wiseman 12–1–54–0; Styris 16–4–46–2; McMillan 1–0–5–0. *Second Innings*—Tuffey 15–3–28–1; Oram 15–4–29–0; Cairns 15–3–48–1; Vettori 34–11–79–0; Wiseman 19–4–68–2; Styris 13–4–29–0; McMillan 5.1–0–15–0.

New Zealand

M. H. Richardson lbw b Pollock	4	
M. H. W. Papps lbw b Kallis	59 – (1) c Boucher b Nel	12
*S. P. Fleming lbw b Adams	27	
S. B. Styris b Pollock	74 – (3) not out	3
C. D. McMillan lbw b Kallis	19	
C. L. Cairns c Boucher b Ntini	28	
J. D. P. Oram not out	119	
†B. B. McCullum c Boucher b Kallis	57 – (2) not out	19
D. L. Vettori b Adams	53	
P. J. Wiseman b Pollock	36	
D. R. Tuffey c Boucher b Pollock	0	
B 12, l-b 11, n-b 10	33	L-b 1, w 1, n-b 3	5

	509	1/34 (1)	**(1 wkt) 39**

1/20 (1) 2/75 (3) 3/127 (2) 4/172 (5)
5/223 (4) 6/225 (6) 7/309 (8)
8/422 (9) 9/509 (10) 10/509 (11)

Bowling: *First Innings*—Pollock 30.4–4–98–4; Ntini 29–9–74–1; Kallis 26–7–71–3; Nel 27–8–91–0; Adams 45–11–118–2; Rudolph 5–0–20–0; Smith 2–0–14–0. *Second Innings*—Pollock 4–2–5–0; Ntini 4–0–15–1; Adams 3–1–2–0; McKenzie 1–0–1–0.

Umpires: S. J. Davis (Australia) and R. B. Tiffin (Zimbabwe).
Third umpire: A. L. Hill.   Referee: C. H. Lloyd (West Indies).

NEW ZEALAND v SOUTH AFRICA

Second Test Match

At Auckland, March 18, 19, 20, 21, 22, 2004. New Zealand won by nine wickets. Toss: New Zealand.

New Zealand gained their first victory in 13 home Tests against South Africa, the only country they had never beaten on their own soil. The win was comprehensive, though that seemed improbable after Fleming inserted the South Africans – only to watch them put on 177 for the first wicket.

South Africa dropped Adams and Nel and replaced them with Boje and Terbrugge. New Zealand, meanwhile, recalled Chris Martin for his first Test appearance since May 2002, ousting the off-spinner Wiseman. Martin proved to be the match-winner, justifying the belief of John Bracewell, the coach, that he could swing the ball away from the trio of left-handers in the South African top six. Martin proved more than useful against the right-handers, too, claiming match figures of 11 for 180, the best for New Zealand against South Africa.

A drop-in pitch helped the fast bowlers early on, but Smith and Gibbs played skilfully as they shared their sixth century opening stand in Tests, equalling the South African record held by Trevor Goddard and Eddie Barlow. Fleming's embarrassment was becoming acute when Gibbs fell to the ball before tea, and Smith to the first delivery afterwards. New Zealand then restricted Rudolph and Kallis to 54 runs in the last session.

Next day the weather was cloudy, and Martin took full advantage of conditions favourable to swing with an inspired, career-best performance. All told, eight South

Angle of attack: Chris Martin took 11 wickets at Auckland to bowl New Zealand to victory, their first over South Africa in home Tests.

Picture by Getty Images

African wickets fell for 65 runs. Martin would have become the first New Zealander to take seven in an innings against South Africa had Fleming held a straightforward chance off Terbrugge at first slip: he settled for six for 76. South Africa's slump from 177 for none to 296 all out was so precipitate that the opening stand accounted for almost 60% of the total – the highest in a completed South African innings.

New Zealand lost Papps – the wicket that took Pollock past Allan Donald's South African record of 330 Test wickets – and Fleming inside eight overs. Stability was restored by Richardson, in typically stoic fashion, and by Styris, who played an exceptional innings, striking the ball crisply, and neatly finding the gaps. Kallis had Richardson caught at gully after they had added 125. It hardly stemmed the flow: McMillan and Styris put on 148 for the fourth wicket and steered New Zealand into a strong position.

MOST TEST INNINGS WITHOUT A RUN

9	C. S. Martin (New Zealand)	0*, 0, 0, 0, 0, 0*, 0, 0, 0	2000-01–2003-04
8	D. Ramnarine (West Indies)	0*, 0, 0, 0*, 0, 0, 0, 0	2001-02
6	J. B. Statham (England)	0, 0*, 0*, 0, 0, 0	1955–1956-57
6	B. S. Chandrasekhar (India)	0, 0, 0*, 0*, 0, 0	1977-78
6	Danish Kaneria (Pakistan)	0, 0, 0, 0*, 0, 0*	2003–2003-04

The record for consecutive Test dismissals for 0 is five, shared by R. G. Holland (Australia) in 1985–1985-86 and A. B. Agarkar (India) in 1999-2000.

On the third morning, Smith surprisingly did not take the new ball when it became available, preferring to persist with Boje. It worked: Styris, in an apparent loss of concentration, nudged the first delivery of the 81st over to slip. His career-best 170 had come off 220 balls with 24 fours and two sixes. Next over Smith did take the new ball – and McMillan and McCullum were gone while the shine was bright. With New Zealand 349 for six, South Africa were still in the game – until a magnificent display of batting from Cairns and Oram.

Their stand of 225, coming in just 190 minutes from 275 balls, was a record for any wicket by New Zealand against South Africa and the sixth-highest for the seventh wicket in Test history. Cairns's career-best 158 was made from 171 balls and included seven sixes. When he was caught at long-on, his career total stood at 79 Test sixes, five behind the record set by Viv Richards.

Rather less productive was Martin who became the first player to fail to hit a run in nine consecutive Test innings. But he did produce a splendid first ball when South Africa batted again, bowling Smith with a full delivery that clipped the leg stump as he tried to play to the on side.

Rudolph, who came in with South Africa still 299 behind, shared century stands with Gibbs and Kallis, raising hopes of a draw. With Tuffey unable to bowl because of a thigh injury, Fleming turned to McMillan. In the final hour of the fourth day and with the deficit down to 50, he broke through, trapping Kallis leg-before, and ending his chance of equalling Bradman by scoring a century in six successive Tests. Next over Martin dismissed Kirsten – having a wretched time in his 100th Test – and McKenzie with successive deliveries.

Boucher also fell that evening, and when South Africa eventually wiped out the arrears next morning, they had just three wickets in hand. Although Rudolph continued to defy the New Zealand bowlers, the match had swung irrevocably their way.

Man of the Match: C. S. Martin.

Close of play: First day, South Africa 231-2 (Rudolph 14, Kallis 39); Second day, New Zealand 201-3 (Styris 118, McMillan 31); Third day, New Zealand 584-8 (Vettori 2, Tuffey 5); Fourth day, South Africa 277-6 (Rudolph 121, Pollock 5).

South Africa

*G. C. Smith lbw b Martin	88	– b Martin	0
H. H. Gibbs b Cairns	80	– lbw b Oram	61
J. A. Rudolph c Papps b Martin	17	– not out	154
J. H. Kallis c McCullum b Martin	40	– lbw b McMillan	71
G. Kirsten b Oram	1	– lbw b Martin	1
N. D. McKenzie c Papps b Martin	27	– c Papps b Martin	0
†M. V. Boucher c McMillan b Martin	4	– c Fleming b Martin	10
S. M. Pollock b Tuffey	10	– c Fleming b Martin	10
N. Boje not out	12	– c McCullum b Cairns	24
M. Ntini c McCullum b Martin	0	– c McMillan b Cairns	6
D. J. Terbrugge lbw b Oram	0	– c sub (J. A. H. Marshall) b Cairns	2
L-b 13, w 1, n-b 3	17	B 6, l-b 1, n-b 3	10

1/177 (2) 2/177 (1) 3/235 (3) 4/236 (5)   296   1/0 (1) 2/103 (3) 3/249 (4)   349
5/240 (4) 6/246 (7) 7/273 (8)   4/250 (5) 5/250 (6) 6/272 (7)
8/289 (6) 9/289 (10) 10/296 (11)   7/290 (8) 8/327 (9)
                                         9/337 (10) 10/349 (11)

Bowling: *First Innings*—Tuffey 24–7–41–1; Martin 31–7–76–6; Oram 28.3–6–60–2; Cairns 21–6–54–1; Styris 14–5–37–0; Vettori 5–1–15–0. *Second Innings*—Martin 23–5–104–5; Oram 27–13–47–1; Tuffey 4–1–13–0; Cairns 13.3–1–63–3; Vettori 24–4–73–0; Styris 13–5–39–0; McMillan 4–1–3–1.

New Zealand

M. H. Richardson c Gibbs b Kallis	45	(2) c Boje b Ntini	10
M. H. W. Papps c Boje b Pollock	0	(1) not out	8
*S. P. Fleming c Kallis b Ntini	4	– not out	31
S. B. Styris c Pollock b Boje	170		
C. D. McMillan b Pollock	82		
†B. B. McCullum b Ntini	13		
C. L. Cairns c Kallis b Smith	158		
J. D. P. Oram b Ntini	90		
D. L. Vettori not out	4		
D. R. Tuffey b Pollock	13		
C. S. Martin b Pollock	0		
L-b 10, n-b 6	16	N-b 4	4

1/5 (2) 2/12 (3) 3/137 (1) 4/285 (4)   595   1/20 (2)   (1 wkt) 53
5/314 (5) 6/349 (6) 7/574 (7)
8/578 (8) 9/595 (10) 10/595 (11)

Bowling: *First Innings*—Pollock 32.5–6–113–4; Ntini 36–7–110–3; Terbrugge 22–4–93–0; Kallis 23–1–108–1; Boje 22–2–108–1; McKenzie 2–0–8–0; Smith 5–0–19–1. *Second Innings*—Pollock 5–1–16–0; Ntini 5–0–31–1; Boje 0.2–0–6–0.

Umpires: Aleem Dar (Pakistan) and E. A. R. de Silva (Sri Lanka).
Third umpire: D. B. Cowie.   Referee: C. H. Lloyd (West Indies).

NEW ZEALAND v SOUTH AFRICA

Third Test Match

At Basin Reserve, Wellington, March 26, 27, 28, 29, 30, 2004. South Africa won by six wickets. Toss: South Africa. Test debut: M. J. Mason.

A crucial fourth-innings stand between Graeme Smith, who made a classy unbeaten hundred, and Gary Kirsten, playing his last Test before retirement, enabled South Africa to hit straight back at New Zealand and tie the series between two well-matched teams.

South Africa replaced McKenzie and Terbrugge with van Jaarsveld and Nel, while New Zealand were forced into two changes. McMillan, the worst affected by a virus that swept through the team, withdrew on the morning of the match and was replaced by Sinclair, while Michael Mason, a 29-year-old right-arm fast-medium bowler, won his first cap in place of the injured Tuffey.

Sinclair soon had a chance to show his worth after both openers fell quickly on a pitch of greater pace and bounce than others used on this tour. But there was also a typical Wellington gale: a strong northerly that made life awkward for the seamers, forcing those bowling upwind to shorten their run-ups. Kallis looked particularly effective doing this, but managed just seven overs before leaving the field with a side strain.

Boje also coped well with the blustery weather, dismissing Fleming and Styris in quick succession and reducing New Zealand to 97 for four. McCullum first supported Sinclair, who struck 74 on his return, and then Cairns, again batting with freedom and power, in a sixth-wicket stand of 85. The new ball worked its magic, though, leaving Oram stranded with last man Martin. Oram hit out before he was stumped off Boje; Martin at least got a single, ending his record sequence of scoreless innings.

With the wind blowing even harder next day, South Africa looked set to take command with Smith and Gibbs, unperturbed by the weather or anything else, moved to their seventh century opening stand, a South African record. And before the day was out, Rudolph and van Jaarsveld had shared another hundred partnership. Once again, though, Martin produced a crucial spell. Armed with the second new ball and in calmer weather, he wrecked South African hopes of a big lead by ripping out three of the middle order in the space of 16 deliveries.

Calling it a day: Gary Kirsten acknowledges the applause of the crowd in his 101st and last Test before retiring.

Rudolph played another impressive innings, but only Boje could stay with him as the last seven wickets fell for 65, to the delight of the third-day crowd of 9,020, the largest of the Test series. South Africa immediately put the pressure back on New Zealand, however, as Pollock removed Papps in the first over with one that cut back sharply. Richardson and Fleming were painstakingly slow, and Fleming admitted afterwards that New Zealand might have been over-cautious in trying to guard their lead in the series. By the end of the third day, things looked bleak: they were five down and only 109 ahead.

Next day initially brought frustration for the tourists as, in bright sunshine, the groundstaff took an age to remove the covers after overnight and early-morning rain. And when play did start, 90 minutes late, New Zealand won the first exchanges. Styris and Cairns scored freely, adding 70 in 15 overs before Cairns was caught at deep mid-wicket. Styris followed next over when Nel held a reflex catch in his follow-through.

Once again Oram found himself batting with Martin with his own innings barely established, and once again he hit effectively to add precious runs, taking the total of his two last-wicket stands with Martin to 61. His partner contributed two. During this partnership, Smith remonstrated furiously with umpire de Silva after he called a wide. At the end of the over, Nel, who had been trying to prevent Oram from keeping the strike, snatched his sweater from the umpire. The referee, Clive Lloyd, fined both for dissent, Nel losing three-quarters of his match fee and Smith half.

South Africa needed 234 to win. Smith and Gibbs started aggressively before Martin, in his last effective burst of the series, had Gibbs caught at first slip and then removed

Picture by Getty Images

the left-handed Rudolph's off stump with a beauty that moved away. Kallis failed for the second time and Kirsten, in his last Test innings, arrived with his side at a crisis point.

From 36 for three, Smith and Kirsten batted soundly until bad light ended the fourth day with another 152 required. The fifth day, though, was all South Africa. Smith scored the majority of his runs on the leg side while his fellow left-hander Kirsten cut and drove through the off. They had taken their fourth-wicket stand to 171 when Kirsten fell lbw for 76 in the last over before lunch. He returned to the dressing-room through a guard of honour formed by his team-mates. The formalities remained, but Kirsten had made a final and successful contribution to his team – and South Africa had still not lost a Test series against New Zealand.

Man of the Match: G. C. Smith.

Close of play: First day, New Zealand 248-6 (Cairns 60); Second day, South Africa 237-3 (Rudolph 60, van Jaarsveld 48); Third day, New Zealand 128-5 (Styris 41, Cairns 7); Fourth day, South Africa 82-3 (Smith 46, Kirsten 19).

New Zealand

M. H. Richardson c Boucher b Kallis	14	– (2) c Smith b Boje	37
M. H. W. Papps lbw b Ntini	7	– (1) lbw b Pollock	0
*S. P. Fleming c Pollock b Boje	30	– c Boucher b Nel	9
M. S. Sinclair lbw b Boje	74	– lbw b Pollock	21
S. B. Styris b Boje	1	– c and b Nel	73
†B. B. McCullum lbw b Pollock	55	– b Boje	3
C. L. Cairns b Pollock	69	– c van Jaarsveld b Boje	41
J. D. P. Oram st Boucher b Boje	34	– lbw b Boje	40
D. L. Vettori c Boucher b Pollock	0	– c van Jaarsveld b Ntini	9
M. J. Mason c van Jaarsveld b Nel	3	– run out	0
C. S. Martin not out	1	– not out	1
B 2, l-b 1, w 1, n-b 5	9	B 1, l-b 9, w 3, n-b 5	18

1/23 (2) 2/23 (1) 3/90 (3) 4/97 (5)   297   1/1 (1) 2/42 (3) 3/73 (4)   252
5/163 (4) 6/248 (6) 7/257 (7)   4/107 (2) 5/111 (6) 6/198 (7)
8/257 (9) 9/264 (10) 10/297 (8)   7/201 (5) 8/220 (9)
    9/224 (10) 10/252 (8)

Bowling: *First Innings*—Pollock 29–2–85–3; Ntini 21–6–63–1; Kallis 7–5–4–1; Nel 27–9–77–1; Boje 20–2–65–4. *Second Innings*—Pollock 22–10–65–2; Ntini 20–6–50–1; Nel 21–5–58–2; Boje 33.2–7–69–4.

South Africa

*G. C. Smith b Cairns	47	– not out	125
H. H. Gibbs c sub (J. A. H. Marshall) b Martin	77	– c Fleming b Martin	16
J. A. Rudolph not out	93	– b Martin	0
G. Kirsten c McCullum b Martin	1	– (5) lbw b Styris	76
M. van Jaarsveld c Oram b Martin	59	– (6) not out	13
J. H. Kallis c McCullum b Martin	0	– (4) lbw b Oram	1
†M. V. Boucher c Papps b Martin	0		
S. M. Pollock c Fleming b Oram	5		
N. Boje b Cairns	25		
M. Ntini c McCullum b Cairns	4		
A. Nel c Oram b Cairns	0		
L-b 1, n-b 4	5	L-b 2, n-b 1	3

1/103 (1) 2/130 (2) 3/136 (4) 4/251 (5)   316   1/29 (2) 2/31 (3)   (4 wkts) 234
5/265 (6) 6/265 (7) 7/270 (8)   3/36 (4) 4/207 (5)
8/304 (9) 9/308 (10) 10/316 (11)

Bowling: *First Innings*—Martin 20–6–55–5; Mason 16–4–73–0; Oram 11–3–21–1; Vettori 26–6–76–0; Cairns 16.5–2–60–4; Styris 10–4–30–0. *Second Innings*—Martin 18.2–2–65–2; Mason 6–1–32–0; Oram 11–3–23–1; Cairns 10–2–19–0; Vettori 18–2–53–0; Styris 9–1–40–1.

Umpires: Aleem Dar (Pakistan) and E. A. R. de Silva (Sri Lanka).
Third umpire: G. A. Baxter.   Referee: C. H. Lloyd (West Indies).

Peace breaks out: for the one-day game at Lahore, supporters of both sides throng the Imran Khan Enclosure.

Picture by Scott Barbour, Getty Images

THE INDIANS IN PAKISTAN, 2003-04

RAHUL BHATTACHARYA

India's tour of Pakistan, their first full one in 14 years, was extraordinary even before a ball was bowled. Two years earlier the two countries had appeared on the brink of nuclear war, but the tour gained impetus from what was popularly described as the "wind of brotherhood" blowing at long last between the nations, and also became an agent of change in itself. Sport, far from being an agent of division, turned out to be the centrepiece for something resembling a peace march. For India, there was another dimension. Their rising cricket team shone as never before in Pakistan, winning the Tests 2–1 and the one-day series 3–2. They had never won even a single Test there in 20 previous attempts.

Few tours had seen such flip-flopping beforehand. In January, news broke that the players had written to the Indian board to express their unease at travelling to Pakistan. They were not alone in their worries. The only team to have completed a full tour since the terrorist attacks of September 2001 was Bangladesh. West Indies and Australia played on neutral territory, and a visit by New Zealand was cut short by a bomb outside the team hotel in

Karachi. As recently as September 2003, South Africa had contemplated cancelling after another bomb in Karachi, but ultimately played a curtailed series at handpicked venues.

For India, the issues went far wider than just the players' safety. Cricket had long been hostage to the political climate between India and Pakistan. This time, the climate was right – but the Indian government harboured absurd theories about possible defeat affecting their chances in the general elections due to begin in April. Mixed signals were leaked to gauge the public mood, and eventually the will-they-won't-they-when-will-they speculation reached the point of silliness, until the Indian prime minister, Atal Behari Vajpayee, decided the plunge ought to be taken.

The itinerary was finalised less than three weeks before the start. Karachi, with its record of terrorism, and Peshawar, by the Afghan border, were not granted Tests, but they did stage one-day games. Given that South Africa had boycotted both cities, this was a minor victory for the Pakistanis. The second compromise hurt the Pakistan Cricket Board, and the tour, considerably more. The Tests were put off until after the one-day games, once again because of the Indian government's election paranoia: they feared losing the one-day series could be more dangerous than losing the Tests. As it was, India won both – and the government was still toppled.

> Hardened ex-players were moved to see the national flags together

The scheduling meant that the notoriously low Test attendances in Pakistan remained poor even for this historic series, the public having sated themselves on one-day razzmatazz. Not only that, but the tight itinerary, designed to include the minimum number of days off and to finish before the elections, meant cricket took place on two of a possible six Sundays, the only full weekly holiday in Pakistan. Even slashed prices could not entice the public, and rows and rows of empty seats made a sad backdrop.

Yet, given all the constraints and pressures, the PCB did a commendable job. They were rewarded with a profit ($21m from TV rights and $1.25m from ticket sales) unparalleled in their history – and badly needed after the spate of cancelled or relocated matches. There was also the intangible gain of having demonstrated to the international cricket community that the most demanding series of all could be staged without a hitch.

The tour could not have had a more nail-biting, or heart-warming, beginning than it did at Karachi's National Stadium. Never had more runs been scored in a one-day international than the 693 made here, and all results were possible at the last ball, when Moin Khan failed to deposit a full toss for six. The tension was not restricted to the cricket. The big question was how the crowds at Karachi would respond; indeed, how the peoples of India and Pakistan would respond. Nearly everybody (though the *Times of India* printed the irresponsibly vulgar headline "Karachi Captured") came through shining. Hardened ex-players were amazed and moved to see the national flags flying together through the match. After an initial shocked silence, the

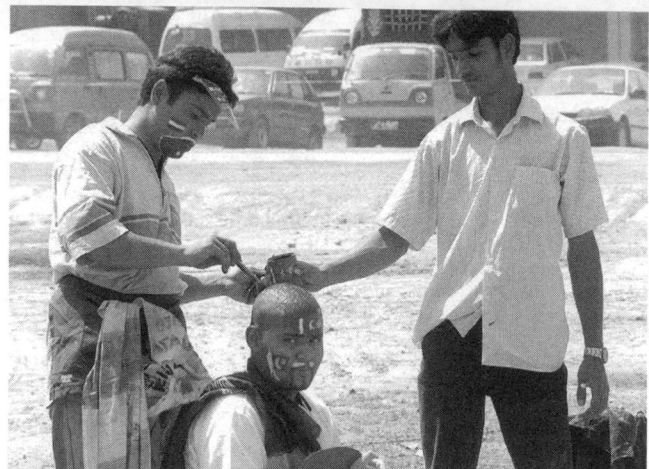

Split allegiance: a cricket supporter in Multan has the flags of both India and Pakistan painted on his head.

Picture by Mueen ud din Hameed

Indians left the pitch to a standing ovation. Quietly, the crowds filed out, obeying instructions to avert the type of riots that had occurred at ticket booths five days before.

Thus was the tone set at Karachi: it never let up. The scent of something like love wafted out of the stands. The people-to-people contact was not phenomenal in terms of numbers, but it was in experience. In total, about 11,000 cricket visas were issued, of which almost half were for the two Lahore one-dayers. Pakistani officials believed this to be the heaviest cross-border traffic since the mass migration brought about by Partition in 1947. For many years, obtaining visas for personal visits had been virtually impossible.

Lahore has a specially poignant position in the subcontinent: it was once the capital of the prosperous northern state of Punjab which was divided by Partition, and stands about 45 minutes from the Indian border. Every effort was made to get Indian spectators there. Airlines, bus companies and railways all put on extra services, and about a thousand people crossed the border on foot. People hunted down old homes, friends, even family; for those who had none, just the hospitality and ancient grandeur of Lahore were overwhelming.

The one-day cricket was splendid, among the best there has been in a bilateral series. Pakistan came from behind to take the lead 2–1, before India did the same to claim the series 3–2. Though batsmen dominated too much for some – the average score was 296 – the game was always afoot, except for the deciding match; even then, Pakistan managed a belated fight. On that night, V. V. S. Laxman made a sublime hundred; later, the 19-year-old left-armer, Irfan Pathan, swung out Pakistan's top order. Laxman had struggled in earlier games, and Pathan was not even picked for the first two. It summed up India's tour: when it came to the crunch, there was always somebody for the job.

Pakistan's captain, Inzamam-ul-Haq, also stood out, but as batsman rather than leader. He stroked two fabulous one-day centuries, both in defeat, and carried this form into the First Test at Multan where he made a seemingly impregnable 77 before being sawn off by a poor decision, and then to Lahore, where he constructed a grinding century, his 19th in Tests, and 14th in a winning cause. In the deciding Test at Rawalpindi, he failed twice, and so did the Pakistan batting around him.

By a quirky symmetry, Rahul Dravid, whose two main one-day innings came in the same matches as Inzamam's, became his opposite number as captain for the first two Tests, after Sourav Ganguly suffered a back injury. Inzamam's second-innings run-out was a pivotal moment in the First Test; and it was a similar run-out of Dravid in the Second that marked India's point of no return. But Dravid trumped Inzamam at Rawalpindi, where he made a momentous 270, gritted out over 740 minutes, to clinch the game for India.

It was a strange Test series, and not as absorbing as it might have been. While results fluctuated wildly – India romping to innings victories in the first and third matches, and Pakistan winning the second by nine wickets – within the life of each Test there were few surprises. They started out on one road and never departed from it. The last two were mirrors of one another: the side batting first was seamed out on the opening day, before the opposition built a lead too heavy to counter. In the First Test, this form of bullying by runs happened in the very first innings. Virender Sehwag flogged 309 in only 375 balls, India's first triple-century in Tests, while Sachin Tendulkar controversially missed a double-hundred when Dravid declared.

The gap between the teams was not merely in batting, which was expected, but also in bowling and fielding. In Anil Kumble, India knew they held the advantage on spin – he was the leading wicket-taker, with 15 – but even their inexperienced seamers, Pathan and Lakshmipathy Balaji, bowled far more incisively than the speedy duo of Shoaib Akhtar and Mohammad Sami. Ganguly later suggested Pakistan had made a mistake by not preparing sparse outfields and dusty pitches to aid reverse swing.

Having seen the Indian seamers nip it about laterally during the one-dayers, Pakistan's batsmen were wary of any green on the pitch. At Multan, Andy Atkinson, the English groundsman acting as consultant to the PCB, was instructed to shave off the grass. But the resounding loss that resulted prompted the PCB to ensure seaming pitches for the remaining Tests – seaming essentially on day one, before the moisture was sucked dry by the pitiless April sun.

On the up: Virender Sehwag springs into action at Multan, where he became the first person to hit a Test triple-hundred for India.

Picture by Scott Barbour, Getty Images

It was not just swing and seam, however, that did the trick for Pathan and Balaji. Quite simply, they bowled in the right area. Young Umar Gul showed the way at Lahore – "the only time when there was some life in our bowling", according to Inzamam – but broke down before the last Test. His example went unheeded.

Shoaib, carrying the reputation of not just the fastest but the most destructive bowler in the world, was the major disappointment, averaging 42 for his seven Test wickets. It did not help that he and Inzamam could not see eye to eye. The discontent was manifest when Tauseef Razzaq, a doctor-cum-trainer attached to the team and a close friend of Shoaib, walked out before the final Test, claiming he had been insulted by Inzamam in front of the players. It prompted the question: what was an international cricket team in 2004 doing with a pair of doctors but no specialist sports fitness trainer?

A combination of all these factors – Shoaib, fitness and internal wrangling – was brought into focus when a medical commission inquired into five non-impact injuries suffered by Pakistan during the Tests, four of them to fast bowlers. The real spur, however, was Shoaib's refusal to bowl after falling in his delivery stride and injuring a thumb and a rib at Rawalpindi. That he batted, lustily, made the authorities wonder if he had faked or over-reacted to his injury. But the commission ascertained nothing

The warmth of the tour radiated beyond cricket

and Imran Khan, the legendary ex-captain with plenty of experience of lawsuits, urged Shoaib to take legal action. Inzamam survived the defeats, unlike some losing captains in India–Pakistan series, but coach Javed Miandad had his contract terminated almost a year early. He was replaced by former South African coach Bob Woolmer, as the PCB sought to usher in an era of modernity.

The spirit of the series was largely pleasant, though there was plenty of needle. Ganguly took a swipe at Shoaib's bowling action and the ICC's regulations on slow over-rates; Moin and Parthiv Patel were both fined for dissent. But India's cricketers were affectionately received everywhere, with Balaji an unexpected hit because of his instant smile and joyful tail-end batting. Wherever possible, goodwill was extended. Inzamam presented T-shirts to the tourists at his home town of Multan. After winning there, the Indians spent time at the SOS Village, a nearby orphanage. At the request of Pakistan's Ministry of Health, Laxman and Tendulkar joined Inzamam and Shoaib in a TV campaign against polio. And the entire Indian team united in an appeal to hospitals back home to offer complicated treatment to a ten-year-old girl with facial cancer.

The warmth of the tour radiated beyond cricket. The governments decided to tone down the aggressive posturing at the daily closing-of-the-gates ceremony on the Wagah border. Bollywood film-makers suggested that Indian films should stop pushing anti-Pakistan propaganda. About 15 Pakistani musical bands crossed the border between January and May. And the business sector brimmed with optimism at the potential for trade. Of course, it would be presumptuous for cricket to take credit. What is irrefutable, however, is that the tour provided the highest possible profile for friendship, and the strongest metaphorical way of saying "peace over conflict". Personalities as diverse as the actor Peter O'Toole and the American secretary of state Colin Powell praised the series' message.

Perhaps the most wearisome aspect of the tour was the media coverage, disproportionate even by the standards of cricket in the subcontinent. Whereas Pakistani newspaper reporters were often unbearably aggressive at press conferences, asking unabashed if lost matches had been fixed, their editors at least kept cricket mainly on the sports pages. Going by the Indian press, you would have thought the world had stopped. About 500 media accreditations were issued by the PCB, more than a hundred for Indian journalists. But the American magazines *Sports Illustrated* and *GQ* were also represented, as was one Chinese news agency.

It was to the Indians' credit that they stayed focused amid all the hoopla. By playing confident, uncompromising cricket, they ensured a place in history as the first Indian team to succeed in Pakistan. "I know there were a lot of things attached to this tour," reflected Ganguly, "but for us in this team it was only cricket. And winning the series, both the series, is the

INDIAN TOURING PARTY

S. C. Ganguly (*captain*), R. Dravid (*vice-captain*), A. B. Agarkar, L. Balaji, A. Chopra, M. Kartik, A. Kumble, V. V. S. Laxman, A. Nehra, P. A. Patel, I. K. Pathan, R. R. Powar, V. Sehwag, S. R. Tendulkar, Yuvraj Singh, Zaheer Khan.

H. K. Badani and M. Kaif took part in the one-day series, and were replaced for the Tests by Agarkar, Chopra and Kumble. A. Bhandari replaced the injured Nehra during the one-day series; Nehra returned when Zaheer Khan was injured during the Tests, and Kaif was recalled as cover for Ganguly.

Coach: J. G. Wright. *Manager:* R. S. Shetty. *Physiotherapist:* A. Leipus. *Trainer:* G. A. King. *Computer analyst:* Ramkrishnan. *Media manager:* A. Mathur.

INDIAN TOUR RESULTS

Test matches – Played 3: Won 2, Lost 1.
One-day internationals – Played 5: Won 3, Lost 2.

TEST MATCH AVERAGES

PAKISTAN – BATTING AND FIELDING

	T	I	NO	R	HS	100s	50s	Avge	Ct/St
†Asim Kamal.	2	3	1	154	73	0	2	77.00	0
Yousuf Youhana	3	5	0	280	112	1	1	56.00	0
Inzamam-ul-Haq.	3	5	0	219	118	1	1	43.80	1
Yasir Hameed.	3	6	1	195	91	0	1	39.00	2
†Imran Farhat	3	6	0	191	101	1	0	31.83	3
†Taufeeq Umar.	3	6	1	92	24	0	0	18.40	4
Kamran Akmal.	2	3	0	45	23	0	0	15.00	7/2
Mohammad Sami	3	5	0	66	49	0	0	13.20	0
Shoaib Akhtar	3	5	0	51	28	0	0	10.20	0
Danish Kaneria.	2	3	2	4	4*	0	0	4.00	1

Played in one Test: Abdul Razzaq 47, 22; Fazl-e-Akbar 25, 12 (1 ct); Moin Khan 17, 5; Saqlain Mushtaq 5, 0; Shabbir Ahmed 19*, 0*; Umar Gul 14.

† *Left-handed batsman.*

BOWLING

	Style	O	M	R	W	BB	5W/i	Avge
Umar Gul	RFM	25	3	96	6	5-31	1	16.00
Imran Farhat	LB	19.1	1	100	3	2-69	0	33.33
Danish Kaneria	LB	81.5	7	248	7	3-14	0	35.42
Shoaib Akhtar	RF	86.2	16	297	7	3-47	0	42.42
Mohammad Sami	RF	123	22	435	7	2-92	0	62.14

Also bowled: Abdul Razzaq (RFM) 15–3–61–0; Fazl-e-Akbar (RFM) 40.4–3–162–1; Saqlain Mushtaq (OB) 43–4–204–1; Shabbir Ahmed (RFM) 31–6–122–0; Yasir Hameed (OB) 1–0–5–0.

INDIA – BATTING AND FIELDING

	T	I	NO	R	HS	100s	50s	Avge	Ct
V. Sehwag	3	4	0	438	309	1	1	109.50	2
R. Dravid	3	4	0	309	270	1	0	77.25	4
S. R. Tendulkar	3	4	1	205	194*	1	0	68.33	1
†P. A. Patel	3	3	1	131	69	0	2	65.50	10
†Yuvraj Singh	3	4	0	230	112	1	1	57.50	2
V. V. S. Laxman	3	4	0	124	71	0	1	31.00	3
†I. K. Pathan	3	3	0	64	49	0	0	21.33	1
A. Chopra	2	3	0	51	42	0	0	17.00	0
A. Kumble	3	3	1	15	9	0	0	7.50	1
L. Balaji	3	3	0	11	11	0	0	3.66	0

Played in one Test: A. B. Agarkar 2, 36; †S. C. Ganguly 77 (1 ct); A. Nehra 1* (1 ct); Zaheer Khan did not bat.

† *Left-handed batsman.*

BOWLING

	Style	O	M	R	W	BB	5W/i	Avge
S. R. Tendulkar . . .	RM/OB/LB	33	4	98	4	2-36	0	24.50
A. Kumble	LBG	130.3	31	389	15	6-72	1	25.93
A. Nehra	LFM	27	6	80	3	2-60	0	26.66
I. K. Pathan	LFM	134	44	342	12	4-100	0	28.50
L. Balaji	RFM	106	24	369	12	4-63	0	30.75

Also bowled: A. B. Agarkar (RFM) 23–5–80–1; S. C. Ganguly (RM) 6–0–27–0; V. Sehwag (OB) 6–0–27–0; Yuvraj Singh (SLA/LM) 9–1–32–1; Zaheer Khan (LFM) 23–6–76–1.

Note: Matches in this section which were not first-class are signified by a dagger.

†PAKISTAN v INDIA

First One-Day International

At Karachi, March 13, 2004. India won by five runs. Toss: Pakistan.

Spectacular batting produced a famous finish in front of an ear-splitting capacity crowd of 33,000. Pakistan wanted nine off the last over, and Nehra bowled it beautifully until his final ball, a full toss – but, with six required, Moin Khan sliced it up for a simple catch. Reminded of India's defeat in similar circumstances at Sharjah in 1985-86, Ganguly rejoiced that "there was no Javed Miandad batting". Put in, curiously, India were kick-started by Sehwag, who hit 79 in 57 balls.

HIGHEST TOTALS BY LOSING SIDE IN ONE-DAY INTERNATIONALS

344-8	**Pakistan lost to India by five runs at Karachi**	**2003-04**
329	Sri Lanka lost to West Indies by four runs at Sharjah.	1995-96
326-3	South Africa lost to Australia by three wickets at Port Elizabeth.	2001-02
325-5	England lost to India by two wickets at Lord's	2002
324-4	West Indies lost to India by five wickets at Ahmedabad	2002-03
317	**India lost to Pakistan by 12 runs at Rawalpindi.**	**2003-04**
315-8	Pakistan lost to Australia by six wickets at Lahore.	1998-99
315	Pakistan lost to Sri Lanka by 34 runs at Singapore	1995-96
314-5	Pakistan lost to India by three wickets at Dhaka	1997-98
312-4	Zimbabwe lost to Sri Lanka by three wickets at New Plymouth	1991-92
312-4	West Indies lost to Sri Lanka by four wickets at Bridgetown	2003
310	India lost to South Africa by ten runs at Nagpur	1999-2000

Note: 24 teams had lost one-day internationals with a total of 300 or more by the end of 2004.

Research: Nirav Malavi

Dravid controlled the middle order before being bowled by Shoaib Akhtar's slower ball for 99. There was no century in a total of 349, but there were 30 runs from wides and no-balls: Naved-ul-Hasan conceded 17 runs before his second legal delivery. Pakistan were 34 for two in the eighth over, but Inzamam-ul-Haq played a great innings, 122 off 102 balls, and they managed seven an over while he was in. Then he fell with 72 required, and Kaif took a champion airborne catch, running from long-on to mid-off and almost colliding with a team-mate, to remove Shoaib Malik. Though they were just short, Pakistan's 344 was the highest total batting second in a one-day international, and 693 the highest ever aggregate.

Man of the Match: Inzamam-ul-Haq.

India

V. Sehwag b Naved-ul-Hasan	79	H. K. Badani not out	8
S. R. Tendulkar c Naved-ul-Hasan		Zaheer Khan b Mohammad Sami	0
b Shoaib Akhtar .	28	M. Kartik not out.	3
*S. C. Ganguly c and b Naved-ul-Hasan.	45	B 1, l-b 7, w 10, n-b 20.	38
†R. Dravid b Shoaib Akhtar	99		
Yuvraj Singh c Yasir Hameed		1/69 (2) 2/142 (1) (7 wkts, 50 overs) 349	
b Naved-ul-Hasan .	3	3/214 (3) 4/220 (5)	
M. Kaif lbw b Mohammad Sami.	46	5/338 (4) 6/344 (6) 7/344 (8)	

L. Balaji and A. Nehra did not bat.

Bowling: Shoaib Akhtar 10–0–55–2; Mohammad Sami 10–0–74–2; Naved-ul-Hasan 10–0–73–3; Abdul Razzaq 9–0–83–0; Shoaib Malik 10–0–50–0; Yasir Hameed 1–0–6–0.

Pakistan

Yasir Hameed b Balaji.	7	Shoaib Malik c Kaif b Zaheer Khan . . .	7
Imran Farhat c Dravid b Zaheer Khan . .	24	Naved-ul-Hasan not out.	3
Yousuf Youhana c sub (I. K. Pathan)		L-b 10, w 7, n-b 2.	19
b Sehwag .	73		
*Inzamam-ul-Haq c Dravid b Kartik . . .	122	1/32 (1) 2/34 (2) (8 wkts, 50 overs) 344	
Younis Khan b Kartik.	46	3/169 (3) 4/278 (4)	
Abdul Razzaq b Zaheer Khan.	27	5/305 (5) 6/322 (6)	
†Moin Khan c Zaheer Khan b Nehra . . .	16	7/340 (8) 8/344 (7)	

Shoaib Akhtar and Mohammad Sami did not bat.

Bowling: Balaji 10–1–56–1; Zaheer Khan 10–0–66–3; Nehra 10–0–58–1; Kartik 10–0–74–2; Ganguly 1–0–14–0; Tendulkar 3–0–34–0; Sehwag 6–0–32–1.

Umpires: S. J. A. Taufel (Australia) and Nadeem Ghauri.
Third umpire: Asad Rauf.   Referee: R. S. Madugalle (Sri Lanka).

†PAKISTAN v INDIA

Second One-Day International

At Rawalpindi, March 16, 2004 (day/night). Pakistan won by 12 runs. Toss: Pakistan. One-day international debut: R. R. Powar.

Once again, the hunters fell tantalisingly short in a high-scoring thriller, with India just failing after needing 16 off the last two overs. Shahid Afridi, out of the Pakistan team for a year since the World Cup, made a glorious comeback, spanking 80 from 58 balls and rattling up 138 in 19 overs with Yasir Hameed. And late hitting by Abdul Razzaq and Shoaib Malik saw 50 runs flow from the final five overs. In between, Nehra braved a swollen ankle to take two in two balls to slow the tempo, then split the webbing of his fingers and had to be sent home. On a pitch that he said became progressively slower, Tendulkar scored a superb century, India's first in a one-day international in Pakistan, and became the first player to reach 13,000 one-day runs. But his dismissal, sweeping to deep mid wicket in the 39th over, galvanised the bowling; seven overs later India slumped to 284 for eight when Shoaib Akhtar fired out two in two. The valiant hitting of Balaji and debutant Ramesh Powar kept the heart of Pakistan's president, Pervez Musharraf, who took tea with the Indians next day. It also kept India in the game until the penultimate over, when Sami theatrically defeated last man Nehra's uncalculated swipe.

Man of the Match: S. R. Tendulkar.

Pakistan

Yasir Hameed run out	86	Abdul Razzaq not out 31
Shahid Afridi b Yuvraj Singh	80	
Yousuf Youhana b Yuvraj Singh	74	L-b 6, w 14, n-b 1 21
*Inzamam-ul-Haq b Nehra	29	
Younis Khan c Dravid b Nehra	28	1/138 (2) 2/191 (3) (6 wkts, 50 overs) 329
†Moin Khan lbw b Nehra	0	3/225 (1) 4/249 (4)
Shoaib Malik not out	30	5/249 (6) 6/284 (5)

Shoaib Akhtar, Mohammad Sami and Shabbir Ahmed did not bat.

Bowling: Balaji 6-0-47-0; Zaheer Khan 7-0-72-0; Nehra 10-0-44-3; Sehwag 5-0-39-0; Yuvraj Singh 10-1-41-2; Powar 6-0-35-0; Tendulkar 6-0-45-0.

India

V. Sehwag b Shoaib Akhtar	26	R. R. Powar not out 18
S. R. Tendulkar c Abdul Razzaq		Zaheer Khan lbw b Shoaib Akhtar..... 0
b Shoaib Malik	141	L. Balaji run out 14
V. V. S. Laxman lbw b Mohammad Sami	4	A. Nehra b Mohammad Sami.......... 0
*S. C. Ganguly st Moin Khan		B 2, l-b 22, w 6, n-b 7...... 37
b Shahid Afridi	15	
†R. Dravid b Mohammad Sami	36	1/56 (1) 2/71 (3) 3/140 (4) (48.4 overs) 317
Yuvraj Singh c Shabbir Ahmed		4/245 (2) 5/260 (5)
b Shahid Afridi	19	6/282 (6) 7/284 (7)
M. Kaif c Shoaib Malik b Shoaib Akhtar	7	8/284 (9) 9/314 (10) 10/317 (11)

Bowling: Shoaib Akhtar 9-1-49-3; Shabbir Ahmed 9-0-65-0; Mohammad Sami 9.4-1-41-3; Shoaib Malik 10-0-59-1; Shahid Afridi 8-0-57-2; Abdul Razzaq 3-0-22-0.

Umpires: S. J. A. Taufel (Australia) and Asad Rauf.
Third umpire: Zamir Haider. Referee: R. S. Madugalle (Sri Lanka).

"A glorious era had ended, and the promise of another was on the horizon. It was one hell of a series."
Indians in Australia, page 1117.

†PAKISTAN v INDIA

Third One-Day International

At Peshawar, March 19, 2004. Pakistan won by four wickets. Toss: Pakistan.

What a difference a bowler's pitch makes. On a rugged surface, much like the surrounding terrain, a target of 245 looked as menacing as 300-plus in the earlier games. India seemed unlikely to get even that when they were condemned to 37 for three by Shabbir Ahmed. His height and high-arm action were perfect for the conditions, though his opening over contained six wides and two no-balls – plus a wicket. Tendulkar, like Sehwag, fell to a splendid delivery that jagged away, while Laxman was worked over and then bowled through the gate. Yuvraj Singh revived the cause with a superbly paced 65, and Balaji thrashed 21 off 12 balls. Pathan extended the fightback with two quick wickets, and Pakistan were soon 65 for four. Yasir Hameed, the home-town boy, scored a 98 of composure and beauty before he too fell to Pathan, at a delicate 173 for six. But Abdul Razzaq made an irresistible run-a-ball fifty and, once he escaped a stinging caught-and-bowled chance to Tendulkar at 200, the match was in the bag.

Man of the Match: Yasir Hameed.

India

V. Sehwag c Shahid Afridi b Shabbir Ahmed .	13	
S. R. Tendulkar c Moin Khan b Shabbir Ahmed.	0	
V. V. S. Laxman b Shabbir Ahmed.	3	
†R. Dravid c Moin Khan b Shoaib Malik	33	
*S. C. Ganguly c Moin Khan b Abdul Razzaq	39	
Yuvraj Singh c Yousuf Youhana b Mohammad Sami .	65	
M. Kaif lbw b Abdul Razzaq	1	
R. R. Powar lbw b Shoaib Malik.	14	
I. K. Pathan b Shoaib Akhtar	16	
L. Balaji not out	21	
Zaheer Khan not out.	6	
B 1, l-b 5, w 23, n-b 4	33	

1/8 (2) 2/30 (1)   (9 wkts, 50 overs) 244
3/37 (3) 4/105 (5)
5/139 (4) 6/140 (7)
7/167 (8) 8/198 (9) 9/237 (6)

Bowling: Shoaib Akhtar 10–0–50–1; Shabbir Ahmed 10–0–33–3; Mohammad Sami 10–0–71–1; Abdul Razzaq 10–1–44–2; Shoaib Malik 10–0–40–2.

Pakistan

Yasir Hameed c Yuvraj Singh b Pathan. .	98
Shahid Afridi b Pathan	6
Yousuf Youhana c Laxman b Pathan . . .	2
Younis Khan run out.	18
Shoaib Malik c Sehwag b Zaheer Khan .	2
*Inzamam-ul-Haq lbw b Tendulkar	28
Abdul Razzaq not out.	53
†Moin Khan not out	22
L-b 11, w 7	18

1/14 (2) 2/29 (3)   (6 wkts, 47.2 overs) 247
3/55 (4) 4/65 (5)
5/156 (6) 6/173 (1)

Shoaib Akhtar, Mohammad Sami and Shabbir Ahmed did not bat.

Bowling: Pathan 10–0–58–3; Balaji 9.2–0–41–0; Zaheer Khan 9–0–56–1; Ganguly 6–0–24–0; Powar 4–0–17–0; Tendulkar 8–1–31–1; Yuvraj Singh 1–0–9–0.

Umpires: D. R. Shepherd (England) and Nadeem Ghauri.
Third umpire: Asad Rauf.   Referee: R. S. Madugalle (Sri Lanka).

†PAKISTAN v INDIA

Fourth One-Day International

At Lahore, March 21, 2004 (day/night). India won by five wickets. Toss: Pakistan.

In front of the biggest contingent of Indian fans on the tour so far, Dravid and Kaif furthered their reputations as men for a crisis. Combining at 162 for five, they levelled the series with an unbroken stand of 132 in 22 overs, an Indian sixth-wicket record. Inzamam-ul-Haq later said it was the series' turning point. On a pitch where even Inzamam wanted to bat first, Pakistan had piled on 293. He himself led with a masterful 123, his tenth one-day century and fourth against India, after the seamers had conceded just 59 in the first 15 overs. India's reply started breathlessly, with wides, no-balls, boundaries, edges and wickets always a moment apart. Half the side was out when Kaif joined Dravid in the 24th over – yet the asking-rate was already down to five an over. With hot heels and cool heads, they left the bowlers' spirits visibly crushed – so visibly that the former whistle-blower Rashid Latif declared on television that the match was rigged.

Man of the Match: Inzamam-ul-Haq.

Pakistan

Yasir Hameed st Dravid b Kartik	45	Mohammad Sami not out	0
Shahid Afridi c Yuvraj Singh b Pathan	3	Shabbir Ahmed not out	0
Yousuf Youhana lbw b Pathan	9		
*Inzamam-ul-Haq b Balaji	123	B 10, l-b 9, w 6, n-b 5	30
Younis Khan c Pathan b Kartik	36		
Abdul Razzaq c Kaif b Tendulkar	32	1/8 (2) 2/39 (3) (9 wkts, 50 overs) 293
†Moin Khan b Balaji	0	3/89 (1) 4/194 (5)
Shoaib Malik c Kaif b Zaheer Khan	13	5/264 (4) 6/264 (7)
Shoaib Akhtar b Zaheer Khan	2	7/283 (6) 8/290 (8) 9/292 (9)

Bowling: Pathan 10–1–53–2; Balaji 10–0–64–2; Zaheer Khan 10–0–43–2; Kartik 10–1–48–2; Tendulkar 8–0–48–1; Yuvraj Singh 2–0–18–0.

India

V. Sehwag c Younis Khan b Mohammad Sami	26	Yuvraj Singh c Yousuf Youhana b Mohammad Sami	36
S. R. Tendulkar c Moin Khan b Shoaib Akhtar	7	M. Kaif not out	71
V. V. S. Laxman b Shoaib Akhtar	20	L-b 9, w 19, n-b 9	37
*S. C. Ganguly c Moin Khan b Abdul Razzaq	21	1/34 (2) 2/69 (3) (5 wkts, 45 overs) 294
†R. Dravid not out	76	3/75 (1) 4/94 (4)
		5/162 (6)

I. K. Pathan, L. Balaji, Zaheer Khan and M. Kartik did not bat.

Bowling: Shoaib Akhtar 9–1–63–2; Shabbir Ahmed 7–0–62–0; Mohammad Sami 10–0–50–2; Abdul Razzaq 7–0–42–1; Shoaib Malik 7–0–38–0; Shahid Afridi 5–0–30–0.

Umpires: S. J. A. Taufel (Australia) and Asad Rauf.
Third umpire: Nadeem Ghauri. Referee: R. S. Madugalle (Sri Lanka).

†PAKISTAN v INDIA

Fifth One-Day International

At Lahore, March 24, 2004 (day/night). India won by 40 runs. Toss: Pakistan.

Finally, a game that was over long before it was over. For the fifth time, Inzamam-ul-Haq won the toss; for the third time, he put India in. Sehwag, Tendulkar and Ganguly were all caught behind trying to tickle to third man. But Laxman, whose best score against Pakistan in six one-day innings was 20, batted 40 overs for a delicious century. India completed 293, the same total they had chased three evenings before – despite the relative discipline of Pakistan, who conceded only 16 extras, down from their series average of 36. Pathan responded with similar discipline and considerable swing, picking up three for 20 in an extended opening spell. When Inzamam was wonderfully caught just inside the long-on fence, a 100th one-day catch for Tendulkar, little hope remained for Pakistan. Shoaib Malik and Moin Khan shared an enterprising stand of 99, but history, in the form of India's first series win in Pakistan, Test or limited-overs, beckoned. Ganguly, who had been stretchered off with a back injury, stepped up to claim the trophy.

Man of the Match: V. V. S. Laxman.　　*Man of the Series:* Inzamam-ul-Haq.

Job done: Lakshmipathy Balaji brings the one-day series to a triumphant conclusion for India by bowling Moin Khan.

Picture by Scott Barbour, Getty Images

India

V. Sehwag c Moin Khan b Shabbir Ahmed	20
S. R. Tendulkar c Moin Khan b Mohammad Sami	37
V. V. S. Laxman c Mohammad Sami b Shoaib Malik	107
*S. C. Ganguly c Moin Khan b Shoaib Akhtar	45
†R. Dravid b Mohammad Sami	4
Yuvraj Singh c Inzamam-ul-Haq b Shabbir Ahmed	18
M. Kaif c Taufeeq Umar b Mohammad Sami	16
I. K. Pathan not out	20
L. Balaji not out	10
B 2, l-b 4, w 5, n-b 5	16

M. Kartik and Zaheer Khan did not bat.

1/34 (1) 2/79 (2)   (7 wkts, 50 overs) 293
3/171 (4) 4/183 (5)
5/227 (6) 6/253 (3)
7/276 (7)

Bowling: Shoaib Akhtar 10–1–47–1; Shabbir Ahmed 10–1–56–2; Mohammad Sami 10–1–63–3; Abdul Razzaq 10–0–54–0; Shoaib Malik 10–0–67–1.

Pakistan

Yasir Hameed b Balaji	2
Taufeeq Umar b Pathan	18
Yousuf Youhana lbw b Pathan	1
*Inzamam-ul-Haq c Tendulkar b Kartik	38
Younis Khan c Yuvraj Singh b Pathan	12
Shoaib Malik c Kaif b Sehwag	65
Abdul Razzaq c Sehwag b Balaji	5
†Moin Khan b Balaji	72
Mohammad Sami b Zaheer Khan	23
Shoaib Akhtar run out	2
Shabbir Ahmed not out	1
B 2, l-b 5, w 4, n-b 3	14

1/8 (1) 2/9 (3) 3/25 (2)   (47.5 overs) 253
4/58 (5) 5/87 (4) 6/96 (7)
7/195 (6) 8/248 (9)
9/250 (10) 10/253 (8)

Bowling: Pathan 10–1–32–3; Balaji 9.5–0–62–3; Zaheer Khan 9–0–54–1; Kartik 10–0–42–1; Tendulkar 5–0–27–0; Sehwag 4–0–29–1.

Umpires: D. R. Shepherd (England) and Nadeem Ghauri.
Third umpire: Zamir Haider. Referee: R. S. Madugalle (Sri Lanka).

PAKISTAN v INDIA

First Test Match

At Multan, March 28, 29, 30, 31, April 1, 2004. India won by an innings and 52 runs. Toss: India.

From about 10 a.m. on March 28, a regular thud, rather than the roars associated with cricket in the subcontinent, began to emerge from Multan Cricket Stadium, a modern ground situated on farmland 45 minutes out of town. The stadium was virtually desolate, and the thumps, from Virender Sehwag's bat, were to resound for a day and a half as he constructed India's first triple-century in Test cricket. It laid the foundation of a historic victory, India's first in Pakistan in 21 Tests spread over 49 years. It was also, briefly, their most substantial win in a largely wretched 72 years of Tests away from home.

HIGHEST TEST SCORES FOR INDIA

309	**V. Sehwag v Pakistan at Multan**	**2003-04**
281	V. V. S. Laxman v Australia at Kolkata	2000-01
270	**R. Dravid v Pakistan at Rawalpindi**	**2003-04**
241*	**S. R. Tendulkar v Australia at Sydney**	**2003-04**
236*	S. M. Gavaskar v West Indies at Madras	1983-84
233	**R. Dravid v Australia at Adelaide**	**2003-04**
231	V. Mankad v New Zealand at Madras	1955-56
227	V. G. Kambli v Zimbabwe at Delhi	1992-93

Sehwag's 309, and his partnership of 336, an Indian third-wicket record, with Tendulkar, who crafted a meticulous century, carried India to their third-highest total, and second-highest away: 675 for five declared. The highest, 705 for seven declared, had come in their previous Test on a similar pitch at Sydney.

Sehwag's glitzy epic was not without luck. He was dropped on 68 and 77 during an opening stand of 160 with Chopra – their third century partnership in as many Tests. Later, he offered two chances behind the wicket off Shabbir Ahmed, one ball either side of the four that took him past the Indian record of 281 held by Laxman. None the less, it was an innings of sustained and versatile violence. He thrashed six sixes and 39 fours in 531 minutes and 375 balls; he went from 99 to 105 with a glided six over third man off Shoaib Akhtar, and from 295 to 301 with a roundhouse blast over wide long-on off Saqlain Mushtaq. That was his 364th ball, just two behind Matthew Hayden's 362-ball treble against Zimbabwe five months earlier. Only while nearing his maiden Test double had Sehwag turned circumspect, perhaps stung by the memory of holing out off a full toss on 195 at Melbourne in December.

Yet despite the continued flowering of the batting, India's real success, as Dravid, acting-captain for the injured Ganguly, explained, was in taking 20 wickets on a grassless, crack-free, crumble-proof surface. To do it virtually in four days (Pakistan's last wicket fell 12 balls into the final day) amid Multan's infamous combination of heat and dust was doubly creditable.

Two bowlers, in their 15th year and fourth month of international cricket respectively, stood out. Leg-spinner Kumble took seven wickets out of 13 on the pivotal fourth day, making it 32 from his last four Tests, all abroad. Left-arm seamer Pathan not only bagged six wickets in the match but bowled 17 maidens in 49 overs, 24 of them on the same day four, when a hamstring injury to Zaheer Khan left India a bowler short. It was Pathan, too, who surprised Abdul Razzaq with a bouncer as soon as he took guard on the fourth morning at 364 for six: the dismissal provided India with just the push they needed to press for the follow-on.

Perhaps the match would have run a different course had Inzamam-ul-Haq, who had scored hundreds in both the previous Tests on his home ground, not been cut short by a poor bat-pad decision by umpire Taufel when 77. It ended a pleasing 160-run stand with Yasir Hameed, who fell ten runs later to a loose stroke, with Pakistan still 432 behind. Their hopes of saving the match diminished with every thrust from Kumble the following day. The final nail was Inzamam's second-innings run-out by a brilliant hit from Yuvraj Singh, swooping at mid-wicket to leave Pakistan 44 for three – 224 short of making India bat again. Yousuf Youhana went on to slash a nothing-to-lose century, his second fifty coming in a mere 35 balls. He and Shoaib added 70 for the ninth wicket, which saw them through all but the last over of the extra half-hour claimed by India as they tried to finish it on the fourth evening.

HIGHEST TEST TOTALS BY INDIA

705-7 dec.	**v Australia at Sydney (drew)**	**2003-04**
676-7	v Sri Lanka at Kanpur (drew)	1986-87
675-5 dec.	**v Pakistan at Multan (won by an innings and 52 runs)**	**2003-04**
657-7 dec.	v Australia at Kolkata (won by 171 runs)	2000-01
644-7 dec.	v West Indies at Kanpur (drew)	1978-79
633-5 dec.	v Australia at Calcutta (won by an innings and 219 runs)	1997-98
628-8 dec.	v England at Leeds (won by an innings and 46 runs)	2002
609-6 dec.	v Zimbabwe at Nagpur (drew)	2000-01
606-9 dec.	v England at The Oval (drew)	1990
600-4 dec.	v Australia at Sydney (drew)	1985-86
600	**v Pakistan at Rawalpindi (won by an innings and 131 runs)**	**2003-04**

Strangely, the biggest of the game's controversies – dwarfing the umpiring and Pakistan's request for a shaved pitch – came from the victorious camp. Dravid stunned observers by declaring when Yuvraj fell an hour before the second-day close. Nothing sensational – except that Tendulkar was 194 not out. Tendulkar did not take the field that evening, claiming a sprained ankle; at a press conference, he made clear his disappointment and surprise.

Back home, some believed Tendulkar had been robbed; others thought his comments were selfish, and demonstrated an obsession with personal milestones. (As it was, the innings put him one ahead of Steve Waugh's 32 Test hundreds, and one behind Sunil Gavaskar's record of 34.) Many in the first group aimed their vitriol at Ganguly, who had no official role as he sat out the game with a back injury, but was seen on television gesturing impatiently.

In fact, Tendulkar had played the perfect innings for his team, a discreet, chanceless companion to Sehwag's theatricals. His pacing was perfect too, each fifty coming quicker than the last, and the final 40 at almost a run a ball. But because he was operating without obvious risk, he seemed not to be pushing on. And Dravid probably erred not in his timing, but in failing to communicate with Tendulkar. The two had an honest discussion next morning to clear the air, which would have been beyond some faction-ridden Indian teams of the past.

Straight after the victory, while the Indians were off to visit orphaned children, Pakistan's beleaguered bowlers were made to go out and practise on the match pitch itself, which looked good for another five days.

Man of the Match: V. Sehwag.

Close of play: First day, India 356-2 (Sehwag 228, Tendulkar 60); Second day, Pakistan 42-0 (Imran Farhat 17, Taufeeq Umar 20); Third day, Pakistan 364-6 (Abdul Razzaq 47); Fourth day, Pakistan 207-9 (Yousuf Youhana 107, Shabbir Ahmed 0).

India

A. Chopra c Imran Farhat b Saqlain Mushtaq .	42
V. Sehwag c Taufeeq Umar b Mohammad Sami .	309
*R. Dravid c Yasir Hameed b Mohammad Sami .	6
S. R. Tendulkar not out	194
V. V. S. Laxman run out	29
Yuvraj Singh c and b Imran Farhat	59
B 8, l-b 20, w 1, n-b 7.	36
1/160 (1) 2/173 (3) (5 wkts dec.) 675	
3/509 (2) 4/565 (5)	
5/675 (6)	

†P. A. Patel, I. K. Pathan, A. Kumble, L. Balaji and Zaheer Khan did not bat.

Bowling: Shoaib Akhtar 32–4–119–0; Mohammad Sami 34–4–110–2; Shabbir Ahmed 31–6–122–0; Saqlain Mushtaq 43–4–204–1; Abdul Razzaq 15–3–61–0; Imran Farhat 6.5–0–31–1.

Pakistan

Imran Farhat lbw b Balaji	38	– c Patel b Kumble	24
Taufeeq Umar c Dravid b Pathan	23	– lbw b Kumble	9
Yasir Hameed c Patel b Pathan	91	– c Sehwag b Yuvraj Singh	23
*Inzamam-ul-Haq c Chopra b Kumble	77	– run out	0
Yousuf Youhana c Patel b Zaheer Khan	35	– c Dravid b Pathan.	112
Abdul Razzaq c Patel b Pathan.	47	– c Chopra b Kumble.	22
†Moin Khan b Tendulkar.	17	– lbw b Pathan	5
Saqlain Mushtaq c Zaheer Khan b Pathan.	5	– (9) lbw b Kumble	0
Mohammad Sami b Kumble.	15	– (8) lbw b Kumble.	0
Shoaib Akhtar c and b Tendulkar	0	– c Laxman b Kumble	4
Shabbir Ahmed not out	19	– not out	0
B 4, l-b 26, n-b 10	40	B 4, l-b 5, w 1, n-b 2, p 5 .	17

1/58 (2) 2/73 (1) 3/233 (4) 4/243 (3) 407	1/33 (1) 2/44 (2) 3/44 (4) 216
5/321 (5) 6/364 (7) 7/364 (6)	4/75 (3) 5/106 (6) 6/113 (7)
8/371 (8) 9/371 (10) 10/407 (9)	7/124 (8) 8/136 (9)
	9/206 (10) 10/216 (5)

Bowling: *First Innings*—Zaheer Khan 23–6–76–1; Pathan 28–5–100–4; Kumble 39.3–12–100–2; Balaji 20–4–54–1; Schwag 2–0–11–0; Tendulkar 14–1–36–2. *Second Innings*—Pathan 21–12–26–2; Balaji 11–3–48–0; Kumble 30–10–72–6; Sehwag 3–0–8–0; Yuvraj Singh 6–1–25–1; Tendulkar 6–2–23–0.

Umpires: D. R. Shepherd (England) and S. J. A. Taufel (Australia).
Third umpire: Asad Rauf. Referee: R. S. Madugalle (Sri Lanka).

PAKISTAN v INDIA

Second Test Match

At Lahore, April 5, 6, 7, 8, 2004. Pakistan won by nine wickets. Toss: India.

A Test lit up brilliantly by youth on the opening day ran a brisk but predictable course, with Pakistan emerging the deserved winners early on the fourth afternoon. It not only levelled the series, but allowed them to get back at their voluble critics, particularly ex-players; Inzamam-ul-Haq dedicated much of his post-match press conference to making the point.

Pakistan made four changes, which worked a charm. The all-rounder Abdul Razzaq (back niggle) was replaced with Asim Kamal, a left-handed batsman who compiled an

Back in business: Umar Gul removes Sachin Tendulkar, and after a heavy defeat in the First Test Pakistan bounce back to win handsomely at Lahore.

Picture by Arko Datta, Reuters

innings of character. Wicket-keeper Moin Khan (groin injury) was swapped with Kamran Akmal, who claimed six dismissals. Saqlain Mushtaq (who conceded 204 runs and played a daft shot at Multan) made way for the leg-spinner Danish Kaneria, who was effective against the lower order. And Shabbir Ahmed (shin pain) sat out for Umar Gul, whose first-day bowling set the game up for Pakistan. India brought in Agarkar for the injured Zaheer Khan.

The pitch, hidden from the media beforehand, showed its nature when Shoaib Akhtar's first ball of the match took Chopra's edge and squirted through for four; the last ball of that over hit Chopra on the shoulder. It was instantly evident that justifying Dravid's decision to bat would be hard work, particularly during the first session when there was moisture in the surface.

Even so, pace without guile, such as Shoaib and Mohammad Sami were dishing out, was a waste. When Gul came on in the 11th over, India were rattling along at six an over. Nine days short of his 20th birthday, Gul was a matchstick-thin seamer from Nawakheli, a village on the Afghan border and birthplace of two of history's greatest squash players, Jahangir and Jansher Khan. Young Gul's idol, however, was Narromine's Glenn McGrath. Though there was little of McGrath in his limby action – described by one observer as that of a flamingo – he showed similar command over line and length, with enough lateral movement for effect.

In a 12-over spell either side of lunch, Gul reaped a harvest that he may be hard-pressed to better: Sehwag, Tendulkar, Laxman, Dravid and Patel. Three were coerced into nicking, the other two lbw to in-swingers. Tendulkar's dismissal was his first in four Test innings in 2004, in which he had amassed a record 497. Gul's five wickets cost a mere 31, but he bowled no further in the first innings because of cramp; his 13 overs in the second left him with a back injury that ruled him out of the Third Test.

Gul's heroics gave 22-year-old Yuvraj Singh, entering at 94 for four, which quickly deteriorated to 147 for seven, a chance to expand his reputation for tackling crises from the one-day to the Test arena. He played a counter-attacking gem, reaching his maiden Test century in 110 balls, unfettered by the situation or the occasional swing-and-miss. Assisting Yuvraj was Pathan, the youngest of the day's young stars at 19 years five months. He made a conscientious 49 in front of his proud parents, who had travelled outside India, and by aeroplane, for the first time.

MOST RUNS BETWEEN TEST DISMISSALS

497	S. R. Tendulkar (India)	241* & 60* v Australia at Sydney	2003-04
		194* v Pakistan at Multan	2003-04
		2 v Pakistan at Lahore	2003-04
490	G. S. Sobers (West Indies)	365* v Pakistan at Kingston	1957-58
		125 v Pakistan at Georgetown	1957-58
473	R. Dravid (India)	41* v Bangladesh at Dhaka	2000-01
		200* & 70* v Zimbabwe at Delhi	2000-01
		162 v Zimbabwe at Nagpur	2000-01
456	J. H. Kallis (South Africa)	157* & 42* v Zimbabwe at Harare	2001-02
		189* v Zimbabwe at Bulawayo	2001-02
		68 v India at Bloemfontein	2001-02

Research: Rajesh Kumar

Pakistan's task was not just to overtake India's 287, but to build enough of a lead to put their batting under pressure second time around. Inzamam, with a dutiful 118, played the main role, sharing century stands with Imran Farhat and Yousuf Youhana. Farhat himself earned a fine hundred, his second in Tests, showing better judgment than usual outside off.

On the third morning, Pakistan lost four for 31, but Kamal shepherded the tail, particularly Shoaib, who hung about for an hour and a half, and extended the lead to 202. By the evening, the game was up for India. Chopra, Tendulkar and Laxman, bowled by a marvellous leg-cutter from Gul, all had their second failure of the match, while Dravid was run out by a fine direct hit from Farhat. It was only Dravid's third duck in 77 Tests, and he had not even faced a ball. India closed five down and still 53 behind. Sehwag remained, on a scintillating 86, but tried too hard to defend the following morning and fell for just four more. A raucous stand between Patel and Agarkar averted an innings defeat – though when the final wicket went Gul ran off the pitch, stumps in hand, before being reminded by his team-mates that they still had to bat again.

Like Pakistan in the last Test, the Indians felt aggrieved at the umpiring. They were particularly aggrieved by Steve Bucknor, who had not endeared himself to them on the tour of Australia; here he rejected several good lbw shouts by Kumble, and reported Patel for excessive appealing, which led to a fine. India's coach, John Wright, marched into the referee's cabin to vent his feelings on the second day.

But as Dravid pointed out, it was efficient batting and bowling, rather than lopsided umpiring, that explained why Pakistan had stormed back into the series.

Man of the Match: Umar Gul.

Close of play: First day, Pakistan 61-1 (Imran Farhat 25, Yasir Hameed 4); Second day, Pakistan 355-3 (Inzamam-ul-Haq 118, Yousuf Youhana 62); Third day, India 149-5 (Sehwag 86, Patel 13).

India

A. Chopra lbw b Mohammad Sami	4	– lbw b Shoaib Akhtar 5
V. Sehwag c Kamran Akmal b Umar Gul	39	– c Kamran Akmal b Shoaib Akhtar . 90
*R. Dravid c Inzamam-ul-Haq b Umar Gul	33	– run out 0
S. R. Tendulkar lbw b Umar Gul	2	– lbw b Mohammad Sami 8
V. V. S. Laxman c Taufeeq Umar b Umar Gul . .	11	– b Umar Gul 13
Yuvraj Singh c Imran Farhat b Danish Kaneria .	112	– c Kamran Akmal
		b Mohammad Sami . 12
†P. A. Patel lbw b Umar Gul	0	– not out 62
A. B. Agarkar c Kamran Akmal b Shoaib Akhtar	2	– (9) c Taufeeq Umar
		b Danish Kaneria . 36
I. K. Pathan c and b Danish Kaneria	49	– (8) c Taufeeq Umar
		b Shoaib Akhtar . 0
L. Balaji c Kamran Akmal b Mohammad Sami .	0	– (11) lbw b Danish Kaneria 0
A. Kumble not out	6	– (10) st Kamran Akmal
		b Danish Kaneria . 0
B 6, l-b 8, w 6, n-b 9	29	L-b 8, w 1, n-b 6 15

1/5 (1) 2/69 (2) 3/75 (4) 4/94 (5)	287	1/15 (1) 2/15 (3) 3/43 (4) 241
5/125 (3) 6/127 (7) 7/147 (8)		4/88 (5) 5/105 (6) 6/160 (2)
8/264 (9) 9/265 (10) 10/287 (6)		7/160 (8) 8/235 (9)
		9/241 (10) 10/241 (11)

Bowling: *First Innings*—Shoaib Akhtar 16–1–69–1; Mohammad Sami 23–1–117–2; Umar Gul 12–2–31–5; Danish Kaneria 13.1–1–56–2. *Second Innings*—Shoaib Akhtar 17–4–62–3; Mohammad Sami 26–6–92–2; Umar Gul 13–1–65–1; Danish Kaneria 6.4–2–14–3.

Pakistan

Imran Farhat c Patel b Balaji	101	– c Yuvraj Singh b Balaji 9
Taufeeq Umar b Balaji	24	– not out 14
Yasir Hameed c Dravid b Agarkar	19	– not out 16
*Inzamam-ul-Haq lbw b Pathan	118	
Yousuf Youhana c Patel b Balaji	72	
Asim Kamal c Patel b Kumble	73	
†Kamran Akmal lbw b Pathan	5	
Mohammad Sami b Pathan	2	
Shoaib Akhtar c Yuvraj Singh b Kumble	19	
Umar Gul hit wkt b Tendulkar	14	
Danish Kaneria not out	0	
B 4, l-b 18, w 4, n-b 16	42	N-b 1 1

1/47 (2) 2/95 (3) 3/205 (1) 4/356 (4)	489	1/15 (1) (1 wkt) 40
5/366 (5) 6/379 (7) 7/386 (8)		
8/432 (9) 9/470 (10) 10/489 (6)		

Bowling: *First Innings*—Pathan 44–14–107–3; Balaji 33–11–81–3; Agarkar 23–5–80–1; Kumble 44.1–5–146–2; Tendulkar 12–1–38–1; Yuvraj Singh 3–0–7–0; Sehwag 1–0–8–0. *Second Innings*—Pathan 4–0–25–0; Balaji 3–0–15–1.

Umpires: S. A. Bucknor (West Indies) and S. J. A. Taufel (Australia).
Third umpire: Nadeem Ghauri. Referee: R. S. Madugalle (Sri Lanka).

> " In a season in which team India were making waves, a quieter revolution was also being ushered in."
>
> Cricket in India, page 1450.

PAKISTAN v INDIA

Third Test Match

At Rawalpindi, April 13, 14, 15, 16, 2004. India won by an innings and 131 runs. Toss: India.

With three and a half days of almost flawless cricket, India not only bettered their thundering victory at Multan for magnitude, but won their first Test series away from home for an entire decade. It was also the first time they had won series in both formats on the same tour, discounting England in 1986, when they won the Tests but were awarded a tied one-day series on run-rate.

INDIAN TEST SERIES VICTORIES AWAY FROM HOME

Captain

Nawab of Pataudi, jun.	3–1	in New Zealand (4 Tests)	1967-68
A. L. Wadekar	1–0	in the West Indies (5 Tests)	1970-71
A. L. Wadekar	1–0	in England (3 Tests)	1971
Kapil Dev	2–0	in England (3 Tests)	1986
M. Azharuddin	1–0	in Sri Lanka (3 Tests)	1993-94
R. Dravid/S. C. Ganguly	**2–1**	**in Pakistan (3 Tests)**	**2003-04**

Ganguly also led India to victory in a one-off Test in Bangladesh in 2000-01.

For Pakistan, the defeat brought to a head the impatience of a nation: two months later, the coach, Javed Miandad, was sacked. Veteran commentator Omar Kureishi described the fourth day, when they finally capitulated, as "the blackest in Pakistan's cricket history", though – match-fixing scandals aside – losing by an innings to Matthew Hayden's bat alone in October 2002 was surely worse.

Like the previous Test, this match was made on day one. Bitten at Lahore, India chose to field when Ganguly, back from injury, continued Dravid's luck with the toss. There, India had been 107 for four at lunch; here, Pakistan were 96 for four. This included the key wicket of Inzamam-ul-Haq, set up beautifully when Nehra (who replaced Agarkar) had him hunch over an in-swinger before slanting one across for the nick.

Any hopes of recovery were thwarted by Balaji, who extracted three wickets in a nine-over spell after the interval, bending away the middle-aged ball late in its trajectory to leave Pakistan tottering at 137 for eight. The top score was a committed 49 from Mohammad Sami, his highest in Tests; that and a comical 25 from Fazl-e-Akbar managed to lift Pakistan to a modest 224. As Ganguly reflected later, extracting the advantage with the ball on the opening day was perhaps the difference between this and his previous quests for an overseas victory. It led to his 15th win as captain, beating Mohammad Azharuddin's record for India.

With Ganguly's return, the debate for India revolved around the second opener. Chopra, Sehwag's regular partner, had failed twice at Lahore, whereas Yuvraj Singh had stroked an exceptional century. Chopra was dropped – but instead of Yuvraj or Ganguly climbing up as was indicated, the wicket-keeper, Patel, was promoted. Though the decision was poorly received, Patel vindicated it with a Test-best 69 while seeing out some crucial hours of play on the first evening and next morning.

It was a colossal 270 from Dravid that put the series beyond Pakistan. In its significance, the innings could stand alongside any ever played by an Indian. Even Dravid agreed, though, that he was not at his most fluent, particularly on the second day, which he ended unbeaten on 134. He was given the benefit of the doubt after an adjacent lbw shout on 21, carelessly dropped at point on 71, and again spared when

Immovable: at Rawalpindi, Rahul Dravid batted 12 hours 20 minutes to take the Test and the series out of Pakistan's reach.

Picture by Arko Datta, Reuters

caught behind off bat-and-boot on 77. In between, he mistimed more than he had sometimes done through entire tours.

Dravid's strength, however, is in raising his game when most needed. The following day he blossomed. He had already glued together the innings through century stands with Patel and, most delightfully, Laxman; he completed a third with Ganguly, and 98 with Yuvraj. It was a phenomenal physical effort. Between his 73 overs in the field and 175 overs at the crease lay a mere ten-minute break: Sehwag had been out first ball. In all, Dravid batted 12 hours 20 minutes – India's longest Test innings – faced 495 balls, and struck 34 fours and a six. His fifth Test double-hundred was an Indian record, one ahead of Sunil Gavaskar.

Dravid's task was made simpler when, late on the second afternoon, Shoaib Akhtar fell in his follow-through and injured his left thumb and a rib, soon after castling Laxman with a rapid out-swinging full toss. He left the field after six further balls and did not return except to bat. It was the last thing Pakistan needed: their bowling had already been depleted by the absence of Umar Gul, whose replacement, Fazl-e-Akbar, churned out dross to the tune of 162 runs for a single wicket in 41 overs.

Dravid finally fell on the third evening attempting, of all things, to reverse-sweep Imran Farhat's part-time leg-spin. Seven runs later, India were out for an even 600. As in the first innings, the Pakistan openers fell in consecutive overs, leaving the others to battle back from 327 runs behind with two days remaining.

They did not even come close, despite the best efforts of India's fielders, who dropped six catches in the first hour next morning, four of them off Balaji. But the potency of his swing, exaggerated by cloud cover, could not be repressed. Before lunch, he added two more wickets, including Inzamam with a peachy away-curler and, between those two, Patel held a superb diving catch down the leg side off Yasir Hameed's glance.

For Pakistan, the only pride came via Asim Kamal, defiantly unbeaten on 60 despite a painful elbow.

There was a final twist when Shoaib came out and smote a manic 14-ball 28, all in boundaries, which contrasted greatly with his mulish obduracy in the previous Test. Eyebrows were raised, Inzamam hurled a few barbs moments after the defeat, and Shaharyar Khan and Ramiz Raja, the PCB chairman and chief executive officer, questioned Shoaib's commitment to the team. They ordered a "medical inquiry commission" to see if he had exaggerated his injury or not; it led to further estrangement and nothing more.

Man of the Match: R. Dravid.   *Man of the Series:* V. Sehwag.

Close of play: First day, India 23-1 (Patel 13, Dravid 10); Second day, India 342-4 (Dravid 134, Ganguly 53); Third day, Pakistan 49-2 (Yasir Hameed 8, Kamran Akmal 10).

Pakistan

Imran Farhat lbw b Nehra	16	– c Sehwag b Balaji	3
Taufeeq Umar lbw b Balaji	9	– lbw b Pathan	13
Yasir Hameed c Laxman b Pathan	26	– c Patel b Nehra	20
*Inzamam-ul-Haq c Patel b Nehra	15	– (5) c Patel b Balaji	9
Yousuf Youhana b Pathan	13	– (6) c and b Kumble	48
Asim Kamal lbw b Balaji	21	– (7) not out	60
†Kamran Akmal c Laxman b Balaji	17	– (4) b Balaji	23
Mohammad Sami run out	49	– c Dravid b Kumble	0
Shoaib Akhtar b Balaji	0	– c Nehra b Kumble	28
Fazl-e-Akbar lbw b Kumble	25	– c Patel b Kumble	12
Danish Kaneria not out	4	– c Ganguly b Tendulkar	0
B 14, l-b 5, w 7, n-b 3	29	B 5, l-b 11, w 2, n-b 11	29
	224		**245**

1/34 (2) 2/34 (1) 3/77 (3) 4/77 (4) 5/110 (5) 6/120 (6) 7/137 (7) 8/137 (9) 9/207 (10) 10/224 (8)

1/30 (1) 2/34 (2) 3/64 (4) 4/90 (3) 5/94 (5) 6/175 (6) 7/179 (8) 8/221 (9) 9/244 (10) 10/245 (11)

Bowling: First Innings—Pathan 22–7–49–2; Balaji 19–4–63–4; Nehra 21–4–60–2; Ganguly 2–0–9–0; Kumble 8.5–2–24–1. *Second Innings*—Pathan 15–6–35–1; Balaji 20–2–108–3; Kumble 8–2–47–4; Nehra 6–2–20–1; Ganguly 4–0–18–0; Tendulkar 1–0–1–1.

India

V. Sehwag c Yasir Hameed b Shoaib Akhtar	0	A. Kumble st Kamran Akmal b Danish Kaneria	9
†P. A. Patel c Kamran Akmal b Fazl-e-Akbar	69	L. Balaji c sub (Shoaib Malik) b Imran Farhat	11
R. Dravid b Imran Farhat	270	A. Nehra not out	1
S. R. Tendulkar c Kamran Akmal b Shoaib Akhtar	1		
V. V. S. Laxman b Shoaib Akhtar	71	B 11, l-b 12, w 6	29
*S. C. Ganguly run out	77		**600**
Yuvraj Singh lbw b Mohammad Sami	47		
I. K. Pathan c Fazl-e-Akbar b Danish Kaneria	15		

1/0 (1) 2/129 (2) 3/130 (4) 4/261 (5) 5/392 (6) 6/490 (7) 7/537 (8) 8/572 (9) 9/593 (3) 10/600 (10)

Bowling: Shoaib Akhtar 21.2–7–47–3; Fazl-e-Akbar 40.4–3–162–1; Danish Kaneria 62–4–178–2; Mohammad Sami 40–11–116–1; Imran Farhat 12.2–1–69–2; Yasir Hameed 1–0–5–0.

Umpires: R. E. Koertzen (South Africa) and D. R. Shepherd (England).
Third umpire: Zamir Haider. Referee: R. S. Madugalle (Sri Lanka).

THE SRI LANKANS IN ZIMBABWE, 2003-04

SPECIAL CORRESPONDENT

Sri Lanka's third Test tour of Zimbabwe, through no fault of their own, was a travesty of international cricket from beginning to end. The civil war between Zimbabwe's administrators and cricketers is reported elsewhere, but it led to the absence of 15 good players in a country desperately short of them. The upshot was a farce in which the Sri Lankans easily won all five one-day internationals and then hammered the team chosen to represent Zimbabwe by record margins in the two Tests.

YOUNGEST TEST CAPTAINS

Years	Days			
20	**358**	**T. Taibu**	**Zimbabwe v Sri Lanka at Harare**	**2003-04**
21	77	Nawab of Pataudi, jun. .	India v West Indies at Bridgetown	1961-62
22	15†	Waqar Younis	Pakistan v Zimbabwe at Karachi	1993-94
22	82	G. C. Smith	South Africa v Bangladesh at Chittagong. .	2003
22	194	I. D. Craig	Australia v South Africa at Johannesburg. .	1957-58
22	260	Javed Miandad	Pakistan v Australia at Karachi	1979-80
22	306	M. Bisset	South Africa v England at Johannesburg . .	1898-99
23	144	M. P. Bowden	England v South Africa at Cape Town. . . .	1888-89
23	169	S. R. Tendulkar	India v Australia at Delhi	1996-97
23	217	G. C. Grant	West Indies v Australia at Adelaide.	1930-31
23	292	Hon. Ivo Bligh	England v Australia at Melbourne	1882-83
23	319	S. P. Fleming	New Zealand v England at Christchurch . .	1996-97
23	354	A. D. R. Campbell. . . .	Zimbabwe v Sri Lanka at Colombo	1996-97

† *Age in dispute.*

The International Cricket Council refused to recognise the extent of the crisis until the results of the Test matches meant that they could bury their heads in the sand no longer. They then stepped in to safeguard the Australian tour that followed from similar abuse of international status; the Zimbabwe Cricket Union agreed to postpone those Tests, before they could be stripped of their official standing. But by that time the Sri Lankan series had become a part of cricket history that could not be revoked.

The shrapnel from the civil war affected the tour from beginning to end. There was a will-they-won't-they saga as to whether the dissident players would make themselves available for the start of the one-day series, then for the final three one-day matches, then the Test series. After the one-day games the players, as a goodwill gesture, returned to practice, and the selectors included the four they considered indispensable in a Zimbabwe A team for a pre-Test warm-up.

This was the only tour game the Sri Lankans failed to win, but then negotiations broke down again, and the team selected for the Tests was basically the one that played in the one-day series. That side had enjoyed a couple of fair games – as well as suffering one humiliation – but Test cricket was a challenge too far, and they were totally outclassed.

Of the team that did play Sri Lanka, only Tatenda Taibu, who became the youngest Test captain in history eight days before his 21st birthday, Dion Ebrahim and Douglas Hondo had been established members of the team before the boycott. The others consisted mainly of black players from the fringe of the full-strength team, some of whom had already tasted international cricket unsuccessfully, and Under-19 players. Two of the latter gave most hope for the future: opening batsman Brendan Taylor, usually the only white left in the team, and pace bowler Tinashe Panyangara.

In the one-day series Zimbabwe averaged 16.75 runs per wicket against Sri Lanka's 36. The disparity would have been greater had the tourists not rested key players after the first couple of games and found difficulty in lifting themselves against opposition so badly below standard. In the two Tests, however, the statistics were ludicrously tilted: Sri Lanka averaged 96.46 runs per wicket against Zimbabwe's 19.

To their credit the young Zimbabweans – Hondo was the grand-daddy at 24 and the average age was just under 20 – never gave up. They were clearly thrilled to be given the chance of playing international cricket, and never really lost heart, although physical and mental exhaustion had its effect. Their batting, though, was horrendously weak, as exemplified by an all-time record low of 35 on the only pitch not prepared with batsmen in mind.

> Taibu remained unfailingly cheerful in his impossible job

The main virtues of their largely medium-paced bowling were enthusiasm and accuracy, which did keep Sri Lankan scoring within bounds in the one-day series, but proved little more than cannon fodder in the Tests. The sole specialist spinner was Prosper Utseya, who kept a brake on the run-rate but failed to take a wicket in his six matches. The fielding was enthusiastic but immature, with the close catching particularly fallible.

Taibu remained unfailingly cheerful and optimistic in his impossible job as captain of a decimated team with no experienced or successful players to support him. He led from the front, with an epic 96 not out on his debut as captain, when both openers had been dismissed without scoring; he even took off his wicket-keeper's pads and bowled to supplement his side's meagre attack.

For Sri Lanka, facing such feeble opposition inevitably meant that they learned little about themselves. Of the newer players, Farveez Maharoof was the most impressive as a seam-bowling all-rounder and valuable batsman. For the others, it was largely a matter of enhancing personal records – when they had the chance. For middle-order batsmen like Tillekeratne Dilshan, that chance did not come often enough – he batted only four times in seven international games.

The new Test captain, Marvan Atapattu, has a good enough reputation against stronger teams; against weak attacks, he fills his boots. He scored big centuries in both Test innings, but did not really enjoy his tour; he complained after his return home about poor organisation and facilities. It seemed the ZCU were so preoccupied with their own crisis that they could not get their act together to take proper care of the tourists.

Kumar Sangakkara played as a specialist batsman in the Tests, passing the wicket-keeper's gloves to Prasanna Jayawardene, who did a fair job, though the Sri Lankan management hinted this arrangement might not be repeated. Sangakkara scored a massive 270 in Bulawayo, where he shared a record-breaking partnership of 438 with Atapattu. But such records were seriously devalued.

Muttiah Muralitharan's seizure of the title of Test cricket's leading wicket-taker was one record likely to have occurred here whatever the quality of the opposition. It was just sad that he could not have overtaken Courtney Walsh's record of 519 wickets in more salubrious circumstances. It was still a memorable occasion, acclaimed rapturously by his team-mates and all of Sri Lanka. Muralitharan said his aim was to play on until the 2007 World Cup, by which time his Test total might be stratospheric. Chaminda Vaas spearheaded the pace attack with skill, as he has done ever since he first toured Zimbabwe almost ten years earlier. He destroyed the top-order batting in the early one-day internationals before being rested, and deserved better figures in the Tests. Nuwan Zoysa gave him good support.

But the entire tour was a mismatch with few memorable moments or worthy records. The exception was a remarkable feat by a remarkable and unique bowler – Murali.

SRI LANKAN TOURING PARTY

M. S. Atapattu (*captain*), D. P. M. D. Jayawardene (*vice-captain*), R. P. Arnold, U. D. U. Chandana, G. I. Daniel, T. M. Dilshan, C. R. D. Fernando, H. M. R. K. B. Herath, W. S. Jayantha, S. T. Jayasuriya, H. A. P. W. Jayawardene, S. H. T. Kandamby, K. M. D. N. Kulasekara, M. F. Maharoof, M. Muralitharan, T. T. Samaraweera, K. C. Sangakkara, W. P. U. J. C. Vaas, D. N. T. Zoysa.

Daniel, H. A. P. W. Jayawardene and Samaraweera arrived for the Test series, replacing Arnold, Jayantha and Kulasekara who had played in the one-day series.

Coach: J. Dyson.   *Manager:* Air Commodore A. N. C. W. Jayasekara.
Physiotherapist: C. J. Clark.   *Computer analyst:* S. Jayasundera.

SRI LANKAN TOUR RESULTS

Test matches – Played 2: Won 2.
First-class matches – Played 3: Won 2, Drawn 1.
One-day internationals – Played 5: Won 5.

Note: Matches in this section which were not first-class are signified by a dagger.

†ZIMBABWE v SRI LANKA

First One-Day International

At Bulawayo, April 20, 2004. Sri Lanka won by 12 runs (D/L method). Toss: Sri Lanka. One-day international debuts: E. Chigumbura, T. Panyangara, B. R. M. Taylor, P. Utseya.

In a heroic performance Tatenda Taibu, international cricket's youngest captain at 20 years 342 days, just missed a maiden international hundred and later bowled four overs of slingy medium-pace after passing the keeper's gloves to Maregwede. Only one other player, Hondo,

YOUNGEST ONE-DAY INTERNATIONAL CAPTAINS

Years	Days			
20	297	Rajin Saleh.	**Bangladesh v South Africa at Birmingham**.	**2004**
20	342	T. Taibu	**Zimbabwe v Sri Lanka at Bulawayo**	**2003-04**
21	354†	Waqar Younis.	Pakistan v West Indies at Sharjah	1993-94
22	71	G. C. Smith.	South Africa v Bangladesh at Chittagong . . .	2003
23	126	S. R. Tendulkar	India v Sri Lanka at Colombo (RPS)	1996-97
23	162	Javed Miandad	Pakistan v West Indies at Karachi	1980-81
23	196	Moin Khan	Pakistan v India at Sharjah	1994-95
23	249	Kapil Dev	India v Sri Lanka at Amritsar	1982-83
23	338	A. D. R. Campbell . .	Zimbabwe v Australia at Colombo (RPS) . . .	1996-97
23	358	S. P. Fleming.	New Zealand v Sri Lanka at Christchurch . . .	1996-97
24	105	W. J. Cronje.	South Africa v New Zealand at Brisbane. . . .	1993-94
24	186	I. T. Botham.	England v West Indies at Leeds.	1980
24	209	C. D. McMillan	New Zealand v Sri Lanka at Sharjah	2000-01

† *Age in dispute.*

Research: Andrew Samson

---

was a certain starter in a full-strength side, and the new-look Zimbabwe lost both openers with only a leg-bye on the board. Once Vaas and Zoysa shattered the early batting, however, Sri Lanka appeared to drift into complacency, allowing Taibu to lead the recovery. A total of 211 for six could be seen as an unexpected triumph. Tinashe Panyangara, hero of the Under-19 World Cup victory over Australia, then dismissed Jayasuriya with his second ball in senior internationals, before rain interrupted Sri Lanka at 31 for two. The new target was 173 off 33 overs. They struggled until Dilshan joined Sangakkara, but were 12 ahead of par when they accepted the offer of bad light.

Man of the Match: T. Taibu.

Zimbabwe

V. Sibanda c Sangakkara b Zoysa	. . . . .	0	A. Maregwede c Dilshan b Chandana. . .	37
B. R. M. Taylor b Vaas	. . . .	0	M. L. Nkala not out	33
D. D. Ebrahim c Jayawardene b Zoysa	. .	13	B 2, l-b 5, w 3, n-b 3	13
*†T. Taibu not out	. . . .	96		
E. Chigumbura c Muralitharan b Zoysa	.	13	1/1 (1) 2/1 (2)	(6 wkts, 50 overs) 211
S. Matsikenyeri st Sangakkara			3/47 (3) 4/64 (5)	
b Muralitharan	.	6	5/79 (6) 6/154 (7)	

P. Utseya, D. T. Hondo and T. Panyangara did not bat.

Bowling: Vaas 10–5–31–1; Zoysa 7–2–21–3; Kulasekara 3–0–26–0; Muralitharan 10–1–47–1; Chandana 10–0–43–1; Jayasuriya 8–0–31–0; Arnold 2–1–5–0.

Sri Lanka

S. T. Jayasuriya c Ebrahim b Panyangara		9	T. M. Dilshan not out	35
*M. S. Atapattu lbw b Hondo.		0		
†K. C. Sangakkara not out		73	L-b 3, w 5	8
D. P. M. D. Jayawardene c Panyangara				
b Hondo	.	5	1/9 (1) 2/9 (2)	(4 wkts, 27 overs) 144
D. N. T. Zoysa c Taylor b Chigumbura	. .	14	3/44 (4) 4/77 (5)	

R. P. Arnold, U. D. U. Chandana, W. P. U. J. C. Vaas, K. M. D. N. Kulasekara and M. Muralitharan did not bat.

Bowling: Hondo 7–1–34–2; Panyangara 5–1–22–1; Chigumbura 5–0–32–1; Nkala 6–0–34–0; Taibu 4–0–19–0.

Umpires: D. J. Harper (Australia) and K. C. Barbour.
Third umpire: R. B. Tiffin. Referee: M. J. Procter (South Africa).

†ZIMBABWE v SRI LANKA

Second One-Day International

At Bulawayo, April 22, 2004. Sri Lanka won by nine wickets. Toss: Sri Lanka.

If Sri Lanka had not known what to expect in the first game, and if Zimbabwe had been running on youthful adrenalin, this match quickly restored the expected pattern. Vaas destroyed Zimbabwe's top order, and this time there was no real recovery from 27 for four, although Taibu threatened again before he was run out by a neat piece of work from substitute fielder Rangana Herath. Muralitharan finished the job with the ball and Sri Lanka began their innings 11 overs before lunch. They had reached 84 before Panyangara dismissed Jayasuriya again, immediately before the interval. Afterwards, a fine maiden international fifty from Jayantha saw Sri Lanka home.

Man of the Match: W. P. U. J. C. Vaas.

Zimbabwe

V. Sibanda lbw b Vaas.	0	D. T. Hondo lbw b Muralitharan	12	
B. R. M. Taylor c Jayantha b Vaas.	2	T. Panyangara b Muralitharan	0	
D. D. Ebrahim c Dilshan b Vaas	16			
*†T. Taibu run out	35	B 1, l-b 2, w 2, n-b 7	12	
E. Chigumbura c Jayawardene b Vaas. . .	0			
S. Matsikenyeri st Sangakkara		1/0 (1) 2/20 (2)	(36.4 overs) 136	
b Muralitharan .	18	3/27 (3) 4/27 (5)		
A. Maregwede lbw b Muralitharan.	10	5/76 (4) 6/80 (6)		
M. L. Nkala b Jayasuriya.	6	7/95 (7) 8/108 (8)		
P. Utseya not out	25	9/134 (10) 10/136 (11)		

Bowling: Vaas 10–1–38–4; Zoysa 6–2–21–0; Chandana 5–0–20–0; Muralitharan 8.4–2–32–4; Jayasuriya 7–0–22–1.

Sri Lanka

W. S. Jayantha not out.	74		
S. T. Jayasuriya c Utseya b Panyangara .	31		
*M. S. Atapattu not out.	21		
W 12, n-b 1	13		
1/84 (2)	(1 wkt, 20.5 overs) 139		

†K. C. Sangakkara, D. P. M. D. Jayawardene, T. M. Dilshan, R. P. Arnold, U. D. U. Chandana, W. P. U. J. C. Vaas, D. N. T. Zoysa and M. Muralitharan did not bat.

Bowling: Hondo 8–1–51–0; Panyangara 6–1–40–1; Chigumbura 2–0–17–0; Utseya 2.5–0–11–0; Matsikenyeri 2–0–20–0.

Umpires: I. L. Howell (South Africa) and K. C. Barbour.
Third umpire: R. B. Tiffin. Referee: M. J. Procter (South Africa).

†ZIMBABWE v SRI LANKA

Third One-Day International

At Harare, April 25, 2004. Sri Lanka won by nine wickets. Toss: Sri Lanka. One-day international debuts: H. M. R. K. B. Herath, M. F. Maharoof.

On a pitch with a grassier surface than usual, Zimbabwe's youngsters suffered the ultimate humiliation: bowled out for 35, one below the previous worst in a one-day international (set by Canada against Sri Lanka in the 2003 World Cup), and three below their own 38, also against Sri Lanka, at Colombo in 2001-02. Ironically, an opening stand of five was their best of the series to date. The second wicket fell at 18, when Ebrahim was caught behind for seven, which was to be Zimbabwe's joint top score – along with Extras. The seamers found life and movement in the pitch: Vaas picked up four for 11, which made him the sixth to achieve 300 one-day international wickets, and Maharoof ended the innings with two in three balls, both caught behind. To their credit, Zimbabwe threw everything into their bowling and fielding, and managed to remove Arnold before the inevitable end came 70 minutes before lunch. Jayantha hit a four and six off successive balls to bring this mismatch to an end in 27.2 overs.

Man of the Match: W. P. U. J. C. Vaas.

Zimbabwe

S. Matsikenyeri run out	4	D. T. Hondo c Sangakkara b Maharoof. .	4	
B. R. M. Taylor c Dilshan b Vaas	4	T. Panyangara c Sangakkara b Maharoof.	0	
D. D. Ebrahim c Sangakkara b Fernando.	7			
*†I. Taibu lbw b Fernando	0	L-b 3, w 4	7	
E. Chigumbura b Vaas	0			
A. Maregwede b Vaas	2	1/5 (1) 2/18 (3) 3/18 (4)	(18 overs) 35	
V. Sibanda c Dilshan b Maharoof	4	4/18 (2) 5/19 (5) 6/27 (6)		
M. L. Nkala not out	3	7/27 (7) 8/28 (9)		
P. Utseya lbw b Vaas	0	9/35 (10) 10/35 (11)		

Bowling: Vaas 9–4–11–4; Fernando 6–2–18–2; Maharoof 3–1–3–3.

Sri Lanka

W S. Jayantha not out	28
R. P. Arnold c Taibu b Hondo	6
D. P. M. D. Jayawardene not out	3
W 3	3

1/23 (2)   (1 wkt, 9.2 overs) 40

S. T. Jayasuriya, *M. S. Atapattu, †K. C. Sangakkara, T. M. Dilshan, W. P. U. J. C. Vaas, M. F. Maharoof, H. M. R. K. B. Herath and C. R. D. Fernando did not bat.

Bowling: Hondo 5–0–11–1; Panyangara 4.2–0–29–0.

Umpires: D. J. Harper (Australia) and I. D. Robinson.
Third umpire: K. C. Barbour. Referee: M. J. Procter (South Africa).

†ZIMBABWE v SRI LANKA

Fourth One-Day International

At Harare, April 27, 2004. Sri Lanka won by 72 runs. Toss: Zimbabwe. One-day international debuts: T. Mupariwa; S. H. T. Kandamby.

Sri Lanka omitted five leading players, including their captain, and still won easily, further illustrating the travesty taking place here. Panyangara bowled a spirited opening spell of eight overs for 23 runs, and Sri Lanka got themselves into a spot of bother at 137 for five – thanks to some careless strokes, two of which benefited Nkala, who took two wickets in an over. A run-a-ball 51 from Chandana prevented major unpleasantness. Sri Lanka's new-ball bowling fell below the standards of Vaas and Zoysa, but Zimbabwe still managed to lose two early wickets. Their sheet-anchor was Ebrahim, playing his 66th one-day international; this was his first fifty against anyone except Bangladesh.

Man of the Match: U. D. U. Chandana.

Sri Lanka

W. S. Jayantha c Chigumbura		H. M. R. K. B. Herath not out	0
b Mupariwa .	23	C. R. D. Fernando b Panyangara	0
†K. C. Sangakkara c Maregwede b Nkala	63	K. M. D. N. Kulasekara not out	0
*D. P. M. D. Jayawardene b Mupariwa . .	26	L-b 2, w 14	16
R. P. Arnold run out	7		
T. M. Dilshan c Taibu b Nkala	18	1/43 (1) 2/106 (3) (9 wkts, 50 overs) 223	
S. H. T. Kandamby c Taibu b Nkala	0	3/118 (4) 4/137 (2)	
U. D. U. Chandana run out	51	5/137 (6) 6/177 (5)	
M. F. Maharoof run out	19	7/220 (8) 8/222 (7) 9/222 (10)	

Bowling: Hondo 10–0–47–0; Panyangara 10–3–32–1; Mupariwa 10–0–44–2; Utseya 10–0–48–0; Nkala 10–1–50–3.

Zimbabwe

S. Matsikenyeri c Sangakkara		T. Mupariwa run out	8
b Kulasekara .	7	D. T. Hondo c Jayawardene b Maharoof .	2
B. R. M. Taylor st Sangakkara		T. Panyangara b Maharoof	0
b Chandana .	38		
M. L. Nkala c Sangakkara b Fernando . .	1	L-b 1, w 1, n-b 5	7
D. D. Ebrahim not out	50		
*†T. Taibu c Sangakkara b Chandana . .	12	1/19 (1) 2/22 (3) 3/65 (2) (43.4 overs) 151	
A. Maregwede c Dilshan b Arnold	18	4/90 (5) 5/115 (6) 6/123 (7)	
E. Chigumbura c and b Arnold	5	7/135 (8) 8/146 (9)	
P. Utseya run out	3	9/151 (10) 10/151 (11)	

Bowling: Kulasekara 7–1–30–1; Fernando 7–1–20–1; Maharoof 8.4–1–19–2; Herath 10–0–37–0; Chandana 7–0–23–2; Arnold 4–0–21–2.

Umpires: I. L. Howell (South Africa) and K. C. Barbour.
Third umpire: I. D. Robinson. Referee: M. J. Procter (South Africa).

†ZIMBABWE v SRI LANKA

Fifth One-Day International

At Harare, April 29, 2004. Sri Lanka won by 25 runs. Toss: Sri Lanka.

A good performance in the field and a maiden international fifty by the Under-19 batsman Taylor, whose nemesis Vaas was again rested, enabled Zimbabwe at least to lose the final one-day game with some honour. Again, complacency affected Sri Lanka's batting; they were 162 for six when Taibu, who once more handed the gloves to Maregwede, took his second wicket. Then Arnold and Maharoof slaughtered the home bowling to the tune of 71 in eight overs, and 13 more came off the last, from Taibu himself. Zimbabwe's openers began confidently: their stand of 79 was the team's best of the series, and Taylor made 74 off 120 balls. Muralitharan was too good for most of the others.

Man of the Match: R. P. Arnold. *Man of the Series:* T. Taibu.

Sri Lanka

W. S. Jayantha c Mupariwa b Hondo	8	M. F. Maharoof c Hondo b Panyangara .	38
*M. S. Atapattu c Matsikenyeri		D. N. T. Zoysa not out	3
b Mupariwa .	38		
D. P. M. D. Jayawardene b Mupariwa . . .	47	L-b 10, w 14	24
†T. M. Dilshan run out	21		
S. H. T. Kandamby b Taibu	13	1/21 (1) 2/93 (2) (7 wkts, 50 overs) 246	
R. P. Arnold not out	51	3/128 (3) 4/137 (4)	
U. D. U. Chandana c Ebrahim b Taibu . .	3	5/146 (5) 6/162 (7) 7/233 (8)	

H. M. R. K. B. Herath and M. Muralitharan did not bat.

Bowling: Hondo 7–1–37–1; Panyangara 8–1–49–1; Mupariwa 10–0–44–2; Nkala 2–0–10–0; Utseya 7–0–39–0; Taibu 10–1–42–2; Matsikenyeri 6–1–15–0.

Zimbabwe

S. Matsikenyeri st Dilshan b Muralitharan	37	
B. R. M. Taylor c Jayantha b Herath	74	
D. D. Ebrahim b Herath	6	
*†T. Taibu c Dilshan b Muralitharan	26	
A. Maregwede c Herath b Chandana	4	
M. L. Nkala c Herath b Chandana	11	
E. Chigumbura c Jayawardene b Muralitharan	19	
P. Utseya c Chandana b Muralitharan	8	

T. Mupariwa not out	12
D. T. Hondo b Muralitharan	5
T. Panyangara not out	2
L-b 2, w 10, n-b 5	17

1/79 (1) 2/92 (3) (9 wkts, 50 overs) 221
3/154 (4) 4/158 (2)
5/163 (5) 6/175 (6)
7/200 (8) 8/200 (7) 9/211 (10)

Bowling: Zoysa 8–0–24–0; Maharoof 8–0–61–0; Muralitharan 10–4–23–5; Herath 10–1–36–2; Chandana 10–0–50–2; Arnold 2–0–14–0; Jayantha 2–0–11–0.

Umpires: D. J. Harper (Australia) and I. D. Robinson.
Third umpire: R. B. Tiffin. Referee: M. J. Procter (South Africa).

At Takashinga SC, Harare, May 1, 2, 3, 2004. **Drawn.** Toss: Zimbabwe A. **Zimbabwe A 294** (S. M. Ervine 75, E. Chigumbura 63) **and 306-8 dec.** (T. R. Gripper 97, P. Utseya 89; U. D. U. Chandana 4-80); **Sri Lankans 461** (T. T. Samaraweera 97, K. C. Sangakkara 95, D. P. M. D. Jayawardene 113, S. H. T. Kandamby 52).

During a brief truce with the 15 white rebels, the ZCU picked four of them – Heath Streak, Trevor Gripper, Sean Ervine and Raymond Price – for Zimbabwe A. Kandamby's 52 in 41 balls consisted of ten fours and two sixes, the only recorded instance in first-class cricket of a completed innings of 50 or more scored entirely in boundaries.

ZIMBABWE v SRI LANKA

First Test Match

At Harare, May 6, 7, 8, 2004. Sri Lanka won by an innings and 240 runs. Toss: Sri Lanka. Test debuts: E. Chigumbura, A. Maregwede, T. Panyangara, B. R. M. Taylor, P. Utseya; M. F. Maharoof.

The one-day embarrassments turned into a three-day humiliation once the Test series began. With the dispute between the Zimbabwe Cricket Union and the 15 dissidents unresolved, the home team was selected from the pool of players who had taken part in the one-day series, plus Mahwire and Vermeulen. In the first and last one-day games, this team had proved moderately competitive, but in Test cricket there is no hiding place. The eleven that took the field had 53 previous Test caps between them, and included five debutants. Taibu – the only man apart from Ebrahim whose Test career ran into double figures – became the youngest-ever Test captain at 20 years 358 days. The result was Zimbabwe's heaviest Test defeat, a record that held for nine days.

Atapattu continued his habit of winning the toss and putting Zimbabwe in, despite the benign appearance of the pitch. The openers began with great caution, taking two runs off the first six overs, but to put on 30 against quality bowling was commendable. Only Taibu, however, had the ability and experience to do more than make a start, scoring a determined 80 before walking for a bat-pad catch. The top-scorer, with 45, was Prosper Utseya, who had been chosen for his accurate off-spin but was wicketless throughout this tour. Muralitharan mopped up the last six, and drew level with Courtney Walsh on 519 Test wickets.

Hondo and Tinashe Panyangara, who had shared a spirited last-wicket stand of 50, caused Sri Lanka some concern for two or three overs when they took the new ball; after that it was one-way traffic. The bowlers exhibited enthusiasm and reasonable accuracy, but had little more to offer as Atapattu and Jayasuriya put on 281, a first-wicket record against Zimbabwe. Jayasuriya scored 157 off 147 balls without ever looking to be forcing the pace. The breakthrough finally came on the second afternoon

520 and counting... Muttiah Muralitharan enjoys the support of his colleagues after taking his record-breaking Test wicket.

Picture by Hamish Blair, Getty Images

when Taibu took off his pads to bowl his skiddy medium-pacers, only to get his third delivery to bounce unexpectedly from the pitch, off Jayasuriya's gloves and into the gully. Atapattu, leaden-footed, was bowled by the second new ball for 170, during a middle-order slump of five for 45. The later batsmen scored usefully, if gratuitously, on the third morning to give Sri Lanka a first-innings lead of 342.

So unbalanced were the teams that the main question was not even whether Zimbabwe could survive the day, but when Muralitharan would break the record – if he had the chance. There were only six overs to go before lunch when Zimbabwe batted, but after just four Atapattu gave Murali the ball, without immediate results.

Either side of the break, Zoysa enjoyed an inspired spell: four for one in 21 balls, reducing Zimbabwe to 18 for five. Maregwede and Nkala fought back, though, and had just drawn level with Zimbabwe's lowest Test score, 63, when Nkala played forward to Murali and was caught off pad and bat at silly mid-off, giving himself a footnote

DESIGNATED WICKET-KEEPERS WHO TOOK WICKETS IN A TEST

Hon. A. Lyttelton	12–5–19–4	England v Australia at The Oval	1884
A. A. Lilley	5–1–23–1	England v Australia at Manchester	1896
W. Storer	16–4–55–1	England v Australia at Melbourne (2nd Test)	1897-98
W. Storer	4–0–24–1	England v Australia at Melbourne (4th Test)	1897-98
C. A. McWatt	4–2–16–1	West Indies v England at Port-of-Spain	1953-54
J. M. Parks	6–0–43–1	England v India at Kanpur	1963-64
Taslim Arif	5–0–28–1	Pakistan v Australia at Lahore	1979-80
S. M. H. Kirmani	2–0–9–1	India v Pakistan at Nagpur	1983-84
T. Taibu	**8–1–27–1**	**Zimbabwe v Sri Lanka at Harare**	**2003-04**

Research: Philip Bailey

in history as Muralitharan's 520th Test wicket. The Sri Lankans erupted and embraced their hero. However, of the 200 spectators present to witness the record, few appreciated its true significance.

Murali was in line for a hat-trick, as he took a sharp return catch from Maregwede with his next delivery, but he hurt his finger in the act and had to go off for treatment; he bowled one more wicketless over on his return. As in the first innings, there was some courageous hitting by the last pair, Hondo and Panyangara, which allowed Zimbabwe to avoid the extra indignity of dismissal for under 100. Panyangara finally gave Mahela Jayawardene his sixth catch of the game, one short of the Test record, but his own all-round form was one of the few positive factors Zimbabwe could take from this match.

Man of the Match: M. Muralitharan.

Close of play: First day, Sri Lanka 67-0 (Atapattu 21, Jayasuriya 43); Second day, Sri Lanka 456-7 (Vaas 28, Maharoof 16).

Zimbabwe

S. Matsikenyeri c D. P. M. D. Jayawardene b Zoysa .		– c D. P. M. D. Jayawardene b Zoysa.	11
B. R. M. Taylor c and b Maharoof	19	– c Muralitharan b Vaas	4
D. D Ebrahim lbw b Zoysa	1	– c H. A. P. W. Jayawardene b Zoysa	2
*†T. Taibu c D. P. M. D. Jayawardene b Muralitharan .	40	– lbw b Zoysa	0
E. Chigumbura c Muralitharan b Zoysa	14	– c H. A. P. W. Jayawardene b Zoysa	0
A. Maregwede lbw b Muralitharan	0	– c and b Muralitharan	22
M. L. Nkala lbw b Muralitharan	2	c D. P. M. D. Jayawardene b Muralitharan .	24
P. Utseya b Muralitharan	45	– b Maharoof	0
N. B. Mahwire b Muralitharan	0	– c D. P. M. D. Jayawardene b Zoysa	2
D. T. Hondo b Muralitharan	19	– not out	15
T. Panyangara not out	32	– c D. P. M. D. Jayawardene b Jayasuriya .	18
B 4, l-b 6, n-b 7	17	L-b 2, n-b 2	4

1/30 (2) 2/32 (3) 3/35 (1) 4/57 (5)   199
5/69 (6) 6/85 (7) 7/118 (4)
8/118 (9) 9/149 (8) 10/199 (10)

1/13 (1) 2/15 (3) 3/17 (2)   102
4/17 (4) 5/18 (5) 6/63 (7)
7/64 (8) 8/64 (6)
9/72 (9) 10/102 (11)

Bowling: *First Innings*—Vaas 19–6–39–0; Zoysa 17–6–53–3; Maharoof 10–3–45–1; Muralitharan 24.2–10–45–6; Jayasuriya 1–0–7–0. *Second Innings*—Vaas 8–2–24–1; Zoysa 9.5–2–20–5; Muralitharan 9.1–1–37–2; Maharoof 4–0–18–1; Jayasuriya 1–0–1–1.

Sri Lanka

*M. S. Atapattu b Hondo	170	M. F. Maharoof lbw b Mahwire	40
S. T. Jayasuriya c Hondo b Taibu	157	D. N. T. Zoysa not out	28
K. C. Sangakkara c Taibu b Matsikenyeri	11	M. Muralitharan c Maregwede b Panyangara .	26
D. P. M. D. Jayawardene c Utseya b Chigumbura .	37	B 2, l-b 13, w 3, n-b 6	24
T. M. Dilshan c Utseya b Mahwire	10		
T. T. Samaraweera c Taibu b Panyangara .	6	1/281 (2) 2/312 (3) 3/369 (4)	541
†H. A. P. W. Jayawardene b Panyangara .	4	4/387 (1) 5/399 (6) 6/403 (7)	
W. P. U. J. C. Vaas c Matsikenyeri b Mahwire .	28	7/414 (5) 8/457 (8)	
		9/496 (9) 10/541 (11)	

Bowling: Hondo 27–6–103–1; Panyangara 26.1–2–101–3; Mahwire 18–1–97–3; Nkala 7–1–41–0; Utseya 12–2–55–0; Matsikenyeri 15–2–58–1; Taibu 8–1–27–1; Chigumbura 12–2–44–1.

Umpires: B. F. Bowden (New Zealand) and R. E. Koertzen (South Africa).
Third umpire: R. B. Tiffin.   Referee: M. J. Procter (South Africa).

ZIMBABWE v SRI LANKA

Second Test Match

At Bulawayo, May 14, 15, 16, 17, 2004. Sri Lanka won by an innings and 254 runs. Toss: Sri Lanka. Test debut: T. Mupariwa.

The First Test showed up the inability of Zimbabwe's reserves to compete at international level; this was even worse. For the second match running, the Zimbabweans suffered the heaviest defeat in their Test history, and this time they managed just three Sri Lankan wickets.

ZIMBABWE'S HEAVIEST TEST DEFEATS

Inns & 254 runs	**v Sri Lanka at Bulawayo**..........................	**2003-04**
Inns & 240 runs	**v Sri Lanka at Harare**	**2003-04**
Inns & 219 runs	v South Africa at Harare........................	1999-2000
Inns & 209 runs	v England at Lord's	2000
Inns & 176 runs	v West Indies at Bulawayo	2001
Inns & 175 runs	v Australia at Perth	2003-04
Inns & 166 runs	v Sri Lanka at Colombo (SSC)	2001-02
Inns & 101 runs	v India at Nagpur	2001-02

Zimbabwe's heaviest defeat by runs alone was by 315 runs v Sri Lanka at Galle in 2001-02. They have also lost six Tests by ten wickets.

Atapattu again put Zimbabwe in on a pitch even better for batting than the one in Harare. Vermeulen, the only contracted white player not to join the dissidents, was included, having finally been declared fit after a head injury in the one-day series in Australia, but he contributed little. Local seamer Tawanda Mupariwa made his debut, a remarkable turnaround after he had been omitted from the Under-19 World Cup team three months earlier. They replaced Mahwire, whose bowling action had been reported to the ICC after the First Test, and Utseya, who had injured his shoulder. So bare was the cupboard that the only slow bowler at a ground reputed to favour them was part-time spinner Matsikenyeri.

Matsikenyeri batted like a millionaire on the first morning, hitting 45 off 64 balls, while Ebrahim put his head down and grafted for 70 in his role as sheet-anchor. But Taibu and Maregwede were cut off in their prime, and Zimbabwe just failed to last the day.

The second day was one for records, none favourable to Zimbabwe. Sri Lanka amassed 425 runs for a single wicket. The bowlers did at least carry out their plan against Jayasuriya, keeping him quiet so that his 48 took 95 balls, but they had no answer to Atapattu or Sangakkara, who piled up 438, the sixth-highest stand for any Test wicket. Shortly before the close, Atapattu reached his sixth Test double-century, his third against Zimbabwe and his second in two Tests on this ground. Sangakkara followed him past 200 next day, and both must have had their eyes on 300 or more. Against such weak opposition, it was perhaps a mercy that neither achieved the coveted landmark. Several hard chances were missed in the field before Atapattu, trying to push a single for his 250, edged to the keeper. He had batted eight hours 36 minutes, and struck 36 fours and a six in 324 balls.

After such a stand, Mahela Jayawardene must have felt like a bear aroused from hibernation as he emerged to bat, but he settled down for a century of his own, with Atapattu delaying his declaration until it was completed. And Brian Lara, who had made 400 not out a month earlier, could breathe again when Sangakkara, who had just beaten the ground record, Dave Houghton's 266 against Sri Lanka in the first Test at Queens Sports Club almost ten years earlier, was well held by the diving Taibu. Sangakkara's 270 occupied seven hours 48 minutes and 365 balls; like Atapattu, he had 36 fours, but he hit a second six. There was one more unwelcome record: it was the first time six bowlers had conceded a century apiece in a Test innings. Taibu did not bowl in this match, but caught all three batsmen who were out.

This time Sri Lanka's lead was 485, and only the pursuit of personal milestones had prevented another three-day victory. A promising 61 by Taylor, studded with handsome off-side strokes, was the fourth day's main feature, Ebrahim again batted well and Panyangara hit merrily at the end. Zimbabwe might have done worse had Muralitharan not been handicapped by a bruised spinning finger – he bowled spells of genuine leg-breaks at times – but another total mismatch finally persuaded the ICC that something had to be done to preserve the integrity of Test cricket.

Man of the Match: K. C. Sangakkara *Man of the Series:* M. S. Atapattu.

Close of play: First day, Sri Lanka 18-0 (Atapattu 7, Jayasuriya 11); Second day, Sri Lanka 443-1 (Atapattu 202, Sangakkara 186); Third day, Zimbabwe 44-2 (Taylor 19, Ebrahim 3).

Zimbabwe

S. Matsikenyeri run out	45	– c H. A. P. W. Jayawardene b Zoysa	14
B. R. M. Taylor c H. A. P. W. Jayawardene		– c D. P. M. D. Jayawardene	
b Vaas	5	b Muralitharan	61
M. A. Vermeulen c Muralitharan b Vaas	0	– c Muralitharan b Zoysa	6
D. D Ebrahim c Dilshan b Maharoof	70	– c Atapattu b Jayasuriya	42
*†T. Taibu c Samaraweera b Maharoof	27	– c Dilshan b Muralitharan	0
A. Maregwede run out	24	– lbw b Vaas	28
E. Chigumbura c D. P. M. D. Jayawardene			
b Vaas	0	– lbw b Muralitharan	12
M. L. Nkala c Sangakkara b Muralitharan	19	– c Dilshan b Vaas	0
T. Panyangara c Vaas b Zoysa	11	– not out	40
T. Mupariwa not out	1	– c Vaas b Jayasuriya	14
D. T. Hondo b Muralitharan	11	– c Atapattu b Muralitharan	3
L-b 2, w 3, n-b 10	15	L-b 7, w 1, n-b 3	11

1/24 (2) 2/31 (3) 3/82 (1) 4/134 (5)   228   1/22 (1) 2/40 (3) 3/125 (2)   231
5/176 (6) 6/176 (7) 7/193 (4)   4/127 (5) 5/143 (4) 6/173 (6)
8/211 (9) 9/216 (8) 10/228 (11)   7/173 (8) 8/173 (7)
                                                                              9/204 (10) 10/231 (11)

Bowling: *First Innings*—Vaas 19–8–41–3; Zoysa 14–0–50–1; Maharoof 16–2–62–2; Muralitharan 22–3–58–2; Jayasuriya 4–0–15–0. *Second Innings*—Vaas 18–6–53–2; Zoysa 13–4–27–2; Muralitharan 28.1–6–79–4; Maharoof 6–0–32–0; Jayasuriya 10–0–33–2.

Sri Lanka

*M. S. Atapattu c Taibu b Chigumbura	249
S. T. Jayasuriya c Taibu b Nkala	48
K. C. Sangakkara c Taibu b Panyangara	270
D. P. M. D. Jayawardene not out	100
T. T. Samaraweera not out	32
L-b 5, w 4, n-b 5	14

1/100 (2) 2/538 (1)   (3 wkts dec.) 713
3/627 (3)

T. M. Dilshan, †H. A. P. W. Jayawardene, W. P. U. J. C. Vaas, M. F. Maharoof, D. N. T. Zoysa and M. Muralitharan did not bat.

Bowling: Hondo 29–5–116–0; Panyangara 25–4–120–1; Mupariwa 34–1–136–0; Nkala 32–3–111–1; Chigumbura 21–2–108–1; Matsikenyeri 23.3–1–112–0; Vermeulen 1–0–5–0.

Umpires: B. F. Bowden (New Zealand) and R. E. Koertzen (South Africa).
Third umpire: R. B. Tiffin.   Referee: M. J. Procter (South Africa).

THE BANGLADESHIS IN THE WEST INDIES, 2003-04

FAZEER MOHAMMED

Bangladesh emerged from their first senior tour of the West Indies with renewed optimism. Although a highly coveted victory over the fallen giants of the game remained tantalisingly out of reach, they made significant progress towards international respectability. In the first one-day international, Bangladesh were within a wicket of a sensational win, and in the First Test, they passed a series of personal and team milestones and secured a hard-fought draw. It was only the third time in 29 Tests they had avoided defeat: both previous draws had been against Zimbabwe and owed everything to the weather. But Habibul Bashar's young squad still lost the rain-affected one-day series 3–0 and the two Tests 1–0. By the ultimate yardstick – winning cricket matches – they failed to counter those who argue they have no right to be playing at this level.

From West Indies there was little celebration, only sighs of relief that another home humiliation had been avoided. England had just emphatically ended a 36-year drought without winning a Test series in the Caribbean, and failure to beat Bangladesh, the whipping boys of world cricket, would have been too much for proud local hearts to bear, not least that of their beleaguered captain Lara.

Lara's world-record 400 not out, against England in Antigua, had erased lingering doubts about his genius as a batsman, but not the justifiable criticism of his leadership. His second coming as captain had not had the messianic impact optimists predicted: when Bangladesh saved the First Test with honour, his overall record was 19 defeats in 35 Tests.

It looked as if he had had enough. On the eve of the Second Test, in Kingston, Lara made an eye-opening proclamation: he would quit the captaincy if West Indies did not win (leaving open the possibility that heavy rain could unseat him). In fact the weather forecast was good, and victory a fairly safe bet. But such a desperate attempt to galvanise himself and his side betrayed the depressing level to which West Indies had plummeted. Increasingly disenchanted, Lara had already used a newspaper column to air his gripes with selectors, administrators, groundstaff, and almost anyone else with a semblance of influence. It added up to a tacit admission that he had failed to halt the agonising decline.

Victory by an innings and 99 runs at Sabina Park may have reassured the less discerning part of the Caribbean population, but those with more insight knew the quality of the cricket betrayed the teams' positions in the bottom three of the ICC Test Championship. Catching, for instance, was embarrassingly poor on both sides.

The frequent errors made the 14 wickets taken by the left-arm seamer Pedro Collins all the more creditable; these included a Test-best six for 53 as Bangladesh capitulated in the last innings of the series. Yet that crash of seven for 22 contrasted sharply with admirable batting efforts in their previous three innings, highlighted by three centuries in the First Test. Before that, Bangladesh had managed only five in their Test history.

West Indies had four centuries in the series, Ramnaresh Sarwan's unbeaten 261 taking the spotlight. Yet almost as important were Sarwan's frequently used rolling leg-spinners: he and the off-spinning all-rounder Omari Banks took 14 wickets between them. That helped reinforce Lara's claim that the quality of West Indian quick bowlers no longer justified an all-pace attack, and that the selectors were languishing in a time-warp, trying to impose the pattern of the past as the solution to the troubling problems of today. "Instead of relying on our dream team we should focus on the current situation," he said.

BANGLADESHI TOURING PARTY

Habibul Bashar (*captain*), Rajin Saleh (*vice-captain*), Abdur Razzaq, Alamgir Kabir, Alok Kapali, Enamul Haque jun., Faisal Hossain, Hannan Sarkar, Javed Omar, Khaled Mahmud, Khaled Mashud, Manjural Islam Rana, Mohammad Ashraful, Mohammad Rafique, Mushfiqur Rahman, Shahriar Hossain, Tapash Baisya, Tareq Aziz.

Coach: D. F. Whatmore. *Manager:* Faruque Ahmed. *Physiotherapist:* J. Gloster. *Fitness adviser:* D. Woodford. *Computer analyst:* Nasir Ahmed.

BANGLADESHI TOUR RESULTS

Test matches – Played 2: Lost 1, Drawn 1.
First-class matches – Played 3: Lost 1, Drawn 2.
One-day internationals – Played 3: Lost 3.
Other non-first-class-match: Played 1: Won 1.

Note: Matches in this section which were not first-class are signified by a dagger.

†At St Vincent, May 12, 2004. **Bangladeshis won by three wickets.** Toss: West Indies Cricket Board XI. **West Indies Cricket Board XI 135** (45.3 overs) (Manjural Islam Rana 4-9); **Bangladeshis 136-7** (41 overs).

†WEST INDIES v BANGLADESH

First One-Day International

At St Vincent, May 15, 2004. West Indies won by one wicket. Toss: West Indies. One-day international debut: T. L. Best.

West Indies' last pair clung on to avoid a humiliating defeat after carelessness and complacency left them nine down, and still 12 runs short, in pursuit of a modest 145. Such a tense finale had seemed unlikely when Bangladesh hobbled to 82 for eight in the 33rd over after Tino Best had emulated Clive Lloyd (at The Oval in 1973) by taking two wickets in his first one-day international over for West Indies. Only an unbroken ninth-wicket stand of 62 brought Bangladesh some respectability. While Powell was hitting a typically robust 52 in reply, it looked as if West Indies would hardly miss Brian Lara, resting his injured finger as a precaution. But then the collapse began: five wickets for 14, two to panicky run-outs. With the tension mounting and the Bangladeshis hardly believing they were so close to such a triumph, Bradshaw and Edwards crawled to victory. Bradshaw's cool head – and his exemplary two for 11 from ten overs – won him the match award.

Man of the Match: I. D. R. Bradshaw.

Bangladesh

Shahriar Hossain c Gayle b Best	0	Khaled Mahmud b Best	0
Manjural Islam Rana lbw b Edwards	1	Mohammad Rafique not out	32
*Habibul Bashar lbw b Best	0	L-b 8, w 17, n-b 1	26
Rajin Saleh c Jacobs b Bradshaw	20		
Mohammad Ashraful c Jacobs b Best	17	1/0 (1) 2/0 (3) (8 wkts, 50 overs) 144	
Alok Kapali c Best b Bradshaw	5	3/5 (2) 4/43 (5)	
Mushfiqur Rahman c Joseph b Best	13	5/51 (4) 6/52 (6)	
†Khaled Mashud not out	30	7/79 (7) 8/82 (9)	

Tapash Baisya did not bat.

Bowling: Best 10–1–35–4; Edwards 10–0–24–2; Bradshaw 10–4–11–2; Bravo 10–2–20–0; Smith 3–0–16–0; Gayle 7–0–30–0.

West Indies

C. H. Gayle c Khaled Mashud b Tapash Baisya	0	†R. D. Jacobs run out	1
R. L. Powell b Khaled Mahmud	52	I. D. R. Bradshaw not out	12
S. C. Joseph c Khaled Mashud b Khaled Mahmud	7	T. L. Best lbw b Manjural Islam Rana	2
		F. H. Edwards not out	4
S. Chanderpaul lbw b Manjural Islam Rana	15	L-b 2, w 9, n-b 1	12
*R. R. Sarwan c Mushfiqur Rahman b Rajin Saleh	22	1/7 (1) 2/46 (3) (9 wkts, 46.4 overs) 145	
D. J. J. Bravo run out	16	3/81 (4) 4/83 (2)	
D. R. Smith st Khaled Mashud b Manjural Islam Rana	2	5/119 (5) 6/123 (7)	
		7/126 (8) 8/126 (6)	
		9/133 (10)	

Bowling: Tapash Baisya 6–1–25–1; Mushfiqur Rahman 6–0–20–0; Khaled Mahmud 10–3–15–2; Mohammad Rafique 9.4–0–35–0; Manjural Islam Rana 10–2–21–3; Alok Kapali 3–0–16–0; Rajin Saleh 2–0–11–1.

Umpires: D. R. Shepherd (England) and E. A. Nicholls.
Third umpire: B. R. Doctrove. Referee: R. S. Mahanama (Sri Lanka).

†WEST INDIES v BANGLADESH

Second One-Day International

At St Vincent, May 16, 2004. West Indies won by 23 runs. Toss: Bangladesh.
West Indies completed only their second series win in the last nine one-day competitions at home. Torrential showers delayed the start, leaving 25 overs a side, and West Indies reached 124 for seven, despite an excellent spell from Tapash Baisya, who took four wickets; Dwayne Smith, the hard-hitting all-rounder, was dropped on 25 and went on to smash an unbeaten 62. Bangladesh needed five an over, but the raw pace of Edwards and Best proved too much. Bradshaw again showed his effectiveness as a first-change, Bangladesh slid to 39 for five in the 12th over, and only battling innings from Hannan Sarkar and Manjural Islam Rana delayed the inevitable.
Man of the Match: D. R. Smith.

> **"** The pitch was grudging, the bowling straight – and in the case of the slingy Edwards terrifying."
>
> The West Indians in England, page 486.

West Indies

C. H. Gayle c Habibul Bashar b Mushfiqur Rahman	7	†R. D. Jacobs b Tapash Baisya	3
R. L. Powell c Habibul Bashar b Khaled Mahmud	20	S. C. Joseph c Hannan Sarkar b Tapash Baisya	0
D. R. Smith not out	62		
S. Chanderpaul c Tapash Baisya b Manjural Islam Rana	10	L-b 4	4
*R. R. Sarwan c Alok Kapali b Tapash Baisya	18		
D. J. J. Bravo c Khaled Mahmud b Tapash Baisya	0		124

1/17 (1) 2/47 (2)   (7 wkts, 25 overs) 124
3/77 (4) 4/109 (5)
5/110 (6) 6/124 (7)
7/124 (8)

I. D. R. Bradshaw, T. L. Best and F. H. Edwards did not bat.

Bowling: Tapash Baisya 5–1–16–4; Mushfiqur Rahman 5–0–24–1; Khaled Mahmud 5–0–31–1; Mohammad Rafique 5–1–21–0; Manjural Islam Rana 5–0–28–1.

Bangladesh

Hannan Sarkar c Smith b Bradshaw	36	†Khaled Mashud b Bravo	9
Mohammad Ashraful c Smith b Edwards	0	Mohammad Rafique not out	4
*Habibul Bashar c Jacobs b Edwards	2	L-b 3, w 3	6
Rajin Saleh c Gayle b Bradshaw	1		
Alok Kapali c Jacobs b Best	1	1/8 (2) 2/10 (3) (8 wkts, 25 overs) 101	
Mushfiqur Rahman c Sarwan b Bravo	8	3/20 (4) 4/21 (5)	
Manjural Islam Rana not out	33	5/39 (6) 6/71 (1)	
Khaled Mahmud c Best b Bradshaw	1	7/78 (8) 8/95 (9)	

Tapash Baisya did not bat.

Bowling: Edwards 5–0–19–2; Best 5–0–15–1; Bradshaw 5–1–15–3; Bravo 5–0–23–2; Gayle 5–0–26–0.

Umpires: D. R. Shepherd (England) and B. R. Doctrove.
Third umpire: E. A. Nicholls. Referee: R. S. Mahanama (Sri Lanka).

†WEST INDIES v BANGLADESH

Third One-Day International

At St George's, Grenada, May 19, 2004. West Indies won by seven wickets. Toss: Bangladesh. One-day international debut: Faisal Hossain.

Devon Smith, dropped and then injured since his last one-day international a year earlier, was given a golden opportunity on his return: chasing 119 in 25 overs against the Bangladeshi attack – and his unbeaten 39 guided West Indies home with five balls to spare. After rain again reduced the match to a 25-over affair (weather interfering for the sixth time in the last ten one-day internationals in the Caribbean), Habibul Bashar hit 42 to give Bangladesh hope of a competitive total. But Dwayne Smith removed him and two others, and Bangladesh's 118 was well within reach. Devon Smith, the first Grenadian to play for West Indies in his home country, rewarded the diehard spectators who braved predictions of a complete washout. This was the first West Indies whitewash in a home one-day series since South Africa's first visit to the Caribbean in 1991-92.

Man of the Match: D. S. Smith.   *Man of the Series:* D. R. Smith.

Bangladesh

Hannan Sarkar c Jacobs b Rampaul	4	Khaled Mahmud c D. S. Smith b Bravo	4
Mohammad Ashraful c Bradshaw b Best	3	Manjural Islam Rana not out	6
*Habibul Bashar c Chanderpaul		L-b 6, w 5	11
b D. R. Smith	42		
Rajin Saleh c Jacobs b D. R. Smith	17	1/11 (1) 2/18 (2) (7 wkts, 25 overs) 118	
Faisal Hossain c Bravo b D. R. Smith	17	3/65 (4) 4/89 (5)	
Mushfiqur Rahman run out	14	5/93 (3) 6/102 (7) 7/118 (6)	

†Khaled Mashud, Mohammad Rafique and Tapash Baisya did not bat.

Bowling: Best 3–0–7–1; Rampaul 5–0–21–1; Bradshaw 5–0–22–0; Bravo 5–0–22–1; Powell 3–0–16–0; D. R. Smith 4–0–24–3.

West Indies

R. L. Powell c Khaled Mahmud		*R. R. Sarwan not out	7
b Mushfiqur Rahman	17		
D. S. Smith not out	39	L-b 2, w 7	9
D. R. Smith lbw b Manjural Islam Rana	23		
S. Chanderpaul c Faisal Hossain		1/21 (1) 2/52 (3) (3 wkts, 24.1 overs) 119	
b Tapash Baisya	24	3/107 (4)	

S. C. Joseph, D. J. J. Bravo, †R. D. Jacobs, I. D. R. Bradshaw, T. L. Best and R. Rampaul did not bat.

Bowling: Tapash Baisya 5–0–28–1; Mushfiqur Rahman 4.1–1–23–1; Khaled Mahmud 5–0–32–0; Mohammad Rafique 5–0–13–0; Manjural Islam Rana 5–0–21–1.

Umpires: D. R. Shepherd (England) and E. A. Nicholls.
Third umpire: B. R. Doctrove. Referee: R. S. Mahanama (Sri Lanka).

At St George's, Grenada, May 22, 23, 24, 2004. **Drawn**. Toss: West Indies Cricket Board XI. **West Indies Cricket Board XI 320-5 dec.** (S. C. Joseph 115, D. J. J. Bravo 100, C. S. Baugh 52*) **and 163-5** (D. R. Smith 103*); **Bangladeshis 161** (Mohammad Ashraful 73; O. A. C. Banks 4-42).

Smith scored 103* in 70 balls, with nine fours and four sixes.

WEST INDIES v BANGLADESH

First Test Match

At Gros Islet, St Lucia, May 28, 29, 30, 31, June 1, 2004. Drawn. Toss: Bangladesh. Test debuts: Faisal Hossain, Tareq Aziz.

Heartened by having competed well in the limited-overs series, Bangladesh showed gutsy resilience to win a deserved, and significant, draw. From a shaky 79 for six on the fourth evening, a lead of 143, they rallied so strongly that by the fifth, Habibul Bashar could enjoy the luxury of their first-ever declaration. And enjoy it he did: his team had avoided defeat in only two of their 28 previous Tests – and both escapes had been down to the weather. For a side still taking small, faltering steps forward, an honourable draw represented triumph.

Having chosen to bat on a sun-drenched opening day, Habibul saw Hannan Sarkar fall to the very first ball, but he himself pulled and hooked merrily en route to a third Test century. His 113 ended, on the first afternoon, as it had so often prospered, with a hook to deep backward square leg. It was Lawson's first wicket after a year out of Test cricket because of a suspect action and a bad back.

Reasons to be cheerful, one, two, three. Habibul Bashar, Mohammad Rafique and Khaled Mashud all hit hundreds for Bangladesh in the St Lucia Test.
Pictures by Sena Vidanagama, Farjana K. Godhuly and Clive Mason, Getty Images

The inevitable wet weather – St Lucia in May receives almost twice as much rain as Manchester in December – meant only 41.1 overs were bowled on the second day and 62.4 on the fourth. For once Bangladesh did not need the assistance. The two Mohammads, Ashraful and Rafique, capitalised on dropped chances and by the third morning had boosted 250 for seven to 416, their highest in Tests (beating 400 in their first Test innings, against India at Dhaka in 2000-01) Though Ashraful's luck ran out on 81, when he was lbw to Lawson, Rafique, batting at No. 9, surged to a maiden first-class hundred in style. He was last out for 111, after an innings spiced with 11 fours and three sixes. Bangladesh's lower order had distinguished themselves, aided by undisciplined bowling and shockingly poor catching.

Bangladeshi spirits soared even higher when Devon Smith, recently recovered from a broken thumb, was run out before scoring on the third morning. But then they too were let down by bad catching. Chance after embarrassingly easy chance was put down, with Gayle chief beneficiary in his innings of 141 – his fifth Test century, decorated with crunching drives off both front and back foot. But, worryingly for West Indies, even after that alarming level of fielding incompetence, Bangladesh still took a lead of 64: Mushfiqur Rahman, having removed Lara, then preyed on a weak-looking tail for Test-best figures of four for 65.

However, all that effort seemed wasted in the midst of a second-innings collapse. Sarwan took three wickets in two overs late on the fourth day with his usually innocuous leg-spin, leaving Bangladesh tottering at 94 for six at the close, a lead of just 158. On the cloudless final morning West Indies walked out strong favourites, only for Khaled Mashud – previous Test-best 61 – to defy every challenge Lara threw at him. He showed a cool temperament and solid technique in trying circumstances, and by the time he reached his hundred, driving Gayle through cover point for a 13th boundary, the match had long since been saved. Lara bowled both part-time spinners, Gayle and Sarwan, and later went public with his unhappiness about the attack the selectors had handed him: "It was evident at quite an early stage that leaving out the spinner was not in our best interests."

With a lead of 335, Habibul proudly declared on the last evening. There were no wickets before the end, as Gayle and Devon Smith built an unbroken stand of 113. But the honours belonged to Bangladesh. Asked about his strategy for the next Test, the delighted Habibul replied: "Jamaica is far away, man. I'm not thinking about Jamaica tonight."

Man of the Match: C. H. Gayle.
Close of play: First day, Bangladesh 278-7 (Mohammad Ashraful 65, Mohammad Rafique 17); Second day, Bangladesh 406-9 (Mohammad Rafique 103, Tareq Aziz 4); Third day, West Indies 262-5 (Gayle 110, Jacobs 1); Fourth day, Bangladesh 94-6 (Rajin Saleh 34, Khaled Mashud 8).

Bangladesh

Hannan Sarkar lbw b Collins	0	– b Edwards	9
Javed Omar c D. S. Smith b Collins	32	– c Jacobs b Collins	7
*Habibul Bashar c D. R. Smith b Lawson	113	– b Best	25
Rajin Saleh c Jacobs b Sarwan	26	– lbw b Edwards	51
Mohammad Ashraful lbw b Lawson	81	– c and b Sarwan	1
Faisal Hossain c Best b Collins	5	– c Gayle b Sarwan	2
Mushfiqur Rahman c Jacobs b Sarwan	1	– lbw b Sarwan	0
†Khaled Mashud st Jacobs b Gayle	2	– not out	103
Mohammad Rafique b Collins	111	– c Jacobs b Sarwan	29
Tapash Baisya c and b Sarwan	9	– c and b Gayle	26
Tareq Aziz not out	6	– not out	1
L-b 10, w 1, n-b 19	30	L-b 5, n-b 12	17

1/0 (1) 2/121 (2) 3/171 (3) 4/227 (4)   416   1/17 (1) 2/21 (2)   (9 wkts dec.) 271
5/238 (6) 6/241 (7) 7/250 (8)   3/70 (3) 4/73 (5)
8/337 (5) 9/370 (10) 10/416 (9)   5/79 (6) 6/79 (7)
                                                      7/123 (4) 8/179 (9) 9/253 (10)

Bowling: *First Innings*—Collins 27.3–8–83–4; Edwards 21–2–78–0; Lawson 16–2–66–2; Best 20–4–64–0; D. R. Smith 4–1–5–0; Gayle 24–3–51–1; Sarwan 23–7–59–3. *Second Innings*—Collins 17–5–42–1; Edwards 19–1–61–2; Lawson 16–0–60–0; Sarwan 20–9–37–4; Best 13–1–33–1; Gayle 19.2–7–33–1; Chanderpaul 1–1–0–0.

West Indies

D. S. Smith run out	0	– (2) not out	40
C. H. Gayle c Habibul Bashar b Tapash Baisya	141	– (1) not out	66
R. R. Sarwan c Mohammad Rafique b Tapash Baisya	40		
*B. C. Lara c Khaled Mashud b Mushfiqur Rahman	53		
S. Chanderpaul c Khaled Mashud b Mohammad Rafique	7		
D. R. Smith c Tareq Aziz b Mohammad Rafique	42		
†R. D. Jacobs not out	46		
T. L. Best b Mohammad Rafique	3		
P. T. Collins c Habibul Bashar b Mushfiqur Rahman	4		
J. J. C. Lawson c Hannan Sarkar b Mushfiqur Rahman	0		
F. H. Edwards lbw b Mushfiqur Rahman	5		
L-b 3, n-b 8	11	B 4, l-b 1, n-b 2	7

1/2 (1) 2/89 (3) 3/162 (4) 4/183 (5)   352   (no wkt) 113
5/253 (6) 6/312 (2) 7/321 (8)
8/336 (9) 9/342 (10) 10/352 (11)

Bowling: *First Innings*—Tapash Baisya 26–5–87–2; Tareq Aziz 23–3–95–0; Mushfiqur Rahman 25.4–8–65–4; Mohammad Rafique 36–12–90–3; Rajin Saleh 6–0–12–0. *Second Innings*—Tapash Baisya 3–0–26–0; Tareq Aziz 6–1–31–0; Mushfiqur Rahman 6–0–25–0; Mohammad Rafique 5–1–7–0; Mohammad Ashraful 3–0–19–0.

Umpires: D. J. Harper (Australia) and J. W. Lloyds (England).
Third umpire: B. E. W. Morgan.   Referee: R. S. Mahanama (Sri Lanka).

❝ 'He is an old man and his judgment in the final was very poor,' Kureishi wrote. Shepherd is 63; Kureishi is 77.**❞**

Asia Cup, page 1345.

WEST INDIES v BANGLADESH

Second Test Match

At Kingston, June 4, 5, 6, 7, 2004. West Indies won by an innings and 99 runs. Toss: Bangladesh.

Before the game, Lara dramatically raised the stakes by promising to step down as captain if West Indies failed to win. Yet his pledge was never really in danger of being tested, even on a placid Sabina Park pitch. Bangladesh's lower order for once failed to produce one of the gutsy fightbacks that characterised their tour, and they collapsed spectacularly to an innings defeat early on the fourth afternoon.

Even before the collapse it would have taken something sensational – or rain-assisted – to save them. When West Indies declared, after tea on the third day, they had a commanding first-innings lead of 275, based on a monumental 261 not out from Sarwan and fluent centuries by Lara and Chanderpaul. Some wondered whether Sarwan should have been allowed to continue; Lara's determination to get the win made that unlikely. In terms of the match it proved the right decision: on the third evening, Bangladesh slipped to 34 for three.

On the overcast fourth morning, the slip was briefly halted but then became a landslide. Habibul Bashar and Manjural Islam Rana added 120 for the fourth wicket, defying an attack that was more controlled than in St Lucia but still unthreatening, until shortly before lunch. Then the dismissal of Rana, cutting to Lara at backward point, triggered a sensational collapse. Habibul, whose 77 underlined him as a player of quality, was lbw to Collins next ball, and with him went the Bangladeshi resistance. A series of loose shots suggested the lower order had exhausted their appetite for a fight, and the last seven wickets fell for 22. They were scattered primarily by Collins, who finished with six for 53 in the innings, nine for 117 in the match. It seemed inevitable he would be given a chance to take ten but, ever one to defy the obvious, Lara tossed the ball after lunch to Sarwan. The vice-captain obliged, Lara himself leaping high at short mid-wicket to take the catch, and with it a 1–0 series win.

Lara's countenance had been far less sunny during Bangladesh's first innings, as West Indies endured yet another opposition rally, from 97 for five to an eventual 284 all out on the second morning. The collapse had begun right at the start when Hannan Sarkar was out to the very first ball for the second Test running. This gave him the share of a strange world record, held by Sunil Gavaskar, the only other batsman to be dismissed three times off the first ball of a Test. No one else had fallen this way more than once; Collins was Sarkar's nemesis on all three occasions. The top-scorer was Tapash Baisya, with 48 from No. 10. On his Test comeback from a bad back injury, the off-spinning all-rounder Banks maintained control, took four wickets and pressed the case, yet again, for a specialist spinner in West Indies' attack.

However, Bangladesh's irksome resistance only awakened Lara. The beleaguered captain made 120, equalling Sir Garfield Sobers's West Indian record of 26 Test centuries, in the commanding manner of a man who had thrown down the gauntlet to his team and himself. And when Lara finished, Sarwan and Chanderpaul just kept going, adding 262 in an unbroken stand. As so often in his decade of Test matches, Chanderpaul was content to lend support, quietly accumulating his tenth Test hundred. Meanwhile, Sarwan made the most of a life on 21 and reached 261, in 573 minutes and 402 deliveries, with 32 fours. He did not flay the ordinary-looking Bangladeshi bowlers, but suffocated them softly with his fluent strokes either side of the wicket. The innings restored his fragile self-confidence (after he had averaged 27.42 against England) and gave West Indies the rare recent experience of an impregnable position, from which they successfully pushed for victory.

After a similar Sabina Park win a year before, which clinched the series against Sri Lanka, Lara's outpourings had been optimistic: "We are working towards a team that is going to do well." But heavy losses in South Africa and at home to England had made that prediction appear decidedly foolish. This time, he studiously avoided fuelling great expectations for campaigns ahead.

Man of the Match: R. R. Sarwan.   *Man of the Series:* R. R. Sarwan.

Close of play: First day, Bangladesh 264-9 (Tapash Baisya 36, Tareq Aziz 4); Second day, West Indies 294-3 (Sarwan 106, Best 1); Third day, Bangladesh 66-3 (Habibul Bashar 28, Manjural Islam Rana 7).

Bangladesh

Hannan Sarkar lbw b Collins	0	– (2) lbw b Collins	10
Javed Omar c Jacobs b Edwards	20	– (1) c D. R. Smith b Best	5
*Habibul Bashar c Banks b Collins	20	– lbw b Collins	77
Rajin Saleh c and b Banks	47	– c D. R. Smith b Collins	0
Mohammad Ashraful c Sarwan b Banks	16	– (6) c Lara b Sarwan	9
Manjural Islam Rana c Jacobs b Best	7	– (5) c Lara b Banks	35
Mushfiqur Rahman st Jacobs b Banks	22	– c D. R. Smith b Collins	0
†Khaled Mashud c Banks b Edwards	39	– c Sarwan b Banks	0
Mohammad Rafique c Collins b Banks	30	– b Collins	2
Tapash Baisya c D. S. Smith b Collins	48	– c Sarwan b Collins	3
Tareq Aziz not out	10	– not out	5
B 4, l-b 7, w 2, n-b 12	25	B 8, l-b 6, w 8, n-b 8	30

1/0 (1) 2/37 (3) 3/54 (2) 4/88 (5)   284
5/97 (6) 6/145 (7) 7/152 (4)
8/192 (9) 9/238 (8) 10/284 (10)

1/16 (2) 2/24 (1) 3/34 (4)   176
4/154 (5) 5/154 (3) 6/154 (7)
7/155 (8) 8/160 (9)
9/164 (10) 10/176 (6)

Bowling: *First Innings*—Collins 19-2-64-3; Edwards 20-5-66-2; Best 20-4-53-1; Banks 31-5-87-4; Sarwan 2-2-0-0; D. R. Smith 3-1-3-0. *Second Innings*—Collins 18-3-53-6; Best 10-0-32-1; Banks 13-2-40-2; Gayle 2-0-9-0; D. R. Smith 5-1-19-0; Sarwan 3-1-9-1.

West Indies

C. H. Gayle c Khaled Mashud b Tareq Aziz	14	S. Chanderpaul not out	101
D. S. Smith run out	44		
R. R. Sarwan not out	261		
*B. C. Lara c Khaled Mashud b Mohammad Rafique	120	B 4, l-b 5, w 1, n-b 7	15
T. L. Best c Khaled Mashud b Tapash Baisya	4	(4 wkts dec.)	559

1/26 (1) 2/109 (2)   (4 wkts dec.) 559
3/288 (4) 4/297 (5)

D. R. Smith, †R. D. Jacobs, O. A. C. Banks, P. T. Collins and F. H. Edwards did not bat.

Bowling: Tapash Baisya 25-5-99-1; Tareq Aziz 19-2-76-1; Mushfiqur Rahman 33-3-127-0; Mohammad Rafique 38-2-124-1; Manjural Islam Rana 28-2-100-0; Mohammad Ashraful 1-1-0-0; Rajin Saleh 7-1-24-0.

Umpires: R. E. Koertzen (South Africa) and J. W. Lloyds (England).
Third umpire: B. R. Doctrove.   Referee: R. S. Mahanama (Sri Lanka).

THE AUSTRALIANS IN ZIMBABWE, 2003-04

Malcolm Conn

If the Australian team thought they knew in advance who and what they might face in Zimbabwe, they got an eye-opener when they changed planes in Johannesburg en route to Harare. At the airport, they met the young Zimbabwean all-rounder Sean Ervine – heading in the other direction.

He said he was on his way to Perth to spend time with his girlfriend, the daughter of the Zimbabwean coach Geoff Marsh. By the time the Aussies returned home, Ervine had pledged his allegiance to Western Australia; he hoped to represent Australia eventually. He left behind the rump of a cricket team and an increasingly sinister country, where cricket has become the victim of politicians.

The failure of the Zimbabwe Cricket Union to reach an agreement with Ervine, sacked captain Heath Streak and 13 other banished white players left them unable to field a team capable of competing against any serious international team, never mind the world champions. This was no ordinary players' dispute; it was obvious to anyone spending time in the country that forces were at work with the aim of getting rid of white cricketers.

> Forces were at work with the aim of getting rid of white cricketers

As it became clear there was no chance of a deal with the players, ICC chief executive Malcolm Speed flew to Harare, apparently to try to save the tour. He was told the ZCU did not want to meet him. He left, furious, to convene an emergency ICC teleconference that was to consider suspending Zimbabwe.

Hours before that was due to happen, and the day before the Test series was scheduled to begin, the ZCU withdrew from all Tests up to the end of 2004. Even this capitulation was painted as some sort of victory by the Zimbabweans, who claimed they remained in control of their own destiny. But the Australians made it clear they were in no hurry to rearrange the two Tests they were supposed to play here; Cricket Australia chief executive James Sutherland said the team was "heavily committed".

Though the ICC was anxious to protect the "integrity of Test cricket", it was unbothered about one-day cricket. So the withdrawal did not affect Zimbabwe's schedule of one-day internationals, and the three planned for this trip were brought forward. Australia won them all easily enough. But with the team under-motivated, they did not inflict anything quite as bad as the 35 all out the young Zimbabwean team suffered against Sri Lanka a month earlier.

However, Australian captain Ricky Ponting made it clear he thought it was not just the integrity of Test cricket that mattered, but the integrity of international cricket generally. His side wanted nothing less then the best versus the best. He described the Zimbabwean team as "pretty ordinary", which is Australian for terrible.

As the tour went on, some of Australia's leading players and officials became increasingly angry about a different kind of integrity, saying they were being continually misled, especially by ZCU members promising that a settlement was imminent. After a while, even the normally bland Sutherland said: "It's got to the point where I won't believe anything until I see it."

The private Australian view was summed up publicly by Tim May, chief executive of the international players' union FICA, who said the ICC had to investigate the allegations of racial discrimination against the missing players and "immoral and unethical behaviour" by ZCU officials.

Claims by the ZCU that they were winning the hearts and minds of the black majority through their development programme bore no resemblance to the evidence of this tour. Despite the strength of the opposition, fewer than 6,000 turned up in total to see the three matches, even though the first was played on a public holiday and the last on a Saturday. Even those crowds were swelled significantly by busloads of schoolchildren in uniform. Without them, the total for the second fixture, played on a Thursday, would have been smaller than a bank queue.

However, only one player declined to make the tour for moral reasons, the leg-spinner Stuart MacGill. Other players were also privately concerned but – despite being assured by Cricket Australia that they would not be penalised for opting out – they were understandably concerned about the possibility of a deputy taking advantage of weak opposition and securing their spot. Some, however, may have shared the view of the ex-player Dean Jones, who happily signed a contract to commentate on the cricket which forbade him to mention any wider issues involving president Robert Mugabe or Zimbabwe: "I'm just there to watch the cricket and I don't give a rat's arse what he does about his country," he said.

What the Australians saw suggested the ZCU did not give a rat's arse about what it was doing to the cricket, and they rapidly lost heart for the whole trip. They did not enjoy the one-sided series much, though the game drives and golf were some consolation. It was all that could be said for a dismal excursion. When asked later what positives the team could take away from Zimbabwe, Ponting's initial response was telling. "Good question," he said.

AUSTRALIAN TOURING PARTY

R. T. Ponting (*captain*), A. C. Gilchrist (*vice-captain*), M. J. Clarke, J. N. Gillespie, I. J. Harvey, M. L. Hayden, G. B. Hogg, M. S. Kasprowicz, S. M. Katich, J. L. Langer, D. S. Lehmann, G. D. McGrath, D. R. Martyn, A. Symonds, S. K. Warne, S. R. Watson, C. L. White, B. A. Williams.

Katich, Langer, Warne and White were selected for the Test series, which was cancelled; they played in a two-day match, and then left. Clarke, Harvey, Hogg, Symonds and Watson had been selected for the one-day series only.

Coach: J. M. Buchanan. *Manager:* S. R. Bernard. *Physiotherapist:* A. Kontouri.

AUSTRALIAN TOUR RESULTS

One-day internationals – Played 3: Won 3.
Other non-first-class-match – Played 1: Drawn 1.

Note: Matches in this section were not first-class.

At Harare Country Club, Harare, May 17, 18, 2004. **Drawn.** Toss: Zimbabwe A. **Zimbabwe A 151** (J. N. Gillespie 4-25); **Australians 448** (J. L. Langer 84, M. L. Hayden 61, R. T. Ponting 87).
Each side named 13 players, of whom 11 could bat and 11 field. Wisdom Siziba made a stumping and three catches in the Australian innings.

ZIMBABWE v AUSTRALIA

First One-Day International

At Harare, May 25, 2004. Australia won by seven wickets. Toss: Zimbabwe.
Three days after the Test series should have started, the Australians finally played a game of international cricket. They expected to take out their frustrations on the field, but found it hard to lift themselves against this second-string opposition: they dropped four catches and missed two run-outs. Taylor, the 18-year-old opener who was one of only two white Zimbabweans playing, made the most of his fortune to etch a fifty, and the captain, Taibu, followed suit. In his first international since ankle surgery in August 2003, McGrath struggled for rhythm but returned respectable figures. Though Hayden went first ball, Ponting and Martyn added 144 in 150 balls and Australia cruised to victory with more than ten overs to spare.
Man of the Match: R. T. Ponting.

Zimbabwe

S. Matsikenyeri c Gilchrist b Gillespie . .	8
B. R. M. Taylor c Ponting b Lehmann . .	59
V. Sibanda b McGrath	18
D. D. Ebrahim b Williams	8
*†T. Taibu c Ponting b Kasprowicz	57
M. A. Vermeulen c Ponting b Kasprowicz	20
A. Maregwede c Clarke b Gillespie	5
M. L. Nkala run out	0
T. Panyangara not out	14
T. Mupariwa run out	3
D. T. Hondo not out	0
B 2, l-b 5, w 4, n-b 2	13

1/9 (1) 2/46 (3)   (9 wkts, 50 overs) 205
3/64 (4) 4/125 (2)
5/172 (6) 6/184 (5)
7/184 (8) 8/188 (7) 9/204 (10)

Bowling: McGrath 10-1-35-1; Gillespie 10-4-21-2; Kasprowicz 10-2-26-2; Williams 5-0-31-1; Lehmann 6-0-32-1; Symonds 9-0-53-0.

Australia

†A. C. Gilchrist c Sibanda b Hondo . . .	26
M. L. Hayden c Mupariwa b Panyangara	0
*R. T. Ponting c Sibanda b Panyangara . .	91
D. R. Martyn not out	74
M. J. Clarke not out	5
L-b 4, w 7	11

1/1 (2) 2/53 (1)   (3 wkts, 39.4 overs) 207
3/197 (3)

D. S. Lehmann, A. Symonds, J. N. Gillespie, M. S. Kasprowicz, B. A. Williams and G. D. McGrath did not bat.

Bowling: Hondo 7-0-40-1; Panyangara 9.4-1-48-2; Nkala 5-1-24-0; Mupariwa 10-1-47-0; Matsikenyeri 6-0-31-0; Sibanda 2-0-13-0.

Umpires: S. A. Bucknor (West Indies) and K. C. Barbour.
Third umpire: R. B. Tiffin. Referee: B. C. Broad (England).

ZIMBABWE v AUSTRALIA
Second One-Day International

At Harare, May 27, 2004. Australia won by 139 runs. Toss: Zimbabwe.

Ponting showed how little he rated this series by dropping down to No. 8. It was his 200th one-day international – he was only the fifth Australian to play so many – and he can rarely have appeared in such low-key circumstances. Only a few hundred spectators witnessed another comprehensive Australian victory, and most of those were schoolchildren, specially bused in. The most memorable moments came from a bowler with the bat and a batsman with the ball. Gillespie clubbed three sixes in a 16-ball 33 which took Australia past 300; Lehmann followed up a bright fifty with a career-best four for seven from his left-arm spin, as Zimbabwe's last seven tumbled in nine overs. Hondo was absent with concussion.

Man of the Match: D. S. Lehmann.

Australia

†A. C. Gilchrist c Mwayenga b Hondo. .	20	J. N. Gillespie not out.	33
M. L. Hayden c Vermeulen b Mupariwa .	87	M. S. Kasprowicz not out	2
M. J. Clarke b Panyangara	16	B 1, l-b 7, w 9, n-b 3	20
D. S. Lehmann b Matsikenyeri	67		
I. J. Harvey c Mupariwa b Matsikenyeri .	22	1/25 (1) 2/43 (3) (8 wkts, 50 overs) 323	
G. B. Hogg c Matsikenyeri b Taylor. . . .	26	3/180 (4) 4/219 (5)	
D. R. Martyn c Panyangara b Mupariwa .	20	5/233 (2) 6/274 (7)	
*R. T. Ponting st Taibu b Mwayenga . . .	10	7/276 (6) 8/314 (8)	
G. D. McGrath did not bat.			

Bowling: Hondo 9.3–1–47–1; Panyangara 6–0–34–1; Mwayenga 9–1–61–1; Mupariwa 8.3–0–64–2; Matsikenyeri 10–0–43–2; Sibanda 2–0–24–0; Taylor 5–0–42–1.

Zimbabwe

S. Matsikenyeri c Hayden b Kasprowicz .	27	W. Mwayenga c McGrath b Lehmann. . .	0
B. R. M. Taylor c Gillespie b Hogg. . . .	65	D. T. Hondo absent hurt	
V. Sibanda c Lehmann b Kasprowicz . . .	23		
M. A. Vermeulen c McGrath b Lehmann .	25	B 4, l-b 8, w 10, n-b 1.	23
*†T. Taibu run out	1		
A. Maregwede not out.	18	1/48 (1) 2/108 (3) (44.3 overs) 184	
D. D. Ebrahim lbw b Hogg	1	3/163 (2) 4/164 (4)	
T. Panyangara c and b Lehmann	1	5/164 (5) 6/168 (7)	
T. Mupariwa c McGrath b Lehmann . . .	0	7/179 (8) 8/180 (9) 9/184 (10)	

Bowling: McGrath 8–1–24–0; Gillespie 8–0–37–0; Harvey 5–0–25–0; Kasprowicz 9–1–23–2; Hogg 10–1–56–2; Lehmann 4.3–1–7–4.

Umpires: S. A. Bucknor (West Indies) and I. D. Robinson.
Third umpire: K. C. Barbour. Referee: B. C. Broad (England).

ZIMBABWE v AUSTRALIA
Third One-Day International

At Harare, May 29, 2004. Australia won by eight wickets. Toss: Australia. One-day international debut: E. C. Rainsford.

Another revamped Australian batting line-up coasted to victory with almost 20 overs to spare. Gillespie took the first five wickets with a devastating spell of pace, and Zimbabwe were 61 for six before a stand of 114 between Chigumbura and Nkala salvaged some respectability. Gillespie finished the series with seven wickets, in contrast to the recovering McGrath, who managed just one in three games. Another Australian making a comeback was Watson: this was his first international for 16 months after back problems, and he was there at the end, but the winning runs came from Clarke, the exciting young batsman from New South Wales. Promoted to open, he blazed a maiden international century, an unbeaten 105 in just 102 balls.

Man of the Match: J. N. Gillespie.   *Man of the Series:* J. N. Gillespie.

Zimbabwe

S. Matsikenyeri c Watson b Gillespie	4	W. Mwayenga lbw b Hogg	1
B. R. M. Taylor lbw b Gillespie	1	E. C. Rainsford not out	1
V. Sibanda c Gilchrist b Gillespie	2		
*†T. Taibu lbw b Kasprowicz	27	L-b 5, w 8, n-b 1	14
M. A. Vermeulen c and b Gillespie	17		
A. Maregwede b Gillespie	1	1/4 (2) 2/9 (1) 3/10 (3) (48.5 overs)	196
E. Chigumbura b Hogg	77	4/42 (5) 5/50 (6) 6/61 (4)	
M. L. Nkala b Hogg	47	7/175 (8) 8/194 (9)	
T. Mupariwa run out	4	9/195 (7) 10/196 (10)	

Bowling: Gillespie 10–2–32–5; Kasprowicz 10–1–27–1; McGrath 8–1–28–0; Watson 8–0–38–0; Hogg 6.5–0–37–3; Symonds 6–0–29–0.

Australia

†A. C. Gilchrist b Mupariwa	44
M. J. Clarke not out	105
A. Symonds c Mwayenga b Mupariwa	20
S. R. Watson not out	18
L-b 4, w 8	12

1/68 (1) 2/115 (3)   (2 wkts, 30.4 overs) 199

*R. T. Ponting, D. R. Martyn, I. J. Harvey, G. B. Hogg, J. N. Gillespie, M. S. Kasprowicz and G. D. McGrath did not bat.

Bowling: Nkala 5–0–27–0; Mwayenga 3–1–22–0; Mupariwa 8–0–48–2; Rainsford 7–0–36–0; Matsikenyeri 5–0–35–0; Chigumbura 2.4–0–27–0.

Umpires: S. A. Bucknor (West Indies) and I. D. Robinson.
Third umpire: R. B. Tiffin.   Referee: B. C. Broad (England).

THE SRI LANKANS IN AUSTRALIA, 2004

Robert Craddock

Officials from the cricketing outposts of Darwin and Cairns thought it would be Christmas in July. Shane Warne and Muttiah Muralitharan were expected in the Australian tropics to duel for one of cricket's most coveted records – most Test wickets. It would have been like Tiger Woods and Ernie Els turning up at the municipal pitch-and-putt to shoot for golf's No. 1 ranking.

Sadly, only half of the fairytale came true. Warne, whose place was threatened when he damaged a finger playing for Hampshire, made the trip, but Muralitharan withdrew for "personal reasons" four days before his side left home. He claimed he needed a break, but there was no doubt sorrowful memories of Australia helped make up his mind.

As incongruous in July as a Christmas carol

Not only had he been no-balled by three Australian umpires on Australian soil for throwing; on his most recent visit, in 2002-03, he was viciously taunted by Australian crowds, the low point being a humid night in Brisbane when he was catcalled after breaking down with a hamstring injury. And the English referee, Chris Broad, who had reported his action after the home series with Australia in March, was to preside again.

Australian prime minister John Howard may have sealed the boycott in May when he branded Murali a chucker at a political lunch. Muralitharan was then touring Zimbabwe, where he claimed top spot by overtaking Courtney Walsh's record of 519 wickets, and told Howard to mind his own business. The Northern Territory government, anxious to entice Murali to Darwin, sent an official to Colombo to beg him to come; he wrote a touching letter saying he appreciated the gesture but needed time away from the game.

The rivalry between Warne and Muralitharan, the most dominant slow bowlers in cricket history, developed an icy edge through long-distance media taunts, as both were inevitably pressed to assess the other. Warne, who needed 11 wickets in two Tests to gain outright ownership of the record, branded Muralitharan "thin-skinned" for pulling out. After taking ten, to finish the series tied on 527, he said he felt they were not on a level playing field – unlike Warne, Muralitharan had home wickets prepared to favour him, and was guaranteed to bowl more overs, given Sri Lanka's weaker attack.

Even the sight of Warne equalling the record gave Cairns's unpretentious Bundaberg Rum Stadium a highlight worthy of Lord's on a balmy July evening or the MCG on Boxing Day. Still, Warne could not claim it outright, or complete the victory that would have given Australia their second whitewash of Sri Lanka in five months. They had crushed the tourists on a seamers' pitch in Darwin, but a friendlier strip at Cairns saw Matthew Hayden score twin hundreds and Sri Lanka hang on for the draw.

The Tests had a curious feel. The sound of willow hitting leather in Australia in July still seemed as incongruous as a Christmas carol. But the ICC's ten-year plan demanded that the Tests be played some time, and there were undoubted pluses. The warm, sunny climates of Australia's two newest Test cities were perfect for winter cricket. Northern fans, starved of top-class sport – the Bangladesh Tests in 2003 fell some way short – rejoiced in the chance to play host, and attendances of 4,000 to 5,000 a day were considered pass-marks. The players enjoyed the warmth of the weather and the people. At a series launch overlooking Darwin harbour, Sri Lankan batsman Kumar Sangakkara delighted local dignitaries when he said: "We were not sure what to expect here, but Darwin reminds us of home... we are loving it." The chief negative was the pitch, dropped in after being prepared off-site, which befriended any bowler who could hit the seam and bedevilled any batsman who was half-committed.

For all their quaint charm, the future of these venues is not assured. Cricket Australia announced in September there would be no further Top End Tests until at least 2007, when Zimbabwe could be posted there. Though the goodwill generated has been substantial, series in the far north are perceived as expensive and awkward to manage. It is a shame, because the northern cities are developing a taste for top-line action.

SRI LANKAN TOURING PARTY

M. S. Atapattu (*captain*), D. P. M. D. Jayawardene (*vice-captain*), R. P. Arnold, U. D. U. Chandana, T. M. Dilshan, C. R. D. Fernando, H. M. R. K. B. Herath, S. T. Jayasuriya, R. S. Kaluwitharana, M. F. Maharoof, S. L. Malinga, T. T. Samaraweera, K. C. Sangakkara, W. P. U. J. C. Vaas, D. N. T. Zoysa.

M. Muralitharan withdrew for personal reasons before the tour.

Coach: J. Dyson. *Manager:* Air Commodore A. N. C. W. Jayasekera. *Physiotherapist:* C. J. Clark. *Trainer:* S. Duff. *Computer analyst:* S. Jayasundera.

SRI LANKAN TOUR RESULTS

Test matches – Played 2: Lost 1, Drawn 1.
Non-first-class match – Played 1: Won 1.

Note: Matches in this section which were not first-class are signified by a dagger.

†At Darwin, June 24, 25, 26, 27, 2004. **Sri Lankans won by five wickets**. Toss: Northern Territory Chief Minister's XII. **Northern Territory Chief Minister's XII 419** (J. L. Langer 151, R. Bowden 75, D. L. Treumer 65; S. L. Malinga 6-90) and **145-9 dec.** (H. M. R. K. B. Herath 4-45). **Sri Lankans 378-7 dec.** (S. T. Jayasuriya 64, K. C. Sangakkara 203*) and **187-5** (T. M. Dilshan 66*).

Each side named 12 players, of whom 11 could bat and 11 field. Sangakkara's 203 lasted 398 minutes and 306 balls and included 21 fours and a six.*

AUSTRALIA v SRI LANKA

First Test Match

At Darwin, July 1, 2, 3, 2004. Australia won by 149 runs. Toss: Sri Lanka. Test debut: S. L. Malinga.

If they couldn't beat Australia at home in March, on purpose-built raging turners, Sri Lanka were odds-on to go belly-up on a soft seamer in Darwin. And so it proved. Rhythmic swing bowler Vaas, who hardly cares about his pace, and explosive newcomer Lasith Malinga, who cares about nothing else, did well to restrict Australia's rusty line-up to barely 200 in either innings. But the difficulties of batting on a slow, seaming, two-toned pitch put even that well out of Sri Lanka's reach.

The state of the pitch caused immense debate. Atapattu chose to field, correctly, but the advantage was nullified because the wicket stayed temperamental throughout. Melbourne curator Tony Ware, who prepared it off-site, said it was never that bad and hinted the batting was dodgier than the deck. But Sri Lankan coach John Dyson said the fact that the biggest total was 207 was candid testimony to its condition and, even when Australia won, their stand-in captain, Gilchrist, said it was not quite up to Test standard: "It was not so much the swing and seam as the variable bounce. All you ask for in a cricket pitch is consistent bounce." If Darwin was to retain its Test status, he added, the issue had to be addressed. After bowling on four pancake-flat wickets against India, however, the home bowlers appreciated favourable conditions like desert explorers sighting a water fountain.

Gilchrist was leading Australia for the third time in Tests, after Ricky Ponting decided to remain in Launceston for his aunt's funeral. He was replaced by Elliott, who had waited five years for a recall after falling from favour in the West Indies in 1998-99. The effect was to give Australia their oldest Test team in more than 71 years, since the infamous Adelaide Bodyline Test of 1932-33.

The main choice facing Gilchrist was how many slips to set to the salivating fast men. Kasprowicz had seven men sweating on the edge during a potent spell on the third day, which became the last.

AGEING AUSTRALIAN TEST SIDES

The team for the Darwin Test was Australia's oldest since 1933.

Australia v England at Adelaide,
January 13, 14, 16, 17, 18, 19, 1933

Australia v Sri Lanka at Darwin,
July 1, 2, 3, 2004

	Years	Days		Years	Days
J. H. Fingleton	24	260	J. L. Langer	33	223
*W. M. Woodfull	35	144	M. L. Hayden	32	246
D. G. Bradman	24	139	M. T. G. Elliott	32	277
S. J. McCabe	22	181	D. R. Martyn	32	254
W. H. Ponsford	32	86	D. S. Lehmann	34	147
V. Y. Richardson	38	128	S. M. Katich	28	315
†W. A. Oldfield	38	126	*†A. C. Gilchrist	32	230
C. V. Grimmett	41	19	S. K. Warne	34	292
T. W. Wall	28	245	J. N. Gillespie	29	73
W. J. O'Reilly	27	24	M. S. Kasprowicz	32	142
H. Ironmonger	50	281	G. D. McGrath	34	143
Average	33	15	Average	32	212

Ages are those on the first day of each Test.

Research: Ric Finlay

Before that, Lehmann's two fifties, full of cheeky footwork and fluent improvisation, were worthy of centuries on batting-friendlier days – no Sri Lankan bettered 44. Australia collapsed from 177 for three to 207 all out on the opening day, when the highly respected Vaas appeared to justify the decision to bowl first with five wickets, including Elliott. He had screamed for joy after being told he would replace Ponting – he was only home from Glamorgan for the birth of his son. But he managed a single run in two innings as Vaas removed him, both times, with centimetre-perfect out-swingers – left-hander to left-hander – which tickled his groping blade.

Vaas was backed up by Malinga, a quietly spoken pocket-sized dynamo whose action drew comparisons with Jeff Thomson and whose pace rattled Australia with six wickets in the match. "He's certainly different – we haven't faced someone like him for a while," said Lehmann, who fell to him twice. His slingshot action was hard to sight, particularly as he delivered the ball from in front of the umpire. But McGrath said he would be tested on flat wickets, where his lack of size meant he would have to drop the ball extremely short to threaten.

McGrath, playing his first Test for almost a year, had been so tentative in his comeback from ankle surgery that he contemplated retirement. But on this pitch he found rhythm. Five first-innings wickets placated his nerves, cemented his short-term future, and took him past Sir Richard Hadlee and Kapil Dev into fourth place in the world wicket-takers' list. Warne moved ahead of Courtney Walsh into second place, while Gillespie took his 200th Test wicket, a notable milestone in a career interrupted seven times by injury. Between them, they dismissed Sri Lanka for 97, their lowest total against Australia.

Second time round, Australia wobbled to 77 for five before Gilchrist took charge and ensured a target of 312. When Sri Lanka began the chase, it was Kasprowicz's turn. He poured sweat into one side of the ball to make it reverse-swing and picked up seven wickets – easily his best international figures on home soil, and the best by any bowler in Australia–Sri Lanka Tests. Five of them were caught by Gilchrist, equalling the Test record for a bowler–keeper combination (shared by Ian Botham and Bob Taylor, for England in Bombay in 1979-80, and Allan Donald and Mark Boucher, for South Africa at Lord's in 1998). Still hunting Muralitharan's world record, Warne found himself elbowed out of proceedings by the fast men.

Man of the Match: G. D. McGrath.   *Attendance:* 13,355.

Close of play: First day, Sri Lanka 43-3 (Jayawardene 12, Zoysa 8); Second day, Australia 201.

Australia

J. L. Langer c Chandana b Samaraweera	30	– c Sangakkara b Vaas	10
M. L. Hayden c Jayasuriya b Vaas	37	– c Sangakkara b Zoysa	2
M. T. G. Elliott c Arnold b Vaas	1	– c Dilshan b Vaas	0
D. R. Martyn c Arnold b Jayasuriya	47	– c Sangakkara b Malinga	7
D. S. Lehmann lbw b Malinga	57	– c Sangakkara b Malinga	51
S. M. Katich c Sangakkara b Vaas	9	– c Dilshan b Chandana	15
*†A. C. Gilchrist c Sangakkara b Malinga	0	– run out	80
S. K. Warne run out	2	– lbw b Malinga	1
J. N. Gillespie lbw b Vaas	4	– c Samaraweera b Chandana	16
M. S. Kasprowicz not out	2	– c and b Malinga	15
G. D. McGrath c Samaraweera b Vaas	0	– not out	0
B 2, l-b 6, w 2, n-b 8	18	L-b 3, n-b 1	4

1/72 (1) 2/73 (3) 3/80 (2) 4/177 (4)   **207**
5/189 (5) 6/189 (7) 7/201 (8)
8/202 (6) 9/207 (9) 10/207 (11)

1/12 (1) 2/12 (2) 3/14 (3)   **201**
4/64 (4) 5/77 (5) 6/114 (6)
7/127 (8) 8/154 (9)
9/201 (7) 10/201 (10)

Bowling: *First Innings*—Vaas 18.3–6–31–5; Malinga 14–3–50–2; Zoysa 13–4–24–0; Samaraweera 9–1–43–1; Chandana 6–0–30–0; Jayasuriya 11–4–21–1. *Second Innings*—Vaas 14–4–51–2; Zoysa 16–3–57–1; Malinga 15.1–3–42–4; Jayasuriya 6–3–9–0; Chandana 11–1–30–2; Arnold 1–0–9–0.

Sri Lanka

*M. S. Atapattu b McGrath	4	– c Warne b Kasprowicz	10
S. T. Jayasuriya lbw b McGrath	8	– lbw b McGrath	16
†K. C. Sangakkara lbw b Gillespie	2	– run out	0
D. P. M. D. Jayawardene c Langer b Gillespie	14	– b McGrath	44
D. N. T. Zoysa c Gilchrist b McGrath	12	– (10) c Gilchrist b Kasprowicz	1
T. T. Samaraweera c Gilchrist b McGrath	1	– (5) c Gilchrist b Kasprowicz	32
T. M. Dilshan not out	17	– (6) c Gilchrist b Kasprowicz	14
R. P. Arnold c Elliott b McGrath	6	– (7) c Gilchrist b Kasprowicz	11
U. D. U. Chandana c Gilchrist b Warne	14	– (8) b Kasprowicz	17
W. P. U. J. C. Vaas c Hayden b Warne	5	– (9) not out	10
S. L. Malinga c Gillespie b Warne	0	– c Gilchrist b Kasprowicz	0
L-b 7, n-b 7	14	L-b 1, w 2, n-b 4	7

1/10 (1) 2/20 (3) 3/33 (2) 4/47 (4)   97   1/23 (1) 2/23 (3) 3/30 (2)   162
5/50 (6) 6/51 (5) 7/59 (8)   4/109 (5) 5/113 (4) 6/132 (7)
8/85 (9) 9/91 (10) 10/97 (11)   7/141 (6) 8/152 (8)
                                    9/162 (10) 10/162 (11)

Bowling: *First Innings*—McGrath 15–4–37–5; Gillespie 13–4–18–2; Kasprowicz 7–1–15–0; Warne 6.5–1–20–3. *Second Innings*—McGrath 16–9–24–2; Gillespie 13–2–37–0; Kasprowicz 17.4–3–39–7; Warne 19–2–61–0.

Umpires: Aleem Dar (Pakistan) and B. F. Bowden (New Zealand).
Third umpire: S. J. A. Taufel. Referee: B. C. Broad (England).

AUSTRALIA v SRI LANKA

Second Test Match

At Cairns, July 9, 10, 11, 12, 13, 2004. Drawn. Toss: Sri Lanka.

There are rare and captivating moments in cricket history when the pursuit of an individual milestone completely overshadows the match going on around it. There are even more special ones when the milestone and the maelstrom go hand in hand. This was such an occasion. Warne needed seven wickets to equal Muralitharan's Test record and eight to beat it. He got seven, after bowling unchanged through the last two sessions, but Sri Lanka held on for a draw.

The record bobbled along in the background for the first four days before surging into focus on that final afternoon – for everyone except Murali. When told, back in Colombo, that Warne had pulled level, he replied "Oh, he's got it, has he? Well done. I've been out practising."

This was a slow-fused game. It started with a romp in the sunshine by Australian openers Hayden and Langer, and finished in near-darkness, with the grim-faced Sri Lankan tail buried in their bunkers.

Atapattu won the toss again and was seduced by predictions of bounce, pace and movement into bowling first. There was bounce, but it was slow, true and hardly vicious; this was a batsman's match for the first four days. Sri Lanka seemed all but out of it after two sessions as Langer and Hayden proceeded in cavalier fashion towards their sixth and biggest double-century stand. It was also the fifth time both had scored a hundred in the same innings, another record. Hayden followed up with 132 in the second innings, his 20th Test century in 95 Test innings, a strike-rate bettered (among batsmen with more than 20 innings) only by Sir Donald Bradman and George Headley.

Australia were 370 for two at stumps on day one but lost seven wickets in 15 overs either side of lunch next day. The unpretentious leg-spin of Chandana took the first of two five-wicket hauls in this match, an admirable effort on a pitch that hardly suited him, even if he did profit from Australian adventure.

527-all: Upul Chandana drags his foot a fraction too far, Adam Gilchrist whips off the bails – and Shane Warne equals Murali's record for most wickets in Tests.

Picture by Hamish Blair, Getty Images

Sri Lanka's batsmen then fought hard. Atapattu led the way, pouring five and a half hours into his 133, and seven of the top eight stayed more than an hour. The decision to relieve Sangakkara of keeping duties saw him emerge fresher at the crease: he batted nearly three hours on the second day, and four and a half on the last to bankroll Sri Lanka's escape. When their first innings finally ended on a rain-delayed fourth day, they had made their highest total in Australia, 455 – which was still 62 behind.

Australia were under pressure to score quickly in a bid to nail a 2–0 victory, but the rush did not start until 67 runs flowed in nine overs on the fourth evening, with Martyn, a cultured blend of power and poise, rocketing to a run-a-ball fifty. Next morning, Hayden completed his second hundred and Ponting, in his first home Test as captain, declared to leave a target of 355 in 85 overs. That never entered Sri Lanka's sights, but Australia's nerves showed when McGrath earned a 25% fine for swearing after an early lbw shout against Jayasuriya was turned down.

By now, Warne needed five wickets to overtake Muralitharan. He focused his talents for a marathon five-hour spell which almost got himself and his country over the line before both contests ended all square. Warne came on in the 12th over, shortly before lunch, and it was obvious at once, as he had the batsmen prodding and scrapping, that his bowling was as good as at any time throughout the series. His first wicket came from his fourth ball after lunch when Jayasuriya, unsure whether to play or leave, meekly edged behind. But Warne had to wait until after tea before his next victim, Kaluwitharana, edged to short leg.

As television executives around Australia mulled over whether to stick with the cricket or go to the game show *The Price is Right*, Warne delved into his magic box to find something special to unseat Sangakkara, whose left-handedness was a buffer between him and the record. He survived everything until a cracking leg-break screwed back from outside off into his middle peg.

The record-equaller was a tight thing. Warne ripped another leg-break past Chandana, whose back foot fatally slid one centimetre too far forward: Gilchrist whipped off the bails. Warne's parents rose in the grandstand, but it was to be Australia's last moment of joy. Try as he did, he could not put the cherry on the pie by claiming the one wicket he needed for outright ownership of the record, or two to win the match, as No. 10 Zoysa stood firm for the final half-hour. It was only the second time Sri Lanka had avoided defeat in eight Tests in Australia.

Man of the Match: M. L. Hayden.   *Attendance:* 20,102.

Man of the Series: M. L. Hayden.

Close of play: First day, Australia 370-2 (Langer 159, Martyn 56); Second day, Sri Lanka 184-2 (Atapattu 75, Jayawardene 9); Third day, Sri Lanka 411-5 (Samaraweera 53, Kaluwitharana 30); Fourth day, Australia 194-2 (Hayden 68, Martyn 52).

Australia

J. L. Langer c Jayawardene b Malinga	162	– c Kaluwitharana b Zoysa	8
M. L. Hayden c Jayasuriya b Samaraweera	117	– b Chandana	132
*R. T. Ponting c Atapattu b Malinga	22	– c Jayasuriya b Zoysa	45
D. R. Martyn lbw b Chandana	97	– st Kaluwitharana b Chandana	52
D. S. Lehmann c Sangakkara b Chandana	50	– c Jayawardene b Chandana	21
S. M. Katich b Chandana	1	– st Kaluwitharana b Dilshan	1
†A. C. Gilchrist c Kaluwitharana b Malinga	35	– b Dilshan	0
S. K. Warne c Samaraweera b Chandana	2	– c Samaraweera b Chandana	4
J. N. Gillespie c Kaluwitharana b Malinga	1	– st Kaluwitharana b Chandana	1
M. S. Kasprowicz c Atapattu b Chandana	9	– not out	3
G. D. McGrath not out	0		
B 7, l-b 3, w 4, n-b 7	21	L-b 20, w 1, n-b 4	25

1/255 (2) 2/291 (3) 3/392 (1) 4/454 (4)   517   1/10 (1) 2/105 (3)   (9 wkts dec.) 292
5/462 (6) 6/469 (5) 7/474 (8)   3/195 (4) 4/261 (5)
8/476 (9) 9/485 (10) 10/517 (7)   5/284 (6) 6/284 (2)
                                          7/288 (8) 8/288 (7) 9/292 (9)

Bowling: *First Innings*—Vaas 27-2-102-0; Zoysa 19-5-72-0; Samaraweera 17-2-55-1; Malinga 29.2-2-149-4; Chandana 26-2-109-5; Jayasuriya 6-0-20-0. *Second Innings*—Vaas 13-3-52-0; Zoysa 14-6-34-2; Malinga 5-0-23-0; Samaraweera 11-0-50-0; Chandana 18.4-1-101-5; Jayasuriya 3-0-8-0; Dilshan 2-0-4-2.

❝It was simple, clear-headed, astute. And it was Hookes's last act in first-class cricket."

Cricket in Australia, page 1402.

Sri Lanka

*M. S. Atapattu c Hayden b McGrath	133	– c Warne b Gillespie	9
S. T. Jayasuriya c Gilchrist b Gillespie	13	– c Gilchrist b Warne	22
K. C. Sangakkara c Gillespie b Warne	74	– b Warne	66
D. P. M. D. Jayawardene c and b Kasprowicz	43	– c Gilchrist b McGrath	6
T. T. Samaraweera c Ponting b Gillespie	70	– run out	0
T. M. Dilshan c Kasprowicz b Warne	35	– c Warne b Gillespie	21
†R. S. Kaluwitharana c Warne b McGrath	34	– c Lehmann b Warne	14
U. D. U. Chandana st Gilchrist b Warne	19	– st Gilchrist b Warne	14
W. P. U. J. C. Vaas c Ponting b Gillespie	2	– not out	11
D. N. T. Zoysa not out	0	– not out	3
S. L. Malinga run out	0		
B 3, l-b 10, w 2, n-b 17	32	B 5, l-b 3, n-b 9	17
	455	**(8 wkts)**	**183**

1/18 (2) 2/156 (3) 3/280 (1) 4/280 (4)   455   1/15 (1) 2/49 (2)   (8 wkts) 183
5/345 (6) 6/420 (7) 7/445 (5)   3/58 (4) 4/64 (5)
8/455 (9) 9/455 (8) 10/455 (11)   5/107 (6) 6/136 (7)
                                          7/159 (3) 8/174 (8)

Bowling: *First Innings*—McGrath 34–10–79–2; Gillespie 37.4–6–116–3; Kasprowicz 32–5–113–1; Warne 38–7–129–3; Lehmann 3–0–5–0. *Second Innings*—McGrath 16–7–31–1; Gillespie 18–6–39–2; Warne 37–14–70–4; Kasprowicz 11–4–34–0; Lehmann 3–2–1–0.

Umpires: Aleem Dar (Pakistan) and B. F. Bowden (New Zealand).
Third umpire: R. L. Parry. Referee: B. C. Broad (England).

ONE-DAY INTERNATIONAL COMPETITIONS

Only competitions involving three or more teams are included.

Competition		Winners	Runners-up	Others
VB Series (A)	January–February	**Australia**	India	Zimbabwe
NatWest Series (E)	June–July	**New Zealand**	West Indies	England
Asia Cup (SL)	July–August	**Sri Lanka**	India	Bangladesh, Pakistan, Hong Kong and UAE
Videocon Cup (Netherlands)	August	**Australia**	Pakistan	India
ICC Champions Trophy (E)	September	**West Indies**	England	All Full Members plus Kenya and USA
Paktel GSM Cup (P)	September–October	**Sri Lanka**	Pakistan	Zimbabwe

THE SOUTH AFRICANS IN SRI LANKA, 2004

Brian Murgatroyd

South Africa set out on their tour of Sri Lanka in July 2004 with the motto "Dare to live the dream." The dream was to re-establish the side as the No. 1 Test and one-day line-up in the world but after a month of defeat, disappointment and disenchantment it had dissolved into a horrible nightmare. For the first time in six attempts Sri Lanka beat them in a Test series, drawing in Galle and winning in Colombo.

Less than two years earlier South Africa had briefly assumed the leadership of the ICC Test Championship; now they slipped to sixth. A subsequent 5–0 drubbing in the one-day series took their run of defeats to ten, equalling their record, and saw them drop to sixth in the one-day table. The last time South Africa endured form like that, in 1994, it cost captain Kepler Wessels and coach Mike Procter their jobs, and while there was no serious suggestion that Graeme Smith's captaincy was under threat – he was still only 23 and had assumed the leadership less than 18 months before – the role of coach Eric Simons began to attract increased scrutiny. Normally extremely supportive of his players in public, Simons took the unusual step of criticising their performance after the Test defeat in Colombo and said he would consider his position if results did not improve. The one-day defeats that followed merely added to his discomfort. He resigned six weeks later, after more failure in the Champions Trophy in England.

South Africa's problems were many and some were fundamental. They failed to find a replacement for the recently retired Gary Kirsten, their leading run-scorer in Tests; the seam bowling, apart from Shaun Pollock, lacked control and penetration; and although spinner Nicky Boje was steady, he never looked likely to run through Sri Lanka's batting line-up. The side looked rusty after the long lay-off that followed the end of their tour of New Zealand in March, and even the fielding, so often a cornerstone of South Africa's performances, was below par. There were also suggestions of discord behind the scenes, with whispers about the commitment of senior players, and Smith admitted to a "clear the air" meeting ahead of the final one-day international.

To watch South Africa in action was to wonder whether any plans had been put in place; and, if they had, whether the players were simply not good enough to execute them. All too often the team's appearance on the pitch was followed by a lengthy delay while the field was set, which suggested that little or nothing had been discussed beforehand. In all fairness, not everything that went wrong could have been helped. Opener Herschelle Gibbs damaged his right ankle before the tour even started and missed the First Test, while Andre Nel, who might have provided a much-needed spark to the seam attack, did not bowl a ball in anger on the trip because of a back spasm. While Gibbs regained fitness he never found any semblance of

Trophy hunters: Kumar Sangakkara (*left*) and Lasith Malinga celebrate victory in
the Colombo Test. With it came Sri Lanka's first series win against South Africa.
Picture by Touchline, Getty Images

form and was frequently made to look like a novice by Chaminda Vaas's
late in-swing. After emerging from the World Cup in 2003 as one of South
Africa's few shining lights, Gibbs's form was so bad that Smith admitted
during the one-day series that he could be dropped.

Pollock, who reached 300 one-day wickets and scored two one-day fifties,
was one of the few players who could look back on the tour with any degree
of satisfaction, although others had their moments. Jacques Rudolph scored
a disciplined hundred in Galle, and Jacques Kallis also reached three figures
in the final one-day international in Colombo. His was the wicket Sri Lanka
wanted most, but his bowling and, surprisingly, his catching, were not up to
his previous standards.

For Sri Lanka the series was of great significance because it showed outsiders and the players themselves that they could win without the services of
Muttiah Muralitharan. The champion spinner played in only the First Test
before succumbing to a shoulder injury that required surgery. But his absence
was never felt, and Sri Lanka revealed a hitherto unheard-of depth in their
fast-bowling resources with Vaas – a worthy man of the series – supported
in particular by Lasith Malinga in the Test series, and Nuwan Zoysa in the
one-dayers. With the bat, Kumar Sangakkara and Mahela Jayawardene were
the stars, although Sangakkara ended the tour with his role in the side still
the subject of debate. He was spared the wicket-keeping duties in the Test
series but resumed the dual role of batsman/keeper in the one-day matches.

SOUTH AFRICAN TOURING PARTY

G. C. Smith (*captain*), M. V. Boucher (*vice-captain*), N. Boje, H. H. Dippenaar, H. H. Gibbs, M. Hayward, J. H. Kallis, L. Klusener, A. Nel, M. Ntini, R. J. Peterson, S. M. Pollock, J. A. Rudolph, M. van Jaarsveld.

A. G. Puttick was called up as cover for Gibbs before the First Test. For the one-day series that followed Dippenaar and Hayward were replaced by A. C. Dawson and J-P. Duminy. When Nel failed to recover from a back injury, he was replaced for the one-day series by C. K. Langeveldt.

Coach: E. O. Simons. *Manager:* T. J. Southey. *Fitness trainer:* A. le Roux.
Physiotherapist: S. Jabaar. *Computer analyst:* G. Obermeyer. *Media manager:* G. de Kock.

SOUTH AFRICAN TOUR RESULTS

Test matches – Played 2: Lost 1, Drawn 1.
One-day internationals – Played 5: Lost 5.
Other non-first-class matches – Played 1: Drawn 1. Abandoned 1.

Note: Matches in this section which were not first-class are signified by a dagger.

†At Colombo Cricket Club, Colombo, July 30, 31, August 1, 2004. **Drawn.** Toss: Sri Lanka Cricket President's XI. **Sri Lanka Cricket President's XI 251** (R. S. Kaluwitharana 51, L. P. C. Silva 68; M. Ntini 5-37) **and 286-3 dec.** (M. G. Vandort 129, R. P. Arnold 83, R. S. Kaluwitharana 54*; **South Africans 226 and 129-2** (G. C. Smith 85*).
Each side named 14 players, of whom only 11 could bat and 11 field.

SRI LANKA v SOUTH AFRICA

First Test Match

At Galle, August 4, 5, 6, 7, 8, 2004. Drawn. Toss: Sri Lanka.

A combination of a pitch that did not deteriorate as much as expected and South African conservatism, when they rejected the chance of chasing 325 in a minimum of 93 overs, condemned this match to a tame finish. South Africa's approach was disappointing but not altogether surprising. They came into the series with only one three-day game behind them after a lengthy break; they were without both Gary Kirsten, who had retired, and the injured Gibbs; and there was an underlying fear that their traditional weakness against spin would be exposed by the home side, including Muralitharan, back in the Test line-up after opting out of the tour to Australia. In reality, that fear proved groundless as Rudolph led them to safety with a painstaking but thoroughly worthy hundred.

For Sri Lanka, Jayawardene and Muralitharan could also reflect on outstanding individual achievements. Jayawardene's second Test double-hundred led his side from 279 for seven at the end of the first day to 486. Muralitharan, in only his second Test since the ICC banned his *doosra*, regained sole possession of the world record for most Test wickets – Shane Warne had drawn level with him on 527 in July – when he had van Jaarsveld caught at slip off bat and pad. But the first two days of the Test belonged to Jayawardene. On day one he renewed his love affair with Galle, reaching his third hundred at the ground. It was a much-needed innings too: Sangakkara's attractive contribution apart, South Africa more than held their own, especially when they claimed two wickets with the new ball in the final two overs of the day.

Galle landmark: Mahela Jayawardene (*facing camera*) is congratulated by Romesh Kaluwitharana on reaching his hundred; he went on to 237.

Picture by Touchline, Getty Images

The match turned in Sri Lanka's favour on day two. Smith was off the field for much of it, suffering from a debilitating virus, and in his absence Jayawardene and Vaas took control. Jayawardene used his feet contemptuously to Boje and, with Vaas an active partner, the pair added a Sri Lanka Test-record 170 for the eighth wicket. South Africa ran out of answers, and it took an impetuous drive to mid-off by Vaas to break the stand, just when he appeared to have a maiden Test hundred for the taking. Not even that dismissal ruffled Jayawardene as he moved to 237 in 563 minutes and 415 balls with 25 fours and three sixes – two driven and one swept off Boje – before he mispulled a delivery from Hayward, returning to Test cricket after a 19-month absence.

With uncertainty surrounding both the lasting qualities of the pitch and Smith's availability to bat, South Africa faced possible meltdown. But the makeshift opening pairing of van Jaarsveld and Dippenaar eased concerns by reaching the close in untroubled fashion. Although both fell in quick succession the following morning, Rudolph emerged to lead the resistance as South Africa passed the follow-on mark of 287 with ease. Selective in his strokeplay and favouring use of the pad, Rudolph could never be described as thrilling during a century which spanned almost seven hours. It went against his aggressive instincts, but there was no doubting either its value to South Africa or his own powers of concentration in sapping heat.

When South Africa were bowled out an hour into the fourth day, Sri Lanka's challenge was to score quickly enough to give themselves time to dismiss them again; by now, it was apparent the pitch was lasting better than most observers had predicted. However, acceleration proved easier said than done as Pollock and Klusener, himself returning to the Test side for the first time in more than two years, proved adept at taking the pace off the ball. Boje bowled a strict defensive line into the footmarks to claim his third five-wicket haul in Tests. Atapattu's closure eventually came with three overs left on day four but, encouraged by their efforts in the first innings and with Smith restored to the top of the order, South Africa felt a little more confident – though not confident enough to contemplate victory.

Man of the Match: D. P. M. D. Jayawardene.

Close of play: First day, Sri Lanka 279-7 (Jayawardene 116); Second day, South Africa 82-0 (Dippenaar 46, van Jaarsveld 30); Third day, South Africa 347-7 (Rudolph 85, Boje 31); Fourth day, South Africa 7-0 (Smith 5, Dippenaar 0).

Sri Lanka

*M. S. Atapattu c Boucher b Pollock	9	– lbw b Klusener	25
S. T. Jayasuriya c Klusener b Pollock	12	– c Boucher b Pollock	74
K. C. Sangakkara c Boucher b Boje	58	– c Hayward b Boje	13
D. P. M. D. Jayawardene lbw b Hayward	237	– c Rudolph b Boje	5
T. T. Samaraweera lbw b Pollock	13	– b Klusener	19
T. M. Dilshan b Hayward	25	– lbw b Pollock	1
†R. S. Kaluwitharana b Pollock	33	– c Pollock b Boje	19
U. D. U. Chandana b Ntini	5	– c Dippenaar b Boje	29
W. P. U. J. C. Vaas c Hayward b Boje	69	– not out	13
M. F. Maharoof not out	6	– (11) not out	3
M. Muralitharan b Hayward	0	– (10) c Dippenaar b Boje	2
B 8, l-b 3, w 2, n-b 6	19	B 4, l-b 1, w 2, n-b 4	11

1/13 (2) 2/22 (1) 3/108 (3) 4/145 (5) 486
5/189 (6) 6/274 (7) 7/279 (8)
8/449 (9) 9/486 (4) 10/486 (11)

1/62 (2) 2/89 (3)   (9 wkts dec.) 214
3/103 (4) 4/140 (2)
5/142 (6) 6/166 (5)
7/172 (9) 8/199 (8) 9/209 (10)

Bowling: *First Innings*—Pollock 23–5–48–4; Ntini 20–1–61–1; Hayward 16.4–0–81–3; Kallis 16–3–52–0; Klusener 19–0–69–0; Boje 42–3–148–2; Rudolph 9–2–16–0. *Second Innings*—Pollock 12–2–19–2; Hayward 6–1–21–0; Klusener 14–2–40–2; Ntini 5–0–19–0; Boje 22–0–88–5; Kallis 8–1–22–0.

South Africa

H. H. Dippenaar run out	46	– (2) c Jayawardene b Muralitharan	11
M. van Jaarsveld c Samaraweera b Muralitharan	37	– (3) lbw b Dilshan	29
J. A. Rudolph c Kaluwitharana b Muralitharan	102	– (5) not out	27
J. H. Kallis c Sangakkara b Muralitharan	59	– not out	52
*G. C. Smith lbw b Jayasuriya	23	– (1) b Chandana	74
†M. V. Boucher c Kaluwitharana b Jayasuriya	6		
S. M. Pollock c Sangakkara b Vaas	25		
L. Klusener c Jayawardene b Dilshan	2		
N. Boje c Kaluwitharana b Vaas	31		
M. Ntini c Chandana b Muralitharan	10		
M. Hayward not out	2		
B 14, l-b 8, w 1, n-b 10	33	B 1, l-b 4, w 2, n-b 3	10

1/84 (1) 2/96 (2) 3/168 (4) 4/213 (5) 376
5/225 (6) 6/287 (7) 7/295 (8)
8/348 (9) 9/363 (10) 10/376 (3)

1/34 (2) 2/98 (3)   (3 wkts) 203
3/135 (1)

Bowling: *First Innings*—Vaas 25–10–50–2; Maharoof 19–9–42–0; Muralitharan 46.4–9–130–4; Chandana 18–0–68–0; Jayasuriya 25–9–40–2; Dilshan 6–0–24–1. *Second Innings*—Vaas 10–3–20–0; Jayasuriya 17–7–30–0; Dilshan 16–5–30–1; Maharoof 5–2–4–0; Muralitharan 20–5–37–1; Chandana 18–5–41–0; Samaraweera 3–0–13–0; Sangakkara 1–0–4–0.

Umpires: D. J. Harper (Australia) and D. R. Shepherd (England).
Third umpire: T. H. Wijewardene. Referee: C. H. Lloyd (West Indies).

SRI LANKA v SOUTH AFRICA

Second Test Match

At Sinhalese Sports Club, Colombo, August 11, 12, 13, 14, 15, 2004. Sri Lanka won by 313 runs. Toss: Sri Lanka.

Sri Lanka recorded their first-ever series win over South Africa by handing out a comprehensive thrashing. The gulf between the two sides in this match was immense and only rain, which all but washed out the fourth day, together with Sri Lanka's reluctance to enforce the follow-on, spared Smith's side from an even greater humiliation.

For South Africa the match was a rude awakening. After surviving on a slow, turning pitch in Galle, they believed they would be well-placed to compete in Colombo at a ground where history suggested fast bowlers would find some assistance. But, after Sangakkara made a high-class double-century and Jayasuriya shredded some paper-thin South African batting, it was Sri Lanka's quick bowlers, Vaas and Malinga, who exploited conditions far better than the visitors. In the fourth innings the pair terrorised South Africa's batsmen: a delicious irony after previous series between the two sides when Sri Lanka's batsmen suffered continually at the hands of South Africa's quicks.

Sangakkara's sixth Test hundred was a superb effort and formed the platform for Sri Lanka's dominance. It was full of the flowing drives that have become his trademark, but he also pounced on anything short, showing a willingness to hook and cut. Together with Jayawardene he added 192 for the third wicket, and although Jayawardene was bowled through the gate with the second new ball late in the day, it was small consolation for South Africa. Their lacklustre display in the field had set the tone for their own performance. Even allowing for the high humidity their over-rate was poor and, crucially, they missed Sangakkara on 57 when Kallis grassed a regulation slip catch off Pollock. Sangakkara was so certain the edge would be caught he had started walking, but a call from his partner made him turn on his heels and resume his innings. He reached his 100th Test double-hundred on day two, sprinting the three runs that took him from 198 to 201 as if to underline Sri Lanka's positive intent. In all he batted for 529 minutes, faced 357 balls and hit 31 fours and a swept six off Boje before edging a drive to slip as South Africa belatedly fought back on day two. It was the only day from which they could derive any satisfaction as they took Sri Lanka's last six wickets for 78, a period that included a last-wicket stand of 33 off 92 balls between Chandana and Malinga, when the match almost ground to a halt.

Atapattu's blushes were spared by the covers

South Africa's fightback in the field continued with the bat as van Jaarsveld and Smith added 108 for the second wicket after Gibbs's return to Test action lasted just one ball, courtesy of a Vaas in-swinger. But the stand was the high-water mark of their efforts and, from the moment when van Jaarsveld drove lazily to short extra, it was all downhill for South Africa. On the third morning they fell in a heap as Jayasuriya and his fellow left-arm spinner Herath ran through some ill-disciplined batting. Jayasuriya, despite the handicap of a side strain, claimed Test-best figures, and the follow-on seemed the natural option for Atapattu. His bowlers were still relatively fresh – Vaas did not bowl on day three – and South Africa's morale was rock-bottom. But rather than risk batting last in pursuit of a small target, Sri Lanka opted to bat again, with Sangakkara helping to extend the lead to 492 by the close.

At that point the weather seemed set fair, but it began to rain in the night. When it continued for much of the following morning the wisdom of Atapattu's decision looked dubious. But his blushes were spared by effective covering that protected virtually the whole ground, and some superb fast bowling by Malinga and Vaas. Only eight overs were possible on day four, but in that time Sri Lanka's fast bowlers tore in. Malinga had Gibbs caught at leg gully as he fended a ball off his rib cage and Vaas bowled van Jaarsveld with a brilliant in-swinging yorker after the batsman had his helmet grille rearranged by a Malinga bouncer. It was brilliant, breathless stuff. When the final day dawned sunny, the bowlers maintained the momentum. Vaas removed Kallis with the third ball of the day thanks to a delivery that disturbed the surface of the pitch and a good low catch by Dilshan at second slip. When Smith and Rudolph fell soon afterwards, both miscuing hook shots, the writing was on the wall. Dippenaar and Boucher showed survival was far from impossible, but Vaas returned to claim his first five-wicket haul against South Africa.

Man of the Match: K. C. Sangakkara.   *Man of the Series:* W. P. U. J. C. Vaas.
Close of play: First day, Sri Lanka 303-3 (Sangakkara 157, Vaas 4); Second day, South Africa 116-3 (Smith 49, Kallis 4); Third day, Sri Lanka 211-4 (Samaraweera 21, Dilshan 23); Fourth day, South Africa 21-2 (Smith 9, Kallis 1).

Sri Lanka

*M. S. Atapattu c Boucher b Pollock	4	– b Rudolph	72
S. T. Jayasuriya lbw b Boje	43	– st Boucher b Boje	19
K. C. Sangakkara c Kallis b Pollock	232	– c Ntini b Kallis	64
D. P. M. D. Jayawardene b Ntini	82	– c Boucher b Kallis	3
W. P. U. J. C. Vaas c van Jaarsveld b Pollock	10		
T. T. Samaraweera c Ntini b Kallis	21	– (5) not out	21
T. M. Dilshan c Kallis b Pollock	3	– (6) not out	23
†R. S. Kaluwitharana c Boucher b Hayward	7		
U. D. U. Chandana st Boucher b Boje	40		
H. M. R. K. B. Herath b Ntini	7		
S. L. Malinga not out	6		
L-b 6, w 1, n-b 8	15	B 6, l-b 1, w 2	9
	470	(4 wkts dec.)	**211**

1/4 (1) 2/99 (2) 3/291 (4) 4/316 (5) 470   1/46 (2) 2/142 (3)   (4 wkts dec.) 211
5/392 (6) 6/399 (7) 7/416 (8)   3/149 (4) 4/179 (1)
8/418 (3) 9/437 (10) 10/470 (9)

Bowling: *First Innings*—Pollock 30–8–81–4; Ntini 33–6–108–2; Hayward 17–4–75–1; Kallis 17–6–54–1; Boje 34.3–5–102–2; Rudolph 4–0–16–0; van Jaarsveld 7–0–28–0. *Second Innings*—Pollock 8–0–46–0; Ntini 4–0–19–0; Boje 23–6–81–1; Hayward 3–1–15–0; Smith 4–0–15–0; Kallis 6–4–6–2; Rudolph 7–2–22–1.

South Africa

*G. C. Smith c and b Jayasuriya	65	– c Samaraweera b Malinga	17
H. H. Gibbs lbw b Vaas	0	– c Samaraweera b Malinga	4
M. van Jaarsveld c Sangakkara b Jayasuriya	51	– b Vaas	2
N. Boje b Jayasuriya	0	– (9) lbw b Vaas	16
J. H. Kallis b Jayasuriya	13	– (4) c Dilshan b Vaas	3
J. A. Rudolph c Kaluwitharana b Malinga	6	– (5) c Malinga b Vaas	1
H. H. Dippenaar c Dilshan b Herath	25	– (6) not out	59
†M. V. Boucher not out	10	– (7) c Kaluwitharana b Vaas	51
S. M. Pollock lbw b Herath	1	– (8) c Atapattu b Dilshan	3
M. Ntini b Herath	0	– c Kaluwitharana b Vaas	0
M. Hayward b Jayasuriya	1	– c and b Malinga	1
B 1, l-b 8, n-b 8	17	B 6, l-b 3, w 1, n-b 12	22
	189		**179**

1/1 (2) 2/109 (3) 3/109 (4) 4/140 (1) 189   1/4 (2) 2/18 (3) 3/24 (4) 179
5/141 (5) 6/166 (6) 7/186 (7)   4/36 (1) 5/36 (5) 6/137 (7)
8/188 (9) 9/188 (10) 10/189 (11)   7/140 (8) 8/163 (9)
                                           9/163 (10) 10/179 (11)

Bowling: *First Innings*—Vaas 7–3–10–1; Malinga 13–1–51–1; Herath 25–6–60–3; Chandana 6–0–21–0; Dilshan 4–1–4–0; Jayasuriya 14.1–4–34–5. *Second Innings*—Vaas 18–8–29–6; Malinga 13–1–54–3; Jayasuriya 9–3–22–0; Herath 8–5–13–0; Chandana 7–1–26–0; Dilshan 12–6–26–1.

Umpires: B. F. Bowden (New Zealand) and S. A. Bucknor (West Indies).
Third umpire: E. A. R. de Silva.   Referee: C. H. Lloyd (West Indies).

†At Moratuwa, August 18, 2004. **Sri Lanka Cricket President's XI v South Africans. No result (abandoned).**

†SRI LANKA v SOUTH AFRICA

First One-Day International

At R. Premadasa Stadium, Colombo, August 20, 2004 (day/night). Sri Lanka won by three wickets. Toss: South Africa. One-day international debut: J-P. Duminy.

A confident Sri Lanka achieved their highest successful run-chase at Premadasa when the recalled Lokuarachchi clipped Pollock for six. For South Africa, by contrast, it was a sixth successive one-day defeat. The turning point of the match came when a well-set Kallis was given out caught and bowled after only the bowler, Chandana, appealed. Most assumed it had been a bump ball; television replays suggested otherwise. In his 150th one-day international, Gibbs was again beaten by Vaas's in-swing.

Man of the Match: W. P. U. J. C. Vaas.

South Africa

*G. C. Smith b Lokurachchi	38	A. C. Dawson not out	3
H. H. Gibbs lbw b Vaas	0	M. Ntini not out	5
J. H. Kallis c and b Chandana	74		
J. A. Rudolph st Sangakkara b Chandana	22	L-b 7, w 4, n-b 1	12
S. M. Pollock b Jayasuriya	30		
†M. V. Boucher c Gunawardene b Vaas	58	1/13 (2) 2/90 (1) (9 wkts, 50 overs) 263	
L. Klusener b Vaas	15	3/138 (4) 4/157 (3)	
J-P. Duminy lbw b Vaas	4	5/209 (5) 6/241 (6)	
N. Boje run out	2	7/249 (7) 8/253 (8) 9/257 (9)	

Bowling: Vaas 7–1–33–4; Zoysa 4–0–20–0; Dilshan 5–0–57–0; Maharoof 2–0–12–0; Lokurachchi 9–1–40–1; Jayasuriya 10–0–47–1; Chandana 9–0–47–2.

Sri Lanka

D. A. Gunawardene c Gibbs b Ntini	51	W. P. U. J. C. Vaas c Klusener b Pollock	18
S. T. Jayasuriya b Dawson	12	K. S. Lokuarachchi not out	11
*M. S. Atapattu c Boucher b Ntini	64		
†K. C. Sangakkara c Gibbs b Boje	24	L-b 12, w 7, n-b 4	23
D. P. M. D. Jayawardene c Boucher b Klusener	19	1/29 (2) 2/95 (1) (7 wkts, 49 overs) 265	
T. M. Dilshan not out	38	3/146 (4) 4/170 (3)	
U. D. U. Chandana run out	5	5/201 (5) 6/211 (7) 7/244 (8)	

M. F. Maharoof and D. N. T. Zoysa did not bat.

Bowling: Pollock 10–1–47–1; Dawson 8–0–42–1; Ntini 9–0–46–2; Klusener 10–0–52–1; Boje 5–0–31–1; Kallis 7–0–35–0.

Umpires: B. F. Bowden (New Zealand) and M. G. Silva.
Third umpire: R. Martinesz.   Referee: C. H. Lloyd (West Indies).

†SRI LANKA v SOUTH AFRICA

Second One-Day International

At R. Premadasa Stadium, Colombo, August 22, 2004. Sri Lanka won by 37 runs. Toss: Sri Lanka.

"We would be lucky to be called club cricketers," said Smith after his side made a mess of chasing an achievable target. But although South Africa's top order batted poorly, credit should still go to Zoysa, who expertly exploited their collective fallibility with bounce, cut and seam movement to secure his first five-wicket haul in one-day internationals the day before his wedding. Sri Lanka's final total owed almost everything to Sangakkara and Chandana, whose stand of 93 in 117 balls was a Sri Lanka record for the sixth wicket against South Africa. Chandana played despite allegedly suffering a road-rage attack by two members of the Sri Lanka army the previous evening. Dilshan ended lower-order resistance to claim career-best figures.

Man of the Match: D. N. T. Zoysa.

Sri Lanka

D. A. Gunawardene c Boucher b Ntini	. .	21	K. S. Lokuarachchi lbw b Kallis	3
S. T. Jayasuriya b Pollock		9	D. N. T. Zoysa b Kallis	6
*M. S. Atapattu c Boucher b Ntini	. . . .	26		
†K. C. Sangakkara run out	. . . .	63	L-b 6, w 2, n-b 4	12
D. P. M. D. Jayawardene c Boucher				
b Klusener	.	0	1/18 (2) 2/45 (1) (9 wkts, 50 overs)	213
T. M. Dilshan c Pollock b Kallis	. . . . . .	5	3/69 (3) 4/72 (5)	
U. D. U. Chandana not out	. . . .	61	5/86 (6) 6/179 (4)	
W. P. U. J. C. Vaas run out	. . . .	7	7/188 (8) 8/198 (9) 9/213 (10)	

H. M. R. K. B. Herath did not bat.

Bowling: Pollock 10–1–35–1; Dawson 8–0–46–0; Ntini 10–1–50–2; Klusener 8–0–26–1; Boje 8–0–30–0; Kallis 6–1–20–3.

South Africa

*G. C. Smith b Zoysa	. . . .	14	L. Klusener c Jayasuriya b Dilshan	40
H. H. Gibbs b Zoysa	. . . .	7	A. C. Dawson c Vaas b Dilshan	15
N. Boje c Dilshan b Zoysa	. . . .	14	M. Ntini not out	0
J. H. Kallis lbw b Zoysa	. . . .	0	W 2	2
J. A. Rudolph c Sangakkara b Zoysa	. . .	4		
S. M. Pollock c Atapattu b Dilshan	. . . .	54	1/15 (2) 2/35 (3) 3/36 (1) (48.5 overs)	176
†M. V. Boucher c Jayawardene			4/37 (4) 5/40 (5) 6/50 (7)	
b Lokuarachchi	.	4	7/94 (8) 8/145 (6)	
J-P. Duminy lbw b Dilshan	. . . .	22	9/176 (10) 10/176 (9)	

Bowling: Vaas 8–0–19–0; Zoysa 8–0–26–5; Lokuarachchi 7–0–17–1; Jayasuriya 5–0–22–0; Chandana 3–0–11–0; Herath 8–0–29–0; Dilshan 9.5–0–52–4.

Umpires: B. F. Bowden (New Zealand) and M. G. Silva.
Third umpire: R. Martinesz. Referee: C. H. Lloyd (West Indies).

†SRI LANKA v SOUTH AFRICA

Third One-Day International

At Dambulla, August 25, 2004 (day/night). Sri Lanka won by four wickets. Toss: South Africa.

A disastrous batting collapse and fielding lapses by South Africa together with a nerveless innings from Atapattu combined to ensure Sri Lanka won the series with two matches in hand. Smith's side were 142 for three with ten overs left, but lost their way completely on a pitch offering sharp turn. Their eventual total might still have been enough. Pollock reached 300 one-day wickets when he dismissed Jayasuriya – the first South African and the seventh player in all to achieve the feat, and only the second after Wasim Akram to combine it with 2,000 runs – and wickets continued to fall steadily. However, both Chandana and Vaas were dropped, and Atapattu eased his side home.

Man of the Match: M. S. Atapattu.

South Africa

*G. C. Smith c Jayasuriya b Vaas	16	N. Boje st Sangakkara b Dilshan	10
H. H. Gibbs st Sangakkara b Herath	49	A. C. Dawson c Herath b Dilshan	11
L. Klusener b Zoysa	0	M. Ntini not out	0
J. H. Kallis c Sangakkara b Herath	52	L-b 6, w 5	11
J. A. Rudolph lbw b Dilshan	18		
†M. V. Boucher c Dilshan b Herath	7	1/44 (1) 2/50 (3) 3/91 (2) (50 overs) 191
S. M. Pollock c Sangakkara		4/144 (5) 5/147 (4) 6/164 (6)
b Lokuarachchi	14	7/170 (7) 8/170 (8)
J-P. Duminy lbw b Lokuarachchi	3	9/189 (10) 10/191 (9)

Bowling: Vaas 8–1–24–1; Zoysa 8–0–33–1; Jayasuriya 7–1–26–0; Dilshan 7–0–25–3; Chandana 7–0–26–0; Herath 8–1–28–3; Lokuarachchi 5–0–23–2.

Sri Lanka

D. A. Gunawardene lbw b Dawson	5	W. P. U. J. C. Vaas not out	16
S. T. Jayasuriya c Gibbs b Pollock	11		
*M. S. Atapattu not out	97	B 3, l-b 2, w 7, n-b 7	19
†K. C. Sangakkara st Boucher b Boje	14		
D. P. M. D. Jayawardene b Duminy	21	1/7 (1) 2/34 (2) (6 wkts, 47.4 overs) 192
T. M. Dilshan b Klusener	3	3/65 (4) 4/111 (5)
U. D. U. Chandana c Duminy b Klusener	6	5/126 (6) 6/145 (7)

K. S. Lokuarachchi, D. N. T. Zoysa and H. M. R. K. B. Herath did not bat.

Bowling: Pollock 9–2–22–1; Dawson 3–0–19–1; Ntini 4–0–16–0; Kallis 6–1–20–0; Boje 9.4–0–46–1; Klusener 9–0–36–2; Duminy 7–0–28–1.

Umpires: B. F. Bowden (New Zealand) and T. H. Wijewardene.
Third umpire: E. A. R. de Silva.   Referee: C. H. Lloyd (West Indies).

†SRI LANKA v SOUTH AFRICA

Fourth One-Day International

At Dambulla, August 28, 2004. Sri Lanka won by seven wickets. Toss: Sri Lanka.

Sri Lanka underlined their growing depth and confidence as they strolled to victory with 23 balls in hand despite resting several key players. The match appeared to be following a familiar pattern when South Africa lost three wickets in 15 balls after a promising start, but power-hitting from the lower-middle order, with Pollock to the fore, produced 49 runs from the final five overs to set what appeared a challenging target on a pitch expected to lose pace as the day progressed. In reality it was South Africa and not the pitch that ran out of steam as Sangakkara and Jayawardene added a carefree, unbroken 98 from just 90 balls to make that target look hopelessly inadequate.

Man of the Match: K. C. Sangakkara.

South Africa

*G. C. Smith lbw b Lokuarachchi	46	L. Klusener st Sangakkara b Dilshan	12
H. H. Gibbs b Fernando	27	N. Boje not out	19
J. H. Kallis b Maharoof	7	L-b 3, w 14, n-b 4	21
J. A. Rudolph run out	24		
†M. V. Boucher b Chandana	27	1/47 (2) 2/61 (3) (7 wkts, 50 overs) 235
J-P. Duminy lbw b Lokuarachchi	0	3/113 (4) 4/115 (1)
S. M. Pollock not out	52	5/115 (6) 6/179 (5) 7/195 (8)

R. J. Peterson and M. Ntini did not bat.

Bowling: Malinga 5–0–40–0; Fernando 5–0–28–1; Maharoof 6–0–20–1; Dilshan 6–0–44–1; Jayantha 1–0–7–0; Jayasuriya 10–2–24–0; Lokuarachchi 10–0–39–2; Chandana 7–0–30–1.

Sri Lanka

D. A. Gunawardene c Boucher b Ntini . .	52
S. T. Jayasuriya run out	8
W. S. Jayantha c Duminy b Peterson . . .	46
†K. C. Sangakkara not out	74
*D. P. M. D. Jayawardene not out	48
L-b 4, w 2, n-b 2	8

1/14 (2) 2/73 (1)   (3 wkts, 46.1 overs) 236
3/138 (3)

T. M. Dilshan, U. D. U. Chandana, C. R. D. Fernando, K. S. Lokuarachchi, M. F. Maharoof and S. L. Malinga did not bat.

Bowling: Pollock 7.1–1–24–0; Kallis 9–0–49–0; Klusener 6–0–38–0; Ntini 8–0–39–1; Boje 8–0–36–0; Peterson 3–0–22–1; Duminy 5–0–24–0.

Umpires: B. F. Bowden (New Zealand) and E. A. R. de Silva.
Third umpire: T. H. Wijewardene.   Referee: C. H. Lloyd (West Indies).

†SRI LANKA v SOUTH AFRICA

Fifth One-Day International

At Sinhalese Sports Club, Colombo, August 31, 2004. Sri Lanka won by 49 runs. Toss: South Africa.

South Africa suffered the final humiliation of a wretched tour by losing their tenth successive match, conceding 300 against Sri Lanka for the first time in one-day cricket, after putting them in to bat. Gunawardene went early but the rest of the top order scored at or around a run a ball, and it took an excellent late spell from Langeveldt to keep Sri Lanka's total even vaguely in bounds. Kallis responded with his 13th one-day hundred, matching Gary Kirsten's South African record, but the pressure eventually told. The last seven wickets tumbled in 46 balls as Chandana took his first five-wicket haul in one-day internationals; he had earlier run out Smith with a throw from deep square leg. Atapattu missed the match to be at the bedside of his daughter Sanjali in hospital with dengue fever.

Man of the Match: U. D. U. Chandana.   *Man of the Series:* K. C. Sangakkara.

Sri Lanka

D. A. Gunawardene b Pollock	0	M. F. Maharoof not out	5
S. T. Jayasuriya c Gibbs b Smith	79	D. N. T. Zoysa not out	1
W. S. Jayantha c Boucher b Klusener . . .	51		
†K. C. Sangakkara c Kallis b Langeveldt	72	L-b 11, w 12, n-b 4	27
*D. P. M. D. Jayawardene			
lbw b Langeveldt .	39	1/0 (1) 2/125 (3) (8 wkts, 50 overs) 308	
T. M. Dilshan b Langeveldt	18	3/164 (2) 4/248 (5)	
U. D. U. Chandana b Pollock	12	5/279 (4) 6/295 (6)	
K. S. Lokuarachchi run out	4	7/302 (8) 8/303 (7)	

H. M. R. K. B. Herath did not bat.

Bowling: Pollock 10–0–58–2; Ntini 6–1–36–0; Langeveldt 7–0–31–3; Smith 7–0–48–1; Boje 9–1–41–0; Klusener 6–0–42–1; Duminy 2–0–10–0; Kallis 3–0–31–0.

South Africa

*G. C. Smith run out	25	N. Boje not out	21

*G. C. Smith run out 25
H. H. Gibbs b Zoysa 6
J. H. Kallis c Sangakkara b Chandana . 101
J. A. Rudolph c Dilshan b Chandana ... 48
†M. V. Boucher st Sangakkara
       b Chandana . 24
S. M. Pollock c Lokuarachchi
       b Jayasuriya . 11
J-P. Duminy c Gunawardene b Chandana 0
L. Klusener c Chandana b Jayasuriya ... 4

N. Boje not out 21
C. K. Langeveldt c Sangakkara
        b Jayasuriya . 2
M. Ntini c sub (S. L. Malinga) b Chandana 7
     B 1, l-b 3, w 6 10

1/11 (2) 2/59 (1) 3/173 (4) (48.1 overs) 259
4/210 (5) 5/221 (3)
6/222 (7) 7/225 (6)
8/239 (8) 9/242 (10) 10/259 (11)

Bowling: Zoysa 8–0–25–1; Maharoof 6–0–42–0; Dilshan 5.5–0–31–0; Jayasuriya 10–0–47–3; Lokuarachchi 6–0–29–0; Herath 3–0–19–0; Chandana 9.1–0–61–5; Jayantha 0.1–0–1–0.

Umpires: B. F. Bowden (New Zealand) and T. H. Wijewardene.
Third umpire: R. Martinesz. Referee: C. H. Lloyd (West Indies).

INTERNATIONAL UMPIRES' PANEL

In 1993, the International Cricket Council formed an international umpires' panel, containing at least two officials from each full member of ICC. A third-country umpire from this panel stood with a "home" country, not necessarily from the panel, in every Test from February 1994 onwards.

In March 2002, an elite panel of eight umpires (contracted to the ICC for two years at a time) was appointed after consultation with the Test captains, who assess umpires' performances after every match. Two elite umpires were to stand in all Tests from April 2002, and at least one in every one-day international. A supporting panel of international umpires was created to provide cover if the Test schedule was unusually crowded, and to provide a second umpire in one-day internationals. The ICC also appointed specialist third umpires to give rulings from TV replays. The panels were sponsored by Emirates Airlines for three years from July 2002.

At the end of 2004, the following umpires were on the elite panel: Aleem Dar (Pakistan), B. F. Bowden (New Zealand), S. A. Bucknor (West Indies), D. B. Hair (Australia), D. J. Harper (Australia), R. E. Koertzen (South Africa), D. R. Shepherd (England) and S. J. A. Taufel (Australia). Aleem Dar was promoted in April 2004, when S. Venkataraghavan (India) retired, E. A. R. de Silva (Sri Lanka) and R. B. Tiffin (Zimbabwe) moved down to the international panel and D. L. Orchard (South Africa) was not offered another contract.

The international panel consisted of A. F. M. Akhtaruddin (Bangladesh), Asad Rauf (Pakistan), K. C. Barbour (Zimbabwe), M. R. Benson (England), D. B. Cowie (New Zealand), S. J. Davis (Australia), E. A. R. de Silva (Sri Lanka), B. R. Doctrove (West Indies), K. Hariharan (India), A. L. Hill (New Zealand), I. L. Howell (South Africa), A. V. Jayaprakash (India), B. G. Jerling (South Africa), J. W. Lloyds (England), Mahbubur Rahman (Bangladesh), Nadeem Ghauri (Pakistan), E. A. Nicholls (West Indies), P. D. Parker (Australia), M. G. Silva (Sri Lanka), R. B. Tiffin (Zimbabwe) and T. H. Wijewardene (Sri Lanka). The specialist third umpires were D. Frost (Zimbabwe), K. H. Hurter (South Africa), N. J. Llong (England), R. Martinesz (Sri Lanka), B. E. W. Morgan (West Indies), Nadir Shah (Bangladesh), R. L. Parry (Australia), I. Sivaram (India), E. A. Watkin (New Zealand) and Zamir Haider (Pakistan). During 2004, Asad Rauf, Lloyds and Silva were promoted from the third umpire list to the main international panel, along with Benson, who was not previously on either. N. A. Mallender (England), P. Manuel (Sri Lanka), I. D. Robinson (Zimbabwe) and P. Willey (England) left the international panel; Frost, Hurter, Llong, Martinesz, Nadir Shah, Watkin and Zamir Haider joined the third umpire list, while G. A. Baxter (New Zealand), G. Cuddumbey (South Africa) and Showkatur Rahman (Bangladesh) left it.

THE ZIMBABWEANS IN PAKISTAN, 2004-05

Zimbabwe had long been scheduled to fly to Pakistan for two Tests and five one-day internationals after competing in the Champions Trophy in England. However, the suspension of Zimbabwe's Test status – the result of the protracted dispute between the Zimbabwe Cricket Union and a group of leading players – left a hole in Pakistan's international programme. Sri Lanka stepped in at short notice to play in the Tests (see pages 1286–1291), and agreed to join the hosts and Zimbabwe in the preceding limited-overs Paktel GSM Cup. The Zimbabweans, who arrived in Pakistan before the Champions Trophy had finished, took part in two warm-up games, one first-class, one not.

ZIMBABWEAN TOURING PARTY

T. Taibu (*captain*), E. Chigumbura, A. G. Cremer, D. D. Ebrahim, D. T. Hondo, A. Maregwede, S. Matsikenyeri, T. Mupariwa, M. L. Nkala, T. Panyangara, E. C. Rainsford, V. Sibanda, B. R. M. Taylor, P. Utseya, M. A. Vermeulen.

Coach: P. V. Simmons. *Manager:* M. A. Meman. *Physiotherapist:* A. Machikicho. *Analyst:* T. Ruswa. *Fitness trainer:* D. Woodford. *Selector:* M. Ebrahim.

ZIMBABWEAN TOUR RESULTS

One-day internationals – Played 3: Lost 3. Abandoned 1. *Losses* – Pakistan (2), Sri Lanka.
    Abandoned – Sri Lanka.
First-class match – Played 1: Lost 1.
Other non-first-class match – Played 1: Drawn 1.

Note: Matches in this section which were not first-class are signified by a dagger.

†At Sheikhupura, September 20, 21, 2004. **Drawn.** Toss: Zimbabweans. **Zimbabweans 215** (E. Chigumbura 81; Mohammad Irshad 4-86); **PCB XI 398-2** (Ashar Zaidi 202*, Asif Zakir 61, Faisal Iqbal 86*).
    The first innings was limited to 90 overs; the Zimbabweans were all out in 79, the PCB XI completed their 90. Their two wickets both fell to Graeme Cremer, a leg-spinner who turned 18 the day before the match.

At Gaddafi Stadium, Lahore, September 23, 24, 25, 26, 2004. **PCB Patron's XI won by an innings and 38 runs.** Toss: Zimbabweans. **PCB Patron's XI 529-9 dec.** (Bazid Khan 94, Naumanullah 56, Misbah-ul-Haq 130, Aamer Bashir 100*, Riaz Afridi 66); **Zimbabweans 324** (B. R. M. Taylor 141) and **167**.
    Brendan Taylor hit his maiden first-class century; Riaz Afridi his highest first-class score.

Zimbabwe's matches against Pakistan and Sri Lanka in the Paktel GSM Cup (September 30–October 11) appear on pages 1357–1363.

THE AUSTRALIANS IN INDIA, 2004-05

Paul Weaver

A boxing promoter might have been proud of the hyperbolic billing that preceded this series. The drum roll carried from Mumbai to Melbourne, but the entire cricket world was aware of a rare frisson of anticipation. Although India were the world's fourth-ranked side when Australia arrived at the end of September, there were many who viewed the meeting of these teams as Test cricket's blue-riband event, based on the epic nature of the preceding two series, in India in 2000-01 and in Australia in 2003-04.

But heavyweight match-ups are often a letdown, and this one never even went the distance, as Australia took an unassailable 2–0 lead in the Third Test. Arguably, the series could have been drawn had it not rained in Chennai with India on top. But by the end of the series Australia had established themselves as much the better side, and the 2–1 scoreline rather flattered the Indians. Steve Waugh's "final frontier" had been breached at last, even if Waugh himself was now back home in Australia watching the series on TV. The Australians had not won here in 35 years, but the modern team could now claim to have beaten everyone everywhere (except Bangladesh away, because they had not yet bothered).

Australia, led for the first three Tests by Adam Gilchrist in place of the injured Ricky Ponting, played the better cricket in the opener at Bangalore, where Michael Clarke made an astonishing debut. Though they could have lost in Chennai, Australia were again the stronger side at Nagpur, on a pitch that could not have been better prepared to assist their fast bowlers. And they outplayed India for most of the final match at Mumbai before showing, once again, that they are perhaps the worst chasers since the Keystone Kops. Their other negative reputation – for losing dead rubbers – has looked a little unfair in recent years, but was also reinforced, even though they lost by just 13 runs on an awful pitch that saw 40 wickets fall for 605 runs in the equivalent of not much more than two days. Even Dilip Vengsarkar, the Mumbai Cricket Association's vice-president and a former Indian captain, said it was unsuitable for Test cricket.

Australia won because of the superiority of their batsmen and fast bowlers. Just one Indian batsman, Virender Sehwag, passed 200 runs in the series. Australia had six, with Damien Martyn (444) and Clarke (400) leading the way. Martyn was voted man of the series. But the award, arguably, should have gone to Clarke, who contributed more in the field and, at Mumbai, with the ball. He also brought a sense of energy and exuberance to the side and was immensely popular. The game might have witnessed the arrival of a great player.

Jason Gillespie, rhythmic, hitting the seam and always making the batsmen play, was the leading fast bowler in the series, with 20 wickets at 16. But the support was massive, with Glenn McGrath, who recorded his 100th Test

Just the start? Michael Clarke, having swapped his helmet for a baggy green, celebrates a hundred on debut during the First Test at Bangalore.

Picture by Hamish Blair, Getty Images

and 450th wicket at Nagpur, taking 14 at 25, and the improved Michael Kasprowicz nine at 28. Contrast that with India's most successful fast bowler, Zaheer Khan, who took ten wickets at nearly 37. The promising Irfan Pathan was second with just two wickets at 84 and simply too much was left to their two admirable spinners, Anil Kumble and Harbhajan Singh, who claimed 48 wickets between them. Australia's fielding, though suspect in the Second Test, was also considerably stronger and often outstanding in the other three.

There was another reason, however, why these Australians won. John Buchanan, their tall, grave and schoolmasterly coach, had been planning this tour with an almost forensic attention to detail since their previous one ended, in April 2001. Then, Australia won the first of the three Tests with some ease – by ten wickets at Mumbai – and thought they had the series wrapped up when India followed on 274 runs behind at Kolkata. But India, remarkably, won, and did so again, narrowly, at Chennai to clinch a famous series victory. Buchanan, aware that India had been beaten in only two home series since the success of David Gower's England side in 1984-85, prepared methodically. Their batsmen learned how to play spin – their success in Sri Lanka earlier in the year was a key – and their fast bowlers decided to work on reverse swing, for the first time, according to McGrath.

They played more thoughtful, patient cricket. Instead of bowling fast and short to an attacking field they varied it more, often bowling fuller and straighter to split fields. "If you are aggressive all the time you can become predictable without having a fall-back position," Buchanan observed. Zsa Zsa Gabor once supposedly declared "Macho doesn't prove mucho." She was probably a duffer at cricket but would have approved of these Australians.

It also helped Australia that they played in the relative cool of October, and not the humid heat of March, as they had done on their previous trip. This time there would be no one-day internationals to distract them from their obsession and they also negotiated a mini-break between the Second and Third Tests, in which the players refreshed themselves in Goa, Mumbai and Singapore. The Australian batsmen wore ice-vests. And during drinks breaks they were given chairs and umbrellas. All their players sipped water constantly, realising, like marathon runners, that drinking is too late once dehydrated. But great players were more important than even this thorough preparation. McGrath and Shane Warne, who had missed the previous, drawn series between the sides in Australia through injury and suspension respectively, were back. Warne, who had never been at his best in India, was something like his old self and at Chennai became the leading wicket-taker in Test history, passing Muttiah Muralitharan's record of 532.

India could argue, with some justification, that the luck went against them, and not only at Chennai: they lost the toss in the first three matches and

THE DUCK HUNTERS

Ducks		Total wickets	Tests
88	**G. D. McGrath (Australia)**	481	106
79	C. A. Walsh (West Indies)	519	132
79	Wasim Akram (Pakistan)	414	104
77	**M. Muralitharan (Sri Lanka)**	532	91
77	**S. K. Warne (Australia)**	566	120
76	C. E. L. Ambrose (West Indies)	405	98
76	Waqar Younis (Pakistan)	373	87

The wicket of Aakash Chopra at Bangalore gave Glenn McGrath a world record that almost passed unnoticed: Chopra was the 80th batsman he had dismissed for a duck in Tests. He had taken this figure to 88 by January 2005.

Research: Rajneesh Gupta

suffered from some ropy umpiring decisions at Bangalore. At Nagpur, they looked as glum as war refugees, the victims of the local Vidarbha Cricket Association's refusal to prepare a pitch according to their requirements. The VCA president, Shashank Manohar, no friend of Jagmohan Dalmiya, the outgoing president of the Board of Control for Cricket in Indian, said five days before the match: "I've got no instructions from either the BCCI or the Indian team management. Even if I do, I'm not going to oblige them." Manohar was as good as his word. When Sourav Ganguly, the India captain, registered his dismay over the way the pitch was shaping up he was magisterially ignored. The surface, with a generous covering of grass, offered bounce and movement, and Gillespie and McGrath took 14 wickets between them. Australia won the match by 342 runs – and with it the series. Ganguly did not play. On the morning of the match he withdrew, handing over to

---

ALL THEIR OWN WORK

C&B		Total wickets	Tests
23	**A. Kumble (India)**	**444**	**92**
22	M. Muralitharan (Sri Lanka)	532	91
20	D. L. Underwood (England)	297	86
20	**S. K. Warne (Australia)**	**566**	**120**
17	R. Benaud (Australia)	248	63
15	L. R. Gibbs (West Indies)	309	79
15	H. Trumble (Australia)	141	32

Anil Kumble acquired a world record when he caught Shane Warne off his own bowling at Chennai, his 23rd caught-and-bowled in Tests. Figures correct up to January 25, 2005.

Research: Rajneesh Gupta

Rahul Dravid who had no time to prepare a strategy. When asked what was wrong with Ganguly, Dravid admitted he didn't know. Some said it was a thigh injury, others that it was a problem with the groin. "I hope it's the groin and not the grass," observed the former Indian all-rounder Ravi Shastri, a little mischievously. Ganguly had appeared fully fit on the eve of the game and his withdrawal caused widespread bewilderment.

The injury may have been real enough but the unfortunate impression he conveyed was that of a general who, denied the munitions he had requested, decided to sulk in his tent. The team's physiotherapist, Andrew Leipus, said the injury was "not very serious". A statement confirmed that there was a problem. The captain was suffering from "intra-articular pathology of the right hip joint noted by increased synovial fluid accumulation". It was difficult to imagine Steve Waugh, that great champion of the primacy of the Border–Gavaskar Trophy, being undone by a little synovial fluid.

Meanwhile, Australia's stricken captain, Ponting, was regularly seen running on the field with drinks and supplies. Australia looked utterly professional and motivated while India appeared demoralised and shambolic. Suddenly, a close series felt terminally one-sided, pivoting on the rain that ended the second match and the pitch preparation that preceded the third. By the time they reached Mumbai both Ganguly and the coach, John Wright, looked vulnerable, despite their impressive records. Again, Ganguly did not play while Wright, his contract almost up, wore the wistful expression of a man who might soon be reacquainted with his treasured fishing-rods.

The selectors were largely responsible for the malaise. They could not decide on Sehwag's opening partner, torn between the strokeless Aakash Chopra and the loose Yuvraj Singh, before finally handing a debut to Gautam Gambhir at Mumbai (between them, the trio managed 34 runs in eight innings). The selectors also decided, too late, to dispense with their wicket-keeper, Parthiv Patel, who had been inept behind the stumps in the first three matches. Essentially, however, it was the failure of their vaunted middle order that hurt India. Dravid, Ganguly and V. V. S. Laxman totalled 349 runs at an average of under 22. Even players as good as these have often seemed mere outriders surrounding the limousine that is Sachin Tendulkar. But the maestro missed the first two Tests with tennis elbow and looked out of sorts in the Third. He produced a thrilling cameo at Mumbai but it was so late it was posthumous.

AUSTRALIAN TOURING PARTY

R. T. Ponting (*captain*), A. C. Gilchrist (*vice-captain*), M. J. Clarke, J. N. Gillespie, N. M. Hauritz, M. L. Hayden, B. J. Hodge, M. S. Kasprowicz, S. M. Katich, J. L. Langer, B. Lee, D. S. Lehmann, G. D. McGrath, D. R. Martyn, S. K. Warne, S. R. Watson, C. L. White.

Hodge was added to the squad after Ponting broke his thumb during the Champions Trophy. *Coach:* J. M. Buchanan. *Team manager:* S. R. Bernard. *Assistant coach:* T. J. Nielsen. *Field/throwing coach:* M. Young. *Physiotherapist:* E. L. Alcott. *Physical performance manager:* J. A. Campbell. *Massage therapist:* L. J. Frostick. *Media manager:* J. D. Rose.

AUSTRALIAN TOUR RESULTS

Test matches – Played 4: Won 2, Lost 1, Drawn 1.
First-class matches – Played 5: Won 2, Lost 1, Drawn 2.

TEST MATCH AVERAGES

INDIA – BATTING AND FIELDING

	T	I	NO	R	HS	100s	50s	Avge	Ct/St
V. Sehwag	4	8	1	299	155	1	1	42.71	0
†I. K. Pathan	2	3	0	100	55	0	1	33.33	0
†P. A. Patel	3	5	0	156	54	0	1	31.20	7/1
M. Kaif	3	5	0	153	64	0	2	30.60	6
R. Dravid	4	7	1	167	60	0	1	27.83	13
†S. C. Ganguly	2	3	0	59	45	0	0	19.66	0
V. V. S. Laxman	4	7	0	123	69	0	1	17.57	7
S. R. Tendulkar	2	4	0	70	55	0	1	17.50	1
A. Kumble	4	7	2	86	26	0	0	17.20	2
†Yuvraj Singh	2	4	1	47	27	0	0	15.66	6
Harbhajan Singh	3	5	0	69	42	0	0	13.80	2
Zaheer Khan	4	7	3	47	25	0	0	11.75	0
†M. Kartik	2	4	0	27	22	0	0	6.75	1
A. Chopra	2	4	0	15	9	0	0	3.75	5

Played in one Test: A. B. Agarkar 15, 44* (1 ct); †G. Gambhir 3, 1; K. D. Karthik 10, 4 (1 ct, 1 st).

† *Left-handed batsman.*

BOWLING

	Style	O	M	R	W	BB	5W/i	Avge
M. Kartik	SLA	73.3	10	207	12	4-44	0	17.25
Harbhajan Singh.	OB	178.5	32	504	21	6-78	3	24.00
A. Kumble	LBG	197.3	30	685	27	7-48	3	25.37
Zaheer Khan	LFM	123.3	22	368	10	4-95	0	36.80

Also bowled: A. B. Agarkar (RFM) 44–9–167–1; S. C. Ganguly (RM) 3–1–2–0; I. K. Pathan (LFM) 57–14–168–2; V. Sehwag (OB) 9–1–45–0; S. R. Tendulkar (RM/OB/LB) 14–2–41–0; Yuvraj Singh (SLA/LM) 4–0–10–0.

AUSTRALIA – BATTING AND FIELDING

	T	I	NO	R	HS	100s	50s	Avge	Ct
M. J. Clarke	4	8	1	400	151	1	2	57.14	7
D. R. Martyn	4	8	0	444	114	2	2	55.50	2
†S. M. Katich	4	8	1	276	99	0	2	39.42	1
†A. C. Gilchrist	4	8	1	218	104	1	0	31.14	16
†M. L. Hayden	4	8	0	244	58	0	1	30.50	3
†J. L. Langer	4	8	0	228	71	0	2	28.50	1
†D. S. Lehmann	3	5	0	132	70	0	1	26.40	1
J. N. Gillespie	4	7	2	66	26	0	0	13.20	0
S. K. Warne	3	5	0	38	31	0	0	7.60	4
G. D. McGrath	4	7	3	27	11*	0	0	6.75	2
M. S. Kasprowicz	4	7	0	46	19	0	0	6.57	0

Played in one Test: N. M. Hauritz 0, 15 (1 ct); R. T. Ponting 11, 12 (2 ct).

† *Left-handed batsman.*

BOWLING

	Style	O	M	R	W	BB	5W/i	Avge
M. J. Clarke	SLA	7.2	0	13	6	6-9	1	2.16
J. N. Gillespie	RF	132.5	33	323	20	5-56	1	16.15
N. M. Hauritz	OB	27	4	103	5	3-16	0	20.60
G. D. McGrath.	RFM	141	51	356	14	4-55	0	25.42
M. S. Kasprowicz. . . .	RFM	108.3	29	255	9	2-11	0	28.33
S. K. Warne	LBG	140	27	421	14	6-125	1	30.07

Also bowled: S. M. Katich (SLC) 2–0–7–0; D. S. Lehmann (SLA) 11–3–40–0.

At Brabourne Stadium, Mumbai, September 30, October 1, 2, 2004. **Drawn.** Toss: Australians. **Australians 302-7 dec.** (M. L. Hayden 67, D. R. Martyn 71 retired ill) **and 207-2** (J. L. Langer 108 retired out, M. J. Clarke 52); **Mumbai 255** (A. A. Muzumdar 52; G. D. McGrath 4-25).

INDIA v AUSTRALIA

First Test Match

At Bangalore, October 6, 7, 8, 9, 10, 2004. Australia won by 217 runs. Toss: Australia. Test debut: M. J. Clarke.

Gilchrist, leading Australia in place of Ponting, who was recovering from a broken thumb, called heads. The tottering coin was going to fall tails but then hit one of the larger cracks on the crazy-paving pitch and flipped over the other way. The luck would remain with Australia throughout the match but they also played the better and more purposeful cricket. Their approach surprised many. Rejecting the nuclear option that had served them so well in recent years, they relied more on conventional warfare: line and length and crease occupation. They played with patient care, sticking to a game plan that had started to evolve since they lost their last series in this country over three years earlier.

"I didn't know what it was like to lose a Test match when we lost here last time," said Gilchrist. "I think it's good to have a little fear, to know what it feels like to lose and what it takes to win." The player of the match, however, was gloriously unscarred by previous battles. Michael Clarke became the 17th Australian to score a century on his Test debut, and the first since Greg Blewett almost a decade earlier. More than that, he played with real audacity, particularly against the spinners, picking the length early and using his feet to get to the pitch of the ball. The opening day was evenly contested until he and Katich put on 107 for the fifth wicket.

When Australia closed on 316 for five, Clarke was unbeaten on 76, of which 56 had come in boundaries. When he reached 98 on the second morning he replaced his helmet with the baggy green, which he kissed with great emotion when he reached his century. Then, if it was possible, he became even more aggressive, striking Kumble for two sixes over mid-wicket on his way to 151. It took 341 minutes and 248 balls, and included 18

> ## Green and gold prevailed over the silk saris

fours and four sixes. Kumble will prefer to recall this match for becoming the ninth bowler and the third spinner to reach 400 Test wickets.

If Clarke's innings swung the game Australia's way it was, as so often, Gilchrist who demoralised the opposition. His 11th Test hundred came from just 103 balls and included 13 fours and three sixes. Kumble and Harbhajan Singh were launched high and hard, and scores of 0, 0, 1 and 1 to finish his last series in India quickly forgotten. Australia's tail was swept away by Harbhajan, who finished with five for 146, but they had scored 474 and were in confident control. When India batted it was Australia's fast bowlers who caused most problems. The ball reversed precociously, helped by the abrasive nature of the pitch, and McGrath and Kasprowicz, who also found cut, exploited this with great skill. India looked out of the match at 150 for six at the end of the second day. On the third, Australia took India's four remaining wickets for 96 runs, though they were held up by an obdurate innings of 46 by the wicket-keeper Patel, who appeared anxious to make up for his maladroitness on the other side of the stumps. Fresh-faced and diminutive and looking even younger than his 19 years – when he toured England in 2002 Alec Stewart asked him whether he bought his pads from Mothercare – Patel batted with fierce concentration for three and a half hours.

India's 246 fell 29 short of the follow-on target. But Australia, perhaps spooked by the ghosts of Kolkata, did not enforce it. Instead, they widened their advantage to 355 runs by the end of the third day. Harbhajan, bowling even better than in the first innings, returned six for 78 in the second as Australia eventually finished on 228, setting India 457, a remote prospect even on a pitch that had not crumbled as many had anticipated. They made an awful start when umpire Bowden, who had an unhappy match, gave Sehwag out lbw despite a thick inside edge. Pathan, who overcame an 87-minute wait on seven to score his maiden Test fifty, put on a defiant 89 for the ninth wicket with Harbhajan, before being given out caught behind – another of the decisions that went against them – and India were bowled out for 239 shortly after lunch on the final day. Green and gold had prevailed over the wonderful silk saris that decorated the concrete of the Chinnaswamy Stadium.

Man of the Match: M. J. Clarke.

Close of play: First day, Australia 316-5 (Clarke 76, Gilchrist 35); Second day, India 150-6 (Patel 18, Pathan 1); Third day, Australia 127-4 (Martyn 29, Clarke 11); Fourth day, India 105-6 (Dravid 47, Pathan 7).

Australia

J. L. Langer b Pathan	52	– lbw b Pathan	0
M. L. Hayden c Yuvraj Singh b Harbhajan Singh	26	– run out	30
S. M. Katich b Kumble	81	– c Dravid b Kumble	39
D. R. Martyn c Chopra b Kumble	3	– c sub (M. Kaif) b Harbhajan Singh	45
D. S. Lehmann c Dravid b Kumble	17	– c Chopra b Harbhajan Singh	14
M. J. Clarke c Patel b Zaheer Khan	151	– c Chopra b Harbhajan Singh	17
*†A. C. Gilchrist c and b Harbhajan Singh	104	– c Chopra b Kumble	26
S. K. Warne c Dravid b Harbhajan Singh	1	– c Yuvraj Singh b Harbhajan Singh	31
J. N. Gillespie not out	7	– c Yuvraj Singh b Harbhajan Singh	8
M. S. Kasprowicz c Yuvraj Singh b Harbhajan Singh	3	– c Dravid b Harbhajan Singh	8
G. D. McGrath lbw b Harbhajan Singh	0	– not out	3
B 5, l-b 15, w 1, n-b 8	29	B 2, l-b 1, w 1, n-b 3	7
	474		**228**

1/50 (2) 2/124 (1) 3/129 (4) 4/149 (5) 5/256 (3) 6/423 (7) 7/427 (8) 8/471 (6) 9/474 (10) 10/474 (11)

1/0 (1) 2/65 (2) 3/86 (3) 4/104 (5) 5/146 (6) 6/167 (4) 7/204 (7) 8/216 (8) 9/217 (9) 10/228 (10)

Bowling: *First Innings*—Pathan 21–6–62–1; Zaheer Khan 22–2–60–1; Harbhajan Singh 41–7–146–5; Kumble 39–4–157–3; Sehwag 5–0–26–0; Yuvraj Singh 2–0–3–0. *Second Innings*—Pathan 12–2–38–1; Zaheer Khan 13–1–45–0; Harbhajan Singh 30.1–5–78–6; Kumble 23–4–64–2.

India

A. Chopra lbw b McGrath	0	– lbw b Gillespie	5
V. Sehwag c Langer b Kasprowicz	39	– lbw b McGrath	0
R. Dravid b McGrath	0	– lbw b Kasprowicz	60
*S. C. Ganguly c Gilchrist b Kasprowicz	45	– run out	5
V. V. S. Laxman c Gilchrist b Warne	31	– lbw b Warne	3
Yuvraj Singh c Gilchrist b McGrath	5	– c Gilchrist b McGrath	27
†P. A. Patel b Gillespie	46	– lbw b Warne	4
I. K. Pathan c Gilchrist b Warne	31	– c Gilchrist b Gillespie	55
A. Kumble b Gillespie	26	– c Kasprowicz	2
Harbhajan Singh c Lehmann b McGrath	8	– c McGrath b Gillespie	42
Zaheer Khan not out	0	– not out	22
B 5, l-b 2, w 5, n-b 3	15	B 6, l-b 5, n-b 3	14
	246		**239**

1/0 (1) 2/4 (3) 3/87 (2) 4/98 (4) 5/124 (6) 6/136 (5) 7/196 (8) 8/227 (7) 9/244 (10) 10/246 (9)

1/1 (2) 2/7 (1) 3/12 (4) 4/19 (5) 5/81 (6) 6/86 (7) 7/118 (3) 8/125 (9) 9/214 (8) 10/239 (10)

Bowling: *First Innings*—McGrath 25–8–55–4; Gillespie 16.2–3–63–2; Warne 28–4–78–2; Kasprowicz 20–4–43–2. *Second Innings*—McGrath 20–10–39–2; Gillespie 14.4–4–33–3; Kasprowicz 14–7–23–2; Warne 32–8–115–2; Lehmann 6–3–14–0; Clarke 1–0–4–0.

Umpires: B. F. Bowden (New Zealand) and S. A. Bucknor (West Indies).
Third umpire: A. V. Jayaprakash. Referee: R. S. Madugalle (Sri Lanka).

INDIA v AUSTRALIA

Second Test Match

At Chennai, October 14, 15, 16, 17, 18, 2004. Drawn. Toss: Australia.

There were some fine performances in this match, most notably the batting of Sehwag and Martyn and the bowling of Kumble. But it will be remembered, chiefly, for the tortured conjecture that followed its soggy ending. The fifth day's play was washed out without a ball bowled and with the match tantalisingly poised.

And then their hopes were drenched... India held the upper hand during the Chennai Test. Virender Sehwag (*left*) drives on towards an aggressive century and Anil Kumble removes Justin Langer in the second innings.

Pictures by Hamish Blair, Getty Images

With all their second-innings wickets in hand, India, probably, would have knocked off the 210 more runs they required to level the series. They certainly thought so, and Australia's acting-captain Gilchrist sheepishly admitted as much. But on the fourth evening McGrath and Warne were still confident the game could be won and wore fierce gleams in their competitive eyes. Still, McGrath had already been lashed for 18 off two overs, and when play was called off at 1 p.m. next day, the Australians departed for their mid-series break in high spirits, clinging to their 1–0 advantage, while the Indian dressing-room looked a sullen place. The happiest man was probably the quick-thinking Australian journalist who opened his curtains early that morning, saw the drenched city and immediately secured odds of 13 to 1 against the draw with a Sydney bookmaker.

Australia had been the more assured side at the start of the match, when Langer and Hayden added 136 for the first wicket. But then they lost ten wickets for 99 runs, the last eight tumbling for a mere 46. They were savaged, as at Sydney ten months earlier, by Kumble's brisk top-spinners. He took seven wickets for 25 runs in 61 balls, doubtless encouraged by a pitch that had more pace and bounce than he had been able to divine at Bangalore. He finished with 13 for 181 in the match, taking his total to 42 in five Tests against Australia since December 2003. India were assisted, though, by Australia's peripatetic tendency. Three of their players – Gilchrist, Gillespie and Kasprowicz – walked without waiting for the umpire's decision. Some interpreted this as an attempt to regain the moral high ground, for their players had been stung by criticism of Sehwag's controversial dismissal in the First Test. Kasprowicz had already been given not out for a catch at silly point, and his decision to go, after a moment's

---

HIGHEST PARTNERSHIPS INVOLVING A NIGHT-WATCHMAN

Runs	Wkt		
197	5th	Nasim-ul-Ghani (101) and Javed Burki (101), P v E at Lord's.....	1962
170	6th	W. W. Davis (77) and C. G. Greenidge (223), WI v E at Manchester	1984
161	2nd	N. Boje (85) and G. Kirsten (79), SA v I at Bangalore.........	1999-2000
157	3rd	H. Carter (72) and C. Hill (98), A v E at Adelaide............	1911-12
155	3rd	A. V. Bedser (79) and W. J. Edrich (111), E v A at Leeds.......	1948
139	3rd	A. L. Mann (105) and A. D. Ogilvie (47), A v I at Perth........	1977-78
139	**5th**	**J. N. Gillespie (26) and D. R. Martyn (104), A v I at Chennai ..**	**2004-05**
131	2nd	R. C. Russell (94) and G. A. Gooch (75), E v SL at Lord's......	1988

In each case, the name of the night-watchman is given first.

Research: Rajneesh Gupta

---

hesitation, so bewildered the umpire, David Shepherd, that he shook his head until perspiration flew from his florid countenance. Shepherd was already chatting to the non-striker Katich when he looked up and saw to his amazement the batsman heading off.

Warne bowled almost as well as Kumble. His record in India had been a poor one, with just 24 wickets at 51 before this match, and a lack of form and fitness had blighted his previous tours. Now, though, he took six for 125. His second wicket came in his fifth over of the second day when he had Pathan caught by Hayden at slip. It was his 533rd Test wicket and for the first time in his wonderful career he was the outright leading wicket-taker in the game, one ahead of his great rival Muttiah Muralitharan. "I would have been happy to take one Test wicket when I started my career," he said afterwards. One of his victims was Sehwag, who scored a blistering 155 out of 233, an innings which included 21 fours. There were also half-centuries for Kaif and Patel, who added 102 for the seventh wicket.

India led by 141. And they had the chance to win inside four days. But they were frustrated by a fine century from Martyn, his eighth in Test cricket, though he was missed behind the wicket before he had scored. His four-hour stand with the night-watchman Gillespie enabled Australia to take the match into the fifth day, when the unexpected arrival of the north-east monsoon confirmed their safety.

Man of the Match: A. Kumble.

Close of play: First day, India 28-1 (Sehwag 20, Pathan 0); Second day, India 291-6 (Kaif 34, Patel 27); Third day, Australia 150-4 (Martyn 19, Gillespie 0); Fourth day, India 19-0 (Yuvraj Singh 7, Sehwag 12).

Australia

J. L. Langer c Dravid b Harbhajan Singh	71	– c Dravid b Kumble 19
M. L. Hayden c Laxman b Harbhajan Singh	58	– c Laxman b Kumble 39
S. M. Katich not out.	36	– (4) lbw b Zaheer Khan 9
D. R. Martyn c Yuvraj Singh b Kumble	26	– (5) c Dravid b Harbhajan Singh. . . 104
D. S. Lehmann c Patel b Kumble	0	– (8) c Patel b Kumble 31
M. J. Clarke lbw b Kumble	5	– (7) not out. 39
*†A. C. Gilchrist c Yuvraj Singh b Kumble.	3	– (3) b Kumble 49
S. K. Warne c and b Kumble	4	– (9) c Laxman b Kumble 0
J. N. Gillespie c Kaif b Kumble	5	– (6) c Dravid b Harbhajan Singh. . . 26
M. S. Kasprowicz c Laxman b Kumble	4	– lbw b Kumble 5
G. D. McGrath run out	2	– b Harbhajan Singh 2
B 7, l-b 4, w 1, n-b 4, p 5	21	B 19, l-b 15, w 3, n-b 4, p 5 46

1/136 (2) 2/136 (1) 3/189 (4) 4/191 (5)   **235**
5/204 (6) 6/210 (7) 7/216 (8)
8/224 (9) 9/228 (10) 10/235 (11)

1/53 (1) 2/76 (2) 3/121 (4)   **369**
4/145 (3) 5/284 (5) 6/285 (6)
7/347 (8) 8/347 (9)
9/364 (10) 10/369 (11)

Bowling: *First Innings*—Pathan 12–3–29–0; Zaheer Khan 11–2–44–0; Harbhajan Singh 29–2–90–2; Kumble 17.3–4–48–7; Sehwag 2–1–8–0. *Second Innings*—Pathan 12–3–39–0; Zaheer Khan 22–6–36–1; Harbhajan Singh 46.5–12–108–3; Kumble 47–8–133–6; Sehwag 1–0–5–0; Yuvraj Singh 2–0–7–0; Ganguly 3–1–2–0.

India

Yuvraj Singh c Gilchrist b Warne	8	– not out 7
V. Sehwag c Clarke b Warne	155	– not out 12
I. K. Pathan c Hayden b Warne	14	
R. Dravid b Kasprowicz	26	
*S. C. Ganguly c Gilchrist b Gillespie	9	
V. V. S. Laxman b Gillespie	4	
M. Kaif run out.	64	
†P. A. Patel c Gilchrist b Warne	54	
A. Kumble b Warne	20	
Harbhajan Singh c and b Warne	5	
Zaheer Khan not out.	0	
B 6, l-b 3, w 2, n-b 6	17	

1/28 (1) 2/83 (3) 3/178 (4) 4/203 (5)   **376**   (no wkt) **19**
5/213 (6) 6/233 (2) 7/335 (8)
8/369 (9) 9/372 (10) 10/376 (7)

In the first innings Kaif, when 60, retired hurt at 363 and resumed at 372.

Bowling: *First Innings*—McGrath 25–4–74–0; Gillespie 35–8–70–2; Warne 42.3–5–125–6; Kasprowicz 25–5–65–1; Lehmann 5–0–26–0; Katich 2–0–7–0. *Second Innings*—McGrath 2–0–18–0; Gillespie 1–0–1–0.

Umpires: R. E. Koertzen (South Africa) and D. R. Shepherd (England).
Third umpire: A. V. Jayaprakash. Referee: R. S. Madugalle (Sri Lanka).

INDIA v AUSTRALIA

Third Test Match

At Nagpur, October 26, 27, 28, 29, 2004. Australia won by 342 runs. Toss: Australia. "Looks like home, don't it?" said umpire David Shepherd, in his familiar West Country burr, as he surveyed the strip at the Vidarbha Cricket Association ground on the eve of this match. And, indeed, it looked like an old-fashioned English green seamer. As Australia prepared to cross what had become known as "the final frontier" and win their first series in India for 35 years, even the return of Tendulkar, who had

Majestic: Damien Martyn glides towards a first-innings hundred at Nagpur. He came within a whisker of making another in the second.

Picture by Hamish Blair, Getty Images

been out of cricket for two months with tennis elbow, was overshadowed by the preparation of the VCA pitch. Ganguly said he had asked the groundsman to remove the grass from the wicket the previous week. "But I don't think he has done much," he said, sounding miffed. "Our strength is our spinners but the pitch is up to him." India seemed dispirited and when Ganguly withdrew injured on the morning of the match they were thrown into disarray. They were also without Harbhajan Singh, who was suffering from gastroenteritis.

The pitch suited tall fast bowlers: Australia had three, India none. McGrath, who became the first Australian fast bowler to win 100 Test caps, bowled with astonishing accuracy, conceding barely a run an over in the first innings. But even he was upstaged by Gillespie, who bowled superbly to take nine wickets and was unlucky not to win the match award.

By the end of the first day Australia had scored 362 for seven. For the fourth time in five innings, Langer and Hayden got them off to a good start, but it was left to Martyn to score a handsome century. Zaheer Khan again bowled with great zest but Agarkar looked uncomfortable at this level, even on a pitch such as this. Kumble seemed disheartened by the nature of the surface, and India badly needed a third seamer; Tendulkar helped out but was more at ease bowling spinners. Apart from Zaheer, India's best bowler in Australia's innings of 398 was Harbhajan's replacement, the left-arm spinner Murali Kartik, who took three wickets and bowled with relative economy.

When India batted they were outclassed not just by McGrath and Gillespie but by Australia's thoughtful field placements. Kaif, whose place was in jeopardy despite his maiden Test fifty in the previous match, top-scored with 55 in India's total of 185. Tendulkar's keenly awaited return yielded just eight diffident runs from 36 balls. Despite a lead of 213, Australia once more declined to enforce the follow-on. When they batted again, they declared on 329 for five just before lunch on the fourth day. Katich was unlucky to fall one short of his century, though he was probably lucky not to be given out lbw before he had scored. Martyn played another elegant innings, failing by just

The Australians in India

1273

three runs to score his third Test century in three innings, a feat last achieved for Australia by Bradman. But the best batting came from Clarke, a jaunty pre-declaration 73, which made up for Langer's curious ponderousness at the top of the order.

India required 543 for victory. They were soon 37 for five, and only a late rally took them to 200. Tendulkar (McGrath's 450th Test victim), Dravid and Laxman made just six runs between them, and Gillespie added four wickets to his first-innings five. Australia, two up with one to play, had won in India for the first time since Bill Lawry's side triumphed against the Nawab of Pataudi's in 1969-70. Acting-captain Dravid conceded that Australia had been the better team at Bangalore and Nagpur. He made the point that a number of Australians had benefited from their numerous visits to the subcontinent since the 1996 World Cup.

Not even the cockroach Gilchrist found in his soy sauce before the match could put Australia off. The restaurant manager quickly swallowed it as if to destroy the evidence. "He took one for the team," said Gilchrist.

Man of the Match: D. R. Martyn.

Close of play: First day, Australia 362-7 (Clarke 73, Gillespie 4); Second day, India 146-5 (Kaif 47, Patel 16); Third day, Australia 202-3 (Martyn 41, Clarke 10).

Australia

J. L. Langer c Dravid b Zaheer Khan	44	– c Laxman b Kartik	30
M. L. Hayden c Patel b Zaheer Khan	23	– b Zaheer Khan	9
S. M. Katich c Chopra b Kumble	4	– lbw b Kartik	99
D. R. Martyn c Agarkar b Kumble	114	– c Patel b Zaheer Khan	97
D. S. Lehmann c Dravid b Kartik	70		
M. J. Clarke c Patel b Zaheer Khan	91	– (5) c Kaif b Kumble	73
*†A. C. Gilchrist c Patel b Kartik	2	– (6) not out	3
S. K. Warne st Patel b Kartik	2		
J. N. Gillespie lbw b Zaheer Khan	9		
M. S. Kasprowicz c Patel b Agarkar	0		
G. D. McGrath not out	11		
B 6, l-b 13, w 1, n-b 8	28	B 1, l-b 15, w 2	18
	398	(5 wkts dec.)	**329**

1/67 (2) 2/79 (1) 3/86 (3) 4/234 (5) 5/314 (4) 6/323 (7) 7/337 (8) 8/376 (9) 9/377 (10) 10/398 (6)

1/19 (2) 2/99 (1) (5 wkts dec.) 3/171 (3) 4/319 (5) 5/329 (4)

Bowling: First Innings—Agarkar 23-2-99-1; Zaheer Khan 26.2-6-95-4; Kumble 25-6-99-2; Kartik 20-1-57-3; Tendulkar 6-1-29-0. *Second Innings*—Zaheer Khan 21.1-5-64-2; Agarkar 21-7-68-0; Kumble 21-1-89-1; Tendulkar 8-1-12-0; Kartik 26-5-74-2; Sehwag 1-0-6-0.

India

A. Chopra c Warne b Gillespie	9	– b Gillespie	1
V. Sehwag c Gilchrist b McGrath	22	– c Clarke b Warne	58
*R. Dravid c Warne b McGrath	21	– b Gillespie	2
S. R. Tendulkar lbw b Gillespie	8	– c Martyn b McGrath	2
V. V. S. Laxman c Clarke b Warne	13	– c McGrath b Kasprowicz	2
M. Kaif c Warne b McGrath	55	– c Gilchrist b Kasprowicz	7
†P. A. Patel c Hayden b Warne	20	– c Gilchrist b Gillespie	32
A. B. Agarkar c Clarke b Gillespie	15	– not out	44
A. Kumble not out	7	– b Gillespie	2
M. Kartik c Clarke b Gillespie	3	– c Gilchrist b McGrath	22
Zaheer Khan b Gillespie	0	– c Martyn b Warne	25
L-b 10, w 1, n-b 1	12	L-b 2, n-b 1	3
	185		**200**

1/31 (2) 2/34 (1) 3/49 (4) 4/75 (5) 5/103 (3) 6/150 (7) 7/173 (8) 8/178 (6) 9/181 (10) 10/185 (11)

1/1 (1) 2/9 (3) 3/20 (4) 4/29 (5) 5/37 (6) 6/102 (2) 7/114 (7) 8/122 (9) 9/148 (10) 10/200 (11)

Bowling: *First Innings*—McGrath 25–13–27–3; Gillespie 22.5–8–56–5; Kasprowicz 21–4–45–0; Warne 23–8–47–2. *Second Innings*—McGrath 16–1–79–2; Gillespie 16–7–24–4; Kasprowicz 7–1–39–2; Warne 14.3–2–56–2.

Umpires: Aleem Dar (Pakistan) and D. R. Shepherd (England).
Third umpire: K. Hariharan. Referee: R. S. Madugalle (Sri Lanka).

INDIA v AUSTRALIA

Fourth Test Match

At Mumbai, November 3, 4, 5, 2004. India won by 13 runs. Toss: India. Test debuts: G. Gambhir, K. D. Karthik; N. M. Hauritz.

India won a thrilling match by a wafer-thin margin to release some of the pressure that had been building on them, though the circumstances surrounding their victory detracted from the celebrations. It was achieved on a pitch which turned square from the start and saw 20 wickets fall on the third and final day after 18 had tumbled on the second. "The wicket was no way near to being Test standard," said Ponting, Australia's returning captain. "Forty wickets in two days is almost unheard of. It's been a fantastic series but this has left a sour taste." Even some Indian players agreed.

India, desperate, shook up their personnel. The left-handed opening bat Gautam Gambhir from Delhi and the Tamil Nadu wicket-keeper Dinesh Karthik came in for their Test debuts in place of Chopra and Patel, who had both lost form and all confidence. Harbhajan returned for Agarkar. Meanwhile, Australia had to do without Warne, who broke his right thumb batting in the nets on the eve of the match. MacGill, the experienced leg-spinner, had been on stand-by for Warne but the lateness of the injury made his call-up impossible. Australia's planning had been meticulous but here, without a seasoned back-up slow bowler, they were exposed. Nathan Hauritz, a tyro off-spinner, played in Warne's place and the switch almost certainly cost them the match. Hauritz bowled tidily, but it was not enough on a pitch so conducive to the spinner's art that the part-timer Clarke took six wickets for nine runs with his slow left-armers.

Ponting returned after missing the first three games through injury. He was anxious to make a belated mark on the series, and also to atone for his wretched experience on his previous tour, when he scored just 17 runs in five innings. It was not to be, and he even lost the toss, breaking Gilchrist's winning sequence. Australia, set 107 to win, were bowled out for 93. As at Headingley in 1981 or Sydney in 1993-94 – to name only the two most memorable examples – a minuscule fourth-innings target was beyond them.

Play had not got under way until 2 p.m. on the first day and lasted just four overs before it was delayed again until 4.30, when they returned for another half hour. Rain had been the problem but they ultimately came off because of the unevenness of the floodlighting, and the difficulties the batsmen had in picking up the red ball in the damp gloom. On the second day India were bundled out for 104 in under 42 overs, with Dravid's unbeaten 31 the only resistance. Tendulkar's 35-ball innings included just one positive stroke. Gillespie was the main destroyer, with four for 29. Australia then placed themselves in a winning position when they scored 203, although only Martyn, with another half-century, played the spinners with any assurance.

When India batted again, Tendulkar briefly found his form for the first time in the series and prospered with Laxman, promoted in the order so his strokeplay could make the most of the harder ball. Their total of 205 gave their bowlers an outside chance. Langer fell to the second ball of Australia's second innings, caught behind off Zaheer, but at 24 for one, with Ponting and Hayden taking the attack to the bowlers, it was difficult to see them losing. Ponting was second out, caught at slip off Kartik, and Martyn fell lbw in the same over. Australia still appeared to be on course even when

Aerial supremacy: at Mumbai on a poor wicket, Australia were brought down to earth by the Indian spinners. Harbhajan Singh is exultant at the fall of Michael Kasprowicz (*out of picture*).

Picture by Hamish Blair, Getty Images

Katich was fourth out at 33. But that changed when they lost two more at 48. Hayden was bowled off his pads and Clarke was deceived by the arm ball as he backed away to cut. It was 58 for seven when Gilchrist swept to deep square leg, and although Gillespie battled hard, it was all over when Glenn McGrath got an outside edge. "No. 11 is the most difficult place to bat because my good innings are always nipped in the bud by others getting out," McGrath had complained a few days before.

Man of the Match: M. Kartik. *Man of the Series:* D. R. Martyn.

Close of play: First day, India 22-2 (Dravid 9, Tendulkar 2); Second day, India 5-0 (Gambhir 1, Sehwag 4).

India

G. Gambhir lbw b Gillespie	3	– c Clarke b McGrath	1
V. Sehwag b McGrath	8	– lbw b McGrath	5
*R. Dravid not out	31	– (5) c Gilchrist b Clarke	27
S. R. Tendulkar c Gilchrist b Gillespie	5	– c Clarke b Hauritz	55
V. V. S. Laxman c Gilchrist b Gillespie	1	– (3) c and b Hauritz	69
M. Kaif lbw b Gillespie	2	– lbw b Clarke	25
†K. D. Karthik b Kasprowicz	10	– c Ponting b Clarke	4
A. Kumble c Ponting b Hauritz	16	– not out	13
Harbhajan Singh c Katich b Hauritz	14	– c Hayden b Clarke	0
M. Kartik c Gilchrist b Hauritz	0	– b Clarke	2
Zaheer Khan b Kasprowicz	0	– lbw b Clarke	0
B 6, l-b 7, n-b 1	14	B 4	4

1/11 (2) 2/11 (1) 3/29 (4) 4/31 (5)   104   1/5 (1) 2/14 (2) 3/105 (4)   205
5/33 (6) 6/46 (7) 7/68 (8)   4/153 (3) 5/182 (5) 6/188 (7)
8/100 (9) 9/102 (10) 10/104 (11)   7/195 (6) 8/195 (9)
                                      9/199 (10) 10/205 (11)

Bowling: First Innings—McGrath 16–9–35–1; Gillespie 12–2–29–4; Kasprowicz 8.3–3–11–2; Hauritz 5–0–16–3. *Second Innings*—Gillespie 15–1–47–0; Hauritz 22–4–87–2; McGrath 12–6–29–2; Kasprowicz 13–5–29–0; Clarke 6.2–0–9–6.

Australia

J. L. Langer c Dravid b Zaheer Khan	12	– c Karthik b Zaheer Khan	0
M. L. Hayden c Kaif b Kartik	35	– b Harbhajan Singh	24
*R. T. Ponting lbw b Kumble	11	– c Laxman b Kartik	12
D. R. Martyn b Kartik	55	– lbw b Kartik	0
S. M. Katich c Kaif b Kumble	7	– c Dravid b Harbhajan Singh	1
M. J. Clarke st Karthik b Kumble	17	– b Kartik	7
†A. C. Gilchrist c Kaif b Kartik	26	– c Tendulkar b Harbhajan Singh	5
J. N. Gillespie c Kaif b Kumble	2	– not out	9
N. M. Hauritz c Harbhajan Singh b Kumble	0	– lbw b Kumble	15
M. S. Kasprowicz c Kumble b Kartik	19	– c Dravid b Harbhajan Singh	7
G. D. McGrath not out	9	– c Laxman b Harbhajan Singh	0
B 2, l-b 4, n-b 4	10	B 8, l-b 5	13

1/17 (1) 2/37 (3) 3/81 (2) 4/101 (5)   203   1/0 (1) 2/24 (3) 3/24 (4)   93
5/121 (6) 6/157 (7) 7/167 (8)   4/33 (5) 5/48 (2) 6/48 (6)
8/171 (4) 9/184 (4) 10/203 (10)   7/58 (7) 8/78 (9)
                                     9/93 (10) 10/93 (11)

Bowling: First Innings—Zaheer Khan 6–0–10–1; Harbhajan Singh 21–4–53–0; Kumble 19–0–90–5; Kartik 15.3–1–44–4. *Second Innings*—Zaheer Khan 2–0–14–1; Harbhajan Singh 10.5–2–29–5; Kartik 12–3–32–3; Kumble 6–3–5–1.

Umpires: Aleem Dar (Pakistan) and R. E. Koertzen (South Africa).
Third umpire: K. Hariharan. Referee: R. S. Madugalle (Sri Lanka).

THE NEW ZEALANDERS IN BANGLADESH, 2004-05

UTPAL SHUVRO

New Zealand's first tour of Bangladesh ended in bitter disappointment for the Bangladeshis. There had been signs in recent series that they were coming to terms with the demands of the international game under their coach, Dav Whatmore. However, any optimism that those results may have engendered evaporated in a comprehensive defeat by the New Zealanders in both the Tests and the one day series.

Bangladesh suffered a heavy blow before the Tests began when Habibul Bashar, their captain, best batsman and the only player to feature in all his country's previous 30 Test matches, was ruled out with a broken thumb. He returned for the one-day series, only to break his toe this time.

Silver lining: Mohammad Rafique bowls during the First Test at Dhaka, where his six wickets gave Bangladesh encouragement. Umpire Mark Benson, standing in his first Test, keeps watch.

Picture by Rafiqur Rahman, Reuters

His replacement was Khaled Mashud, the wicket-keeper/batsman who had stepped down from the captaincy after Bangladesh's dismal performance in the 2003 World Cup. New Zealand also employed a stand-in captain for the one-day series, left-arm spinner Daniel Vettori replacing Stephen Fleming, who returned home after the Tests to recharge his batteries in readiness for his country's tour of Australia.

Vettori, who had taken only 16 wickets in his last nine Tests before arriving in Bangladesh, had a rewarding time in both the Test series and the one-day games. He captured 20 wickets in the two Tests, more than twice as many as any other player, and was a unanimous choice for the Man of the Series award. He might have been presented with a more serious challenge had his counterpart Mohammad Rafique bowled in more than two innings. However, that was enough for Rafique to become his country's first bowler to claim 50 Test wickets, in only 13 games, reaching the landmark faster than any of his contemporaries in the left-arm spinning fraternity. Given that Rafique rarely gets the chance to bowl in the fourth innings of a match, he can claim to be a serious challenger to Vettori's status as the best left-arm spinner in the game.

Not even the skills of Rafique could compensate for some feeble batting displays by his team-mates, however. The failure of the top order has been haunting Bangladesh for some time, and a tally of just two half-centuries, from Mohammad Ashraful and Javed Omar, among the top six tells its own sorry story. Nor was the New Zealand batting entirely convincing, but major innings from Brendon McCullum and Fleming proved decisive. McCullum's maiden Test century, in his seventh appearance, turned the first match on its head after Rafique had threatened to bowl Bangladesh back into contention. And in the Second Test, a flawless double-century from Fleming effectively put the game beyond Bangladesh's reach by lunch on the second day.

NEW ZEALAND TOURING PARTY

S. P. Fleming (*captain*), D. L. Vettori (*vice-captain*), N. J. Astle, I. G. Butler, J. E. C. Franklin, B. B. McCullum, H. J. H. Marshall, C. S. Martin, K. D. Mills, J. D. P. Oram, M. H. Richardson, M. S. Sinclair, S. B. Styris, P. J. Wiseman.

M. H. W. Papps withdrew through injury and was replaced by Sinclair. A. R. Adams, C. L. Cairns, P. G. Fulton, C. Z. Harris and C. D. McMillan replaced Fleming, Martin, Oram, Richardson and Wiseman for the one-day internationals, when Vettori took over the captaincy.

Coach: J. G. Bracewell.   *Manager:* R. A. Dykes.   *Physiotherapist:* D. F. Shackel.   *Conditioner:* G. Owen.   *Video analyst:* P. Mayell.

NEW ZEALAND TOUR RESULTS

Test matches – Played 2: Won 2.
One-day internationals – Played 3: Won 3.
Other non-first-class match – Played 1: Drawn 1.

Note: Matches in this section which were not first-class are signified by a dagger.

†At Savar, October 14, 15, 16, 2004. **Drawn.** Toss: New Zealanders. **New Zealanders 344-6 dec.** (S. P. Fleming 129 retired hurt, H. J. H. Marshall 51, B. B. McCullum 52*) **and 351-4 dec.** (M. S. Sinclair 113 retired hurt, N. J. Astle 113 retired hurt, J. E. C. Franklin 62); **BCB President's XII 208 and 27-1.**

This match did not have first-class status as each side named 12 players, of whom only 11 could bat and 11 field.

BANGLADESH v NEW ZEALAND

First Test Match

At Dhaka, October 19, 20, 21, 22, 2004. New Zealand won by an innings and 99 runs. Toss: Bangladesh. Test debut: Nafis Iqbal.

The first seven overs of the opening day set the tone for the match and the series. Having opted to bat in ideal conditions, Bangladesh lost their first three wickets for just five runs in the space of 39 deliveries, handing New Zealand an initiative they never relinquished.

Hannan Sarkar, who shares with Sunil Gavaskar the dubious distinction of having been dismissed off the first ball of a Test three times, narrowly missed claiming the record outright, edging the third ball of the match from Oram to first slip. Javed Omar and debutant Nafis Iqbal soon followed, to leave Bangladesh in disarray.

Pulling away: a maiden Test hundred from Brendon McCullum ensures New Zealand stretch clear of Bangladesh at Dhaka. Tapash Baisya takes more punishment.

Picture by Rafiqur Rahman, Reuters

A partial recovery was effected by Rajin Saleh and Mohammad Ashraful, who added 115. Ashraful was the more aggressive: though he was dropped on five, his fluent 67 featured three sixes and eight fours before he became Vettori's first victim of what was destined to be a profitable series. His departure heralded some painfully slow batting for the rest of a mainly forgettable first day.

Any hope of sustained late-order resistance on the second morning evaporated when the left-arm seamer Franklin became only the second New Zealander to achieve a Test hat-trick, emulating off-spinner Peter Petherick's feat on his debut at Lahore in 1976-77. Franklin, following his impressive form in England, dismissed Manjural Islam Rana and Mohammad Rafique with the last two deliveries of his 14th over and Tapash Baisya with the first ball of his 15th.

New Zealand fared little better at first themselves. Only Sinclair, who scored 76 from 173 balls, looked at ease against the left-arm spin combination of Rafique and Manjural. When he was fifth out, at 139, Bangladesh entertained reasonable hopes of restricting the deficit to manageable proportions. However, McCullum had other ideas. Under pressure to get runs, like all modern wicket-keepers, he had set himself the target of scoring a maiden Test century during the series and fulfilled his ambition in splendid fashion, with 143. When he was ninth out at 371 he had given his side complete control. McCullum, who survived two chances, played the leading role in three crucial stands, as the last five wickets contributed a decisive 263 runs.

The only consolation for Bangladesh was the performance of Rafique, who claimed his fourth five-wicket haul on a pitch taking increasing spin, and Vettori wasted little time in exploiting the conditions when Bangladesh batted again, 225 behind. He had endured a lean spell prior to this match, with just 16 wickets in his last nine Tests, but this was an opportunity he was unlikely to miss, and he claimed his first five-for since December 2001.

Once again, the Bangladesh top order failed, Vettori grabbing the first three wickets in the opening 22 overs with just 41 on the board. Iqbal and Ashraful stemmed the tide for a while. But the dismissal of Iqbal, run out one short of a maiden half-century, sparked a collapse in which the last seven wickets fell for 39. Vettori, backed up by Wiseman's off-spin, sealed victory with five sessions to spare.

Man of the Match: B. B. McCullum.

Close of play: First day, Bangladesh 165-6 (Khaled Mashud 12, Manjural Islam Rana 16); Second day, New Zealand 207-5 (Oram 18, McCullum 48); Third day, Bangladesh 41-2 (Nafis Iqbal 24, Rajin Saleh 0).

Bangladesh

Hannan Sarkar c Fleming b Oram	0	– (3) c and b Vettori 1
Javed Omar b Franklin	1	– c McCullum b Vettori 14
Nafis Iqbal c McCullum b Oram	1	– (1) run out 49
Rajin Saleh c Oram b Franklin	41	– c McCullum b Vettori 0
Mohammad Ashraful c Astle b Vettori	67	– c Styris b Vettori 26
Alok Kapali c McCullum b Vettori	14	– c McCullum b Wiseman 0
*†Khaled Mashud not out	23	– c Styris b Wiseman 2
Manjural Islam Rana c McCullum b Franklin	16	– c Richardson b Vettori 1
Mohammad Rafique c Styris b Franklin	0	– c Fleming b Wiseman 24
Tapash Baisya b Franklin	0	– (11) not out 0
Tareq Aziz c Astle b Oram	0	– (10) lbw b Vettori 0
L-b 7, w 1, n-b 6	14	B 6, n-b 3 9

1/0 (1) 2/5 (2) 3/5 (3) 4/120 (4) 177   1/27 (2) 2/33 (3) 3/41 (4) 126
5/124 (5) 6/136 (6) 7/165 (8)   4/87 (1) 5/88 (6) 6/92 (7)
8/165 (9) 9/165 (10) 10/177 (11)   7/101 (8) 8/112 (5)
                                          9/122 (10) 10/126 (9)

Bowling: *First Innings*—Oram 22.5–9–36–3; Franklin 17–7–28–5; Styris 2–1–4–0; Butler 12–3–34–0; Vettori 29–15–26–2; Wiseman 16–5–42–0. *Second Innings*—Oram 7–4–6–0; Franklin 5–1–14–0; Butler 4–1–8–0; Vettori 22–13–28–6; Wiseman 16.5–1–64–3.

New Zealand

M. H. Richardson c Khaled Mashud b Mohammad Rafique .	15	
M. S. Sinclair lbw b Mohammad Rafique	76	
*S. P. Fleming c Khaled Mashud b Manjural Islam Rana .	29	
S. B. Styris c Rajin Saleh b Manjural Islam Rana .	2	
N. J. Astle c Manjural Islam Rana b Mohammad Rafique .	11	
J. D. P. Oram c Manjural Islam Rana b Mohammad Rafique .	23	
†B. B. McCullum c Alok Kapali b Mohammad Rafique .	143	

D. L. Vettori c Nafis Iqbal b Manjural Islam Rana .	23
J. E. C. Franklin c Rajin Saleh b Tapash Baisya .	23
P. J. Wiseman b Mohammad Rafique . . .	28
I. G. Butler not out.	15
B 3, l-b 5, w 4, n-b 2	14
	—
	402

1/34 (1) 2/97 (3) 3/99 (4)
4/122 (5) 5/139 (2) 6/223 (6)
7/294 (8) 8/351 (9)
9/371 (7) 10/402 (10)

Bowling: Tapash Baisya 28–4–112–1; Tareq Aziz 12 1 59 0; Mohammad Rafique 59.1–18–122–6; Manjural Islam Rana 42–12–84–3; Rajin Saleh 1–0–4–0; Alok Kapali 2–0–6–0; Mohammad Ashraful 1–0 7 0.

Umpires: M. R. Benson (England) and D. J. Harper (Australia).
Third umpire: Mahbubur Rahman. Referee: A. G. Hurst (Australia).

BANGLADESH v NEW ZEALAND

Second Test Match

At Chittagong, October 26, 27, 28, 29, 2004. New Zealand won by an innings and 101 runs. Toss: New Zealand. Test debut: Aftab Ahmed.

Bangladesh suffered another humiliating defeat, the 18th time they had lost by an innings in their 32 Tests. They were outplayed in all departments and, once again, the match ended five sessions early. Vettori, who had claimed eight wickets in the First Test, played a crucial role again, recording match figures of 12 for 170. Even he was upstaged by Fleming, who celebrated his 87th Test appearance, surpassing the New Zealand record held by all-rounder Sir Richard Hadlee, with a double-century. He also passed Martin Crowe's record of 5,444 runs for New Zealand.

Fleming chose to bat first on another typically low, slow subcontinental wicket, but there was an element of encouragement for the home side when both openers went. Then Fleming and Styris assumed control.

Styris struggled at first. He was missed behind the wicket, survived two loud lbw appeals and took 87 balls to register his first boundary. However, he grew more fluent as time wore by and it was a surprise when he was caught and bowled by Mohammad Rafique 11 short of his century, with the stand worth 204.

By that time, Fleming had already reached his eighth Test hundred. Particularly powerful on the on side, he added 99 more with Astle and reached his double-century soon after lunch on the second day. He had batted for 446 minutes, faced 318 balls and hit a six and 21 fours when he scooped a ball from part-time off-spinner Rajin Saleh to mid-off. New Zealand were already a formidable 447 for five, but the torment was not over for Bangladesh: Marshall and Oram added another 70 before Fleming finally called a halt.

Requiring 346 to make New Zealand bat again, Bangladesh desperately needed a solid start. But despite an early flurry of boundaries, they were soon in disarray. Not surprisingly, it was Vettori who made the breakthrough, having Nafis Iqbal well caught by the diving Styris in the gully. From that point, only Javed Omar, who during his sixth Test half-century became the second Bangladesh batsman after Habibul Bashar to score 1,000 runs, offered sustained resistance. Despite some late hitting by Rafique, Vettori wrapped up the innings with Bangladesh still 363 in arrears.

They fared little better second time around, losing their first five wickets for 74. Mohammad Ashraful, one of the few batsmen to show any fight in the previous Test, collected the second pair of his Test career in the space of three hours. Bangladesh finished the third day 153 runs behind with only two wickets standing and no prospect of avoiding yet another innings defeat.

Surprisingly, a crowd of around 2,000 turned up to witness the last rites, and their enthusiasm was rewarded by some enterprising play from tailender Tapash Baisya, who threw caution to the winds as he raced to his half-century from just 36 balls, the fastest by a Bangladesh batsman. He hammered Wiseman for a six and four fours in three overs, and even Vettori came in for punishment. When he was finally stumped off Vettori, Tapash had plundered 51 from only 30 balls in the morning session and his whirlwind 66 from 47 deliveries featured two sixes and ten fours.

It was fun while it lasted, but could not disguise the grim reality that, once again, Bangladesh had been completely outplayed.

Man of the Match: S. P. Fleming.　*Man of the Series:* D. L. Vettori.

Close of play: First day, New Zealand 338-3 (Fleming 137, Astle 34); Second day, Bangladesh 82-3 (Javed Omar 45); Third day, Bangladesh 210-8 (Mohammad Rafique 30, Tapash Baisya 15).

New Zealand

M. H. Richardson c Mushfiqur Rahman b Enamul Haque .	28
M. S. Sinclair b Mohammad Rafique . . .	23
*S. P. Fleming c Mushfiqur Rahman b Rajin Saleh .	202
S. B. Styris c and b Mohammad Rafique .	89
N. J. Astle lbw b Mohammad Rafique . . .	39
H. J. H. Marshall c Tapash Baisya b Enamul Haque .	69
J. D. P. Oram not out	38
†B. B. McCullum not out	17
B 9, l-b 11, w 2, n-b 18	40

D. L. Vettori, J. E. C. Franklin and P. J. Wiseman did not bat.

1/49 (2) 2/61 (1) 3/265 (4) (6 wkts dec.) 545
4/364 (5) 5/447 (3) 6/517 (6)

Bowling: Tapash Baisya 17–0–82–0; Mushfiqur Rahman 15–1–68–0; Mohammad Rafique 55–12–130–3; Enamul Haque 42–4–142–2; Rajin Saleh 19–0–81–1; Mohammad Ashraful 1–0–5–0; Alok Kapali 3–0–17–0.

Bangladesh

Nafis Iqbal c Styris b Vettori	13	– b Wiseman	9
Javed Omar c Sinclair b Wiseman	58	– c and b Franklin	1
Aftab Ahmed lbw b Vettori	20	– b Vettori	28
Rajin Saleh c Sinclair b Wiseman	2	– c Sinclair b Vettori	35
Mohammad Ashraful c Astle b Wiseman	0	– c Styris b Vettori	0
Alok Kapali c Fleming b Vettori	13	– c Astle b Wiseman	13
*†Khaled Mashud lbw b Vettori	18	– b Oram	51
Mushfiqur Rahman c McCullum b Franklin	15	– b Vettori	20
Mohammad Rafique c Wiseman b Vettori	32	– c Sinclair b Vettori	31
Tapash Baisya c Sinclair b Vettori	0	– st McCullum b Vettori	66
Enamul Haque, jun. not out	0	– not out	0
B 4, l-b 2, w 2, n-b 3	11	B 4, l-b 3, w 1	8

1/34 (1) 2/66 (3) 3/82 (4) 4/82 (5)　　　　　182
5/108 (6) 6/128 (2) 7/142 (7)
8/181 (9) 9/182 (8) 10/182 (10)

1/9 (2) 2/25 (1) 3/47 (3)　　　　　262
4/51 (5) 5/74 (4) 6/123 (4)
7/161 (8) 8/183 (7)
9/217 (9) 10/262 (10)

Bowling: *First Innings*—Oram 5–0–20–0; Franklin 5–0–17–1; Vettori 32.2–12–70–6; Wiseman 27–5–68–3; Astle 2–1–1–0. *Second Innings*—Oram 10–4–33–1; Franklin 8–3–16–1; Wiseman 24–4–106–2; Vettori 28.2–9–100–6.

Umpires: M. R. Benson (England) and D. J. Harper (Australia).
Third umpire: A. F. M. Akhtaruddin.　Referee: A. G. Hurst (Australia).

†BANGLADESH v NEW ZEALAND

First One-Day International

At Chittagong, November 2, 2004. New Zealand won by 138 runs. Toss: New Zealand. One-day international debut: P. G. Fulton.

Not for the first time, Cairns changed the course of the match with some powerful hitting. New Zealand had stuttered to 94 for five when he strode to the crease in the 24th over. Cairns was content to accumulate quietly at first, but accelerated to reach his half-century from 76 balls, with two sixes and a solitary four. Then, with the end of the innings in sight, he hit a further three sixes before he was last out, dismissed by 17-year-old seamer Nazmul Hossain. His 74 came from 83 deliveries. Bangladesh lost Aftab Ahmed to the third ball of the innings, and thereafter only captain Habibul Bashar, restored to the side after missing the Test series through injury, batted with any confidence. Bangladesh's 86 was their fourth-lowest one-day score. Mills claimed four wickets in his opening spell to finish with four for 14.

Man of the Match: C. L. Cairns.

New Zealand

P. G. Fulton b Nazmul Hossain	9	*D. L. Vettori b Tapash Baisya	12
N. J. Astle b Nazmul Hossain	27	A. R. Adams c Khaled Mahmud	
H. J. H. Marshall st Khaled Mashud		b Nazmul Hossain	4
b Manjural Islam Rana	7	K. D. Mills not out	0
S. B. Styris run out	43		
C. D. McMillan c Khaled Mashud		L-b 4, w 11, n-b 3	18
b Tapash Baisya	17		
†B. B. McCullum b Mohammad Rafique	8	1/11 (1) 2/49 (2) 3/50 (3) (49.2 overs) 224
C. L. Cairns b Nazmul Hossain	74	4/77 (5) 5/94 (6) 6/143 (4)
C. Z. Harris c Rajin Saleh		7/168 (8) 8/191 (9)
b Manjural Islam Rana	5	9/224 (10) 10/224 (7)

Bowling: Tapash Baisya 10–0–58–2; Nazmul Hossain 8.2–1–40–4; Manjural Islam Rana 10–0–35–2; Khaled Mahmud 5–0–28–0; Mohammad Rafique 10–2–28–1; Rajin Saleh 6–0–31–0.

Bangladesh

Aftab Ahmed lbw b Mills	4	Mohammad Rafique c Styris b Harris	11
Javed Omar c Fulton b Mills	3	Tapash Baisya c Adams b Vettori	2
Rajin Saleh c McMillan b Mills	4	Nazmul Hossain not out	0
*Habibul Bashar lbw b Styris	22	L-b 1, w 7, n-b 1	9
Mohammad Ashraful c McCullum			
b Mills	2	1/4 (1) 2/10 (2) 3/23 (3) (31.5 overs) 86
Manjural Islam Rana c Styris b Vettori	13	4/27 (5) 5/45 (4) 6/51 (7)
†Khaled Mashud lbw b Styris	2	7/68 (6) 8/79 (9)
Khaled Mahmud st McCullum b Vettori	14	9/83 (8) 10/86 (10)

Bowling: Mills 7–2–14–4; Adams 6–1–24–0; Cairns 4–2–5–0; Styris 6–3–13–2; Harris 5–0–21–1; Vettori 3.5–0–8–3.

Umpires: M. R. Benson (England) and A. F. M. Akhtaruddin.
Third umpire: Nadir Shah. Referee: A. G. Hurst (Australia).

" Inzamam was so mortified by his mistake that he could not face breakfast the next morning."
Pakistanis in New Zealand, page 1139.

†BANGLADESH v NEW ZEALAND

Second One-Day International

At Dhaka, November 5, 2004 (day/night). New Zealand won by three wickets. Toss: Bangladesh.
A splendid spell of seam bowling from Aftab Ahmed raised the prospect of an unlikely victory for Bangladesh after they had been dismissed for only 146. Aftab, who had not bowled in any of his three previous one-day internationals or his only Test appearance, claimed five for 31 in ten overs to reduce New Zealand from 74 without loss to 125 for six. However, Cairns again settled his team-mates' nerves. Bangladesh had batted meekly and suffered the added blow of losing captain Habibul Bashar with a fractured toe before Rajin Saleh and Khaled Mashud had a sixth-wicket partnership of 57. New Zealand openers Sinclair and Astle appeared to be on cruise control before Aftab's unexpected contribution.

Man of the Match: Aftab Ahmed.

Bangladesh

Nafis Iqbal c Styris b Mills	0	Tapash Baisya c Sinclair b Styris 7
Javed Omar b Franklin	12	Nazmul Hossain not out 4
Aftab Ahmed c McCullum b Mills	4	
*Habibul Bashar b Franklin	0	L-b 1, w 8, n-b 8 17
Mohammad Ashraful c Franklin b Styris	17	
Rajin Saleh c McCullum b Cairns	28	1/1 (1) 2/5 (3) 3/22 (4) (43.4 overs) 146
†Khaled Mashud c Harris b Cairns	41	4/25 (2) 5/51 (5) 6/108 (7)
Manjural Islam Rana lbw b Styris	12	7/125 (6) 8/135 (9)
Mohammad Rafique c Franklin b Vettori	4	9/139 (8) 10/146 (10)

Bowling: Mills 8–0–25–2; Franklin 4–0–34–2; Styris 7.4–1–16–3; Harris 10–4–19–0; Vettori 9–0–36–1; Cairns 5–1–15–2.

New Zealand

M. S. Sinclair st Khaled Mashud b Mohammad Rafique	62	C. Z. Harris c Nazmul Hossain b Tapash Baisya	7
N. J. Astle c Javed Omar b Aftab Ahmed	29	*D. L. Vettori not out 3
H. J. H. Marshall lbw b Aftab Ahmed	2	L-b 4, w 4, n-b 1 9
S. B. Styris b Aftab Ahmed	12	
C. D. McMillan lbw b Aftab Ahmed	7	1/74 (2) 2/76 (3) (7 wkts, 44.4 overs) 148
C. L. Cairns not out	17	3/102 (1) 4/114 (4)
†B. B. McCullum lbw b Aftab Ahmed	0	5/125 (5) 6/125 (7) 7/133 (8)

K. D. Mills and J. E. C. Franklin did not bat.

Bowling: Nazmul Hossain 6–1–30–0; Tapash Baisya 10–2–33–1; Manjural Islam Rana 8.4–2–24–0; Mohammad Rafique 10–1–26–1; Aftab Ahmed 10–0–31–5.

Umpires: M. R. Benson (England) and Mahbubur Rahman.
Third umpire: Nadir Shah.   Referee: A. G. Hurst (Australia).

†BANGLADESH v NEW ZEALAND

Third One-Day International

At Dhaka, November 7, 2004 (day/night). New Zealand won by 83 runs. Toss: New Zealand.
Bangladesh failed to build on their near miss in the previous match, slumping to another comprehensive defeat. Astle and Sinclair shared a second successive half-century opening partnership before Cairns, whose 34 took only 16 balls, led a middle-order charge. New Zealand scored 99 from the last ten overs and 57 from the last five. Bangladesh sent in Mohammad Rafique first in an attempt to raise their strike-rate, but he did not last long and the innings soon developed into another damage-limitation exercise. They succeeded in batting for the full 50 overs, thanks to Nafis Iqbal and Khaled Mashud. Both scored 40, Mashud in just 44 balls, Iqbal in a painstaking 87. But a New Zealand whitewash was never in doubt.

Man of the Match: S. B. Styris.   *Man of the Series:* S. B. Styris.

New Zealand

N. J. Astle run out	27	
M. S. Sinclair c and b Mohammad Rafique	66	
C. Z. Harris lbw b Aftab Ahmed	9	
H. J. H. Marshall c Rajin Saleh b Mohammad Rafique	0	
S. B. Styris c Alok Kapali b Mohammad Rafique	51	
C. D. McMillan c and b Mohammad Rafique	39	

C. L. Cairns c Rajin Saleh
b Tapash Baisya . 34
*D. L. Vettori not out 18

L-b 3, w 3 6
—
1/72 (1) 2/99 (3)   (7 wkts, 50 overs) 250
3/102 (4) 4/105 (2)
5/191 (6) 6/207 (5) 7/250 (7)

†B. B. McCullum, K. D. Mills and J. E. C. Franklin did not bat.

Bowling: Tapash Baisya 5–0–35–1; Mushfiqur Rahman 8–1–28–0; Manjural Islam Rana 9–0–46–0; Aftab Ahmed 10–0–36–1; Mohammad Rafique 10–0–63–4; Rajin Saleh 4–0–18–0; Alok Kapali 4 0 21–0.

Bangladesh

Javed Omar lbw b Franklin	8	
Mohammad Rafique lbw b Mills	21	
Nafis Iqbal c Sinclair b Vettori	40	
Rajin Saleh lbw b Styris	0	
Mohammad Ashraful c Sinclair b Vettori	13	
Aftab Ahmed c Harris b Vettori	8	
*†Khaled Mashud not out	40	

Alok Kapali b Cairns 17
Manjural Islam Rana not out 8
L-b 4, w 4, n-b 4 12

1/15 (1) 2/42 (2)   (7 wkts, 50 overs) 167
3/48 (4) 4/86 (3)
5/96 (5) 6/109 (6) 7/138 (8)

Mushfiqur Rahman and Tapash Baisya did not bat.

Bowling: Mills 10–1–39–1; Franklin 9–2–29–1; Styris 10–1–31–1; Cairns 7–0–21–1; Vettori 10–0–25–3; Harris 4–0–18–0.

Umpires: M. R. Benson (England) and A. F. M. Akhtaruddin.
Third umpire: Nadir Shah.   Referee: A. G. Hurst (Australia).

THE SRI LANKANS IN PAKISTAN, 2004-05

Brian Murgatroyd

The major frustration arising from this series, which like the Paktel Cup that preceded it was slotted into the schedule to replace Zimbabwe's Test tour of Pakistan, was that it was only two matches long. Both sides played some outstanding cricket for a win each, and the situation cried out for a decider. The absence of one called into question the value of a two-match series.

For Pakistan there was satisfaction at the way they fought back to level the series at Karachi without three of their leading fast bowlers, Mohammad Sami, Shoaib Akhtar and Shabbir Ahmed, who had been sidelined since suffering a knee injury in the lead-up to the Champions Trophy in September. Bob Woolmer, in his first Test series as Pakistan coach, could also point to the continued development of their spinners and the triumphant return to Test cricket for Younis Khan.

There was still the need to find a stable opening pairing, and the failure to ram home the advantage earned on the first morning at Faisalabad was also disturbing. But overall Pakistan could take heart, especially as the win at Karachi came under the sort of intense pressure on the final day that had caused them to fold in several recent one-day matches.

Sri Lanka, too, could derive plenty of positives. As against South Africa two months earlier, they showed they were more than capable of coping in the continued absence of the injured Muttiah Muralitharan. The slow left-armer Rangana Herath revelled in the role of leading spinner and played a useful role with the bat. Sanath Jayasuriya made two superb hundreds and Thilan Samaraweera scored his first Test century outside Sri Lanka.

Both sides ended the series with question-marks over the wicket-keeping position. Moin Khan, 33, was dropped by Pakistan after the First Test and replaced by 22-year-old Kamran Akmal who did a tidy job at Karachi. But there were suggestions that Rashid Latif was ready to make himself available again a year after dropping out of international cricket following a five-match ICC ban. And, breathing hard on them all, Zulqarnain Haider, Pakistan's Under-19 World Cup-winning wicket-keeper, was attached to the squad throughout the series, though he did not play.

On the Sri Lankan side, Romesh Kaluwitharana announced his retirement from international cricket after the series when he was left out of the training squad ahead of the tour of New Zealand. Kaluwitharana kept moderately in his one match behind the stumps before injuring himself while batting in Karachi, but the fact the selectors had opted for him in Pakistan suggested they were desperate to avoid burdening Kumar Sangakkara with the dual roles of No. 3 batsman and wicket-keeper.

Morning dew and a lack of daylight hours meant only five and a half hours of play could be scheduled per day, which is allowed in Pakistan under a special ICC dispensation.

SRI LANKAN TOURING PARTY

M. S. Atapattu (*captain*), U. D. U. Chandana, G. I. Daniel, C. R. D. Fernando, H. M. R. K. B. Herath, S. T. Jayasuriya, D. P. M. D. Jayawardene, R. S. Kaluwitharana, S. H. T. Kandamby, M. F. Maharoof, S. L. Malinga, J. Mubarak, T. T. Samaraweera, K. C. Sangakkara, W. P. U. J. C. Vaas.

Coach: J. Dyson. *Manager:* D. S. B. P. Kuruppu. *Physiotherapist:* C. J. Clark. *Fitness trainer:* S. Duff. *Computer analyst:* R. S. Kalpage.

PAKISTAN v SRI LANKA

First Test Match

At Faisalabad, October 20, 21, 21, 23, 24, 2004. Sri Lanka won by 201 runs. Toss: Sri Lanka.

If ever a Test could be said to have turned on one delivery, this was it. At 15 for one in their second innings, Sri Lanka still trailed by six runs, when Jayasuriya, on nine, was caught behind off Shoaib Akhtar. It was signalled a no-ball, and Jayasuriya went on to score a wonderfully authoritative, match-winning 253, a record in this fixture.

It would, however, be wrong to put Sri Lanka's success simply down to one man. Samaraweera scored his first Test hundred outside Sri Lanka to help rescue them from nine for three on the first morning; Herath excelled with ball and, more surprisingly, bat; Sangakkara and Jayawardene played important innings on the third day; and Fernando produced an outstanding spell of fast bowling on the fourth evening.

Sweeping all before him: Sanath Jayasuriya heads towards a commanding double-hundred in the First Test at Faisalabad – and Sri Lanka head for victory.

Picture by Mohsin Raza, Reuters

A crushing Sri Lanka win looked a million miles away in the first half-hour of the match as Shoaib Akhtar and Mohammad Sami took advantage of early assistance both in the air and off the seam to cut a swathe through the visitors' top order. Mubarak dug in for over an hour and a half, but with Sri Lanka staggering to 147 for six, Pakistan were in charge. Samaraweera, however, was in characteristically dogged mood, found some allies and overcame a bout of cramp. He moved to his fourth Test hundred, off 231 balls, from the first delivery of the second day but perished almost immediately to signal a swift end to the innings, Shoaib Akhtar claiming his ninth five-wicket haul in only his 33rd Test.

By now the pitch appeared benign, but disciplined Sri Lankan bowling and careless batting from Pakistan ensured the match remained evenly poised. The pressure exerted

---

LOWEST CONTRIBUTIONS TO A TEST 100 PARTNERSHIP

1	C. R. D. Fernando . .	101 with S. T. Jayasuriya (253), SL v P at Faisalabad.	2004-05
12	D. R. Parry	100 with A. I. Kallicharran (98), WI v I at Madras	1978-79
13	P. I. Pocock	109 with G. A. R. Lock (89), E v WI at Georgetown. . .	1967-68
14*	D. K. Morrison	106* with N. J. Astle (102*), NZ v E at Auckland	1996-97
17	D. Ganga	126 with C. H. Gayle (116), WI v SA at Cape Town . .	2003-04

Research: Andrew Samson

---

by Vaas and Herath in particular proved too much for Pakistan and although every one of the top seven reached double figures, only Yasir Hameed, in his first Test as an opener, passed 50. The dismissals of Inzamam-ul-Haq, miscuing a slog-sweep tamely to mid-on, and Shoaib Malik, run out as he ran at an angle seeking a needless single to mid-on, were the two most glaring examples of poor judgment. With the last five wickets going down for 37, Pakistan's lead was only 21.

With Atapattu completing his fourth Test pair, that advantage might still have been important had Shoaib Akhtar not overstepped when he found the edge of Jayasuriya's bat. Instead, Sri Lanka galloped along at more than four an over and by tea, in just 43 overs, they had hit 28 fours. Jayasuriya bludgeoned the ball with customary force and reached his 13th Test hundred with a six over mid-wicket off Danish Kaneria. The following day he reached his third double-century with another six – a pull off Shoaib Akhtar – to become the first player to pass both landmarks in one innings with sixes. To make matters worse for Pakistan, Jayasuriya added 101 for the ninth wicket with Fernando – a Sri Lankan record – and shielded his partner so well that he faced just 23 balls of 102. Fernando did not get off the mark until they had added 70.

By the time Jayasuriya was last man out, having faced 348 balls and hit 33 fours and four sixes in eight hours ten minutes, it was simply a question of whether Pakistan could bat for just over four sessions to save the match. They started positively enough, but then came up against an inspired Fernando, who bowled fast and straight. He found the perfect length, with batsmen unsure whether to go forward or back, and knocked the stuffing out of Pakistan's top order with a spell of four for nine in 36 balls.

Sri Lanka wrapped up the match 40 minutes after lunch on the final day. Herath made the important breakthroughs, trapping Yousuf Youhana and Abdul Razzaq leg-before with successive deliveries, and he also had the satisfaction of claiming his best figures when he finished the match by having Shoaib Akhtar stumped. For Pakistan, Malik scored his maiden fifty but there was little else for them to cheer.

Man of the Match: S. T. Jayasuriya.

Close of play: First day, Sri Lanka 233-7 (Samaraweera 97, Herath 28); Second day, Pakistan 256-8 (Mohammad Sami 2, Shoaib Akhtar 6); Third day, Sri Lanka 285-3 (Jayasuriya 131, Samaraweera 15); Fourth day, Pakistan 114-4 (Yousuf Youhana 23, Shoaib Malik 3).

Sri Lanka

*M. S. Atapattu lbw b Shoaib Akhtar	0	– lbw b Shoaib Akhtar	0
S. T. Jayasuriya c Asim Kamal b Mohammad Sami	38	– lbw b Danish Kaneria	253
K. C. Sangakkara c Imran Farhat b Shoaib Akhtar	2	– c Moin Khan b Shoaib Akhtar	59
D. P. M. D. Jayawardene c Moin Khan b Mohammad Sami	0	– c Moin Khan b Danish Kaneria	57
T. T. Samaraweera c Mohammad Sami b Shoaib Akhtar	100	– run out	21
J. Mubarak c Inzamam-ul-Haq b Mohammad Sami	34	– c Moin Khan b Shoaib Akhtar	0
†R. S. Kaluwitharana c and b Danish Kaneria	4	– c sub (Naved-ul-Hasan) b Danish Kaneria	1
W. P. U. J. C. Vaas c Yousuf Youhana b Shoaib Akhtar	22	– b Shoaib Malik	4
H. M. R. K. B. Herath not out	33	– lbw b Danish Kaneria	5
C. R. D. Fernando b Shoaib Akhtar	0	– run out	1
S. L. Malinga b Mohammad Sami	1	– not out	0
L-b 3, n-b 6	9	B 12, l-b 5, w 3, n-b 12, p 5	37
	243		438

1/0 (1) 2/6 (3) 3/9 (4) 4/77 (2)
5/142 (6) 6/147 (7) 7/180 (8)
8/237 (5) 9/242 (10) 10/243 (11)

1/0 (1) 2/98 (3) 3/216 (4)
4/309 (5) 5/314 (6) 6/319 (7)
7/330 (8) 8/337 (9)
9/438 (10) 10/438 (2)

Bowling: *First Innings*—Shoaib Akhtar 19–3–60–3; Mohammad Sami 21.4–5–71–4; Abdul Razzaq 15–5–33–0; Danish Kaneria 18–3–53–1; Shoaib Malik 8–1–23–0. *Second Innings*—Shoaib Akhtar 25–1–115–3; Mohammad Sami 12–1–48–0; Abdul Razzaq 22–7–78–0; Danish Kaneria 38.2–4–117–4; Shoaib Malik 12–1–58–1.

Pakistan

Yasir Hameed c Mubarak b Fernando	58	– lbw b Fernando	17
Imran Farhat c Mubarak b Malinga	11	– lbw b Fernando	53
Asim Kamal c Jayawardene b Fernando	17	– b Fernando	1
*Inzamam-ul-Haq c Malinga b Herath	32	– b Fernando	3
Yousuf Youhana c Kaluwitharana b Herath	17	– lbw b Herath	44
Shoaib Malik run out	48	– c and b Herath	59
Abdul Razzaq c Jayawardene b Vaas	39	– lbw b Herath	0
†Moin Khan b Jayasuriya	5	– c Kaluwitharana b Vaas	1
Mohammad Sami not out	5	– run out	6
Shoaib Akhtar lbw b Herath	9	– st Kaluwitharana b Herath	12
Danish Kaneria run out	1	– not out	0
B 6, l-b 4, n-b 12	22	B 4, l-b 1, w 6, n-b 9	20
	264		216

1/28 (2) 2/94 (3) 3/109 (1) 4/134 (5)
5/188 (4) 6/227 (6) 7/246 (8)
8/248 (7) 9/262 (10) 10/264 (11)

1/59 (2) 2/65 (3) 3/86 (2)
4/91 (4) 5/154 (5) 6/158 (7)
7/159 (8) 8/187 (9)
9/215 (6) 10/216 (10)

Bowling: *First Innings*—Vaas 26–5–62–1; Malinga 10–1–50–1; Fernando 16–0–65–2; Herath 27.1–6–68–3; Samaraweera 1–0–5–0; Jayasuriya 4–1–4–1. *Second Innings*—Vaas 16–4–54–1; Malinga 6–2–13–0; Herath 32.2–10–64–4; Fernando 20–4–77–4; Jayasuriya 4–2–2–0; Mubarak 1–0–1–0.

Umpires: B. F. Bowden (New Zealand) and S. A. Bucknor (West Indies).
Third umpire: Nadeem Ghauri. Referee: J. J. Crowe (New Zealand).

PAKISTAN v SRI LANKA

Second Test Match

At Karachi, October 28, 29, 30, 31, November 1, 2004. Pakistan won by six wickets. Toss: Pakistan. Test debuts: Naved-ul-Hasan, Riaz Afridi.

This was a fantastic Test full of feats of individual brilliance, littered with landmarks and complete with a result that could have gone either way. Pakistan won to square the series, but Sri Lanka – 270 behind on first innings – showed real fighting spirit and might have pulled off an astonishing victory had Sangakkara clung on to an edge offered by Abdul Razzaq when Pakistan were 59 for four in pursuit of 137.

Inzamam-ul-Haq's brave decision to bowl first set the ball rolling. Without the injured Mohammad Sami (groin) and Shoaib Akhtar (shoulder), he had to throw the new ball to a pair of debutants: Naved-ul-Hasan, who had already played one-day internationals, and the 19-year-old Riaz Afridi.

The Sri Lankans made the better start as Jayasuriya and Atapattu became only the second opening pair in Tests, after Gordon Greenidge and Desmond Haynes, to add 4,000 runs together. But Kaneria removed both, and Pakistan chipped away afterwards with some disciplined bowling in helpful conditions, especially from Razzaq, who completed a maiden five-for. Sri Lanka lost all ten for 142 with only Kaluwitharana passing 50, and even that came at a price – Razzaq hit him on the right hand, forcing him to pass the wicket-keeping gloves to Sangakkara for the entire match.

On day two Younis Khan, playing his first Test for more than a year, set about building a big lead for Pakistan, combining clever drop-and-run tactics with some thumping off-side strokeplay. He added 122 with Imran Farhat, 149 with Inzamam, and reached his sixth Test hundred before walking for a catch at silly point. Inzamam completed his hundred on the third morning with the pitch now playing easily.

When Sri Lanka batted again on the third evening, they trailed by 270 and seemed set for an uncomfortable 28 overs. Jayasuriya, however, had other ideas. Starting with the first ball of the innings, which he clubbed through mid-wicket for four, he launched into a thrilling counter-attack. By the close he had 97, and had passed Aravinda de Silva's Sri Lankan record of 6,361 Test runs – this in the same match in which he beat de Silva's tally of 93 caps, a national record held jointly with Arjuna Ranatunga.

Jayasuriya completed his 14th Test hundred from just 110 deliveries on the fourth morning but fell to a top-edged sweep soon after. The day then took on an air of attrition as Sri Lanka's batsmen dropped anchor in the face of a marathon spell from Danish Kaneria, who bowled all but eight overs out of 42 from the Pavilion End and finished the day with six wickets and a bleeding spinning finger. Sangakkara steadily compiled his seventh Test century, and it was not until Kaneria lured the strokeless Samaraweera into a rare loose drive halfway through the final session that the wickets tumbled. Four fell for 27, including Sangakkara, who provided Naved with a maiden Test scalp when he edged a tired drive after almost six hours at the crease. In sheer frustration Sangakkara tossed his bat in the air and down on to the stumps, a gesture that cost him 30% of his match fee.

Sloppy fielding by Pakistan on the final morning meant they had to chase 137 in around two sessions. It proved trickier than it should have done, and when Atapattu dived brilliantly at mid-off to dismiss Younis, they were 57 for four. With Inzamam not certain to bat after missing the previous day with a sore back, nerves were jangling. But Sangakkara had already dropped Razzaq, and with Vaas tiring towards the end of a 14-over spell broken only by tea, Pakistan regrouped. Shoaib Malik eventually secured victory when he hammered 22 in an over off Herath.

Man of the Match: Danish Kaneria. *Man of the Series:* S. T. Jayasuriya.

Close of play: First day, Sri Lanka 208; Second day, Pakistan 298-4 (Inzamam-ul-Haq 79); Third day, Sri Lanka 134-1 (Jayasuriya 97, Sangakkara 3); Fourth day, Sri Lanka 361-7 (Vaas 2, Maharoof 0).

Sri Lanka

S. T. Jayasuriya lbw b Danish Kaneria	26	– c Shoaib Malik b Danish Kaneria	107
*M. S. Atapattu c Younis Khan b Danish Kaneria	44	– c Yasir Hameed b Danish Kaneria	25
K. C. Sangakkara c Danish Kaneria b Riaz Afridi	13	– c Kamran Akmal b Naved-ul-Hasan	138
D. P. M. D. Jayawardene c Inzamam-ul-Haq b Riaz Afridi	16	– c Yasir Hameed b Danish Kaneria	32
T. T. Samaraweera c Imran Farhat b Abdul Razzaq	13	– c Younis Khan b Danish Kaneria	22
J. Mubarak c Yasir Hameed b Abdul Razzaq	13	– c Imran Farhat b Danish Kaneria	2
†R. S. Kaluwitharana c Kamran Akmal b Danish Kaneria	54	– b Danish Kaneria	7
W. P. U. J. C. Vaas b Imran Farhat b Abdul Razzaq	7	– not out	32
M. F. Maharoof c Kamran Akmal b Abdul Razzaq	2	– b Danish Kaneria	3
H. M. R. K. B. Herath c Kamran Akmal b Abdul Razzaq	12	– c and b Naved-ul-Hasan	6
C. R. D. Fernando not out	0	– c Kamran Akmal b Naved-ul-Hasan	4
B 4, l-b 3, w 1	8	B 6, l-b 10, n-b 12	28

1/66 (1) 2/79 (2) 3/97 (3) 4/106 (4)   208
5/126 (5) 6/140 (6) 7/158 (8)
8/164 (9) 9/208 (7) 10/208 (10)

1/117 (2) 2/170 (1) 3/253 (4)   406
4/333 (5) 5/351 (3) 6/359 (6)
7/360 (7) 8/364 (9)
9/387 (10) 10/406 (11)

Bowling: *First Innings*—Naved-ul-Hasan 17–2–52–0; Riaz Afridi 19–7–42–2; Abdul Razzaq 23.1–9–35–5; Danish Kaneria 23–3–72–3. *Second Innings*—Naved-ul-Hasan 24.5–4–83–3; Riaz Afridi 12–3–45–0; Abdul Razzaq 29–8–99–0; Danish Kaneria 60–20–118–7; Shoaib Malik 16–5–45–0.

Pakistan

Yasir Hameed c Sangakkara b Maharoof	3	– c Atapattu b Herath	15
Imran Farhat lbw b Vaas	72	– c Jayawardene b Vaas	19
Younis Khan c Samaraweera b Herath	124	– c Atapattu b Vaas	14
*Inzamam-ul-Haq c Jayawardene b Vaas	117		
Riaz Afridi b Vaas	9		
Yousuf Youhana c Sangakkara b Fernando	46	– (4) lbw b Herath	1
Shoaib Malik lbw b Fernando	44	– (5) not out	53
Abdul Razzaq c Fernando b Jayasuriya	16	– (6) not out	35
†Kamran Akmal c Jayawardene b Herath	15		
Naved-ul-Hasan b Fernando	11		
Danish Kaneria not out	5		
L-b 9, n-b 7	16	L-b 1, n-b 1	2

1/13 (1) 2/135 (2) 3/284 (3) 4/298 (5)   478
5/372 (6) 6/387 (4) 7/437 (8)
8/462 (7) 9/464 (9) 10/478 (10)

1/31 (1) 2/43 (1)   (4 wkts) 139
3/47 (4) 4/57 (3)

Bowling: *First Innings*—Vaas 33.5–106–3; Maharoof 23–4–62–1; Fernando 22.1–1–96–3; Herath 33–3–125–2; Mubarak 9–2–33–0; Jayasuriya 11–3–35–1; Samaraweera 6.0–12–0. *Second Innings*—Vaas 14–0–45–2; Maharoof 2–0–13–0; Herath 15–2–63–2; Jayasuriya 3–1–6–0; Fernando 3–0–11–0.

Umpires: B. F. Bowden (New Zealand) and S. A. Bucknor (West Indies).
Asad Rauf deputised for Bowden on the 3rd day.

Third umpire: Asad Rauf. Referee: J. J. Crowe (New Zealand).

THE SOUTH AFRICANS IN INDIA, 2004-05

Dileep Premachandran

Ultimately, this tour of India proved too much for a South African side with only four players who had experience of local conditions. They arrived with a new coach in Ray Jennings, who threatened to give some of his squad "a good kick up the backside", but he also showed he could put a caring arm round those who needed it.

He combined this philosophy of "love and care" with an attritional strategy, and it worked for eight days, until Harbhajan Singh twirled his arm like a dervish to gift-wrap an Indian win at Eden Gardens. A side in transition, and wrestling with the intricacies of racial balance, was finally overpowered by one still smarting after losing to Australia a month earlier.

Despite preparation that involved training in specially recreated shirt-soaking humidity, and playing on ripped-up pitches with scuffed-up balls, not to mention 4.30 a.m. wake-up calls, South Africa never suggested they had the ambition or nerve to push for victory. The safety-first approach was exemplified by Andrew Hall, a normally ebullient strokeplayer who out-barnacled Trevor Bailey as South Africa crawled to 510 in the First Test at Kanpur. The lack of aggressive intent was all the more perplexing given that among India's batsmen only Virender Sehwag was in form, after the abysmal collapses which coloured the defeats by Australia.

India did themselves no favours by selecting only one specialist pace bowler on a snooze-inducing Kanpur pitch, but the balance was righted in Kolkata where Irfan Pathan and Zaheer Khan bowled beautifully in tandem to supplement the efforts of Harbhajan. On the batting front, there were positives in the encouraging form of Gautam Gambhir, and the runs made by Rahul Dravid and Sourav Ganguly, despite neither being anywhere near their best.

With Graeme Smith playing only one substantial innings, it was left to Jacques Kallis to shepherd a callow batting line-up. The likes of Zander de Bruyn and Hashim Amla showed glimpses of promise in trying conditions, and de Bruyn's canny medium-pace also gave South Africa an extra bowler, though there was a distressing sameness to an attack without a quality spinner.

Nicky Boje had spun them to a massive victory in Bangalore four and a half years earlier, but both he and Herschelle Gibbs declined the trip this time, fearing interrogation by Delhi police over their alleged roles in the match-fixing scandal which disfigured that tour. Their absence stoked the ire of Jennings. "It doesn't help to hide," he said. "If they were involved in the things they are accused of, they must face the music so the air can be cleared once and for all." But this did not annoy him as much as the axing of Mark Boucher, a veteran of 76 Tests, in favour of Thami Tsolekile, who appeared out of his depth on surfaces with erratic bounce and turn.

Still, the coach with a penchant for the headline quote nearly coaxed a stalemate from his wards, but his best-laid plans were thwarted by the sheer brilliance of Sehwag and especially Harbhajan, who continued his happy knack of running through sides on the brown, brown grass of home.

SOUTH AFRICAN TOURING PARTY

G. C. Smith (*captain*), H. H. Dippenaar (*vice captain*), H. M. Amla, Z. de Bruyn, A. J. Hall, J. H. Kallis, M. Ntini, J. L. Ontong, R. J. Peterson, S. M. Pollock, J. A. Rudolph, A. C. Thomas, T. L. Tsolekile, M. van Jaarsveld.

N. Boje was selected in the original party but withdrew after failing to receive assurances that the Delhi police would not detain him as part of their match-fixing investigation. Boje was replaced by C. K. Langeveldt, who pulled out on November 5 with a back injury, and was replaced by Peterson.

Coach: R. V. Jennings. *Manager:* Goolam Rajah. *Assistant coach:* V. A. Barnes. *Physiotherapist:* S. Jabaar. *Fitness trainer:* A. le Roux. *Doctor:* M. Mossajee.

SOUTH AFRICAN TOUR RESULTS

Test matches – Played 2: Lost 1, Drawn 1.
First-class matches – Played 3: Lost 1, Drawn 2.

At Sawai Mansingh Stadium, Jaipur, November 14, 15, 16, 2004. **Drawn.** Toss: South Africans. **South Africans 226-5 dec.** (G. C. Smith 86, J. L. Ontong 70; S. V. Bahutule 4-64) **and 172-8; Indian Board President's XI 361-6 dec.** (D. Mongia 148, H. K. Badani 74*).

Mongia's 148 lasted 289 balls and included 18 fours. Jacques Kallis suffered a side strain, which prevented him bowling in either Test.

INDIA v SOUTH AFRICA

First Test Match

At Kanpur, November 20, 21, 22, 23, 24, 2004. Drawn. Toss: South Africa. Test debuts: Z. de Bruyn, T. L. Tsolekile.

Two utterly disparate innings grabbed the headlines in a match that meandered to a predictable draw, on a pitch where eternity might have been too short to produce a result. Virender Sehwag careered past 1,000 runs for the year with an innings of staggering virtuosity and impudence, while Andrew Hall – whose big-hitting credentials were amply displayed in the Headingley Test of 2003 – eked out a painstaking 163 after being asked to open.

In the absence of Herschelle Gibbs, Hall – who had never opened even at provincial level – was expected to provide a similarly cavalier approach at the top of the order. He did anything but, exterminating any trace of flair to construct an innings remarkable for its patience and cast-iron discipline. By the time he was finally bowled behind his pads by Kumble, Hall had thwarted the Indians for almost ten hours, allowing South Africa to reach a total that virtually ruled out defeat, and declare on the third morning. Only three batsmen had spent longer at the crease for South Africa.

In for the long Hall: asked to open for the first time in senior cricket, Andrew Hall batted almost ten hours for his 163. Umpire Simon Taufel looks on from square leg.

Picture by Getty Images

But Hall was not the only one whose attritional approach frustrated India. Zander de Bruyn, the all-rounder from Easterns, produced a stolid and composed 83 on debut, and even the indefatigable Kumble could only make intermittent inroads on a surface that gave few signs of life.

If South Africa's innings had been a methodical crawl, India's burst into life with a fusillade of strokes. Sehwag carved the bowlers apart, as is his wont, but the fact that Gambhir, playing only his second Test, matched him shot for shot unnerved even the usually metronomic Pollock. It didn't help that Thami Tsolekile, picked in place of Mark Boucher, goofed a stumping off Peterson when Sehwag had just 29.

The two openers, team-mates for Delhi, had put on 218 when Gambhir edged a Pollock delivery and fell four short of a maiden Test hundred. It was India's best opening stand in 49 years. Sehwag carried on and on, thumping 46 from three overs after lunch on the fourth day with some exhilarating drives and hoicks. But once he departed for 164 off 228 balls (Hall faced 454 for one run less), the momentum was lost, and a fiery burst from Ntini helped South Africa take six wickets for 65, giving them the satisfaction of a 44-run first-innings lead.

But by then it was already the fifth morning, so it meant nothing. As the South African batsmen withstood some fine left-arm spin from Kartik, the bored crowd were left to serenade Tendulkar to amuse themselves, though not everyone found such innocent distractions. With the match dribbling to a draw, a TV cameraman spotted a young man sitting near the boundary, cradling a .38 calibre revolver. When he was apprehended, the authorities were embarrassed to discover he was Taslimuddin Pasha,

LONGEST TEST INNINGS FOR SOUTH AFRICA

Hrs	Mins	Runs		
14	38	275	G. Kirsten v England at Durban	1999-2000
10	59	211*	H. H. Gibbs v New Zealand at Christchurch	1998-99
10	58	275*	D. J. Cullinan v New Zealand at Auckland	1998-99
10	50	210	G. Kirsten v England at Manchester	1998
9	48	**163**	**A. J. Hall v India at Kanpur**	**2004-05**
9	40	189*	J. H. Kallis v Zimbabwe at Bulawayo	2001-02
9	35	105†	D. J. McGlew v Australia at Durban	1957-58
9	34	180	G. Kirsten v Sri Lanka at Durban	2000-01
9	34	259	G. C. Smith v England at Lord's	2003

† McGlew's innings was the second-slowest Test century (9 hours 5 mins).

Research: Andrew Samson

---

son of the president of the Kanpur Cricket Association, and had been granted an access-all-areas pass. His intentions remained unclear – he claimed carrying a gun was simply the done thing in that part of the world – but police confirmed he had breached ground regulations by bringing in a firearm. It provided a late frisson in a game that neither Sehwag's ebullience nor Hall's obduracy could raise from a morass of mediocrity.

Man of the Match: A. J. Hall.

Close of play: First day, South Africa 230-4 (Hall 78, Dippenaar 46); Second day, South Africa 459-7 (Pollock 31, Tsolekile 5); Third day, India 185-0 (Sehwag 85, Gambhir 85); Fourth day, India 401-4 (Dravid 52, Laxman 4).

South Africa

*G. C. Smith b Kumble	37	– c Gambhir b Kartik.	47
A. J. Hall b Kumble	163	– c Karthik b Harbhajan Singh	26
M. van Jaarsveld lbw b Kumble	2	– lbw b Kartik	13
J. H. Kallis lbw b Kumble	37	– not out	28
J. A. Rudolph b Kumble	0	– c Karthik b Harbhajan Singh	2
H. H. Dippenaar c Karthik b Ganguly	48	– not out	31
Z. de Bruyn c Dravid b Harbhajan Singh	83		
S. M. Pollock not out	44		
†T. L. Tsolekile lbw b Kumble	9		
R. J. Peterson b Harbhajan Singh	34		
B 9, l-b 22, w 1, n-b 16, p 5	53	B 12, l-b 5, n-b 5.	22

1/61 (1) 2/69 (3) 3/154 (4)   (9 wkts dec.) 510   1/67 (2) 2/100 (3)   (4 wkts) 169
4/154 (5) 5/241 (6) 6/385 (2)   3/110 (1) 4/115 (5)
7/445 (7) 8/467 (9) 9/510 (10)

M. Ntini did not bat.

Bowling: *First Innings*—Zaheer Khan 29–7–59–0; Ganguly 12–2–45–1; Kumble 54–13–131–6; Harbhajan Singh 44.4–9–127–2; Kartik 42–12–76–0; Tendulkar 9–0–36–0. *Second Innings*—Zaheer Khan 8–2–26–0; Kumble 21–8–52–0; Harbhajan Singh 16–5–39–2; Kartik 14–6–17–2; Tendulkar 5–0–18–0.

" " Hussain was distraught after 'doing a Boycott' on the local lad."
The New Zealanders in England, page 456.

India

V. Sehwag lbw b Hall	164	Zaheer Khan b Hall 30
G. Gambhir c Tsolekile b Pollock	96	M. Kartik not out 0
R. Dravid c Tsolekile b Ntini	54	
S. R. Tendulkar b Hall	3	B 10, l-b 9, n-b 7 26
*S. C. Ganguly c Peterson b de Bruyn	57	
V. V. S. Laxman c Ntini	9	1/218 (2) 2/294 (1) 3/298 (4) 466
†K. D. Karthik lbw b Pollock	1	4/394 (5) 5/407 (3) 6/408 (7)
A. Kumble c Tsolekile b Ntini	9	7/419 (8) 8/420 (6)
Harbhajan Singh c Dippenaar b Peterson	17	9/456 (9) 10/466 (10)

Bowling: Pollock 38–11–100–2; Ntini 39–0–135–3; Peterson 21–2–90–1; Hall 25.4–7–93–3; de Bruyn 11–3–29–1.

Umpires: D. J. Harper (Australia) and S. J. A. Taufel (Australia).
Third umpire: A. V. Jayaprakash. Referee: J. J. Crowe (New Zealand).

INDIA v SOUTH AFRICA

Second Test Match

At Kolkata, November 28, 29, 30, December 1, 2, 2004. India won by eight wickets. Toss: South Africa. Test debut: H. M. Amla.

Harbhajan Singh revisited the scene of his greatest triumph to inspire India to an ultimately comfortable victory, but they were made to toil by a South African side that owed much to the obduracy of Kallis and the tireless efforts of their quicker bowlers. In March 2001, Harbhajan had taken 13 Australian wickets, in a match remembered more for Laxman's glorious 281; this time, his second-innings seven for 87 snuffed out the last South African resistance.

LEADING TEST WICKET-TAKERS FOR INDIA

Test bowling figures for Anil Kumble and Kapil Dev at the end of the matches in which they took their 434th Test wicket.

	M	O	R	W	BBI	BBM	Avge	ER	SR	5W/i	10W/m
A. Kumble	90	4,779	12,227	434	10-74	14-149	28.17	2.55	66.06	28	6
Kapil Dev	131	4,623.2	12,867	434	9-83	11-146	29.64	2.78	63.91	23	2

South Africa still had a ray of hope heading into the final day with a lead of 66, and five wickets in hand. But once Harbhajan deceived Kallis in the flight to take a simple return catch, the last glimmer faded. Their cause was not helped by a dubious bat-pad decision against Pollock, after the ball struck his ribcage and then appeared to be caught on the bounce by Gambhir.

Demolition job complete, Harbhajan yielded centre-stage to Kumble, who winkled out the last two batsmen to join Kapil Dev as India's highest Test wicket-taker, with 434 victims. India were left to chase just 117 and despite losing Sehwag early they eased to victory with time to spare.

The eyes have it: a doleful Graeme Smith departs for 71, caught by V. V. S. Laxman (*foreground*) at first slip off Harbhajan Singh.

Picture by Getty Images

Sehwag had done his work in the first innings. He helped set the game up for India with a dazzling 88, after South Africa managed just 305 on a placid track. As at Kanpur, his was a virtuoso effort, full of thrilling strokes; Ontong, given the role of premier spinner, suffered most. He conceded 19 in one dramatic over, where a huge leg-before shout was followed by a waspish cover-drive, two biffs over mid-wicket and the deftest of reverse sweeps.

Luckily for South Africa, Ntini zeroed in on Sehwag's discomfort against the short ball, having him caught at slip off a snorter that was shooting straight for the nose. It ended an innings that was once again a cut above any other played, and a total contrast to Kallis's adept effort on the opening day. Kallis had arrived at the crease early, after both Smith — passed fit at the last minute after his chauffeur drove over his foot — and Hall had given the keeper catching practice.

With the other Jacques, Rudolph, crafting a dogged 61, Kallis motored to a 17th Test century. As usual, he was utterly implacable against both pace and spin — driving and cutting with authority and panache after a few ill-judged sweeps early on. But Zaheer Khan bowled Rudolph with one that straightened, and Pathan knocked over Hashim Amla, who looked set for more than 24 on debut: after that Kallis was always waging a lone battle. It ended inexplicably on the second morning when he shouldered arms to the innocuous medium-pace of Ganguly.

South Africa were left 100 short of a par score, and India then overcame the challenge posed by the fiery Ntini and the support seamers. Dravid chiselled out a valuable but scarcely fluent 80 to buttress Sehwag's effort, and the middle order ensured a healthy lead. Despite second-innings resistance from Smith, who played quite beautifully for 71 before Harbhajan snaffled him with a magnificent off-break, India never relinquished their grip.

Later on the fourth day Ganguly copped yet another fine for dissent after a bat-pad spat involving the resolute Kallis. However, such penalties were far from his mind the following afternoon, when India closed a disappointing home season with a victory that provided some balm for the bruising suffered at Australian hands.

Man of the Match: Harbhajan Singh.   *Man of the Series:* V. Sehwag.

Close of play: First day, South Africa 227-5 (Kallis 103, de Bruyn 15); Second day, India 129-1 (Sehwag 82, Dravid 33); Third day, India 359-6 (Karthik 35, Pathan 21); Fourth day, South Africa 172-5 (Kallis 52, de Bruyn 9).

South Africa

*G. C. Smith c Karthik b Pathan	0	– c Laxman b Harbhajan Singh	71
A. J. Hall c Karthik b Zaheer Khan	7	– c Karthik b Harbhajan Singh	21
J. A. Rudolph b Zaheer Khan	61	– lbw b Harbhajan Singh	3
J. H. Kallis b Ganguly	121	– c and b Harbhajan Singh	55
H. M. Amla b Pathan	24	– c Laxman b Harbhajan Singh	2
H. H. Dippenaar c Karthik b Pathan	1	– c Sehwag b Kumble	2
Z. de Bruyn c Karthik b Zaheer Khan	15	– not out	32
S. M. Pollock c Dravid b Kumble	18	– c Gambhir b Harbhajan Singh	6
J. L. Ontong not out	16	– c Karthik b Harbhajan Singh	0
†T. L. Tsolekile c and b Harbhajan Singh	15	– b Kumble	1
M. Ntini c Pathan b Harbhajan Singh	0	– c Dravid b Kumble	12
L-b 17, n-b 10	27	B 12, l-b 2, n-b 3	17

1/0 (1) 2/21 (2) 3/130 (3) 4/176 (5)	305	1/77 (2) 2/81 (3) 3/126 (1)	222
5/182 (6) 6/230 (7) 7/261 (4)		4/138 (5) 5/147 (6) 6/183 (4)
8/273 (8) 9/305 (10) 10/305 (11)		7/193 (8) 8/193 (9)
		9/194 (10) 10/222 (11)

Bowling: First Innings—Pathan 31–7–72–3; Zaheer Khan 27–7–64–3; Kumble 30–6–76–1; Ganguly 9–3–14–1; Harbhajan Singh 21.3–6–54–2; Tendulkar 3–0–8–0. *Second Innings*—Pathan 5–1–17–0; Zaheer Khan 5–0–22–0; Kumble 34.4–7–82–3; Harbhajan Singh 30–3–87–7.

India

V. Sehwag c Smith b Ntini.	88	– c Smith b Ntini	10
G. Gambhir lbw b Pollock.	7	– lbw b Rudolph.	26
R. Dravid b Hall	80	– not out	47
S. R. Tendulkar b de Bruyn	20	– not out	32
*S. C. Ganguly lbw b de Bruyn	40		
V. V. S. Laxman c Ontong b Ntini	38		
†K. D. Karthik lbw b Pollock.	46		
I. K. Pathan c Smith b Ntini	24		
A. Kumble c Kallis b Ntini	8		
Harbhajan Singh c Dippenaar b Ontong	14		
Zaheer Khan not out.	11		
L-b 19, w 6, n-b 10.	35	L-b 1, n-b 4	5
	411	(2 wkts)	**120**

1/17 (2) 2/144 (1) 3/189 (4) 4/238 (3)   **411**   1/15 (1) 2/60 (2)   (2 wkts) 120
5/267 (5) 6/308 (6) 7/366 (8)
8/382 (9) 9/387 (7) 10/411 (10)

Bowling: *First Innings*—Pollock 45 13–101–2; Ntini 44–9–112–4; Ontong 18.1–1 79–1; Hall 27–5–68–1; de Bruyn 16–4–32–2. *Second Innings*—Pollock 7–1–22–0; Ntini 4–0–11 1; Ontong 10.4–1–44–0; Rudolph 8–1–24–1; Smith 7–1–16–0; Hall 3–2 2–0.

Umpires: D. J. Harper (Australia) and S. J. A. Taufel (Australia).
Third umpire: I. Sivaram. Referee: J. J. Crowe (New Zealand).

THE NEW ZEALANDERS IN AUSTRALIA, 2004-05

PETER ENGLISH

New Zealand's tour began under clouds of injury and illness and finished under heavier ones at Brisbane, when rain ruined the gripping conclusion to the one-day series. In between there was an initially competitive but ultimately lop-sided Test series. Despite their lowly world ranking, many thought New Zealand would again perform their traditional trick of ruffling their mighty neighbours. They didn't.

Winning the series with a depleted team was too ambitious, but to challenge in every session was a reasonable target for the tourists. Instead, the world champions, who defeated India away for the first time since 1969 less than two weeks before the First Test, spectacularly roused themselves after two days of slumber in Brisbane to toy with and humiliate their opponents. "Every time they play this well they send tremors round the world," was Fleming's summation of the series.

The two-Test Trans-Tasman Trophy was squeezed in over 13 days and effectively decided at the Gabba when New Zealand were run over for 76. The visitors had arrived for the tour to a terse description of their attack from *The Australian*: "Kiwi popguns". But at that stage their problem was getting a side on the field at all. Fleming was struggling with a mysterious virus contracted in Bangladesh; Nathan Astle had a back injury and Daniel Vettori (crucial to an attack definitely without Shane Bond, Daryl Tuffey and the retired Chris Cairns) a shoulder problem.

All three eventually played in all the international matches, and Vettori enhanced his reputation in both forms. But the injuries did have one significant knock-on effect: Craig McMillan, who was called in as emergency cover and played the First Test ahead of the original squad member Hamish Marshall, made his greatest impact during a heated argument with Adam Gilchrist over the merits of walking.

As the outcome of the series became inevitable, batsmen standing their ground became the month's big moral issue. It rumbled when Mathew Sinclair stayed put at Brisbane and was pilloried for not accepting Ponting's word that he had taken a third-slip chance off Jason Gillespie, which was confirmed by the video umpire. Then on the fourth afternoon at Brisbane, it exploded. McMillan appeared to inside-edge Gillespie to Gilchrist, but stood his ground and was given not out by Steve Bucknor. A less-than-cordial exchange ensued.

Yet there was barely a ripple when Matthew Hayden leaned on his bat after a clean caught-and-bowled to Paul Wiseman in the next match. McMillan continued the debate with a more cordial – and public – discussion with Gilchrist on the boundary's edge when the match finished. "Just because one or two guys are on a crusade doesn't mean it changes the way of 95% of the other cricketers," Fleming said. Throughout the series, players were

Australia's latest all-rounder? Glenn McGrath is congratulated by his team-mates after reaching his first international fifty; he had gone 101 Tests and 193 one-day internationals without one.

Picture by Hamish Blair, Getty Images

asked for their stance on walking: Gilchrist does, Ponting doesn't, Hayden won't, Fleming might. "An individual's right to decide should be respected," he continued.

Fleming missed the first tour match, a nine-wicket defeat by New South Wales, but joined the squad for the opening Test, and his demeanour was bright. That lasted until Australia, as so often, produced a string of devastating partnerships to reply to New Zealand's challenging first-innings score. Michael Clarke, playing his first home Test, and Gilchrist pounced with centuries, and a last-wicket stand of 114 from Glenn McGrath and Gillespie, who both reached maiden Test fifties, pushed the match out of reach even if New Zealand had batted respectably second time round, which they didn't.

"It probably happened a bit easier than we thought," Ponting said of the innings-and-156-run victory. He made it harder at Adelaide, sadistically extending New Zealand's torture into a fifth day. Justin Langer's double-century and an all-round bowling performance set up a 213-run win. It could have ended a day earlier if Ponting had enforced the follow-on with a lead of 324. He decided to protect his bowlers and inflict more misery on a side Australia would face again in March. The tour was barely three weeks old; for New Zealand it felt much, much longer.

The mood altered when the one-day specialists turned up and the versatile players changed from whites to colours. As Cairns arrived at the hotel, the New Zealanders must have wanted to hang like a toddler from the hem of his trousers. Cairns had become a one-day-only player following the 2004 England tour, and his giant bowling and batting shadows hung over New Zealand's efforts in the Tests. The first reminder of his talent came during the opening match of the inaugural Chappell–Hadlee one-day series at the Telstra Dome.

Suddenly, New Zealand had upgraded from easy-beats to upbeat and were one win away from taking the best-of-three series. Australia restored parity at Sydney with a display that was convincing at times and worryingly jittery at others. The series was poised for an appetising finale, but any hope of a satisfying conclusion was drowned in unseasonal rain.

NEW ZEALAND TOURING PARTY

S. P. Fleming (*captain*), N. J. Astle, I. G. Butler, J. E. C. Franklin, B. B. McCullum, H. J. H. Marshall, C. S. Martin, K. D. Mills, J. D. P. Oram, M. H. Richardson, M. S. Sinclair, S. B. Styris, D. L. Vettori, P. J. Wiseman.

G. J. Hopkins and C. D. McMillan were later added to the Test squad. A. R. Adams, C. L. Cairns, T. K. Canning and C. Z. Harris replaced Franklin, Hopkins, Martin, Richardson and Wiseman in the squad for the one-day internationals.

Coach: J. G. Bracewell. *Manager:* R. A. Dykes. *Physiotherapist:* D. F. Shackel.

NEW ZEALAND TOUR RESULTS

Test matches – Played 2: Lost 2.
First-class matches – Played 3: Lost 3.
One-day internationals – Played 2: Won 1, Lost 1. Abandoned 1.
Other non-first-class match – Played 1: Won 1.

Note: Matches in this section which were not first-class are signified by a dagger.

At Sydney, November 11, 12, 13, 14, 2004. **New South Wales won by nine wickets.** Toss: New Zealanders. **New Zealanders 213** (M. S. Sinclair 88, S. C. G. MacGill 4-57) and **201** (M. H. Richardson 50, M. S. Sinclair 79; S. C. G. MacGill 4-52); **New South Wales 286** (D. J. Thornely 59, J. J. Krejza 54) and **129-1** (P. A. Jaques 70*).

AUSTRALIA v NEW ZEALAND

First Test Match

At Brisbane, November 18, 19, 20, 21, 2004. Australia won by an innings and 156 runs. Toss: New Zealand.

Fleming left the field at stumps on day two with much to smile about. After a preparation hampered by his mystery illness and the late withdrawal of Franklin with a groin injury, he had four Australian wickets and a lead of 156. They were riches of which he would not have dared dream. Oram, a tall all-rounder with immense power, had rescued the side from No. 7 with an innings using guile to reach his second Test century and serious bite once past it. The bowlers had stuck together while batting and were further rewarded with indents into Australia's top order.

By lunch the next day Fleming's control had been loosened by a spectacular innings from Clarke, who added a memorable home debut to his stunning first Test at Bangalore a month earlier, and 216 runs in with Gilchrist. Worse was to follow when Gillespie and McGrath combined in an outrageous display. Both notched half-centuries in a 114-run partnership that was just 13 short of Australia's highest last-wicket stand, between Arthur Mailey and Johnny Taylor in 1924-25. The change was so swift that, in just three sessions, Fleming had gone from plotting a fifth-day target to an almost impossible match-saving assignment. New Zealand's second-innings resistance lasted less than three hours.

Australia dawdled through days one and two. The opening sessions were moderately successful as Kasprowicz, playing his first Test on his home ground for six years, bowled with speed and purpose, enjoying bounce not found on the subcontinent's pitches. He delivered a double blow in his third over when he induced edges from Richardson and Fleming.

Astle, smartly run out by Clarke, and Sinclair (whose nick to Ponting was referred to the third umpire Peter Parker) went with the score on 138. New Zealand were five down and staring at trouble, but Oram, the logical all-round replacement for Chris Cairns, found enough partners to boost his side to 353.

Oram, on 92 when Martin, a definite No. 11, arrived, cleverly worked the field – which had as many as eight fielders on the boundary – for twos as he neared his hundred. Then he opened up with three sixes, including two in a row from Kasprowicz.

It took a while for Australia to get going. Clarke began the third day on 31 and waited until the third over to assert himself with two pulls off Mills; as lunch neared, he was at full pace. Joined by Gilchrist after Martyn lofted a cut to third man, Clarke accelerated with cover-drives off both feet, and wanted 11 from the last over of the morning to reach his century. After taking a four and a three from Martin's first two deliveries, Clarke watched Gilchrist engineer a single, as he had for Steve Waugh against England at Sydney in 2002-03, and had one ball to move off 96.

Men were sent to the square and fine-leg boundaries, and Martin provided the requisite short ball, which Clarke pulled in front of square and celebrated with air-punches and helmet kisses. Some observers compared it to Doug Walters's six off Bob Willis to get a century in a session at the WACA in 1974-75. Bowled attempting a wild swipe that ended his 200-ball stay, including 21 fours and a six, Clarke became one of Vettori's four victims. The innings of Gilchrist, who had also taken a supporting role at Bangalore, was overlooked, but with 13 fours and four sixes in 151 balls, he had scored at a faster rate than his partner.

The innings was expected to end quickly, but McGrath and Gillespie drained New Zealand with a frolicking partnership that spanned 36.1 overs. Ponting shelved plans for a declaration, and the pair reached stumps, by which time McGrath had his first half-century. His 61 boasted a hooked six and was the highest score by an Australian No. 11, beating the 52 by Rodney Hogg at Georgetown in 1983-84. That was one record no one ever expected McGrath to break.

Gillespie reached his fifty and celebrated by riding his bat like a jockey to satisfy a promise to club team-mates at the Adelaide Buffalos. The ridicule ended when McGrath became Martin's fifth wicket, but New Zealand surrendered meekly in 165 minutes with their lowest total against Australia since their first meeting at Wellington in 1945-46.

Man of the Match: M. J. Clarke.   *Attendance:* 52,082.

Close of play: First day, New Zealand 250-7 (Oram 63, Vettori 13); Second day, Australia 197-4 (Martyn 59, Clarke 31); Third day, Australia 564-9 (Gillespie 44, McGrath 54).

New Zealand

M. H. Richardson c Ponting b Kasprowicz	19	– c Gilchrist b McGrath	4
M. S. Sinclair c Ponting b Gillespie	69	– lbw b McGrath	0
*S. P. Fleming c Warne b Kasprowicz	0	– c Langer b McGrath	11
S. B. Styris c Gilchrist b Kasprowicz	27	– lbw b Warne	7
N. J. Astle run out	19	– c Warne b Kasprowicz	17
C. D. McMillan c Gilchrist b Warne	23	– lbw b Gillespie	9
J. D. P. Oram not out	126	– c Hayden b Warne	8
†B. B. McCullum st Gilchrist b Warne	10	– c Gilchrist b Gillespie	8
D. L. Vettori c Warne b Kasprowicz	21	– c Hayden b Warne	2
K. D. Mills c Hayden b Warne	29	– not out	4
C. S. Martin c Ponting b Warne	0	– lbw b Warne	0
B 1, l-b 2, w 3, n-b 4	10	L-b 2, n-b 4	6

1/26 (1) 2/26 (3) 3/77 (4) 4/138 (5)   353   1/6 (1) 2/7 (2) 3/19 (3) 4/42 (4)   76
5/138 (2) 6/180 (6) 7/206 (8)   5/44 (5) 6/55 (7) 7/69 (8)
8/264 (9) 9/317 (10) 10/353 (11)   8/72 (6) 9/72 (9) 10/76 (11)

Bowling: *First Innings*—McGrath 27–4–67–0; Gillespie 29–7–84–1; Kasprowicz 28–5–90–4; Warne 29.3–3–97–4; Lehmann 4–0–12–0. *Second Innings*—McGrath 8–1–19–3; Gillespie 10–5–19–2; Kasprowicz 8–2–21–1; Warne 10.2–3–15–4.

Australia

J. L. Langer lbw b Vettori	34	M. S. Kasprowicz c Mills b Martin	5
M. L. Hayden lbw b Mills	8	G. D. McGrath c Astle b Martin	61
*R. T. Ponting c Astle b Martin	51		
D. R. Martyn c McMillan b Martin	70	B 1, l-b 7, w 1, n-b 8	17
D. S. Lehmann c McCullum b Vettori	8		
M. J. Clarke b Vettori	141	1/16 (2) 2/85 (1) 3/109 (3)	585
†A. C. Gilchrist c Styris b Martin	126	4/128 (5) 5/222 (4) 6/438 (6)	
S. K. Warne lbw b Vettori	10	7/450 (7) 8/464 (8)	
J. N. Gillespie not out	54	9/471 (10) 10/585 (11)	

Bowling: Martin 39.5–7–152–5; Mills 26–8–99–1; Styris 8–1–33–0; Oram 25–4–116–0; Vettori 50–9–154–4; McMillan 5–1–23–0.

Umpires: Aleem Dar (Pakistan) and S. A. Bucknor (West Indies).
Third umpire: P. D. Parker.   Referee: M. J. Procter (South Africa).

AUSTRALIA v NEW ZEALAND

Second Test Match

At Adelaide, November 26, 27, 28, 29, 30, 2004. Australia won by 213 runs. Toss: Australia.

Having given as good as they got before being blown away in the second half at Brisbane, New Zealand faced five days of relentless punishment at Adelaide. Australia's performance was cruelly efficient; New Zealand could find no improvement in the four days' rest between Tests.

Langer began the first day with a boundary off Martin and ended it with a century that even he called "gritty" – a term he usually despises when used to describe his batting. With the Adelaide weather approaching its most scorching, and the pitch looking as enticing to batsmen as ever, Australia kept the same side while New Zealand opted to strengthen their bowling. The off-spinner Wiseman, on the tour with this match in mind, was preferred to McMillan, who failed twice at Brisbane, while the left-arm seamer Franklin, recovered from the groin strain that ruled him out of the First Test, replaced Mills.

But Franklin overpitched far too often, and in the second over Langer hit him for four boundaries, a display repeated before stumps during Franklin's second over with the new ball. New Zealand's fast bowlers failed to take a single wicket in the match: the ten Australian wickets to fall were shared by Vettori and Wiseman, although Warne took only three of the 20 New Zealand wickets.

Langer and Hayden took their combined opening-partnership record past 4,000 runs with their 13th century stand, and the batting almost became a carnival: Martyn and Clarke were the only two of the top eight not to reach half-centuries. Hayden stood his ground when caught by the bowler Wiseman – and the video umpire was consulted to give an easy decision; Ponting again looked in too much of a rush to make his first hundred as captain; Lehmann, narrowly missing a home-ground hundred, found another strange way of getting out when bowled by Wiseman off his pads playing outside leg stump; Gilchrist faced some tricky moments against Vettori before freeing his arms, and Warne hit out as the declaration approached.

Vettori's five-wicket haul was New Zealand's highlight, but his second only came when Langer, who brought up his double-century with one of three sixes to go with 25 crashed fours, departed at 445 for four after 499 minutes and 368 balls at the crease. Vettori talked about copying India's performance here the previous year, when Australia opened with 556 and lost by four wickets, but that dream ended quickly. The crucial wicket came when Fleming, having played his one fluent innings of the series, was caught behind off McGrath, who led the way with four wickets. But all the front-line bowlers made telling contributions, and Warne broke the untrodden ground of 550 Test wickets when Franklin played back and was lbw.

Leading by 324, Ponting decided against the follow-on and ordered tactics to crush any possible fightback. The top four plodded to 139 from 56 overs, sparking unusual hurry-ups from the crowd to a home captain. Ponting even batted on four overs after lunch on the fourth day, from which he and Martyn made four: arithmetically neat but turgid to watch. "We've entertained a lot better than any other side in the history of the game, but with one two-hour period it's all over the papers," Ponting said doggedly. "We achieved what we wanted to achieve."

Australia did then turn it on, producing a bowling performance that Fleming described as facing "three Richard Hadlees and the greatest leg-spinner of all". Within 21 overs New Zealand were 34 for four and Fleming, the only batsman capable of leading any lengthy resistance, had again fallen to McGrath. He tried to leave the ball alone but it darted back, deceiving not only him but McGrath too, who appealed for an lbw even though the off bail had been dislodged.

Contributions from Oram and McCullum, whose bright attack on Warne centred on lifting him out of the heavy rough, eased the contest into a fifth day, and a half-century by Vettori dragged it into the second session. Australia took six balls to capture the final wicket after lunch. Thereafter, the main interest was in the end-of-series race between Lehmann and Richardson, the slowest men on each team. Richardson broke the tape, but his batting spirit was also torn. He went home, waited a week and then announced his retirement from all cricket. With four failures Richardson had suffered as much as anyone in a series Fleming correctly called a "hiding".

Man of the Match: J. L. Langer.   *Attendance*: 60,689.

Man of the Series: G. D. McGrath.

Close of play: First day, Australia 327-3 (Langer 144, Lehmann 28); Second day, New Zealand 56-2 (Fleming 38, Wiseman 4); Third day, Australia 57-0 (Langer 31, Hayden 21); Fourth day, New Zealand 149-5 (Oram 40, McCullum 34).

    ❝Now, the bin wheeled back."

The New Zealanders in England, page 462.

Australia

J. L. Langer c Oram b Vettori.	215	– lbw b Wiseman	46
M. L. Hayden c and b Wiseman	70	– c McCullum b Vettori	54
*R. T. Ponting st McCullum b Vettori	68	– not out	26
D. R. Martyn c Fleming b Wiseman	7	– not out	6
D. S. Lehmann b Wiseman	81		
M. J. Clarke lbw b Vettori	7		
†A. C. Gilchrist c and b Vettori	50		
S. K. Warne not out	53		
J. N. Gillespie c Richardson b Vettori.	12		
B 4, l-b 4, n-b 4	12	L-b 6, n-b 1	7

1/137 (2) 2/240 (3) 3/261 (4)   (8 wkts dec.) 575   1/93 (1) 2/119 (2)   (2 wkts dec.) 139
4/445 (1) 5/457 (6) 6/465 (5)
7/543 (7) 8/575 (9)

M. S. Kasprowicz and G. D. McGrath did not bat.

Bowling: *First Innings*—Martin 27–4–118–0; Franklin 17–2–102–0; Oram 24–7–55–0; Vettori 55.2–10–152–5; Wiseman 32–7–140–3. *Second Innings*—Martin 6–1–11–0; Oram 5–1–17–0; Franklin 5–0–18–0; Wiseman 22–3–52–1; Vettori 18–2–35–1.

New Zealand

M. H. Richardson b Kasprowicz	9	– c Langer b Kasprowicz	16
M. S. Sinclair c Warne b Gillespie	0	– lbw b Gillespie.	2
*S. P. Fleming c Gilchrist b McGrath	83	– b McGrath.	3
P. J. Wiseman lbw b Kasprowicz.	11	– (10) not out.	15
N. J. Astle c Langer b McGrath	52	– c Langer b Lehmann	38
J. D. P. Oram c Gilchrist b Gillespie	12	– c Gilchrist b McGrath.	40
†B. B. McCullum lbw b Gillespie	10	– lbw b Gillespie.	36
D. L. Vettori lbw b McGrath	20	– c Gillespie b Lehmann.	59
J. E. C. Franklin lbw b Warne	7	– c Gilchrist b Kasprowicz.	13
S. B. Styris c Clarke b McGrath	28	– (4) c Clarke b Warne.	8
C. S. Martin not out	2	– c Ponting b Warne	2
B 3, l-b 5, n-b 9	17	B 1, l-b 12, n-b 5	18

1/2 (2) 2/44 (1) 3/80 (4) 4/153 (3)   251   1/11 (2) 2/18 (3) 3/34 (1)   250
5/178 (5) 6/183 (6) 7/190 (7)   4/34 (4) 5/97 (5) 6/150 (6)
8/213 (9) 9/242 (8) 10/251 (10)   7/160 (7) 8/206 (9)
                                              9/243 (8) 10/250 (11)

Bowling: *First Innings*—McGrath 20.1–3–66–4; Gillespie 19–4–37–3; Warne 28–5–65–1; Kasprowicz 16–3–66–2; Lehmann 5–2–9–0. *Second Innings*—McGrath 12–2–32–2; Gillespie 16–5–41–2; Kasprowicz 14–4–39–2; Warne 27.3–6–79–2; Lehmann 13–0–46–2.

Umpires: S. A. Bucknor (West Indies) and D. R. Shepherd (England).
Third umpire: S. J. Davis.   Referee: M. J. Procter (South Africa)

†At Albert Ground, Melbourne, December 2, 2004. **New Zealanders won by 34 runs.** New Zealanders batted first by mutual consent. **New Zealanders 277-7** (40 overs) (S. P. Fleming 67, N. J. Astle 66); **Victoria Invitational XII 243** (38.3 overs) (I. S. L. Hewett 82).
Victoria Invitational fielded a 12-man team, of whom 11 could bat and 11 field.

†AUSTRALIA v NEW ZEALAND

First One-Day International

At Colonial Stadium, Melbourne, December 5, 2004 (day/night). New Zealand won by four wickets. Toss: New Zealand.

Beaten by New Zealand for the first time in eight one-day internationals, Australia did not enjoy the first in-season match under the Telstra Dome's retractable roof, which stayed firmly shut though it was a fine evening. Many of the spectators were unhappy even before the result. "The wind should dictate the bowling. The light should influence the batsman. In here we don't know if it's day or night, hot or cold. I'm part of some controlled experiment," grumbled one. "Where's the smell of sunscreen? Where's the breeze? Where's the atmosphere?" asked another. Australia had appeared untouchable when Gilchrist, with 68 from 54 balls, raced them to 113 in the 20th over. But Cairns and Vettori instigated a collapse of four wickets for ten. Australia then used three spinners in Hogg, Symonds and Lehmann to take advantage of a slow pitch, but Lee, playing only because McGrath and Gillespie were rested, was the stand-out, removing Fleming with the second ball of the innings, which topped the 150kph mark. With three overs to go, New Zealand were still 32 short. But the 48th over, bowled by Kasprowicz, went for 22, including a leg-side full-toss that cost five wides. Marshall and McCullum took them to victory with two balls to spare.

Man of the Match: H. J. H. Marshall. *Attendance:* 30,753.

Australia

†A. C. Gilchrist c Cairns	68		B. Lee b Cairns		8
M. L. Hayden c Sinclair b Oram	13		M. S. Kasprowicz not out		9
*R. T. Ponting lbw b Vettori	29				
D. S. Lehmann c Butler b Oram	50		B 2, l-b 2, w 2, n-b 3		9
D. R. Martyn lbw b Vettori	1				
A. Symonds c Mills b Vettori	0		1/64 (2) 2/113 (1)	(9 wkts, 50 overs)	246
M. J. Clarke b Cairns	36		3/121 (3) 4/123 (5)		
S. R. Watson c McCullum b Butler	3		5/123 (6) 6/194 (7)		
G. B. Hogg not out	20		7/198 (8) 8/220 (4) 9/236 (10)		

Bowling: Mills 4–0–28–0; Butler 8–0–58–1; Oram 9–0–51–2; Cairns 10–0–39–3; Vettori 10–1–31–3; Styris 9–0–35–0.

New Zealand

*S. P. Fleming lbw b Lee	0		†B. B. McCullum not out		20
N. J. Astle c Ponting b Lehmann	70				
M. S. Sinclair run out	48		L-b 9, w 7		16
S. B. Styris c Lee b Lehmann	5				
H. J. H. Marshall not out	50		1/0 (1) 2/128 (3)	(6 wkts, 49.4 overs)	247
J. D. P. Oram c Gilchrist b Kasprowicz	24		3/131 (2) 4/140 (4)		
C. L. Cairns b Lee	14		5/189 (6) 6/208 (7)		

D. L. Vettori, K. D. Mills and I. G. Butler did not bat.

Bowling: Lee 8–0–40–2; Kasprowicz 9–1–53–1; Watson 8.4–0–42–0; Hogg 7–0–33–0; Lehmann 9–0–35–2; Symonds 8–0–35–0.

Umpires: R. E. Koertzen (South Africa) and S. J. Davis.
Third umpire: R. L. Parry. Referee: M. J. Procter (South Africa).

" 'It was the most touching thing I have ever seen or heard, almost orchestral in its sound and feeling. Whenever I think of it, tears still come to my eyes.'"

Richie Benaud, The Man Who Made Cricket Glow, page 44.

†AUSTRALIA v NEW ZEALAND

Second One-Day International

At Sydney, December 8, 2004 (day/night). Australia won by 17 runs. Toss: Australia.

Cairns and Mills maintained New Zealand's interest until the 48th over, but Australia squared the series. Australia were in control after another explosive Gilchrist half-century, which at one stage included eight fours and a six from three overs. But they again relaxed and lost five wickets for 21. Lehmann and Hogg led the rescue with a 74-run stand, and New Zealand needed a record chase on the ground to secure the series. The middle order folded after a promising start. Cairns heaved 50 from 40 balls, and Mills walloped four sixes to bring the asking-rate to a run a ball with six overs remaining. Harris, who tore a rotator cuff while fielding, walked out at No. 11 with the target 26. His hope of a courageous upset in his 250th one-day international was ended by McGrath.

Man of the Match: G. B. Hogg.   *Attendance:* 28,484.

Australia

†A. C. Gilchrist c Astle b Styris	60		G. B. Hogg not out	41
M. L. Hayden run out	43		B. Lee not out	10
*R. T. Ponting c Fleming b Mills	32		L-b 2, w 2, n-b 8	12
D. R. Martyn lbw b Mills	5			
A. Symonds lbw b Vettori	0		1/86 (1) 2/140 (3) (7 wkts, 50 overs)	261
D. S. Lehmann run out	52		3/147 (2) 4/148 (4)	
M. J. Clarke c McCullum b Cairns	6		5/148 (5) 6/161 (7) 7/235 (6)	

J. N. Gillespie and G. D. McGrath did not bat.

Bowling: Mills 10–0–49–2; Oram 10–0–77–0; Cairns 10–0–60–1; Styris 10–0–37–1; Vettori 10–1–36–1.

New Zealand

*S. P. Fleming lbw b Hogg	34		K. D. Mills not out	44
N. J. Astle c Gilchrist b Lee	11		C. Z. Harris b McGrath	4
M. S. Sinclair c Hayden b Gillespie	17			
S. B. Styris lbw b Symonds	5		L-b 5, w 6, n-b 3	14
H. J. H. Marshall b Lee	9			
J. D. P. Oram lbw b Hogg	2		1/27 (2) 2/63 (3) 3/68 (4) (47.1 overs)	244
C. L. Cairns c McGrath b Gillespie	50		4/78 (1) 5/84 (6) 6/86 (5)	
†B. B. McCullum lbw b Hogg	21		7/154 (7) 8/166 (8)	
D. L. Vettori run out	33		9/236 (9) 10/244 (11)	

Bowling: McGrath 7.1–0–27–1; Lee 9–0–48–2; Gillespie 10–1–41–2; Symonds 10–1–47–1; Hogg 8–0–45–3; Lehmann 3–0–31–0.

Umpires: R. E. Koertzen (South Africa) and P. D. Parker.
Third umpire: S. J. A. Taufel.   Referee: M. J. Procter (South Africa).

†AUSTRALIA v NEW ZEALAND

Third One-Day International

At Brisbane, December 10, 2004 (day/night). No result (abandoned).

The final match of the first Chappell–Hadlee Series was abandoned without a ball bowled. Heavy rain throughout the week had forced the curator Kevin Mitchell junior to switch wickets, but neither was required as showers continued. Ian Chappell and Sir Richard Hadlee presented the captains with the trophy which will next be contested in New Zealand in 2005-06.

Man of the Series: D. L. Vettori.

THE PAKISTANIS IN AUSTRALIA, 2004-05

GEOFFREY DEAN

Pakistan were expected to mount a more serious challenge to Australia's hegemony of the international game than New Zealand had a month earlier. In the event, however, they were beaten with equal ease by the world champions, who won all three Tests inside four days despite losing the toss each time. Pakistan did manage to start every Test promisingly, only to fall away with numbing predictability – never more so than at Perth, where they were skittled in the equivalent of just over a session in their second innings. Australia's winning margin of 491 runs was the biggest in terms of runs in a Test since the Second World War.

Pakistan's young touring party had arrived in Australia as early as the end of November to give themselves plenty of time to get used to Perth's notorious extra bounce and pace. But the preparation did not go well: they were bowled out for 83 in pursuit of 94 to be humbled by Western Australia's Second XI. And against the full state side they lost by ten wickets. After the debacle in the First Test at Perth, their captain Inzamam-ul-Haq complained that his players had needed even longer to prepare. But the reality was that, with their poor techniques against the rising ball on a quick pitch, no amount of time would have made much difference.

The gamble of playing only six batsmen at Perth to allow room for a fifth bowler also backfired, and collapses were a recurrent theme. However, Pakistan were highly unfortunate that, against such unforgiving opposition, Inzamam, their best batsman, was ruled out of the last two Tests with a back problem. And by the time the touring party got to Sydney for the third game, the injury list had grown: Abdul Razzaq went to hospital during the third day's play at Melbourne with dizziness reported to be caused by eating too much spinach, while other casualties included Mohammad Sami, who suffered severe bruising to the heel, and Shoaib Malik, who split the webbing in his hand. It was an unhappy tour for Malik, the off-spinner whose action was deemed to be in need of remedial action after it was filmed at 250 frames per second by the specialist unit at the University of Western Australia. The findings were not reported to the ICC until after the series, but Pakistan elected not to bowl him at Melbourne.

Fitness problems also afflicted their spearhead Shoaib Akhtar at Sydney, where he was restricted by a sore hamstring to 15 overs out of 133. With the help of Sami, Akhtar had given Australia a fright on the opening day of the series by reducing them to 78 for five. Not for the first time, Adam Gilchrist, later described as "a genius" by the Pakistan coach Bob Woolmer, came to the rescue with the first of three important innings. Justin Langer also compiled his second big score in successive Tests to go clear as the leading run-scorer in Test cricket in 2004; he finished with 1,481 at a shade under 55. Damien Martyn, who was named Man of the Series, finished second in that list: two hundreds in this series gave him six for the calendar year and a total of 1,353 runs at 56. That represented a remarkable turnaround by Martyn, whose previous Test century had been in the 2001-02 season in South Africa. Conversely, Ricky Ponting, after his extraordinary year in 2003, when he averaged 100 in Tests, failed to score a century in 2004, although he began 2005 with a double-hundred at Sydney. Matthew Hayden, meanwhile, became the first man to make 1,000 Test runs in four successive calendar years.

CONSECUTIVE TEST WINS AGAINST ONE TEAM

10	West Indies v England.		1984 to 1985-86
9	Australia v West Indies		1998-99 to 2002-03
9*	**Australia v Pakistan**		**1999-2000 to 2004-05**
8	Australia v England		1920-21 to 1921
8	England v South Africa.		1888-89 to 1898-99
7	Australia v South Africa		1921-22 to 1935-36
7	England v Australia		1884-85 to 1887-88
7	England v New Zealand		1950-51 to 1958
7	England v South Africa.		1909-10 to 1913-14
7	West Indies v India.		1961-62 to 1966-67

* *Unbroken.*

Note: Australia have not played a Test in Pakistan during the current sequence. Six have been in Australia and Pakistan's three home Tests in 2002-03 were played on neutral grounds because of security fears.

Australia's bowling was led, once again, by Glenn McGrath and Shane Warne, who shared 32 wickets in the series. McGrath took the first seven in Pakistan's second innings at Perth, and was only one wicket short of the best-ever Test figures by an Australian: his analysis of eight for 24 was second only to Arthur Mailey's nine for 121 against England at Melbourne in 1920-21. Jason Gillespie bowled much better than a series haul of seven wickets suggests, and suffered from a number of dropped catches. Michael Kasprowicz, in the form of his life at 32, provided valuable back-up as third seamer, condemning Brett Lee to an unwanted national record of six consecutive stints as twelfth man. When Kasprowicz was left out at Sydney to accommodate a second spinner on a turning pitch, Stuart MacGill, who had been in outstanding form for New South Wales, claimed eight wickets and the match award.

After Pakistan's shambles in Perth, Cricket Australia feared that the public might lose interest. But the traditionally huge Boxing Day crowd (61,552) still turned out, and in Sydney the first two days were watched by 37,854 and 35,185. Gate receipts were down, however, on the India series the season before, partly explaining Cricket Australia's heavy loss for the financial year (projected at $A14m in December). Officials said they had expected a major deficit because of reduced income from overseas TV rights, but were not alarmed because they were in profit over a four-year cycle.

PAKISTANI TOURING PARTY

Inzamam-ul-Haq (*captain*), Yousuf Youhana (*vice-captain*), Abdul Razzaq, Asim Kamal, Danish Kaneria, Imran Farhat, Kamran Akmal, Mohammad Asif, Mohammad Khalil, Mohammad Sami, Naved-ul-Hasan, Salman Butt, Shahid Afridi, Shoaib Akhtar, Shoaib Malik, Yasir Hameed, Younis Khan.

For the one-day international VB series (which will be covered in *Wisden 2006*), Azhar Mahmood, Iftikhar Anjum, Mohammad Hafeez and Taufeeq Umar replaced Asim Kamal, Danish Kaneria, Imran Farhat, Mohammad Asif and Mohammad Sami.

Coach: R. A. Woolmer. *Manager:* Haroon Rashid. *Physiotherapist:* D. Lifson.

PAKISTANI TOUR RESULTS

Test matches – Played 3: Lost 3.
First-class matches – Played 4: Lost 4.
One-day internationals – Played 8: Won 3, Lost 5. *Wins* – West Indies (2), Australia. *Losses* – Australia (4), West Indies.
Other non-first-class matches – Played 6: Won 4, Lost 2.

TEST MATCH AVERAGES

AUSTRALIA – BATTING AND FIELDING

	T	I	NO	R	HS	100s	50s	Avge	Ct/St
D. R. Martyn	3	4	1	310	142	2	1	103.33	2
R. T. Ponting	3	6	2	403	207	1	2	100.75	4
†A. C. Gilchrist	3	4	1	230	113	1	1	76.66	12/2
†J. L. Langer	3	6	0	390	191	1	2	65.00	0
J. N. Gillespie	3	3	1	74	50*	0	1	37.00	3
†M. L. Hayden.	3	6	2	128	56*	0	1	32.00	3
M. J. Clarke.	3	4	0	83	35	0	0	20.75	3
S. K. Warne.	3	3	0	38	16	0	0	12.66	5
†D. S. Lehmann	2	3	0	28	12	0	0	9.33	1
G. D. McGrath.	3	3	1	18	9	0	0	9.00	2

Played in two Tests: M. S. Kasprowicz 4, 4 (2 ct). Played in one Test: S. C. G. MacGill 9*; S. R. Watson 31.

BOWLING

	Style	O	M	R	W	BB	5W/i	Avge
G. D. McGrath	RFM	107	35	260	18	8-24	1	14.44
M. S. Kasprowicz	RFM	56	17	142	9	5-30	1	15.77
S. C. G. MacGill.	LBG	47	7	170	8	5-87	1	21.25
S. K. Warne.	LBG	124.3	24	402	14	4-111	0	28.71
J. N. Gillespie.	RF	91.2	24	258	7	3-77	0	36.85

Also bowled: M. J. Clarke (SLA) 3–0–24–0; D. S. Lehmann (SLA) 6–2–18–0; R. T. Ponting (RM/OB) 3–1–15–0; S. R. Watson (RFM) 19–5–60–1.

PAKISTAN – BATTING AND FIELDING

	T	I	NO	R	HS	100s	50s	Avge	Ct/St
Younis Khan	3	6	0	259	87	0	1	43.16	2
†Salman Butt.	3	6	0	225	108	1	1	37.50	0
Yasir Hameed.	2	4	0	146	63	0	2	36.50	1
Yousuf Youhana	3	6	0	189	111	1	0	31.50	2
Abdul Razzaq	2	4	1	45	21	0	0	15.00	0
Mohammad Sami	2	4	0	54	29	0	0	13.50	1
Kamran Akmal.	3	6	0	77	47	0	0	12.83	3/4
†Imran Farhat	2	4	0	44	20	0	0	11.00	1
Shoaib Akhtar	3	6	0	42	27	0	0	7.00	2
Danish Kaneria.	3	6	3	18	9*	0	0	6.00	0

Played in one Test: †Asim Kamal 10, 87; Inzamam-ul-Haq 1, 0 (2 ct); †Mohammad Asif 0*, 12* (1 ct); †Mohammad Khalil 0, 5; Naved-ul-Hasan 0, 9; Shahid Afridi 12, 46; Shoaib Malik 6, 41 (2 ct).

BOWLING

	Style	O	M	R	W	BB	5W/i	Avge
Shoaib Akhtar.	RF	77.3	8	334	11	5-99	2	30.36
Danish Kaneria.	LBG	149.2	18	560	15	7-188	2	37.33
Abdul Razzaq.	RFM	31.3	1	130	3	2-55	0	43.33
Naved-ul-Hasan.	RM	29	3	135	3	3-107	0	45.00
Mohammad Sami	RF	67.5	6	283	5	3-104	0	56.60

Also bowled: Imran Farhat (LBG) 19–2–82–0; Mohammad Asif (RFM) 18–3–88–0; Mohammad Khalil (LM) 25.2–0–97–0; Shahid Afridi (LBG) 29–3–115–0.

Note: Matches in this section which were not first-class are signified by a dagger.

†At James Oval, Perth, December 1, 2, 3, 2004. **Western Australia Second XI won by ten runs.** Toss: Western Australia Second XI. **Western Australia Second XI 158** (L. Ronchi 66) **and 192** (C. J. Simmons 65; Danish Kaneria 7-45); **Pakistanis 257** (Younis Khan 142; J. P. Coetzee 5-66, M. J. Petrie 4-29) **and 83** (J. P. Coetzee 5-23).
　　Western Australia Second XI fielded 12 players, Pakistan 15.

†At James Oval, Perth, December 3, 2004. **Pakistanis won by 126 runs.** Toss: Pakistanis. **Pakistanis 273-8** (40 overs) (Abdul Razzaq 55); **Western Australia Second XI 147** (38.1 overs) (A. K. Heal 53).
　　The match was arranged on the scheduled last day of the three-day fixture, which ended with enough time to fit in a 40-over-a-side match. Western Australia Second XI fielded 12 players, Pakistan 11.

†At Lilac Hill, Perth, December 7, 2004. **Pakistanis won by 43 runs.** Toss: Pakistanis. **Pakistanis 256-9** (50 overs) (Salman Butt 115*); **Cricket Australia Chairman's XI 213** (45.2 overs) (C. J. L. Rogers 61, L. Ronchi 51).
　　Both teams fielded 12 players.

At Perth, December 9, 10, 11, 2004. **Western Australia won by ten wickets.** Toss: Pakistanis. **Pakistanis 262** (Yousuf Youhana 77, Abdul Razzaq 83*) **and 174** (B. R. Dorey 5-41); **Western Australia 404-9 dec.** (M. E. K. Hussey 124, M. J. North 79) **and 34-0.**

AUSTRALIA v PAKISTAN

First Test Match

At Perth, December 16, 17, 18, 19, 2004. Australia won by 491 runs. Toss: Pakistan. Test debut: Mohammad Khalil.

Australia's largest victory in terms of runs for over 70 years was achieved on the stroke of lunch on the fourth day after McGrath returned career-best figures of eight for 24. Pakistan lost their last nine wickets in 21 overs for just 38 in a display their coach Bob Woolmer described as disgraceful. "There are no excuses," he said. "We just batted badly." Against outstanding fast bowling on a quick, bouncy pitch, Pakistan's batsmen failed to move their feet and played with their bats well away from their bodies.

AUSTRALIA'S BIGGEST WINS BY RUNS

Margin		
562	beat England at The Oval	1934
530	beat South Africa at Melbourne	1910-11
491	**beat Pakistan at Perth**	**2004-05**
409	beat England at Lord's	1948
384	beat England at Brisbane	2002-03
382	beat England at Adelaide	1894-95
382	beat West Indies at Sydney	1968-69
377	beat England at Sydney	1920-21
365	beat England at Melbourne	1936-37
352	beat West Indies at Melbourne	2000-01

It was the first time McGrath had taken more than four wickets in an innings in ten Tests at Perth. In temperatures pushing 34°C, he bowled all that last morning despite feeling "pretty ordinary" at the end of his first over. "My energy levels were down a bit, but it's amazing how when you get a few overs and wickets under your belt, things turn around," he said. "Towards the end, that was as good as I've ever felt bowling." Six of his victims were caught in the cordon from wicket-keeper to gully.

Shoaib Akhtar and Mohammad Sami had likewise caused the Australians problems with their pace and movement on the first day, but the supporting seamers, including the debutant left-armer Mohammad Khalil, were ineffective. Pakistan were perhaps one wicket away from dismissing Australia cheaply after reducing them to 78 for five, but then bowled poorly at Langer and Gilchrist, who repaired the innings with a stand of 152 in less than 29 overs. Gilchrist's fine counter-attack of 69 off 78 balls with ten fours was ended when he unluckily played on off his thigh. But Langer then found staunch support from Gillespie, one of the most improved tailenders in world cricket, as the pair added an important 80 in 20 overs for the eighth wicket.

Langer narrowly missed carrying his bat, sacrificing himself to be last out for 191 off 280 balls. His cutting and pulling were a feature of his 413-minute stay, which included three sixes, two of them over long-on off Danish Kaneria, as well as 18 fours.

Firing line: the close fielder cowers as Justin Langer pulls hard en route to his 21st Test hundred.

Picture by Hamish Blair, Getty Images

Curiously, he said he had never felt truly "in", even at the end of an innings in which he was hit several times by the fiery Shoaib, to whom the wicket-keeper stood back some 30 yards. Shoaib collected not just a five-wicket haul but also a fine worth 40% of his match fee from Ranjan Madugalle, the series referee, for pointing Hayden towards the pavilion on the first morning – an act deemed a Level 1 offence under the ICC code of conduct.

Pakistan's fate in the match was sealed by an abject batting performance in their first innings against persistent bowling. Of the top-order batsmen, only Younis Khan, who resisted 138 minutes for his 42, seemed to have much stomach for a fight, and he was one of three batsmen to get out to ugly slog-sweeps at Warne. Kasprowicz was the pick of the Australian seamers, maintaining an ideal length to return only his second five-wicket haul in a home Test. Had the Australians not dropped five catches, admittedly all difficult, the Pakistanis might barely have reached three figures. Ponting said afterwards that, at 111 for eight, he envisaged enforcing the follow-on, but when it took 30 overs to claim the last two wickets, he decided against. No doubt, he also wanted his top order to have some batting practice, after all bar Langer had failed in the first innings.

With Shoaib suffering from a foot problem, Australia's second innings became something of a run-feast against dispirited opposition. Langer took his match aggregate to 288, while Ponting, who came within two runs of a first Test hundred in 2004, delayed the declaration longer than needed so Martyn could complete his century. After bowling their overs at a funereal pace in the first innings, Pakistan hustled through 43 overs of spin in the second, thereby precluding any possibility of fines, or the suspension of their captain for a slow over-rate.

Man of the Match: J. L. Langer.   *Attendance:* 42,193.

Close of play: First day, Australia 357-8 (Langer 181, Kasprowicz 4); Second day, Australia 15-0 (Langer 3, Hayden 7); Third day, Pakistan 18-1 (Salman Butt 8, Younis Khan 7).

Australia

J. L. Langer c Younis Khan b Mohammad Sami	191	– b Abdul Razzaq	97
M. L. Hayden lbw b Shoaib Akhtar	4	– b Shoaib Akhtar	10
*R. T. Ponting b Mohammad Sami	25	– st Kamran Akmal b Danish Kaneria	98
D. R. Martyn c Kamran Akmal b Mohammad Sami	1	– not out	100
D. S. Lehmann b Shoaib Akhtar	12	– b Danish Kaneria	5
M. J. Clarke c Inzamam-ul-Haq b Shoaib Akhtar	1	– c Inzamam-ul-Haq b Mohammad Sami	27
†A. C. Gilchrist b Abdul Razzaq	69	– not out	0
S. K. Warne c Yousuf Youhana b Abdul Razzaq	12		
J. N. Gillespie c Kamran Akmal b Shoaib Akhtar	24		
M. S. Kasprowicz lbw b Shoaib Akhtar	4		
G. D. McGrath not out	8		
B 1, l-b 14, w 5, n-b 10	30	L-b 15, w 2, n-b 7	24
	381	(5 wkts dec.)	**361**

1/6 (2) 2/56 (3) 3/58 (4) 4/71 (5)   381
5/78 (6) 6/230 (7) 7/253 (8)
8/333 (9) 9/362 (10) 10/381 (1)

1/28 (2) 2/191 (1)   (5 wkts dec.) 361
3/271 (3) 4/281 (5)
5/360 (6)

Bowling: *First Innings*—Shoaib Akhtar 22–1–99–5; Mohammad Sami 25.5–3–104–3; Mohammad Khalil 16–0–59–0; Abdul Razzaq 12–0–55–2; Danish Kaneria 15–2–49–0. *Second Innings*—Shoaib Akhtar 6.3–1–22–1; Mohammad Sami 14–1–55–1; Abdul Razzaq 12.3–1–48–1; Mohammad Khalil 9.2–0–38–0; Danish Kaneria 32–3–130–2; Imran Farhat 11–0–53–0.

Pakistan

Salman Butt c Gilchrist b Kasprowicz	17	– c Hayden b McGrath	9
Imran Farhat c Gilchrist b Gillespie	18	– lbw b McGrath	1
Younis Khan c Gillespie b Warne	42	– c Warne b McGrath	17
*Inzamam-ul-Haq b Kasprowicz	1	– (6) c Gilchrist b McGrath	0
Yousuf Youhana c Gilchrist b Kasprowicz	1	– (4) c Gilchrist b McGrath	27
Abdul Razzaq b Warne	21	– (5) c Gilchrist b McGrath	1
†Kamran Akmal b Kasprowicz	2	– c Clarke b McGrath	0
Mohammad Sami c Clarke b Kasprowicz	29	– b Kasprowicz	2
Mohammad Khalil b Warne	0	– (10) c and b Kasprowicz	5
Shoaib Akhtar c Warne b McGrath	27	– (9) c Lehmann b McGrath	1
Danish Kaneria not out	6	– not out	0
B 1, l-b 3, w 7, n-b 4	15	L-b 7, w 2	9
	179		**72**

1/32 (2) 2/45 (1) 3/55 (4) 4/60 (5)   179
5/108 (3) 6/110 (6) 7/110 (7)
8/111 (9) 9/171 (10) 10/179 (8)

1/5 (2) 2/34 (1) 3/43 (3)   72
4/49 (5) 5/49 (6) 6/61 (7)
7/64 (4) 8/66 (8) 9/72 (9) 10/72 (10)

Bowling: *First Innings*—McGrath 19–7–44–1; Gillespie 14–2–43–1; Kasprowicz 16.3–6–30–5; Warne 21–9–38–3; Lehmann 4–2–5–0; Ponting 3–1–15–0. *Second Innings*—McGrath 16–8–24–8; Gillespie 13.2–3–37–0; Kasprowicz 3.3–2–4–2.

Umpires: B. F. Bowden (New Zealand) and R. E. Koertzen (South Africa).
Third umpire: S. J. Davis.   Referee: R. S. Madugalle (Sri Lanka).

AUSTRALIA v PAKISTAN

Second Test Match

At Melbourne, December 26, 27, 28, 29, 2004. Australia won by nine wickets. Toss: Pakistan.

Australia's ability to extricate themselves from a tight corner was well illustrated by a victory that clinched their fifth successive series win over Pakistan. When Clarke was fifth out at 171 shortly before the end of the second day, they faced the likelihood of a first-innings deficit, possibly a large one, and the prospect of a difficult run-chase in the fourth innings. Barely five sessions later, they had won the series.

Pakistan had entered the match full of uncertainty, after angry criticism of their performance in Perth had culminated in the burning of effigies of Inzamam-ul-Haq, Yousuf Youhana, Bob Woolmer and selector Wasim Bari on the streets of Karachi. When Inzamam was ruled out by a back injury, thus handing the captaincy to Youhana, Pakistan's first Christian captain, their new leader responded by making a brilliant 111 off 134 balls, sharing a national record fourth-wicket stand against Australia of 192 in 46 overs with Younis Khan. Both played Warne particularly well, mainly off the back foot: Youhana hit him for three of his four sixes.

The platform for a competitive total – on a pitch much more to Pakistan's liking than Perth – was laid by an opening stand of 85. It was dominated by the 20-year-old

Nice and easy does it: never in a hurry, Damien Martyn glides Australia towards a series win. Kamran Akmal watches from behind the stumps.

Picture by Hamish Blair, Getty Images

stroke-playing left-hander Salman Butt, whose 70 took just 99 balls. But he threw away his wicket when chancing an unlikely second run on Clarke's throw from third man. It was symptomatic of Pakistan's profligacy, which later returned when their last seven wickets went down for 55. Abdul Razzaq's strokeless stay played completely into Australia's hands, his unbeaten four spanning 110 minutes and 76 balls. His innings compared with the slowest in Test history: only Geoff Allott's nought in 101 minutes for New Zealand against South Africa in 1998-99 was comparably painstaking.

Australia were no less guilty of some poorly conceived and executed strokes in the first half of their innings. Hayden slapped a long-hop to point, and Ponting hooked to the squarer of two men back for the miscue. Langer reached a solid fifty off 80 balls but then tried to sweep from well outside off. Lehmann fended tamely to short leg, a third successive failure that would cost him his place.

Martyn, however, barely committed a single indiscretion in his 370-minute vigil, an expert innings from a player in the form of his life. His fourth hundred in seven Tests shepherded his side to an unlikely first-innings lead of 38, which lifted Australia's bowlers and badly demoralised Pakistan's batsmen. Martyn never dominated the bowling, hitting only 12 fours in 245 balls, but nor did he try to. Avoiding waste and concentrating on effect, he presented the tightest of defences while scoring at a steady pace. When Gilchrist joined him, he sensibly acted as a foil while his partner reaped 48 off 51 balls out of a stand of 59. Valuable support later came from Gillespie, who reached a second Test fifty, from 107 balls, and helped him add an important 93 for the eighth wicket. Shoaib Akhtar and Danish Kaneria fully deserved their five-wicket hauls, but they lacked support: Razzaq could bowl only seven overs due to dizziness.

Confronted by some excellent Australian bowling in their second innings, Pakistan succumbed to pressure on a drop-in pitch still playing well. The openers perished to ill-advised shots, Imran Farhat hooking straight to deep backward square. If Yasir was the victim of fine bowling by McGrath, then Youhana was particularly unlucky to be given caught off bat-pad against Warne. Younis played too early, toe-ending a pull to gully. From 68 for five, there was no way back, although Shoaib Malik resisted stoutly after he had retired hurt with split webbing. Australia made short work of their target, and Ponting sealed victory with a straight six. His side promptly donated their prize money to the Asian tsunami relief appeal.

Man of the Match: D. R. Martyn. *Attendance*: 129,079.

Close of play: First day, Pakistan 318-6 (Abdul Razzaq 1, Kamran Akmal 16); Second day, Australia 203-5 (Martyn 67, Gilchrist 26); Third day, Pakistan 85-5 (Shoaib Malik 11, Mohammad Sami 8).

Pakistan

Salman Butt run out	70	– c Kasprowicz b McGrath	0
Imran Farhat c Ponting b Kasprowicz	20	– c Martyn b Gillespie	5
Yasir Hameed lbw b Gillespie	2	– c Gilchrist b McGrath	23
Younis Khan c Gilchrist b Gillespie	87	– c Hayden b Kasprowicz	23
*Yousuf Youhana st Gilchrist b Warne	111	– c Ponting b Warne	12
Shoaib Malik c Ponting b Gillespie	6	– c Gillespie b Warne	41
Abdul Razzaq not out	4	– (8) c Gilchrist b McGrath	19
†Kamran Akmal c Gilchrist b McGrath	24	(9) lbw b Warne	0
Mohammad Sami lbw b Warne	12	– (7) lbw b Gillespie	11
Shoaib Akhtar st Gilchrist b Warne	0	– b McGrath	14
Danish Kaneria run out	0	– not out	9
L-b 4, w 1	5	B 4, l-b 1, n-b 1	6

1/85 (2) 2/93 (3) 3/94 (1) 4/286 (5)	**341**	1/0 (1) 2/13 (2) 3/35 (3)	**163**
5/298 (4) 6/301 (6) 7/326 (8)		4/60 (5) 5/68 (4) 6/98 (7)
8/341 (9) 9/341 (10) 10/341 (11)		7/101 (6) 8/140 (6)
		9/140 (8) 10/163 (10)

In the second innings Shoaib Malik, when 15, retired hurt at 91 and resumed at 101.

Bowling: *First Innings*—McGrath 28–12–54–1; Gillespie 26–7–77–3; Kasprowicz 20–6–66–1; Warne 28.3–2–103–3; Clarke 3–0–24–0; Lehmann 2–0–13–0. *Second Innings*—McGrath 11.2–1–35–4; Gillespie 12–7–15–2; Kasprowicz 16–3–42–1; Warne 25–7–66–3.

Australia

J. L. Langer c Imran Farhat b Danish Kaneria . .	50	– c Kamran Akmal
		b Mohammad Sami . 5
M. L. Hayden c Shoaib Malik b Shoaib Akhtar .	9	– not out 56
*R. T. Ponting c Shoaib Malik b Shoaib Akhtar .	7	– not out 62
D. R. Martyn lbw b Danish Kaneria	142	
D. S. Lehmann c Yasir Hameed b Shoaib Akhtar	11	
M. J. Clarke c Shoaib Akhtar b Danish Kaneria .	20	
†A. C. Gilchrist c Mohammad Sami		
b Danish Kaneria .	48	
S. K. Warne c and b Danish Kaneria	10	
J. N. Gillespie not out	50	
M. S. Kasprowicz c sub b Shoaib Akhtar	4	
G. D. McGrath lbw b Danish Kaneria	1	
B 1, l-b 2, w 5, n-b 19	27	L-b 2, n-b 2 4

1/13 (2) 2/32 (3) 3/122 (1) 4/135 (5)   379   1/11 (1)   (1 wkt) 127
5/171 (6) 6/230 (7) 7/254 (8)
8/347 (4) 9/368 (10) 10/379 (11)

Bowling: *First Innings*—Shoaib Akhtar 27–4–109–5; Mohammad Sami 23–2–102–0; Abdul Razzaq 7–0–27–0; Danish Kaneria 39.3–5–125–5; Imran Farhat 3–0–13–0. *Second Innings*—Shoaib Akhtar 7–0–35–0; Mohammad Sami 5–0–22–1; Danish Kaneria 10.5–1–52–0; Imran Farhat 5–2–16–0.

Umpires: R. E. Koertzen (South Africa) and J. W. Lloyds (England).
Third umpire R. L. Parry.   Referee: R. S. Madugalle (Sri Lanka).

AUSTRALIA v PAKISTAN

Third Test Match

At Sydney, January 2, 3, 4, 5, 2005. Australia won by nine wickets. Toss: Pakistan. Test debuts: S. R. Watson; Mohammad Asif.

Australia completed their third successive 3–0 whitewash of Pakistan, who had begun the match with their first century opening stand in this fixture for 22 years, before fading away yet again. From 193 for one they subsided to a below-par 304 all out on a slowish pitch, despite a fine maiden Test hundred from Salman Butt. After that they were always struggling to save the game. MacGill took a five-wicket haul in his first Test for nearly ten months, to take his record at Sydney to 40 wickets in six Tests, but no less decisive were outstanding innings by Ponting (who became only the third Australian, after Don Bradman and Greg Chappell, to score four Test double-hundreds) and Gilchrist, whose 13th century passed Andy Flower's Test record for a wicket-keeper.

Pakistan were given every encouragement at the start of their innings when Yasir Hameed was dropped off successive balls – by Warne at first slip, and Gilchrist – in Gillespie's opening over, and it was not until the 32nd that Warne finally broke through,

Horses for courses. At Sydney, leg-spinners grabbed 21 of the 31 wickets to fall; Stuart MacGill, who took eight, celebrates the departure of Yousuf Youhana.

Picture by Hamish Blair, Getty Images

inducing a top-edged sweep from Yasir. Younis Khan joined Salman to add 91 in just 20 overs before lofting a lax drive off MacGill to mid-off. It proved a turning-point. MacGill, spinning the ball generously on a pitch that started a little damp, produced a superb leg-break to have Yousuf Youhana taken at slip, and McGrath, strangely ignored in the afternoon session, unearthed a fine leg-cutter with the third ball of a new spell after tea to get rid of Salman, who had cut and pulled impressively. His dismissal kick-started a collapse in which Pakistan's last seven wickets fell for 63. A pair of dreadful shots accounted for Asim Kamal and Shahid Afridi, who shovelled a full toss to deep mid-wicket; McGrath conjured up some reverse swing; and five wickets fell in five overs. Only a plucky 47 from Kamran Akmal took Pakistan past 300.

Australia's first-innings lead was never in doubt once Ponting and Martyn added 174 in 45 overs for the third wicket. Heavily favouring the leg side, Ponting completed his first Test hundred for 13 months off 143 balls, and his eventual 207 contained 30 fours, the bulk of which were made up of on-drives, whips, clips and pulls. It was the third time in succession he had converted a century into a double, following his two against India late in 2003. When he eventually played on, he had batted for eight hours 11 minutes and faced 332 balls.

Then Gilchrist completely took the game away from Pakistan with a scintillating 109-ball hundred. After playing himself in carefully, he rushed to his fifty as Pakistan gave him too much width. Devastating throughout off the back foot, he went from 82 to 94 with successive pulled sixes off the debutant seamer, Mohammad Asif. He then drove Asif's next ball one bounce into the sightscreen and reached his hundred two overs later when he struck Afridi for a straight six. Danish Kaneria, who eventually beat him in the flight to earn a third stumping from the gifted young wicket-keeper Akmal, won praise from the Australians, notably Warne, for probing bowling throughout the series, and his seven-wicket haul was his third in Test cricket. With Shoaib able to bowl only fitfully after the second day, Kaneria delivered more than a third of Pakistan's overs. However, his use of obscene language after dismissing Clarke cost him his entire match fee.

MOST TEST HUNDREDS BY A WICKET-KEEPER

A. C. Gilchrist (Australia)	13	K. C. Sangakkara (Sri Lanka)	5
A. Flower (Zimbabwe)	12	M. V. Boucher (South Africa)	4
L. E. G. Ames (England)	8	I. A. Healy (Australia)	4
A. J. Stewart (England)	6	Moin Khan (Pakistan)	4
P. J. L. Dujon (West Indies)	5	J. H. B. Waite (South Africa)	4
A. P. E. Knott (England)	5		

Note: Stewart hit nine other hundreds, and Sangakkara two, when not keeping wicket.

Research: Philip Bailey

Trailing by 264 on the first innings, Pakistan again made a hash of a promising beginning. All the top six got starts, but none apart from Kamal, who was last out for a doughty 87, went on to a major innings. Yasir and Afridi batted positively, but Australia whittled their way through the batting, and only a last-wicket stand of 55 in 16 overs stretched proceedings into the last hour of the fourth day. Australia's third seamer, Shane Watson, finally took a maiden wicket on debut when Younis played across a straight one.

Man of the Match: S. C. G. MacGill.   *Attendance:* 105,692.
Man of the Series: D. R. Martyn.
Close of play: First day, Pakistan 292-9 (Kamran Akmal 35, Mohammad Asif 0); Second day, Australia 340-4 (Ponting 155, Gilchrist 17); Third day, Pakistan 67-1 (Yasir Hameed 40, Younis Khan 5).

Pakistan

Salman Butt c Gilchrist b McGrath	108	– c Warne b MacGill	21
Yasir Hameed c Clarke b Warne	58	– lbw b Warne	63
Younis Khan c McGrath b MacGill	46	– lbw b Watson	44
*Yousuf Youhana c Warne b MacGill	8	– b MacGill	30
Asim Kamal c Gillespie b MacGill	10	– c Ponting b Gillespie	87
Shahid Afridi c McGrath b MacGill	12	– run out	46
†Kamran Akmal c Warne b McGrath	47	– c Hayden b Warne	4
Naved-ul-Hasan lbw b McGrath	0	– lbw b Warne	9
Shoaib Akhtar b McGrath	0	– c Martyn b Warne	0
Danish Kaneria c Gilchrist b MacGill	3	– b MacGill	0
Mohammad Asif not out	0	– not out	12
B 6, l-b 2, w 1, n-b 3	12	B 4, l-b 3, n-b 2	9

1/102 (2) 2/193 (3) 3/209 (4) 4/241 (1)   **304**   1/46 (1) 2/104 (2) 3/164 (4)   **325**
5/241 (5) 6/261 (6) 7/261 (8)   4/164 (3) 5/238 (6) 6/243 (7)
8/261 (9) 9/280 (10) 10/304 (7)   7/261 (8) 8/269 (9)
                                   9/270 (10) 10/325 (5)

Bowling: *First Innings*—McGrath 16.4–5–50–4; Gillespie 14–3–47–0; Watson 10–3–28–0; Warne 24–4–84–1; MacGill 22–4–87–5. *Second Innings*—McGrath 16–2–53–0; Gillespie 13.2–2–39–1; Warne 26–2–111–4; MacGill 25–3–83–3; Watson 9–2–32–1.

Australia

J. L. Langer b Naved-ul-Hasan	13	– b Danish Kaneria	34
M. L. Hayden b Danish Kaneria	26	– not out	23
*R. T. Ponting b Naved-ul-Hasan	207	– not out	4
D. R. Martyn st Kamran Akmal b Danish Kaneria	67		
M. J. Clarke st Kamran Akmal b Danish Kaneria	35		
†A. C. Gilchrist st Kamran Akmal b Danish Kaneria	113		
S. R. Watson c Mohammad Asif b Danish Kaneria	31		
S. K. Warne c Younis Khan b Danish Kaneria	16		
J. N. Gillespie lbw b Naved-ul-Hasan	0		
G. D. McGrath c Yousuf Youhana b Danish Kaneria	9		
S. C. G. MacGill not out	9		
B 6, l-b 13, w 3, n-b 20	42	N-b 1	1
	568		62

1/26 (1) 2/83 (2) 3/257 (4) 4/318 (5)   568   1/58 (1)   (1 wkt) 62
5/471 (6) 6/529 (3) 7/535 (7)
8/537 (9) 9/556 (10) 10/568 (8)

Bowling: First Innings—Shoaib Akhtar 15–2–69–0; Naved-ul-Hasan 26–3–107–3; Mohammad Asif 16–3–72–0; Danish Kaneria 49.3–7–188–7; Shahid Afridi 27–3–113–0. *Second Innings*—Naved-ul-Hasan 3–0–28–0; Mohammad Asif 2–0–16–0; Danish Kaneria 2.3–0–16–1; Shahid Afridi 2–0–2–0.

Umpires: B. F. Bowden (New Zealand) and D. R. Shepherd (England).
Third umpire: S. J. Davis.   Referee: R. S. Madugalle (Sri Lanka).

†At Adelaide, January 12. **Pakistanis won by 13 runs.** Toss: Australia A. **Pakistanis 279-8** (50 overs) (Mohammad Hafeez 61, Abdul Razzaq 89*); **Australia A 266** (48.4 overs) (B. J. Haddin 129).

†At Adelaide, January 13. **Australia A won by 56 runs.** Toss: Australia A. **Australia A 185-5** (20 overs) (D. J. Hussey 50, C. L. White 58*); **Pakistanis 129-7** (20 overs).
   This was the first international Twenty20 match in Australia.

Pakistan's matches against Australia and West Indies in the VB Series (January 16–February 6) will appear in Wisden 2006.

†At Canberra, January 25. **Pakistanis won by five wickets.** Toss: Pakistanis. **Prime Minister's XI 191** (46.4 overs); **Pakistanis 192-5** (42.5 overs) (Yousuf Youhana 50, Younis Khan 62*).

THE INDIANS IN BANGLADESH, 2004-05

Amit Varma

India won both series, but the headlines were stolen by Bangladesh's stunning one-day victory at Dhaka, when they upset a second-string Indian side to achieve only their third victory over Test-playing opposition in 90 matches. Yet India's first full tour of Bangladesh might never have happened. When a carelessly scribbled letter was faxed to the Indian High Commission in Dhaka, from the Islamic group Harkat-ul-Jihad, the departure of the Indian squad from Kolkata was delayed by two days. The letter reportedly contained a death threat to the team, but after assessments by a governmental security delegation, the trip was given the green light.

Such was the predictability of the results that initial interest focused on the milestones approached by Anil Kumble and Sachin Tendulkar. Kumble needed one wicket to pass Kapil Dev's Indian record of 434 in Tests, while Tendulkar required a single Test century to equal Sunil Gavaskar's world mark of 34. Both tasks were dealt with deftly on the first two days of the tour.

Bangladesh's place in the order of Test-playing nations was under constant scrutiny, and the fact that they lost the two matches convincingly – both by an innings in a little over three days – did nothing to further their cause. Their coach Dav Whatmore pleaded for the cricket world to be patient, but that plea fell on deaf ears – at least until the third day of the Second Test at Chittagong, when Mohammad Ashraful answered the clarion-call of a cricket-mad nation with an innings so pure in its freedom of strokeplay that it invited comparisons to a young Tendulkar. His footwork was stunning, his shot-selection impeccable, and his complete disdain for the bowlers a breath of fresh air. Ashraful's unbeaten 158 suggested that the talent on the streets of Dhaka was not necessarily inferior to that in Colombo, Karachi or Kolkata. That Bangladesh failed to avoid the follow-on, and collapsed to another humiliating defeat, paled in comparison to the self-belief and inspiration they drew from Ashraful's innings.

It proved a catalyst for their one-day victory, when they played out of their skins against a depleted and amateurish Indian side. Ultimately, the tour will be remembered not for Irfan Pathan's five-fors or the centuries from Rahul Dravid, Tendulkar and Gautam Gambhir, but for this single defeat. If critics insist that Bangladesh do not deserve to play international cricket, then the result left India's claims to be the second-best side in the world sounding a touch hollow.

INDIAN TOURING PARTY

S. C. Ganguly (*captain*), R. Dravid (*vice-captain*), Gagandeep Singh, G. Gambhir, Harbhajan Singh, M. Kaif, K. D. Karthik, M. Kartik, A. Kumble, V. V. S. Laxman, I. K. Pathan, S. S. Paul, V. Sehwag, S. R. Tendulkar, Zaheer Khan.

For the one-day internationals, A. B. Agarkar, M. S. Dhoni, Joginder Sharma, D. Mongia, S. Sriram and Yuvraj Singh replaced Gagandeep Singh, Gambhir, Karthik, Kumble, Laxman and Paul.

Coach: J. G. Wright. *Manager:* Sudhakar Rao. *Physiotherapist:* A. Leipus.

INDIAN TOUR RESULTS

Test matches – Played 2: Won 2.
One-day internationals – Played 3: Won 2, Lost 1.

Note: Matches in this section which were not first-class are signified by a dagger.

BANGLADESH v INDIA

First Test Match

At Dhaka, December 10, 11, 12, 13, 2004. India won by an innings and 140 runs. Toss: India.

That India would win, and easily, was never in doubt. Two of their greatest ever – Tendulkar and Kumble – were chasing records and hungry to do well, perhaps against the weakest opposition of their long and distinguished careers. And when India put Bangladesh in on a Bangabandhu Stadium pitch with a bit of bounce in it, one sensed Kumble would be among the wickets. But even he had to wait, as Pathan immediately hit his stride – and line and length to go with perfect shape into the right-hander – to scythe through the top order. Before the batsmen could come to terms with what was swerving at them, they were 50 for five.

But Mohammad Ashraful looked a cut above his team-mates and bolstered the middle order with a crisp unbeaten 60. With the gutsy Mohammad Rafique, he pushed the score from 106 for seven to 171, before Kumble claimed his slice of history, trapping Rafique in front with a typical fizzing slider to give him his 435th Test wicket – one more than Kapil Dev, India's previous record holder, but in 40 fewer Tests. Bangladesh had clawed their way back to some extent, but 184 all out on the first day, with Pathan claiming his maiden Test haul of five wickets, was never going to be enough.

Sure enough, the second day was a roaring Indian bat-fest. The fall of seven wickets did not stop them from racking up 348, with Tendulkar drawing level with Sunil Gavaskar as Test cricket's most prolific centurion. An unbeaten 159, his 34th hundred, was not the toughest test of his career, yet he was dropped three times – two of them

---

HIGHEST TEST SCORES BY NUMBER 11

75	Zaheer Khan	India v Bangladesh at Dhaka	**2004-05**
68*	R. O. Collinge	New Zealand v Pakistan at Auckland	1972-73
62*	A. E. E. Vogler	South Africa v England at Cape Town...........	1905-06
61	**G. D. McGrath**	Australia v New Zealand at Brisbane	**2004-05**
60*	Wasim Bari	Pakistan v West Indies at Bridgetown	1976-77
59*	J. A. Snow	England v West Indies at The Oval..............	1966
59	Mushtaq Ahmed	Pakistan v South Africa at Rawalpindi..........	1997-98
54	P. L. Symcox	South Africa v Australia at Adelaide	1997-98
52	R. M. Hogg	Australia v West Indies at Georgetown	1983-84

Research: Philip Bailey

sitters – before he reached 50. For Tendulkar, who had been battling a painful tennis elbow for at least four months, the century was reconfirmation that a day would come when strength would return to his left arm, and with it the range of strokes.

On the third day, India romped to 526. Tendulkar's final contribution was a Test-best 248 not out, from 379 balls and including 35 fours in nine hours 12 minutes. "Forget about the record, forget the double-hundred, the very fact that I could bat this long was a relief and joy," he said. Zaheer Khan rollicked his way to 75, the highest score by a Test No. 11. When India's bowlers were let loose a second time, Pathan, the star of the first innings, just needed to run in and bowl with a strong wrist position, and the swinging ball took care of the rest. From 36 for five Bangladesh could forge no meaningful reply, and despite half-centuries from Nafis Iqbal and Manjural Islam Rana at either end of the innings, they were bowled out for 202, as Pathan secured victory with match figures of 11 for 96.

Man of the Match: I. K. Pathan.

Close of play: First day, Bangladesh 184; Second day, India 348-7 (Tendulkar 159, Kumble 0); Third day, Bangladesh 170-8 (Manjural Islam Rana 50, Tapash Baisya 17).

Bangladesh

Javed Omar lbw b Pathan	4	– lbw b Pathan	4
Nafis Iqbal lbw b Pathan	20	– lbw b Kumble	54
*Habibul Bashar c Tendulkar b Zaheer Khan	8	– c Zaheer Khan b Pathan	12
Rajin Saleh lbw b Pathan	0	– lbw b Pathan	0
Mohammad Ashraful not out	60	– lbw b Pathan	0
†Khaled Mashud c Karthik b Zaheer Khan	8	– c Karthik b Pathan	5
Manjural Islam Rana c Karthik b Pathan	24	– c Karthik b Zaheer Khan	69
Mushfiqur Rahman lbw b Pathan	0	– c Dravid b Harbhajan Singh	6
Mohammad Rafique lbw b Kumble	47	– c Sehwag b Kumble	11
Tapash Baisya c Dravid b Kumble	0	– c Tendulkar b Pathan	29
Mashrafe bin Mortaza run out	7	– not out	0
L-b 4, n-b 2	6	L-b 5, w 2, n-b 5	12

1/8 (1) 2/29 (2) 3/29 (4) 4/35 (3)   184   1/4 (1) 2/24 (3) 3/24 (4)   202
5/50 (6) 6/106 (7) 7/106 (8)   4/24 (5) 5/36 (6) 6/100 (2)
8/171 (9) 9/171 (10) 10/184 (11)   7/117 (8) 8/133 (9)
    9/202 (10) 10/202 (7)

Bowling: *First Innings*—Pathan 16–5–45–5; Zaheer Khan 15–2–51–2; Ganguly 4–2–16–0; Kumble 13.5–2–45–2; Harbhajan Singh 9–1–23–0. *Second Innings*—Pathan 15–5–51–6; Zaheer Khan 13.2–2–60–1; Kumble 13–4–42–2; Harbhajan Singh 12–3–44–1.

India

G. Gambhir run out	35	A. Kumble b Mashrafe bin Mortaza	1
V. Sehwag lbw b Tapash Baisya	13	Harbhajan Singh c Habibul Bashar	
R. Dravid b Mashrafe bin Mortaza	0	b Mushfiqur Rahman	8
S. R. Tendulkar not out	248	Zaheer Khan st Khaled Mashud	
*S. C. Ganguly b Tapash Baisya	71	b Mohammad Ashraful	75
V. V. S. Laxman		B 2, l-b 11	13
lbw b Mohammad Rafique	32		
†K. D. Karthik c Mashrafe bin		1/19 (2) 2/24 (3) 3/68 (1)	526
Mortaza b Mushfiqur Rahman	25	4/232 (5) 5/291 (6) 6/339 (7)	
I. K. Pathan c Mushfiqur Rahman		7/348 (8) 8/368 (9)	
b Mohammad Rafique	5	9/393 (10) 10/526 (11)	

Bowling: Tapash Baisya 29–4–114–2; Mashrafe bin Mortaza 31–8–125–2; Mushfiqur Rahman 24–4–104–2; Mohammad Rafique 40–9–113–2; Manjural Islam Rana 12–1–55–0; Mohammad Ashraful 0.4–0–2–1.

Umpires: Aleem Dar (Pakistan) and J. W. Lloyds (England).
Third umpire: A. F. M. Akhtaruddin. Referee: B. C. Broad (England).

BANGLADESH v INDIA

Second Test Match

At Chittagong, December 17, 18, 19, 20, 2004. India won by an innings and 83 runs. Toss: India. Test debut: Nazmul Hossain.

After the canter to victory in the First Test, the Indian team, and its latest hero, Pathan, would have been forgiven for thinking the Second would be no harder. But results did not come quite as quickly as they anticipated after they had won the toss and chosen to bat on a Chittagong pitch that had none of the pace or bounce of Dhaka. The ball did not come on to the bat, and big shots did not fetch their reward – at least not until Mohammad Ashraful showed how it was done with a sparkling century to ease the pain of another defeat for Bangladesh.

Mashrafe bin Mortaza, the one Bangladeshi bowler who would push for a spot in most Test teams, was playing his first series in more than a year after a knee injury, and he made an impact by dismissing Sehwag cheaply. Then India dug deep. Gambhir, anxious for his maiden Test hundred, and Dravid, keen to score a century in Bangladesh to become the first man to reach three figures in all ten Test-playing countries, put on 259 for the second wicket, and ground Bangladesh's bowlers into the dust. Gambhir fell towards the end of the first day, having faced 196 balls for his 139, but this only heightened the anticipation, as Sachin Tendulkar helped himself to 36, and, with four full days to play, looked almost certain to go past Gavaskar's tally of 34 Test centuries. Then, with the first ball of the second day, a corker that pitched on line and darted in just enough to beat Tendulkar's defence and trap him plumb in front, Mashrafe raised Bangladesh's sagging morale. But it was a false dawn, for with Tendulkar's record hunt out of the way, India were free to bat normally. Dravid scored 160 from 304 balls with 24 fours, Ganguly hit 88, and India racked up 540.

TEST CENTURIES IN MOST COUNTRIES

10   R. Dravid
9   S. R. Tendulkar, S. R. Waugh
8   Inzamam-ul-Haq, G. Kirsten
7   M. Azharuddin, K. F. Barrington, A. R. Border, M. C. Cowdrey, M. D. Crowe, B. C. Lara, Saeed Anwar, G. P. Thorpe, Yousuf Youhana.

Note: Tendulkar has not scored a Test century in Zimbabwe; Waugh did not score a century in either Sri Lanka or Bangladesh, but did get one in the United Arab Emirates (v Pakistan at Sharjah in 2002-03); Inzamam is missing South Africa and India; Kirsten Sri Lanka and Bangladesh.

Barrington and Cowdrey scored centuries in all countries that hosted Tests during their career.

Bangladesh responded with their usual inconsistency, resisting at first, then slumping to 54 for three, before Ashraful played the innings of the tour. His forthright biffing of the fast bowlers – hooking while hopping on one leg *à la* Gordon Greenidge – and his effervescent thwacking of the spinners got the crowd to its feet. He paced his way to 50 from 70 balls, then needed just 55 more to reach his second Test century, racing from 76 to three figures with seven consecutive scoring shots. If anything, that spurred him on, for he unfurled such authoritative and audacious strokes that India were forced to spread the field to him, close it in to his partners, and hope for a mistake. The mistake never came from Ashraful, who scored 158 not out from only 194 balls with 24 fours and three sixes, beating the previous best by Bangladesh: Aminul Islam's 145 in the inaugural Test, also against India. But he ran out of partners, and eight runs short of the follow-on mark of 341, the last man was sent back. India's bowlers regrouped for the kill. Bangladesh duly capitulated without so much as a whimper.

Pathan, who probed without instant success in the first innings, found his groove, and Bangladesh were teetering on the brink of defeat at 118 for nine when the third day ended. It took India just four balls on the fourth to wrap things up.

Man of the Match: Mohammad Ashraful.   *Man of the Series:* I. K. Pathan.

Close of play: First day, India 334-2 (Dravid 145, Tendulkar 36); Second day, Bangladesh 54-3 (Habibul Bashar 0); Third day, Bangladesh 118-9 (Nazmul Hossain 8, Talha Jubair 25).

India

V. Sehwag c Habibul Bashar	I. K. Pathan c Khaled Mashud
b Mashrafe bin Mortaza . 10	b Mohammad Rafique . 4
G. Gambhir b Nazmul Hossain 139	A. Kumble st Khaled Mashud
R. Dravid c Khaled Mashud	b Mohammad Ashraful . 23
b Mashrafe bin Mortaza . 160	Harbhajan Singh c Manjural Islam Rana
S. R. Tendulkar	b Nazmul Hossain . 47
lbw b Mashrafe bin Mortaza . 36	Zaheer Khan not out 0
*S. C. Ganguly c Talha Jubair	
b Mohammad Rafique . 88	B 5, l-b 4, w 2, n-b 2 13
V. V. S. Laxman	
c and b Mohammad Rafique . 9	1/14 (1) 2/273 (2) 3/334 (4) 540
†K. D. Karthik c Khaled Mashud	4/371 (5) 5/384 (6) 6/402 (7)
b Mohammad Rafique . 11	7/412 (8) 8/465 (9) 9/540 (5) 10/540 (10)

Bowling: Masrafe bin Mortaza 26–5–60–3; Nazmul Hossain 25.5–4–114–2; Talha Jubair 19–1–95–0; Mohammad Rafique 50–2–156–4; Manjural Islam Rana 16.3–0–63–0; Aftab Ahmed 4–0–14–0; Mohammad Ashraful 7–0–29–1.

Bangladesh

Nafis Iqbal c Gambhir b Harbhajan Singh	31	– lbw b Pathan	0
Javed Omar c Dravid b Kumble	10	– c Karthik b Pathan	6
Mashrafe bin Mortaza lbw b Kumble	4	– (9) c Harbhajan Singh b Tendulkar .	6
*Habibul Bashar st Karthik b Kumble	22	– (3) lbw b Pathan	17
Mohammad Ashraful not out	158	– (6) lbw b Kumble	3
Aftab Ahmed lbw b Kumble	43	– (4) c Karthik b Pathan	4
Manjural Islam Rana lbw b Zaheer Khan	0	– c Gambhir b Kumble	0
†Khaled Mashud c Karthik b Zaheer Khan	22	– c Dravid b Harbhajan Singh	0
Mohammad Rafique c Dravid b Pathan	4	– (5) c Sehwag b Pathan	22
Talha Jubair b Pathan	0	– (11) c Pathan b Harbhajan Singh . .	31
Nazmul Hossain run out	0	– (10) not out	8
B 17, l-b 8, w 3, n-b 11	39	B 9, l-b 7, w 7, n-b 4	27

1/48 (2) 2/54 (1) 3/54 (3) 4/124 (4)   333   1/0 (1) 2/30 (2) 3/34 (4)   124
5/239 (6) 6/240 (7) 7/300 (8)   4/75 (5) 5/76 (3) 6/77 (7)
8/312 (9) 9/312 (10) 10/333 (11)   7/78 (6) 8/80 (8) 9/84 (9) 10/124 (11)

Bowling: *First Innings*—Pathan 23–7–86–2; Zaheer Khan 18–3–76–2; Kumble 26–9–55–4; Harbhajan Singh 22–5–79–1; Tendulkar 2–0–12–0. *Second Innings*—Pathan 9–2–32–5; Zaheer Khan 6–1–28–0; Kumble 4–2–2–2; Harbhajan Singh 4.4–0–19–2; Tendulkar 3–0–27–1.

Umpires: Aleem Dar (Pakistan) and M. R. Benson (England).
Third umpire: Mahbubur Rahman. Referee: B. C. Broad (England).

†BANGLADESH v INDIA

First One-Day International

At Chittagong, December 23, 2004. India won by 11 runs. Toss: Bangladesh. One-day international debuts: M. S. Dhoni, Joginder Sharma.

Even with an experimental team, India were simply too good for Bangladesh, and the apparent slimness of the margin was misleading: in reality, Bangladesh were never in the hunt. India quickly slumped to 45 for three, but careful half-centuries from Dravid and Kaif lifted them to 245. Bangladesh's reply showed their mindset: they never really believed victory was possible. Habibul

Bashar, the captain, blatantly ignored the scoreboard and the match situation, and helped himself to a 96-ball 65, steering his team to 156 when he was sixth out in the 41st over. Khaled Mashud entertained the crowd with a 39-ball half-century full of sweeps and lofted drives, but victory was never really within striking distance.

Man of the Match: M. Kaif.

India

*S. C. Ganguly b Tapash Baisya	0	A. B. Agarkar c Mushfiqur Rahman	
S. R. Tendulkar c Khaled Mashud		b Tapash Baisya	25
b Nazmul Hossain	19	I. K. Pathan not out	21
Yuvraj Singh lbw b Mushfiqur Rahman	21	Joginder Sharma not out	5
R. Dravid c Khaled Mashud		L-b 6, w 11, n-b 1	18
b Khaled Mahmud	53		
M. Kaif c and b Nazmul Hossain	80	1/0 (1) 2/37 (2) (8 wkts, 50 overs) 245	
S. Sriram st Khaled Mashud		3/45 (3) 4/173 (4)	
b Mohammad Rafique	3	5/180 (6) 6/180 (7)	
†M. S. Dhoni run out	0	7/203 (5) 8/232 (8)	

Harbhajan Singh did not bat.

Bowling: Tapash Baisya 10–0–67–2; Mushfiqur Rahman 6–0–29–1; Nazmul Hossain 9–1–39–2; Khaled Mahmud 10–0–43–1; Mohammad Rafique 10–0–39–1; Aftab Ahmed 5–0–22–0.

Bangladesh

Nafis Iqbal run out	9	Mushfiqur Rahman lbw b Agarkar	2
Mohammad Rafique c Yuvraj Singh		Khaled Mahmud c Kaif b Agarkar	21
b Pathan	8	Tapash Baisya not out	7
*Habibul Bashar c Dravid b Sriram	65		
Mohammad Ashraful c Ganguly		L-b 2, w 17, n-b 7	26
b Joginder Sharma	2		
Aftab Ahmed c Harbhajan Singh		1/11 (2) 2/40 (1) (8 wkts, 50 overs) 234	
b Sriram	30	3/44 (4) 4/108 (5)	
Rajin Saleh c Joginder Sharma b Sriram	14	5/143 (6) 6/156 (3)	
†Khaled Mashud not out	50	7/160 (8) 8/200 (9)	

Nazmul Hossain did not bat.

Bowling: Pathan 9–0–45–1; Joginder Sharma 8–2–28–1; Agarkar 10–0–51–2; Ganguly 4–0–19–0; Harbhajan Singh 10–1–46–0; Sriram 9–0–43–3.

Umpires: Aleem Dar (Pakistan) and Mahbubur Rahman.
Third umpire: Nadir Shah.   Referee: B. C. Broad (England).

†BANGLADESH v INDIA

Second One-Day International

At Dhaka, December 26, 2004 (day/night). Bangladesh won by 15 runs. Toss: Bangladesh.

This was the most startling day of India's tour, as a depleted side – missing Tendulkar, Dravid, Harbhajan and Pathan – slid to a sensational 15-run defeat. Bangladesh had never won before at home, and this was only their third victory against a Test-playing nation, following victories over Pakistan at the 1999 World Cup and Zimbabwe in 2003-04. For once, 40,000 baying fans at the Bangabandhu had their dreams realised. The upset seemed entirely improbable when Bangladesh slipped to 88 for five, but the tail wagged vigorously, thanks to 67 from the supple-wristed Aftab Ahmed. Even a second-string Indian side should have had no difficulty chasing 230 on an easy pitch against gentle bowling. But they did not factor in the Bangladeshi spirit: their fielders fought for every run, clawed every catch, and struck the stumps every time they had to. The top order failed, and the middle order, led by Sriram, eked out a painful existence. Suddenly, the required rate climbed to a run-a-ball, and when Kaif ran himself out, the wheels came off, and Dhaka went wild. But even this triumph was badly timed: it was the day of the Asian tsunami, and the result was barely noticed across a traumatised continent.

Man of the Match: Mashrafe bin Mortaza.

Elation: the Bangladesh players are exultant at beating India in the second one-day international, at Dhaka. It was their first major win on home soil.

Picture by Rafiqur Rahman, Reuters

Bangladesh

Nafis Iqbal c Dhoni b Agarkar	9
Mohammad Rafique lbw b Zaheer Khan	0
*Habibul Bashar b Agarkar	17
Mohammad Ashraful c and b Kartik	28
Aftab Ahmed b Kartik	67
Rajin Saleh run out	0
†Khaled Mashud c Joginder Sharma b Sriram	20
Khaled Mahmud run out	17

Mashrafe bin Mortaza not out	31
Tapash Baisya b Zaheer Khan	17
Nazmul Hossain not out	3
L-b 4, w 6, n-b 10	20

1/1 (2) 2/26 (1)   (9 wkts, 50 overs) 229
3/37 (3) 4/81 (4)
5/88 (6) 6/132 (7)
7/168 (5) 8/187 (8) 9/226 (10)

Bowling: Agarkar 9–1–31–2; Zaheer Khan 8–1–53–2; Joginder Sharma 10–1–51–0; Kartik 10–0–43–2; Sriram 10–1–37–1; Mongia 3–0–10–0.

India

V. Sehwag b Mashrafe bin Mortaza	0
*S. C. Ganguly c Mashrafe bin Mortaza b Khaled Mahmud	22
Yuvraj Singh c Rajin Saleh b Tapash Baisya	4
S. Sriram st Khaled Mashud b Mohammad Rafique	57
M. Kaif run out	49
D. Mongia lbw b Tapash Baisya	12
†M. S. Dhoni c Habibul Bashar b Mashrafe bin Mortaza	12

A. B. Agarkar c Aftab Ahmed b Mohammad Rafique	9
Joginder Sharma not out	29
Zaheer Khan c Mashrafe bin Mortaza b Khaled Mahmud	10
M. Kartik run out	3
L-b 4, w 3	7

1/0 (1) 2/5 (3) 3/51 (2)   (47.5 overs) 214
4/114 (4) 5/131 (6) 6/155 (7)
7/170 (5) 8/172 (8) 9/204 (10) 10/214 (11)

Bowling: Mashrafe bin Mortaza 9–2–36–2; Tapash Baisya 10–2–35–2; Nazmul Hossain 7–0–26–0; Khaled Mahmud 9.5–0–40–2; Mohammad Rafique 10–0–57–2; Aftab Ahmed 2–0–16–0.

Umpires: Aleem Dar (Pakistan) and A. F. M. Akhtaruddin.
Third umpire: Nadir Shah. Referee: B. C. Broad (England).

†BANGLADESH v INDIA

Third One-Day International

At Dhaka, December 27, 2004 (day/night). India won by 91 runs. Toss: India.

After their shock defeat, India came storming back, foaming at the mouth. Sehwag, who had failed all tour, blistered an angry 70 in 52 balls and Tendulkar belligerently knocked out 47, as India sped away to a flyer in the series decider. Dravid and Ganguly then took over, nursing their way through the middle overs, taking no chances and sparing no loose balls. They added 98 in 19 overs before leaving it to Yuvraj Singh to finish things off with a brutal 69 in 32 balls, with eight fours and three sixes. Bangladesh responded as best they could to India's 348 for five, with Rajin Saleh compiling a workmanlike 82, but the task was far too steep.

Man of the Match: V. Sehwag.   *Man of the Series:* M. Kaif.

India

V. Sehwag c Mohammad Ashraful b Khaled Mahmud	70	M. Kaif not out	29
S. R. Tendulkar c Khaled Mashud b Khaled Mahmud	47	Yuvraj Singh c Aftab Ahmed b Khaled Mahmud	69
*S. C. Ganguly c Khaled Mahmud b Rajin Saleh	55	†M. S. Dhoni not out	7
		L-b 4, w 7	11
R. Dravid c Mashrafe bin Mortaza b Mohammad Rafique	60	(5 wkts, 50 overs)	348

1/106 (2) 2/125 (1) (5 wkts, 50 overs) 348
3/223 (3) 4/247 (4) 5/340 (6)

A. B. Agarkar, Joginder Sharma, Zaheer Khan and Harbhajan Singh did not bat.

Bowling: Mashrafe bin Mortaza 10–0–60–0; Hasibul Hussain 6–0–53–0; Mushfiqur Rahman 6–0–52–0; Khaled Mahmud 10–0–62–3; Mohammad Rafique 10–1–63–1; Aftab Ahmed 2–0–16–0; Rajin Saleh 6–0–38–1.

Bangladesh

Nafis Iqbal c Dhoni b Agarkar	10	Mashrafe bin Mortaza st Dhoni b Tendulkar	39
Rajin Saleh st Dhoni b Tendulkar	82	Hasibul Hossain not out	1
Mohammad Rafique c Dravid b Zaheer Khan	0	L-b 8, w 17, n-b 6	31
*Habibul Bashar c Dhoni b Agarkar	2		
Mohammad Ashraful run out	32	(9 wkts, 50 overs)	257
Aftab Ahmed c Dhoni b Harbhajan Singh	9	1/31 (1) 2/32 (3)	
†Khaled Mashud lbw b Tendulkar	10	3/41 (4) 4/102 (5)	
Khaled Mahmud c Joginder Sharma b Tendulkar	14	5/138 (6) 6/163 (2) 7/164 (7) 8/198 (8)	
Mushfiqur Rahman not out	27	9/246 (10)	

Bowling: Agarkar 7–0–32–2; Zaheer Khan 6–1–15–1; Joginder Sharma 3–0–20–0; Harbhajan Singh 8–0–48–1; Ganguly 5–0–25–0; Yuvraj Singh 6–0–24–0; Tendulkar 9–2–54–4; Sehwag 6–1–31–0.

Umpires: Aleem Dar (Pakistan) and Mahbubur Rahman.
Third umpire: Nadir Shah. Referee: B. C. Broad (England).

VB SERIES, 2003-04

Soumya Bhattacharya

Coming on the back of one of the hardest fought and most compelling Test series of recent times, the VB had much to live up to. India had been tantalisingly close to defeating Australia in the Tests, and hopes were high that the one-day games would produce similarly dramatic cricket. But though the Indians started well, and in their early games against Australia retained the fierce competitiveness that lit up the Tests, they ran out of steam even before the finals – in which they were hammered.

Another factor in a disappointing tournament was that the third team, Zimbabwe, merely made up the numbers, losing seven games with their eighth ruined by the weather, though they did once come within a boundary of surprising India.

Perhaps the Indians were weary at the end of a long and demanding tour, but great sides overcome fatigue and lift their game when it matters – as Australia showed, time and again. And quite simply, the Indians were outclassed by a team who, when it came to crunch matches, were in a different league: Australia beat India five times out of six.

One of the Australian stars, Adam Gilchrist, ran into superb form after a disappointing run in the Tests, but he was far from alone. Matthew Hayden was savage at the top, Ricky Ponting brutal in the middle and Andrew Symonds devastating at the death. (Symonds usually batted No. 5, but in this company there was no guarantee he would see more than the closing overs.) Michael Clarke, aged just 22, also showed why many believed he would assume Steve Waugh's place in the Test side. Brett Lee was caned early in the tournament – against India at Brisbane, he conceded 83 runs – but he soon regained his lethal reputation. The rest of the pace attack all showed that they had more than enough control and guile to prevent the Indians rebuilding an innings.

Despite some sublime batting from V. V. S. Laxman, who hit three hundreds in the series, India never matched the world champions for urgency, athleticism, improvisation or in exerting pressure. They were also unable to make as much impact with the new ball as the Australians, though Irfan Pathan, the 19-year-old Indian left-armer, did take 16 wickets – more than anyone else – if at a cost of more than five and a half an over.

The Test series had been close because it celebrated the classicism of Laxman, Rahul Dravid and (in Sydney) Sachin Tendulkar. In the abbreviated form of the game, it soon became clear that those same Indian batsmen simply could not produce the ferocity of their Australian counterparts. Laxman hit his 443 runs at a respectable strike-rate of 83 per 100 balls, but he was eclipsed by Gilchrist, whose 498 came at a hum-dinging 122. The combination of plentiful runs and coruscating speed – Symonds added 349 at 94 for good measure – was irresistible.

Note: Matches in this section were not first-class.

AUSTRALIA v INDIA

At Melbourne, January 9, 2004 (day/night). Australia won by 18 runs. Australia 5 pts, India 1 pt. Toss: Australia. One-day international debut: I. K. Pathan.

Tendulkar rediscovered the cover-drive (unused during his double-hundred in the Sydney Test), Ganguly the blend of aggression and discipline he showed at Brisbane – and Australia the habit of clinging on to half-chances. In the end, the catches prevented India making the highest successful run-chase in a one-day international at the MCG. Tendulkar was brilliantly taken at mid-wicket for a belligerent 63, but India's hopes lived on until the 46th over, when they reached 257 for four. Then Yuvraj Singh and Ganguly, who was run out by Bangar, departed to successive deliveries, and within 20 balls India had lost their last six wickets for 13. In Australia's innings, Symonds and Clarke – who made a stroke-filled 63 and later took four catches – added 143 to steady the ship. Agarkar, India's deceptively amiable trundler, took six for 42, but could not prevent Australia from setting a daunting total.

Man of the Match: A. Symonds.   *Attendance:* 63,271.

Australia

†A. C. Gilchrist c Pathan b Agarkar	34	J. N. Gillespie not out	8
M. L. Hayden c Yuvraj Singh b Agarkar	20	B. A. Williams c Yuvraj Singh b Agarkar	0
*R. T. Ponting c and b Balaji	18		
D. R. Martyn c Balaji b Agarkar	0	L-b 10, w 14, n-b 3	27
A. Symonds c Kumble b Agarkar	88		
M. J. Clarke c Laxman b Kumble	63	1/59 (1) 2/70 (2) 3/70 (4) (48.3 overs) 288
M. G. Bevan c Ganguly b Sehwag	1	4/89 (3) 5/232 (6) 6/233 (7)
I. J. Harvey c Tendulkar b Agarkar	28	7/258 (5) 8/272 (9)
A. J. Bichel run out	1	9/287 (8) 10/288 (11)

Bowling: Agarkar 9.3–1–42–6; Pathan 10–0–61–0; Balaji 9–0–52–1; Kumble 10–0–56–1; Bangar 3–0–19–0; Ganguly 5–0–40–0; Sehwag 2–1–8–1.

India

V. Sehwag b Harvey	35	A. Kumble c Clarke b Williams	5
S. R. Tendulkar c Ponting b Symonds	63	L. Balaji not out	0
*S. C. Ganguly run out	82		
V. V. S. Laxman c Clarke b Symonds	16	B 1, l-b 8, w 11, n-b 1	21
†R. Dravid c Harvey b Clarke	16		
Yuvraj Singh c Clarke b Harvey	25	1/103 (1) 2/134 (2) (49 overs) 270
S. B. Bangar c Ponting b Harvey	3	3/168 (4) 4/195 (5)
A. B. Agarkar c Clarke b Gillespie	1	5/257 (6) 6/257 (3) 7/260 (8)
I. K. Pathan c Hayden b Williams	3	8/263 (7) 9/266 (9) 10/270 (10)

Bowling: Gillespie 10–1–50–1; Williams 9–0–52–2; Bichel 6–0–38–0; Harvey 10–1–52–3; Symonds 10–0–47–2; Clarke 4–0–22–1.

Umpires: S. A. Bucknor (West Indies) and S. J. A. Taufel.
Third umpire: R. L. Parry.   Referee: C. H. Lloyd (West Indies).

AUSTRALIA v ZIMBABWE

At Sydney, January 11, 2004 (day/night). Australia won by 99 runs. Australia 6 pts. Toss: Australia.

Brad Williams, another blond bomber in the Brett Lee mould, snatched five for 22 to secure Australia a crushing victory and a bonus point. Batting first, they were in trouble at 118 for five as Zimbabwe bowled with spirit and threw themselves around in the field. Then Symonds and Clarke – for the second time in two games – put the innings back on track, this time with a 66-run stand. Symonds hit a measured 42, Clarke a more rapid 40 from 57 balls, though 225 was the lowest 50-over total Australia had made against Zimbabwe. It still proved more than enough. Zimbabwe lost their top five for 17 (four to Williams), and although Taibu and Streak shared a 73-run stand, they never posed much of a threat.

Man of the Match: B. A. Williams.   *Attendance:* 20,538.

Australia

†A. C. Gilchrist c Taibu b Blignaut	34	A. J. Bichel not out	11	
M. L. Hayden b Streak	14	J. N. Gillespie not out	1	
*R. T. Ponting c Carlisle b Blignaut	21	L-b 4, w 6, n-b 6	16	
D. R. Martyn c and b Flower	21			
A. Symonds c Hondo b Ervine	42	1/42 (2) 2/73 (3) (8 wkts, 50 overs)	225	
M. G. Bevan c and b Flower	3	3/77 (1) 4/112 (4)		
M. J. Clarke c Sibanda b Ervine	40	5/118 (6) 6/184 (5)		
I. J. Harvey c and b Ervine	22	7/192 (7) 8/222 (8)		

B. A. Williams did not bat.

Bowling: Streak 10–2–36–1; Hondo 5–1–35–0; Ervine 10–0–53–3; Blignaut 5–0–21–2; Price 10–0–34–0; Flower 10–0–42–2.

Zimbabwe

V. Sibanda c Williams b Gillespie	7	R. W. Price b Gillespie	0	
S. V. Carlisle c Hayden b Williams	1	D. T. Hondo not out	1	
M. A. Vermeulen b Williams	5			
G. W. Flower lbw b Williams	0	B 1, l-b 6, w 12	19	
S. Matsikenyeri c Gilchrist b Williams	0			
†T. Taibu c Gilchrist b Symonds	29	1/2 (2) 2/13 (1) 3/13 (4) (37.3 overs)	126	
*H. H. Streak st Gilchrist b Clarke	46	4/14 (5) 5/17 (3) 6/90 (6)		
S. M. Ervine c Ponting b Symonds	14	7/119 (8) 8/122 (7)		
A. M. Blignaut c Ponting b Williams	4	9/124 (10) 10/126 (9)		

Bowling: Gillespie 8–0–21–2; Williams 8.3–2–22–5; Bichel 6–2–24–0; Harvey 4–0–14–0; Symonds 6–1–24–2; Clarke 5–0–14–1.

Umpires: R. E. Koertzen (South Africa) and S. J. A. Taufel.
Third umpire: R. L. Parry.   Referee: C. H. Lloyd (West Indies).

INDIA v ZIMBABWE

At Hobart, January 14, 2004. India won by seven wickets. India 6 pts. Toss: Zimbabwe.

Sehwag grabbed a catch and two wickets and batted with his inimitable mixture of method and madness to score a quickfire 90 and run the opposition to ground almost single-handedly. Almost the only thing Zimbabwe won in this game was the toss. Choosing to bat, they subsided to 114 for six before Streak and Ervine restored a shred or two of respectability. Those shreds were ripped off as Sehwag, launching five sixes and five fours, and Tendulkar clattered 129 for the first wicket. With the result a formality, Ganguly, who contributed a 26-ball 32, took the opportunity to shuffle the batting order, but Badani did not grab his chance.

Man of the Match: V. Sehwag.   *Attendance:* 3,109.

Zimbabwe

V. Sibanda run out	12	S. M. Ervine not out	48	
S. V. Carlisle lbw b Sehwag	36			
S. Matsikenyeri c Badani b Pathan	9	L-b 4, w 6, n-b 1	11	
M. A. Vermeulen b Kumble	2			
G. W. Flower c and b Sehwag	15	1/14 (1) 2/36 (3) (6 wkts, 50 overs)	208	
†T. Taibu b Badani	16	3/48 (4) 4/78 (2)		
*H. H. Streak not out	59	5/83 (5) 6/115 (6)		

A. M. Blignaut, R. W. Price and D. T. Hondo did not bat.

Bowling: Agarkar 8–2–39–0; Pathan 8–0–30–1; Balaji 7–2–26–0; Kumble 10–1–38–1; Sehwag 10–0–40–2; Badani 7–0–31–1.

India

V. Sehwag c Flower b Price	....	90
S. R. Tendulkar b Ervine	....	44
H. K. Badani c Taibu b Hondo	....	15
V. V. S. Laxman not out	....	13
*S. C. Ganguly not out	....	32
L-b 4, w 7, n-b 6	....	17

1/130 (2) 2/158 (1) (3 wkts, 37.4 overs) 211
3/172 (3)

†R. Dravid, Yuvraj Singh, A. B. Agarkar, I. K. Pathan, A. Kumble and L. Balaji did not bat.

Bowling: Streak 5–2–23–0; Hondo 8–0–39–1; Ervine 8–0–42–1; Blignaut 5–0–28–0; Price 10–0–67–1; Flower 1.4–0–8–0.

Umpires: S. A. Bucknor (West Indies) and P. D. Parker.
Third umpire: S. J. Davis. Referee: C. H. Lloyd (West Indies)

AUSTRALIA v ZIMBABWE

At Hobart, January 16, 2004. Australia won by 148 runs. Australia 6 pts. Toss: Australia.

Gilchrist, who had hardly got bat on ball all summer, now got a lot of bat on the 126 balls he faced. His 172, including 13 fours and three sixes, fell one short of the record one-day score for Australia, set by Mark Waugh against West Indies at Melbourne in 2000-01. And when Gilchrist reached 150 from his 110th ball, making it the fastest international 150, he also reached 6,000 runs in limited-overs internationals. The middle order registered three ducks and a seven but, with the top four rattling up 319, Australia closed at 344 – a total that shut the opposition out of the match. When Zimbabwe batted, they did so with the ineptitude that typified their recent form: half the side had gone with the score at 93. Not for the first time, Streak had to carry the team, following his three wickets with a combative 64.

Man of the Match: A. C. Gilchrist.   *Attendance:* 12,715.

Australia

†A. C. Gilchrist b Ervine	....	172	A. J. Bichel b Streak	....	0
M. L. Hayden c Sibanda b Streak	....	63	G. B. Hogg not out	....	6
*R. T. Ponting c Matsikenyeri b Flower	.	37	B 1, l-b 5, w 4, n-b 2	......	12
D. R. Martyn not out	....	47			
A. Symonds run out	....	0	1/140 (2) 2/246 (3) (7 wkts, 50 overs) 344		
M. G. Bevan c Streak b Ervine	......	7	3/310 (1) 4/310 (5)		
M. J. Clarke c Vermeulen b Streak	....	0	5/326 (6) 6/332 (7) 7/333 (8)		

B. Lee and B. A. Williams did not bat.

Bowling: Streak 10–1–50–3; Hondo 6–0–41–0; Blignaut 8–0–66–0; Ervine 9–0–65–2; Price 10–0–59–0; Flower 6–0–40–1; Matsikenyeri 1–0–17–0.

Zimbabwe

D. D. Ebrahim c Gilchrist b Symonds	..	21	S. Matsikenyeri not out	....	1
V. Sibanda c Gilchrist b Lee	....	1			
M. A. Vermeulen c Gilchrist b Williams	.	1	L-b 11, w 5	....	16
G. W. Flower run out	....	40			
S. M. Ervine c Bichel b Hogg	....	8	1/15 (2) 2/19 (3) (6 wkts, 50 overs) 196		
*H. H. Streak not out	....	64	3/36 (1) 4/52 (5)		
†T. Taibu c Hayden b Bichel	....	44	5/93 (4) 6/195 (7)		

A. M. Blignaut, R. W. Price and D. T. Hondo did not bat.

Bowling: Lee 10–1–29–1; Williams 8–0–25–1; Bichel 9–0–31–1; Symonds 10–0–48–1; Hogg 10–0–36–1; Clarke 3–0–16–0.

Umpires: R. E. Koertzen (South Africa) and S. J. Davis.
Third umpire: P. D. Parker. Referee: C. H. Lloyd (West Indies).

AUSTRALIA v INDIA

At Brisbane, January 18, 2004 (day/night). India won by 19 runs. India 5 pts, Australia 1 pt. Toss: India. One-day international debut: R. S. Gavaskar.

India's highly rated top order gave a polished performance to give them their first one-day win over Australia in Australia for 12 years. Tendulkar, cramped by an ankle injury, refused a runner and had to cut back on twos – but he cracked eight magnificent boundaries for 86; Laxman played only orthodox cricket shots, all of them delightful, for an unbeaten 103; Dravid made an unobtrusive 74 from just 64 balls; and India passed 300 for the first time on Australian soil. Lee's ten overs cost 83. In their reply, Australia got off to a galloping start – they were 86 for one in the 11th over – but then slowed to a canter, and finally lost too many wickets. Hayden hit an imperious run-a-ball 109, but his departure, at 204 for five in the 34th over, spelt the end. On debut, Rohan Gavaskar, son of Sunil, bowled nine overs of left-arm spin for 56 but had his moment of glory with his fifth ball when he brought off a fine diving return catch to dismiss Symonds.

Man of the Match: V. V. S. Laxman.   *Attendance:* 35,052.

India

*S. C. Ganguly c and b Williams	18	R. S. Gavaskar not out	2
S. R. Tendulkar c and b Symonds	86	B 4, l-b 2, w 6, n-b 3	15
V. V. S. Laxman not out	103		
†R. Dravid c Williams b Harvey	74	1/37 (1) 2/147 (2) (4 wkts, 50 overs) 303
Yuvraj Singh b Lee.	5	3/280 (4) 4/295 (5)	

H. K. Badani, I. K. Pathan, A. Kumble, L. Balaji and A. Nehra did not bat.

Bowling: Gillespie 10–0–40–0; Williams 8–0–40–1; Lee 10–0–83–1; Harvey 10–0–61–1; Symonds 8–0–47–1; Clarke 4–0–26–0.

Australia

†A. C. Gilchrist c Balaji b Pathan	21	J. N. Gillespie c Pathan b Balaji	6
M. L. Hayden c Dravid b Pathan.	109	B. A. Williams run out	0
*R. T. Ponting c Laxman b Balaji	7		
D. R. Martyn c Yuvraj Singh b Balaji . .	1	B 1, l-b 8, w 12, n-b 2.	18
A. Symonds c and b Gavaskar	20		
M. J. Clarke c Dravid b Pathan.	42	1/46 (1) 2/86 (3) 3/94 (4) (49.4 overs) 284
M. G. Bevan not out.	41	4/141 (5) 5/204 (2)	
I. J. Harvey c Gavaskar b Nehra	13	6/224 (6) 7/249 (8)	
B. Lee c Kumble b Balaji	6	8/266 (9) 9/282 (10) 10/284 (11)	

Bowling: Nehra 10–0–53–1; Pathan 9.4–0–64–3; Balaji 10–0–48–4; Kumble 10–0–53–0; Gavaskar 9–0–56–1; Ganguly 1–0–6–0.

Umpires: S. A. Bucknor (West Indies) and P. D. Parker.
Third umpire: S. J. Davis.   Referee: C. H. Lloyd (West Indies).

INDIA v ZIMBABWE

At Brisbane, January 20, 2004 (day/night). India won by 24 runs. India 5 pts, Zimbabwe 1 pt. Toss: India.

India stumbled en route to victory in a game they found more problematic than expected, and Zimbabwe picked up their first point of the series. But the game was overshadowed by a horrific injury to Vermeulen, who suffered a hairline fracture of the skull for the second time in a year: he had suffered a similar injury in the nets at the World Cup ten months earlier. Vermeulen top-edged a ball from Pathan into his head: it squeezed between his helmet and visor and he had to undergo a three-and-a-half-hour operation to reconstruct the impact area above his right eye. India were without Tendulkar, who had injured his ankle in the win against Australia, and were in some trouble before Dravid and Yuvraj Singh rebuilt the innings with a stand of 114 in 24 overs, helping India to a respectable, if gettable, total. Zimbabwe then stumbled too, lurching to 148 for six – effectively seven after Vermeulen was hurt. Ervine and Ebrahim kept Zimbabwe in the game but could not quite sustain the pace. Dravid was fined half his match fee for rubbing a cough lozenge on to the shiny side of the ball. John Wright, India's coach, maintained it was "an innocent mistake".

Man of the Match: Yuvraj Singh.   *Attendance:* 9,638.

Through the batsman's defences: Mark Vermeulen is in agony after top-edging the ball on to his head.

Picture by Jonathon Wood, Getty Images

India

†P. A. Patel b Streak	19	I. K. Pathan not out	5
*S. C. Ganguly c Hondo b Ervine	33		
V. V. S. Laxman c Taibu b Ervine	12	L-b 3, w 6, n-b 1	10
R. Dravid c Streak b Ervine	84		
Yuvraj Singh b Price	69	1/41 (1) 2/67 (2) (6 wkts, 50 overs) 255	
R. S. Gavaskar b Streak	22	3/74 (3) 4/188 (5)	
H. K. Badani not out	1	5/249 (6) 6/249 (4)	

A. Kumble, L. Balaji and A. Nehra did not bat.

Bowling: Streak 10–1–48–2; Blignaut 7–1–44–0; Hondo 6–0–39–0; Ervine 10–0–47–3; Price 10–0–43–1; Flower 7–0–31–0.

Zimbabwe

G. W. Flower c Laxman b Nehra	36	R. W. Price not out	18
M. A. Vermeulen retired hurt	14	D. T. Hondo run out	0
T. J. Friend run out	7		
S. V. Carlisle c Patel b Ganguly	34	L-b 11, w 13, n-b 1	25
A. M. Blignaut c Yuvraj Singh b Balaji	1		
*H. H. Streak b Ganguly	3	1/66 (3) 2/70 (1) 3/73 (5) (47.1 overs) 231	
†T. Taibu c Laxman b Ganguly	15	4/81 (6) 5/128 (7)	
S. M. Ervine c Ganguly b Balaji	39	6/148 (4) 7/197 (8)	
D. D. Ebrahim c Ganguly b Pathan	39	8/231 (9) 9/231 (11)	

Vermeulen retired hurt at 28.

Bowling: Nehra 9–1–44–1; Pathan 9–2–40–1; Balaji 9.1–0–37–2; Kumble 10–1–44–0; Ganguly 10–0–55–3.

Umpires: R. E. Koertzen (South Africa) and S. J. Davis.
Third umpire: P. D. Parker. Referee: C. H. Lloyd (West Indies).

AUSTRALIA v INDIA

At Sydney, January 22, 2004 (day/night). Australia won by two wickets (D/L method). Australia 5 pts, India 1 pt. Toss: India.

Lee hit a last-over six as Australia, arguably helped by Duckworth/Lewis recalculations, scampered home with a ball to spare in the tightest game of the series. Earlier, Laxman hit his second century against Australia within five days – all four of his limited-overs international hundreds had come against them – though his innings was leisurely compared to Yuvraj Singh's 122-ball 139. Even with both Tendulkar and Sehwag injured, India set a formidable target. But Gilchrist reached 50 from 31 balls, as if aiming to settle matters before the forecast storm arrived. It came, and, when play resumed, he fell five short of a blistering century. Ponting stroked a brisk 42, but wickets fell regularly, and 11 were needed off the final over, from Balaji. Lee hit a six off the fourth ball to level the scores, and clinched victory off the next. In the second over of the day, Gilchrist became the first wicket-keeper to 300 dismissals in one-day internationals; Ganguly, his victim, was later fined for India's shocking over-rate, which referee Clive Lloyd said crossed the line into time-wasting.

Man of the Match: Yuvraj Singh.   *Attendance:* 39,088.

India

*S. C. Ganguly c Gilchrist b Lee	1	R. S. Gavaskar not out	2
†P. A. Patel c Gilchrist b Gillespie	28	L-b 1, w 5, n-b 2	8
V. V. S. Laxman not out	106		
R. Dravid c Gilchrist b Bichel	12	1/1 (1) 2/63 (2) (4 wkts, 50 overs) 296	
Yuvraj Singh b Lee	139	3/80 (4) 4/293 (5)	

H. K. Badani, A. B. Agarkar, I. K. Pathan, M. Kartik and L. Balaji did not bat.

Bowling: Gillespie 10–0–50–1; Lee 9–0–46–2; Bichel 9–0–60–1; Harvey 10–0–68–0; Symonds 7–0–42–0; Clarke 5–0–29–0.

Australia

†A. C. Gilchrist c and b Kartik	95	A. J. Bichel not out	2
S. M. Katich c Ganguly b Pathan	2	B. Lee not out	12
*R. T. Ponting c Patel b Pathan	42	L-b 7, w 15	22
D. R. Martyn c Patel b Pathan	0		—
A. Symonds c Agarkar b Ganguly	16	1/24 (2) 2/150 (3) (8 wkts, 33.5 overs) 225
M. G. Bevan b Ganguly	12	3/150 (4) 4/154 (1)
M. J. Clarke c Badani b Ganguly	21	5/176 (5) 6/195 (6)
I. J. Harvey run out	1	7/202 (8) 8/210 (7)

J. N. Gillespie did not bat.

Bowling: Agarkar 7–1–47–0; Pathan 7–1–51–3; Balaji 5.5–0–40–0; Ganguly 7–0–41–3; Kartik 7–0–39–1.

Umpires: S. A. Bucknor (West Indies) and D. J. Harper.
Third umpire: S. J. A. Taufel.   Referee: C. H. Lloyd (West Indies).

INDIA v ZIMBABWE

At Adelaide, January 24, 2004 (day/night). India won by three runs. India 5 pts, Zimbabwe 1 pt.
Toss: India.

Laxman had another peerless day. After a run-filled Test series and two one-day hundreds against Australia, he hit another, against this less testing attack, and also held two spectacular catches as India, pushed to the brink for two games running, shoved Zimbabwe aside in a thrilling, final-over finish. Dravid and Gavaskar gave Laxman, who faced 138 balls, good support, enabling India – three down for four at one stage – to rattle up 280. But Zimbabwe's reply was built on resolve, determination and two classic innings: an even-ball hundred from Ervine and a slightly slower one from Carlisle. It was the first time two batsmen had made centuries in a Zimbabwe one-day innings but, as in India's last game against Australia, twin hundreds could not bring victory. Ervine and Carlisle's beautifully paced stand was worth 202 – a Zimbabwean record for any wicket – but once Ervine was run out at the end of the 46th over, with 33 needed, the chase lost momentum. The result confirmed that Australia and India would contest the finals.

Man of the Match: V. V. S. Laxman.   *Attendance:* 8,680.

India

S. B. Bangar c Carlisle b Streak	0	A. B. Agarkar not out	12
†P. A. Patel c Taibu b Streak	0	I. K. Pathan not out	5
V. V. S. Laxman c Friend b Hondo	131	L-b 4, w 8, n-b 4	16
*S. C. Ganguly c Ebrahim b Blignaut	1		—
R. Dravid c Blignaut b Price	56	1/0 (1) 2/3 (2) (7 wkts, 50 overs) 280
R. S. Gavaskar c Blignaut b Hondo	54	3/4 (4) 4/137 (5)
H. K. Badani b Streak	5	5/255 (6) 6/261 (7) 7/271 (3)

M. Kartik and L. Balaji did not bat.

Bowling: Streak 10–1–53–3; Blignaut 5–0–25–1; Ervine 6–0–48–0; Hondo 10–0–59–2; Price 10–0–43–1; Flower 9–0–48–0.

Zimbabwe

V. Sibanda c and b Balaji	12	D. D. Ebrahim not out	2
G. W. Flower c Patel b Agarkar	10		
I. J. Friend c Laxman b Agarkar	0	B 3, l-b 12, w 12	27
S. V. Carlisle b Kartik b Agarkar	109		—
S. M. Ervine run out	100	1/14 (2) 2/25 (3) (6 wkts, 50 overs) 277
A. M. Blignaut c Laxman b Bangar	12	3/46 (1) 4/248 (5)
*H. H. Streak not out	5	5/261 (4) 6/274 (6)

†T. Taibu, R. W. Price and D. T. Hondo did not bat.

Bowling: Agarkar 10–0–39–3; Pathan 10–0–47–0; Balaji 10–1–52–1; Bangar 8–0–42–1; Kartik 7–0–49–0; Ganguly 5–0–33–0.

Umpires: R. E. Koertzen (South Africa) and D. J. Harper.
Third umpire: S. J. Davis.   Referee: C. H. Lloyd (West Indies).

AUSTRALIA v ZIMBABWE

At Adelaide, January 26, 2004 (day/night). Australia won by 13 runs. Australia 5 pts, Zimbabwe 1 pt. Toss: Australia.

Australia took advantage of a meaningless game to rest Gilchrist and shuffle their batting order. Martyn's promotion to open was not a success, but Bevan's move to No. 4 was, even though he had broken a rib in practice. After four failures from five innings, he anchored Australia's total with 75. Meanwhile, Ponting exploded, hitting 11 fours to Bevan's six. Zimbabwe were set a target that was possible but, given their form so far, improbable. Flower stroked his way to 94 but had little support from the top order. A gutsy 31 not out from Blignaut narrowed the margin of defeat, but Australia never looked in danger.

Man of the Match: G. W. Flower.   *Attendance:* 27,612.

Australia

M. L. Hayden c Ebrahim b Blignaut . . .	20	
D. R. Martyn c Ebrahim b Streak	9	
*R. T. Ponting run out	63	
M. G. Bevan c Ervine b Hondo	75	
M. J. Clarke run out	36	
A. Symonds c Hondo b Streak	34	
†B. J. Haddin lbw b Streak	14	

G. B. Hogg not out	1
B. Lee not out	6
B 1, l-b 9, w 9, n-b 2	21
1/25 (2) 2/84 (1) (7 wkts, 50 overs)	279
3/128 (3) 4/205 (5)	
5/230 (4) 6/271 (7) 7/272 (6)	

J. N. Gillespie and B. A. Williams did not bat.

Bowling: Streak 10–0–45–3; Blignaut 9–0–53–1; Ervine 5–0–41–0; Hondo 6–0–45–1; Price 10–0–40–0; Flower 10–0–45–0.

Zimbabwe

G. W. Flower c Haddin b Gillespie	94	
†T. Taibu b Williams	9	
T. J. Friend b Lee	8	
S. V. Carlisle c sub (I. J. Harvey) b Williams .	15	
S. M. Ervine c Lee b Hogg	33	
*H. H. Streak c and b Symonds	28	
D. D. Ebrahim st Haddin b Symonds . . .	11	
S. Matsikenyeri b Clarke	5	

A. M. Blignaut not out	31
R. W. Price not out	13
B 11, l-b 1, w 5, n-b 2	19
1/29 (2) 2/55 (3) (8 wkts, 50 overs)	266
3/90 (4) 4/159 (5)	
5/169 (1) 6/191 (7)	
7/206 (8) 8/229 (6)	

D. T. Hondo did not bat.

Bowling: Gillespie 10–2–40–1; Lee 8–0–32–1; Williams 8–1–38–2; Hogg 10–0–40–1; Clarke 7–0–57–1; Symonds 7–0–47–2.

Umpires: S. A. Bucknor (West Indies) and S. J. Davis.
Third umpire: D. J. Harper. Referee: C. H. Lloyd (West Indies).

AUSTRALIA v ZIMBABWE

At Melbourne, January 29, 2004 (day/night). No result. Australia 3 pts, Zimbabwe 3 pts. Toss: Zimbabwe. One-day international debut: N. B. Mahwire.

Persistent rain ruined this match but, with the finalists long since decided, it scarcely mattered. The weather did allow time for the Australian innings – and also gave Zimbabwe as many points as in their past six games combined. Bevan, still suffering from the broken rib that would rule him out of the rest of the series, produced another rescue act with a run-a-ball 56, while Martyn – under pressure after a string of poor scores – showed a glimmer of his true ability in a stroke-filled 42. Next day he also showed that the pressure might have been getting to him: leaving the team hotel he made an offensive gesture to a TV cameraman, earning him a reprimand from Ponting.

Attendance: 15,218.

Australia

M. L. Hayden b Hondo	23	B. Lee c Blignaut b Ervine	3
D. R. Martyn lbw b Streak	42	B. A. Williams not out	0
*R. T. Ponting c Mahwire b Price	35		
M. J. Clarke b Mahwire	11	L-b 7, w 4, n-b 4	15
I. J. Harvey run out	23		
M. G. Bevan run out	56	1/59 (2) 2/69 (1) (9 wkts, 50 overs) 263	
†B. J. Haddin b Streak	32	3/97 (4) 4/139 (5)	
G. B. Hogg run out	0	5/155 (3) 6/213 (7)	
A. J. Bichel not out	23	7/214 (8) 8/252 (6) 9/257 (10)	

Bowling: Streak 10–0–47–2; Blignaut 4–1–23–0; Hondo 4–0–35–1; Mahwire 6–1–35–1; Ervine 7–0–36–1; Flower 9–0–42–0; Price 10–0–38–1.

Zimbabwe

V. Sibanda, G. W. Flower, S. V. Carlisle, S. M. Ervine, †T. Taibu, *H. H. Streak, D. D. Ebrahim, A. M. Blignaut, R. W. Price, D. T. Hondo and N. B. Mahwire.

Umpires: R. E. Koertzen (South Africa) and P. D. Parker.
Third umpire: R. L. Parry. Referee: C. H. Lloyd (West Indies).

AUSTRALIA v INDIA

At Perth, February 1, 2004. Australia won by five wickets. Australia 6 pts. Toss: India. One-day international debut: M. E. K. Hussey.

Australia produced a slick performance in a dress rehearsal for the final. With Ponting rested and Bevan injured, Mike Hussey made his debut on his home ground after a decent – if unspectacular – season for Western Australia. Tendulkar and Sehwag returned for India, who might have looked the stronger team on paper, but on the pitch were thrashed. On a WACA strip offering as much pace and bounce as ever, Lee bowled magnificently. In the face of his genuine speed and movement, the Indian batting keeled over, losing their sixth wicket at 101. Australia also lost quick wickets before Gilchrist and Symonds, in a merciless assault, put on 122 in 16 overs. Australia thundered home with 18 overs to spare.

Man of the Match: A. C. Gilchrist. *Attendance:* 18,858.

India

V. Sehwag c Lee b Gillespie	32	M. Kartik not out	32
S. R. Tendulkar c Hayden b Lee	5	L. Balaji run out	11
V. V. S. Laxman c Gilchrist b Lee	1		
†R. Dravid c Hussey b Williams	13	L-b 7, w 16, n-b 3	26
*S. C. Ganguly c Gilchrist b Bichel	1		
Yuvraj Singh c Gilchrist b Symonds	47	1/20 (2) 2/32 (3) 3/50 (1) (49 overs) 203	
R. S. Gavaskar b Lee	6	4/57 (5) 5/79 (4)	
A. B. Agarkar run out	9	6/101 (7) 7/129 (8)	
I. K. Pathan c Bichel b Symonds	20	8/142 (6) 9/172 (9) 10/203 (11)	

Bowling: Gillespie 10–0–51–1; Lee 10–2–22–3; Williams 7–2–23–1; Bichel 7–0–44–1; Symonds 10–0–37–2; Hussey 3–0–15–0; Clarke 2–0–4–0.

Australia

*†A. C. Gilchrist c Balaji b Pathan	75	M. E. K. Hussey not out	17
M. L. Hayden c Gavaskar b Agarkar	0	B 1, l-b 2, w 14	17
D. R. Martyn c Laxman b Agarkar	2		
M. J. Clarke c Sehwag b Balaji	2	1/14 (2) 2/16 (3) (5 wkts, 32 overs) 204	
A. Symonds c Laxman b Pathan	73	3/37 (4) 4/159 (5)	
S. M. Katich not out	18	5/165 (1)	

A. J. Bichel, B. Lee, J. N. Gillespie and B. A. Williams did not bat.

Bowling: Agarkar 9–0–56–2; Pathan 8–0–69–2; Balaji 10–1–37–1; Kartik 5–0–39–0.

Umpires: S. A. Bucknor (West Indies) and D. J. Harper.
Third umpire: S. J. A. Taufel. Referee: C. H. Lloyd (West Indies).

INDIA v ZIMBABWE

At Perth, February 3, 2004 (day/night). India won by four wickets. India 6 pts. Toss: Zimbabwe.
Zimbabwe finished the tournament with another heavy defeat – and without a win in seven completed games. Even so, in a low-voltage match, India's stumbling efforts inspired little confidence ahead of the finals. Pathan, at least, bowled beautifully, grabbing four wickets and confirming that he was India's find of the tour. Zimbabwe found his pace and bounce as testing as India had found Brett Lee's, and could put up only a modest target. However, India lost half the side for 105, and it was left to Badani, playing a sensible, unhurried innings, to see them home.

Man of the Match: I. K. Pathan.   *Attendance:* 4,053.

Zimbabwe

V. Sibanda c Laxman b Pathan	0	A. M. Blignaut c Sehwag b Nehra	2
†T. Taibu lbw b Pathan	0	R. W. Price c Laxman b Pathan	0
D. D. Ebrahim c Laxman b Pathan	7	N. B. Mahwire not out	8
S. V. Carlisle run out	28	L-b 9, w 15	24
S. M. Ervine c sub (M. Kartik)			
b Bhandari	23	1/0 (1) 2/1 (2) 3/11 (3) (34.4 overs) 135
*H. H. Streak c Laxman b Balaji	6	4/74 (4) 5/79 (5) 6/85 (6)
S. Matsikenyeri c Dravid b Bhandari	36	7/103 (8) 8/114 (9)
T. J. Friend c Gavaskar b Bhandari	1	9/115 (10) 10/135 (7)

Bowling: Pathan 10–1–24–4; Balaji 10–1–32–1; Nehra 7–1–39–1; Bhandari 7.4–0–31–3.

India

V. Sehwag c Matsikenyeri b Blignaut	23	I. K. Pathan not out	3
S. R. Tendulkar c Taibu b Streak	3		
V. V. S. Laxman b Ervine	32	L-b 6, w 15, n-b 2	23
*†R. Dravid b Blignaut	10		
Yuvraj Singh c Friend b Ervine	4	1/28 (2) 2/34 (1) (6 wkts, 30.3 overs) 136
H. K. Badani not out	34	3/61 (4) 4/73 (5)
R. S. Gavaskar run out	4	5/105 (3) 6/115 (7)

L. Balaji, A. Bhandari and A. Nehra did not bat.

Bowling: Streak 7–0–36–1; Blignaut 10–0–41–2; Ervine 8.3–2–29–2; Friend 5–0–24–0.

Umpires: R. E. Koertzen (South Africa) and S. J. A. Taufel.
Third umpire: D. J. Harper.   Referee: C. H. Lloyd (West Indies).

QUALIFYING TABLE

	Played	Won	Lost	No result	Bonus Points	Points	Net run-rate
Australia	8	6	1	1	4	37	1.10
India	8	5	3	0	4	29	0.28
Zimbabwe	8	0	7	1	3	6	–1.32

Win = 5 pts, no result = 3 pts. One bonus point awarded either to the winning team for achieving victory with a run-rate 1.25 times that of the opposition, or to the losing team for denying the winners a bonus point. Net run-rate is calculated by subtracting runs conceded per over from runs scored per over.

AUSTRALIA v INDIA

First Final Match

At Melbourne, February 6, 2004 (day/night). Australia won by seven wickets. Toss: India.

Australia imposed themselves on India, proving – as so often in the recent past – that they were the team for the big occasion. The seam attack bowled intelligently on a largely unresponsive pitch by varying their line, length and pace, and reduced India to 75 for six before a spirited 102-run stand between Agarkar and Badani helped them to pass 200. In reply, the Australian batsmen made their intentions clear right away, crashing 12 boundaries in the first 12 overs. Gilchrist began the onslaught at a rate of around two runs a ball; Ponting then scored 88 off 80 balls with consummate ease. The bowlers were simply incapable of defending a modest total, and defeat came with almost ten overs to spare; in this sort of mood, Australia would have threatened a total of 300 or more.

Man of the Match: R. T. Ponting.   *Attendance:* 44,737.

India

V. Sehwag c Gilchrist b Gillespie	3	A. Kumble run out		2
S. R. Tendulkar b Lee	8	L. Balaji b Gillespie		2
V. V. S. Laxman c Symonds b Williams	24			
†R. Dravid c Hayden b Harvey	12	L-b 6, w 2, n-b 4		12
*S. C. Ganguly c Gilchrist b Harvey	6			
Yuvraj Singh c Gilchrist b Lee	21	1/6 (1) 2/14 (2) 3/48 (3)	(49 overs)	222
H. K. Badani not out	60	4/48 (4) 5/75 (5) 6/75 (6)		
A. B. Agarkar c Lee b Clarke	53	7/177 (8) 8/209 (9)		
I. K. Pathan run out	19	9/217 (10) 10/222 (11)		

Bowling: Gillespie 10–0–39–2; Lee 9–0–34–2; Williams 10–1–38–1; Harvey 10–0–40–2; Symonds 7–0–47–0; Clarke 3–0–18–1.

Australia

†A. C. Gilchrist c Tendulkar b Balaji	38
M. L. Hayden c and b Balaji	50
*R. T. Ponting c Dravid b Balaji	88
D. R. Martyn not out	20
A. Symonds not out	10
B 6, l-b 2, w 8, n-b 2	18

1/48 (1) 2/187 (2)   (3 wkts, 40.1 overs) 224
3/193 (3)

M. J. Clarke, S. M. Katich, I. J. Harvey, B. Lee, J. N. Gillespie and B. A. Williams did not bat.

Bowling: Agarkar 9.1–0–58–0; Balaji 10–0–52–3; Pathan 8–0–36–0; Kumble 7–0–36–0; Sehwag 5–0–29–0; Ganguly 1–0–5–0.

Umpires: S. A. Bucknor (West Indies) and S. J. A. Taufel.
Third umpire: D. J. Harper.   Referee: C. H. Lloyd (West Indies).

AUSTRALIA v INDIA

Second Final Match

At Sydney, February 8, 2004 (day/night). Australia won by 208 runs. Toss: Australia.

For the third time in less than a year these teams met in a tournament final, and for the third time Australia prevailed. In the first of these meetings, at the climax of the World Cup, Australia had made a massive 359 – their highest in one-day internationals – and they equalled that total now. Hayden was lethal in his run-a-ball 126, Martyn kept up the tempo, and it was nicely set up for the savagery of Symonds. He smashed 66 off 39 balls and was largely responsible for 70 coming from the last five overs. Against controlled bowling, India could not offer even token resistance. By the 17th over, they were 59 for six (including Dravid for his first duck for 121 one-day international innings), and no one could pass 30. The margin of 208 was India's second-heaviest defeat by runs in limited-overs cricket – and Australia had wrapped up the VB Series in the most emphatic style.

Man of the Match: M. L. Hayden. *Attendance:* 39,760.
Man of the Series: A. C. Gilchrist.

Australia

†A. C. Gilchrist c Ganguly b Nehra....	29	S. M. Katich not out.............. 11
M. L. Hayden b Tendulkar..........	126	L-b 6, w 15, n-b 2......... 23
*R. T. Ponting c Dravid b Pathan	4	—
D. R. Martyn c Badani b Pathan......	67	1/62 (1) 2/73 (3) (5 wkts, 50 overs) 359
A. Symonds b Nehra..............	66	3/230 (4) 4/248 (2)
M. J. Clarke not out..............	33	5/347 (5)

I. J. Harvey, B. Lee, J. N. Gillespie and B. A. Williams did not bat.

Bowling: Pathan 10–0–75–2; Balaji 9–0–65–0; Nehra 10–0–63–2; Kartik 7–0–51–0; Sehwag 5–0–30–0; Ganguly 1–0–9–0; Tendulkar 8–0–60–1.

India

V. Sehwag c Lee b Gillespie........	12	L. Balaji b Williams.............. 2
S. R. Tendulkar c Lee b Gillespie	27	A. Nehra not out 14
V. V. S. Laxman c and b Lee	5	
*S. C. Ganguly c Symonds b Harvey...	3	L-b 7, w 4, n-b 2 13
†R. Dravid run out...............	0	—
Yuvraj Singh c Gilchrist b Harvey.....	4	1/22 (1) 2/49 (2) 3/49 (3) (33.2 overs) 151
H. K. Badani run out	18	4/52 (5) 5/56 (6) 6/59 (6)
I. K. Pathan b Lee	30	7/99 (7) 8/123 (8)
M. Kartik c Gilchrist b Williams......	23	9/136 (9) 10/151 (10)

Bowling: Gillespie 9–1–52–2; Lee 10–1–39–2; Williams 6.2–1–12–2; Harvey 5–2–30–2; Symonds 3–1–11–0.

Umpires: R. E. Koertzen (South Africa) and D. J. Harper.
Third umpire: S. J. A. Taufel. Referee: C. H. Lloyd (West Indies).

ASIA CUP, 2004

CHARLIE AUSTIN

Improved relations between the governments of India and Pakistan paved the way for the resumption of the Asia Cup in July 2004 after a four-year gap. The 2002 tournament had been a casualty of the animosity between the subcontinental powers but, providing the India–Pakistan rapprochement continued, the Asia Cup was now to be staged every two years. The eighth edition of the one-day jamboree was slotted into a small window in the international calendar and hosted by Sri Lanka, who won the competition for the third time.

As a fund-raising vehicle for the development of Asian cricket, the Asia Cup was a resounding success: some estimates put the price paid by ESPN Star Sports for the broadcasting and sponsorship rights for the 13 matches at a staggering $19m. But as a spectacle, the event struggled. The decision to invite both the United Arab Emirates and Hong Kong was an old one – they had qualified in 2000 to play at the 2002 Asia Cup, had it happened – but a flawed one. The participation of these two sides, as well as a weak Bangladesh team, ensured that of the first six games just one, between Sri Lanka and India, was not utterly predictable. A long-winded three-stage format made matters worse. Those six games made up the first stage, whose main purpose was to weed out the two weakest teams, inevitably the UAE and Hong Kong. But because the second phase involved Bangladesh, the mismatches continued. All told, the outcomes of eight of the tournament's 13 games were, to put it politely, wholly foreseeable. The ICC gave all the matches official one-day international status.

The organisers also foresaw a flood of overseas supporters, but tripling normal ticket prices had an effect even more predictable than much of the cricket – and the anticipated rush did not happen until the final. Then Colombo's first-class hotels and restaurants bulged to the seams with visiting Indians, and prices were too expensive for many locals. The result was that most of the matches were played out in front of depressingly empty stands.

However, local disenchantment with the ticketing was assuaged by the performance of a rejuvenated Sri Lanka. Despite only 90 or so hours to travel from Cairns to Dambulla, switch from five-day to one-day mode, and fight off a flu virus that swept through a tired squad, Sri Lanka still dominated the competition. They deservedly won the final against India, the pre-tournament favourites, thanks to an electric bowling and fielding performance.

Sri Lanka welcomed back Muttiah Muralitharan, who had opted out of the Australia tour after the controversy surrounding his *doosra*, but their success was built on an all-round team effort. Nuwan Zoysa was a revelation with the new ball, winning two match awards and playing an important role in the final, as did the leg-spinner Upul Chandana. All the batsmen chipped in, including Sanath Jayasuriya, who ended a lean one-day run with back-to-back hundreds, while at times the fielding, particularly the catching, was brilliant.

After a three-month break, India's return to international cricket proved disappointing. They were hampered by injuries to Zaheer Khan (hamstring) and V. V. S. Laxman (bruised knee), and the absence of specialist batting back-up in the squad unbalanced the team. Although Irfan Pathan was the most successful bowler in the competition, with 14 wickets – Sachin Tendulkar came next with 12 – their fast bowlers were often wayward. Their star-studded batting line-up coughed and spluttered through the games, struggling most when chasing, never easy in the day/night matches as the new ball zipped around after dark.

Pakistan, playing their first tournament with Bob Woolmer as coach, unsurprisingly breezed past Hong Kong and Bangladesh in the first phase. But in the second they found Sri Lanka a different proposition and were skittled out for just 122 – their lowest in 100 meetings. Pakistan bounced back in the India game, winning convincingly thanks to a magnificent 143 from Shoaib Malik, the tournament's highest run-scorer. But crucially, it was not quite convincing enough: India's ninth-wicket pair filched a bye off the last ball, and with it a bonus point. Had they not, Pakistan would almost certainly have reached the final.

Improved performances earlier in the year against Zimbabwe and West Indies should have given Bangladesh a fillip. Arriving early for extra time to acclimatise was sensible, and Dav Whatmore's intimate knowledge of conditions after six years coaching Sri Lanka should also have helped. However, they were hindered by an injury to their opener, Javed Omar, their only batsman to make an impression. Morale also suffered when, after two encouraging performances, the left-arm spinner Abdur Razzaq was reported for a suspect action. In the end, what self-belief they had dripped away, and they left with a meaningless victory over Hong Kong and not much else.

Hong Kong's first appearances in one-day international cricket produced two unsurprisingly heavy defeats, but the UAE's disciplined and spirited performance against India and Sri Lanka – they lost to both by a margin of 116 runs – was an eye-opener. A 25-day training camp before the tournament paid dividends and, having already won the 2004 Asian Cricket Council Trophy, the UAE, along with the hosts, were perhaps the only sides to make gains in this tournament.

Note: Matches in this section were not first-class.

GROUP A

BANGLADESH v HONG KONG

At Sinhalese Sports Club, Colombo, July 16, 2004. Bangladesh won by 116 runs. Bangladesh 6 pts. Toss: Hong Kong. One-day international debuts: Abdur Razzaq; Hong Kong (all).

Hong Kong's first senior game gave Bangladesh just their second win in 52 completed one-day internationals, spanning more than five years. However, the Bangladeshi batting looked worryingly shaky against such inexperienced opponents. The exception was Javed Omar, who constructed a steady 68 from 113 balls before being run out. The Hong Kong batsmen found life even trickier as Abdur Razzaq, a tight left-arm spinner, grabbed three for 17 on debut. Captained by the 43-year-old Rahul Sharma, they were hustled out for 105. (Sharma was the third-oldest player to make a one-day international debut, beaten only by 47-year-old Nolan Clarke of Holland and Norman Gifford of England, who was six days short of his 45th birthday.) Hong Kong's last wicket fell to Mohammad Rafique, who had unwittingly embarked upon an 11th over. The incident caused alarm at the ICC – terrified that something similar could occur in a close match – who reprimanded the umpires, saying both they and the third umpire should have been keeping count, and communicating. The umpires said the official scorers had lost track.

Man of the Match: Javed Omar.

Bangladesh

Javed Omar run out	68
Mohammad Ashraful c French	
b Afzaal Haider .	9
*Habibul Bashar c Sharma	
b Najeeb Aamer .	32
Rajin Saleh c Smart b Ilyas Gul	10
Alok Kapali lbw b Ilyas Gul	2
Mushfiqur Rahman c Smart b Ilyas Gul .	18
†Khaled Mashud c Najeeb Aamer	
b Khalid Khan .	26

Mohammad Rafique b French	3
Khaled Mahmud run out	22
Tapash Baisya not out	6
Abdur Razzaq not out	5
L-b 4, w 13, n-b 3	20

1/10 (?) 2/95 (3)   (9 wkts, 50 overs) 221
3/123 (4) 4/127 (5)
5/145 (1) 6/167 (6)
7/174 (8) 8/198 (7) 9/212 (9)

Bowling: Afzaal Haider 8–1–31–1; Khalid Khan 8–1–31–1; Lamsam 4–0–20–0; Najeeb Aamer 10–2–38–1; French 10–0–51–1; Ilyas Gul 10–0–46–3.

Hong Kong

†T. Smart lbw b Abdur Razzaq	9
M. Cheruparambil b Mushfiqur Rahman .	0
A. N. French c and b Mushfiqur Rahman	10
Tabarak Dar lbw b Khaled Mahmud . . .	20
J. P. R. Lamsam c Khaled Mashud	
b Khaled Mahmud .	8
*R. Sharma c Khaled Mashud	
b Mohammad Rafique .	10
Ilyas Gul c Mohammad Rafique	
b Abdur Razzaq .	16
Najeeb Aamer run out	0

S. B. Lama not out	16
Afzaal Haider lbw b Abdur Razzaq	0
Khalid Khan c Khaled Mashud	
b Mohammad Rafique .	3
L-b 3, w 9, n-b 1	13

1/2 (2) 2/15 (3) 3/38 (1)   (45.2 overs) 105
4/49 (4) 5/65 (5) 6/65 (6)
7/67 (8) 8/96 (7)
9/98 (10) 10/105 (11)

Bowling: Tapash Baisya 8–2–21–0; Mushfiqur Rahman 8–3–21–2; Abdur Razzaq 9–2–17–3; Khaled Mahmud 7–2–17–2; Mohammad Rafique 10.2–3–21–2; Alok Kapali 3–1–5–0.

Umpires: E. A. R. de Silva (Sri Lanka) and T. H. Wijewardene (Sri Lanka).
Third umpire: A. V. Jayaprakash (India).   Referee: R. S. Mahanama (Sri Lanka).

BANGLADESH v PAKISTAN

At Sinhalese Sports Club, Colombo, July 17, 2004. Pakistan won by 76 runs. Pakistan 6 pts. Toss: Pakistan.

Bob Woolmer, the former England player and South Africa coach, made a successful start to his tenure with Pakistan, who strolled to a straightforward win. Yasir Hameed won the match award for a controlled 102 from 123 balls on a slow pitch, and Shoaib Akhtar silenced the long-running debate over his fitness with three for 30 from a full ten overs. Bangladesh's faltering run-chase was stopped in its tracks when Javed Omar departed at 114 for four in the 30th over. For the second game running, he was run out in the 60s; each time he was comfortably Bangladesh's top-scorer. In his second international, Abdur Razzaq took another two wickets, only to discover afterwards that he had been reported to the ICC for a suspect action.

Man of the Match: Yasir Hameed.

Pakistan

Yasir Hameed c Mushfiqur Rahman		Abdul Razzaq	
b Khaled Mahmud .	102	c and b Mohammad Rafique .	5
Imran Farhat lbw b Abdur Razzaq	28	†Moin Khan not out	3
Shoaib Malik run out	3	L-b 5, w 6	11
*Inzamam-ul-Haq st Khaled Mashud			
b Abdur Razzaq .	58	1/86 (2) 2/91 (3) (6 wkts, 50 overs) 257	
Yousuf Youhana not out	29	3/200 (4) 4/200 (1)	
Younis Khan b Tapash Baisya.	18	5/241 (6) 6/248 (7)	

Mohammad Sami, Shoaib Akhtar and Danish Kaneria did not bat.

Bowling: Tapash Baisya 10–0–59–1; Mushfiqur Rahman 10–1–50–0; Abdur Razzaq 10–1–36–2; Khaled Mahmud 10–0–56–1; Mohammad Rafique 10–0–51–1.

Bangladesh

Javed Omar run out	62	Khaled Mahmud c Abdul Razzaq	
Mohammad Ashraful c Moin Khan		b Shoaib Akhtar .	0
b Mohammad Sami .	12	Tapash Baisya b Shoaib Malik	13
*Habibul Bashar lbw b Mohammad Sami	2	Abdur Razzaq not out	1
Rajin Saleh c and b Shoaib Malik	15		
Alok Kapali c Yasir Hameed		L-b 9, w 6, n-b 5	20
b Imran Farhat .	28		
Mushfiqur Rahman lbw b Shoaib Akhtar.	2	1/48 (2) 2/52 (3) 3/97 (4) (45.2 overs) 181	
†Khaled Mashud b Shoaib Akhtar	8	4/114 (1) 5/118 (6)	
Mohammad Rafique c Yasir Hameed		6/136 (7) 7/148 (5)	
b Danish Kaneria .	18	8/150 (9) 9/178 (10) 10/181 (8)	

Bowling: Shoaib Akhtar 10–1–30–3; Mohammad Sami 8–0–30–2; Abdur Razzaq 6–0–27–0; Danish Kaneria 8.2–1–26–1; Shoaib Malik 10–0–41–2; Imran Farhat 3–0–18–1.

Umpires: B. G. Jerling (South Africa) and M. G. Silva (Sri Lanka).
Third umpire: A. V. Jayaprakash (India).   Referee: R. S. Mahanama (Sri Lanka).

HONG KONG v PAKISTAN

At Sinhalese Sports Club, Colombo, July 18, 2004. Pakistan won by 173 runs (D/L method). Pakistan 6 pts. Toss: Pakistan. One-day international debuts: Nadeem Ahmed, Nasir Hameed.

Pakistan hammered Hong Kong in an inevitably one-sided contest. Shoaib Malik repaid the confidence shown in his elevation to No. 3 with a brisk hundred, and Younis Khan gorged himself with 144 from 122 balls, Pakistan's second-highest one-day score. These two added 223 for the third wicket and guided Pakistan to 343, their fourth-highest one-day total. Malik also shone with the ball, snapping up four wickets with his dinky off-breaks. Rain interrupted both innings, resulting in Hong Kong's target being reduced, not very helpfully, to 339 off 47 overs.

Man of the Match: Shoaib Malik.

Pakistan

Imran Nazir lbw b Khalid Khan	10	Mohammad Sami not out.	9
Imran Farhat c French b Khalid Khan . .	20		
Shoaib Malik run out	118	L-b 3, w 8, n-b 2	13
Younis Khan c Nadeem Ahmed			
b Afzaal Haider .	144	1/33 (1) 2/51 (2) (5 wkts, 50 overs) 343	
Abdul Razzaq c Smart b Ilyas Gul	18	3/274 (3) 4/313 (5)	
†Moin Khan not out	11	5/327 (4)	

*Inzamam-ul-Haq, Yousuf Youhana, Shabbir Ahmed and Naved-ul-Hasan did not bat.

Bowling: Afzaal Haider 9–0–73–1; Khalid Khan 10–1–62–2; Najeeb Aamer 10–1–59–0; Ilyas Gul 9–0–67–1; Nadeem Ahmed 10–0–63–0; French 2–0–16–0.

Hong Kong

T. Smart c Younis Khan b Abdul Razzaq	25	Khalid Khan st Moin Khan	
†Nasir Hameed lbw b Mohammad Sami	0	b Shoaib Malik	2
A. N. French b Imran Farhat	14	Nadeem Ahmed not out	1
Tabarak Dar b Shoaib Malik	36		
*R. Sharma b Imran Farhat	1	L-b 4, w 18, n-b 7	29
Najeeb Aamer lbw b Imran Farhat	4		—
Ilyas Gul lbw b Mohammad Sami	1	1/1 (2) 2/45 (1)	(44.1 overs) 165
M. Cheruparambil c Imran Farhat b Shoaib Malik	30	3/95 (4) 4/95 (3) 5/101 (6) 6/102 (5)	
Afzaal Haider c Mohammad Sami b Shoaib Malik	22	7/102 (7) 8/149 (9) 9/156 (10) 10/165 (8)	

Bowling: Mohammad Sami 7–2–16–2; Shabbir Ahmed 6–2–12–0; Abdul Razzaq 6–0–30–1; Naved-ul-Hasan 8–0–45–0; Shoaib Malik 9.1–1–19–4; Imran Farhat 4–2–10–3; Imran Nazir 4–0–29–0.

Umpires: E. A. R. de Silva (Sri Lanka) and B. G. Jerling (South Africa).
Third umpire: A. F. M. Akhtaruddin (Bangladesh). Referee: R. S. Mahanama (Sri Lanka).

GROUP B

INDIA v UNITED ARAB EMIRATES

At Dambulla, July 16, 2004 (day/night). India won by 116 runs. India 6 pts. Toss: India. One-day international debuts: United Arab Emirates (all).

India displayed signs of rustiness in their first match for three months, slipping to 65 for three before being rescued by a superb 104 off 93 balls from Dravid. Asim Saeed, a trundling left-armer, won $1,000 for the prized scalp of Tendulkar, who edged on to his pads and was caught at short mid-wicket. Tendulkar and Pathan then sealed the game with the ball, sharing six wickets, but not before the UAE had shown some spirit: Mohammad Tauqir, at No. 8, smacked an entertaining fifty to drag his side past 100. They had some help from the Indian bowlers: all five contributed wides.

Man of the Match: R. Dravid.

India

V. Sehwag run out	0	Yuvraj Singh b Khurram Khan	22
S. R. Tendulkar c Fahad Usman b Asim Saeed	18	M. Kaif not out	31
*S. C. Ganguly c Naeemuddin Aslam b Rizwan Latif	56	I. K. Pathan not out	1
		L-b 10, w 4	14
V. V. S. Laxman c and b Mohammad Tauqir	14		—
†R. Dravid b Rizwan Latif	104	1/0 (1) 2/30 (2)	(6 wkts, 50 overs) 260
		3/65 (4) 4/153 (3)	
		5/195 (6) 6/254 (5)	

A. Kumble, L. Balaji and Zaheer Khan did not bat.

Bowling: Ali Asad 10–1–38–0; Asim Saeed 7–2–25–1; Syed Maqsood 4–0–24–0; Mohammad Tauqir 10–0–46–1; Khurram Khan 10–0–48–1; Rizwan Latif 9–0–69–2.

United Arab Emirates

Asim Saeed c Kaif b Pathan	12	Ali Asad not out	9
Arshad Ali c Dravid b Pathan	0	Rizwan Latif c Laxman b Tendulkar	0
Fahad Usman lbw b Balaji	9		
Naeemuddin Aslam lbw b Pathan	0	B 8, l-b 1, w 21, n-b 4	34
*Khurram Khan lbw b Balaji	5		—
Syed Maqsood c Laxman b Zaheer Khan	5	1/1 (2) 2/26 (1) 3/26 (4)	(35 overs) 144
Asghar Ali lbw b Kumble	14	4/29 (3) 5/36 (5) 6/45 (6)	
Mohammad Tauqir b Dravid b Tendulkar	55	7/97 (7) 8/121 (9)	
†Abdul Rehman b Tendulkar	1	9/144 (8) 10/144 (11)	

Bowling: Pathan 8–0–28–3; Balaji 8–2–28–2; Zaheer Khan 8–1–42–1; Kumble 7–1–16–1; Tendulkar 4–0–21–3.

Umpires: B. R. Doctrove (West Indies) and I. L. Howell (South Africa).
Third umpire: Nadeem Ghauri (Pakistan). Referee: M. J. Procter (South Africa).

SRI LANKA v UNITED ARAB EMIRATES

At Dambulla, July 17, 2004 (day/night). Sri Lanka won by 116 runs. Sri Lanka 6 pts. Toss: Sri Lanka. One-day international debuts: S. L. Malinga; Ramveer Rai, Sameer Zia.

Sri Lanka, who rested Atapattu and Vaas, began their tournament with a jetlagged display after racing back from Cairns, where they had drawn their Test against Australia less than four days before. Gunawardene, playing his first one-day international for 15 months, anchored the Sri Lankan innings with 73, though the UAE captain, Khurram Khan, caused an embarrassing middle-order slide with his left-arm spin. But on a dry pitch, Chandana and Muralitharan proved too much for the UAE's batsmen. For the third time in four games, the margin of victory was 116 runs.

Man of the Match: Khurram Khan.

Sri Lanka

W. S. Jayantha b Syed Maqsood	18	D. N. T. Zoysa c Sameer Zia b Arshad Ali . . 21
S. T. Jayasuriya lbw b Ali Asad	21	M. Muralitharan b Khurram Khan 3
D. A. Gunawardene c Sameer Zia b Khurram Khan	73	S. L. Malinga not out 5
†K. C. Sangakkara lbw b Sameer Zia	17	B 10, l-b 4, w 10 24
*D. P. M. D. Jayawardene run out	26	
T. M. Dilshan b Khurram Khan	6	1/39 (1) 2/41 (2) 3/105 (4) (50 overs) 239
S. H. T. Kandamby c Syed Maqsood b Khurram Khan	4	4/143 (5) 5/151 (6) 6/161 (7)
U. D. U. Chandana b Ali Asad	21	7/190 (3) 8/214 (8) 9/222 (10) 10/239 (9)

Bowling: Ali Asad 10–0–35–2; Asim Saeed 2–0–15–0; Syed Maqsood 7–0–60–1; Sameer Zia 10–0–44–1; Mohammad Tauqir 10–1–34–0; Khurram Khan 10–0–32–4; Arshad Ali 1–0–5–1.

United Arab Emirates

Ramveer Rai b Chandana	39	Mohammad Tauqir c Dilshan b Chandana . 6
Arshad Ali lbw b Zoysa	7	Ali Asad b Chandana 12
Fahad Usman c Sangakkara b Zoysa	0	Sameer Zia not out 2
Naeemuddin Aslam c sub (M. F. Maharoof) b Chandana	12	B 3, l-b 4, w 14, n-b 3 24
Syed Maqsood c Chandana b Muralitharan	13	1/14 (2) 2/14 (1) 3/43 (4) (47.5 overs) 123
*Khurram Khan b Malinga	8	4/71 (5) 5/91 (6) 6/98 (7)
Asghar Ali c and b Muralitharan	0	7/98 (8) 8/99 (1)
†Asim Saeed c Chandana b Muralitharan	0	9/113 (9) 10/123 (10)

Bowling: Zoysa 8–3–11–2; Malinga 10–2–39–1; Dilshan 9–1–22–0; Muralitharan 10–3–21–3; Chandana 9.5–2–22–4; Jayantha 1–0–1–0.

Umpires: I. L. Howell (South Africa) and P. D. Parker (Australia).
Third umpire: Nadeem Ghauri (Pakistan). Referee: M. J. Procter (South Africa).

SRI LANKA v INDIA

At Dambulla, July 18, 2004 (day/night). Sri Lanka won by 12 runs. Sri Lanka 5 pts, India 1 pt. Toss: Sri Lanka.

The only high-profile clash of the first round sparked an engrossing contest, though the tournament's structure meant the winners gained nothing more than a psychological edge, since both teams had already qualified for the next phase. In the end, it was Sri Lankan confidence that enjoyed a boost. They piled up 282 on a sluggish pitch thanks to a frenetic late-innings stand between Jayawardene and Sangakkara, who put on 116 at almost eight an over. Zoysa then burst through with the new ball and followed up with a laser-like throw from third man to run out Sehwag. India, without the injured Laxman, were in disarray on 71 for four. But Dravid cobbled together 133 with Yuvraj Singh to resuscitate the run-chase. However, Muralitharan bowled Dravid via an inside edge for 82 just when he was upping the tempo. The lower order provided a late flourish, but with Sri Lanka's death bowlers holding their nerve, the rate grew too steep.

Man of the Match: D. N. T. Zoysa.

Sri Lanka

W. S. Jayantha c Patel b Balaji	34	T. M. Dilshan not out	7	
D. A. Gunawardene run out	49	B 2, l-b 9, w 12, n-b 4	27	
*M. S. Atapattu run out	50			
†K. C. Sangakkara c Ganguly b Pathan	57	1/63 (1) 2/128 (2)	(4 wkts, 50 overs)	282
D. P. M. D. Jayawardene not out	58	3/156 (3) 4/272 (4)		

U. D. U. Chandana, M. F. Maharoof, W. P. U. J. C. Vaas, D. N. T. Zoysa and M. Muralitharan did not bat.

Bowling: Pathan 10–0–49–1; Balaji 9–1–60–1; Zaheer Khan 9–0–39–0; Ganguly 2–0–15–0; Kumble 10–1–46–0; Sehwag 7–0–45–0; Yuvraj Singh 3–0–17–0.

India

S. R. Tendulkar c Jayantha b Zoysa	11	L. Balaji c Sangakkara b Vaas	10	
†P. A. Patel c Sangakkara b Zoysa	6	Zaheer Khan not out	0	
V. Sehwag run out	37	B 1, l-b 6, w 21, n-b 6	34	
*S. C. Ganguly c Muralitharan b Zoysa	6			
R. Dravid b Muralitharan	82	1/16 (1) 2/33 (2)	(8 wkts, 50 overs)	270
Yuvraj Singh c Sangakkara b Vaas	47	3/71 (3) 4/71 (4)		
M. Kaif b Maharoof	22	5/204 (6) 6/234 (5)		
I. K. Pathan not out	15	7/243 (7) 8/266 (9)		

A. Kumble did not bat.

Bowling: Vaas 10–0–51–2; Zoysa 10–2–49–3; Maharoof 10–0–46–1; Muralitharan 10–0–46–1; Chandana 5–0–39–0; Dilshan 3–0–25–0; Jayantha 2–0–7–0.

Umpires: B. R. Doctrove (West Indies) and P. D. Parker (Australia).
Third umpire: Nadeem Ghauri (Pakistan). Referee: M. J. Procter (South Africa).

GROUP TABLES

Group A	Played	Won	Lost	Bonus points	Points	Net run-rate
PAKISTAN	2	2	0	2	12	2.56
BANGLADESH	2	1	1	1	6	0.40
Hong Kong	2	0	2	0	0	2.97

Group B	Played	Won	Lost	Bonus points	Points	Net run-rate
SRI LANKA	2	2	0	1	11	1.28
INDIA	2	1	1	2	7	1.04
United Arab Emirates	2	0	2	0	0	−2.32

Win = 5 pts. One bonus point awarded either to the winning team for achieving victory with a run-rate 1.25 times that of the opposition, or to the losing team for denying the winners a bonus point. Net run-rate is calculated by subtracting runs conceded per over from runs scored per over.

SECOND PHASE

BANGLADESH v INDIA

At Sinhalese Sports Club, Colombo, July 21, 2004. India won by eight wickets. India 6 pts. Toss: India.

The first phase of the tournament might have ended, but the mismatches continued. India, defeated in Dambulla three days earlier, knuckled down against Bangladesh and eased to an eight-wicket win in which Tendulkar starred with bat and ball. First he gobbled up three wickets with his leg-breaks to help bowl out Bangladesh for 177 and then, in partnership with Ganguly, he guided India towards victory with 82 not out. It was not vintage Tendulkar – he started hesitantly against some niggardly left-arm spin from Abdur Razzaq, who opened the bowling – but he had blown away his early-season cobwebs by the close. Nehra proved an effective replacement for Zaheer Khan, who had picked up a hamstring injury against Sri Lanka, but it was Pathan who grabbed the initiative with a fine new-ball spell of swing bowling.

Man of the Match: S. R. Tendulkar.

Bangladesh

*Habibul Bashar b Pathan	2	Abdur Razzaq b Pathan	21
Mohammad Ashraful run out	35	Tareq Aziz not out	0
Rajin Saleh lbw b Pathan	0		
Alok Kapali c Dravid b Nehra	10	B 4, l-b 4, w 23, n-b 6	37
Faisal Hossain lbw b Harbhajan Singh	17		—
†Khaled Mashud c Dravid b Tendulkar	12	1/10 (1) 2/10 (3) 3/56 (4) (49.1 overs) 177	
Manjural Islam Rana b Tendulkar	21	4/92 (5) 5/92 (2) 6/117 (6)	
Mohammad Rafique b Tendulkar	0	7/117 (8) 8/141 (7)	
Khaled Mahmud c Laxman b Sehwag	22	9/176 (9) 10/177 (10)	

Bowling: Pathan 8.1–0–32–3; Balaji 7–0–32–0; Nehra 9–0–26–1; Harbhajan Singh 10–2–20–1; Tendulkar 10–0–35–3; Sehwag 5–0–24–1.

India

V. Sehwag c Alok Kapali b Tareq Aziz	16	V. V. S. Laxman not out	1
S. R. Tendulkar not out	82	L-b 9, w 4, n-b 6	19
*S. C. Ganguly c Alok Kapali b Mohammad Rafique	60	1/19 (1) 2/173 (3) (2 wkts, 38.3 overs) 178	

†R. Dravid, Yuvraj Singh, M. Kaif, I. K. Pathan, Harbhajan Singh, L. Balaji and A. Nehra did not bat.

Bowling: Tareq Aziz 7–0–49–1; Abdur Razzaq 10–0–40–0; Khaled Mahmud 8–1–28–0; Mohammad Rafique 7–2–30–1; Manjural Islam Rana 6.3–0–22–0.

Umpires: B. R. Doctrove (West Indies) and D. R. Shepherd (England).
Third umpire: M. G. Silva (Sri Lanka). Referee: R. S. Mahanama (Sri Lanka).

SRI LANKA v PAKISTAN

At R. Premadasa Stadium, Colombo, July 21, 2004 (day/night). Sri Lanka won by seven wickets. Sri Lanka 6 pts. Toss: Pakistan.

After the easiest of rides in the first round, Pakistan self-destructed in spectacular fashion. Sri Lanka were near-flawless in the field on a sticky afternoon, fielding like dervishes and bowling with military discipline, especially Zoysa and Vaas with the new ball. Pakistan were bundled out for 122, their lowest total against Sri Lanka. Bob Woolmer, Pakistan's bemused coach, summed it up afterwards: "Inzamam kicked the ball on to his stumps, Youhana tried to take a single to silly mid-off, Imran Nazir gave catching practice and Younis Khan played too early." Pakistan's pace attack did their best, bowling their hearts out and unleashing a steady flow of unplayable, lightning-fast deliveries, but the total was simply too small. Sri Lanka cruised home with 18 overs to spare, collecting a bonus point – and denying one to Pakistan.

Man of the Match: D. N. T. Zoysa.

Pakistan

Imran Nazir c Jayawardene b Zoysa....	14	Shoaib Akhtar run out............	1	
Yasir Hameed run out..........	22	Shabbir Ahmed not out...........	0	
Shoaib Malik c Dilshan b Zoysa......	4			
*Inzamam-ul-Haq b Muralitharan	9	L-b 7, w 8, n-b 1	16	
Yousuf Youhana run out	0			
Younis Khan c Jayawardene b Maharoof.	1	1/19 (1) 2/25 (3) 3/45 (4)	(39.5 overs)	122
Abdul Razzaq c Dilshan b Maharoof ...	43	4/46 (5) 5/52 (6) 6/72 (2)		
†Moin Khan c Sangakkara b Zoysa .	3	7/88 (8) 8/120 (7)		
Mohammad Sami b Jayasuriya	9	9/122 (9) 10/122 (10)		

Bowling: Vaas 7–3–14–0; Zoysa 10–3–29–3; Maharoof 6–0–25–2; Muralitharan 8–1–14–1; Chandana 7–0–28–0; Jayasuriya 1.5–0–5–1.

Sri Lanka

D. A. Gunawardene c Imran Nazir		†K. C. Sangakkara not out.........	14	
b Abdul Razzaq .	26	D. P. M. D. Jayawardene not out	19	
S. T. Jayasuriya c Younis Khan		L-b 4, w 17, n-b 4	25	
b Mohammad Sami .	20			
*M. S. Atapattu c Shoaib Malik		1/51 (2) 2/84 (3)	(3 wkts, 32 overs)	123
b Abdul Razzaq .	19	3/88 (1)		

T. M. Dilshan, U. D. U. Chandana, M. F. Maharoof, W. P. U. J. C. Vaas, D. N. T. Zoysa and M. Muralitharan did not bat.

Bowling: Shoaib Akhtar 8–1–29–0; Mohammad Sami 9–0–34–1; Shabbir Ahmed 8–1–25–0; Abdul Razzaq 6–2–21–2; Shoaib Malik 1–0–10–0.

Umpires: B. F. Bowden (New Zealand) and P. D. Parker (Australia).
Third umpire: A. F. M. Akhtaruddin (Bangladesh). Referee: M. J. Procter (South Africa).

SRI LANKA v BANGLADESH

At R. Premadasa Stadium, Colombo, July 23, 2004 (day/night). Sri Lanka won by ten wickets. Sri Lanka 6 pts. Toss: Bangladesh.

Faced with snowballing media criticism for a 30-match run without a century, Jayasuriya burst back to something like his devastating best against a demoralised Bangladesh. Sri Lanka were in control throughout, and on a placid batting track Bangladesh's 190 was far from enough. Mohammad Ashraful anchored their innings, eking out 66 from 120 balls, but they never fully recovered from 31 for four. Gunawardene and Jayasuriya – who pummelled his first fifty from 38 balls and finished with 107 from 101 – powered home with all ten wickets and more than 16 overs in hand.

Man of the Match: S. T. Jayasuriya.

Bangladesh

Mohammad Ashraful run out	66	Mohammad Rafique run out.........	5	
Rajin Saleh c Sangakkara b Malinga ...	5	Khaled Mahmud not out	7	
*Habibul Bashar c Sangakkara b Vaas ..	7	Tapash Baisya not out	6	
Alok Kapali run out	1	B 5, l-b 11, w 2, n-b 2.......	20	
Faisal Hossain b Maharoof..........	1			
Manjural Islam Rana c Sangakkara		1/6 (2) 2/21 (3)	(9 wkts, 50 overs)	190
b Muralitharan .	43	3/23 (4) 4/31 (5)		
†Khaled Mashud c and b Vaas	19	5/131 (6) 6/151 (1)		
Abdur Razzaq b Vaas	10	7/172 (8) 8/175 (8) 9/182 (9)		

Bowling: Vaas 10–3–30–3; Malinga 9–1–24–1; Muralitharan 10–2–26–1; Maharoof 8–0–33–1; Chandana 7–0–39–0; Jayasuriya 6–0–22–0.

Sri Lanka

D. A. Gunawardene not out 64
S. T. Jayasuriya not out 107
    L-b 2, w 18 20
                         —
    (no wkt, 33.3 overs) 191

*M. S. Atapattu, †K. C. Sangakkara, D. P. M. D. Jayawardene, T. M. Dilshan, U. D. U. Chandana, W. P. U. J. C. Vaas, M. F. Maharoof, S. L. Malinga and M. Muralitharan did not bat.

Bowling: Tapash Baisya 7–0–32–0; Khaled Mahmud 5–0–40–0; Abdur Razzaq 6–0–41–0; Mohammad Rafique 8–0–42–0; Manjural Islam Rana 7–0–30–0; Mohammad Ashraful 0.3–0–4–0.

Umpires: P. D. Parker (Australia) and D. R. Shepherd (England).
Third umpire: Nadeem Ghauri (Pakistan). Referee: M. J. Procter (South Africa).

INDIA v PAKISTAN

At R. Premadasa Stadium, Colombo, July 25, 2004 (day/night). Pakistan won by 59 runs. Pakistan 5 pts, India 1 pt. Toss: Pakistan.

The bye India's ninth-wicket pair stole off the last ball gave them and not Pakistan a place in the final. Losing by 59 runs rather than 60 ensured India gained – and Pakistan lost – a bonus point. And results in the remaining second-phase games meant India finished two points ahead of Pakistan – though behind on net run-rate. The game itself, however, was a triumph for a Pakistani team who somersaulted back to their best form. Leading the way was Shoaib Malik, who hit 143, a career-best in all cricket. His unorthodox century, which came from 127 balls, included some audacious strokes and two grassed chances in the slips. Malik was well supported by Inzamam-ul-Haq and Yousuf Youhana, and they set a mountainous challenge. India quickly lost Sehwag, but Tendulkar and Ganguly weathered a terrifyingly hostile spell from Shoaib Akhtar to keep them in the hunt. However, the run-out of Kaif at 151 for five opened up the tail, and India swapped the quest for victory for the easier goal of achieving a bonus point. They cut that fine, too, but just made it, meaning Pakistan's fate was no longer in their own hands: they would progress only if Sri Lanka, already guaranteed a place in the final, beat India.

Man of the Match: Shoaib Malik.

Pakistan

Imran Nazir lbw b Pathan 1
Yasir Hameed b Kumble 31
Shoaib Malik c Kaif b Tendulkar. 143
*Inzamam-ul-Haq c Yuvraj Singh
        b Harbhajan Singh . 34
Yousuf Youhana c Kaif b Kumble 29
Abdul Razzaq b Pathan 22
†Moin Khan c Harbhajan Singh b Pathan 14
Younis Khan b Tendulkar. 4

Mohammad Sami c Kaif b Tendulkar . . . 1
Shoaib Akhtar not out 0

      L-b 6, w 11, n-b 4. 21
                      —

1/2 (1) 2/105 (2)   (9 wkts, 50 overs) 300
3/171 (4) 4/234 (5)
5/277 (3) 6/286 (6)
7/296 (7) 8/300 (9) 9/300 (8)

Shabbir Ahmed did not bat.

Bowling: Pathan 10–0–52–3; Balaji 7–0–61–0; Nehra 8–1–54–0; Harbhajan Singh 10–0–50–1; Kumble 10–0–49–2; Tendulkar 5–0–28–3.

" The Maharaja of Porbandar achieved the unique feat of being the only visiting captain to own more Rolls-Royces than he scored runs on tour."

Ramachandra Guha, Cricket Books, page 1675.

India

V. Sehwag c Moin Khan b Shabbir Ahmed .	1
S. R. Tendulkar c Imran Nazir b Shoaib Malik .	78
*S. C. Ganguly b Mohammad Sami. . . .	39
†R. Dravid lbw b Abdul Razzaq	5
Yuvraj Singh c and b Shoaib Malik	28
M. Kaif run out	3
I. K. Pathan c Imran Nazir b Shoaib Akhtar .	38

Harbhajan Singh c Younis Khan b Shabbir Ahmed . 2
L. Balaji not out 5
A. Kumble not out 4
B 2, l-b 13, w 10, n-b 13 38

1/17 (1) 2/79 (3) (8 wkts, 50 overs) 241
3/94 (4) 4/139 (5)
5/151 (6) 6/214 (2)
7/223 (8) 8/233 (7)

A. Nehra did not bat.

Bowling: Shoaib Akhtar 10–0–51–1; Shabbir Ahmed 10–0–38–2; Mohammad Sami 10–0–57–1; Abdul Razzaq 10–2–38–1; Shoaib Malik 10–0–42–2.

Umpires: B. F. Bowden (New Zealand) and B. R. Doctrove (West Indies).
Third umpire: M. G. Silva (Sri Lanka). Referee: M. J. Procter (South Africa).

INDIA v SRI LANKA

At R. Premadasa Stadium, Colombo, July 27, 2004 (day/night). India won by four runs. India 5 pts, Sri Lanka 1 pt. Toss: India.

The situation for India was simple. Win, and they were in the final; lose, and Pakistan (assuming they beat Bangladesh) would play Sri Lanka instead. Preparing the team sheet was more challenging: the match started seven minutes late after Ganguly inadvertently included Ashish Nehra rather than Harbhajan Singh, but Atapattu sportingly agreed to the last-minute change. India then stacked up a handsome 271, Sehwag firing for the first time in the tournament, if in unusually measured style. India seemed set for 300 while he and Ganguly were sharing a 134-run stand, though they went off the boil in the slog overs. Jayasuriya then carried Sri Lanka to within touching distance of a remarkable victory with 130 from 132 balls. However, on a crumbling surface Ganguly persisted with his part-time slow bowlers, especially Sehwag and his off-spin. Extracting sharp turn, Sehwag broke a 103-run stand between Jayasuriya and Dilshan to leave Sri Lanka needing 35 off 37 balls. Then, with 18 required from 18, Sehwag caught and bowled an exhausted Jayasuriya. It came down to 11 off the last over, and the cool-headed Zaheer Khan held his nerve.

Man of the Match: V. Sehwag.

India

S. R. Tendulkar lbw b Zoysa	18
V. Sehwag c Sangakkara b Jayasuriya. . .	81
*S. C. Ganguly c Chandana b Malinga. .	79
R. Dravid c Sangakkara b Maharoof . . .	1
Yuvraj Singh c Gunawardene b Malinga .	50
M. Kaif run out.	1
†P. A. Patel not out.	13

I. K. Pathan not out 8

L-b 2, w 14, n-b 4 20

1/34 (1) 2/168 (2) (6 wkts, 50 overs) 271
3/169 (4) 4/240 (3)
5/248 (6) 6/255 (5)

Harbhajan Singh, Zaheer Khan and A. Kumble did not bat.

Bowling: Zoysa 8–0–49–1; Malinga 10–0–56–2; Dilshan 10–0–49–0; Maharoof 8–0–37–1; Chandana 7–0–42–0; Jayasuriya 4–0–17–1; Jayantha 3–0–19–0.

Sri Lanka

D. A. Gunawardene c Pathan		
	b Zaheer Khan .	7
S. T. Jayasuriya c and b Sehwag		130
W. S. Jayantha c Patel b Pathan		5
*M. S. Atapattu c Yuvraj Singh		
	b Harbhajan Singh .	8
†K. C. Sangakkara c Tendulkar b Sehwag		15
D. P. M. D. Jayawardene b Tendulkar		18
T. M. Dilshan b Sehwag		39
U. D. U. Chandana c Yuvraj Singh		
	b Pathan .	11

M. F. Maharoof b Zaheer Khan.		4
D. N. T. Zoysa not out		3
S. L. Malinga not out		1
B 4, l-b 14, w 8		26
1/20 (1) 2/36 (3)	(9 wkts, 50 overs)	267
3/76 (4) 4/103 (5)		
5/134 (6) 6/237 (7)		
7/254 (2) 8/261 (8) 9/266 (9)		

Bowling: Pathan 9–0–34–2; Zaheer Khan 9–1–63–2; Harbhajan Singh 10–0–41–1; Sehwag 9–0–37–3; Kumble 10–0–51–0; Tendulkar 3–0–23–1.

Umpires: B. R. Doctrove (West Indies) and D. R. Shepherd (England).
Third umpire: A. F. M. Akhtaruddin (Bangladesh). Referee: M. J. Procter (South Africa).

BANGLADESH v PAKISTAN

At R. Premadasa Stadium, Colombo, July 29, 2004 (day/night). Pakistan won by six wickets. Pakistan 5 pts, Bangladesh 1 pt. Toss: Bangladesh.

India's victory two days earlier left these sides fighting for pride only, and Pakistan were far too strong. Yet again, Bangladesh folded against the new ball, and inside eight overs they were staring down the barrel at 42 for five. Had Mohammad Sami not conceded 22 runs in the third over, Bangladesh's position would have been even more woeful. Sami had begun the match with a wicket maiden, so it came as a surprise when his second over proved so expensive. It included

SAMI GOING WEST

Mohammad Sami's 17-ball over:

Wd 4 2 NB Wd NB • Wd Wd • Wd NB Wd Wd NB • 4

seven wides and four no-balls, lasted a world-record 17 balls, and raised a few eyebrows, especially given the meaningless nature of the contest. ICC anti-corruption officials are understood to have investigated, but took no action. The Pakistani explanation was that Sami was remodelling his action and struggling for rhythm. Thanks to 37 from Extras and a dogged half-century from Khaled Mashud, Bangladesh eventually cobbled together 166. Pakistan's top order made heavy weather of their target, using 41 overs and four wickets in the process. Once again Shoaib Malik, who top-scored with 48 and bowled ten economical overs earlier on, clinched the match award.

Man of the Match: Shoaib Malik.

Bangladesh

Mohammad Ashraful		
	lbw b Mohammad Sami .	0
Rajin Saleh c Younis Khan		
	b Abdul Razzaq .	23
*Habibul Bashar lbw b Shabbir Ahmed .		10
Alok Kapali c Younis Khan		
	b Shoaib Akhtar .	3
Faisal Hossain lbw b Shabbir Ahmed		0
Manjural Islam Rana c Moin Khan		
	b Shabbir Ahmed .	0
†Khaled Mashud b Mohammad Sami		54

Mushfiqur Rahman lbw b Shoaib Akhtar.		21
Abdur Razzaq b Shoaib Malik		2
Tapash Baisya lbw b Abdul Razzaq		14
Tareq Aziz not out		2
B 1, l-b 2, w 21, n-b 13		37
1/0 (1) 2/30 (3) 3/41 (4)	(45.2 overs)	166
4/42 (5) 5/42 (6) 6/75 (2)		
7/118 (8) 8/121 (9)		
9/147 (10) 10/166 (7)		

Bowling: Mohammad Sami 8.2–2–38–2; Shabbir Ahmed 10–2–32–3; Shoaib Akhtar 9–1–33–2; Abdul Razzaq 8–0–41–2; Shoaib Malik 10–1–19–1.

Pakistan

Yasir Hameed c Manjural Islam Rana		Younis Khan not out..............	16
b Tapash Baisya .	11	Abdul Razzaq not out.............	16
Imran Nazir c Faisal Hossain b Tareq Aziz	27	B 2, l-b 1, w 4, n-b 3	10
Shoaib Malik b Abdur Razzaq	48		
Yousuf Youhana c Mushfiqur Rahman		1/35 (1) 2/52 (2) (4 wkts, 41 overs) 167	
b Manjural Islam Rana .	39	3/118 (3) 4/137 (4)	

*Inzamam-ul-Haq, †Moin Khan, Mohammad Sami, Shabbir Ahmed and Shoaib Akhtar did not bat.

Bowling: Tapash Baisya 10–1–42–1; Tareq Aziz 7–1–32–1; Mushfiqur Rahman 6–0–26–0; Abdur Razzaq 10–1–29–1; Manjural Islam Rana 8–1–35–1.

Umpires: B. F. Bowden (New Zealand) and P. D. Parker (Australia).
Third umpire: A. V. Jayaprakash (India).   Referee: M. J. Procter (South Africa).

QUALIFYING TABLE

Second Phase ...	Played	Won	Lost	Bonus points	Points	Net run-rate
SRI LANKA	3	2	1	3	13	1.14
INDIA.............	3	2	1	2	12	0.02
Pakistan............	3	2	1	0	10	0.16
Bangladesh..........	3	0	3	1	1	−1.19

Win = 5 pts. One bonus point awarded either to the winning team for achieving victory with a run-rate 1.25 times that of the opposition, or to the losing team for denying the winners a bonus point. Net run-rate is calculated by subtracting runs conceded per over from runs scored per over.

FINAL

SRI LANKA v INDIA

At R. Premadasa Stadium, Colombo, August 1, 2004 (day/night). Sri Lanka won by 25 runs. Toss: Sri Lanka.

Sri Lanka saved their best performance till last, rising to the occasion as crowds poured through the turnstiles for the first time. For India, cheered on by thousands of horn-blowing supporters, defeat stretched their run in one-day finals to a solitary win in their last 19 attempts. Midway through the match, though, India looked the likely winners after restricting Sri Lanka to 228. But the pitch was far drier than the teams had expected, and at times the ball spun viciously. Tendulkar, delivering his leg-breaks from around the wicket into the rough, had been fiendishly difficult to play. By the evening, the surface had deteriorated further and, after Vaas and Zoysa imposed early pressure with miserly spells, Sri Lanka's spin bowlers slowly throttled the Indian run-chase. Tendulkar kept the innings together for a while, but received scant support from a batting line-up restored to full strength by Laxman's recovery. Sri Lanka's approach was highly aggressive, a tactic that unsettled India's lower order, but led to three players – Sangakkara, Chandana and Dilshan – being fined for verbal abuse. Fittingly, it was Atapattu, responsible for the new togetherness, focus and intensity of the team, who won the match award for a crucial 65 earlier in the day.

Man of the Match: M. S. Atapattu.   *Man of the Series:* S. T. Jayasuriya.

ONE-DAY CHOKERS

India's record in recent one-day tournament finals: P 19, W 1, L 14, NR 4.

Pepsi Cup	lost to Pakistan by 123 runs at Bangalore	1998-99
Coca-Cola Cup	lost to Pakistan by eight wickets at Sharjah	1998-99
Coca-Cola Singapore Challenge	no result v West Indies at Singapore	1999-2000
Coca-Cola Singapore Challenge	lost to West Indies by four wickets at Singapore .	1999-2000
LG Cup	lost to South Africa by 26 runs at Nairobi	1999-2000
ICC Knockout	lost to New Zealand by four wickets at Nairobi .	2000-01
Coca-Cola Champions Trophy	lost to Sri Lanka by 245 runs at Sharjah	2000-01
Coca-Cola Cup	lost to West Indies by 16 runs at Harare	2001
Coca-Cola Cup	lost to Sri Lanka by 121 runs at Colombo	2001
Standard Bank Triangular	lost to South Africa by six wickets at Durban . . .	2001-02
NatWest Series	*beat* England by two wickets at Lord's	2002
ICC Champions Trophy	no result v Sri Lanka at Colombo.	2002
ICC Champions Trophy	no result v Sri Lanka at Colombo.	2002
ICC World Cup	lost to Australia by 125 runs at Johannesburg . . .	2002-03
TVS Cup	no result v South Africa at Dhaka	2003
TVS Cup	**lost to Australia by 37 runs at Kolkata**	**2003-04**
VB Series	**lost to Australia by seven wickets at Melbourne**	**2003-04**
VB Series	**lost to Australia by 208 runs at Sydney**	**2003-04**
Asia Cup	**lost to Sri Lanka by 25 runs at Colombo**	**2004**

Note: The finals of the 1999-2000 Singapore Challenge and the 2002 Champions Trophy were
replayed from scratch on the reserve day. The 2003-04 VB Series final was a best-of-three affair.

Sri Lanka

D. A. Gunawardene c Ganguly b Nehra .	8
S. T. Jayasuriya lbw b Pathan	15
*M. S. Atapattu run out.	65
†K. C. Sangakkara b Sehwag	53
D. P. M. D. Jayawardene c Yuvraj Singh	
b Tendulkar .	0
T. M. Dilshan st Dravid b Tendulkar . . .	22
U. D. U. Chandana lbw	
b Harbhajan Singh .	8
M. F. Maharoof run out.	9

W. P. U. J. C. Vaas c Yuvraj Singh
               b Pathan .   6
D. N. T. Zoysa not out   6
M. Muralitharan not out   4
          B 4, l-b 14, w 11, n-b 3 32

1/28 (2) 2/31 (1)   (9 wkts, 50 overs) 228
3/147 (4) 4/150 (5)
5/174 (3) 6/194 (6)
7/202 (7) 8/213 (8) 9/219 (9)

Bowling: Pathan 7–0–33–2; Nehra 6–0–22–1; Zaheer Khan 7–0–35–0; Harbhajan Singh
10–0–48–1; Sehwag 10–2–32–1; Tendulkar 10–0–40–2.

India

V. Sehwag lbw b Vaas.	5
S. R. Tendulkar b Dilshan	74
*S. C. Ganguly c Jayawardene b Zoysa .	4
V. V. S. Laxman c Dilshan b Jayasuriya .	12
†R. Dravid c Dilshan b Chandana	16
Yuvraj Singh b Chandana.	8
M. Kaif c Jayawardene b Chandana	5
I. K. Pathan run out	2
Harbhajan Singh st Sangakkara	
b Jayasuriya .	16

Zaheer Khan not out. 28
A. Nehra not out   8

       B 12, l-b 8, w 3, n-b 2 25
                           —

1/15 (1) 2/26 (3)   (9 wkts, 50 overs) 203
3/62 (4) 4/96 (5)
5/119 (6) 6/135 (7)
7/140 (2) 8/147 (8) 9/193 (9)

Bowling: Vaas 7–1–24–1; Zoysa 8–2–18–1; Maharoof 2–0–16–0; Muralitharan 9–0–46–0;
Jayasuriya 10–0–34–2; Chandana 10–0–33–3; Dilshan 4–0–12–1.

Umpires: B. F. Bowden (New Zealand) and D. R. Shepherd (England).
Third umpire: A. F. M. Akhtaruddin (Bangladesh).   Referee: M. J. Procter (South Africa).

THE PAKTEL GSM CUP, 2004-05

Brian Murgatroyd

This triangular tournament, together with the two-Test series between Pakistan and Sri Lanka that followed, was arranged to fill a gap in Pakistan's international programme following the removal of Zimbabwe's Test status. Sri Lanka played thanks to Bangladesh's willingness to postpone their own series against them, and although the weakness of the Zimbabwe side meant the identity of the two finalists was never in doubt, there was still some hard-fought and, at times, compelling cricket on offer.

Sri Lanka lost both group games to Pakistan but saved their best for last with a crushing win in the final – a real shot in the arm for the players' self-belief in the continuing absence of their injured off-spinner Muttiah Muralitharan. That victory was especially satisfying for the Sri Lankans as it came in the wake of stinging criticism of the team's management and, by implication, its senior players, from the chairman of selectors, Ashantha de Mel. De Mel claimed on the eve of the final that the team's management was "selfish" for not giving extended opportunities to the younger squad members. Atapattu kept his own counsel at first, but after the win said de Mel's criticisms had spurred his side on to victory. Both Atapattu and Kumar Sangakkara batted beautifully throughout the series, while Chaminda Vaas led the attack impressively.

For the third time in seven weeks – after losing the Videocon final in the Netherlands and the Champions Trophy semi-final in England – Pakistan fluffed their lines on the big occasion after looking impressive in the build-up. Yet their unbeaten form up to the final did disguise some fundamental problems. The absence of Taufeeq Umar, suffering from a lack of match practice, and Imran Farhat, out of favour since making a duck against India in the Champions Trophy, meant Pakistan were left searching desperately for an ideal opening combination. Although Salman Butt hinted at a promising future, the decision to open with Yasir Hameed exposed his short-comings outside off stump.

Shoaib Malik, however, was a worthy man of the series thanks to his continued development as a one-day batsman and his increasingly useful off-spin, which formed an effective combination with Shahid Afridi's leg-breaks in the middle of the innings. But the gloss was taken off when Malik's action was reported to the ICC the day after the final. Another area of concern was the one-day role of Shoaib Akhtar. The debate, which ran throughout the tournament, centred on whether he should open the bowling or come on as first change. Shoaib, for his part, appeared listless for much of the time, even operating off a short run on several occasions.

Zimbabwe started the tour before the Champions Trophy in England had finished, which was an indication of the low expectations of a side still shorn of its experienced "rebels". Tinashe Panyangara's form was outstanding, especially with the new ball, but the tour also highlighted the lack of depth and penetration in Zimbabwe's bowling and, in many cases, a lack of batting technique. They were never short of enthusiasm, however.

Note: Matches in this section were not first-class.

PAKISTAN v ZIMBABWE

At Multan, September 30, 2004. Pakistan won by 144 runs. Pakistan 6 pts. Toss: Pakistan. One-day international debuts: Bazid Khan, Iftikhar Anjum.

Only eight days after facing fierce criticism for defying conventional wisdom and batting first in the Champions Trophy semi-final at Southampton, Pakistan appeared to repeat the error half a world away. Only an amazing blitz by Abdul Razzaq and Shahid Afridi put Zimbabwe's limited resources into perspective and got them out of trouble after they had slumped to 36 for four. Panyangara immediately removed Yasir Hameed to become the second Zimbabwean (after Everton Matambanadzo) to take a wicket with the first ball of a one-day international. And when he dismissed the debutant Bazid Khan, son of the former Pakistan captain Majid Khan, in his seventh over, Pakistan were staring into the abyss. With ten overs to go they had advanced to only 147 for six but, as conditions became more batsman-friendly, Razzaq and Afridi cashed in, adding 107 from 45 deliveries. Razzaq had survived a simple return catch to Matsikenyeri on 33, and went on to score his second one-day international hundred from 111 balls. In all, he hit five fours and five sixes and reached his second fifty in just 21 deliveries. Afridi faced only 26 balls, bludgeoning five fours and four sixes. The last ten overs cost Zimbabwe 145 runs – and with it the match. Sibanda's stylish 57 from 69 balls merely delayed the inevitable.

Man of the Match: Abdul Razzaq.

Pakistan

Yasir Hameed c Taibu b Panyangara	0	Shahid Afridi b Hondo	58
Bazid Khan c Taibu b Panyangara	12	Naved-ul-Hasan not out	16
Shoaib Malik lbw b Hondo	1	L-b 3, w 11, n-b 3	17
Yousuf Youhana c Taibu b Hondo	1		
*Inzamam-ul-Haq lbw b Utseya	73	1/0 (1) 2/2 (3)	(7 wkts, 50 overs) 292
Abdul Razzaq not out	107	3/6 (4) 4/36 (2)	
†Moin Khan st Taibu b Taylor	7	5/131 (5) 6/146 (7) 7/253 (8)	

Iftikhar Anjum and Shoaib Akhtar did not bat.

Bowling: Panyangara 10–3–52–2; Hondo 10–1–54–3; Chigumbura 6–0–64–0; Utseya 10–1–31–1; Nkala 6–0–47–0; Matsikenyeri 6–0–35–0; Taylor 2–0–6–1.

Zimbabwe

B. R. M. Taylor b Shoaib Akhtar	5	T. Panyangara b Shoaib Malik	9
S. Matsikenyeri lbw b Naved-ul-Hasan	1	P. Utseya not out	0
V. Sibanda c Moin Khan b Shoaib Malik	57	D. T. Hondo b Shahid Afridi	1
D. D. Ebrahim b Abdul Razzaq	29		
M. A. Vermeulen c Bazid Khan b Iftikhar Anjum	10	L-b 3, w 7, n-b 1	11
*†T. Taibu b Shahid Afridi	3	1/4 (2) 2/8 (1) 3/64 (4)	(38.3 overs) 148
E. Chigumbura lbw b Shahid Afridi	9	4/81 (5) 5/96 (6) 6/117 (3)	
M. L. Nkala c Abdul Razzaq b Shoaib Malik	14	7/122 (7) 8/144 (8)	
		9/145 (9) 10/148 (11)	

Bowling: Shoaib Akhtar 6–0–14–1; Naved-ul-Hasan 5–0–15–1; Iftikhar Anjum 7–1–41–1; Abdul Razzaq 6–1–20–1; Shoaib Malik 8–0–37–3; Shahid Afridi 6.3–0–18–3.

Umpires: M. R. Benson (England) and Nadeem Ghauri.
Third umpire: Asad Rauf. Referee: J. J. Crowe (New Zealand).

PAKISTAN v ZIMBABWE

At Peshawar, October 3, 2004. Pakistan won by three wickets. Pakistan 5 pts, Zimbabwe 1 pt. Toss: Pakistan.

This was Zimbabwe's best performance of the tournament but the final margin of defeat flattered them: they lacked the bowling resources to put pressure on Pakistan once Panyangara and, to a lesser extent, Hondo were out of the attack. Their batting was positive, with Ebrahim and Taibu adding an unbroken 91 from 65 balls to build on the foundation laid by a stand of 87 between openers Matsikenyeri and Taylor – their best in ten one-day matches together. But Shoaib Malik and Younis Khan, who kept wicket for the first time in place of the ailing Moin Khan, added an untroubled 114 from 128 balls to ease Pakistan's nerves. The Zimbabwe players wore black armbands following the death of Dawson Mutsekwa, the Zimbabwe Cricket Union's provincial development manager for Mashonaland.

Man of the Match: Younis Khan.

Zimbabwe

S. Matsikenyeri c Mohammad Sami		M. A. Vermeulen b Naved-ul-Hasan	1
b Shahid Afridi	41	*†T. Taibu not out	46
B. R. M. Taylor c Yousuf Youhana		L-b 2, w 11, n-b 7	20
b Naved-ul-Hasan	73		
V. Sibanda run out	0	1/87 (1) 2/87 (3) (4 wkts, 50 overs) 252
D. D. Ebrahim not out	71	3/159 (2) 4/161 (5)

E. Chigumbura, M. L. Nkala, T. Panyangara, P. Utseya and D. T. Hondo did not bat.

Bowling: Mohammad Sami 10–1–43–0; Iftikhar Anjum 8–1–32–0; Naved-ul-Hasan 10–0–82–2; Shahid Afridi 10–0–39–1; Shoaib Malik 10–1–43–0; Bazid Khan 2–0–11–0.

Pakistan

Salman Butt c Chigumbura b Panyangara	30	Shahid Afridi not out	16
Yasir Hameed c Taibu b Panyangara	0	Naved-ul-Hasan not out	0
Bazid Khan lbw b Panyangara	0	L-b 3, w 14, n-b 1	18
Shoaib Malik c Matsikenyeri b Nkala	80		
Misbah-ul-Haq c Taibu b Hondo	23	1/1 (2) 2/25 (3) (7 wkts, 48.1 overs) 258
†Younis Khan run out	77	3/48 (1) 4/89 (5)
*Yousuf Youhana b Hondo	14	5/203 (4) 6/240 (7) 7/252 (6)

Mohammad Sami and Iftikhar Anjum did not bat.

Bowling: Panyangara 9–1–28–3; Hondo 10–0–61–2; Chigumbura 5–1–31–0; Utseya 10–2–34–0; Matsikenyeri 4–0–23–0; Taylor 3–0–23–0; Nkala 5.1–0–41–1; Sibanda 2–0–14–0.

Umpires: M. R. Benson (England) and Asad Rauf.
Third umpire: Nadeem Ghauri. Referee: J. J. Crowe (New Zealand).

PAKISTAN v SRI LANKA

At Karachi, October 6, 2004. Pakistan won by eight wickets. Pakistan 5 pts, Sri Lanka 1 pt. Toss: Sri Lanka.

An unbroken partnership of 200 from 224 balls between Shoaib Malik and Yousuf Youhana, a record for all wickets in one-day internationals at Karachi, ensured a comfortable win for Pakistan, as they became the first side to play 600 one-day internationals. Youhana scored his tenth one-day international hundred, passing 6,000 runs in the process. That landmark took him 168 innings, a rate bettered by only Saeed Anwar (162) for Pakistan. Both batsmen took advantage of an outfield that quickened up as the day went on following heavy rain in the week before the match. Several Sri Lankan batsmen got starts but a combination of disciplined mid-innings bowling by Pakistan and, in Jayasuriya's case, apparent fatigue caused by the high humidity, meant they did not push on. Jayasuriya, dropped by Inzamam at mid-wicket on 38, failed to regain his ground at the non-striker's end when the bowler Malik gathered a straight-drive from Atapattu.

Man of the Match: Shoaib Malik.

Sri Lanka

D. A. Gunawardene b Naved-ul-Hasan . .	1	W. P. U. J. C. Vaas b Shoaib Akhtar. . . .	11
S. T. Jayasuriya run out.	53	M. F. Maharoof b Mohammad Sami . . .	15
*M. S. Atapattu c Inzamam-ul-Haq		K. S. Lokuarachchi not out	4
b Shoaib Malik .	46	B 4, l-b 11, w 14, n-b 4	33
†K. C. Sangakkara b Mohammad Sami .	38		
D. P. M. D. Jayawardene b Shoaib Malik	18	1/4 (1) 2/113 (2) (9 wkts, 50 overs) 232	
T. M. Dilshan c Younis Khan		3/129 (3) 4/165 (5)	
b Shoaib Malik .	4	5/177 (6) 6/194 (4)	
U. D. U. Chandana b Shahid Afridi	9	7/196 (7) 8/222 (9) 9/232 (8)	
D. N. T. Zoysa did not bat.			

Bowling: Mohammad Sami 10–1–41–2; Naved-ul-Hasan 7–0–30–1; Shoaib Akhtar 8–0–46–1; Shahid Afridi 10–0–42–1; Abdul Razzaq 5–0–26–0; Shoaib Malik 10–0–32–3.

Pakistan

Salman Butt c Atapattu b Zoysa 17
Yasir Hameed lbw b Vaas 13
Shoaib Malik not out 86
Yousuf Youhana not out 107
      L-b 6, w 4 10

1/33 (2) 2/33 (1)   (2 wkts, 48.4 overs) 233

*Inzamam-ul-Haq, †Younis Khan, Abdul Razzaq, Shahid Afridi, Mohammad Sami, Naved-ul-Hasan and Shoaib Akhtar did not bat.

Bowling: Vaas 10–0–24–1; Zoysa 8–0–31–1; Maharoof 7.4–0–41–0; Lokuarachchi 6–0–36–0; Jayasuriya 7–0–40–0; Chandana 4–0–31–0; Dilshan 6–0–24–0.

Umpires: M. R. Benson (England) and Asad Rauf.
Third umpire: Nadeem Ghauri.   Referee: J. J. Crowe (New Zealand).

SRI LANKA v ZIMBABWE

At Rawalpindi, October 9, 2004. Sri Lanka won by seven wickets. Sri Lanka 6 pts. Toss: Sri Lanka.

After their promising display at Peshawar this was a dreadful performance by Zimbabwe, which called into question their right to be in this company. On a blameless pitch they lost their last nine wickets for 50 thanks to a mix of ill-discipline and poor technique, and Sri Lanka could even afford to juggle around their batting order. The match finished 35 minutes into the scheduled second session, which was a relief to everyone bar the Zimbabweans: strong winds had whipped up a dust storm around the ground, forcing the bails to be removed after only five overs of Sri Lanka's reply.

Man of the Match: M. F. Maharoof.

Zimbabwe

S. Matsikenyeri b Maharoof	37	P. Utseya b Fernando	1
B. R. M. Taylor c Sangakkara b Zoysa . .	3	E. C. Rainsford b Chandana	5
V. Sibanda c Jayantha b Maharoof.	7		
D. D. Ebrahim not out.	24	L-b 1, w 11, n-b 4	16
M. A. Vermeulen c Atapattu b Fernando.	7		
*†T. Taibu lbw b Vaas.	0	1/10 (2) 2/54 (1) 3/55 (3) (33 overs) 104	
E. Chigumbura c and b Chandana	1	4/72 (5) 5/72 (6) 6/73 (7)	
M. L. Nkala c Atapattu b Vaas	1	7/76 (8) 8/84 (9)	
T. Panyangara lbw b Chandana	2	9/94 (10) 10/104 (11)	

Bowling: Vaas 8–0–20–2; Zoysa 6–1–24–1; Maharoof 5–3–11–2; Fernando 8–1–33–2; Chandana 6–0–15–3.

Sri Lanka

W. S. Jayantha c Taibu b Chigumbura	21
S. T. Jayasuriya b Chigumbura	40
T. M. Dilshan not out	26
U. D. U. Chandana b Panyangara	7
M. F. Maharoof not out	7
L-b 1, w 6	7

1/49 (1) 2/70 (2)   (3 wkts, 18.1 overs) 108
3/96 (4)

*M. S. Atapattu, †K. C. Sangakkara, D. P. M. D. Jayawardene, W. P. U. J. C. Vaas, C. R. D. Fernando and D. N. T. Zoysa did not bat.

Bowling: Panyangara 8–1–36–1; Rainsford 5–0–31–0; Chigumbura 3–0–18–2; Nkala 2.1–0–22–0.

Umpires: S. J. A. Taufel (Australia) and Aleem Dar.
Third umpire: Zamir Haider. Referee: J. J. Crowe (New Zealand).

SRI LANKA v ZIMBABWE

At Rawalpindi, October 11, 2004. No result (abandoned). Sri Lanka 3 pts, Zimbabwe 3 pts.
Heavy rain on the day before the match left areas surrounding the square and the bowlers' landing area extremely damp, and the umpires, Aleem Dar and Simon Taufel, abandoned the match in mid-afternoon. That meant Sri Lanka's place in the final alongside Pakistan was confirmed.

PAKISTAN v SRI LANKA

At Lahore, October 14, 2004 (day/night). Pakistan won by six wickets. Pakistan 5 pts, Sri Lanka 1 pt. Toss: Pakistan.
Pakistan geared up for the final with their highest-ever successful run-chase in a home one-day international, beating the 292 for seven they made against New Zealand at the same venue in November 2003. The pursuit was built around consistent batting, with the left-handed Salman Butt scoring his maiden international fifty, and Inzamam clobbering eight fours and a six from 59 balls. Sri Lanka were not helped by the onset of a heavy dew, which made gripping the ball tough, but they did themselves no favours by failing to take at least four chances. Shoaib Malik alone should have been stumped on 12 and run out on 23. Play continued at the start of the Pakistan innings even though one bank of floodlights went off for four overs. Sri Lanka's total was built around Atapattu's first one-day hundred as captain, an innings spanning 114 balls and including eight fours and two sixes. He added 146 in 159 balls with Sangakkara.
Man of the Match: M. S. Atapattu.

Sri Lanka

W. S. Jayantha c Moin Khan b Naved-ul-Hasan	9	S. H. T. Kandamby c Shahid Afridi b Abdul Razzaq	6
S. T. Jayasuriya lbw b Naved-ul-Hasan	10	U. D. U. Chandana not out	10
*M. S. Atapattu run out	111		
†K. C. Sangakkara st Moin Khan b Shahid Afridi	69	L-b 4, w 18, n-b 6	28
D. P. M. D. Jayawardene c Shoaib Malik b Mohammad Sami	18	1/18 (1) 2/26 (2) (6 wkts, 50 overs) 293	
		3/172 (4) 4/233 (5)	
T. M. Dilshan not out	32	5/244 (3) 6/270 (7)	

W. P. U. J. C. Vaas, C. R. D. Fernando and D. N. T. Zoysa did not bat.

Bowling: Mohammad Sami 8–1–35–1; Naved-ul-Hasan 10–1–65–2; Shoaib Akhtar 4–0–30–0; Shoaib Malik 10–0–45–0; Abdul Razzaq 10–0–57–1; Shahid Afridi 8–0–57–1.

Pakistan

Salman Butt c Sangakkara b Vaas		57
Yasir Hameed b Chandana		48
Shoaib Malik b Fernando		56
*Inzamam-ul-Haq not out		76
Yousuf Youhana c Chandana b Vaas		30

Abdul Razzaq not out	4
B 3, l-b 9, w 9, n-b 5	26

1/99 (2) 2/139 (1)   (4 wkts, 48.5 overs) 297
3/210 (3) 4/285 (5)

Shahid Afridi, †Moin Khan, Mohammad Sami, Naved-ul-Hasan and Shoaib Akhtar did not bat.

Bowling: Vaas 9.5–1–62–2; Zoysa 7–0–44–0; Fernando 10–0–57–1; Chandana 10–1–45–1; Dilshan 5–0–25–0; Jayasuriya 7–0–52–0.

Umpires: S. J. A. Taufel (Australia) and Nadeem Ghauri.
Third umpire: Zamir Haider.   Referee: J. J. Crowe (New Zealand).

QUALIFYING TABLE

	Played	Won	Lost	No result	Bonus points	Points	Net run-rate
Pakistan	4	4	0	0	1	21	0.89
Sri Lanka	4	1	2	1	3	11	1.05
Zimbabwe	4	0	3	1	1	4	−2.29

Win = 5 pts, no result = 3 pts. One bonus point awarded either to the winning team for achieving victory with a run-rate 1.25 times that of the opposition, or to the losing team for denying the winners a bonus point. Net run-rate is calculated by subtracting runs conceded per over from runs scored per over.

FINAL

PAKISTAN v SRI LANKA

At Lahore, October 16, 2004 (day/night). Sri Lanka won by 119 runs. Toss: Pakistan.

Sri Lanka ripped up the script in sensational fashion to outclass the home side with bat and ball. The match began amid suggestions it would be decided by the toss because of the expected onset of dew in the second innings. But in reality the dew was minimal, and Jayasuriya took full advantage of a turning pitch and some increasingly nervous Pakistan batting to record his fourth five-wicket haul in one-day internationals. Sri Lanka owed their total to a partnership of 106 in 118 balls between Atapattu and Sangakkara and late impetus from Dilshan, who already knew he had been left out of the squad for the Test series that followed. In all, 85 runs came from the final ten overs. Sangakkara became the first player to reach 1,000 one-day international runs in the calendar year when he reached 59. In an unfortunate postscript, Shoaib Malik was reported to the ICC by the match referee Jeff Crowe for having a potentially flawed action.

Man of the Match: K. C. Sangakkara.   *Man of the Series:* Shoaib Malik.

Sri Lanka

W. S. Jayantha run out		0
S. T. Jayasuriya c Inzamam-ul-Haq b Naved-ul-Hasan		21
*M. S. Atapattu st Moin Khan b Shoaib Malik		66
†K. C. Sangakkara b Abdul Razzaq		68
D. P. M. D. Jayawardene b Shahid Afridi		49
T. M. Dilshan b Shahid Afridi		39

U. D. U. Chandana b Mohammad Sami	7
W. P. U. J. C. Vaas not out	18
M. F. Maharoof not out	2
L-b 5, w 6, n-b 6	17

1/0 (1) 2/35 (2)   (7 wkts, 50 overs) 287
3/141 (3) 4/181 (4)
5/244 (6) 6/257 (7) 7/275 (5)

C. R. D. Fernando and D. N. T. Zoysa did not bat.

Bowling: Shoaib Akhtar 7–1–41–0; Naved-ul-Hasan 7–0–29–1; Mohammad Sami 9–0–53–1; Shahid Afridi 10–0–60–2; Shoaib Malik 10–0–56–1; Abdul Razzaq 7–0–43–1.

Pakistan

Salman Butt b Chandana	40	Mohammad Sami c Atapattu b Jayasuriya	4
Yasir Hameed b Fernando	18	Naved-ul-Hasan not out	14
Shoaib Malik st Sangakkara b Chandana.	37	Shoaib Akhtar b Jayasuriya	0
*Inzamam-ul-Haq lbw b Vaas	4	W 7, n-b 4	11
Yousuf Youhana st Sangakkara			
b Jayasuriya .	7	1/40 (2) 2/85 (1) 3/91 (4) (38 overs) 168	
†Moin Khan c Sangakkara b Chandana .	14	4/108 (5) 5/124 (3) 6/134 (7)	
Abdul Razzaq c Dilshan b Jayasuriya. . .	8	7/149 (8) 8/150 (6)	
Shahid Afridi c Maharoof b Jayasuriya. .	11	9/168 (9) 10/168 (11)	

Bowling: Vaas 7–0–42–1; Zoysa 4–1–12–0; Maharoof 4–0–20–0; Fernando 5–1–21–1; Chandana 10–0–56–3; Jayasuriya 8–2–17–5.

Umpires: S. J. A. Taufel (Australia) and Aleem Dar.
Third umpire: Asad Rauf. Referee: J. J. Crowe (New Zealand).

THE DUCKWORTH/LEWIS METHOD

In 1997, the ECB's one-day competitions adopted a new method to revise targets in interrupted games, devised by Frank Duckworth of the Royal Statistical Society and Tony Lewis of the University of the West of England. The method was gradually taken up by other countries and, in 1999, the ICC decided to incorporate it into the standard playing conditions for one-day internationals.

The system aims to preserve any advantage that one team has established before the interruption. It uses the idea that teams have two resources from which they make runs – an allocated number of overs, and ten wickets. It also takes into account when the interruption occurs, because of the different scoring-rates typical of different stages of an innings. Traditional run-rate calculations relied only on the overs available, and ignored wickets lost.

After modifications, the system now uses one table with 50 rows, covering matches of any length up to 50 overs, and ten columns, from nought to nine wickets down. Each figure in the table gives the percentage of the total runs in an innings that would, on average, be scored with a certain number of overs left and wickets lost.

If overs are lost, the table is used to calculate the percentage of runs the team would be expected to score in those missing overs. This is obtained by reading off the figure for the number of overs left and wickets down when play stops and subtracting from it the corresponding figure for the number of overs remaining when it resumes.

If the suspension of play occurs between innings, and the second team's allocation of overs is reduced, then their target is obtained by calculating the appropriate percentage for the reduced number of overs with all ten wickets standing. For instance, if the second team's innings halves from 50 overs to 25, the table shows that they still have 66.5% of their resources left, so have to beat two-thirds of the first team's total rather than half.

If the first innings is complete and the second innings is interrupted or prematurely terminated, the score to be beaten is reduced by the percentage of the innings lost. In the World Cup match between South Africa and Sri Lanka at Durban on March 3, 2003, South Africa's run-chase was ended by rain after 45 overs, when they were 229 for six. The Duckworth/Lewis tables showed that, with five overs left and four wickets standing, South Africa has used 85.7% of their run-scoring resources, and 14.3% remained unused. Multiplying Sri Lanka's 50-over total, 268, by 85.7% produced a figure of 229.67. This was rounded down to 229 to give the par score (the runs needed to tie), and the target to win became par plus one – 230 in 45 overs. Under old-fashioned average run-rate per over, the target would have been 242; South Africa benefited because they had preserved wickets into the final stages. (If they had lost one more wicket, par would have been 233; one fewer, 226). As South Africa had equalled par exactly, the match was tied, the points were split, and they failed to qualify for the Super Six stage of the tournament.

The system also covers interruptions to the first innings, multiple interruptions and innings terminated by rain. The tables were revised slightly in September 2002, taking account of rising scoring-rates; the average 50-over total in a one-day international is now taken to be 235, rather than 225.

The version known as the "Professional Edition" was introduced into one-day internationals from October 1, 2003 and subsequently into several national one-day competitions. Based on a more advanced mathematical formula (it is entirely computerised), in effect it adjusts the tables to make allowance for the different scoring-rates that emerge in matches with above-average first-innings scores. The former version, now known as "Standard Edition", continues to operate in some national competitions and lower levels.

BCCI PLATINUM JUBILEE MATCH, 2004-05

This game, squeezed into the brief hiatus between India's home Test series against Australia and South Africa, marked two significant events, but was overshadowed by a third. The ostensible cause was to celebrate the 75th anniversary of the founding of the Board of Control for Cricket in India, while the choice of Pakistan as India's opponents was further proof of the rapprochement between the subcontinental cricketing superpowers. There was no such rapprochement, however, between Sourav Ganguly, the headstrong Indian captain, and the ICC. Soon after play had finished – almost an hour late – the result was forgotten in a huge argument stemming from a two-Test ban for Ganguly. The referee, Clive Lloyd, incensed at India's slow over-rate and mindful that he had fined Ganguly for a similar offence ten months earlier, imposed a penalty that would have ruled the captain out of both South African Tests. India immediately appealed, citing extenuating circumstances, such as heavy dew causing countless ball changes. The appeal was heard by Tim Castle, a New Zealand barrister, who rescinded the ban, though still upbraiding Ganguly: "On any analysis, the delay of nearly an hour... is out of an acceptable range... I am of the opinion that the circumstances were particularly unusual in this game and a large number of them conspired to cause the delays." Ganguly was still fined 50% of his match fee for the slow over-rate.

Note: This match was not first-class.

INDIA v PAKISTAN

One-Day International

At Kolkata, November 13, 2004 (day/night). Pakistan won by six wickets. Toss: India.

Around 90,000 spectators watched a match that turned out to be a cracker, as both sets of batsmen made the most of a belting pitch. First, Yuvraj Singh underlined his value to India's one-day side with a lightning 78 in 62 balls, helping his side to 105 runs from the last 11 overs. Then Salman Butt, in his sixth limited-overs international, played a beautiful innings to reach a maiden hundred. He faced only 130 balls but, thanks to the many delays in Pakistan's innings, batted nearly four and a half hours, despite retiring briefly with cramp. On returning, Salman hit 40 off his last 36 balls, steering Pakistan to their fourth successive one-day victory over India.

Man of the Match: Salman Butt.

India

V. Sehwag b Shahid Afridi	53	M. Kaif not out		14
S. R. Tendulkar run out	16	I. K. Pathan not out		0
V. V. S. Laxman c Kamran Akmal b Shahid Afridi	43			
*S. C. Ganguly c Kamran Akmal b Shoaib Akhtar	48			
†R. Dravid c Shahid Afridi b Abdul Razzaq	16	B 4, l-b 6, w 11, n-b 3		24
Yuvraj Singh c Younis Khan b Naved-ul-Hasan	78	1/29 (2) 2/111 (3) (6 wkts, 50 overs)		292

3/124 (1) 4/163 (5)
5/237 (4) 6/290 (6)

Harbhajan Singh, Zaheer Khan and A. Nehra did not bat.

Bowling: Shoaib Akhtar 9–1–55–1; Naved-ul-Hasan 9–1–67–1; Mohammad Sami 6–0–51–0; Shahid Afridi 10–0–29–2; Shoaib Malik 6–0–31–0; Abdul Razzaq 10–0–49–1.

Pakistan

Salman Butt not out	108	Abdul Razzaq not out	1
Younis Khan c Sehwag b Zaheer Khan	0	L-b 5, w 23, n-b 2	30
Shoaib Malik c Kaif b Sehwag	61		
*Inzamam-ul-Haq c Sehwag b Nehra	75	1/15 (2) 2/128 (3) (4 wkts, 49 overs)	293
Yousuf Youhana c Dravid b Nehra	18	3/186 (5) 4/284 (4)	

Shahid Afridi, †Kamran Akmal, Mohammad Sami, Naved-ul-Hasan and Shoaib Akhtar did not bat.

Salman Butt, when 68, retired hurt at 155 and resumed at 186.

Bowling: Pathan 10–1–48–0; Zaheer Khan 10–1–47–1; Nehra 10–0–65–2; Harbhajan Singh 10–0–51–0; Sehwag 6–0–43–1; Tendulkar 1–0–15–0; Ganguly 1–0–9–0; Yuvraj Singh 1–0–10–0.

Umpires: S. J. A. Taufel (Australia) and K. Hariharan.
Third umpire: I. Sivaram.   Referee: C. H. Lloyd (West Indies).

ONE-DAY INTERNATIONAL RATINGS

The One-Day International Ratings, introduced in August 1998 and sponsored by PricewaterhouseCoopers until January 2005, when they were taken over by the International Cricket Council, follow similar principles to the Test Ratings (see page 1112).

The leading 20 batsmen and bowlers in the One-Day International Ratings on December 31, 2004, were:

	Batsmen	Rating		Bowlers	Rating
1	A. C. Gilchrist (*Australia*)	775	1	S. M. Pollock (*South Africa*)	853
2	J. H. Kallis (*South Africa*)	757	2	W. P. U. J. C. Vaas (*Sri Lanka*)	847
3	S. R. Tendulkar (*India*)	740	3	M. Muralitharan (*Sri Lanka*)	833
4	R. R. Sarwan (*West Indies*)	738	4	J. N. Gillespie (*Australia*)	832
5	R. T. Ponting (*Australia*)	735	5	G. D. McGrath (*Australia*)	777
6	M. E. Trescothick (*England*)	734	6	J. D. P. Oram (*New Zealand*)	759
7	A. Flintoff (*England*)	732	7	A. Flintoff (*England*)	751
8	C. H. Gayle (*West Indies*)	723	8	M. Ntini (*South Africa*)	730
9	S. P. Fleming (*New Zealand*)	719	9	B. Lee (*Australia*)	727
10	K. C. Sangakkara (*Sri Lanka*)	716	10	D. Gough (*England*)	710
11	M. L. Hayden (*Australia*)	702	11	D. L. Vettori (*New Zealand*)	705
12	Yousuf Youhana (*Pakistan*)	700	12	D. R. Tuffey (*New Zealand*)	686
13	A. Symonds (*Australia*)	685	13	Harbhajan Singh (*India*)	680
14	M. S. Atapattu (*Sri Lanka*)	676	14	D. N. T. Zoysa (*Sri Lanka*)	679
15	S. T. Jayasuriya (*Sri Lanka*)	674	15	A. F. Giles (*England*)	678
16	B. C. Lara (*West Indies*)	668	16	J. M. Anderson (*England*)	676
17	R. Dravid (*India*)	663	17	Shoaib Malik (*Pakistan*)	673
18	G. C. Smith (*South Africa*)	648	18	Shoaib Akhtar (*Pakistan*)	660
19	Inzamam-ul-Haq (*Pakistan*)	643	19	I. K. Pathan (*India*)	655
20	D. R. Martyn (*Australia*)	635	20	G. B. Hogg (*Australia*)	649

THE SRI LANKANS IN NEW ZEALAND, 2004-05

Of all the cricketing nations, Sri Lanka was the worst affected by the tsunami that overwhelmed Indian Ocean coastlines on December 26, 2004. The disaster struck while the Sri Lankan team were batting in the tour's opening one-day international in Auckland.

That evening, the still unsuspecting Sri Lankans returned to the reports on their hotel-room televisions. The next game was quickly postponed, but the Sri Lankan board initially rejected the idea of abandoning the tour for fear of being fined by the ICC. Three days later, as the scale of the tragedy and the ICC's position became clear, the four remaining one-day games and both Tests were called off, and eventually rescheduled for April 2005. It left New Zealand with unfulfilled obligations to spectators and commercial partners, and no midsummer international programme. After India confirmed they could not plug the gap, a one-day series was hastily arranged against a FICA World XI led by Shane Warne. New Zealand won the series (not given full one-day international status) 2–1.

SRI LANKAN TOURING PARTY

M. S. Atapattu (*captain*), R. P. Arnold, U. D. U. Chandana, T. M. Dilshan, C. R. D. Fernando, H. M. K. R. B. Herath, W. S. Jayantha, S. T. Jayasuriya, D. P. M. D. Jayawardene, K. M. D. M Kulasekara, M. F. Maharoof, S. L. Malinga, K. C. Sangakkara, W. P. U. J. C. Vaas, D. N. T. Zoysa.

Chandana, Jayantha and Kulasekara were part of the one-day squad, and were due to be replaced by G. I. Daniel, M. Muralitharan and T. T. Samaraweera for the Tests.

Coach: J. Dyson. *Manager:* D. S. B. P. Kuruppu. *Physiotherapist:* C. J. Clark. *Trainer:* S. Duff.

Note: Matches in this section were not first-class.

At Yarrow Stadium, New Plymouth, December 21, 2004. **No result.** Toss: Sri Lankans. **Central Districts 220-7** (49 overs) (J. D. P. Oram 74); **Sri Lankans 20-2** (5 overs).

Each side fielded 12 players, of whom 11 could bat and 11 field. Rain cut Central Districts' innings to 49 overs and eventually ended the game.

At Hamilton, December 23, 2004 (day/night). **Northern Districts v Sri Lankans. No result** (abandoned).

†NEW ZEALAND v SRI LANKA

First One-Day International

At Auckland, December 26, 2004. New Zealand won by seven wickets. Toss: New Zealand.

The sight of the white ball jagging past outside edges briefly reignited criticism of New Zealand's drop-in pitches, and their fitness for international cricket. Inserted under grey cloud, Sri Lanka hobbled to 70 for five, then 141 all out: Cairns removed Jayasuriya on his way to four for 33. He made clever use of his variations, but they were hardly necessary: bowling a good line was usually enough. When New Zealand took their turn, the sun peeped out and conditions were easier: Fleming hit two elegant straight sixes in a decisive unbeaten 77, made against an attack short of Muralitharan – recovering from a shoulder injury – and match practice. But the hubbub about the pitch soon shrank to silence as the news from Sri Lanka came through.

Man of the Match: S. P. Fleming.

Sri Lanka

W. S. Jayantha lbw b Tuffey	0	M. F. Maharoof c Fleming b Cairns	2
S. T. Jayasuriya c Marshall b Cairns	43	K. M. D. N. Kulasekara not out	4
*M. S. Atapattu c McCullum b Tuffey	4	C. R. D. Fernando run out	3
†K. C. Sangakkara c McCullum b Mills	1	L-b 4, w 9, n-b 1	14
D. P. M. D. Jayawardene c Sinclair b Oram	2		

T. M. Dilshan c Fleming b Cairns 48
U. D. U. Chandana run out 20
W. P. U. J. C. Vaas b Cairns 0

1/1 (1) 2/17 (3) 3/18 (4) (42 overs) 141
4/35 (5) 5/70 (2) 6/114 (7)
7/116 (8) 8/120 (9)
9/134 (6) 10/141 (11)

Bowling: Tuffey 8–1–17–2; Mills 8–3–24–1; Oram 7–0–23–1; Cairns 8–1–33–4; Vettori 6–0–22–0; Styris 5–0–18–0.

New Zealand

*S. P. Fleming not out 77
N. J. Astle lbw b Vaas 6
M. S. Sinclair c and b Chandana 31
S. B. Styris run out 12
H. J. H. Marshall not out 14
 B 2, l-b 1, n-b 1 4

1/7 (2) 2/64 (3) (3 wkts, 33 overs) 144
3/101 (4)

J. D. P. Oram, C. L. Cairns, †B. B. McCullum, D. L. Vettori, D. R. Tuffey and K. D. Mills did not bat.

Bowling: Vaas 8–1–31–1; Kulasekara 8–3–13–0; Maharoof 3–0–31–0; Fernando 5–0–22–0; Chandana 7–1–29–1; Jayasuriya 2–0–15–0.

Umpires: P. D. Parker (Australia) and B. F. Bowden.
Third umpire: D. B. Cowie. Referee: M. J. Procter (South Africa).

WORLD CRICKET TSUNAMI APPEAL MATCH, 2004-05

PETER ENGLISH

ICC WORLD XI v ACC ASIAN XI

At Melbourne, January 10, 2005 (day/night). World XI won by 112 runs. Toss: ICC World XI.

Ricky Ponting, who made 140 not out in the 2003 World Cup final, confirmed his love of the big occasion with a valuable and delightful century in the first international to raise money for the Boxing Day tsunami victims. The contest, hastily arranged with volunteer labour staffing much of the ground, was also a rare opportunity to showcase the globe's playing pearls, representing not their countries but the ICC and the Asian Cricket Council. It was a success on both counts as a cheque for \$A14.6m (about £6m) was presented to the ICC's chosen charity, World Vision, at the conclusion of a game delivering relaxed brilliance and a guest fielding stint from Steve Waugh, the nominal World XI coach. The match was awarded full one-day international status (to the irritation of some statisticians) and South Africa and Zimbabwe were the only two Test nations not represented (though England's sole representative, Darren Gough, was available only because he was no longer a Test player, and Bangladesh merely rated a twelfth man, Alok Kapali).

WORLD CRICKET TSUNAMI APPEAL MATCH TEAMS

The two teams that met at the MCG for the world cricket tsunami appeal one-day international. *Back row* (ICC World XI players in italics, ACC Asian XI in bold): *Matthew Hayden, Adam Gilchrist, Glenn McGrath*, **Kumar Sangakkara, Zaheer Khan, Alok Kapali, Muttiah Muralitharan, Sanath Jayasuriya**. *Middle row:* Bob Parry *(third umpire)*, Billy Bowden *(umpire)*, *Chris Gayle, Dwayne Bravo, Stephen Fleming, Daniel Vettori, Chris Cairns*, **Virender Sehwag, Abdul Razzaq, Chaminda Vaas**, Rahul Dravid, Paul Reiffel *(fourth umpire)*, *Anil Kumble*, Chris Broad *(referee)*, Rudi Koertzen *(umpire)*. *Seated:* Shane Warne, Darren Gough, Brian Lara, Steve Waugh *(World XI coach)*, Ricky Ponting, **Sourav Ganguly**, Bob Woolmer *(Asian XI coach)*, **Sachin Tendulkar, Yousuf Youhana**.

Picture by Hamish Blair, Getty Images

Ponting, preferred as captain to Stephen Fleming, faced a difficult task positioning his batting order – Matthew Hayden was the No. 8, while the competitiveness was devalued by Glenn McGrath at No. 6 – but found no such problem with his footwork. Full of crisp drives and pulls, Ponting's 115 off 102 balls, including eight fours and three sixes, was worth more than runs alone. Sponsors paid $A1,000 for every single and $A50,000 for each six, so Ponting collected a match-winning century and $265,000 for the charity. Chris Cairns rattled the tins with two sixes in his 47-ball 69 and Brian Lara scored a half-century as the World XI prepared an impenetrable defence.

Muttiah Muralitharan had taken a front-line role in Sri Lanka following the disaster, and his bowling appearance on the ground where Darrell Hair no-balled him for throwing provoked cheering and flag-waving from united nations. After taking three wickets, Muralitharan was welcomed to Australia by John Howard, the prime minister who had publicly questioned his action in May 2004. Some of the Asian XI brought tales of loved ones' deaths and near misses – Sanath Jayasuriya's mother was badly hurt but survived by clinging on to a tree – but the inspiration did not help them succeed against a dream attack. Shane Warne returned from two years out of one-day internationals with two wickets, including Virender Schwag's to curb his dangerous flow, while Daniel Vettori further stifled the chase. A gripping finish was missing, but it was a memorable tribute from the cricket community. *See also The Tragedy that Brought Us Together, page 85.*

Man of the Match: R. T. Ponting.   *Attendance:* 70,101.

ICC World XI

C. H. Gayle c Sangakkara b Zaheer Khan	1	M. L. Hayden st Sangakkara	
†A. C. Gilchrist c Sangakkara		b Muralitharan .	2
b Zaheer Khan .	24	D. L. Vettori not out	27
*R. T. Ponting st Sangakkara b Kumble .	115	S. K. Warne not out	2
B. C. Lara c Vaas b Kumble.	52		
C. L. Cairns st Sangakkara		L-b 3, w 7, n-b 12.	22
b Muralitharan .	69		
G. D. McGrath c Yousuf Youhana		1/1 (1) 2/50 (2) (8 wkts, 50 overs) 344	
b Muralitharan .	0	3/172 (4) 4/263 (3) 5/264 (6)	
S. P. Fleming b Vaas.	30	6/286 (5) 7/292 (8) 8/337 (7) 15 overs: 78-2	
D. Gough did not bat.			

Bowling: Vaas 9–1–59–1; Zaheer Khan 8–0–46–2; Abdul Razzaq 5–0–50–0; Muralitharan 10–0–59–3; Kumble 10–0–73–2; Sehwag 7–0–46–0; Jayasuriya 1–0–8–0.

ACC Asian XI

S. T. Jayasuriya c Fleming b Cairns. . . .	28	A. Kumble b McGrath	11
V. Sehwag c Gayle b Warne	45	M. Muralitharan run out	0
*S. C. Ganguly c Gough b Vettori	22	L-b 2, w 2, n-b 1	5
R. Dravid not out	75		
Yousuf Youhana c Ponting b Warne	4	1/59 (1) 2/76 (2) (39.5 overs) 232	
†K. C. Sangakkara c Gilchrist b Gough .	24	3/107 (3) 4/114 (5)	
Abdul Razzaq st Gilchrist b Vettori	11	5/156 (6) 6/173 (7)	
W. P. U. J. C. Vaas c McGrath b Vettori .	7	7/197 (8) 8/199 (9)	
Zaheer Khan run out.	0	9/226 (10) 10/232 (11) 15 overs: 85-2	

Bowling: McGrath 7–0–37–1; Gough 8–0–55–1; Cairns 6–0–37–1; Warne 7–0–27–2; Vettori 10–0–58–3; Gayle 1.5–0–16–0.

Umpires: B. F. Bowden (New Zealand) and R. E. Koertzen (South Africa).
Third umpire R. L. Parry (Australia).   Referee: B. C. Broad (England).

ENGLAND A IN INDIA, 2003-04

KATE LAVEN

After three months in the gyms, classrooms and nets at the ECB's new academy in Loughborough, the 2003-04 squad left for a tour of Malaysia and India, where they had been invited to compete in the Duleep Trophy, in theory the premier Indian first-class tournament.

The invitation was unprecedented in the competition's history, and was a brave move on the part of the Indian board since they had no idea whether the young side, strengthened by the Test discard Ed Smith, would humiliate or be humiliated. The latter turned out to be nearer the mark. England played two Duleep matches and suffered heavy defeats in both, having lost five of their six previous matches in India. It proved to be a disappointing experiment.

The side went under the name of England A, a title last used three years earlier. The Indians apparently thought it sounded grander than the intended England Academy.

The scorecards told a sorry tale of inexperience and inconsistency, and the return of captain Alex Gidman to England without playing a game, after his broken hand refused to mend, helped expose the flaws of the squad. Several players had only a handful of first-class appearances, which showed, especially among the batsmen. They also seemed unable to summon the mental discipline their coach, the academy director and England selector Rod Marsh, deemed necessary. Marsh said they played like "millionaires".

Only Nottinghamshire's Kevin Pietersen, South African-born and not yet England-qualified, wholly escaped Marsh's wrath, demonstrating a striking maturity and versatility in the way he sized up bowlers, pitches and conditions. He piled on runs, scoring 708 in eight matches, and emerged as a near-certainty for England caps. His talent was no longer in question and his reputation for being self-centred and obtuse was dispelled by a sustained show of spirited camaraderie, on and off the field.

The Sussex wicket-keeper Matt Prior also staked a claim, with a string of persuasive innings. He made an unbeaten 82 in the final match against East Zone but ran out of partners. However, his keeping was less convincing.

Smith, offered a place as compensation for his exclusion from the main winter tours, missed out by too often adopting a siege mentality when run-making became difficult. His sluggishness served neither him nor his side well in the one-day games and, by the time the four-day matches started, the runs had dried up altogether.

The absence of Gidman contributed to the inability to construct big innings or fight back. Without him, the side lacked adhesion in the batting order and cohesion as a team. While his deputy, James Tredwell, impressed as a tactician and wicket-taking spinner, he was not a natural leader and proved unable to prevent factions forming, which was disruptive.

So the emergence of the Lancashire pace bowler Sajid Mahmood as a quality performer who refused to be distracted was a big plus. He was quick and disciplined and, despite a laid-back demeanour, displayed a willingness to learn, a characteristic not shared by many of his colleagues.

Mahmood benefited from the presence of Simon Jones, included in the Academy's winter programme as part of his rehabilitation from the cruciate-ligament injury he sustained at Brisbane more than a year before. Reports of his progress at Loughborough had been encouraging but the true test, which would decide whether he was fit enough for the senior tour of the West Indies, lay in India.

Alarm bells sounded when he missed the opening games with a sore and swollen knee, but he returned for a gentle workout in the last two one-day games against India A, then booked his flight to the Caribbean with a blistering ten wickets in the friendly against Tamil Nadu at Chennai. After a second four-day workout, against South Zone, Marsh decided he was ready, and should leave immediately.

Getting Jones fit again allowed the management to tick one all-important box. The emergence of Pietersen and Mahmood as strong England contenders filled two more. But the generally poor standards led Marsh to a blunt conclusion: "There aren't many of this group that will be successful Test-match or one-day players." It raised important issues about the Academy's selection process, which Marsh and his team were quick to address.

In June it was announced that the average age of future squads would increase, and that the academy would increasingly fulfil a role more like that played by the old England A tours. "Rather than projecting for six or seven years' time," said chairman of selectors David Graveney, "we'll address specific, immediate needs of the England team."

ENGLAND A TOURING PARTY

A. P. R. Gidman (Gloucestershire) (*captain*), J. C. Tredwell (Kent) (*vice-captain*), Kadeer Ali (Worcestershire), S. R. G. Francis (Somerset), S. P. Jones (Glamorgan), S. A. Khalid (Worcestershire), M. J. Lumb (Yorkshire), S. I. Mahmood (Lancashire), G. R. Napier (Essex), S. A. Newman (Surrey), K. P. Pietersen (Nottinghamshire), M. J. Prior (Sussex), B. M. Shafayat (Nottinghamshire), E. T. Smith (Kent), G. G. Wagg (Warwickshire).

Gidman returned home injured after the one day games. Jones joined the senior England party in the West Indies before the last match, and was replaced by S. P. Kirby (Yorkshire).

Coach: R. W. Marsh. *Manager:* N. E. F. Laughton. *Physiotherapist:* S. Osborne.

ENGLAND A TOUR RESULTS

First-class matches – Played 2: Lost 2.
Non-first-class-matches – Played 7: Won 2, Lost 5.

Note: Matches in this section which were not first-class are signified by a dagger.

†At Royal Selangor Club, Kuala Lumpur, January 29, 2004. **England A won by 112 runs.** Toss: England A. **England A 213-8** (46 overs) (S. A. Newman 50); **Malaysia CA Invitational XI 101** (33.5 overs) (N. M. Krishnamurthi 52).
Man of the Match Graham Wagg scored 38 and had figures of 5–2–4–3.

†At Indian Air Force Ground, Bangalore, February 6, 2004. **Karnataka won by eight wickets.** Toss: England A. **England A 116** (35.1 overs) (S. T. R. Binny 4-29); **Karnataka 120-2** (23.3 overs).
England A slumped from 44-2 to 61-7.

†At Jain International Residential School Ground, Bangalore, February 7, 2004. **Karnataka won by four wickets.** Toss: Karnataka. **England A 203-7** (50 overs) (E. T. Smith 52); **Karnataka 206-6** (45.3 overs) (B. M. V. Uthappa 101*).
England's coach, Rod Marsh, requested this unscheduled rematch after England's heavy defeat the previous day. Karnataka recovered from 11-3.

†At M. Chinnaswamy Stadium, Bangalore, February 9, 2004. **India A won by 55 runs.** Toss: England A. **India A 324-4** (50 overs) (D. Mongia 116, S. Sriram 92); **England A 269-9** (50 overs) (G. R. Napier 61).

†At M. Chinnaswamy Stadium, Bangalore, February 10, 2004. **India A won by two wickets.** Toss: England A. **England A 228** (46 overs) (K. P. Pietersen 131); **India A 229-8** (41.1 overs) (D. Mongia 88, S. Sriram 50; S. I. Mahmood 4-51).
The England management suspended Bilal Shafayat for one game after he swore loudly when dismissed, the first of three England batsmen to be run out. India A collapsed from 189-2 to 226-8.

†At M. A. Chidambaram Stadium, Chennai, February 12, 2004. **India A won by five wickets.** Toss: England A. **England A 210** (42.1 overs) (S. A. Newman 68, E. T. Smith 76*); **India A 213-5** (45.1 overs) (S. Sriram 105*, Y. Venugopal Rao 66).
Sriram and Rao rescued India A from 34-4 with a stand of 155. India A won the series 3–0.

†At M. A. Chidambaram Stadium, Chennai, February 14, 15, 16, 17, 2004. **England A won by 187 runs.** Toss: Tamil Nadu. **England A 368** (K. P. Pietersen 147 retired hurt, M. J. Prior 81) **and 295-9 dec.** (S. A. Newman 57, Kadeer Ali 56; V. Sivaramakrishnan 5-74); **Tamil Nadu 333** (K. Vasudevadas 98; S. P. Jones 5-57) **and 143** (S. P. Jones 5-31).
Pietersen and Prior put on 182 together in the first innings.

DULEEP TROPHY, 2003-04

The Duleep Trophy table, and details of matches not involving England A, can be found in Cricket in India (see pages 1450–1466).

ENGLAND A v SOUTH ZONE

At TERI Oval, Gurgaon, February 21, 22, 23, 24, 2004. South Zone won by six wickets. South Zone 4 pts. Toss: South Zone.
Pietersen scored two outstanding hundreds, but could not prevent England A sliding to an implausible defeat when South Zone managed to become the seventh team in history to reach 500 or more to win a first-class match. Set 501, they scored 503 for four, then larger than the record set by Central Province in Sri Lanka the previous month and surpassed on only two other occasions in cricket history. Until midway through the final afternoon, an England defeat looked out of the question. But Venugopal Rao led South Zone to an astonishing victory. After seven balls, they were one for two, but reached 171 by the close of play without further damage and Rao took his stand with Sriram to 226, before adding another 212 with Badrinath, taking full advantage of a flat, flat pitch and England's lack of discipline in the field. England coach Rod Marsh was infuriated by the outcome. "We had no one to blame but ourselves," he said. "I don't know whether it's arrogance or what, but it's pretty dumb. When you bowl with so little discipline, miss easy

The prosperous South: (*left to right*) Sridharan Sriram, S. Badrinath and Y. Venugopal Rao all hit hundreds for South Zone to send England A to a humiliating defeat.
Photo by Gulu Ezekiel, GE Features

opportunities in the field, you don't expect to win cricket matches at this level. If they've got any pride, some of them will take a lot of heartache away. Others will have forgotten about it already. That doesn't upset me, but it's going to upset their cricket careers, I think." The pitch, carved out of a forest as part of an ecological project, was easy-paced from the start and Pietersen's first-innings 104 was reinforced by Prior and Napier, as England made 377. South Zone's captain, Ramesh, had split his finger while fielding at slip, and in his absence his batsmen faltered, mustering just 174 in reply, Tredwell's off-spin doing most damage. In the second innings, Pietersen reached 115, including several improvised reverse sweeps, which afforded England the luxury of a declaration and an apparently theoretical target. Rao, lucky to survive a fluffed run-out early in his innings, was unbeaten on 228, lasting 457 minutes and 394 balls, 32 of them hit for four.

Close of play: First day, England A 308-7 (Napier 43, Mahmood 2); Second day, England A 88-3 (Pietersen 65, Prior 0); Third day, South Zone 171-2 (Sriram 78, Venugopal Rao 88).

England A

S. A. Newman run out	31	– c Khaleel b Santh	10
E. T. Smith b Singh	27	– run out	10
M. J. Lumb c Khaleel b Joshi	1	– b Santh	0
K. P. Pietersen c Singh b Joshi	104	– b Sriram	115
†M. J. Prior lbw b Joshi	66	– lbw b Santh	0
B. M. Shafayat c Khaleel b Ramkumar	0	– st Khaleel b Joshi	34
G. R. Napier c Khaleel b Ramkumar	76	– not out	64
*J. C. Tredwell c Joshi b Santh	15	– c Venugopal Rao b Joshi	36
S. I. Mahmood lbw b Singh	14	– c sub (S. A. Asnodkar) b Joshi	8
S. P. Jones c Khaleel b Joshi	23	– not out	1
S. R. G. Francis not out	0		
B 6, l-b 7, w 1, n-b 6	20	B 9, l-b 8, n-b 2	19

1/50 (1) 2/55 (3) 3/98 (2) 4/241 (4)   377   1/10 (1) 2/10 (3)   (8 wkts dec.) 297
5/242 (6) 6/244 (5) 7/306 (8)   3/85 (2) 4/89 (5) 5/168 (6)
8/321 (9) 9/377 (7) 10/377 (10)   6/188 (4) 7/245 (8) 8/264 (9)

Bowling: *First Innings*—Singh 24–5–93–2; Santh 13–1–58–1; Joshi 34.2–7–106–4; Ramkumar 22–4–67–2; Venugopal Rao 5–1–17–0; Sriram 4–0–23–0. *Second Innings*—Santh 19–2–79–3; Singh 6–2–11–0; Joshi 33–4–91–3; Ramkumar 15–0–71–0; Sriram 5–0–21–1; Venugopal Rao 1–0–7–0.

South Zone

†I. Khaleel lbw b Francis	1	– (2) lbw b Mahmood	0
B. M. Rowland c Lumb b Mahmood	0	– (1) b Francis	1
S. Sriram b Tredwell	44	– c Prior b Mahmood	117
Y. Venugopal Rao not out	58	– not out	228
S. Sharath c Lumb b Jones	0	– c Pietersen b Napier	28
S. Badrinath lbw b Jones	2	– not out	100
Sunil B. Joshi c Francis b Tredwell	6		
R. Ramkumar b Tredwell	43		
N. P. Singh c Francis b Tredwell	4		
S. Santh c Prior b Napier	4		
*S. Ramesh absent hurt			
B 2, l-b 3, w 2, n-b 5	12	B 17, l-b 8, n-b 4	29

1/3 (2) 2/3 (1) 3/77 (3) 4/78 (5)   174   1/1 (2) 2/1 (1)   (4 wkts) 503
5/86 (6) 6/96 (7) 7/166 (8)   3/227 (3) 4/291 (5)
8/170 (9) 9/174 (10)

Bowling: *First Innings*—Mahmood 11–1–36–1; Francis 8–1–49–1; Napier 4.3–0–19–1; Jones 9–0–24–2; Tredwell 10.2–2–41–4. *Second Innings*—Mahmood 20.1–1–85–2; Francis 13–3–40–1; Jones 13.5–0–89–0; Tredwell 36–3–122–0; Napier 23–5–63–1; Pietersen 9–0–50–0; Lumb 1–0–1–0; Shafayat 8.2–2–28–0.

Umpires: M. S. Mahal and S. K. Porel.

EAST ZONE v ENGLAND A

At Gandhi Ground, Amritsar, February 27, 28, 29, March 1, 2004. East Zone won by 93 runs. East Zone 4 pts. Toss: England A.

Needing a win to reach the final, England A replaced Simon Jones – promoted to the Caribbean tour – with Steve Kirby of Yorkshire, called up from Dennis Lillee's pace foundation in Chennai. Kirby's exuberance buoyed flagging spirits, and a first five-wicket haul from Tredwell earned England the advantage. On another flat, dry track East Zone made 283, 124 from the steadfast Das, who carried his bat. But in reply, only Prior resisted the strike bowler Paul for long, with a vibrant, unbeaten 82. Although Mahmood then maintained great control on the hot third day, taking five wickets, two robust middle-order partnerships extended East Zone's lead and left England 367 to win. Pietersen produced another quality innings, falling six short of a fifth century of the tour, and victory looked possible at lunch on day four, with England 211 for four. But the other contributions were too meagre. The spinner Lahiri removed five England batsmen, and their Indian tour ended as it began, with defeat against an average side.

Close of play: First day, East Zone 283; Second day, East Zone 65-3 (Powar 16, Lahiri 7); Third day, England A 78-2 (Smith 23, Pietersen 29).

East Zone

S. S. Das not out	124	– (9) c Kirby b Mahmood	55
M. S. Dhoni c Smith b Kirby	52	– c Napier b Mahmood	24
A. S. Das lbw b Napier	0	– c Prior b Kirby	7
†D. Dasgupta lbw b Napier	0	– (1) b Mahmood	7
*D. J. Gandhi c Pietersen b Tredwell	7	– (6) c Ali b Tredwell	59
K. R. Powar lbw b Tredwell	13	– (4) b Tredwell	40
L. R. Shukla c Newman b Tredwell	8	– c Wagg b Tredwell	60
S. S. Lahiri run out	17	– (5) b Mahmood	40
U. Chatterjee c and b Tredwell	23	– (8) b Tredwell	1
D. S. Mohanty c Pietersen b Tredwell	0	– c Kirby b Mahmood	0
S. S. Paul b Napier	9	– not out	1
B 5, l-b 9, n-b 16	30	B 2, l-b 4, n-b 8	14

1/93 (2) 2/99 (3) 3/99 (4) 4/147 (5)   283   1/27 (2) 2/34 (1) 3/49 (3)   308
5/171 (6) 6/183 (7) 7/227 (8)   4/112 (4) 5/132 (5) 6/238 (7)
8/272 (9) 9/272 (10) 10/283 (11)   7/249 (8) 8/270 (6)
                                         9/271 (10) 10/308 (9)

Bowling: *First Innings*—Mahmood 19–7–42–0; Kirby 15–6–41–1; Napier 18–6–54–3; Tredwell 24–0–101–5; Wagg 12–3–31–0. *Second Innings*—Mahmood 23.1–9–62–5; Kirby 16–5–47–1; Napier 11–1–48–0; Tredwell 26–1–130–4; Wagg 4–1–15–0.

England A

S. A. Newman b Paul	20	– b Paul	0
E. T. Smith c A. S. Das b Mohanty	0	– st Dasgupta b Lahiri	42
M. J. Lumb lbw b Paul	33	– lbw b Lahiri	13
K. P. Pietersen c Mohanty b Chatterjee	32	– c Dasgupta b Powar	94
†M. J. Prior not out	82	– c Dasgupta b Paul	46
Kadeer Ali lbw b Paul	0	– not out	34
G. R. Napier c Powar b Chatterjee	28	– c and b Lahiri	17
G. G. Wagg c Dasgupta b Powar	8	– (9) c Paul b Chatterjee	13
*J. C. Tredwell c A. S. Das b Chatterjee	1	– (8) lbw b Paul	0
S. I. Mahmood b Paul	12	– b Lahiri	1
S. P. Kirby b Paul	0	– c Dhoni b Lahiri	0
L-b 3, w 6	9	B 8, l-b 1, n-b 4	13

1/0 (2) 2/36 (1) 3/87 (4) 4/104 (3)   225   1/0 (1) 2/25 (3) 3/124 (2)   273
5/106 (6) 6/171 (7) 7/187 (8)   4/176 (4) 5/222 (5) 6/251 (7)
8/188 (9) 9/217 (10) 10/225 (11)   7/253 (8) 8/272 (9)
                                    9/273 (10) 10/273 (11)

Bowling: *First Innings*—Paul 18.5–4–61–5; Mohanty 9–1–23–1; Lahiri 8–0–57–0; Chatterjee 22–3–55–3; Powar 6–0–21–1. *Second Innings*—Paul 20–5–53–3; Mohanty 10–4–19–0, Lahiri 37.4–9–118–5; Chatterjee 20–6–54–1; Powar 6–0–20–1.

Umpires: V. Chopra and I. Sivaram.

OTHER A-TEAM TOURS

SRI LANKA A IN SOUTH AFRICA AND KENYA, 2003-04

Sri Lanka A toured South Africa in October 2003. They lost a two-match first-class series with South Africa A 1–0, and the three-match one-day series 2–1. They subsequently toured Kenya, where they won a five-match one-day series 5–0. The squad of 15 was as follows: R. P. Arnold (*captain*), M. N. Nawaz (*vice-captain*), G. I. Daniel, S. K. L. de Silva, L. J. P. Gunaratne, D. A. Gunawardene, H. M. R. K. B. Herath, H. A. P. W. Jayawardene, M. T. T. Mirando, J. Mubarak, H. G. D. Nayanakantha, M. G. Vandort, K. Weeraratne, O. L. A. Wijesiriwardene, D. N. T. Zoysa. *Coach:* H. H. Devapriya. *Manager:* E. R. Fernando. *Physiotherapist:* C. J. Clark.

At Potchefstroom, October 3, 4, 5, 2003. **Drawn.** Toss: Sri Lanka A. **Sri Lanka A 311-9 dec.** (D. A. Gunawardene 64, H. M. R. K. B. Herath 70*) **and 211-6 dec.** (G. I. Daniel 81, J. Mubarak 56); **South Africa Academy 291-7 dec.** (M. M. Matika 74, M. R. Sekhoto 81) **and 102-1** (G. M. Smith 56*).

At Benoni, October 7, 8, 9, 2003. **South Africa A won by nine wickets.** Toss: South Africa A. **Sri Lanka A 127** (R. Telemachus 4-40) **and 266** (D. A. Gunawardene 95, H. M. R. K. B. Herath 50*); **South Africa A 361** (A. G. Puttick 97, M. van Jaarsveld 114; H. G. D. Nayanakantha 4-75) **and 33-1.**

At Potchefstroom, October 12, 13, 14, 15, 2003. **Drawn.** Toss: South Africa A. **South Africa A 450-8 dec.** (M. van Jaarsveld 87, A. G. Prince 182*) **and 176-2 dec.** (M. van Jaarsveld 67*, A. G. Prince 56*); **Sri Lanka A 239** (S. K. L. de Silva 58) **and 170-3** (S. K. L. de Silva 81*, J. Mubarak 52*).

SRI LANKA A IN INDIA, 2003-04

Sri Lanka A toured India in November–December 2003, and drew a three-match first-class series with India A 1–1. They subsequently took part in a triangular one-day tournament with India A and Pakistan A, winning the final, against India A, by seven wickets. The squad of 15 was as follows: M. N. Nawaz (*captain*), S. K. L. de Silva (*vice-captain*), G. I. Daniel, H. M. R. K. B. Herath, H. A. P. W. Jayawardene, S. H. T. Kandamby, A. B. T. Lakshitha, S. L. Malinga, J. Mubarak, C. R. B. Mudalige, N. T. Paranavitana, A. S. Polonowita, P. S. A. N. Shiroman, K. Weeraratne, O. L. A. Wijesiriwardene. *Coach:* H. H. Devapriya. *Manager:* N. Mohamed. *Physiotherapist:* C. J. Clark.

At Sardar Patel (Gujarat) Stadium, Ahmedabad, November 23, 24, 25, 26, 2003. **Drawn.** Toss: India A. **Sri Lanka A 244** (H. M. R. K. B. Herath 51; A. Bhandari 6-55) **and 308** (H. A. P. W. Jayawardene 76, M. N. Nawaz 92; M. M. Patel 4-70, R. R. Powar 4-60); **India A 369** (M. Kaif 53, H. K. Badani 50, R. S. Gavaskar 60; H. M. R. K. B. Herath 6-89) **and 102-5** (M. Kaif 50*).

At Nehru Stadium, Pune, November 29, 30, December 1, 2, 2003. **India A won by an innings and 92 runs.** Toss: Sri Lanka A. **Sri Lanka A 340** (G. I. Daniel 111, J. Mubarak 64; A. Bhandari 5-70) **and 124** (M. Kartik 4-27); **India A 556-7 dec.** (G. Gambhir 131, R. S. Gavaskar 173, A. Ratra 68, R. R. Powar 64*).

At Brabourne Stadium, Mumbai, December 6, 7, 8, 2003. **Sri Lanka A won by three wickets.** Toss: India A. **India A 172** (H. M. R. K. B. Herath 4-34) **and 206; Sri Lanka A 226** (S. H. T. Kandamby 60; S. K. Trivedi 4-23) **and 155-7** (S. H. T. Kandamby 64*).

India A's first innings reached 138-2 before they lost eight for 34 in 14 overs, with Herath claiming four in seven balls. In the final innings, Sri Lanka A collapsed to 57-5 chasing 153 before Kandamby steered them to victory and a tied series.

SRI LANKA A IN NEW ZEALAND, 2003-04

Sri Lanka A toured New Zealand in March–April 2004, and were whitewashed 3–0 in a three-match first-class series with New Zealand A. They also lost both games played in a three-match one-day series, with the third abandoned because of the weather. The squad of 16 was as follows: M. N. Nawaz (*captain*), S. H. T. Kandamby (*vice-captain*), G. I. Daniel, K. A. D. M. Fernando, K. H. R. K. Fernando, T. C. B. Fernando, D. Hettiarachchi, R. P. Hewage, H. A. P. W. Jayawardene, S. Kalawithigoda, A. B. T. Lakshitha, S. L. Malinga, J. Mubarak, W. M. B. Perera, L. P. C. Silva, M. S. Villavarayan. *Coach:* H. H. Devapriya. *Manager:* R. G. C. E. Wijesuriya. *Physiotherapist:* C. J. Clark.

At Alexandra, March 7, 8, 9, 2004. **Drawn.** Toss: Sri Lanka A. **Sri Lanka A 308-6 dec.** (G. I. Daniel 94, S. H. T. Kandamby 64) **and 170-7 dec.** (R. P. Hewage 67, K. H. R. K. Fernando 66*; W. C. McSkimming 5-16); **Otago 246-8 dec.** (N. L. McCullum 80; D. Hettiarachchi 4-65) **and 208-5** (C. D. Cumming 92; D. Hettiarachchi 5-74).

In Sri Lanka A's second innings, Hewage's first five partners fell to McSkimming for 19 runs between them.

At Queenstown, March 11, 12, 13, 14, 2004. **New Zealand A won by an innings and 237 runs.** Toss: New Zealand A. **Sri Lanka A 212** (K. A. D. M. Fernando 53; I. G. Butler 4-64, C. S. Martin 5-54) **and 148** (M. J. Mason 5-21); **New Zealand A 597-9 dec.** (M. D. Bell 173, M. S. Sinclair 133, L. Vincent 56, R. G. Hart 51, Extras 54).

Bell and Sinclair added 250 for New Zealand A's second wicket.

At Bert Sutcliffe Oval, Lincoln, March 19, 20, 21, 22, 2004. **New Zealand A won by an innings and 66 runs.** Toss: New Zealand A. **Sri Lanka A 276** (G. I. Daniel 124) **and 228** (G. I. Daniel 66, W. M. B. Perera 70); **New Zealand A 570** (M. D. Bell 92, J. M. How 92, M. S. Sinclair 50, L. Vincent 107, H. J. H. Marshall 60, J. E. C. Franklin 64*; S. L. Malinga 4-163).

At Village Green, Christchurch, March 27, 28, 29, 30, 2004. **New Zealand A won by an innings and 258 runs.** Toss: Sri Lanka A. **New Zealand A 537** (J. M. How 50, P. G. Fulton 60, H. J. H. Marshall 65, P. J. Wiseman 107, B. P. Martin 113*; D. Hettiarachchi 4-121); **Sri Lanka A 154 and 125** (G. I. Daniel 59; J. E. C. Franklin 4-31).

Wiseman and Martin added 209 for the ninth wicket to take New Zealand A past 500 for the third match running and set up a third successive innings win.

ZIMBABWE A IN BANGLADESH, 2003-04

Zimbabwe A toured Bangladesh in March–April 2004. They lost a two-match first-class series with Bangladesh A 1–0, and a five-match one-day series 3–2. The squad of 14 was as follows: A. Maregwede (*captain*), R. J. Bennett, E. Chigumbura, C. K. Coventry, G. M. Ewing, T. R. Gripper, W. Mwayenga, J. S. Nicolle, T. Panyangara, H. P. Rinke, S. Matsikenyeri, V. Sibanda, R. W. Sims, B. R. M. Taylor. *Coach:* P. V. Simmons. *Manager:* E. Sembezeya. *Physiotherapist:* A. Machikicho. *Selector on tour:* S. Mangongo.

At Fatullah Stadium, Dhaka, March 12, 13, 14, 2004. **Zimbabwe A won by 223 runs.** Toss: Zimbabwe A. **Zimbabwe A 328** (V. Sibanda 68, T. R. Gripper 81, G. M. Ewing 57; Arafat Sunny 6-79) **and 203-4 dec.** (T. R. Gripper 68, E. Chigumbura 59*, A. Maregwede 50*); **Bangladesh Under-23 157 and 151** (G. M. Ewing 4-31).

At Rajshahi, March 17, 18, 19, 2004. **Bangladesh A won by five runs.** Toss: Zimbabwe A. **Bangladesh A 200** (Tushar Imran 103) **and 195; Zimbabwe A 229** (T. R. Gripper 59; Alamgir Kabir 4-76) **and 161** (Alamgir Kabir 4-63, Enamul Haque, jun. 5-64).

The match started and ended with collapses. Bangladesh A recovered from 53-5 on the first morning. Zimbabwe A were 146-5 chasing 167 in the final innings, but lost five wickets for 15 runs in 7.3 overs.

At Bogra, March 23, 24, 25, 26, 2004. **Drawn.** Toss: Bangladesh A. **Zimbabwe A 407** (R. W. Sims 80, A. Maregwede 90, G. M. Ewing 100; Tareq Aziz 5-91) **and 267-3 dec.** (T. R. Gripper 59, E. Chigumbura 130*); **Bangladesh A 378** (Rajin Saleh 86, Mohammad Ashraful 82, Faisal Hossain 83, Dhiman Ghosh 54) **and 99-7.**

In their first innings, Maregwede and Ewing added 170 for Zimbabwe A's seventh wicket.

INDIA A IN ZIMBABWE AND KENYA, 2004

India A toured Zimbabwe in July–August 2004. They won all their three first-class matches, including the one against Zimbabwe A, and a one-day game against Zimbabwe A. They subsequently travelled to Kenya for a triangular one-day tournament, beating Pakistan A in the final by six wickets on Duckworth/Lewis method. Afterwards, they played a two-match first-class series against Kenya, winning 1–0. The original squad of 15 was as follows: S. V. Bahutule (*captain*), H. Badani, A. Bhandari, A. Chopra, M. S. Dhoni, G. Gambhir, R. S. Gavaskar, Y. A. Golwalkar, D. S. Jadhav, K. D. Karthik, M. M. Patel, S. S. Paul, R. R. Powar, A. M. Salvi, S. Sriram. *Coach:* S. M. Patil. *Manager:* Professor R. R. Rohi. *Physiotherapist:* V. Daga. N. V. Ojha, A. T. Rayudu and Y. Venugopal Rao joined the party in Kenya when Gavaskar and Karthik were called up by the senior Indian side.

At Harare Sports Club, Harare, July 22, 23, 24, 2004. **India A won by nine wickets.** Toss: India A. **India A 420** (D. S. Jadhav 93, G. Gambhir 103, K. D. Karthik 96; E. C. Rainsford 4-96) **and 50-1; Zimbabwe Select XI 259** (B. R. M. Taylor 56, V. Sibanda 51, E. Chigumbura 57; S. V. Bahutule 4-71) **and 208** (E. Chigumbura 71, I. M. Chinyoka 62; S. V. Bahutule 6-43).
Zimbabwe A's second innings collapsed to 88-7 before Chigumbura and Chinyoka added 109 for the eighth wicket.

At Harare Sports Club, Harare, July 29, 30, 31, 2004. **India A won by ten wickets.** Toss: India A. **Zimbabwe Select XI 152** (S. V. Bahutule 4-27) **and 131** (S. V. Bahutule 4-11); **India A 259** (R. S. Gavaskar 60, K. D. Karthik 52, S. V. Bahutule 57; T. Panyangara 5-60) **and 26-0.**
India A keeper Mahendra Dhoni made 11 dismissals in the match (seven caught, four stumped).

At Country Club, Harare, August 5, 6, 7, 8, 2004. **India A won by ten wickets.** Toss: Zimbabwe A. **Zimbabwe A 200** (T. Taibu 53, A. Maregwede 50; S. S. Paul 6-46, A. Bhandari 4-65) **and 221** (A. Maregwede 68, E. Chigumbura 69; S. S. Paul 6-56); **India A 413-9 dec.** (R. S. Gavaskar 127, S. V. Bahutule 101*; T. Panyangara 4-87) **and 12-0.**
Shib Paul took 12-102 in the match.

At Ruaraka, Nairobi, August 26, 27, 28, 2004. **India A won by an innings and 233 runs.** Toss: Kenyans. **Kenyans 116** (S. V. Bahutule 5-37) **and 168** (S. V. Bahutule 5-58, R. R. Powar 4-73); **India A 517-4 dec.** (S. Sriram 118, Y. Venugopal Rao 200*, A. T. Rayudu 102*).
Venugopal Rao's 200, his second double-hundred, lasted 365 balls and included 24 fours and a six. He added 199 for the fourth wicket with Sriram and an unbroken 229 for the fifth with Rayudu.*

At Simba Union, Nairobi, September 1, 2, 3, 2004. **Drawn.** Toss: India A. **India A 492** (D. S. Jadhav 260*, M. S. Dhoni 78, A. T. Rayudu 50; P. J. Ongondo 5-90); **Kenyans 356** (M. A. Ouma 58, S. O. Tikolo 156).
Jadhav carried his bat for 260, his fourth double-hundred – all in the space of nine months – which lasted 386 balls and included 22 fours.*

PAKISTAN A IN KENYA, 2004

Pakistan A toured Kenya in August 2004. They drew both their first-class matches with Kenya, and subsequently took part in a triangular one-day tournament also involving India A; they lost the final to India A by six wickets on Duckworth/Lewis method. The squad of 14 was as follows: Misbah-ul-Haq (*captain*), Taufeeq Umar (*vice-captain*), Bazid Khan, Faisal Iqbal, Iftikhar Anjum, Junaid Zia, Kamran Akmal, Mansoor Amjad, Naved Ashraf, Naved Latif, Qaiser Abbas, Riaz Afridi, Salman Butt, Zahid Saeed. *Coach:* Aqib Javed. *Manager:* Sultan Rana.

At Simba Union, Nairobi, July 31, August 1, 2, 2004. **Drawn.** Toss: Pakistan A. **Pakistan A 495-7 dec.** (Taufeeq Umar 144, Faisal Iqbal 119, Naved Latif 81) **and 129-2** (Salman Butt 54*); **Kenyans 371-8 dec.** (R. D. Shah 124, S. O. Tikolo 109).
Shah and Tikolo added 216 for the second Kenyan wicket.

At Sir Ali Muslim Club, Nairobi, August 5, 6, 7, 8, 2004. **Drawn.** Toss: Pakistan A. **Kenyans 502** (R. D. Shah 247, S. O. Tikolo 80, M. O. Odumbe 52; Iftikhar Anjum 4-123) **and 286** (H. S. Modi 95, M. O. Odumbe 106; Junaid Zia 4-82, Mansoor Amjad 4-98); **Pakistan A 375** (Salman Butt 104, Misbah-ul-Haq 151) **and 55-2.**

Ravindu Shah scored his third hundred in three first-class innings, his maiden double-century. Kenyan keeper Kennedy Otieno made six catches in Pakistan A's first innings.

SOUTH AFRICA A IN ZIMBABWE, 2004

South Africa A toured Zimbabwe in August 2004. They won a two-match first-class series with Zimbabwe A 1–0, and a three-match one-day series 3–0. The original squad of 13 was as follows: A. G. Prince (*captain*), P. R. Adams, H. M. Amla, L. L. Bosman, Z. de Bruyn, A. B. de Villiers, G. J-P. Kruger, C. K. Langeveldt, N. D. McKenzie, J. A. Morkel, A. C. Thomas, T. L. Tsolekile, C. M. Willoughby. *Coach:* R. V. Jennings. *Manager:* O. Nkagisang. *Physiotherapist:* D. Jackson. H. D. Ackerman, H. H. Dippenaar, J. M. Kemp and M. N. van Wyk joined the party for the one-day matches.

At Bulawayo, August 11, 12, 13, 14, 2004. **South Africa A won by seven wickets.** Toss: South Africa A. **Zimbabwe A 186** (M. A. Vermeulen 62; P. R. Adams 5-51) **and 286** (B. R. M. Taylor 57, S. Matsikenyeri 66, M. A. Vermeulen 77; P. R. Adams 5-99); **South Africa A 307** (A. B. de Villiers 91, J. A. Morkel 76, G. J-P. Kruger 55*; E. C. Rainsford 6-67) **and 168-3** (A. B. de Villiers 84).

South Africa A's first innings reached 154-7 before the last three wickets all but doubled the score.

At Bulawayo, August 17, 18, 19, 20, 2004. **Drawn.** Toss: South Africa A. **South Africa A 272** (J. A. Morkel 94; D. T. Hondo 4-46) **and 309-5 dec.** (N. D. McKenzie 126*, H. M. Amla 74); **Zimbabwe A 278** (B. R. M. Taylor 68, D. D. Ebrahim 97*; A. C. Thomas 4-60) **and 290-8** (B. R. M. Taylor 59, V. Sibanda 59, M. L. Nkala 65*; Z. de Bruyn 4-52).

Morkel and Charl Langeveldt rescued South Africa A's first innings from 169-9 with a last-wicket stand of 103.

THE ICC SIX NATIONS CHALLENGE, 2003-04

The United States achieved their greatest cricketing triumph of modern times when they overcame five other associate members with far more pedigree and thus secured the last place in the 2004 ICC Champions Trophy in England, where they would play their first official one-day internationals. The result was achieved by the merest sliver: they finished ahead of Scotland in the final table by 0.03 of a run. But that was more decisive than their right to take part in this tournament in the first place.

They had been confirmed as the sixth team in the competition, held in the Gulf states of Dubai and Sharjah, barely two months before it began. The other participants had filled the top five places at the last ICC Trophy, the tournament for associate members, in Canada in 2001, and some assumed the final place would go to Denmark, who came sixth there. But Denmark only finished ahead of Ireland and the Americans on run-rate, and an ICC spokesman said Ireland had beaten the Danes since then, so that ranking was probably out of date. That did not open the way for Ireland, however. The spokesman said the USA had been included "to help the development of the sport in that country".

Still, their opponents could hardly claim they were unworthy entrants. The Americans' old rivals Canada lost all five matches, but the other five teams all finished level on points, having each won three games and lost two. While the Americans headed for The Oval and the Rose Bowl, their opponents could only curse a missed single here and a dropped catch there that would have changed the arithmetic. This was especially true for the Scots, beaten by the Americans in the final match with 16 balls to spare, which was the nick of time because an over later would have been too late for the USA. The win was secured with 60 from 42-year-old Clayton Lambert, who played five Tests for West Indies. Lambert was the leading scorer in the competition, with 214 and an average of 107.

QUALIFYING TABLE

	Played	Won	Lost	Points	Net run-rate
USA	5	3	2	6	0.55
Scotland.	5	3	2	6	0.52
Namibia.	5	3	2	6	0.15
Holland	5	3	2	6	0.12
United Arab Emirates. . .	5	3	2	6	−0.05
Canada	5	0	5	0	−1.21

Net run-rate is calculated by subtracting runs conceded per over from runs scored per over.

Note: Matches in this section were not first-class.

At Dubai (Ground No 1), February 29, 2004. **Holland won by 35 runs.** Toss: Scotland. **Holland 198-9** (50 overs) (L. P. van Troost 58); **Scotland 163** (47 overs). *Holland 2 pts.*

At Sharjah, February 29, 2004. **USA won by five wickets.** Toss: USA. **Namibia 254-8** (50 overs) (G. Snyman 62); **USA 258-5** (46.5 overs) (S. Massiah 71, C. B. Lambert 64*). *USA 2 pts.*
  Lambert scored his 64 in 49 balls.*

At Dubai (Ground No 2), February 29, 2004. **United Arab Emirates won by five wickets.** Toss: United Arab Emirates. **Canada 157-9** (50 overs) (A. Bagai 53); **United Arab Emirates 160-5** (33.3 overs) (Khurram Khan 53*). *United Arab Emirates 2 pts.*

At Sharjah, March 1, 2004. **Holland won by 67 runs.** Toss: Canada. **Holland 236-7** (50 overs) (J. F. Kloppenburg 52); **Canada 169** (41.4 overs). *Holland 2 pts.*

At Dubai (Ground No 1), March 1, 2004. **Scotland won by 93 runs.** Toss: Scotland. **Scotland 160-8** (50 overs) (B. O. van Rooi 4-40); **Namibia 67** (22.5 overs) (P. J. C. Hoffmann 4-14). *Scotland 2 pts.*
   Namibia's 67 was the lowest total of the tournament.

At Dubai (Ground No 2), March 1, 2004. **United Arab Emirates won by five wickets.** Toss: United Arab Emirates. **USA 245-6** (50 overs) (R. Alexander 53, S. Massiah 92*, C. B. Lambert 57); **United Arab Emirates 246-5** (46 overs) (Syed Maqsood 65, Khurram Khan 103*). *United Arab Emirates 2 pts.*
   Pakistan-born Khurram Khan scored the tournament's only century, in 104 balls, with eight fours and a six, and added 159 for the fifth wicket with Syed Maqsood. Earlier, Massiah and Lambert added 119 for the USA's fifth wicket.

At Dubai (Ground No 1), March 3, 2004. **USA won by six wickets.** Toss: USA. **Canada 126** (48.4 overs); **USA 127-4** (24 overs) (M. Johnson 67). *USA 2 pts.*

At Dubai (Ground No 2), March 3, 2004. **Namibia won by 71 runs.** Toss: Namibia. **Namibia 247-5** (50 overs) (D. Keulder 81, D. B. Kotze 81*); **Holland 176** (46.3 overs). *Namibia 2 pts.*
   Keulder and Kotze added 173 for Namibia's fourth wicket.

At Sharjah, March 3, 2004. **Scotland won by 48 runs.** Toss: United Arab Emirates. **Scotland 258-6** (50 overs) (G. M. Hamilton 70, D. R. Brown 80); **United Arab Emirates 210** (45.1 overs) (R. R. Watson 4-47). *Scotland 2 pts.*

At Sharjah, March 4, 2004. **Scotland won by 36 runs.** Toss: Canada. **Scotland 214** (49.4 overs) (I. M. Stanger 84; A. Codrington 4-39); **Canada 178** (45.1 overs). *Scotland 2 pts.*

At Dubai (Ground No 2), March 4, 2004. **Holland won by eight wickets.** Toss: Holland. **USA 248** (48.3 overs) (R. W. Staple 94, C. A. Reid 55; E. Schiferli 5-45); **Holland 249-2** (48.1 overs) (D. J. Reekers 67, D. L. S. van Bunge 79*, B. Zuiderent 64*). *Holland 2 pts.*
   Schiferli claimed the only five-wicket return of this tournament. Van Bunge and Zuiderent shared an unbroken stand of 137 for Holland's third wicket.

At Dubai (Ground No 1), March 4, 2004. **Namibia won by 70 runs.** Toss: United Arab Emirates. **Namibia 177** (46.4 overs) (D. Keulder 64; Khurram Khan 4-35); **United Arab Emirates 107** (40 overs). *Namibia 2 pts.*
   UAE wicket-keeper Mohammad Nadeem made two catches and three stumpings.

At Dubai (Ground No 1), March 6, 2004. **Namibia won by five runs.** Toss: Canada. **Namibia 195** (49.4 overs); **Canada 190** (49.2 overs). *Namibia 2 pts.*

At Dubai (Ground No 2), March 6, 2004. **USA won by five wickets.** Toss: Scotland. **Scotland 206** (49.4 overs) (G. M. Hamilton 60; Nasir Javed 4-39); **USA 208-5** (47.2 overs) (C. B. Lambert 60). *USA 2 pts.*
   The USA's victory put them ahead of the Scots in the final table by less than 0.03 on run-rate. American wicket-keeper Mark Johnson made four catches and a stumping in Scotland's innings.

At Sharjah, March 6, 2004. **United Arab Emirates won by three wickets.** Toss: Holland. **Holland 290** (45.5 overs) (D. J. Reekers 85, T. B. M. de Leede 73); **United Arab Emirates 295-7** (49.1 overs) (Asim Saeed 55, Syed Maqsood 93). *United Arab Emirates 2 pts.*
   This match featured the two highest totals of the tournament.

ICC INTERCONTINENTAL CUP, 2004

The International Cricket Council introduced a new competition for its Associate Members in 2004 – a global tournament for a dozen countries, running from March to November. The most important difference from the ICC Trophy, in which the Associates gather for a few weeks in a single country, was that matches would be played over three days, rather than one, with four regional groups leading to a knockout in the Gulf. The aim was to raise playing standards by encouraging the teams to adapt to the longer game.

"Batsmen will learn to build an innings, spend more time at the crease and thereby increase their confidence and ability," explained Bob Woolmer, the ICC's high performance manager when the tournament was launched. "Bowlers too will get fitter and more accurate, and learn more skills." It was perhaps ironic that the only match which did not last three days was the final, in which Scotland thrashed Canada in five sessions.

The competition was given first-class status, which raised some eyebrows, but ensured Canada's John Davison another entry in the record books. In February 2003, he had astonished everyone by taking a 67-ball hundred, the fastest in World Cup history, off West Indies. This time, Davison made headlines with the ball, bowling Canada to victory over the USA with 17 for 137. He was only the second man, after Jim Laker, to claim so many wickets in a match since the Second World War. Sadly for Canada, he returned to his other job, playing for South Australia, before the finals.

Scotland's title made up for their disappointment on their last trip to the Gulf, in March, when they had narrowly missed qualifying for the ICC Champions Trophy. In this event, they led the European group after beating Ireland at Clontarf, thanks to nine wickets from Asim Butt. And their strong batting – Fraser Watts was the tournament's leading scorer with 413, including two hundreds – gave them a decisive advantage over Kenya, who collapsed for 95 in the semi-final.

Kenya, whose leading batsman Ravindu Shah also scored two hundreds, had headed the African group through an innings win over Uganda, who surprisingly beat Namibia, one of the teams from the 2003 World Cup. United Arab Emirates were the Asian group winners, though home advantage was not enough to see them through their semi-final with Canada.

The ICC announced that the tournament would return in 2005 on similar lines, with Hong Kong replacing Malaysia in the Asian group.

QUALIFYING TABLES

Africa	Played	Won	Lost	Drawn	Batting	Bowling	Points
					Bonus points		
KENYA	2	1	0	1	16	15.5	45.5
Uganda	2	1	1	0	14	13	41
Namibia	2	0	1	1	18.5	14	32.5

Americas	Played	Won	Lost	Drawn	Bonus points Batting	Bowling	Points
CANADA	2	1	0	1	16.5	19.5	50
USA	2	1	1	0	14	19	47
Bermuda	2	0	1	1	13	16	29

Asia	Played	Won	Lost	Drawn	Bonus points Batting	Bowling	Points
UNITED ARAB EMIRATES . .	2	1	0	1	19	17.5	50.5
Nepal	2	1	0	1	10.5	17	41.5
Malaysia	2	0	2	0	9.5	13.5	23

Europe	Played	Won	Lost	Drawn	Bonus points Batting	Bowling	Points
SCOTLAND	2	1	0	1	18	16.5	48.5
Ireland	2	1	1	0	13	16	43
Holland	2	0	1	1	15.5	11.5	27

Semi-finals
Scotland drew with Kenya, and Canada drew with United Arab Emirates; Scotland and Canada qualified for the final by virtue of gaining more points in their respective matches.

Final
Scotland beat Canada by an innings and 84 runs.

Win = 14 pts. Bonus points were awarded, over both innings, as follows: 0.5 pts for every 25 runs, to a maximum of six points (in the first innings restricted to the first 90 overs); 0.5 pts for every wicket taken (no restriction in either innings).

Africa Group

At Windhoek, April 23, 24, 25, 2004. **Uganda won by five wickets.** Toss: Namibia. **Namibia 165 and 289** (D. Keulder 67, D. B. Kotze 60; K. Kamyuka 5-83); **Uganda 274** (N. Kishore 74, F. Nsubuga 62) **and 183-5** (B. Musoke 72). *Uganda 32 pts, Namibia 16 pts.*

At Gymkhana, Nairobi, July 23, 24, 25, 2004. **Kenya won by an innings and four runs.** Toss: Kenya. **Uganda 152 and 151** (J. Olweny 51); **Kenya 307-6 dec.** (R. D. Shah 135, H. S. Modi 85; K. Kamyuka 4-83). *Kenya 30 pts, Uganda 9 pts.*

At Aga Khan, Nairobi, October 1, 2, 3, 2004. **Drawn.** Toss: Kenya. **Namibia 357-6 dec.** (D. Keulder 90, L. J. Burger 50, D. B. Kotze 62, G. Snyman 67*) **and 202-5 dec.** (A. J. Burger 50, S. J. Swanepoel 74*); **Kenya 258** (H. S. Modi 53, L. N. Onyango 67) **and 259-3** (R. D. Shah 187*). *Kenya 15.5 pts, Namibia 16.5 pts.*
   Ravindu Shah's 187, his second century of the tournament and his fourth in five first-class matches, was the Intercontinental Cup's highest score. He hit 27 fours.*

Americas Group

USA v CANADA

At Fort Lauderdale, May 28, 29, 30, 2004. Canada won by 104 runs. Canada 30.5 pts, USA 15 pts. Toss: Canada. First-class debuts: Aijaz Ali, Z. A. Amin, D. L. Blake, H. R. Johnson, M. R. Johnson, S. J. Massiah, C. A. Reid; A. Bagai, D. Chumney, H. Dhillon, A. Patel, E. Sinnathamby, Z. Surkari.

SIXTEEN WICKETS IN A MATCH SINCE THE SECOND WORLD WAR

19-90	J. C. Laker	England v Australia at Manchester	1956
17-137	**J. M. Davison**	**Canada v USA at Fort Lauderdale**	**2004**
16-83	B. Dooland	Nottinghamshire v Essex at Nottingham	1954
16-83	G. A. R. Lock	Surrey v Kent at Blackheath	1956
16-84	C. Gladwin	Derbyshire v Worcestershire at Stourbridge	1952
16-99	A. Kumble	Karnataka v Kerala at Thalassery	1994-95
16-112	J. H. Wardle	Yorkshire v Sussex at Hull	1954
16-119	M. P. Bicknell	Surrey v Leicestershire at Guildford	2000
16-130	A. R. Tait	Northern Districts v Auckland at Hamilton.	1996-97
16-136	N. D. Hirwani	India v West Indies at Madras	1987-88
16-137	R. A. L. Massie	Australia v England at Lord's	1972
16-154	P. Sunderam	Rajasthan v Vidarbha at Jodhpur	1985-86
16-167	R. Dhanraj	Trinidad & Tobago v Leeward Islands at Charlestown . .	1995-96
16-215	T. P. B. Smith	Essex v Middlesex at Colchester	1947
16-220	M. Muralitharan	Sri Lanka v England at The Oval.	1998
16-225	J. E. Walsh	Leicestershire v Oxford University at Oxford	1953

John Davison devastated the USA with 17 wickets for 137, the best match analysis since Jim Laker's 19 for 90 against Australia in 1956. A new turf pitch at Brian Piccolo Park, in Florida, proved perfect for his off-spin. All but one of his victims were caught. Davison was also the game's top-scorer, with 84, though he had to retire on the first morning. He had been vomiting with a stomach bug shortly before he won the toss and decided to bat. Resuming after lunch, he added 88 with Hani Dhillon before Nasir Javed, a leg-spinner from Lahore, wound up the innings; by the close, Davison had already grabbed six wickets. He finished the Americans off next morning to establish a lead of 85. The Canadian batsmen struggled too, and were 54 for six when Davison, batting down the order, was out, but Sunil Dhaniram, formerly of Guyana, made a career-best 65. An American target of 231 looked possible at 87 for two overnight; in the morning, however, Davison routed them even more conclusively.

Man of the Match: J. M. Davison.

Close of play: First day, USA 110-8 (Aijaz Ali 24, Nasir Javed 0); Second day, USA 87-2 (M. R. Johnson 37, Massiah 25).

Canada

D. Chumney c H. R. Johnson b Amin	33	– c M. R. Johnson b H. R. Johnson .	0
*J. M. Davison run out	84	– (7) c H. R. Johnson b Staple	3
Z. Surkari c M. R. Johnson b Nasir Javed	1	– c Blake b Reid.	0
I. S. Billcliff c Amin b Nasir Javed	3	– c Reid b Amin.	23
†A. Bagai b Amin	0	– run out	20
N. A. De Groot c Massiah b Blake	11	– (2) c M. R. Johnson b Reid	2
H. Dhillon c Aijaz Ali b Lambert	69	– (6) c M. R. Johnson b Amin.	2
S. Dhaniram c H. R. Johnson b Nasir Javed . . .	0	– not out	65
Zahid Hussain lbw b Nasir Javed	0	– c M. R. Johnson b Lambert	8
A. Patel not out.	8	– c Staple b Nasir Javed.	7
E. Sinnathamby c Blake b Nasir Javed	2	– lbw b H. R. Johnson	1
B 1, l-b 1, w 2, n-b 6	10	B 4, l-b 1, n-b 4, p 5	14

1/57 (1) 2/67 (3) 3/69 (5) 4/69 (4) **221**	1/0 (1) 2/1 (3) 3/21 (2) **145**
5/106 (6) 6/194 (7) 7/194 (8)	4/41 (4) 5/45 (6) 6/54 (7) 7/63 (5)
8/209 (9) 9/209 (2) 10/221 (11)	8/96 (9) 9/131 (10) 10/145 (11)

In the first innings Davison, when 28, retired ill at 66 and resumed at 106.

Bowling: First Innings—H. R. Johnson 8–1–25–0; Reid 4–0–22–0; Amin 20–7–35–2; Nasir Javed 23.5–7–78–5; Massiah 2–0–11–0; Blake 5–1–17–1; Lambert 11–0–31–1. *Second Innings*—H. R. Johnson 7.5–2–24–2; Reid 6–2–10–2; Nasir Javed 13–3–24–1; Staple 17–4–32–1; Amin 19–7–20–2; Massiah 3–0–12–0; Blake 2–1–4–0; Lambert 5–0–9–1.

USA

L. C. Romero c Billcliff b Davison	33	– (2) c Bagai b Zahid Hussain	14
†M. R. Johnson lbw b Patel	0	– (1) b Davison	41
*R. W. Staple c Sinnathamby b Davison	30	– c Surkari b Davison	1
S. J. Massiah c Billcliff b Davison	7	– c Dhaniram b Davison	37
C. A. Reid c Davison b Dhaniram	4	– c Dhaniram b Davison	2
C. B. Lambert c Dhillon b Davison	2	– c Chumney b Davison	11
Aijaz Ali c Zahid Hussain b Davison	36	– c sub (M. Chaudhury) b Davison	4
Z. A. Amin c De Groot b Davison	2	– c Chumney b Davison	1
D. L. Blake c De Groot b Davison	0	– c Billcliff b Davison	0
Nasir Javed not out	11	– c De Groot b Davison	2
H. R. Johnson c Zahid Hussain b Davison	2	– not out	2
B 5, w 2, n-b 2	9	B 8, l-b 2, w 1	11

1/1 (2) 2/43 (3) 3/64 (4) 4/77 (5)   136   1/37 (2) 2/38 (3) 3/93 (1)   126
5/83 (1) 6/90 (6) 7/92 (8)   4/105 (5) 5/107 (4) 6/111 (7)
8/92 (9) 9/134 (7) 10/136 (11)   7/112 (8) 8/112 (9)
   9/114 (10) 10/126 (6)

Bowling: *First Innings*—Patel 6–1–12–1; Sinnathamby 3–0–11–0; Zahid Hussain 3–0–16–0; Davison 14.4–2–61–8; Dhaniram 14–4–31–1. *Second Innings*—Davison 21.2–3–76–9; Zahid Hussain 7–2–15–1; Dhaniram 15–6–18–0; Sinnathamby 1–0–7–0.

Umpires: B. R. Doctrove (West Indies) and N. A. Malcolm (West Indies).
Referee: J. J. Crowe (New Zealand).

At Hamilton, July 13, 14, 15, 2004. **USA won by 114 runs. Toss:** USA. **USA 297-9 dec.** (S. J. Massiah 104) **and 183** (D. Leverock 7-57); **Bermuda 201-8 dec.** (C. J. Smith 62) **and 165** (C. J. Smith 65; H. R. Johnson 5-38). *USA 32 pts, Bermuda 16.5 pts.*

At Toronto, August 13, 14, 15, 2004. **Drawn.** Toss: Bermuda. **Canada 250-9 dec.** (A. Bagai 66) **and 250-4 dec.** (J. M. Davison 78, H. Dhillon 102*); **Bermuda 107** (J. M. Davison 5-19) **and 221-9** (C. J. Smith 63; K. Sandher 6-68). *Canada 19.5 pts, Bermuda 12.5 pts.*

Asia Group

At Sharjah, March 25, 26, 27, 2004. **Drawn.** Toss: Nepal. **United Arab Emirates 293-9 dec.** (Arshad Ali 143, Khurram Khan 75; B. K. Das 5-61) **and 253-6 dec.** (Fahad Usman 102*); **Nepal 213** (R. Khadka 67; Ali Asad 9-74) **and 141-5** (S. Vesawkar 50*; Ali Asad 4-52). *United Arab Emirates 18 pts, Nepal 14 pts.*
    Arshad Ali scored 143 on first-class debut. Ali Asad's 9-74 was the best innings return of the tournament, beating Davison by two runs; he finished with 13-126 on first-class debut.

At Kathmandu, April 23, 24, 25, 2004. **Nepal won by nine wickets.** Toss: Malaysia. **Malaysia 132** (R. M. Selvaratnam 56) **and 99; Nepal 198** (S. P. Gauchan 69*; S. Navaratnam 5-61) **and 34-1.** *Nepal 27.5 pts, Malaysia 9.5 pts.*

At Kuala Lumpur, September 17, 18, 19, 2004. **United Arab Emirates won by 124 runs.** Toss: Malaysia. **United Arab Emirates 231-9 dec.** (Khurram Khan 66) **and 211-7 dec.** (Arshad Ali 78); **Malaysia 173** (R. M. Selvaratnam 53; Mohammad Tauqir 4-34) **and 145** (R. Madhavan 60; Mohammad Tauqir 6-17). *United Arab Emirates 32.5 pts, Malaysia 13.5 pts.*

Europe Group

At Aberdeen, June 11, 12, 13, 2004. **Drawn.** Toss: Scotland. **Scotland 314-7 dec.** (C. V. English 65, C. M. Wright 88*) **and 250-8 dec.** (B. M. W. Patterson 51, D. F. Watts 79; S. F. Gokke 4-77); **Holland 257** (B. Zuiderent 78, L. P. van Troost 71; R. R. Watson 5-74) **and 207-3** (T. N. de Groth 59, B. Zuiderent 68*). *Scotland 17.5 pts, Holland 16.5 pts.*

At Deventer, July 13, 14, 15, 2004. **Ireland won by an innings and 47 runs.** Toss: Ireland. **Holland 200** (D. T. Johnston 4-34) **and 141** (Naseer Shaukat 5-30); **Ireland 388-8 dec.** (A. R. White 152*, D. T. Johnston 60; E. Schiferli 4-70). *Ireland 30 pts, Holland 10.5 pts.*
    Andrew White scored 152 on first-class debut, with 17 fours and three sixes.*

At Clontarf, August 6, 7, 8, 2004. **Scotland won by eight wickets.** Toss: Scotland. **Ireland 193** (Asim Butt 4-25) **and 178** (A. R. White 67; Asim Butt 5-47); **Scotland 167** (Naseer Shaukat 5-60) **and 206-2** (D. R. Lockhart 53*, D. F. Watts 118*). *Scotland 31 pts, Ireland 13 pts.*

Fraser Watts hit 17 fours and three sixes to reach 118*, his maiden first-class century, in 136 balls.

Semi-finals

At Abu Dhabi, November 17, 18, 19, 2004. **Drawn.** Scotland qualified for the final by virtue of gaining more points in the match. Toss: Scotland. **Scotland 300-5 dec.** (D. F. Watts 146, R. R. Watson 57) **and 401-7 dec.** (R. R. Watson 56, C. J. O. Smith 93, K. J. Coetzer 133*, C. M. Wright 59); **Kenya 95** (P. J. C. Hoffmann 5-5) **and 163-4** (A. K. P. Bhudia 79). *Kenya 10.5 pts, Scotland 19 pts.*

Fraser Watts batted six hours for a career-best 146, his second century in successive first-class innings, hitting 11 fours and a six; Kyle Coetzer followed up with 133*, including 15 fours and three sixes, on the final day. Paul Hoffmann's first-innings analysis was 5.5–4–5–5.

At Sharjah, November 17, 18, 19, 2004. **Drawn.** Canada qualified for the final by virtue of gaining more points in the match. Toss: Canada. **Canada 337-6 dec.** (Z. Surkari 139, D. E. S. Maxwell 88; Ali Asad 4-59) **and 253-8 dec.** (I. S. Billcliff 63, S. Dhaniram 53; Zahid Shah 4-53); **United Arab Emirates 254-8 dec.** (Arshad Ali 57, Syed Maqsood 100*) **and 194-9** (Kashif Khan 56; U. Bhatti 5-43). *United Arab Emirates 15.5 pts, Canada 19.5 pts.*

FINAL

CANADA v SCOTLAND

At Sharjah, November 21, 22, 2004. **Scotland won by an innings and 84 runs.** Scotland 29 pts, Canada 7.5 pts. Toss: Canada. **Canada 110 and 93** (Blain 4-28, Asim Butt 4-10); **Scotland 287-8 dec.** (D. R. Lockhart 64, G. M. Hamilton 115, R. R. Watson 56; U. Bhatti 4-49).

Scotland won with four sessions to spare. The one-time Test cap Gavin Hamilton shared century partnerships with Dougie Lockhart and Ryan Watson. Canada were reeling at 24-8 in their second innings; one run later a ninth batsman retired hurt. Umar Bhatti and Ashish Patel, Canada's last pair, held out for an hour before Watson removed Bhatti for 41.

> **“**Not even the cockroach Gilchrist found in his soy sauce before the match could put Australia off. The restaurant manager quickly swallowed it as if to destroy the evidence. ‘He took one for the team,’ said Gilchrist.”
>
> Australians in India, page 1273.

ENGLAND UNDER-19 IN MALAYSIA AND BANGLADESH, 2003-04

England Under-19 won both their matches against Malaysia during a six-day tour aimed at acclimatising the players to conditions before the Under-19 World Cup in Bangladesh in February 2004. They also won both warm-up games in Chittagong. Durham fast bowler Mark Turner injured his ankle in Malaysia and was replaced by his county colleague Ben Harmison, younger brother of the Test bowler Steve Harmison.

ENGLAND UNDER-19 TOURING PARTY

A. N. Cook (Essex) (*captain*), R. S. Bopara (Essex), T. T. Bresnan (Yorkshire), D. L. Broadbent (Yorkshire), S. M. Davies (Worcestershire), A. J. Harrison (Glamorgan), J. C. Hildreth (Somerset), M. A. K. Lawson (Yorkshire), T. J. New (Leicestershire), S. R. Patel (Nottinghamshire), L. E. Plunkett (Durham), D. A. Stiff (Kent), M. I. Turner (Durham), L. J. Wright (Sussex).

B. W. Harmison (Durham) replaced the injured Turner.

Coach: R. A. Pick.   *Manager:* J. Abrahams.   *Physiotherapist:* N. A. Kent.

Note: Matches in this section were not first-class.

At Royal Selangor Club, Kuala Lumpur, February 3, 2004. **England Under-19 won by 58 runs.** Toss: England Under-19. **England Under-19 197** (44.1 overs) (R. S. Bopara 77 retired out); **Malaysia 139** (44 overs) (G. P. Gopinath 72*).
   Each side named 12 players, of whom 11 could bat and 11 field. Gopinath carried his bat through the Malaysian innings.

At Royal Selangor Club, Kuala Lumpur, February 7, 2004. **England Under-19 won by 75 runs.** Toss: England Under-19. **England Under-19 203-7** (45 overs) (A. N. Cook 72, T. T. Bresnan 59*); **Malaysia 128** (36.5 overs).
   Each side named 12 players, of whom 11 could bat and 11 field.

At M. A. Aziz Stadium, Chittagong, February 12, 2004. **England Under-19 won by ten wickets.** Toss: England Under-19. **Chittagong Division B 132** (40 overs); **England Under-19 135-0** (22 overs) (A. N. Cook 69*).

At Chittagong Divisional Stadium, Chittagong, February 13, 2004. **England Under-19 won by 84 runs.** Toss: England Under-19. **England Under-19 274-7** (50 overs) (Extras 56); **Chittagong Division B 190-9** (50 overs).

UNDER-19 WORLD CUP, 2003-04

BENEDICT BERMANGE

The fifth Under-19 World Cup set new standards for the tournament. The quality of the cricket was not necessarily higher than before, but the ICC's decision to award the biennial competition to Bangladesh proved a masterstroke. In total, more than 350,000 spectators saw the 54 matches; attendances at the last World Cup in New Zealand were minute. And the competition ended with a close final between the two best teams – West Indies and Pakistan – and a 30,000 crowd acclaiming the victorious Pakistanis almost as their own, despite the animosity still lingering in Bangladesh from their war of independence 33 years earlier.

The up-and-coming stars were also able to parade their skills in front of a far wider audience than before: many games were televised across the world, and press boxes were regularly packed. After handing the trophy to Pakistan's captain, Khalid Latif, the ICC president Ehsan Mani said: "This has been the most spectacular Under-19 World Cup the world has ever seen." For once the platitude rang true.

The local fans revelled as hosts. The players, from the ten Test countries and six other nations, were feted wherever they went, and the appetite for cricket was remarkable: even Zimbabwe v Canada sold out. All the original 28,000 tickets for group matches in Bogra, a small town in northern Bangladesh, went well in advance, and more had to be printed. An easy-to-understand format helped too. As in the last competition, four groups of four produced two groups of four in the Super League, which in turn produced four semi-finalists. The parallel Plate competition catered for teams finishing in the bottom half of the first-round tables.

Future stars? Shikhar Dhawan of India, the tournament's most prolific batsman (*left*), and Tariq Mahmood, Pakistan's answer to Murali?

Almost incredibly, that consolation competition was where Australia, the defending champions, were dumped. Their place in the main competition was taken by Zimbabwe, who skittled them for 73 on their way to a massive upset in the first group stage. And on the same day, February 18, South Africa were humiliated by Nepal. But they scraped through on run-rate. Australia, meanwhile, did not even win the Plate, losing the final to Bangladesh amid thumping drums and gleeful celebrations. That unexpected victory, their success as organisers, and the construction or redevelopment of five grounds were all welcome steps forward for Bangladeshi cricket.

Still, the quality of some of the cricket left something to be desired. On slow, low pitches, offering little sideways movement, the bowlers tended to rely on batsmen gifting their wickets. The running was often shambolic, with five run-outs in the final. And six unnamed bowlers were reported for having suspicious actions by an ICC group including Bruce Elliott, a biomechanics expert from the University of Western Australia. They were referred to their home boards for remedial work.

> West Indies had several spinners and no out-and-out quicks

The tournament was held at one of the drier times of year in Bangladesh, and most of the leading bowlers were spinners. Bangladesh's Enamul Haque junior – a left-armer with two Tests against England in October 2003 – was leading wicket-taker, with 22. But it was the Pakistani off-spinner Tariq Mahmood who had commentators waxing lyrical. His arm and wrist action were remarkably similar to Muttiah Muralitharan's – and subject to similar murmurings. But few denied his effectiveness: his *doosra* (or wrong 'un) turned even further than Murali's and, in the semi-final against arch-rivals India, he hit a match-winning 45 not out from the middle order. Pakistan's coach Sultan Rana said he hoped to see Tariq in the senior team soon.

Few quick bowlers stood out. A notable exception was Shahadat Hossain of Bangladesh. Discovered at a talent-spotting camp, he had the height, pace and aggression that could bring some welcome penetration to his country's Test attack. Among batsmen, the strongest case for promotion was made by the Indian opener Shikhar Dhawan, also voted player of the tournament. He hit three hundreds, averaged 84.16 and had a robust-looking technique.

The strength of the victorious **Pakistan** side lay in their bowling. No team managed a higher total against them than West Indies' 205 in the final, and the opening attack of the pacy Ali Imran and Riaz Afridi almost always made early inroads. It was then left to a triumvirate of spinners – Tariq, Mansoor Amjad, and Salman Qadir, off-spinning son of the legendary Abdul – to restrict the scoring, though they took regular wickets too. Although its depth was rarely tested, the batting delivered under pressure in both the semi-final against India and in the final. But for a hiccough against England – when both teams had already qualified for the semis – Pakistan would have swept home unbeaten.

The other finalists, **West Indies**, were superbly captained by their wicket-keeper Denesh Ramdin, tipped to break into the senior squad when Ridley

Jacobs retires. He was one of six players of Indian descent in the side for the semi-final and final. They had several spinners and no out-and-out quicks, a departure from tradition that could be mirrored in the senior attack in a few years' time. The fast-medium of Ravi Rampaul, one of the tournament's few full internationals, was a little disappointing.

After an unhappy and unsuccessful 2001-02 World Cup, the progress of **England** to the semi-finals was a comparative success. Here they were viewed as potential winners, and they beat three Test countries, against a total of one in the two preceding World Cups. The captain, Alastair Cook of Essex, hit two centuries and 87 in successive Super League games, and looked a class apart. But in the semi-final, the bowlers struggled on an unresponsive pitch, Cook became bogged down by the accuracy of the West Indian spinners and four run-outs contributed to his side's demise. Tim Bresnan, the Yorkshire seamer, took 17 wickets in the tournament, but there were no obvious candidates for swift promotion.

India completed the semi-finalists. Dhawan and Suresh Raina were the backbone of a strong batting line-up, and Raina's 90 from just 38 balls against the hapless Scots was as brutal an innings as one will see at any level. Both looked international-class already, though faced with a tough task breaking into their senior side's formidable top order. The captain Ambati Rayudu had been hailed as the next great batting hope, having scored a century and a double in a first-class match at the age of 17. But he did not score the runs promised and was banned by the referee John Morrison from the semi-final after allowing a funereal over-rate during the Super League win against Sri Lanka: eight overs were bowled in the first 50 minutes.

Judged against the last World Cup, when they blazed to victory unbeaten, **Australia** had a terrible tournament. After being bowled out for 73 by Zimbabwe, and humiliatingly defeated, they took the earliest possible exit, in the first group phase. It was an honest Zimbabwean win, not a fluke. "Everything about their game was perfect," said the Australian coach, Bennett King, "I can't remember a game where we were so completely dominated." Australia lost to **Bangladesh** too, in the final of the Plate. "We have several promising players," King said, "but they still have a lot to learn." He perhaps had a point: in the Plate final five of the Bangladeshis, but none of the Australians, had first-class experience.

Of the sides that did reach the Super League, **New Zealand** and **Sri Lanka** both fell below the standard they hoped for, but fielded some useful cricketers. Sri Lanka's captain Farveez Maharoof controlled the team with aplomb, and made his Test debut in Zimbabwe in May. Their off-spinner Mohamed Suraj also looked useful. New Zealanders Bradley-John Watling and Brad Wilson flayed Scotland, but generally the batsmen were unable to support their battery of medium-pacers.

A close-run victory against India was the highlight for **South Africa**, who otherwise underperformed, even ignoring the Nepal result. Jaco Booysen's 120 against Sri Lanka might have been the innings of the tournament, but it was unable to bring victory, and their bowlers' lack of firepower was exploited throughout.

Judging by their team's performance, **Zimbabwe** cricket was not short of young talent, which made the grim state of their domestic game all the more poignant. Given proper support, batsmen Brendan Taylor and James Cameron looked good bets for the future, and the fast bowler Tinashe Panyangara took six for 31, the second-best figures in the competition's history, to destroy Australia. Zimbabwe also beat New Zealand. Shortly after the tournament, several of their Under-19s made a full international debut against Sri Lanka, though it was a bittersweet experience because they were part of a squad drastically weakened by the absence of 15 senior players, which was thrashed.

Nepal traditionally takes mountaineers, not cricketers, for sporting heroes. But Shakti Gauchan's unbeaten 51, which secured the one-wicket victory over South Africa, was the spark that brought the whole tournament alive. Not content with one match-winning performance, he followed up with an undefeated 80 in the victory against Uganda. After those wins Nepal, cheered on by locally-based Nepalese students, only missed the Super League on run-rate. But their coach Roy Dias was realistic about the future in a country with just one turf pitch: "There are two international-standard fields in Chittagong and you need infrastructure like that in Nepal."

There were a few outstanding performances from the other non-Test sides, all of whom were permitted players a year over age. Emmanuel Isaneez of **Uganda** took six for 37 in a losing effort against Bangladesh; his team-mate Martin Ondeko was stranded on 99 not out during the win over Canada. And a century from Eoin Morgan, contracted to Middlesex, helped **Ireland** beat Uganda. In fact Ireland beat all their non-Test opponents convincingly, competed well against West Indies and Australia, and should have a good core of young players when they host the 2005 ICC Trophy, with a place in the next full World Cup at stake. Compared with that extravaganza, the Under-19 World Cup remains small-scale. But, thanks to the cricket supporters of Bangladesh, the gap got a little smaller in 2004.

Note: Matches in this section were not first-class.

Group A

At Shaheed Chandu Stadium, Bogra, February 15, 2004. **Sri Lanka won by two wickets.** Toss: Sri Lanka. **Zimbabwe 161** (49.3 overs) (M. F. Maharoof 4-28); **Sri Lanka 162-8** (38.2 overs). *Sri Lanka 2 pts.*

At Rajshahi Stadium, Rajshahi, February 16, 2004. **Australia won by six wickets.** Toss: Australia. **Canada 164** (45.1 overs) (S. Anjaria 50); **Australia 165-4** (28.4 overs) (T. P. Doropoulos 57). *Australia 2 pts.*

At Rajshahi Stadium, Rajshahi, February 17, 2004. **Sri Lanka won by nine wickets.** Toss: Sri Lanka. **Canada 81** (31.1 overs) (C. K. B. Kulasekara 5-27); **Sri Lanka 84-1** (16 overs) (H. E. Vithana 52*). *Sri Lanka 2 pts.*

At Shaheed Chandu Stadium, Bogra, February 18, 2004. **Zimbabwe won by seven wickets.** Toss: Australia. **Australia 73** (19 overs) (T. Panyangara 6-31, E. Chigumbura 4-17); **Zimbabwe 74-3** (17.1 overs). *Zimbabwe 2 pts.*

Tinashe Panyangara's aggressive spell brought figures of 9–1–31–6, the second-best in an Under-19 World Cup, after 7-19 by B. M. A. J. Mendis of Sri Lanka against Zimbabwe in 2001-02.

At Shaheed Chandu Stadium, Bogra, February 19, 2004. **Zimbabwe won by eight wickets.** Toss: Zimbabwe. **Canada 180-9** (50 overs) (A. Keshvani 63; P. Utseya 4-41); **Zimbabwe 183-2** (36.2 overs) (J. G. Cameron 84*). _Zimbabwe 2 pts._

At Rajshahi Stadium, Rajshahi, February 20, 2004. **Australia won by two runs.** Toss: Sri Lanka. **Australia 186-9** (50 overs); **Sri Lanka 184** (49.1 overs) (M. F. Maharoof 56). _Australia 2 pts._

Sri Lanka 4 pts, Zimbabwe 4 pts, Australia 4 pts, Canada 0 pts. Sri Lanka and Canada qualified for the Super League ahead of Australia on net run-rate, as all three were equal on points and wins, and each had beaten one of the other two.

Group B

At M. A. Aziz Stadium, Chittagong, February 15, 2004. **England won by eight wickets.** Toss: Nepal. **Nepal 191-8** (50 overs) (S. Vesawkar 82); **England 192-2** (43 overs) (R. S. Bopara 59, S. M. Davies 78*). _England 2 pts._

At Chittagong Divisional Stadium, Chittagong, February 16, 2004. **South Africa won by eight wickets.** Toss: Uganda. **Uganda 125** (48.4 overs) (W. E. September 4-14); **South Africa 126-2** (28 overs) (A. Birch 56*). _South Africa 2 pts._

At M. A. Aziz Stadium, Chittagong, February 17, 2004. **England won by 213 runs.** Toss: Uganda. **England 259-7** (50 overs) (L. J. Wright 70, S. R. Patel 55); **Uganda 46** (30.4 overs) (T. T. Bresnan 4-7, D. A. Stiff 4-7). _England 2 pts._

 Uganda's 46 was the second-lowest completed innings in an Under-19 World Cup, before Scotland sunk even lower against Australia.

NEPAL v SOUTH AFRICA

At Chittagong Divisional Stadium, Chittagong, February 18, 2004. Nepal won by one wicket. Nepal 2 pts. Toss: South Africa.

Unfancied Nepal pulled off one of the biggest shocks in the competition's history, and certainly the biggest since they beat Pakistan in the previous tournament. In a tense finish they squeezed home with two balls left and just one wicket to fall. Earlier, their opening bowler Manjeet Shrestha cut a swathe through the South African top order with accurate right-arm seam bowling, helping to reduce them to 11 for four. The change bowlers built further pressure, and it was only a quickfire 52 not out from Keagan Africa at No. 9 that saved South Africa from total humiliation. Nepal made steady progress in reply, and at 118 for four appeared to be heading for a comfortable victory. However, a middle-order wobble, in which five wickets fell in quick succession, left them needing 19 with only one wicket in hand. But their captain Shakti Gauchan, who had held firm for more than three hours, struck the winning boundary in a nerve-shredding final over.

 Man of the Match: S. P. Gauchan.

South Africa

C. Bowyer c and b Khadka	3	K. Africa not out	52
A. Birch b M. Shrestha	0	W. E. September st Katuwal b Lama	1
J. Booysen lbw b M. Shrestha	3	C. Alexander b Lama	0
*D. van Wyk c Katuwal b Khadka	26	L-b 1, w 16	17
V. B. van Jaarsveld c Khatri			
b M. Shrestha	0	1/2 (2) 2/6 (1) 3/11 (3) (50 overs) 156
†R. van der Merwe c Katuwal b Gauchan	14	4/11 (5) 5/37 (4) 6/59 (6)
V. D. Philander st Katuwal b Lama	11	7/62 (7) 8/141 (8)
G. Stevens c Khatri b M. Shrestha	29	9/151 (10) 10/156 (11)

Bowling: M. Shrestha 10–4–15–4; Khadka 10–2–22–2; Khatri 5–0–34–0; Gauchan 10–1–28–2; Kesari 5–0–22–0; Lama 10–2–34–2.

Nepal

K. Chaugai c September b Alexander . . .	0	L. Lama c and b van Jaarsveld	7
M. K. Shrestha lbw b Alexander	11	S. Kesari not out	13
*S. P. Gauchan not out	51		
S. Vesawkar b September	27	L-b 4, w 15, n-b 8	27
Y. Subedi c van der Merwe b Birch	11		
P. Khadka c Bowyer b Africa	8	1/0 (1) 2/21 (2) (9 wkts, 49.4 overs) 158
M. Shrestha c van der Merwe b Africa . .	3	3/63 (4) 4/83 (5)
†M. Katuwal b Africa	0	5/118 (6) 6/123 (7)
D. J. Khatri lbw b Alexander	0	7/123 (8) 8/124 (9) 9/138 (10)

Bowling: Alexander 10–1–23–3; Africa 10–2–36–3; Philander 7–2–9–0; Birch 10–1–38–1; September 8–0–24–1; van Jaarsveld 3.4–0–19–1; Bowyer 1–0–5–0.

Umpires: A. F. M. Akhtaruddin (Bangladesh) and K. C. Barbour (Zimbabwe).
Referee: R. S. Mahanama (Sri Lanka).

At M. A. Aziz Stadium, Chittagong, February 19, 2004. **Nepal won by five wickets.** Toss: Uganda. **Uganda 194** (49.5 overs) (L. Lama 4-40); **Nepal 195-5** (48.1 overs) (S. P. Gauchan 80*). *Nepal 2 pts.*

At Chittagong Divisional Stadium, Chittagong, February 20, 2004. **South Africa won by one wicket.** Toss: South Africa. **England 189** (48.3 overs) (S. M. Davies 63); **South Africa 190-9** (47.3 overs) (V. B. van Jaarsveld 76). *South Africa 2 pts.*
South Africa's last pair added 20 to win the game and take their side into the Super League.

England 4 pts, South Africa 4 pts, Nepal 4 pts, Uganda 0 pts. England and South Africa qualified for the Super League ahead of Nepal on net run-rate, as all three were equal on points and wins, and each had beaten one of the other two.

Group C

At Bangabandhu National Stadium, Dhaka, February 15, 2004. **New Zealand won by two wickets.** Toss: New Zealand. **Bangladesh 202** (46.3 overs) (Nafis Iqbal 67; C. Smith 4-43); **New Zealand 204-8** (49.2 overs). *New Zealand 2 pts.*

At Bangabandhu National Stadium, Dhaka, February 16, 2004. **India won by 270 runs.** Toss: Scotland. **India 425-3** (50 overs) (R. V. Uthappa 97, A. T. Rayudu 53, S. Raina 90); **Scotland 155-8** (50 overs) (K. J. Coetzer 62). *India 2 pts.*
India's 425 was the second-highest score in Under-19 one-day internationals after Australia's 480-6 against Kenya in 2001-02. Raina's 90 was smashed from 38 balls, with 14 fours and two sixes.

At Fatullah Khan Saheb Osman Ali Stadium, Dhaka, February 17, 2004. **Bangladesh won by nine wickets.** Toss: Bangladesh. **Scotland 95** (30.2 overs) (Enamul Haque, jun. 4-21); **Bangladesh 96-1** (12.2 overs). *Bangladesh 2 pts.*

At Bangabandhu National Stadium, Dhaka, February 18, 2004. **India won by 69 runs.** Toss: India. **India 215** (47.2 overs) (Sunny Singh 68*; B. Findlay 4-36); **New Zealand 146** (44.5 overs) (B-J. Watling 55). *India 2 pts.*

At Bangladesh Krira Shikkha Protisthan Ground, Savar, February 19, 2004. **New Zealand won by 240 runs.** Toss: Scotland. **New Zealand 389-2** (50 overs) (B-J. Watling 154, B. Wilson 144*); **Scotland 149** (33 overs) (K. Farid 60). *New Zealand 2 pts.*
Watling and Watson put on 273 for the second wicket in 28.5 overs.

At Bangabandhu National Stadium, Dhaka, February 20, 2004. **India won by 131 runs.** Toss: Bangladesh. **India 309-7** (50 overs) (R. V. Uthappa 59, S. Dhawan 120); **Bangladesh 178** (40.3 overs). *India 2 pts.*

India 6 pts, New Zealand 4 pts, Bangladesh 2 pts, Scotland 0 pts. India and New Zealand qualified for the Super League.

Group D

At Khulna Divisional Stadium, Khulna, February 15, 2004. **Pakistan won by eight wickets.** Toss: Pakistan. **Papua New Guinea 60** (17.5 overs) (Riaz Afridi 4-15); **Pakistan 63-2** (14.5 overs). *Pakistan 2 pts.*

At Khulna Divisional Stadium, Khulna, February 16, 2004. **West Indies won by six runs.** Toss: West Indies. **West Indies 265-8** (50 overs) (X. M. Marshall 83; G. Thompson 5-49); **Ireland 259-9** (50 overs) (G. Wilson 64, K. O'Brien 95). *West Indies 2 pts.*

At Khulna Divisional Stadium, Khulna, February 17, 2004. **Pakistan won by eight wickets.** Toss: Pakistan. **Ireland 142** (47.5 overs) (Mansoor Amjad 4-28); **Pakistan 146-2** (25.2 overs) (Khalid Latif 50, Adnan Zaheer 64*). *Pakistan 2 pts.*

At Khulna Divisional Stadium, Khulna, February 18, 2004. **West Indies won by 152 runs.** Toss: West Indies. **West Indies 371-3** (50 overs) (X. M. Marshall 52, T. Maraj 117, L. M. P. Simmons 107, A. B. Fudadin 59*); **Papua New Guinea 219** (44.2 overs) (A. Vala 84*). *West Indies 2 pts.*

At Khulna Divisional Stadium, Khulna, February 19, 2004. **Ireland won by 70 runs.** Toss: Papua New Guinea. **Ireland 212** (49 overs) (V. Vali 4-40); **Papua New Guinea 142** (38.2 overs). *Ireland 2 pts.*

At Khulna Divisional Stadium, Khulna, February 20, 2004. **Pakistan won by 163 runs.** Toss: West Indies. **Pakistan 251-9** (50 overs) (Jahangir Mirza 92); **West Indies 88** (27.3 overs) (Riaz Afridi 5-28). *Pakistan 2 pts.*

Pakistan 6 pts, West Indies 4 pts, Ireland 2 pts, Papua New Guinea 0 pts. Pakistan and West Indies qualified for the Super League.

Super League Group One

At Bangabandhu National Stadium, Dhaka, February 22, 2004 (day/night). **South Africa won by three runs.** Toss: South Africa. **South Africa 226-5** (50 overs) (R. van der Merwe 54); **India 223** (47.1 overs) (S. Dhawan 66). *South Africa 2 pts.*

At Fatullah Khan Saheb Osman Ali Stadium, Dhaka, February 22, 2004. **West Indies won by 19 runs.** Toss: Sri Lanka. **West Indies 200-7** (50 overs) (D. Ramdin 51); **Sri Lanka 181** (49 overs) (C. K. B. Kulasekara 64; L. S. Baker 6-39). *West Indies 2 pts.*
 Sri Lanka recovered from 71 for seven.

At Bangabandhu National Stadium, Dhaka, February 24, 2004 (day/night). **India won by 96 runs.** Toss: India. **India 253-9** (50 overs) (S. Raina 66); **West Indies 157** (39.1 overs) (A. B. Fudadin 51; A. Sharma 4-28). *India 2 pts.*

At Fatullah Khan Saheb Osman Ali Stadium, Dhaka, February 24, 2004. **Sri Lanka won by 29 runs.** Toss: Sri Lanka. **Sri Lanka 277-5** (50 overs) (W. U. Tharanga 117, N. P. Nawela 56); **South Africa 248** (48.3 overs) (J. Booysen 120; M. F. Maharoof 4-49). *Sri Lanka 2 pts.*

At Bangabandhu National Stadium, Dhaka, February 26, 2004 (day/night). **India won by 56 runs.** Toss: India. **India 316-5** (50 overs) (S. Dhawan 146, S. Raina 54, K. D. Karthik 70*); **Sri Lanka 260** (46 overs) (W. U. Tharanga 61). *India 2 pts.*

At Fatullah Khan Saheb Osman Ali Stadium, Dhaka, February 26, 2004. **West Indies won by 34 runs.** Toss: West Indies. **West Indies 284-6** (50 overs) (X. M. Marshall 106); **South Africa 250** (50 overs). *West Indies 2 pts.*

India 4 pts, West Indies 4 pts, Sri Lanka 2 pts, South Africa 2 pts. India and West Indies qualified for the semi-finals.

Super League Group Two

At Bangabandhu National Stadium, Dhaka, February 23, 2004 (day/night). **England won by 97 runs.** Toss: England. **England 306-2** (50 overs) (A. N. Cook 108*, S. R. Patel 102*); **New Zealand 209** (42.2 overs). *England 2 pts.*

At Bangladesh Krira Shikkha Protisthan Ground, Savar, February 23, 2004. **Pakistan won by nine wickets.** Toss: Pakistan. **Zimbabwe 141** (47.4 overs) (J. G. Cameron 68; Tariq Mahmood 4-33); **Pakistan 143-1** (30 overs) (Khalid Latif 84*). *Pakistan 2 pts.*

At Bangladesh Krira Shikkha Protisthan Ground, Savar, February 25, 2004. **England won by six wickets.** Toss: England. **Zimbabwe 218-9** (50 overs); **England 219-4** (49 overs) (A. N. Cook 108*, L. J. Wright 79). *England 2 pts.*

At Bangabandhu National Stadium, Dhaka, February 25, 2004 (day/night). **Pakistan won by eight wickets.** Toss: Pakistan. **New Zealand 181-8** (50 overs); **Pakistan 184-2** (34.2 overs) (Khalid Latif 90, Adnan Zaheer 72*). *Pakistan 2 pts.*

At Fatullah Khan Saheb Osman Ali Stadium, Dhaka, February 27, 2004. **England won by five runs.** Toss: Pakistan. **England 196** (50 overs) (A. N. Cook 87, S. M. Davies 53; Riaz Afridi 5-42); **Pakistan 191** (47.4 overs). *England 2 pts.*

At Bangabandhu National Stadium, Dhaka, February 27, 2004 (day/night). **Zimbabwe won by 92 runs.** Toss: Zimbabwe. **Zimbabwe 272-8** (50 overs) (B. R. M. Taylor 127); **New Zealand 180** (42 overs). *Zimbabwe 2 pts.*

England 6 pts, Pakistan 4 pts, Zimbabwe 2 pts, New Zealand 0 pts. England and Pakistan qualified for the semi-finals.

Semi-finals

At Bangabandhu National Stadium, Dhaka, February 29, 2004 (day/night). **Pakistan won by five wickets.** Toss: India. **India 169** (47.3 overs); **Pakistan 171-5** (44.5 overs).
The match was wide open with Pakistan 83 for five, but Tariq Mahmood (45) and Fawad Alam (43*) saw them home.*

At Bangabandhu National Stadium, Dhaka, March 2, 2004 (day/night). **West Indies won by 94 runs.** Toss: West Indies. **West Indies 249-6** (50 overs) (A. B. Fudadin 51, D. Ramdin 72, Z. Khan 60*); **England 155** (39.1 overs).
West Indies scored 88 from their last ten overs. England suffered four run-outs.

FINAL

PAKISTAN v WEST INDIES

At Bangabandhu National Stadium, Dhaka, March 5, 2004 (day/night). Pakistan won by 25 runs. Toss: Pakistan.

Pakistan won the Under-19 World Cup for the first time, to the delight of a packed house. Electing to bat first, they made a steady start before the introduction of left-arm spinner Rishi Bachan brought three quick wickets. Asif Iqbal – playing his first match of the tournament – and Salman Qadir rebuilt the innings, as they added 97 in 20.5 overs. Some lusty late blows from wicket-keeper Zulqarnain Haider lifted the score to a competitive 230 for nine on a good pitch. Xavier Marshall and Tishan Maraj set off in hot pursuit as the Pakistani opening bowlers for once had little success, and the captain Khalid Latif had to turn to his spinners early to stem the flow. As in previous matches, they did not let him down, and Pakistan gradually clawed back the initiative. Still, at 197 for six, West Indies needed only 34 from 38 balls. But Mansoor Amjad and Tariq Mahmood turned the screw and, after some chaotic running between the wickets, West Indies were all out in the 48th over, prompting massive celebrations. Intriguingly, the final was a repeat of the final 2000 Under-15 World Challenge. Five West Indians, but no Pakistanis, survived from that game.

Man of the Match: Asif Iqbal. *Player of the Tournament:* S. Dhawan (India).

Coming of age? Pakistan celebrate winning the Under-19 World Cup in Dhaka, along with their compatriot, ICC president Ehsan Mani (in suit).

Picture by Farjana K. Godhuly, AFP/Getty Images

Pakistan

*Khalid Latif st Ramdin b Bachan	20	Mansoor Amjad c Ramdin b Matthew	9
Adnan Zaheer b Bachan	33	Ali Imran not out	5
Jahangir Mirza c Ramdin b Khan	11		
Tariq Mahmood st Ramdin b Bachan	10	L-b 3, w 6, n-b 3	12
Asif Iqbal run out	54		
Salman Qadir c Matthew b Sebastien	42	1/53 (2) 2/58 (1) (9 wkts, 50 overs) 230	
Fawad Alam c Augustus b Rampaul	10	3/79 (4) 4/81 (3)	
†Zulqarnain Haider not out	23	5/178 (5) 6/179 (6)	
Riaz Afridi b Matthew	1	7/195 (7) 8/197 (9) 9/211 (10)	

Bowling: Rampaul 10–0–54–1; Matthew 10–2–35–2; Simmons 2–0–25–0; Bachan 10–0–34–3; Khan 10–0–35–1; Sebastien 8–0–44–1.

West Indies

X. M. Marshall c Zulqarnain Haider b Tariq Mahmood	26	L. A. Sebastien run out	0
T. Maraj run out	32	M. Matthew c Zulqarnain Haider b Tariq Mahmood	2
L. M. P. Simmons lbw b Jahangir Mirza	5	R. Bachan run out	1
A. B. Fudadin c Salman Qadir b Jahangir Mirza	13	B 4, l-b 16, w 9, n-b 2	31
*†D. Ramdin lbw b Riaz Afridi	36		
J. C. Augustus run out	25	1/69 (2) 2/72 (1) 3/84 (3) (47.1 overs) 205	
Z. Khan c Zulqarnain Haider b Tariq Mahmood	10	4/94 (4) 5/144 (6) 6/169 (7)	
R. Rampaul not out	24	7/197 (5) 8/200 (9)	
		9/203 (10) 10/205 (11)	

Bowling: Riaz Afridi 6–0–39–1; Ali Imran 5–0–23–0; Salman Qadir 10–1–33–0; Mansoor Amjad 9.1–1–27–0; Tariq Mahmood 10–1–34–3; Jahangir Mirza 7–0–29–2.

Umpires: J. W. Lloyds (England) and P. D. Parker (Australia).
Third umpire: B. G. Jerling (South Africa). Referee: J. F. M. Morrison (New Zealand).

UNDER-19 WORLD CUP WINNERS

1987-88	AUSTRALIA beat Pakistan by five wickets at Adelaide.
1997-98	ENGLAND beat New Zealand by seven wickets at Johannesburg.
1999-2000	INDIA beat Sri Lanka by six wickets at Colombo (SSC).
2001-02	AUSTRALIA beat South Africa by seven wickets at Lincoln, New Zealand.
2003-04	PAKISTAN beat West Indies by 25 runs at Dhaka.

Plate Championship Group One

At M. A. Aziz Stadium, Chittagong, February 22, 2004. **Australia won by ten wickets.** Toss: Scotland. **Scotland 22** (22.3 overs) (G. D. Putland 4-9, C. S. Huckett 4-7); **Australia 23-0** (3.5 overs). *Australia 2 pts.*
   After Australia's humiliating exit from the main competition, Scotland reaped the whirlwind. Their innings of 22 was the lowest in Under-19 one-day internationals.

At Chittagong Divisional Stadium, Chittagong, February 22, 2004. **Nepal won by seven wickets.** Toss: Nepal. **Papua New Guinea 168-9** (50 overs) (L. Lama 4-51); **Nepal 169-3** (39.2 overs) (K. Chaugai 90*). *Nepal 2 pts.*

At Chittagong Divisional Stadium, Chittagong, February 24, 2004. **Australia won by nine wickets.** Toss: Australia. **Papua New Guinea 83** (35 overs) (J. P. Mangan 4-30); **Australia 85-1** (18.2 overs). *Australia 2 pts.*

At M. A. Aziz Stadium, Chittagong, February 24, 2004. **Scotland won by three wickets.** Toss: Scotland. **Nepal 200-9** (50 overs) (S. Vesawkar 51); **Scotland 204-7** (49.5 overs) (M. M. Iqbal 67). *Scotland 2 pts.*

At Chittagong Divisional Stadium, Chittagong, February 26, 2004. **Australia won by six wickets.** Toss: Nepal. **Nepal 154-9** (50 overs); **Australia 158-4** (36.2 overs) (A. J. Crosthwaite 50*). *Australia 2 pts.*

At M. A. Aziz Stadium, Chittagong, February 26, 2004. **Scotland won by seven wickets.** Toss: Scotland. **Papua New Guinea 114** (32.2 overs); **Scotland 115-3** (26.4 overs). *Scotland 2 pts.*

Australia 6 pts, Scotland 4 pts, Nepal 2 pts, Papua New Guinea 0 pts. Australia and Scotland qualified for the semi-finals.

Plate Championship Group Two

At Chittagong Divisional Stadium, Chittagong, February 23, 2004. **Bangladesh won by four wickets.** Toss: Canada. **Canada 136** (37.2 overs); **Bangladesh 139-6** (34.5 overs) (S. Keshvani 5-29). *Bangladesh 2 pts.*

At M. A. Aziz Stadium, Chittagong, February 23, 2004. **Ireland won by 123 runs.** Toss: Ireland. **Ireland 329-9** (50 overs) (E. J. G. Morgan 117, K. O'Brien 70); **Uganda 206** (45.2 overs). *Ireland 2 pts.*

At Chittagong Divisional Stadium, Chittagong, February 25, 2004. **Bangladesh won by four wickets.** Toss: Uganda. **Uganda 78** (33.3 overs) (Nazmul Hossain 5-30, Enamul Haque, jun. 4-18); **Bangladesh 79-6** (19.5 overs) (E. Isaneez 6-37). *Bangladesh 2 pts.*

At M. A. Aziz Stadium, Chittagong, February 25, 2004. **Ireland won by 155 runs.** Toss: Ireland. **Ireland 265-9** (50 overs) (K. O'Brien 51); **Canada 110** (34.3 overs). *Ireland 2 pts.*

At Chittagong Divisional Stadium, Chittagong, February 27, 2004. **Bangladesh won by eight wickets.** Toss: Ireland. **Ireland 141** (46.4 overs) (Nadif Chowdhury 4-14); **Bangladesh 143-2** (30 overs) (Nafis Iqbal 86*). *Bangladesh 2 pts.*

At M. A. Aziz Stadium, Chittagong, February 27, 2004. **Uganda won by five wickets.** Toss: Canada. **Canada 231** (50 overs) (S. Keshvani 65); **Uganda 235-5** (47.2 overs) (M. Ondeko 99*, H. S. Almuzahim 50). *Uganda 2 pts.*

Bangladesh 6 pts, Ireland 4 pts, Uganda 2 pts, Canada 0 pts. Bangladesh and Ireland qualified for the semi-finals.

Plate Semi-finals

At M. A. Aziz Stadium, Chittagong, February 29, 2004. **Australia won by 49 runs.** Toss: Australia. **Australia 340-5** (50 overs) (T. P. Doropoulos 83, M. M. Harrison 91); **Ireland 291-9** (50 overs) (E. J. G. Morgan 65).

At Chittagong Divisional Stadium, Chittagong, March 1, 2004. **Bangladesh won by 91 runs.** Toss: Bangladesh. **Bangladesh 197** (49.5 overs); **Scotland 106** (33.3 overs) (Nazmul Hossain 4-11).

Plate Final

At Fatullah Cricket Stadium, Dhaka, March 4, 2004. **Bangladesh won by eight runs.** Toss: Bangladesh. **Bangladesh 257-9** (50 overs) (Nafis Iqbal 59, Naeem Islam 66, Aftab Ahmed 57); **Australia 249** (49.3 overs) (A. R. Beadle 54, S. N. J. O'Keefe 65; Enamul Haque, jun. 5-31).
   Roared on by a crowd of 15,000, Test spinner Enamul Haque, jun. bowled out the Australians with three balls left. The Australians recovered from 108 for five in the 28th over thanks to Beadle and O'Keefe, but their work was undone in four astonishing balls, which produced three run-outs. Bangladesh's top three all made fifties, and they were 204 for two with ten overs to go – a "new situation for us" according to their Australian coach Richard McInnes.

ENGLAND WOMEN IN SOUTH AFRICA, 2003-04

CAROL SALMON

Charlotte Edwards

After Test and one-day victories over South Africa in 2003, England's women visited the Republic for a one-day series in February 2004. The trip was useful preparation for the Women's World Cup, to be staged in South Africa the following year, and the team made encouraging progress in a comprehensive 4–1 win.

Their star was opener Charlotte Edwards. Despite recent knee surgery, she averaged 95, amassing 380 runs – more than twice the next best aggregate, Claire Taylor's 172. Her lowest score was 55 in the first one-day international, when South Africa recovered from 68 for five, and their last pair scrambled the winning run off the final delivery. The hugely talented Johmari Logtenberg, a week short of her 15th birthday, masterminded the run-chase with 67.

England coach Richard Bates said his side had let themselves down by scoring only 151: they needed to bat with more purpose, and stick to the game plan. They bounced back three days later with 281 for seven, after Edwards and Laura Newton opened with a stand of 142. Newton had an amazing let-off: a direct hit saw her comfortably run out, but the bails resettled on the stumps after rising five centimetres in the air. Still, the batting needed to improve before the World Cup. Only Edwards, Taylor and Newton made half-centuries, and the form of captain Clare Connor and Arran Brindle (née Thompson) was disappointing.

Jenny Gunn enjoyed a fine debut series. A 17-year-old seamer who had played football like her father, Nottingham Forest's Bryn Gunn, she had given it up for cricket. Opening the bowling, she conceded just 2.77 an over. Off-spinner Rosalie Birch, who had made an outstanding debut the previous summer, was the leading wicket-taker, with 11 at 12.18.

South Africa had a new coach, Stephen Jones, formerly of Western Province and Boland. He would have been disappointed that, apart from Logtenberg's fifties in the first and last internationals, they managed only one half-century, from Daleen Terblanche – and embarrassed that South Africa conceded 142 extras in five innings, including 99 in wides.

ENGLAND TOURING PARTY

C. J. Connor (Sussex) (*captain*), R. A. Birch (Sussex), A. Brindle (Lancashire), C. M. Edwards (Kent), L. Greenway (Kent), I. T. Guha (Berkshire), J. L. Gunn (Nottinghamshire), B. L. Morgan (Middlesex), L. K. Newton (Lancashire), L. C. Pearson (Staffordshire), J. Smit (Nottinghamshire), C. E. Taylor (Yorkshire), S. C. Taylor (Berkshire), H. Wardlaw (Yorkshire).

  Coach: R. T. Bates. *Assistant coach and manager:* N. Rider.

ENGLAND TOUR RESULTS

Matches – Played 9: Won 8, Lost 1.

Note: Matches in this section were not first-class.

At Harlequins, Pretoria, February 8, 2004. **England XI won by 115 runs.** Toss: England XI. **England XI 238-7** (50 overs) (L. K. Newton 84); **Northerns 123** (43.3 overs).

At University No. 1 Oval, Port Elizabeth, February 12, 2004. **England XI won by 154 runs.** Toss: England XI. **England XI 207-6** (50 overs); **Western Province-Boland Invitation XI 53** (46.5 overs) (L. C. Pearson 4-10).

At University No. 1 Oval, Port Elizabeth, February 14, 2004. **England XI won by 124 runs.** Toss: England XI. **England XI 225** (42.2 overs) (S. C. Taylor 90); **Eastern Province-Border Invitation XI 101-9** (50 overs).

At University No. 1 Oval, Port Elizabeth, February 15, 2004. **First one-day international: South Africa won by one wicket.** Toss: England. **England 151-9** (50 overs) (C. M. Edwards 55); **South Africa 152-9** (50 overs) (J. Logtenberg 67; C. J. Connor 4-25).
  One-day international debuts: S. Pillay; J. L. Gunn.
  Debutant wicket-keeper Shafeeqa Pillay took five catches, a South African one-day international record.

At East London, February 18, 2004. **Second one-day international: England won by 119 runs.** Toss: England. **England 281-7** (50 overs) (C. M. Edwards 102, L. K. Newton 65); **South Africa 162** (42.5 overs).
  Edwards and Newton put on 142 for the first wicket, setting up England's highest total against South Africa. Edwards reached her fourth one-day century in 112 balls; in all, she hit 13 fours in 117 balls.

At Sinoville, Pretoria, February 20, 2004. **England XI won by 51 runs.** Toss: England XI. **England XI 212** (49.4 overs) (L. K. Newton 60; K. Blair 4-32); **Northerns 161-8** (50 overs).

At Laudium Oval, Pretoria, February 22, 2004. **Third one-day international: England won by seven wickets.** Toss: South Africa. **South Africa 157-5** (50 overs) (M. Terblanche 81); **England 159-3** (40.5 overs) (C. M. Edwards 84*).

At Lenasia Stadium, Johannesburg, February 29, 2004. **Fourth one-day international: England won by 100 runs.** Toss: England. **England 242-5** (50 overs) (C. M. Edwards 58, S. C. Taylor 82); **South Africa 142-9** (50 overs).
  This was originally scheduled as the fifth one-day international, but the fourth game at Benoni was washed out. Claire Taylor and Lydia Greenway added 97 for England's fourth wicket.

At North West Cricket Stadium, Potchefstroom, March 1, 2004. **Fifth one-day international: England won by 38 runs.** Toss: England. **England 254-9** (50 overs) (C. M. Edwards 81); **South Africa 216** (48.5 overs) (J. Logtenberg 76; R. A. Birch 5-50).
  This match replaced the originally scheduled fourth one-day international, at Benoni on February 26; rain prevented any play on that date or the reserve day. England won the series 4–1.

CRICKET IN AUSTRALIA, 2003-04

CHRISTIAN RYAN

Matthew Elliott

Every so often, an Australian summer comes along that stirs the senses. Days feel longer, traffic queues shorter, distractions like war and football slip away. The season of 2003-04 was one such, destined to resound down the ages alongside some of the great Ashes and West Indian summers. Two graceful and attacking sides, Australia and India, fought out a titanic drawn series before packed stadiums. A couple of forgettable Tests against Zimbabwe were made fantastic by Matthew Hayden's buccaneering 380. Overhanging it all was the month-long, cross-country, tear-jerking farewell lap by Steve Waugh.

Meanwhile, one of the most captivating and emotional domestic summers in living memory quietly unfolded. It, too, was a season of records and retirements. New South Wales said goodbye to two worldly Waughs and Michael Slater, while elsewhere three giants of the domestic game, who played five Tests between them but eagerly shed blood for their states, walked into the sunset. Victoria's Darren Berry departed as the most successful wicket-keeper in Sheffield Shield/Pura Cup history, with 546 dismissals. Gentle Jo Angel waved a friendly cheerio in Western Australia as the competition's most prolific fast bowler, with 419 wickets – only Clarrie Grimmett's leg-spin had claimed more. And Stuart Law, Queensland's inaugural Shield-winning captain, signed off with one final, freewheeling, four-figure season which made him the state's greatest run-scorer, just 80 short of 10,000.

The great pity was that all this went on largely unnoticed. Radio coverage was minimal, and not a single four-day match graced Australian TV. Even the broadsheets have stopped sending reporters to games more than a ten-minute bus trip from their offices. This seems the most disturbing trend of all. It has long been claimed that far more people follow Australian domestic cricket than the handful of desperados who actually go. How much longer this comforting cliché will ring true is questionable. Soon nobody may care.

Crowds, to borrow the term loosely, often consisted of mums, wives and friends. Only 166 people saw Victoria end a 20-year hoodoo at the Gabba with a thrilling win over Queensland. A mere 466 watched one of the most rollicking last-day run-chases in the SCG's long history as Steve Waugh bulldozed a century and New South Wales helter-skeltered 303 in 48 overs to edge out Western Australia.

The funny thing was that these two games took place in a November free, for once, of home internationals – Australia's elite were in India for a one-day tournament. It was a one-off chance to make the Pura Cup the hottest ticket in town. Quite the reverse happened. Those two momentous final days fell on Wednesday and Friday respectively, when the masses could not have gone even if they had wanted to. Cricket Australia, having shortened its name from the Australian Cricket Board in June, appeared to have lopped several points off its IQ too.

Yet if ever a summer should be bottled as an advertisement for the domestic game, this was it. Thirteen years had passed, the longest drought in **Victoria's** history, since Simon O'Donnell thrust the Sheffield Shield skywards. Few titles have been so overdue. None, surely, can have been so emotional.

On January 19, their coach David Hookes died, aged 48, after an incident outside St Kilda's Beaconsfield Hotel, where he and some players had been celebrating a one-day win over his old state South Australia. To say that the Victorian players "did it for Hookesy" is too schmaltzy and simplistic: the team were already on top of the table. The effect of Hookes's death was to give everything that followed a shimmering sense of romance and destiny. His name came up constantly, as when David Hussey said: "I guess I'm a bit like Hookesy in that I'm always trying to hit the ball to the fence. It certainly beats running."

The clean-hitting Hussey, the discovery of the season, had played the innings of the season a week before Hookes died: 212 not out in 218 balls at Newcastle, enabling Victoria to scale a bewildering fourth-innings 455 to overhaul New South Wales. It was the second-steepest winning chase in the competition's 111-year history. Needing 452 on the last day, Hookes advised breaking it down into two one-day targets: they needed 226 in 50 overs twice. It was simple, clear-headed, astute. And it was Hookes's last act in first-class cricket.

Hussey and Brad Hodge, inching ever closer to national honours, underpinned Victoria's middle order. The 26-year-old Hussey, younger brother of Western Australia's Mike, had fled to Victoria in 2001-02 after being overlooked by his home state. His rise underlined the extraordinary richness of Australia's batting reserves – a depth emphasised by the relative shallowness of the bowling pool.

Victoria's attack, led by Mick Lewis, exuded unexpected menace courtesy of Allan Wise, a 25-year-old left-armer with a hitherto patchy club record, and young all-rounder Andrew McDonald. Jon Moss sneaked handy wickets while jumping ahead in leaps and bounds as a batsman. Cameron White, a vintage Hookes hunch, became Victoria's youngest captain when he assumed command of the one-day side, aged 20, and was named to succeed Berry as four-day captain in 2004-05. Lauded for his cool handling of craggier comrades, White is tipped by admirers to lead Australia some day. First, he must make the team: primarily a skidding leg-spinner, he averaged 37 with the ball, only slightly less than his 40 with the bat.

Berry left the game as sweet and sound a gloveman as ever, with 603 first-class dismissals. In the keeper/batsman era he might have played several dozen Tests; in the age of the batsman/keeper he never even played for Australia A.

Above them all, lean and big-beaked at the top of the order, crouched Matthew Elliott. He started the season a self-confessed international has-been; he finished it with seven hundreds and an emergency Test SOS against Sri Lanka. His 1,381 Pura Cup runs, uncoiled with a spectacular flourish and watertight defence, trashed fellow-Victorian Graham Yallop's all-time competition record of 1,254 in 1982-83. Elliott's triumph had as much to do with emotion as technique. Crowned Pura Cup player of the year a record third time, he told his team-mates: "You have helped me find a love of the game again."

While love, death and emotion infiltrated the fusty corridors of Victorian cricket, it paid to keep things in perspective. They were overachievers in an underappreciated competition. Shane Warne elicited more headlines and hoopla in three-quarters of a game for Victoria's Second XI – the end of his drugs suspension ruled him out of the first day – than the First XI managed all summer.

As the infinite fascination of Warne entered a new era, the man who averaged infinity – thanks to a solo Test innings of 54 not out against Sri Lanka in 1995-96 – marked the passing of an old one. Stuart Law, who broke one of cricket's longest-running curses by captaining Queensland

> **Cheeky and aggressive, ruthless and forever graceful...**

to Sheffield Shield glory in 1994-95, announced his retirement from Australian cricket, aged 35; he intended to see out his playing days in England. Cheeky and aggressive, ruthless and forever graceful, Law was both the glue that held Queensland's batting together and the polish that set them apart through 16 summers. His form of the previous two seasons had been ropey; this time, he passed 1,000 runs and his final first-class innings at his beloved Gabba was an emotional 203 against Western Australia.

That triumphant farewell helped soothe **Queensland** frustrations at reaching two finals but winning neither. Martin Love, the Test fringe-dweller, slammed 300 not out against Victoria but only one other century. The rest of the batting might best be described as a team effort. Twelve players chalked up hundreds, equalling the record for an Australian domestic season. The bowling lacked its trademark firepower. The 33-year-old quick Joe Dawes, whose 30 victims cost 36 runs apiece, was the leading wicket-taker. Nathan Hauritz's output – 16 at 63 – suggested the national selectors might have done him more harm than good by blooding him so abruptly in the one-day side.

For all that, Queensland were good enough to reach the Pura Cup final yet again, making it six in a row. They left it later than usual, beating New

South Wales under the SCG floodlights on the last evening of the last round. **Tasmania** would have qualified had they beaten Victoria that same evening. They were four wickets short with ten overs left when play at Bellerive Oval, where there are no floodlights, was called off. Level with Queensland on points and outright victories, they missed the final by a difference in quotient of 0.19.

Unusually, Tasmania's success centred on a rugged trio of fast bowlers – Damien Wright, Andrew Downton and Gerard Denton – rather than their batsmen. Jamie Cox struggled again and Ricky Ponting did not play a single four-day match, skipping the one game for which he was available to attend his wife Rianna's university graduation. Their shining lights were Dan Marsh and Shane Watson, unable to bowl until January because of a back injury, who hit four centuries from No. 3. His apparent coming of age was tarnished, for Tasmanians, by the news he was moving home to Queensland.

Western Australia's golden years of the 1970s and 1980s felt a distant memory. Their success back then hinged on a seemingly never-ending well of fast men, long since dried up. So thin were the ranks that when Brad Williams was summoned by Australia, halfway through the last day of a match against Tasmania, his replacement was debutant Ben Edmondson. A Queenslander unable to grasp a regular spot in that state's Second XI, Edmondson had been living in Perth only five days. But he nailed three wickets in a dramatic final session and, with Tasmania needing seven runs from the last over, conceded six. He was the only Western Australian bowler to reach 20 wickets. Michael Clark was barely sighted because of back troubles; Angel, his knees buckling, was followed into retirement by Paul "Blocker" Wilson; Beau Casson, the precocious 21-year-old chinaman bowler, missed half the season with a hand injury.

There was better news with the return of Michael's popular and accomplished father, Wayne Clark, as coach. Murray Goodwin's 1,183 runs were a Shield/Pura state record and talented left-handers Marcus North and Chris Rogers were close behind. But Shaun Marsh, the exhilarating son of Geoff, averaged only 16 with the bat and tumbled out of favour. Western Australia's season at least ended with a bang: three wins in the last four Pura Cup matches and an upset with two balls to spare in a mesmerising one-day final with Queensland, when Kade Harvey, a journeyman all-rounder, was the star turn.

For defending champions **New South Wales** it was a summer of melancholy upheaval, with a constant expectation that the Waughs might engineer one last miracle. Indeed, despite winning only one of their last nine games, they entered the final round with vague ambitions of tiptoeing into the final. It was not to be. Steve, presumably exhausted by his elongated international farewell, scratched out only two Pura Cup half-centuries after Christmas. Mark could not shake a lifetime habit of wasting exquisite starts with extravagant get-out shots: he failed to reach double figures only twice in 18 innings, yet never bettered his 90 at the Gabba.

At least their fans had ample opportunity to say goodbye; the twins, glimpsed only fleetingly in domestic cricket in recent times, appeared in 18

Pura Cup matches between them. Michael Bevan and Michael Slater played three apiece – Bevan averaging 101, Slater 17 – then departed in the off-season. Bevan, whose 9,309 runs made him the most prodigious scorer in the state that produced Don Bradman and Victor Trumper, packed his bags for Tasmania, where more dollars and the assistant coaching position were on offer. Slater, quick of foot and sharp of wit, quit the game at 34 because of ankylosing spondylitis, a form of arthritis also suffered by Mike Atherton.

Of the rest, Greg Mail exceeded and Phil Jaques fell short of expectations. Simon Katich, recalled to the Test team largely because of his bowling, blazed away as never before with the bat. Michael Clarke, Australia's most eye-catching prodigy since Ponting, was restricted to two Pura Cup games as the selectors continued their risky strategy of grooming him within the national one-day side instead of letting him grow up in first-class cricket.

Matt Nicholson, back home from Western Australia, was the Pura Cup's overall leading wicket-taker with 39 scalps. Stuart MacGill headed the one-day charts, bewitching 20 wickets at 15 but, though he remained in the Test side, was never asked to add to his career total of three one-day internationals. It seemed an inexplicable waste. Another leg-spinner, Adrian Tucker, was plucked from grade anonymity for the final match against Queensland – ten years and 54 days after his last first-class appearance. A season bubbling with nostalgia started with Alan Davidson calling stumps after 33 years as association president. Among his proudest achievements he cited the success of Geoff Lawson, Mark Taylor, Glenn McGrath, Adam Gilchrist, Slater and Bevan: six country lads made good.

South Australia looked to Zimbabwean exile Andy Flower for inspiration. Sadly, their most glittering recruit since Joel Garner failed to hit a hundred and averaged only 24. The team recorded two victories and a draw in their first three games, and not a single point thereafter. Their ING Cup campaign fizzled out in similar fashion, undone by four consecutive narrow defeats.

Greg Blewett and Darren Lehmann scored one century apiece – though Lehmann's 237 in 238 balls against New South Wales meant he averaged 53 when available. More encouraging signs came from youth, notably Ben Cameron and the 19-year-old Mark Cosgrove, a Lehmann-like left-hander who looked assured and aggressive in his first full season. The three standout bowlers – Paul Rofe, Mark Cleary and Shaun Tait – were all 23 or under. The man turning heads was Tait, a 21-year-old with a slinging action, who bowls out-swing and reverse swing at a sharp clip. He took eight for 43, a one-day tournament record, against Tasmania – including three in four balls, all bowled, in his tenth over.

It was the highlight of a one-day summer of firsts, bests, fastests, highests. Law's 69-ball century against Tasmania, the quickest on record, was soon upstaged by the biggest, Jimmy Maher's 187 against Western Australia. Maher propelled his Queensland side past 400, another competition first. Umpires wore microphones. Batsmen were gifted free hits to punish the bowlers for front-foot no-balls. And crowds, if they didn't quite flock, were at least increasingly drawn to a competition that has had seven names in 35 years without ever tickling the public's imagination. More than 26,000 ventured to Sydney's Olympic Stadium one gloomy evening to watch Queensland pip New South Wales. An equally implausible 16,238 spectators witnessed the Waughs' farewell frolic at the WACA. An all-time high of 161,000 people crept inquisitively through the turnstiles.

The trick now is to achieve something similar – by staging more weekend matches, by taking the Pura Cup out bush – in the four-day game. For the moment it is roundly ignored, an anachronism, and a dusty and unwelcoming one at that. But they were saying the same thing about five-day cricket not so long ago. And look what happened to that in 2003-04.

Christian Ryan is the editor of Wisden Cricketers' Almanack Australia 2004-05. *John MacKinnon has retired after 18 distinguished years as our Australian correspondent.*

FIRST-CLASS AVERAGES, 2003-04

BATTING

(Qualification: 600 runs)

	M	I	NO	R	HS	100s	Avge	Ct/St
R. T. Ponting (*Australia*)	6	11	2	965	257	3	107.22	3
†M. L. Hayden (*Australia & Queensland*) . . .	7	12	2	961	380	3	96.10	13
†S. M. Katich (*Australia & New South Wales*)	11	19	4	1,301	182*	4	86.73	10
†M. T. G. Elliott (*Victoria*)	12	21	3	1,429	182	7	79.38	11
B. J. Hodge (*Victoria & Australia A*)	12	22	3	1,282	264	5	67.47	5
S. G. Law (*Queensland*)	11	20	4	1,053	203	2	65.81	9
M. W. Goodwin (*Western Australia*)	10	20	2	1,183	201*	4	65.72	4
J. Moss (*Victoria*)	12	18	3	972	172*	1	64.80	6
M. L. Love (*Queensland & Australia A*)	11	20	3	998	300*	2	58.70	11
D. J. Hussey (*Victoria*)	12	17	2	878	212*	4	58.53	10
D. J. Marsh (*Tasmania*)	10	18	5	751	111*	2	57.76	11
†M. J. North (*Western Australia*)	11	21	2	1,074	130*	3	56.52	8
M. G. Dighton (*Tasmania*)	10	18	1	944	152	3	55.52	5
S. R. Watson (*Tasmania*)	10	19	1	983	157	4	54.61	9
†C. J. L. Rogers (*W. Australia & Australia A*).	10	20	1	982	142	4	51.68	9
†J. L. Langer (*Australia & W. Australia*)	12	22	1	1,027	163*	3	48.90	7
G. J. Mail (*New South Wales*)	10	18	2	754	152*	3	47.12	6
†M. J. Di Venuto (*Tasmania*)	9	15	1	649	174*	1	46.35	12
†M. J. Cosgrove (*South Australia*)	8	15	1	639	144	2	45.64	10
S. R. Waugh (*Australia & New South Wales*) .	14	24	2	966	157	1	43.90	6
†M. E. K. Hussey (*W. Australia & Australia A*)	11	22	0	920	138	1	41.81	17
R. J. Campbell (*Western Australia*)	11	21	2	723	134	1	38.05	29/8
C. T. Perren (*Queensland*)	11	20	1	721	141	1	37.94	5
†P. A. Jaques (*New South Wales*)	10	20	0	636	146	1	31.80	6

† *Left-handed batsman.*

BOWLING

(Qualification: 20 wickets)

	Style	O	M	R	W	BB	5W/i	Avge
M. S. Kasprowicz (*Queensland*)	RFM	196.1	54	559	24	5-84	1	23.29
J. N. Gillespie (*Australia & S. Australia*) .	RF	253.4	71	627	26	5-54	1	24.11
A. B. Wise (*Victoria*)	LFM	284	88	801	33	5-47	2	24.27
D. G. Wright (*Tasmania & Australia A*) . .	RFM	386.5	114	1,030	39	5-43	1	26.41

	Style	O	M	R	W	BB	5W/i	Avge
A. B. McDonald (*Victoria*)	RFM	270.1	67	889	33	6-67	1	26.93
P. C. Rofe (*South Australia & Australia A*)	RFM	328.5	83	989	36	7-66	2	27.47
M. L. Lewis (*Victoria*)	RFM	312.3	74	947	34	6-59	2	27.85
M. W. H. Inness (*Victoria*).	LFM	229.4	69	669	24	4-26	0	27.87
M. J. Nicholson (*NSW & Australia A*) . . .	RFM	372.5	82	1,228	43	6-76	2	28.55
S. W. Tait (*South Australia & Australia A*)	RFM	256	40	957	33	5-85	1	29.00
M. F. Cleary (*South Australia*)	RFM	261.1	45	893	30	5-102	1	29.76
A. J. Bichel (*Australia & Queensland*) . . .	RFM	313.2	62	1,158	37	6-61	1	31.29
B. M. Edmondson (*Western Australia*) . . .	RFM	212.2	24	885	28	5-90	1	31.60
G. J. Denton (*Tasmania*)	RFM	276.3	60	994	30	4-60	0	33.13
N. W. Bracken (*Australia & NSW*)	LFM	290	98	747	22	5-38	1	33.95
J. H. Dawes (*Queensland*)	RFM	364.2	94	1,081	30	4-83	0	36.03
A. G. Downton (*Tasmania*)	LFM	373.5	76	1,353	37	5-71	1	36.56
C. L. White (*Victoria & Australia A*)	LBG	294.1	39	1,105	30	4-27	0	36.83
S. R. Clark (*New South Wales*)	RFM	289.2	57	882	23	4-52	0	38.26
B. Lee (*Australia & New South Wales*). . .	RF	268.5	48	1,041	24	5-124	1	43.37
S. C. G. MacGill (*Australia & NSW*). . . .	LBG	475.1	76	1,866	41	5-79	2	45.51
X. J. Doherty (*Tasmania*)	SLA	306.2	41	1,132	22	6-149	1	51.45

Note: Averages do not include Bangladesh's tour in July 2003 or Sri Lanka's in July 2004.

PURA CUP, 2003-04

	Played	Won	Lost	Drawn	1st-inns Points	Points	Quotient
Victoria	10	6	0	4	4	40	1.457
Queensland	10	3	3	4	6	24	1.108
Tasmania.	10	3	1	6	6	24	0.917
Western Australia . . .	10	3	3	4	4	21*	0.934
New South Wales . . .	10	2	6	2	6	17*	0.927
South Australia. . . .	10	2	6	2	0	12	0.802

Final: Victoria beat Queensland by 321 runs.

Queensland finished ahead of Tasmania by virtue of a superior quotient.
* One point deducted for slow over-rate.
Outright win = 6 pts; lead on first innings in a drawn or lost game = 2 pts.
Quotient = runs scored per wicket divided by runs conceded per wicket.

Full scores, match reports and statistics of the 2003-04 Australian season can be found in *Wisden Cricketers' Almanack Australia 2004-05.*

At Perth, October 19, 20, 21, 22, 2003. **South Australia won by 56 runs.** Toss: Western Australia. **South Australia 327** (G. S. Blewett 85, M. C. Miller 79) **and 221** (P. C. Worthington 6-59); **Western Australia 178** (M. W. Goodwin 89; S. W. Tait 4-61) **and 314** (M. J. North 80, P. C. Worthington 50; P. C. Rofe 5-89). *South Australia 6 pts.*
Jo Angel became Western Australia's leading wicket-taker, overtaking Terry Alderman's 433.

At Brisbane, November 2, 3, 4, 5, 2003. **Victoria won by five wickets.** Toss: Victoria. **Queensland 277** (C. P. Simpson 83; C. L. White 4-27) **and 256** (S. G. Law 81); **Victoria 374** (J. L. Arnberger 89, D. J. Hussey 106; S. J. Jurgensen 4-72) **and 160-5** (J. R. Hopes 4-63). *Victoria 6 pts.*
White made six catches in the field in the match, equalling Victoria's record. This was Victoria's first win in a first-class match in Queensland since 1983-84.

At Hobart, November 3, 4, 5, 6, 2003. **Drawn.** Toss: South Australia. **South Australia 236** (M. F. Cleary 58; A. G. Downton 5-71) **and 482-6** (D. A. Fitzgerald 202*, G. S. Blewett 171); **Tasmania 420** (J. Cox 119, S. R. Watson 103, M. J. Di Venuto 50; D. J. Marsh 76*; M. F. Cleary 5-102). *Tasmania 2 pts.*
Cox and Watson added 213 for Tasmania's second wicket. Fitzgerald's 202, his maiden double-hundred, lasted 607 minutes and 493 balls, and included 29 fours; he added 281 for South Australia's second wicket with Blewett.*

At Sydney, November 4, 5, 6, 7, 2003. **New South Wales won by five wickets.** Toss: Western Australia. **Western Australia 376** (M. W. Goodwin 201*) **and 362-8 dec.** (J. L. Langer 163*, M. E. K. Hussey 53, R. J. Campbell 58; M. J. Nicholson 4-69); **New South Wales 436** (S. M. Katich 182*, N. S. Pilon 78; B. Casson 4-141) **and 303-5** (S. R. Waugh 117*, S. M. Katich 71*). *New South Wales 6 pts.*

Goodwin's 201*, his fourth double-hundred (after three for Sussex), lasted 434 minutes and 320 balls and included 33 fours; Western Australia's next highest score was 34. In the second innings, he was out fourth ball for nought. New South Wales scored 303 in 47.2 overs to win.

At St Kilda, November 11, 12, 13, 14, 2003. **Drawn.** Toss: Victoria. **Victoria 381-9 dec.** (M. T. G. Elliott 106, J. Moss 80; J. H. Dawes 4-89) **and 208-2** (M. T. G. Elliott 79, B. J. Hodge 111*); **Queensland 605-7 dec.** (C. T. Perren 95, M. L. Love 300*, J. R. Hopes 97, W. A. Seccombe 57). *Queensland 2 pts.*

Love's 300*, his first triple-hundred but his eighth double, lasted 610 minutes and 489 balls and included 32 fours; he added 236 with Hopes, a Queensland fifth-wicket record, to set up their highest total against Victoria.

At Hobart, November 12, 13, 14, 15, 2003. **Tasmania won by six wickets.** Toss: New South Wales. **New South Wales 453-5 dec.** (S. M. Katich 171, S. R. Waugh 157) **and 208-8 dec.** (G. J. Mail 107*; D. G. Wright 4-50); **Tasmania 276** (S. R. Mason 58, D. J. Marsh 68; S. C. G. MacGill 5-79) **and 386-4** (M. J. Di Venuto 174*, D. J. Marsh 107*). *Tasmania 6 pts, New South Wales 2 pts.*

Mark Waugh played his 100th first-class match for New South Wales. His brother Steve scored his 79th first-class hundred, which was to be his last before retirement, and added 270 with Katich for the third wicket. Di Venuto and Marsh shared an unbroken stand of 220 for Tasmania's fifth wicket.

At Adelaide, November 18, 19, 20, 21, 2003. **South Australia won by five wickets.** Toss: New South Wales. **New South Wales 267** (G. J. Mail 94; P. C. Rofe 4-62) **and 267** (S. M. Katich 69; J. N. Gillespie 5-54); **South Australia 400** (S. A. Deitz 66, M. J. Cosgrove 118, J. M. Davison 84; M. J. Nicholson 6-76) **and 137-5** (G. S. Blewett 65*). *South Australia 6 pts.*

Gillespie finished New South Wales's second innings with four wickets in eight deliveries.

At St Kilda, November 19, 20, 21, 22, 2003. **Drawn.** Toss: Western Australia. **Western Australia 273** (C. J. L. Rogers 103, M. W. Goodwin 70; A. B. McDonald 4-35) **and 265** (M. E. K. Hussey 57, J. L. Langer 96, C. J. L. Rogers 52; M. L. Lewis 5-58); **Victoria 355-9 dec.** (M. T. G. Elliott 71, B. J. Hodge 100, J. Moss 52, C. L. White 58*; J. J. Taylor 4-70) **and 35-1.** *Victoria 2 pts.*

Hodge scored his 25th first-class hundred.

At Brisbane, November 20, 21, 22, 2003. **Tasmania won by 174 runs.** Toss: Queensland. **Tasmania 233** (M. J. Di Venuto 79; D. R. MacKenzie 4-43) **and 213** (D. G. Wright 60; S. J. Jurgensen 4-52); **Queensland 104** (D. G. Wright 4-30) **and 168** (G. J. Denton 4-60). *Tasmania 6 pts.*

Queensland wicket-keeper Wade Seccombe made five catches in each innings. Queensland recovered from 41-5 but 104 was their lowest total against Tasmania.

At Adelaide, November 27, 28, 29, 30, 2003. **Queensland won by 61 runs.** Toss: Queensland. **Queensland 310** (S. G. Law 75, W. A. Seccombe 67*) **and 274** (S. G. Law 72, W. A. Seccombe 115); **South Australia 301** (G. S. Blewett 62, A. Flower 82; A. J. Bichel 6-61) **and 222** (A. Flower 56, M. A. Higgs 71; A. J. Bichel 4-52, M. S. Kasprowicz 5-84). *Queensland 6 pts.*

Kasprowicz became Queensland's leading wicket-taker, overtaking Carl Rackemann (425).

At Perth, December 7, 8, 9, 10, 2003. **Drawn.** Toss: Tasmania. **Western Australia 437** (M. E. K. Hussey 138, M. W. Goodwin 72, M. J. North 90; G. J. Denton 4-94) **and 329-5 dec.** (C. J. L. Rogers 120, M. E. K. Hussey 61, M. W. Goodwin 104*); **Tasmania 380** (S. R. Mason 52, S. G. Clingeleffer 79, D. G. Wright 65; B. A. Williams 4-115) **and 386-7** (M. G. Dighton 88, D. J. Marsh 111*). *Western Australia 2 pts.*

Clingeleffer made seven catches in Western Australia's first innings, which equalled the Tasmanian record. Chasing 387 in 75 overs, Tasmania levelled the scores in the final over, when Ben Edmondson, making his first-class debut as a full playing substitute for Williams, restricted them to six runs.

At Melbourne, December 12, 13, 14, 15, 2003. **Victoria won by two wickets.** Toss: New South Wales. **New South Wales 287** (B. J. Haddin 76, B. Lee 74*) **and 268** (M. G. Bevan 106, M. E. Waugh 58; A. B. Wise 5-59); **Victoria 326** (D. J. Hussey 120, C. L. White 78) **and 230-8** (J. Moss 63, D. J. Hussey 50; S. R. Clark 4-52). *Victoria 6 pts.*

White made four catches in the field in New South Wales's first innings and six in the match, equalling the Victorian record for the second time in the season. Dominic Thornely of New South Wales took two wickets in his first over on first-class debut. New South Wales were penalised one point for a slow over-rate.

At Sydney, December 19, 20, 21, 22, 2003. **Drawn.** Toss: Tasmania. **Tasmania 322** (S. R. Mason 51, M. G. Dighton 69, S. G. Clingeleffer 53; B. Lee 5-124) **and 315** (S. R. Watson 157; S. M. Katich 4-42); **New South Wales 462** (M. G. Bevan 216, S. M. Katich 53, D. J. Thornely 81; X. J. Doherty 4-142) **and 175-3** (P. A. Jaques 85, M. G. Bevan 53). *New South Wales 2 pts.*

Australian captain Ricky Ponting turned down a rare chance to play for Tasmania so that he could attend his wife's graduation at the nearby University of Wollongong. Bevan's 216, his fifth and highest double-hundred, lasted 484 minutes and 416 balls and included 30 fours and a six. It made him the first player to score 9,000 first-class runs for New South Wales. This was the second successive Tasmanian match which finished with the scores level.

At Brisbane, December 19, 20, 21, 2003. **Queensland won by an innings and 137 runs.** Toss: South Australia. **South Australia 204** (S. A. Deitz 74, G. A. Manou 51; A. A. Noffke 4-48) **and 156; Queensland 497-7 dec.** (J. P. Maher 97, A. Symonds 102, C. D. Hartley 103, A. A. Noffke 114*; M. F. Cleary 4-133). *Queensland 6 pts.*

Chris Hartley scored 103 on first-class debut and added 218 with Noffke for Queensland's seventh wicket.

At Perth, December 20, 21, 22, 2003. **Victoria won by an innings and 158 runs.** Toss: Victoria. **Western Australia 151** (S. W. Meuleman 53) **and 304** (S. W. Meuleman 106, R. J. Campbell 54; A. B. McDonald 6-67); **Victoria 613-3 dec.** (M. T. G. Elliott 182, M. P. Mott 78, J. Moss 172*, D. J. Hussey 160*). *Victoria 6 pts.*

Moss and Hussey shared an unbroken stand of 309 for the fourth wicket, a Victorian record, to set up Victoria's highest total against Western Australia.

At Newcastle, January 9, 10, 11, 12, 2004. **Victoria won by three wickets.** Toss: New South Wales. **New South Wales 317** (P. A. Jaques 56, S. M. Katich 76, B. J. Haddin 50; M. L. Lewis 4-68) **and 396** (S. M. Katich 126, D. J. Thornely 143); **Victoria 259** (D. J. Hussey 51; S. C. G. MacGill 5-94) **and 455-7** (J. Moss 76, D. J. Hussey 212*, C. L. White 60). *Victoria 6 pts, New South Wales 2 pts.*

Hussey's 212, his maiden double-hundred, lasted 310 minutes and just 218 balls and included 26 fours and five sixes, helping Victoria score 455 in 102 overs to win – the second-biggest successful fourth-innings run-chase in Sheffield Shield/Pura Cup cricket.*

At Adelaide, January 11, 12, 13, 14, 2004. **Tasmania won by 213 runs.** Toss: Tasmania. **Tasmania 207** (M. F. Cleary 4-41) **and 334** (S. R. Watson 61, S. G. Clingeleffer 74); **South Australia 112 and 216** (M. J. Cosgrove 54, M. C. Miller 53*; D. G. Wright 5-43). *Tasmania 6 pts.*

Jamie Cox played his 150th Sheffield Shield/Pura Cup match. South Australia's 112 was their lowest total against Tasmania.

At Perth, January 11, 12, 13, 14, 2004. **Drawn.** Toss: Western Australia. **Western Australia 427-9 dec.** (C. J. L. Rogers 94, M. W. Goodwin 156, M. J. North 67; M. S. Kasprowicz 4-74) **and 312-6 dec.** (J. L. Langer 92, R. J. Campbell 50); **Queensland 434** (J. P. Maher 60, C. T. Perren 95, M. L. Love 66, A. A. Noffke 55, N. M. Hauritz 94; B. Casson 5-109) **and 247-6** (C. T. Perren 61, M. L. Love 63, S. G. Law 54*). *Queensland 2 pts.*

Goodwin scored his 30th first-class hundred.

At Hobart, January 21, 22, 23, 24, 2004. **Drawn.** Toss: Tasmania. **Queensland 400-8 dec.** (M. L. Love 100, S. G. Law 99) **and 322** (C. A. Philipson 101*, J. R. Hopes 111; A. G. Downton 4-59); **Tasmania 402-4 dec.** (S. R. Watson 53, M. J. Di Venuto 91, M. G. Dighton 127*, D. J. Marsh 80*) **and 8-1.** *Tasmania 2 pts.*

Mike Kasprowicz played his 100th first-class match for Queensland. Craig Philipson scored 101 on first-class debut.*

At Perth, January 23, 24, 25, 26, 2004. **Western Australia won by 126 runs.** Toss: New South Wales. **Western Australia 474-6 dec.** (M. E. K. Hussey 76, C. J. L. Rogers 142, M. J. North 87, R. J. Campbell 87) **and 279** (J. L. Langer 94, M. E. K. Hussey 71, J. J. Taylor 50; N. W. Bracken 5-38, M. J. Nicholson 4-62); **New South Wales 367-7 dec.** (S. M. Katich 82, D. J. Thornely 59, S. R. Waugh 51; B. M. Edmondson 4-78) **and 260** (P. A. Jaques 56). *Western Australia 6 pts.*

Hussey took over as wicket-keeper when Campbell was injured, and caught three in each innings. Jo Angel retired after the match with 485 first-class wickets, a record 445 of them for Western Australia and 419 in the Sheffield Shield/Pura Cup, behind only Clarrie Grimmett (513). Western Australia were penalised one point for a slow over-rate.

At Brisbane, February 1, 2, 3, 4, 2004. **Drawn.** Toss: Queensland. **Queensland 431-5 dec.** (J. P. Maher 116, M. L. Love 68, S. G. Law 146*) **and 124-2 dec.** (C. T. Perren 57); **New South Wales 229-7 dec.** (P. A. Jaques 53, M. E. Waugh 90) **and 277-8** (G. J. Mail 50, P. A. Jaques 146; M. S. Kasprowicz 4-74). *Queensland 2 pts.*

Law became Queensland's leading run-scorer, overtaking Sam Trimble's 9,465. Mark Waugh made his 450th first-class catch, and Mike Kasprowicz took his 800th wicket.

At Adelaide, February 1, 2, 3, 4, 2004. **Victoria won by 197 runs.** Toss: Victoria. **Victoria 343** (M. T. G. Elliott 111, M. P. Mott 53, B. J. Hodge 81; P. C. Rofe 7-66) **and 272** (B. J. Hodge 86, C. L. White 75; J. M. Davison 4-72); **South Australia 262** (C. L. White 4-43) **and 156** (M. W. H. Inness 4-26, A. B. Wise 5-47). *Victoria 6 pts.*

This was Victoria's 1,000th first-class match (385 wins, 296 defeats, 316 draws and three ties); Hodge had played in 100 of them. Darren Lehmann passed 20,000 first-class runs. Victoria completed their fourth successive win, in their first first-class game since the death of coach David Hookes.

At Hobart, February 4, 5, 6, 7, 2004. **Drawn.** Toss: Tasmania. **Western Australia 562-6 dec.** (M. E. K. Hussey 82, M. W. Goodwin 77, M. J. North 118, R. J. Campbell 134, K. M. Harvey 100*) **and 270-6 dec.** (J. L. Langer 84, M. J. North 87); **Tasmania 384-5 dec.** (S. R. Watson 139, M. G. Dighton 101, D. J. Marsh 51*) **and 396-9** (S. R. Mason 126, S. R. Watson 92, M. J. Di Venuto 50, M. G. Dighton 62). *Western Australia 2 pts.*

Goodwin passed 10,000 first-class runs. Campbell scored 102 before lunch on the second day.

At Melbourne, February 8, 9, 10, 11, 2004. **Drawn.** Toss: South Australia. **South Australia 225** (B. P. Cameron 54, M. C. Miller 84) **and 122-2** (B. P. Cameron 58*); **Victoria 331-8 dec.** (M. T. G. Elliott 154*, B. J. Hodge 73). *Victoria 2 pts.*

This match was postponed from January 23 after the death of David Hookes, who played for South Australia and coached Victoria. Victorian wicket-keeper Darren Berry played his 150th first-class match.

At Brisbane, February 15, 16, 17, 18, 2004. **Western Australia won by seven wickets.** Toss: Western Australia. **Queensland 362** (J. P. Maher 92, C. A. Philipson 63, J. R. Hopes 71) **and 445-8 dec.** (C. T. Perren 141, S. G. Law 203; D. J. Wates 4-77); **Western Australia 523** (C. J. L. Rogers 73, M. J. North 130, S. W. Meuleman 50, R. J. Campbell 91; N. M. Hauritz 4-95) **and 287-3** (C. J. L. Rogers 119*, M. W. Goodwin 119). *Western Australia 6 pts.*

Law's 203, his 65th hundred and fifth double, lasted 297 minutes and 233 balls and included 26 fours and a six; he added 369 with Perren, a Queensland second-wicket record. Rogers and Goodwin added 234 for Western Australia's third wicket.

At Melbourne, February 16, 17, 18, 19, 2004. **Victoria won by 218 runs.** Toss: Victoria. **Victoria 494** (M. T. G. Elliott 166, B. J. Hodge 121; X. J. Doherty 6-149) **and 194-2 dec.** (M. T. G. Elliott 102*, J. Moss 79*); **Tasmania 249-7 dec.** (M. G. Dighton 50) **and 221** (M. G. Dighton 54; S. K. Warne 4-51). *Victoria 6 pts.*

This was Warne's first first-class match since his 12-month drugs ban ended. Elliott's twin hundreds gave him three in consecutive innings; he added 251 with Hodge for Victoria's second wicket in the first innings.

At Sydney, February 17, 18, 19, 20, 2004. **New South Wales won by 25 runs.** Toss: New South Wales. **New South Wales 350-9 dec.** (G. J. Mail 128, N. S. Pilon 50; S. W. Tait 5-85) **and 299-4 dec.** (G. J. Mail 152*, M. J. Phelps 62); **South Australia 129** (M. J. Nicholson 5-36) **and 495** (G. A. Manou 130, D. S. Lehmann 237, M. A. Higgs 50; S. C. G. MacGill 4-144). *New South Wales 6 pts.*

There were six ducks in South Australia's first innings, equalling the Sheffield Shield/Pura Cup record; in their second, chasing 521 to win, they were all out for 495 – the fifth-highest fourth innings in Australian history – in the 118th over. Lehmann's 237, his 65th hundred and ninth double, lasted 314 minutes and just 238 balls and included 34 fours and two sixes; he added 210 for the third wicket with Manou and became the second player after David Hookes to score 10,000 runs for South Australia.

At Sydney, March 4, 5, 6, 7, 2004. **Queensland won by 37 runs.** Toss: New South Wales. **Queensland 418-9 dec,** (C. P. Simpson 75, M. L. Love 52, A. J. Nye 102, A. J. Bichel 112) **and 54-1 dec.; New South Wales 196-4 dec.** (M. G. Bevan 79*, S. R. Waugh 65) **and 239** (M. E. Waugh 72, B. J. Haddin 62*; A. J. Bichel 4-69). *Queensland 6 pts.*

This was the final first-class appearance of the Waugh twins. Steve ended his career with 24,052 first-class runs at 51.94, and Mark with 26,855 at 52.04. In this match, Steve reached 50 for the 176th time, and Mark for the 214th. Aaron Nye became the third Queensland batsman to score a hundred on first-class debut in 2003-04. Glenn McGrath, seeking match fitness after an ankle injury, made his first Pura Cup appearance since October 2001.

At Adelaide, March 4, 5, 6, 7, 2004. **Western Australia won by 87 runs.** Toss: Western Australia. **Western Australia 335** (M. W. Goodwin 55, M. J. North 130*) **and 302** (G. B. Hogg 75, D. J. Wates 99; S. W. Tait 4-59); **South Australia 300** (S. A. Deitz 51, M. J. Cosgrove 144) **and 250** (B. P. Cameron 81, M. J. Cosgrove 88; B. M. Edmondson 5-90). *Western Australia 6 pts.*

At Hobart, March 4, 5, 6, 7, 2004. **Drawn.** Toss: Tasmania. **Tasmania 341** (M. G. Dighton 152; A. B. McDonald 4-69) **and 222-9 dec.** (J. Cox 54, S. R. Watson 117; J. Moss 4-60); **Victoria 252-7 dec.** (B. J. Hodge 125, A. B. McDonald 51*) **and 212-6** (J. Moss 77*, B. R. Joseland 51). *Tasmania 2 pts.*

Darren Berry became the fourth Australian wicket-keeper to make 600 first-class dismissals. Debutant Brendan Joseland took a wicket with his fourth ball in first-class cricket. Had Tasmania won, they would have joined Victoria in the final instead of Queensland.

FINAL

VICTORIA v QUEENSLAND

At Melbourne, March 12, 13, 14, 15, 16, 2004. Victoria won by 321 runs. Toss: Queensland.

On day three, the rule that the team heading the table need only draw the final to win looked to have produced a farce. Victoria's curator prepared a featherbed pitch, Victoria's selectors included an extra batsman, and the Victorian XI spent nearly 14 hours stacking up 710. They had put Queensland's hopes to bed and any onlookers to sleep. Or so it seemed. It was the fifth afternoon when Berry – the sole survivor from Victoria's last title 13 years earlier – dived to pouch the winning catch, his final leap as a first-class cricketer. Queensland captain Maher had fielded first in the hope of exploiting early moisture, but soon regretted it. Elliott played and missed once all day as he cut and pulled his way to a Shield/Pura seasonal record of 1,381 runs; six others passed fifty. Queensland's reply lasted half as long, White's leg-spin sparking a middle-order collapse. Berry waived the follow-on and, after Arnberger heaved Hauritz for three straight sixes, declared 575 ahead. Maher implored his men to fight to the death, then got out first ball. The last-day crowd, let in free, saw Lewis collect a career-best six for 59, as only Law, in his final Queensland innings, stood unflustered. As the Victorians sang their victory song they cleared a space for David Hookes and John Scholes, their much-loved coaches who had both died in the previous 12 months. Maher said he felt Queensland had been playing 13 men, in a season when beating 11 Victorians had proved problematic enough.

Man of the Match: M. T. G. Elliott.   *Attendance:* 25,644.

Close of play: First day, Victoria 322-1 (Elliott 140, Hodge 85); Second day, Victoria 592-6 (Harvey 34, McDonald 37); Third day, Queensland 177-6 (Love 22, Bichel 2); Fourth day, Queensland 56-2 (Perren 32, Law 8).

Victoria

M. T. G. Elliott c Hartley b Bichel	155	– (2) not out	55
J. L. Arnberger lbw b Hauritz	90	– (1) c and b Hauritz	72
B. J. Hodge c Hopes b Dawes	89	– not out	5
J. Moss c Law b Hauritz	98		
D. J. Hussey c Hartley b Noffke	16		
C. L. White c Hartley b Simpson	54		
I. J. Harvey b Noffke	62		
A. B. McDonald c sub (A. J. Nye) b Dawes	42		
*†D. S. Berry c Law b Hauritz	61		
M. L. Lewis lbw b Noffke	11		
A. B. Wise not out	1		
B 3, l-b 14, w 2, n-b 12	31	L-b 5, w 2, n-b 1	8

1/165 (2) 2/336 (3) 3/342 (1) 4/369 (5)   710   1/119 (1)   (1 wkt dec.) 140
5/504 (6) 6/516 (4) 7/614 (8)
8/656 (7) 9/708 (10) 10/710 (9)

Bowling: *First Innings*—Bichel 37–4–170–1; Dawes 38–9–97–2; Noffke 31–4–104–3; Hopes 24–5–80–0; Hauritz 50–13–145–3; Simpson 22–5–66–1; Law 9–2–26–0; Perren 1–0–5–0. *Second Innings*—Dawes 7–2–22–0; Bichel 6–0–22–0; Hopes 9–2–37–0; Hauritz 8–0–54–1.

Queensland

*J. P. Maher lbw b Moss	72	– c White b Lewis	0
C. T. Perren c Berry b Lewis	40	– lbw b Lewis	32
S. G. Law c Hussey b White	18	– (4) b White	72
C. P. Simpson lbw b White	8	– (5) c Berry b Lewis	15
J. R. Hopes lbw b White	5	– (6) c White b Harvey	31
M. L. Love not out	65	– (3) lbw b Lewis	14
†C. D. Hartley lbw b Moss	0	– not out	31
A. J. Bichel lbw b White	19	– c Elliott b Lewis	3
A. A. Noffke c Lewis b Moss	13	– lbw b McDonald	13
N. M. Hauritz b McDonald	0	– c Lewis b McDonald	33
J. H. Dawes b Harvey	21	– c Berry b Lewis	2
B 3, l-b 5, n-b 6	14	B 4, n-b 4	8

1/85 (2) 2/122 (3) 3/132 (4) 4/148 (5)   275   1/0 (1) 2/31 (3) 3/56 (2) 4/86 (5)   254
5/157 (1) 6/157 (7) 7/201 (8)   5/152 (6) 6/174 (7) 7/177 (8)
8/228 (9) 9/229 (10) 10/275 (11)   8/211 (9) 9/249 (10) 10/254 (11)

Bowling: *First Innings*—Wise 10–4–21–0; Harvey 14.5–3–41–1; Lewis 24–10–66–1; McDonald 16–4–55–1; White 30–6–66–4; Moss 11–4–18–3. *Second Innings*—Lewis 17.3–4–59–6; Harvey 14–4–43–1; McDonald 15–5–34–2; Moss 5–2–19–0; White 13–1–83–1; Hodge 4–1–12–0.

Umpires: P. D. Parker and R. L. Parry.   Referee: R. W. Stratford.

CHAMPIONS

1913-14	New South Wales		1965-66	New South Wales
1914-15	Victoria		1966-67	Victoria
1915-19	No competition		1967-68	Western Australia
1919-20	New South Wales		1968-69	South Australia
1920-21	New South Wales		1969-70	Victoria
1921-22	Victoria		1970-71	South Australia
1922-23	New South Wales		1971-72	Western Australia
1923-24	Victoria		1972-73	Western Australia
1924-25	Victoria		1973-74	Victoria
1925-26	New South Wales		1974-75	Western Australia
1926-27	South Australia		1975-76	South Australia
1927-28	Victoria		1976-77	Western Australia
1928-29	New South Wales		1977-78	Western Australia
1929-30	Victoria		1978-79	Victoria
1930-31	Victoria		1979-80	Victoria
1931-32	New South Wales		1980-81	Western Australia
1932-33	New South Wales		1981-82	South Australia
1933-34	Victoria		1982-83	New South Wales
1934-35	Victoria		1983-84	Western Australia
1935-36	South Australia		1984-85	New South Wales
1936-37	Victoria		1985-86	New South Wales
1937-38	New South Wales		1986-87	Western Australia
1938-39	South Australia		1987-88	Western Australia
1939-40	New South Wales		1988-89	Western Australia
1940-46	No competition		1989-90	New South Wales
1946-47	Victoria		1990-91	Victoria
1947-48	Western Australia		1991-92	Western Australia
1948-49	New South Wales		1992-93	New South Wales
1949-50	New South Wales		1993-94	New South Wales
1950-51	Victoria		1994-95	Queensland
1951-52	New South Wales		1995-96	South Australia
1952-53	South Australia		1996-97	Queensland
1953-54	New South Wales		1997-98	Western Australia
1954-55	New South Wales		1998-99	Western Australia
1955-56	New South Wales			
1956-57	New South Wales		*Pura Milk Cup*	
1957-58	New South Wales		1999-2000	Queensland
1958-59	New South Wales			
1959-60	New South Wales		*Pura Cup*	
1960-61	New South Wales		2000-01	Queensland
1961-62	New South Wales		2001-02	Queensland
1962-63	Victoria		2002-03	New South Wales
1963-64	South Australia		2003-04	Victoria
1964-65	New South Wales			

New South Wales have won the title 43 times, Victoria 26, Western Australia 15, South Australia 13, Queensland 5, Tasmania 0.

ING CUP, 2003-04

Note: Matches in this section were not first-class.
Each side had 12 players of whom 11 could bat and 11 field.

	Played	Won	Lost	Tied	No result	Bonus points	Points	Net run-rate
Queensland	10	7	3	0	0	4	32	0.70
Western Australia	10	6	3	0	1	3	29	0.14
Victoria	10	6	3	1	0	2	28	0.11
New South Wales	10	5	4	1	0	1	23	0.13
South Australia	10	3	7	0	0	1	13	−0.29
Tasmania	10	1	8	0	1	0	6	−0.86

Final

At Brisbane, February 29, 2004. **Western Australia won by four wickets.** Toss: Queensland. **Queensland 244** (49.1 overs) (S. G. Law 50, C. T. Perren 57; K. M. Harvey 4-28); **Western Australia 248-6** (49.4 overs) (S. W. Meuleman 71, K. M. Harvey 53*).

Law hit his 50 in 40 balls; he and opening partner Jimmy Maher (46) raised 100 in 12 overs before both fell to man of the match Kade Harvey, who later hit a match-winning 53 in 42 balls.*

SHEFFIELD SHIELD/PURA CUP FINALS

1982-83	NEW SOUTH WALES* beat Western Australia by 54 runs.
1983-84	WESTERN AUSTRALIA beat Queensland by four wickets.
1984-85	NEW SOUTH WALES beat Queensland by one wicket.
1985-86	NEW SOUTH WALES drew with Queensland.
1986-87	WESTERN AUSTRALIA drew with Victoria.
1987-88	WESTERN AUSTRALIA beat Queensland by five wickets.
1988-89	WESTERN AUSTRALIA drew with South Australia.
1989-90	NEW SOUTH WALES beat Queensland by 345 runs.
1990-91	VICTORIA beat New South Wales by eight wickets.
1991-92	WESTERN AUSTRALIA beat New South Wales by 44 runs.
1992-93	NEW SOUTH WALES beat Queensland by eight wickets.
1993-94	NEW SOUTH WALES beat Tasmania by an innings and 61 runs.
1994-95	QUEENSLAND beat South Australia by an innings and 101 runs.
1995-96	SOUTH AUSTRALIA drew with Western Australia.
1996-97	QUEENSLAND* beat Western Australia by 160 runs.
1997-98	WESTERN AUSTRALIA beat Tasmania by seven wickets.
1998-99	WESTERN AUSTRALIA* beat Queensland by an innings and 31 runs.
1999-2000	QUEENSLAND drew with Victoria.
2000-01	QUEENSLAND beat Victoria by four wickets.
2001-02	QUEENSLAND beat Tasmania by 235 runs.
2002-03	NEW SOUTH WALES* beat Queensland by 246 runs.
2003-04	VICTORIA beat Queensland by 321 runs.

Note: The team that finished top of the table had home advantage over the runners-up. In a drawn final, the home team won the title.

* *Victory for the away team.*

PURA CUP PLAYER OF THE YEAR

The Pura Cup Player of the Year Award for 2003-04 was won by Matthew Elliott of Victoria, for a record third time. He also won in 1995-96 and 1998-99. Elliott was awarded 21 points, three more than his team-mate David Hussey and six ahead of Queensland's Stuart Law. The Award, instituted in 1975-76, is adjudicated by the umpires over the course of the season.

ALLAN BORDER MEDAL

Australia's new Test captain Ricky Ponting won the Allan Border Medal in February 2004 with 139 votes, 48 ahead of his nearest rival, Matthew Hayden. Team-mates, umpires and journalists voted for the best Australian international player of the past 12 months. Previous winners were Glenn McGrath, Steve Waugh, Hayden and Adam Gilchrist. In the remaining awards, voted on by fellow players, Ponting was also named Test Cricketer of the Year, with Gilchrist One-day International Player of the Year for the second year running. Simon Katich of New South Wales was State Player of the Year, and Shaun Tait of South Australia won the Bradman Young Player of the Year award. Cathryn Fitzpatrick was the Women's International Cricketer of the Year.

CRICKET IN SOUTH AFRICA, 2003-04

Colin Bryden and Andrew Samson

Zander de Bruyn

While the national team struggled, with mixed results, to maintain South Africa's previously acknowledged position as the leading threat to Australia's supremacy, the country saw the beginnings of an internal revolution designed to transform domestic cricket. At the end of the 2003-04 season South Africans had a first taste of the new professional franchise system during a 20-overs competition, modelled on the English version so successfully introduced less than a year earlier.

More than 153,000 spectators watched 17 matches in the Pro20 tournament, which served a dual purpose, forging an identity for six new teams and reversing a fall in domestic attendances. The United Cricket Board hoped the crowds would return when the franchise system started in earnest in 2004-05, with the same teams playing four-day and 45-overs cricket.

The new structure arose from a review prompted by South Africa's failure against Australia in 2000-01 and a perceived decline in provincial standards. Independent consultants recommended cutting the number of professional teams from 11 to six, with the aim of strengthening the game below Test level and providing better preparation for the national side.

Cricket SA, the body set up by the UCB to run the professional game, awarded six franchises, mostly incorporating the 11 existing teams, in February 2004. Northerns and Easterns combined as the Titans, based at Centurion. At Johannesburg, Gauteng and North West formed the Lions. KwaZulu-Natal won a sole franchise, and would play at Durban as the Dolphins. Western Province plus Boland covered the Western Cape from Cape Town. The Eastern Cape took in Eastern Province and Border, whose headquarters, rather unexpectedly, were to be at Border's ground in East London rather than Port Elizabeth. Free State and Griqualand West could not agree a joint proposal, and bid separately; Free State won and named themselves the Eagles, based at Bloemfontein, while Griqua supporters staged a peaceful but unavailing pitch invasion during a one-day game to protest against the decision.

First impressions from the 2004-05 season were that the new system seemed to be fulfilling the cricketing objectives without making much impact on the public.

Free State Eagles became the first franchise side to win a trophy. Led by Nicky Boje and including Loots Bosman and Deon Kruis, signed from Griqualand West, they beat Eastern Cape in the rain-affected Pro20 final. Bosman was named Pro20's "Master Blaster" after scoring 219 at a strike-rate of 120.99.

The league phase was dominated by the Titans and the awkwardly titled Western Province Boland: the name, combined with the sponsor, took up so much space that the players had to let their shirts hang out of their trousers for it to be visible in full. With Western Province dominating the partnership, it was expected that "Boland" would eventually disappear.

The Lions finished last, but drew the biggest crowd when 18,221 turned up at the Wanderers and saw them lose with a ball to spare against the Dolphins – who failed to reach the semis despite fielding Shaun Pollock and Lance Klusener.

The true value of the new system would be tested when the sides played first-class cricket. A challenge for all of them, and a potential conflict with the principle of raising standards, was a UCB target for 40% of squads and four players on the field in each match to be "players of colour". Meanwhile, below the professional level, the 11 provincial unions affiliated to the UCB would continue to play amateur cricket with, for the time being, first-class status. Five further unions – Limpopo, Mpumalanga, South Western Districts, Border-Kei and KwaZulu-Natal Inland – would play in a third, non-first-class tier.

Western Province were the last first-class champions under the old system, beating KwaZulu-Natal in the SuperSport Series final despite Klusener taking 12 wickets. It was a deserved victory: the business end of the season took place while five of their players were with the Test squad in New Zealand. They also headed the league in the one-day Standard Bank Cup, but were knocked out in the semi-finals.

Two left-handers, 23-year-old Andrew Puttick and Jean-Paul Duminy, who turned 20 in April, between them scored more than 1,200 first-class runs for Western Province. Left-arm seamer Charl Willoughby was the competition's leading wicket-taker, with 42 at 20, one ahead of Klusener, with 41 at 21 for KwaZulu-Natal. Claude Henderson, the left-arm spinner, took 38 but decided to move on after six seasons for a new career with Leicestershire. Also tempted abroad was Arthur Turner, one of the country's leading administrators, to be commercial director of Glamorgan after 11 years as chief executive at Newlands. And the captain, Gary Kirsten, retired. Test calls meant he took charge in only two first-class matches; in his absence, Ashwell Prince proved a capable leader.

KwaZulu-Natal started in rampant form, winning five of their first six SuperSport games before losing the last three, including the final. Bad weather washed away their one-day chances. All was not well in their camp: coach Eldine Baptiste, the former West Indies Test player, left, and Dale

Benkenstein resigned the captaincy after eight largely successful seasons. Phil Russell, the former Derbyshire player who had stepped down when Baptiste took the job, moved up again, and the new captain was 21-year-old Hashim Amla.

Amla led the batting, with 647 runs; Benkenstein and opener Doug Watson also passed 550. On the bowling front, the Natalians gained immensely from Klusener's determination to play himself back into the national side, with support from West Indian Nixon McLean and fellow seamer Andrew Tweedie. Off-spinner Imraan Khan, who led South Africa Under-19 in England in 2003, showed promise on debut.

North West enjoyed their best season since elevation to the top flight in 1999-2000, finishing third in the SuperSix, but lost their first seven one-day matches. They greeted the franchise system without enthusiasm, as minor partners with Gauteng. Only two North West players, seamer Garth Roe and spinner Werner Coetsee, were offered contracts with the Lions; others were lured to rival franchises. **Border** were fourth, thanks to fast-medium bowler Tyron Henderson, who took 38 SuperSport wickets and had the season's highest first-class aggregate with 44. He was also an aggressive pinch-hitter in the one-day competition, where Border finished mid-table.

Free State, captained by Allan Donald who had retired from national duty, had hopes of reaching the SuperSport final until bad light denied them in their penultimate game, with North West eight down. Losing the last match to Western Province bumped them down to fifth, and they could not win a single one-day fixture before their re-emergence as the Eagles when the new system began. **Griqualand West**, who as Kimberley were the second winners of the Currie Cup in 1890-91, at the height of the diamond rush, were the big losers in the franchise shake-up; they did well to reach the Super Six but, disillusioned by rejection, lost their remaining games.

Defending champions **Easterns** built some large totals, but failed to win in the pool phase and did not reach the Super Six. Three victories in the Shield Series for non-qualifiers placed them top of that table by more than 27 points, and they also got to the one-day final. New captain Daryll Cullinan and Zander de Bruyn were in prolific form. De Bruyn set an Easterns record with 266 not out against Griqualand West and, with 1,015 runs at 72.50, became only the second man after Barry Richards to score 1,000 in a season in Currie Cup/SuperSport cricket. De Bruyn scored 1,048 in all first-class matches. Sven Koenig, formerly of Western Province and Gauteng, appeared as an overseas player for Easterns, having joined Middlesex on a European passport.

Boland's last season as an independent professional team ended with farewells to some of their best players. Henry Williams, who had played seven one-day internationals in 1999 and 2000, retired, aged 36, while Justin Ontong joined the Lions. Bad weather and some bad luck contributed to a disappointing campaign by **Northerns**, without their three Test batsmen for much of the season. Seamers Alfonso Thomas and Ethy Mbhalati compensated for the failure of West Indies' Reon King, while all-rounder Justin Kemp regained some of the form which earned him international selection in 2000-01. Batsman A. B. de Villiers was one of the most promising newcomers to provincial cricket.

Eastern Province, whose time among the giants had become a distant memory, ended a streak of 18 first-class matches without victory when they defeated Northerns in March, but it was a rare highlight. Captain Carl Bradfield resigned mid-season and was replaced by Robin Peterson. Some problems were solved when a properly constituted board was elected in December; the union had been in "judicial management" for almost 18 months after endless wrangling between officials and the transformation monitoring committee. But there was a further unhappy incident when Kepler Wessels, the coach, was accused of racism by two disaffected players. An inquiry cleared him.

Gauteng did not have a single player in the top 20 of the batting or bowling averages and had not qualified for the Super group of the first-class competition since their last title in 1999-2000. They did win the one-day Standard Bank Cup. In the semi-final, an opening stand of 175 between Adam Bacher, nephew of Ali, and Stephen Cook, son of Jimmy, set up victory over Northerns, and they went on to beat Easterns in a final postponed for two days because of heavy rain.

Off the field, Diteko Modise, the United Cricket Board's financial manager, was suspended after an audit, arrested and, in May, charged with irregularities reportedly involving more than seven million rand (about £600,000).

FIRST-CLASS AVERAGES, 2003-04

BATTING

(Qualification: 500 runs)

	M	I	NO	R	HS	100s	Avge	Ct
J. H. Kallis (*Western Province & S. Africa*) .	5	7	2	817	177	5	163.40	7
H. H. Gibbs (*Western Province & S. Africa*).	5	9	2	644	192	3	92.00	6
†J-P. Duminy (*Western Province*)	8	11	4	508	105*	2	72.57	11
M. van Jaarsveld (*SA A, Northerns & SA*) . .	7	13	2	730	128	2	66.36	8
Z. de Bruyn (*Easterns*).	10	17	1	1,048	266*	3	65.50	6
†A. G. Prince (*S. Africa A & W. Province*) . .	9	14	4	646	182*	2	64.60	4
†A. G. Puttick (*S. Africa A & W. Province*) . .	9	16	3	831	250*	2	63.92	12
D. J. Jacobs (*North West*)	7	14	0	767	181	3	54.78	14
D. J. Cullinan (*Easterns*).	10	17	1	866	161	3	54.12	18
†S. G. Koenig (*Easterns*)	8	14	1	662	105	2	50.92	3
H. M. Amla (*KwaZulu-Natal*)	9	14	1	647	159	1	49.76	6
†G. V. Grace (*North West*).	7	14	1	647	102*	2	49.76	1
P. de Bruyn (*Easterns*)	9	15	3	573	159*	2	47.75	9
D. M. Benkenstein (*KwaZulu-Natal*)	9	14	2	569	112	2	47.41	9
J. L. Ontong (*South Africa A & Boland*) . .	9	15	0	684	166	3	45.60	3
B. Hector (*Griqualand West*)	8	16	2	610	143*	2	43.57	3
D. J. Watson (*KwaZulu-Natal*)	8	14	1	559	147	2	43.00	5
†J. G. Strydom (*Boland*).	9	17	1	682	151	1	42.62	10
†C. C. Bradfield (*Eastern Province*)	9	14	0	563	145	2	40.21	2
†G. Toyana (*Easterns*)	10	16	2	558	113	1	39.85	9
M. L. Bruyns (*Border*).	8	15	0	523	101	1	34.86	4
A. N. Petersen (*South Africa A & Northerns*)	9	16	0	551	95	0	34.43	4

† *Left-handed batsman.*

BOWLING

(Qualification: 20 wickets)

	Style	O	M	R	W	BB	5Wi	Avge
C. M. Willoughby (*Western Province*). .	LFM	335.4	103	844	42	7-56	1	20.09
T. Henderson (*Border*).	RFM	328.5	93	889	44	5-57	2	20.20
A. C. Dawson (*Western Province*).	RFM	222	66	528	26	6-55	1	20.30
J. J. van der Wath (*Free State*).	RF	260.4	67	666	32	5-59	1	20.81
L. Klusener (*KwaZulu-Natal*).	RFM	340.4	79	868	41	7-70	3	21.17
A. C. Thomas (*Northerns*).	RFM	300.4	99	767	36	7-63	2	21.30
M. Ntini (*South Africa*)	RF	186.5	45	620	29	5-49	3	21.37
C. K. Langeveldt (*Border*).	RFM	195.3	53	622	28	5-42	2	22.21
C. W. Henderson (*SA A & W. Province*)	SLA	424	120	989	41	5-71	1	24.12
N. A. M. McLean (*KwaZulu-Natal*) . . .	RFM	276	71	741	30	5-32	2	24.70
Q. Friend (*S. Africa A & W. Province*). .	RFM	171.1	45	547	21	5-34	1	26.04
H. S. Williams (*Boland*).	RFM	187.4	58	530	20	3-44	0	26.50
A. Nel (*Easterns & South Africa*)	RFM	288.1	65	871	32	5-87	1	27.21
G. J. Kruis (*Griqualand West*).	RFM	273	84	670	24	5-46	2	27.91
A. N. W. Tweedie (*KwaZulu-Natal*) . . .	RFM	274.3	77	736	26	5-61	1	28.30
A. A. Donald (*Free State*)	RFM	228	60	653	23	5-40	2	28.39
I. Khan (*KwaZulu-Natal*).	OB	214.1	52	625	22	6-43	1	28.40
C. D. de Lange (*Boland*)	SLA	194.3	40	610	21	7-48	2	29.04
N. E. Mbhalati (*Northerns*).	RFM	217	52	676	23	4-37	0	29.39
G. A. Roe (*North West*)	RFM	311.1	84	869	29	5-54	3	29.96
G. J-P. Kruger (*S. Africa A & Gauteng*)	RFM	178.2	28	707	23	6-112	2	30.73
J. M. M. Malao (*Easterns*).	SLA	451	97	1,216	39	5-50	3	31.17
F. van der Merwe (*North West*)	RFM	204	32	665	20	5-45	2	33.25
W. A. Albertyn (*Boland*)	RFM	277.1	65	803	23	4-29	0	34.91
M. Zondeki (*South Africa A & Border*)	RF	245.2	53	800	22	4-53	0	36.36
J. F. Venter (*Free State*)	OB	234.5	31	804	21	7-83	1	38.28
C. Pietersen (*Griqualand West*)	LFM	226.5	41	857	22	4-24	0	38.95

SUPERSPORT SERIES, 2003-04

First Round

Pool A

					Bonus Points		
	Played	Won	Lost	Drawn	Batting	Bowling	Points
KwaZulu-Natal	5	4	0	1	18.48	16	74.48
Griqualand West	5	2	2	1	16.24	13	49.24
Free State	5	2	2	1	14.22	14	48.22
Boland.	5	1	2	2	14.60	12	36.60
Easterns.	5	0	1	4	21.66	12	33.66
Eastern Province	5	0	2	3	14.34	13	27.34

Pool B

					Bonus Points		
	Played	Won	Lost	Drawn	Batting	Bowling	Points
Western Province	4	2	0	2	13.66	15	48.66
Border	4	2	2	0	12.20	13	45.20
North West	4	2	1	1	12.82	7	39.82
Northerns	4	1	1	2	12.36	16	38.36
Gauteng	4	0	3	1	12.06	8	20.06

The top three teams from each pool advanced to the Super Six; the remaining five contested the Shield Series.

Super Six

	Played	Won	Lost	Drawn	Batting	Bowling	Points
					Bonus Points		
Western Province	5	5	0	0	17.72	16	83.72
KwaZulu-Natal	5	3	2	0	15.38	20	65.38
North West	5	2	2	1	17.58	16	53.58
Border	5	2	3	0	13.20	17	50.20
Free State	5	2	2	1	13.94	16	49.94
Griqualand West	5	0	5	0	9.42	13	22.42

Super Six teams carried forward results and points gained against fellow-qualifiers in the first round, but not those gained against the teams eliminated.

Final

Western Province beat KwaZulu-Natal by 108 runs.

Shield Series

	Played	Won	Lost	Drawn	Batting	Bowling	Points
					Bonus Points		
Easterns	4	3	0	1	20.56	14	71.292
Boland	4	1	2	1	16.52	10	43.84
Northerns	4	1	2	1	7.86	14	41.45
Eastern Province	4	1	0	3	12.38	9	36.848
Gauteng	4	0	2	2	8.10	7	20.115

Teams carried forward their average points gained per match in the first round.

Outright win = 10 pts.
Bonus points awarded for the first 100 overs of each team's first innings. One batting point was awarded for the first 150 runs and 0.02 of a point for every subsequent run. One bowling point was awarded for the third wicket taken and for every subsequent two.

Pool A

At Paarl, October 17, 18, 19, 20, 2003. **KwaZulu-Natal won by ten wickets.** Toss: Boland. **Boland 244** (J. L. Ontong 66; L. Klusener 5-52) **and 182** (J. G. Strydom 78; L. Klusener 4-40); **KwaZulu-Natal 403** (D. L. Brown 152*) **and 24-0.** *KwaZulu-Natal 17.62 pts, Boland 5.88 pts.*

At Benoni, October 17, 18, 19, 20, 2003. **Drawn.** Toss: Easterns. **Easterns 498-9 dec.** (S. G. Koenig 98, Z. de Bruyn 63, D. J. Cullinan 161, A. J. Hall 70); **Free State 273** (J. F. Venter 51, J. J. van der Wath 66) **and 84-2.** *Easterns 9.64 pts, Free State 5.46 pts.*

At Kimberley, October 17, 18, 19, 20, 2003. **Griqualand West won by five wickets.** Toss: Eastern Province. **Griqualand West 411** (B. Hector 98, L. L. Bosman 85; M. Hayward 4-99, J. Botha 4-85) **and 67-5; Eastern Province 70** (G. J. Kruis 4-17, C. Pietersen 4-24) **and 404** (J. D. C. Bryant 56, A. Jacobs 102, J. Louw 56*). *Griqualand West 18.68 pts, Eastern Province 3 pts.*
   This was the first time Griqualand West had made Eastern Province follow on, in 31 matches dating back to 1890-91.

At Port Elizabeth, October 24, 25, 26, 27, 2003. **Drawn.** Toss: Eastern Province. **Boland 534-6 dec.** (C. Baxter 86, J. L. Ontong 166, R. Magiet 92, C. D. de Lange 51*, G. C. Marais 52*) **and 109-5; Eastern Province 426** (J. Louw 124, C. A. Thyssen 56; W. J. du Toit 4-97). *Eastern Province 4.54 pts, Boland 5.92 pts.*
   Ontong and Magiet added 243, a Boland fourth-wicket record, to set up the province's highest total in Currie Cup/SuperSport cricket.

At Kimberley, October 24, 25, 26, 27, 2003. **Drawn.** Toss: Easterns. **Easterns 528** (S. G. Koenig 51, Z. de Bruyn 266*, D. J. Cullinan 125; Shahid Afridi 5-92) **and 215-5 dec.** (S. G. Koenig 100, D. J. Cullinan 61*); **Griqualand West 485** (M. I. Gidley 143, Shahid Afridi 111; J. M. M. Malao 4-129) **and 140-9.** *Griqualand West 3.9 pts, Easterns 6.34 pts.*

De Bruyn's 266*, his maiden double-hundred, the highest individual score for Easterns, and the highest of the season, lasted 501 minutes and 408 balls and included 39 fours and a six. He added 243 for the third wicket, another Easterns record, with Cullinan, who passed 15,000 first-class runs. Gidley became the second player to score 5,000 first-class runs for Griqualand West, after Mike Doherty, and equalled Doherty's record of 12 centuries. Afridi scored 111 in 83 balls, with 15 fours and three sixes. Griquas No. 11 Deon Kruis survived the last five balls to deny Easterns.

At Durban, October 24, 25, 26, 2003. **KwaZulu-Natal won by an innings and 115 runs.** Toss: KwaZulu-Natal. **Free State 93** (L. Klusener 4-27, R. P. Symcox 4-13) **and 185** (I. Khan 4-37); **KwaZulu-Natal 393-6 dec.** (H. M. Amla 159, D. M. Benkenstein 50, I. Khan 53*). *KwaZulu-Natal 17.62 pts, Free State 2 pts.*
  Amla's 159 lasted nine hours 16 minutes.

At Paarl, October 31, November 1, 2, 3, 2003 **Griqualand West won by 110 runs.** Toss: Boland. **Griqualand West 475** (G. M. Smith 50, B. Hector 114, Shahid Afridi 70, W. Bossenger 93*, M. A. Mashimbyi 61; R. L. Groeneveld 5-112) **and 131-5 dec.; Boland 205** (R. Magiet 91; G. J. Kruis 5-46) **and 291** (C. D. de Lange 89; G. J. Kruis 5-73). *Griqualand West 19.36 pts, Boland 4.1 pts.*
  Groeneveld (37*) and Henry Williams (49) added 81 for the last wicket in Boland's second innings, a provincial record.

At Benoni, October 31, November 1, 2, 3, 2003. **KwaZulu-Natal won by an innings and 102 runs.** Toss: KwaZulu-Natal. **KwaZulu-Natal 495-6 dec.** (D. J. Watson 147, J. C. Kent 73, D. M. Benkenstein 112, L. Klusener 98); **Easterns 215** (G. Toyana 72; I. Khan 6-43) **and 178** (S. G. Koenig 53, A. M. van den Berg 57; N. A. M. McLean 4-41). *KwaZulu-Natal 17.7 pts, Easterns 3.3 pts.*
  This was Easterns' first defeat at Benoni in 11 first-class matches since they lost to North West in March 2001.

At Bloemfontein, October 31, November 1, 2, 3, 2003. **Free State won by ten wickets.** Toss: Free State. **Eastern Province 331** (C. C. Bradfield 145; A. A. Donald 5-95) **and 103; Free State 237** (J. F. Venter 61; J. Louw 4-58) **and 198-0** (M. N. van Wyk 106*, J. A. Beukes 83*). *Free State 14.32 pts, Eastern Province 6.24 pts.*
  Donald passed 1,200 first-class wickets. Free State wicket-keeper van Wyk made four catches in each innings and then steered them to victory without losing a wicket in the final innings.

At Paarl, November 7, 8, 9, 10, 2003. **Drawn.** Toss: Easterns. **Easterns 558-8 dec.** (Z. de Bruyn 174, A. J. Hall 89, G. Toyana 113, P. de Bruyn 80) **and 95-9** (W. A. Albertyn 4-29); **Boland 241** (J. L. Ontong 102; J. M. M. Malao 5-50) **and 416** (M. D. Sanders 57, J. G. Strydom 151, C. D. de Lange 109). *Boland 3.82 pts, Easterns 8.02 pts.*
  Zander de Bruyn and Hall added 201, an Easterns fourth-wicket record, to set up what was briefly their highest total. Strydom and de Lange added 190, a Boland fifth-wicket record. Dylan Jennings became the first wicket-keeper to make 100 dismissals for Easterns. Boland finished one wicket short of victory and Easterns five runs.

At Port Elizabeth, November 7, 8, 9, 10, 2003. **Drawn.** Toss: Eastern Province. **Eastern Province 326** (C. C. Bradfield 99, B. H. Tucker 67; I. Khan 4-73) **and 281-6 dec.** (R. J. Peterson 108, J. D. C. Bryant 69*); **KwaZulu-Natal 305** (D. J. Watson 134, D. M. Benkenstein 64, D. L. Brown 84; R. J. Peterson 5-136) **and 241-5** (D. M. Benkenstein 73*). *Eastern Province 4.26 pts, KwaZulu-Natal 3.62 pts.*

At Kimberley, November 7, 8, 9, 2003. **Free State won by an innings and 16 runs.** Toss: Griqualand West. **Griqualand West 215** (L. L. Bosman 86; J. J. van der Wath 4-35) **and 195** (L. L. Bosman 52; A. A. Donald 5-40); **Free State 426** (M. N. van Wyk 122, J. A. Beukes 69, G. F. J. Liebenberg 52). *Free State 19.12 pts, Griqualand West 4.3 pts.*

At Benoni, November 14, 15, 16, 17, 2003. **Drawn.** Toss: Eastern Province. **Eastern Province 457** (R. J. Peterson 118, J. D. C. Bryant 163, I. Mitchell 61; A. J. Hall 4-69, Z. de Bruyn 4-84) **and 145** (J. M. M. Malao 5-54); **Easterns 318** (A. J. Seymore 52, D. J. Cullinan 95, G. Toyana 64, Extras 52) **and 42-0.** *Easterns 6.36 pts, Eastern Province 9.3 pts.*

At Bloemfontein, November 14, 15, 16, 17, 2003. **Boland won by 23 runs.** Toss: Free State. **Boland 244** (J. L. Ontong 150; J. J. van der Wath 5-59) **and 250** (J. G. Strydom 68; J. F. Venter 7-83); **Free State 266** (H. H. Dippenaar 87; R. L. Groeneveld 4-39) **and 205** (J. A. Beukes 70). *Boland 16.88 pts, Free State 7.32 pts.*

Gerhardus Liebenberg made four catches in the field in Boland's first innings, when the next highest score after Ontong's 150 was 19.

At Durban, November 14, 15, 16, 2003. **KwaZulu-Natal won by ten wickets.** Toss: Griqualand West. **Griqualand West 112** (N. A. M. McLean 5-32, L. Klusener 4-29) **and 287** (B. Hector 143*; N. A. M. McLean 5-85); **KwaZulu-Natal 383** (H. M. Amla 81, L. Klusener 66; Z. A. Abrahim 4-48) **and 17-0.** *KwaZulu-Natal 17.92 pts, Griqualand West 3 pts.*

Pool B

At East London, October 17, 18, 19, 20, 2003. **Border won by seven wickets.** Toss: Gauteng. **Gauteng 290** (S. Conrad 60; M. Zondeki 4-73) **and 309-8 dec.** (S. C. Cook 109, A. M. Bacher 138; S. C. Pope 4-45); **Border 380** (S. C. Pope 84, J. P. Kreusch 91, L. L. Gamiet 61, Extras 51; G. J-P. Kruger 6-112) **and 223-3** (M. L. Bruyns 96). *Border 17.5 pts, Gauteng 5.3 pts.*

Cook and Bacher shared an opening stand of 238 in Gauteng's second innings.

At Centurion, October 17, 18, 19, 20, 2003. **Drawn.** Toss: Western Province. **Northerns 198** (A. N. Petersen 95, A. B. de Villiers 58; C. M. Willoughby 7-56) **and 259-7 dec.** (A. B. de Villiers 61, M. van Jaarsveld 90; C. M. Willoughby 4-67); **Western Province 173** (N. E. Mbhalati 4-37) **and 11-0.** *Northerns 5.96 pts, Western Province 5.46 pts.*

At Johannesburg, October 24, 25, 26, 27, 2003. **Northerns won by 223 runs.** Toss: Northerns. **Northerns 402** (A. N. Petersen 89, A. B. de Villiers 62, G. Dros 54, J. M. Kemp 143; D. B. Powell 4-125, C. E. Eksteen 4-80) **and 227-7 dec.** (A. B. de Villiers 54, J. M. Kemp 77); **Gauteng 217** (S. C. Cook 63; N. E. Mbhalati 4-55, A. C. Thomas 4-48) **and 189** (A. M. Bacher 51, H. D. Ackerman 52; P. L. Harris 6-59). *Northerns 18.84 pts, Gauteng 5.34 pts.*

De Villiers became the first player to reach 50 in each of his first four innings in Currie Cup/SuperSport cricket. This was Northerns' fourth consecutive win at the Wanderers, and their fifth in six games since their inaugural victory on the ground (as Northern Transvaal) in 1991-92.

At Potchefstroom, October 24, 25, 26, 27, 2003. **North West won by five wickets.** Toss: Border. **Border 369** (J. P. Kreusch 56, P. C. Strydom 53, L. L. Gamiet 116; F. van der Merwe 5-94) **and 215** (M. L. Bruyns 59, L. L. Gamiet 57*); **North West 443** (D. J. Jacobs 110, J. M. Henderson 84, G. Celliers 54; T. Henderson 4-74) **and 145-5.** *North West 16.94 pts, Border 4.76 pts.*

Jacobs and Henderson put on 216 for North West's first wicket, a provincial record. Gamiet made his maiden century nearly eight years after his first-class debut.

At Centurion, October 31, November 1, 2, 3, 2003. **Border won by six wickets.** Toss: Border. **Northerns 197** (M. van Jaarsveld 63; T. Henderson 5-73) **and 317** (M. van Jaarsveld 71, J. A. Rudolph 64, A. C. Thomas 52); **Border 230** (P. C. Strydom 53; A. C. Thomas 7-63) **and 286-4** (S. C. Pope 146*). *Border 16.6 pts, Northerns 5.94 pts.*

At Cape Town, October 31, November 1, 2, 3, 2003. **Western Province won by ten wickets.** Toss: North West. **Western Province 480-5 dec.** (A. G. Puttick 101, D. J. Bassage 69, A. G. Prince 50, N. C. Johnson 135, J-P. Duminy 80*) **and 16-0**; **North West 266** (T. A. Bula 60*) **and 229** (R. T. Bailey 87; C. W. Henderson 4-61). *Western Province 16.9 pts, North West 3.86 pts.*

At East London, November 7, 8, 9, 10, 2003. **Western Province won by 176 runs.** Toss: Border. **Western Province 239** (A. G. Puttick 64; T. Henderson 4-74, C. K. Langeveldt 4-61) **and 304** (G. Kirsten 78, J-P. Duminy 70; T. Henderson 4-62); **Border 217** (M. L. Bruyns 101, J. P. Kreusch 59; R. Telemachus 4-59) **and 150** (C. W. Henderson 4-59). *Western Province 16.78 pts, Border 6.34 pts.*

Kirsten passed 16,000 first-class runs.

At Johannesburg, November 7, 8, 9, 10, 2003. **North West won by 169 runs.** Toss: North West. **North West 369** (G. Rowley 69, R. T. Bailey 80; G. J-P. Kruger 5-82) **and 300-6 dec.** (J. M. Henderson 143*, G. V. Grace 64); **Gauteng 375** (E. T. Nkwe 51, H. D. Ackerman 73, D. N. Crookes 82; G. A. Roe 5-108) **and 125** (F. van der Merwe 5-45). *North West 16.78 pts, Gauteng 5.92 pts.*

At Potchefstroom, November 14, 15, 16, 17, 2003. **Drawn.** Toss: Northerns. **North West 212** (D. J. Jacobs 66; P. L. Harris 4-41) **and 495-4** (D. J. Jacobs 181, G. V. Grace 78, G. Rowley 106*, Extras 68); **Northerns 518-6 dec.** (J. A. Rudolph 96, A. N. Petersen 62, M. van Jaarsveld 128, N. D. McKenzie 101; F. van der Merwe 4-137). *North West 2.24 pts, Northerns 7.62 pts.*
  Jacobs and Grace added 243, a North West second-wicket record.

At Cape Town, November 14, 15, 16, 17, 2003. **Drawn.** Toss: Western Province. **Western Province 520-6 dec.** (A. G. Prince 84, J. H. Kallis 105, G. Kirsten 125, J-P. Duminy 105*); **Gauteng 225** (J. M. Otto 91; P. R. Adams 4-50) **and 505-7** (S. C. Cook 135, A. M. Bacher 65, H. D. Ackerman 54, U. Abrahams 134*). *Western Province 9.52 pts, Gauteng 3.5 pts.*
  Duminy, aged 19 years 215 days, was the second youngest player to score a hundred for Western Province; Kepler Wessels was 100 days younger in 1976-77. Western Province wicket-keeper Thami Tsolekile made six catches in Gauteng's first innings and eight in the match. Gauteng's 505-7 was the second highest total by a team following on in Currie Cup/SuperSport cricket (after 581-7 by Western Province v Northerns in 1997-98).

Super Six

At Bloemfontein, March 4, 5, 6, 2004. **Free State won by four wickets.** Toss: Border. **Border 153** (J. J. van der Wath 4-34) **and 183; Free State 196** (T. Henderson 4-46) **and 141-6** (G. F. J. Liebenberg 50). *Free State 15.92 pts, Border 5.06 pts.*

At Durban, March 4, 5, 6, 7, 2004. **KwaZulu-Natal won by five wickets.** Toss: KwaZulu-Natal. **North West 255** (G. V. Grace 102) **and 242-7 dec.** (G. V. Grace 102*, E. O. Moleon 66*); **KwaZulu-Natal 227** (G. A. Roe 5-57) **and 273-5** (D. M. Benkenstein 102*). *KwaZulu-Natal 16.54 pts, North West 7.1 pts.*
  Of the three scores of 102 in the match, two belonged to Grace, while Benkenstein's came in his 100th first-class match, and he reached his hundred in 100 balls. The only previous recorded case of three 102s in a first-class match came in Otago v Canterbury at Dunedin in 1966-67, when K. Thomson scored 102 and 102* and G. T. Dowling 102, all for Canterbury.

At Cape Town, March 4, 5, 6, 7, 2004. **Western Province won by an innings and 186 runs.** Toss: Western Province. **Griqualand West 185** (W. Bossenger 68; A. C. Dawson 6-55) **and 183** (B. Hector 70; A. C. Dawson 4-37, Q. Friend 5-34); **Western Province 554-2 dec.** (A. G. Puttick 250*, L. D. Ferreira 130, J-P. Duminy 100*). *Western Province 18.78 pts, Griqualand West 1.7 pts.*
  Martyn Gidley became Griqualand West's highest run-scorer, passing Mike Doherty's 5,238. Puttick's 250*, his second double-hundred, lasted 596 minutes and 479 balls and included 36 fours and a six, and helped Western Province win the match with the loss of only two wickets.

At East London, March 11, 12, 2004. **Border won by seven wickets.** Toss: Border. **Griqualand West 169** (C. K. Langeveldt 5-42, J. P. Kreusch 4-52) **and 134** (M. Zondeki 4-53, C. K. Langeveldt 5-42); **Border 266** (C. B. Sugden 93; C. Pietersen 4-79) **and 41-3.** *Border 17.32 pts, Griqualand West 5.38 pts.*
  The entire match lasted 153.3 overs.

At Potchefstroom, March 11, 12, 13, 14, 2004. **Drawn.** Toss: North West. **Free State 267** (M. N. van Wyk 77, J. J. van der Wath 68; G. A. Roe 5-54) **and 337-6 dec.** (G. F. J. Liebenberg 72, H. H. Dippenaar 115*, J. J. van der Wath 55); **North West 349** (D. J. Jacobs 164, W. L. Coetsee 56) **and 148-8** (J. F. Venter 4-60). *North West 8.42 pts, Free State 5.34 pts.*

At Cape Town, March 11, 12, 13, 14, 2004. **Western Province won by 154 runs.** Toss: KwaZulu-Natal. **Western Province 311** (N. C. Johnson 58, T. L. Tsolekile 63, C. W. Henderson 71; N. A. M. McLean 4-53) **and 371-4 dec.** (D. J. Bassage 61, L. D. Ferreira 100, A. G. Prince 110*); **KwaZulu-Natal 332** (D. J. Watson 58, H. M. Amla 50, A. M. Amla 75, D. M. Benkenstein 65) **and 196** (L. Klusener 80*). *Western Province 16.22 pts, KwaZulu-Natal 7.74 pts.*

Charl Willoughby of Western Province reached 300 first-class wickets, well ahead of his 222 first-class runs. KwaZulu-Natal wicket-keeper Duncan Brown made eight catches in the match. Klusener and Jon Kent were suspended from the next match for dissent.

At Bloemfontein, March 19, 20, 21, 2004. **Western Province won by eight wickets.** Toss: Free State. **Free State 322** (H. H. Dippenaar 69, W. A. Deacon 59; C. W. Henderson 5-71) **and 78**; **Western Province 202** (T. L. Tsolekile 56; J. J. van der Wath 4-35) **and 199-2** (D. J. Bassage 79). *Western Province 15.04 pts, Free State 7.56 pts.*

At Kimberley, March 19, 20, 21, 22, 2004. **North West won by 139 runs.** Toss: Griqualand West. **North West 263** (D. J. Jacobs 61, G. V. Grace 61, D. J. J. de Vos 62) **and 431-9 dec.** (G. V. Grace 70, D. J. J. de Vos 51, G. Rowley 136, R. T. Bailey 62); **Griqualand West 302** (W. Bossenger 71, A. K. Kruger 56) **and 253** (J. Brooker 110). *North West 17.26 pts, Griqualand West 8.04 pts. Rowley and Bailey added 130, a North West fifth-wicket record.*

At Durban, March 19, 20, 21, 2004. **Border won by eight wickets.** Toss: Border. **KwaZulu-Natal 178** (T. Henderson 4-42) **and 185** (D. J. Watson 50; T. Henderson 4-54); **Border 236** (M. L. Bruyns 76; A. N. W. Tweedie 5-61) **and 128-2.** *Border 16.72 pts, KwaZulu-Natal 5.56 pts.*
Duncan Brown beat Keigh Forde's KwaZulu-Natal record of 41 wicket-keeping dismissals in a season.

FINAL

WESTERN PROVINCE v KWAZULU-NATAL

At Cape Town, March 31, April 1, 2, 3, 4, 2004. Western Province won by 108 runs. Toss: Western Province. First-class debut: V. D. Philander.

Western Province, losing finalists a year earlier, secured a convincing victory after Willoughby and Dawson skittled KwaZulu-Natal's middle order with the second new ball. The previous evening, makeshift opener Khan and Hashim Amla had shared a slow but solid second-wicket stand of 123, making the quest for 346 look feasible. But they were parted one run later, and the last eight wickets fell for 70. By the first afternoon, Klusener had demolished six Western Province wickets for 82 but Puttick held firm for three hours, and then Dawson got them to 217. KwaZulu-Natal mustered only 187 in reply, though Amla batted over five hours for an unbeaten 79. Duminy made the game's top score, a fine 89, as Western Province extended their lead on the third day, adding 126 with Henderson, who was playing his last game for the side. Klusener finished with 12 wickets, a career-best; Brown completed seven catches to become the first wicket-keeper to make 50 first-class dismissals in a Currie Cup/SuperSport season.

Man of Match: L. Klusener.

Close of play: First day, KwaZulu-Natal 33-1 (Khan 9, H. M. Amla 2); Second day, Western Province 62-1 (Tsolekile 27, Ferreira 1); Third day, Western Province 260-6 (Duminy 89, Philander 3); Fourth day, KwaZulu-Natal 127-1 (Khan 62, H. M. Amla 53).

Western Province

A. G. Puttick lbw b Tweedie	70	– lbw b Tweedie 28
†T. L. Tsolekile c A. M. Amla b Klusener	0	– lbw b Klusener............ 36
L. D. Ferreira c H. M. Amla b Klusener......	21	– c Brown b McLean........... 9
*A. G. Prince c Brown b Klusener	0	– lbw b MacQueen 14
J-P. Duminy lbw b Klusener..............	3	– c Brown b McLean........... 89
N. C. Johnson c Brown b Klusener	3	– c Benkenstein b Klusener....... 4
V. D. Philander c Watson b Klusener	0	– (8) c Tweedie b Klusener 18
C. W. Henderson c Brown b Tweedie........	21	– (7) lbw b Tweedie.......... 53
A. C. Dawson b Kent	56	– b Brown b Klusener 1
Q. Friend c Brown b Klusener	23	– not out 38
C. M. Willoughby not out	8	– c McLean b Klusener 0
L-b 6, w 2, n-b 4	12	B 8, l-b 12, w 4, n-b 1 25
	217	**315**

1/16 (2) 2/54 (3) 3/54 (4) 4/64 (5)
5/82 (6) 6/82 (7) 7/123 (1)
8/124 (8) 9/177 (10) 10/217 (9)

1/50 (1) 2/84 (2) 3/84 (3)
4/119 (4) 5/126 (6)
6/252 (7) 7/260 (5)
8/261 (9) 9/308 (8) 10/315 (11)

Bowling: *First Innings*—McLean 15–2–52–0; Klusener 21–3–70–7; Tweedie 14–4–38–2; Kent 6.5–2–15–1; MacQueen 8–1–31–0; Khan 2–1–5–0. *Second Innings*—McLean 31–8–90–2; Klusener 32.4–8–90–5; MacQueen 32–15–48–1; Tweedie 18–4–39–2; Kent 8–4–15–0; Khan 4–1–13–0.

KwaZulu-Natal

D. J. Watson lbw b Willoughby	18	– c Johnson b Dawson	4
I. Khan b Dawson	35	– c Tsolekile b Willoughby	62
H. M. Amla not out	79	– c Tsolekile b Willoughby	72
A. M. Amla c Puttick b Philander	4	– lbw b Dawson	20
*D. M. Benkenstein c Johnson b Henderson	0	– lbw b Henderson	9
J. C. Kent c Johnson b Henderson	0	– c Puttick b Dawson	32
L. Klusener c Ferreira b Friend	17	– c Prince b Willoughby	0
†D. L. Brown c Tsolekile b Friend	2	– lbw b Henderson	0
R. B. MacQueen lbw b Philander	3	– not out	12
N. A. M. McLean c Puttick b Henderson	9	– c Willoughby b Dawson	2
A. N. W. Tweedie b Philander b Willoughby	15	– c Philander b Willoughby	15
L-b 3, w 2	5	B 1, l-b 3, w 5	9

1/28 (1) 2/74 (2) 3/88 (4) 4/89 (5)   187   1/4 (1) 2/128 (2) 3/167 (3)   237
5/89 (6) 6/120 (7) 7/123 (8)   4/169 (4) 5/198 (5) 6/199 (7)
8/132 (9) 9/143 (10) 10/187 (11)   7/200 (8) 8/208 (6)
                                        9/210 (10) 10/237 (11)

Bowling: *First Innings*—Dawson 14–4–34–1; Willoughby 24.5–5–75–2; Friend 16–4–30–2; Henderson 25–12–27–3; Philander 10–5–18–2. *Second Innings*—Dawson 30–10–51–4; Willoughby 33.2–10–71–4; Friend 12 4–33–0, Henderson 34–8–74–2; Philander 3–1–4–0.

Umpires: K. H. Hurter and M. Z. Nanabhay.
Third umpire: B. G. Jerling. Referee: D. T. Lindsay.

CHAMPIONS

Currie Cup		1947-48	Natal
1889-90	Transvaal	1950-51	Transvaal
1890-91	Kimberley	1951-52	Natal
1892-93	Western Province	1952-53	Western Province
1893-94	Western Province	1954-55	Natal
1894-95	Transvaal	1955-56	Western Province
1896-97	Western Province	1958-59	Transvaal
1897-98	Western Province	1959-60	Natal
1902-03	Transvaal	1960-61	Natal
1903-04	Transvaal	1962-63	Natal
1904-05	Transvaal	1963-64	Natal
1906-07	Transvaal	1965-66	Natal/Transvaal (Tied)
1908-09	Western Province	1966-67	Natal
1910-11	Natal	1967-68	Natal
1912-13	Natal	1968-69	Transvaal
1920-21	Western Province	1969-70	Transvaal/W. Province (Tied)
1921-22	Transvaal/Natal/W. Prov. (Tied)	1970-71	Transvaal
1923-24	Transvaal	1971-72	Transvaal
1925-26	Transvaal	1972-73	Transvaal
1926-27	Transvaal	1973-74	Natal
1929-30	Transvaal	1974-75	Western Province
1931-32	Western Province	1975-76	Natal
1933-34	Natal	1976-77	Natal
1934-35	Transvaal	1977-78	Western Province
1936-37	Natal	1978-79	Transvaal
1937-38	Natal/Transvaal (Tied)	1979-80	Transvaal
1946-47	Natal	1980-81	Natal

1981-82	Western Province	1993-94	Orange Free State
1982-83	Transvaal	1994-95	Natal
1983-84	Transvaal	1995-96	Western Province
1984-85	Transvaal		
1985-86	Western Province	*SuperSport Series*	
1986-87	Transvaal	1996-97	Natal
1987-88	Transvaal	1997-98	Free State
1988-89	Eastern Province	1998-99	Western Province
1989-90	E. Province/W. Province	1999-2000	Gauteng
	(Shared)	2000-01	Western Province
Castle Cup		2001-02	KwaZulu-Natal
1990-91	Western Province	2002-03	Easterns
1991-92	Eastern Province	2003-04	Western Province
1992-93	Orange Free State		

Transvaal/Gauteng have won the title outright 25 times, Natal/KwaZulu-Natal 21, Western Province 18, Orange Free State/Free State 3, Eastern Province 2, Easterns and Kimberley 1. The title has been shared five times as follows: Transvaal 4, Natal and Western Province 3, Eastern Province 1.

Shield Series

At Port Elizabeth, March 5, 6, 7, 8, 2004. **Drawn.** Toss: Easterns. **Easterns 515-7 dec.** (S. G. Koenig 71, A. J. Seymore 102, Z. de Bruyn 84, D. J. Cullinan 117) **and 117-4 dec.; Eastern Province 379** (C. C. Bradfield 123, W. R. Wingfield 88; J. M. M. Malao 4-104) **and 147-4** (C. A. Thyssen 60*). *Eastern Province 4.32 pts, Easterns 6.26 pts.*
   De Bruyn beat Shakeel Ahmed's Easterns record of 679 runs in a season.

At Centurion, March 5, 6, 7, 8, 2004. **Drawn.** Toss: Northerns. **Gauteng 194-5 dec.** (A. M. Bacher 89, H. D. Ackerman 56*) **and 109-4** (V. B. van Jaarsveld 53*); **Northerns 219-6 dec.** (M. A. Aronstam 63, J. M. Kemp 71*; J. T. Mafa 4-42). *Northerns 4.38 pts, Gauteng 3.88 pts.*

At Paarl, March 12, 13, 14, 15, 2004. **Northerns won by 147 runs.** Toss: Boland. **Northerns 451-7 dec.** (A. N. Petersen 57, M. A. Aronstam 201*, G. Dros 66; R. L. Groeneveld 4-49) **and 173-6 dec.** (A. B. de Villiers 85); **Boland 259** (J. G. Strydom 67; A. C. Thomas 7-91) **and 218** (J. G. Strydom 52; G. Dros 5-17). *Northerns 17.82 pts, Boland 5.18 pts.*
   Maurice Aronstam's 201, in his second first-class match, lasted 577 minutes and 448 balls and included 19 fours and four sixes. He added 131* with Pierre Joubert (48*), equalling the Northerns eighth-wicket record.*

At Johannesburg, March 12, 13, 14, 15, 2004. **Drawn.** Toss: Eastern Province. **Gauteng 34-1 v Eastern Province.**

At Port Elizabeth, March 19, 20, 21, 22, 2004. **Eastern Province won by 45 runs.** Toss: Eastern Province. **Eastern Province 233** (J. Botha 56*, I. Mitchell 56; P. Joubert 6-28) **and 158** (P. Joubert 6-19); **Northerns 128** (G. Dros 67; B. B. Kops 5-36) **and 218** (J. Botha 6-42). *Eastern Province 16.66 pts, Northerns 4 pts.*
   Joubert's full match analysis was 47.3–31–47–12, the best of the season. This was Eastern Province's first first-class win since they beat Border in October 2001; in between, they had lost nine matches and drawn nine.

At Benoni, March 19, 20, 21, 22, 2004. **Easterns won by an innings and six runs.** Toss: Easterns. **Easterns 563-9 dec.** (S. G. Koenig 105, A. J. Seymore 51, Z. de Bruyn 64, P. de Bruyn 117, D. J. Cullinan 70, G. Toyana 73; J. L. Ontong 4-150); **Boland 364** (H. Davids 54, J. G. Strydom 64, J. L. Ontong 77, W. J. Smit 59, W. Euley 50) **and 193** (M. D. Sanders 66, W. J. Smit 58; A. M. van den Berg 5-49). *Easterns 20.08 pts, Boland 6.28 pts.*
   Easterns' 563-9 was their fourth total of 500-plus in 2003-04, and beat their all-time record of 558-8, against Boland in November.

At Randjesfontein, March 26, 27, 28, 2004. **Boland won by nine wickets.** Toss: Gauteng. **Gauteng 228** (C. D. de Lange 7-48) **and 193** (C. D. de Lange 5-68); **Boland 279** (H. Davids 67, W. J. Smit 104; C. E. Eksteen 4-60) **and 143-1** (M. D. Sanders 65*, J. G. Strydom 62*). *Boland 17.58 pts, Gauteng 6.56 pts.*

De Lange's 7-48 was the best innings return of the season.

At Centurion, March 26, 27, 28, 29, 2004. **Easterns won by 60 runs.** Toss: Easterns. **Easterns 306** (S. G. Koenig 51, Z. de Bruyn 51, D. J. Cullinan 61, D. Jennings 50; A. C. Thomas 4-67) **and 149;** **Northerns 183 and 212** (J. M. Kemp 65; B. L. Reddy 5-39). *Easterns 18.12 pts. Northerns 5.66 pts.*

At Paarl, April 2, 3, 4, 5, 2004. **Drawn.** Toss: Eastern Province. **Eastern Province 432** (C. C. Bradfield 60, W. R. Wingfield 146*, I. Mitchell 92); **Boland 324** (M. D. Sanders 87, W. C. Swan 65*; G. T. Love 5-92). *Boland 7.48 pts, Eastern Province 10.4 pts.*

At Benoni, April 2, 3, 4, 5, 2004. **Easterns won by 228 runs.** Toss: Easterns. **Easterns 405-4 dec.** (Z. de Bruyn 159, P. de Bruyn 159*) **and 338-9 dec.** (Z. de Bruyn 88, G. Toyana 63, D. J. Cullinan 65; B. Mathebula 5-56); **Gauteng 286** (R. I. Coutts 77; J. M. M. Malao 5-82) **and 229** (B. Snijman 64, D. R. Gain 68*). *Easterns 20.1 pts, Gauteng 4.66 pts.*

Gauteng fielded four debutants as their first-choice players prepared for the ensuing Pro20 tournament. Zander de Bruyn added 244 with namesake Pierre, an Easterns third-wicket record, and reached 1,000 runs in the Currie Cup/SuperSport season, a feat achieved twice before, by Barry Richards in both 1971-72 and 1972-73.

Note: Matches in the following sections were not first-class.

STANDARD BANK CUP, 2003-04

	Played	Won	Lost	No Result	Bonus Points	Points	Net run-rate
Western Province	10	8	1	1	4	47	0.93
Gauteng	10	7	2	1	6	44	0.80
Northerns	10	6	0	4	2	44	1.31
Easterns	10	5	2	3	3	37	0.20
Griqualand West	10	5	5	0	5	30	0.04
Border	10	3	4	3	4	28	−0.10
Boland	10	3	6	1	4	22	−0.69
KwaZulu-Natal	10	1	5	4	4	21	−0.49
Eastern Province	10	3	6	1	2	20	−0.74
North West	10	3	7	0	4	19	−0.67
Free State	10	0	6	4	6	18	−0.15

Gauteng finished ahead of Northerns by virtue of more wins.

Semi-finals

At Cape Town, February 20, 2004 (day/night). **Easterns won by four wickets.** Toss: Western Province. **Western Province 197-8** (45 overs) (J-P. Duminy 51; Z. de Bruyn 5-44); **Easterns 198-6** (43.5 overs) (S. G. Koenig 95*).

At Johannesburg, February 22, 2004. **Gauteng won by six wickets.** Toss: Gauteng. **Northerns 233** (44 overs) (A. B. de Villiers 99; D. N. Crookes 4-49); **Gauteng 234-4** (44.4 overs) (S. C. Cook 88, A. M. Bacher 96).

Final

At Johannesburg, February 29, 2004. **Gauteng won by seven wickets.** Toss: Gauteng. **Easterns 144** (43.3 overs); **Gauteng 146-3** (33.3 overs) (S. C. Cook 64).

STANDARD BANK PRO20 SERIES, 2003-04

	Played	Won	Lost	No Result	Bonus Points	Points	Net run-rate
Titans	5	4	1	0	2	22	1.49
Western Province Boland.	5	3	1	1	2	19	0.76
Eastern Cape	5	2	3	0	3	13	−0.14
Eagles	5	2	2	1	1	13	−1.11
Dolphins	5	2	3	0	3	12*	−0.47
Lions	5	1	4	0	3	8	−0.58

* Dolphins were penalised 1 point for a slow over-rate.
Eastern Cape finished ahead of Eagles by virtue of winning their head-to-head match.

Semi-finals

At Cape Town, April 27, 2004. **Eastern Cape won by seven wickets.** Toss: Eastern Cape. **Western Province Boland 128-7** (20 overs) (P. C. Strydom 4-11); **Eastern Cape 129-3** (18.5 overs).

At Centurion, April 28, 2004 (day/night). **Eagles won by seven wickets (D/L method).** Toss: Titans. **Titans 47** (14.3 overs); **Eagles 48-3** (11.1 overs).
   Titans' top score was nine by Daryll Cullinan. Eagles' target was revised to 48 in 16 overs.

Final

At East London, May 1, 2004 (day/night). **Eagles won by seven runs (D/L method).** Toss: Eastern Cape. **Eagles 131-6** (20 overs); **Eastern Cape 108-9** (17 overs).
   Eastern Cape's target was revised to 116 in 17 overs.

CRICKET IN THE WEST INDIES, 2003-04

Tony Cozier

Devon Smith

Between November 2003 and August 2004, West Indies cricket passed through the most agonising period in its history, even by recent distressing standards. The optimism created by a record-breaking last-Test win over Australia in May 2003, followed by victory over Sri Lanka, rapidly evaporated during five tightly packed series.

In 16 Tests, West Indies suffered ten defeats, one by an innings, three by ten wickets, and two by over 200 runs. They beat Zimbabwe and Bangladesh – the only teams ranked below them in the ICC's Test Championship – in one Test each. Even these two enjoyed the better of West Indies in their other, drawn matches. South Africa, at home, and England, in the Caribbean, were denied clean sweeps only by two exceptional innings – Dwayne Smith's last-day, run-a-ball hundred in Cape Town, and Brian Lara's unbeaten Test-record 400 in Antigua. There were no such heroics in the return series: England completed the dreaded whitewash at The Oval, where West Indies had formalised their own "blackwash" 20 years earlier. The ICC Champions Trophy final brought a timely triumph only a month later, on the same ground as their Test match humiliation. But this euphoria was soon dissipated in an acrimonious row between the board and the players.

The difficulties had been compounded by Sir Viv Richards's exit after two years as chairman of selectors, before the tour of England. It reflected his frustration at the team's performances and the players' sensitivities. A formal letter of protest to the West Indies Cricket Board from the West Indies Players' Association had alleged that he and other selectors "verbally belittled and threatened" some of its members in public.

Stung by the realisation that, after five years of failure, the situation was getting worse, not better, and the fear that West Indies were losing their global appeal, the board announced drastic changes to the running of the Test team and to the domestic tournaments. "If it is true that there is no stronger force than cricket to unify us regionally and give us pride, then we must be prepared to go to bat for the regional game," said Teddy Griffith,

TWO YEARS TO GO...

In June 2005, the Kensington Oval in Bridgetown will start the transformation designed to make the familiar, homely ground a suitable stadium to host the climax of the Caribbean's greatest ever sporting event.

Kensington was chosen by the ICC last July to host the final of the 2007 World Cup, and also six matches at the quarter-final stage, the so-called Super Eights. After this year's Test, a new pavilion and stands will be constructed to create a permanent capacity of 15,000, to be increased to 27,000 for the tournament itself.

The main architect is Dipesh Patel of the British firm Arup Associates, who also worked on the City of Manchester Stadium and the Hull Super Stadium. The plan involves knocking down everything except the Mitchie Hewitt stand in the south-western corner. The ground itself is to change from oval to circular, with longer boundaries, which means the square will shift about ten yards east. The time frame is tight, but at least West Indian grounds do not have the problems new English grounds face. The soil here is such that you can almost cut a strip one day and expect it to play respectably the next.

Whether this is the right way to proceed is another matter: about 20 houses round the ground will have to go, and traffic round Kensington is an increasing headache. A series of flyovers is due to be built by 2006, which may help. But many Barbadians believe Kensington – in a prime commercial location – could have been sold off and a new stadium built in a more practical spot.

Seven other countries will also stage matches: Guyana and Antigua (which are building completely new stadiums), Grenada (where the ground should recover from hurricane devastation), Jamaica, Trinidad and Tobago, St Kitts-Nevis and St Lucia. The ICC chose not to add the United States to that list for fear of creating similar security and political problems to those created by the games scheduled for Zimbabwe and Kenya in 2003. The other big losers are the Trinidadians. Queen's Park Oval, which has staged more Tests than any other ground in the region, was assumed by some to be the natural venue for the final. Instead the country has been allotted just six first round games, the same as tiny St Kitts-Nevis.

The prime minister Patrick Manning said in advance that Trinidad and Tobago would not compete to stage matches: it would take what it got. So it ended up without even a quarter-final. A former sports minister, now in opposition, Manohar Ramsaran, said the outcome was "the price we pay for incompetence". What the *Trinidad Guardian* described as the "cavalier approach" to the bidding was typified by the fact that Trinidad and Tobago's bid book was received two hours past deadline. All the others were on time.

the WICB president. "There will be no gain without pain, and the way forward must entail the involvement of those with the skills, talents and ideas to lift us up."

But unity seemed a long way off. In November 2004, most of the players invited to prepare for the one-day triangular in Australia in the New Year initially refused to sign the proposed tour contracts, under advice from the players' association, which accused the board of "an attempt to exploit the players for commercial purposes". This was a similar dispute to the one that afflicted India before the 2003 World Cup, and it required the intervention of the prime minister of Grenada, Keith Mitchell, and arbitration to allow the selected team to go to Australia. But even this was only a temporary solution: the board asserted that "there were still a number of issues unresolved". It was a worrying indication that further confrontation was likely with the revitalised players' association, which had already called a strike of its members before the domestic Carib Beer semi-finals in 2003 and had threatened two others.

The latest dispute coincided with the appointment of Bennett King, director of the Australian academy, as new head coach, the first foreigner at the helm of the West Indies team. This followed a report from a committee headed by the board's vice-president, Val Banks, which recommended increasing the head coach's powers, appointing a full-time manager, and establishing "distinct and discrete roles for the manager, coach, captain and selectors, with clear reporting lines and accountability". The coach would have a full-time contract, serve on the selection panel, and have the casting vote on the final eleven. The captain would carry out strategy and tactics in collaboration with him. "The coach will be accountable for the team's performance," Griffith said. Compounded by the choice of an outsider, which some saw as an insult to the great legacy of West Indies cricket, it was a radical switch.

But it was not unexpected. The board had prematurely announced King as its choice in March 2003, only for him to then turn it down. In the circumstances, Gus Logie, the successful youth team coach, was elevated by default. His contract was terminated "by mutual agreement" in September – immediately after the Champions Trophy success – to accommodate King. The WICB's position was that King came free of the insular baggage that had hindered the seven West Indians who preceded him in the post, none of whom lasted more than three years. As the buck would stop with him, King insisted on choosing his support staff: he brought along an assistant coach, David Moore, and a physiotherapist, Stephen Partridge, fellow Queenslanders who worked under him in Australia.

Yet another Queenslander, Darren Holder, had been recruited earlier as coaching manager, to devise specialist coaching programmes, oversee the Cricket Academy's curriculum and organise an agenda for emerging players. It was a significant position, but the new head coach would be the one expected to make a difference. At least he had an unexpected breathing space to assert himself. A Test series in Australia in 2004-05 was postponed for a year, meaning that West Indies would play no Test cricket between The Oval in late August 2004 and Georgetown in April, against South Africa.

At domestic level, the first-class and one-day tournaments were both to be overhauled. For four seasons, a foreign team and an Under-23 development side had taken part in the first-class competition; since 1996-97, a series of non-first-class teams such as Bermuda, Canada, the USA and the University of the West Indies had joined the one-day competition. Both expansions had burdened a financially insecure organisation with heavy running costs, while adding little to general standards. From 2004-05, both tournaments would feature only the six traditional regional teams: Barbados, Guyana, Jamaica, the Leewards, Trinidad & Tobago and the Windwards. The first-class competition would become a home-and-away league, instead of a single round leading to semi-finals and a final.

Meanwhile, two major sponsorships changed hands. Cable & Wireless ended its association with the Test team after 18 years, preferring involvement with the 2007 World Cup and agreements with individual players, most prominently Lara. They were replaced by a rival telecommunications company, Digicel, in a five-year deal. Red Stripe Beer, a sponsor since 1988, withdrew from the one-day tournament which, in the absence of a replacement for 2004-05, had to be called the President's Cup.

> # The national board might have sought advice from Barbados

The change from Cable & Wireless to Digicel led directly to the impasse between the board and players' association. The board's tour contract required players not to endorse a competitor of its major sponsor unless they had a pre-existing agreement that it had approved. The players' objection was that the board wanted "to unilaterally assume infinite ownership of the players' endorsement rights".

As the board sought solutions to West Indies' decline, it might have sought advice from its Barbados representatives. After failing to reach the first-class semi-finals in 2001-02, **Barbados** had turned things round so swiftly that they comfortably won both stages of the competition, the league (Carib Beer Cup) and the knockout (International Challenge), in the next two seasons. They extended their unbeaten sequence in the first-class tournament to 21 matches. Though they could not keep the one-day trophy, the Red Stripe Bowl, which they won in 2002-03 – they lost the final to Guyana – their side were Under-15 champions in April and Under-19 one-day champions in August.

The senior Barbados side won all seven first-round matches, a record for the expanded competition. No other team won more than three. It gave them the Cup by a margin of 32 points over Jamaica. But it was in the Challenge that their resilience was most severely tested. In the semi-final, they claimed a hard-fought first-innings lead over Guyana in a drawn match; in the final, they staged a spirited fightback to defeat Jamaica.

Their success once more revolved around their confidence, their preparation, the captaincy of long-serving wicket-keeper Courtney Browne, and a combination of proven experience and enthusiastic youth. Of three batsmen with Test caps, Sherwin Campbell and Ryan Hinds amassed over 500 runs in the competition, and Floyd Reifer was only nine short. Pedro Collins, the left-arm swing bowler, was the tournament's leading wicket-taker with 43 at 18 runs each, while the pacy Tino Best had 37 at 13. It was enough to earn both a Test recall. The left-hander Ian Bradshaw had solid returns either side of his call-up for the one-day squad in South Africa. Indeed, all 17 players used by Barbados made some kind of worthwhile contribution.

The other teams lacked their consistency and relied on too few key players. **Jamaica** reached their fifth successive final, but were handicapped by the absence through injury of their Test men, Wavell Hinds, Marlon Samuels and Jermaine Lawson, and had to wait for Chris Gayle's return from South Africa to boost their batting. Seamer Andrew Richardson, aged 22, who played for West Indies B in 2002-03, stepped up to claim 36 wickets.

The **Windward Islands**, whose third place was their highest league finish for 21 years and put them in the semis, had the batsman of the season in the Grenadian left-handed opener Devon Smith. He scored 842 runs at an average of 76 in the tournament, 283 more than anyone else, including four hundreds – three in successive innings. He followed that with his first Test century when recalled to play England, before a broken thumb put him out. His opening stand of 309 with Rommel Currency against Kenya was a Windwards all-wicket record. In the same match, Fernix Thomas's lively pace brought him the season's best figures, eight for 28.

Guyana and **Trinidad & Tobago** had 40 points each but Guyana advanced to the Challenge round by virtue of winning their head-to-head fixture. Their batting was so brittle that no one scored a hundred until Ramnaresh Sarwan returned from South Africa to reel off two (plus a 95) in three matches. In the semi-final against Barbados, he shared a double-century partnership with Test colleague Shivnarine Chanderpaul, who had been controversially installed as captain, in spite of Sarwan's position as West Indies' vice-captain.

If Smith was the season's outstanding batsman and Best the finest bowler, Dwayne Bravo was the top all-rounder. The 20-year-old Trinidadian, born in the same Santa Cruz district as Lara, confirmed his long-recognised potential with 481 runs at 37 and 28 wickets at 13, and made his debut for West Indies. Amit Jaggernauth, an off-spinner with variations of flight and turn who had played for West Indies B the previous season, collected 30 wickets, but Trinidad & Tobago's overall performance was again disappointing.

The **Leeward Islands**, a powerhouse in the 1990s, languished at the bottom of the table with the **Kenyans**, who followed A-teams from England, Bangladesh and India as the fourth foreign side in the regional tournament. The Leewards were undermined by much the same insularity that affects West Indian cricket as a whole; Kenya simply found seven four-day matches in less than seven weeks too demanding.

Neither side won a match and both were beaten by **West Indies B**, the Under-23 team, but they did produce a run glut when they met on a perfect pitch at The Valley in Anguilla. Kenya's Maurice Odumbe scored 207, out of 564, and Sylvester Joseph 195 in Leewards' reply, which reached 718 for seven, a tournament record.

FIRST-CLASS AVERAGES, 2003-04

BATTING

(Qualification: 350 runs)

	M	I	NO	R	HS	100s	Avge	Ct/St
R. R. Sarwan (*Guyana & West Indies*)	9	13	1	917	261*	3	76.41	11
†B. C. Lara (*Trinidad & Tobago & West Indies*)	7	11	1	698	400*	2	69.80	4
†D. S. Smith (*Windward Islands & West Indies*)	13	22	3	1,109	180	5	58.36	14
†R. D. Jacobs (*Leeward Islands & West Indies*)	7	10	3	377	107*	1	53.85	17/2
†C. H. Gayle (*Jamaica & West Indies*)	9	16	1	792	219	2	52.80	8
S. C. Joseph (*Leeward Islands*)	9	15	0	718	195	2	47.86	4
S. L. Campbell (*Barbados*)	9	15	2	559	211*	1	43.00	0
C. M. Tuckett (*Leeward Islands*)	7	11	1	413	142	1	41.30	0
†R. O. Hinds (*Barbados & West Indies*)	12	19	1	677	84	0	37.61	9
D. R. Smith (*Barbados & West Indies*)	8	11	1	372	114	2	37.20	9
†S. Chanderpaul (*Guyana & West Indies*)	8	12	1	404	101*	1	36.72	4
K. O. Otieno (*Kenyans*)	8	15	0	540	104	1	36.00	4/1
D. J. J. Bravo (*Trinidad & Tobago*)	10	20	2	641	197	2	35.61	8
†F. L. Reifer (*Barbados*)	9	14	0	491	133	1	35.07	20
R. N. Lewis (*Windward Islands*)	8	12	1	366	82	0	33.27	3
†S. Chattergoon (*Guyana*)	8	13	2	365	85	0	33.18	6
T. L. Lambert (*Jamaica*)	9	16	1	493	82	0	32.86	9
S. O. Tikolo (*Kenyans*)	8	14	1	405	94	0	31.15	1
K. H. Hibbert (*Jamaica*)	8	14	2	368	102*	1	30.66	21/2
C. O. Browne (*Barbados*)	9	14	0	419	98	0	29.92	42/1
T. M. Dowlin (*Guyana*)	8	13	0	370	94	0	28.46	11
D. E. Bernard (*Jamaica*)	10	17	1	449	120	1	28.06	9
R. R. Ramdass (*West Indies B & Guyana*)	8	15	1	386	91	0	27.57	3
T. A. Willett (*Leeward Islands*)	9	16	1	406	93	0	27.06	5

† *Left-handed batsman.*

BOWLING

(Qualification: 20 wickets)

	Style	O	M	R	W	BB	5W/i	Avge
M. O. Odumbe (*Kenyans*)	OB	151.2	40	333	24	6-64	3	13.87
D. J. J. Bravo (*Trinidad & Tobago*)	RFM	180.4	50	421	29	6-70	1	14.51
A. P. Richardson (*Jamaica*)	RM	210.5	47	666	36	5-42	1	18.50
T. L. Best (*Barbados & West Indies*)	RF	341.5	65	992	52	7-33	3	19.07
P. T. Collins (*Barbados & West Indies*)	LFM	452.3	112	1,304	68	6-53	2	19.17
R. O. Cunningham (*Jamaica*)	SLA	199.5	61	425	21	4-27	0	20.23
F. Thomas (*Windward Islands*)	RF	227.5	56	647	30	8-28	2	21.56
R. R. Emrit (*Trinidad & Tobago*)	RFM	180	57	453	21	5-12	2	21.57
D. M. Washington (*West Indies B*)	RF	168.5	47	455	21	3-23	0	21.66
A. Jaggernauth (*Trinidad & Tobago*)	OB	272.4	68	671	30	5-63	1	22.36
D. J. G. Sammy (*Windward Islands*)	RM	205	44	506	22	5-20	2	23.00
G. R. Breese (*Jamaica*)	OB	273.4	60	590	25	3-30	0	23.60
M. V. Nagamootoo (*Guyana*)	LBG	288.5	74	723	28	5-45	3	25.82
N. C. MacGarrell (*Guyana*)	SLA	341	125	630	24	4-28	0	26.25
J. P. Bennett (*West Indies B*)	RFM	236.1	39	729	26	5-45	2	28.03
R. N. Lewis (*Windward Islands*)	LBG	246.1	56	595	21	4-82	0	28.33
F. H. Edwards (*Barbados & West Indies*)	RF	197	28	719	23	4-48	0	31.26
V. A. Browne (*Leeward Islands*)	SLA	215.4	34	635	20	8-129	1	31.75

Note: Averages include Bangladesh's tour in May–June 2004.

CARIB BEER CUP, 2003-04

	Played	Won	Lost	Drawn	1st-inns Points	Points
Barbados.........	7	7	0	0	0	84
Jamaica..........	7	3	1	3	7	52
Windward Islands...	7	3	2	2	6	48
Guyana..........	7	3	3	1	1	40
Trinidad & Tobago...	7	2	3	2	10	40
West Indies B	7	2	4	1	0	27
Leeward Islands	7	0	3	4	4	16
Kenyans	7	0	4	3	7	16

Win = 12 pts; draw = 3 pts; 1st-innings lead in a drawn match = 3 pts; 1st-innings lead in a lost match = 4 pts; no 1st-innings lead in a drawn match = 1 pt each.

Barbados won the Carib Beer Cup and became regional champions. The top four teams qualified for the Carib Beer International Challenge. Guyana were placed ahead of Trinidad & Tobago by virtue of winning their head-to-head game. Matches involving the Kenyans and West Indies B counted for points but neither of these teams could win the Carib Beer Cup.

At Kensington Oval, Bridgetown, January 9, 10, 11, 12, 2004. **Barbados won by ten wickets.** Toss: Barbados. **Guyana 108** (P. T. Collins 4-31) **and 321** (S. Chattergoon 85, K. Arjune 97; I. D. R. Bradshaw 4-69); **Barbados 422-7 dec.** (K. J. Wilkinson 116, F. L. Reifer 133, I. D. R. Bradshaw 65*; L. J. Cush 4-122) **and 8-0.** *Barbados 12 pts.*
   Guyana were awarded five penalty runs in their second innings after the umpires reported that Barbados had tampered with the ball.

At Guaracara Park, Pointe-à-Pierre, January 9, 10, 11, 12, 2004. **Drawn.** Toss: Leeward Islands. **Trinidad & Tobago 335** (I. H. Jan 55, T. Maraj 61, S. Babwah 94; V. A. Browne 8-129) **and 255** (I. H. Jan 58, R. L. Powell 77); **Leeward Islands 324** (S. M. Jeffers 74, T. A. Willett 93, W. W. Cornwall 57; D. J. J. Bravo 6-70) **and 56-3.** *Trinidad & Tobago 6 pts, Leeward Islands 3 pts.*
   Virgil Browne took 8-129 on first-class debut.

At Edgar Gilbert Sporting Complex, Molyneux, St Kitts, January 9, 10, 11, 2004. **West Indies B won by 12 runs.** Toss: Kenyans. **West Indies B 97** (M. O. Odumbe 5-11) **and 149** (M. O. Odumbe 5-32); **Kenyans 149** (M. O. Odumbe 61; J. P. Bennett 5-45) **and 85.** *West Indies B 12 pts, Kenyans 4 pts.*
   Odumbe became the first bowler to take ten wickets for Kenya in a first-class match. Bennett followed up five wickets in the first Kenyan innings with a hat-trick in the second.

At Beausejour Stadium, Gros Islet, St Lucia, January 9, 10, 11, 12, 2004. **Drawn.** Toss: Windward Islands. **Jamaica 266** (M. D. Ventura 50) **and 296-8 dec.** (K. H. Hibbert 50, D. E. Bernard 55, T. L. Lambert 76); **Windward Islands 273** (D. J. G. Sammy 55, S. Shillingford 63; R. O. Cunningham 4-27) **and 223-5** (D. S. Smith 118*, C. W. Emmanuel 55). *Windward Islands 6 pts, Jamaica 3 pts.*

At Mount Gay North Stars, Crab Hill, Barbados, January 16, 17, 18, 2004. **Barbados won by an innings and 90 runs.** Toss: Barbados. **Windward Islands 113** (J. R. Murray 57*; T. L. Best 4-33) **and 92** (T. L. Best 7-33); **Barbados 295** (F. L. Reifer 86, S. A. Graham 68). *Barbados 12 pts.*

At Sabina Park, Kingston, January 16, 17, 18, 2004. **Jamaica won by six wickets.** Toss: Guyana. **Guyana 222** (S. Chattergoon 68, N. Deonarine 69) **and 150** (N. C. McGarrell 66*); **Jamaica 270** (D. E. Bernard 51, T. L. Lambert 55; M. V. Nagamootoo 4-70, N. C. McGarrell 4-45) **and 107-4.** *Jamaica 12 pts.*

At Ronald Webster Park, The Valley, Anguilla, January 16, 17, 18, 19, 2004. **Drawn.** Toss: Leeward Islands. **Kenyans 564** (R. D. Shah 99, K. O. Otieno 54, S. O. Tikolo 94, M. O. Odumbe 207); **Leeward Islands 718-7** (F. A. Adams 90, S. C. Joseph 195, S. C. Williams 105, C. M. Tuckett 142, E. J. Powell 61*). *Leeward Islands 6 pts, Kenyans 3 pts.*
   Odumbe's 207, which lasted 225 balls and included 23 fours and two sixes, was the first first-class double-hundred for Kenya, and 564 was their highest first-class total. In reply, 718-7 was

a Leewards record and the fourth-highest total in West Indian domestic cricket. Joseph batted ten hours 35 minutes. Eight men bowled for the Leewards and nine for Kenya.

At National Cricket Centre, Couva, Trinidad, January 16, 17, 18, 19, 2004. **Trinidad & Tobago won by seven wickets.** Toss: Trinidad & Tobago. **West Indies B 238** (R. R. Ramdass 91, L. M. P. Simmons 59; A. Jaggernauth 4-76) **and 256** (A. B. Fudadin 55; A. Jaggernauth 5-63); **Trinidad & Tobago 359** (D. J. J. Bravo 197; J. P. Bennett 5-113) **and 138-3** (T. Maraj 68*, A. Kanhai 53). *Trinidad & Tobago 12 pts.*

At Sabina Park, Kingston, January 23, 24, 25, 26, 2004. **Barbados won by 40 runs.** Toss: Barbados. **Barbados 198** (R. O. Hinds 56; R. O. Cunningham 4-49) **and 251** (M. A. Nurse 77; A. P. Richardson 4-36); **Jamaica 205** (D. E. Bernard 81; T. L. Best 5-44) **and 204** (M. O. Kepple 65, K. H. Hibbert 51). *Barbados 12 pts, Jamaica 4 pts.*
  Both wicket-keepers, Courtney Browne and Hibbert, made ten dismissals (nine catches and a stumping each) in the match. Browne made six catches and a stumping in Jamaica's second innings.

At Grove Park, Charlestown, Nevis, January 23, 24, 25, 2004. **West Indies B won by eight wickets.** Toss: West Indies B. **West Indies B 339** (D. P. Hyatt 65, P. A. Browne 83) **and 59-2**; **Leeward Islands 171** (D. M. George 4-49) **and 224.** *West Indies B 12 pts.*

At Shaw Park, Scarborough, Tobago, January 23, 24, 25, 26, 2004. **Drawn.** Toss: Trinidad & Tobago. **Trinidad & Tobago 257** (D. J. J. Bravo 69, S. Babwah 100; P. J. Ongondo 5-60) **and 103** (M. A. Suji 4-23); **Kenyans 150** (D. J. J. Bravo 4-20) **and 88-8** (R. R. Emrit 5-12). *Trinidad & Tobago 6 pts, Kenyans 3 pts.*

At Botanical Gardens, Roseau, Dominica, January 23, 24, 25, 26, 2004. **Windward Islands won by 131 runs.** Toss: Windward Islands. **Windward Islands 204** (R. Wilkinson 64, R. N. Lewis 56; M. V. Nagamootoo 4-79) **and 242** (D. S. Smith 52, D. J. G. Sammy 87; R. L. Griffith 6-44); **Guyana 192** (T. M. Dowlin 78) **and 123** (D. J. G. Sammy 5-20, D. C. Butler 4-17). *Windward Islands 12 pts.*
  Guyana lost all ten wickets for 50 runs on the final day to go down to their third successive defeat. Afterwards, it was reported that a fight broke out on their team bus, and the Windwards scorer, who was also the mayor of Roseau, had to threaten two players with arrest.

At Three Ws Oval, Bridgetown, January 30, 31, February 1, 2, 2004. **Barbados won by 162 runs.** Toss: West Indies B. **Barbados 217 and 215-8 dec.** (S. A. Graham 66, R. O. Hinds 55); **West Indies B 131** (P. T. Collins 4-38, R. P. O. Nurse 4-19) **and 139** (R. P. O. Nurse 7-41). *Barbados 12 pts.*
  Ryan Nurse's 11-60 was the best match analysis of the season.

At Enmore, Demerara, January 30, 31, February 1, 2, 2004. **Drawn.** Toss: Leeward Islands. **Leeward Islands 350** (S. M. Jeffers 63, S. C. Williams 79, W. W. Cornwall 59*; T. M. Dowlin 4-59); **Guyana 270-9** (N. Deonarine 70; A. Sanford 4-64). *Guyana 4 pts, Leeward Islands 4 pts.*

At Queen's Park, St George's, January 30, 31, February 1, 2, 2004. **Drawn.** Toss: Jamaica. **Kenyans 302** (K. O. Otieno 104, M. A. Suji 59, S. O. Tikolo 63; A. P. Richardson 5-42) **and 170-7** (K. O. Otieno 68); **Jamaica 199** (S. O. Tikolo 4-33). *Kenyans 6 pts, Jamaica 3 pts.*

At Queen's Park Oval, Port-of-Spain, January 30, 31, February 1, 2004. **Trinidad & Tobago won by 81 runs.** Toss: Trinidad & Tobago. **Trinidad & Tobago 203** (C. E. Cuffy 4-32, D. J. G. Sammy 5-37) **and 160** (S. Shillingford 4-39); **Windward Islands 73 and 209** (R. K. Currency 57, D. S. Smith 60; D. J. J. Bravo 4-39). *Trinidad & Tobago 12 pts.*
  Windwards' 73, which occupied 37.4 overs, was the lowest total of the season.

At Windward Park, Lucas Street, Barbados, February 6, 7, 8, 9, 2004. **Barbados won by six wickets.** Toss: Barbados. **Kenyans 171** (K. O. Otieno 52; P. T. Collins 5-57) **and 202** (S. O. Tikolo 76*; T. L. Best 5-54); **Barbados 221** (F. L. Reifer 50; M. O. Odumbe 6-64) **and 153-4** (M. A. Nurse 77). *Barbados 12 pts.*

At Albion, Berbice, February 6, 7, 8, 9, 2004. **Guyana won by seven wickets.** Toss: Trinidad & Tobago. **Trinidad & Tobago 143** (I. H. Jan 73; D. Dasrath 4-17) **and 193** (D. J. J. Bravo 68*); **Guyana 270** (N. Deonarine 71, T. M. Dowlin 67; R. R. Emrit 5-48) **and 67-3.** *Guyana 12 pts.*

At Carib Ground, Philipsburg, St Maarten, February 6, 7, 8, 9, 2004. **Drawn.** Toss: Leeward Islands. **Leeward Islands 378-9 dec.** (T. A. Willett 65, S. C. Williams 74; R. N. Lewis 4-82) and **153-6** (C. M. Tuckett 53*); **Windward Islands 435** (D. S. Smith 159, C. W. Emmanuel 73, R. N. Lewis 82; W. W. Cornwall 4-98). *Leeward Islands 3 pts, Windward Islands 6 pts.*

The Carib Ground became the 56th first-class venue in the West Indies. The 34-year-old former Test batsman Stuart Williams had the little finger on his right hand amputated after it was broken in the field, and gangrene set in. The Players' Association took up Williams's case on the grounds that he had received questionable medical attention.

At Airport Ground, St John's, February 6, 7, 8, 9, 2004. **Drawn.** Toss: Jamaica. **West Indies B 242** (D. P. Hyatt 55); **Jamaica 299-9** (C. S. Baugh 115, G. R. Breese 72). *West Indies B 3 pts, Jamaica 6 pts.*

Baugh and Breese added 200 for Jamaica's sixth wicket after they slumped to 61-5.

At Enmore, Demerara, February 12, 13, 14, 15, 2004. **Guyana won by an innings and four runs.** Toss: West Indies B. **Guyana 419** (R. R. Sarwan 95, T. M. Dowlin 94, D. Dasrath 56, M. V. Nagamootoo 58; J. P. Bennett 4-83); **West Indies B 228** (M. V. Nagamootoo 5-100) and **187** (D. M. Washington 58; N. C. McGarrell 4-28). *Guyana 12 pts.*

Washington scored his maiden fifty, West Indies B's top score, at No. 11.

At Alpart Sports Club, St Elizabeth, February 12, 13, 14, 15, 2004. **Jamaica won by three wickets.** Toss: Jamaica. **Trinidad & Tobago 229** (S. Ganga 64, A. Kanhai 111) and **182** (D. Ganga 77; A. P. Richardson 4-35, O. V. Brown 4-50); **Jamaica 147 and 266-7** (M. O. Kepple 55, D. J. Pagon 94; D. J. J. Bravo 4-32). *Jamaica 12 pts, Trinidad & Tobago 4 pts.*

At Addelita Cancryn Ground, Charlotte Amalie, St Thomas, February 12, 13, 14, 2004. **Barbados won by an innings and 48 runs.** Toss: Barbados. **Barbados 432** (S. L. Campbell 211*); **Leeward Islands 161** (S. J. Benn 4-33) and **223** (S. C. Joseph 50, T. A. Willett 63). *Barbados 12 pts.*

Campbell carried his bat for a career-best 211, his second double-hundred, which lasted 435 minutes and 336 balls and included 29 fours. Benn took a hat-trick in Leewards' first innings.*

At Arnos Vale, St Vincent, February 12, 13, 14, 2004. **Windward Islands won by an innings and 26 runs.** Toss: Windward Islands. **Kenyans 152** (F. Thomas 8-28) and **179; Windward Islands 357-1 dec.** (D. S. Smith 180, R. K. Currency 121*). *Windward Islands 12 pts.*

Thomas's figures of 18.2–6–28–8 were the best of the season. Openers Smith and Currency put on 309, Windwards' first triple-century stand for any wicket.

At Guaracara Park, Pointe-à-Pierre, February 18, 19, 20, 21, 2004. **Barbados won by 246 runs.** Toss: Trinidad & Tobago. **Barbados 285** (R. O. Hinds 50, C. O. Browne 98) and **372** (K. J. Wilkinson 82, R. O. Hinds 83, C. O. Browne 82); **Trinidad & Tobago 265** (S. Ganga 59, R. L. Powell 115; R. O. Hinds 4-51) and **146** (F. H. Edwards 4-48). *Barbados 12 pts.*

Floyd Reifer took four catches in Trinidad & Tobago's first innings.

At Bourda, Georgetown, February 19, 20, 21, 22, 2004. **Guyana won by an innings and 114 runs.** Toss: Guyana. **Guyana 444** (S. Chattergoon 60, R. R. Sarwan 199, S. Chanderpaul 75; R. G. Aga 4-71); **Kenyans 139** (B. J. Patel 59; M. V. Nagamootoo 5-45) and **191** (K. O. Otieno 70, H. S. Modi 50). *Guyana 12 pts.*

At Alpart Sports Club, St Elizabeth, February 19, 20, 21, 22, 2004. **Jamaica won by 260 runs.** Toss: Jamaica. **Jamaica 200** (C. S. Baugh 87*; C. J. K. Hodge 4-67) and **394-3 dec.** (C. H. Gayle 219, M. O. Kepple 58, T. L. Lambert 60*); **Leeward Islands 190** (S. C. Joseph 89; D. B. Powell 5-40) and **144** (A. P. Richardson 4-23, O. V. Brown 4-44). *Jamaica 12 pts.*

Gayle's 219, his fourth double-hundred and the highest score in the 2003-04 tournament, lasted 396 minutes and 272 balls and included 31 fours and a six.

At Queen's Park, St George's, February 19, 20, 21, 22, 2004. **Windward Islands won by ten wickets.** Toss: West Indies B. **West Indies B 197** (A. C. L. Richards 74; S. Shillingford 5-50) and **237** (A. C. L. Richards 59, K. D. Williams 55; F. Thomas 5-49); **Windward Islands 427** (D. S. Smith 154, D. J. G. Sammy 61) and **11-0.** *Windward Islands 12 pts.*

Smith scored his third hundred in successive innings.

REGIONAL CHAMPIONS

Shell Shield		1980-81	Combined Islands	1995-96	Leeward Islands
1965-66	Barbados	1981-82	Barbados	1996-97	Barbados
1966-67	Barbados	1982-83	Guyana		
1967-68	No competition	1983-84	Barbados	*President's Cup*	
1968-69	Jamaica	1984-85	Trinidad & Tobago	1997-98	{Leeward Islands
1969-70	Trinidad	1985-86	Barbados		{Guyana
1970-71	Trinidad	1986-87	Guyana		
1971-72	Barbados			*Busta Cup*	
1972-73	Guyana	*Red Stripe Cup*		1998-99	Barbados
1973-74	Barbados	1987-88	Jamaica	1999-2000	Jamaica
1974-75	Guyana	1988-89	Jamaica	2000-01	Barbados
1975-76	{Trinidad	1989-90	Leeward Islands	2001-02	Jamaica
	{Barbados	1990-91	Barbados		
1976-77	Barbados	1991-92	Jamaica	*Carib Beer Cup*	
1977-78	Barbados	1992-93	Guyana	2002-03	Barbados
1978-79	Barbados	1993-94	Leeward Islands	2003-04	Barbados
1979-80	Barbados	1994-95	Barbados		

Barbados have won the title outright 18 times, Jamaica 6, Guyana 5, Leeward Islands and Trinidad/Trinidad & Tobago 3, Combined Islands 1. Barbados, Guyana, Leeward Islands and Trinidad have also shared the title.

CARIB BEER INTERNATIONAL CHALLENGE, 2003-04

Semi-finals

At Kensington Oval, Bridgetown, February 26, 27, 28, 29, 2004. **Drawn.** Barbados qualified for the semi-final by virtue of their first-innings lead. Toss: Barbados. **Guyana 310** (R. R. Sarwan 121, S. Chanderpaul 81, D. Dasrath 51; P. T. Collins 4-85) **and 148-8** (R. R. Ramdass 60; D. R. Smith 4-46); **Barbados 395** (S. L. Campbell 91, R. O. Hinds 56, D. R. Smith 114, I. D. R. Bradshaw 50*; M. V. Nagamootoo 5-116).

In Guyana's first innings, Sarwan and Chanderpaul added 203 for the fourth wicket.

At Alpart Sports Club, St Elizabeth, February 26, 27, 28, 29, 2004. **Drawn.** Jamaica qualified for the semi-final by virtue of their first-innings lead. Toss: Windward Islands. **Jamaica 338** (D. E. Bernard 120) **and 372-5** (C. H. Gayle 71, T. L. Lambert 82, K. H. Hibbert 102*); **Windward Islands 249** (D. S. Smith 51).

All the Windwards players except the keeper bowled in Jamaica's second innings; the game ended early when some spectators threw bottles on to the field in protest at Jamaica's refusal to declare.

FINAL

BARBADOS v JAMAICA

At Mount Gay North Stars, Crab Hill, Barbados, March 25, 26, 27, 28, 2004. Barbados won by 84 runs. Toss: Jamaica.

This match was staged during the blank week halfway through the Test series with England, and the return of five internationals confirmed Barbados's position as favourites. But they crumbled when they were put in; only a 24-ball blast from Best got them to 142, which Jamaica overtook with eight wickets in hand. Gayle struck 12 fours and a six and, though he last five went for 53 runs on the second afternoon, they took a first-innings lead of 116. That looked enough when Barbados ended the day only 33 ahead with half their side gone again. Then Reifer, who had held four first-innings catches but was himself dropped twice, began to steady the innings. A stand of 80 with Browne began to give Barbados hope, and they finally left a target of 200. Collymore quickly removed both openers, including Gayle, and in the last over of the third day Bradshaw had Lambert caught behind, at 69 for six. Barbados were celebrating their second successive double before lunch on the final day.

Man of the Match: F. L. Reifer.

Close of play: First day, Jamaica 135-2 (Gayle 57, Lambert 19); Second day, Barbados 149-5 (Reifer 18, Collymore 0); Third day, Jamaica 69-6 (Brown 1).

Barbados

K. J. Wilkinson b Richardson	18	– lbw b Richardson	6
M. A. Nurse c Baugh b Richardson	0	– c Richardson b Powell	32
S. L. Campbell b Powell	0	– lbw b Richardson	49
R. O. Hinds c Hibbert b Gayle	43	– c Baugh b Gayle	25
F. L. Reifer st Baugh b Gayle	18	– c Hibbert b Powell	83
D. R. Smith c Gayle b Powell	1	– c Baugh b Powell	7
*†C. O. Browne b Powell	11	– (8) b Richardson	47
I. D. R. Bradshaw c Gayle b Perry	12	– (9) run out	17
T. L. Best c Baugh b Richardson	30	– (10) c Bernard b Perry	7
P. T. Collins c Richardson b Perry	2	– (11) not out	1
C. D. Collymore not out	2	– (7) c and b Perry	10
B 1, l-b 1, n-b 3	5	B 8, l-b 6, w 6, n-b 11	31

1/9 (2) 2/19 (3) 3/21 (1) 4/68 (5)   142   1/36 (1) 2/41 (2) 3/93 (4)   315
5/83 (6) 6/85 (4) 7/106 (8)   4/137 (3) 5/148 (6) 6/174 (7)
8/112 (7) 9/120 (10) 10/142 (9)   7/254 (8) 8/307 (9)
    9/313 (5) 10/315 (10)

Bowling: *First Innings*—Powell 13–3–36–3; Richardson 7.5–1–29–3; Gayle 13–2–33–2; Bernard 5–0–27–0; Perry 3–0–15–2. *Second Innings*—Powell 20–3–66–3; Richardson 22–3–90–3; Gayle 19–5–49–1; Bernard 15–6–30–0; Brown 8–0–29–0; Perry 24.2–10–37–2.

Jamaica

*C. H. Gayle lbw b Collins	76	– lbw b Collymore	17
M. O. Kepple c Reifer b Collymore	16	– c Hinds b Collymore	1
D. J. Pagon lbw b Collins	20	– c Wilkinson b Bradshaw	10
T. L. Lambert c Reifer b Bradshaw	33	– c Browne b Bradshaw	21
K. H. Hibbert c Reifer b Collymore	32	– c Browne b Collymore	0
D. E. Bernard b Bradshaw	6	– hit wkt b Collins	7
†C. S. Baugh c Browne b Bradshaw	12	– (8) lbw b Collins	0
N. O. Perry not out	14	– (9) lbw b Best	13
D. B. Powell b Collins	13	– (10) c Reifer b Collymore	20
O. V. Brown c Reifer b Best	3	– (7) c Wilkinson b Bradshaw	8
A. P. Richardson b Collins	1	– not out	0
B 8, l-b 12, n-b 12	32	B 2, l-b 4, n-b 12	18

1/44 (2) 2/86 (3) 3/163 (1) 4/177 (4)   258   1/3 (2) 2/33 (1) 3/40 (3) 4/41 (5)   115
5/195 (6) 6/220 (5) 7/226 (7)   5/63 (6) 6/69 (4) 7/77 (7)
8/243 (9) 9/255 (10) 10/258 (11)   8/77 (8) 9/107 (9) 10/115 (10)

Bowling: *First Innings*—Collins 18.3–5–56–4; Best 12–2–52–1; Collymore 21–4–46–2; Bradshaw 24–8–58–3; Smith 5–0–7–0; Hinds 6–2–19–0. *Second Innings*—Collins 13–2–41–2; Collymore 10.3–3–32–4; Best 3–0–16–1; Bradshaw 12–6–20–3.

Umpires: G. T. Johnson and B. E. W. Morgan. Third umpire: D. Holder.

RED STRIPE BOWL, 2003-04

Note: Matches in this section were not first-class.

Zone A (in Jamaica)	Played	Won	Lost	No result	Points	Net run-rate
Jamaica	4	4	0	0	16	1.73
Trinidad & Tobago	4	2	1	1	11	1.09
Leeward Islands	4	2	2	0	10	-0.05
Windward Islands	4	1	2	1	8	0.16
Canada	4	0	4	0	4	-2.34

Zone B (in Antigua)

	Played	Won	Lost	No result	Points	Net run-rate
Barbados	4	3	1	0	13	0.62
Guyana	4	3	1	0	13	0.39
Antigua & Barbuda	4	2	1	1	11	0.60
West Indies Under-19	4	1	3	0	7	−0.36
University of the West Indies . .	4	0	3	1	5	−1.70

Win = 4 pts, no result = 2 pts, loss = 1 pt. Net run-rate was calculated by subtracting runs conceded per over from runs scored per over.

Semi-finals

At Kaiser Sports Club, Discovery Bay, October 16, 2003. **Guyana won by four runs.** Toss: Jamaica. **Guyana 183** (49.5 overs); **Jamaica 179** (49.1 overs) (C. H. Gayle 67).

At Kaiser Sports Club, Discovery Bay, October 17, 2003. **Barbados won by 61 runs.** Toss: Barbados. **Barbados 175** (48.2 overs) (D. J. J. Bravo 4-34); **Trinidad & Tobago 114** (36 overs) (I. D. R. Bradshaw 5-22).

Final

At Kaiser Sports Club, Discovery Bay, October 19, 2003. **Guyana won by 27 runs (D/L method).** Toss: Guyana. **Guyana 212-9** (50 overs); **Barbados 156** (36 overs).

    Barbados's target was revised to 184 in 37 overs. Their wicket-keeper, Courtney Browne, made four dismissals (one stumped, three caught), just as he had in the zonal game against Guyana (all caught).

CRICKET IN NEW ZEALAND, 2003-04

Don Cameron

Michael Papps

In the bad old days, the fact that New Zealand lost two home Tests, to Pakistan at Christmas and South Africa before Easter, would have consigned 2003-04 to the rubbish tip of lost hopes. Instead, even as Graeme Smith struck South Africa's winning run at Wellington, New Zealanders were rejoicing in a season that repaired some old weaknesses and produced some brilliant new prospects for a game they still cherish, even if few attend.

Every now and then all of New Zealand erupts with joy at some brave, unexpected milestone – conquering Everest, winning the Rugby World Cup or the America's Cup. Nothing lately could quite compare with all the Oscars for the New Zealand-made *Lord of the Rings* films, but the win over South Africa at Auckland in March captured something of the Everest spirit. The players were on cloud nine.

Various commentators tried to classify the worth of their achievement. Was this New Zealand's greatest Test win? Was the team the best they had ever fielded? Probably not. Very likely the 1955-56 victory over West Indies on the same ground was the best, simply because it was the first. And the 1985-86 side that defeated Australia at Brisbane and Perth very likely rates as the most talented. But this nine-wicket win had brilliant batting, effective bowling, fluctuating fortunes, rich summer sun, and Stephen Fleming completing it with a lovely straight six. Chris Martin was recalled and took 11 wickets, Scott Styris made a blistering 170, and Chris Cairns hit the century of his life, with seven sixes.

South Africa pulled level at Wellington, where New Zealand had also lost to Pakistan thanks to an explosive 11-wicket performance from Shoaib Akhtar. Apart from that, the New Zealand and Pakistan Test sides were evenly balanced, and those two defeats should not disguise all the good things that happened during the season. A year before, New Zealand Cricket had been embroiled in a dangerous fight with the new Cricket Players Association. But common sense on both sides eventually allowed them to work in harmony, with never a bitter word from what had been warring camps.

There were encouraging signs that the struggle to produce consistent pitches was being won, despite the handicaps of a fickle climate and heavy rugby traffic at the stadiums in Auckland and Christchurch. In 2003-04, international pitches in the North Island were variable, but Christchurch and Dunedin could be relied on for good strips catering equally for batsmen and bowlers. The next objective must be to develop pitches giving slow bowlers as much chance as fast men and seamers. This was all the more necessary as New Zealand's long-established spinner, Daniel Vettori, was less effective since remodelling his action after back problems: in five home Tests, Vettori took seven wickets at 96 each and he was ineffective in the three one-day games he played for Northern Districts.

...this may be seen as the season's greatest legacy

With the international players on duty from mid-December to the end of March, the six major associations had to draw on new talent, but sadly this did not mark the arrival of any especially talented new spinners. Paul Wiseman, the Canterbury off-spinner, returned again to the Test ranks, but he was 34 in May. And two leggies, Brooke Walker of Auckland, tried by New Zealand a couple of seasons earlier, and Aaron Redmond of Canterbury (son of Test batsman Rodney) were little more than occasional bowlers in domestic cricket.

One thoughtful piece of planning did help some fringe players, producing a group of a dozen cricketers of past international experience or exceptional promise who could move in and out of the extended national squad. Sri Lanka A toured in March, playing three unofficial Tests (all innings wins for New Zealand A) and a one-day series. But intelligent scheduling meant each of the A-team Tests started a day after one of the South African Tests, so players omitted from the senior squad could immediately transfer to New Zealand A. Lou Vincent, trying to rediscover his international form, James Franklin, whose quickish left-arm bowling and promising batting deserved encouragement, Mathew Sinclair, out of the national side since December, and Kyle Mills all benefited, while players recovering from injury, such as fast bowler Shane Bond, could be slipped into a game to test their fitness. In future, this may be seen as the season's greatest legacy.

The format of the first-class State Championship was revised again. For the past three seasons, it had been played strictly as a round-robin league, with each of the six teams playing ten matches. In 2003-04, they played eight: one full round of five matches, after which the top three teams played each of the bottom three once more. The two leaders after this second partial round met in a final, restored for the first time in four years.

Canterbury made a flying start, and were easy leaders when the full round ended in January, with 20 points to Wellington's 14. Michael Papps scored 119, 192 and 130 in six innings during this phase, earning promotion to the national side, while Peter Fulton followed a triple-century in 2002-03 with 114 and 113 in his first two matches; they were the only batsmen from any team to pass 600 runs in this tournament, though captain

Chris Harris was close with 580 and provided all-round support. Warren Wisneski took 29 Championship wickets and Chris Martin 28, boosted by his international bowling to 53 – the season's best in all first-class cricket.

Wellington pulled ahead of Canterbury in an unusually wet February, when they beat Central Districts for a second time. Leading the table meant they earned home advantage in the final, and needed only a draw to become champions. The match was staged in between the South African one-day and Test series, and Canterbury were still fancied, with three players from New Zealand's one-day squad returning (Fleming, attached to Wellington, was rested). But they lost six wickets on the first morning and, though they fought back to what could have been a winning position, Wellington held firm for the title-clinching draw. Wellington opening bowlers James Franklin and Mark Gillespie were the Championship's leading wicket-takers, with 36 and 31 respectively; Matt Walker and Chris Nevin, who were there at the end in the final, both passed 500 tournament runs.

Defending champions **Auckland** started with a win over Northern Districts, and were only a point behind Wellington after the first round, but lost ground and slipped to fourth. Matt Horne, averaging 18 in his first half-dozen matches, finally found top gear with 118 and 209 not out against Northern Districts, then dropped out with a debilitating virus. Aaron Barnes helped Horne add 347, a national fifth-wicket record, in that game, and contributed another century in the next match, but both were drawn.

Otago could not win a game in the first round, then beat Auckland and Canterbury in February to leap into third place. Only Chris Gaffaney completed a century; seamers Warren McSkimming and Bradley Scott picked up 28 Championship wickets apiece.

Central Districts managed only one win, over Otago, thanks to 169 from Jamie How, and Sinclair scored consistently, gaining a Test recall against South Africa via New Zealand A, and finishing as the leading first-class run-scorer with 851. Ross Taylor, 20 in March, looked a dashing batsman of uncommon promise, but needed to work on his four-day game. **Northern Districts** had a desperate season – in their first six matches, the top half of the batting contributed only five fifties – and the bowling lacked bite. Bruce Martin showed promise as a slow left-armer who could bat, but still lived in Vettori's shadow. They never won a match in the four-day State Championship, and had a solitary win in the one-day State Shield.

The Shield provided another disappointment for Canterbury. They entered the final against Central Districts with everything in their favour – it was a home game, and they fielded seven players who appeared for New Zealand at some point during the season. They put Central Districts in to bat – and Central simply put their bowling to the sword. Craig Spearman, the Gloucestershire opener, plundered an astonishing 85 from 48 balls, with ten fours and five sixes; How, Taylor and Sinclair continued the murderous assault. Chasing 355, a stunned Canterbury side succumbed in 42 overs. It was a triumphant conclusion to Mark Greatbatch's two-year stint as Central Districts coach.

FIRST-CLASS AVERAGES, 2003-04

BATTING

(Qualification: 400 runs)

	M	I	NO	R	HS	100s	Avge	Ct
M. D. J. Walker (*Wellington*)	8	12	4	582	126*	1	72.75	9
†J. D. P. Oram (*New Zealand*)	5	8	2	412	119*	1	68.66	4
C. J. Nevin (*Wellington*).	8	12	4	524	143*	2	65.50	24
†C. Z. Harris (*Canterbury*).	7	12	2	580	103	1	58.00	8
M. S. Sinclair (*C. Districts, NZ A & NZ*) .	10	16	1	851	133	2	56.73	7
M. J. Horne (*Auckland*).	8	12	1	516	209*	2	46.90	3
S. B. Styris (*Northern Districts & NZ*) . .	7	12	1	502	170	1	45.63	2
M. D. Bell (*Wellington & NZ A*)	12	17	0	775	173	2	45.58	14
M. H. W. Papps (*Canterbury & NZ*) . . .	9	17	1	719	192	3	44.93	17
P. G. Fulton (*Canterbury & NZ A*).	11	19	2	728	114	2	42.82	8
A. C. Barnes (*Auckland*)	8	12	1	456	134*	2	41.45	7
†J. E. C. Franklin (*Wellington & NZ A*) .	11	16	4	492	108*	1	41.00	3
C. B. Gaffaney (*Otago*).	9	14	1	528	160	1	40.61	9
L. Vincent (*Auckland, NZ & NZ A*)	10	14	1	503	156	2	38.69	3
P. J. Wiseman (*Canterbury, NZ & NZ A*) .	12	17	3	535	107	1	38.21	5
J. M. How (*Central Districts & NZ A*) . . .	12	19	1	682	169	1	37.88	18
R. A. Lawson (*Otago*).	9	13	1	412	69	0	34.33	5
R. L. Taylor (*Central Districts*)	9	15	0	489	66	0	32.60	6
†N. K. W. Horsley (*Northern Districts*). . .	8	13	0	420	101	1	32.30	2
†M. H. Richardson (*Auckland & NZ*). . . .	12	19	0	564	82	0	29.68	5
Mohammad Wasim (*Otago*)	9	15	1	415	94	0	29.64	3

† *Left-handed batsman.*

BOWLING

(Qualification: 20 wickets)

	Style	O	M	R	W	BB	5W/i	Avge
K. D. Mills (*Auckland & NZ A*)	RM	153	60	369	25	5-50	1	14.76
E. P. Thompson (*Central Districts*)	LFM	134.2	34	419	25	7-55	2	16.76
J. W. Wilson (*Otago*).	RFM	144.5	40	390	23	5-71	2	16.95
W. A. Wisneski (*Canterbury*).	RM	215.5	52	575	29	5-35	2	19.82
J. E. C. Franklin (*Wellington & NZ A*) .	LFM	334	79	937	47	5-36	1	19.93
C. S. Martin (*Canterbury, NZ A & NZ*) .	RFM	448	142	1,144	53	6-76	6	21.58
A. R. Adams (*Auckland*).	RFM	170	48	525	24	5-40	2	21.87
M. R. Gillespie (*Wellington & NZ A*) . .	RFM	279.5	84	799	34	5-23	1	23.50
W. C. McSkimming (*Otago*)	RM	317.3	95	798	33	5-16	4	24.18
B. G. K. Walker (*Auckland*)	LB	157.5	30	554	22	5-55	1	25.18
B. E. Scott (*Otago*)	LFM	315.4	84	800	31	5-97	1	25.80
S. J. Cunis (*Canterbury*)	RFM	202	49	569	21	4-69	0	27.09
L. J. Hamilton (*Central Districts*)	LFM	289.1	65	826	29	4-67	0	28.48
B. P. Martin (*Northern Districts & NZ A*)	SLA	265.5	61	756	25	5-73	2	30.24
I. G. Butler (*N. Districts, NZ & NZ A*) .	RFM	202.3	36	707	23	6-46	1	30.73
P. J. Wiseman (*Canterbury, NZ & NZ A*)	OB	358	91	961	31	5-67	1	31.00
M. J. Mason (*C. Districts, NZ & NZ A*)	RFM	235.1	70	636	20	5-21	2	31.80

STATE CHAMPIONSHIP, 2003-04

	Played	Won	Lost	Drawn	1st-inns Points	Points	Net avge runs per wkt
Wellington	8	3	0	5	6	24	3.68
Canterbury	8	2	1	5	10	22	5.02
Otago	8	2	2	4	8	20	−0.30
Auckland	8	1	1	6	10	16	1.71
Central Districts . . .	8	1	2	5	7	13	−1.61
Northern Districts . .	8	0	3	5	7	7	−7.43

Final: Wellington drew with Canterbury, but took the title by virtue of heading the table.

Outright win = 6 pts; lead on first innings = 2 pts; no result or tie on first innings = 1 pt each. Net average runs per wicket is calculated by subtracting average runs conceded per wicket from average runs scored per wicket.

At Aorangi Park, Timaru, December 1, 2, 3, 4, 2003. **Canterbury won by seven wickets.** Toss: Canterbury. **Canterbury 375** (P. G. Fulton 114, N. T. Broom 53, J. W. Wilson 5-82) **and 68-3; Otago 212** (R. A. Lawson 59; P. J. Wiseman 4-82) **and 230** (C. B. Gaffaney 76; W. A. Wisneski 5-40). *Canterbury 8 pts.*

At Seddon Park, Hamilton, December 1, 2, 3, 2003. **Auckland won by nine wickets.** Toss: Auckland. **Northern Districts 130** (A. R. Adams 4-41) **and 120** (A. R. Adams 4-41); **Auckland 141** (M. H. Richardson 55) **and 112-1** (L. Vincent 70*). *Auckland 8 pts.*

At Basin Reserve, Wellington, December 1, 2, 3, 2003. **Wellington won by eight wickets.** Toss: Wellington. **Central Districts 139** (E. P. Thompson 55*; A. J. Penn 4-46) **and 195** (R. L. Taylor 64; A. J. Penn 4-55); **Wellington 105** (R. R. Sherlock 4-33) **and 230-2** (M. D. Bell 112, G. T. Donaldson 96). *Wellington 6 pts, Central Districts 2 pts.*

At Eden Park Outer Oval, Auckland, December 7, 8, 9, 10, 2003. **Drawn.** Toss: Auckland. **Auckland 424** (M. H. Richardson 56, L. Vincent 65, T. G. McIntosh 146; J. W. Wilson 5-71); **Otago 131-6.** *Auckland 1 pt, Otago 1 pt.*

At Harry Barker Reserve, Gisborne, December 7, 8, 9, 10, 2003. **Drawn.** Toss: Central Districts. **Central Districts 191 and 220-3** (J. M. How 97*); **Northern Districts 445-9 dec.** (J. A. H. Marshall 59, S. B. Styris 80, G. G. Robinson 65, J. A. F. Yovich 59, I. G. Butler 52*). *Northern Districts 2 pts.*

At Basin Reserve, Wellington, December 12, 13, 14, 15, 2003. **Drawn.** Toss: Wellington. **Canterbury 499-8 dec.** (B. B. McCullum 76, M. H. W. Papps 119, G. R. Stead 105, P. J. Wiseman 75, C. Z. Harris 65) **and 247-6 dec.** (P. G. Fulton 113*); **Wellington 393** (M. D. Bell 75, C. J. Nevin 143*, M. D. J. Walker 68; P. J. Wiseman 5-67) **and 291-7** (R. A. Jones 82, G. T. Donaldson 71). *Canterbury 2 pts.*

At Eden Park Outer Oval, Auckland, December 18, 19, 20, 21, 2003. **Drawn.** Toss: Auckland. **Wellington 201** (K. P. Walmsley 4-45) **and 372** (L. J. Woodcock 86, J. E. C. Franklin 61, M. D. J. Walker 62*); **Auckland 226** (P. A. Hitchcock 51) **and 268-7** (T. G. McIntosh 104). *Auckland 2 pts.*

At Fitzherbert Park, Palmerston North, December 18, 19, 20, 21, 2003. **Drawn.** Toss: Canterbury. **Central Districts 196** (M. S. Sinclair 52; S. J. Cunis 4-69) **and 318** (J. M. How 53, M. S. Sinclair 52, G. P. Sulzberger 59; C. Z. Harris 4-37); **Canterbury 190** (G. P. Sulzberger 6-54) **and 194-7.** *Central Districts 2 pts.*

At Carisbrook, Dunedin, December 18, 19, 20, 21, 2003. **Drawn.** Toss: Northern Districts. **Northern Districts 121** (W. C. McSkimming 5-56) **and 242-5** (N. K. W. Horsley 69, H. J. H. Marshall 65*, B. P. Martin 54*); **Otago 305-8 dec.** (Mohammad Wasim 60, R. A. Lawson 69, M. N. McKenzie 74; J. A. F. Yovich 4-80). *Otago 2 pts.*

At Eden Park Outer Oval, Auckland, December 27, 28, 29, 30, 2003. **Drawn.** Toss: Auckland. **Central Districts 201** (P. J. Ingram 105*; K. D. Mills 5-50) **and 346-6 dec.** (M. S. Sinclair 127*, C. M. Spearman 133); **Auckland 231** (E. P. Thompson 5-43) **and 185-9** (R. J. Nicol 77; B. E. Hefford 4-38). *Auckland 2 pts.*

In the second innings, Sinclair and Spearman added 224, a Central Districts third-wicket record.

At Hagley Oval, Christchurch, December 27, 28, 29, 30, 2003. **Canterbury won by an innings and 109 runs.** Toss: Northern Districts. **Northern Districts 206 and 137** (J. A. F. Yovich 52; C. S. Martin 5-46); **Canterbury 452** (M. H. W. Papps 192, P. G. Fulton 83; B. P. Martin 5-81). *Canterbury 8 pts.*

Canterbury wicket-keeper Brendon McCullum made five catches in Northern Districts' second innings, and seven plus a stumping in the match.

At Carisbrook, Dunedin, December 27, 28, 29, 30, 2003. **Drawn.** Toss: Wellington. **Otago 465** (C. B. Gaffaney 160, G. J. Hopkins 53, N. L. McCullum 63, N. D. Morland 56) **and 91-2** (Mohammad Wasim 50*); **Wellington 381** (M. D. Bell 55, G. T. Donaldson 92, J. E. C. Franklin 108*). *Otago 2 pts.*

At Hagley Oval, Christchurch, January 3, 4, 5, 6, 2004. **Drawn.** Toss: Canterbury. **Canterbury 443** (M. H. W. Papps 130, P. G. Fulton 68, C. Z. Harris 103; A. C. Barnes 4-55) **and 58-1; Auckland 403** (L. Vincent 156). *Canterbury 2 pts.*

At Pukekura Park, New Plymouth, January 3, 4, 5, 6, 2004. **Central Districts won by 134 runs.** Toss: Otago. **Central Districts 350** (J. M. How 169, M. S. Sinclair 62, B. B. J. Griggs 53*; B. E. Scott 5-97) **and 291-7 dec.** (J. M. How 51, M. S. Sinclair 61, R. L. Taylor 52); **Otago 209** (N. W. Rushton 59; M. J. Mason 5-70) **and 298** (C. B. Gaffaney 53, M. N. McKenzie 58, N. L. McCullum 53). *Central Districts 8 pts.*

Otago wicket-keeper Gareth Hopkins took five catches in Central Districts' first innings.

At Seddon Park, Hamilton, January 3, 4, 5, 6, 2004. **Wellington won by 94 runs.** Toss: Wellington. **Wellington 250** (M. D. J. Walker 94*; G. W. Aldridge 4-31) **and 190** (M. D. Bell 60; B. P. Martin 5-73, G. L. West 4-23); **Northern Districts 125** (J. E. C. Franklin 4-34) **and 221.** *Wellington 8 pts.*

Matthew Walker took four catches in Northern Districts' second innings.

At Dudley Park, Rangiora, February 14, 15, 16, 17, 2004. **Drawn.** Toss: Canterbury. **Canterbury 303** (C. Z. Harris 78, P. J. Wiseman 68; L. J. Hamilton 4-71) **and 96-5; Central Districts 178** (M. S. Sinclair 54, R. L. Taylor 66; W. A. Wisneski 5-35). *Canterbury 2 pts.*

At University Oval, Dunedin, February 14, 15, 16, 17, 2004. **Otago won by nine wickets.** Toss: Otago. **Auckland 198** (W. C. McSkimming 5-60) **and 126** (T. K. Canning 66; W. C. McSkimming 5-56); **Otago 154** (A. C. Barnes 5-24) **and 172-1** (C. D. Cumming 63*, Mohammad Wasim 94). *Otago 6 pts, Auckland 2 pts.*

This was the first first-class match at the University Oval since Otago played an England XI 20 years earlier.

At Basin Reserve, Wellington, February 14, 15, 16, 17, 2004. **Drawn.** Toss: Northern Districts. **Northern Districts 155-4** (G. G. Robinson 61) **v Wellington.** *Wellington 1 pt, Northern Districts 1 pt.*

There was no play after the first day.

At Eden Park, Auckland, February 20, 21, 22, 23, 2004. **Drawn.** Toss: Northern Districts. **Auckland 283** (M. J. Horne 118; B. P. Martin 4-34) **and 381-4 dec.** (M. J. Horne 209*, A. C. Barnes 134*); **Northern Districts 388** (J. A. H. Marshall 78, M. G. Orchard 97) **and 269-8** (J. A. H. Marshall 77, N. K. W. Horsley 75). *Northern Districts 2 pts.*

Horne's 209, his second hundred of the match and the second double of his career, lasted 289 minutes and 232 balls and included 26 fours and eight sixes; he shared an unbroken stand of 347, a national fifth-wicket record, with Barnes. Horne later complained that he had been "feeling queasy all day", was taken to hospital and put on a drip, and missed the rest of the season.*

At McLean Park, Napier, February 20, 21, 22, 2004. **Wellington won by 231 runs.** Toss: Central Districts. **Wellington 181** (E. P. Thompson 7-55) **and 310** (C. J. Nevin 65, M. R. Gillespie 76*; E. P. Thompson 4-94); **Central Districts 63** (M. R. Gillespie 5-23, J. E. C. Franklin 5-36) **and 197** (R. L. Taylor 66; M. R. Gillespie 4-71). *Wellington 8 pts.*

At Molyneux Park, Alexandra, February 20, 21, 22, 23, 2004. **Otago won by 108 runs.** Toss: Canterbury. **Otago 336** (Mohammad Wasim 66, R. A. Lawson 50; A. M. Ellis 5-63) **and 143** (G. J. Hopkins 50; W. A. Wisneski 4-45); **Canterbury 219** (C. Z. Harris 63) **and 152.** *Otago 8 pts.*

At Pukekura Park, New Plymouth, February 26, 27, 28, 29, 2004. **Drawn.** Toss: Central Districts. **Auckland 316** (R. J. Nicol 88, A. C. Barnes 108); **Central Districts 268-8** (G. P. Sulzberger 56, R. L. Taylor 52; A. R. Adams 4-110). *Central Districts 1 pt, Auckland 1 pt.*

At Harry Barker Reserve, Gisborne, February 26, 27, 28, 29, 2004. **Drawn.** Toss: Northern Districts. **Northern Districts 434** (N. K. W. Horsley 101, M. N. Hart 64, I. G. Hatwell 68, J. A. F. Yovich 65); **Canterbury 215** (P. G. Fulton 90, P. J. Wiseman 65; M. G. Orchard 5-10) **and 136-3** (S. L. Stewart 78). *Northern Districts 2 pts.*

At Basin Reserve, Wellington, February 26, 27, 28, 29, 2004. **Drawn.** Toss: Otago. **Wellington 482-9 dec.** (N. R. Parlane 62, C. J. Nevin 124*, M. D. J. Walker 126); **Otago 231-3** (C. D. Cumming 57, C. B. Gaffaney 69, R. A. Lawson 62*). *Wellington 1 pt, Otago 1 pt.*
Nevin and Walker added 250 in 253 minutes, a Wellington seventh-wicket record.

FINAL

WELLINGTON v CANTERBURY

At Basin Reserve, Wellington, March 4, 5, 6, 2004. Drawn. Wellington won the State Championship by virtue of heading the table. Toss: Wellington.

Canterbury had to win outright to take the title from Wellington, and were further set back when they lost the toss on a pitch with early life. The match looked over on the first morning, when Gillespie and Franklin routed six men for 27. But determined fifties from Harris and Ellis (his first) winched them to 192, and Wellington had their own problems when Martin reduced them to 62 for five. Walker came in at an uncomfortable 143 for seven, and helped add 158 for the last three wickets. The third day belonged to Papps, who just missed his fourth century of the season, and a 75-ball 64 from No. 10 Cunis enabled Harris to declare, setting a target of 227. Canterbury glimpsed the victory they needed when Wisneski claimed three wickets and Cunis made it 83 for five, but Bell, who had taken six catches, dug in, and Nevin and Walker ensured a championship-clinching draw.

Close of play: First day, Wellington 53-4 (Franklin 1, Gillespie 0); Second day, Wellington 288-9 (Walker 73, Turner 14); Third day, Canterbury 283-8 (Harris 18, Cunis 35).

Canterbury

M. H. W. Papps b Gillespie	0	– c Nevin b Walker	91
S. L. Stewart c Nevin b Franklin	0	– c Walker b Franklin	2
P. G. Fulton lbw b Gillespie	1	– c Bell b Walker	58
G. R. Stead c Nevin b Franklin	7	– (6) c Bell b Franklin	6
*C. Z. Harris c Bell b Turner	79	– (7) not out	38
†B. B. McCullum b Franklin	0	– (4) c Nevin b Gillespie	17
P. J. Wiseman b Turner	0	– (5) c Bell b Turner	7
A. M. Ellis lbw b Walker	65	– c Bell b Franklin	3
W. A. Wisneski c Nevin b Turner	4	– lbw b Franklin	33
S. J. Cunis c Bell b Gillespie	13	– not out	64
C. S. Martin not out	7		
B 5, l-b 10, n-b 1	16	B 2, l-b 6, w 5, n-b 3	16
	192	(8 wkts dec.)	**335**

1/0 (1) 2/2 (3) 3/2 (2) 4/25 (4) 5/26 (6) 6/27 (7) 7/151 (5) 8/171 (9) 9/171 (8) 10/192 (10)

1/12 (2) 2/119 (3) 3/155 (4) 4/174 (5) 5/188 (1) 6/190 (6) 7/196 (8) 8/239 (9)

Bowling: *First Innings*—Gillespie 17.2–8–52–3; Franklin 20–5–32–3; Turner 16–5–48–3; Walker 21–6–38–1; Woodcock 4–1–7–0. *Second Innings*—Gillespie 27–4–98–1; Franklin 24–4–75–4; Turner 25–2–84–1; Walker 26–3–70–2.

Wellington

*M. D. Bell run out	17	– c McCullum b Harris	57
R. A. Jones c McCullum b Wisneski	13	– c McCullum b Wisneski	8
G. T. Donaldson c Ellis b Martin	14	– c McCullum b Wisneski	0
J. E. C. Franklin b Martin	62	– lbw b Wisneski	4
N. R. Parlane c Ellis b Martin	4	– lbw b Cunis	11
M. R. Gillespie c Stead b Martin	7		
M. E. Parlane c McCullum b Wisneski	30	– (6) lbw b Cunis	0
†C. J. Nevin lbw b Ellis	1	– (7) not out	43
M. D. J. Walker not out	84	– (8) not out	29
L. J. Woodcock b Ellis	26		
A. D. Turner c McCullum b Martin	16		
L-b 9, w 11, n-b 7	27	B 15, l-b 12, w 2, n-b 1	30
	301		**182**

1/23 (2) 2/44 (1) 3/47 (3) 4/53 (5)   301   1/23 (2) 2/23 (3)   (6 wkts) 182
5/62 (6) 6/134 (7) 7/143 (8)   3/53 (4) 4/83 (5)
8/170 (4) 9/243 (10) 10/301 (11)   5/83 (6) 6/113 (1)

Bowling: *First Innings*—Martin 36–10–101–5; Wisneski 23–3–75–2; Wiseman 12–5–17–0; Cunis 14–5–39–0; Ellis 30–13–41–2; Harris 10–5–15–0; Stewart 4–2–4–0. *Second Innings*—Wisneski 25–8–54–3; Martin 19–6–24–0; Harris 10–5–11–1; Wiseman 17–9–19–0; Ellis 7–3–11–0; Cunis 12–1–36–2.

Umpires: D. M. Quested and E. A. Watkin.

CHAMPIONS

Plunket Shield					
1921-22	Auckland	1953-54	Central Districts	1980-81	Auckland
1922-23	Canterbury	1954-55	Wellington	1981-82	Wellington
1923-24	Wellington	1955-56	Canterbury	1982-83	Wellington
1924-25	Otago	1956-57	Wellington	1983-84	Canterbury
1925-26	Wellington	1957-58	Otago	1984-85	Wellington
1926-27	Auckland	1958-59	Auckland	1985-86	Otago
1927-28	Wellington	1959-60	Canterbury	1986-87	Central Districts
1928-29	Auckland	1960-61	Wellington	1987-88	Otago
1929-30	Wellington	1961-62	Wellington	1988-89	Auckland
1930-31	Canterbury	1962-63	Northern Districts	1989-90	Wellington
1931-32	Wellington	1963-64	Auckland	1990-91	Auckland
1932-33	Otago	1964-65	Canterbury	1991-92	{ Central Districts / Northern Districts
1933-34	Auckland	1965-66	Wellington		
1934-35	Canterbury	1966-67	Central Districts	1992-93	Northern Districts
1935-36	Wellington	1967-68	Central Districts	1993-94	Canterbury
1936-37	Auckland	1968-69	Auckland	1994-95	Auckland
1937-38	Auckland	1969-70	Otago	1995-96	Auckland
1938-39	Auckland	1970-71	Central Districts	1996-97	Canterbury
1939-40	Auckland	1971-72	Otago	1997-98	Canterbury
1940-45	No competition	1972-73	Wellington	1998-99	Central Districts
1945-46	Canterbury	1973-74	Wellington	1999-2000	Northern Districts
1946-47	Auckland	1974-75	Otago	2000-01	Wellington
1947-48	Otago				
1948-49	Canterbury	*Shell Trophy*		*State Championship*	
1949-50	Wellington	1975-76	Canterbury	2001-02	Auckland
1950-51	Otago	1976-77	Otago	2002-03	Auckland
1951-52	Canterbury	1977-78	Auckland	2003-04	Wellington
1952-53	Otago	1978-79	Otago		
		1979-80	Northern Districts		

Auckland and Wellington have won the title outright 20 times, Canterbury 14, Otago 13, Central Districts 6, Northern Districts 4. Central Districts and Northern Districts also shared the title once.

STATE SHIELD, 2003-04

Note: Matches in this section were not first-class.

	Played	Won	Lost	No result	Bonus points	Points	Net run-rate
Canterbury	10	6	2	2	2	30	0.50
Central Districts	10	5	2	3	1	27	0.31
Auckland	10	4	3	3	2	24	0.34
Wellington	10	4	4	2	1	21	−0.14
Otago.	10	4	5	1	0	18	−0.23
Northern Districts. . . .	10	1	8	1	0	6	−0.58

Play-off

At Pukekura Park, New Plymouth, February 3, 2004. **Central Districts won by three wickets.** Toss: Central Districts. **Auckland 107** (39.5 overs); **Central Districts 108-7** (20.1 overs) (R. T. Taylor 56).

Final

At Lancaster Park, Christchurch, February 6, 2004. **Central Districts won by 99 runs.** Toss: Canterbury. **Central Districts 354-5** (50 overs) (C. M. Spearman 85, J. M. How 92, R. L. Taylor 95); **Canterbury 255** (41.2 overs) (P. G. Fulton 59, P. J. Wiseman 51).

Spearman hit ten fours and five sixes in 48 balls; he and How put on 155 in 17.1 overs, including 30 runs off the 14th over, bowled by Wiseman.

CRICKET IN INDIA, 2003-04

R. MOHAN AND MOHANDAS MENON

Dheeraj Jadhav

In a season in which Team India were making waves and surprising critics, pundits and even bookmakers with their performances in Australia and on a ground-breaking visit to Pakistan, a quieter revolution was also being ushered in. This regenerated the domestic game after years when it has been overwhelmed by the rush to grab cash from international cricket.

The Ranji Trophy had been reformed a year earlier. In 2003-04 the Duleep Trophy, supposedly a step up from the Ranji towards Test cricket, was finally given a lift. It had undergone many sporadic revisions over the years without really getting anywhere: it was at its desultory worst as a five-team league, with ten four-day matches in some corner of the country where players, officials and caterers were just about the only people present. The previous season, the traditional regional teams had been replaced by three drawn from the Ranji's Elite division and two from the Plate, but the structure was unchanged.

Switching to two mini-leagues followed by a final, and inviting England A to join the reinstated regional sides, gave the tournament the kiss of life. This was the first time a foreign side had taken part, though in 1962-63 four West Indian fast bowlers had been imported and each attached to a team to broaden the Indians' experience. There was a further boost when the national selectors demanded Yuvraj Singh play in the Duleep final to prove his fitness; he made a century in each innings and was recalled for the Pakistan tour, where he scored a memorable Test hundred.

In the endless debate over how much cricket is too much, India's stars have invariably taken the easy route and stayed away from domestic cricket. But this season was well planned. September was set aside for the limited-overs Challenger Series and the Irani Cup, and the board made the international players take part as preparation for fixtures with New Zealand and Australia. The Ranji group games occupied November and December, the Duleep Trophy started in February and the Ranji knockout provided a ceremonial end in March.

Another major reform by the board was increasing exponentially domestic players' pay. In the past, most had played in the hope of finding fame and fortune with the national team. They were paid by their state associations; the poorest of these could offer as little as Rs500 (about £6) per match. A few associations had sponsors, and could pay up to Rs10,000 (£120). The board is now paying players a fee for each Ranji or Duleep game, expected to be up to Rs35,000 (£420) in 2004-05, with a proportion going into a benevolent fund. It is a huge leap for some cricketers, though those with more successful sides like Mumbai or Tamil Nadu may see less of a difference.

Mumbai and Tamil Nadu were the Ranji finalists for the second year running, but the quality of cricket in their encounter gave the lie to those who believe the national selectors have an embarrassment of riches to pick from. Mumbai pulled above their weight to claim their 36th title. With their top players touring Pakistan, the team consisted mostly of has-beens and a few wannabes; their triumph came through team-oriented cricket. Tamil Nadu were younger, but with less new talent,

The stakes have risen in Indian cricket

and their irresponsible first-day batting wasted the advantage of the toss on a true pitch. Mumbai made no such error, building a massive first-innings lead to retain the Trophy, although Tamil Nadu did hang on for a draw. The selectors in attendance may have concluded that the cream they have chosen for India faces very little competition.

Back in September, Mumbai had also taken first-innings lead in the Irani Cup match, but came a cropper as Rahul Dravid and V. V. S. Laxman guided Rest of India to a tricky target. But Mumbai did set up a double by winning the one-day competition for Ranji teams, heading a five-team super league, recently added to rekindle interest. The games did not draw the kind of crowds generated by Twenty20 in England, nor did they rouse the partisan emotions associated with Indian cricket.

Another western team, Maharashtra, won the Plate final, thanks to 251 from Dheeraj Jadhav. This match, too, looked like being settled on first innings, until the Madhya Pradesh leg-spinner Yogesh Golwalkar woke things up with five wickets – only for his side to be bowled out on the last day.

North Zone won all their three matches in the new-look Duleep Trophy: the highlight was the dazzling display by Yuvraj in the final with East Zone. The visitors, England A, lost both their games. The South African migrant Kevin Pietersen did his prospects of a future international career no harm, scoring twin centuries against South Zone to set a target of 501. But his team's reputation was dented when South got home with six wickets in hand, to the fury of coach Rod Marsh. The A-team's sojourn was never dull. Indeed, they may have been surprised at the aggressively vocal behaviour of some opponents – a sign of how much the stakes have risen in Indian cricket.

East Zone made up for losing a close Duleep final by annexing the one-day Deodhar Trophy with 18 points – twice as many as the closest challengers, West and South – and India A won the Challenger Series back in September. To spread the talent under scrutiny, the board had demanded three balanced teams, rather than allowing Indian Seniors to dominate. It was India B, captained by Dravid, who headed the league, beating the Seniors, led by Test captain Sourav Ganguly, and India A. But in the final, India A, led by an enthusiastic Anil Kumble, proved the importance of batting first in friendly conditions and piling on a total.

In a season of many positives, the case of Abhijit Kale of Maharashtra, accused of offering cash for a spot in India's squad in Australia, was a discordant note. The hearings dragged through the season, with fears that another instance of corruption might be the tip of an iceberg. Finally, with "cogent proof" that Kale had tried to influence two selectors, though the evidence that this involved money was not conclusive, he was suspended until the end of 2004.

Kale had already missed the 2003-04 season during the investigation, and his absence paid extraordinary dividends for another Maharashtra batsman, the opener Jadhav. His career previously amounted to 386 runs in 11 matches over four seasons, with one fifty. Called on to fill the gap, he responded with 1,066 Ranji runs, including three double-hundreds, and 1,245 in all at 103.75. A patient left-hander, Jadhav made up in temperament what he lacked in style, but at 24 was not considered much of an international prospect. The leading wicket-takers were two leg-spinners, Mumbai captain Sairaj Bahutule and Narendra Hirwani of Madhya Pradesh, with 52 wickets each. That the 35-year-old Hirwani – who first played for India in 1987-88 – remained so successful on the national circuit may be a comment on the state of spin bowling in the land.

FIRST-CLASS AVERAGES, 2003-04

BATTING

(Qualification: 600 runs, average 40.00)

	M	I	NO	R	HS	100s	Avge	Ct/St
†D. S. Jadhav (*Maharashtra & West Zone*)....	9	15	3	1,245	251	5	103.75	10
†H. H. Kanitkar (*Maharashtra & West Zone*)..	9	13	2	935	207*	4	85.00	7
S. V. Saravanan (*Assam*)................	6	11	3	604	123	2	75.50	2
†Yuvraj Singh (*Punjab, North Zone & India*)..	8	12	2	698	148	3	69.80	7
Y. Venugopal Rao (*Andhra & South Zone*)....	9	14	2	785	228*	3	65.41	10
D. S. Bundela (*Madhya Pradesh & Central Z.*).	9	15	3	782	167*	2	65.16	8
V. R. Mane (*Mumbai & West Zone*)	11	17	3	832	154	3	59.42	14
B. M. Rowland (*Karnataka & South Zone*)....	8	15	3	710	210	3	59.16	8
†G. Gambhir (*Delhi, North Zone & India A*) ..	10	16	1	877	147	4	58.46	9
A. A. Muzumdar (*Mumbai*)..............	9	12	1	643	146	2	58.45	3
Wasim Jaffer (*Mumbai*)	10	15	3	684	143	3	57.00	24
A. A. Christian (*Gujarat*)	6	11	0	611	112	3	55.54	2
S. Badrinath (*Tamil Nadu & South Zone*).....	10	18	3	822	190	4	54.80	5
†D. Mongia (*Punjab & North Zone*)	9	12	0	632	185	2	52.66	12
N. V. Ojha (*Madhya Pradesh & Central Zone*) .	8	14	0	695	79	0	49.64	16/5
†T. P. Singh (*Railways*)...............	8	15	1	675	168	2	48.21	4
†V. G. Kambli (*Mumbai*)................	10	13	0	613	114	3	47.15	2
S. S. Das (*Orissa, East Zone & India A*)	10	16	2	650	124*	3	46.42	4
J. J. Martin (*Baroda & West Zone*)	9	16	2	616	149	1	44.00	5
†S. Sriram (*Tamil Nadu, South Z. & India A*)..	11	17	0	692	172	2	40.70	9

† *Left-handed batsman.*

BOWLING

(Qualification: 25 wickets)

	Style	O	M	R	W	BB	5W/i	Avge
S. O. Mathur (*Rajasthan*)	RFM	178.2	46	484	30	6-52	3	16.13
F. Mohammad (*Services*)	RFM	191.2	51	471	28	5-58	3	16.82
Gagandeep Singh (*Punjab & North Zone*)	RFM	334.1	102	831	45	5-11	5	18.46
S. V. Bahutule (*Mumbai & West Zone*) . . .	LB	422.1	113	971	52	6-48	3	18.67
D. S. Mohanty (*Orissa & East Zone*)	RM	294.4	85	643	34	5-24	2	18.91
S. S. Paul (*Bengal & East Zone*)	RM	348.4	93	979	50	7-44	6	19.58
N. D. Hirwani (*Madhya Pradesh &*								
Central Zone)	LBG	464.4	101	1,063	52	7-66	2	20.44
D. Ganesh (*Karnataka*)	RM	252.5	45	745	36	6-91	3	20.69
A. W. Zaidi (*Uttar Pradesh*)	RFM	235	55	575	27	4-36	0	21.29
A. Bhandari (*Delhi, North Z. & India A*) .	RFM	322.3	69	918	42	6-55	2	21.85
S. K. Trivedi (*Gujarat, West Z. & India A*)	RM	213	44	590	26	4-23	0	22.69
Harvinder Singh (*Railways & Central Z.*) .	RFM	318	83	790	34	5-40	2	23.23
P. P. Gupta (*Uttar Pradesh*)	SLA	265.4	70	629	27	5-143	1	23.29
R. D. Khirid (*Maharashtra*)	RM	238	70	589	25	7-45	1	23.56
N. P. Singh (*Hyderabad & South Zone*) . .	RM	265.1	78	693	29	6-31	3	23.89
Sunil B. Joshi (*Karnataka & South Zone*).	SLA	418.4	122	1,001	41	6-59	2	24.41
K. S. Sahabuddin (*Andhra*)	RFM	260.3	75	612	25	5-52	3	24.48
R. Ramkumar (*Tamil Nadu & South Zone*)	SLA	381.1	106	891	36	6-62	2	24.75
Joginder Sharma (*Haryana & North Zone*)	RFM	300.5	74	804	32	6-49	1	25.12
M. M. Patel (*Mumbai, West Z. & India A*)	RFM	281.4	61	834	33	4-70	0	25.27
N. M. Kulkarni (*Mumbai & West Zone*) . .	SLA	364.3	85	740	29	6-83	1	25.51
Y. A. Golwalkar (*Madhya Pradesh*)	LB	272.1	68	665	25	6-95	2	26.60
R. B. Patel (*Baroda & West Zone*)	RFM	357	80	1,021	36	5-54	2	28.36
R. R. Powar (*Mumbai, West Z. & India A*)	OB	373.4	80	994	35	4-16	0	28.40
Sarandeep Singh (*Delhi & North Zone*) . .	OB	365.1	75	859	29	5-64	2	29.62
I. R. Siddiqui (*Maharashtra*)	RFM	250.2	57	751	25	5-65	2	30.04
K. S. Parida (*Railways & Central Zone*) . .	OB	402.1	97	961	31	5-27	2	31.00
U. Chatterjee (*Bengal & East Zone*)	SLA	362.2	102	836	26	8-54	1	32.15

IRANI CUP, 2003-04

Ranji Trophy Champions (Mumbai) v Rest of India

At M. A. Chidambaram Stadium, Chennai, September 18, 19, 20, 21, 2003. **Rest of India won by three wickets.** Toss: Rest of India. **Mumbai 297** (S. R. Tendulkar 94, S. V. Bahutule 58; Zaheer Khan 5-77) **and 244** (S. R. Tendulkar 50, R. R. Powar 57; Harbhajan Singh 4-79); **Rest of India 202** (R. R. Powar 4-61) **and 340-7** (R. Dravid 121, V. V. S. Laxman 99).

Rest of India were set 340 in just over two days. Dravid, who batted nearly seven hours, and Laxman took them to 291-3 before they lost four wickets in 34 balls, but their captain, Sourav Ganguly, steered them home with more than a day to spare.

RANJI TROPHY, 2003-04

Elite Group A	Played	Won	Lost	Drawn	1st-inns Points	Bonus Points	Points
Mumbai	7	3	0	4	8	2	22
Railways.	7	3	0	4	2	0	14
Uttar Pradesh	7	2	1	4	4	1	13
Punjab	7	1	0	6	6	1	11
Andhra.	7	1	1	5	2	0	6
Delhi	7	0	2	5	6	0	6
Baroda	7	0	4	3	4	0	4
Kerala	7	0	2	5	2	0	2

Elite Group B	Played	Won	Lost	Drawn	1st-inns Points	Bonus Points	Points
Tamil Nadu.........	6	3	0	3	2	1	15
Hyderabad	6	3	1	2	2	1	15
Karnataka..........	6	3	2	1	2	1	15
Bengal............	6	1	1	4	4	1	9
Gujarat............	6	2	2	2	0	0	8
Assam............	6	1	3	2	2	0	6
Rajasthan..........	6	1	5	0	0	0	4

Hyderabad qualified for the semi-finals ahead of Karnataka because of a better run-quotient.

Semi-finals

Mumbai beat Hyderabad by an innings and 152 runs; Tamil Nadu drew with Railways but qualified for the final by virtue of their first-innings lead.

Final

Mumbai drew with Tamil Nadu but won the Ranji Trophy by virtue of their first-innings lead.

Plate Group A	Played	Won	Lost	Drawn	1st-inns Points	Bonus Points	Points
Madhya Pradesh......	5	2	0	3	4	0	12
Haryana............	5	1	1	3	4	0	8
Vidarbha	5	1	1	3	2	1	7
Bihar.............	5	1	2	2	2	0	6
Jammu and Kashmir...	5	1	2	2	0	0	4
Tripura............	5	0	0	5	4	0	4

Plate Group B	Played	Won	Lost	Drawn	1st-inns Points	Bonus Points	Points
Maharashtra	5	2	0	3	4	2	14
Orissa	5	2	0	3	4	1	13
Services	5	1	1	3	2	0	6
Goa...............	5	1	3	1	2	0	6
Saurashtra..........	5	1	1	3	0	0	4
Himachal Pradesh	5	1	3	1	0	0	4

Semi-finals

Maharashtra beat Haryana by ten wickets; Madhya Pradesh beat Orissa by five wickets.

Final

Maharashtra beat Madhya Pradesh by 40 runs.

Maharashtra and Madhya Pradesh were promoted to the Elite Groups, replacing Kerala and Rajasthan.

Outright win = 4 pts; lead on first innings in a drawn match = 2 pts; win by an innings or ten wickets = 1 bonus pt.

Elite Group A

At Fort Maidan, Palakkad, November 7, 8, 9, 10, 2003. **Drawn.** Toss: Punjab. **Punjab 541-7 dec.** (R. S. Ricky 125, D. Mongia 151, R. S. Sodhi 57, C. Madan 67); **Kerala 344** (C. Hemanth Kumar 61, S. C. Oasis 82, A. N. Kudva 53; D. Mongia 4-34) **and 131-2.** *Punjab 2 pts.*
    Fort Maidan was a new first-class venue in Palakkad (formerly Palghat).

At Wankhede Stadium, Mumbai, November 7, 8, 9, 10, 2003. **Mumbai won by five wickets.** Toss: Mumbai. **Baroda 213** (N. R. Mongia 74; A. M. Salvi 5-42) **and 270** (C. C. Williams 50, S. S. Parab 121; A. M. Salvi 4-61, N. M. Kulkarni 4-69); **Mumbai 324** (V. R. Mane 50, V. G. Kambli 114, R. F. Morris 51; Shekhar B. Joshi 4-81) **and 160-5** (Wasim Jaffer 86*). *Mumbai 4 pts.*

At Karnail Singh Stadium, Delhi, November 7, 8, 9, 10, 2003. **Drawn.** Toss: Andhra. **Andhra 262** (M. S. K. Prasad 61, G. Shankar Rao 53) **and 337-7** (M. S. K. Prasad 58*, G. Shankar Rao 53*; Harvinder Singh 4-76); **Railways 441-8 dec.** (A. A. Pagnis 58, S. B. Bangar 116, T. P. Singh 77, Siddharth Verma 79*; G. Shankar Rao 4-96). *Railways 2 pts.*

At Modi Stadium, Green Park, Kanpur, November 7, 8, 9, 10, 2003. **Drawn.** Toss: Delhi. **Delhi 478** (S. Oberoi 80, G. Gambhir 147, M. Manhas 56, Sarandeep Singh 51*; P. P. Gupta 5-143); **Uttar Pradesh 243** (G. K. Pandey 84) **and 141-1** (Jyoti P. Yadav 79*). *Delhi 2 pts.*
Former Test player Ajay Jadeja, banned for five years from December 2000 over match-fixing, made his debut for Delhi after an arbitrator ruled he should be allowed to play domestic first-class cricket.

At Alembic Ground, Vadodara, November 15, 16, 17, 2003. **Andhra won by seven wickets.** Toss: Andhra. **Baroda 216** (S. A. Gaekwad 68) **and 105; Andhra 230** (Y. Venugopal Rao 76; R. B. Patel 5-54) **and 92-3.** *Andhra 4 pts.*
Shatrunjay Gaekwad, whose father Anshuman and grandfather Datta both played for India, scored 68 on first-class debut.

At Jamia Millia Cricket Ground, Delhi, November 15, 16, 17, 18, 2003. **Mumbai won by ten wickets.** Toss: Delhi. **Delhi 199** (G. Gambhir 96; N. M. Kulkarni 4-62, S. V. Bahutule 5-45) **and 224** (G. Gambhir 105; N. M. Kulkarni 4-76, S. V. Bahutule 4-77); **Mumbai 239** (V. R. Mane 52, B. J. Thakkar 71*; Sarandeep Singh 5-107, R. L. Sanghvi 4-72) **and 185-0** (V. R. Mane 63*, Wasim Jaffer 117*). *Mumbai 5 pts.*
Jamia Millia was a new first-class venue.

At Fort Maidan, Palakkad, November 15, 16, 17, 18, 2003. **Drawn.** Toss: Railways. **Railways 295** (S. N. Khanolkar 72; K. N. A. Padmanabhan 4-46) **and 320** (S. B. Bangar 86, T. P. Singh 50, Harvinder Singh 50; K. N. A. Padmanabhan 7-104); **Kerala 321** (C. Hemanth Kumar 131, S. R. Nair 69, M. Suresh Kumar 56*; Harvinder Singh 5-57, M. S. Yadav 5-101) **and 142-3** (A. N. Kudva 50*, S. C. Oasis 53*). *Kerala 2 pts.*
Slow left-armer Madan Yadav took 5-101 on first-class debut.

At Bhamashah Stadium, Meerut, November 15, 16, 17, 18, 2003. **Drawn.** Toss: Uttar Pradesh. **Uttar Pradesh 471** (R. P. Srivastava 186, Jyoti P. Yadav 72, R. Shamshad 65, G. K. Pandey 65*; Gagandeep Singh 4-97, R. Sharma 4-97) **and 32-0; Punjab 441** (R. S. Ricky 115, D. Mongia 185; A. W. Zaidi 4-88). *Uttar Pradesh 2 pts.*
Bhamashah was a new first-class venue. In their first innings, Punjab were 1-2 before Ricky and Mongia added 284 for the third wicket, the highest stand for any wicket in the 2003-04 Ranji Trophy.

At Trishna Stadium, Visakhapatnam, November 23, 24, 25, 26, 2003. **Drawn.** Toss: Andhra. **Andhra 458-7 dec.** (Y. Venugopal Rao 115, I. G. Srinivas 116, R. V. C. Prasad 82*, Extras 51; S. C. Oasis 4-61); **Kerala 354** (C. Hemanth Kumar 94, S. C. Oasis 51; K. S. Sahabuddin 4-94, G. Shankar Rao 4-54). *Andhra 2 pts.*

At IPCL Sports Complex Ground, Vadodara, November 23, 24, 25, 26, 2003. **Drawn.** Toss: Baroda. **Baroda 369** (R. A. Parab 54, J. J. Martin 149) **and 247-6** (R. A. Parab 56, S. A. Gaekwad 72*); **Punjab 334** (D. Mongia 60, P. Dharmani 98, R. S. Sodhi 66; R. B. Patel 5-98). *Baroda 2 pts.*
Baroda wicket-keeper Nayan Mongia made six catches in Punjab's first innings.

At Karnail Singh Stadium, Delhi, November 23, 24, 25, 26, 2003. **Railways won by three wickets.** Toss: Railways. **Delhi 195** (M. Manhas 62) **and 278** (V. Dahiya 61, P. Chawla 82; Harvinder Singh 4-58); **Railways 234 and 244-7** (Jai P. Yadav 101). *Railways 4 pts.*

At K. D. Singh Babu Stadium, Lucknow, November 23, 24, 25, 26, 2003. **Drawn.** Toss: Uttar Pradesh. **Uttar Pradesh 205** (G. K. Pandey 77*) **and 205-7** (S. Raina 50; S. V. Bahutule 6-48); **Mumbai 332** (B. J. Thakkar 71, R. F. Morris 93*; P. P. Gupta 4-79). *Mumbai 2 pts.*

At Indira Gandhi Stadium, Vijayawada, December 1, 2, 3, 4, 2003. **Drawn.** Toss: Mumbai. **Mumbai 504-6 dec.** (Wasim Jaffer 143, A. A. Muzumdar 115, V. G. Kambli 86) **and 25-0; Andhra 298** (M. S. K. Prasad 72). *Mumbai 2 pts.*

At IPCL Sports Complex Ground, Vadodara, December 1, 2, 3, 4, 2003. **Drawn.** Toss: Kerala. **Kerala 231** (C. Hemanth Kumar 66; R. B. Patel 4-85, T. B. Arothe 4-50) **and 337-9 dec.** (S. Somasunder 93, C. M. Deepak 53, S. R. Nair 86); **Baroda 411** (R. A. Parab 104, R. B. Patel 67). *Baroda 2 pts.*

At PCA Stadium, Mohali, December 1, 2, 3, 4, 2003. **Drawn.** Toss: Punjab. **Delhi 310** (M. Manhas 129, Varun Kumar 50; Gagandeep Singh 5-55) **and 264-5** (R. Bhatia 75, A. Jadeja 54*); **Punjab 385** (Yuvraj Singh 138, P. Dharmani 79; S. Gill 4-109, N. S. Negi 4-87). *Punjab 2 pts.*

At Dr Sampurnanda Stadium, Varanasi, December 1, 2, 3, 2003. **Railways won by 152 runs.** Toss: Railways. **Railways 137** (S. B. Bangar 51; A. W. Zaidi 4-36) **and 208; Uttar Pradesh 71** (K. S. Parida 5-27) **and 122** (K. S. Parida 5-47). *Railways 4 pts.*

At IPCL Sports Complex Ground, Vadodara, December 9, 10, 11, 12, 2003. **Drawn.** Toss: Baroda. **Delhi 510-7 dec.** (G. Gambhir 52, M. Manhas 57, A. Jadeja 206*); **Baroda 223** (J. J. Martin 92; A. Bhandari 4-57) **and 286-3** (S. S. Parab 126, R. K. Solanki 65, J. J. Martin 69*). *Delhi 2 pts.*
Jadeja's 206, his seventh double-hundred, lasted 505 minutes and 383 balls and included 23 fours and two sixes.*

At Wankhede Stadium, Mumbai, December 9, 10, 11, 2003. **Mumbai won by an innings and 91 runs.** Toss: Kerala. **Kerala 165 and 94** (R. R. Powar 4-16); **Mumbai 350** (A. A. Muzumdar 85, V. G. Kambli 102; P. Chandran 7-71). *Mumbai 5 pts.*
For Mumbai, Wasim Jaffer made six catches in the match.

At Karnail Singh Stadium, Delhi, December 9, 10, 11, 12, 2003. **Drawn.** Toss: Railways. **Railways 390** (S. B. Bangar 79, T. P. Singh 168; Gagandeep Singh 5-61) **and 114-4** (A. A. Pagnis 51*); **Punjab 472** (Yuvraj Singh 80, A. Kakkar 124*, Gagandeep Singh 50; Jai P. Yadav 5-82). *Punjab 2 pts.*
Kakkar and Gagandeep Singh added 104 for Punjab's eighth wicket.

At Modi Stadium, Green Park, Kanpur, December 9, 10, 11, 12, 2003. **Drawn.** Toss: Uttar Pradesh. **Uttar Pradesh 267** (S. Raina 106, G. K. Pandey 97; K. S. Sahabuddin 5-67) **and 223** (S. Raina 79; K. S. Sahabuddin 5-72); **Andhra 237** (Y. Ganeswara Rao 111; A. W. Zaidi 4-92) **and 129-6.** *Uttar Pradesh 2 pts.*

At IPCL Sports Complex Ground, Vadodara, December 17, 18, 19, 20, 2003. **Uttar Pradesh won by an innings and seven runs.** Toss: Uttar Pradesh. **Uttar Pradesh 473** (S. Raina 66, R. Shamshad 168, Extras 51); **Baroda 249** (N. R. Mongia 85; A. W. Zaidi 4-75) **and 217** (N. R. Mongia 88*; N. Chopra 4-75). *Uttar Pradesh 5 pts.*

At Harbax Singh Stadium, Delhi, December 17, 18, 19, 20, 2003. **Drawn.** Toss: Delhi. **Kerala 371** (A. N. Kudva 123, S. C. Oasis 63*; Sarandeep Singh 4-83, R. L. Sanghvi 4-83); **Delhi 375-6** (G. Gambhir 78, R. Bhatia 104, A. Jadeja 60). *Delhi 2 pts.*

At Wankhede Stadium, Mumbai, December 17, 18, 19, 20, 2003. **Drawn.** Toss: Railways. **Mumbai 388** (A. A. Muzumdar 95, R. R. Powar 131) **and 168** (V. G. Kambli 64; Jai P. Yadav 4-41); **Railways 198** (R. R. Powar 4-69) **and 121-4** (Raja Ali 58*). *Mumbai 2 pts.*

At PCA Stadium, Mohali, December 17, 18, 2003. **Punjab won by an innings and 95 runs.** Toss: Punjab. **Andhra 30** (Gagandeep Singh 5-11, Vineet Sharma 5-3) **and 84** (Gagandeep Singh 5-32, Vineet Sharma 4-32); **Punjab 209** (K. S. Sahabuddin 5-52). *Punjab 5 pts.*

Andhra's first innings lasted 17.4 overs, and only Yalaka Ganeswara Rao (11) reached double figures. The highest score of the match was 39 by Punjab's Pankaj Dharmani.

At IPCL Sports Complex Ground, Vadodara, December 25, 26, 27, 28, 2003. **Railways won by 57 runs.** Toss: Railways. **Railways 353** (T. P. Singh 114, Y. K. T. Goud 54; R. B. Patel 4-40) **and 103; Baroda 217** (A. P. Bhoite 55; Harvinder Singh 5-40) **and 182** (S. N. Khanolkar 5-21). *Railways 4 pts.*

At Fort Maidan, Palakkad, December 25, 26, 27, 28, 2003. **Uttar Pradesh won by 90 runs.** Toss: Uttar Pradesh. **Uttar Pradesh 214** (S. Raina 74; S. R. Nair 4-43) **and 255** (R. P. Srivastava 79, R. B. Elahi 74*); **Kerala 247** (S. Somasunder 66; N. Chopra 4-69) **and 132.** *Uttar Pradesh 4 pts.*

At PCA Stadium, Mohali, December 25, 26, 27, 28, 2003. **Drawn.** Toss: Punjab. **Mumbai 224** (A. A. Muzumdar 55, R. F. Morris 81; Gagandeep Singh 5-68) **and 181-4** (V. R. Mane 60, B. J. Thakkar 50); **Punjab 153** (A. Uniyal 56*; U. R. Malvi 4-55, S. P. Hazare 5-45). *Mumbai 2 pts.*

At ACA-VDCA Stadium, Visakhapatnam, December 26, 27, 28, 29, 2003. **Drawn.** Toss: Andhra. **Andhra 438** (Y. Venugopal Rao 142, M. S. K. Prasad 71, Y. Ganeswara Rao 53, R. V. C. Prasad 54*; S. Gill 4-87); **Delhi 386-7** (V. Dahiya 93, Varun Kumar 75).

The Andhra Cricket Association–Visakhapatnam District Cricket Association Stadium had staged only one previous first-class match, between the Board President's XI and the New Zealanders in September. This game started a day late because the Delhi team could not arrive in time.

Elite Group B

At Sardar Patel (Gujarat) Stadium, Ahmedabad, November 7, 8, 9, 10, 2003. **Hyderabad won by 150 runs.** Toss: Hyderabad. **Hyderabad 245** (D. Vinay Kumar 76; L. A. Patel 5-58) **and 185** (S. K. Trivedi 4-45); **Gujarat 129** (N. P. Singh 6-33) **and 151** (S. Vishnuvardhan 4-44, S. L. V. Raju 4-15). *Hyderabad 4 pts.*

At Indian Air Force Ground, Bangalore, November 7, 8, 9, 10, 2003. **Tamil Nadu won by four wickets.** Toss: Karnataka. **Karnataka 208** (L. Balaji 4-51, R. Ramkumar 4-42) **and 235** (S. T. R. Binny 54; R. Ramkumar 6-62); **Tamil Nadu 184** (B. K. V. Prasad 6-51) **and 261-6** (S. Sharath 57). *Tamil Nadu 4 pts.*

The Air Force Ground was a new first-class venue. Ramkumar took a hat-trick to finish Karnataka's first innings.

At K. L. Saini Ground, Jaipur, November 7, 8, 9, 10, 2003. **Rajasthan won by 152 runs.** Toss: Bengal. **Rajasthan 253** (G. K. Khoda 86; S. S. Paul 6-68) **and 268-5 dec.** (V. A. Saxena 59, R. B. Jhalani 85, A. S. Jain 53*); **Bengal 118** (Sanjeev Sharma 6-18) **and 251** (R. S. Gavaskar 96, S. C. Sanyal 60; Shamsher Singh 4-52). *Rajasthan 4 pts.*

At Nehru Stadium, Guwahati, November 15, 16, 17, 18, 2003. **Gujarat won by seven wickets.** Toss: Assam. **Assam 180** (S. B. Saikia 56, S. V. Saravanan 58; H. A. Majmudar 5-47) **and 312-3 dec.** (K. R. Powar 108, S. V. Saravanan 100*); **Gujarat 234** (A. A. Christian 73) **and 260-3** (A. A. Christian 104, N. K. Patel 55). *Gujarat 4 pts.*

At PET Cricket Stadium, Mandya, November 15, 16, 17, 18, 2003. **Drawn.** Toss: Karnataka. **Karnataka 411** (J. Arun Kumar 63, B. M. Rowland 151, V. S. T. Naidu 71; S. S. Paul 6-90); **Bengal 228** (L. R. Shukla 86; D. Ganesh 4-54) **and 318-7** (A. P. Chakraborty 56, N. L. Haldipur 66, R. S. Gavaskar 64*, L. R. Shukla 87; D. Ganesh 4-74). *Karnataka 2 pts.*

The People's Education Trust Cricket Stadium was a new first-class venue.

At K. L. Saini Ground, Jaipur, November 15, 16, 2003. **Tamil Nadu won by an innings and nine runs.** Toss: Tamil Nadu. **Rajasthan 97** (R. Ramkumar 4-41) **and 107** (L. Balaji 7-42); **Tamil Nadu 213.** *Tamil Nadu 5 pts.*

At North-East Frontier Railway Stadium, Guwahati, November 23, 24, 25, 26, 2003. **Drawn.** Toss: Assam. **Assam 537-9 dec.** (P. K. Das 71, S. V. Saravanan 89, S. Z. Zuffri 53, R. Sathish 133*, Sukhvinder Singh 112; J. S. Yadav 5-140); **Hyderabad 410-9** (Anirudh Singh 68, D. Vinay Kumar 53, A. S. Yadav 91, I. Khaleel 89; A. Konwar 6-141).

At K. L. Saini Ground, Jaipur, November 23, 24, 25, 26, 2003. **Karnataka won by 69 runs.** Toss: Rajasthan. **Karnataka 145 and 350** (J. Arun Kumar 58, B. M. Rowland 81, R. V. Bharadwaj 50; S. O. Mathur 4-64); **Rajasthan 168** (G. K. Khoda 61, R. J. Kanwat 54; B. K. V. Prasad 4-51, D. Ganesh 5-72) **and 258** (P. R. Gupta 58, R. J. Kanwat 84; D. Ganesh 6-91). *Karnataka 4 pts.*

At Indian Cement Company Ground, Tirunelveli, November 23, 24, 25, 26, 2003. **Drawn.** Toss: Bengal. **Bengal 400** (A. P. Chakraborty 58, N. L. Haldipur 100, S. C. Sanyal 89); **Tamil Nadu 188** (S. Badrinath 86; S. S. Paul 7-44) **and 397-4** (S. Badrinath 190, S. Sharath 101*). *Bengal 2 pts.*

At Eden Gardens, Kolkata, December 1, 2, 3, 4, 2003. **Drawn.** Toss: Assam. **Bengal 246** (N. L. Haldipur 67, L. R. Shukla 82) **and 250; Assam 347** (S. V. Saravanan 123, Sukhvinder Singh 115*; S. S. Paul 5-106) **and 130-4** (R. Sathish 74). *Assam 2 pts.*

At Sardar Patel (Gujarat) Stadium, Ahmedabad, December 1, 2, 3, 4, 2003. **Drawn.** Toss: Tamil Nadu. **Tamil Nadu 372** (S. Sharath 155, V. Sivaramakrishnan 50; S. G. Bhatt 4-93) **and 208-5** (S. S. Viswanathan 56*, V. Sivaramakrishnan 68, S. Ganesh Kumar 55*); **Gujarat 323** (A. A. Christian 112, M. H. Parmar 82, T. K. Patel 51; R. Ramkumar 5-66). *Tamil Nadu 2 pts.*

At Gymkhana Ground, Secunderabad, December 1, 2, 3, 2003. **Hyderabad won by 297 runs.** Toss: Hyderabad. **Hyderabad 177** (D. Vinay Kumar 65) **and 309** (D. S. Manohar 57, I. Khaleel 72*); **Karnataka 100** (N. P. Singh 6-31) **and 89** (M. Faiz Ahmed 6-29). *Hyderabad 4 pts.*

At Eden Gardens, Kolkata, December 9, 10, 11, 12, 2003. **Bengal won by an innings and one run.** Toss: Hyderabad. **Hyderabad 252** (I. Khaleel 66; U. Chatterjee 8-54) **and 135** (S. S. Lahiri 4-26); **Bengal 388** (A. S. Das 91, S. C. Sanyal 59; J. S. Yadav 5-124). *Bengal 5 pts.*
   Chatterjee's 8-54 was the best innings return of the Indian season.

At K. L. Saini Ground, Jaipur, December 9, 10, 11, 12, 2003. **Gujarat won by six wickets.** Toss: Gujarat. **Rajasthan 259** (V. A. Saxena 80, R. J. Kanwat 65; L. A. Patel 4-55) **and 110; Gujarat 196** (A. A. Christian 56; S. O. Mathur 6-52) **and 176-4** (N. K. Patel 77*). *Gujarat 4 pts.*

At M. A. Chidambaram Stadium, Chennai, December 9, 10, 11, 12, 2003. **Tamil Nadu won by 269 runs.** Toss: Assam. **Tamil Nadu 310** (K. D. Karthik 71, V. Sivaramakrishnan 53, R. Ramkumar 73) **and 277-6 dec.** (S. Suresh 73, S. Badrinath 115*); **Assam 134** (R. Ramkumar 4-24) **and 184** (S. V. Saravanan 62; D. T. Kumaran 5-57). *Tamil Nadu 4 pts.*
   Medium-pacer Tamil Kumaran took 5-57 on first-class debut.

At Nehru Stadium, Guwahati, December 17, 18, 19, 20, 2003. **Assam won by seven wickets.** Toss: Rajasthan. **Rajasthan 288** (A. P. K. Sharma 92) **and 115** (R. Raghuram 5-25); **Assam 306** (P. K. Das 50, R. Sathish 108*, Extras 61; S. O. Mathur 5-36) **and 102-3** (S. V. Saravanan 52*). *Assam 4 pts.*
   The 61 extras in Assam's first innings included five penalty runs when Rajasthan sent on a substitute without the umpires' permission.

At Sardar Patel (Gujarat) Stadium, Ahmedabad, December 17, 18, 19, 20, 2003. **Karnataka won by ten wickets.** Toss: Gujarat. **Gujarat 210** (B. D. Thaker 50; D. Ganesh 5-61) **and 172** (N. D. Modi 63; Sunil B. Joshi 6-59, U. B. Patel 4-53); **Karnataka 353** (B. M. Rowland 150; S. K. Trivedi 4-89) **and 30-0.** *Karnataka 5 pts.*

At Gymkhana Ground, Secunderabad, December 17, 18, 19, 20, 2003. **Drawn.** Toss: Tamil Nadu. **Hyderabad 447** (D. S. Manohar 54, D. Vinay Kumar 93, I. Khaleel 75, S. Vishnuvardhan 59); **Tamil Nadu 240** (S. Sriram 58, S. S. Viswanathan 50; S. Vishnuvardhan 5-79) **and 239-4** (S. Badrinath 56, S. S. Viswanathan 70*). *Hyderabad 2 pts.*

At Sardar Patel (Gujarat) Stadium, Ahmedabad, December 25, 26, 27, 28, 2003. **Drawn.** Toss: Bengal. **Gujarat 179** (B. D. Thaker 87*; R. R. Bose 5-55) **and 384-3** (A. A. Christian 103, N. K. Patel 118, A. Y. Sood 100*); **Bengal 479** (A. S. Das 215*, D. J. Gandhi 90). *Bengal 2 pts.*
Das carried his bat for 215, his maiden double-hundred, which lasted 658 minutes and 488 balls and included 23 fours and a six. Saurasish Lahiri (40) helped him add 106 for Bengal's ninth wicket.*

At Gymkhana Ground, Secunderabad, December 25, 26, 27, 2003. **Hyderabad won by an innings and nine runs.** Toss: Rajasthan. **Hyderabad 389** (Anirudh Singh 50, A. T. Rayudu 124, A. S. Yadav 52, M. Faiz Ahmed 65*; S. O. Mathur 5-124); **Rajasthan 235** (V. A. Saxena 62; N. P. Singh 6-70) **and 145** (S. Vishnuvardhan 4-51). *Hyderabad 5 pts.*

At M. Chinnaswamy Stadium, Bangalore, December 25, 26, 27, 28, 2003. **Karnataka won by seven wickets.** Toss: Karnataka. **Assam 285 and 308** (P. K. Das 56, K. R. Powar 51, S. V. Saravanan 50, R. Sathish 100; D. Ganesh 4-69, Sunil B. Joshi 5-100); **Karnataka 475** (B. M. Rowland 210, Sunil B. Joshi 110, D. Ganesh 55; A. Konwar 5-150) **and 119-3.** *Karnataka 4 pts.*
Rowland's 210, his second double-hundred, lasted 567 minutes and 434 balls and included 26 fours. Joshi scored 110 in Karnataka's first innings and took five wickets in Assam's second.

Semi-finals

At Wankhede Stadium, Mumbai, March 14, 15, 16, 2004. **Mumbai won by an innings and 152 runs.** Toss: Hyderabad. **Hyderabad 166** (A. T. Rayudu 95; S. V. Bahutule 4-42) **and 158** (A. T. Rayudu 53; S. V. Bahutule 6-53); **Mumbai 476** (V. R. Mane 154, V. G. Kambli 100, A. A. Muzumdar 51; S. L. V. Raju 6-139, J. S. Yadav 4-162).

At M. A. Chidambaram Stadium, Chennai, March 14, 15, 16, 17, 18, 2004. **Drawn.** Tamil Nadu qualified for the final by virtue of their first-innings lead. Toss: Tamil Nadu. **Tamil Nadu 481** (S. Sriram 172, K. D. Karthik 122) **and 306** (S. Ramesh 97; M. S. Yadav 4-117, K. S. Parida 4-65); **Railways 342** (Jai P. Yadav 116, Raja Ali 61) **and 117-5.**
In Tamil Nadu's first innings, Sriram and Karthik added 212 for the seventh wicket.

FINAL

TAMIL NADU v MUMBAI

At M. A. Chidambaram Stadium, Chennai, March 26, 27, 28, 29, 30, 2004. Drawn. Mumbai won the Ranji Trophy by virtue of their first-innings lead. Toss: Tamil Nadu.

The previous year's finalists were reunited but, even with home advantage, Tamil Nadu could not loosen Mumbai's grip on the trophy. They prepared a plumb pitch and won first use, only for their batsmen to throw it away. The approach was epitomised by the reverse sweep Sriram played into the hands of slip – one of five catches for Wasim Jaffer – to make it 123 for five. As in the semi-final, Karthik fought back with a century, but Kulkarni's left-arm spin accounted for six victims out of an inadequate 294. It looked as if Mumbai would capture the lead without losing a wicket. Mane made his third hundred in successive first-class innings and Jaffer added another before the breakthrough came at 243. Muzumdar outground them with a remorseless seven-and-a-half-hour 146, while Bahutule contributed a livelier 92. A lead of 319 virtually guaranteed Mumbai's 36th Ranji title; Tamil Nadu clung on for a face-saving draw, thanks to an unbroken stand between Badrinath and Badani.
Close of play: First day, Tamil Nadu 269-9 (Karthik 102, Srinivas 2); Second day, Mumbai 236-0 (Mane 105, Wasim Jaffer 121); Third day, Mumbai 513-5 (Muzumdar 119, Bahutule 64); Fourth day, Tamil Nadu 163-3 (Ramesh 31, Badrinath 17).

Tamil Nadu

*S. Suresh c Wasim Jaffer b Kulkarni	38	– c and b Bahutule		36
S. Ramesh c Samant b Patel	1	– (4) lbw b Patel		35
S. Sriram c Wasim Jaffer b Kulkarni	51	– st Samant b Bahutule		5
S. Badrinath c Joglekar b Kulkarni	0	– (5) not out		110
H. K. Badani c Wasim Jaffer b Kulkarni	27	– (6) not out		77
S. Sharath c Wasim Jaffer b Bahutule	29			
†K. D. Karthik not out	109			
V. Sivaramakrishnan c Wasim Jaffer b Bahutule	6	– (2) st Samant b Kulkarni		70
R. Ramkumar c Mane b Bahutule	5			
C. Ganapathy c Joglekar b Kulkarni	1			
M. R. Srinivas lbw b Kulkarni	17			
B 6, l-b 3, n-b 1	10	B 1, l-b 7, w 2, n-b 10		20
	294	(4 wkts)		353

1/5 (2) 2/74 (1) 3/74 (4) 4/122 (5)   294   1/80 (1) 2/94 (3)   (4 wkts) 353
5/123 (3) 6/207 (6) 7/219 (8)   3/135 (2) 4/180 (4)
8/227 (9) 9/238 (10) 10/294 (11)

Bowling: *First Innings*—Patel 19–3–62–1; Salvi 17–2–58–0; Thakkar 3–0–8–0; Kulkarni 32.2–5–83–6; Bahutule 26–4–74–3. *Second Innings*—Salvi 10–1–38–0; Patel 18–1–60–1; Kulkarni 40–8–85–1; Bahutule 32–8–77–2; Mane 15–4–32–0; Joglekar 21–5–28–0; Thakkar 11–8–22–0; Muzumdar 2–0–3–0.

Mumbai

V. R. Mane c Karthik b Suresh	106	M. M. Patel c sub (R. Jesuraj)		
Wasim Jaffer c and b Suresh	133	b Sivaramakrishnan		10
B. J. Thakkar lbw b Ganapathy	9	A. M. Salvi not out		12
A. A. Muzumdar c Karthik b Ganapathy	146	B 6, l-b 3, w 1, n-b 20		30
V. G. Kambli c Srinivas b Badrinath	55			
M. V. Joglekar c Karthik b Badrinath	0	1/243 (1) 2/257 (2) 3/266 (3)		613
*S. V. Bahutule c and b Sivaramakrishnan	92	4/379 (5) 5/382 (6) 6/563 (7)		
N. M. Kulkarni lbw b Sivaramakrishnan	4	7/569 (4) 8/575 (8)		
†V. R. Samant c Ramesh b Ramkumar	16	9/590 (9) 10/613 (10)		

Bowling: Ganapathy 34–3–131–2; Srinivas 29–13–74–0; Ramkumar 38–8–106–1; Suresh 27–5–77–2; Sivaramakrishnan 42.5–5–146–3; Sriram 11–2–17–0; Badrinath 17–2–51–2; Badani 2–0–2–0.

Umpires: M. S. Mahal and S. K. Porel. Referee: R. Desraj.

RANJI TROPHY WINNERS

1934-35	Bombay	1951-52	Bombay	1968-69	Bombay
1935-36	Bombay	1952-53	Holkar	1969-70	Bombay
1936-37	Nawanagar	1953-54	Bombay	1970-71	Bombay
1937-38	Hyderabad	1954-55	Madras	1971-72	Bombay
1938-39	Bengal	1955-56	Bombay	1972-73	Bombay
1939-40	Maharashtra	1956-57	Bombay	1973-74	Karnataka
1940-41	Maharashtra	1957-58	Baroda	1974-75	Bombay
1941-42	Bombay	1958-59	Bombay	1975-76	Bombay
1942-43	Baroda	1959-60	Bombay	1976-77	Bombay
1943-44	Western India	1960-61	Bombay	1977-78	Karnataka
1944-45	Bombay	1961-62	Bombay	1978-79	Delhi
1945-46	Holkar	1962-63	Bombay	1979-80	Delhi
1946-47	Baroda	1963-64	Bombay	1980-81	Bombay
1947-48	Holkar	1964-65	Bombay	1981-82	Delhi
1948-49	Bombay	1965-66	Bombay	1982-83	Karnataka
1949-50	Baroda	1966-67	Bombay	1983-84	Bombay
1950-51	Holkar	1967-68	Bombay	1984-85	Bombay

1985-86	Delhi	1992-93	Punjab	1999-2000	Mumbai
1986-87	Hyderabad	1993-94	Bombay	2000-01	Baroda
1987-88	Tamil Nadu	1994-95	Bombay	2001-02	Railways
1988-89	Delhi	1995-96	Karnataka	2002-03	Mumbai
1989-90	Bengal	1996-97	Mumbai	2003-04	Mumbai
1990-91	Haryana	1997-98	Karnataka		
1991-92	Delhi	1998-99	Karnataka		

Bombay/Mumbai have won the Ranji Trophy 36 times, Delhi and Karnataka 6, Baroda 5, Holkar 4, Bengal, Hyderabad, Madras/Tamil Nadu and Maharashtra 2, Haryana, Nawanagar, Punjab, Railways and Western India 1.

Plate Group A

At Mecon Sail Stadium, Ranchi, November 23, 24, 25, 26, 2003. **Madhya Pradesh won by 159 runs.** Toss: Madhya Pradesh. **Madhya Pradesh 133** (N. V. Ojha 58; M. S. Diwakar 4-36) **and 353-8 dec.** (D. S. Bundela 167*); **Bihar 85** (S. P. Pandey 7-23) **and 242** (M. Goel 81*, S. Pandu 62; N. D. Hirwani 4-86). *Madhya Pradesh 4 pts.*

At Vishkarma High School Ground, Rohtak, November 23, 24, 25, 26, 2003. **Haryana won by eight wickets.** Toss: Haryana. **Haryana 304** (Sunny Singh 66, I. Ganda 57, Shafiq Khan 71; S. Khajuria 5-117) **and 102-2** (Jitender Singh 56*); **Jammu and Kashmir 96** (G. Vashisht 6-32) **and 309** (D. Mahajan 63, Majid Dar 50; G. Vashisht 6-102). *Haryana 4 pts.*

At Maharaja Bir Bikram College Stadium, Agartala, November 23, 24, 25, 26, 2003. **Drawn.** Toss: Vidarbha. **Vidarbha 287** (N. S. Gawande 60; A. R. Kapoor 4-101) **and 220** (S. A. Khare 56; A. R. Kapoor 6-84); **Tripura 336** (R. R. Jaiswal 76, C. Y. Sachdev 110; M. S. Acharya 6-65) **and 70-4.** *Tripura 2 pts.*
Khare made five catches in Tripura's first innings.

At Vaish College Ground, Rohtak, December 1, 2, 3, 4, 2003. **Drawn.** Toss: Haryana. **Haryana 461-6 dec.** (Chetan Sharma 74, Sunny Singh 67, I. Ganda 95, M. Rawat 68, Joginder Sharma 52*, Extras 57; Sonu Sharma 4-89) **and 110-2** (Sunny Singh 61*); **Tripura 325** (T. Roy 118, S. B. Dahad 55, C. Y. Sachdev 67*; P. Sahu 6-96). *Haryana 2 pts.*

At Molana Azad Stadium, Jammu, December 1, 2, 3, 2003. **Jammu and Kashmir won by five wickets.** Toss: Bihar. **Bihar 172** (M. S. Dhoni 64) **and 159** (S. Khajuria 4-48); **Jammu and Kashmir 115** (Shahid Khan 7-25) **and 217-5** (A. Gupta 51*, Vijay Sharma 61*; Shahid Khan 4-42). *Jammu and Kashmir 4 pts.*

At Maharani Usharaje Trust Cricket Ground, Indore, December 1, 2, 3, 4, 2003. **Drawn.** Toss: Vidarbha. **Vidarbha 387** (A. V. Deshpande 126, A. S. Naidu 50, V. C. Naidu 100; N. D. Hirwani 4-80) **and 250-3** (A. V. Deshpande 80, P. R. Londase 64, R. S. Paradkar 66*); **Madhya Pradesh 327** (N. V. Ojha 79, D. S. Bundela 85; M. S. Acharya 4-84). *Vidarbha 2 pts.*

At Molana Azad Stadium, Jammu, December 9, 10, 11, 12, 2003. **Drawn.** Toss: Jammu and Kashmir. **Tripura 235** (R. R. Jaiswal 66, T. K. Chanda 50) **and 266-8 dec.** (S. Mahesh 65, A. R. Kapoor 59; Jagtar Singh 5-71); **Jammu and Kashmir 210** (D. Mahajan 64, Majid Dar 51; A. R. Kapoor 5-87) **and 96-4** (Sonu Sharma 4-37). *Tripura 2 pts.*

At Captain Roop Singh Stadium, Gwalior, December 9, 10, 11, 12, 2003. **Madhya Pradesh won by four wickets.** Toss: Haryana. **Haryana 278** (Joginder Sharma 56; N. D. Hirwani 7-66) **and 148** (Jitender Singh 71; N. D. Hirwani 6-41); **Madhya Pradesh 220** (D. S. Bundela 100*; Joginder Sharma 6-49) **and 207-6** (Sachin M. Dholpure 62). *Madhya Pradesh 4 pts.*
Hirwani's 13-107 was the best match analysis of the Indian season.

At VCA Ground, Nagpur, December 9, 10, 11, 2003. **Bihar won by seven wickets.** Toss: Vidarbha. **Vidarbha 244** (R. S. Paradkar 56, S. A. Khare 65; S. S. Rao 6-58) **and 146** (S. S. Rao 4-40); **Bihar 337** (Rajiv Kumar 124, M. S. Dhoni 68; M. S. Acharya 4-81) **and 55-3.** *Bihar 4 pts.*
Bihar wicket-keeper Dhoni made six catches in Vidarbha's first innings and nine in the match.

At Keenan Stadium, Jamshedpur, December 17, 18, 19, 20, 2003. **Drawn.** Toss: Bihar. **Bihar 238** (Rajiv Kumar 100) **and 324** (Rajiv Kumar 56, M. Goel 70, M. S. Diwakar 50; G. Vashisht 4-69); **Haryana 349** (Sunny Singh 130, I. Ganda 51, Shafiq Khan 62; M. S. Diwakar 5-58) **and 12-1.** *Haryana 2 pts.*

At Maharani Usharaje Trust Cricket Ground, Indore, December 17, 18, 19, 20, 2003. **Drawn.** Toss: Madhya Pradesh. **Madhya Pradesh 454** (S. Abbas Ali 109, N. A. Patwardhan 106; A. Sarkar 4-72); **Tripura 266** (T. K. Chanda 74; N. D. Hirwani 4-81, Y. A. Golwalkar 4-75) **and 177-7** (S. Mahesh 59; N. D. Hirwani 4-52). *Madhya Pradesh 2 pts.*

At VCA Ground, Nagpur, December 17, 18, 19, 2003. **Vidarbha won by an innings and 112 runs.** Toss: Jammu and Kashmir. **Vidarbha 379** (A. V. Deshpande 66, F. Y. Fazal 151); **Jammu and Kashmir 104** (S. R. Singh 5-56) **and 163** (D. Mahajan 51; P. V. Gandhe 5-49). *Vidarbha 5 pts.*
  Faiz Fazal, aged 18 years 101 days, made a hundred on first-class debut.

At Keenan Stadium, Jamshedpur, December 25, 26, 27, 28, 2003. **Drawn.** Toss: Tripura. **Tripura 187 and 233-6** (S. B. Dahad 58*); **Bihar 356** (Rajiv Kumar 155*, M. Goel 56; A. R. Kapoor 4-105). *Bihar 2 pts.*

At TERI Oval, Gurgaon, December 25, 26, 27, 28, 2003. **Drawn.** Toss: Haryana. **Vidarbha 226** (V. C. Naidu 54, A. S. Naidu 57; A. Mishra 4-73); **Haryana 215-8.**

At Molana Azad Stadium, Jammu, December 25, 26, 27, 28, 2003. **Drawn.** Toss: Madhya Pradesh. **Madhya Pradesh 443** (N. V. Ojha 50, D. S. Bundela 89, N. A. Patwardhan 62, H. S. Sodhi 54; S. Khajuria 5-115) **and 190-2** (N. V. Ojha 65, S. Abbas Ali 100*); **Jammu and Kashmir 263** (Kavaljit Singh 119, A. Gupta 54; S. P. Pandey 6-121, N. D. Hirwani 4-55). *Madhya Pradesh 2 pts.*

Plate Group B

At Barabati Stadium, Cuttack, November 23, 24, 25, 26, 2003. **Orissa won by an innings and 99 runs.** Toss: Orissa. **Goa 235** (S. A. Asnodkar 126*; D. S. Mohanty 5-44) **and 132** (Bipin Singh 5-46); **Orissa 466-8 dec.** (B. B. C. C. Mohapatra 83, S. Behera 87, P. M. Mullick 134*; S. B. Jakati 5-99). *Orissa 5 pts.*
  Swapnil Asnodkar carried his bat through Goa's first innings.

At Madhavrao Scindia Cricket Ground, Rajkot, November 23, 24, 25, 26, 2003. **Maharashtra won by an innings and 79 runs.** Toss: Saurashtra. **Saurashtra 177** (A. B. Kamalia 50, R. V. Dhruv 79; R. D. Khirid 7-45) **and 187; Maharashtra 443** (D. S. Jadhav 67, H. H. Kanitkar 60, K. R. Khadkikar 104, S. A. Satbhai 66). *Maharashtra 5 pts.*

At Model Sports Complex, Delhi, November 23, 24, 25, 26, 2003. **Himachal Pradesh won by five wickets.** Toss: Services. **Services 233** (M. P. Reddy 66, Sanjay Verma 58; V. S. Malik 5-56) **and 175** (K. G. Chawda 56; V. S. Malik 6-42); **Himachal Pradesh 291** (Virender Sharma 134; F. Mohammad 5-73, Arun Sharma 4-90) **and 118-5** (M. S. Bisla 76*). *Himachal Pradesh 4 pts.*
  Fast medium-pacer Fazil Mohammad took 5-73 on first-class debut.

At Bhausaheb Bandodkar Ground, Panaji, December 1, 2, 3, 4, 2003. **Services won by 78 runs.** Toss: Goa. **Services 212 and 179** (M. P. Reddy 55; S. B. Jakati 6-42); **Goa 142** (S. V. Ghag 6-34) **and 171** (S. V. Ghag 4-53, Arun Sharma 4-46). *Services 4 pts.*

At Barabati Stadium, Cuttack, December 1, 2, 3, 4, 2003. **Drawn.** Toss: Maharashtra. **Maharashtra 77** (D. S. Mohanty 5-24) **and 439-8 dec.** (D. S. Jadhav 200*, K. D. Aphale 100); **Orissa 204** (R. R. Parida 81, N. Behera 62*; I. R. Siddiqui 5-65, R. D. Khirid 4-51) **and 219-9** (S. Behera 57, R. R. Parida 70*). *Orissa 2 pts.*
  Jadhav, who had scored only two first-class fifties since his debut four years earlier, batted throughout Maharashtra's second innings for 200, which lasted 635 minutes and 409 balls and included 17 fours and a six.*

At Madhavrao Scindia Cricket Ground, Rajkot, December 1, 2, 3, 4, 2003. **Saurashtra won by seven wickets.** Toss: Himachal Pradesh. **Himachal Pradesh 214 and 324-7 dec.** (Sandeep Sharma 96, Virender Sharma 78, A. Mannu 67); **Saurashtra 309** (S. H. Kotak 69, P. J. Bhatt 62; V. Bhatia 5-93) **and 230-3** (S. H. Kotak 73*, F. U. Bambhaniya 58*). *Saurashtra 4 pts.*

At Nehru Stadium, Pune, December 9, 10, 11, 12, 2003. **Maharashtra won by ten wickets.** Toss: Maharashtra. **Goa 326** (V. V. Kolambkar 66, M. D. Phadke 78; K. R. Khadkikar 4-72) **and 175** (M. D. Phadke 56; K. R. Khadkikar 5-51); **Maharashtra 500-2 dec.** (D. S. Jadhav 89, K. D. Aphale 215*, H. H. Kanitkar 123*) **and 4-0.** *Maharashtra 5 pts.*
 Aphale's 215, his maiden double-hundred, lasted 452 minutes and 318 balls and included 20 fours and two sixes; he and Kanitkar shared an unbroken third-wicket stand of 273.*

At Barabati Stadium, Cuttack, December 9, 10, 11, 12, 2003. **Orissa won by 180 runs.** Toss: Himachal Pradesh. **Orissa 246** (Sangram Singh 4-39) **and 309-8 dec.** (R. R. Parida 50; Sangram Singh 4-28); **Himachal Pradesh 116** (D. K. Mangaraj 7-42) **and 259** (Sandeep Sharma 53, Sangram Singh 78, A. Mannu 51*; D. K. Mangaraj 4-69). *Orissa 4 pts.*
 Medium-pacer Deepak Mangaraj took 11-111 on first-class debut.

At Harbax Singh Stadium, Delhi, December 9, 10, 11, 12, 2003. **Drawn.** Toss: Saurashtra. **Saurashtra 214** (P. J. Bhatt 93, R. V. Dhruv 58; F. Mohammad 5-58) **and 201-9 dec.** (R. V. Dhruv 51); **Services 216** (Yashpal Singh 77; N. D. Doshi 5-41) **and 107-4.** *Services 2 pts.*

At HPCA Stadium, Dharmasala, December 17, 18, 19, 20, 2003. **Goa won by six wickets.** Toss: Himachal Pradesh. **Himachal Pradesh 111** (A. I. Aware 5-63, A. P. Dani 5-45) **and 280** (Sandeep Sharma 53, A. Mannu 97; A. P. Dani 5-73, S. B. Jakati 4-45); **Goa 312** (R. T. D'Souza 74, S. B. Jakati 66; A. K. Thakur 4-61) **and 80-4.** *Goa 4 pts.*
 The Himachal Pradesh Cricket Association Stadium was a new first-class venue.

At N2 Stadium, Aurangabad, December 17, 18, 19, 20, 2003. **Drawn.** Toss: Services. **Maharashtra 403** (H. H. Kanitkar 112, R. D. Khirid 117; F. Mohammad 5-104) **and 325-4** (H. H. Kanitkar 207*, S. A. Shah 78); **Services 299** (A. P. Singh 144, Yashpal Singh 58; C. P. Kulkarni 8-59). *Maharashtra 2 pts.*
 Kanitkar's 207, his second hundred of the match and the third double of his career, lasted 296 minutes and just 211 balls, and included 28 fours and one six. Kulkarni took 8-59 in his fourth first-class match.*

At Barabati Stadium, Cuttack, December 17, 18, 19, 20, 2003. **Drawn.** Toss: Orissa. **Saurashtra 228** (K. Waghela 95*; D. K. Mangaraj 4-79) **and 206-6** (K. Waghela 93, S. H. Kotak 50); **Orissa 320-8 dec.** (S. Behera 50, S. S. Raul 107, P. M. Mullick 60). *Orissa 2 pts.*
 Waghela carried his bat through Saurashtra's first innings and narrowly missed his maiden hundred twice.

At Arlem Breweries Ground, Margao, December 25, 26, 27, 28, 2003. **Drawn.** Toss: Goa. **Saurashtra 220** (K. Waghela 86; A. I. Aware 6-85) **and 379-5 dec.** (K. Waghela 83, S. H. Kotak 118, J. N. Shah 86; S. B. Jakati 4-120); **Goa 434** (V. V. Kolambkar 120, M. D. Phadke 132, A. P. Dani 80). *Goa 2 pts.*
 Waghela took his sequence to 357 in four innings, without a hundred.

At Municipal Rajaram Maidan, Ichalkaranji, December 25, 26, 27, 28, 2003. **Drawn.** Toss: Maharashtra. **Maharashtra 564** (D. S. Jadhav 207, K. D. Aphale 95, K. R. Khadkikar 75, S. A. Satbhai 54; V. Bhatia 5-179) **and 2-0; Himachal Pradesh 219 and 392** (Sandeep Sharma 135, Sangram Singh 70, M. S. Bisla 83; M. J. Dalvi 7-93). *Maharashtra 2 pts.*
 The only previous first-class match at this ground was in December 1980. Jadhav's 207, his second double-hundred in four weeks, lasted 512 minutes and 368 balls and included 20 fours and a six.

At Model Sports Complex, Delhi, December 25, 26, 27, 28, 2003. **Drawn.** Toss: Orissa. **Services 268** (C. D. Thomson 53; D. S. Mohanty 4-64); **Orissa 173-4** (S. S. Das 100*).

Plate Semi-finals

At Nehru Stadium, Pune, March 14, 15, 16, 17, 18, 2004. **Maharashtra won by ten wickets.**
Toss: Haryana. **Haryana 236** (Shafiq Khan 114) **and 364** (Chetan Sharma 61, Sunny Singh 87,
Shafiq Khan 66; K. R. Adhav 5-125, K. R. Khadkikar 4-85); **Maharashtra 592** (D. S. Jadhav
132, H. H. Kanitkar 180, S. A. Satbhai 119; Joginder Sharma 4-126) **and 11-0.**

At Barabati Stadium, Cuttack, March 14, 15, 16, 17, 18, 2004. **Madhya Pradesh won by five
wickets.** Toss: Orissa. **Orissa 318** (P. M. Mullick 142*; Y. A. Golwalkar 6-95) **and 253** (R. R.
Parida 74, S. S. Raul 87; Y. A. Golwalkar 4-102, N. D. Hirwani 4-79); **Madhya Pradesh 258**
(N. V. Ojha 74, N. A. Patwardhan 71; S. K. Satpathy 4-75) **and 315-5** (N. V. Ojha 54, S. Abbas
Ali 90*).

Plate Final

At Nehru Stadium, Pune, March 26, 27, 28, 29, 30, 2004. **Maharashtra won by 40 runs.** Toss:
Maharashtra. **Maharashtra 501** (D. S. Jadhav 251, H. H. Kanitkar 55, D. Mohan 77; S. K. Pitre
4-91, N. D. Hirwani 4-140) **and 202** (D. S. Jadhav 79; Y. A. Golwalkar 5-73); **Madhya Pradesh
370** (N. V. Ojha 79, D. S. Bundela 83; I. R. Siddiqui 5-101) **and 293** (N. V. Ojha 70, Sachin
M. Dholpure 56, S. K. Pitre 57).

   *Jadhav batted throughout Maharashtra's first innings; he was last out for 251, the highest
individual score of the Indian season and his third double of 2003-04. It lasted 731 minutes and
536 balls, included 28 fours, and made him the only player to complete 1,000 first-class runs in
the season.*

DULEEP TROPHY, 2003-04

Group A	Played	Won	Lost	Drawn	1st-innings Points	Points
North Zone	2	2	0	0	0	8
Central Zone . . .	2	0	1	1	0	0
West Zone.	2	0	1	1	0	0

Group B	Played	Won	Lost	Drawn	1st-innings Points	Points
East Zone	2	1	0	1	2	6
South Zone	2	1	0	1	0	4
England A.	2	0	2	0	0	0

Outright win = 4 pts; lead on first innings in a drawn match = 2 pts.

Final

North Zone beat East Zone by 59 runs.

Group A

At Devi Lal Stadium, Gurgaon, February 14, 15, 16, 17, 2004. **Drawn.** Toss: Central Zone. **Central
Zone 549** (G. K. Khoda 156, R. P. Srivastava 73, D. S. Bundela 72, Jai P. Yadav 80, V. A. Saxena
69); **West Zone 352-4** (D. S. Jadhav 154, H. H. Kanitkar 96, J. J. Martin 50*).
   The Devi Lal stadium was a new first-class venue.

At Devi Lal Stadium, Gurgaon, February 21, 22, 23, 24, 2004. **North Zone won by five wickets.**
Toss: Central Zone. **Central Zone 154 and 211** (V. A. Saxena 51); **North Zone 249** (M. Manhas
68; N. D. Hirwani 4-62) **and 118-5.** *North Zone 4 pts.*

At HPCA Stadium, Dharmasala, February 27, 28, 29, March 1, 2004. **North Zone won by 21
runs.** Toss: North Zone. **North Zone 279** (P. Dharmani 73; R. R. Powar 4-62) **and 191**
(G. Gambhir 111*); **West Zone 172** (V. R. Mane 54) **and 277** (V. R. Mane 127*, J. J. Martin 50;
Sarandeep Singh 4-99). *North Zone 4 pts.*
   In the second innings, Gambhir carried his bat for North Zone and Mane for West Zone.

Group B

At HPCA Stadium, Dharmasala, February 14, 15, 16, 17, 2004. **Drawn.** Toss: East Zone. **East Zone 388** (S. S. Das 120, A. S. Das 55, L. R. Shukla 84; N. P. Singh 4-66) **and 216-9 dec.** (D. J. Gandhi 87); **South Zone 331** (S. Ramesh 57, Sunil B. Joshi 51) **and 7-0.** *East Zone 2 pts.*

At TERI Oval, Gurgaon, February 21, 22, 23, 24, 2004. SOUTH ZONE beat ENGLAND A by six wickets (see England A tour section).

At Gandhi Ground, Amritsar, February 27, 28, 29, March 1, 2004. EAST ZONE beat ENGLAND A by 93 runs (see England A tour section).

FINAL

NORTH ZONE v EAST ZONE

At PCA Stadium, Mohali, March 4, 5, 6, 7, 8, 2004. North Zone won by 59 runs. Toss: East Zone. Yuvraj Singh tipped a well-balanced game North Zone's way with twin hundreds. He had missed their previous game with a sore shoulder, but the national selectors demanded he prove his fitness. Put in on a grassy pitch, North reached 285 for two through Yuvraj and Mongia. Then Yuvraj was run out, the second new ball accounted for four more, and the rest followed next morning. Powar dominated East Zone's reply with a four-hour century, putting them in sight of first-innings lead, until, running short of partners, he holed out to deep mid-wicket. Yuvraj reprised his first-day feats, sharing another big stand, 230 with Chopra, and the tail managed to raise the target to a challenging 409. East Zone glimpsed a historic first Duleep Trophy as Powar and Gavaskar reached 200 for two, but faltered on the final day and lost hope when Powar, three short of a second hundred, offered a simple catch to cover. North Zone were soon celebrating a record 14th outright Duleep title.

Close of play: First day, North Zone 304-7 (Ratra 8); Second day, East Zone 287-8 (Powar 69, Mohanty 0); Third day, North Zone 292-3 (Mongia 14, Manhas 11); Fourth day, East Zone 213-3 (Powar 51, Lahiri 1).

North Zone

A. Chopra lbw b Paul	27	– c Shukla b Lahiri	95
G. Gambhir lbw b Lahiri	46	– b Lahiri	9
Yuvraj Singh run out	106	– c Dhoni b Paul	148
*D. Mongia c Shukla b Mohanty	84	– b Chatterjee	48
M. Manhas lbw b Paul	1	– lbw b Chatterjee	11
†A. Ratra b Paul	13	– c A. S. Das b Chatterjee	2
Joginder Sharma c Dhoni b Paul	0	– c Dhoni b Paul	25
Gagandeep Singh c Dhoni b Mohanty	4	– (9) b Mohanty	19
Sarandeep Singh c Lahiri b Paul	14	– (8) c and b Chatterjee	2
A. Nehra not out	4	– c Dhoni b Mohanty	17
A. Bhandari b Mohanty	0	– not out	2
B 4, l-b 7, n-b 20	31	B 8, l-b 2, n-b 12	22

1/82 (1) 2/88 (2) 3/285 (3) 4/285 (4)	**330**	1/30 (2) 2/260 (3) 3/278 (1)	**400**
5/288 (5) 6/288 (7) 7/304 (8)		4/292 (5) 5/316 (6) 6/335 (4)
8/325 (6) 9/326 (9) 10/330 (11)		7/341 (8) 8/367 (7)
		9/385 (9) 10/400 (10)

Bowling: *First Innings*—Paul 27–8–83–5; Mohanty 24.1–3–52–3; Lahiri 20–5–61–1; Shukla 8–3–28–0; Chatterjee 12–0–66–0; Powar 6–0–24–0; Gavaskar 2–1–5–0. *Second Innings*—Paul 23–4–108–2; Mohanty 13–3–44–2; Lahiri 33–2–128–2; Chatterjee 27–7–63–4; Powar 6–0–34–0; Gavaskar 2–0–4–0; Gandhi 1–0–9–0.

East Zone

S. S. Das c Yuvraj Singh b Nehra	12	– (7) b Manhas	0
†M. S. Dhoni c Chopra b Joginder Sharma	21	– c Yuvraj Singh b Gagandeep Singh	60
A. S. Das b Sarandeep Singh	70	– (1) lbw b Sarandeep Singh	35
R. S. Gavaskar lbw b Joginder Sharma	1	– c Ratra b Bhandari	49
*D. J. Gandhi c Manhas b Sarandeep Singh	42	– (6) c Ratra b Mongia	9
K. R. Powar c Gambhir b Sarandeep Singh	102	– (3) c Mongia b Manhas	97
L. R. Shukla c Yuvraj Singh b Sarandeep Singh	8	– (8) c Nehra b Bhandari	17
S. S. Lahiri st Ratra b Sarandeep Singh	6	– (5) c Mongia b Sarandeep Singh	27
U. Chatterjee c Yuvraj Singh b Nehra	39	– c Gagandeep Singh b Manhas	0
D. S. Mohanty lbw b Gagandeep Singh	2	– c Manhas b Bhandari	26
S. S. Paul not out	0	– not out	0
L-b 2, w 1, n-b 16	19	B 6, l-b 9, n-b 14	29

1/34 (2) 2/44 (1) 3/46 (4) 4/139 (5)   322
5/174 (3) 6/182 (7) 7/200 (8)
8/286 (9) 9/302 (10) 10/322 (6)

1/77 (2) 2/116 (1) 3/200 (4)   349
4/264 (5) 5/284 (6) 6/285 (7)
7/311 (8) 8/313 (9)
9/335 (8) 10/349 (10)

Bowling: *First Innings*—Nehra 20–7–50–2; Bhandari 20–1–86–0; Joginder Sharma 11–0–59–2; Gagandeep Singh 17–3–54–1; Sarandeep Singh 22.5–6–64–5; Mongia 1–0–7–0. *Second Innings*—Nehra 15–3–44–0; Bhandari 18.5–1–71–3; Joginder Sharma 13–1–60–0; Gagandeep Singh 10–1–44–1; Sarandeep Singh 27–1–71–2; Mongia 13–3–29–1; Manhas 10–3–15–3.

Umpires: Jasbir Singh and I. Sivaram.   Referee: S. Bhagwandas.

DULEEP TROPHY WINNERS

1961-62	West Zone	1976-77	West Zone	1991-92	North Zone
1962-63	West Zone	1977-78	West Zone	1992-93	North Zone
1963-64	{ South Zone	1978-79	North Zone	1993-94	North Zone
	{ West Zone	1979-80	North Zone	1994-95	North Zone
1964-65	West Zone	1980-81	West Zone	1995-96	South Zone
1965-66	South Zone	1981-82	West Zone	1996-97	Central Zone
1966-67	South Zone	1982-83	North Zone	1997-98	{ Central Zone
1967-68	South Zone	1983-84	North Zone		{ West Zone
1968-69	West Zone	1984-85	South Zone	1998-99	Central Zone
1969-70	West Zone	1985-86	West Zone	1999-2000	North Zone
1970-71	South Zone	1986-87	South Zone	2000-01	North Zone
1971-72	Central Zone	1987-88	North Zone	2001-02	West Zone
1972-73	West Zone	1988-89	{ North Zone	2002-03	Elite C
1973-74	North Zone		{ West Zone	2003-04	North Zone
1974-75	South Zone	1989-90	South Zone		
1975-76	South Zone	1990-91	North Zone		

DEODHAR TROPHY, 2003-04

Note: Matches in this tournament were not first-class.

	Played	Won	Lost	Bonus Points	Points
East Zone	4	4	0	2	18
West Zone	4	2	2	1	9
South Zone	4	2	2	1	9
Central Zone	4	2	2	–1	7
North Zone	4	0	4	–3	–3

Win = 4 pts; no result = 2 pts. One bonus point awarded for achieving victory with a run-rate 1.25 times that of the opposition, and one subtracted for conceding a bonus point.

CRICKET IN PAKISTAN, 2003-04

ABID ALI KAZI

Aamer Bashir

The highlight of the season was the return of India for their first full tour of Pakistan in 14 years. They brought the crowds back to the stadiums and much-needed revenue to the Pakistan Cricket Board – but, to the disappointment of the masses, Pakistan eventually lost the one-day and the Test series. Both times they entered the final game level, only for India to clinch the decider. That summed up a season in which Pakistan's performances remained mediocre, though studded with strokes of brilliance.

Before India arrived in March 2004, Pakistan had won their previous three Test series, though the only whitewash was against Bangladesh; they beat South Africa (at home) and New Zealand (away) 1–0 while losing the associated one-day series. Their results in three one-day tournaments after India's visit – the Asia Cup, Videocon Cup and ICC Champions Trophy – were uneven; they beat India in each of them, but lost the crunch games and picked up no trophies.

Losing the series with India cost Javed Miandad his job as national coach for the fourth time; Bob Woolmer replaced him in June, before the Asia Cup. Inzamam-ul-Haq retained the captaincy, which he had taken over from Rashid Latif during Bangladesh's tour, and Haroon Rashid carried on as manager. But there were two changes at the top of the PCB. The chairman, General Tauqir Zia, had stepped down in December, after four years in command, tired by rows over Pakistan's performances on the pitch, television rights, and the selection of his son Junaid for the national one-day side. Shaharyar Khan, a career diplomat, took over, and soon found out that foreign policy was a piece of cake compared with running the PCB. He and the board's chief executive, Ramiz Raja, were given a torrid time by the senate after the defeats by India; in August, Ramiz finally caved in after barely a year in office and resigned to concentrate on his career as a television commentator.

An overhaul of the game's domestic structure has become something of a PCB tradition. In 2002-03, the regional and departmental sides had competed alongside each other for the Quaid-e-Azam Trophy; this time, they were separated again, with the Patron's Trophy revived for the departmental teams after a season's gap. The Quaid-e-Azam Trophy reverted to a regional tournament, in a new format. The PCB divided the country into nine regions, with some first-class teams losing their identity as they merged into larger neighbours, and the players were picked by the board's own selectors. The nine sides were Faisalabad (absorbing Sargodha), Hyderabad (including Dadu), Karachi, Lahore, Multan (Bahawalpur), Peshawar, Quetta, Rawalpindi (Islamabad) and Sialkot (Gujranwala and Sheikhupura); they were scheduled to play eight four-day matches apiece in a round-robin league with no knockout.

But there was some resentment at the imposition of the PCB's selections. One player who thought he should have been chosen for Hyderabad sued; the court temporarily barred Hyderabad from taking part in the competition. Meanwhile the Cricket Association of Baluchistan, the province represented by Quetta, went to court against the PCB, alleging biased selection. Hyderabad's opening three matches and Quetta's first two were cancelled (these included the game between the two of them). Though they did eventually play their remaining fixtures, the PCB announced that these would not be counted in the final championship table; all points earned by other teams against Hyderabad and Quetta were wiped out, and though the games retained first-class status the league was effectively reduced to seven teams playing six matches each.

> **It was no suprise when the board rewrote the rules**

Faisalabad were clear first-time champions with five victories – their only defeat was in the discounted game with Quetta. Faisalabad completed a double triumph by winning all the seven fixtures they played in the one-day Quaid-e-Azam Cup. In 2004-05, the first-class competition remained regionally based, but expanded to 11 teams as the two biggest cities, Karachi and Lahore, were once again allowed to field two teams each.

The intention was that the Patron's Trophy should be contested by the top eight teams from an Inter-Department Qualifying Tournament for 27 sides in October and November, with Bangladesh A invited as a ninth. But when Habib Bank and National Bank failed to reach the last eight, they pleaded to be allowed in anyway, arguing that many senior players would otherwise be deprived of first-class match practice. It was no surprise when the PCB rewrote the rules and invited four more teams to take part. The 13 sides included three making their first-class debuts: the Defence Housing Authority, Karachi Port Trust and Pakistan Telecom Company Limited. They were divided into two pools, won by the Water and Power Development Authority and Zarai Taraqiati Bank Limited (until recently known as the Agricultural Development Bank of Pakistan); these two met in a final, which ZTBL won to clinch the title for the first time since 1995-96. Habib Bank, one of the original non-qualifiers, beat PIA in the final of the one-day Patron's Cup.

The non-first-class Cornelius and Kardar Trophies, which functioned as the second divisions of the Quaid-e-Azam and Patron's competitions, were scrapped, but the board introduced a regionally based tournament, the Inter-District Seniors, for 79 district teams playing two-day cricket.

The season's leading batsman was Aamer Bashir, of Pakistan Customs and Multan, who made 1,260 runs, including five centuries, culminating in a career-best 205 against Hyderabad. Shoaib Khan scored 1,249 including an unbeaten 300 for Peshawar against Quetta, the 13th first-class triple-hundred by a Pakistani. The leading wicket-takers were Nasir Khan of DHA and Karachi with 62, and Zahid Saeed of National Bank and Sialkot with 60.

FIRST-CLASS AVERAGES, 2003-04

BATTING

(Qualification: 600 runs)

	M	I	NO	R	HS	100s	Avge	Ct/St
Shoaib Khan (*WAPDA & Peshawar*)	14	22	4	1,249	300*	3	69.38	14
Naved Ashraf (*ZTBL & Rawalpindi*)	13	20	3	1,089	184	5	64.05	11
Aamer Bashir (*Pakistan Customs & Multan*)	13	24	2	1,260	205	5	57.27	15
Shehzad Malik (*PTCL & Sialkot*)	13	19	2	956	111*	2	56.23	10
Inzamam-ul-Haq (*Pakistan & Multan*)	8	14	2	654	138*	2	54.50	4
Hasan Raza (*Habib Bank & Karachi*)	10	16	1	805	182	4	53.66	17
†Salman Butt (*Pakistan, Nat. Bank & Lahore*)	9	17	0	875	137	3	51.47	5
†Shadab Kabir (*Karachi Port Trust & Karachi*)	10	19	0	945	176	2	49.73	9
†Ashar Zaidi (*PTCL & Rawalpindi*)	12	20	3	839	110*	1	49.35	15
Yasir Hameed (*Pakistan & Peshawar*)	10	18	4	670	170	2	47.85	3
†Nasim Khan (*Pakistan Customs & Quetta*)	11	20	1	896	125	4	47.15	8
Naved Latif (*PTCL & Faisalabad*)	10	18	1	799	129	2	47.00	5
†Taufeeq Umar (*Pakistan & Lahore*)	9	17	1	717	111	1	44.81	17
Shahid Yousuf (*ZTBL & Sialkot*)	11	16	2	625	118	1	44.64	17
Ijaz Ahmed, jun. (*Allied Bank & Faisalabad*)	12	19	0	836	146	3	44.00	9
†Adil Nisar (*WAPDA & Lahore*)	14	25	3	889	157	2	40.40	12
†Babar Naeem (*PTCL & Rawalpindi*)	14	24	1	873	149	4	37.95	7
Mohammad Ramzan (*KRL & Faisalabad*)	12	20	3	601	161	2	35.35	14
Asif Zakir (*DHA & Karachi*)	10	19	0	650	136	3	34.21	3/1
Atif Ali (*Karachi Port Trust & Quetta*)	11	21	0	667	98	0	31.76	6
†Usman Tariq (*Allied Bank & Multan*)	12	22	0	684	101	1	31.09	6

† *Left-handed batsman.*

BOWLING

(Qualification: 30 wickets)

	Style	O	M	R	W	BB	5W/i	Avge
Shahid Nazir (*Habib Bank & Faisalabad*)	RFM	231.1	52	585	37	6-42	3	15.81
Saeed Ajmal (*KRL & Faisalabad*)	OB	342.3	98	803	42	6-26	2	19.11
Iftikhar Anjum (*ZTBL & Rawalpindi*)	RM	319.2	59	1,028	52	7-85	4	19.76
Stephen John (*Pakistan Customs & Quetta*)	LFM	309.4	64	1,061	51	6-44	4	20.80
Sarfraz Ahmed (*WAPDA & Sialkot*)	LFM	373.2	114	917	43	6-46	3	21.32
Mohammad Siddiq (*ZTBL & Peshawar*)	RFM	272.5	51	978	42	5-70	2	23.28
Naved-ul-Hasan (*WAPDA & Sialkot*)	RM	434.2	87	1,261	54	6-38	3	23.35
Wasim Khan (*Sui Gas & Lahore*)	RFM	338.2	55	1,107	47	7-70	4	23.55
Fahad Khan (*Karachi Port Trust & Karachi*)	RFM	209.3	30	759	32	5-55	1	23.71
Fazl-e-Akbar (*Pakistan, PIA & Peshawar*)	RFM	283.2	48	1,029	42	7-30	2	24.50
Zahid Saeed (*National Bank & Sialkot*)	LFM	362.2	48	1,499	60	6-144	5	24.98

	Style	O	M	R	W	BB	5W/i	Avge
Nasir Khan (*DHA & Karachi*)	LFM	442	86	1,559	62	6-65	8	25.14
Tahir Mughal (*Allied Bank & Sialkot*)	RFM	254	55	833	33	6-54	4	25.24
Umar Gul (*Pakistan & Peshawar*)	RFM	228.1	33	830	31	5-31	2	26.77
Yasir Arafat (*KRL & Rawalpindi*)	RM	281.5	54	978	36	5-57	1	27.16
Jaffar Nazir (*KRL & Sialkot*)	RFM	273.1	47	882	32	5-52	1	27.56
Riaz Afridi (*PTCL & Peshawar*)	RFM	283.2	75	886	32	6-68	2	27.68
Abdur Rauf (*Allied Bank & Multan*)	RFM	283.5	44	1,004	35	6-94	2	28.68
Danish Kaneria (*Pakistan & Karachi*)	LBG	361.3	78	969	33	5-46	1	29.36
Najaf Shah (*PIA & Rawalpindi*)	LFM	317.1	73	890	30	5-57	1	29.66
Aqeel Ahmed (*WAPDA & Faisalabad*)	OB	271.4	39	893	30	5-70	1	29.76
Wahab Riaz (*Karachi Port Trust & Hyderabad*)	LFM	247.2	47	957	32	6-76	2	29.90
Saqlain Mushtaq (*Pakistan, PIA & Lahore*)...	OB	291.3	50	916	30	6-80	2	30.53
Mohammad Asif (*KRL & Quetta*)	RFM	385	62	1,394	44	5-141	1	31.68

PCB PATRON'S TROPHY, 2003-04

Pool A

	Played	Won	Lost	Drawn	1st-inns Points	Points
WAPDA	6	4	0	2	12	36
KRL.	6	3	1	2	12	30
PIA	6	2	2	2	12	24
PTCL	6	2	0	4	9	21
Pakistan Customs	6	1	2	3	9	15
DHA	6	0	3	3	3	3
Bangladesh A.	6	0	4	2	3	3

Pool B

	Played	Won	Lost	Drawn	1st-inns Points	Points
ZTBL.	5	3	0	2	6	24
National Bank	5	1	0	4	9	15
Allied Bank	5	1	1	3	9	15
Habib Bank	5	1	1	3	6	12
Karachi Port Trust.	5	1	3	1	3	9
Sui Gas	5	0	2	3	3	3

Outright win = 6 pts; lead on first innings in a won or drawn game = 3 pts.

Final: ZTBL beat WAPDA by three wickets.

Pool A

At UBL Sports Complex, Karachi, December 8, 9, 10, 2003. **PIA won by an innings and 90 runs.** Toss: PIA. **DHA 167** (Sharjeel Ashraf 63; Fazl-e-Akbar 7-30) **and 194** (Asmatullah Mohmand 63; Asif Mujtaba 4-18); **PIA 451-5 dec.** (Ghulam Ali 64, Faisal Iqbal 167, Asif Mujtaba 109, Mahmood Hamid 50*). *PIA 9 pts.*

At National Stadium, Karachi, December 8, 9, 10, 2003. **WAPDA won by an innings and 155 runs.** Toss: WAPDA. **KRL 124** (Naved-ul-Hasan 6-38) **and 139** (Sarfraz Ahmed 5-53); **WAPDA 418** (Tariq Aziz 172, Farooq Iqbal 65*). *WAPDA 9 pts.*

At Quaid-e-Azam Park, Karachi, December 8, 9, 10, 11, 2003. **Drawn.** Toss: Pakistan Customs. **Pakistan Customs 431** (Kashif Siddiq 82, Bilal Khilji 69, Aamer Bashir 115) **and 113-7; PTCL 419** (Naved Latif 129, Shehzad Malik 111*; Junaid Zia 4-83). *Pakistan Customs 3 pts.*
    This was the first first-class match at Quaid-e-Azam Park, which became Karachi's 17th first-class ground.

At National Stadium, Karachi, December 15, 16, 17, 18, 2003. **Drawn.** Toss: DHA. **Bangladesh A 452-9 dec.** (Shahriar Hossain 218, Extras 78; Rizwan Saeed 4-116); **DHA 158** (Rizwan Qureshi 62; Tareq Aziz 4-36) **and 473-6** (Mohtashim Ali 107, Sharjeel Ashraf 103*, Aamer Iqbal 129). *Bangladesh A 3 pts.*

Shahriar Hossain's 218, his maiden double-hundred, lasted 469 minutes and 352 balls and included 36 fours. Sharjeel Ashraf and Aamer Iqbal came together when DHA were still 63 behind with five wickets left following on, and added 229 for the sixth wicket.

At UBL Sports Complex, Karachi, December 15, 16, 17, 18, 2003. **KRL won by three wickets.** Toss: KRL. **PIA 127** (Mahmood Hamid 66; Mohammad Asif 4-67) **and 286** (Ghulam Ali 56, Zahid Fazal 68; Saeed Ajmal 4-112); **KRL 285** (Intikhab Alam 60; Saqlain Mushtaq 4-77, Asif Mujtaba 5-34) **and 129-7.** *KRL 9 pts.*

At Niaz Stadium, Hyderabad, December 15, 16, 17, 18, 2003. **WAPDA won by 112 runs.** Toss: Pakistan Customs. **WAPDA 343** (Tariq Aziz 112; Stephen John 5-78) **and 157** (Stephen John 4-40); **Pakistan Customs 294** (Nasim Khan 77; Naved-ul-Hasan 4-91, Sarfraz Ahmed 4-86) **and 94** (Sarfraz Ahmed 4-38). *WAPDA 9 pts.*

Customs wicket-keeper Hanif Malik made nine dismissals in the match – eight caught, one stumped.

At UBL Sports Complex, Karachi, December 22, 23, 2003. **KRL won by an innings and 28 runs.** Toss: Pakistan Customs. **Pakistan Customs 95** (Yasir Arafat 4-25) **and 156** (Saeed Ajmal 6-26); **KRL 279** (Mohammad Ramzan 51, Zulfiqar Jan 83). *KRL 9 pts.*

At Niaz Stadium, Hyderabad, December 22, 23, 24, 25, 2003. **Drawn.** Toss: PIA. **WAPDA 283** (Hassan Adnan 81; Najaf Shah 4-68) **and 203-3** (Shoaib Khan 75*, Hassan Adnan 72*); **PIA 417-9 dec.** (Kamran Sajid 68, Ghulam Ali 50, Bazid Khan 134). *PIA 3 pts.*

At National Stadium, Karachi, December 22, 23, 24, 25, 2003. **PTCL won by eight wickets.** Toss: Bangladesh A. **Bangladesh A 223** (Shahriar Hossain 84; Riaz Afridi 4-39) **and 339** (Mohammad Ashraful 108, Rajin Saleh 114; Nauman Habib 4-66); **PTCL 327** (Sheraz Khalid 99, Shehzad Malik 87, Zulqarnain Haider 63*; Anwar Hossain Monir 7-81) **and 238-2** (Babar Naeem 118*, Ashar Zaidi 80*). *PTCL 9 pts.*

At Quaid-e-Azam Park, Karachi, December 29, 30, 31, 2003, January 1, 2004. **Drawn.** Toss: Pakistan Customs. **Pakistan Customs 370** (Aamer Bashir 108, Fahad Iqbal 73; Nasir Khan 6-99) **and 263-8 dec.** (Kashif Siddiq 62, Aamer Bashir 100*; Nasir Khan 6-93); **DHA 211** (Asif Zakir 68, Wajid Ali 68; Mohtashim Rasheed 5-38) **and 372-7** (Asif Zakir 136, Asmatullah Mohmand 55, Mohtashim Ali 68). *Pakistan Customs 3 pts.*

Aamer Bashir scored a century in each innings for the first time, and Nasir Khan took 12-192 in the match.

At National Stadium, Karachi, December 29, 30, 31, 2003, January 1, 2004. **PTCL won by seven wickets.** Toss: PTCL. **PIA 218** (Kamran Sajid 72; Riaz Afridi 6-68) **and 116** (Riaz Afridi 4-45); **PTCL 239** (Mohammad Fayyaz 65; Kamran Sajid 4-45) **and 96-3.** *PTCL 9 pts.*

At UBL Sports Complex, Karachi, December 29, 30, 31, 2003, January 1, 2004. **WAPDA won by ten wickets.** Toss: WAPDA. **Bangladesh A 166** (Hannan Sarkar 64; Naved-ul-Hasan 4-51, Sarfraz Ahmed 4-31) **and 337** (Hannan Sarkar 57, Jamaluddin Ahmed 50, Manjural Islam Rana 84; Naved-ul-Hasan 4-95); **WAPDA 502-8 dec.** (Asif Hussain 139, Adil Nisar 157, Shoaib Khan 88; Alamgir Kabir 4-113) **and 4-0.** *WAPDA 9 pts.*

At National Stadium, Karachi, January 5, 6, 7, 2004. **KRL won by an innings and 27 runs.** Toss: KRL. **DHA 63** (Yasir Arafat 4-17) **and 343** (Aamer Iqbal 76, Mohtashim Ali 123*); **KRL 433-9 dec.** (Saeed Anwar, jun. 104, Yasir Arafat 100, Zulfiqar Jan 101*; Nasir Khan 5-144). *KRL 9 pts.*

DHA wicket-keeper Aamer Iqbal caught six of the nine KRL wickets to fall.

At Quaid-e-Azam Park, Karachi, January 5, 6, 7, 8, 2004. **PIA won by an innings and 15 runs.** Toss: Bangladesh A. **Bangladesh A 203** (Rashidul Haque 110; Saqlain Mushtaq 6-80) **and 284** (Tushar Imran 61, Jamaluddin Ahmed 81; Saqlain Mushtaq 5-79); **PIA 502-9 dec.** (Faisal Iqbal 125, Asif Mujtaba 126, Mahmood Hamid 62, Ahmed Zeeshan 100*). *PIA 9 pts.*

Faisal Iqbal and Asif Mujtaba added 221 for PIA's fourth wicket, and Ahmed Zeeshan and Saqlain Mushtaq 107 for the eighth.

At UBL Sports Complex, Karachi, January 5, 6, 7, 8, 2004. **Drawn.** Toss: WAPDA. **PTCL 426** (Ashar Zaidi 61, Naved Latif 124, Shehzad Malik 50, Zulqarnain Haider 61*) **and 135** (Babar Naeem 50; Naved-ul-Hasan 4-70, Sarfraz Ahmed 6-46); **WAPDA 366** (Adil Nisar 149, Hassan Adnan 70; Riaz Afridi 5-125) **and 127-6** (Shoaib Khan 60*). *PTCL 3 pts.*

At Quaid-e-Azam Park, Karachi, January 12, 13, 14, 15, 2004. **WAPDA won by ten wickets.** Toss: DHA. **DHA 242** (Aamer Iqbal 91; Naved-ul-Hasan 5-77, Aqeel Ahmed 4-84) **and 238** (Mohtashim Ali 56; Aqeel Ahmed 5-70); **WAPDA 409** (Mohammad Zaman 148, Shoaib Khan 64; Nasir Khan 5-138) **and 72-0.** *WAPDA 9 pts.*

At Niaz Stadium, Hyderabad, January 12, 13, 14, 15, 2004. **Drawn.** Toss: KRL. **PTCL 223** (Ashar Zaidi 53, Shehzad Malik 63; Saeed Ajmal 4-73) **and 221-9** (Ashar Zaidi 110*; Saeed Ajmal 4-57); **KRL 431-8 dec.** (Mohammad Ramzan 111, Saeed Anwar, jun. 76, Saeed Bin Nasir 122, Intikhab Alam 53; Tabish Nawab 4-142). *KRL 3 pts.*
   Aqeel Mukhtar and Irfan Haider appeared for PTCL as full playing substitutes for Zulqarnain Haider and Riaz Afridi, who were called up by Pakistan Under-19.

At National Stadium, Karachi, January 12, 13, 2004. **Pakistan Customs won by an innings and 41 runs.** Toss: Pakistan Customs. **Bangladesh A 118** (Stephen John 6-44) **and 30** (Junaid Zia 7-7); **Pakistan Customs 189** (Nasim Khan 69). *Pakistan Customs 9 pts.*
   Customs wicket-keeper Shahbaz Butt made five catches in Bangladesh A's first innings. Their second lasted 14.4 overs; only Extras (16) passed six. Junaid Zia, son of the former PCB chairman Tauqir Zia, had figures of 7.4-4-7-7.

At Niaz Stadium, Hyderabad, January 19, 20, 21, 22, 2004. **Drawn.** Toss: DHA. **PTCL 367** (Babar Naeem 65, Ashar Zaidi 96, Sheraz Khalid 87; Nasir Khan 6-97); **DHA 377-4** (Asif Zakir 129, Aamer Iqbal 79*, Rizwan Qureshi 55*). *DHA 3 pts.*

At UBL Sports Complex, Karachi, January 19, 20, 21, 22, 2004. **Drawn.** Toss: Bangladesh A. **Bangladesh A 198** (Nasiruddin Faruque 64*; Yasir Arafat 4-26, Saeed Ajmal 5-50); **KRL 160-5** (Saeed Anwar, jun. 76; Fahim Muntasir 4-38).

At National Stadium, Karachi, January 19, 20, 21, 22, 2004. **Drawn.** Toss: Pakistan Customs. **PIA 431** (Bazid Khan 193*) **and forfeited second innings; Pakistan Customs 175-7 dec.** (Aamer Bashir 69) **and 154-3.** *PIA 3 pts.*

Pool B

At KRL Ground, Rawalpindi, December 15, 16, 17, 18, 2003. **Drawn.** Toss: Habib Bank. **Allied Bank 297** (Ijaz Ahmed, jun. 139; Kabir Khan 4-58) **and 98-2; Habib Bank 267** (Aftab Alam 55, Hasan Raza 120; Tahir Mughal 5-108, Taimur Khan 5-77). *Allied Bank 3 pts.*

At Arbab Niaz Stadium, Peshawar, December 15, 16, 17, 18, 2003. **ZTBL won by nine wickets.** Toss: ZTBL. **Karachi Port Trust 240** (Atif Ali 70, Rashid Hanif 56) **and 322** (Atif Ali 98, Farhan Iqbal 53*; Iftikhar Anjum 7-94); **ZTBL 512** (Shahid Yousuf 118, Naved Ashraf 176*, Iftikhar Anjum 78) **and 54-1.** *ZTBL 9 pts.*
   Naved Ashraf and Iftikhar Anjum added 182 for ZTBL's ninth wicket.

At Rawalpindi Cricket Stadium, Rawalpindi, December 15, 16, 17, 18, 2003. **Drawn.** Toss: National Bank. **Sui Gas 353-5 dec.** (Sufyan Munir 175, Misbah-ul-Haq 111, Saleem Mughal 50*); **National Bank 136-4** (Naumanullah 55*).
   The first two days were washed out. Sufyan Munir and Misbah-ul-Haq added 230 for Sui Gas's third wicket.

At Rawalpindi Cricket Stadium, Rawalpindi, December 22, 23, 24, 25, 2003. **Drawn.** Toss: Allied Bank. **Karachi Port Trust 225** (Tahir Mughal 6-54) **and 258-7 dec.** (Shadab Kabir 87, Atif Ali 76; Tahir Mughal 5-95); **Allied Bank 263-9 dec.** (Wajahatullah Wasti 56, Farhan Adil 75*) **and 55-2.** *Allied Bank 3 pts.*

At KRL Ground, Rawalpindi, December 22, 23, 24, 25, 2003. **Drawn.** Toss: Habib Bank. **Sui Gas 152** (Umar Javed 54; Kabir Khan 4-20, Waqas Chughtai 4-54) **and 94-2** (Sufyan Munir 59*); **Habib Bank 291** (Khaqan Arsal 90, Abdur Rehman 59; Wasim Khan 4-83, Adnan Farooq 4-75). *Habib Bank 3 pts.*

At Arbab Niaz Stadium, Peshawar, December 22, 23, 24, 25, 2003. **Drawn.** Toss: ZTBL. **National Bank 334** (Qaiser Abbas 64, Sajid Ali 97, Mohammad Javed 82; Mubashir Nazir 4-91) **and 181-7** (Naumanullah 74); **ZTBL 207** (Shahid Yousuf 88; Imran Javed 4-32). *National Bank 3 pts.*

At KRL Ground, Rawalpindi, December 29, 30, 31, 2003, January 1, 2004. **Drawn.** Toss: National Bank. **Allied Bank 501-9 dec.** (Manzoor Akhtar 107, Ijaz Ahmed, jun. 146, Tahir Mughal 55); **National Bank 313-5** (Naumanullah 146*, Sajid Ali 54).

At Arbab Niaz Stadium, Peshawar, December 29, 30, 2003. **Habib Bank won by an innings and 15 runs.** Toss: Habib Bank. **Karachi Port Trust 100** (Kabir Khan 4-38, Sajid Shah 4-30) **and 166** (Iqbal Sheikh 50; Shahid Nazir 5-57, Sajid Shah 4-41); **Habib Bank 281** (Khaqan Arsal 136; Fahad Khan 5-55). *Habib Bank 9 pts.*

At Rawalpindi Cricket Stadium, Rawalpindi, December 29, 30, 31, 2003, January 1, 2004. **Drawn.** Toss: ZTBL. **ZTBL 245** (Faisal Naved 63, Javed Hayat 58; Adnan Farooq 4-62) **and 169-8** (Sajid Ali 4-31); **Sui Gas 372** (Asim Munir 68, Misbah-ul-Haq 168). *Sui Gas 3 pts.*

At Rawalpindi Cricket Stadium, Rawalpindi, January 5, 6, 7, 8, 2004. **ZTBL won by an innings and nine runs.** Toss: ZTBL. **Allied Bank 205** (Iftikhar Anjum 4-60) **and 60** (Iftikhar Anjum 5-27); **ZTBL 274** (Naved Ashraf 114*; Abdur Rauf 4-95). *ZTBL 9 pts.*

At KRL Ground, Rawalpindi, January 5, 6, 7, 8, 2004. **Drawn.** Toss: National Bank. **Habib Bank 253** (Hasan Raza 59; Zahid Saeed 4-101) **and 151-5** (Hasan Raza 74*); **National Bank 277** (Sajid Ali 81, Kamran Akmal 74; Shahid Nazir 5-49). *National Bank 3 pts.*

At Arbab Niaz Stadium, Peshawar, January 5, 6, 7, 8, 2004. **Karachi Port Trust won by an innings and 146 runs.** Toss: Sui Gas. **Karachi Port Trust 518** (Maisam Hasnain 108, Shadab Kabir 176, Atif Ali 92; Wasim Khan 5-119, Adnan Farooq 4-90); **Sui Gas 304** (Asim Munir 67, Sufyan Munir 101; Wahab Riaz 4-117) **and 68** (Shahid Iqbal 7-19). *Karachi Port Trust 9 pts.*
   Sui Gas's second innings lasted 28.5 overs; only Asim Munir (43) passed six.

At Arbab Niaz Stadium, Peshawar, January 12, 13, 14, 15, 2004. **Allied Bank won by eight wickets.** Toss: Allied Bank. **Sui Gas 267** (Misbah-ul-Haq 69, Saleem Mughal 59; Tahir Mughal 6-72) **and 261** (Abdur Rauf 6-94); **Allied Bank 459-8 dec.** (Usman Tariq 81, Wajahatullah Wasti 59, Farhan Adil 78, Bilal Asad 92, Mohammad Salman 52) **and 70-2.** *Allied Bank 9 pts.*
   Shahid Khan appeared for Sui Gas as a full playing substitute for Tariq Mahmood, who was called up by Pakistan.

At KRL Ground, Rawalpindi, January 12, 13, 14, 15, 2004. **ZTBL won by nine wickets.** Toss: ZTBL. **Habib Bank 366** (Hasan Raza 182, Atiq-uz-Zaman 64; Iftikhar Anjum 5-102) **and 108** (Imran Sabir 5-25); **ZTBL 317** (Zeeshan Mohsin 54, Atif Ashraf 50, Shahid Yousuf 56, Naved Ashraf 63; Waqas Chughtai 4-58) **and 158-1** (Atif Ashraf 65*, Faisal Naved 73*). *ZTBL 6 pts.*

At Rawalpindi Cricket Stadium, Rawalpindi, January 12, 13, 14, 15, 2004. **National Bank won by nine wickets.** Toss: National Bank. **Karachi Port Trust 386** (Shadab Kabir 98, Wajihuddin 120, Rashid Hanif 58; Mohammad Javed 5-76) **and 180** (Imran Javed 5-49); **National Bank 502** (Naumanullah 169, Qaiser Abbas 81, Kamran Akmal 73, Naeem Tayyab 50) **and 67-1.** *National Bank 9 pts.*
   Wajihuddin scored 120 on first-class debut.

Final

At National Stadium, Karachi, January 26, 27, 28, 29, 2004. **ZTBL won by three wickets.** Toss: ZTBL. **WAPDA 308** (Adil Nisar 57, Hassan Adnan 85; Iftikhar Anjum 7-85) **and 147; ZTBL 280** (Abdul Razzaq 65, Extras 52; Sarfraz Ahmed 5-66) **and 177-7** (Shahid Yousuf 78; Naved-ul-Hasan 5-96).
   WAPDA keeper Zahid Umar made five catches in ZTBL's first innings.

WINNERS

Ayub Trophy		1974-75	National Bank	1990-91	ADBP
1960-61	Railways-Quetta	1975-76	National Bank	1991-92	Habib Bank
1961-62	Karachi	1976-77	Habib Bank	1992-93	Habib Bank
1962-63	Karachi	1977-78	Habib Bank	1993-94	ADBP
1964-65	Karachi	1978-79	National Bank	1994-95	Allied Bank
1965-66	Karachi Blues	†1979-80	IDBP		
1967-68	Karachi Blues	†1980-81	Rawalpindi	*PCB Patron's Trophy*	
1969-70	PIA	†1981-82	Allied Bank	1995-96	ADBP
		†1982-83	PACO	1996-97	United Bank
BCCP Trophy		1983-84	Karachi Blues	1997-98	Habib Bank
1970-71	PIA	1984-85	Karachi Whites	1998-99	Habib Bank
1971-72	PIA	1985-86	Karachi Whites	†1999-2000	Lahore City Blues
		1986-87	National Bank	2000-01	Pakistan Customs
BCCP Patron's Trophy		1987-88	Habib Bank	2001-02	National Bank
1972-73	Karachi Blues	1988-89	Karachi	2003-04	ZTBL
1973-74	Railways	1989-90	Karachi Whites		

† *The Patron's Trophy was not first-class between 1979-80 and 1982-83, when it served as a qualifying competition for the Quaid-e-Azam Trophy, or in 1999-2000; it was not held in 2002-03.*

QUAID-E-AZAM TROPHY, 2003-04

	Played	Won	Lost	Drawn	1st-inns Points	Points
Faisalabad..........	7	5	1	1	15	45
Sialkot............	8	4	3	1	9	33
Karachi	6	3	2	1	12	30
Peshawar	8	3	3	2	9	18*
Lahore............	8	3	4	1	9	15*
Multan............	8	3	5	0	6	9*
Rawalpindi	8	2	4	2	3	6*
Quetta	6	3	3	0	9	0*
Hyderabad	5	1	2	2	0	0*

Outright win = 6 pts; lead on first innings in a won or drawn game = 3 pts.

* *Four matches involving Hyderabad and Quetta were cancelled, and points gained against Hyderabad and Quetta were not included in the final totals. The other seven teams were ranked on the six matches each of them played against each other. Peshawar and Rawalpindi's totals exclude nine points each from the discounted games, Lahore 12 and Multan 15. Quetta's total excludes 27 points from their surviving matches and Hyderabad six.*

At Iqbal Stadium, Faisalabad, February 9, 10, 11, 12, 2004. **Drawn.** Toss: Sialkot. **Faisalabad 381** (Ijaz Ahmed, jun. 96, Naved Latif 88) **and 242-7** (Mohammad Hafeez 58, Misbah-ul-Haq 52; Shoaib Malik 4-76); **Sialkot 360** (Imran Nazir 83, Shehzad Malik 93; Saeed Ajmal 4-102). *Faisalabad 3 pts.*

At Niaz Stadium, Hyderabad, February 9, 10, 11, 12, 2004. **Hyderabad v Quetta. Cancelled.**

At Gaddafi Stadium, Lahore, February 9, 10, 11, 12, 2004. **Lahore won by ten wickets.** Toss: Lahore. **Multan 186** (Rehan Rafiq 54) **and 140** (Abdul Razzaq 5-27); **Lahore 322-7 dec.** (Salim Elahi 85, Adil Nisar 83) **and 8-0.** *Lahore 9 pts.*

At Arbab Niaz Stadium, Peshawar, February 9, 10, 11, 12, 2004. **Drawn.** Toss: Peshawar. **Rawalpindi 403-8** (Bilal Asad 54, Naved Ashraf 121*; Noor-ul-Amin 5-112) **v Peshawar.** *The first two days were washed out.*

At Niaz Stadium, Hyderabad, February 16, 17, 18, 19, 2004. **Hyderabad v Faisalabad. Cancelled.**

At National Stadium, Karachi, February 16, 17, 18, 19, 2004. **Karachi v Quetta. Cancelled.**

At Sheikhupura Stadium, Sheikhupura, February 16, 17, 18, 2004. **Peshawar won by nine wickets.** Toss: Peshawar. **Lahore 236** (Salman Butt 122; Arshad Khan 6-57) **and 163** (Umar Gul 5-69); **Peshawar 363** (Ahmed Said 106, Shoaib Khan 116; Wasim Khan 4-67, Mohammad Khalil 6-106) **and 37-1.** *Peshawar 9 pts.*

At Multan Cricket Stadium, Multan, February 16, 17, 18, 2004. **Sialkot won by nine wickets.** Toss: Sialkot. **Multan 234** (Usman Tariq 53, Aamer Bashir 71; Zahid Saeed 4-37) **and 215** (Inzamam-ul-Haq 91); **Sialkot 405** (Imran Nazir 122, Faisal Naved 50, Shoaib Malik 55, Naved-ul-Hasan 65; Mohammad Irshad 4-107, Tahir Maqsood 4-76) **and 50-1.** *Sialkot 9 pts.*

At National Stadium, Karachi, February 17, 18, 19, 20, 2004. **Faisalabad won by 78 runs.** Toss: Karachi. **Faisalabad 311** (Ijaz Ahmed, jun. 54, Naved Latif 91, Tauqeer Hussain 97*; Tanvir Ahmed 6-112) **and 215** (Misbah-ul-Haq 115; Mohammad Sami 5 62); **Karachi 246** (Asim Kamal 53, Moin Khan 58; Ahmed Hayat 5-69) **and 202** (Asim Kamal 82; Tauqeer Hussain 5-55). *Faisalabad 9 pts.*

At LCCA Ground, Lahore, February 23, 24, 25, 26, 2004. **Lahore won by five wickets.** Toss: Lahore. **Rawalpindi 494** (Babar Naeem 149, Azhar Mahmood 75, Yasir Arafat 64; Irfan Fazil 4-119) **and 259** (Ashar Zaidi 65, Sheraz Khalid 60, Azhar Mahmood 54; Wasim Khan 5-72); **Lahore 460** (Taufeeq Umar 86, Salman Butt 137, Adil Nisar 62*; Yasir Arafat 4-118) **and 294-5** (Abdul Razzaq 126*, Kamran Akmal 99*; Azhar Mahmood 4-82). *Lahore 6 pts.*
   Junaid Zia was out handled the ball in Rawalpindi's second innings. Abdul Razzaq and Kamran Akmal shared a match-winning stand of 246 in two and a half hours for Lahore's sixth wicket. The match saw 1,507 runs scored for the loss of 35 wickets.*

At Multan Cricket Stadium, Multan, February 23, 24, 25, 26, 2004. **Multan won by 139 runs.** Toss: Quetta. **Multan 297** (Yasir Arafat 50, Rehan Rafiq 78*; Irfanuddin 4-94) **and 272** (Usman Tariq 54; Stephen John 4-61); **Quetta 304** (Nasim Khan 125, Stephen John 50, Extras 54; Abdur Rauf 4-56) **and 126** (Abdur Rauf 5-42). *Multan 6 pts.*

At Jinnah Stadium, Sialkot, February 23, 24, 25, 2004. **Sialkot won by eight wickets.** Toss: Sialkot. **Sialkot 348** (Faisal Khan 61, Shehzad Malik 71, Qaiser Abbas 54; Fazl-e-Akbar 4-92) **and 86-2; Peshawar 195** (Zahid Saeed 5-46) **and 238** (Shoaib Khan 57, Wajahatullah Wasti 74). *Sialkot 9 pts.*

At Iqbal Stadium, Faisalabad, March 8, 9, 10, 11, 2004. **Faisalabad won by nine wickets.** Toss: Multan. **Faisalabad 445** (Imran Ali 52, Asif Hussain 63, Ijaz Ahmed, jun. 115, Mohammad Zaman 107) **and 92-1; Multan 283** (Usman Tariq 54, Rehan Rafiq 53) **and 253** (Usman Tariq 60, Rehan Rafiq 64*; Mohammad Hafeez 4-51). *Faisalabad 9 pts.*
   Multan wicket-keeper Aamer Atta made five catches in Faisalabad's first innings.

At National Stadium, Karachi, March 8, 9, 10, 11, 2004. **Karachi v Hyderabad. Cancelled.**

At Sheikhupura Stadium, Sheikhupura, March 8, 9, 10, 2004. **Lahore won by an innings and 59 runs.** Toss: Lahore. **Quetta 157** (Irfan Fazil 6-54) **and 244** (Nasim Khan 106, Mohammad Javed 52; Aizaz Cheema 5-61); **Lahore 460** (Khaqan Arsal 51, Intikhab Alam 147*, Extras 57; Mohammad Asif 5-141). *Lahore 9 pts.*

At Jinnah Stadium, Sialkot, March 8, 9, 10, 11, 2004. **Rawalpindi won by six runs.** Toss: Sialkot. **Rawalpindi 170** (Sarfraz Ahmed 4-38) **and 348** (Afaq Raheem 71, Bilal Asad 63); **Sialkot 212** (Mohammad Ayub 88) **and 300** (Faisal Naved 73, Shehzad Malik 64; Bilal Asad 5-37). *Rawalpindi 6 pts.*
   Rawalpindi wicket-keeper Mohammad Shehbaz made four catches in each of Sialkot's innings.

At Iqbal Stadium, Faisalabad, March 15, 16, 17, 18, 2004. **Faisalabad won by 83 runs.** Toss: Peshawar. **Faisalabad 171** (Naved Latif 73) **and 443** (Mohammad Ramzan 161, Imran Ali 81, Mohammad Zaman 57); **Peshawar 240** (Wajahatullah Wasti 107; Shahid Nazir 4-75) **and 291** (Aftab Alam 58, Shoaib Khan 67, Wajahatullah Wasti 60*). *Faisalabad 6 pts.*

In Faisalabad's second innings, Mohammad Ramzan and Imran Ali added 236 for the second wicket.

At Bahawal Stadium, Bahawalpur, March 15, 16, 17, 18, 2004. **Karachi won by three wickets.** Toss: Karachi. **Multan 220** (Aamer Bashir 69; Nasir Khan 5-74) **and 441-6 dec.** (Aamer Bashir 151, Rehan Rafiq 100, Asif Iqbal 71*); **Karachi 352** (Shadab Kabir 70, Naumanullah 56 retired hurt; Abdur Rauf 4-93) **and 310-7** (Saeed Bin Nasir 118, Faisal Iqbal 81). *Karachi 9 pts.*

Karachi wicket-keeper Ahmed Zeeshan made five catches in Multan's first innings.

At KRL Ground, Rawalpindi, March 15, 16, 17, 2004. **Rawalpindi won by an innings and two runs.** Toss: Rawalpindi. **Hyderabad 213** (Faisal Athar 91; Najaf Shah 5-57, Alamgir Khan 4-62) **and 237** (Faisal Athar 95*; Yasir Arafat 5-57); **Rawalpindi 452** (Babar Naeem 102, Naved Ashraf 150, Yasir Arafat 99*; Kashif Ali 4-84). *Rawalpindi 9 pts.*

At Saga Cricket Ground, Sialkot, March 15, 16, 17, 2004. **Quetta won by nine runs.** Toss: Sialkot. **Quetta 256** (Zahid Saeed 5-80) **and 192** (Kamran Niazi 57; Jaffar Nazir 5-52, Zahid Saeed 5-71); **Sialkot 233** (Sufyan Munir 68; Stephen John 5-92) **and 206** (Mohammad Asif 4-85, Faisal Irfan 4-71). *Quetta 9 pts.*

At Sargodha Stadium, Sargodha, March 22, 23, 2004. **Quetta won by 25 runs.** Toss: Faisalabad. **Quetta 136** (Shahid Nazir 6-42) **and 183** (Nasim Khan 50, Naseer Khan 50; Shahid Nazir 4-68, Samiullah Khan 4-81); **Faisalabad 134** (Stephen John 6-47) **and 160** (Naved Latif 53, Saeed Ajmal 53; Mohammad Asif 4-88, Stephen John 4-52). *Quetta 9 pts.*

Quetta wicket-keeper Zulqarnain Haider made four catches in each of Faisalabad's innings.

At LCCA Ground, Lahore, March 22, 23, 24, 25, 2004. **Karachi won by seven wickets.** Toss: Lahore. **Karachi 392** (Asif Zakir 102, Shadab Kabir 148; Wasim Khan 7-70) **and 220-3** (Asif Zakir 58, Faisal Iqbal 82*); **Lahore 201** (Kashif Siddiq 55; Nasir Khan 4-77) **and 407** (Salman Butt 87, Intikhab Alam 75, Adil Nisar 61, Kamran Akmal 54; Nasir Khan 4-83). *Karachi 9 pts.*

Asif Zakir and Shadab Kabir opened with 233 in Karachi's first innings. Karachi wicket-keeper Ahmed Zeeshan made five catches in Lahore's second innings. Farhan Adil appeared for Karachi as a full playing substitute for Danish Kaneria, who was called up by Pakistan.

At Abbottabad Cricket Stadium, Abbottabad, March 22, 23, 24, 25, 2004. **Drawn.** Toss: Peshawar. **Hyderabad 457** (Akram Khan 52, Shahid Qambrani 106, Rizwan Ahmed 149); **Peshawar 286-6** (Aftab Alam 150*; Kashif Raza 4-67).

This was the first first-class match played at Abbottabad.

At KRL Ground, Rawalpindi, March 22, 23, 24, 25, 2004. **Multan won by four wickets.** Toss: Multan. **Rawalpindi 213** (Yasir Arafat 70; Tahir Maqsood 4-69) **and 394** (Usman Saeed 141); **Multan 333** (Usman Tariq 80, Aamer Bashir 76, Kamran Hussain 61) **and 275-6** (Mohammad Shafiq 82). *Multan 9 pts.*

Usman Saeed scored 141 on first-class debut.

At Sheikhupura Stadium, Sheikhupura, March 29, 30, 31, April 1, 2004. **Drawn.** Toss: Hyderabad. **Lahore 324** (Salman Butt 70, Rizwan Ahmed 58; Wahab Riaz 4-97) **and 519-9 dec.** (Salman Butt 132, Rizwan Aslam 151, Ashraf Ali 101*); **Hyderabad 273** (Rizwan Ahmed 58; Shehzad Butt 5-83) **and 92-3.** *Lahore 3 pts.*

Salman Butt and Rizwan Aslam opened with 114 in Lahore's first innings and 182 in their second.

At Arbab Niaz Stadium, Peshawar, March 29, 30, 31, April 1, 2004. **Peshawar won by 280 runs.** Toss: Peshawar. **Peshawar 260** (Jannisar Khan 55, Shoaib Khan 166*) **and 383-6 dec.** (Ahmed Said 105, Shoaib Khan 166*); **Multan 172** (Fazl-e-Akbar 4-67) **and 191** (Usman Tariq 101, Azhar Shafiq 60; Fazl-e-Akbar 6-39, Mohammad Siddiq 4-67). *Peshawar 9 pts.*

At KRL Ground, Rawalpindi, March 29, 30, 31, April 1, 2004. **Quetta won by six wickets.** Toss: Quetta. **Quetta 456** (Samiullah Agha 70, Nasim Khan 110, Atif Ali 72, Zulqarnain Haider 78; Saad Altaf 5-161) **and 169-4** (Nasim Khan 66*); **Rawalpindi 173** (Irfanuddin 5-37) **and 448** (Naved Ashraf 184, Yasir Arafat 52). *Quetta 9 pts.*

At Jinnah Stadium, Sialkot, March 29, 30, 31, April 1, 2004. **Sialkot won by five wickets.** Toss: Sialkot. **Karachi 495** (Shadab Kabir 96, Saeed Bin Nasir 53, Hasan Raza 114, Tanvir Ahmed 88*) **and 142** (Zahid Saeed 4-52); **Sialkot 438** (Shehzad Malik 101, Khalid Mahmood 178) **and 202-5** (Shehzad Malik 63*). *Sialkot 6 pts.*
  Shehzad Malik and Khalid Mahmood added 277 for Sialkot's seventh wicket.

At UBL Sports Complex, Karachi, April 5, 6, 7, 8, 2004. **Drawn.** Toss: Rawalpindi. **Rawalpindi 406** (Babar Naeem 114, Naved Ashraf 94; Azam Hussain 5-123) **and 242** (Ashar Zaidi 66, Mohammad Fayyaz 52; Azam Hussain 8-113); **Karachi 423** (Shadab Kabir 53, Agha Sabir 64, Hasan Raza 150) **and 171-7** (Shadab Kabir 72; Alamgir Khan 4-60). *Karachi 3 pts.*
  Karachi left-arm spinner Azam Hussain took 13-236 in the match.

At LCCA Ground, Lahore, April 5, 6, 7, 8, 2004. **Faisalabad won by six wickets.** Toss: Faisalabad. **Lahore 327** (Ashraf Ali 141) **and 267** (Ashraf Ali 65, Adnan Akmal 53; Mohammad Hafeez 5-46); **Faisalabad 492** (Imran Ali 131, Asif Hussain 105, Naved Latif 77; Salman Butt 4-82) **and 104-4.** *Faisalabad 9 pts.*

At Arbab Niaz Stadium, Peshawar, April 5, 6, 7, 2004. **Peshawar won by an innings and 145 runs.** Toss: Quetta. **Peshawar 561-4 dec.** (Jannisar Khan 159, Shoaib Khan 300*, Wajahatullah Wasti 51), **Quetta 195** (Samiullah Agha 69; Mohammad Siddiq 5-78, Arshad Khan 5-33) **and 221** (Nasim Khan 107, Zulqarnain Haider 72; Mohammad Siddiq 5-70). *Peshawar 9 pts.*
  Shoaib Khan's 300 lasted 505 minutes and 377 balls and included 50 fours. His previous highest score was 166* against Multan the previous week. Shoaib added 343 for Peshawar's third wicket with Jannisar Khan and 160 for the fourth with Wajahatullah Wasti.*

At Jinnah Stadium, Sialkot, April 5, 6, 7, 8, 2004. **Hyderabad won by seven wickets.** Toss: Sialkot. **Sialkot 419** (Faisal Khan 79, Shehzad Malik 76, Kamran Younis 71, Khalid Mahmood 68; Wahab Riaz 5-114) **and 189** (Kashif Raza 4-56, Wahab Riaz 6-76); **Hyderabad 390** (Hanif Malik 69, Faisal Athar 126, Wahab Riaz 62; Zahid Saeed 5-121) **and 220-3** (Akram Khan 80, Shahid Qambrani 61*). *Hyderabad 6 pts.*

At National Stadium, Karachi, April 12, 13, 14, 2004. **Karachi won by nine wickets.** Toss: Peshawar. **Karachi 297** (Mohammad Ghazan 51, Zeeshan Pervez 98, Rashid Latif 54; Riaz Afridi 4-90) **and 68-1; Peshawar 110** (Nasir Khan 5-58, Fahad Khan 4-44) **and 252** (Ahmed Said 93, Jannisar Khan 75; Nasir Khan 6-65). *Karachi 9 pts.*
  Karachi wicket-keeper Rashid Latif made five catches in Peshawar's first innings; Hasan Raza took over behind the stumps when they followed on and held another five.

At Multan Cricket Stadium, Multan, April 12, 13, 14, 15, 2004. **Multan won by ten wickets.** Toss: Multan. **Hyderabad 197** (Hanif-ur-Rehman 97) **and 419** (Akram Khan 147, Hanif-ur-Rehman 52, Zulfiqar Ali 58, Hanif Malik 65*; Mohammad Tanvir 6-115); **Multan 610-7 dec.** (Nazir Ahmed 102, Yasir Arafat 69, Aamer Bashir 205, Asif Iqbal 51, Mohammad Fazil 69; Zulfiqar Ali 4-108) **and 10-0.** *Multan 9 pts.*
  Aamer Bashir's 205, his fifth century of the season and his maiden double, lasted 380 minutes and 281 balls. He shared successive century partnerships with Rehan Rafiq, Asif Iqbal and Mohammad Fazil.*

At KRL Ground, Rawalpindi, April 12, 13, 14, 15, 2004. **Faisalabad won by 100 runs.** Toss: Rawalpindi. **Faisalabad 329** (Tauqeer Hussain 100, Ijaz Ahmed, jun. 54, Mohammad Salman 79*; Rizwan Akbar 6-87) **and 246-9 dec.** (Usman Arshad 92; Nadeem Sikander 4-78); **Rawalpindi 229** (Afaq Raheem 110, Aqeel Ahmed 4-51) **and 246** (Afaq Raheem 79; Ijaz Ahmed, jun. 5-49). *Faisalabad 9 pts.*

At Jinnah Stadium, Sialkot, April 12, 13, 14, 15, 2004. **Sialkot won by six wickets.** Toss: Sialkot. **Lahore 309** (Ashraf Ali 115; Zahid Saeed 4-108, Ali Imran 5-84) **and 427** (Salman Butt 96, Azhar Ali 53, Extras 72; Zahid Saeed 6-144); **Sialkot 585** (Faisal Naved 73, Faisal Khan 62, Qaiser Abbas 160, Kamran Younis 90; Wasim Khan 5-91) **and 154-4** (Shahid Yousuf 87*). *Sialkot 9 pts.*

QUAID-E-AZAM TROPHY WINNERS

1953-54	Bahawalpur	1974-75	Punjab A	1990-91	Karachi Whites
1954-55	Karachi	1975-76	National Bank	1991-92	Karachi Whites
1956-57	Punjab	1976-77	United Bank	1992-93	Karachi Whites
1957-58	Bahawalpur	1977-78	Habib Bank	1993-94	Lahore City
1958-59	Karachi	1978-79	National Bank	1994-95	Karachi Blues
1959-60	Karachi	1979-80	PIA	1995-96	Karachi Blues
1961-62	Karachi Blues	1980-81	United Bank	1996-97	Lahore City
1962-63	Karachi A	1981-82	National Bank	1997-98	Karachi Blues
1963-64	Karachi Blues	1982-83	United Bank	1998-99	Peshawar
1964-65	Karachi Blues	1983-84	National Bank	1999-2000	PIA
1966-67	Karachi	1984-85	United Bank	2000-01	Lahore City Blues
1968-69	Lahore	1985-86	Karachi	2001-02	Karachi Whites
1969-70	PIA	1986-87	National Bank	2002-03	PIA
1970-71	Karachi Blues	1987-88	PIA	2003-04	Faisalabad
1972-73	Railways	1988-89	ADBP		
1973-74	Railways	1989-90	PIA		

The competition has been contested sometimes by regional teams, sometimes by departments, and sometimes by a mixture of the two. Karachi teams have won the Quaid-e-Azam Trophy 17 times, PIA 6, National Bank 5, Lahore teams and United Bank 4, Bahawalpur, Punjab and Railways 2, ADBP, Faisalabad, Habib Bank and Peshawar 1.

Note: Matches in the following sections were not first-class.

PCB PATRON'S CUP, 2003-04
Final

At National Stadium, Karachi, January 25, 2004. **Habib Bank won by 131 runs.** Toss: PIA. **Habib Bank 266-7** (50 overs) (Salim Elahi 85, Younis Khan 73); **PIA 135** (39.1 overs) (Bazid Khan 51).

QUAID-E-AZAM CUP, 2003-04

	Played	Won	Lost	Cancelled	Points	Net run-rate
Faisalabad	7	7	0	1	24*	0.52
Karachi	6	4	2	2	16	0.07
Lahore	8	5	3	0	12*	0.83
Sialkot	8	5	3	0	12*	0.61
Peshawar.	8	5	3	0	12*	0.33
Rawalpindi	8	4	4	0	8*	0.48
Multan	8	2	6	0	0*	−0.43
Quetta	6	0	6	2	0	−1.56
Hyderabad	5	0	5	3	0	−1.61

Win = 4 pts.
Net run-rate is calculated by subtracting runs conceded per over from runs scored per over.

* *Four matches involving Hyderabad and Quetta were cancelled, and points gained against Hyderabad and Quetta were not included in the final totals, so that the other seven teams were ranked on the six matches each of them played against each other. Faisalabad's total excludes four points from the discounted games, and Lahore, Sialkot, Peshawar, Rawalpindi and Multan eight each.*

CRICKET IN SRI LANKA, 2003-04

SA'ADI THAWFEEQ AND GERRY VAIDYASEKERA

Tillekeratne Dilshan

The routine worries of Sri Lankan cricket shrivelled away at the end of 2004 when the Indian Ocean tsunami struck the island with full venom, destroying many thousands of lives. (See The Tragedy that Brought Us Together, pages 85–90.) The stadium at Galle was just one of the sites wrecked by the wave, and the consequences of the disaster will test the island's resilience to the full in the months and years ahead. Before that, the country's cricketing news had been dominated more than ever by Muttiah Muralitharan.

He very nearly became the first bowler to take 100 first-class wickets in a Sri Lankan season; he was reported for his controversial delivery, the *doosra*, after the home series with Australia; and in May he broke Courtney Walsh's record of 519 Test wickets in Zimbabwe. Shane Warne was breathing down his neck, however, and gained an extra chance to catch up when Muralitharan decided to withdraw from the tour of Australia in July. The two exchanged places twice before the year was out, but Warne was playing more Tests and eventually took a substantial lead.

By publicising his new delivery before the England series, Muralitharan had attracted unnecessary attention. A report by referee Chris Broad eventually led to a ban on his *doosra* while the International Cricket Council gathered evidence on its legality. But at home, he ruled unchallenged. He topped the first-class averages with 96 wickets at 14.40, 54 in six Tests against England and Australia and 42 in six domestic games; he also led Central Province to victory in an interprovincial tournament.

The national team did not match Muralitharan's personal success, winning only one of six home Tests and losing all three against Australia, usually from promising positions. The results proved that countries such as England and Australia, who once preferred to shun the subcontinent, were learning to master the conditions and beat Sri Lanka at their own game. Many blamed the captaincy of Hashan Tillekeratne, who had been given the Test side while Marvan Atapattu led the one-day team. Critics felt Sri Lanka could have whitewashed Michael Vaughan's England but for Tillekeratne's defensive approach, which allowed them to escape with draws in the first two Tests. Though Arjuna Ranatunga had favoured Tillekeratne as his successor when he stood down after the 1999 World Cup, it was widely believed that he owed his belated appointment – after Sanath Jayasuriya gave up in 2003 – to his former Nondescripts team-mate, Aravinda de Silva, an influential member of the selection committee. Tillekeratne resigned after the Australian defeats to be replaced by Atapattu, whose more positive approach brought a fresh outlook.

Former Australian opener John Dyson, who had become national coach in September 2003 after Dav Whatmore left for Bangladesh, also faced some criticism for his handling of the team. But a 100% record in Zimbabwe, albeit tainted by the absence of most of the home side's white players, a 1–0 defeat in Australia – not entirely disappointing on their territory – a Test series win over South Africa and successes in the one-day Asia Cup and Paktel Cup looked to have put him firmly in the saddle for the time being.

Another dominant figure, Thilanga Sumathipala, also continued to produce his share of headlines. Held in custody over alleged serious passport offences, Sumathipala decided to surrender his position as president of Sri Lanka Cricket when the elections came round in April; Mohan de Silva, who had served under him as secretary, moved up. SLC decided, however, that Sumathipala should continue to represent them on the ICC's executive board, and he managed to obtain bail and have his passport released by the court so he could attend an ICC meeting in Lahore in October 2004. None the less, the allegations against Sumathipala remained extremely murky. In January 2004, the central figure in the case against him, Dammika Amarasinghe, had been shot dead. Amarasinghe was a suspected underworld figure, facing trial for a series of contract killings, who is alleged to have travelled to the 1999 World Cup as a guest of the cricket board on a fake passport. Sumathipala is accused of using £1,500 of the board's money to help fund the trip.

Meanwhile, Ashantha de Mel, the 1980s Test seamer, succeeded Lalith Kaluperuma as chairman of selectors, though Kaluperuma remained on the seven-member committee. But Aravinda de Silva stepped down as a selector to concentrate on his work as SLC vice-president. His principal achievement was to reintroduce the provincial tournament, providing a higher level of competition in domestic first-class cricket. Replacing the invitation quad-rangular played in the previous two seasons, it proved a great success, with virtually all the national players taking part in advance of Australia's visit.

The Ten Sports Interprovincial Tournament was contested in January and February by five of Sri Lanka's seven provinces, playing four-day cricket rather than the three days of the club competition. North Central Province headed the league table, but lost the final to Central Province, captained by Muralitharan, with a day to spare. Muralitharan took 20 wickets at 12.69 in three matches; Kumar Sangakkara, tipped as a future Test captain, deputised for him in the other two games, and emerged as the tournament's leading scorer with 544 at 68.

The competition produced some of the best cricket of the season, most notably on the final day of the opening match between Central Province and Southern Province at Kandy. Challenged to score 512, Central reached 513 with one wicket to spare, a world record for a successful fourth-innings run-chase, beating Cambridge University's 507 for seven at Lord's in 1896. Sangakkara played a captain's innings of 101, while Sajith Fernando made 111 and Hasantha Fernando and Thilan Samaraweera fell just short of centuries; Sanath Jayasuriya sent down a marathon 43 overs, claiming four for 173.

In club cricket, Kumar Dharmasena led Bloomfield to a double triumph: victory in the Premier Trophy, when they defeated Colombo Colts by five wickets in December, and in the Premier Limited-Overs Tournament a month later, beating Colts again. Dharmasena himself took 17 wickets in the Premier Trophy, one behind 19-year-old seamer Udara Varuna, while Tillekeratne Dilshan and Jayasuriya both passed 400 runs.

The tournament was shortened in the previous season's format. Instead of the top ten teams from the early stages advancing to a Super League, the top four went straight into semi-finals, where Bloomfield crushed Nondescripts, and Colts took first-innings lead in a draw with Galle, who later won a third-place play-off. Though the title was decided in December, before the Interprovincial Tournament began, the remaining 12 teams continued to play in the Plate Championship, which included their results from the earlier phase and lasted into February. Moors, who had beaten Bloomfield in the previous season's Premier Trophy final but failed to reach the semi-finals this time, did get to the Plate final, only to lose to Sinhalese.

Six batsmen passed 1,000 runs, led by Dilshan, whose 1,284 included five hundreds; he earned a recall against England, his first Test since England's previous visit in early 2001, and never looked back.

FIRST-CLASS AVERAGES, 2003-04

BATTING

(Qualification: 500 runs, average 30.00)

	M	I	NO	R	HS	100s	Avge	Ct/St
R. S. Kaluwitharana (*Colts & W. Province*)	9	14	3	682	166	2	62.00	20/6
T. T. Samaraweera (*Sinhalese, SL & C. Prov.*) . . .	17	27	7	1,236	165	3	61.80	12
†R. P. A. H. Wickremaratne (*Sinhalese*)	7	11	0	628	171	2	57.09	10
T. M. Dilshan (*Bloomfield, SL & N. C. Prov.*)	16	26	1	1,284	151	5	51.36	18/1
D. P. M. D. Jayawardene (*Sinhalese, SL & NCP*) .	15	26	1	1,196	177	3	47.84	29
U. C. Hathurusinghe (*Moors*).	11	19	4	705	191	2	47.00	11
M. S. Atapattu (*Sinhalese, Sri Lanka & S. Prov.*) .	14	23	0	1,061	198	4	46.13	6
S. Kalawithigoda (*Colts & N. C. Province*)	12	19	2	774	126	4	45.52	18
†S. T. Jayasuriya (*Bloomfield, SL & S. Prov.*)	15	27	0	1,229	185	4	45.51	12
†K. C. Sangakkara (*Nondescripts, SL & C. Prov.*) .	16	28	1	1,191	125	3	44.11	43/12
†W. N. M. Soysa (*Police & C. Province*)	13	23	4	822	147	2	39.14	5
†S. I. Fernando (*Colts & C. Province*)	15	23	1	849	160	3	38.59	12
L. P. C. Silva (*Sinhalese & S. Province*)	12	21	2	733	110	2	38.57	5
†M. M. D. N. R. G. Perera (*Chilaw M. & S. Prov.*)	12	18	2	548	102	1	34.25	9
†W. M. G. Ramyakumara (*Chilaw M. & NCP*) . . .	9	17	2	513	148	1	34.20	2
W. S. Jayantha (*Bloomfield & S. Province*).	9	16	0	539	121	1	33.68	2
M. N. Jaymon (*Kurunegala Youth*)	8	16	1	502	150*	2	33.46	14/6

	M	I	NO	R	HS	100s	Avge	Ct/St
R. R. Wimalasiri (_Police & S. Province_)	10	17	1	514	101	1	32.12	9
R. P. Hewage (_Nondescripts & W. Province_).	13	24	2	700	78*	0	31.81	13
W. M. B. Perera (_Moors & C. Province_)	12	19	2	531	83	0	31.23	8
K. R. P. Silva (_Air Force_).	12	22	0	686	171	2	31.18	14
†H. P. Tillekeratne (_Nondescripts, SL & W. Prov._) .	16	26	5	637	122*	1	30.33	15

† _Left-handed batsman._

BOWLING

(Qualification: 30 wickets, average 25.00)

	Style	O	M	R	W	BB	5W/i	Avge
M. Muralitharan (_Tamil U., SL & C. Prov._). . . .	OB	636.4	213	1,383	96	7-46	7	14.40
M. K. G. C. P. Lakshitha (_Air Force & Uva P._).	RFM	263	45	834	52	6-27	3	16.03
T. C. B. Fernando (_Colombo & S. Province_). . . .	RFM	270.2	62	727	41	6-19	2	17.73
P. N. Ranjith (_Moors & N. C. Province_).	LFM	196.4	37	625	35	6-42	2	17.85
K. T. G. D. Prasad (_Sinhalese & S. Province_) . .	RFM	244.5	47	804	42	6-25	2	19.14
M. S. Villavarayan (_Colombo & C. Province_) . .	RFM	293.4	77	812	41	5-44	2	19.80
P. D. R. L. Perera (_Sinhalese & S. Province_). . .	LFM	222.4	33	916	45	7-90	3	20.35
G. S. Dananjaya (_Air Force_)	SLA	218.2	35	782	38	6-76	1	20.57
S. Weerakoon (_Burgher_)	SLA	260.5	73	619	30	5-123	1	20.63
M. R. C. N. Bandaratilleke (_Colts & Uva Prov._)	SLA	362.3	88	875	42	6-19	2	20.83
A. Rizan (_Air Force_)	OB	179.3	20	683	32	6-99	2	21.34
G. A. S. Perera (_Panadura & S. Province_)	SLA	269.2	62	689	32	5-71	1	21.53
K. R. P. Silva (_Air Force_)	RFM	187	33	672	31	7-41	2	21.67
A. W. Ekanayake (_Kurunegala Youth_).	SLA	268.3	39	874	40	5-60	2	21.85
W. P. U. J. C. Vaas (_Colts, Sri Lanka & Uva P._)	LFM	417.3	88	1,174	53	6-29	2	22.15
K. H. R. K. Fernando (_Chilaw M. & C. Prov._)	RFM	239.1	50	711	32	6-45	1	22.21
D. G. R. Dhammika (_Chilaw M. & C. Prov._) . .	SLA	277.2	49	871	39	6-50	2	22.33
M. D. K. Perera (_Panadura_).	OB	260.1	58	721	32	6-78	2	22.53
D. Hettiarachchi (_Sinhalese & W. Province_). . . .	SLA	354.1	92	1,024	42	5-41	4	24.38
H. P. A. Priyantha (_Police_).	LM	277.1	64	741	30	7-77	2	24.70

PREMIER TROPHY, 2003-04

Group A	Played	Won	Lost	Drawn	1st-inns lead	Bonus points Batting	Bonus points Bowling	Points
Nondescripts CC	7	2	1	4	3	13.165	9.5	70.665
Galle CC	7	1	1	5	4	10.105	10.5	64.405†
Sinhalese SC	7	2	0	5*	2	11.63	8.8	59.78†
Chilaw Marians CC . .	7	2	0	5	1	11.615	11.3	54.915
Tamil Union C & AC . .	7	2	2	3*	1	8.89	8.8	49.69
Moors SC.	7	1	0	6	2	8.905	11.7	48.605
Air Force SC.	7	0	4	3	2	10.44	9.2	35.64
Police SC	7	0	2	5	1	11.475	8.3	27.775

Group B	Played	Won	Lost	Drawn	1st-inns lead	Bonus points Batting	Bonus points Bowling	Points
Colts CC	7	2	0	5	3	11.765	11.5	71.265
Bloomfield C & AC . .	7	0	0	7*	5	11.735	6.8	58.535
Colombo CC	7	1	0	6	3	10.465	9.5	55.815†
Ragama CC.	7	0	1	6	4	11.28	8.0	51.28
Panadura SC	7	1	2	4	1	8.39	9.2	37.59
Sebastianites C & AC .	7	0	0	6	1	9.45	8.1	37.35†
Burgher RC.	7	1	1	5	1	8.99	8.1	37.09
Kurunegala Youth CC .	7	1	1	5*	1	10.455	8.1	26.555

* _Includes one match abandoned without a ball bowled._
† _Points deducted for slow over-rate: Galle –0.2, Sinhalese –0.65, Colombo –0.15, Sebastianites –0.2._

Outright win = 12 pts; lead on first innings in a drawn game = 8 pts. Bonus points were awarded as follows: 0.1 pt for each wicket taken and 0.005 pt for each run scored, up to 400 runs per innings.

The top two teams in each group qualified for the semi-finals; the others took part in the Plate Championship and carried forward their results and points to the Plate table.

Semi-finals: Bloomfield beat Nondescripts by 276 runs; Colts drew with Galle but qualified for final by virtue of their first-innings lead.

Third-place play-off: Galle beat Nondescripts by nine wickets.

Final: Bloomfield beat Colts by five wickets.

PLATE CHAMPIONSHIP, 2003-04

Group A	Played	Won	Lost	Drawn	1st-inns lead	Batting	Bowling	Points
Sinhalese SC	9	2	0	7*	4	17.065	11.8	84.215†
Burgher RC	9	1	1	7	2	14.455	10.7	53.155
Panadura SC	9	1	2	6	1	11.175	12.9	44.075

Group B	Played	Won	Lost	Drawn	1st-inns lead	Batting	Bowling	Points
Chilaw Marians CC	9	3	0	6	2	16.445	15	83.445
Tamil Union C & AC	9	2	3	4*	1	13.135	11.8	56.935
Kurunegala Youth CC	9	0	2	7*	2	14.25	11.7	41.95

Group C	Played	Won	Lost	Drawn	1st-inns lead	Batting	Bowling	Points
Moors SC	9	2	0	7	3	14.475	14.7	77.175
Colombo CC	9	2	1	6	3	15.03	12.3	75.18†
Air Force SC	9	0	5	4	2	13.78	12.2	41.98

Group D	Played	Won	Lost	Drawn	1st-inns lead	Batting	Bowling	Points
Ragama CC	9	0	1	8	6	16.32	11.3	75.62
Sebastianites C & AC	9	2	0	7	1	12.985	12.1	56.885†
Police SC	9	0	3	6	1	15.11	10.8	33.91

* Includes one match abandoned without a ball bowled.
† Points deducted for slow over-rate: Sinhalese –0.65, Colombo –0.15, Sebastianites –0.2.
Outright win = 12 pts; lead on first innings in a drawn game = 8 pts. Bonus points were awarded as follows: 0.1 pt for each wicket taken and 0.005 pt for each run scored, up to 400 runs per innings.

Semi-finals: Moors beat Chilaw Marians by ten wickets; Sinhalese drew with Ragama but qualified for the final by virtue of their first-innings lead.

Final: Sinhalese beat Moors by 103 runs.

PREMIER TROPHY

Group A

At Air Force Ground, Katunayake, October 10, 11, 12, 2003. **Chilaw Marians won by 198 runs.** Toss: Chilaw Marians. **Chilaw Marians 247** (M. M. D. N. R. G. Perera 70*; W. P. Wickrama 6-61) **and 259-4 dec.** (W. M. G. Ramyakumara 57, C. S. Fernando 56, K. H. R. K. Fernando 55*, P. C. Jayasundera 50*); **Air Force 119** (P. C. Jayasundera 5-23) **and 189** (D. G. R. Dhammika 6-50). *Chilaw Marians 16.53 pts, Air Force 2.94 pts.*

At Moors Sports Club, Braybrooke Place, Colombo, October 10, 11, 12, 2003. **Sinhalese won by ten wickets.** Toss: Sinhalese. **Galle 139** (T. K. D. Sudarshana 52) **and 213; Sinhalese 329-7 dec.** (M. S. Atapattu 107, L. P. C. Silva 106; N. C. Komasaru 4-94) **and 24-0.** *Sinhalese 15.765 pts, Galle 2.46 pts.*

At Nondescripts Cricket Club, Maitland Place, Colombo, October 10, 11, 12, 2003. **Drawn.** Toss: Moors. **Nondescripts 213** (U. D. U. Chandana 53; P. N. Ranjith 6-42) **and 282-7 dec.** (R. P. Hewage 74, K. C. Sangakkara 67); **Moors 206** (C. R. B. Mudalige 5-54) **and 0-0.** *Nondescripts 11.475 pts, Moors 2.73 pts.*

At P. Saravanamuttu Stadium, Colombo, October 10, 11, 12, 2003. **Tamil Union won by an innings and 146 runs.** Toss: Police. **Tamil Union 412-8 dec.** (R. R. Tissera 143, P. B. Ediriweera 65, C. P. Handunnettige 88; P. Serasinghe 4-129); **Police 83** (K. G. A. S. Kalum 4-26, M. Muralitharan 4-5) **and 183** (R. R. Wimalasiri 55*; W. J. M. R. Dias 5-34, M. Muralitharan 5-41). *Tamil Union 16 pts, Police 2.13 pts.*
Muralitharan's first-innings figures were 6–2–5–4.

At Air Force Ground, Katunayake, October 17, 18, 19, 2003. **Tamil Union won by five wickets.** Toss: Air Force. **Air Force 114** (C. M. Bandara 4-12) **and 126** (M. Muralitharan 5-29); **Tamil Union 104** (M. K. G. C. P. Lakshitha 6-27) **and 139-5.** *Tamil Union 15.215 pts, Air Force 2.7 pts.*

At Moors Sports Club, Braybrooke Place, Colombo, October 17, 18, 19, 2003. **Drawn.** Toss: Galle. **Moors 174** (M. N. R. Cooray 57) **and 208** (H. M. S. Jayawardene 76); **Galle 125** (P. N. Ranjith 5-34) **and 209-5** (A. Rideegammanagedera 76). *Moors 11.41 pts, Galle 3.67 pts.*

At Nondescripts Cricket Club, Maitland Place, Colombo, October 17, 18, 19, 2003. **Drawn.** Toss: Sinhalese. **Sinhalese 309** (M. S. Atapattu 198) **and 130-3; Nondescripts 226** (R. P. Hewage 56, K. C. Sangakkara 55). *Nondescripts 2.43 pts, Sinhalese 11.195 pts.*

At Police Park, Colombo, October 17, 18, 19, 2003. **Chilaw Marians won by nine wickets.** Toss: Police. **Chilaw Marians 410-8 dec.** (C. S. Fernando 96, M. M. D. N. R. G. Perera 102, C. U. Jayasinghe 52, D. G. R. Dhammika 54*) **and 25-1; Police 157** (P. C. Jayasundera 4-36) **and 277** (W. N. M. Soysa 101; D. G. R. Dhammika 5-58). *Chilaw Marians 16.125 pts, Police 3.07 pts.*

At Bloomfield Cricket and Athletic Club, Reid Avenue, Colombo, October 24, 25, 26, 2003. **Drawn.** Toss: Moors. **Sinhalese 232** (T. T. Samaraweera 56; P. N. Ranjith 4-45) **and 126-5** (D. P. M. D. Jayawardene 61); **Moors 288** (W. M. B. Perera 80, U. C. Hathurusinghe 52, M. N. R. Cooray 58*; P. D. R. L. Perera 4-68). *Moors 10.94 pts, Sinhalese 2.79 pts.*

At Nondescripts Cricket Club, Maitland Place, Colombo, October 24, 25, 26, 2003. **Galle won by an innings and 26 runs.** Toss: Nondescripts. **Galle 400** (T. K. D. Sudarshana 106, M. K. P. B. Kularatne 80, K. M. D. N. Kulasekara 95; W. C. A. Ganegama 5-94); **Nondescripts 73** (S. L. Malinga 4-21) **and 301** (H. P. Tillekeratne 57, K. C. Sangakkara 91; S. L. Malinga 5-80). *Galle 16 pts, Nondescripts 2.87 pts.*

At Police Park, Colombo, October 24, 25, 26, 2003. **Drawn.** Toss: Police. **Police 205** (W. N. M. Soysa 52; M. K. G. C. P. Lakshitha 6-65) **and 322-6** (W. N. M. Soysa 69, R. R. Wimalasiri 79, R. G. D. Sanjeewa 61); **Air Force 474** (K. R. P. Silva 171, T. R. Peiris 98, S. N. Wijesinghe 54; H. P. A. Priyantha 5-120). *Police 3.635 pts, Air Force 11.6 pts.*

At P. Saravanamuttu Stadium, Colombo, October 24, 25, 26, 2003. **Drawn.** Toss: Tamil Union. **Tamil Union 298** (P. B. Ediriweera 136) **and 240** (P. B. Ediriweera 61, N. A. N. N. Perera 69; D. G. R. Dhammika 4-41); **Chilaw Marians 199** (P. C. Jayasundera 50; M. Muralitharan 4-50) **and 101-7** (C. M. Bandara 4-38). *Tamil Union 12.39 pts, Chilaw Marians 3.5 pts.*

At FTZ Sports Complex, Katunayake, October 31, November 1, 2, 2003. **Drawn.** Toss: Galle. **Galle 244** (D. G. R. Dhammika 4-56) **and 96-5; Chilaw Marians 216** (K. H. R. K. Fernando 50, P. C. Jayasundera 71; S. L. Malinga 5-69). *Chilaw Marians 2.58 pts, Galle 10.65 pts.*

At Moors Sports Club, Braybrooke Place, Colombo, October 31, November 1, 2, 2003. **Drawn.** Toss: Moors. **Police 132** (H. M. R. K. B. Herath 8-43) **and 148** (W. N. M. Soysa 61); **Moors 105** (T. A. V. H. K. Ranaweera 4-30) **and 153-7** (H. P. A. Priyantha 4-50). *Moors 3.29 pts, Police 11.1 pts.*

At Nondescripts Cricket Club, Maitland Place, Colombo, October 31, November 1, 2, 2003. **Nondescripts won by an innings and 130 runs.** Toss: Nondescripts. **Nondescripts 379-9 dec.** (H. A. P. W. Jayawardene 131, R. P. Arnold 89, U. D. U. Chandana 66); **Tamil Union 118 and 131.** *Nondescripts 15.895 pts, Tamil Union 2.145 pts.*

At P. Saravanamuttu Stadium, Colombo, November 1, 2, 3, 2003. **Sinhalese won by 150 runs.** Toss: Air Force. **Sinhalese 304-7 dec.** (D. P. M. D. Jayawardene 116, L. P. C. Silva 83; G. S. Dananjaya 4-52) **and 174-5 dec.** (R. P. A. H. Wickremaratne 110); **Air Force 215** (T. R. Peiris 73) **and 113** (T. T. Samaraweera 4-35). *Sinhalese 16.39 pts, Air Force 2.84 pts.*

At FTZ Sports Complex, Katunayake, November 7, 8, 9, 2003. **Drawn.** Toss: Moors. **Moors 146** (W. M. G. Ramyakumara 4-36) **and 172-4** (W. M. B. Perera 76*); **Chilaw Marians 274** (L. J. P. Gunaratne 98). *Chilaw Marians 10.77 pts, Moors 2.59 pts.*

At Nondescripts Cricket Club, Maitland Place, Colombo, November 7, 8, 9, 2003. **Nondescripts won by 133 runs.** Toss: Air Force. **Nondescripts 214-7 dec.** (M. N. Nawaz 68, K. C. Sangakkara 59; G. S. Dananjaya 6-76) **and 123-7 dec.** (K. C. Sangakkara 66; G. S. Dananjaya 4-46); **Air Force 109 and 95** (D. H. S. Pradeep 5-27). *Nondescripts 15.685 pts, Air Force 2.42 pts.*

At Police Park, Colombo, November 7, 8, 9, 2003. **Drawn.** Toss: Police. **Galle 254** (M. M. D. P. V. Perera 57; U. M. G. U. Karunaratne 5-76) **and 11-1; Police 51** (W. R. S. de Silva 4-25, S. L. Malinga 6-17) **and 220** (S. A. Wijeratne 57; N. C. Komasaru 5-48). *Police 2.455 pts, Galle 11.325 pts.*

At P. Saravanamuttu Stadium, Colombo, November 7, 8, 9, 2003. **Tamil Union v Sinhalese. Abandoned.**

At Moors Sports Club, Braybrooke Place, Colombo, November 14, 15, 16, 2003. **Drawn.** Toss: Air Force. **Air Force 144** (L. H. D. Dilhara 6-24) **and 117** (L. L. Fernando 4-26); **Moors 67** (K. R. P. Silva 7-41) **and 29-1.** *Moors 2.48 pts, Air Force 10.405 pts.*

At Nondescripts Cricket Club, Maitland Place, Colombo, November 14, 15, 16, 2003. **Drawn.** Toss: Chilaw Marians. **Nondescripts 152** (K. H. R. K. Fernando 4-23) **and 114-3** (R. P. Hewage 78*); **Chilaw Marians 135** (K. R. Pushpakumara 5-39). *Nondescripts 10.33 pts, Chilaw Marians 1.975 pts.*

At Police Park, Colombo, November 14, 15, 16, 2003. **Drawn.** Toss: Police. **Police 286** (R. R. Wimalasiri 101, H. P. A. Priyantha 76; P. D. R. L. Perera 6-71); **Sinhalese 229-8** (T. T. Samaraweera 114*; U. M. G. U. Karunaratne 4-57). *Police 2.23 pts, Sinhalese 2.095 pts.*

At P. Saravanamuttu Stadium, Colombo, November 14, 15, 16, 2003. **Drawn.** Toss: Galle. **Galle 142** (P. S. Jayaprakashdaran 6-46) **and 30-0; Tamil Union 119** (A. Rideegammanagedera 4-24). *Tamil Union 1.595 pts, Galle 9.86 pts.*

At Air Force Ground, Katunayake, November 28, 29, 30, 2003. **Drawn.** Toss: Galle. **Air Force 134** (N. C. Komasaru 4-48) **and 213-8** (W. R. D. Dissanayake 57, H. E. Vithana 6-60); **Galle 158** (W. R. D. Dissanayake 5-35). *Air Force 2.735 pts, Galle 10.59 pts.*

At FTZ Sports Complex, Katunayake, November 28, 29, 30, 2003. **Drawn.** Toss: Chilaw Marians. **Sinhalese 412-6 dec.** (W. M. S. M. Perera 119, B. M. A. J. Mendis 152*, D. N. T. Zoysa 66) **and 69-5 dec.; Chilaw Marians 207** (M. M. D. N. R. G. Perera 66; P. D. R. L. Perera 4-45) **and 260-8** (M. K. Gajanayake 95, K. H. R. K. Fernando 61; P. D. R. L. Perera 4-70). *Chilaw Marians 3.435 pts, Sinhalese 11.995 pts.*

At Moors Sports Club, Braybrooke Place, Colombo, November 28, 29, 30, 2003. **Moors won by eight wickets.** Toss: Moors. **Tamil Union 96** (A. C. Wettasinghe 4-24) **and 133** (M. N. R. Cooray 4-29); **Moors 154 and 79-2.** *Moors 15.165 pts, Tamil Union 2.345 pts.*

At Police Park, Colombo, November 28, 29, 30, 2003. **Drawn.** Toss: Police. **Nondescripts 215** (K. M. H. Perera 78, H. P. Padmasanka 51; H. P. A. Priyantha 7-77) **and 341** (J. K. Silva 50, H. P. Padmasanka 106, W. C. A. Ganegama 67); **Police 195** (W. N. M. Soysa 58; D. H. S. Pradeep 6-41) **and 36-2.** *Police 3.155 pts, Nondescripts 11.98 pts.*

Padmasanka scored 51 and 106 on first-class debut.

Group B

At Colombo Cricket Club, Maitland Crescent, Colombo, October 10, 11, 12, 2003. **Drawn.** Toss: Colombo. **Burgher 191** (V. S. K. Waragoda 60, A. C. Pathirana 57; T. C. B. Fernando 6-19) **and 200** (B. C. M. S. Mendis 52; B. S. M. Warnapura 4-40); **Colombo 292** (A. S. A. Perera 62; R. C. R. P. Silva 5-74) **and 26-1.** *Colombo 11.59 pts, Burgher 3.055 pts.*

At Colts Cricket Club, Havelock Park, Colombo, October 10, 11, 12, 2003. **Drawn.** Toss: Colts. **Bloomfield 361** (S. T. Jayasuriya 123, H. D. P. K. Dharmasena 74) **and 98-6** (M. Pushpakumara 4-27); **Colts 345** (S. I. Fernando 103, D. K. Liyanage 50; D. M. G. S. Dissanayake 4-47). *Colts 3.325 pts, Bloomfield 11.295 pts.*

At Panadura Esplanade, Panadura, October 10, 11, 12, 2003. **Sebastianites won by an innings and seven runs.** Toss: Panadura. **Panadura 117** (K. A. D. M. Fernando 5-35) **and 169; Sebastianites 293** (P. S. A. N. Shiroman 65, K. A. D. M. Fernando 100; G. A. S. Perera 5-71). *Sebastianites 15.465 pts, Panadura 2.43 pts.*

At Bloomfield Cricket and Athletic Club, Reid Avenue, Colombo, October 17, 18, 19, 2003. **Drawn.** Toss: Burgher. **Bloomfield 347** (T. M. Dilshan 151) **and 77-2; Burgher 210** (V. S. K. Waragoda 60). *Bloomfield 11.12 pts, Burgher 2.25 pts.*

At Colombo Cricket Club, Maitland Crescent, Colombo, October 17, 18, 19, 2003. **Drawn.** Toss: Colts. **Colombo 215** (A. S. A. Perera 66) **and 243** (A. S. Polonowita 106*; D. K. Liyanage 5-34); **Colts 198** (T. C. B. Fernando 4-62) **and 28-0.** *Colombo 11.14 pts, Colts 3.13 pts.*

At Welagedera Stadium, Kurunegala, October 17, 18, 19, 2003. **Drawn.** Toss: Kurunegala Youth. **Sebastianites 175** (P. S. A. N. Shiroman 103; A. W. Ekanayake 5-60) **and 209-7 dec.** (P. S. A. N. Shiroman 101, K. A. D. M. Fernando 56*; A. W. Ekanayake 5-94); **Kurunegala Youth 130 and 151-7** (D. M. Ramanayake 56; A. P. Dalugoda 4-52). *Kurunegala Youth 3.105 pts, Sebastianites 11.62 pts.*

Shiroman scored a hundred in each innings.

At Panadura Esplanade, Panadura, October 17, 18, 19, 2003. **Drawn.** Toss: Panadura. **Ragama 210** (K. S. Rodrigo 50; N. Quintaz 4-49) **and 225-9** (K. S. Rodrigo 77; M. D. K. Perera 6-78); **Panadura 192.** *Panadura 2.86 pts, Ragama 11.175 pts.*

At Colombo Cricket Club, Maitland Crescent, Colombo, October 24, 25, 26, 2003. **Drawn.** Toss: Colombo. **Colombo 238** (K. G. N. Randika 66; H. S. H. Alles 4-31) **and 236-6** (D. N. Hunukumbura 91, A. S. A. Perera 67*); **Bloomfield 370** (S. T. Jayasuriya 129, S. I. de Saram 59). *Colombo 3.37 pts, Bloomfield 11.45 pts.*

At Colts Cricket Club, Havelock Park, Colombo, October 24, 25, 26, 2003. **Colts won by an innings and 123 runs.** Toss: Colts. **Colts 338** (H. G. J. M. Kulatunga 52, K. E. A. Upashantha 55, P. S. Liyanage 55*; D. F. Arnolda 5-87); **Burgher 112 and 103** (M. R. C. N. Bandaratilleke 6-19). *Colts 15.69 pts, Burgher 2.075 pts.*

In Colts' first innings, Upashantha and Liyanage added 114 for the last wicket.

At Panadura Esplanade, Panadura, October 24, 25, 26, 2003. **Panadura won by 207 runs.** Toss: Kurunegala Youth. **Panadura 251** (R. Soysa 76; H. M. Maduwantha 4-43) **and 264-5 dec.** (T. N. S. Warusamana 86, J. S. K. Peiris 102*); **Kurunegala Youth 128** (G. A. S. Perera 4-51, M. D. K. Perera 4-18) **and 180** (N. Quintaz 4-52, G. A. S. Perera 4-58). *Panadura 16.575 pts, Kurunegala Youth 3.04 pts.*

At Tyronne Fernando Stadium, Moratuwa, October 24, 25, 26, 2003. **Drawn.** Toss: Ragama. **Sebastianites 142** (W. D. D. S. Perera 5-37) **and 214-8** (K. A. D. M. Fernando 62; R. D. Dissanayake 5-66); **Ragama 439-6 dec.** (K. S. Rodrigo 58, W. D. D. S. Perera 128, E. F. M. U. Fernando 102*, K. A. S. Jayasinghe 63). *Sebastianites 2.38 pts, Ragama 11.8 pts.*

At Bloomfield Cricket and Athletic Club, Reid Avenue, Colombo, October 31, November 1, 2, 2003. **Drawn.** Toss: Sebastianites. **Bloomfield 402-7 dec.** (T. M. Dilshan 150*, D. M. G. S. Dissanayake 61) **and 232-4** (T. M. Dilshan 54, S. H. T. Kandamby 69, H. D. P. K. Dharmasena 52*); **Sebastianites 202.** *Bloomfield 12.16 pts, Sebastianites 2.11 pts.*

At Burgher Recreation Ground, Havelock Park, Colombo, October 31, November 1, 2, 2003. **Burgher won by eight wickets.** Toss: Burgher. **Kurunegala Youth 221** (N. M. Ramzi 64; S. Weerakoon 4-52) **and 163; Burgher 271** (D. M. Perumal 112*, D. N. Pathirana 102; A. W. Ekanayake 4-76, K. K. S. Jayasinghe 4-15) **and 114-2** (R. H. S. Silva 55*). *Burgher 15.925 pts, Kurunegala Youth 3.12 pts.*

At Colombo Cricket Club, Maitland Crescent, Colombo, October 31, November 1, 2, 2003. **Colombo won by an innings and 32 runs.** Toss: Colombo. **Ragama 171** (S. Arangalla 53; M. S. Villavarayan 4-34, B. S. M. Warnapura 4-24) **and 168** (E. F. M. U. Fernando 69); **Colombo 371-4 dec.** (D. N. Hunukumbura 82, J. Mubarak 169, A. S. Polonowita 69). *Colombo 15.855 pts, Ragama 2.095 pts.*

At Colts Cricket Club, Havelock Park, Colombo, October 31, November 1, 2, 2003. **Colts won by 140 runs.** Toss: Colts. **Colts 273** (R. S. Kaluwitharana 100; M. D. K. Perera 4-68) **and 149-1 dec.** (D. P. Samaraweera 87*); **Panadura 127** (M. R. C. N. Bandaratilleke 5-42, S. I. Fernando 5-32) **and 155** (S. I. Fernando 5-47, M. Pushpakumara 4-40). *Colts 16.11 pts, Panadura 2.51 pts.*

At Bloomfield Cricket and Athletic Club, Reid Avenue, Colombo, November 7, 8, 9, 2003. **Bloomfield v Kurunegala Youth. Abandoned.**

At Burgher Recreation Ground, Havelock Park, Colombo, November 7, 8, 9, 2003. **Drawn.** Toss: Burgher. **Sebastianites 214; Burgher 313-6** (D. M. Perumal 64, R. H. S. Silva 100*, V. S. K. Waragoda 63*, Extras 50; K. A. D. M. Fernando 5-84). *Burgher 10.565 pts, Sebastianites 1.47 pts.*

At Colombo Cricket Club, Maitland Crescent, Colombo, November 7, 8, 9, 2003. **Drawn.** Toss: Panadura. **Colombo 105** (N. Quintaz 6-43) **and 14-2; Panadura 111-8 dec.** *Colombo 1.395 pts, Panadura 9.755 pts.*

At Colts Cricket Club, Havelock Park, Colombo, November 7, 8, 9, 2003. **Drawn.** Toss: Ragama. **Colts 222-8 dec.** (S. Kalawithigoda 110*, M. Pushpakumara 57); **Ragama 91** (W. P. U. J. C. Vaas 6-29) **and 18-2.** *Colts 10.31 pts, Ragama 1.345 pts.*

At Kadirana Cricket Grounds, Gampaha, November 14, 15, 16, 2003. **Drawn.** Toss: Ragama. **Ragama 190** (K. S. Rodrigo 83*; H. G. D. Nayanakantha 5-87) **and 62-1; Bloomfield 114** (S. Arangalla 4-28). *Bloomfield 1.67 pts, Ragama 10.26 pts.*
  Rodrigo carried his bat through Ragama's first innings.

At Colombo Cricket Club, Maitland Crescent, Colombo, November 14, 15, 16, 2003. **Drawn.** Toss: Sebastianites. **Sebastianites 274** (S. H. S. M. K. Silva 92, K. A. D. J. Siriwardene 63; M. S. Villavarayan 5-57, N. S. Rupasinghe 4-73); **Colombo 79-4.** *Colombo 1.395 pts, Sebastianites 1.77 pts.*

At Welagedera Stadium, Kurunegala, November 14, 15, 16, 2003. **Drawn.** Toss: Colts. **Kurunegala Youth 124** (D. K. Liyanage 5-31) **and 170-7; Colts 263** (S. Kalawithigoda 114; A. W. Ekanayake 4-78, M. P. G. D. P. Gunatilleke 4-43). *Kurunegala Youth 2.47 pts, Colts 11.015 pts.*

At Panadura Esplanade, Panadura, November 14, 15, 16, 2003. **Drawn.** Toss: Panadura. **Panadura 146-6** (J. S. K. Peiris 51*; S. Weerakoon 4-45) **v Burgher.** *Panadura 0.73 pts, Burgher 0.6 pts.*

At FTZ Sports Complex, Katunayake, November 21, 22, 23, 2003. **Drawn.** Toss: Ragama. **Kurunegala Youth 296** (M. N. Jaymon 113) **and 143** (R. H. Sureshchandra 62; R. D. Dissanayake 5-39); **Ragama 172** (S. A. Perera 52; A. W. Ekanayake 4-55) **and 161-8** (C. M. Withanage 67). *Kurunegala Youth 11.995 pts, Ragama 3.665 pts.*

At Bloomfield Cricket and Athletic Club, Reid Avenue, Colombo, November 28, 29, 30, 2003. **Drawn.** Toss: Panadura. **Bloomfield 178** (D. M. G. S. Dissanayake 51; G. A. S. Perera 4-47) **and 170** (W. S. Jayantha 50; G. A. S. Perera 4-54); **Panadura 144** (J. S. K. Peiris 57*) **and 2-1.** *Bloomfield 10.84 pts, Panadura 2.73 pts.*

At Burgher Recreation Ground, Havelock Park, Colombo, November 28, 29, 30, 2003. **Drawn.** Toss: Ragama. **Ragama 322** (C. M. Withanage 61, E. F. M. U. Fernando 86, S. A. D. U. Indrasiri 52; S. Weerakoon 4-60) **and 66-2; Burgher 284** (D. W. A. N. D. Vitharana 63, B. C. M. S. Mendis 95*). *Burgher 2.62 pts, Ragama 10.94 pts.*

At Welagedera Stadium, Kurunegala, November 28, 29, 30, 2003. **Drawn.** Toss: Colombo. **Kurunegala Youth 230** (R. H. Sureshchandra 51, B. M. S. N. Mendis 61; N. S. Rupasinghe 4-41) **and 155-7; Colombo 274-9 dec.** (D. N. Hunukumbura 54, T. C. B. Fernando 60*; A. W. Ekanayake 4-91). *Kurunegala Youth 2.825 pts, Colombo 11.07 pts.*

At Tyronne Fernando Stadium, Moratuwa, November 28, 29, 30, 2003. **Drawn.** Toss: Colts. **Colts 327-9 dec.** (S. Kalawithigoda 110, D. P. Samaraweera 105; B. C. N. Amarasinghe 4-84) **and 210-8; Sebastianites 167** (W. J. S. D. Perera 50; D. K. Liyanage 4-26, M. Pushpakumara 4-51). *Sebastianites 2.535 pts, Colts 11.685 pts.*

Kalawithigoda scored his third hundred in successive innings.

Semi-finals

At Colts Cricket Club, Havelock Park, Colombo, December 5, 6, 7, 2003. **Bloomfield won by 276 runs.** Toss: Bloomfield. **Bloomfield 213** (D. M. G. S. Dissanayake 50; D. H. S. Pradeep 4-26) **and 334** (M. T. Gunaratne 51, W. S. Jayantha 121, T. M. Dilshan 57; J. Saverimuttupillai 5-133); **Nondescripts 148** (T. M. Dilshan 4-22) **and 123** (D. M. G. S. Dissanayake 4-27).

At Nondescripts Cricket Club, Maitland Place, Colombo, December 5, 6, 7, 2003. **Drawn.** Colts were declared winners by virtue of their first-innings lead. Toss: Colts. **Galle 134** (D. K. Liyanage 4-35) **and 137-5** (C. R. P. Galappathy 53*); **Colts 683** (S. Kalawithigoda 126, S. I. Fernando 160, R. S. Kaluwitharana 53, H. G. J. M. Kulatunga 54, M. Pushpakumara 56, M. R. C. N. Bandaratilleke 68; M. M. D. P. V. Perera 4-139).

Kalawithigoda scored his fourth hundred in five innings, in four successive matches. Six batsmen passed 50 in Colts' 683, the highest total in Sri Lankan domestic first-class cricket.

Third-place play-off

At Moors Sports Club, Braybrooke Place, Colombo, December 26, 27, 2003. **Galle won by nine wickets.** Toss: Galle. **Nondescripts 138** (A. Rideegammanagedera 4-30) **and 127** (A. Rideegammanagedera 4-37); **Galle 205** (T. K. D. Sudarshana 82) **and 62-1.**

FINAL

BLOOMFIELD v COLTS

At Sinhalese Sports Club, Maitland Place, Colombo, December 26, 27, 28, 2003. Bloomfield won by five wickets. Toss: Bloomfield.

Bloomfield won a low-scoring match after a scare on the last afternoon, when they lost five wickets for 31. Bandaratilleke's left-arm spin claimed three in 20 balls, Dilshan was brilliantly run out by Kulatunga, and Vaas claimed a fifth with 57 still required. But Lokuarachchi hit 48 in

40 balls to clinch the title. Asked to bat, Colts had toppled to 38 for six in the game's first 14 overs. Liyanage, at No. 8, salvaged something with an unbeaten 76, and was soon back in action with the ball, removing both openers, while Vaas coupled three wickets with a run-out to leave Bloomfield on a shaky 103 for seven. They too were rescued by their No. 8, Dissanayake, whose 83 was the top score of the match. The spinners took charge when Colts resumed on the second afternoon. Kaluwitharana resisted longer than most, but became Jayasuriya's fourth victim just before the close. Despite another lengthy tail-end partnership in the morning, Daniel and Jayasuriya took Bloomfield halfway to their target before the final wobble.

Close of play: First day, Bloomfield 100-5 (de Saram 28, Lokuarachchi 2); Second day, Colts 158-8 (Upashantha 0).

Colts

D. P. Samaraweera b Nayanakantha	0	– lbw b Lokuarachchi.		31
C. Mendis c Dilshan b Varuna	15	– b Lokuarachchi.		3
S. I. Fernando c Dilshan b Nayanakantha	0	– st Dilshan b Dharmasena		29
†R. S. Kaluwitharana lbw b Nayanakantha	11	– lbw b Jayasuriya.		72
*H. G. J. M. Kulatunga c Dilshan b Nayanakantha	37	– c Lokuarachchi b Jayasuriya		16
M. Pushpakumara b Varuna	1	– (7) lbw b Jayasuriya		1
W. P. U. J. C. Vaas lbw b Varuna	0	– (8) c and b Dharmasena.		0
D. K. Liyanage not out	76	– (6) c Weeraratne b Jayasuriya		0
K. E. A. Upashantha c Jayasuriya b Lokuarachchi	21	– c Dissanayake b Dharmasena		20
M. R. C. N. Bandaratilleke c Jayasuriya b Dharmasena	1	– c Weeraratne b Dharmasena		48
M. K. D. I. Amerasinghe c Daniel b Dharmasena	6	– not out		0
L-b 1, w 1, n-b 5	7	B 13, l-b 6		19
	175			**239**

1/4 (1) 2/4 (3) 3/25 (4) 4/36 (2)
5/38 (6) 6/38 (7) 7/80 (5)
8/132 (9) 9/151 (10) 10/175 (11)

1/26 (2) 2/53 (1) 3/91 (3)
4/130 (5) 5/130 (6) 6/139 (7)
7/158 (8) 8/158 (4)
9/239 (10) 10/239 (9)

Bowling: *First Innings*—Nayanakantha 16–2–54–4; Varuna 12–4–53–3; Weeraratne 5–0–22–0; Lokuarachchi 10–3–35–1; Dharmasena 4–1–10–2. *Second Innings*—Nayanakantha 5–0–26–0; Varuna 2–0–9–0; Lokuarachchi 25–4–77–2; Dharmasena 24.4–5–56–4; Jayasuriya 21–5–46–4; Dissanayake 1–0–6–0.

Bloomfield

G. I. Daniel c Vaas b Liyanage	10	– c sub b Bandaratilleke		42
S. T. Jayasuriya c Upashantha b Liyanage	36	– c Liyanage b Bandaratilleke		52
M. T. Gunaratne c Kaluwitharana b Amerasinghe	9	– c Fernando b Bandaratilleke		4
S. I. de Saram run out	28	– (5) not out		22
†T. M. Dilshan c Kaluwitharana b Vaas	2	– (4) run out		4
*H. D. P. K. Dharmasena c Kaluwitharana b Vaas	4	– c Mendis b Vaas		5
K. S. Lokuarachchi lbw b Vaas	2	– not out		48
D. M. G. S. Dissanayake c Amerasinghe b Upashantha	83			
K. Weeraratne c Bandaratilleke b Fernando	25			
H. W. U. Varuna not out	18			
H. G. D. Nayanakantha c Fernando b Amerasinghe	4			
L-b 7, n-b 11	18	L-b 2		2
	239	(5 wkts)		**179**

1/51 (2) 2/57 (1) 3/79 (5) 4/83 (5)
5/96 (6) 6/100 (7) 7/103 (4)
8/191 (9) 9/223 (8) 10/239 (11)

1/88 (2) 2/94 (3)
3/98 (4) 4/104 (1)
5/119 (6)

Bowling: *First Innings*—Vaas 21–6–60–3; Liyanage 9–1–30–2; Bandaratilleke 14–3–50–0; Amerasinghe 15.1–4–51–2; Pushpakumara 2–1–7–0; Fernando 9–0–24–1; Upashantha 3–0–10–1. *Second Innings*—Vaas 7–2–19–1; Liyanage 4–1–14–0; Fernando 14–1–41–0; Pushpakumara 6–0–35–0; Bandaratilleke 11–1–59–3; Amerasinghe 1–0–9–0.

Umpires: P. G. Liyanage and M. G. Silva.
Third umpire: R. Martinesz. Referee: S. D. Anurasiri.

CHAMPIONS

Lakspray Trophy

1988-89	{ Nondescripts CC
	{ Sinhalese SC
1989-90	Sinhalese SC

P. Saravanamuttu Trophy

1990-91	Sinhalese SC
1991-92	Colts CC
1992-93	Sinhalese SC
1993-94	Nondescripts CC
1994-95	{ Bloomfield C and AC
	{ Sinhalese SC

1995-96	Colombo CC
1996-97	Bloomfield C and AC
1997-98	Sinhalese SC

Premier Trophy

1998-99	Bloomfield C and AC
1999-2000	Colts CC
2000-01	Nondescripts CC
2001-02	Colts CC
2002-03	Moors SC
2003-04	Bloomfield C and AC

Sinhalese have won the title outright 4 times, Bloomfield and Colts 3, Nondescripts 2, Colombo and Moors 1. Sinhalese have also shared the title twice, and Bloomfield and Nondescripts once each.

Plate Group A

At Sinhalese Sports Club, Maitland Place, Colombo, January 16, 17, 18, 2004. **Drawn.** Toss: Panadura. **Sinhalese 431** (N. T. Paranavitana 58, B. M. A. J. Mendis 52, W. L. P. Fernando 124, F. H. S. M. Silva 78; M. D. K. Perera 5-127) **and 287-7** (M. U. Dissanayake 85, R. P. A. H. Wickremaratne 75); **Panadura 259** (R. Soysa 88, K. L. K. Fernando 71; P. D. R. L. Perera 5-96). *Sinhalese 12.435 pts, Panadura 2.995 pts.*
    In Sinhalese's first innings, Fernando and Silva added 186 for the eighth wicket.

At Panadura Esplanade, Panadura, January 23, 24, 25, 2004. **Drawn.** Toss: Panadura. **Burgher 331** (B. C. M. S. Mendis 51, D. N. Pathirana 80, V. S. K. Waragoda 58; S. Gayan 4-58) **and 171; Panadura 225** (M. D. K. Perera 92; S. Weerakoon 4-64) **and 73-5** (R. C. R. P. Silva 4-39). *Panadura 3.49 pts, Burgher 12.01 pts.*

At Burgher Recreation Ground, Havelock Park, Colombo, January 30, 31, February 1, 2004. **Drawn.** Toss: Sinhalese. **Burgher 370** (D. M. Perumal 51, R. H. S. Silva 73, B. C. M. S. Mendis 78, V. S. K. Waragoda 76*; C. W. Vidanapathirana 4-75) **and 221; Sinhalese 374** (W. M. S. M. Perera 128, L. P. C. Silva 88, R. P. A. H. Wickremaratne 53; S. Weerakoon 5-123) **and 26-1.** *Burgher 4.055 pts, Sinhalese 12 pts.*

Plate Group B

At FTZ Sports Complex, Katunayake, January 16, 17, 18, 2004. **Chilaw Marians won by six wickets.** Toss: Chilaw Marians. **Tamil Union 117** (K. H. R. K. Fernando 6-45) **and 337** (N. A. N. N. Perera 64, K. M. Fernando 111*); **Chilaw Marians 247** (T. M. I. Mutaliph 57; P. S. Jayaprakashdaran 5-58) **and 210-4** (W. A. D. A. P. Perera 89*, C. U. Jayasinghe 55*). *Chilaw Marians 16.285 pts, Tamil Union 3.67 pts.*

At P. Saravanamuttu Stadium, Colombo, January 24, 25, 26, 2004. **Drawn.** Toss: Kurunegala Youth. **Tamil Union 173** (N. N. Weeraman 56; H. M. Maduwantha 5-31) **and 222** (K. S. D. Kumara 56, R. R. Tissera 61; H. M. Maduwantha 6-70); **Kurunegala Youth 187** (S. P. West 6-41) **and 99-6.** *Tamil Union 3.575 pts, Kurunegala Youth 11.43 pts.*

At Welagedera Stadium, Kurunegala, January 30, 31, February 1, 2004. **Drawn.** Toss: Chilaw Marians. **Chilaw Marians 323** (W. A. D. A. P. Perera 54, M. S. R. Wijeratne 63; A. W. Ekanayake 4-89) **and 186-6 dec.** (W. A. D. A. P. Perera 58); **Kurunegala Youth 143 and 330-7** (M. N. Jaymon 150*). *Kurunegala Youth 3.965 pts, Chilaw Marians 12.245 pts.*

Plate Group C

At Colombo Cricket Club, Maitland Crescent, Colombo, January 16, 17, 18, 2004. **Moors won by ten wickets.** Toss: Colombo. **Colombo 291** (D. K. Ranaweera 92, B. G. U. N. Seneviratne 51; U. W. M. B. C. A. Welagedera 5-53) **and 161** (B. S. M. Warnapura 55; U. W. M. B. C. A. Welagedera 4-36, W. M. B. Perera 4-27); **Moors 434-8 dec.** (H. M. S. Jayawardene 57, U. C. Hathurusinghe 148, A. C. Wettasinghe 70; B. S. M. Warnapura 4-85) **and 22-0.** *Moors 16.11 pts, Colombo 3.06 pts.*

At Air Force Ground, Colombo, January 23, 24, 25, 2004. **Colombo won by ten wickets.** Toss: Air Force. **Air Force 298** (S. N. Wijesinghe 91; M. I. Ratnayake 5-82) **and 226** (K. A. Kumara 60; M. I. Ratnayake 4-47, B. S. M. Warnapura 6-86); **Colombo 464** (D. K. Ranaweera 56, S. K. L. de Silva 181, K. G. N. Randika 79; G. S. Dananjaya 4-96) **and 61-0.** *Colombo 16.305 pts, Air Force 3.62 pts.*

This was the first first-class match on this ground. De Silva and Randika added 186 for Colombo's seventh wicket.

At Moors Sports Club, Braybrooke Place, Colombo, January 30, 31, February 1, 2004. **Drawn.** Toss: Moors. **Moors 292** (M. M. Dunusinghe 82) **and 622** (M. M. Dunusinghe 55, U. C. Hathurusinghe 191, W. R. Fernando 150, A. C. Wettasinghe 108; A. Rizan 4-176); **Air Force 144** (U. W. M. B. C. A. Welagedera 4-55). *Moors 12.46 pts, Air Force 2.72 pts.*

In Moors' second innings, Hathurusinghe added 106 for the third wicket with Dunusinghe and 215 for the fourth with Fernando, then Fernando and Wettasinghe added 186 for the fifth.

Plate Group D

At Police Park, Colombo, January 16, 17, 2004. **Sebastianites won by an innings and 119 runs.** Toss: Sebastianites. **Police 76** (M. N. T. H. Kumara 6-33, U. L. K. D. Fernando 4-41) **and 213** (R. G. D. Sanjeewa 76, M. Y. Kudagodage 75*; M. N. T. H. Kumara 4-45, U. L. K. D. Fernando 4-57); **Sebastianites 408-8 dec.** (U. L. K. D. Fernando 81, K. A. D. J. Siriwardene 109, A. S. N. Fernando 55, A. P. Dalugoda 51*). *Sebastianites 16 pts, Police 2.245 pts.*

At Kadirana Cricket Grounds, Gampaha, January 23, 24, 25, 2004. **Drawn.** Toss: Ragama. **Police 175** (B. A. R. S. Priyadarshana 5-37) **and 263** (P. H. K. S. Nirmala 57, R. G. D. Sanjeewa 52); **Ragama 295** (C. M. Withanage 73, W. D. D. S. Perera 86; Y. A. N. Mendis 5-47) **and 119-7** (Y. A. N. Mendis 4-25). *Police 3.89 pts, Ragama 12.07 pts.*

At Police Park, Colombo, February 1, 2, 3, 2004. **Drawn.** Toss: Sebastianites. **Ragama 302** (C. G. Wijesinghe 51, K. A. S. Jayasinghe 72; B. C. N. Amarasinghe 4-49) **and 292** (C. M. Withanage 81, W. D. D. S. Perera 64*; B. C. N. Amarasinghe 4-67); **Sebastianites 248** (R. D. Dissanayake 4-33) **and 59-3.** *Ragama 12.27 pts, Sebastianites 3.535 pts.*

Plate semi-finals

At FTZ Sports Complex, Katunayake, February 6, 7, 2004. **Moors won by ten wickets.** Toss: Moors. **Chilaw Marians 91** (K. K. A. K. Lakmal 4-42) **and 223** (W. A. D. A. P. Perera 67, T. M. I. Mutaliph 70); **Moors 303** (H. M. S. Jayawardene 94, U. C. Hathurusinghe 50) **and 12-0.**

At Colts Cricket Club, Havelock Park, Colombo, February 6, 7, 8, 2004. **Drawn.** Sinhalese were declared winners by virtue of their first-innings lead. Toss: Ragama. **Sinhalese 287** (R. P. A. H. Wickremaratne 96, G. D. D. Indika 85; A. A. D. H. Nilantha 7-92) **and 455-9** (R. P. A. H. Wickremaratne 171, W. L. P. Fernando 110, F. H. S. M. Silva 59*); **Ragama 236** (C. M. Withanage 59, W. M. P. N. Wanasinghe 58; C. W. Vidanapathirana 4-43, D. Hettiarachchi 4-80).

In Sinhalese's second innings, Wickremaratne and Lasith Fernando came together at 93-5 and added 271 for the sixth wicket. Ten Ragama players bowled, including wicket-keeper Upul Fernando.

Plate final

At P. Saravanamuttu Stadium, Colombo, February 13, 14, 15, 2004. **Sinhalese won by 103 runs.** Toss: Sinhalese. **Sinhalese 220** (M. S. Atapattu 66, L. P. C. Silva 57) **and 223-8 dec.** (D. A. Gunawardene 69); **Moors 233** (H. M. S. Jayawardene 58; K. T. G. D. Prasad 4-70) **and 107** (D. Hettiarachchi 4-14).

Sinhalese wicket-keeper Malintha Perera made five dismissals in each Moors innings.

Promotion/Relegation League

The two least successful teams in the Plate Championship, Air Force and Police, played the finalists from the non-first-class Sara Trophy for the right to compete in the next year's Premier Trophy.

At Air Force Ground, Katunayake, February 27, 28, 2004. **Police won by nine wickets.** Toss: Moratuwa. **Moratuwa 104** (I. D. Gunawardene 5-45) **and 224** (M. A. P. Salgado 51; H. M. Jayawardene 6-52); **Police 247** (H. P. A. Priyantha 52) **and 82-1** (S. A. Wijeratne 65*). *Police 15.645 pts, Moratuwa 2.74 pts.*

At Police Park, Colombo, February 28, 29, March 1, 2004. **Air Force won by 314 runs.** Toss: Singha. **Air Force 373** (P. H. K. de Silva 63, K. R. P. Silva 62, T. R. Peiris 66; K. S. S. de Silva 5-91, L. Ranasinghe 4-77) **and 255** (P. H. K. de Silva 86); **Singha 248** (H. W. M. Kumara 127*; M. K. G. C. P. Lakshitha 4-78) **and 66** (K. R. P. Silva 6-22). *Air Force 17.14 pts, Singha 3.57 pts.*

At Police Park, Colombo, March 5, 6, 2004. **Air Force won by 69 runs.** Toss: Air Force. **Air Force 226** (K. R. P. Silva 62, S. N. Wijesinghe 68; M. H. R. M. Fernando 5-61) **and 118;** **Moratuwa 113 and 162** (M. R. Fernando 66; A. Rizan 5-60). *Air Force 15.72 pts, Moratuwa 3.375 pts.*

At Air Force Ground, Katunayake, March 5, 6, 7, 2004. **Police won by four wickets.** Toss: Police. **Singha 237** (T. R. D. Mendis 54) **and 117;** **Police 204** (W. N. M. Soysa 73) **and 151-6.** *Police 15.775 pts, Singha 3.37 pts.*

At Air Force Ground, Katunayake, March 12, 13, 14, 2004. **Air Force won by 41 runs.** Toss: Air Force. **Air Force 230** (K. R. P. Silva 145) **and 220** (W. C. R. Tissera 87; Y. A. N. Mendis 4-78); **Police 152** (A. Rizan 4-33) **and 257** (H. P. A. Priyantha 53, M. M. Rasmijinan 62; A. Rizan 6-99). *Air Force 16.25 pts, Police 4.045 pts.*

At Police Park, Colombo, March 12, 13, 2004. **Singha won by nine wickets.** Toss: Singha. **Moratuwa 73 and 193** (W. D. J. Abeywardene 71; G. I. Dilshan 5-72); **Singha 238** (H. T. P. Premaratne 124; D. Seneviratne 4-48) **and 29-1.** *Singha 15.335 pts, Moratuwa 2.43 pts.*

Leg-spinner Kalumarakkala Tharaka of Singha had first-innings figures of 2–2–0–3 on first-class debut.

Air Force 49.110 pts, Police 35.465 pts, Singha 22.275 pts, Moratuwa 8.545 pts.

"He could have been out in three different ways off the same delivery."

Northamptonshire in 2004, page 713.

TEN SPORTS INTERPROVINCIAL TOURNAMENT, 2003-04

	Played	Won	Lost	Drawn	1st-inns lead	Bonus points Batting	Bonus points Bowling	Points
North Central Province	4	3	1	0	0	10.49	7.6	54.09
Central Province	4	2	1	1	1	10.2	6.2	48.15*
Western Province	4	2	1	1	0	9.165	6.5	39.665
Southern Province	4	1	3	0	0	9.915	7.9	29.815
Uva Province	4	1	3	0	0	8.72	6.2	26.92

* *Central Province had 0.25 points deducted for a slow over-rate.*

Outright win = 12 pts, lead on first innings in a drawn game = 8 pts. Bonus points were awarded as follows: 0.1 pt for each wicket taken and 0.005 pt for each run scored, up to 400 runs per innings.

Final: Central Province beat North Central Province by 176 runs.

CENTRAL PROVINCE v SOUTHERN PROVINCE

At Asgiriya Stadium, Kandy, January 3, 4, 5, 6, 2004. Central Province won by one wicket. Central Province 15.815 pts (after 0.25 penalty for slow over-rate), Southern Province 5.32 pts. Toss: Southern Province.

Central Province's last pair rewrote a 108-year-old record when they reached 513 on the final evening – the seventh-highest fourth-innings total in first-class cricket, and the highest to win. The previous best was Cambridge University's 507 for seven to beat MCC and Ground in 1896. Southern Province had led by 219 on first innings, after Charitha Buddhika Fernando bowled out Central for a mere 173, and centuries from Atapattu and Rodrigo stretched their advantage to 511 before the declaration. Central were already one down in the fifth over. But Sajith and Hasantha Fernando added 198 before Jayasuriya removed both, and a stand of 140 between Sangakkara and Samaraweera took them past tea. At 475 for four, they needed only 37. Then the loss of Samaraweera triggered a collapse of five wickets, with Jayasuriya taking his haul to four in a marathon 43 overs. Four overs remained, with 13 runs or one wicket required: Zoysa hit three fours to see Central to the record with 15 balls to spare.

Close of play: First day, Southern Province 306-7 (Silva 63, Mudalige 0); Second day, Southern Province 36-0 (Atapattu 12, Jayasuriya 22); Third day, Central Province 77-1 (S. I. Fernando 37, K. H. R. K. Fernando 18).

Southern Province

*M. S. Atapattu st Sangakkara b Dhammika	74	– c P. D. R. L. Perera b Dhammika . . 126
S. T. Jayasuriya c Sangakkara b P. D. R. L. Perera	4	– c Sangakkara b K. H. R. K. Fernando . 23
K. S. Rodrigo c K. H. R. K. Fernando b P. D. R. L. Perera	0	– not out 106
W. S. Jayantha lbw b Dhammika	98	
L. P. C. Silva c Paranavitana b P. D. R. L. Perera	110	
†H. A. P. W. Jayawardene c Sangakkara b P. D. R. L. Perera	20	
M. M. D. N. R. G. Perera b Weeraratne	29	– (4) not out 24
T. C. B. Fernando lbw b P. D. R. L. Perera	2	
C. R. B. Mudalige c S. I. Fernando b P. D. R. L. Perera	24	
A. B. T. Lakshitha not out	1	
S. L. Malinga b P. D. R. L. Perera	0	
B 12, l-b 10, n-b 8	30	B 4, l-b 3, w 1, n-b 5 13
1/14 (2) 2/16 (3) 3/174 (1) 4/191 (4) 5/241 (6) 6/289 (7) 7/305 (8) 8/385 (9) 9/386 (5) 10/392 (11)	392	1/37 (2) 2/248 (1) (2 wkts dec.) 292

Bowling: _First Innings_—Zoysa 27–9–68–0; P. D. R. L. Perera 26.5–3–90–7; Samaraweera 9–1–35–0; Weeraratne 15–0–73–1; K. H. R. K. Fernando 14–3–34–0; Dhammika 20–2–64–2; S. I. Fernando 1–0–6–0. _Second Innings_—Zoysa 14–4–44–0; P. D. R. L. Perera 8–1–50–0; K. H. R. K. Fernando 12–4–43–1; Weeraratne 3–0–27–0; Dhammika 17–2–101–1; Samaraweera 5–1–20–0.

Central Province

N. T. Paranavitana lbw b Fernando	0	– c Lakshitha b Fernando 7
S. I. Fernando c Fernando b Jayasuriya	48	– c Silva b Jayasuriya 111
*†K. C. Sangakkara lbw b Lakshitha	6	– (4) c Jayawardene b Malinga..... 101
T. T. Samaraweera b Fernando	6	– (5) c Perera b Fernando 90
W. M. B. Perera b Jayasuriya	51	– (7) c Malinga b Jayasuriya 5
S. H. T. Kandamby c Jayasuriya b Fernando	2	– c Jayantha b Malinga.......... 38
K. H. R. K. Fernando c Jayawardene b Fernando	3	– (3) c Mudalige b Jayasuriya 92
K. Weeraratne b Mudalige	21	– c Silva b Jayasuriya 0
D. N. T. Zoysa c Mudalige b Fernando	6	– not out 20
D. G. R. Dhammika b Mudalige	12	– c Jayawardene b Malinga 3
P. D. R. L. Perera not out	0	– not out 0
L-b 5, n-b 13	18	B 14, l-b 11, w 9, n-b 12.. 46

1/0 (1) 2/8 (3) 3/15 (4) 4/123 (2)   173   1/10 (1) 2/208 (2)   (9 wkts) 513
5/126 (6) 6/134 (7) 7/134 (5)   3/264 (3) 4/404 (4)
8/155 (9) 9/168 (8) 10/173 (10)   5/475 (5) 6/484 (6)
                                                 7/487 (8) 8/488 (7) 9/499 (10)

Bowling: _First Innings_—Fernando 15–3–46–5; Lakshitha 8–1–46–1; Malinga 7–0–32–0; Mudalige 5.5–1–21–2; Jayasuriya 10–2–23–2. _Second Innings_—Fernando 21–2–65–2; Lakshitha 11–0–56–0; Malinga 14.3–0–81–3; Mudalige 27–4–83–0; Jayasuriya 43–5–173–4; Perera 4–1–17–0; Jayantha 2–0–13–0.

Umpires: P. T. Manuel and R. Martinesz. Referee: C. T. M. Devaraj.

At Sinhalese Sports Club, Maitland Place, Colombo, January 3, 4, 5, 6, 2004. **North Central Province won by an innings and 19 runs.** Toss: Western Province. **Western Province 330** (H. P. Tillekeratne 122*) **and 198** (R. S. Kaluwitharana 65; H. D. P. K. Dharmasena 5-77); **North Central Province 547** (D. P. M. D. Jayawardene 177, T. M. Dilshan 123, H. D. P. K. Dharmasena 99; D. Hettiarachchi 5-163). _North Central Province 16 pts, Western Province 3.64 pts._
   Kaluwitharana conceded no byes in North Central Province's 547.

At Galle International Stadium, Galle, January 9, 10, 11, 12, 2004. **North Central Province won by 19 runs.** Toss: Southern Province. **North Central Province 365** (W. M. G. Ramyakumara 58, H. M. R. K. B. Herath 50*; S. L. Malinga 4-115) **and 309** (D. P. M. D. Jayawardene 53, L. J. P. Gunaratne 56); **Southern Province 184** (W. S. Jayantha 50; H. D. P. K. Dharmasena 5-66) **and 471** (S. T. Jayasuriya 185, M. S. Atapattu 57, G. A. S. Perera 51; H. M. R. K. B. Herath 5-120). _North Central Province 17.37 pts, Southern Province 4.92 pts._
   Six days after conceding 513 in the fourth innings to Central Province, Southern Province scored 471 in the fourth innings chasing 491.

At R. Premadasa Stadium, Colombo, January 9, 10, 11, 12, 2004. **Western Province won by seven wickets.** Toss: Western Province. **Uva Province 235** (D. A. Gunawardene 89; C. R. D. Fernando 4-33) **and 363** (T. K. D. Sudarshana 105, G. I. Daniel 125; D. Hettiarachchi 5-86); **Western Province 507-9 dec.** (R. P. Hewage 64, J. Mubarak 61, R. P. Arnold 126, R. S. Kaluwitharana 166; M. R. C. N. Bandaratilleke 4-94) **and 92-3.** _Western Province 16.46 pts, Uva Province 4.19 pts._
   In Western Province's first innings, Arnold and Kaluwitharana added 313 for the fourth wicket, a national record. Kaluwitharana made six wicket-keeping dismissals in the second innings and eight in the match. His opposite number Rashan Peiris conceded no byes in Western Province's total of 507-9.

At Rangiri Dambulla International Stadium, Dambulla, January 17, 18, 19, 20, 2004. **Uva Province won by four wickets.** Toss: Uva Province. **North Central Province 405** (W. M. G. Ramyakumara 148, D. P. M. D. Jayawardene 84; M. K. G. C. P. Lakshitha 6-101) **and 135** (W. P. U. J. C. Vaas 4-40); **Uva Province 442** (M. N. Nawaz 56, W. P. U. J. C. Vaas 104, M. R. C. N. Bandaratilleke 80) **and 99-6** (W. M. G. Ramyakumara 4-54). *Uva Province 16.495 pts, North Central Province 4.275 pts.*

In Uva Province's first innings, Vaas and Bandaratilleke added 154 for the ninth wicket.

At P. Saravanamuttu Stadium, Colombo, January 17, 18, 19, 2004. **Western Province won by 38 runs.** Toss: Southern Province. **Western Province 244** (R. S. Kaluwitharana 90*; A. B. T. Lakshitha 5-59) **and 205** (R. P. Hewage 73, K. S. Lokuarachchi 62; K. T. G. D. Prasad 5-35); **Southern Province 237** (D. Hettiarachchi 5-67) **and 174** (S. T. Jayasuriya 56; K. S. Lokuarachchi 4-41, D. Hettiarachchi 5-41). *Western Province 16.245 pts, Southern Province 4.055 pts.*

At Rangiri Dambulla International Stadium, Dambulla, January 24, 25, 26, 27, 2004. **Drawn.** Toss: Western Province. **Central Province 276** (T. T. Samaraweera 91, W. M. B. Perera 83; M. T. T. Mirando 4-57) **and 306-5 dec.** (K. H. R. K. Fernando 69, K. C. Sangakkara 125, S. H. T. Kandamby 67*); **Western Province 97** (R. P. Hewage 56; P. D. R. L. Perera 4-18) **and 267-9** (H. P. Tillekeratne 96; M. Muralitharan 4-68). *Central Province 12.81 pts, Western Province 3.32 pts.*

At Galle International Stadium, Galle, January 24, 25, 26, 2004. **Southern Province won by eight runs.** Toss: Uva Province. **Southern Province 166** (M. M. D. N. R. G. Perera 59; W. P. U. J. C. Vaas 6-31) **and 138** (M. R. C. N. Bandaratilleke 4-32); **Uva Province 91** (K. T. G. D. Prasad 6-25) **and 205** (H. G. J. M. Kulatunga 51, W. P. U. J. C. Vaas 58; K. T. G. D. Prasad 4-73). *Southern Province 15.52 pts, Uva Province 3.48 pts.*

At Sinhalese Sports Club, Maitland Place, Colombo, January 30, 31, February 1, 2, 2004. **Central Province won by an innings and 166 runs.** Toss: Uva Province. **Uva Province 238** (H. G. J. M. Kulatunga 51, M. Pushpakumara 64; M. Muralitharan 4-73) **and 113** (M. S. Villavarayan 5-44); **Central Province 517** (W. N. M. Soysa 147, T. T. Samaraweera 165). *Central Province 16 pts, Uva Province 2.755 pts.*

At Nondescripts Cricket Club, Maitland Place, Colombo, February 5, 6, 7, 2004. **North Central Province won by seven wickets.** Toss: North Central Province. **Central Province 305** (K. H. R. K. Fernando 54, K. C. Sangakkara 104*) **and 180** (K. C. Sangakkara 78); **North Central Province 386-8 dec.** (S. K. L. de Silva 59, T. M. Dilshan 97) **and 103-3.** *North Central Province 16.445 pts, Central Province 3.525 pts.*

Final

At R. Premadasa Stadium, Colombo, February 11, 12, 13, 2004. **Central Province won by 176 runs.** Toss: Central Province. **Central Province 235** (S. I. Fernando 73, K. C. Sangakkara 56; K. M. D. N. Kulasekara 5-46) **and 258** (T. T. Samaraweera 82; P. N. Ranjith 5-57); **North Central Province 120** (M. Muralitharan 4-33, M. S. Villavarayan 4-35) **and 197** (D. N. T. Zoysa 4-36).

Note: Matches in the following section were not first-class.

PREMIER LIMITED-OVERS TOURNAMENT, 2003-04

Final

At R. Premadasa Stadium, Colombo, January 22 (day/night), 2004. **Bloomfield won by 189 runs.** Toss: Bloomfield. **Bloomfield 299-7** (50 overs) (W. S. Jayantha 108, S. H. T. Kandamby 69, T. M. Dilshan 63*); **Colts 110** (28.3 overs).

Dilshan took two catches as wicket-keeper, then took off his pads and bowled six overs for three wickets.

CRICKET IN ZIMBABWE, 2003-04

SPECIAL CORRESPONDENT

Tatenda Taibu

The world has looked on helplessly for several years now as the Zimbabwean government has ruined the country's economy and manipulated elections in its thirst to retain power. In 2004, a similar disaster unfolded in the nation's cricket community, as politically motivated administrators with little love for the game destroyed the competitiveness of the national side – and, potentially, the future of cricket in Zimbabwe – when most of the top players rebelled against their rule.

Though the final outcome of the dispute, as with the country's wider political crisis, remains unclear, there is no question that the reputation and health of Zimbabwean cricket has been damaged, perhaps irreparably, by the very people supposed to safeguard it.

Conflict was perhaps inevitable from 2000 when the Zimbabwe Cricket Union, under political pressure, set up an integration task force to draw up a plan for "the rapid evolution of Zimbabwean cricket". Headed by an American management consultant, Dr Richard Zackrison, the group found that "racism was right at the heart of Zimbabwe cricket" and added "Zimbabwe cricket was sitting on a powder keg that was ready to explode." This turned out to be true, but not for the reasons Zackrison thought.

His plan offered a route not merely to fast-track blacks in cricket but effectively to force whites out. Whites dominated cricket at the time, which was hardly a surprise: historically, non-whites in Rhodesia (in contrast to South Africa) barely touched the game, and it takes many years to build a cricket culture. The aim of the task force was to ensure that by 2005 blacks would be in the majority in every area of the game. The intention was that these "goals"– the term "quotas" was never used – should be carried out with "the least possible reduction in individual and team performance". This, unfortunately, was not to be.

Over the next three years, a steady stream of white faces departed the cricketing scene. Most said they were simply disillusioned with ZCU policy and unsatisfactory working conditions, which was perhaps an easy way of getting rid of them. But some were forced out, such as the national team's fitness trainer, Malcolm Jarvis, and the assistant coach, Kevin Curran. The most devastating repercussions, however, were felt in the national team. Murray Goodwin and Neil Johnson quit in 2000. Other white players saw the task force as a direct threat to their careers, and, amid an atmosphere of increasing paranoia, fringe members of the squad – such as Alistair Campbell, Bryan Strang, Gavin Rennie, Douglas Marillier, Brian Murphy and Dirk Viljoen – opted for early retirement rather than fight for a place they feared they would not be able to claim anyway.

It was not only the whites: pace bowlers Everton Matambanadzo and

THE ZIMBABWE REBELS

	Age†	Tests	ODIs		Age†	Tests	ODIs
A. M. Blignaut	26	15	47	T. J. Friend	23	13	51
G. B. Brent	28	4	48	T. R. Gripper	29	20	8
S. V. Carlisle	32	35	108	R. W. Price	28	18	26
S. M. Ervine	22	5	42	B. G. Rogers	22	0	7
G. M. Ewing	23	2	0	R. W. Sims	25	0	3
N. R. Ferreira	25	0	0	H. H. Streak	30	59	183
G. W. Flower	34	67	219	C. B. Wishart	30	25	89

† At January 1, 2005.

Note: C. K. Coventry, usually listed as a rebel, later said he did not consider himself part of the group. Ewing and Rogers have both returned to the Zimbabwe team. Subsequently, Ewing has played one one-day international; Rogers has played five as well as two Tests.

Brighton Watambwa left the game in that period too. Many former Academy players, of all colours, were also lost. Yet at the start of 2004, Zimbabwe had a promising young side, with talented players such as Tatenda Taibu, Andy Blignaut, Sean Ervine and Raymond Price. However, Taibu was still the only non-white, with the seamer Douglas Hondo not far behind, who was unquestionably worth his place. It was a situation some black nationalists were unable to stomach. So they brought the house crashing down.

At the age of 29, the captain, Heath Streak, was enjoying the best all-round season of his outstanding career. A fluent Ndebele speaker, he was idolised by the young black cricketers he coached in the township. After a tough start, he had settled into the captaincy and won the respect of the players, although some, such as Andy Flower, thought him too malleable. This may have been true, but also understandable: the Streaks' farm was in danger of being overrun by the "war veterans" unleashed by President Robert Mugabe, and any outspokenness could have had serious consequences for his family.

Even so, Streak and his players were unhappy, and in March 2004 he took a list of the team's grievances to the board. Streak said he threatened retirement if the board failed to act. The ZCU announced he had resigned – although Streak later claimed he had been sacked – and in his place

HOW THE ZIMBABWE CRISIS UNFOLDED IN 2004

Compiled by Lawrence Booth

January 20 ECB marketing chairman Des Wilson submits report to his board calling for a "moral dimension" when deciding if a tour should go ahead.

January 21 The ICC reminds England politics are not a factor in considering tours.

January 23 British foreign secretary Jack Straw refuses to order the ECB not to tour Zimbabwe but reiterates he would rather they did not.

March 4 Cricket Australia confirms Australia's tour will go ahead after declaring itself satisfied with security arrangements.

March 10 The ICC rules that tours may only be cancelled for reasons of safety and security, or because a government explicitly orders its players should not go.

March 13 ICC president Ehsan Mani says the ECB must decide by April whether or not to tour. If England refuse to go, they could face a $2m fine and suspension.

April 2 Streak ceases to be captain of Zimbabwe. The ZCU says he resigned; Streak says he was sacked.

April 8 Zimbabwe's senior players issue an ultimatum to the ZCU, saying they will quit unless Streak is reinstated.

April 11 The chairman of the ECB, David Morgan, says England will tour Zimbabwe because of the ICC's threats.

April 15 The selectors omit 13 white players from their squad for the first one-day international against Sri Lanka at Bulawayo.

April 16 The rebels and the ZCU begin legal proceedings against each other after the players are sacked for failing to turn up to a training session.

April 20 *Daily Telegraph* journalist Mihir Bose is deported from Zimbabwe after arriving to cover the series with Sri Lanka. The ZCU claims Bose's application for accreditation arrived late and was incorrectly completed.

April 21 Leg-spinner Stuart MacGill withdraws from Australia's trip to Zimbabwe, citing moral reasons.

April 24 South African journalist Telford Vice is deported from Zimbabwe, because of a late application for accreditation.

April 25 Zimbabwe are dismissed for 35 in the third game against Sri Lanka at Harare, the lowest-ever total in one-day internationals.

April 27 Des Wilson resigns from the ECB after his report is rejected.

April 29 Sri Lanka complete a 5–0 clean sweep of the one-day series.

May 1 Four rebels are included in the Zimbabwe A team to play the Sri Lankan tourists. But any hope of a rapprochement with the board is ruined when it emerges that the others are not being considered for the First Test.

May 5 British prime minister Tony Blair says he would "prefer" England not to tour Zimbabwe. "But there is a difference between doing that and ordering them not to go," he adds, "which I think would step over the proper line." Mani says: "Mr Blair is seeking to divert attention away from his own inaction in dealing with Zimbabwe by attempting to exert inappropriate pressure on an international sporting body."

May 8 A Zimbabwe team containing only one white player loses the First Test to Sri Lanka by an innings and 240 runs at Harare.

May 10 The ZCU says it has sacked 15 rebels after they failed to return to training on May 7, the deadline imposed by the board.

May 16 Zimbabwe coach Geoff Marsh says he will not renew his contract when it expires in September.

May 17 Sri Lanka win the Second Test at Bulawayo by an innings and 254 after making 713 for three declared. The ICC chief executive, Malcolm Speed, flies to Harare for a meeting with the ZCU, which refuses to let him attend a full meeting.

May 21 Cricket Australia accepts the ZCU's offer to cancel their two-Test series after it becomes clear that the ICC would have stripped it of Test status anyway. The sides agree to play three one-day internationals. The rebels ask the ICC to apply their own disputes-resolution process.

June 4 A statement from 13 rebels suggests they have had enough of the dispute and wish "the current Zimbabwe cricket team the best of luck for the future".

June 8 Streak calls for Zimbabwe to be banned from all cricket pending an investigation from the ICC.

June 10 The ZCU and the ICC agree to withdraw Test status from Zimbabwe until 2005. They may continue to play one-day internationals.

June 14 ZCU chairman Peter Chingoka angrily denies that it has been guilty of discrimination. "Nothing could be further from the truth," he says.

June 17 ZCU managing director Vince Hogg announces his resignation.

July 9 Lawyers representing the ZCU and the rebels resume talks.

July 14 Rebels begin tour of England, playing club games as "the Red Lions". The ZCU agrees to arbitration by a tribunal.

July 20 The players agree to arbitration too.

August 10 ICC appoint India's Solicitor-General, Goolam Vahanvati, and South African judge Steven Majiedt to investigate claims of racism within the ZCU.

September 9 England agree to play five one-day internationals on their tour of Zimbabwe after the ECB decides there is no threat to the players' security.

September 11 England beat Zimbabwe by 152 runs in the Champions Trophy opener at Edgbaston.

September 19 England fast bowler Steve Harmison says he is opting out of the Zimbabwe tour for moral reasons.

September 29 England all-rounder Andrew Flintoff, "rested" from the tour party, says he would not have gone if he had been chosen. The first day of the ICC hearing in Harare into alleged ZCU racism ends early when Chris Venturas, the players' lawyer, requests the removal from the room of three ZCU officials while the players are giving evidence, for fear of intimidation.

September 30 The ICC scraps the hearing because of what it calls "the inflexible attitudes of both parties". It says it will now consider written evidence only.

October 17 The ICC says it found no evidence of racism in Zimbabwe cricket, and blames Streak for the dispute with the players.

November 6 The ZCU renames itself Zimbabwe Cricket and adopts a new logo.

November 16 The three remaining rebels in Zimbabwe – Stuart Carlisle, Trevor Gripper and Streak – withdraw from disputes tribunal because of the cost.

November 23 On the eve of England's tour, 13 British journalists are denied entry into Zimbabwe. "Bona fide media organisations in the UK have been cleared, but those that are political have not. This is a game of cricket, not politics," says a government official. ECB chairman Morgan instructs the England team not to board its flight from Johannesburg to Harare.

November 25 All the journalists are allowed to enter after Morgan threatens to scrap the tour. The first of the five one-day internationals is cancelled.

November 26 England arrive in Harare.

November 27 England captain Michael Vaughan says England will pull out of the tour if they are forced to meet President Mugabe.

December 1 The England management reacts angrily after the Harare newspaper, *The Herald*, claims: "One by one, England's players are queuing up to give their approval of their tour to this country."

December 5 Mani announces Zimbabwe will regain Test status in time for January's tour of Bangladesh. England complete a 4–0 whitewash in the one-day series.

appointed Taibu. Leading Zimbabwe on to the field before his 21st birthday, he became the youngest-ever Test captain.

Many viewed his appointment as premature and racially motivated. The players were outraged, and within two weeks most of the regular team, along with several on the fringe, had decided on what was in effect a strike. They demanded not only the reinstatement of their captain, but a reconstruction of both the selection panel and the ZCU board itself, as they believed both were now dominated by those with a political or racial agenda. Their decision to strike rather than pursue the matter through official channels did not help their cause, but years of frustration and aggravation had come to a head. However, all the rebel players were white. They said three "players of colour" had planned to join them, but had been intimidated into withdrawing their support. They were not alone in reporting threats: a Bulawayo reporter, Mehluli Sibanda, wrote an article critical of the ZCU and claimed to have received menacing phone calls from two board members.

The officials named were the two leading "hawks" cited by the rebel players: Ozias Bvute, appointed to the board after the task force report and a man whose cricketing background was negligible; and Maqsood Ebrahim, chairman of Universals Sports Club cricket section, and another with virtually no playing career to speak of. Throughout this time, there were numerous reports of mismanagement and outrageous behaviour by those charged with running Zimbabwe cricket, including an actual fight between Bvute and the newly appointed convener of selectors, Stephen Mangongo. In October 2003, the entire board and their wives went off to Australia, for "networking" purposes. And in late 2004 the ZCU was expensively rebranded as Zimbabwe Cricket, for reasons that did not appear to match the urgency of the situation or the financial state of either the country or the organisation.

In the past Peter Chingoka, the ZCU chairman, had generally been regarded as a benign figurehead, but as the rift widened he became more hawkish. His claims that Zimbabwe cricket was totally non-racial and, at the AGM in August 2004, that "the future for Zimbabwe cricket has never been brighter" were met with widespread derision. The board was racially balanced, with four black, four white and four Asian members, but there was little doubt that it was dominated by Bvute and Ebrahim. Talks between the rebels and administrators rumbled on, but they were further apart than ever when Sri Lanka arrived in April to play a Zimbabwe team shorn of most of its leading players. Sri Lanka duly won all five one-day internationals, skittling Zimbabwe for a world-record low of 35 in the third match, at Harare, and inflicted on the home side their two heaviest defeats in Test cricket. Zimbabwean cricket would have been a laughing stock, except that tears were more appropriate.

The rebel players pressed for arbitration. At first, the ICC did not want to get involved: they said they could not intervene in a domestic dispute, and were all too ready to accept the ZCU version of events. But the one-sided nature of the Sri Lanka visit concerned them; ICC chief executive Malcolm Speed flew to Harare, and the ZCU, bizarrely, refused even to meet him. When the players were eventually given a hearing, both sides accused the other of racism and threatened to sue for breach of contract – a situation which placed the financially less secure rebels at a disadvantage.

By the time the Australians arrived in May, Zimbabwe were fielding something close to a third eleven. Anticipating farce, the ZCU agreed with the Australian authorities to postpone the two Tests, although the three one-day internationals went ahead, with predictable results. Eventually, Zimbabwe were forced to cease playing Tests for the rest of 2004 although, mystifyingly, they were allowed to resume Test cricket in January 2005, when they gave

---

RECOMMENDATIONS OF ICC RACISM INQUIRY

1. There must be broad-based selection in terms of the integration policy and without any regional bias.

2. The ZCU should take immediate steps to ensure that competent selectors are appointed, who should be hands-on.

3. The ZCU should immediately investigate and attend to the complaint that national selectors do not attend matches in certain regions.

4. The ZCU should take steps to set up a players' association, if not already in place, and to provide for a players' representative who shall act as chief liaison between the players and the ZCU.

5. Channels of communication between the players and the ZCU must be improved without delay so that all concerned are treated respectfully and act together in the best interests of Zimbabwean cricket.

6. The policy of integration should be implemented with tact and restraint rather than in an aggressive or confrontational manner and there should be uniformity in the approach of all members of the ZCU board in this regard.

7. Criticism should be viewed in the right spirit and not taken personally.

8. A proper, clear and transparent grievance process must be put in place so that all stakeholders in Zimbabwe cricket can seek redress.

Bangladesh their first Test victory, in Chittagong. The team were outmatched even against these opponents. Caught in the crossfire were managing director Vince Hogg and the coach, Geoff Marsh. Both departed, with the former West Indian Test player Phil Simmons replacing Marsh, though perhaps not for long, since he was blamed for the defeat in Bangladesh. "Phil must be held responsible," said selector Richie Kaschula.

It was not only the players who resented the ZCU. The provincial boards were fed up with having to be accountable to the national selectors for their own teams; there were disputes involving local officials at both main associations, Mashonaland and Matabeleland, and at many clubs, resentful at the high-handedness of Bvute, above all. And when the ZCU held their AGM in August, they pre-empted the potential removal of their hardline members by manipulating the constitution. Several ZCU employees were then sacked, including the long-serving umpire Ian Robinson, who had been the board's International Tours Manager.

The ICC did send two judges to Harare to hold an inquiry into racism in Zimbabwean cricket which held two farcical days of hearings, gave up, and resorted to written submissions. In October they told the ICC: "We do not find any evidence of racism" in the game from April 2003 to July 2004. They said the ZCU board had no option but to accept Streak's threat of retirement, and that the other rebels were mistaken in believing Streak had said he would only "consider" retirement. They added: "the ZCU policies for the integration of cricket in Zimbabwe are based on sound principles and are generally accepted by all stakeholders in Zimbabwe cricket".

The upshot was that in late 2004 the ZCU board appeared as firmly entrenched as Mugabe himself, despite the alarming decline presided over by both. The board still claimed it would accept what amounted to unconditional surrender on the part of individual players, but most had had enough. The Australians, heading towards Zimbabwe, met Sean Ervine flying out – to try his luck in Perth; Andy Blignaut signed for Tasmania. Others headed for county cricket, and it seemed a number of international careers had abruptly come to an end. It was true that the players had at times done themselves no favours over the years. During the Bangladesh tour in early 2004, for example, they demanded a meeting with Hogg to press for pay rises, only to weaken their case by losing a one-day international to a team then seen as much inferior. The players were also less than solid as a group: Charles Coventry, named all year as one of the 15 rebels, said later he was never among them and was merely away fulfilling his club contract in England; Gavin Ewing and Barney Rogers rejoined the fold; and in early 2005 there were rumours that Ervine and Blignaut, having failed to set Australian cricket alight, might be open to the idea of returning.

The former Rhodesia captain Ray Gripper believes that the problems came about because of poor communication, a lack of man-management skills and weak leadership by the ZCU over the years. Originally a white-dominated organisation under a militant black government, they were forever struggling to maintain the principle of merit selection, but their efforts at compromise satisfied no one.

On the field, Zimbabwe endured a chequered season, although there had been definite signs of hope for the future: players like Ervine, Blignaut and Price began to make their names on the international scene, and more experienced figures, such as Stuart Carlisle and Craig Wishart, were playing better than ever before. Streak had taken over the mantle of Andy Flower and had a superb all-round season. His bowling figures did not do him justice, as opponents made it their policy to see him off and then score from the bowlers at the other end. But when Price was also operating, Zimbabwe could hold their own with the ball. Streak was also Zimbabwe's most reliable batsman, saving many a difficult situation with watchful consolidation and, when free to do so, powerful attack. He deserved wider recognition as an all-rounder of true world class.

The 2003-04 season began painfully at Perth, where Zimbabwe conceded the world Test batting record to Matthew Hayden and were overwhelmed by Australia, although they were much more competitive in the second game at Sydney. And they almost picked up their first Test victory in over two years against a side other than Bangladesh when they just failed to take the final West Indian wicket at Harare. In the Second Test they matched the visitors before falling apart in the final innings. They also led the one-day series 2–1, before losing the last two matches and once again laying themselves open to charges of choking. Returning to Australia for the VB Series, Zimbabwe failed to win a match in a three-way tournament which also included India, although they improved as the competition progressed. Back home again, they took on their juniors, Bangladesh, in two intriguing series. After initial tension, Zimbabwe took control of the Test series but, perhaps a little overconfident going into the one-day series – another regular accusation – and on the back of some questionable selections, they lost to Bangladesh after the first two matches had been washed out. Only the skill and determination of Streak allowed them to claw their way to two tense victories and claim an unconvincing series win. Then came the crisis.

At domestic level, Mashonaland won the Logan Cup for the fifth successive year, but they were not the force of old and were beaten, for the first time since 1995-96, by both Midlands and Matabeleland. Midlands might well have won the competition, as they were ahead of Mashonaland on points before the final round of matches, but at this point the rebels quit, and Midlands were far worse affected than Mashonaland, as they relied heavily on Wishart, Ervine and Travis Friend. With a superb all-round performance by Taibu (175 not out and eight for 43), Mashonaland won the match and the tournament.

The four Logan Cup teams as a whole were more evenly matched than they had ever been, as many of the leading Harare players were again seconded to strengthen the other provinces, despite having no qualification to play for them. The most successful of those transferred players was opening batsman Trevor Gripper, who scored most runs in the season and marked his Manicaland debut with 234 against his old province. Overall, the standard of play was weaker, though, and this was made even more obvious when the final four rounds were played without the Zimbabwe A players, who were touring Bangladesh. This time, Manicaland were worst affected, and they lost each of their last four matches.

In *Wisden 2004,* it was noted that unless certain issues could be resolved, not all of them within the power of the ZCU or the players, the future of Zimbabwe cricket looked bleak. How much worse it appears a year later. Early in 2005, there were hints of a deal. Not all the players were succeeding in their new homes, and rapprochement with some rebels was in the air. But this is only one part of the story. Just as it may be decades before the country as a whole recovers from its political misrule, Zimbabwe's fragile cricket culture will take many years to overcome the effects of this disastrous year.

FIRST-CLASS AVERAGES, 2003-04

BATTING

(Qualification: 300 runs)

	M	I	NO	R	HS	100s	Avge	Ct/St
H. H. Streak (*Matabeleland*)	8	13	4	593	131	3	65.88	5
S. V. Carlisle (*Mashonaland*)	6	11	3	503	181*	2	62.87	5
G. M. Strydom (*Matabeleland*) . . .	6	12	1	681	216	3	61.90	4
C. B. Wishart (*Midlands*)	6	10	1	554	154	2	61.55	5
T. R. Gripper (*Manicaland*)	8	15	1	739	234	1	52.78	7
†A. M. Blignaut (*Mashonaland*) . .	5	9	0	465	194	1	51.66	2
G. B. Brent (*Manicaland*)	4	8	0	379	121	1	47.37	0
†S. M. Ervine (*Midlands*)	8	11	0	504	110	1	45.81	7
G. M. Ewing (*Matabeleland*)	5	10	1	406	82	0	45.11	2
A. D. Soma (*Mashonaland*)	4	8	0	317	204	1	39.62	3
T. Taibu (*Mashonaland*)	12	20	1	678	175*	1	35.68	34/5
D. D. Ebrahim (*Mashonaland*) . . .	10	18	0	629	121	1	34.94	11
M. L. Nkala (*Matabeleland*)	8	16	1	524	124*	1	34.93	6
T. J. Friend (*Midlands*)	8	12	1	361	183	1	32.81	5
M. A. Vermeulen (*Matabeleland*) . .	8	16	0	467	118	1	29.18	7
S. Matsikenyeri (*Manicaland*)	9	17	2	391	84*	0	26.06	8
P. Utseya (*Manicaland*)	8	15	2	331	89	0	25.46	4
N. B. Mahwire (*Manicaland*)	13	20	3	300	115	1	17.64	3

† *Left-handed batsman.*

BOWLING

(Qualification: 10 wickets)

	Style	O	M	R	W	BB	5W/i	Avge
T. Taibu (*Mashonaland*)	RM	113.3	37	302	21	8-43	1	14.38
N. Chari (*Midlands*)	RFM	80.3	19	324	17	5-27	1	19.05
H. H. Streak (*Matabeleland*)	RFM	254	89	633	33	7-55	1	19.18
E. C. Rainsford (*Midlands*)	RFM	130.4	29	416	19	5-44	1	21.89
J. S. Nicolle (*Mashonaland*)	RFM	47.4	5	227	10	4-61	0	22.70
R. W. Price (*Midlands*)	SLA	347.3	83	981	42	6-73	4	23.35
S. M. Ervine (*Midlands*)	RM	136.4	30	469	20	4-28	0	23.45
D. T. Mutendera (*Mashonaland*) . . .	RFM	91.1	10	379	16	5-62	1	23.68
D. T. Hondo (*Mashonaland*)	RFM	242.5	59	666	27	4-29	0	24.66
T. Mupariwa (*Matabeleland*)	RFM	142	42	421	16	3-26	0	26.31
T. J. Friend (*Midlands*)	RF	175.4	52	452	17	5-16	1	26.58
G. B. Brent (*Manicaland*)	RFM	129.4	34	409	14	4-66	0	29.21
A. M. Blignaut (*Mashonaland*)	RFM	153.2	30	591	20	4-86	0	29.55
T. R. Gripper (*Manicaland*)	OB	123.2	36	328	11	3-22	0	29.81
L. J. Soma (*Manicaland*)	RFM	80.5	17	331	11	5-58	1	30.09
T. P. Ruswa (*Mashonaland*)	OB	98.1	23	376	10	3-56	0	37.60
G. M. Ewing (*Matabeleland*)	OB	176.4	38	574	14	4-54	0	41.00
N. B. Mahwire (*Manicaland*)	RM	314.1	57	1,210	29	3-17	0	41.72
M. L. Nkala (*Matabeleland*)	RFM	150	28	507	11	4-60	0	46.09

Note: All of the above players except Brent, Chari, Mutendera, Nicolle, Rainsford, Ruswa, A. D. Soma, L. J. Soma and Strydom played Test cricket for Zimbabwe during the home season. Averages do not include India A's tour in July–August 2004.

LOGAN CUP, 2003-04

	Played	Won	Lost	Drawn	Bonus points Batting	Bowling	Penalty	Points
Mashonaland	6	3	2	1	13	23	0	78
Matabeleland	6	3	2	1	12.5	22	0	76.5
Midlands	6	3	2	1	9.5	22	0	73.5
Manicaland	6	1	4	1	14.5	20	3.5	49

Outright win = 12 pts; drawn match = 6 pts.

Bonus points are awarded for the first 100 overs of each team's first innings. Half a batting point is awarded for the first 175 runs and for every subsequent 25 to a maximum of four points. One bowling point is awarded for the third wicket taken and for every subsequent two.

Penalty points are imposed for slow over-rates.

At Mutare Sports Club, Mutare, September 12, 13, 14, 15, 2003. **Drawn.** Toss: Mashonaland. **Manicaland 523** (T. R. Gripper 234, Extras 52) **and 288-8 dec.** (T. R. Gripper 61, G. B. Brent 82); **Mashonaland 448** (C. N. Evans 50, A. M. Blignaut 194, D. T. Hondo 85*) **and 96-2.** *Manicaland 13 pts, Mashonaland 13 pts.*
   In Manicaland's first innings, Flower broke a finger attempting a slip catch, which put him out of the Test tour of Australia. Gripper's 234, his maiden double-hundred, lasted 492 minutes and 371 balls and included 37 fours. Blignaut and Hondo added 237, a national eighth-wicket record; both scored career-bests.

At Queens Sports Club, Bulawayo, September 12, 13, 14, 15, 2003. **Drawn.** Toss: Matabeleland. **Matabeleland 161 and 479** (G. M. Ewing 67, H. H. Streak 131, M. L. Nkala 124*; R. W. Price 5-148); **Midlands 220** (V. Sibanda 69, C. B. Wishart 67; A. P. Hoffman 5-6) **and 326-5** (C. B. Wishart 52*, S. M. Ervine 110). *Matabeleland 10 pts, Midlands 11 pts.*

At Mutare Sports Club, Mutare, September 19, 20, 21, 22, 2003. **Manicaland won by nine wickets.** Toss: Manicaland. **Manicaland 435** (T. R. Gripper 65, R. W. Sims 148, B. G. Rogers 117; A. Maungwa 5-61) **and 152-1** (T. R. Gripper 72*, R. W. Sims 56*); **Midlands 153** (H. P. Rinke 6-43) **and 433** (S. M. Ervine 57, A. Maregwede 90, R. W. Price 117*). *Manicaland 20 pts, Midlands 2 pts.*

At Harare Sports Club, Harare, September 19, 20, 21, 22, 2003. **Mashonaland won by 131 runs.** Toss: Matabeleland. **Mashonaland 270** (C. N. Evans 60; G. M. Ewing 4-54) **and 442-6 dec.** (D. D. Ebrahim 70, S. V. Carlisle 181*); **Matabeleland 289** (M. A. Vermeulen 53, G. M. Ewing 82, G. M. Strydom 59) **and 292** (M. L. Nkala 64, G. M. Ewing 62; J. S. Nicolle 4-61). *Mashonaland 18 pts, Matabeleland 6.5 pts.*

At Harare Sports Club, Harare, March 19, 20, 2004. **Midlands won by nine wickets.** Toss: Midlands. **Mashonaland 103 and 183** (S. M. Ervine 4-28); **Midlands 157 and 130-1** (T. J. Friend 57*). *Midlands 16 pts, Mashonaland 4 pts.*
   This two-day defeat was Mashonaland's first loss in a first-class match since 1995-96.

At Queens Sports Club, Bulawayo, March 19, 20, 21, 22, 2004. **Matabeleland won by 190 runs.** Toss: Manicaland. **Matabeleland 442** (G. M. Strydom 216, M. L. Nkala 84) **and 334-7 dec.** (W. T. Siziba 56, M. A. Vermeulen 83); **Manicaland 283** (G. B. Brent 53, N. B. Mahwire 115) **and 303** (G. B. Brent 121). *Matabeleland 20 pts, Manicaland 6.5 pts.*
   Strydom's 216, his maiden double-hundred, lasted 204 minutes and 140 balls and included 35 fours and six sixes; he added 276 for the fourth wicket with Nkala.

At Harare Sports Club, Harare, March 26, 27, 28, 2004. **Mashonaland won by an innings and 31 runs.** Toss: Manicaland. **Manicaland 137** (T. Taibu 4-26) **and 191** (D. R. Matambanadzo 72; G. W. Flower 4-23); **Mashonaland 359** (D. D. Ebrahim 94, T. Taibu 72; G. B. Brent 4-66). *Mashonaland 18.5 pts, Manicaland –1.5 pts.*
   Manicaland's two bowling points were wiped out by a 3.5-point penalty for a slow over-rate.

At Kwekwe Sports Club, Kwekwe, March 26, 27, 28, 29, 2004. **Midlands won by an innings and 103 runs.** Toss: Matabeleland. **Matabeleland** 143 (T. J. Friend 5-16) **and** 81 (R. W. Price 5-41); **Midlands** 327-9 dec. (D. A. Marillier 89, R. W. Price 70, E. C. Rainsford 50*). *Midlands 19.5 pts, Matabeleland 4 pts.*

At Queens Sports Club, Bulawayo, April 2, 3, 4, 2004. **Matabeleland won by five wickets.** Toss: Matabeleland. **Mashonaland** 285 (D. D. Ebrahim 121; H. H. Streak 4-49) **and** 190 (H. H. Streak 7-55); **Matabeleland** 274 (H. H. Streak 107; D. T. Mutendera 4-60) **and** 205-5 (G. M. Strydom 94*). *Matabeleland 18 pts, Mashonaland 6.5 pts.*
    Streak scored a century and took 11 for 104 in the match.

At Kwekwe Sports Club, Kwekwe, April 2, 3, 4, 2004. **Midlands won by an innings and 181 runs.** Toss: Manicaland. **Manicaland** 156 (B. G. Rogers 52; N. Chari 5-27) **and** 218 (S. Chioza 63; E. C. Rainsford 5-44); **Midlands** 555 (T. Duffin 64, T. J. Friend 183, C. B. Wishart 154, C. R. Ervine 59; B. G. Rogers 4-108). *Midlands 20 pts, Manicaland 3 pts.*
    Friend and Wishart added 286 for Midlands' third wicket.

At Mutare Sports Club, Mutare, April 9, 10, 11, 12, 2004. **Matabeleland won by 16 runs.** Toss: Matabeleland. **Matabeleland** 390 (W. T. Siziba 66, G. M. Strydom 128, M. L. Nkala 57, Extras 60; L. J. Soma 5-58) **and** 359 (H. Masakadza 67, G. M. Strydom 104, R. T. Kasawaya 50); **Manicaland** 526 (R. N. Manyande 148, A. D. Soma 204, N. B. Mahwire 51) **and** 207 (P. Utseya 77; M. L. Nkala 4-60). *Matabeleland 18 pts, Manicaland 8 pts.*
    Both matches in the final round were weakened by the absence of the rebel players. Strydom hit two centuries in the match: 128 in 92 minutes and 78 balls, including 12 fours and ten sixes, and 104 in 116 minutes and 90 balls, including eight fours and six sixes. Andre Soma's 204, his maiden century, lasted 231 minutes and 213 balls and included 31 fours and two sixes; he added 288 for Manicaland's third wicket with Manyande.

At Kwekwe Sports Club, Kwekwe, April 9, 10, 11, 2004. **Mashonaland won by 329 runs.** Toss: Mashonaland. **Mashonaland** 258 (E. Chauluka 105, J. Marumisa 66; E. C. Rainsford 4-37) **and** 460-3 dec. (J. Marumisa 101, T. Taibu 175*, T. V. Mufambisi 101*); **Midlands** 204 (C. R. Ervine 51; D. T. Mutendera 5-62) **and** 185 (C. H. Brewer 53, C. R. Ervine 100; T. Taibu 8-43). *Mashonaland 18 pts, Midlands 5 pts.*
    Taibu recorded career-bests with bat and ball; he had also stumped one and caught three as wicket-keeper in Midlands' first innings. Mufambisi became the youngest Zimbabwean to score a first-class century at 17 years 116 days and took over the keeper's gloves from Taibu on the final day.

LOGAN CUP WINNERS

1993-94	Mashonaland Under-24	1999-2000	Mashonaland
1994-95	Mashonaland	2000-01	Mashonaland
1995-96	Matabeleland	2001-02	Mashonaland
1996-97	Mashonaland	2002-03	Mashonaland
1997-98	Mashonaland	2003-04	Mashonaland
1998-99	Matabeleland		

Mashonaland have won the title eight times, Matabeleland twice and Mashonaland Under-24 once.

CRICKET IN BANGLADESH, 2003-04

By UTPAL SHUVRO

Faisal Hossain

Bangladesh's form under coach Dav Whatmore followed an upward curve for most of the season, only to take a nosedive in July and September, with miserable performances in the one-day Asia Cup and ICC Champions Trophy. It was January 2005 before they finally achieved their first Test win, at the 35th attempt, and that against troubled Zimbabwe. As usual, their demolition by other sides prompted questions about the wisdom of granting Bangladesh full status. The International Cricket Council has been considering a plan to reduce the amount of top-level cricket they play, but this was still meeting resistance. Though that is seen as an insult in certain quarters, it might not prove a bad idea in the long run. Many believe Bangladesh have been too busy, and their players have not had enough time to recover and learn from their games.

They had enjoyed some moments in the sun, however. Despite being whitewashed in series with Pakistan and England in late 2003, they gave both some scares. In February, they travelled to Zimbabwe, lost the First Test in one bad session, drew the Second thanks to rain, and then took the lead in the one-day series through only their fourth victory at this level – their first since beating Pakistan in the 1999 World Cup. In between, Bangladesh had started 47 matches without winning, losing 45. Even allowing for two washouts, this created the longest losing streak in one-day international history. Bangladesh could even have won the one-day series with Zimbabwe, but for a superlative performance from home captain Heath Streak. The improvement continued on the tour of the West Indies: it was hard to believe they lost the one-day games 3–0 after having West Indies on the ropes in the first game and being unlucky in the second.

But Bangladesh's greatest glory came in the First Test at St Lucia. By building their highest-ever score, 416, in the first innings, they earned a well-deserved draw. It was only their third in Test cricket, after two with Zimbabwe, but the first one they had secured through their playing abilities rather than inclement weather. Before St Lucia, Bangladeshi batsmen had scored only five centuries in 28 Tests. Here, they added another three.

Remarkably, two came from the lower order, with Mohammad Rafique scoring 111 at No. 9 and Khaled Mashud adding an unbeaten 103 at No. 8 in the second innings.

Bangladesh hosted the Under-19 World Cup in February and March 2004, and it was a stupendous success. For the first time in the competition's history, almost every match attracted a full house. Impressed by the colourful opening ceremony and the crowd's enthusiasm, ICC president Ehsan Mani said, "This exceeds any previous show." Bangladesh's own team played their part in making it a memorable tournament, their disappointment at failing to qualify for the Super League evaporating when they defeated defending champions Australia in the Plate final.

On the domestic front, it was a chaotic season. The Dhaka Premier Cricket League, traditionally the most popular competition, did not take place at all. It was initially delayed because of the Under-19 World Cup, and scheduled to start in April. But the main clubs were reluctant to play, arguing that the rainy season was fast approaching. Their withdrawal spelled disaster for about 700 cricketers who depend on the league for their livelihood. They protested to the president of the Bangladesh Cricket Board, but the clubs could not be forced to change their minds. The board did come up with a solution, however: a hastily-arranged Corporate Cricket League. Twelve leading companies formed teams and provided many cricketers with contracts. A BCB Development XI also took part, and international stars including Shahid Afridi of Pakistan and Yuvraj Singh of India joined in the later stages. The weather was better than expected, and ARAF Apparels won the final, against Bashundhara. The new venture was so successful that the BCB decided to make it a regular event.

The Ispahani Mirzapore Tea National Cricket League, the country's only first-class competition, reverted to a home-and-away league between the six divisions, after a season when they played a single round of five matches each. Even in its fifth year (the inaugural season in 1999-2000 was not first-class), the tournament left much to be desired. There were regular complaints about poor pitches, one of the main problems of Bangladeshi domestic cricket, which makes a mockery of its supposed purpose of preparing players for the international game. Another flaw is that most of the cricketers are based in Dhaka, so very few have a sense of belonging to their regional sides, which seriously reduces the tournament's competitive intensity. Moreover, the leading players barely featured, as they were getting ready for the tour of Zimbabwe.

Despite all these handicaps, the tournament was a live race until the last day. From the early stages, Dhaka and Sylhet had left the rest of the pack behind, and they entered the final round level pegging. Both won their closing fixtures convincingly, to tie on five wins and 42 points each. Over their ten games, Sylhet had scored more heavily, with 4,446 runs to Dhaka's 3,805. But the tie-breaker was runs per wicket, and Dhaka edged past Sylhet to become the first team to win the title twice.

It was a disastrous season for holders Khulna; they won only one match. To rub salt in their wounds, Dhaka shot them out for 67 in a four-day game, and a few days later Rajshahi sent them packing for 41 in the one-day tournament, which was won by Chittagong, with Rajshahi second. Tragically, Khulna lost a promising left-arm spinner and improving batsman, Tamim Bashir, when he died of cerebral malaria in June, aged 19. Bashir had finished third in the season's batting averages

In the first-class National League, Dhaka's triumph was a real team effort: only one of their batsmen featured among the tournament's top ten run-scorers (Sanwar Hossain, with 503), and none of their bowlers among the ten leading wicket-takers. The leading scorer in the League was Nuruzzaman of Rajshahi with 633, but Chittagong's Faisal Hossain scored 809 in all first-class cricket, including a tour by Zimbabwe A. The left-handed Faisal was the find of the season, and earned a call-up for the West Indies tour. On the bowling front, Rajshahi's left-arm spinner Saifullah Khan was far ahead of the rest, with 63 first-class wickets at 16.33.

The Emirates National Championship, contested by districts and some corporate teams, preceded the National League, but was hampered by rain; with no reserve days in the earlier rounds, several matches were decided by the flip of a coin, and batsmen struggled on slow pitches. Bangladesh Biman clinched their seventh title by defeating Comilla District in a low-scoring final.

FIRST-CLASS AVERAGES, 2003-04

BATTING

(Qualification: 300 runs)

	M	I	NO	R	HS	100s	Avge	Ct/St
Tushar Imran (*Khulna & Bangladesh A*) ..	4	7	2	306	103*	2	61.20	1
Golam Rahman (*Sylhet*)	4	7	1	327	115*	1	54.50	1
Tamim Bashir (*Khulna*)	9	13	4	475	98*	0	52.77	4
Nuruzzaman (*Rajshahi*)	10	16	3	633	139*	1	48.69	4
Al Sahariar (*Dhaka*)	5	8	1	328	92	0	46.85	5
Arif Ahmed (*Chittagong*)	7	11	1	387	122	2	38.70	3
Sanwar Hossain (*Dhaka*)	9	13	0	503	117	1	38.69	8
†Faisal Hossain (*Chittagong & Bang. A*) . .	13	24	3	809	100	1	38.52	6
Shafiul Alam (*Khulna*)	6	9	0	343	77	0	38.11	2
Anisur Rahman (*Rajshahi*)	8	12	2	362	76*	0	36.20	9
Khaled Mashud (*Bangladesh & Dhaka*). . .	5	10	1	322	86	0	35.77	11/3
Towhid Hossain (*Barisal*)	8	14	3	383	63	0	34.81	3
†Mohammad Mostadir (*Barisal*).	9	14	4	346	72*	0	34.60	4
Parvez Ahmed (*Sylhet*)	10	20	2	556	106	1	30.88	8
Anisul Hakim (*Chittagong*)	10	18	0	531	118	1	29.50	7
Rafiqul Islam (*Rajshahi*).	9	16	0	460	99	0	28.75	7
Prosenjit Joy (*Barisal*)	7	11	0	309	105	1	28.09	1
Mehrab Hossain (*Dhaka*)	9	14	0	393	169	1	28.07	7
Nasirul Alam (*Sylhet*)	10	18	0	493	89	0	27.38	11
Imran Ahmed (*Barisal & Bangladesh U23*)	11	19	1	486	152*	1	27.00	8
Rana Miah (*Sylhet*)	7	12	0	322	73	0	26.83	5
Golam Mawla (*Sylhet*)	10	18	0	456	68	0	25.33	5
Imtiaz Hossain (*Sylhet*)	10	20	2	418	73	0	23.22	13
Shabbir Khan (*Chittagong*)	9	15	1	320	100	1	22.85	8
†Nahidul Haque (*Barisal*).	9	15	1	310	47	0	22.14	2
Jahangir Alam (*Dhaka*)	9	15	1	301	95	0	21.50	6
Golam Mabud (*Sylhet*).	8	16	0	316	64	0	19.75	16/2

† *Left-handed batsman.*

BOWLING

(Qualification: 15 wickets)

	Style	O	M	R	W	BB	5W/i	Avge
Rezaul Haque (*Sylhet*)	LFM	210.5	74	460	32	6-60	2	14.37
Naimur Rahman (*Dhaka*)	OB	136.3	40	353	23	5-16	1	15.34
Saifullah Khan (*Rajshahi*).	SLA	416.4	107	1,029	63	7-22	7	16.33
Nabil Samad (*Sylhet*).	SLA	375.1	114	803	49	6-43	3	16.38
Ashraful Khan (*Dhaka*)	RFM	134.3	44	285	17	5-6	1	16.76
Mohammad Rafique (*Bang. & Dhaka*) . .	SLA	280.5	87	621	30	6-45	1	20.70
Syed Russell (*Khulna & Bangladesh U23*)	LFM	272.4	79	655	31	8-67	2	21.12
Neeyamur Rashid (*Dhaka*)	RFM	151	34	405	19	3-35	0	21.31
Khaled Mahmud (*Dhaka*)	RM	125.3	45	325	15	5-32	1	21.66
Sanwar Hossain (*Dhaka*)	OB	119.5	26	354	16	4-12	0	22.12
Mohammad Shahzada (*Rajshahi*)	RM	229	55	622	28	4-64	0	22.21
Arafat Sunny (*Dhaka & Bangladesh U23*)	SLA	142.3	31	382	17	6-79	1	22.47
Elias Sunny (*Dhaka*)	SLA	245.1	63	571	25	4-52	0	22.84
Yasin Arafat (*Chittagong*)	OB	328.1	97	789	33	7-62	1	23.90
Gazi Alamgir (*Chittagong & Bang. U23*).	RFM	145.5	36	433	18	5-44	1	24.05
Abdur Razzaq (*Khulna & Bang. U23*). .	SLA	510	142	1,154	47	7-11	2	24.55
Ahsanullah Hasan (*Chittagong*)	SLA	332	121	690	28	5-55	2	24.64
Imtiaz Hossain (*Sylhet*)	OB	152.5	22	499	20	3-60	0	24.95
Shabbir Khan (*Chittagong*)	OB	517	177	1,017	40	6-72	2	25.42
Tariqul Islam (*Barisal*).	OB	283.2	64	745	29	7-116	2	25.68
Tamim Bashir (*Khulna*)	SLA	279	63	636	22	5-43	2	28.90
Mohammad Mostadir (*Barisal*)	SLA	225.2	50	635	15	3-78	0	42.33

ISPAHANI MIRZAPORE TEA NATIONAL CRICKET LEAGUE, 2003-04

	Played	Won	Lost	Drawn	1st-inns Points	Points	Runs per wkt
Dhaka	10	5	1	4	4	42	27.17
Sylhet	10	5	1	4	4	42	25.55
Khulna	10	1	3	6	6	24	24.19
Rajshahi	10	2	3	5	2	24	23.90
Chittagong	10	1	4	5	6	22	23.55
Barisal	10	1	3	6	2	20	23.21

Win = 6 pts; draw = 2 pts; 1st-innings lead in a drawn match = 2 pts.

Teams tied on points were separated by dividing runs scored by wickets lost.

At Comilla Stadium, Comilla, December 10, 11, 12, 13, 2003. **Chittagong won by eight wickets.** Toss: Rajshahi. **Rajshahi 234** (Yasin Arafat 7-62) **and 194** (Khaled Mashud 59); **Chittagong 300** (Anisul Hakim 53, Faisal Hossain 99*; Saifullah Khan 6-91) **and 129-2** (Faisal Hossain 65*). *Chittagong 6 pts.*

At Dhanmondi Cricket Stadium, Dhaka, December 10, 11, 12, 2003. **Dhaka won by an innings and 63 runs.** Toss: Barisal. **Barisal 193** (Shahin Hossain 55; Mohammad Rafique 4-60) **and 118** (Khaled Mahmud 4-19, Fahim Muntasir 4-31); **Dhaka 374** (Halim Shah 119, Khaled Mahmud 51, Neeyamur Rashid 62, Fahim Muntasir 58; Kamaluddin 4-76). *Dhaka 6 pts.*

At Sylhet Stadium, Sylhet, December 10, 11, 12, 13, 2003. **Khulna won by 76 runs.** Toss: Khulna. **Khulna 160** (Rezaul Haque 5-45) **and 156;** **Sylhet 80** (Abdur Razzaq 7-11) **and 160** (Tamim Bashir 5-43). *Khulna 6 pts.*

Khulna wicket-keeper Hasibul Haque made four catches and two stumpings in Sylhet's second innings.

At Bangabandhu National Stadium, Dhaka, December 18, 19, 20, 21, 2003. **Dhaka won by 226 runs.** Toss: Chittagong. **Dhaka 143** (Gazi Alamgir 5-44) **and 318-9 dec.** (Al Sahariar 87, Sanwar Hossain 52; Shabbir Khan 4-106, Yasin Arafat 4-126); **Chittagong 134** (Faisal Hossain 52; Mohammad Rafique 6-45) **and 101** (Mohammad Rafique 4-39, Naimur Rahman 5-16). *Dhaka 6 pts.*

Al Sahariar was out handled the ball in Dhaka's first innings. He defended a delivery from Debabrata Barua into the ground, and then pushed the ball aside with his hand once he realised it was heading for the stumps.

At Shamsul Huda Stadium, Jessore, December 18, 19, 20, 21, 2003. **Drawn.** Toss: Barisal. **Khulna 219-7 dec.** (Tushar Imran 103*); **Barisal 112-4.** *Khulna 2 pts, Barisal 2 pts.*

The first two days were washed out.

At Cricket Garden, Rangpur, December 18, 19, 20, 21, 2003. **Sylhet won by 13 runs.** Toss: Sylhet. **Sylhet 102** (Saifullah Khan 4-41) **and 233** (Parvez Ahmed 91); **Rajshahi 200-9 dec.** (Hasanuzzaman 77; Nabil Samad 5-41) **and 122** (Tapash Baisya 4-28). *Sylhet 6 pts.*

At Abdur Rab Serniabad Stadium, Barisal, December 26, 27, 28, 29, 2003. **Drawn.** Toss: Barisal. **Rajshahi 190** (Khaled Mashud 86; Tariqul Islam 4-67) **and 232-5** (Anisur Rahman 54, Khaled Mashud 73*); **Barisal 266** (Imran Ahmed 152*; Mohammad Shahzada 4-64). *Barisal 4 pts, Rajshahi 2 pts.*

Imran Ahmed carried his bat through Barisal's innings.

At Comilla Stadium, Comilla, December 26, 27, 28, 29, 2003. **Drawn.** Toss: Chittagong. **Chittagong 389-9 dec.** (Faisal Hossain 100, Arif Ahmed 107, Shabbir Khan 57); **Khulna 215-5** (Hasibul Haque 75*, Asadullah Khan 61). *Chittagong 2 pts, Khulna 2 pts.*

At Sylhet Stadium, Sylhet, December 26, 27, 28, 29, 2003. **Drawn.** Toss: Sylhet. **Sylhet 331** (Alok Kapali 85, Tapash Baisya 59, Rezaul Haque 56*) **and 66;** **Dhaka 250** (Sanwar Hossain 88; Tapash Baisya 4-42, Rezaul Haque 4-52) **and 16-0.** *Sylhet 4 pts, Dhaka 2 pts.*

At Cricket Garden, Rangpur, January 3, 4, 5, 6, 2004. **Drawn.** Toss: Rajshahi. **Chittagong 104** (Saifullah Khan 5-30, Imran Parvez 4-34) **and 218-8 dec.** (Anisul Hakim 93, Akram Khan 73; Saifullah Khan 6-69); **Rajshahi 175** (Anisur Rahman 50; Shabbir Khan 6-72) **and 85-3.** *Rajshahi 4 pts, Chittagong 2 pts.*

At Sylhet Stadium, Sylhet, January 3, 4, 5, 6, 2004. **Sylhet won by nine wickets.** Toss: Barisal. **Barisal 130 and 275** (Towhid Hossain 63, Extras 50; Nabil Samad 4-83); **Sylhet 355** (Tariqul Islam 7-116) **and 51-1.** *Sylhet 6 pts.*

At Dhanmondi Cricket Stadium, Dhaka, January 4, 5, 6, 7, 2004. **Dhaka won by five wickets.** Toss: Dhaka. **Dhaka 224** (Al Sahariar 92, Mehrab Hossain 57; Syed Russell 7-55) **and 155-5** (Elias Sunny 54*; Syed Russell 4-54); **Khulna 67** (Ashraful Khan 5-6) **and 311** (Salahuddin Ahmed 55, Tamim Bashir 76*; Naimur Rahman 4-86). *Dhaka 6 pts.*

The match started a day late because of a general strike in Dhaka. Ashraful Khan's first-innings figures were 10–7–6–5.

At Comilla Stadium, Comilla, January 10, 11, 12, 13, 2004. **Barisal won by three wickets.** Toss: Chittagong. **Chittagong 300** (Shabbir Khan 100) **and 136** (Minhazul Abedin 59; Anisur Rahman 4-26); **Barisal 239** (Jamal Faisal 54; Shabbir Khan 4-82, Ahsanullah Hasan 5-55) **and 199-7** (Prosenjit Joy 72, Towhid Hossain 51; Shabbir Khan 4-80). *Barisal 6 pts.*

At Dhanmondi Cricket Stadium, Dhaka, January 10, 11, 12, 13, 2004. **Drawn.** Toss: Sylhet. **Sylhet 247** (Golam Mabud 50, Golam Mawla 68, Ejaj Ahmed 51) **and 324** (Parvez Ahmed 106; Ashraful Khan 4-53); **Dhaka 326** (Sanwar Hossain 117, Jahangir Alam 57, Neeyamur Rashid 55*; Rezaul Haque 6-60) **and 40-2.** *Dhaka 4 pts, Sylhet 2 pts.*

At Shamsul Huda Stadium, Jessore, January 10, 11, 12, 13, 2004. **Rajshahi won by six wickets.** Toss: Khulna. **Khulna 220** (Abdur Razzaq 83) **and 146** (Shafiul Alam 59; Saifullah Khan 6-73); **Rajshahi 297** (Nuruzzaman 68, Anisur Rahman 64, Hasanuzzaman 62*; Abdur Razzaq 6-70) **and 70-4.** *Rajshahi 6 pts.*

At Abdur Rab Serniabad Stadium, Barisal, January 17, 18, 19, 20, 2004. **Drawn.** Toss: Sylhet. **Sylhet 375** (Parvez Ahmed 55, Nasirul Alam 89, Rana Miah 73) **and 183-7 dec.** (Nasirul Alam 65); **Barisal 217** (Arafat Salahuddin 54; Jakwan Ahmed 4-83) **and 201-5** (Jamal Faisal 90). *Barisal 2 pts, Sylhet 4 pts.*

At Dhanmondi Cricket Stadium, Dhaka, January 17, 18, 19, 20, 2004. **Drawn.** Toss: Dhaka. **Rajshahi 249** (Anisur Rahman 76*; Naimur Rahman 4-76) **and 250** (Jamiul Alam 54, Nuruzzaman 62; Elias Sunny 4-52); **Dhaka 374** (Mehrab Hossain 169, Sajjad Kadir 67; Saifullah Khan 5-113) **and 103-6.** *Dhaka 4 pts, Rajshahi 2 pts.*
  Mehrab Hossain's 169 was the highest individual score of the season.

At Shamsul Huda Stadium, Jessore, January 17, 18, 19, 20, 2004. **Drawn.** Toss: Chittagong. **Khulna 285** (Tamim Bashir 98*, Niaz Morshed 51; Ahsanullah Hasan 5-107) **and 187** (Shabbir Khan 4-65); **Chittagong 358** (Anisul Hakim 118, Gazi Salahuddin 66, Arif Ahmed 68). *Khulna 2 pts, Chittagong 4 pts.*

At Comilla Stadium, Comilla, January 24, 25, 26, 27, 2004. **Drawn.** Toss: Chittagong. **Chittagong 254** (Gazi Salahuddin 64) **and 299** (Anisul Hakim 79, Shabbir Khan 85*; Elias Sunny 4-75); **Dhaka 148** (Shabbir Khan 5-62) **and 203-8** (Jahangir Alam 51*). *Chittagong 4 pts, Dhaka 2 pts.*

At Shamsul Huda Stadium, Jessore, January 24, 25, 26, 27, 2004. **Drawn.** Toss: Sylhet. **Sylhet 181 and 266** (Golam Mabud 64, Nasirul Alam 59; Tamim Bashir 5-56); **Khulna 245** (Salahuddin Ahmed 64; Nabil Samad 5-55). *Khulna 4 pts, Sylhet 2 pts.*

At Cricket Garden, Rangpur, January 24, 25, 26, 27, 2004. **Drawn.** Toss: Rajshahi. **Barisal 175-6** (Prosenjit Joy 51) **v Rajshahi.** *Rajshahi 2 pts, Barisal 2 pts.*
  Only 85.2 overs were played in the match; play was initially delayed by a wet pitch, and was then interrupted and finally ended by a general strike.

At Abdur Rab Serniabad Stadium, Barisal, February 7, 8, 9, 10, 2004. **Drawn.** Toss: Khulna. **Barisal 193** (Arafat Salahuddin 59; Syed Russell 8-67) **and 247-6** (Prosenjit Joy 105); **Khulna 375** (Shafiul Alam 61, Sanjay Chakrabarty 63, Salahuddin Ahmed 55, Jamaluddin Ahmed 113). *Barisal 2 pts, Khulna 4 pts.*
  Syed Russell was the only bowler to take eight wickets in an innings in the season.

At Cricket Garden, Rangpur, February 7, 8, 2004. **Rajshahi won by eight wickets.** Toss: Dhaka. **Dhaka 90** (Saifullah Khan 5-30) **and 108** (Saifullah Khan 7-22); **Rajshahi 148** (Khaled Mahmud 5-32) **and 53-2.** *Rajshahi 6 pts.*
  Saifullah Khan's match figures of 12-52 were the best of the season.

At Sylhet Stadium, Sylhet, February 7, 8, 9, 10, 2004. **Sylhet won by 124 runs.** Toss: Sylhet. **Sylhet 235** (Ahmed Sadiqur 59, Golam Mawla 59) **and 278-6 dec.** (Golam Rahman 115*); **Chittagong 93** (Rezaul Haque 4-15) **and 296** (Gazi Salahuddin 71, Faisal Hossain 79; Nabil Samad 4-78). *Sylhet 6 pts.*

At Abdur Rab Serniabad Stadium, Barisal, February 23, 24, 25, 2004. **Dhaka won by an innings and 25 runs.** Toss: Dhaka. **Dhaka 352-7 dec.** (Sanwar Hossain 53, Jahangir Alam 95, Sajjad Kadir 52*); **Barisal 161** (Towhid Hossain 59) **and 166.** *Dhaka 6 pts.*

At Comilla Stadium, Comilla, February 23, 24, 25, 2004. **Sylhet won by ten wickets.** Toss: Chittagong. **Chittagong 170** (Masumud Dowla 56) **and 163** (Ahsanullah Hasan 51; Nabil Samad 4-21); **Sylhet 271** (Rezaul Haque 52) **and 64-0.** *Sylhet 6 pts.*

At Cricket Garden, Rangpur, February 23, 24, 25, 26, 2004. **Drawn.** Toss: Rajshahi. **Khulna 420** (Shafiul Alam 77, Salahuddin Ahmed 50, Jamaluddin Ahmed 53, Tamim Bashir 85; Rezwanul Islam 4-93); **Rajshahi 185** (Anisur Rahman 53) **and 348-5** (Rafiqul Islam 99, Nuruzzaman 139*). *Rajshahi 2 pts, Khulna 4 pts.*

At Abdur Rab Serniabad Stadium, Barisal, March 4, 5, 6, 7, 2004. **Drawn.** Toss: Barisal. **Barisal 251** (Mohammad Mostadir 72*) **and 293** (Imran Ahmed 62, Ali Arman 76); **Chittagong 289** (Arif Ahmed 122; Tariqul Islam 5-85) **and 36-2.** *Barisal 2 pts, Chittagong 4 pts.*

At Shamsul Huda Stadium, Jessore, March 4, 5, 6, 7, 2004. **Dhaka won by 152 runs.** Toss: Dhaka. **Dhaka 358-8 dec.** (Elias Sunny 94, Sanwar Hossain 52, Halim Shah 91*) **and 223-5 dec.** (Rashidul Haque 65, Moniruzzaman 53); **Khulna 252** (Tamim Bashir 60; Mahbubul Alam 4-61) **and 177** (Sanwar Hossain 4-12). *Dhaka 6 pts.*

At Sylhet Stadium, Sylhet, March 4, 5, 6, 7, 2004. **Sylhet won by 138 runs.** Toss: Sylhet. **Sylhet 371** (Imtiaz Hossain 73, Golam Rahman 78) **and 273** (Imtiaz Hossain 53, Golam Rahman 52); **Rajshahi 329** (Rafiqul Islam 82, Raqibul Islam 72, Nuruzzaman 61; Ahmed Sadiqur 4-47) **and 177** (Nuruzzaman 55; Nabil Samad 6-43). *Sylhet 6 pts.*

NATIONAL CRICKET LEAGUE WINNERS

†1999-2000	Chittagong	2002 03	Khulna
2000-01	Biman Bangladesh Airlines	2003-04	Dhaka
2001-02	Dhaka		

† *The National Cricket League was not first-class in 1999-2000.*

Note: Matches in the following section were not first-class.

ISPAHANI MIRZAPORE TEA NATIONAL ONE-DAY CRICKET LEAGUE, 2003-04

	Played	Won	Lost	Points	Net run-rate
Chittagong	10	8	2	16	−0.06
Rajshahi	10	7	3	14	0.98
Dhaka	10	5	5	10	0.21
Sylhet	10	4	6	8	−0.22
Barisal	10	3	7	6	−0.38
Khulna	10	3	7	6	−0.52

CRICKET IN KENYA, 2004

MARTIN WILLIAMSON

If an appearance in the semi-finals of the 2003 World Cup seemed to herald the arrival of Kenya as a force in world cricket, then 2004 was a year of regression. Far from building on their achievement in Southern Africa, Kenya's development was undermined by infighting and scandal. Sadly, most of the headlines in 2004 centred on off-field events.

The most public low was the five-year ban handed down to former captain Maurice Odumbe after an ICC hearing in Nairobi in July. Odumbe was accused and found guilty of frequenting with a known bookmaker, damned largely by the evidence of his ex-wife. The ramifications of that rumbled on for the rest of the year, and in December the ICC began to question another 15 past and present players as its investigations widened.

Meanwhile, behind the scenes the battle between the Kenyan Cricket Association and the country's stakeholders grew increasingly bitter. The KCA and Sharad Ghai – the controversial former fixture secretary who took over as the board's chairman from Jimmy Rayani in May – appeared at odds not only with many of the national team, but also almost all the country's clubs and players. A legal case, brought by the powerful Coast Cricket Association, questioning the board's constitution, dragged through the courts for much of the year and prevented new elections being held.

In October the KCA announced it was holding a thorough review of its own constitution, with Bob Merriman, the chairman of Cricket Australia, overseeing it. Hopes that this represented a real breakthrough were soon dashed, with opponents claiming that the members were hand-picked and that the very review itself was unconstitutional. Merriman's role, which upon closer investigation appeared less than hands-on, also attracted criticism.

The board's questionable financial management – it was reported to be close to broke – resulted in October's strike, with players, led by Steve Tikolo, who stood down as captain after the Champions Trophy, claiming they were owed money from as far back as the 2003 World Cup. The disharmony was fuelled by the board's refusal to offer anything other than two-month contracts to players who had already taken considerable pay cuts throughout the year. The shortage of cash was exacerbated when the ICC put a stop to the practice of using money allocated for development to pay the players' salaries. The KCA's deteriorating reputation made sponsorship hard to attract: the culture of corruption pervades Kenyan society and – though the facts are murky – it is obvious cricket has not been immune.

The ICC intervention was a sign that the outside cricketing world was growing impatient, and in April, ICC president Ehsan Mani visited Nairobi and warned the KCA that it had to put its house in order. That visit coincided with the government, which had previously been concentrating on sorting out Kenyan football, turning the spotlight on cricket. In November the ICC requested a meeting with Ochillo Ayacko, the sports minister, to discuss the growing crisis. Less than a fortnight into 2005 the minister suspended the KCA and appointed a multi-party Normalisation Committee to run the game pending the outcome of the constitutional review.

Meanwhile, the essential cricketing problem remained. Though a handful of players, now ageing, have brought Kenyan cricket to the world's attention, there is a huge gulf between Nairobi club cricket and one-day internationals, and it has been hard to find ways of bridging that: the major countries, with their packed fixture lists, do not always have time to be helpful. The ICC is finding ways round the problem, but Kenyan mismanagement means it may be some time before a new generation arises capable of making the leap.

Nonetheless, Kenya played 14 first-class matches in the calendar year, a total few teams other than English counties ever match, and one which the Kenyans may not approach again. Seven of these games came in the Carib Beer Cup, the West Indies' domestic first-class competition; there were also two home fixtures against both India A and Pakistan A, and three fixtures in the ICC's inaugural Intercontinental Cup.

In the Caribbean, Kenya were outclassed. They lost four and drew three matches, finishing bottom of their group. There were positives – Kennedy Otieno scored 512 runs at 39.38 and the soon-to-be banned Odumbe made a double-hundred and took 24 wickets. But there was little depth in the side, and the bowling was especially threadbare. There was another double-century when Ravindu Shah hit 247 in the second fixture against Pakistan A, having hit 124 in the first a week earlier. He also made a superb unbeaten 187 to take Kenya to the brink of victory in their match against Namibia, and began to attract some interest from English counties.

But the showcase one-day internationals in the Champions Trophy, Kenya's only ones of the year, resulted in two defeats. While both were expected, the Pakistan game was particularly dismal, as Kenya crumbled from 67 for one to 94 all out. Against India, the front-line batting again failed, although the scale of the defeat was not so great. The Intercontinental Cup, the ICC's new first-class competition for the non-Test nations, promised much, and Kenya started with a good win over Uganda (the only one of the year). But by the time of their second match, against Namibia in October, the side was in chaos with a dozen of the leading African players on strike. It was to the credit of a hastily assembled young team that they did enough against Namibia to qualify for the finals. But in the semi-final at Abu Dhabi, against a well-drilled Scotland team, they were completely outclassed.

Hitesh Modi took over the captaincy at a difficult time and handled the responsibility capably. When Modi missed the Scotland match because of his wedding, Rageb Aga, who made his Kenyan debut only in January, took over as the side's third captain of the year. None of this helped, and the future fixture list – with only two games pencilled in for 2005 – was discouraging.

So were events at home. As 2004 drew to a close, the KCA's claim to be representative of Kenyan cricket was further undermined when its own national league and cup competitions fell apart before they started. Almost all clubs opted to stay with the estranged Nairobi Provincial Cricket Association, and only four sides entered the official competition. Even one of those subsequently claimed that its entry had been made without its knowledge, and it is unclear whether the other entrants actually play cricket or even have pitches. It was a sorry and messy end to a deeply disappointing and divisive year. The KCA's suspension on January 14 gave renewed hope to those inside Kenya, but it also ensured more short-term unrest as the ruling executive sought to defend their position.

Jasmer Singh writes from Nairobi In contrast to the brilliance of 2003, this was a much-troubled year for Kenyan cricket. Test cricket, which once looked so close, now seems to be moving further and further away.

Despite everything, many strides were made on the development front. Age-group cricket at every level from Under-13 to Under-9 was begun, with organised coaching programmes and tournaments at all levels. Twenty local coaches were working under development manager Mark Lane.

The National Academy has also been active under the former Pakistani Test player Mudassar Nazar. Academy players enabled Kenya to reach the semi-finals of the Intercontinental Cup, even after the 13 national squad players went on strike, refusing to accept temporary two-month contracts. The KCA were unable to offer annual contracts because of the absence of a sponsor after the five-year deal with Kenya Breweries expired in June 2003. Breweries failed to renew this contract, as they did with soccer as well, and the KCA were landed with the burden of footing the players' salaries themselves.

One encouraging development was that in September, the Friends of Kenya Cricket Society in the UK was inaugurated, with a launch in Southall during the Champions Trophy. It is intended to launch similar organisations for Africa, Asia and America in the future.

KENYAN FIRST-CLASS AVERAGES, 2004

BATTING AND FIELDING

	M	I	NO	R	HS	100s	Avge	Ct/St
R. D. Shah	12	19	1	1,036	247	4	57.55	7
S. O. Tikolo	12	20	1	823	156	2	43.31	5
M. O. Odumbe	8	13	0	473	207	2	36.38	7
K. O. Otieno	12	20	0	653	104	1	32.65	17/1
†H. S. Modi	11	18	1	458	95	0	26.94	5
L. N. Onyango	10	15	4	196	67	0	17.81	6
M. A. Suji	10	16	3	217	59	0	16.69	4
C. O. Obuya	8	12	1	161	43	0	14.63	5
M. A. Ouma	8	14	0	204	58	0	14.57	4/1
T. O. Suji	4	5	2	35	18	0	11.66	2
R. G. Aga	7	14	2	129	43	0	10.75	5
T. M. Odoyo	4	5	0	43	14	0	8.60	1

	M	I	NO	R	HS	100s	Avge	Ct/St
M. L. Patel	6	10	0	84	35	0	8.40	3
B. J. Patel	9	16	1	121	59	0	8.06	5
F. N. Otieno	4	7	2	26	8*	0	5.20	6
P. J. Ongondo	11	15	2	48	12	0	3.69	8

Played in three matches: A. S. Luseno 1*, 0*, 7* (1 ct). Played in two matches: J. S. Ababu 3, 10, 1, 5* (1 ct); †J. L. Bhimji 1*, 1*; A. K. P. Bhudia 9, 31, 6, 79; R. V. Bhudia 29, 0 (1 ct); A. M. T. Janmohamed 18, 1 (6 ct, 1 st); K. A. Patel 17, 13, 23* (1 ct). Played in one match: J. O. Angara 0*, 1*; T. Mishra 1, 32 (1 ct); S. D. Okumu 2*.

† *Left-handed batsman.*

BOWLING

	Style	O	M	R	W	BB	5W/i	Avge
M. O. Odumbe	OB	195.2	50	433	27	6-64	3	16.03
T. M. Odoyo	RFM	86.3	18	283	11	3-27	0	25.72
R. G. Aga	RFM	123.1	22	395	13	4-71	0	30.38
S. O. Tikolo	RM	247.3	44	738	24	4-33	0	30.75
P. J. Ongondo	RFM	259.5	59	825	24	5-60	2	34.37
M. A. Suji	RFM	191.2	57	466	11	4-23	0	42.36
T. O. Suji	RM	63	10	220	5	3-74	0	44.00
C. O. Obuya	LB	120	12	477	8	2-3	0	59.62
L. N. Onyango	RM	186	35	665	10	2-17	0	66.50

Also bowled: J. S. Ababu (RFM) 41–13–114–3; J. O. Angara (RFM) 4–0–20–0; J. L. Bhimji (SLA) 68–11–223–3; R. V. Bhudia 55–14–210–3; A. S. Luseno (RM) 37–0–172–1; H. S. Modi (OB) 24.4–3–101–2; S. D. Okumu (RFM) 9–0–48–0; F. N. Otieno (RM) 48–6–150–3; K. A. Patel (RM) 54.3–4–227–3; B. J. Patel (SLA) 83.3–10–282–1; R. D. Shah (RFM) 21–1–68–1.

These averages include all of Kenya's 14 first-class matches in 2004: seven in the Carib Beer Cup in the West Indies (January–February), three in the ICC Intercontinental Cup (July–November), two v Pakistan A in Kenya (July–August) and two v India A in Kenya (August–September).

CRICKET IN THE NETHERLANDS, 2004

David Hardy

"The mere thought of a triangular series between India, Pakistan and Australia on Dutch soil caused my adrenalin level to rise to unknown proportions." This is how René van Ierschot, chairman of the Royal Dutch Cricket Association, described the moment when it was confirmed that the Videocon Cup – a warm-up for the Champions Trophy in England – would be held at Amstelveen in August. Holland, hosts of just one previous official one-day international (Kenya v South Africa in the 1999 World Cup), now had four in a week.

Stands for around 10,000 spectators were erected at the picturesque VRA ground, Holland's premier grass wicket, situated in woodland just outside Amsterdam. For the opening game, between India and Pakistan, they were full as supporters converged from across Europe. There was so much congestion at turnstiles that some spectators had to be admitted free – bad news for the Dutch board, who stood to profit only from gate receipts.

Understandably, crowds then dwindled, partly because of a clash with the Athens Olympics (ensuring almost no media exposure in the Netherlands, though hundreds of millions watched in the subcontinent), and partly because the weather was terrible. Australia did not bowl a ball in their two rainy group games, but still qualified for the final, where they beat Pakistan on a damp pitch.

All in all, though, 2004 proved a disappointment for Holland after their impressive performances at the World Cup the previous year. It began with an unsuccessful tour of South Africa in February: Holland lost two one-day matches against provincial sides, though in their first three-day game since 1980 they did defeat the Western Cape Academy.

Over the summer, they played two more three-dayers in the new Intercontinental Cup, a first-class tournament for emerging nations. However, Holland never made it out of the European group: in two moderate displays, they drew with the eventual champions Scotland and lost to Ireland by an innings.

And, at the all-important ICC Six Nations Challenge in February and March, they just missed out on the big prize: a chance to play the Test nations in the Champions Trophy later in 2004. That went instead to the USA. Gallingly, Holland actually beat the USA, and Canada and Scotland, but slipped up against Namibia and UAE.

Those lukewarm performances did not improve much across the summer. At the one-day European Championship, held in Holland in July, the hosts finished a disappointing third, losing narrowly to the ECB Amateur XI, the eventual winners, and Ireland. They also went out of the C&G Trophy at the first opportunity. When plans were announced to reorganise the tournament for 2006, Holland had been dropped.

The underwhelming year ended with changes. In November, Emmerson Trotman left by mutual agreement, after eight years as coach, during which he guided Holland to an ICC Trophy win, two European Championships and their first victory in a World Cup match. "We and the players felt it was time," said van Ierschot, "for a new broom to sweep the floor." In an impressive signing for Dutch cricket, Bobby Simpson, the former coach of Australia, was appointed Trotman's replacement.

Simpson inherited a team stronger in batting than bowling. Bas Zuiderent returned in 2004 after five years as a Sussex batsman, and Daan van Bunge flourished for MCC Young Cricketers. He hit a century in 38 balls, earned a Twenty20 contract at Middlesex and became the fifth Dutchman to play county cricket. But the attack featured a surfeit of ordinary medium-pacers now that Roland Lefebvre has retired.

Lefebvre was succeeded as captain by Luuk van Troost of Excelsior from Schiedam. His runs – 770 at 51.33 – helped Excelsior to the Dutch premier league (*Hoofdklasse*) for the seventh time in 14 seasons. Van Troost also took 25 wickets, with other big contributions from Wade Seccombe, the Queensland wicket-keeper/batsman, and South African Billy Stelling. VVV of Amsterdam were promoted to the *Hoofdklasse* for the first time.

A significant trend in 2004 was the appearance of more grass pitches: there are now four in Holland, though only two in the top league. One, at Utrecht, hosted a new triangular tournament in June, featuring two-day games between representative teams from Amsterdam, Rotterdam and The Hague. Longer games and turf wickets should both strengthen the game. Meanwhile, a new field was unveiled at the HCC club in The Hague which was completely covered in artificial grass. This may become common in a country where all cricket grounds double as hockey or football pitches in winter.

The Dutch Lions Project, involving the establishment of national teams from Under-12 through to Under-23, continued to flourish. The Under-15 tour of South Africa was a highlight, providing hope that Holland will meet their goal of qualification for the 2008 Under-19 World Cup.

CRICKET IN THE UNITED STATES, 2004

Deb K. Das

As the twilight gathered over Woodley Field in Los Angeles, Dr Tony Verity, at 78 one of the oldest living cricketers to have represented the United States, looked at the 20-odd youngsters who had assembled for a group picture of the All-Stars of the first US Under-19 National Tournament. "There," he said. "Look at them. There is our future."

This was a sight unique in the annals of American cricket: there had never been a national Under-19 tournament before. Until late August, there was no guarantee it would happen. Then, miraculously, everything fell into place: the venue was decided, and 60 youngsters headed for their first encounter with national cricket – and each other. The organisers had carefully selected youngsters who were "nearly eligible" to represent the country, i.e. who stood a good chance of meeting ICC eligibility criteria by the 2007 World Cup. The effect was that the standard was very encouraging. Two centuries were scored in the tournament, by Bill Perkins of New Jersey and Renaldo Francis of Florida, with a near-miss by Akeem Dodson of New York. The bowling and fielding, too, matched the best in the senior US Nationals, which were being played next door.

By any reckoning, more things happened in US cricket in 2004 than in the previous decade. But, while the overall outlook has altered dramatically, the outcomes have not all been positive. Two events in 2004 substantially raised the profile of the country's cricket. The first was Team USA's unexpected victory over all the major Associate Members at the Six Nations Challenge in Sharjah, which put them into the Champions Trophy in England and the international limelight. The second was the advent of US ProCricket, the first professional league in North America, which invited first-class cricketers from all over the world to join in a modified Twenty20 format along with the best home-grown players. Both went badly wrong.

Team USA, which had been mired in dissension over issues such as selection, player morale and team mismanagement, arrived in England totally unprepared to face up to the rigours of world competition. Although winning handily over Zimbabwe in a warm-up, they were thoroughly humiliated by New Zealand and Australia in their two competitive matches. The team's sole distinction was to turn out the oldest side ever to participate in a one-day international tournament. It will take some time to live down the image of a geriatric squad flailing away helplessly against the world's best. The blame for the situation rested partly with the ICC, whose eligibility regulations had ruled out many of the best young players. But the side's abysmal performance left little room for excuses.

On top of everything, there was a nasty dispute that grew out of the USA Cricket Association's decision to remove one squad member, Imran Awan, from the pre-tournament training camp in Jamaica. Awan then alleged he had paid an official several thousand dollars to secure his place, and he wanted his money back. Soon there were other claims of similar payments. An enquiry was promised, but failed to materialise.

US ProCricket got off to an even worse start. It had counted on participation from first-class players from all the major countries, but the Indian board barred its players, and only West Indians took part in significant numbers. Pitches and facilities were inadequate: the organisers had to use minor league baseball stadiums and other readily available grounds, and many of these were badly prepared. It was a little hard to work out exactly who did turn out for whom, due to a scheme whereby the 15 to 20 overseas players who appeared were rotated among various teams.

These mainly comprised West Indians like Wavell Hinds, Daren Ganga, Merv Dillon and also 51-year-old Larry Gomes, plus a few Zimbabwean exiles such as Craig Wishart. Some Indians surfaced, including Ajay Jadeja and Vinod Kambli, but insisted they were only playing exhibition games. The Twenty20 format was Americanised in only one significant respect: five ball overs rather than six, which effectively reduced each innings to 16.4 overs. Despite all the glitches, the tournament did show signs of coming right. It finished the season, attendances were averaging 500 by the end, and the first-ever TV broadcasts of live US cricket on North American soil were secured, via Dish Network, which covers international cricket for US-based enthusiasts. But unless attitudes in other countries change, ProCricket will never attract the stars who might fulfil the organisers' dreams.

Another major disappointment for American cricket was the failure to secure any matches for the 2007 World Cup. The US had submitted a well-supported bid for a proposed site at Fort Lauderdale in Florida, and they believed that at least a few matches could be arranged on American soil. But they were shut out of the proceedings, and this was seen by many in this country as a calculated, and deliberate, snub.

Meanwhile, Project USA, ICC's plan to promote the development of cricket in the world's richest market, woke up from its state of dormancy and a CEO, Gary Hopkins, was appointed. Hopkins, an American businessman with extensive experience in sports development (he is credited with putting US professional soccer on a viable financial footing), is an energetic and dynamic individual who knows what is expected of him and seems well-equipped to take on the task. The USA Cricket Association is not too enthusiastic about this, because it sees the Project as an encroachment on its turf and fears a siphoning off of revenues into ICC's offshore coffers.

Another highlight of 2004 was the successful staging of the Third National Championships in Plano, Texas and Los Angeles. The 40-odd leagues and 600 clubs dotted across the country are an impressive demonstration of the growth of US cricket in the past decade, but it had remained Balkanised by geography and demographics. But an inter-zone format was tried two years ago, and it seems to be working at last. New York beat Central West (i.e. Texas) in the finals, thanks to a devastating spell of spin bowling by veteran Zamin Amin. The best batsman in the tournament was young Steve Massiah of New York, the only Team USA player to have performed well against Australia.

The one unchanging element in American cricket is the USA Cricket Association, which has continued to display the ineptitude, authoritarianism, secretiveness and unwillingness to deal with the facts that has characterised it for the past decade. And in January 2005 this view received official backing when the ICC wrote formally to the association, describing the American performance in the Champions Trophy as "abysmal". The letter, sent to Gladstone Dainty, the USACA president, and signed by both the ICC president and chief executive, Ehsan Mani and Malcolm Speed, went on to say: "We have seen numerous sporting organisations in various states of disarray throughout our period of involvement as sports administrators. We have never seen a sporting organisation that combines such great potential and such poor administration as USACA. From our observations, much of the blame for this lies with the current office bearers of USACA including yourself. We question whether the current administration of USACA can play any constructive role in taking the game forward in the United States."

CRICKET ROUND THE WORLD

Edited by Tony Munro

The Cricket Round the World feature began in Wisden 1993. *The inclusion of Congo, Jordan, Mali, North Korea and Peru this year takes the total of countries, regions and territories featured in the past 13 almanacks to 95, girdling the globe from Norway to Antarctica. Reliable reports of cricket in improbable places are always welcome. Please contact Tony Munro at wcrtw2005@yahoo.com.au.*

AFGHANISTAN

Though the politics of Afghanistan remain fraught, it has been another good year for cricket. The ICC has agreed to release funds for the building of a new cricket stadium in Kabul; exact funding is under negotiation. Already, the academies in Khost and Jalalabad are prospering, and a third, part-funded by the Asian Cricket Council (ACC), is being built in Kabul. At the ACC Trophy in Kuala Lumpur the senior team beat both Bahrain, with Karim Khan scoring 100, and Malaysia. Abdul Khalil and Andrew Banks

ARGENTINA

The ancient cricketing traditions of Argentina are reviving, with 400 active players, three divisions of league cricket and 25 schools involved. The big change is that, in contrast to the game two decades ago, English is rarely heard on the field: some of the ten touring teams who visited the country in 2004 found themselves confused when fielding and bowling instructions are barked in Spanish. However, the visiting coaches – Mike Hesson from New Zealand and Chris Anderson from South Africa – gave their advice in English. The classic North v South fixture was played for the 105th time on a new turf wicket at Corimayo. The three-day game was drawn, but a superb century by Matías Paterlini was a highlight. E. J. Cartledge

BELGIUM

An Australian who will remain anonymous, reputedly a deft wicket-keeper/batsman, drove the 100 miles from Lille, France, to play in Antwerp, but could not work out how to unlock the gate. Meanwhile, inside the ground, his team, Antwerp Indians, were losing by one wicket to Royal Brussels CC. Another gate on the other side of the ground, used by all the other players, was open throughout. Colin Wolfe

BRUNEI DARUSSALAM

Alas, there was very little cricket played in Brunei during 2004. There are now only four teams, which means there is insufficient cricket to maintain the interest of the remaining players. Derek Thursby

CANADA

Has a country's fortunes ever been more closely aligned to a single player than Canada's in 2004 to new captain John Davison? Davison was crucial to Canada's year, in which they put together a seven-game unbeaten streak to end a run of 14 straight defeats since their upset win over Bangladesh in the 2003 World Cup. The winning sequence began with Davison's amazing performance against the USA at the start of the new first class Intercontinental Cup (see page 1382), when he took 17 for 137, the best first-class match figures anywhere since Jim Laker's Test in 1956. Davison was then the centre of a tug-of-war between Canada and South Australia over his availability for the semi-final and final, and he ultimately had to be replaced by New Zealand-based Ian Billcliff as captain. Unfortunately, two inept batting performances in

Putting others in the shade: Canada's John Davison claimed the best match figures for almost 50 years when he routed the USA.
Picture by Stu Forster, Getty Images

the final gave Scotland the trophy. The national side also qualified for next year's ICC Trophy in Ireland after regaining the Americas Cup, going unbeaten in the round-robin series in Bermuda. RON FANFAIR

CHINA

This year was a watershed for China cricket. The government-run China Cricket Association was founded and subsequently admitted as an affiliate member of the Asian and International Cricket Councils. Government official Li Gaochao met ICC president Ehsan Mani at the Hong Kong Sixes and was promised assistance with coaching and equipment for schools in Beijing, Guangzhou and Shanghai, and even the possibility of a full one-day international, provided a suitable ground was available. Li's portfolio title didn't survive translation though: all sports in China are run by the government, and ball sports are divided into two portfolios: basketball, netball, volleyball etc into one and others such as cricket, tennis and hockey into another. Li was known as the deputy director-general for Small Balls until the joke dawned on the Chinese and they changed the department's name to Multi-Sports. Locally, the first-ever league began in Shanghai, with the Van Hessen Hot Dogs winning the O'Malleys league title, and Maharajahs the grand final. The International Sixes was again rain affected, but guests Sir Viv Richards and Doug Walters were entertaining both on the field and at the gala dinner. CBB from Chiang Mai won the final, after home favourites the Shanghai Dragons were knocked out in a match that finished in complete darkness... at one point the batsmen had run six before a spectator discovered that the ball had crossed the boundary. The Interport Series with Hong Kong CC, which dates back to 1866, was resurrected. The Dragons made the trip south for the first fixture since the Communist takeover, but narrowly lost in a high-scoring contest. Earlier in the year a Hong Kong ladies representative side had made the trip to Shanghai, losing to the Shanghai Pearls by one run. MIKE TSEMELIS

DEMOCRATIC REPUBLIC OF CONGO

Goma Stadium in the eastern Congo (formerly Zaire) is not the most obvious setting for a one-day international, however unofficial. In March 2004 it was the venue for a match between India and Pakistan, as intensely contested as if it were in Karachi or Kolkata. The players were members of the 12,000-strong UN peacekeeping mission, which is trying to end the long war in Congo. The outfield was black, due to lava from the eruption of Mount Nyriangongo in 2002. The boundary markers were old gun boxes covered in gleaming white. The umpire's job was less to worry about the lbw law (which was interpreted liberally) than to stop UN soldiers from non-cricketing countries walking behind the arm, or even on the wicket. In the words of one Swedish soldier: "The UN warned me about gorillas attacking us but not cricket balls!" The match was a 20-over slog so that the soldiers could return to barracks in time to start night patrols: genuine night-watchmen. India won, having avoided any attacks by gorillas. A Pakistani outfielder, however, had to make a run for it as a herd of goats from the prison farm dashed across the outfield, followed by the prisoners and their guards. DAVID TURNER

CUBA

Before Fidel Castro came to power in 1959 there was plenty of cricket in Cuba. Thanks largely to the efforts of Leona Ford (see *Wisden 2004*, page 1607), a revival is under way with 19 adult teams, including six made up of overseas students. There are also 55 age-group teams. So far, however, there has been no organised inter-club competition; the fact that cricket is only recognised as a recreation and not a sport limits the amount of support that it obtains from INDER, the Cuban Sports Ministry. However, there are hopes of a Cuban national championship in 2005. The best-organised province is the Isle of Youth (*Isla de la Juventud*) where an INDER employee, Daniel Garcia, has obtained funding from the provincial government to set up a ground with a pitch based on sand and scoria (solidified lava). Garcia has brought in teams from the local prison (cricket is considered good for self-discipline, I was told), the fire station and a dog club. Apparently, the dog club was holding a trial when Daniel and a friend started to play with a kanga cricket set. The dog lovers were smitten, and the rest is history. GERRY BEATON

DENMARK

Frederik Klokker of the MCC Young Cricketers was the lone star of Danish cricket internationally in 2004. Klokker broke new ground when he fielded for England as a substitute for Nasser Hussain during the Lord's Test against New Zealand. He also kept wicket for Middlesex for a session in their match against Gloucestershire, and was the only Dane to perform with credit in the European Cricket Championship. The side failed to win any of their four matches. The future is now very dependent on the next generation, and the Danish team, all aged under 19, again won the European indoor title in Holland. They also beat Holland in the European Under-19 outdoor tournament. Domestically, Skanderborg repeated their 2003 success as champions and took the knock-out cup to achieve the double. PETER S. HARGREAVES

FIJI

There was embarrassment when Suva Rangers' star batsman Joeli Mateyawa accepted an offer of bad light in the last over of their tight Dewar Prasad Shield final against Nadi. His team lost on scoring-rate by 0.7 of a run.

FRANCE

The year's sweetest moment came in front of Channel 4 cameras at Lord's in May, when Janet Gough presented France Cricket patron Richie Benaud with a silver rosebowl, originally given to her father Jack as founder of the Northern France Cricket League, in 1922. But it was a troubled year for cricket in France. With the Baseball & Softball Federation, to which France Cricket is affiliated, mired in financial crisis, cricket's state subsidy fell to its lowest level since 1988. Federation hopes of an Olympic sports complex near Charles de Gaulle Airport – including a 10,000-seater cricket stadium – were abandoned, and cricket was written out of France's bid to host the 2012 Olympics (the last time cricket was an Olympic sport was in Paris in 1900). France's leading all-French club, Chauny, collapsed, and the national league was again dominated by Pakistani sides. Gymkhana beat Dreux in the final – the last game played at Ed Cannon's scenic ground at St Astier in the Dordogne before it was redeveloped as a supermarket. The national junior championships, splendidly organised at Entrecasteaux in Provence, were marred when the South-West turned up with half a side – and again when it transpired that the player of the tournament, Thushora Koralangamaga, was over-age. But France's national sides brought brighter news. The Under-21 indoor team beat Kent at the annual international tournament in Le Touquet; five days later, at the European Cricket Council Indoor Championships, they were denied promotion, earned in 2003, after three countries cried off and the ECC reduced Division One from six teams to five. France were left in Division Two, which they topped again. SIMON HEWITT

HONG KONG

"Marvellous," said the president, T. E. Smith, in his speech at the opening reception for the 2003 Hong Kong Sixes. The only trouble was that he went on to use the word a further 19 times in a two-minute speech. He has not been allowed to forget this. For the record, though, the event continues to be, well, marvellous, and England have now established themselves as the dominant team, having won both the 2003 and 2004 events. In November 2004, England, led by Matthew Maynard, easily overcame Sri Lanka in the final, thanks to a sterling all-round performance from Kabir Ali. Domestically, cricket has continued to thrive, though the team failed to progress in the qualifying rounds of the World Cup. We now have an extended lease on our Po Kong village ground, which supports two pitches, and will continue to develop it. Women's cricket is now under way, and we were delighted that China became an Affiliate Member of ICC in 2004: we look forward to helping their cricketing development. We have translated a short version of the Laws into Chinese and are working on the full version. There are some who say that "Zenmayang!" will be the Mandarin term for "Howzat!" but our view is that Howzat will be Howzat in whatever language the game is played. JOHN CRIBBIN

IRAQ

Regardless of how close it is, the reaction is always the same when an explosion reverberates during our regular Friday games at the newly constituted Baghdad Cricket Ground, a converted playground at the back of an old school that is now the British Embassy. There is initial fear, panic and a dash for the nearest hard cover, the interior of the embassy building itself. The scorebook normally reads "Mortar Stopped Play", although the loudest explosion came from a car bomb at a nearby checkpoint. Conveniently, it just so happens that the corridor where we shelter leads to the appropriately named Mortar Inn, the perfect location for a soothing post-match or post-mortar drink. The only time anyone has ever played on was in a different sport – touch rugby – when our commercial officer ran through to score a try after the rest of us had legged it back inside.

A Foreign Office CC colleague had the foresight to bring a beach cricket set to Baghdad. The plastic bat is used against a tennis ball specially adapted by Pakistani construction workers, who wrapped it tightly in builders' tape to give it extra weight and reduce the bounce; the playground gives some lift just short of a length, occasionally necessitating body armour. The security situation is such that all play is confined to the BCG – there is no way we could play outside the International Zone (too much of a target) – even if we could find a pitch. And the ground the Americans use for football and touch rugby has a pipe running across it. The BCG is enclosed by a 12ft fence, itself surrounded by an outer wall topped by razor wire. For obvious reasons, what would normally be a six out of the ground is deemed out, although there was conjecture about interpretation of that rule when one of my beautifully flighted off-breaks was despatched on to the roof of the canteen, and ricocheted back to safety off the satellite dish.

Other local rules vary, depending on numbers, but are loosely based on indoor cricket: so batsmen can be caught off the wire fence, batsmen bat for a set number of overs losing runs each time they're out, and everyone bowls. The quirkiest obstacle on the field is a ripped and battered pool table by the cover-point boundary. It is used by off-duty Gurkha guards – even during matches. Spectators' facilities include (in addition to the Mortar Inn) two picnic tables, with a small palm tree for shade. We call the table area the Edward Chaplin Stand after the current Ambassador. KEITH SCOTT

ISRAEL

Cricket's growing profile in Israel gained an unexpected boost in 2004 – thanks to the movies. Avi Nesher's *Turn Left at the End of the World*, described by the *Hollywood Reporter* as "one of the most successful Israeli films of the past decade", has cricket as central to the plot. It concerns an Indian Jew, just arrived in the Promised Land: in reality a desolate Israeli town of the early 1960s. To ward off homesickness, he builds a cricket pitch in the middle of the desert and attracts the locals to play with him. The Israeli Cricket Association provided technical assistance, coaching, and some of the actors. In real life, the form of our Under-17 squad in the tournament held in Italy was especially gratifying: the batting, inspired by Danny Hotz and the captain Gal Matz, produced large totals, and all five opponents were easily defeated. The senior squad was, however, very disappointing at the World Cup qualifier in Belgium, and we look forward to the progress of this crop of juniors into the senior ranks. The league was won in style by Lions Lod, for the fifth time in six years. STANLEY PERLMAN

ITALY

The Italian national team easily won the European qualifying series for the 2007 World Cup, held in Belgium. This took them to the tournament in Malaysia in February 2005 which would determine the final place for the ICC Trophy in Ireland next summer. The Italians did everything right in the first stage: they were the youngest side in the tournament but swept away opposition from Norway, France, Germany, Israel and Gibraltar. The 22-year-old wicket-keeper Gabriele Passaretti, from the small town of Guidonia, just outside Rome, was named player of the tournament on the strength of his 19 victims. Pianoro retained the championship, their ninth in 11 years. But, as in 2003, they had to thank their opponents for letting them back in. The Sicilian team, Murri, beat Pianoro twice, and it looked as though the pennant was destined for the foot of Mount Etna. However, the Sicilians lost their way. And in the last round Pianoro recovered from 33 for seven against Gallicano to win the most closely fought championship in Italy's brief cricketing history. SIMONE GAMBINO

Spiritual home? Cricket beneath Mount Fuji.

JAPAN

Mumtaz Alam's Giants XI completed the Japanese cricket season by winning their fourth consecutive Kanto Cricket League championship in late October. They beat YCAC from Yokohama in the crucial game by six wickets, thanks mainly to an excellent spell from off-spinner Hamid Saeed, who took five for 12 off his eight overs. MCC are due to tour Japan in September 2005.

JORDAN

Cricket has acquired royal patronage in an unlikely setting. In Britain, none of Prince Philip's children have shown an interest in the game to match his, but HRH Prince El Hassan bin Talal of Jordan remains keen. The prince, younger brother of the late King Hussein and uncle of the present king, learned the game at Harrow and has maintained an interest in the Pakistan team: his wife, Princess Sarwath, comes from Pakistan, and he is friendly with Imran Khan. Unfortunately, there is no established cricket scene in Jordan, but occasional games are played by expats. In 1995 the Australian Embassy outplayed the British Embassy for the "Jordan Ashes", created from burning the silk shorts the Aussies had sported during the match. The British regained the trophy in 2004 but the Australians failed to hand over the Ashes. In May, the British Ambassador, Christopher Prentice, challenged Prince El Hassan, and a match was arranged at the Amman Baccalaureate School. Aged 57, the prince excused himself from playing, but tossed the coin and bowled the first ball. The Prince's XI beat the British team by three wickets. PATRICK FORBES

Royal assent: Prince El Hassan bin Talal of Jordan presides over the toss before his team takes on the British Ambassador's XI.

MALI

Cricket has now nudged closer to what might be its ultimate destination: Timbuktu. From unlikely beginnings in one school's English Club in 2001 (following a chance remark by the British consul, Violet Diallo), cricket has been introduced into ten schools across Bamako, the capital of Mali. Unfortunately, few people have a clue where Mali is. ("You mean Bali?" "No, it's in Africa." "Ah, Malawi!" "No! M-A-L-I. It's in *West* Africa!") It's a poor, sand-rich, land-locked country with an extraordinarily rich cultural heritage. But since it's a former French colony, that heritage does not include cricket. Or it didn't. Malians established their cricket association, AMaCrik, in 2003, and the first inter-school tournament took place in 2004. When shown models of bats and asked to produce something similar, a local carpenter said "Yes, of course... but what are they?" The carpenter, Yacouba Coulibaly, has since scaled a steep learning-curve, producing wooden bats and wickets for us; and thanks to some generous donations we now have some sets of "real" kit. But they are hard to get and expensive to transport here. The climate is unyielding, and we play a lot on sand and rock. Even so, regular turnout at Saturday morning training sessions in Bamako now exceeds 90 people and there are early developments in other towns. "When you hear it explained, you may not see why people like cricket," said one teacher, "but once you start playing, then you get hooked." This teacher is now AMaCrik's president. Timbuktu? (Officially it's Tombouctou.) It's more than 900km from Bamako, but we are heading in that direction. PHIL WATSON

NAMIBIA

England's visit to Namibia in November 2004, which they regarded as both a pleasure and more of a severe test than the controversial trip to Zimbabwe that followed, came at the end of an eventful year for Namibian cricket. But these were just two out of 49 matches arranged for the national team in a strenuous 2004-05 season. The sport continued to progress: a sponsorship deal with MTC allowed the appointment of the country's first full-time coach, the Zimbabwean Andy Waller, who was given the job of ensuring qualification for the 2007 World Cup. He cleared the first hurdle when the team won the African qualifier, held in Lusaka. The development programme is mainly focused in the north of the country, where there are 7,500 young players. And the prize for cricketing enthusiasm must go to the players of Oshakati Cricket Club, in the far north of the country near the Angolan border, whose players have to travel at least 1,400km every weekend to play in the "local" leagues. They have not missed a game yet. LAURIE PIETERS

NORWAY

A troubled year for Norwegian cricket was guaranteed when a promised grant of £20,000 from the Sports Council was cancelled, due to a miscalculation in their budget figures. This was a severe blow to the development planned on the back of a very successful 2003. Some clubs blamed the board for this. There was further upheaval after a disappointing year on the field: an under-prepared national side did not fulfil its high hopes. And so Norwegian cricket had its second new president in just six months. BOB GIBB

NORTH KOREA

Cricket exists even in this isolated country. Matches in Pyongyang are very social occasions, a chance for some of the resident expats to escape the city and head for a nice picnic site by a lake which happens to have a suitable patch of land near by. Although our game is very much improvised, and the exact form often depends on whether there are any locals picnicking nearby, it does involve two sets of stumps and real bats, if not whites. We do, however, have our own "Pyongyang Cricket Club" shirt. Numbers depend on availability: it can be up to 30. But despite the rapid turnover of expats, we somehow seem to be able to maintain a hard core of Brits and Aussies to provide instant coaching for the newcomers. Last year, some of the keenest players moved on to a faster-moving six-a-side game on a football pitch. These included the North Korean groundsman, who, it turned out, had in his youth been a professional baseball player in Japan. Once he had worked out that the bowler is supposed to pitch the ball, he did well, even if his action fell outside ICC guidelines. To satisfy local curiosity, and build a few bridges with our contacts, we organised a match involving Korean embassy staff, which was a very good social event. When we play, a few Koreans will sometimes stand and watch from a distance, very respectfully. DAVID SLINN

PERU

The Lima Cricket and Football Club has now completed 15 years play without losing a single minute to rain (which is a good reason to visit for our annual Easter tournament). We play from February to April, and our pitch is pretty rough because football is played in winter. It is a grass surface, but a broadleaf grass which forms a mat under the leaves. It is not conducive to driving, and many a fine innings has been played without a single cover-drive but plenty of lusty blows over the boundary. We now have a hard core of 25 players (plus tourists, who are welcome), more than at any time in my 15 years here. There has not been an influx, but the Brits at the cricket club have now joined forces with local Asians. When I had been here a year or two and was driving past the cliff-top park in Lima, I saw a couple of what I assumed were locals playing tip and run with a cricket bat. Good God, I thought, dived out of the car and talked to them. Of course, they turned out to be Indians and were immediately invited along. We now have a regular hotly contested fixture: India & Pakistan v Rest of the World, whose team includes our one Peruvian, Jorge Pancorvo, an excellent wicket-keeper (aged 51, but still fit). VIVIAN ASH

RWANDA

Rwanda won their first international match in 2004, saw a century scored on Rwandan soil for the first time, shared the ground with a BBC film crew, and continued the struggle with the authorities to get the game established. The ICC approved Rwanda as an affiliate member, enabling the team to appear in the World Cup qualifier in South Africa. The team won one and lost four of their five matches, trouncing The Gambia. Despite concerns expressed by the South African Embassy in Kigali, who were unenthusiastic about issuing visas, all the players returned to Rwanda after the tournament. The ICC presented equipment for use in schools but yet again the Rwanda Revenue Authority impounded the kit, where, as this report goes to press, it still remains. The ICC, in their infinite wisdom, gave with one hand and took with the other, presenting us with an unannounced bill for some $5,000 for participating in the South Africa event. For an Association which relies on the wallets of players, this sort of money is pie in the sky. The National League was run again (with Kigali CC again the champions) despite the sponsor, MTN, deciding they could not afford the £500 cost. The centurion was Edward Kataha, a Rwandan playing for Right Guards, who had lived in Uganda for many years. The BBC connection came from their feature film, *Shooting Dogs*, starring John Hurt and based on true events during the Rwandan genocide of 1994. Kicukiro Oval, now the home of Rwandan cricket, is at a school where many people were massacred, and the BBC wanted to use the actual site. This meant "Filming Stopped Play" several times, with crowd scenes affecting the outfield and vehicles often being parked at third man. However, in October the ICC sent coach William

Kamonyi to work with youngsters, and it was most gratifying to see a few dozen kids from local schools taking lessons. All we need now is to get the Revenue Authority to release the kit. CHRIS FREAN

SWEDEN

There cannot be many greater pleasures in life than undertaking an epic journey in the knowledge that at the other end there is a cricket pitch being prepared. In May 2004, Rain Men, a more than averagely shambolic travelling XI, flew to Sweden for a game against Guttsta WCC, who are based in Kolsva, a small industrial town 60km west of Stockholm. The pitch was a converted field, with a matting wicket, and a ramshackle shed of a pavilion that smelt comfortingly of old pads. Forests and mountains rose up on all sides; the greens were every bit as vivid as English greens, but from a different palette; the weather was surprisingly gentle, given that we were further north than Orkney. Guttsta are run by an Englishman, but the bulk of their side is Swedish. They suggested an interesting format: two innings each in an afternoon. This suited the Swedish style of play, which was madcap and agricultural. Guttsta needed 15 to win in their second innings and still lost five wickets. The air was a joy to breathe, our hosts were generous, funny and utterly obsessed, and the beer was not as expensive as everyone had warned. We return in 2005. MARCUS BERKMANN

VANUATU

Having secured the sponsorship of Sharman Networks to support Vanuatu's community cricket programme, we have seen the number of children playing rise from 200 to 4,000. MARK STAFFORD

WORLD CUP QUALIFYING SERIES

The World Cup Qualifying Series, theoretically at least, provided an opportunity for almost all the ICC's 89 members to qualify for the 2007 World Cup in the West Indies. Ten regional tournaments were held to determine the 12 teams who will contest the ICC Trophy in Ireland this June. This in turn will produce five teams to join the ten Test-playing countries and Kenya, who have special status.

Oman created the greatest shock, becoming the first affiliate (the third tier of ICC membership, below full member and associate) to qualify for the ICC Trophy by reaching the final of the Asian Cricket Council Trophy, where they lost to the United Arab Emirates. In a Persian Gulf whitewash, such long-term Associates as Hong Kong, Malaysia and Singapore all failed to reach the semi-finals. Afghanistan also caused a surprise, beating Hong Kong.

But the gap between the world's leading countries and the rest was exposed when a South African Country Districts team was drafted in to replace Morocco in the African Affiliates tournament: cricketing carnage ensued. Ghana (18), Mozambique (29), Rwanda (60) and Malawi (20) were all demolished before the South Africans won the final against Botswana by 235 runs. Morocco had been forced to withdraw after the national handball team went AWOL on a tour of Germany. The sheer joy of participation was enough for some, though: 15 countries made their official international debuts.

Eight teams were due to contest the final ICC Trophy qualifying place in Malaysia in February 2005 in a repechage event. The winner will join Bermuda, Canada, Denmark, Holland, Ireland, Namibia, Oman, Scotland, Uganda, United Arab Emirates and the US.

TOURNAMENTS CONTESTED BY NON-TEST NATIONS, 2003-04 AND 2004

Competition	Winners	Runners-up	Others
African ICC Affiliates World Cup Qualifying Series (March)	**South African Country Districts**	Botswana	Ghana, Malawi, Mozambique, Sierra Leone, Gambia, Rwanda
African ICC Associates World Cup Qualifying Series (August)	**Namibia**	Uganda	Zambia, Botswana Nigeria, Tanzania
Americas Championship (July)	**Canada**	United States	Bermuda, Cayman Islands, Argentina, Bahamas
Americas ICC Affiliates World Cup Qualifying Series (March)	**Bahamas**	Panama	Belize, Turks & Caicos Islands, Suriname
Asian Cricket Council Fast-Track Countries (3-day)	(Hong Kong meet UAE in final, Feb. 2005)		Nepal, Singapore, Malaysia
Asian Cricket Council Trophy (June)	**United Arab Emirates**	Oman	Kuwait, Qatar, Nepal, Afghanistan, Malaysia, Bhutan, Singapore, Saudi Arabia, Hong Kong, Bahrain, Thailand, Maldives, Iran
East Asia Pacific Challenge (May)	**Fiji**	Tonga	Japan, Indonesia
European Championship Division 1 (July)	**ECB XI**	Ireland	Holland, Scotland, Denmark
European Championship Division 2 (July)	**Italy**	France	Germany, Norway, Gibraltar, Israel
European Cricket Council Representative Festival (August)	**Croatia**	Finland	Switzerland, Slovenia, Luxembourg, Bulgaria
Gulf Cup (December 2003– January 2004)	**Kuwait**	Bahrain	Oman, Qatar, Saudi Arabia
ICC Six Nations Challenge (March)	**USA**	Scotland	Namibia, Holland, United Arab Emirates, Canada

Competition	Winners	Runners-up	Others
Middle East Gulf Cup (September)	**Oman**	Bahrain	Qatar, Saudi Arabia, Kuwait Reds, Kuwait Blues
Tuanku Ja' Afar Trophy (May)	**Malaysia**	Hong Kong	Singapore, Thailand
South American Championships (December)	**Miami Masters**	Puerto Rico	Argentina A, Chile, Brazil, Peru, Andean Masters, Chile A
West African Championships (May–June)	**Sierra Leone**	Ghana	Gambia

Opposite: Straight to the point. Muttiah Muralitharan, in a steel brace allowing no elbow movement, bowls at Shenley Park in July to prove that his action is legal.
Picture by Gary Prior

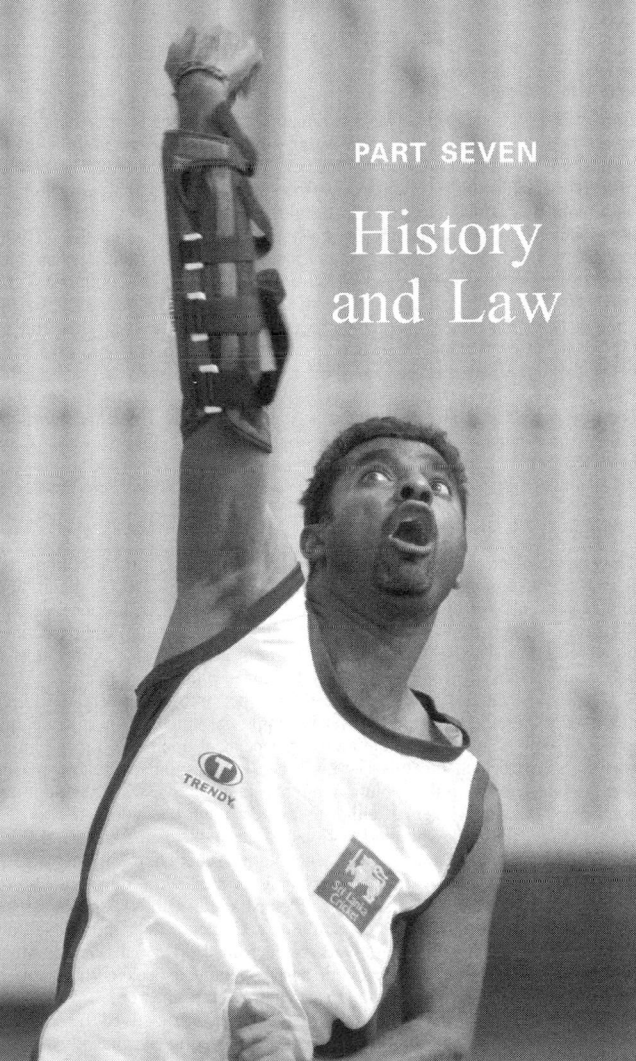

HISTORY OF CRICKET

What is cricket?

Cricket is a game played between two teams, generally of 11 members each. In essence, it is single combat, in which an individual batsman does battle against an individual bowler, who has helpers known as fielders. The bowler propels the ball with a straight arm from one end of the 22-yard pitch in an attempt to dismiss the batsman by hitting a target known as the wicket at the other end, or by causing the batsman to hit the ball into the air into a fielder's grasp, or by inducing one of a number of other indiscretions. The batsman attempts to defend the wicket with the bat and to score runs – the currency of the game – by striking the ball to the field boundary, or far enough from the fielders to allow the batsman to run to the other end of the pitch before the ball can be returned. At least two bowlers must take turns, from alternating ends; also, there are always two batsmen on the field, each to take a turn as required. When all but one of the batting team have been dismissed – or after an agreed period – the teams' roles are reversed. After all the players required to bat on both sides have done so either once or twice (which can take from a few hours to five days) the total number of runs accumulated determines the winner. But sometimes there isn't one.

Origins of the game

The origins of cricket lie somewhere in the Dark Ages – probably after the Roman Empire, almost certainly before the Normans invaded England, and almost certainly somewhere in Northern Europe. All research concedes that the game derived from a very old, widespread and uncomplicated pastime by which one player served up an object, be it a small piece of wood or a ball, and another hit it with a suitably fashioned club.

How and when this club–ball game developed into one where the hitter defended a target against the thrower is simply not known. Nor is there any evidence as to when points were awarded dependent upon how far the hitter was able to despatch the missile; nor when helpers joined the two-player contest, thus beginning the evolution into a team game; nor when the defining concept of placing wickets at either end of the pitch was adopted.

Etymological scholarship has variously placed the game in the Celtic, Scandinavian, Anglo-Saxon, Dutch and Norman-French traditions; sociological historians have variously attributed its mediaeval development to high-born country landowners, *emigré* Flemish cloth-workers, shepherds on the close-cropped downland of south-east England and the close-knit communities of iron- and glass-workers deep in the Kentish Weald. Most of these theories have a solid academic basis, but none is backed with enough evidence to establish a watertight case. The research goes on.

What is agreed is that by Tudor times cricket had evolved far enough from club–ball to be recognisable as the game played today; that it was well established in many parts of Kent, Sussex and Surrey; that within a few years it had become a feature of leisure time at a significant number of schools; and – a sure sign of the wide acceptance of any game – that it had become popular enough among young men to earn the disapproval of local magistrates.

Dates in cricket history

c. **1550**	Evidence of cricket being played in Guildford, Surrey.
1598	Cricket mentioned in Florio's Italian–English dictionary.
1610	Reference to "cricketing" between Weald and Upland near Chevening, Kent.
1611	Randle Cotgrave's French–English dictionary translates the French word "crosse" as a cricket staff. Two youths fined for playing cricket at Sidlesham, Sussex.
1624	Jasper Vinall becomes first man known to be killed playing cricket: hit by a bat while trying to catch the ball – at Horsted Green, Sussex.
1676	First reference to cricket being played abroad, by British residents in Aleppo, Syria.
1694	Two shillings and sixpence paid for a "wagger" (wager) about a cricket match at Lewes.
1697	First reference to "a great match" with 11 players a side for fifty guineas, in Sussex.
1700	Cricket match announced on Clapham Common.
1709	First recorded inter-county match: Kent v Surrey.
1710	First reference to cricket at Cambridge University.
1727	Articles of Agreement written governing the conduct of matches between the teams of the Duke of Richmond and Mr Brodrick of Peperharow, Surrey.
1729	Date of earliest surviving bat, belonging to John Chitty, now in the pavilion at The Oval.
1730	First recorded match at the Artillery Ground, off City Road, central London, still the cricketing home of the Honourable Artillery Company.
1744	Kent beat All England by one wicket at the Artillery Ground. First known version of the Laws of Cricket, issued by the London Club, formalising the pitch as 22 yards long.
c. **1767**	Foundation of the Hambledon Club in Hampshire, the leading club in England for the next 30 years.
1769	First recorded century, by John Minshull for Duke of Dorset's XI v Wrotham.
1771	Width of bat limited to 4¼ inches, where it has remained ever since.
1774	LBW law devised.
1776	Earliest known scorecards, at the Vine Club, Sevenoaks, Kent.
1780	The first six-seamed cricket ball, manufactured by Dukes of Penshurst, Kent.

1787	First match at Thomas Lord's first ground, Dorset Square, Marylebone – White Conduit Club v Middlesex. Formation of Marylebone Cricket Club by members of the White Conduit Club.

1788 First revision of the Laws of Cricket by MCC.

1794 First recorded inter-schools match: Charterhouse v Westminster.

1795 First recorded case of a dismissal "leg before wicket".

1806 First Gentlemen v Players match at Lord's.

1807 First mention of "straight-armed" (i.e. round-arm) bowling: by John Willes of Kent.

1809 Thomas Lord's second ground opened at North Bank, St John's Wood.

1811 First recorded women's county match: Surrey v Hampshire at Ball's Pond, London.

1814 Lord's third ground opened on its present site, also in St John's Wood.

1827 First Oxford v Cambridge match, at Lord's. A draw.

1828 MCC authorise the bowler to raise his hand level with the elbow.

1833 John Nyren publishes his classic *Young Cricketer's Tutor* and *The Cricketers of My Time*.

1836 First North v South match, for many years regarded as the principal fixture of the season.

c. **1836** Batting pads invented.

1841 General Lord Hill, commander-in-chief of the British Army, orders that a cricket ground be made an adjunct of every military barracks.

1844 First official international match: Canada v United States.

1845 First match played at The Oval.

1846 The All-England XI, organised by William Clarke, begins playing matches, often against odds, throughout the country.

1849 First Yorkshire v Lancashire match.

c. **1850** Wicket-keeping gloves first used.

1850 John Wisden bowls all ten batsmen in an innings for North v South.

1853 First mention of a champion county: Nottinghamshire.

1858 First recorded instance of a hat being awarded to a bowler taking three wickets with consecutive balls.

1859 First touring team to leave England, captained by George Parr, draws enthusiastic crowds in the US and Canada.

1864 "Overhand bowling" authorised by MCC. John Wisden's *The Cricketer's Almanack* first published.

1868 Team of Australian aborigines tour England.

1873   W. G. Grace becomes the first player to record 1,000 runs and 100 wickets in a season.
First regulations restricting county qualifications, often regarded as the official start of the County Championship.

1877   First Test match: Australia beat England by 45 runs in Melbourne.

1880   First Test in England: a five-wicket win against Australia at The Oval.

1882   Following England's first defeat by Australia in England, an "obituary notice" to English cricket in the *Sporting Times* leads to the tradition of The Ashes.

1889   Present Lord's pavilion begun.
South Africa's first Test match.
Declarations first authorised, but only on the third day, or in a one-day match.

1890   County Championship officially constituted.

1895   W. G. Grace scores 1,000 runs in May, and reaches his 100th hundred.

1899   A. E. J. Collins scores 628 not out in a junior house match at Clifton College, the highest individual score in any match.
Selectors choose England team for home Tests, instead of host club issuing invitations.

1900   Six-ball over becomes the norm, instead of five.

1909   Imperial Cricket Conference (ICC – now the International Cricket Council) set up, with England, Australia and South Africa the original members.

1910   Six runs given for any hit over the boundary, instead of only for a hit out of the ground.

1912   First and only triangular Test series played in England, involving England, Australia and South Africa.

1915   W. G. Grace dies, aged 67.

1926   Victoria score 1,107 v New South Wales at Melbourne, the record total for a first-class innings.

1928   West Indies' first Test match.
A. P. Freeman of Kent and England becomes the only player to take more than 300 first-class wickets in a season: 304.

1930   New Zealand's first Test match.
Donald Bradman's first tour of England: he scores 974 runs in the five Ashes Tests, still a record for any Test series.

1931   Stumps made higher (28 inches not 27) and wider (nine inches not eight – this was optional until 1947).

1932   India's first Test match.
Hedley Verity of Yorkshire takes ten wickets for ten runs v Nottinghamshire, the best innings analysis in first-class cricket.

1932-33   The Bodyline tour of Australia in which England bowl at batsmen's bodies with a packed leg-side field to neutralise Bradman's scoring.

1934   Jack Hobbs retires, with 197 centuries and 61,237 runs, both records.
First women's Test: Australia v England at Brisbane.

1935	MCC condemn and outlaw Bodyline.
1947	Denis Compton of Middlesex and England scores a record 3,816 runs in an English season.
1948	First five-day Tests in England. Bradman concludes Test career with a second-ball duck at The Oval and a batting average of 99.94 – four runs short of 100.
1952	Pakistan's first Test match.
1953	England regain the Ashes after a 19-year gap, the longest ever.
1956	Jim Laker of England takes 19 wickets for 90 v Australia at Manchester, the best match analysis in first-class cricket.
1957	Declarations authorised at any time.
1960	First tied Test, Australia v West Indies at Brisbane.
1963	Distinction between amateur and professional cricketers abolished in English cricket. The first major one-day tournament begins in England: the Gillette Cup.
1969	Limited-over Sunday league inaugurated for first-class counties.
1970	Proposed South African tour of England cancelled: South Africa excluded from international cricket because of their government's apartheid policies.
1971	First one-day international: Australia v England at Melbourne.
1975	First World Cup: West Indies beat Australia in final at Lord's.
1976	First women's match at Lord's, England v Australia.
1977	Centenary Test at Melbourne, with identical result to the first match: Australia beat England by 45 runs. Australian media tycoon Kerry Packer, signs 51 of the world's leading players in defiance of the cricketing authorities.
1978	Graham Yallop of Australia wears a protective helmet to bat in a Test match, the first player to do so.
1979	Packer and official cricket agree peace deal.
1980	Eight-ball over abolished in Australia, making the six-ball over universal.
1981	England beat Australia in Leeds Test, after following on with bookmakers offering odds of 500 to 1 against them winning.
1982	Sri Lanka's first Test match.
1991	South Africa return, with a one-day international in India.
1992	Zimbabwe's first Test match. Durham become the first county since Glamorgan in 1921 to attain first-class status.
1993	The ICC ceases to be administered by MCC, becoming an independent organisation with its own chief executive.
1994	Brian Lara of Warwickshire becomes the only player to pass 500 in a first-class innings: 501 not out v Durham.

2000 South Africa's captain Hansie Cronje banned from cricket for life after admitting receiving bribes from bookmakers in match-fixing scandal.
Bangladesh's first Test match.
County Championship split into two divisions, with promotion and relegation.
The Laws of Cricket revised and rewritten.

2001 Sir Donald Bradman dies, aged 92.

2003 Twenty20 Cup, a 20 over-per-side evening tournament, inaugurated in England.

2004 Lara becomes the first man to score 400 in a Test innings, against England.

THE ASHES

"In affectionate remembrance of English cricket which died at The Oval, 29th August, 1882. Deeply lamented by a large circle of sorrowing friends and acquaintances, R.I.P.
N.B. The body will be cremated and the Ashes taken to Australia."

Australia's first victory on English soil over the full strength of England, on August 29, 1882, inspired a young London journalist, Reginald Shirley Brooks, to write this mock "obituary". It appeared in the *Sporting Times*.

Before England's defeat at The Oval, by seven runs, arrangements had already been made for the Hon. Ivo Bligh, afterwards Lord Darnley, to lead a team to Australia. Three weeks later they set out, now with the popular objective of recovering the Ashes. In the event, Australia won the First Test by nine wickets, but with England winning the next two it became generally accepted that they brought back the Ashes.

It was long believed that the real Ashes – a small urn thought to contain the ashes of a bail used in the third match – were presented to Bligh by a group of Melbourne women. In 1998, Lord Darnley's 82-year-old daughter-in-law said they were the remains of her mother-in-law's veil, not a bail. Other evidence suggests a ball. The certain origin of the Ashes, therefore, is the subject of some dispute.

After Lord Darnley's death in 1927, the urn was given to MCC by Lord Darnley's Australian-born widow, Florence. It can be seen in the cricket museum at Lord's, together with a red and gold velvet bag, made specially for it, and the scorecard of the 1882 match.

OFFICIAL BODIES

INTERNATIONAL CRICKET COUNCIL

The ICC is world cricket's governing body. It is responsible for managing the playing conditions and Code of Conduct for international fixtures, expanding the game and organising the major international tournaments, including the World Cup.

Its mission statement says the ICC "will lead by promoting the game as a global sport, protecting the spirit of cricket and optimising commercial opportunities for the benefit of the game."

Ten national governing bodies are currently Full Members of the ICC; full membership qualifies a nation (or geographic area) to play official Test matches. A candidate for full membership must meet a number of playing and administrative criteria, after which elevation is decided by a vote among existing Full Members. There are also currently 27 Associate Members (non-Test-playing nations or geographic areas where cricket is firmly established and organised) and 55 Affiliate Members (other countries or geographic areas where the ICC recognises that cricket is played in accordance with the Laws).

The ICC was founded in 1909 as the Imperial Cricket Conference by three Foundation Members: England, Australia and South Africa. Other countries (or geographic areas) became Full Members and thus acquired Test-match status as follows: India, New Zealand and West Indies in 1926, Pakistan in 1952, Sri Lanka in 1981, Zimbabwe in 1992 and Bangladesh in 2000. South Africa ceased to be a member on leaving the Commonwealth in 1961, but was re-elected as a Full Member in 1991.

In 1965, the Conference was renamed the International Cricket Conference and new rules permitted the election of countries from outside the Commonwealth for the first time. The first Associate Members (Fiji and USA), who had diluted voting rights, were admitted. However, Foundation Members retained a veto over all resolutions.

In 1989, the Conference was again renamed without changing its initials. The new International Cricket Council adopted revised rules, aimed at producing an organisation which could make a larger number of binding decisions, rather than simply make recommendations to national governing bodies. In 1993, the Council, which had previously been administered by MCC, gained its own secretariat and chief executive, though its headquarters remained at Lord's. The category of Foundation Member was abolished. Sir Clyde Walcott became the first non-British chairman.

In 1997, the Council became an incorporated body, with an executive board, and a president instead of a chairman. One Australian, Malcolm Speed, succeeded another, David Richards, as chief executive in July 2001. The ICC remained at Lord's, with a commercial base in Monaco, but by 2004 it was considering unifying its offices, most probably in Dubai, where it is believed there would be organisational and tax advantages.

Officers

President: Ehsan Mani (2003–05). *Vice-President:* P. H. F. Sonn. *Chief Executive:* M. W. Speed.

Chairmen of Committees: Chief Executives' Committee: M. W. Speed; *Cricket:* S. M. Gavaskar; *Development:* M. W. Speed; *Audit Committee:* Sir John Anderson.

Executive Board: The president, vice-president and chief executive sit on the board and all committees *ex officio*. They are joined by Ali Asghar (Bangladesh), Sir John Anderson (New Zealand), P. F. Chingoka (Zimbabwe), J. Dalmiya (India), E. H. C. Griffith (West Indies), R. Mali (South Africa), R. F. Merriman (Australia), F. D. Morgan (England), S. Perlman (Israel), J. Rayani (Kenya), Shaharyar Khan (Pakistan), T. Sumathipala (Sri Lanka), HRH Tunku Imran (Malaysia).

General Manager – Cricket: D. J. Richardson. *Cricket Operations Manager:* C. D. Hitchcock. *Umpires and Referees Manager:* C. S. Kelly. *Umpires' High Performance Manager:* K. T. Medlycott. *Global Development Manager:* M. R. Kennedy. *General Manager – Corporate Affairs:* B. F. McClements. *Chief Financial Officer:* F. Hasnain. *Commercial Manager:* D. C. Jamieson. *Human Resources and Administration Manager:* J. Moore. *In-house Lawyer:* U. Naidoo.

Constitution

President: Each Full Member has the right, by rotation, to appoint ICC's president. In 1997, India named J. Dalmiya to serve until June 2000, when M. A. Gray of Australia took over. Ehsan Mani of Pakistan succeeded M. A. Gray in June 2003; he and subsequent presidents will serve for two years. P. H. F. Sonn, elected vice-president in July 2004, was due to take over in 2005.

Chief Executive: Appointed by the Council. D. L. Richards served from 1993 to 2001, and was succeeded by M. W. Speed.

Membership

Full Members: Australia, Bangladesh, England, India, New Zealand, Pakistan, South Africa, Sri Lanka, West Indies and Zimbabwe.

Associate Members*: Argentina (1974), Bermuda (1966), Canada (1968), Cayman Islands (2002), Denmark (1966), Fiji (1965), France (1998), Germany (1999), Gibraltar (1969), Hong Kong (1969), Ireland (1993), Israel (1974), Italy (1995), Kenya (1981), Malaysia (1967), Namibia (1992), Nepal (1996), Netherlands (1966), Nigeria (2002), Papua New Guinea (1973), Scotland (1994), Singapore (1974), Tanzania (2001), Uganda (1998), United Arab Emirates (1990), USA (1965), Zambia (2003).

Affiliate Members*: Afghanistan (2001), Austria (1992), Bahamas (1987), Bahrain (2001), Belgium (1991), Belize (1997), Bhutan (2001), Botswana (2001), Brazil (2002), Brunei (1992), Chile (2002), China (2004), Cook Islands (2000), Costa Rica (2002), Croatia (2001), Cuba (2002), Cyprus (1999), Czech Republic (2000), Finland (2000), Gambia (2002), Ghana (2002), Greece (1995), Indonesia (2001), Iran (2003), Isle of Man (2004), Japan (1989), Kuwait (1998), Lesotho (2001), Luxembourg (1998), Malawi (2003), Maldives (2001), Malta (1998), Mexico (2004), Morocco (2001), Mozambique (2003), Norway (2000), Oman (2000), Panama (2002), Philippines (2000), Portugal (1996), Qatar (1999), Rwanda (2003), St Helena (2001), Samoa (2000), Saudi Arabia (2003), Sierra Leone (2002), South Korea (2001), Spain (1992), Suriname (2002), Sweden (1997), Switzerland (1985), Thailand (1995), Tonga (2000), Turks & Caicos Islands (2002) and Vanuatu (1995).

* *Year of election shown in parentheses.*

The following governing bodies for cricket shall be eligible for election.

Full Members: The governing body for cricket (recognised by the ICC) of a country, or countries associated for cricket purposes, or a geographical area, from which representative teams are qualified to play official Test matches.

Associate Members: The governing body for cricket (recognised by the ICC) of a country, or countries associated for cricket purposes, or a geographical area, which does not qualify as a Full Member but where cricket is firmly established and organised.

Affiliate Members: The governing body for cricket (recognised by the ICC) of a country, or countries associated for cricket purposes, or a geographical area (which is not part of one of those already constituted as a Full or Associate Member) where the ICC recognises that cricket is played in accordance with the Laws of Cricket. Affiliate Members have no right to vote or to propose or second resolutions at ICC meetings.

ICC: M. W. Speed, The Clock Tower, Lord's Cricket Ground, London NW8 8QN (020 7266 1818; fax 020 7266 1777; website www.icc-cricket.com; email enquiry@icc-cricket.com).

ENGLAND AND WALES CRICKET BOARD

The England and Wales Cricket Board (ECB) became responsible for the administration of all cricket – professional and recreational – in England and Wales on January 1, 1997. It took over the functions of the Cricket Council, the Test and County Cricket Board and the National Cricket Association which had run the game in England and Wales since 1968. The Management Board is answerable to the First-Class Forum on matters concerning the first-class game and to the Recreational Forum on matters concerning the non-professional game. The First-Class Forum elects five members to the Management Board and the Recreational Forum elects four.

Officers

Chairman: F. D. Morgan. *Chief Executive:* D. G. Collier.

Management Board: F. D. Morgan *(chairman),* D. L. Acfield, D. L. Amiss, R. G. Bransgrove, C. G. Clarke, D. G. Collier, D. E. East, P. W. Gooden, B. W. Havill, R. Jackson, R. D. V. Knight, Sir Bill Morris, R. C. Moylan-Jones, J. B. Pickup, M. J. Soper, D. P. Stewart.

Chairmen of Committees: First-Class Forum: M. J. Soper; *Recreational Forum:* J. B. Pickup; *Cricket Advisory Committee:* D. L. Acfield; *International Teams Management Group:* D. L. Amiss; *Finance Advisory Committee:* D. P. Stewart; *Marketing Advisory Committee:* C. G. Clarke; *Discipline Standing Committee:* G. Elias QC; *Registration and Contracts Standing Committee:* D. S. Kemp.

Finance Director: B. W. Havill; *Director of Cricket Operations:* J. D. Carr; *Commercial Director:* vacant; *Director of Communications:* vacant; *Performance Director:* H. Morris; *National Development Director:* K. R. Pont; *Executive Director for Women's Cricket:* G. E. McConway; *Director of Legal Affairs and Business Development:* M. N. Roper-Drimie; *Cricket Operations Manager (First-Class):* A. Fordham; *Cricket Operations Manager (Recreational):* F. R. Kemp.

ECB: D. G. Collier, Lord's Ground, London NW8 8QZ (020 7432 1200; fax 020 7289 5619; website www.ecb.co.uk).

THE MARYLEBONE CRICKET CLUB

The Marylebone Cricket Club evolved out of the White Conduit Club in 1787, when Thomas Lord laid out his first ground in Dorset Square. Its members revised the Laws in 1788 and gradually took responsibility for cricket throughout the world. However, it relinquished control of the game in the UK in 1968 and the International Cricket Council finally established its own secretariat in 1993. MCC still owns Lord's and remains the guardian of the Laws. It calls itself "a private club with a public function" and aims to support cricket everywhere, especially at grassroots level and in countries where the game is least developed.

Patron: HER MAJESTY THE QUEEN

Officers

President: 2004–05 – T. W. Graveney.

Club Chairman: C. A. Fry. *Treasurer:* O. H. J. Stocken.

Trustees: A. C. D. Ingleby-Mackenzie, Sir Michael Jenkins, M. O. C. Sturt.

Hon. Life Vice-Presidents: Sir Alec Bedser, Lord Bramall, D. G. Clark, E. R. Dexter, G. H. G. Doggart, Lord Griffiths, D. J. Insole, M. E. L. Melluish, C. H. Palmer, D. R. W. Silk, J. J. Warr, J. C. Woodcock.

Secretary and Chief Executive: R. D. V. Knight. *Deputy Chief Executive:* D. N. Batts.

Head of Cricket: J. P. Stephenson. *Assistant Secretary (Membership):* C. Maynard. *Personal Assistant to Secretary and Chief Executive:* Miss S. A. Lawrence. *Curator:* A. Chadwick

MCC Committee: J. R. T. Barclay, A. N. W. Beeson, L. J. Dowley, J. A. Fingleton, M. W. Gatting, M. G. Griffith, R. Heyhoe-Flint, R. P. Hodson, P. L. O. Leaver, T. J. G. O'Gorman, N. M. Peters, D. R. Walsh.

Chairmen of committees: A. R. Lewis (Cricket); M. J. de Rohan (Estates); J. A. F. Vallance (Membership); A. W. Wreford (Marketing); *Additional member of the cricket committee:* G. J. Toogood.

MCC: R. D. V. Knight, Lord's Ground, London NW8 8QN (020 7289 1611; fax 020 7289 9100. Tickets 020 7432 1066; fax 020 7432 1061).

PROFESSIONAL CRICKETERS' ASSOCIATION

The Professional Cricketers' Association was formed in 1967 (as the Cricketers' Association) to represent the first-class county playing staffs, and to promote and protect professional players' interests. During the 1970s, it succeeded in establishing pension schemes and a minimum wage. In 1995, David Graveney became the Association's general secretary and first full-time employee; in 1998, he became chief executive. In 1997, the organisation set up its own management company to raise regular revenue and fund improved benefits for members of the PCA during and after their playing careers.

President: M. W. Gatting. *Chairman:* M. C. J. Ball. *Group Chief Executive:* R. H. Bevan. *Group Chairman:* T. J. G. O'Gorman. *Group Directors:* S. A. Marsh, T. A. Munton, G. C. Small.

PCA: R. H. Bevan, 3rd Floor, 338 Euston Road, London NW1 3BT (020 7544 8668; fax 020 7544 8515; email admin@pcaml.co.uk; website www.cricnet.com).

FEDERATION OF INTERNATIONAL CRICKETERS' ASSOCIATIONS

The Federation of International Cricketers' Associations was established in 1998 to co-ordinate the activities of all national players' associations. It aims to protect the interests of professional cricketers throughout the world. In 2003 FICA was recognised as an official representative body by the ICC, and FICA representatives now sit on the ICC's Cricket Committee.

President: B. A. Richards. *Chief Executive:* T. B. A. May. *Secretary:* T. J. G. O'Gorman. *Director of Operations:* R. H. Bevan.

EUROPEAN CRICKET COUNCIL

On June 16, 1997, the eight-year-old European Cricket Federation was superseded by the European Cricket Council, bringing together all European ICC members, plus Israel. In February 2005, the Council consisted of Denmark, France, Germany, Gibraltar, Ireland, Israel, Italy, Netherlands and Scotland (Associate Members); and Austria, Belgium, Croatia, Cyprus, Czech Republic, Finland, Greece, Isle of Man, Luxembourg, Malta, Norway, Portugal, Spain, Sweden and Switzerland (Affiliate Members). The ECC also supports development initiatives in non-member countries Belarus, Bulgaria, Estonia, Guernsey, Iceland, Jersey, Latvia, Poland, Russia, Slovakia, Slovenia, Turkey and Ukraine.

Chairman: D. J. Insole. *European Development Manager:* R. Holdsworth. *European Development Officer:* P. Hudson.

ECC: R. Holdsworth, Europe Office, Lord's Ground, London NW8 8QN (020 7616 8635; fax 020 7616 8634; website www.ecc-cricket.com).

THE LAWS OF CRICKET

(2000 CODE)

World copyright of MCC and reprinted by permission of MCC. Copies of the "Laws of Cricket" are obtainable from Lord's Cricket Ground.

INDEX OF THE LAWS

THE PREAMBLE – THE SPIRIT OF CRICKET

Cricket is a game that owes much of its unique appeal to the fact that it should be played not only within its Laws, but also within the Spirit of the Game. Any action which is seen to abuse this spirit causes injury to the game itself. The major responsibility for ensuring the spirit of fair play rests with the captains.

1. There are two Laws which place the responsibility for the team's conduct firmly on the captain.

Responsibility of captains

The captains are responsible at all times for ensuring that play is conducted within the Spirit of the Game as well as within the Laws.

Player's conduct

In the event of a player failing to comply with instructions by an umpire, or criticising by word or action the decisions of an umpire, or showing dissent, or generally behaving in a manner which might bring the game into disrepute, the umpire concerned shall in the first place report the matter to the other umpire and to the player's captain, and instruct the latter to take action.

2. Fair and unfair play

According to the Laws the umpires are the sole judges of fair and unfair play. The umpires may intervene at any time, and it is the responsibility of the captain to take action where required.

3. The umpires are authorised to intervene in cases of

- Time-wasting.
- Damaging the pitch.
- Dangerous or unfair bowling.
- Tampering with the ball.
- Any other action that they consider to be unfair.

4. The Spirit of the Game involves respect for

- Your opponents.
- Your own captain and team.
- The role of the umpires.
- The game's traditional values.

5. It is against the Spirit of the Game

- To dispute an umpire's decision by word, action or gesture.
- To direct abusive language towards an opponent or umpire.
- To indulge in cheating or any sharp practice, for instance:

    (a) To appeal knowing that the batsman is not out.

    (b) To advance towards an umpire in an aggressive manner when appealing.

    (c) To seek to distract an opponent either verbally or by harassment with persistent clapping or unnecessary noise under the guise of enthusiasm and motivation of one's own side.

6. Violence

There is no place for any act of violence on the field of play.

7. Players

Captains and umpires together set the tone for the conduct of a cricket match. Every player is expected to make an important contribution to this.

The players, umpires and scorers in a game of cricket may be of either gender and the Laws apply equally to both. The use, throughout the text, of pronouns indicating the male gender is purely for brevity. Except where specifically stated otherwise, every provision of the Laws is to be read as applying to women and girls equally as to men and boys.

LAW 1.   THE PLAYERS

1. Number of players

A match is played between two sides, each of 11 players, one of whom shall be captain. By agreement a match may be played between sides of more or less than 11 players, but not more than 11 players may field at any time.

2. Nomination of players

Each captain shall nominate his players in writing to one of the umpires before the toss. No player may be changed after the nomination without the consent of the opposing captain.

3. Captain

If at any time the captain is not available, a deputy shall act for him.

    (a) If a captain is not available during the period in which the toss is to take place, then the deputy must be responsible for the nomination of the players, if this has not already been done, and for the toss. See 2 above and Law 12.4 (The toss).

    (b) At any time after the toss, the deputy must be one of the nominated players.

4. Responsibility of captains

The captains are responsible at all times for ensuring that play is conducted within the spirit and traditions of the game as well as within the Laws. See The Preamble – The Spirit of Cricket and Law 42.1 (Fair and unfair play – responsibility of captains).

LAW 2. SUBSTITUTES AND RUNNERS; BATSMAN OR FIELDER LEAVING THE FIELD; BATSMAN RETIRING; BATSMAN COMMENCING INNINGS

1. Substitutes and runners

    (a) If the umpires are satisfied that a player has been injured or become ill after the nomination of the players, they shall allow that player to have:

        (i) A substitute acting instead of him in the field.

        (ii) A runner when batting.

    Any injury or illness that occurs at any time after the nomination of the players until the conclusion of the match shall be allowable, irrespective of whether play is in progress or not.

    (b) The umpires shall have discretion, for other wholly acceptable reasons, to allow a substitute for a fielder, or a runner for a batsman, at the start of the match or at any subsequent time.

    (c) A player wishing to change his shirt, boots, etc. must leave the field to do so. No substitute shall be allowed for him.

2. Objection to substitutes

The opposing captain shall have no right of objection to any player acting as a substitute on the field, nor as to where the substitute shall field. However, no substitute shall act as wicket-keeper. See 3 below.

3. Restrictions on the role of substitutes

A substitute shall not be allowed to bat or bowl nor to act as wicket-keeper or as captain on the field of play.

4. A player for whom a substitute has acted

A player is allowed to bat, bowl or field even though a substitute has previously acted for him.

5. Fielder absent or leaving the field

If a fielder fails to take the field with his side at the start of the match or at any later time, or leaves the field during a session of play:

    (a) The umpire shall be informed of the reason for his absence.

(b) He shall not thereafter come on to the field during a session of play without the consent of the umpire. See 6 below. The umpire shall give such consent as soon as is practicable.

(c) If he is absent for 15 minutes or longer, he shall not be permitted to bowl thereafter, subject to (i), (ii) or (iii) below, until he has been on the field for at least that length of playing time for which he was absent.

    (i) Absence or penalty for time absent shall not be carried over into a new day's play.

    (ii) If, in the case of a follow-on or forfeiture, a side fields for two consecutive innings, this restriction shall, subject to (i) above, continue as necessary into the second innings but shall not otherwise be carried over into a new innings.

    (iii) The time lost for an unscheduled break in play shall be counted as time on the field for any fielder who comes on to the field at the resumption of play. See Law 15.1 (An interval).

6. Player returning without permission

If a player comes on to the field of play in contravention of 5(b) above and comes into contact with the ball while it is in play:

    (i) The ball shall immediately become dead and the umpire shall award five penalty runs to the batting side. See Law 42.17 (Penalty runs). The ball shall not count as one of the over.

    (ii) The umpire shall inform the other umpire, the captain of the fielding side, the batsmen and, as soon as practicable, the captain of the batting side of the reason for this action.

    (iii) The umpires together shall report the occurrence as soon as possible to the executive of the fielding side and any governing body responsible for the match, who shall take such action as is considered appropriate against the captain and player concerned.

7. Runner

The player acting as a runner for a batsman shall be a member of the batting side and shall, if possible, have already batted in that innings. The runner shall wear external protective equipment equivalent to that worn by the batsman for whom he runs and shall carry a bat.

8. Transgression of the Laws by a batsman who has a runner

(a) A batsman's runner is subject to the Laws. He will be regarded as a batsman except where there are specific provisions for his role as a runner. See 7 above and Law 29.2 (Which is a batsman's ground).

(b) A batsman with a runner will suffer the penalty for any infringement of the Laws by his runner as though he had been himself responsible for the infringement. In particular he will be out if his runner is out under any of Laws 33 (Handled the ball), 37 (Obstructing the field) or 38 (Run out).

(c) When a batsman with a runner is striker he remains himself subject to the Laws and will be liable to the penalties that any infringement of them demands.

    Additionally, if he is out of his ground when the wicket is put down at the wicket-keeper's end, he will be out in the circumstances of Law 38 (Run out) or Law 39 (Stumped) irrespective of the position of the non-striker or of the runner. If he is thus dismissed, runs completed by the runner and the other batsman before the dismissal shall not be scored. However, the penalty for a no-ball or a wide shall stand, together with any penalties to be awarded to either side when the ball is dead. See Law 42.17 (Penalty runs).

(d) When a batsman with a runner is not the striker:

    (i) He remains subject to Laws 33 (Handled the ball) and 37 (Obstructing the field) but is otherwise out of the game.

    (ii) He shall stand where directed by the striker's end umpire so as not to interfere with play.

    (iii) He will be liable, notwithstanding (i) above, to the penalty demanded by the Laws should he commit any act of unfair play.

9. Batsman leaving the field or retiring

A batsman may retire at any time during his innings. The umpires, before allowing play to proceed, shall be informed of the reason for a batsman retiring.

(a) If a batsman retires because of illness, injury or any other unavoidable cause, he is entitled to resume his innings subject to (c) below. If for any reason he does not do so, his innings is to be recorded as "Retired – not out".

(b) If a batsman retires for any reason other than as in (a) above, he may resume his innings only with the consent of the opposing captain. If for any reason he does not resume his innings it is to be recorded as "Retired – out".

(c) If after retiring a batsman resumes his innings, it shall be only at the fall of a wicket or the retirement of another batsman.

10. Commencement of a batsman's innings

Except at the start of a side's innings, a batsman shall be considered to have commenced his innings when he first steps on to the field of play, provided "Time" has not been called. The innings of the opening batsmen, and that of any new batsman at the resumption of play after a call of "Time", shall commence at the call of "Play".

LAW 3.   THE UMPIRES

1. Appointment and attendance

Before the match, two umpires shall be appointed, one for each end to control the game as required by the Laws, with absolute impartiality. The umpires shall be present on the ground and report to the executive of the ground at least 45 minutes before the start of each day's play.

2. Change of umpire

An umpire shall not be changed during the match, other than in exceptional circumstances, unless he is injured or ill. If there has to be a change of umpire, the replacement shall act only as the striker's end umpire unless the captains agree that he should take full responsibility as an umpire.

3. Agreement with captains

Before the toss the umpires shall:

(a) Ascertain the hours of play and agree with the captains:

(i) The balls to be used during the match. See Law 5 (The ball).

(ii) Times and durations of intervals for meals and times for drinks intervals. See Law 15 (Intervals).

(iii) The boundary of the field of play and allowances for boundaries. See Law 19 (Boundaries).

(iv) Any special conditions of play affecting the conduct of the match.

(b) Inform the scorers of the agreements in (ii), (iii) and (iv) above.

4. To inform captains and scorers

Before the toss the umpires shall agree between themselves and inform both captains and both scorers:

(i) Which clock or watch and back-up timepiece is to be used during the match.

(ii) Whether or not any obstacle within the field of play is to be regarded as a boundary. See Law 19 (Boundaries).

5. The wickets, creases and boundaries

Before the toss and during the match, the umpires shall satisfy themselves that:

(i) The wickets are properly pitched. See Law 8 (The wickets).

(ii) The creases are correctly marked. See Law 9 (The bowling, popping and return creases).

(iii) The boundary of the field of play complies with the requirements of Law 19.2 (Defining the boundary – boundary marking).

6. Conduct of the game, implements and equipment

Before the toss and during the match, the umpires shall satisfy themselves that:

(a) The conduct of the game is strictly in accordance with the Laws.

(b) The implements of the game conform to the requirements of Laws 5 (The ball) and 6 (The bat), together with either Laws 8.2 (Size of stumps) and 8.3 (The bails) or, if appropriate, Law 8.4 (Junior cricket).

(c) (i) No player uses equipment other than that permitted.

(ii) The wicket-keeper's gloves comply with the requirements of Law 40.2 (Gloves).

7. Fair and unfair play

The umpires shall be the sole judges of fair and unfair play.

8. Fitness of ground, weather and light

The umpires shall be the final judges of the fitness of the ground, weather and light for play. See 9 below and Law 7.2 (Fitness of the pitch for play).

9. Suspension of play for adverse conditions of ground, weather or light

(a) (i) All references to ground include the pitch. See Law 7.1 (Area of pitch).

(ii) For the purpose of this Law the batsmen at the wicket may deputise for their captain at any appropriate time.

(b) If at any time the umpires together agree that the condition of the ground, weather or light is not suitable for play, they shall inform the captains and, unless

(i) in unsuitable ground or weather conditions both captains agree to continue, or to commence, or to restart play, or

(ii) in unsuitable light the batting side wish to continue, or to commence, or to restart play,

they shall suspend play, or not allow play to commence or to restart.

(c) (i) After agreeing to play in unsuitable ground or weather conditions, either captain may appeal against the conditions to the umpires before the next call of "Time". The umpires shall uphold the appeal only if, in their opinion, the factors taken into account when making their previous decision are the same or the conditions have further deteriorated.

(ii) After deciding to play in unsuitable light, the captain of the batting side may appeal against the light to the umpires before the next call of "Time". The umpires shall uphold the appeal only if, in their opinion, the factors taken into account when making their previous decision are the same or the condition of the light has further deteriorated.

(d) If at any time the umpires together agree that the conditions of ground, weather or light are so bad that there is obvious and foreseeable risk to the safety of any player or umpire, so that it would be unreasonable or dangerous for play to take place, then notwithstanding the provisions of 9(b)(i) and 9(b)(ii) above, they shall immediately suspend play, or not allow play to commence or to restart. The decision as to whether conditions are so bad as to warrant such action is one for the umpires alone to make.

Merely because the grass and the ball are wet and slippery does not warrant the ground conditions being regarded as unreasonable or dangerous. If the umpires consider the ground is so wet or slippery as to deprive the bowler of a reasonable foothold, the fielders of the power of free movement, or the batsmen of the ability to play their strokes or to run between the wickets, then these conditions shall be regarded as so bad that it would be unreasonable for play to take place.

(e) When there is a suspension of play it is the responsibility of the umpires to monitor the conditions. They shall make inspections as often as appropriate, unaccompanied by any of the players or officials. Immediately the umpires together agree that conditions are suitable for play they shall call upon the players to resume the game.

(f) If play is in progress up to the start of an agreed interval then it will resume after the interval unless the umpires together agree that conditions are or have become unsuitable or dangerous. If they do so agree, then they shall implement the procedure in (b) or (d) above, as appropriate, whether or not there had been any decision by the captains to continue, or any appeal against the conditions by either captain, prior to the commencement of the interval.

10. Exceptional circumstances

The umpires shall have the discretion to implement the procedures of 9 above for reasons other than ground, weather or light if they consider that exceptional circumstances warrant it.

11. Position of umpires

The umpires shall stand where they can best see any act upon which their decision may be required. Subject to this over-riding consideration the umpire at the bowler's end shall stand where he does not interfere with either the bowler's run-up or the striker's view.

The umpire at the striker's end may elect to stand on the off side instead of the on side of the pitch, provided he informs the captain of the fielding side, the striker and the other umpire of his intention to do so.

12. Umpires changing ends

The umpires shall change ends after each side has had one completed innings. See Law 14.2 (Forfeiture of an innings).

13. Consultation between umpires

All disputes shall be determined by the umpires. The umpires shall consult with each other whenever necessary. See also Law 27.6 (Consultation by umpires).

14. Signals

(a) The following code of signals shall be used by umpires.

(i) Signals made while the ball is in play:

Dead ball	– by crossing and re-crossing the wrists below the waist.
No-ball	– by extending one arm horizontally.
Out	– by raising the index finger above the head. (If not out the umpire shall call "Not out.")
Wide	– by extending both arms horizontally.

(ii) When the ball is dead, the signals above, with the exception of the signal for "Out", shall be repeated to the scorers. The signals listed below shall be made to the scorers only when the ball is dead.

Boundary 4	– by waving an arm from side to side finishing with the arm across the chest.
Boundary 6	– by raising both arms above the head.
Bye	– by raising an open hand above the head.
Commencement of last hour	– by pointing to a raised wrist with the other hand.
Five penalty runs awarded to the batting side	– by repeated tapping of one shoulder with the opposite hand.
Five penalty runs awarded to the fielding side	– by placing one hand on the opposite shoulder.
Leg-bye	– by touching a raised knee with the hand.
New ball	– by holding the ball above the head.
Revoke last signal	– by touching both shoulders, each with the opposite hand.

Short run   — by bending one arm upwards and touching the nearer shoulder with the tips of the fingers.

(b) The umpires shall wait until each signal to the scorers has been separately acknowledged by a scorer before allowing play to proceed.

15. Correctness of scores

Consultation between umpires and scorers on doubtful points is essential. The umpires shall satisfy themselves as to the correctness of the number of runs scored, the wickets that have fallen and, where appropriate, the number of overs bowled. They shall agree these with the scorers at least at every interval, other than a drinks interval, and at the conclusion of the match. See Laws 4.2 (Correctness of scores), 21.8 (Correctness of result) and 21.10 (Result not to be changed).

LAW 4. THE SCORERS

1. Appointment of scorers

Two scorers shall be appointed to record all runs scored, all wickets taken and, where appropriate, number of overs bowled.

2. Correctness of scores

The scorers shall frequently check to ensure that their records agree. They shall agree with the umpires, at least at every interval, other than a drinks interval, and at the conclusion of the match, the runs scored, the wickets that have fallen and, where appropriate, the number of overs bowled. See Law 3.15 (Correctness of scores).

3. Acknowledging signals

The scorers shall accept all instructions and signals given to them by the umpires. They shall immediately acknowledge each separate signal.

LAW 5. THE BALL

1. Weight and size

The ball, when new, shall weigh not less than 5½oz/155.9g, nor more than 5¾oz/163g, and shall measure not less than 8¹³⁄₁₆in/22.4cm, nor more than 9in/22.9cm in circumference.

2. Approval and control of balls

(a) All balls to be used in the match, having been approved by the umpires and captains, shall be in the possession of the umpires before the toss and shall remain under their control throughout the match.

(b) The umpire shall take possession of the ball in use at the fall of each wicket, at the start of any interval and at any interruption of play.

3. New ball

Unless an agreement to the contrary has been made before the match, either captain may demand a new ball at the start of each innings.

4. New ball in match of more than one day's duration

In a match of more than one day's duration, the captain of the fielding side may demand a new ball after the prescribed number of overs has been bowled with the old one. The governing body for cricket in the country concerned shall decide the number of overs applicable in that country, which shall not be less than 75 overs.

The umpires shall indicate to the batsmen and the scorers whenever a new ball is taken into play.

5. Ball lost or becoming unfit for play

If, during play, the ball cannot be found or recovered or the umpires agree that it has become unfit for play through normal use, the umpires shall replace it with a ball which has had wear comparable with that which the previous ball had received before the need for its replacement. When the ball is replaced the umpires shall inform the batsmen and the fielding captain.

6. Specifications

The specifications as described in 1 above shall apply to men's cricket only. The following specifications will apply to:

    (i) *Women's cricket*
       Weight   – from 4¹⁵⁄₁₆oz/140g to 5⁵⁄₁₆oz/151g.
       Circumference – from 8¼in/21.0cm to 8⅞in/22.5cm.

    (ii) *Junior cricket – Under-13*
       Weight   – from 4¹¹⁄₁₆oz/133g to 5¹⁄₁₆oz/144g.
       Circumference – from 8¹⁄₁₆in/20.5cm to 8¹¹⁄₁₆in/22.0cm.

LAW 6. THE BAT

1. Width and length

The bat overall shall not be more than 38in/96.5cm in length. The blade of the bat shall be made solely of wood and shall not exceed 4¼in/10.8cm at the widest part.

2. Covering the blade

The blade may be covered with material for protection, strengthening or repair. Such material shall not exceed ¹⁄₁₆in/1.56mm in thickness, and shall not be likely to cause unacceptable damage to the ball.

3. Hand or glove to count as part of bat

In these Laws,

    (a) Reference to the bat shall imply that the bat is held by the batsman.

    (b) Contact between the ball and either
       (i) the striker's bat itself, or
      (ii) the striker's hand holding the bat, or
     (iii) any part of a glove worn on the striker's hand holding the bat

    shall be regarded as the ball striking or touching the bat, or being struck by the bat.

LAW 7. THE PITCH

1. Area of pitch

The pitch is a rectangular area of the ground 22yds/20.12m in length and 10ft/3.05m in width. It is bounded at either end by the bowling creases and on either side by imaginary lines, one each side of the imaginary line joining the centres of the two middle stumps, each parallel to it and 5ft/1.52m from it. See Laws 8.1 (Width and pitching) and 9.2 (The bowling crease).

2. Fitness of the pitch for play

The umpires shall be the final judges of the fitness of the pitch for play. See Laws 3.8 (Fitness of ground, weather and light) and 3.9 (Suspension of play for adverse conditions of ground, weather or light).

3. Selection and preparation

Before the toss the ground authority shall be responsible for the selection and preparation of the pitch. During the match the umpires shall control its use and maintenance.

4. Changing the pitch

The pitch shall not be changed during the match unless the umpires decide that it is unreasonable or dangerous for play to continue on it and then only with the consent of both captains.

5. Non-turf pitches

In the event of a non-turf pitch being used, the artificial surface shall conform to the following measurements:

> Length – a minimum of 58ft/17.68m.
> Width – a minimum of 6ft/1.83m.

See Law 10.8 (Non-turf pitches).

LAW 8.   THE WICKETS

1. Width and pitching

Two sets of wickets shall be pitched opposite and parallel to each other at a distance of 22yds/20.12m between the centres of the two middle stumps. Each set shall be 9in/22.86cm wide and shall consist of three wooden stumps with two wooden bails on top.

2. Size of stumps

The tops of the stumps shall be 28in/71.1cm above the playing surface and shall be dome-shaped except for the bail grooves. The portion of a stump above the playing surface shall be cylindrical, apart from the domed top, with a circular section of diameter not less than 1³/₈in/3.49cm nor more than 1½in/3.81cm.

3. The bails

(a) The bails, when in position on the top of the stumps:

  (i) Shall not project more than ½in/1.27cm above them.

  (ii) Shall fit between the stumps without forcing them out of the vertical.

(b) Each bail shall conform to the following specifications.

Overall length	– 4⁵/₁₆in/10.95cm.
Length of barrel	– 2⅛in/5.40cm.
Longer spigot	– 1³/₈in/3.49cm.
Shorter spigot	– ¹³/₁₆in/2.06cm.

4. Junior cricket

In junior cricket, the same definitions of the wickets shall apply subject to the following measurements being used:

Width	– 8in/20.32cm.
Pitched for Under-13	– 21yds/19.20m.
Pitched for Under-11	– 20yds/18.29m.
Pitched for Under-9	– 18yds/16.46m.
Height above playing surface	– 27in/68.58cm.

Each stump

Diameter	– not less than 1¼in/3.18cm nor more than 1³/₈in/3.49cm.

Each bail

Overall	– 3¹³/₁₆in/9.68cm.
Barrel	– 1¹³/₁₆in/4.60cm.
Longer Spigot	– 1¼in/3.18cm.
Shorter Spigot	– ¾in/1.91cm.

5. Dispensing with bails

The umpires may agree to dispense with the use of bails, if necessary. If they so agree then no bails shall be used at either end. The use of bails shall be resumed as soon as conditions permit. See Law 28.4 (Dispensing with bails).

LAW 9. THE BOWLING, POPPING AND RETURN CREASES

1. The creases

A bowling crease, a popping crease and two return creases shall be marked in white, as set out in 2, 3 and 4 below, at each end of the pitch.

2. The bowling crease

The bowling crease, which is the back edge of the crease marking, shall be the line through the centres of the three stumps at that end. It shall be 8ft 8in/2.64m in length, with the stumps in the centre.

3. The popping crease

The popping crease, which is the back edge of the crease marking, shall be in front of and parallel to the bowling crease and shall be 4ft/1.22m from it. The popping crease shall be marked to a minimum of 6ft/1.83m on either side of the imaginary line joining the centres of the middle stumps and shall be considered to be unlimited in length.

4. The return creases

The return creases, which are the inside edges of the crease markings, shall be at right angles to the popping crease at a distance of 4ft 4in/1.32m either side of the imaginary line joining the centres of the two middle stumps. Each return crease shall be marked from the popping crease to a minimum of 8ft/2.44m behind it and shall be considered to be unlimited in length.

LAW 10. PREPARATION AND MAINTENANCE OF THE PLAYING AREA

1. Rolling

The pitch shall not be rolled during the match except as permitted in (a) and (b) below.

(a) Frequency and duration of rolling

During the match the pitch may be rolled at the request of the captain of the batting side, for a period of not more than seven minutes, before the start of each innings, other than the first innings of the match, and before the start of each subsequent day's play. See (d) below.

(b) Rolling after a delayed start

In addition to the rolling permitted above, if, after the toss and before the first innings of the match, the start is delayed, the captain of the batting side may request to have the pitch rolled for not more than seven minutes. However, if the umpires together agree that the delay has had no significant effect on the state of the pitch, they shall refuse the request for the rolling of the pitch.

(c) Choice of rollers

If there is more than one roller available the captain of the batting side shall have the choice.

(d) Timing of permitted rolling

The rolling permitted (maximum seven minutes) before play begins on any day shall be started not more than 30 minutes before the time scheduled or rescheduled for play to begin. The captain of the batting side may, however, delay the start of such rolling until not less than ten minutes before the time scheduled or rescheduled for play to begin, should he so desire.

(e) Insufficient time to complete rolling

If a captain declares an innings closed, or forfeits an innings, or enforces the follow-on, and the other captain is prevented thereby from exercising his option of the rolling permitted (maximum seven minutes), or if he is so prevented for any other reason, the extra time required to complete the rolling shall be taken out of the normal playing time.

2. Sweeping

(a) If rolling is to take place the pitch shall first be swept to avoid any possible damage by rolling in debris. This sweeping shall be done so that the seven minutes allowed for rolling is not affected.

(b) The pitch shall be cleared of any debris at all intervals for meals, between innings and at the beginning of each day, not earlier than 30 minutes nor later than ten minutes before the time scheduled or rescheduled for play to begin. See Law 15.1 (An interval).

(c) Notwithstanding the provisions of (a) and (b) above, the umpires shall not allow sweeping to take place where they consider it may be detrimental to the surface of the pitch.

3. Mowing

(a) The pitch

The pitch shall be mown on each day of the match on which play is expected to take place, if ground and weather conditions allow.

(b) The outfield

In order to ensure that conditions are as similar as possible for both sides, the outfield shall be mown on each day of the match on which play is expected to take place, if ground and weather conditions allow.

If, for reasons other than ground and weather conditions, complete mowing of the outfield is not possible, the ground authority shall notify the captains and umpires of the procedure to be adopted for such mowing during the match.

(c) Responsibility for mowing

All mowings which are carried out before the match shall be the responsibility of the ground authority.

All subsequent mowings shall be carried out under the supervision of the umpires.

(d) Time of mowing

(i) Mowing of the pitch on any day of the match shall be completed not later than 30 minutes before the time scheduled or rescheduled for play to begin on that day.

(ii) Mowing of the outfield on any day of the match shall be completed not later than 15 minutes before the time scheduled or rescheduled for play to begin on that day.

4. Watering

The pitch shall not be watered during the match.

5. Re-marking creases

The creases shall be re-marked whenever either umpire considers it necessary.

6. Maintenance of footholes

The umpires shall ensure that the holes made by the bowlers and batsmen are cleaned out and dried whenever necessary to facilitate play. In matches of more than one day's duration, the umpires shall allow, if necessary, the re-turfing of footholes made by the bowler in his delivery stride, or the use of quick-setting fillings for the same purpose.

7. Securing of footholds and maintenance of pitch

During play, the umpires shall allow the players to secure their footholds by the use of sawdust provided that no damage to the pitch is caused and that Law 42 (Fair and unfair play) is not contravened.

8. Non-turf pitches

Wherever appropriate, the provisions set out in 1 to 7 above shall apply.

LAW 11.   COVERING THE PITCH

1. Before the match

The use of covers before the match is the responsibility of the ground authority and may include full covering if required. However, the ground authority shall grant suitable facility to the captains to inspect the pitch before the nomination of their players and to the umpires to discharge their duties as laid down in Laws 3 (The umpires), 7 (The pitch), 8 (The wickets), 9 (The bowling, popping and return creases) and 10 (Preparation and maintenance of the playing area).

2. During the match

The pitch shall not be completely covered during the match unless provided otherwise by regulations or by agreement before the toss.

3. Covering bowlers' run-ups

Whenever possible, the bowlers' run-ups shall be covered in inclement weather, in order to keep them dry. Unless there is agreement for full covering under 2 above the covers so used shall not extend further than 5ft/1.52m in front of each popping crease.

4. Removal of covers

(a) If after the toss the pitch is covered overnight, the covers shall be removed in the morning at the earliest possible moment on each day that play is expected to take place.

(b) If covers are used during the day as protection from inclement weather, or if inclement weather delays the removal of overnight covers, they shall be removed promptly as soon as conditions allow.

LAW 12.   INNINGS

1. Number of innings

(a) A match shall be one or two innings of each side according to agreement reached before the start of play.

(b) It may be agreed to limit any innings to a number of overs or by a period of time. If such an agreement is made then:

(i) In a one-innings match it shall apply to both innings.

(ii) In a two-innings match it shall apply to either
the first innings of each side, or
the second innings of each side, or
both innings of each side.

2. Alternate innings

In a two-innings match each side shall take their innings alternately except in the cases provided for in Law 13 (The follow-on) or Law 14.2 (Forfeiture of an innings).

3. Completed innings

A side's innings is to be considered as completed if:

(a) The side is all out, or

(b) At the fall of a wicket, further balls remain to be bowled, but no further batsman is available to come in, or

(c) The captain declares the innings closed, or

(d) The captain forfeits the innings, or

(e) In the case of an agreement under 1(b) above, either

(i) the prescribed number of overs has been bowled, or

(ii) the prescribed time has expired.

4. The toss

The captains shall toss for the choice of innings on the field of play not earlier than 30 minutes, nor later than 15 minutes, before the scheduled or any rescheduled time for the match to start. Note, however, the provisions of Law 1.3 (Captain).

5. Decision to be notified

The captain of the side winning the toss shall notify the opposing captain of his decision to bat or to field, not later than ten minutes before the scheduled or any rescheduled time for the match to start. Once notified the decision may not be altered.

LAW 13.   THE FOLLOW-ON

1. Lead on first innings

(a) In a two-innings match of five days or more, the side which bats first and leads by at least 200 runs shall have the option of requiring the other side to follow their innings.

(b) The same option shall be available in two-innings matches of shorter duration with the minimum required leads as follows:

(i) 150 runs in a match of three or four days.

(ii) 100 runs in a two-day match.

(iii) 75 runs in a one-day match.

2. Notification

A captain shall notify the opposing captain and the umpires of his intention to take up this option. Law 10.1 (e) (Insufficient time to complete rolling) shall apply.

3. First day's play lost

If no play takes place on the first day of a match of more than one day's duration, 1 above shall apply in accordance with the number of days remaining from the actual start of the match. The day on which play first commences shall count as a whole day for this purpose, irrespective of the time at which play starts.

Play will have taken place as soon as, after the call of "Play", the first over has started. See Law 22.2 (Start of an over).

LAW 14.   DECLARATION AND FORFEITURE

1. Time of declaration

The captain of the batting side may declare an innings closed, when the ball is dead, at any time during a match.

2. Forfeiture of an innings

A captain may forfeit either of his side's innings. A forfeited innings shall be considered as a completed innings.

3. Notification

A captain shall notify the opposing captain and the umpires of his decision to declare or to forfeit an innings. Law 10.1 (e) (Insufficient time to complete rolling) shall apply.

LAW 15.   INTERVALS

1. An interval

The following shall be classed as intervals:

(i) The period between close of play on one day and the start of the next day's play.

(ii) Intervals between innings.

    (iii) Intervals for meals.

    (iv) Intervals for drinks.

    (v) Any other agreed interval.

All these intervals shall be considered as scheduled breaks for the purposes of Law 2.5 (Fielder absent or leaving the field).

2. Agreement of intervals

(a) Before the toss:

    (i) The hours of play shall be established.

    (ii) Except as in (b) below, the timing and duration of intervals for meals shall be agreed.

    (iii) The timing and duration of any other interval under 1(v) above shall be agreed.

(b) In a one-day match no specific time need be agreed for the tea interval. It may be agreed instead to take this interval between the innings.

(c) Intervals for drinks may not be taken during the last hour of the match, as defined in Law 16.6 (Last hour of match – number of overs). Subject to this limitation the captains and umpires shall agree the times for such intervals, if any, before the toss and on each subsequent day not later than ten minutes before play is scheduled to start. See also Law 3.3 (Agreement with captains).

3. Duration of intervals

(a) An interval for lunch or for tea shall be of the duration agreed under 2(a) above, taken from the call of "Time" before the interval until the call of "Play" on resumption after the interval.

(b) An interval between innings shall be ten minutes from the close of an innings to the call of "Play" for the start of the next innings, except as in 4, 6 and 7 below.

4. No allowance for interval between innings

In addition to the provisions of 6 and 7 below:

(a) If an innings ends when ten minutes or less remain before the time agreed for close of play on any day, there will be no further play on that day. No change will be made to the time for the start of play on the following day on account of the ten minutes between innings.

(b) If a captain declares an innings closed during an interruption in play of more than ten minutes duration, no adjustment shall be made to the time for resumption of play on account of the ten minutes between innings, which shall be considered as included in the interruption. Law 10.1(e) (Insufficient time to complete rolling) shall apply.

(c) If a captain declares an innings closed during any interval other than an interval for drinks, the interval shall be of the agreed duration and shall be considered to include the ten minutes between innings. Law 10.1(e) (Insufficient time to complete rolling) shall apply.

5. Changing agreed times for intervals

If for adverse conditions of ground, weather or light, or for any other reason, playing time is lost, the umpires and captains together may alter the time of the lunch interval or of the tea interval. See also 6, 7 and 9(c) below.

6. Changing agreed time for lunch interval

(a) If an innings ends when ten minutes or less remain before the agreed time for lunch, the interval shall be taken immediately. It shall be of the agreed length and shall be considered to include the ten minutes between innings.

(b) If, because of adverse conditions of ground, weather or light, or in exceptional circumstances, a stoppage occurs when ten minutes or less remain before the agreed time for lunch then, notwithstanding 5 above, the interval shall be taken immediately. It shall be of the agreed length. Play shall resume at the end of this interval or as soon after as conditions permit.

(c) If the players have occasion to leave the field for any reason when more than ten minutes remain before the agreed time for lunch then, unless the umpires and captains together agree to alter it, lunch will be taken at the agreed time.

7. Changing agreed time for tea interval

(a) (i) If an innings ends when 30 minutes or less remain before the agreed time for tea, then the interval shall be taken immediately. It shall be of the agreed length and shall be considered to include the ten minutes between innings.

(ii) If, when 30 minutes remain before the agreed time for tea, an interval between innings is already in progress, play will resume at the end of the ten-minute interval.

(b) (i) If, because of adverse conditions of ground, weather or light, or in exceptional circumstances, a stoppage occurs when 30 minutes or less remain before the agreed time for tea, then unless

either there is an agreement to change the time for tea, as permitted in 5 above,

or the captains agree to forgo the tea interval, as permitted in 10 below,

the interval shall be taken immediately. The interval shall be of the agreed length. Play shall resume at the end of this interval or as soon after as conditions permit.

(ii) If a stoppage is already in progress when 30 minutes remain before the time agreed for tea, 5 above will apply.

8. Tea interval – nine wickets down

If either nine wickets are already down when two minutes remain to the agreed time for tea, or the ninth wicket falls within these two minutes or at any later time up to and including the final ball of the over in progress at the agreed time for tea, then not withstanding the provisions of Law 16.5 (b) (Completion of an over) tea will not be taken until the end of the over in progress 30 minutes after the originally agreed time for tea, unless the players have cause to leave the field of play or the innings is completed earlier.

9. Intervals for drinks

(a) If on any day the captains agree that there shall be intervals for drinks, the option to take such intervals shall be available to either side. Each interval shall be kept as short as possible and in any case shall not exceed five minutes.

(b) (i) Unless both captains agree to forgo any drinks interval, it shall be taken at the end of the over in progress when the agreed time is reached. If, however, a wicket falls within five minutes of the agreed time then drinks shall be taken immediately. No other variation in the timing of drinks intervals shall be permitted except as provided for in (c) below.

(ii) For the purpose of (i) above and Law 3.9(a)(ii) (Suspension of play for adverse conditions of ground, weather or light) only, the batsmen at the wicket may deputise for their captain.

(c) If an innings ends or the players have to leave the field of play for any other reason within 30 minutes of the agreed time for a drinks interval, the umpires and captains together may rearrange the timing of drinks intervals in that session.

10. Agreement to forgo intervals

At any time during the match, the captains may agree to forgo the tea interval or any of the drinks intervals. The umpires shall be informed of the decision.

11. Scorers to be informed

The umpires shall ensure that the scorers are informed of all agreements about hours of play and intervals, and of any changes made thereto as permitted under this Law.

LAW 16.   START OF PLAY; CESSATION OF PLAY

1. Call of "Play"

The umpire at the bowler's end shall call "Play" at the start of the match and on the resumption of play after any interval or interruption.

2. Call of "Time"

The umpire at the bowler's end shall call "Time" on the cessation of play before any interval or interruption of play and at the conclusion of the match. See Law 27 (Appeals).

3. Removal of bails

After the call of "Time", the bails shall be removed from both wickets.

4. Starting a new over

Another over shall always be started at any time during the match, unless an interval is to be taken in the circumstances set out in 5 below, if the umpire, after walking at his normal pace, has arrived at his position behind the stumps at the bowler's end before the time agreed for the next interval, or for the close of play, has been reached.

5. Completion of an over

Other than at the end of the match:

(a) If the agreed time for an interval is reached during an over, the over shall be completed before the interval is taken except as provided for in (b) below.

(b) When less than two minutes remain before the time agreed for the next interval, the interval will be taken immediately if either

(i) a batsman is out or retires, or

(ii) the players have occasion to leave the field

whether this occurs during an over or at the end of an over. Except at the end of an innings, if an over is thus interrupted it shall be completed on resumption of play.

6. Last hour of match – number of overs

When one hour of playing time of the match remains, according to the agreed hours of play, the over in progress shall be completed. The next over shall be the first of a minimum of 20 overs which must be bowled, provided that a result is not reached earlier and provided that there is no interval or interruption in play.

The umpire at the bowler's end shall indicate the commencement of this 20 overs to the players and the scorers. The period of play thereafter shall be referred to as the last hour, whatever its actual duration.

7. Last hour of match – interruptions of play

If there is an interruption in play during the last hour of the match, the minimum number of overs to be bowled shall be reduced from 20 as follows:

(a) The time lost for an interruption is counted from the call of "Time" until the time for resumption of play as decided by the umpires.

(b) One over shall be deducted for every complete three minutes of time lost.

(c) In the case of more than one such interruption, the minutes lost shall not be aggregated; the calculation shall be made for each interruption separately.

(d) If, when one hour of playing time remains, an interruption is already in progress:

(i) Only the time lost after this moment shall be counted in the calculation.

(ii) The over in progress at the start of the interruption shall be completed on resumption of play and shall not count as one of the minimum number of overs to be bowled.

(e) If, after the start of the last hour, an interruption occurs during an over, the over shall be completed on resumption of play. The two part-overs shall between them count as one over of the minimum number to be bowled.

8. Last hour of match – intervals between innings

If an innings ends so that a new innings is to be started during the last hour of the match, the interval starts with the end of the innings and is to end ten minutes later.

    (a) If this interval is already in progress at the start of the last hour, then to determine the number of overs to be bowled in the new innings, calculations are to be made as set out in 7 above.

    (b) If the innings ends after the last hour has started, two calculations are to be made, as set out in (c) and (d) below. The greater of the numbers yielded by these two calculations is to be the minimum number of overs to be bowled in the new innings.

    (c) Calculation based on overs remaining:

        (i) At the conclusion of the innings, the number of overs that remain to be bowled, of the minimum in the last hour, to be noted.

        (ii) If this is not a whole number it is to be rounded up to the next whole number.

        (iii) Three overs to be deducted from the result for the interval.

    (d) Calculation based on time remaining:

        (i) At the conclusion of the innings, the time remaining until the agreed time for close of play to be noted.

        (ii) Ten minutes to be deducted from this time, for the interval, to determine the playing time remaining.

        (iii) A calculation to be made of one over for every complete three minutes of the playing time remaining, plus one more over for any further part of three minutes remaining.

9. Conclusion of match

The match is concluded:

    (a) As soon as a result, as defined in sections 1, 2, 3 or 4 of Law 21 (The result), is reached.

    (b) As soon as both

        (i) the minimum number of overs for the last hour are completed, and

        (ii) the agreed time for close of play is reached

unless a result has been reached earlier.

    (c) If, without the match being concluded either as in (a) or in (b) above, the players leave the field, either for adverse conditions of ground, weather or light, or in exceptional circumstances, and no further play is possible thereafter.

10. Completion of last over of match

The over in progress at the close of play on the final day shall be completed unless either

    (i) a result has been reached, or

    (ii) the players have occasion to leave the field. In this case there shall be no resumption of play except in the circumstances of Law 21.9 (Mistakes in scoring), and the match shall be at an end.

11. Bowler unable to complete an over during last hour of match

If, for any reason, a bowler is unable to complete an over during the last hour, Law 22.8 (Bowler incapacitated or suspended during an over) shall apply.

LAW 17. PRACTICE ON THE FIELD

1. Practice on the field

    (a) There shall be no bowling or batting practice on the pitch, or on the area parallel and immediately adjacent to the pitch, at any time on any day of the match.

(b) There shall be no bowling or batting practice on any other part of the square on any day of the match, except before the start of play or after the close of play on that day. Practice before the start of play:

> (i) Must not continue later than 30 minutes before the scheduled time or any rescheduled time for play to start on that day.

> (ii) Shall not be allowed if the umpires consider that, in the prevailing conditions of ground and weather, it will be detrimental to the surface of the square.

(c) There shall be no practice on the field of play between the call of "Play" and the call of "Time", if the umpire considers that it could result in a waste of time. See Law 42.9 (Time-wasting by the fielding side).

(d) If a player contravenes (a) or (b) above he shall not be allowed to bowl until either at least one hour later than the contravention or until there has been at least 30 minutes of playing time since the contravention, whichever is sooner. If an over is in progress at the contravention he shall not be allowed to complete that over.

2. Trial run-up

No bowler shall have a trial run-up between the call of "Play" and the call of "Time" unless the umpire is satisfied that it will not cause any waste of time.

LAW 18.   SCORING RUNS

1. A run

The score shall be reckoned by runs. A run is scored:

> (a) So often as the batsmen, at any time while the ball is in play, have crossed and made good their ground from end to end.

> (b) When a boundary is scored. See Law 19 (Boundaries).

> (c) When penalty runs are awarded. See 6 below.

> (d) When "Lost ball" is called. See Law 20 (Lost ball).

2. Runs disallowed

Notwithstanding 1 above, or any other provisions elsewhere in the Laws, the scoring of runs or awarding of penalties will be subject to any disallowance of runs provided for within the Laws that may be applicable.

3. Short runs

> (a) A run is short if a batsman fails to make good his ground on turning for a further run.

> (b) Although a short run shortens the succeeding one, the latter if completed shall not be regarded as short. A striker taking stance in front of his popping crease may run from that point also without penalty.

4. Unintentional short runs

Except in the circumstances of 5 below:

> (a) If either batsman runs a short run, unless a boundary is scored the umpire concerned shall call and signal "Short run" as soon as the ball becomes dead and that run shall not be scored.

> (b) If, after either or both batsmen run short, a boundary is scored, the umpire concerned shall disregard the short running and shall not call or signal "Short run".

> (c) If both batsmen run short in one and the same run, this shall be regarded as only one short run.

> (d) If more than one run is short then, subject to (b) and (c) above, all runs so called shall not be scored.

If there has been more than one short run the umpire shall inform the scorers as to the number of runs scored.

5. Deliberate short runs

Notwithstanding 4 above, if either umpire considers that either or both batsmen deliberately runs short at his end, the following procedure shall be adopted:

(a) (i) The umpire concerned shall, when the ball is dead, warn the batsmen that the practice is unfair, indicate that this is a first and final warning and inform the other umpire of what has occurred. This warning shall continue to apply throughout the innings. The umpire shall so inform each incoming batsman.

(ii) The batsmen shall return to their original ends.

(iii) Whether a batsman is dismissed or not, the umpire at the bowler's end shall disallow all runs to the batting side from that delivery other than the penalty for a no-ball or wide, or penalties under Laws 42.5 (Deliberate distraction or obstruction of batsman) and 42.13 (Fielders damaging the pitch), if applicable.

(iv) The umpire at the bowler's end shall inform the scorers as to the number of runs scored.

(b) If there is any further instance of deliberate short running by any batsman in that innings, when the ball is dead the umpire concerned shall inform the other umpire of what has occurred and the procedure set out in (a)(ii) and (iii) above shall be repeated. Additionally, the umpire at the bowler's end shall:

(i) Award five penalty runs to the fielding side. See Law 42.17 (Penalty runs).

(ii) Inform the scorers as to the number of runs scored.

(iii) Inform the batsmen, the captain of the fielding side and, as soon as practicable, the captain of the batting side of the reason for this action.

(iv) Report the occurrence, with the other umpire, to the executive of the batting side and any governing body responsible for the match, who shall take such action as is considered appropriate against the captain and player or players concerned.

6. Runs scored for penalties

Runs shall be scored for penalties under 5 above and Laws 2.6 (Player returning without permission), 24 (No-ball), 25 (Wide ball), 41.2 (Fielding the ball), 41.3 (Protective helmets belonging to the fielding side) and 42 (Fair and unfair play).

7. Runs scored for boundaries

Runs shall be scored for boundary allowances under Law 19 (Boundaries).

8. Runs scored for lost ball

Runs shall be scored when "Lost ball" is called under Law 20 (Lost ball).

9. Batsman dismissed

When either batsman is dismissed:

(a) Any penalties to either side that may be applicable shall stand but no other runs shall be scored, except as stated in 10 below.

(b) 12(a) below will apply if the method of dismissal is caught, handled the ball or obstructing the field. 12(a) will also apply if a batsman is run out, except in the circumstances of Law 2.8 (Transgression of the Laws by a batsman who has a runner) where 12(b) below will apply.

(c) The not out batsman shall return to his original end except as stated in (b) above.

10. Runs scored when a batsman is dismissed

In addition to any penalties to either side that may be applicable, if a batsman is:

(a) Dismissed handled the ball, the batting side shall score the runs completed before the offence.

(b) Dismissed obstructing the field, the batting side shall score the runs completed before the offence.

If, however, the obstruction prevents a catch from being made, no runs other than penalties shall be scored.

(c) Dismissed run out, the batting side shall score the runs completed before the dismissal. If however, a striker with a runner is himself dismissed run out, no runs other than penalties shall be scored. See Law 2.8 (Transgression of the Laws by a batsman who has a runner).

11. Runs scored when ball becomes dead

(a) When the ball becomes dead on the fall of a wicket, runs shall be scored as laid down in 9 and 10 above.

(b) When the ball becomes dead for any reason other than the fall of a wicket, or is called dead by an umpire, unless there is specific provision otherwise in the Laws, the batting side shall be credited with:

    (i) All runs completed by the batsmen before the incident or call, and

    (ii) the run in progress if the batsmen have crossed at the instant of the incident or call. Note specifically, however, the provisions of Law 34.4(c) (Runs permitted from a ball lawfully struck more than once) and 42.5(b)(iii) (Deliberate distraction or obstruction of batsman), and

    (iii) any penalties that are applicable.

12. Batsman returning to wicket he has left

(a) If, while the ball is in play, the batsmen have crossed in running, neither shall return to the wicket he has left, except as in (b) below.

(b) The batsmen shall return to the wickets they originally left in the cases of, and only in the cases of:

    (i) A boundary

    (ii) Disallowance of runs for any reason.

    (iii) The dismissal of a batsman, except as in 9(b) above.

LAW 19.   BOUNDARIES

1. The boundary of the field of play

(a) Before the toss, the umpires shall agree the boundary of the field of play with both captains. The boundary shall if possible be marked along its whole length.

(b) The boundary shall be agreed so that no part of any sightscreen is within the field of play.

(c) An obstacle or person within the field of play shall not be regarded as a boundary unless so decided by the umpires before the toss. See Law 3.4(ii) (To inform captains and scorers).

2. Defining the boundary – boundary marking

(a) Wherever practicable the boundary shall be marked by means of a white line or a rope laid along the ground.

(b) If the boundary is marked by a white line:

    (i) The inside edge of the line shall be the boundary edge.

    (ii) A flag, post or board used merely to highlight the position of a line marked on the ground must be placed outside the boundary edge and is not itself to be regarded as defining or marking the boundary. Note, however, the provisions of (c) below.

(c) If a solid object is used to mark the boundary, it must have an edge or a line to constitute the boundary edge.

    (i) For a rope, which includes any similar object of curved cross section lying on the ground, the boundary edge will be the line formed by the innermost points of the rope along its length.

    (ii) For a fence, which includes any similar object in contact with the ground, but with a flat surface projecting above the ground, the boundary edge will be the base line of the fence.

(d) If the boundary edge is not defined as in (b) or (c) above, the umpires and captains must agree, before the toss, what line will be the boundary edge. Where there is no physical marker for a section of boundary, the boundary edge shall be the imaginary straight line joining the two nearest marked points of the boundary edge.

(e) If a solid object used to mark the boundary is disturbed for any reason during play, then if possible it shall be restored to its original position as soon as the ball is dead. If this is not possible, then:

  (i) If some part of the fence or other marker has come within the field of play, that portion is to be removed from the field of play as soon as the ball is dead.

  (ii) The line where the base of the fence or marker originally stood shall define the boundary edge.

3. Scoring a boundary

(a) A boundary shall be scored and signalled by the umpire at the bowler's end whenever, while the ball is in play, in his opinion:

  (i) The ball touches the boundary, or is grounded beyond the boundary.

  (ii) A fielder, with some part of his person in contact with the ball, touches the boundary or has some part of his person grounded beyond the boundary.

(b) The phrases "touches the boundary" and "touching the boundary" shall mean contact with either

  (i) the boundary edge as defined in 2 above, or

  (ii) any person or obstacle within the field of play which has been designated a boundary by the umpires before the toss.

(c) The phrase "grounded beyond the boundary" shall mean contact with either

  (i) any part of a line or a solid object marking the boundary, except its boundary edge, or

  (ii) the ground outside the boundary edge, or

  (iii) any object in contact with the ground outside the boundary edge.

4. Runs allowed for boundaries

(a) Before the toss, the umpires shall agree with both captains the runs to be allowed for boundaries. In deciding the allowances, the umpires and captains shall be guided by the prevailing custom of the ground.

(b) Unless agreed differently under (a) above, the allowances for boundaries shall be six runs if the ball having been struck by the bat pitches beyond the boundary, but otherwise four runs. These allowances shall still apply even though the ball has previously touched a fielder. See also (c) below.

(c) The ball shall be regarded as pitching beyond the boundary and six runs shall be scored if a fielder:

  (i) Has any part of his person touching the boundary or grounded beyond the boundary when he catches the ball.

  (ii) Catches the ball and subsequently touches the boundary or grounds some part of his person beyond the boundary while carrying the ball but before completing the catch. See Law 32 (Caught).

5. Runs scored

When a boundary is scored:

(a) The penalty for a no-ball or a wide, if applicable, shall stand together with any penalties under any of Laws 2.6 (Player returning without permission), 18.5(b) (Deliberate short runs) or Law 42 (Fair and unfair play) that apply before the boundary is scored.

(b) The batting side, except in the circumstances of 6 below, shall additionally be awarded whichever is the greater of:

  (i) The allowance for the boundary.

  (ii) The runs completed by the batsmen, together with the run in progress if they have crossed at the instant the boundary is scored. When these runs exceed the boundary allowance, they shall replace the boundary for the purposes of Law 18.12 (Batsman returning to wicket he has left).

6. Overthrow or wilful act of fielder

If the boundary results either from an overthrow or from the wilful act of a fielder the runs scored shall be:

(i) The penalty for a no-ball or a wide, if applicable, and any penalties under Laws 2.6 (Player returning without permission), 18.5(b) (Deliberate short runs) or Law 42 (Fair and unfair play) that are applicable before the boundary is scored, and

(ii) the allowance for the boundary, and

(iii) the runs completed by the batsmen, together with the run in progress if they have crossed at the instant of the throw or act.

Law 18.12(a) (Batsman returning to the wicket he has left) shall apply as from the instant of the throw or act.

LAW 20.   LOST BALL

1. Fielder to call "Lost ball"

If a ball in play cannot be found or recovered, any fielder may call "Lost ball". The ball shall then become dead. See Law 23.1 (Ball is dead). Law 18.12(a) (Batsman returning to wicket he has left) shall apply as from the instant of the call.

2. Ball to be replaced

The umpires shall replace the ball with one which has had wear comparable with that which the previous ball had received before it was lost or became irrecoverable. See Law 5.5 (Ball lost or becoming unfit for play).

3. Runs scored

(a) The penalty for a no-ball or a wide, if applicable, shall stand, together with any penalties under any of Laws 2.6 (Player returning without permission), 18.5(b) (Deliberate short runs) or Law 42 (Fair and unfair play) that are applicable before the call of "Lost ball".

(b) The batting side shall additionally be awarded either

(i) the runs completed by the batsmen, together with the run in progress if they have crossed at the instant of the call, or

(ii) six runs,

whichever is the greater.

4. How scored

If there is a one-run penalty for a no-ball or for a wide, it shall be scored as a no-ball extra or as a wide as appropriate. See Laws 24.13 (Runs resulting from a no-ball – how scored) and 25.6 (Runs resulting from a wide – how scored). If any other penalties have been awarded to either side, they shall be scored as penalty extras. See Law 42.17 (Penalty runs).

Runs to the batting side in 3(b) above shall be credited to the striker if the ball has been struck by the bat, but otherwise to the total of byes, leg-byes, no-balls or wides as the case may be.

LAW 21.   THE RESULT

1. A win – two-innings match

The side which has scored a total of runs in excess of that scored in the two completed innings of the opposing side shall win the match. Note also 6 below.

A forfeited innings is to count as a completed innings. See Law 14 (Declaration and forfeiture).

2. A win – one-innings match

The side which has scored in its one innings a total of runs in excess of that scored by the opposing side in its one completed innings shall win the match. Note also 6 below.

3. Umpires awarding a match

(a) A match shall be lost by a side which either

(i) concedes defeat, or

(ii) in the opinion of the umpires, refuses to play

and the umpires shall award the match to the other side.

(b) If an umpire considers that an action by any player or players might constitute a refusal by either side to play then the umpires together shall ascertain the cause of the action. If they then decide together that this action does constitute a refusal to play by one side, they shall so inform the captain of that side. If the captain persists in the action the umpires shall award the match in accordance with (a)(ii) above.

(c) If action as in (b) above takes place after play has started and does not constitute a refusal to play:

(i) Playing time lost shall be counted from the start of the action until play recommences, subject to Law 15.5 (Changing agreed times for intervals).

(ii) The time for close of play on that day shall be extended by this length of time, subject to Law 3.9 (Suspension of play for adverse conditions of ground, weather or light).

(iii) If applicable, no overs shall be deducted during the last hour of the match solely on account of this time.

4. A tie

The result of a match shall be a tie when the scores are equal at the conclusion of play, but only if the side batting last has completed its innings.

5. A draw

A match which is concluded, as defined in Law 16.9 (Conclusion of a match), without being determined in any of the ways stated in 1, 2, 3 or 4 above, shall count as a draw.

6. Winning hit or extras

(a) As soon as a result is reached, as defined in 1, 2, 3 or 4 above, the match is at an end. Nothing that happens thereafter, except as in Law 42.17(b), shall be regarded as part of it. Note also 9 below.

(b) The side batting last will have scored enough runs to win only if its total of runs is sufficient without including any runs completed before the dismissal of the striker by the completion of a catch or by the obstruction of a catch.

(c) If a boundary is scored before the batsmen have completed sufficient runs to win the match, then the whole of the boundary allowance shall be credited to the side's total and, in the case of a hit by the bat, to the striker's score.

7. Statement of result

If the side batting last wins the match without losing all its wickets, the result shall be stated as a win by the number of wickets still then to fall. If the side batting last has lost all its wickets but, as the result of an award of five penalty runs at the end of the match, has scored a total of runs in excess of the total scored by the opposing side, the result shall be stated as a win to that side by penalty runs. If the side fielding last wins the match, the result shall be stated as a win by runs.

If the match is decided by one side conceding defeat or refusing to play, the result shall be stated as "Match conceded" or "Match awarded" as the case may be.

8. Correctness of result

Any decision as to the correctness of the scores shall be the responsibility of the umpires. See Law 3.15 (Correctness of scores).

9. Mistakes in scoring

If, after the umpires and players have left the field in the belief that the match has been concluded, the umpires discover that a mistake in scoring has occurred which affects the result, then, subject to 10 below, they shall adopt the following procedure.

(a) If, when the players leave the field, the side batting last has not completed its innings, and either

(i) the number of overs to be bowled in the last hour has not been completed, or

(ii) the agreed finishing time has not been reached,

then unless one side concedes defeat the umpires shall order play to resume.

If conditions permit, play will then continue until the prescribed number of overs has been completed and the time remaining has elapsed, unless a result is reached earlier. The number of overs and/or the time remaining shall be taken as they were when the players left the field; no account shall be taken of the time between that moment and the resumption of play.

(b) If, when the players leave the field, the overs have been completed and time has been reached, or if the side batting last has completed its innings, the umpires shall immediately inform both captains of the necessary corrections to the scores and to the result.

10. Result not to be changed

Once the umpires have agreed with the scorers the correctness of the scores at the conclusion of the match – see Laws 3.15 (Correctness of scores) and 4.2 (Correctness of scores) – the result cannot thereafter be changed.

LAW 22.   THE OVER

1. Number of balls

The ball shall be bowled from each wicket alternately in overs of six balls.

2. Start of an over

An over has started when the bowler starts his run-up or, if he has no run-up, his delivery action for the first delivery of that over.

3. Call of "Over"

When six balls have been bowled other than those which are not to count in the over and as the ball becomes dead – see Law 23 (Dead ball) – the umpire shall call "Over" before leaving the wicket.

4. Balls not to count in the over

(a) A ball shall not count as one of the six balls of the over unless it is delivered, even though a batsman may be dismissed or some other incident occurs before the ball is delivered.

(b) A ball which is delivered by the bowler shall not count as one of the six balls of the over:

(i) If it is called dead, or is to be considered dead, before the striker has had an opportunity to play it. See Law 23 (Dead ball).

(ii) If it is a no-ball. See Law 24 (No-ball).

(iii) If it is a wide. See Law 25 (Wide ball).

(iv) If it is called dead in the circumstances of Law 23.3(b)(vi) (Umpire calling and signalling "Dead ball").

(v) When five penalty runs are awarded to the batting side under any of Laws 2.6 (Player returning without permission), 41.2 (Fielding the ball), 42.4 (Deliberate attempt to distract striker) or 42.5 (Deliberate distraction or obstruction of batsman).

5. Umpire miscounting

If an umpire miscounts the number of balls, the over as counted by the umpire shall stand.

6. Bowler changing ends

A bowler shall be allowed to change ends as often as desired, provided only that he does not bowl two overs, or parts thereof, consecutively in the same innings.

7. Finishing an over

(a) Other than at the end of an innings, a bowler shall finish an over in progress unless he is incapacitated, or he is suspended under any of Laws 17.1 (Practice on the field), 42.7 (Dangerous and unfair bowling – action by the umpire), 42.9 (Time-wasting by the fielding side), or 42.12 (Bowler running on the protected area after delivering the ball).

(b) If for any reason, other than the end of an innings, an over is left uncompleted at the start of an interval or interruption of play, it shall be completed on resumption of play.

8. Bowler incapacitated or suspended during an over

If for any reason a bowler is incapacitated while running up to bowl the first ball of an over, or is incapacitated or suspended during an over, the umpire shall call and signal "Dead ball". Another bowler shall complete the over from the same end, provided that he does not bowl two overs, or parts thereof, consecutively in one innings.

LAW 23.   DEAD BALL

1. Ball is dead

(a) The ball becomes dead when:

    (i) It is finally settled in the hands of the wicket-keeper or the bowler.

    (ii) A boundary is scored. See Law 19.3 (Scoring a boundary).

    (iii) A batsman is dismissed.

    (iv) Whether played or not it becomes trapped between the bat and person of a batsman or between items of his clothing or equipment.

    (v) Whether played or not it lodges in the clothing or equipment of a batsman or the clothing of an umpire.

    (vi) It lodges in a protective helmet worn by a member of the fielding side.

    (vii) There is a contravention of Law 41.2 (Fielding the ball) or Law 41.3 (Protective helmets belonging to the fielding side).

    (viii) This is an award of penalty runs under Law 2.6 (Player returning without permission).

    (ix) "Lost ball" is called. See Law 20 (Lost ball).

    (x) The umpire calls "Over" or "Time".

(b) The ball shall be considered to be dead when it is clear to the umpire at the bowler's end that the fielding side and both batsmen at the wicket have ceased to regard it as in play.

2. Ball finally settled

Whether the ball is finally settled or not is a matter for the umpire alone to decide.

3. Umpire calling and signalling "Dead ball"

(a) When the ball has become dead under 1 above, the bowler's end umpire may call "Dead ball", if it is necessary to inform the players.

(b) Either umpire shall call and signal "Dead ball" when:

    (i) He intervenes in a case of unfair play.

    (ii) A serious injury to a player or umpire occurs.

    (iii) He leaves his normal position for consultation.

    (iv) One or both bails fall from the striker's wicket before he has the opportunity of playing the ball.

(v) He is satisfied that for an adequate reason the striker is not ready for the delivery of the ball and, if the ball is delivered, makes no attempt to play it.

(vi) The striker is distracted by any noise or movement or in any other way while he is preparing to receive or receiving a delivery. This shall apply whether the source of the distraction is within the game or outside it. Note, however, the provisions of Law 42.4 (Deliberate attempt to distract the striker).

The ball shall not count as one of the over.

(vii) The bowler drops the ball accidentally before delivery.

(viii) The ball does not leave the bowler's hand for any reason other than an attempt to run out the non-striker before entering his delivery stride. See Law 42.15 (Bowler attempting to run out non-striker before delivery).

(ix) He is required to do so under any of the Laws.

4. Ball ceases to be dead

The ball ceases to be dead – that is, it comes into play – when the bowler starts his run-up or, if he has no run-up, his bowling action.

5. Action on call of "Dead ball"

(a) A ball is not to count as one of the over if it becomes dead or is to be considered dead before the striker has had an opportunity to play it.

(b) If the ball becomes dead or is to be considered dead after the striker has had an opportunity to play the ball, except in the circumstances of 3(b)(vi) above and Law 42.4 (Deliberate attempt to distract striker), no additional delivery shall be allowed unless "No-ball" or "Wide" has been called.

LAW 24.   NO-BALL

1. Mode of delivery

(a) The umpire shall ascertain whether the bowler intends to bowl right-handed or left-handed, and whether over or round the wicket, and shall so inform the striker.

It is unfair if the bowler fails to notify the umpire of a change in his mode of delivery. In this case the umpire shall call and signal "No-ball".

(b) Underarm bowling shall not be permitted except by special agreement before the match.

2. Fair delivery – the arm

For a delivery to be fair in respect of the arm the ball must not be thrown. See 3 below.

Although it is the primary responsibility of the striker's end umpire to ensure the fairness of a delivery in this respect, there is nothing in this Law to debar the bowler's end umpire from calling and signalling "No-ball" if he considers that the ball has been thrown.

(a) If, in the opinion of either umpire, the ball has been thrown, he shall:

(i) Call and signal "No-ball".

(ii) Caution the bowler, when the ball is dead. This caution shall apply throughout the innings.

(iii) Inform the other umpire, the batsmen at the wicket, the captain of the fielding side and, as soon as practicable, the captain of the batting side of what has occurred.

(b) If either umpire considers that after such caution, a further delivery by the same bowler in that innings is thrown, the umpire concerned shall repeat the procedure set out in (a) above, indicating to the bowler that this is a final warning. This warning shall also apply throughout the innings.

(c) If either umpire considers that a further delivery by the same bowler in that innings is thrown:

(i) The umpire concerned shall call and signal "No-ball". When the ball is dead he shall inform the other umpire, the batsmen at the wicket and, as soon as practicable, the captain of the batting side of what has occurred.

(ii) The umpire at the bowler's end shall direct the captain of the fielding side to take the bowler off forthwith. The over shall be completed by another bowler, who shall neither have bowled the previous over nor be allowed to bowl the next over. The bowler thus taken off shall not bowl again in that innings.

(iii) The umpires together shall report the occurrence as soon as possible to the executive of the fielding side and any governing body responsible for the match, who shall take such action as is considered appropriate against the captain and bowler concerned.

3. Definition of fair delivery – the arm

A ball is fairly delivered in respect of the arm if, once the bowler's arm has reached the level of the shoulder in the delivery swing, the elbow joint is not straightened partially or completely from that point until the ball has left the hand. This definition shall not debar a bowler from flexing or rotating the wrist in the delivery swing.

4. Bowler throwing towards striker's end before delivery

If the bowler throws the ball towards the striker's end before entering his delivery stride, either umpire shall instantly call and signal "No-ball". See Law 42.16 (Batsmen stealing a run). However, the procedure stated in 2 above of caution, informing, final warning, action against the bowler and reporting shall not apply.

5. Fair delivery – the feet

For a delivery to be fair in respect of the feet, in the delivery stride:

(i) The bowler's back foot must land within and not touching the return crease.

(ii) The bowler's front foot must land with some part of the foot, whether grounded or raised, behind the popping crease.

If the umpire at the bowler's end is not satisfied that both these conditions have been met, he shall call and signal "No-ball".

6. Ball bouncing more than twice or rolling along the ground

The umpire at the bowler's end shall call and signal "No-ball" if a ball which he considers to have been delivered, without having previously touched the bat or person of the striker, either

(i) bounces more than twice, or

(ii) rolls along the ground

before it reaches the popping crease.

7. Ball coming to rest in front of striker's wicket

If a ball delivered by the bowler comes to rest in front of the line of the striker's wicket, without having touched the bat or person of the striker, the umpire shall call and signal "No-ball" and immediately call and signal "Dead ball".

8. Call of "No-ball" for infringement of other Laws

In addition to the instances above, an umpire shall call and signal "No-ball" as required by the following Laws.

Law 40.3   – Position of wicket-keeper.
Law 41.5   – Limitation of on-side fielders.
Law 41.6   – Fielders not to encroach on the pitch.
Law 42.6   – Dangerous and unfair bowling.
Law 42.7   – Dangerous and unfair bowling – action by the umpire.
Law 42.8   – Deliberate bowling of high full-pitched balls.

9. Revoking a call of "No-ball"

An umpire shall revoke the call of "No-ball" if the ball does not leave the bowler's hand for any reason.

10. No-ball to over-ride wide

A call of "No-ball" shall over-ride the call of "Wide ball" at any time. See Law 25.1 (Judging a wide) and 25.3 (Call and signal of "Wide ball").

11. Ball not dead

The ball does not become dead on the call of "No-ball".

12. Penalty for a No-ball

A penalty of one run shall be awarded instantly on the call of "No-ball". Unless the call is revoked this penalty shall stand even if a batsman is dismissed. It shall be in addition to any other runs scored, any boundary allowance and any other penalties awarded.

13. Runs resulting from a no-ball – how scored

The one-run penalty for a no-ball shall be scored as a no-ball extra. If other penalty runs have been awarded to either side, these shall be scored as in Law 42.17 (Penalty runs). Any runs completed by the batsmen or a boundary allowance shall be credited to the striker if the ball has been struck by the bat; otherwise they also shall be scored as no-ball extras.

Apart from any award of a five-run penalty, all runs resulting from a no-ball, whether as no-ball extras or credited to the striker, shall be debited against the bowler.

14. No-ball not to count

A no-ball shall not count as one of the over. See Law 22.4 (Balls not to count in the over).

15. Out from a no-ball

When "No-ball" has been called, neither batsman shall be out under any of the Laws except Laws 33 (Handled the ball), 34 (Hit the ball twice), 37 (Obstructing the field) or 38 (Run out).

LAW 25. WIDE BALL

1. Judging a wide

(a) If a bowler bowls a ball, not being a no-ball, the umpire shall adjudge it a wide if, according to the definition in (b) below, in his opinion the ball passes wide of the striker where he is standing and would also have passed wide of him in a normal guard position.

(b) The ball will be considered as passing wide of the striker unless it is sufficiently within his reach for him to be able to hit it with his bat by means of a normal cricket stroke.

2. Delivery not a wide

The umpire shall not adjudge a delivery as being a wide:

(a) If the striker, by moving, either

  (i) causes the ball to pass wide of him, as defined in 1(b) above, or

  (ii) brings the ball sufficiently within his reach to be able to hit it with his bat by means of a normal cricket stroke.

(b) If the ball touches the striker's bat or person.

3. Call and signal of "Wide ball"

(a) If the umpire adjudges a delivery to be a wide he shall call and signal "Wide ball" as soon as the ball passes the striker's wicket. It shall, however, be considered to have been a wide from the instant of delivery, even though it cannot be called wide until it passes the striker's wicket.

(b) The umpire shall revoke the call of "Wide ball" if there is then any contact between the ball and the striker's bat or person.

(c) The umpire shall revoke the call of "Wide ball" if a delivery is called a "No-ball". See Law 24.10 (No-ball to over-ride wide).

4. Ball not dead

The ball does not become dead on the call of "Wide ball".

5. Penalty for a wide

A penalty of one run shall be awarded instantly on the call of "Wide ball". Unless the call is revoked (see 3 above), this penalty shall stand even if a batsman is dismissed, and shall be in addition to any other runs scored, any boundary – allowance and any other penalties awarded.

6. Runs resulting from a wide – how scored

All runs completed by the batsmen or a boundary allowance, together with the penalty for the wide, shall be scored as wide balls. Apart from any award of a five-run penalty, all runs resulting from a wide shall be debited against the bowler.

7. Wide not to count

A wide shall not count as one of the over. See Law 22.4 (Balls not to count in the over).

8. Out from a wide

When "Wide ball" has been called, neither batsman shall be out under any of the Laws except Laws 33 (Handled the ball), 35 (Hit wicket), 37 (Obstructing the field), 38 (Run out) or 39 (Stumped).

LAW 26.   BYE AND LEG-BYE

1. Byes

If the ball, not being a no-ball or a wide, passes the striker without touching his bat or person, any runs completed by the batsmen or a boundary allowance shall be credited as byes to the batting side.

2. Leg-byes

(a) If a ball delivered by the bowler first strikes the person of the striker, runs shall be scored only if the umpire is satisfied that the striker has either

   (i) attempted to play the ball with his bat, or

   (ii) tried to avoid being hit by the ball.

If the umpire is satisfied that either of these conditions has been met, and the ball makes no subsequent contact with the bat, runs completed by the batsmen or a boundary allowance shall be credited to the batting side as in (b). Note, however, the provisions of Laws 34.3 (Ball lawfully struck more than once) and 34.4 (Runs permitted from ball lawfully struck more than once).

(b) The runs in (a) above shall

   (i) if the delivery is not a no-ball, be scored as leg-byes.

   (ii) if no-ball has been called, be scored together with the penalty for the no-ball as no-ball extras.

3. Leg-byes not to be awarded

If in the circumstances of 2(a) above the umpire considers that neither of the conditions (i) and (ii) therein has been met, then leg-byes will not be awarded. The batting side shall not be credited with any runs from that delivery apart from the one run penalty for a no-ball if applicable. Moreover, no other penalties shall be awarded to the batting side when the ball is dead. See Law 42.17 (Penalty runs). The following procedure shall be adopted.

(a) If no run is attempted but the ball reaches the boundary, the umpire shall call and signal "Dead ball", and disallow the boundary.

(b) If runs are attempted and if:

   (i) Neither batsman is dismissed and the ball does not become dead for any other reason, the umpire shall call and signal "Dead ball" as soon as one run is completed or the ball reaches the boundary. The batsmen shall return to their original ends. The run or boundary shall be disallowed.

(ii) Before one run is completed or the ball reaches the boundary, a batsman is dismissed, or the ball becomes dead for any other reason, all the provisions of the Laws will apply, except that no runs and no penalties shall be credited to the batting side, other than the penalty for a no-ball if applicable.

LAW 27. APPEALS

1. Umpire not to give batsman out without an appeal

Neither umpire shall give a batsman out, even though he may be out under the Laws, unless appealed to by the fielding side. This shall not debar a batsman who is out under any of the Laws from leaving his wicket without an appeal having been made. Note, however, the provisions of 7 below.

2. Batsman dismissed

A batsman is dismissed if either

(a) he is given out by an umpire, on appeal, or

(b) he is out under any of the Laws and leaves his wicket as in 1 above.

3. Timing of appeals

For an appeal to be valid it must be made before the bowler begins his run-up or, if he has no run-up, his bowling action to deliver the next ball, and before "Time" has been called.

The call of "Over" does not invalidate an appeal made prior to the start of the following over provided "Time" has not been called. See Laws 16.2 (Call of "Time") and 22.2 (Start of an over).

4. Appeal "How's that?"

An appeal "How's that?" covers all ways of being out.

5. Answering appeals

The umpire at the bowler's end shall answer all appeals except those arising out of any of Laws 35 (Hit wicket), 39 (Stumped) or 38 (Run out) when this occurs at the striker's wicket. A decision "Not out" by one umpire shall not prevent the other umpire from giving a decision, provided that each is considering only matters within his jurisdiction.

When a batsman has been given not out, either umpire may, within his jurisdiction, answer a further appeal provided that it is made in accordance with 3 above.

6. Consultation by umpires

Each umpire shall answer appeals on matters within his own jurisdiction. If an umpire is doubtful about any point that the other umpire may have been in a better position to see, he shall consult the latter on this point of fact and shall then give his decision. If, after consultation, there is still doubt remaining the decision shall be "Not out".

7. Batsman leaving his wicket under a misapprehension

An umpire shall intervene if satisfied that a batsman, not having been given out, has left his wicket under a misapprehension that he is out. The umpire intervening shall call and signal "Dead ball" to prevent any further action by the fielding side and shall recall the batsman.

8. Withdrawal of an appeal

The captain of the fielding side may withdraw an appeal only with the consent of the umpire within whose jurisdiction the appeal falls and before the outgoing batsman has left the field of play. If such consent is given the umpire concerned shall, if applicable, revoke his decision and recall the batsman.

9. Umpire's decision

An umpire may alter his decision provided that such alteration is made promptly. This apart, the umpire's decision, once made, is final.

LAW 28.   THE WICKET IS DOWN

1. Wicket put down

(a) The wicket is put down if a bail is completely removed from the top of the stumps, or a stump is struck out of the ground by:

   (i) The ball.

   (ii) The striker's bat, whether he is holding it or has let go of it.

   (iii) The striker's person or by any part of his clothing or equipment becoming detached from his person.

   (iv) A fielder, with his hand or arm, provided that the ball is held in the hand or hands so used, or in the hand of the arm so used.
   The wicket is also put down if a fielder pulls a stump out of the ground in the same manner.

(b) The disturbance of a bail, whether temporary or not, shall not constitute its complete removal from the top of the stumps, but if a bail in falling lodges between two of the stumps this shall be regarded as complete removal.

2. One bail off

If one bail is off, it shall be sufficient for the purpose of putting the wicket down to remove the remaining bail, or to strike or pull any of the three stumps out of the ground, in any of the ways stated in 1 above.

3. Remaking the wicket

If the wicket is broken or put down while the ball is in play, the umpire shall not remake the wicket until the ball is dead. See Law 23 (Dead ball). Any fielder, however, may:

   (i) Replace a bail or bails on top of the stumps.

   (ii) Put back one or more stumps into the ground where the wicket originally stood.

4. Dispensing with bails

If the umpires have agreed to dispense with bails, in accordance with Law 8.5 (Dispensing with bails), the decision as to whether the wicket has been put down is one for the umpire concerned to decide.

(a) After a decision to play without bails, the wicket has been put down if the umpire concerned is satisfied that the wicket has been struck by the ball, by the striker's bat, person, or items of his clothing or equipment separated from his person as described in 1(a)(ii) or 1(a)(iii) above, or by a fielder with the hand holding the ball or with the arm of the hand holding the ball.

(b) If the wicket has already been broken or put down, (a) above shall apply to any stump or stumps still in the ground. Any fielder may replace a stump or stumps, in accordance with 3 above, in order to have an opportunity of putting the wicket down.

LAW 29.   BATSMAN OUT OF HIS GROUND

1. When out of his ground

A batsman shall be considered to be out of his ground unless his bat or some part of his person is grounded behind the popping crease at that end.

2. Which is a batsman's ground?

(a) If only one batsman is within a ground:

   (i) It is his ground.

   (ii) It remains his ground even if he is later joined there by the other batsman.

(b) If both batsmen are in the same ground and one of them subsequently leaves it, (a)(i) above applies.

(c) If there is no batsman in either ground, then each ground belongs to whichever of the batsmen is nearer to it, or, if the batsmen are level, to whichever was nearer to it immediately prior to their drawing level.

(d) If a ground belongs to one batsman, then, unless there is a striker with a runner, the other ground belongs to the other batsman irrespective of his position.

(e) When a batsman with a runner is striker, his ground is always that at the wicket-keeper's end. However, (a), (b), (c) and (d) above will still apply, but only to the runner and the non-striker, so that that ground will also belong to either the non-striker or the runner, as the case may be.

3. Position of non-striker

The non-striker, when standing at the bowler's end, should be positioned on the opposite side of the wicket to that from which the ball is being delivered, unless a request to do otherwise is granted by the umpire.

LAW 30. BOWLED

1. Out Bowled

(a) The striker is out *Bowled* if his wicket is put down by a ball delivered by the bowler, not being a no-ball, even if it first touches his bat or person.

(b) Notwithstanding (a) above he shall not be out bowled if before striking the wicket the ball has been in contact with any other player or with an umpire. He will, however, be subject to Laws 33 (Handled the ball), 37 (Obstructing the field), 38 (Run out) and 39 (Stumped).

2. Bowled to take precedence

The striker is out bowled if his wicket is put down as in 1 above, even though a decision against him for any other method of dismissal would be justified.

LAW 31. TIMED OUT

1. Out Timed out

(a) Unless "Time" has been called, the incoming batsman must be in position to take guard or for his partner to be ready to receive the next ball within three minutes of the fall of the previous wicket. If this requirement is not met, the incoming batsman will be out, *Timed out*.

(b) In the event of protracted delay in which no batsman comes to the wicket, the umpires shall adopt the procedure of Law 21.3 (Umpires awarding a match). For the purposes of that Law the start of the action shall be taken as the expiry of the three minutes referred to above.

2. Bowler does not get credit

The bowler does not get credit for the wicket.

LAW 32. CAUGHT

1. Out Caught

The striker is out *Caught* if a ball delivered by the bowler, not being a no-ball, touches his bat without having previously been in contact with any member of the fielding side and is subsequently held by a fielder as a fair catch before it touches the ground.

2. Caught to take precedence

If the criteria of 1 above are met and the striker is not out bowled, then he is out caught even though a decision against either batsman for another method of dismissal would be justified. Runs completed by the batsmen before the completion of the catch will not be scored. Note also Laws 21.6 (Winning hit or extras) and 42.17(b) (Penalty runs).

3. A fair catch

A catch shall be considered to have been fairly made if:

(a) Throughout the act of making the catch:

(i) Any fielder in contact with the ball is within the field of play. See 4 below.

(ii) The ball is at no time in contact with any object grounded beyond the boundary.

The act of making the catch shall start from the time when a fielder first handles the ball and shall end when a fielder obtains complete control both over the ball and over his own movement.

(b) The ball is hugged to the body of the catcher or accidentally lodges in his clothing or, in the case of the wicket-keeper, in his pads. However, it is not a fair catch if the ball lodges in a protective helmet worn by a fielder. See Law 23 (Dead ball).

(c) The ball does not touch the ground, even though the hand holding it does so in effecting the catch.

(d) A fielder catches the ball after it has been lawfully struck more than once by the striker, but only if the ball has not touched the ground since first being struck.

(e) A fielder catches the ball after it has touched an umpire, another fielder or the other batsman. However, it is not a fair catch if the ball has touched a protective helmet worn by a fielder, although the ball remains in play.

(f) A fielder catches the ball in the air after it has crossed the boundary provided that:

(i) He has no part of his person touching, or grounded beyond, the boundary at any time when he is in contact with the ball.

(ii) The ball has not been grounded beyond the boundary.

See Law 19.3 (Scoring a boundary).

(g) The ball is caught off an obstruction within the boundary, provided it has not previously been decided to regard the obstruction as a boundary.

4. Fielder within the field of play

(a) A fielder is not within the field of play if he touches the boundary or has any part of his person grounded beyond the boundary. See Law 19.3 (Scoring a boundary).

(b) Six runs shall be scored if a fielder:

(i) Has any part of his person touching, or grounded beyond, the boundary when he catches the ball.

(ii) Catches the ball and subsequently touches the boundary or grounds some part of his person over the boundary while carrying the ball but before completing the catch.

See Laws 19.3 (Scoring a boundary) and 19.4 (Runs allowed for boundaries).

5. No runs to be scored

If the striker is dismissed caught, runs from that delivery completed by the batsmen before the completion of the catch shall not be scored, but any penalties awarded to either side when the ball is dead, if applicable, will stand. Law 18.12(a) (Batsman returning to wicket he has left) shall apply from the instant of the catch.

LAW 33.   HANDLED THE BALL

1. Out Handled the ball

Either batsman is out *Handled the ball* if he wilfully touches the ball while in play with a hand or hands not holding the bat unless he does so with the consent of the opposing side.

2. Not out Handled the ball

Notwithstanding 1 above, a batsman will not be out under this Law if:

(i) He handles the ball in order to avoid injury.

(ii) He uses his hand or hands to return the ball to any member of the fielding side without the consent of that side. Note, however, the provisions of Law 37.4 (Returning the ball to a member of the fielding side).

3. Runs scored

If either batsman is dismissed under this Law, any runs completed before the offence, together with any penalty extras and the penalty for a no-ball or wide, if applicable, shall be scored. See Laws 18.10 (Runs scored when a batsman is dismissed) and 42.17 (Penalty runs).

4. Bowler does not get credit

The bowler does not get credit for the wicket.

LAW 34.   HIT THE BALL TWICE

1. Out Hit the ball twice

(a) The striker is out *Hit the ball twice* if, while the ball is in play and it strikes any part of his person or is struck by his bat and, before the ball has been touched by a fielder, he wilfully strikes it again with his bat or person, other than a hand not holding the bat, except for the sole purpose of guarding his wicket. See 3 below and Laws 33 (Handled the ball) and 37 (Obstructing the field).

(b) For the purpose of this Law, "struck" or "strike" shall include contact with the person of the striker.

2. Not out Hit the ball twice

Notwithstanding 1(a) above, the striker will not be out under this Law if:

(i) He makes a second or subsequent stroke in order to return the ball to any member of the fielding side. Note, however, the provisions of Law 37.4 (Returning the ball to a member of the fielding side).

(ii) He wilfully strikes the ball after it has touched a fielder. Note, however, the provisions of Law 37.1 (Out obstructing the field).

3. Ball lawfully struck more than once

Solely in order to guard his wicket and before the ball has been touched by a fielder, the striker may lawfully strike the ball more than once with his bat or with any part of his person other than a hand not holding the bat.

Notwithstanding this provision, the striker may not prevent the ball from being caught by making more than one stroke in defence of his wicket. See Law 37.3 (Obstructing a ball from being caught).

4. Runs permitted from ball lawfully struck more than once

When the ball is lawfully struck more than once, as permitted in 3 above, only the first strike is to be considered in determining whether runs are to be allowed and how they are to be scored.

(a) If on the first strike the umpire is satisfied that either

(i) the ball first struck the bat, or

(ii) the striker attempted to play the ball with his bat, or

(iii) the striker tried to avoid being hit by the ball,

then any penalties to the batting side that are applicable shall be allowed.

(b) If the conditions in (a) above are met then, if they result from overthrows, and only if they result from overthrows, runs completed by the batsmen or a boundary will be allowed in addition to any penalties that are applicable. They shall be credited to the striker if the first strike was with the bat. If the first strike was on the person of the striker they shall be scored as leg-byes or no-ball extras, as appropriate. See Law 26.2 (Leg-byes).

(c) If the conditions of (a) above are met and there is no overthrow until after the batsmen have started to run, but before one run is completed:

    (i) Only subsequent completed runs or a boundary shall be allowed. The first run shall count as a completed run for this purpose only if the batsmen have not crossed at the instant of the throw.

    (ii) If in these circumstances the ball goes to the boundary from the throw then, notwithstanding the provisions of Law 19.6 (Overthrow or wilful act of fielder), only the boundary allowance shall be scored.

    (iii) If the ball goes to the boundary as the result of a further overthrow, then runs completed by the batsmen after the first throw and before this final throw shall be added to the boundary allowance. The run in progress at the first throw will count only if they have not crossed at that moment; the run in progress at the final throw shall count only if they have crossed at that moment. Law 18.12 (Batsman returning to wicket he has left) shall apply as from the moment of the final throw.

(d) If, in the opinion of the umpire, none of the conditions in (a) above has been met then, whether there is an overthrow or not, the batting side shall not be credited with any runs from that delivery apart from the penalty for a no-ball if applicable. Moreover, no other penalties shall be awarded to the batting side when the ball is dead. See Law 42.17 (Penalty runs).

5. Ball lawfully struck more than once – action by the umpire

If no runs are to be allowed, either in the circumstances of 4(d) above, or because there has been no overthrow and:

(a) If no run is attempted but the ball reaches the boundary, the umpire shall call and signal "Dead ball" and disallow the boundary.

(b) If the batsmen run and:

    (i) Neither batsman is dismissed and the ball does not become dead for any other reason, the umpire shall call and signal "Dead ball" as soon as one run is completed or the ball reaches the boundary. The batsmen shall return to their original ends. The run or boundary shall be disallowed.

    (ii) A batsman is dismissed, or if for any other reason the ball becomes dead before one run is completed or the ball reaches the boundary, all the provisions of the Laws will apply except that the award of penalties to the batting side shall be as laid down in 4(a) or 4(d) above as appropriate.

6. Bowler does not get credit

The bowler does not get credit for the wicket.

LAW 35.   HIT WICKET

1. Out Hit wicket

(a) The striker is out _Hit wicket_ if, after the bowler has entered his delivery stride and while the ball is in play, his wicket is put down either by the striker's bat or person as described in Law 28.1(a)(ii) and (iii) (Wicket put down) either

    (i) in the course of any action taken by him in preparing to receive or in receiving a delivery, or

    (ii) in setting off for his first run immediately after playing, or playing at, the ball, or

    (iii) if he makes no attempt to play the ball, in setting off for his first run, provided that in the opinion of the umpire this is immediately after he has had the opportunity of playing the ball, or

    (iv) in lawfully making a second or further stroke for the purpose of guarding his wicket within the provisions of Law 34.3 (Ball lawfully struck more than once).

(b) If the striker puts his wicket down in any of the ways described in Law 28.1(a)(ii) and (iii) (Wicket put down) before the bowler has entered his delivery stride, either umpire shall call and signal "Dead ball".

2. Not out Hit wicket

Notwithstanding 1 above, the batsman is not out under this Law should his wicket be put down in any of the ways referred to in 1 above if:

(a) It occurs after he has completed any action in receiving the delivery, other than as in 1(a)(ii), (iii) or (iv) above.

(b) It occurs when he is in the act of running, other than in setting off immediately for his first run.

(c) It occurs when he is trying to avoid being run out or stumped.

(d) It occurs while he is trying to avoid a throw-in at any time.

(e) The bowler, after entering his delivery stride, does not deliver the ball. In this case either umpire shall immediately call and signal "Dead ball". See Law 23.3 (Umpire calling and signalling "Dead ball").

(f) The delivery is a no-ball.

LAW 36. LEG BEFORE WICKET

1. Out LBW

The striker is out *LBW* in the circumstances set out below.

(a) The bowler delivers a ball, not being a no-ball, and

(b) the ball, if it is not intercepted full pitch, pitches in line between wicket and wicket or on the off side of the striker's wicket, and

(c) the ball not having previously touched his bat, the striker intercepts the ball, either full pitch or after pitching, with any part of his person, and

(d) the point of impact, even if above the level of the bails, either

   (i) is between wicket and wicket, or

   (ii) is either between wicket and wicket or outside the line of the off stump, if the striker has made no genuine attempt to play the ball with his bat, and

(e) but for the interception, the ball would have hit the wicket.

2. Interception of the ball

(a) In assessing points (c), (d) and (e) in 1 above, only the first interception is to be considered.

(b) In assessing point (e) in 1 above, it is to be assumed that the path of the ball before interception would have continued after interception, irrespective of whether the ball might have pitched subsequently or not.

3. Off side of wicket

The off side of the striker's wicket shall be determined by the striker's stance at the moment the ball comes into play for that delivery.

LAW 37. OBSTRUCTING THE FIELD

1. Out Obstructing the field

Either batsman is out *Obstructing the field* if he wilfully obstructs or distracts the opposing side by word or action. It shall be regarded as obstruction if either batsman wilfully, and without the consent of the fielding side, strikes the ball with his bat or person, other than a hand not holding the bat, after the ball has touched a fielder. See 4 below.

2. Accidental obstruction

It is for either umpire to decide whether any obstruction or distraction is wilful or not. He shall consult the other umpire if he has any doubt.

3. Obstructing a ball from being caught

The striker is out should wilful obstruction or distraction by either batsman prevent a catch being made.

This shall apply even though the striker causes the obstruction in lawfully guarding his wicket under the provisions of Law 34.3 (Ball lawfully struck more than once).

4. Returning the ball to a member of the fielding side

Either batsman is out under this Law if, without the consent of the fielding side and while the ball is in play, he uses his bat or person to return the ball to any member of that side.

5. Runs scored

If a batsman is dismissed under this Law, runs completed by the batsmen before the offence shall be scored, together with the penalty for a no-ball or a wide, if applicable. Other penalties that may be awarded to either side when the ball is dead shall also stand. See Law 42.17(b) (Penalty runs).

If, however, the obstruction prevents a catch from being made, runs completed by the batsmen before the offence shall not be scored, but other penalties that may be awarded to either side when the ball is dead shall stand. See Law 42.17(b) (Penalty runs).

6. Bowler does not get credit

The bowler does not get credit for the wicket.

LAW 38.   RUN OUT

1. Out Run out

(a) Either batsman is out *Run out*, except as in 2 below, if at any time while the ball is in play

   (i) he is out of his ground and

   (ii) his wicket is fairly put down by the opposing side.

(b) (a) above shall apply even though "No-ball" has been called and whether or not a run is being attempted, except in the circumstances of Law 39.3(b) (Not out Stumped).

2. Batsman not Run out

Notwithstanding 1 above, a batsman is not out run out if:

(a) He has been within his ground and has subsequently left it to avoid injury, when the wicket is put down.

(b) The ball has not subsequently been touched again by a fielder, after the bowler has entered his delivery stride, before the wicket is put down.

(c) The ball, having been played by the striker, or having come off his person, directly strikes a helmet worn by a fielder and without further contact with him or any other fielder rebounds directly on to the wicket. However, the ball remains in play and either batsman may be run out in the circumstances of 1 above if a wicket is subsequently put down.

(d) He is out stumped. See Law 39.1(b) (Out Stumped).

(e) He is out of his ground, not attempting a run and his wicket is fairly put down by the wicket-keeper without the intervention of another member of the fielding side, if "No-ball" has been called. See Law 39.3(b) (Not out Stumped).

3. Which batsman is out

The batsman out in the circumstances of 1 above is the one whose ground is at the end where the wicket is put down. See Laws 2.8 (Transgression of the Laws by a batsman who has a runner) and 29.2 (Which is a batsman's ground).

4. Runs scored

If a batsman is dismissed run out, the batting side shall score the runs completed before the dismissal together with the penalty for a no-ball or wide, if applicable. Other penalties to either side that may be awarded when the ball is dead shall also stand. See Law 42.17 (Penalty runs).

If, however, a striker with a runner is himself dismissed run out, runs completed by the runner and the other batsman before the dismissal shall not be scored. The penalty for a no-ball or a wide and any other penalties to either side that may be awarded when the ball is dead shall stand. See Laws 2.8 (Transgression of the Laws by a batsman who has a runner) and 42.17(b) (Penalty runs).

5. Bowler does not get credit

The bowler does not get credit for the wicket.

LAW 39.   STUMPED

1. Out Stumped

(a) The striker is out *Stumped* if

  (i) he is out of his ground, and

  (ii) he is receiving a ball which is not a no-ball, and

  (iii) he is not attempting a run, and

  (iv) his wicket is fairly put down by the wicket-keeper without the intervention of another member of the fielding side. Note Law 40.3 (Position of wicket-keeper).

(b) The striker is out stumped if all the conditions of (a) above are satisfied, even though a decision of run out would be justified.

2. Ball rebounding from wicket-keeper's person

(a) If the wicket is put down by the ball, it shall be regarded as having been put down by the wicket-keeper, if the ball

  (i) rebounds on to the stumps from any part of his person, other than a protective helmet, or

  (ii) has been kicked or thrown on to the stumps by the wicket-keeper.

(b) If the ball touches a helmet worn by the wicket-keeper, the ball is still in play but the striker shall not be out stumped. He will, however, be liable to be run out in these circumstances if there is subsequent contact between the ball and any member of the fielding side. Note, however, 3 below.

3. Not out Stumped

(a) If the striker is not out stumped, he is liable to be out run out if the conditions of Law 38 (Run out) apply, except as set out in (b) below.

(b) The striker shall not be out run out if he is out of his ground, not attempting a run, and his wicket is fairly put down by the wicket-keeper without the intervention of another member of the fielding side, if "No-ball" has been called.

LAW 40.   THE WICKET-KEEPER

1. Protective equipment

The wicket-keeper is the only member of the fielding side permitted to wear gloves and external leg guards. If he does so, these are to be regarded as part of his person for the purposes of Law 41.2 (Fielding the ball). If by his actions and positioning it is apparent to the umpires that he will not be able to discharge his duties as a wicket-keeper, he shall forfeit this right and also the right to be recognised as a wicket-keeper for the purposes of Laws 32.3 (A fair catch), 39 (Stumped), 41.1 (Protective equipment), 41.5 (Limitation of on-side fielders) and 41.6 (Fielders not to encroach on the pitch).

2. Gloves

If, as permitted under 1 above, the wicket-keeper wears gloves, they shall have no webbing between fingers except joining index finger and thumb, where webbing may be inserted as a means of support. If used, the webbing shall be

  (a) a single piece of non-stretch material which, although it may have facing material attached, shall have no reinforcement or tucks.

  (b) such that the top edge of the webbing.

  (i) does not protrude beyond the straight line joining the top of the index finger to the top of the thumb.

  (ii) is taut when a hand wearing the glove has the thumb fully extended.

3. Position of wicket-keeper

The wicket-keeper shall remain wholly behind the wicket at the striker's end from the moment the ball comes into play until

  (a) a ball delivered by the bowler either

  (i) touches the bat or person of the striker, or

  (ii) passes the wicket at the striker's end, or

  (b) the striker attempts a run.

In the event of the wicket-keeper contravening this Law, the umpire at the striker's end shall call and signal "No-ball" as soon as possible after the delivery of the ball.

4. Movement by wicket-keeper

It is unfair if the wicket-keeper standing back makes a significant movement towards the wicket after the ball comes into play and before it reaches the striker. In the event of such unfair movement by the wicket-keeper, either umpire shall call and signal "Dead ball". It will not be considered a significant movement if the wicket-keeper moves a few paces forward for a slower delivery.

5. Restriction on actions of wicket-keeper

If in the opinion of either umpire the wicket-keeper interferes with the striker's right to play the ball and to guard his wicket, Law 23.3(b)(vi) (Umpire calling and signalling "Dead Ball") shall apply. If, however, the umpire concerned considers that the interference by the wicket-keeper was wilful, then Law 42.4 (Deliberate attempt to distract striker) shall apply.

6. Interference with wicket-keeper by striker

If, in playing at the ball or in the legitimate defence of his wicket, the striker interferes with the wicket-keeper, he shall not be out, except as provided for in Law 37.3 (Obstructing a ball from being caught).

LAW 41.   THE FIELDER

1. Protective equipment

No member of the fielding side other than the wicket-keeper shall be permitted to wear gloves or external leg guards. In addition, protection for the hand or fingers may be worn only with the consent of the umpires.

2. Fielding the ball

A fielder may field the ball with any part of his person but if, while the ball is in play, he wilfully fields it otherwise:

(a) The ball shall become dead and five penalty runs shall be awarded to the batting side. See Law 42.17 (Penalty runs). The ball shall not count as one of the over.

(b) The umpire shall inform the other umpire, the captain of the fielding side, the batsmen and, as soon as practicable, the captain of the batting side of what has occurred.

(c) The umpires together shall report the occurrence as soon as possible to the executive of the fielding side and any governing body responsible for the match who shall take such action as is considered appropriate against the captain and player concerned.

3. Protective helmets belonging to the fielding side

Protective helmets, when not in use by fielders, shall only be placed, if above the surface, on the ground behind the wicket-keeper and in line with both sets of stumps. If a helmet belonging to the fielding side is on the ground within the field of play, and the ball while in play strikes it, the ball shall become dead. Five penalty runs shall then be awarded to the batting side. See Laws 18.11 (Runs scored when ball becomes dead) and 42.17 (Penalty runs).

4. Penalty runs not to be awarded

Notwithstanding 2 and 3 above, if from the delivery by the bowler the ball first struck the person of the striker and if, in the opinion of the umpire, the striker neither

    (i) attempted to play the ball with his bat, nor

    (ii) tried to avoid being hit by the ball,

then no award of five penalty runs shall be made and no other runs or penalties shall be credited to the batting side except the penalty for a no-ball if applicable. See Law 26.3 (Leg byes not to be awarded).

5. Limitation of on-side fielders

At the instant of the bowler's delivery there shall not be more than two fielders, other than the wicket-keeper, behind the popping crease on the on side. A fielder will be considered to be behind the popping crease unless the whole of his person, whether grounded or in the air, is in front of this line.

In the event of infringement of this Law by the fielding side the umpire at the striker's end shall call and signal "No-ball".

6. Fielders not to encroach on the pitch

While the ball is in play and until the ball has made contact with the bat or person of the striker, or has passed the striker's bat, no fielder, other than the bowler, may have any part of his person grounded on or extended over the pitch.

In the event of infringement of this Law by any fielder other than the wicket-keeper, the umpire at the bowler's end shall call and signal "No-ball" as soon as possible after the delivery of the ball. Note, however, Law 40.3 (Position of wicket-keeper).

7. Movement by fielders

Any significant movement by any fielder after the ball comes into play and before the ball reaches the striker is unfair. In the event of such unfair movement, either umpire shall call and signal "Dead ball". Note also the provisions of Law 42.4 (Deliberate attempt to distract striker).

8. Definition of significant movement

    (a) For close fielders anything other than minor adjustments to stance or position in relation to the striker is significant.

    (b) In the outfield, fielders are permitted to move in towards the striker or striker's wicket, provided that 5 above is not contravened. Anything other than slight movement off line or away from the striker is to be considered significant.

    (c) For restrictions on movement by the wicket-keeper see Law 40.4 (Movement by wicket-keeper).

LAW 42. FAIR AND UNFAIR PLAY

1. Fair and unfair play – responsibility of captains

The responsibility lies with the captains for ensuring that play is conducted within the spirit and traditions of the game, as described in The Preamble – The Spirit of Cricket, as well as within the Laws.

2. Fair and unfair play – responsibility of umpires

The umpires shall be sole judges of fair and unfair play. If either umpire considers an action, not covered by the Laws, to be unfair, he shall intervene without appeal and, if the ball is in play, shall call and signal "Dead ball" and implement the procedure as set out in 18 below. Otherwise the umpires shall not interfere with the progress of play, except as required to do so by the Laws.

3. The match ball – changing its condition

(a) Any fielder may:

(i) Polish the ball provided that no artificial substance is used and that such polishing wastes no time.

(ii) Remove mud from the ball under the supervision of the umpire.

(iii) Dry a wet ball on a towel.

(b) It is unfair for anyone to rub the ball on the ground for any reason, interfere with any of the seams or the surface of the ball, use any implement, or take any other action whatsoever which is likely to alter the condition of the ball, except as permitted in (a) above.

(c) The umpires shall make frequent and irregular inspections of the ball.

(d) In the event of any fielder changing the condition of the ball unfairly, as set out in (b) above, the umpires after consultation shall:

(i) Change the ball forthwith. It shall be for the umpires to decide on the replacement ball, which shall, in their opinion, have had wear comparable with that which the previous ball had received immediately prior to the contravention.

(ii) Inform the batsmen that the ball has been changed.

(iii) Award five penalty runs to the batting side. See 17 below.

(iv) Inform the captain of the fielding side that the reason for the action was the unfair interference with the ball.

(v) Inform the captain of the batting side as soon as practicable of what has occurred.

(vi) Report the occurrence as soon as possible to the executive of the fielding side and any governing body responsible for the match, who shall take such action as is considered appropriate against the captain and team concerned.

(e) If there is any further instance of unfairly changing the condition of the ball in that innings, the umpires after consultation shall:

(i) Repeat the procedure in (d)(i), (ii) and (iii) above.

(ii) Inform the captain of the fielding side of the reason for the action taken and direct him to take off forthwith the bowler who delivered the immediately preceding ball. The bowler thus taken off shall not be allowed to bowl again in that innings.

(iii) Inform the captain of the batting side as soon as practicable of what has occurred.

(iv) Report the occurrence as soon as possible to the executive of the fielding side and any governing body responsible for the match, who shall take such action as is considered appropriate against the captain and team concerned.

4. Deliberate attempt to distract striker

It is unfair for any member of the fielding side deliberately to attempt to distract the striker while he is preparing to receive or receiving a delivery.

(a) If either umpire considers that any action by a member of the fielding side is such an attempt, at the first instance he shall:

(i) Immediately call and signal "Dead ball".

(ii) Warn the captain of the fielding side that the action is unfair and indicate that this is a first and final warning.

(iii) Inform the other umpire and the batsmen of what has occurred.

Neither batsman shall be dismissed from that delivery and the ball shall not count as one of the over.

(b) If there is any further such deliberate attempt in that innings, by any member of the fielding side, the procedures, other than warning, as set out in (a) above shall apply. Additionally, the umpire at the bowler's end shall:

(i) Award five penalty runs to the batting side. See 17 below.

(ii) Inform the captain of the fielding side of the reason for this action and, as soon as practicable, inform the captain of the batting side.

(iii) Report the occurrence, together with the other umpire, as soon as possible to the executive of the fielding side and any governing body responsible for the match, who shall take such action as is considered appropriate against the captain and player or players concerned.

5. Deliberate distraction or obstruction of batsman

In addition to 4 above, it is unfair for any member of the fielding side, by word or action, wilfully to attempt to distract or to obstruct either batsman after the striker has received the ball.

(a) It is for either one of the umpires to decide whether any distraction or obstruction is wilful or not.

(b) If either umpire considers that a member of the fielding side has wilfully caused or attempted to cause such a distraction or obstruction he shall·

(i) Immediately call and signal "Dead ball".

(ii) Inform the captain of the fielding side and the other umpire of the reason for the call.

Additionally:

(iii) Neither batsman shall be dismissed from that delivery.

(iv) Five penalty runs shall be awarded to the batting side. See 17 below. In this instance, the run in progress shall be scored, whether or not the batsmen had crossed at the instant of the call. See Law 18.11 (Runs scored when ball becomes dead).

(v) The umpire at the bowler's end shall inform the captain of the fielding side of the reason for this action and, as soon as practicable, inform the captain of the batting side.

(vi) The ball shall not count as one of the over.

(vii) The batsmen at the wicket shall decide which of them is to face the next delivery.

(viii) The umpires shall report the occurrence as soon as possible to the executive of the fielding side and any governing body responsible for the match, who shall take such action as is considered appropriate against the captain and player or players concerned.

6. Dangerous and unfair bowling

(a) Bowling of fast short-pitched balls

(i) The bowling of fast short-pitched balls is dangerous and unfair if the umpire at the bowler's end considers that by their repetition and taking into account their length, height and direction they are likely to inflict physical injury on the striker, irrespective of the protective equipment he may be wearing. The relative skill of the striker shall be taken into consideration.

(ii) Any delivery which, after pitching, passes or would have passed over head height of the striker standing upright at the crease, although not threatening physical injury, shall be included with bowling under (i) both when the umpire is considering whether the bowling of fast short-pitched balls has become dangerous and unfair and after he has so decided. The umpire shall call and signal "No-ball" for each such delivery.

(b) Bowling of high full-pitched balls

(i) Any delivery, other than a slow-paced one, which passes or would have passed on the full above waist height of the striker standing upright at the crease is to be deemed dangerous and unfair, whether or not it is likely to inflict physical injury on the striker.

(ii) A slow delivery which passes or would have passed on the full above shoulder height of the striker standing upright at the crease is to be deemed dangerous and unfair, whether or not it is likely to inflict physical injury on the striker.

7. Dangerous and unfair bowling – action by the umpire

(a) As soon as the umpire at the bowler's end decides under 6(a) above that the bowling of fast short-pitched balls has become dangerous and unfair, or, except as in 8 below, there is an instance of dangerous and unfair bowling as defined in 6(b) above, he shall call and signal "No-ball" and, when the ball is dead, caution the bowler, inform the other umpire, the captain of the fielding side and the batsmen of what has occurred. This caution shall continue to apply throughout the innings.

(b) If there is any further instance of such dangerous and unfair bowling by the same bowler in the same innings, the umpire at the bowler's end shall repeat the above procedure and indicate to the bowler that this is a final warning.

Both the above caution and final warning shall continue to apply even though the bowler may later change ends.

(c) Should there be any further repetition by the same bowler in that innings, the umpire shall:

(i) call and signal "No-ball".

(ii) Direct the captain, when the ball is dead, to take the bowler off forthwith. The over shall be completed by another bowler, who shall neither have bowled the previous over nor be allowed to bowl the next over.

The bowler thus taken off shall not be allowed to bowl again in that innings.

(iii) Report the occurrence to the other umpire, the batsmen and, as soon as practicable, the captain of the batting side.

(iv) Report the occurrence, with the other umpire, as soon as possible to the executive of the fielding side and to any governing body responsible for the match, who shall take such action as is considered appropriate against the captain and bowler concerned.

8. Deliberate bowling of high full-pitched balls

If the umpire considers that a high full pitch which is deemed to be dangerous and unfair, as defined in 6(b) above, was deliberately bowled, then the caution and warning prescribed in 7 above shall be dispensed with. The umpire shall:

(a) Call and signal "No-ball".

(b) Direct the captain, when the ball is dead, to take the bowler off forthwith.

(c) Implement the remainder of the procedure as laid down in 7(c) above.

9. Time-wasting by the fielding side

It is unfair for any member of the fielding side to waste time.

(a) If the captain of the fielding side wastes time, or allows any member of his side to waste time, or if the progress of an over is unnecessarily slow, at the first instance the umpire shall call and signal "Dead ball" if necessary and:

(i) Warn the captain, and indicate that this is a first and final warning.

(ii) Inform the other umpire and the batsmen of what has occurred.

(b) If there is any further waste of time in that innings, by any member of the fielding side, the umpire shall either

(i) if the waste of time is not during the course of an over, award five penalty runs to the batting side (See 17 below), or

(ii) if the waste of time is during the course of an over, when the ball is dead, direct the captain to take the bowler off forthwith. If applicable, the over shall be completed by another bowler, who shall neither have bowled the previous over nor be allowed to bowl the next over in that innings. The bowler thus taken off shall not be allowed to bowl again in that innings.

(iii) Inform the other umpire, the batsmen and, as soon as practicable, the captain of the batting side, of what has occurred.

(iv) Report the occurrence, with the other umpire, as soon as possible to the executive of the fielding side and to any governing body responsible for the match, who shall take such action as is considered appropriate against the captain and team concerned.

10. Batsman wasting time

It is unfair for a batsman to waste time. In normal circumstances the striker should always be ready to take strike when the bowler is ready to start his run-up.

(a) Should either batsman waste time by failing to meet this requirement, or in any other way, the following procedure shall be adopted. At the first instance, either before the bowler starts his run-up or when the ball is dead, as appropriate, the umpire shall:

(i) Warn the batsman and indicate that this is a first and final warning. This warning shall continue to apply throughout that innings. The umpire shall so inform each incoming batsman.

(ii) Inform the other umpire, the other batsman and the captain of the fielding side of what has occurred.

(iii) Inform the captain of the batting side as soon as practicable.

(b) If there is any further time-wasting by any batsman in that innings, the umpire shall, at the appropriate time while the ball is dead:

(i) Award five penalty runs to the fielding side. See 17 below.

(ii) Inform the other umpire, the other batsman, the captain of the fielding side and, as soon as practicable, the captain of the batting side, of what has occurred.

(iii) Report the occurrence, with the other umpire, as soon as possible to the executive of the batting side and to any governing body responsible for the match, who shall take such action as is considered appropriate against the captain and player or players, or, if appropriate, the team concerned.

11. Damaging the pitch – area to be protected

(a) It is incumbent on all players to avoid unnecessary damage to the pitch. It is unfair for any player to cause deliberate damage to the pitch.

(b) An area of the pitch, to be referred to as "the protected area", is defined as that area contained within a rectangle bounded at each end by imaginary lines parallel to the popping creases and 5ft/1.52m in front of each and on the sides by imaginary lines, one each side of the imaginary line joining the centres of the two middle stumps, each parallel to it and 1ft/30.48cm from it.

12. Bowler running on the protected area after delivering the ball

(a) If the bowler, after delivering the ball, runs on the protected area as defined in 11(b) above, the umpire shall at the first instance, and when the ball is dead:

(i) Caution the bowler. This caution shall continue to apply throughout the innings.

(ii) Inform the other umpire, the captain of the fielding side and the batsmen of what has occurred.

(b) If, in that innings, the same bowler runs on the protected area again after delivering the ball, the umpire shall repeat the above procedure, indicating that this is a final warning.

(c) If, in that innings, the same bowler runs on the protected area a third time after delivering the ball, when the ball is dead the umpire shall:

(i) Direct the captain of the fielding side to take the bowler off forthwith. If applicable, the over shall be completed by another bowler, who shall neither have bowled the previous over nor be allowed to bowl the next over. The bowler thus taken off shall not be allowed to bowl again in that innings.

(ii) Inform the other umpire, the batsmen and, as soon as practicable, the captain of the batting side of what has occurred.

(iii) Report the occurrence, with the other umpire, as soon as possible to the executive of the fielding side and to any governing body responsible for the match, who shall take such action as is considered appropriate against the captain and bowler concerned.

13. Fielders damaging the pitch

(a) If any fielder causes avoidable damage to the pitch, other than as in 12(a) above, at the first instance the umpire shall, when the ball is dead:

(i) Caution the captain of the fielding side, indicating that this is a first and final warning. This caution shall continue to apply throughout the innings.

(ii) Inform the other umpire and the batsmen of what has occurred.

(b) If there is any further avoidable damage to the pitch by any fielder in that innings, the umpire shall, when the ball is dead:

(i) Award five penalty runs to the batting side. See 17 below.

(ii) Inform the other umpire, the batsmen, the captain of the fielding side and, as soon as practicable, the captain of the batting side of what has occurred.

(iii) Report the occurrence, with the other umpire, as soon as possible to the executive of the fielding side and any governing body responsible for the match, who shall take such action as is considered appropriate against the captain and player or players concerned.

14. Batsman damaging the pitch

(a) If either batsman causes avoidable damage to the pitch, at the first instance the umpire shall, when the ball is dead:

(i) Caution the batsman. This caution shall continue to apply throughout the innings. The umpire shall so inform each incoming batsman.

(ii) Inform the other umpire, the other batsman, the captain of the fielding side and, as soon as practicable, the captain of the batting side.

(b) If there is a second instance of avoidable damage to the pitch by any batsman in that innings:

(i) The umpire shall repeat the above procedure, indicating that this is a final warning.

(ii) Additionally he shall disallow all runs to the batting side from that delivery other than the penalty for a no-ball or a wide, if applicable. The batsmen shall return to their original ends.

(c) If there is any further avoidable damage to the pitch by any batsman in that innings, the umpire shall, when the ball is dead:

(i) Disallow all runs to the batting side from that delivery other than the penalty for a no-ball or a wide, if applicable.

(ii) Additionally award five penalty runs to the fielding side. See 17 below.

(iii) Inform the other umpire, the other batsman, the captain of the fielding side and, as soon as practicable, the captain of the batting side of what has occurred.

(iv) Report the occurrence, with the other umpire, as soon as possible to the executive of the batting side and any governing body responsible for the match, who shall take such action as is considered appropriate against the captain and player or players concerned.

15. Bowler attempting to run out non-striker before delivery

The bowler is permitted, before entering his delivery stride, to attempt to run out the non-striker. The ball shall not count in the over.

The umpire shall call and signal "Dead ball" as soon as possible if the bowler fails in the attempt to run out the non-striker.

16. Batsmen stealing a run

It is unfair for the batsmen to attempt to steal a run during the bowler's run-up. Unless the bowler attempts to run out either batsman – see 15 above and Law 24.4 (Bowler throwing towards striker's end before delivery) – the umpire shall:

(i) Call and signal "Dead ball" as soon as the batsmen cross in any such attempt.

(ii) Return the batsmen to their original ends.

(iii) Award five penalty runs to the fielding side. See 17 below.

(iv) Inform the other umpire, the other batsman, the captain of the fielding side and, as soon as practicable, the captain of the batting side of the reason for the action taken.

(v) Report the occurrence, with the other umpire, as soon as possible to the executive of the batting side and any governing body responsible for the match, who shall take such action as is considered appropriate against the captain and player or players concerned.

17. Penalty runs

(a) When penalty runs are awarded to either side, when the ball is dead the umpire shall signal the penalty runs to the scorers as laid down in Law 3.14 (Signals).

(b) Notwithstanding the provisions of Law 21.6 (Winning hit or extras), penalty runs shall be awarded in each case where the Laws require the award. Note, however, that the restrictions on awarding penalty runs in Laws 26.3 (Leg-byes not to be awarded), 34.4(d) (Runs permitted from ball struck lawfully more than once) and Law 41.4 (Penalty runs not to be awarded) will apply.

(c) When five penalty runs are awarded to the batting side, under either Law 2.6 (Player returning without permission) or Law 41 (The fielder) or under 3, 4, 5, 9 or 13 above, then:

(i) They shall be scored as penalty extras and shall be in addition to any other penalties.

(ii) They shall not be regarded as runs scored from either the immediately preceding delivery or the following delivery and shall be in addition to any runs from those deliveries.

(iii) The batsmen shall not change ends solely by reason of the five-run penalty.

(d) When five penalty runs are awarded to the fielding side, under Law 18.5(b) (Deliberate short runs), or under 10, 14 or 16 above, they shall be added as penalty extras to that side's total of runs in its most recently completed innings. If the fielding side has not completed an innings, the five penalty extras shall be added to its next innings.

18. Players' conduct

If there is any breach of the Spirit of the Game by a player failing to comply with the instructions of an umpire, or criticising his decisions by word or action, or showing dissent, or generally behaving in a manner which might bring the game into disrepute, the umpire concerned shall immediately report the matter to the other umpire.

The umpires together shall:

(i) Inform the player's captain of the occurrence, instructing the latter to take action.

(ii) Warn him of the gravity of the offence, and tell him that it will be reported to higher authority.

(iii) Report the occurrence as soon as possible to the executive of the player's team and any governing body responsible for the match, who shall take such action as is considered appropriate against the captain and player or players, and, if appropriate, the team concerned.

REGULATIONS OF THE INTERNATIONAL CRICKET COUNCIL

Extracts

1. Standard playing conditions

In 2001, the ICC Cricket Committee amended its standard playing conditions for all Tests and one-day internationals to include the new Laws of Cricket. The following playing conditions were in force from October 1, 2004:

Duration of Test Matches

Test matches shall be of five days' scheduled duration and of two innings per side. The two participating countries may:

(a) Provide for a rest day during the match, and/or a reserve day after the scheduled days of play.

(b) Play on any scheduled rest day, conditions and circumstances permitting, should a full day's play be lost on any day prior to the rest day.

(c) Play on any scheduled reserve day, conditions and circumstances permitting, should a full day's play be lost on any day. Play shall not take place on more than five days.

(d) Make up time lost in excess of five minutes in each day's play due to circumstances outside the game, other than acts of God.

Hours of Play and Minimum Overs in the Day in Test Matches

A. Start and Cessation Times: The home board shall determine the hours of play, subject to there being six hours' scheduled play per day (Pakistan, a minimum of five and a half hours).

1. Minimum Overs in the Day:

(a) On days other than the last day, play shall continue on each day until the completion of a minimum target of 90 overs (or 15 overs per hour) or the completion of the scheduled or rescheduled cessation time, whichever is the later, provided that play shall not continue for more than 30 minutes beyond the scheduled or rescheduled cessation time (permitted overtime). For the sake of clarity, if any of the minimum target number of overs have not been bowled at the completion of the permitted overtime, play shall cease upon completion of the over in progress. The overs not bowled shall not be made up on any subsequent day.

(b) On the last day, a minimum of 75 overs (or 15 overs per hour) shall be bowled during the playing time other than the last hour of the match where a minimum of 15 overs shall be bowled. All calculations with regard to suspensions of play or the start of a new innings shall be based on one over for each full four minutes. If however, at any time after 30 minutes of the last hour have elapsed, both captains (the batsmen at the wicket may act for their captain) accept that there is no prospect of a result to the match, they may agree to cease play at that time. If any of the minimum of 75 overs (or as recalculated) have not been bowled when one hour's scheduled playing time remains, the last hour of the match shall be regarded as the hour immediately following the completion of these overs.

2. Reduction in minimum overs: except in the last hour of the match, if play is suspended due to adverse weather or light or any other reason (other than normal intervals) for more than one hour on any day, the minimum number of overs shall be reduced by one over for each full four minutes of the aggregate playing time lost. For the avoidance of doubt, the aggregate of one hour shall be inclusive of any time that may have been brought forward from previous days due to playing time lost on such previous days under clause 3(b) below.

3. Making up lost time:

(a) On the day: subject to weather and light, except in the last hour of the match, in the event of play being suspended for any reason other than normal intervals, the playing time on that day shall be extended by the amount of time lost up to a maximum of one hour. For the avoidance of doubt, the maximum of one hour shall be inclusive of any time that may have been added to the scheduled playing time due to playing time having been lost on previous days under clause 3(b) below.

(b) On subsequent days: if any time is lost and cannot be made up under clause 3(a) above, additional time of up to a maximum of 30 minutes per day shall be added to the scheduled playing hours for the next day, and subsequent day(s) as required (to make up as much lost time as possible). Where appropriate this additional time shall be added prior to the scheduled start of the first session. In circumstances where this is not possible, the additional time may be added to the second and/or the third sessions (see also 4). When such time is added, the minimum overs for that day shall be increased by one over for each four minutes of additional time or part thereof.

(c) On the last day only: Clause 3(a) applies, but the definition of playing time shall be the time up to the most recently scheduled time for the start of the last hour. Should an interruption in play commence prior to the most recently scheduled time for the last hour and continue past this time:

    (i) Only the playing time lost prior to this last hour start time will be made up (subject to the maximum of one hour described in (a) above), with the start time for the last hour rescheduled accordingly

    (ii) The period between the scheduled last-hour start time at the start of the interruption and the time of the resumption of play will not be made up. The minimum number of overs to be bowled prior to the last hour at the start of the interruption will be reduced by one over for each full four minutes of aggregate time lost.

    (iii) The start time for the last hour will thus be the later of the rescheduled time (as defined at the end of (i) above) and the time at which the minimum overs prior to the last hour have been completed, or reduced to zero.

    (iv) No time is made up in respect of any interruptions that commence after the start of the last hour.

B. Extra Time: The umpires may decide to play 30 minutes (a minimum of eight overs) extra time at the end of any day (other than the last day) if requested by either captain if, in the umpires' opinion, it would bring about a definite result on that day. If the umpires do not believe a result can be achieved no extra time shall be allowed. If it is decided to play such extra time, the whole period shall be played out even though the possibility of finishing the match may have disappeared before the full period has expired. Only the actual amount of playing time up to the maximum 30 minutes' extra time by which play is extended on any day shall be deducted from the total number of hours of play remaining, and the match shall end earlier on the final day by that amount of time.

Use of Lights:

If, in the opinion of the umpires, natural light is deteriorating to an unfit level, they shall authorise the ground authorities to use the available artificial lighting so that the match can continue in acceptable conditions.

    The lights are only to be used to enable a full day's play to be completed as provided for in Clause A above. In the event of power failure or lights malfunction, the existing provisions of Clause A shall apply.

Dangerous and Unfair Bowling: The Bowling of Fast, Short-Pitched Balls: Law 42.6(a)

1.   (a) A bowler shall be limited to two fast, short-pitched deliveries per over.

    (b) A fast, short-pitched ball is defined as a ball which passes or would have passed above the shoulder height of the striker standing upright at the crease.

    (c) The umpire at the bowler's end shall advise the bowler and the batsman on strike when each fast short-pitched ball has been bowled.

    (d) For the purpose of this regulation, a ball that passes above head height of the batsman that prevents him from being able to hit it with his bat by means of a normal cricket stroke shall be called a wide.

    (e) Any fast, short-pitched delivery called a wide under this condition shall count as one of the allowable short-pitched deliveries in that over.

(f) In the event of a bowler bowling more than two fast, short-pitched deliveries in an over, the umpire at the bowler's end shall call and signal "no-ball" on each occasion. The umpire shall call and signal "no-ball" and then tap the head with the other hand.

(g) If a bowler delivers a third fast, short-pitched ball in an over, the umpire must call no-ball and then invoke the procedures of caution, final warning, action against the bowler and reporting as set out in Law 42.7. The umpires will report the matter to the ICC referee who shall take such action as is considered appropriate against the captain and bowler concerned.

The above Regulation is not a substitute for Law 42.6 (as amended below), which umpires are able to apply at any time:

The bowling of fast, short-pitched balls is unfair if the umpire at the bowler's end considers that, by their repetition and taking into account their length, height and direction, they are likely to inflict physical injury on the striker, irrespective of the protective clothing and equipment he may be wearing. The relative skill of the striker shall also be taken into consideration.

The umpire at the bowler's end shall adopt the procedures of caution, final warning, action against the bowler and reporting as set out in Law 42.7. The ICC referee shall take any further action considered appropriate against the captain and bowler concerned.

New Ball: Law 5.4

The captain of the fielding side shall have the choice of taking a new ball any time after 80 overs have been bowled with the previous ball. The umpires shall indicate to the batsmen and the scorers whenever a new ball is taken into play.

Ball Lost or Becoming Unfit for Play: Law 5.5

The following shall apply in addition to Law 5.5

However, if the ball needs to be replaced after 110 overs for any of the reasons above, it shall be replaced by a new ball. If the ball is to be replaced, the umpires shall inform the batsmen.

Judging a Wide: Law 25.1

Law 25.1 will apply, but in addition

For bowlers attempting to utilise the rough outside a batsman's leg stump, not necessarily as a negative tactic, and for bowlers whom umpires consider to be bowling down the leg side as a negative tactic, the strict limited-overs wide interpretation shall be applied.

Practice on the Field: Law 17

In addition to Law 17.1:

The use of the square for practice on any day of any match will be restricted to any netted practice area on the square set aside for that purpose.

Fieldsman Leaving the Field: Law 2.5

If a fielder fails to take the field with his side at the start of the match or at any later time, or leaves the field during a session of play, the umpire shall be informed of the reason for his absence, and he shall not thereafter come on to the field during a session without the consent of the umpire. The umpire shall give such consent as soon as practicable. If the player is absent from the field longer than eight minutes, he shall not be permitted to bowl in that innings after his return until he has been on the field for at least that length of playing time for which he was absent. This restriction will, if necessary, be carried over into a new day's play, and in the event of a follow-on or a forfeiture, it will continue into the second innings. Nor shall he be permitted to bat unless or until, in the aggregate, he has returned to the field and/or his side's innings has been in progress for at least that length of playing time for which he has been absent or, if earlier, when his side has lost five wickets. The restrictions shall not apply if he has suffered an external blow (as opposed to an internal injury such as a pulled muscle) while participating earlier in the match and consequently been forced to leave the field, nor if he has been absent for very exceptional and acceptable reasons (other than injury or illness).

2. Classification of first-class matches

1. Definitions

A match of three or more days' duration between two sides of 11 players played on natural turf pitches on international standard grounds and substantially conforming with standard playing conditions shall be regarded as a first-class fixture.

2. Rules

(a) Full Members of the ICC shall decide the status of matches of three or more days' duration played in their countries.

(b) In matches of three or more days' duration played in countries which are not Full Members of the ICC, except Kenya (see 2.3 (l) below):

    (i) If the visiting team comes from a country which is a Full Member of the ICC, that country shall decide the status of matches.

    (ii) If the visiting team does not come from a country which is a Full Member of the ICC, or is a Commonwealth team composed of players from different countries, the ICC shall decide the status of matches

Notes

(a) Governing bodies agree that the interest of first-class cricket will be served by ensuring that first-class status is not accorded to any match in which one or other of the teams taking part cannot on a strict interpretation of the definitions be adjudged first-class.

(b) In case of any disputes arising from these Rules, the Chief Executive of the ICC shall refer the matter for decision to the Council, failing unanimous agreement by postal communication being reached.

3. First-Class Status

The following matches shall be regarded as first-class, subject to the provisions of 2.1 (Definitions) being complied with:

(a) **In Great Britain and Ireland:** (i) County Championship matches. (ii) Official representative tourist matches from Full Member countries unless specifically excluded. (iii) MCC v any first-class county. (iv) Oxford, Cambridge, Durham and Loughborough University Centres of Excellence against first-class counties. (v) Oxford v Cambridge. (vi) Scotland v Ireland.

(b) **In Australia:** (i) Pura Cup matches. (ii) Matches played by Australia A or an Australian XI and teams representing states of the Commonwealth of Australia between each other or against opponents adjudged first-class.

(c) **In Bangladesh:** (i) Matches between Bangladesh and a Full Member. (ii) Matches between Full Member teams adjudged first-class and Bangladesh. (iii) Matches between teams adjudged first-class and a Full Member. (iv) Matches between Bangladesh and Kenya. (v) Matches between teams adjudged first-class and Kenya. (vi) National League three-day matches between the Divisions of Barisal, Chittagong, Dhaka, Khulna, Rajshahi and Sylhet.

(d) **In India:** (i) Ranji Trophy matches. (ii) Duleep Trophy matches. (iii) Irani Trophy matches. (iv) Matches played by teams representing state or regional associations affiliated to the Board of Control between each other or against opponents adjudged first-class. (v) Matches of three days or more against representative visiting sides.

(e) **In New Zealand:** (i) State Championship matches. (ii) Matches played by New Zealand A or major associations affiliated to New Zealand Cricket, between each other or against opponents adjudged first-class.

(f) **In Pakistan:** (i) Quaid-e-Azam Trophy (Grade 1) matches. (ii) Patron's Trophy (Grade 1) matches. (iii) A-team matches played in Pakistan between Pakistan and other Full Members and Kenya.

(g) **In South Africa:** (i) SuperSport Series four-day matches between Dolphins, Eagles, Lions, Titans, Warriors and Western Province Boland. (ii) UCB Provincial Cup three-day matches between Boland, Border, Eastern Province, Easterns, Free State, Gauteng, Griqualand West, KwaZulu-Natal, Northerns, North West, Western Province. (iii) Matches played by

South Africa A, South Africa Academy, a franchise or provincial team against a fully representative or A-team, from a Full Member Country.

(h) **In Sri Lanka:** (i) Matches of three days or more against touring sides adjudged first-class. (ii) Premier League Division I matches played over three or more days for the Premier Trophy. (iii) Matches of three days or more against visiting A teams of Full Member countries by Sri Lanka A or senior development squad teams or Sri Lanka Cricket representative teams (except Under-19 and below).

(i) **In West Indies:** Matches played by teams representing Barbados, Guyana, Jamaica, the Leeward Islands, Trinidad & Tobago and the Windward Islands, either for the Carib Beer Cup or against other opponents adjudged first-class.

(j) **In Zimbabwe:** (i) Logan Cup matches. (ii) Matches played by teams representing associations affiliated to Zimbabwe Cricket, between each other or against opponents adjudged first-class.

(k) **In all Full Member countries represented on the Council:** (i) Test matches and matches against teams adjudged first-class played by official touring teams. (ii) Official Test Trial matches. (iii) Special matches between teams adjudged first-class by the governing body or bodies concerned.

(l) **In Kenya:** (i) Matches between a Full Member and Kenya. (ii) Matches between teams adjudged first-class and Kenya.

3. Classification of Test matches

Any match of not more than five days' scheduled duration played between teams selected by Full Members as representatives of their member countries and accorded the status of Test match by the ICC.

Only Full Members of ICC can participate in Test matches.

4. Classification of one-day international matches

The following shall be classified as one-day internationals:

(a) All matches played in the official World Cup and ICC Champions Trophy competitions, including matches involving Associate Member countries.

(b) All matches played between the Full Member countries of the ICC as part of an official tour itinerary.

(c) All matches played as part of an official tournament between Full Member countries, at an ICC-approved Associate or Affiliate Member venue.

(d) All matches between the Full Members and Kenya.

(e) All matches played in the Asia Cup with a format consisting of four Full Members and two Associate Members.

Note: Matches involving the A team of a Full Member country shall not be classified as one-day internationals.

5. Player qualification rules for ICC matches, series and competitions

(a) A cricketer is qualified to play representative cricket for an ICC Member country of which he is a national or, in cases of non-nationals, in which he was born, provided that he has not played representative cricket for any other Member country during the four immediately preceding years.

(b) Where the country is an Associate or Affiliate Member, the cricketer must satisfy one or more of the following additional Development Criteria:

  (i) he shall have played 50% or more of the scheduled games for his team in a national cricket competition in the relevant Member country in any three of the preceding five years.

  (ii) he shall have spent a cumulative total of 100 days or more during the preceding five years coaching, playing or working in the administration or development of cricket in the relevant Member country.

(iii) he shall have played representative cricket for the relevant Member country.

(iv) he shall have dedicated a reasonable period of time to activities which, in the opinion of the Chairman of the Cricket Committee, constitute a sufficient demonstration of his genuine commitment to the development of cricket in the relevant Member country.

He must also satisfy the quota requirement for deemed nationals (see below).

(c) A player who has resided for a minimum of 183 days in a Member country in each of the four immediately preceding years shall be a "deemed national" of that country for the purpose of these rules. Affiliate and Associate Members may not field more than two players in any one team who are deemed nationals, but a player who has resided in an Affiliate or Associate Member country for a minimum of 183 days in each of the seven immediately preceding years shall be classified as a national rather than a deemed national of that Member country.

(d) Where an Associate or Affiliate Member country is fielding a team against a Full Member or in any tournament or competition involving teams from one or more Full Members, the requirements relating to having played a representative cricket match for any other Member country during the four immediately preceding years, the Development Criteria and the quota rules shall not apply.

(e) A cricketer qualified to play for a Member country can continue to represent that country without negating who eligibility or interrupting his qualification period for another Member country until he has played for the first Member country at Under-19 level or above.

(f) A cricketer qualified to play for an Associate or Affiliate Member can continue to represent that country without negating his eligibility or interrupting his qualification period for a Full Member country until he has played for the Full Member Country at Under-19 level or above.

(g) Associate and Affiliate Members shall be limited to two players per team who have formerly played representative cricket for a Full Member country, except when fielding a team against a Full Member or in any tournament or competition involving teams from one or more Full Members.

Notes: "Representative cricket" means any cricket match in which a team representing a Member country at Under-19 level or above takes part, including Tests and one-day internationals.

The governing body for cricket of any Member country may impose more stringent qualification rules for that country.

ICC CODE OF CONDUCT

1. Players and/or team officials shall at all times conduct play within the spirit of the game as well as within the Laws of Cricket, and the captains are responsible at all times for ensuring that this is adhered to.

2. Players and/or team officials shall at no time engage in conduct unbecoming to their status which could bring them or the game of cricket into disrepute.

3. Players and/or team officials shall be required to report to the captain and/or team manager or to a senior board official or to the Anti-Corruption and Security Unit any approach made to them by a bookmaker or any other corrupt approach made to any other player or team official.

4. Players and/or team officials shall not bet on matches nor otherwise engage in any conduct of the nature described in the paragraphs below. For conduct in breach of this rule, the penalties to be considered are set out below, for individuals who have:

   i. Bet on any match or series of matches, or on any connected event, in which such player, team official or administrator took part or in which the Member country or any such individual was represented (penalty (a));

   ii. Induced or encouraged any other person to bet on any match or series of matches or on any connected event or to offer the facility for such bets to be placed (penalty (b));

   iii. Gambled or entered into any other form of financial speculation on any match or on any connected event (penalty (a));

iv. Induced or encouraged any other person to gamble or enter into any other form of financial speculation on any match or any connected event (penalty (b));

v. Was a party to contriving or attempting to contrive the result of any match or the occurrence of any connected event (penalty (c));

vi. Failed to perform on his merits in any match owing to an arrangement relating to betting on the outcome of any match or on the occurrence of any connected event (penalty (c));

vii. Induced or encouraged any other player not to perform on his merits in any match owing to any such arrangement (penalty (c));

viii. Received from another person any money, benefit or other reward (whether financial or otherwise) for the provision of any information concerning the weather, the teams, the state of the ground, the status of, or the outcome of, any match or the occurrence of any connected event unless such information has been provided to a newspaper or other form of media in accordance with an obligation entered into in the normal course and disclosed in advance to the cricket authority of the relevant Member country (penalty (b));

ix. Received any money, benefit or other reward (whether financial or otherwise) which could bring him or the game of cricket into disrepute (penalty (d));

x. Provided any money, benefit or other reward (whether financial or otherwise) which could bring the game of cricket into disrepute (penalty (d));

xi. Received any approaches from another person to engage in conduct such as that described above, and has failed to disclose the same to his captain or team manager, or to a senior board official or to the Anti-Corruption and Security Unit (penalty (e)); or

xii. Is aware that any other player or individual has engaged in conduct, or received approaches, such as described above, and has failed to disclose the same to his captain or team manager, or to a senior board official or to the Anti-Corruption and Security Unit (penalty (e));

xiii. Has received or is aware that any other person has received threats of any nature which might induce him to engage in conduct, or acquiesce in any proposal made by an approach, such as described above, and has failed to disclose the same to his captain or team manager, or to a senior board official or to the Anti-Corruption and Security Unit (penalty (e));.

xiv. Has engaged in any conduct which, in the opinion of the Executive Board, relates directly or indirectly to any of the above paragraphs (i to xiii) and is prejudicial to the interests of the game of cricket (penalty (e)).

Penalties:

(a) Ban for a minimum of two years and a maximum of five years. In addition, a fine may be imposed, the amount to be assessed in the circumstances.

(b) Ban for a minimum of two years and a maximum of five years if a bet was placed directly or indirectly for the benefit of the individual; otherwise, a ban for a minimum of 12 months. In addition, a fine may be imposed, the amount to be assessed in the circumstances.

(c) Ban for life (a minimum of 20 years).

(d) Ban for a minimum of two years and a maximum of life. In addition, a fine may be imposed, the amount to be assessed in the circumstances.

(e) Ban for a minimum of one year and a maximum of five years. In addition, a fine may be imposed, the amount to be assessed in the circumstances.

5. A valid defence may be made to a charge in respect of any prohibited conduct in paragraphs 4 (xi) to (xiii) above if a person proves that this conduct was the result of an honest and reasonable belief that there was a serious threat to the life or safety of himself or any member of his family.

6. Players and/or team officials shall not use or in any way be concerned in the use or distribution of illegal drugs. Illegal drugs shall mean those drugs which are classified as unlawful in the player's or team official's home country or in the country in which he is touring. Any such conduct shall constitute behaviour prohibited under paragraph 2 and shall be dealt with as such. Players and team officials shall also be subject to any doping policy which is applied by their home board and such policies which are introduced for ICC events. Any breach of such doping policy shall be dealt with under the terms of such policy itself and not under this code.

CRIME AND PUNISHMENT

ICC Code of Conduct – Breaches and Penalties in 2003-04 to 2004-05

A. Nel   South Africa v West Indies, First Test at Johannesburg.
Obscene language and gesture. Fined 50% of match fee and reprimanded by R. S. Madugalle.

K. D. Mills   New Zealand v Pakistan, one-day international at Napier.
Excessive appealing. Officially reprimanded and warned of future conduct by B. C. Broad.

R. Dravid   India v Zimbabwe, one-day international at Brisbane.
Changing ball's condition in breach of Law 42.3. Fined 50% of match fee by C. H. Lloyd.

S. C. Ganguly   Australia v India, one-day international at Sydney.
Failed to ensure spirit of the game maintained. Fined 50% of match fee by C. H. Lloyd.

I. K. Pathan   Australia v India, one-day international at Sydney.
Conduct contrary to the spirit of the game. Officially reprimanded by C. H. Lloyd.

A. C. Gilchrist   Sri Lanka v Australia, one-day international at Dambulla.
Dissent after dismissal of Symonds. Fined 50% of match fee by M. J. Procter.

Inzamam-ul-Haq   Pakistan v India, one-day international at Rawalpindi.
Conduct contrary to the spirit of the game. Fined 50% of match fee by R. S. Madugalle.

B. C. Lara   West Indies v England, Second Test at Port-of-Spain.
Dissent at umpire's decision. Fined 50% of match fee by M. J. Procter.

S. P. Jones   West Indies v England, Second Test at Port-of-Spain.
Conduct bringing the game into disrepute. Fined 50% of match fee by M. J. Procter.

G. C. Smith   New Zealand v South Africa, Third Test at Wellington.
Dissent at umpire's decision. Fined 50% of match fee by C. H. Lloyd.

A. Nel   New Zealand v South Africa, Third Test at Wellington.
Serious dissent at umpire's decision. Fined 75% of match fee by C. H. Lloyd.

Moin Khan   Pakistan v India, First Test at Multan.
Serious dissent at umpire's decision. Fined 75% of match fee by R. S. Madugalle.

P. A. Patel   Pakistan v India, Second Test at Lahore.
Serious dissent at umpire's decision. Fined 60% of match fee by R. S. Madugalle.

D. D. Ebrahim   Zimbabwe v Sri Lanka, Second Test at Bulawayo.
Offensive comment on opponent's bowling. Banned for one Test by M. J. Procter.

T. L. Best   West Indies v Bangladesh, First Test at Gros Islet, St Lucia
Inappropriate physical contact with batsman. Fined 75% of match fee by R. S. Mahanama.

G. D. McGrath   Australia v Sri Lanka, Second Test at Cairns.
Obscene, offensive or insulting language. Fined 25% of match fee by B. C. Broad.

Nasir Hameed   Pakistan v Hong Kong, one-day international at Colombo (SSC)
Dissent at umpire's decision. Officially reprimanded by R. S. Mahanama.

K. C. Sangakkara   Sri Lanka v India, one-day international at Colombo (RPS).
Obscene, offensive or insulting language. Fined 100% of match fee by M. J. Procter.

U. D. U. Chandana   Sri Lanka v India, one-day international at Colombo (RPS).
Obscene, offensive or insulting language. Fined 50% of match fee by M. J. Procter.

T. M. Dilshan   Sri Lanka v India, one-day international at Colombo (RPS).
Obscene, offensive or insulting language. Fined 50% of match fee by M. J. Procter.

G. C. Smith   West Indies v South Africa, one-day international at The Oval.
Failed to ensure spirit of the game maintained. Fined 50% of match fee by B. C. Broad.

M. P. Vaughan   England v West Indies, one-day international at The Oval.
Failed to ensure spirit of the game maintained. Fined 50% of match fee by R. S. Madugalle.

V. Sehwag   India v Australia, First Test at Bangalore.
Serious dissent at umpire's decision. Fined 65% of match fee by R. S. Madugalle.

K. C. Sangakkara   Pakistan v Sri Lanka, Second Test at Karachi.
Hurled bat into air when given out. Fined 30% of match fee by J. J. Crowe.

S. B. Styris   Bangladesh v New Zealand, one-day international at Dhaka.
Conduct contrary to spirit of the game. Severely reprimanded by A. G. Hurst.

C. D. McMillan   Bangladesh v New Zealand, one-day international at Dhaka.
Dissent at umpire's decision. Fined 25% of match fee by A. G. Hurst.

S. C. Ganguly   India v Pakistan, one-day international at Kolkata.
Failed to ensure spirit of the game maintained. Banned for two Tests by C. H. Lloyd; ban overturned
on appeal.

I. K. Pathan   India v Pakistan, one-day international at Kolkata.
Inappropriate physical contact with another player. Fined 50% of match fee by C. H. Lloyd.

Yousuf Youhana   India v Pakistan, one-day international at Kolkata.
Inappropriate physical contact with another player. Fined 75% of match fee by C. H. Lloyd.

S. C. Ganguly   India v South Africa, Second Test at Kolkata.
Dissent at umpire's decision. Fined 30% of match fee by J. J. Crowe.

Shoaib Akhtar   Australia v Pakistan, First Test at Perth.
Aggressive gesturing towards pavilion when batsman out. Fined 40% of match fee by R. S.
Madugalle.

A. J. Hall   South Africa v England, First Test at Johannesburg.
Aggressive gesturing towards pavilion when batsman out. Officially reprimanded by C. H. Lloyd.

H. H. Gibbs   South Africa v England, Second Test at Durban.
Conduct contrary to spirit of the game. Fined 40% of match fee by C. H. Lloyd.

Danish Kaneria   Australia v Pakistan, Third Test at Sydney.
Obscene, offensive or insulting language. Fined of 100% of match fee by R. S. Madugalle.

M. P. Vaughan   South Africa v England, Fourth Test at Johannesburg.
Public criticism of umpires. Fined 100% of match fee by C. H. Lloyd.

REGULATIONS FOR FIRST-CLASS MATCHES IN BRITAIN, 2004

Hours of play

1st, 2nd [and 3rd in 4-day matches] days. . .   11.00 a.m. to 6.30 p.m.
Final day. . . . .   11.00 a.m. to 6.00 p.m.
(Tourist matches, all days . . . .   10.45 a.m. to 5.45 p.m.)

Intervals

Lunch: 1.15 p.m. to 1.55 p.m. (1st, 2nd [3rd] days)
        1.00 p.m. to 1.40 p.m. (final day)
        (Tourist matches) 12.45 p.m. to 1.25 p.m.
        Where an innings concludes or there is a break in play within ten minutes of the scheduled lunch interval, the interval will commence at that time and be limited to 40 minutes.

Tea: (Championship matches) A tea interval of 20 minutes shall normally be taken at 4.10 p.m. (3.40 p.m. on final day), or at the conclusion of the over in progress at that time, provided 32 overs or less remain to be bowled (except on the final day). The over in progress shall be completed unless a batsman is out or retires either within two minutes of, or after, the scheduled time for the interval. In the event of more than 32 overs remaining, the tea interval will be delayed.

      If an innings ends or there is a stoppage caused by weather or light, or the players have cause to leave the field, within 30 minutes of the scheduled time, the tea interval shall be taken immediately. There will be no tea interval if the scheduled timing for the cessation of play is earlier than 5.30 p.m.

    (Tourist matches) 3.25 p.m. to 3.45 p.m.

    (Other matches) 4.10 p.m. to 4.30 p.m. (1st, 2nd [3rd] days), 3.40 p.m. to 4.00 p.m. (final day).

Note: The hours of play, including intervals, are brought forward by half an hour for matches scheduled to start in September.

Minimum Overs in the Day

(i) Play shall continue on each day until the completion of a minimum number of overs or until the scheduled cessation time, whichever is the later. The minimum number of overs, unless an innings ends or an interruption occurs, shall be 104 (90 in tourist matches) on days other than the last day, and 80 (75) on the last day before the last hour.

(ii) Where there is a change of innings during a day's play (except during an interval or suspension of play or exceptional circumstances or during the last hour of domestic matches), two overs will be deducted from the minimum number, plus any over in progress at the end of the completed innings (in domestic matches).

(iii) If interruptions for weather or light occur, other than in the last hour of the match, the minimum number of overs shall be reduced by one over for each full 3¾ minutes (four minutes in tourist matches) of the aggregate playing time lost.

(iv) On the last day, if any of the minimum of 80 (75) overs, or as recalculated, have not been bowled when one hour of scheduled playing time remains, the last hour of the match shall be the hour immediately following the completion of those overs.

(v) Law 16.6, 16.7 and 16.8 will apply except that a minimum of 16 six-ball overs (15 in tourist matches) shall be bowled in the last hour, and all calculations with regard to suspensions of play or the start of a new innings shall be based on one over for each full 3¾ (four) minutes. If, however, at 5.30 p.m. both captains accept that there is no prospect of a result or (in Championship games) of either side gaining any further first-innings bonus points, they may agree to cease play at that time or at any time after 5.30 p.m.

(vi) (Domestic matches). The captains may agree or, in the event of disagreement, the umpires may decide to play 30 minutes (a minimum eight overs) extra time at the end of any day other than the last day if, in their opinion, it would bring about a definite result on that day. The whole period shall be played out even though the possibility of finishing the match may have disappeared before the full period has expired. The time by which play is extended on any day shall be deducted from the total number of hours remaining, and the match shall end earlier on the last day by the amount of time by which play was extended. If there is a change of innings immediately prior to the start of, or during the period of extra time, then two overs shall be deducted.

(vii) Notwithstanding any other provision, there shall be no further play on any day, other than the last day, if a wicket falls or a batsman retires, or if the players leave the field during the last minimum over within two minutes of the scheduled cessation time or thereafter.

(viii) An over completed on resumption of a new day's play shall be disregarded in calculating minimum overs for that day.

(ix) The scoreboard shall show the total number of overs bowled with the ball in use and the minimum number remaining to be bowled in a day. In Championship matches, it shall show the number of overs up to 130 in each side's first innings and subsequently the number bowled with the current ball, and the minimum remaining to be bowled. In addition it shall indicate the number of overs that the fielding side is ahead of or behind the over-rate.

Substitutes

(Domestic matches only) Law 2.1 will apply, but in addition:

No substitute may take the field until the player for whom he is to substitute has been absent from the field for five consecutive complete overs, with the exception that if a fieldsman sustains an obvious, serious injury or is taken ill, a substitute shall be allowed immediately. In the event of any disagreement between the two sides as to the authenticity of an injury or illness, the umpires shall adjudicate. A substitute shall be allowed immediately for all head or blood injuries. If a player leaves the field during an over, the remainder of that over shall not count in the calculation of the five complete overs.

The umpires shall have discretion, for other wholly acceptable reasons, to allow a substitute for a fielder, or a runner for a batsman, at the start of the match or at any subsequent time subject to consent being given by the opposing captain.

A substitute shall not be allowed to bat or bowl, or to act as captain. The opposing captain shall have no right of objection to any player acting as substitute, or to where the substitute shall field, with the exception of the position of wicket-keeper. However, with the agreement of both captains (not to be unreasonably withheld), any substitute may act as wicket-keeper. In the event of the captains' disagreement, the substitute shall not be allowed to act as wicket-keeper.

A substitute shall be allowed by right immediately in the event of a cricketer currently playing in a Championship match being required to join the England team for a Test match (or one-day international). Such a substitute may be permitted to bat or bowl in that match, subject to the approval of the ECB. If the cricketer substituted is batting at the time, he shall retire "not out" and his substitute may be permitted to bat later in that innings subject to the approval of the ECB. If the cricketer is subsequently not required by England then, subject to the approval of the ECB, he may return and resume a full part in the match, taking over from the player that substituted for him. If the substitute is batting, he shall complete his innings and the cricketer shall take over thereafter. If the substitute is bowling when the cricketer is ready to take the field, the substitute shall complete any unfinished over and the cricketer shall take the field thereafter.

If a player is released by England prior to the teams being named in a Championship match, his county may have a fielding-only substitute until the cricketer is able to join the Championship team. If a player is released by England after the teams have been named in his county match, then he may return to that match and take the place of a nominated player, who may or may not have already participated. Each county that has representation in the England squad must, if it wishes that a specified England player shall participate in a Championship match if released, specify which player will be replaced. This shall be done at the nomination of the teams to the umpires.

If the England player is released, then he must make all reasonable efforts to take his place in the county side at the earliest opportunity. No replacement will be allowed if the England player is not available to take his place in the county side until after the start of play on the third scheduled day. There is no option for the county to refuse the England player if they have nominated a player to be replaced.

If the nominated player is batting, he shall complete his innings and the England player shall take over thereafter. If the nominated player is bowling when the England player is ready to take the field, then the nominated player shall complete any unfinished over, and the England player shall take the field thereafter.

Fieldsman leaving the field

ICC regulations apply (see page 1507) but, in domestic matches, it is explained that "external blow" should include, but not be restricted to, collisions with boundary boards, clashes of heads, heavy falls etc and, in the case of "exceptional and acceptable reasons", consent for a substitute must be granted by the opposing captain.

New ball

The captain of the fielding side shall have the choice of taking the new ball after 90 overs (80 in tourist matches) have been bowled with the old one.

Covering of pitches and surrounding areas

The whole pitch shall be covered:

(a) The night before the match and, if necessary, until the first ball is bowled; and whenever necessary and possible at any time prior to that during the preparation of the pitch.

(b) On each night of the match and, if necessary, throughout any rest days.

(c) In the event of play being suspended on account of bad light or rain, during the specified hours of play, and at lunch, tea and between innings on account of rain.

The bowler's run-up shall be covered to a distance of at least ten yards, with a width of four yards, as will the areas 20 feet either side of the length of the pitch.

Declarations

Law 14 will apply, but if, due to weather conditions, play in a County Championship match has not started when less than eight hours' playing time remains, the first innings of each side shall automatically be forfeited and a one-innings match played.

MEETINGS AND DECISIONS, 2004

ICC CRICKET COMMITTEE – MANAGEMENT

The ICC's Cricket Committee – Management (renamed the Chief Executives' Committee later in the year) met in Dhaka on February 14 and 15. Delegates reviewed measures to increase umpires' consistency by keeping comprehensive records of umpiring decisions in all international cricket. The meeting was briefed on discussions between ICC management and the World Anti-Doping Authority on an Anti-Doping Code for cricket. It was agreed to recommend that the administration of men's and women's cricket at international level should be integrated.

ICC EXECUTIVE BOARD

The ICC's Executive Board met in Auckland on March 9 and 10. It ruled that teams refusing to fulfil scheduled tours could face a minimum fine of $2m and possible suspension from international cricket, unless they could cite valid security concerns or were told by their government not to tour. The ICC stated that national boards "should not be drawn into making political decisions when assessing their future tour commitments".

It was agreed to release more of the money withheld from ICC members after the 2003 World Cup. This had been kept in a reserve pool to cover compensation claims from the ICC's commercial partner, the Global Cricket Corporation; England and New Zealand were penalised after refusing to play in Zimbabwe and Kenya respectively, and India because their players had declined to sign ICC contracts, but South Africa had also missed out because, as World Cup hosts, they had contributed more money to the pool and could not be immediately repaid.

The board decided that matches in the new ICC Intercontinental Cup, a tournament for the top Associate Members, should have first-class status.

ENGLAND SUMMER CONTRACTS

On April 15, after England's successful Test series in the West Indies, the ECB awarded six-month summer contracts for the 2004 English season to Steve Harmison, Matthew Hoggard, Simon Jones and Graham Thorpe. Eight other players had been awarded 12-month contracts in September 2003: James Anderson, Mark Butcher, Paul Collingwood, Andrew Flintoff, Ashley Giles, Nasser Hussain, Michael Vaughan and Marcus Trescothick.

MCC ANNUAL GENERAL MEETING

The 217th AGM of the Marylebone Cricket Club was held on May 5, with the president, Charles Fry, in the chair. He announced that his successor, from October, would be Tom Graveney. The meeting adopted updated and revised rules, and approved a programme of works for the conservation, restoration and upgrading of the pavilion the following winter. Membership of the club on December 31, 2003, totalled 22,539, made up of 18,032 full members, 3,972 associate members, 296 honorary members, 183 senior members and 56 out-match members. In 2003, 515 vacancies arose.

ECB FIRST-CLASS FORUM

On May 11, the ECB's First-Class Forum met at Loughborough and rejected the Domestic Structure Review Group's proposals on the county programme, which included amalgamating the County Championship and one-day league. It agreed to set up an Interim Review Group, headed by the forum's chairman, Mike Soper, to examine alternatives. The group was to focus on developing Twenty20 cricket, the format for the one-day League, the scheduling of all first-class cricket, promotion and relegation, and the extension of floodlit cricket. The forum also decided that counties should be allowed two overseas players for one further season in 2005, pending the review's outcome.

ICC CRICKET COMMITTEE

The ICC Cricket Committee (formerly known as the Cricket Committee – Playing) met in Dubai on May 13 and 14 and agreed not to change the current two-stage process for dealing with potentially illegal bowling actions until research was completed at the Champions Trophy in September. The committee also recommended several playing innovations to be tested in one-day domestic cricket, such as allowing more than one batsman to be dismissed off the same ball, allowing teams of 12 in which 11 players would bat and 11 field, and allowing the batting team to choose the 15 overs for which fielding restrictions would apply. They discussed regulations on making up time lost in Tests. The committee proposed that, in future, Tests and one-day internationals abandoned without a ball bowled should be included in the records if the toss had taken place, and that, where one-day internationals continued into a reserve day, the toss and the teams named should stand unless both captains agreed otherwise. They opposed earpiece communications between players on the field and staff off it, and recommended further tests of stump microphone technology to assist umpires.

ZIMBABWEAN CRISIS – STATUS OF TESTS

Following the removal of Heath Streak as Zimbabwean captain on April 2, 14 white players including Streak had withdrawn from representing Zimbabwe during the Sri Lankan tour in April and May and were sacked by the ZCU. After attempts at mediation broke down and a weakened Zimbabwean side was overwhelmed by Sri Lanka, ICC chief executive Malcolm Speed travelled to Harare to express ICC fears for the integrity of Test cricket, as Zimbabwe prepared to face Australia in a Test series beginning on May 22. He was not permitted to speak to the full ZCU board, though he met officials as well as the rebel players.

The ICC announced that its Executive Board would hold a teleconference on May 21, which was widely expected to strip the matches with Australia of Test status. Hours before the teleconference was due, the ZCU announced it would postpone the Tests with Australia; it was agreed the one-day series should go ahead with full international status, while the rebel players appealed to the ICC's Disputes Resolution Committee. The ZCU said it would not recognise the committee's authority, though it softened its position at a meeting with an ICC subcommittee in Dubai on June 10.

ICC ANNUAL MEETING

The ICC held its annual meeting at Lord's between June 27 and July 1. The ICC board confirmed that Zimbabwe's scheduled Test series against Pakistan and England in late 2004 should be postponed, but that Zimbabwe should continue to play one-day internationals. Their Test programme would resume in January 2005 in Bangladesh. In the meantime, the A-teams of India and South Africa would tour to increase Zimbabwe's exposure to first-class cricket. The board also told the ZCU and its players to agree a process to resolve their dispute in the next 14 days, after which the ICC would decide whether to apply its own disputes resolution process. The ICC agreed to investigate allegations of ZCU racism.

A decision on whether to move the ICC headquarters from London to Dubai or Malaysia was deferred when the UK government submitted a new proposal on possible tax concessions.

It was decided that all matches at the 2004 Asia Cup, including those involving Associate Members Hong Kong and the United Arab Emirates, would have full international status.

China, Mexico and the Isle of Man were granted ICC affiliate membership, bringing total membership to 92.

Percy Sonn, the former president of the United Cricket Board of South Africa, was elected ICC vice-president on South Africa's nomination, to succeed Ehsan Mani as president at the annual conference in 2005.

2007 WORLD CUP – AWARD OF MATCHES

The venues for the 51 matches in the 2007 World Cup were announced in Jamaica on July 14. Barbados would host seven matches including the final; Jamaica won seven including one semi-final, plus the opening ceremony; St Lucia seven including one semi-final; Antigua & Barbuda, Grenada, Guyana, Trinidad & Tobago and St Kitts & Nevis six each.

ZIMBABWEAN CRISIS – ALTERNATIVE DISPUTE RESOLUTION TRIBUNAL

On July 20, the rebel Zimbabwean players agreed to the ICC's proposed alternative to the formal disputes resolution process: a three-person tribunal to deal with the dispute over the captaincy, the selection of the Zimbabwe team, and relations between directors and players. The ZCU and the rebel players should each nominate one person, who would together nominate a third as chairman. The ZCU nominated Norman Arendse, and the players Justice Hungwe; former Test player John Traicos was named chairman. The tribunal was dissolved on November 16, however, when the players withdrew, apparently feeling that the process was too lengthy and expensive, and unlikely to produce a satisfactory result.

CODE OF CONDUCT HEARING

On August 17, former Kenyan captain Maurice Odumbe was banned by the Kenya Cricket Association for five years. At a four-day hearing in Nairobi in July, presided over by Justice Ahmed Ebrahim of Zimbabwe, witnesses had testified that Odumbe accepted money and hotel accommodation from Indian bookmaker Jagdish Sodha in 2002 and 2003 in order to fix matches. Justice Ebrahim found most of the charges proved, though Odumbe was neither charged with nor convicted of actually fixing games.

ZIMBABWEAN CRISIS – RACISM HEARING

On September 29, India's Solicitor General, Goolam Vahanvati, and South African High Court Judge Steven Majiedt opened a hearing in Harare into allegations of racism in Zimbabwean cricket. It was adjourned on the first day when Vahanvati and Majiedt reluctantly accepted the players' request that three ZCU members should not be present while the players' evidence was recorded. The ZCU objected and, with both sides threatening to withdraw, the panel announced on the second day that oral submissions were concluded, though further written submissions were invited.

At the ICC board meeting at Lahore in October, Vahanvati and Majiedt presented a 73-page report stating they found no "direct or credible evidence of racism on the part of the ZCU as an institution", but that discontent over selection and the functioning of some ZCU directors needed to be addressed. They recommended broad-based selection, without any regional bias; appointing competent, hands-on selectors; investigation of the complaint that selectors did not attend matches in certain regions; setting up a players' association, with a players' representative to liaise with the ZCU; improving communication between the players and the ZCU; implementing the policy of integration "with tact and restraint rather than in an aggressive or confrontational manner"; and a transparent grievance process.

ECB CHIEF EXECUTIVE

On October 13, the England and Wales Cricket Board named David Collier as its next chief executive, succeeding Tim Lamb. Collier, chosen from a shortlist of eight, had been Nottinghamshire's chief executive for five years. He took office on January 1, 2005.

In September, David Morgan had been confirmed in his position as chairman of the ECB for a second two-year term, no other candidate being nominated.

ICC EXECUTIVE BOARD

The ICC board met in Lahore on October 16 and 17 and considered alternatives to the current five-year international programme, including extending the timescale to six years and modifying the programme for Zimbabwe and Bangladesh. It was agreed that each country should consider the proposals before further discussions in March 2005. The decision on the location of the ICC offices was again deferred.

It was decided that players currently banned for match-fixing and related activities should not be granted media accreditation for international matches and events. It was also agreed that the ICC Code of Conduct should be amended to make it clear national selectors were among the team officials bound by the code.

The board agreed to review the format of the Champions Trophy before its return in 2006.

ECB FIRST-CLASS FORUM

On October 21, the ECB announced that a meeting of the First-Class Forum the previous week had agreed that, from 2005, a percentage of the fees paid to the 18 first-class counties would reward counties on criteria including the number of England players produced by the county, the number of players provided for England A and age-group sides, the number of Under-23 England-qualified players contracted by the county, the number of England-qualified contracted players appearing in the Championship and the one-day League, the implementation of a county academy and the qualifications of coaching staff.

The forum also approved an England Development Squad of up to 25 of the best England-qualified players, both centrally contracted and county contracted, who would fall under the control of the England head coach.

It was agreed that in 2006 counties could still sign two overseas players, who could be substituted if required by their home boards, but all overseas players and their substitutes must be nominated by July 1, and no substitutes would be allowed to replace injured players or other substitutes.

ICC CRICKET COMMITTEE

The ICC Cricket Committee, chaired by Sunil Gavaskar, met in Dubai on November 9 and 10 to consider a report on dealing with flawed bowling actions. A subcommittee of former Test players – Aravinda de Silva, Angus Fraser, Michael Holding, Tony Lewis, Tim May and David Richardson – had reviewed research carried out by Dr Paul Hurrion during the ICC Champions Trophy in September and by two other biomechanics specialists, Professor Bruce Elliot and Marc Portus. They recommended that the starting point for any report should be the suspect action's appearance to the naked eye. The review process should be reduced from two stages to one, managed by the ICC from the outset; the gap between reporting and assessment should be cut from six to four weeks, during which the bowler could still play. If the action was then found illegal, the player should be automatically suspended until it was remedied; a second report during the following two years could result in a year-long ban. The rules should concentrate on bowlers straightening their arms from a flexed position rather than involuntarily moving the arm backwards, or sideways at the elbow joint. They preferred one standard limit of 15 degrees straightening for all bowlers rather than different figures for different types of bowler.

ECB BROADCASTING RIGHTS

On December 15, the ECB announced that it had sold TV rights for 2006 to 2009 to BSkyB and Channel Five. The satellite company BSkyB gained exclusive rights to live coverage of all international and domestic cricket in England and Wales, with a commitment to provide uninterrupted coverage of all international cricket, while terrestrial Channel Five won the rights to highlights of Tests and one-day internationals, to be broadcast between 7.15 and 8 p.m. BBC Radio retained radio commentary rights for all home international cricket and non-exclusive rights to domestic cricket, including the Cheltenham & Gloucester Trophy and the Twenty20 Cup. TalkSPORT Radio was also given non-exclusive rights to the Twenty20 Cup. The various deals were expected to provide a combined total of £220m over four years.

ECB DOMESTIC COMPETITIONS REFORM

On December 23, the ECB announced changes in the structure of domestic one-day cricket from 2006 after the First-Class Forum approved the recommendations of the Domestic Structure Interim Working Party the previous week. To increase the amount of 50-over county cricket, the knockout format of the Cheltenham & Gloucester Trophy would be replaced by a league format. The 18 first-class counties plus Scotland and Ireland would be divided into two conferences, north and south; the Minor Counties would no longer take part. During the first half of the season, the conferences would play round robins, with nine 50-over matches for each team; the northern winner would meet the southern winner in a Lord's final in August. All games would be played in coloured clothing, with a white ball.

The existing one-day league (currently the totesport League) would begin in mid-July. Two divisions would be retained, but teams would play eight matches not 16, and 40 overs a side not 45. There would be automatic two-up two-down promotion and relegation between divisions, but the third team in the second division would host a play-off against the seventh team from the first to settle the remaining place.

The Twenty20 Cup, to be held in between these two competitions, would retain its new 2005 format: eight group matches for each county, followed by quarter-finals and a Finals Day. The ECB was investigating adding two overseas teams.

The County Championship would retain its current format. From 2006, however, prize money would be paid to the top three counties in the first division plus the second-division winners, rather than the top two counties in each division.

From 2006, England A would play two first-class matches – or one first-class match and two one-day matches – against the tourists.

To encourage player development during the winter, the ECB urged counties to contract players for longer periods of the year (preferably 12 months).

Opposite: Mightier than the bat?
Retired Australian captain Steve Waugh
signs copies of his latest book.
Picture by Adam Pretty, Getty Images

PART EIGHT

The Wisden Review

CHRONICLE OF 2004

JANUARY

6 Steve Waugh's last Test ends in draw and an enthralling series finishes 1–1, with India retaining Border–Gavaskar Trophy. In Sri Lanka, Central Province score the highest fourth-innings total to win a first-class match – 513 for nine v Southern Province. **9** In Colombo, a key witness in fraud case against Sri Lankan board president, Thilanga Sumathipala, is shot dead. **16** Graeme Smith and Herschelle Gibbs complete a record third 300 Test partnership, v West Indies at Centurion. **17** Sumathipala detained on charges of fraud and passport forgery. **19 David Hookes dies after a fracas outside a Melbourne hotel.**

FEBRUARY

10 Shane Warne plays for Victoria Second XI in comeback from one-year drugs ban. **18** At the Under-19 World Cup in Bangladesh, Zimbabwe beat Australia, and Nepal beat South Africa.

MARCH

5 Pakistan beat West Indies to win Under-19 World Cup. **7** The Waugh twins retire from first-class cricket. **8** Warne returns to Test cricket, v Sri Lanka at Galle. **10** Bangladesh beat Zimbabwe at Harare, their first international win since May 1999. **12** Warne becomes second man to 500 Test wickets and ends his comeback with a match-winning ten for 159. **13** India and Pakistan renew normal cricketing relations as India win the one-day international at Karachi: the match contains a record 693 runs. **14** Steve Harmison takes seven for 12 at Kingston to skittle West Indies for 47, their record low. Jacques Kallis becomes first man since Don Bradman to hit centuries in five successive Tests. **16** Muttiah Muralitharan reaches 500 Test wickets. **22** New Zealand complete first home Test match win over South Africa. **23** England retain Wisden Trophy with win at Port-of-Spain. **28** In Colombo, Australia complete 3–0 Test white-wash; Muralitharan reported for throwing his *doosra*; Hashan Tillekeratne resigns as Sri Lankan captain. **29** Virender Sehwag hits 309 at Multan, India's first Test triple-century. **31** Marvan Atapattu named Sri Lankan Test captain; Sumathipala stands down as board president.

APRIL

2 Heath Streak loses Zimbabwean captaincy, after ZCU refuse his demands for change in selection personnel and policies. **3** At Bridgetown, Matthew Hoggard takes England's tenth Test hat-trick and England win series. **12 In Antigua, Brian Lara makes 400 not out, reclaiming the Test record.** Waqar Younis retires from international cricket. **15** Streak and 14 other white rebel players ignored for one-day series v Sri Lanka. **16** India beat Pakistan at Rawalpindi to take Test series 2–1. **25** In Harare, Zimbabwe dismissed for 35 by Sri Lanka, a record low for one-day internationals.

> ❝'I'm just there to watch the cricket and I don't give a rat's arse what he does about his country,' Jones said."
>
> The Australians in Zimbabwe, page 1237.

MAY

8 In Harare, Muralitharan breaks Courtney Walsh's world record of 519 Test wickets. 11 After testing Muralitharan's action, ICC tell him not to bowl his *doosra*. Alf Valentine, hero of West Indies' 1950 tour of England, dies. **14** Australian Prime Minister John Howard claims that Murali throws. **21** Zimbabwe cancel Test series v Australia, pre-empting ICC moves to suspend their Test status. **24** England successfully chase 282 to beat New Zealand at Lord's, with Nasser Hussain hitting memorable century. **27** Hussain announces retirement from all cricket. Tim Lamb announces he will step down as ECB chief executive in September. **30** John Davison has best first-class bowling figures in 48 years: 17 for 137 for Canada v USA at Fort Lauderdale.

JUNE

1 In St Lucia, Bangladesh declare for the first time – and draw for the third – in their 29 Tests. **2** Abhijit Kale, an Indian batsman accused of trying to bribe two national selectors, is banned until 2005. **10** ICC suspend Zimbabwe's Test schedule until end of 2004. **11** Craig Spearman hits 341 for Gloucestershire against Middlesex, breaking W. G. Grace's 128-year-old county record. **13** England win Third Test v New Zealand at Nottingham, their first 3–0 whitewash since 1978. **15** Muralitharan withdraws from Sri Lanka's forthcoming tour of Australia, citing "personal reasons". **16** Javed Miandad loses job as Pakistan coach; Bob Woolmer succeeds him. **17** Ireland beat West Indies in Belfast. Vince Hogg resigns as managing director of Zimbabwe Cricket Union. **20** Sir Viv Richards resigns as West Indies chairman of selectors. **22** Jack Russell retires.

JULY

13 Warne equals Muralitharan's record 527 Test wickets. **15** First Twenty20 match at Lord's is a sell-out. **25** Michael Vaughan becomes the first man since Graham Gooch in 1990 to hit two centuries in a Lord's Test.

AUGUST

1 England retain Wisden Trophy again. **5** New Zealand women win cricket's first Twenty20 international, v England at Hove. **6** Murali pulls ahead of Warne again. **15** Sri Lanka complete first Test series win over South Africa, in Colombo. At Manchester, Lara becomes fourth batsman to 10,000 Test runs. **17** Kenyan Maurice Odumbe found guilty of taking bookmakers' money and banned from cricket for five years. **21** England complete 4–0 series whitewash over West Indies; their run of seven successive wins equals record of 1884-85 to 1887-88 and 1928 to 1928-29. **26** ECB chairman David Morgan chosen unopposed for new two-year term. **28** Gloucestershire win C&G Trophy for fourth time in six years.

SEPTEMBER

5 Essex lose to Glamorgan after scoring 642. **6** Warwickshire win County Championship. **7** Rahul Dravid named Player of the Year at ICC's first awards ceremony; Andrew Flintoff wins the one-day award. **8** Hurricane Ivan destroys Grenada's National Stadium. **10** Champions Trophy in England begins with USA's one-day international debut, a 210-run defeat by New Zealand. **17** Pre-season favourites Lancashire relegated from

Championship's first division. **21** England reach Champions Trophy final, after beating Australia for first time in 15 one-day internationals. **22** West Indies beat Pakistan in second semi-final at the Rose Bowl. **25** West Indies win Champions Trophy at The Oval thanks to a ninth-wicket stand of 71 in near-darkness. **29** ICC hearing into alleged racism in Zimbabwean cricket begins in Harare. The Wanderers Club in Johannesburg burns down.

OCTOBER

4 Gus Logie steps down as West Indies coach. **7** In Bangalore, Michael Clarke hits 151 on Test debut for Australia. **11 Keith Miller dies, aged 84.** **13** David Collier named ECB's new chief executive. **15** Warne takes his 533rd Test wicket and pulls ahead of Murali again. Eric Simons resigns as South Africa coach; Ray Jennings named as caretaker. **17** ICC investigation rejects allegations of racism in Zimbabwe. **26** Bennett King appointed West Indies' first foreign coach. **29** At Nagpur, Australia thrash India by 342 runs to regain the Border–Gavaskar Trophy and secure their first series win in India since 1969-70.

NOVEMBER

3 Nicky Boje withdraws from South Africa's squad to tour India because of fears of arrest over past match-fixing allegations. **5** India bowl out Australia for 93, their lowest in 20 years, to end series 2–1, after Clarke takes six for nine on much-criticised Mumbai pitch. **7** Stephen Fleming claims to have been offered £200,000 in 1999 to join a match-fixing syndicate. **10** ICC investigation into illegal bowling actions announces that most bowlers exceed the permissible degree of straightening and says it should be increased to 15 degrees. **22** Scotland win inaugural Intercontinental Cup for ICC Associates, beating Canada in two days at Sharjah. **23** Zimbabwe government bans 13 British journalists from entering the country to cover England tour. **24** England cancel flight to Harare. After a contract dispute, West Indies drop 16 players – including Brian Lara – for forthcoming one-day series in Australia. **25** Zimbabwe government backs down over journalists; England agree to play all but first scheduled one-day international. **30** At Adelaide, Australia complete 2–0 series win over New Zealand.

DECEMBER

2 At Kolkata, South Africa lose Second Test to India, and the series 1–0. At Sydney, New South Wales bowl South Australia out for 29. **5** England wrap up 4–0 win in one-day series with Zimbabwe. South Africa sack Omar Henry as convenor of selectors. **8** Neck injury forces Allan Donald to retire from all cricket. **10** At Dhaka, Anil Kumble overtakes Kapil Dev's Indian-record 434 Test wickets. **11 Tendulkar equals Sunil Gavaskar's world-record 34 Test centuries. 15** Sky TV awarded rights to show all England's home Tests from 2006 to 2009. **18** Former Indian captain Vijay Hazare dies aged 89. **19** Australia beat Pakistan by 491 runs at Perth, the fourth-biggest Test win by runs; Glenn McGrath takes eight for 24, the second-best Test figures by an Australian. **20** India take series against Bangladesh 2–0; Harbhajan Singh reported for allegedly throwing his *doosra*. **21** At Port Elizabeth, England stretch their run of Test wins to eight, a national record. **25** West Indies board announce full-strength squad for one-day series in Australia after settling dispute. **26** A tsunami devastates Indian Ocean coasts, killing many thousands across Asia; Test ground at Galle severely damaged. Bangladesh beat India in one-day international at Dhaka. **30** England's winning run ended in Durban when bad light helps South Africa to a draw. **31** Justin Langer of Australia ends 2004 as highest Test run-scorer of the year and India's Kumble as leading wicket-taker. Warne has 561 wickets and Murali 532.

The following stories were also reported in the media during 2004:

SYDNEY MORNING HERALD   January 7

Police have clamped down on one of the Sydney Cricket Ground's newest and most popular institutions: the beer wench. For the second summer running, busty bikini-wearing women have been serving beer for spectators who don't want to queue. But Inspector Mark Szalajko yesterday said the

wenches promoted irresponsible drinking: "So far this week we have ejected four of them, all for serving alcohol to intoxicated persons, and one lady for acting in an offensive manner. My message to potential beer wenches is 'Stay home or face fines of up to $550.'"

THE GUARDIAN   January 23

Comedian Jimmy Tarbuck included a tape of the *Test Match Special* "legover" giggle between Brian Johnston and Jonathan Agnew in 1991 in his eight-disc selection for *Desert Island Discs* on BBC Radio Four.

DAILY MIRROR, COLOMBO   January 23

An 18-year-old youth was hit on the head with a stump and died while umpiring a game in Colombo. A 21-year-old bowler in the match was arrested. Eyewitnesses said the suspect had claimed he was bowling like Mushtaq Ahmed; the umpire, Mohamed Aboosali Pasreen, scoffed.

THE SUN-HERALD, SYDNEY   January 25

A bolt of lightning killed a cricketer yesterday with a shock so intense it shattered his bat. David Evans was playing for the Bomaderry Fourth Grade team in southern New South Wales when the bolt hit out of a clear sky. "The bat just exploded," said Bomaderry secretary Graeme Sawkins. "It left a hole in the ground next to the wicket where he was standing and six or seven other players got knocked down with the impact." Evans, 31, came from a well-known local cricketing family.

AUSTRALIAN ASSOCIATED PRESS   January 26

Steve Waugh has been named as Australian of the Year 2004, prime minister John Howard announced. He is the third successive Test captain to be given the award after Allan Border (1989) and Mark Taylor (1999).

ABC RADIO: THE WORLD TODAY   January 30

Former Australian captain Greg Chappell said the order he gave to his brother Trevor in 1981 to bowl the last ball of a one-day international underarm was the product of a mental breakdown. "I was mentally wrung out, I was physically wrung out and I was fed up with the whole system," Chappell said. "Things seemed to be just closing in on us, and I suppose in my case they were closing in on me, and it was a cry for help... I thought 'I've had a gutful of this.'"

ROTORUA POST   January 31

A Rotorua cricketer found himself fielding at deep, deep fine leg after the ground gave way beneath his feet and trapped him in a hole filled with hot water. The unnamed man, who was fielding in an inter-business match in Kuirau Park, was treated for burns. The area is full of thermal springs.

SYDNEY MORNING HERALD   February 5

Research at the University of New South Wales School of Optometry suggested short sight might not be a disadvantage while batting. David Mann used a bowling machine to fire balls at batsmen wearing contact lenses that blurred their vision and found they performed as well as they normally did. He speculated that short-sightedness may compel batsmen to play strokes later or concentrate harder to compensate for poorer vision.

DAILY MIRROR, COLOMBO   February 10

Sohan Boralessa, 18, of St Peter's College took all ten wickets for 30 against Wesley College.

AGENCE FRANCE-PRESSE   February 17

Police arrested nine white cricketers for dancing nude in the rain on the cricket pitch at Hwange, Zimbabwe, during celebrations marking the anniversary of the Wankie Cricket Club. Inspector Andrew Phiri said: "They were all playing cricket, following the normal cricket rules and when it started raining all the officials and players left the ground. All of a sudden these nine undressed, rushed back and started dancing round naked... nude, nude." He added that some spectators took photographs.

OUTLOOK   February 23

Two youths from the village of Santagarh, Uttar Pradesh were murdered because the upper-caste Hasanpur cricket team resented the lower-caste Santagarh players' regular victories over them, according to civil liberties campaigners. "The cricket team from Hasanpur, made up mostly of Rajputs, seems to have taken the defeats as an insult to their pride and honour," said Pushkar Raj of the People's Union for Civil Liberties.

PRESS GAZETTE   February 27

The *News of the World* launched a furious attack on the England and Wales Cricket Board after it wrecked an exclusive interview with England captain Michael Vaughan by emailing an advance copy of the text to two rival papers. Cricket correspondent David Norrie had sent the board a copy of the interview as "a courtesy". Norrie said: "It's outrageous. After being immersed in the totally professional world of the England rugby set-up for the past few months, I'd happily forgotten the antics of the Carry on Cricket bunch at Lord's."

INDIAN EXPRESS   February 28

The Indian government waived customs duty and the requirements for a road-worthiness certificate so Sachin Tendulkar could import a £90,000 Ferrari Modena 360. Bharat Petroleum also blended special fuel so the car could run on Indian roads; the 97-octane petrol the car requires is not sold in India.

THE TELEGRAPH, CALCUTTA   March 5

The Gujarat government refused to allow Indian wicket-keeper Parthiv Patel and fast bowler Irfan Pathan to defer their 12th standard exams after they were selected for the tour of Pakistan. "A lot of other students may queue up citing various reasons," said a spokesman.

DAILY MIRROR, COLOMBO   March 15

A 19-year-old prefect at Royal College was drowned in a ducking ritual at the end of the annual fixture between the college and St Thomas's. Students traditionally jump into the pool on the last day of the game. The father of the dead boy, Isharath Dawood, told the Colombo city coroner that his son could not swim.

THE WISDEN CRICKETER   April

A memorial has been erected at the unmarked Godalming grave of Julius Caesar, who was a member of the first overseas tour by an England team, to North America in 1859.

THE TIMES   April 7

David Graveney, the chairman of the England selectors, has accepted an insurance settlement after his son, Adam, lost most of the vision in his right eye due to an accident in the nets. Adam was 17 when he was struck by a shot hit from an adjoining net at Colston's School in Bristol in 2000. The ball was bowled by John Sexstone, whose father Colin was then Gloucester-shire's chief executive. Graveney had originally threatened to sue the school and both batsman and bowler, but eventually accepted that Adam was outside the net at the time and no one was to blame.

TIMES OF INDIA   April 15

A group of young cricketers playing in Naroda, Ahmedabad, stumbled across 23 signal rockets, which are normally used by ships in distress. One was inadvertently launched, the ensuing explosion triggering panic in the streets and bringing a bomb disposal unit rushing to the field. Police are mystified as to how the rockets found their way 100 miles inland.

THE TIMES *April 15*

Wearing a helmet may seriously affect quick thinking at the crease, according to a research paper presented to the British Psychological Society. Co-author Dr Mick Neave of Northumbria University said: "When your head gets too hot, the higher cognitive functions such as accuracy, response time and vigilance, are the first things to go."

TIMES OF INDIA *April 21*

Parthiv Patel and Irfan Pathan, billed as "the most celebrated first-time voters in Gujarat", were denied a chance to cast their vote when the two Test players discovered that they were not on the electoral roll. Constant touring prevented Patel from registering in time; Pathan's father applied on his behalf but his name was still omitted.

PRESS TRUST OF INDIA *April 22*

All India's 174 retired Test players and umpires are to receive a pension of 5,000 rupees a month.

SUSSEX CCC NEWSLETTER *May*

An electric buggy stopped play during a match between West Blatchington and St Matthias in East Sussex, when a spectator parked himself on the extra-cover boundary. Taking exception when one of the fielders requested that he move the vehicle, the driver allegedly tried to run down the cricketers, then parked on the pitch and steadfastly refused to budge. Only after a plea from a relative did the invader vacate and play resume.

TIMES OF INDIA   May 2

Research by zoologists at St Joseph's College, Bangalore, showed that many professional cricketers exhibit the same fingerprint patterns. Almost all those they surveyed had the "ulnar loop" pattern on the right little finger. Their study was hindered because many Indian players refused to co-operate.

LEICESTER MERCURY   May 4

Martin Crowson of Leicester Ivanhoe took a hat-trick with the first three balls of a Leicestershire County League match at Kibworth. He went on to take seven for 15.

BOLTON EVENING NEWS   May 4

Two women umpires took charge of a first-team Bolton League match for the first time. Karen Knott and Gail Ashton umpired Farnworth v Heaton.

CRICINFO   May 7

The South African Civil Aviation Authority has concluded that bad weather and human error caused the plane crash that killed former Test captain Hansie Cronje. He was travelling on a cargo plane that crashed into a mountainside near George in June 2002.

DAILY MAIL   May 12

Carlisle Cricket Club held a minute's silence in memory of their former player and groundsman, Leonard Brunton, and then rang his home to ask if flowers should be sent. Mr Brunton answered the phone; there had been a misunderstanding.

WELLINGTON WEEKLY NEWS   May 13

Henry, a golden Labrador, held up play for seven minutes in the match between Nynehead and Wombats in Somerset by fielding the ball with his mouth and refusing to drop it.

PRESS ASSOCIATION May 25

A Pakistan fan from Leicester has had to remortgage his house after losing a £50,000 bet on the recent India–Pakistan Test and one-day series. The loser was not named but winner Jake Caratella, who says he is not a cricket fan, was happy to parade his good fortune. "My friend was saying Pakistan this and Pakistan that so I asked him to put his money where his mouth is. He shook my hand and we drew up a contract later that night. I did not watch it because I am not into cricket. I just went around getting on with my life."

CRICINFO May 26

Sachin Tendulkar is now on the Indian curriculum: children in schools in and around Delhi will study the life and times of the nation's idol. New textbooks for those in the 10–12 age group include an interview with Tendulkar, where he talks about his own childhood and what it takes to be a successful cricketer. Krishna Kumar, an education official, said that the move to include a first-person account of Tendulkar's life was part of an effort to make education "a more pleasurable experience".

THE GUARDIAN May 28

Richie Benaud, 74, won the Royal Television Society lifetime achievement award, having just commentated on the England–New Zealand Test at Lord's, his 500th Test as player, journalist, spectator or broadcaster.

WEST BRITON May 28

Play was interrupted in the Cornwall League Division Five West fixture between Praze and Chacewater because a runner was wearing the wrong-coloured helmet. When Chacewater's Chris Gould joined the limping Steve Moyle, umpire Gordon Butcher halted proceedings because his helmet was blue: Moyle's was red. "It was just the fact that both players have to be dressed exactly the same," explained Butcher. "We were all looking for a pot of paint on the sidelines," said Moyle's father John, the next man in.

THE WISDEN CRICKETER June

The radio station, TalkSPORT, has been censured by the Advertising Standards Authority after running an advertising campaign for its coverage of England's Caribbean tour that linked cricket with drugs. The headline used in the ad which appeared in the *Daily Telegraph* read "Splat, splat, spliff". It attracted one complaint from the public.

DAILY NEWS, COLOMBO June 2

Police raided a unique brothel in Templers Road, Mount Lavinia, which for the past ten years had been catering only for professional cricketers. A policeman posing as a cricketer had made a booking and paid 5,000 rupees (about £25). His colleagues then moved in; eight girls in their twenties and their 78-year-old madame were arrested.

THE TIMES June 2

Will Prozesky, a 24-year-old South African playing for Purbrook in the Southern League, hit an unbeaten 214 against Leckford, then took a hat-trick – all bowled. Two balls later, he pulled a hamstring, limped off and took no further part.

BBC ONLINE June 3

First-class umpires have been offered free eye tests and prescription glasses under a sponsorship deal for the Twenty20 Cup signed between the ECB and lens manufacturers Sola.

DAILY MAIL June 4

Ten-year-old Sam Bate, chosen as the England mascot on the opening day of the Headingley Test against New Zealand, got all the home team's autographs. But the New Zealanders asked for a fee of £10 for them to sign.

PRESS GAZETTE June 4

The day after announcing his retirement from Test cricket, Nasser Hussain took his family out for what he hoped would be a quiet pub lunch, away from the press. He then discovered that almost everyone at the General's Arms, Little Baddow, was a journalist. The pub was hosting the Essex Journalist of the Year Awards.

BBC ONLINE June 6

Indian cricketer Abhijit Kale has been banned for the rest of the year after an inquiry into claims that he offered money to selectors Kiran More and Pranab Roy in the hope of being picked for the 2003-04 tour of Australia. Kale denied trying to bribe them, but admitted he had approached the selectors in an attempt to influence them. Roy said he had been offered a million rupees (£12,800) but he and More were criticised for saying nothing for three months.

NORTHERN ECHO, DARLINGTON June 7
Martin Gill, with 23, was the only batsman to score as Seaham Harbour collapsed for 29 against Eppleton in a Durham Senior League match. The other ten batsmen all made nought, Sean Birbeck taking eight for 12.

THE SPIN June 8
Sid the Shark, the Sussex mascot, fell dramatically with victory in sight in the Sport Relief Mascot Derby at Epsom. Sid trod on a fin, got tangled up and fell flat on his face, to be beaten by Sting, representing Wasps rugby club. "I didn't realise I'd outsprinted everyone, but by the end I was getting knackered," explained Sid.

BIGGLESWADE CHRONICLE June 11
The match between Ickwell and Kimbolton in the Bedford Hospital Cup was repeatedly interrupted by BBC production staff running on the pitch prior to broadcasting a weather forecast for the regional news programme *Look East* from the outfield. There were a string of hold-ups to the Kimbolton innings while the camera crew made sound and lighting checks and the programme's host tried to hit a ball against an oak tree.

THE GUARDIAN June 11
Former England captain and Lord's eminence Sir Pelham Warner was famous in his family for his minimal appetite, his eldest grandchild, the author Marina Warner has recalled: "One evening, when he was asked if he would like a second helping, he replied: 'One pea, please.'"

SIFY.COM/PRESS TRUST OF INDIA June 15/November 15
Indian captain Sourav Ganguly's new Kolkata restaurant – Sourav's, The Food Pavilion – was opened by his team-mate and fellow restaurateur Sachin

Tendulkar, who owns two similar establishments in Mumbai. Sourav's is described as "Kolkata's first four-storeyed multiplex restaurant". Ganguly had earlier reportedly been alarmed that Tendulkar was planning to beat him to it by opening a branch in Kolkata.

HEREFORD TIMES   June 17

Openers Alan Jones and Jon Andrews of Garnons put on 349 for the first wicket against Hay in Division Two of the Marches League.

THE TIMES   June 23

Imran Khan announced that his high-society marriage to Jemima, daughter of the late tycoon Sir James Goldsmith, has ended in divorce. Imran admitted that his wife had not been happy living in Pakistan. Mrs Khan has recently been linked with the actor Hugh Grant.

DAILY MAIL   July 6

Former Conservative Party leader Iain Duncan Smith was left covered in blood after being hit near the eye while batting No. 11 in the Fathers v Sons match at Sunningdale School. He gallantly returned to the crease and helped secure the draw. "The boys must have thought I looked quite horrifying, covered in gore," he said.

YORKSHIRE POST   July 10

A cricketer in the Bassetlaw League has been given an eight-week ban, thought to be the longest in the league's history, for making a sexist remark. Mark Barlow of Cutthorpe sledged the England women's player Kate Lowe, who was batting for NSK Newark, telling her: "Go home and make your husband's tea." Barlow said: "This is a case of political correctness gone bananas."

THE TIMES   July 28

The 41-year-old former England fast bowler Devon Malcolm achieved his one remaining cricketing goal, by scoring a century. Playing for Bantham Exiles against Lashings, he reached his hundred off 41 balls, with 11 fours and seven sixes.

THE SUN   August 5

Thieves stole jewellery worth £70,000 from Ian Botham's Yorkshire home during a party.

DAILY TELEGRAPH   August 7

MCC have sacked their caterers Sodexho from 2005. "We've decided to do the catering ourselves," said deputy chief executive David Batts. "So if standards aren't up to scratch, it'll be our feet in the fire."

SUNDAY TELEGRAPH   August 8

A 37-year-old MCC member is being investigated by the police after allegedly drawing a knife on a fellow-member he saw using a mobile phone. The club has a zero tolerance policy on mobile-phone use during matches, but officials were far more shocked about the knife. "I am horrified that anyone should bring a knife when coming to watch cricket," said former president Colin Ingleby-Mackenzie, "unless it was for a delicious picnic."

DAILY TELEGRAPH   August 9

A factory in Catania, Sicily, is producing pasta in the shape of cricket balls to honour Italy's reaching the ICC Trophy qualifying tournament in Malaysia in February 2005.

CRICINFO   August 12

Australia's leading cricketers have been asked to return more than $A500,000 (about £200,000) after they were overpaid due to "administrative error".

DAILY TELEGRAPH   August 13

A rabbit accidentally set alight by a cricket club bonfire took refuge in the groundsman's hut and caused a blaze that ruined £60,000 worth of equipment. A volunteer was using paraffin to burn branches at Devizes Cricket Club, Wiltshire when the rabbit, on fire, shot out from the pile. The club's two big mowers were destroyed, as was the rabbit. "It's very sad for the poor thing," said fire station commander Pip Flowers.

EVENING POST, BRISTOL   August 17

Fifteen hot air balloons stopped play in the Bristol & District League match between University Staff and YMCA at the Coombe Dingle sports complex. The cricketers directed all but one of them to neighbouring fields, but the well-known balloonist Don Cameron landed on the pitch to avoid crashing into the pavilion. The game was further delayed as they helped him pack up.

DAILY MAIL   August 23

Imran Khan was held for three hours at Dulles Airport, Washington, for a second time, because his name was similar to someone on a list of terrorist suspects.

DAILY POST, LIVERPOOL   September 6

Pwllhelli Cricket Club suffered a double whammy in the North Wales League. Their first team were going well against Gwersyllt Park, who fielded only nine players but then left at tea without explanation. The Second XI did complete their game, unfortunately: they were bowled out for five by Castell Alun.

DAILY TELEGRAPH   September 7

What is thought to be the world's shortest scheduled cricket match may have to be abandoned forever because of global warming. The annual match between the Royal Southern Yacht Club and the Island Sailing Club is staged on a sandbank in The Solent for 40 minutes a year when it is exposed by the tide. As sea levels rise, the pitch may be forever waterlogged. "The cricketers are lucky that they have been able to play for this long," said oceanographer Professor Carl Amos.

BBC ONLINE   September 8

Three thousand white umpiring jackets have been stolen from a garage in Kent. An official of the Association of Cricket Umpires & Scorers was storing them in a garage in Rainham and returned there to find they had vanished. Kent police said the jackets were very distinctive, with a green association badge and a red Post Office sponsorship logo. "Maybe they should try looking on Ebay," said MCC spokeswoman Clare Skinner.

THE TIMES   September 9

The Committee of Tattersalls, which adjudicates on unpaid betting bills on British racecourses, has quietly deleted the name of Sir Garfield Sobers from its Excluded Persons List, on which he had apparently languished since the 1960s. Sobers has now settled his unpaid debts from his cricketing days.

THE SUN   September 10

England wicket-keeper Chris Read was the victim of an attack by armed raiders who burst into his home at 3 a.m. and threatened him, his fiancée and his parents, ordering him to hand over the keys to his car: a limited-edition Ford Focus Rally Sport. Read complied, and they took the car.

DAILY NEWS, COLOMBO   September 14

A 15-year-old schoolboy at Trinity College, Kandy, Sachith Pathirana, scored 228 out of his team's 294 for six declared against Rahula College. He is believed to be Sri Lanka's youngest double-centurion.

DORSET ECHO   September 15

Weymouth fast bowler Glen Dawson was banned for the whole of 2005, and the team were docked 35 points, after Dawson stuck a picture of Colehill's Carl Brissett on the dressing-room wall with the caption "Kill the ****" before the teams met. Brissett spotted the picture and complained.

THE BOOKSELLER   September 17

An Australian coalminer flew to London to attend a book launch and then went straight home again. Kip Barr was determined not to miss the party for *Test Cricket Grounds*, written by his friend John Woods, and set out from Sydney on Tuesday morning to attend the Thursday evening party, and went back on Friday in readiness for his shift at the pit on Sunday morning.

"He's a mate," said Mr Barr. "John would do the same for me if I ever wrote a book."

MAIL ON SUNDAY   September 26

Gypsies have moved their caravans on to the pitch at 150-year-old Bulwell Cricket Club, Nottingham, causing damage which some locals believe will be impossible to repair. "I can't see how we'll survive this," said club chairman Fred Bramley. Nottingham City Council spent £40,000 relaying the pitch in 2003.

AGENCE FRANCE-PRESSE   October 8

A Hyderabad court has ordered Pepsi-Cola to withdraw an advert showing a boy serving Pepsi to the Indian cricket team because it depicts child labour.

DAILY TELEGRAPH   October 9

Hugh Cornwell, lead singer of the rock band The Stranglers, says in his autobiography that he experienced a life-changing moment and decided to leave the band after watching Devon Malcolm hit a six against India in the Old Trafford Test of 1990. "Unexpectedly I suddenly identify with this character and recognise that the effort being made to fight his way out of the straitjacket situation in which the Indian bowlers have placed him perfectly mirrors my own current, repressed state within the group. As I watch the ball soar high over the turf, it comes to me in a flash that I should leave The Stranglers tonight, after the gig."

FREE PRESS JOURNAL, MUMBAI   October 12

Rahul Dravid has been voted sexiest Indian sports personality in the 2004 Durex global sex survey. Yuvraj Singh was second with Sachin Tendulkar third.

THE ADVERTISER, ADELAIDE   October 18

"Fashion police" were installed outside the members' enclosure at the Adelaide Oval after the South Australian Cricket Association imposed a ban on jeans with designer tears, "revealing" tops, thongs [flip-flops] and T-shirts. "The members love it," said SACA marketing manager Terry Davies.

CRICINFO   October 24

The Queen's Park Cricket Club in Port-of-Spain has finally voted to admit women members after a seven-year campaign led by journalist Vaneisa Baksh. The Trinidad & Tobago prime minister had hinted that unless the club relented, he might not help fund 2007 World Cup matches at the stadium, supporting a new facility in San Fernando instead. After the vote, by 346–194, club president Willie Rodriguez said women would still have to join the long waiting list.

SUNDAY TELEGRAPH   October 31

Club batsmen in Melbourne have been warned by local councils not to hit sixes for fear that they might hit passers-by who will then demand compensation. More than 100 clubs in the Eastern Cricket Association are affected by the ban. Batsmen who hit sixes will be awarded no runs and warned for the first offence; five runs will be deducted for any subsequent six. Canterbury fast bowler Henry Gregory said people should wear helmets or stay at home.

THE ADVERTISER, ADELAIDE   November 5

An Adelaide advertising agency is hunting body-doubles for members of the Australian team. A "top secret" ad campaign is due to feature the players, but they are only available for a short time.

THE TIMES   November 8

Tim Hudson, the pony-tailed entrepreneur who was briefly Ian Botham's agent at the height of his fame, has put his ten-acre ground, Birtles Bowl near Prestbury in Cheshire, up for sale. Hudson was forced to sell his 18th-century house, Birtles Old Hall, when he went broke in 1990 but hung on to the cricket ground, even though it became covered in weeds. "Cricket was the most incredible trip I ever had," said Hudson from his home in California. "Then, unfortunately, I ran out of money."

SOUTH CHINA MORNING POST   November 14

Hong Kong Cricket Club have suspended fixtures because of fears that big-hitting batsman Hussain Butt is a safety threat to passing traffic. Butt scored 311 not out for Hong Kong University with 36 sixes, two of which hit passing cars. The club intend to raise the safety nets by an additional three metres.

AGENCE FRANCE-PRESSE   November 30

A diamond and gold cricket ball, made in Sri Lanka and brought to Australia for the opening of a new jewellery store in Melbourne, is reported to be the first of its kind. Composed of 2,704 diamonds and an 18-carat gold stitch, it weighs 53.83 carats and has a 125-gram gold seam. The material used to keep the diamonds on the ball is similar to one used on the wings of NASA space shuttles.

BBC ONLINE   December 1

England coach Duncan Fletcher has been awarded the Mussabini Medal, which acknowledges "the contribution of coaches to UK performers who have achieved success on the world stage".

THE TELEGRAPH, CALCUTTA   December 3

The Speaker of the Indian Parliament, Somnath Chatterjee, summoned senior broadcasting officials and reprimanded them for showing the India v South

Africa Test instead of parliamentary question hour. The officials offered an unconditional apology; Chatterjee said he was granting "conditional pardon".

The Anjuman-I-Islam Fort English School scored 1,121 in a match in the Harris Shield in Mumbai, the same competition in which Sachin Tendulkar once put on 664 with Vinod Kambli. This time, Shishir Tiwari and Sufian Shaikh added 531 for the fifth wicket against St John the Baptist School from Thane. Tiwari made 318. The total was 989 for six but, under competition rules, the fielding team were penalised 132 runs (12 per over) for bowling 11 overs less than their allotment.

Later reports suggested that this score should be regarded as suspicious. Other school coaches claimed the fielders were not trying. The Mumbai School Sports Association absolved the teams of match-fixing but said this should not be regarded as any kind of record.

New Zealand schoolboy Matt Nelson, 12, clean bowled five successive victims in an Under-13 match for Taradale against Central Hawke's Bay.

Playing for St Benedict's College in an Under-12 competition in Colombo, left-arm wrist-spinner Shannon Patterson picked up seven for nine in the first innings and nine for 23 in the second, against Maha Bodhi College.

A match in Dhanmodi was halted by an army helicopter crash-landing on the outfield. No one was hurt, though the tailbone of the helicopter broke in two. Players in the First Division match between Surjatarun and Jatrabari Krira Sangha watched in disbelief as it came down barely 50ft from the umpire and bowler. Groundsman Habibur Rahman Habib said he heard a long bang, and saw the helicopter heading for the players. Then everyone started running for cover.

A crowd estimated at 8,000 turned up at the Windy Hill football ground in Melbourne to watch an hour-long exhibition match between six Australian Test players and the Essendon Australian Rules football team.

The search engine MSN reported that "cricket" was the eighth most requested word or phrase among British users in 2004. It was behind Big Brother, Inland Revenue, Horoscopes, EastEnders, Football, Alton Towers and Jordan (thought to mean the model more often than the country) but ahead of, among others, Barbie, Harry Potter, Arsenal and Wedding dresses.

THE GUARDIAN December 31

Andrew Flintoff was named joint winner in Britain's Beard of the Year competition, sharing the title with Paul Mackney, leader of the lecturers' union, NATFHE.

Cartoons by Nick Newman

Chronicle is compiled by Rob Steen and Matthew Engel. We welcome contributions from readers, especially for items from local or non-UK papers. Please send newspaper cuttings to Matthew Engel at Fair Oak, Bacton, Herefordshire HR2 0AT (always including the paper's name and date) and weblinks to almanack@wisdengroup.com.

OBITUARIES

ABELL, JOHN NORMAN, who died on May 26, 2004, aged 72, kept wicket in three first-class matches for Oxford University. He failed to emulate his father George by winning a Blue. But in his final match he did manage to stump both the Richardson brothers, Peter and Dick, who were playing for his father's old county, Worcestershire.

AINLEY, ANTHONY, who died on May 3, 2004, aged 71, was an actor and a keen club cricketer for The Stage and London Theatres CC. "He was an eccentric and very effective opening bat who appeared in full body padding, sunblock, helmet and swimming goggles," according to his fellow-actor Christopher Douglas, "and he had a penchant for charging down the track and smashing the ball back over the bowler's head." Ainley followed his father Henry on to the stage, but found his greatest success on television as The Master, the arch-enemy of Doctor Who, in the 1980s. At one club game at the time, Ainley's fame preceded him, and the *Sutton & Cheam Herald* ran a headline above its match report proclaiming that "Inter-Galactic Terror" had been visited upon Surrey. A complex character, he usually took his cricket teas alone in his car – possibly because, according to one report, he "despised cheeses of all kinds".

ALLEY, WILLIAM EDWARD, died on November 26, 2004, aged 85. Bill Alley became a Somerset legend, although he was born in Australia and did not make his county debut until 1957, when he was 38. In 1961 he was the last man ever to score 3,000 first-class runs in a season. He later became a Test umpire, and one of the game's most durable characters.

Alley arrived in Sydney in the 1940s, working as a labourer, nightclub bouncer, blacksmith's assistant and oyster fisherman. He was also making a name as a New South Wales batsman, and as a boxer: he was unbeaten in 28 fights as a welterweight. But boxing – and almost cricket too – came to an end after a gruesome accident in the Adelaide nets in 1946. His team-mate Jock Livingston hooked a ball that went through the net and poleaxed Alley in the adjacent one. He needed 60 stitches in his jaw and was in a coma for two days. He pulled through, but the accident set back his hopes of touring England in 1948. A year earlier, Bradman had hinted that Alley was likely to win a spot on Australia's first post-war tour, to New Zealand early in 1946 – but Ron Hamence went instead. Alley had even acquired a dozen new white shirts for the trip.

After his first wife died in childbirth (their son, Ken, also died young in an army accident), Alley decided to take up an offer to play in the Lancashire leagues, and enjoyed ten prolific seasons with Colne and Blackpool. Apart from a tour of India with a strong Commonwealth XI in 1949-50, when he plundered two unbeaten double-centuries, it appeared that Alley's first-class days were over: some counties made offers, but the sums involved were hardly more for six-days-a-week cricket than for Saturdays only in the leagues. Finally, though, he decided to give county cricket a go – with Somerset, he later wrote, "because of the sheer magic of the name".

Alley was no stylist, a left-hander who favoured the leg side and the horizontal bat; but every now and then he would play a beautiful cover-drive. The man himself summed up his own philosophy succinctly: "If the ball is there to be hit, for Christ's sake hit it." And in 1961 he hit it everywhere. "The crease was his

Bill Alley, born in Australia but a Somerset legend.

Picture by Patrick Eagar

God-given territory," wrote David Foot. "He occupied it with the mannerisms of a lusty, lovable black-sheep squire." In 1960, Alley had made only 807 runs at 23. But now, aged 42, he was relentless. His 3,019 runs at 56.96 included 11 centuries, among them his career-best 221 not out against Warwickshire at Nuneaton. His Somerset team-mate Roy Virgin preferred his 156 at Northampton: "Malcolm Scott, the left-arm spinner, was bowling, and Bill was almost placing his field for him. He'd say 'No, you want that bloke at mid-wicket a bit squarer', and then he'd smash the ball over the chap's head anyway." He even made 134 and 95 against the touring Australians.

The following year Alley persuaded his captain to use his right-arm seamers rather more, and he finished with 112 wickets (at only 20.74 apiece) to go with 1,915 runs. He was record-conscious enough to rue the missing 85 runs that cost him an even rarer double. His bowling fell away a little in later seasons, though team-mates remember how nimbly he would run in. And he continued to field brilliantly in the gully ("Bill just plucked legitimate cut-shots out of the air," said Virgin) and collect his annual 1,000 runs every year bar one until 1968. Bill kept talking too. Once he waved a handkerchief at Fred Trueman, and said it would do as a thigh-pad against him. His forthright manner offended some of his team-mates, and this appears to have cost him the chance of the county captaincy in 1965 after he had deputised the previous year. He played on and would have been there after his 50th birthday, except that Somerset offered him terms for one-day games only. He angrily turned them down and stomped off to join the umpires' list. Fearless in that role too, he stood in ten Tests and nine one-day internationals between 1974 and 1981. But he was too trigger-happy for some batsmen and he had several seasons off the international list, which he put down to aggrieved captains' reports; he finally retired in 1984.

Alley retreated to a smallholding in Somerset with Betty, his second wife, and was happy raising chickens and shooting rabbits. Ill-health marred his later years, although knee replacements gave him temporary relief: spotted striding up the pavilion stairs at Lord's in his mid-seventies, he announced that his brand-new knees were tempting him to make a comeback. To umpiring? "Stuff that, mate – I'm talking about playing!" His funeral service was held in St James's Church, next to the ground in Taunton. Merv Kitchen, another Somerset player-turned-umpire, observed that the setting was appropriate, as Alley had hit so many balls into the graveyard.

APPERLEY, FRANK HOCKENHULL, who died on June 3, 2004, aged 75, was an opening bat, and Shropshire's captain for the first seven seasons after they joined the Minor Counties Championship in 1957.

ATTWELL, ROBERT HILLMAN, died on May 19, 2004, aged 92. Bob Attwell played a lot of club cricket, mostly for Cranleigh in Surrey, for whom he took all ten wickets for 49 with his slow left-armers against Nigel Paul's XI in 1956. He was the non-striker in the 1942 match at Lord's when the former Surrey and England player Andy Ducat collapsed and died, aged 56, while batting for the Surrey Home Guard against their Sussex counterparts. Attwell recalled: "In the dressing-room before the game we all remarked how fit he looked."

BALDWIN, JEREMY MICHAEL SYDNEY, who died on March 19, 2004, aged 73, was a batsman who played 19 matches for Rhodesia in the 1950s, scoring 639 runs at 19.36.

BASKERVYLE-GLEGG, Major-General JOHN MBE, who died on November 30, 2004, aged 64, was Eton's opening batsman and, after Henry Blofeld was seriously injured in a road accident in 1957, wicket-keeper. He had a long career in the Grenadier Guards and became commander of the 24th Infantry Brigade. He played one first-class match, for Combined Services against Ireland, in 1962.

BEAMES, PERCY JAMES, who died on March 28, 2004, aged 92, was one of Australia's best-known cricket writers, covering 119 Tests for the Melbourne newspaper, *The Age*, from the war until his retirement in 1976. Beames was also the paper's Australian Rules football correspondent. His knowledge – regarded as profound in cricket and encyclopaedic in footy – was based on considerable playing ability. He was one of the leading footballers of his era, and a powerful and prolific batsman for the Melbourne club. However, he was only rarely given opportunities for Victoria, mainly in the secondary fixtures against Tasmania, clobbering their attack for an unbeaten 226 in 1938-39, an innings that helped him to an overall first-class average of 51.56 in his 18 matches. Beames was made state captain for the non-Sheffield Shield season in 1945-46 before concentrating on journalism. His daughter Adrienne became, in 1971, the first woman to run a marathon in under three hours.

BICHEL, DONALD ALAN, who died of cancer on October 11, 2004, aged 69, was an off-spinner who played three games for Queensland in the 1960s. "Snowy" Bichel's bowling was highly regarded by contemporaries, but he was overshadowed by his fellow-Queenslander Tom Veivers, who was a far better batsman, and Bichel also refused to leave his farm to play club cricket in Brisbane. He was the uncle of Andy, the Australian Test player.

BLAKEMORE, DAVID BARRY, who died on June 2, 2004, aged 71, was the driving force behind the Warwick Pool. This transformed Warwickshire into the richest club in the country and, in the days when lotteries were a novelty, revolutionised sports fund-raising. Blakemore was working at Edgbaston when the Warwickshire player Ray Hitchcock founded his pool in 1953 and he gradually took over the shilling-a-time weekly game, with Winnie Crook; they married in 1959, and continued the joint venture under the aegis of the club's Supporters' Association. Soon the number of subscribers rocketed from 50,000 to 800,000. At the Pool's peak, there were 10,000 agents, including 100 in the Longbridge motor plant alone, and thousands of punters, many living miles from Birmingham with no interest in cricket, helped the development of Edgbaston into a major venue. Blakemore remained secretary of the Supporters' Association until 1998; by then what he called "lottery fatigue" had set in and the punters had drifted away. Blakemore, however, remained a tireless worker.

BOOTH, ARTHUR, who died on September 12, 2004, aged 78, played only four first-class matches for Lancashire in 1950 and 1951, but scored 253 in the Minor Counties Championship against Lincolnshire at Grimsby in 1950, which was a Lancashire Second XI record for 48 years. His highest first-class score was 49. He had spells as a professional with Dukinfield and Haslingden.

BORRETT, NORMAN FRANCIS, who died on December 10, 2004, aged 87, was a batsman and slow left-armer who took a hat-trick in the 1939 Cambridge Seniors' Match, then considered an important trial. He never played a first-class match for the university, though he did play three times for Essex, before and after the war, and regularly for Devon until 1959, shining both as batsman and cover point. His more significant sporting achievements came elsewhere: he captained England to the hockey silver medal at the 1948 Olympics, but he was an even more outstanding squash player, winning the English Amateur Championship every year from 1946 to 1950, almost without practice, because he lived in Devon where he had no serious opposition. He played golf off four, reputedly failed to play at Wimbledon only because he was too busy, and turned down an invitation to be a co-driver at Le Mans. *The Times* called him "probably Britain's most talented post-war all-round amateur sportsman". He taught at Framlingham College for 30 years.

BROOKS, GORDON VICTOR, who died of cancer on January 31, 2004, aged 65, was a South Australian fast bowler of sharp pace with an action that generated whispers at a time of sensitivity over throwing, though he was never called. He was also an old-fashioned tail-ender: in 26 first-class matches, he had 61 wickets – but only 41 runs. Brooks was a useful member of the cast when Garry Sobers inspired South Australia to the Sheffield Shield in 1963-64, and the prime mover of the reunion to mark the 40th anniversary of the triumph. He died on the day of the celebration.

BROWNLOW, BERTIE, who died on October 22, 2004, aged 84, was a left-hand bat and wicket-keeper who played eight matches for Tasmania in their pre-Sheffield Shield days in the 1950s. He was on the management committee of the Tasmanian Cricket Association for many years before being made a life member in 1981, and often joked about his first-ball duck, inflicted by Trevor Bailey, when he played against the 1954-55 England tourists.

BUULTJENS, DOOLAND PHILIP, who died on April 25, 2004, aged 70, was a Sri Lankan umpire who stood in three Tests and 18 one-day internationals. These included the England v South Africa qualifier at Melbourne in the 1992 World Cup, the teams' first meeting in 27 years. He represented Sri Lanka at both cricket and football, and later opened his own coaching school.

CAPEL-CURE, GEORGE NIGEL, died on August 8, 2004, aged 95. Nigel Capel-Cure was an Etonian leg-spinner and left-hand bat who played one match for Essex in 1929. He represented Cambridge at squash, but never at cricket.

CARTLEDGE, BRIAN LEWIS, who died on October 22, 2004, aged 63, played four first-class matches for Tasmania in the 1970s, the first of them against Ray Illingworth's England tourists in 1970-71. He made only 53 runs at 7.57, but did manage an innings of 56 in a one-day game against Western Australia at Launceston.

CARTWRIGHT-JONES, RICHARD HENRY, who died on July 14, 2004, aged 87, played one match for Warwickshire (as R. H. Jones), in a two-wicket victory over Somerset at Edgbaston in 1946. Unusually, he opened both the batting (scoring 9 and 23) and the bowling, without taking a wicket.

CHAMBERLAIN, WILLIAM RICHARD FRANK, died on April 7, 2004, aged 78. After a war spent as a Fleet Air Arm pilot guarding Arctic convoys, Frank Chamberlain had a less distinguished career as a batsman in six matches for Northamptonshire in 1946. He disappeared from the professional game into the family leather business for the next three decades while at the same time running his old boys' team, the Uppingham Rovers. He reappeared as a member of the club committee in 1977 and had an improbably meteoric career in cricket administration, becoming chairman of Northamptonshire in 1985 and, five years later, starting a four-year stint as chairman of the Test and County Cricket Board, which then ran the English game. Chamberlain was a courtly, low-key chairman chosen by the counties as an antidote to his activist predecessor, Raman Subba Row. "He had endeared himself to the other chairmen and they chose him more or less unanimously," recalled A. C. Smith, then the chief executive. "They acknowledged his business experience and thought he would chair the meetings in an accomplished manner, which indeed he did." He operated as a non-executive, encouraging officials to take their own decisions. And though the England team lost a lot of games and the TCCB were outmanoeuvred by an Asian-led alliance that transformed the game's international politics, English cricket maintained its financial strength under Chamberlain, and has rarely been better-natured.

CLEVERLEY, DONALD CHARLES, died on February 16, 2004, aged 94. When he died, Don Cleverley was the oldest surviving Test cricketer – a mantle he passed on to a fellow New Zealander, Eric Tindill. Cleverley was a fast-medium bowler with the ability to generate surprising lift, and played two Tests for New Zealand, more than 14 years apart. His first cap came against South Africa in 1931-32, when he went wicketless in an innings defeat, a pattern repeated when he was called up for the ill-starred inaugural Test against Australia in March 1946, in which New Zealand were shot out for 42 and 54. He played on for Auckland until 1951, and rounded off his career in 1952-53 with one match for Central Districts, by which time he was 43. To his delight, his new side polished off his old one by an innings. Cleverley took eight for 75 for Auckland at Wellington in January 1946, a performance that sparked his selection against Australia. He was also a national amateur boxing champion, and eventually established a gym in one of the hotels he managed. His brother Alf boxed for New Zealand at the 1928 Olympics.

CLINGLY, MICHAEL THOMAS, died on August 16, 2004, aged 72. Mick Clingly was a left-arm medium-pacer who could drop his speed and bowl orthodox spin when required; he played five Sheffield Shield matches for South Australia in the late 1950s – and also represented the state at Australian Rules football.

COGHLAN, TIMOTHY BOYLE LAKE, died on February 11, 2004, aged 64. Tim Coghlan was a fastish bowler who took a hat-trick at Lord's while captaining Rugby against Marlborough in 1956. He played 19 times for Cambridge University between 1958 and 1960, winning a Blue in his final year, when his two victims were a future Pakistan Test captain (Javed Burki) and a future MCC president (Charles Fry). He toured the Far East in 1964 with a strong side, raised by E. W. Swanton, which also included Richie Benaud and Garry Sobers.

COLLIS, GERALD FRASER, who died on May 6, 2004, aged 82, was president of Gloucestershire from 2001 until his death, having undertaken many committee jobs over the years. An RAF pilot, architect and pub landlord, Gerry Collis was one of the most versatile and popular figures at Nevil Road.

COVILL, REGINALD JOHN, who died on March 18, 2002, aged 96, was a fast bowler who played a dozen first-class matches in the 1930s, mostly for MCC while on the groundstaff at Lord's, and took five for 31 against The Army there in 1931.

COX, NICHOLAS GEORGE, who died on December 13, 2004, aged 62, was the son and grandson of the two George Coxes who between them played more than a thousand matches for Sussex between 1895 and 1960. The third generation Cox became instead a historian, and senior official at the Public Record Office; *The Guardian* called him an "unsung hero" of contemporary history and "a passionate believer in freedom of information". Among his researches was the discovery that, owing to a transcription error in the 1901 census, his grandfather had been described as a professional "ticketer". He said it made it sound as though his forefathers worked on the Underground.

DARKS, GEOFFREY CHALTON, who died in late 2004, aged 78, played seven matches for Worcestershire as a fast-medium bowler between 1946 and 1950, taking five for 49 against Combined Services at New Road in 1950. Darks umpired the youth Test between England and West Indies at Stone in 1974.

DAVIES, IAN STUART, who died on December 20, 2004, aged 71, was sports editor of the BBC World Service from 1982 to 1990. His passion for cricket ensured the game remained a central part of the sporting coverage. He cheerfully filled in as Northamptonshire correspondent for *Wisden 1998.*

de ANDRADO, HAROLD, who died on November 6, 2004, aged 76, was a well-known Sri Lankan cricket writer from the 1950s onwards. He was also a regular player for the Nondescripts club before Sri Lanka had first-class domestic cricket.

DENMAN, HENRY WYNNE, who died on December 28, 2002, aged 73, was a wicket-keeper/batsman from Oundle School who played seven matches for Cambridge University in the early 1950s, without winning a Blue. He managed only four runs in five innings.

de VILLIERS, PETER, died on June 4, 2004, aged 63. "Sam" de Villiers played two Currie Cup matches for Griqualand West in 1967-68, scoring 24 runs in his three innings.

DICK, WILLIAM ALLAN AO, died on March 27, 2004, aged 81. Allan Dick played 18 matches as a leg-spinner for Victoria in the decade from 1946-47. His five for 31 at Melbourne in 1954-55 – on a pitch on which Richie Benaud had struggled – helped set up a narrow victory over New South Wales. He had a long career in grade cricket, and was awarded the Order of Australia for his work for the Anti-Cancer Council of Victoria.

DUDMAN, LEONARD CHARLES, died on February 12, 2004, aged 70. Len Dudman was an opening bat who played 49 games for Scotland, and almost gave them their first-ever victory over a first-class county when he made 161 against Warwickshire at Edgbaston in 1956. He made another 91 against them in Edinburgh seven years later. Dudman played football for Falkirk and Forfar.

DUNN, WALLACE PETER, died on February 1, 2004, aged 82. Peter Dunn was a left-arm fast-medium bowler who played 18 times for Western Australia. His first wicket, in 1948-49, was that of Keith Miller; his last, four years later, was Alan Davidson. In between there were 46 others, nine of them for 58 in one match, against South Australia at Perth in 1949-50.

EDRICH, GEOFFREY ARTHUR, died on January 2, 2004. He was 85. One of the famous Norfolk family (his brother Bill and cousin John played for England, while brothers Brian and Eric also played county cricket), Geoff Edrich was a Lancashire stalwart for a dozen seasons after the Second World War, which he had ended weighing only six stone after being captured by the Japanese. He was a consistent, determined right-hander and in 1950 was talked of as an England possible. "There is a good deal of his distinguished brother in him," wrote E. W. Swanton. "A similar physique, a similar predilection for the drive, and among other mannerisms that trick of remaining poised after the stroke, with the bat following full through pointing the direction of the ball." But this Edrich was solid rather than stellar, reaching 1,000 first-class runs in eight of his 11 full seasons, and falling just short in the other three. In 1952 he passed 2,000 runs, and in all scored more than 15,000, with 26 hundreds. He was also a fine close fielder, especially to the off-spin of Roy Tattersall. In his later years Edrich occasionally captained Lancashire when Cyril Washbrook was away. "Geoff was a much more aggressive captain," remembered Geoffrey Howard, Lancashire's secretary at the

Geoff Edrich: after retiring from Lancashire, he became groundsman and coach at Cheltenham College.

Picture by EMPICS

time. "He always played to win; Cyril played not to lose." Edrich's tenure included the match against Leicestershire at Old Trafford in 1956 which Lancashire won without losing a wicket, the first such instance in first-class cricket. But his association with the county ended bitterly in 1959 when, as captain of the Second XI, he was blamed after his players damaged a guesthouse. Edrich, who had recently received a drink-driving caution, was sacked, and struggled for some time. He bounced back to become a respected groundsman/coach at Cheltenham College, presiding over Gloucestershire's annual festival there until his retirement.

ELLIOTT, CHARLES STANDISH MBE, died on January 1, 2004, aged 91. Charlie Elliott had a long career as a county batsman – he played in Derbyshire's only Championship-winning side, in 1936 – Test umpire, selector, and county administrator. He started at Derby in 1932, joining his uncle Harry, their long-serving wicket-keeper. He was not quite a regular in the 1930s; although he did play over half the matches in the title-winning year, he was released a year later, and played league cricket before being re-engaged after the war. Once established, he passed 1,000 runs every year from 1947 to 1952. The highest of his nine centuries was 215 at Trent Bridge in 1947, when he put on 349 for the second wicket with John Eggar, which remained a record for any Derbyshire wicket until 1997. Elliott's career batting average of 27 was better than it looks, because Derbyshire pitches were notoriously green. After a poor season in 1953, he took up umpiring, and quickly rose to the top, standing in 42 Tests between 1957 and 1974, then second only to Frank Chester, including one (very rare at the time) in New Zealand, in 1970-71, when he was there on a Churchill Fellowship. "He was one of the old school of umpires," said the England wicket-keeper Bob Taylor, "and all the players had a lot of respect for him." In addition to the other umpiring paraphernalia, Elliott always kept a big cigar in his top pocket. After stepping down, he had seven years as an England selector, until 1981, "He was a great fellow, very reliable," remembered Alec Bedser, his chairman, "and a sound judge of a player." Elliott later became chairman of Derbyshire's cricket committee and, more than 60 years after first arriving there as a player, was the county's president in 1994. He also played soccer, as a defender for Coventry City, whom he managed in 1954-55. In his 90th year he was still running a memorabilia-festooned guesthouse in Nottingham.

FLAVELL, JOHN ALFRED, died suddenly on February 25, 2004, aged 74. Jack Flavell was a masterful fast bowler in an era when England had an excess of them. He won only four Test caps – all against Australia – but formed, with Len Coldwell, one of the most successful of all county opening attacks. Together, they were largely responsible for bowling Worcestershire to the Championship in 1964 and 1965.

Flavell was a Staffordshire man who hardly played cricket until he was a teenager; he seemed more likely to make a career in football. But while he was playing full-back for Walsall, after his National Service, his fast bowling in the Birmingham League began to attract more attention. Worcestershire signed him in 1949. At the time he was fast and often furious: red hair, red face and, at regular intervals, red mist – which extended to throwing the cards out of the coach window when he got cross during games of whist. He was known in the dressing-room as "Bottle" (as in bluebottle) because he could never sit quietly. And for his first six years in county cricket he was a bowler of intermittent brilliance and frequent back injuries.

By 1957, however, he had succeeded Reg Perks as the county's main strike bowler, and cut down his run. With a strong arm action, natural out-swing and increasing accuracy, he became one of the most consistent and lethal bowlers in the country, expecting to bowl around 1,000 overs a season and take 100 wickets. "He attacked the stumps, and he was quicker than he looked," said wicket-keeper Roy Booth, who had a share in many of Flavell's 1,529 wickets. By 1961 the in-swing bowler Coldwell had emerged as his regular partner and Worcestershire had become contenders for the Championship. Flavell was picked for the last two Tests, being preferred to Fred Trueman at The Oval, and performed respectably without justifying his elevation. Over the next two seasons, he had Achilles tendon trouble while Coldwell got into the Test team instead. But by 1964 they were fully back in harness, and Flavell led the way to Worcestershire's first title, taking 101 Championship wickets even though he missed nine games, partly through injury and partly due to selection for two more Tests. His England career ended abruptly, however, after a disaster at Headingley when Ted Dexter took the new ball with

Jack Flavell, a mainstay of the Worcestershire attack, played at a time when quality fast bowling was thick on the ground.

Picture by EMPICS

England in control, and Trueman and Flavell were carted all round Leeds by Peter Burge, who led Australia to victory and the Ashes. Flavell returned to Worcester and in 1965, aged 36, had his most triumphant season, playing in every Championship match for the first time and collecting 142 wickets.

He retired two years later, ran a restaurant, and then the Panorama Hotel in Barmouth, on the west Welsh coast, where he became a pillar of the local garden and golf clubs. He also maintained his friendship with his old partner, Coldwell. At Worcester, he had been the senior man ("I'm bowling this end. Which end do you want, Len?") but they remained staunch buddies – the families would take holidays together – until Coldwell's death in 1996. Flavell was much saddened by this, and left bereft by the death of his only child, Cindy, who had a heart attack in her early thirties.

GOFFET, GORDON, who died on July 29, 2004, aged 63, was an opening bat who played 17 matches for New South Wales in the 1960s. On his debut, against the 1965-66 MCC team, he was bowled for nought by David Brown, but the following season collected his only first-class century, 122 against Western Australia.

GRIFFITHS, COLIN, who died on September 14, 2004, aged 73, was an attacking amateur batsman who played 27 times for Essex in the early 1950s. In 1952, he spanked what turned out to be the fastest hundred of the summer, 105 in 90 minutes against Kent at Tunbridge Wells. Ten days later Griffiths hit a rapid 89 against Middlesex at Colchester which, like his century, was scored from No. 9. Promoted in the second innings, he pulled a back muscle while hitting a six. The family demolition business intruded, and he played little cricket of any kind after that. He tried mountaineering and scuba diving, and later became the chairman of the Cricketers' Club of London, a retreat with a well-stocked bar off Baker Street.

HARBIN, Dr LEONARD, who died in 2002 aged 87, was an off-spinner and handy batsman who played eight matches for his native Trinidad – he was part of the team that won the Inter-Colonial title in 1936-37 – before moving to England, where he made four appearances for Gloucestershire while qualifying as a doctor in Bristol. On his debut in 1949, he took nine wickets in the match against a strong Combined Services team (Peter May, with 80 and 90 not out, eluded him). However, Harbin took only one wicket in his three Championship outings in 1951, and faded from the scene. Arthur Milton remembered "a useful cricketer, with an endearing habit of rushing down the wicket for a word – cheery, not sledging – with a batsman who'd just been in trouble with his off-spin".

HARTY, JOHN PATRICK, who died on April 27, 2004, aged 67, was Eastern Province's first-choice wicket-keeper for ten seasons from 1956-57, making 129 dismissals, 19 of them stumpings.

HAZARE, VIJAY SAMUEL, died on December 18, 2004, aged 89. Vijay Hazare was one of the few Indian batsmen of his time who could translate prolific domestic form into success at Test level, and who could perform equally well on turf and on matting pitches. Despite coming late to international cricket because of the war – he was 31 when he made a subdued debut in England in 1946 – Hazare went on to play 30 Tests and score seven centuries and, above all, skipper India to their first Test victory, over England at Madras in 1951-52.

Hazare was one of eight children of a Maharashtra schoolteacher and, unusually in India, was not merely Christian but Protestant. He was picked for the first unofficial Test at Lahore against the very strong touring team brought over by Lord Tennyson in 1937-38, mainly for his medium-paced bowling, but was only allowed two overs, and batted No. 9. He soon, however, became a protégé of the Maharaja of Dewas, who took him on his personal staff and brought Clarrie Grimmett over as well, hoping he might make Hazare into a leg-spinner. Grimmett soon decided that would not work; but what he did teach Hazare, according to the historian Mihir Bose, was patience and judgment as a batsman.

He succeeded in that. In January 1940, Hazare became the first Indian (excluding Duleepsinhji, who was playing as an Englishman) to hit a triple-century: 316 not out for Maharashtra against Baroda at Poona. He made 619 runs in five Ranji Trophy innings that season, and Indians proclaimed that the great Vijay Merchant had a rival. It was the age of the two Vs. Unlike the silky, stylish Merchant, Hazare was a functional batsman with few flourishes, and his habit of tucking the bat between his pads in the stance worried the purists. But he liked to hook and

Vijay Hazare captained India to their first Test win over England in 1951-52. Here he tosses with Len Hutton during the less successful return series in 1952.

Picture by Getty Images

cut, and in an age of formidably high scores in Indian domestic cricket vied with Merchant on the topmost peaks. They exchanged the batting record in the Bombay Pentangular tournament – then as important as the Ranji Trophy – four times in the early 1940s, including three times in a week late in 1943. Hazare was helped by a move to Baroda, where princely patronage enabled him to devote himself to cricket. This paid off when he put together an extraordinary sequence from March 1943 to February 1944 of 264, 81, 97, 248, 59, 309, 101, 223 and 87.

That 309, in the Bombay Pentangular final, was an extraordinary innings, made out of a total of only 387 as the Rest followed on against the Hindus. He shared (if that is the word) a stand of 300 with his brother Vivek, who scored just 21. The Hindus still won by an innings. Three years later, playing for Baroda in the Ranji final against Holkar, Hazare made 288, and put on 577 for the fourth wicket with Gul Mahomed, the highest partnership in all first-class cricket.

When Test cricket returned to England in 1946, Hazare made his debut in front of a packed Lord's; his first real flourish as a Test batsman came at Adelaide in 1947-48 when he scored two centuries in the match. These also came in an understandably losing cause: Bradman had made 201, and Hazare's second-innings 145 was more than half the total. But this made him a member of what was then a very exclusive club, and the feat enhanced both his own reputation and India's. A century at Bombay against West Indies a year later left India six runs short of their maiden Test victory.

It was nearly three years before they had a chance to try again, and by now Hazare was captain against what was not much more than England's third team. He made big but slow centuries in the first two Tests, at Delhi and Bombay, and India's win finally came – at the 25th attempt in all – in the Fifth, at Madras. But this was the prelude to their disastrous 1952 tour when the full England team blew them away, and Hazare's reputation as a leader never recovered. "With all due respects to Hazare, a thorough gentleman and a great cricketer," said *Wisden*, "he was far from the ideal captain. His shy, retiring disposition did not lend itself to forceful authority." Indeed, according to Bose, he was a ditherer, taking 15 minutes to decide whether to bat or field before he scored his century against England at Bombay, and then being ordered back on to the field by the chairman of selectors, C. K. Nayudu, after hooking a bouncer from the fiery Fred Ridgway on to his pith helmet and trying to retire hurt.

Merchant later observed: "Hazare was always a disciplined soldier, never a commander. Captaincy affected his otherwise unflagging concentration and he was never the same batsman again. It was a tragedy of Indian cricket." But he made another Test century, at Bombay against Pakistan, and regained the captaincy for the 1952-53 tour of the West Indies, when the team performed respectably, though his batting indeed went to pieces. He still averaged more than 47 in Tests overall and 58 in first-class cricket, and was also an underrated bowler, whose 20 Test wickets included Bradman twice in 1947-48. But he will be remembered above all for his batting. "He had an impregnable defence and a wide array of strokes," said the Indian cricket eminence Raj Singh. "The manner in which he held the bat, hands spread slightly apart, made him different. He had great hands, and could move them up or down the handle, like a flute player."

HENDERSON, JAMES DOUGLAS, who died on August 14, 2004, aged 85, was a noted Scottish all-rounder in the decade after the war. He was a left-handed bat and useful left-arm medium-pacer who played 18 times for Scotland, 14 times in first-class matches. His three best innings all came against Ireland, including his highest first-class score, a sparkling 121 at Paisley in 1954. Henderson was rooted in Forfar, one of Scotland's cricketing hotbeds, and represented Forfarshire for many years.

HILLS, Captain STUART FABER MC, who died on May 29, 2004, aged 80, was the leading run-scorer and wicket-taker at Tonbridge School in 1942. Two years later, as a tank commander, he won an immediate Military Cross for his role in the capture of a ridge above the River Noireau. Hills was later in the Malaysian Civil Service and the oil industry.

HOOKES, DAVID WILLIAM, died on January 19, 2004, aged 48, after becoming involved in an argument with a bouncer outside a Melbourne pub, where, as coach of the Victorian state team, he had been celebrating a victory with his players. Hookes was allegedly hit in the face and smashed his head on the road. News of his death stunned Australia and the cricketing world, partly because of its brutal suddenness and partly because of his larger-than-life personality. He had an impact on the game as cricketer, coach and character that transcended his patchy career record, and more than 10,000 mourners attended his funeral at Adelaide Oval which was televised across Australia.

After a spectacular career in Adelaide schoolboy cricket and a low-key start with South Australia, Hookes burst to fame in his second season of first-class cricket. In 17 days in February 1977, he scored five centuries in six innings at the Adelaide Oval, all at blistering speed. The first, 163 against Victoria, contained four sixes in an over. A week later he smashed 185 in 191 minutes and 105 in 101 minutes against Queensland. The next week produced 135 and 156 against New South Wales. Less than a month later, he joined the greats in perhaps the most famous cricket match ever played: the Melbourne Centenary Test. Aged just 21, he strode to the crease looking full of confidence. Then he hit the England captain Tony Greig for five successive fours; he matched him in the lip department as well. Greig had taunted him at the pre-match cocktail party: "Not another Australian left-hander who can't bat"; Hookes said that at least he was an

---

ON HOOKESY...

"Hookesy told me before the 1999 World Cup final that bowlers were attacking me from round the wicket and targeting my off stump... His observation was simple: adjust my stance slightly, then think only of playing those bowlers back down the ground. Forget the horizontal bat shots. In the end, he was spot-on – I finished the World Cup with a winner's medal and the satisfaction of scoring a quickfire 50."

Adam Gilchrist

"We must live life to the full and make the most of each day, otherwise David will be on your back shouting 'C'mon mate, you're here for a good time, not a long time.' "

Caprice Gellman, stepdaughter, at his funeral.

"If all the people that came and spoke to him and said 'I was there the day you ploughed Greigy for five fours in a row at the MCG,' Hookesy's calculations had it that meant there would have been a crowd of 384,000 people."

Wayne Phillips

"For Hookes... valour was the better part of discretion."

Warwick Franks, *Wisden Australia*

"He enjoyed being provocative and at times he was impetuous, intemperate, even outrageous. At the same time he was thoughtful and insightful and able to mentor young men, enthuse children about a glorious game and provoke intelligent debate about important issues of sport."

Mike Coward, *The Australian*

HOOKESY ON...

Australian selection policy: "When they give out the baggy blue cap in New South Wales, they give you a baggy green one in a brown paper bag as well to save making two presentations."

The woman who accused Shane Warne of telephone harassment: "Some dopey hairy-backed Sheila trying to dob him in."

Not being a cricket administrator: "I haven't got a blue blazer and I don't have dandruff."

His Centenary Test innings: "I made Tony Greig famous."

Australian, not "an effing import". After he was out for 56, Greig brought a beer to the dressing-room, and said: "Mind if I sip with you, son?"

Hookesy had the cricketing world at his mercy, but a greater game was afoot, and less than two months later it became known that Hookes had joined Greig and most of the Australian team in the rebel venture sponsored by Kerry Packer that became known as World Series Cricket. Logically, his career would have flourished more had he stuck with the official game. But the leading rebel Ian Chappell was his hero, and safety first was never the Hookes style, in cricket or in life.

On the strange, shadowed tour of England that followed, he faded into the general mediocrity of a distracted Australian side, though he made a sweet 85 in the rain-ruined finale at The Oval. When the Packer circus came back, he seemed to be running into form and had reached 81 at the Sydney Showground when he was felled by a bouncer from Andy Roberts which broke his jaw. Some felt his batting never recovered its carefree innocence; despite his name, he gave up hooking. Certainly he never recaptured his automatic place in the Australian team. After peace broke out in 1979, he played only two Tests in three years, cast into the wilderness after a pair at Karachi. But in 1981-82 South Australia made him captain, and he led them with panache to their first Shield title in six years. The next year his old batting form came back, and with it his Test place, though his steady performances in the Ashes series were overshadowed by one blazingly angry innings against Victoria. Incensed by a belated declaration by Graham Yallop, Hookes promoted himself and struck a century in 43 minutes off 34 deliveries – the fastest-ever uncontrived hundred in terms of balls received. He made South Australia's target, 272 off 30 overs, look momentarily plausible; he also made his point, and made it again in the return fixture when he scored an even-time 193. His star was rising again; he was appointed vice-captain to Greg Chappell for Australia's inaugural tour of Sri Lanka, and smacked an unbeaten 143 in the one Test, at Kandy, the last 100 coming in a session. It was his first, and only, Test century.

But Hookesy had to be Hookesy. He criticised Chappell's successor, Kim Hughes, on air at a time when he was not scoring enough runs to ride the storm. From then on, his Test appearances were intermittent and indifferent, though he played on until 1991-92, breaking the Shield run-scoring record with the occasional amazing innings, like his unbeaten 306 off 330 balls against Tasmania in 1986-87.

"For David Hookes, valour was the better part of discretion."

Picture by Patrick Eagar

His batting was always distinctive: "Gowerish but more brutal" according to Alan Shiell, who helped write his autobiography: "He could be elegant and he was just as vulnerable outside off stump, but he played shots Gower wouldn't have bothered with, flogging bowlers over wide mid-wicket or hoicking them over square leg." The egg-shaped Adelaide Oval, with its inviting square boundaries, was made for the Hookes style, and it gave him an edge throughout his career.

Since he was articulate as well as forthright, he became a radio star in Adelaide, and in 1995 moved to the bigger market of Melbourne. Seven years later, Victoria appointed him their coach; when he died, the team he moulded was on the way to their first title in 13 years. They were celebrating a win over South Australia at a pub in St Kilda. Outside, a bouncer, Zdravko Micevic, 21, allegedly threw a punch at Hookes – he was charged with manslaughter.

At Hookes's funeral, his bat was placed against the stumps, with his cap and gloves alongside; it was a trademark gesture of his when he was batting at an interval, a sign that he would be back. In these circumstances, it was almost unbearably poignant.

HOTCHKIN, NEIL STAFFORD, died on February 6, 2004, two days after his 90th birthday. He was the last survivor of the first team fielded by the Arabs, the wandering club side founded by E. W. Swanton in 1935. At a dinner to mark his own 90th birthday, in 1997, Swanton spoke of Hotchkin in an affectionate address: "The most extraordinary thing about him is that as a cricketer he got worse and worse. In the Eton and Harrow match he made 153 in the first year [1931], 109 and 96 in the second year, and 88 and 12 in the third. So he obviously left school thinking he'd get a pair in the next year if he played on… 458 he made, and that's the most that have ever been made in the Eton and Harrow match." Hotchkin did play a little more first-class cricket than that suggests – he opened the batting for Cambridge in the 1935 Varsity match. But apart from three wartime games in India, and a handful of matches for Middlesex, the last of them in 1948, he concentrated on club cricket – and golf, in which he rose to become president of the European Golf Union. He owned the Woodhall Spa golf club in Lincolnshire, where the main course is now named after him.

HOWDEN, ROBERT, who died on May 1, 2004, aged 87, played three matches for Natal in 1939-40. He made only 85 runs, 64 of them in one innings against Eastern Province. Howden's sister, Edith, married Andrew "Mac" Pollock and was the mother of Peter and Graeme, and the grandmother of Shaun.

HYAM, Judge MICHAEL JOSHUA, collapsed and died of a heart attack at a legal dinner on July 8, 2004, aged 66. At Westminster School in the mid-1950s, Hyam was an accurate and persistent medium-pacer – though an unathletic fielder – who took 84 wickets for the First XI in his last three years. He later captained Cambridge Crusaders and played club cricket for many years, especially for Esher, turning into an off-spinner renowned for changing his field between every ball. Hyam was appointed Recorder of London (the senior judge at the Old Bailey) in 1998 and presided over many high-profile cases, including the trial of Jane Andrews, the Duchess of York's former assistant, who was convicted of murder. He was a humorous and highly regarded judge.

IRONTON, BARRY, who was killed in a road accident, aged 62, on August 7, 2004, was a popular wicket-keeper for Barnet and then a well-respected umpire in Hertfordshire. In 2003 he achieved an ambition by umpiring the national village final at Lord's. His name was mistakenly given in *Wisden 2004* as Ireton.

JAYASURIYA, JALIYA, was killed in the Indian Ocean tsunami in Sri Lanka on December 26, 2004. He was briefly secretary of the Sri Lankan cricket board in 2002 when an interim committee was running the game. Jayasuriya (no relation of the Test player) had previously been promotions manager for Singer, long-time sponsors of Sri Lankan cricket. He was killed with two of his sons while on holiday; his wife survived.

JENKINS, VIVIAN GORDON JAMES, who died on January 5, 2004, aged 92, was an outstanding Welsh sportsman of the inter-war years. Viv Jenkins played in the 1933 Varsity Match as a late replacement, and held out, with F. G. H. Chalk, to prevent Oxford being routed after they had collapsed to 32 for six against the pace of Ken Farnes. He also appeared in 44 matches for Glamorgan in the 1930s, mainly as a wicket-keeper. Jenkins's fame rests on his rugby, however: he appeared 14 times for Wales as the prototype of a modern attacking full-back, and was vice-captain of the 1938 Lions team in South Africa. He then switched to journalism, starting with the *News of the World* before moving to the *Sunday Times* after the war. Interspersed with the rugby, Jenkins covered three MCC tours, starting in 1946-47 when he went to Australia by flying boat. Frank Keating described him as "the trail-blazing paragon" of the sports-star-turned-journalist, adding: "He was an appealingly vivid writer, the goodness of the game always paramount."

JONES, RICHARD HENRY, *see* Cartwright-Jones.

KAMALASURIYA, SUJEEWA PRIYANTHA, was killed by the Indian Ocean tsunami at Unawatuna, Sri Lanka, on December 26, 2004. He was 39. Kamalasuriya was a left-handed bat who played three first-class matches for Tamil Union in 1988-89, scoring 69 against Galle, and also appeared in two Under-19 Tests. He had moved to Australia and was showing his home country to a friend; they had arrived at the beach to go snorkelling when the wave struck.

KUMAR, DILEEP, died after he was hit on the chest during a college match in Srikakula, near Visakhapatnam in India, on July 31, 2004. He was 18. A promising opening batsman, he was a junior intermediate student at Nalanda College, and was playing for East Bengal against a team from Vizianagram when he collapsed after being hit by a rising delivery. He died on the way to hospital.

LANGDON, CHRISTOPHER WALTER, died on May 2, 2004, aged 81. Wally Langdon was a legendary figure in Western Australian cricket, and a member of the side that sensationally claimed the Sheffield Shield at their first attempt, in 1947-48. They did not win it again for 20 years, by which time he was their coach. Langdon was a classy left-hander regarded in Perth as unlucky to miss out on Test selection, then dominated by players from the Eastern states. Langdon had to content himself with state cricket, and a tour of India with Jock Livingston's Commonwealth XI in 1949-50. All Langdon's five first-class hundreds came for Western Australia, two as captain in his last full season, 1952-53. His first was a boundary-studded 112 against Don Bradman's Australian team who stopped off in Perth in March 1948 before boarding the boat to England. The Don was impressed, and invited Langdon to play in one of his farewell testimonial matches the following season. In front of huge crowds at the MCG, Langdon scored 60 and 42 in a match that ended as a tie. Langdon, who was also a handy left-arm medium-pacer, was Burnley's professional in the Lancashire League in 1955 and 1956, and later became a familiar voice as a commentator for ABC Radio. Richie Benaud recalled his "gift of painting the picture of the play for the listeners".

LARKHAM, WILLIAM TREVOR, died on April 3, 2004, aged 74. Trevor Larkham was a leg-spinner who played one match for Worcestershire in 1952 when Roly Jenkins was in the Test team. He was a stalwart of the Kidderminster club in the Birmingham League.

LEGARD, ANTONY RONALD, who died on August 22, 2004, aged 92, produced a devastating piece of bowling in the 1935 Varsity Match. Opening the bowling for Oxford and swinging the ball both ways, he bowled out a very strong Cambridge side and took seven for 36. It was not enough to save Oxford from a heavy defeat. He was also their most successful bowler in the 1932 game, with match figures of six for 64, but was dropped for the Varsity Match in 1933 and did not play at all in 1934. He appeared in a solitary match for Worcestershire after his success at Lord's, and played sporadically thereafter for the Europeans in India, the Free Foresters and for MCC in Ireland.

LEGGAT, ALICK J., who died aged 98 on January 23, 2004, served on the Lancashire committee from 1961 to 1987, the last 15 years as treasurer. He returned, however, as club president for 1991–1992, shortly after the admission of women to full membership. A man of strongly held and traditional opinions, he struggled to remember to add "Ladies" to "Gentlemen" when addressing the AGM. A friend of the artist L. S. Lowry, he collected many of his paintings, including *A Cricket Match and a Cricket Sight Board*, whose sale for £600,000 is reported in Cricketana, page 1699.

LEWIS, WILLIAM IAN, died suddenly on November 20, 2004, aged 69. Ian Lewis was a right-hand bat who represented Ireland 20 times between 1955 and 1973, playing in five first-class matches without much success. He was president of the Irish Cricket Union in 1989, and his son Alan became Ireland's most capped player.

MACKENNA, ROBERT OGILVIE, died on November 22, 2004, aged 91. An opening bowler, Ogilvie MacKenna played two first-class matches for Scotland, against Yorkshire in 1938 and Ireland in 1946, taking two wickets. He became a librarian, and was keeper of the Hunterian Books and Manuscripts at Glasgow University from 1951 to 1978. He was president of the Scottish Cricket Union in 1968.

MACKERDHUJ, KARAMCHUND, died in a Durban hospital on May 26, 2004, aged 64, having suffered a heart attack after a knee operation. Krish Mackerdhuj was president of South Africa's United Cricket Board from 1992 to 1998 and played a major role in the post-apartheid unification of the game there. A member of the Durban Indian community, Mackerdhuj had been a staunch campaigner against the half-hearted integration of sport under the old regime and as late as 1989 was arrested at a demonstration against a touring rugby team. But his mixture of a sharp mind and genial manner made him a highly effective operator in the new South Africa and he forged a constructive, if wary, partnership with the board's chief executive, Ali Bacher, and useful alliances with cricket's emerging Asian partners. Mackerdhuj felt flashes of his old anger when South Africa were welcomed to England and Australia after the end of the boycott as though the tours were merely a resumption of the old apartheid-era connections. He described the programme for the 1994 Lord's Test as "the most deplorable, disgusting document that was ever produced" for making no reference to the unity process. He gave up cricket administration to become South Africa's ambassador to Tokyo for five years, but before he died was being whispered as a possible president of ICC in 2005. "South African cricket has lost a visionary leader," said the current board president Ray Mali.

McLEAN, Sir TERENCE POWER, who died on July 10, 2004, aged 90, is believed to be the only person knighted specifically for his sports journalism (Sir Neville Cardus was partly recognised for his music writing). Terry McLean was mainly famous for his knowledgeable and incisive work on rugby; he was a tireless writer on the game in the *New Zealand Herald* and produced a stream of books.

Krish Mackerdhuj led South African cricket in the post-apartheid era.
Picture by Patrick Eagar

He was also a welcome visitor to cricket press boxes. In 1965-66 he covered the MCC tour of New Zealand, but the tedium of the cricket – every game was drawn – did not encourage him to repeat the experience.

MAKER, ELIZABETH JEAN, died on February 2, 2004, aged 78. Betty Maker, born in Australia, was a left-arm medium-pace bowler for Wellington who played three women's Tests for New Zealand, all in England in 1966, when she was past 40. She made a 29-minute duck in her first Test, and opened the bowling in the last, at The Oval, where she took four for 60 in the match.

MARA, Ratu Sir KAMISESE KAPAIWAI TUIMACILAI, who died on April 18, aged 83, was hereditary paramount chief of the island of Lau and the founding father of modern Fiji, as its first prime minister and later president. He was also a fast-medium bowler who was vice-captain of the 1953-54 Fijian touring team in New Zealand, and played two matches which were given first-class status. He performed impressively in both games, taking seven wickets against Otago, and scoring 44 in 46 minutes against Canterbury, before breaking his arm in the second innings. He also led the Fijian team to victory over the West Indians in Suva in 1956. His imposing stature – 6ft 6in – helped both his bowling and his political authority, and he cut an especially impressive figure in his *sulu* (traditional skirt) at Commonwealth Conferences. Under his leadership, the country became a beacon of stability in the South Pacific, but this broke down later, leading to three coups and lasting damage to Mara's reputation.

MARSHAM, ALGERNON JAMES BULLOCK, who died on February 11, 2004, aged 84, was the last of the Marshams to play for Kent; the family had been associated with cricket in the county since the 18th century, and his father was captain from 1904 to 1908. Algernon Marsham played just six games for Kent in the two seasons after the war without much success, but he scored an unbeaten 74 for Combined Services against Oxford in 1946.

MARTIN, EDMUND JOHN, died on June 9, 2004, three months short of his 102nd birthday. Teddy Martin was a Western Australia leg-spinner in the days before the state joined in the Sheffield Shield. As a result he only played two first-class matches, but they were memorable: the first two games of the 1932-33 MCC tour when Douglas Jardine's team faced a state side and then a Combined XI at the WACA. Martin took six for 165 in the opening match, and had Freddie Brown dropped four times. Batting at No. 9, he was also roughed up by Harold Larwood and Bill Bowes in a short bouncer barrage that was a harbinger of the Bodyline strategy. Martin retired to concentrate on accountancy and worked for BP until he was 72, remaining sprightly until after he reached his 100th birthday, a milestone never previously achieved by an Australian first-class player. "It's nice to have beaten Bradman at something," he said.

MARTIN, RUTH, *see* Symons.

MATTHEWS, ALEXANDER ANGUS, died on January 30, 2004, aged 73. Sandy Matthews, from Port Elizabeth, umpired 35 first-class matches in South Africa between 1969-70 and 1986-87, when his final match involved Kim Hughes's rebel Australians. He wrote more than a thousand columns on chess for the *Eastern Province Herald*.

MELLE, MICHAEL GEORGE, died on December 28, 2003, aged 73. South African fast bowler Michael Melle took five for 113 against Australia on his Test debut, at Johannesburg in 1949-50. It was only his fifth first-class match, and he had taken just six previous wickets. He played seven Tests in all, six against Australia and one at The Oval in 1951, when he mopped up the tail for the startling figures of 10–6–9–4 in England's first innings. Melle topped the bowling averages on that tour, with 50 wickets at 20.28, but a hernia operation cost him six weeks halfway through, and he appeared only in the final Test. The previous home season he recorded the astonishing analysis of 12–7–8–8 for Transvaal as Griqualand West were bundled out for 29. In Australia in 1952-53 he played in the first four Tests, taking six for 71 in the First at Brisbane, but overall he was not quite quick enough to trouble the best batsmen. The Australian commentator Johnnie Moyes, reviewing the tour, said that Melle "in general lacked the extra life and fire so necessary for Test match fame. This likable chap had the bulk, power and probably the ambition to bowl fast, but... lacked the ability to use body and arms as the great fast bowlers have done." Melle's father Basil played for Western Province, Hampshire and Transvaal.

MEULEMAN, KENNETH DOUGLAS, died on September 10, 2004, aged 81. A prolific and consistent opener whose fluid foot-movement led Arthur Mailey to nickname him "Pavlova", Ken Meuleman played just one Test for Australia, against New Zealand at Wellington in 1945-46, where he was out for a duck in his only innings, a dishonour he shares with five other Australians. He was selected for that tour, which only later gained Test status, after just five first-class matches for Victoria, which included two centuries. He was twelfth man for the first two Tests of the 1946-47 Ashes series, but could not force himself back into the strong Australian side, although he did tour India with Ben Barnett's Commonwealth XI in 1953-54, and struck centuries in the last two unofficial Tests. He had moved across to Perth the season before, and became something of a legend there, not least because his son, Bob, and grandson, Scott, both played for the state too. But Meuleman initially earned that respect with his runs – scoring over 3,000 for Western Australia at an average of 51.48, and half his 22 first-class hundreds. The highest was a gritty 234 not out in nearly eight hours against South Australia in 1956-57, the state's first double-century. Richie Benaud recalled his "great sporting gesture" during the deciding Sheffield Shield match of 1959-60 when Meuleman, as fielding captain, could have gone off in light rain and prevented New South Wales from winning the Shield. After his retirement, Meuleman turned to coaching, setting up an indoor school and shop in Perth, where he had a hand in the development of many notable local players, including Justin Langer.

MICHAEL, REGINALD GILBERT, who died on August 30, 2004, aged 97, was secretary of Ewyas Harold Cricket Club, Herefordshire, for 78 years, from 1924 until 2002. It is thought he was performing most of the secretarial functions from about 1922. Reg Michael played regularly as an all-rounder until he was 65, and was also secretary of the village football team for more than 70 years, and the village's *Hereford Times* correspondent for 77 years until his death. He lasted a trifling 40 years as clerk to the parish council. "Ewyas Harold was the centre of my dad's universe," said his son Robin.

MILLER, KEITH ROSS MBE, AM, died on October 11, 2004, aged 84. He was, Neville Cardus wrote, "Australia *in excelsis*". Free-spirited, generous, sometimes bloody-minded, altogether bonzer, Miller was the most colourful cricketer of his post-war generation, driving sixes beyond imagination, bowling fearsomely fast and catching with a predatory instinct, playing to and for the crowd. Off the field, his zest for life and natural charm attracted friendship from every quarter, be it country house or street-corner bar. He was, moreover, Hollywood handsome, over six feet tall, broad-shouldered, with dark brown hair worn longer than the times approved. Little wonder women wanted to be with him and men wanted to be him.

Associated mainly with New South Wales and captaining them to three successive Sheffield Shield titles, Miller was in fact Melbourne-born and raised. He was named after Australian aviators Keith and Ross Smith who at the time were making the first flight from England to Australia. His hard-hitting batting for South Melbourne led to selection for Victoria Second XI while he was still attending Melbourne High, where Bill Woodfull, the former Australian captain, taught maths. Miller's earlier dreams of becoming a jockey had been dashed when he grew almost a foot taller in his mid-teens, although those extra inches did give

Keith Miller: "a young eagle among crows and daws," said Neville Cardus.
Picture by EMPICS

him the physique to star in Australian Rules football for St Kilda and win state honours. Not that the lure of the track ever left him; odds always mattered more than averages.

Two months after turning 18, in 1937-38, he made an impressive if restrained first-class debut, scoring 181 (with only five fours) against Tasmania at the MCG. But his Shield debut was held back another two years until 1939-40. He made a century when South Australia came to Melbourne, but war soon took priority over cricket, and in 1942 Miller enlisted in the RAAF, qualifying as a pilot. A stopover in America en route to England led to him meeting his first wife Peg. By night, "Dusty" Miller flew first Beaufighters and then Mosquito fighter-bombers in raids over Germany; on summer days, he played cricket. "Flight Sergeant Keith Miller... revealed the ability and temperament of a champion and showed every promise of developing into one of Australia's best all-rounders," *Wisden* forecast in 1944. He had left Australia little more than an occasional bowler. When Lindsay Hassett's Australian Services team set sail for India in 1945, *Wisden* was rating Pilot Officer Miller "the liveliest opening bowler seen in England during the summer". There were eulogies, too, for his upright, full-flowing batting that had *The Times* correspondent musing whether Lord's was big enough for his mighty hitting. Unimpressed with Lord's on first sight – a crummy little ground, he thought – he subsequently blessed it with his best. His three hundreds there in 1945 included a magnificent 185 to set up the Dominions' victory over England. The first of his seven sixes carried to the top tier of seats between the Pavilion turrets; an on-drive crashed into the roof of the broadcasting box above the England dressing-room. Albert Trott's unique 1899 drive over the Pavilion was mentioned in despatches and Miller returned home with a brand new name: "Nugget", the golden boy.

NUGGETS

"A young eagle among crows and daws."

Sir Neville Cardus

"He's the best all-rounder, along with Garry Sobers, who ever lived."

Alan Davidson

"He could bat, bowl, field, and he could fly an airplane."

Bill Brown

"Keith was a genuine legend. He understood that the game, great as it is, is just a game, and he played it that way."

Bob Merriman, chairman of Cricket Australia

"Sorry, Godfrey, but I have to do it – the crowd are a bit bored at the moment."

Miller's apology after bowling successive bouncers to Evans in 1946-47

"I'll tell you what pressure is. Pressure is a Messerschmitt up your arse. Playing cricket is not."

Miller on the modern game

"No regrets. I've had a hell of a good life. Been damned lucky."

Miller at 75

The first of Miller's 55 Tests – the 1946 annihilation of New Zealand at Wellington – was not recognised as such until March 1948. By then he had returned Test-best figures of seven for 60 at Brisbane against England, made a maiden Test hundred at Adelaide, and forged the hostile pairing with Ray Lindwall that spearheaded Bradman's Invincibles through England in 1948. At least Lindwall was orthodox. All a batsman had to think about was searing pace, late swerve, skiddy bouncer, the phalanx of fielders behind the bat and a new ball every 55 overs. Miller was unpredictable. A pitch-perfect ball, snaking off the seam, might easily be followed by a leg-break or googly or a round-arm off-cutter. His run-up comprised nine easy paces – ostensibly. As likely as not he would come off a few yards and let loose a snorting bouncer that sucked the crowd breathless – or, when he bounced Len Hutton five times in eight balls at Trent Bridge, encouraged

Keith Miller bowls in early-season nets at Lord's in 1948, admired by young boys and women.

Picture by EMPICS

a protracted chorus of booing. Miller's response was a toss of his thick mane and, next day in atrocious light, bumping Denis Compton, supposedly a mate, back on his stumps to end a rearguard innings of 184.

But his seven Trent Bridge wickets had a price. Miller's pace, the product of immense torque, put a terrible strain on a back damaged when he crash-landed late in the war. (Bored with hanging about the airfield, he had taken his mechanic up for a "flip" and an engine caught fire. "Nearly stumps drawn that time, gents," he said as they walked away from the wreckage.) He did not bowl at Lord's or in the first innings at Old Trafford. When Bradman threw him the ball, Miller tossed it back, kindling rumours of a rift between them and embellishing the rebellious Miller image. He took only six more wickets in the series, and failed to top his 74 at Lord's.

Who cared? His style counted more, contrapuntal to Bradman's relentless advance into immortality. "He'll learn," Bradman muttered to Trevor Bailey at Southend after Miller, coming in at 364 for two, disdained the plunder and gave his wicket away first ball. Bradman was wrong. War, and with it the death of friends, had taught Miller there was more to life than easy runs. But Bradman, godfather of Australian cricket, was unforgiving. Miller was omitted from the 1949-50 side to South Africa. And for all his success as New South Wales captain, he was never appointed to lead his country in Tests. The stories of Miller telling his players to "scatter", instead of setting a field, masked New South Wales's pre-match planning and his intuitive leadership.

Bill Johnston's motor accident early in the South African tour got Miller there as a replacement, and he played in all five Tests. One of his six sixes against Eastern Province travelled some 130 yards before splashing into the St George's Park duckpond. When MCC toured in 1950-51, he headed Australia's batting averages and was second in the bowling behind mystery spinner Jack Iverson. "Good as they were," *Wisden* said, "figures could not indicate Miller's worth to Australia." West Indies buckled before the Lindwall–Miller–Johnston pace barrage in the 1951-52 "cricket championship of the world", but a year later Jack Cheetham's young South Africans arrested Australia's momentum in a drawn rubber. England would have the upper hand in Miller's last three Ashes series. He began the 1953 tour with 220 not out at Worcester and closed with 262 not out against Combined Services; in between, he put Australia in a winning position at Lord's with a selfless 109, only for Bailey and Watson's famous stand to thwart them on the final day. But his ten wickets at 30 in that series were his costliest yet, as were his 20 at 32 in the Caribbean in 1954-55. Those, however, came in a winning cause given impetus by his three centuries. In the First Test at Kingston he also led Australia to victory after Ian Johnson injured his foot on the second day.

But the West Indies pitches were easy-paced, and the home attack had no one approaching the speed of Tyson and Statham, who had recently rolled Australia over at home. In 1956, Jim Laker and spin-friendly pitches made Miller's final tour a nightmare, reducing his classical batting to mockery as hair, pad and bat flopped forward in futile defensive lunges. Yet there were consolations. At Lord's, ignoring his 36 years, he bowled Australia to victory with peerless fast-medium bowling and his only ten-wicket return in Tests. It came as no surprise to team-mates who, seven months earlier, had witnessed his seven-for-12 demolition of South Australia at Sydney; showman to the last, he acknowledged the Lord's ovation by picking the umpire's pocket and tossing the bails into the crowd.

A fortnight later, while captaining the tourists against Hampshire, he was invited to nearby Broadlands by Lord Mountbatten, whose guests included Princess Margaret. Miller had met the princess in 1948 when the Australians visited Balmoral; now he found himself being asked to sit beside her during the after-dinner film. "The bluest eyes I have ever seen," Miller noted, but rumours of an affair gained no currency from him. "No gentleman ever discusses any relationship with a lady," he chastised the curious.

He continued to visit England every summer, working initially as a journalist for the *Daily Express*, maintaining friendships and pursuing his love of classical music. A cousin had introduced him to Beethoven early on – returning from a wartime mission he reputedly diverted over Bonn to see Beethoven's birthplace – and music, as much as cricket, was integral to his friendship with Sir Neville Cardus. Hallé maestro Sir John Barbirolli wrote the foreword to one of Miller's books. But passing years and ill-health took their toll, and he was wheelchair-bound when the statue of him at the MCG was unveiled in February 2004. It didn't matter. The legend and the memories were intact; the mourners who packed Melbourne's cathedral for his state funeral testified to that.

MILLS, DAMIAN, who died in his sleep on November 17, 2003, aged 24, was a promising young player in the Canadian high-performance programme. He captained Winnipeg Juniors, scoring over 1,100 runs for them in 2003, the sixth year in seven that he had been the leading run-scorer in Manitoba. He played three times for Canada in the West Indian Red Stripe Bowl, in 1999 and 2000, opening the innings each time, but with limited success.

MOONEY, FRANCIS LEONARD HUGH, died on March 8, 2004, aged 82. A polished wicket-keeper who won 14 caps for New Zealand, Frank Mooney was serious on the field, rarely smiling or speaking, but a changed man off it, where his exploits earned him the nickname "Starlight". He first appeared for Wellington in 1941-42, and hammered 180 against Auckland in his second match a year later, but his batting was generally moderate, so it was a shock when he was chosen as the first-choice keeper for the 1949 tour of England. It caused outrage in Dunedin, where dockers threatened strike action in support of their local man, George Mills of Otago. But Mooney was a success, scoring 102 against MCC at Lord's, and kept his place for almost five years. Soon after he retired, Mooney made the news when he won a hefty bet that he could drive the 410 miles on the then primitive roads from Auckland to Wellington in less than seven hours. He started at midnight, had his powerful Jaguar further souped up, arranged for garages to be open in the small hours and rocketed through the night. There was widespread embarrassment when news leaked out and Mooney paid a small fine out of the winnings to cover the police's certainty that he must have exceeded 100mph at some point. In his forties he won another big bet that he could run a five-minute mile. He later became a Test selector.

MOUNTGARRET, Rt Hon the 17th Viscount, who died on February 7, 2004, was regarded as a comically eccentric aristocrat until events thrust him into the centre of Yorkshire's turbulent cricket politics of the 1980s. In 1984, Mountgarret – owner of a huge swathe of countryside near Harrogate – was nominated out of the blue as Yorkshire president in the midst of the club's civil war between supporters and opponents of Geoff Boycott. His arrival was farcical: the chairman, Reg Kirk, introduced him as "Viscount Mountbatten". But Mountgarret, himself just an enthusiastic but indifferent cricketer for the smarter touring clubs, was so far above the Yorkshire battle that he proved the ideal choice. He said he intended to "bang heads together", and he succeeded in doing so: during his six years as president, the situation became far calmer. He was helped by being rather deaf, which meant he never had to listen to the overheated nonsense talked on both sides of the dispute. Earlier, he had been best known for a bizarre incident when he took pot-shots at a hot-air balloon that flew over his grouse moor; he was found guilty of recklessly endangering an aircraft, and fined £1,000.

NEASOM, MICHAEL, died on March 15, 2004, aged 69, after a long illness. Mike Neasom grew up in Sussex, where he watched Harold Gimblett's 310 at Eastbourne in 1948 and faced the young John Snow, who bowled him for a duck, playing for Midhurst against Bognor. He later crossed the border and covered Hampshire (and Portsmouth FC) for *The News*, Portsmouth, from 1974 to 1997. Neasom was a stalwart local journalist, trusted by the players but honest and critical whenever necessary. He was *Wisden's* Hampshire correspondent from 1990 to 1998.

NORTON, ERIC BERTRAM, died on February 23, 2004, aged 84. "Pop" Norton was an Eastern Province batsman who toured Australia in 1952-53 without breaking into the Test side. He was, at 32, the oldest member of a South African party notable for its tigerishly youthful fielding. He captained the Junior Springbok rugby team in 1950, and was regarded as an outstanding rugby coach at his old school, St Andrew's College in Port Elizabeth, where he eventually became headmaster. His uncle, Norman Norton, played one Test for South Africa in 1909-10.

OGIRAL, ARUN MURALIDHAR, died on February 26, 2004, aged 61. He was an off-spinner who played for Vidarbha and India's Central Zone, and took eight for 39 against Madhya Pradesh at Nagpur in 1967-68. In his one appearance against a major touring side – for Central Zone against Clive Lloyd's West Indians in 1974-75 – he took five for 186 including Viv Richards, caught behind for 45.

OUTRIDGE, THOMAS MICHAEL, who died on July 21, 2003, aged 75, was a left-hand batsman who played 19 matches for Western Australia in the late 1940s and early 1950s. Outridge passed 90 twice without ever making a first-class century, scoring a rapid 92, with three sixes off Brian Close, in a run-chase against Freddie Brown's England tourists in 1950-51. He also took 21 wickets with his left-arm wrist-spin.

PATON, ERIS A., who died on November 23, 2004, aged 76, was an all-rounder from Otago who played four women's Tests for New Zealand between 1954 and 1960-61. She made an undefeated 77 out of 130 (the next-highest score was 14) against England at Auckland in 1957-58, and had match figures of six for 55 in her last match, against Australia at Dunedin.

PETRIE, ERIC CHARLTON, who died on August 14, 2004, aged 77, was an unfussy wicket-keeper with soft hands, and one of the few successes of New Zealand's 1958 tour of England. This was when a largely untried side was outclassed – only rain in the final Test prevented a 5–0 whitewash. But Petrie was unfailingly enthusiastic, and his contribution was acknowledged when he was selected for the Gentlemen against the Players at Scarborough that September, a very rare honour for a touring player. It was somehow appropriate: fellow-player Roger Harris remembered him as "in my time, the great gentleman of New Zealand cricket". Petrie came from Waikato, outside the mainstream of New Zealand cricket at the time, which contributed to his late start. As early as 1949 he had made 138 in a trial match before the tour of England, but did not make his first-class debut for another two seasons, when he was nearly 24. He played for Auckland, captaining them in 1954-55, before moving back home to Northern Districts when they gained first-class status in 1956-57. One of his happiest moments was taking part in their first Plunket Shield title, in 1962-63. He toured India and Pakistan in 1955-56, sharing the gloves in the eight Tests played with Wellington's Trevor McMahon. After that season New Zealand had no Test cricket for more than two years, which may account for some of the zanier selections for the 1958 England tour. Petrie was the cheerleader, and his team-mate Bert Sutcliffe described him as "a superb wicket-keeper, regarded by English critics as perhaps the best in the land that summer". Petrie played both Tests against England at home that winter, and was then overlooked for seven years, before returning for the home series against England in 1965-66, his penultimate season, when he scored his only fifty in 14 Tests. The competition for club sides in Northern Districts is named after him.

PRETZLIK, NICHOLAS CHARLES, died suddenly on July 11, 2004, aged 58. Nick Pretzlik was in the Eton XI for three years and played an outstanding innings for Public Schools against Combined Services at Lord's in 1963 when he made an unbeaten 90 at almost a run a minute. "He reminded me of Colin Ingleby-Mackenzie," recalled Richard Gilliat, his captain in that match. "Played for fun and hit the ball like stink." Pretzlik became a protégé of E. W. Swanton, who recruited him for his wandering club, the Arabs, and hoped he would become a fine county cricketer. Pretzlik indeed devoted himself to the Arabs, but not in the way Swanton intended. He gave up cricket, reputedly after his kit was stolen from the back of his Jaguar and he never bothered to replace it. After working in the family business he became engrossed in the plight of the Palestinians and, turning away from his reputation as a *boulevardier*, became a vocal activist on their behalf in the 1990s. He wrote passionate articles for political websites and regularly interceded with the Israeli authorities on behalf of refugees. He died when training for a London–Jerusalem cycle ride for peace.

RADFORD, ROBERT MICHAEL AM, died on February 28, 2004, aged 60. Bob Radford was one of cricket's most remarkable and original administrators, described by Don Bradman as the best in Australia – before lunch. Radford became secretary of the New South Wales Cricket Association in 1976 and ruled the game there in individualistic style for the next 19 years. He was an enthusiastic networker and was particularly successful at linking the game to the community at large, as well as insisting on sentimental touches: thanks to him, New South Wales now keep in touch assiduously with former players. But his successes were often overshadowed by his self-destructive lifestyle. The near-vegan Greg Chappell remonstrated with him and warned him he would not reach 60 unless he changed. This turned into a bet, and when Radford made it – just – Chappell was forced to eat a huge steak. "Radford was an outstanding administrator – sharp, efficient, decisive – who also possessed a deep love for the game and its history," wrote Philip Derriman in the *Sydney Morning Herald.*

REID, SEYMOUR CHARLTON, died on January 13, 2004, aged 89. "Sibby" Reid played five matches for Border in the first two seasons after the Second World War, scoring only 93 runs in ten innings. His career included the famous match at East London when Border, chasing 42 to win after bowling Eastern Province out for 52, were shot out for 34 themselves. Reid, as opener, scored one. His older brother, Bernard, also represented Border.

RICKETTS, MICHAEL RODNEY, who died on November 21, 2004, aged 81, was a batsman who played one first-class game for Free Foresters against Oxford in 1948 and scored a solitary run. He played eight seasons for Suffolk.

ROBINS, DERRICK HAROLD, who died on May 1, 2004, aged 89, was a wicket-keeper who played just two first-class matches for Warwickshire in 1947, but then became a successful businessman and one of the game's most significant patrons. Starting with a cement-mixer in a field, he turned his firm Banbury Buildings into a major public company. In 1960, he became chairman of Coventry City FC and hired Jimmy Hill as manager, and their combined acumen and innovative drive made a failing club into one that stayed in the top division for 34 successive seasons and became a model for progressive thinking. Cricket was a harder game in which to find room for a man of Robins's determination, though he did take charge of the Eastbourne Festival, first organising the matches played by Colonel L. C. Stevens's XI, then taking over the fixtures in his own right. In 1969, D. H. Robins's XI played the opening match against the West Indian tourists with Robins

Derrick Robins at the Eastbourne Festival in 1978 with New Zealanders Bruce
Edgar (*left*) and John Wright.

Picture by Patrick Eagar

as captain of a team containing eight Test players; he was then 54 and it had been
22 years since his last first-class match. He captained another star-studded team
against the Indians in 1971, when he was already 57. (No one older has appeared
in a first-class match in England since the war; his nearest rival R. E. S. Wyatt
was 56 when he turned out for Free Foresters in 1957.) But the following year
he had six heart attacks in a week – he was not a man to do things by halves –
which put paid to his cricket, his chairmanship of Coventry, and his business
career. The South African administrator Jack Cheetham, however, asked him to
start organising tours to South Africa. The four Robins teams, in successive seasons
from 1972-73, were early busters of the anti-apartheid boycott and included many
of the era's leading players. Robins insisted that the parties were multi-racial (John
Shepherd of Kent was on the middle two trips) and shrugged off the political flak,
organising trips elsewhere in the cricketing world as well. But the South African
link was strongest, and he made his winter home there from 1975 onwards. Some
players found the Robins style a little overbearing; most enjoyed the ride. He
continued to organise golf tours long afterwards, involving many of the players
from those 1970s trips. The Robins's XI maintained its own arcane rituals and
joky hierarchy, with such positions as Keeper of the Chair (Robins himself), Senior
Keeper (Peter Parfitt), Keeper of the Peace and – most intriguingly – Keeper of
the Liaison.

SALEEM AKHTAR, the father of the Pakistan Test cricketers Wasim and Ramiz Raja, died on April 22, 2004. He was 73. Saleem Akhtar was a leg-spinner who captained Multan and Sargodha, taking five for 34 for Sargodha against Peshawar in 1961-62. Another son, Zaeem, also played first-class cricket.

SAMARASINGHE, THAMMAHETTI MUDALIGE, died on June 4, 2004, aged 61. T. M. Samarasinghe umpired seven Tests and 14 one-day internationals in Sri Lanka in the 1990s. His health problems (which culminated in a fatal third heart attack) started when he suffered a slight stroke during a match in 1994 – the players noticed something was wrong when he tried to stand at the bowler's end for successive overs.

SAULEZ, GEOFFREY GORDON ALFRED, who died on December 23, 2004, aged 88, was the England scorer on a succession of tours from the 1970s to the mid-1980s. Saulez was chosen partly because he did the job very efficiently, and partly because he was a retired accountant, a bachelor and a cricket obsessive who was happy to do the job on an amateur basis. He also scored for Sussex and, briefly, Surrey. Saulez maintained a file with about 40,000 index cards showing career records of players from round the world; this was an invaluable resource for statisticians until it was superseded by the computerised records of CricketArchive. He took special delight in finding obscure errors in past scorecards. Somewhat dishevelled in his appearance but meticulous in his statistics, he had been a good enough player to open the batting with Reg Simpson in a wartime tournament in Lahore. He was disappointed when his fellow-statisticians decided it did not warrant first-class status.

SHUTTLEWORTH, NORMAN, who died on June 18, 2004, aged 94, was a Yorkshire businessman who became chairman of one of the famous Leeds menswear stores: J Hepworth & Son, which grew into a chain of 350 shops. He was also a useful all-rounder, who captained the Leeds club after the war and later became chairman of Leeds CF&A, owners of Headingley. He worked hard to preserve the ground as a viable Test venue, and is credited with introducing bucket seats, at a time when Lord's still made spectators sit on benches, and the novel (if not always reliable) Mark 1 electronic scoreboard. He was also briefly a crucial figure in Yorkshire administration, when the club was in meltdown over the future of Geoff Boycott. He was obliged to chair the 1984 annual meeting, and held together the warring factions. "Without his sure touch," according to Yorkshire journalist John Callaghan, "a sad situation may well have declined into disaster."

SMITH, DONALD JAMES, who died on December 3, 2004, aged 75, was a left-arm swing bowler who gave up his job as a bank clerk to play for Lancashire. But after his debut against the 1951 South Africans, he was picked only twice more and retreated to the leagues and Cheshire, alongside his brother Colin, who also played for Lancashire. Smith became a successful businessman, and eventually bought as his home the large double-fronted bank where he first worked.

SMITH, MICHAEL JOHN, died after a heart attack on November 12, 2004, aged 62. Mike Smith of Middlesex was a popular and respected county pro who has two footnotes in cricket history: he was the first man to appear for England in one-day internationals without playing a Test match; later he became the last (perhaps for all time) of the distinguished line of ex-pros who moved from the

Mike Smith: "when he batted, something interesting was always likely to happen," said his Middlesex captain, Mike Brearley.

Picture by Getty Images

dressing-room to the scorers' box. Smith first played for Middlesex as a 17-year-old slow left-arm bowler. His bowling never developed, but ten years later he finally established himself as Eric Russell's opening partner and was a fixture at the top of the Middlesex order throughout the 1970s. By 1972 he was rated highly enough to be chosen in the England 13 for the Headingley Test, and narrowly missed selection for the 1973-74 West Indies tour. Those calls never came, but in 1973 he did play against West Indies in the first two of his five one-day internationals. The concept of a one-day specialist was unknown, but Middlesex already recognised that he was ideally equipped for the game. Even in three-day cricket he would often get them off to a tearaway start. "He would get a good audience of fellow players out on the balcony when he batted," said Mike Brearley. "Something interesting was always likely to happen." But, though Smith scored 37 centuries for Middlesex, a figure beaten by only ten players, his career average was a mere 31, and some felt he stuck over-rigidly to a flawed technique that did insufficient justice to his talent. This involved shuffling across the stumps and hitting almost everything square of the wicket. "It's done me all right," he would say when challenged. After retirement, he started a business selling Swedish Army thermal underwear but sold up and in 1994 replaced Harry Sharp as the Middlesex scorer. This was the year after computerised scoring was introduced, and Sharp had seen the writing on the screen and retired. It was an unfamiliar discipline for Smith too. "He struggled at first," said one colleague, Tony Kingston of Northamptonshire, "but Mike was such a lovely bloke that everyone helped him out."

SOKELL, JACK MBE, who died on April 2, aged 77, was for many years the secretary of the Wombwell Cricket-Lovers' Society, which he and a group of friends founded in 1951. Sokell, a Barnsley journalist who covered cricket and football for the *South Yorkshire Times* and was on the Yorkshire committee from 1974 to 2002, publicised the society well, and its various awards received widespread coverage. It also ran coaching classes, attended over the years by several future Yorkshire and England players. Michael Parkinson wrote in his tribute to the society's magazine *The Twelfth Man:* "To say Jack loved cricket was a bit like saying Romeo fancied Juliet. It misses the point. Jack's passion was all-consuming and all-embracing. If they don't play cricket in heaven there is going to be an unholy row." Another Barnsley man, Dickie Bird, said that Sokell built Wombwell "into the finest cricket society in the world".

STEEL, Sir DAVID EDWARD CHARLES DSO, MC, TD, who died on August 9, 2004, aged 87, was chairman of BP from 1975 to 1981. At Rugby School, he was captain of cricket and in 1933 shared a century opening stand in each innings against Marlborough at Lord's.

STURGESS, ERIC WILLIAM, who died on January 14, 2004, aged 83, appeared in two wartime first-class matches in South Africa in 1942-43. In the first, playing for the Air Force under Walter Hammond's captaincy, he scored 0 and 45 and, opening the bowling, took three wickets in each innings. In the second game, for the Rest of South Africa under the national captain Alan Melville, he made 43 from No. 8 and dismissed the Test players Eric Rowan and Ossie Dawson. Shortly afterwards his Spitfire was shot down near Boulogne, and he spent the rest of the war as a prisoner in the notorious Stalag Luft III camp. When peace broke out, cricket was supplanted by tennis. Sturgess, an elegant baseliner with solid ground-strokes but a modest serve, won the mixed doubles at Wimbledon in 1949 with his fellow South African Shirley Summers, and retained the title the following year, partnering the great American Louise Brough. He won four other major doubles titles, and reached the singles final in Paris twice and New York (where he lost to Pancho Gonzales in 1948) once. At the British Hard Court Championships in Bournemouth in 1949, he won five matches and three titles in a day.

SYMONS, RUTH (later Mrs Ruth Martin), died on September 11, 2004, aged 90. She was New Zealand's first captain in a women's Test, leading them against England in her home town of Christchurch in 1934-35. It was a terrible start. New Zealand were bowled out on the first morning for 44 (Symons resisted for more than 50 minutes for her five). They lost by an innings and 337. It was Symons's only Test appearance, although she did tour New South Wales three years later under the captaincy of Ina Lamason. New Zealand Cricket's annual batting award, the Ruth Martin Trophy, is named after her.

TAMIM BASHIR, who died of cerebral malaria on June 18, 2004, aged 19, was a promising left-arm spinner who had already played 15 first-class matches for Bangladesh's Khulna Division. He had been training with the Bangladesh high-performance unit, and his father criticised the coaching staff there after his death, claiming they had forced his son to keep training even though he was feeling ill. This was denied by Richard McInnes, the Bangladesh Under-19 coach, who said he only knew Tamim was ill when he was in hospital. Tamim Bashir, who was nicknamed "Tushar", took 44 wickets at 24.52, and was also a handy batsman, being stranded on 98 not out against Chittagong at Jessore in January 2004. His best bowling, six for 41, came against Dhaka at Jessore in 2001-02, when he was only 16.

TRESIDDER, PHILLIP LYLE, died on October 19, 2003, aged 75. Phil Tresidder was one of Australia's most prominent sports writers. In the 1960s he covered cricket extensively for Sydney newspapers, but was later more identified with golf. His passion was the Randwick Cricket Club, where he was a member for more than 60 years.

TURNER, ALFRED LOUIS, died on April 29, 2004, aged 82. Alf Turner umpired six first-class matches in Otago, and also stood in two games in the women's World Cup in New Zealand in 1981-82. But his main claim to fame was as father of Glenn Turner, the leading New Zealand batsman of the 1970s and later the national coach. Another son, Brian, played international hockey, and became a well-known writer and poet, while the youngest, Greg, was a well-known golfer. Asked once what he himself was good at, Turner indicated his children and said: "I would have thought that was fairly obvious."

ULUIVITI, NACANIELI MATAIKA, died in Fiji on May 6, 2004, shortly before his 72nd birthday. A big-hitting batsman who once smote a 35-minute century in a minor game, Nat Uluiviti appeared in eight first-class matches, the first four on Fiji's tour of New Zealand in 1953-54. He went to university in New Zealand, and played four matches the following season for Auckland, hitting 48 not out in his first match for them, at Wellington. Back in Fiji, he was called up for the national rugby side and scored 59 points from full-back on their tour of New Zealand in 1957, including six conversions in a famous victory over the Maori All-Blacks.

VALENTINE, ALFRED LOUIS, died in Orlando, Florida, on May 11, 2004, shortly after his 74th birthday. He had suffered a stroke while recovering from a back operation, and spent his last days in a wheelchair. A toothy Jamaican, Alf Valentine had a meteoric rise to fame, being selected for West Indies' 1950 tour of England aged just 20, after only two first-class matches, and then, along with the Trinidadian off-spinner Sonny Ramadhin, spinning West Indies to three successive and sensational victories. This was the first hint of the new world order that would dominate the game for much of the next half-century. It also spawned perhaps cricket's most famous song: Lord Beginner's calypso about

> *Those two little pals o' mine,*
> *Ramadhin and Valentine.*

Valentine's two previous matches were both selection trials. He made little impact in them – he took two for 190 and was rather flummoxed by the matting pitches – but he impressed the tour captain, John Goddard, and was boosted by a recommendation from the former Glamorgan fast bowler Jack Mercer, who had coached him in Jamaica. Valentine was a brisk left-armer who gave the ball a prodigious tweak and sometimes made it fizz audibly. On that tour, he bowled nearly 1,200 overs and took 123 wickets, but he started steadily rather than spectacularly, and might not have played in the First Test at Old Trafford had it not been preceded by a match there against Lancashire, in which he took 13 wickets for 67.

Alf Valentine catches up on a backlog of autographs; he later devoted his life to helping underprivileged children.

Picture by Getty Images

Understandably retained for the Test, he grabbed five wickets before lunch on the first day and, uniquely, claimed the first eight to fall on his debut. He finished with eight for 104, took three more in the second innings, and 33 in all in a four-match series. West Indies lost at Old Trafford but then took command. At Lord's, he bowled 71 overs in the second innings, then 92 in the second innings at Trent Bridge, a Test record later beaten by Ramadhin. Doug Insole played in that game, and had his Test debut rather ruined by the two spinners as he made 21 and nought: "Valentine wasn't a graceful-type bowler, he'd chunter up to the wicket and rip it." Clyde Walcott was keeping wicket: "Val in 1950 was extremely accurate, and he concentrated on pure spin with no gimmicks. The result was that he turned the ball more in helpful conditions than any left-arm bowler I have ever seen," he said. "Those who thought that batsmen got out to Valentine merely in reaction to playing Ramadhin at the other end underrated Val badly."

Halfway through the tour a team-mate asked him the score, but he couldn't read the board. He was despatched for some National Health specs, which he wore from then on, secured by sticking-plaster when he bowled. They did little for his batting – he ended up with more first-class wickets (475) than runs (470). The big rip Valentine gave the ball took its toll on his fingers, which he bathed in surgical spirit and later, following a tip from Richie Benaud, a mixture of calamine lotion and boracic acid powder. England 1950 remained the pinnacle of his career: although he took 24 Test wickets in Australia in 1951-52, the harder pitches allowed the batsmen to combat the spin twins more effectively.

Valentine had little subtlety beyond the fizzing spin, and rarely bothered top batsmen again, although he was still a fine containing bowler (Frank Worrell wrote: "No matter what sort of field the skipper places to suit the team's tactics at that time, Valentine can and will bowl to it"). At Georgetown in February 1954 he became the first West Indian to reach 100 Test wickets, in only three years and eight months, on his way to a final tally of 139. But a youngster called Garfield Sobers made his debut in the last match of that England series, and although his left-arm spin was altogether gentler than Valentine's, the other aspects of his game were infinitely superior. Valentine carried on, touring England in 1957, when a broken nose and loss of confidence hampered him, and played in the tied Test at Brisbane in 1960-61, where his sensible piece of backing-up in the final over saved what would have been the winning overthrows. He faded out of Test cricket, still only 31, after the final match of West Indies' clean sweep over India in 1961-62, although he toured England one last time without making the Test team in 1963.

After a few years in the Birmingham League, he returned home, and moved to Florida in 1978 with his second wife Jacquelyn (his first wife Gwendolyn, who bore him four daughters, had died). A chance visit to a Sydney care home during that 1960-61 tour had made him want to devote his life to helping underprivileged children, and the Valentines became foster parents to a succession of what are known in Florida as "adjudicated children" – those in need of special care and counselling while their parents are in prison or rehabilitation. Sometimes they would have as many as 12 at a time, and Valentine lost count of the total number who passed through their care.

VIGAR, FRANK HENRY, who died on May 31, 2004, aged 86, was a tall, Somerset-born leg-spinner who turned into one of Essex's most reliable batsmen in the decade after the war. Vigar's batting came to the fore when he went in as night-watchman against Gloucestershire at Westcliff, and scored 121 the next day after Jack O'Connor, the man he had been promoted to protect, was out for a duck. When cricket resumed after the war, he was a regular and made 1,735 runs in the golden summer of 1947, with five hundreds. One of those came in an extraordinary match at Chesterfield, when Essex were up against it – 104 for seven, then 199 for nine when last man Peter Smith came in to join Vigar, who was just past his half-century. Vigar tried to protect Smith at first but then, noticing how well he was playing, let him have his head. The result was that Smith clattered 163 – the highest score by a No. 11 in first-class cricket – and, with Vigar making 114 not out in five hours, the last pair put on 218, to set up an unlikely five-wicket victory. Trevor Bailey remembered him as: "a very unusual mix – a very sound batsman, solid and stubborn, and a useful leg-spinner." But Essex had a better leggie in Smith, so Vigar rarely got the most helpful end. His highest score of 145 also came in 1947 – oddly, in the only one of his 257 first-class matches that wasn't for Essex: he was playing for a combined Middlesex and Essex XI against Surrey/Kent in a festival match at Kingston-upon-Thames. Vigar also took 64 wickets in 1947, but both his batting and bowling fell away later, and he was released in 1954.

WALTER, KENNETH ALEXANDER, died on September 13, 2003, aged 63. Ken Walter was a fast bowler from Transvaal who played two Tests for South Africa, both against New Zealand in 1961-62. Walter, a notable dragger of the

Willie Watson with bat for Yorkshire and ball for Sunderland.
Pictures by Getty Images and EMPICS

back foot through the bowling crease, had come to prominence the previous season, claiming 44 wickets at 15, and in the first innings of his Test debut, he took four for 63. But Walter managed only one wicket in his second Test, and was dropped.

WATSON, WILLIE, died in Johannesburg on April 23, 2004, aged 84. Willie Watson was the last-but-one of the long-gone breed of all-round sportsmen who played cricket and football for England. He played 23 Tests, scoring 879 runs at 25.85, but will be best remembered for his century in the 1953 Ashes Test at Lord's, when his defiant four-hour partnership with Trevor Bailey on the final day staved off what had seemed certain defeat. Coming together at 12.40 p.m., they survived until 40 minutes before the close. Watson, who had come in the previous evening at 12 for three, briefly entertained thoughts of going for the victory target of 343, and asked Bailey mid-pitch whether they should. "Trevor just turned his back on me and walked away," he recalled.

Watson's 109, in 346 minutes, came in his first Test against Australia – but did not secure him a place for long. He was dropped before the end of the series, and missed the Ashes-winning triumph at The Oval. He was, however, named as one of *Wisden*'s Five Cricketers of the Year: Bill Bowes's 1954 essay observed that "unfortunately, a quiet modesty – perhaps until recently an inferiority complex – prevented him making full use of his ability".

His England debut came against South Africa at Trent Bridge in 1951, and Watson scored 57 in his first match and 79 in his second. But it was a golden era of English batting, and he found it difficult to nail down a regular place. Watson toured the West Indies in 1953-54, and added a second Test century in Jamaica. He flitted in and out of the England side until the end of the decade, playing his last Tests in 1958-59. He was a graceful and correct left-hander who scored over 25,000 runs in a first-class career that spanned 25 years, first for

Yorkshire, starting in 1939, and later for Leicestershire, whom he joined as assistant secretary-cum-captain in 1958. His second season there, immediately after what proved to be his final Test appearance, turned out to be his most prolific, and he passed 2,000 runs for the first time.

As a footballer, he played for Huddersfield, Sunderland and Halifax, and won four England caps as an attacking wing-half. He was part of the first England squad that took part in the World Cup, in Brazil in 1950, when they famously lost 1–0 to the unfancied United States, although he didn't actually play a match. Doug Insole recalled Watson in both guises: "He was as graceful a player at cricket and football as you could imagine. He glided around at soccer, with a lovely left foot and a spot of acceleration." Arthur Milton, the 12th and last of those double internationals, never played against Watson at football, but remembered him kindly as a cricketer and a man: "He played well off both feet, and always seemed to be in charge of himself. He was a delightful chap." Milton also remembered him as a skilful bridge player on the boat to Australia in 1958-59.

Watson did better financially from cricket than football: he was paid £60 for that trip to Brazil but missed out on payments of around £300 from Yorkshire while he was away – and got "hopping mad" when the Football Association sent him a bill for 16/3d (81p): "I'd taken a first-class rail supplement travelling to London to avoid standing all the way from Huddersfield." He was player-manager of Halifax for a time in the 1950s, and had a second stint in charge in the 1960s, going on to be manager of Bradford City. He was also a Test selector for three years from 1962. But in the late 1960s he emigrated to Johannesburg to become manager of the Wanderers sports club. He saw out his twilight years in South Africa in somewhat straitened circumstances, but Scyld Berry observed in the *Sunday Telegraph*: "Though not much wealthier than a church mouse he was far from bitter, happy indeed that he could play cricket and football when both were fun." He enjoyed a final reunion with Bailey at Lord's in 2003, 50 years after their famous stand.

WEST, GORDON HARRY SINCLAIR, who died in December 2002, aged 79, was an opener who played two matches for Essex, in 1949 and 1953.

WHITE, EDMUND, who died in February 2004, aged 76, was a right-hand bat who played a match for Northamptonshire in each of the three seasons after the war.

WIGHT, GEORGE LESLIE, died in Toronto on January 4, 2004, aged 74. Leslie Wight was a member of a famous cricketing family from British Guiana (now Guyana): three of his brothers also played first-class cricket, and one, Peter, had a long career in England, firstly with Somerset and then as an umpire. Leslie's most famous innings came when he batted nearly 12 hours to amass 262 not out for British Guiana against Barbados at Georgetown in 1951-52, putting on 390 with Glendon Gibbs, who also made a double-century. The stand remained a West Indian first-wicket record for 49 years. Wight was on the field throughout that match, which British Guiana won by an innings, and early in 1953 he was called up for the Fourth Test against India at Georgetown. He batted as slowly as he did against Barbados, but less effectively: his first dozen runs took two hours, and he was out for 21. Although he helped Clyde Walcott put on 71, he was never selected again. But his first-class average remained outstanding: 1,260 runs at 66.31.

WILMOT, ANTHONY LORRAINE, shot himself on his farm near Grahamstown, South Africa, on February 29, 2004. He was 60, and was facing a jail term after being convicted of raping a 13-year-old girl. Lorrie Wilmot was a powerful batsman whose first-class career lasted 28 years – from his debut at 17 for Eastern Province in January 1961, via a couple of short-lived retirements, to his final match for Border in March 1989, when he was almost 46.

There were early signs of the big-hitting that was to become his trademark: when New Zealand toured in 1961-62, Wilmot blasted the off-spinner Jack Sparling for a six at Port Elizabeth that carried about 120 yards, bouncing on top of the 60ft-high stand beyond mid-wicket, and vanishing into the pine trees. Wilmot put on 136 that day with his old school-mate Graeme Pollock, who was a year younger at 17. They were to share many a rip-roaring stand for Eastern Province, several notable for tragicomic running between the wickets. The largest was a partnership of 338 against Natal at Port Elizabeth in January 1976, when they came together at 15 for four. Pollock scored 194 and Wilmot 152. At Salisbury in 1965-66 Wilmot reined in his attacking instincts and grafted to 222 not out, the first of his two double-centuries. It was not the last time he annoyed Rhodesia. In 1972-73, by then Eastern Province's captain, he led his team off the field at Bulawayo when Rhodesia – with Mike Procter in full flight – were six short of the victory that would probably have given them their only Currie Cup title. Wilmot argued that the compulsory last 20 overs had already been bowled, and refused to resume. At first the match was forfeited, but then the South African authorities ruled that it should be considered a draw.

Wilmot never played an official Test, but in 1975-76, to mark his 100th first-class match, he was made captain of a Board President's XI that took on a strong International Wanderers side skippered by Greg Chappell. Wilmot's explosive hitting would have made him a natural for one-day cricket, which was in its infancy in South Africa when he was at his peak. In the South African Gillette Cup final at the Wanderers in 1972-73 he landed another famous blow, smashing Eddie Barlow into the nearby golf course. The *Eastern Province Herald* summed him up: "He plundered runs off the bowlers the way the old Caribbean pirates sacked a town." His last years were shadowed by the case against him, which dated back to 1998, and he was on bail pending an appeal against his seven-year sentence. His counsel had argued that Wilmot, who was divorced, had lost "everything" during the trial, including the farm which had been in the family for many years.

WILSON, Lt-Gen Sir JAMES ALEXANDER KBE, MC, died on December 17, 2004, aged 84. Jim Wilson was an effective all-rounder for Winchester immediately before the war and also played for Oxford in wartime matches, including the 1940 12-a-side game when they beat the British Empire by ten wickets. During a long military career he commanded the UN force in Cyprus, and rose to be GOC South-East District, but he was best-known for combining this with a sideline as a football reporter: he covered matches for the *Sunday Times* for 33 years.

WILSON, OWEN NEVILLE, who died on January 26, 2004, aged 77, kept wicket in six matches for Orange Free State in 1958-59 and 1959-60.

WILSON, RICHARD, died on December 3, 2004, aged 90. Dick Wilson was a member of the Wrea Green club, near Preston, for 75 years, 20 as captain of the First XI. He was brought up in his father's pub, next to the village green, and first played for their colts side in 1922. More recently he was Wrea Green's chairman, then president, and had been hoping to take part in their centenary celebrations in 2005.

WOLTON, MICHAEL JOHN, died on March 20, 2004, after being knocked down by a car on his way to work at Lord's the day before. He was 39, the father of twins, and had been personal assistant to the curator in the MCC library for more than seven years. Always helpful to researchers, and less serious browsers, he took a particular interest in MCC's revamped publishing programme, helping to promote the books by arranging for signing sessions at big matches. An MCC member who was a regular on the real-tennis court, he was also the secretary of London's Britain-Australia Society. Journalist Murray Hedgcock, a regular at the library, said: "I know 'nice' is seen as a silly word these days, but he was a genuinely nice bloke."

WOOLLETT, ANTHONY FRANK, died on January 26, 2004, aged 76. Tony Woollett was a left-hand batsman who joined Kent in 1950. He played 44 matches for them over the next five seasons, without ever quite establishing himself, and without ever quite scoring a century, although he did make 96 against Yorkshire at Dover in 1953 – his best season. After leaving Kent he played and coached at the Wokingham club in Berkshire for more than 40 years.

WREDE, NEIL ALBERT, who died on May 8, 2004, aged 61, was an accurate left-arm spinner who played 13 matches for Border in the 1960s, taking 38 wickets at 27.52. He was rarely collared, and his best figures were four for 61 against Natal B at Pietermaritzburg in 1967-68, when his victims included the future Test umpire Dave Orchard.

YOUNGER, ALAN CHRISTOPHER WYRILL, who died in May 2004, aged 71, was in the same Alleyn's School side as Micky Stewart, and was described in *Wisden 1952* as "a useful off-spinner and sound opening batsman". He became one of the most famous stained-glass artists in Britain, and was responsible for work at several cathedrals, including Westminster Abbey, where he designed a window in the Henry VII Chapel.

CAREER FIGURES OF TEST CRICKETERS

	Tests				First-class			
	Runs	Avge	Wkts	Avge	Runs	Avge	Wkts	Avge
D. C. Cleverley. . . .	19	19.00	0	–	159	5.30	99	29.08
J. A. Flavell	31	7.75	7	52.42	2,032	6.53	1,529	21.48
V. S. Hazare.	2,192	47.65	20	61.00	18,621	58.19	595	24.61
D. W. Hookes.	1,306	34.36	1	41.00	12,671	43.99	41	58.02
M. G. Melle.	68	8.50	26	32.73	544	11.33	160	24.93
K. D. Meuleman . . .	0	0.00	–	–	7,855	47.60	19	50.31
K. R. Miller.	2,958	36.97	170	22.97	14,183	48.90	497	22.30
F. L. H. Mooney* . .	343	17.15	0	–	3,143	23.11	0	–
E. C. Petrie*	258	12.90	–	–	2,788	17.98	0	–
A. L. Valentine . . .	141	4.70	139	30.32	470	5.00	475	26.21
K. A. Walter.	11	3.66	6	32.83	594	13.50	217	21.22
W. Watson	879	25.85	–	–	25,670	39.86	0	–
G. L. Wight	21	21.00	–	–	1,260	66.31	–	–

* Wicket-keepers: Mooney 22 ct, 8 st in Tests and 168 ct, 54 st in first-class cricket; Petrie 25 ct in Tests and 198 ct, 37 st in first-class cricket.

CRICKET BOOKS, 2004

Inking in the White Pages

RAMACHANDRA GUHA

With one significant exception, the spread of good cricket literature has followed the spread of good cricket. As the home of the game, England also produced its first fine writers; this a long line, extending from John Nyren at one end through Neville Cardus and R. C. Robertson-Glasgow on to our contemporaries Frank Keating and John Woodcock. Meanwhile, its great rival, Australia, was producing cricket books in bulk and, from the middle decades of the last century, also in quality – consider only the works of Ray Robinson and Jack Fingleton.

Next came the Caribbean, whose rise to cricketing greatness was nicely timed to coincide with the publication of C. L. R. James's *Beyond a Boundary*. Likewise, it is scarcely an accident that India's first major cricketing victories, from the 1960s onwards, were accompanied by the first serious cricket books written by Indians – by, in particular, Sujit Mukherjee and N. S. Ramaswami.

The exception, of course, is South Africa. Although the third country to be granted Test status, its traditions of cricket literature have been undistinguished. One reason was the absence of a strong sense of sporting nationalism. Those who played Test cricket for South Africa were often of English extraction; and even when not, best described as honorary Englishmen. This was in contrast to Australia and the West Indies, where the cricketers defined themselves against the Mother Country, as, to good effect, did the cricket writers. A more important reason is that for its first hundred years South African cricket was wholly unrepresentative. "White" writers were prone to bypass rather than confront the fact that their team was chosen from a fraction of the population. They could thus publish (as they did) bland accounts of matches won and lost, but they could not give us works of evocative literature or solid social history.

Things are now changing. With the dismantling of apartheid have come some superb studies – by Andre Odendaal, Vishnu Padayachee and Ashwin Desai, among others – of the cost to good cricket of that horrific system of social discrimination. And this year, 2004, sees the publication of biographies of two cricketers whose careers reflected, at every turn, the troubles and torments of South African history. The books are a study in contrast, but so, indeed, were the cricketers.

Rodney Hartman's **Ali: The Life of Ali Bacher** starts with an artless attempt at winning the reader's sympathy; in a lengthy prologue about a Holocaust that Ali Bacher's father escaped by emigrating to South Africa two decades before it had been conceived. Growing up in a Johannesburg suburb, Ali was a precocious boy batsman. When he was 17, he was compared by an Australian critic to the Don himself. Bacher, wrote R. S. Whitington, has "Bradman's stature, Bradman's lack of grace... Bradman's time to play all his strokes – even Bradman's ability and time to correct a mistake and escape from it". These are remarks more prescient than Hartman acknowledges. While Bacher never matched Bradman's feats with the bat, off the field he has matched him in the ability to extract advantage from any situation and to be on the winning side in any dispute – and, indeed, to "correct a mistake and escape from it".

Hartman provides a useful account of Bacher's first-class and Test career. The main focus, however, is on his later work as a full-time cricket administrator. He was the architect of the notorious rebel tours of the 1980s, which took much plotting and planning: secret visits to London, Colombo and Australia, fictitious companies floated, huge international phone bills run up – real cloak-and-dagger stuff. In the 1990s, as the African National Congress came overground, Bacher forged a close friendship with Steve Tshwete, later to be Minister of Sport in Nelson Mandela's cabinet. Together they helped form the United Cricket Board of South Africa. Still to come was the "resounding success" of the 2003 World Cup, at the culmination of which Bacher "received a resounding cheer" from the crowd at the final.

The most original part of the book deals with Bacher's relationship with Hansie Cronje and Makhaya Ntini: two cricketers of the new South Africa plagued by controversy. There are fascinating excerpts from the testimonies given to the King Commission set up to enquire into Cronje's corruption. But overall the narrative drags; at 450 pages, this must be one of the fattest cricketing biographies ever.

> Oborne breaks new ground in his account of D'Oliveira's career in South Africa

More subtle by far is Peter Oborne's **Basil D'Oliveira: Cricket and Conspiracy: The Untold Story**. Its opening chapter exquisitely captures D'Oliveira's dilemma when a letter arrived from England asking him to join Middleton as its cricket pro, when he was already 28, settling into his career at a printing press, with his adored wife expecting their first child. He walked across town to consult his friend Damoo Bansda, who insisted that he go, and set about raising the money to pay for his air fare.

Oborne breaks new ground in his account of his hero's cricketing career in South Africa. As he writes, D'Oliveira's "extraordinary exploits were invisible" to white South Africa. He pays proper respect to the other remarkable black cricketers whom apartheid consigned to penury and obscurity: the bowler Eric Petersen, the all-rounder Cec Abrahams, the wicket-keeper Lobo Abed. There is an excellent chapter on the matches played between Kenya and a non-racial South African team of which D'Oliveira was captain. His career in England, from Middleton to Worcestershire to the Test team, is well-known, but here too Oborne adds the telling cameo, such as the reception D'Oliveira got back in Cape Town after his first season in England: being driven in an open car to the City Hall to meet the mayor, the streets lined with cheering crowds.

Using freshly released records, Oborne shows how the South African government worked overtime to stop D'Oliveira from being chosen for the projected winter tour of 1968-69: by lobbying Tory grandees, blackmail, and even an outright attempt at bribery. Johannes Vorster and his cabinet showed a quite amazing level of interest in the case; their personal stakes in not having D'Oliveira come were very high indeed. Senior MCC men tacitly encouraged them, some asking the cricketer to back out on his own (which he refused to do). In the midst of all this D'Oliveira was dropped from the England side in the ongoing series against Australia, then recalled for the final Test at The Oval. Here he played what Oborne considers the most remarkable innings in Test history, 158 runs scored "against an attack comprising Prime Minister

Johannes Vorster and South African apartheid at its most savage and corrupt, supported by the weight of the British establishment".

Despite that innings, he was not chosen for the tour of South Africa. Oborne, scrupulously fair-minded, sees this as a case (as Ted Dexter wrote at the time) of "honest bungling by honest men". But when Tom Cartwright withdrew, the selectors, "bowing to public opinion", chose D'Oliveira, thus sparking the cancellation of the tour, and the beginning of South Africa's cricketing isolation.

Reading these two books in conjunction, one cannot but see the contrasts. Where the young D'Oliveira walked miles lugging a mat to play on a bare and uneven ground, Bacher went by motorcycle to bat on immaculately groomed turf wickets. No blacks or coloureds figure in the narrative of Bacher's playing career; the subject, like his biographer, was oblivious of other forms of cricket in the South Africa of the 1950s and 1960s. However, Oborne always writes about the cricket played by D'Oliveira in the context of contemporary white cricket as well.

A bit player in the D'Oliveira story was E. W. Swanton. I grew up hearing Swanton's plummy voice on *Test Match Special*; for me he embodied the British cricket establishment, as, apparently, he did for David Rayvern Allen. In **Jim: The Life of E. W. Swanton**, Allen relates how, when he first met

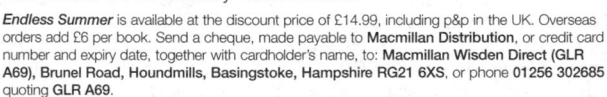

the great man, Swanton looked over his shoulder for someone more important. Later, they became friends, but yet he approaches his subject with a mixture of awe and animosity – there is not that instinctive empathy which marked, for example, his life of Arlott. But the book is all the better for these ambivalences.

An autobiography is a pre-emptive strike against a prospective biographer. Swanton wrote two of those, with which Allen wisely does not seek to compete. Instead, he fills in their silences, writing at some length about Swanton's childhood, his war experiences and his deep Christian faith. He describes his early breaks in Fleet Street, providing some useful embellishment on the way. (Thus we are told that the Maharaja of Porbandar came to England in 1932 "with his fleet of white Rolls-Royces in tow". Actually, there were only three, still enough for him to achieve the unique feat of being the only visiting captain to own more Rolls-Royces than he scored runs on tour – there being only two of *those*.) There is a detailed account of Swanton's ascendancy in the post-war cricket world, with extensive excerpts from his correspondence.

This is an affectionate but not uncritical book. We learn of Jim's social ambition – he was an energetic lobbyist on his own behalf – his tendency to cut corners, his temper. On the other side, we learn of Swanton's admirable efforts to eliminate bad behaviour on the cricket field. By the evidence of this book the first cricketers to sledge were Len Hutton's Englishmen, on the West Indies tour of 1953-54, when, to Swanton's disgust, the cricketers at times treated their hosts with a condescension that bordered on arrogance. Swanton's own pomposity was counterbalanced by his principled anti-racism, often on display in this book, as in a heartfelt tribute to Frank Worrell, or an angry letter of protest at Enoch Powell's "Rivers of Blood" speech.

If a book by David Rayvern Allen comes, can one by David Frith be far behind? These are writers who are both gifted and prolific, in a class whose only other member is the brilliant young Australian Gideon Haigh. This year Frith gives us **The Ross Gregory Story**, his biography of an ill-fated Australian cricketer.

Gregory, who grew up in a Melbourne suburb, was an outstanding schoolboy cricketer who made his debut for Victoria at 17. A string of good scores in the Sheffield Shield catapulted him into the Australian side. He played a more than modest role in the last two Tests of one of the more exciting series in cricket history, played in the winter of 1936-37, when Australia recovered from a 0–2 deficit to win the rubber. These were the only two Tests Gregory appeared in. He was desperately unlucky not to be chosen for the 1938 tour of England. The next year war broke out. Gregory enlisted in the Air Force, serving in Europe and the Middle East, before dying in a crash over the floodplains of what is now Bangladesh.

The cricketing parts of the book bear marks of the author's characteristically careful research. I once wrote of Frith that he "probably knows more cricket facts than any man alive". Here are some new ones. When Gregory made his Test debut, the Ashes rivals were tied at 54 wins apiece; but with that match the Aussies went into a lead which they have never since

relinquished. In Gregory's second Test, he was caught by Hedley Verity off the bowling of Ken Farnes. This was a "uniquely tragic treble Test scoreline", for batsman, bowler and fielder were *all* to perish in the Second World War.

The press box's other celebrated Anglo-Australian has this year published his autobiography. Peter Roebuck's **Sometimes I Forgot to Laugh** is the work of a sensitive and deeply intelligent man. The controversies that have peppered his life are recounted with a remarkable detachment and lack of bitterness; notably the "Somerset Affair", when, during Roebuck's captaincy, Ian Botham, Viv Richards and Joel Garner all left the club. He is penetrating on Richards's batsmanship and even more so on Botham's character ("far more vulnerable than he pretends – that's why he must always take the masses with him". Or again: "Rejection and isolation were his greatest fears and they drove him towards the light"). Also recalled, and with some nostalgia, are the days before the fight, when Somerset were united, and plenty of silverware came to adorn a previously bare cupboard.

Roebuck writes well about his adopted homeland and its contemporary cricketers – though I remain unconvinced by the claim that sledging is merely a manifestation of the Aussie love of democracy. This will be read as a cricket book, but it is also, in its own way, a contribution to social history. From the accounts of his family, in particular, we sense how sport and education were the great vehicles of social mobility in the 20th century.

A sort of semi-autobiography is Farokh Engineer's **From the Far Pavilion**, which rehearses the career of this much-loved wicket-keeper/batsman with Bombay, India, and (not least) Lancashire. The memories are warm – particularly of his early days in the Dadar Parsi Colony – and the sepia photographs very fine. Some stories strain one's credulity, as of the time 40,000 Indians apparently queued up outside the Taj Mahal, not to view the monument, but to garner autographs of their cricketers. Withal, this is a valuable account of one of the few players of Indian cricket's Golden Age whose life story was not yet in print (now we all await, some with anticipation, others with alarm, the autobiography of Bishan Bedi).

Jorge Luis Borges once wrote that there were two kinds of anthologies: the idiosyncratic and the encyclopaedic. Decidedly of the first kind is Graeme Wright's **A Wisden Collection**, a little yellow book made out of hundreds of big fat ones. The editor displays both a prodigious knowledge of earlier *Wisdens* and a sharp understanding of how best to deploy it. The first entry is about John Wisden; the last, about another cricketing entrepreneur (Hansie Cronje). The excerpts in between cover an astonishing variety of themes – though I did detect a welcome bias towards bowlers (for so long the game's underclass). To this Indian, the Antipodean editor seemed to have a strange fascination with cold climes. There is a whole chapter on cricket on ice, for example, and a too-loving mention of the Gondwanaland Occasionals, who play occasionally – in Antarctica.

By contrast, David Rayvern Allen and Hubert Doggart, the editors of **A Breathless Hush: the MCC Anthology of Cricket Verse**, throw in everything as well as the kitchen sink. There are some very good poems here, but far too many dull or mediocre ones. The editors have laboured mightily – as shown by their excellent biographical notes – but the subject itself is not worthy of their labours. Much cricket verse is far too agreeable to count as good poetry. This extract, from a poem called *A New Season*, is representative:

> *A member sets aside his beer*
> *And cheerfully applauds*
> *Will this one be the golden year*
> *With glory won at Lord's?*

Even more embarrassing are the selections from my neck of the woods, as in a piece of juvenilia from Dom Moraes, otherwise the finest English-language poet produced by the subcontinent. (This was probably the only poem on cricket that Moraes published, for as he got older he got on to worthier subjects.)

An anthology that seeks to be both exhaustive and eccentric is John Woods's **Test Cricket Grounds**. This is a sort of Lonely Planet guide for the cricket lunatic who seeks to follow his side to the farthest corners of the world. He can learn here how to get to the ground – be this Chittagong or Christchurch – where (and where not) to stay, what (and what not) to eat, and which local monuments to see before the match or if it is rained out. The writing is lively, although the spelling is somewhat cavalier, as befits a compatriot of the late James Joyce.

The year's best illustrated book is Ken Piesse's **Cricket Colosseum: 125 Years of Test Cricket at the MCG**, with a lively text to match the rare pictures. This is a handsome tribute to the ground where the first three Test matches were played, a ground next only to Lord's in its significance to cricket history. Piesse provides crisp accounts of every Test played at the MCG. Bradman looms large in the narrative (he scored nine hundreds here), but there is also much interesting information on the social background of other Aussie cricketers.

Another informative local history is Vedam Jaishankar's **Casting a Spell: the Story of Karnataka Cricket**, this, astonishingly, the first-ever history of a Ranji Trophy side. The pictures are less distinctive (a consequence perhaps of the notorious Indian disregard for archiving), but the word portraits as loving. Jaishankar writes of the great international stars who graced Karnataka cricket – from B. S. Chandrasekhar and G. R. Viswanath to Dravid and Kumble – but also of the lesser heroes who have helped the state to as many as six Ranji Trophy triumphs.

Having surveyed the globe, we return, in the end, to where cricket and its literature began: the village green in England. Tim Heald's **Village Cricket** presents a cheerful romp through the game as played in places as dissimilar as Cornwall and Lancashire. This is a chatty, conversational, unfailingly good-humoured book, determined to see the best in everyone – even the squire and the parson. "The importance of tea in this class of cricket can never be overstated," writes Heald. Elsewhere he says: "The nearer one gets to London and the stockbroker belt the further one gets from traditional village cricket."

Rather more elevated in scope and manner are two autobiographies published by famous England cricketers. As one would expect, **As It Was**, the memoirs of the ageless Freddie Trueman, is rich in stories true and apocryphal, all told to the advantage of the teller – but many very good none the less, like the one about his first entry in *Wisden*, as a "slow left-arm spinner". There are vivid accounts of his boyhood in pre-war Yorkshire, of his first sight of Headingley, and of the great Yorkshire cricketers who helped him on his way up (memories of the Yorkshire committee and MCC, naturally, are less pleasant). There are some fine throwaway lines, although to think of Fiery Fred quoting Euripides when sacked from his *Sunday People* column (as he claims he did) does rather boggle the mind.

Nasser Hussain's **Playing with Fire** is also very good on his boyhood, this time in a close-knit Asian family shuttling between Madras and Ilford. He too writes with much affection of his early mentors, such as Keith Fletcher and Graham Gooch, and at some length about the important Test matches of his career. Particularly valuable is Hussain's account of the tension produced by living and playing in close proximity, which sometimes leads to superb collective work and at other times to nasty brawls.

The Hussain and Trueman memoirs are essential reading, because of who they are and what they did. Both are long books, and yet somewhat parochial. Trueman can, it seems, praise only players from Yorkshire. There is not even an appreciation of his mate Brian Statham. Hussain is more generous in his acclaim of his England colleagues. But it is disappointing to see him so comprehensively reproduce Trueman's disregard of the great foreign players of his generation. A dose of internationalism would have made his book far more interesting in a purely cricketing sense. What did it mean to face Curtly Ambrose on a bouncing track, or Shane Warne on a turning wicket? What was it like to field while Steve Waugh or Sachin Tendulkar batted? Sadly, questions such as these are not even posed, still less answered.

Nicely complementing the above are two books written by honest county professionals, both Test cricketers, but only just. Steve James's **Third Man**

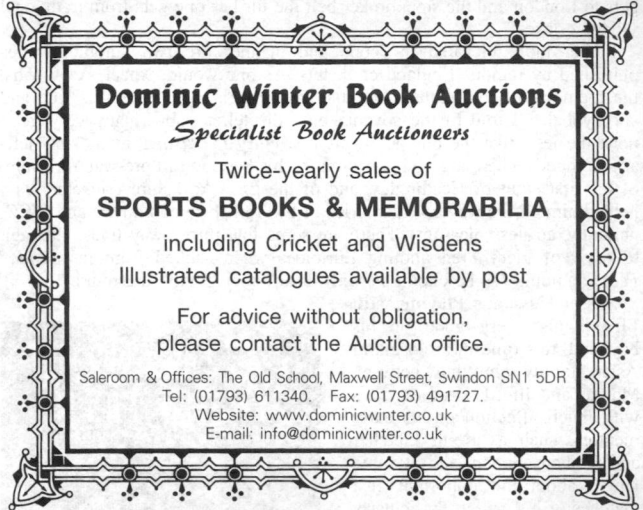

To Fatty's Leg (its title explained in the preface) has an appealing, self-deprecatory style. The man was anxious, even paranoid, before every innings he played – and honest enough to say so. He is often acute on the dilemmas of his nationhood: is he English, or Welsh, or both? At other times the tone is jokey, or should one say blokey; the humour, such as it is, tends towards the slapstick.

Like James, Ed Smith has written every word of **On and Off the Field**, an account, however, of a single year in his life (2003), rather than a two-decade-long career. The book begins in Mumbai, where Smith spent his winter improving his technique against spin bowling, and ends in Boston, where he was sent to cover the Harvard–Yale football match. In between we have a wry, detached, if occasionally too introspective account of an English cricket season.

Smith is rightly sceptical of too much jogging and weight-training. The pre-season routine at Kent is almost as wearying as life at a Gandhian *ashram*, where prayer would take the place of a team-meeting and spinning substitute for modern exercise. (Admittedly, Smith's day ended on an un-Gandhian note: "9 p.m., hit the night spots of Maidstone".) And it didn't help. The season started disastrously, with Smith slow to strike his best form and Kent going down to a series of defeats. But, as he played more cricket and jogged less, the runs began to flow. Later in the summer Smith scored four centuries on the trot, a feat rewarded by his being picked for England.

This book is like an innings by an orthodox England batsman (Vaughan, say, rather than Flintoff). It starts slowly, but as it goes on picks up speed. The reader gets drawn into Smith's fate and that of his county too. Hardy and Wagner pop up almost as often as Thorpe and Trescothick, as one would expect from the son of a novelist and a double first from Cambridge. This is a formidable intelligence indeed. The analysis of what makes good "timing" is exceptionally acute. And which other cricketer could describe technology as "that headless horseman of history, capable of changing everything without intention or care"? Ed Smith's *On and Off the Field* is *Wisden's* Book of the Year.

Ramachandra Guha's A Corner of a Foreign Field *won the Cricket Society Literary Award in 2003. His other books include* Environmentalism: A Global History *and* Savaging the Civilized: Verrier Elwin, His Tribals, and India. *He lives in Bangalore.*

> **"** Added piquancy was given to the situation by the fact that, the following weekend, London's Afro-Caribbean population had swayed through Notting Hill in a well-organised burst of merry-making. The carnival was going strong, but cricket was neither invited nor included."
>
> Robert Winder, Cricket's Migrant Soul, page 27.

BOOKS RECEIVED IN 2004

GENERAL

Appleby, Matthew **Durham County Cricket Club** 100 Greats (Tempus, £12.99)

Bassano, Brian **Mann's Men** The MCC Team in South Africa 1922-23 (limited edition, J. W. McKenzie, 12 Stoneleigh Park Road, Ewell, Epsom, Surrey KT19 0QT, Tel: 020 8393 7700, £18.99)

Baum, Greg **The Waugh Era** The Making of a Cricket Empire 1999–2004 (ABC Books, \$A32.95)

Coward, Mike **Rookies, Rebels & Renaissance** Cricket In The '80s (ABC Books, \$A49.95)

Eason, Alan **The A–Z of Bradman** Foreword by David Frith (ABC Books, \$A29.95)

Fernando, M. L. ed. **125: History of the Royal–St. Thomas' Cricket Match** (Lake House Printers and Publishers, 41 W. A. D. Ramanayake Mawatha, Colombo 2, Sri Lanka, RsSL1,000)

French, Stanley **Come in, my Lords, Come in!** (PO Box 887, Castries, St Lucia, West Indies or email french@candw.lc, no price given) *Celebration of St Lucia's much-admired new stadium and the island's cricketing traditions*

Gibbs, David **Summers by the Sea** The Centenary of the Sussex Martlets Cricket Club 1905–2005 (available from S. Ross, Birchwood, Twitten Lane, Felbridge, East Grinstead, Sussex RH19 2NZ, £20)

Goble, Ray and Sandiford, Keith A. P. **75 Years of West Indies Cricket 1928-2003** Foreword by Clive Lloyd (Hansib, £20)

Hart-Davis, Duff ed. **Pavilions of Splendour** An Architectural History of Lord's Foreword by HRH The Duke of Edinburgh (Methuen, £20)

Heald, Tim **Village Cricket** (Time Warner Books, £16.99)

Henderson, Nigel **The Worst of Cricket** Run outs to riots: Malice and misfortune in the world's cruellest game (Pitch, £9.99)

Hignell, Andrew **Gloucestershire County Cricket Club** Fifty of the Finest Matches (Tempus, £12.99)

Jones, Trevor **Two In Blue** Surrey's Double-Winning 2003 Season (Sporting Declarations, available from The Oval Shop, Kennington, London SE11 5SS, £14.99)

Lodge, Jerry **Into the Second Century** Surrey CCC: A History Since 1945 (Tempus, £20)

Lynch, Steven comp. **The Wisden Cricket Quiz Book** (John Wisden & Co, £7.99)

McCann, Timothy J. **Sussex Cricket in the Eighteenth Century** (Sussex Record Society, £20)

Piesse, Ken **Cricket's Colosseum** 125 Years of Test Cricket at the MCG Foreword by Bill Lawry (Hardie Grant Books, available in UK from Roundhouse Publishing, Millstone, Limers Lane, Northam, North Devon EX39 2RG, Tel: 01237 474474, £35)

Ryan, Christian ed. **Inside Edge presents The Greatest** Top 50 Innings by Australian Batsmen 1877–2004 (ACP, \$A9.95)

Ryan, Christian ed. **Inside Edge presents Fast Men** The Real Story behind Australia's Top Guns (ACP, \$A9.95)

Wade, Tim **Village Idiots?** An Affair with English Cricket (Trafford, available from www.trafford.com, £9.60)

Wallace, John **Glorious Summer** The Sussex CCC Championship 2003 (Tempus, £12.99, paperback)

Weaver, Paul and Talbot, Bruce **The Longest Journey** The Inside Story of Sussex's Championship Triumph Foreword by John Barclay (Sutton, £16.99)

Woods, John **Test Cricket Grounds** The Complete Guide to the World's Test Cricket Grounds (SportsBooks, £12.99, paperback)

AUTOBIOGRAPHY

Collins, Jared E. **Not Out: Impossible** The Recollections of a North Devon Cricketer (available from Peter Adams, Amberley, Limers Lane, Northam, Bideford, North Devon EX39 2RG, Tel: 01237 472 338, £9.99, paperback)

Engineer, Farokh and Cantrell, John **Farokh Engineer: From the Far Pavilion** Foreword by John Major (Tempus, £20)

Flintoff, Andrew (with Patrick Murphy) **My Life in Pictures** (Orion, £16.99)

Halbish, Graham **Run Out** My Dismissal and the Inside Story of Cricket Foreword by Rod Nicholson (Lothian Books, available in UK from Roundhouse Publishing, Millstone, Limers Lane, Northam, North Devon EX39 2RG, Tel: 01237 474474, £13.99)

Hassan, Basharat (ed. Peter Wynne-Thomas) **Basher** The Autobiography of Basharat Hassan Foreword by Sir Garry Sobers (from Nottinghamshire CCC or Association of Cricket Statisticians (ACS)/Sport in Print, 3 Radcliffe Road, West Bridgford, Nottingham NG2 5FF, £14.99)

Hussain, Nasser (with Paul Newman) **Playing with Fire** The Autobiography (Michael Joseph, £17.99)

James, Steve **Third Man To Fatty's Leg** (First Stone, £16.99)

Luckhurst, Brian **Boot Boy to President** A celebration of 50 years with Kent and England, as told to Mark Baldwin Foreword by Derek Underwood (KOS Media, £10.95)

O'Keeffe, Kerry **According to Skull** An Entertaining Stroll Through the Life of Kerry O'Keeffe (ABC Books, $A29.95)

Ponting, Ricky and Murgatroyd, Brian **Ricky Ponting's World Cup Diary** (HarperCollins, £14.99)

Roebuck, Peter **Sometimes I Forgot to Laugh** (Allen & Unwin Australia, available in UK from June 2005 from Orion Publishing, £12.99, paperback)

Smith, Ed **On and Off the Field** (Viking, £18.99)

Trueman, Fred **As It Was** The Memoirs of Fred Trueman (Macmillan, £18.99)

Tyson, Frank **In the Eye of the Typhoon** Recollections of the Marylebone Cricket Club Tour of Australia 1954/55 (Parrs Wood Press, £20)

Waugh, Steve **Never Say Die** (HarperCollins, £14.99)

BIOGRAPHY

Allen, David Rayvern **Jim** The Life of E. W. Swanton (Aurum Press, £20)

Frith, David **The Ross Gregory Story** (Lothian Books, available in UK from Roundhouse Publishing, Millstone, Limers Lane, Northam, North Devon EX39 2RG, Tel: 01237 474474, paperback, £14.99)

Hartman, Rodney **Ali** The Life of Ali Bacher Foreword by Nelson Mandela (Viking, paperback, £14.99)

Miller, Douglas **Born to Bowl** The Life and Times of Don Shepherd Foreword by Tony Lewis (Fairfield Books, 17 George's Road, Fairfield Park, Bath BA1 6EY, Tel: 01225 335813, £15)

Oborne, Peter **Basil D'Oliveira** Cricket and Conspiracy: The Untold Story (Little, Brown, £16.99)

Sharpham, Peter **Charlie Macartney** Cricket's 'Governor-General' Foreword by Bill Brown (Walla Walla Press, $A39.95)

FICTION

Knox, Malcolm **Adult Book** (Bloomsbury, £10.99, paperback)

Morrison, Paul **Wondrous Oblivion** A Wide-Eyed Boy in a Narrow-Minded World (Hodder Children's Books, paperback, £5.99)

Panckridge, Michael (with Brett Lee) **Toby Jones and the Secret of the Missing Scorecard** (Angus&Robertson, Australia, $A14.95)

ANTHOLOGIES

Allen, David Rayvern and Doggart, Hubert (eds) **A Breathless Hush** The MCC Anthology of Cricket Verse Preface by Lord Alexander of Weedon Foreword by Sir Tim Rice (Methuen, £20)

Wright, Graeme ed. **A Wisden Collection** (Bloomsbury, £16.99)

STATISTICAL

Ambrose, Don comp. **1879: A Statistical Survey** (Association of Cricket Statisticians (ACS)/Sport in Print, 3 Radcliffe Road, West Bridgford, Nottingham NG2 5FF, www.acscricket.com, £7)

Bailey, Philip comp. **Bangladesh First-Class Matches 2001/02; 2002/03 and 2003; and 2003/04** (ACS, £6 for 2001/02, £5 for 2002/03 and 2003, £6 for 2003-04)

Bailey, Philip comp. **First-Class Cricket Matches 1907** (ACS, £16)

Bailey, Philip comp. **Sri Lanka First-Class Matches 2002/03** (ACS, £9.50)

Crofton, Philip and Bartlett, Kit **Derek Underwood** His Record Innings-by-Innings (ACS, £10.50)

Garrod, Hugh **G. L. Jessop** His Record Innings-by-Innings (ACS, £8.50)

Hudd, Gerald **C. W. L. Parker** His Record Innings-by-Innings (ACS, £9.50)

Hudd, Gerald **Ian Botham** His Record Innings-by-Innings (ACS, £9.50)

Leopard, Mark comp. **Philadelphia and North American Cricketers 1878-1972** (ACS, £5)
Rogers, Norman **H. E. 'Tom' Dollery** His Record Innings-by-Innings (ACS, £6)
Warsop, Keith **E. G. Wynyard** His Record Innings-by-Innings (ACS, £7.50)
Webb, Tony ed. **The Minor Counties Championship 1895** (ACS, first of new series, £6)

HANDBOOKS AND ANNUALS

All first-class counties produce handbooks of varying quality. Details available from each club.
Agnew, Jonathan **C&G Cricket Year 2004** 23rd edition (Bloomsbury, £22.50)
Bailey, Philip ed. **ACS International Cricket Year Book 2004** (ACS, address as above, £12.95)
Bryden, Colin ed. **Mutual & Federal South African Cricket Annual 2004** (UCBSA, available from cricket@mf.co.za, R95)
Frindall, Bill ed. **Playfair Cricket Annual 2004** (Headline, £6.99, paperback)
Gerrish Keith, comp. **First Class Counties Second Eleven Annual 2004** (ACS, address as above, £5.95)
Irish Cricket Annual 2003 (from Irish Cricket Union, Sport HQ, Joyce Way, Parkwest Dublin 12, £3/Euros 5)
Marshall, Chris ed. **The Cricketers' Who's Who 2004** (Queen Anne Press, £16.99)
Payne, Francis and Smith, Ian ed. **2004 New Zealand Cricket Almanack** (Hodder Moa Beckett, Auckland, no price given)
Ryan, Christian ed. **Wisden Cricketers' Almanack Australia 2004-05** Seventh Edition (Hardie Grant, Victoria, $A49.95, in UK from Macmillan Wisden Direct, Brunel Road, Houndmills, Basingstoke, Hampshire RG21 6XS, Tel: 01256 302 685, £22.50; abridged pocket paperback $A14.95)
Viswanath, G. comp. **Indian Cricket 2004** (Kasturi & Sons, Chennai, Rs100)

REPRINTS AND UPDATES

Allen, David Rayvern **Arlott** The Authorised Biography (paperback edition, Aurum, £8.99)
Arthur Haygarth's/Marylebone Club Cricket Scores and Biographies Volumes XIV (1877–1878) and XV (final volume – Biographies and Index) A continuation of Frederick Lillywhite's Scores and Biographies from 1772 to 1854. (Facsimile editions, from Roger Heavens, 2 Lowfields, Little Eversden, Cambridgeshire CB3 7HJ; limited edition of 500, Volume XIV £68 inc. p&p, Volume XV £65 inc. p&p)
This represents the end of Roger Heavens's massive project to make these rare books available in facsimile. He is working on further volumes from Haygarth's manuscripts.
Bird, Dickie **Dickie Bird's Britain** Photographs by Derry Brabbs (paperback edition, Hodder & Stoughton, £14.99)
John Wisden's Cricketers' Almanack for 1880, 1881, 1882, 1883, 1884 and 1886 (second facsimile editions, Willows Publishing, 17 The Willows, Stone, Staffordshire ST15 0DE, fax: 01785 615867, email: jenkins.willows@ntl.com, £60 plus p&p)
Johnston, Barry **Johnners** The Life of Brian (paperback edition, Coronet Books, £8.99)
Lewis, Tony **Taking Fresh Guard** A Memoir (paperback edition, Headline, £7.99)
Lillee, Dennis **Menace** The Autobiography (Headline, paperback, £7.99)
Tom Smith's New Cricket Umpiring and Scoring Jubilee edition. Introduction by Richie Benaud (Weidenfeld & Nicolson, £9.99)

PERIODICALS

Allout cricket (ten per year) ed. Andy Afford, Matt Thacker (PCA Management, £3.50. Subscriptions: 0870 4583778 or via www.cricnet.com)
The Cricket Statistician (quarterly) ed. Philip J. Bailey (ACS, £2, free to ACS members)
The Journal of the Cricket Society (twice yearly) ed. Clive W. Porter (from D. Seymour, 13 Ewhurst Road, Crofton Park, London, SE4 1AG, £5 to non-members)
The Scottish Cricketer (electronic monthly) ed. Neil Leitch and Mike Stanger (subscribe online via sales@cricketscotland.com or www.cricketscotland.com)
Wisden Asia Cricket (monthly) ed. Sambit Bal (Spenta Management, Rs30, £2.75 in UK. Subscriptions: + 91 22 24960102 or subs.wac@wisdengroup.com)

The Wisden Cricketer (monthly) ed. John Stern (Wisden Cricketer Publishing, £3.40.
   Subscriptions: The Pavilion, Lamberhurst Vineyard, Tunbridge Wells, Kent TN3 8ER, 01892
   893030 or subclub@wisdengroup.com)
The Wisden Cricketer (South African edition) ed. Robert Houwing (Touchline Media, R22.95.
   Subscriptions: + 27 860 007827 or subs@touchline.co.za)
The Yorker (quarterly) ed. James Greenfield   Official Magazine of Yorkshire CCC (Yorkshire
   CCC, £2.50)

EDITORS OF WISDEN, 1864–2005

W. H. Crockford* and W. H. Knight*	1864–1869
W. H. Knight*	1870–1879
George H. West*	1880–1886
Charles F. Pardon	1887–1890
Sydney H. Pardon	1891–1925
C. Stewart Caine	1926–1933
Sydney J. Southerton	1934–1935
Wilfrid H. Brookes	1936–1939
Haddon Whitaker	1940–1943
Hubert Preston	1944–1951
Norman Preston	1952–1980
John Woodcock	1981–1986
Graeme Wright	1987–1992, 2001–2002
Matthew Engel	1993–2000, 2004–
Tim de Lisle	2003

* Exact dates and roles unconfirmed.

WISDEN BOOK OF THE YEAR

Since 2003, *Wisden's* reviewer has selected a Book of the Year. The winners have been:
2003 *Bodyline Autopsy* by David Frith
2004 *No Coward Soul* by Stephen Chalke and Derek Hodgson
2005 *On and Off the Field* by Ed Smith

THE CRICKET SOCIETY LITERARY AWARD

The Cricket Society Literary Award has been presented since 1970 to the author of the cricket
book judged best of the year. The 2004 award, sponsored by *The Times* and the Sir Tim Rice
Charitable Trust, was won by David Frith for **The Ross Gregory Story**.

CRICKET AND THE MEDIA, 2004

A Year of Stundays

ANDREW NICKOLDS

Appropriately enough it was on the Ides of March that readers of the sporting press got an inkling of future events in 2004 which nobody could have seriously predicted: six months of virtually unbroken England Test success. The ten-wicket win against West Indies made headlines on both the front and back pages of the *Daily Mirror*, though typically "The Day Sport Turned Upside Down" and "Stunday" referred to both Sabina Park and Manchester, where City beat local rivals United 4 1 in the football Premiership.

For British tabloid newspaper editors cricket is something of a Cinderella sport, most useful when it can be put together with a couple of Ugly Sisters wearing different England shirts, to present a grimly dysfunctional family portrait. Another Stunday in July 2001 comes to mind, when England lost by an innings to Australia at Edgbaston, Tim Henman succumbed after three rain interrupted days to Goran Ivanisevic at Wimbledon, the British Lions were overrun by the Wallabies in Melbourne… and the whole country could look forward to a bout of enjoyable self-flagellation on the Monday morning.

Of course, it helped that Steve Harmison, chief architect of the England victory with figures of seven for 12, was able to give free and full rein to the collective sports-writing imagination. So, "Grievous Bodily Harmison" bellowed *The Sun*, with the letters G, B and H reversed out in case anybody missed the point.

"Grievous Bodily Harmison" echoed the *Daily Mirror* twice in the text, though this was outscored by three uses of "Harmy Army", and outdone by one of those bursts of sentimental prose that erupt whenever the subject is sport in the North-East: "The Geordie pilgrim… Wor Harmy, who comes from the Northumberland sporting gold mine of Ashington, where Sir Bobby Charlton and Jack Charlton were also raised."

By the time the series in the Caribbean was won, cricket was back below stairs wearing its familiar rags. Not even talkSPORT, the series' official broadcaster in England, could be persuaded to interrupt its regular football programme to cover Matthew Hoggard's hat-trick (it was also Grand National day – bad luck Hoggy), much less Brian Lara's record-breaking 400 on Easter Monday, another big day for the Premiership.

Even when the media noticed England, they were not always complimentary, especially when ex-England players were doing the noticing. The relationship between the game's past and present stars has often been touchy, never more so than when the present lot are doing well. As far as Geoffrey Boycott was concerned in his weekly column in the *Daily Telegraph*, only seven of the England team on the West Indies tour were pulling their weight, which said much about the quality of the opposition. Therefore a 3–0 victory could hardly be counted as an achievement (despite the definitive statement "the achievement that this team has achieved is a fantastic achievement" from captain Michael Vaughan in the post-Barbados press conference).

Vaughan was actually one of Boycott's four underachievers, but luckily by the time of the return visit the "Worst Indies" (headline in the *Daily Mirror*) themselves were down to only three achievers by Boycott's reckoning: Lara, Chanderpaul and Gayle, a convincing 7–3 scoreline.

This must have been confusing for the likes of poor Dwayne Bravo, a newcomer pilloried by Boycott one moment for not being up to the job, then encouraged in his Channel 4 commentaries the next, along the lines of "he's got a bit about him this lad, I like the look of him". But that's only to be expected when you hire "The great entertainer", the headline to a hymn of praise written in *The Times* by Tim de Lisle. His argument was that while remaining polar opposites, the media personalities of Boycott and Ian Botham had turned out completely contrary to expectations.

"If you had looked at them 20 years ago, you'd have said that the one who was in danger of turning into another Fred Trueman, better known to the younger generation for being a grumpy old lag than a great cricketer, was Boycott. It has turned out to be Botham." After assessing their respective strengths (Boycott beating throat cancer) and weaknesses (Botham appearing in panto) in the "Tale of the Tape" style of boxing journalism, de Lisle concluded that "It is Boycott who plays more shots, takes more risks, has more to say. The tortoise has overtaken the hare."

So it was inevitably to t'tortoise that the *Observer Sports Monthly*, for example, would regularly turn when in need of a bit of salty wisdom on topics ranging from slow over-rates ("I wrote in 1990 that we need to combat this, but what did the ICC do? They pissed around for 14 years, that's what") to politicians ("I don't respect them because I don't think they give a shit about us") to being stopped from providing one of the quintessential sounds of an English summer to rank alongside leather on willow – car-key on earth ("If you ask me, groundsmen have become too precious about their pitches. It's all bloody stupid").

Grumpiness can also be used as a force for good, some might argue, and Botham was one of the few who risked being unrestrained in his criticism of the forthcoming England tour of Zimbabwe, a subject which rumbled on through the summer and autumn, a tummy bug threatening to strike at inopportune moments. "As long as [Zimbabwe] is run by a barbaric regime who sponsor genocide and starvation, we shouldn't be going near the place," Botham told the *Daily Mirror*. "There are some government ministers and cricket administrators whose appeasement of an appalling regime is sickening and they should hang their heads in shame. I haven't met a single person yet who thinks England should be going to Zimbabwe this winter."

He apparently was not far wrong: an unscientific BBC Radio 5 Live poll in November had 98% of listeners in favour of England withdrawing. Naturally, a few days later they arrived in Harare.

By midsummer Botham had been joined in the Sky commentary box by another grumpy former England captain: Nasser Hussain, who never quite gained the affectionate status of "Wor Nass", despite his Durham University connections. He confirmed in an interview with the *Daily Mail* online edition that he had retired for good: "I won't pick up a cricket bat ever again, unless I'm shopping," Hussain said. Yes, I suppose it can get quite rough at times at the Lakeside Mall.

He was also candid on the main difficulty of being captain. This – Michael "Achievement" Vaughan, take note – was more than merely dealing with the Australians, or a recalcitrant Jimmy Anderson: "The toughest thing was you are always wary of what you say because of your quotes. You might do a piece in a newspaper and things get taken out of context, and then someone else has to comment on it because the England captain has commented on it and it goes round in circles."

But there were more experienced commentators on hand, often the target of angry Hussain gestures from out in the middle, who were now ready to put his five-year period of captaincy into generous perspec-

United's crisis hits a new low as they crash to rivals City

Harmison makes history to blow out the Windies

tive. Not all of them were as colourful as Simon Barnes in *The Times*: "Let us find the roadside corpse of some luckless car-struck weasel, cremate it, place the ashes in a small urn and present it to Hussain – the man that slew the weasel of defeatism, the greatest achievement of any England captain in history."

Yet all acknowledged that Hussain had, with the help of Duncan Fletcher, turned the side around since the World Cup and New Zealand humiliations of 1999. Hussain's departure, marked by a match-winning century at Lord's, was encapsulated by Marcus Trescothick in the *Daily Telegraph*: "I don't know who writes his scripts." For sports journalists, in both print and broadcasting, this was 2004's must-bestow accolade, honouring heroes as varied as Colin Montgomerie and Wayne Rooney after their unlikely exploits.

It was also a useful shorthand when the superlatives were drying up, and thus invaluable for summing up Andrew Flintoff's season, or the "Summer of (Seven) Love" as the new *All Out Cricket* magazine called it in psychedelic lettering. Advertised on the cover as "The Players' View", this was produced

by the Professional Cricketers' Association and pitched somewhere in the corridor of uncertainty between *The Wisden Cricketer* and a county fanzine – its editors include the former Nottinghamshire bowlers Andy Afford and Jimmy Hindson. There was not an awful lot of meat in this magazine, though it may have all been cut to make way for pictures of Flintoff – inevitably "the people's champion". I counted 29 in the October issue.

Maybe cricket reporting really was getting more lazily tabloid in tone, because England players' proud fathers were much in evidence throughout the year, from Jimmy Harmison in *The Sun* who was over the moon, to Emrys Jones in *The Guardian* who listened to Geraint's hundred at Headingley and woke the neighbours in Toowoomba, Queensland with his shouting. Even Joe Hussain was credited by Nasser in the *Daily Mail* with having a hand in his son's decision to retire. Needless to say the Unknown Scriptwriter weighed in again when it came to Colin Flintoff, who was caught on camera doing the opposite, dropping one of Freddie's sixes which made it to an upper tier at Edgbaston where his mum and dad were sitting. Exclusive to all newspapers, as they say in *Private Eye*.

This was counterbalanced by a story sympathetically reported by Sybil Ruscoe in the *Daily Telegraph* of equally proud father John Wagg, who had worked night shifts at a pet food factory so that he could drive his promising youngster to matches in a clapped-out Ford Escort (the money saved being spent on new kit) and then slept in the car instead of splashing out on bed-and-breakfasts before watching his son play. Now that same son, Graham Wagg, is serving a 15-month suspension for failing a drugs test and is back living with his dad after being sacked by Warwickshire.

And every so often a piece came along which made me think that perhaps cricket writing hadn't all gone the way of *Hello!* magazine. "What Happened to the Black Cricketer?" was a well-researched analysis by Rob Steen in *The Wisden Cricketer*. Steen's report tackled head-on the question of racial stereotyping in the media ("Tudor? Soft slacker. Cowans? Mouthy slacker. Chris Lewis, the most gifted new Botham of all? Daft slacker").

Of course, put race, cricket and the media all together and you get strange outcomes. Even after the Summer of (Seven) Love, it would have been hard to imagine the England team threatening to pull out of a tour because journalists were not being allowed to report it. It happened over Zimbabwe. And some of those hacks were ex-England players. Who wrote that script?

Andrew Nickolds is still the back half of Dave Podmore, the cricketer inexplicably ignored by the England selectors in good years and bad. He is also co-author of the Radio 4 comedy series, Ed Reardon's Week.

CRICKET EQUIPMENT, 2004

With Lord's on their Side

NORMAN HARRIS

There was a touch of the surreal in two recent moves on the equipment front: MCC became agents for an Australian-made helmet, and a famous German sports company entered the world of willow. Two separate actions, but together they suggest that what was once a cottage industry has moved on from flowerbeds and thatch.

Helmets have dramatically altered not only the look of cricket over the past quarter-century, but also the sound. Last summer the clang of ball on supposedly protected heads seemed to grow more frequent. Northampton-shire's Graeme Swann took one full-on at Old Trafford that split his helmet and left him dramatically rubber-legged, like a boxer about to go down. Even more worrying was a blow on the left side of the head for Glen Chapple of Lancashire, during the Championship match against Sussex: it brought a delayed reaction that indicated brain bruising and required several weeks' rest.

International batsmen also featured in the new ball-to-head game. Andrew Strauss got a ball wedged hard in the grille of his visor and extracted it with a somewhat comical-looking pull, as if removing a mote from his eye; and Nathan Astle of New Zealand was shaken by a hit on the side of the head by a fiery Steve Harmison on home soil at Chester-le-Street. Once again the question was prompted: why are batsmen being hit more often than they were before helmets?

Perhaps the answer is in research presented to the British Psychological Association in April 2004 which showed that wearing a helmet made batsmen measurably less alert. Reaction times were slowed by a tiny fraction of a second – quite enough for the head to fail to get out of the way. And, though no studies have been done on this, it seems pretty obvious that a helmet's weight, in itself, is going to slow down reactive head movement.

This does not make a case for not wearing helmets. It just underlines the need for the best possible materials, for more research and development, and, perhaps, for radical redesign. The present British Standard for helmets clearly focuses on protection of the *crown* of the head. Indeed, a drawing specifies the area to be protected as being above a line drawn (in profile) from the eyes to the top of the ears.

Little thought seems to have been given to protection against blows when a batsman turns his head – as he commonly does, when in trouble – and is struck in the area of ear and jaw. According to one manufacturer of (non-cricketing) helmets: "The rivets that join the visor to the helmet have the potential to cause injury, and a blow there can greatly magnify the shock waves. Cricket helmets should be shaped to encompass the ears and back of the head."

How did that get there? A delivery from Daniel Vettori lodges inside Andrew Strauss's helmet during the Lord's Test v New Zealand.

Picture by Patrick Eagar

Such innovation as there has been focuses on high-tech materials that are both lighter and stronger, like the titanium used for the grille of Gray-Nicolls' top-of-the-range helmet, and in better ventilation. Beyond that, there seems to be little drive to radically improve cricketers' head protection. Most helmets are made in India for cricket goods "manufacturers" in Australia and England, and the market is not of a size to warrant massive R&D.

It is a little puzzling, therefore, that a helmet should be the one item of cricket equipment to be officially endorsed by the ECB, who announced last summer that it had agreed a three-year deal to make C&D Albion, of Australia, the "preferred supplier of cricket helmets to the ECB". One might imagine that this indicated a special interest by the ECB in player-protection, and that perhaps the Albion product had been judged to meet higher safety standards than other helmets. Perhaps the different shape of the Albion helmet (as worn by Andrew Strauss, and by most of the Australian team), being somewhat like an upturned saucer, has a better ball-deflection capability? But the ECB do not appear to be making this claim. Nor do MCC.

One might ask: why should they? Well, MCC turn out to be the UK and European agents for the Albion helmet. The idea that the guardians of cricket should ally themselves to one commercial product has shocked English cricket manufacturers. One said: "I'm very surprised, to put it mildly. Surely there's a conflict of interest there? The MCC had always been very careful not to be allied to any particular commercial interest."

MCC do not accept that the move was controversial, and are unapologetic in confirming their new commercial agenda: "We are strongly committed to increasing our commercial activities, so as to invest in cricket and to provide year-round income," said the club spokesman, Iain Wilton. "Representing Albion brings further welcome income. We're happy to have a relationship with a company who are market leaders in innovation and quality, and we don't see it affecting our relationships with a wide variety of equipment companies."

Commercial, pragmatic cricket is further heralded by the arrival of a bat bearing the brand-name of Puma: the name established in 1948 by Rudi Dassler, when he started making sporting footwear in competition with his brother Adi's eponymous brand, Adidas. These days it would be surprising if there were much market resistance to a name once synonymous with Germany and athletics. After all, there are many other non-traditional brand names, at least at the economy end of the market. Further, many – if not most – "English" bats are now made (from English willow) in India.

A consequence of this process is that there are fewer "leading brands" – that is to say, the sort of bat that a serious club cricketer might purchase on a regular basis. In 1976, a *Sunday Times* survey found nine such bats in a representative selection of stores countrywide – the top prices of the bats ranging from £15 to £21. Now just three of those brands dominate the market: Gray-Nicolls, Gunn & Moore and County, with Kookaburra offering the strongest challenge. Club batsmen these days are likely to pay between £150 and £200 (and the top list price of any bat is £275).

But one bat-maker from outside the leading group continues to survive: Warsop-Stebbing, who sell direct from their Essex factory. From them, a top-of-the-range bat is now around £110. Their willow comes from just down the road, from the long-established firm of Wrights of Great Leighs. And they have been making bats since 1870. Without any official endorsement.

CRICKET AND THE WEATHER, 2004

Ah, Yes, But it Could have been Worse

PHILIP EDEN

One consequence of the proliferation of international cricket in recent years has been the scheduling of tours and competitions outside the various traditional cricket seasons. Another has been the appearance of many new venues, from Durham to Darwin, mainly – as *Wisden* pointed out last year – used to host "less attractive opposition on unseasonable dates".

It is surely obvious that this trespassing into unknown territory, both geographical and temporal, has implications as far as the weather is concerned. And one would have expected the various authorities to have sought climatological advice in advance. Two examples – England's spring tour of the West Indies and the Champions Trophy in September – suggest that the ECB either (a) failed to do that, (b) received poor advice, or (c) received good advice and ignored it.

Colin Cowdrey's team played a Test in Trinidad on January 19, 1968. In 2004, England tourists did not start playing until early March, and came back in May. Of the seven one-day internationals scheduled between April 18 and May 5, three were abandoned and one other seriously rain-affected. A climatologist would scarcely have raised an eyebrow at the news: both rainfall duration and amount in the region increase sharply in April and May, while rising humidity and lower sunshine duration inhibit the drying process once the rain has stopped. The seasonal progression is especially marked in Jamaica where twice as much rain falls in April compared to February, and in May *seven times* as much.

The danger of holding a major international tournament in England in the second half of September was highlighted on this page last year. A grey competition under grey skies it was, but only great good fortune allowed them to get away with it at all: September 2004 was appreciably drier, sunnier and warmer than average in London, Birmingham and Southampton. Had the Champions Trophy been held at the same time in 2001, 2000, 1999 or 1998 it would have been unceremoniously drowned. The quantity of rain that falls is, on average, less in September than in August but this is heavily outweighed by a rise in rainfall duration, much reduced evaporation (grounds dry more slowly and wickets remain damp), as well as less sunshine and lower temperatures.

Our faulty memories are already traducing the summer of 2004. It was, of course, much poorer than its predecessor. But, just as the ten-day August heatwave dominates our image of the 2003 season, 18 days of rain in August 2004 are all that many remember from last summer. If it was such a washout, how on earth did England manage to win seven successive Test matches?

From grey to gold: England's glorious summer begins under Lord's leaden skies in May.

Picture by Patrick Eagar

For the record, widespread rain fell during April 17–21, April 27–May 5, June 22–July 8, August 9–26, and September 16–20. Who remembers now the outstanding weather that dominated May and the first two-thirds of June?

The meteorological statistics averaged over England and Wales for the 2004 season, are as follows:

	Average max temperature (°C)	Difference from normal for 1971–2000	Total rainfall (mm)	% of normal	Total sunshine (hours)	% of normal
April	13.6	+1.3	86	152	146	93
May	16.9	+1.3	51	79	217	105
June	19.8	+1.1	63	97	209	102
July.	20.4	−0.5	74	126	177	90
August.	22.1	+1.4	157	183	181	99
September	19.1	+1.2	57	69	163	116
2004 season	**18.7**	**+1.0**	**488**	**117**	**1,093**	**101**

Each summer has slightly different regional variations, although in most years northern and western counties are cooler, cloudier and damper than those in the east and south. The Wisden Summer Index allows us to compare the summer county by county, and incorporates rainfall amounts and frequency, sunshine, and temperature, in a single figure. The formula is explained in *Wisden 2004* (page 1597). The final index ranges from zero for the theoretical worst possible summer to 1,000 for the theoretical best.

The score for an average recent summer ranges from 525 at Chester-le-Street and 530 at Old Trafford to 670 at Lord's and 675 at The Oval. Broadly speaking, an index over 650 indicates a good summer whereas one below 500 clearly describes a poor one. Values for each county for the summer of 2004 against the average for the standard reference period of 1971–2000 are given below:

	2004	Normal	Difference		2004	Normal	Difference
Derbyshire	488	580	−92	Middlesex	653	670	−17
Durham	462	525	−63	Northamptonshire .	560	615	−55
Essex	589	640	−51	Nottinghamshire . .	503	590	−87
Glamorgan	565	555	+10	Somerset	599	620	−21
Gloucestershire . .	578	595	−17	Surrey	657	675	−18
Hampshire	662	645	+17	Sussex	669	665	+4
Kent	611	655	−44	Warwickshire	540	555	−15
Lancashire	419	530	−111	Worcestershire . . .	591	615	−24
Leicestershire . . .	512	585	−73	Yorkshire	512	560	−48

Perhaps surprisingly, three counties had above average scores, but there were large negative totals in Lancashire, Derbyshire and Nottinghamshire. Old Trafford was not the wettest ground in terms of rainfall amount, but it easily topped the list for rainfall frequency and lack of sunshine. Southampton was only 44 points behind last year, but 14 counties were 100 points or more lower than 2003, and Lancashire were 168 lower. Not surprisingly, their dreams of the Championship were dashed.

Averaged nationally, last season's index of 541 was 106 points lower than that of 2003, and in the last 20 years only the summers of 1985, 1987, 1988, 1991 and 2002 were poorer.

1993	573	1996	663	1999	637	2002	506
1994	651	1997	601	2000	556	2003	647
1995	777	1998	565	2001	632	2004	541

Highest: 812 in 1976   Lowest: 309 in 1879

With the enticing prospect of England entertaining the Australians this season, cricket followers started asking me what sort of summer it would be even before Christmas. Forecasting at such long range remains the province of the fool and the fraud, but climatologists do recognise a phenomenon known as the biennial oscillation, meaning summers tend to alternate between good and bad. This oscillation was strong between 1946 and 1962, and again since 1997, so I think I am on fairly safe ground if I suggest that it could well be better than 2004 but probably not as good as 2003.

Philip Eden is weather expert for BBC Radio Five Live, and the Daily *and* Sunday Telegraph.

CRICKETANA IN 2004

Big Match for Matchstick Men

DAVID RAYVERN ALLEN

People are often shocked by the amounts paid for cricketing artefacts, but when cricket and art come together, prices can move into areas even Bradman caps cannot reach. And at the Christie's saleroom in November, L. S. Lowry's unique view of the game had a magical effect.

The Cricket Match and a Cricket Sight Board made an amazing £600,000, which is not merely one of the highest prices ever paid for a cricketing artefact (one or two 18th-century portraits may have fetched more) but believed to be the second-highest for a Lowry.

The work was sold from the estate of Alick Leggat, an industrialist, former Lancashire president and a friend and patron of Lowry's. It is an unusual picture, split into two by the artist (see overleaf and the colour section). One version of the story is that Lowry knew little about cricket, that Leggat took him to a league game somewhere in Lancashire (the exact venue is unknown), that Lowry stayed about ten minutes under protest and went away to paint the crowds incongruously, either behind or in front of the sightscreen. Leggat mocked him, so Lowry turned it into two separate, but related, pictures.

If he did only stay ten minutes, his cricket career would now be worth £60,000 a minute, which even Tendulkar cannot match. The truth appears to be less colourful. Lowry said he had artistic difficulties resolving the two parts of the painting, which is why he split it. He later considered the lower part to be one of his most successful crowd scenes. And he certainly produced other works depicting children playing cricket, if not of formal matches. Lowry was such a prodigious worker that no one knows exactly how many paintings he produced, let alone where they are, so it is possible another cricket picture will appear one day.

The sale was not good news for Lowry enthusiasts. The work was previously on long-term loan from Leggat to the Lowry gallery in Salford. But Christie's sold it to an unidentified woman bidder, who was (or was representing) "a private buyer in the UK". The painting's present whereabouts – and chances of being seen in public – are unknown. MCC sent a representative to the auction, and would have loved to buy it, but the bidding was too ferocious. The Lowry record is £1,750,000 for his football picture, *Going to the Match*. But that was paid by the Professional Footballers' Association, and is now on long loan to the Lowry for everyone's enjoyment. Football is a richer game than cricket.

For the more average collector, the highlight of the year came in an improbable corner of Somerset. "West of London and east of New York there is only one Laurences," says the sign on the lavatory wall of the biggest

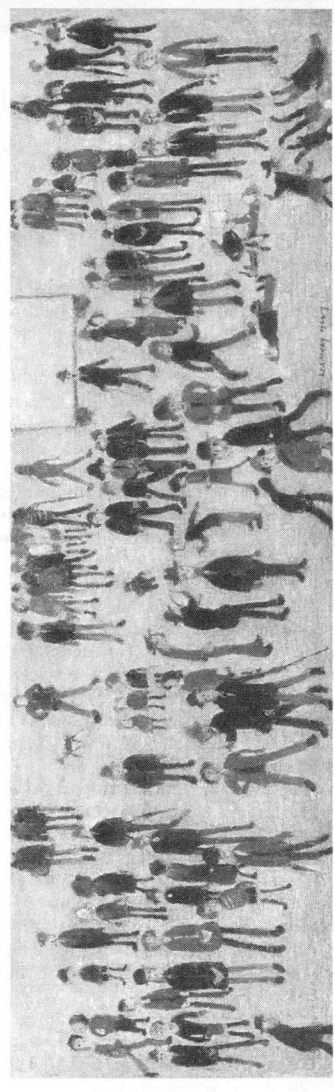

A Cricket Sight Board: L. S. Lowry painted this and *The Cricket Match* (see colour section) as a single work.
By permission of the Lowry Estate; image supplied by Christie's Images Limited 2004

auction house in the whole of Crewkerne. For those of us who had managed to get there on a January day, there was a real sense of achievement just arriving, as well as a sense of keen anticipation.

The occasion was a landmark sale to place alongside those that broke up two other great cricket book collections: Joe Goldman's in 1966 and Tony Winder's in 1985. The library of that doyen of booksellers, Leslie Gutteridge (who until he emigrated to Canada in the mid-1960s was the ever-welcoming face of Epworth Press in London's City Road), was being sold three and a half years after his death. Gutteridge specialised in some of the great 19th-century rarities, and many of them reached healthy prices.

But to general disbelief, an incomplete set of Fred Lillywhite's *Young Cricketer's Guide* from the mid-19th century climbed to stratospheric levels. These guides (not to be confused with the publications produced by other members of the family) are a nightmare for bibliophiles because no one is sure how many were actually produced. This set had 19 of the roughly two dozen volumes that were published between 1849 and 1866. They are very rare; even so, no one expected the feverish contest between a mysterious phone bidder, known to the rest of us only as No. 894, and a well-known London dealer, which left the estimate of £8,000–£10,000 far behind. The hammer eventually came down in favour of the phone bidder at £70,000 (£80,500 with 15% buyer's premium).

Everyone at Crewkerne was speculating who No. 894 might be. There are suspicions, but the mystery has still not been wholly solved, except presumably by visitors to his or her library. There was astonishment all round, and particularly from the delighted beneficiary, John Gutteridge, Leslie's son. The total for the cricket collection (there were other Gutteridge collections on the following days, including Natural History and Antarctica) came to over £265,000, including premiums. Almost certainly that amount would have been increased by well over 20% had not about 25 items been stolen from the Gutteridge home in Canada. They included a unique copy of the *Laws of Cricket*, 1845, with additional material by a member of the Toronto Club. How sad that the collection could not parade in all its glory! Many of us are convinced we know who the thief is, and let us hope that at some stage justice prevails and the books are resurrected.

The rest of the year could easily have been anticlimactic, but somehow it was not. In June, Christie's sold another Bradman cap, this time from 1930, though the date was not in evidence. It fetched £35,850 with 19.5% – yes, 19.5% – buyer's premium. The situation with Bradman's caps is rapidly acquiring the madness traditionally associated with hatters. Since his death in 2001, there have been a shop-full of his caps: those worn for a season, for a few minutes, dated, undated, pristine, faded, with moth holes. Where will it end? At the September sale at Lawson Menzies in Sydney, his 1946-47 Ashes baggy failed to realise the \$A30,000–\$A50,000 (about £12,000–£20,000) estimate, so maybe sense has prevailed at last. Although it can be argued anything is worth what somebody will pay for it, a cap – anybody's cap – should not have the intrinsic worth of, say, a precious book or beautiful painting where intellect and artistry have been involved.

Bat madness was calming down too. One of Sir Jack Hobbs's bats, also from 1930 (the one with which he overtook W. G. Grace's first-class run aggregate), made £13,145 with premium. But the one Sir Garry Sobers used to score the then Test record of 365 not out in 1957-58 failed to make its reserve of £32,000. And a silver bat presented to Farokh Engineer for his performance against England at Bombay in February 1973 did not reach its minimum of £10,000 in November.

And there were chances elsewhere to buy cricketana at quite modest prices. In April at Old Trafford, the Cricket Memorabilia Society auctioned attractive items from the collection of the late Burt Rhodes, a genial man who for many years was musical director at the old Talk of the Town in London, and, at Edgbaston in October, there was another sale of caps, county shields and *Wisdens* owned by the Lancashire and England spinner Bob Berry. The more modest prices, and lack of buyer's premium, were a boon for stretched pockets.

Perhaps the most unconventional item to appear on the market anywhere was a hand-carved boomerang used by Murrumgunarrim ("Twopenny") to entertain the English spectators during the Aborigines' tour of 1868, which appeared in Lawson Menzies' July sale. The buyers, for $A11,000 ($A13,106 with premium), were the National Museum of Australia, who also bought an original 1867 composite photograph by Peter Dawson showing individual portraits of the Aboriginal cricketers. This fetched $A14,000 ($A16,681 with premium).

So, overall, were there any noticeable trends during the year? Well, certainly there were two. Those auction houses that commenced business at midday, as opposed to 10 a.m., tended to have a larger attendance because it was far easier for potential buyers travelling long distances to get there. And with their new swingeing buyer's premiums (which allow the auctioneers to get commission from the purchaser as well as the vendor) of around 20%, and lack of interest in any item valued at under several hundred pounds, the big London houses are in danger of losing potential clientele. There is now a discernible improvement in quality and wider range of material at some provincial houses such as Knight's and Vennett-Smith, who charge more reasonable amounts.

In his will, Leslie Gutteridge had stipulated that his collections should be auctioned by Sotheby's. But in the present climate, understandably, his widow Norma had looked further afield in search of greater accommodation and flexibility. Surely, there is a lesson to be learned here.

CRICKET AND BETTING, 2004

Dead Cert? Flat Broke!

PAUL HAIGH

Cricket began as a gambling medium. Only after The Great Lord's Scandal of 1817 did betting on the game that became synonymous with all the bourgeois virtues begin to seem disgraceful: stooped to only by bounders, and later Bodyliners, ball-tamperers, bribers, and bump-ball claimers.

In the past ten years the game has endured a betting scandal with global ramifications that far outstripped 1817. The ICC now boasts a group of sleuths who can sniff out a player making a dubious call on his mobile from a thousand paces. But still the gambling goes on. And it always will. No game's scoring system lends itself so perfectly to betting as cricket, and the volume of cricket business conducted in the various types of betting outlet now available to the unapologetic punter continues to reflect this fact.

Cricket betting is now a serious industry, and the amount of money changing hands is such that corrupt results can only be a tiny fraction of the total. In Britain cricket fans cheerfully bet on anything from the fall of the next wicket to the fall of the next raindrop. If they had the chance and some means of verifying the result, they would probably be quite happy to bet on whether Billy Bowden acts like that at home.

India's illegal bookmaking industry regularly turns over more than $1 billion (yes, that's a "b" not an "m", and the guess isn't mine: it comes from Britain's own legal bookmakers) on well-contested one-day internationals. And only the great ogre, football, can begin to compete with that.

The rise in betting on cricket has been synchronous with a revolution in betting worldwide – but the coincidence is not entirely coincidental. Eight years ago I suggested in *Wisden* that the invention of spread betting (a system like that of the stock market, but in which one buys a stake in sports teams' and individual players' performances) was likely to change the face of betting in general and of cricket betting in particular. I was nearly right, too – which makes a pleasant change – but not quite right enough. Spread betting has largely been superseded by the invention of the internet-based exchanges, in which individuals make their own odds and offer the chance for other punters to take them on as they think fit.

The trouble with spread betting is that you can lose very large sums indeed if the bet goes wrong. If you "sell" a Test team's runs at, say, 250, thinking they will get less than that, the losses can theoretically be infinite if they are 350 for no wicket at the close of the first day. An innocent might put a fiver on, without realising that's £5 *per run* above or below the figure offered by the spread firms. That's why people say you need balls of steel to bet the cricket spreads.

For exchange betting, titanium testicles are an advantage, but not an absolute prerequisite. On the exchanges, you can bet all the time on a cricket match, but you can only lose your stake, not your house. And there are plenty of opportunities to hedge your bets. You are only up against other punters, who might react less quickly than the pros employed by the spread firms.

Cricket lends itself to what the exchange boys call "in and out" betting, which really just means changing positions as the game's flow changes. That's also why the exchanges don't like it much, because they make their profits on commission charged on the profits on settled bets. But it's only taken on the net profit at the end of the contest. So huge amounts can be "matched" on cricket without much of it sticking to the exchange's fingers.

More than £23m was placed on Betfair, the biggest exchange, on England's Test at Johannesburg, compared with only £7m on the England–France football match at Euro 2004. Soccer punters, being the simple folk they are, tend to go in hard for their team and then stick with the bet through thick or thin, maybe even going in again at big odds if the situation starts to look desperate. Cricket punters, apparently more pragmatic, are quite happy to back all possible outcomes at huge odds in order to protect themselves from the financial consequences of the freak result.

The slow pace of the game, of course, makes such self-protection possible. In soccer, a goal can change a game instantly. In cricket, a single wicket – even if it's Lara's, Tendulkar's or Flintoff's – hardly ever does quite that. Just as exchange betting on cricket makes it possible for the prudent to protect themselves, however, it also makes it possible for the very greedy to get badly damaged. The final of the Champions Trophy is a case in point. West Indies 147 for eight, needing another 70 or so, with Harmison bowling at 95mph in the dark? People fell over themselves to back England at odds of 1-10, 1-20, 1-33, even 1-99. Money for old rope really, wasn't it? Well, as it turned out, not.

So too the famous county one-day game last season in which two supposedly no-hope Kent batsmen snatched victory from the champions Glamorgan. Someone, hoping to shave a little more profit from what seemed a certainty, laid 1,000-1 against Kent on Betfair in that game with just two overs to go. We can only guess at their sentiments when the leg-side full toss that was Adrian Dale's last ball in county cricket before emigration to New Zealand (which was already planned, in case you were wondering) was planted straight on to the roof of the dressing-rooms.

You're probably thinking that there's scope for corruption here (not by Ade, who was devastated) if only someone – an umpire perhaps – could predict such fluctuations in advance. Maybe a scratched right ear could mean the next appeal's going to be given, for example, and then an accomplice at a computer... Well, yes. But because there is no cash betting on the exchanges, Betfair Know Who You Are, and have agreed to sneak to the ICC if they suspect anything. Actually, this development may make life harder for the match-fixers, not easier.

Paul Haigh is chief columnist of the Racing Post.

CRICKET PEOPLE IN 2004

The Slovak Goalie Who Changed Cricket

TANYA ALDRED, LAWRENCE BOOTH AND SIMON BRIGGS

EVERY COUNTY cricketer in England knows about **MAROS KOLPAK**, but Maros Kolpak can't name a single one of them. "I know what cricket is," he says, "I've seen it on TV, but I can't play." Then again, most cricketers can only name the one handball player, who happens to be a Slovak goalkeeper playing for Ostringen in the second division of the German league.

Kolpak won a battle at the European Court in 2003 to be allowed to play in Germany without being classed as a foreigner. In the process he transformed county cricket. The judgment was the corollary to the Bosman ruling of 1995, which allowed free movement of players within the EU, but did not affect cricket much. The Kolpak ruling applied this to all countries that have trade agreements with the EU, allowing South Africans and others to make their living unrestricted in the UK.

Kolpak was not thinking about Northamptonshire or Leicestershire when he brought his case. "I did it for myself," he admits. Like county cricket, German handball restricted clubs to two foreign players, and his fight against that took six years. Other handball players were waiting for the judgment, and there has since been an influx of players from Eastern Europe into Germany.

"Are the foreign players thought of as a good thing in cricket?" he asked, to which there is no short answer. He has looked his name up on the internet and has seen it linked with other sports, but when he was told that cricketers are known as "Kolpak players" he roared with laughter.

The winding road to Lord's (1)

WHEN **TOM GRAVENEY** became MCC president last autumn he broke the mould: he is the first ex-professional cricketer to hold the post. Elegant and distinguished though his cricket career was, you could have got long odds when he retired 35 years ago against his latest achievement.

Any other man might have left cricket vowing never to return. Graveney exited the big time unceremoniously in 1969, after he played in one of his own benefit matches on the rest day of a Test against West Indies. He was dropped and banned, even though – just shy of his 42nd birthday – he had scored 75 in what *Wisden* described as "a careful mood".

Actually, he could have been more careful. "I'm an easy-going sort of bloke but I had a couple of run-ins," Graveney says now with the mellow good nature that has become his trademark. "I left Gloucester under a bit of a cloud. Also I played this benefit game. I did ask the chairman of selectors, and assumed that when I was picked he knew what I was going to do. But it didn't really make a difference, I was getting very close to retirement age. Cricket is only a game and I didn't bear any grudges."

Rising to the top: Tom Graveney *(left)* and Sir Bill Morris both accepted jobs at Lord's during 2004.

Pictures by Patrick Eagar and Mike Hewitt, Getty Images

After retiring, he coached Queensland, became a relaxed-sounding TV commentator for the BBC and landlord of the Royal Oak in Prestbury, close to Cheltenham racecourse. "My wife said it was the first proper job I had. I've never worked so hard."

Graveney had been involved with the MCC for a while, but the presidency was a complete surprise. "It has been fantastic – a real eye-opener. The MCC has taken over all sorts of things, especially backing up grass-roots cricket, and I've met so many people, good people."

He grew up in the game amid the old divide between professionals and amateurs, when a Player could not call a Gentleman by his first name. All that is long gone, and the ex-Player is now coming up from Cheltenham every week to represent the most famous Gentlemen's club of all. He has been given four different MCC ties, and he loves every one.

The winding road to Lord's (2)

FEW HAVE addressed both the ECB and the TUC. But **SIR BILL MORRIS** has a habit of tramping through boundaries. Morris, the former leader of the Transport and General Workers Union, joined the management board of the ECB in 2004. It was not an invitation he was expecting.

"My love of the game is a matter of public record," he says. "Cricket has been a formative part of my life and character. But it was a bolt from the blue. I thought long and hard about accepting because I've been critical of the authorities in the past, but I hope to be a view from the boundary."

Morris was born in Jamaica and came to England as a 16-year-old in 1954, getting a job at a car-parts manufacturer in Birmingham. Thirty-seven years later, he was representing 900,000 workers. He stood down as general secretary of the T&G in 2003, but is still heavily involved in a variety of public offices: he is, for instance, a director of the Bank of England (a long-standing bastion of cricket lovers).

It was not until England's last tour of the Caribbean that Morris first went to Sabina Park, which he had walked past but not entered as a boy – and he loved it. But his favourite place to watch cricket is on village greens near his home in Hertfordshire: "Just youngsters giving 100%, with no prima donnas."

Though he is now an Establishment figure, he hopes to bring something of a radical perspective to the game. "We have moved a long way from Gentlemen and Players, but people from university and public schools are still dominant. We have to develop better facilities and opportunities for all."

The coach with the golden touch

WHEN ANDREW Strauss cracked Chris Martin through extra cover to reach his debut century at Lord's last summer, up in the Allen Stand sat a very proud, but not at all surprised, octogenarian. The man was **BERT ROBINSON**, cricket coach at Radley College. It is nearly half a century since he watched one of his charges, Ted Dexter, blossom into an England batting star. Now Strauss had repeated the trick. "The best day of my life," he said. "I knew he was special: the boy had first-class cricket stamped all over him."

Robinson played for Northamptonshire either side of six long years in the RAF, and then brought his bowling boots to Radley in 1949, when tea was still rationed. But for Bert, now aged 88, not too much has changed. He still lives in the same village, in the same house, with the same wife (Doris) and, wearing the same tie, does the same job, if at a slightly more leisurely pace. And, if Strauss's progress is anything to go by, he still has the same touch. Nor, after coaching 55 Radley first elevens in succession, does he think that boys have changed much either. "They are pretty well behaved, and I don't stand any nonsense."

"I've been a pretty hard task master at times but I don't think that any boy who has passed through my hands would have a bad word to say about me." The current crop of first-class cricketers moulded by Bert includes Robin Martin-Jenkins, Ben Hutton and, Robinson's favourite for success, Jamie Dalrymple. How long will he go on? "For as long as the college will tolerate me. I've got the right sort of bones." And the secret of his longevity? "Loving the game and accepting it as part and parcel of my life."

Europe's enemy within

THERE HAVE BEEN many cricket nuts in politics before now, but few with a background in the game to match **ASHLEY MOTE**, Member of the European Parliament for south-east England and author of *The Glory Days of Cricket*, a history of the Hambledon Club and winner of the Cricket Society Literary Award in 1997.

"I started researching *The Glory Days* as a 2,000-word pamphlet for the landlord of the Bat and Ball, on Broadhalfpenny Down," he says. "Two years and 160,000 words later, and after discovering John Nyren's manuscript, there was my labour of love." The book led to the reformation of Hambledon, with membership fees set at three guineas, unchanged from the 18th century.

Politics was another passion. Mote flirted with the Liberal Party in the late 1950s and early 1960s, "when they were proper Liberals, a free trade, free enterprise party". But by the 1990s, his biggest bugbear had become the EU. He wrote two books about the European Union, *Vigilance: A Defence of British Liberty* and *Overcrowded Britain* (his stance can be guessed from the titles) and was soon being asked to speak at public meetings. Then last June he was elected as an MEP on a UK Independence Party platform, with the political stance of "the turkey voting for Christmas".

Unfortunately, Mote's political career has not gone quite as well as his cricket writing. Immediately after his election, the *Daily Telegraph* reported that he was facing ten charges at Chichester Crown Court relating to an allegedly fraudulent claim for housing benefit. He vigorously denies the allegations.

UKIP removed the whip from him, so he now sits as an Independent, which perhaps makes the lonely life of being an anti-European within the parliament even lonelier. "I do have Sky Television in Brussels, and like to keep an eye on the score. There are a number of cricket-mad MEPs from all sides, though we don't yet have a team."

He was once squashed nose to nose next to a Polish representative in a lift who said he had a tie identical to the one Mote was wearing. Mote said that it was unlikely as it was a Primary Club tie, and the man replied: "I was out first ball playing for Oxford University." "Little things like that make one's day," said Mote.

The captain's lady

HE WAS LOSING the Test match and the series. He was out of form. He was in dispute with the selectors. He was suffering from concussion because his coach had just whacked a ball on to his temple during fielding practice. Could the Wanderers Test against England get worse for South African captain Graeme Smith?

Oh, yes, it could, according to the local papers. They had got hold of the story that Smith's high-profile relationship with swimwear model **MINKI VAN DER WESTHUIZEN** might be on the rocks.

Graeme and Minki have become the southern hemisphere version of Posh and Becks. And like Victoria Beckham, wife of England footballer David, "Slinky Minki" tends to attract the cameras whenever she shows up at the ground – often in the company of Jacques Kallis's girlfriend, ex-Miss South Africa Cindy Nel. Also like Mrs Beckham, Minki has independent celebrity status, thanks to the American tank regiment in Iraq who made her their unofficial mascot. Commissions in various lads' mags ensued, followed by dinner with Smith – who had cemented his reputation as one of cricket's

Desert attraction: a poster of Minki van der Westhuizen decorates a military
vehicle in Iraq.

Picture by Damir Sagolj, Reuters

boldest captains by demanding her number from *South Africa Sports
Illustrated*. At the end of 2004, *FHM* named Minki as South Africa's sexiest
woman (up from 36th place), while another poll rated her and Smith the
nation's cutest couple.

Sources suggested that the 18-month-old relationship had run into trouble
in the lead up to the Fourth Test. After a difficult year, Smith was said to
be distracted and on edge. On the evening before the match, all seemed lost,
but then Smith asked South African team manager Goolam Raja to get Minki
on a flight from Cape Town. He drove to meet her at the airport and talks
continued into the evening, with the upshot that the affair was declared
neither off nor on, but temporarily on ice.

CRICKET AND SLOWCOACHES IN 2004

The Last Shall be First

LAWRENCE BOOTH

Speed was never really part of Mark Richardson's repertoire. In 38 Tests as New Zealand's opener, he cheerfully played the role of sheet anchor, eking out his 2,776 runs at a rate of one every three minutes and 37 seconds, or 33 per two-hour session. But Richardson was nothing if not self-deprecating, and decided to make a virtue of his lack of speed – this time across the turf – by challenging the slowest member of the opposition to a 100-metre sprint at the end of every Test series. By the time he announced his retirement in December 2004 at the age of 33, the sight of Richardson failing to burn up a section of some outfield had become as synonymous with New Zealand cricket as Richard Hadlee's white wristbands.

The ritual was born during banter in the Auckland dressing-room, where Richardson and his team-mate Aaron Barnes were arguing over who was faster – or, to be more precise, less slow. Richardson proved his point by winning the ensuing race, and on Boxing Day 2003 took the challenge to the Test arena, leaving the Pakistan leg-spinner Danish Kaneria (his captain Inzamam presumably being quicker over 100 metres than he is over 22

Wacky races: Mark Richardson and Darren Lehmann go head to head at the Adelaide Oval.

Picture by Hamish Blair, Getty Images

yards) for dead at Wellington. Over the course of the following year, he took on fellow slowcoaches from South Africa, England and Australia, and achieved as much notoriety for his brown-and-beige Lycra suit as for the slowness of his batting.

After seeing off Kaneria, Richardson came up against swifter opposition in March in the form of Neil McKenzie. Suspicions that South Africa had actually put forward their hare instead of their tortoise were confirmed when McKenzie literally zig-zagged his way to the line – and still won with time to spare. But when Richardson lined up against Ashley Giles at Trent Bridge in June, the foot-race had become serious business. The Beige Brigade – a small but vociferous group of New Zealand fans whose badge of honour is their country's prototype sickly weak-tea-and-milk-chocolate one-day strip – provided Richardson with his streamlined Lycra. "It didn't leave much to the imagination," said an observer. And it didn't help, either: although Richardson controversially dived for the line, later arguing that because the race was his idea he could make up the rules, he was still beaten by a head. Worse was to follow, when Giles claimed he was not the slowest member of the England side at all. "Five of them wouldn't do it," he said, "so the sixth-slowest took him on, which was me."

There was little doubt that Darren Lehmann was the slowest Australia had to offer when the two waited for the gun at the Adelaide Oval in November. Lehmann had been provided with a Lycra suit of his own – green and gold, of course – by the ever-helpful Beige Brigade, but discreetly wore a long T-shirt over the top, reportedly on his mother's instructions. By now this was becoming sponsored big business. Two kegs of Toohey's beer placed in the middle of the course turned the sprint into a mini-steeplechase, but Richardson's hurdling proved superior and some pride was restored after defeat in the Tests. "We needed a win," said Richardson. "He was too quick for me," admitted Lehmann.

Richardson received \$A2,000 for his win, which he donated to Intellectually Handicapped Children, while Lehmann gave his loser's cheque of \$A1,000 to the Shane Warne Foundation, which helps seriously ill and underprivileged children. Before retiring, Richardson admitted: "I guess the only thing I'm remembered for in Australia is stupidity." That, and out-sprinting Lehmann.

THE BACKROOM IN 2004

On the Cutting Edge

SIMON BRIGGS

If 2004 was a triumphant year for England's national team, it was no less rewarding for the coaching staff who finally saw their efforts bearing fruit. Yet before the end of the year, one of the key figures in the set-up – National Academy director Rod Marsh – announced he would not be renewing his contract when it expired in September 2005.

It was no secret that Marsh had had his differences with Duncan Fletcher, the England coach, whose preference for experience over youth had occasionally blocked the path of an Academy graduate. But this appeared to have had little to do with the decision. For all that Marsh likes to cultivate a tough-as-teak image, he actually decided to return to Australia because he misses his grandchildren – or "grandies", as he likes to call them.

Since his appointment in 2002, Marsh had been instrumental in forming the Academy's ethos of intense fitness training and self-help; he deliberately avoided what he viewed as prescriptive coaching, believing that the only way to further a player's development was to give him the tools and let him work out the best way to use them himself.

His greatest legacy may come to be seen in the appointments he made – especially the signing of Australian Academy bowling coach Troy Cooley in June 2003. Immediately liked and trusted by the top Test bowlers, Cooley's patient methods played a significant part in transforming England's attack from the "pie-throwers" once famously derided by Marsh (before his defection from Australia) into the hit squad that demolished New Zealand and West Indies.

Cooley's influence was rated so highly that some newspapers started asking why he only visited the dressing-room for the two days of pre-Test training, rather than the match itself. Cooley himself shrugged off such suggestions, saying "I can't go out there and bowl the ball for them." But he did agree to stick around in future until at least the end of the first day.

There were plenty of other duties to attend to. Early in 2004, Cooley set up the Elite Fast Bowling Group (EFBG) to nurture the next generation of Harmisons and Hoggards. Using technology that would surely boggle Fred Trueman's mind, he invited a group of 40 quicks to Loughborough – men, women and teenagers – to be filmed by 20 simultaneous high-speed cameras. They were then assessed for efficiency and potential injury problems.

"All this data is enabling us to do some really interesting work," Cooley said. "One of the things we've been looking at is front-foot impact, and its connection with back problems – it's not much more than an intuitive leap at the moment, but we're hoping we can chase it down with numbers." For once, it seemed that English coaching was setting the pace rather than following it.

Troy's battleground: the England bowling coach Troy Cooley at Lord's.
Picture by Patrick Eagar

The same could not be said of Mike Young's contribution as a fielding coach. A former professional baseball player in the US, Young had previously spent four years developing the Australian Test team's fielding skills. Still, the exercise was clearly valuable to the National Academy squad. As Simon Hughes reported in the *Daily Telegraph*: "After ten minutes even I was throwing faster and more accurately."

Young has little time for the traditional out-fielding tactic of walking in with the bowler. He said: "I've seen some guys take 14 steps in, then after the ball's bowled they take 14 steps back again. Fourteen steps! There and back every ball for three hours: that's three kilometres. No wonder a guy's a bit tired when he comes back on to bowl." Though it took him some time, he eventually persuaded the Australians to settle for a single "split-step", similar to the movement a tennis player makes as he waits to receive serve.

Meanwhile, the Academy was also developing its links with the counties. Fast-bowling specialists from around the country gathered for a workshop with Cooley, designed to spread the word about the EFBG. Meanwhile, all county grounds were encouraged to mount video cameras to record their home matches so that the data could be shared. Five counties went further still and bought the eCricket software package, developed by New Zealand's former video analyst Zach Hitchcock, and used by England (see Goodbye Gin and Tonic, page 37).

Essex coach Graham Gooch described it as "a massive help". But he also admitted that it was difficult to find a full-time analyst to work the computer throughout four days of Championship cricket. "It would be very handy if every county had it," Gooch said, "because then you could just cover your home matches and swap DVDs. We couldn't afford to do it for away games this year, but if you look at other sports this sort of thing is standard practice. Ipswich Town have three people working their computer analysis during a match – though obviously a football match takes up far less time."

Only a few days after announcing his departure, Marsh gave a positive assessment of England's future potential. "I would expect everyone who plays for England in the next 20 years to spend time at Loughborough, either through youth cricket, the Academy or specialist camps. The organisation of youth cricket in England is fantastic. All people ever do is put it down by saying cricket's not played in schools, but England has the best coaching system in the world. A group of highly qualified coaches is starting to come through at the lower levels and that's very encouraging."

CHARITIES IN 2004

The Brian Johnston Memorial Trust

The Trust (run through the Lord's Taverners) was launched in 1995 to support causes dear to the late Brian Johnston: cricket for the blind, and talented young players in financial need. In 2004, the ECB Wrist-Spin Programme – which aims to produce an England leg-spinner by 2007 – received £15,000. This helped Yorkshire's Mark Lawson, the scheme's first graduate to play first-class cricket, spend three months in Adelaide with Shane Warne's coach, Terry Jenner. The Trust also provides playing kit for the England blind team.

Secretary: Richard Anstey, The Lord's Taverners, 10 Buckingham Place, London SW1E 6HX. Tel: 020 7821 2828; email: richard.anstey@lordstaverners.org; website: www.lordstaverners.org.

The Bunbury Cricket Club

Pop songwriter and entrepreneur David English launched the Bunbury Club in 1986. Although not a registered charity, by 2004 the club had raised around £8.5m, mainly through its famous celebrity games, which are half cricket match, half jamboree. Beneficiaries include youth cricket – in 2004 the club stepped in when the schools' Under-13 cup was left sponsorless – and other deserving causes. In December, English chartered a plane to take seriously ill children to visit Father Christmas in Lapland; and in 2005 the Indian Ocean tsunami appeal will benefit. The club raised around £400,000 in 2004, and English was awarded an honorary doctorate by the University of Middlesex.

Founder: David English MBE, 1 Highwood Cottages, Nan Clark's Lane, London NW7 4HJ.

CHASE Ben Hollioake Fund

The Fund was established in 2002 by the family of the late Ben Hollioake, the Surrey and England all-rounder who was killed in a car crash. Their goal is to raise enough money to build a second centre for CHASE, a hospice caring for terminally ill children and their families in the south of England; by the end of 2004, £250,000 had been raised. That sum included the proceeds of an Eric Clapton concert at the Royal Albert Hall in May. Plans for 2005 include an adventure race, involving running, cycling, navigating and rowing, a mass sponsored abseil from a prominent building, and many cricket and golf matches.

Fund Manager: Karen Thurston, CHASE, Loseley Park, Guildford, Surrey GU3 1HS. Tel: 01483 447753; email: karen.thurston@chasecare.org.uk; website: www.benhollioakefund.com.

The Cricket Foundation

The Foundation was reconstituted in 1996 and exists to provide cricketing opportunities for young people throughout Britain. Although the ECB has traditionally provided much of its funding, it operates independently of the board, with Ossie Wheatley as chairman of trustees. Since 1996, the foundation has spent around £25m on cricket development officers, county youth teams, cricket in clubs and schools, and training for coaches, umpires, groundsmen and teachers. In May 2005, the Foundation is due to launch an ambitious campaign to bring competitive cricket back to state schools.

Director: Nick Gandon, Lord's Cricket Ground, London NW8 8QZ. Tel: 020 7432 1259; email: nickgandon.cricketfoundation@ecb.co.uk.

The Cricket Society Trust

The Trust was founded in 1958 and became a registered charity in 1992. It helps young cricketers by providing equipment for schools and clubs; the Trust also pays for children from deprived areas in London, including some who have never left the city, to spend a day playing various ball games at Arundel Castle in Sussex. The aim is to target the small projects and problems often overlooked by bigger donors.

Hon. Secretary: Ken Merchant, 16 Louise Road, Rayleigh, Essex SS6 8LW. Tel: 01268 747414.

The Hornsby Professional Cricketers Fund

The Fund was established in 1928 from the estate of J. H. J. Hornsby, who played for Middlesex, MCC and the Gentlemen. It provides money to assist "former professional cricketers [not necessarily first-class] or their wives, widows until remarriage, children and other dependants, provided the persons concerned shall be in necessitous circumstances". Assistance is given by monthly allowances, special grants or, in certain cases, loans. Donations, requests for help or information about potential recipients are all welcome.

Clerk to the Trustees: John Light, 14 St Albans Villas, London NW5 1QU. Tel: 020 7485 7712.

ICC World Cricket Tsunami Appeal

Days after the Indian Ocean tsunami of December 26, 2004, the ICC began an appeal to raise money to help the victims. The planned centrepieces were two matches between an ICC World XI and an ACC Asian XI. The first was played on January 10 in front of 70,101 at the Melbourne Cricket Ground. Many concessionaires donated their products free to the organisers, Travelex gave $A1m, and in total the game generated around $A15m (£6.2m) for World Vision, a Christian relief charity working especially with children. The second match was scheduled for Kolkata in April.

ICC contact: Jon Long, ICC, Lord's Cricket Ground, London NW8 8QN. Tel: 020 7266 7912; email: jon.long@icc-cricket.com.

Joint United Nations Programme on HIV/AIDS (UNAIDS)

Over 12m of the estimated 40m people infected with HIV live in cricket-playing countries, and in 2003 the ICC entered an alliance with the United Nations Programme on HIV/AIDS. The partnership aims to educate the public, using cricketing icons to help overcome the stigma attached to the disease. At many matches in 2004 players wore a red ribbon – a symbol of solidarity with sufferers; during the Third Test of the Pakistan v India series, the captains were each accompanied at the toss by someone who was HIV-positive. On December 1, World Aids Day, the ICC supported a mass distribution of information in Africa, and the Test captains pledged to raise awareness of a disease that remains a taboo in many countries.

ICC contact: Jon Long, ICC, Lord's Cricket Ground, London NW8 8QN. Tel: 020 7266 7912; email: jon.long@icc-cricket.com; website: www.icc.cricket.org/unaids.

The Lord's Taverners

The Taverners, founded in 1950 by a group of actors enjoying a pint in the old Lord's Tavern, raises money to "give young people, particularly those with special needs, a sporting chance". Since then, the Club has raised more than £35m, and in 2004 it distributed £2m: half went to youth cricket and special projects recommended by the ECB; the rest to provide special sports equipment and 59 minibuses for young disabled people. In March 2004 the Taverners raised more than £150,000 at a Royal Albert Hall concert, involving Eric Clapton and Bill Wyman. They almost matched that during a series of events held in the Caribbean to tie in with England's 2003-04 tour.

Chief Executive: Mark Williams, The Lord's Taverners, 10 Buckingham Place, London SW1E 6HX. Tel: 020 7821 2828; email: hq@lordstaverners.org; website: www.lordstaverners.org.

NatWest Cricket with the Prince's Trust

The scheme, launched in 2003, links groups of disadvantaged people aged 16 to 25 with county cricket clubs. Each group spends 12 weeks based at a county ground, where they complete a self-development course run by the Prince's Trust. The clubs provide work placements, motivational talks from players, training facilities and cricket coaching. The aim is to develop confidence, purpose and skills, with a view to getting work afterwards. Fourteen counties are now involved: at Surrey one member of the

2004 scheme, Stephanos Yohannes, acted as twelfth man for a day. The programme is funded by NatWest and organised through the PCA.

Prince's Trust contact: Joe Howes, Prince's Trust, 18 Park Square East, Regent's Park, London NW1 4LH. Tel: 020 7543 7340; email: joseph.howes@princes-trust.org.uk.

The Primary Club

The Primary Club began in 1955 when four club players, depressed by their poor performance with the bat, vowed to raise money for blind cricketers. The Club continues to provide sporting and recreational facilities for the blind and partially sighted. Membership is nominally restricted to those who have been dismissed first ball in any form of cricket, and around 12,500 currently admit to it. In total, the club has raised over £1.5m – through donations and members' events, and by selling its famous tie, popularised by *Test Match Special*. In 2004, grants included £45,000 toward a canal boat for the Royal London Society for the Blind, and smaller sums for county blind cricket. In 2005, the Club is planning a gala dinner to celebrate its 50th anniversary.

Hon. Secretary: Chris Larlham, PO Box 12121, Saffron Walden, Essex CB10 2ZF. Tel: 01799 586507; email: secretary@primaryclub.org.

The Professional Cricketers' Association Charity

The PCA Charity was founded in 1983 by Harold Goldblatt. It aims to relieve financial hardship among present or former members of the Association (or anyone who has played cricket for a first-class county) along with their dependants. At present the charity is helping more than 30 people. Donations are very welcome, as are requests for help and information about past or present cricketers (or dependants) who may be in need.

Chairman of Trustees: David Graveney, 34 High Street, Westbury-on-Trym, Bristol B59 3DZ. Tel: 0117 950 8676; fax: 0117 959 0227; email: david.graveney@thepca.net.

CRICKET AND THE LAW, 2004

DISGRUNTLED BATSMAN JAILED FOR ASSAULT

Mahmood Akhtar, a 38-year-old shopkeeper from Leeds, was jailed for three years at York Crown Court in March for assaulting a player in a Yorkshire club fixture. The case was described by *The Times* as "one of Britain's first recorded cases of cricket rage". Incensed by an lbw decision given against him by a stand-in umpire Qadeer Hussain, Akhtar waited until the next match before retaliating. This time, Hussain was keeping wicket in a West Riding Sunday Cricket Council game between Harehills and Nafees in Keighley, when Akhtar and his brother, Zaqar, marched out to confront him; Zaqar was armed with a baseball bat. The victim was left with a badly broken arm that required a plate. Andrew Semple, for the defence, said the incident had a "cultural background" and that it was totally out of character. Sentencing Akhtar, Judge James Spencer QC said he was the instigator of the attack. "The fact that you didn't wield the baseball bat serves you not a jot."

PROFESSIONAL GETS LIFE SENTENCE AFTER KILLING LOVER

A professional cricketer was jailed for life in July after stabbing his lover to death in an alleyway in front of her four-month-old son and his own ten-month-old daughter. Bevon Williams, 27, murdered Melanie Horridge in Chorley, Lancashire, after she threatened to expose their secret affair, Preston Crown Court heard. Three teenagers later found her in a pool of blood; she had been stabbed 24 times. Mr Justice Leveson recommended that Williams should serve a minimum of 11½ years. He pleaded guilty but said he had picked up the knife from the ground rather than taken it with him, a claim rejected by the judge. Williams had arrived in the UK from Tobago to play for a team in Cambridgeshire, before joining Euxton in Chorley. He was reportedly due to sign for West Leigh when the murder occurred.

FORMER ENGLAND CAPTAIN'S SON JAILED ON COUP CHARGE

Former SAS officer Simon Mann, whose father George captained England in seven Test matches in the late 1940s, was given a seven-year jail sentence in Harare in September for buying weapons. These were allegedly to be used to overthrow Obiang Nguema, the dictator of the West African state of Equatorial Guinea. Mann, an old Etonian, had been held in jail by the Zimbabweans since being arrested at Harare airport in March. Sir Mark Thatcher, Lady Thatcher's son, was also implicated in the plot and arrested in South Africa, but was eventually allowed to leave the country after reaching a deal with the authorities.

OFFICIAL HAD CHILD PORNOGRAPHY ON COMPUTER

Derbyshire's former membership secretary was given an eight-month jail sentence after admitting having child pornography on his home and work computers. John Grainger, 61, possessed 246 indecent images, including 16 video files, Derby Crown Court heard in November. Police raided Grainger's home and workplace after he had used a credit card to subscribe to an illicit website. He pleaded guilty to 16 charges of making, possessing or distributing indecent pictures. Grainger initially said that some of the images were received via a virus and others were downloaded by his family, but later admitted sole responsibility.

WOMAN STOLE COUNTY FUNDS

Northamptonshire's former finance administrator was jailed for 20 months for stealing £82,000 from the club. Susan Woodward, 54, admitted 19 charges of theft and asked for 58 other offences to be taken into consideration. Between November 2002 and March 2003 she cashed 77 fake cheques, using the proceeds to buy property in Spain and take her family on lavish holidays. "She was an utterly trusted employee," Anwen Rowe, prosecuting, told Northampton Crown Court in November. "She had access to all the club's accounts. She kept the books: she was the accounting system." Michael Ellis, defending, said she stole the money because she was unable to cope with the pressure of her job. Northamptonshire said they would sue Woodward, who they blame for a £240,000 black hole in the accounts.

BOTHAM AND LAMB v KHAN (AGAIN)

Ian Botham and Imran Khan returned to the High Court in November to argue over the costs from the high-profile libel action that took place there in 1996. Imran, who won the original verdict, is claiming £250,000 but says that he will settle for £75,000 less. Botham and Lamb say his claim should be struck out because of the delay. In the original action Botham and Lamb unsuccessfully claimed that Imran had libelled them by saying that they were racists and lacked class, and had called Botham a cheat (see *Wisden 1997*, page 1378). Mr Justice Richards told the players to give up the "folly" of their eight-year battle, warning that the extra costs could easily exceed the amount fought over. But he said he was obliged to allow proceedings to continue.

AUSTRALIAN OFFICIAL IN THEFT CASE

Martin Whitely, a former accountant with the Western Australia Cricket Association (WACA), pleaded guilty to 53 counts of theft and was sentenced to 20 months in jail. The district court in Perth heard in November that Whitely, 32, stole almost $160,000 (about £65,000) from the WACA over a three-year period and gambled it away.

BOUNCER FACES TRIAL OVER HOOKES DEATH

Zdravko Micevic, a bouncer at the Beaconsfield Hotel, St Kilda, was committed for trial in November by Melbourne magistrates for the manslaughter of former Test cricketer David Hookes. Micevic admitted to police that he had felled Hookes with "a haymaker" outside the pub on January 18, but said Hookes had hit him first. He also told them: "I wish I was dead." Hookes smashed his skull when he fell, and died in hospital. After a six-day committal hearing, magistrate Ian McGrane said there were many different accounts of the incident but there was enough evidence for the case to go to trial. Micevic was released on bail to appear before the Supreme Court in March.

FORMER TEST PLAYER JAILED

Yograj Singh, 46, who played one Test and six one-day internationals for India, was sentenced to six months jail for "negligent and rash driving". Singh was found guilty by a Chandigarh magistrate in November, more than four years after the crash in which a scooter rider was seriously injured. Yograj is the father of the current Indian star, Yuvraj Singh.

DIRECTORY OF BOOKSELLERS AND AUCTIONEERS

BOOKSELLERS

AARDVARK BOOKS, 19 Vanwall Drive, Waddington, Lincoln, Lincolnshire LN5 9LT. Tel/fax: 01522 722671. Peter Taylor specialises in *Wisdens*, including rare hardbacks and early editions. Quarterly catalogues sent on request. *Wisdens* purchased. Cleaning, gilding and restoration undertaken.

ACUMEN BOOKS, Nantwich Road, Audley, Staffordshire ST7 8DL. Tel: 01782 720753; fax: 01782 720798; e-mail: wca@acumenbooks.co.uk; website: www.acumenbooks.co.uk. Everything for umpires, scorers and others; textbooks, equipment, Duckworth/Lewis etc; import/export.

TIM BEDDOW, 66 Oak Road, Oldbury, West Midlands B68 0BD. Tel: 0121 421 7117; email: wisden1864@hotmail.com; website: www.edgbastonbooks.co.uk. Large stock of cricket/football books, programmes and signed material. Items purchased. Send SAE for catalogue. Stall at Thwaite Gate, Edgbaston, every first-team match.

BODYLINE BOOKS, 150a Harbord Street, London SW6 6PH. Tel: 020 7385 2176; fax: 020 7610 3314; e-mail: info@bodylinebooks.com; website: www.bodylinebooks.com. We are the only specialist dealer in London for old copies of *Wisden Cricketers' Almanack*. Most years always in stock. Catalogue issued free on request.

BOUNDARY BOOKS LTD, 507 Castle Quay, Manchester M15 4NT. Fax: 01925 858237; e-mail: mike@boundary-books.demon.co.uk. Publishers of high-quality limited-edition books, and specialists in rare and hard-to-find books and memorabilia, particularly from great collectors of the past.

CRICKETBOOKS.CO.UK, Ian Dyer Cricket Books, 29 High Street, Gilling West, Richmond, North Yorkshire DL10 5JG. Tel: 01748 822786; fax: 08707 051561; website: cricketbooks.co.uk. For *Wisdens*, annuals, books, programmes, tour guides, scorecards, benefit brochures, magazines, memorabilia. Keyword search; automatic postage calculation. Paypal/credit cards accepted.

K. FAULKNER, 65 Brookside, Wokingham, Berkshire RG41 2ST. Tel: 0118 978 5255. Book room open by appointment. E-mail: kfaulkner@bowmore.demon.co.uk; website: www.bowmore.demon.co.uk. Cricket books, *Wisdens*, memorabilia, bought and sold. Also at Gloucestershire CCC shop, Nevil Road, Bristol BS7 9EJ.

GEOFF FREEMAN, 51 Noah's Ark Lane, Lindfield, Haywards Heath, West Sussex RH16 2LU. Tel: 01444 484195; e-mail: geoff.freeman@btinternet.com; website: www.geoff-freeman.com. Antiquarian books, *Wisdens*, 19th-century material, Australiana, postcards, photographs, letters, yearbooks, autographs, scrapbooks, albums, brochures, teamsheets and all signed material bought and sold. Catalogues issued.

GRACE BOOKS AND CARDS (TED KIRWAN), 3 Pine Garden, Oadby, Leicester LE2 5UT. Tel: 0226 271 6363 (weekdays) and 0116 271 4267 (evenings and weekends). Second-hand and antiquarian cricket books, *Wisdens*, autographed material and cricket ephemera of all kinds. Now also modern postcards.

ROGER HEAVENS, 2 Lowfields, Little Eversden, Cambridge CB3 7HJ. Tel: 01223 262839; fax: 01223 262033; Mobile: 0796 709 6924; e-mail: roger@ahaygarth.fsnet.co.uk; website: www.booksoncricket.net. Cricket publisher specialising in the works of Arthur Haygarth and early history of cricket. Send for free catalogue. Order direct – all major credit cards accepted.

*J. W. MCKENZIE, 12 Stoneleigh Park Road, Ewell, Epsom, Surrey KT19 0QT. Tel: 020 8393 7700; fax: 020 8393 1694; email: jwmck@netcomuk.co.uk; website: www.mckenziecricket.co.uk. Specialists in antiquarian second-hand books, particularly *Wisdens*, and memorabilia. Established 1969. Catalogues issued. Publishers of cricket books. Shop premises open regular business hours.

MACMILLAN WISDEN DIRECT, Brunel Road, Houndmills, Basingstoke, Hampshire RG21 6XS. Tel: 01256 302685. New *Wisdens* for 1996–2005 and the first seven editions of *Wisden Cricketers' Almanack Australia* available from Wisden's mail-order supplier. Prices from £19.99, including p&p.

ROGER PAGE, 10 Ekari Court, Yallambie, Victoria 3085, Australia. Tel: (+61) 3 9435 6332; fax: (+61) 3 9432 2050; email: rpcricketbooks@unite.com.au. Dealer in new and second-hand cricket books. Distributor of overseas cricket annuals and magazines. Agent for Association of Cricket Statisticians and Cricket Memorabilia Society.

RED ROSE BOOKS, Brook Mill Complex – Office Block, Branch Road, Lower Darwen, Lancashire BB3 0PR; Tel: 01254 776767; e-mail: info@redrosebooks.co.uk; website: www.redrosebooks.co.uk. Office/bookroom open by appointment. Specialist cricket booksellers and publishers. Second-hand/antiquarian cricket books and memorabilia bought and sold. Regular catalogues issued.

WILLIAM H. ROBERTS, The Crease, 113 Hill Grove, Salendine Nook, Huddersfield, West Yorkshire HD3 3TL. Tel/fax: 01484 654463; email: william.roberts2@virgin.net; website: www.williamroberts-cricket.com. Second-hand/antiquarian cricket books, *Wisdens*, autograph material and memorabilia bought and sold. Catalogues sent on request.

ST MARY'S BOOKS & PRINTS, 9 St Mary's Hill, Stamford, Lincolnshire PE9 2DP. Tel: 01780 763033; e-mail: cricket@stmarysbooks.com; website: www.stmarysbooks.com. Dealers in *Wisdens* 1864–2005, second-hand, rare cricket books and *Vanity Fair* prints. Also search service offered.

CHRISTOPHER SAUNDERS, Kingston House, High Street, Newnham-on-Severn, Gloucestershire GL14 1BB. Tel: 01594 516030; fax: 01594 517273; email: chrisbooks@aol.com; website: www.cricket-books.com. Office/bookroom open by appointment. Second-hand/antiquarian cricket books and memorabilia bought and sold. Regular catalogues issued containing selections from over 10,000 items in stock.

*SPORTS BOOKS DIRECT, Sportspages Bookshop at Caxton Walk, 94–96 Charing Cross Road, London WC2H 0JW. Tel: 020 7240 9604; and at Barton Square, St Ann's Square, Manchester M2 7HA. Tel: 0161 832 8530. Mail order – Sports Books Direct, tel: 020 7836 7817; fax: 020 7836 0104; website: www.sportsbooksdirect.co.uk. New cricket books, especially Australian imports. Retail through Sportspages and worldwide mail-order service, including regular catalogues of new books, through Sports Books Direct.

STUART TOPPS, 40 Boundary Avenue, Wheatley Hills, Doncaster, South Yorkshire DN2 5QU. Tel: 01302 366044. Our 120-page plus catalogue of cricket books, *Wisdens*, booklets, brochures and county yearbooks is always available.

*WILLOWS PUBLISHING CO., 17 The Willows, Stone, Staffordshire ST15 0DE. Tel: 01785 814700; email: jenkins.willows@ntlworld.com. *Wisden* reprints 1879–1889, 1900–1920 and 1940–1945. Send SAE for prices.

MARTIN WOOD CRICKET BOOKS, 1c Wickenden Road, Sevenoaks, Kent TN13 3PJ. Tel/fax: 01732 457205; e-mail: martin@martinwoodcricketbooks.co.uk; website: www.martinwoodcricketbooks.co.uk. Catalogue, available only online, lists all my cricket books which, standing, fill 160 yards of shelving. Established 1970.

AUCTIONEERS

*CHRISTIE'S, 85 Old Brompton Road, South Kensington, London SW7 3LD. Tel: 020 7752 3355; email: mdunbar@christies.com. Christie's highly successful cricket memorabilia auctions have been held every year since the inaugural MCC Bicentenary sale in 1987. For enquiries, please contact Max Dunbar.

*T. VENNETT-SMITH, 11 Nottingham Road, Gotham, Nottinghamshire NG11 0HE. Tel: 0115 983 0541. Auctioneers and valuers. Twice-yearly auctions of cricket and sports memorabilia. The cricket auction is run by cricketers for cricket-lovers worldwide.

DOMINIC WINTER BOOK AUCTIONS, Specialist Book Auctioneers & Valuers, The Old School, Maxwell Street, Swindon, Wiltshire SN1 5DR. Tel: 01793 611340; fax: 01793 491727; email: info@dominicwinter.co.uk; website: www.dominicwinter.co.uk. Twice-yearly auction sales of sports books and memorabilia, including *Wisdens*.

Asterisks indicate businesses that have display advertisements elsewhere in the Almanack. See Index of Advertisements (page 1726) for details.

CRICKET SUPPLIERS

CRICKET EQUIPMENT

CENTURION CRICKET, 1550 London Road, Leigh-on-Sea, Essex SS7 2TA. Tel: 01702 554801; fax: 01702 553747. The gentleman's choice in cricket equipment.

DUKE SPORTSWEAR, Unit 4, Magdalene Road, Torquay, Devon TQ1 4AF. Tel/fax: 01803 292012. Test-standard sweaters to order in your club colours, using the finest yarns.

EXITO SPORTS COMPANY, Unit C1, Burley Heyes, Arley Road, Appleton Thorn, Warrington, Cheshire, WA16 0JL; Tel: 01565 777300; e-mail: info@exitosports.com; website: www.exitosports.com. Manufacturers and suppliers of quality cricket clothing and leisurewear to first-class and minor counties, amateur clubs, schools and colleges.

FORDHAM SPORTS LTD, 81/85 Robin Hood Way, Kingston Vale, London SW15 3PW. Tel: 020 8974 5654; email: fordham@fordhamsports.co.uk; website: fordhamsports.co.uk. Cricket and rugby equipment specialist with largest range of branded stock in London at discounted prices. Mail order worldwide. Free catalogue.

GRAYS SPORTS, 36 Sidney Street, Cambridge CB2 3HX. Tel: 01223 362428. Specialist sports retailers offering a great range of products to cricketers of all levels.

KANON BOWLING MACHINE, Tesson Ltd, 4 Holdenby Court, Anchorage Park, Portsmouth, Hampshire PO3 5US. Tel: 07749 786845 or 07802 175142; email: sales@kanonball.co.uk; website: www.kanonball.co.uk. The UK's sole agent for the **Kanon Bowling** machine, the perfect machine for recreational and coaching purposes. Endorsed by Robin Smith, ex-Hampshire and England.

NOMAD PLC. Tel: 01858 464878. Nomad manufacture coffins to suit all levels. The new "International" range has aluminium edging on all sides, wheels, and is available in ten different colours.

STUART & WILLIAMS (BOLA), 6 Brookfield Road, Cotham, Bristol BS6 5PQ. Email: info@bola.co.uk; website: www.bola.co.uk. Manufacturer of bowling machines and ball-throwing machines for all sports. Machines for recreational and commercial application for sale to the UK and overseas.

CRICKET TOURS

ALL WAYS SPORTS TOURS, 7 Whielden Street, Old Amersham, Buckinghamshire HP7 0HT. Tel: 01494 432747; email: sales@all-ways.co.uk; website: www.all-ways.co.uk. Specialist tour operators for supporters' tours following rugby, cricket and golf worldwide. Also escorted and tailor-made tours to New Zealand, Australia and the South Pacific.

BARBADOS JOURNEYS. Tel: 08707 082010; e-mail: barbadosjournies@wwj.uk.com. Specialist tour operators to the Caribbean. Schools, club sides, benefit tours, testimonials, intensive coaching academy – founders of Sir Garry Sobers School Tournament.

QUIES HOTEL, NEWQUAY. Tel: 01637 872924; e-mail: quieshotel@btconnect.com; website: www.quieshotelnewquay.co.uk. A two-minute walk from Newquay town centre, storage areas available, private car park, help given with fixtures; stags, hens, teams welcome.

RIVERDALE HALL HOTEL, Bellingham, Nr Hexham, Northumberland NE48 2JT. Tel: 01434 220254; fax: 01434 220457; e-mail: iben@riverdalehall.demon.co.uk. Country House Hotel with cricket pitch, indoor pool, gold nearby, real ales, "Gold Plate" Les Routiers restaurant. Up to 20 visiting teams annually. Cocker's 27th year.

SUN LIVING, 8a Milton Court, Ravenshead, Nottingham NG15 9BD. Tel: 01623 795365; fax: 01623 797421; email: sun.living@virgin.net. 25 years' experience arranging great-value escorted tailor-made worldwide cricket/general sports tours for schools, colleges, clubs, seniors and supporters. ABTA and ATOL bonded.

SUNSPORT TOURS & TRAVEL, Hamilton House, 66 Palmerston Road, Northampton NN1 5EX. Tel (UK): 08707 427014; fax (UK): 01604 631628; email: paul@sunsport.co.uk; website: www.sunsport.co.uk. High-quality tailor-made tours to Kenya, South Africa, West Indies and subcontinent. Clients include counties, clubs, colleges, senior/prep schools. ATOL bonded. Contact Barry Dudleston/Paul Bush.

TITAN GROUPS LTD, HiTours House, Crossoak Lane, Redhill, Surrey RH1 5EX. Tel: 01293 450600; fax: 01293 450602; e-mail: cricket@titantravel.co.uk; website: www.titangroups.co.uk. Tailor-made sports tours for supporters, schools, clubs, and universities to any destination in the world. ABTA, ATOL and IATA bonded. ECB official tour operator.

VINTAGE CRICKET TOURS. Vintage Cricket, PO Box 28 656, 349 Remuera Rd, Remuera, Auckland, New Zealand. Tel: (64) 9 522 1310; fax: (64) 9 522 6856; email: mail@vintagecricket.com; website: www.vintagecricket.com. Carnivals, fun and friendship for cricketers over 35 of all ages, experience and ability; next carnival in Barbados October 2006.

GIFTS AND MEMORABILIA

BUCKINGHAM COVERS, Church House, 136 Sandgate Road, Folkestone, Kent CT20 2BY. Tel: 01303 850672; fax: 01303 850687. Autographed cricket photographs and covers; if you collect memorabilia make sure we know your details so we can send you our FREE colour magazines.

DD DESIGNS, 62 St Catherine's Grove, Lincoln, Lincolnshire LN5 8NA. Tel: 01522 800298; email: ddprints@aol.com. Specialists in genuinely signed limited-edition prints. Official producers of *Wisden's* "Five Cricketers of the Year" sets, and other signed cricket portfolios. Free information leaflet available.

JOCELYN GALSWORTHY, The Studio, 39 Latimer Road, St Helens, Isle of Wight PO33 1TG. Tel: 020 7591 0698 (London), 01983 873741 (IoW) or 07885 542652 (mobile); fax: 01983 874182; email: theartist@jocelyngalsworthy.co.uk; website: www.jocelyngalsworthy.co.uk. Limited-edition cricket prints signed and numbered by the artist. Original cricket paintings and drawings of cricket personalities for sale. Free catalogue.

PAVILION AND GROUND EQUIPMENT

ALL WEATHER SPORTS COVER. Tel: (+31) 615 241 408; email: sales@allweathersportscover.com; website: www.allweathersportscover.com. New Zealand's leading automated groundcover since 1988, now sold in the UK/Europe. No major breakdowns in 16 years, and 40% more cost effective than UK/European competitors.

AUTOGUIDE EQUIPMENT LTD, Stockley Road, Heddington, Nr Calne, Wiltshire SN11 0PS. Tel: 01380 850885; fax: 01380 850010; e-mail: sales@autoguide.co.uk. Manufacturers of the world-famous Auto-Roller for cricket wickets. We now supply bolt-in Re-Power packs that include power steering for older rollers.

CRICKET COVERS LTD, Carpenters Cottage, Forton, Longparish, Hampshire SP11 7AL. Tel: 01256 896574. In our opinion Cricket Covers Ltd simply make the best mobile net, sight screens and mobile covers. For a better product, give us a call.

CRICKET NETTING from ROMBULL (UK) LIMITED. Unit 1, Field End, Crendon Industrial Park, Long Crendon, Buckinghamshire HP18 9EJ. Tel: 01844 203870; fax: 01844 203871; e-mail: enquiries@rombull.co.uk; website: www.rombull.co.uk. Wide range of durable, high-quality knotless polypropylene and knotted polyethylene netting products. Practice enclosures, ball-stop netting and boundary ropes.

FSL SCOREBOARDS. Tel: 028 8676 6131; website: www.fslelectronics.com. UK designed and manufactured. FSL offer complete range of electronic scoreboards in portable and self-install kits. Leasing options from less than £12 per week!

HUCK NETS (UK) LTD, Gore Cross Business Park, Bridport, Dorset DT6 3UX. Tel: 01308 425100; fax: 01308 458109; e-mail: sales@hucknet.com; website: www.hucknet.com. Manufacturers and direct suppliers of outdoor/indoor knotless netting, mobile/fixed net cages, sightscreens, pitch covers, roll-out matting, slip cradles, boundary ropes, scoreboards etc. FREE colour catalogue.

JMS CRICKET LTD, Parkside Works, Parkwood Street, Keighley, West Yorkshire BD21 4PJ. Tel: 08700 116144; fax: 01535 606777; e-mail: sales@jmscricket.com; website: www.jmscricket.com. Buy direct from the manufacturer. Mobile covers, flat sheets, sightscreens, mobile nets, slip cradles, plus much, much more. We've got cricket covered.

POWEROLL ROLLERS by Power Precision & Fabrication Ltd, Greenhill, Gunnislake, Cornwall PL18 9AS. Tel: 01822 832608; website: www.poweroll.com. Manufacturers of a comprehensive range of grass rollers to suit different budgets and applications.

PROCTOR NETS LTD of Worcester Park, Surrey. Tel: 020 8337 2554; fax: 020 8337 2558. For nets, artificial wickets, scoreboards and boxes, covers, sightscreens, ball-stop installations.

STUART CANVAS PRODUCTS, Warren Works, Hardwick Grange, Warrington, Cheshire WA1 4RF. Tel: 01925 814525; fax: 01925 831709; email: sales@stuartcanvas.freeserve.co.uk. Designers, manufacturers and suppliers of flat sheets, mobiles, roller and hover covers – sold throughout the world, including Test and county grounds.

TILDENET LIMITED, Hartcliffe Way, Bristol BS3 5RJ. Tel: 0117 966 9684; fax 0117 923 1251; email: enquiries@tildenet.co.uk; website: www.tildenet.co.uk. Extensive range of equipment… grass germination sheets, ball-stop fencing, mobile practice nets, static nets and frames, sightscreens, layflat, mobile and automatic rain covers, practice netting.

PITCHES (TURF AND NON-TURF)

BOUGHTON LOAM LTD, Telford Way Industrial Estate, Telford Way, Kettering, Northamptonshire NN16 8UN. Tel: 01536 510515; fax: 01536 510691; email: enquiries@boughton-loam.co.uk; website: www.boughton-loam.co.uk. Boughton Loam offer the full range of cricket loams, grass seeds and fertilisers for construction and maintenance of cricket grounds, also contracting services including the Koro "Field Topmaker".

FLICX UK LTD, Walltree House Farm, Steane, Brackley, Northamptonshire NN13 5NS. Tel: 01295 816765; fax: 01295 810298; e-mail: flicxuk@flicx.com; website: www.flicx.com. Manufacturers and suppliers of portable cricketing equipment, including *Flicx* cricket pitches, *Brel* bowling machines, portable nets and coaching equipment. Call for brochure and video.

NOTTS SPORT®, Premier House, 18 Mandervell Road, Oadby, Leicester LE2 5LQ. Tel: 0116 272 0222; fax: 0116 272 0617; email: info@nottssport.com; website: www.nottssport.com. Notts Sport® offers a free design and advisory service for non-turf cricket pitches. Their Envelope System® and NottsBase D® System designs are ECB approved

PEAK SPORTS LTD, Unit 4, Ford Street, Brinksway, Stockport SK3 0BT. Tel: 0161 480 2502; fax: 0161 480 1652; website: www.pscricket.com. Agents for Wimbledon Unreal Grass pitches. Glue to concrete, nail to tarmac or unroll on gym floor. Guaranteed ten years. Write for brochure. Installed at Radley, Winchester, Manchester GS, etc.

TECHNICAL SURFACES LTD, Standards House, Meridian East, Meridian Business Park, Leicester, LE19 1WZ. Tel: 08702 400 700; fax: 08702 400 701; email: cricket@ technicalsurfaces.co.uk; website: www.technicalsurfaces.co.uk. Nationwide maintenance of artificial cricket pitches. Over 20 years' experience of all types and systems. Block hole repairs to complete resurfacing.

TOTAL TURF SOLUTIONS (tts), PO Box 250, Northampton, NN5 5WZ. Tel: 01604 750555/07973 885775; email: enquiry@totalturfsolutions.co.uk; website: www. totalturfsolutions.co.uk. Independent consultants and lecturers to the sports turf industry. Specialist cricket contractors. Suppliers of "Climate Cover" a revolution in sports turf covering.

SOCIETIES

CRICKET MEMORABILIA SOCIETY. Honorary Secretary: Steve Cashmore, 4 Stoke Park Court, Stoke Road, Bishops Cleeve, Cheltenham, Gloucestershire GL52 8US. Email: cms87@btinternet.com. For collectors worldwide: magazines, meetings, auctions, speakers, and – most of all – friendship.

INDEX OF ADVERTISEMENTS

Opposite: A century ago. The Oval during the Fifth Test of England's successful Ashes summer of 1905.
Picture by Getty Images

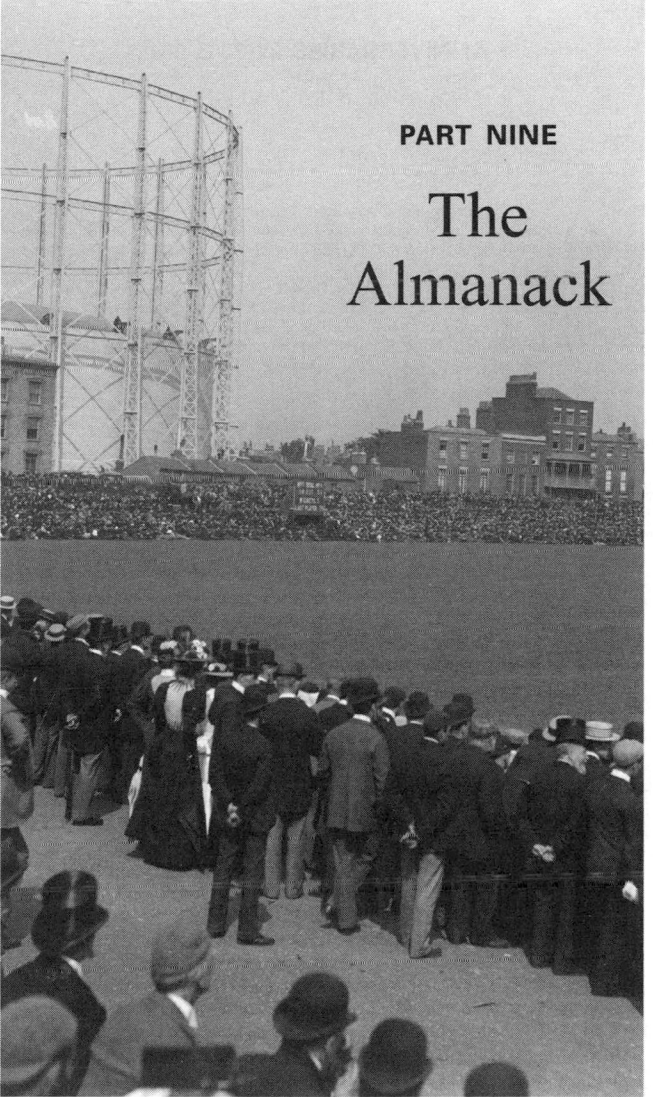

PART NINE

The Almanack

ANNIVERSARIES IN 2005-06

COMPILED BY STEVEN LYNCH

2005

May 14   Peter Kirsten (South Africa) born, 1955

May 17   Leslie Hylton (West Indies) died, 1955
The only Test cricketer to be executed: he was hanged in Jamaica for the murder of his wife. A fast bowler, born March 29, 1905, he played six Tests in the 1930s.

May 18   Hedley Verity (England) born, 1905
One of the greatest of left-arm spinners, he took 15 wickets in the 1934 Lord's Test, England's only 20th-century Test win there over Australia. Verity also claimed ten for ten for Yorkshire against Nottinghamshire at Headingley in 1932, the best innings analysis in first-class history. He died of war wounds in 1943. "Judged by any standard, Verity was a great bowler," observed Wisden. *"Merely to watch him was to know that."*

May 20   George Hirst scored 341 at Leicester, 1905
The highest individual innings for Yorkshire.

May 30   Archie MacLaren scored 140 for England v Australia, 1905
The first Test century scored at Trent Bridge.

June 13   K. S. Duleepsinhji (England) born, 1905
Silky right-hander who emulated his uncle, Ranjitsinhji, by scoring a century in his first Test against Australia, 173 at Lord's in 1930. The Duleep Trophy, India's first-class competition for zonal teams, is named after him.

June 15   Australia scored 758 for eight against West Indies, 1955
Five batsmen scored centuries in the innings at Kingston, a Test record. In the same match, Clyde Walcott scored his fourth and fifth hundred of the rubber, another record, but finished on the losing side.

June 21   West Indies won the first World Cup final, 1975
Clive Lloyd's 102 set up a 17-run victory in a match that lasted until nearly 9 p.m.

June 25   Vic Marks (England) born, 1955

July 5   Dick Pilling (England) born, 1855
"The Prince of Wicket-keepers".

July 14   Warwick Armstrong reached 303 not out, 1905
... for the Australians against Somerset at Bath, "his driving being almost perfect", according to Wisden.

July 26   England retain Ashes, 1905
England won the Old Trafford Test against Australia, after a second century in three innings by their captain, the Hon. F. S. Jackson, to take an unbeatable 2–0 lead in the series. Jackson won all five tosses.

July 27   Allan Border (Australia) born, 1955
Captained Australia in 93 of his 156 Tests, scoring 11,174 runs and averaging 50.56.

August 28   Cyril Walters (England) born, 1905
Elegant batsman for Glamorgan and Worcestershire. Captained England v Australia at Trent Bridge, 1934.

September 15   Abdul Qadir (Pakistan) born, 1955
Took 236 wickets in 67 Tests, including nine for 56 v England at Lahore in 1987-88.

October 3   Errol Hunte (West Indies) born, 1905
A Trinidadian who, for more than 20 years, was credited in record books (including, alas, this one) with two separate Test careers after a copytaker mistook his first name for the initials "R. L.".

October 29   Dennis Brookes born, 1915
Elegant batsman who played one Test for England. Associated with Northamptonshire for more than 70 years.

November 17   Arthur Chipperfield (Australia) born, 1905
Scored 99 on Test debut against England at Trent Bridge in 1934.

November 19   Willie Bates (England) born, 1855
Yorkshireman who took England's first Test hat-trick, against Australia at Melbourne in 1882-83.

November 23   W. W. Read (England) born, 1855
Captained England v Australia at Sydney 1887-88.

November 24   Ian Botham (England) born, 1955
England's finest all-rounder and the scourge of Australia in the 1981 Ashes series, he scored 5,200 runs in 102 Tests, and also took 383 wickets and 120 catches.

December 3   Leslie Ames (England) born, 1905
"The greatest wicket-keeper/batsman the game has so far produced,"– Wisden 1991. Ames scored 102 first-class hundreds, most of them for Kent, and also made 1,121 dismissals, including a record 418 stumpings.

December 20   Bill O'Reilly (Australia) born, 1905
"Tiger" O'Reilly took 144 wickets in only 27 Tests, 102 against England, with brisk, high-bouncing leg-breaks. Sir Donald Bradman once said: "To my mind there has never been a bowler to equal O'Reilly. To play with him was an education – to play against him usually a lesson."

December 28   The Maharaja of Vizianagram (India) born, 1905
"Vizzy" – captain of the Indian team to England, 1936.

2006

January 7   Vinoo Mankad and Pankaj Roy complete stand of 413, 1956
The highest opening partnership in Test history, for India v New Zealand at Madras.

January 15   W. H. Scotton (England) born, 1856
The most relentlessly defensive English batsman of the 19th century: he batted nearly four hours for 34 in The Oval Test of 1886, prompting a famous Punch parody: "Block, block, block, at the foot of thy wicket, O Scotton!..." Committed suicide, 1893.

February 15   Desmond Haynes (West Indies) born, 1956

March 13   New Zealand beat West Indies at Auckland, 1956
Their first Test victory, after 45 matches and 26 years of trying.

March 16   Maurice Turnbull (England) born, 1906
Great all-round sportsman who played cricket for England, and rugby and hockey for
Wales. He was killed in action in France in 1944.

March 23   Maurice Allom (England) born, 1906
Took four wickets in five balls, including a hat-trick, on his Test debut against New
Zealand at Christchurch in 1929-30.

April 6   Mudassar Nazar (Pakistan) born, 1956

April 6   Dilip Vengsarkar (India) born, 1956

April 11   Arthur Shrewsbury (England) born, 1856
"The greatest professional batsman of his day," said Wisden. W. G. Grace, when asked
to choose his opening partner, replied "Give me Arthur."

ERRATA

WISDEN, 1956

Page 812   F. H. Tyson should have been listed as playing for Northamptonshire, not
                      Lancashire.

WISDEN, 1978

Page 539   G. P. Howarth, not G. R. J. Roope, was the non-striker when J. H. Edrich
                      reached his 100th hundred.

WISDEN, 2004

Pages 56 and 57   The first Duke of Richmond was involved in cricket from 1702, but it is not
                      known when Goodwood, his country seat, hosted its first match. It was
                      definitely played by the 1720s.
Page 481   R. S. Gavaskar batted before A. T. Rayudu against Nottinghamshire.
Page 602   Sir Dennis Landau replaced J. F. Blackledge as president of Lancashire in
                      2003.
Page 657   Nottinghamshire's promotion run was in 2002.
Page 675   Somerset's first-class record should read Played 18, Won 4, Lost 8, Drawn 6.
Page 951   Shoaib Malik completed the match double for PIA v ZTBL at Rawalpindi in
                      2002-03 when he scored 100 and took 4-24 and 6-73.
Page 1005   The scorebook for India v Zimbabwe at Tunbridge Wells in 1983 is unavailable,
                      but research suggests Kapil Dev's hundred was closer to 100 balls than 72.
Page 1087   Sutcliffe was stumped in both innings while playing West Indies, not India.
Page 1135   Kallis's unbeaten run in Tests did not stretch to 1,138 minutes at Centurion,
                      as he was out in the previous Test at Johannesburg.
Page 1139   In the fourth one-day international, Gibbs's second six lifted him to his century
                      and his third completed South Africa's victory.
Page 1562   Billy Wade was the first South African-born player to play and umpire in Test
                      cricket, but Frank Hearne, who was born in Middlesex and played two Tests
                      for England and four for South Africa, umpired six South African Tests from
                      1898-99 to 1905-06.
Page 1580   The ACS book on Bill Edrich was compiled by Jerry Lodge, and not by his
                      late brother Derek.

2005 FIXTURES

NWS	NatWest Series between England, Australia and Bangladesh
NWC	NatWest Challenge between England and Australia
NWWS	NatWest Women's Series between England and Australia
FCC Div 1/Div 2	Frizzell County Championship Division 1/Division 2
C&G	Cheltenham & Gloucester Trophy
TL Div 1/Div 2	totesport League Division 1/Division 2
UCCE	University Centre of Cricketing Excellence
♇	Day/night game

Note: All matches of three days or more are first-class, except those involving Bradford/Leeds UCCE, Cardiff UCCE and England Women.

April 8–11	Friendly	MCC	v Warwickshire	Lord's
April 9–11	**Universities**	Cambridge UCCE	v Essex	Cambridge
		Glamorgan	v Cardiff UCCE	Cardiff
		Northamptonshire	v Brad/Leeds UCCE	Northampton
		Oxford UCCE	v Gloucestershire	Oxford
		Somerset	v Durham UCCE	Taunton
		Sussex	v Lough UCCE	Hove
April 13–15	**Universities**	Kent	v Cardiff UCCE	Canterbury
		Nottinghamshire	v Lough UCCE	Nottingham
April 13–16	**FCC Div 1**	Hampshire	v Gloucestershire	Southampton
		Surrey	v Sussex	The Oval
		Warwickshire	v Glamorgan	Birmingham
	FCC Div 2	Derbyshire	v Worcestershire	Derby
		Essex	v Yorkshire	Chelmsford
		Lancashire	v Somerset	Manchester
		Leicestershire	v Durham	Leicester
April 17	**TL Div 1**	Hampshire	v Essex	Southampton
		Lancashire	v Glamorgan	Manchester
		Northamptonshire	v Worcestershire	Northampton
		Nottinghamshire	v Middlesex	Nottingham
	TL Div 2	Derbyshire	v Kent	Derby
		Leicestershire	v Durham	Leicester
		Surrey	v Yorkshire	The Oval
		Warwickshire	v Somerset	Birmingham
April 20–22	**Universities**	Oxford UCCE	v Derbyshire	Oxford
		Surrey	v Brad/Leeds UCCE	The Oval
April 20–23	**FCC Div 1**	Kent	v Warwickshire	Canterbury
		Middlesex	v Nottinghamshire	Lord's
		Sussex	v Hampshire	Hove
	FCC Div 2	Durham	v Worcestershire	Chester-le-Street
		Northamptonshire	v Leicestershire	Northampton
		Yorkshire	v Somerset	Leeds
April 22	**TL Div 1**	Glamorgan	v Essex	Cardiff ♇
April 24	**TL Div 1**	Gloucestershire	v Northamptonshire	Bristol
		Middlesex	v Lancashire	Lord's
	TL Div 2	Durham	v Surrey	Chester-le-Street
		Kent	v Leicestershire	Canterbury
		Sussex	v Derbyshire	Hove
		Yorkshire	v Somerset	Leeds

April 27–30	FCC Div 1	Glamorgan	v Surrey	Cardiff
		Gloucestershire	v Kent	Bristol
		Nottinghamshire	v Sussex	Nottingham
		Warwickshire	v Middlesex	Birmingham
	FCC Div 2	Derbyshire	v Northamptonshire	Derby
		Somerset	v Essex	Taunton
		Worcestershire	v Lancashire	Worcester
April 27–29	Universities	Hampshire	v Cardiff UCCE	Southampton
		Leicestershire	v Durham UCCE	Leicester
May 1	TL Div 1	Lancashire	v Nottinghamshire	Manchester
		Middlesex	v Worcestershire	Lord's
		Northamptonshire	v Hampshire	Northampton
	TL Div 2	Scotland	v Durham	Edinburgh
		Somerset	v Leicestershire	Taunton
		Warwickshire	v Kent	Birmingham
		Yorkshire	v Sussex	Leeds
May 2	TL Div 1	Hampshire	v Gloucestershire	Southampton
		Nottinghamshire	v Glamorgan	Nottingham
	TL Div 2	Durham	v Sussex	Chester-le-Street
		Somerset	v Surrey	Taunton
May 3	C&G	Berkshire	v Gloucestershire	Reading
	Round 1	Buckinghamshire	v Lancashire	Wormsley
		Denmark	v Northamptonshire	Brondby
		Devon	v Essex	Exmouth
		Durham	v Derbyshire	Chester-le-Street
		Ireland	v Yorkshire	Belfast
		Northumberland	v Middlesex	Jesmond
		Wiltshire	v Kent	Salisbury
May 4	C&G	Bedfordshire	v Sussex	Luton
	Round 1	Leicestershire	v Somerset	Leicester
		Holland	v Warwickshire	Rotterdam
		Scotland	v Worcestershire	Edinburgh
		Shropshire	v Hampshire	Whitchurch
		Staffordshire	v Surrey	Stone
		Suffolk	v Glamorgan	Bury St Edmunds
		Wales Minor Co	v Nottinghamshire	Swansea
May 6–9	FCC Div 1	Glamorgan	v Gloucestershire	Cardiff
		Hampshire	v Middlesex	Southampton
		Surrey	v Nottinghamshire	The Oval
	FCC Div 2	Durham	v Somerset	Chester-le-Street
		Essex	v Leicestershire	Chelmsford
		Lancashire	v Derbyshire	Manchester
		Yorkshire	v Northamptonshire	Leeds
May 8–10	Universities	Worcestershire	v Lough UCCE	Kidderminster
May 8	TL Div 2	Scotland	v Kent	Edinburgh
		Sussex	v Warwickshire	Horsham
May 10–13	FCC Div 1	Sussex	v Warwickshire	Horsham
May 10–12	Tour Match	British Universities	v Bangladeshis	
May 11–14	FCC Div 1	Kent	v Hampshire	Canterbury
		Middlesex	v Gloucestershire	Lord's
		Surrey	v Glamorgan	The Oval

May 11–14	FCC Div 2	Lancashire	v Durham	Manchester
		Leicestershire	v Yorkshire	Leicester
		Northamptonshire	v Essex	Northampton
		Worcestershire	v Derbyshire	Worcester
May 11	TL Div 2	Scotland	v Somerset	Edinburgh
May 15	TL Div 1	Essex	v Glamorgan	Chelmsford
		Lancashire	v Northamptonshire	Manchester
		Middlesex	v Hampshire	Lord's
		Worcestershire	v Nottinghamshire	Worcester
	TL Div 2	Durham	v Yorkshire	Chester-le-Street
		Leicestershire	v Surrey	Leicester
May 15–17	Tour Match	Sussex	v Bangladeshis	Hove
May 17	C&G	Berks/Glos	v Staffs/Surrey	
	Round 2	Bucks/Lancs	v Devon/Essex	
		Durham/Derbys	v Wiltshire/Kent	
		Ireland/Yorks	v Scotland/Worcs	
		Holland/Warwicks	v Leics/Somerset	
		Northumb/Middx	v Denmark/Northants	
		Suffolk/Glam	v Shrops/Hants	
May 18	C&G Rd 2	Beds/Sussex	v Wales/Notts	
May 20–22	Tour Match	Northamptonshire	v Bangladeshis	Northampton
May 20–23	FCC Div 1	Hampshire	v Glamorgan	Southampton
		Nottinghamshire	v Kent	Nottingham
	FCC Div 2	Durham	v Yorkshire	Chester-le-Street
		Essex	v Worcestershire	Chelmsford
		Somerset	v Lancashire	Taunton
May 20	TL Div 2	Derbyshire	v Warwickshire	Derby
		Scotland	v Surrey	Edinburgh
May 21–23	Universities	Cambridge UCCE	v Warwickshire	Cambridge
May 22	TL Div 1	Gloucestershire	v Middlesex	Bristol
May 25–28	FCC Div 1	Gloucestershire	v Nottinghamshire	Bristol
		Kent	v Surrey	Tunbridge Wells
		Sussex	v Middlesex	Hove
		Warwickshire	v Hampshire	Stratford-upon-Avon
	FCC Div 2	Northamptonshire	v Somerset	Northampton
		Yorkshire	v Essex	Leeds
May 25–27	Universities	Durham UCCE	v Durham	Durham
		Oxford UCCE	v Lancashire	Oxford
May 26–29	FCC Div 2	Derbyshire	v Leicestershire	Derby
May 26–30	1st npower Test Match			
		ENGLAND	**v BANGLADESH**	**Lord's**
May 27	TL Div 1	Glamorgan	v Worcestershire	Cardiff ♀
May 29	TL Div 2	Kent	v Durham	Tunbridge Wells
		Warwickshire	v Scotland	Birmingham

Championship debut: Stratford-upon-Avon's Swan's Nest Lane ground was new to the circuit in 2004.

Picture by Graham Morris

May 30	TL Div 1	Gloucestershire	v Lancashire	Bristol
		Hampshire	v Northamptonshire	Southampton
		Nottinghamshire	v Essex	Nottingham
		Worcestershire	v Middlesex	Worcester
	TL Div 2	Derbyshire	v Leicestershire	Derby ♀
		Somerset	v Sussex	Taunton
		Surrey	v Durham	The Oval
		Yorkshire	v Scotland	Leeds
June 1–3	Universities	Cambridge UCCE	v Middlesex	Cambridge
		Yorkshire	v Brad/Leeds UCCE	Leeds
June 1–4	FCC Div 1	Glamorgan	v Sussex	Swansea
		Kent	v Gloucestershire	Maidstone
		Nottinghamshire	v Hampshire	Nottingham
		Surrey	v Warwickshire	Whitgift School
	FCC Div 2	Essex	v Derbyshire	Chelmsford
		Lancashire	v Northamptonshire	Manchester
		Leicestershire	v Somerset	Oakham School
		Worcestershire	v Durham	Worcester
June 3–7	2nd npower Test Match			
		ENGLAND	**v BANGLADESH**	**Chester-le-Street**
June 5	TL Div 1	Glamorgan	v Nottinghamshire	Swansea
		Lancashire	v Hampshire	Manchester
		Middlesex	v Essex	Lord's
	TL Div 2	Kent	v Derbyshire	Maidstone
		Leicestershire	v Somerset	Oakham School
		Surrey	v Warwickshire	Whitgift School
June 8–11	FCC Div 1	Glamorgan	v Kent	Cardiff
		Middlesex	v Surrey	Lord's
	FCC Div 2	Somerset	v Worcestershire	Bath
		Yorkshire	v Lancashire	Leeds
June 9–12	FCC Div 2	Durham	v Essex	Chester-le-Street
June 10–13	FCC Div 1	Gloucestershire	v Warwickshire	Gloucester
June 10	Tour Match	Derbyshire	v Bangladeshis	Derby
June 10	TL Div 2	Scotland	v Sussex	Edinburgh
June 11	Friendly	Hampshire	v England	Southampton
June 11	Tour Match	Leicestershire	v Australians	Leicester
June 12	Tour Match	Worcestershire	v Bangladeshis	Worcester
June 12	TL Div 1	Northamptonshire	v Middlesex	Northampton
		Nottinghamshire	v Lancashire	Nottingham
	TL Div 2	Leicestershire	v Yorkshire	Leicester
		Somerset	v Kent	Bath
June 13	NWS Twenty20	**ENGLAND**	**v AUSTRALIA**	**Southampton**
June 13	TL Div 2	Durham	v Derbyshire	Chester-le-Street
June 15–18	FCC Div 1	Hampshire	v Surrey	Southampton
		Middlesex	v Glamorgan	Southgate
		Sussex	v Nottinghamshire	Arundel
		Warwickshire	v Kent	Birmingham

June 15–18	FCC Div 2	Derbyshire	v Lancashire	Derby
		Leicestershire	v Worcestershire	Leicester
		Northamptonshire	v Durham	Northampton
June 15	Tour Match	Somerset	v Australians	Taunton
June 16	NWS	**ENGLAND**	**v BANGLADESH**	**The Oval**
June 17	TL Div 1	Essex	v Gloucestershire	Chelmsford ♀
	TL Div 2	Somerset	v Scotland	Taunton
June 17	Varsity Match	Cambridge Univ	v Oxford Univ	Lord's
June 18	NWS	**AUSTRALIA**	**v BANGLADESH**	**Cardiff**
June 19	NWS	**ENGLAND**	**v AUSTRALIA**	**Bristol**
June 19	TL Div 1	Hampshire	v Glamorgan	Southampton
		Middlesex	v Nottinghamshire	Southgate
		Northamptonshire	v Gloucestershire	Stowe School
		Worcestershire	v Essex	Worcester
	TL Div 2	Derbyshire	v Scotland	Derby
		Sussex	v Durham	Arundel
		Warwickshire	v Leicestershire	Birmingham
June 20	Twenty20 International	**ASIAN XI**	**v INTERNATIONAL XI**	**The Oval**
June 20	TL Div 2	Leicestershire	v Scotland	Leicester
June 21	NWS	**ENGLAND**	**v BANGLADESH**	**Nottingham** ♀
June 22	UCCE Challenge Final			Lord's
June 22	Twenty20 Cup	Derbyshire	v Durham	Derby
		Glamorgan	v Somerset	Cardiff ♀
		Hampshire	v Middlesex	Southampton
		Kent	v Surrey	Beckenham
		Leicestershire	v Nottinghamshire	Leicester
		Northamptonshire	v Gloucestershire	Milton Keynes
		Sussex	v Essex	Hove
		Worcestershire	v Warwickshire	Worcester
		Yorkshire	v Lancashire	Leeds
June 23	NWS	**ENGLAND**	**v AUSTRALIA**	**Chester-le-St** ♀
June 23	Twenty20 Cup	Middlesex	v Surrey	Lord's
		Somerset	v Worcestershire	Taunton
June 24	Twenty20 Cup	Derbyshire	v Leicestershire	Derby
		Essex	v Kent	Chelmsford ♀
		Gloucestershire	v Glamorgan	Bristol
		Hampshire	v Sussex	Southampton
		Northamptonshire	v Warwickshire	Northampton
		Nottinghamshire	v Lancashire	Nottingham
June 25	NWS	**AUSTRALIA**	**v BANGLADESH**	**Manchester**
June 25	Twenty20 Cup	Glamorgan	v Warwickshire	Swansea
		Kent	v Middlesex	Beckenham
		Surrey	v Hampshire	The Oval
June 26	NWS	**ENGLAND**	**v BANGLADESH**	**Leeds**
June 26	Twenty20 Cup	Essex	v Sussex	Chelmsford
		Gloucestershire	v Worcestershire	Bristol
		Leicestershire	v Durham	Leicester
		Nottinghamshire	v Yorkshire	Nottingham

June 27	Twenty20 Cup	Hampshire	v Kent	Southampton
		Lancashire	v Leicestershire	Manchester
		Somerset	v Glamorgan	Taunton
		Worcestershire	v Northamptonshire	Worcester
June 28	**NWS**	**ENGLAND**	**v AUSTRALIA**	**Birmingham** ♀
June 28	Twenty20 Cup	Durham	v Nottinghamshire	Chester-le-Street
		Gloucestershire	v Warwickshire	Bristol
		Hampshire	v Essex	Southampton
		Surrey	v Middlesex	The Oval
		Yorkshire	v Derbyshire	Leeds
June 28	Varsity Match	Cambridge Univ	v Oxford Univ	Cambridge
June 29	Twenty20 Cup	Essex	v Hampshire	Chelmsford ♀
		Lancashire	v Derbyshire	Manchester
		Middlesex	v Kent	Uxbridge
		Northamptonshire	v Somerset	Northampton
		Sussex	v Surrey	Hove ♀
June 30	**NWS**	**AUSTRALIA**	**v BANGLADESH**	**Canterbury**
June 30	Twenty20 Cup	Nottinghamshire	v Leicestershire	Nottingham
		Warwickshire	v Glamorgan	Birmingham
		Yorkshire	v Durham	Leeds
July 1	Twenty20 Cup	Durham	v Leicestershire	Chester-le-Street
		Glamorgan	v Northamptonshire	Cardiff ♀
		Gloucestershire	v Somerset	Bristol
		Lancashire	v Yorkshire	Manchester
		Middlesex	v Essex	Southgate
		Nottinghamshire	v Derbyshire	Nottingham
		Surrey	v Kent	The Oval
		Sussex	v Hampshire	Hove ♀
		Warwickshire	v Worcestershire	Birmingham
July 2	**The NatWest Series Final**			Lord's
July 2	Twenty20 Cup	Somerset	v Northamptonshire	Taunton
		Worcestershire	v Gloucestershire	Worcester
July 3	Twenty20 Cup	Lancashire	v Durham	Manchester
		Yorkshire	v Nottinghamshire	Leeds
July 4	Twenty20 Cup	Derbyshire	v Lancashire	Derby
		Durham	v Yorkshire	Chester-le-Street
		Sussex	v Middlesex	Hove ♀
		Warwickshire	v Somerset	Birmingham
July 5	Twenty20 Cup	Essex	v Surrey	Chelmsford ♀
		Glamorgan	v Gloucestershire	Cardiff ♀
		Kent	v Sussex	Canterbury
		Leicestershire	v Derbyshire	Leicester
		Northamptonshire	v Worcestershire	Northampton
July 6	Twenty20 Cup	Derbyshire	v Nottinghamshire	Derby
		Durham	v Lancashire	Chester-le-Street
		Kent	v Essex	Canterbury
		Leicestershire	v Yorkshire	Leicester
		Middlesex	v Hampshire	Richmond
		Somerset	v Gloucestershire	Taunton
		Surrey	v Sussex	The Oval

	Warwickshire	v Northamptonshire	Birmingham
	Worcestershire	v Glamorgan	Worcester
July 7	**NWC**	**ENGLAND**	**v AUSTRALIA**	**Leeds**

July 8–11	**FCC Div 1**	Gloucestershire	v Surrey	Bristol
		Middlesex	v Hampshire	Southgate
		Nottinghamshire	v Glamorgan	Nottingham
	FCC Div 2	Durham	v Lancashire	Chester-le-Street
		Somerset	v Leicestershire	Taunton
		Worcestershire	v Yorkshire	Worcester
July 8	**TL Div 1**	Essex	v Northamptonshire	Chelmsford ☂
	TL Div 2	Sussex	v Kent	Hove ☂
		Warwickshire	v Derbyshire	Birmingham
July 10–13	**FCC Div 1**	Kent	v Sussex	Canterbury
	FCC Div 2	Essex	v Northamptonshire	Chelmsford
July 10	**NWC**	**ENGLAND**	**v AUSTRALIA**	**Lord's**
July 12	**NWC**	**ENGLAND**	**v AUSTRALIA**	**The Oval**
July 13	**TL Div 2**	Yorkshire	v Surrey	Leeds ☂
July 15–17	**Tour Match**	Sussex/Leics/Som	v Australians	
July 15	**C&G Trophy Quarter-Finals**			
July 16	**C&G Trophy Quarter-Finals**			
July 17	**TL Div 1**	Middlesex	v Gloucestershire	Lord's
		Northamptonshire	v Lancashire	Northampton
		Nottinghamshire	v Hampshire	Nottingham
		Worcestershire	v Glamorgan	Worcester
	TL Div 2	Durham	v Warwickshire	Chester-le-Street
		Surrey	v Derbyshire	The Oval
July 18	**Tour Match**	British Universities	v Bangladesh A	Oxford
July 18	**Twenty20 Cup Quarter-Finals**			
July 19	**TL Div 1**	Lancashire	v Essex	Manchester ☂
July 20–23	**FCC Div 1**	Hampshire	v Sussex	Southampton
		Surrey	v Kent	Guildford
		Warwickshire	v Nottinghamshire	Birmingham
	FCC Div 2	Northamptonshire	v Worcestershire	Northampton
		Yorkshire	v Leicestershire	Scarborough
July 20–22	**Tour Match**	Gloucestershire	v Bangladesh A	Bristol
July 20	**TL Div 1**	Glamorgan	v Middlesex	Cardiff ☂
	TL Div 2	Derbyshire	v Durham	Derby ☂
July 21–24	**FCC Div 1**	Glamorgan	v Middlesex	Cardiff
	FCC Div 2	Derbyshire	v Durham	Derby
		Lancashire	v Essex	Manchester
July 21–25	**1st npower Test Match**			

		ENGLAND	**v AUSTRALIA**	**Lord's**
July 24	**Tour Match**	Hampshire	v Bangladesh A	Southampton
July 24	**TL Div 1**	Gloucestershire	v Worcestershire	Bristol
		Nottinghamshire	v Northamptonshire	Nottingham
	TL Div 2	Kent	v Somerset	Canterbury
		Scotland	v Leicestershire	Edinburgh
		Surrey	v Sussex	Guildford
		Yorkshire	v Warwickshire	Scarborough
July 25–27	**Frizzell Women's County Championship Finals**			Cambridge
July 26–28	**Tour Match**	Glamorgan	v Bangladesh A	Abergavenny
July 26–29	**FCC Div 1**	Nottinghamshire	v Surrey	Nottingham
		Sussex	v Gloucestershire	Hove
	FCC Div 2	Leicestershire	v Essex	Leicester
		Somerset	v Durham	Taunton
		Yorkshire	v Derbyshire	Leeds
July 26	**TL Div 1**	Hampshire	v Worcestershire	Southampton ♀
July 27	**TL Div 2**	Kent	v Warwickshire	Canterbury ♀
July 30–Aug 1	**Tour Match**	Wor/Gla/Glo/Nor	v Australians	
July 30	**Twenty20 Cup Semi-Finals and Final**			The Oval ♀
July 31	**TL Div 2**	Leicestershire	v Warwickshire	Leicester
		Yorkshire	v Kent	Leeds
August 1	**TL Div 2**	Sussex	v Somerset	Hove ♀
August 1	**Tour Match**	Lancashire	v Bangladesh A	Liverpool
August 2	**TL Div 1**	Worcestershire	v Northamptonshire	Worcester ♀
August 3–5	**Tour Match**	Yorkshire	v Bangladesh A	Leeds
August 3–6	**FCC Div 1**	Gloucestershire	v Hampshire	Cheltenham
		Kent	v Glamorgan	Canterbury
		Middlesex	v Warwickshire	Lord's
		Sussex	v Surrey	Hove
	FCC Div 2	Essex	v Durham	Southend
		Leicestershire	v Lancashire	Leicester
August 3	**TL Div 2**	Derbyshire	v Somerset	Derby ♀
August 4–7	**FCC Div 2**	Derbyshire	v Somerset	Derby
		Worcestershire	v Northamptonshire	Worcester
August 4–8	**2nd npower Test Match**			
		ENGLAND	**v AUSTRALIA**	**Birmingham**
August 7	**Tour Match**	Durham	v Bangladesh A	Chester-le-Street
August 7	**TL Div 1**	Essex	v Middlesex	Southend
		Gloucestershire	v Hampshire	Cheltenham
	TL Div 2	Kent	v Surrey	Canterbury
		Scotland	v Yorkshire	Edinburgh

		Sussex	v Leicestershire	Hove

| **August 9–12** | **1st npower Women's Test Match** | | | |
| | | **ENG WOMEN** | **v AUST WOMEN** | **Hove** |

| **August 9** | **TL Div 1** | Gloucestershire | v Nottinghamshire | Cheltenham |
| | **TL Div 2** | Surrey | v Leicestershire | The Oval ♀ |

| **August 10–12** | **Tour Match** | Surrey | v Bangladesh A | The Oval |

August 10–13	**FCC Div 1**	Glamorgan	v Warwickshire	Colwyn Bay
		Gloucestershire	v Sussex	Cheltenham
		Nottinghamshire	v Middlesex	Nottingham
	FCC Div 2	Northamptonshire	v Derbyshire	Northampton
		Somerset	v Yorkshire	Taunton

| **August 10** | **TL Div 1** | Hampshire | v Lancashire | Southampton ♀ |

| **August 11–13** | **3rd npower Test Match** | | | |
| | | **ENGLAND** | **v AUSTRALIA** | **Manchester** |

| **August 12–15** | **FCC Div 1** | Hampshire | v Kent | Southampton |
| | **FCC Div 2** | Durham | v Leicestershire | Chester-le-Street |

| **August 14–17** | **FCC Div 1** | Nottinghamshire | v Warwickshire | Nottingham |

August 14	**TL Div 1**	Glamorgan	v Lancashire	Colwyn Bay
		Gloucestershire	v Essex	Cheltenham
	TL Div 2	Derbyshire	v Sussex	Derby
		Somerset	v Yorkshire	Taunton

| **August 15** | **NWWS** | **ENG WOMEN** | **v AUST WOMEN** | **Cheltenham** |

| **August 15** | **TL Div 1** | Middlesex | v Northamptonshire | Lord's |

August 16–19	**FCC Div 1**	Middlesex	v Sussex	Lord's
		Surrey	v Gloucestershire	The Oval
	FCC Div 2	Derbyshire	v Essex	Derby
		Lancashire	v Yorkshire	Manchester
		Worcestershire	v Somerset	Worcester

| **August 16** | **TL Div 2** | Durham | v Leicestershire | Chester-le-St ♀ |

| **August 16–18** | **Tour Match** | Kent | v Bangladesh A | |

| **August 17** | **TL Div 1** | Northamptonshire | v Glamorgan | Northampton ♀ |

| **August 18** | **Tour Match** | Scotland | v Australians | Edinburgh |

| **August 19** | **NWWS** | **ENG WOMEN** | **v AUST WOMEN** | **Kidderminster** |

| **August 20–21** | **Tour Match** | Northants/Middx | v Australians | |

| **August 20** | **C&G Trophy Semi-Finals** | | | |

| **August 21** | **NWWS** | **ENG WOMEN** | **v AUST WOMEN** | **Stratford-on-Avon** |

August 21	**TL Div 1**	Lancashire	v Gloucestershire	Manchester
		Worcestershire	v Hampshire	Worcester
	TL Div 2	Leicestershire	v Sussex	Leicester

		Somerset	v Durham	Taunton
		Warwickshire	v Yorkshire	Birmingham
August 22	**TL Div 1**	Essex	v Nottinghamshire	Chelmsford ♥
	TL Div 2	Surrey	v Kent	The Oval ♥
August 23	**TL Div 1**	Glamorgan	v Gloucestershire	Cardiff ♥
	TL Div 2	Warwickshire	v Sussex	Birmingham ♥
August 24–27	**2nd npower Women's Test Match**			
		ENG WOMEN	**v AUST WOMEN**	**Worcester**
August 24–27	**FCC Div 1**	Kent	v Middlesex	Canterbury
		Surrey	v Hampshire	The Oval
	FCC Div 2	Essex	v Somerset	Colchester
		Leicestershire	v Northamptonshire	Leicester
		Yorkshire	v Durham	Scarborough
August 24	**TL Div 1**	Lancashire	v Worcestershire	Manchester ♥
August 25–28	**FCC Div 1**	Gloucestershire	v Glamorgan	Bristol
		Warwickshire	v Sussex	Birmingham
	FCC Div 2	Lancashire	v Worcestershire	Blackpool
August 25–29	**4th npower Test Match**			
		ENGLAND	**v AUSTRALIA**	**Nottingham**
August 26	**TL Div 2**	Scotland	v Derbyshire	Edinburgh
August 28	**TL Div 1**	Essex	v Hampshire	Colchester
		Northamptonshire	v Nottinghamshire	Northampton
	TL Div 2	Durham	v Scotland	Chester-le-Street
		Surrey	v Somerset	The Oval
		Yorkshire	v Derbyshire	Scarborough
Aug 30–Sept 2	**FCC Div 1**	Glamorgan	v Nottinghamshire	Cardiff
		Gloucestershire	v Middlesex	Bristol
		Hampshire	v Warwickshire	Southampton
	FCC Div 2	Durham	v Derbyshire	Chester-le-Street
		Northamptonshire	v Lancashire	Northampton
		Worcestershire	v Leicestershire	Worcester
August 30	**NWWS**	**ENG WOMEN**	**v AUST WOMEN**	**Taunton**
August 30	**TL Div 2**	Kent	v Yorkshire	Canterbury ♥
		Sussex	v Scotland	Hove
August 31	**TL Div 2**	Sussex	v Surrey	Hove ♥
Sept 1	**NWWS**	**ENG WOMEN**	**v AUST WOMEN**	**Taunton**
Sept 1	**TL Div 2**	Kent	v Scotland	Canterbury
Sept 2	**NWWTwenty20**	**ENG WOMEN**	**v AUST WOMEN**	**Taunton**
Sept 3	**C&G Trophy Final**			Lord's
Sept 3–4	**Tour Match**	Essex/Sussex/Notts	v Australians	
Sept 4	**TL Div 1**	Glamorgan	v Northamptonshire	Cardiff
		Hampshire	v Middlesex	Southampton

	TL Div 2	Worcestershire	v	Gloucestershire	Worcester
		Derbyshire	v	Surrey	Derby
		Durham	v	Kent	Chester-le-Street
		Yorkshire	v	Leicestershire	Leeds
Sept 5–8	FCC Div 1	Nottinghamshire	v	Gloucestershire	Nottingham
Sept 5	TL Div 2	Somerset	v	Warwickshire	Taunton ☂
Sept 6	TL Div 2	Leicestershire	v	Derbyshire	Leicester ☂
Sept 7–10	FCC Div 1	Middlesex	v	Kent	Lord's
	FCC Div 2	Sussex	v	Glamorgan	Hove
		Somerset	v	Northamptonshire	Taunton
		Yorkshire	v	Worcestershire	Leeds
Sept 7	TL Div 1	Essex	v	Lancashire	Chelmsford ☂
Sept 8–11	FCC Div 2	Leicestershire	v	Derbyshire	Leicester
Sept 8–12	**5th npower Test Match**				
		ENGLAND	**v**	**AUSTRALIA**	**The Oval**
Sept 9–12	FCC Div 2	Essex	v	Lancashire	Chelmsford
Sept 9	TL Div 1	Nottinghamshire	v	Gloucestershire	Nottingham ☂
Sept 10–13	FCC Div 1	Warwickshire	v	Surrey	Birmingham
Sept 11	TL Div 1	Middlesex	v	Glamorgan	Lord's
		Nottinghamshire	v	Worcestershire	Nottingham
	TL Div 2	Yorkshire	v	Durham	Leeds
Sept 13	TL Div 1	Glamorgan	v	Hampshire	Cardiff ☂
Sept 14–17	FCC Div 1	Kent	v	Nottinghamshire	Canterbury
	FCC Div 2	Durham	v	Northamptonshire	Chester-le-Street
Sept 14	TL Div 2	Derbyshire	v	Yorkshire	Derby ☂
		Warwickshire	v	Surrey	Birmingham ☂
Sept 15–18	FCC Div 1	Glamorgan	v	Hampshire	Cardiff
Sept 16–19	FCC Div 2	Derbyshire	v	Yorkshire	Derby
Sept 18	TL Div 1	Essex	v	Worcestershire	Chelmsford
		Lancashire	v	Middlesex	Manchester
	TL Div 2	Durham	v	Somerset	Chester-le-Street
		Kent	v	Sussex	Canterbury
		Scotland	v	Warwickshire	Edinburgh
Sept 21–24	FCC Div 1	Hampshire	v	Nottinghamshire	Southampton
		Surrey	v	Middlesex	The Oval
		Sussex	v	Kent	Hove
		Warwickshire	v	Gloucestershire	Birmingham
	FCC Div 2	Lancashire	v	Leicestershire	Manchester
		Northamptonshire	v	Yorkshire	Northampton
		Somerset	v	Derbyshire	Taunton
		Worcestershire	v	Essex	Worcester
Sept 25	TL Div 1	Gloucestershire	v	Glamorgan	Bristol
		Hampshire	v	Nottinghamshire	Southampton

INTERNATIONAL SCHEDULE, 2005–2011

In February 2001, the International Cricket Council unveiled a ten-year schedule of Tests and one-day internationals. It initially runs from May 2001 to April 2011; all of the ICC's ten Test-playing members are intended to play each other in home and away Test series (with a minimum of two matches to a series) during each five-year period.

The programme is based around Tests, but there will usually be associated one-day internationals. Countries may revise dates as long as they do not disrupt other series.

Other fixtures include a Super Series (Australia v the Rest of the World) in October 2005; the Champions Trophy, October 2006; and the World Cup, March–April 2007.

	Australia	Bangladesh	England	India	New Zealand	Pakistan	South Africa	Sri Lanka	West Indies	Zimbabwe
Australia	–	9/10	11/06 11/10	12/07	11/06	11/08	**12/05** 12/09	**1/06** 11/07	**10/05** 12/08	11/09
Bangladesh	**4/06**	–	2/07 2/11	10/06	10/07	1/10	3/08	2/08	10/09 11/10	1/09
England	**6/05** 6/09	**5/05** 5/10	–	6/07	5/09	**6/06**	6/08	**5/06**	5/07 6/10	5/08
India	10/10	**4/05** 12/10	**2/06**	–	10/09	**4/05** 3/09	10/08	**11/05** 12/09	2/08	10/07
New Zealand	**12/05** 2/09	12/06	2/08	2/07	–	12/08	2/11	**4/05** 12/07	**2/06** 12/09	**12/05** 2/10
Pakistan	2/08	9/09	**11/05** 11/09	**1/06** 1/11	10/08	–	10/07	2/10 3/11	12/06	10/06 11/10
South Africa	**2/06** 2/10	4/09	12/08	12/06 1/09	**10/05** 10/10	2/07 12/10	–	10/09	12/07	2/08
Sri Lanka	9/08	**2/06**	10/07	7/08	8/07	**3/06** 8/10	10/06	–	**7/05** 7/09	2/07
West Indies	2/07 2/11	11/08	2/09	**4/06** 3/10	4/08	**5/05** 4/10	**4/05** 4/11	5/08	–	**5/06** 4/09
Zimbabwe	9/06	12/07	10/09	**10/05** 3/11	**9/05** 9/10	9/07	8/06	12/08	9/08	–

Home teams listed on left, away teams across top. Tours between April 2005 and July 2006 shown in bold.

ENGLAND'S INTERNATIONAL SCHEDULE, 2005–2010

Home		**Away**	
2005	Tests and ODIs v Bangladesh and Australia	2005-06	Tests and ODIs v Pakistan and India
2006	Tests and ODIs v Sri Lanka and Pakistan	2006-07	ICC Champions Trophy; Tests and ODIs v Australia and Bangladesh
2007	Tests and ODIs v West Indies and India		WORLD CUP in the West Indies
2008	Tests and ODIs v Zimbabwe and South Africa	2007-08	Tests and ODIs v Sri Lanka and New Zealand
2009	Tests and ODIs v New Zealand and Australia	2008-09	Tests and ODIs v South Africa and West Indies
2010	Tests and ODIs v Bangladesh and West Indies	2009-10	Tests and ODIs v Zimbabwe and Pakistan

All tours subject to confirmation.

INDEX OF FILLERS

INDEX OF UNUSUAL OCCURRENCES